# THE

# Encyclopædia of Missions.

*DESCRIPTIVE, HISTORICAL, BIOGRAPHICAL,*
*STATISTICAL.*

WITH A FULL ASSORTMENT OF MAPS, A COMPLETE BIBLIOG-
RAPHY, AND LISTS OF BIBLE VERSIONS, MISSIONARY
SOCIETIES, MISSION STATIONS, AND A
GENERAL INDEX.

## VOL. II.

EDITED BY

## REV. EDWIN MUNSELL BLISS.

FUNK & WAGNALLS:
NEW YORK,
LONDON,     1891     TORONTO.
*All Rights Reserved.*
PRINTED IN THE UNITED STATES.

## Printing Statement:

Due to the very old age and scarcity of this book,
many of the pages may be hard to read due to the
blurring of the original text, possible missing pages,
missing text, dark backgrounds and other issues
beyond our control.

Because this is such an important and rare work, we
believe it is best to reproduce this book regardless of
its original condition.

Thank you for your understanding.

# LIST OF MAPS.

# ENCYCLOPÆDIA

OF

# MISSIONS

---

**Mabang,** a town of Sierra Leone, West Africa, east of Freetown. Station of the Wesleyan Methodist Missionary Society (England), with 1 native missionary, 6 local preachers, 85 church-members, 30 day-scholars.

**Maboulela** (Mabolela), a town in Orange Free State, South Africa, north of Berea, and almost due east of Bloemfontein. Mission station of Paris Evangelical Society (1859); 1 missionary, 5 evangelists, 372 communicants, 151 scholars.

**Macarthy's Island,** an island in the mouth of the Gambia, Senegambia, West Africa. The Wesleyans founded a station here in 1832, but so many white missionaries died on account of the climate, that in 1848 it had to be left to the charge of native preachers from Sierra Leone. They have 86 church-members, a congregation of 300, and the Gospel of Matthew has been translated into Wolof. English, however, is generally understood.

**Macao,** a colony of Portugal, on the southeast extremity of Hiung-shang Island, Canton province, China, 60 or 70 miles southeast of Canton. This place was formerly the shipping station for the coolies sent to South America. It is noted now principally for its healthfulness, and for the gambling which is there carried on. A station of the Presbyterian Board (North), with 1 missionary and wife, from which out-stations in the Canton province are worked. The work is mainly among the districts from whence emigrants go to the United States and other countries.

**Macassar Version.**—The Macassar belongs to the Malaysian languages, and is spoken in the island of Celebes. A version of the Gospel of Mark, which Dr. Leyden had prepared with the help of some learned scholars, was never printed. In 1840 Dr. B. F. Matthess of the mission house at Rotterdam was sent to Celebes, and after having studied the language, he translated parts of the New Testament, which were published by the Netherlands Bible Society between 1863 and 1874. The first part of the New Testament was published at Macassar and

Amsterdam in 1875, and the second in 1888 by the above Bible Society.

**Macedonia,** a section of European Turkey, bounded on the north by Bulgaria, on the south by Greece, on the west by Albania, while on the east there are no definite boundaries to separate it from the rest of European Turkey. It is in the main coincident with the old kingdom of Macedonia. The chief cities are Salonica (Thessalonica), Uscup, and Monastir. The population is chiefly Bulgarian and Greek, though there are large numbers of Albanians. Mission work is carried on by the A. B. C. F. M., with a station at Monastir; and the Presbyterian Board (South), with a station at Salonica. A missionary of the Committee of the Free Church of Scotland for the Conversion of the Jews resides at Salonica. (See Turkey, and Bulgarian Mission of the A. B. C. F. M.)

**Macedonian-Rouman Version.**—The Rouman or Roumanian belongs to the Græco-Latin branch of the Asian family of languages, and is divided into two dialects: the one is the standard Rouman, and is vernacular in Roumania and part of Transylvania; the other is the Macedonian dialect, and is spoken by the Roumans or Vlachs, as they are called, of Macedonia, Albania, and Thessaly. All former efforts made in behalf of the British and Foreign Bible Society to procure a translation into this dialect having failed, the Society at last succeeded in procuring the services of Lazar Demetrins, a teacher in the Roumanian Academy at Monastir, who translated the Gospel of St. Matthew into this dialect, which after a careful revision was printed under the direction of Mr. Kyrias, a good Rouman scholar, at Bucharest in 1889. The edition consists of 5,000 copies.

**Maceio,** a city of Brazil, South America, on the coast in the province of Alagoas. Its harbor is protected from the ocean by a reef of rocks. Population, 10,000. Mission station Southern Baptist Connection; 1 native pastor.

**Macfarlan,** a town in East Kaffraria, South Africa, northwest of King William's Town. Mission station of the Free Church of Scotland;

1 missionary, 1 church, 326 communicants, 6 out-stations, 4 schools, 218 scholars.

**Mackay, Alexander M.,** b. Rhynie, Aberdeenshire, Scotland, October 13th, 1849; was a son of a minister of the Free Church. At three years of age he read the New Testament; at seven, Milton's "Paradise Lost," Gibbon's "Decline and Fall of the Roman Empire," and Robertson's "History of the Discovery of America." His father taught him geography, astronomy, and geometry; stopping in their walks to demonstrate a proposition of Euclid, or illustrate the motions of the heavenly bodies, or trace the course of a newly-discovered river of the Dark Continent with his cane in the sand. He listened with interest to letters and conversations of men of science, as Hugh Miller, Sir Roderick Murchison, and others, who were sometimes visitors at the manse, sometimes in correspondence with his father. At eleven he for a time discarded books, and gave himself to the study of engines, gas-making, carpentry, blacksmithing, saddlery, etc. At thirteen he again began to devour books, and made great progress in the classics and mathematics, but for recreation watched the processes of photography and ship-building. At sixteen his mother's death, and her dying request that he would "search" the Scriptures, deeply impressed him. At eighteen he entered the training-college for teachers, and was distinguished in many departments of study. He afterwards studied for three years, at Edinburgh University, applied mechanics, engineering, higher mathematics, physics, to which he added one year of surveying and fortification. At twenty-four he went to Germany to acquire the language, and thus have access to the stores of lore in that land. He soon secured a position in a large engineering establishment in Berlin as *constructeur* or draughtsman. Here he was a missionary among the ungodly workmen in the institution, and was preparing in heart and purpose to go as an engineering missionary to carry the gospel with civilization to some dark corner of the heathen world. At twenty-six, in 1875, in response to an appeal from the Church Missionary Society for a practical business man to go to Mombasa, he offered himself, but another person had been secured. Later in the year an offer of a highly lucrative secular position was made him; but he declined it, that he might be ready, when the Lord should permit him, to go to the heathen. Early the next year he was accepted by the Church Missionary Society; embarked April 25th, 1876, for Victoria Nyanza, reaching Zanzibar May 29th. In November, on the march through Ugogo, he was taken very ill, and was sent back by Dr. Smith, but recovered before reaching the coast. Instructed by the secretary not to return before the close of the rainy season, he constructed 230 miles of road to Mpwapwa. In November, 1878, he reached Uganda. Alluding to the kind treatment he had received from the natives, he says: "Wherever I find myself in Stanley's track, I find his treatment of the natives has invariably been such as to win from them the highest respect for the face of a white man." Mr. Mackay had acquired a knowledge of the Swahili language, and was able immediately to print portions of the Scriptures, and to read and explain them to the king and his people. Mtesa showed much interest in the truth. Children

were much drawn to Mr. Mackay, and constantly surrounded him. Many were learning to read the Bible, and the Sabbath began to be partially observed at Court. Soon Roman Catholic teachers came, and bitterly opposed his teaching. Mohammedans also began to withstand him. He labored daily at the printing-press, having to cut his own types, and also repaired tools, and did other work for the natives, thereby supplying his own wants. He expressed regret that so much of his time was thus taken from religious teaching, but hoped his example would be useful, as labor was so much despised by the heathen. November 1st, 1879, he wrote: "Hosts of people come every day for instruction, chiefly in reading." Again he mentions having men read to him while he works at the lathe or forge. His journal shows intense zeal and incessant labor in making known the gospel with prayer and faith. In 1882 five converts were baptized, and in 1884 the native church consisted of 86 members, including two daughters and a grand-daughter of the king. But in that year Mtesa died, and was succeeded by his young son Mwanga, who proved to be weak and vacillating, and a tool in the hands of his crafty courtiers. Political events in Africa stimulated suspicion of foreigners, and he soon began to persecute the Christians and oppose the missionaries. Three lads were burned for their adhesion to Christianity, and many others were slain. Mr. Mackay was repeatedly threatened with expulsion, but held his ground, and was allowed for a time to continue his work, his skill as an engineer and mechanic, of which the king often availed himself, helping to secure his favor. In 1886 the persecution broke out again, many under great tortures exhibiting a Christian fortitude and heroism unsurpassed in apostolic times. In 1887 the Arabs succeeded in persuading Mwanga to expel Mr. Mackay. Having locked the mission premises, he embarked July 20th for the southern end of the lake, making his abode at Usambiro. Here he remained for three years, translating and printing the Scriptures, teaching the Christian refugees from Uganda, instructing the natives of the district, as far as he could with an imperfect knowledge of their language, and working at house-building, brick-making, and the construction of a steam-launch with which to navigate the lake. He was attacked with malarial fever, and died February 8th, 1890, after five days' illness. Mr. Ashe, his companion, says: "I have lost my best and most loving earthly friend. A born leader, as gentle as he was brave. One part of his character was his earnestness in prayer and the study of the Bible." Colonel J. A. Grant, companion of Speke in his journeys, thus writes: "The blow to civilization in Central Africa which has fallen on us all is not easily repaired, for a score of us would never make a Mackay." Mr. Stock remarks: "Mackay is identified in most minds with the industrial, material, and civilizing side of missions. It would indeed be most unjust to think of him entirely in that aspect. A man who was one day grappling with Mohammedans in strenuous theological argument, and preaching Christ, that He is the Son of God; who the next day was content to sit for hours teaching boys to read, and explaining to them simple texts; and who the third day was patiently translating the blessed words of life into a language that had no grammar or dictionary

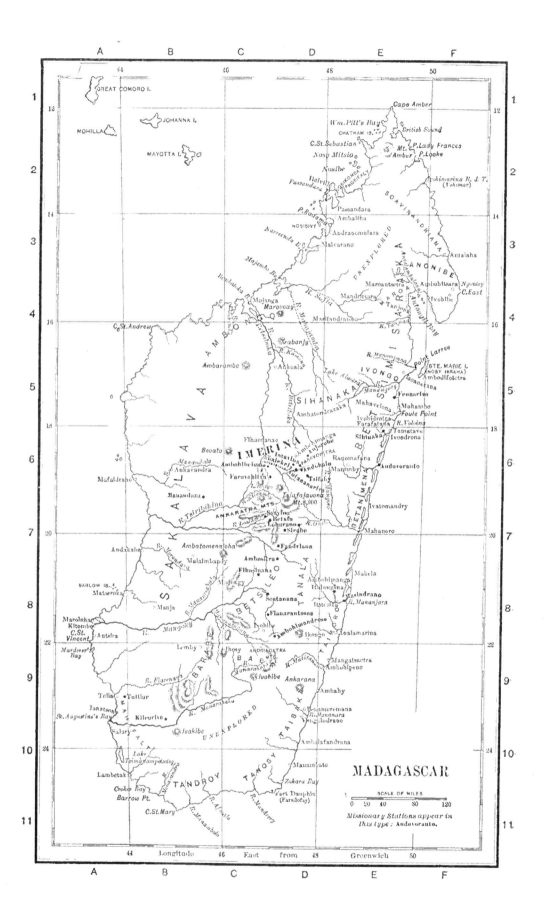

MADAGASCAR

—such a man was no mere industrial and civilizing missionary." The Society thus records its estimate of Mr. Mackay: "His talents were of a very high order, and he brought to bear upon the cause of the spread of Christianity and civilization in Africa not only remarkable practical resourcefulness as an accomplished engineer, but the powers of a vigorous and cultivated mind, and a devotion and perseverance unsurpassed by any African missionary. Moreover, he took a leading part in the direct work of the mission, teaching and preaching the Word of God; and he utilized the knowledge of both classical and modern languages in reducing the vernacular of Uganda to writing, and rendering into it portions of Scripture, prayers, etc."

**Mackenzie, J. Kenneth, M.D.,** a medical missionary of the London Missionary Society: was first appointed to Hankow; he took charge of the mission hospital there till 1878, when in the autumn he was transferred to Tientsin. He was called in to prescribe for the illness of the wife of the powerful Viceroy of Chihli, Li Hung Chang, and his success in curing her attracted the attention of the Viceroy to his work. A dispensary was opened in the Viceroy's theatre, with a female department, and large subscriptions were made by him and other high officers towards the building of a hospital. In 1881 the hospital, on the premises of the London Mission, was opened by the Viceroy, and plans were adopted for a medical school, to which the students formerly sent to the United States of America by the government were sent to be trained as doctors, and a thorough organization of a medical staff for the Chinese army and navy was in course of formation. Amid his arduous duties, Dr. Mackenzie found time to pursue evangelistic work, both among the poor patients and those "in Cæsar's household," for the favor of the Viceroy secured him access to many of the high officials. The work at Tientsin grew and enlarged, so that in his last report, 1887, he gave the number in attendance at the dispensary as 13,799, in-patients in the hospital 591, and 9 medical students. He was called suddenly away from his work by death, April 1st, 1888. He was universally admired and beloved by his associates, and was said to be the "most important man in Tientsin." The London Missionary Society report speaks of him thus: " A skilful physician, he was also, and above all, an earnest evangelist." A handsome slab of stone, bearing a brief motto on one side, and on the other a short biographical sketch, built into the outer wall of the courtyard of his old dispensary at Tientsin, is the mark of the esteem and loving memory of his college students and some of the native Christians who knew and loved him well.

**Macleag,** a settlement on Lake Alexandrina, South Australia; was founded in 1858 by the Scotchman Taplin, who translated parts of the Bible into Narrinjeri, wrote a grammar of the tongue, and made a careful study of 22 native languages. Station of the Hermannsburg Evangelical Lutheran Mission.

**Macmillanpatna,** town in Orissa, India, two miles from Cuttack, the capital. A sub-station of the General Baptist Missionary Society (established 1868), worked from Cuttack. It has one chapel, supplied by preachers from Cuttack, 32 church-members, and a Christian community of 115.

**Madagascar,** an island of the Indian Ocean, nearly parallel with the eastern coast of South Africa, from which it is separated by the Mozambique Channel, which varies in width from 220 to 540 miles. Its northernmost point is in 11° 57′ 30″ south latitude, and the southernmost is in 25° 38′ 55″ south latitude. Its breadth is at the widest point over 7° of longitude. Its extreme length is 975 miles, and its breadth varies from 250 to 350 miles. Its area is about 230,000 English square miles. It is the third largest island in the world, ranking only below Borneo and New Guinea.

Madagascar has a coast-line of over 2,000 miles, and on the northwestern, northern, and northeastern coasts there are many good and some excellent harbors; but south of latitude 19° there are very few roadsteads where a vessel can ride in safety, either on the east or west coasts. At the north, Diego Suarez Inlet is its finest harbor. The ports best known on the east coast are: Port Choiseul in Antongil Bay, Ports Ste. Marie, Fenoarivo, Foule Point, Tamatave, Mahanoro, Vatomandry, Mohila. On the south are Fort Dauphin and two or three less important ports. On the west the important harbors are: Nosy-Vé, Morondava, Maintirano, Mojanga, the largest port on the island; Helleville, in the French island of Nòsy-Bé; Bavatòby, and Pasindava.

*Surface and Productions.*—The island is of volcanic origin, and has many extinct volcanoes and some which, if not now active, have been so within the historic period. Its general structure includes three or four ranges of mountains, not parallel, but extending from north to south, with many spurs; these are in the central portions of the island, though nearer to the east than the west coast. Some of the ranges extend nearly to the northern limit of the island, and others to the southern coast. Ankaratra mountains, mostly in Imerina, whose principal summits rise between 8,000 and 9,000 feet; the Angàvo range, forming the water-shed of the island, about 70 miles from the east coast, and 200 from the west, having five summits with an elevation of 6,000 to 7,300 feet; the Andringitra ranges, mostly in Betsileo, and others farther south. The mountain summits, lofty as they are, do not in this latitude reach the snow-line. This mountainous region is known as the Highland provinces, and constitutes the finest portion of the island in healthfulness, delightful climate, productiveness, and the intelligence of its inhabitants. Immediately below these highlands is a belt or perhaps two belts of forest, extending nearly around the island. This forest belt varies in altitude from 1,800 to 4,000 feet. Portions of it are dense jungle, with the llianas or climbing plants rendering it almost impassable; other portions are park-like groves, with stately and valuable timber-trees; toward the south there are extensive prairies and desert lands. The forest belt varies from 30 to 50 miles in breadth.

From the forest belt to the coast extends the littoral or alluvial region, having a flat, low-lying, sandy, and marshy soil, washed down through the ages, from the rocks and forests, and bordered on the east coast by a long line of lagoons or sounds. This littoral region is from 20 to 30 miles wide on the east coast, but from 40 to 60 on the west coast. It is sickly and hot, the decaying vegetation producing fevers and miasmatic diseases.

*Climate.*—Temperate and healthy in the Highland provinces, the temperature rarely above 85° F. or below 40° F., except in the mountains, where it sinks to 32° at night perhaps once or twice in a year. In the forest belt, less healthy and more moist, and at times hot; in the more open timber the climate is delightful. In the littoral region the heat is intense, and the Malagasy fever prevails, and very often proves fatal to those who are not fully acclimated.

*Natural History and Products.*—Madagascar is remarkable in its zoölogy. There are no great beasts of prey. The lemur takes the place of the various families of monkeys and apes; there are several species of ant-eaters, two or three civet cats; the aye-aye, an animal allied to the sloth family, but found nowhere else; and there are several rodents. Reptiles are numerous, but, except the crocodile and three or four species of pythons, are generally harmless. Birds are numerous, and many of them of beautiful plumage. The birds of prey are large and powerful, but not abundant; and a species, just become extinct, the æpyornis, is believed to have been the largest bird on the earth. About two thirds of the known species of birds on the island are peculiar to Madagascar.

The fish are plentiful, and many of them of edible species. Most of the domestic animals have been introduced, and cattle and sheep are raised and exported in great numbers. Wild dogs are so numerous as to be a pest.

The flora of Madagascar is abundant, and about 700 out of 3,000 species are peculiar to the island. Many of them are of exquisite beauty. It is a paradise for the orchids; more, and more beautiful species being found here than in all other countries. The forests abound in peculiar and valuable timber, some of it the finest known; and caoutchouc trees and vines, the copal-tree, the sago-palm, the bread-fruit, the Rofia palm, the pepper-tree, the tallow-tree, the traveller's-tree, the pomegranate and other trees of the Citrus family, the tamarind, the quassia, the lace-leaf shrub, the sugar-cane, the manioc—an indigenous arrow-root, etc., etc., are plentiful in the forests and highlands. Most of the cereals are largely cultivated.

*Ethnology and Tribal Divisions.*—The origin of the Malagasy and their race affinities with the other oriental nations have led to great controversies among the most eminent ethnologists of our century.

It is generally agreed that the original inhabitants of the island were from some of the African races, and most probably from southeastern Africa—Zulus or Kafirs. Though dark, they seem to have been negritos rather than negroes. They were known by the Malagasy as Vazimba. Investigations show that they were of low stature; their heads were narrow and elongated; they were physically weaker than the invading tribes, had no knowledge of the use of iron, and fled before the superior weapons of their adversaries. A small remnant of them were still living in 1843, and it is believed that a few are yet to be found in the southwest.

In regard to the present inhabitants of the island, known as the Malagasy, these facts are settled: They all speak the same language, the dialects differing no more than the Yorkshire and Lancashire do in England; and this language is of very close kindred with the Malay, and has many Malay words. There is a marked difference in color, features, and hair among the different tribes: some are of fine stature and physique, but very dark, with curly or frizzly black hair; their features are more Polynesian than negro; others are of lighter complexion, with straight or very slightly curled hair, generally of good height, and well-formed. The Hovas, who are the ruling tribe, are generally somewhat below the middle stature, of a light-olive complexion, frequently fairer than the Spanish, Portuguese, or Italians. Their hair is black, but soft, fine, and straight or curling; their eyes are hazel, their figures erect, and though small, well-proportioned; the hands and feet small, and their gait and movements agile, free, and graceful.

The theory of their origin which is best supported seems to be that these tribes are of Malayan or Malayo-Polynesian stock; that they came to Madagascar at different times, and probably not in large numbers at first; that the first invaders landed on the south-southeast or east coasts, and gradually crowded the Vazimba into the interior or highland regions; that other companies came later, and landed upon the southern and western coasts, and they also forced the aborigines away from the coasts; that these invaders, engaging largely in the slave-trade (bringing negroes from the Mozambique coast), and trading with Arabs, Phœnicians, and Syrians, and being of loose morals, became gradually a mixed race, having the physical characteristics of the several races thus commingled. At a period about 1,000 years ago, a fresh irruption came from Malaysia, a more intelligent tribe than their predecessors, and finding the coasts occupied, pushed forward into the interior, and driving the Vazimba before them, possessed themselves of their lands, and grew strong and great there. These were the Hovas, and perhaps also the Bètsimisàrakas, the Bètànimèna, and the Sihànakas of the eastern coast and forest regions. The Betsileo, who occupy the province south of Imerina, though in intelligence and political ability they strongly resemble the Hovas, are physically very different from them, being of large stature, very dark complexion, and crisp or woolly hair, and with a low and broad forehead and thick lips, resembling the negro race more strongly than any other of the Malagasy tribes. Yet their language is substantially the same with that of the Hovas, and they take as readily to the arts of civilization. They were probably earlier immigrants, and perhaps had intermarried with the Vazimba or the Mozambique slaves. They were divided into three clans, and these were often at war with each other, and the captives became the slaves of the captors.

In 1810 the principal tribes of Madagascar were: 1. The Sàkalàva, divided into the northern and southern tribes, occupying the western coast, and including many smaller clans; their members were estimated at 1,500,000. 2. The Bètsimisàraka, with several clans, and including the Bètànimèna, occupying the east coast. about 1,500,000 more. 3. The Sihanaka and Tankarana, northeast provinces; about 500,000. 4. The Bara and Tanala and some smaller tribes, in the southeast, 500,000. 5. Imerina, the land of the

Hovas, then about 600,000 ; and 6. The Betsileo, 1,200,000. The last two were the Highland provinces.

*Social and Religious Condition before Missions were established.*— Though discovered in mediæval times, no effort was made by Europeans to explore or colonize Madagascar till 1506, when the Portuguese, after some exploration in 1540, undertook to enslave and Christianize its inhabitants. They made repeated efforts to this end in the next hundred years, landing small colonies on its shores, establishing trading-posts, from whence they sold the people who came under their power as slaves. These natives were Sàkalàvas, who did not choose to be the prey of European slave-dealers, and massacred the Portuguese colonists and priests in 1548, 1585, 1600, and 1615. The English and Dutch made several attempts to plant colonies at various points on the coast of the island, between 1595 and 1640. Both nations were at that time engaged in the slave trade.

In 1642 the French undertook to colonize Madagascar, and within the next 170 years they had organized several great companies or societies, and planted many colonies, in which Lazarist and Jesuit priests were always conspicuous and often evil advisers, but owing to their maintenance of the slave-trade, and their treacherous dealings with the natives, four or five of these colonies were attacked and massacred by the chiefs. From their own misconduct and the deadly character of the climate on the coast, the last of these societies was obliged, in 1686, to surrender its charter and its whole property to Louis XIV., King of France, who claimed, but never exercised, authority over it. For the next thirty or thirty-five years the northern part of the island was the most formidable rendezvous of the pirates, who infested the Indian Ocean and bade defiance to all the European powers. They treated the natives well, and several of the tribes were on friendly terms with them; but their rendezvous was finally broken up in 1723. It was not until 1754 that another attempt was made by the French to plant a colony in Madagascar, and this was broken up by a massacre. In the 57 years which followed, occasional attempts were made to establish trading-posts at different points on the island—at Fort Dauphin in the south, Tamatave and Foule Point on the east coast, and Nòsy-Bé and Ste. Marie Islands; but these were one after another abandoned, till, in 1811, the only two remaining trading-posts, Tamatave and Foule Point, with a mere handful of men in each, were surrendered to the English, as their sole possessions in Madagascar. These settlements and trading-posts, maintained with fitful irregularity from 1642 to 1811, had professed to have, for one of their objects, the conversion of these heathen to Christianity; they had had at all times Roman Catholic priests, generally Lazarist or Jesuit Fathers, at their stations; but the rapacity and licentiousness of the officials and their men, and in many cases of the priests themselves, had disgusted the Malagasy, and made them despise a religion so much worse in their sight than their own idolatry. In all these 160 years there is no mention of more than one Malagasy convert, who had been taken to France, and educated by Vincent de Paul; and he, while acting as a servant of two of the belligerent priests, was slain with them by his own countrymen in 1663.

The social and religious condition of these tribes at the beginning of this century was most deplorable. Not only were the different tribes almost constantly at war with each other, for the double purpose of obtaining spoil, and of securing captives who were reduced to slavery and sold to the slave-ships of the Arabs, Turks, Portuguese, Spanish, French, and (alas, that it should be necessary to say it!) English, and possibly Americans. Their principal chiefs also carried on a considerable trade with the Arab *dhows*, or slavers, from Zanzibar, Mozambique, and Sofala, purchasing negro slaves from Mozambique and rum from Zanzibar, and paying for them in rice, bullocks, timber, and other products of the island, and often in their own countrymen whom they had enslaved. As might be supposed, the state of morals was as low as it well could be: polygamy was the rule with the chiefs and nobles; chastity was unknown in the towns, and little regarded in the country. Many of the large tribes were adroit thieves, cheats, and liars. This was particularly true of the Sàkalàva (long the ruling tribe), the Bara, and the Betsileo. One of the best of the Sàkalàva said to Mr. Sibree: " All the Sàkalàva steal; I myself also." They were also the most treacherous and vindictive of the tribes. Some of the tribes were industrious and skilful, so far as their opportunities admitted, in the mechanic arts; others were indolent, averse to work, but ready to steal. The coast tribes were generally, though with some exception, fond of aquatic pursuits, skilful as fishermen, turtle-catchers, or rowers, and imitated the Malays in their long and well-handled *proas* or canoes with outriggers; the interior tribes were generally agriculturists, when not engaged in war.

Their religious system was not as artificial or philosophical as that of many heathen nations. They believed in a supreme being who ruled over all; they also had an idea of subordinate deities, who ruled over certain places, persons, or interests. There were no idol temples, few idolatrous processions, no priestly class in rich robes and exerting almost regal power, no pilgrimages, penances, castes, no costly offerings or sacrifices (this at least among the Hovas, though it is said that among some of the coast tribes, on important occasions, human sacrifices were offered), and while there was some superstition, and occasionally attempts at divination, there seems to have been little tendency to fetichism or voodooism. Mr. William Pool was present when, at the destruction of the national idols in 1869, their chief idol, Rakèlimalàza, was dissected before being burned. It was of small size—a piece of wood two or three inches long, and as large as the middle finger of a man's hand, wrapped in two thicknesses of scarlet silk about three feet long and three inches wide, the wood pointed at one end and movable in the silk, and two silver chains about three inches in length at either end of the silk. It was placed in a small case made of a portion of the trunk of a young tree hollowed out. There was no carving or ornamental work upon it. This idol was the guardian of the sovereign and the kingdom; others, as that protecting against serpents, that preserving the rice crop from harm, etc., were still more rude than that already described. One of the sovereign's idols was a small quantity of sand tied up in a cloth; another was an imitation of shark's teeth in silver; others, pieces of coral or bone. The worship of these idols was not very general or reverent. The Malagasy were not a devout people; they did not like to retain God in their knowledge. They paid a sort of homage to their deceased ancestors, but reared no temples or statues to them. The idol-keepers, who by custom held the rank and privileges of nobles, were not very numerous, and were disliked by the people. They resorted to divination at the demand of the rulers, and generally the ordeal of the *tangena* was administered by them. This ordeal, which consisted in the administration of a portion of the nut of the *Tanghinia Veneniflua* in a part of a ripe banana, with many ceremonies and prayers and much mystery, was a very potent instrument of evil in the hands of these idol-keepers. From one third to one fourth of those who took it died. It was a powerful emetic poison.

The religious system of the Malagasy exerted no influence on their moral natures, and indeed made no pretence of doing so. It was simply supposed to confer upon them temporal benefits; why or for what service on their part does not appear.

There were no days or seasons for the public worship of the idols; indeed they seem to have been only or mainly used for purposes of divination. On certain occasions, such as the accession of a new sovereign, the coronation or public showing (*fisehoana*) of the new ruler to the people, and the observance of the Malagasy new year, which usually took place in the spring, they were brought out. The Malagasy year was a lunar year, and consisted of only 354 days. This observance of the new year was a feast of five days; the sovereign bathed publicly in the palace, and each of the principal families in their own homes. There was great feasting in all the capital villages, many thousands of bullocks being slain and their flesh distributed. The idols were carried in procession, all laws being in abeyance for the time, and drunkenness and the most horrible licentiousness prevailed everywhere during these public days, as on the other occasions already mentioned.

The government of the various tribes was, like that of most savage nations, by chiefs. It was not necessarily hereditary, though confined to the class of nobles (Andriana), and was as often, perhaps, in the female as in the male line. The succession was not often conferred upon the eldest son or daughter, and there was much intrigue, and sometimes bloodshed, before the ruler was selected. Once on the throne, however, his government was an absolute despotism, though sometimes "tempered by assassination." There was no written language in any of the tribes; the decrees of the sovereign were promulgated by heralds, and however unjust, could only be changed by his will. The government was feudal in its character; the chief and the nobles held the tribe in bondage; they owned all the land, and the people as well; if either the ruler or the nobles required any work done, as the cultivation of the fields, the preparation of clothing, or arms and munitions of war, or if they desired to go to war with a neighboring tribe, the clansmen were called out and required to perform the service, providing themselves with food and clothing, for the time required. The chief or nobles were only required to furnish the necessary arms. This forced service was called *fanompoana*, and it exists, in a modified form, to this time.

There was no military organization, no drill, and nothing but an ignorant mass or rabble of men, ill provided with weapons, and each fighting "on his own hook." There was always, of course, immense loss of life, more from starvation and fever than from wounds in battle. The raids, which were very frequent between the tribes, were started for purposes of plunder, the theft of cattle, and the capture of slaves, either for purposes of lust or for sale —not infrequently for both.

For the most part, during the 17th and 18th centuries, the Sàkalàva, who were divided into two great tribes,—the Northern and Southern Sàkalàva,—seem to have been in the ascendancy, and to have controlled, though with many revolts, the tribes of the forests and the highlands. The yoke they imposed was a heavy one, and the Hovas and Betsileos were restless under it; but their conquerors treated them with contempt, calling them dogs, outcasts, and denying that they were true Malagasy.

The Hovas and Betsileos were at this time unknown to the outside world. Neither the Portuguese, the French, the Dutch, nor the English had ever heard of them except in terms of contempt. They were the dogs, the slaves of the Sàkalàvas; of less account than the Bètanimena, the Betsimisaraka, the Bàra, or the Anòsy. But in 1785 an *Andrian*, or chief, of the Hovas, called Impoinimerina (the desire of Imerina), succeeded in uniting the divided clans of the province of Imerina under his own authority, and by his superior abilities and diplomacy gained to his cause several of the smaller adjacent tribes; but while he proceeded to subdue most of the forest tribes, he was yet compelled to pay tribute to the Sàkalàva of the western coast. Between 1808 and 1810 he was attacked with a mortal sickness, and summoned home his son Radama, born in 1792 and trained in part by Arab teachers. This young chief, not over 17 years of age, at his father's death was proclaimed as Radama, King of the Hovas.

Radama was a very remarkable man. He had no faith in the idols of his countrymen, but he was ambitious, intelligent, capable of reading character, shrewd and politic, and possessed of that magnetic power over men which would compel them to do his will. He had in the Hovas a people who were thoroughly fitted for his purpose, obedient, teachable, and capable of being made good soldiers. In some way he had provided them with a considerable quantity of firearms. It was his purpose from the day he ascended the throne to throw off the yoke of the Sàkalàvas, and become King of Madagascar. He knew that for this purpose he must have a very large army, well trained in European tactics and discipline, and supplied with European arms and ammunition. Great Britain was at war with France in all parts of the world; and in 1810 her squadrons captured the two islands Mauritius or the Isle of France, and Bourbon (afterwards called Rèunion). Mauritius had been actively engaged in commerce, and the French settlements or trading-posts in Madagascar had been placed under the control of the French commandant, or governor of Mauritius, and were known as dependencies of the Mauritius government. The surrender of these two islands to Great Britain involved also that of the dependencies in Madagascar, of which there were but two, Tamatave and Foule Point.

The French were not disposed, however, to give up their claims on Madagascar, and a long controversy, involving much treachery on the part of some of the coast chiefs, ensued. The new governor of the Mauritius, Sir Robert Farquhar, was exceedingly hostile to the slave-trade, of which Madagascar had been the chief seat in the Indian Ocean; and he sought, in this surrender of the French power in Madagascar, to strike a crushing blow at the slave-trade there, of which the French had been the strong supporters. Learning of the increasing power of the Hovas and the ability of their king, Radama, he resolved to make a treaty with him, as the representative of the Malagasy, by which, under terms favorable to both parties, the slave-trade in Madagascar should be broken up. The time was favorable, for Radama needed the help which the English Government could give him, and was ready to make large concessions to obtain it. There were many difficulties in the way of the negotiation. Radama wished to be recognized as King of Madagascar, yet it was only by receiving arms and money by means of this treaty that he could conquer the formidable tribes to which he was now paying tribute. He hoped, also, that by reducing the language to writing, educating his people, and giving his soldiers military instruction, he should be able to retain the ascendency over the whole island, which he was endeavoring to acquire. Sir Robert Farquhar believed that Radama would soon become sovereign of Madagascar, and while he knew the craftiness and treachery of most savage chiefs, he felt satisfied that the young king would keep faith with him. The great objects he sought to gain were the breaking up of the slave-trade, the securing of the commerce of the island to England, the elevation of these savages to civilization, education, and a better life; and the introduction of Christianity among a people wholly given over to vice. At the same time he knew that if this treaty was made with Radama alone it would be repudiated by some or all of the coast tribes, who together were possibly stronger than Radama. Sir Robert Farquhar sent Captain Le Sage and Mr. Hastie to Antananarivo, the Hova capital, to negotiate the terms of the treaty; and on January 14th, 1817, Captain Le Sage took the oath of blood with Radama; and the treaty between them was concluded on the 4th of February, in which it was stipulated that Radama should cause the cessation and extinction of the export slave-trade throughout the island, either by himself or parties under his control, any aiding or abetting in such sale in any way being punishable by the reduction of the person or persons so offending to slavery themselves. In consideration of this concession on the part of Radama, the commissioners on the part of the Governor of Mauritius and of the King of England agreed to pay to Radama yearly $1,000 in gold, $1,000 in silver, 100 barrels of powder, 100 English muskets, 400 uniforms, a complete uniform for the king, swords and belts, two horses, etc., etc. Further it was stipulated that officers should be sent for the instruction of the Malagasy troops in military tactics; that there should be no attacks made on the Sultan of the Comoro Islands; that the language should be reduced to writing, and that schools should be established.

Sir Robert Farquhar did not deem it safe to conclude definitively the treaty until he had secured the acquiescence of other chiefs who were partially independent of Radama. Accordingly he instructed his agent Mr. Pye to bring to Tamatave, if possible, two younger brothers of Radama, one of them heir-presumptive; the two chiefs of the Bètsimisaraka (one a French half-breed, who called himself King of Tamatave), two of the southern chiefs, a son of one of the chiefs of the Bètanimèna, and Radama's two chief ministers, and reconciling them with Radama, to have the treaty signed and approved by all. This was accomplished after many delays, October 23d, 1817, and Captain Stanfell and Mr. T. R. Pye signed on the part of Sir Robert Farquhar; and Mr. James Hastie, as agent, went to Antananarivo and continued to instruct the young princes and aid in enforcing the treaty for preventing the exportation of slaves. Many untoward circumstances, including the treachery of some of the parties and the stupidity of others, delayed the ratification of this treaty until October 11th, 1820.

Meanwhile, early in 1818, without waiting for the final ratification of the treaty, the LONDON MISSIONARY SOCIETY sent two missionaries, Rev. S. Bevan and D. Jones, with their families, as their first missionaries to Madagascar. They had attempted to plant a mission there in 1811, but their missionary, Dr. Vanderkemp, had died on his way from the Cape of Good Hope to Mauritius. Messrs. Bevan and Jones reached Port Louis (Mauritius) in July, 1818, and landed at Tamatave August 18th, leaving their families in Mauritius. They were kindly received by some of the chiefs, and collected together a number of children, whom they taught, and made some studies in regard to the language. About October 1st they revisited Port Louis, but soon returned with their families. Soon after landing on the coast, where a station was established at Andovoranto, all were attacked with the deadly Madagascar fever, and before two months had passed Mr. Jones was the sole survivor of the two families. In April he attempted to resume his labors, but frequent relapses rendered it necessary for him to return to Mauritius in July. He remained there for fourteen months, but when the troubles with Radama had been adjusted and Mr. Hastie was about to return to Antananarivo, Mr. Jones accompanied him, Sir Robert Farquhar doing all in his power to secure for him a favorable reception. He arrived there October 4th, 1820. King Radama welcomed him cordially, and gave the fullest permission for English Protestant missionaries to settle at his capital; and by his personal kindness to Mr. Jones showed his people how desirous he was that they should be instructed. On the 8th of December, 1820, the first school was opened at Antananarivo. The London Missionary Society, awake to their great opportunity, sent forward their missionaries, teachers, and artisans as rapidly as practicable, and very soon the mission work was actively prosecuted in all directions. The first work, of course, was the acquisition of the language and its reduction to writing; then, in their schools, the children were taught the written language, and elementary instruction by means of it. The missionary teachers were preparing books in the Malagasy language; the artisans were teaching the people carpentry, weaving, tanning, and blacksmith work; and a printing-press having been sent out, and fonts of Malagasy type cast in England, they were soon printing school-books and portions of the Scriptures, and instructing the young and teachable Malagasy boys in the art of printing. The missionaries were engaged in translating the Scriptures, and in preaching as soon as they could command the language. No missionaries ever worked harder, and none had more evident manifestations of the divine blessing on their labors. Necessarily, the schools held a prominent position in their work for the first few years. The king, though engaged with his army and his wars, encouraged the instruction of his people to the utmost of his power. Nearly 100 schools were established in the capital and its vicinity, and between 4,000 and 5 000 pupils of both sexes passed through them before 1828, having received the elements of a good education. The instruction in the arts and trades was also making great progress. At first it was difficult to overcome the strong prejudices of the people against foreigners and their teaching, and it was still more difficult to teach those who had been the bond-servants of sin and addicted to the grossest vices, to become temperate, chaste, pure, and Christ-like. The missionaries found, after they became able to preach, that it was necessary to have the Word of God circulated among the people as far as possible; and hence they redoubled their efforts to translate the Scriptures quickly, and have them printed and circulated, at the same time multiplying as rapidly as they could the number of readers.

A church was organized from the English residents in the capital, and though small in numbers, it was very active in Christian work; and those who understood the Malagasy tongue were encouraged to gather the young Hovas for religious instruction and singing. Two congregations of natives for Christian worship were formed in Antananarivo, and very fully attended; others were formed in villages around the capital, and two or three in Vonizongo, a district about a day's journey to the west. In January, 1828, the Gospel of St. Luke in Malagasy was put to press, and other portions of the Scriptures were printed as rapidly as they could be properly prepared. In the autumn of 1827 a permission had been received from the king allowing any to be baptized who desired to receive that rite; but though none came, there was evidence in abundance that many had abandoned their idols, and were seeking after God, and that His truth was finding an entrance into their hearts.

It was at this time, when the missionaries were beginning to feel encouraged at the great success which seemed to be within their grasp, that King Radama died, on the 27th of July, 1828. Radama was not a Christian; indeed he was a man of many and heinous faults, and his death, at the early age of thirty-six, was undoubtedly due to his excesses and self-indulgence. But he had many good traits: he was patriotic, manly, and truthful; he was far-sighted, and even his ambition led him to desire the improvement and elevation of his people. He saw that a written language, education and general intelligence, the promotion of industry, and thorough military discipline would make the Hovas superior to all adjacent tribes or nations; he had no faith in the national idols or in divination; and without any convictions of the necessity of personal religion, he was persuaded that Christianity would be

better for his people than heathenism. The loss of such a ruler, at such a time, seemed the severest blow which could be inflicted upon this infant mission; but God made it eventually the means of the greatest good. Radama had selected his nephew as his successor, if he left no son, but one of his twelve wives, by no means the favorite wife, conspired to secure the throne to herself, and succeeded. Her name was Rabodo, and she was of a family of nobles of the first rank; but she was of violent temper, utterly unscrupulous and bloodthirsty, devoted to the worship of idols, and given to all the vices of the Hovas. She ascended the throne as Ranavalona I.; and her first official act was the putting to death of all the near relatives of the late king, and all the officers who had been most attached to him. Some of these were spared, but others of the highest rank, and among them the mother and sister of Radama, and the husband of the latter, were starved to death. No one was left alive who could contest her claim to the throne. Mr. Hastie, the British resident and warm friend of the missionaries, had died at Antananarivo in 1826; but his successor, Mr. Lyall, was ordered to leave the country at a few hours' notice, and his family were subjected to gross insults. The missionaries and their followers were naturally alarmed; but though there were indications of a coming storm of persecution, it pleased God that its fury should be averted for nearly seven years, and that the new converts should be gathered into churches, and encouraged and instructed by the missionaries till they could bear up against persecution and death In 1829, '30, and '31 the queen was engaged in a controversy, and a sort of guerilla warfare with the French. Their war-ships had bombarded Tamatave, Foule Point, and Point Larrée, but had been severely repulsed at Foule Point, and the French commander and six sailors captured, beheaded, and their heads put on poles on the shore of the town. The revolution in France prevented a continuance of the war; but Queen Ranavalona, to show her brutal nature, had sent out her armies against the coast tribes north, south, and west, and at a fearful cost of the lives of her own subjects had, by deceit and trickery, caused the surrender of great numbers of the innocent inhabitants, on the promise that their lives should be spared; and then butchering the men, had taken the women and youth captives, and sold them into slavery. In 1831, '32, '33, and '34 there were about 25,000 people murdered in these raids, while more than 50,000 were captured and sold into slavery. In one district on the west coast the headmen of a clan of Sákaláva were accused of concealing arms, seized and crucified, to the number of some hundreds, the crosses surrounding the village; and some thousands of the people, whom they had tried to defend, were seized and sold as slaves. So great was the reign of terror, that the people of Vohilena, in the forest belt, escaped to the forests, and became brigands, plundering all who came that way.

During this period the queen found little time to persecute the Christians, among whom she believed there were very few natives; while she hated the missionaries, she was disposed for a time to allow them to teach in the schools, to print school-books, to prosecute scientific studies, and in other ways to improve the condition of the people. Accordingly, at the end of six months after Radama's death the missionaries were permitted to resume their labors, and the schools, the translation of the Scriptures and other books, and their printing went forward rapidly; the New Testament translation was completed, and soon after, by the aid of the British and Foreign Bible Society, its printing was commenced. Portions of the Old Testament, and particularly of the Psalms, were prepared for the press, and the translation of the whole of the Old Testament was pushed forward. Through the children in the schools, and those who had gone out from them, these portions of the Scriptures were widely circulated; and when in 1832 all the boys above thirteen years of age in the schools were drafted into the army, large quantities of these and other good books were widely circulated. In 1833 not less than 15,000 copies of parts of the Scriptures were finished, and upwards of 6,000 of them were sent out. Mr. and Mrs. Atkinson were sent home in July, 1832, on the plea that their permit to remain had expired, and Mr. Canborn in 1833; but there were about a dozen missionaries and their families left, and none of these were ordered away till 1835, when Messrs. Cameron, Freeman, Chick, and Kitching were dismissed. During these years the missionaries who were able to preach had been very active, and their labors had been greatly blessed. No native church had been formed, and no Malagasy had been baptized until 1831; but on the 22d of May of that year the queen issued a message, granting permission for the baptism of converts. Regarding this as the direct answer to prayer, the missionaries proceeded to avail themselves of it. There were many converts, and on the 29th of May, 1831, Mr. Griffiths baptized twenty, and the first native church was formed. Baptisms were almost constant, other churches were formed; and in a few months there were between one and two thousands of members of these churches. At the end of six months the permission to baptize was withdrawn in the case of those who were in the government service, and a month or two earlier the use of wine at the Communion was prohibited to the same class. About three months later, in January, 1832, these prohibitions were extended to all the people. Before 1833 the attempt was made to divest the education given in the schools of any religious character, and those who had been baptized were put into inferior positions. The queen was proceeding cautiously, but it was evident that a decided reactionary policy had commenced. Liberty to preach and print still remained, and great exertions were made to prepare a large number of books for circulation, and to instruct the increasing congregations which pressed forward to hear the Word of God. The Christian soldiers, who had formed part of the army of the queen, had carried their portions of the Scriptures with them, and all over the island little groups were learning to read, meeting together for worship, and trusting in Christ for salvation. The more promising of the converts were seeking for instruction to enable them to preach Christ to their countrymen. In June, 1834, the missionaries, though looking forward to the rapid approach of the storm of persecution, were still able to praise God that so many were savingly converted and that the work was going forward with such power. In July, 1834, the queen forbade any native except those in the government service to learn to read or write; it was evident that still greater trials were in store for the Christians. This and other proclamations indicated that the whole force of the queen's displeasure was to be visited on the native Christians; and a few who, from unworthy motives, had manifested some friendship for the Christians (though, to their honor be it said, not one of those who had received baptism), began to withdraw from them, and associate with the heathen portions of the community.

Ratsimanisa, who had been the commander-in-chief of the army, and about this time became prime-minister to the queen, was the chief persecutor, and prompted her to greater cruelties than even her brutal nature demanded. It was clear to him that if Christianity was not arrested the idolatry of the country would be overturned, and the customs of their ancestors forgotten; and in January, 1835, at his instigation, a formal accusation was made against the Christians, before the chief judges of the Hovas, and the following charges were preferred: 1st. They despise the idols; 2d. They are always praying; 3d. They will not swear, but merely affirm; 4th. Their women are chaste; 5th. They are of one mind with regard to their religion; 6th. They observe the Sabbath as a sacred day. It seems that their enemies could allege nothing against them, "except it were concerning the law of their God."

The queen formed the opinion that their despising the idols of their fathers, and ceasing to pray to the royal ancestors by whom the kingdom had been founded, would surely lead them in time to despise her, and treat her, their living sovereign, with contempt, reserving all their reverence and love for the Lord Christ. Thus jealousy was added to her hostility to Christianity.

The crisis which came so suddenly was said to have been brought about by the following incident: An influential chief appeared before the queen, and requested that a bright and sharp spear might be brought, saying "that he could not but see with grief the dishonor done, both to the idols and the memory of the queen's predecessors, by the doctrines of the foreigners, and how the ancient customs were being destroyed, and the new faith was spreading on every hand; that this would soon be followed by the invasion of Madagascar by the Europeans; and as he would rather die than see his sovereign and country so disgraced, he asked for a spear to pierce his heart before that evil day came."

It is said that the queen was so affected with grief and rage that she remained silent for a considerable time, and then vowed that she would put a stop to Christianity if it cost the life of every Christian on the island. She issued an order on the 15th of February, 1835, for a grand *kabary* (a mass-meeting of the people), to assemble on Sunday, the 1st of March, on the plain of Mahamasina, west of the capital, and great preparations were made for the assembly. On the same day (February 15th), all the "heads of hundreds" were assembled on the same plain, where the judges met them, and conveyed the queen's command that they should forthwith summon all who were able to walk—men, women, children, and slaves—to attend the kabary to be held that day fortnight, on the 1st of March. None were to remain at home in Imerina except one individual in each house, to take charge of the property. On the 26th of February several officers, headed by Ratsimanisa, entered the chapel at Ambatonakanga in the capital and read a letter from the queen addressed to the missionaries, forbidding religious worship, the rite of baptism, and the assembling of a society, to her subjects. The Europeans were permitted to follow their own customs and religious practices, but they could not be allowed to teach them to the subjects of Ranavalona. They would be allowed to teach such arts and sciences as would be beneficial to her subjects, but nothing beyond these.

At the great kabary of March 1st there was firing of cannon and musketry, and the soldiers surrounded the multitude to inspire them with terror, and then the principal judge addressed the kabary, delivering a long message from the queen, calling upon all who had been baptized, all who had worshipped and kept the Sabbath, or had entered into a Christian society, to come forward and accuse themselves, and confess such crimes, under pain of death. Ratsimanisa repeated the substance of the queen's royal message, and some of the head men replied to it with servility. Others seemed reluctant to make reply; when Rainiharo, one of the queen's chief officers, and for twenty-five years a prime-minister, the bitterest of persecutors, said that unless the guilty came forward within a month to accuse themselves, the officers and judges would cut off their heads. The queen reduced the time for confession to a week. About two thousand confessed, and on the 9th of March, 1835, she pronounced sentence on them. The twelve senior teachers were reduced in rank, and four hundred of the officers of the army were degraded, some of them to the condition of common soldiers. Among the people, those who did not hold offices under the government were fined according to the extent to which they had avowed their attachment to Christianity. There were about 1,600 of these. There was no shedding of blood at this time; but as an answer to the earnest petition of the missionaries and teachers to be permitted to teach and preach under certain restrictions, the queen ordered that any Malagasy who was seen in company with any of the missionaries should be arrested and put in chains.* All portions of the Scriptures and other religious books were ordered to be given up, under the severest penalties; but many were concealed, and gave comfort to the persecuted ones in after years. All religious meetings were prohibited, and spies commissioned to hunt the Christians and their forbidden books.

In June and August Messrs. Cameron, Freeman, Chick, and Kitching left Madagascar by order of the queen, but Rev. Messrs. D. Johns and E. Baker remained to give what comfort and help they could to the little band of faithful disciples. They also determined to complete the translation and printing of the entire Scriptures and of the "Pilgrim's Progress." Their Malagasy printers and compositors had been compelled to leave them, but they toiled on till they had completed both books, and printed an edi-

tion of about one thousand copies, which were soon absorbed by the Christians, who concealed them, as far as possible, from the government spies. Probably the larger part were eventually confiscated, but a considerable number came to light after Ranavalona's death. Being again ordered to leave the island, Messrs. Johns and Baker departed in July, 1836, but not till they had bid the converts an affectionate farewell, preaching at great risk in the old chapel at Ambatonakanga from the text, "Lord, save us! we perish." They retreated to Mauritius, but Mr. Johns, at least, visited the island more than once, and in 1840 penetrated to the capital, where he found to his sorrow that many of the disciples had been called to suffer martyrdom, while nine at the time of his visit were put to death at Ambohipotsy. More than two hundred Christians were scattered over the country, many of them in chains, others hiding from their enemies, but all "destitute, afflicted, tormented," yet full of faith and trust in God, "enduring as seeing Him who is invisible" to mortal eyes. Mr. Johns made great efforts to secure the escape of some of these to Nòsy Bè, and thence to Mauritius. A few did escape, but the strict watch kept up by the queen rendered it almost impossible for them to evade her spies. In 1843 Mr. Johns, who had again visited Nòsy-Bè on one of these errands of mercy, succumbed to the fever, and died a martyr to his zeal for the rescue of these Malagasy converts.

Greatly to the astonishment of Queen Ranavalona, her plan for extinguishing Christianity in Madagascar had signally failed. She had closed the schools; prohibited all religious meetings; sent away all the missionaries; confiscated all the portions of Scriptures and religious books she could find by her spies; degraded, fined, and whipped the Christians, and threatened them with severer punishments; and yet the number of Christians was increasing every day, and quietly but persistently all her decrees were set at naught. She determined upon severer measures, for she had sworn a solemn oath to root out Christianity if she had to put every Christian to death.

Early in 1836 Rafaravavy, a woman of high rank, was accused of Christianity, and was condemned to death; but the queen, being alarmed by a great fire in the capital, spared her life but fined her heavily.

The queen's bloody wars and reckless disregard of the lives of her soldiers, who perished by tens of thousands, had led to a famine and to uprising in some portions of Imerina; these she put down with a strong hand, and if those accused were Christians, there was no mercy for them. In the eight months following Messrs. Johns' and Baker's departure in July, 1836, 1,016 persons were put to death in the capital on various charges, 900 of them having been declared guilty by the *tangena* ordeal, and either dying from the poison or being speared, 56 being burned to death, and 60 killed by crucifixion or other means. That a considerable number of these were Christians was certain; but the avowed executions for professing Christianity did not begin till August, 1837, when a prayer-meeting was discovered and broken up, those who had attended it arrested and punished: one of these, a young woman named Rasalama, one of the earliest converts, who had been baptized by Mr. Griffiths, was reserved

---

* The Malagasy punishment of putting an accused person in chains was one of great severity: the prisoner had bands or collars of iron around his neck, waist, and ankles, the latter being sometimes bound together. These bands were connected together by heavy bars of iron, so that sitting was impossible, locomotion difficult, and the torture was constant.

for death by the queen. She was first chained in the way to produce the utmost torture, and the next morning led to the place of execution at Ambòhipòtsy, where, while praying that the Lord would receive her spirit and that this sin might not be laid to the charge of her murderers, she was thrust through by the fatal spear, and her body left to be devoured by the wild dogs. In 1837 Rafaralahy, a young but devoted Christian man, suffered martyrdom on the same spot, and with the same holy confidence and joy. The storm of persecution now increased in violence, and a large number of Christians were apprehended and condemned to death. Among the number were six (four men and two women, one of the latter being Rafaravavy, already mentioned), who escaped from the island and reached England. Most of those who were condemned suffered death by the spear. Many were sentenced to take the *tangena* ordeal, and being generally declared guilty, were speared, if they did not die first from the poison. Many were deprived of their honors and rank, and if in the army, whatever their rank, were degraded to the position of common soldiers. Heavy fines were exacted from others; many were sold into perpetual slavery, and some were sent to the most unhealthy portions of the coast to die from the fatal marsh fevers.

There were many hundreds of these sufferers for Christ's sake, but none of them turned back to idols, or to the vile life of the heathen; and what was especially astonishing to the queen, there were scores of adherents to the new faith for every one whom she put to death. The persecution raged fiercely in 1839, 1840, 1841, and 1842.

The years from 1843 to 1848 were marked by a decided lull in the persecution. The queen was in difficulties with both England and France, and her attention was diverted from the Christians by the incidents of the war. In this lull of the persecuting spirit the gospel made great progress. The queen's son, Rakòto (afterward Radama II.), took a great interest in the Christians, and it is said professed conversion; Prince Ramonja, his cousin, was already an active Christian, and had suffered for the faith, and among others of noble rank the son of Rainiharo, the prime-minister of the queen, and the most violent persecutor among the Hovas, had joined the Christians. The native preachers preached and baptized almost openly in the suburbs of the capital, and very many were added to the churches. Another fiery baptism came in the early months of 1849. The queen finding that her realm was becoming largely Christian in spite of her previous efforts, resolved now to try still severer means of fulfilling her vow. On the 28th of March, 1849, nineteen Christians, all of them of excellent families and four of them at least from the highest nobles, were condemned to die for the crime of being Christians. Fifteen were to be hurled over the cliffs at Ampàmarìnana, a perpendicular wall of rock 159 feet high, and with a rocky ravine or cañon at the bottom. This is now known as the Rock of Hurling of Antananarivo. The queen looked down from her palace windows and saw her subjects dashed to pieces because they were Christians. The idols were taken to the place of execution, and each victim was lowered by a rope a little way over the precipice, and the demand made, "Will you

worship this god? or will you cease to pray to Christ?" The answer in each case was an emphatic "No!" and the rope was cut, and the martyrs, often singing as they went, were hurled down upon the rocks below. Only one of the condemned was spared—a young girl of fifteen, a relative and favorite of the queen, who finding her firm caused her to be taken away and sent to a distant village on the charge that she was insane. This noble girl, Raviva by name, lived to found a large Christian church in the place where she was exiled, and to bring her father and her relatives to Christ. Mr. Ellis saw her in 1862.

Four of the nineteen who were condemned to death that day were andrians or nobles of the highest rank, and as, by the Hova custom, their blood could not be shed, the queen resolved to put them to death by burning them at the stake. The sentence was executed at Faravòhitra, a level summit of the northern ridge of hills of the city, just where it begins to slope down to the great plain. Of these four, two were husband and wife, the latter about to become a mother. They walked calmly to the place of execution, singing the sweet Malagasy hymns which had been their joy in the past and were their solace now. Arrived at the place they meekly surrendered themselves to be fastened to the stakes. Amid a terrific storm of rain and lightning the fires were kindled and mounted higher and higher, but no cry of pain proceeded from the funeral pyres, but only songs of praise, and these prayers, recorded by a faithful disciple who witnessed their martyrdom: "O Lord, receive our spirits; for Thy love to us has caused this to come to us; but, O Lord! lay not this sin to the charge of our rulers." The Christian lady had the pangs of maternity added to the terrors of the flame, but she uttered no cry of anguish even when the brutal executioner with his spear thrust the new-born babe back into the flames. When their bodies were consumed the bodies of those who had been hurled over the cliff at Ampàmarìnana, or such portions of them as had not been devoured by the wild dogs, were brought to Faravòhitra and burned in the same fires which had consumed the other martyrs.

This was only the beginning. The queen's rage increased every day, and she was constantly inventing some new torture. Her prime-minister, Rainiharo, was equally ferocious with his mistress as a persecutor—both had sons who were converts, or at least fearless advocates of the Christians. They resorted to crucifixion, and fearing lest the agony of this form of death should not be sufficient, when they were nearly dead with hunger and thirst and exhaustion, fires were lighted under the crosses, and these and the martyrs were consumed together. At Fiadàna, a plain adjacent to the capital, scores of victims were put to death by stoning, and the horrors of this form of death as committed by Malagasy hands were said to have exceeded all others. The friends of those put to death at Fiadàna stole forth at night, and at the imminent peril of their lives carried off for interment all that could be collected of their remains.

Every possible indignity was inflicted upon those who were condemned to death. These executions were continued till hundreds had perished. In addition to those who endured the extreme penalty of death by these various modes of destruction, a far larger number suffered in other ways, and in very many cases their sufferings terminated in death or helplessness. Thirty-seven preachers, with their wives and families, were consigned to a life of irredeemable slavery. The property of those who were sold into slavery, as well as of those who were executed, was allowed to become the prey of the rabble, who were thus encouraged to become spies. Over 100 were flogged terribly with whips, and then sentenced to work in chains for life. Many who had property were heavily fined, and the nobles who had professed Christianity were not only deprived of their rank, but were forced to the hardest and most menial labor. Officers of the army were reduced to the ranks and condemned to severe labor in building a large stone house as a government factory, and were branded with the words *Tsi-huhárana,*—" That which is not to be imitated,"—to prevent others from following their example. "Altogether, in the early spring of 1849," says the Rev. E. Prout, one of the missionaries of the London Missionary Society, " 1,900, according to the lowest estimate, but more probably upwards of 2,000, were thus severely punished and tortured because they had either professed or favored the religion of Jesus."

This cruel persecution went on for years. The judges were incessantly occupied with examinations, and the least act or word, the vaguest suspicion, exposed all, from the highest to the lowest, to be dragged before them. The country was scoured in all directions by the spies of the queen and the idol-keepers. Domiciliary visits were of daily, often of hourly, recurrence, and slaves—usually an affectionate class of the inhabitants—watched their owners' every movement, and, for the first time, found themselves listened to in a court of justice. Numbers fled to the mountains, or hid themselves in the depths of the neighboring forests, eking out a scanty subsistence, until want and exposure put an end to their lives. Others constructed hiding-places in their own houses, in their rice-pits, and on their own farms, and were there tended and supplied with food by their relatives for years, reappearing long after they had been accounted dead.

The four principal places of execution, Ambohipotsy, Ampàmarinana, Ambàtonakànga, and Faravòhitra, have, since the queen's death, been made the sites of four memorial churches of stone, capable of seating about one thousand worshippers. The money for erecting these was furnished by English friends of the Malagasy Christians, but the Christians have themselves erected excellent and commodious churches on other sites, where the blood of the martyrs was shed. All the testimony, both heathen and Christian, shows that not only was there no recantation among these converts to Christianity, many of whom were illiterate and but recently brought to Christ, but that they bore the gross indignities, and the cruel and terrible deaths to which they were subjected, with quiet heroism and unfaltering trust in God. "Let us go and see how these Christians behave; they are said not to be afraid to die," were the words of some of the principal officers of the royal household. The same officers said afterward, "We were near, and saw all that took place. The Christians were not afraid, and did not recant."

Their fortitude and courage produced a deep impression on the minds of the people. The cruelty of the queen was beginning to defeat its own purpose. The heathen saw that there was a power in the Christian religion which overcame all earthly opposition, and that the Christians were the most truly loyal of all the queen's subjects. Many felt and said: "This is the finger of God; there must be something divine in this belief;" and they were led to become Christians notwithstanding the peril to which it exposed them.

This persecution continued with great fury till 1852, when the death of Rainihàro, the prime-minister (who had been even more bitter in his persecuting spirit than the queen herself); the influence of the young prince, which was exerted in favor of Christianity; and of his cousin Ramonjà, who was an active Christian—were instrumental in producing greater toleration. But the discovery of a plot to dethrone the queen, instigated by a French adventurer, and maliciously charged against the Christians, furnished a pretext for the commencement of a new and still more bloody persecution by the queen in 1857.

During this period of comparative quiet, Rev. William Ellis, Foreign Secretary of the London Missionary Society, made three visits to Madagascar, in the hope of bringing comfort to the suffering, faithful disciples in Imerina, in 1853, 1854, and 1856. He reached Tamatave and other towns on the east coast in 1853 and 1854, and Antánanarivo in 1855. Again in March, 1856, he visited the island. In these visits he was able to cheer and comfort many of the Christians, to distribute many copies of the Malagasy New Testament, and in his third visit to make the acquaintance of the young Prince Rakoto (later Radàma II.), of whom he formed a high opinion. He was also presented to the queen, who treated him courteously, but coldly. He returned to England in March, 1857, and three months later, the last great persecution was commenced. On the 3d of July, 1857, the population of the capital were driven from their homes by the soldiers to a great kabary or National Assembly. The queen announced her determination to stamp out Christianity. All suspected persons were imprisoned, and daily kabarys (assemblies) were held in the city and its neighborhood to denounce the Christians. A few days after the first great assembly, twenty-one were stoned and then beheaded; many others suffered at the "Rock of Hurling;" and it was believed that this was the most fatal of all the persecutions. A large number were sentenced to the tangena ordeal, by which many died, and many more were put in chains and reduced to slavery. This persecution was maintained for nearly three years. But deliverance was now at hand. On the 15th of August, 1861, the queen died. She had reigned thirty-three years, and twenty-five of those years had been marked by cruel persecution of the saints of God, and vain efforts to root out Christianity from the island. The result had been that those who were persecuted "went everywhere, preaching the Word." Christian life had attained a depth, power, and reality which would have been impossible in a time of ease and prosperity. All that an absolute sovereign, backed by a powerful government and a numerous army, could do to dislodge Christianity from the country had been done. Several thousands had been put to death in various ways. Yet the little company of believing men and women left by their English pastors and teachers, as sheep without a shepherd, in 1836, had multiplied at least twenty-fold in 1861, and had attained to a fulness of faith and love, which brought their heathen fellow-country-men to Christ more surely than any preaching could do. They had studied the Word of God very faithfully, and, like Paul, they knew in whom they had believed. Their patient trust in God, their forgiving spirit, had often melted the hearts of their persecutors. Their purity of life and morals was attested by their enemies; their religion was their only crime. On the 18th of August the Prince Rakòto, the son of Ranavalona I., succeeded his mother with the title of Radama II. Mr. Ellis says: " The sun did not set on the day on which Radama II. became King of Madagascar before he had proclaimed equal protection to all its inhabitants, and declared that every man was free to worship God according to the dictates of his own conscience, without fear or danger." Prison doors were opened, the fetters were knocked off from the prisoners, messengers were dispatched to the remote and pestilential districts, to which many of the Christians had been banished, to save alive those who had not already perished from disease and exhaustion, to remove the heavy and cruel chains they had worn so long, and to set free those who had been consigned to hopeless slavery. The exiles hastened home. Men and women, wan and wasted with suffering and want, reappeared in the city, to the astonishment of their neighbors, who had deemed them long since dead, and to the grateful joy of their friends. The long-desired jubilee had come, and gladness and rejoicing everywhere prevailed; while even the heathen, who had sympathized with the Christians in their sufferings, now congratulated them on their deliverance.

Within a month after the queen's decease eleven houses were opened for the worship of God in the capital and great numbers in the adjacent country, and churches were being erected everywhere, and filled Sabbath after Sabbath with rejoicing worshippers. Within a very few years the memorial churches were erected, which rendered Antananarìvo famous alike for its churches and palaces.

Radama II. invited the missionaries of the London Missionary Society, and especially his friend Rev. William Ellis, to return. Mr. Ellis reached the capital in June, 1862, and was followed in August by three ordained ministers, a medical missionary, a teacher and a printer, who were all soon busy resuming the work laid down in 1836. Christianity had triumphed. The 2,000 adherents to the Christian cause who then braved the rage of the persecuting queen had become a host of 40,000, only about one fifth of them baptized believers, but all witnesses for Christ, and ready to suffer and die for Him. In this jubilee of deliverance many were daily added to the churches. Back of these were more than 100,000 who, though not believers, had rejected idols and were ready to embrace Christianity. Provision was made as rapidly as possible for reopening the schools, and the king gave his sanction and aid, for he desired that the children should be educated, and that the nation should make progress. The

printing was also actively resumed, and this was of great service to the king.

Radama II. was a man of fair abilities, and of a kindly and amiable disposition. He had, in the later years of his mother's life, been very heartily in sympathy with the Christians, and had boldly defended them, sometimes at the peril of his own life. He had never united with any of the churches, nor did he profess to be a Christian after he came to the throne, though he had often said he hoped to become one. His earliest proclamations were very favorable to Christianity, giving perfect religious freedom to all, and inviting religious teachers to come to the country. He also invited traders and foreigners to come to the island and establish trade there. He also abolished all export and import duties. The immediate result of this was that the cheap, vile rum of the Mauritius was poured into the island in immense quantities, and the great trade in bullocks and other commodities was paid for in this horrible stuff. The natives, especially of the coast tribes, who had previously been addicted to the use of their own rum, which was more costly, now became utterly besotted and ruined, both in body and estate. He made many other decrees which were wise and good. He restored the lands and property to the Christians which had been confiscated by his mother's orders. He diminished very greatly the *fanompòana* or unrequited service, which had been exacted from the common people by the government or nobles, and set the example of paying for labor in money. He set free all the captives of the Betsileo, Sàkalava, and other tribes which his mother had raided; and not only restored their property so far as he could, but sent back the bones of those who had perished. He endeavored to make treaties with foreign nations, and to secure for his people the advantages of foreign inventions.

But with these good laws and decrees he made many bad ones, which worked great injury to himself and his country. He became very intimate with a wily and unscrupulous French adventurer named Lambert, the same one who had conspired against his mother, who led him into intemperance and other vices, that he might have more power over him. While intoxicated, the king conceded to Lambert over one third of the arable lands of the island, the privilege of working all its mines, and of conducting manufactures, and of bringing in as many Jesuits as he pleased. These concessions were all violations of the long-established "customs" of the Hova rulers, but Lambert induced him to sign contracts for them, without any compensation. He had also surrounded himself with young men, many of them heathen, and of dissolute habits, with whom he engaged in gross excesses, and who controlled the appointments to offices, and really governed the realm. These young favorites were called the *Mènamàso*. At their prompting, and in the interest of the idol-keepers, he promulgated a decree that all differences of opinion of individuals or of villages and towns, might be settled by open battle between the parties, and that the successful party should not be called to account for any deaths which might result. This was really opening the way to civil war, and the wiser nobles and leaders would not permit this law to go into effect, nor the Mènamáso to continue to rule. The most powerful of the nobles went to the king and, on their knees, begged him to revoke this decree and give up the Mènamáso. He obstinately refused to do either; a revolution ensued; the Mènamáso were secured, and most of them put to death; and the king, still continuing obstinate, was strangled. No other deaths and no riots ensued, and the next day the queen, Rabòdo, was proclaimed as a constitutional sovereign, ruling in connection with the body of nobles and the heads of the people. The new queen was called to the throne as Rasoherina. The constitutional provisions were few and simple, but very effective. These are samples: 1. "The sovereign shall not drink spirituous liquors." 2. "Perfect freedom and protection is guaranteed to all foreigners who are obedient to the laws of the country." 3. "Friendly relations are to be maintained with all other nations." 4. "Protection and liberty to worship, teach, and promote Christianity are secured to the native Christians as well as to foreigners." 5. "The sovereign or any other person may not sell to foreigners any lands, or mines, or waterfalls." This last was the revival of an old law.

Queen Rasoherina was not a Christian, but an idolater; but she was a woman of good sense and integrity, and she carried out, in perfect good faith, the agreement she had made, and even added many favors to the Christians. She had difficulties at first with the Sàkalàvas and some of the other tribes, who would not believe that Radama II. was dead; later she had troubles with Lambert, who insisted on his concession, and threatened to cause the French squadron to bombard Tamatave unless it was yielded. He was finally quieted by the payment of $240,000 by the Hova government. She was also greatly annoyed by the Jesuit priests, who were really French spies. They demanded sites for churches, and the recognition of their schools, and were given to intruding into the palace, and administering their ritual and rites, without asking anybody's permission. They claimed to have crowned Radama II., and when Queen Rasoherina was dying, and had been for many hours unconscious, to have administered extreme unction and ushered her, all unknown to herself, into heaven as a devout Catholic queen. She found it necessary to depose her first prime-minister for intemperance, and replaced him by his brother, Rainilaiarivony, who became later distinguished as the ablest of Oriental statesmen.

But in all her relations with the missionaries and Christians she was a good and just ruler, and during her reign the churches prospered, and the mission work went on very satisfactorily. From 1864 to 1866, the Society for the Propagation of the Gospel had planted some missions at Tamatave and at Foule Point, but owing to the climate did not for some time meet with great success, and after the withdrawal of the Church Missionary Society from the coast in 1874 they transferred their headquarters to the capital, though still maintaining a mission at Tamatave and its vicinity, and going forward with the work in Betsileo. They now have a bishop at the capital. The Church Missionary Society, after many misfortunes, established a mission at Andevorànto, 70 miles south of Tamatave, and in 1868 extended their labors into the Betsileo province.

Their missions in Madagascar were transferred to the S. P. G. in 1874. There are more than 10,000 adherents in these combined missions, and 112 native preachers and teachers. The Society of Friends, both of England and America, established schools and labored zealously with the missionaries of the London Missionary Society from 1867, and soon established a printing establishment. They have many schools, and are doing a great and good work. The Norwegian Missionary Society commenced their labors in 1867 at Bìtàfo, in North Betsileo. Their work here has been productive of excellent results. They had in 1888 23 stations, including several among the Sàkalàva of the west coast, established in 1874, but not very successful; and three established in 1888 among the Tanála and Anòsy of the southeast coast, which are promising. They have more than 20,000 adherents, and 304 schools with nearly 33,000 scholars.

The last days of Queen Rasoherina were darkened by a conspiracy and insurrection, headed by the ex-prime-minister, Rainivonina-hitriàniony, to place a young Christian king on the throne, with himself as his prime-minister. The scheme failed signally, and the conspirators were arrested and put in irons. Queen Rasoherina died April 1st, 1868. On the 2d of April, 1868, Ramoma, a niece or cousin of the late queen, was proclaimed Queen of Madagascar under the title of Ranavàlona II. On this occasion, for the first time in the history of Madagascar, no idols were brought forth to greet the new queen as she stood before the people on the balcony of the great palace. The popular leaders of the Malagasy were shrewd enough to see that the attempted revolution after the death of Radama II. had partly failed because it had not gone far enough, and that if they would retain their position, and make Madagascar a real and permanent power among the eastern nations, the reform must go forward, and Christianity must be recognized as a real power in the state, and its government and policy must be changed with that end in view. The prime-minister, Rainilaiàrivony, a man of extraordinary ability, who was at the head of this movement, was not, probably, at that time a Christian, though he had been for years a student of the Scriptures. One after another, changes were made, and it soon became understood that Madagascar was to be a Christian kingdom, and that Ranavalona II. was to be the first Christian queen of the island. On the 3d of September, 1868, the coronation (literally the *fischoina*, or "ceremony of showing"), the first public occasion when the sovereign showed herself to the people, took place. It was celebrated with great pomp and ceremony: the royal canopy was emblazoned with Scripture texts, and a copy of the Malagasy Scriptures, elegantly bound, was placed conspicuously by her side under the canopy, and on her return to the palace prayers were offered by one of the native pastors. The next month the queen, the prime-minister, and the household of the palace met together for Christian worship, and this practice was maintained daily during her whole reign. On the 19th of February, 1869, Ranavalona II., following the example of former queens, was married to the prime-minister, Rainilaiàrivòny. It was in their case a love-match; he had been converted since her accession to the throne. Two days later, after a very careful and thorough examination, the queen and prime-minister were baptized and received into the palace church by Andrìambèlo, one of the most eloquent and devoted of the native pastors. It was the custom with each sovereign of Madagascar to erect at the beginning of the reign some stately building, usually a palace, in the royal enclosure. Queen Ranavalona II. commenced the erection of a stone church in the palace enclosure in July, 1869.

The idol-keepers and the idol-worshippers of Imerina saw that the power would soon pass out of their hands, and they were enraged. Their anger was increased by the notice given them that they were degraded from their rank as nobles, and would be compelled henceforth to render the *fanìmpoìna* or forced government service. The principal idol-keepers came to the palace and demanded that the queen should return to the worship of her ancestors: when this was refused, they declared that the idol had medicine that killed. The language was treasonable, and after a hasty consultation a deputation of the chief officers of the government was sent to Ambòhimànambòla, the place where the national idols were kept, to burn them; the queen replying meanwhile to the idol-keepers at the gate: "I will burn all the idols of my ancestors; but as to yours, they are your concern." They were burned on the 8th of September, 1869, in the presence of many witnesses. On the following day officers were despatched to destroy the royal idols in other parts of the country; the people followed the example of the queen, though with many apprehensions of evil and disaster, and the greater part of the idols were destroyed.

In a few days requests came from all parts of the island: "You have destroyed our gods, and we know not how to worship according to the new religion; send us teachers." So many requests of this sort came to the prime-minister that he called the missionaries together, and after deliberation 126 teachers were sent out, all selected by the missionaries of the London Missionary Society; the government released them from the forced government service, and the mission guaranteed their support.

Thus was the final blow struck which insured the supremacy of Christianity in the island of Madagascar. Fifty years before, they were in the darkest depths of heathenism; forty years before, there was not a native Christian among the millions of the Malagasy; now, there were probably 50,000 communicants, 150,000 adherents, many thousand scholars in the schools, and a population of at least 1,500,000 asking for Christian instruction. On the borders, among the Sàkalàva, the Bàra, the Betanimèna, the Betsìmisaràka, and many of the smaller tribes, and even among the Betsileo and Antsihànaka, darkness yet reigned, and idolatry, though waning, was yet rife; but the time was not far off when they too would abandon their idols and come to the light. During her whole administration of fifteen years this wise Christian queen sought to do that which would please God, and make her people an intelligent, civilized Christian nation. She had many difficulties to encounter, and serious obstacles to surmount. The coast tribes, numbering at least two thirds of the whole population, were still savages and idolaters of the worst sort, liars, thieves, bloodthirsty, and lustful; they persisted in making raids for plunder and

slaves, until the queen's firm and gentle management made them ashamed. As soon as possible she sent missionaries and teachers among them. Even of her own Hova and Betsileo, nearly 2,500,000 in number, only 150,000 were nominally Christians; and the rest, though their idols were burned, were liable to lapse into idolatry again if they had a determined leader. Their tendencies in this direction must be overcome.

The French, under the influence of Lambert and the Jesuits, continually harassed the queen by their demands and intrigues to gain possession of the island, expel the Protestants, and establish the Roman Catholic Church there. At one time they demanded indemnity for a pretended loss; at another they required an unconditional surrender, giving her eight days to comply with their ultimata, the alternative being the bombardment of all her ports. After six or seven years of such conduct the queen was driven into a defensive war with the French nation, and through the two years of life which remained to her she carried it on with a dignity and patriotism which commanded the admiration of other nations.

While thus resisting evil from without, she carried forward reforms and measures of Christian civilization within her own realm, which transformed the Malagasy, in those fifteen years, into an enlightened Christian nation, worthy to take its place among the nations of Christendom. She established schools everywhere, drawing upon the London Missionary Society and its native pastors and teachers for the men for the work; made attendance upon the schools compulsory; established and promoted normal schools, high-schools, and aided the theological schools; built many churches, and aided in the building of others; fully organized the government in ten bureaus, all subordinate to the prime-minister; promoted agriculture and commerce; established schools of training and drill for the army; codified, revised, and enlarged the laws; abolished forever the *tangena* ordeal, and established a judiciary system with trials by jury; organized a constabulary force, the officers of which had also the powers of justices of the peace, and were drawn from the best of the petty officers of the army and the most intelligent graduates of the schools. Above all her other acts of patriotism were those relating to slavery. She, by severe edicts, prohibited the importation or sale of any slaves in Madagascar; and finding these edicts evaded, she ordered that every Mozambique (as the slaves from the east coast of Africa were called) should be set free, and be at liberty to return to Africa or remain on the island. As there were about 150,000 of these, the cost of this liberation was borne by her husband and herself from their own private fortunes. They had previously emancipated all their own personal slaves. This heavy sacrifice was made for the good of her country, and to please God. This royal example was followed by a number of nobles of the highest rank. In all these reforms her husband, the prime-minister, went hand in hand with her, and many of them could not have been accomplished without his powerful influence. In several of them, especially those relating to the schools, the Jesuits and nuns prompted the people to disobey the new laws, telling them that they would make it all right. The queen, while promoting these reforms, was tenacious on one point. There are no roads or highways on the island, except in the large cities; the whole internal commerce of the island is conducted through bridle-paths, and all burdens are transported either on the shoulders of men, or the backs of animals—generally mules. The French ridiculed the queen and the Malagasy government for this condition of things, insisting that it was absurd to call any people even half-civilized who had no roads. But the queen was firm. There were inconveniences, she acknowledged, in not having roads; but situated as they were, with a wily enemy ready to take advantage of them, their marshes, forests, mountains, and bridle-paths were their defences and safeguards. And so it proved in the war which followed.

When the French commissioner and admiral made their last demands upon the queen, she received their threatening messages, and replied quietly that she could not yield to their demands; and then, like Hezekiah, she laid their letters before the Lord. She knew that He was mighty to save, and she trusted Him fully. She then sent an embassy to England, France, Germany, and the United States, pleading with France not to do this great wrong, and with the other nations to intervene and prevent it. Her embassadors were treated by the French Government with contempt and gross insults; by the other nations with civility and some expressions of sympathy, but no active measures of intervention. France was too near and too strong, Madagascar was too far away and too weak. Our own government, which had the largest commerce at stake, was pitifully apathetic. The queen immediately took measures to arm and increase her military force, to have them instructed in military tactics ; and calling her people together in a grand kabary, or assembly, she laid before the assembled myriads the demands of the French, and her reply, and all that she had done, and asked them to say if she had done rightly. Her whole speech was quiet, just, and Christian, but determined. She could not manifest a hostile or bitter spirit, but she must defend and protect the land God had given to her fathers, and she did this, trusting only in God, who had made her the sovereign of this people. He was her God and their God. Would they trust in Him, and when they went to the battle, marching side by side with their queen, would they contend valiantly for their country? The whole assembly (over 100,000, it is said) were ready to lay down their lives for their queen, and begged for the privilege of fighting in her behalf. The bombardment of Mojanga, Tamatave, Foulé Point, etc., by the French, without a formal declaration of war, and after giving the inhabitants only an hour's notice, made it necessary for the Queen to send away the French missionaries, teachers, and residents of the capital. They were about 90 in number, and the greater part of them had been actively engaged as spies of the French Goverment, conveying to the French commissioner everything they could pick up, whether true or false, in regard to the queen's movements. It was evident that they must go at once, and the government officers were urgent to send them off *sans ceremonie;* but the queen said : " No! they sent our people away from Mojanga at an hour's notice, and with the loss of all their effects; we will give them five days (from May 25th to May 30th), to pack up

their goods." The Jesuits proposed to walk and carry their goods, intending to pose as martyrs, but the queen, from her own private purse, furnished an ample supply of bearers and provisions, and as the way was long and dangerous (about 200 miles), she detailed an escort of Christian soldiers to protect them. Such was her understanding of the law of Christ. It hardly seems possible, but the records of the French commissioner show, that these Jesuit missionaries made bitter complaint of the manner in which they had been treated by the queen, alleged that they had been robbed by the escort, and put in a claim against the Malagasy Government for $50,000 (which they subsequently increased to $250,000, as a part of the indemnity in 1885-86) for the losses they had sustained. And these Jesuit missionaries immediately after the war came back and demanded their schools and privileges !

The queen's health had been failing for some months, and she herself knew that death was approaching. She had been, during all these fifteen years, a most devoted Christian. Whatever might be the cares of state, she would spend two or three hours of every day in reading the Scriptures and in communion with God. She took no important step without asking counsel of the Most High. As she approached death, her faith and trust never faltered. She declared that she should die fully trusting in Jesus Christ as her Saviour. After joining in the evening prayers, she summoned the prime minister, her husband, and her niece who was to be her successor, to her side, and assuring them that she felt no anxiety for her beloved country, charged them to remember that her kingdom was resting upon God, and that they were to continue as before in all matters of religion. She begged them to remember that not one foot of her land was to be given to the French. Having thus given her testimony, she fell asleep. By her own request she was buried quickly and without unnecessary pomp or display, in order that no interruption should occur in the preparations for resisting the French.

The death of Ranavalona II. took place in the early morning of July 13th, 1883, and the accession of her niece, Razâfindrahèty, as Ranavalona III. was announced on the evening of the same day. She was about twenty years of age, a widow and childless. She was a graduate of the Friend's Foreign Mission Association School, and of the London Missionary Society's Girls' High School at Ambodin-Andohalo, near the capital. She was well educated and an active Christian.

The war went on, the French as boastful and insolent as ever; but the fever and the excesses of the men caused from 50 to 60 per cent of the force to be on the sick-list all the time, and brought the death-rate up to 40 per cent, while the expenditure was enormous. With all their boasting, they had never been able to penetrate into the island farther than the guns of their warships could protect their men, and every attempt to extend their lines, for even eight or ten miles inland, was followed by a swift and bloody repulse.

On the other hand, the Malagasy were not losing ground, and their expenditures, though large, did not seriously impoverish them; their loss of men on the field was small; it was greater from fever, especially in the lowland camps; but they were learning the art of war very rapidly under the instruction of able and experienced English and American officers. The sick had excellent nursing in their camps from the nurses of the Geneva Red Cross Association, a branch of which Ranavalona II. had established. They could go on with the war for years, if necessary, and make the condition of the French forces constantly more untenable. They were fast becoming as formidable a military force as the Sepoys of India. There was no moral or religious deterioration of either the army or the people, during the four years of the war. In all modern history, even among Cromwell's Ironsides, no such statement could be made with truth; but under the wise management of the Christian leaders of the Hovas, it was not difficult to maintain this high moral and religious standard. The soldiers were massed in large camps at the strategic points, and their families were encamped with them. Intoxicating drinks were rigidly prohibited. No camp-followers of either sex were permitted. The Christian soldiers and their families were organized into churches (of which there were twenty in some of the largest camps), each with its native pastor, who was usually himself an officer or soldier. They had regularly two services on the Sabbath and frequent prayer and praise meetings during the week. The Sunday and day schools were kept up in all the camps, and the soldiers, when called into action, marched singing hymns.

The queen and the venerable prime-minister did much to keep up the faith and courage of the people. Every few months, kabarys were held on the great plain, usually attended by 100,000 or more, at which the situation was rehearsed, and the queen and prime-minister expressed their complete trust in God, and their fervent love for their country. The responses of the people were always thoroughly loyal and hearty. On one occasion, when the skies were darkest and the people anxious, the queen requested the prime-minister to voice the nation's petitions to God for deliverance. It was an impressive scene! The venerable man, standing upon the "Sacred Stone," with bared head, gave utterance to their petitions in a prayer, humble, earnest, and fervent, and which showed that he was accustomed to commune with God, while from myriads of hearts and lips in the great congregation went up the deep and hearty Amens like the voice of many waters. Not only in these great assemblies were prayers for God's blessing and deliverance offered. Mr. H. E. Clark, a missionary of the Friends F. Mission Association, was in the Highland provinces of Madagascar during the whole of the war. At the London Missionary Conference in 1888, he said: "In the time of the war the central provinces (Imerina and Betsileo) may be said to have been almost one large prayer-meeting. . . . I have seen a young man kneel down in his pulpit, and I have heard him pray, with tears running down his cheeks, that God would be pleased to take the French soldiers back again safe and sound to their wives and children in France. I do not mean to say that they did not pray that God would help them to conquer the French; but they did also, in some degree, carry out the words of the Saviour when He commanded them 'to love their enemies.'" Mr. Clark said further, that it was during the years of the war that the Sunday-school movement in Antananarivo took firm hold upon the

people; and that now, in the capital, it has become almost as much an institution as it is in London, and that the Home Missionary Society established by the native churches increased in strength so much during the war that they were constantly sending out missionaries to the heathen tribes who were employed by the French to make war upon them. The church of God, all the missionaries say, is every way stronger and more robust in its spiritual life than before the war. God did hear these fervent and earnest prayers of the Malagasy churches and of Christian people in other lands, and He sent deliverance.

The time had come when the French Government found themselves compelled to give up the conflict, and withdraw from it on the best terms they could. The Madagascar question had already aided in overthrowing two cabinets. The expenditures in men and means had been enormous—over 100,000,000 francs and about 12,000 of their best troops, and they had gained neither lands, goods, nor reputation. Their allies, as they called the savage Sâkalâvas, were cowardly, indolent, and thievish; they would not fight the Hovas, but in midnight raids would steal cattle and slaves, keeping the former for their own use and selling the latter to the Arabs. On an average, 6.000 French soldiers were sent out annually, but they had never been able to bring 1,200 effective men into the field at any one time. They held no cities, for they could not capture any; and the reputation they had acquired by their cruelties and barbarities during the war, was so unsavory that they could no longer endure it. The Society of Friends in England, America, and France, and all Protestants everywhere, were making vigorous demonstrations against it, and the English and Italian governments were offering to mediate. So, though the French consul, commissioner, and admiral were blustering more loudly than ever, and threatening to capture the island, to loot the capital, and to carry off the queen to France as a prisoner, the French war minister put an end to their vaporing, recalled them in disgrace, sent a special commissioner to Madagascar, and ordered him to negotiate a peace.

The terms offered were hard and unjust, and ought not to have been sanctioned by England or the United States; yet France was by far the greatest loser, as she deserved to be. They were: The cession of the harbor of San Diego Suarez and a moderate amount of territory around it (the harbor is good, but the territory ceded is barren, and very sparsely inhabited); the payment by the Malagasy Government of an indemnity of 10,000,000 francs ($2,000,000); and the concession to France of the complete control of all the foreign affairs of the kingdom. The internal management of the nation's affairs was to be in the hands of the Malagasy Government, but a French minister resident was to reside at the capital, with a staff and military escort, and no transaction with any foreign government was to be permitted without his approval. The Catholic churches and schools were to be placed on the same footing as the Protestant churches and schools. The French professed great solicitude for their ancient allies and protégés, the Sâkalâvas, and requested that the queen's government would treat them with the greatest benevolence, and not subject them to any of those tortures or punishments which they had been in the habit of practising on these tribes. Base and false as this insinuation was in every respect, the queen passed it over in silence, ordered the treaty signed, and awaited the result. The French forces left the island, rejoiced to get away; but they made no provision for the payment or care of the Sàkalàvas, who had, according to their capacity, served them faithfully, but left them on the lowlands of the coast to die of their wounds, of the fever, or of starvation. The queen, learning their condition, at once sent supplies, physicians, and nurses of the Red Cross Association, and even visited some of their camps in person to minister to their needs. Though her enemies, they were sick and in distress, and she visited and cared for them. It is safe to say that during the lifetime of the present queen these northern and western Sàkalàvas will never be hostile to her.

The Malagasy Government has complied with the provisions of the treaty in good faith, and accepted the situation. They have paid the indemnity, and the Jesuit priests and nuns in charge of the churches and schools, though not welcome, are tolerated. What the future may have in store remains to be seen. Meantime the close of the war in the early part of 1886 brought new duties to the Christians of Madagascar. New missions to the Sàkalàvas, the Bara, the Anòsy, and the Antsihànaka have been undertaken, and some of the ablest of the young Hova preachers have volunteered to go and preach to them the way of salvation. There have been extensive revivals in several of these missions as well as in the capital, and in the principal towns of Imerina and Bétsileo.

It is the testimony of the missionaries as well as of those Christian visitors who have been there, that the churches have since the war manifested a higher type of Christianity than before. They are more zealous after a holy life, more anxious to bring souls to Christ and to convert the heathen, more hearty in their determination to support not only their pastors and churches, but missionary operations on their own island and elsewhere.

Of course, among so many converts from heathenism in less than sixty years there will be some who will fall away. Temptations to intemperance, to licentiousness, to theft and falsehood, surround them, and some of the professed converts are not strong enough to resist. It has been so in all the Christian ages. The Apostolic churches suffered largely from such apostasies; so did the mediæval churches; so do the churches in Japan, in Burma, in Siam, and in India. A rigid discipline is maintained in all these missions, but we are inclined to believe that the defections in India and in Japan are quite as large in proportion to the membership of the churches as in Madagascar. The influence of a pure and holy example, and great activity in Christian work, will do much to prevent the weak from falling into sin; and these safeguards they have in the lives of their pastors, teachers, and superintendents and rulers. No more saintly woman has occupied any throne in modern times than Ranavalona II., and her successor seems to be imbued with the same spirit.

Intelligence has come within the past year that at the ports of the island, particularly on the west and northwest coasts, intemperance and licentiousness prevail to a fearful extent, and that the slave-trade has been renewed at some of those ports with the Arab traders, and that the French colony of Réunion (Isle Bourbon) is now, as in the time of Ranavalona I., profiting by it. We fear that these reports are partially true; but though they are very sad, they do not reflect upon the government of Ranavalona III., nor should they be quoted against it. The ports and foreign commerce of Madagascar are, by the treaty, wholly under the control of the French resident. No vessels can trade at those ports without a permit from him; and if the slave-trade is reöpened there, it is by his permission or connivance, and for the benefit of the French colonies of Réunion, Nòsy-Bè, etc. He knows what sacrifices the present queen and her predecessors have made to extinguish the slave-trade, and that the queen is hostile to it in heart and soul; but both the Arabs and the Creoles of Réunion are thoroughly wicked and unscrupulous. As to the depravity at the ports, the French soldiers and sailors, and the Arab, Portuguese, and other sailors, at any ports where there is free license, and among such a class as the heathen women of those ports, will reach depths of depravity which would make even the denizens of the pit of destruction recoil with horror.

The apprehensions of the missionary friends of Madagascar in regard to the results of French interference with its church and educational work have been unhappily verified within the year 1890. Though France is not now professedly a Catholic state, and two of its recent premiers have been Protestants, yet in its intercourse with foreign nations in Asia and Africa Jesuits have always been its representatives, and they have always wielded the whole power of the French Government for the prosecution of their often nefarious schemes. They have, since 1886, determined to capture the schools and the educational institutions of the capital, Antananarivo, although they knew that the queen and prime minister were decided Protestants. They grew more and more aggressive, till in the autumn of 1890 their action became so treasonable that the prime minister arrested them and broke up their establishment. They at once appealed to the French Resident, with what result has not yet transpired, though it can hardly be doubted that he would insist upon their reinstatement and upon other concessions, and this may lead to another war.

For the summarization of the mission work in Madagascar, we refer to the statistical tables and the notes appended to them. The provinces of Imerina and Bétsileo are Christianized, and there are Christian churches among a vast mass of heathenism in the other provinces, but the rulers and government are Christian.

**Madampitiya,** a station of the Wesleyan Methodist Missionary Society in the Colombo district, South Ceylon, with 2 chapels, 1 preaching-place, 1 native assistant, 6 day-schools, 65 church-members, and a congregation of 150.

**Madanapalli,** a town in Cuddapah district, Madras, South India, 154 miles northwest of Madras City. Climate hot, 60°–110° F. Population of city and circuit, 550,000, Brahmins, Dravidians, Hindus, Moslems. Languages, Telugu, Hindustani, Kanarese, Marathi, Tamil. Natives of higher classes comfortably off; lower, very poor; education at a low ebb. Mission station Reformed Church in America (1863); 2 ordained missionaries, 1 missionary's

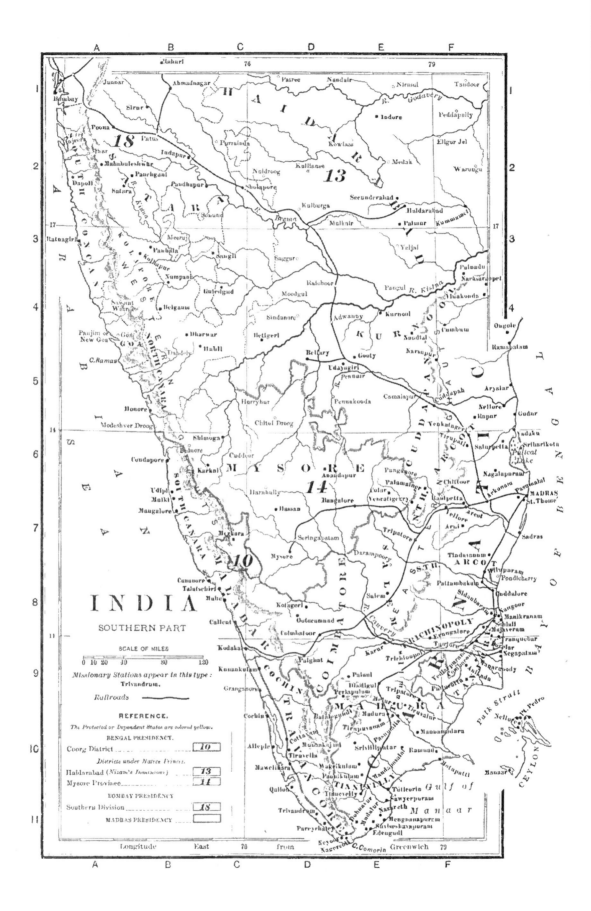

wife, 1 other lady, 45 native helpers, 13 out-stations, 1 church, 128 church-members, 18 schools, 589 scholars.

**Madhepur** (Madhupur), a town in Bengal, East India, 25 miles east of Darbhangah. Admirably situated for trade with all parts of Tirhût and Purniah, it will probably become an important commercial town. Population, 5,054, Hindus and Moslems. Station of the Wesleyan Methodist Missionary Society; 1 native assistant, 5 Christians, 1 school, 14 pupils.

**Madjalengka,** settlement on the north coast of Java, west of Cheribon. Mission station of the Dutch Missionary Society.

**Madras,** a city of British India, capital of the Madras presidency (see next article), and the third city in size and importance in all India, being outranked only by Bombay and Calcutta; situated in north latitude 13° 4′ and east longitude 80° 17′, on the east coast of the peninsula of India. Population (1881), 405,848. The first settlement was begun in 1639, when a grant of land was obtained by Mr. Francis Day, a servant of the East India Company, from the Hindu prince who possessed jurisdiction in that region. A factory (as it was then the custom to term the headquarters of the Company's mercantile establishments in India) and slight fortifications were at once erected, and the city of Madras was begun. The origin of the name is exceedingly uncertain. The word "Madrissa" signifies a Mohammedan school, and some scholars consider the name of the city to have been derived from that. In 1653 Madras was made the seat of the local government or presidency of the East India Company's territory in South India. In 1746, during the time when the French power in South India threatened to eclipse the English, it was taken by the French commander La Bourdonnais, but was restored two years later by the treaty of Aix-la-Chapelle. Within a century of the first settlement Madras had become the largest city in South India. Its growth since then has been great, though far less than that either of Calcutta or Bombay; but its natural advantages are far less than those enjoyed by its sister cities. It has no harbor; vessels are obliged to lie off at a distance of a mile, more or less, from the shore; and until very recently all freight and passengers have been transported back and forth between the shore and the ships in surf-boats, for skilful management of which, through the surf which breaks unceasingly on the beach, the boatmen of Madras are famed. In 1862 a pier was constructed, which extends out 300 yards into the sea; and more recently still the construction was undertaken of an artificial harbor, consisting of two parallel breakwaters curving towards each other at the outer end. The city is by no means compact, but stretches along the shore of the Bay of Bengal for more than 9 miles, and its territory extends 3 miles inland. Of the population more than three fourths are Hindus. The Mohammedans number only one eighth—a little over 50,000, Christians nearly 40,000, 3,205 Europeans, 12,659 Eurasians (half-castes of mixed European and Indian descent). Tamil is spoken by more than half of the entire population; Telugu by a little less than a quarter.

MISSION WORK.—Danish missionaries had been operating at Tranquebar and other points south of Madras for a number of years early in the last century before any form of Christian work was attempted in Madras itself. In the year 1716, with the help of the English chaplain at Madras, they commenced a Christian school in that city, which however languished, and soon ceased altogether. In 1726 Schultze, one of the missionaries at Tranquebar, made a journey to Madras, began the school work again, and laid the foundations of the first Protestant mission in the capital of South India. A few years afterwards the Society for Propagation of Christian Knowledge, of England, undertook its support, though Schultze continued in charge of it. The missionary labored hard, preaching, teaching, translating, and writing. Results were not slow in appearing. In the one year 1729 Schultze baptized 140 persons; by the end of 1736 the converts numbered 415. The mission was encouraged by the Madras government. Other missionaries arrived from Europe, and the work went on apace. In 1746 the capture of the city by the French was the occasion of much distress to the mission; its work was interrupted, its buildings destroyed, and its church used by the French conquerors as a magazine. In 1748, when the city was returned to the English, the missionaries and Christians who had fled during the troubles came back, and operations were resumed—still under the fostering care of the government. By the end of the last century some 4,000 persons had been received into the Christian church. With all this apparent success it may be doubted if the real achievements were very great. These numerical results were not carried over into the present century; on the other hand, when the first converts died off there seemed to be no vital Christianity behind them as a basis for further progress. With all their devotion and industry the earlier missionaries did not have the best methods of labor, and the churches which they founded lacked accordingly that sound and efficient vitality which would have ensured their permanence.

With the beginning of this century began the new era of missionary work in Madras and throughout all India. Of the great missionary societies which were formed near the year 1800 the London Missionary Society was first on the ground at Madras in 1805. Their collegiate institution was begun in 1852, and has had a most successful and useful career. The mission has also maintained a girls' boarding-school. The Church Missionary Society began work in 1815. From the first this mission paid much attention to education as well as to preaching, and schools for both sexes were carried on with vigor. The Wesleyans came in 1816. About the year 1826—just 100 years after its establishment by Schultze—the original mission of the Christian Knowledge Society was transferred to the care of the Society for the Propagation of the Gospel. The American Board entered the field in 1836, but withdrew in 1864 in order to concentrate its strength more effectively on other stations. During its existence great attention had been devoted by it to the work of translating and publishing. The Leipsic Lutheran Society entered Madras in 1848. The Established Church of Scotland began a mission in 1837, and devoted its energies, as in Calcutta and Bombay, especially to the higher education, through the medium of the English language. The fervid eloquence of Dr. Duff of Calcutta during his first visit home is said to have been the exciting cause of the beginning of the Madras work. The Scotch institution was begun in 1837 with 59 pupils, but had 277 on its rolls before the end of the following year. After the disruption of the Scotch Church the Madras missionaries sided with the Free Church; so that in 1843 another mission of a similar character was begun by the Old Kirk, and since then the two have worked on harmoniously and successfully side by side. The Free Church has also had much success among high-caste women in Madras, and girls' schools have prospered greatly under their care. The Strict Baptists have a small mission in Madras, begun in 1866, and the Danish Lutherans another dating from 1878. The Christian Vernacular Education Society has here its central station, though its three schools for the training of vernacular teachers are in other parts of India. Zenana mission work is conducted, not only by the ladies connected with the societies just mentioned and by their women's auxiliaries, but also by other ladies connected with the Female Normal School Society. There is also a mission especially for lepers, over 400 of whom were reported in the census of 1881. The usual missionary agencies are reinforced by the Bible and Tract Societies and by the Society for the Propagation of Christian Knowledge—the venerable organization which so long supported the mission started by Schultze, but which now works wholly through the press. The American Methodists, under the lead of Rev. Wm. Taylor, began work in 1872, at first directing their efforts especially to unevangelized Europeans and Eurasians, though not neglecting persons of other races who might be brought under their influence.

Besides the mission chapels the city is well provided with Protestant churches for the accommodation of Europeans, and with Roman Catholic churches for persons of all nationalities who adhere to that form of Christianity. The usual institutions of a philanthropic or literary character which spring up everywhere in the path of enlightened and liberal government, such as hospitals, libraries, and the like, are not wanting in Madras. Education is in a fair state of progress. In 1881 over 24 per cent of the city's population were able to read and write or were under instruction. This was a gain during the preceding ten years of 6 per cent. In 1882–3 there were in operation 5 colleges, also 3 others for professional training, an art school, and a medical college. There were 14 English high-schools as well as many of lower grade; there were 54 high-schools for girls. There were several normal and special institutions. In all, 495 institutions were in that year teaching 26,234 pupils. Missionary institutions are included in these statistics.

*Missionary Societies* at present at work in the city: American Baptist Missionary Union; 4 missionaries and wives, 2 female missionaries, 6 native preachers, 2 self-supporting churches, 107 church-members, 200 Sabbath-scholars. Methodist Episcopal Church (North), U. S. A.; 3 missionaries (2 married), 1 female missionary, 138 church-members, 827 Sabbath-scholars. London Missionary Society; 2 missionaries and wives, 4 female missionaries, 8 native preachers, 206 church-members, 153 Sabbath-scholars. Society for the Propagation of the Gospel (the Society's report gives the individual

congregations in Madras separately, but in such a way that it is impossible to give the sum of all). Strict Baptist Mission (England); 2 workers, 20 church-members, 25 scholars. Wesleyan Missionary Society (England); 8 missionaries and wives, 5 catechists, 524 church-members, 1,459 scholars. Established Church of Scotland; 2 missionaries and wives, 2 lay teachers, 4 female missionaries, 4 native preachers, 104 communicants, 608 scholars. Free Church of Scotland; 10 missionaries, 2 female missionaries, 3 medical missionaries, 25 communicants, 6,376 scholars. Evangelical Lutheran Society of Leipsic; 2 native preachers, 553 communicants, 533 scholars.

**Madras Presidency** is one of the general divisions into which British India is divided. It is ruled by a governor and council appointed by the crown, subject to the supervision of the governor-general and viceroy of India. This presidency covers the southern portion of the Indian peninsula—with the exception of the territory still under native princes. Its eastern boundary is the Bay of Bengal; its western, the Indian Ocean. But the territory of the presidency extends along the coast of the former for some 1,200 miles, while its western shore-line, along the Indian Ocean, extends only 540 miles. On the north and northwest it joins (proceeding from east to west) Orissa, a part of the Bengal presidency; then the Central Provinces; then the dominions of the Nizam of Haidarabad; and finally, as its boundary-line nears the Indian Ocean, the presidency of Bombay. Near the centre of this irregular triangular territory is the great native state of Mysore, including five smaller native states which are very closely related to the Madras government, and directly subordinated to it. The total area of the presidency is 149,092 square miles, and the population 34,172,067 souls. The presidency may be divided, as to its physical aspects, into three well marked areas. Along the eastern coast, between the range of hills known as the Eastern Ghats and the sea, is a broad strip of low country. A similar, though narrower and more diversified, strip of land extends along the western coast, between the Western Ghats and the Indian Ocean. The interior consists of a table-land, supported on its western edge by the Western Ghats, and sloping down gradually towards the Bay of Bengal on the east, its boundary on that side being the eastern range just alluded to. Much of the high interior is occupied by the native state of Mysore. The mountains rise to greater heights as they go south: the highest peaks of Southern India are those of the Nilgiri and Anamalai groups, several of which are between eight and nine thousand feet high. Just south of the Anamalais, the group known as the Palanis rise to a height of nearly 8,000 feet. Three large rivers, with a number of tributary and minor streams, traverse the presidency from west to east, having their sources in the Western Ghats, and discharging their waters through deltas into the Bay of Bengal. These are the Godavari, the Krishna, and the Caveri. Each of them has a number of affluents, some of which are of considerable size. The only rivers on the west are the small and short streams which can crowd their short course into the narrow strip of land between the foot of the western range and the sea. Neither of the larger rivers is navigable to any extent; all are impetuous torrents during the rains, but dwindle away greatly in volume during the hot months. Their waters, however, diverted by dams and weirs into canals, are useful for irrigation. The surface of the agricultural districts is dotted with tanks and reservoirs of greater or less extent, some being immense artificial lakes, others covering but a few acres, wherein the water is stored during the rains, and in the dry season distributed to the fields by ingenious systems of canals and ducts. Many of these reservoirs were constructed by Hindu governments ages ago; some have fallen into disrepair, and others are kept up and still serve their fertilizing purpose. Recently the government has paid much attention to the matter of irrigation, and some great canal systems have been devised and perfected by government during the past forty or fifty years. Rice in some districts is the staple food; and elsewhere, where rice cannot be grown, other cheap grains are eaten. Tea and coffee are cultivated successfully in several of the mountainous districts. Cocoanuts grow plentifully along the western coast, and the mountains are often covered with dense growth of timber, some of it valuable. Pepper is grown on the hills at the south. On the whole, however, the presidency can hardly be considered favorable for the agriculturist, although the larger part of the people depend upon agriculture for their maintenance. But it is in many places only moderately fertile; over much of the presidency the rainfall is deficient and irregular, and sometimes irrigation is difficult or impossible. The average density of the population—221 per square mile, as opposed to 443 in Bengal and 416 in the Northwest Provinces—indicates with tolerable clearness the smaller power of the soil in the southern presidency as compared with the fertile richness of the Ganges valley.

The population is chiefly Hindu; over 91 per cent were thus classified in the census of 1881; Mohammedans claim only a trifle over 6 per cent. Christians numbered in that year 711,072—nearly 2¼ per cent. About 25,000 reported themselves as Jains, and the unclassified number was exceedingly small. Probably most of the aboriginal tribes were classed among the Hindus.

The Hindus of this presidency, and some of the so-called aboriginal tribes also, belong to the Dravidian family, of which the strongest subdivision is that now known as the Tamil. People of this race appear, in prehistoric times, to have occupied the Gangetic valley, and to have been pushed south by the invading Aryans as they moved down the valley and spread over the peninsula. Portions of the Dravidic population declined to accept the lordship of these Aryan invaders, and, retiring to mountain and jungle tracts, gave rise to some of the aboriginal tribes still found in Central India, of which the Khonds and the Gonds are the most important, though two smaller tribes are still found occupying land within the limits of the Bengal presidency, one of them in the very centre of the valley (the Oraons and the Rajmahalis); but for the most part the Dravidians were absorbed into the social system of their conquerors, were fused with them into Hinduism, and furnished the main stock of the population of Southern India. The language of the Dravidians still exists, though differentiated into the distinct modern tongues of South

India, viz.: the Tamil (most important) spoken by over 12,000,000 in the presidency; the Telugu, used by almost as large a number; the Kanarese, spoken by about 1,300,000; the Tulu (preserved only by a remnant of the people among the mountains in the west of the presidency, and doomed doubtless to disappear as a spoken language; the Coorg (see that article) and the Malayalim (2,400,000). The languages of the aboriginal tribes above mentioned are also Dravidian. The original religion of the Dravidians, before the coming of the Aryans, was probably some form of demon-worship, such as the jungle tribes still preserve. Doubtless many of these demon-deities were admitted to the Hindu Pantheon by the Brahmans as time went on; the popular Hinduism of South India still shows many marks of this early kinship with the religious ideas of a more barbarous time, and preserves in its rites and superstitions marks of the primeval demonolatry. Though the civilization, language, and religion in South India bear profound evidence of Aryan influence, yet the fusion between the Aryan and original elements is probably less perfect here than in the north. The debt of the modern Dravidian languages to Sanskrit is not so great; the proportion of Brahmans and the other Aryan castes to the entire population is smaller (less than half as great as in the Bombay presidency); while the separation between the Brahmans and the lower castes is wider than in the north, thus showing that the union between the two classes is less complete. The number of Mohammedans also is much less here than in most parts of India: 6 per cent of the population were thus classed in 1881; while in the Bombay presidency the percentage was about 20 per cent, and throughout India as a whole it is somewhat greater even than that. The distance of the Madras presidency from the Ganges valley, where the Mohammedan empires erected their chief stronghold, accounts for this. Their power over the outlying provinces dwindled with increasing distance. The native states within the territorial limits of the presidency which were overthrown by the English and absorbed into the fabric of the present government, were mostly Hindu, and not Mohammedan.

A word must be said as to the connection of the English with the presidency. Calicut and Cranganore on the west coast were occupied by the East India Company as places of trade in 1616. The Company had been preceded, first by the Portuguese, and as their power waned, by the Dutch. But finally the former concentrated themselves at Goa, and the Dutch withdrew. On the east coast, Masulipatam, north of Madras, was occupied by the English traders in 1611. The first English settlement on the site of Madras City was in 1639 (see Madras City). The French occupied Pondicherri, south of Madras, in 1672. It was not until the middle of the 18th century, when the English and French powers were in armed rivalry in Europe, that the thought of a possible rivalry for supremacy in India began to be realized. In 1746 Madras was overpowered and captured by the French commander La Bourdonnais; but restored to the English two years later, at the peace of Aix-la-Chapelle. But the country was occupied with weak and tottering dynasties of native princes. In their contests among themselves, the English would

befriend one princeling, and the French another. The strife between the Oriental principals could not fail to extend itself to the European powers by which they were respectively seconded; and for half a century the fate of South India hung undecided between the French and English. Dupleix undertook to unite the native powers into one combination under French protection; but his plans were defeated by the military skill, first of Lord Clive, afterwards of Sir Eyre Coote. Haidar Ali, and his son Tippu Sultan, the only members of a Mohammedan dynasty which erected itself on the ruins of a Hindu principality in Mysore, withstood the progress of English power with a fierceness which at one time threatened to stop it altogether. But in 1799 Tippu Sultan died in the breach at his capital, Seringapatam, the English entered the fort in triumph, and military opposition, from whatever quarter, to the English power in South India was at an end. Since then the English Government has had hardly any use for its Madras army, save for police purposes.

To the historian of Indian Christianity the Madras Presidency is the most interesting portion of India. Tradition says that the Apostle Thomas preached the gospel here; and Mount St. Thome, near Madras, is his traditional burial-place. A branch of the Syrian Church settled on the west coast, near Cape Comorin, centuries ago, and this "Syrian Church of Malabar" still preserves its ancient liturgies, and still acknowledges subjection to the patriarch of Antioch. Here also Xavier preached and baptized in the 16th century, and the Jesuit missionaries of Madura in the 17th. And here was the beginning of the Protestant missionary movement in India, by the hands of two young Danish missionaries (Bartholomew Ziegenbalg and Henry Plutschau), in 1705. Tranquebar (on the coast south of Madras) was the first station occupied. The Society for Promoting Christian Knowledge (English) in a few years assumed support of the mission. But it was long before a distinctively English mission was founded. Schultze came in 1719, and in 1726 began the first really successful mission in Madras City. Kiernander came in 1740; but in 1746, when the French were besieging Cuddalore, where he was stationed, and rendering his operations there impossible, he removed to Calcutta, and became the father of Protestant missions in the Bengal presidency. (See Calcutta). In 1750 Christian Frederic Schwartz landed in South India, and until his death in 1798 labored uninterruptedly for the good of the people and the progress of the cause of Christ. No better or greater name adorns the history of Protestant missions in India than his. His influence as a missionary was great; his influence as a man was felt all over South India, by all classes. The Rajah of Tanjore, a Maratha principality, though far removed from the original seat of Maratha power, revered him as a father, followed his advice in the conduct of his kingdom and in his relations with the English Government and other powers around him, and finally on his death virtually constituted him guardian over his son during the latter's minority. By the labors of these great and good men and their associates congregations were gathered, schools established, and churches founded at Tranquebar, Madras, Trichinopoli, Tanjore, and other places. Converts were baptized by the

hundred and the thousand. Yet with all their excellences of character, their ability, their piety, and their zeal, these men did not plant a self-sustaining, manly, and vigorous Christianity. Their churches exist, but with diminished numbers and enfeebled strength. The Protestant Christianity of the present day, in South India, rests chiefly on foundations independently laid, not on those laid by the Danish and German laborers of the last century. The churches gathered by them have in many cases been surpassed by those more recently organized, not alone in numbers, but in aggressive character and influence. For the most part the work begun by the missionaries of the last century was subsidized by the Society for the Propagation of Christian Knowledge, which to a large extent furnished the funds, while the missionaries themselves came from Denmark and Germany. Early in the present century this Society transferred the missions to the Society for the Propagation of the Gospel, and in due time the *personnel* of the mission staff came to be recruited wholly from the English Church, even as the money came from the same source.

The introductory labors of the missionaries of the 18th century were followed by work on a larger scale, more systematically and energetically pursued, during the present century. We record here the principal agencies operating in this more recent era. The London Missionary Society leads the way. Two missionaries of this Society occupied Vizagapatam, on the east coast, far north of Madras, in 1805, during a period when the Indian Government, taught by the directors of the East India Company at home, was bitterly opposed to the entrance of missionaries into India. The missionaries at Vizagapatam, however, were not molested, and when in 1814 Parliament, in the new charter granted that year to the company, inserted a clause favoring missionary operations, and the opposition of the government ceased in consequence, the London Society was all ready to establish a station in Madras City. Bellari, northwest of Madras, near the boundary-line now separating the presidency from that of Bombay, had been occupied in 1810, and Coimbatoor was occupied in 1830. The Church Missionary Society entered Madras City in 1815, and took over the Palamcotta station (in the Tinnevelli district) from the Danish missionaries, who had planted it in 1785, in 1817. In the same year the Society for the Propagation of the Gospel began work at Cuddalore, and assumed, during the years 1820-29, charge, from the Society for Propagating Christian Knowledge, of most of the old Danish missions. The Wesleyan Missionary Society appeared upon the scene at Madras in 1816, and at Trichinopoli two years later. The Basle Evangelical Missionary Society began its work, which since has spread over all the western portion of the presidency, and into many of the Kanarese districts of the Bombay presidency, in 1834. The English Baptists planted a station in the Ganjam district, the most northerly of those bordering on the Bay of Bengal, in 1837. The American Board of Commissioners for Foreign Missions, whose mission among the Tamil-speaking people of Jaffna, in North Ceylon, had been begun soon after 1820, colonized thence, first to Madura in 1834, to Madras in 1836; Arcot was occupied by this Society in 1855, but its work there was a year or two afterwards transferred to the Dutch Reformed Church (as it was then called) of the United States, by which church it has since been maintained with much vigor. The mission in Madras City was discontinued, but that in the city and district of Madura is one of the most flourishing of all the missions sustained by the American Board. The Church of Scotland came to Madras in 1837, and after the Disruption in 1843 two Scotch missions have worked there side by side, and to some extent also in the interior. The American Baptist Missionary Union began its work—now of large proportions and of extraordinary success—in Nellore, and other parts of the Telugu portion of the the presidency, in 1840. The Leipsic Lutherans came in 1841 to Tranquebar and adjacent stations, where the Lutherans of the preceding century, whose places were now filled by missionaries of the English Church, had labored with such assiduity. There are also small German missions elsewhere in the presidency—that of the Hermannsburg Lutherans at Nellore, (1865), of the American German Lutherans in the Krishna district (1842), and an independent though successful German mission in the Godaveri Delta, which dates from 1838. (See also Madras City.)

The chief successes of this army of Christian laborers have been won in the Tinnevelli district, where the Christian churches and communities are very numerous, and where the native Christians are numbered by thousands. In the Telugu districts, also, under the charge of the American Baptists, there have been ingatherings of surprising vastness and power; the American missionaries in the Arcot and Madura districts have also been very successful. Probably in no other part of India has Christianity taken so firm a hold. Elsewhere individuals have been reached and converted, but in many parts of the Madras presidency the converts have come in families, in groups, sometimes by whole villages. People of the Dravidian races seem disposed to move gregariously.

The statistics of education during the past forty years show great progress. In 1852–3 the Madras Government expended in all for educational purposes only £4,556. Beyond the indigenous schools, where the children of the upper castes—so far as they wished to learn—were taught to read and write their own vernacular and to keep accounts, by old Brahman pedagogues, and the educational operations of the missionaries, nothing was done for popular education. The present system of government education dates from 1855. In that year the Madras University was remodelled, and systematic operations begun by the government to promote the education of the people. In 1882–3 the total number of schools of all kinds in the presidency was 17,494; attendance, 446,324. These institutions were all in some way under governmental inspection; and besides these were an unknown number of indigenous and uninspected schools. The census of 1881 reported 514,872 boys and 39,104 girls under instruction, besides 1,515,061 males and 94,013 females able to read and write. In 1882–3 it was estimated that the total number of schools of all sorts, inspected and uninspected, was about 20,000, which would give only one school for every 1,550 of population—estimating the latter at 31,000,000. Between 1853 and 1883

the Madras government has spent about £1,250,000 sterling on the higher education,—how much upon all grades of educational operations is not stated. With the educational system of the presidency are connected 29 colleges; also 3 professional colleges, and over 100 high-schools, of which 16 are for girls. The extent to which the young men of the presidency are influenced by the higher education is roughly indicated by the fact that during the 10 years 1873–1883, 28,575 candidates appeared for the entrance examination of the Madras University, of whom over one third succeeded in passing. The distribution of these candidates among the several classes of population may be indicated by the figures for 1876, when of the students who matriculated at the University (1,250 in all), 59 per cent were Brahmans, 26 per cent Hindus of other castes, 1½ per cent Mohammedans, and nearly 7 per cent native Christians. The remainder were Eurasians and Europeans.

**Madura**, a city (and district, the city being the capital of the district) in the Madras presidency (British India); situated in north latitude 9° 55′ and east longitude 78° 10′, about 275 miles south southwest from Madras. The population of the city is 73,807, divided as follows: Hindus, 64,823; Mohammedans, 6,701; Christians, 2,281; others, 2. The language of the Hindus is Tamil, though with the progress of education the rising generation of natives is more and more familiar with English. Madura has long been the most important place in South India. It was the seat of an ancient dynasty of Hindu kings (the Pandyan), whose history stretches back into prehistoric times, and is adorned with the usual wealth of myth and legend. As the Mohammedan power stretched south in the 15th and 16th centuries this Hindu kingdom was overthrown, though no Mohammedan dynasty took its place; but on the ruins of the old state rose another Hindu dynasty,—that of the Nayaks,—which culminated in the 17th century, when most of the architectural works at Madura, which still attest the power and wealth of this line of princes, were completed. During the political chaos of the last century the Nayak kingdom in its turn crumbled. Maratha and Mohammedan armies successively overran the region, until at last the British came, and in 1801 Madura passed into their possession. The religious history of the place chiefly concerns us now. It contains one of the most famous Hindu temples—that of the goddess Minakshi—in India. The temple enclosure is 847 ft. long and 744 ft. broad, and contains, besides the shrines of the goddess and of the god Siva, a vast collection of buildings,— halls, bazaars, etc.,—occupied by the priests and temple attendants. The conspicuous features of the temple are the great towers, 9 in number, which rise above its outer walls, in one case reaching to the height of 152 feet.

The Christian history of Madura is of much interest. The famous Roman Catholic missionary Francis Xavier gathered a little church here in the 16th century. In 1606 a Jesuit mission was begun here by Robert de Nobilis, who lived as an ascetic, was renowned for his sanctity and learning, and his complete mastery of the Tamil language. Following him were men of like spirit, notably John de Britto, who suffered martyrdom in 1693, and Beschi, who pre pared the first Tamil grammar, and whose writings are regarded as models of pure Tamil style. The native converts in the region about Madura were estimated at a million or more, won largely by the great concessions to Hinduism which the missionaries made. The number of Catholic Christians now in the district has greatly dwindled, hardly 70,000 being returned in the census of 1881.

The history of Protestant effort begins in 1834, when the place was occupied by Messrs. Todd and Hoisington, connected with the Board's Mission in Jaffna, Ceylon, which had been founded in 1816. The work of the American missionaries has been carried on vigorously and successfully ever since. In process of time they occupied most of the important towns in the district round Madura as mission stations, established schools of different grades, gathered congregations of Christian adherents, and founded churches, composed of such as gave credible evidence of piety. They have labored as preachers on their tours and in the churches, as teachers in their schools, as writers and editors through the medium of the press, as physicians through their labors in hospitals and dispensaries. They have hospitals at Madura and Dindigul, 38 miles north; a training-school for teachers and preachers, with which a collegiate department is now connected, at Pasumalai, just out of Madura; a boarding-school for girls in Madura, besides churches and schools of different grades at all the mission stations, and in many villages through the district. The latest statistics show that in the mission of which Madura is the centre there are 12 stations and 259 out-stations, 13 missionaries with their wives, 8 other American ladies, 17 ordained native preachers, 431 other native laborers, preachers and teachers, etc.; nearly 13,000 adherents, 36 churches with 3,562 members, and 4,628 in Sunday-schools, and nearly 5,500 pupils in the schools of all grades. The contributions of the native Christians for religious purposes amounted to $6,192. These figures represent the state of the work in 1889-90.

**Madura District,** a district or collectorate in the Madras presidency, of which Madura is the capital. It covers an area of 8,401 square miles, extending from the straits separating Ceylon from the mainland on the east, to the mountains on the west (known as the Palnais) which form the boundary between British territory and the native state of Travancore. Other districts of the Madras presidency bound it on the north and south. The population is (1881) 2,168,680; 90 per cent are Hindus; 6½ per cent Mohammedans; 4 per cent Christians (Roman Catholic Christians number a little over 67,000). Since the census of 1871 Christians had increased nearly 20 per cent, and the Hindus have lost nearly 6 per cent.

The history of the district has been sufficiently indicated for our purposes in the article on "Madura City," where will also be found statements relative to present missionary work within the district.

**Madurantakam,** a station of the Wesleyan Methodist Missionary Society in the Madras district, India; 1 missionary, 1 assistant, 3 preaching places, 1 chapel, 26 church-members, 395 scholars.

**Mafeking,** a small English town in British Bechuanaland, South Africa, where there are 1 missionary with 3 native assistants of the Wesleyan Methodist Missionary Society, 355 church-members, a congregation of 1,275, and 250 Sunday-school scholars.

**Mafubé,** a station of the Paris Evangelical Society (Société des Missions Évangéliques) in the Orange Free State, Africa (1883); 1 missionary, 325 church-members, and 315 pupils.

**Mágadhi Version.**—The Mágadhi is a dialect of the Behari language, differing radically from Hindi and Bengali. It is vernacular of the country-folk in the district of Patna and Gaya, Monghyr, and the greater part of Chhota Nagpur. It is spoken by probably 4,000,000 people. A version of the New Testament was made by the late Dr. Carey, and published at Serampore 1824-26. It was not reprinted. More recently portions of the Gospels were translated by the Rev. E. Start of Patna, of which the Gospel of Matthew was published by the British and Foreign Bible Society in 1867. In 1887 the same Society issued at Calcutta, at the request of Mr. Grierson, a magistrate of Gaya, the Gospel of Mark from Carey's New Testament. As there is no missionary who now knows the language, the version will be circulated tentatively among the people.

**Magalle,** a station in the South Ceylon district of the Wesleyan Methodist Missionary Society; 1 native assistant, 6 church-members, 174 pupils.

**Magdala.**—1. A station of the Moravian Brethren at a village on Pearl Key Lagoon, Moskito Coast, Central America (1853). There were many negroes, mulattoes, and Indians in the vicinity of the station.—2. An out-station of the Moravian Brethren, worked from Bethesda among the Hlubi Kafirs in Griqualand, South Africa. Has 1 native pastor.

**Magila,** a station of the Universities Mission in Usambara, on the continent opposite Zanzibar, East Africa, founded in 1869 by Bishop Tozer. In 1882 the Moslems of the place closed their mosque and became Christians. It has 1 missionary and 4 laymen.

**Magomero,** on Lake Scherwa, East Africa. In 1861 Bishop Mackenzie, leader of the Universities Mission, on his way up the Sambesi, met a gang of slaves. He liberated them, settled them at Magomero, and began their education and conversion. But the situation was too difficult. He died in 1862, and in 1864 his successor, Bishop Tozer, moved the colony to Zanzibar. (See Mbweni.)

**Magyar:** see Hungarian.

**Mahabeleshwar,** a town in Bombay presidency, West India, 80 miles southeast of Bombay. Principal sanitarium of the presidency, and during some seasons of the year one of the most lovely spots on earth, owing to the beauty of its scenery, and the great variety and luxuriance of its foliage and flowers. Population, 3,248. Mission station A. B. C. F. M. with Satara (q.v.).

**Mahaena,** station of the Paris Evangelical Society in Tahiti; 1 native pastor, 67 church-members.

**Mahanad,** station of the Free Church of Scotland, in Bengal, India; 1 missionary, 1 native teacher, 1 colporteur.

**Mahanaim,** station of the Hermannsburg Missionary Society in South Transvaal, East South Africa; church-members, 102.

**Mahanoro,** on the east coast of Madagascar, about latitude 20° south, was occupied by the S. P. G. in 1884; 1 missionary, 1 native pastor, 1 physician.

**Mahé,** one of the Seychelles Islands, East Africa. A station of the C. M. S., which works principally by its schools among the Creole negroes.

**Mahraoli,** a town in the Lahore district, Punjab, India. A station of the S. P. G.; 3 native workers, 6 communicants.

**Mai,** a small island belonging to the middle group of the New Hebrides, Melanesia; is visited by the Melanesian Mission, and looks promising. Three entirely different languages are spoken in this island.

**Maiana,** one of the Gilbert Islands, Micronesia. Population, 1,900; 1 missionary and wife under the Hawaiian Evangelical Association; 57 church-members.

**Main,** mission station of the Free Church of Scotland, in Kafraria, Africa; 16 preaching places, 1 missionary, 9 native assistants, 377 communicants, 7 schools, 338 pupils.

**Mainpuri** (Mynpuri), station of the American Presbyterian Board (North), in the Northwest Provinces, India (1843); 1 missionary and wife, 7 native assistants, 32 church-members, 260 pupils.

**Maiwo,** an island in the central group of the New Hebrides, Melanesia; was opened for the Melanesian missionaries in 1874, and has now over 70 Christians.

**Makewitta,** Ceylon, station of the Baptist Missionary Society; 2 evangelists, 58 church-members, 310 pupils.

**Makhabeng** (Makchabeng), town in North Transvaal, East South Africa, on a branch of the Limpopo River, northwest of GaMatlale. Mission station of Berlin Evangelical Lutheran Society (1868); 1 missionary, 3 native helpers, 190 church-members.

**Makhaleh,** station of the United Presbyterian Church of U. S. A. (1869), in the province of Assiout, Egypt.

**Makodweni,** town in East Central Africa, near the coast, 16 miles west of Mongwe. Mission station of A. B. C. F. M.; 1 missionary and wife.

**Mala,** a town in Southeast Lapland, southeast of Sorsele and north of Lucksele. Station of the Friends of the Mission to the Lapps, Sweden.

**Malacca,** a portion of the Straits Settlements of Great Britain, lying along the western coast of the Malay peninsula between Singapore and Penang, consists of a strip of territory about 42 miles in length, and from 8 to 24½ miles in breadth. Its surface is hilly, but not mountainous; and it is drained by five navigable rivers, making the soil alluvial and rich. The climate is equable and healthful. In 1881 the population numbered 93,579, of whom there were 67,523 Malays, 19,741 Chinese, 1,891 natives of India. Missions: S. P. G., stations at Singapore and elsewhere; 8 missionaries. Presbyterian Church of Scotland, stations at Singapore, Bukit-Timat, Serangoon, Tekkha, and Johor; 2 churches, 1 missionary and wife, 2 single ladies.

**Malagasi Version.**—The Malagasi belongs to the Malayan languages, and is spoken on the island of Madagascar. The Revs. Jones and Griffiths of the London Missionary Society translated the entire Bible, which was printed at Antananarivo between the years 1828 and 1835. In 1865 the British and Foreign Bible Society published at London another edition of the Malagasi Bible, which was prepared for the press by the Revs. Jones, Griffiths, and Meller. In 1869 the same Society published, at London, a revised edition of the New Testament with marginal references, under the care of the Rev. R. G. Hartley, of the London Missionary Society; and in 1871 an edition of the Bible was issued under the editorship of the Rev. R. Toy, who corrected the orthography of the Old Testament to make it harmonize as far as possible with the New. In order to secure as far as possible a thoroughly accurate and idiomatic version of the Bible in the Malagasi tongue, a joint board, representing all the missions on the island, was formed in 1873. In 1882 an interim edition of the Bible was published at London, under the care of the Rev. J. J. Sibree. The preliminary revision of the Bible, forming the basis of the revision committee's work, was completed by the Rev. W. E. Cousins, the chief reviser, September 15th, 1884. The work was begun December 1st, 1873, and the actual time which he has spent on it has been about eight years, and two days per week of that time have been given to the revision committee. On October 28th, 1885, the completion of the first revision of the Bible was made. The revision committee sat 433 days, and held 771 sittings, chiefly of three hours each. A second revision, for the purpose of harmonizing the different parts of the whole Bible, was begun on November 4th, 1885. The changes made in the second revision were chiefly from the native standpoint, to render the translation more easily understood, and more pleasant to the ear. The last meeting was held in the committee-room of the London Missionary Society, Madagascar, on April 30th, 1886. On May 2d, two days after the completion of the revision, a thanksgiving service was held in the Memorial Church, attended by missionaries, native pastors, and a large number of the Christians. The prime-minister was present, with a special message of thanks from Queen Ranavalona III., and this he delivered with his own congratulations on the very spot where, 38 years before, 14 Christians were hurled over the precipice at the command of Ranavalona I., for their adherence to the Word of God. The revised edition was printed at London under the care of the Rev. W. E. Cousins, assisted by others, and published in an edition of 8,000 copies 8vo, in 1888; an edition of the

New Testament in 32mo, consisting of 25,000, was also issued at London in 1887. Up to March 31st, 1889 there were disposed of 426,-434 portions of the Scriptures.

*(Specimen verse.* John 3 : 16.)

Fa lzany no nitiavan' Andriamanitra izao tontolo izao, fa nomeny ny Zanani-lahi-tokana, mba tsy ho very izay rehetra mino Azy, fa hahazo fiainana mandrakizay.

**Malan,** district in East Kaffraria, south Africa, south of Duff, 100 miles from King William's Town. Temperate, healthy. Population, 25,000, Kafir. Language, Xosa-Kafir. Religion, belief in spirits and an Almighty Maker—a sort of worship of ancestors. Natives very degraded. Mission station United Presbyterian Church of Scotland (1882); 1 missionary and wife, 19 native helpers, 12 out-stations, 8 churches, 342 members, 5 schools, 9 teachers.

**Malang,** a town in Southeast Java, southeast of Kediri. Mission station of the Netherland Missionary Society (Reformed Church); has 750 members and a medical mission. Missionaries from this station have of late begun to visit the inhabitants of the neighboring Tenger mountains, who annually offer sacrifices to the volcano Bromo.

**Malanha,** one of the Solomon Islands, Melanesia. A station of the Melanesian Missionary Society.

**Malay Versions.**—The Malay belongs to the Malaysian languages, and is spoken in the isles of Sumatra and Malacca. It is divided into the Standard and Low Malay.

1. *The Standard Malay.*—More than fifty years before the first complete New Testament in the Malay was published, parts of the Bible by different translators had been published. In 1668 the New Testament was printed in Roman letters at Amsterdam, translated by Daniel Bower, a Dutch minister who lived and died in the East. His translation of the Book of Genesis was also printed in 1662, and again in 1687. In 1685 Dr. M. Leidekker, a Dutch minister of Batavia, commenced a translation of the Bible, which became the standard Malay version. Upon the death of Dr. Leidekker, in 1701, Petrus von der Vern was appointed to complete the work of his predecessor, which he did during the same year. In 1722 a revision committee was appointed by the Dutch Government, which completed its work in 1728. Two editions were made—one in Roman characters, printed at Amsterdam 1731–33; the other in Arabic characters, published at Batavia in 1758. An edition of the New Testament from the Amsterdam text was published at Serampore in 1814, for the benefit of the Christians at Amboyna, by the Calcutta Auxiliary Bible Society, which in 1817 also issued an edition of the entire Bible from the Amsterdam text. An edition in Arabic characters from the Batavia text, carefully revised, was also issued by the same Society in 1822, and forwarded to Penang, Malacca, Java, and Bencoolen, for distribution. In the same year the British and Foreign Bible Society and the Netherlands Bible Society republished the Antwerp text, and in 1824 the latter Society also issued an edition from the Batavia text, under the care of Professor Wilmet. The same Society published between the years 1868

and 1872 a translation of the New Testament, and of the Book of Genesis, made by the Rev. H. C. Klinkerl; while the National Bible Society of Scotland issued an edition of the New Testament at Haarlem in 1877, under the care of Mr. Roskott, the translator. A new version of the Malay Scriptures, in Roman and Arabic characters, was undertaken by the Rev. B. P. Keasberry, and an edition of the New Testament was published in 1863. Some parts of the Old Testament, also translated by Mr. Keasberry, were issued by the British and Foreign Bible Society; the translator's death in 1875 put a stop to the work of completing the Old Testament. In 1885 the British and Foreign Bible Society issued, under the editorship of Dr. Rost of the India Office, a corrected edition of 5,000 copies of the four Gospels, and also an edition of 5,000 copies of the Books of Genesis, Psalms, and Proverbs, of Keasberry's translation. The Acts of the Apostles were edited in a slight revision by Mr. Klinkerl, of Leiden, the edition consisting of 5,000 copies. A new edition of the Malay Bible, lithographed from the translator's (Mr. Klinkerl's) own writing, was published by Netherlands Bible Society at Amsterdam, 1886–9, 4 vols.

2. *Low Malay or Sourabayan.*—An edition of the New Testament, prepared by Robinson and Medhurst, was published in 1816 and 1833 at Singapore. In 1846 the Netherlands Bible Society published an edition of the Psalms, and in 1853 the New Testament. The Book of Exodus, translated by the Rev. J. L. Marten, was published by the British and Foreign Bible Society in 1877 at Edinburgh, under the care of the Rev. E. W. King. An edition of the four Gospels and the Acts were published by the same Society in 1887, under the care of Mr. Klinkerl, whose second edition of the New Testament was issued by the Netherlands Bible Society in 1888.

*(Specimen verse.* John 3 : 16.)

*Standard.*

كرنا دميكين قربس الله سرده مغاسيهي ايسي دنيا. سهيڠت كرنيٱكن انقڽ يڠ توڠڬل سڤايٻ بارڠسيٻڠ يڠ ڤرچاي اكن دي. نياد اكن بناس. هان مندٱقت كهيدوڤن يڠ ككل.

*Roman.*

Kŭrna dŭmkianlah halnya Allah tŭlah mŭngasihi orang isi dunia ini, sahingga dikurniakannya Anaknya yang tunggal itu, supaya barang siapa yang pŭrchaya akan dia tiada iya akan binasa, mŭlainkan mŭndapat hidop yang kŭkal.

*Low Malay, or Sourabayan.*

Karna sabagitoe sangat Allah soedah mengasehi isi doenia, sahingga ija soedah membri Anaknja laki-laki jang toenggal, soepaja sasaorang jang pertjaja akan dia, djangan binasa, hanja beroleh kahidoepan kakal.

**Malayalam Version.**—The Malayalam or Malayalim belongs to the Dravidian family of non-Aryan languages, and is spoken in Travancore and Malabar. The New Testament was translated by Timapah Pillay, and published at Madras in 1810 by the British and Foreign

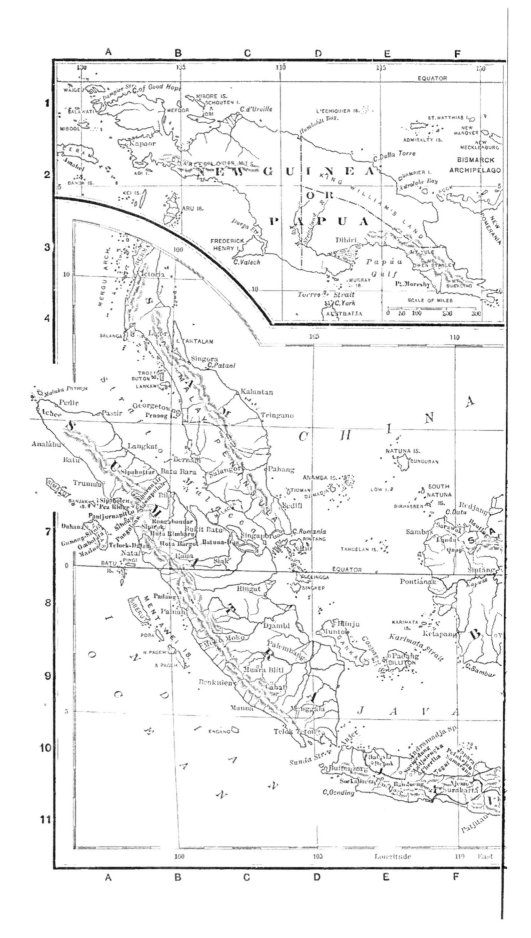

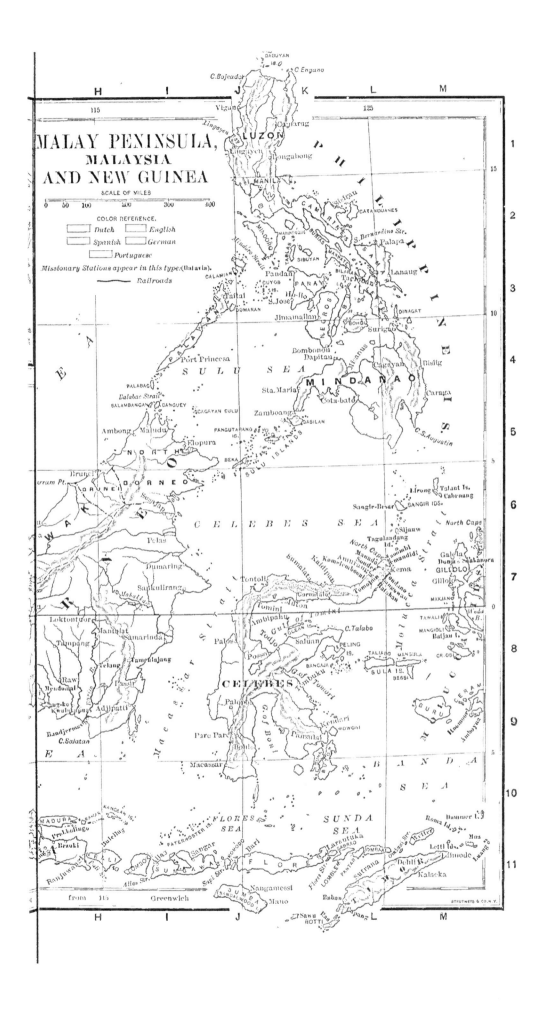

MALAY PENINSULA,
MALAYSIA
AND NEW GUINEA

SCALE OF MILES

COLOR REFERENCE.

Dutch          English
Spanish        German
        Portuguese

Missionary Stations appear in this type:(Batavia).
—— Railroads

Bible Society. A new translation was undertaken by Mr. Bailey of the Church Missionary Society, for Travancore, and another by Mr. Spring for Malabar. The former's version of the New Testament was published at Cattayam by the Madras Auxiliary. When the first edition of the entire Bible was published is not known, but probably between 1832 and 1856. A new translation of the New Testament was made by Mr. Gundert, and published at Mangalore in 1868 by the Basle Bible Society. A reprint of the Old Testament was issued by the British and Foreign Bible Society in 1863.

In 1870 a joint committee representing the different missionary societies and including members of the Syrian Church, was formed for the purpose of revising the New Testament. Dr. Gundert's version is to be taken as the basis, and an attempt will be made to adopt such terms as may render one version intelligible both among the northern and southern Malayalim-speaking people. The revision of the New Testament which was begun in 1870 was completed on September 19th, 1882, and printed under the care of the Rev. J. Knoblauch. In 1885 the Revision Board resolved to revise again the revised New Testament but to meet a pressing demand an interim edition of 2,500 copies each of the old and the revised versions of the New Testament was issued. In 1888 an interim edition of 5,000 copies of Bailey's New Testament was published to meet present wants. The work of re-revision is steadily progressing.

Mr. Gundert continues his translation of the Old Testament in Germany.

(*Specimen verse.* John 3 : 16.)

എന്തുകൊണ്ടെന്നാൽ ദൈവം തന്റെ ഏകജാതനായ പുത്രനെ, അവനിൽ വിശ്വസിക്കുന്ന വൻ ഒരുത്തനും നശിച്ചുപൊകാതെ, നിത്യ ജിവൻ ഉണ്ടാകെണ്ടന്നതിന, തരുവാൻ തക്ക വണ്ണം ഏത്രയും ലൊകത്തെ സ്നേഹിച്ചു.

**Malays.**—1. In its strictest sense, the name given to the inhabitants of the Malay peninsula, Penang, and Sumatra, who belong to the Mongoloid race, being closely allied anthropologically to the Chinese. In physical appearance they are of somewhat short stature; brown complexion—not so light as the Chinese or so dusky as the Hindu; have straight black, coarse hair; no beard; large mouth; flat nose; large, dark eyes; somewhat thick lips; small hands and feet, with thin, weak legs. In temperament the Malays are thoroughly Asiatic—taciturn, undemonstrative, cunning, treacherous, and at times cruel. Their passions are easily aroused, and under special exciting circumstances, such as love, jealousy, or stimulants, they reach a height of frenzy during which they "run amuck," assailing violently all whom they meet.

We find three principal classes: the *Orang benua*, "men of the soil," or hill-tribes; the *Orang laut*, "men of the sea," who are the daring, skilful, adventurous seafaring men of the Indian Archipelago; and the *Orang Malyeru*, or Malays proper, the civilized class, who exhibit more of refinement, and are courteous and kind to their families and friends. The Malay sailors were the formidable pirates who formerly menaced commerce and were the dread scourge of the Indian seas. Their deeds of cruelty, treachery, and cunning, aided by their daring, brave, audacious seamanship, are still the theme of stories of adventure. Even at the present time few ship-captains care to have a crew composed entirely of Malays, though they form the largest part of the sailors on the Indian and China coast.

Mohammedanism was embraced by the Malays in the 13th and 14th centuries, the fierce, uncompromising, aggressive spirit of the False Prophet attracting them at once to the faith.

*Language.*—The Malay language is the *lingua franca* of the Indian Archipelago. Its phonetic elements are simple, the grammatical structure is regular, and its vocabulary, especially in nautical terms, is very copious. It has the five vowels, *a, e, i, o, u,* short and long, with one diphthong. The consonants are, *b, d, g, h, j, k, l, m, n, ñ, p, r, s, t, w, y, ng, ch.* Malay is a dissyllabic language, with the accent as a rule on the penultimate, except where that syllable is open and short. Derived words are formed by prefixes, affixes, infixes, and reduplication. Much skill is displayed in the idiomatic use of the hundred or more derivative forms. There are no inflectional forms to distinguish number, gender, or case. Number is denoted only when absolutely necessary by the use of the adjectives *sagála,* all, and *bañak,* many, or by *sa* or *satu,* one, with a classifier. As in the Chinese language, classifiers are numerous, such as *orang,* used in speaking of persons; *képing,* piece, for flat things. Gender is distinguished by the use of auxiliary words. Case is indicated by position. Verbs have no person, number, mood, or tense. Long sentences are avoided, and in a sentence first comes the subject, then the verb followed by the object, and qualifying words follow the words they qualify.

The Perso-Arabic alphabet is used for writing Malay; it was introduced at the time of the Mohammedan conquest. A great number of Arabic words have also been introduced into the vocabulary.

The literature of the Malays consists mainly of proverbs, and love poems of four lines. Their religious literature is remarkable mainly for its independence, and the fact that it does not show the influence of Islam.

2. In a wider sense the term is applied to the races inhabiting the Indian Archipelago and many of the islands of the Pacific, embracing an area 13,000 by 5,000 miles, or from Easter Island to Madagascar, from New Zealand to the Hawaii Islands. This wide dispersion of the race has been the subject of much study and theory; but the causes of it, and proof as to the fact, are not within the limits of this article. A classification of this wider definition is as follows: (1) Malay. (2) Malay Javanese: the inhabitants of the Ladrones, Formosa, Philippine Islands, the Malagassi, the Javanese. (3) Melanesian: Fiji Islands. (4) Polynesian: the Hawaiians, Marquesas Islanders, Tahitians, Rarotongans, Samoans, Tonguans, Maoris. To these Wallace adds the Papuans, who are the farthest removed from the Malays, yet whom he considers to be of the same stock. They represent the extreme difference in type, due to the mingling of other races with the Malays, and have frizzly hair, are tall and black, bearded, and hairy-bodied. The mental

characteristics of the Papuan are also modified, and they are bold, excitable, impetuous, and noisy. Between the two extremes every gradation is found, varying with the preponderance of either the Malay or Papuan type. In some of the provinces of China, in Formosa, and Hainan, the aborigines are closely allied if not identical with the Malays. The special characteristics of the Malay are modified in the various islands by the lapse of time and the influences of environment, so that each island race has peculiarities of its own. In Borneo we find the fierce spirit of the passionate Malay cropping out in the grim hunt for human heads; in other islands cannibalism is the form it assumes. Mohammedanism does not accompany the Malays in their dispersion, and low forms of superstition, of fetichism, and of demonolatry take its place in the religion of the races.

For mission work, see Malacca and Singapore.

**Malegaon** (Malegam), town in Bombay, India, on the Mosam River, about 100 miles northeast of Bombay City. It is the headquarters for the work of the Church Missionary Society in the Khandesh district, which covers an area of 13,000 square miles, with a population of 1,227,000. The people are eager to hear the gospel, which is being preached to them by a small force of workers: 1 missionary and wife, 18 native teachers, 8 schools, 143 Christians, 65 communicants. A "triple chain of caste, custom, and debt" holds the people in bondage, and keeps them heathen.

**Malekula**, one of the New Hebrides Islands; has three foreign missionaries under the general direction of the Presbyterian Church in Canada, though they are supported by the Presbyterian Church in Victoria, Australia. These islands are now in monthly communication with Australia by the establishment of a line of steamers running between Melbourne and Sydney, and the principal islands.

**Maliseet Version.**—The Maliseet belongs to the languages of America, and is spoken by an Indian tribe in New Brunswick. A translation of the Gospel of John was made by the Rev. S. T. Rand, aided by a native, who was confined to his couch, by a broken thigh, during the whole time that he was engaged on this important work. An edition of the Gospel was printed by the British and Foreign Bible Society at London in 1870.

(*Specimen verse.* John 3 : 16.)

Eebŭchŭl Nŭkskam ĕdooche-moosajĭtpŭn oos-kĭtkŭmĭkw wĕjemelooĕtpŭn wihwebu Ookwŏŏsŭl, welaman 'msea wĕn tan wĕlämsŭtŭk oohŭkĕk, skatŭp ŭksekăhăwe, kănookŭloo ootelnp askŭmowsooagŭn.

**Malmesbury**, town in Southeast Cape Colony, South Africa, north of Cape Town. Station of S. P. G.; 1 missionary.

**Malokong**, town in Transvaal, East South Africa, on a branch of the Limpopo, south of GaMatlale. Mission station Berlin Evangelical Lutheran Society (1867); 1 missionary, 5 other helpers, 6 out-stations, 71 church-members.

**Malta**, an island in the Mediterranean, south of Italy; a British crown colony, and an important naval station. Area, 95 square miles. Population, 162,423 (English, 2,138; foreigners, 1,097, the remainder natives). Language, a patois of Arabic. Religion, Roman Catholic.

Malta was for many years the most important missionary station in the Mediterranean, and was occupied by all the missionary societies seeking to work in the Levant. The mission press of the A. B. C. F. M., was established here prior to its removal to Smyrna, and it was here that Wm. Goodell and his associates studied the Turkish and Armenian before establishing themselves at Smyrna, Constantinople, and Beyrout. It is now occupied as a preaching station by several of the Colonial Societies of England and Scotland, especially the Scotch Free Church.

**Maltese Version.**—The Maltese is a dialect of the Arabic, belonging to the Semitic family of languages, and is spoken by the natives of Malta, the ancient Melita. In writing, the Roman letters are used, Arabic characters being unknown to the Maltese. The first attempt to translate the Scriptures into Maltese was made in the early part of the present century by the Rev. W. Jowett of the Church Missionary Society aided by a native. In 1882 a small edition of the Gospel of John was published at London as a specimen of the work. In 1827 the four Gospels and the Acts were published by the Society for Promoting Christian Knowledge; and in 1847 the entire New Testament in Maltese. The translation was for the greater part made by Mr. Camilleri, a native of Malta, but afterwards a minister of the Church of England. The book, however, did not meet with that acceptance which had been hoped for, owing not so much to any defects in the translation as to the bigoted ignorance of the people, and also in part to the difficulty of expressing Arabic gutturals in Roman characters. About eight different systems of orthography have been tried at various times, but the uncouth letters which have been adopted to represent certain sounds failed to give satisfaction. A deep interest having been taken by a few Englishmen living in the island in the spiritual welfare of this priest-ridden people, a revised translation of the Gospel of Matthew was prepared by Mr. Bonavia, and sent over to England. After due examination and revision it was printed, under the editorship of Dr. Camilleri, at London in 1870. In 1872 the Gospel of John and the Acts were also issued by the British and Foreign Bible Society.

(*Specimen verse.* John 3 : 16.)

Ghallex Allā hecca hab id dinia illl tā l'Iben tighu unigenitu, sabiex- collmin jemmen bih ma jintilifx, izda lcollu il haja ta dejem.

**Malto, Pahari, or Rajmahal Version.**—The Malto belong to the Dravidian family of non-Aryan languages, and is spoken by the Paharis in the Rajmahal district of North India. Methodist Episcopal missionaries of North India translated the Gospel of Matthew, which was published by the American Bible Society in 1875. A translation of the Gospels of Luke and John was prepared by the Rev. E. Droese of the Church Missionary Society, who for more than twenty years lived among the Paharis.

The former was published by the British and Foreign Bible Society in 1882, the latter in 1883. Mr. Droese also translated the Gospels of Matthew and Mark and the Acts, which were published by the Calcutta Auxiliary in 1887. An edition of the Psalms was issued in 1888 at the Secundra Orphanage Press, under the care of the same auxiliary in 1888. The version was also made by Mr. Droese.

**Malua,** town in Upolu, one of the Samoan Islands, Polynesia : is occupied by the work of the London Missionary Society (1836). It has a training institute for young men, with 96 students in full course, 11 in preparatory; 3 missionaries, 1 lady, 8 native ministers, 14 native preachers, 478 church members, with an attendance of 1,596. Contributions, £161 7s. 2d. A movement to promote higher education among the girls and women has recently been inaugurated. The late political troubles, added to the severe ravages of a hurricane, have been great hindrances to the work; but it is now progressing very favorably. The Samoan Christians give striking proof of the efficacy of the gospel in changing natural vices to Christian virtues.

**Mamboe,** a town in the Sherbro country, West Africa, on the Mamboe River, east of Yoruba. Station of the United Brethren in Christ (U. S. A.); 1 teacher, 1 itinerant, 16 church-members, 1 school, 18 pupils.

**Mamboia,** town in East Central Africa, inland, due west of Zanzibar Island, north of Usagara. Mission station C. M. S. (1879); 1 missionary, 1 native assistant, 2 communicants, 1 school. The work here is carried on with great danger on account of the hostility between the Arabs and Germans. Communication with England is often interrupted, so that five months passed at one time without any word from the coast.

**Mamgaia,** one of the Hervey Islands, Polynesia, south of Rarotonga. Mission station L. M. S.; 1 missionary and wife, 3 native pastors. Communication with this station is most difficult, five months sometimes elapsing between the sending and receipt of a letter.

**Mamre,** a town in Cape Colony southeast of Malmesbury, South Africa. Mission station of the Moravians (1808); 3 missionaries and their wives, 1 assistant missionary, 1,843 church-members.

**Mamusa,** a city in the Orange Free State, on the river Hart, South Africa. In 1841 a Paris missionary founded a station here among the Kovas, which for a long time was maintained by their pious chief. It is now an outstation of the work of the London Missionary Society at Taung (q.v.).

**Manaar,** a station of the Wesleyan Methodist Missionary Society in the Jaffna district, Ceylon; 1 native preacher, 1 chapel, 6 preaching-places, 28 church-members, 127 pupils.

**Manado,** a city of Minahassa, the northeastern peninsula of Celebes, East Indies, and noted as a great coffee emporium. From 1830 to 1874 it was the chief seat of the Netherland-ische Zendingsvereeniging, which worked with great success among the heathen Alifures. Out of a population of 114,000 no less than 95,000 were converted, and the great difficulty arising from the different languages spoken by the Alifures was happily overcome by the introduction of the Malayan language in church and school. But lack of money and the discoveries of the Dutch Government compelled the missionaries to enter the service of the state church in 1870, and now Islam is making great headway.

**Manamadura,** city in Tamil country, Madras, British India, 30 miles southeast of Madura. Climate very hot and dry, 80°–100° F. Language, Tamil. Religions, Brahminism, Moslemism. Natives ignorant, degraded. Mission station A. B. C. F. M. (1864); 1 missionary and wife, 33 native helpers, 1 church, 27 out-stations, 3 churches, 219 church-members, 20 schools, 628 scholars.

**Manandona,** town in West Central Madagascar, northeast of Morondava. Mission station of the Norwegian Missionary Society (1870).

**Manargudi,** town in the south-central part of the district of Trichinopoly, East Madras, India, south of Combaconam and southwest of Negapatam. Mission station of the Wesleyan Methodists; 3 missionaries, 32 native helpers, 26 church-members, 1 chapel, 7 schools, 570 scholars, and a high-school.

**Manchentuduvy,** a station of the Wesleyan Methodist Missionary Society in the Jaffna district, Ceylon; 1 native minister, 23 church-members, 378 pupils.

**Manchuria,** one of the divisions of the Chinese Empire (see China), lying north of China proper, between latitude 42° and 53° north. In accordance with the treaty of 1860 between Russia and China, nearly one half of the former territory was given over to Russia, and the present limits are the Amoor on the north, the Usuri and Sunga-Cha on the east, Kirin on the south, from which it is separated by the Shan-Alin range; and on the west the Khingan Mountains, the Sira-Muren River, and the district of Upper Sungari separate it from the desert of Gobi. Its area is about 378,000 square miles. Population estimated from 11,-000,000 to 12,000,000. Physically, the country is divided into the mountain ranges on the north and east, among which lie numerous fertile valleys; and the plain which stretches south from Moukden to the Gulf of Liao-tung. There are three principal rivers—the Amoor, the Usuri, and the Sunagari. The latter is over 1,200 miles long, and along its fertile banks is the most populous region of the country. Manchuria is divided into three provinces: Shing-King, or Liao-tung, of which Moukden is the capital (q.v.); Newchwang (Ying-tse), at the head of the Gulf of Liao-tung, is the treaty port;—Kirin (Central Manchuria); capital, Kirin, on the Sungari, 200 miles from its source, has a population of about 150,000, mostly Chinese;—and Tsi-tsi-har (Northern Manchuria), sparsely populated, with few cities of importance. The climate varies from extremes of heat and cold, from 90° F. in the summer to 10° below zero in the winter. During four months of the year the rivers are frozen up, a short spring is followed by the heat of summer, and a few weeks of autumn usher in the snow and ice of the winter. Minerals are abundant. The agricultural products are mainly indigo and opium, though cereals, cotton, and tobacco are also grown. The reigning race of China are Manchus, but though they have subjugated China, Manchuria is gradually losing its native language and system of education under the influence of the Chinese, who are overrunning the country and bringing its customs into conformity with those of China. The native Manchus are a finer race physically, mentally, and morally than the Chinese; they are of larger frame, lighter color, and have greater intellectual capacity. Mission work in this part of China is carried on by the Presbyterian Church of Ireland, with stations at Newchwang, Jiu-jow, Kwan-cheng-tszu, and Kirin (q.v.); and by the United Presbyterian Church of Scotland, with stations at Newchwang, Haichung, Liaoyang, Moukden, Tieling, Kaiyuen, Taiping Kow (q.v.).

**Manduilung,** a dialect of the Batta language (q.v.), spoken in Southern Sumatra. Seven thousand and ten copies of the New Testament and portions in this dialect were put in circulation previous to March 31st, 1889.

**Mandalay,** the capital (and district) of Upper Burma, on the Irawaddy, 380 miles north of Rangoon. The climate is tropical and dry. In the district there are 150,000 to 200,000 people. Burmese is the language spoken; Buddhism the prevailing religion. Station of A. B. M. U.; 1 missionary and wife, 4 other ladies, 1 physician, 3 native assistants, 1 church, 80 church-members, 95 pupils. S. P. G.; 2 missionaries, 4 native assistants, 53 communicants. Wesleyan Methodist (1886); 1 missionary, 1 native pastor, 1 Anglo-vernacular school, 85 pupils, 4 church-members.

**Mandapasalai,** a city in the Madura district, South India, Population, 200,000. Language, Tamil. Religions, Hinduism and Mohammedanism. A station of the Madura mission of the A. B. C. F. M. (1851); 1 missionary and wife, 10 out-stations, 2,493 adherents, 10 churches, 723 communicants, 3 native preachers, 32 assistants, 25 Sunday-schools, 400 scholars, 2 girls' schools, 80 scholars. Contributions (1888), $595.

**Mandari Version.**—The Mandari belongs to the Kolarian group of non-Aryan languages, and is used by the Kohls of Chota Nagpur, Central India. A translation of the Scriptures into this language was undertaken by the Rev. N. Nottrott of the German Missionary (Gossner's) Society, who prepared the Gospel of Mark, which was issued by the Calcutta Auxiliary Society in 1876. The Gospel of Luke was added as prepared by the Rev. L. Beyer of the same missionary society in 1879. The Gospels of Matthew (by Nottrott) and of John (by Beyer) were published in 1880. Each revised the work of the other by the help of native assistants, and thus they provided the four Gospels for the 25,000 Christians of their own mission, and the 10,000 Christians of the Society for the Propagation of the Gospel mission, and the still larger number of non-Christian Kohls of Chota Nagpur. In 1885 an edition of 2,000 copies of the Acts of the Apostles, translated by Mr. Beyer, was issued by the Calcutta Auxiliary; and in 1887 the Epistles of Peter and James, translated by Mr. Nottrott. Thus far 32,570 portions of the Scriptures have been disposed of.

(*Specimen verse.* Mark 3 : 35.)

विसिष परमेश्वरा मेंने ठेका सेनतन होइंटे इनांगे चांटगा हाग। कोंड़े मिसो कोंड़े बइंगा दंगा मेनैद ॥

**Mandarin Colloquial Version.**—The Mandarin is one of the most important dialects of the Chinese, because it is the colloquial medium of a large proportion of the people of Northern China. In general two branches of the Mandarin Colloquial are distinguished: the Pekin or Northern, and the Nankin or Southern.

1. *The Pekin or Northern.*—The New Testament into this dialect was translated by Revs. Burdon, Blodgett, Schereschewsky, Edkins, and Martin, and was published by the American and British Bible Societies in 1872. The Old Testament, translated by Dr. Schereschewsky, was also published by both Societies in 1875 and 1877.

The British and Foreign Bible Society also published, in 1888, a reference edition of 3,000 copies of the New Testament in the Roman alphabet. About the year 1875 the China Inland Mission brought out an edition of the four Gospels and Acts. This portion was revised by the Rev. W. Cooper, who has transliterated the remaining books of the New Testament, and added the references. The text is a rendering, word for word, into Roman character of the Northern Mandarin version. The term used for God is Shang-ti, and the transliteration has followed the system in use in the China Inland Mission for twenty years. Several missionaries assisted in the final preparation of the copy, and the edition was edited by Mr. Cooper.

2. *The Nankin or Southern.*—A New Testament translation into this dialect was made by the Revs. Medhurst and Stronach, and published by the British and Foreign Bible Society in 1856.

(*Specimen verse.* John 3 : 16.)

1. Pekin colloq.

上帝把獨生的兒子賜給世人使那信他的人，免得永遠受苦可以得着長久的生命上帝愛惜世人如此。

2. Nankin colloq.

天主憐愛世人甚至將獨生子賜給他們，凡信他的不至滅亡必得永生。

**Mandawar** (Mandaur), a town and station of the Methodist Episcopal Church (North), U. S. A., in the Rohilkund district, Northwest Provinces, India; 1 native preacher, 85 Christians, 15 day-schools, 250 pupils.

**Manchu,** the language of Manchuria, North China (q.v.), akin to the Mongolian. The New Testament has been translated and published by the British and Foreign Bible Society.

(*Specimen verse.* John 3 : 16.)

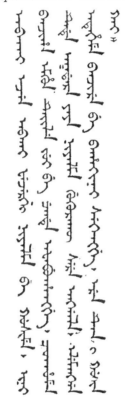

**Mande** or **Mandingo Version.**—The Mande belongs to the Negro group of African languages, and is used in Mandingo country, south of Gambia River. The Rev. Macbrair, of the Wesleyan Missionary Society, translated the four Gospels, of which the Gospel of Matthew only was published by the British and Foreign Bible Society in 1838.

(*Specimen verse.* John 3 : 16.)

Katuko Alla ye dunya kannu nyinuyama, an ading wulukilering di, mensating mo-omo men lata ala, ate tinyala, barri asi balu abadaring sotto.

**Mandla,** town in the Central Provinces, India, on the Nerbudda River, 1,770 feet above the sea. Population, 4,732, Hindus, Moslems. Station of the Church Missionary Society (1878); 2 missionaries, 6 native teachers, 21 communicants, 2 schools, 13 pupils. Contributions, 45 rupees.

**Mandomai** (Mentowei), town in Southeast Borneo, on the Little Dyak River. Station of the Rhenish Missionary Society (1869); 1 missionary, 5 native agents, 94 communicants. The Rhenish Mission in Borneo, founded in 1839, ceased entirely in 1859 on account of a conspiracy between the Malays and the Dyaks against the whites, in which several missionaries and their wives were killed. The Dutch Government tried to make the missionaries responsible for the rebellion, but allowed them, nevertheless, to resume work in 1866.

**Mandridrano,** a country station in Madagascar, occupied by the Friends Foreign Missionary Association, 1888; 1 medical missionary and wife. The medical services of the missionary have been in great demand, and four cottages have been put up as a hospital, to which the natives subscribed £5.

**Manchnodu,** station of the Leipsic Evangelical Lutheran Missionary Society in Madras, India; 197 communicants.

**Manepy,** town in Northern Ceylon, five miles from Jaffnapatam. Climate tropical, average $82\frac{1}{2}°$ Fahrenheit. Population, 11,672. Race and language, Tamil. Religion, Brahman-Sivaism. Natives rude, uncultivated farmers. Mission station of the A. B. C. F. M. (1831); 1 missionary and wife, 84 native helpers, 8 out-stations, 3 churches, 401 church-members, 42 schools, 2,613 scholars.

**Mangaia,** one of the Hervey Islands, Polynesia; a station of the L. M. S. Of the five chiefs ruling over 2,266 souls, only one is still averse to Christianity. Numangatini, a chief who at one time was a heathen priest and offered human sacrifices, was after his conversion very zealous for the prohibition of the importation of English whiskey. It has 1 missionary, 3 native pastors.

**Mangalore,** chief town of South Kanara, district of Madras, India; picturesque, clean, with good streets and nicely-built houses. It is buried amid groves of cocoa-nut palms, with water on three sides and a harbor good for small vessels. Population, 32,099, Hindus, Moslems, and Christians. Station of the Basle Missionary Society; 13 missionaries, 9 missionaries' wives, 1 other lady, 55 native assistants, 3 out-stations, 1,047 communicants.

**Manikramam,** station of the Leipsic Evangelical Lutheran Missionary Society (1859), in Madras presidency, India; 1 missionary, 11 out-stations, 166 communicants.

**Manihihi,** the principal island of the Penrhyn group, Polynesia. It was almost depopulated by slave-hunters from Peru. It is visited by missionaries of the L. M. S. from Rarotonga (q.v.).

**Manipuri Version.**—The Manipuri belongs to the Tibeto-Burman group of non-Aryan languages, and is spoken in Manipur, a small independent kingdom south of Assam. A version of the New Testament was undertaken by Dr. Carey in 1814; he procured some learned natives from Manipur, and superintended their labors. When the translation was completed it was printed in the Bengali character in 1824 at Serampore, but never reprinted.

**Manisa,** a city of Asia Minor, about 50 miles east of Smyrna. The ancient Magnesia, it is still a large and important city. Population about 40,000, chiefly Turks, Greeks, and Armenians For many years it was an out-station of the A. B. C. F. M., worked from Smyrna. Then for a few years it was occupied as a missionary residence, on account of the heat and difficulty of mission work in Smyrna. A flourishing church was established. It is now again an out-station of Smyrna.

**Mannoh,** town in Sherbro, West Coast, Africa, a little north of Avery. Station of the United Brethren (U. S. A.); 19 church-members, 1 day-school, 18 scholars, 1 Sunday-school, 18 scholars.

**Mansinam,** town on island of Manaswari, New Guinea. Station of the Utrecht Missionary Society (1863); 2 missionaries, 1 female missionary, 1 native assistant, 40 communicants, 1 school, 40 scholars.

**Mansura** (Monsoora), town in Upper Egypt, near the apex of the Delta, north of Cairo, south of Damietta. Station of the United Presbyterian Church of America (1866); 2 missionaries and wives, 1 female missionary, 7 native assistants, 37 communicants, 2 schools, 241 scholars.

**Manchu Version.**—The Manchu belongs to the Tungus branch of the Ural-Altaic family of languages, and is spoken in Manchuria, and is also the court language of Pekin. Into this language Mr. Lipofzoff translated the Gospel of Matthew, which was printed in 1822 at St. Petersburg, by the British and Foreign Bible Society. An edition of the entire New Testament was issued by the same Society in 1835, the translation having been made by Mr. Swan of the London Missionary Society. In 1857 an edition of the Gospels of Mark and Luke in Manchu and Chinese, in parallel columns, was published at Shanghai, under the care of Mr. Wylie.

**Manua,** one of the Samoan Islands, Polynesia. The people have their own king and government, and have been undisturbed by the political troubles in the other islands. None of their land is alienated to foreigners. The people are noted for the simplicity and purity of their Christian life. The London Missionary Society began work in 1837, but now the native ministry carry on the work, with an occasional visit from the missionaries on the other islands. There are 8 native ministers, 412 communicants, 1,612 adherents, 7 Sunday-schools, 592 scholars, 7 boys' schools, 327 pupils, 7 girls' schools, 265 pupils. Contributions, £12 1s. 0d.

**Manuane,** a Hermannsburg station in the circle of Mariko, Transvaal, South Africa, with 517 members.

**Manx Version.**—The Manx belongs to the Keltic branch of the Aryan family of languages, and is used in the Isle of Man. Between the years 1771 and 1775 a version of the Bible was published at Whitchaven. In 1815 the British and Foreign Bible Society published an edition, followed by another in 1819, which was probably the last, since the islanders are now supplied with the Bible in English.

*(Specimen verse. John 3 : 16.)*

Son lheid y ghraih shen hug Jee da'n theihll, dy dug eh e ynrycan Vac v'er ny gheddyn, nagh jinnagh quoi-erbee chredjagh aynsyn cherraghtyn, agh yn vea ta dy bragh farraghtyn y chosney.

**Maoombi** (Maumby), a town in Northwest Celebes between Manado and Talawan, west by northwest from Ajimandidi. Mission station of the Netherlands Missionary Society.

**Maori Version.**—The Maori or New Zealand belongs to the Polynesian languages, and is spoken in New Zealand. The first edition of the New Testament was printed by the British and Foreign Bible Society in 1837. The translation was made by the Revs. Williams and Yate of the Church Missionary Society. Soon the edition of 5,000 copies was exhausted, and a second and a third edition, each of 20,000 copies, were reprinted in a few years. In 1859 the Old Testament, as translated by the Rev. R. Maunsell of the Church Missionary Society, was published at London in 1858. An edition carefully revised by Mr. Maunsell and members of the Church Missionary and Wesleyan Missionary Societies was published at London in 1868, under the editorship of the Rev. T. W. Meller. In 1885 an edition of the Maori Bible, corrected and slightly revised by Messrs. Maunsell and Williams, with the numbers of the verses prefixed to the verses and not placed in the margins, and with chapter and page readings, was commenced in 1885 by the British Bible Society, and was completed at press in 1888, the edition consisting of 6,000 copies of the complete Bible, 4,000 New Testaments, and 2,000 each, of the four Gospels and Acts, as portions. Thus far 141,150 portions of the Scriptures have been disposed of.

*(Specimen verse. John 3 : 16.)*

Na, kola ano te aroha o te Atua ki te ao, homai ana e ia tana Tamaiti ko tahi, kia kahore ai e mate te tangata e whakapono ana ki a ia, engari kia whiwhi ai ki te oranga tonutanga.

**Maoris,** the aboriginal inhabitants of New Zealand, who belong to the Malay family of mankind. They claim to have migrated to New Zealand 500 years ago from "Hawaiki," which is supposed to be either Hawaii or Savaii of the Samoan Islands. They are a fine race, of average stature, with olive-brown skins, and their heads exhibit a high order of intellectual development. They are beardless as a rule, but that is due in part to the custom of plucking out the beard with shells. Most of the race have long black hair, but some have reddish hair, and in others it is frizzly. Large eyes, thick lips, and large, irregular teeth are characteristic. The women are smaller than the men, and generally inferior to them. Tattooing was a universal practice previous to the introduction of Christianity. The custom of *taboo*, which has given a word in universal use among English-speaking people, was practised by the priests to make any person or thing sacred and inviolable. Such regard was paid to the sanctity of the taboo, that even in war time tabooed persons or things were not harmed. Cannibalism was practised by the heathen

Maoris, but has disappeared, together with infanticide, slavery, and polygamy, under the enlightening influences of Christianity.

The Maoris, like most races in tropical climates, marry young, but they are not a very prolific race. Their language belongs to the Malay family. Fourteen letters, *a, e, h, i, k, m, n, o, p, r, t, u, w,* and *ng,* are all that the alphabet contains. Seven dialects are recognized. The language is sonorous, and adapted to lyrics and poems, and the popular literature consists largely of metrical proverbs, legends, and traditions. The people are very fond of music and songs. (For mission work, see New Zealand.)

**Mapumulo,** town in Natal, East South Africa, near Port Natal. Station of A. B. C. F. M.; 1 missionary and wife, 1 out-station.

**Marakei,** one of the Gilbert Islands, Polynesia. The work in the island is under the native preacher, in the employ of the Hawaiian Evangelical Association since 1887, and a missionary of the L. M. S. makes an annual visit to the islands. The population of the island is 2,000; and 70 are church-members.

**Maran,** one of the Solomon Islands, Melanesia. Has a station of the Melanesian Mission.

**Maranhao,** city in Northeast Brazil. A place of great mercantile importance. Climate hot, unhealthy. Population, 34,023. Mission station Presbyterian Church (South); 1 missionary and wife.

**Marash,** a city of Northern Syria, at the foot of the Taurus Mountains, 90 miles northwest of Aleppo. Population about 40,000, Turks and Armenians. Mission station of the A. B. C. F. M., with 4 missionaries and wives and 2 female missionaries, 3 large churches with fine buildings and over 2,000 church-members. Here is located the theological seminary of the Central Turkey Mission and a flourishing girls' boarding-school of high grade. The graded schools of the city are most excellent—not surpassed by those of any city in Turkey. Missionary work commenced with bitter persecution, but after repeated attempts a foothold was obtained, and then the work progressed very rapidly. The Foreign Christian Missionary Society (U. S. A.) also have a preacher, a school, and 25 scholars.

**Marathi Version.**—The Marathi belongs to the Indic branch of the Aryan family of languages, and is spoken by the educated natives in the Bombay presidency. A version of the Scriptures was undertaken in 1804, and the entire Bible was published at Serampore between 1811 and 1820, and a second revised edition in 1825. A new version was undertaken by the Rev. John Taylor, but he only lived to complete the Gospel of Matthew, which was printed at Bombay in 1819.

American missionaries (Messrs. G. Hall and S. Newell) commenced a version in 1817, and the New Testament was published at Bombay in 1826; a revised edition was printed in 1831, and a second revision, to which Rev. H. Ballantine devoted several years, in 1845. In 1858 a New Testament with references was published, and again in 1868. The Bible was issued in 1847, and a thorough revision in 1855. In 1857 and 1871 other editions of the Bible followed, published by the American Bible So-

ciety. In 1881 the British and Foreign Bible Society issued an edition of the Old Testament with paragraph headings prepared by the Rev. Baba Padmonji, and in 1888 the New Testament.

All these editions are printed in the so-called Balboodh or Balborah character, which appears to be almost if not quite the same as the Devanagari itself. But there is also the Modhi character, which is most generally understood, and is employed in all transactions of business. In this latter character the Gospels and the Acts, as prepared by Mr. Farrar, are also published.

In 1881 an edition of 500 copies of the Gospel of John in Roman characters was carried through the press by Dr. Murray Mitchell.

The Marathi Bible is now undergoing a thorough revision.

(*Specimen verses.* John 3 : 16.)

कां तर देवाने जगावर एवढी प्रीति केली
की, त्याने आपला एकुलता पुच दिल्हा,
यासाठीं कीं जो कोणी त्यावर विश्वास
ठेवितो त्याचा नाश होऊं नये, तर त्याला
सर्वकालचें जीवन व्हावें.

(*Modhi.*)

[Modhi script specimen verses]

**Marburg,** a small town on the east coast of Natal, Africa, south of Durban and northeast of Queenstown. Mission station of the Hermannsburg Missionary Society.

**Marden, Henry,** b. New Boston, N. H., U.S.A., December 9th, 1837; graduated at Dartmouth College 1862, and Andover Theological Seminary 1869; ordained September, 1869; sailed for Turkey as a missionary of the American Board September 21st, the same year. He was stationed at Marash, Central Turkey. He visited the United States in 1878, and his health having failed, he again left for home April 17th, 1890, with Mrs. Marden and his daughter. In a letter written from Marash, May 2d, he said: "I find that during the year ending to-day I have been absent from home 189 days, and have travelled over 1,500 miles on horseback, visiting 43 cities and towns which have Christian communities. Only a part of these places as yet have Protestant congregations, but I have personal relations with the people in them all." On reaching Athens, May 4th, he was seriously ill, and by the advice of friends was removed to the "Hospital Evangelismos." His disease proved to be a malignant form of typhus. The best medical skill and nursing failed to arrest it, and he died Tuesday, May 13th. He was buried in the beautiful Greek cemetery at Athens. Great sympathy was expressed by the Greek Prime Minister, the American Minister, and Mr. Manatt, the United States Consul at Athens, who writes of the sympathy awakened throughout the American community at Athens, and of their purpose to endow an American ward in the

"Hospital Evangelismos" in honor of Mr. Marden. His associates bear witness to his earnestness and fidelity, and his courage in pursuing the evangelistic work, often requiring great wisdom and physical endurance. A native paper speaks of him as "a man of fine culture, and of true Christian spirit, honored and loved by all;" and a fellow-missionary, who was with him for years, speaks of him as "truly the people's friend." Rev. H. G. Clark of New Hampshire, a classmate and intimate friend, says: "He was regarded by his classmates and missionary associates as a man of sound sense, and the results of methods of work he adopted usually proved the wisdom of his judgment and foresight." He gives the following extracts from a letter written in 1881 and 1890: "I am satisfied to spend my life here, and though I long inexpressibly for the home land and the home friends, I am sure that nothing could induce me to leave the work while I am able to stay." In speaking of the long tours made among the mountain villages and the preaching in the private houses of the Armenians, he says: "I ask for no nobler work than this hovel preaching, notwithstanding its discomforts." Just before leaving his work last April he wrote: "I long for home at times more than tongue can tell, yet I am sorry to leave the work here even for a year."

**Mardin,** a city of Eastern Turkey, about 60 miles southeast of Diarbekir; most picturesquely situated on a bluff of the Taurus Mountains, commanding a magnificent view over the Mesopotamia plain. On a clear day the hills nearly a hundred miles away to the south are clearly visible. In spring the plain several thousand feet below looks like a broad carpet beautifully diversified with rich colors. The climate is trying, the summer being long and hot; the winter pleasant, but lacking in any tonic which can repair the waste of the summer's work. The population of the city is about 15,000, chiefly Arabs and Syrian Jacobites, though there are Chaldeans, Armenians, Koords, and Jews. Mission station of the A. B. C. F. M. (1839); 4 missionaries and wives, 3 female missionaries, 37 native helpers, 20 out-stations, 8 churches, 330 church-members, 28 schools, 708 scholars. There is a large and flourishing high-school, virtually a college (see A. B. C. F. M. Assyrian and Eastern Turkey missions; also Armenia). Since the giving up of the station at Mosul, Mardin has been the centre of the Arabic work of the A. B. C. F. M. Of late years, however, it has been decided to reopen the Mosul station.

**Maré,** on the Loyalty Islands, Southwest Polynesia, off the coast of New Caledonia, southeast of Lifu. Mission station of the L. M. S.; 15 native pastors, 688 church-members. The London Missionary Society brought teachers hither from Samoa and Rarotonga in 1841, and in 1855 a congregation was formed at Maré, which now numbers 3,117 members under 15 pastors. The New Testament, the Psalms, and the Pentateuch have been translated. Nevertheless, when the French took possession of the Loyalty Islands in 1864, the Roman Catholic priests began their intrigues and chicaneries immediately, and in 1884 they obtained a decree from the governor by which all Protestants were placed under the supervision of French priests, all schools in which the instruction was not carried on in French were closed, and the Maré Bible was forbidden.

**Maré** or **Nengone Version.**—The Maré belongs to the Polynesian languages, and is spoken in the Loyalty Islands. The first part of the Scriptures printed was the Gospel of Mark, and in 1867 the New Testament was printed on the spot. In 1867 Mr. Jones carried through the press in London a revised edition of the New Testament at the expense of the British and Foreign Bible Society. The edition consisted of 4,000 copies. During Mr. Jones' absence Mr. Creagh translated the Books of Genesis, Exodus, Leviticus, Isaiah, and Jeremiah, and printed Genesis and Exodus at the mission press in Maré. Mr. Creagh having removed to the neighboring island of Lifu, Mr. Jones carried on the translation of the Old Testament. He translated the Psalms, which Mr. Creagh, during a visit which he made to England in 1876, carried through the press. In 1887 Mr. Jones was expelled by the French from the island, and thus for the present the work of translation is interrupted.

(*Specimen verse.* John 3:16.)

Wen' o re naeni Makaze hna raton' o re ten' o re aw, ca ile nubonengo me nunuone te o re Tei nubonengo sa so, thu deko di ma tango-ko re ngome me sa ci une du nubon, roi di nubone co numu o re waruma tha thu ase ko.

**Maripastoon.**—A town on the left bank of the river Saramacca, in Surinam, South America, a station of the Moravians. The Matuari tribe of Bush-negroes reside here, among whom a work was commenced by John King, the native evangelist. A native minister is in charge here, as it would be impossible, it is said, for any European to live at Maripastoon.

**Marquesas Islands.**—A group of islands in the South Pacific, northwest of the Society Islands. Since 1841 a possession of France. Area, 480 square miles. Population, 5,250. Occupied by the Hawaiian Evangelical Society.

**Marquesas Version.**—The Marquesas belongs to the Polynesian languages, and is spoken in the Marquesas Islands. The Marquesan language was first reduced to writing by English missionaries early in this century, and the Gospel of Matthew was printed at Honolulu in 1853, and in 1857 the Gospel of John followed. American missionaries took up the work in a more thorough manner, and the New Testament appeared in 1873, and in a second edition in 1878.

(*Specimen verse.* John 3:16.)

Ua kaoha nui mai te Atua i to te aomaama nei, noela, ua tuu mai oia i taia Tama fanautahi, ia mate koe te enata i haatia la ia, atia, ia koaa ia la te pohoe mau ana'tu.

**Maronites.**—The Maronites of Syria take their name from John Maron, their political leader and first patriarch, who died 701 A.D. During the sixth and seventh centuries of our era the Monophysite (*monos*, one; *phusis*, nature) controversy was raging throughout the Eastern church. Armenia, Syria, and Egypt, frontier lands of the Byzantine Empire, were deeply infected by the heresy. The Emperor

Heraclius (610-640 A.D.) was anxious to reunite the church that he might the more effectually ward off the Saracen invasion from Arabia, which threatened to despoil the empire of its south-eastern provinces. With the help of Sergius, Patriarch of Constantinople, a Syrian, he arranged a compromise doctrine which he hoped would put a stop to the rancorous theological dispute. The statement proposed was, that whatever might be said, Christ having one (divine) or two (human and divine) natures, all ought to agree that he has but one will (divine and therefore sinless). Honorius, Bishop of Rome, assented to this proposition, and many of the Monophysites agreed to accept it. But no imperial decree could stop the quarrel; and after a long controversy (during which the Saracens conquered Syria, Egypt, and all North Africa) the case was decided against the Monethelites (*monos*, one, *thelem*, to will), and Bishop Honorius (afterwards called "Pope") was declared heretical.

Among many who accepted the Monothelite heresy were the Christians of Syria, who fled to the mountains before the Saracen invader. John Maron was their leader. High up on the shoulders of Lebanon and Anti-Lebanon these vigorous people managed for five hundred years to maintain their independence in the face of Byzantine, Greek, and Saracen. Defended by tremendous ravines and snowy mountain passes, they were never seriously in danger. The long contest developed manly qualities and industry. They spoke Syriac, and used it in all their services. A sort of feudal system developed itself. The government was theocratic, the head of the state being styled "The Patriarch of Antioch and all the East." The episcopal dioceses were Aleppo, Ba'albek, Jebeil, Tripoli, Ehden, Damascus, Beyrout, Tyre, and Cyprus. Village sheikhs were elected, as were all the officers, secular and religious.

The Crusaders brought to light this interesting people, so long cut off from Christendom. William of Tyre and Jacob de Nitry have left us accounts of the Maronites, who leagued themselves with the Crusaders, and in 1182 opened communications with the papal hierarchy. They gradually dropped their heretical tendencies, adopted the Arabic language as their vernacular, and in 1445 at the Council of Florence were taken entirely under the wing of the Roman Church. They were allowed to retain their Syriac liturgy, the celebration of the communion in both kinds, the marriage of the lower clergy, their own fast-days, and their own saints. In 1596 the decrees of Trent were accepted; transubstantiation, prayers for the Pope, and other novelties were introduced. A special college was established at Rome (Collegium Maronitarum) for investigation by Maronite scholars, which gave to the world the learned Assemani. Schools for the clergy and printing-presses were established in Syria. A papal legate was sent to Beyrout, and to-day the Maronites are submissive followers in the Latin Church.

There are about 250,000 of this sect scattered all over the Lebanon range and the Anti-Lebanon. They are massed somewhat in the northern districts of Lebanon (Kesrawan and Bsherreh), and have complete control of local affairs. They are found as far south as Mt. Hermon, in the heart of the Druze country. The growing hostility of Druze and Maronite, fostered by the Turkish soldiery, culminated in the massacre of 1860, in which thousands of the Maronites were butchered. European intervention compelled the Sultan to redistrict Syria, and form the pashalik of Mt. Lebanon, which must have a Christian pasha to rule it, and which is under the protection of the Great Powers. The stronghold of the Maronites in the North Lebanon region is high up on the mountains, with surpassing views over the Mediterranean to the west. It is a bit of the Middle Ages left over. The priests have complete control, and the people are frugal and industrious. They are illiterate for the most part, and schools are established only when they are required to ward off Protestant influences. The rough mountain sides are terraced, and every available bit of soil utilized. The raising of cattle, silk culture and weaving, vineyards, grain, maize, and potatoes (Irish) occupy the attention of the people. Hundreds of monasteries are scattered over the mountains, the most notable one being the monastery of Kennôbin (the Greek word for monastery), which is romantically situated in the gorge of the Kadisha (Holy) River, and is the summer home of the Patriarch. At the head of this profound ravine is the famous group of 400 ancient cedars, which are carefully guarded as sacred. Some of them are 40 ft. in circumference, and over 100 ft. high.

When the American missionaries entered Syria, in 1823, the Roman Catholic authorities became alarmed, and have put forth every effort to hold the Maronites true to their papal allegiance. In the early days of this rivalry a young Maronite, Asaad Shidiak, who had adopted the evangelical faith, was imprisoned in the Kennôbin monastery, where he died from rigorous treatment. He has been called "The Martyr of Lebanon." The Jesuits and Lazarists have in hand the task of holding the Maronites to the Latin faith. A fine school for boys is found at Antura, conducted by the Lazarites, not far from Bkurkeh, the winter home of the Patriarch. The Jesuit College at Beyrout is an imposing institution, with a fine library and a very complete scientific apparatus. The Jesuits were forced to issue an Arabic Bible, and it is interesting to note that they made the translation from the original Greek and Hebrew Scriptures.

At the time of the massacre of 1860 the Protestant missionaries had the privilege of endearing themselves to the Maronites by caring for thousands of orphans and other fugitives in Sidon and Beyrout. But as yet the northern portions of the Lebanon range have been impervious to Protestant influence. Rev. Isaac Bird, in the early days of the mission, was driven from the region, and no attempt has since been made to permanently reside in the Kesrawan and in Bsherreh. Missionaries occasionally have summered in the mountains above Tripoli, and the prejudice against them is gradually subsiding. The potatoes which Mr. Bird left behind in his garden have spread all over the mountains, and form a staple of agriculture along with maize. Other societies besides the Presbyterian Board are reaching the Maronites. The Free Church of Scotland have occupied the Metn region just south of Kesrawan for some years. The English schools for girls, established after 1860, and which are scattered over the mountains to the south, are doing very efficient work. The mission of the Irish

Presbyterian Church in Damascus is reaching the Maronites in that region. In spite of the great care of the Roman Catholics, education is transforming the whole sect, and evangelical truth is more and more winning its way among them.

**Marshall,** a town of Sierra Leone, West Africa, centre of a circuit of Bishop Taylor's work. It has 5 local preachers and 84 church-members.

**Marshall Islands,** Micronesia, two chains of lagoon islands, called Ratack (13) and Ralick (11); comprise an area of 1,400 square miles with an estimated population of 10,000. A missionary of the A. B. C. F. M. is located at Kusaie (q.v.), and the work among the various islands is carried on by native preachers and teachers under his supervision. Ten islands have schools or preaching-places; there are 8 churches, 6 pastors, and 12 native preachers. The German occupation of the islands has not improved the morals of the natives.

**Marshman, Joshua,** b. April 20, 1768, Westbury-Leigh, Wiltshire, England. When young, he showed a great passion for reading. His parents being poor, his school education was defective, and he followed the occupation of a weaver till 1794. Removing then to Bristol, he taught a small school, and at the same time became a student in Bristol Academy, where he studied Latin, Greek, Hebrew, and Syriac. Having decided to be a missionary to the heathen, he offered himself to the Baptist Missionary Society, and 1799 was sent with three others to join Dr. Carey in his mission north of Bengal. As the East India Company prohibited missions in its territories, they were advised not to undertake to land at Calcutta, but to go direct to the Danish settlement of Serampore on the Hugli, 16 miles above Calcutta. They reached Serampore October 13th, 1799, and were cordially received by the governor, Colonel Bie. Carey soon joined them. Dr. Marshman, finding the support granted by the Society insufficient, with the aid of his wife, opened two boarding-schools for European children, and a school for natives. The income from these, supplemented by that of Carey as professor in the Fort William Government College, rendered their mission nearly independent of support from the Society. The Committee disapproved of this course, and censured the missionaries. Dr. Marshman in 1822 sent his son John to England to make explanations and endeavor to restore harmony; but being unsuccessful, he himself went in 1826 in order to confer with the Committee. But failing in his object, the Serampore Mission was separated from the Society, and was for several years an independent mission. He returned in 1829 to Serampore. The death, from cholera, of Mr. Ward, with whom he had labored for twenty-three years, and the treatment he received from the parent Society, greatly distressed him, so that his strength of body and mind was much impaired. Other afflictions followed. The death of Dr. Carey in 1834 left him alone. In 1836 his daughter, wife of General Havelock, barely escaped with her life from her burning bungalow, losing one of her three children in the flames. The nervous excitement from these afflictions completely prostrated him, and he died December 5th, 1837. A few days before his death the Society in London had arranged for a reunion with the Serampore Mission, and the appointment of Dr. Marshman as superintendent.

In addition to his more special missionary duties, he applied himself to the study of Bengâli, Sanskrit, and Chinese. Dr. Carey wrote to Andrew Fuller: "Brother Marshman is a prodigy of diligence and prudence; learning the language is mere play for him." He translated into Chinese the Book of Genesis, the Gospels, and the Epistles of Paul to the Romans and Corinthians. In 1811 he published "A Dissertation on the Characters and Sounds of the Chinese Language." "The Works of Confucius, containing the Original Text, with a Translation;" "Clavis Sinica: Elements of Chinese Grammar, with a Preliminary Dissertation on the Characters and Colloquial Mediums of the Chinese." He was associated with Dr. Carey in preparing a Sanskrit grammar and Bengâli-English dictionary, and published an abridgment of the latter. Raja Rammohun Roy having assailed the miracles of Christ in a work entitled "The Precepts of Jesus the Guide to Peace," Dr. Marshman replied in a series of articles in the "Friend of India," afterwards published in a volume entitled "A Defence of the Deity and Atonement of Jesus Christ." To this Rammohun Roy replied. The degree of D.D. was conferred on Mr. Marshman by Brown University, 1811.

**Marsovan,** a city of Asia Minor, Turkey, 350 miles east of Constantinople, and 60 miles south of Samsun, its port on the Black Sea. Climate mild and healthy. Population of the city about 30,000; of the district 800,000; mostly Turks and Armenians, though there are a number of Greeks. Of late years large companies of Circassians from the Caucasus have been located in the villages of the plain, causing much disturbance. Mission station of the A. B. C. F. M. (1853); 4 missionaries and wives, 4 female missionaries, 14 native helpers, 5 churches, 776 church-members, 27 schools, 2,000 scholars. These cover the district. In the city itself there is a large self-supporting church.

Marsovan is also the seat of Anatolia College, which is the outgrowth of the theological seminary of the Mission, originally established in Constantinople, but removed to Marsovan. In 1881, it was divided into two parts, one for strictly theological training and the other a high-school. This has developed into a college since 1885. The course of study is very full, and of high grade. There are 10 professors and instructors, and 117 undergraduates, 58 in the college and 59 in the preparatory department; 80 are Armenians, 34 Greeks, 2 Germans, and 1 an Israelite. (See Armenia).

**Martyn, Henry,** b. Truro, Cornwall, England, February 18th, 1781; attended the grammar school of Dr. Carden in his native town; entered St. John's College, Cambridge, 1797; received in 1801 the highest academical honor of "senior wrangler," and also the prize for the greatest proficiency in mathematics. In 1802 he was chosen fellow of his college, and took the first prize for the best Latin composition. He was twice elected public-examiner. It was his intention to devote himself to the bar, but the sudden death of his father and the faithful preaching and counsels of Mr.

Simeon, the university preacher, led to his conversion and dedication to the ministry. In 1802 a remark of Mr. Simeon on the good accomplished in India by a single missionary,—William Carey,—and a subsequent perusal of the "Life of David Brainerd," led him to devote himself to the work of a Christian missionary. He was ordained deacon October 22d, 1803, then priest, and served as curate of Mr. Simeon. But his heart was still set on work in heathen lands, and he designed to offer himself to the Church Missionary Society. A sudden disaster in Cornwall deprived him and his unmarried sister of the property their father had left for them, and it was necessary he should obtain a position that would support them both. His friends applied for a chaplaincy under the East India Company, and being appointed, he embarked for India July 5th, 1805, reaching Calcutta May, 1806. Detained at Calcutta a few months, he applied himself to the study of Hindustani, which he had begun in England, and pursued on board ship, and preached the gospel to his own countrymen. In October he went to his station, Dinapore. On the boat he studied Sanskrit, Persian, and Arabic, and translated the Parables. At Dinapore and Cawnpore most of his work in India was done in the space of four and a half months. He not only labored among the soldiers and English residents as chaplain, but preached to the natives in their vernacular, established schools, and spent much time in the work of translation. He studied Sanskrit, soon became fluent in Hindustani, and had religious discussions daily with the moonshee and pundit. In February, 1807, he finished the translation of the Book of Common Prayer in Hindustani, and soon after a Commentary on the Parables. In September he was urged by the Rev. M. Brown to take charge of the mission church at Calcutta, but declined, because he wished to labor among the natives. His Sunday service was reading prayers and preaching at 7 A.M. to Europeans, to Hindus at 2 P.M. and attendance at the hospital, and in the evening he met privately the pious and inquiring soldiers. In March, 1808, he completed the version of the New Testament in Hindustani, which was pronounced by competent judges to be idiomatic, and intelligible by the natives.

In April, 1809, he was removed to Cawnpore, 628 miles from Calcutta. He went in a palankeen in the hottest season. In his journey of 400 miles from Chunar, the intense heat nearly proved fatal to him. On his arrival he fainted away. There being no church-building at Cawnpore, he preached to a thousand soldiers, drawn up in a hollow square in the open air, with the heat so great that before sunrise many were overpowered. At the end of this year he made his first attempt to preach to the heathen in his own compound, "amidst groans, hissings, curses, blasphemies, and threatenings;" but he pursued his work among the hundreds who crowded around him, comforting himself with the thought that if he should never see a native convert, God "might design by his patience and continuance to encourage other missionaries." He now translated the New Testament into Hindi, and the Gospels into Judæo-Persic. Having perfected himself in the Persian, he prepared, by the advice of friends, with the assistance of the moonshee Sabat, a version of the New Testament in that language. His health

being seriously impaired, the doctors ordered him to take a sea-voyage; and his version not being sufficiently idiomatic, he decided to go to Persia and correct it with the aid of learned natives, and also revise the Arabic version, which was nearly finished. After preaching in the new church, whose erection he had accomplished, he left Cawnpore October 1st, 1810. Delayed at Calcutta a month, he preached, though in great weakness, nearly every Sabbath, and also at the anniversary of the Calcutta Bible Society. He left, January 7th, 1811, for Bombay, and after a five months' journey reached Shiraz June 9th, 1811, where, with the help of learned natives, he revised his Persian and Arabic translations of the New Testament. He made also a version of the Psalms from the Hebrew into Persian. He held frequent discussions with the mollahs and sufis, many of whom were greatly impressed. "Henry Martyn," said a Persian mollah, "was never beaten in argument; he was a good man, a man of God." To counteract the effect of these discussions and of his translation of the New Testament into Persian, the preceptor of all the mollahs wrote an Arabic defence of Mohammedanism, to which Martyn replied in Persian. He had also a public discussion with a professor of Mohammedan law, and another with Mirza Ibraheem, in a court of the palace of one of the Persian princes in the presence of a large body of mollahs. Having ordered two splendid copies of his manuscript of the Persian New Testament to be prepared, one for the Shah of Persia, the other for Prince Abbas Mirza, his son, he left Shiraz for the Shah's camp to present them. The Shah refused to receive them without a letter from the British ambassador, and he proceeded to Tabriz to obtain one from Sir Gore Ousley. On this journey he suffered much from fever; but after arriving at Tabriz, he was tenderly cared for by the ambassador and his lady. Being too ill to make the presentation to the Shah, Sir Gore kindly performed this service, and received from his majesty a letter of acknowledgment, with appreciative mention of the excellence of the translation. After a temporary recovery, he found it necessary to seek a change of climate. On September 12th, 1812, he left on horseback, with two Armenian servants, for England via Constantinople, 1,300 miles distant. Though the plague was raging at Tokat, he was compelled to stop there from utter prostration, and after a week's illness, died, October 16th, 1812, in the thirty-second year of his age, among strangers, with no friendly hand to care for his wants. His body rests in the Armenian cemetery. A monument was erected over the grave in 1813 by Mr. Claudius James Rich, the accomplished British resident at Bagdad, with an inscription in Latin. The East India Company had another constructed, bearing on its four sides an inscription in English, Armenian, Turkish, and Persian.

He published "Sermons Preached in Calcutta and Elsewhere" (1822); "Controversial Tracts on Christianity and Mohammedanism" (1824); "Journals and Letters" (1837). The great work of Martyn's life was the translation of the Bible. His versions of the New Testament in Hindustani and Persian, spoken by many millions of people, are enduring monuments not only to his scholarship, but to his zeal for extending the knowledge of the Christian Scriptures.

**Maruthuvambadi,** a town of Arni district, Madras, India. Out-station of the Reformed (Dutch) Church, U. S. A.; 22 communicants, 65 scholars.

**Marwari Version.**—The Marwari is a dialect of the Hindi, and belongs to the Indic branch of the Aryan family of languages. It is spoken in the province of Jaipur, or Marwar, north of Mewar. The New Testament as translated into this dialect was published at Serampore in 1821. In 1866 the Bombay Auxiliary Bible Society published an edition of the Gospel of Luke, to be used in Rajputana generally.

**Masinandriana,** a town in South Central Madagascar, a little west of Sirabe. Mission station of the Norwegian Missionary Society.

**Mason, Francis,** b. York, England, April 2d, 1799. His grandfather was rightful heir to an estate worth £200 per annum, but religious scruples prevented his going to law to secure it. So his father, a lay-preacher of the Baptist denomination, was under the necessity of supporting his family as a shoemaker, and Francis followed the same trade. The son's opportunities for schooling were small, but his father's conversations enlightened him in history, and his mother aided him to the books he craved for the study of trigonometry, algebra, navigation, and optics. Of religious controversy he heard much. He became skeptical. At the age of nineteen he came to America, travelled through many States, and settled in Massachusetts. He boarded with Mr. Putnam, the Baptist minister of Randolph, who sought in personal conversation to show him his need of a Saviour. He also married an excellent Christian woman, whose influence and prayers were blessed to his conversion. The reading of "Butler's Analogy" he mentions as having overcome his skeptical difficulties. "One of my first petitions in the corner of my workshop was," he says: "'O God, give me religion, if there be any truth in religion.' Theologians might say God would not hear such unbelieving prayer, but He did hear and answer too, and I soon was a praying man." "I had been moving through the world," he said, "with an aching want at my heart, but when I believed in Jesus I entered into rest." Again: "I had wandered over the world like a lost child yearning for its mother, but when I found God I felt that I had got home." He struggled for months against a conviction which grew in his mind that he ought to preach, but left it to the decision of the church in Canton, which was that he should become a minister. He was licensed to preach October, 1827, and the next month entered the Newton Theological Seminary, having previously studied Greek and Hebrew. In his second year his wife died of consumption. In connection with his first thoughts of preaching the Gospel, his mind was directed to the missionary work. In regard to this he says that the story of the conversion of the Saxon king Edwin from heathenism, told him in childhood, had much influence in turning his thoughts to heathen lands in after-years. He was appointed by the American Baptist Missionary Convention as a missionary December 17th, 1819, ordained May 23d, 1830, married Miss Helen Griggs of Brookline, and sailed May 26th for Burmah. After spending a short time at Moulmein, he was stationed, January, 1831, at Tavoy, a town with from ten to fifteen thousand inhabitants. The province contained fifty Burmese villages. He was met at the wharf by Mr. Boardman, who, unable to walk, was carried in a chair to the jetty to welcome him. He accompanied Mr. Boardman on his last tour among the Karens, and witnessed his triumphant death. Entering upon the work in his new field, he labored earnestly among the Karens, visiting them in their jungle homes, preaching, organizing churches, establishing schools. The rainy season was occupied in translating the Scriptures, and instructing in the theological seminary established for training Karen preachers. One evening, on his return from a preaching tour among the Burmans, he found a Sgau chief sitting like a child at Mrs. Mason's feet, and earnestly imploring her to visit the Karens in his village and neighborhood. "We have heard of Christianity, and it seems to us something wonderful. We do not understand it, yet it seems the thing we want. Come to our jungle homes, and preach to us. Many will believe. I have a wife, daughters, daughters-in-law, brothers and nephews, all of whom will become Christians, as well as myself, as soon as we really understand it."

Mr. Mason was not only a preacher among the Karens, he was also a man of science and a great linguist. He translated the Bible into the two principal dialects of the Karen, the Sgau and Pwo, and also Matthew, Genesis, and Psalms into the Bghai, another dialect. He wrote and printed a grammar of the first two for the use of missionaries. Wishing to give the pupils of his theological school some scientific knowledge, he wrote an original treatise on "Trigonometry, with its Applications to Land Measuring, etc." This was printed in Sgau and Burmese, and the government paid for an edition in Bghai Karen. In 1832 he received the degree of M.A. from Colby University. At the request of English residents at Moulmein he prepared and had printed a work on the natural productions of the country, entitled "Tennasserim; or, Notes on the Fauna, Flora, Minerals, and Nations of British Burmah and Pegu," of which "The Friend of India" says: "It is one of the most valuable works of the kind which has ever appeared in this country, not only for the complete originality of its information, but also for the talent exhibited in collecting and arranging it." His motive in investigating these subjects was the more accurate translation of the Scriptures. He had observed the difficulty met by translators of correctly rendering the terms used in the original Scriptures to designate beasts, birds, fishes, insects, trees, gems, and many other natural objects, the misinterpretation of which often made the sense obscure, sometimes to the native mind absurd. He studied medicine after reaching Burmah, and wrote a small work on "Materia Medica and Pathology," in three languages. His greatest literary work was a "Pali Grammar with Chrestomathy and Vocabulary," which was received by scholars with great favor. In 1842 he started a Karen periodical, the first native paper published east of the Ganges, and the next year a similar monthly in Burmese at Moulmein. The Karens had no books but many traditions, among which were many remarkable Scripture traditions, all of which Mr.

Mason collected. Those relating to Scripture were published in an appendix to his "Life of Ko-Thah-Byu." In 1846 Mrs. Mason died. His health having failed, he yielded to the advice of the mission to return for a season to America. Arriving in Calcutta with health improved, he concluded to return to Burmah and work on the translation of the Old Testament, stopping at Moulmein in order to have the advice of the missionaries there. While there he was married to Mrs. Bullard. The translation was finished in 1853, and returning to Tavoy he had the entire Bible printed. In appreciation of his marked literary and Biblical attainments the degree of D.D. was conferred upon him in 1853 by Brown University. After the printing of the Karen Bible he took his final departure from Tavoy for England and America. On reaching Moulmein with health improved, he decided to visit Toungoo, the ancient capital, and begin a new mission. He started with Mrs. Mason in a canoe, and found the people, who had never heard the gospel message, wonderfully eager listeners. Dr. Mason continued to labor until utter exhaustion compelled him to leave. But God had raised up from the Karen nation a man qualified by talent and Christian character to take charge of the new mission. San Quala had been since 1830 a consistent Christian and a faithful worker among his people in Tavoy. For fifteen years he had accompanied Dr. Mason in his jungle tours, and in 1844 was ordained. He had often desired to carry the gospel to the province of Toungoo, and soon followed Dr. Mason thither. Committing the mission to Quala, Dr. Mason left for Calcutta January 18th, 1854, and there took a steamer for England. He visited America in October, 1854, where he again embarked for Burmah July 2d, 1856. Reaching Calcutta after a long and perilous voyage, he arrived at Toungoo January 2d, 1857. The progress during his absence through the labors of Quala and three assistants was wonderful. He found 2,600 baptized Christians and 35 churches. Three years before not one in those jungles had heard of the Saviour. "When I look around me," he says, "I find myself in a Christian country, raised up as if by magic from the darkness of heathenism in three years." After his return Pwaipan, who had been a member of his theological school in Tavoy, was ordained. In his youth Dr. Mason had a great desire to be a printer. That desire was gratified in Toungoo after he was sixty years of age. Living next door to Mr. Bennett's printing-office, he learned the trade himself, taught the Karens, and soon his printing, done in English, Burmese, Karen, Old Pali, and Sanskrit, was pronounced equal to that done in the best printing-offices in India. Dr. Mason's last missionary labor was a visit to Bhamo in Upper Burmah, on the Irrawaddy, to endeavor to establish a mission among the Ka Khyens. In this he failed, but was permitted by the king to live and work in Mandalay. Having entered into a contract with the E. I. C. to print a new edition of one of his books on Burmah, he started for Calcutta, but was attacked with fever at Rangoon, and after a short illness died March 3d, 1874, aged 74.

Besides the works mentioned, he published a memoir of his second wife, Mrs. Helen M. Mason, "Life of Ko-Thah-byu, the Karen Apostle," a collection of Karen hymns, "The Story of a Workingman's Life," an autobiography.

**Massett,** Queen Charlotte's Islands, North Pacific, U. S.; a town on one of Queen Charlotte's Islands, which lie in the North Pacific Ocean about 70 miles off the coast of British Columbia. Climate healthy and temperate; rainfall very great. Population, 1,000, composed of people of the Haida race. Language, Haida, a strange tongue totally different from the languages of the coast. Religion, pagans up to 1876; now Christian. Station of the Queen Charlotte Islands' Mission. C. M. S. occupied it in 1876 by Rev. W. H. Collison; present missionary, Rev. Charles Harrison; 1 out-station with 350 adherents, 1 organized church, 132 communicants, 2 preaching-places with an average attendance of 350, 3 unordained preachers, 1 Sabbath-school, 60 scholars; 1 other school, 63 scholars, 2 teachers.

**Massitissi,** a small town in Cape Colony, South Africa, on a southern branch of the Orange River, southeast of Bethesda. Mission station of the Paris Evangelical Society (1866), 1 missionary, 7 evangelists, 511 communicants, 293 scholars.

**Massowa** (Massawah), a town on the coast of Abyssinia, brought into special notice by its occupation by the Italian forces. Occupied at one time by missionaries of the Swedish Missionary Society. They were, however, driven away, and remained in Syria until the Italian troops went to Massowa, when they went with them, hoping thus to get access to the interior, a hope which has been in a measure fulfilled. (See Abyssinia.)

**Masulipatam,** city in Madras, British India, Kistna district, 215 miles north of Madras, with 37,000 inhabitants. Mission station C. M. S.; 8 missionaries, 2 missionaries' wives, 31 native helpers, 366 communicants, 26 schools, 423 scholars, a seminary, a printing establishment, and active zenana mission.

**Matale,** town in Ceylon, 15 miles north of Kandy. Population, 3,529. Mission station of Baptist Missionary Society (1868); 1 missionary, 3 out-stations, 59 school-children, 17 church-members. S. P. G.; 1 missionary, 40 communicants, 2 schools, 4 teachers, 115 scholars. The coffee-plantations here are mostly owned by European planters, and worked by coolies imported from the continent, as the natives are very lazy. The mission among the coolies receives much encouragement from the planters, but has to stand a good deal from the trickery of the natives.

**Matamoras,** city on the northeast Mexican frontier, 450 miles north of the city of Mexico. Climate, semi-tropical. Population, 12,000, Mexicans, Spaniards, Aztecs. Language, Spanish. Religion, Roman Catholic. Natives poor, ignorant, superstitious, lazy. Mission station of Presbyterian Church (South) (1874); 1 missionary and wife, 3 other ladies, 9 native helpers, 6 out-stations, 7 churches, 500 church-members, 1 theological seminary, 4 students, 2 schools, 175 scholars. Methodist Episcopal Church (South); 1 native preacher.

**Matara,** a town in the district of Colombo, Ceylon, northeast of Colombo. Mission station of the S. P. G.; 2 missionaries, 1 native agent,

3 out-stations, 3 churches, 121 church-members, 12 schools, 1,166 scholars. Wesleyan Methodist Missionary Society (England); 3 missionaries and assistants, 3 local preachers, 100 church-members, 841 scholars.

**Matara,** on the Berbice, British Guiana, South America, is the seat of a Plymouth Brethren's station, which works with great success among the Indians, negroes, and Chinese.

**Matautu,** a town on the island of Savaii, Samoan Islands, Polynesia. Mission station of the L. M. S.; 1 missionary, 17 native preachers, 1,024 church-members, 1,450 Sunday-school scholars, 1,400 other scholars. The Wesleyan Methodists (England) also carry on work here, but no statistics are available.

**Matawankumman,** a station of the C. M. S. in the Moosonee district, Canada; 3 native workers, 62 church-members, 1 school, 24 scholars, among the Ojibwa Indians.

**Matchuala,** a city of Mexico, State of Coahuila. Mission station of the Southern Baptist Convention; 1 missionary and wife.

**Mather, Robert Cotton,** b. November 8th, 1808, at New Windsor, Manchester, England; educated at Edinburgh, Glasgow, and Hamerton College; sailed July 9th, 1833, for India, as a missionary of the L. M. S. He was stationed at Benares for four years, and then removed with his family to Mirzapore, founding a new station. In 1844 he went to England for his health. Returning in 1846, he continued his work in and around Mirzapore, and prepared Christian vernacular literature. He again visited England in 1857, where he was occupied for three years, at the request of the North India and the British and Foreign Bible Societies, engaged in making a revision, with marginal references, of the whole Bible in Urdu. This was carried through the press, and the New Testament in English and Urdu was reprinted. He re-embarked for India November 20th, 1860, with Mrs. Mather. In 1862 he received the degree of LL.D. from the University of Glasgow. In 1869 he left Mirzapore for Almora, seeking to benefit his health. He aided in mission work while carrying on his literary work, completing a new edition of the entire Bible in Urdu-Roman. He commenced work on an edition in Urdu-Arabic with references. He returned to Mirzapore in 1870. In 1873 he left India on his final return to England. At the request of the Religious Tract Societies of North India and London, he undertook to prepare and carry through the press a Hindustani version of the New Testament portion of the Tract Society's Annotated Paragraph Bible. This was completed in two years. He then undertook the preparation of a similar version of the Old Testament portion of the same work. Unable to resume foreign missionary work, he thus continued in England to work for India with his pen. He died at Finchley, near London, April 21st, 1877.

**Matsumoto,** Japan, a town in the Nagoya district, on the main island (Nippon), south of Tokyo. Mission station of the Methodist Episcopal Church, (North); 2 native preachers, 30 church-members, 1 school, 35 scholars.

**Matsushiro,** Japan, a town in the Nagoya district, South Nippon Island. Mission station of the Methodist Episcopal Church (North); 1 native preacher, 35 church-members.

**Matsuyama,** Japan, a town in the Hiroshima district, in the extreme southwestern part of the island of Nippon. Mission station of the Methodist Episcopal Church (South), U. S. A.; 1 missionary and wife.

**Matsuye,** Japan, a town on the northern coast of the southwestern extremity of the island of Nippon, northeast of Hiroshima. Mission station of the C. M. S.; 1 native pastor, 16 church-members.

**Mattisudden,** a town in Central Lapland, southeast of Joknok. Mission station of the Friends of the Mission to the Lapps (Sweden).

**Mattoon, Stephen,** b. Champion, N. Y., U. S. A., May 5th, 1816; graduated at Union College 1842, at Princeton Theological Seminary 1846; ordained as an evangelist by the Troy Presbytery; sailed for Siam as a missionary of the Presbyterian Board July 20th, 1846, reaching Bangkok March 22d, 1847. Bitterly opposed at first, he soon won the confidence of the people, and carried forward the missionary work with great success. A treaty having been negotiated between the United States and Siam in 1856, at the solicitation of the American Government and the Siamese authorities, and for the good of the mission cause, he consented to act as United States consul until some person should be sent to take his place. He held the office for three years. Meanwhile his mission work was not intermitted. He was the first to translate the gospels into the Siamese tongue, and his last great work before returning home was the revision of the entire New Testament in that language. "The records show that he was a leader in all the details and enterprises connected with the mission, and that his prudent counsel was sought and his advice accepted by all." He resided and labored mainly in Bangkok, and was pastor of the First Presbyterian Church in that city from 1860 to 1866. In the latter year, on account of the failure of Mrs. Mattoon's health, he returned home. In 1867 he was settled as pastor of the Presbyterian Church at Ballston Spa, N. Y., from which he was released, December 2d, 1869, to accept the presidency of Biddle Institute, (chartered in 1877 as Biddle University), at Charlotte, N. C., which position he held till 1885, still retaining his chair as Professor of Theology and Church Government till near the time of his death in 1889. He was at the same period stated supply of several churches. He was an indefatigable worker in his class-rooms, and on Sundays would often ride 25 miles to preach the gospel to some little colored church. During the last year of his life his health failed rapidly from organic disease of the heart, but having somewhat improved from a visit to Clifton Springs, he started for his Southern home, stopping on the way with his daughter, Mrs. Thomas, at Marion, Ohio. There he rapidly grew worse, and died August 15th, 1889, aged 75. To the great educational work among the freedmen he gave himself with ardor, and with it to the labor of preaching the gospel to the colored people throughout that region. Commencing his work in the reconstruction period, when passion and prejudice controlled public sentiment, he soon by his prudence and wisdom won the confidence and support of the community, and the universal grief at his funeral attested the esteem in which he was held. He was interred at Charlotte, N. C. Dr. Mattoon was honored with the degree of D.D. by his Alma Mater, Union College, in 1870.

**Maubin,** town in Thongwa district, Irawadi Division, Burma, directly west of Rangoon. Climate warm, unhealthy. Population, 1,589, Burmese, Karens, Shans, Chinese, Hindus of all castes. Languages: 42 different tongues used by the various races represented in Burma. Religion, Buddhism, demon-worship, and various other idolatrous forms. Mission station of the American Baptist Missionary Union among the Pwo Karens (1880); 1 missionary and wife, 1 other lady, 22 native helpers, 15 out-stations, 15 churches, 635 church-members among the Pwos.

**Maui,** one of the Hawaiian Islands, between Hawaii and Oahu. The inhabitants, 12,109 in number, are all nominally Christians. Station of the Hawaiian Evangelical Society, which has taken up the work commenced by the A. B. C. F. M.

**Maupiti,** one of the Society Islands, South Pacific, 60 miles northwest of Raiatea. Mission station L. M. S.; 1 native pastor.

**Mauritius,** Island of, lies in the Indian Ocean, 500 miles east of Madagascar. Area, 708 square miles. Together with its dependencies, the Seychelles group, Rodriguez, and Diego Garcia (total area, 172 square miles), it forms a colony of Great Britain. Climate tropical, and very malarious and unhealthy on the coast. Population, 1889, 369,302; of this number 251,550 are Indians, and the remainder are Africans, mixed races, and whites. The Chinese number 3,935. The people are divided in their religious belief as follows: Hindus, 200,000 ; Roman Catholics, 108,000; Mohammedans, 35,000; and Protestants, 8,000. State aid is granted to both Roman Catholics and Protestants. English, French, and the languages of the different races represented are spoken there. The island was originally a French colony, and a stronghold of the pirates in the Indian Ocean. In 1810 the English took possession of it, and in 1834 the 90,000 negro slaves were emancipated. The island is one of the foremost sugar-producing places of the globe, and the emancipation of the slaves necessitated the importation of labor from China and India, with the resulting conglomerate population. Education is conducted partly in government and partly in state-aided schools, 144 in number, with an average attendance (1888) of 10,143. There is also a Royal College. Missionary work was commenced here in 1814 by the L. M. S. (q.v.). After the Society gave up the mission in 1832 Mr. Le Brun, their missionary, returned to the island and took the pastoral care of the people, and the church of 50 members. When persecution in Madagascar (1836) drove out both Christians and missionaries, one of the latter, Mr. Johns, went to Mauritius, and continued to labor among the Malagasy. A plot of land was procured, and a congregation of Malagasy refugees was gathered together in 1845, after Mr. Johns' death, and theological instruction was given to young men from Madagascar, to prepare them for work, as soon as the persecution ceased. In the meantime Mr. Le Brun continued his labors among the natives, and in 1850 there were 173 church-members at the stations of Port Louis and Moka. At the present time there is a native church council, who number 2,221 Christians on the rolls of their churches.

The S. P. G. station (1836) now numbers 4 missionaries, 383 communicants, 10 schools, 455 scholars. The C. M. S. Mission (1856) is carried on among (1) the Tamil-speaking coolies, (2) Bengali and Hindus, (3) the Chinese, (4) Seychelles Islanders. They number 5 pastorates (exclusive of Chinese and Seychelles Missions), 3 missionaries, 1 layman, 3 native pastors, 542 communicants, 25 schools, 1,562 scholars. Much hindrance to the work of the Protestant missions is caused by the efforts of the Church of Rome to get the larger part of the state grants in aid of education.

**Mauritius Creole Version.**—The Mauritius Creole is a dialect of the French, belonging to the Græco-Latin branch of the Aryan family of languages, and is spoken by about 350,000 Creoles in Mauritius, East Africa. It is the only medium of communication among all the languages and dialects of the island. A translation of the Gospel of Matthew into this language was made by the Rev. T. H. Anderson, a native of Mauritius, and after having been revised by several Mauritius scholars it was published by the British and Foreign Bible Society in 1884. Encouraged by the reception given to the version of Matthew, the same Society issued in 1887 a tentative edition of 500 copies of the Gospel of Mark, also prepared by Mr. Anderson.

**Mavelikara,** town in Travancore, Madras, India. Mission station of the C. M. S. The church council centred here includes 8 pastorates.

**Mawphlang,** a city of Assam, India, among the Khasia and Jaintia Hills. Mission station of the Welsh Presbyterian Church; 1 missionary and wife. The district contains 2 churches, 3 preaching stations, 123 church-members, 159 Sunday-scholars and teachers, and 103 day-scholars. A successful medical mission is also carried on.

**Maya Version.**—The Maya belongs to the languages of South America, and is vernacular to the Yucatan Indians. The Gospel of Luke was translated and published between the years 1862 and 1866 by the British and Foreign Bible Society. In 1870 an edition of the Gospel of John was published at London, the translation having been made by the Rev. R. Fletcher of the Wesleyan Missionary Society.

*(Specimen verse. John 3 : 16.)*

Tumen bay tu yacuntah Dioz le yokolcab, ca tu caah u pel mehenan Mehen, utial tulacal le max cu yoczictuyol ti leti, ma u kaztal, uama ca yanacti cuxtal minanuxul.

**Mayaguana,** a station of the Baptist Missionary Society in the Bahama Islands, West Indies; 3 evangelists, 3 out-stations, 66 communicants, 40 pupils.

**Mayaveram** (Majaveram), a town of the Tanjore district, Madras, India, northwest of Tranquebar, northeast of Combaconam, between the Cauvery River and the sea. Mission station of the Evangelical Lutheran Society of Leipsic, founded in 1845; 1 missionary, 1 native pastor, 771 communicants, 223 scholars.

**Mayhew, Experience,** b. Martha's Vineyard, R I., U.S.A., 1673. He was the oldest son of Rev. John Mayhew and great-grandson of Gov. Thomas Mayhew. In 1694, at the age of twenty-one, he began to preach to the Indians, having the oversight of six congregations, which continued until his death, a period of sixty-four years. Though not liberally educated, Dr. Cotton Mather, in a sermon printed in Boston 1698, and reprinted in his "Magnalia," London, after speaking of more than "thirty hundred Christian Indians," and "thirty Indian assemblies," adds: "A hopeful and worthy young man, Mr. Experience Mayhew, must now have the justice done him of this character, that in the evangelical service among the Indians there is no man that exceeds this Mr. Mayhew, if there be any that equals him." He learned the Indian language in his infancy, and having afterwards thoroughly mastered it he was employed by the Commissioners to make a new version of the Psalms and the Gospel of John. This was accomplished in 1709, in parallel columns of English and Indian. He was offered the degree of Master of Arts by Cambridge University, which he declined; but it was conferred at the public commencement July 3d, 1723. He published in 1727 "Indian Converts," comprising the lives of 30 Indian preachers and 80 other converts ; also a volume entitled "Grace Defended." He died 1758.

**Mazatlan,** a town in the Sonora district, Mexico. Mission station of the Methodist Episcopal Church (South), U. S. A.; 1 missionary, 1 native preacher.

**Mbau,** a city in Witi-Lewu, one of the two large islands in the Feejee group, Polynesia. One of the chief stations of the Wesleyan Missionary Society in this region. It was the residence of King Thakombau, who in 1854 was converted to Christianity, after many feuds with the French, who introduced a Roman Catholic Mission in Awalau, and with European and American traders finally brought peace and order to the islands by placing them in 1874 under English protection. He sent the queen a silver-inlaid club as token of his submission, and she accepted it. Mbau has given its name to the principal dialect spoken in the Feejee Islands, that one in which Calvert and Hunt translated the Bible.

**Mbulu,** city in Cape Colony, South Africa, 70 miles northeast of King William's Town, 10 miles southeast of Queenstown, 70 miles inland from the mouth of the Kei River. Climate very healthy. Population, 50,000. Race, Fingo. Language, Abantic. Religion, Fetichism; fast becoming Protestant Christianity. Social condition barbarous; polygamy, circumcision, and tattooing common. Mission station (1868) United Presbyterian Church of Scotland; 1 lady, 45 native helpers, 9 out-stations, 9 churches, 590 church-members, 12 school children.

**Mbweni,** a city of Zanzibar, East Africa. Mission station of the Universities Mission to Central Africa, with 2 clergy, 7 laity, 1 native reader, 6 native teachers. There is a home for 71 girls, and a separate building for an industrial school with 21 girls. A village of 300 released slaves, with permanent church, domestic chapel, workshop, traction engine, lime kiln, etc

**McAll Mission,** known also as the "Mission Populaire Évangélique de France." Headquarters, 28 Villa Molitor, Auteuil, Paris.—The first thought of this "Mission to the Workingmen of France" was suggested to the founder, Dr. Robert W. McAll, by the urgent request of a French workingman to come over and teach them "a religion of freedom and earnestness," in place of the imposed religion of the Church of Rome, which he and thousands of his fellows in the turmoil of the revolution had cast off. These words, spoken in August, 1871, led Dr. McAll to leave his English home and pastorate, and devote himself to those who through their comrade had made this appeal.

Plans of work were formed, and a suitable place of meeting found, and opened January 17th, 1872, in Belleville, the capital of the Commune, where Miss De Broen had already established her work. The constitution of the mission has been developed as circumstances have indicated. At first a purely personal and private effort to make known the love of God in Christ, it soon gathered to itself willing helpers, who were rejoiced to find that there was so ready a hearing for the truth. Soon appeals came from distant parts of the city that meetings might be held there too. Gradually new halls were opened ; at present there are 42 in and around Paris, and 88 scattered throughout 33 out of the 86 Governmental Departments into which France is divided.

The mission is guided by a Board of Directors, and is carried on among the French, in their own country and the adjacent colonies, Corsica, Algiers, and Tunis. The workers from Paris have been sent for to inaugurate efforts in other places, and thus the work has radiated to the extreme points of the land, until more than 60 cities and towns have received the light of God's truth.

In connection with its halls it has established Bible-schools on Sundays and week-days, mothers' meetings, dispensaries, libraries, societies for Bible study and Christian converse, domestic visitation, tract distribution and circulation of the Scriptures, besides the regular services and preaching of the gospel.

Forming no separate churches of its own, it helps all evangelical workers, and knits its converts to the existing churches. At the same time all evangelical pastors assist in its meetings, and in many cases find there the people who will not enter their churches.

The workers in this mission do not attack any forms of Christian life around them, but freely proclaim God's truth, leaving it to meet the errors of the past. In contrast with the constant demands for payment of service in the Church of Rome, the mission has from the first presented the message of the gospel freely to the people. Its support has been derived from generous gifts of Christians in Great Britain, Ireland, America, and many parts of Europe. No development of the work of sustaining the mission has been so remarkable and interesting as the growth of the American McAll Association, which numbers more than 60 auxiliaries.

Extensive work has been done this year (1889) in halls close to the main entrance to the

Exposition. Co-operating with the British and Foreign Bible Society, and the Religious Tract Societies of London and Paris, these halls have been used for the distribution of the Scriptures and tracts, as well as for the regular preaching of the gospel.

There are now open 130 mission halls, having 20,000 sittings. More than 20,000 meetings have been held during the past year, with an attendance of 1,155,000; 26,000 visits to the homes of the people have been paid, and more than 500,000 Scriptures, tracts, and illustrated papers circulated.

A maritime branch of this mission carries on very interesting work among the seaboard towns of France. By means of the "Herald of Mercy," a missionary boat lent to the mission by Mr. Henry Cook, of the Portsmouth and Gosport's Seamen's Mission, services are held in many places otherwise inaccessible. The chief part of the time available in 1888 was divided between the northern seaports Cherbourg and Morlaix. In both places crowds of all ages and classes flocked to the vessel on each occasion when a meeting was to be held. None were more eager listeners than the soldiers of the garrison at Cherbourg. A permanent mission hall was the result of the visit of the ship. Morlaix, a town in the very midst of Popish Brittany, was an entirely new and untried sphere for such efforts. The preaching was conducted in the native Breton, as well as as in French. On every occasion the people crowded around the vessel, filled the cabin and the deck, and stood on the quay seeking to hear. The pure gospel of Christ came as a new and surprising discovery to multitudes, and on all sides the earnest desire was expressed that another season the "Herald of Mercy" might visit Morlaix again.

In connection with the mission are also free lending libraries, dispensaries, etc. During the year 9,000 persons have been prescribed for at the latter; the very poorest make use of them, and many come from long distances, so much do they prize the kind aid offered them. To all the gospel is spoken, and many weary and troubled hearts are comforted.

The mission in Tunis embraces "foreign mission" work, in addition to its work for the French and German residents, through its connection with the Kabyle Mission, whose evangelist, Mr. Jocelyn Bureau, was one of the early converts at Belleville.* In Algiers, also, meetings are held for the purpose of reaching the Arab population.

The mission is greatly aided in its work of distributing tracts, etc., by the large grants made to it by various societies. Among these the "Feuillets Illustrés," published by the Children's Special Service Mission, are greatly prized.

**McKullo,** a town in Eastern Abyssinia, North Africa, just inland from Massowa. Mission station of the Swedish Evangelical National Society.

* Owing to the fact that Mr. McAll's Mission had its first station at Belleville, it is often confounded with "Miss De Broen's Belleville Mission" (q.v.). As will be seen, the two missions are entirely distinct in origin, organization, and scope, having in common only the earnest desire to bring the gospel to the multitudes who are destitute of it. Miss De Broen, knowing from experience the magnitude of the work, urged Mr. McAll to listen to the appeal of the French workingman, and establish a mission for them.

**McMullin, Robert,** b. Philadelphia, Pa., U. S. A., November 30th, 1832; graduated at the University of Pennsylvania 1850, and at Princeton Theological Seminary 1854; ordained July 27th, 1856, and sailed for India September 11th, the same year, as a missionary of the Presbyterian Board of Foreign Missions. He was stationed at Futtehgurh. A few months before his capture by the Sepoy rebels he wrote: "We are trying to be calm and trustful, but this cloud is fearfully dark. No matter whether our lives be prosperous or adverse, God has some gracious purpose, which will sooner or later be made manifest." When the mutiny broke out, he with other missionaries endeavored to reach Allahabad, a British station, but was made prisoner, and put to death at Cawnpur by order of the rebel chief Nana Sahib, June 13th, 1857.

**Medak,** a city of the Hyderabad district, India. Station of Wesleyan Methodist Missionary Society (England); 2 missionaries, 13 church-members, 1 school, 7 scholars.

**Medhurst, Walter Henry,** b. London, England, 1796; learned the trade of a printer; was educated for the ministry, and, having decided to be a missionary to the heathen, was appointed by the London Missionary Society, and sailed as its missionary in 1816 for Malacca. He was ordained there in 1819. In 1822 he was established at Batavia in Java, remaining there eight years, during which time and for several years afterwards he performed missionary work in Borneo and on the coasts of China. Having spent two years in England, he was in 1843, after the conclusion of the first war with China, stationed at Shanghai, where he remained till his final return to England in 1856. This was the earliest Protestant mission in that city. The printing-press owned by this Society, which had to this time been worked at Batavia, was now removed to Shanghai, and was under the charge of Mr. Medhurst. He preached three times a week to the patients in the hospital, and distributed tracts to readers. While in Shanghai he performed much mission work in the interior of China amid great peril. The mission was much opposed by Romanists, but it grew so rapidly that in 1847, 34,000 copies of various works were printed and 500 tracts widely distributed. A union chapel was built, and Mr. Medhurst wrote: "Our sanctuary opened August 24th, 1846, when every part of it was crowded with hearers who listened attentively to the preached word." In 1847 three Chinese were baptized, one of them a literary graduate. The University of New York conferred on Mr. Medhurst in 1843 the degree of D.D. In 1847 delegates from several missions convened in Shanghai for the revision of the Chinese versions of the Sacred Scriptures. After the completion of the New Testament Messrs. Medhurst, Milne, and Stronach, by instruction of the directors, withdrew from the general committee, and prosecuted the work of revision of the Old Testament. This was completed in 1853. The result of this revision was virtually a new version of the Bible, very correct in idiom and true to the meaning of the original.

Dr. Medhurst left Shanghai in 1856 in impaired health for England, and died two days after reaching London, January 24th, 1857. A remarkable linguist, he was a proficient in

Malay, well versed in the Chinese, Japanese, Javanese, and other Eastern languages, besides Dutch and French, in all of which he wrote. "Strong, sprightly, versatile, and genial, he was a man of extraordinary gifts and generous soul. No efforts (and many were made) could draw him from his devotion to the work of missions."

**Mediæval Missions.**—We include in this title all missions of Catholic Christendom from A.D. 500 till the Reformation. The missions of the Nestorians in Central and Eastern Asia, although in their bloom during this period, are so entirely detached from the rest that they form a subject apart.

We can hardly speak of missions of the Catholic Church in the East, in the Middle Ages. Russia, it is true, embraced Christianity in the 10th century. But this fundamentally important transition (we can hardly say that, to this day, it is a conversion) was not induced by missionary persuasion, but by a deliberate determination of the monarch, who issued orders to his subjects to be baptized and was implicitly obeyed.

The conversion of Ireland took place in the century previous to our *terminus a quo*. It was the real foundation of Mediæval Missions. To Ireland, much more certainly than to Rome, the Christianization of both England, Scotland, and Germany was due.

South Britain, under the Romans, of course shared in the general Christianity of the Empire. But when the heathen English came over from northern Germany and Jutland, they, in their slow, stubbornly contested advance, swept the land clean, as of its civilization and historical remembrances, so of its religion. The still unconquered Britons, retreating into the Welsh mountains, with difficulty maintained there a Christianity which the conquering English utterly despised. And when, in 597, the Benedictine abbot Augustine, and his companions, sent by Pope Gregory the Great, persuaded the men of Kent to accept the gospel, which from Kent spread among the West, East, and Middle Saxons, the Middle and Northern English remained but little affected. It is true, Paulinus, a companion of Augustine, accompanying a Kentish queen of Northumbria to York, prevailed on the Northumbrian king, her husband, and on his priests and nobles, to accept baptism, which the peasantry likewise received out of deference to their superiors. Yet, as Professor Green remarks, these latter remained profoundly indifferent to their new religion. The real Christianization of Northumbria came from Ireland. Columba, a youth of the royal blood of Ulster, having, as a penance for a civil war kindled through his fiery Celtic temper, been required to exile himself to Caledonia, and to spend the rest of his life in laboring for the conversion of the Picts, founded the famous monastery of Iona in the Hebrides, from which he and his disciples poured out with irresistible zeal and with complete success over the lands of the Northern Picts, the Southern Picts being already largely Christian. They were aided by the fact that western Caledonia was largely occupied by Christian Scots of Irish extraction. The Scottish kings, succeeding through intermarriage to the Pictish throne, gave the name of Scotia to the whole land, and withdrew it from Ireland, which was the original Scotia.

From Iona came the humble and zealous bishop Aidan to Northumbria, where he labored with great success. But the full Christianization of the country was accomplished through his disciple Cuthbert, who, himself a Northumbrian Englishman of humble birth, understood the inmost heart of his rude but strong and really tender-hearted countrymen, whose race extended from the Humber to the Forth. Of simple habits, dauntless courage, strong sense, ready wit, tenderness of heart, deep devotion, and of a missionary zeal inflamed by the example of his Irish masters, he became the Apostle of the North. From York the tide of Irish and Northumbrian missionary zeal rolled down upon Middle England, which then formed the kingdom of Mercia. Here the Mercian king, Penda, finding his political account in becoming the champion of heathenism, made a desperate stand against the new religion. But heathenism being already undermined in men's convictions, collapsed entirely at Penda's defeat and death in battle against the Northumbrians. Thenceforth the Mercians likewise gave up the old gods with one consent, and England was now Christian from the Forth to the Channel, being bounded by the Christian Scots on the north and the Christian Welsh on the west, which latter, however, in their implacable animosity against their conquerers, had refused to take the slightest share in the work of conversion.

East Anglia (now Norfolk and Suffolk) meanwhile had also become Christian, by contagion from the two great Anglian realms of Northumbria and Mercia, as well as by direct Roman efforts from the south. But so little is it true that Middle and Northern England were mainly converted by the Romans that even Sussex, on the British Channel, became Christian through the efforts of the exiled northern bishop Wilfrid, who preached to the rude fishermen at the same time that he won their hearts by teaching them greater skilfulness in plying their art. It is true, Rome and Iona may be said to have wrought conjointly in him, as he was an adherent of the Roman discipline.

The merits of Rome in the conversion of England are, however, great: (1) she initiated it; (2) she mainly converted the Saxons, as distinguished from the Anglians; (3) she introduced the gospel among the Anglians; (4) she undertook and carried through, with general consent of the English, that to which the Irish were everywhere utterly incompetent, namely, the organization and practical conduct of the English Church, which she thus held in unity with the general body of Christendom, and preserved it from erratic developments and from final disintegration and anarchy, such as befell the Irish Church, and finally induced even her to submit herself to the organizing skill of Rome.

The Irish Church was, during the early Middle Ages, equally zealous and equally effective in the work of conversion on the Continent. She was, indeed, the great missionary church of this era. The reception of the gospel in Ireland, although it did nothing to control the intertribal anarchy and to remove the moral rudeness of the people generally, evoked unbounded enthusiasm in thousands of elect spirits, who gathered around their abbots in multitudes of monasteries, surrounded by pious families, and gave themselves up to an extravagant asceticism, but also to noble intellectual pursuits, and a deep study of the Scriptures. Irish piety, says Green, had (as it still has) a very imperfect control over the passions of anger and wrath; it was deficient in that moral dignity which was congenial to Roman, and is still more congenial to the higher English piety; but, on the other hand, it was ethereal, full of tender and delicate sentiment, and pervaded with the glow of a fiery enthusiasm, which, finding insurmountable obstacles at home in an anarchy which it knew not how to reduce into order, poured itself in an irresistible flood upon Western and Middle Europe. The Irish at this time were incomparably superior to the Romans in point of knowledge, while the Irish temperament and the Irish mind, perhaps the finest didactic mind in the world, had an extraordinary power of communicating its convictions. The Irish monks, caring little for the secular clergy, allowed them to marry. They honored an abbot vastly more than a bishop. But they themselves, in their unsparing asceticism, presented to the wretched Continental populations of that era, succeeding the fearful devastations of barbarian conquest, the impressive spectacle of men living, by their own free will, a more wretched life than the wretched peasants, and yet making not the least account of this destitution of earthly comforts. No wonder then that they were listened to with profoundest reverence, and contributed mightily to the fuller Christianization of their fellow-Celts (of the Cymric branch, it is true), the rural populations of Gaul, and to the rooting of the gospel in Switzerland and in various parts of Germany, especially the south.

The great Irish missionary on the Continent was Columban (not to be confounded with the earlier Columba, of Iona), who established his monastery in 590 among the Vosges Mountains in Eastern Gaul. The monastic rule known as his, with its intolerable severities, is judged to be of later date. His own rule was severe, but practical, combining ascetic self-discipline, manual labor in various forms, and study, especially of the Scriptures. He laid great stress on the inward state, and subordinated all observances to this. But his courageous opposition to the wickedness of Queen Brunehild caused his expulsion from Frankish Gaul into what is now Switzerland. His enemies, however, following him up, expelled him after three years from his missionary labors here also. He withdrew into Italy, where he died in 613, in the monastery which he had founded at Bobbio, near Pavia.

He left behind, however, (detained by sickness, like St. Paul among the Galatians), a beloved pupil, a young Irishman of good family, named Gallus. Gallus sought out a retreat in the deep woods of Eastern Switzerland, where he founded the monastery famous for so many centuries as St. Gall, the nucleus of the present canton of that name. It became a great centre of population, civilization, learning, and Christianity for Eastern Switzerland, the Tyrol, and Southern Germany. Somewhat later came the Irish Fridolin, laboring in Alsace, Switzerland, and Suabia; and the Irish Thrudpert (whom the Germans call St. Hubert), laboring in the Black Forest. The Irish Cilian, after 650, labored in West Thuringia, towards the middle of Germany.

And these are only shining examples of an endless succession of missionary monks, that poured out for two or three centuries from Ireland into Gaul, Switzerland, Southern and Middle Germany. Before Boniface began his labors, about 720, Southern Germany seems to have been mainly, and Middle Germany largely, Christianized. The Saxons, who filled the great northern plain of Germany, gave not the slightest heed to the gospel, the acceptance of which they regarded as the mark of subjection to their rivals, the Catholic Franks.

From of old, along the Rhine and the Danube, and even farther in the heart of Germany, there had been Christian congregations. And though these had been ravaged and trodden down in the tumultuous movements of the Migration of the Nations, which overthrew the Roman Empire, they still offered a good many points of attachment for the Irish missionaries. Holy men, whose hearts were moved with compassion for the unspeakable miseries of this age, offered themselves as centres of consolation, both spiritual and temporal. The most illustrious of these were, on the Danube, Severinus, whom some held to be a North African and some a Syrian, and, near the Rhine, Eligius, of an old Christian family of the Franks, originally a goldsmith, afterwards a bishop. Both these men distinguished themselves by boundless compassion and works of mercy, sometimes redeeming captives, sometimes interceding successfully for the wretched people with their barbarian conquerors, and thus laying foundations the traces of which still subsisted when the Irish missionaries subsequently began their labors. Eligius, indeed, was later than the earliest of these missionaries.

There was, however, the same difficulty with Irish missionary work on the continent that there had been in England, namely, a want of unity and of organizing power. In Ireland itself, beyond a general deference paid to the abbey and bishopric of Armagh, there was no ecclesiastical unity. The priests had no defined parishes, the bishops no defined dioceses. The abbots were the real ecclesiastical rulers, but every abbot only of his own monastic sept. And this confusion and jarring individualism was reflected in the Irish work abroad. Ireland, moreover, having been for a long while cut off by the wall of English heathenism from the rest of Western Europe, had diverged in various particulars, not so much of doctrine (for both parties stood on the foundation of the great councils, including the Council of Orange) as of ecclesiastical usage in discipline, worship, and polity, points which necessarily occasioned a perpetual friction. Especially was it intolerable that while the Romans had adopted a corrected Easter cycle, the Irish still adhered to the earlier, unreformed cycle. Thus, before Oswiu of Northumbria had wisely decided to accept the Roman discipline, the Northumbrian kings had sometimes been holding the Easter rejoicings while their Kentish or Saxon queens were still in the sadness of the Passion-week.

Germany, therefore, compelled like England to commit her Christian future either to the erratic uncertainty of Irish impulse or to the steady, though certainly much harder, hand of Roman discipline, decided, and doubtless on the whole decided wisely, for the latter. Many free influences and simpler Christian apprehensions were, it is true, compelled to give way for a time. But in reality the Irish national spirit was as distinctly alien from Germany as the Roman. And, except in some casual particulars, the spiritual depth and evangelical freedom of the future Protestantism were no more anticipated in Celtic than in Latin Christianity. Protestantism was, as to its human source, an entirely original creation of the Teutonic genius, which first really apprehended the full significance of the apostolate of Paul. That Rome prevailed, and Ireland gave way in the final settlement of the German Church, cannot, therefore, be regarded on the whole otherwise than as a providential good. The more we learn of the Middle Ages, the more fully we become aware that there were never absent from them seething forces of spiritual and social anarchy, which Rome could hardly control, and which Ireland, herself anarchical, could not have controlled at all. There were, moreover, still latent in the Saxons of Northern Germany, and yet more terribly in the brooding cloud of Scandinavian piracy that was one day to burst forth over Europe, aggressive forces of heathenism, which could not have been withstood by any fabric less firm than that great organism owning Rome as its centre, which finally extended to the very Orkneys, and at last took in Ireland herself, and grappled with the most formidable enemy by incorporating the Scandinavian North. Neander, regretfully as he recounts the ultimate prevalence of Rome, acknowledges that the rude nations needed a rigorous discipline of centuries before they would be ripe for spiritual and national independence.

The conference at York, in the year 664, before King Oswiu, between Bishop Colman, of the Irish use, and the presbyter Wilfrid, of the Roman use, decided the Northumbrians and Mercians to join with the Saxons and Jutes of Southern England in accepting Rome, rather than Iona, as their future spiritual metropolis. It decided no less the ecclesiastical destiny of Germany. For it was an Englishman that was finally to bring Germany into conformity with Rome, and away from conformity with Ireland.

Winfrid, as he was properly called, was born in Kirton, Devonshire, in the year 680. His father, a man of wealth, destined him for some secular profession, but, humbled by a reverse of fortune, yielded at length to his son's ardent desire for a monastic life. In this, Winfrid developed the same qualities of fervent piety, deep disinterestedness, unquailing courage, practical skill, monkish narrowness of mind, and intolerant orthodoxy which distinguished him subsequently when acting, under the name of Boniface, as the papally invested missionary archbishop of Germany. As a Saxon he had, of course, an affinity of race with the Germans which doubtless came into play in his long contest with the Irish missionaries of the Continent. To him the Roman discipline and the Roman supremacy were of the very essence of the gospel. He was incapable of making the slightest concession to the Irish monks, although they had converted so much of Germany, for in his eyes the Irish hardly deserved to be called Christians at all, and he suffered grievous troubles of conscience that he could not altogether avoid an intercourse of social civility with them.

He began his missionary labors in 715, among the Frisians of the German coast. His elder countryman Willibrord, after twelve years of study in Ireland, had begun a mission in Friesland, aided by various other Englishmen. Willibrord, although of Irish education, yet, as an Englishman, conformed to the Roman discipline, and visited Rome to solicit the papal sanction on his new mission. He was there ordained by the pope himself Bishop of Utrecht, where he died after thirty years of not ineffective work. Winfrid first came to Friesland during one of the many intervals of adversity in the mission. He afterwards, however, returned and labored for three years under Willibrord with encouraging results. Declining the aged bishop's offer to consecrate him as his successor, he journeyed to Thuringia, in Middle Germany, where he baptized two princesses, and in various visits admitted at least 100,000 persons to the Church. In Hesse, his boldness in felling the sacred oak of Donar (whom the Scandinavians called Thor) so appalled the heathen that large numbers forsook the worship of gods who seemed unable to defend their own honor. He had already twice visited Rome, and at his second visit, in 723, had been ordained regionary bishop by the pope, with what we might call a roving commission, taking an oath of obedience and conformity to the Apostolic See, which became the keynote of his whole subsequent policy. Turning away from his nearest German kinsmen, the Saxons (who were, indeed, at this time wholly insensible to Christianity), he spent most of the rest of his life in incessant, sincere, intolerant, and finally successful efforts to bring Middle and Southern Germany under the Roman obedience. His double controversy with Virgil, the learned Irish abbot, subsequently bishop of Salzburg, was, it is true, unsuccessful. Rome, though a great admirer of her servant Boniface, decided both points against him, not without some gentle quizzing of his hyperbolical orthodoxy. But Virgil was willing to come under the new system, and after his death was impartially canonized by the Apostolic See.

In 738 Boniface visited Rome a third time, and received the fullest legatine powers, as archbishop of Germany. He held numerous synods, supported at length by Pepin, who, having been authorized by Pope Zachary to set aside the outworn Merovingian line and to assume the royal dignity for himself, was then, in the pope's name, anointed by Boniface, and thus stood committed to the closest union with Rome. Henceforth Boniface had good assurance of complete success in his effort to transform the German Christianity from the Irish to the Roman type. His veneration for Rome, however, had in it nothing of the slavishness of modern Ultramontanism. He did not apprehend the pope as Universal Bishop, but as the court of highest instance in a graduated scale of episcopal pre-eminence. He himself meant to establish the German primacy at Cologne, but being disappointed of this by an intrigue, fixed it, less suitably, at Mentz. He also founded the renowned Benedictine abbey of Fulda, which for 1,000 years was the Monte Cassino of Germany. In all his organizing plans and administrative acts, his unsympathetic, heresy-hunting, Romanizing orthodoxy was accompanied by a large forecast of cool statesmanship, which in him decidedly prevailed over enthusiasm. Not even his most admiring disciples, says Neander, ascribed to him a single miracle. It is the judgment of one who has given much attention to his course that the deepest instinct of his heart was, after all, not that of the ecclesiastical administrator, but of the monastic missionary. To this his early life agrees, and much of his middle life, and above all his end. For in 755, abandoning his great see of Mentz, he set out for his early mission-field of Friesland, and there, having fixed a day on which many of his baptized converts should return to him for confirmation, was, on that very day, surprised by a heathen band, and, in his seventy-fifth year, with many of his companions, joyfully received the crown of martyrdom.

It may be disputed, in view of the earlier successes of Ireland, whether we have a right to call him the Apostle of Germany. Nor can we be blind to his deep defects or at least to his narrow limitations. Yet after all abatements he stands forth as one of the great characters of Christian, of German and English, and of missionary history.

Germany was now two-thirds Christian. Its full Christianization, in the abandonment of heathenism by the mighty Saxon race of the northern plain, was accomplished, not by the missionary, but by the crowned soldier, Charles the Great. His spiritual adviser, the English abbot Alcuin, bitterly remonstrated against his unevangelical employment of force, and against his imposition of the tithe. But Charlemagne persisted, being convinced that his empire could never have peace until the Saxons were brought into the national and spiritual communion of his great realm. And though they were thus compelled into the Church, yet, so soon as the national pride of their adherence to paganism had been broken, they rapidly assimilated Christianity, and soon became perhaps the most staunchly Christian of all the German tribes. And when the fulness of the time had come, at the Reformation, for the complete emancipation of the gospel, it was in Northern Germany that the adult Christianity of Protestantism found its home. Luther himself, it is true, though called a Saxon, was only such by that curious territorial lapse which had transferred the ancient name from its proper seat, and made it the designation of a Middle German race.

The conversion of Northern Germany laid the basis for the Christianization of the three Scandinavian realms. The Apostle of Scandinavia, St. Ansgar, is a character of peculiar beauty. He was a native of the Frankish kingdom, having been born in the diocese of Amiens, A D. 801. The delicacy of his imagination, and the sweet courtesy of his character, make it probable that he was a Roman rather than a German Frank; in other words, that he was a Frenchman proper. He early became a monk in the neighboring Corbie, under the abbot Adalhard and the learned teacher Paschasius Radbert. But when Charles the Great (Charlemagne), having forcibly converted the Saxons, wished to instruct them in their new religion, and removed a colony of monks from Corbie to the Weser, calling the daughter-abbey Corvey, Ansgar was one of the colonists. He had early been sensible of a vocation to the missionary life. Once he seemed to be lifted up to the Source of all light.

" All the ranks of the heavenly host, standing around in exultation, drew joy from this fountain. The light was immeasurable, so that I could trace neither beginning nor end to it. And although I could see far and near, yet I could not discern what was embraced within that immeasurable light. I saw nothing but its outward shining, yet I believed that He was there of whom St. Peter says that even the angels desire to behold Him. He Himself was in a certain sense in all, and all around Him were in Him. He encompassed them from without, and, supplying their every want, inspired and guided them from within. . . . And from the midst of that immeasurable light a heavenly voice addressed me saying, ' Go and return to Me again crowned with martyrdom.' " Ansgar's whole life showed that he " was not disobedient to the heavenly vision." The pious and statesmanlike Ebbo, archbishop of Rheims, having gained over to Christianity King Harold of Denmark, on a visit to the Emperor Lewis, deputed Ansgar to accompany the king on his return to his fierce heathen subjects, a journey then so much dreaded that Ansgar could only find a single monk, Authbert, to go with him, who, soon dying, left him alone. After two years of residence, and some initial successes, he and King Harold were both expelled. But now better prospects began to open in Sweden. Seeds of Christianity had already begun to germinate there. Ansgar, therefore, during some two years' residence, found much encouragement. His favorable report, on his return from Sweden, induced the Emperor Lewis to establish the archbishopric of Bremen-Hamburg as the basis of the Northern Mission, and to despatch Ansgar to Rome, where he received episcopal consecration and was invested with the archiepiscopal pallium. During many years, from the basis of his metropolitan see, with a flexible patience that knew no discouragement, that availed itself of every opportunity, and recovered itself after every shock of heathen aggression, such as once laid his own diocese waste, Ansgar steadily pursued his great purpose. He was aided by suffragan bishops in Denmark and Sweden, whom he supported as occasion required by personal visits. At last, the heathen having already become accustomed, by many instances of deliverance after invoking the name of Christ, to regard Him as a mighty deity, Ansgar visited the national assembly of Gothland, in the south of the peninsula, and that of Sweden proper, in the middle, and obtained from each a decree that the preaching and acceptance of the gospel should be freely permitted. Ansgar, having made arrangements for the more effective prosecution of the missions, returned to Bremen. There were many subsequent vicissitudes, especially in Denmark, for the gospel seemed to cohere more intimately with the nature of the milder and perhaps more thoughtful Swedes, who, moreover, are of a deeply devotional turn. But the foundations laid by Ansgar remained. Danish conquest in England, moreover, reacted for the evangelization of Denmark, especially through the influence of the mighty Canute. The process of conversion was slow but steady. By the year 1100 it is doubtful whether any traces of avowed heathenism remained in either Denmark or Sweden.

" After having labored," says Neander,

"more than thirty-four years for the salvation of the heathen nations of the north, when past the age of sixty-four he was attacked by a severe fit of sickness, under which he suffered for more than four months. Amidst his bodily pains, he often said they were less than his sins deserved, repeating the words of Job, 'Have we received good from the hand of the Lord, and shall we not receive evil?' His only regret was to find that the hope of dying as a martyr, with which that early dream had inspired him, was not to be fulfilled. An anxious concern for his diocese, for the souls of the individuals who stood round him, and especially for the salvation of the Danes and Swedes, occupied his mind to the last. In a letter written during his sickness he recommended in the most earnest terms, to the German bishops and to King Lewis, strenuous efforts for the continuance of these missions. At last, having received the holy supper, he prayed that God would forgive all who had done him wrong. He repeated over, as long as he could speak, the words, 'Lord, be merciful to me, a sinner; into Thy hands I commend my spirit;' and died, as it had been his wish to do, on the feast of the Purification of the Virgin, February the third, 865."

Ansgar's character seems to have the effectiveness of Boniface without his hardness, and the zeal of the Irish missionaries without the wrathful impatience adhering to some of them, —a most winning embodiment, certainly, of missionary excellence.

The Christianization of the Mongolian Finns resulted in part from the conquest of Finland by St. Eric, the first Swedish king of that name, but still more from the evangelical labors of St. Henry, the first bishop of Abo. St. Henry's day is still a conspicuous festival of the Lutheran Church of Finland.

The introduction of Norway within the Christian pale resembles in its earlier stage a chapter of Moslem and in its later stage of Buddhist propagandism, more than any chapter of genuinely Christian missionary effort. It seems to have had very little root in the religious instincts of the people, although genuine Christian influences are by no means absent. But the kings who finally subdued the whole of Norway under them, and rooted out the power of the petty local monarchs, being convinced, and very justly, that effective government could only rest on the foundation of a wider and richer civilization, and that this could only be supported by Christianity (thoughts such as are now working so vigorously among Japanese statesmen), really forced Christianity on their subjects at the point of the sword. And when these were once baptized, the Roman missionaries unfolded the utmost magnificence of their ritual,—here again like the Buddhist missionaries in Japan. And as the Norsemen, says Herder, had the profoundest faith in the efficacy of magical rites, and regarded the Roman ceremonies (not altogether unjustly) as a more exalted and a purer kind of magic, they finally surrendered themselves to the new worship without any further thought of resistance. But the fact that so few Norwegian kings or heroes have cared to be buried in the metropolitan cathedral of Trondjhem, is noted by Mr. Froude as signifying that they had little heart in their professed Christianity until the Reformation gave them a form of it which they could really believe. Lutheran Norway is now a genuinely and zeal-

ously Christian country, though somewhat stiffly and narrowly such. But the religious development of Sweden, both under Latin and under Lutheran Christianity, has been (as is natural, in view of its much greater population), a far richer and more conspicuous one. In the 14th century St. Brigitta, the widowed Swedish princess, may be regarded as "the bright consummate flower" of the Scandinavian race, showing, it is said, almost equal vigor of the practical, the poetical, and the prophetic instinct, and under the veil of an extravagant devotion to the Virgin revealing many deep evangelical perceptions, true harbingers of the Reformation. And although her ashes rest in Rome, and her name stands in the Roman calendar, yet her prediction is on record that "the throne of the Pope shall yet be cast into the abyss."

By this time Germany, France, Great Britain, Denmark, Sweden and Norway, were all included within the pale of Latin, and Russia within that of Greek Christianity. Poland and Bohemia and the other Slavonian countries were thus morally certain, sooner or later, to yield to the irresistible influence of what was becoming the religion alike of Southern and of Northern Europe. Moravia and Bohemia, indeed, the two principal Slavonic countries of Middle Europe, rather antedated than followed the conversion of Scandinavia. By an unusual providence, they were Christianized by two Greek missionaries, Cyril and his brother Methodius. These had already been active among the Bulgarians, who also received missionaries from the Pope, but after some wavering settled down under the patriarchal rule of Constantinople. Cyril and Methodius then labored among the Mongolian Chazars in the Crimea, with a good deal of success. They then came up into Central Europe, among the Moravians, not far from the year 850, and therefore while Ansgar was still laboring in the north. German missionaries sent out by the Archbishop of Salzburg had already effected a good many conversions. But their foolish obstinacy in adhering to the Latin liturgy was in the way. Methodius (for Cyril soon became a monk in Rome), with his more flexible Greek character, boldly introduced the Slavonian tongue into worship. The German bishops murmured; but the Pope, who had already consecrated Methodius Archbishop of Moravia, stood forth as his defender. Bohemia, then dependent on Moravia, was Christianized from it. The Germans still wrangled with Methodius over his independent jurisdiction and over his Slavonic liturgy, so that at last he went to Rome and seems to have followed his brother Cyril into retirement. But the Christianizing impulse had now become so strong among the Slavonians, that, by somewhat obscure stages, the whole Slavonic race from Bohemia to the Adriatic is found to be Christian. It is interesting to note that, after long interruption, the use of the Slavonic liturgy has lately been conceded again, by the present Pope, to the Slavonic Illyrians.

The propagation of Christianity among the Slavonic Wends, between Bohemia and the Baltic, is a confused history of genuine missionary successes, of armed proselytism by over-zealous princes, and of violent and persecuting heathen reactions. Yet ultimately Christianity prevailed here also, by an historical necessity. Poland, like its great Slavonian sister and rival, Russia, was Christianized mainly from above, not far from the year 1000. But while Russia took Constantinople for her spiritual capital, Poland, as might have been expected from her rivalry, chose Rome. The Teutonic order of military monks had much to do with the suppression of Paganism along the Baltic.

The Magyars, of Mongolian race, who wrought fearful devastations in Germany in the earlier Middle Ages, but were finally shut up to their new kingdom of Hungary, of which they still form the dominant race, were found after this check not altogether inaccessible to German missionaries. St. Adalbert, Archbishop of Prague, who afterwards died a missionary martyr among the Slavonic Prussians (near Poland), spent some time in Hungary. Prince Geisa and his wife were baptized, but remained about as much pagans as before. Their son Stephen, however, (St. Stephen), was a thorough and zealous Christian. He married a German princess, received the rank of king from the Christian Emperor Otto, and succeeded in impressing on the kingdom of Hungary that deep character of mediæval yet kindly Catholicism which it still retains. Protestantism is there powerful, and honorably considered; but nowhere in Europe does the ecclesiastical magnificence of the Middle Ages remain so little disturbed. The Archbishop of Gran, the Primate of Hungary, is the only primate of actual jurisdiction in the Latin Church. And at a coronation the lines of splendid horsemen wearing the insignia of mitred abbots show that in Hungary the illustrious Benedictine order still retains its ancient pre-eminence. The Hungarian Christianity, which glories in the monarch's title of Apostolical King, has been the anvil that has worn out the Moslem hammer of the kindred Turks. But this Mongolian Christianity has shown its zeal rather in the field of war than of spiritual achievement, in which the Mongolian race has seldom been pre-eminent.

The latest surrender of a whole European nation to the profession of Christianity took place in 1384, when Ladislaus Jagiello, Grand Duke of the then very extensive and powerful principality of Lithuania, obtained the hand of Hedwig, Queen of Poland, and went over, with all his people, from paganism to the Church.

Such were the missions, proselytizing crusades, and proselytizing compacts of Catholic Europe, Eastern and Western, between the year 500 and the year 1500. The principles of the gospel seem to have been most thoroughly carried out in the Christianization of England, Scotland, Switzerland, Southern and Middle Germany, and Sweden, and to have been the farthest departed from in the cases of Northern Germany and Norway, the former of which, however, became soon, and the latter ultimately, sincerely and zealously Christian. Not even the gospel, accepted in this wholesale way as a national creed, can avoid large complications with uncivilized rudeness, with violence, and with selfish policy. The Reformation brought in that sifting process which is every day becoming more rapid, and setting Christ more distinctly over against Antichrist. Yet we have great occasion to thank God that over so large a proportion of mediæval Europe so great a number of humble and self-devoted men of God secured the genuine conversions of so many individuals and nations to the gospel of Christ.

Apostolic preaching was the root; mediæval missions were the trunk; and modern missions, going abroad into all the world, will appear, we trust, the fair and widely-extending crown.

**Medical Missions.**—"The history of Medical Missions is the justification of Medical Missions."

One of the oldest Buddhist writings recognizes the close connection between body and soul, and that the doctor should also be a missionary. We find the following expression: "No physician is worthy of waiting on the sick unless he has five qualifications for his office: 1, The skill to prescribe the proper remedy; 2, The judgment to order the proper diet; 3, The motive must be life and not greed; 4, He must be content and willing to do the most repulsive office for the sake of those whom he is waiting upon; and 5, He must be both able and willing to teach, to incite, and to gladden the hearts of those whom he is attending by religious discourse."

In view of the fact that healing was made so prominent in the Apostolic Church, we cannot but wonder at the extent to which, in the ages after the apostles, it dropped out of the Church's work.

The Roman Catholics of the sixteenth and seventeenth centuries used medicine largely as an aid to mission work. It is to them largely that we owe the use of cinchona, which has rendered mission work possible in fever-stricken lands; as well as ipecacuanha and many other remedies which we probably should not have known so soon had it not been for their labors.

America has been the foremost nation in this cause. Her sons, and later her daughters, have been among the earliest to enter the field. The first medical missionary to leave the United States was Dr. John Scudder, who, with his wife, sailed in 1819 from New York for India, where he labored until his death in 1855. In 1849 there were just forty medical missionaries in the world—26 from America, 12 from Great Britain, 1 from France, and 1 from Turkey or Arabia, at Jaffa. It was not until 1879 that the value of this agency for reaching the outcast and depraved in our large cities was realized sufficiently to lead to action. In this particular Great Britain has taken the lead, forming a large number of separate medical missions.

In 1876 Dr. William H. Thomson, with the desire of aiding medical missionary students, succeeded in establishing seven scholarships at the University of the City of New York, U.S.A. In April, 1879, Mr. E. F. Baldwin opened in Philadelphia the first organized medical mission in America, which was followed in 1881 by the International Medical Mission Society (q.v.) in New York City.

The need of medical missions is now universally recognized.

In all the heathen world the practice of medicine is marked by the densest superstition and characterized by the most extreme cruelties.

Even the Chinese have no doctors worthy of the name; they have absolutely no reliable knowledge of anatomy, physiology, chemistry, physics, surgery, or of obstetrical practice, and their "doctors" often do more harm than good. The sick are often left to die in the streets and not even a drink of water is given to the wounded after a battle, who, if unable to drag themselves away, are abandoned to perish. In India charms and incantations are a common resort, the sick are dosed with putrid Ganges water, and patients are suffocated with charcoal-fires.

The Arab resorts with the greatest confidence to the most ridiculous, severe, or disgusting remedies. A slip of paper, containing certain written words, is swallowed with avidity; a man in the last stages of consumption takes a prescription directing him to feed, for a fortnight, upon the raw liver of a male camel, and fresh liver not being attainable, he continues the use of this diet in a putrid state until he dies; while the Arab's most common remedy for all diseases is the "kei," or the burning of the skin, entirely around the seat of pain, with a red-hot iron.

To the missionary himself a knowledge of medicine is sometimes of essential importance, for he may find himself removed many days' journey from a physician, even, as it has happened in some cases, 250 to 800 miles. Let missionaries possess medical education, to enable them (1) to look after their own health; (2) to relieve the physical suffering around them; (3) to obtain ready entrance for the gospel; and (4) to enable them to support themselves as far as possible. At Melange, in Africa, 400 miles from the coast, Mr. Heli Chatelain, a few days after his arrival, was offered by a trader a home in his house and $1,200 a year to look after his family alone, and he was assured that others in the town would increase the sum to $5,000 per annum if he would consent to remain.

The benefits of medical missions may be well-nigh placed beyond computation in value. "It will not strike you with surprise," said Dr. J. L. Maxwell of Formosa, "when I tell you that again and again the lives of valued missionaries in China have escaped destruction at the hands of evil and fanatic mobs just because they were providentially recognized to be the associates of the mission doctor at this or that missionary hospital. During the Afghan war the tribe of the Wazaris destroyed the town of Tank, and even the government hospital, but spared the mission hospital of the Church Missionary Society, because of their esteem and affection for the Medical Missionary. In the Chinese village of Na-than, 100 miles to the north of Swatow, a most remarkable work has been carried on without the agency of a resident missionary. It is the dwelling-place of a leper who, after having visited the hospital at Swatow, where he was converted, returned to his home and gathered about him a congregation of men and women whom he instructed in the Word and in the worship of the living God." "In South Formosa I could point to four different congregations which lie far removed from each other, and at a distance from the mission headquarters, each of which sprang from men who had received their first religious impressions in the mission hospital, and these congregations have established flourishing schools."

The hospital is the secret of success in the foreign field. The influence of a dispensary is fleeting; but in the hospital the patient can attend the prayer-meetings and have time for thought and conversation. Even itinerating work is of less value. Such is the testimony of Dr. A. Sims.

"When young men go out as M. D.'s," said F. K. Saunders from Ceylon, "the field is almost boundless in the influence they may exert. They get a hold on the people as no other missionaries can. What they can do in five or ten years, he can do in one."

"The medical missionary dispensaries are bringing," says Miss Patterson of Benares, "the different castes and peoples together—the Hindu and Mohammedan, Brahmin and Sudra, Jew and native Christian, Eurasian, Parsi and European. To some dispensaries the admission is by ticket, on which is also written a verse of Scripture. If the poorest outcast gets the first ticket of admission, she is the first attended to."

### Statement of Medical Work in Foreign Fields.

CHINA.—Of the Rev. Peter Parker, M.D., who arrived at Canton October 26th, 1834, it was said, "he opened China to the gospel at the point of his lancet." It would be difficult to estimate what Dr. Parker has accomplished in behalf of medical missions; not only has he furthered the cause in China, but in other countries also; and of him it has been said, he has done more to advance the cause of medical missions than any other man. He was instrumental in the founding of the Edinburgh Medical Missionary Society (q.v.)

It is in China that hospital work can be pursued to the best advantage as an aid to the mission cause, for a hospital in China is not troubled by any of the caste difficulties of India, and it can be carried on at a minimum of expense, being a kind of medical mission work which commends itself most powerfully to the Chinese people.

In one village a successful church of a hundred or more members resulted from the restoration of sight to a mother and her two daughters, the operations having been performed by Dr. Mackenzie. The Chinese are so accessible to the medical missionary that he has no need to take up any distinct clerical work at all as his time can be wholly occupied in treatment of pressing cases awaiting his skill.

Native assistants have now become so expert and trustworthy that they have been left in full charge of a hospital containing between fifty and one hundred patients.

In February, 1838, the Canton Medical Missionary Society was formed. Dr. Parker was elected Vice-President, and his hospital was taken under its patronage. Over 12,000 patients were treated at the Canton Hospital during one year; of these 703 were in-patients and there were 797 surgical operations. The number of patients increased in 1884 to 15,405 there having been 975 surgical operations performed. The new Christian College being founded by Rev. A. P. Happer, D.D., M.D., at Canton, will have a preparatory, a collegiate, and a medical department, under American professors, to raise up educated men to become Christian ministers, teachers, and physicians among the hundreds of millions of that empire.

At the various points where missionary work is carried on, experiences such as the following are constantly repeated. "During the summer months our work largely increased. It was not uncommon to see ten or twelve carts outside, crowded with sick people. The blind, the maimed, the halt, alike sought relief, many being beyond all hope of recovery. As numerous cases require operative interference and careful treatment, we look about for some premises we may hire, and convert into a temporary hospital. In some cases it is an inn, where the utmost publicity is allowed; and frequently it is difficult to come near our patient for the crowd, and even after succeeding, all the available light is carefully excluded."

The cities furnish a field for medical work not unlike that of any large city in the United States. The most frequent diseases met with are those relating to the digestive organs. The Chinaman whose "heart's mouth" has never pained is seldom to be met with. This "heart's mouth" is a favorite locality with the Chinese as a seat of disease. The native doctors know nothing of the dissection of the human body, and they rely chiefly upon their imaginations. The brain is put in the stomach; the seat of courage is in the liver; the bladder communicates directly with the mouth by a tube into which all liquids find their way; while a hole in the heart has mysterious relations with the stomach, and to this orifice is ascribed much of the pain consequent upon indigestion, which is exceedingly common, in consequence of the universal habit of rapid eating.

*The Hankow* native hospital was opened on the 27th of September, 1880, with a Christian dedicatory service. Gospel preaching and teaching have been continuously sustained. It is a Chinese building, supported by Chinese money. Opposite the doorway is the inscription in gilt letters, "To God be all the glory." Dr. Yang, a native who was educated at the hospital, is not only a skilful physician, but a most eloquent speaker, and will prove an effective instrument in furthering the great work in his native city.

*Canton.*—In this city the hospital, dispensary, and college attract wide-spread and deserved attention, 20,000 patients being treated annually. Associated with Dr. J. G. Kerr is an efficient staff of native doctors and surgeons whom he has trained. He has instructed scores of pupils, thirty of whom have taken the full course and received certificates. Most of these educated native doctors are Christians, and engage in evangelistic labors. The blessings of the Institution have been manifest in diminishing the power of superstition and lessening the anti-foreign feeling of the Chinese. The hospital was founded in 1838, and up to 1889 had treated three quarters of a million of cases, many of them demanding the highest possible surgical skill and experience. A small charge for medicines reduced (1886) the number of out-patients, but the number of in-patients has been very large. At times every ward has been crowded, from 150 to 175 being inmates at one time. The number of out-patients treated was 13,041; in-patients, 1,287; and the number of operations, 2,318, for the year.

*Shanghai.*—In this city there is an efficient hospital doing a work similar to that of Canton, the aggregate attendance having reached, as early as 1860, over 20,000. The most difficult cases are those of patients addicted to the opium-habit. Dr. James Henderson, soon after his arrival in 1860, had 15,000 copies of a small tract printed in Chinese, containing a short epitome of the gospel. Each patient who could read (the Chinese generally are taught to read) received a copy, and by this means Christian truth was widely diffused. In St. Luke's Hospital

(Episcopal Mission) there were treated (1887), in-patients, 601; other patients (seen for the first time), 8,627; total number of visits by these, 23,505.

*Peking.*—The beginning of medical missionary work in this city dates from the arrival of W. Lockhart, M.R.C.S., at the British Legation in September, 1861. From two or three daily applicants for medicine the number rapidly increased, and at the close of 1863 there were treated during the year 10,251 separate cases. In 1865 the hospital was removed to a Buddhist temple, where for over twenty years it has been accomplishing its noble work. In 1886 the visits at the dispensary were over 15,000, and four medical students were under instruction. Students from the Imperial College attend a weekly clinic at the hospital. The year 1873 was made notable by the arrival of the first lady physician, Miss Combs, M.D. (of the Methodist Episcopal Mission), who has since been followed by 25 doctors of her own sex. Dr. B. C. Atterbury in 1879 began medical work under the Presbyterian Board. First, a dispensary was opened in connection with the street chapel, and afterwards buildings were added. The An Ting Hospital now has room for about 45 patients, and in one year the attendance of patients has reached 16,318, the in-patients having been 111. There is also an opium refuge, in which 105 cases were treated.

*Hankow* presents a most important field for medical missions, as it is called by the Chinese "the mart of nine provinces," i.e., the half of all China. Within a five-mile radius they have a population of perhaps 1,500,000, and here the missionary comes in contact with traders from most distant parts. "During the more than twenty years" (Dr. Gillison reports in 1888) of the hospital's existence, many hundreds of patients from various provinces have been treated in our dispensary and wards, and have afterwards returned to their homes; and we may confidently hope that the kindness here shown them may help toward breaking down anti-foreign prejudice, which exists so intensely in the province of Hunan. Number of patients registered during the year (1887): out-patients, 5,415; patients making more than one visit, 3,875; seen in the country, 200; in-patients, 938; seen at home, 15; total, 10,443.

*Hangchow.*—In this large city Dr. Duncan Main, of the English Church Mission, has lately (1887) built a fine hospital. One of the Chinese newspapers said: "At the opening of the hospital all the mandarins came to congratulate Dr. Main. Chinese and foreign all came together, there not being a person in Hangchow who did not praise the work." The doctor treats more than 10,000 cases yearly; during the last year 79 cases of attempted suicide by opium were brought to him, in 60 of which life was saved. In 1888 there were 652 victims to the opium habit treated. Thirteen persons made a profession of their faith and were baptized.

*Swatow* has the largest mission hospital in the world, treating 3,592 in-patients in a year. The hospital buildings consist of three two-storied blocks, one being administrative, and the other two having each four large wards—two up-stairs and two downstairs. There are also small wards for special cases, private wards, students' rooms, and the former leper hospital. One ward is for opium-smokers, free treatment of whom proving unsatisfactory, they are now charged $1 each as a guarantee of good faith. This has reduced the numbers one half, but the treatment of those who do come is much more satisfactory. A class of six students has been under instruction.

*Tien-tsin* furnishes a romance in the history of medical missions. When Dr. J. Kenneth Mackenzie reached this city in March, 1879, everything looked dark for the medical missions. While at prayer with the native converts a member of the English Legation learned that the wife of the viceroy was seriously ill, the doctors having wholly despaired of her case. The Englishman entering an earnest plea for the foreign doctors, the viceroy committed his wife's case to the care of Dr. Mackenzie, who was speedily summoned to the vice-regal palace, and in a few weeks Lady Li was quite well. Her treatment was followed by successful surgical operations in the presence of the viceroy. The court was stirred, and great public interest excited. The viceroy agreed to pay the current expenses of both a hospital and dispensary when erected. In a short time a building was completed, with wards for 60 patients, the Chinese themselves contributing the sum of $10,000. The viceroy now believing in western medicine, he commissioned Dr. Mackenzie to select eight young men from among over 100 of those who had been educated in America, and enter them upon a three years' course in medicine and surgery, the viceroy building them a house in the mission compound, and the government answering for their support and furnishing all needed apparatus. The missionary stipulated that he should be entirely free in his religious intercourse with these young men. The practical results of the viceroy's interest are now showing themselves in the formation of various semi-recognized schools of medicine within China itself, and in the new school of medicine at Hong Kong, which was inaugurated October 1st, 1887. The medical profession and the colony generally have entered into the work of the college, which has already begun with 13 scholars. Several residents have made subscriptions to this worthy scheme.

*Han Chung-fuh* has a commodious house rented (1887), large waiting-rooms for men and women, and a long room fitted up for dispensary and consulting-room.

The following Chinese cities are fields of medical mission work: Tung-chau, dispensary, annual cases 3,474; Sio Khe; Han Chung; Tai-wan, Formosa, with three divisions of the work—healing, evangelistic, and educational; Chin-chew, hospital in charge of Dr. Grant; Che-foo, hospital and dispensary, 79 in-patients, 7,648 out-patients; Wei Hien, the "Mateer Memorial Hospital," the gift of ladies in Minneapolis and St. Paul; Fat-shan; Pao-ting-fu, hospital; Tai-ku, hospital; Wei Hien, hospital in private house; Nodoa, Hainan, hospital given by a grateful mandarin; Che-fu, hospital; Formosa.

*Moukden* (Manchuria) has a hospital with the following apartments: waiting-room, consulting-room, dispensary, minor operating room and ophthalmic room, reception and class rooms, assistants' room, etc., all large, airy, and well lighted. The hospital proper, which is situated behind and quite distinct from the front building, consists of two large compounds after the ordinary native style. During

a period of four and a half years 17,389 individual cases have been treated, 40,859 visits were made, and 54 of the patients have been received into the church by baptism.

There is much itinerating work done by the missionaries. On one excursion " we had," says Rev. A. A. Fulton, " a thousand applications for medical aid, and every patient heard the gospel." Up to the close of 1889, 200 medical missionaries have gone to the Chinese field; there being now (1889) 82 such workers, the majority of whom are from the United States, 16 being lady physicians. In no part of the world is the medical missionary more highly appreciated than within the Chinese Empire. A great part of the current expenses of the hospitals and dispensaries are borne by Chinese officials, the gentry and the merchants, foreign residents also contributing with liberality.

INDIA.—It is not generally known that to the magnanimity of an English physician England owes, in great part, her influence and possessions in the East. In 1636 Dr. Gabriel Boughton, having cured a princess of the Great Mogul's court, who had been badly burned, asked, as his only reward, leave for his countrymen to trade with India. This was the beginning of English power and civilization in the East.

In Northwest India and Oude missionary physicians are doing a great work. Nearly 72,000 cases (1887) were treated at 11 missionary dispensaries, 11,000 women sought relief at Mrs. Wilson's dispensary at Agra, and 18,850 women and children were treated at the Thomas Dispensary at Agra, the lady doctors performing some very important surgical operations.

North India Conference of the Methodist Episcopal Church reports (1886) at *Bareilly :* patients in the hospital, 49, of whom 24 are Hindus; patients in dispensary, 10,025; prescriptions, 17,875; donations, 239 rupees. The Conference has (1886) 15 medical Bible readers, 50 patients in the zenanas, 45 hospital patients, dispensary patients 21,920, and prescriptions made 31,858.

Dr. Morrison of the Presbyterian Mission writes: "Our two dispensaries were kept open the entire year (1886), having had 10,231 visits, 3,681 making one visit each, and 6,550 making more than one. A portion come from a great distance, but the large majority live within a radius of ten miles from the station. Every patient hears the gospel message, receives a tract, and frequently makes purchase of a copy of a portion of the Bible or one of the Gospels, which are sold separately at less than a halfpenny."

As early as 1847 Dr. Bacheler had treated 2,407 cases and performed 126 surgical operations, 12 of them under the influence of chloroform. Dr. Chamberlain, in giving an account of their itinerating work, says: "Patients come from hundreds, from thousands of towns and villages, and there is scarcely a day that we do not have those from more than 100 miles distant, who hear the gospel and upon departing receive a ticket upon the back of which is printed a concise statement of Christian truth, ending with the declaration, 'This is what the true *Veda,* the Holy Bible, teaches.'"

The fact that now (1889) there are 200 young

Hindu women studying medicine in the medical schools of India, affords increasing encouragement to the friends of this great cause.

*Calcutta.*—Babu Sagore Dutt left an estate of 30 lacs of rupees, or $3,000,000. of which he bequeathed (1886) 12, or $1,200,000, to establish and maintain an almshouse, hospital, and school for the benefit of the native community.

*Lucknow.*—Here the Government of India has made (1890) a free grant of land to the Indian Female Normal School and Instruction Society to build a hospital as a memorial of the late Dowager Lady Kinnaird.

*Bombay.*—Free dispensary opened (1888) by Dr. Lydia J. Wyckoff. "The India people are most generous; their gratitude oftentimes overcomes me."

*Amritsar* (Punjab).—The work of the medical mission here is enormous—40,000 patients last year (1886), 52,000 the year before, besides operations, in-patients, training of students, itineration, inspection of 3 dispensaries, etc. "The fame of our hospital has gone abroad, so that now patients come to us from all parts of the Punjab. Three dispensaries have been maintained in the district during 1886—at Jandiala, Sultanvind, and Narowal."

*Neyoor* (South Travancore).—Dr. Lowe fairly entered his mission hospital work in 1862, beginning at once a medical class for young Christian men, and opening three branch dispensaries in different parts of the field. In 1872 Dr. T. Thomson enlarged the training-school and branch work so that at the time of his death in 1884 there were 7 branch dispensaries and as many medical evangelists, and now (1889) there are nine dispensaries outside the Central hospital and dispensary at Neyoor. "The experience of this mission has shown conclusively the necessity and value of a native agency to carry on the branch dispensaries, for it is by these that heathen prejudices are broken down, accessions made to distant congregations, and the influence of the medical missionary increased tenfold."

*Jeypore.*—Here great results ensued from the successful treatment of the Maharani by Dr. Colin S. Valentine. The Maharajah, Ram Singh, expressed his gratitude in most liberal plans for the furtherance of the mission cause. The college and educational institutions were transferred to Dr. Valentine, and a grant of 10,000 rupees was made for a college library and scientific instruments. The European members of the station were formed into a church, and through his Highness the Maharajah Dr. Valentine was enabled to establish several institutions for the physical and moral improvement of the people, among which are the school of arts, the public library, the philosophical institute, a museum, a medical hall, branch dispensaries, jail discipline, the introduction of prison works.

*Benares.*—In 1864 Dr. Valentine was appointed civil surgeon to this station and medical officer to the Ajmere and Marwara police corps, the duties of which appointments he carried on in conjunction with those of the mission, handing over the whole of the emoluments derived from the government appointments to the funds of the mission. In town and country he had from 12,000 to 14,000 patients and a large number of surgical cases. His labors were abundant here and in the vicinity, extending to the examination of government schools, publishing books, attendance upon jail and regimental hospitals, vaccinating, with assistants, 7,000 children, etc. Miss Patterson of Benares emphasizes among the benefits of medical work: 1. It is understood and appreciated by the people. 2. It helps to educate a native agency, and to raise up a band of workers among India's own daughters. 3. It raises Christian missions and missionaries in the regard of the people, and our spiritual teachers are more willingly received for the sake of their medical sisters' skill.

*Calicut.*—A German-Swiss medical missionary began work in 1887, and treated in the first three months 640, 950, and 1,332 cases, respectively.

Medical mission work is also carried on in the following places: *Madras*—medical college hospital and dispensary, the expenses of which are assumed by the government. *Palamanair*—two hospitals and dispensaries, also a preaching place, the heathen insisting that pills and prayers cured more people than pills alone. *Delhi*—dispensary by the Church of England: $2,400 contributed in 1886. *Baduar* (Northwest Province)—dispensary, 3,500 cases; attendance, 9,000. *Srinagar*—dispensary, 5,000 attendances. *Madura* and *Dindigul*—dispensaries and hospital, 42,111 cases treated, of which 4,995 were Christians, and 17,079 Hindus and Mohammedans. Patients come from more than 500 different villages, and from their first establishment, twenty-four years ago, these institutions have cost the mission nothing. *Biloches*—hospital, 112 in-patients, 6,755 out-patients. *Arcot*—hospital and dispensary, and mission, founded by Dr. H. M. Scudder and wife. *Agra*—dispensary, 12,000 in attendance. *Kashmir*—dispensary, opened May 9th, 1865, by Dr. W. J. Elmslie; to June, 1867, 310 patients, next season 759, and made 15,000 visits. *Rahuri*—dispensary, a heathen committee donating 400 rupees, the patients, Hindus, willing to pay a small fee. *Midnapore*—free government dispensary, with a corps of able doctors, a European surgeon and four or five native assistants; also the mission dispensary for patients who prefer to pay rather than to apply at the free government institution. *Lucknow*—two dispensaries in 1886; 2,712 new cases; number of attendances, 6,930. *Behar*—the Maharajah of Durhanga established (for females) a hospital and dispensary at a cost of 55,000 rupees. This is the third hospital he has endowed, and in addition to many charitable works, he has built and maintained twenty-three schools, and has given (to 1888) $1,750,000.

*Zenana Work.*—The lady physician when visiting her patient is always attended by her Bible-reader, who reads the Bible to the women while the doctor is attending to the sick. In all the dispensaries each prescription paper has printed upon one side a Scripture text. In the waiting-rooms of the hospitals and dispensaries the Bible-women read and expound the Bible to those waiting their turn in the consulting-room. At Miss Robert's dispensary there were, during the year 1886, 10,776 cases treated, most of the women being Hindus, and belonging to every caste.

## SYRIA.

*Jerusalem.*—Here is the oldest field of labor of the (Prussian) "Sisters." In 1851, on Mt. Zion, near the Anglican Church, they opened, under the direction of Fliedner, a hospital "for the sick of all religions and confessions." This hospital, after successive enlargements, now (1887) receives over 450 patients yearly, while 8,200 visit the clinics. Four "Sisters" are in charge. The original aversion of the Mohammedans to the "dogs' house" was soon overcome. At present over one third of all treated are Moslems. As a traveller was telling a Mohammedan—a former patient—about the German victories, the latter replied: "It is the Prussian Sisters who have conquered us."

Leper's Asylum.—In this institution German love has of late also extended its compassionate care to the lepers of Palestine. This asylum was erected 22 years ago by the Countess von Keffenbrink, and is conducted and served by the Unitas Fratrum. The imposing new building, situated not far from the Templar Colony, and dedicated in 1886, with room for about 30 patients, has been occupied mostly by men. An Arab evangelist gives a Bible lecture twice a week, which the inmates willingly attend, the word of God often conveying the deepest consolation to these sorely afflicted ones.

*Beirut.*—The medical school was organized on the graded system of Edinburgh, not on the usual American model. Its course of instruction extends through four years and is eminently practical. Students on entering must pass an examination in arithmetic, algebra, geometry, physics, and English, which is the basis of instruction. During their medical course they study elementary Latin, mineralogy, geology, botany, and zoölogy. This most thorough course has reacted on the whole system of medical education in the land, and is steadily advancing the standard of medical learning. The catalogue for 1886-7 has the names of 167 students, of whom 29 are in the medical department, which, with the pharmaceutical, has graduated 103 students since 1871.

Hospital of St. John.—Hospital under the care of the German sisters from Kaiserswerth, the American faculty of surgeons and physicians in charge, where the students receive their practical training. In 1888 there were 8,000 patients treated.

*Sea-of-Galilee Medical Mission.*—Dispensary, with a daily average of between 30 and 40, the number being limited; chiefly Jews. A colporteur and Bible-woman speak on religious subjects to the patients awaiting their turn.

*Jaffa Medical Mission.*—New hospital opened October 19th, 1886; total attendance from November 1st, 1885, to December 31st, 1886, was 11,176, and 231 nursed in the hospital, of whom 12 have died, 7 having been admitted in a hopeless condition.

In the wards every evening the Holy Scriptures are read in Arabic, and, as a recent report says, "the black eyes of the sick women fix themselves eagerly upon the reader as if they would devour every word she utters."

*Nazareth.*—Here and in the branch dispensaries were recorded (1887) 52,000 cases, 1,300 operations performed, 130 in-patients fed and cared for, and the spiritual aim continually kept in view.

### TURKEY.

*Constantinople*—The Free Church of Scotland has a medical mission and dispensary, reporting as patients, Jews, 6,026; Mohammedans, 140; other creeds, 755—total, 6,921, and 592 visits to patients at home. The Friends' Medical Mission to the Armenians reports 200 to 250 patients a week, and the purchase of premises for a meeting-house, day-school, and dispensary.

*Aintab.*—The Azariah Smith Memorial Hospital, from funds given by Dr. Smith's classmates and from a grant in England, was erected in 1878, with a house for a medical professor. In the ninth year the number of patients was 3,130, of whom 150 were in-door cases; 200 surgical operations were performed, and great numbers had to be turned away for want of room. The people of the vicinity are now contributing to its support.

*Mardin.*—A dispensary under charge of a medical missionary of the A. B. C. F. M. Plans for a hospital have been made but not completed.

In almost every city of Turkey there are a number of physicians, most of them Armenians educated in America or in the college at Aintab, or by Dr. West, for many years a medical missionary of the A. B. C. F. M. at Sivas. The Turkish Government has a large medical college, and compels all physicians who wish to practice medicine in the empire to pass an examination and receive diplomas.

### AFRICA.

*Wathen on the Congo.*—Medical mission opened in 1886, and also at Banana; another at Banza Manteke, where, after 1,000 conversions, the missionary was immediately thronged with patients, necessitating an increase of help when 300 to 400 patients weekly were recipients of medical skill. "Conversions, not medicine, brought the patients at this station." "As the natives give up fetiches and belief in Satanic origin of sickness, they come for medical assistance in great numbers." Drs. A. Sims, Clark Smith, W. R. Summers, and Mary R. M. Davenport are (1886) opening medical missions in Central Africa at Loanda, Cashilange, Melange, and a hospital at Leopoldville; thousands of cases having been treated by a single practitioner.

*Cairo.*—Dispensary for poor Moslems and others, built by Miss Whately in 1879, and relieving annually more than 7,000 of the sick and suffering poor.

*Livingstonia Mission* sustains (1886) a competent physician at Blantyre, another at Bandawe, a third at Mweniwanda, between the two great lakes. The attendances were, in 1882, 3,300; in 1883, 7,000; in 1884, 10,000.

*Livlezi Valley* (above the entrance to Lake Nyassa), overwhelming number of medical cases: in March and April, 1889, 1,270, of which 563 were men, 776 being surgical; 3 physicians in attendance.

*Lake Nyassa.*—On the north shore in 1886 an important medical mission was founded by Rev. David Kerr Cross, who subsequently performed heroic and important services as a noncombatant in the war between the African Lakes Company and the Arab slave-traders. The result was that, at the close of 1889, the Arabs signed a treaty by which the white men gained the concessions they demanded. During the war Dr. Cross tendered his medical aid to the wounded on both sides, meanwhile caring for the sick and needy of the natives.

## MADAGASCAR.

The medical mission was first begun in 1862 by the London Missionary Society, through Dr. Davidson, and in 1866 it was greatly extended under Dr. Thomson. In 1873 there existed a ' Royal Medical Missionary College," with 41 students, with a hospital for 80 patients, three dispensaries, 14 native Christian women in training for nurses, and in which over 10,000 cases were annually treated.

*Antananarivo.*—Medical Missionary Academy inaugurated July, 1886; ten lads have obtained (1888) their diplomas. Arrangements have been made for a very full course of five years' study, preceded by an examination in general education. The hospital was reopened in 1881; in six years 1,755 in-patients have been treated in its wards, of whom 945 were cured and 546 relieved; the average attendance of out-patients is about 100 weekly, and all, except the poorest, willingly pay a moderate charge. Several native students are pursuing a course of medicine.

*Analakely.*—A hospital was built in 1864. "I do honestly and firmly believe," writes Dr. Andrew Davidson at the close of 1863, "that if I had at command a moderate sum per annum, I could reach within a few years every tribe in the country. My plan is this: to select suitable Christian young natives, train them in medicine and in the faith of Christ, and send them out as pioneers of the clerical missionary."

## JAPAN.

*Tokyo.*—The Cottage Hospital, founded in memory of Anna L. Whitney, who died in Tokyo April 17th, 1883, was commenced November, 1886, and as soon as the roof was on and floors laid, began to receive and treat the thronging patients. The beds are English made, with spring mattresses. The institution has consulting and medicine rooms. There are several native training-schools for nurses, and many asylums for the blind and afflicted. Japan is not far behind some of the more backward States of America. The sanitary condition of the people is more satisfactory than in any other city of the Orient. At the two dispensaries in Tokyo under the charge of Dr. Harrell (1887) 11,903 calls have been made—an increase of 2,500 over the year before; 61 in-patients were treated in temporary quarters.

*Osaka.*—The medical mission has been more than self-supporting; in-patients in St. Barnabas Hospital (1887) 105, out-patients 1,292, who made 6,985 visits. A Bible-teacher is employed daily to instruct the patients in Christianity. The fees from the patients amounted to $2,890, and after all expenses of the year were paid a balance remained of $445.

## KOREA.

*Seoul*—The rapidly developed work here grew out of the treatment of the wounded prince, Min Yong Ik, by Dr. H. N. Allen, who arrived just prior to the *émeute* of 1884. The superiority of Western medical skill, made manifest by the treatment of both the prince and the wounded Chinese soldiers, induced the king to order at once the building of a new hospital (opened April, 1885) and the purchase of a compound of buildings adjoining the hospital to be fitted for a school-house. Money was appropriated for needed apparatus, and a complete outfit of surgical instruments. Grand total of cases for the year, 10,460; operations, 394, by only two physicians, Drs. Allen and Heron. Venereal disorders among these basely sensual people present a terrible showing; no less than 1,686 cases, chiefly syphilitic, were treated, and there were 845 cases of skin disease, due in the main to want of cleanliness. It is estimated by the native faculty that about fifty per cent of the deaths in Korea are caused by small-pox. (Dr. Allen, sent out by the Presbyterian Board on a salary of $1,500, soon earned from $5,000 to $8,000 a year, which he turned over to the Board; he has also been sent with the embassy to the United States by the king.) Twelve students (1887), who are supported by the government, are preparing for medical work. During the third year 1,970 hospital cases were treated.

## PERSIA.

" Dr. Grant, the first physician sent to Persia, found that his medical practice gave him twenty times as much intercourse with the Mohammedans as the clerical missionary could secure." His treatment of the governor of Tabriz prepared the way for the mission at Oroomiah. This remarkable man, by his patience, consummate skill, and eminent character, won universal favor in Persia and opened the door for the founding of various mission enterprises in this ancient land.

*Oroomiah.*—The hospital, in spacious grounds (16 acres), well-shaded, near the city, has been built (1886), equipped, and is in full operation. The dispensary has been thronged with sick (1887); as many as 100 a day are sometimes treated, besides numerous visits made far and near. Dr. Holmes' appointment as consulting physician to the heir-apparent to the throne, has greatly aided the work.

*Hamadan.*—Number of cases treated (1887) over 5,000, while the number of visitors was double that number.

*Teheran.*—By imperial firman (1887), his majesty has authorized the American missionaries to establish a hospital, where, without regard to religion or nationality, all seeking relief shall be received for treatment, and his majesty has conferred upon Dr. Torrence, director, the title of Grand Officer of the Order of the Lion and Sun of Persia.

*Tabriz* also has a dispensary, and at *Teheran* the Ferry Hospital is (1887) being built.

## ARABIA.

See Keith Falconer Mission.

## SIAM.

In 1828 Dr. Carl Gutzlaff, the famous German missionary, with Rev. Mr. Tomlin, visited Bangkok, treated thousands of patients who applied for medical aid, and distributed boxes of books and tracts in the Chinese tongue. They were so impressed with the needs of Siam and the open door to the missionary, that they appealed to the churches of America to send forth laborers into this new harvest field.

*Bangkok.*—The hospital here resulted (1887), from the efforts of foreign citizens to take care of sick seamen in the port, the king himself contributing four acres, containing buildings suitable for a hospital, physicians' dwellings, and servants' quarters. The first year 1,300 cases came under the care of Dr. Hays. To the Baptist Mission the king has recently given the sum of $240,000 for a hospital and schools.

*Petchaburi.*—Here the king and queen have contributed to the medical missionary work (to 1890) $25,000, and his majesty has presented Dr. J. B. Thompson with a silver medal for services rendered to his subjects. In 1888 additions were made to the hospital, consisting of two wings erected in front of the old building : one wing containing the dispensary and operating-room, the other to provide a ward for women and children. Dr. Thompson treated 2,838 cases during 1887.

*Rathboree* (the third city in importance).—Here the prime-minister gave to the Mission a large and well-built brick house, which was the result of medical mission work, as he and his family had been under treatment at Petchaburi and Bangkok.

*Chieng Mai.*—A new dispensary has been (1888) completed, and a small temporary hospital erected, while much material has been prepared for the permanent hospital. In seven months Dr. Cary treated 670 patients, much of the medicine used being paid for by themselves. Surgical cases were treated with almost uniform success.

### ZANZIBAR.

Here the munificent sum of Rs. 2,300,000 has been given (1887) by Mr. Taria Tophan for the building of the hospital and its permanent maintenance ; the British Government holding in trust the sum of Rs. 1,500,000 for the support of this charitable institution.

Medical missions are also carried on at the following named places: *Morocco* (Fez and Tangier) ; *Fiji*, *Madeira*, *Formosa*, etc.; also in *Melbourne*, where, in the Mission House next the Dispensary, some 1,500 (1886) have been brought to Christ, and over 35,000 have attended the free medical dispensary.

MEDICAL MISSIONS ESPECIALLY FOR THE JEWS are carried on in Jerusalem, Tiberias, Constantinople, Buda-Pesth, Smyrna, Rabat, Morocco, and London, all of which are supported by British Societies.

*Jerusalem.*—Here is the oldest and by far the largest organization. The hospital admitted (in 1887) 849 patients (417 males, 432 females), while the out-patient department dealt with no fewer than 17,480 cases.

*Tiberias.*—Begun by Dr. Torrance in 1884. From November, 1887, to February, 1888, there were 601 dispensary patients, of whom 382 were Jews, 144 Moslems, and 75 Christians. The visits of these patients were 2,105, being an average of 3½ times for each. Many patients were visited at their own homes of whom no record has been kept.

*Constantinople.*—In an airy hall (for 100 people) one may see Scripture verses in many languages so placed as to catch the eyes of the Jews, who come from many lands to visit the dispensary. In 1887 of the cases treated there were 6,026 Jews, 140 Mohammedans, and 755 of other creeds,—total 6,921,—and 592 visits to patients at their own homes.

*Buda-Pesth.*—The work was established in 1841. Patients (in 1887) 312 (of whom 128 were Jews) and 1,091 visits.

*Smyrna.*—Hospital established, and during the first year 77 cases (56 Jews) were treated.

*Rabat-Saleh* (Morocco).—During 1887 there were treated 1,835 cases; of whom 219 were Jews, 1,338 were Moors, Europeans, Arabs, and Berbers ; visits to homes, 278. None of the indoor patients had ever before heard of the name of Jesus. This mission work is also conducted at Safed.

*London.*—The mission here is associated with much other work in behalf of Israel, extending to the Continent, and also to North Africa. The attendances in 1887 were 13,822, including 5,000 individual patients, revealing the immense scope of this mission. Among the various agencies attached to the mission is a convalescent home for the Jews who have been treated in the hospital.

*Advantages and Benefits.*—1. Medical missionaries, as far as possible, become self-supporting, and go out on an unsectarian basis.

2. This plan does not conflict with the work of the regular mission boards, but on the contrary its purpose is to supplement their efforts, and pioneer where they may follow.

3. Where a dispensary has been located a church has soon been formed.

4. Medical mission work destroys caste. In the waiting-room may be seen, day after day, sitting side by side, the Brahmin, Sudra and Shanar, the Pulayar and Pariah, the devil-worshipper, the worshipper of Siva, the Mohammedan, the Roman Catholic, and Protestant; men, women, of all castes and creeds, while waiting their turn to be examined, listening attentively to the reading of God's Word, and the preaching of the gospel, thousands of whom, otherwise, would never have an opportunity of hearing the tidings of salvation.

5. Medical mission work secures protection and provision. Dr. Summers, with thirty-six carriers, penetrated Africa 1,500 miles in a direct line, securing from his grateful patients all the means and material which they needed upon the long and difficult tour, and during his whole career of three and a half years he did not received one dollar from the Home Society.

6. Medical missions are far reaching in their results. "As many as 1,200 to 1,400 towns and villages have been represented in a single year among the in-patients of one hospital, who, returning to their homes, carry with them some of the truth received. In nine years more than 100,000 patients had been treated in the dispensaries under the charge of the New York Medical Mission. The hospitals and dispensaries of the Presbyterian Board reach 50,000 patients every year.

7. Medical mission work (especially in China) is lessening the anti-foreign feeling, is diminishing the power of superstition which connects disease with evil spirits, and is giving constant proof of the unselfish character of the Christian religion.

8. "One thing is perfectly certain," said Dr. Post of Syria, "namely, that medical mission work never fails. Other work may fail, but this affording of relief for physical suffering goes on the debit side of Christianity in all cases, and opens the way for other work to follow."

For additional references to medical work see articles on the different countries and stations mentioned above, the Missionary Societies and Methods of Missionary work.

*Medical Mission of Chicago.* Headquarters, 7 and 9 Jackson Street. Organized March, 1885. Incorporated July, 1885. *Title* —"American Medical Missionary Society."

This Society is interdenominational in character, and comprises three departments:

First, a board of managers having the supreme control.

Second, a board of honorary directors having advisory functions.

Third, an executive committee, composed of the officers of the board of managers having the power to transact the business of the Society during the recess of the board.

It is no part of the object of this organization to establish foreign missions or to send either physicians or ministers into the missionary fields of labor under its own superintendence, but to furnish systematic and well-directed aid in securing a full medical education to such young men and women belonging to any of the recognized evangelical Christian denominations as can comply with the following:

*Requirements.*—1. Every applicant must furnish the executive committee satisfactory testimonials of earnest Christian character and ability for Christian work from his or her church, society, or board of missions.

2. Every applicant must be a graduate of some college, or produce evidence of having received a fair, liberal education.

3. Every applicant must pass a physical examination, as is required by our good insurance companies.

4. Every applicant must agree to take a full medical course of three years, and to graduate.

5. Every applicant must bind himself or herself, on completion of the course of medical education furnished by the Society, to go out to the foreign fields as a medical missionary, or else to pay back to the Society the cost of the medical education provided.

These rules, besides exacting evidence of Christian character and other needed qualifications, also guard against the tendency to send out, as medical missionaries, men and women with only an inadequate amount of medical knowledge.

The Society does not intend to devote any part of the money received to the establishment of any medical college, as the work can be more economically and efficiently done in the best class of medical colleges already established in various parts of the country. As none of the officers receive salaries, all the money contributed can be devoted directly to the work of education, except a very limited amount for stationery, printing, etc., for the secretary and general agent.

The various bodies composing the Society share in its benefits in proportion to their gifts to its funds.

AIMS AND OBJECTS.—The great object of the Society shall be to endeavor to promote the consecration of the healing art to the service of Christ:

1. By making use of a dispensary and training institution, in addition to the medical instruction in the colleges, where the principle of medical missions may be seen in practical operation—the sick and suffering receiving appropriate surgical and medical treatment, and at the same time having the gospel faithfully proclaimed to them by those who minister to their bodily wants and infirmities.

2. By aiding financially and otherwise young men who may offer themselves for this department of the Lord's work, and who, after careful examination, are approved for their piety and capacity, and by providing them with the means of becoming fully equipped, thoroughly qualified, and well-educated medical men, as well as practically acquainted with evangelistic work while prosecuting their professional studies.

3. By endeavoring to promote the employment of female medical mission agency in the foreign field where such an auxiliary to evangelistic work is urgently required.

4. By furnishing other missionary boards with medical missionaries who shall be highly educated medical men, worthy representatives of the profession.

5. By establishing, either independently or in co-operation with other societies, medical mission stations and dispensaries abroad; by supporting as many medical missionaries in the foreign field as the funds at its disposal and the demand by other missionary societies for our medically trained missionaries will allow; by assisting medical missionaries laboring abroad in connection with other societies with grants of medicines, instruments, etc.; and by diffusing medical missionary intelligence as widely as possible, and enforcing the many considerations fitted to promote the cause of medical missions.

The board of managers is so proportioned, denominationally, as to represent the catholicity of the Society's constitution.

Actual cost of medical mission training is $100 and upwards for each of three courses, making a total of $300, or as much more as one is able and willing to spend for a better style of living, or luxuries not necessary.

Life-membership in the American Medical Missionary Society costs only $100, which entitles the member to a place in the honorary board of directors. Those paying $500 and upward shall be, in addition to life-membership, constituted honorary members of the board of managers of the Society. A life-membership fee pays the necessary expenses of one student for one year at the minimum rate as above noted.

The Society is now (October, 1890) furnishing eight young men with their medical education free in the "Rush" and "Chicago" Medical Colleges, and the Society has thus given a regular medical education in these colleges to over thirty young men. In this feature the Society takes a leading position.

As early as 1887 the Society had its workers in Africa on the east and west coasts, and also one in India.

The "Medical Missionary Journal" is the authorized publication of the Society. It is published monthly in the interest of medical missionary training and labor throughout the world.

**Medingen,** town of North Transvaal, East South Africa, north of Mphome, south of the Limpopo River. Mission station of the Berlin Evangelical Lutheran Society; 1 missionary, 10 native helpers, 5 out-stations, 76 church-members, of whom 52 are communicants, 31 scholars.

The station was founded in 1881, and in 1884 the preacher and his helper were murdered. At present, however, the station is flourishing.

**Meerut** (Mirat), a city of the Northwest Provinces, India, halfway between the Ganges and Jumna rivers. Climate variable, subject to extremes. Population, 81,000, Hindus, Moslems, Jains, Christians. Language, Urdu, Hindi. Mission station C. M. S.: 1 missionary, 2 female missionaries, 10 native helpers, 5 outstations, 372 adherents, 3 churches, 186 communicants, 5 schools, 400 scholars.

**Meigs, Benjamin Clark,** b. Bethlehem, Conn., U. S. A., August 9th, 1789; graduated 1809; was converted in college and joined the college church. After graduation he taught school at Bedford, N. Y., and spent two years and a half at Andover Theological Seminary. While there he was a member of the select band that was formed for inquiry and prayer in reference to their personal duty to engage in mission work among the heathen, and determined to devote himself to a missionary life. He was ordained June 21st, 1815, and sailed October 23d following as one of the original founders of the American Board's mission in Jaffna, Ceylon. There he labored forty years. In 1840, after an absence of twenty-five years, he visited the United States, and sailed again from Boston October 17th, 1841, to resume his mission labors. Failure of health in 1858 compelled him to relinquish the mission work and return again to America. He died in New York City, May 12th, 1862, aged sixty-three. He possessed a kind, conciliatory spirit, excellent judgment, and was highly esteemed by the natives, as well as by his missionary associates.

**Meiktila,** a city of Burma, recently occupied as a station of the American Baptist Missionary Union. Has 1 missionary and wife.

**Meisei,** a town of Japan, near Tokyo. Station of the United Church of Japan; 1 preacher, 176 church-members.

**Megnanapuram,** a town of Madras, India. Centre of a church council of the C.M.S.; 63 churches, 20 native pastors, 4,004 communicants, 3,400 scholars.

**Melanesia,** the name given to that part of Australasia which lies south of the equator, including New Guinea, New Ireland, Solomon Islands, the New Hebrides, New Caledonia, the Louisiade group, and many small groups of islands. The inhabitants of Melanesia have more of the negro characteristics, as distinguished from the more typical Malay races of Microesia. (See special articles.)

**Melanesian Mission.**—Headquarters, Norfolk Island, Melanesia.

The diocese of the first Anglican bishop of New Zealand extended over 84° of latitude and 20° of longitude, and thus embraced a large number of the islands of the South Pacific; and Bishop Selwyn, occupied as he was with the duties of his colonial diocese—so extensive that it has since been divided into six—at once endeavored to carry out a suggestion made to him upon the occasion of his consecration as bishop of New Zealand in 1841 by Archbishop Howley—viz., that he should establish an Island Mission apart from that of New Zealand. He made many voyages along the coast of New Zealand, and became quite as expert in managing small craft at sea as the Cambridge boat in his university days, but was not able to visit any of the heathen islands of the South Seas until 1847, when he set sail in H. M. S. "Dido" on a voyage of inspection, which resulted, two years later, in a second voyage in his own small schooner, the "Undine," of twenty-one tons. Ten days after leaving Auckland he reached Aneityum, 1,000 miles to the north, the most southerly island of the New Hebrides, where he met Captain (now Admiral) Erskine of H. M. S. "Havannah," in whose company he proposed to make his trial voyage, the object of which was to get young lads from the New Hebrides, the Loyalty Islands, and New Caledonia, to take back with him to Auckland, where they would be instructed in reading, writing, and the elementary truths of the Scriptures. The vessels proceeded on their way through the various groups of islands, the Bishop developing a wonderful art in gaining the confidence of the savage people. Each of the many islands has a language of its own, but he picked up a few words in each, and carefully noted down the names of the chiefs whom he met on one voyage, and as carefully inquired for them when he next visited their island. Human nature being the same all the world over, these chiefs liked to be remembered by name, and in this way, and by his great tact and never-failing kindness, Bishop Selwyn gained the affections even of the cannibals of the South Seas. From year to year, as his acquaintance with the seas and the people increased, and as he obtained a larger vessel, he extended his voyages towards the north, and most of the islands between New Zealand and the Santa Cruz group were visited; all of them, with the exception of the Loyalty Islands and the southern portion of the New Hebrides group, being without European missionaries or even native teachers. With a courage and enterprise never surpassed, and with zeal and wisdom equal to his peculiar trials and difficulties, the bishop pioneered the way for those who were to follow. Few men have braved so many dangers, with less means of defence, in the service of Christ. In his first voyages he had no charts, and for a long time had to rely upon his own drawings and some old Spanish and Russian charts. He had to command his vessel, take observations, calculate distances, pull a rope, and manage people on board speaking perhaps ten languages. The natives who came on board sometimes brought their wives with them, and the bishop made dresses for the women, and when they were sick, "he even washed their babies." Thus was the Melanesian Mission founded, and at a meeting of the bishops of Australasia held in Sydney in 1850 it was adopted by them as the mission work of their churches.

By contributions from Australia, the "Border Maid," a schooner of 100 tons, was furnished for the mission; and in 1851 Dr. Tyrrell, the Bishop of Newcastle, New South Wales, who had been Bishop Selwyn's comrade in the Cambridge University boat, accompanied him on a voyage. At Mallicollo, one of the largest of the New Hebrides,—where very little intercourse could have been held with white men, since the natives did not know the words "tobacco" and "missionary," usually the first two English words known in the South Seas,— Bishop Selwyn and his men had a narrow es-

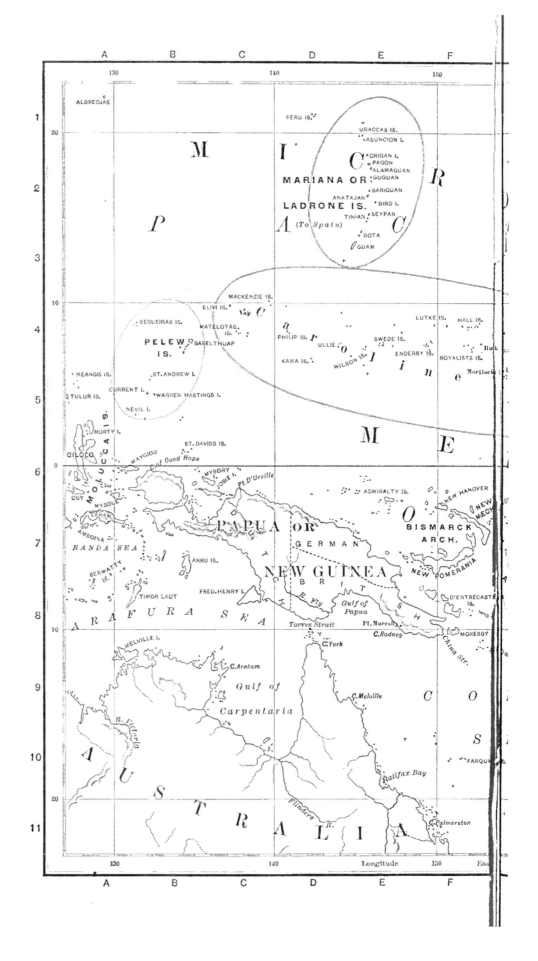

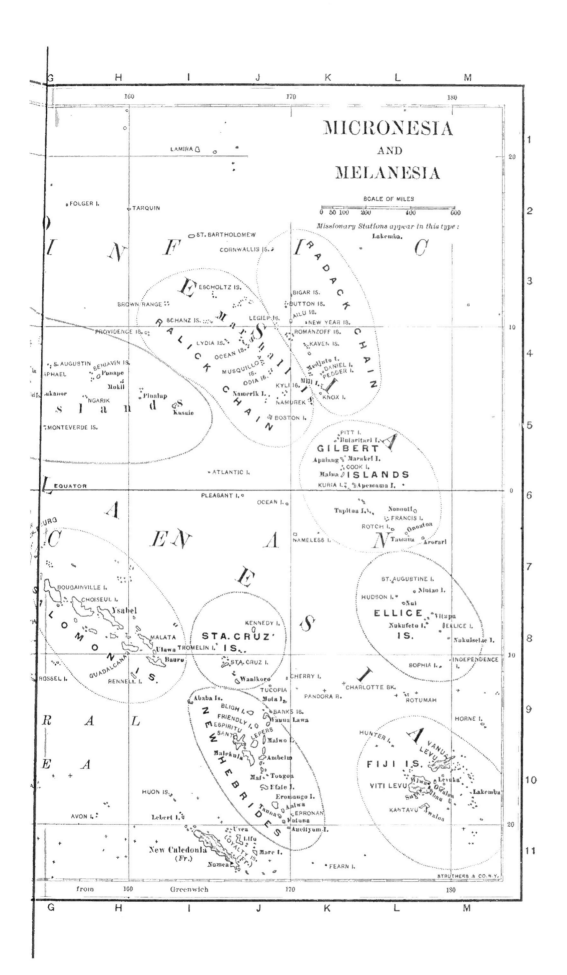

MICRONESIA
AND
MELANESIA

cape. Leaving the Bishop of Newcastle on the "Border Maid," the Bishop of New Zealand landed, as he almost always did when near any island, and walked about, making special acquaintance with a very pleasing elderly man and his son, a fine intelligent lad. Finding a well of good water, the bishop returned the next morning with a party, to replenish his water-casks. The work was fraught with some danger, and, had it not been for the extraordinary presence of mind, which never seemed to be absent from the Bishop of New Zealand, the men might never have returned to the boat. The people were bent on mischief, but the bishop kept his eye on the chief, told his men to go on with the water, and thus got all in safety to the boats,—greatly to the relief of the Bishop of Newcastle, who had been watching the state of affairs with his glass. The canoes, which had in the meantime surrounded the ship, when the bishop's party arrived were got away, and no harm was done.

In 1855 the Rev. John Coleridge Patteson, M.A., joined the mission at his own charges, was trained by Dr. Selwyn to take complete charge of it, and in 1861 was consecrated Bishop of Melanesia. Carrying on the work as the Bishop of New Zealand had planned it, Bishop Patteson collected bands of young men, who were trained first at Auckland and afterwards at Norfolk Island (to which the headquarters of the mission were removed in 1867). Bishop Patteson was joined by Rev. R. H. Codrington, M.A., of Wadham College, Oxford, who also labored gratuitously, and together they trained young men to be missionaries to their fellow-countrymen. The chief sphere of Bishop Patteson's labors was in the Northern New Hebrides, the Banks, and Solomon groups. Between the latter are the Santa Cruz and Swallow Isles, where he eagerly sought openings; and it was at Nukapu in the Swallow group that he, with Rev. J. Atkin and a native teacher, was murdered in 1871. But the work was carried on. Dr. Codrington, while declining the bishopric, continued the mission, which now owes more than can be said to his labors in every field of the work, but especially to his management of the school at Norfolk Island, and to his unwearied researches into the philology of the island languages and his application of them to the practical work of translations. In 1873 Rev. J. R. Selwyn, M.A., a son of the pioneer bishop, and Rev. John Still volunteered for the work, and the former was, in 1877, consecrated Bishop of Melanesia. He had been a crack oarsman at Cambridge, and has proved a fine oceanic missionary. The present field of the Melanesian Mission embraces groups of islands from the northern part of the New Hebrides to the Solomon Islands, and extends from 17° to 7° south latitude and from 168° to 158° east longitude. In the Banks group the mission has won its greatest success, but it is pushing on to the Santa Cruz Islands, and has obtained a good footing on Nukapu, where Bishop Patteson perished.

*Mode of Working.*—From the earliest days of the mission the Bishop of New Zealand hoped to work these islands by means of native teachers and a native ministry. To use his own phrase, "The white corks were only to float the black net." To carry out this purpose, the islands are divided into districts, each headed by a white clergyman or member of the staff, and from these districts boys are brought every year to Norfolk Island, where they are trained to be teachers of their own people. The mission estate on this island comprises 1,000 acres, for which £2,000 were paid by the Government, and contains several blocks of buildings for the bishop, clergy, and scholars, chapel, schools, and workshops. Towards the cost of these Bishop Patteson contributed £1,000, and Miss Yonge, the authoress, gave the profits of "Daisy Chain," and other sums amounting to £1,000. Farm work and mechanical operations are carried on, whereby the island youths and their wives (for many are married) are instructed and civilized. Lessons, in an almost endless variety of dialects and languages, alternate with work, and religious exercises are daily observed. As opportunity offers, these teachers are placed at stations in their own homes, or, as is often the case, on neighboring islands. Here they are superintended by the white clergymen, and the bishop makes a tour of inspection and examination every year. The young men are not allowed to become ministers, or even church-members, until after long trial. The school is considered the great work of the mission, and it is sought to form the characters of the boys by close and personal instruction. Each member of the European staff has a separate house, and the boys are lodged with them, and are encouraged to be friendly and to speak openly with their teachers. The students number about 200, and to feed and clothe them is no slight undertaking. Sweet potatoes and maize and very much of the meat, which form the staple food, are produced on the place, and their production is looked upon as a large part of the training of the Melanesians, but even under favorable circumstances of weather and crops, large quantities of biscuit, rice, and sugar have to be imported, and, as has recently been the case, when the crops fail through drought, the expense of importing makes heavy demands upon the mission funds. The Melanesian party breaks up in April, when the island voyages begin, and is not made up again till they are over, in November.

These winter voyages are the most arduous part of the work connected with the mission, and are prosecuted under circumstances of continual hardship and danger over seven months of the year and 18,000 miles of sea; but without them and the mission vessel, the "Southern Cross," the mission, which has now 83 stations and schools on the islands, could not be maintained.

The income of the mission, about £6,500, is derived from subscriptions from England, Australia and New Zealand, and from an endowment fund, a large portion of which was bequeathed by Bishop Patteson, and which produces about £1,500 a year. In New Zealand the mission is adopted as a work of the church, and collections are made for it in every parish. In Australia the help is less definite, and comes largely from Sunday-schools, which support scholars at the mission.

### Mission Fields.

*The New Hebrides.*—Many islands in the New Hebrides group were visited by the Bishop of New Zealand on his first voyage, and a few natives were induced to return with him to Auckland. Afterwards he and Bishop Patteson repeatedly stopped at one and another island on their annual voyages in the "Southern Cross," and the Presbyterian missionaries on Aneityum, Futuna, Eromanga, and other islands of the group were many times cheered and helped by their visits, and the great interest which they always manifested in their mission. Many young men were trained at Auckland in the early days, and later at Norfolk Island, and returned to be teachers on their own or neighboring islands, and five or six languages were reduced to writing by Bishop Patteson; but gradually as the Presbyterian Mission increased in strength and enlarged its borders, the Melanesian Mission confined its labors in this group to the most northern islands, while extending its efforts towards Santa Cruz and the Solomon Islands. Its present stations in the New Hebrides are on Maewo, Opa, and Arahga.

1. Maewo, or Aurora, situated between 168° 3' and 168° 15' east longitude, and 14° 51' and 15° 21' south latitude: is about 30 miles long from north to south, and 7 miles broad. It is mountainous and richly wooded, and there are some picturesque waterfalls in the mountain streams. It was discovered by Bougainville in 1768, and in 1774 Captain Cook visited it. Bishop Patteson, after the visit to Leper's Isle (q. v.), went ashore here, and his men filled up their water-tanks at a beautiful waterfall. A few young men were obtained on this occasion, and subsequently for the institution at New Zealand and Norfolk Island, who were regularly returned to their friends; thus friendly relations were established, and the vessel called from year to year. When upon his last cruise in 1871 the bishop landed in two places. In the end of the same year H. M. S. "Rosario" sailed near the island, and the commander sent off a boat, under charge of the paymaster, for the purpose of obtaining fresh provisions. The paymaster, while offering beads to a native in exchange for coconuts, was treacherously struck from behind with a club, and apparently killed. The commander, seeing the occurrence from the ship, ordered a shell to be fired, and a party of seamen and marines landed for the purpose of punishing the wretches, who, however, made their escape; but four villages were burned and some canoes destroyed. The paymaster ultimately recovered, and Commander Markham admitted that it was possible that the treachery had been perpetrated in retaliation for some previous wrong inflicted on these islanders by his own countrymen. The attack may have been made in requital for the kidnapping of some of their tribe. (Cruise of the "Rosario," p. 200.) At the same end of Aurora, in November, 1874, Captain King, of a Fiji cutter in the labor trade, was clubbed to death. These cases indicate what sort of inhabitants are on Maewo; yet even here the "Southern Cross" wintered without any danger in 1874; the natives evidently distinguishing between a mission vessel and other vessels. The visits of the "Southern Cross" have greatly conciliated them; and the young men who had been taken to Norfolk Island and returned, prepared the way for the residence of a missionary during the winter months, and in June, 1878, Bishop Selwyn resolved to spend some time there. He had a house erected of closely-laced reeds, for which he paid 3 axes, 7 knives, and 14 pipes and tobacco. The little shanty, which he jokingly called his "palace," was only two feet off the

ground at the sides, so that he could not stand erect, except when under the ridge-pole. The people were friendly to his residence among them, and the bishop kept up daily service and taught the people, kept school in the mornings and evenings, and in the afternoons visited the villages. The language of the island is akin to that of Mota, which the bishop knew, so that he could generally follow his interpreter (he had two boys with him). He had a school of 25 children at a village near his "palace," and made a tour of all the villages, and was everywhere well received.

2. Opa, or Leper's Isle.—This island was also discovered by Bougainville, and was the only one of the New Hebrides upon which he landed. Although apprehensive of an attack, he remained long enough to take possession of the islands in the name of the King of France, and to bury underground a plank of oak upon which was an inscription telling what he had done. As he went off, the natives sent after him a shower of arrows and stones, and he retaliated in powder and shot. His impressions of the people were not favorable. "The islanders," he says, "are of two colors: black and mulatto. Their lips are thick, their hair woolly, and sometimes of a yellowish color. They are short, ugly, ill-proportioned, and most of them infected with leprosy, a circumstance from which we called the island they inhabit, Isle of Lepers." He saw few huts, but many people. Captain Cook, in 1774, was visited by two canoes from the island, but they did not remain long. From his ship he saw many beautiful cascades pouring down from the mountains, which are about 3,000 feet high. The island is about 15 miles long and is 8 miles from Aurora.

Bishop Patteson had a much higher opinion of the island and islanders than had Bougainville. "This magnificent island," he wrote, "is inhabited by a singularly fine race of people. Never was a place more completely misnamed." Many times he praised its beautiful scenery and interesting people, and regretted much that it should have been called the Isle of Lepers. Skin diseases common to the South Sea Islands are there, but not leprosy. Its native name is Opa. Bishop Patteson's first visit here was in 1857. At three different places he landed in his boat, and at a fourth waded ashore to meet the people. Things did not look favorable to him or his cause, but he showed no fear, and soon calmed the alarm of the natives, who were fingering their bows and arrows, from a suspicion that their food might be the object sought by the visitor. Upon another visit in 1864, he succeeded in getting two boys to go with him to Auckland, but was in very great peril from the club of an enraged man, which was lifted to strike him. He held out a few fish-hooks to the man, and at the same moment two of the natives, among whom the bishop was sitting, seized the man by the waist. This attempt to kill the bishop was owing to the fact that a young man had been shot dead by a trader two months before for stealing a bit of calico. "The wonder was," said the bishop, "not that they wanted to avenge the death of their kinsman, but that the others should have prevented it. How could they possibly know that I was not one of the wicked set? Yet they did discriminate; and here again, always by the merciful providence of God, the plan of going among the people unarmed and unsuspiciously has been seen to dis arm their distrust and to make them regard me as a friend." Some pupils were obtained from the island, and were taken to their home again. "The natives live in a very sad way among themselves," the bishop says in the record of a visit in 1868, "but they know us now in many parts of the island, and a visit to them has become far less anxious work than it once was." In 1869, he writes again, "I have learned enough of the Leper Island tongue to talk with some degree of fluency. . . . It fits into its place as a very friendly neighbor of Aurora, and still more Espiritu Santo and Whitsuntide; and all these go along with the Banks Islands." Thus a hope is held out that comparative philology may yet do something to reduce the babel of these island languages into unity. The bishop felt now that if a missionary were resident among the natives of Opa much good might result, and accordingly, by way of experiment, the Rev. C. Bice was left there for a fortnight in 1871, and was taken up again by the "Southern Cross," and seven boys, who had been for some time under instruction at Norfolk Island, were left. Thus the work began on Opa. Mr. Bice returned several times for a month's stay, and has now for many years been in charge of the mission on the island, where he has his residence during the winter months. Schools and churches have been established, and a wonderful work has been accomplished. The language of Mota, the common tongue at Norfolk Island, is now well understood, and is likely to become the vernacular.

3. Aragha or Pentecost Island.—Bougainville sighted the island of Aragha on Whitsunday (May 22d, 1768), and named it Ile de Pentecôte. He did not land on this island, and little was known of it even after Cook's voyage through the group, until the days of the bishop of New Zealand, who, with Mr. Patteson, visited it in 1857. They rowed to the shore, where they found a most friendly party, sixty in number, with a chief named Mankau at their head, who met them in the water up to his knees and presented the bishop with his bunch of bright colors, a compliment which was acknowledged by a gift of a hatchet, and then the bishop and Mr. Patteson stepped into the water and walked with him to land. The bishop had already acquired a few words of the Ambrym (an island south of Pentecost) language, and made the chief understand that he wanted water for his vessel. A supply was at once furnished, and thus the first visit passed off satisfactorily. The island is 36 miles long and less than 10 miles wide; its elevation is about 2,000 feet, and at some places the cliffs are very steep, but at the extreme northwest there is a landing-place called Van Marana. At this point Bishop Patteson frequently called, and acquired the language in use there, printing a vocabulary with many words arranged grammatically and with illustrative sentences. He soon became well known to the natives, and in 1862 sat for two hours alone among a crowd of people, and a young man afterward went with him to spend a year at Auckland. The natives continued to be friendly, and occasionally lads went in the schooner to the institute. There is a considerable population on the island, affording great opportunity for missionary operations, and Bishop Selwyn has followed up the work of his predecessor here as elsewhere. There are now in these three islands of the New Hebrides group several churches, and 12 schools with 23 teachers and over 300 scholars.

*Solomon Islands.*—This group of islands, discovered by Mendana in 1568, and called by him the Solomon Isles, because he supposed them to be the source of King Solomon's "gold, ivory, apes, peacocks," lies about 200 miles to the northwest of the New Hebrides group. They were first visited by Bishop Selwyn and Mr. Patteson in 1857, and from that time until his death in 1871 Bishop Patteson put forth every effort to extend to them the blessings of Christianity. Stations and schools are now established upon most of the islands of the group. At Isabel, the most northerly of the Solomon Isles, there are three schools, and Christianity has gained a great hold on the people. Native preachers and teachers in charge here are aided by the presence and advice of the missionaries, when they stop at the islands upon their annual voyages. At Florida, the history of the rise and progress of Christianity may be indicated by a slight sketch of the life and labors of Charles Sapibuana, a native of Gaeta, southeast of Florida. He was a very small boy, perhaps twelve years of age, when Bishop Patteson in 1866 took him to New Zealand. There, at Kohimarama, and afterwards at St. Barnabas, Norfolk Island, he received the teaching which bore such abundant fruit; the course of training, broken only by the holiday spent among his own people once in two years, was continued until 1877, when he, with his wife and child, settled at Gaeta, to begin work as a teacher. The ground there was entirely unbroken, save for such attempts at school work as he and other Gaeta scholars had been able to make during their holidays.

Setting himself with quiet and unflinching determination against what was wrong, his power began to be felt, and of course met with bitter and most dangerous opposition, but he passed unhurt through all, though the threats of vengeance and the plans to kill him and destroy his property might well have daunted a less determined man. It is not strange that his work should soon have begun to tell. In 1878 he gathered the first-fruits of his labors in the baptism of his brother and his brother's wife, with their two small children. Then several others joined the little party for daily prayers. In the following year a great change took place at Gaeta, the remarkable feature of which was the evident presence of something working in the minds of the people—something, the missionaries said, easier to be conscious of than to describe. As a result of it, more than thirty adults were baptized. After three years of hard work Sapibuana went to Norfolk Island for rest and medical treatment, but was compelled to return home, although his health was far from restored, owing to the troubles brought upon his people by the massacre of H. M. S. "Sandfly's" boat's crew. His influence with Kalekona, the Gaeta chief, was of the greatest assistance in bringing about the settlement which was finally secured. In 1882 he was ordained deacon in the presence of his people, and from that time until he left Gaeta in 1885, for another much-needed period of rest at Norfolk Island, and to receive his ordination as priest, his work became even more remarkable, and his influence among all, whether Christian or heathen, was greatly felt. Each year saw a large and increasing number received into the church, while the lives of the people, delivered from the dread of their native superstitions and the fear of treachery, expanded into brighter and happier channels. Loved, respected, and obeyed, Charles Sapibuana was the guiding power among his people; and his death at Norfolk Island in October, 1885, seemed to the missionaries an irreparable loss; but his work was taken up by others, and is carried on with good success. Other islands in the Solomon Isles. upon which many schools and churches have been established, are San Christobal, Ulawa, and Malanta.

*Banks Islands.*—In this group, lying to the north of the New Hebrides, the mission, as has been said, has been most successful. Mota is now a Christian island, under the charge of a native pastor. There are six schools on the island. Moblav and Ra are also under the charge of a native pastor, and under his able and active superintendence Christian work is progressing favorably. The schools, well attended and well taught, fairly encircle the islands, so that the people almost everywhere have an opportunity of attending one or other of them within reasonable distance. At a recent confirmation service on Ra the church was too small to hold the congregation, so a place was prepared in the village under the large spreading banians. Mats were spread for the candidates (36 in number) in front, whilst the congregation sat behind. The whole scene was beautiful in the setting sunlight, and everything tended to make the occasion a bright and happy one. At Vanua Lava five schools are progressing favorably, and at Ureparapara a school under the charge of a teacher from Mota is doing satisfactory work. Many baptisms have taken place on this island. At Santa Maria there are eight schools; many of the natives have been baptized, and there has been a universal demand for teachers. Excellent work of great power and extent has been done by the native deacon in charge. At Merlav earnest work had been begun by a native teacher, but the bishop on his yearly visit in 1886 was met by the sad and disheartening news of his ill-conduct and the consequent breaking up of his school; but had the comfort of finding the other and older school, one of the best taught in the group, well attended, and the scholars earnest and well-behaved under their able and earnest Christian teacher. The little reef island of Rowa, with a population of 29 souls, is under the charge of a native teacher, and the people are well taught, industrious, and well behaved. The little church building recently completed is a great credit to them. Having little or no timber for the purpose, the walls, seats, communion-table, and altar-rails were all made of coral, plastered very smoothly and evenly with lime. The whole is excellently finished, considering that it is entirely native design and work. A great event throughout the Banks group was the recent visit of Mrs. Selwyn, who landed on most of the islands and visited many of the schools. Her presence excited an intense interest, and was productive of much good as well as much pleasure.

In 1888 a number of canoes were blown away from the island of Ticopia (northeast of the Banks Islands) in a gale, and three of them found their way to Banks Islands. The occupants were most hospitably received by the people of Mota and Motalava, and were eventually taken home by the bishop in his vessel. Two most friendly visits were paid to the island, and volunteers were readily forthcoming from

Motalava to establish a station there; but the people were afraid, saying that if these teachers should come, disease and death would follow. They were afraid also to have any boys go to Norfolk Island; but the bishop thinks there will be little difficulty in overcoming this natural hesitation, and hopes this year to establish a station on an island to which the path has been so providentially made clear.

In the Torres Islands very little progress has been made of late years, but a very good teacher and his wife, natives of Lo, have been established there, and their influence already is being felt.

*Santa Cruz Islands.*—For nearly three centuries the Santa Cruz Islands have borne a tragic relation to European life. Mendana died near Santa Cruz in 1595. Captain Carteret's expedition in H. M. S. "Swallow" had experience of sorrow there in 1797, in which his master was mortally wounded, and his lieutenant, gunner, and 30 men rendered incapable of duty. Several of them died there. The great French navigator, La Perouse, perished with all his company at Vanikora, the southern island of the group, in 1788. D'Entrecasteaux, sent to search for La Perouse in 1793, died as he sailed from Santa Cruz to the Solomon Islands. In 1864 Bishop Patteson's boat was attacked, and two of his faithful assistants in the mission, sons of Norfolk Islanders, died from the wounds inflicted by the savage natives. In September, 1871, Bishop Patteson was murdered by the heathen a short distance off in the Swallow group, while his thoughts were full of Santa Cruz and its people. Rev. J. Atkin and a native teacher were also killed, and, lastly, Commodore Goodenough, when on a mission of humanity to the natives of the same islands, died by their hostile arrows. As in the Hawaiian Islands, in Samoa, Fiji, the New Hebrides, and the Banks group, "the blood of the martyrs in the Santa Cruz Archipelago and in the Solomon Islands will also be the seed of the Church, and the Melanesian Mission will reap the harvest." Already sheaves have been gathered, and Bishop Selwyn, in his report for 1888, says that Santa Cruz, although as yet without many Christians, is open and friendly to mission work, and the erection of a cross on the spot where Commodore Goodenough was killed proves how completely the people have accepted the proffer of peace and friendship. In 1888, 17 Santa Cruzians were under instruction at Norfolk Islands.

The report of the mission for 1888 (the latest received) shows 766 baptisms, 96 confirmations, 83 stations, 145 teachers, and 2,514 scholars.

**Mela Seithali,** a town in the Tuticorin district, Madras, India. Station of the S. P. G.; 1 missionary, 7 native workers, 16 out-stations, 197 church-members.

**Melkaon,** a district of Cochin, India. Station of the C. M. S.; 3 churches, 1 native pastor, 541 communicants, 222 scholars.

**Mellawi,** a town in Lower Egypt. Mission out-station of the United Presbyterian Church of America (1872); 2 native workers, 42 church-members, 1 school, 50 scholars.

**Melnattan,** a town in the Negapatam district, India. Station of the Wesleyan Methodist Missionary Society (England); 1 missionary, 86 communicants, 570 scholars.

**Melorane,** a town in the Transvaal, South Africa. Station of the Herrmansburg Missionary Society.

**Memikan,** a village west of Oroomiah, Persia, on the border of Turkey and Persia. At various times missionaries from Oroomiah have been stationed there for work among the mountain Nestorians, but the work has been chiefly conducted by the native church and pastor.

**Mendi,** a mission in West Africa, in the Mendi country, on the coast near Sherbro Island, lying between latitude 7° and 8° north, and longitude 10° and 13° east

In 1839 a Spanish slaveship called the "Amistad" was captured by the United States off Long Island. Forty-two Africans were found on the vessel, of which they had taken possession, and they were committed to jail on the charge of murder made by the Spanish captain. Anti-slavery men were aroused in their behalf, a committee was appointed to raise the funds and fight the case in the courts, and finally the slaves were declared free by the order of the Supreme Court of the United States in March, 1841. The committee was then empowered to return them to Africa and settle them as a colony, and with the funds in hand to establish a mission among them. The party, consisting of the Africans and two missionaries (one married), landed at Freetown, Sierra Leone, in January, 1842, and soon after a site was occupied near the village of KaMendi, on the Little Boom River. After their departure the "Amistad" committee was merged into the Union Missionary Society, which afterwards was united with two other kindred societies to form the American Missionary Association.

In spite of the war which broke out in 1845 in the Sherbro country and continued several years, the mission prospered, and in 1849 the church, organized in 1845, numbered 40 members. Through the mediation and wise counsels of one of the missionaries the war was finally brought to a close, and peace was once more known in the Mendi country. From that time till 1853 the work prospered, reinforcements of missionaries arrived, and a station was established at Tecongo. Tissana on the Big Boom River, Good Hope on Sherbro Island, and Avery Station in the Bargroo country, were successively opened as mission stations, the latter being in a most healthy location and having an industrial school connected with it. The mortality among the missionaries was so great that Africans or descendants of Africans were thought to be the best for the work, and a body of missionaries sailed in 1877, and an additional party of two Fisk University graduates, with their wives, was sent out in 1878; all of these took at once a vigorous part in the work.

In 1883 the American Missionary Association withdrew from its work in Africa. The Mendi mission was offered to the A. B. C. F. M., but on their declination it was transferred to the United Brethren in Christ, whose missionaries had long been laboring in close proximity to the mission, and the mission is now in their hands. (For present condition of the work see Shaingay.)

**Mendi Version.**—The Mendi belongs to the Negro group of African languages, and is spoken by the Mendi tribe, near Sierra Leone. The Rev. J. F. Schön, of the Church Missionary Society, translated the four Gospels, aided by a native of the Mendi country, named Harvey Ritchell. The version, for which the alphabet of Dr. Lepsius has been adopted, was published at the request of the Church Missionary Society by the British and Foreign Bible Society in 1870. In addition to the Gospels, the Bible Society printed in 1871 the Acts of the Apostles, which the Rev. H. Johnson, a native African clergyman, had translated for the Church Missionary Society. In 1872 the Epistle to the Romans was added to the already published parts of the New Testament. The four Gospels were on exhibition at Calcutta.

**Mendoza,** South America, capital of Mendoza, a southwestern province of Argentine Republic, surrounded by several canals, one of which traverses the town, and the banks of all of which are fringed with poplars. Every available spot of land in the vicinity is highly cultivated. Population, 8,124. Mission circuit of the Methodist Episcopal Church (North); 1 ordained preacher, 1 unordained preacher, 81 church-members.

**Mennonite Missionary Society** (De doopsgezinde Vereeniging).—De doopsgezinde Vereeniging tot bevordering van Evangelieverbreiding, or, as it is generally called, The Mennonite Missionary Society, was founded in Amsterdam in 1840 and works, according to its last annual report, March 31st, 1889, in the Dutch colonies in the East Indies, maintaining one station at Pakanten, Sumatra, and one at Mergaredja, Java.

The coast-lands of Sumatra, mostly low, swampy, hot, but extremely fertile, are inhabited by Mohammedans who, as shown by a number of temples now falling into ruins, have been converted from Buddhism. On the plateaus in the interior heathen savages are found who were not wholly subdued by the Hollanders until 1878. The Rhenish Missionary Society has a great number of flourishing stations both among the Mohammedans and among the heathen. The Mennonite station, Pakanten or Huta Bargot, situated at the head of the Batany Gadis River, was founded in 1871, and has gathered a congregation of about 200 Christians, principally from among the Mohammedans. An out-station will probably very soon be established in the vicinity of Pakanten.

Java, "the pearl in the crown of Holland," was heathen throughout when, in 1594, the Dutch expelled the Portuguese and built Batavia. Now it is Mohammedan throughout, in spite of the exertions of the Christian missionaries. The population consists of 13,000,000 Javanese, into whose language the Bible was translated by Guericke in 1856; 8,000,000 Sundanese, into whose language the New Testament was translated in 1878; 3,000,000 Madureses and Malayans, 207,000 Chinese, and 33,700 Europeans. Most of these people are lively and alert, and the country they inhabit is one of the most luxuriant spots on the globe. But the constitution under which they live makes progress an impossibility. According to this constitution the Dutch Government is the sole proprietor of the soil. It gives to each native, when he comes of age and can marry, a rice-field or a coffee-garden, for which he as tenant must pay a certain rent or he will be sent to the galleys. What surplus he raises above the rent is his, but he is not allowed to sell his products to anybody but the agents of the Dutch Government, and the price which they give is fixed in Amsterdam. In a good year the Dutch Government draws a revenue of about 50,000,000 fl. from Java, for which the Hollanders have built their railroads. In a bad year the natives are left to die like fish in a dried-up stream. This system, which is nothing but a clumsily masked slavery, explains with sufficient plainness why the natives have sought refuge in a stagnant Mohammedan fatalism, though Christianity was offered them.

In this teeming population of about 25,000,-000 people there are at present 23 Christian missionaries at work under the direction of 1 German and 8 Dutch societies, and it is estimated that they have made about 10,000 converts among the natives. The Mennonite station at Mergaredja has 99 members and 5 out-stations: Teyalamba with 64 members, Kedung-pendjalin with 147, Bondo with 46, Bangutawa with 30, and Japara with 2—in all 388 members. The New Testament, translated by the missionary Jansz, has already been printed, and a translation of the Old Testament is in preparation.

**Mennonites, Foreign Missionary Society of.** Headquarters, Milford Square, Penn., U. S. A.—The mission work carried on by the Mennonite General Conference of North America is solely amongst the Cheyenne and Arapahoe Indians in Indian Territory. The work was begun during the summer of 1880 by S. S. Henry, sent out under the auspices of the Mennonite Mission Board, elected by the General Conference. A mission station was first established near the Cheyenne and Arapahoe agency at Darlington, I. T. A mission-house was built and an industrial boarding-school for young Indians established. In February, 1882, this mission-house was destroyed by fire and a larger and more substantial dwelling erected in its place.

A year or two later another station was opened, about 55 miles northwest of the first, at Cantonment, I. T. Here also a school was started similar to the one in Darlington. Both have been carried on since and are well filled with pupils.

Besides these two stations another is to be established near the Washita River about 60 miles southwest of Darlington, where a day-school is to be opened in connection with other mission work. In addition to the schools in Indian Territory, the Board maintains a government contract school for Indians at Halstead, Kansas.

Besides the missionaries and their wives there are a number of male and female helpers, among whom are several natives. One great drawback to the work is the sickly condition of the Indians, many of the most promising of the young men being called away by death when about to enter upon careers of usefulness. There are 3 Sabbath-schools with a total attendance of 125, and 2 places for stated preaching, though as yet no churches have been organized.

**Mercara** (Merkara), a town of Coorg, India, 67 miles west of Seringapatam, 72 miles northeast from Kannanore, 155 miles southwest of Bangalore. A pleasant town, comparatively well built and well kept. Climate cool, damp, healthy. Population, 6,227, Hindus, Moslems, Christians, etc. Mission-station Basle Missionary Society; 2 missionaries and wives, 4 other helpers, 58 communicants, 1 out-station, 2 schools, 55 scholars.

**Mergaredja,** a town of Java, East Indies. Mission station of the Mennonite Missionary Society (Holland); has 99 church-members and 5 out-stations with 388 church-members.

**Meriam, William B.,** b. Princeton, Mass., U. S. A., September 15th, 1830; graduated at Harvard University 1855; Andover Theological Seminary 1858; ordained November 29th of that year; sailed as a missionary of the A. B. C. F. M. January 17th, 1859, for Turkey, reaching Smyrna February 22d, Adrianople April 22d. After spending a few months at the latter place in studying Turkish, he went with Mr. Clark to the new station of Philippopolis, where he remained till his death. Returning from Constantinople with his wife he was met by five mounted brigands, and as he was alighting from his horse he fell, pierced by two balls in his right side. His death was almost instantaneous. Mrs. Meriam proceeded with the body to Philippopolis, where the funeral took place July 5th, 1862. Then followed a long and tedious struggle to bring the murderers to justice. Every conceivable excuse for delay was brought forward by the Turkish Government, but at last a conviction was secured, and the men were executed. This was a matter of special moment, as it was one of the few instances where Moslems have suffered the death penalty for the murder of a Christian, and the prompt, energetic action of the American Legation, supported by the English Consul, undoubtedly did much to insure the safety of Americans in travelling through the country. The universal esteem in which Mr. Meriam was held by all who knew him made his loss widely felt, and attracted the notice of many to the action of the government.

**Merrick, James Lyman,** b. at Munson, Mass., U. S. A.; graduated at Amherst College 1830, and the Theological Seminary, Columbia, S. C., 1833; ordained as a missionary to Persia 1834, and arrived at Tabriz 1835. After laboring among the Mohammedans for two years he joined the Nestorian Mission at Oroomiah. He returned to America in 1845, and became pastor of the Congregational Church at Amherst, where he died in 1866. He was well versed in Persian, Arabic, Hebrew, Turkish, Greek, Latin, and French. He was interested in the Persian language and literature, and bequeathed his property for the formation of four Persian scholarships in Amherst College and Columbia Seminary. He published "Life and Religion of Mohammed," translated from the Persian; "Keith's Evidences of Prophecy," translated into Persian; "A Friendly Treatise on the Christian Religion," and a full work on Astronomy, left in manuscript and translated into Persian.

**Mersine,** a city on the southern coast of Asia Minor, about 30 miles from Tarsus. Originally a mere landing-place for steamers to receive the merchandise brought by caravans from Southern Asia Minor, it has become a port of considerable importance. It lies very low, and is very malarious, so that the better class of the inhabitants reside in villages on the slope of the mountains a few miles distant, at least through the hot summer months. The population includes representatives of every race on the border of the Mediterranean. The greater part, however, are of the Nusairyeh sect, and speak the Arabic language.

Mission work was commenced by the A. B. C. F. M. missionaries at Adana, and a small congregation was gathered. Later the Reformed Presbyterian or Covenanter Church of America transferred the Rev. David Metheny, M.D., to this place from Latakiyeh, and he commenced work among the Nusairyeh. Flourishing schools have been started, and the work is progressing, although the missionaries have been compelled to remove their residence to Tarsus and Adana on account of the prevalence of fever.

**Mesopotamia,** originally the country "between the rivers," i.e., the Tigris and the Euphrates. It is not now a political division, and the term is used differently by different writers, but in general it may be said to include the whole plain of the valley of the Tigris from Mardin in the north to Bagdad or even Bassora on the south, and from the Euphrates on the west to the Zagros Mountains of the Persian border on the east. It comprises the cities of Mardin, Jezireh, Mosul (Nineveh), Suleimaniyeh, and Bagdad. The land is extraordinarily fertile, and even now if properly cultivated would yield a wonderful increase. The population are chiefly Arabs and Christians of the Jacobite and Chaldæan sects. The Koords live mostly on the mountains, and come into the plains for their winter pasturage. Mission work is carried on by the A. B. C. F. M. (see Eastern Turkey and Assyria missions of that Board), with stations at Mardin and Mosul. The Presbyterian Board (North) is enlarging its work among the Syriac Nestorians, found in large numbers near Mosul and extending up the valleys of Koordistan. The C. M. S. has a missionary at Bagdad.

**Metaremba,** station of the Wesleyan Methodist Missionary Society in the Galle district, Ceylon; 1 chapel, 1 missionary, 25 communicants, 257 pupils.

**Methodist Church in Canada, Missionary Society.** Headquarters, Toronto, Canada.—The Missionary Society of the Methodist Church was organized 1824. At that time, in addition to work among the white settlers, some efforts were being made to reach the scattered bands of Indians in Ontario with the gospel message, and it was with a view of extending the work that the Society was formed. The income for the first year was less than $150. Nearly 66 years have passed away, and the missionary force of the church now numbers some 596 persons, including missionaries, teachers, interpreters, and native assistants, but not including their wives. The field of operation has extended until it includes the whole of the Dominion, Newfoundland, Bermuda, and Japan, while the income has increased to over $215,000. This includes both Home and Foreign work, and the entire fund is administered by one General Board.

Although there is but one fund and one management, the work itself is divided into several distinct departments. The Home work (called Domestic missions) embraces all the dependent fields of the church among the English-speaking people throughout the Dominion, in Newfoundland and Bermuda. These fields are 396 in number, with 416 missionaries and 40,376 communicants. The expenditure on the Home work last year was a little over $87,594. This department of missionary effort is constantly changing, inasmuch as every year some of the Home missions become self-sustaining charges, while on the other hand new fields are being constantly added, especially in the new settlements of the older provinces, in the northwest, and British Columbia.

The Indian missions are in Ontario, the Northwest, and British Columbia. They are 44 in number, with 43 missionaries, 20 native assistants, 28 teachers, and 12 interpreters, or a total missionary force of 103. The number of communicants is 4,697. There is a large Industrial Institute at Muncey, Ontario, where about 100 Indian youth of both sexes are educated and trained in various industrial pursuits; also a Home for Indian girls at Port Simpson, B. C., and an Orphanage at Morley, N. W. T. There are two Industrial Institutes being organized in the Northwest, which it is hoped will be in operation in the near future. The expenditure on the Indian work last year was $48,508.

The results of mission work among the Indians have been of the most encouraging kind. Whole tribes have been reclaimed from barbarism and superstition, and many of them walk worthy of their high calling as followers of the Lamb. A significant illustration of the value of these missions is found in the fact that not one member or adherent of the Methodist Church among the Indians, nor, so far as is known, of any Protestant mission, was implicated in the revolt that occurred a few years ago.

The French missions are entirely in the province of Quebec. They are 6 in number, with 6 missionaries, 4 teachers, and several colporteurs. Buildings to accommodate 100 pupils of both sexes have been erected at a cost of $40,000 in the suburbs of Montreal, and this Institute bids fair to be a powerful agency for good. The work among the French is peculiarly trying and difficult, but is not without many encouraging signs. Unquestionably, Quebec is the great problem in Canada's future; but the problem will be solved, if at all, along evangelical rather than political lines.

The only Foreign work of the Methodist Church is in Japan. This mission was begun in 1873, when two men were sent to the field. At the present time there are 14 missions, with 51 missionaries, 29 of whom are native assistants. The expenditure last year on this branch of the work, was over $23,987. Over five years ago a college was established in Tokyo, designed as training-school for a native ministry, and also to afford a good education, under Christian auspices, to young men who might be disposed to avail themselves of its advantages. So popular did this school become during the first year, the building had to be enlarged, and the latest reports show about 200 young men on the register, and the work of the school limited only by the extent of the buildings and the number of teachers on the staff. The Woman's Missionary Society of the Methodist Church is also doing good work in Japan. They have an excellent ladies' school in Tokyo, which is patronized to the full capac ity of the buildings and staff. They have also charge of two schools supported by the natives, one at Kofu, and the other at Shidzuoka. These schools are not only valuable as an educational force, but are centres of growing evangelistic power.

A few years ago the church had a providential call to begin work among the Chinese of British Columbia. There are now 3 missions, 2 missionaries, and 6 teachers. There are 76 communicants. Commodious buildings have been erected in Vancouver, and a site in Victoria secured, on which buildings are being erected.

*Methods in raising and disbursing funds.* In this, as in other matters, the Society proceeds upon the connexional principle. It is not left to the voluntary action of individual congregations to raise or expend money for missionary purposes, but in every congregation collections and subscriptions are taken once a year for the missionary work of the church. The usual custom is for missionary sermons to be preached and a public meeting held at which information from the Annual Report is presented, and the claims of the mission urged upon the people. The sympathy and co-operation of the young people are also utilized, and from this source alone nearly $28,000 came into the treasury last year. The amounts collected are forwarded from time to time to the General Treasurer, and payments are made in accordance with the amounts fixed by the General Missionary Board.

In regard to disbursements, there is a General Board of Missions representing the whole church, which meets annually in the month of October. They have before them tabulated reports from every district in the connexion, giving the name of each mission, the amount which it is proposed to pay to the missionary, the amount which the mission is able to raise for this purpose, and the grant recommended from the fund by the district meeting. These reports are carefully scrutinized by the Missionary Board, and grants are then made on the basis of the preceding year's income.

It may be safely said that the missionary cause has a stronger hold upon the sympathy and liberality of the Methodist Church than any other interest. Conviction is growing that missions are not a side issue, but the main question, and that blessings upon the home churches may be expected just in proportion as they are faithful to the Master's command to preach His gospel "to every creature." The signs of the times all indicate the approach of a great missionary revival, and a speedy and large increase in missionary givings, as well as a large extension of the missionary field, are confidently anticipated.

**Methodist Episcopal Church (North), U. S. A.**—*Missionary Society.* Headquarters, 150 Fifth Avenue, New York, N. Y., U. S. A.—As in so many cases, the impulse for the formation of this Society came from an incident of church work. A drunken negro (John Stewart) in the town of Marietta, O., on his way to the river to drown himself, was arrested by the voice of Marcus Lindsey, a noted Methodist preacher of his day. The sermon resulted in his conversion. An impulse—who will say it was not the same that sent Paul to Macedonia?—moved him to bear his message

among the savage tribes of the Northwest. He reached the Wyandotte Agency. His simple story touched the heart of the agent, and his preaching resulted in the conversion of several chiefs and a number of the people. This work, demonstrating the gospel to be the power of God unto salvation of those savage tribes, stirred the entire church, and was among the leading agencies which led to the organization of the Missionary Society. Nathan Bangs, Joshua Soule, and other leaders of the Methodist churches in the city of New York, after earnest counsel and prayer, decided that the time had come when American Methodism should join in the organized missionary movements for the conversion of the human race. The Wesleyans of England had organized a society. The Baptists and Congregationalists of this country had entered the mission field, and like responsibilities rested on the Methodist Episcopal Church.

At a meeting of the preachers of the Methodist Episcopal Church in New York City, held in 1818, the Rev. Laban Clark proposed the organization of a Bible and Missionary Society in the church of which they were members. The subject having been fully discussed, the formation of such a society was resolved upon, and Messrs. Clark, Nathan Bangs, and Freeborn Garrettson were appointed a committee to draft a constitution, which was approved by the Preachers' Meeting, and subsequently submitted to a public meeting of members of the church and friends of the missionary cause convened by the Preachers' Meeting, and held in the Forsyth-street Church, on the evening of April 5th, 1819. The constitution was adopted, and "The Missionary Society of the Methodist Episcopal Church" was organized, with Bishop McKendree as its first president, Rev. Thomas Mason as secretary, and Rev. Joshua Soule, treasurer.

The objects of the Society are charitable and religious; it is designed "to diffuse more generally the blessings of education and Christianity, and to promote and support missionary schools and Christian missions throughout the United States and Territories, and also in foreign countries, under such rules and regulations as the General Conference of the Methodist Episcopal Church may from time to time prescribe."

Until 1844 the Society represented all the churches of the denomination. In that year, however, a division was made, and the Methodist Episcopal Church (South) was formed, and established its own Missionary Society.

*Constitution and Organization.*—The Missionary Society of the Methodist Episcopal Church (North) is really the church itself acting through its various forms of organization. These will require special definition. First, the General Conference is composed of delegates from the different annual conferences. These delegates are ministerial and lay. The ministerial delegates consist (1890) of one delegate for every 45 members of each annual conference; the lay delegates of two laymen for each annual conference, except that when a conference has but one ministerial delegate, it shall be entitled to no more than one lay delegate. Second, the annual conferences are composed of not less than twenty effective members, that is, of ministers in a certain territorial district. Of these there are now (1890) one hundred and eleven.

The General Conference for the prosecution of its missionary work appoints two bodies, one a Board of Managers, and the other a General Missionary Committee.

The Missionary Committee is composed of the bishops, as ex-officio members, one representative from each of fourteen districts, and the secretaries and treasurers; also fourteen members of the Board of Managers.

The Board of Managers is composed of the bishops as ex-officio members, thirty-two laymen, and thirty-two travelling ministers of the church elected by the General Conference.

The General Conference meets once in four years; the General Missionary Committee once every year, and the Board of Managers monthly, or oftener, as may be required.

Originally the Missionary Society was composed of members who had contributed a certain sum, not less than $20 at one time, to the funds of the Society, and who had the right of voting at the annual meetings. When the charter was changed, and the General Conference assumed the supervision of the missionary work, the system was continued of acknowledging as members, honorary managers and patrons, those who contributed not less than $20 to $150, or $500, respectively, at one time. This membership is practically merely honorary, though honorary managers and patrons have the right of attending the meetings of the Board of Managers, but do not vote.

The General Missionary Committee determines what fields shall be occupied as foreign missions, the number of persons to be employed in them, and the amount necessary for their support; it also determines the amount which each bishop shall draw for the domestic missions of the conference over which he shall preside. The appropriation of money rests entirely with the General Missionary Committee, except that the Board of Managers may provide for any unforeseen emergency that may arise in any of the missions, and meet any demands to an amount not exceeding $25,000. Wherever a foreign mission is organized into a conference, they receive the notice of appropriations directly from the General Missionary Committee. Wherever missions are not thus organized as a conference, they receive their information of appropriations through the Board of Managers. For those missions that are organized as a conference the Board of Managers acts simply as the executive body of the Missionary Committee. All funds, however, for all missions pass through the hands of the Board of Managers, who account to the General Missionary Committee, and they to the General Conference.

Each mission, whether it be organized as a conference or not, is divided into districts over which certain ministers are appointed by the bishop as presiding elders, who superintend the work of that district and are in a sense sub-diocesan bishops.

Whenever any appropriation is made to a mission, whether it comes directly from the General Missionary Committee to the mission as a conference, or from the Board of Managers to the mission, the bishop calls together the members of the conference in annual meeting, and the amount of money appropriated by the General Committee or the Board of Managers is apportioned among the different stations or departments of missionary work. The bishop has the right of veto over the decision of the annual conference.

*Development of Foreign Work.*—1. *Africa.*—In March, 1819, President Monroe approved an act of Congress by which all Africans recaptured from slavers should be restored to the coast of Africa and committed to the care of agents of the government of the United States. The depot of the United States for this purpose determined also the selection of the same section by the Colonization Society, and that, in turn, determined the location of the first Methodist mission at Sherbro, Liberia, in 1820. The utter unfitness of Sherbro became apparent in a few days, in the general prostration by fever and the speedy death of numbers, including two of the agents. The fragment of the colony returned disheartened to Sierra Leone. In November, 1821, Dr. Eli Ayres was instructed to visit the survivors and proceed down the coast in search of a new location. The party went about 250 miles until they came to a high point of land called Cape Montserrado. With address and firmness they secured by purchase a valuable tract, including the cape, consisting of 36 miles along the shore with an average breadth of two miles. They paid in exchange goods worth about $300. On April 28th, 1822, the emigrants passed over and occupied the cape, having, however, to meet and overcome the hostility of the natives, who had repented of their bargain. Mr. Ashmun arrived the following August and became the instrument of giving form and permanence to Liberian institutions. He established a civil polity, purchased additional land, and in fact founded Monrovia. We now have, as a result, the Republic of Liberia.

Melville B. Cox, the first foreign missionary of this Society, arrived at Monrovia, March 7th, 1833. He entered heroically upon his work, but was very soon prostrated (April 12th) by the African fever. On June 26th he made his last record in his journal, and expired July 21st, having uttered these words: "Let a thousand fall before Africa be given up." Re-inforcements arrived on January 1st, 1834, and on the 10th was organized "The Liberia Annual Conference," which was also constituted a temperance society.

The Rev. John Seys was appointed superintendent, and arrived October 18th, 1834. He was born on the island of Santa Cruz and had lived and labored on fifteen of the West India Islands; he was thus better adapted to the African climate. Under his superintendency the work rapidly advanced, not less than 10,000 pagans having put themselves, during the year, under the care of the colony. The important acquisition of a thoroughly educated physician was enjoyed by the colony in the arrival (October, 1836) of Dr. S. M. E. Goheen.

The selection of Jackstown, Junk, Sinoe, and Boporto, in 1857, as missionary stations indicates the enterprise of the mission. The little host were pressing far down the coast and into the interior. It had now 15 missionaries, besides Dr. Goheen, and 7 school-teachers, instructing 221 pupils; it had 6 Sabbath-schools with 300 scholars. The next year there were 17 missionaries, 10 teachers, a physician, a missionary steward, and a printer; and the church numbered 421 members. The mission also entered upon the work of publication, issuing a bi-monthly named "Africa's Luminary." The next year the "Liberia Conference Seminary" was opened, and the superintendent obtained permission and aid from the Board to erect a saw-mill and a sugar-mill, there being neither in the colony. In addition to these the "White Plains Manual Labor School" had been successfully instituted to teach agriculture and various kinds of handicraft to the natives.

In 1839 the Heddington station was blessed with a great revival, the first-fruits of a harvest of souls from the natives, among whom was King Tom himself.

At this time arose a series of difficulties with the government, and although the mission was completely exonerated from all blame, it was for a long time subject to annoyances from the government and the Colonization Society. Worse than these, however, were the dissensions between the missionaries themselves, which led to the dismantlement of the mission for a time. Matters were soon adjusted, and the work was taken up with renewed activity. Tours into the interior were undertaken, and new stations were established at various points. Bishop Levi Scott visited Africa in 1853, and met one of the great needs of the work by ordaining the preachers in the field. The Liberia Conference (January, 1858) elected Francis Burns to the bishopric, and he proceeded promptly to the United States for ordination. He was succeeded by Bishop Roberts, after whose death no "missionary bishop" was chosen to succeed him, and Bishops Burns and Roberts are the only colored bishops the church has had.

Bishop Haven, arriving at Monrovia December 16th, 1876, made an extensive tour among the mission stations, greatly encouraging the laborers and stimulating the work.

The General Conference of 1884 placed all the mission work in Africa under Wm. Taylor, who was elected and ordained as "Missionary Bishop for Africa." (See Bishop Taylor's Missions.)

In 1887–8 there were probationers, 161; full members, 2,641; local preachers, 60; churches, 36 (value, $31,000); Sabbath-schools, 40; officers and teachers, 376; scholars, 2,342; collections, $1,270.

2. *South America.*—The Rev. Fountain E. Pitts, appointed by the bishops (who were recommended by the Board to make the appointment which the General Conference had advised), sailed July, 1835, to South America with the view of examining fields for the establishment of mission-stations. His report recommended the establishment of missions at Rio de Janeiro and Buenos Ayres, where the American and English residents had especially encouraged the work. At the latter place he rented and furnished a room, and began preaching to the people.

BRAZIL.—At Rio de Janeiro Mr. Pitts formed a small society of religious people, with a promise that a pastor should be sent at no distant day. Rev. Justin Spaulding, by appointment, went to Rio, sailing in March, 1836, and Rev. John Dempster, appointed to Buenos Ayres, sailed in October.

There were indications that the grasp of Rome upon Brazil was rapidly loosening. The pope had refused to acknowledge a bishop ordained in Brazil, and the prince regent, in a speech before parliament, more than intimated that they could get on quite well without the pope's approbation. The message proved very popular. There was a large English-speaking population who welcomed the missionaries. The Bible could be distributed, and the American Bible Society and the British and Foreign Bible Society generously supplied Spanish and Portuguese Bibles and Testaments for this purpose, the people eagerly receiving a book which, until recently, had been interdicted.

Mr. Spaulding rented and fitted a private room for public worship, and gathered a congregation. In November, 1837, Rev. Daniel P. Kidder and R. M. McMurdy, a local preacher, and wife, as teachers, sailed from Boston. Mr. Kidder entered upon extensive itinerations, preaching and scattering Bibles and tracts as he journeyed. In Rio the work grew; a Sunday-school was begun, and larger accommodations were needed. There were there 1,000 priests, but rarely was prayer or sermon heard in the language of the people. No interest was taken in the advancement of education, morality, or religion. Not one in five hundred of the natives had seen a Bible. The hostility of the Roman priests was awakened, and the superintendent (Mr. Spaulding) was subjected to every possible annoyance and hindrance. Journals and pamphlets were issued dealing in vituperation, violent abuse, and perversions of historic truth as against Protestantism and Methodism. But these efforts were short-lived and served to advertise the mission. The missionaries claimed their rights under the toleration act of the constitution. So eager were the people for the Scriptures that it was at first feared there was a general plan to secure copies to destroy them, but it was found that nearly every copy was appropriately used. Preaching services were held also on decks of vessels for the benefit of the thousands of seamen who frequent the harbor of Rio. Excursions to various points were undertaken, at different times, by Messrs. Spaulding and Kidder, the latter going alone to more distant parts, he being the first Protestant minister to visit San Paulo. In the interior a liberal *padre* declared that Catholicism was well-nigh abandoned, and that infidel principles and infidel books had, for the most part, taken its place. Mr. Kidder extended his visits to Andradas, to Santos, northward to Bahia, Maceio, Pernambuco, Orlinda, Maranham, and Para.

Through financial embarrassment the Board abandoned Brazil at the close of 1841, and the field is now occupied by the missions of the Presbyterian Boards and of the Methodist Episcopal Church (South).

BUENOS AYRES AND MONTEVIDEO.—The first Protestant worship in the city of Buenos Ayres was held by Mr. James Thompson, a Scotchman, at the home of Mr. Dickson, an English gentleman, on Sunday, November 19th, 1820. These private meetings were continued for two years, and the first Sunday school was opened on March 23d, 1821. In October, 1823, Messrs. Brigham and Parvin, who were Presbyterians, arrived from the United States. They re-established preaching March, 1824, at the house of Mr. Tate. Mr. Parvin opened a Sunday-school, in which was a class of Spanish children taught by an American named Gilbert. This work excited great interest in the city, but was discontinued in 1836. Just as Mr. Torry was closing his labors (1836) Mr. Pitts arrived in the field, and from the time of his arrival the missionaries of the M. E. Church have been the sole representatives of American Protestantism in this part of South America.

The mission was reinforced, and the interest

rapidly increased until the place of assemblage could not contain the worshippers. The Board appropriated $10,000 for the erection of an edifice, and $1,500 was subscribed in Buenos Ayres.

Rev. Wm. H. Norris arrived at Montevideo October 12th, 1839, and found two opposing armies within a few miles of the city, and the garrison fully manned. Not being able to land, Mr. Norris held his first services on a vessel in the harbor. An important step forward was secured when he obtained from the governor a decree authorizing the consuls of England, Sweden, and the United States " to erect a temple which may serve for the exercise of the worship of their countrymen, as also for the establishment of a public school for the children of the same nations." In October, 1841, the debt of the Society compelled the recall of the missionaries from Montevideo, and the work was retarded in Buenos Ayres by the terrible confusion, violence, robbery, and slaughter in that city (1840). " During this reign of terror a sepulchral gloom veiled the city." Mission work was resumed in Buenos Ayres in December, 1842, upon the return of Mr. Norris, for whose support the people had pledged $1,000, petitioning for his return. On January 3d, 1843, the new church was dedicated and the Sunday-school reorganized. During the greater part of Mr. Norris's term of service a bloody civil war raged in the country.

New laborers continued to strengthen the mission and school work, and during the superintendency (13 years—beginning February, 1856) of Rev. Wm. Goodfellow the city was twice besieged, once visited by yellow-fever, twice decimated by cholera, and once shaken fearfully by a foreign war ; but conversions continued and prosperity increased.

In 1860 the work was extended by cottage prayer-meetings and Bible-readings. John F. Thompson, after years of preparation in the United States, returned, ably equipped for the work in Buenos Ayres and Montevideo, and confronted with great success the errors and superstitions of Romanism and infidelity by delivering lectures on " Evidences of Christianity, Darwinism, the Elements of National Progress, and other themes of world-wide or local interest." On a notable occasion of a public discussion between Mr. Thompson and a *padre*,—Mansueto,—presided over by Don Ambrosio Velazio, L.L.D., a prince among jurists, Mr. Thompson appealed to the crowded audience to decide between the two (for Father Mansueto had before declared he would accept the people as his judges) ; and when Mr. Thompson said. " I ask all those who think Father Mansueto entitled to the name of conqueror, to rise," not a man stood up. But when he said, " I now ask those who think he is not entitled to that name to rise," apparently every man in the house was instantly on his feet ; and about 200 followed the *padre* fourteen blocks to his own door, loudly expressing their disapprobation and contempt for the manner in which he had treated Mr. Thompson and conducted the controversy ; for he had publicly caricatured Mr. Thompson when he was ill and absent, and had offered to settle the controversy by a bet.

In Rosario (1864) after the visit of Rev. Thomas Carter a church was erected, the English and Spanish citizens contributing $1,800 in gold, and friends in Buenos Ayres giving $1,200 more.

So this church was reared without aid from the missionary treasury. An important part of the work here is that which is done in a Protestant educational institution. Rosario is the headquarters of higher education for the whole province.

*India.*—In 1852, $7,500 was appropriated to the work of opening a mission in India. It was not, however, until 1856 that a beginning was actually made. The Rev. Wm. Butler, a native of Ireland, who had for four years before his appointment to the India field been laboring in the United States, arrived in Calcutta on September 25th, 1856.

After most careful investigation and much conference with others more familiar with India, the Northwest seemed to be the most needy and promising field. " Our field," wrote Dr. Butler, " is the valley of the Ganges with the adjacent hill range, a tract nearly as large as England, being nearly 450 miles long, with an average breadth of 150 miles, containing more than 18,000,000 people." On his way to Bareilly (a city of 100,000), selected as mission headquarters, Dr. Butler was greatly favored by the American Presbyterian Church at Allahabad giving him as a native interpreter and helper Joel T. Janvier, whom they had trained and educated, and who subsequently became the first native preacher of the Methodist Episcopal Church in India. A few native converts had been gathered in Bareilly through the zeal of an English chaplain, and religious services were at once begun.

Before much could be accomplished the " Mutiny" burst upon the country. A fortnight later, May 31st, 1857, the native soldiers in Bareilly mutinied, and attempted to assassinate their officers and exterminate every foreigner in the city. Dr. Butler and family, with other civilians, and all the women and children connected with the English residents, were sent away to Naini Tal, in the Himalayas. Scenes of fright and horror followed; yet after exposure, hunger, racking travel, perils from wild beasts in the jungle, and constant apprehension of sudden death at the hands of assassins, experiencing on occasion prompt deliverance through prayer, they arrived in safety at Naini Tal. Reinforcements for the mission arrived on September 22d, 1857, but were obliged to remain at Calcutta until the rebellion was over.

The faithful Joel Janvier and his family were preserved, and found their way to Naini Tal by way of Mussoree and the mountains.

Mr. Josiah Parsons, who had been five years in the employ of the Church Missionary Society, joined (with his wife) the missionaries at Naini Tal, and work was immediately begun. During the summer of 1858 religious services in both English and Hindustani were held ; and a school for boys was opened in the Bazaar, and one for girls in one of the mission houses. In an admirable location a house, with a small tract of land, was purchased, a chapel begun, the corner-stone of which was laid in October, by Major (now Sir Henry) Ramsay, who has continued a fast friend of the mission through all its history. Mr. Parsons, who was soon joined by Rev. J. and Mrs. Humphrey removed January, 1859, to Moradabad, which, early in the season, had been reoccupied by the English. Naini Tal was left in charge of Mr. S. Knowles and an English brother who had been an English officer and had joined the mission in 1858.

The missionaries at Moradabad were soon surprised by a deputation from the Mozhabee Sikhs, who begged them to visit their village, twenty miles away, and explain to their people the nature of the Christian religion. Some of them had heard American Presbyterian missionaries preach at the great *melas* on the banks of the Ganges, before the mutiny, and had been deeply impressed. This opening field was promptly occupied. Converts from these Mozhabee Sikhs have been doing service at the large stations, and are also scattered through the mission as preachers, catechists, colporteurs, and teachers; those in their villages support themselves without aid from the missionaries. Up to 1871 eight-tenths of all the Christians in this mission were from these Sikhs. They are living in over 100 villages; their work is divided into eight circuits, each under a pastor, and all under an ordained preacher of the same class as the people. These pastors have an average of 15 villages each and receive a salary of about ten rupees a month; the ordained preacher in charge of all getting 35 rupees (about $17) per month. The rule among the people is to pay toward the support of their pastors as much, at least, as they expended on their own religion before their conversion.

Public preaching was begun March 18th, 1859, in the Bazaar at Bareilly by Dr. Humphrey. On July 24th he baptized the first convert (Zahur-ul-Huqq). Young men from the Sikhs came to Bareilly, worked for their food, and applied themselves to learning more of the Christian religion, and also to learning to read.

The *methods of work* adapted to India were already indicating themselves. Public preaching in the streets of towns and cities, and at great gatherings of the people, so common in India, at fairs or *melas*, seemed most important. It is not unusual to find two millions of people gathered at certain festivals by the sacred Ganges, for purposes of barter, and bathing, and for burning up some portions of the bodies of their deceased friends, to cast their ashes into the river. The missionaries also make tours through the country. There are no isolated houses. Agriculture being carried on co-operatively, the natives live in villages, and are easily accessible at the close of day, when they can be gathered in the public square, which is left vacant for purposes of assemblage. After preaching, the people are invited to the tent for books and conversation. Many respond, to whom, in the quiet of the camp, the missionary gives careful instruction.

Oudh.—The wretched government of Oudh was swept out of existence by the British authorities just before the "Mutiny," and the mission entered as a part of the new order of things at a time when Mohammedanism was broken and Christianity was politically triumphant. Much of the property of the mutineers had come into the possession of the British Government by confiscation, and was ready for disposal. In Lucknow, Commissioner Montgomery (a noble Christian) made over the large grounds and buildings of the "Asfee Kotee" (which had belonged to the Nawab of Oudh) for the use of the missionaries. He had the premises thoroughly refitted at the expense of the government, and the mission entered, free of charge, into possession of property which cost about 40,000 rupees.

Missionaries began work in September, 1858;

in November Mr. Pierce, Goel and Azim Ali had four preaching services, weekly, in the bazaars of Lucknow, a class-meeting, and two small schools. The soldiers were also included in their work. July, 1859, found two schools in the mission compound, one for boys and one for girls, and a third in the southern part of the city. Five missionaries arrived August 21st, 1859; they proceeded at once to the first general gathering of the missionaries, which took place at Lucknow.

The "Boys' Orphanage" began in September, 1858, in Lucknow (afterwards removed to Shahjehanpore), where children of those slain in the mutiny, or destroyed by the famine and pestilence that followed, were cared for by the missionaries.

This year, also, at Bareilly a printing-office was fitted up and the issue of publications begun. This was the foundation of the "Mission Press" or "Book Concern," now at Lucknow, to which place it was removed in 1886.

At Badaon a mission station was established in 1859, and premises for mission residence and school were purchased. Great scarcity followed a drought. Children were sold by their parents in the streets of the city for two or three rupees apiece. Men assaulted and pretended to rob others merely to get into prison, where they could be fed. Children were found whose protectors and friends had all perished of starvation. Many of these waifs were made over to the mission at various points. The girls were gathered together at Lucknow (1861) and constituted the "Girls' Orphanage."

From the lowest class of *mehters* (sweepers) were raised up efficient helpers, who, having been educated at the Theological Seminary, are now engaged in preaching the gospel in various mission fields. A valuable accession came from Mohammedanism. Mahbub Khan had been a teacher in a government vernacular school. As a boy he had been for a short time in a mission school in Sialkot. Interested in the search for truth he read all the Mohammedan books he could find, but his unrest continued. In that state of mind he wandered into a government school to ask the teacher if he had any books which could dispel a "fit of blues." The man replied he had only a New Testament which had been left by a missionary. Finding no other book, he took this to his home. He read; laid it aside; took it up again. The fifth chapter of Matthew interested him deeply. The beatitudes fascinated him, and so did the simple narrative. While reading the account of the Saviour's sufferings, in Matthew, 27th chapter, a profound conviction of the truth of the narrative and of the divinity of Christ came like a flash to his soul. He and his wife were baptized, several of his relatives following his example.

The year 1870 marked an era of unprecedented success in the Badaon field: 149 adults and 66 children were baptized. In summing up the results of labor done during his six years of residence, Mr. Hoskins states that over 450 have been baptized, of whom 300 are communicants.

In 1860 much attention was given to the English in Lucknow, and among the soldiers there was a continuous revival, and a chapel was built.

At Moradabad (1860) Sabbath services were conducted in English and among the soldiers.

Shahjehanpore (an important post in Rohilkund, near the borders of Oudh) was formally opened as a mission station October 1st, 1859, and a chapel was dedicated, January, 1861.

In October, 1861, J. T. Gracey and wife arrived, and were appointed to open the work at Seetapore, organizing the first school under the shade of a tree. January 15th, 1862, a mission school was opened in Haidarabad, and soon had 40 pupils. The war having occasioned the abandonment of large tracts in the province of Oudh, the government disposed of these tracts, and Dr. Butler was prompt to secure a section for the Christian village community, and the "grant" was named Wesleypore—"pore" meaning place. This spot was the only one of equal size in all India where there was "not an idol, nor an idol temple, nor a Mohammedan mosque to be found," said the superintendent. There was also secured (1869) a tract or jungle of 887 acres, 12 miles east of Shahjehanpore, to provide homes for needy Christians, and within 50 days 25 families (95 souls) were settled in straw houses on this tract; better houses soon followed, and also a chapel and schoolhouse. In 1872, when Mr. Thomas endowed the theological school at Bareilly, this village was given by him as part of the endowment.

In 1874 floods came and crops were destroyed, but the work went on. An industrial school was opened in Bareilly, July 16th, 1868, men and women manufacturing cloth, carpets, and furniture. A school was also kept up for the children, and so, while thousands were perishing with hunger, these poor Christians were both clothed and fed.

At the annual meeting (February, 1864), upon his resignation, Dr. Butler gave a summary of the work done: 9 of the most important of the cities of India had been occupied; 19 mission houses built or purchased; 16 schoolhouses erected, and 10 chapels; 2 large orphanages and a publishing-house established; 12 congregations had been gathered, and 10 small churches organized; 1,321 youths were under daily instruction; 161 persons had attained a Christian experience, 4 of whom had become preachers and 11 of them exhorters; $55,186 had been contributed in India for the work, and property accumulated worth $73,188. Such were the results in so short a period.

Gurwhal.—The work here owes its origin to General Sir Henry Ramsay, who promised $1,500, with $25 monthly for current expenses, —November, 1864.

The government school in Streenugger was now offered to the mission and accepted.

The year 1872 was made memorable by the establishment of a Theological Seminary, the donation of the Rev. D. W. Thomas amounting to $20,000, the largest sum ever given by a missionary, Eliphalet Remington, Esq., giving $5,000, to which the Board added $5,000. The India Conference was organized in 1864 by Bishop Thompson; and in January, 1877, Bishop Andrews presiding, the instructions of the preceding Conference were carried out by organizing a second conference in Hindustan; the former one to be styled the North India Conference, embracing the old mission field; the new one, South India Conference, covering the work under the superintendence of William Taylor. In 1886 the Bengal Conference was organized; and in 1889 the Malaysian Mission.

EDUCATION has immense power in breaking down the idolatry of India, inasmuch as false science is everywhere wrought into the very fibre of their religious text-books and systems, and to this false science geography and astronomy are fatal. Lord Halifax was the author of the developed system which was embodied in the great Educational Dispatch from the Court of Directors to the Governor-General of India, dated July 19th, 1854. Universities were established at Calcutta, Bombay, and Madras; all other schools (private, government, or church) were to be affiliated with these universities and lead up to them.

Among the important schools founded was the Centennial school of Lucknow, its history dating from the year 1866, the centennial year of American Methodism.

Practically the Mohammedan ignores the connection between religion and morality, hence the great need of religion in the schools.

MEDICAL INSTRUCTION was begun by Dr. Corbyne, civil surgeon of Bareilly, who taught, 1868, a class of midwives who were in practice in that city.

Dr. Humphrey had charge of seven different dispensaries, and gave treatment, during the year, to 24,652 out-door patients, 341 in-door, performed 21 capital operations and 411 minor ones, and the next year his patients exceeded 35,000.

When his Highness, the Nawab of Rampore, was approached by a proposition to grant his premises, he arrested the conversation and promptly presented the estate as a free gift, to be used for medical purposes in behalf of women, Miss Swain, M.D., taking charge of the work. As is well known, almost the only possible means of reaching the women of India is through women missionaries, and it is of great consequence that many of these should be possessed of the knowledge and practice of medicine.

Amid all the magnificence of Mohammedan and Hindu rule, neither system contains one thought calculated to relieve the wants, mitigate the sufferings, or improve the condition of humanity. Christian civilization, however, has dotted all India with schools, dispensaries, hospitals, asylums, and almshouses. Prominent among these are the orphanages, with their schools and industrial departments; the children being required to spend five hours daily in school and three hours at their trades.

THE MISSION PRESS was founded by Rev. James Walter Waugh, he beginning work in Bareilly (1860) with an antiquated hand-press and inferior material, himself having to boil the molasses and glue, and cast the inking rollers. In the course of five years, by taking in jobwork, the business yielded a net profit of 5,000 rupees, and the press, which had been started on $1,000, became worth $3,500. In 1865 the press was removed to Lucknow, where there are greater facilities for shipment of material and securing of skilled laborers.

The widespread revival in South India dates its beginning from the labors of the noted evangelist, Rev. Wm. Taylor, who arrived (from Australia) at Bombay November 20th, 1870. Pressed by necessity for the nursing and building up of his converts, he everywhere formed them into "Fellowship Bands," societies within and around the churches, after the manner of Mr. Wesley. During his extensive tours, after beginning at Lucknow, he pursued his great work in Cawnpore, Bombay, Poona, Calcutta (where a chapel was built, soon succeeded by a large church), Hyderabad, Madras (to the surrounding towns, where societies arose, as at Berhampore, Mount St. Thome, Palaveram, Arconum, Jollarpet, Salem, etc.), and Bangalore. The evangelist, preaching through interpreters or not, preaching in theatres, in halls, in streets, in squares, in houses, preaching through converts and assistants, founded many churches and "Fellowship Bands," and multitudes of converts, from among not only the natives, but the English and other foreign residents, and the Eurasian English-speaking people, crowned his labors.

3. *China.*—The origin of the Methodist Mission in the great empire may be traced, in its first movement, to discussions which were conducted in the "Missionary Lyceum" of the Wesleyan University, at Middletown, Conn., during April and May of 1835. The question, "What country now presents the most promising field for missionary exertions?" was debated. The Chinese Empire was warmly advocated, and the Lyceum resolved that the Methodist Episcopal Church should send missionaries and a press at once to the field. A committee prepared an address upon the subject, which appeared in the "Christian Advocate" of May 15th, 1835, with a full exhibit of the field and its claims. China was placed on the list of foreign missions May 20th, 1846, with an appropriation of $3,000 for two missionaries, half of this sum being for their outfit and travelling expenses. Previous to this a young man, Judson Dwight Collins, converted in the great revival at Ann Arbor, Michigan (1837–38), was ardently moved to enter upon work in China; and when told there had been nothing done 'oward beginning such a work, he replied to Bishop James: "Engage me a place before the mast, and my own strong arm will pull me to China and support me while there."

Months of hesitation and delay ensued, and it was not until April 15th, 1847, that the first company of Methodist missionaries for China departed, setting sail in the "Heber" from Boston harbor. On September 4th they entered the mouth of the river Min, and on the 6th they were hospitably received by the brethren of the American Board in Foochow. On a small island (Tong Chin) abreast of the city of Foochow, and densely inhabited, the missionaries were able to secure premises for their occupation. Quietly housed, they set themselves to the study of the language, and carefully used their little stock of medicines in administering to the sick, and were marvellously successful. They also distributed many tracts and portions of Scripture, which had been translated by Dr. Medhurst of the L. M. S. The Kian San House and the Kalan Orchard House were erected south of the river. In October Mr. Collins made a vigorous effort to obtain a foothold within the city walls. He rented quarters in a house and afterwards in a temple, but thought it prudent to retire because of the public excitement. Rev. Henry Hickok and wife and Rev. R. S. Maclay reinforced the mission, arriving April 15th, 1848.

As soon as possible the missionaries opened schools, employing native teachers, the missionaries giving religious instruction and conducting the devotions. The first of these schools was begun February 28th, 1848, but was suspended because much of the mission force became disabled. The first Sunday-school was organized in 1848, most of the children coming an hour before the appointed time. A small chapel in Nantai (outside the walls and on the north bank) was rented, and the crowds surging by supplied an ever-changing congregation. The Chinese are fond of hearing public discourse, and connect audience-rooms with their restaurants in which public talks are invited. Of these rooms the missionaries took advantage; but it was not until 1855 that the first church-building was erected, the churches of New York and vicinity giving $5,000 to aid the project. The church was named "Ching Sing Tong" —Church of the True God—which title, ever inviting the attention of the passing throngs, was carved on a tablet of porphyry over the door. Another church (called "Heavenly Rest") was built close to the homes of the missionaries, where there was a large foreign community, they contributing $1,500 on the condition that an audience-room should be added for English speaking. This church was dedicated October 18th, 1856, and the English part December 28th, 1856.

Mr. Collins's health rapidly declining, soon after his appointment to the superintendency he set sail for the United States (April 23d, 1851), and went to California, wishing to establish a mission among the Chinese of that State, being impressed with the incalculable reflex power upon China of a Chinese mission in California. But his strength rapidly declined, and he died on May 13th, 1852, in the thirtieth year of his age.

Though the mission was reinforced, yet, in consequence of the Taiping rebellion, sickness, and other troubles, it suffered a period of great depression. The schools were deserted; the missionaries scattered; death had been relentless, and all was dark and unpromising; but the Board courageously said in their report to the Church: "Let us hold fast our faith in the China mission, and trust in God."

July 14th, 1857, was a memorable day at the Tienang church. Ting Ang, 47 years of age, having a wife and five children, was received as the first convert, and was baptized. For two years he had been carefully instructed at the mission. Messrs. Maclay and Gibson found his home stripped of idols, blessed with religious books, and their examination of him was scrutinizing and satisfactory. On October 18th Ting Ang's wife and two of their children were baptized. During the year 13 were baptized. Converts increased in number, a surprising proportion being of mature age. Some of these endured persecution, losing all things for Christ's sake, but to a man they remained steadfast.

The Foundling Asylum was established in 1858, friends in Foochow contributing $670. In 1859 the work of the mission began to extend westward. Fifteen miles northwest of Foochow the To-Cheng (Peach Farm) appointment was begun. This year, also, native helpers were licensed and employed. Hu Po Mi became pastor at the Peach Farm, and the first native itinerant in China. At a visit to To-Cheng (February, 1859) nine of the Li family gave their names for baptism. Alarm at the success of the new work spread through all the valley, and though personal violence was proposed, the better class of people discountenanced all resorts to open persecution, and converts multiplied. In 1859 the mission was reinforced by the arrival of Rev. and Mrs. **S. L.**

Baldwin, the Misses Willston and Miss Potter, and on November 28th a female school was opened.

After the circulation among the churches in Baltimore of a powerful appeal by Dr. Wentworth, emphasizing the debased condition of females in China, the need of Christian wives for the male converts, the influence of Christianized and educated young women returning to their homes, the liberal readiness of English and American residents at Foochow to assist, the funds were promptly forthcoming, and the "Waugh Female Seminary" and the "Baltimore Female Academy" were succeeded permanently by "The Girls' Boarding-school." The year 1861 was marked by the still further extension of the work to the westward. After years of collisions between China on the one hand and England and France on the other, treaties were ratified in which the Chinese Government agreed to receive resident ministers from other nations, to tolerate Christianity, to protect missionaries, to open other ports, and to make the Yangtz River free to all nations. Foreign intercourse with the interior received a powerful impulse, and the way was thus opened for the advancement of the gospel. At this time a class (of 13) was formed at Kang Chia, ten miles west of Ngu Kang, hitherto our most westerly outpost, and a chapel was built. A press was obtained, and a font of Chinese type, and important tracts and parts of the Scriptures were printed and put into circulation—reaching 500,000 pages annually.

In 1862 the first annual meeting of the mission assembled. A course of study for the native helpers was ordained, examinations established, appointments regularly announced as at conference, and statistics were reported.

The appointments included eight fields never before occupied.

A membership of 87, mission property worth $30,115, and collections amounting to $70,000, including $20,000 for the poor, were reported.

A signal triumph marked the year 1863. After many attempts a station was finally secured within the walls of Foochow, a house and lot having been purchased on East Street; but the following year persecution raged, the East Street Church was destroyed by a mob, and also the house of the missionary (Rev. C. R. Martin), who with his wife and children effected a marvellous escape. In 1865 Bishop Thomson visited the mission. In the same year the new Reference Testament of Mr. Gibson was completed, and became the standard from Canton to Pekin. Preparations were also made for a similar version of the Old Testament. A colloquial New Testament was also begun, and new editions of the hymn-book, ritual and catechism, and many valuable pamphlets, were issued. . The work rapidly advanced in 1866, and 1867 was a great revival year. The harvest was seen in 451 members reported; yet literary labors were not interrupted. The dictionary of the Fokien dialect, in the Anglo-Chinese alphabet, was rapidly advanced (since that time it has been completed, and is a standard work); the issues of the press increased to 5,000,000 pages.

Pekin and Kiukiang.—On December 1st, 1867, Revs. V. C. Hart and E. S. Todd entered Kiukiang, an important city in the Kiang Si province. They opened a chapel 40 miles north of the city, and extended their labors 60 miles to the westward and 70 miles to the eastward. Converts were gathered rapidly in.

Pekin, occupied at a later date, is the capital of the empire, having a population of about 2,000,000, and the field north of the Yangtz comprises an area half as large as the United States, and contains a population of about 200,-000,000, nearly all of whom can be addressed in the Mandarin or court dialect. (This is also understood in Tibet, Mongolia, and Manchuria.) The great plain lying northeast of Pekin forms the richest and most productive part of the empire, girt about by mountains in which are buried coal and iron without limit, with lead, silver, and gold in abundance. It is traversed on its whole eastern part by the Grand Canal, and is for many reasons one of the grandest mission fields on earth.

These inland people everywhere regarded the missionaries with intense curiosity. "I stopped," writes Mr. Hart, "at a large trading-place over Sunday, and called upon an officer for a little quiet and rest; but crowds pressed into the building, making holes through the paper windows to secure a look at me."

Mr. Wheeler with his family sailed for the north, and reached Tientsin early in March, 1869. Thence they made their way by mule-carts to Pekin, and were hospitably received by the missionaries of the American Board. Exposure and hardships of travel caused the death of Mr. Wheeler's only son. On April 15th Mr. Lowry and family arrived to share in the work. Premises were secured just inside one of the city gates, not far from the foreign legations.

Bishop Kingsley upon his visit (1869) divided the work into three missions, appointing Dr. Maclay superintendent at Foochow, Mr. Hart at Kiukiang, and Mr. Wheeler at Pekin. Self-support was systematically provided for, and, with the advice of the mission, Bishop Kingsley ordained from the native helpers 7 deacons, 4 of whom were also ordained elders. At this time the board sent out six single young ministers. The year 1870 brought severe trials. A plot originated with the gentry of Canton to drive all foreigners from the land. Many were massacred under circumstances of atrocious cruelty. At Tientsin (80 miles from Pekin) 100 native Catholics, several Protestants, and 22 foreigners were killed. The first violent blows caused a reaction, and the plot could not be carried out.

The mission having been re-enforced, the system of itinerating was put in practice. Thus has the gospel been preached and Christian literature been scattered in hundreds of cities and villages from the steppes of Mongolia on the north, to the city of Confucius, 400 miles to the south, and from the sacred mountains of Shansi on the west, to where the Great Wall of China reaches the sea on the east.

As from time to time the missions received new laborers from the United States and raised up helpers from among the native converts, the work was extended. New preaching-places were secured, new stations established; native congregations arose upon their feet, voting in favor of self-support. In 1874 four districts supported their presiding elders, and one circuit their bachelor preacher. Hu Po Mi, presiding elder of Hok Chiang district, presented to the annual meeting deeds of eleven chapels, all paid for and vested in the Methodist Episcopal Church.

Medical mission work was entered upon and carried forward with most gratifying results.

Bishop Wiley upon his first episcopal visit (24 years after he left the field as a missionary) uses such language as the following: "Then not a soul had been converted. We were simply met with prejudice and opposition. We did not dare to venture five miles from the city of Foochow. Now our work extends through five districts, over many hundreds of miles in length and breadth. I confess I would feel alarmed at the very magnitude of this work if I did not see the most satisfactory evidence of its genuineness and thoroughness in every respect."

As at present arranged, the missions of the Methodist Episcopal Church in China are four in number: the Central China Mission, established in 1868, including the districts of Kiukiang, Nanking, Chinkiang, and Wuhu, with a total of 11 missionaries and a church-membership of 339; North China (1869), including the districts of Pekin, Tientsin, Shantung, Tsunhua, and Lanchou, with 15 missionaries and a church-membership of 782; Foochow (1877), with the districts of Foochow, Hokchiang, Hinghwa, Ingchung, Kucheng, Yongping, and Haitang, under the care of 6 missionaries and with a church-membership of 2,441; West China (1881), with a station at Chunking, where still 2 missionaries are holding the outpost in the hope that with increased means and reinforcements they shall be able to go forward and enlarge their work. (See also article China.)

*Japan.*—The General Missionary Committee at its annual session in New York (November 1872) authorized the establishment of the Japan Mission. Rev. Dr. R. S. Maclay (formerly of the mission in Foochow, China), Rev. J. C. Davison, Rev. Julius Soper, Rev. M. C. Harris, were appointed to Japan. Dr. Maclay and family arrived in Yokohama June 11th, 1873, having been accompanied from San Francisco by Dr. J. P. Newman and wife, who remained for weeks aiding in opening the mission. Bishop Harris, accompanied by Rev. Messrs. Waugh, Houghton, and Spencer, as visiting brethren, arrived in Yokohama July 9th, 1873.

The meeting for formal organization convened August 8th, 1873, in the rented Mission House at No. 60, Bluff, Yokohama; Bishop Harris was chairman, and some fifteen others, including the wives of the missionaries and several visitors, were present. It was proposed that the mission proceed at once to establish stations at Yokohama, Yedo (Tokyo), Hakodati, and Nagasaki, which proposition was unanimously adopted, and missionaries were appointed to the work.

There was no Protestant mission as yet on the Island of Yesso, so in occupying Hakodati the missionaries of the Methodist Episcopal Church were the first to preach the gospel to the nations of that region.

The second year was marked by the beginning of missionary work in Japan by the Woman's Foreign Missionary Society of the Methodist Episcopal Church (q.v.). Rev. John Ing, from the mission in Kiukiang, China, began his labors in Hirosaki, Japan.

The first chapel occupied by the mission in Yokohama was rented by Mr. Correll, through his teacher, August 11th, 1874, in the native portion of the town, and was first opened for public preaching on the 16th, when the audi-ence-room was filled with attentive hearers, Mr. Correll speaking in Japanese, from Matthew 1: 18–25.

The first baptisms in Tokyo occurred in 1875. The first purchase of land in Yokohama for the use of the mission was made in 1875, when lot No. 222 on the Western Bluff was obtained. Outside the Foreign Concession Mr. Soper began holding Sabbath services in a portion of the city called Kanda.

The third year was marked by the beginning of public day-schools, the organization of church-classes, the introduction of quarterly meetings, love-feasts, and quarterly conferences, the erection of suitable dwelling-houses for the members of the mission resident in Yokohama and Tokyo, the erection of an excellent chapel in Nagasaki, and other work that showed the advance of the mission.

In Nagasaki, upon an eligible lot donated by the government, a mission chapel was erected in a portion of the city called Desima, and was opened for religious services in 1876. In the same year, after two years of faithful labor, Mr. Davison baptized his first approved candidates in Nagasaki—Mr. Asuga Kenjiro, together with his wife and two children.

The work advanced in the several stations. In Tokyo a handsome mission chapel was built in 1876; also a handsome Home by the Woman's Missionary Society; out-stations were commenced, and tours to the interior cities begun. In January, 1877, another neat chapel, built on a portion of the lot owned in Tokyo by the Missionary Society, was completed and occupied, at a cost of $1,600.

In the sixth year of the mission the Satsuma Rebellion broke out in the southern portion of Japan, which during the closing part of 1876 and the former half of 1877 depressed business, suspended commerce, devastated the fairest portion of the country, and was one of the most formidable dangers that had ever confronted the civil authorities of Japan. In the autumn of 1877 the severe prevalence of the cholera in Yokohama caused the suspension of the public work of the mission in that city. At other stations, where the disease was less violent, the labors of the missionaries were not interrupted. All the missionaries escaped the pestilence.

On Mr. Correll's tour (October, 1877), the inhabitants of Matsumoto described themselves to him as being a people without a religion. They had destroyed their idols, pulled down their temples, had removed all traces of their former faith (Buddhism), and had determined to live destitute of any system of religion. But finding such a life without satisfaction, they expressed an earnest desire to receive Christian instruction. About 300 persons gave their names as candidates for Christian baptism. Mr. Correll arranged at once to send a native helper to instruct these eager and ready people.

In some places, as in Hirosaki (population 33,631), so eager are the people to hear the gospel that crowds will stand outside in winter snows to catch the words as they may be heard through the windows and doors and over the heads of the crowds within.

On Bishop Wiley's visit to Japan (1878) he dedicated the new church edifice, (completed by Mr. Harris), and ordained the Rev. Yoitsu Honda at Hakodati. He is now president of the Anglo-Japanese College at Tokyo.

Within five years the missionaries established mission stations at five important centres of population and political influence; procured church buildings, school and dwelling houses, the estimated value of which is $25,000; translated into Japanese the Catechism, portions of the Discipline, about 50 hymns, and prepared an original tract; planted out-stations extending from about 25 miles northeast of Tokyo to 220 miles west of Yokohama; established a first-class seminary for young ladies in Tokyo; organized five flourishing day-schools for boys and girls; matured plans for a mission training school and a theological seminary; and gathered under their care a native church of 200 members, of whom 10 are candidates for the Christian ministry. (See Japan.)

*Mexico.*—The commencement of the work of the Methodist Episcopal Church in Mexico was at an auspicious time. Louis Napoleon had been defeated and was dead. Austrian schemes had failed. The temporal power of the Pope had been denied, and the Juarez Government had expelled from the country, as enemies and conspirators against the government, the various orders of nuns, Jesuits, sisters of charity, and had confiscated their properties.

On February 6th, 1873, Rev. Dr. Wm. Butler (whose work in India is elsewhere recorded) arrived at Vera Cruz, and journeyed to the city of Mexico over the railway which had just been opened. There he found Bishop Haven, who had preceded him to the capital.

In addition to the appropriation made by the General Committee in November, the Hon. Washington C. De Pauw had placed at the disposal of the Missionary Society the sum of $5,000, to aid in the purchase of property, to enable the mission to secure two or three centres in which to begin its work.

The bishop had visited Puebla, where he examined a property which was formerly part of the Romish Inquisition. This property included the chapel, and also the cells where the victims of the Inquisition were confined or walled in to die. These premises passed into the possession of the Missionary Society by purchase from a Jew, for the sum of $10,000.

The bishop, returning with Dr. Butler to Mexico City, opened negotiations for the purchase of what was called "The Circus of Chiarinic."

Romanism had seized the great palace of Montezuma, and in it founded the vast and wealthy monastery of San Francisco. The monks held it as their headquarters for about three hundred years. Such was its extent that it was capable of luxuriously accommodating 4,000 monks, rich revenues being wrung from a people who were kept in ignorance, debasement, and superstition.

Notwithstanding the efforts of the Romanists to prevent the transfer of the property, the Methodist Episcopal Church acquired her title by honest purchase from the Mexican people, through their government, at a cost of $16,300.

Four months of toil transformed the costly court from its theatrical condition into a beautiful church. Thus on the site of Montezuma's paganism and the institutions of Romanism evangelical Methodism entered, and holds the place as the headquarters of her missions in the Republic of Mexico. Within these premises the church room was dedicated on Christmas, 1873, 600 persons being present. The premises extend 180 feet by 100, and are in the best part of one of the widest streets in the city of Mexico. Besides the church edifice, there are class-rooms and vestries, a book-store, a printing establishment, two parsonages, and a school-room; also the orphanage and school of the ladies' mission, and a home for their missionary, with room still to spare. It forms to-day one of the most complete mission establishments in the world.

By the arrival of Rev. Dr. Thomas Carter, who had a knowledge of the Spanish language, the mission was able to begin divine service, and also to start a school, in March, 1873. At the end of the first quarter the mission was able to report four Mexican congregations in the capital and two English services; also both day and Sabbath scholars, numbering 55.

Dr. Cooper of the Protestant Episcopal Church (April, 1873) formerly of Spain, more recently sent by the American and Foreign Christian Union for Spanish work in Mexico, concluded to unite his English congregation with the Methodists, and give himself wholly to Spanish work in connection with the mission. Invitations poured in upon the mission from various parts of the country from earnest inquirers, urging the missionaries to visit them, and preach the gospel, marry them, baptize their children, and give them the Word of God. The fruit of three hundred years of Catholicism was everywhere seen in the degradation, ignorance, and immorality of the people, living without lawful marriage, their children growing up in illegitimacy and shame.

Near the close of 1873 the Romish clergy were peculiarly excited and sanguinary in temper. Threats were made and intimidation tried. Nine of the leading Protestants, as was alleged, were marked for assassination. Elsewhere their plots were in a degree successful. At Ahualulco, Mr. Stevens of the Presbyterian Mission and his native preacher were murdered. Then followed assaults upon the Methodist Mission; some were wounded, and the churches at Mixcoac were burned. On January 26th, 1875, followed the horrible assassination (in their chapel, and during public worship) of nine of the congregation at Acapulco, Rev. Mr. Hutchinson escaping and finding refuge on board a United States ship-of-war then in the harbor. Within a few months followed the deadly assault on Rev. Mr. Phillips in Queretaro, violence on the missions in Guanajuato and Puebla, the plundering of some of the places of worship, and the murder of other missionaries near the City of Mexico. The public journals of the country denounced, in concert, these religious murders and outrages of Romish fanatics, and boldly held the Church responsible for these violent acts of persecution.

Reinforcements arrived, and the work was carried on at Puebla, Miraflores, Orizaba, Guanajuato. At the last-named place the persecutions were most bitter and violent; infuriated and drunken mobs of thousands of men again and again assailed the mission house and premises, but they were dispersed through the energy of the police and the determination of the authorities.

In 1876, upon his visit to the United States, Dr. Butler obtained subscriptions to the extent of $13,000 to enable the mission to provide itself with a complete outfit for a printing establishment, including a steam-press and stereo type machinery. During 1877 it issued over 700,000 pages of evangelical truth in the Spanish language. It prints the beautifully illustrated and highly successful "El Abogado Christiano Illustrado."

Bishop Merrill having inspected, in 1878, the entire work in Mexico, concluded his report as follows: "We have in all 17 congregations in Mexico. . . . We are preaching the gospel regularly to from 2,000 to 2,500 people. We have several hundred children under training in day and Sunday-schools, and circulating religious tracts, books, and papers far beyond the range of our congregations and the reach of our ministry. We have seven English-speaking missionaries and ten Mexican preachers, besides a few local preachers. The ladies have two representatives. Besides a school in Amecca, the Woman's Foreign Society of the M. E. Church (q.v.) have a complete establishment in the city of Pachuca for the education of girls, valued at $6,000, and in the capital is the Girls' Orphanage.

At present the Mission is divided into four districts: The Central district including the circuits of Mexico City, Ayapango, Pachuca, Tezontepec, Tulancingo, Miraflores, San Vicenti, Santa Ana, and Zacualtipan. The Coast district including the circuits of Cordoba, Tehuacan, Orizaba, Oaxaca, Tuxtla, and Tuxpan. The northern district with the circuits of Guanajuato, Salamanca, Cortazar, Queretaro, Cueramero, and San Juan del Rio. The Puebla district with the cities of Puebla Tetela, Tezuitlan, and the Xochiapulco circuit.

*Malaysian Mission.*—This youngest daughter of Methodism in foreign lands was born on April 29th, 1889, when Bishop Thoburn read the appointments and closed the first annual meeting of the Malaysian Mission.

The territory covered by it is wide, populous, needy, and presents some features that are unique and most interesting. For the present but one point is occupied—Singapore; but this is the strategic point of the archipelago, and England, with her keen eye for the nerve centres of the commercial world, is happily the mistress of this key to the trade of Southern Asia.

The work at Singapore comprises the following branches: First, an English church, which gathers at its services many English-speaking residents, American visitors, and ship-captains as they pass through the port. Second, a Chinese mission consisting of—first, a medical and evangelistic mission, and, second, the Anglo-Chinese school. The former is in its infancy, but is already giving promise of great good. Hundreds of cases have been treated, and much access gained to the hearts of the people. The Anglo-Chinese school is already the largest of the Chinese schools, with an average of three hundred and fifty boys on the rolls. Third, the Malaysian Mission. A work among the Malays of Singapore is particularly difficult, for they are Mohammedans, and largely believe that the white man is godless. Still they are more or less accessible, and some of the ladies have succeeded in visiting the Malay women in their homes. They need a man to go and live in their midst, and itinerate among the villages outside. Fourth, the Tamil Mission. Thousands of these people are employed on the sugar estates of the peninsula; many of them, nominally Christians when they leave their homes, lapse into heathenism on these unfriendly shores.

The missionaries of the A. B. C. F. M. have sent a Tamil local preacher from their school in Ceylon, and there is now a small Tamil church and a school, and the mission promises well. The woman's work is very successful, some fifty households being regularly visited and taught the Scriptures. The other points will soon be opened. In Borneo and in Java several stations have been tentatively selected in consultation with the Dutch missionaries.

*Bulgaria.*—During the meeting of the General Committee in November, 1852, the corresponding secretary reported voluminous correspondence concerning a mission to Bulgaria, and among the Greeks in Constantinople; whereupon it was

"*Resolved*, that a fund be created and placed at the disposal of the Board and bishops superintending foreign missions, for the commencement of a mission in Bulgaria, to the amount of $5,000." An appropriation was made from year to year, till the mission was actually opened in 1857.

Rev. Wesley Prettyman and Rev. Albert L. Long were appointed with joint authority to institute the mission, and conduct it until a superintendent should be appointed.

Upon their arrival at Rustchuk, on the south side of the Danube, they found the country was beautiful, fruitful, and populous. The Turkish authorities were kind and tolerant, and the Protestant population everywhere gave them a cordial reception. They fixed upon Varna and Shumla as their mission stations. After advice they determined to occupy but one central location, Shumla, a city of 40,000 population, 8,000 of whom were Bulgarians. Rev. F. W. Flocken was added to the mission, November, 1858. September 17th, 1859, Tirnova was occupied as a mission station. The missionaries were received with special favor, as it was understood that they came not to displace anything that was good, but to vitalize and purify the dead formalism of the Bulgarian Church.

On December 24th, 1859, in his home at Tirnova, Mr. Long began regular public religious services exclusively in the Bulgarian language. He was not left without encouragement. Two Bulgarian priests called, one of whom had at a previous visit complained with tears of the lapsed condition of Christianity among his people: "They call themselves Christians, but they do not love God: they neither love the Saviour nor keep his commandments."

He now begged the loan of a Bible, for the senior or superior priest had refused him one, asking what business he had with a Bible, and declaring that the Bible was not a book for him to read.

At this juncture Gabriel Elieff, a devoted Bulgarian, the first Protestant convert of the land, who was converted through the reading of a Bulgarian Testament, joined Mr. Long as colporteur and assistant.

The work of the missionaries was everywhere largely one of personal effort, and in such labors their chief successes were found.

Mr. Prettyman, at Shumla, was surprised at his own constantly increasing influence. Even the Bulgarian priests were not slow to manifest their good will. From fifty miles around they called upon him, often inviting him to go with them to the sick, having more confidence in a little of his medicine than in their own holy oil and other sacerdotal rites.

The Molokans of Tultcha had a most singular origin. Some ninety years ago, they told Mr. Long, there were with a Russian embassador a young Russian man and woman, who, during their stay in England,attended religious services, and upon their return to Russia informed their nearest friends of the modes of worship in England; of those who met, not in temples, but in dwelling-houses, and had at their places of worship no sort of images, not even a cross or candle; who did not fast or cross themselves, yet were pious and earnest people. These communications led their friends to adopt similar modes of worship, though retaining their membership in the Russo-Greek Church. They abolished images, cross-making, weekly fastings, etc. Their use of milk on fast-days (the Russian word for milk being moloko) induced their enemies to call them Molokans. Persecution broke out against them, and when summoned to appear before the Emperor, Alexander I., they begged to be permitted to conduct their worship in his presence. He consented and permitted them to return unmolested, and they continually increased in numbers until they have reached about a million. Mr. Flocken was immediately invited by the Molokans of Tultcha to attend their simple services, they then expressing their earnest desire that he would instruct them more fully in the truths and forms of the gospel. In April, 1860, he removed to Tultcha.

The lack of a printing-press left the mission powerless against the assaults of the Bulgarian organ of the Greek patriarchate and Russian embassy, and the Jesuit organ, which was ably edited. These journals poured forth, through the year, a torrent of falsehood and abuse, while the mission had no means with which to respond.

Mr. Prettyman slowly concluded that the task of reviving the ancient and corrupt church was hopeless, and that a separate church organization was necessary.

Constantinople being the centre of Turkish influence, it was thought best to remove the superintendency of the mission to that city. In 1864 the publication of the "Zornitza"— The Day Star—was begun, and was received with great favor by the Bulgarians.

Persecutions and discouragements followed; the mission passed through many vicissitudes, and the missionaries through a great variety of severe trials because of the Russo-Turkish war, and by reason of pestilence and other causes which resulted, for a time, in greatly weakening and almost destroying the work. Yet in 1878 the mission was re-enforced; complete separation from the Greek Church was effected in Bulgaria; fifteen Bulgarian bishops occupied the frontier Greek dioceses and 500 Bulgarian priests conducted the services of the land; yet dissatisfaction was widespread, and circumstances did not favor the missionary work.

The last report (1888) uses the following language: "Bulgaria has long been the battleground for sharp contests in the General Missionary Committee, as well as for contending hosts on her own soil. It has been a hard field to cultivate under the great difficulties it has had to meet. It has so often seemed to be on the eve of abandonment that the few workers have had to contend with the depressing effects of uncertainty as to the continuance of the mission, as well as with the complicated difficulties of the field itself. The reports of this year, however, are more filled with encouragement and hope than ever before."

*Korea.*—The work in Korea was begun in the year 1885, and is under the supervision of Bishop Ninde, H. G. Appenzeller being the nearest superintendent.

A small house was purchased in the southern part of Seoul to be used for church work. Within this building, in a room 8 feet by 8, and 6 feet high, with but four persons present, was the first formal service held by Methodism in Korea. On October 9th, 1887, a woman was baptized, being the first baptism by a Protestant missionary in that land. A week later, at night, in the same room, Dr. Scranton and Mr. Appenzeller, with five communicants, celebrated the Lord's Supper. In this quiet way Methodism began her public work in the Hermit nation.

A few weeks later the house adjoining was purchased, and regular services were held there every Sabbath until May, when they were stopped by a royal edict.

During the fall of 1887 two colporteurs were sent out to travel in the northwestern part of the peninsula. The first one was absent about a month, was robbed by highwaymen, but met a few who listened to his words. The other brother was gone three months, and for telling the people to "cease to do evil and learn to do well" he was arrested and cast into prison. After confinement for three days in a cold, damp room, he was brought before the magistrate, who, when he heard the charges preferred against him, promptly dismissed him.

In the spring of 1887 the superintendent, with the Rev. H. G. Underwood of the Presbyterian Mission, started to visit the work in the north of Korea. Medicines, books, and tracts were sold. They were everywhere cordially received; some inquirers being found, they were provided with books.

Notwithstanding the edict prohibiting public religious services, the work went forward. Some of the best men in the school spent their vacation in visiting their friends with the view of bringing them to Christ. Their efforts were successful in leading a number of inquirers to the mission.

The *Pai Chai Hak Dang* (school for rearing useful men) had (report of 1888) a very successful year. Sixty-three students were enrolled. The new college hall is completed. In the fall an industrial department was established, and after that no aid was given to any one unless he earned it by work. The students proved themselves willing laborers.

About the same time Dr. Scranton opened a school for medical students, the young men working in the dispensary, being taught the theory and practice together.

With July 1st, 1887, closed the third year and a quarter of medical work in Korea, and the second of the hospital. There is no doubt that the medical work of the two societies has had marked effect upon the reception foreigners have received in Korea. Schools, as they now stand, could not have effected a like result.

The first quarter of 1887 the number of cases was 481, the same quarter in 1888 the number rose to 1,427, and for the year, reckoning the last two quarters of 1887, was 4,930.

All classes accept medical aid with readiness, among them being patients from the highest orders in the land who count themselves among the friends of the misson.

*Italy.*—Methodist mission work for Italy found an early and zealous advocate in the Rev. Charles Elliott, D.D., who began the public agitation of the subject in 1832. It was not, however, until January 18th, 1870, that the Board appointed a committee to consider and report upon the proposition to institute a mission in that country.

At the St. Louis Conference (March, 1871) Bishop Ames appointed Rev. Dr. Leroy M. Vernon missionary and superintendent of the mission work of the Methodist Episcopal Church in Italy. He was directed to make a thorough and extensive canvass before fixing upon a place in which to locate a permanent centre for operations. In August Dr. Vernon and family arrived in Genoa, and early visited twelve of the chief cities of Italy, and made his report as directed. Bologna was fixed upon (December, 1872) as headquarters, but subsequently Rome was chosen in its place.

Vigorous prosecution of the work excited the opposition of the Romish priesthood. In June, 1873, the church in Bologna was inaugurated. A pamphlet against Protestantism was directed against the chapel, and Protestantism was charged with being atheistic, immoral, and retrogressive.

Public meetings were immediately appointed for confutation of the libels, and the priesthood was challenged, but no representative appeared. People came in crowds, the charges against Protestantism were shown to be true of Romanism, and the tables were turned.

A valuable acquisition was gained in the person of Signor Teofilo Gay, who had graduated from the Genevan Theological School, the last year of Dr. Merle d'Aubigné's presidency. He was a man of talent, activity, and culture, who had served at The Hague, afterwards in London at the French Church, and then returned to Italy. Also at this time a successful work among the Italian soldiers in Rome came into the hands of the superintendent.

With the close of 1873 Methodism entered Florence; a hall was rented, and the Rev. A. Arrighi, who had been educated in America, was put in charge and began the public services. The building was attacked, the doors broken in, the lights extinguished, the sexton assaulted, and an attempt made to harm Mr. Arrighi. Next day six of the rioters were lodged in jail.

The most important advance of 1874 was the occupancy of Milan. Two places of worship were opened in different parts of the city, and five or six services were conducted weekly.

Converts now began to come from distinguished ranks. Prof. Aleeste Lanna, D.D., Ph.D., was then (1874) professor in the Appolinare, the most popular Catholic college in Rome, and two years previous, in the face of strong remonstrance, had resigned his chair of philosophy in the Vatican Seminary. He had been in a state of agitation and religious inquiry. He frankly recounted his struggles to Dr. Vernon, was encouraged and aided; then he resolved to forsake Romanism, to give up his professorship and associations, and give himself henceforth to Christ and His work.

In January, 1875, followed, in Milan, the conversion and introduction into the church of Prof. E. Caporali, LL.D., son of a Viennese baroness. An industrious student of wide range,

he was engaged in writing an elaborate encyclopædia of geography and all its cognate sciences, to number about 30 volumes. He abandoned all his worldly prospects, and entered upon the work of preaching salvation to his countrymen.

In April, 1875, a station was opened in Perugia; from the first the work met with favor. In May, Rev. Vincenzo Ravi of Rome, and his entire congregation, united with the M. E. Church. Mr. Ravi had taken a full course of theology at Florence, and afterward had studied a year in Scotland, where he married a Scotch lady.

Dr. Vernon (April 5th, 1875) in the city of Rome secured an eligible site for a church edifice, and the Missionary Society promptly appropriated the funds necessary for the erection of a small church and mission residence. And on Christmas day, 1875, St. Paul's M. E. Church, on Via Poli, Rome, was dedicated.

The work went on; converts were added, new stations were established. The uprising and firmness of the liberals disconcerted and defeated the violence of Romish devotees. The Woman's Foreign Missionary Society entered the field (1877) and began their work. In January, 1878, "The Torch" ("La Fiacola") began its issue, and Sunday-schools, in face of many and formidable obstacles, were established in the principal stations.

*Germany.*—In the year 1844 Rev. Wm. Nast was authorized to visit Germany and inspect its condition, with a view to the founding of a mission there by the Methodist Episcopal Church.

In a providential manner the way was being prepared by the zealous and successful labors of a Mr. Müller, who, in order to escape military service, had fled at twenty years of age, to England, where he was converted and became a local preacher. After twenty-five years' absence (1830) he returned to his native Würtemberg, and at Winnenden began to preach the necessity of the new birth. Such success crowned his labors that in 1833 he reported to the Wesleyan Missionary Society that there were villages where all the inhabitants came to the meetings, that in places he was detained until ten and eleven o'clock at night, after the meetings, for religious conversation, and that new doors were everywhere opening to him which he could not enter.

By 1839 the membership had increased to 600, and 60 assistants were employed. From this period the statistics appear in the British minutes.

In 1844 Mr. Nast found the crowds at Müller's meetings so great that there was no room for kneeling, and their shadows darkened the rooms in which they met. Worn out by his excessive labors, Müller died (March 17th, 1858), and in 1859 Dr. Lythe was sent out as his successor.

At the annual meeting (May, 1849) the Board of Managers and the General Committee of the Missionary Society of the Methodist Episcopal Church made arrangements for the establishment of the mission. Mr. Ludwig S. Jacoby was appointed, and was directed to begin work in either Bremen or Hamburg, two of the four free cities of Germany. He selected Bremen, and preached his first sermon on December 9th, 1849, 20 miles distant from Bremen, and on December 23d he occupied in the city a rented hall, called Krameramthus.

Preaching was also begun among the lowest classes of a suburb of Bremen, and Mr. Jacoby also went to Baden, there addressing large congregations. Great numbers were converted at these services, many of whom remained in the churches to which they already belonged, making, however, public confession of the new life they had experienced.

On Easter, 1850, the first class was organized, the Lord's Supper administered for the first time, and the first love-feast was held the next evening, and on May 21st the first Quarterly Conference was held. Mr. Jacoby considered this the birthday of the mission.

Even as early as this 1,000 Methodist hymn-books had been sold in Germany, besides tracts and copies of Wesley's sermons, and on May 21st, 1850, a Methodist religious journal, "Der Evangelist," began its issue, the prominent house of J. G. Heyse undertaking the publishing for the mission. About this time Christian Feltman, hoping to spread a knowledge of Evangelical Christianity, opened a library, and loaned books free of charge.

June 7th, 1850, the mission was reinforced by the arrival from the United States of Rev. C. H. Doering and Rev. Louis Nippert. The latter preached his first sermon in the mission at a country place two miles from Bremen, on the open floor of a farm-house, great crowds, anxious to hear, filling all the vacant space. On one side were horses and pigs, on the other were bellowing cows, while overhead were flying and cackling hens : but the congregation listened with the greatest attention.

Rev. Dr. John McClintock, who had accompanied these brethren, preached in the parlor of the American Consul, probably the first English Methodist sermon ever preached in Bremen, while Mr. Doering preached on the same Sabbath to crowds in the Krameramthus.

On June 16th, 1850, a Sabbath-school (such as heretofore had not been introduced into Germany) was opened in Bremen, 80 children being present at the first session. It met with favor, and soon there were 300 present.

A circuit was now formed in and around Bremen, having 15 appointments. Letters from converts in the United States, sometimes read in public assemblies and even from State Church pulpits, served to fan the flame and quicken the work. Converts were active; some were engaged as colporteurs, and Wessel Fiege (August, 1850) was licensed as exhorter.

Persecutions met the missionaries in the Grand Duchy of Saxe-Weimar and in the Kingdom of Hanover and the Duchy of Brunswick. In the latter place the congregations were especially large and the conversions numerous, but many times the missionaries barely escaped imprisonment. They were assailed and abused through the press, and accused of foul heresies and absurd abuses. At Vegesack (a town of Bremen) a crowded hall was attacked by a half-drunken mob, instigated by the State clergy; every window was broken by flying stones, yet no one was hurt.

The work grew rapidly, and the prosperity was more than equal to the opposition. Crowds attended upon the ministry of the Word. In some places persecution was exceedingly bitter. Erhardt was forbidden to preach. He persisted and was fined; was brought before magistrates, banished from some places and imprisoned in others. In one jail he found three infidel fellow-prisoners, who thought it strange indeed that they should be in prison because they did not pray, and he imprisoned because he prayed too much.

Only in the Grand Duchy of Oldenburg and the free cities of Germany were the missionaries at full liberty to preach the gospel and to form congregations.

Prohibition of meetings was so general that Mr. Riemenschneider's labors were confined chiefly to Frankfort and its environs. Mr. Nippert, though greatly embarrassed by the State Church authorities, without whose consent he could do nothing, had access to eight places.

The year 1858 was notable for the origination of the Book Concern of Germany, called "Verlag des Tractathauses," also for an institute for Biblical instruction which was the germ of the Martin Mission Institute, founded by the centennial gift of John T. Martin, Esq., of Brooklyn, N. Y., of $25,000, to which he afterwards added $1,000 for a library, built at Roederberg, an elevated suburb of the city of Frankfort.

In 1860 the mission, having bought types and press, began to do its own printing, and the "Evangelist" and "Kinderfreund" became self-supporting.

At the conference in Basle (July 7th–12th, 1864) it was found that the work had so expanded that there were not enough preachers to supply the demand.

Enlargement and development continued in every direction. In 1886 Switzerland was formed into a separate conference. The best results are those indicating that not only are the Methodist churches themselves growing in spirituality and strength, but the State Church itself is awakening to its duty, and its pastors are taking to heart Dr. Christlieb's reminder—"The best method against Methodism is to do the same as it is doing." This, however, does not indicate that Methodism is no longer necessary. It stands as a help to the State Church and a constant witness for aggressive Christianity unbound by State relations.

*Scandinavian Missions.*—The successful work carried on in Sweden, Norway, and Denmark owed its origin and impulse to fruitful mission work done among the Scandinavian sailors and immigrants in the United States, beginning in New York City in 1845, under the superintendency of the zealous Olof Gustaf Hedstrom.

The Bethel Ship, "John Wesley," in which Pastor Hedstrom held the first service, May 25th, 1845, became the headquarters of the mission in the United States. Here the work was carried forward with great success.

The ship became an asylum for destitute immigrants, supplying for them, at once, bed, table, wardrobe, and sanctuary, and also a labor agency for hundreds. There was a constant work of grace going on among the mingled Germans, Belgians, Swedes, Finns, Norwegians, English, and Americans.

Wherever these converts went they testified to what God had done for them in New York. In one year (1847) 3,000 were directed to homes in the West, societies were formed, and the work rapidly extended.

In 1850 about 12,000 Scandinavian seamen visited the port of New York and 15,000 Bibles and Testaments were distributed from the ship.

Besides the formation of churches and building of edifices in the West, great interest began to spring up in Sweden and Norway, excited by letters written and visits paid by converts to their friends at home.

Mr. O. P. Petersen left New York for Norway (May, 1849) bent upon an evangel to his kindred. A wide awakening followed the work of Mr. Petersen, and he remained nearly a year. He was appointed a missionary to Norway and returned, arriving at Fredericks-hald in December, 1853. Opposition was encountered. Methodists were looked upon as a low and despised people. The State Church and its priests left nothing untried to annoy and hinder them and their work.

Many souls were saved, and the interest spread so rapidly that Mr. Petersen soon felt the need of help, and Rev. C. Willerups was sent out in the summer of 1856.

In Sarpsborg (1857) an excellent church building was erected without aid from the Missionary Society, and a second edifice, the same year, was built at Frederickshald.

Christiania was occupied in 1864 by S. A. Steensen; but the work continued feeble for some time for want of a suitable building.

One thing became patent to all, namely, that these Methodist intruders had excited the Lutherans to work. They were aroused to the building of chapels and meeting-houses, besides their churches, in almost every town. They took to sending out colporteurs, with a warning, it is true, against Methodist books and preachers; but through them, after all, Christ was preached. It was a new life for Lutheranism.

In 1872, poor as the members were, they gave on an average $5 each to the benevolent objects of the church; one lady offering $4,500 to build a church at Christiania. This church, with a seating capacity of 1,200, was dedicated in 1874, when, as a result of A. Olsen's labors, there were 177 probationers and 120 persons in full connection with the church. The mission was organized (August 17th, 1876) by Bishop Andrews into an annual conference; at which time the membership numbered 2,798, who, amid the greatest financial embarrassment, gave for benevolent objects $1,500 more than they had done the preceding year.

"I am compelled to believe," said Bishop Andrews, "that the Lutherans of this land urgently need the aid which Methodism can give and is giving. The coming of Methodism has been the signal for discussion and strife. It has encountered the most violent opposition, and has advanced with difficulty. But far beyond its organized and numerical success, it has quickened religious thought; has made manifest the defects of existing church life; has stirred the pastors to greater activity; has introduced, in many places, better measures for the religious improvement of the people (the prayer-meeting societies are an evidence), and thus, beyond its own limits, has done great good. I believe that this result is of incalculable value, and amply repays all our efforts."

*Sweden.*—In the year 1857 the king, greatly in advance of his people, made an earnest effort to obtain more liberal legislation on the subject of religion, but the State Church officials were too strong for him. All Sweden rocked with the agitation of this subject of granting the privileges of religious worship to others than the members of the State Church.

In the year 1865 Rev. A. Cederholm went over from the mission in Norway and unfurled the banner of Methodism in Gotland, an island in the Baltic. The work rapidly grew, and aid was required.

Persecutions and troubles, similar to those experienced in Norway, were encountered in Sweden, but the triumphs were many and the fruits encouraging.

In 1868 Bishop Kingsley on his visit made this a separate mission, appointing Victor Witting superintendent. The year was one of general and constant revival. Large societies sprung up at Gottland, Stockholm, Gottenburg, Orebro, and Carlskrona. At the latter place a chapel was built, many of the people living on two meals daily and others pawning clothing and furniture in order to give. The chapel at Carlskrona was the first Methodist church in Sweden.

The whole country seemed to open to this new faith. In 1871 eight chapels were built and dedicated, eight more were in process of erection, and four had been built.

Bishop Foster, upon his visit (1872), found fifty ministers employed, and the work in every department prosperous.

In 1874, at the annual meeting, Bishop Harris presiding, it was decided, with great unanimity, to withdraw from the state church under the new law for dissenters. A petition, signed by 1,400, was presented to the king, who received the deputation with great consideration, was much moved, and dismissed them with his blessing, saying, "God be with you, my people."

A training-school for candidates for the ministry was originated and located at Orebro, having 11 to 17 students.

The Swedish Conference was organized at Upsala August 2d, 1876, by Bishop Andrews.

*Denmark.*—Mr. Willerup, a Dane, removed to Copenhagen in 1857 from his labors in Norway and Sweden.

The great want of the mission was a church building, but an early convert surprised all Scandinavia by proposing to give 3,000 rixdollars (about $1,500) toward building an edifice. The General Committee of 1861 appropriated $5,000, and Harold Dollner, a merchant of New York, offered to add $1,000 more.

Political troubles and the war cloud delayed the work, but by January 6th, 1866, the church was dedicated. In 1872 a church was dedicated at Hornsyld, which was built and presented by Niels Simonsen. Since then a good church has been built and dedicated at Viele, without aid from abroad.

Similar inspiriting effects were exerted by the mission upon the state church in Copenhagen, as in other parts of Scandinavia. They began Sunday-schools, and in a section of the city where, for a hundred years, no church had been built, they at once began to provide church accommodation for the people.

At Langeland a wealthy farmer donated a hall for public worship, and then gave himself to the church.

**Methodist Episcopal Church (South), U. S. A.—*Board of Missions.*** Headquarters, Nashville, Tennessee, U. S. A. The beginning of the work of this Society is coincident with that of the Methodist Episcopal Church (North) (q.v.), until the separation of the two churches in 1844. Up to that time each branch had a share in all the missions, but subsequent to that date the Southern churches organized their own board and carried on separate missions.

At its first General Conference, held in 1846, a Home and Foreign Missionary Society was organized. Its operations were committed to a Board of Managers, who, in conjunction with the bishops, determined the fields that were to be occupied, selected the missionaries, and distributed the amount to be collected among the annual conferences. The home and the foreign fields were under the management of the same Board. In 1866 the General Conference placed the work of the Missionary Society under two, one having charge of the foreign, and the other of the home field. In 1870 the missions of the church were again placed under one Board. In 1874 the constitution was again changed, giving to the work its present organization. The General Board has charge of the foreign missions, and all others not provided for by the Annual Conferences. It consists of a president, vice-president, three secretaries, and twenty-five managers. The bishops and treasurer are *ex officio* members of the Board. The Board meets annually, to determine what fields shall be occupied, and the number of persons to be employed in each; to estimate the amount that may be necessary for its missions; and to divide the same among the Annual Conferences. The revenue of the Board is derived from annual collections in every congregation and Sunday-school, and from such other plans as may be adopted by the church and congregation, by the Sunday-schools and by such societies as may be formed to raise money for this object, and by special collections by the secretaries and bishops, and from donations and legacies.

Each Annual Conference is required to provide for the mission work within its bounds. Each one is authorized to organize a Board of Missions auxiliary to the General Board. Said Conference Board appoints its own officers, regulates its own affairs, and has control over the missions it may establish, with the consent of the president, within its bounds, and of the funds raised for their support.

The first work of the Board was among the colored people and Indians of the United States. The latter was especially important, but is treated of under the article Indians.

### Foreign Missions.

CHINA.—The offer made by Charles Taylor in 1843 to go to China as a missionary of the Church was the origin of the action of the first General Conference, held at Petersburg, Va., in May, 1846, when it was decided to commence a mission to China, and Charles Taylor was appointed missionary. It was deemed best that he should have an associate, and during the year and a half which elapsed before one could be secured, Mr. Taylor studied and took a degree in medicine. In April, 1848, Dr. Taylor and his colleague, Mr. Jenkins, sailed for China with their families.

Shanghai was the place selected, after much thought by Dr. Taylor, as the best location for the mission. On arriving at Hong Kong after a four months' voyage, the illness of Mrs. Jenkins prevented Mr. Jenkins from going any farther, and Dr. Taylor began work in Shanghai, in September, alone. Nine months later, May, 1849, Mr. Jenkins arrived, and so soon as

a sufficient knowledge of the language had been acquired, the two missionaries opened a preaching place and talked and preached to the many who came, attracted more by the strange appearance of the foreigners than by any desire to learn. Few Christian books were published in Chinese at that time, and the work for quite a while was entirely oral; but as the language was acquired more perfectly and intelligibly, converts were made and the nucleus of a church was formed. Liew-seen-sang and his wife were the first converts, and the man's name has been familiar to Southern Methodists ever since, until his death in 1866, as the eloquent and useful native preacher, whose vigorous mind, quick apprehension, ready and fluent utterance, and noble piety made him so universally beloved and heeded.

The mission was strengthened in 1852 by the arrival of Rev. W. G. E. Cunnyngham and his wife; but the work and the climate began to tell on the pioneers, and in that same year ill-health caused the return of Mrs. Taylor in the spring, and in the fall Dr. Jenkins took his wife and family for a visit home, hoping to restore Mrs. Jenkins' health by the change, but she died at sea. In September, 1853, Dr. Taylor joined his family in the United States, as his wife was still in bad health, and the mission was left in the care of one inexperienced missionary. Then was the time of the Taiping rebellion, and in that year Shanghai was captured, and remained in the power of the insurgents for eighteen months. During all this time little work could be done. Fire and the ravages of the contending armies were fatal obstacles to the spread of the gospel, and the only chapel, together with two mission houses, was burned.

Dr. Jenkins returned in 1854 with a large reinforcement of three married missionaries, and the hope was that the cessation of the war, the increased number of workers, and the new strength thus given the mission would result in a great degree of prosperity. But the war continued, and the missionaries were attacked by sickness. The following year one left the field and died soon after reaching home, and in the next year another of the missionaries was forced to leave. But in spite of difficulties arising from lack of suitable buildings and lack of means, amid bodily weakness and privation, the work was carried on, inquirers increased, and several were received into the church.

In 1860 two more missionaries were sent out, but in 1861 Mr. Cunnyngham and his family were forced to leave, after nine years' work in that trying climate. Another of the workers was forced to take a furlough in 1861, and in 1862 Dr. Jenkins withdrew from the mission; so that in 1869 the record of the mission during the twenty-one years of its existence showed that eight missionaries with their families had been sent out. Death had removed one missionary and two missionaries' wives; one had withdrawn from the work, four returned, and two were left in the field. About sixty natives had been baptized, and among them were two native preachers of great gifts and usefulness. In 1870 three stations had been occupied— Shanghai, Soochow, and Nantziang, of which Shanghai remained the principal station, having good mission houses, and two chapels. Good earnest work was beginning to have its effect, and the mission was as strong and aggressive a power for good as any other of the missions in China. Rev. Y. J. Allen took charge of an Anglo-Chinese school under the patronage of the Chinese Government, and gave up his support from the Board for the benefit of the work. In addition to his work of instruction, two papers, one religious, the other scientific and literary, were edited by him, and were patronized by missionaries and native Christians of all denominations. The lack of good periodical literature for the Chinese has been largely remedied by the indefatigable and valuable efforts of this missionary.

Until 1875 Rev. Y. J. Allen and Dr. J. W. Lambuth carried on the work. Bible-women and native assistants were trained and put to work, itinerating tours were made in the surrounding country, a church was gathered together at each of the three stations, boarding and day-schools were opened, the work grew in importance, and the circulation of the papers published by Dr. Allen was greatly enlarged.

In 1875 another missionary was added to the force, and in 1877 Bishop Marvin visited Shanghai, and presided over the quarterly Conference. That same year a missionary and his wife arrived at Shanghai. The Women's Board entered the field in 1879, and sent two female missionaries. From this time on the history of the mission has been one of steady and encouraging growth along all the lines as laid down in the beginning, with most encouraging results. Trials and reverses have been met with, but have only been temporary. In 1889 the report showed the following statistics: 18 missionaries and wives, 14 female missionaries, 6 stations, 7 sub-stations, 468 church-members, 3 Anglo-Chinese schools, 205 pupils, 1 boys' boarding-school, 78 boys, 3 girls' boarding-schools, 63 girls, 31 day-schools, 579 pupils, 20 Sunday-schools, 666 scholars, 2 hospitals, 10,427 patients.

CENTRAL MEXICAN MISSION.—The conversion of an educated Mexican, Alijo Hernandez, was the providential beginning of the work in Mexico. Under the appointment of Bishop Marvin, Hernandez labored one year on the Rio Grande River, bordering on Mexico. He was re-appointed to the same field for 1872. "Bishop Keener, who presided at the West Texas Conference, which convened in Victoria in the month of December, 1872, was favorably impressed with Hernandez, and became much interested in view of establishing a mission in the city of Mexico; consequently, early in the year 1873 the bishop visited the city, purchased property suitable for a house of worship, made arrangements for the organization of a mission, and sent Hernandez to enter at once upon the work in this new field of toil." Later the bishop appointed Rev. Joel T. Dawes, of the Louisiana Conference, superintendent of the mission in the city of Mexico. He pushed the work with energy. Bishop Keener visited the city and his judgment was confirmed as to the opening for mission-work presented to the church. In 1879 the work had extended from the city of Mexico to the cities of Leon, Cuernavaca, Cuautla, Toluca, and Orizaba. Guadalajara and the region about it was taken under the care of the mission in 1883, as a missionary who had been working independently in that region united with the mission. The Central Mexican Mission Conference was organized in 1886. The latest statistics, (1889) show that

missions are now carried on in the States of Mexico, Hidalgo, San Luis Potosi, Morelos, Puebla, Vera Cruz, Oaxaca, Guanajuato, Mechoacan, Agnas, Calientes, Colima, and the territory of Tepic, with a total of 17 local preachers, 1,633 members, 55 Sunday-schools, 1,245 attendants. There is a theological seminary at San Luis Potosi, and the mission press issues regularly "El Evangelista," the organ of the mission, besides lesson-leaves and, during the past year, 800,000 pages of tracts.

MEXICAN BORDER MISSION.—This mission was also an outcome of the work of Hernandez in the valley of the Rio Grande. The mission district was established in December, 1874, with missions at Brownsville and Rio Grande City. In 1881 there were four missionaries, and the mission was divided into two districts—the San Diego and the San Antonio districts. Two schools were opened in 1882 under the charge of missionaries of the Woman's Board, one at Concepcion and the other at Laredo. By 1883 the work had extended two hundred miles into Mexico, and of the 23 missions, 9 were in Texas, 4 were on both sides of the Rio Grande, and 10 were in Mexico. In 1886 the mission was formed into an Annual Conference, which reported in 1889, 20 local preachers, a membership of 1,819, 14 church-buildings, 76 Sunday-schools, 1,860 scholars, six day-schools: Laredo Seminary, 83 scholars; Monterey Institute, 18 students; Nogales Seminary, 57 scholars; Saltillo Colegio Ingles, 60 scholars; Chihuahua School, 18 scholars; Durango school, 36 scholars. The work is carried on in five districts: Durango, including the states of Durango and Chihuahua in Mexico and part of Texas and New Mexico, has a population of 1,000,000, and is 700 miles long by 300 wide; Sonora includes the states of Sonora, Sinaloa, and Lower California, and part of Arizona, with a population of 500,000 in its area of 200,000 square miles; Monterey, with mission stations at strategic points along the Texan border; Tamaulipas, and Monclova.

BRAZIL MISSION.—In 1875 the Mission Board constituted Rev. J. E. Newman, for some years a resident in Brazil, its first missionary in that country, and early in the following year Rev. J. J. Ransom joined him. The province of São Paulo was first occupied, but in 1877 work was commenced in Rio de Janeiro. Two missionaries went out under the Woman's Board in 1881. In 1887 the conference was organized, and in 1889 the statistics were: 9 foreign missionaries, 359 church-members, 10 Sunday-schools, 257 scholars, and a college and seminary at Juiz de Fora.

JAPAN.—At the annual meeting in 1885 the following resolution, offered by Bishop Keener, was adopted by the Mission Board:

"Resolved, That we establish a mission in Japan, and that we appropriate therefor the sum of $3,000."

By request of the authorities at home Dr. J. W. Lambuth visited Japan, and reported favorably respecting a mission. April 20th, 1886, Bishop McTyeire, in charge of the China Mission, appointed J. W. Lambuth, W. R. Lambuth, and O. A. Dukes to Japan. On the 25th of July Dr. J. W. Lambuth and wife and Dr. Dukes landed in Kobe, Japan. Dr. W. R. Lambuth followed as soon as his duties in China would permit, and on the 17th of September, thirty-two years after the landing of Dr. J. W.

Lambuth in China, they held the inauguration meeting of the Japan Mission in Kobe. A field of most inviting character around the great Inland Sea of Japan was found open, and with apostolic zeal our missionaries entered on their work. Their first Church Conference was held in Kobe December 3d, 1886. In 1887 they reported 6 foreign members, 1 Chinese, and 1 Japanese. Rev. W. B. Palmore, visiting Japan, had contributed $100 annually for a supply of sound religious literature, and the Palmore Institute, having that end in view, was projected. A Sunday-school with 20 scholars was opened. A weekly collection for a church-building was started. The wives of the three missionaries entered fully into the work. Sixty women of good families were gathered for Bible-reading and study. The whole length of the Inland Sea was visited. Inquirers had increased to 27; three circuits—Lake Biwa, Kobe, and Hiroshima—were mapped out and manned by O. A. Dukes, J. W. Lambuth, and W. R. Lambuth in the same order. From the lower end of the great island of Shikoku came appeals for instruction which were answered in 1887. In 1888 a native missionary society and a church extension society were formed, and in the same year resolutions were adopted favoring an organic union of the various Methodist bodies in Japan. A "Basis of Union" was subsequently drawn up and referred to the home Board. At the third annual meeting of the mission held in Kobe September 4th, 1889, the report gave the following statistics: 5 stations, 12 out-stations, 5 missionaries and wives, 3 single men, 1 single woman; 232 church-members, 12 theological students, 18 Sunday-schools, 485 scholars, 250 pupils in various schools, and 1 church.

**Methodist New Connexion Missionary Society.**—Secretary, Rev. W. J. Townsend, Richmond Hill, Ashton-under-Lyne, England.—The Methodist New Connexion, the earliest offshoot from the stem of the parent Wesleyan body in 1797, was for some years occupied in laying its own foundations and organizing its forces, but in 1824 it took its first steps in missionary enterprise. It looked with pitying eyes to the sister-island of Ireland, and the Conference passed a resolution to the effect that: "Sincerely deploring the ignorance, superstition, and misery prevalent in Ireland, an effort be made to diffuse the blessings of Protestant Christianity in that island." The plan was developed at the Conference of 1825, and the following year the mission was established in Belfast and contiguous towns. Since that time important and useful operations have been continued with considerable success.

In 1835 the attention of the Conference was directed to Canada as an urgent sphere for missionary operations, and in 1837 the Rev. John Addyman went as the first agent of the Connexion to the Dominion. He was joined in 1839 by Rev. H. O. Crofts, D.D., and great prosperity attended their labors. The mission expanded until in 1875 it united with the other Methodist bodies in Canada, and became the one powerful Methodist Church of that country. When the union took place the Mission comprised 396 churches, 7,661 church-members, 167 Sunday-schools, and 9,259 scholars.

In 1859 a long-cherished wish of the Connexion was realized by the formation of a mission to the heathen. China was selected as the field of labor, and Revs. John Innocent and William N. Hall were the first agents of the Society sent there. They worked at Shanghai, until they had opportunity to choose deliberately their location, and eventually they settled in Tientsin, the great seaport of North China. Here they opened several stations and met with encouraging success.

In 1862 a mission to Australia was commenced and churches were raised in Adelaide and Melbourne. In 1887, these churches not having developed resources to make them independent, and the energies of the Society being demanded by the increasing claims of the Chinese work, they were given up. The church in Adelaide united with the Bible Christians, and that in Melbourne with the Wesleyans.

The Society is managed by a committee, consisting of a president, a treasurer, and a secretary, with 16 ministers and 16 laymen, appointed annually by the Conference.

The mission in China is its only foreign sphere, but it actively pursues its work in Ireland, and also in opening fresh stations in large manufacturing centres in England. In China it has three circuits. The first and earliest, in Tientsin, has a fine establishment in the British Compound, consisting of a college for the training of young men for the native ministry and which is complete, with residences and appliances for the principal, the native tutor, and 18 students; also a female college for the education and training of 12 native girls and 4 women for Christian work, with residence for a lady principal and native helpers. There are two chapels in the city where daily preaching of the Word is carried on, and the English church, in which united services are held, stands on ground owned by the Society. In addition to these there are a chapel and native church in Taku, and the same in Hsing Chi, a city to the west of Tientsin. This society was the first to enter this great city, but it has been joined since by the agents of several other societies.

In 1866 an aged man took his seat in the principal chapel of the Society in the main street of the city, and listened with earnest attention to the address of the missionary. He remained after the service as an inquirer, and told a wonderful story. He was a farmer from the village of Chu Chia Tsai, in the Shantung province, 140 miles south of Tientsin. Under the influence of a marvellous dream he had travelled to the great city to listen to the foreign teachers of religion. He became an earnest believer in Jesus, and went to his home carrying with him Bibles, hymn-books, and other Christian publications. He invited his neighbors to his house, announcing to them his conversion and reading to them the Bible. A great awakening took place in the village, which spread by degrees over the district, with the result that a pressing appeal was sent to Tientsin for a missionary to come down and take charge of the great work. Thus a second circuit was formed by the Society which now spreads over about 300 miles of the province and consists of more than 40 native churches.

In recent years a third sphere of labor has been occupied in the neighborhood of Kai Ping, north of Tientsin. Near this city extensive mines are being worked by a syndicate of Chinese mandarins, who applied to the Society for a medical missionary, offering to afford facilities for the teaching of Christian doctrine amongst the workmen. An extensive circuit is now being worked round the neighborhood of the Tang San collieries, extending to Yung Ping Fu, an ancient and important city near the old wall. These are the particular localities at present occupied by the agents of the Society.

It has been a special aim of this Society to work the mission as much as possible by native help. The number of foreign agents has been small, but it has been blessed with and owes much of its success to a large number of faithful and devoted native helpers. It numbers at present 52 chapels, besides smaller preaching places, 6 foreign ordained missionaries, 40 native preachers and catechists, about 3,000 adherents, 1,268 church-members, 227 candidates for membership, 19 schools, and 178 scholars. In addition to these, in Tientsin it has a lady agent in charge of the college for training women and girls, in Shantung it has a medical missionary who has charge of a dispensary, and a hospital, with beds for 30 in-patients. This institution is crowded with patients, who come on the appointed days from all parts of the district, often to the number of 120 or more, and it is exercising a very happy influence on the success of the mission.

The missionaries have no methods of work peculiar to themselves. The chapels are open daily for reading the Scriptures and preaching the gospel, and generally in the large cities and towns, large audiences assemble to listen to the foreigners. After the public service audience is given and conversation held with inquirers who may remain for further information. In the Shantung circuit the area covered by the mission is so wide that the foreign missionaries have to take frequent tours round the churches, exercising a general superintendence over them, and directing the native agents in charge of them. In connection with the work in this circuit several pious native women have been employed for some years in ministering the gospel to women with great success. These have not been able to read or write, but having retentive memories, they are able to repeat the principal portions of the New Testament, hymns, catechisms, etc., and so are well prepared to speak to congregations of women with great effect. It is to cultivate this branch of essential mission work that the college for women and girls has been opened in Tientsin, and it is intended to prepare females there who may carry the gospel to their own sex in all portions of the mission.

The organ of the mission is "Gleanings in Harvest Fields," which is published every other month, and is edited by Rev. W. J. Townsend, the general secretary of the Society. The income of the Society for 1889 was £6,038, the expenditure was £6,206.

## Methodist Protestant Church, Board of Foreign Missions. Head-

quarters, Easton, Maryland, U. S. A.—The organized missionary work of the Methodist Protestant Church began in 1882. Previous to that time the money received by the church for foreign missions was given to other Boards, at the direction of the pastor who secured it. Some of this money went to Japan, where Miss L. M. Guthrie was employed by the Woman's Union Missionary Society of New York. By this means Miss Guthrie learned of the Methodist Protestant Church, and subsequently when she was in this country she put herself in communication with some ladies of the church in Pittsburg, Pa., through whom she had received funds for her work. Before her return to Japan she had an interview with these ladies, which resulted in the organization of the Woman's Board of the Methodist Protestant Church. Soon after the General Conference of the Church elected a Board of Missions, Rev. F. C. Klein of Baltimore being appointed superintendent of the mission work in Japan. Under his management the work developed to its present proportions. Rev. F. T. Tagg, being elected corresponding secretary, organized methods for the collection of funds, and the church became more interested in the work, and it became possible to send more workers into the field.

*Development of its Foreign Work.*—The organization of a Board of Missions was due to the interest aroused by Miss Guthrie, and Japan, her field of work, was most naturally chosen. Yokohama was the first station opened by the Board. The work at Fugisama and Nagoya was organized in response to the call from the natives for Christian teaching and evangelistic work.

*Constitution and Organization.*—The Board of Missions is organized under the discipline of the church, which provides for the collection of funds, the employment of missionaries, the establishment of missions, the erection of schools and church buildings, etc. The Society is permitted to do all that its finances will permit, but it cannot go into debt. It has no special lines of work; its general methods are like the Boards of other churches, in the organization of schools for the education and churches for the evangelization of the natives.

## Methods of Missionary Work. Un-

der this head it is proposed to give a brief survey of missionary work as it is actually being conducted, with special reference to the methods used. Under the head "Organization of Mission Work" the agencies employed in the conduct of these methods will be considered.

The first thing to be clearly stated is the object of missions. A missionary society is formed, funds are collected, missionaries are appointed and sent out to some foreign land. What is it that these men and women seek to accomplish? Have they any definite thing in mind, or do they go out under some great, if rather vague, impulse of doing good and obeying the last command of the ascending Saviour?

Ordinarily the constitution of a society gives the answer to such a question. In the case of missionary societies many make no reference to it at all, or mention it in only the most general way, e. g., "the diffusion of the knowledge of the religion of Jesus Christ;" "the diffusion of the blessings of education and Christianity;" "to preach Christ and Him crucified, and as an after result to lift the natives to a higher level," etc.

Scarcely more particular on this point are the instructions to the missionaries as they go to their fields. So far as published statements are concerned, there is little or no precise definition of the work of the foreign missionary. It is undoubtedly partly for this reason that so many are skeptical of the value and results of missions. Were a clearer statement made and widely known, there might be less misapprehension. It does not, however, follow that the actual work of missionary societies is vague or scattering. Except in rare instances, it is sharply defined and steadily directed to a well-understood end. That end is twofold: first the conversion, second the sanctification and development, of individual souls. The second, indeed, involves their relations as members of the Church of Christ, as component parts of society and the nation, but the basis is always the individual. Missionaries go, not to Africa, but to the Africans; not to Persia, but to the Persians. The Church of Christ in Japan is made up of men, women, and children, in each one of whom the missionary is interested and for whom he labors, that the likeness of Christ may be developed in them. Undoubtedly other ends are sought: the spread of the comforts of civilization, the emancipation of thought from the thrall of false systems of belief, the establishment of better social conditions, government, etc. But these are subsidiary, and in a degree accidental. Wherever they seem to take the precedence, a more careful examination will in almost every case reveal the fact that they are means to an end, and that the end is the individual soul to be converted and built up in likeness to Christ. And this is not mere theory, but actual fact. Let any one look carefully at the reports of the societies, and whether or not he approves of their general organization, he will find that their methods tend always toward individual, personal work.

According to this, the methods adopted in missionary work may be considered as, 1st, Evangelistic; 2d, Pastoral. The first has primary reference to the conversion of men, the second to their development into a likeness to Christ.

As expressed in a letter received from the secretary of the Church Missionary Society, we have: "1. The preaching of the gospel to the unconverted; 2. The building up of the native church as it is pictured to us in the concluding chapter of St. John's Gospel, where Christ's servants are represented in figure, first as fishers casting the gospel net, and then as shepherds feeding and tending the flock. Education is a part of each. For the heathen and the Mohammedan it is undertaken solely as a means of evangelization. For the Christian population, whether elementary for the children or professional for the future pastor or teacher or evangelist, it is a department of pastoral work. So, too, publication is a department of each. Medical work is primarily evangelistic, its benefit to converts is rather incidental."

We will therefore consider first these two classes more fully and then take up the particular methods—first, those that really belong to both; second, those that are distinctive of each.

1. *Evangelistic.*—The missionary as an evangelist meets with four classes of men: 1st. Those who are greatly dissatisfied with themselves and their condition, and are not only ready but anxious for a change. 2d. Those who are bitterly opposed to change because of their relation to the existing order of things. 3d. Those who are willing enough to change but wish to have the advantage of change made evident. 4th. Those who are absolutely indifferent, content to let well enough alone. The first constitute a very small minority, and the classes increase in number to the last, which includes in every case the immense majority of every land where missionary work is undertaken.

The problem of the evangelist missionary is to find the first, disarm the second, convince the third, arouse the fourth, and bring all to an acceptance of the gospel of Christ as a Saviour from sin, and their repentance and conversion.

2. *Pastoral.*—The evangelist having accomplished his work, that of the pastor commences. First, the individual Christian is to be established in the faith, to be guided and assisted as he endeavors to throw off old habits of thought and of life and put on new ones; to be instructed, that he may be enabled to recognize and overcome temptation now meeting him under entirely unaccustomed forms; to be strengthened, that he may become an aggressive power to bring others to Christ.

He is then to be associated with his fellow-Christians, to be looked upon no longer merely as an individual but as a member, first, of the organic church, and, second, of a community and nation which he is to help to bring into accord with the precepts of the gospel.

The church is to be established as a permanent institution for the work of Christ. It must first be organized in all its different departments, placed on a firm foundation of faith, self-support, activity; be provided with the various means essential to its continued existence and growth. The community is to be permeated with Christian ideas, its social life freed from its evil associations, brought into accordance with the spirit of the gospel, its customs purified, its aims enlightened, its national life made to include a genuine and true patriotism. And so on in all the endless lines that open up before us as we look out over all that is involved in the establishment of the kingdom of God upon earth.

Each division is a mighty task, more perplexing even than the corresponding duty of the churches at home. And retrospect only makes its difficulties stand out more prominently. No one can travel in the Levant, over the roads where Paul led the way in Christian work, recall the story of those first centuries of growth, remember the subsequent centuries of stagnation, decay, and almost death, and not wonder whether the story is to be repeated in the churches now gathering in every city and town, and almost in every village. Modern Christians are no more sincere or devoted than those of earlier ages; modern missionaries no more earnest or skilled than the apostles and fathers. The problem of the missionary, especially in his pastoral work, is one of permanency and growth. The question he is constantly striving to solve is that of how to hold the vantage-ground gained, and make it the point of departure for new achievements. Here certain essentials must be kept in mind: 1. The development and growth of the individual church and community must be natural, not forced. The genius of the people must be studied, and that line of development found which will bring out the best that is in them. South Sea islanders cannot be transformed into Europeans or Americans, and every effort to so transform them results in harm. At the same time they must be something different from what they have been. While it is doubtless true that the Asiatic must remain an Asiatic, it is also true that the Christian Asiatic must be as different from the heathen or Mohammedan Asiatic as the modern Englishman is from his Norman-Saxon progenitors. 2. The element of time is very essential. Occasionally a sudden transformation will come; but this is the exception rather than the rule, and he works best who is not disturbed if he has to work slowly. 3. The methods adopted must be primarily constructive, not destructive. Their object is to build up rather than to tear down. They do not attack systems, but seek to help individuals. It is not that Islam, Hinduism, Shintoism, or Fetichism is to be overthrown, but that individual Moslems, Hindus, Japanese, Africans, are to be guided and assisted into a higher life. It is not so much that corrupted, degenerate Christian churches, as churches, are to be brought back to a pristine, or even better than pristine, purity; but individual Armenians, Nestorians, Copts, Roman Catholics, Bulgarians, Greeks, are to be helped to lead Christian lives, to understand better the full force of the truths that their lips profess, the full love of the God that they so often ignorantly worship. Undoubtedly the false systems will fall, the old churches be purified; but that is not the end in itself. Attacks are at times necessary. Fearless exposure of false teaching has its place, but missionary polemics as a rule are directed not against false thought so much as against sinful life. There is no shirking in the declaration of the truth, but the truth attractive, not repellent, is the great theme.

I. Taking up now the different methods, we mention first those that are common to both evangelistic and pastoral work, not undertaking to be exhaustive in the statement of them, but rather to indicate the lines along which the missionary works.

1. *Personal Conversation.*—The prime element in all missionary work is the personal. Men are drawn to men. Just as it was Christ's personality that drew men to Him, so it is largely the personality of the missionary that draws men to him, and through him to the Saviour. This has been most markedly shown in the lives of the great leaders Henry Martyn, Judson, Livingstone, Goodell, Hannington, and others. Indeed, almost all who have had success in missionary work have found their greatest power in the close, intimate relation of personal conversation, personal contact, where the needy soul felt the touch of the full soul, drew strength from it, and was satisfied; where the hard soul felt the power of the magnetic soul, and despite itself was drawn away into a higher life; where the cold, indifferent soul felt the heat of a soul on fire with the love of God, and expanded into a nature purer far than it had dreamed of.

It is no easy thing for an Occidental to come in contact with Oriental ideas, prejudice, and habits, and seek to exert such influences as shall bring about change without doing harm. It is easier to create repulsion than attraction, to harden than to soften, especially in public. Men, too, are swayed by the power of association with their fellow-men. A single soul in a multitude may be overwhelmed, in private conversation it may be developed.

Thus the fundamental method of missionary work in every land is intercourse with persons. Not only is this true of the historical inception of any work, but also of its continuance. It is just as important and universal to-day as when mission work was commenced. It is employed by every different agency, foreign and native, missionary, pastor, catechist; especially by zenana-workers, and almost exclusively by Bible-readers; it is adapted to every class, and is almost the only means of reaching some.

In the pastoral division of missionary work the element of personal influence is, if anything, stronger than in the evangelistic—certainly so far as the missionary himself is concerned; and it is here that personal genius makes itself felt most markedly. It not infrequently happens that to a passing traveller the missionary appears to be doing little missionary work. He seldom preaches, he may not be an educator or a translator. Hour after hour and day after day he is in his study, or among the people, talking, talking, talking. Could the observer hear and understand the conversation, he would marvel at the range of topics, covering every department of human life and every phase of religious doctrine. Shall tithes be given? How shall a church be organized? What is a Christian's duty toward an unjust, tyrannical government? The following, jotted down in a few moments by a missionary, will give an idea of the keenness of the questioners: "Why has Christian civilization not accomplished in America what you preachers claim that it is fitted to accomplish?" "Why are your Indians so bitter against you, and repressible only by force?" "If friends pray for us on earth, why should their hearts be dried up and their mouths be stopped when they go to heaven?" "Can a man be a believer who has not been an infidel? Must he not first challenge, then establish, then believe?"

Any one can give instance after instance where he has had to call up every line of study that he has ever pursued, to meet the difficulties that occur to the minds of those he seeks to help. But not only does he have to meet personal queries. The missionary must be a statesman. Church quarrels occur on mission ground as well as in Christian lands, and it is often owing chiefly to the missionaries' personal power that they are overcome. Conflicts with persecuting relatives furnish some of the most difficult cases. But instances need not be repeated to show that personal individual influence is one of the mightiest forces of modern as of ancient missions.

2. *Public Preaching.*—This is the development of personal conversation—is, in fact, personal conversation on a somewhat extended scale. It is not oratorical, but conversational; not instructive, so much as hortatory. And it is universal. Not a few have the idea that preaching is taking a secondary place in the importance of modern mission work. In the large cities, schools, colleges, Bible houses, printing-presses, are often more prominent than the preaching places, and many a traveller passes through and reports that mission work, which is primarily concerned with saving souls, has become a means of diffusing education and civilization—all good in its way, but a departure from fundamental ideas. Thus a Christian man visited the city of Constantinople, saw Robert College, the Bible House, the American College for Girls, the school and dispensary of the Scotch Free Church Mission, etc., and said he was glad to see such good work being done, but was sorry to see so little preaching! The missionary said: "Come with me on Sun-

day." Then he took him from one end of the city to another, and in Stamboul, Scutari, Galata, Hasskeuy, showed him gathering after gathering, where preaching to audiences numbering from 75 to 300 was going on in Turkish, Armenian, Greek, Spanish, and English. The traveller went away, satisfied that missions had not made a new departure in that line. The same thing is true of every mission station in the world. Comparatively few of the missionary societies report the number of preaching places, partly for the reason that accurate statistics are almost impossible, partly because there is such a wide divergence of usage. If we take the term preaching place to mean a place where divine service is held regularly, whether conducted by a pastor, preacher, evangelist, or catechist, it is probable that the number will somewhat exceed the number of stations and out-stations. Thus, the A. B. C. F. M. reports 1,058 stations and out-stations, and 1,402 preaching places. Other societies, however, make the term station synonymous with preaching place, so that the proportion of the A. B. C. F. M. would not hold through the whole list. We may estimate the whole number of stations and out-stations at about 12,000. (The statistical tables of the "Missionary Review," December, 1889, give 10,609; but there were a number of societies from which no returns were secured, so that the above estimate is probably not far out of the way.) If we increase that by 10 per cent, it is probable that we shall strike a fair estimate as to the number of places where there is regular preaching, and this would give 13,200. In addition to these there are a large number of places where preaching services are held in connection with evangelistic tours, and in many sections of India and China there is not a little of public street-preaching. The fact, too, that there are fully 1500 to 1600 ordained preachers, and a very much larger number of unordained evangelists, catechists, etc., whose chief work is preaching, shows that it is relied upon as the great means of bringing the knowledge of the gospel within the reach of men.

Passing to the pastoral division, we find the preaching assuming more the character of that in our home churches. It is less conversational, more rhetorical; less hortatory, more educational. Its range of topics widens, and it touches upon every and all the various needs of society and the nation, as well as of individuals. Yet always and everywhere it is intensely personal: the man is never lost sight of in the community.

3. *Sunday-schools.*—These need no special description. They are carried on in much the same way as in home lands, exert much the same influence, and hold much the same general position, both in their evangelistic and pastoral use. An idea of the universality of their use is gained in the fact that in the report of the A. B. C. F. M. they are not classified apart from the churches and attendance, the rule being that wherever there are services there is a Sunday-school, with not far from the same average attendance. The American Baptist Missionary Union shows 521 Sunday-schools, with 9,072 pupils; the Methodist Episcopal Church (North), 1,944 Sunday-schools, with 112,928 pupils (including 710 schools and 43,569 scholars in the European missions, being 1,234 schools and 69,359 scholars in their dis-

tinctively foreign work). Of the British Societies the London Missionary Society reports 381 schools with 22,415 scholars; the Wesleyan Methodist, 694 schools, 35,698 scholars (in their foreign work as distinct from the Colonial and Continental); the Baptist Missionary Society does not give the number of schools, but reports 3,746 scholars. The Basle and Rhenish Societies report large numbers. The fact that they do not appear in most of the reports is by no means an indication that they are not widely used as an evangelizing agency. The chief hindrance lies in the lack of competent teachers, but that is constantly diminishing in force.

4. *Education.*—This is a broad term, and as used indefinitely creates not a little misapprehension. As used in regard to missions, it comprehends the whole system of schools, from the primary to the college, in which (except in the case of the theological seminary) the instruction is general, and covers the same subjects as are covered in the public schools, academies, and colleges of America and Europe, but always including some direct religious instruction. In the earlier stages of missionary enterprise this form of work was, at least in most cases, not thought to be consistent with its distinctive character as evangelistic. As the pastoral element increased, it became readily recognized as an essential, especially for those who were to take up the work that so increased upon the missionary's hands that he simply could not do it. Converts implied churches; churches needed pastors, and the contrast between pastor and missionary must not be so great that the people should not be willing to look to the former as their leader. And so on in all the grades of active work and church development. Education as a direct means of evangelization has come, however, to hold a more and more prominent place in the minds and plans of missionaries.

1st. It is an essential to the reading and understanding of the Bible, and upon the knowledge of the Bible conversion must depend in a great degree. Illiteracy in mission lands is extreme, and involves not merely ignorance of letters, but of words, as expressive of ideas. The child in a primary school who has learned to read has a higher grade of knowledge of Bible truth than his parent.

2d. It is a great assistant in the correction of false ideas, thus opening the mind to receive the truth. In many cases it is almost an absolute prerequisite to such appreciation of truth as must precede conversion.

3d. It secures a certain time during which positive religious influence can be brought to bear upon the individual, whether child or adult. This element of time, in which the old prejudices may be softened and new ambitions and hopes aroused, is one of the most important elements in the influence of education as an evangelizing agency, especially as it takes chiefly the young at a period when they are under formative influences.

Looking now at education as it is actually conducted, it is so similar to that in Christian lands as to scarcely need description. The concomitants of rooms, seats, floor, walls, windows, etc., are often different; but the text-books are much the same, the methods are very similar. The kindergarten has not been confined to the Occident, but helps the Orient as well; and every form of modern advance in style of instruction is adapted to the needs of Arabs, Hindus, Japanese, and Kafirs.

Grading is conducted on much the same principle as in other lands. Small villages have little more than the primary school, where children (and sometimes grown people) learn to read and write, and get some idea of the great realm of knowledge that opens before them. The larger towns and the cities have every grade up to the high-school. Boarding-schools are established for those who, having passed the lower grades in village schools, are anxious for higher education, or may be fitted for work as teachers. Colleges, too, with courses of study that may be most favorably compared with those of England and America, are founded everywhere, and exert not a little influence among those classes that do not attend the lower grades of schools.

In the same general line is the movement for industrial education carried out so fully by the Basle Missionary Society, and at Lovedale, South Africa (q.v.), by the Presbyterian churches of Scotland.

It is, however, in the second division of missionary work that the value of education is seen in its fullest degree, and in which it is carried to its highest grade of efficiency; and it is here that there has been the most discussion as to the wisdom of allowing it so prominent a place in missionary work. Without entering into the discussion, or even undertaking to give a detailed statement of the extent to which higher education is carried by the different societies, it is sufficient to say that it has been developed in direct proportion to the appreciation of this second part of missionary work. As long as it was felt that the work of the missionary proper ceased when a man was converted, so long it was felt and held that the higher education, while advantageous in itself, formed no legitimate part of the missionary society's work, but must be left to local organization or individual effort. When, however, it became more and more evident that the only salvation for the convert himself lay in his opportunity and ability to grow, and that that opportunity could not and would not be given or the ability developed unless the society lent a helping hand, then the high-schools and colleges sprang up on every side, until there is scarcely a society that has not one or more, while many have several. These are in many cases semi-missionary, i.e., they are under missionary auspices and general missionary direction, though supported partly if not entirely by distinct funds.

Looking at the special objects in view in this second division of pastoral work, we note especially—1. The furnishing of an educated ministry, which not only takes the place of the missionary, leaving him free for the work of superintendence, but enables the churches to be placed upon a more substantial basis of self-development and fits them for aggressive work. 2. It supplies an element of support to the ministry in the form of an educated laity, able to hold its own in matters of faith, resist any undue desire for ministerial authority (very natural in lands where the hierarchical idea has held a most prominent place), and exert a powerful influence in the community. 3. It helps to solve the question of social customs by bringing the community in contact with the best results of society in other lands. This has its dangers as well as its advantages, yet it is a positive necessity. Customs of social life a people must have. If heathen ones are discarded, something must be provided to take their place. It is chiefly through the higher education that the best of Christian usages in social intercourse reach the people of non-Christian lands. 4. It places women in their proper relation in the home, the church, and the community. The occasion for the development of one of the finest institutions for girls on mission ground (the American College for Girls at Constantinople) was the feeling, as expressed by parents of the wealthier classes, that they wanted a Christian education for their daughters, which should fit them, not only for teaching, but for presiding in their homes. Any one who would accurately judge of the effects of this line of missionary work should follow those young ladies not only to the village life of Asia Minor and Bulgaria, but to the more pretentious homes of the cities. 5. It gives a proof unexcelled by any other, to the great mass of the indifferent in mission lands, that the gospel takes in the whole man and develops the best that there is in him. In these days of the telegraph and quick and easy communication, Christianity is judged by its ability to develop as well as to impart. Islam, Buddhism, etc., are losing their hold upon men largely by reason of their failure in this very regard, and Christianity is being watched most closely to see whether it meets the need. Robert College at Constantinople, the Syrian Protestant College at Beyrout, the Doshisha in Japan, the almost numberless institutions in India, are testifying to an element of power in Christianity before which old systems must soon give way.

5. *Publication* (see also Bible Distribution).— As an evangelizing agency the preparation and dissemination of Christian literature has always held a foremost place, and need not be discussed here. Its object is: 1. The presentation of Christian truth in such form as to attract the notice, stir the thought, and arouse the conscience of those who for one reason or another do not come under the personal influence of Christian workers. 2. To guide the thoughts of those who are already inquiring. Here especially the constructive spirit rather than the destructive is kept prominent. To put into the hands of a Moslem a tract attacking the character of Mohammed or the truth of the Koran would in most cases do more harm than good. Such tracts are indeed powerful instruments in the hands of those who know how to use them. The sledge-hammer will do what nothing else can, but it must not be allowed to work indiscriminately, without special direction. The lines of publication followed by missionaries with a special view to evangelistic work are: 1. Tracts, setting forth in simple and attractive style some gospel truth, often in the form of narrative, so as to bring out forcibly the personal element. 2. Books explanatory of the Bible and Christian doctrine, emphasizing such points as have special relevancy to the needs of that particular people and place. 3. Periodicals, weekly and monthly. These latter are in many cases in the form of illustrated child's papers. The weekly papers have more of secular matter, but are always not merely evangelical, but evangelistic

in tone, and reaching, as they do, multitudes who hold aloof from direct missionary influences, are powerful means for Christian work.

In pastoral work missionary publications include the higher lines of theological and other text-books, and some general literature. There is not as much of this as there ought to be, chiefly because, in the great strain upon the time and strength of missionaries, only that is done which at the moment is most essential. As, however, higher education provides mature minds among the natives, this want is being supplied more fully.

II. Turning now to those methods which are distinctively evangelistic or pastoral, we notice, as belonging to the former class, —

*Attention to physical and social needs*, including especially medical work. The relief of physical suffering, the supplying of social wants, is a department of missionary work where, except in the single item of medical work, classification is impossible. Acting upon the general principle that the state of the body affects most vitally the condition of the mind, missionaries in every land have adopted the various means now used so freely and successfully in the large cities of Europe and America. "The gospel of a clean shirt," or even of any shirt at all, has proved in many cases a most powerful one in lands where social customs were of the lowest. But even in communities where that particular form of evangelization was not called for there has almost invariably been need of more or less attention to these wants, in order to secure entrance to and appreciation of divine truth.

In the earlier history of missions, far more than now, persecution took a form that left the convert without even the means of subsistence. An excommunication that forbade the baker to sell him bread, meant more than trial: it meant starvation to the man who was bold enough to accept the new faith. In such circumstances the missionary was compelled to meet the emergency in such way as he best could. Of recent times that has not been so true; but the need has come in the form of widespread distress from deluge, famine, and pestilence. India, Turkey, Persia, and notably China, have repeatedly furnished instances where the supplying of material food has prepared the way for the reception of the spiritual, and hunger, cold, and nakedness have unbarred many a door hitherto held tight closed by prejudice and hostility.

Undoubtedly there is danger in this, and none are so quick to recognize it as the missionaries. How to give help without pauperizing, how to avoid the appearance of a bribe to accept Christianity, has required the most careful judgment.

Medical missions have of late come to the front as a direct element of missionary evangelization with a rapidity that makes one wonder that the church was so slow to recognize their value and power. Their general character is noted elsewhere (see Medical Missions); here we have simply to mention the varied forms in which they effect their work.

1. The most important end that they meet is the alleviation of physical pain, so that the soul can comprehend the force of the divine message. No one who has been in mission lands can have failed to see instance after instance where preacher and teacher have failed, but the doctor has succeeded, primarily by re-

moving the obstacles inherent in a diseased body, and by the positive attraction of gratitude for the kindness rendered.

2. The medical missionary is often a pioneer, securing entrance and acceptance where a preacher or teacher would be immediately rejected. This is especially true in such countries as China, where the prejudice against foreign influence is so strong as to yield to almost nothing else. Another notable example is found in the history of missions in Korea (q. v.).

3. The physician is often able to exert an indirect influence in favor of evangelical work by the prevention of hostility on the part of influential men. Notable instances of this have occurred in Persia, where the personal influence of such men as Dr. Asahel Grant and later of Dr. J. P. Cochran with the wild chiefs of the Koordish Mountains have undoubtedly availed much to prevent bloodshed, secure gratitude, and disarm prejudice.

The distinctively pastoral methods of mission work are chiefly connected with organization and superintendence, and cover the church, the family, and social and community life.

*Church organization* is one of the first of the distinctively pastoral duties of the missionary. The new converts cannot stand alone. For their own growth they need mutual support, and for their position in an unfriendly and often hostile community they need organization. It is not only natural but inevitable that that organization should take the form to which the missionary himself has been accustomed; and thus it happens that mission churches are in most cases the extension of the denominational differences of the home lands. It is, however, to be said that those differences are seldom if ever as sharply defined in foreign fields as at home; and except in case of divisions in the churches resulting from rival teaching, the members look upon them as formal rather than substantial. There are some cases where the form of church organization has been left almost entirely to the choice of the native community, with the result of an occasional departure from the denominational usage of the missionary. This is especially true of the missions conducted by the Congregational Churches of England and the United States. As a rule, however, the idea of the missionary has prevailed, not because he has felt tied to it, but because in it he can work to better advantage for the best growth of the church. The question of church organization has come up with some sharpness in reference to the work among the Oriental churches and in Papal lands. When missions were commenced in the Levant among the Armenians, Nestorians, Greeks, etc., there was no plan for a separate church organization. The old one, it was thought, was good enough, and it was far better to utilize that, introducing whatever of reform was necessary or practicable, but not severing historic associations, especially in view of the fact recognized by all, that their creeds were essentially in accord with modern faith. This, however, was found to be impracticable (see especially article Armenia); and as a matter of fact Protestant church organizations have been formed wherever Protestant missionaries have gone.

*Family life* on mission ground has always received the attention which has only recently been given to it in Christian countries as a direct method of exercising Christian influence. This is true in almost every land, but is especially marked in those sections where the change has been from a complete paganism. The relations and mutual duties of husbands and wives, parents and children, form not only the theme of much earnest thought on the part of the missionary, but of much careful counsel. To raise the wife from the position of a slave to that of an associate; to develop in the husband and father the sense of responsibility for something more than the provision of the physical needs of those dependent upon him; to educate the children to a genuine reverence rather than an unthinking obedience; to give the home an identity as a centre of Christian life,—these are some of the problems which can only be met by the recognition of family life as a distinct method of pastoral work. The mere statement of 'hem indicates their broad scope, but gives very little idea of the perplexity attending them. The transition from the old to the new must not be too abrupt or do too much violence to established customs. However much the missionary may deprecate the marriage of a Christian man to a heathen woman, it may be better to allow, or even to encourage it, than to give occasion for the charge that Christianity disregards the sanctity of the betrothal vow entered into before conversion. Even polygamy has to be treated carefully, lest the impression be given that the marriage relation itself is of light moment in the missionary's eye compared with the observance of customs with which he is familiar, but which seem to the convert unnecessarily harsh, especially in view of the biographies of the Old Testament. And so on in all the numerous relations which come out in bold relief when seen in the light of unaccustomed habits. Here we can merely indicate, not discuss or even explain in detail the different forms in which missions must work as they seek to confirm the new churches in their works as well as their faith.

*Social life*, or the relations of families with each other, may perhaps be considered as one of the problems rather than a method of missionary work or influence. It is, however, gaining increased importance in the eyes of those who are watching the development of Protestant Christianity in foreign lands. A man leaves his old faith and accepts the new one. He cannot, however, break away entirely from his old associations, which may include those dependent upon him—certainly those to whom he has duties. He meets them daily in home, in business, in the social circle, is bound together with them in many ways. He cannot if he would isolate himself from them. It is the old question of the times of the apostles, and creates as much perplexity now as then. To meet it wisely, and place the settlement on a firm, enduring basis, requires that the missionary make a specialty of its study in all its bearings, and be able not merely to show where the old is wrong or weak, but to present something that shall commend itself to all as taking its place. That this is being done increasingly is evident to all who watch carefully the progress of thought as indicated in the discussions of missionary methods.

*Community and national life* are in most cases but the development of the social. There are fields, however, where they involve ques-

tions of still greater perplexity. Instances of this occur in Africa and the islands of the Pacific, and even in the Levant, wherever church and state are united, and political privileges depend upon ceremonial observances. In some cases practically new states have been formed, with their entire paraphernalia of offices and officers. When this has not been the case, still the new Christian community has invariably had a distinct if not a corporate existence, which has come to be recognized as an important element in rendering the position of the church complete and permanent. Here the missionary meets the questions of accord to unjust laws and the demands of unchristian governments. Each case cannot be settled merely upon its own merits: the very idea of a Christian's relation to the "powers that be" must be thoroughly thought out and clearly stated. Most marked instances of this have occurred recently in connection with the French and Spanish occupation of islands in the Pacific, where the firm, patient influence of the missionaries has been the only thing that prevented hostilities, which would inevitably have ended in loss of life if not of national existence. The Christian state, not so much as an accomplished fact, but as an ideal, is a most practical and important element in the methods by which Christianity is to be ultimately established.

That this statement of the methods of missionary work is complete, is not claimed. Many things will occur to those intimately acquainted with the subject which should have been mentioned. If, however, the impression shall have been given that missionary work is no mere haphazard carrying out of a vague although noble impulse, but a calm, determined, well-considered effort on the part of the churches through their representatives to establish Christian faith, worship, and life on a sure foundation in every section of the globe, the chief end of the writer will have been attained. Some special items, such as the work of laymen, the community life, etc., will be mentioned under the head "Organization of Mission Work."

**Metla Kahtla,** northwest coast British Columbia, 30 miles south of Alaskan boundary. Fairly healthy, though damp and very changeable. Population chiefly Indians. Language, Zimshian. Religion, pagan. Condition of natives low. Mission station C. M. S. (1862); 6 ordained missionaries and wives, 1 bishop, 5 unordained missionaries, 17 native helpers, 8 out-stations, 7 churches, 250 church-members, 1 theological seminary, 6 students, 8 schools, 310 scholars.

The mission was begun by Mr. Duncan, a C. M. S. teacher at Fort Simpson, in 1857. The Zimshians are a very simple-minded, single-hearted people, a little credulous, very superstitious, and therefore very open to the seductive influences of the whiskey and vices of the white man. In order to protect his flock, Mr. Duncan moved with his converts in 1862 to Metla Kahtla, where he led them in the pursuit of agriculture, deep-sea fishing, etc. Good artisans of his acquaintance were induced to join the colony, which was at that time a well-ordered, progressive, and prosperous congregation of about 1,200.

**Mexican** or **Aztec Version.**—The Mexican belongs to the South American lan-

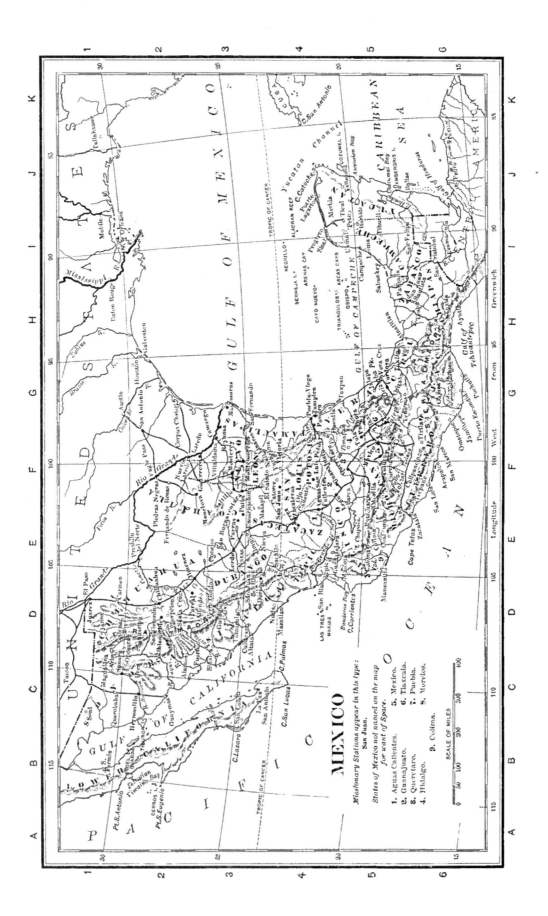

guages, and is used by the Mexicans, for whom some priests are said to have translated portions of the Scripture at a very early period. But nothing is known of these translations. A version of the Gospel of Luke was made by Dr. Pazos Kanki, under the care of Mr. Thomson, the agent of the British and Foreign Bible Society, and printed in 1832. Latterly a fresh demand having arisen for the Scriptures in Mexico, a reprint was made by the American Bible Society in Mexico.

(*Specimen verse.* Luke 15 : 18.)

Mexican, or Aztec.

Ni mehuaz yhuan ni az campa câ in no tâtzin yhuan nic ilhuiz: No tâtzin é, oni tlàtlacô ihui- copa in ilhuicatl yhuan mixpan têhuatl.

**Mexico.**—*Physical Geography.*—In form Mexico is shaped like a cornucopia, whose mouth opens toward the United States. As seen on the map it hangs as a receptacle below the great sister republic, and not as a ripening fruit above, destined to fall into its possession.

Mexico anticipated the United States as a European colony by about a century. Yet seventy years ago it was glad to copy our national institutions, and from that time to this, in spite of the restrictions of papal bigotry, it has continued to receive some of its choicest blessings from this country,—at the same time, as must be confessed, yielding up some of its most valuable territories by the arbitrament of war.

Mexico, as it now stands, is a country with nearly 6,000 miles of coast-line, more than two thirds of which are on the Pacific and the great Gulf of California. It has no navigable rivers. The east coast is peculiarly lacking in good harbors. It is, moreover, low-lying, and as a rule insalubrious. Mexico can boast but few islands, and those are insignificant in character or extent. The mountain ranges, which seem to form a sort of vertebral column throughout this hemisphere from Alaska to Patagonia, are prominent in Mexico, though cut off from the South American chain by the low-lying Isthmus of Darien. The high table-land intervening between the eastern and western branches of this great mountain range constitutes an admirable highway for railroad development and for international traffic—a fact which did not escape the eye of the great explorer and philosopher Humboldt. There is a vast portion of land in the country that can never become arable, but for this deficiency there are partial compensations: first, in the prevalence of mineral resources; and, second, in the fact that the coast is everywhere easily reached. With the establishment of artificial harbors and breakwaters, access can be found for maritime commerce, both on the Pacific and on the Gulf of Mexico. Yet the whole situation indicates that the chief commerce of the country must be carried on with the United States.

In the northern portions of the republic there are great barren expanses, which, though sufficiently level for tillage, are so lacking in fertility as to promise but a slender reward to agriculture. Farther south, and along the east coast, however, there is an affluence of fertility; and although the climate is often unhealthful, the fruitfulness of the country is such as to supply a large population, if need be, and a

lucrative commerce. In Michoacan and other still more southern States there are extensive forests of all the most valuable timber-trees.

The great lacustrine basins of Anahuac and Chihuahua, lying at elevations of from 4,000 to 7,000 feet, undergo great vicissitudes from alternate floods and droughts. But a general process of desiccation, due, undoubtedly, to the destruction of forests on the mountain tops, has gone on until in the valley of Mexico what was once an extended lake or a series of lakes is well-nigh dry.

The country is in many places volcanic, and from an elevated position in the city of Mexico one can behold several greater or smaller cones which are manifestly of volcanic origin, and near them extended plains of flinty lava. About the middle of the last century the mountain known as Jorullo, in the State of Michoacan, was thrown up about 1,600 feet above the plain by volcanic action.

A great transverse range running nearly at right angles with the northern and southern trend, and presenting the great peaks of Popocatapetl, Orizaba, and Ixtaccihuatl, though very old, is thought to be of more recent origin than the general ranges extending north and south.

The mines of Mexico, especially those of silver, have long been regarded as the richest in the world. It is said that for two or three centuries Mexico has produced at least one half of the entire yield of silver possessed by mankind. From 1537 to 1880 the total yield of this metal is said to have been nearly three thousand millions. The yield of gold in the same time has been nearly one thousand millions of dollars.

*Population.*—The entire area of the country is 763,804 square miles. The population was reckoned in 1880 to be 9,577,279. It has undoubtedly now reached 10,000,000, and may be divided as follows: Persons of pure Spanish lineage, 1,000,000; descendants of aborigines, 5,500,000; persons of mixed blood, 3,500,000; total, 10,000,000. In speaking of the Indian population, an able writer has justly said: "A wide difference exists between the Indians of the United States and British America and the so-called Indians of Mexico. They are a different race. The Mexican Indians are docile and industrious; they engage in agriculture, in mining, and in such rude arts as are practised in countries which do not enjoy the advantages of modern transportation. In all the wars in which Mexico has been engaged the Indians have constituted largely the rank and file of her armies. They are now enfranchised citizens under the laws of their country, and to the extent to which they are taxed they enjoy equal political rights with those of the Spanish race. While the Indians and the inhabitants of mixed blood comprise the menial class, yet from the ranks of the aborigines have sprung men of mark—men who have risen to distinction in science, in arts, in letters, in educational employments, in the church, in military life, and in the conduct of state affairs. Benito Juarez, the deliverer of his country from the Austrian usurper, was an Indian of full blood, and as a statesman and military leader he stood peerless among his countrymen. Morelos, who achieved fame in the early efforts of his countrymen to secure their liberty from the Spanish yoke, was also an Indian of full blood."

*The Ancient Inhabitants.*—The Toltecs, who preceded the Aztecs in the valley of Mexico, are supposed to have migrated from the north. Like other Indian races on the Western Hemisphere, they probably passed over the narrow channel known as Behring's Straits from northern Asia, and were attracted southward by more friendly climates and more abundant supplies of food. Ebrard has given good reasons for supposing that other migrations also occurred—perhaps in some instances by accidents—from Japan across the Pacific, and from Europe and Africa across the Atlantic. The Aztec civilization and that of the Mayas of Yucatan have many things in common with Eastern cults, and particularly with the hieroglyphic inscriptions of ancient Egypt.

The Toltecs were in some respects more highly civilized than the Aztecs, who finally conquered them. Their strength lay in the arts of peace as that of the Aztecs was developed by war. The terrible system of bloody sacrifice was established in connection with the warlike spirit of the Aztec conquerors. The Tezcucans, who entered into a triple league with the Aholcuans and the Aztecs, and were finally betrayed and conquered by the latter, presented the highest perfection of the ancient Mexican civilization. One of their kings was one of the grandest figures in history.

The Aztecs were characteristically a warlike race; and, like the Lombards in the Roman Empire, they took on the culture of the vanquished peoples. Like the Venetians, who, when driven by northern barbarians into the Adriatic, built upon the very lagoons and marshes a mighty dominion,—more invincible because built upon the marshes,—so the Aztecs, harassed at first by other tribes, took refuge upon a small island in the shallow lake of Tezcuco. This, gradually enlarged by driven piles and the dredging of their canals, became the impregnable stronghold from which they at length dictated terms to all their neighbors, till they had built up a great empire, extending from sea to sea.

At the time of the Spanish conquest this little island had become another Venice, intersected by numerous canals, having 300,000 inhabitants, and subsidizing the best civilization of all the tribes of Anahuac. And but for the one sanguinary blot of their religious system, we should think of the Aztecs with unmingled wonder and admiration. There is not space to speak of their early industries and skill, their agriculture and ingenious floating gardens, their jewelry and feather-work, their aqueducts and architecture, their chronology and their marvellous calendar whose intercalations quite equal our own in accuracy, their picture language and poetry, their humane laws and local courts, their kindness toward women, and their hospitals for their wounded soldiers; and after all the long history of bondage, many of these elements still remain in the character of their Indian descendants. No chapter of history is more pathetic than that which describes the invasion of Cortez and his followers in the early part of the 16th century. The combination of prowess and treachery, and the heartless cruelty inflicted in the alleged service of the Cross, have left an indelible blot upon the Christian name, and the Aztecs, in spite of their bloody religion, have the sympathy of mankind.

The three centuries which followed the conquest are historically a barren waste.

Cortez became an object of mean jealousy, and was misrepresented at the court of Spain, was baffled and persecuted till he had drunk the dregs of the very cup of ingratitude and heartlessness which he had given to the generous monarch of the Aztecs. The Indians were reduced to peonage on the great estates of the Spanish planters. Foreign bishops amassed fortunes, while the lower clergy of the native priesthood were allowed a pittance.

Immense estates were gathered into the hands of the church, which finally became the chief creditor of the nation. By deed or by mortgage one third of all real property was thus held, and the nation came under the thrall of the Church. This state of things existed till the spirit of liberty and independence was awakened within a comparatively recent period.

THE DAWN OF POLITICAL LIBERTY.

It seems wonderful that Napoleon I. should have been the man to strike at last the keynote of liberty among all Spaniards on both hemispheres; but so it was. There had been in all the colonies a sort of chivalric loyalty to the sovereigns of Castile, however severe their oppression. But when in 1808 Napoleon sent his armies into Spain and dethroned Ferdinand VII., placing the sceptre in the hands of a Bonaparte, the spell of loyalty was forever broken. In 1810 the standard of independence was raised, a patriotic priest leading the movement. By the year 1821 the independence of Mexico and several other Spanish-American states had been won, and by the year 1828 all the Spanish colonies on the Western Hemisphere had become free republics. But the work of reform was as yet only partial—religious liberty had not been achieved. The people had not learned that republicanism and ultramontanism cannot coexist; that the one encourages the enlightenment and free thought of the people, and cannot exist without them; while the other must exist by authority and repression. The result has been a succession of pronunciamentos, and a general insecurity.

But we come to another series of providences in relation to Mexico, and those too which have to do with our own history and with the general advancement of civilization.

In the year 1835 Santa Anna, then President of Mexico, brought about a *coup d'état*, by which the governments of the different States were abolished, and all the power was concentrated in the central government under his dictatorship.

Yucatan on the south and Texas on the north at once rebelled; and so grave was the Texan rebellion that Santa Anna himself was compelled to take the field. His armies attacked and dispersed the Texan Legislature; and prisoners of war whom they captured were mercilessly shot by his orders, thus rendering the reconciliation of the people of Texas forever impossible.

At the battle of San Jacinto, Santa Anna was vanquished and taken prisoner by General Houston, and for nine years Texas maintained her independence. In 1846 Texas applied for admission to our union and was admitted, and Mexico thereupon declared war upon the United States. The oppressive acts of the Mexican dictator were considered a first-rate pretext.

And besides, the fashion of our English cousins in making conquered nations pay the expense of conquering them was also thought to be the right thing to do; and so we concluded to defend Texas all the way from the Gulf of Mexico to the Pacific.

General Taylor appeared on the battlefields of Matamoras and Monterey. General Scott marched triumphantly from Vera Cruz to Mexico city. General Kearney was heard from in Arizona, and Fremont in California.

THE ADVENT OF RELIGIOUS FREEDOM.— Up to the year 1867 there was no religious liberty in Mexico. It is true that the Liberal party had in 1857 drafted a constitution demanding liberty of faith, abolishing conventual establishments, and confiscating church properties in mortmain; but they were not able to enforce them. Juarez, the president of the republic, was a fugitive, and the Reactionists were in arms against him.

How, then, was religious freedom at length established, and what were the influences which finally united the discordant political elements of the country, and achieved the more stable government of the present time? As Napoleon I. had unconsciously promoted the political independence of all the Spanish-American states a half-century before, so Napoleon III. became the unconscious leader in this later movement for religious freedom and political consolidation. He also attempted the dispensing of crowns and sceptres; and he also saw his efforts overruled for the very opposite results. The War of the Rebellion in the United States had furnished the opportunity. A Swiss banker had an exaggerated financial claim against the Mexican Government, which by the adoption of the banker as a citizen of France furnished the emperor with a pretext. England and Spain also had claims, and an alliance was formed for an armed intervention.

In 1862 the united fleets appeared at Vera Cruz with their contingents of men. But England and Spain soon withdrew from the enterprise and returned home. The French army under Generals Forey and Bazaine fought their way over the Cordilleras to the capital, where they established a provisional government known as the "Regency of the Empire." This virtual French Assembly submitted the choice of a ruler to the patronizing French emperor, who was politic enough to give it to the house of Austria, which he had defeated on the plains of Lombardy.

In the beautiful palace of Miramar, on the shores of the Adriatic, resided an Archduke of Hapsburg with his young and accomplished wife, daughter of King Leopold of Belgium and granddaughter of Louis Philippe. There the evil genius of French ambition sought him, and thither strange ambassadors, half Spanish and half Indian, came to offer him a crown. On the 10th of April, 1864, amid all the pomp of royalty, this ill-starred couple left their charming abode and embarked for Mexico. Stopping at Civita Vecchia, they paid a visit to the Holy City, where they received the communion and the Papal benediction, and were honored with a private breakfast with Pius IX. and Cardinal Antonelli.

They arrived in May at Vera Cruz. Their journey to Mexico City was one series of ovations from the clerical party. Having proceeded first of all to the great cathedral to celebrate mass, they were escorted to the old Vice-regal palace, amid the ringing of bells and the rejoicing of the Reactionists that the republic was dead, and an empire was once more established.

But General Sherman was already on his march to the sea; and within four months General Grant received a sword presentation at Appomattox, which attracted the attention of France, and of all the courts of Europe. From that day everything went wrong with the French power in Mexico. It was patent to all men that the empire would prove a failure; and the French people especially were vexed at the stupendous blunder of their ambitious and meddling emperor.

Meanwhile, Maximilian and Carlotta had both sincerely endeavored to conciliate the people— he by special franchises, she by indefatigable charities.

But in July, 1866, matters had assumed so grave an aspect that the young empress, then only twenty-six years of age, set out with a few attendants to visit the court of France and remonstrate with Napoleon against the withdrawal of his support.

Receiving only discouragement, she passed on to her deserted castle of Miramar, which she reached in the midst of a dismal storm, as if the very skies would point the contrast of her return and symbolize the ruin of her fortunes. She next sought solace in a visit to the Pope; but even before she reached Rome her reason began to sink under its heavy burdens, and her wild fancy was that Napoleon had bribed her friends to poison her.

Meanwhile no means were left untried to reconcile the people to the empire. Efforts were made especially to excite jealousy toward the United States. The ravings of a subsidized Roman Catholic press on this subject were sometimes tragic and sometimes amusing. A favorite line of argument was that the United States were only impeding the imperial cause in order to secure the country for themselves. "You will soon hear," said one of these papers, "of schemes of annexation. The sordid and aggressive Yankees will overrun your land with their railroads and their sharp speculations. Your mines will be exhausted by adventurers, and all positions of profit will be monopolized."

Meanwhile the republic, which for ten years had existed, we might almost say in the person of a single man,—Benito Juarez,—had returned from its exile at El Paso to San Luis Potosi, and it became apparent that the final conflict would centre at Queretaro, half way between the latter place and the capital.

During all the years of the struggle with France this man, with a cabinet composed of Lerdo, Iglecias, and Mareshal, and with Senor Romero as his Minister at Washington, kept alive the cause of liberty among the people. Even when they were driven to El Paso on the northern border, they still held their organization as President and Cabinet of the Republic; and sending letters through the United States to friends in all lands, they assured them that their republican cause was not dead, but would certainly triumph in the end.

Their sublime faith and devotion doubtless had great influence in shaping diplomacy at Washington and in creating a reactionary sentiment against the empire even in Europe.

The spring of 1867 brought the beginning of the end. Maximilian's chief forces, with himself among them, were at Queretaro under siege. In an attempt to escape he was betrayed by one of his generals, placed under arrest, tried by a military tribunal, and with Generals Miramon and Mexia were sentenced to be shot.

In the trying scenes which followed, the character of this typical Indian president was well illustrated. Efforts were made by the United States and by the European consuls to secure a change of sentence. And when the wife of Prince Salm Salm, a member of Maximilian's staff, threw herself at the president's feet and clung to his knees as she poured out her entreaties, he wept in sympathy, while he declared himself powerless as a mere executive under the behests of the law.

It is a strange spectacle, a European princess at the feet of an Indian patriot pleading for the life of an emperor, and both weeping as the solemn fiat is uttered. And this is the man —this full-blooded American Indian—this is the man who for ten years of hard struggles had carried a republic in his head and heart, and who, both before and after that solemn hour, did more than any other to restore order to his distracted country. When, in a public reception, a captured French tricolor was spread for him to walk upon, he stepped aside. "No," he said, "the French are not our enemies—it is only their emperor. The French are our friends, and depend upon it that flag will yet wave over a republic." A prophecy which Juarez lived to see fulfilled!

With the establishment of the republic under Juarez in 1867 that religious liberty which had been proclaimed in 1857 was fully realized, and notwithstanding the efforts and the bitter persecutions of the Roman Catholic clergy, it has been maintained till the present time.

THE RECORD OF THE PAPACY IN MEXICO.— Even by the judgment of candid Roman Catholics, the religion of Mexico from the very beginning of the Spanish conquest has been a mixture of Christianity and heathenism, the latter often predominating. Abbe Dominic, chaplain of the Emperor Maximilian, a native of France, did not hesitate to pronounce the religion of the country a baptized heathenism, a mixture of superstitions, unworthy of the name of Catholic. Some of his utterances against the ignorance and immorality of the priesthood and their degrading ceremonies, as quoted in Abbott's "Mexico and the United States," are quite equal to the strongest denunciations which have been expressed by even the most prejudiced Protestant writers. For ages no religion except that of the Roman Catholic Church was known in Mexico. When the republic was established in 1823, and thence onward to the proclamation of religious liberty in 1857, an express provision in the constitution declared that the Roman Catholic faith was the religion of the state, and that no other could be tolerated.

One third of the real property of the republic came at length into the possession of the hierarchy. Conventual establishments for either sex were greatly multiplied. Mexico City might almost have been said to be a city of convents at the time when religious liberty was established. The people, wearied with the long dominion of an unscrupulous hierarchy, and remembering that the church had been implicated in all the measures designed to overthrow the popular liberty, carried reform to an opposite extreme of intolerance. It confiscated a large portion of the church property, silenced the clangor of convent-bells which the public patience had so long endured, ordered the long robes and shovel-hats and other insignia of the priesthood and other sacred orders to be laid aside when appearing upon the public streets, and suppressed all public processions and various childish pageants. The Jesuits were banished from the country, as they had been at various times from so many nations of Europe. It is difficult for any who desire to be entirely candid, to decide whether the papacy, as it existed in Mexico fifty years ago, was on the whole a blessing or a curse.

It can hardly be doubted that although the Virgin Mary was almost made to take the place of Deity, yet enough of Christ was communicated to many souls to save them from sin and death. Yet the influence of the priesthood was declared by many who were residents in the country to be positively corrupting to the public morals. The licentiousness of their lives was scarcely disguised, and their exactions for the performance of the marriage ceremony were so oppressive, that to a large extent the masses dispensed with the sacred rite altogether, and with the poor, concubinage became the rule. The Bible was strictly kept from the people, or if found in their possession was burned as a poisonous and pestilent thing. In the desecration of the Sabbath the priesthood, by example at least, might be said to take the lead. The perfunctory ceremonies of the morning mass once over, they were among the promptest and most enthusiastic at the bull-fights. Gambling was a favorite pastime within the monasteries, and that excessive wine-drinking took the place of vigils and of fasting was too plainly indicated by the rotund figures and sodden faces of the padres whenever they appeared in public.

This easy-going life was not inconsistent with the most fiery zeal for dogma, and the bitterness that could persecute even unto death.

The priesthood of Mexico was in touch with the priesthood of Spain in the palmy days of the Inquisition. This institution was established in Mexico by Philip II., and the spirit of the infamous Torquemada did not fail to stamp itself upon the new continent, as upon the old.

When the Northern Methodist Mission purchased a confiscated monastery in Puebla in 1872, and proceeded to adapt it to their missionary uses, they found in the substructure skeletons of Christian martyrs who had been walled into their cells to perish from the sight and memory of men.

The people of Mexico, two thirds of whom were of Indian blood, were on the whole easily managed in matters of religion. The race had been thoroughly quelled and cowed by the bloodthirsty Spaniards, and after three centuries of oppression and toilsome bondage, coupled with dense ignorance, submission had become hereditary. Although revolts were frequent enough after the establishment of the republic, they were generally instigated by those who were wholly or in part of Spanish blood. The masses of the Indian population were spiritless, though there were noble exceptions, as in the person of Juarez, who was of pure Indian blood. The old superstitions of the people were largely countenanced and utilized. To these were added the pleasing effects of the Catholic pageantry, of which the Spanish Mexican Church was so complete a master. Enlightenment was the last thing thought of, and truth was invariably sacrificed whenever circumstances required. An example is furnished in the legend of Our Lady of Guadaloupe, whose miracle-working image is still seen in a church situated three miles from the city of Mexico. Candid Mexicans do not hesitate to relate how, when the Indians of the early day still bore a grudge against the conquering and oppressive Spaniards, against their religion and all that belonged to them, even against their fair-faced Queen of Heaven, the happy device was planned of miraculously producing the image of an Indian Virgin Mary. Through all changes this dusky goddess has remained one of the most popular of all images. She has performed no end of wonders, all of a merciful type. One apartment of the church above named bears witness to the miracles which she has performed for the distressed. Her picture is on the wall, and around it many other pictures illustrative of her wonderful works. In a corner is a stack of crutches said to have been left by cripples whom she had instantly healed. The whole scene is almost an exact counterpart to an apartment in the Buddhist Temple of Osakasa, in Tokyo, Japan, where an image of Quan Yen, the Buddhist Goddess of Mercy, is surrounded by similar trophies of her miraculous power. Meanwhile, even before the proclamation of religious liberty in 1857, the more enlightened statesmen of Mexico had come to feel the degradation which papal superstition had brought upon the country; and when upon the death of Maxamilian the republic was restored under Juarez as president, the general protest of enlightened men became outspoken. Juarez was from the first in favor of the more enlightened influence of Protestantism, and every president since 1867 has exerted his influence for freedom of opinion. Among those of liberal sentiments there have been two classes—some undoubtedly mere freethinkers, who cared for no religious faith, but were stanch supporters of freedom. Others, even though Catholics, have advocated liberty of thought, and welcomed Protestantism, not only because such freedom is the dictate of wise government, but because they believe that the disintegration of the one dominant mass of the papacy is more favorable to national liberty. Of this class was General Esquibedo, who in 1879 was heard to express his satisfaction at the introduction of Protestantism, because he believed that its influence, even its rivalries, would prove a benefit to the Mexican Catholic Church, and make it more like the Catholic Church in the United States.

THE POLITICAL ATTITUDE OF THE PAPAL CHURCH.—A Mexican's estimate of the part taken by the church in the achievement of political independence is as follows. While speaking of the past struggle for liberty he says: " Over against the leaders of the national uprising, bigotry reveals to us the haughty clergy united most intimately and firmly with our would-be oppressors, hurling their anathemas against the defenders of independence, and making their own the cause of the throne and of foreign do-

minion during the second decade of this century.

" It shows us also the real secret of that sudden desire for the independence of Mexico which in 1821, at the last moment of the struggle, seized upon our infuriated enemies. It was the hope of transferring hither the persecuted dynasty (of Castile) which was on the point of disappearing entirely amid the revolutionary convulsions of Europe; the intention of strengthening still more the dependence of the ancient colony upon the mother-country, converting it into a fief of the Spanish crown. Then came the war with the United States, a nation eminently Protestant,—more so then than now,—representing in 1847 in religious matters the most marked contrast with our country, which had not even yet rid itself of its uniformity of creed and of worship. What efforts, what diligence, what sacrifices were manifested in that epoch, a thousand times to be deplored, by these jealous partisans of religious uniformity!

" Did they summon their compatriots to arms in defence of the sacred cause of religion and their native land ? Did they fly to the battlefields and fight heroically against the invader and the Protestant ? No; the only thing which they did was to seduce to revolution the battalions of the National Guard, who, as the result, fought many days in the effort to overthrow the Liberal administration which was at the head of affairs, and these battalions actually were fighting in the streets of Mexico, covered with shame, at the very time when the North American squadron was bombarding night and day the port of Vera Cruz, that noble city which covered herself with glory in this struggle.

"Afterward came the French invasion, invited to our land by these same zealous partisans of religious uniformity who to-day figure as champions of national independence; and while the true and constant defenders of this noble and divine cause of the nation's liberty succumbed before the invader on the battle-field, or under the terrible sentences of court-martial, or amid the unspeakable horrors of exile, these false defenders of independence were receiving under a gorgeous canopy, at the gates of the capital, Marshal Forey, and were being appointed as regents by the invader, and were crowding their newspapers with the praises of the enemy. . . . "

Referring to the constant efforts of the church party in recent years to arouse the patriotism of the Mexican in the interest of the papacy, that historic foe of patriotism in all the struggles of the past, the same writer says:

" A party of this sort, which has always opposed the national independence, which has always sympathized with invaders, which indeed has united itself with them, even if it did not defend intolerance, has no right to invoke a cause so sacred and noble as that of national liberty. Let it set forth, at the right time and in the right place, its private interests, its opinions with reference to sect and its animosities; but let it not invoke that which it has never loved nor defended, not even when to do so would have been to defend also religious uniformity, as in 1847. For the rest, they have as absolute a right to defend their religious beliefs as the Protestants have to diffuse their principles."

THE PRESENT STATUS OF THE REPUBLIC.
—A great advance in industrial and commercial resources has been made since the more complete establishment of the republican government in 1867 at the close of the Maximilian empire. The cause of public education has also greatly advanced since the separation of church and state. It certainly is not creditable to the Roman Catholic Church, which for more than three centuries had held dominion over the country, that the breaking of its dominion was the signal for a great advance in the education of the people. In the year 1857 the University of Mexico was abolished, and was replaced by special schools of law, medicine, letters, agriculture, mines, science, and a military college. There are now said to be 200 schools of the lower class in the capital alone, where formerly there were innumerable pageants and the constant din of church and convent bells, but very little that could promote the intelligence of the people. All this is changed.

In 1886 there were in the republic 11,000 primary schools with 600,000 pupils. Of these schools 9,236, with 470,000 scholars, were sustained by the federal or state governments, or by municipalities. The Lancasterian Society had 39 schools with 5,000 students; the Catholic parishes maintained about 1,000 schools with 100,000 children; the Protestant societies and missions were credited with 260 schools with 12,000 pupils, and there were 731 private schools in the republic with 26,000 pupils. There are not far from 2,500,000 persons in Mexico who can read and write. Mexico can now boast a larger proportion of her whole population in school than Austria, Greece, Portugal, or Brazil.

In an article entitled "Europeans in Mexico," published in November, 1882, by Señor Romero, Mexican Minister to the United States, he says in regard to his country: "From a bigoted, intolerant country, it has been changed into a liberal, progressive nation, and this could not have been effected without great effort, and without commotion and bloodshed to some extent. Neither England, nor France, nor other countries standing now at the head of the civilized world, could establish civil and religious freedom without revolution and bloodshed; but, once accomplished, all the purposes of revolution—freedom of religion, freedom of education, equality before the law, trial by jury, etc.—established, there is no political reason for revolution."

In an official report to the State Department of the United States, dated December 23d, 1882, Hon. David H. Strother, United States consul-general at the city of Mexico, said: "After fifty years of almost continuous wars and revolutions, the party of liberal opinions has at last definitely triumphed. The results of this triumph have been the complete separation of church and state, and the absolute subjection of the ecclesiastical to the civil authority; a political constitution based on the broadest republican principles; a free press, free schools, and universal religious toleration. Indeed the laws of the reform proclaimed in 1857, under Comonfort, and executed by Benito Juarez in 1867, after the downfall of the empire, are more thorough and radical in their character than those promulgated by any government of modern times."

All that was said of the stability and prosperity of the country in 1882 has been more than verified in the subsequent years. The railroad systems which had then connected the chief cities with the great lines of international traffic have been extended in all directions, and have given decided impulse to commerce, mining, and manufactures.

The country has so long been exempt from serious political disturbances, that the confidence of capitalists has been fully established, and the wealth which springs up with stable government has of itself become a strong conservative factor, and a new warrant for future prosperity.

The capitalists of the country cannot afford the luxury of the old-time pronunciamento, and they are now a more influential class than the impecunious adventurers who follow political revolution as a profession.

The Catholic party have not ceased to re-echo the old cry of "patriotism" as a means of opposition to Protestant missions and all American influence, but the most enlightened statesmen have learned long ere this, that Protestantism is a better friend to Mexico than the Papacy. Nothing is more foreign to the purpose of Protestant missions than to promote annexation to the United States. The more free thought and general enlightenment of the people are promoted, the better are they prepared to maintain their independence. Such a result is the desire and hope of all Protestant missionaries for Mexico.

*The Era of Protestant Missions.*—For the beginning of the Protestant movement, we must go back to a period anterior to the proclamation of religious liberty. The seed-sowing of the truth followed immediately the rude ploughshare of the so-called Mexican war. The Bible was borne into the country by General Scott's army. This divine talisman, that had wrought such marvels in the civil and religious institutions of the Northern republic, was a stranger on Mexican soil. It was as novel as a falling meteor from another planet. The simple truths of the gospel were received by the people with a sort of hunger.

The American Bible Society had from an early period cherished a deep interest in Mexico, but almost nothing could then be done for the spread of the truth. But after the Mexican war direct effort was made to introduce the Word of God.

Rev. Mr. Thompson was employed as a Bible agent in Brownsville in 1860. Bible distribution was carried on in connection with the missionary work of Miss Melinda Rankin in Brownsville, Texas, in 1854. In 1866 she established a school in Monterey, Mexico. As an example of the way in which this word found its way and began to work like leaven, we may cite Ville de Cos, a mining community, in the State of Zacatecas.

An "ecclesia" like those of New Testament times was formed in a private house, where people met to read the Word of God in secret. The proclamation of liberty of thought in 1857 gave them courage, and the little company grew in numbers and in knowledge. Sending to Monterey for a clergyman, they received the rite of baptism, and organized themselves into a church.

They appointed one of their own number to conduct services and administer the sacraments. They were instructed and variously assisted from time to time by Dr. G. W. Provost, an American physician of Zacatecas. By the year 1872 they had erected a church, and the number of communicants had risen to over a hundred.

A similar example of the leaven of Bible-distribution was found years later in Zitacuaro, in the State of Michoacan. A Presbyterian native preacher, Rev. Mr. Forcada, on commencing missionary work at that point in 1877, learned that a Bible depository had been opened there by a Mexican six years before, and that four hundred Bibles and many religious tracts had been sold. Thus the way had been prepared for an unexpected welcome to the missionary, and a most gratifying success. At present, within a radius of forty miles, there are sixteen congregations of Protestant Christians.

*Undenominational Missionary Work.* — Through the influence of Miss Rankin at Monterey the attention of Rev. Henry A. Riley was called to Mexico as a promising missionary field, and in 1869 he proceeded to the capital, where he found the harvest ripe beyond his expectations. He began his labors under the auspices of the American and Foreign Christian Union, and he succeeded in purchasing at a low price a valuable confiscated church property. Meanwhile an important movement had already begun in the city of Mexico, where a few prominent priests openly avowed their renunciation of the Roman Catholic dogmas and corruptions.

The first was Francisco Aguilas, a man of great fervor and eloquence. Alarmed at his boldness and success, a fellow-priest, Manuel Aguas, set out to prepare himself to refute the teachings of Aguilas, who had already been joined and encouraged by Mr. Riley. While Aguas pursued his investigations in search of arguments, he himself became a convert, and a most successful preacher of the gospel. Unfortunately for the cause which they had espoused, both of these eloquent men died after a brief career. The converts who were gathered by Father Aguas were organized into a church based upon the doctrines and order of American Episcopacy, and known as the Church of Jesus.

This church now reports "29 mission stations, served by five ministers (of whom 4 are natives) and 9 teachers (of whom 6 are natives). It embraces about 700 communicants and 2,700 members. In the mission schools there are 68 boarders and 121 day scholars. Mrs. M. J. Hooker is in charge of the girls' orphanage, and Mr. Hernandez in charge of the training school."

The Advisory Committee in the United States, appointed by the Right Rev. H. C. Potter, D.D., L.L.D., Bishop of New York, consists of Revs. Henry Y. Satterlee (president); Geo. F. Flichtner (secretary); G. Williamson Smith, J. H. Eccleston, David H. Greer; lay members, Thos. P. Fowler, Alexander Orr, E. P. Dutton and John H. Boynton (treasurer).

*The Missions of the Presbyterian Church (North).* — In 1872 the Presbyterians sent three men and four ladies to establish stations at San Luis Potosi and Zacatecas. While stopping at the capital they were requested to adopt and assist a congregation then worshipping under the care of a convert from Romanism, Senor Palacios.

This led to the establishment of a station in Mexico City. In January, 1873, Rev. M. N. Hutchinson and wife were sent to take charge of the station. Rev. Henry C. Thomson was in the beginning stationed at San Luis Potosi and Rev. Messrs. Paul Pitkin and Maxwell Phillips and their wives established themselves at Zacatecas, where a prosperous work had already been begun by Dr. G. W. Provost. The Presbyterian Mission in Mexico has had a checkered history, often diversified by persecution, mob violence, and martyr deaths. In two instances the lives of missionaries have been attempted, but in both the mob failed of their purpose. Many native Christians, however, and three or four native preachers, have fallen as martyrs to their faith. In all cases the ignorant murderers have been instigated by the priests, who were only careful to accomplish their murderous purposes in such a way as to save themselves from the hands of justice.

Characteristic features of the Presbyterian Mission have been the large number and the ability of its native ministry. A prosperous theological seminary is now conducted by Rev. Messrs. Thomson and Brown at Tlalpam, twelve miles from the capital. Two flourishing girls' seminaries are also in full operation — one in Mexico City under the care of Misses Bartlett and De Baun, the other conducted by Wheeler and Elliott at Saltillo. This institution has sprung from the germ planted by Miss Melinda Rankin at Monterey. It was placed by her under the care of the American Board of Foreign Missions, by which it was subsequently transferred to the Presbyterian Board.

The present statistics of the Presbyterian Mission in Mexico are as follows:

Ordained missionaries, 7; lady missionary helpers, 4; ordained natives, 25; licentiates, 25; native preachers and helpers, 53; churches, 90; communicants, 5,165; added during the year, 388; boarding-schools, 2, with 88 pupils; day-schools, 40, for boys and girls, with 1,270 pupils; theological seminaries, 1, with 15 students; pupils in Sabbath-schools, 1,709; contributions, $3,627. The press, under the able management of Dr. J. M. Green, has issued 13,000,000 pages during the year, and the bi-weekly paper, "El Faro," has been widely read. The missions of the Board extend to 12 States.

*Mission of the Methodist Episcopal Church (North).* — This mission was established in 1873 in Mexico City. Fortunate purchases of property were secured at an early day in the capital, at Puebla, Cordova, Pachuca, and at other important points. The policy pursued has been the always wise one of laying strong and permanent foundations. Great attention has been paid to education and to the work of the press. An attractive illustrated Christian paper has been among the most effective agencies. The Mexican report of the Missionary Society of the Methodist Episcopal Church (North) for January, 1890, gives: foreign missionaries, 10; assistant missionaries, 9; missionaries of the Woman's Foreign Missionary Board, 8; native ordained preachers, 10; native unordained preachers, 27; foreign teachers, 3; native teachers, 26; workers of the Woman's Foreign Missionary Society, 27; other helpers, 27; communicants, 1,286; probationists, 757; adherents, 4,599; converts during year, 120; adults baptized, 143; infants baptized, 123; theological seminaries, 1, with 2 instructors and 5 students; high-schools, 3, with 12 teachers and 147 pupils; day-schools, 36, with 2,199 pupils; churches and chapels, 19. The press has issued over 3,000,000 pages. The estimated value of churches and chapels is $89,200; there are 35 places of worship and 15 parsonages. Parsonage property is reported at $100,800; property in orphanages, hospitals, schools, etc., $106,240; making a total of nearly $300,000 ; 8 different states are occupied.

*The Methodist Church (South)*.—This branch of the Methodist Episcopal Church began missionary work in the city of Mexico in 1873, under the general direction of Bishop Keener. Olijo Hernandez, a converted Mexican, was an active laborer. Rev. J. T. Davis was soon appointed. In 1878 W. M. Patterson, D.D., was appointed superintendent of the mission. Evangelistic work has been pushed forward with great vigor. It has greatly multiplied its stations, and the number of its evangelists—not without corresponding results. Its roll of communicants is relatively large. The reports of 1888 show in the Central and the Border Mission: missionaries, 10; native preachers of all grades, 89; communicants, 3,095; Sunday-schools, 90; 17 States are occupied.

*The American Board Mission*.—The opening history of the work of this Board in Mexico was marked by sad disaster. Its first missionary, Mr. Stevens, was killed by a mob at Almaluco in 1874. One of his first converts shared his martyr's crown. Nevertheless a strong mission has grown up from that sanguinary beginning. The American Board has 16 missionaries, 10 churches, 323 communicants, of whom 74 were received last year, 6 schools, with 176 pupils.

*The Southern Baptist Convention* reported in its missions in Mexico in 1889, 15 missionaries including wives of missionaries and unmarried ladies. Its stations are located in the States of Coahuila, Zacatecas, Aguascalientes and Jalisco. The statistics of the work show 16 churches, with 572 communicants, and 102 pupils in schools. This mission has not escaped the fires of persecution. Many assailments have been made with a view of breaking up its religious services, and in December, 1881, Rev. J. D. Westrup, a newly appointed missionary, was murdered by the Indians. On the other hand, this mission has received some special encouragements. The governor of Coahuila has shown much sympathy with its efforts in the line of female education. A large and flourishing girls' school is now maintained at Saltillo.

*The Presbyterian Church (South)* has a mission in Mexico in which, according to the report for 1889, there are 6 missionaries, including ladies—communicants, 400; native ministers, 8; pupils in day-schools, 150; Sunday-school pupils, 250; contributions, $875. Its chief work is on or near the northern border. The stations are Brownsville, Matamoras, Montemorelos and Linares.

*The Society of Friends* established a mission in Mexico in 1871. It is now carrying forward work in the state of Tamaulipas.

*The Associated Reformed Presbyterian Synod of the South* has also a mission extending to two of the Mexican States.

There are in all 150 foreign Protestant missionaries in the country, 360 native laborers, 400 congregations, 15,000 communicants, 4,000 pupils in schools, and 6,000 Sunday-school pupils.

**Mexico**, the capital of the republic of Mexico, is beautifully situated on a plateau 7,500 feet above the level of the sea, in the Tenochtitlan valley, not far from the lake Tezcuco. Population, 241,100 (1880), comprising Spaniards, Aztec Indians, and all gradations of mixed races. In the midst of lofty mountains, the climate is temperate and healthy. The streets are well-paved, broad, and well-lighted, and raised paved roads, called *paseos*, which lead out into the country, and are shaded on either side by fine trees, add much to the natural beauties of the place. The Roman Catholic religion is the state religion, but other religions are tolerated. In addition to the many churches, monasteries, convents, and other religious or benevolent institutions are plentiful. Schools and colleges, theatres, and the buildings for the government offices give the city the usual modern appearance. Street railways are in operation. Of the railroads, the Mexican Central, Mexican National, Mexican, and Morelos railroads run into the city. Protestantism is represented by the following missions: Methodist Episcopal Church. (South) (1886); 3 missionaries and their wives, 21 outstations; 17 churches, 445 communicants, 18 Sunday-schools, 337 scholars, 7 other schools, 269 students, 1 theological seminary, 10 students, 5 girls' schools, 110 scholars. Methodist Episcopal Church (North). 1873; 1 missionary and wife, 2 other ladies, 219 church-members, 145 Sabbath-scholars, 128 day-scholars. Presbyterian Church (North); 2 missionaries and wives, 2 other ladies, 2 native preachers.

**Meyer, Philip Lewis Henry**, b. at Neuwied-on-the-Rhine, Germany, November 13th, 1826, of earnest Christian parents. At his confirmation in 1840 the love of Christ mightily took possession of his heart. Successively a cabinet-maker, a school-teacher, a student of medicine, he was thus variously qualified for mission service, and received a call to South Africa in 1854. He was ordained July 16th, 1854, married Louisa Gregor, daughter of a missionary, and reached Cape Town November 3d the same year. He found the mission stations at Shiloh and Goshen in ashes by a recent Kafir war, and commenced rebuilding at once, studying the Kafir language, teaching the natives handicraft, and inculcating gospel truths. In 1859 he built a new station, not far from Shiloh, in a plain watered by the river Engoti, and called it Engotine. "The desert was changed into a beautiful village surrounded with gardens and fields, and the outward change was a type of the spiritual transformation." Now he might be seen at the hardest manual labor, now hastening to a Kafir kraal to tell the glad tidings of salvation. Disease and drought brought great hardship to the natives, in which the missionaries gladly shared, seeing that the Lord used these means to open the hearts of the people to their influence, and the reception of the gospel. In 1869 a call came from Zibi, chief of the Hlubi Kafirs, 240 miles from Engotine, to come and teach his people. Receiving this as a call from the Lord, he set out with Samuel and Luke, native Christians. They went through great dangers and hardships to settle with him. War followed, and its worst perils threatened them. The chief and people, after being routed, forsook the region, and for two years the missionary and his family dwelt in solitude, except as Mr. Meyer went from time to time to preach to the chief and his people in their mountain fastnesses. A great work of grace followed, and when peace was restored many from neighboring tribes came to listen to the gospel. A church-building was erected, a church formed, a school followed; in all things the missionary was friend and counsellor, and his house was thronged with people seeking advice in things spiritual and temporal. Mr. Meyer was permitted to found one more mission, but his health failed, and he was obliged to return to Europe. After severe suffering he received his release at Marburg, Germany, August 2d, 1876.

**Mhow** (Mhau), city in Malwa, Central India, 13½ miles from the city of Indore. Population, 27,227. Hindus, Moslems, etc. Mission station Methodist Episcopal Church (North); 2 missionaries, 11 native helpers, 2 schools, 95 scholars, 19 church-members. Presbyterian Church in Canada; 1 missionary, 2 ladies, 300 Sabbath-scholars, 320 day-scholars.

**Micronesia,** a section of Australasia, north of the equator and between 130° and 180° east longitude, including the Gilbert (Kingsmill), Marshall (Mulgrave), and Caroline Islands, the Marianas (or Ladrones), and Bonin Island, the Radack and Ralick chains, and many other small atolls and groups. These latter have been colonized by the Spaniards, and the native races are nearly extinct. With few exceptions the islands are low atolls of coral formation. The groups vary in extent—from the single islet half a mile long to the extensive archipelago enclosed by a coral reef 200 miles or more in circumference. The depth of the island-studded lagoon thus enclosed varies from 5 to 100 fathoms. Some islands are accessible to the largest ships, having good channels through breaks in the reef, and furnishing commodious harbors; while some have channels which cannot be entered with the prevailing winds, and others are entirely enclosed by reefs and have no anchorage. Ocean currents with frequent calms render navigation very uncertain and often dangerous. The area of land in any of these atolls is insignificant compared with the size of the lagoon or the extent of the supporting reef. The land, ranging in elevation from 5 to 20 feet above high-water mark, is composed of coral rocks and sand washed up by the waves, and forms a series of islets resting at varying distances from one another upon the reef. At high tide the waves roll over the reef at a depth of 4 to 10 feet and between the islets into the lagoon, while at ebb tide the reef is bare, and furnishes a connecting pathway from islet to islet, except where it is broken by a channel. (Ebon, of the Marshall Islands, for example, is a ring of reef 25 miles in circumference. Upon it rest 18 islets, the longest being about 6 miles and the shortest but a few yards in length, while the width of land averages about one half mile, and the fringe of reef on either side is 1 or 2 furlongs more.) Some of the islets are 20 miles in length, and in some cases there are long stretches of reef with no land upon it. The average area of land in the atolls is probably from 5 to 10 square miles.

The flora of the atolls is exceedingly poor, but varies according to situation with reference to the belt of precipitation. The cocoa-nut palm abounds everywhere, and thrives even where the roots are washed by the sea-water.

It furnishes the natives food, shelter, and sometimes clothing. It is the principal article of commerce, copra being shipped in large quantities from all the islands. The pandanus is also found everywhere, and furnishes food in its season; while the leaf, green and ripe, is used for braiding mats, hats, sails, etc., and is the principal roofing material on the atolls. Except on the Gilbert Islands, the bread-fruit is plentiful, and bananas are cultivated. The timber of the bread-fruit is valuable for the construction of canoes and for some building purposes. A coarse kind of taro is also cultivated. The islands are all wooded, and those within the belt of constant precipitation have a dense growth of (mostly) low trees and shrubs. On some there are wells rising and falling with the tides, but foreigners depend upon rain-water, there being no fresh-water streams.

The high islands of volcanic origin are Kusaie (or Strong's Island), 2,300 feet; Ponape (Ascension), 2,800 feet; Ruk (Hogolu); and Yap. These have the physical peculiarities of the atolls, only that the lagoon is replaced by elevated land. Ruk is an immense lagoon about 100 miles by 40, with 10 large islands (some nearly 300 feet high), and many islets. These are very fertile, and are well supplied with food. Besides the flora already enumerated, we find on the high islands yams, taro, pineapples, sweet potatoes, sugar-cane, and a great variety of bananas. Many tropical trees and plants have been introduced, and all the tropical flora would flourish. On Ponape and Kusaie are many beautiful streams and cascades, furnishing abundance of pure water. The fauna of the atolls consists of a few birds (mostly aquatic), lizards, and rats. Pigs and chickens have been introduced, and everywhere thrive. The fauna of the high islands is much richer, including many varieties of birds, some of beautiful plumage and some good for food. Pigs and chickens have there relapsed into the wild state. Dogs and cats have been introduced, but deteriorate rapidly. Goats thrive and cattle to some extent, but only on the high islands. The temperature ranges from 72° to 90°. (On Apaiang, 80° to 90°; Ebon, 75° to 87°; Ponape, 74° to 87°.) Fish are taken in great abundance in their seasons, and the most beautiful shells in the world are found on the reefs. The people are of the brown Polynesian race, but bear traces of a constant addition from a variety of sources. The languages are quite distinct in the different groups, but have some peculiarities pointing to a common origin. They are simple in construction, easily acquired, yet quite difficult to reduce to writing because of the shading of sounds, and also on account of the presence of close consonants at the end of words. Five of these languages have been reduced to writing. Portions of the Bible, hymn-books, and various school-books have been printed. Some of the dialects are very expressive, and though not having extended vocabularies, are rendered flexible by the use of pronominal suffixes, verbal directives, and terminations to indicate place and to express comparison. Degraded in past usage, the introduction of Christian ideas means resurrection to the language no less than life to the people.

The religion of the islanders was not greatly unlike modern spiritism, and their social usages imposed no family ties. Polygamy was tolerated among the chiefs, but not very extensively practised. No marriage ceremony was known. Men and women lived together until the caprice of one or the other separated them. The children belong as much to all the sisters of the mother and brothers of the father as to their own parents; and the children of brothers or of sisters continue to be counted brothers and sisters through all generations. The chiefs received their rank from the mother. On Ponape and some other islands the language varies in its use, according to the rank of the one addressed.

The forms of government varied, but were all founded on the idea of the aggrandizement of the chief rather than the good of the subject. Human life was lightly regarded, and even petty chiefs sent many a victim to the executioner.

Licentiousness prevailed, and chastity was almost unknown. The seeds of disease planted in such soil by vile white men resulted in such a spread of disease that none escaped, and the taint reappears in the successive generations. Cannibalism was not practised, except on rare occasions in time of war.

The people wore little if any clothing, though the habits of different groups show great variety. In the Gilbert Islands men had no covering of any kind; the women wore a fringed skirt 10 or 12 inches long, the children being nude. In the Marshall Islands men wore a fringe skirt 25 to 30 inches long, and the women two mats, about a yard square each, belted about the waist. Upon the Caroline Islands some covering was used. The dwelling-houses were mere shelters of simple construction, though the council-houses were large. Their canoes vary greatly in construction. Those of the Marshall and Mortlock Islands are large, and adapted to making long sea-voyages. An outrigger is always used. These sea-going crafts were all of hewn timber, the pieces fitted together and fastened with cord made of the cocoa-nut fibre. Ropes were made of the same and the sails of matting. The natives were skilful navigators, some of them seeming to have an intuitive perception of locality, and an instinct of the proximity of land while yet many miles out of sight of it; yet whole fleets have been often lost, and canoes sometimes drift about for days and weeks to reach land at last hundreds of miles from home. Such occurrences suggest how the islands may have been peopled at first, and account for the mixed character of the population. Missionary work was begun on Ponape and Kusaie (Caroline group) in 1852 by three American missionaries (L. H. Gulick, A. A. Sturges, and B. G. Snow) with their wives. They were accompanied by two Hawaiian missionary helpers with their wives. The first five years were discouraging. Many times the enterprise seemed ready to fail. Opposition of foreigners (self-exiled and more degraded than the natives), small-pox on Ponape, insurrection on Kusaie, disastrous results of contact with the whaling fleets, and the dense paganism of the natives themselves had all to be overcome by the faith of earnest men. Three more missionaries (G. Pierson, E. T. Doane, and H. Bingham) with their wives joined the mission, and the first "Morning Star" was built. The year 1857 saw Apaiang (Gilbert Islands), Ebon (Marshall Islands), and Kusaie and Ponape (Caroline Islands) occupied by six mission families with two Hawaiian helpers.

During the next five years (1857 to 1862) the harvest began. Three churches were organ-

ized. The one on Kusaie, with 30 members, was left in care of a native helper. The missionary force was reduced to three men with their wives and five Hawaiian assistants. During the next nine years the work of teaching, translating, and laying foundations went on. The churches on Kusaie and Ponape witnessed a steady growth. Five of the Marshall and five of the Gilbert Islands were occupied by Hawaiian missionaries under the direction of the Board of the Hawaiian Evangelical Association (see Hawaiian Board). In 1870 the number of church-members was as follows: Ponape, 250; Kusaie, 226; Marshall Islands, 140; Gilbert Islands, 51: a total of 667. There had been printed for these missions nearly 2,500,000 pages of Scripture, hymn-books, etc. (2,408,218; viz., Ponape, 381,-600; Kusaie, 223,200; Marshall Islands, 381,726; and for Gilbert Islands, 1,050,192).

From 1869, when the second "Morning Star" was wrecked, till 1871, there was only one white missionary in the field (Rev. E. T. Doane, Ponape). This was a time of preparation for the advance to be made during the next decade.

In 1871 the third "Morning Star" carried as passengers from Honolulu the three veterans, Messrs. Sturges, Snow, and Bingham, one new family from America (F. T. Whitney and wife), and three Hawaiians—these last for Gilbert Islands. In 1873 the "Morning Star" visited the Mortlock Islands and stationed three Ponapeans with their wives, inaugurating that movement which in later years yielded such wonderful results.

In 1874 three more men (H. J. Taylor for Gilbert Islands, R. W. Logan and F. E. Rand for Ponape) with their wives joined the mission. More attention was given to establishing training-schools and developing the native agency. In 1877 E. M. Pease, M.D., and wife were sent to take the place of Mr. Snow, who was taken from the work by a paralytic stroke; and in 1880 A. C. Walkup and wife accompanied Mr. Taylor, returning to his work on the Gilbert Islands. The same year the Marshall Islands training-school was removed to Kusaie. The reports for 1880 give nearly 2,000 church-members, 45 pupils in the two training-schools, and 1,500 in other schools.

During the last decade there has been a constant increase of both hearers and converts. The training-school for the Gilbert Islands was removed to Kusaie. Girls' schools were established at Kusaie and Ponape under the care of lady missionaries sent out by the various woman's boards. Political changes during this period greatly affected the missions. In 1885 Germany annexed the Marshall Islands. She attempted at the same time to take possession of the Caroline Islands, but was prevented by Spain's claim of long standing. The Spanish occupation of Ponape resulted in such acts of injustice and persecution that the natives arose in self-defence. The governor had already sent one of the American missionaries (Rev. E. T. Doane) to Manila under arrest. When he was released and returned to Ponape it was found that the governor and many of his soldiers had been slain, and the natives were in possession of the Spanish quarters. A new governor was sent out, who, after investigating the matter, recognized the injustice of his predecessor, and proposed terms that the mission was able to indorse, and thus peace was restored without further bloodshed. The scattered churches were gathered again, and the schools opened; some of the converts under pressure renounced the truth, but the steadfast faith of many of them greatly encouraged the missionaries.

In the Marshall Islands the German rule is oppressive. The heavy taxation is impoverishing the people, while frequently the assertion of their rights by the people is regarded as an offence, and punished with heavy fines. The result so far of foreign intervention has not been beneficial to the natives. The sale of liquor, tobacco, and firearms by unscrupulous foreigners, both before and since annexation, has fostered old and developed new vices among the people.

The latest reports of the mission (January, 1890) give a total membership of 4,509; three training-schools with 79, and 48 other schools with 2,035 pupils.

The estimated population of Micronesia is 84,000: Gilbert Islands, 25,000; Marshall Islands, 15,000; Ponape and adjacent islands using the same language, 5,000; Ruk and Mortlocks, 15,000; islands lying between Ruk and Yap, 7,000; Yap, 10,000; Palau, 7,000. Of these perhaps 50,000 have heard the gospel; about 8,000 have become converts, and twice as many more call themselves Christians. This work has been accomplished in less than 40 years. There have been employed of American missionaries and assistants a total of 40, viz., 15 ordained missionaries, 17 wives of missionaries, and 8 single women. Three missionaries and 5 wives of missionaries have died; 6 missionaries, 6 wives of missionaries, and 1 single woman have withdrawn. The present force (May, 1890) is 20, of whom 2 are at the Hawaiian Islands, and 6 others are in America on account of failure of health.

The changes which have been wrought through the efforts of the missionaries are truly wonderful. The transforming power of the Word of God has never been more manifest than in this field. There has been a marked development of stability in the character of the natives. Formerly they were dishonest and untruthful. There was a belief among them that the Great Spirit used deceitful means for the accomplishment of His plans or for maintaining His authority, and the people accordingly cultivated deceit. Ships were often pillaged and the crews murdered. But the gospel has in many islands effected a complete revolution. Social ideas have been changed. The family has been built up, and the ceremony of marriage is becoming more and more common. The practice of family worship has done much to purify and crystallize social ideas, and a strong sentiment of his duty to guard the household and defend his family from the lust of even the chiefs is rising in the mind of the head of the household.

Drunkenness has prevailed to some extent on all the islands—more on the Gilbert Islands than elsewhere. On the Marshall Islands this vice was unknown until the advent of foreigners, and became prevalent only after many years of contact with them. Prohibitory enactments have been made by some of the chiefs of the Marshall Islands against the traffic in ardent spirits. These still serve a salutary purpose, though they have been greatly modified and weakened under German rule. Some of the disputes with the German authorities have grown out of the desire of the natives to stop the traffic in fermented as well as distilled liquors.

Better dwellings, greater personal cleanliness, and tidiness have also followed the moral reformation. Intellectual progress is quite marked. The schools are well attended. Native teachers have done very efficient work. The mother-tongue has become the vehicle of blessing. From the first a missionary spirit has been cultivated, and the young convert has been taught to keep in view the prospect of becoming a teacher of the new doctrine on his own island, or, if need be, on other islands. When the work was to be pushed westward from Ponape it was done by native missionaries, furnishing one of the most interesting chapters in the annals of missionary work. Going forth to a people of diverse tongue, these men and women prepared themselves for the work, and soon gathered in large numbers of converts.

The type of Christianity on the islands is eminently biblical. The Word of God is held in great reverence. The instability of native character is often exhibited by the converts, and large numbers have retrograded, usually, however, to return with a juster estimate of their weakness and a humbler and more tenacious trust in God.

The "Morning Star," provided by the Sabbath-school children of America and thrice rebuilt, has been an invaluable aid to the missionary work.

**Midnapur,** a town of India, 70 miles west of Calcutta. Climate hot. Population, 33,624. Race and language, Bengali Santhal. Religion, Hindu. Social condition of the masses, corrupt, ignorant, very poor. Station of the Bengal Mission American Free Baptists, occupied 1844, reopened 1863; 3 missionaries and wives, 2 other ladies, 4 out-stations, 462 adherents, 6 churches, 245 communicants, 17 additions in 1888, 2 preaching places, 150 average attendance, 2 ordained preachers, 5 unordained, 6 Sabbath-schools, 2,268 scholars, 1 theological seminary, 1 female school, 516 scholars, 1 other school, 73 scholars.

**Midyat,** a town of Koordistan, in the Jebel Tur district, about 50 miles northeast of Mardin. The people are a hardy, energetic race, belonging to the old Jacobite (Monophysite) Church, and speaking both Arabic and Koordish. Mission work among them, conducted by the missionaries of the A. B. C. F. M. at Mardin, has been very successful. Schools have been established and a flourishing church formed.

**Mier,** a town of the Tamaulipas district, Mexico. Mission station of the Methodist Episcopal Church (South).

**Mikmak Version.**—The Mikmak belongs to the American languages, and is used by the Mikmak Indians of Nova Scotia. The Gospels of Matthew and John were published by the British and Foreign Bible Society in 1854. Two years later the Gospel of Luke, prepared by the Rev. S. T. Rand, was published at Halifax; and in 1871 there were printed at the same place the Book of Exodus, the Epistles to the Romans, Galatians, and Hebrews, by the same person.

(*Specimen verse.* John 3 : 16.)

Mŭdu Nicscąm teliksatcuə məsitcumŭ · wedjį
igunum-ŭedəgub-unŭ nɛukţu-bistadjul ŭewisul,
cŭląmąn m'sit wen tąn kedlamsito ŭtįnincu, mą
mnŭmadtjinpŭc, cądŭ uscərtʋ apçŭąwɛ mįmadjŭocuɱ.

## Mildmay Missions.

Headquarters, the Conference Hall, Mildmay Park, London, England.—The work of the Mildmay Mission radiates from the "Conference Hall," near Mildmay Park, the corner-stone of which was laid, 4th August, 1869, by the founder and superintendent of the work, the Rev. William Pennefather, Vicar of St. Jude's, Mildmay Park. The first "Conferences," which led to the formation of the mission, assembled at Barnet in 1856. The "Iron Room," in which they were held, was afterwards removed to London, and used as a conference hall for many years, giving place in 1870 to the larger hall. The main object of this hall, which seats 2,500 people, is to provide a place for holding conferences, but it is also designed to be a centre of union for Christians of all denominations, and to facilitate the prosecution of a variety of evangelistic and missionary enterprises.

The large hall is used for preaching every Sunday afternoon and evening throughout the year, and for many public and evangelistic meetings: the five basement rooms are used for Bible-classes and special services, including one for deaf-mutes on Sundays, and for unceasing efforts during the week to benefit the poor, both temporally and spiritually. Adjoining the hall, on the west, is the Deaconess House, the centre for an extensive field of "woman's work." The deaconesses reside on the premises, and without taking vows give their whole time to ministry among the poor and ignorant, their work comprising house-to-house visitation, mothers' meetings, night-schools, and classes of many kinds, conducted in some room or house set apart for the purpose; these missions are at Bethnal Green, Hackney Road, Hoxton, Pentonville, Caledonian Road, St. James's, Islington, Stratford, West Ham, Lambeth, Bermondsey, Old Kent Road, etc., etc. Others, south of the river, are worked in connection with a Branch Deaconess House at Brixton, established in 1879, in response to appeals from ministers in South London; it is on the same plan and under the same supervision as that at Mildmay. An important branch of the Mildmay work is the home for nurses in Mildmay Road, whence trained nurses are sent to hospitals in London and provincial towns, and to private cases and other work, as directed.

Opposite the Nursing Home is the Cottage Hospital, with ten beds for the reception of patients from the parish of St. Jude. Other branches of work are the Home for Invalid Ladies, the Orphanage, Invalids' Kitchen, Dorcas Society, Servants' Registry, and Mothers' Meeting.

A Men's Night-school is held in one of the rooms in the Conference Hall. The 46 classes are taught by ladies; the branches taught range from the most elementary to the higher branches of general and practical knowledge. Coffee and bread and butter may be purchased by scholars before leaving. A Lending Library is attached to the school. The highest attendance in 1888 was 570, the lowest 443. In connection with the work carried on by the deaconesses in one of the poorest parts of Bethnal Green is the Medical Mission, opened in 1875. Its hospital contains 30 beds, and out-patients are cared for two days weekly. Attached to this mission are a coffee-house and a lodging-house for men, which is almost always full. In other localities, too, coffee-houses have been opened, with comfortable sitting and reading rooms, library, etc.

Missions to cabmen and to railway employés are carried on. "Special Teas" are provided for policemen, postmen, cabmen, etc. The Bible Flower Mission, established in 1876, has now four depots in London. From the depot at Conference Hall from 1,500 to 2,000 bouquets, with Scripture texts, are sent out weekly to the hospitals and infirmaries assigned to it. The Mildmay Mission to the Jews was commenced in 1876; it embraces a medical mission, services in Hebrew twice a week, sewing-meetings for Jewesses, a night-school for Jewish children, etc. An itinerant mission to Jews living in towns and cities of Great Britain is a distinct feature of the mission. Hebrew New Testaments are distributed in Russia, Austria, Hungary, Galicia, Morocco, etc., and grants are made to missionaries of other societies in all parts of the world.

The Medical Mission at Jaffa is under the care of Mildmay (see Jaffa Medical Mission and Hospital). The Mildmay Association for Female Workers has now 1,400 members, many of whom reside in distant parts of the earth.

From £22,000 to £24,000 is required annually for the whole work of the mission, of which Jas. E. Mathieson, Esq., is the present superintendent.

## Mills, Cyrus Taggart,

b. Paris, N. Y., U. S. A., May 14th, 1819. From the day of his conversion, at the age of nineteen, he dedicated himself to the missionary work. He graduated at Williams College 1844, and Union Theological Seminary, New York, 1847. While pursuing his theological course he was active in mission work among the poor of the city. He also studied the Tamil language a year with a returned missionary from Ceylon. In September, 1848, he was married to Miss Susan Tolman of Ware, who had been for six years in Mount Holyoke Seminary with Miss Mary Lyon as pupil and teacher. Sailed October 10th, the same year, as a missionary of the A. B. C. F. M. for Ceylon. He was appointed, by the Jaffna Mission, Professor in the Batticotta Seminary in 1848, and in 1849 succeeded Mr. Hoisington as president, which position he filled till 1853, when utter failure of health compelled him to resign and return home. He spent two years in the service of the board among the churches; was settled as pastor in Berkshire, N. Y. His health again failed, and resigning his charge, he spent two years in business in Ware, Mass., in which he was successful. Dr. Mark Hopkins having suggested him as a suitable person for the presidency of Oahu College, Honolulu, Hawaiian Islands, he was appointed, and in 1860 sailed for that field. This position he held for four years, when ill-health obliged him to resign, and he returned home. In 1865 he purchased Miss Atkins' school at Benicia, California, with which he was connected for seven years. Having purchased land in Oakland that rapidly appreciated, and generous contributions having been made by friends of education to induce him to remove to that city, he decided to erect buildings there, and in 1871 the seminary was reopened in Oakland. In 1877 the seminary was incorporated and deeded by Dr. Mills to a Board of Trustees. He made additions of buildings and improvements until the property increased to the value of $275,000.

About two months before his death he had a severe pain in his right arm, and it was found to be necessary to amputate it to save his life. When the preparations were going forward he was perfectly tranquil, saying to his physician: "I cannot think just now, but I can trust; I am simply clinging to the cross." He seemed to rally for a while after the operation, but soon began to fail, and died April, 1884. The Trustees of Mills Seminary passed the following resolution: "We record our appreciation of the true Christian character and manliness of our deceased friend. Associated with him in our official relations, we bear testimony to the wisdom of his counsels, the soundness of his judgment, his financial skill, his clear foresight, his genial manners, his earnest purposes, and his transparent rectitude." The Presbytery of San Francisco also testified in the highest terms to Dr. Mills' long and useful life in the "active work of the ministry in both the home and foreign mission fields of the church, and an honored career in the grand work of woman's education."

Dr. Mills was honored with the degree of D.D. from Williams College in 1870.

**Mills, Samuel John,** b. at Torringford, Conn., U. S. A., April 21st, 1783, was the son of a minister. He was a subject of earnest Christian instruction and of early deep religious impressions. In childhood he heard his mother say to a friend, "I have consecrated this child to the service of God as a missionary;" and from the time of his conversion he cherished the desire to go to heathen lands to make known the gospel. He entered Williams College in 1806 and graduated in 1809. After entering college he was accustomed to meet with a few students in a grove for prayer and religious conference, and on a memorable afternoon, when driven by a thunderstorm to continue their conference under a haystack, he first suggested the idea of sending the gospel to the benighted portions of the earth, and declared that they could and ought to send them the gospel. They formed a society, whose object was stated to be "to effect in the persons of its members a mission to the heathen." In 1810 he entered Andover Theological Seminary, where he found Hall, Newell, Judson, and Nott deeply interested in the same subject, and with them he united in a memorial to the General Association of Massachusetts soon to meet at Bradford. This memorial led to the formation of the American Board. He was licensed to preach in 1812, and spent two years in the Southern and Western States, distributing Bibles, and organizing Bible and other benevolent societies. On his return he was ordained, June 21st, 1815, and spent the next two years in New York and other cities, laboring to promote the missionary cause. In behalf of the American Colonization Society, in whose organization he largely shared, he was appointed to visit England, and to explore the western

coast of Africa for a site for a colony of colored people from America. Having had extensive intercourse with chiefs, and collected much important and encouraging information, he embarked for home May 22d, 1818. Having taken a severe cold, which was followed by fever, he rapidly declined, till on the 16th of June he ceased to breathe. His body was committed to the ocean near the west coast of Africa.

Though not permitted to engage personally in a foreign mission on which his heart was set, he accomplished much for the conversion of the world. Dr. Griffin, president of the college, speaking of the society formed by him and his associates at Williams College, says: "I have been in situations to know that from the counsels formed in that sacred conclave, or from the mind of Mills himself, arose the American Board of Commissioners for Foreign Missions, the American Bible Society, the United Foreign Missionary Society, and the African School under the care of the Synod of New York and New Jersey; besides all the impetus given to Domestic Missions, to the Colonization Society, and to the general cause of benevolence in both hemispheres." He then adds: "If I had any instrumentality in originating any of those measures, I here publicly declare that in every instance I received the first impulse from Samuel John Mills."

**Millsburg,** town in Monrovia, Liberia, west coast of Africa, on the St. Paul's River, northeast of Clay-Ashland. Mission station Methodist Episcopal Church (North); 2 native workers, 60 church-members.

**Milne, William,** b. Aberdeenshire, Scotland, in 1785. He was converted at the age of sixteen, and joined the church in Huntley. His fixed purpose to engage in missionary work was formed in 1805, at the age of twenty. After this he spent five years in securing a support for his mother and sisters. His early opportunities for education were meagre. Entering the missionary college at Gosport, he went through the regular course of study, under the direction of the Rev. David Bogue. He was ordained in July, 1812, received his appointment to China, married, and sailed for China, arriving at Macao July 4th, 1813, where he was welcomed by Dr. Morrison. China being closed against missionaries, and the Portuguese, who controlled the neighboring islands and points on the mainland, being hostile, he was ordered in ten days to leave Macao.

Leaving Mrs. Milne with Mrs. Morrison, he went to Canton, almost the only place in China where he could remain in safety. Here he remained six months, engaged in the study of the language. The next eight months he spent in a tour through Java and other points of the Indian Archipelago, distributing among Chinese residents copies of the New Testament, and some tracts and catechisms Dr. Morrison had translated into Chinese.

At the end of the eight months' tour he rejoined Dr. Morrison at Canton, September 27th, and spent the winter of 1814 in studying Chinese, and at the same time holding religious service in his own rooms for the foreign residents and sailors. As preaching was prohibited, and little could be done to circulate religious literature in China at that time, it was decided to open a mission to the Chinese in Malacca. Dr.

Milne was appointed to this work, and in 1815 he and his wife went to Penang, taking up their residence at Malacca, where they were received by the Dutch residents, to whom he preached every Sunday. He obtained from the government land for a missionary establishment at Malacca. Soon a free school was established, Christian books were cautiously introduced, and the pupils induced to attend religious service. He began now to publish "The Chinese Monthly Magazine," which was continued till his death, and thousands of copies were circulated through the Chinese communities in the Dutch East Indies and in China also. In 1817 he began to issue an English Quarterly, "The Indo-Chinese Gleaner." He also gave much time and thought to the founding of the Anglo-Chinese College. Dr. Morrison in 1818 gave £1,000 for this object, and a yearly gift of £100 for five years thereafter. But the entire work of planning and executing the details fell to Dr. Milne. The corner-stone was laid at Malacca, November 11th, 1818, and in 1820 the first class was formed. The main work of Dr. Milne from 1815 to the close of his life was the preparation of religious literature. He aided Morrison in the work of translating the Bible into Chinese, the Books of Deuteronomy and onward to Job being translated by him. He prepared also a Commentary on the Epistle to the Ephesians, an "Essay on the Soul," in two volumes, and fifteen tracts, all acceptable to the Chinese. He had great skill and readiness in the use of the language, and in addition to his literary labors performed much evangelistic work. His first convert, Leang-Afa, whom he baptized, was the first ordained Chinese evangelist, and was in the service of the London Missionary Society for many years. The University of Glasgow conferred upon him the degree of doctor of divinity in 1820. Mrs. Milne died in March, 1819, leaving four children, one of whom, William, became a missionary to China in 1839, and labored some years at Ningpo and Shanghai. Dr. Milne's health failing, he took a voyage to Penang, but returned weaker, and died in 1822, at the early age of thirty-seven, and but ten years in the missionary work.

Besides the works mentioned, he published "Retrospect of the Protestant Mission to China."

**Minas Geraës,** town in Brazil, S. A., not far from Rio de Janeiro. Mission station of the Southern Baptist Convention, recently started; 2 missionaries and wives, 1 native preacher.

**Minchinpatna,** a town of Bengal, India, 25 miles from Cuttack. Mission station of the General Baptist Missionary Society (England); 1 native preacher, 31 church-members, 63 scholars.

**Mingrelia,** a district of Asiatic Russia, in the lieutenancy of the Caucasus, lying between Tiflis and the Black Sea. Area, 2,600 square miles. Surface generally mountainous, sloping towards the south. Climate warm and damp; fevers are prevalent; soil exceedingly fertile, and vegetation rapid. The mountains are covered with magnificent forests, and much good land lies waste. The district is without external improvement, and has a savage and deserted appearance. Population, 240,000,

most of whom belong to the Georgian race, but are generally inferior in appearance to the mountaineers of the Caucasus. The dominant religion is that of the Greek Church. Mingrelia corresponds with ancient Colchis. It was long a part of the kingdom of Georgia, was afterwards independent under a long line of native princes, and became subject to Russia in 1804, but its prince remained nominally sovereign till 1867, when he sold all his rights to the emperor of Russia for 1,000,000 roubles.

There is no distinctive mission work carried on among the Mingrelians, though colporteurs of the British and Foreign Bible Society go through the country occasionally.

**Minuangoda,** a town in Kandy district, Ceylon. Station of the Wesleyan Methodist Missionary Society; 1 missionary, 27 church-members, 374 scholars.

**Mirzapur,** city in Northwest Provinces, British India, on the Ganges River, 45 miles west of Benares, 56 southeast of Allahabad. As viewed from the river, the city presents a very striking appearance, exhibiting numerous mosques, Hindu temples, and dwelling-houses of the wealthy merchants, all of which make the town better than many in India. Population, 56,378, Hindus, Moslems, Jains, Christians. Mission station London Missionary Society: 4 missionaries, 3 missionaries' wives, 2 native helpers, 20 church-members, 2 schools, 48 scholars.

**Missionary Conferences.**—When the revival of missions commenced at the close of the last century, the great effort at home was to find enough of those interested in the work to justify making a beginning, and the great aim abroad was to find a field where missionaries could labor unmolested. The whole undertaking was then so novel that those engaged in it had not yet begun to know their ignorance. For to carry on the work of missions with success requires not merely a spirit of obedience to Christ, but some knowledge of the difficulties to be met and the best method of overcoming them, and only an actual advance could indicate the points on which they needed light. They found, moreover, that the further they went on the more the questions multiplied. Even success only furnished new problems to be solved, that had not occurred to them before. For the solution of these they went, first of all, to the Lord Jesus, and then as in apostolic times, when an unlooked-for emergency arose, "the apostles and elders were gathered together to consider the matter" (Acts 15: 6), so now in the constantly recurring inquiries, "How can we remove this evil, and secure that result?" each group of laborers felt the need of counsel from others who encountered similar obstacles. Hence missionary conferences came into existence naturally and unavoidably—now among those laboring in the same heathen land, and now among the societies at home; the former seeking to discover the best ways of presenting the truth to heathen minds, and the latter how to secure the greatest interest in the work among the churches. At first a few deprecated such conventions lest some utopian scheme should be broached by unpractical men, or some impracticable organic union of different societies, instead of the cordial co-operation of independent bodies. These fears happily proved groundless, for those interested in missions are too earnest to be satisfied with anything that does not push forward the work.

The first union missionary conference was held in the United States May 4th, 1854, the various missionary societies then existing there being moved by the presence of the celebrated Dr. Alexander Duff among them to propose such a convention in order to manifest the real unity of Christians, increase interest in the work, and secure a more intelligent co-operation in carrying it on. So 11 missionaries, 18 officers of missionary societies, and 150 persons in all, met in the chapel of Dr. Alexander's church in New York, and continued together a day and a half. They considered the comparative advantages of concentration and diffusion in missionary work on the field, and came to the conclusion that the best way was to equip commanding centres of operation thoroughly, and then operate from those centres by itinerating in the regions round about.

They expressed their satisfaction also that so little interference with each other had occurred among different societies, and recommended that it be understood that as soon as an evangelical society had occupied any field it should be left in undisturbed possession of the ground.

In the matter of raising up candidates they were unanimous in the opinion that much depended on pastors taking an intelligent interest in the work.

The next conference met that same year in London, October 12th and 13th, and was somewhat limited in the range of its discussions, for unfortunately at that time only a few secretaries of missionary societies were able to be present.

*India.*—Another form of missionary conference was inaugurated at the close of that same year. At that same time the American Board sent out its senior secretary, Rev. Rufus Anderson, D.D., with Dr. A. C. Thompson, a member of its Prudential Committee, as a Deputation to consult with the missions in India and Turkey. They discussed with the several missions such topics as "The governing object of missions," and this they found to be the preaching of the gospel. Then "Preaching,"—how is this connected with schools, and how can they be made most promotive of evangelization? Next, "Native churches and pastors,"—how can they be brought into existence and made most efficient for good? Also, "Caste and Polygamy;" "Schools of all grades for both sexes;" "Native helpers," other than pastors and teachers; "Correspondence;" "Printing establishments,"—should they be owned and managed by the mission, or by natives independently? "Provision for invalids, for children and widows of missions,"—how can this be made most effective, and at least cost? "Medical missions and instruction of natives in medicine;" "Visits home,"—how can these be made most subservient to success in the work? and "Mission property,"—how much? how managed? and in whose name invested? "Government grants;" "Estimates and appropriations;" "Aid to poor converts," etc.,—were also considered. The results of these discussions appeared in the form of papers drawn up by the missionaries, and letters commenting on them by the deputation, and the whole form a volume of 600 pages, full of most valuable information in these details of missionary work. The title is "Reports

and Letters connected with Special Meetings of the India and Syria Missions of the American Board in 1855. Printed for the use of the Prudential Committee, Boston." See also Dr. Anderson's Missions to India, pp. 240-265.

About the same time E. B. Underhill, Esq., Secretary of the Baptist Missionary Society (England), rendered a similar service to their missions in India. The title of the volume recording the results is "Minutes and Reports of the Baptist Missionaries in Bengal, the Northwest Provinces, Behar, and Ceylon, in 1885-6. Printed for the use of the Committee and the Missionaries." Mr. Underhill was a fellow passenger with Drs. Anderson and Thompson from England to India.

More than a year before this, the Executive Committee of the American Baptist Missionary Union had deputed Rev. Solomon Peck, D.D., and Rev. J. N. Granger to visit their mission in Burmah and consult with the missionaries. They met at Moulmein April 4th, 1853, and continued in session till May 17th. Their proceedings were printed for the use of the Executive Committee in a volume of 116 pages.

Dr. Anderson left copies of the printed minutes of the conferences with Dr. Mullens (L. M. S.) at Calcutta; and the latter, in his "Brief Review of Ten Years' Missionary Labor in India. London, 1863," states that the idea of a general conference of missionaries of all societies for consultation sprung from these meetings of the Deputation in India.

The Bengal Missionary Conference met in Calcutta September, 1855. It was composed of nearly 50 missionaries of various societies, sat four days, held eight sessions besides meetings for prayer, and discussed "The progress and the peculiar difficulties in Bengal," "Preaching in the vernacular," "Education in English," "Influence of the Indigo and Zemindary Systems on the Work in Rural Districts," "Vernacular Literature and Schools," and "Female Education." Each topic was set forth in a paper, and after discussion the opinions of the brethren were embodied in resolutions, and the whole published in a volume entitled "Proceedings of a General Conference of Bengal Protestant Missionaries held in Calcutta, September, 1855. Dalton, London"

Another Conference of missionaries in the Northwest Provinces was held in Benares January, 1857. Thirty missionaries were present from seven societies. A sketch of the proceedings appeared in the "Calcutta Christian Observer," March, 1857; but the records of the Conference were destroyed when the Allahabad Mission press was burnt during the mutiny, June, 1857.

A third Conference of South India missionaries was held at Ootacamund, in the Nilgiri Hills; thirty-two missionaries met, and spent a pleasant fortnight in comparing notes. The results were published in "The Proceedings of the South India Missionary Conference held at Ootacamund, April, 1858. London." This volume contains twenty-seven narratives of missionary labor, and thirty papers on different themes, followed by resolutions embodying the general views of the Conference on "Native Agencies," "Education," "Vernacular Preaching," "Village Congregations," "Industrial Institutions," "Caste," "Government and Morality," and "Government Education," with a number of valuable statistical tables. See "Conference on Missions at Liverpool, 1860," pp. 365-374.

Next in order comes the Conference on Missions at Liverpool, March 19th to 23d, 1860, where 25 British societies were represented by their officers. Two missionaries from America were present, and nearly one hundred other members took part in the proceedings. Two sessions of three and a half hours each were held daily, preceded by a meeting for prayer in the morning, and followed by a soirée in the evening. The whole ended in a large public meeting in Philharmonic Hall. Two stenographers reported the discussions, and the whole proceedings were published in an octavo of 428 pages; of these the index alone fills 38. Papers were read on "European Missionaries abroad," "Best Means for producing and maintaining a Missionary Spirit." Three papers were read "On Missionary Education." The next topic was "How to call forth Liberality at Home." "Native Agency" followed; then "Candidates for the Work," "Indian Converts in the Mutiny," and "Native Churches," Addresses supplemented these papers, with others on "The Missionary Lectureship," "The Peshawar Mission," "Missions in South Africa," "Missions in Turkey," "Education of Woman in the East," and "Medical Missions in China and Japan." The discussions are also summarized in "minutes" on the several themes.

The "Proceedings of the Conference at Lahore, in the Punjab, December, 1862, and January, 1863," fill 398 octavo pages.

At Allahabad, where the records of a previous Conference were burned in 1857, another was held in 1872-73, at which 136 missionaries were present from nineteen societies. Among these were 21 Presbyterians, 18 Methodists, 4 represented the American Board, 2 the United Presbyterian Church, and 1 the Reformed—all these from the United States. The English Baptists sent 10, Church Missionary Society 25, London Missionary Society 13, Free Church 12, Church of Scotland 3, Irish Presbyterians 3, United Presbyterian Church 3, and Gossner's Mission 2; 96 foreigners and 28 natives.

Several missionary Conferences have been held in China. The first important one was at Shanghai in 1877. This is often quoted as authority in matters pertaining to missions in that empire. (See below.)

Eighteen years passed away after the Conference at Liverpool before another was held in England, in the large hall of Mildmay Park, on the north side of London, October 21st to 26th, 1878. The Conference at Liverpool represented only 25 British Societies, but this one 37 in all—26 British, 6 American, and 5 from the continent of Europe. This one not only dealt more thoroughly with particular fields, but also viewed each in its relations to the whole world, noting what had been accomplished, and searching to see what might be brought to pass in the near future. Besides a general review of missionary education, Christian literature, and Bible translation, it gave a list of recent versions of Scripture covering 15 pages. There was a looking forward to the completion of the work in some fields, and a passing on to the regions beyond. It inquired for the readjustments that would secure the largest aggressive evangelization. The topics discussed were such as these: Increased Co-operation of all Agencies, by Rev.

Dr. Mullens; Results of Emancipation, by E. B. Underhill, LL.D.; Discovery and Missions in South Africa, by Sir T. Fowell Buxton, Bart.; Lovedale, South Africa, by Rev. Dr. Stewart; Medical Missions, by Rev. Dr. Lowe; Claims of Foreign Missions, by Rev. Daniel Wilson and Rev. Dr. Herdman; the Missionary Character of the Church, by Rev. Dr. A. C. Thompson; the Gospel in Turkey, by Rev. Dr. N. G. Clark; Growth of Christianity in India, by Rev. M. A. Sherring; Education in India, by Rev. Dr. Murray Mitchell; Dutch India, by Rev. Dr. Schreiber; Netherlands Missionary Society, by the Secretary; Islam and Hinduism as related to the Gospel, by Rev. E. E. Jenkins; The Work in China and its Future, by Rev. Dr. Legge; Work in the Zenana, by Mrs. Weitbrecht; The Karen Mission, by Rev. Dr. Murdock; Dr. Maxwell, Rev. J. Hudson Taylor, and Rev. W. F. Stevenson spoke on Missions in China, and Rev. Dr. Legge on the Opium Traffic; The Bible Work of the World was set forth by the Assistant Secretary of the British and Foreign Bible Society; Missions in Japan, by Rev. Dr. Ferris; The Provinces of China, by Rev. J. H. Taylor and others; Polynesia, by Rev. S. J. Whitmee; The Influence of Colonization on Native Races, by Rev. G. Blencowe; New Guinea, by Rev. W. G. Lawes; Madagascar, by H. Clark and Rev. J. Sibree, Jr.; New Hebrides, by Rev. J. Inglis; Education of Woman in the East, by Miss E. J. Whately of Egypt, Mrs. Urmston of North India, Mrs. Ferguson of Bengal, Mrs. Etherington of Benares, Rev. J. E. Payne of Calcutta, and Miss M. A. West of Turkey; Missions among the Moslems, by Rev. T. P. Hughes, B.D., of Peshawar; English Mission Schools at Cairo, by Miss E. J. Whately; Mission Work in Egypt, by Rev. Dr. Watson; Mission Work among the Afghans, by Rev. T. P. Hughes; Foreign Work of the Religious Tract Society, by its Secretary; British Syrian Schools, by a sister of Mrs. Bowen Thompson; The American Mission in Syria, by Rev. Dr. H. Jessup; Sabbath-schools on the Continent, by F. J. Hartley, Esq.; Continental Missions, by Rev. R. S. Ashton; Mission Work in Paris, by Rev. D. M. Berry; The McAll Mission, by Pastor Dumas; Missions to the Jews, by Rev. J. C. Brenan. Interspersed among these were many short addresses on the topics presented. And in almost every case both the paper and the address were from men who had been on the ground, and could speak from personal observation. The Conference closed with a general meeting in Exeter Hall, which seemed to gather into a focus the interest and energy that had been steadily increasing during all its ten sessions.

But these previous conventions only prepared the way, and rendered possible the Centenary Conference on Foreign Missions that met in London June 9th to 19th, 1888.

For years men had been asking, What is the result of so vast expenditure? What lessons are taught by a century of missionary experience in all parts of the world? What victories have been won among savage races, and what among those whose civilization and literature antedates our own? For the first time Protestant missionary societies gave an authoritative answer to these questions, having devoted fifty meetings to a searching scrutiny of every department of missionary work, and to the public record of the results. The great object was to encourage the churches to press forward in obedience to the last command of Christ, by setting forth the experience of evangelical missions during the last hundred years, and to confer together on those numerous questions which the large expansion of the work had brought into the foreground. The Conference made no attempt to legislate for the churches, nor to stir up temporary excitement by a mass meeting. The work of Christ is not to be carried forward in either of these methods. But the kingdom of truth advances by the spread of information concerning the principles of that kingdom and the facts connected with its progress in the past.

The Mildmay Conference was a great advance on that at Liverpool, but this was a still greater advance on that. Even though it accomplished nothing else, the great number of men and women that it drew together from all parts of the world was a grand testimony to the advance that had taken place in the work. In 1860 about 129 met together; in 1878 about 158; and in 1888, 1,576—nearly ten times as many. In 1860 there is not one name of a woman in the entire list; and in 1878 only two appear, though more than that number (5) took part in the proceedings; but in 1888 the names of 429 women appear on the roll—much more than the entire membership of previous Conferences. In 1860 none were present from the United States. In 1878 one attended from the United States and one from Canada. In 1888, 183 names appear from the United States and 30 from Canada. Indeed, the numbers were so large that two simultaneous meetings were held in the forenoon and evening, and generally three at the same hour in the afternoon. The Conference being divided into sections for that purpose, nine meetings were devoted exclusively to prayer; twenty-four meetings of members in section, for the discussion of important principles; six meetings for open Conference; and, including the opening meeting, eighteen public assemblies. The published report of the Conference fills two octavo volumes of 560 pp. and 624 pp., the Indices alone filling 46 pages with double columns. In the first volume is a Missionary Bibliography of 48 pages, prepared by Rev. S. M. Jackson of New York, giving the works published on Missionary Ethnology, Heathen Religions, Miscellany, History of Missionary Societies, Jewish Missions, Papal Missions, Missionary Biography general and individual, Missionary Biography of Converts, Travels in Missionary Lands in general and in each one severally. This last occupies 28 pages.

The number of missionary societies represented in the Conference was 139; of these, 57 belonged to the United States, 9 to Canada, 18 to the continent of Europe, and 2 to the colonies; leaving 53 to the kingdom of Great Britain.

Many topics discussed at previous Conferences were also discussed at this, but with much greater thoroughness; e.g., Missionary Comity was the subject of two papers, and a prolonged discussion filling 59 pages. Instead of repeating these again, some new topics are more worthy of mention, such as, The Increase and Influence of Islam; Buddhism compared with Christianity, by Sir Monier M. Williams; Papal Foreign Missions; Reaction of Foreign Missions on the Church; The State of the World a Hundred Years ago with Reference to the Missionary Work as compared with the Present; Mission-

ary Methods, (1) The Agents, (2) Modes of Working, (3) Dealing with Social Customs, (4) Dealing with Religious Beliefs. The entire two volumes are full of both very interesting and instructive reading.

The "Allgemeine Missions Zeitschrift" for November, 1889, contains a report of the Third Scandinavian Missionary Conference July 2d to 5th, at Christiania, Norway. The next meeting is appointed for 1893. At this session 553 members were present—400 from Norway, 105 from Denmark, 61 from Sweden, and 1 from Finland. Scandinavian societies support over 100 missionaries, and spend annually $200,000. The same class of topics discussed in the London Conference were prominent here; and so the work goes on till there shall remain no more lands to be won for Christ ("Missionary Herald," 1890, 28).

Even in Japan, though it was not accessible to Christendom till 1854, and missionaries were unknown there till 1859, and even then could only employ themselves in learning the language, a missionary Conference was held at Osaka on the large island of Nippon, April 16th to 21st, 1883.

It is interesting to note the progress of the work in those islands up to that date. The first convert, Yano Riû, was baptized in October, 1864. The first church of nine young men was organized at Yokohama, March 10th, 1872. In 1876 the converts numbered 1,004; in 1879, 2,965; in 1882, 4,987; and in 1883, the year of the Conference, 6,598. Twenty-two societies were represented in it by 106 delegates, 48 of whom were women. The A. B. C. F. M. had 32 representatives, the largest number from any one society. Next to that came the American Presbyterians with 12. The Church Missionary Society, The American Episcopal Church, and The Reformed (Dutch) Church had 8 each; and other societies had smaller representations. The opening sermon was preached by Rev. James H. Ballagh, from Acts 1 : 8; and a History of Protestant Missions in Japan, by Rev. G. F. Verbeck, D.D., fills 163 of the 566* pages of the volume of Proceedings of the Conference, which was printed and published at Yokohama. Other topics discussed were: The Obstacles to the Reception of the Gospel in Japan; among which were specified, The Influence of Buddhism, on which Rev. M. L. Gordon, M.D., read an instructive paper; The Influence of Confucianism, on which Rev. H. Waddell read another paper; and the Influence of Modern Antichristian Literature,—Rev. D. C. Greene, D.D., read on this topic, and divided it into (1) that which gives expression to an atheistic philosophy, (2) that based on objections to the Bible, and (3) that which opposed the gospel on political grounds.

Education was considered (1) as to the object of missionary education in Japan, (2) its methods, (3) the training needed for native pastors and evangelists, and (4) the distinctive claims of education for women. Two papers on this last topic were read by women—Mrs. L. H. Pierson and Mrs. E. R. Miller.

The self-support of the native church was discussed, with special reference to some extreme views on this subject entertained by one of the missionaries.

---

* The pages number only 468, but are duplicated from 88 to 186 to make room for the first paper.

Medical missions came in for their usual share of attention; and a unique paper by J. C. Berry, M.D., on Missionary Health, Vacations, and Furloughs, gave a great deal of valuable information on that subject, and on the practice of the different societies in that regard. Another paper on a subject unusual though practical, viz., The Health of the Missionary as affected by his Work, by Rev. W. Taylor, M.D., took up the various causes of ill-health in Japan, and gave counsel which, intelligently carried out, may greatly promote missionary health and usefulness in that interesting field.

Other topics were also discussed, such as: The Preparation of a Christian Literature for Japan; The Principles of Translation into Japanese; The Matter and Method of Preaching to the Heathen; How best to conduct Sunday-schools in that Field; etc.

On two evenings the topics that had been discussed during the day were further elucidated by papers read by the native Japanese pastors, Rev. T. Matsuyama, J. T. Ise, P. Sawayama, and P. Kanamori, though no Japanese name appears on the roll of the Conference. Perhaps in the next Conference the natives will have it all to themselves.

In the paper on missionary health is a large colored chart of temperature and humidity, giving the elastic force of vapor in inches for the twelve months of the year, at Sapporo, Kiyoto, Hakodate, Tokyo, Kobe, Nagasaki, and Yokohama in Japan, and the mean annual temperature and relative humidity of fourteen other cities in various parts of the world, four of them in the United States of America.

*China.**—I. The first Conference of the missionaries laboring in China was held in Shanghai, May 10th–24th, 1877. The origin of this meeting was at a meeting of the Presbyterian Synod of China, held at Chefoo in August, 1874, at which many delegates of other Presbyterian bodies were present; and so beneficial were the meetings, so much good was accomplished by the mutual interchange of views and the discussion of methods, that the desire for a meeting of representatives of all the missionaries in China took form in the appointment of a committee to confer with the missionaries and secure a universal opinion on the practicability and advisability of holding a general Conference. This committee consisted of Rev. J. L. Nevius, D.D., Rev. A. Williamson, LL.D., and Rev. J. B. Hartwell. A circular was issued by the committee, stating the object of the Conference, and asking opinions as to the time, place, subjects for discussion, writers, and delegates to such a conference. Amid the variety of opinions received the committee were unable to decide, and a new circular was issued, giving the results of the first circular; when replies to this were received the result was published in the "Chinese Recorder" for May–June, 1875, the holding of the Conference was advised, and the following committee of arrangements was appointed:

A. Wylie, Esq., representing Hong Kong and Canton Province; Revs. C. Douglas, LL.D., Formosa and Fokien Province; J. Butler, Chekiang; W. Muirhead, Kiangsu; G. John, Yangtz Ports; C. W. Mateer, Newchwang and Shantung; J. Edkins, Chihli.

This committee met at Shanghai, October 25th, 1875, and finding that fully two thirds of the missionaries were in favor of the meeting, called the Conference for the 10th of May, 1877.

The attendance on the Conference was very gratifying to those who had labored for its success. There were in all 126 members—74 gentlemen, 52 ladies. Five of this number had arrived in China in 1847. Twenty different missionary societies were represented: 10 American, 1 German, and 9 of Great Britain, besides the British and Foreign Bible Society. Ten different provinces claimed the delegates, and Presbyterians, Baptists, Congregationalists, Episcopalians, Methodists, and Lutherans united in fraternal discussion and worship. Papers were read and discussed which dealt with the practical details as well as the general policy of the missionary work, such as: The Field in all its Magnitude; Buddhism and Taouism; Itinerancy; Medical Missions; Woman's Work for Woman; Schools; Christian Literature; Self-support; Opium; Ancestral Worship; Treaty Rights of Native Christians; Principles of Translation; and the Training of a Native Agency. In addition to those who were at the Conference, papers were prepared by such well-known missionaries as Dr. James Legge, Rev. A. P. Happer, D.D., Rev. W. A. P. Martin, D.D., and J. G. Kerr, M.D., who were unable to be present.

A delightful spirit of harmony and brotherly kindness prevailed throughout all the meetings of the Conference, so that subjects likely to create spirited and perhaps unpleasant discussion were harmoniously considered in a calm and Christian way. The influence of this meeting was felt in greater harmony between the different missionaries, in a spirit of unity which pervaded the whole body, not only those who had been in attendance upon the Conference, but among their associates, and in the resulting friendships, the mutual encouragement, the increased wisdom, and the greater zeal in missionary work which was the inevitable result of such a meeting.

The tabulated results of the Conference of 1877 were a full table of statistics and the publication in a volume of the papers read, together with the discussion which followed them; and this formed a valuable treasury of facts in regard to mission work, as well as the views held in regard to methods of work.

A summary of the statistics will be found on the next page.

The work thus tabulated was done by a force of 473 missionaries, divided thus: married men, including wives, 344; single men, 66; single women, 63; total, 473. This large number was connected with 11* American societies, 13 † British, 2 ‡ Continental, 3 § Bible Societies, and 7 were unconnected with any society.

---

* The conferences in China have been so important that a special and somewhat enlarged statement of them is appended.)

---

* A. B. M. U., South. Bap. Conven., Seventh Day Baptists, A. B. C. F. M., P. E. Mission, M. E. (North), M. E. (South), Presbyterian (North), Presbyterian (South), Reformed (Dutch), Woman's Union Mission.

† Baptist, China Inland, Church Missionary Society, S. P. G., London Mission, Methodist New Connexion, United Methodist Free Church, Wesleyan Mission, Canadian Presbyterian, English Presbyterian, Irish Presbyterian, Scotch United Presbyterian, Society for Promotion of Female Education.

‡ Basle Mission, Rhenish Mission.

§ American Bible Society, British and Foreign Bible Society, National Bible Society of Scotland.

| | American. | British. | Conti-nental. | Totals. |
|---|---|---|---|---|
| Mission stations. . . . . . . . . . . . . . . . . . . . . . . . . . | 41 | 42 | 8 | 91 |
| Out-stations. . . . . . . . . . . . . . . . . . . . . . . . . . . . | 215 | 269 | 27 | 511 |
| Organized churches . . . . . . . . . . . . . . . . . . . . . | 150 | 150 | 12 | 312 |
| Wholly self-supporting. . . . . . . . . . . . . . . . . . . | 11 | 7 | . . . . . . . . . . | 18 |
| Partially     "     . . . . . . . . . . . . . . . . . . . . | 115 | 128 | . . . . . . . . . . | 243 |
| Communicants. . .    . . . . . . . . . . . . . . . . . . | 5,300 | 6,464 | 1,271 | 13,035 |
|    "    Males . . . . . . . . . . . . . . . . . . . . | 3,117 | 4,264 | 687 | 8,068 |
|    "    Females . . . . . . . . . . . . . . . . . . . . | 2,183 | 2,200 | 584 | 4,967 |
| Boys' boarding-schools . . . . . . . . . . . . . . . . . . | 19 | 8 | 3 | 30 |
| Pupils. . . . . . . . . . . . . . . . . . . . . . . . . . . . | 347 | 118 | 146 | 611 |
| Girls' boarding-schools . . . . . . . . . . . . . . . . . | 24 | 12 | 2 | 38 |
| Pupils . . . . . . . . . . . . . . . . . . . . . . . . . . | 464 | 189 | 124 | 777 |
| Boys' day-schools. . . . . . . . . . . . . . . . . . . . . . | 93 | 70 | 14 | 177 |
| Pupils. . . .   . . . . . . . . . . . . . . . . . . . . | 1,255 | 1,471 | 265 | 2,991 |
| Girls' day-schools. . . . . . . . . . . . . . . . . . . . . | 57 | 24 | 1 | 82 |
| Pupils . . . . . . . . . . . . . . . . . . . . . . . . . . | 957 | 335 | 15 | 1,307 |
| Theological schools . . . . . . . . . . . . . . . . . . . . | 9 | 9 | 2 | 20 |
| Sunday-schools . . . . . . . . . . . . . . . . . . . . . . . | 92 | 23 | . . . . . . . . . . | 115 |
| Scholars. . . . . . . . . . . . . . . . . . . . . . . | 2,110 | 495 | . . . . . . . . . . | 2,605 |
| School-teachers . . . . . . . . . . . . . . . . . . . . . . . | 178 | 88 | 24 | 290 |
| Ordained preachers and pastors. . . . . . . . . . . . | 42 | 28 | 3 | 73 |
| Assistant preachers . . . . . . . . . . . . . . . . . . . . | 212 | 265 | 34 | 511 |
| Colporteurs. . . . . . . . . . . . . . . . . . . . . . . . . . | 28 | 45 | 3 | 76 |
| Bible-women . . . . . . . . . . . . . . . . . . . . . . . . | 62 | 26 | 2 | 90 |
| Church buildings for Christian worship . . . . . . . . | 113 | 115 | 15 | 243 |
| Chapels and other preaching places . . . . . . . . . . | 183 | 229 | 25 | 437 |
| Hospitals. . . . . . . . . . . . . . . . . . . . . . . . . . . | 6 | 10 | . . . . . . . . . . | 16 |
| In-patients for year 1876 . . . . . . . . . . . . . . . . | 1,390 | 2,340 | . . . . . . . . . . | 3,730 |
| Out-patients for 1876. . . . . . . . . . . . . . . . . . . | 47,635 | 39,870 | . . . . . . . . . . | 87,505 |
| Dispensaries . . . . . . . . . . . . . . . . . . . . . . . . | 14 | 4 | 6 | 24 |
| Patients treated in 1876 . . . . . . . . . . . . . . . . . | 25,107 | 16,174 | . . . . . . . . . . | 41,281 |
| Medical students . . . . . . . . . . . . . . . . . . . . . | 19 | 10 | 1 | 30 |
| Total contributions of native Christians in 1876. . . . | $4,482.84 | $4,789.08 | . . . . . . . . . . | $9,271.92 |

II. *The Conference of 1890* met at Shanghai May 7th–17th, pursuant to a resolution of the Conference of 1877 calling for another conference. Over 400 representatives of the various missions from almost every province of China were assembled at the meetings. Nearly seventy papers were prepared for presentation. In most cases the papers were printed beforehand, and each member of the Conference was supplied with a copy, so that intelligent discussion could take place after a brief résumé of the essay had been given. The subjects of these papers embraced almost every topic that was relevant to mission wants or work. The Bible, the Church, Education, Literature, Relation of Christian Missions to the Chinese Government, Hospitals, Orphanages, Opium, Aboriginal Tribes, Woman's Work, Self-support, Ancestral Worship, and other subjects were treated of in a manner varying from a brief synopsis of general principles to an exhaustive treatise. The meetings were characterized by the greatest harmony and unanimity of opinion, such dangerous topics as the Term Question having been excluded from consideration. Forty missionary societies were represented, and almost all Protestant denominations, yet the key-note of the whole Conference was unity. Diversity of opinion there was, of course; but kindly Christian forbearance dominated the entire meeting.

A wide range of experience was represented in the Conference. Side by side sat the hoary-headed veteran of over thirty years' service in China, and the recruit who had but just landed. Fourteen members had served over thirty years, the Nestor of them all, Rev. A. P. Happer, D.D., of the American Presbyterian Church, having seen forty-six years of service. This group of seniors represented a combined service of more than five hundred years in the mission field. Such being the case, one of the most interesting meetings of the whole session was the inquiry and experience meeting, where practical questions were asked and answered

out of the fulness of the experience there represented. Many of these questions were of universal interest, as the following: "The safety and advisability of adopting the Chinese costume: it is perfectly safe, and expediency alone is to be considered." "The length of time necessary for acquiring the language: that depends on individual gifts,—at least a year is considered necessary." "Is a slight amount of medical training beneficial or otherwise?—'a little knowledge is a dangerous thing,' but used with common-sense it would be of great help, especially in the interior, when separated from physicians." "Is the need of a greater number of foreign missionaries a real one?—the present need can only be met by foreign workers."

The practical results of the Conference were:

1. The crowning work was the agreement upon a union version of the Sacred Scriptures, in three styles—the high classical, the easy classical, and the Mandarin; this version to supersede the various translations which have been made during the last forty years. Committees were appointed to elect the translators and superintend the entire work. Thus the question of Bible translation in China has been simplified, unified, and perfected.

In addition to this chief action, committees were appointed with reference to the rendering of the Scriptures into the various vernaculars of China, and for the publication of editions for the blind, and deaf and dumb. The use of the Roman letter was indorsed, and recommended for the vernacular translations.

2. The wealth of information contained in the papers and the discussions of the Conference form a most valuable result of the meeting: as an argument for foreign missions it is unanswerable.

3. Steps were taken for securing a Bible in Chinese, with summaries, chapter headings, and brief explanations, the need of which has long been felt.

4. A committee was also appointed to prepare

a union annotated Bible; this ranks next in importance to the union version.

5. A resolution was adopted, expressing in well-chosen, temperate language a protest against the growth and use of opium (and the abuse of anti-opium pills containing morphia), calling upon the Christian Church to make more earnest efforts against this great evil.

6. The use of alcoholic liquors among the native Christians was made the subject of inquiry for a committee who will report at the next Conference.

7. The Educational Association of Practical Teachers, which has been formed in China for the promotion of educational matters, especially the matters of text-books and scientific terminology, was recognized by the Conference, and the work and material assets—books, maps, blocks, etc., of the school and text-book committee of the last Conference—were turned over to it.

8. Harmonious working in literary effort is desired, and a permanent committee was elected with a great many important duties to perform in regard to the classification, storage, and sale of standard books at important centres.

9. In order that Christianity should not appear to be inimical to government and those in authority, a committee was appointed to present to the Chinese Government a statement as to what Christianity is, and what its aims are; and while thanking the government for the protection of the past, to ask for the suppression of libellous charges against Christian missions.

10. Strong appeals for reinforcements were issued by the Conference, not in the enthusiasm of the moment, but as a measure made necessary by the results already accomplished, by what is now in hand, and by the needs of the future. One appeal was framed on behalf of the two hundred lady-members, asking for more lady missionaries for China. An appeal for more lay missionaries, and another appeal which called for large reinforcements of ordained workers, were drafted into one grand appeal for a thousand more men in the next five years.

11. Comity between missions and a division of the field was made the subject of the work of a permanent committee, whose object is to promote harmony between individuals as well as societies.

12. A permanent committee of correspondence was elected to serve as a medium of communication on subjects of interest common to missionaries, and to provide for the next Conference.

13. The importance of periodical literature was recognized, and a resolution passed urging upon all missionaries to support and spread the publications already in existence.

14. Full statistics were gathered together, but as yet only abstracts are available. At the close of 1889 the number of missionaries in China was 1,295, belonging to 42 different organizations. The increase of 1889 over 1888 was 172. At the end of 1889 the number of native communicants was 37,287, an increase of more than 286 per cent since 1876. The contributions of the native Christians (only) for the year 1889 were $36,884.54, which lacks a little less than $403 of being an average of one dollar a member for all the native communicants in the empire. Organized churches numbered 520, 94 of which are wholly self-supporting, 49 others partly so, while 61 hospitals and numerous dispensaries treated a total of 348,439 patients.

In the short space at the disposal of this article the above summary of the results of this most important Conference must suffice. Acknowledgment is due to the "North China Herald," whose full reports of the meetings have been availed of, and its closing comment on the Conference is well worthy of repetition: " Whatever it may have done or left undone, the Shanghai Conference of 1890 is both a prophecy and a promise of the day hinted at in the Latin verse found in some editions of Bagster's Testament: '*Multæ terricolis linguæ cælestibus una*,' —To the dwellers upon earth there are many tongues; to those in heaven, but one."

**Missionary Leaves Association.** Headquarters, 20 Compton Terrace, Upper Street, Islington, London, N., England.—The work of the Association originated in the needs called forth by the success vouchsafed to the Church Missionary Society. The organization of native churches resulted in the formation at each missionary station of a sort of parish with all the wants of any poor out-of-the-way English parish, with some needs peculiar to itself. While these mission stations were comparatively few, private friends were able to meet their wants; but with the growth of the work of the Society came the need of organized help. Thus, in 1868, by the advice of Rev. Henry Venn, Honorary Secretary of the Church Missionary Society, was formed the Missionary Leaves Association for the purpose of furnishing information to friends at home, and of conveying their aid to recipients abroad. It is the object of the Association to supply the missionaries and stations of the Church Missionary Society with help in money and material towards such requisites as it is not the province of the Society to supply, but which aid nevertheless is found to be most helpful in the various works undertaken by the missionaries.

*Organization.*—To insure, as far as possible, that the administration of the Missionary Leaves Association shall be in harmony with that of the C. M. S., it has been arranged that some members of the committee of the former shall be nominated by the committee of the latter. As a matter of fact, all the present members of the Association committee are members of the Society committee. The Association possesses an organization peculiarly adapted for placing private gifts where they are most needed, and affords advantages in acknowledging gifts, which the C. M. S. has not been able to do, owing to the immense amount of correspondence and other work involved in the general management of the missions.

**Mizpah,** a Moravian Brethren station in Jamaica, West Indies. Formerly an out-station of Bethany, known then as Cheapside. It lies about ten miles northeast of Bethany, on the Blue Ridge Mountains. It is pleasantly situated 1,800 feet above the level of the sea, surrounded by a well-wooded district. In 1866 a formal separation from the mother-church was effected, and an independent congregation organized. It is one of the most promising of the Jamaica congregations. Moravia and Bohemia, with schools and regular preaching services, are two flourishing out-stations belonging to Mizpah.

**Mkunazini,** town in Zanzibar, Africa. Station of the Universities Mission; 2 missionaries, boys' school, 43 pupils, dispensary, and medical work among the natives.

**Moab Mission,** or Methodist Mission to Palestine. Established 1884. Conducted by Mr. and Mrs. Lethaby. Supported by Wesleyan Methodists in England. Secretary, Rev. George Piercy, 267 Burdett Road, London, E.—Much courage and determination were needed to effect an entrance into the town of Kerak in Moab, and to maintain the position when it had been won. Mr. and Mrs. Lethaby have been subjected to personal violence, robberies, insults, and intimidation of every kind. The two missionaries have now to a great degree lived down opposition, and their work has so far developed as to render further assistance absolutely necessary. The difficulties of the work are still very great, owing to the isolation of the place, the dangers attending communication with Jerusalem and the outside world, and the lawless character of the people. There is one great advantage—Kerak is still a purely Arab state, independent of Turkish control. From its position on the top of the mountains of Moab it may be plainly seen from Jerusalem, which is in a direct line only fifty miles away; the actual travelling distance is about ninety miles. The journey from Jerusalem occupies four days of hard travel, and is attended with considerable danger of pillage or worse treatment at the hands of the Bedouin who infest the way. Kerak is a very old town, is elevated 3,500 feet above the sea, and must have been before the invention of gunpowder almost impregnable. All the fortifications are now in ruins. There is a population of 8,000. About one sixth of this number are Greek Christians.

Day and Sunday-school teaching form a very important part of the work of this mission, because it is only through the children that the parents can be reached. The Moslem school has enabled Mrs. Lethaby to gain access to twelve Moslem homes, where she conducts evangelistic services. The medical work and house to house visiting are also important agencies.

The present attendance on the day-school is 30; on the Sunday-school, 40.

**Modimolle** or **Waterburg,** a town in North Transvaal, East South Africa, not far from Ga Matlale. Mission station of the Berlin Evangelical Missionary Society (1867); 2 missionaries, 12 native helpers, 237 communicants.

**Modjovarno,** city in Java, East Indies, northwest of Malang. Mission station of the Netherlands Missionary Society, Rotterdam, with 10 churches and 2,816 members; also a medical station.

**Moffat, Robert,** b. Ormiston, East Lothian, Scotland, December 21st, 1795, of humble parentage. His mother had carefully trained him in the Bible, and told him much of the early Moravian Brethren. He learned the craft of gardening. While in England he saw a placard on the wall announcing a missionary meeting. He attended, listened with great interest, and that night in his quiet chamber he prayed that if it were God's will He would send him forth to preach the gospel to the heathen. Having resolved to be a missionary, he offered himself at the age of nineteen to the L. M. S.; was accepted, and after spending some time in special study, was ordained; sailed from England for South Africa October 31st, 1816, and arrived at Cape Town in 1817. His request to proceed inland being refused by the Governor of Natal, he remained several months at the Cape, studying in the meantime the Dutch language with a Christian Hollander. This tongue was chiefly spoken at that time by Europeans in South Africa. At length permitted to proceed, Moffat set out from Cape Colony, through the territory of the Boers, for Namaqualand, in the Orange River country, and especially for the district controlled by Africaner. This chief had been outlawed for barbarous crimes, and his name had been a terror to all the region. But he had become a convert to Christianity. The farmers did not believe the reported conversion, and predicted Moffat's destruction. After incredible perils and difficulties he reached a mission station called Warm Baths, where the native Christian teacher and the people insisted on his remaining, the women declaring that they would block the wheels of his wagon with their own bodies, when a party from Africaner's men appeared and carried him off to the kraal of Africaner, beyond the Orange River. He arrived January 26th, 1818, and was cordially received by the chief, who ordered some women to build a house for the missionary. In this hut he remained six months, exposed to the sun, rain, dogs, snakes, and cattle, doing his own sewing and cooking, and often having nothing to cook, consoling himself with his violin and the Scotch Psalms, but with all his hardships maintaining regular day-schools and preaching services. Africaner was a regular attendant, and proved himself to be a true Christian, very docile, a firm friend and efficient helper of the mission. In 1819 Moffat visited the Cape for the double purpose of getting supplies and introducing Africaner to the governor. The chief hesitated to go, since he was an outlaw; but when assured of safety he consented. The presence of Moffat was a surprise to the people, who supposed he had long since been murdered by Africaner, and even his testimony to the entire reformation of the chief was utterly disbelieved. On Moffat's arrival at Cape Town the governor received Africaner with great kindness, and expressed his pleasure at seeing one who had been the "scourge of the country, and the terror of the border colonists." He was also much struck with this result of missionary enterprise. As a testimony of good feeling he presented to Africaner a wagon worth £80. The people who had been for twenty years familiar with Africaner's deeds were struck with the mildness of his demeanor, also with his knowledge of the Scriptures. Mr. Moffat had intended to return at once to his station with the purchased supplies, but was prevailed upon by the deputation from the L. M. S., Rev. J. Campbell and Dr. Philip, who had just arrived, to accompany them in their visits to the mission stations. While at Cape Town he was married to Miss Mary Smith, to whom he had long been engaged, and who had come from England to meet him. In 1820 he left the Cape with his wife for Griqua Town, and eventually was appointed to the Bechuana tribes lying west of the Vaal River. In 1821 he commenced a mission at Kuruman, where for many years he labored, preaching, teaching, translating Scripture, composing hymns and books, without seeing the people converted. In 1829 he visited the Matabele tribes lying south of the Zambesi, and in 1835 established a mission there. The results of these journeys were published in England. About 1830 he completed a translation of Luke, and printed it at Cape Town. He returned with this and a hymn-book in the native language, a printing-press, type, paper, and ink, having learned to print while at the Cape. After this the mission greatly prospered. He made frequent excursions into the interior to visit other tribes, where, amid great perils and strange adventures, he made known the gospel, and prepared the way for other laborers. By 1838 the entire New Testament was translated, and in 1839 he went to England to get it printed. He made there a deep impression by his addresses. He published also in 1842, while at home, "Missionary Scenes and Labors in South Africa." Returning to his station in 1843, he says: "Many were the hearty welcomes we received, all appearing emulous to testify their joy. Some whose hearts had sickened with deferred hope would ask again and again, 'Do our eyes indeed behold you?'" In 1857 he completed single-handed the translation of the whole Bible into Bechuana, which was printed at Kuruman. In 1858 he went to Cape Town, returning with a reinforcement for the new Matabele Mission. His son was at Matabele, and afterwards took up his father's work at Kuruman, where his sister was engaged in teaching. The first church was formed in 1829, at Kuruman. His eldest daughter was married in 1844 to Dr. Livingstone. In 1870, enfeebled by age and work, Mr. Moffat returned to England. Mrs. Moffat, who for more than a half-century had been a sharer of his labors and trials, died in 1871. In 1872 he received from the University of Edinburgh the degree of doctor of divinity, and a testimonial of about £6,000. He died at Leigh, near Tunbridge Wells, August 9th, 1883.

Moffat sought not only to Christianize the natives, but to induce them to abandon their savage modes of life, and adopt the arts of civilization. By precept and example he succeeded in turning murderous savages into a "people appreciating and cultivating the arts and habits of civilized life, with a written language of their own." "The discouragements and dangers which Moffat met were overcome by his strong will, heroic faith, and genial humor."

**Mofuss,** town in East Sherbro country, West Coast, Africa, southeast of Mambo and northeast of Toungkoloh. Mission station of the United Brethren in Christ (U. S. A.); 33 church-members, 21 scholars.

**Mogadore,** a city of Morocco, Barbary States, North Africa, on the Atlantic coast, 130 miles southwest of Morocco City. Substantially built; houses large, flat-roofed; some of the mosques fine; the harbor is the best on the coast of Morocco. Population, 20,000, many of them Jews. Mission station of the London Society for the Jews; 1 missionary.

**Mograhat,** town in Bengal, East India, 32 miles southeast of Calcutta, 12 from Barripur. Mission station S. P. G. with Barripur.

**Moge-Mirim** or **Mogy Mirim,** town in Southeast Brazil, northwest of Campinas and Sao Paulo, southwest of Espirito Santo. Mission station of the Presbyterian Church (South), U. S. A.; 1 native pastor, 1 church, 30 members.

**Mohammedanism. — I. *The Problem.***—Islam is the greatest organized opponent of Christianity. Geographically it has an unbroken field from the Philippine Islands in the Pacific to Sierra Leone on the Atlantic, and from the snows of Crimea to the Equator. It has been successful with every race type—Semitic, Aryan, Turanian. It has won to its banners polytheists, pantheists, Jews, and Christians. It has steadily grown in war and peace for over a thousand years, and to-day controls the religious life of two hundred million human beings. It has a common religious language (Arabic), which is rich and expressive, and which is the medium of a literature of wide range and enduring power. It is the language of commerce throughout two thirds of the continent of Africa, and is preparing the way for the extension of a Moslem civilization. There is a simplicity of practice in Islam which easily adapts itself to its environment wherever it has gone. Although politically Mohammedanism has always tended toward despotism, there is running through it all a democratic spirit, which recognizes the brotherhood of man, and which places all believers on a common level. Its ethical and doctrinal code is lofty and pure as contrasted with all other extra-biblical religions; and even when contrasted with many degraded forms of Judaism and Christianity, it does not take a secondary place. It develops strong individuality, and yet binds the faithful together as few religions have been able to do as effectively. In the earlier days Islam was a political as well as a religious unit. As a type of the ancient life which fashioned the nation on the war principle, Islam was a success for centuries; but under the new conditions, when nations are being more and more fashioned on the industrial principle, it can never succeed politically. Moslem powers are steadily weakening as civilization advances. In the endeavor to keep in line with the progressing nations, Moslem rulers invariably impoverish their lands to the last degree and make industrial progress impossible. Moslems flourish best under Christian rule or under a controlling Christian influence. Syria under the Sultan is growing poorer every day, while Egypt under English guidance is growing richer. The tendency to revert to a nomad civilization in Mohammedan countries has about reached its limit.

But while the political power of Islam is weakening, and as far as civilization is concerned may be counted as dead, the last few years have witnessed a great religious revival in the Moslem world, especially in Turkey, Russia (Caucasus and Central Asia), India (Bengal), Australasia (Java and Sumatra), and Africa. Steamship lines make Mecca more accessible, and religious zeal, fanned to a white heat at the pilgrim festivals, is making surer and even more rapid conquests than did the sword. In 1888 Sumatra alone had 50,000 Moslems who had made the pilgrimage to Mecca. Loss of political power seems to bring unity of religious life to the Mohammedan world, the like of which has not been witnessed since the Ommeiads from Damascus ruled an unbroken territory from the Indus to the Atlantic. Islam is throwing itself with all its combined forces upon the inferior races of Asia, Australasia, and Africa, and is winning them to its faith. It is its last opportunity. Another century must see vast transformations, and a Christian civilization is sure to win.

Mohammed, by accepting Jesus as the promised Messiah of the Old Testament, allied himself with Christianity rather than with Judaism. He gave all credit to the original text of the Scriptures, and claimed to have been predicted by Christ as the fulfiller of the New Testament dispensation. His rejection of the crude tri-theistic Christianity about him shows the vitality of his religious instinct. The minutiæ of detailed ceremonial in Islam undoubtedly was the result of Jewish influence, while its missionary fervor was Christian. The genius of Mohammed coined the metals at his hand and put his own image and superscription on the mixed resultant. His admissions as to Jesus and the original Scriptures will in the coming struggle be the open door for the Christian apologetic. In 627 A.D. Mohammed sent from Medina the following letter to Heraclius, Emperor at Constantinople. It was his first strictly foreign missionary effort, and speaks of peace.

"In the name of God the Compassionate, the Merciful. Mohammed, who is the servant of God, and is His apostle, to Heragl the Qaisar of Rum; peace be on whoever has gone on the straight road. After this I say, verily I call you to Islam (resignation or submission). Embrace Islam, and God will reward you twofold. If you turn away from the offer of Islam, then on you be the sins of your people. O people of the Book (Christians), come toward a creed which is fit both for us and for you. It is this —to worship none but God, and not to associate anything with God, and not to call others God. Therefore, O ye people of the Book, if ye refuse, beware! But we are Moslems, and our religion is Islam.

(Seal.) Mohammed, The Apostle of God."

This letter reveals the sober sense of Moslems to-day as they look over into the Christian camp. It is not unlike the letter sent by the Mahdi to Emin Pasha a short time ago. We must prove to these 200,000,000 votaries of Islam that we do "worship none but God," and that we do not "associate anything with God" and "call others God." It was a misconception from the first (natural enough when we consider the phase of Christianity presented to Mohammed), and it is a misconception emphasized by a thousand years of contact with half-idolatrous Christian sects in a state of decadence. The problem before the Christian Church is to sweep away this misconception, to present the gospel in its simplicity, and to lead this great unitarian disaffection back to the truth. The doctrine of the Trinity is vitally involved, and the Arian controversy must be fought all over again. The Incarnation must be shown, even more clearly than the thought of a millennium and a half has been able to do, to be not only a fact, but a reasonable fact, though still a mystery.

Recent controversy over the usefulness and power of Islam has called attention away from the true issue. Moslems can never be won over to Christianity by a series of wholesale maledictions, nor by a weak yielding of the vital facts of a true faith. The truths contained in the Koranic creeds should be readily granted, but it must be understood by way of caution that truths may be so connected that the result may be a great falsehood. Good bricks may be used in putting together useless structures. Islam has happily been characterized as a "broken cistern,"—so badly broken that it must be all torn down, and many new bricks added before it may hold water; but it is a cistern still. The historic relations of Islam with Judaism on the one hand and with Christianity on the other will be considered later on, but there cannot be a question but that Mohammed and his early followers looked upon the Abyssinian Christians as their religious neighbors and kinsmen. From the first that peculiar relationship has been noted. Dean Stanley calls special attention to this when he says: "Springing out of the same Oriental soil and climate, if not out of the bosom of the Oriental church itself, in part under its influence, in part by way of reaction against it, Mohammedanism must be regarded as an eccentric heretical form of Eastern Christianity. This, in fact, was the ancient mode of regarding Mohammed. He was considered not in the light of the founder of a new religion, but rather as one of the chief heresiarchs of the church." Döllinger agrees with this, and says: "Islam must be considered at bottom a Christian heresy, the bastard offspring of a Christian father and a Jewish mother, and is indeed more closely allied to Christianity than Manichæism, which is reckoned a Christian sect." (Lect. "Reunion of Churches," p. 7, translated by Oxenham, 1872). Ewald calls it "the last and most powerful offshoot of Gnosticism." John of Damascus, who did his work early in the eighth century, at the very seat of the Ommeiad dynasty, did not consider Islam a new religion, but only a Christian heresy. The same was true of Samonas of Gaza, Bartholomew of Edessa, Peter Abbot of Clugny, Thomas Aquinas, Savonarola, and most of the mediæval writers. Radulfus de Columna, who wrote about 1300 A.D., says: "The tyranny of Heraclius provoked a revolt of the Eastern nations. They could not be reduced, because the Greeks at the same time began to disobey the Roman Pontiff, receding, like Jeroboam, from the true faith. Others among these schismatics (apparently with the view of strengthening their political revolt) carried their heresy further, and founded Mohammedanism." The very errors in this statement are instructive. Dante consigned Mohammed to the company of heresiarchs in the "Inferno" (canto 28). Turning to the early Protestant confessions, we find similar notions. The Augsburg Confession condemns as heresies Manichæism, Valentinianism, Arianism, Eunomianism, Mohammedanism, "and all similar to these." The second Helvetic Confession condemns Jews, Mohammedans, and all those heresies teaching that the Son and the Spirit are not God.

Doubtless there has been a tendency to carry this idea of the identity between Islam and Christianity too far, and we are in a reactionary period just now. But without a certain sympathy and an open acknowledgment of the truth in Mohammedanism, the missionary can never hope to win Moslems. When once the principles of higher criticism are understood in the Mohammedan world, Mohammed's admissions as to the inspiration of the original Christian Scriptures will be used with effect, for we have manuscripts of the New Testament older by several centuries than the rise of Islam. His admission of the miraculous birth of Jesus, of His miraculous power, of His deathlessness, and that He will be the Judge at the last great day will also play an important part in the controversy.

The great difficulty is that Islam has not preserved its early simplicity, and tradition plays a prominent part in Moslem belief and practice. Any movement like that of the Wahabees is a good symptom. A larger number of sects have arisen within the pale of Mohammedanism than can be found in Christendom. Saint-worship has sprung up in many forms, and monastic orders have been established. Fanaticism crops out at frequent intervals. It is death for any but Moslems to visit Mecca, and except under Christian law, it is death for a Mohammedan to change his religion.

It is into this vast field that the Christian Church is sent by its Master. Already the field has been cultivated a long while, and the harvest is as yet insignificant. The problem is as various as the sects and nationalities in the Moslem world. Patient labor, instruction in fundamental questions of philosophy and religion, the cultivation of an historic sense, the example of pure lives and a Christlike self-denial must at last give effect to the striving of the Spirit upon these hearts of flint.

II. *Pre-Islamic Arabia* (see Arabia).—Arabia, cut off from the rest of the world by deserts and seas, unconquered by Assyrian, Babylonian, Persian, Egyptian, Greek, or Roman, was the last place to which a prophet would have looked for the rise of such a phenomenon as Islam. It was not always thus isolated, for the latest research gives evidence of a very ancient civilization, which was the connecting link between Egypt and Babylonia in the earliest periods. But up to the time of Mohammed the Arabs had remained free. The peninsula, together with adjacent regions, inhabited by Arabs, covered about 800,000 square miles, or an area as large as the United States east of the Mississippi. Throughout the early centuries its inhabitants probably averaged from 9,000,000 to 10,000,000 people, divided up into tribes, some of which were nomadic, while the large majority were settled. The southern portion of the peninsula was well cultivated, and furnished many valuable articles of commerce. The tribes were for the most part independent, or were loosely bound by confederacies. There was no nation of Arabs until the genius of Mohammed welded together the heterogeneous mass and gave Arabia a distinct mission, which harmonized with a latent pride and love of conquest.

In the earliest days commerce seems to have been a predominant occupation in Arabia. The caravan trade furnished occupation to a large proportion of the inhabitants. At that era commerce was almost entirely confined to the land. The influence of Rome, and the development of a merchant marine under government protection and patronage, and the disturbed condition of the Persian frontier, broke up the monopoly of the Arabs, and many tribes were compelled to betake themselves to a nomad life. We have traditions of great emigrations from the more crowded south northwards, which occurred before the historic period, which removals were doubtless caused by the interruption of the caravan trade.

The story of Arabia until the period of Mohammed is confused. Putting aside conjecture, which has taken great license with the mysterious peninsula, we learn of a number of kingdoms which wielded considerable power. The Himyarites in the southwest formed the most prominent political combination in Arabia. Their king, Abd Kelâl, who reigned about 275 A.D., is said to have been converted to Christianity by a Syrian stranger, and was murdered by his subjects. His son, Marthad, was famous for his religious toleration. He is reported to have said: "I reign over men's bodies, not over their opinions. I exact from my subjects obedience to my government; as to their religious doctrine, the judge of that is the great Creator." Constantius, the Byzantine emperor, about the middle of the fourth century sent an embassy to the Himyarites, wishing to strengthen his alliance with them and to attract them to Christianity. Two hundred Cappadocian horses of the purest breed were sent as a present, and Bishop Theophilus undertook the mission work. Churches were built at the capital, Tzafar, at Aden, and one on the Persian Gulf. Arabian historians make no mention of this mission. A little later the Himyarites began to decline, and became a sort of dependency of Abyssinia, a Christian kingdom across the Red Sea. Between 490 and 525 A.D. Dhu Nowas, in the district of Najran, took the reins of power in his hands. He was a recent convert to Judaism, and persecuted Christians bitterly in that region. They were offered Judaism or death, and twenty thousand are said to have perished. One intended victim, Tholaban, escaped to Hira, and holding up a half-burnt copy of the Gospel, invoked, in the name of outraged Christendom, retribution. Justin I. sent a message to the Abyssinian monarch, asking him to inflict punishment on the usurper. Dhu Nowas was defeated, and the Najran became an Abyssinian dependency. A zealous Christian, Abraha, had become Abyssinian viceroy somewhat later in Yemen. Bishop Gregentius was sent by the Patriarch of Alexandria to assist in pushing the interests of Christianity. A cathedral was built at Sana, and an attempt made to make it the Mecca of the peninsula. The Meccans were displeased, and killed one of the Christian missionaries. A Koreishite from Mecca defiled the cathedral at Sana, whereupon Abraha set out on an expedition, about 570 A.D., to destroy the Kaaba. His army was destroyed, and the episode has come down in Mohammedan story as the affair of "The Elephant." Mohammed was born a few months after. By the aid of the Persians the Abyssinians were finally expelled, in 603 A.D., and Southern Arabia became thereafter loosely dependent upon that eastern rival of the Byzantine empire, until it was absorbed, in 634, by Moslem conquest.

Along the Persian frontier was another considerable political power—the kingdom of Hira, founded in the second century of our era, and having political autonomy until the spread of Islam. It looked to Persia for help in its various wars, and tended more and more towards a dependent condition. Along the Syrian border, and more or less under Byzantine influence, was the kingdom of the Ghassanides, which early came under the influence of the western civilization. Christianity had a strong following in this region from the first, and the whole kingdom was under Christian influence. The kingdom of the Kindites, in Central Arabia, was another political unit, but much weaker than the other three. At Mecca we find the powerful Koreish tribe, which had control of the Kaaba, the religious centre of native Arabian religion.

The religion of Pre-Islamic Arabia may be called heathen, with constant tendencies in the nobler minds toward a conception of one supreme God. Mohammed speaks of the era before him as "the times of ignorance," which he came to do away with. At the Kaaba there were said to have been three hundred and sixty-five images of the gods, who were looked upon as the children of Allah, the creator of all. The wife of Allah was Al-hat, or Al-Ozza, and the Meccans looked upon their local gods as daughters of this union. Sexual dualism thus was the fundamental religious notion of the Arabs. Idols were found in every house, and formed an important article of manufacture. Religion was a sort of barter, which the individual carried on with the gods or goddesses whose aid he desired or whose vengeance he wished to avert. Festivals and pilgrimages, punctiliously attended to, made up a large part of religious life and worship. There was a considerable stir of literary life, and renowned poets contested at the annual fairs for pre-eminence. The successful poems were displayed on the walls of the Kaaba. These poems, some of which have come down to us, show the lowest grade of morals. Drunkenness, gambling, gross love intrigues, vengeance, theft, the loosest possible family ties, the degrading of woman to a mere animal existence —all these traits, common throughout Arabia, make plain the utter inadequacy of the prevailing faith to elevate the life. Add to this the widespread tendency toward atheism and indifference.

Such a state could not last long. Serious minds turned in every direction for help. There arose an ascetic fraternity who called themselves Hanifs (penitents). They sought to go back to the simple faith of Abraham, whom they styled the first Hanif. They proclaimed themselves as seekers after truth, and adopted the life which had been set before them for centuries by Christian hermits, whose rigid vigils had impressed the Oriental mind. Among these Hanifs were Obaydallah, own cousin of Mohammed, Waraqah and Othman, cousins of Khadijah; all three of whom found their way to Christianity. Zaid ibn Amr, an aged Hanif, was seen leaning against the Kaaba, and sadly stretching his hands upward, and praying: "O God, if I knew what form of worship is most pleasing to Thee, so would I serve Thee; but I know it not." Mohammed was touched when this was reported to him, and said: "I will pray for him; in the resurrection he, too, will gather a church around him." It cannot be said that these Hanifs were Jews or Christians, yet they could not have arisen without these two religions as forerunners. They anticipated the central idea contained in the word "Islam" (resignation), and their conception of God was summed up in the word "Judgment." We shall see later how Mohammed became a Hanif, and gave shape, proportion, and continuity to a half-faith which was floating about Mecca and Medina (Yathrib), and how he originated a church polity in closest union with a political organization, the combination of which was destined to make him the moral ruler over more human beings than have ever been controlled by any other man.

The whole question of Christianity in Arabia is very obscure. Christians fled for refuge from the Roman persecutions to the fastnesses of the Syrian desert in the early days of Christianity. Paul himself spent three years among Arabs, whether on the Sinaitic peninsula or along the border of the desert south of Damascus. A local church council at Bostra shows a large growth of Christianity east of the Jordan before the close of the third century. The Ghassanides were first reached, and bishops were appointed to follow the wandering tribes in their migrations. The faith penetrated into the desert south and east along caravan routes, and we may be sure that by the middle of the third century Christianity was well known in many parts of Arabia. We have seen how the Himyarites were reached in the succeeding century. Hira and Kufa, along the Persian frontier, about the same time learned of Christianity through Nestorian missionaries. A king of Hira was converted in the sixth century. Other tribes, such as the Beni Taghlib of Mesopotamia, the Beni Haris of Najran, the Beni Tay, and various tribes about Medina (Yathrib) became nominally Christian. Ali Saad sneeringly said, "The Beni Taghlib are not Christians: they have borrowed from Christianity only the custom of drinking wine." In the first wars between the Persians and the rising Moslem power the Christian Arabs of the northeastern frontier joined the Persians. But in spite of this spread of Christian knowledge throughout the peninsula it did not seem to take any vital hold. It was swept away at the first onset of Islam. The nomad life in the desert was not conducive to Christianity. Hostile Judaism to some extent neutralized its efforts. Northern Arabia was the battlefield between Persian and Byzantine. The form of Christianity which penetrated into Arabia was of the most inferior type. The apocryphal gospels were held as of equal value with the real gospels. The doctrine of the trinity was travestied by a crude tri-theism, in which the three persons of the Godhead were God the Father, God the Son, and the "Virgin Mary." This sounded to Mohammed like the sexual dualism of the "times of ignorance." Jacobite and Nestorian influences predominated. It is doubtful whether the Bible or any portions were put into the vernacular. The haughty nature of the Arabs could with difficulty accept the humble and forgiving spirit of the gospel. The Abyssinians, although making up a powerful Christian kingdom, were of negro blood, and hence uninfluential. "In fine," says Muir, in summing up this subject, "viewed thus in a religious aspect the surface of Arabia had been now and then gently rippled by the feeble efforts of Christianity; the sterner influence of Judaism had been occasionally visible in a deeper and more troubled current; but the tide of indigenous idolatry and of Ishmaelite superstition, setting from every quarter with an unbroken and unebbing surge towards the Kaaba, gave ample evidence that the faith and worship of Mecca held the Arab mind in a thraldom rigorous and undisputed. Yet, even amongst a people thus enthralled, there existed elements which a master mind, seeking the regeneration of Arabia, might work upon. Christianity was well known; living examples of it were amongst the native tribes; the New Testament was respected, if not reverenced, as a book that claimed to be divine; in most quarters it was easily accessible, and some of its facts and doctrines were admitted without dispute. The tenets of Judaism were even more notorious, and its legends, if not its sacred writings, were familiar throughout the peninsula. The worship of Mecca was founded upon patriarchal traditions believed to be common both to Christianity and Judaism. Here, then, was a ground on which the spiritual fulcrum might be planted; here was a wide field, already conceded by the inquirer at least in close connection with the truth, inviting scrutiny and improvement. . . . The material for a great change was here. But it required to be wrought, and Mohammed was the workman."

Jews had made their homes in the Arabian peninsula in the earliest times. From the days of Solomon the Red Sea was the avenue of a thrifty commerce, and Hebrews had probably located at the trading ports. Later the conquests of Palestine by Assyrians, Babylonians, Persians, Egyptians, Greeks, and Romans had sent waves of Jewish immigration into the desert. The fall of Jerusalem and the rebellion of Bar Cochab had driven thousands of Jews in the footsteps of their brethren. A number of native Arab tribes embraced Judaism, and in the time of Mohammed we find this people scattered all over the peninsula, in small compact colonies. There were a large number of colonies near Medina, and from their teachers Mohammed drew much of the material found in the Koran. At first he hoped to win them to Islam, and contemplated making Jerusalem the Kibla. Their obduracy changed his temper, and in the conflicts that ensued thousands of Jews were butchered, and most of the others submitted to Islam. Communities of Jews are still to be found in Southern Arabia who have clung to their faith all these centuries.

III. *The Life of Mohammed.*—Into this world of conflicting dogmas Mohammed was born in the year 570 A.D., at Mecca. This city, situated on the caravan route between Yemen and Syria, had for centuries been famous for the Kaaba, which contained the sacred Black Stone and formed the centre of the Arabian peninsula. The leading tribe had for years been the Koreish, and Mohammed sprang from the Beni Hashim, a noble though somewhat waning branch of this tribe. His father's name was Abdallah. Returning from a mercantile trip to Syria, Abdallah was taken sick at Medina, and died some months before the birth of Mohammed. His mother, Amina, according to the prevailing custom, put the infant out to nurse with Halima, a woman of the Beni Sâd, one of the Bedawin tribes, where he remained four or five years, acquiring the free manners and the pure tongue of the nomads. His Bedawin nurse was more than once alarmed by epileptic symptoms in her charge, and at the age of about five years he was given back to the keeping of Amina. The following year,

while travelling toward Medina with her boy, Amina died, and the orphaned Mohammed was taken up by his uncle, Abu Tâleb, who became his faithful guardian. At the age of twelve years Mohammed accompanied his uncle on a mercantile trip to Syria, when he first came in contact with the rites and symbols of Oriental Christianity. As a youth he lived for the most part quietly, keeping the flocks of Abu Tâlib, and at the age of twenty-five, his uncle being poor, he entered the service of a rich widow named Khadîja. He was sent by her on a trading journey to Syria, and superintended the caravan. Khadija was delighted with her agent's service, and though almost double his age, soon became his wife. She bore him four daughters and two sons. Both sons died. The youngest daughter, Fatima, married Ali, and thus became the ancestress of all the Moslem nobility.

When approaching his fortieth year Mohammed began to retire from his family for the purpose of meditation. The gross idolatry of Arabia oppressed his mind. He was aroused but not satisfied by his slight knowledge of Judaism and Christianity. For days at a time he would continue in a lonely cave on Mount Hira. Ecstatic reveries accompanied his meditations, and he finally came to believe himself called to be the reformer of his people. After a period of silence known as the *fatrah*, these revelations continued with more or less frequency till the end of his life.

Khadija was his first convert. The first three years of his preaching resulted in the conversion of some forty of his relatives and friends, among whom were Ali, Zeid, Abu Bekr, and Othman. His teaching against idolatry developed fierce opposition, in which Mohammed was safe under the protection of Abu Tâleb, but others suffered persecution, and in 615 eleven men fled to Abyssinia. In 620 Abu Tâleb and Khadija died. Mohammed afterward married other wives, nine of whom survived him. Proceeding to Tâif, he was unsuccessful in his appeal to the people there, but returned strengthened by a dream of a journey to heaven. In 621 his cause was greatly advanced by the addition of twelve pilgrims from Medina, and the following year the band was increased to seventy, who were pledged to receive and defend the prophet in Medina. His brightest hopes now centred about the northern city. Abandoning Mecca, he and 150 followers in little bands fled to Medina. This date marks the era of the Hégira (migration), A.D. 622.

At Medina Mohammed built a mosque, instituted rites of worship, and declared war against unbelievers. The Jews rejecting his claims, he became their bitter foe. In 623 the battle of Bedr resulted in a signal victory for the Moslems over the Meccans. A year later he was defeated by the Koreish at Ohod, and Medina was unsuccessfully besieged by 4,000 Meccans. About this time the Beni Koreitza, the last of the Jewish tribes in the neighborhood, surrendered to the power of Mohammed, and over 600 men were beheaded by his order. In the sixth year of the Hégira Mohammed, with 1,500 followers made a pilgrimage to Mecca, but was refused admittance. A truce was signed at Hodeibia, near the city, suspending hostilities for ten years, and granting permission for a pilgrimage the following year. Discontent was allayed among the Moslem converts by an expedition against the Jews of Kheibar, yielding rich booty.

His plans now widened, and the same year he sent written demands to the Persian king, Chosroes II., Emperor Heraclius, the Governor of Egypt, the Abyssinian king, and several Arab tribes.

Chosroes tore up the letter and Muta killed the envoy. To revenge this insult Mohammed fought a losing battle at Muta, on the Syrian border, where his friend Zeid was killed.

A breach of the truce at this time by the Koreish gave grounds for attack, and Mohammed at the head of 10,000 men entered Mecca in triumph in 630.

In the course of the year Tâif submitted, and this ended opposition in the peninsula. In 632 Mohammed with his wives and 40,000 adherents performed the "Farewell Pilgrimage" to Mecca. The rites of this pilgrimage are still scrupulously followed. Three months after Mohammed fell sick and died in the house of his favorite wife, Ayesha, after having liberated his slaves and distributed alms to the poor. He was buried in the room where he died, which is now included within the Great Mosque.

The person of Mohammed was attractive. Though little above the ordinary height, his presence was stately and commanding. His expression was always pensive and contemplative. His eyes and hair were black, and a beard reached to his breast. His gait was quick, and is said to have resembled a man descending a hill.

As to his character, up to the end of his life in Mecca his sincerity cannot be doubted, and his conduct seems beyond reproach. He believed himself to be the divinely appointed messenger for the overturning of idolatry, and he suffered for years the taunts of a nation with apparently no ulterior motive but the reformation of his people. Secular history can furnish no more striking example of moral courage than Mohammed bearing patiently the scorn and insults of the Koreish. From the beginning of life in Medina temporal power and the acquisition of wealth and glory mingled with the Prophet's motives. Cruelty, greed, and gross licentiousness were justified by special "revelations." His conduct during the last ten years of his life seems to bear out this estimate of his character, "that he was delivered over to the judicial blindness of a self-deceived heart."

IV. *The Korân.*—Like Christianity, Islam centres about a book. This book is the Korân ("reading" or "that which is to be read"). This title is applied by the Moslems to the whole book or to such selections as may be used at one time. The Korân is the foundation of Islam. The faithful believe that the original text existed in heaven as a "concealed book," "a well-guarded tablet." By a process of "sending down," one piece after another was communicated to the Prophet, who in turn proclaimed them to his immediate circle of followers, and so to the world. The Mohammedan idea of God excludes the thought of direct intercourse between God and the Prophet, and this rendered necessary a mediator, who is sometimes known as the "Spirit" and again as "Gabriel," who dictated the words directly to Mohammed. This being the origin and nature of the Korân, all Moslems hold to its absolute

verbal inspiration, and regard it as the rule of faith and practice, from which there can be no appeal.

The Korân as given to the Moslem world is in Arabic, a volume slightly smaller than the New Testament. It is divided into 114 chapters or *suras*, of very unequal length, a *sura* literally meaning a row or series. This collection constitutes the Revelation proclaimed by Mohammed as received during the last twenty-three years of his life. The heading of each sura indicates whether it was revealed at Mecca or Medina, though it must be noted that these headings are the work of commentators, and form no part of the inspired text. Every sura is in turn divided into verses, though it is doubtful if these subdivisions are actually numbered in any manuscript copies.

The 114 chapters are arranged seemingly in a most artless manner, without regard to chronology or doctrine, the only order discernible being that the longest are placed first, with the notable exception of Sura I., called the *Fatihat*. So far as is known, Mohammed himself never wrote anything down, and if he was acquainted with the arts of reading and writing (which some have disputed), it seems that he found it more convenient to employ an amanuensis whenever he had anything to commit to writing. At the time of his death the revelations existed only in scattered fragments, on bits of stone, leather, and thigh-bones. The great repository of truth was in the minds of his followers. With the marvellous tenacity of the Arab memory, large numbers of Moslems at the time of their Prophet's death could repeat the principal suras, and soon after some are mentioned who could recite the whole without an error. With Mohammed's death the canon was closed, but up to this time no attempt had been made to systematically arrange or even to collect the contents. In the second year after this event a vast number of the best reciters of the Korân were slain at the battle of Yemâna, and Omar became convinced that the divine revelation ought to be put on a less precarious footing. The attention of Abu Bekr being called to the matter, he speedily appointed Zeid, the chief amanuensis of the Prophet, to make the collection.

Zeid worked diligently, and brought together the fragments of the Korân from every quarter, gathering them from "palm-leaves, stone tablets, the breast-bones of sheep and camels, from bits of leather, but most of all from the breasts of men." The tablets of the Arab memory were at that time the reliable source of much of the revelation. The manuscript thus formed was given into the keeping of Haphsa, one of the Prophet's widows, and remained during the caliphate of Omar the standard text.

As transcripts of this original were made variety crept in, and in the caliphate of Othmân, sometime a little later than 33 A.H., Zeid was appointed to make a recension of his former text. With a committee of three Koreish to act as final judges in disputed cases, the new collection was made in the pure Meccan dialect, which Mohammed himself used. The former copies were called in and burned, and the recension of Othmân has remained down to the present day unaltered. All the facts warrant us in supposing that the Korân as now existing contains the very words as delivered by the Prophet. Various readings are practically unknown.

One source of the Korân's power is the simplicity of its doctrine. The unity of God, Judgment, and Islam (that is, submission to His will) are the fundamental teachings. The whole substance of the religion is comprehended under two propositions, which are sometimes spoken of as the Mohammedan "Confession of Faith," viz., "There is no God but God, and Mohammed is His Prophet." The former sweeps away idolatry, and the latter at once lends divine authority to every precept of Mohammed. The portion of confession pertaining to faith embraces six branches: Belief in God; in His angels; in His scriptures; in His prophets; in the resurrection and the day of judgment; in God's absolute decree, and predestination of both good and evil.

Relating to practice, there are four points: prayer, alms, fasting, and the pilgrimage to Mecca.

Salvation depends on belief, and "the believer is at the same time bound to do good works, and, in particular, to observe the ordinances of Islam." Large portions of the Korân deal with the narratives of the Jewish and Christian Scriptures, showing that Mohammed had come in contact with the corrupt forms of these religions then in Arabia. The Old Testament characters, especially the Patriarchs and Prophets, and Our Lord Himself, are regarded with the greatest reverence. His narratives taken from the Jewish and Christian sources are, however, often garbled, and many are drawn from later apocryphal accounts. The Korân prescribes an ethical code, dealing with the relation of the sexes, inheritance, the indulgence of appetites, etc. If we may trust the opinion of some of the most learned of modern scholars, the Korân is to-day the most widely-read book in existence.

V. *The Hadeeth or Traditions.*—All Mohammedans regard the Koran as the only divine book, but along with it they place what they consider to be the well-authenticated sayings of the prophet, which they call "an unread revelation." The utterances that have in this way come down purport to be authoritative declarations on religious, ethical, and ceremonial subjects, "uninspired records of inspired sayings." They inform us not only what Mohammed said and did, but what he allowed others to say and do unrebuked. Mohammed was much afraid that he would be misreported, and commanded his adherents as follows: "Convey to other persons none of my words except those ye know of a surety. Verily he who represents my words wrongly shall find a place for himself in the fire." How poorly this injunction was followed is evident from the fact that Abu Daud received only 4,800 traditions out of 500,000. Thus it appears why there is such a diversity of opinion among Mohammedans. Various canons of criticism have been laid down by learned Moslems by which these traditions may be sifted—such as the integrity of the persons transmitting the saying, the number of links in the chain of narrators, the style of composition, etc. The first attempts to collect these traditions were made in the 8th century. The work of Imam Malik is held in the greatest esteem. The six standard collections (out of 1465 in all) are by (1) Mohammed Ismail al Bukhari, A.H. 256;

(2) Muslim ibnu'l Hajjaj, A.H. 261; (3) Abu 'Isa Mohammed at-Tirmizi, A.H. 279; (4) Abu Da'ud as-Sajistani, A.H. 275; (5) Abu 'Abdi'r-Rahman an Nasa'i, A.H. 303; and (6) Abu 'Abdi 'llah Mohammed Ibn Majah, A.H. 273.

All the Moslem sects receive the traditions, although the Sunnites arrogate to themselves the title of "Traditionists." The following are a few characteristic sayings of Mohammed:

"I am no more than a man, but when I enjoin anything respecting religion, receive it, and when I order anything about the affairs of the world, then I am nothing more than a man."—"I have left you two things, and you will not stray as long as you hold them fast. The one is the book of God, and the other is the law (Sunnah) of his prophet."—"Some of my injunctions abrogate others."—"My sayings do not abrogate the Word of God, but the Word of God can abrogate my sayings."

The following is a specimen of the way a tradition was handed down in the collection of at-Tirmizi:

"Abu Kuraib said to us that Ibrahim ibn Yusuf ibn Abi Ishaq said to us from his father, from abu Ishaq, from Tulata ibn Musarif, that he said, I have heard from Abdu'r-Rahman ibn Ausajah that he said I have from Bara ibn 'Azib that he said I have heard that the prophet said, 'Whoever shall give in charity a milch-cow, or silver, or a leathern bottle of water it shall be equal to the freeing of a slave.'" (See "Tradition" in Hughes' Dict. of Islam, and Muir's Life of Mahomet, Vol. 1., Introd., p. xxviii.)

VI. *Islam and the Bible.*—Mohammedans profess to receive the Old and New Testament Scriptures, as well as the Koran, as the revealed Word of God. Mohammed and his immediate followers seem to have considered the Koran as being in perfect harmony with the Bible. When the discrepancies were pointed out somewhat later, the learned Moslem doctors claimed that the current Scriptures had been corrupted since Mohammed's time. They claimed that the Koran was in perfect accord with the original Scriptures to which their prophet had access. The modern discovery of texts of the New Testament older than Mohammed's times has seriously weakened that argument. When once they are compelled to admit the genuineness and antiquity of the uncial manuscripts, they will be compelled to show reason for the discrepancies.

The Koran gives a large part of the Old Testament history in a garbled form. Adam, created out of earth, the "chosen one of God," was the first man. Eve, his wife, was created by God from a rib of Adam's left side. Iblees (Satan) tempted them, they fell and were cast out of Paradise. The story of Abel and Cain is embellished with rabbinical additions. Noah, "the Prophet of God," is a prominent person in the Koran, and the narrative of the flood is told with many amusing details. Abraham, "the Friend of God," is mentioned very freely, together with Ishmael and Isaac. The story of the conversion of Abraham is of a high order. "When the night overshadowed him he saw a star and he said, This is my Lord. But when it set he said, I like not those that set. And when he saw the moon rising he said, This is my Lord; but when it set he said, Verily if my Lord direct me not I shall assuredly be of the erring people. And when he saw the sun rising, he said, This is my Lord. This is greater. But when it set he said, O my people, I am clear of the objects which ye associate with God. Verily I turn my face unto Him who hath created the heavens and the earth; following the right religion I am not of the polytheists." The story of his sojourn in Babylonia is given elaborately. His journey to Palestine, his dealings with corrupt Lot, the half-miraculous birth of Isaac, the destruction of the cities of the plain, the attempted sacrifice of Isaac, together with apocryphal incidents, are tediously set forth. Abraham gives direction to his children as to Islam, the true religion, and is accounted the first "Hanif," the founder of the Moslem faith in its present form. The stories of Isaac, Ishmael, Joseph, the life and bondage of the Hebrews in Egypt, Moses and the wanderings in the desert, Joshua (slightly mentioned), Samuel, Saul, David, Solomon, Job, Elijah, Elisha, Isaiah, Jonah, Ezra, are given in a prolix fashion. Turning to the New Testament we find mention of Zacharias, with John the Baptist, his son, and Gabriel. There is no evidence in the Koran that Mohammed ever saw a copy of the New Testament, but he constantly mentions it as the "Injil which was given to Jesus." The Koran says: (57 : 27) "We caused our Apostles to follow in their (i.e. Noah and Abraham) footsteps, and We caused Jesus the son of Mary to follow them, and We gave him the Injil, and We put into the hearts of those who followed him kindness and compassion, but as to the monastic life, they invented it themselves." Again (3 : 2): "He has sent thee a book (Koran) confirming what was sent before it, and has revealed the Law and the Gospel before, for the guidance of men." (See also 7 : 156; 3 : 43; 3 : 58; 48 : 29; 9 : 112; 5 : 50, 51, 70, 72, and 110; 19 : 31.)

Very full statements are made concerning Jesus Christ. He is called Jesus ('Isa), Jesus the Son of Mary, the Messiah, the Word of God, the Word of Truth, a Spirit from God, the Messenger of God, the Servant of God, the Prophet of God and illustrious in this world and the next. Mohammed taught that Jesus was miraculously born of the "Virgin" Mary (Sura 3:37–43; 19:16–21) who was the sister of Aaron. The infant vindicated the chastity of its mother miraculously by speaking in its cradle (19 : 22–34; 23 : 52). Jesus performed miracles in his youth (Apocryphal Gospels) and in his maturity (3 : 43–46; 5 : 112–115). He was commissioned as a Prophet of God to confirm the Law and reveal the Gospel (57 : 26, 27; 5 : 50, 51; 2 : 81, 254; 61 : 6; 6 : 85; 4 : 157; 3 : 44). The Koran affirms that Jesus did not die, but ascended to heaven miraculously, and another victim was, unknowingly to the Roman soldiers, substituted for Jesus on the cross. (3 : 47–50; 4 : 155, 156.) After he left the earth his disciples disputed as to whether he was a prophet, like Moses or Isaiah, or a part of the Godhead, making up the Trinity as "The Father, the Mother, and the Son." (19 : 35, 36; 3 : 51; 52; 43 : 57–65; 9 : 30; 3 : 72, 73; 5 : 19; 5 : 76–79; 4 : 169; 5 : 116, 117). The Traditions teach that Jesus will come a second time, and that he will be the Judge at the last great day, and that even Mohammed will be judged by him. Jesus, it is claimed, was more than a prophet or an apostle, he was a Spirit of God. He predicted one that should come after him who should carry out his mission, and Moslem theologians affirm that Mo-

hammed was that person. Mohammed himself calls himself "Ahmad," (Sura 61 : 6), "The Praised," to adapt his name to the title used by Christ which Moslems claim had been perverted from "Paraclitos" to "Paracletos," the former meaning "the Praised" and thus designating Mohammed ("The Praised").

Sir William Muir says : "After a careful and repeated examination of the whole Koran I have been able to discover no grounds for believing that Mohammed himself ever expressed the smallest doubt at any period of his life in regard either to the authority or the genuineness of the Old and New Testaments as extant at his time. He was profuse in his assurances that his system entirely corresponded with both, and that he had been foretold by former prophets; and as perverted Jews and Christians were at hand to confirm his words, and as the Bible was little known among the generality of his followers, those assurances were implicitly believed." (Muir's Life of Mahomet; Lond. ed. Vol. I. p. lxx.)

VII. *History of Mohammedan Conquests.*—At the time of Mohammed's death (June 8th, 632 A.D., in the 11th year of the Moslem era) the whole of the Arabian peninsula had embraced Islam, with the exception of a few southern tribes which preferred Moseylemah, the "false prophet" of the Nejd. The few hours that succeeded the death of Mohammed were critical for Islam. Ali, the nephew and son-in-law of the prophet, a young man, and Abu Bekr, the old staunch follower of Mohammed, and the father of Ayesha, the prophet's favorite wife, were the natural candidates for the leadership. Abu Bekr was at last proclaimed caliph ("successor"), and the wisdom of the election was made plain by the vitality which characterized his reign of two years. The rebellious tribes of Arabia were subdued, the government was thoroughly organized and centralized, and the long career of victory was begun. Under Khaled the armies crossed the Syrian frontier, occupied Bosrah, overran the Hauran, defeated the Byzantine army on the plains of Eznadin, and invested Damascus. After a seventy days' siege this capital of Southern Syria fell August 3d, 634 A.D. (13 A.H.). Sweeping eastward and northward, Khaled defeated a second Byzantine army at Yamook. In the meanwhile Omar succeeded to the caliphate, August 22d, 634 A.D. Jerusalem was conquered, and all Syria was in the hands of Moslems. In the mean time an army was pushing across the Persian frontier. At the battle of Kadisiya the initial failure of the Arabs was retrieved, Ctesiphon and Susa fell, Mesopotamia was gained, and on the field of Mahavend (641 A.D.) the Sassanid dynasty of Persia received a death blow. The whole of Persia, Khorasan, Kerman, Mekran, Seistan, and Balkh were conquered and assimilated. The century had not passed before the Oxus was the eastern boundary of the caliph's empire.

In 641 A.D. Amr invaded Egypt, which fell with hardly a struggle, the Monophysite Christians throwing in their lot with the Arabs as against the orthodox Byzantines. Othman succeeded to the caliphate in 644 A.D. The armies steadily pushed westward. Libya, Tripoli, Tunis, Algeria, and Morocco fell successively. A Christian civilization made a firm stand at Carthage, but in the battle of Utica (698 A.D.) the Byzantine power was broken, and Musa rode to his saddle-girths into the Atlantic, and with raised sword took possession of the regions beyond in the name of Allah.

Othman had been assassinated in 656 A.D., and Ali, Mohammed's nephew, was at last raised to the caliphate. A rebellion was put down at the battle of the Camel, fought at Basra, November, 656 A.D. The murder of Othman aroused the Koreishite faction. Mo'awiya of this tribe, the Syrian governor, did not recognize Ali as caliph, and Ali saw it was a hopeless task to subdue him. The strength of Ali was in Kufa. The Syrians gained the battle of Siffin by fastening copies of the Koran to their lances (657). Disaffection arose among the caliph's forces, and he was murdered in January, 661 A.D., becoming a martyr in the eyes of a large part of the Moslem world, and occasioning that great split in the faith which has ever since divided Shiite (Ali's faction) from Sunnite (traditionists). Mo'awiya was proclaimed caliph by his soldiers. Moslem Persia proclaimed Hassan, a son of Ali, as caliph; but on being defeated in battle, Hassan retired from the struggle. Hossein, another son of Ali, was not so tractable. The Syrian caliph showed great statesmanship in the management of his empire, which was expanding in every direction. Armenia, Cyprus, Cos, and Crete were conquered, and even Constantinople was invested. Mo'awiya died at Damascus, which he made the capital of the Ommeiad dynasty, of which he was the founder, 680 A.D., and was succeeded by his son, Yazid I. This voluptuous caliph ordered the prefect of Medina to strike off the head of Hossein, a son of Ali, if he would not yield. Hossein fled toward Kufa with all his family. The Ommeiad army met him in the plain of Kerbela, near Kufa, and surrounded his little company. Hossein declared himself ready to renounce all pretension to the caliphate, but on October 9th, 680 (9th of Moharram, A.H. 61), on his refusal to surrender his person to the enemy, he and all his followers were cut to pieces. The Shiites observe the 10th of Moharram as a day of public mourning. The news of this bloody ending of the son of Ali spread consternation far and wide. Revolts were with difficulty put down. Ali, son of Hossein, wisely refused to put himself at the head of the opposition. Medina was plundered, and Mecca was in a state of siege, when news came of the death of the caliph at Damascus (November 11th, 683). Mo'awiya II., Merwan I., Abd al Melik, al Walid, and the other caliphs in the Ommeiad dynasty saw Islam extending in every direction. Tarik crossed the strait, ever after called from him Jebel Tarik (Gibraltar), into Spain in 711 A.D.; Roderick, the last of the Visigothic kings, lost his crown and life in the battle of Xeres; Malaga, Granada, Cordova, Seville, Toledo, Saragossa, Barcelona, and the whole Spanish peninsula, except a few mountain retreats, were rapidly conquered. In 731 Abder-Rahman crossed the Pyrenees and swept up as far as Tours, where his host was defeated by Charles Martel in 732.

In the meanwhile the Ommeiad dynasty at Damascus began to decline. Ibrahim, great-grandson of Abbas, the uncle of the Prophet, of the house of Hashem, put himself at the head of a revolt, which under his son Abd Allah Abu-Abbas, the "Blood-shedder," was successful. The Ommeiad dynasty gave place to the Abbassides, and the newly-built city of Baghdad became the capital of the Moslem world.

The year 750 A.D. was the turning-point in Islam. There were still further conquests to be made in Central Asia, India, and Central Africa, but the unity of the Moslem world was broken politically forever. The Abbassides controlled affairs in the east, but the Ommeiads held on in Spain. In 755 Abder-Rahman founded the caliphate of Cordova, which ran a brilliant career until 1013 A.D., when Moslem power in Spain was broken up into various factions. Christians were treated with great leniency, universities were established, libraries collected, literature, science, and art fostered, and from these centres went forth light which hastened the dawning of modern civilization. The "Mozarabes" ("Arabs by adoption") were Christians living under this mild rule, who were the instruments of this wide diffusion of Arab learning throughout Europe.

The Saracens did not long remain in France. In 760 Pepin the Short drove them over the Pyrenees. Charles the Great (Charlemagne) drove them back in Spain beyond the Ebro. By the year 1030 A.D. the kingdom of Leon was well established. Navarre, Aragon, Castile, and Portugal were gathering headway. Sardinia in 1017 was reclaimed from the Arabs, and Corsica in 1050. The Balearic Islands were won by Aragon. By the middle of the fourteenth century the Saracens had nothing left in Spain but the little mountainous kingdom of Granada. In 1492 the combined forces of Castile and Aragon under the lead of Ferdinand the Catholic extinguished this last faint glimmer of Moslem rule in Southwestern Europe, at the close of a crusade lasting eight centuries.

With the downfall of the Ommeiad dynasty at Damascus Arabia lost political power in the Moslem world. The Abbassides at Baghdad were non-Arab in tendency. The subtile scepticism of Persia brought a looseness and indifference in sharp contrast with the strict and fanatical Arab type. Founded in 750, this dynasty existed until 1258. For a hundred years it ran a brilliant career. Baghdad was the resort of learned men from every region. Greek letters and philosophy were cultivated. Haroun er-Rasheed (768–809 A.D.) gathered at his court an assemblage of the wisest and wittiest minds in his empire. Arabic literature expanded under his patronage. He sent an embassy to the court of Charles the Great, and gathered information from every quarter. But the first century of Abbasside rule was followed by four centuries of decay. The Karmathian revolt in Arabia greatly weakened the central organization. Turkish mercenaries at Baghdad, called in as a body-guard of the caliph, acquired more and more power, and the last caliphs were mere puppets in their hands. Province after province was dismembered. In 1258 Holagoo, grandson of Genghis Khan, overthrew Baghdad and extinguished the Abbasside rule.

In 909 A.D. the Fatimite dynasty was founded in Egypt by Obeidallah, a supposed descendant of Ali and Fatima. The story of this mystic rule in Egypt is revolting to the extreme. Cairo was founded and made the capital. Saladin put an end to this dynasty in 1171 A.D.

In the mean time Islam had been pushing steadily eastward. Large bodies of Mongols were converted, among them several tribes of Turks, members of which served in the body-guard at Baghdad and learned the arts of civilization. The Seljuk Turks appeared as an independent body of marauders as early as 1035 A.D., and pushed south and west to the Mediterranean. After conquering Armenia, they set up a powerful kingdom in Central Asia Minor, threatening destruction to the Byzantine empire. Their discontinuance of the mild treatment of Christian pilgrims to the holy places about Jerusalem excited the Crusades, which held the attention of Europe from 1095 to 1291, and which resulted in the checking of the onset of the Seljuk Turk, but left Syria a prey to discord. A little later the Ottoman Turk appeared, and by 1300 A.D. had a firm position on the border of the Byzantine empire. After absorbing all the Greek territory in Asia, the Ottoman armies entered Europe in 1354; Constantinople fell a century later (1453), and the whole Balkan peninsula was under the crescent. The armies of the sultans pressed up the Danube as far as Vienna, but from the last part of the 17th century the Ottoman has been receding, until he has only a precarious foothold in Europe.

Islam obtained a firm foothold in India as early as 1000 A.D. An attempt to conquer Sindh in the eighth century had failed. It was not until the Moslem Turk appeared that Islam made headway. Seventeen invasions and twenty-five years of fighting under the leadership of Mahmud of Ghazni (1001–1030) had reduced only the western portions of the Punjab. Bengal was conquered in 1203. By 1306, as a result of the barbarous conquests of three centuries, there was a powerful Mohammedan rule in Northern India. The story of Islam in India is one of constant revolts, or uninterrupted invasions and steady aggrandizement. There were a large number of independent Mohammedan states when the Mogul dynasty (1526–1761) put in appearance. Babar (1482–1530), having gathered headway on the Afghan side of the Indian passes, pushed through in 1526 and conquered right and left, until at his death his empire stretched from the river Amu in Central Asia to the delta of the Ganges. This vast power began to decline as early as 1707. Independent Moslem kingdoms were detached from the main body. The Marhattas grew in power until they were able to break the Mogul Empire into pieces. The English East India Company was already at work in India, backed by the British army. The first governor, Lord Clive, took the helm in 1758. The Company grew until nothing less than a great military power could properly care for the immense territory and the millions under its control. Since 1858 the Mohammedans of India have been directly under English rule.

The spread of Islam in China, Australasia, and Central Africa cannot be traced historically. During the last hundred years its extension has been promoted very largely by peaceful measures. Having conquered the Mediterranean coast of Africa Mohammedanism pushed up the Nile valley and across the Sahara. Abyssinia alone has been able to withstand the Moslem civilization, and remains like an island in a sea of Islam. The native terminology of the geography of all Northern Africa as far south as the equator is Arabic. Misr (Egypt), Sahara, Soudan, Bahr el Abyad (White Nile), Bahr el-Asrak (Blue Nile), Bahr el Ghasel, are specimen names. The Arabic has penetrated south beyond the Zambesi River, as is shown in "Kafir" (Caffre), which means infidel or unbeliever. In Zanzibar and throughout Central Africa the

Swahili dialect of the Arabic is the language of commerce. Islam has spread in Africa by three agencies—the sword, commerce, and the missionary.

VIII. *The Extent of Islam To-day.*—It is impossible to estimate accurately the numerical strength of the Mohammedan world. For many years it was reckoned at 160,000,000, but the latest investigations push it up to 200,000,000. The following table is drawn from the most recent data (see Statesman's Year Book, 1890):

EUROPE.

| | | |
|---|---|---|
| Roumania | 2,000 | |
| Bulgaria | 668,173 | |
| Servia | 14,569 | |
| Bosnia and Herzegovina | 492,710 | |
| Montenegro | 10,000 | |
| Greece | 24,000 | |
| Turkey in Europe | 2,000,000 | |
| Russia in Europe | 2,600,000 | |
| Total for Europe | | 5,811,452 |

ASIA

| | | |
|---|---|---|
| Turkey in Asia (including Arabia) | 22,000,000 | |
| Persia | 7,560,600 | |
| Bokhara | 2,500,000 | |
| Russia in Caucasus | 2,000,000 | |
| Khiva | 700,000 | |
| Russia in Central Asia | 3,000,000 | |
| Siberia | 61,000 | |
| Afghanistan | 4,000,000 | |
| India | 50,121,595 | |
| Ceylon | 197,775 | |
| Baluchistan | 500,000 | |
| China | 30,000,000 | |
| Australasia | 15,000,000 | |
| Total for Asia | | 137,640,970 |

AFRICA.

| | | |
|---|---|---|
| Egypt | 6,000,000 | |
| Zanzibar | 200,000 | |
| Morocco | 5,000,000 | |
| Tripoli | 1,000,000 | |
| Tunis | 1,500,000 | |
| Algeria | 3,000,000 | |
| Bornu (Lake Tsad) | 5,000,000 | |
| Wadai | 2,600,000 | |
| Baghirmi | 1,500,000 | |
| Egyptian Soudan | 10,400,000 | |
| Sokoto and feudatory states | 14,000,000 | |
| Sahara and scattered | 10,000,000 | |
| Total for Africa | | 60,200,000 |
| Total for Europe | 5,811,452 | |
| Total for Asia | 137,640,970 | |
| Total for Africa | 60,200,000 | |
| Total Moslems | | 203,652,422 |

It is believed that these figures will fall below rather than above the facts. Let us examine more in detail the various countries. Roumania, Servia, Montenegro, and Greece have nearly rid themselves of the Turk. Those who remain are scattered about as land-owners and merchants. It is said that they are moving towards Asia Minor slowly, and before long will not be an appreciable part of the population. The same is true of Bosnia, Herzegovina, and Bulgaria, although over a million Moslems still remain in these lands. Turkey in Europe has two million Mohammedans, scattered from the

Adriatic to the Bosphorus. These are more stationary, although it is a common feeling among the Turks that Anatolia (Asia Minor) is their true home, and there is a constant movement that way as European civilization more and more pervades the Balkan peninsula. It should be remembered, however, that by far the greater number of the Moslems of European Turkey, etc., are not Turks, but natives of the land who accepted Islam, and have always identified themselves with the Turkish government. What course they will take is by no means certain.

Mohammedanism in European Russia has of late attracted considerable attention, especially since the last census. It is largely confined to Southern and Eastern Russia—territory which for centuries has been occupied by Tartars, Mongols and Turks (synonyms). In 1886, 50,955 roubles were dispensed by the Russian Government to the Mussulman clergy. There are said to be 20,000 muftis, mollahs, and other teachers in European Russia. A majority of the population of the Transcaucasus district are Moslems, as might have been expected. As Russia has pushed down toward the Persian and Afghanistan borders she has taken in more and more tribes of Mohammedans. Professor Arminius Vambéry, a witness of the highest intelligence, in writing of these Moslem portions of the Russian Empire, has said ("Nineteenth Century," February, 1890, pp. 203-4): "In the cities of Central Asia, where Islam has taken much firmer root than in the Caucasus or the other parts of the Mohammedan world, there can be no probability of the old and knotty trunk of religious education being soon shaken. On the whole, Islam stands everywhere firmly on its feet, nor can Christianity succeed in weakening it. Indeed, when subjected to Christian rule it seems to become stronger and more stubborn, and to gain in expansive force. This we see in India, where, in spite of the zeal of the Christian missionaries and the millions spent in their support, the conversions to Islam become daily more frequent. We see this too in Russia, where statistics prove that the number of mosques has considerably increased in the course of this century, and that the heathen among the Ural-Altaic people are more easily converted by the Mollah than by the Pope. . . . Bokhara will still long continue to boast of being the brightest spot in Islam, and her colleges will not soon lose their attraction for the studious youth among the Moslems of Inner Asia."

The British Empire is the greatest Mohammedan power in the world, in that it rules over more followers of the Prophet than does any other one sovereignty. The statistics for India are elaborately worked out. The figures given in the table were those for 1881, and probably several millions should be added (one authority putting the number of Moslems in India as 80,000,000). They are massed in Bengal (22,000,000), Punjab (12,000,000), Northwest Provinces, including Oudh (6,000,000), Bombay (4,000,000), Madras (2,000,000), Assam (1,000,000), Hyderabad (1,000,000), Rajputana (1,000,000), Central India (50,000), and the others are in Ajmere, Berar, British Burmah, Central Provinces, Coorg, Baroda, Cochin, Mysore, and Travancore. Mohammedanism has considerable influence in Ceylon. In speaking of the growth of Islam in India, Sir William Hunter says: "Islam is progressing in India neither

more quickly nor more slowly than the rest of the population. If you take a hasty view of India and add up totals, you will find that Islam now has a great many more followers than it had 10 years ago. But you will find that the whole population has increased." He places the increase of Mohammedans at 10½ per cent. during the nine years for which we have comparative statistics.

The extent of Islam in China must remain conjectural for many years. Thirty millions may seem too high a figure (see Statesman's Year-Book, 1890, p. 412). Moslems are found in dense masses in the Province of Yunnan and in Western Chinese Tartary, and they are also scattered in communities throughout the Empire. The Mohammedan name for China is Tung Tu ("Land of the East"). There stands a Mohammedan mosque in the southwestern angle of Pekin, in the midst of the Moslem quarter, where are found 200,000 Mohammedans. Hangchau is also a stronghold of Islam. Between 1865-73 there was a bloody insurrection among the Mohammedans of the Kansuh Province. According to Dr. S. Wells Williams ("The Middle Kingdom," rev. ed. 1883, vol. ii. p. 268), the introduction of Islam into China was very gradual. It began at the sea-ports of Canton and Hangchau. "The number throughout the region north of the Yangtz River cannot be stated, but it probably exceeds 10,000,000. In some places they form a third of the population. A missionary in Sz'chuen reckons 80,000 living in one of its cities." This being so, it is probable that 30,000,000 of Moslems is a conservative estimate for China.

The wide spread of Mohammedanism in Australasia is becoming more and more evident. It is spreading rapidly among the whole Malay race, and assumes a peculiar type. It established itself in the Malay Peninsula in the 14th century, and crossed into Sumatra, Java, and adjacent islands in the 15th century, thus anticipating the Portuguese by only a few years. There are a large number of Malay Moslems on the Malay Peninsula, in the native states, and under the English flag. Sumatra (128,560 square miles) has a population of 2,000,000, nearly all of whom are strict Mohammedans. Java before 1478 A.D. was Hindu in religion. In that year Islam overthrew the chief Hindu principality of Majapahit, and the conversion of the whole island to Mohammedanism followed within the century. The census for 1886 shows on this island of 50,000 square miles a population of 21,997,560 (see Statesman's Year-Book 1890, p. 770), and of these only 11,229 were Christians. Mohammedanism claims the majority of the remainder. The Celebes, with a population of over 800,000, is largely Mohammedan in religion. Islam had just been introduced when the Portuguese landed in 1525. It spread in a hundred years over all the districts it now occupies. The south peninsula is divided into nine native Moslem states, which form a kind of Bugis confederacy. They are in alliance with the Dutch. North of this is a smaller Mandar confederacy of states, only partly Mohammedan. There are Moslems also along the north coast of Celebes. Concerning Islam in the Dutch possessions, the Rev. Dr. Schreiber of the Rhenish Missionary Society says: "Wherever Mohammedans and heathen are in contact, Islam is winning ground, sometimes slowly, sometimes more speedily. . . . Only a small portion of the whole population remains still heathen, and those only small and insignificant tribes scattered in the forests of Sumatra and Borneo. There are some strong and unmistakable signs of the increasing vigor of Islam in Dutch India. According to the official statements there were in 1886 not less than 48,237 Hadjis (pilgrims to Mecca) in Java alone, against 33,802 in 1874; thus an increase of 40 per cent within 12 years. In Sumatra—not including Atcheen—there were 8,342 Hadjis in 1874 and 15,287 in 1886; thus an increase of 83 per cent. In Borneo and Celebes they increased from 3,019 to 5,074; thus 66 per cent. . . . Those Mohammedan sects whose well-known hostile and aggressive tendencies make them so dangerous, are more and more supplanting the more placable-spirited folks, formerly so common amongst the Mohammedans of Dutch India, especially of Java. Another hardly less ominous sign is the astonishing growth of Mohammedan schools. In 1882 there were in Java 10,913 of those schools, numbering 164,667 pupils; in 1885 we are told there were 16,760 schools, with not less than 225,148 pupils: thus within 3 years an increase of not less than 55 per cent. Even in the residency of Tapanoeli in Sumatra, where the whole of Mohammedanism is of comparatively recent date, we find 210 such schools and 2,479 pupils." (Report of the Missionary Conference, London, 1888, vol. i. pp. 21–2.)

Turning eastward from the Dutch possessions, we find Mohammedanism constantly pushing forward. The large islands of Bouton and Moona are inhabited by Moslem Malays. The coast villages of Bouru, west of Ceram, are inhabited by semi-civilized Mohammedans. In Ceram we have villages nominally Mohammedan. In Amboyna, Banda, Goram, Manowolke, Ké, Mysol, Lombok, and Sumbawa there are considerable numbers of Moslems. Bali and Lombok are the only islands in the Malay Archipelago which maintain their old Hindu religion. The Sulu Archipelago, still further eastward, comprises 150 islands, inhabited by Mohammedans of the Malay race, speaking a peculiar language, which they write with the Arabic character. They are ruled over by a sultan, who claims sovereignty over part of western Borneo. Piracy is prevalent in this region. The Philippine Islands have 7,500,000 inhabitants, 4,000,000 of which are unsubdued Mohammedan and pagan tribes. The Moslems are mostly in the southern portions of this group. Taking all these facts into consideration the figures set down in the table for Islam in Australasia are probably too small. There are at least 150,000,000 Moslems in Asia alone.

Turning to Africa, we find ourselves in still greater difficulty. The data for Egypt, Zanzibar, Morocco, Algeria, Tunis, and Tripoli are correct enough. For the interior we are obliged to use the estimates of travellers (see Statesman's Year-Book, 1890). We can get even these rough estimates for only a few of the tribes. It does not seem exorbitant to put down 10,000,000 for those unaccounted for. Crossing the Atlantic to South America, we find the Protestant missionaries asking for Arabic Bibles to use with Moslems who have immigrated for purposes of trade.

IX. *Sects in Islam.*—It is related that Mohammed said, "Verily it will happen to my people as it did to the children of Israel. The children of Israel were divided into seventy-two sects, and my people will be divided into seventy-three. Every one of these will go to hell except one sect." If the number was put too low for the Christian sects (probably confused with the Jews), the corresponding number is far too low for the Moslem world, and the bitterness of feeling indicated by the traditional utterance of the prophet holds true to-day in the fanatical world of Islam. Shaykh Abdu 'l-Qadir says there are 150 sects in Islam; but there are infinite shades between them which make them practically innumerable. The two grand divisions of the Moslem world are Sunnites ("traditionists"), who account Abu Bekr, Omar, and Othman legitimate caliphs; and the Shiites("followers"), who consider the first three rulers after Mohammed as illegitimate rulers, and account Ali, the prophet's nephew and the husband of Fatima, the first true caliph. The Sunnites embrace by far the larger part of the Moslem world, the Shiites being mainly confined to Persia. Upon the death of Mo'awiya (A.H. 60), Yazid obtained the position of Imam or caliph without the form of election, and hence arose the great schism, which is as strong to-day as ever. The Shiites trace the true Imam down through Ali, Al-Hassan, Al-Hussin, Ali Zainu'l-Abidin, Mohammed el-Baqir, Ja'far as-Sadiq, Musa al-Kazim, Ar-Raza, Mohammed at-Taqi, Ali an-Naqi, Al-Hassan, Al-Askari, and Mohammed, the Imam al-Mahdi. This last Imam is believed by the Shiites to be still alive, although absent for a time, and they claim that he will appear in the last days as the Mahdi ("Director"), after which the judgment day will soon follow. Many of the Shiites carry their veneration for Ali so far as to account him a divine being, and even greater than Mohammed. Besides these differences as to the doctrine of Imams and the person of Ali, the Shiites differ from the Sunnites in observing the ceremonies of the Muharram in commemoration of the cruel death of the sons of Ali, Hassan and Hossein, while the Sunnites observe only the tenth day of Muharram as the day on which God created Adam. The Shiites receive the "fire-worshippers" as a people who have received an inspired record from God, while the Sunnites acknowledge only Jews, Christians, and Moslems as such. The Shiites allow pious fraud when in danger of persecution. The other differences have to do with liturgies and civil law.

Although the Shiites number only about fifteen millions out of two hundred millions, they have about as many subordinate schisms and sects as the Sunnites. It is hard to account for this except on the principle that Persia is the nationality which holds the influential Shiites. The Persians are Aryans, and it may be the outcropping of peculiar Aryan tendencies, and that Persia is the Germany of the Moslem world. The Persians have always had sceptical tendencies, and have demanded a high order of religion. The Sunnites are divided into many sects, the following of which are the most important: (1) the Hanafiyahs (in Turkey, Central Asia, and Northern India); (2) the Shafi'iyahs (Southern India and Egypt); (3) the Malakiyahs (Morocco, Barbary, and other parts of Africa); (4) the Hambaliyahs (Eastern Arabia and some parts of Africa).

In India we find Sikhism (Sikh = "a disciple" or "pupil"). It is confined to the Punjab, and is a strange mixture of Hindu and Mohammedan ideas, and is pantheistic in its tendency. Nanak seized the idea of the unity of God, and reduced the Hindu gods to the subordinate position of angels. The soul of man is a ray of light from the divine Light, and hence naturally sinless. Sin and misfortune are the result of delusion. The object before the believer is to attain the total cessation of individual existence. There are five leading sects among the Sikhs.

In Persia we have a powerful and growing sect, the Sufi, which are subdivided into innumerable divisions or sub-sects. They all inculcate blind submission to an inspired guide. Sufism is Mohammedanism engrafted on the primeval mysticism of Persia. God only is existent; all things are an emanation from Him; religions are matters of indifference; there is no real difference between good and evil; the will of man is fixed by God; the soul existed before the body; and meditation is the method by which the soul may progress along the journey of life so as to attain unification with God.

In Arabia we find the Wahhabees, founded in 1691 A.D., by Mohammed, son of Abdu 'l Wahhab. This sect grew out of the Hambaliyah sect. Its founder was the Luther of Mohammedanism, calling Moslems back to the original Scriptures of Islam. He proposed to do away with saint-worship, which permeated the Moslem world. The Wahhabees call themselves "unitarians," and claim that any man who can read the Koran and sacred traditions can judge for himself in matters of doctrine. They forbid prayers to any prophet, wali, pir, or saint. They hold that at the judgment-day Mohammed will obtain permission of God to intercede for his people. They forbid the illumination of shrines, or prayers and ceremonies in or about them, not excepting Mohammed's shrine. Women must not visit graves, because they weep so violently. This sect has always been fanatical. The sword was appealed to. Abdu 'l Aziz, the leader after 1765 A.D., pushed his conquest to the limits of Arabia. He was assassinated in 1803. His son Sa'ud carried the victorious banner beyond the peninsula, and threatened the Turkish empire. Mecca was conquered in 1803. All sorts of ornaments and pipes were burned. Tobacco was prohibited on pain of death. Sa'ud sent commands to Mohammedan sovereigns in every direction that pilgrims to Mecca must conform to these puritan regulations. Missionaries were sent out. Disturbances were occasioned in Northern India. A little later, Mahomet Ali of Egypt sent a strong force into Arabia under Ibrahim Pasha. The Wahhabees were thoroughly subdued, and Mecca released from the strict rule of this Protestant phase of Islam. The sect since that day has made little if any progress.

X. *Agencies in use to reach Mohammedans.*—Such being the state of the Moslem world, what means are being used to win these millions to Christ, and what success has up to this time attended the efforts of the church? We must believe that God has some beneficent aim in view even when He allows Islam to arise and spread from the Pacific to the Atlantic. Could we fully understand, we should probably see some underlying scheme of Providence which is being worked out before our

eyes, even though the conversion of idolaters and fetich-worshippers to Islam seems to fill them with a gloomy fanaticism which resists Christianity far more successfully than does heathendom itself. Mohammedanism has undoubtedly an elevating influence upon the heathen it wins. It develops a strong individuality, it theoretically and most frequently practically frees from drunkenness, cannibalism, gambling, and the more degrading heathen practices. It elevates womanhood and the family to a certain degree. It gives a regular order of life, and has introduced letters everywhere it has gone. Its use of the sword recalls the method by which Christianity has made its largest territorial conquests (Germany, Spain, South and Central America, Siberia, etc.). With the exception of the Mahdi movement on the upper Nile, its method of propaganda to-day is peaceful and successful. The startling fact is that, although Christian missions have been in contact with Islam for so many years, so little real progress has been made in winning individual Mohammedans to Christ. The task has appeared so formidable, that no great missionary society has been organized with the special object of reaching them, although we have several societies for the conversion of the Jews, who number at most eight millions as contrasted with two hundred million Moslems. We are dealing with Islam incidentally. The best that can be said is that up to this time we have been laying foundations, and perhaps this is all that could have been done. At any rate some of our foundation-stones will be abiding. In the first place, we have put into the sacred language of the Koran the Christian Scriptures. The Arabic Bible, translated by Drs. Eli Smith and Van Dyck, and published at Beyrout, Syria, is accounted one of the finest translations in existence, and is being distributed all over the Moslem world from Sierra Leone to Java. When Mohammedans can be convinced that this Bible is practically the original Scriptures which Mohammed considered to be inspired records, a great deal will have been gained. In lands where Arabic is not the vernacular this Arabic translation is read more freely by Mohammedans than in countries where that language is in common use, for they do not appear to be yielding a point to the Christian missionaries, who do their main work with the masses by means of a local vernacular translation. The Arabic Bible is far more effective than any missionary society we could organize, and which might send forth an army of missionaries.

The second great agency for reaching Islam is the Christian schools and colleges scattered now all over the Mohammedan world. Robert College on the Bosphorus, Anatolia College at Marsovan, Euphrates College at Harpoot, Central Turkey College at Aintab, Oroomiah College in Persia, the Syrian Protestant College at Beyrout, Assiout College in Egypt, and Jaffna College in Ceylon are a few of the list. In Western Africa at Sierra Leone and in Liberia, and in Eastern Africa at Mombasa, we have similar institutions. The great universities of India carried on by the government and by the missionary agencies are reaching Mohammedans. All of these institutions, and thousands of others, especially of a lower grade, are constantly adding to a Christian literature which is bringing a Christian civilization effectively before the Mohammedans, who in the Middle Ages were leaders in science, philosophy, literature, and art.

A third agency to be mentioned is the personal influence of the Christian missionary, whose home is an example of what Christianity can do. Silent influences are sometimes the most effective. The medical missionary is especially successful in reaching all grades of society. Mohammedans rarely attend religious Christian services, but they are respectful on the streets, as a rule, and welcome the missionary to their homes. In many cases they are convinced that Christianity is the true religion, but are afraid to acknowledge Christ openly for fear of social ostracism, if not of legal persecution and martyrdom.

Without attempting to exhaust the catalogue of agencies in use in reaching Mohammedans, we will mention lastly Protestantism or evangelical Christianity as the only phase of Christianity likely to be successful in this great work. Pictures and images used in the service of the Greek Orthodox, Roman Catholic, Coptic, Nestorian, Abyssinian, and other decayed forms of Christianity are utterly revolting to followers of Mohammed, and churches using these can never hope to make headway among Mohammedans. The simple gospel simply proclaimed, must be the effective weapon.

The number of sincere Mohammedans who have been reached successfully is small. In the Turkish Empire it is still death to these religionists to embrace Christianity. In Africa a few individuals have become Christians. A few in Persia and still more in India have turned to Christ. The interesting successes that give us hope, have been achieved in Dutch India (Java and Sumatra). According to Dr. Schreiber, "Of the eleven thousand converted in Java, all of them, with very few exceptions, were won from amongst the Mohammedans. And in Sumatra also, where the number of Christians since 1878 has increased from 2,500 to 12,000, there are hundreds of Mohammedans who have been baptized by our missionaries during the past few years, or are under instruction for baptism just now (1888). I am not aware of any other country where so many converts have been won from Islam in our days as is the case in Dutch India, or where it seems more easy to win many more of them. Notwithstanding the increased vigor of Islam in this region, it is not growing in the same ratio as Christianity; and although the numbers of Mohammedans are swelled yearly, very considerably indeed by the natural increase of the population, the number of converts from heathenism to Islam is very probably far below that of converts made by the Christian missionaries; and whereas conversions from Christianity to Islam are almost never heard of, thousands of Mohammedans are coming over from the adherents of the False Prophet to Jesus Christ, our only Saviour." (See Report Miss. Conference, Lond. 1888, vol. i. pp. 22–3.)

Sir William Hunter, an authority on the statistics of India, says that while Mohammedanism is increasing in that peninsula at the rate of $10\frac{1}{2}$ per cent in nine years, the Christian population has increased at the rate of 64 per cent in the same time.

In Persia Mohammedanism seems to be disintegrating through internal forces. That country stands midway in the Mohammedan world. Over a hundred conflicting Moslem sects are found among the seven or eight millions of this Aryan race dwelling between the Caspian and the Persian Gulf. Russian and English influences are predominant. The naturally sceptical Persian mind is open to new influences. In some important respects Persia is a strategic point in Islam. If it could be won to Christ Islam would be cut in two. There are indications that great transformations may take place in Persia at a not distant date.

On the whole there is everything to encourage the Christian Church to move forward upon this its greatest organized enemy. In the near future the battle must be squarely joined. Civilization is slowly but surely opening the way. Before long all political opposition to the propagation of Christianity in Moslem lands will be over. The followers of Christ never had a more serious undertaking on hand when looked at from the theological, social, ethical, or political standpoint. It calls for the keenest minds and the most consecrated hearts. We shall succeed. " Deus vult."

**Mohawk Version.**—The Mohawk belongs to the languages of North America, and is spoken by Indians west of Niagara Falls. In 1700 the Rev. Mr. Freeman translated the Gospel of Matthew, and some chapters were printed by the Gospel Propagation Society, New York, 1714. In 1787 another translation of Matthew by Joseph Brant, a Mohawk chief, was printed in London at the cost of the crown; and another with English in parallel columns, by the New York District Bible Society, in 1829. The Gospel of John was translated by John Norton, a chief of the Mohawks, and published at London, 1805, by the British and Foreign Bible Society. Another edition was published by the American Bible Society at New York in 1818. In 1832 the three Epistles of John, translated by Rev. Mr. Williams, and the Gospel of Luke, translated by A. Hill, a Mohawk chief, were printed at New York by the Young Men's Bible Society, and in 1835 the Acts of the Apostles and the Epistles to the Romans and Galatians by the same translator. In 1836 the same Society published the Epistles to the Philippians, Colossians, Thessalonians, Timothy, Titus, and Philemon, translated by an educated Mohawk. The latter also translated the Book of Isaiah, which was published in 1843 by the British and Foreign Bible Society, and also by the American Bible Society in 1848.

*(Specimen verse.  John 3 : 16.)*

Iken ne Yehovah egh ne s'hakonoronghkwa n'ongwe, nene rodewendeghton nene raonhâon rodewedon rohhàwàk, nene onghka kiok teyakaweghdaghkon raonhage yaghten a-onghtonde, ok denghnon aontehodiyendane ne eterna adonhëta.

**Molepolole,** town in the Transvaal, East South Africa, on a branch of the Limpopo, northwest of Pretoria. Mission station of L. M. S.; 1 missionary and wife, 174 church-members, 1 out-station, 2 schools, 208 scholars.

**Molokans,** a sect of Russian dissenters, many of whom, having been expelled from Russia, have settled in the Caucasus and Bulgaria. (See M. E. Church (North), Bulgarian Mission.)

**Moluccas** or **Spice Islands,** a group of the Indian or Malay Archipelago, scattered over the sea from Celebes on the east to Papua on the west, and from the Philippines to Timor. Area, 42,946 square miles. The number of these islands is said to be several hundreds. Many of them are small and uninhabited. The large islands are Ceram, Gilolo, and Booro. Nearly all are mountainous. The climate is hot, but not excessively so. Population (estimated 1888) 370,248 natives and over 2,000 Europeans. The native population consists of two races, the Malays and the Papuans. The Malay is the common language, and the Arabic character is employed in writing it. Mohammedanism is the prevailing religion, but some few profess Christianity. The laws are chiefly founded on the precepts of the Koran. The chief power is in the hands of the Dutch. Missionary work is carried on by the Netherlands Missionary Society, especially in Ceram (q.v.).

**Molung,** village of Assam, bordering on the plain of Assam, 35 miles south of Sibsagar. Climate cooler than usual for Assam. Population, 450 to 500, As-Nagas. Religion, demon worship. Social condition good; family relations distinct; woman respected. Mission station A. B. M. U. (1876); 1 missionary and wife, 13 native helpers, 8 out stations, 3 churches, 69 church-members, 160 school-children. Contributions, $28.90.

**Mombasa,** a small island on the east coast of Africa, 4° south latitude, which was the first station of the C. M. S. in East Africa (1844), and is now with two other stations the Mombasa district. A medical work is carried on among the slaves of the Swahili people, and the Arabs and rich Hindus are very willing to assist the doctor. There are 91 communicants, 2 schools, 280 scholars.

**Monastir,** city in Macedonia, European Turkey, in a valley 1,700 feet above the sea, 100 miles northwest of Salonica. Climate temperate. Population, 35,000, Bulgarians, Turks, Wallachs, Albanians, Gypsies. Social condition, civilized. Mission station A. B. C. F. M. (1873); 2 missionaries and wives, 2 other ladies, 8 native helpers, 5 out-stations, 112 communicants, 1 school, 35 scholars. (See Bulgaria and Macedonia.)

**Monclova,** town in Central North Mexico, southeast of Chihuahua, northwest of Bilbao. Mission station Methodist Episcopal Church (South); 1 missionary.

**Monghyr** (Mungir), a town of Bengal, India, on the Ganges. Being very old, it is not in a good condition; but its numerous temples, etc., give it a very pretty appearance, and its picturesque scenery and healthy climate make it a great resort for invalids. Population, 55,372, Hindus, Moslems, etc. Mission station Baptist Missionary Society; 3 missionaries, 1 evangelist, 81 church-members, 1 out-station, 340 school-children.

**Mongol Versions.**—The Mongol language belongs to the Mongol branch of the Ural-Altaic family of languages, and is spoken in Mongolia. There exist four different versions in the Mongol.

1. *The Literary Mongol,* used in Mongolia. A translation of the Old Testament into the Literary Mongol was effected by Messrs. E. Stallybrass and W. Swan of the London Missionary Society, and printed at St. Petersburg in 1840. A translation of the New Testament was made by the same scholars, and printed in 1846 at the expense of the British and Foreign Bible Society. The same Society published in 1880 an edition of the New Testament in Mongolian characters, under the editorship of Antoine Schiefner and Prof. Pozdnieff, and in 1881 an edition in Manchu character.

2. *The Northern or Buriat Colloquial,* which is used by the Buriats on Lake Baikal, to the number of about 150,000, of whom only some are Christians. At the beginning of the present century Dr. Schmidt, aided by two Buriat nobles, commenced a translation of the New Testament into the Buriat Colloquial, which was printed at St. Petersburg in 1824.

3. *The Southern or Kalkhas Colloquial.*—A translation into this dialect, which is spoken in Chinese Mongolia, was undertaken by the Rev. J. Edkins of the London Missionary Society, and J. J. Schereschewsky of the American Missions. The Gospel of Matthew was published at Pekin in 1872.

4. *The Western Mongolian or Kalmuk.*—The Kalmuks or Western Mongols occupy a large steppe in the southeast of Russia in Europe. It stretches from the bend of the Volga at Sarepta westward toward the Don, and southward toward the Kuban. As early as 1808 the aid of the British and Foreign Bible Society in providing Scriptures in Kalmuk for the Moravian Mission at Sarepta was sought. The preparation of a version was entrusted to N. James Schmidt of the mission, and in 1812 the Gospel of Matthew was ready. It was printed at St. Petersburg in 1815 for the British and Foreign Bible Society, and was the first book ever printed in that language. A second edition followed in 1817, and in 1820 the Gospel of John was added, the Emperor Alexander I. sharing the cost of its preparation. In 1822 the Gospels and Acts were put to press, and conversions to Christianity were appearing as the fruit of the previous circulation of the two Gospels. The suppression of the mission brought all this good work to an abrupt end.

In 1877 a new edition of the above-named Gospel of John was greatly needed, but the necessary type and a competent proof-reader were no longer to be had. So an old copy was taken to pieces and photographed upon zinc plates, from which a new edition was printed and bound in a more attractive and serviceable form than before. This book has not been circulated in Siberia. However, a fresh version has been for some years in progress for the good of the Kalmuks. Prof. Pozdnieff, of the University of Petersburg, was authorized by the British Bible Society to prepare a translation of the New Testament. The four Gospels were published in 1887, and the entire New Testament in 1888. The edition was large, since according to statistics in 1869 the number of Kalmuks in European Russia should be 119,866, in Asiatic Russia 40,000, in China 253,000 souls, or a grand total of 434,366, possessed of a common language, not indeed devoid of dialectical peculiarities, but mutually intelligible, and having a common literature.

(*Specimen verses.* John 3 : 16.)

Literary.

Colloquial.    Buriat Colloqural.

Western Mongolian or Kalmuck.

**Mongolia,** "the land of the Mongols," is a vast part of the empire of China (q.v.) lying in the interior of Asia, comprising 1,300,000 square miles of territory between latitude 37° and 54° north, and longitude 85° and 125° east. On the north it is bounded by Siberia, on the east by Manchuria, on the south by China proper, and on the west by East Turkestan and Jungaria. Its population is estimated at 2,500,000, one fifth of whom are Chinese. A high plateau 3,000 feet above sea-level occupies the greater part of the region. In the centre is the Desert of Gobi, where sand and stones, dust in summer and snow in winter, render habitation unbearable. The northern part is occupied by ranges of mountains forming part of the Altai chain. On its slopes rise the Selenga, the Kerlow, and Onon, which form the Amoor. In the south are rich meadow-lands, which afford food for cattle. Chinese have introduced agriculture to some extent. Mountain ranges are again found on the west. On the east is a strip of fertile land. On the southeast of the desert of Gobi is the mountain range of Alashan, which reaches in some places the height of 15,000 feet above the sea. Along its hills pasture-land is found. The climate is in general cold, subject to sudden changes, and in summer intolerably hot.

Mission work in Mongolia is carried on by the A. B. C. F. M. (See Kalgan.)

**Mongols,** the term given to a large branch of the human family, which has been designated Turanian by late ethnologists. It comprises, in its proper limitation, the hordes of Central Asia, the Buriats, Bashkirs, and Kalmucks and, more widely, the Chinese, Indo-Chinese, Tibetans, Burmese, Siamese, Japanese, Eskimo, Samoieds, Finns, Lapps, Turks, Tartars, and Magyars. In very ancient times they formed the Median Empire in Chaldea, though they are the characteristic nomadic people. Another offshoot settled in the plains of China at a remote period. To the Greeks the Mongols were known as Scythians, to the Romans as Huns. Under Genghis Khan, in the 13th century, they overran and conquered the greater part of Asia, and Russia and Hungary in Europe. The Mongols proper are divided into three branches: the East Mongols, the West Mongols, and the Buriats. Of the East Mongols the Khalkas inhabit the region north of the Gobi, the Shara Mongols are found south of the Gobi along the Great Wall, and the Shairagut are found in Tangut and North Tibet. The West Mongols are found in Kokonor, Kansuh, on the eastern slope of the Thianshan Mountains, and many of them under the name of Kalmucks are under the rule of Russia. The Buriats are in the Russian province of Irkutsk, around Lake Baikal.

The original Mongols are thus described by Dr. Latham: "Face broad and flat; the cheek-bones stand out laterally and the nasal bones are depressed. The eyes are oblique; the distance between them is great, and the carunculæ are concealed. The iris is dark, the cornea yellow. The eyebrows form a low and imperfect arch, black and scanty. The complexion is tawny, the stature low. The ears are large, standing out from the head; the lips thick and fleshy, forehead low and flat, and the hair lank and thin." In the more civilized nations of Mongol origin these original characteristics have been modified more or less.

The language of the Mongols is found in three dialects corresponding to the division of the race as above given. It is written perpendicularly from above down and from left to right. Seven vowels and seventeen consonants are represented (see Mongol Versions). Buddhism is the most prevalent form of religion, though Confucianism and Mohammedanism have had their influence upon the races nearest to China and India.

**Mongwe,** East Central Africa, north of the Limpopo River, very near Inhambane. Mission station A. B. C. F. M.; 2 missionaries and wives. The headquarters of the East Central Africa Mission, with a training-school of 23 members. The organization of a church has been delayed, although there are a number desiring church-membership.

**Monrovia,** the capital of the republic of Liberia, west coast of Africa, so named in honor of President Monroe of the United States, stands at the foot of Cape Mensurado, in Monrovia Bay. The town is laid out in American style, but cocoa-nut palms and mango-trees give a tropical aspect to the place. The climate is not excessively hot; the mean annual temperature is not more than 81° F., with daily variations between 77° and 86°. In the dry season the intense heat of the day is followed by cooler nights. But the climate is considered very dangerous for Europeans, on account of the prevalence of marsh-fever. The population is estimated at 3,400, nearly all of whom are negroes. Mission station of the Methodist Episcopal Church (North); 2 missionaries, 353 church-

members. Protestant Episcopal Church, 4 missionaries, 2 ladies, 4 out-stations, 76 communicants. Presbyterian Church (North); 1 missionary, 53 communicants.

**Monte Allegre,** a city of Northern Brazil, in the district of Pernambuco. Station of the Presbyterian Church (South), U. S. A.; 1 native pastor, 20 church-members, 25 Sunday-scholars.

**Monte Christi,** station of the Baptist Missionary Society in San Domingo, West Indies; 2 evangelists, 24 church-members, 62 scholars

**Montego Bay,** town in Jamaica, West Indies, on the north coast. Population, 6,000. Mission station of U. P. Church of Scotland; 1 missionary, 224 church-members.

**Montemorelos,** capital of a district of the same name, in the State of Nuevo Leon, Mexico, 2,000 feet above the sea. Climate hot, but healthful. Population about 9,000, chiefly mixed Spanish and Indian. Language, Spanish. Religion, Roman Catholic. Social condition, civilized. An out-station of Matamoras, Mexico, Presbyterian Church (South); 1 organized church (18 added during 1888), 4 preaching places, 1 Sabbath-school.

**Montenegro,** an independent principality in European Turkey. It is bordered on the south or southeast by Scutari and Kossovo, vilayets of Turkey, on the east by the Sanjak of Novi Bazar, and on the northwest by Herzegovina. A narrow strip of Austrian territory separates it from the Adriatic on the west, excepting where the newly acquired districts of Antivari and Dulcigno give it a seaboard of 28 miles in length. The entire area is estimated at 3,630 square miles, with an extreme length of 100 miles and a width of 80. The population is estimated at 236,000. The principal cities are: Cettinjé, the capital; Podgoridza, Dulcigno, Danilograd.

The government is a limited monarchy, according to the constitution dating from 1852. The prince holds the executive authority, and a state council has the legislative power; practically the will of the prince is law.

The religion of the kingdom is the Greek Church, and that too is under the direct influence of the prince, who appoints the bishops. Nominally, church and state are independent. The number of adherents is 222,000; the Mohammedans number 10,000, and the Roman Catholics 4,000. Elementary education is compulsory and free, government supporting the schools. In 1889, 3,000 male and 300 female pupils attended 70 elementary schools.

The Montenegrins are Slavs of the Servian (q. v.) stock, and have many noble characteristics. A dialect of the Servo-Illyrian Slavonic is the language spoken. Agriculture is the leading occupation of the people, and live-stock of all kinds are reared.

There are no missionary societies at work in Montenegro. The British and Foreign Bible Society have translated the Bible into Servian and Croatian.

**Monterey,** capital of the State of Nuevo Leon, Mexico, 450 miles north-northwest from Mexico City, and 6 miles from the base of the Sierra Madre Mountains. Climate comparatively mild, but subject to sudden changes, and to extremes of heat and cold, drought and rain. Population (1869), 13,534, chiefly people of mixed Spanish and Indian descent. Language, Spanish. Religion, Roman Catholic, in its most degraded form. Social condition not good, but improving; morals and manners very lax indeed. Principal station of the Mexican Border Mission, Methodist Episcopal Church (South); first touched by missionary influence in 1846–48, at the time of the Mexican war; occupied permanently in 1874. Including all the other stations and out-stations of the Mexican Border Mission, the statistics are as follows: 8 ordained missionaries, 1 unordained, 6 missionaries' wives, 24 other ladies, 36 stations and out-stations, 60 organized churches, 1,640 communicants (134 added in 1888), 144 preaching places, with an average attendance of about 3,600 for all; 21 ordained preachers, 7 unordained, 77 Sabbath-schools, 1,651 scholars, 6 female schools, 275 scholars, 3 other schools, 75 scholars, 6 theological students, 5 teachers.

**Montevideo, San Felipe de,** the capital of Uruguay, South America, is situated on the north bank of the River Plate, near its mouth, where it is 60 miles wide. It is said to be the cleanest and most healthy city in South America, though the water-supply is limited. A wall surrounds the city, with its one-storied, flat-roofed houses. A university and other schools for secondary and higher education are located here. In 1887 the population, including the suburbs, was 134,346, one third of whom were foreigners. With a fine bay, it has quite a trade—principally with Great Britain; but lines of steamers run also to the United States, Brazil, and Genoa; and France and Spain share in the traffic. Mission station of the Methodist Episcopal Church (North); 2 missionaries, 5 schools, 501 scholars, 203 communicants.

**Montgomery,** a town on the island of Tobago, West Indies, beautifully situated on an elevation of considerable height in the western part of the island, commanding a fine view over that portion of the country which is most thickly populated and best cultivated. Mission station of the Moravians, opened in 1789, but after one year closed on account of the death of the missionaries; reopened in 1827; now under the charge of 1 missionary and wife.

**Montgomery, Giles Foster,** b. Walden, Vermont, U. S. A., November 8th, 1835; graduated at Middlebury College 1860, Lane Theological Seminary 1863; sailed as a missionary of the A. B. C. F. M., and reached Aintab, December 23d, 1863. He was the first missionary to enter Marash after being driven away three times and almost killed in 1865, but was afterwards stationed at Adana. It was chiefly due to his courage, skill, and great personal influence that a division in the large church at Adana was healed, and the esteem in which he was held in the city could not be too highly rated. At the time of the famine in Adana he worked very hard, and his health was greatly impaired. The heat, too, was greater than was ever known before in Turkey, and he was too much reduced in strength to rally. He died at Adana December 4th, 1888. The native brethren, when permitted to come into the room to look upon his face a minute before the end came, wept like children. "Notwithstanding the rain and mud, 3,000 at the time of the funeral occupied the paved yard and verandas

of the house, and some 2,000 were on the house-tops and standing in the street. An Armenian priest made an address, in which he said: 'The Armenians as a community wished to express their thanks to God for giving such a man to the work here; that his life would still speak to us, and help us to live for others, and not for self.' A Greek priest wished to speak, but did not, as he knew no language but Greek, which the people do not understand." Most of the large crowd walked through the mud to the Protestant cemetery a mile distant. "Mr. Montgomery was one of the strongest men in Turkey, a good business man, a strong preacher, and unusually successful in the management of men."

**Montserrat,** one of the Leeward Islands, West Indies; 10,083 inhabitants. Mission station of the Baptist Missionary Society (England); 1 evangelist, 12 church-members.

**Moosh,** a city of Eastern Turkey, 83 miles southeast of Erzroom, in a large plain, one of the most populous of the whole section. The population is Koordish and Armenian. The Koords are very fierce, and treat the Christians most oppressively. This plain is the home of Moussa Beg, a famous Koordish chief, who attacked two American missionaries, and committed such assaults on the Armenians that he was called to Constantinople, and despite the most active efforts of his friends, was exiled. Mission out-station of the A. B. C. F. M., worked from Bitlis.

**Moradabad,** British India, a town in the Rohilkund district, Northwest Provinces. Mission station of the Methodist Episcopal Church (North); 1 missionary, 1 assistant missionary, 2 single ladies, 2 other European assistants, 76 native helpers, 3 churches, 237 church-members, 31 schools, 1,363 scholars.

**Moratummulla,** a town of Ceylon, in the district of Colombo. Mission station of the Wesleyan Methodist Missionary Society; 1 missionary, 12 local preachers, 386 church-members, 405 scholars.

**Moravian Hill,** a station of the Moravian Brethren in Cape Town, Cape Colony, South Africa. Owing to droughts and scarcity of employment, many of the members of the Moravian congregation at Gnadendal, Mamre, etc., wandered to Cape Town and settled there, finding shelter chiefly in Malay lodging-houses. Their spiritual life suffered much from the loss of church privileges, and the brethren determined to follow them. At first they visited Cape Town once a week; but this being found insufficient, one of the missionaries and his wife removed thither, and purchased a piece of property, which they named Moravian Hill, where they settled, and soon brought about the building of a church, which is well and faithfully attended by quite a large congregation.

**Moravian Missions.—***History.*—The Unitas Fratrum, or the Moravian Church, as it is commonly called, was founded in the year 1457 by followers of John Huss, the Bohemian reformer and martyr. In spite of frequent and severe persecutions it flourished in Bohemia and Moravia for a century and three quarters, and was then forcibly overthrown by Ferdinand II., a bigoted Romanist, in the so-called Bohemian Anti-Reformation, at the beginning of the Thirty Years' War. Their episcopate, however, was carefully preserved in the event of a resuscitation of their church, and a "hidden seed" remained in Bohemia and Moravia.

In 1722 some descendants of the brethren belonging to the "hidden seed" emigrated to an estate of Count Zinzendorf in Saxony, and founded Herrnhut, which grew to be a flourishing settlement.

As early as the year 1715 Count Zinzendorf, while yet at the academy at Halle, had entered into a covenant with the friend of his youth, Fred. de Watteville, to establish missions, especially among those heathen tribes which were totally neglected by others. He had an opportunity, while at the house of Professor Franke, to hear accounts relative to the mission established by Fred. W. King of Denmark, among the Malabars at Tranquebar, in the East Indies; he became acquainted there with some missionaries whom Mr. Franke was preparing for their intended situation, for which they were soon to set out by way of Copenhagen, as well as with others who happened to be on a visit at his house. This excited in him an earnest desire to further, as far as he could, the increase of the kingdom of God by the conversion of heathen nations, as soon as a door should be opened for that purpose. This opportunity presented itself in the year 1731, when Count Zinzendorf undertook a journey to Copenhagen in order to be present at the coronation of Christian VI. For on this occasion some of the brethren who belonged to the household of the count became acquainted with a negro from the West Indies, named Anthony, who was then employed in the service of Count de Laurwig at Copenhagen. The brethren, and especially David Nitschmann (who in the sequel assisted in the commencement of the first mission, and was consecrated a bishop in 1735, chiefly with a view to the establishment and furtherance of the Brethren's missions among the heathen), were informed by this negro, that while yet on the island of St. Thomas he had often felt an ardent longing after a full revelation of the divine truth, in consequence of which he had prayed to God to give him an insight into the nature of that doctrine which the Christians professed to believe in. God had in His providence led him to Copenhagen, where he had received instruction in the Christian faith, and been added to the church by baptism. He then described in a lively manner the lamentable situation of the negro slaves on that island, both as to temporal and spiritual things; and deplored more especially the wretched condition of his own sister there, who, like himself, had entertained an earnest desire to become acquainted with God, but had neither time nor opportunity for obtaining instruction in consequence of her being in a state of slavery, and who frequently offered up prayers to God that he would send some messenger to instruct her in the way of salvation. He concluded his representations on this subject by expressing a confident hope, that if instruction could be conveyed to them, she, and many other negroes who were of the same mind with her, would be converted to Christianity. Count Zinzendorf being informed of this subject, deemed it of so much importance, that he wished to send David Nitschmann immediately to St. Thomas, to carry the consolatory tidings of the gospel to this distressed negro woman and her fellow-slaves. But as this was found to be impracti-

cable, he returned as soon as possible to Herrnhut, whither he desired the negro Anthony and David Nitschmann to follow him, in order that the former might himself make known his request. Soon after his return to Herrnhut, the Count related, according to his usual practice, July 23d, 1731, to the assembled congregation, the most remarkable incidents of his journey, and acquainted them particularly with what he had heard of the negroes in St. Thomas. His narrative excited in the hearts of two young and lively brethren, John Leonhard Dober and Tobias Leupold, an earnest desire to go and preach the gospel of Jesus Christ to these poor slaves. They were intimate friends, yet they did not, on that day, communicate to each other their sentiments and views.

It was Leonhard Dober's custom every evening to converse with Tobias Leupold concerning the day that was now passed, and to engage with him in prayer; and having fixed his mind on him as a suitable fellow-traveller and fellow-worker among the negroes in St. Thomas, he determined to mention to him the impulse he felt, and if he found him to be of the same mind to consider the affair as settled and to give it further publicity. How great then was his astonishment when he learned from his friend that he himself had felt the same impulse to go among the slaves in St. Thomas, and that he had not been able to fix his mind on any other than his intimate friend to be his companion and assistant in this undertaking.

July the 29th the negro Anthony arrived at Herrnhut; and soon after an opportunity was given him to make known his request to the congregation, on which occasion the count acted as his interpreter, for his address was delivered in the Dutch language. In this address he described, in feeling terms, the miserable condition of the blacks in the West Indies, who not only were groaning under the yoke of the most oppressive slavery, but lived in the commission of the most heinous vices, in consequence of that gross darkness in which they walked, not knowing anything of God and of His Christ. He expressed a hope that as soon as the crucified Saviour should be preached to the negroes many of them would be converted, and mentioned in this view his own sister more particularly; but added that it would be almost impossible for a teacher to have any intercourse with them, except he would himself submit to a state of slavery; for the negroes were so overwhelmed with labors that there would be no access to them with a view to give them instruction, except in the hours they were doomed to spend in their labors.

Leonhard Dober and Tobias Leupold, however, were not intimidated by this representation, but declared their willingness to sacrifice their lives in the service of our Saviour, and to be sold as slaves if they could win but one soul for Him. Their whole project, however, met with little encouragement from the congregation: in the first instance, most of them considered it as a well-meant but impracticable intention of youths who, being full of ardor and courage, did not sufficiently take into account the insurmountable obstacles connected with it. Leonhard Dober drew up a memorial addressed to the congregation, in which he says: "You require me to state the reason I have to assign for my proposed undertaking. I have therefore to make the following declaration: It was not my intention for the time present to go from home, but rather to tarry, with a view to get more firmly rooted and grounded in our Lord Jesus Christ; but when the count returned from his journey to Denmark, and explained to us the condition of the slaves, so deep an impression was made on my mind that nothing could erase it. It was then I formed the resolution, that, if another brother should be found willing to accompany me, I would offer myself to be a slave in order to tell these poor beings what I knew and had experienced of the love and grace of our blessed Saviour; for I am fully persuaded that the word of the cross, though preached by the weakest and poorest of His followers, must have a divine influence upon the souls that hear it. As to myself, my earnest desire was that should I even be of benefit to none, I might thereby show my love and obedience to our Lord and Saviour. I leave my proposal to the decision of the congregation, and have no other reason to urge it but this—that I think there are yet souls on that island who cannot believe because they have never heard."

After a whole year's delay spent in weighing and examining the proposal of Leonhard Dober, it was finally decided to permit him to go. Tobias Leupold was unable at that time to accompany him, and the congregation feeling unwilling to let Dober travel alone, the latter requested that they would allow David Nitschmann, who had first become acquainted with the negro at Copenhagen, to accompany him. The congregation consenting, the proposal was made to this brother, and he willingly accepted it, though he had to leave a wife and children behind him.

At 3 o'clock in the morning of the 21st of August the count set out with Leonhard Dober and David Nitschmann, and accompanied them as far as Bautzen, where he commended them and their important undertaking to the grace of the Lord, and blessed the former in a solemn manner with imposition of hands. All the instruction he gave to him was comprised in the advice in all things to suffer himself to be guided by the Holy Spirit. At taking leave the count gave each of them a ducat (about $2.50) for their journey-money, in addition to the sum of $3, which they had before. And with this scanty provision they continued their route on foot, by way of Wernigerode, Brunswick, and Hamburg, to Copenhagen.

All along their journey and in Copenhagen they met with much discouragement and many difficulties and hardships; eventually they succeeded in securing a passage on board a Dutch vessel bound for St. Thomas, no captain belonging to the Danish West India Company being willing to take them. The voyage lasted upwards of 10 weeks, during which they encountered many difficulties and perils, but turned on all occasions to the Lord, whose help they constantly experienced.

They reached St. Thomas on the 13th of December. The next day after their arrival being Sunday, they began to put into execution the design which had induced them to leave their homes and cross the ocean to St. Thomas. In the afternoon of that day they went in search of Anna, the sister of Anthony. They found her and a second brother named Abraham, and delivered the letter received from Anthony for them. The letter contained an account of Anthony's baptism, and an admonition urging them also to believe in Christ. This admonition gave the brethren an opportunity to begin there and then their labors by preaching to Anna and her brother, and some others who had gathered with them, the universal redemption wrought out by Jesus Christ.

This was the beginning of the mission work of the Brethren's Church, which has been owned and blessed of the Lord until the present time.

*The Government of the Foreign Missions.*—The General Synod.—The Foreign Missions are carried on by the Moravian Church as such, and constitute a cause in which all its three provinces are conjointly engaged. Hence the missions stand directly under the control of the General Synod, which meets every ten or twelve years, and consists of delegates from Germany, Great Britain, America, and the Foreign Missions.

The Unity's Elders' Conference.—The General Synod elects an Executive Council or Board of Bishops and other ministers, styled "The Unity's Elders' Conference," to superintend the general affairs of the Unitas Fratrum in the interval between two Synods. To this body is committed the entire control of the Foreign Missions, including the general management of the finances, and the appointment of the superintendents and other missionaries, who are all responsible to it. It has its seat at Berthelsdorf, near Herrnhut, in Saxony, and is divided into three Boards or Departments, as they are technically called, namely, the Department of Education, the Department of Finance, and the Department of Missions.

The Mission Board Proper.—The Department of Missions is the Mission Board proper, directing the details of the work and its finances. Matters of importance, however, such as the appointment of missionaries and the organization of stations, are brought before the whole body.

Agents and other Officers.—The Unity's Elders' Conference appoints a treasurer of missions, a secretary of missions in England, and agents of missions in Germany, England, and America. These officers are empowered to receive contributions, to draw on the mission treasury, and to represent the cause in other ways.

*Methods of Work.*—Long experience has taught the Brethren that the doctrine of Christ crucified is the power and wisdom of God unto salvation to every one that believeth. Without, therefore, first endeavoring to prepare the minds of the heathen for the reception of the gospel, by instructing them in natural religion, they at once declare unto them the record that God gave of His Son. This they have found, whenever received in faith, to be the most efficacious means of turning the Gentiles from darkness to light, and from the power of Satan unto God. Yet there is no part of revealed truth, whether of doctrine or practice, which the missionaries do not endeavor to inculcate on the minds and hearts of their hearers and converts. In a word, their constant aim is to humble the sinner, to exalt the Saviour, and promote holiness.

The internal regulations are the same in every mission. Besides preaching the gospel, the missionaries are diligently employed in visiting the heathen in their dwellings, or in receiving visits from them, for the purpose of discoursing with them in a familiar manner on spiritual subjects, or administering comfort, advice, or reproof, as the case may require. If any heathen are led to serious reflection, and desire their names to be put down for further instruction, they are called New People, and included in the class of catechumens. If they remain steadfast in their resolution to forsake heathenism, and in their desire after baptism, they are considered as candidates for baptism: and, after previous instruction respecting this ordinance, are baptized. If their conduct afterwards proves that they have not received the grace of God in vain, they become candidates for the Communion, and are admitted to be present as spectators at the celebration of the Lord's Supper. Separate meetings are held with each of these divisions. This is likewise done with other divisions of the congregation, with the children, the single men, the single women, the married people, the widowers and widows. These meetings, besides affording the missionaries an opportunity of instructing them, in a practical manner, in those precepts of the gospel which have a more immediate reference to their circumstances, and in exhorting them to make their calling and election sure, have a pleasing tendency to cement the bond of brotherly love, and maintain the spirit of unity among all the members of the congregation.

In most missions, especially when the number of converts is very large, assistants are chosen, consisting of persons of both sexes, whose good understanding and exemplary conduct have made them respected by the whole congregation. In the discharge of their duty they have particular districts assigned them, in which they visit the people from house to house, attend to the poor, the sick and infirm, endeavor to remove dissensions and promote harmony, etc. They are occasionally employed to hold meetings on week-days, and to preach in the out-places. The assistants, at stated times, meet the missionaries in conference, to report to them and receive their counsel and advice. Servants are also appointed to have the care of the chapel, and attend to everything relating to external order. A council, consisting of a number of persons, chosen by the whole congregation, meets occasionally to confer on all subjects involving the general welfare of the congregation or settlement.

*Statement of Missions.*—DANISH WEST INDIA ISLANDS.—*St. Thomas.*—The island of St. Thomas, being the scene of the first labors of the Moravian missionaries, the history of the commencement of the mission on that island is necessarily included in the account of the beginning of the missions of the Moravian Church.

St. Thomas was the home of Anthony, the negro whose pathetic account of the condition of the slaves in that island, which he related to the congregation in Herrnhut, Saxony, moved the hearts of Leonhard Dober and Tobias Leupold to determine to preach the gospel to these destitute souls if God would permit them to carry out their desire.

St. Thomas was a place of considerable commercial importance at that time. Lying, as it does, between the Greater and Lesser Antilles, and having the advantage of a safe and magnificent harbor, it was a port of call for vessels of all kinds seeking cargo, and at the same time a depot for many of the neighboring islands.

It was at one time the rendezvous of the noted

Carribbean buccaneers, and there are towers still standing bearing the names of Bluebeard and Blackbeard, said to have been the homes of these pirates.

The moral and spiritual condition of the slaves was deplorable in the extreme. The missionaries, however, found them willing to listen to the gospel, and the poor creatures clapped their hands for joy when they understood the glad tidings that Jesus had died for them also.

*St. Croix.*—In the mean time a mission had been opened on the adjacent island of St. Croix, the largest of the Danish group, which is often called the Garden of the West Indies, on account of its rich, fruitful soil and fine vegetation. At the time when the Brethren first went there (1733), the island was covered with forests; a very small portion of it had been brought under cultivation, and the climate was exceedingly insalubrious, especially for a European constitution. Eighteen persons went out on the invitation of Count Pless; they were to settle down as colonists and managers of his estates there, and at the same time to avail themselves of every opportunity that would offer for carrying on mission work among the negroes. In less than a year nine were dead, and the rest, perplexed and disheartened, made their way back to Europe, with the exception of one man, Freundlich, who joined Frederick Martin in his work. It soon became evident that the attempt in this form had been a mistake, and that the seed of failure was in it from its commencement. A few years later (1740) Martin visited here and found entrance to many hearts, especially on the Great Princess estate, the property of the West India Trading Company, where the first church was built by the blacks in 1749. Some natives of his training proved, even at this early stage, very valuable helpers in the missionary work.

*St. Jan.*—In the neighboring small and mountainous island of St. Jan or St. Johns the gospel had found entrance by means of some Christian slaves who had been sold from an estate in St. Thomas, where they had belonged to Martin's flock. Visits of the missionary to his scattered members led to a spread of the truth here as elsewhere, and it was soon possible to receive converts into the church by baptism. With the exception of a small Lutheran congregation which is occasionally visited by the minister from St. Thomas, there are no churches besides the Moravian in St. Jan, and the whole population, which does not greatly exceed 1,000 persons, is under the care of the Moravian missionaries.

GREENLAND.—The occasion for sending Brethren to Greenland was nearly the same, and took place at the same time, with that which proved the cause of the commencement of the mission among the negroes in the West Indies. While Count Zinzendorf and some other Brethren were at Copenhagen in the year 1731, they saw there two baptized Greenlanders, and heard much of Mr. Egede's endeavors to preach the gospel to the heathen dwelling in that remote country. The count being informed at the same time of the many difficulties this pious man had already encountered, and of the small success which had as yet attended his zealous exertions, was much distressed to learn that serious thoughts were entertained of relinquishing the mission in Greenland altogether. He therefore resolved, if possible, to procure help for this faithful servant of the Lord, and the missionary spirit which at that time began to manifest itself among the inhabitants of Herrnhut promoted his design. For when, after his return thither, the mission to St. Thomas was taken into consideration, the Brethren who had been with him related at the same time what they had heard at Copenhagen concerning the Danish mission in Greenland. The Brethren Matthew Stach and Frederic Böhmisch immediately felt a powerful impulse to go thither and preach the gospel to the Greenlanders. Matthew Stach himself gives us the following account of the impulse then excited in him, and the manner in which it was carried into effect: "While I was attending the meeting at which the letter of the two Brethren who offered themselves to go to St. Thomas was communicated, the impulse I had felt, when I heard for the first time the accounts received concerning the state of Greenland, was forcibly renewed in my mind, for hitherto I had entertained serious misgivings about making that impulse known to any one, in consideration of my disqualifications for such an undertaking, and my great inexperience, as having been only two years an inhabitant of Herrnhut. I was working at that time with Frederic Böhmisch in the new burial-ground on the Hutberg; to him I first unbosomed myself, and found that in him also a desire had been excited to promote the salvation of the heathen. We entered into a simple and confidential conversation on the subject, and each of us felt an uncommon desire to go to Greenland; yet we knew not whether we were to consider this inclination as produced by a divine impulse and should on that account make it known to the congregation, or ought rather to wait till a call should be given us. But being of one mind, and simply believing that our Saviour will at all times fulfil His promise, that if two agree as touching anything that they shall ask, it shall be done for them (Matth. 18:19), we kneeled down before Him in the little grove hard by, and entreated Him to fill our minds with clearness as to this important matter, and to lead us in the right way. We felt on that occasion an extraordinary degree of cheerfulness and alacrity, and we hesitated no longer to declare our mind in writing to the congregation, leaving it entirely undecided to what heathen tribe we should be called, though we ourselves had the greatest inclination to go to Greenland."

About five months after the departure of Dober and Nitschmann for St. Thomas—January 19th, 1733—the second missionary company left Herrnhut to proceed to Greenland. The little information about this land that had reached Herrnhut was anything but cheering and calculated to awaken hopeful enthusiasm; the country barren and unfruitful, the people indescribably repulsive in their savage barbarism, their language very difficult even for a man of learning and education. The few European colonists in the employ of a Danish trading company were about to be withdrawn, as the trade-returns proved far less than had been expected, and the heroic labors of the Norwegian clergyman, Hans Egede, and his noble wife, which had been carried on without interruption since the year 1721, had resulted in no real spiritual fruit, although a few children had been baptized. Those who knew most about Greenland were the most eloquent in

dissuading the two volunteers—Frederic Böhmisch and Matthew Stach—from adhering to their offer of service. But all in vain. When the church at Herrnhut gave its sanction to the attempt, the men were ready to start. Böhmisch was away on a long journey when the decision was given, and could not go till the following year, but his place was taken by Christian Stach; and with them went Christian David, the carpenter, whose axe had felled the first tree for the building of Herrnhut, and was now to be used in the construction of a missionary abode in distant Greenland, while his wisdom and Christian experience were for the first year or two to be a guide and support to the unlettered novices in the work. "There was no need of much time," wrote one of these men, "or expense for our equipment. The congregation consisted chiefly of poor exiles, who had not much to give, and we ourselves had nothing but the clothes on our backs. The day before our departure a friend in Venice sent a donation, and part of this we received for our journey to Copenhagen. Now we considered ourselves richly provided for, believing that He who had procured us something for our journey at the very critical moment, would also supply us with everything requisite for accomplishing our purpose, whenever it should be needful." Their instructions were to offer themselves as assistants to that apostle of the Greenlanders, Mr. Egede, in case he would and could make use of them; but if he did not want their assistance, then not to disturb him in the least.

At Copenhagen Count Pless, First Lord of the Bedchamber of King Christian VI., after a while pleaded their cause; and they received much kindness from many persons in high positions, including the royal family, the king giving them a letter in his own handwriting to Mr. Egede, in which he warmly commended them to his kind assistance.

By the 20th of May, after a voyage of seven weeks, they reached the coast of Greenland, and were warmly welcomed by Egede at Godhaab, the most northerly of the Danish colonies in South Greenland. (The sphere of labor of the Moravian Mission is restricted to South Greenland; in North Greenland there is only the Danish Mission.) An eligible spot, about a mile away, was selected, a sod-hut raised, and an old boat bought for the purpose of travelling along the coast, and fishing. By and by a wooden house brought from Denmark was put together, the place was called New Herrnhut, and the Moravian Mission in Greenland had begun.

In the year 1738 the first Greenlander was awakened by the preaching of Jesus' sufferings. They give the narrative of this pleasing event. "On the 2d of June, many of the natives of the South, passing by our dwelling, visited us. John Beck was just then employed in making a fair copy of part of a translation of the Evangelists. The heathen wished to know what were the contents of that book. He read part of it to them, and took the opportunity to enter into conversation with them. Having put the question whether they had immortal souls, they replied, yes. He further asked whither their souls would go when their bodies must die. Some said up above, others down below. After setting them to rights, he inquired who had made heaven and earth, mankind and everything visible. Their answer was that they did not know, nor had ever heard, but supposed it must be some mighty and opulent lord. He then related to them how God had created all things good, and man in particular; and how man had rebelled against Him through disobedience, and thereby plunged himself into extreme misery and perdition: but, added he, God had pity on him, and was manifested in the flesh to redeem man by suffering and dying. In Him, said he, we must believe if we wish to be saved. The Holy Ghost, on this occasion, prompted this brother impressively to describe the sufferings and death of Jesus. He exhorted them, with great energy, to consider well how much it cost our Saviour to redeem us; and to give up their hearts to Him, as His reward so dearly gained by all that He suffered, and especially by the travail of His soul, which caused His sweat to be as it were great drops of blood falling down to the ground. He then read to them the history of our Saviour's sufferings on the Mount of Olives. It was then that the Lord opened the heart of one of these savages called Kajarnak, who stepped up to the table, and said with a loud voice that trembled with emotion: 'How was that? Tell me that once more, for I would fain be saved too.' 'These words,' says the missionary, 'which I had never heard from any Greenlander before, pierced my very soul, and affected me so much that with tears in my eyes I related to them the whole history of the sufferings of Christ, and the counsel of God for our salvation.' Meanwhile, the other brethren returned home from their occupations, and entered, full of joy, into a still farther explanation of the doctrines of the gospel. Some of the savages laid their hands upon their mouths, as is their custom when much surprised at anything they hear; others, who had no relish for the subject, sneaked away; but some desired that we would teach them also how to pray; and, when we did so, they repeated our words several times, lest they should forget them. In short, there was such an emotion amongst them as we had never seen before. At taking leave, they promised soon to repeat their visit, because they wished to hear more of this matter, and to tell it also to their acquaintance."

THE NORTH AMERICAN INDIANS.—The history of the Moravian Missions among the North American Indians is one full of sadness, of faithfulness, and of discouragement. From the year 1735 efforts were made to carry on missions in the north and west among the Delawares, Iroquois, Mahikanders, Nantioks, Shawanos, Monseys, Chippewas, and other tribes in Pennsylvania, Ohio, Canada, and the Western States, and also among the Creek and Cherokee Indians, first in Georgia, then in North Carolina, and finally in the far west.

In the year 1735 Moravian missionary work was commenced in North America. A colony of pious men from Herrnhut and neighborhood were sent out to Georgia, with the assistance of Count Zinzendorf and the Government of that State, in the hope that they might there obtain that religious liberty which was denied them at home. Some brethren resolved to go with them, in order to preach the gospel to the Creek, Chickasaw, and Cherokee Indians, who were understood to reside in the neighborhood of Savannah. Here the colony was soon successfully established, under the patronage of General Oglethorpe, and faithfully tended for a time by Brother Peter Böhler as its pastor. On an isl-

and in the river Ogeechee a school for Creek Indian children was commenced, and many natives listened with interest and pleasure to "the great Word" which was proclaimed. Three years later the demand that the colonists should take up arms in order to resist an attempt of the Spaniards to expel the English from Georgia, to which they conscientiously refused compliance, led them to abandon their flourishing plantations and retire to Pennsylvania.

In Pennsylvania a settlement was erected, which was called Bethlehem, and which soon developed into an important centre of Christian activity among nominal Christians, and especially among the aborigines. Spangenberg's account of the wretched condition of the Indians on his return from America awakened so great an interest on their behalf that several young men at once volunteered their services as missionaries. From these, Christian Henry Rauch was selected to commence the work. On reaching New York in the summer of 1740, he was quite in the dark as to the course and means he should adopt for executing his commission, but firmly assured by faith that the Lord would be his Guide and Counsellor. At that time successful missionary work among the Indians was deemed an impossibility even by Christian people. The Romanists had been attempting it with not a little self-denial and heroism from the year 1649; the Puritans had labored in it with such men as Eliot and Mayhew; but the results were anything but encouraging, and the work was regarded with little sympathy or hope. "Heathen they are, and heathen they must remain," was the sad exclamation of a missionary who had labored for six years among them.

One day Rauch met two Mohicans, Shabash and Wasamapah by name, who had come to negotiate with the government; and he requested permission to accompany them to their village and become the teacher of their tribe. Half intoxicated, they consented, but eventually slunk off to their village without him. Rauch at once followed them to Shekomeko, where his two acquaintances and the rest of the tribe listened to his message, and permitted him to visit them. Residing on the farm of a settler, to whose children he acted as tutor, Rauch continued his work, preaching and visiting from house to house; and by degrees, in spite of the most determined opposition of the white men in the district, the hard hearts became softened under the influence of God's Word and Spirit, and some of the worst characters in the tribe were converted. (Among the first converts was Wasamapah, commonly called Choop, who had been notorious for his violence, drunkenness, and profligacy. This word, pronounced Chōpe, is supposed to be a German corruption of the name Job, which the man appears to have borne among the European settlers round Shekomeko. At his baptism he received the name John.) Nor was the effect of a transitory character; on the contrary, the power of the grace of God was singularly manifested in the rapid growth to manhood in Christ Jesus, which marked the course of these firstfruits from among the Indians. On February 11th, 1742, the first three were baptized at Oley in Pennsylvania, and a few weeks afterwards Job (or Wasamapah) at Shekomeko. Under Rauch's faithful care the little church here grew in numbers and in grace, and natives from a considerable distance came to hear his "good words of the God who died to save the Indians." By the close of the year there were thirty-one baptized converts, and Count Zinzendorf, who visited there in the month of August, was filled with wonder and amazement at the change which God had wrought in these degraded savages.

In this year, 1742, the Indian congregation was dispersed by the enemies of the gospel. About this time Count Zinzendorf made many heart-stirring visits among the Indians; but the white inhabitants showed their enmity towards the gospel so that the missionaries were driven from place to place. In the following years the Indian congregations endured great persecutions until their settlement in Fairfield, Canada, in 1792. Among the many noteworthy events during this period may be mentioned the following: In 1755, when war broke out between the English and French, the Indian tribes were more or less concerned in it. The missionaries and Christian Indians remained neutral, thus incurring the odium of both parties. On the evening of November 24th the mission-house near Gnadenhütten, on the Mahanoy (now Lehighton, Carbon County, Pa.), was attacked by the Indians, and individuals either shot or burnt to death in the house.

In 1772, under the lead of the venerable and devoted missionary David Zeisberger, the Christian Indians removed to the Tuscarawas valley, Ohio, and built two stations, Schönbrunn and Gnadenhütten. Here the congregations flourished for some ten years; many Indians were awakened, and brought to know Jesus as their Saviour; but in 1781 the peaceable Indian congregations were suddenly attacked by 300 Hurons, at the instigation of the English, who believed the Christian Indians to be allied with the Americans; the lives of the missionaries were endangered, and all the inhabitants were dragged for trial to Sandusky, and the missionaries to Detroit. In 1782 many of the famished Indians who had been brought to Sandusky returned to Gnadenhütten to secure the corn which they had left in their fields. They were surprised by a band of 160 armed Americans, imprisoned, and on the 8th of March cruelly massacred on the pretence of their being British spies; their bodies were then burnt. Of 96 Indians only one youth escaped to tell the ghastly tale. (A monument now marks the scene of this tragedy.)

In 1797 the American Government having offered land on the Muskingum (now called Tuscarawas), where Schönbrunn and Gnadenhütten had once flourished as a garden of the Lord, Zeisberger at once and for the last time took the pilgrim's staff in hand, and led a party of his Indians to the much-beloved spot. Here Zeisberger closed his pilgrimage, and his sixty years of mission work among the Indians, on the 17th of November, 1808. The weeping Indians stood round his death-bed, exclaiming, "Father, we will cleave to the Saviour, and live to Him alone." After his death many of the Indians returned to Fairfield, Canada; others migrated westward in 1837, and founded Westfield, on the river Kansas. Of the many congregations founded by the Brethren among the Indian tribes in New York, Connecticut, Massachusetts, Pennsylvania, Ohio, Michigan, Canada, Kansas, and Arkansas, the only re-

maining stations at the present time are Fairfield and New Westfield.

In the South renewed efforts were made to commence a mission among the Cherokees, and with this view several visits were paid from the Moravian congregation at Salem, in North Carolina, to the ancient seats of the tribes in the upper valley of the Tennessee River, and among the mountains of Georgia, Western Carolina, and Alabama. Here, in 1801, the brethren Steiner and Byhan commenced a station, called Spring Place; the Indians gave the missionaries a kindly welcome, but lent a deaf ear to the gospel which they preached. The school proved useful in many respects, but years elapsed before visible results of the labor expended were granted. In 1819 a second station was opened at Oochgelogy. In 1830 the troubles began between the citizens of Georgia and the Indians, which resulted in the forcible expulsion of the latter from the State to the Indian Territory, west of the Mississippi. This took place in 1837 and 1838. The missionaries went with the emigrants, of whom many died on the arduous journey; but the missionary work was for the time ended, as regular systematic effort was impossible. After various vain attempts, stations were formed at Canaan (1840), and New Spring Place (1842), and the work revived and prospered.

The civil war between the Northern and Southern States again put an end to the mission, as the Cherokees from their geographical position were involved in the struggle. The nation was convulsed, old feuds were revived, lawless bands wandered through the country, plundering and murdering without restraint, and many of the inhabitants sought safety in flight. A native assistant, James Ward, was murdered by some Indians belonging to the Union party, and the missionaries were in considerable peril. The station at Canaan was entirely destroyed, New Spring Place greatly damaged, and all hope of a renewal of the Cherokee Mission seemed vain.

At the close of the war, however, in 1866, Brother Mack returned to New Spring Place, and subsequently another station was occupied at Tahlequah, in the Parkhill district. These two are still maintained, and only these, as the result of seventy years of labor, hindrances, and trials, and have still been persevered in, often in hope against hope.

SOUTH AMERICA.—Between the 5th and 6th degrees of north latitude the territory of Guiana stretches in southeasterly direction from the mouth of the river Orinoco towards that of the Amazon. Formerly entirely a Dutch possession, a portion of it is now held by the French, and contains their well-known penal colony of Cayenne, and the largest part by the English, who gave the names of Demerara and Berbice to the two counties of British Guiana. The Dutch colony goes by the name of Surinam. In British Guiana only the flat land along the shore, extending from ten to fifty miles inland, is cultivated; in Dutch Guiana the swamp is on the coast, and the cultivated land generally follows the course of the rivers up to the border of the colonial territory; beyond that, in virgin forests on higher land, are the homes of the bush-negroes, or maroons, as they are called in Jamaica, and of some Indian tribes. For Europeans the climate is very unhealthy, and the death-roll of missionary brethren and sisters in this land is exceptionally long. The sphere of the operations of the Moravian Church is almost entirely within the borders of the Dutch colony, as the work among the negroes in Demerara is as yet comparatively insignificant, and that among the Indians, although begun in English, had most of its stations in Dutch territory. For the sake of clearness it is well to distinguish four separate branches, which, although in more or less close connection with each other, and to some extent worked by the same men, have yet their own characteristic features and separate history.

I. *Arawack Indians.*—Of several Indian tribes resident in Berbice, the Arawacks, at the time the mission began, were the chief in point of numbers and influence. They occupied a considerable territory, and were under a sort of royal government, which, however, was materially limited by the untamed independence of the Indian nature. Their religion was distinguished by dark superstitions and revolting rites. Their character was marked by strong sensual tendencies, hypocritical deceitfulness, revengeful cruelty. The work among the Indians proved almost throughout its whole course a "sowing in tears;" with wonderful perseverance, and often with heroic endurance, it was maintained for seventy years, and then sorrowfully abandoned.

The following are some of the principal events in connection with this mission. In 1748 the gospel was already beginning to exercise its blessed influence on the poor heathen, when Theophilus Solomon Schuman, called the "Apostle of the Arawacks," arrived. His great talents rendered him, after an abode of four months among the Indians, capable of preaching in the difficult language of the natives; whilst a wonderful combination of wisdom and firmness enabled him to triumph over the opposition of the whites in Berbice. Three hundred converts were a proof of the success of his labors. But in 1757 difficulties of every description, and among the rest famine and epidemics, thickened around and almost dispersed this little flock. The Brethren therefore sought a more peaceful abode, which they found at Sharon on the Saramacca, about two hundred miles east from Pilgerhut in Berbice, and in Ephrem on the Correntyn, about forty miles east from Pilgerhut. In 1761 Sharon was burnt by the bush-negroes on a marauding excursion, and the converts dispersed for a time; and in 1779 it was given up, as continual incursions of the bush-negroes, combined with difficulty in procuring a maintenance, had compelled the Indians to emigrate.

As Ephrem was unfavorably situated, a new station about twelve miles higher up the river was commenced, and called Hoop (Dutch for Hope); but in 1808 this station was burnt to the ground by enemies, and thus ended the Brethren's mission among the South American Indians.

II. *Mission among the Negroes in Surinam.*—The river Correntyn separates Surinam from Demerara. The products and general aspect of the two colonies are alike, only that the latter has far outstripped the former in development. With an area of 60,000 square miles, the population is estimated at 70,000, including 17,000 bush-negroes. Paramaribo, the capital of Surinam, on the river Surinam, is a thoroughly Dutch town of 23,000 inhabitants, with

an atmosphere which is described as "like that of a hot-house and vapor-bath combined, having blown over the great moist plains, brimming river-marshes, and dense forests which constitute nine tenths of the Guianas and Brazil." Fifteen miles of swamp and forest separate the larger part of the cultivated districts from the sea-breeze. The town itself is said to be healthy. It contains a Lutheran, a Reformed, and a Roman Catholic Church, besides the large Moravian places of worship, and also two synagogues.

In the year 1735, when the first Moravian missionaries landed in Surinam, the town was not more than half its present size: it afforded convenient headquarters for those Brethren who soon afterward came out to commence a mission in Berbice. Four years later a company of five Brethren arrived, and began to work at their trades, in order by the labor of their hands to support both themselves and the mission in Berbice; for the latter their services as a kind of local agents were of great value. At first they had to face a good deal of opposition, but they gradually overcame ill-grounded prejudice, and were permitted to purchase a piece of land in the town. For a considerable time their missionary work continued very limited: indeed it was almost entirely restricted to those persons with whom business connections brought them into close and frequent intercourse. By slow degrees, however, they became more untrammelled in their evangelistic operations, and Paramaribo became a genuine mission station. In 1776 Christian Cupido, the first negro convert, was baptized; he was followed by eight more in the same year. Two years later a church was built in the garden surrounding the missionaries' abode: at that time fifty-two negroes and mulattoes were under the spiritual care of the brethren, of whom eighteen were baptized. Some influential white residents, including the governor, occasionally attended the services, and showed themselves favorably disposed towards the new work, but not a few proprietors punished their slaves for entering the church.

In 1779 it became necessary to enlarge the church, and at the same time a new sphere of usefulness was opened for the missionaries, which in years to come was destined to assume great importance as one of the most extensive departments of Surinam missionary work. The proprietor of the "Fairfield" estate on the river Commewyne, some 30 miles from Paramaribo, having requested the Brethren to supply his negroes with the gospel, the latter gladly accepted the invitation. For many years this was the only estate, out of some 400 then in cultivation, to which they had access with the gospel, but here it was received with joy.

With the year 1821 an era of more marked progress began. A few additional estates were thrown open to the missionaries,—by the year 1826, 6; in the following year, 13; during the next ten years, 90,—and the negroes on them were supplied with the gospel, as far as was possible, under very disadvantageous circumstances. The visits to the estates could only be paid about once in eight weeks, and the want of trustworthy native helpers made it very difficult for the missionaries to become thoroughly acquainted with their people, and to ensure their being well-grounded in Scripture truth. The negroes themselves complained that "they could understand what the teacher said as long as he spoke, and that they heartily rejoiced over it; but that they were too dull to remember it or repeat it." This drawback was to some extent remedied by the publication and distribution in the Negro-English language of the "Harmony of the Four Gospels (1821);" but, although mitigated by the creation of central stations, at which missionaries reside, and to which the negroes have, of course, free access, it remains a serious obstacle down to the present day.

Up to this time no entire portion of the Scriptures had been printed for circulation among the negroes; indeed the number of those who were able to read was so few that it would scarcely have seemed worth while to publish an edition of the Bible or even the New Testament for them. The New Testament existed in manuscript in the Negro-English language, and was used in this imperfect form, but along with the preaching of the gospel education had made way among the slaves; wherever permitted, the Brethren commenced schools, in which, at all events, the first rudiments of learning were taught. Hence, when in 1831 the British and Foreign Bible Society sent out a supply of printed New Testaments in the Negro-English language, they at once came into the hands of such as could use them intelligently. Naturally much good resulted. In not a few instances older persons were brought to the knowledge of the truth as it is in Jesus, and became consistent Christians from hearing their children read out of the Testaments which they had learnt to read in the mission school. Thus the work rapidly expanded; at the close of the year 1831 the congregation at Paramaribo numbered 3,089 souls, while 264 persons on the plantations were under the spiritual care of the missionaries.

In the year 1862 the first step towards the emancipation of the slaves was taken by the passing of a law by the Legislative Assembly in Holland. On the 1st of July, 1863, proclamation was made that at the close of ten years of apprenticeship, to date from the passing of the Act of Parliament, all bondsmen in Surinam should become free, and there was great rejoicing in every humble home. Everywhere order and decorum were maintained. The effects of emancipation on the mission were awaited with feelings of anxiety, for it could scarcely be expected that the 27,000 persons who professed church connection with the Moravian Church in the year 1863, all would prove stable against the temptation to convert liberty into license.

The anticipations of the Brethren were in part fulfilled when in 1872 the term of apprenticeship ended. A recent report sums up the position in a few words: "Social relations have greatly changed, and with them the aspect of the missionary work. Formerly the blacks, being attached to the soil, could always be found by the visiting missionary on the estate to which they belonged; now they are scattered abroad: some have become possessors of land themselves, and often reside at great distances, beyond his reach; others have no settled abode, but wander about from place to place. Under these circumstances pastoral intercourse and supervision, which constitute an important part of our missionary work, as well as preaching the gospel, are rendered very difficult."

III. *Bush-negroes or Free Negroes in Suri-*

nam.—"Bushland," the home of these representatives of the negro race, comprises the more elevated tracts of forest land through which the rivers Surinam, Saramacca, and Marowyne wend their early course. The name merely distinguishes this district from the cultivated portion of the colony, which is itself, to a large extent, covered with forests. As early as the 17th century bands of fugitive slaves ranged through these regions, but their permanent occupation on a large scale is to be traced to the following circumstances: In the year 1712 a detachment of a French fleet appeared at the mouth of the river Surinam, with hostile intentions towards the colony. The Dutch proprietors, as a matter of precaution, removed their slaves up the country out of reach of the enemy. But when the danger was over the slaves very naturally refused to return to bondage, and every attempt to compel them only drove them deeper into the recesses of the forest. Warlike operations proved not only useless but disastrous, as most of the European soldiers perished, struck down by the hardships of the campaign in the deadly climate of those forests and swamps, or by the poisoned arrows of unseen foes. After several years peace was concluded in 1761, and the independence of the Bush-negroes was formally proclaimed.

Soon after this settlement of affairs the colonial authorities requested the Brethren to extend their operations to the Bush-negroes on the river Surinam, and the invitation was at once accepted. Thus began a mission which is unique in some of its features. Unaffected by the obstacles which are inseparable from a state of slavery, this mission had to struggle against the darkest heathenism and to encounter the most violent resistance from the idolatrous priests and sorcerers; and this, too, under the depressing influence of a climate which proved fatal to a large number of missionaries, and disabling to almost every European who engaged in the service.

In the year 1813 Brother and Sister Mähr, who had labored at Bambey for 18 years, and were unable to continue in active service, were recalled, and no successor was appointed, partly in consequence of the urgent claims of other mission fields for all the available missionary resources of the church. During the 48 years of the mission's existence nine Brethren and six Sisters had sacrificed their lives in its service. The number of converts was only 50, and of these some were of doubtful character.

Among the Matuari tribe of Bush-negroes a remarkable work had begun in 1858, through the instrumentality of a man named King, who lived at Maripastoon. Led to inquiry by remarkable dreams, he visited the missionaries at Paramaribo, and on his return home at once stood forward as a bold antagonist of the dark horrors of heathenism. The impression made was very powerful indeed—so much so that no hand or voice was raised in opposition when he ventured to overthrow the wretched idol-temples and cast the idols with their paraphernalia into the river. Other branches of the tribe were visited, and even the chieftain Kalkoen listened respectfully to the eloquent protests of this singular "prophet." A goodly number of his countrymen, following his example, made their way to town to inquire further about the strange things they had heard. In 1861 (August 11th) King was baptized, receiving the name John. A church was built at Maripastoon, exactly suited to the people's means and notions—in fact a native house on an enlarged scale; John King acted as teacher and native helper, the missionaries visited there as frequently as they could, and the little band of converts grew in number and in grace. King seemed to feel it his calling to work as an evangelist among his countrymen, and undertook long journeys to the Auka, Matuari, and Bouy negroes, everywhere preaching Christ, and meeting with a very favorable reception for his message. When a missionary from Paramaribo or Bergendal, the station which is the "key of the bush-country," travels up the river, it almost always happens that King brings some converts to be added to the church by baptism, who are the fruit of his own faithful testimony as a witness for Christ to his dark countrymen.

IV. *Demerara.*—In the year 1835 Brother and Sister Coleman were sent to commence a mission among the negroes on the Anna Regina estate, the proprietors of which defrayed the entire expense. Hopeful at first, the aspect of things seemed soon to change, and unexpected difficulties arose, which led to the withdrawal of Brother Coleman after two years of service. The effort was resumed by Brother and Sister Hamann, and the work appeared to prosper, but Sister Hamann's suddenly failing health necessitated a second abandonment of the field in the year 1838.

At the request of Quintin Hogg, Esq., in the year 1878 a similar mission was commenced at his expense for the benefit of the negroes on his estates. Brother Henry Moore and Brother A. Pilgrim occupied two stations,—Graham's Hall and Reliance,—and reported, in general, gratefully of the measure of success which marked the past and hopefully as to future prospects, although not concealing sundry very serious drawbacks.

In 1884 Mr. Q. Hogg informed the Directing Board that he could no longer continue to pay the full amount he had at first given for the support of the work, and in consequence Reliance, one of the newly-founded stations in Demerara, had to be abandoned.

SOUTH AFRICA.—Since the year 1869 this extensive sphere of labor has been divided into a western and an eastern province. The former used to be called the Oberland or Upper District, and embraced the stations near Cape Town, and also those in the vicinity of Algoa Bay. The latter was called Unterland or Lowlands; it embraces all the stations in Kaffraria. In the former the people are mostly a mixed race of Hottentots and negroes, the pure Hottentots being generally supposed to have dwindled down to a very small number; in the latter they are mainly Kafirs of various tribes.

I. *The Western Province.*—The work at the Cape of Good Hope began in the year 1737, when George Schmidt reached Cape Town as the first representative of the Moravian Church in the colony. Two and a half centuries earlier Christianity had begun to touch the country, as the Portuguese successors of the bold Bartholomew Diaz often paid short visits to its shores on their way to and from India. Crosses were reared here and there on the shore, but little more was done to bring Christianity to the notice of the inhabitants. In 1620 two English captains took possession of the country in the name of their sovereign, hoping that "the savage inhabitants would soon become servants of his Majesty, and then worshippers of the true God." Thirty years later the Dutch built a fort at the Cape, and claimed the land as theirs, and in their record of the transaction expressed the desire that "their rule might tend to uphold righteousness, and plant and further pure Christian teaching among the wild and savage natives of the country."

When Schmidt arrived at the Cape, the condition of the natives, and their relations to the white colonists, who embraced French and German elements as well as Dutch, painfully showed that very little had been done to carry out the wishes of the early occupants of the colony. Both Hottentots and Bushmen had been disgracefully treated, robbed of their lands, regarded as beasts rather than as human beings, and reduced to hard servitude or the wild life of the brigand, hiding in rocks and caves, and preying on the white man as opportunity offered. The Dutch Boer or farmer, combining in his character the most contrary qualities, and strongly tinged with a peculiar puritan form of religion, persistently regarded the natives as doomed to destruction, like the people in Canaan in olden times, and treated them with contempt and loathing, and with terrible cruelty. To offer Christian teaching to these "zwarte schepsels" (black creatures), was not to be dreamt of : Christianity was intended for white people, but not for "black cattle." To buy land, however absurdly low the price paid might be, was of course out of the question, if it could safely be taken by force. The curse of civilization they were welcome to, and they had become to a terrible extent slaves to the vice of drunkenness, with all its concomitant evils; diseases, too, previously unknown, raged with fearfully fatal effects, decimating the population of the country. Thus it came about that the colonists as they increased in number and power seized the whole land, while the poor natives were reduced to a condition of moral and physical degradation and wretched servitude. Christian churches existed in the country and Christian doctrine was preached—often, alas! by men who were mere hirelings; but woe be to the native who would dare to venture near the white man's house of prayer. Under these circumstances G. Schmidt entered upon his work.

Two gentlemen residing in Amsterdam, who had become interested in the natives of the Cape Colony by Ziegenbalg's account of them, and had been led to the duty of taking part in Christian missions by intercourse with some of the gospel messengers who had embarked for their destination at Amsterdam, suggested to the Brethren at Herrnhut the commencement of a mission among the Hottentots. The man selected for the office of pioneer was a devoted servant of God whose zeal and steadfastness had already stood a severe test. Although only twenty-seven years of age when setting forth for Africa, he had spent six years in chains in a Bohemian prison " for the sake of the gospel," and one year (immediately on his release) in travelling on foot through several countries of Europe in order to become acquainted with awakened souls, and to proclaim, wherever he could find an opportunity, the glad tidings of salvation in Jesus. He was a poor man, earning his living by his daily labor; his education had been exceedingly limited, but his heart was full of love and devotion, and he longed to be spent in the Master's service.

Arriving at Cape Town on July 9th, 1739, he and his projects soon became common topics of conversation: in all sorts of circles of society the missionary was sneered at and derided, or spoken of with angry scorn. Scarcely any one gave him credit for the most ordinary honesty of purpose, not to speak of lofty enthusiasm for his work and calling, and no one believed in his achieving any success. In two months' time, however, he was making his way to a Hottentot kraal on the river Zonderend, about fifty miles to the east of Cape Town, under the guidance of Afriko and Kybodo, natives from that place whom he had met there. The former was master of the Dutch language and of great use as interpreter. Having built himself a hut near Afriko's dwelling, round which a garden was soon laid out, he at once began to preach with the help of the interpreter. His attempts to learn the Hottentot language with its singular variety of "click" sounds and most peculiar intonations, which travellers compared with the "cries of turkeys, owls, or magpies," proving a failure, he wisely resolved to teach the people Dutch. In imperfect fashion he told the story of the cross; but before long a Dutch corporal living near was won for Christ by his testimony, and became his stanch friend and faithful helper in the work.

In the following year (1738) some hostile farmers procured an order transferring him to a spot some ten miles off, a wild locality, called Bavianskloof, or Ape Valley, from the large number of those animals which frequented the place. Eighteen Hottentots followed him, who were surprised to see how soon he had built himself a new hut and laid out a garden; at once he resumed his work of preaching and teaching, and training the natives to habits of industry and all kinds of agricultural pursuits. The people liked the only kindly white being they had ever seen; they had such confidence in him that even several of those who did not come to reside near him sent their children to school to him. The number of pupils soon grew to fifty, among whom the most promising was Willem (William), who was the first to be baptized (in the year 1742), and subsequently Schmidt's valued assistant. With the Hottentots' tendency to lead a roving life and to indulge in gross vice, the office of a faithful missionary was no sinecure; on the contrary, it required an inexhaustible supply of love and patience, and Schmidt appears to have possessed this. In a short time the Christian flock at Bavianskloof numbered seven Hottentots, and a considerably larger number of natives had become very warmly attached to the good teacher.

As soon as the tidings of the baptism of natives reached Cape Town, great opposition was excited; the chaplain of the fort summoned some of the candidates to an examination, and was amazed to find that they could read fairly well, and give sensible and even correct answers to his questions on Christian doctrines. His favorable testimony, however, had no weight with those who could not endure that these natives should be regarded and treated as human beings, and they succeeded in inducing the governor to forbid Schmidt to baptize. Thus obstructed in his work, he returned to Europe in 1744, in the hope that negotiations there would clear the way for missionary operations at the Cape. The hope was vain: no petitions availed with the government in Holland, and the small flock of converts, which had grown to forty-seven persons, after keeping together for a time in the hope that their teacher would return to them, gradually dispersed or died. Bavianskloof was abandoned and became a wilderness. Schmidt returned to his humble calling of day-laborer, but to the last day of his life never lost faith in the eventual success of the Mission in South Africa, and never wearied of frequent prayer for his beloved Hottentots. While on his knees the Master's welcome summons called the faithful servant home.

*Eastern Province.*—The Kafir Mission proper dates back to the year 1828, when, at the request of Lord Somerset, the Brethren consented to commence a mission in a tract on the northeast frontier of the colony, which owned the sway of the Tambookie Bowana as its chief. At that time the London Missionary Society, the Glasgow Missionary Society, and the Wesleyans were already at work among portions of the Kafir tribes. The brethren Lemmertz, Hoffmann, and Fritsch, some twenty Hottentots, and Wilhelmina Stompjes, a Kafir woman, who seems in God's providence to have been specially raised up as an invaluable help to the missionaries in their difficult and often perilous work, formed the little company, which set out from Gnadendal on February 21st, 1828. Not before May 20th did they reach their destination, and fix on a site for the new station on the river Klipplaat. (Its position is 120 miles northeast of Port Elizabeth, and 60 or 70 northwest of East London.) In a month's time building operations were so far advanced that services could be held in a room which served as a church, and the natives were surprised and delighted to see the happy effects of an irrigation scheme, which the brethren at once recognized as a necessity if good harvests were to be looked for. Spiritual work had hard rocky ground to deal with. Bowana and his Tambookies were by no means eager to hear the gospel, and very loath to accept it. "The Word of God is for the white people," they said, "not for us: it will not enter our ears and hearts." And their statement seemed only too true.

They would come, and listen stolidly, and beg most pertinaciously; yielding to the infectious example of the missionaries, whom they saw leading the way in hard manual labor in garden, field, or water-conduit, they would even handle a spade for a while in a dilettanti fashion, but the gospel appeared to make no impression. The missionaries labored under the great disadvantage of being obliged to carry on all communications through an interpreter. But Wilhelmina proved a host in herself, teaching a number of native girls, interpreting with great readiness, though frequently interspersing comments and additional remarks from her own warm heart, using all the gifts and graces she possessed with singular humility and earnestness for the furtherance of the Lord's work. Employed in the kitchen of the mission-house, she liberally dispensed the Word of Life along with the dole of bread to the throng of beggars which daily crowded round the door: there, too, she received the messengers of many a proud Kafir chief, who could not resist the powerful weight of her noble, upright, unselfish character, and her words of wisdom and discretion. At the close of the year things looked far from promising, however; locusts had devastated the gardens, thievish Fetkamcas had stolen the herds, and most of the Tambookies had left the neighborhood.

In the following year Bowana and his savage son Mapasa, enraged at a well-deserved fine inflicted on them by government for an unwarrantable act of violence towards another tribe, and attributing the action of government to the advice of the missionaries, suddenly appeared at Shiloh at the head of fifty armed men with the intention of murdering all its inhabitants. Working in the garden, Wilhelmina at once recognized, from the war-costume of her countrymen, the object of the visit, and hastened to the rescue of her teachers. With undaunted courage she faced the fierce and cruel chiefs, and with scathing eloquence upbraided them with their abominable treachery and wicked designs. Instead of killing the missionaries and the woman who had dared to intrude in the assembly of men, they withdrew peacefully with their followers, and in a few days actually sent to apologize. Mapasa's hatred continued unabated, but so did the Lord's care for Shiloh and its people, and faithful Wilhelmina was often used by Him as the channel for His protection and blessing. Through many difficulties, hindrances, and trials the missionaries persevered until the work was fairly established on a solid foundation and began to spread to the surrounding tribes.

BARBADOES (WEST INDIES).—Except the force of Christian sympathy and compassion, there appears to have been no cause of a special character to induce the authorities of the Brethren's Church to commence a mission in this island. But its circumstances might well claim both. Churches and schools there were, but exclusively for the whites, who were more numerous in proportion to the black population than in any other West Indian island. Even the members of the Society of Friends, at that time numerous in Barbadoes, appear to have been mainly, if not exclusively, concerned with the improvement of the external condition of the slaves; these were at that time intellectually lower than in some other islands, but of a restless turn, which not unfrequently led to opposition against the ruling class, and severity of treatment by way of check or retaliation.

It was in the year 1765 that John Wood and Andrew Rittmansberger were sent to commence operations in Barbadoes. They reached Bridgetown in safety, but within a month of their landing Rittmansberger had died of fever, and before the end of the year Wood had lost courage, and abandoned his vocation. Another brother, sent out in the following year, fell a victim to fever a week after reaching the island. In 1767 Brother B. Brookshaw, who was subsequently in Antigua, arrived, and was permitted at length to lay a foundation to the spiritual building, which it was proposed to erect to the glory of God. Though not possessed of great learning, he was gifted with practical good sense, and above all was devoted to our Saviour, and full of eager zeal for the spread of His kingdom on earth. To his simple faith no obstacle proved insuperable, and his genuine humility and loving nature won the hearts of all with whom he came in contact. His first address to the slaves was delivered in the yard surrounding the "great house" on an estate belonging to a Quaker gentleman, Mr. Jackman. A week later the spacious saloon of the residence was used, and several white persons were present. The proprietor was astonished at the attention of the negroes, who seemed eagerly to swallow the words as they fell from the preacher's lips. An effect was soon perceived, the work of evangelization had begun, and if there were opponents around who invoked vengeance on the ship's captain who had brought out "this Moravian preacher," or threatened to throw him into the water if they came across him, there were several stanch friends who rallied round him. Among the latter were several clergymen of the Church of England, of whom Brookshaw says in his diary that "their doctrine is more in accordance with the truth of the gospel, and the articles of the Church of England, than what one is accustomed to hear in churches at home."

JAMAICA (WEST INDIES).—It was at the request of two wealthy proprietors—the brothers William Foster and Joseph Foster Barham—that a mission was commenced on their estates in this island. Through the preaching of John Cennick in England they had been converted, and were desirous of conferring the blessings of the gospel on their slaves; hence they brought all their influence to bear on the missionary work which Brother Zacharias George Caries and two others went out to commence in the year 1754. For the attainment of this object they were willing to make no inconsiderable pecuniary sacrifice; but this was of small account to persons of their condition, in comparison with the loss of reputation, the ridicule and ill-will to which they cheerfully subjected themselves from relatives, friends, and fellow-proprietors. Their object was in the first instance to provide religious instruction, but then also to promote the temporal and social well-being of the negroes, for whom they held themselves responsible. In the case of some of the subsequent promoters, Christian philanthropic motives may have been tinged with a hope of improving their property, especially after it became known—as was publicly stated by a Jamaica proprietor in the House of Commons—that a "Moravian negro" by reason of his industry, obedience, and faithfulness was worth considerably more than an ordinary one. But it is fair to state that many Jamaica estate-owners, resident and non-resident, especially during the past fifty years, have been ready to make real sacrifices to secure the spiritual, moral, and temporal well-being of their negroes.

On the 18th of October, 1754, Caries reached the Bogue estate in the parish of St. Elizabeth. The negroes heard his message gladly, and the Word of the Cross soon found its way into some hearts, and proved itself a regenerating divine power. In April of the following year the first convert was baptized, and the preaching of Caries attracted white men as well as blacks, from a distance of twenty to thirty miles even, so that the faithful and truly humble servant of God began to be anxious concerning the favor he was obtaining from men. By the end of the year 1755 there were already 77 baptized negroes and 400 candidates or inquirers on the estates under the care of the brethren.

ANTIGUA (WEST INDIES).—Samuel Isles was the honored founder of the mission in this island. He had labored for eight years in the island of St. Thomas, when he was sent on to Antigua with instructions to commence work there among the neglected black population, if an opening could be found. On April 1st, 1756, he landed at St. John's, alone, friendless, without introduction. Placing his trust in God, and seeking for His guidance, he straightway called on the governor, to whom he presented a copy of the Act of the British Parliament of 1749 recognizing the Moravian Church and encouraging its labors in the British colonies. Permission to commence work was at once granted, and on the 12th of January of the following year the first convert was baptized. But the work progressed very slowly. For the exercise of the public ministry among the slaves there was little scope, the opposition of most of the planters was strong and bitter, and the efforts of the missionaries were greatly impeded by having to labor for their own maintenance, which was the common practice among the early Moravian messengers. Isles died at his post in 1764, having seen but little fruit of his labor. In the years immediately following, the number of baptized members dwindled down from thirty-six to fourteen. This was the state of the mission when in 1769 Brother Peter Brown (or Braun), commonly known among the negroes as "Massa Brown," arrived from Bethlehem in Pennsylvania, through whose influence, with God's blessing, a wonderful change was soon effected.

Brown is described as "undistinguished by either shining abilities or superior knowledge, by dignity of manner or elegance of delivery; yet possessed of gifts and graces which the most talented among his fellow-servants would do well earnestly to covet." Brother Bennet Harvey, who followed him in his service after an interval of forty years and had ample opportunity of forming a just estimate of his character and labors, wrote of him as follows: "Simplicity and unction marked the genuine character and earnest labors of Brother P. Brown. Rightly discerning his call to be a disciple of the cross and a preacher of the gospel to the poor, he minded not high things, but condescended to men of low estate; even to those who were esteemed the weak, base, foolish, and despised of this world. Even by such he was himself at first despised; but he pitied and bore with their ignorance and the mockery of their children, until by the Christian meekness and gentleness of his demeanor he overcame their obstinacy, obtained from them a patient hearing, and prevailed with them to be reconciled to God. He visited them in their huts, followed them in their hours of rest in the field, ate with them out of their calabash, talked the gospel to them, and with equal grace and wisdom, as a father with his children, drew their hearts to himself as the negro's friend, and the messenger of the Church desirous of their salvation. His heart was in his work and in his words. . . . With a wisdom which the world counts foolishness, and a lowliness of mind which it despises, he suited himself to their capacity and condition; and thus by word and deed preached the gospel to the poor. . . . Truly blessed continues to be his memory."

ST. KITTS (WEST INDIES).—Tidings of the happy results of the mission in Antigua, easily transmitted to the adjacent island of St. Kitts, soon awakened a desire on the part of some well-meaning proprietors in the latter to try the experiment of Moravian missions on their own estates. Self-interest was, no doubt, a leading motive with several of the intelligent gentlemen who promoted the scheme. But in the case of the main mover, Mr. Gardiner, an eminent solicitor and planter, there was a true desire to advance the Saviour's kingdom among the black population on his own property and throughout the island. On his invitation the Brethren Gottwalt and Birkby were sent out in the year 1777, and received a very kind welcome from Mr. and Mrs. Gardiner, who introduced them to some of the leading officials, including the governor and the commander-in-chief of the Leeward Islands. A house in the outskirts of the town of Basseterre was hired as headquarters, and the work of preaching began here and at Palmetto Point, the estate of Mr. Gardiner. Supported by this friend and the governor, the Brethren were able to successfully cope with the hostility of some ill-disposed whites, and they soon found that their words were beginning to take effect on the hearts of the negroes.

TOBAGO (WEST INDIES).—The whole population of this island is about 17,000 souls, considerably less than that of the single town of Bridgetown in Barbadoes. It lies about 24 miles northeast of Trinidad, and rather more than 50 miles from the South American Continent. Its landscapes are very picturesque, river-scenery frequently enhancing their beauty. A large portion of the central districts is still uncultivated. Situated nearer to the equator, its hot and damp climate is generally found to be more unhealthy for Europeans than that of the other islands; but it is stated that cases of yellow fever in its most dangerous type are of rare occurrence. Hurricanes, too, are seldom mentioned in the island records.

The missionary work of the Moravian Church in this beautiful tropical island may be dated from the year 1787; but permanent footing was not actually obtained until 1826. In the former year Brother and Sister Montgomery (the parents of the poet) proceeded from Barbadoes to Tobago on a visit to Mr. Hamilton, the proprietor of several estates, who was anxious to do more than he had done for his numerous slaves. Mr. Hamilton, at that time not the decided Christian he subsequently became, was a man of great benevolence, and an exception to the majority of the planters of that day, among whom the rule was to make as much money as possible out of the labor of oppressed and helpless slaves, and spend it in reckless profligacy and debauchery. He was deeply impressed by the consistent Christian words and work of the Brethren, whom he had learnt to know in London and Barbadoes, and became very urgent in his wish to have Moravian missionaries for his people. He was favored to see good fruits produced among his slaves, and several members of his family continue to the present day to manifest their interest in the mission work.

Montgomery returned to Barbadoes, with a report which was very hopeful of good results for a missionary effort in Tobago. But men were so scarce, and the requirements of the rapidly growing mission elsewhere so multiplied, that it was not till 1790 that the first missionary could be sent in the person of Brother Montgomery himself. His work was begun with great vigor, but was sadly hindered by a formidable outbreak of soldiers and people on receipt of the tidings of the French Revolution, by a disastrous hurricane a month or two later, and the failing health of his wife which ended in her happy departure before the year closed. In March of the following year Montgomery, with his health completely shattered, had to return to Barbadoes, where, in the month of July, his brief missionary career was terminated by his death.

Twenty-four years later the mission was reopened by Brother Peter Ricksecker, from the congregation at Bethlehem in Pennsylvania, with prospects not less favorable than on the previous occasions. The son of Mr. Hamilton, who had inherited not only his father's estate, but also his ardent desire for the temporal and spiritual welfare of his slaves, was ready to give them every assistance, and the island seemed now to be permanently settled in English hands. At Riseland a building was soon arranged as a temporary church; and as the missionary became acquainted with the people, he was delighted to find that the fruits of the earlier missions had not altogether disappeared. At first the blacks came from all parts to see and hear him, but the charm of novelty soon wore away, and then it became needful for him, with patient and self-denying love, to seek them out and press the gospel on their attention: the children especially were objects of his warm interest and tender care. In 1827 twenty estates were visited and provided with services, and the need of a mission station with its own church became pressing.

MOSQUITO COAST, CENTRAL AMERICA.— About the year 1847 the Mosquito Coast was much spoken of in public papers in connection with an attempt of the Prussian Government to establish a colony there and to direct the tide of emigration to those parts. The project proved abortive, chiefly on account of the universally prevailing belief that the climate was unhealthy for Europeans. As a field for missionary labor this region was first commended to the consideration of the Moravian Directing Board by Prince Schönburg Waldenburg, a munificent helper in their missionary work in various climes, whose generous gifts were always characterized by practical wisdom and a very real and intelligent interest.

The country in question, comprising a narrow strip of coast, about one degree in breadth and two in length (west longitude 83° 31' to 84° 40', north latitude 11° 45' to 14° 15'), is bounded on the north by Honduras, on the west and south by Nicaragua. A reconnoitring visit was made in 1847 by the Brethren H. G. Pfeiffer and A. A. Reinke, at that time missionaries in Jamaica.

A four days' sail from Kingston brought the explorers to St. Juan de Nicaragua, on account of its harbor the most important town on the coast. It is now also called Greytown, after Sir George Grey, formerly governor of Jamaica. Colored Spaniards from Nicaragua and Costa Rica were the inhabitants of the place; the Christian religion was represented by a Roman Catholic Church in course of erection at the expense of the Nicaraguan Government, to which, however, as yet no priest was attached. Truly characteristic it was that the missionaries were forbidden to preach in public, and ordered to restrict their worship to the precincts of their own bedrooms. Greytown is still Nicaraguan, but such restrictions are happily no

longer enforced. Between this town and Blewfields, the capital of the Mosquito territory, early experience was made of the delays which often attend these coasting trips: it took four days to accomplish seventy miles, as the rough state of the sea obliged the travellers frequently to seek safety on shore. On May 2d Blewfields was reached, where the Brethren, on presentation of a letter of introduction from Lord Palmerston, received a cordial welcome from Mr. Walker, the British consul-general, who, during the whole visit, did all that lay in his power to aid them in the attainment of their object.

The town of Blewfields was found to contain about 600 inhabitants, the majority of whom were whites and colored men, with a good many negroes and a very small number of Indians. Of the whites about 80 were German immigrants. Most of the residents professed to be Christians, although there was very little pretence of Christian knowledge and still less of Christian life. A catechist of the English Church, recently arrived from Jamaica, read prayers and a sermon on Sunday, and conducted a school during the week; but these advantages were confined to the white and colored people, and no manner of provision was made for the moral and religious instruction of the blacks and Indians. Of the latter a considerable number often visited Blewfields to do homage to their chief or "king," or to sell turtle, tortoise-shell, deer-skins, and other articles of traffic. Under the general term of Moscos or Mosquito Indians, a number of tribes were included, Woolwas, Ramahs, Summoos, and others, differing from one another in outward features, in dialect, manners and customs, but all understanding the Mosco language, yielding willing obedience to the one chief, and inspired with a firm determination to defend their country against all efforts of Nicaragua to annex it.

Gross darkness covered the people; but while scarcely a semblance of religious belief was to be found, there existed a great dread of evil spirits, whose influence could only be controlled by the Sukias, or witch-doctors; these wily impostors therefore held unrivalled sway over the poor deluded natives. Polygamy was commonly practised, and the vice of drunkenness was terribly prevalent. Even a brief examination sufficed to show that there was here abundant scope for missionary effort, while the gentle, pliable, impressible nature of the Indians furnished ground for a fair hope of successful evangelization of the tribes who lived scattered along the coast. Before the two missionaries concluded their visit (July 10th), the king and his council of state begged them to commence a mission in the country, at the same time offering for their use a small island inhabited by Ramah Indians, and a plot of land in the town of Blewfields.

The General Synod of the Moravian Church, which met at Herrnhut in the summer of 1848, recognizing in a variety of providential circumstances an indication of the Lord's will that they should go forward to occupy fresh fields of heathendom for the Saviour, almost unanimously passed a resolution to send missionaries to the Mosquito Coast. Before the end of the year Brother H. G. Pfeiffer, who had spent twenty-two years in the service of the Jamaica Mission, was on his way to this new sphere of labor, accompanied by the young Brethren J. E. Lundberg and E. G. Kandler as his assistants.

LABRADOR.—The first attempt to commence a mission among the Eskimos was made in the year 1752. The chief originator of the work was John Christian Erhardt, a sailor, who, by God's blessing on the faithful preaching of Frederick Martin, had come to the knowledge of the Saviour in the year 1741, on a visit to St. Thomas. Having visited Greenland in the Brethren's ship "Irene," under the command of Captain Garrison, and there heard of the Eskimos living on the western shores of Davis' Straits, he most persistently urged the Brethren at Herrnhut to send the gospel there. The request that missionaries might be allowed a passage on board of one of the Company's vessels to the territory of the Hudson's Bay Company, was not acceded to; but a London merchant, Mr. Nisbet, with two other gentlemen, volunteered to fit out a trading vessel for Labrador, in which, after some delay, Erhardt with four companions sailed from London on May 17th, 1752. A suitable spot for a station was selected, to which they gave the name of Nisbet Harbor, and a wooden hut was soon put up. Continuing his journey up the coast, Erhardt, with the captain and five of the crew, were treacherously murdered by the natives, and the other missionaries had to help to work the ship on her homeward voyage.

Deep sympathy with the fate of this brave Christian sailor, and the accounts received from the survivors of the party, stimulated to many prayers on behalf of these savage heathen, and a carpenter, Jens Haven, resolved to take up Erhardt's work as soon as the Lord would open the way. After spending two years in the Greenland Mission, where he learned the language, while assisting in establishing the station at Lichtenfels, he made his way to London in the spring of the year 1764, with the intention of getting to Labrador by working his passage out as ship's carpenter or sailor on board of one of the Hudson's Bay Company's vessels. Eventually he was allowed to sail with the British fleet to St. John, whence he succeeded in procuring a passage in a small coasting schooner to Labrador, landing in Chateau Bay (north latitude 52°) towards the end of August. On hearing the stranger speak in their own language, the Eskimos vociferously bade him welcome, and he trusted himself without any escort in their midst. They hailed him as their countryman, listened to his message with interest, and begged him to renew the visit.

The success of this attempt to open up friendly communication with the Eskimos induced the Brethren of the Directing Board to continue the effort. Three other Brethren were associated with Haven, one of whom, Drachart, before joining them had been a clergyman in the employ of the Danish Mission in Greenland, where he had displayed singular tact and power in the treatment of the natives—gifts which stood him in admirable stead during his service in Labrador. Drachart was then fifty years old, but full of youthful courage and enthusiasm—the very man for the work.

A British man-of-war conveyed them from St. John's, Newfoundland, to Pitt's Harbor, where by and by some 300 natives assembled, who were extremely friendly in their demeanor, and singularly attentive to the words of Haven

and Drachart, and open to their quiet Christian influence. In September they returned to London, to prepare for a permanent occupation of Labrador, by obtaining from the Board of Trade in England ensured possession of a piece of land on the coast. Four years elapsed before a decision was reached, as suspicion was entertained in certain influential quarters as to the real intentions of the Brethren. In the mean time Haven and Drachart lived in England, chiefly at the Moravian settlement Fulneck, in Yorkshire. Here they had the privilege of bringing the first Eskimo from Labrador to the knowledge of the truth, and seeing him baptized as the first-fruits from that nation. This was a youth of fifteen, named Karpik, who with other natives had been brought to England by Commodore Sir Hugh Palliser, and intrusted to the care of these two Brethren. On the day after his baptism, after having given satisfactory proof of his faith in Jesus, he died of small-pox.

In 1769 the obstacles were removed, and Haven, Drachart, and eight others went out in the "Jersey Packet," a small sloop of eighty tons, under the command of Captain Mugford, purchased and fitted out by the "Ship's Company," which consisted principally of members of the "Brethren's Society for the Furtherance of the Gospel among the Heathen." After touching at several points on the coast, a suitable place for a station was selected on Nunengoak Bay, which afforded the advantage of a fair harbor. There were about 700 natives here, who flocked round the ship in their kayaks, and were especially delighted to see their "little Jens," as they called him, his small stature, like their own, being a strong recommendation in their eyes; their affectionate familiarity did not, however, interfere with the respect and veneration entertained for him. On August 16th possession was taken of a plot of land in the name of George III., and presents were distributed. Two days later the ship was on her way home.

Communication between Europe and the mission stations in Labrador has been maintained since the work commenced, in the year 1770, by means of a vessel which makes annual voyages each way. During this long period (of 120 years) no fatal accident has been permitted to befall the favored bark, or those whom she was conveying across the boisterous and often ice-bound deep, and along a coast bristling with rocks, and abounding with peculiar perils; nor has the communication between the missionaries and their brethren in Europe been in a single instance interrupted. To the praise of God, the Society can record with grateful hearts that his preserving mercies have been graciously vouchsafed in rich measure and with unchanging faithfulness, in answer to many prayers of His children.

Since the year 1770 nine vessels have been employed in this mission service—the "Amity," the "Good Intent" (1776), the first "Harmony" (1788), the "Resolution" (1802), the "Hector" (1808), the "Jemima" (1809), the second "Harmony" (1819), the third "Harmony" (1831), the fourth or present "Harmony" (1861). The ship now in use is a bark of about 250 tons register, built at Yarmouth, and has proved a sound, strong vessel and a very good sailer. She has a slightly raised quarterdeck, by which additional height is gained for the cabins. The latter, though small, are neat and commodious.

Though furnished with every additional protection required in case of contact with the ice, the outline of the ship is elegant. Her usual crew consists of twelve hands, besides the captain. The present commander, Captain Linklater, fills his important post in such a manner as to enjoy in the highest degree the esteem and confidence of his employers, being thus a worthy successor to those whose names are recorded with grateful respect in the history of the Society, as "faithful, experienced, and energetic seamen, in whom a degree of confidence has been placed, which could only have been inspired by the belief that they considered themselves the servants of the cause, rather than of the Society; that they acknowledged their entire and continued dependence on that Lord whom winds and waves obey, and were disposed at all times, and especially in seasons of difficulty and peril, to seek His counsel, help, and blessing."

ALASKA.—1. *Bethel.*—On the 18th of May, 1885, a party consisting of the Rev. William H. Weinland and wife, Rev. J. H. Killbuck (a Delaware Indian who had been educated in the theological college at Bethlehem, Pa.) and wife, and Mr. Hans Torgersen, a mechanic and lay assistant, sailed from San Francisco, carrying with them lumber, sashes, doors, hardware, furniture, etc., for mission buildings. A spot had been selected on a previous exploratory tour on the Kuskokwim River, one hundred and fifty miles from its mouth, near the native village of Mumtrekhlagamute. On the 20th of June the little company landed on the shores of Alaska, and in the course of the month began their mission work at the station, which had been previously selected, and which was named Bethel.

The mission met with a sad loss on the 10th of August by the accidental drowning of Mr. Torgersen. The other brethren felt his loss keenly, as their house was only in the course of erection, and there was much to be done before they would be ready for the long and severe Alaska winter. Gradually they became acquainted with the people, and learned something of the language. The latest intelligence from this station mentions awakenings and conversions, and a general desire on the part of the surrounding heathen for religious instruction. In 1888 an unmarried Brother was added to the staff in Bethel, and in 1889 an unmarried Sister.

2. *Carmel.*—In 1886 the Moravian Brethren were requested by the Commissioners of Education to commence a station at Nushagak, near Fort Alexander. They were first to establish a school, but hoped and expected also to reach the adult Eskimos. The Rev. Frank Wolff, with his wife and two children and Miss M. Huber, arrived there in May, 1886. A school was established, and the missionaries have been much encouraged. The school is appreciated, and there are prospects of the work being enlarged and extended. In 1889 an unmarried Brother was added to the force at this station.

AUSTRALIA.—It was about the year 1834 that for the first time the attention of the Moravian Church was directed to the needs of the aborigines of Australia, especially in the "district of Port Philip," now the prosperous colony of Victoria. Missionary efforts had been undertaken by various churches or societies from the days of Samuel Marsden, of the Church Missionary Society, in 1795. But none had been maintained for more than a few years,

and the results were very trifling. It was, therefore, scarcely a matter of surprise that repeated calls addressed to the Church to enter this field of labor failed to move the Directing Board. They had the effect, however, of creating and fostering a deep, prayerful interest in the proposed work among various circles in the German congregations. Associations were formed to keep up constant intercession for the Australian blacks, and to provide a fund for the maintenance of the mission, whenever it should be undertaken. A repetition of the call in a letter addressed by the London Association in aid of the Moravian Missions to the General Synod assembled at Herrnhut in 1848, led to the unanimous resolution to enter upon this field without delay.

In the autumn of 1849 the Brethren Taeger and Spieseke sailed for Australia, and reached Melbourne in February, 1850. Here they received a cordial welcome from all classes, and not least from C. J. La Trobe, Esq., at that time superintendent of Port Philip and soon afterwards first lieutenant-governor of the Colony of Victoria.

The aborigines of Australia, called Australnegroes or Papoos, are said to be a branch of the negro race; socially, morally, physically, they would seem to stand on the lowest stage of humanity. Their clothing at most an opossum-skin or a bit of grass-matting; their home a hut of branches, affording scarcely any shelter or protection; their food the flesh of kangaroo, opossum, wild dog, fish-grubs, lizards, snakes, rats, and occasionally that of a human foe, with scarcely any pretence of religion or worship,—they seemed to have no object to live for except to sustain gross animal life and indulge their sensual and cruel instincts. The women were slaves and beasts of burden; the children, if troublesome, were killed; if not, left to care for themselves as best they could. Wherever else the "noble savage" might be found—if to be found at all—in Australia he certainly did not exist.

In April (1850) the missionaries went up the country to Mount Franklin, the station of Mr. Parker, Assistant-Protector of Aborigines, where they sojourned for eight months, perfecting themselves in English, and studying the natives and their language. This place, about eighty miles from Melbourne, afforded good opportunities for reconnoitring the district in search of a suitable site for a station, and welcome facilities for intercourse with the blacks, who were induced to attend a small school, maintained at the charge of the government.

Eventually, at a distance of some two hundred miles from Melbourne, a piece of land on the shores of Lake Boga, south of the police-station, Swanhill, on the river Murray, was fixed on, and, after wearisome negotiations with government, and not a few perilous journeys to and fro, occupied by the missionaries in October, 1851.

CENTRAL ASIA.—At an early date in the history of the missions of the Moravian Church interest was manifested in the nations of the old world, and especially in the Mongolian race. Count Zinzendorf looked with a longing eye to the countries of Eastern Asia, and in one of his hymns speaks of the communication of the gospel to the Persians and Mongols as no improbable event. Several attempts were made in this direction, which may be regarded as introductory to the mission now in progress in the Himalayan Mountains.

The memory of these past efforts of the church to convert the Mongol race, with their many details calculated to interest both mind and heart, was revived in the year 1850 by a prolonged visit of the well-known and zealous missionary to China, Dr. Gützlaff, at Herrnhut. Responding to his urgent representation of the desirableness and the hopeful prospects of a renewed attempt for the accomplishment of this great object, the Directing Board after much serious consideration resolved to take measures for the establishment of a mission to the Mongols inhabiting the northern provinces of the Chinese Empire, as soon as qualified candidates could be found, and the best mode of commencing the work ascertained. An appeal for volunteers for this missionary service brought forward several applicants, from whom J. E. Pagell and A. W. Heyde were selected to go forth as pioneers; both of them men of courage and endurance, with a fair education, but without theological training.

On August 1st, 1853, they set out for their field of labor by sailing-vessel to Calcutta. It had been their plan to proceed through Russian territory to Mongolia, but it was frustrated by the refusal of the Russian Government to provide the needful passports.

Early in April, 1854, the missionaries had reached Kotgur, a station of the Church Missionary Society, situated about a week's journey to the northeast of Simla, but separated from that delightful retreat by two or three lofty mountain ranges crossed by passes at an elevation of about 11,000 feet. The Rev. Mr. Prochnow gave them a warm welcome, and assisted them by all the means in his power in the work of equipping themselves for their difficult task. Hindustani had to be learnt for conversing with Hindus, and their knowledge of English perfected for negotiating with British officials; the study of the Mongolian language, of which a beginning had been made, was continued; but special effort directed to mastering the Tibetan, which is the language of a large portion of the people inhabiting the provinces adjacent to the Chinese frontier. A Tibetan lama, employed by Mr. Prochnow as interpreter, proved most serviceable as linguistic teacher.

In March, 1855, Heyde and Pagell set out on their first great missionary journey, which they hoped would take them right into Mongolia. At Sultanpur, the capital of Kullu, a stay of some weeks had to be made until the passes across the mountains were open. Then the Rotang Pass (13,600 feet) was crossed, and the province of Lahoul entered. Thence they proceeded on perilous paths to Leh, the capital of Ladak, and residence of the native potentate, Goolab Singh. To their great surprise not a single Mongol was to be found amongst its 4,000 inhabitants. Turning eastwards in pursuance of their mission, the missionaries then crossed the Kailas range (18,000 feet), and, after skirting the extensive Pangong Lake, reached the borders of the Chinese province of Ruduk. Entrance into Chinese territory was at once and peremptorily refused. Separating, in order to more effectually reconnoitre the unknown country, each renewed the attempt to cross the Chinese borders, and actually pushed forward through a few villages. But they were soon stopped, and compelled to return by the determined re-

fusal of the authorities to allow the people to provide any food for man or beast. By different routes they made their way back to Kotgur, where they arrived in October.

The result of the seven months' journey was disappointing as far as its main object was concerned. It was not possible to reach the Mongols from the side of British India, or the provinces of neighboring states standing more or less under British influence or protection.

In other respects the results of the tour were very satisfactory. The ground covered by the travellers embraced the provinces of Lahoul, Kunawur, Spitti, Kullu, Rupchu, which, with some extension to the north and west, have ever since formed the principal sphere of missionary operations. Much information was obtained respecting the country and its inhabitants, which proved of very great service when the question came to be discussed where they should settle down to work, pending the opening of Chinese Tibet to their advance. Ladak seemed to offer a good field, especially Leh and its neighborhood; but the ruler, Goolab Singh, had let them distinctly understand that he would not give his sanction to their permanent settlement under his rule. Eventually, on the advice of Mr. Prochnow, the province of Lahoul was selected, and a suitable site for a station fixed on in the village of Kyelang, situated on the banks of the river Bhaga, about 10,000 feet above the level of the sea. Although scarcely 150 miles distant from both Leh and Simla—a little to the west of a line joining these two towns—Kyelang is separated from both by such lofty mountain ranges that a journey to either is an undertaking of at least a fortnight. The population in the district is sparse; but as the village lies on the main commercial route between India, Yarkand, Ladak, and other regions to the north, it affords an opportunity for intercourse with representatives of a great variety of nations.

BOHEMIA.—Bohemia is the birth-place and original home of the Church of the Brethren's Unity (Unitas Fratrum; Bohemian, Jedrota bratrska). The Ancient Church, begun in 1457 by earnest, peace-loving followers of John Huss, had, in spite of severe trials and bitter persecutions, spread over a large part of Bohemia and Moravia, and into Poland. Within fifty years she had some two hundred congregations with many thousand members.

After a period of one hundred and sixty years of much prosperity and influence, she was destroyed in the cruel and bloodthirsty triumph of the Roman Catholic power in the great Thirty Years' War. Then for one hundred and sixty years the darkness of popery held sway over the fair lands of her home.

Gradually some of the restrictions against Protestantism were removed. In 1781 the "Edict of Toleration" was issued, and in 1861 a kind of general religious liberty was introduced by the Austrian Government.

At once, on the door being thus partially opened, the missionary evangelists of the Renewed Church pushed in, and busily traversed the accessible parts of Bohemia and Moravia. They were gladly welcomed by the people at large, and found many traditions of the Ancient Unity still alive and held in loving reverence; many earnest appeals were made to them to come and renew its life and work. Owing to political considerations the work had to be carried on with quietness and caution. At length the General Synod of the Church in 1869 took up the claims of Bohemia. Steps were taken for the evangelizing and forming congregations of the Brethren's Church in Bohemia wherever openings for the same should be presented.

Pottenstein, a village in the picturesque northeast of Bohemia, where four hundred years before there had been a congregation of the Unitas Fratrum, was the first to be occupied, and in 1870 a number of persons hitherto Roman Catholics, earnestly awakened, applied for admission and were formed into a congregation.

In 1872 the second congregation was begun at Dauba. These two places and congregations have continued to be the centres of the ever-growing and hopeful, ever-difficult and trying, but ever-devoted labors of the missionaries and their assistants.

Prague is now occupied by an agent, and services are held in a building secured for the purpose, with good hopes of progress.

At Landskron, Tschenkowitz, Leutomischel, and Reichenau hopeful work is opening out.

At Pottenstein a girls' orphanage is in a promising condition.

UNSUCCESSFUL MISSIONS.—Some of the Moravian Missions proved unsuccessful, and were abandoned from time to time.

*Lapland.*—In 1734 and 1735 an attempt was made by Andrew Grassman, Daniel Schneider, and John Nitschmann to establish a mission among the Swedish Laplanders, but relinquished because they were found to be under the supervision of the Lutheran state church.

*Shores of the Arctic Ocean.*—In 1737 and 1738 Andrew Grassman, Daniel Schneider, and Micksh proceeded to Archangel, in order to begin a mission among the Samoyedes on the shores of the Arctic Ocean. But the missionaries were arrested and thrown into prison, falsely charged with being Swedish spies, and after an imprisonment of five weeks conveyed to St. Petersburg, where they were examined, and, their innocence having been established, sent back to Germany.

*Algiers.*—In 1740 Ehrenfried Richter, at one time a wealthy merchant of Stralsund, but subsequently a resident of Herrnhut, felt constrained, although far advanced in years, to undertake a mission among the Christian slaves of Algiers, where he labored with great zeal and some success, until he was carried off by the plague, five months after his arrival.

*Ceylon.*—In 1740 David Nitschmann, known as the Syndic, and subsequently a bishop of the church, accompanied by Dr. Eller of Berlin, inaugurated a mission among the natives of Ceylon, which work, however, just when it began to prosper, was relinquished on account of the persistent opposition of the colonial authorities and the Dutch clergy.

*Guinea.*—In 1737 Christian Protten, a converted mulatto and native of Guinea, together with Henry Hukuff, undertook a mission on that coast. Hukuff died, and Protten met with no success. Hence the work was abandoned in 1741. In 1767, however, it was renewed, and continued until 1770, in which period nine missionaries were sent out, who all died, so that the enterprise was finally given up.

*Persia.*—In 1747 Dr. Frederick William Hocker and Dr. J. Rueffer attempted a mission among the Guebres, or the so-called fire-wor

shippers of Persia, which country they penetrated as far as Ispahan. They could, however, effect nothing, and abandoned the field in 1748. On their way home Rueffer died at Damietta, in Egypt.

*Egypt.*—From 1752 to 1783 three attempts were made by Hocker, George Pilder, John Danke, and John Antes to begin a mission in Abyssinia; but, in each case, they could penetrate no farther than Egypt, where some of them labored among the Copts, especially at Benesse, on the Nile. Owing to a want of success in this work, and political disturbances, the field was abandoned in 1783.

*East Indies.*—In this country a mission was carried on for thirty-seven years, from 1759 to 1796, and stations were established at the so-called "Brethren's Garden" near Tranquebar, at Serampore, at Patna, and on the Nicobar Islands. But the work did not prosper, the cost of it was enormous, and the mortality among the missionaries and Moravian settlers very great, nearly forty of them being carried off by disease. Hence this enterprise was finally given up in 1796.

*The Countries of the Kalmucks.*—For more than half a century, from 1768 to 1823, repeated attempts were made to begin missions among the Kalmucks, but they all proved unsuccessful.

### *Chronological Table of Moravian Missions:*

| | |
|---|---|
| 1732 | Mission to St. Thomas, West Indies. |
| 1733 | Mission to Greenland. |
| 1734 | Mission to North American Indians. |
| 1734 | Unsuccessful attempt in Lapland. |
| 1735 | Mission to Surinam. |
| 1736 | Mission to South Africa. The work here had to be suspended in 1743, and was not resumed till 1792. |
| 1737 | Attempt among the Samoyedes, Arctic Ocean, lasting till 1741. |
| 1738 | Mission to the Arawack Indians, Surinam. Abandoned in 1816. |
| 1740 | Attempt in Ceylon, which proved unsuccessful. |
| 1740 | Unsuccessful attempt in Algiers. |
| 1742 | Unsuccessful attempt in China. |
| 1747 | Unsuccessful attempt in Persia. |
| 1752 | Between this date and 1783 three attempts were made in Abyssinia. |
| 1752 | Failure of attempt to commence a mission in Labrador. |
| 1754 | Mission in Jamaica begun (West Indies). |
| 1756 | Mission in Antigua begun (West Indies). |
| 1759 | Mission in the East Indies (Nicobar Islands, Tranquebar, and Serampore). Abandoned in 1796. |
| 1765 | Mission in Barbadoes begun (West Indies). |
| 1768 | Mission among the Kalmucks, repeated attempts up to 1823. |
| 1771 | Mission in Labrador begun. |
| 1775 | Mission in St. Kitts begun (West Indies). |
| 1782 | Unsuccessful attempt in the Caucasus. |
| 1790 | Unsuccessful attempt in Tobago (West Indies). |
| 1792 | Mission in South Africa renewed. |
| 1818 | Kafir Mission begun, South Africa. |
| 1822 | Work among lepers at Hemelen Aarde, South Africa. |
| 1827 | Tobago (West Indies) permanently occupied after three attempts. |
| 1828 | Shiloh, the first station in Kaffraria proper, South Africa, founded. |

1835 Unsuccessful attempt in Demerara, South America.
1838 Training school at Gnadendal, South Africa, commenced.
1842 Training school at Fairfield (Jamaica) begun.
1846 Leper hospital transferred to Robben Island, South Africa.
1847 Training Institution at Cedar Hall, Antigua, begun.
1849 Mosquito Coast Mission begun (Central America).
1849 Australian Mission begun on Lake Boga.
1851 Training school at Beekhuizen, Surinam.
1853 Central Asian Mission begun.
1856 Suspension of work in Australia.
1859 Australia reoccupied.
1867 Leper Mission at Jerusalem commenced.
1869 Bohemian Mission begun.
1878 Demerara reoccupied (South America).
1885 Mission to the Alaska Eskimos commenced.

**Mordwin Version.**—The Mordwin belongs to the Finn branch of the Ural-Altaic family of languages, and is used by a tribe on the banks of the Oka and Volga, in the governments of Nijni-Novgorod and Kazan, Russia, supposed to number about 400,000. The Russian Bible Society published at St. Petersburg a New Testament under the care of the Archbishop of Kazan, in 1820. It has never been reprinted, though the Mordwins profess Christianity. The Gospel of Matthew was printed in 1865 for Prince L. L. Bonaparte.

(*Specimen verse*, John 3 : 16.)

Секс псшй вечкизе Пазъ масшôронь эрпцяшъ, мякс мáксызе цёранзо сонзé скáмонъ шáчшумань, шшобы эрьвá кéмнцѣ лáнгозонзо авбль юма, но улевель пицѣ гень эрямосо.

**Moresby, or Port Moresby,** a station of the London Missionary Society, on the southern coast of New Guinea, Melanesia, under English authority. It was founded in 1873, and has a college in which natives from Tahiti, Rarotonga, Samoa, etc., are educated, and from which 17 stations are provided with teachers. There are 2 missionaries, 14 native ordained preachers, 314 church-members, 927 scholars.

**Moriah,** a mission station of the Moravians on the island of Tobago, West Indies. It was begun in 1842, and the work has been blessed from the very beginning. Its situation is very picturesque, standing as it does on an eminence surrounded by a labyrinth of sharp ridges and deep ravines, over which grow the luxuriant tropical vegetation. It is ten miles from Montgomery.

**Moriaro,** town in Chota Nagpur, Bengal, India. Mission station of the Gossner Missionary Society; an out-station of Muzaffarpur.

**Morija,** a town of Cape Colony, South Africa, 160 miles east of Caledon. Population about 4,000. Mission station of the Paris Evangelical Society (1833); 5 missionaries. Is, since 1883, the chief seat of the missions, and has a normal school, with a theological class, and 853 church-members.

**Morioka,** a town in Japan, north part of Nippon, southeast of Honjo. Station of A. B. M. U.; 1 missionary and wife, 4 out-stations, 43 church-members, 70 pupils. Methodist Episcopal Church (North); 1 native pastor, 36 church-members, 2 Sunday-schools, 60 scholars.

**Morocco,** a country of Africa on the Atlantic and Mediterranean. Area about 260,000 square miles. Population, 5,000,000, chiefly of the Berber race, though there are large numbers of Arabs. Religion Mohammedan. Mission work is carried on by the North Africa Mission, with stations at Tangier, Tetuan, and Sifroo. (See Africa and North Africa Mission.)

**Morrison, John Hunter,** b. Wallkill Township, New York, U. S. A., June 29th, 1806; fitted for college at Bloomfield Academy with Dr. Armstrong; graduated at Princeton College 1834, and Theological Seminary 1837; ordained as an evangelist by the Presbytery of New York the same year; sailed as a missionary of the Presbyterian Board for North India and the Punjâb 1838. He was stationed at Allahabad, Agra, and other places. He was characterized by great earnestness and boldness in the presentation of truth. On account of his fearlessness he was in mission circles styled "the lion of the Punjab." Yet no one was more affable than he, more genial in personal intercourse. Dr. Morrison made two brief visits to the United States, during one of which he was Moderator of the General Assembly at Peoria, Illinois. It was he who, after the Sepoy mutiny in 1857, proposed to the Lodiana Mission to call upon all Christians to observe an annual week of prayer for the conversion of the world. He died of cholera at Dehra Doon September 16th, 1881, aged 76, and in the 44th year of mission work. His dying words were, "It is perfect peace. I know whom I have believed." Dr. Morrison left a wife and several children, of whom a son and daughter are engaged in the work of the Lodiana Mission.

**Morrison, Robert,** b. Morpeth, Northumberland, England, January 15th, 1782, of humble Scotch parentage, his father being a maker of lasts and boot-trees. After receiving an elementary education he was apprenticed at an early age to his father. So eager was he to acquire knowledge, that he not only devoted all his leisure to close study, but had his book open before him while he worked, and removed his bed to his workshop, that he might study late into the night. At the age of fifteen he joined the Scotch Church. As early as 1801 he began the study of Latin, Hebrew, and theology with the minister of Newcastle, and after fourteen months' study entered the Independent Theological Academy at Hoxton, to prepare for the ministry. Soon after his admission he decided to become a missionary to the heathen. In May, 1804, he offered himself to the London Missionary Society, was accepted, and appointed its first missionary to China. Entering the Mission College at Gosport, he spent two years not only in special preparatory studies, but also in acquiring Chinese under a native teacher. He devoted also some hours daily to copying from a Chinese manuscript in the British Museum. He was ordained, and sailed for China January 31st, 1807, but the Chinese being hostile to the English on account of the opium difficulties, he was obliged to go via New York instead of going direct from London. He received from Mr. Madison, Secretary of State, a letter of introduction to our consul at Canton, which was of great advantage to him. Reaching Canton September 7th, he secured lodgings in the basement story of an American factory used as a wareroom, but soon removed to a more comfortable and convenient French factory. At first he adopted the Chinese dress, diet, and habits, but soon resumed his usual mode of life. An edict being issued about this time by the Chinese Government prohibiting the printing of religious books and the preaching of the gospel, Mr. Morrison set himself at once to study the language and translate the Bible. His health having suffered from incessant study and too rigid economy, he went, June 1st, 1808, to Macao, a Portuguese colony below Canton, where he had to remain in seclusion because of the jealousy of the Roman Catholic priests. His health being restored, he returned to Canton. But difficulties having arisen between the Chinese Government and the British Government, he went again to Macao. He resided here a year with an English family named Martin, and in 1809 married the eldest daughter. On the same day he was offered the position of translator to the East India Company's factory at Canton. As it relieved him of pecuniary anxiety, secured for him a permanent residence in China, ready access to some of the people, and time for the translation of the Scriptures and preparation of his dictionary, he accepted the appointment. This office he held to the day of his death—twenty-five years. To the end he had the confidence of the E. I. C., and they advanced large sums at different times for the publication of his various works. Though much occupied with office-work, he found time for Bible translation and the preparation of religious books. In 1810 a revised and amended version of the Acts of the Apostles, based on his copy of the manuscript in the British Museum, was printed—the first portion of the Scriptures in Chinese printed by any Protestant missionary. In 1812 the Gospel of Luke was printed. Early in 1814 the whole of the New Testament was ready, and the E. I. C. furnished a press and materials, also a printer to superintend its printing. In this year he baptized his first Chinese convert, Tsai-A-Ko, the first Chinese convert to Protestant Christianity, who continued steadfast in his faith till his death in 1818. In 1815 a Chinese grammar of 300 quarto pages, prepared in 1805, was printed at the Serampore press. In 1815 Mrs. Morrison went to England for her health, remaining five years, and died in 1822, two years after her return to China. In 1816 Mr. Morrison acted as interpreter to Lord Amherst. In 1817 he published "A View of China for Philological Purposes." In this year the University of Glasgow conferred upon him the degree of doctor of divinity. In 1818 the translation of the entire Bible, in part with the aid of Dr. Milne, was completed, and printed in 1821. This version is said to be too literal, and not idiomatic. But it was the first attempt, and the difficulties were enormous. Dr. Morrison says he studied "fidelity, perspicuity, and simplicity," "common words being preferred to classical." He was convinced of the necessity of a thorough revision, and hoped to be able to revise the work. From 1810 to 1818 the British

and Foreign Bible Society appropriated £6,000 at several different times towards the printing and publication of the Chinese Bible. The Old Testament formed 21 volumes 12mo. In 1818 the Anglo-Chinese College at Malacca (removed in 1844 to Hong Kong) was founded for "the reciprocal cultivation of Chinese and European literature." Dr. Morrison gave £1,000 for the buildings, and £100 annually for its support. With Dr. Milne he established this year a monthly magazine in Malacca. His most laborious literary work was the Chinese dictionary, published in 1821 by the East India Company at an expense of £15,000. In 1824, for the purpose of recruiting his health and awakening an interest in the mission, he visited England, where he spent two years. Previous to his departure for home he ordained to the ministry Leang-Afa, having had eight years' experience of his fitness for the work. He was elected while at home a Fellow of the Royal Society. Everywhere he was received with distinction by civil and religious bodies. He had an audience with George IV., to whom he presented a copy of the Sacred Scriptures in Chinese, and a map of Pekin. In 1826 he married Miss Armstrong of Liverpool, embarked for China, and reached Macao the September following. Though not vigorous, he continued his public labors for nine years more. He devoted himself more than ever to the missionary work, preaching, translating, and distributing printed works among the Chinese. He conducted religious services on the Sabbath, both in English and Chinese. He baptized Choo-Tsing, a Chinese teacher once employed at the Malacca College. In 1832 he writes: "I have been 25 years in China, and am now beginning to see the work prosper. By the press we have been able to scatter knowledge far and wide." He was cheered by the arrival in 1830 of Messrs. Abeel and Bridgman from America. He accompanied Lord Napier as interpreter to Canton, and died there August 1st, 1834. His remains were taken to Macao, where they still rest, the site being marked by an appropriate inscription. "He endeavored," says his biographer, "in the employment of such expedients as he could command, to relieve the wants, to mitigate the sufferings, and heal the diseases of the poor Chinese around him. In order to secure to the natives the means of a liberal and religious education, as well as to furnish facilities to foreigners for prosecuting the study of the Chinese language, he projected the establishment of the Anglo-Chinese College."

Besides the works mentioned, he published "Horæ Sinicæ," being translations from the popular literature of the Chinese, and "Chinese Miscellany."

**Mortlock Islands,** a group in Micronesia, 300 miles west-southwest of Ponape. Mission station of A. B. C. F. M., with Ruk; 1 missionary, 2 ladies, 1 lay helper, 13 churches, 3 native pastors. A geography has recently been translated by Mr. and Mrs. Logan, and is now in use; and Genesis, Exodus, and "Story of the Gospels," translated by Mr. Logan, are now in the press. A population greater than at any other point in Micronesia awaits the efforts of the missionaries.

**Mortlock Islands Version.**—The language used in Mortlock Islands belongs to the

Micronesian languages. In 1880 the American Bible Society published at Honolulu the Gospel of Mark, translated by the Rev. R. W. Logan.

(*Specimen verse.* John 3:16.)

Pue an Kot a *tane* fanufan mi *rapur*, ie mɫ a nanai na an Alaman, pue monison mi luku i´ra te pait mual la, pue ra pue uerai manau samur.

**Mosetla,** a town in South Transvaal, East South Africa. Mission station of the Hermannsburg Missionary Society, with 435 members.

**Mosquito Coast,** a territory on the Caribbean coast, Central America, extending from latitude 10° 30´ to 13° N, with a width of about 40 miles, was for a long time an independent reserve of native Indians, under the protection of Great Britain, 1655-1850. By the Clayton-Bulwer treaty of 1850, England resigned all claims to the Mosquito Coast, and by the treaty of Managua, 1860, the territory was ceded to Nicaragua (q.v.), which country exercises a supervision over the native administration. A chief elected by the natives is assisted by an administrative council. Mission field of the Moravian Brethren, with stations at Blewfields, Magdala, Ramah, Bethany, etc.

**Mosquito Version** (Moskito).—The Mosquito belongs to the South American languages, and is spoken by the Mosquito Indians, a people dwelling along the coast from Blewfields northward to Cape Gracias à Dios, and thence to Truxillo. The Rev. Alexander Henderson of Belize, a Baptist missionary, resolved the language to writing and grammatical principles. Parts of the Bible were published at Stuttgart in 1864 by the Moravian Missionary Society of Herrnhut, the translation having been made by Mr. Grünwald. A translation of the four Gospels and the Acts of the Apostles, made by the Rev. W. Sieberge of the Moravian Mission, is now being carried through the press by the translator, for the British and Foreign Bible Society.

**Mossel Bay,** a town in Cape Colony, South Africa, on Mossel Bay, 25 miles west-southwest of Georgetown. Mission station of the S. P. G., with 2 missionaries, 365 church-members. Berlin Evangelical Society (1879); 1 missionary, 4 native helpers, 208 members, 77 communicants.

**Mosul,** a city of Mesopotamia, on the western bank of the Tigris, 160 miles southeast of Mardin. Just across the river are the ruins of Nineveh. The city covers a great extent of ground, but is poorly built, and large sections are almost uninhabited. Population about 50,000, Arabs, Jacobite and Chaldean Christians, Jews, Turks, Koords, etc. The summers are very hot, and those who remain in the city are compelled to live in the cellars. The result is that it is very unhealthy, except as great care is taken. Mission station of the A. B. C. F. M., at first belonging to the Assyria and now to the Eastern Turkey Mission. It was the point of departure for Dr. Asahel Grant in his journeys among the mountain Nestorians. So many of the missionaries died from the effect of the climate that it was given up as a station, and the force was transferred to Mardin. Of late years, however, as people have learned better to guard against the evil effects of the cli-

mate, it is being occupied again as a permanent station. The Protestant church is a strong church, and increasing in numbers and influence.

The Presbyterian Board (North), U. S. A., have taken Mosul also as their headquarters for their work among the Nestorians in the valleys of Koordistan.

Near Mosul is the chief shrine of the Yezidees (q.v.).

**Mota,** one of the Banks' Islands, the northernmost group of the New Hebrides, Melanesia, has 700 inhabitants, all Protestants. It was the first island of the New Hebrides which was visited by Christian missionaries, in 1857, from Melbourne. Infanticide and polygamy have entirely disappeared in Mota, and in 1884 the natives built a church of stone themselves, though none of them had ever seen a stone building before. They have sent out 12 teachers to the other islands.

**Mota Version.**—The Mota belongs to the Melanesian languages, and is used in Banks' Islands. A translation of the New Testament into the Mota was published in 1884 by the Society for Promoting Christian Knowledge.

**Motu** or **Port Moresby** or **New Guinea Version.**—The Motu belongs to the Melanesian languages, and is spoken in New Guinea. The first connected portion of Scripture that was printed was the Gospel of Mark, translated by the Rev. W. G. Lawes. It was printed at Sydney, New South Wales, under the superintendence of the Rev. J. T. Sunderland, and at the expense of the Sydney Auxiliary. In 1884 the four Gospels were also printed in Sydney, under Mr. Lawes' personal supervision.

**Motupatti,** in the Trichinopoli district, Madras, India, on or near the north bank of the Coleroon River, between Trichinopoli and Puducottai. Mission station of the Evangelical Lutheran Society of Leipsic (1863); 1 native preacher, 282 communicants, 81 scholars.

**Moukden,** the capital of Shing-King, Manchuria, (called Shing-Yang by the Chinese), is situated on the river Shin, a tributary of the Liaou. It has a wall around it, pierced by twelve gates, and is a city of some grandeur. Broad streets, well laid out, and numerous shops for native and foreign goods, add to its commercial importance. It is distant 120 miles from the treaty port of Newchwang. The population is estimated at 200,000, and Koreans, Tartars, Manchus, as well as a large number of Chinese, give variety to the streets. Several Korean scholars helped Mr. Ross in the translation of the New Testament, which was made here. Mission station of the United Presbyterian Church of Scotland (1876); 3 missionaries and wives, 15 native helpers, 4 out-stations, 3 churches, 500 members, 257 communicants, 4 schools, 57 scholars.

**Moulmein** (Maulmain), a city of Burmah, at the mouth of the Salwin River. Population, 53,107, chiefly Buddhists, Hindus, and Moslems. Mission station of the American Baptist Missionary Union. It has been and is one of the most important stations of that Society. The work is carried on in three departments—Burman, Karen, and Telugu and Tamil. There are 3 missionaries and wives, 9 female missionaries,

1 physician, 15 out-stations, 17 churches (15 self-supporting), 10 ordained, 22 unordained preachers, 1,757 church-members, 1,070 scholars (see article American Baptist Missionary Union). S. P. G.: 1 missionary, 54 communicants, 230 scholars.

**Mount Olive,** town in Monrovia, Liberia, West Coast of Africa, on or near the Junk River, north of Fish Town. Mission circuit of Methodist Episcopal Church (North); 2 missionaries, 8 native helpers, 80 church-members.

**Mount Scott,** town in Maryland, Liberia, West Coast of Africa, near Cape Palmas. Mission circuit of Methodist Episcopal Church (North); 59 native helpers, 3 out-stations, 339 church-members.

**Mount Tabor,** a town in Barbadoes, West Indies, 10 miles from Bridgetown, on an elevated plateau 900 feet high, thus commanding an extensive and beautiful view over the surrounding country. Mission station of the Moravians (1825); 1 native missionary and wife. The site for this station was granted by the pious proprietor, Edmund Haynes, Esq., who also gave liberally towards erecting the mission buildings.

**Mozambique.**—1. A part of the east coast of Africa, between Cape Delgado and Delagoa Bay, nominally subject to Portugal. It contains 80,000 square miles, with a population of 600,-000. It is administered by a governor-general and 9 district governors. Along the coasts are large tracts of fertile lands; but between Delagoa Bay and Cape Corrientes, and from Mozambique to Cape Delgado, the shores are steep and lofty. Ornamental woods, ivory, gold, and copper are the principal products. The climate is good in the highlands, but the coast is full of fever and malaria. From November to March is the rainy season, and the heat of summer is intense. The Arab traders visited the coast long before the first visit of the Portuguese in 1498, and carried on a brisk slave-trade, which was not entirely suppressed, even after Portuguese power was enforced, until 1857 and after.

2. The capital, on a small coral island in latitude 15° 2' south, was the original fortress of the Portuguese. It has three strong forts. The population consists largely of slaves and Arabs, with a few Christians and Hindustanis. Since the abolition of the slave-trade its export trade, principally with India, is of little importance. Education and religion are under the control of the Roman Catholics, and are at a very low ebb.

**Mphome,** a town in North Transvaal, Africa, south of Limpopo River. Mission station Berlin Evangelical Lutheran Society (1878); 2 missionaries, 20 native helpers, 12 out-stations, 604 church-members, 205 scholars.

**Mpongwe** or **Pongua Version.**—The Mpongwe belongs to the Bantu family of African languages, and is vernacular in the region of the Gaboon River. The Gospel of Matthew, as translated by the Rev. W. Walker, was printed by the American Bible Society at Gaboon in 1850. The Gospel of John translated by Rev. A. Bushnell, and revised by N. J. L. Wilson, was printed in New York. Proverbs, Genesis, Exodus, and the Acts, translated by Mr. Walker, were printed in New York under the translator's supervision. Paul's Epistles appeared at New York in 1867. A third edition of the Gospels, the Epistles of Paul, Ecclesiastes, Song of Songs, the Minor Prophets, and Isaiah i-xxix., appeared in 1879 from the press of the American Bible Society, which also published the entire Bible in two volumes.

(*Specimen verse.* John 3 : 16.)

Kănde Anyambiŏ·arăndi ntye yiulă nli ntăndinli mŏ avenliŏ Oŋwanli yŏ wikika, inlŏ om' edu o bekeliŏ avere, ndo e be doanla nl'emĕnlă zakănlaka.

**Mpwapwa,** town in Eastern Central Africa, inland west of Zanzibar, south of Mamboia, the starting-point of Stanley on his first expedition. Mission station C. M. S.; 2 missionaries, 1 missionary's wife, 1 out-station, 1 school, 51 scholars. A printing establishment is issuing the first books in Kigogo.

**Mudalur** (Moodaloor), town in India, in the Tuticorin district, Madras. Mission station of the S. P. G (1835); 1 missionary, 22 native helpers, 2.745 church-members.

**Muden,** a town in North Natal, South Africa, northeast of Emakabeleni, and northwest of Hermannsburg. Mission station of the Hermannsburg Missionary Society.

**Muhlenberg,** town in Liberia, West Africa, on the St. Paul River, 20 miles northeast of Monrovia. Climate tropical. Religions, fetichism, devil-worship. Natives very low. degraded. Mission station Evangelical Lutheran General Synod (1860); 2 missionaries and wives, 6 other missionaries, 7 native workers, 2 churches, 175 members, 70 communicants, 2 schools, 100 scholars.

**Mukimvika,** town in West Africa, southwest of Underhill, at the mouth of the Congo. Mission station of the Baptist General Association of the Western States and Territories (U. S. A.), worked under the general direction of the American Baptist Missionary Union; 2 missionaries and a flourishing Sunday-school.

**Mulki,** town in South Kanara, Madras, British India, on an inlet of the sea, 19 miles north of Mangalore. Mission station Basle Missionary Society: 2 missionaries and wives, 28 native helpers, 329 church-members, 7 schools, 460 scholars.

**Mullens, Joseph,** b. London, England, 1820; entered Coward College 1837; graduated 1841 at the London University; ordained 1843, and embarked the same year for Calcutta as a missionary of the London Missionary Society. In 1858 he visited England, and returning to India remained till 1865, when, after visiting the missions in India and Ceylon, he sailed for England to be assistant secretary with Dr. Tidman. On Dr. Tidman's death he became sole foreign secretary. In 1870 he visited the United States as delegate of the London Society to the American Board. In 1873 and 1874 he visited Madagascar in the interest of the missionary work. Mr. Arthington of Leeds having made a liberal donation in 1875 for a new mission on Lake Tanganyika in Central Africa, Dr. Mullens accompanied several missionaries to assist in the organization of the mission. Starting from Zanzibar for the interior, he reached Mwapwa, where from exposure and fatigue he died of peritonitis July 10th. There his remains were buried. He was a man of great earnestness, and an eloquent speaker. The degree of doctor of divinity was conferred upon him in 1851 by Williams College, Mass., and in 1868 by the University of Edinburgh. He published "Twelve Months in Madagascar," "A Brief Review of Ten Years' Missionary Labor in India between 1852 and 1863," "London and Calcutta compared in their Heathenism," "Privileges and Prospects."

**Multan.**—1. City in Punjab, India, 193 miles southwest of Lahore, with which it is connected by railway. One of the oldest cities of India, having some very interesting ruins, also many modern buildings of note. A very important commercial centre. Population, city and suburbs, 57,471, Moslems, Hindus, Sikhs, Jains, etc. Mission station C. M. S. (1856); 1 missionary and wife, 1 native pastor, 24 communicants, 2 schools, 450 scholars, (with Bahawalpur.)—2. (Mooltan), town in Mussoorie district, Bengal, India. Mission station Methodist Episcopal Church (North); 1 missionary, 20 church-members.

**Mundakayam,** a town in Travancore, Madras, India. Mission district of the C. M. S.; 4 Pukka churches, 19 preaching places, 497 communicants.

**Munger, Sendol B.,** b. Fair Haven, Vermont, U. S. A., October 5th, 1802; graduated at Middlebury College 1828, and Andover Theological Seminary 1833; was for a time agent of the A. B. C. F. M. in Vermont; ordained 1834; sailed May 21st the same year as a missionary of the same Society for Bombay. He was first stationed at Bombay, but in 1837 removed to Jalna. In 1842 he returned to the United States for his wife's health; re-embarked January 3d, 1846. Mrs. Munger died on the passage, and was buried in the Indian Ocean. Mr. Munger was then stationed for a time at Ahmadnagar, then for some years at Bhingar, and in 1855 removed to Satara, where he remained till 1866, when the wants of Bombay required his return to that, his first field in India. He made before this two other visits to the United States, in 1853 and 1860.

Mr. Munger was an able preacher, and continued to preach to the last. He held meetings but a few weeks previous to his illness at his own house Sabbath evenings for a few families that found it difficult to attend upon regular services. A few days before his death, when his strength allowed him to speak but one or two minutes, he was at the preaching place in front of the American mission house. The meeting of the mission, July 21st, was held at Bombay to secure the benefit of his counsels and prayers, and he was to have preached the sermon; but on the first day of the session he was partly paralyzed and not able to speak, and did not speak afterwards except once, when he was heard to say, "None but Christ." He died July 23d, 1868, and native Christians bore his body to the Scotch Cemetery at Bombay. A biographical notice in "Bombay Guardian" soon after his death, says: "While Mr. Munger was in Jalna and Ahmadnagar he spent much time in itineracies, traversing on horseback the whole region of country from Sholapoor to Nagpoor, and preaching in every village on the route. He delighted in the work of an evan-

gelist. He had an admirable command of the Marathi language, great facility, earnestness, and power in preaching, and a powerful voice. Men heard him gladly." In preaching to Europeans, an officer to whom the message had been blessed, desired, as a thank-offering to the Lord, to place in the hands of the Board a large sum of money for establishing a new mission at Nagpoor. The Board then not being able to avail itself of the offer, it was subsequently made to the Committee of the Free Church of Scotland's Mission, and they established the Nagpoor Mission. Mr. Munger had an extensive acquaintance with Marathi literature. He published several valuable books and tracts in the vernacular, and left others in manuscript.

**Mungeli,** town in Chattisgarh, Central Provinces, India, on the banks of the Shironath River, 200 miles northeast of Nagpur. Climate hot, dry. Religion, Hindu; Kabir, Perathi, Satwami sects. Languages, Hindu, Chatdisgarhi. Natives poor, miserable, dwelling in huts of mud and grass. Mission station Foreign Christian Missionary Society (1888), worked from Bisrampur; 2 missionaries and wives, 1 native preacher, 1 church, 6 members, 1 school, 15 scholars.

**Munkeu-liang,** town in South China, province of Kwangtung, near Swatow. Mission station American Baptist Missionary Union; 1 missionary and wife, 1 other lady, 2 ordained, 2 unordained preachers, 40 church-members.

**Munson, Samuel,** b. New Sharon, Maine, U. S. A., March 23d, 1804; graduated at Bowdoin College 1829, Andover Theological Seminary 1832; ordained October 10th; sailed June 10th, 1833, as a missionary of the A. B. C. F. M. with Rev. Henry Lyman, under instructions to explore the Indian Archipelago, especially Java, Sumatra, Borneo, Celebes, the Moluccas, and the neighboring islands, and reached Batavia September 30th. In April, 1834, they embarked for Padang, on the island of Sumatra, and thence sailed for the Battas group of 122 islands. War raging in the interior, they were attacked by the Battas, and both fell, Mr. Lyman being shot, and Mr. Munson pierced with a spear. For an account of their expedition and death, see the article on Mr. Lyman.

**Murray Island,** an island in the Gulf of Papua, south of New Guinea, east of York Island. Mission station of the London Missionary Society; 3 missionaries, 2 missionaries' wives, 18 native pastors, 256 church-members, 1,148 catechumens, and a seminary with 93 scholars. It is the chief seat of the mission in the western districts.

**Murray Island Version.**—The Murray Island belongs to the Melanesian languages, and is used in Torres Straits, New Guinea. A translation of the Gospels of Mark and John, translated by the Revs. McFarlane and H. Scott, was published in 1865 by the Sydney Auxiliary, under the care of the Rev. J. P. Sunderland.

**Music and Missions.**—Missions touch music at two points: 1. The missionary as an intelligent man studies the poetry and songs of the people among whom he labors. Those investigations are carried on during the earlier period of a mission, and contrary to what some might expect, among savage races, as well as in more civilized communities. 2. After a mission has become successful the newly formed churches must be helped in their worship, especially in the department of Praise, and this we shall see sometimes demands a very deep and thorough knowledge of the foundation principles of music.

DAKOTA MUSIC.—Rev. A. L. Riggs ("Gospel among the Dakotas," pp. 450–484) gives a very interesting *résumé* of Dakota music, with specimens of songs of love and war, songs of sacred mysteries, and social songs. They are extremely simple, and abound with the repetitions so natural to untutored minds. A widow's lament expresses the deepest heartweariness and despair.

Their music is also very simple. It consists of melody alone, with rude accompaniment, mainly for marking time. The men sing, while the women sound one single falsetto note *ai, ai, ai*, keeping time with drums. They do not appreciate harmony. The minor key is their favorite, though the major key occurs in their war songs. Their instruments are the drum, rattle, and pipe. The drum is more than a foot in diameter, and from three to ten inches deep. The rattle is made of segments of deer hoops tied to a tapering rod of wood. The conjuror uses a gourd shell with a few pebbles inside. The usual pipe is a sumac flageolet, nineteen inches long, with a diameter of five eighths of an inch. A peculiar partition forms the whistle. Six notes are burnt on the upper side, and a brass thimble forms the mouthpiece. The pitch is A Prime, changed to G Prime by a seventh hole. Sometimes the pipe is made of the long wing or thigh bone of a crane or swan. Dakota music is rude, but its power is measured by the adaptation of its wild melody to savage life in the wilderness, where in the misty moonlight the night air bears the plaintive sounds, with the hollow bass of the drum-beat, along the waste, full of possible war-whoops, and where each bush may hide an enemy.

CHINESE MUSIC.—Dr. S. Wells Williams ("The Middle Kingdom," new edition, vol. ii. 94–104) gives a graphic description of Chinese music and musical instruments. However small their attainments in both theory and practice, no nation gives to music a higher place. Confucius taught that it was essential to good government, harmonizing the different ranks in society, and causing them all to move on in unison. The Chinese have sought to develop instrumental rather than vocal music.

The names of the notes, ascending regularly from the first line of the staff to the third space above it, are as follows: first line, *ho;* first space, *sz´;* then *i, chang, ché, kung, fan, liu, wu;* first space above, *i;* then *chang, ché, kung, fan,* the last being on the third space above.

The real tone cannot be represented by our staff. The second octave is denoted by affixing the sign *jin,* a man, to the simple notes. No chromatic scale exists—at least no instrument is made to express flat and sharp notes.

There are two kinds of music in China—the northern and the southern. The octave in the former seems to have had only six notes, while the eight-tone scale prevails in more cultivated circles. Music is written for only a few instruments, and the notation good for one is

useless for another, because marks meaning to push, fillip, hook, etc., are added to denote the mode of playing; indeed, the combinations are so complicated that the Chinese usually play by ear. All music is in common time; no triple measures are used. Of harmony and counterpoint they know nothing. Marks to regulate the expression are unknown, nor are tunes set to any key.

No description can do justice to their vocal music, and few can imitate it. Some notes seem to issue from the larynx and nose; tongue, teeth, and lips having little to do with them. Singing is usually in a falsetto key, somewhere between a squeal and a scream, and yet it is plaintive and soft, and not without a certain sweetness.

Chinese musical literature is voluminous. A work on beating the drum dates from A.D. 860, and contains a list of 129 symphonies. Among 12 instruments described in the chrestomathy are 17 drums of various sizes, then gongs, cymbals, tambourines, musical vases in considerable variety. Stringed instruments are not so numerous. They have nothing that resembles the lyre. The *kin* or scholar's lute is deemed the finest. "Easy Lessons" for this lute is a work in two volumes, explains 109 terms, and has 29 pictures of the position of the hand in playing. The instrument itself is ancient, and is named *kin,* "to prohibit," because it restrains evil passions. It is a board, four feet long and eighteen inches wide, convex above and flat below, where two holes open into hollows. Seven strings of silk pass over a bridge through the board at the wide end, and are fastened by nuts beneath. They are fastened to two pegs at the smaller end. The sounding-board is divided by thirteen studs, so placed that the strings are divided into halves, thirds, quarters, fifths, sixths, and eighths, but no sevenths. The seven strings enclose the compass of a ninth, or two fifths, the middle one being treated like A on the violin, and the outer ones tuned one fifth from that. The interval is treated like our octave in the violin, for the compass of the *kin* is made up of fifths. Each of the outer strings is tuned a fourth from the alternate string within the system, so that there is a major tone, and interval tone less than a minor third, and a major tone in the fifth. The Chinese leave the interval entire and skip the half-tone, while we divide it into two unequal parts; so the mood of the music of the *kin* is different from our instruments, and for that reason none of them can do justice to Chinese airs. There are other instruments like the *kin,* one with 30 and another with 13 strings. Some resemble the guitar, lute, and spinet, with strings of silk or wire, but never of catgut. The *pipa,* a balloon-shaped guitar, has four strings, is three feet long, with twelve frets to guide the player. The strings are tuned to the intervals of a fourth, a major tone, and a fourth, so that the outer strings are octaves to each other. The *san hien* or three-stringed guitar resembles a rebeck in shape, but the head and neck is three feet in length. The strings are tuned as fourths to each other, and their sound is low and dull. The *yueh kin,* or full-moon guitar, has four strings in pairs that are unisons with each other, with an interval of a fifth between the pairs. It is struck briskly, and used for lively tunes.

The two-stringed fiddle is merely a bamboo split stuck into a bamboo cylinder, with two strings fastened on pegs at one end of the stick and passing over a bridge on the cylinder to the other end. They are tuned at intervals of a fifth. As the bow passes between the two strings, much care is needed in playing not to scrape the wrong string. The harsh grating of this wretched machine is very popular among the natives. The *ti kin* (crowing lute) has a cocoa-nut shell for its body, and is even more dissonant than the last. The *yang kin* is an embryo piano, consisting of brass wires of different lengths, tuned at proper intervals, and fastened on a sounding-board. The sounds are very attenuated. The *sang*, in like manner, is an embryo organ, a cone-shaped box, with a mouthpiece to blow in, and thirteen reeds of different lengths, inserted in the top, the valves of some opening upwards and others downwards. They are provided with holes also that may be opened or closed by the player. It is very ancient. Some think it the organ invented by Jubal (Gen. 4 : 21). The Chinese think it more curious than useful.

Their wind instruments are numerous. The *hwang tih* (flute) is twice the length of our pipe, made of bamboo, and pierced with ten holes. The two near the end are not used. The mouth hole is one third of the way from the top. The *shu tih* (clarionet) takes the lead in musical performances. It has seven holes, but no keys. Its tones are shrill and deafening, and therefore popular. A street musician fits a flageolet, or small clarionet, to his nose, slings a small drum under one shoulder, hangs a frame of four cymbals on his breast, and with a couple of monkeys sallies forth, a peripatetic choir and orchestra.

The stem of the horn is retractible, like a trombone. There are other varieties, however.

The *lo* (gong) is the standing type of Chinese music. A crashing harangue of rapid blows on this, with a rattling accompaniment of drums, and a crackling symphony of shrillness from clarionet and cymbal, is their beau ideal of music. They have heard good Portuguese music for ages, but have never adopted either an instrument or a tune.

A Chinese band makes the European think of Hogarth's "Enraged Musician." Each performer seems to have his own time, and bent on drowning the noise of all the rest; yet they keep good time, only no two of them are tuned on the same key. (See G. T. Lay in "Chinese Repository," vol. viii. 30–54; Doolittle's "Social Life of the Chinese," ii. 216; "Mémoires concernant les Chinois," tomes i., iii., vi., etc.; "Barrow's Travels," 313–323; "Chinese Chrestomathy," 356–365.)

ARAB MUSIC.—Dr. Eli Smith of Beirut found that hymns composed in Arabic measures could seldom be sung in our tunes, and our musicians were puzzled by the intervals in Arab music. On the other hand, Arabs could not repeat our scale. A treatise on Arab music by Michael Mishakah of Damascus explained the difficulty; and from that, with Kosegarten's edition of Ispahany's "Book of Odes," and Faraby on "Ancient Arab Music," Dr. Smith wrote a valuable paper which was published in the "Journal of the American Oriental Society" (i. 171–210), with notes by Prof E. C. Salisbury.

He says that sounds are naturally divided into groups of seven, rising one above the other, each the response to the one below, and the base of the one above. The group is called an octave, *diwan*, and the octaves are composed of tones, *burj*, pl. *buruj*. The first is called *yegáh*, then *ösheiran, árak, rest, dugáh, sigáh*, and *jehárgáh*. This is the first octave. The second is *nawa, huseiny, auj, máhúr, muhaiyar, buzrek*, and *mahúrán*. The last is the response to *jehárgáh*. The first of the third octave is *remel túty*, the response to *nawa*. The next octave is the response to the response of *nawa*, and so on ad infinitum. So in the first series below *yegáh* they say the base to *jehárgáh*, to *sigáh*, and so through the list, then the base to the base of *jehárgáh*, etc. The intervals between these notes are unequal. They are divided into two classes, one containing four quarters, and the other three. The former are from *yegáh* to *ösheiran*, from *rest* to *dúgáh*, and from *jehárgáh* to *nawa*. The latter from *ösheiran* to *arak*, from *arak* to *rest*, from *dúgáh* to *sigáh*, and from *sigáh* to *jehárgáh*. The first class then has three intervals with twelve quarters, and the second four intervals with twelve quarters. The modern Greeks divide the intervals into seconds, and make three classes. One class, corresponding to the first of the Arabs, divides the interval into twelve seconds; the second class divides it into nine seconds, and is from *dugáh* to *sigáh*, and from *huseiny* to *auj*. The third class, from *sigáh* to *jehárgáh*, and from *auj* to *mahur*, has seven seconds to the interval. So their octave contains seven intervals, and sixty-eight seconds. The Arab and Greek scales coincide only at four out of the sixty-eight seconds.

This is the substance of only four of the thirty pages of the paper. Chapter II describes Arab melodies now in use, and Chapter III is devoted to musical rhythm, and Chapter IV to musical instruments, describing stringed instruments like *el ud* (literally the wood, whence our word "lute"), the Arab guitar, the *kemenjeh*, or Arab fiddle, with a cocoanut shell for its body, like the Chinese *ti kin;* the *tambur*, a kind of mandolin, and the *kanún*, corresponding to the *yang kin* of the Chinese orchestra, only, it would seem, a better instrument. Then of wind instruments, the *nay* or flute, *kerift, mizmar, sunnáy, urghan* (organ, see Chinese *sang*), and *jenah*. For a full description of Arab musical instruments with illustrations, see Lane's "Modern Egyptians," vol. 2, in small edition, pp. 66–82.

INDIA.—In India music was formerly much more scientific than at present. There idolatry has degraded music, and the martial music of the country has changed with its government. Its religion now has little to do with music, except in connection with the dancing girls of the temples. Operas are unknown, and theatrical music is of a low order. Marriages furnish the chief occasions for musical display. There are many kinds of musical instruments, as drums, trumpets, horns, cymbals, hautboys, and violins, but the performers have little skill and less taste. The wedding orchestra varies from six to twenty performers. Singing is an accomplishment of women of doubtful morality, who are much employed for this purpose by the wealthy.

Christianity is changing all this, not generally, it is true, but gradually and permanently, for the native convert must give vent to his new joy in songs of praise, and they do this not only in the church, but also in their families and when alone. Even before conversion, music does much to prepare the way.

Miss Mary Leitch in visiting the schools in Ceylon used to take her little organ with her, as it could easily be carried by coolies, and sing translations of our best English hymns, in the soft Tamil tongue. One day she asked a teacher whether he taught English. "Why should we teach it? Sanskrit is the primitive language." "Are there not valuable books in English?" "English books are not true. The most valuable are in Tamil. The works of the greatest scholars are in Sanskrit." "But the most valuable books in science are in English." "What do we care for science? Our religious books are in Sanskrit." Meantime the coolies had brought in the organ, which soon became the centre of eager curiosity, and when she sang with the organ in Tamil, "There's a land that is fairer than day," she had the hearts of the children at least, who pressed up close to the singer in the fulness of their enjoyment. ("Life and Light," 1881, p. 322.)

A favorite and most successful mode of introducing the gospel in western India is the *kirttan*, i.e. solo singing by native evangelists with orchestral accompaniment. In September, 1880, Rev. Mr. Bruce of Satara visited Wai with his kirttan choir. The people crowded to hear, especially as the leader had been a Moslem. Hundreds stood outside of the building in the rain, and listened for the first time to the way of salvation through a Redeemer. The whole city was moved, and Christ was the great topic of conversation for many days. ("Missionary Herald," 1880, pp. 521, 526.)

Rev. H. Ballantine, called the Dr. Watts of the Marathi Mission, prepared a hymnal for the churches, and another for the children, which met with great acceptance among the people.

Rev. E. Webb was an enthusiast in his researches into the laws of Tamil poetry. It is extremely elaborate in its rhythmical construction. The whole Ramanayam is rendered into rhyme and sung throughout the country. Our tunes do not suit Tamil taste, nor are our metres adapted to the language. In 1853 he published a Tamil hymn-book, containing hymns in our metre, children's hymns, and chants with music, but the largest part of the volume was made up of hymns in native metres. Many copies were taken at once by the English missions in Tanjore and Tinnevelly, and singing was introduced in congregations of the American missions in places where it had been unknown before. An edition of 2,000 copies was soon exhausted, and a new one was issued in 1858. Though the people hear listlessly the most important truth in prose, they give eager attention to the same truth when versified and sung. In October, 1860, Mr. Webb gave an account of Tamil versification to the American Oriental Society, defining the two kinds of syllables, then the feet and the stanzas in which they were combined. Though the natives could see no measure in our verses, or melody in our music, yet hymns written in their own metres, and set to their own melodies, were extremely popular. He read some of them in Tamil with elaborate rhyme assonance and alliteration. He described also the music of the Hindus, known all over India under the same Sanskrit titles, and indicated its relation to our own scale. ("Journal of the American Oriental Society," vol. 271, and "Missionary Herald," 1854, p. 150; 1858, p. 59.) Rev. G. T. Washburn carried on the work thus begun by Mr. Webb. In 1863 he published two volumes of Tamil lyrics. They were hymns by natives in native metres. Ancient India excelled Greece in her cultivation of music; and though no new tunes have appeared for centuries, those of the best periods still exist, and for these the hymns were composed. Rev. W. W. Howland prepared the tunes for the Tamil hymn-book of Dr. Spaulding. ("Missionary Herald," 1870, p. 130.)

OTHER LANDS.—Though in other missions there may not have been the same zeal for native music, yet in them all, as soon as men receive "the light of the knowledge of the glory of God in the face of Jesus Christ," they feel impelled to praise the name of the Lord, and missionaries are glad to assist the effort to praise as soon as the spirit of praise appears.

It is interesting to look over the record of missions in this line. In Turkey, though at that time they had few hymns ready for use, yet they could not wait to prepare more, but in 1850 issued an Armenian hymn-book of only 55 pages. This was followed in 1853 by one in Armeno-Turkish, i.e. Turkish in Armenian letters, of 112 pages, and the next year saw an Armenian "Hymn and Tune Book" of 300 pages, so rapidly grew their hymnology. That same year (1854) the Greek hymn-book appeared, of 100 pages, though 16 pages of hymns had been printed as early as 1833. All these were 16mo, but in 1855 appeared a work on church music, in Armenian, of 44 pages 8vo. Then in the same language a hymn and tune book for children was published in 1860, 40 pages 8vo. This was followed by 24 8vo pages of additional hymns and music in 1863. It seemed as though good men kept on composing hymns, and, as fast as they did so, the churches could not wait, but had them printed for use at once. Next year (1864) appeared a hymn-book of 104 16mo pages in Arabo-Turkish, i.e. Turkish in Arabic type. The following year four hymns were printed on one 8vo sheet, and in 1866 a supplement to the Armeno-Turkish hymn-book, of 88 pages 16mo, made its appearance. Next came an Armenian Sunday-school hymn-book of 184 16mo pages, followed next year by a Sunday-school hymn and tune book in the same language of 128 8vo pages. The year 1869 saw a volume of Armenian hymns and prayers of 192 pages 16mo. The same year welcomed a Greco-Turkish hymn-book of 264 16mo pages, and a second edition came out ten years later. In 1869 the Armenian hymn-book had grown to 426 pages, and four years later a fresh edition contained 430 pages. This was followed by a supplement of 56 8vo pages to the Armenian hymn and tune book in 1877, and as though that was not enough, an appendix of 16 pages more was issued the same year. Such a list of publications indicates an abounding spiritual life that makes what would otherwise be the driest of statistics an occasion of great joy to all who love the prosperity of Zion. In Bulgarian, three pages of hymns and tunes were printed in 1861, the year following a hymn-book of 24 12mo pages, and in 1865 a hymn and tune book of 64 8vo pages. The hymn-book in 1872 had grown to 154 16mo pages. In Syria, while the mission was still under the care of the American Board, 200 pages of versified Psalms were printed about 1868. The same year gave 200 pages of children's hymns to the Sunday-schools, and before the mission passed into the hands of the Presbyterians a hymn-book appeared first of 300 pages, and after that of 500. About 1874 a hymn and tune book was print. ed, containing an introduction teaching how to read our musical notation. This was afterwards printed separately, 30 pages 8vo. In 1882 the Psalms in verse were printed for the use of the United and Reformed Missions, hymns alone, 400 18mo pages; with tunes, 500 12mo pages; and with tonic Sol Fa notation, 600 12mo pages. In 1885 a new 8vo hymn and tune book, containing 327 hymns and 280 tunes, was prepared by Rev. Samuel Jessup and Rev. George Ford, and a second edition was called for in 1889. A hymn-book without tunes appeared in 1885, of 418 pages 18mo. This advanced to a second edition in 1887, and a third in 1889, showing a very encouraging demand for such a work.

In the Persian Mission the hymn-books have gone through several editions. The last, issued in 1886, has about 300 hymns, mostly translations, but adapted to the expression of Christian feeling in Persia, and also to the wants of the young in their Oriental homes.

Music has been taught by the missionaries. The popular tunes are those used in congregations in the United States. The chants of the Ancient Syriac are used in religious worship, and are very popular. The words, of course, are in the vernacular, and so the congregation can join in the responses. They are used especially in chanting the Psalms, and also some other portions of the Scripture, such as are found in books for responsive reading at home.

The writer has material for similar statements concerning other missions, but these may suffice to show how in our day those words of the Psalmist were fulfilled (Ps. 67 : 3) : "Let the peoples praise Thee, O God. Let all the peoples praise Thee." And again (Ps. 145: 10–13): "All Thy works shall give thanks unto Thee, O Lord, and Thy saints shall bless Thee. They shall speak of the glory of Thy kingdom, and talk of Thy power. To make known to the sons of man His mighty acts, and the glory of the majesty of His kingdom. Thy kingdom is an everlasting kingdom, and Thy dominion endureth throughout all generations."

**Muskoki,** or **Cree Version.**—The Muskoki belongs to the languages of America, and is spoken by the Indians in the United States. They were provided by the American Bible Society with several parts of the New Testament,—Matthew, John, the Epistles of John, of James, to Titus and Philemon,—which were published since 1867. In 1879 the same Bible Society published at New York the Acts of the Apostles, translated by Mrs. E. W. Robertson, and in 1885 the Epistle to the Hebrews. In 1886 the New Testament was completed by Mrs. Robertson, who also revised the version of Matthew which had been in use since 1867.

*(Specimen verse.* John 3 : 16.)

Hesaketvmese ekvnv vnokece mahet omekv, Eppuce hvmkuse heckuecvte emvtes, mvn estlmvt oh vkvsamat estemerkekot, momis hesaketv yuksvsekon oevren.

**Mussooree,** a town and sanitarium of Dehra-Dun district, Northwest Provinces, Bengal, India, 7,433 feet above the sea, on a Himalayan peak, among beautiful and varied scenery. Population fluctuates with the season of the year, the maximum reached being 7,652; Hindus, Moslems, Christians, and Jews. Mission station of Methodist Episcopal Church (North); including Rajpore, 2 missionaries and wives, 7 native helpers, 2 out-stations, 2 churches, 21 church-members, 2 girls' schools, 28 scholars, 5 Sunday-schools, 100 scholars.

**Musquiz,** Mexico; two towns in the State of Coahuila, near Saltillo. Mission station of the Southern Baptist Convention; 1 missionary and wife. Methodist Episcopal Church (South); 1 native pastor.

**Muttra** (Mattra), town in the Rohilkund district, Northwest Provinces, India, between Agra and Aligarh, east of Alwar. Mission station of the C. M. S.; 14 native agents, 28 church-members, 1 school, 8 scholars. Methodist Episcopal Church (North); 1 missionary and wife, 24 native helpers, 15 church-members, 12 schools, 300 scholars.

**Mutwal,** Southeast Ceylon, very near Colombo. Mission station of the S. P. G.; 1 missionary, 1 church, 77 church-members, 3 chapels, 9 native helpers, 3 schools, 162 scholars.

**Mutyalapad,** town in Madras, South India, near Secunderabad. Mission station of the S. P. G.; 1 missionary, 35 native helpers, 727 communicants.

**Muzaffarnagur,** town of Muzaffarnagur district, Northwest Provinces, Bengal, India; station on the Sind, Punjab and Delhi Railroad. Population (1881), 15,080, Hindus, Mohammedans, Jains, and a few Christians. Climate formerly very unhealthy and malarious, but lately, owing to modern sanitary improvements, it has been made much more salubrious. Station of the Bengal Mission, Methodist Episcopal Church (North); 1 foreign missionary, 1 missionary's wife, 2 out-stations with 10 adherents, 1 organized church, 6 communicants, 2 preaching-places with an average attendance for each of 65, 1 ordained preacher, 2 unordained, 1 Sabbath-school, 50 scholars, 1 female school, 20 scholars, 3 teachers.

**Muzaffarpur,** or **Muzufferpoor,** a town in Bengal, India, 35 miles north-north-east of Patna. Population, 38,223. It is well built and clean, with good schools, temples, court-houses, and other public buildings. Has a large trade. Mission station of the Gössner Missionary Society and of the Methodist Episcopal Church (North).

**Myingyan,** town in Burma, on the Irrawaddy River, 100 miles south of Mandalay. Healthy, hot, very dry. Population, 20,000 to 30,000, Burmans, Chinese, Hindus. Language, Burman. Religion, Buddhism. Social condition unusually good for Burma. Mission station of the A. B. M. U. (1887); 1 missionary and wife, 2 native helpers, 1 out-station, 1 church, 7 church-members, 1 school, 22 students, 1 Sunday school, 40 pupils.

**Mymensing** (Maimansingh), town in Dacca division, Bengal, India, same as Nasirabad. Mission station of the Baptist Missionary Society (England); 1 missionary, 5 evangelists, 44 church-members, 89 scholars.

**Mynpuri,** a town in the district of Furukhabad, Bengal, Northeast India, 40 miles west of Futehgurh. Mission station of the Presbyterian Church (North) (1843); 1 missionary and wife, 2 foreign helpers, 8 native workers.

**Mysore,** a large and important native principality in South India. Its territory is entirely surrounded by the British dominions belonging to the presidency of Madras. It lies at the point where the ranges of the Western and Eastern Ghats come together, and most of its territory is on the elevated plateau lying between these ranges. Its limits of north latitude are 11° 40′ and 15°, and of east longitude 74° 40′ and 78° 30′. The area is 24,723 square miles and the population 4,186,188, according to the last census (1881). Its surface is much broken by rocky hills and ravines; the drainage of the country is almost wholly to the east; in the northwest one river falls in a fine cascade over the precipitous wall of the Western Ghats and seeks the Indian Ocean. Otherwise the streams all reach the Bay of Bengal through the Tungabhadra on the north, which itself is an affluent of the Krishna, the Kaveri on the south, and several smaller rivers between these two more important streams. These rivers, like almost all those of India, while useless for navigation, support large systems of artificial irrigation. Water is also stored in artificial reservoirs wherever the configuration of the country renders their construction possible. Of these tanks there are nearly 38,000. The rainfall of the wet season, stored up behind their walls, is slowly let out into the fields during the arid months of the year and insures the crops of the agriculturists. Mysore was included in the territories ruled from time immemorial by old prehistoric Hindu dynasties of South India, whose existence can dimly be traced in the uncertain light of early Indian times. The Mohammedan invasions of the 14th and 15th centuries subverted these and afforded opportunity for the rise of others; one of the most important of these newer kingdoms was that of Vijayanagar; this, of which the capital just mentioned lay to the north of Mysore, near the banks of the Tungabhadra, was overthrown by surrounding Mohammedan powers in 1565. During the feeble years of waning power which remained to this dynasty after the battle some of the local chieftains began to assert their independence; prominent among these was the representative of a family known as the Wodeyar of Mysore, who, in 1610, seized the fort of Seringapatam and became the founder of the present Mysore principality. This dynasty was most powerful in the 17th century. During the latter part of the 18th it suffered total eclipse by the rising power of a Mohammedan usurper named Haidar Ali, who displaced the Hindu line and made himself sole master of the state. The English arms in India have never had a fiercer, a more determined, nor an abler antagonist than he. But his son, Tippu Sultan, though animated with his father's spirit, had not the latter's ability nor success. After making the name of the Mysore dynasty a terror, and more than once ravaging South India with fire and sword, this usurping line came to an end in 1799, when the English laid siege to Seringapatam. Tippu Sultan was slain in the breach, and the English conquerors replaced the old Hindu line upon the throne. Between the years 1831 and 1881, owing to the incapacity of one Hindu prince and the minority of his successor, the English administered the country in the name of the House of Wodeyar. But in the latter year, when the young chief came to his majority, the administration was handed back to him. The town of Bangalore, however, and a small area adjacent to it is assigned to the British for a cantonment, where the necessary troops are quartered and where the English officials have their headquarters. Bangalore is thus, to all intents and purposes, in British dominions, and as such is the natural starting-point of Christian missions within the principality.

Of the entire population the Hindus amount to nearly 95 per cent, Mohammedans to a little less than 5 per cent. The total number of Christians was returned as 29,249. Of these 21,021 were native converts. About one-fourth of the Christians are Protestants, the others Roman Catholics. The language almost universally used is Kanarese. The Jains were once very numerous in Mysore. Their tenets are in some particulars akin to those of the Buddhists. They are very scrupulous in their regard for all forms of animal life, do not follow the Brahmans, nor worship the usual gods of Hinduism, but pay reverence to certain deified saints of their own sect. An unorthodox sect of Hindus, known as the Lingaits, are numerous in Mysore, and are also found in adjacent districts of the Bombay presidency. They do not observe caste, nor adhere to Brahmanical rites; they worship the God Siva, and get their name from their custom of wearing upon their persons, usually in little silver boxes suspended from their necks, the *ling*, or emblem of their God. They are prominent in mercantile pursuits. Mysore is for the most part an agricultural country. Some iron is found, and of late years there has been no little excitement over the existence of gold in quantities which it is thought will make gold-mining profitable. The progress of education since 1854 has been fairly good. In 1880–81 the total outlay was £29,939. In 1883–4 there were in all 2,388 schools in Mysore with 63,490 pupils. Of the pupils 3,828 were girls, and female education is said to be growing in popularity.

The first Protestant mission in Mysore was that of the Society for the Propagation of the Gospel, established at Bangalore in 1817. In 1820 the London Missionary Society planted a station at the same city. The Hindu Government seems to have been unfriendly to the work of the missionaries, and opportunities for preaching in Kanarese—the vernacular of the people—were are first greatly curtailed by this fact. The first few years of the mission were not prosperous; but since its earlier difficulties have been overcome, it has had a career of much success. The Wesleyans also entered Mysore, planting their principal station in the city of that name, shortly after the London Society entered Bangalore. Both these missions have now many stations throughout the State. The cultivation of the Kanarese language is greatly indebted to the missionaries; grammars and dictionaries, as well as translations of the Bible, and a Christian literature generally are due to their labors.

**Mysore** (City), the capital of Mysore native state, situated in north latitude 12° 18′ and east longitude 76° 42′. The population (1881) was 60,292. Of these 45,699 were Hindus, 13,288 Mohammedans (a much larger proportion than throughout the State of Mysore as a whole), 1,289 Christians, and 46 unspecified. The Hindu prince or rajah has a palace here, though since 1831, when the English assumed control of the government on account of the incapacity of the then reigning prince, Bangalore has been actually the capital, as it was the headquarters of the English officials, and the prince now resides there a portion of the year. The Wesleyan Missionary Society has a mission here, as well as at other points in the state.

# N.

**Nablous** (Shechem), town in Palestine, 30 miles north of Jerusalem. A very ancient town, noted now chiefly as the possessor of several valuable manuscripts, the most important of which is the copy of the Pentateuch known as the Samaritan Codex. Population from 10,000 to 20,000, Christians, Samaritans. Mission station, Church Missionary Society; 1 missionary and wife, 12 native helpers, 162 scholars. Baptist Missionary Society; 1 native missionary, 8 helpers, 4 out-stations, 48 school-children.

**Nagalapuram,** town in India, in the Tuticorin district, Madras. Mission station of the S. P. G.; 7 missionaries (5 of them native), 47 native helpers, 993 communicants.

**Nagarkoil** (Nagercoil), a station of the London Missionary Society, in Travancore, India (1809). It is one of the most important stations in India. With 60 out-stations, the gospel is carried by preaching, by distribution of handbills, and by personal visitation to the many heathen villages and to the coolies on the coffee plantations. On the first Sunday of the year a general meeting of Christians in the district is held at Nagarkoil, and at the last reported meeting 925 communicants were present —an imposing array and great contrast to the demon-worship of 100 years before. There are 3 missionaries, 5 native ministers, 32 preachers, 1,401 church-members, 59 boys' schools, 2,468 pupils, 13 girls' schools, 1,112 pupils.

**Nagasaki,** on the island of Kiu-Shiu, the principal seaport of the western coast of Japan, is picturesquely situated at the head of a small inlet four miles long and a mile wide. It has thus one of the finest harbors in the world. The surrounding hills, 1,500 feet high, and the numerous small islands with which the harbor is dotted, add greatly to its beauty. The city is laid out with great regularity, in rectangles. A stream of water flows through it. There is a foreign concession separated from the main city by an arm of the bay. A hospital was established here in 1861—the oldest now in Japan, and there is a fine government school, in which hundreds of young Japanese are instructed in European languages and sciences. The population numbers 40,187 (1887). The climate is salubrious, and the city is a pleasant one in which to live. Regular steamship communication connects it with Shanghai. Mission station of the South Japan Mission of the Reformed (Dutch) Church, U. S. A. (1872); 4 missionaries (3 married), 2 female missionaries, 9 out-stations, 3 churches, 200 communicants, 10 Sunday-schools, 370 scholars, 7 theological students. Methodist Episcopal Church (North); 4 missionaries, 4 assistant missionaries; 4 missionaries W. F. M. S.; Cobleigh Seminary (W. F. M. S.), 185 pupils; 238 church-members, 1 theological school, 11 students, 4 Sunday-schools, 242 scholars. C. M. S.; 1 missionary and wife, 45 communicants, 1 girls' school, 11 scholars.

**Nagoya,** a city on the main island of Japan, situated on the railroad midway between Tokyo and Kyoto. It is in the midst of a broad, fertile plain, surrounded by an innumerable number of thriving towns and villages, and is the fourth largest city of the empire, with a population of 360,000. Such a strategic position for missions was early availed of by the Reformed (Dutch) Church (U. S. A.), but there is no representative of that mission there at present. The Methodist Episcopal Church (North) have a flourishing mission. It is the central point of the Nagoya district, and its importance as a base of operations is fully recognized. A fine church building has been erected; 1 missionary, 1 preacher, 207 church-members. The Presbyterian Church (South) has a mission there since 1887 with 3 missionaries, 3 out-stations, 2 churches, 2 Sunday-schools, 100 scholars, 4 theological students, 141 church-members. The Methodist Protestant Church has occupied Nagoya since 1887; 3 missionaries, 3 ladies, 70 church-members, 1 girls' school, 20 scholars. The Cumberland Presbyterian Church has one female missionary in this centre of work.

**Nagpur** (Nagpore), city in Central Provinces, India, 42 miles east-northeast of Bombay. It is a large city, but not a very fine one, although there are many relics of its former greatness still to be seen, and the handsome tanks and gardens outside the city and the pretty scenery give the place a very attractive appearance. Trade is good and steadily increasing. Climate healthy. Population, 98,299, Hindus, Moslems, Christians, Jains, Kaberpanthis, Satnamis, Parsis, Brahmos, Buddhists, Jews, etc. Mission station Methodist Episcopal Church (North): 1 missionary, 1 native helper. Free Church of Scotland; 4 missionaries, 10 native helpers, 3 out-stations, 3 churches, 15 schools, 1,017 scholars. S. P. G.: see Chota Nagpur.

**Nain,** town in Labrador; the principal and oldest station of the Moravian Brethren in Labrador, on a good harbor on the east coast. Population, 270. Occupied by the mission since 1771; 4 missionaries, 3 missionaries' wives.

**Naini Tal,** town in Kumaon district, North-west Provinces, India, picturesquely situated on the banks of a lovely little lake which nestles among the spurs of the Himalayas. Favorite sanitarium and summer resort of Europeans from the plains. Population fluctuates; maximum, 10,054, Hindus, Moslems, Europeans, etc. Mission station Methodist Episcopal Church (North); 5 missionaries, 2 missionaries' wives, 2 other ladies, 34 native helpers, 15 schools, 665 scholars, 115 church-members.

**Nama Version.**—The Nama belongs to the Hottentot group of African languages, and is spoken in Great Namaqualand. The first parts of Scripture which were published in the Nama were the four Gospels, translated by the Rev. Mr. Schmelen of the L. M. S. and printed at Capetown in 1826 at the expense of the British and Foreign Bible Society. Twenty years later (1846) the Gospel of Luke, translated by Rev. Mr. Knûdsen of the Rhenish Missionary Society, was printed at Capetown. A new translation was undertaken by the Rev. G. Kronlein, also of the Rhenish Missionary Society, and when completed, the director of that Society, Dr. Fabri, addressed a communication to the British and Foreign Bible Society in 1863, of which the following extract is of interest:

"The Rhenish Missionary Society has its oldest and most extensive field of labor in South Africa. The stations stretch from Capetown to Walfisch Bay. The central part of this region forms (Little and Great) Namaqualand, peopled by the rest of those Hottentot tribes that were formerly living in the Cape Colony, but were afterwards dislodged by the Dutch farmers of that colony. The Rhenish Missionary Society is at present laboring among those Hottentots having the chief stations, so that this extensive though thinly-peopled country is already brought under the sound of the gospel. A considerable number of converts have already been incorporated into the church of Christ by baptism. Fifty years ago the London Missionary Society commenced work in that country, but afterwards committed its few stations to the Rhenish Missionary Society. Several very satisfactory revivals, followed by good fruits, have taken place there even up to the present time. But strange as it appears, the lingual labors in that mission field are still very little advanced. The chief reason for this is the difficulty of the language, containing four singular smacking sounds which can scarcely be mastered by any European; only a few have succeeded in acquiring them. To these few belongs Mr. Kronlein, missionary at the station Bersaba, in Great Namaqualand. He has at last, after many years' preliminary work, succeeded in translating the whole New Testament into Namaqua. Several conferences of missionaries have examined this translation and made the necessary remarks. The missionaries intend to meet ere long at the station Houchanas, in order to examine it verse by verse. This will be the last revisal. Thus you see that this translation has been performed with all possible care and circumspection, as the importance of the matter and the difficulty of the language require."

After the British and Foreign Bible Society had consented to defray the expense of the printing of the New Testament, the translator left his station and betook himself to Berlin, where he carried his work through the press in 1866, the translation being based on the "Textus Receptus," with references made also to the German, English, French, and Dutch versions.

Mr. Kronlein, who prosecuted the work of translation, issued the Psalms at Capetown in 1872, and on October 25th, 1881, he completed at Stellenbosch the translation of the Old Testament, early portions of which had been begun on May 23d, 1873. The translator is now revising into one harmonious whole the entire books of the New Testament.

(*Specimen verse.* John 3 : 16.)

‖Natigoseb gum Eloba ǀhûb-eiba‾gye ǀnamo, ob gye ‖ĕib di ǀguise ǀnai hā ǀgôaba gye‿ma, ‖ĕib ǀna ra ǂgomn hoan‿gã-‖ŏ tite se, χawen nĭ lamö ûiba û-ha se.

**Namkyung,** a town in the province of Kwangtung, China. Station of the Berlin Missionary Society, with 2 out-stations under a native deacon; 3 native helpers, and 100 members.

**Nanchang,** capital of the province of Kiang-si, China, 285 miles southwest of Nanking. Mission circuit of the Methodist Episcopal Church (North).

**Nandial,** or **Kurnool-Nandyal,** is a prosperous town in Madras, India, surrounded by highly cultivated rice-fields. Population, 78,282. Mission station of the S. P. G.; 1 missionary, 5 native helpers, 108 communicants.

**Nangur** (Nangoor), India, in the Trichinopoli district, Madras, near Tranquebar. Mission station of the S. P. G. (1878), worked with Tranquebar; 1 missionary, 459 communicants, 1 boys' boarding-school, 10 boys, 1 girls' boarding-school, 15 girls, 2 day schools.

**Nankang,** a town in the province of Kiang-si, China, between Kiu-kiang and Nan-chang. Mission station of the China Inland Mission (1887); 3 female missionaries, 1 native helper, 1 church, 1 chapel, 28 church-members; also a station of the Kiu-kiang circuit, Central China Mission of the M. E. Church (North).

**Nanking,** "southern capital," so-called from its having been the seat of government during the Ming dynasty (1368–1644), is one of the principal cities of China. It is situated on the south bank of the Yangtsz, which makes a right angle, and borders the city on the north and west, in the province of Kiang-su, 223 miles west of Shanghai, and almost midway between Canton and Pekin. It formerly possessed one of the finest walls known, 20 miles in circuit, 70 ft. high, 30 ft. wide, and pierced with 13 gates. The interior of the city has much unoccupied ground. The famous Porcelain Tower, built by the Emperor Yung Loh (1403–28), was an object of the wonder and admiration of Europeans, until it was destroyed by the Tai-ping rebels during their occupancy of the city in 1853–6, at which time most of the public buildings were ruthlessly destroyed. It was formerly a literary centre, and was noted also for its industries. Cotton cloth, called nankeen, from the name of the city, satin, crêpe, and pottery were all manufactured. An arsenal is now located at Nanking under European superintendence, where fire-arms and vessels of war are manufactured. Sir Henry Pottinger signed here the famous Nanking Treaty in 1842.

Not far from the city are the tombs of the emperors of the Ming dynasty, with an avenue leading to them guarded by gigantic stone figures of men and animals.

By a treaty made with France in 1858, this port was thrown open, but practically no commerce is carried on with foreigners. The climate is warm and dry, and not unhealthy. Population, 150,000, with 100,000,000 who use the Nanking dialect. Its importance as a centre for educational work has been appreciated by the Methodist Episcopal Church, who have established here a university with an endowment of $200,000. The Disciples of Christ are also about to erect a college. The medical work in connection with the Methodist Episcopal Hospital, said to be the largest in China, is most important. Mission of the Presbyterian Church (North), 1876; 2 missionaries and wives, 2 female missionaries, 1 native minister, 1 girls' boarding-school, 1 boys' boarding-school. Methodist Episcopal Church (North); 3 missionaries, 3 assistant missionaries, 2 female missionaries, 24 church-members, 1 Sunday-school, 60 scholars, 43 high-schools, 43 scholars, 2 day-schools, 35 scholars. Foreign Christian Missionary Society (Disciples); 2 missionaries, 4 church-members, 24 Sabbath-scholars, 24 day-scholars.

**Nanking Colloquial,** a dialect of the Mandarin, sometimes called the South Mandarin, in distinction from the North Mandarin, spoken in Pekin. The New Testament has been published in this dialect by the B. and F. Bible Society. See Mandarin Colloquial.

**Nantai,** city in Southeast China, near the coast, south of Foochow. Mission station A. B. C. F. M. with Foochow.

**Nantziang,** city in Eastern China, in the Shanghai district, province of Chehkiang. Mission station of the Methodist Episcopal Church (South); 1 missionary, 2 native pastors.

**Narasaraopet** (Nursaravapetta), a subdivision of a district of Madras. Area, 712 square miles. Population, 128,791, Hindus, Moslems, Christians, etc. Town of Athern or Narasaraopet; population, 3,928. Mission station American Baptist Missionary Union; 1 missionary and wife, 59 native helpers, 157 out-stations, 12 churches, 4,268 church-members, 70 schools, 724 scholars.

**Nardupett,** a town in the Nizam's Dominions, India, 29 miles southeast of Hyderabad. Mission station of the Hermannsburg Missionary Society.

**Narowal,** a station of the Church Missionary Society in the Punjab, India, the centre of an important work among the villages near by. A medical mission is meeting with success. There are 5 native helpers, 40 communicants, 5 schools, 559 scholars.

**Narrinyeri Version.**—The Narrinyeri belongs to the Australian languages and is spoken by aborigines of South Australia. For their benefit parts of the Old and New Testaments were translated by Mr. Taplin, and were published at Adelaide in 1865 by the British and Foreign Bible Society.

(*Specimen verse,* John 3 : 16.)

Lun ellin Jehovah an pornun an Narrinyeri: pempir ile ityan kinauwe Brauwarate, ungunuk korn wurruwarrin ityan, nowaiy el itye moru hellangk, tumbewarrin itye kaldowamp.

**Narsinghpur,** a maritime town of Madras, India, 40 miles east of Masulipatam. Population, 6,819. Mission station of the Swedish Evangelical National Society (1878); 2 missionaries, 2 native assistants, 2 schools, 153 scholars.

**Nasa,** a village on Speke Gulf, southeast corner of Lake Victoria Nyanza, Africa, occupied for a while by two missionaries of the Church Missionary Society, who left it in August, 1889, on an urgent summons to work elsewhere.

**Nasik,** an important town and district in Bombay, India. Occupied in 1832 by the Church Missionary Society; 2 missionaries, 12 native helpers, 107 communicants, 14 schools, 289 pupils.

**Nasirabad,** (1) town in Bengal, India, mission station of the Baptist Missionary Society (see Mymensing); (2) town and cantonment in Ajmere-Merwara, Rajputana, India, situated on a bleak, open plain, which slopes eastward from the Aravalli Hills. Population of town (1881), 18,482; of cantonment, 2,838, chiefly Hindus and Mohammedans. The people are poverty-stricken and in debt. Station of the Rajputana Mission, United Presbyterian Church of Scotland (1861); 3 missionaries and wives, 2 other ladies, 1 out-station, Ashapura; 2 churches, 77 communicants, 8 Sunday-schools, 335 scholars, 8 schools, 676 pupils.

**Nassau,** the capital of New Providence, one of the Bahamas, West Indies, with a population of 5,000. Station of the Baptist Missionary Society (1833); 1 missionary, 1 native assistant, 412 church-members (including entire island), 57 day-scholars, 330 Sabbath-scholars. The Wesleyan Methodist Missionary Society (1811) have on the island 6 chapels, 3 missionaries and assistants, 1 day-school, 1,000 church-members. Nassau is a diocese of the S. P. G. mission (1732), with a resident bishop. In the whole diocese there are 20 clergy, 80 stations, 4,000 communicants.

**Natal,** a section of the southeastern coast country of Africa, lying between Kaffraria and Zululand, is, since 1856, a crown colony of Great Britain; formerly it was part of the Cape of Good Hope settlement. It has a seaboard of 200 miles, with an estimated area of 21,150 square miles; some of the districts are not yet accurately delimited. (See Natal, under Africa.)

**Nateta,** capital of Uganda, on the northern shore of Victoria Nyanza, and formerly a station of the C. M. S.

**National Bible Society of Scotland.** Headquarters, 5 St. Andrew Square, Edinburgh, Scotland.—The National Bible Society of Scotland was formed by the union, in 1861, of the Edinburgh and the Glasgow Bible societies, founded respectively in 1809 and 1812, together with other leading Bible societies of Scotland. Although these societies accomplished great work alone, yet the advantageous results of the union may be seen by the progress since 1861. Since that time the auxiliary societies have increased from 52 to 335, the total income from £8,000 to £33,000, the yearly issues from 103,610 to 562,151, and the total circulation since 1861 now reaches 10,673,126 copies.

The Society carries on a large work both at home and in foreign countries. The Home

Mission supplies large numbers of the Scriptures annually at reduced rates to the poor and to various missionary and benevolent associations; it circulates the Gaelic Bible throughout the Highlands and islands of Scotland and in the regions of North America where Gaelic is spoken; and aids the distribution of the Scriptures in Ireland. Over 9,000 Bibles, Testaments, and portions of the Bible in Gaelic are distributed annually. As a Colonial Mission it distributes the Scriptures throughout all the British colonies and dependencies. As a Continental Mission it works in nearly all European countries.

As a more distinctively Foreign Mission the National Bible Society of Scotland publishes in the vernacular and distributes by means of colporteurs the Scriptures in Africa, China, India, Japan, South America, and Turkey. In Asia it has begun work among the Bedouins of the Syrian desert; it has distributed thousands of Scriptures among the Tartar tribes of Mongolia; it was the first to establish regular colportage in Korea.

The Society has recently published the Bible in the Efik for Old Calabar, Africa; the New Testament in one of the Malay dialects and in Chinyanja, the language spoken by 500,000 in Central Africa, translations in the Tannese (New Hebrides), and Mandarin (China) are also in preparation, and the Society has had its share in the Japanese version of the Scriptures, and in the Wen-li version, an idiomatic translation intelligible to the great mass of the Chinese.

The Society takes its stand upon the two great Protestant truths that the Bible is God's message to all men, and that it is the right of every man to have it in his own language and judge of it for himself. It is impossible to estimate all the results of the Society's work, but, mainly through the influence of its colporteurs, not a few Protestant congregations have been formed in Roman Catholic countries and Christian churches in heathen lands.

This Society has not carried on its work chiefly through specially appointed agents, but has worked in connection with the various missionary societies, finding this method productive of good results, especially in view of the principle and practice of allowing its colporteurs to circulate unsectarian tracts together with the Scriptures in Roman Catholic and heathen countries. It was, however, the first Society to appoint a special agent for Japan, Mr. Robert Lilley, who served there for ten years.

The circulation for 1889 was as follows:

| | Bibles. | Tests. | Parts. | Total. |
|---|---|---|---|---|
| Foreign | 29,789 | 95,407 | 337,884 | 463,080 |
| Colonies | 18,564 | 11,766 | 2,328 | 32,658 |
| United Kingdom | 111,682 | 62,789 | 19,606 | 194,077 |
| Total | 160,035 | 169,962 | 359,818 | 689,815 |

**Native States** (British India).—The collective term applied to those portions of India which are not under the direct control of the Anglo-Indian Government, but are still ruled by native princes and chiefs. These states are scattered over the whole of Hindustan. Some of them are large and important districts, covering hundreds and thousands of square miles, with millions of inhabitants, with military and civil departments of administration, with mints, postal establishments, educational systems, courts, and all the machinery of modern government; some of them are hardly large enough to be noted upon an ordinary map, and consist simply of a village or so with a handful of inhabitants, under the control of some petty descendant of the old chief of an aboriginal clan. Between these two extremes the native states range themselves in all degrees of importance. They vary greatly with reference to their populations. Some of them consist almost wholly of Hindus, under a Hindu prince. In others, the ruling family will be Mussulman—though the population will consist of persons of all the races usually found in the districts of Hindustan. Others again are made up almost wholly of the aboriginal tribes, still owning the headship of the hereditary chieftain. The manner in which it has come about that, in the midst of territory under the authority of the Anglo-Indian Government, these islands of native rule should be left, may be briefly and generally explained as follows: The English acquired their territory in India little by little. As they were brought into contact and relation with the old native chiefs and princes, conflicts more or less bitter were natural. The result of these conflicts often was that the territory of the native prince passed wholly into the hands of the British. Some of these wars were waged by the English in self-defence; some of them, it is also to be feared, were little else than wars of aggression. Sometimes the territories of a prince joining English districts would be so ill-governed and mismanaged that that fact of itself would be made by the English authorities the pretext for annexation. Thus by degrees the possessions of the English in India assumed their present far-spreading area, but among the native rulers with whom the English power has been brought in contact there have been those whose original authority over their hereditary domains there was no valid reason for disturbing. Some such reigning families have been allied to the growing British power for tens and even hundreds of years by treaty, and have always been faithful friends and allies. Some native principalities are too far removed from the march of British power to render interference with them at all natural. Some princes and chiefs have been confirmed in their possessions simply because in the absence of glaring reasons for annexation such a step would provoke hostility which it would be inconvenient to experience. Thus it has happened that while, as the result of conquest, almost all India has now passed under British rule, many native principalities still retain their existence, and many purely native governments still continue in enjoyment of their ancient power. Yet the English Government sustains very close and influential relations with all these states. They are all bound by treaty to that government, which in its relation to them is styled the "paramount power;" and which undertakes to guarantee to them all protection against foreign enemies. No one of them is permitted to enter into any treaty relations with any other power save through the English Government; and though some of the states maintain small military establishments, these are rather for display than for any serious purpose. In order to prevent the populations of these states from misgovernment, as well as to insure a due degree of subjection to the paramount power, they are all closely supervised by the Anglo-Indian Government, acting through a class of officials designated to that duty. These officials are known as "residents," or "political agents," or "political superintendents." A resident is one appointed to reside permanently at the court of a native prince, and to be the medium of communication and influence between the prince and the paramount power. Political agents and superintendents usually have supervision over groups of smaller states not large and important enough to require each the services of a resident. There are many such groups of inferior states or chieftainships, connected with all the presidencies and lieutenant-governorships. The political superintendent will often be the nearest British magistrate, who discharges the duties of supervision in connection with the general duties of his official station in British territory. Under the supervision of these officers the internal affairs of the several states are usually left to be managed by their own princes. Continuous and incorrigible incompetence will generally result in the deposition of a prince by the English Government; in this case the government of his state will often be administered by the English until his successor—if a minor—be of age; or some successor will be at once placed upon the throne.

The most important native states—some of which have been made the subject of separate treatment in this work—are Cashmir, in the far north; Nepal, along the slopes of the Himalaya; Baroda, in the northern part of the Bombay presidency; the dominions of Holkar and of Sindia in Central India; of the Nizam of Haidarabad in the Central Deccan; of Mysore, in the midst of the Madras presidency; and of Travancore and Cochin at the extreme south of the peninsula.

In some of these states missionary operations are carried on successfully. This is notably the case with Travancore and Cochin; also with Mysore. In others the degree of independent action which the chieftain or prince is suffered to exercise, united with the fact that these princes are usually Hindus or Mohammedans who consider themselves set, as it were, for the defence of their respective faiths, is sufficient to prevent any large and effective exercise of evangelistic agencies. Of late years, however, the more important native states have become more and more tolerant. Missions have within recent years been begun in several of them, and though very discreet and cautious conduct is necessary on the part of the missionaries, their work is yearly becoming more secure and influential. Often some of the smaller states will be found the most backward, the most difficult to enter, and the most impervious to all new influences of enlightenment.

**Navulon,** on the Fiji Islands, Polynesia, has a training institution under the Wesleyan Methodist Missionary Society. From it in 1875 nine young men of Navulon went to New Britain to carry the gospel. In 1889 four students came to the institute from New Britain—one result of the labors of the nine Navuloans. In the district there are 5,000 local preachers and 28,000 full members.

**Nazareth.**—1. Town in Palestine, 65 miles north of Jerusalem. It is beautifully situated in a valley surrounded by hills on all sides. The houses are mostly well built of stone. The population has a more prosperous appearance than in most parts of the country, and the women of Nazareth are famous for their beauty. Population, 4,000, Greek Catholics, Moslems, Latins, Maronites. Mission station of C. M. S.; 1 missionary and wife, 1 native pastor, 12 helpers, 8 schools, 365 scholars. Edinburgh Medical Mission; 1 physician.—2. A town on the island of Jamaica, West Indies, near Fairfield. One of the most healthy locations on the whole island, and is much used as a sanitarium by missionaries whose health has been impaired by residence in the lower and less healthy stations. Mission station of the Moravians before 1838; an out-station of Fairfield, but now has a large and flourishing congregation under one missionary and his wife.—3. District in Madras, India, which contains 44 villages. Climate tropical. Hindus, Moslems, demon-worshippers. Language, Tamil. Mission station S. P. G. (1798); 2 missionaries, 1 missionary's wife, 1 other lady, 145 native helpers, 1,698 communicants, 35 schools, 1,484 scholars.—4. A town in South Transvaal, Africa. Mission station of the Hermannsburg Missionary Society, with 136 members.

**Neemuch,** a town of the Indore State, Central Provinces, India, near Mhow and Indore. Mission station of the Presbyterian Church in Canada; 1 missionary and wife, 2 female missionaries, 1 Anglo-vernacular school.

**Neesima, Joseph Hardy,** b. Japan, February, 1844,—ten years before Commodore Perry's fleet awaited in the Bay of Yeddo the opening of Japan to the world. When in his teens, having never seen a Christian nor heard of the gospel, Neesima had some conviction of His presence who is not far from any one, and of the vanity of idols. When he met in a Chinese book the words, "In the beginning God created the heaven and the earth," he said: "This is the God for whom I am looking;" "This is the true God," and secretly determined to know more of that God, even if he left all to find him. These words from the Bible as he understood were brought by an American, and to America he must go. To leave his country was unlawful, and punishable with death. But this he risked, concealed himself among some produce in a boat, and reached Shanghai and ultimately America, working his way as a sailor. A prayer, which he committed to paper, after an Oriental usage, shows his state of mind. It was: "O God, if Thou hast got eyes, please look upon me. O God, if Thou hast got ears, please hear for me. I wish heartily to read the Bible, and I wish to be civilized with the Bible." The owner of the vessel in which he sailed was the late Hon. Alpheus Hardy of Boston, who, on his reaching America, received him into his family, and provided for his education, giving him nine years in Phillips Academy, Amherst College, and Andover Theological Seminary. The elevation of his countrymen became his absorbing purpose.

While in his course of study, the Japanese Embassy that visited this country and Europe in 1871, to observe the condition of education in western countries, summoned Mr. Neesima to act as its interpreter. He replied that he was an outlaw from his country, and was subject to no ruler save the King of kings. He thereupon received formal pardon for leaving his country. He visited with the embassy the principal colleges and universities of the United

States, Canada, and Europe. Not only was he thus brought into close and friendly relations with Japanese officials of high character and position and of enlarged views, but his wish to devote his life to the Christian education of his countrymen was greatly strengthened. He was ordained, September 24th, 1874, in Mount Vernon Church, Boston. In response to his modest but moving plea at the meeting of the American Board in Rutland, nearly $4,000 were pledged for the school which he proposed to establish in Japan. After ten years' absence, he arrived in his native land, in November, 1874, "cherishing," as he says, "in my bosom this one great purpose, i.e., the founding of an institution, in which the Christian principles of faith in God, love of truth, and benevolence towards one's fellow-men" should "train up not only men of science and learning, but men of conscientiousness and sincerity." In the following January, Mr. Neesima writes in a paper prepared by him, and published simultaneously, November 10th, 1888, in twenty of the leading periodicals of Japan, "I met Mr. Kido, counsellor to the cabinet, and told him of my purpose, who approved of it, and gave me much aid. I also received much aid from Mr. Tanika, minister of education, and from Mr. Makimura, governor of the Kyoto Fu. On November 8th, 1875, I opened the school in Kyoto, which was the beginning of the present Doshisha College. There were only six pupils in a room little better than a shed. Against much prejudice on the part of the people the school won its way." Mr. Neesima employed foreign teachers, himself taught daily classes in philosophy and theology, acted in person in all the critical relations of the school with the government, where his utmost wisdom, patience, and skill were often taxed. With the teachers he was courteous adviser, mediator, and friend; with the students, as a father or elder brother. In ten years there were two hundred and thirty pupils in commodious buildings. He was almost equally interested in evangelistic work, planning for its extension, and preaching wherever he went. A remarkable revival occurred in the Doshisha in 1884, during which the strain upon his health was such as obliged him to leave the country for a while. "My heart burns," he wrote, "for Japan, and I cannot check it." He revisited the United States in 1885. On returning to Japan in 1886, he formed a plan for the enlargement of the Doshisha, so that it might have the rank of a university. Not in any wise concealing his purpose to make it a Christian institution, he yet appealed for aid to the non-Christian statesmen and influential men of Japan. He so won their confidence that he secured contributions from those in high social and official positions amounting to nearly $60,000, and also the gift of $100,000 from an American gentleman for the same purpose. In 1889 he received from Amherst College the degree of Doctor of Laws.

In the fall of 1889 he was in Tokyo working to interest leading men at the capital, and secure funds for his enlarged plans. He took a severe cold, and, renewing his efforts too soon, was prostrated. His wife and other friends were summoned, and pastors, teachers, and students flocked from east and west to catch some farewell word. Maps were brought at his request to his bedside, and eagerly, almost with dying breath, he pointed out places which ought at once to be filled by the Christian teacher. He passed away, January 23d, 1890, saying, "Peace." "Joy," "Heaven." A booth capable of holding three thousand persons had to be built to accommodate the crowds who came to his funeral. All classes united to show him respect. The governor, the chief-justice for the district, and many other officials were present. The students from one government school and one private school were in the procession. One banner from Tokyo was inscribed with one of Mr. Neesima's own sentences: "Free education and self-governing churches: if these go together, the country will stand for all generations." Another was inscribed, "From the Buddhists of Osaka."

**Negapatam** (Nagapatnam), Snake-town, city and port in Madras, India, on the Bay of Bengal, 162 miles southeast of Madras city. It is a large, irregularly built place, containing many fine public buildings. Climate healthy, 66° F. in shade. Population, 53,855, Hindus, Moslems, Christians. Mission station S. P. G. (1835); 1 missionary, 4 native helpers, 3 schools, 93 scholars. Wesleyan Methodist Missionary Society; 1 missionary, 63 native helpers, 2 out-stations, 87 church-members, 16 schools, 942 scholars, 1 college. Evangelical Lutheran Society of Leipsic (1864); 150 communicants, 5 schools, 121 scholars.

**Negombo,** a town on the west coast of Ceylon, 20 miles north of Colombo. Mission station S. P. G.; 1 missionary, 10 native helpers, 5 out-stations, 4 churches, 4 schools, 216 scholars. Wesleyan Methodist station of Tamil Mission; 4 church-members, 1 school, 52 scholars.

**Negro Race.**—Much ignorance and confusion attend the use of the word Negro, and there is much trouble in properly classifying the race. In its widest sense the term is applied to those sections of the human race who have black or distinctly dark skins as opposed to those who have yellow or brown complexions. In this somewhat ill-defined use it designates the inhabitants (1) of Africa south of the Sahara, (2) of the peninsula of India south of the Indo-Gangetic plains, (3) of Malaysia and the greater part of Australasia. In this wide dispersion the peculiar characteristics of the pure Negro have been modified by contact with the Mongol on one side and the Caucasian on the other.*

In a more restricted sense, the Negro race includes two classes: the true Negro of African type, and the Papuan or Melanesian type.

I. *African Negro.*—While it is true that all Negroes of this class are Africans, it is not true that all Africans are Negroes, and the two terms should not be used synonymously. The geographical distribution of the true Negro race includes all of the West Coast lying along the Niger, the Senegal, and Gambia rivers, and the country between them, together with parts of the Soudan. This area is thus a thin belt of territory along the centre of Africa, not all of which is inhabited solely by Negroes, and forms but a very small part of the whole continent. Here and there, scattered through other sec-

---

* In the preparation of this article use has been made of the "History of the Negro Race in America" by G. W. Williams.

tions, especially to the south, occasional tribes of Negroes may be met with, but the limits above given are in the main correct. The home of the race in its purity is in the district between the Volta and Niger, the Kong Mountains and the coast, where are found the Negro kingdoms of Benin, Dahomey, and Yoruba, while just west of the Volta is Ashanti. Different tribes are found throughout this whole territory, such as the Jolofs and Mandingoes in Senegambia, the Susu on the Rio Pongas, the Temne inland from Lagos, the Ibo on the Lower Niger, the Hausa north of the Niger confluence, besides the tribes about Lake Tchad and in the parts about Darfur.

*History.*—It is the generally accepted opinion that the Negroes were the aborigines; or, at least, the first settlers in the region they occupy. If, as seems plausible, they belong to some branch of the Hamitic family, the indications are that they were among the first to come from Asia into Africa. The Bantu race followed, crowding the Negro to the south and west, and pushing the Hottentot Bushmen ahead until the three divisions of the African races occupied their respective localities as now defined. Within these limits, however, the negroes have been subject to much unrest and change. The slave trade diminished their numbers, and in later years the return of the descendants of former slaves has perhaps modified in a slight degree their racial characteristics.

*Racial Characteristics.*—Physical.—The true Negro is marked by an unusual length of arm; projecting jaws; small brain; black eye; flat, short nose; thick, red, protruding lips; thickness of skull; weak legs, prehensile great toe, and projecting heel; black or brown skin, thick and velvety, with a strong odor; and short, woolly hair.

Mental.—In their native home the race is regarded as naturally inferior in mental development to many of the races of the world. The possibilities of development are affirmed and denied by writers of equal weight. In the aboriginal state the Negro is a mere savage. His nature is sunny and childlike; inordinately susceptible to flattery, he can easily be influenced. While rendered cruel by the lust for gold, he is naturally gentle. He appreciates the beautiful, and is fond of songs and mirth. The victim of gross superstition, he retains the belief in a supreme being. He is indolent, slothful, and improvident; if his animal wants are satisfied, he is content. He knows how to conceal his real feelings, and can be an enigma hard to solve if he so chooses.

He responds quickly to kindness, and will prove his gratitude by great devotion. Morally, his standard is very low. Polygamy is practised, and marriage ties are almost unknown. The women are the slaves of the men, and in Dahomey are cruel and bloodthirsty soldiers. Cannibalism is sometimes indulged in, and human sacrifices have been offered to the fetich objects of their worship, some of which are most hideous (see Fetichism). Some of the tribes have a great degree of skill in the arts of life and in the manufactures. Buildings, manufactures in iron and other metals, clothes made of skins,—all show a degree or civilization which is proof of the capabilities of the race. Mungo Park found Sego, the capital of Bambasu, a city of 30,000 people, with two-story houses, containing mosques in every quarter, with ferries over the

Niger for men and beasts. To sum up, in the words of Dr. Cust: "Many great races in ancient times have had their day of greatness, exhausted the power that was in them, and have been completely broken up, trodden down, or utterly effaced by younger and more powerful races. But this cannot be said of the Negro race; they are not broken, fewer in number, or poorer in resources: though pressed upon from without, they have proved to be the only race suitable to the climate. Their soil is wonderfully fertile, their minerals abundant, their power of reproduction exceeding calculation. We know now from the instances of men who have had the advantages of culture, that they are not deficient in intelligence, probity, and even genius, yet they have left absolutely not a monument to tell of the material greatness of any particular tribe, or of any ancient civilization, as in Central America and Asia; not a written or sculptured document; they have but a scant store of proverbs and traditions."

*Language.*—The zone occupied by the Negro presents a greater diversity of tongue than is to be found elsewhere in the world, except perhaps in parts of America, in Melanesia, or Caucasia. In the Cust-Müller classification of African languages the Negro is one of six divisions, and in it are included four sub-classes such as the Atlantic, Niger, Central, and Nile; in the entire group 195 languages are recognized, and 49 dialects. They belong to the agglutinating type, and are often characterized by an intricacy of structure and delicate alliterativeness. The Grebo language on the coast of northern Guinea is monosyllabic, and is spoken with great rapidity. The Mandingo language, spoken in Senegal and Gambia, is a smooth tongue, with a predominance of vowels, and a remarkable minuteness in defining the time of an action.

*Missions.*—In the latter part of the 15th century Roman Catholicism was propagated in Benin by the Society of Jesus, but its hold on the people was soon relaxed. Protestant missions were commenced by the Moravian Brethren on the Gold Coast in 1736, but on account of the unhealthfulness of the climate the field was abandoned after thirty years of patient labor. The Church Missionary Society commenced their work in West Africa, and now have missions in Sierra Leone (q. v.), together with a strong native church. In Yoruba their work was commenced in 1843, and the stations and the date of their occupancy are: Badagry, 1845; Abeokuta, 1846; Ibadan, Lagos, Otta, 1852; Leke, 1875; Ode Ondo, 1876. The Niger Mission was commenced in 1857, and the stations are Onitsha, Lokoja, Bonny, Brass, Asaba, Kipo Hill, Gyebe, Okrika, and Ida.

The Wesleyan Methodist Missionary Society soon followed the C. M. S., and have now four missions among the Negroes: Sierra Leone, with 10 stations; Gambia, 4 stations; Lagos and Yoruba Mission; and the Gold Coast, 7 stations. Numerous other societies have also conducted missions among them, for an account of which see article on Africa, under Slave Coast. In the interior very little work has so far been attempted.

II. *Papuan Negro.*—The name Papua is a Malay term meaning "frizzled," and points at once to the mark which distinguishes the frizzly-haired Negro from the straight-haired Malay. The purest type of the Papuan is found on the western part of the island of New Guinea or

Papua, but their influence is felt throughout the whole of Melanesia and parts of Polynesia, where they mingle and amalgamate with the Malay or Mongoloid race. In the words of Mr. Wallace: "The Papuans are well-made, have regular features, intelligent black eyes, small white teeth, curly hair, thick lips and large mouth, the nose is sharp but flat beneath, the nostrils large, and the skin dark brown." The Polynesians are considered by some ethnologists as differing in no fundamental particular from the Papuans, while others class them with the Malay, as an intermediate type between the Malay and the Negro.

In their temperament and customs the Papuans show many traits similar to those of the African Negro. Their belief in sorcery, their superstitions in regard to bits of wood and stone as causes of disease, their easy-going, listless life, light-hearted and boisterous moods, all point to similarity of origin. In their architecture, rude as it is, they follow the Malay fashion of building on piles. They show a great degree of skill in agriculture. The men build the houses, hunt, and fish, leaving the heavier work to be done by the women. The latter are more modest than the rest of the Polynesian races. The Papuan languages form a class by themselves, differing widely from the Malayo-Polynesian languages. (See Papua.)

III. *Mixed Races.*—The slave-trade has scattered the Negro race throughout the globe. In most countries of the eastern hemisphere they do not assimilate. The Negro is lost in the general population, and although a trace of black blood is seen in Morocco, in Arabia, Malabar, and Ceylon, and in the various races lying between India and New Guinea, where the Papuan type is met with, they have left no distinctive mark, and no statistics are available to indicate the number of Negroes, or the proportion of the population which they form.

The degree of intermingling which has gone on in the western hemisphere has given rise to many mixed races, with more or less of Negro blood in them. The terms Creole, Quadroon, Octoroon, or Mulatto are well known and generally understood, but there are other less common terms, such as: *Mestizo,* half-breed, of either white and Negro, or Indian and Negro; *Creole,* in addition to the common meaning of one born in Spanish America, of European parents, is also applied in Peru to the children of Mestizoes; *Zambo,* half-breed, but usually the issue of Negro and Indian, or Negro and Mulatto; *Zambo Preto,* progeny of Negro father and Zambo mother. In the South American countries these terms are multiplied until almost every shade of mixture has its appropriate term.

Though the slave-trade is carried on in a few places still, yet practically slavery is extinct, and the many Negroes who are in the countries to which they have been taken as slaves are now freedmen.

*The Negro in America.*—1. *In the United States.*—From the time of the first arrival of Negroes as slaves in the colony of Virginia in 1619 till the Emancipation Act in 1865, Negro slavery has been identified with and has greatly influenced the history of the nation. The final solution of the great question of slavery left the country with a greater question confronting it, which is called the Negro Question. During the first half of the present century the number

of Negroes brought to the United States was from 60,000 to 70,000 annually, and the number multiplied until in 1880 the Negro or colored element numbered 6,581,000, or 13 per cent of the whole population. Comparatively few of this number are of unmixed blood, while many retain but a trace of Negro origin, and are in their mental and physical characteristics almost entirely Caucasian. In the Southern States, the purer type of Negro is found, and they exhibit the same characteristics already described. A jovial, light-hearted race, fond of a laugh, living only in the present, contented with mere animal pleasures, full of superstition which in some has taken the form of religious fervor, not strict in their ideas as to the rights of property, possessing a low order of cunning rather than intelligence, full of moral sentiment and lofty emotions, but prone to immoral actions and low crimes; fearing the Voodoo woman with her fetiches, and yet shouting amen in Christian services with much unction—the Negro, as modified by his environment in the United States, presents a mixture of good and evil, of childlike simplicity and shallow cunning, of deep feeling and weak character, of hopelessness and of possibility, which may well stagger the faith and try the patience of those who are trying to educate and Christianize him. Notable instances of full-blooded Negroes there are who have shown an intelligence, a strength of mind and executive ability, a steadfast faith and upright life, equal to that of the Caucasian; and these instances, when viewed in connection with their as yet meagre opportunities, may fairly be placed in comparison with the great majority which seem to give weight to the opinion that the Negro is mentally and morally inferior to and can never be on an equality with the white race which surrounds him.

It has been suggested that the Negro is not so much immoral as non-moral, for there seems to be such a lack of the perception of right and wrong that a Negro will stop on his way to or from a prayer-meeting, at which he takes a fervid part, to lift a chicken from a neighbor's hen-roost. The Rev. Dr. Tucker, at the American Church Congress in 1883, brought out this side of the American Negro character when he spoke of Negro missionaries who were earnest and successful, unconscious of hypocrisy, but who were guilty of lives of the grossest immorality, were addicted to lying and thieving, and yet were respected and heeded by their flocks.

The Negro question is looked at in two distinct ways, not only by the politician but by the Christian, and the difference is due mainly to presence or absence of perspective. By those who live away from the daily contact with the Negro, who look at him idealized, as a man entitled to the rights of men, to all the privileges of citizenship, and to all the yearning love which a fallen image of God should excite in the Christian heart, the practical difficulties in the way of civilizing, Christianizing, and elevating the Negro to the landed plane of equality are ofttimes overlooked, and theory takes the place of practice, sentiment of common-sense, and faith and hope overpower "works." To those who live among the Negroes, who daily see the deficiencies in their character, in their capabilities, in their morals, there is an absence of perspective, and they take the other extreme view, that there is little that can be done for them, that liberty and equality should for some time, at least, be mere words without any practical meaning so far as they are concerned. This is not only true of upright and honorable men who are not distinctively Christian, but men who are anxious to save the souls of the Negroes are just as averse as their political neighbors to contact with Negroes on terms of equality, or to recognition of their political rights. Among the men who are ready to keep the Negro from the polls by violence if necessary, are men who are active in Christian work; (this the writer knows from actual conversation with such a one). Between these two widely divergent views of the Negro there is, without doubt, as in all things, a middle ground, and to that mean the opinion of wise men is turning; but as yet it cannot be clearly defined, nor is the question yet solved.

While the political part of the Negro question is taxing the thought of the statesmen, the Church is doing her part to aid in the solution. (See article on United States.) In addition to the missionary work of the different churches, and that of the American Missionary Association (q.v.), there is a large and flourishing church among the Negroes themselves. The African Methodist Episcopal Church was organized in 1816, and in 1880 it had a total membership of over 400,000, and supported a missionary society which was organized in 1844 as the Parent Home and Foreign Missionary Society. In 1888 nearly 300 missionaries were engaged in the home work of the church, though it has been only within the last ten years that any successful mission has been established in foreign lands. (See article African Methodist Episcopal Church.) In addition to their own church, the Negroes form fifteen conferences of the Methodist Episcopal Church (South). Of the Baptists, a large proportion in the Southern States are Negroes, and many of the ministers have been men of great power and of great zeal in religious life.

2. *In Mexico.*—It is difficult to calculate the number of Negroes in Mexico, for there the mixture is so blended that Negro ancestry is hard to trace. Of the population of nearly 10,000,000, the Negro element is put at 60,000, and by the constitution of 1824 all distinctions of race were abolished, and they are virtually amalgamated with the rest of the people. About 43 per cent of the people are of mixed race, Negroes and Indians.

3. *Central America.*—The number of the colored or Negro population in Central America has been estimated at 50,000. In this section of the country intermingling with the Indians and other races is very great, and there is little social distinction between them.

4. *South America.*—Brazil was the last country in America to abolish slavery. In 1850 the slaves were estimated at 2,500,000; in 1887 the slaves were given on the official returns as numbering 723,419, and by a law passed in 1888 slavery was abolished. The Negroes are found principally in the provinces of Pernambuco, Bahia, Rio de Janeiro, and Minas, and according to the census of 1872 numbered 1,954,452. In the other countries of South America the Negroes are so mixed with the other races (as in Peru), or form so small an element in the population, that no definite statement as to their numbers can be attempted.

5. *West Indies.*—The number of Negroes in the West Indies is about 3,000,000. Slavery was abolished in the British West Indies in 1834, in the French possessions in 1848, and in Cuba in 1886. (See article West Indies).

The vitality of the race is surprising and is unaltered by their location, except when they leave the tropics or sub-tropics. The farther north they go, the greater the mortality, and their stability as a race, in constitution and numbers, depends upon the restriction of their habitation to the warm climates.

**Nellore.**—1. The capital of a district of the same name, Madras, India, stands on the Tenner, and has been since 1840 a station of the A. B. M. U.; 5 out-stations, 3 missionaries, 10 native preachers, 2 churches, 605 church-members, 5 Sunday-schools, 165 scholars, 7 day-schools, 217 pupils. Out-station of the mission of Free Church of Scotland at Madras (q.v.).—2. A pastorate in the Jaffna district of the C. M. S. Mission in Ceylon (1818), where there are 557 communicants, in the 4 pastorates. A girls' boarding-school at Nellore has an attendance of 54, of whom 39 are Christians. There is 1 married missionary.

**Nembe,** an inland town in the Niger Valley, West Africa, 55 miles from the sea, and 1,500 miles from Sierra Leone. Climate humid; quite unhealthy for foreigners. Population, 10,000 of mixed races, principally Ijo. Language, Ijo. Brass dialect. Religion, seven eighths heathen. Social condition very degraded. Government, hereditary monarchy. Political condition very distressing. Mission station of the Church Missionary Society (1876); 1 unordained missionary, 1 church, 283 church-members. 1 school, 78 scholars.

In 1876 King Arkija surrendered his idols and built a church. His children were educated by the missionaries, and he was baptized and gave up polygamy. He died in 1879. Since that time Christianity is speedily spreading, and, as a rule, the chiefs of the households come to the church. Nevertheless in 1885 one instance of cannibalism occurred.

**Nepal,** independent kingdom, lying along the southern slopes of the Himalayas, in North India; it is not one of the so-called "protected" or feudatory states, ruled by its own chieftain, but supervised by British officials, and so practically a part of British India; but it is still independent, under its own sovereign, and though there are treaty stipulations between its government and that of British India, it is outside of the immediate circle of British influence. To the north its territory extends up the sides of the Himalayan range until it meets that of Tibet along an unsurveyed and indefinite frontier. Its southern boundary is usually about 30 miles from the foot of the Himalayas. On the west a small stream separates it from the sub-Himalayan British province of Kumaon; and its eastern limit is the small mountain state of Sikkim, north of Calcutta. Its greatest length northwest and southeast is 512 miles; its breadth varies from 70 to 150 miles. The total area has been computed at about 54,000 square miles. No census of population has ever been taken. The Nepalese estimate is about 5,500,000; the soberer, and probably more correct, opinion of Anglo-Indian officials places the population at 2,000,000. There are many aboriginal tribes in Nepal, most of whom seem to be of Tartar or Chinese origin. But the regnant tribe is that of the Gurkhas, who are descended from the Rajputs of Northwestern India, and who migrated in the 12th century from the original home of their people during the early ascendancy of one of the invading Mussulman dynasties. In process of time they intermarried largely with the women of the mountain tribes where they took up their new abodes, though still adhering tenaciously to the Hindu religion. Most of these aboriginal tribes are Buddhists, but Buddhism is gradually disappearing before the stronger Hinduism of the ruling race. Rice is the staple food of the people. The highest known mountain in the world,—Mt. Everest, 29,002 ft. high,—as well as many Himalayan peaks inferior only to that, lie within the limits of Nepalese territory. Since the subjugation of the country by the Gurkha dynasty, several bloody revolutions, marked by the true Oriental features of assassination and usurpation, have occurred. The last was in 1885, when the prime-minister and two other prominent men were murdered by the head of a rival faction. The murderer at once made himself prime-minister. Violent as the revolution was, it was considered a probable step towards much-needed reforms within the kingdom. Nepal has never been open to the entrance of Europeans, though the Indian Government has usually maintained a resident there. Accordingly missionary operations have not yet been begun. The capital is Khatmandu, north latitude 27° 42′, east longitude 85° 12′. Population supposed to be about 50,000.

**Nepali Version.**—The Nepali belongs to the Indic branch of the Aryan family of languages, and is spoken in the kingdom of Nepal. A translation of the New Testament into this language was made by Serampore missionaries, and published at Serampore in 1821. This version has never been reprinted. A new translation was undertaken by Rev. W. Starb, and the Gospel of Luke and the Acts were published at Calcutta in 1850, 1871, and 1877. Of the translations made by Scotch missionaries at Darjeeling, Genesis, Exodus, Proverbs, the Gospels, and Acts have been published.

(*Specimen verse.* John 3 : 16.)

क्याहा ईश्वरले दुनियाहार रहो पिचारो गऱ्या कि उसल आफुना रकपेदा दोराहाइ दियो कि जो हरेक मानिस उसमाथो विश्वास गर्छन् सो नाश न होइन तर धनजजिन्दगी पाउन ।

**Nestorians,** a people living in the mountains of the Perso-Turkish frontier and on the plain of Oroomiah in Northwestern Persia. They are akin to the Jacobites of Eastern Turkey and Mesopotamia, and are sometimes spoken of as the Assyrian Christians. (See articles Persia; A. B. C. F. M.; Presbyterian Board (North); Archbishop's Mission; Historical Geography of Missions; and China.)

**Netherlands Missionary Society.** Headquarters, Rotterdam, Holland.—The Netherlands Missionary Society was established in December, 1797, at Rotterdam, Holland, through the influence of Dr. Vanderkemp, a celebrated missionary of the London Missionary Society to South Africa. On a visit to his home he translated into Dutch and published an address to the religious people of Holland, which led to the establishment of the Society. The members are confined almost entirely to the Established Church. The General Synod, however, has no control over the missionaries or the funds collected, yet the missionaries sent out are examined and ordained by a committee of ministers appointed by the General Synod. The Society is supported by regular subscriptions, donations, and legacies. A body of directors, both lay and clerical, is annually appointed from among the subscribers to control the affairs of the Society. The Society has a college of its own for the preparation of candidates for the missionary work, a large number of whom are not Dutch, but German and Swiss. For a time the funds of the Society did not permit the sending out of missionaries, but were expended in home work, especially in publication, the establishment of Sunday-schools, etc. In the year 1800 they began to turn their attention more especially to foreign lands. Their funds increased rapidly, and numbers of young men offered their services. Political complications, however, at that time rendered it wiser for them to enter into a friendly agreement with the L. M. S., by which missionaries supported by the N. M. S. were under the general direction of the L. M. S. The first missionaries, Vos, Erhardt, and Palm, were sent to Ceylon, but they were unable to accomplish very much in that field, owing perhaps to the hostility of the Dutch Consistory of the island. In 1812 three missionaries, Kam, Supper, and Bruckner, were sent to Java. Mr. Kam established himself at Amboyna, in the Molucca Islands, Mr. Bruckner at Samarang, and Mr. Supper at Batavia. Two years later, Holland having regained its independence from France, the N. M. S. commenced its operations independently, reorganized the seminary, and sent out five missionaries to work with Mr. Kam. These established themselves at Celebes, Ceram, Ternati, Banda, and Timor, and found abundant opportunity for labor. In 1833 Mr. Kam, who had endured much exposure in his efforts to travel from island to island, and had been often employed, even by the government, as a peacemaker among the tribes, died from the effects of overwork. In 1826 the same Society sent out Mr. Gutzlaff to China (see biographical sketch). A mission was also established at the Dutch colony of Surinam in Guiana, and Alphonse F. Lacroix was sent to the Dutch territory in India (see biographical sketch). When in 1825 the Dutch settlements on the continent of India were ceded to the Dutch Government, their four missionaries connected themselves with the different English societies, thinking it better not to render their time and labor and knowledge of the languages of the people of no avail. At present the N. M. S. carries on its work in Java, Amboyna, and Celebes, and reports 18 missionaries, 184 native workers, 136 schools, with 20,000 communicants.

**Nevis,** one of the Leeward Islands, West Indies, is a colony of Great Britain. Area, 50 square miles. Population (1881) 11,864. Formerly a station of the Wesleyan Methodist Missionary Society. It is now under the care of the West Indian Conference. Congregations of the Anglican and Moravian churches are also the fruit of former missionary labors.

**New Calabar,** town in West Africa, in the valley of the Lower Niger, on the Bight of Biafra. Climate mild, somewhat unhealthy. Population, 12,000. Race and language, Ibo. Religion, Fetichism. Government, native kingdom. Mission station of the C. M. S.; 1 missionary and wife, 1 church, 1 out-station.

**New Caledonia,** together with its dependency, the Loyalty Islands, is a French penal colony, lying about 720 miles northeast of Australia, in latitude 20°–22° 30′ south, and longitude 164°–167° east. It is 200 miles long, 30 broad, with an area of 6,000 square miles, and a population (1887) of 62,752; 41,874 natives; the remainder are colonists, soldiers, and convicts. The natives belong to or resemble the Papuans. The Roman Catholics have established missions at various points on the island, but so far no Protestant work has been commenced. It was occupied by the French in 1853, and has been a penal settlement since 1872.

**Newchwang,** called also Ying-tze, one of the treaty ports of China, in the Manchurian province Shing-king, is situated on a branch of the Liau-ho, 35 miles from the Gulf of Liantung. The real port is Ying-tze, farther down the river, to which the name of Newchwang is also applied. The port is closed by ice for four or five months in the year. The product of pulse (beans) is the principal export. Population, 60,000. Mission station of the Irish Presbyterian Church (1868); 4 missionaries and wives, 1 female missionary, 12 native helpers, 6 out-stations, 76 church-members, 1 school, 11 scholars. United Presbyterian Church of Scotland; 1 missionary works in harmony and union with the Irish Presbyterian Mission.

**Newell, Samuel,** b. Durham, Me., U. S. A., July 24th, 1784; graduated at Harvard College and Andover Seminary; one of those whose memorial called the American Board into existence. He married Harriet Atwood, and sailed February 19th, 1812, as a missionary of the American Board for Calcutta. Forbidden by the East India Company to remain in its territory, he sailed with his wife for Mauritius to establish a mission for that island and Madagascar. After a long and perilous voyage they reached Port Louis, where Mrs. Newell died soon after their arrival. Mr. Newell went to Ceylon, the opening there for a mission being favorable; but in January, 1814, he joined his brethren Hall and Nott at Bombay. He died of cholera May 30th, 1821, being violently attacked while ministering to the sick, and was buried in the English cemetery. He was greatly endeared to the friends of missions by his devotedness and his peculiarly amiable character.

**New England Company.** Headquarters, 1 Furnival's Inn, Holborn, London, E. C., England.—In the early part of the 17th century the English colonists of New England, headed by the renowned John Eliot, "the Apostle to the North American Red Men," began the work amongst the Indians which laid the foundations for the New England Company. The accounts of the work among the Red Men, circulated throughout London in writings called "tracts," aroused so much interest in the great city that the needs of the Indians were brought before Parliament, and on July 27th, 1649, an Act was passed with this title: "A Corporation for the Promoting and Propagating the Gospel of Jesus Christ in New England." In this Act was recognized the necessity of work amongst the Indians for the purposes of evangelization and civilization, and provision was made for the expenditure involved in the furtherance of such work. The Ordinance enacted that there should be a Corporation in England consisting of a president, treasurer, and fourteen assistants, and invested the Corporation with power to acquire lands, goods, and money.

*History.*—Soon after the action of Parliament and the appointment of the members of the Corporation, a general subscription was directed by Cromwell, the Lord Protector, and nearly £12,000 was raised for the purposes of the Corporation. Commissioners and a treasurer were appointed in New England, and work was carried on by itinerant missionaries and school-teachers, chiefly near Boston. On the restoration of Charles II. in 1660, the Corporation created by the Long Parliament became defunct, but through the efforts of the Hon. Robert Bryle a new charter was granted by the king. This charter was completed in 1662. By it the Company was limited to forty-five members; the first forty-five named; the object defined; the name decided as "The Company for the Propagation of the Gospel in New England and the parts adjacent in America:" the duties and powers of the officers defined; and in fact the complete constitution was made and adopted.

The work progressed in the New England states until the outbreak of the War of American Independence, when the Company was obliged to cease its labors there. The field was therefore transferred to New Brunswick, but after a fair attempt was found unprofitable, and was again changed to British America, where since 1822 the work has been permanently maintained.

*Present Work.*—The funds of the Company are derived from three sources, the original charter fund and two legacies. The money coming from two of these sources may be used only for work amongst the American Indians and work in American dependencies of the British crown, while that from the third may be used for spreading the gospel in any British colonies. The work carried on now by the Company is evangelistic and educational amongst the Indian tribes of Canada and British America. Between the years 1823 and 1840 large sums were contributed toward aiding the Missions in the West Indies, but the increase of the work in North America of late years has necessitated the withdrawal of funds from that quarter, and all have been devoted to the missions of the Company. The principal stations at the present time are:

1. Among the Mohawks, Oneidas, Onondagas, Cayugas, Senecas, and Tuscaroras, settled on the banks of the Grand River between Brantford and Lake Erie.

2. Among the Missasaguas of Chemong or Mud Lake and Rice Lake, in the county of Peterborough, Ontario.

3. On the banks of the Garden River in the district of Algoma, near the rapids between Lake Superior and Lake Huron.

4. On Kuper Island in the Strait of Georgia, British Columbia.

**New Fairfield,** a town among the Delaware Indians, Ontario, Canada. The oldest station of the Moravian Brethren in this region (1792); 2 missionaries and wives.

**Newfield,** a mission station of the Moravians in Antigua, West Indies. It was opened in 1782, when the numbers of hearers at Grace-hill increased so largely that it was impossible for the missionaries to exercise the needful supervision, or for the negroes to be accommodated. So it was very desirable to establish an out-station near by; and as the Moravian Brethren were too poor to do this, the planters gave them a grant of land, a considerable sum of money for building materials, much help in the way of lending them slaves who were skilled as masons and carpenters, and promised a yearly salary for a missionary, while the slaves gave all their leisure time to the work. Under these circumstances the station was begun, and is now continued under the care of a missionary and wife.

**Newfoundland,** a British North American colony, comprising an island of that name and the coast of Labrador from Blanc Sablon bay, at the west entrance to the Strait of Belle Isle, to Cape Chudleigh, at the east entrance of Hudson Strait, a distance of about 750 miles. The island lies at the mouth of the Gulf of St. Lawrence, and is separated from Labrador on the northwest by the Strait of Belle Isle, 12 miles wide, and is rugged and for the most part barren. The principal range of hills is the Long Range Mountains, which run in a northeast direction from Cape Ray to the Humber River, which with the Exploits, Terra Nova, and some other streams, are the principal rivers of Newfoundland, and are navigable by canoes or flats. The soil is not very productive, and poorly cultivated; but it is rich in minerals, and there are fine quarries of building stone and marble found. The climate, being tempered on the one hand by the Gulf Stream and on the other by the Arctic Current, is neither so cold in winter nor hot in summer as might be expected, but the weather is very variable; dense fogs are prevalent, and fierce and sudden gales render navigation along its coast dangerous, and bring into use the many good harbors which its rugged coast line affords. Population, in 1874, 161,455, chiefly made up of English and French colonists and a few Indians. The aborigines, a tribe of Indians called Beoths, are extinct. The chief occupations are fishing and trapping. Religion, Protestant and Roman Catholic. The executive power in Newfoundland is a governor appointed by the British crown, and a council of not more than 7 members appointed by the governor. The legislative power is vested in a council of not more than 15 members and a house of assembly of 31 members. The chief towns and commercial centres are St. Johns, the capital and emporium, on the southeast coast, Harbor Grace and Carbonear on Conception Bay.

**New Guinea:** see Papua.

**New Guinea Version,** or South Cape dialect.—This dialect belongs to the Melanesian languages and is vernacular at South Cape, New Guinea. A translation of the Gospel of Mark into this dialect, made by one of the teachers and revised by the missionaries, was published by the British and Foreign Bible Society at Sydney in 1885 under the care of the Rev. J. P. Sunderland.

**New Halle,** town in South Central Transvaal, East South Africa, southeast of Waterburg, northeast of Kana. Mission station of the Berlin Evangelical Lutheran Society (1873); 1 missionary, 7 other helpers, 11 out-stations, 506 church-members, 206 communicants.

**New Hanover,** a town in Natal, East South Africa, on a branch of the Umvoti River, north of Pietermaritzburg and south of Greytown. Mission station of the Hermannsburg Missionary Society.

**New Hebrides Islands,** a group in the South Pacific, part of Melanesia (q.v.), lying between latitude 21° and 15° south, and longitude 171° and 166° east, about 1,000 miles north of New Zealand, 400 miles west of Fiji, 200 miles east of New Caledonia, and 1,400 miles northeast of Sydney, Australia. There are about 30 islands of volcanic origin, mountainous, with wooded ridges and fertile valleys, nearly all of them inhabited. Santo, the largest and most northerly of the group, is especially beautiful and picturesque. The principal other islands are Aurora, Eromanga, Tanna, Fotuna, Aneityum, Pentecost, Mallicollo, Ambrim or Lopevi, and Efate or Vati. Lopevi has a conical volcano 5,000 feet high. Tanna has the mountain of Yoswa, the largest and most active volcano in the group. Cocoa-nuts and other magnificent trees grow in profusion, and the soil, like that of most volcanic islands, is very fertile, and fruits and vegetables are raised in abundance. A small group lies to the north of the above islands, and is called the Banks Islands or North New Hebrides. The population number perhaps 50,000, and belong in general to the Papuan race (q.v.). The general type is rather ugly: below the middle height, fairer than the typical Papuan, with low, receding foreheads, broad faces, and flat noses. Bracelets, ear-rings, and nose-rings made out of shells are very often their only clothing, though oil and red clay is smeared over the body in some of the islands. Kava, a kind of intoxicating drink made from the pepper-plant, is drunk by the men, but women and boys are not allowed to drink it. The characteristics and habits of the people differ greatly in the various islands; at Aneityum and most of the southern islands the people have become Christianized, while on some of the other islands cannibalism is prevalent. The languages of the islands are about twenty in number, and sometimes two or three are used on the same island, so that the missionaries laboring at opposite sides of the island are unable to use each other's books for their respective congregations. These languages are alike in grammatical construction, and belong to the Melanesian class. The natives are very superstitious, and worship idols. Large carved images are found in the north, while rude, uncarved stones of all shapes and sizes were the objects of worship in Aneityum and Tanna. The fear of the taboo prevails, and their sacred men are supposed to be able to bring rain, wind, disease, and death. The cruel, treacherous, and savage characteristics of the people,—who believe that strangers are the cause of storms, disease, and death,—the exigencies of the climate, and the utter remoteness from the world's traffic, unite to make the New Hebrides one of the most dangerous of all mission fields. Mission work is carried on in the main islands by the New Hebrides Mission. The Banks Islands are visited by missionaries of the Melanesian Mission, with schools at Santa Maria and the other islands.

**New Hebrides Mission.**—This is a synodical union of missionaries of several different Presbyterian Boards carrying on mission-work in the New Hebrides Islands. I. HISTORY. —The New Hebrides Mission was begun in 1848 by a solitary missionary settled on the island of Aneityum, but the origin of the mission antedates that event by a good many years. The islands were named by Cook in 1774, though they had previously been discovered by Spanish sailors, who named Santo "Espiritu Santo;" and Bougainville, in 1768, had proved it to be but an island instead of a great southern continent, as the Spanish supposed. Cook's "Narrative" of his voyage was the source of the great missionary zeal manifested at that time in England. William Carey (see biographical sketch) was anxious to go to Polynesia, but went to India. The L. M. S., which was formed through his influence (see article), sent its missionaries to the Tahiti and Samoan Islands. John Williams longed to extend the work to the New Hebrides, and expressed this desire as early as 1824 to the directors of the L. M. S. The United Presbyterian Church of Scotland (then the United Secession Church) placed £500 at his disposal to take the gospel to New Caledonia (q.v.) and the New Hebrides. His tragic death at Eromanga is part of the martyr history of the church, and the funds were used in Africa instead. Between that time and the arrival of Mr. Geddie (1839–1848) the missionary ship of the L. M. S. visited the islands several times, and left native Samoan teachers on some of them, many of whom suffered persecution and even death.

Since 1848 the mission work has been distinctively Presbyterian. In that year the Presbyterian Church of Nova Scotia sent out the Rev. John Geddie of Prince Edward's Island. (See biographical sketch.) The United Secession Church made over to the Nova Scotian Church their claim to the South Seas, so this mission is the legitimate successor of the attempt of John Williams.

II. DEVELOPMENT OF THE WORK.—1. *Aneityum.*—This, the most southerly island of the group, was not visited by Cook, but he saw it from Tanna. It is very picturesque, and has a good harbor. The climate is somewhat humid, but in general agreeable, and, to those who exercise care, not unhealthy. It was visited as early as 1830, and soon after that became quite a resort for traders who sought sandalwood. Their ill-treatment by these traders had much to do with the hostility shown to strangers by the savages. The native teachers left by the L. M. S. ship "Camden" had to flee for their lives at one time, and were always in jeopardy, but they prepared the way for the work of Mr. Geddie when he arrived in 1848. Two years after his arrival, forty-five natives assembled for worship on the Sabbath, and the first convert afterwards went as missionary to Fotuna. In May, 1852, the first church was formed, and in July of that year Rev. John Inglis and wife arrived and shared the work. Mr. Geddie had labored at Anelgahat, on the south side of the island, but Mr. Inglis commenced work at Aname, on the north side, where he labored for twenty-three years. In

1854 there were 30 schools, and 2,600 people attended worship. Mr. Geddie translated and printed at Aneityum the Gospel of John, the Acts and the Epistles of Paul; the Gospel of Mark was printed at Sydney, and Luke was sent to England to be printed by the British and Foreign Bible Society. Mr. Inglis took the whole New Testament to England to be printed (see Aneityum Version). The history of the succeeding years at Aneityum is summed up in the inscription on the memorial tablet to Mr. Geddie in the church at Anelgahat: "When he landed in 1848 there were no Christians here, and when he died in 1872 there were no heathen."

In 1872 Rev. J. D. Murray joined the mission, but was forced to leave it in 1876, on account of the health of his wife. Mr. Inglis left the station in 1877 after the arrival of a new missionary, but continued his work by superintending the publication of the Old Testament at London. So wise was he in counsel, so generous in friendship, liberal in help, pacific in manner, so trusted by all, and so charitable in his dealings with other missions, that his absence was much lamented, and his memory is ever living in the hearts of his people. He has since published attractive and interesting narratives of his work, which crown an able and honorable career as missionary for thirty years. The Rev. J. H. Lawrie, from Scotland, joined the mission in 1879, and after a furlough at the end of ten years is now at this post.

2. *Fotuna.*—The Rev. John Williams visited Fotuna, and succeeded in conciliating the natives, but his death prevented his carrying out his purpose to send teachers to them. Samoan teachers were left by the "Camden" in 1841, but they were killed and eaten or thrown in the sea two years later. Two Aneityumese were the pioneers from the work at Aneityum, and they were taken to this island by the "John Williams" in 1853. In the face of persecution, they stuck to their post, were joined later on by another teacher from Aneityum, and one from Rarotonga, and in 1866 the Rev. Joseph Copeland and his wife arrived at this island, where work has been carried on faithfully ever since, though it is still one of the most difficult fields. A medical mission has been established.

3. *Aniwa.*—In 1840 Christians from Samoa settled here as teachers, but little progress was made, and the arrival of reinforcements from Aneityum was the cause of an outburst of long-smouldering hatred on the part of the natives, who held a grudge against Aneityum on account of former cruel practices. The two Aneityumese teachers were attacked, and one was killed but the other escaped and fled to Aneityum. Other native teachers took up the work, undeterred by the fate of Nemeian, as the fallen teacher was called, and in 1866 the Rev. J. G. Paton found on his arrival that the people were in some measure prepared for his teachings. The mission house stands on a spot long used for cannibal feasts. After eight years of labor the island was completely Christianized.

4. *Tanna.*—The "lighthouse of the Southern Pacific," as this island has been called, was a very hard and trying field, and the work here was accompanied with unusual disaster and death. John Williams' native teachers had to flee, and Turner and Nesbit of the L. M. S. were also forced to escape for their lives in 1843. From that time till 1858 Samoan teachers repeat-

edly tried to introduce the gospel. Once in 1853 an outbreak of an epidemic of small-pox, carelessly introduced by a Californian ship, incensed the natives against foreigners, and the Samoan teacher with his family fled in an open boat to Aneityum. In 1854 the visit of a party of Tannese to Aneityum, where they noted with wonder the improvements of Christian civilization, gave a favorable turn to the work, for they requested teachers, and two were sent; many listened to their instruction and it seemed as though heathenism would be given up. But the recurrence of an epidemic led to the old superstitious fears of the baneful influence of the teachers, and for a time the lives of the teachers were in danger, but they remained faithfully at work. In 1858 Rev. John Paton and Rev. Mr. Copeland landed on the island; Rev. J. W. Matheson and the Rev. S. F. Johnston and wife joined them soon from Nova Scotia. In 1859 Mr. Copeland left to take Mr. Inglis' work in Aneityum, and within three years Messrs. Johnston and Matheson, Mrs. Paton and child, Mrs. Matheson and child, were dead, and Mr. Paton, distressingly ill himself, after passing through harrowing scenes of death and in peril from the natives, was forced to flee from the island. The Rev. Thomas Neilson resumed work here in 1868, and by his medical skill, and the exercise of common-sense and Scotch caution, he has been able to continue in the work, and encouraging results are seen.

5. *Eromanga.*—Not only by the blood of Williams was this mission field watered: it is the scene of other martyrdoms as well. Christian teachers from Samoa placed here in 1840 suffered much persecution, and were forced to leave the following year. Eight years later some young men were taken from this island to Samoa, and there instructed in Christianity. They returned in 1852 to work among their people; one went back to heathenism, but the others remained faithful till their death. The Bishop of New Zealand, who spoke the Eromangan language and felt deeply interested in the work, secured several natives to study in the training-school at Auckland, who were Christianized and sent back to labor for their countrymen. Christian influence was exerted from Aneityum as well. In 1857 Rev. G. N. Gordon of Nova Scotia was stationed at Eromanga. For four years he labored with untiring zeal and devotion. He translated Jonah, the Gospel of Luke, Acts, and a catechism and hymn-books. But a hurricane swept over the island, doing great damage; the measles, introduced by a trading-vessel, caused the death of hundreds of the people; and the old superstitions in regard to the evil influences of foreigners took possession of the natives, and stirred up by an enemy of the mission, the angry people murdered Mr. and Mrs. Gordon on the 20th of May, 1861. Some of the Christians fled to Aneityum and told the tragic story. Bishop Patteson, himself a martyr afterwards, was the first to visit the island after the murder. He felt the loss of his friend very deeply. He was accustomed to stop and visit him, as he made his annual visits to the islands. Now all he could do was to read the burial-service over the grave where the mangled remains had been buried by the faithful Christians before they sought safety in flight.

The Rev. J. D. Gordon came out from Nova Scotia in 1864 to take up the work of his brother. He found a scattered but still faithful flock of Christians, who had been brave enough to keep up the services on the Sabbath. In 1868 Mr. J. McNair joined the mission from Scotland, but he died in 1870, and after a few years Mr. Gordon severed his connection with the mission. He still remained in Eromanga, and hoped to establish a mission to Santo, and perhaps New Guinea, before he died; but in March, 1872, while revising the translation of the seventh chapter of Acts, where the martyrdom of Stephen is recorded,—the same passage which occupied Bishop Patteson on the morning of the day he fell a martyr at Nackapu,—he was murdered by a native who had come to him upon an apparently friendly errand. In the same year Rev. Hugh Robertson and his brave young wife arrived from Nova Scotia. Knowing well the danger, they deliberately chose Eromanga as their field of labor. Since then the blood of the martyrs has borne rich fruit, for the report for 1889 says: "The work on Eromanga was never more encouraging; the converts are doing all in their power to help on the work of the mission, and under constant training they are growing in liberality and other graces with gratifying rapidity."

In the church at Dillon's Bay is a tablet whose brief record is a fitting close to this slight sketch of the work at Eromanga:

> Sacred to the Memory of Christian Missionaries
> who died on this island:
> JOHN WILLIAMS,
> JAMES HARRIS,
> Killed at Dillon's Bay by the Natives, 30th November, 1839;
> GEORGE N. GORDON,
> ELLEN C. GORDON,
> Killed on 20th of May, 1861;
> JAMES McNAIR,
> Who died at Dillon's Bay, 16th July, 1870; and
> JAMES D. GORDON,
> Killed at Portinia Bay, 7th March, 1872.
> They hazarded their lives for the name of the Lord Jesus.—Acts 15:26.
> It is a faithful saying and worthy of all acceptation, that Christ Jesus came into the world to save sinners.—1 Tim. 1:15.

The other islands are visited by means of the "Dayspring," a vessel given by the Sunday-school children of Nova Scotia. The tragic history of the mission has interested many in it, and at present there are eight branches of the Presbyterian Church represented in the New Hebrides Missions, with 18 missionaries and 130 native teachers.

III. *Organization.*—The eight churches supporting this mission are: the Presbyterian Church in Canada (formed by the union in 1876 of the various branches of Scotch Presbyterians in Canada and the Maritime Provinces); the Free Church of Scotland, including now the Reformed Presbyterian Church of Scotland; and the Presbyterian Churches of Victoria, New Zealand, Otago, Tasmania, South Australia, and New South Wales. The Established Church of Scotland also renders support in connection with the church in Canada.

The representatives of these various branches of the Presbyterian Church have formed themselves into one Synod, called the "New Hebrides Mission Synod," which meets annually, and is the supreme authority in the mission in all general matters, each missionary being under the Synod in a general way, while personally responsible only to the church by which he is supported. Although each man is translating the Bible into and preaching in a language as different from that of any other man as English is from French or French from German, unity of method is aimed at and achieved. Old associations are forgotten in the New Hebrides; "Establishment" men and "Voluntaries," men from the mother-church and the colonies, work together with one interest, and form indeed a "United Presbyterian Church" in reality and practice.

**New Herrnhut.**—1. A town on the island of St. Thomas, West Indies, which was the scene of the earliest direct effort made by any Christian community for the conversion of the ignorant, debased, and enslaved West Indian negro. New Herrnhut is pleasantly situated on high ground, backed by hills of yet greater elevation. Its distance from the town of St. Thomas is nearly four miles in a northeasterly direction. For several years the missionaries on St. Thomas occupied a very humble and unhealthy tenement in the village of Tappas, now the town of St. Thomas, and preached the gospel here and on the neighboring estates; but in 1737 they purchased a small plantation on an elevated and healthier locality, to which they gave the name of Pozaunenberg, which was shortly after formed into a settlement, and in 1753 received the name of New Herrnhut. It has at present only a small congregation, the majority of the inhabitants having removed nearer to the town.—2. A town on southwest coast of Greenland, south of Umanak. Mission station of the Moravians. Originally a group of huts built by Moravian missionaries, which now has grown to be quite an extensive settlement. Occupied 1733 by Matthew and Christian Stach, the first missionaries to Greenland. Has 1 missionary.

**New Providence Island,** Bahamas, West Indies, 17 miles long, 7 broad. More hilly than most islands of the group. Has fertile lands and produces good fruit. Population, 10,000. Chief town, Nassau. Mission field Baptist Missionary Society; 1 missionary, 2 evangelists, 5 out-stations, 412 church-members, 57 day and 430 Sabbath-scholars. Wesleyan Methodist Missionary Society; 2 missionaries, 73 native helpers, 962 church-members, 6 chapels, 1 school, 26 scholars.

**New Rotterdam,** an out-station of the Moravian station of Waterloo, in Surinam, South America, built on a narrow peninsula north of the river Nickeris, in the village of New Rotterdam. The sea has made such encroachments on this peninsula that the church and mission buildings have been twice removed farther inland.

**New Zealand.**—The colony of New Zealand consists of three islands, viz., North, South, and Stewart's Islands, together with certain small islets. The North Island is 44,000 square miles, the South Island 55,000, and Stewart's Island 1,000 square miles. Thus the area of the three islands in round numbers is about 100,000 square miles. The principal islands are separated by Cook's Straits, and Stewart's Island by Foveaux Straits. The entire length of the colony is 1,100 miles, and resembles Italy in form, while in size it is somewhat less than Great Britain and Ireland. In the North Island the mountains occupy one tenth of the surface, and vary in height from 1,500 to 6,000 feet in height. There are a few loftier volcanic mountains, as Tongariro (6,500 feet), which is occasionally active; Ruaperhui (9,100 feet), and Mount Egmont are extinct volcanoes above the snow-line. In the South Island Mount Cook rises to about 13,000 feet in height. New Zealand is situated in the South Pacific Ocean, 1,200 miles south of the Australian continent, and about 8,000 miles from San Francisco. The entire group lies between 34° and 48° S. latitude and 166° and 179° E. longitude.

The climate of New Zealand is unquestionably one of the finest in the world. "The climate's delicate, the air most sweet, fertile is the isle." The mean annual temperature of the different seasons for the whole colony is, in spring 55°, in summer 63°, in autumn 57°, and in winter 48°. In future it will become the favorite resort of persons seeking health from all parts of the world, possessing, as it does within a limited area, the most charming scenery and most desirable climate. The death-rate is only 10.29 per 1,000.

The natives are of Malay origin, and superior to other inhabitants of the Pacific, intellectually and physically. The Maori is the average size of a European, viz., 5 ft. 6 in., but not so well developed. Mentally the natives are capable of very considerable development, and may hereafter fulfil Lord Macaulay's prediction of them.

The government is administered by a Governor appointed by the crown, and a Ministry, a Legislative Council nominated by the crown, and a House of Representatives elected by the people. Though the provincial system of government is abolished, the colony is divided, as heretofore, into the following provincial districts:

Auckland, population 130,379; Taranaki, population 17,999; Wellington (seat of government), 77,536; Hawke's Bay, 24,568; Marlborough, 11,113; Nelson, 30,203; Westland, 15,931; Canterbury, 121,400; Otago, 140,154; Chatham Islands, 199; total, including Chinese and half-castes, 578,482. A census is taken every three years. The last census, in December, 1888, estimated the population in round numbers, exclusive of aborigines, at 607,380. The Maoris, estimated in 1835 at 2,000,000, now number about 40,000, divided into many tribes, and scattered over an area of 45,156 square miles. They are chiefly located in the North Island. Only some 2,000 are found living on the reserves provided by the government in the South Island. The king (nominal) resides in Waikato, in the provincial district of Auckland. His influence is paramount within a limited radius. Occasionally he emerges from his solitude and reaches the confines of civilization, and learns European vices. He donned the blue ribbon some years ago, and the outside world has not heard much of him since. Recently, too, there has been a disposition to resort to pagan forms of worship. Gradually, however, the barriers are giving way before the rising, advancing tide of Christian influences, and though the social condition of the aborigines is far from satisfactory, there is an undoubted movement upward in some districts of New Zealand. It is a wise provision of government to give them power to elect members to represent them in the legislature, which meets yearly to make laws for the peace, order, and good government of the colony.

New Zealand was first discovered by Tasman in 1642, and surveyed by Captain Cook in 1770. Thereafter it was frequently visited by whalers; and eventually the first missionary of the cross landed in 1814, and entered upon his labor of love at the close of that year. The apostle of the Maoris is the Rev. Samuel Marsden, and to him belongs the honor of having publicly unfurled the banner of the cross in the "Greater Britain" of the South.

Marsden was the chaplain at the penal settlement of Port Jackson, and he was greatly struck by the Maoris, who used occasionally to visit Sydney as working hands in whalers and small merchantmen. He built a hut in his parsonage grounds for their reception, and had as many as thirty staying with him at one time. He was greatly impressed by their superiority over other savages, and in 1807, when he visited England, he persuaded the Church Missionary Society to undertake the establishment of a mission in this colony. Delays of various kinds took place. Just as the mission party were about to leave Sydney on one occasion, news arrived of what is known as the "Massacre of the Boyd" at the harbor of Whangaroa. The natives attacked the vessel out of revenge for indignities suffered by one of their chiefs at the hands of the captain, the vessel was burned, and the crew and passengers, amounting to nearly seventy persons, were killed, only eight having escaped. The general horror caused by this event was greatly increased by the "o'er true tale" of cannibalism connected with it. In 1814 Marsden purchased the brig "Active," of 110 tons burden, to be mainly used for the purpose of the mission. After she had paid a preliminary visit to New Zealand to reconnoitre, Marsden, on the 19th November, 1814, embarked on board to formally open the mission. He took with him three lay missionaries, Kendall, Hall, and King, with their wives and children, an adventurous friend named Nicholas, and eight Maoris, including a chief named Ruatara, whom he had befriended in Sydney, and his uncle, the far-famed Hongi, destined ere long to become the most powerful man in New Zealand. The "Active" first went to Whangaroa, the scene of the Boyd massacre, where Marsden succeeded in winning the confidence of the natives, and afterwards to Rangihoua, Ruatara's village in the Bay of Islands. We have a graphic account of the first service, which was held on Christmas Day. Ruatara enclosed about half an acre of land with a rough fence, erected a reading desk and pulpit in the centre, and covered the erection with some black cloth he had brought from Sydney for the purpose. He also arranged some old canoes on each side of the pulpit as seats for the English; the native portion of the congregation was to sit, according to custom, on the ground. Finally he rigged up a flagstaff and ran up the English colors. The service was begun by singing the Old Hundredth Psalm. While the service was being read the natives stood up, and sat down at the signals given by Korokoro's switch, which was regulated by the movements of the Europeans. Marsden preached from the text, "Behold, I bring you glad tidings of great joy," and at the end of the sermon Ruatara told the natives in their own language what the missionary had been talking about. "In this manner," says Marsden in his journal, "the

gospel has been introduced into New Zealand, and I fervently pray that the glory of it may never depart from its inhabitants till time shall be no more." The whole scene must have been as dramatic and affecting as anything recorded in the romance of missions.

The work thus inaugurated by Mr. Marsden and his coadjutors under the auspices of the Church Missionary Society advanced through various vicissitudes until in the year of grace 1841 Bishop Selwyn was consecrated Bishop of New Zealand (see Melanesian Mission). He was a prince of missionaries, and with apostolic zeal and fidelity consecrated his noble talents to the cause of his divine Lord. There are many at this hour in the colony whose lives have been influenced for good by his wise and truly Christian counsel. He was a true friend to more than one missionary outside the pale of the Church of England. The next to enter the field were the Wesleyans.

It was in 1822 that the pioneers of Methodism first set foot in New Zealand. In February of that year the Rev. Samuel Leigh commenced a mission in the North Island, under the auspices of the Standing Committee of the Wesleyan Methodist Church in London. The first station was planted at Kaeo, Whangaroa, in the northernmost part of what is now the Auckland Provincial District. Here the Rev. Nathaniel Turner, father of Mr. C. W. Turner of Christchurch, took charge in 1823. For over four years the work was carried on; but the soil was stubborn, little progress was made, and at last disaster overtook the mission. On January 9th, 1827, Hongi Hika, the famous chief of the Ngapuhis, "The Napoleon of New Zealand," advanced on Whangaroa, and the station was destroyed. Mr. Turner and his family, alarmed in the night, fled through the bush for twenty miles, to Keri-Keri, the Church of England mission station on the Bay of Islands. The fugitives were in serious peril during their flight, but their lives were saved by the chief Patuone, known afterwards in colonial days as Edward Marsh, and near Keri-Keri they were met by the Episcopalian missionary, the Rev. Mr. Williams, who with a party of natives went out to succor them. On January 31st the members of the Wesleyan Mission left for New South Wales. They did not long allow the ground to lie idle, however, for towards the end of the year they had re-established a mission in New Zealand. The station was at Hokianga, and was under the charge of the Revs. John Hobbs and Stack. The progress of the work was at first slow. Up to the middle of 1830 the missionaries had obtained no success, and were apprehensive that orders would be received from England to break up the station. Under this impression Mr. Hobbs wrote home requesting permission to be allowed to remain alone. But a reaction was at hand. Later in the year the missionaries were able to report that twenty-eight young men and boys and six young women were living in the station under instruction. By the end of 1831 there were some converts, and the first class, of five men, was formed. The Rev. John Whiteley, who met a martyr's death in the last war, arrived at the Bay of Islands on May 21st, 1833. The mission work was now extending, and needed more laborers. In the school there were four hundred scholars, chiefs, old and young men and women, and even slaves. The first great success of the mission occurred in 1834. On one Sunday in that year eighty-one converts were baptized, and fourteen couples married in the mission chapel at Mangungu. In December of the same year there arrived at Hokianga the Rev. James Wallis, still living at Auckland, after more than fifty years' service in the Wesleyan ministry. In 1835, with Mr. Whiteley, he founded a station at Kawhia. In 1836 the Rev. J. Buller, well remembered in Canterbury, came to New Zealand as tutor to Mr. Turner's family. At the end of 1837 there were fifteen chapels or out-stations in connection with the parent chapel at Mangungu and on the Hokianga River. A printing-press had been set up at the mission station, and thousands of small books, in Maori, were issued therefrom. In 1838 the mission house and store at Mangungu were accidentally burned, their inmates escaped with difficulty, and but little of their contents was saved, despite the gallant efforts of the Maoris. This year the worshippers at the mission chapel at the same place had increased to a thousand.

*The Wesleyan Church in the Colony.*—On March 19th, 1839, the Rev. J. H. Bumby, who was drowned little more than a year later in the Waitemata, arrived from England to take charge of the mission. He was accompanied by Miss Bumby and by the Revs. C. Creed and S. Ironsides. Next year it was announced that there were connected with the mission 1,300 communicants or accredited church-members, and 600 catechumens or persons on trial. In 1844 the Rev. Walter Lawry landed at Auckland, and was instrumental in establishing a college in that town, and a native model school at the Three Kings. In 1855 the Australian Conference was formed, the first session being held in Sydney, under the presidency of the Rev. W. B. Boyce. This Conference undertook the control of the New Zealand Missions. By that time the Wesleyan Church in this colony had 16 circuits or stations, 20 European ministers, 508 European and 3,070 Maori members, 2,514 European and 7,590 Maori adherents, 733 European and 4,418 Maori Sunday-scholars, 19 churches for Europeans and 74 for Maoris, 21 other preaching places for Europeans, and 121 for Maoris. The history of the English Wesleyan Church, under the Australian Conference, is one of steady progress ; that of the Maori Church one of disaster. Through the spread of the Hau-hau (a tribe living in the Waikato valley south of Auckland) superstition, and the diminution in the numbers of the native race, the membership fell from thousands to a few hundreds. The brave Whiteley was shot at Whitecliffs in 1869, by the men to whose welfare he had devoted a lifetime, and for a time the Maori Wesleyan Church, like the other native churches, in the North Island at all events, seemed in danger of being almost swept away.

It is a strange coincidence, and yet not strange, that both societies should have almost analogous experience. Early in the field, and enjoying signal blessing in their work, we find the Wesleyan missionaries full of gladness; anon they were, in 1869, filled with sorrow and dismay at the disasters brought on by war and superstition. Very similar was the ordeal through which the Church Missionary Society had to pass. The first bishop of that Society (Selwyn) traversed the colony by land and sea, and wrote home: "Everywhere I see the people eager for instruction, meeting for daily prayers, keeping the Sabbath, learning to read portions of God's Word translated into their language: in short, I seem to see a nation born in a day." Then followed the war and its attendant evils, which seemed for a time to completely arrest missionary operations in New Zealand. It was not until 1841 that the Presbyterian Church entered upon this field of labor. The Reformed Presbyterian Church of Scotland sent out two saintly men, Messrs. Duncan and Inglis. The former is the patriarch minister of Foxton, who takes a warm interest in the evangelization of the natives; the latter is the ex-missionary of the New Hebrides who has translated the New Testament into the language of that interesting people. Both the Presbyterian Church of New Zealand and the Church of Otago and Southland take a deep interest in the aborigines, and for many years have employed agents specially among them. The Rev. Mr. Blake, M.A., labored successfully in the South, while Messrs. Honoré and Milson have toiled in the North Island amid many discouragements, but not without some measure of encouragement. Mr. Honoré, in 1889, reported to the committee that "the moral and religious life of the Maoris in some parts of his district would compare favorably with that of an equal number of Europeans." From many directions prayers ascend in behalf of the Maoris that they may be saved. The Baptists of New Zealand were not unmindful of the Maoris, but could not well overtake the work. However, a Christian friend communicated with Mr. Spurgeon and succeeded in having a missionary sent from the Pastor's College to labor in the North Island. The Salvation Army also has penetrated into the dark places of heathenism, and in its own way arrested the attention of the natives. How far it has influenced the native mind and heart it is difficult to conjecture. Enough has been stated to make it evident that the gospel through diverse agencies has been brought within the reach of all classes of society, both European and native. The desideratum in the colony at this moment is the moving of God's Spirit upon the people. Meantime the work of organization progressed steadily. The Church of England, under the able guidance of Bishop Selwyn, had its foundations laid firmly. The Free Church of Scotland in its infancy turned its thoughts to the "Brighter Britain of the South" as a suitable field for emigration. Hither, therefore, her wise sons came under the pastoral care of Dr. Burns, and under the serene southern sky unfurled the blue banner of Presbyterianism. Hence Otago and Southland bear the impress of Knox on the educational and ecclesiastical systems formulated in the southern part of the colony. Happily from one end of New Zealand to the other the leading Presbyterian churches of the world are blended into one brotherhood, and the antipodes present to the world an undivided and sacred oneness, except in so far as Otago and Southland are geographically and otherwise a distinct and separate synod for a time. The Wesleyan Church, as already indicated, developed marvellously. From being an outpost it began to assume the form of a duly constituted organization.

In 1874 the Wesleyan Church in this colony had grown to such dimensions that the New Zealand Conference was formed, with administrative but not legislative functions. The first session was held in Christ Church, and the late Rev. Thomas Buddle, a veteran of the early days, was elected president. There were then 114 European and 12 native churches, with 148 other preaching places. The ministers, including supernumeraries, missionaries, and probationers, numbered 56. There were 198 local preachers, 170 class-leaders, 2,937 church-members, 23,793 attendants at public worship, and 8,460 Sunday-scholars, with 900 teachers.

Since the establishment of the New Zealand Conference the church has more than doubled its membership, and the work among the Maoris has shown signs of revival. According to the statistics presented to the last Conference, there were, at the end of 1888, 192 European and 16 native Wesleyan churches, 274 European and 33 Maori other preaching places, 85 ministers, 343 European and 46 Maori local preachers, 236 European and 13 Maori class-leaders, 7,121 European and 294 Maori church-members, 5,059 persons on trial for membership, 47,999 European and 2,766 native attendants at public worship, and 18,633 Sunday-scholars with 2,039 teachers. What a contrast these figures present to those of 1855, when the European Church members were but 500, while those of the Maori race numbered 3,000.

The principal feature of Wesleyan Church history of recent years has been the movement for separation from the Australasian General Conference, and for the establishment of a conference with legislative powers in New Zealand. A proposition to effect this was rejected at the meeting of the General Conference in Christ Church in 1884. The principal reforms which the advocates of separation wished to effect in the church were two—firstly, the extension of the term of the itinerancy, so as to enable ministers, with the consent of their congregations, to remain at one station for more than three years; and, secondly, the recognition as church-members of godly persons who do not meet in class. After the rejection of the proposals for independence in 1884 it was hoped that the General Conference would grant these reforms to the whole of the Wesleyan Church in Australasia. The last meeting of that conference, however, passed over without this being done, and it remains to be seen what action will be taken by the New Zealand Wesleyans in consequence.

Nor did the Congregationalists and Baptists fail to organize themselves into unions. The manifold advantages of these unions and conferences are recognized specially in relation to work in other parts of the world. It is a pleasing feature in the colony to find the missionary spirit universally diffused through all the evangelical denominations. In every instance aid is given to missions in other parts of the world while eagerly prosecuting evangelistic work and building up the cause of Christ in New Zealand itself. Home-mission work is best fostered by evangelizing the regions beyond.

The churches of New Zealand have sought from the beginning to make the adjacent islands of the Pacific the chief centre of evangelization. Bishop Selwyn not only attended to the spiritual wants of the colony, but established successfully an important mission in Melanesia, with Norfolk as headquarters. In 1855 the martyr Bishop Patteson was appointed to take the oversight thereof. It is now a diocese of New Zealand,

and the present bishop (son of Bishop Selwyn) has a seat in the General Synod.

The Presbyterian Church has devoted its attention specially to work among the aborigines of the New Hebrides. This field is sacred, not only by the blood of Williams, but also by the blood of the devoted Gordons. The Rev. W. Watt and his wife have labored there on the island of Tanna for twenty-one years, and at length the cheering intelligence reaches the colony of spiritual quickening. The island of Ambrim was occupied by the faithful missionary Charles Murray and his devoted wife, who was taken from his side. This island is now to be occupied by another laborer. Besides these Messrs. Milne and Michelsen are toiling at Nguna and Spi, and Mr. Smail was recently ordained and appointed to this promising field of labor. The group of islands which bear this name are situated to the northeast of New Caledonia and to the west of the Fijis, in south latitude between 14° and 20°, estimated at 2,500 square miles. The group embraces Espiritu Santo, Mallicollo, Ambrim, Aneityum, Eromanga, Tanna, etc. The inhabitants, variously estimated at from 50,000 to 150,000, are largely savage, though a goodly number are in touch with the gospel. There are in all 17 European missionaries connected with the mission. Besides these more than 100 native teachers perform the offices of preachers, evangelists, and teachers on twenty different islands.

Thus the churches of New Zealand co-operate with the Free Church of Scotland and the Presbyterian Churches of Canada and Australia in evangelizing the New Hebrideans. The Word of God has been translated in the languages of several islands. The climate is trying in some parts, and the French for a time menaced the mission, but hitherto the Lord has blessed and protected His work in these islands of the sea.

The Wesleyan Church dispatched the Rev. G. Brown to New Britain, with some helpers from Tonga and Fiji. Unfortunately four of these men were murdered. Still the work was prosecuted with zeal and firmness, and now solid progress has been made.

The Congregationalists have co-operated with the London Missionary Society, and in a general way gave monetary help, though they have no distinct organization otherwise of their own in the Pacific, nor do they employ any missionaries of their own. The Baptists, on the other hand, are specially interested in India, and have sent two ladies to engage in zenana work. Considering the limited membership of this church, they have done noble service for the Lord in establishing this important mission.

From the above outline it will appear that New Zealand is not unmindful of her duty to the heathen in the South Sea Islands. The results achieved may not appear to critics commensurate with the treasure and blood expended, nevertheless real progress has been made by the various organizations employed in preaching the gospel to the heathen. The church, however, is only now fully awakening to the magnitude and urgency of the work to be done in the Pacific for the Lord Jesus. Meanwhile the wonder is to see so many islands which a few years ago were the habitations of horrid cruelty now enjoying the light and love of heaven. The results cannot be tabulated by pen and ink. There shall come from these southern seas an innumerable company which no man can number, of all nations and kindreds and people and tongues. Even so, come, Lord Jesus, and reign over these lovely isles of the sea !

Missionary societies at work in New Zealand: C. M. S., with 38 stations in the three dioceses of Auckland, Waiapu, and Wellington; 15 ordained missionaries, 2 unordained, 515 church-members. Their work is among the Maoris. Wesleyan Methodist Missionary Society, with a large number of stations; 204 churches. Primitive Methodist Missionary Society, with stations at Auckland, Dunedin, Oamaru, Waimate, South Invercargill; 279 church-members, 33 native workers, 10 schools, 901 scholars. United Methodist Free Churches, with stations at Addington, Auckland, Christchurch, Malvern, Napier, Oxford, Rangiora, Reefton, Richmond, Wellington, Westport and Charleston, and Woodville; 80 native workers, 898 church-members. Colonial and Continental Society, North German Missionary Society, Seventh Day Adventists (America).

**Newton, John, Jr.,** b. Lodiana, India, 1838. He was the eldest of the four sons of Rev. John Newton, Sr., who were all born in India and educated in America. John, the subject of this sketch, graduated at the medical college in the University of Pennsylvania, went to India independently of the Board, became a member of the mission in 1860, and was afterwards ordained to the ministry by the Presbytery of Lodiana. His first regular work as a doctor was at Kupoorthula, but from 1866 to 1880 he was stationed at Sabathoo, where he had a dispensary. After Dr. Newton was posted there, the poor-house, established forty years before, became the Leper Asylum. As a physician, he took special interest in the lepers, and experimented with the view of discovering some medicine that might arrest the progress of the disease. He built several houses near the mission-house that he might the more effectively minister to his patients. Considering them not as medical patients only, but as the poor who needed the gospel, he had a small building erected, which served the double purpose of a dispensary and a chapel, and there the lepers assembled daily for worship, on the Lord's Day holding special services. Dr. Newton was an earnest preacher, skilful physician, and an excellent writer. Though of scholarly turn, he was much engaged in itineration, bazaar preaching, and labor among the soldiers of the local garrison. His most responsible charge was that of the Leper Asylum, having 89 inmates. A missionary associate thus speaks of him after his death: "No love in this dark world has ever seemed to me so much like the Saviour's as that of Dr. Newton for his lepers." A correspondent of one of the Indian newspapers says: "He was a true missionary, obeying in the letter and in the spirit the command given to the first missionaries, not only, 'preach, saying the kingdom of heaven is at hand,' but, 'heal the sick, cleanse the lepers.' He did this so far as medical skill and sanitary science enabled him."

Dr. Newton died July 29th, 1880, of cancer of the stomach, after a period of great suffering. The funeral was numerously attended by Europeans and natives. Soldiers who loved him carried the coffin from the house to the cemetery.

His father, who had been fifty years a missionary in India, read a part of the Episcopal service, closing with an address. The hymn, "Home at last, my labor's done," was sung. The mission say: "His fine endowments, thorough knowledge of the language, great devotion to the work, make his removal a severe loss to the missionary cause."

**Neyoor,** a city in South Travancore, India, 300 miles south of Madras. Hinduism, Mohammedanism, devil worship, and various forms of degrading superstitions are met with among the Hindus, Pulyars, and aborigines who compose the population. The caste system prevails, and the marriage ties are very loose. The climate is hot, and in some parts very unhealthy; average temperature 80° F.; annual rainfall, 50 inches. Mission station London Missionary Society (1828); 1 missionary, 1 layworker and wife, 1 female missionary, 60 outstations, 4 native ministers, 1,112 church-members, 47 Sabbath-schools, 2,140 scholars, 42 dayschools, 2,678 scholars.

**Nez Perces Version.**—The Nez Perces belongs to the languages of North America, and is spoken by the Indians of Idaho. A translation of the Gospel of Matthew was made by the Rev. H. H. Spaulding of the Oregon Mission of the A. B. C. F. M., was first printed in Oregon in 1845, and was reprinted by the American Bible Society in 1871. A translation of the Gospel of John was made by the Rev. George Ainslee, and printed by the Presbyterian Board of Publication at Philadelphia in 1876.

(*Specimen verse.* Matthew 28 : 19.)

Kunki wiwihnath, awltaaishkaiikith, uyikashliph, wiwatashph, Awibaptainaiikith immuna Pishitpim wanikitph, wah Miahspim. Wanikitph, Wah Holy Ghostnim wanikitph.

**Ng'anga** or **Chinyana Version.**—The Ng'anga belongs to the Bantu family of African languages, and is spoken by tribes living around Lake Nyassa. In 1886 the National Bible Society of Scotland published the New Testament in that language.

**Ngkangphu,** in the province of Kwangtung, China. Station of the English Presbyterian Mission among the Hakkas.

**Ngombe,** town in the Congo, West Africa, between Lukolela and Equator station. Mission station Baptist Missionary Society; 3 missionaries, 15 church-members, 36 scholars, 38 Sabbath-scholars.

**Nguna,** a volcanic isle among the southernmost New Hebrides, Melanesia; has 800 inhabitants. Station of the New Hebrides Mission, supported by the Church of Otago. A congregation of 40 church-members, among whom is the chief, who had to dismiss 9 wives before baptism.

**Nguna Version.**—The Nguna belongs to the Melanesian languages, and is spoken in the New Hebrides. In the year 1870 the Rev. Peter Milne from the Presbyterian Church of New Zealand settled there. In 1882 he published his translation of the Gospels of John and Matthew at the expense of the British and Foreign Bible Society. Besides these two Gospels, the same Society published in 1886 the other two Gospels, and the Acts, also translated by Mr. Milne, who claims that his translations are intelligible to about 7,000 people. Of the Nguna version about 2,020 portions of the Scripture have thus far been disposed of.

**Nias Islands**, a small group lying to the west of Sumatra, in latitude 1° north, is composed of one large island and several islets, and is part of the Dutch Residency of east coast, Sumatra. Area, 2,523 square miles. The Rhenish Missionary Society has 2 stations on the main island, at Gunong Sitoli and Fagulo, both on the east coast of the island. The population is estimated at 230,000, who speak a distinctive language, into which portions of the Bible have been translated.

**Nias Version.**—The Nias belongs to the Malaysian languages, and is spoken in the island of Nias, near Sumatra. Rev. J. Deminger recently undertook a translation of the Scriptures into this language. He was especially fitted for such a work, for he had committed the language to writing, and had prepared a grammar in Nias. At the request of the Rhenish Missionary Society, the British and Foreign Bible Society printed at London, in 1874, an experimental edition of the Gospel of Luke. The Book of Genesis has also been prepared for the press by the same translator.

(*Specimen verse.* Luke 22 : 70.)

Ando͡ wa lawá'o ira ma'afefu: Ya'ŭgŏ hŭlŏ dä sogi O'no Löwaläni? Ba mañuä'o Ia hŏrä ando: Iämi ande mañuä'o, mŏ Ia'ŏdo ande só Ia andó.

**Nicaragua**, a republic of Central America, bounded north by Honduras, east by the Caribbean Sea, south by Costa Rica, and west by Pacific Ocean. Area, about 49,500 square miles. The principal mountains are in a range from 10 to 20 miles back of the west coast, and running parallel to it, sometimes rising in high volcanic cones, sometimes subsiding into low plains or places of slight elevation; it seems to have been the principal line of volcanic action, and Nicaragua is marked by some very high volcanoes. The Coco River, which rises in the Segovia Mountains, is the longest of Central America, its course being about 350 miles. The San Juan River, 120 miles long, is the only outlet of the beautiful lakes of Managua and Nicaragua. The country is rich in minerals, especially gold and silver. Climate, except in the very highest portions, is essentially tropical; the northeast part is very damp, rainfall is moderate. The soil is very rich, particularly on the Pacific slope, where all tropical fruits and plants thrive abundantly. Population is about 350,000, consisting of aborigines, mulattoes, negroes, and mixed races. The full-blooded Indians, who are civilized, are a sober and industrious race, but the half-breeds are lazy, vicious, and ignorant. Education is at a low ebb. The state religion is Roman Catholic, and other religions are not publicly tolerated. The chief industry is cattle-raising.

The capital, Managua, has 8,000 inhabitants. Other cities are: St. Leon, the former capital, 25,000; and Nicaragua, 8,500. The constitution was proclaimed 1858. It provides for a congress, the members of both houses to be elected by universal suffrage. The President is elected for four years. The Nicaragua Canal, when completed, will add greatly to the importance and prosperity of the republic.

Mission work in Nicaragua is carried on by the Moravian Brethren in the coast region called the Mosquito Coast (q.v.), which was formerly an independent territory under the protectorate of Great Britain, but is now, by treaty of 1860, a part of Nicaragua. Recently (1890) permission has been given the Moravians by the Nicaraguan Government to follow their converts into the interior, from which the missionaries have been jealously excluded.

**Nicobar Islands** are a small group of islands attached to British India, lying in the Bay of Bengal, northeast of Sumatra, and south of the Andaman Islands. There are 8 large islands and 12 small ones. Great Nicobar is 30 miles long, and from 12 to 15 miles wide. The islands are well wooded and fertile. Cocoa-nuts are raised in great abundance. The aborigines are allied to the hill-tribes of Formosa. The Nicobar swallow is the builder of the edible birds' nests, so highly prized by the Chinese, and they are the principal exports together with bêche-de-mer, tortoise-shell, and ambergris.

Mission work is carried on in these islands by the Danish Mission Society.

**Nicobar Version.**—The Nicobar belongs to the Malaysian languages, and is spoken in the Nicobar Islands, Bay of Bengal. The Rev. F. A. Ralpstorff of the Moravian Brethren Missionary Society is preparing for the British and Foreign Bible Society a translation of the New Testament.

**Nicomedia**, a city of Bithynia, Western Turkey, 60 miles from Constantinople, at the head of the gulf of the same name. It was the ancient capital of Bithynia, being built by Nicomedes I. in 264 B.C., and during the Roman Empire it was frequently used as an imperial residence. Under Turkish rule it decreased very much in importance, but has grown again since the extension of the railway from Constantinople into the interior of the province. Its Turkish name is Ismidt.

Mission station of the Western Turkey Mission of the A. B. C. F. M. (1840). It is a number of years since any missionary families have resided there, largely on account of the prevalence of malaria; Bardezag, just across the bay, and Adabazar, about 30 miles inland, being more healthy. There is a successful work in Nicomedia, and a church with a native pastor.

**Niigata**, a seaport and the place of greatest commercial importance on the west coast of the main island of Japan; population, 44,470 (1887). The city is neatly laid out; the streets levelled, paved with gravel, well drained, cleaned, and lighted with coal-oil obtained in the neighborhood. It has a flourishing inland trade, and contains national and private banks, a government hospital, and a school of foreign languages. Mission station of the A. B. C. F. M. (1883); 5 missionaries, 4 missionaries' wives, 5 other ladies, 15 native helpers, 7 out-stations, 2 churches, 226 church-members, 3 schools, 385 scholars. Reformed (Dutch) Church, U. S. A. 15 church-members.

**Ninghsia**, prefectural city in extreme north part of province of Kan-suh, Northwest China, situated on the Yellow River. Mission station China Inland Mission (1885); 5 missionaries.

**Ningkwoh,** prefectural city in the province of Nganhwui, Eastern China, northwest of Hangchau and south of Nanking. Mission station of the China Inland Mission (1874); 4 missionaries, 2 native helpers, 1 church, 43 church-members, 5 chapels, 4 out-stations, 1 school, 10 scholars.

**Ningpo,** one of the five treaty ports of China, opened to foreigners by the treaty of 1842, is one of the most important cities of the empire, and the principal emporium of the Chekiang province. It stands east of the mountains, in a plain on the left bank of the Takia or Ningpo River, 16 miles from its mouth. The old wall surrounding it, 25 feet high and 16 feet broad, is in a good state of preservation. There are the usual gates of all Chinese walled cities, north, east, south, and west, and two others, besides two passages for boats, in the 5 miles circuit. The principal striking buildings are the large ice-houses; the Ningpo pagoda, 160 feet high; and the Drum-tower, built earlier than the 15th century. Temples and monasteries are numerous, and very handsome. The houses are mostly built of brick, and are usually of but one story. The city suffered from the ravages of the insurgents during the Taiping rebellion, when it was occupied for six months (1864).

The foreign trade of Ningpo is quite considerable. Silks, cottons (Nankeen takes its name from this city), straw hats, white-wood carvings, are the principal products. It was occupied by the English forces on the 12th of October, 1841, after the fort at the mouth of the river, Chinhai, was successfully stormed.

The climate of Ningpo is variable: the usual range of temperature is from 20°–100° F. The rainfall is excessive. The population of the city and surrounding plain is estimated at 500,000. A distinctive dialect is spoken, called the Ningpo.

Mission station of: A. B. M. U. (1843); 1 missionary and wife, 2 physicians and wives, 3 other ladies, 14 out-stations, 15 native preachers, 7 churches, 248 church-members, 3 Sunday-schools, 160 scholars, 9 schools, 125 scholars. Presbyterian Church (North), 1844; 2 missionaries and wives, 2 other ladies, 37 native assistants, 21 out-stations, 10 churches, 5 self-supporting, 760 communicants, 9 schools, 141 scholars. C. M. S. (1848); 3 missionaries, 2 female missionaries, 4 native ministers, 100 Christians, 1 college, 3 schools, 71 scholars. China Inland Mission (1857); 2 out-stations with a total of 107 communicants. Free Methodists, 2 itinerant preachers, 10 local preachers, 279 church-members, 4 chapels, 9 preaching places, 3 Sunday-schools, 23 scholars.

**Ningpo Colloquial Version.** — The Ningpo belongs to the languages of China, and is spoken in Ningpo and vicinity. An edition of the Chinese New Testament in the Ningpo colloquial was published at London in 1868 under the care of the Rev. Messrs. F. F. Gough and Hudson Taylor. The American Bible Society published a re-revised edition in 1880. An edition in Roman characters, prepared by the Rev. E. C. Lord of the A. B. M. U. Mission (who had previously issued a translation of Isaiah in 1870), was published in 1874. In

1871 the American Bible Society published the Books of Genesis and Exodus, both translated by the Rev. H. V. Rankin. The American Bible Society, which had already published the New Testament between 1853 and 1859, intends to publish the Old Testament in this dialect. At present a representative committee is at work revising the New Testament.

(*Specimen verse.* John 3 : 16.)
Roman.

Ing-we Jing-ming æ-sih shū-kœn-zông tao ka-go din-dj, we s-lôh Gyi-zi-go doh-yiang ng-ts, s-teh væn-pah siang-sīng Gyi cū-kwu feh-we mih-diao, tu hao teh-djôh üong-yün web-ming.

**Ningtaik,** district in the province of Fuhkien, China. Station of the C. M. S.; 376 communicants, 91 scholars.

**Nisbet, Henry,** b. September 2d, 1818, at Laurieston, Glasgow, Scotland; studied at Glasgow University, Relief Divinity Hall, Paisley, and Chesnut College; sailed August 11th, 1840, as a missionary of the L. M. S. to Tanna, one of the New Hebrides Islands. The natives were so hostile that he went to Upolu, where he settled soon at Fasitoonta, and had the charge of ten villages. He spent much time in visiting the out-stations, and was one of the missionaries who accompanied the Nova Scotia brethren to select their station in the New Hebrides, on the island of Aneityum. He was one of the revisers of the Samoan Bible.

On the death of Mr. Stallworthy in November, 1859, he removed to Malua and took charge of the mission seminary during Mr. Turner's absence. When Mr. Ellis left Samoa in 1862, in addition to the work of the seminary he took charge of the station and mission press. During his residence at Malua he prepared for the students many lectures, sermons, notes of Scripture, etc., which were subsequently published in England under his supervision. He spent some eight years longer in the mission field in various departments of usefulness, and died at Malua May 9th, 1876. He received the degree of LL.D. from the University of Glasgow.

**Nishiwo,** a city in the Nagoya district, Japan. Mission station of the Methodist Episcopal Church (North), U. S. A.; 1 native ordained pastor, 21 church-members, 20 Sabbath-scholars.

**Nisky** (Niesky), a town on south coast of St. Thomas Island, Virgin Group, West Indies, 1½ miles from St. Thomas town. Mission station of the Moravians (1753); 1 missionary and wife. A theological seminary for the natives was opened here in 1886.

**Niue or Savage Island,** one of the Tonga group, Eastern Polynesia, between the Hervey and Samoan Isles. Climate hot; temperature 75°–98° Fahr. Population, 4,726 stationary, and 363 away in ships, etc. Race, light copper-colored Malays, Polynesians, "Hawaiori." Language, a combination of Tongese and Samoan. Religion, Protestant. Government, a kingdom, ruled by head of clans under the king. Social condition now civilized, and very comfortable. The people are peaceable and good subjects, live in good houses, and are neatly clothed. Mission field of the L. M. S.;

1 missionary and wife, 11 native pastors, 25 other helpers, 11 stations, 11 churches, 1,450 church-members, 1 theological seminary, 20 students, 11 schools, 1,599 scholars.

**Niue Version.**—The Niue belongs to the Polynesian languages, and is vernacular to the people of Savage Island, who number about 5,000; of these 1,500 are now professing Christians. In 1861 the Rev. W. G. Lawes of the L. M. S. settled on the island, together with the Rev. George Pratt. Parts of the New Testament were printed at Sydney in 1863 by the New South Wales Auxiliary to the British and Foreign Bible Society, and in 1867 the entire New Testament was printed at Sydney in an edition of 3,500. The Book of Psalms was published in 1870. In 1873 a revised edition of the New Testament, and Psalms, Genesis, and Exodus, were carried through the press in England by Mr. Lawes; another edition of the New Testament and Psalms, and an edition of the Pentateuch was published by the British and Foreign Bible Society in 1881. Mr. Lawes continued the work of translating the Old Testament, and during the year 1888 Genesis to 2 Kings, with Isaiah, Jeremiah, and Jonah, were printed at Sydney, Mr. Pratt reading the proofs.

(*Specimen verse* John 3 : 16.)

Nukua pihia mai e fakaalofa he Atua mai ke he lalolagi, kua ta mai ai hana Tama fuataha, kia nakai mate taha ne tua kia ia, ka kia moua e ia e moui tukulagi.

**Nizam's Territories** (British India), one of the largest and most important of the so-called "protected" or feudatory states of India, governed by its own native prince (in this case a Mohammedan, the descendant of the "Nizam-ul-Mulk," or viceroy of the Deccan, who ruled the country as viceroy of the Mogul emperors of Delhi nearly two centuries ago, but in the decadence of the Delhi power rebelled and set up as an independent prince). A British resident is maintained at the Nizam's court (see article Native States). This state is officially known as the Haidarabad State—from the name of its chief city and capital. Among the people it is popularly spoken of as "the Mogalai,"—in allusion to the Mogul origin of its rulers. It lies in the centre of the great table-land which occupies almost all of India south of the Vindhya Mountains. The limits of the state are north latitude 15° 10' to 20° 4', and east longitude 74° 35' to 81° 25'. This does not include the district of Berar (which see), which is under British control, though nominally belonging to the Nizam's state. The area of the state without Berar is about 80,000 square miles. The population (1881), 9,845,594. Of this number about 10 per cent are Mohammedans; and as the ruling dynasty is Mohammedan, persons of that faith occupy not only the principal positions of trust and authority, but also pervade the lower ranks of both civil and military employment. The state lies just where several language areas meet; accordingly there is a great diversity of dialect within its borders. Marathi is spoken by the Hindu population of the west and northwest; Kanarese by the Hindus of the southwest; Telugu by those of the eastern districts; Hindustani by the Mohammedans throughout, though Persian is the court language; and the aboriginal tribes (Gonds, etc.) have, as elsewhere, each its own tongue. The chief city and capital is Haidarabad (north latitude 17° 22', east longitude 78° 30'), with a population, including suburbs, of 231,287, largely Mohammedan, though hardly any other city in India presents so great a variety of race. The people of the city are very warlike, and have the habit of going armed with an imposing number and variety of weapons, some of which, it is true, are antiquated, though on occasion capable of effective use. The same habit of carrying weapons is quite universal among Mohammedans throughout the state; to some extent Hindus also adopt it. It is not unusual to see, in some village bazaar, a man with a long matchlock musket over his shoulder, a curved sword in his hand, two or three daggers and knives of different patterns stuck into his girdle, and a shield of ancient pattern hanging down his back. The presence everywhere of these walking arsenals, together with the violent and bitter fanaticism of the average Mohammedan, and the feeling prevailing in the minds of the Moslem inhabitants of the Haidarabad state that it is a territory sacred to their faith and power, often renders missionary work there difficult, not to say dangerous; no Christian preacher has ever been actually assailed, though sometimes threats of violence are made. It is not considered safe for Europeans to venture into Haidarabad City without the permission of the authorities, or without adequate protection. In other parts of the territory life and property are usually safe. Secunderabad, a city closely adjoining Haidarabad, is assigned to the British as the headquarters of the Haidarabad subsidiary force,—furnished and officered by the British Government and paid for from the revenues of Berar. Secunderabad being thus directly under British control is a perfectly safe place for missionary operations, which have been for some time in progress under the care of the Wesleyans. The American Methodists also have stations in the Nizam's dominions, as well as the S. P. G. The American Board's Mission among the Marathas has extended its operations into some of the villages in the western part of the state, adjacent to the British districts in which the work of that mission chiefly lies. Their work in the Nizam's territory has been largely done by native itinerants and pastors, and has affected principally persons of the Mang caste—one of the lowest of the outcaste classes of the Maratha country. Education in the Nizam's State is rather backward, and the general condition of the country, as shown by its roads, postal system, and other appliances of civilization, attests the inefficiency and carelessness of Oriental rule. Yet the constant example of the British Government is not lost upon the leading men in the Haidarabad state, and the government is striving, not altogether without success, to pattern its operations after the model thus set before it. The railway uniting Bombay and Madras passes through the Nizam's state, and about 15 years ago a branch line to Haidarabad City was constructed by the Nizam's Government,—though not without opposition from some of the older and more bigoted Mohammedans,—and thus his capital city is brought into direct communication with outside civilization. On the whole, although this Mohammedan area in the midst of territories under the control of an enlightened

Christian nation is still to a degree benighted, yet rays of light are beginning to dawn over it, and civilizing influences are slowly penetrating it from all sides.

**Njcmo** or **Wonoredjo,** a station of the Netherlands Missionary Society, Evangelical Church, in Java, East Indies. It has 257 church-members. (See Wonoredjo.)

**Njenhangli,** a station of the Basle Missionary society in the province of Kwangtung, China; 3 missionaries, 16 native helpers, 453 church-members, 197 scholars.

**Nogai Turki,** also called the Karass Turki, a dialect spoken by the Tartars in Ciscaucasia and on the lower Volga in Russia. The Pentateuch and New Testament have been translated and published by the B. and F. Bible Society.

**Nongkhyllem,** station of the Welsh Calvinistic Methodists, in the Shillong district, Assam, India; 3 churches, 68 communicants, 176 Sunday-scholars, 56 day-scholars.

**Nongrymai,** a village in the Khasia Hills, Assam, India, containing only 40 houses. Together with Nongrang it is a mission station of the Welsh Calvinistic Methodists; 2 churches, 46 communicants, 154 Sabbath-scholars, 63 day-scholars. One missionary and his wife are in charge of the district, which includes eight villages.

**Nongsawlia,** a station of the Welsh Calvinistic Methodist Church in the Cherra district, Assam, India; 2 native preachers, 131 communicants, 296 Sabbath-scholars.

**Nongtrai,** mission station of the Welsh Calvinistic Methodists, in Shella district, Assam, India; 1 church, 1 preacher, 13 communicants, 35 Sabbath-scholars, 46 day-scholars.

**Nongwah.**—1. Station of the Welsh Calvinistic Methodists in the Shillong district, Assam, India; 3 churches, 45 communicants, 194 Sabbath-scholars, 67 day-scholars.—2. Station of the Welsh Calvinistic Methodists in the Shella district.

**Nongwar,** station of the Welsh Calvinistic Methodists in the Shella district, Assam, India; 1 church, 1 preacher, 31 communicants, 56 Sabbath-scholars, 29 day-scholars.

**Nononti,** one of the Gilbert Islands, Micronesia. Mission station of the Hawaiian Evangelical Society (1887). Population, 2,500; 2 native teachers.

**Nonpareil,** a station of the S. P. G. in British Guiana, South America, with 171 Chinese and 172 Hindu Christians.

**Norfolk Island,** a dependency of New South Wales, Australia; the largest and finest of a small cluster of islands consisting of Norfolk, Nepean, and Philip Islands. Area, 14 square miles; elevation, 400 feet. Population, 500. Mission station of the S. P. G.; 1 missionary. Headquarters of the Melanesian Mission (q. v.).

**North Africa Mission.** Headquarters, 19 and 21 Linton Road, Barking, England.—With the fall of the French Empire and the establishment in its place of the French Republic, religious liberty was granted not only to France, but also to Algeria, which was sub-

duced by her in 1830. Thus was North Africa opened for the introduction of the gospel. Mr. George Pearce, who was providentially led to visit Algeria in 1876, revisited it in 1880, and returning to England aroused considerable interest in the Kabyles, a portion of the Berber tribes inhabiting the mountains a little to the east of the city of Algiers. A mission to these interesting people was started. Mr. Grattan Guinness, who paid a brief visit to Algeria, and Mr. Edward Glenny, who had independently been making investigations as to the condition of Morocco and Algeria, united in forming a committee for its management. In November of 1881 Mr. Pearce accompanied by Mr. Glenny returned to Algeria, taking with them two young brethren to work under Mr. Pearce's direction. They settled at Djemmâa Sahrij, but met with so much difficulty through the suspicion and opposition of the French local administrator, that one of the young men, a Syrian, retired from the work, and the other returned in the summer of 1882 to Europe to seek a fellow-laborer with a French diploma who might be more favorably received by the local authorities. After encountering many difficulties, which threatened again and again to destroy the whole work, the mission was reorganized in 1883. Several other friends joined in forming a council, and a fresh band of workers was taken out by Mr. Glenny, who then proceeded to Tangier, the council having determined to widen its sphere to the other aboriginal or Berber races of North Africa. Since then it has step by step extended its work, establishing stations in various places in Morocco, Algeria, Tunis, and Tripoli, and a branch mission to the Bedouins in Northern Arabia. It now no longer confines itself to the Berbers, but seeks to evangelize among all the Moslems, and is hoping to do definite work also among Europeans and Jews. There are seven fields into which the work is divided, which though they are small are each worked under distinct direct control from London.

The character of the mission is, like that of the Young Men's and Young Women's Christian Associations, evangelical, and embraces members of all denominations who are sound in their views on fundamental truths. The missionaries seek, by itinerant and localized work, to sell or distribute the Scriptures far and wide; and by conversation in the houses, streets, shops, and markets, in town and country, to teach Christian doctrine, encouraging to profession of faith and baptism.

Educational work is not a prominent feature in this mission, but is subordinate to evangelistic work. Medical aid has been found most useful in removing prejudices. A hospital and dispensary are established at Tangier and a dispensary at Fez, but in Algeria much difficulty has been experienced through the law forbidding the practice of medicine without a French diploma. Stations have been formed at Tangier, Tetuan, and Sifroo, in Morocco; Tlemcen, Oran, Mostaganem, Akbou, Djemmâa Sahrij, and Constantine, in Algeria; Tunis and Tripoli, and at Homs, in Syria, northeast of Beyrout. This is the only mission seeking to fill the great field of Northwest Africa.

**North German Missionary Society.** Headquarters, 26 Ellhorn Street, Bremen, Germany.—From the early years of this century missionary unions have existed in North Germany. The first one—not to speak of a loosely organized company, the "mustard-seed," in East Friesland—was formed in Bremen in December, 1819. Their first collections were sent to Janicke in Berlin, and to Basle; during the very first year of the organization two men presented themselves to be sent as missionaries, and this led to vigorous work to support them. The establishment of this union is attributed to the interest awakened by Janicke's work in Berlin, and the visit of Missionary La Roche to Bremen on his way from Basle to London.

In the following years unions were formed in Lübeck (1820) and in Hamburg (1823), both sending their contributions to Basle. In these early years great opposition was experienced from the authorities and mockery from the people. No church could be secured for their annual meetings, and notices of them could not be inserted in the papers in connection with other religious announcements.

The first movement towards a work in common was an invitation extended by the State Bible and Missionary Union to the neighboring Hanover and Hanseatic Unions to attend its annual meeting in 1834. An organic union was not contemplated, but it was hoped that the conference would be repeated in subsequent years. A young theological student resolved at the time to go as a missionary, stated his determination, and expressed the wish that he might in some way retain close connection with the unions. This led to consultation as to the advisability of forming a society for independent work. In June, 1835, a preliminary conference in Stade decided to make the proposal to the various unions to assemble for the sake of organizing into a society. This occurred April 9th, 1836—the date of the organization of the North German Missionary Society. The unions that thus united were Stade, Bremen, Hamburg, Lauenburg, Ritzebuttel, Lehe, and Bremerhaven. Before October, when the next meeting took place, Elmshorn and Holstein had joined the number. In this October meeting the permanent form of government was adopted, whereby the current affairs of the Society should be carried on by the committee in Hamburg, but its direction should remain in the hands of the unions that comprised the Society; these should assemble yearly, and all decisions should be by majorities. This confessedly clumsy form of management is thus accounted for by the history of the organization of the Society, as a federation of independent unions.

A second noticeable feature of the early period of the Society, and one destined to involve it in serious difficulties, was its confessional position. By § 2 of the statutes both Lutherans and Reformed were recognized as its supporters; the existing relations of the two churches were to be in no way prejudiced; denominational differences caused by the historical development of the two home churches were not to be propagated in the mission churches, but they were to be left to develop in their own ways. This section was adopted in October, 1836, in lieu of a statement agreed upon in April that the Augsburg Confession should be the norm. The Stade Union (Lutheran) objected to the earlier, as it might give offence to the Reformed. Such was the liberal spirit of the Lutherans at that time.

In 1837 the Missionary Institute was determined upon, and was established in Hamburg. Five years later the first men were sent out to New Zealand; in 1843 a temporary mission was started in India; in 1847 Western Africa was entered by missionaries of the Society.

We conclude first the sketch of the work at home. Before 1850 the unions in Altona, Rostock, Celle, Ludvigslust, Glückstadt, Neustrelitz, and Heide had joined the Society. The thirteen supported this organization exclusively, and had a vote in the general assembly. In addition, about thirty others sent contributions, extending from the Russian Baltic provinces westward, including Danzig, Leipsic, and Cassel, to East Friesland, and reaching northward to Alpenrade in Schleswig. Especially in Holstein and Schleswig, in Hanover and Bückeburg, did the Society find support. The year 1846 was perhaps the summit of the prosperity under the old régime, when the income reached 8,210 thalers, and West Africa was determined upon as the chief field of activity.

The confessional question from the first developed differences of opinion among the unions. As early as 1838 it was feared that the attitude of the statutes might be interpreted as one of indifference, and might allow doctrinal caprice on the field, and the assembly of that year directed two men to prepare an interpretation of the section. The discussion in 1839 was a friendly one, and resulted in the following resolutions: Section 2 was to remain unchanged; it was to determine the instruction in the institute, and the ordination of the missionaries; further, it was declared that confessional questions were not to be discussed in the Society. In spite of this, in 1841, similar questions arose. The Altona Union insisted that at one station there should be men of but one confession. In 1844 the Augsburg Confession of 1530 was adopted as the basis of work and of doctrine. But these concessions to the Lutherans failed to ward off the division. In 1849 a reorganization of the institute was resolved upon. The next year the situation at home was such, complicated as it was by discouragement in the field, that the very continuation of the Society became a matter of debate. While the possibility of maintaining it on the existing basis was unanimously conceded, the Mecklenburg Union announced that they would have to withdraw on confessional grounds. After their withdrawal, with the express statement that it was not on account of the leaders, but out of regard to other friends of missions in their territory and that of Harms, though in this case on other grounds than the confessional question, chiefly because of the peculiar character of the man, the Society's headquarters were removed to Bremen. The Union there assumed the direction, only on condition that the form of government be altered; the committee have now full powers. Only in case of closing or opening a mission field are all the unions to be consulted. Soon after the Stade and Hanover Unions withdrew, and the constituency gradually assumed its present character.

The radical change in the constituency of the Society is due partly to personal causes, partly to the clumsy democratic mode of government, that precluded the predominance of a single energetic man as an executive, but chiefly to the gradual growth, marked all over Germany, of an ardent confessional sentiment among Lutherans. The Society did not, however, become exclusively Reformed: it still "combines members of the Lutheran and of the Reformed Church, for the spread of the gospel among the heathen." Accordingly Lutheran members are on the committee as well as Reformed.

The school at Hamburg suffered by reason of these conflicts. In 1848 it was transferred to Bremen, but was even then ready to expire. Louis Harms had in 1837 been chosen as Inspector, but he declined the call because of his work in Lauenburg; in 1842 he was called as second teacher; but he again declined, as he could not leave his aged father. He now proposed to undertake at Hermannsburg the education of the missionaries; this proposal was accepted, but in 1859, as has been said, he left the Society, and the relation was abandoned. So the Society is without a school. In 1851 the decision to prosecute the work in Western Africa was occasioned by the offer of the Basle Society to supply men from its Institute; since then the men have been educated at Basle—an arrangement not entirely satisfactory, because of the lack of local sympathy between Society and men. So far as possible, however, North Germans are selected for the work.

In 1862 the office of Inspector was created, and F. M. Zahn was elected to fill it; he still holds the position.

The organ of the Society is the "Monatsblatt der Norddeutschen Missionsgesellschaft" (from 1846 to 1851 under the title "Mittheilungen der Norddeutschen Missionsgesellschaft").

After careful examination of various proposed fields of work, it was decided to begin in India among the Telugu tribes. A man was sent out in 1843, followed by two more in 1846; but it was thought necessary to have university trained men in India; the difficulties at home decreased the income; other missions must be continued; so very soon it was decided to give up the work there. Rajahmundri (Rajamahendri) was assumed by the American Lutheran Society, and since then numerous other organizations have continued the work.

Two young men who were intended for India at the first were unable to go there on account of poor health, and were sent instead to New Zealand, to which there was at that time much emigration. A share in the New Zealand Colonization Company was bought for the missionaries, which should furnish location for the station in the northern part of South Island; but the work there in Nelson, so far as any was practicable, was in the hands of other societies; so one of the men went to Taranaké in North Island, where he stayed until 1861; then the revolt of the Maoris drove him away, and he worked at Otago on South Island till his death in 1866. The second missionary went to the little island of Ruapuké, just south of South Island, where he is yet located. Money is still sent him, but the work is not any longer among the heathen, but among natives already nominally Christians.

Further detachments of men were not needed; so in 1846 Western Africa was decided upon, and in the following year four men were sent out. The location assigned them was in the French possessions, just under the equator. The French Government refused to give them permission to work, and they returned, disappointed, to Accra, farther north and west, on the Gold Coast, where was a station of the Basle Society. Here they learned that missionaries were desired by the king of the Peki, an Ewe tribe east of the Volta River, some distance from the coast. The work soon began, but with only one of the four men sent out; three had died of the fever. This sad experience of sickness and death has been constantly repeated through the history of this mission. In 1886 it was stated that out of 110 missionaries sent to the coast 40 had returned broken in health, 56 had died from the effects of the climate, and 30 of the 56 children born to the missionaries on the field had died.

Other men were sent out, but discouragement and sickness was so great that in 1851 all suddenly returned to Germany; one of the number died in the harbor of Hamburg. Encouraged by the Basle Society, a second attempt was made to occupy Peki, but this also failed. One man remained in Accra, waiting for permission to alter the plan and begin first at the coast; this was not deemed advisable in Bremen, and work was again begun in the interior. After but a few months all were driven out by a war. This led finally to the adoption of the plan suggested by the missionary, and a station was opened in 1853, on the coast at Keta, which was then simply a harbor, where a large settlement was planned. The plan was slow of execution, and in order to reach the natives a second station was opened in 1856 at Waya, about 50 miles in the interior. In 1857 a third, Anyako, was begun between the two. A fourth was opened in 1859–1860 at Ho, formerly Wegbe. In addition to hindrances from climate, other causes have brought great tribulation to the mission: the language was utterly strange, and must be learned and reduced to writing; wars have been frequent—one especially, that lasted from 1869 to 1874, caused the temporary abandonment of Waya, the total destruction of Ho, and much damage to Anyako. Ho was entered again in 1875, and the year 1889 witnessed the formal completion of the station. Keta has been less unfortunate; it is the seat of a seminary, a middle school, and of a newly organized deaconess' foundation.

The state of the mission as given in the report for 1889 is as follows: There are two central stations already occupied, Ho and Keta, and a third, Amedschovhe, just begun in the north, on higher and healthier land. At Ho, which is since 1888 in German territory, ten Europeans are stationed,—6 men and 4 women,—and 21 native helpers. At Keta are 10 Europeans and 63 native helpers. These number an increase of 12 workers during the year. In the Keta parish are 201 members, with 125 communicants. At Ho, 516 members, with 283 communicants. The numbers are small, but the rapid increase of the last few years is full of promise. In 1880, after 32 years of work, there were 202 Christians. Ten years before that, 126. The 717 members at the present time are distributed in 10 parishes, varying from 4 to 142 in number.

In connection with the central stations are 12 out-stations, with native helpers, schools, and chapels; the great liability to sickness among European missionaries has led the Society to emphasize the training of natives to the work. Some are being trained in Germany, others at the schools in the field. The number of scholars in the seminary at Keta is 5 at present; 25 are in the middle school there. The total number of pupils in all classes of schools—the above mentioned, the regular station schools, those of the out-stations, and the evening schools —is 315.

The receipts during the year were 82,000 marks, an increase of nearly 4,000 over those of the preceding year.

In 1880 the Society started a General Missionary Conference of the different organizations of Germany, Scandinavia, the Netherlands, and France. It meets at Bremen every three or four years, to consult upon topics of general interest. The decisions of the Conference are in no way binding, but its influence is of greatest value to the cause of foreign missions.

**Northwest Provinces** (British India), one of the great divisions or provinces of the Anglo-Indian Empire, and one of the five provinces which go to make up the Bengal presidency. Its ruler is the lieutenant-governor of the Northwest Provinces, who is appointed by the viceroy and governor-general of India, to whom he is directly subordinate. The province (formerly the kingdom) of Oudh is almost wholly surrounded by the territories of the Northwest Provinces, of which it is practically a part, since the lieutenant-governor of the provinces is also chief commissioner of Oudh. The judicial administration of the two provinces, however, is separate, but they are sufficiently one to be considered together here. Their territory extends from north latitude 23° 52' to 31 7', and from east longitude 77° 5' to 84° 41'. It reaches from Bengal on the southeast to the Jumna River on the northwest (which is the boundary between the Northwest Provinces and the Punjab). On the northeast the independent kingdom of Nepal forms part of the boundary, while farther west the area extends clear up into the Himalayas themselves, and impinges at last on Tibet. Near the southern edge runs the great Ganges, though some of the territory of the province lies south of that river. Thus a vast extent of the Upper Ganges valley is included in these provinces, and the great tributaries of that river flow through it. The area of the provinces is 106,104 square miles. The population of the Northwest Provinces is 32,720,128; of Oudh, 11,387,741; in all, 44,107,869. The country is largely flat, sloping gradually towards the southeast. In the extreme northwest, however, it becomes mountainous as it approaches the Himalayan region, and several mighty peaks of that great range lie within the limits of these provinces, the highest being Nandi Devi (25 661 feet). In this vicinity are located several sanitaria and favorite places of European resort and residence. In this same region also, at the locality known as Haridwar, far among Himalayan defiles, the Ganges takes its rise. This is a famous point of Hindu pilgrimage, as being the source of their most sacred river. On the mountain-slopes hereabouts tea is grown in large quantities; this industry is mainly in the hands of Europeans, and supported by European capital. The Jumna River has its rise like the Ganges in the Himalayas; and, after describing a southerly, takes a southeasterly course, nearly parallel to the Upper Ganges, though gradually approaching it, and farther west it joins the greater river at Allahabad, which is now the capital city of the provinces. This point of union is another famous place of Hindu pilgrimage. The district enclosed between these two rivers (known as the "Doab," or Two Waters), is described as the granary of the Northwest. The rainfall of the whole territory is only twenty-five inches a year, and confined within three or four months. This fact renders artificial irrigation necessary to ensure the fertility of the soil. The government has supplemented the smaller labors of the native husbandmen in this direction by establishing large canal systems fed by the great rivers of the provinces, and large enough often to be of use for navigation as well as for irrigation. Besides wheat and the other cereals usual to Indian agriculture, large quantities of opium are grown near Benares, and in other parts of the provinces, and in Oudh. Two hundred and fifty thousand acres, or six per cent of all the land under cultivation, was reported a few years since as devoted to opium. It is a government monopoly here as elsewhere in India.

The population may be thus summarized: 86 per cent are Hindus, 13 per cent Mohammedan. The small remainder contains nearly 80,000 Jains, nearly 48,000 Christians, and a sprinkling of Parsis, Jews, Buddhists, Sikhs (a sect which has separated from Hinduism, but which still presents most of the traits peculiar to Hinduism), etc. The Christian population included in 1881, the year of the enumeration, over 13,000 natives, the results of missionary work. Of these 1,782 were Romanists, and the rest Protestants of the several denominations sustaining missions in the province.

Historically, these provinces present many points of great interest. Of the very earliest inhabitants few remnants now are left; the aboriginal tribes (Kols and others of this and adjacent regions) are almost certainly their representatives. The Aryan invasion pouring in from the northwest through the Punjab dispossessed the former dwellers on the soil, founded great cities, of which the ruins of some remain (such as Hastinapur and Kanauj), and established kingdoms and dynasties, whose wars and achievements form the basis of fact for the great Hindu poem of the Mahabharat. At Kapila, in Oudh, Gautama Buddha was born early in the 6th century before Christ, and at Kasia he died half a century later. The territory of this province formed a part of the realms of the great King Asoka, who in the third century before Christ gave his political support to Buddhism and made it the prevailing religion of Hindustan. In the 11th century after Christ the Mohammedans began to invade the land, through the same northwestern door as the Aryans before them. The upper portion of these provinces became a few centuries later the central seat of their power; though the city of Delhi, their greatest capital, once just within the northwestern boundary of the Northwest Provinces, has more recently been transferred to the Punjab. Late in the last century, when the great Mogul power had sensibly declined and was disintegrating into weak and petty principalities, the English authority, then firmly established in Bengal under Warren Hastings, began to creep up the Ganges. Benares became theirs in 1775; a part of Oudh was ceded in 1801; other districts followed; but the details we need not here repeat. A British cantonment was established at Cawnpur as early as 1778, which became the nucleus of the present great city (see Cawnpur). The districts thus annexed to the English territory were first governed from Bengal; but in 1833 the plan was formed of erecting them into a fourth presidency; this plan was abandoned two years later in favor of that still in force, by which they constitute a province of similar rank to the province of Bengal, and like that governed by a lieutenant-governor, subject to the governor-general. In 1856 the continued misgovernment of the King of Oudh caused that territory to be annexed and placed under the charge of a chief-commissioner, as above explained.

The great Indian mutiny of 1857 raged more fiercely within the borders of this province than elsewhere in all India. It was at Mirat in its northwestern part that a native regiment of cavalry broke into open and violent rebellion on the 10th of May, 1857. After massacring their officers and many others, they started for Delhi. There the native infantry joined them. The city was seized by them, the old Mogul Empire was proclaimed, and the fire of rebellion spread rapidly over the whole province. In September of the same year Delhi was recaptured, and Lucknow was relieved the next March. The rebellion was wholly quelled before the end of 1858. But the siege of Delhi, the defence of Lucknow under Lawrence and his little band, with its subsequent relief by Havelock, and the massacres at Cawnpur, are destined to perpetual memory.

Besides the cities already mentioned, all of which are famous on account of the great events just mentioned in connection with them, these provinces contain the city of Agra, celebrated as the capital of the later Mogul emperors, and adorned by Akbar in the 16th century, and Shah Jehan in the 17th, with architectural works which are the admiration of mankind. The Taj Mahal (built by the last-named emperor) is said by some to be the most beautiful structure standing on the earth. Allahabad, the capital of the provinces, is a city of nearly or quite 150,000 population. Benares, the most sacred place in Hindustan in the Hindu's esteem, is also within the limits of these provinces.

Hindi is the principal language, subject in different localities to marked dialectic variation. The Mohammedans mostly use Urdu or Hindustani, as they do generally throughout India,—a fact which constitutes that form of speech the *lingua franca* of India. The following description of the people may be quoted from Rev. Mr. Sherring's history of Protestant missions in India: "In place of the stunted, dark races of Bengal, of great vivacity, and of considerable keenness of intellect, you have a fine, stalwart people, tall, strong-limbed, often powerful, of noble presence, ready to fight, independent, of solid rather than sharp understanding, and of somewhat duller brain than their neighbors of Bengal. By reason of the contrariety between the two nationalities there is no friendship between them, nor is ever likely to be. The Bengali is proud; but it is because he is subtle and quickwitted, and thinks he is capable of overreaching you. The Hindustani is proud; but it is because of his trust in his strong arm, because of his long pedigree, because of his well-cultivated manly habits. The

Bengali has no royal tribes to be compared for a moment with the Rajput clans of the northwest, with lineages stretching back for a thousand or even two thousand years."

Christian missionary work dates back to 1807, when Rev. Mr. Corrie, chaplain of the East India Company, was stationed at Chunar, and undertook a little evangelistic work in addition to his regular duties; and to 1809, when Henry Martyn, also a chaplain, residing at Cawnpur, made full proof of his ministry among the natives. But no regular missionary work by any agency specially existing for that purpose was undertaken until 1811, when the Baptist Society undertook to occupy Agra, sending thither Rev. Messrs. Chamberlain and Peacock from Serampore. The opposition of the government interfered, and the station was broken up, and not resumed by the Baptists until 1834. In 1813 Rev. Mr. Corrie, who had removed to Agra, gave the Church Missionary Society a hold there which it has never relinquished. The Baptists occupied Allahabad in 1816 or 1817, but abandoned the station after a few years, only to resume it still more recently. The same Society began work in Benares in 1816, and was followed in due time by others (see Benares). The Church Missionary Society has stations at Gorakpur, Azimgarh, Benares, Chunar, Allahabad, Agra, Aligarh, Mirat, Dehra Dun, Fyzabad, Lucknow, and Barelli, and at a few smaller places. The American Presbyterians occupy Allahabad, Fatehpur, Fatehgarh, Mainpuri, Etawa, Muzaffarnagar, Saharanpur, Rurki, and Dehra Dun. It sustains at Allahabad a theological school. The American Methodists began their work just before the mutiny. Lucknow is their chief station. Others are at Amroha, Bijnour, Moradabad, Budaon, Shajehanpur, Sitapur, Baraich, Rai Barelli, Gonda, Naini Tal, Paori, and Cawnpur. The London Missionary Society, besides its station at Benares, has work at Mirzapur, Almora, and Rani Khet in the hill region. There is a German Mission at Ghazipur. Ladies' missionary societies co-operate with the missionaries at many of these stations, attending specially to work in the zenanas and schools. Education, promoted both by the missions and by government, is making fair progress.

**Norway.**—The missionary activity of the Norwegian people began with Hans Egede. But as Norway at that time was united to Denmark, and as Egede was supported and controlled by the mission department of the royal government in Copenhagen, it is proper to refer his labor to the Danish Mission. Entirely national both in origin and operation are the three Norwegian Mission Societies now at work,—the Norwegian Mission to the Finns, the Norwegian Mission Society, and the Mission of the Norwegian Church by Schreuder.

*The Norwegian Mission to the Finns.* Headquarters, Stavanger, Norway.— The Finns, who occupy the northernmost part of Norway, from Roraas to North Cape, are allied to the Tshudi and Samoyedes of Russia, to the Magyars and the Turks, and belong to a race entirely different from the Scandinavian. A distinction is made between the Sea-Finns, located along the fjords and the ocean, and engaged in fishing and a little agriculture, and the Flik-Finns, who, with their herds of reindeers, roam about on the inland plateau;

but neither the former nor the latter understand the Norwegian language well enough to follow a Norwegian sermon, and even if they did, a visit to a Norwegian place of worship would, for most of them, mean a journey of from 50 to 100 miles over tracts of wild and weird land. Since the beginning of the 17th century they have been Christians, but only nominally; and for the last two centuries it has been a heavy task for the Norwegian Church—during the union with Denmark poorly supported by the royal government, yet never given up by the Norwegian clergy—to awaken a truly Christian life among them. Many venerable names are connected with that labor, but not until very recently has the problem been attacked in a systematic and effective way. February 28th, 1888, Bishop Skaar of Tromsö, to whose diocese the Finns mostly belong, sent out an appeal to the Norwegian people, that missionaries or itinerant preachers who could speak the Finnish language should be sent out among them. This appeal was promptly taken up, and by means of a yearly subscription of about 4,000 crowns it has already been possible to set two Finnish-speaking Norwegian preachers to work among them.

**The Norwegian Mission Society** (Det Norske Missions Selskab). Headquarters, Stavanger, Norway.—In the third decade of the present century, after Norway had become an independent state by the separation from Denmark in 1814, there were formed all over the country, but more especially among the followers of the great revivalist, Hans Nilsen Hauge, a number of minor mission associations, the first and the largest among which was that of Stavanger, 1826. These associations sent their money and their missionaries, if any they had, to Basle: the Stavanger Association, however, placed its first missionary, Hans Christian Knudsen, in the service of the Rhenish Mission Society. As a striking sign of the energy of the movement may be mentioned, that the " Norsk Missionsblad," which in 1852 became the organ of the mission to the Jews, was founded at Christiania in 1827, and in 1845 followed " Norsk Missionstidende," which still is the organ of the mission to the heathen. Then, in 1841, Jon Hougvaldstad, a small tradesman from Stavanger, but a personal friend of Hauge and seventy-one years of age, went to Germany to see with his own eyes what mission societies and missionary schools really were; and the result of his journey was, that August 8th, 1842, all the minor associations in Western Norway consolidated into one society. In 1843 they were joined by all the minor associations of Eastern Norway, and thus was formed the Norwegian Mission Society. It should be noticed, however, that the movement was carried on almost exclusively by laymen, while the Norwegian church, in its official position as a state institution, assumed a very cool and reserved attitude towards it—a circumstance which later proved of importance for the formation of the Mission of the Norwegian Church by Schreuder.

The Norwegian Mission Society is, as might be inferred from its origin, thoroughly democratic in its organization. The minor associations, numbering 900, besides 2,300 woman's societies, still exist, and have retained a considerable proportion of autonomy. They form eight circles, with their administrative centres respectively in the following cities: Christiania,

Hamar, Drammen, Christianssand, Stavanger, Bergen, Trondhjem, and Tromsö. Each circle holds a conference two years in succession in June or July, and the third year the General Assembly meets, deciding all the more important questions for the following three years. The central administration, consisting of the director of the Mission School, a secretary and eight members elected by the Conferences, has its seat in Stavanger. It must consult the Conferences on all important business, and it must carry out the decision of the majority of the General Assembly, irrespective of its own opinion.

In 1887–88 the revenue of the Society amounted to 349,514 kroners, its expenses to 337,464 kroners. It receives an annual support of about 30,000 kroners from the Norwegian churches in the United States. It owns a fund of 200,000 kroners, a donation from Mr. P. von Möller at Helsingborg, Sweden, from which it pensions old and worn-out missionaries, or missionaries' widows and children; but its missionaries are not allowed to marry without the permission of the Central Board. It maintains a mission-school at Stavanger, founded in 1843, closed in 1847, but reopened in 1858, and is now in a flourishing condition, with 14 pupils, and now and then visited by Zulus and Malagasses. It also owns a mission-steamer, presented to it by special subscription, and usually stationed at Madagascar.

The denominational character of the Society is strictly Lutheran. According to its laws its missionaries must receive ordination from a bishop of the Lutheran State Church, and in order to obtain that they must, curiously enough, first have a license from the king, which, still more curiously, is valid only for a certain field. No harm, however, appears to have been caused by this requirement.

The Society is engaged in two different fields: (1) Zululand and (2) Madagascar.

(1) The Zulu Mission was begun in 1844 by Schreuder. To the Norwegians, as to other missionaries, Zululand proved a very hard, but after the first hindrances were overcome, a very promising field. The first station was founded there at Umpumulo, in 1850. In 1858 the first convert, a Zulu girl, was baptized at Umpumulo. When Bishop Schreuder in 1876 transferred his services to the Mission of the Norwegian Church, he carried with him a part of the field already under cultivation, namely Entumeni. But the Society continued its labor with great energy and considerable success. In 1887–88 the full members of the congregations numbered 500, church-visitors 2,000, children in the schools 448, catechumens 110, stations 11, ordained Norwegian pastors 14, unordained native preachers and teachers 16.

(2) The Madagascar Mission was begun in 1866, and soon assumed very large proportions, including now not only the Hovas in the inland, with a station in the capital, Antananarivo, a city of about 100,000 inhabitants, but also, since 1874, the Sakalavas, " wild-cats," on the western coast, and since 1888 some points on the southern coast never before visited by Europeans. In 1887–88 the full members of the congregations numbered 16,-555, church-visitors 44,000, children in the schools 37,500, ordained native pastors 16, native teachers and evangelists 900. There are in the inland 20 stations with 17 ordained Nor-

wegian pastors, among the Sakalavas 5 stations with 4 ordained Norwegian pastors, and on the southern coast 4 stations with 4 Norwegian pastors.

*The Norwegian Church Mission by Schreuder* (Den Norske Kirkes Mission ved Schreuder). Headquarters, Christiania, Norway.—Hans Palludan Smith Schreuder, b. at Sogndal, Norway, June 18th, 1817; d. at Untumjambili, Natal, Africa, January 27th, 1882, consecrated bishop in the Cathedral of Bergen 1866, was the father of the Norwegian Mission. His " A few words to the Church of Norway," 1842, had an effect throughout the whole country as if a mighty lamp had been lit. He started the Zulu Mission under tremendous difficulties, and it is indebted for its success to his eminent energy, his lofty enthusiasm, and powerful personality. During the war between the English and the Zulus most of the English and German mission stations were disturbed or fully destroyed. But Entumeni was not touched; King Cetewayo had too deep a respect for Schreuder to dare such a thing. The Madagascar Mission he also directed and superintended at its beginning. Nevertheless, although he served the Norwegian Mission Society for thirty years, it was always his wish to be the missionary of the Church of Norway, of the official state institution, and not the missionary of any private association. In 1873 he separated from the Society and a committee was formed, with Bishop Tandberg at its head, and representing the Church of Norway. He took Entumeni with him, and shortly after a new station was founded at Untumjambili in Natal, where a church was built and consecrated in 1881. After his death the mission was continued by his pupils, among whom are several natives, under the direction of the above-mentioned committee, which has its seat in Christiania. In 1888–89 its revenue amounted to 7,072 kroners, and its expenses to 8,864 kroners.

**Norwegian Version.**—The Norwegian belongs to the Teutonic branch of the Aryan family of languages, and is spoken in Norway, whose population numbers 1,925,000. Under the patronage of King Hakon V. Magnussons' (1294–1319), parts of the Old Testament, with notes, were translated into the old Norwegian (Pentateuch–Chronicles were edited by Prof. Unger, Christiania, 1853–1862). In late times the Danish Bibles were used. Since the formation of the Norwegian Bible Society in 1816, the New Testament, edited by Bishop Beck, Professors Hersleb and Stevenson, and the court-preacher (afterwards Bishop) Pavols, was published. A revised and corrected edition prepared by Prof. Hersleb was published in 1830. A new translation of the Old Testament was also undertaken by Prof. Hersleb 1842–1873. In 1873 an edition of the New Testament revised by Professors Dietrichson, Johnson, and Esseldorp was also published by the Norwegian Bible Society. Some change was made in the language of this edition in order to conform to modern usage. The Old Testament was also revised in the same form and was completed in 1888. An edition of the entire Bible in this revised form was issued in the same year.

**Norwegian-Lapp** or **Quanian Version.**—The Quanes, a wandering people for whom this version is made, inhabit that most northerly part of Lapland which is called Finmark or Norwegian Lapland. This dreary region, having for its northern boundary the Arctic or Frozen Ocean, is the habitation of about 6,000 Quanes who until the beginning of this century were left without any version of the Bible in their vernacular dialect. The Bible Society of Finland sent them copies of the Finnish New Testament, but they could not understand it, nor could they read intelligibly the Lappish Testament, though they speak a dialect of Laplandish. In 1822 the British and Foreign Bible Society voted a sum of money for a Quanian version, and at last in 1842 the Norwegian Bible Society published at Christiania a translation of the New Testament, made by a missionary among the Laplanders. The Psalms were published in 1856. In 1875 a revised translation of the 1842 version, prepared by Lars Haetta, with the aid of Bishop Hersleb and Prof. Friis, was published by the Norwegian Bible Society. The British and Foreign Bible Society has of late years undertaken the publication of a version of the Bible, to be prepared by Prof. Jens Andreas Friis, for the Lapps, who number about 30,000, of whom 17,000 live in Norway, and have never had the Bible in their own tongue. They do not understand the Bible of the Swedish Lapps. The Book of Genesis in this new version was printed by the local Bible Society in 1887, and Isaiah in 1888.

*(Specimen verse. John 3 : 16.)*

Dastgo nuft rakkasen ani Ibmel nailme, atte barnes sån addi, dam aino, amas juokkaš, gutte su ala åssko, lapput, mutto vai agalaš ællesån åžuši.

**Nott, Henry,** b. England 1774; sailed 1796 for the South Seas as a missionary of the L. M. S.; stationed at Tahiti, Eimeo, and Huahine. Early in 1802, he with Mr. Elder made the first missionary tour of the island, and in thirty days he preached in nearly every district. During the war of rebellion in 1808 Mr. Nott remained at Eimeo. In 1825 he visited England, married, and returned to Tahiti in 1827. Having after twenty-seven years' labor completed the translation of the Scriptures into the Tahitian language, and being in ill-health, he returned to England in 1836. He there revised the translation and had it published at the expense of the British and Foreign Bible Society. In 1838 he re-embarked for Tahiti, and soon after his arrival in 1840 retired from active service. He died at Tahiti, May 2d, 1844.

**Nott, Samuel,** b. Franklin, Conn., U. S. A., 1788; son of Rev. Samuel Nott of Franklin, and nephew of Rev. Dr. Eliphalet Nott, President of Union College; graduated at Union College 1808, Andover Theological Seminary 1810; ordained 1812 with Newell, Judson, Hall, and Rice, the first company of missionaries sent out by the American Board; embarked with Gordon Hall February 24th. After some delays from the East India Company, they reached Bombay, where they commenced the first mission of the Board in India. In 1815 Mr. Nott was taken seriously ill, and the physicians decided that he could not remain in that country, and that he should return to his native land or to Europe. He embarked for America by the way of England. He died, July 1st,

1869, at the residence of his son in Hartford, Conn., aged 81.

**Nowgong,** a town of Central Assam, south of the Brahmaputra, between Gauhati and Tezpore. Mission station of the American Baptist Missionary Union; 1 missionary, 2 ladies, 26 native helpers, 1 church (self-supporting), 89 church-members, 12 schools, 251 scholars.

**Nuba-Fulah Race.**—A very considerable number of tribes, some in Egyptian Soudan, and some over against them on the west coast of North Central Africa, are found to differ so much, both linguistically and ethnographically, from the several races into which the Africans have been heretofore divided, that some of the ablest recent writers on these subjects, such as F. Müller and Dr. R. N. Cust, have added a new class or group, with two sub-groups which they call Nuba and Fulah. This twofold race, Nuba-Fulah, is evidently very ancient,—doubtless aboriginal in the lower basin of the Nile, which still continues to be the headquarters of the Nuba portion of the general group. As the old Egyptian race was doubtless divided by the incoming of the Bantu family at an early age (see articles on the Bantu and on the Hottentot), and a part of it carried southward until it came to the extreme south angle of the continent, and there took the name of Khoi-Khoi and then Hottentot, so the same incoming family doubtless proved an entering wedge, on its way up the Nile valley, to split the original Nuba race, through which it passed, on the south of Egypt, causing a portion of it to move first southward, then westward, till it lodged, a part of it on the sources of the Nile, part east of Lake Nyanza, and a part on the Niger, while another part moved on till it finally came to have its headquarters in the lower basin of the Senegal, and there came to be known as the Filatah, Fuladu, Pulah, or Fulah people, being so called because they were of a light brown, and thus in strong contrast with the Negroes of a pure black around them. The present scattered or fragmentary condition of the Nuba-Fulah race, a portion of it being found on the east of Lake Nyanza, as the Kwafi and Masai, other portions on the sources of each of the two Niles, and yet other portions in different parts of Nigritia, all the way from Dar-Fur to the Senegal, as in groups here and there among the Hausa and other mid-African tribes, all goes to support the idea that the original Nuba-Fulah race was broken and scattered, as already indicated, by the divisive and propelling force of another powerful race, as the Bantu, at an early age of African history.

One important branch of the Nuba stock still has its home in the original abode of the race—the basin of the Nile from the first to the second cataract. The earliest account we have of them represents them as a powerful, superior race, of good features, not so dark on the northern border as farther south, and quite distinct from both the Egyptian and the Negro. They were once Christians, but now, like all their neighbors, profess the Islam faith, and speak, some the Arabic, and some their own vernacular language. Some live as nomads in tents, and some as a settled, industrious, thriving people, in well-built houses. There is also a tribe or group of tribes, evidently related to the Nuba

family in both blood and language, in Kordofan and Dar-Fur. They differ from the Negroes around them, believe in Islam, and speak, some of them, what is called the Koldagi dialect, some of them the Tumale, and some the Konjara. Other tribes of this class, as the Kwafi and Masai, who call themselves Loikob, and designate their language as the Enguduk, are found on or near the equator. The Kwafi have the Victoria Nyanza on their west and the Masai on their south. Both tribes, differing materially, as they do, from the Hamitic race on the north, and from the Bantu on other sides, are counted as belonging to the Nuba-Fulah group. They are represented as the most savage of all East African tribes. Still another group of tribes, as the Berta and Kamail, belonging to the Nuba-Fulah race, has its home on the Blue Nile, north of the Galla and west of Abyssinia. In this race are included also the Nyam-Nyam, together with the Golo and the Monbutto on the sources of the White Nile and the Shary.

Turning now and going westward between the 10th and 15th degrees of north latitude, we come upon several families of the sub-Fulah group, scattered here and there all along from Dar-Fur through the Hausa and Mandingo countries, till we come to where they abound in Bundu, Futa Jalo and Futa Toro, south of Lower Senegal, where "they dominate," says Dr. Cust, "as Mohammedan foreign conquerors. They have placed their foot firmly down in the land of the Wolof, and the people of the coast have come under their influence as far as the river Nunez. They are numerous and powerful in Mandingo-land and in the kingdom of Massina, south of Timbuktu. In Hausa-land the kingdom of Sokoto and Gando is their creation, including the whole of the Hausa territory. Far to the east we find them in Bornu, Mandara, Logon, Baghirmi, Wadai, and even in Dar-Fur. Their tendency to expand is not on the wane, and they have made a powerful impression on the Negro population; from the union of the two races a mixed population has sprung up, called Torodo, Jhalonki, Toucouleur, and other names." It is unnecessary here to detail their history or speculate on their origin. Their movement has been comparatively of late date, by force of arms, and coupled with the spread of the Mohammedan religion. They are spoken of by a recent writer as " an interesting Mohammedan people of the Western Soudan in Africa, remarkable for their enterprise, intelligence, and religious zeal. They are a race, and not a nation; have many tribes, several shades of color and varieties of form, probably from the fact that they have blended with various subject races. They cultivate Mohammedan learning with much enthusiasm. Their history is quite obscure. Saccatoo is their principal state, but they are the predominant people of many countries in the Soudan."

Very little mission work of a Protestant Christian character has been as yet done or even attempted for this race; but the eyes of not a few are on the great region they occupy, with high purpose and hope of reaching them soon. (See article on "The Soudan" in this work; also article on "Mahdism and Missions," in "Missionary Review of the World," New Series, vol. iii.)

**Nuba Version.**—The Nuba belongs to the Nuba-Fulah group of African languages, and is vernacular in Nubia. For the Mohammedans about Dongola, East Africa, the British and Foreign Bible Society published in 1884 the Gospel of Mark, which the late Prof R. Lepsius of Berlin had translated into the Fadidja dialect of the Nubian. Prof. Lepsius prepared his translation originally for his Nubian grammar, from which it was republished in Roman characters and edited by Prof. Rheinisch of Vienna. Steps are now being taken, according to the Report for 1888, by Rev. R. H. Weakley to have a part of the Society's version transliterated into the Arabic character, and to have its value tested by the Nubians resident in Alexandria and Cairo.

**Nubia,** a country of Eastern Africa, south of Egypt, and forming a part of the Egyptian or Eastern Soudan (see Africa and Soudan).

**Numadzu,** town in Japan. A mission station of the Methodist Church of Canada, in Southeastern Nippon, not far from Shidzuoka; 1 native pastor, 105 church-members. Protestant Episcopal Church; 1 church, 4 communicants, 11 Sabbath-scholars.

**Numpani** (Nimpani, Nipani), British India. A town in the Belgaum district, Bombay, 40 miles north of Belgaum. Population, 9,777, Hindus, Moslems, Jains, Christians. Mission station of the Swedish Evangelical National Society (Swedish Fatherland's Association).

**Nundi Gopee, Nath.,** b. in Calcutta, India. While a student in Dr. Duff's school he became a Christian, and was baptized by Dr. Duff in 1832. He afterwards, at the recommendation of Dr. Duff, went to the Northwest to became a teacher in the orphan-school at Futtehpore, supported by the British residents. He was licensed to preach by the Presbytery of Furrukabad in 1843, and the following year was ordained to the work of an evangelist. In the Sepoy mutiny he escaped with his family from Futtehpore, to fall into the hands of the insurgents, and suffered much before he was finally released. He died in 1861, while pastor of the church at Futtehpore, under a severe surgical operation. When the hour of trial came, he said: "I am not afraid to die; I can trust that Jesus whom I have so often preached to others." Dr. Duff wrote, on hearing of his death: "I mourn over him as I would over an only son, till at times my eyes are sore with weeping. When shall we have scores and hundreds clothed with his mantle and imbued with his spirit?"

**Nupé Version.**—The Nupé belongs to the Negro group of African languages and is spoken by the Nupé tribe on the Niger, West Africa, for whom the Revs. Messrs. C. Crowther and J. F. Schön translated the first seven chapters of Matthew, which the British and Foreign Bible Society published in 1860 at the request of the Church Missionary Society. Since 1884 the four Gospels have been published as translated by Archdeacon Johnson, and edited by Rev. J. F. Schön of the C. M. S. In 1886 an edition of 500 copies each of the Gospels of Luke and John as translated by Mr. Johnson was published in the new orthography as rendered by Dr. Schön.

(*Specimen verse.* Matt. 5 : 16.)

*Lugo ebayetinye un nán atsi eye ezabo, a-a-le etun wangi 'yeye, a-fe dzin yebo ndaye nan dan alidzana nan.*

**Nusairiyeh, The.**\*—The origin of the Nusairiyeh people seems lost in the obscurity of antiquity. In asking one of their chiefs concerning their origin the most he could say was that it was very ancient. Another says that they descended from the Persians; others, from the Philistines, or from the tribes that Joshua drove out of Palestine. They have dwelt for hundreds of years where they now are, and it is probable that ethnologists and historians have taken little or no notice of them because of their political insignificance and low state of civilization. However, their religious practices sustain the theory that they are descended from some of the ancient heathen tribes of Palestine. At present they are a mixed race, just like many other races bordering on the Mediterranean, owing, no doubt, to the Crusades, when many thousands of Europeans were lost and became mingled with the inhabitants of the country, and this fact probably accounts for the existence of so many blonde complexions among the swarthy aborigines. They receive their name from Nusair, who, with his son Abu Shaeeb, was a renowned leader and teacher among them, and who flourished some centuries ago. They inhabit Northern Syria and Cilicia, and number about three hundred thousand souls. As to their religion, they are a branch of the Shiites who broke off under the leadership of Nusair, and their religious system was brought to perfection by one of his descendants named Khusaib. They are practically pagans, although they claim to be followers of Mohammed. They reject the caliphate of "Abu Bekr" and his successors down to "Abd ul Hamid," the present incumbent, and claim that the succession belonged of right to Ali. The contest for the caliphate was between these two after the death of Mohammed. Ali was Mohammed's son-in-law, having married Fatima, his daughter by Khadijah, his first wife; and Abu Bekr was his father-in-law, Mohammed having taken Ayesha, the daughter of Abu Bekr, as one of his fourteen wives. Tradition says that Abu Bekr compassed the death of his rival by strategy, the circumstances being that Ali was praying in a mosque, and Abu Bekr learning of it, sent two of his retainers to simulate a deadly quarrel outside of the mosque, knowing that Ali, hearing the disturbance, would rush out to separate the combatants, when they were to fall on him and kill him. The result was as anticipated, and the deadly feud which continues to this day was then precipitated. The followers of Ali devised a religion of their own, and being in the minority, and fearing persecution, they bound themselves by the most horrid oaths to keep it secret. None are initiated into its mysteries under 18 years of age, and women not at all, except that they are taught one short prayer to purify them. The applicant for initiation to the secrets of the Nusairiyeh religion must bring twelve men as security, and these must

\* This article is based largely upon an Arab book entitled "A Revelation of the Secrets of the Nusairiyeh Religion," by Suleyman Effendi of Adana.

be secured by two others; and not satisfied with this, the applicant is required to swear by all the heavenly bodies that he will never reveal the mysteries he is about to receive under penalty of having his hands, head, and feet severed from his body, and this same penalty will be visited upon him should he fail to complete what he has now begun. Consequently all the Nusairiyeh are extremely reticent, and will never converse on the subject of their religion. Some years ago one of their number, Suleyman Effendi of Adana, revealed their mysteries, at least in part, and after a time mysteriously disappeared, and no doubt he suffered the penalty. Their religion is a conglomeration of almost all religions, ancient and modern, false and true. They have introduced the beliefs and the ceremonies of the Jews, the Greeks, the Egyptians, the Phenicians, the Mohammedans, and the heathen in general. They worship Ali Ibn Abu Taulib, the prophet Mohammed, and Suleyman the Persian. They consider Ali the Father, Mohammed the Son, and Suleyman the Holy Spirit,—a perfect Trinity; but they pay their chief adoration to Ali, ascribing to him the divine nature and attributes and also creative power, and the devout worshipper is represented as supplicating "his Lord, Ali Ibn Abu Taulib, with a reverent heart and a humble spirit, to deliver him from his wickedness." They teach that Ali created Mohammed, and that Mohammed created Suleyman, and that Suleyman created five great angels, and that the angels created the universe, and that each angel is entrusted with the management of some particular part thereof, viz.. One has charge of thunder, lightning, and earthquakes; another, of the heavenly bodies; another, of the winds, and receives the spirits of men at death; another has charge of the health and sickness of human beings; and another furnishes souls for the bodies of men at birth. They assign to Fatima a place very much like that assigned by Catholics to the Virgin Mary. They consider that the moon is Ali's throne, and that the dark part commonly called the man in the moon is Ali with a veil thrown over his form, but in the hereafter the veil will be removed and all true believers will see him as he is. Hence they worship the moon. They believe that the sun is Mohammed, and pay divine honors to it. They worship fire, the wind, the waves of the sea,—anything that manifests power; the shades of the dead, the living, even men of influence and renown among them. These last they consider to be possessed of the spirits of the prophets, it may be of Ali himself. They profess to have a warfare, and it consists of two parts. The first is to revile and curse Abu Bekr, Omar, Othman, and all others who believe that Ali or any of the prophets ate or drank, or married, or were born of women, because the Nusairiyeh believe that the prophets descended from heaven without bodies, and that the bodies in which they appeared were not real, but illusory. The second part of their warfare consists in keeping their religion secret from strangers, and in refusing to reveal it under any circumstances whatever, even in the face of death. They believe in the transmigration of souls, and hold that the Moslem sheikhs enter the bodies of asses at death, that the souls of Christian priests enter the bodies of swine, that the souls of Jewish rabbis enter the bodies of apes, that the souls of the wicked among

themselves enter the bodies of clean animals. Those among themselves who disbelieve their religion enter the bodies of apes. Those who are part evil and part good enter the bodies of those who belong to sects other than the Nusairiyeh, while all good Nusairiyeh enter the bodies of Nusairiyeh each one according to his grade and station. If one of another belief should unite with them, they claim that in past generations he was of them, but for some sin he was compelled to enter a strange sect and remain a stated time as a punishment, when he was allowed to transmigrate to his own religion. Formerly they received no proselytes except from the Persians, and they were thus favored because they confess the divinity of Ali. Should one backslide from their religion, they declare that his mother committed adultery with one of the sect with which he has united, and that he has returned to his source. They have numerous feasts, and some of their religious rites are vile and abominable. The Nusairiyeh easily distance all competitors in lying and hypocrisy. They always accommodate themselves to their surroundings, provided they are not able to overcome them. For example, should one enter a mosque with a Moslem, he performs the prostrations and genuflexions just as his companion; but instead of praying as does the Moslem, he inwardly curses Abu Bekr and all his successors, and likewise him who bows at his side. He argues that the Nusairiyeh religion is the body, while all other religions are clothing to be worn and thrown aside at pleasure; and it matters not what a man wears, it does him no injury; and he who does not dissemble thus lacks good sense, for no sensible person will walk through the streets naked. The unpardonable sin with him is to reveal his own religion, for to reveal it is equivalent to forsaking it. In regard to women, they teach that Ali created the devils from the sins of men, and that he created women from the sins of devils; and that is the reason why they do not teach women their religion. They believe that Ali has appeared in human form at various times during the history of the world. As a people, the Nusairiyeh are revengeful, and practice blood atonement in righting wrongs among themselves. They are thievish, and consider stealing, especially from infidels, a virtue. Nevertheless they are cowardly, and will not attempt either revenge or theft unless assured of personal safety. Their deep deceitfulness is no doubt due to the fact that they are sworn to eternal secrecy in regard to their religion. They will not acknowledge that they believe in Ali, for to acknowledge it is to reveal a part of their religion. They will rather deny it with an oath. Considering this fact one can imagine the difficulty of carrying on mission work among them. Socially they are semi-barbarous, and there are many feuds among them, tribe against tribe. They often have bloody encounters, and the hyenas and jackals feast upon the bodies of the slain. Their morality is low. All classes practise polygamy. Social purity is disregarded among the upper classes—as when one chief becomes the guest of another of like rank the host sends his wife to share the bed of his guest. This abomination is not practised among the common people. Politically they are a nonentity, being under the absolute sway of the Turk, and are therefore much oppressed; and were it not that the Turkish Goverment places every available obstacle in the way of their enlightenment and advancement in civilization, the rising generation would soon be brought under the influence of the gospel.

*The Mission of the Covenanter Church of America to the Nusairiyeh People.*—As early as 1818 the Covenanter Church of America began to consider the expediency of establishing a Foreign Mission. But various providential dispensations hindered the realization of their hopes until 1856, when the cause of missions was again revived, and Syria was selected as the field of operations. The Rev. R. J. Dodds and Mr. Joseph Beattie, licentiate, accepted appointments as missionaries. The latter was ordained, and both set sail for Syria with their newly married wives in October, 1856. After they had spent some time in Damascus studying the Arabic language, Mr. Dodds settled in Zahleh, a large town in Mount Lebanon, while Mr. Beattie continued to pursue his studies in Damascus. In May, 1858, Mr. Dodds was compelled to abandon Zahleh because of the hostility of the Catholic priests, who instigated persecutions against him, and the people threw his goods into the street. Mr. Beattie then joined him, and they spent the following year in B'hamdûn and Beirût. After several explorations, Latakia, a town of about 15,000 inhabitants, situated on the shore of the Mediterranean, 36° north latitude, was chosen, and there the mission was permanently established in October, 1859. It was intended to operate principally among the Nusairiyeh people, consisting of a number of semi-barbarous tribes who occupy the neighboring Nusairiyeh mountains; but the Moslems and the nominally Christian sects were all found to be legitimate subjects of missionary operations, because of the ignorance and superstition that prevail among them. The Moslems however, were practically inaccessible because of the bigotry and intolerance of their leaders, and so remain to this day. Three native teachers were employed, and a school opened with a bright outlook. But little opposition was encountered until the effects of their teaching began to be apparent, when the prejudices of the people began to loom up in the pathway of the missionaries. The Rev. Mr. Lyde, an English missionary, a gentleman of high attainments and great benevolence, was operating in this field when Mr. Dodds went thither on a prospecting tour, and his health having failed, he presented the property that he had acquired to Messrs. Dodds and Beattie for missionary purposes, and withdrew from the field. The first convert, Hammâd, a Nusairiyeh, was baptized by Mr. Dodds in December, 1861, and then it was felt that the mission had not only been planted, but had taken root. The first convert from any of the Christian sects was Salim Saleh, a youth who was in attendance on the mission school, and whose parents were members of the Orthodox Greek Church. This young man suffered shameful persecution from the members of his own family, and was compelled for a time to take refuge with the missionaries. On account of sickness Mr. Beattie and family visited America in 1863, and having recuperated returned in 1864, accompanied by David Metheny, M.D., and family, who had in the mean time been appointed as a medical missionary. The mission was making steady progress, striking deeper root and stretching out

its branches, and about this time four schools were established in the mountains among the Nusairiyeh, manned by native teachers. The Medical Department added much to the efficiency and influence of the mission by introducing the healing art. Mr. Dodds and family visited America in 1865, in order to recruit their failing energies, and returned the following year with Miss Rebecca Crawford, who took charge of a newly established girls' school. Much difficulty was encountered in persuading the Nusairiyeh to patronize this school. Two influences worked against it: they hold peculiar ideas in regard to women, considering them inferior creatures, and consequently not susceptible of instruction; and again, they were suspicious of the designs of the missionaries thinking that they wished to gain possession of the girls, and after a time to transport them. A building for a girls' boarding-school was erected in 1868, and by this means the girls were separated more from their heathen surroundings, and were brought under the influence of Christian home life, and much more efficient work was done. In May, 1867, Mr. Dodds took charge of a mission station in Aleppo. It had formerly been under the care of the United Presbyterian Church of Scotland. The station consisted of two schools and one hundred pupils. Other schools were opened in various places,—notably in Idlib, a small town in a fertile plain, a day's journey southwest of Aleppo, where there is still a small congregation of Protestants. Dr. Dodds died in December, 1870, and the field was abandoned, the mission not having the force to occupy it. Latterly the Rev. James Martin, M.D., of Antioch, has occupied Idlib, and is meeting with flattering success. Dr. Dodds was admirably adapted to be a successful missionary. He was a classical scholar, and became very proficient in the Arabic tongue. In his day he was ranked with Dr. Van Dyck, who has since become the accomplished author and translator. He was habitually cheerful, possessed of great equanimity of temper, and of a sympathetic disposition; of keen intellect, retentive memory, and great ability of concentration. He died at the early age of forty-six, in the midst of his usefulness, and his loss was deeply felt, both at home and abroad. In the autumn of 1871 the Rev. S. R. Galbraith and his wife and Miss Mary E. Dodds, daughter of the lately deceased missionary, departed for Latakia. They had been there but a few months when Mr. Galbraith fell a victim to fever, and his wife and child returned to America. It was a severe trial for the mission—two deaths following one another in such quick succession, one a veteran and the other a fresh recruit; but one had no sooner fallen than another stepped forward into the ranks, and in 1872 the Rev. Henry Easton accepted an appointment to this field, and arrived on the ground with his family in January, 1873. Dr. Metheny visited America the same year, was ordained a minister, and returned in the autumn. While at home the missionaries were not idle, but did some very effective work by way of instructing the people, and stirring them up to a higher appreciation of mission work. The mission was not without its troubles, since a number of the Nusairiyeh converts were cruelly treated by the Turkish authorities because they had the effrontery to change their religion. Some of them were imprisoned and others sent to the army, the authorities thus hoping to destroy the germs of Christianity that had taken root among the Nusairiyeh; and in this they were aided and abetted by the chiefs of the people themselves, who began to fear for the consequences. But the result showed that it was the planting of the Lord, and when He plants, who shall pluck up? One of the converts, David Makhloof, was very sorely tried. He was in the army during the Turco-Russian war. His Bible was taken from him. He was flogged and imprisoned in a dungeon with the design of forcing him to deny Christ; but with all the fortitude of the early Christian martyrs, he stood firm and remained true, holding fast the profession of his faith without wavering. He was wonderfully preserved, having several horses shot from under him while in action. He was in the siege of Plevna, but was providentially spared to return to his family, and he is now a burning and a shining light in his own native mountains. And thus the work continued to grow apace. God had brought to naught the machinations of evil men against the spread of His glorious gospel. In the autumn Miss M. R. Wylie went to Latakia as a teacher in the girls' school. The following year the Rev. Dr. Beattie and family visited America to arrange for the education of the children. The girls' school was now enlarged to meet the growing need, and Mrs. Emma G. Metheny also erected a handsome chapel on the mission premises. Shortly after—December, 1875—she was called to rest, and the chapel is now her memorial. In April, 1875, Suadea was included in the mission field. This station is 60 miles north of Latakia, at the mouth of the Orontes, and had been operated by Dr. William Holt-Yates and his wife. The Doctor having died, Mrs. Holt-Yates desired to return to London, her home; and having erected a commodious building upon the mission premises, she donated the entire property to the Latakia Mission, who have since operated the post, Mrs. Yates furnishing £200 a year to sustain a boys' boarding-school there, and a very successful work has been prosecuted. Shortly after Dr. Beattie's return to Syria in June, 1878, he received telegraphic news of the death of his wife, and he immediately sailed for America to take charge of his motherless children. He resigned his connection with the mission, and remained in America. About this time two more vacancies were created in the mission by the marriage of Miss Mary E. Dodds to Rev. D. Metheny, M.D., and Miss Rebecca Crawford to Rev. James Martin, M.D., of Antioch. In 1878 Dr. Metheny and family visited America in search of health. He returned in November, 1879, accompanied by Rev. William J. Sproull and wife, and Miss Mary E. Carson. An effort was then made to expand the work, and eight or ten new schools were opened in the mountain districts. These schools are preaching stations as well, and form centres whence light is shed on the surrounding communities. The nature of the instruction given is intensely evangelistic, and whenever a school is visited by a missionary or a district superintendent, a short religious service is held. In favorable weather the people usually assemble under the shade of some friendly tree, but in foul weather the school building is utilized, and ordinarily every available spot is occupied, while on special occasions the doors and windows are adorned

with eager, expectant faces. Every year adds converts to the Protestant body, and the mission has acquired a strong and beneficent influence throughout the entire field. Miss Carson's health failed, and Miss Wylie returned with her to America in the summer of 1880. Dr. Beattie was persuaded to return to Syria in December of the same year, and opened a theological school for the training of a native ministry. Miss Wylie also returned in May, 1881, and steps were then taken to enlarge the curriculum of the girls' boarding-school, and render it more efficient. The school had grown so much in public favor that many applicants for admission were turned away for lack of accommodations. A boys' boarding-school was also being conducted in Latakia on a small scale, and the need of an industrial department for their benefit was sorely felt. In the autumn of 1881 A. J. Dodds, M.D., and Miss Evadne M. Sterrett, having accepted appointments on the mission staff, repaired to Latakia. Dr. Dodds had recently been graduated from Jefferson Medical College, Philadelphia, with high honors. He was a son of the late Dr. Dodds of Aleppo, and was born in Damascus. He resided in Syria until he was fourteen years of age, and having considerable knowledge of the Arabic language, he entered immediately upon his labors as a physician. He was united in marriage with Miss Mizpah E. Metheny September 26th, 1882. In December, 1882, Rev. D. Metheny, M.D., and Miss E. M. Sterrett were transferred to Cilicia to establish a mission, and they opened schools in Tarsus, Adana, Mersine, and Alexandretta. In 1886 a building was erected in Mersine, and the efforts put forth have met with encouraging success. The population of this section consists of Nusairiyeh, Turks, Armenians, and Greeks. Considerable opposition has been manifested by the authorities, and one teacher was thrown into prison on pretence of having violated the school law—and a Turkish prison is not to be judged by prisons in Christian lands. In October, 1883, the mission was sorely tried by the death of Dr. Beattie. His loss was deeply deplored by all. He was a model missionary, amiable, urbane, and keenly sympathetic, and will always occupy a chief place in the hearts of those who knew him. He was an effective preacher, and in him the last of the pioneers was laid in the tomb. At his demise the theological school was discontinued for a time. During the years 1883 and '84 the boys' boarding-school was enlarged, and a normal department added with the design of training teachers, and commendable progress was made toward the plane of a higher education. In April, 1885, Mrs. A. J. Dodds departed this life, necessitating the return of her husband to America with their child. And now the saddest calamity that ever befell the mission occurred in the loss of Dr. Dodds, who on his return to Syria went down with the steamer "Sidon," that was wrecked off the coast of Spain October 26th, 1885. He was an amiable gentleman, a proficient scholar, well read in general literature, and thoroughly conversant with the various departments of medical science. He was a devoted missionary, a conscientious worker, and eminently successful in the Master's cause. In May, 1886, Rev. William J. Sproull, having resigned his position on the mission staff, sailed for America with his family. In the following November Miss Maggie B.

Edgar arrived in Latakia as a teacher, and Miss Lily B. Joseph in Mersine April, 1887; and in September of the same year the Mission at Latakia was still further reinforced by the arrival of J. M. Balph, M.D., and family, thus supplying the vacancy created by the death of Dr. Dodds, and Miss Willia A. Dodds arrived at the same place in November, to engage in zenana work among the Moslem population. An addition was made to the ministerial force by the appointment of licentiate J. S. Stewart, who was subsequently ordained, and he landed at Latakia with his family in the autumn of 1888. In the mean time the work of the mission was flourishing most encouragingly, and it was becoming more firmly fixed in the affections of the people. A wall of dense prejudice met the pioneer missionaries at the outset; but as the continued dropping of water will wear away the adamantine rock, so persistent effort, personal contact, uniform kindness, and patient forbearance for Christ's sake wore away the prejudices of the people, and if the mission were blotted out of existence to-day it would be considered a public calamity. By aiding the destitute, by healing the sick, by sympathizing with the sorrowing, a way was made for the gospel of peace, and, notwithstanding the dogged, determined, persistent opposition of the authorities in closing the schools and otherwise hindering the work, last year (1889) the mission enjoyed more encouraging success than any year since it was founded. The statistics show an increase of 51 communicants,—almost double that of any previous year,—an increase of 27 per cent. The Suadea station, which has not had a resident missionary since it came under the control of the Latakia Mission, is now amply provided for in this respect. Miss Martha Cunningham, M.D., of Belfast, who formerly labored in Antioch, Syria, 20 miles inland, now occupies this important post. Her salary is paid by the Scotch and Irish Covenanters, and she operates the station in connection with the Latakia Mission. Her presence and energy have given the work a fresh impulse, and bright hopes are entertained for the future of that field where Paul once preached and whence he sailed on his first missionary tour.

The statistical report of the mission for January, 1890, gives the following facts: Number of out-stations 3, ordained missionaries 9, unordained 6, physicians 2, missionaries' wives 4, other ladies 5. Native workers: 6 evangelists, 47 male and female teachers, 11 male and female helpers; preaching places 7, organized churches 2, communicants 230, added during the year 51, Sabbath schools 29, scholars 843, girls' schools 5, scholars 216, other schools 20, scholars 759 (see Ref. Presb. Church of America).

**Nyanja** (sometimes called Chinyanja), a dialect of East Equatorial Africa, spoken on the borders of Lake Nyassa. The New Testament has been translated and published by the National Bible Society of Scotland.

**Nylander, J. C.,** sent out by "Church Missionary Society" to West Africa, from Germany; embarked for Sierra Leone, February 12th, 1806. Here Mr. Nylander became chaplain of the colony till about 1816, when he went to Yongroo Pomah, opposite Free Town, and seven miles from it, where he commenced a mission among the Bulloms. He labored among this superstitious people with unremitting zeal, teaching and preaching. He translated into the Bullom language the four Gospels, the Epistles of St. John, morning and evening prayers of the Church of England, hymns, and elementary books. The mission was abandoned on account of the slave-trade, but Mr. Nylander transferred his flourishing school to the colony, taking his scholars with him. He died in 1825.

# O.

**Oaxaca.**—1. A state on the coast of Mexico. The physical features of this country include some of the grandest scenery on the globe. Stately, picturesque mountains, beautiful plains, deep gorges, roaring cataracts, and luxurious vegetation are everywhere found. Area, 33,582 sq. miles. Population, 761,274. There are 26 towns and cities of over 10,000 inhabitants. Eleven distinct families of Indians are found, among whom an important work is carried on by the Methodist Episcopal Church (North).—2. The capital of the state. It is a live, progressive city of 30,000 inhabitants. An important station and circuit of the Methodist Episcopal Church (North), at present without any missionary; 1 native pastor, 1 assistant, 47 church-members, 1 day-school with 40 scholars.

**Odaiputty Puthur,** a station of the Madras Mission, India, of the S. P. G.; 17 villages are included in this field; 1 clergyman, 100 communicants, 1 boys' school, 3 mixed schools, 111 scholars.

**Ode Ondo,** town in Yoruba, Africa, near Abeokuta. Mission station of the C. M. S. (1876); 2 out-stations, 1 native pastor, 2 other native workers, 80 church-members, 1 school, 34 scholars.

**Odonga,** a region north of Herero, West Africa, very fertile but full of fever, inhabited by the Ovamboes, a negro race. In 1870, 10 Finnish missionaries were allowed to settle here, and formed three stations at Omandongo, Olukonda, and Omulonga. The king liked them better than his own medicine-men, and when in 1883 they translated Luther's Catechism and some extracts from the Bible, and converted six young men, he decided to investigate the affair thoroughly, the result of which was, that he ordered the Finns to instruct his whole people. In the same year he died, but his successor proved also favorable to the missionaries, and for their sake he ordered that the dead king's wives and councillors should not be killed.

**Odumase,** a town on the Amu or Volta River, Gold Coast, West Africa, in the extreme northern part of the district of Adangme, northeast of Akropong. Mission station of the Basle Missionary Society. In 1856 two of the king's sons were converted, and now the station has 461 members, 236 communicants.

**Ogbomoshaw,** town in Yoruba, West Coast Africa, 200 miles inland from Lagos, on the Gulf of Guinea. Climate tropical, though not oppressively hot; unhealthy, but better than on the coast. Population, 75,000. Religions, idolatry and fetichism; a few Moslems. Many gods, but few carved idols; certain trees, nuts, shells, rocks, etc., used as symbols. Social condition very low, but improving. Polygamy and domestic slavery common. Mission station Southern Baptist Convention (1851); 2 missionaries and wives, 1 church, 18 church-members, 1 school, 20 scholars. Missionaries of the C. M. S. from Ode Ondo visit it occasionally.

**Ohneberg, George,** a missionary of the United Brethren to St. Croix, West Indies. He was one of the first of the United Brethren who succeeded in establishing himself on this island. He went from the island of St. Thomas to St. Croix in April, 1751. The Christian negroes welcomed him with open arms, for since the mission was suspended in 1742 they had received only occasional visits from the missionaries at St. Thomas. He was hardly settled there before both himself and the Christian slaves had to endure many persecutions from the pagans by whom they were surrounded. The huts of the negroes were set on fire, and sometimes entirely destroyed. Mr. Ohneberg's house was burned, but his furniture was saved by the efforts of the Christian negroes. When these pagan people found they could do nothing to unsettle Mr. Ohneberg, and that he went on with his work, they gave up their persecutions and left him in peace. An estate of four acres was soon purchased by the Brethren, where they built a church and dwelling-house, and named the place "Freidensthal." The work increased more and more till the little church at Friedensthal could not contain the hearers, and service for nearly twelve months was held in the open air. As many as a hundred negroes were annually baptized into the church.

**Oita,** a town of the Matsuyama circuit, in the district of Hiroshima, South Nippon, Japan. Mission station of the Methodist Episcopal Church (South); 1 missionary and wife, 10 communicants, 2 Sunday-schools, 37 scholars.

**Ojibwa Version.**—The Ojibwa belongs to the Indian languages of British North America and the United States. The first part of the Scriptures published for the Ojibwa Indians was the Gospel of John, issued by the British and Foreign Bible Society in London in 1832, translated by John and Peter Jones, two Ojibwas in the service of the Methodists. In 1838 the American Bible Society issued an edition of the same Gospel, and in 1844 the same Society published the entire New Testament. A revised edition under the superintendence of the Rev. Sherman Hall followed in 1856. At the expense of the Society for Promoting Christian Knowledge, the Psalms, translated by Dr. O'Mearar, were published at Toronto in 1854. The British and Foreign Bible Society published in 1874 the Minor Prophets, translated by the Rev. R. McDonald of the Church Missionary Society, and in 1886 the Book of Genesis.

This tribe is sometimes confounded with the Chippewas of Athabasca, an entirely different tribe.

*(Specimen verse. John 3 : 16.)*

Gaapij shauendy sv Kishemanito iu aki, ogion jimigiuenvn iniu baiezhigonijin Oguisvn, aueguen dvsh getebueienimaguen jibvnatizisig, jiaiat dvsh iu kagige bimatiziuin.

**Okahandya,** a town in Hereroland, West Africa, east by northeast from Ojimbingue, and north of North Barmen. Mission station of the Rhenish Missionary Society; 2 ordained missionaries, 3 salaried and 5 volunteer native helpers, 180 church-members.

**Okayama,** a town in South Japan, 100 miles west of Kobe, on the highway thence to Hiroshima, 5 miles from Inland Sea. Climate mild, humid. Population, 35,000. Mission station A. B. C. F. M.; 2 missionaries and wives, 3 other ladies, 43 native helpers, 48 out-stations, 6 churches, 1,122 church members, 6 schools, 401 scholars.

**Okrika,** town in West Africa, on an island near the mouth of the Niger River, 30 to 35 miles northwest of Bonny. Climate unhealthy, owing to the surrounding dense mangrove-swamps. Population, 15,000. Race and language, Ibo or Idso. Religion, fetich-worship, now declining under the influence of Christianity. Government in the hands of a king and chiefs. Mission station of the C. M. S. (1885); 1 unordained missionary and wife, 1 out-station, 1 church, 10 communicants, 1 school.

**Ombolata,** a station of the Rhenish Missionary Society in Nias, Sumatra, East India, founded in 1873; 1 missionary, 4 native helpers, 283 church-members, 81 communicants.

**Omburo,** a town in Hereroland, Southwest Africa. Station of the Rhenish Missionary Society; 1 missionary, 3 native helpers, 145 members, 50 communicants.

**Ongole,** a town of 9,200 inhabitants in the Nellore district, east coast of Madras, India, half-way between Nellore and Masulipatam. Mission station of the A. B. M. U. The mission in the Nellore district was begun in 1842. From 8 members in 1867 it increased to 3,269 in 1877. Then the famine came. Idols were prayed to, but in vain. The missionaries came to the rescue, and with the aid of English money a canal was built, which will prevent the recurrence of any similar famine. The grateful Ongolites then came in large numbers to listen to the preaching of their benefactors. The station has now (1890) 2 missionaries, 3 female missionaries, 143 native helpers, 236 out-stations, 16 self-supporting churches, 17,159 church-members, 242 schools, 2,130 scholars, 1 high-school, 101 students.

**Onitsha,** a town on the upper course of the Niger River, West Africa, northeast of Aleuso. Mission station of the C. M. S.; 4 native workers, 200 church-members, 1 school, 80 scholars. In 1882 the king ordered that Sunday should be kept holy in all his dominions.

**Onomabo** (Anamabu), a circuit of the Wesleyan Missionary Society in the Gold Coast, West Africa, which contains 30 chapels, 84 preaching places, 4 missionaries and assistants, 1,928 church-members, 5 Sunday-schools, 598 scholars, 5 day-schools, 438 scholars.

**Oodeypore,** a town in the Merwar district, Rajputana, North India, northwest of Neemuch and south of Todgurh. Mission station of the United Presbyterian Church of Scotland; 1 missionary, 2 native workers, 14 church-members, 4 schools, 12 teachers, 421 scholars, medical mission.

**Oodoopitty,** town in Jaffna district, Ceylon. Station of the A. B. C. F. M. (1816); 1 missionary and wife, 1 native pastor, 1 church, 109 church-members, 1 girls' school, 25 scholars. The educational work carried on here and in other parts of the Ceylon Mission is almost independent of aid from the Board. In all departments of church work "there is genuine progress in Ceylon."

**Oodooville,** town in Jaffna district, North Ceylon, 5¼ miles north of Jaffnapatam. Hot, but healthy. Population, 2,354. Race and language, Tamil. Religion, Sivaism. Natives, half-civilized farmers. Mission station A. B. C. F. M. (1831); 1 ordained missionary, 1 female missionary, 54 native helpers, 2 out-stations, 3 churches, 380 church-members, 15 schools, 1,013 scholars.

**Ooshooia,** a town in Terra del Fuego, South America, on the north shore of the Beagle Channel. Mission station of South American Missionary Society (1869); 1 superintendent, 2 assistant missionaries, 1 female missionary, 3 native helpers. The work in these islands was commenced by Captain Allen Gardiner, who visited the place in 1851. Not only have the natives been improved morally, but the cause of civilization in general has been aided; for shipwrecked crews are now taken care of and guided to places of safety, instead of being massacred—a direct result of missionary labor.

**Ootacamund** (Utacamund), a town in Madras, South India, in the Coimbatoor district, in the hill country, near Coimbatoor, and southeast of Tillicherri. Mission station of the C. M. S. (1870); 1 native pastor, 5 other agents, 391 church-members, 9 schools, 425 scholars.

**Opium in China.**—In the millennium one of the most incomprehensible facts of history will be the way in which opium was forced upon the Chinese Empire. If heathen had done it, it had not been so strange, nor would it excite such surprise had it been the work of a papal power, for under that the Word of God is not allowed to mould the national character; but that England should be the guilty one—that source whence the gospel flows to so many lands, that home of Bible-societies—will be the wonder of that day.

One of her own citizens, Archdeacon Moule of Shanghai, says: "British authorities in India, well aware of the attitude of the Chinese Government, deliberately prepared and sent opium to China, with only two years' intermission, for sixty years" ("Missionary Review," 1889, 36). The Shanghai Conference of 1877 says emphatically: "We know that opium is a curse, both physically and morally, to the Chinese. We must appeal to the great heart of England, and when her heart beats warmly on this question this foul blot on her fair name will be wiped away." Mr. Alexander Wylie of the British and Foreign Bible Society says: "Unless some means be found to check the practice, it bids fair to accomplish the utter destruction of that great empire." Rev. George Piercy, for thirty years a missionary, says: "No one can fully comprehend all the evil that the English nation has done by manufacturing and supplying this death-dealing poison to the millions of China." Rev. Howard Malcom, of U. S. A., says: "No one can describe the horrors of the opium trade. That the government of British India should be the prime mover in it is one of the wonders of the 19th century. The escutcheon of England is made to bear a blot darker than any other in the Christian world" (Report of London Missionary Conference, 1888, vol. i. p. 472). Rev. J. Hudson Taylor says: "In China are tens of thousands of villages with small trace of Bible influence, but hardly a hamlet where the opium pipe does not reign. It does more harm in a week than all our missionaries are doing good in a year. The slave-trade was bad, the drink is bad, but the opium traffic is the sum of villanies. It debauches more families than drink, and it makes more slaves than the slave-trade."

Such testimonies might be multiplied, but we want facts; and from an article by Rev. G. L. Mason of Huckow we glean the following ("Missionary Review of the World," 1889, pp. 36-40):

Previous to the 18th century opium was used in China only in small quantities as a medicine. Till 1767 the trade with India was through the Portuguese, who imported annually about 200 chests, each weighing 140 lbs. Even as late as 1830 a large city like Hangchow had no opium-dens. Now it has 2,000. The rapid growth of the evil dates from 1773, when the East India Company entered on the business. In 1790, 4,054 chests were imported; in 1799, 5,000; in 1826, 9,969; in 1830, 16,800. In 1834 the East India Company closed its factory, but British officials continued the traffic, bringing 34,000 chests in 1836. After that, piculs of 133⅓ lbs. each were substituted for chests, and in 1850 52,925 piculs were imported, the number steadily increasing to 75,308 in 1880; in 1887 it reached 96,746 piculs, thus growing from 12 tons in 1767 to 5,312 tons in 1887 (London Missionary Conference, 1888, vol. ii. 546).

Let us try to catch a glimpse of the work of death wrought by this immense amount of opium. The opium-smoker can be detected in a crowd by his hollow eyes, sunken cheeks, emaciated frame, and sallow complexion. He needs three hours a day to inhale the drug, and then he cannot work more than two hours before he must repeat the dose. If he has not time for his vice and opium, he chooses the last. If he has not money enough for both, he buys only opium. If he has no money he pawns his clothes. If they are already pawned, he steals. He even sells his children into slavery, or his daughters to a life of shame, that his accursed appetite may be fed. Often wives are sold that the husband may have his opium. If he cannot get the drug, water flows from his eyes, his throat burns, his extremities are cold, and he dies in agony (London Missionary Conference, 1888, vol. i. 128).

One missionary reports that in three years he was called to attend thirty-six attempts at suicide caused by opium ("Missionary Herald," 1889, p. 255).

An opium-smoker came to another missionary from a distant city to be cured of the habit. Soon he became so sick that the missionary feared he would die, and told him so. He thought it all over, and said, "Teacher, I take the responsibility: live or die, do for me what you can;" and by the blessing of God on the means employed, and in answer to prayer, the poor wretch was brought back from the very gates of death (London Missionary Conference, 1888, vol. i. 136).

The traffic has doomed to death as many as would repeople London were its four millions to leave their houses empty to-day (Id., vol. ii. 546).

Up to 1860 opium was smuggled into China. In 1780 (because they could not take it on shore) it was stored on two vessels anchored near Macao, and thence taken in charge by Chinese smugglers. The Abbé Raynal (Tract i. p. 424) writes in 1770: "The Chinese emperors have condemned to the flames every vessel that imports it." It was prohibited in 1796, 1799, 1809, 1820, 1836, and 1837, and always on moral grounds. In 1828 the severity of the laws almost destroyed the trade. In 1831 and 1834 England sent men-of-war to Canton and armed the lorchas of the smugglers. In 1830 strangling was the penalty for selling the drug, and an offender was thus executed at Macao in 1832, in the presence of a crowd of foreigners. Still Chinese prohibition did not prohibit; but this was no excuse for England, for the Chinese did what they could to defend their country from this onslaught. A crisis came in 1839. The imperial commissioner, Lin, wrote to Queen Victoria, imploring her to put an end to the traffic, and for twenty days committed to the flames 20,283 chests of British opium, thus destroying $10,000,000 worth of the drug in the vain effort to save their country from English rapacity. This brought on the war of 1840, and at its close, besides ceding the island of Hong Kong, China paid $12,000,000 for the expenses of the war, besides the price of the opium. But when Sir Henry Pottinger demanded the legalization of the trade, the Emperor Ko Twang replied: "True, I cannot prevent the introduction of the poison, but nothing will induce me to raise a revenue from the vice and misery of my people." It would seem as though a Christian nation would have thanked God for such words from a heathen monarch, and rallied to his help. Instead of that, for fourteen years England stubbornly pursued her course of ruin, till in 1857 a smuggler bearing the British flag was fired on, and this was made the pretext for bombarding Canton, while England and France advanced together up the Peiho toward Pekin, and the emperor was forced to legalize the destruction of his people by British opium in the treaty of 1860, negotiated by Lord Elgin, besides paying $10,800,000 to England and $6,000,000 to France. This opened five ports to opium and the gospel; and in 1887, eighty years after the arrival of Robert Morrison in China, there was a total of 32,000 converts to Christianity in the empire, and 150,000,000 who were victims of opium either in their own persons or in their families ("Missionary Review," 1888, 678; and London Missionary Conference, 1888, vol. i. 131). If any ask for the secret of so great wickedness on the part of a Christian nation, let a member of its own Parliament give

the answer. The late Mr. Henry Richards said in the House of Commons: "It might be true that England spread among the Chinese demoralization, disease, and death; but there was the Indian revenue. The traffic might create an enormous amount of hatred against England; but there was the Indian revenue. The traffic might constitute a most formidable obstacle to the evangelization of China; but there was the Indian revenue. It might prevent the development of all legitimate commerce, and dishonor England before the world, but there was, etc., etc. ("Missionary Review," 1888, p. 679; London Missionary Conference, 1888, vol. i. 473).

The second opium war only intensified the evil. The government after 1860 made few efforts to discourage the cultivation of the poppy; for if opium must be used, they preferred not to enrich those who had so persistently fastened the plague upon the country. In the province of Sichuan government interference with raising opium ceased in 1865. In July, 1861, the government made a pathetic appeal to England, and in October a supplementary convention was signed at Pekin, allowing China to raise the import duty from 30 to 50 taels; but even this England refused to ratify, lest her Indian revenue should suffer.

In 1876 the Chefoo convention opened four more ports to trade, in return for which England agreed that the inland transit duty on opium should differ from that on other goods, so as if possible to check the trade. The additional ports were opened, but this other clause was not ratified. After seven years of evasion China proposes 80 taels transit dues, in addition to the import duty. Earl Granville proposes 70, and insists that China must guarantee not to hinder the trade by further taxes. Next year (1884) the Marquis Tseng claims that China may tax it as she pleases after it has passed into Chinese hands. The agreement, such as it was, was not signed till July, 1885, and went into effect February 1, 1887. By this a total revenue of $1.10 per lb. brings a little more money into the treasury, but intensifies the evil. The cancer strikes deeper into the heart of the nation. The customs reports for 1887 tell how the new rule "benefits the trade." The trade "acquires stability" and "increased facility." One commissioner reports: "The native dealers send it to markets more distant than before." Forty-five million dollars spent in one year (1887) for foreign opium, half of it by those unable to buy both opium and good food, means immense suffering. In that part of Shanghai under European control more than 1,200 opium saloons were licensed in 1887, and a burglar would be received into the church as soon as a smoker of opium. A missionary preaching on a street in China mentioned the word hell. "Yes," replied a respectable elderly man, "since you foreigners came China has become hell." Some may claim that the concessions of China to England in this matter have been voluntary. Yes, in the light of these facts, as voluntary as the giving up of one's purse to a midnight highwayman.

God grant that England may not persist in this evil course. The United States of America put slavery in the Constitution, and seemed to prosper for nearly eighty years, but retribution did not sleep, and three billions of national debt, 300,000 wounded men, and 500,000 graves bear witness that it is not safe for a nation to persist in wrong.

**Orange Free State,** one of the Boer republics in South Africa, north of Cape Colony, west of Natal, and south of the Transvaal. (See Africa.)

**Organization of Missionary Work.** —The methods of missionary work are much the same wherever or by whomever they are carried on. Personal influence, public preaching, education, pastoral supervision, do not vary greatly whether found in Africa, Japan, or Turkey, or conducted by Moravians, Episcopalians, Baptists, or Methodists. The agencies by which the methods are conducted do, however, vary not a little, and differences of organization merely, not infrequently seem to imply differences of method and even of aim and purpose.

The purpose of this article is to furnish a statement of the different forms of organization used in mission work, and the agencies employed both at home and on the foreign field.

1. *At Home.*—Into the question of the degree of organization needed, it is not necessary to enter here. It is sufficient to say that the present forms have been the direct outgrowth of the pressing needs of the situation. 1. Missionaries in foreign lands must be supported (the instances of self-support being so few and so exceptional as to be practically ruled out of the question), and money must be raised and forwarded to them. 2. It is not every man or woman who, however willing, can advantageously work in foreign lands; there must be some means for selecting those who are best qualified. 3. In the conduct of foreign work two things are essential: first, that expenditure be proportioned to receipts; second, that different sections of the great work shall not clash, or one assume relatively undue importance over another. It thus becomes necessary that there be some central authority to keep, so far as practicable, an even hand over the whole wide extent. 4. Those who give for the support of missions have a natural and righteous desire to know what is accomplished by them, and there must be the means of collecting and imparting that information. 5. As mission work in most instances involves the holding of property, there must be some corporate body having a recognized existence before the law.

The necessity of meeting these demands has resulted in the formation of Missionary Societies or Boards, so organized as to provide for these varied departments.

As full a list of these as it has been practicable to secure is printed in Appendix C. For convenience there they have been divided into sections.

I. Those societies which are engaged directly in general foreign missionary work by sending out missionaries, and which are not confined by their constitutions to any particular phase of that work or to any special country. They are either interdenominational, i.e., drawing their support from different churches, or represent some one of the different denominations.

II. Woman's Boards. Societies organized by women, with special reference to work among women, and either independent, i.e. sending out their own missionaries, or acting in connection with some general society.

III. Special Societies which are confined by their constitutions to specific forms of work or to distinct territories. These include: (*a*) Aid societies, which merely collect funds to assist other societies, especially from people who are interested in their work, but are not naturally included in their constituency. (*b*) Bible and Publication Societies, which engage directly in foreign work by the employment of colporteurs and distributing agents. (*c*) Seamen's Societies, which undertake foreign work for seamen. (Many local organizations are not included in this list.) (*d*) Medical Missionary Societies, whose object is to train and furnish physicians (male and female) who shall enter the foreign work, either independently or in connection with some general Society.

IV. Individual efforts and miscellaneous organizations, including many of the "Faith" missions.

All of these with regard to which it has been practicable to secure any statement either from headquarters or from published accounts, will be found described under their several headings. We are concerned in this article chiefly with the general statement of the organization and agencies.

ORGANIZATION. I. *Organized Missionary Societies or Boards.*—These may be classed under three general heads: 1. Those directly controlled by some ecclesiastical organization. 2. Those ecclesiastically connected with some denomination, but not controlled by it. 3. Those independent of any ecclesiastical connection.

1. Those directly controlled by some ecclesiastical organization. Among these are the Presbyterian Boards; the Missionary Society of the Methodist Episcopal Church (North), U. S. A.; the Domestic and Foreign Missionary Society of the Protestant Episcopal Church in the United States; the Missionary Society of the Moravian Church; and most of the Lutheran Boards of America and Europe. In them the society or board is a committee appointed by and responsible to the general governing body of the church or denomination. These are: The General Assemblies of the various Presbyterian Churches; the General Conference of the Methodist Episcopal Church (North); the General Convention of the Protestant Episcopal Church in the United States; and the General Synod of the Moravian Church. Whenever there are so-called members, directors, etc., the term is merely honorary, indicating that such persons have by virtue of certain grants of money been allowed certain privileges, e.g. of receiving regularly the Society's publications, or attending certain regular meetings. They do not indicate any right to vote upon any action of the Society or Board. Officials are required to belong to the denomination, and missionaries must have received ordination from authorities recognized by the Church. In case of difference between the missions and the Board there is an appeal to the General Assembly, etc.

2. Those ecclesiastically connected with some denomination, but not directly controlled by it. Among these are the Church Missionary Society, the Society for the Propagation of the Gospel, and the various Baptist, Methodist, and Wesleyan Societies of England, the United States, and Canada. In these the societies or boards are composed of members of the denomination which they represent, either by virtue of grants of money, or by appointment to represent certain churches. Their officials and

missionaries are members of the denomination, and are required to conform to its customs and discipline. So far as the direction of the affairs of the society or mission is concerned, the authority of the board itself is final—there is no appeal.

3. Those independent of ecclesiastical relations. Among these are the American Board of Commissioners for Foreign Missions, the London Missionary Society, the Paris Evangelical Society, the Basle and Berlin Missionary Societies, the British and Foreign and American Bible Societies, and most of the special societies. Here, however, we find again two classes: (1) Those which are general in their membership; and (2) those that are self-perpetuating, or close corporations.

The first class includes the London Missionary Society, the Bible Societies, and most of the special societies. In them the membership is absolutely unlimited in number, and any person can become a member by acceding to certain conditions. He then has the right to vote in the annual or general meetings of the society when the special committees or boards are elected.

The second class includes the A. B. C. F. M., the Paris Evangelical Society, and the Basle and Berlin Missionary Societies. In them the membership is restricted in number, and the right to vote at any meeting of the society is confined to the actual members of the society, who alone have the right to elect other members.

In neither class is there any restriction of denominational connections or of special ordination and discipline, though, as a matter of fact, both the A. B. C. F. M. and the London Missionary Society have become Congregational societies.

The decision of the general society in every case is final—there is no appeal.

II. *Faith Missions.*—These in general are mission enterprises, in which the missionaries go to the foreign field without the assurance of any definite or continued support from the home land. They usually claim to put forth no efforts to secure such support, beyond the offering of prayer to God. In some cases they seek to support themselves by some occupation on the ground; but as a rule they give themselves entirely to their work, relying solely upon whatever gifts may come to them from friends at home, or may be given by travellers and others who visit them. In most instances they are carried on by individuals, but occasionally they have a more or less elaborate organization. The most prominent instance of these is the China Inland Mission. (For a full statement see article.) There is no formal organization, but a committee or council receives and forwards funds, publishes reports, and renders accounts. The same thing is practically done by individual friends for all the smaller Faith Missions. Public appeals are seldom made, as in the case of the organized societies, and the missionaries are absolutely independent (in most cases) of any ecclesiastical direction, though they are always connected with some religious body.

AGENCIES.—The agencies employed by the organized societies in the prosecution of the work of the five departments, viz., collection and forwarding of funds, selection of missionaries, direction of the foreign work, furnishing reports, and holding of property, are, 1. A committee; 2. Executive officers.

1. *The Committee.*—In the case of the societies of the first class enumerated above, viz., those directly under the control of an ecclesiastical organization, the committee and the board are identical. In the other classes they are generally appointed by the general society, though in some cases, as in the American Baptist Missionary Union, the society appoints a Board of Managers, which in its turn appoints an Executive Committee. However appointed or however named,—Board of Managers, Executive Committee, Prudential Committee, Advisory Committee, etc.,—its duties are to conduct the affairs of the society under the general direction of the society or the church. All matters pertaining to the particular policy or active operations both at home and abroad, are discussed and decided in its meetings, and it is rarely the case that an appeal is taken to the general society or church, or, if taken, sustained. In fact these committees are, for all practical purposes, the societies, the latter doing, as a rule, little more than mark out general lines of policy. Each committee appoints sub-committees for the special departments. These vary greatly in their form, according to the differing customs of each society.

2. *The Executive Officers.*—These are the secretaries, treasurers, agents, etc. Scarcely any two societies apportion their duties in the same way, but those duties are so familiar that they need no special mention. They are never voting members of the committee, but merely executive officers. The definition of a few of the terms in general use among such of the societies as make a distinction between the different officers will suffice.

A *foreign* secretary has charge of the correspondence with the missions, presents to the committee all questions relating to the conduct or interests of the foreign work, and the estimates for the missions. A *home* secretary has general charge of the home department, with special reference to the raising of funds, and the relations of the committee or board to the churches. In some cases all applications for appointment to the foreign field pass through his hands, in other cases they go to the foreign secretaries. An *editorial* secretary has general charge of the publications of the society, edits the periodicals and the annual reports, and superintends, when he does not prepare, the various leaflets, tracts, etc., by which the knowledge of the society's operations is disseminated. A *field* secretary is one, whose special work it is to visit the churches, attend meetings of ministers, and arrange plans for public presentations of the needs of the society. This work of visiting is shared by all the secretaries, according to their time and ability. In some cases there is a *recording* secretary, as a permanent official whose special duty it is to keep the record of all the transactions of the committee. In other cases that work is divided up among the other secretaries. Some societies also employ *district* secretaries, who have special charge of certain sections of country, gather the subscriptions, arrange for visits and addresses, and reports to the committee, generally through the home or the recording secretary. The *treasurer* has charge of all moneys and accounts. He receives all remittances, makes all payments, keeps all accounts, and receives and disburses the appropriations after the estimates have been passed upon in committee. He furnishes to the monthly periodicals full statements of moneys received, and his accounts are submitted to auditors for careful examination. In some instances the office of treasurer is honorary, the regular work being conducted by an assistant treasurer or a financial secretary. Usually there is also a general or business agent, who has charge of the publishing department, and the purchase and forwarding of outfits, supplies, etc., for missionaries.

The term *honorary* secretary, etc., is at times applied to persons who serve in the office, but without receiving any renumeration.

The executive officers are the only persons connected with the society who receive salaries. Members of committees or of boards invariably serve gratuitously.

In the case of some of the smaller societies, where the duties are not numerous or heavy, they are performed freely by some minister or layman, but in all the large societies, where the duties require the whole time of the officers, salaries are paid.

Taking up now the different departments as carried on by the boards in their home work, we notice:

1. The collection of funds and their remittance to the foreign field.

The income of a missionary society includes (*a*) all donations, collections, subscriptions, whether by individuals, churches, Sunday-schools, auxiliaries, bands, etc. These are sent either direct to the treasurer, or through some local or church organization, and are, as a rule, applied to the general purposes of the board.

(*b*) Legacies. These are usually payable in full by the executors of a will, but are in some instances subject to conditions of annuity or application to some distinct purpose.

(*c*) The income of invested funds (usually legacies). In some cases these funds have been by their donors set apart for special objects, e.g., the payment of the salaries of the executive officers, or the support of certain departments of mission work. Here also may be classed the income from certain buildings owned by the societies. It has become increasingly the custom for the societies to own the premises where their offices are located. The original erection or purchase of these has been in almost if not in every case from moneys contributed for that special purpose, and entirely apart from the ordinary donations to the missionary work of the society. Heavy rents have thus been saved, and in some instances the additional income is sufficient to meet the ordinary expenses of home management.

The remittance of money to the missionaries on the field is generally through some well-known banking-house of New York or London which has commercial dealings with the country where the mission is located, and is in the form of bills of exchange or letters of credit such as are issued to travellers. These are sold on the field either to representatives of the banking-house that issues them or to local traders who have dealings with England or America.

2. The selection of missionaries. This is one of the most difficult duties that devolves on a mission board. The peculiar elements that enter into foreign life, the strain of changed climate, food, habits of life, unaccustomed forms of thought and language, the necessity of very close and intimate relations with associates, the demands of sudden emergencies, etc., all enter into the consideration. Then, again, the strange misconceptions as to the nature of missionary work, the idea that personal consecration is all that there is to be considered, often cause great perplexity to the officers of the board. Without entering into the discussion of the qualifications necessary for missionaries, it will be sufficient here to indicate the course pursued in their selection and appointment.

This course varies greatly in different societies, and even in the same society there is no iron-clad rule. There are, however, certain points of examination that are common to all. The most important of these are: 1. Examination on doctrinal beliefs and ecclesiastical relations. In certain denominations this amounts to no more than the ascertaining of the antecedent action of church authorities (Episcopal or Presbyterian ordination is accepted as final), and in all it is in the great majority of cases more formal than minute, with a view to securing that the missionary shall be in substantial harmony with those whose representative he is, and with those who are to be his associates. 2. Physical examination. This is with a view to secure those only whose physical health is such that there is a reasonable probability that they will be able to endure the strain of life in a foreign land, and not be obliged to return home after all the expense incidental to their being sent out is incurred. 3. What may be called a general examination, including the circumstances of the candidate. Are there relatives who may be compelled to look to him for support? Is there ability to acquire with comparative ease a foreign and difficult language; such a temperament as will make it easy to co-operate with others; the faculty of adapting one's self to circumstances, etc. These examinations are conducted with great courtesy, kindness, frankness, and thoroughness, as is instanced by the small number of failures on the foreign field, and the few examples of those who have felt aggrieved by the refusal of the board to grant an appointment.

The examinations finished, the appointment is given, and preparations are made for the departure. In the case of some societies, especially in England and Germany, there comes then a period of special training and preparation with a view to fitting the missionary for the special work that is before him. In America there is often something of the same kind done by the appointee's taking special courses in language, medicine, etc. The whole question of the preparation of missionary candidates is under discussion.

3. The conduct of the foreign works. It is in place here to make a brief statement of the general scope of the business included in the foreign work of a Missionary Society, as indicated in the article on Methods of Missionary Work. It is (1) a great evangelistic agency, employing hundreds of men and women whose chief, almost sole, duty it is to preach the gospel. (2) A bureau of education supplying every grade of instruction to thousands who would otherwise be absolutely ignorant of the most ordinary truths of religion and science. (3) A publishing society with all its different departments of translation, editing, publication, and

distribution. (4) A building society for the erection of churches, colleges, hospitals, etc. (5) An aid and charitable society for the assistance of the suffering poor, the diseased, the widowed and orphaned. All the various departments that in Europe and America are divided among a dozen different organizations are here combined into one.

As a rule, the decision in regard to the detailed conduct of the missions is committed into the hands of the missionaries on the field. Questions, however, are constantly arising which can only be decided by the home authority. Such are: 1. The question of expenses to be incurred in different departments, and the accounting for payments made. 2. The beginning of new work. 3. Relations between different missions and different societies in the same field. 4. General questions of policy in regard to the conduct of the work in its different departments. These are all perplexing questions, and questions in regard to which there is much division of opinion even among those best informed on the field. Perhaps the most difficult one is the first. Each mission prepares every year an estimate of the amount of money needed for the ensuing year. These estimates, while varying greatly in form, may in general be classed under three heads: (a) Expenses absolutely necessary, e.g., salaries of missionaries and certain native pastors and teachers, rental of buildings, etc.; (b) expenses that may possibly be curtailed, though needful to the best progress of the work, e.g., travelling expenses, publications, certain helpers and teachers; (c) new work. With these estimates comes a detailed statement explanatory of the different items. Then all from the various missions go to the foreign secretaries, are examined by them, and then presented, with their comments, to the committee. The committee, making a careful estimate of the probable receipts of the board from donations, legacies, etc., or else acting under general instructions from the Society, fixes a limit of the sum total to be appropriated, and then sets itself to the work of "cutting the coat to fit the cloth." New work, however attractive, must not be allowed to supplant the old, even if the churches are a little anxious "to see or hear of some new thing." At the same time old work cannot claim to itself such a monopoly as shall close the doors opening into new fields. At last the apportionment is made, and the appropriations are returned to the field. Then arise emergencies. "It is the unexpected that is always happening" on mission ground as well as elsewhere, and items of expenditure are always coming up that require immediate action. In these days of the telegraph consultation with the home board is far more frequent than formerly, but still there are many cases where the missionaries simply must take the responsibility of action. Then comes the question of allowing the expense. The rule is, of course, to stand by them as agents, yet there are times when the board is compelled to refuse certain items, and throw the responsibility back upon the missionaries.

To enter into detail more fully is beyond the limits of this article. Enough has already been said to show that the position of the committee is no sinecure, and that the men who meet weekly or oftener to consider and decide these varied questions are no less earnest and conse-crated in their labor than those who go to the foreign field.

4. The imparting to the churches of the information that they call for in regard to the foreign work, its ends, successes, difficulties, etc., is becoming more and more an important branch of the home work of the societies. There is a marked difference between them in every particular. Some societies publish very full reports, some very meagre. Some most carefully arrange and index everything; others give interesting general statements, but are not explicit in details.

5. The question of property-holding has assumed increasing importance in the prosecution of missionary work. The fact that it is in most mission fields simply impossible to rent premises suitable for the work has necessitated the purchase and erection of such buildings. The laws relating to the holding of property are very different in different lands; but whatever be the form of title, the actual ownership rests with the committee at home.

II. *On the Foreign Field.* Turning now to the organization of mission work abroad and the agencies employed, we find that the organization is: 1st. Territorial; 2d. Ecclesiastical. The agencies are: 1. Missionaries; 2. Native Helpers.

ORGANIZATION. 1st. *Territorial organization.* 1. Missions; 2. Stations; 3. Out-stations or sub-stations.

Missions.—The word "mission" is used in a great variety of senses, denoting sometimes a single undertaking, but as found in the majority of the reports of the missionary societies it indicates an organized (or simply associated) body of missionaries occupying a certain territory, e.g., the North Africa, the Mid-China, the Japan Mission. It includes a number of stations, with their out-stations and fields, and its extent is usually regulated by the ease of communication between the different parts. Thus the A. B. C. F. M. divides its general mission in Turkey between four distinct missions: the European, Western, Eastern, and Central Turkey Missions. The Church Missionary Society has its West Africa, Yoruba, Niger, and Eastern Equatorial Africa Missions. The American Baptist Missionary Union combines territorial and racial divisions, having the Japanese and Chinese Missions, but also the Burman, Karen, Shan, etc., missions in Burma. In the usage of the Methodist Episcopal Churches of the United States the term mission has the same meaning as in the A. B. C. F. M. until the formation of a regular ecclesiastical organization, when the mission becomes a conference. The Wesleyan Methodists of England limit the use of the word so that it is practically synonymous with district, having (e.g.) four missions in the island of Ceylon. The Society for the Propagation of the Gospel uses the term in the most restricted sense, combining its individual missions in dioceses.

Speaking now of missions in the general sense, as organizations or associations of missionaries occupying a certain territory or working for a special race, we find them, in the majority of cases, including the Baptist, Congregational, Presbyterian, Methodist, and most of the Episcopal Societies, having a more or less complete form of organization. They have regular meetings, conferences, or councils annually or semi-annually, with permanent officers, treasurer, secretary, or presiding elder. Action affecting the mission as a whole is transacted in these meetings, and transmitted to the home department through the appropriate office. Thus the estimates arranged (see above) at the annual meeting are transmitted by the secretary of the mission to the foreign secretary of the board; the appropriations made by the board return to the treasurer of the mission, who keeps all the accounts. This does not prevent personal correspondence or relations between the missionaries and the home officers, but it is found to be essential that matters of general importance should pass through regular stages, both that there may be no confusion and that clear record of action may be kept.

Stations.—This word also has varied meanings. Usually it denotes some city or large town occupied by one or more missionaries, from which the work extends to the surrounding territory. Sometimes it includes the whole field worked from that place as a centre, but the restricted use is the more common, and is that usually adopted in this Encyclopædia. In the stations too there is, as a rule, some organization, especially when there are a number of missionaries, an extended field, and many departments (see below).

Out-stations or Sub-stations.—These are places—sometimes an important city, more often a town or village, where there is mission work carried on. Usually there is a church or congregation ministered to by native preachers, and the schools are under native teachers. It is seldom the case that an out-station is the residence of a missionary. In the usage of the Methodist and some Baptist boards there is really no distinction between stations and out-stations, except as the most important centres of work are called principal stations and the remainder stations; the missionaries frequently reside at the different stations in turn. They also use the term circuit in the foreign field as at home, to indicate what other societies mean by station field.

2d. *Ecclesiastical Organization.*—This varies greatly with the different societies, is governed by the rules of the denominations at home, and follows the lines of the three classes mentioned above. Wherever the missionary societies are organically connected with the church, the missions, whether as Presbyterian Synods, Conferences, etc., are organic parts of the church. They are thus entitled to representation in the governing body of the church, and as a matter of fact are usually so represented.

In the second class, where the relation of the board to the church is not organic, the missionaries are under the ecclesiastical discipline of the church or churches at home, by the laws of the Society. In the third class individual missionaries are free to arrange their own ecclesiastical relations, entirely independent of the board.

With regard to the native churches, there is a wide difference of custom. As a rule they follow the lead of the missionaries, though except in the Episcopal churches there is no law governing them; and there is a large liberty left by almost all the societies to their representatives in the field in regard to the details of formal organization.

AGENCIES.—These are foreign missionaries and native workers.

1. *Foreign Missionaries.*—These are ordained, lay, female, and medical.

The great majority of foreign missionaries are, and except in special instances always have been, ministers, regularly ordained according to the laws of the churches to which they belonged. Specific instances in the history of the early missions of the London Missionary Society and the Moravians of the sending out of entirely or comparatively uneducated persons, to encounter the perplexities, trials, and hardships of missionary life, made it all the more evident that the rule must be that a man to be a successful foreign missionary must be a man of education and special training. This was for many years synonymous with preparation for the ministry, and probably it was due as much to this as to the special work of preaching that it became so decided a rule that all missionaries should be ordained preachers. There were instances where laymen went out as printers, but that was considered exceptional, and in some instances they afterwards received ordination. Another element in the case was the fact that the people of many foreign lands could not understand how a man who was not a "priest" could administer spiritual help and counsel, and they were somewhat unwilling to apply to any one whose ministerial status was not of the highest. As, however, missionary work has developed its different departments, as education in the home lands has become more general and in foreign lands more exacting; as medical work opened up; as the general work has extended to include many lines of business, such as publication, treasury work, etc.; as also the supply of ministers at home available for foreign fields did not equal the increasing demand, —the question of other agencies came up, and the lay element in mission service became more prominent.

At the present time, in all the organized societies, lay missionaries are employed chiefly as business agents, printers, instructors in the higher schools and colleges, and in medical work. It is increasingly the custom to put a layman in charge of the treasury, the accounts, and the publication work of the different missions. The lay element in education is enlarging constantly; and in medical work it is becoming increasingly evident that a physician who prepares himself for his profession thoroughly has no time to study theology, and in his practice he finds less and less need of it: indeed, it is in many cases a positive hindrance to be known as a preacher or priest.

Female missionaries have taken an increasingly important position, both in their numbers and in the amount of work that is done by them. Whether as wives or as single ladies, they have done and are doing some of the best work, both pioneer and constructive, that is found. They are not always mentioned in the tables of statistics, unless they carry separate commissions, though it is increasingly the custom in the annual reports to indicate them, either in separate columns as "wives" or "assistant missionaries," or by the letter (*m*) placed after the husband's name. Their work is threefold. First in order of time, and in the judgment of many, of actual importance, is that of furnishing and exhibiting a Christian home. The power of this no one can realize who has not had occasion to study into it, and note its relation to the establishment of a Christian community on a firm foundation.

Many a missionary wife and mother who has had little or no opportunity to go out among the villages or homes of the people has exerted through her home an influence that cannot be easily calculated. Second comes the work of visiting in families, reaching the women in their own homes, or as it is called in some countries, zenana work. Third in order of time is the special work of female education, conducted by women who have themselves received the best that modern education can provide. (See also article Woman's Work.)

It is in place here to speak of the association and manner of life adopted by the missionaries in the field.

1. It has been the custom in most countries to send and locate two or more missionaries and their families together. The reasons for this are so obvious that they only need to be mentioned: Mutual consultation in cases of perplexity, sympathy in trial, support in anxiety, social relief from the strain of work, division of labor. In much the same way as it has been found to be wise for missionaries, as a rule, to be married, so it is wise for families to be associated. When female missionaries, whether as teachers or zenana workers, are sent out, they also, as a rule, go "two and two" together, and establish a home of their own, or else join with the families of the stations. Thus a mission station almost invariably calls to mind a social circle of educated, refined Christian people, whose individual labors are scarcely more important than their combined power as a Christian community. Since the increase in numbers and importance of lay workers, there has risen a "community" method of life which is somewhat peculiar. Without being in any sense monastic, it seeks to reap the advantage of association. This is primarily economy, both of funds and of men. Under the community method a number of lay workers can be supported for the same sum that it costs to maintain a single missionary family. Another advantage lies in the possibility it offers of utilizing agencies that otherwise would hardly be available. The China Inland Mission and the Salvation Army have largely adopted it; and other societies, notably the Church Missionary Society, are considering it.

2. Manner of Life.—It is the universal custom in foreign missions to provide for the missionaries, so that their manner of life shall differ as little as possible from their home life. The limitations of surrounding customs, etc., are of course considered, and great expense is avoided; but so far as is practicable it is the policy of the societies to enable their missionaries to have such comforts as a family in moderate circumstances is accustomed to have at home. These are: a substantial, healthy dwelling, comfortably furnished; clothing and food adapted to the climate and their habits of life; service sufficient to enable them to give their whole time to the mission work, so much of adornment of the home as shall make it home-like. It is primarily a question of economy. To send a man or a man and wife to Africa, India, or Japan, and compel them to live as the natives do, would, in the immense majority of cases, doom them to early death, or at least to permanent disability. It pays for a mission board to keep its missionaries in good health. But there is an additional reason. With rare exceptions, a missionary has influence in proportion as he preserves his own individuality. In pioneer work it may be wise to conform to the customs of the land, and sink the foreigner in the native; but after his position is once established, the rule is that his own national and racial individuality should assert itself. This is matter of experience, as well as of theory; and notwithstanding the constant reappearance of the other idea, it has a stronger hold to-day than ever before. But the subject is too wide a one for discussion here. It should be said that in some cases missionaries have funds of their own or receive additional help from friends, and in this fact would be found the explanation of much adverse criticism.

3. Method of Support.—This is usually by a fixed allowance, arranged either by or in consultation with the missionaries themselves, and graded according to circumstances of location or of family. Some experience will show the actual cost of comfortable living, and then a unit is often adopted. That is increased according to the size of the family, and the demands upon it. In the large cities it is often imperative that the missionary maintain a certain social position, and carry an attendant expense which his associate in a smaller place does not need. The basis is an adequate support from year to year for the missionary and his family. In most instances it becomes essential for the children of missionary families to go to the home-land for education, in some cases for the preservation of health. For such, as also for those who are left widows or fatherless, the board are under obligation to provide, at least in a good degree, in case there are no other resources from which they can draw.

4. Vacations.—It is the custom in most if not all missionary societies to allow the missionaries to return to the home land once in a certain number of years. This, too, is the result of experience, and is found to be economy in the long run. It is needful for the missionaries: first, for rest from the unintermitting strains of missionary life; second, for recuperation by contact with the life of our rapidly advancing countries, and for the purpose of retaining a sympathetic relation with the growth of the churches whose representatives they are; third, for the strength that comes from free intercourse with friends and relatives; fourth, for the care of children and arrangements for their education. It is advantageous for the churches, too, to come face to face with those who know the problem of mission work from experience.

II. *Native Workers.*—These constitute naturally the great body of the working force. Not only is it impossible, but it is undesirable, for the missionary to undertake to do all the work of his field. His chief aim, next to the conversion of individual souls, is the establishment of the Christian Church on its own distinct basis, with all its different departments. As soon as there are converts they are utilized as workers, each with some responsible share in the work of the missionary,—at first as Bible-readers; then as catechists, teachers, preachers; and at last as pastors, in full charge of the general work of an organized body of believers. The relation of each of these to the missionary force is, as a rule, that of assistants, not subordinates. The missionary is the organizer and superintendent, and thus, in a degree, director; yet those who in a sense work under him still work with him, and follow rather than obey him. It has been the custom of many missionary societies to keep the missionary and native force entirely distinct. This has been due not to any lack of appreciation of the value of native work, or to any desire to exalt the missionary, but rather to the feeling that it was not advantageous from the point of view of the best development of the native churches to a position of independence of all missionary direction and assistance. In those societies where the work is but the extension of the home church this becomes less noticeable, and in them it is frequently the case that native clergy are placed on the same official basis as the missionary. A marked instance of the success of this is the great work done by Bishop Crowther of the Church Missionary Society in Africa. In every case there is the fullest mutual consultation, not only in regard to plans, but estimates; and it is very seldom a step is taken by the missions without the full concurrence of the native workers.

The question of their support is one of varying difficulty in different fields. At first it is usually assumed by the mission, but as the churches grow they are urged to take the entire support of their preachers and teachers, and also of those who do the aggressive work. In some missions the custom is adopted of requiring that a certain proportion of the pastor's salary be met by the people before they can have a distinct organization. There is, however, no rule, different arrangements being made according to circumstances of time, place, and condition of the people. In the older-established communities in many cases the entire running expenses of preaching and teaching are met by the native churches, the mission only assuming the support of those engaged in distinctively mission work, e.g., Bible, book, and tract translation, colportage, etc. Even this work is in some cases assumed by native organizations, such as the Bulgarian Evangelical Alliance, the Church Councils of Travancore under the auspices of the Church Missionary Society, etc. In some countries, notably in Japan, the churches commence their life with a good degree of self-support, and such an organization as the United Church of Christ in Japan is a wonderful power for good by reason of its development of native workers, identified with the native church.

Innumerable questions come up in this connection with regard to the amount of education to be given, the salaries to be paid, etc., which can only have a mention here, with the simple statement that whatever rules are adopted by different societies working in different fields, they all have one specific end in view—the training up, as rapidly as possible, but not too hastily, of a body of workers native to the land and in perfect sympathy with their churches, so that in due time the foreign element may retire and take up other work, confident that the church thus left dependent upon itself will grow stronger rather than weaker, until it becomes able to itself cope with the problems of Christ's kingdom in its own land.

The classification of native workers is not essentially different from that of Christian workers in America or Europe. Pastors, preachers, evangelists, catechists, colporteurs, Bible-readers, teachers, are essentially the same, and have similar duties and relations, wherever they are found.

As in the article on Methods of Missionary Work, so in this, there has been no attempt to give more than an outline of the organizations and agencies upon which the representatives of the churches rely for the great work committed to them. Special attention is called to the articles on the China Inland Mission, Moravian Missions, and Salvation Army, where many of these points are treated somewhat fully.

**Orissa** (British India), one of the four subdivisions of the lieutenant-governorship of Bengal; the other three being Bengal Proper (or Lower Bengal), Behar, and Chota Nagpur. The administration of each of these divisions is through a commissioner under the jurisdiction of the lieutenant-governor. It constitutes the southwestern part of Bengal; and its territory is thus limited: The divisions of Chota Nagpur and Bengal Proper touch it on the north; the Bay of Bengal bounds it on the east and southeast; south, it impinges upon the Madras Presidency, and west upon the Central Provinces. Its extent as defined by latitude and longitude is from 19° 28' to 22° 34' north latitude, and from 83° 36' to 87° 32' east longitude. The area is 9,053 square miles, and the population (1881) 3,730,735 souls. Several tributary states (see the general character of these defined in article "Native States") lie adjacent to the territory now described, and are under the political supervision of the Orissa officials. The area of these is 15,187 square miles, and the population about a million and a half, largely consisting of Aborigines, Kandhs, and others. This native district occupies the northwestern part of the territory, a hilly region, with a sparse population as indicated by the figures just given. British Orissa consists largely of fertile alluvial plains formed out of the deltas of three large rivers—the Mahanadi on the south, the Baitarani on the north, and the Brahmani between them. The people are almost exclusively agricultural; rice is the staple food. Over 95 per cent of them are Hindus, and only 2¼ per cent Mohammedans. The number of aborigines in British Orissa is over 130,000, most of them being included among the Hindus; only about 7,000 still practice their ancient aboriginal religion; nearly 4,000 were returned as Christians. These include 3,246 natives, most of whom are connected with one or other of the missions in the province, hereafter to be noticed. The million and a half in the tributary states consists of a fraction less than 75 per cent of Hindus, and a fraction less than 25 per cent of aborigines, many of whom have professed Hinduism, though still ethnically distinct. The most important of these aboriginal tribes are the Kandhs, the Savars, the Gonds, the Bhumijs, the Bhuiyas, and the Pans; there are also some Kols and Santals who are more numerous elsewhere. Some of the larger tribes also spread beyond the borders of Orissa into adjacent districts of the Central Provinces or Madras Presidency. A few Mohammedans, Buddhists, and Christians make up the fraction of 1 per cent left unaccounted for in the division of the population just made into Hindus and aborigines. The aborigines—it need hardly be said—for the most part cling to the hills, while the Hindus inhabit the valleys lying between. It was among the Kandhs that the practice of semi-annual human sacrifices to their earth-god prevailed, until the entrance of the British authority into these districts in 1835 put a stop to it. Kidnapping for this purpose—for the victims were usually obtained by violent raids among the quiet inhabitants of the valleys—was then made a capital offence; and the Kandh priests were induced to substitute buffaloes for human beings in their sacrificial rites. The Kandhs are described as finely developed and intelligent specimens of humanity, possessing capabilities of civilization which it may be confidently believed will before long be fully brought out by the agencies of Christianity and education. The language of Orissa among the Hindus is the Uriya, an Aryan dialect, closely related to the Bengali: sometimes it has been classed simply as a dialect of that tongue; but the latest scholars regard it as distinct. Among the aboriginal tribes different languages prevail; those of the Kandhs and the Gonds belong to the Dravidian family of South India (like the Tamil, Telugu, and Kanarese). The Kols, Santals, and Bhumijs speak languages of still another family, now called, from the name of the Kols, the Kolarian family. Many dialects are in use by as many distinct tribes inhabiting Orissa and other regions.

A word as to the history of this province will be sufficient. Brahmanical records in the Great Temple of Jagannath profess to trace the chronology of the earliest Hindu kings to the year 1807 B.C. Little reliance can be put upon these dates; but this much they make clear, that for many centuries before Christ Orissa was governed by Hindu rulers. Doubtless it was under these kings that the Kols, and the Gonds, and the Santals, and the Kandhs were pushed back from the plains to the mountains. Then from about 500 B.C. to the Christian era is the period of Buddhist development and dominion. Buddhist caves, dug out during this period (probably, though some assign a date as low as 1000 A.D.) still exist at Raninur. Then followed the period of the Yavana invasions, though just who the Yavanas were, is a problem not fully settled. They came, however, from some northern quarter. They were at last expelled, and Orissa was governed by two successive Hindu dynasties from the fifth century of our era until well on into the sixteenth. The worship of Jagannath, which according to tradition had long been practised in Orissa, was restored, after the Buddhist and Yavana eras, by the one of these dynasties, and the present Great Temple at Puri built by the other, in the twelfth century. During the sixteenth century the Mohammedans came, and Orissa became a part of the Mogul Empire of Delhi. In the eighteenth century, when the Mogul power faded before the rising Marathas, the latter ruled for a time over this province. From them it was taken by the English in 1803, by whom it has since been governed as a part of Bengal, as before explained.

The Hindus of Orissa are excessively religious. Temples and shrines abound. But the chief one, and one of the most famous in all India, is the one already named, sacred to Jagannath ("Lord of the World," one of the titles of Vishnu), at Puri. To this temple 300,000 pilgrims have been known to come in one year. The great Car Festival alone sometimes draws to it as many as a third of that number. The excessive crowding of these persons, under the most unsanitary conditions, has often given rise to cholera, and their dispersal to all parts of India has disseminated it. It is estimated that from an eighth to a fifth of the pilgrims die from exposure, exhaustion, and similar causes on the home journey. The government has done all in its power to prevent the outbreak and spread of disease, and to enable the pilgrims to reach home safely. But nothing short of an absolute prohibition of the pilgrimage would wholly prevent suffering, and such a prohibition could not be enforced. It would be too great an interference with the religious customs of the people. The popular thought of this great festival is associated with that of the self-immolation of devotees under the ponderous wheels of Jagannath's car as it is dragged along from the temple to the "Summer-house" of the god, a mile away. Doubtless the descriptions of these religious suicides have been exaggerated. The cult of Jagannath is opposed to the sacrifice of life; though it is probably the case that some devotees in moments of religious frenzy have caused themselves thus to be destroyed. Doubtless also many have perished through accident. But self-immolation during recent years may be said to be almost wholly unknown; and under the more careful police regulations introduced by English rule, accident is less frequent than formerly. The long traditional connection of Jagannath with Orissa helps to make his worship popular within the province itself; the popularity of it beyond the limits of Orissa is maintained, and within the province is still further helped by the fact that he is represented as a god of the people, without reference to caste or sect: he is the "Lord of the World." Prince and peasant are alike at his shrine; caste lines disappear there. The holy food, prepared at the great festival within the temple, is given without distinction to all pilgrims of whatever caste, race, or even alien faith. His worship is made to include every species of divine homage which any Hindu pays to any manifestation of the deity by whatever name addressed. This wide catholicity still further promotes the widespread devotion to him. Still another cause may lie in the fact that of late years a theory of sensuous worship has been advocated by the followers of Vallabha Swami (North India, 1520), who held that God was to be sought and honored in the enjoyment of the good things of the flesh. Vishnu or Jagannath was to be adored under the incarnation of Krishna, leading a life of sensuous pleasure. In the wake of such teaching, licentious and obscene rites easily followed and incorporated themselves in the system of permitted observances at Puri. In short, the religious history of Orissa is of the utmost interest; the Jagannath worship in which it has culminated involves some of the noblest as well as some of the most corrupting features of Hinduism; and its historic development is associated with the memory of some of the noblest souls in all the annals of Hindustan.

Education, at least in British Orissa, is making good progress. One boy in every three of school age is under instruction. The province is destitute of rail communication, though in 1885 a line was projected from Benares to Cuttack. It would be of great help to the pilgrim traffic. Traffic by sea is difficult, as the coast-line has no good harbors, and passage from the shore to the vessels is dangerous during the rainy season. It is therefore difficult to supply the province with food when famines occur, and much suffering has been the consequence of this state of things in times of scarcity. Owing to the exposed situation of Orissa it also suffers occasionally from inundations from the sea: vast tidal-waves, impelled by the tremendous cyclones which sweep at times over the Bay of Bengal, accompanied often by heavy falls of rain which aggravate the disaster by swelling the rivers, will devastate several hundred square miles of low-lying territory, and cause enormous destruction of life and property.

The Baptist missionaries at Serampore undertook, previous to the year 1820, evangelistic work in Orissa, but they withdrew in favor of the General Baptist Society (formed in England in 1816), which began work in this province in 1822. Cuttack, the chief city, was first occupied, and later Puri, the seat of Jagannath's temple and worship. The American Freewill Baptist Missionary Society (dating from 1835) sent its first missionaries, Revs. Eli Noyes and Jeremiah Phillips, to Orissa in 1835. Their stations are at Balasore (1836), Jellasore (1840), Midnapur (1863), Bhimpur (1873), and at seven other principal points. Their work is both among Hindus and Santals—evangelistic, educational (through both schools and printing-press), and medical. They have a training-school, a Bible-school, and an industrial school, as well as others of the usual character.

**Orizaba,** a large city in the heart of the mountains in the State of Oaxaca, Mexico; is the centre of an important work among the Indians, carried on by the Methodist Episcopal Church (North); has 1 missionary, 168 church-members, 1 school, 20 scholars. Methodist Episcopal Church (South); 1 local preacher.

**Oroomiah** (Urmia), a city of Persia, in the plain and west of the northern part of the lake of the same name. Population about 35,000, chiefly Moslems and Nestorians, though there are some Armenians. It is the centre for the Nestorians, who are found in large numbers in the city and the villages of the plain, and has been the seat of mission work among them for many years. (See A. B. C. F. M.; Presbyterian Board (North); and Persia.) The city itself is much like other cities of Persia, but the surroundings are especially beautiful. The extensive irrigation of the gardens and fields render it very malarious, and for many years the missionaries suffered a great deal from sickness. The village of Seir (q.v.), about six miles from the city, on the mountain, was chosen for a summer residence, and for the theological school during the whole year. Within a few years, however, advantageous sites have been secured nearer the city, and the general health has been better. Oroomiah was the scene of the great Koordish insurrection under Sheikh Obeidullah. The city itself was not taken, but the surrounding villages were pillaged and in many cases destroyed.

The present (1890) missionary force consists of 4 ordained missionaries and their wives, 1 lay missionary, 1 medical missionary, 6 female missionaries, 34 ordained native preachers, 29 licentiates, 126 teachers and helpers, 20 organized churches, 1,941 communicants, 2,021 scholars. Oroomiah is also occupied by representatives of the Archbishops' Mission to the Assyrian Christians (q.v.).

**Osaka,** one of the large cities of Japan, is situated on the main island, 25 miles southwest of Kyoto. It is one of the three imperial cities, is well built and clean, and is the centre of large tea-districts. A government college and academy are located here. The climate is mild. Population, 432,000. Its importance as a centre of influence has been fully recognized by the missionary societies, of which there are seven represented. A. B. C. F. M. (1876); 1 missionary and wife, 1 physician and wife, 3 single ladies, 20 out-stations, 7 churches, 1 girls' school, 403 scholars, boys' school, medical work. Methodist Episcopal Church (South), Osaka circuit; 6 stations. Protestant Episcopal Church, U. S. A.; 2 missionaries and wives, 1 physician and wife, 5 female missionaries, 2 churches, 100 communicants, 115 Sunday-scholars, 20 out-stations. Presbyterian Church (North), 1881; 6 missionaries and wives, 4 female missionaries. Cumberland Presbyterian (1878); 2 churches, girls' school, 65 pupils. C. M. S. (1874); 5 missionaries, 4 female missionaries, 2 native ministers, 220 communicants, 2 schools, 81 scholars.

**Osgood, Dauphin William,** b. Nelson, N. H., U. S. A., November 5th, 1845; studied medicine at Brunswick, Me., and Lowell, Mass., graduating at the University of New York in 1869; sailed as a medical missionary of the A.B.C.F.M. for Foochow, China, December, 1869. He soon mastered the intricacies of the Chinese language, acquiring a knowledge of both the Mandarin and local dialects. One of his earliest efforts was the establishment of the Foochow Medical Missionary Hospital. During the ten years of its existence medical aid was given gratuitously to 51,838 patients among the poorer classes. He established also in connection with the mission an asylum for the victims of opium, and in two years 1,500 patients received treatment, a large number of whom were cured. He was frequently called as a consulting physician by his medical confrères.

Dr. Osgood died at the Sanitarium, near Foochow, August 17th, 1880. The funeral was attended by many foreign residents, as well as by Chinese.

Dr. Baldwin thus writes of his worth and labors: "His mind was strong and active. He possessed good common-sense and a clear, practical judgment, not caring to spend much time in discussing theories. He seemed to be engrossed in his profession as a healer of bodily ailments. But to his missionary and native Christian friends he was well known as a devoted Christian worker, placing the good of the souls of patients far above bodily health." The "Foochow Herald" contained an article written by an English gentleman connected with a banking institution in Foochow, closing thus: "The energy, skill, patience, and never-ceasing care manifested by Dr. Osgood in the management of his hospital and asylum, and the value of his good work, compelled the admiration of the whole community of Foochow, and gained him the sympathy and support of every one."

Every hour he could spare from the active duties of his profession for the last four years of his life was devoted to the translation into Chinese of a standard work on anatomy. The finishing touches were put to it only on the day before his departure. The work has been published in five volumes, illustrated by numerous plates. It is the first of its kind in the Chinese language, and has been much used in China.

**Osmanli-Turkish.** Turkish printed in Arabic characters as distinct from Turkish printed in Armenia or Greek characters. See Turkish.

**Ossét Version.**—The Ossét belongs to the Iranic branch of the Aryan family of languages, and is vernacular in the Caucasus range, Russia. A translation of the four Gospels was made by a certain Jalgusidse, a nobleman who in 1821 joined the Greek Church with about 30,000 of his former co-religionists, and published by the Russian Bible Society at St. Petersburg in 1824, with the aid of the British and Foreign Bible Society. In 1869 the Psalms and in 1882 the Epistle of James were added.

(*Specimen verse.* John 3 : 16.)

Цӕмӕйдӕрідӕр Хẏпаẏ аѳӡӕ баẏарота лẏпеі, ӕмӕ
Jӕ jẏпӕггẏрл Фврӡẏлӕр радта ẏмӕп, цӕмӕj Ẏj ӡӕj
ура, ẏj ма ѳесӕѳа, ѳӕлӕ іп ẏа ӕпẏсоп пард.

**Ostyak Version.**—The Ostyak belongs to the Finn branch of the Ural-Altaic family of languages, and is spoken by the Ostyaks, who live in the province of Tobolsk and Tomsk, Russia, and number about 24,000 souls. There is a translation of the Gospel of Matthew extant in the famous collection of Prince Louis Bonaparte. Very recently the Rev. William Nicolson, the agent of the British and Foreign Bible Society at St. Petersburg, has called the attention of the Society to the Ostyaks, and a Gospel is now being prepared for them.

**Otaki,** a town on the southwestern coast of New Zealand. Station of the C. M. S. The "Book of Mormon" has recently been published in the Maori language, and a majority of the inhabitants of a small village in this district have gone over to the Mormons. This Mormon movement has interfered somewhat with the success of the Church Mission. Has 1 missionary, 150 communicants.

**Otaru,** a town in the Hakodate district, in the south part of the island of Yezo, Japan. Mission station of the Methodist Episcopal Church (North); 42 church-members. Worked by the two missionaries at Hakodate. Money is being collected to build a church.

**Otshi** or **Ashanti Version.**—The Otshi belongs to the Negro group of African languages, and is spoken on the Gold Coast and in Ashanti. As early as 1846 missionaries of the Basle Missionary Society undertook a translation of the Scriptures into this language. Parts of the New Testament were prepared. Since the year 1855 the work of translation has entirely devolved on the Rev. J. G. Christalles of the Basle Mission, and in 1871 the entire Bible was printed at Basle by the British and Foreign Bible Society.

(*Specimen verse.* John 3 : 16.)

Nà senca Onyańkōpoń do ẃiasc ni, se ode
ne ba a owoo no koro mãe, na obiara a ogye
no di no anyera, na wanyã dã ŭkwã.

**Otyikango,** a town in Herero-land, Southwest Africa, a little northeast of North Barmen, south of Okahandye. Mission station of the Rhenish Missionary Society; 1 missionary, 1 single lady, 3 native helpers, 406 members, 171 communicants.

**Otyimbingue,** a town in Herero-land, Southwest Africa, northeast of Salem, and southwest of North Barmen and Okahandye. Mission station of the Rhenish Missionary Society; 2 missionaries and wives, 2 single ladies, 7 native helpers, 380 members, 182 communicants.

**Otyosazu,** a town in Herero-land, Southwest Africa. Mission station of the Rhenish Missionary Society; 1 missionary, 9 native helpers, 140 church-members.

**Oua,** a station of the Micronesian Mission, on the island of Ponapi, Micronesia (1872). Of the 200 people on this island 124 are churchmembers, and their contributions for 1889 averaged $1.00 per member.

**Oudh** (British India), a province of the Anglo-Indian Empire, governed by a chief commissioner, who is directly subordinate to the Governor-General of India. Formerly an independent native kingdom, annexed by English in 1856. Practically a part of the Northwest Provinces, which see. Chief city, Lucknow, the fifth city in India. Population (1881), 261.303. Missions since 1857 mostly under direction of American Methodists.

**Oudtshoorn,** a mission station of the S. P. G. in Cape Colony, Africa. The mission field covers 1,780 square miles, with a population of 21,000; has 2 missionaries, 242 communicants.

**Owen, Joseph,** b. Bedford, New York, U. S. A., June 14th, 1814; graduated at Princeton College 1835, and theological seminary 1839; ordained as an evangelist by Presbytery of Westchester October 2d, 1839; sailed as a missionary of the Presbyterian Board for the Northern Provinces, India, August 5th, 1840. Most of his life was spent at Allahabad (1840–68). His labors, like those of most missionaries in India, were various—preaching, teaching, translating, and revising former translations of the Scriptures, and preparing commentaries on different books of the Bible. He was president of the Allahabad Missionary College, and professor in the Allahabad Theological Seminary. After 28 years of continuous labor he left in ill health for America via Scotland, intending after spending a few days in Edinburgh to visit his native land, and then return to India, but died in Edinburgh December 4th, 1870. He took high rank as a scholar. Of him an English resident wrote: "One of the most learned missionaries the American Societies have sent to India." When he left India he had just completed a second revision and edition of the Old Testament in Hindi, and a commentary on Isaiah in the Urdu language for the American Tract Society. He wrote a new translation of the Psalms in Hindustani, and several commentaries in the same language.

**Oxford,** a circuit in New Zealand, of the United Methodist Free Church Mission; 4 native workers, 2 chapels, 31 church-members, 2 Sunday-schools, 114 scholars.

**Oxford Mission to Calcutta.** Headquarters, 9 Keble Road, Oxford, England.—

The mission was founded in 1880 in answer to an appeal from the Bishop of Calcutta to the University of Oxford to "send out men to work among the natives of that city who have received or are receiving the advantages of the system of education provided by the English Government." The form selected for the mission was that which was suggested by the late Bishop Douglas of Bombay—that of a "missionary brotherhood." It was decided, therefore, that the Oxford Mission should form a community under a superior, although its members would not be bound by any vows for life, but would be allowed to withdraw at pleasure. The rules of the community were tested by two years' work in Calcutta; after which the bishop incorporated the first members of "The Oxford Brotherhood of the Epiphany."

*Foreign Work.*—The mission now consists of a head and three other members, all Oxford University men, who carry on work in three lines:

1. Interviews with the natives, lectures, and discussions. 2. The conduct of a school for native Christian boys. 3. The editing of a weekly paper called "The Epiphany," in which free discussion of all religious questions is carried on between members of the mission and inquirers.

The work is carried on at present only in Calcutta, but it is desired to start branches at Dacca and Patna.

An association has been started in connection with the mission under the name of the "Oxford Mission Association," which endeavors to aid the mission by any means in its power.

**Oye,** a district of Asaba, Upper Niger, Africa; is reached by the mission of the C. M. S. Owing to their influence, the market-day, which usually comes every five days, is postponed a day whenever it will come on the Sabbath, and thus the native Christians are enabled to keep the fourth commandment.

**Oyo,** a station of the C. M. S. in the interior district of the Yoruba mission, Africa. Has 1 native pastor, 29 communicants, 1 school, 16 scholars.

# P.

**Padang,** town on the west coast of Sumatra, East Indies. Population, 10,000. Mission station of the Rhenish Missionary Society; 1 missionary, 1 native helper, 31 church-members.

**Padre-Polli,** town in North Madras, British India, northwest of Berhampur. A purely agricultural village. Mission station of the General Baptist Missionary Society (1849); 1 native pastor, 1 chapel, 69 church-members.

**Pakhoi,** a city at the head of the Gulf of Tonkin, Kwantung, China, is a treaty port, with a population of 25,000. Mission station of the C. M. S. (1886); 2 missionaries and wives, 23 communicants, 1 school, 28 scholars.

**Pakur** (Pakour), a town of the Calcutta district, Bengal, India, is a centre of influence for many villages. Mission station of the Methodist Episcopal Church (North); 1 missionary and wife, 10 church-members, 5 schools, 120 scholars, 6 Sunday-schools, 130 scholars.

**Palaballa,** a town in the Congo country, West Africa, at the foot of Livingstone Falls, 110 miles from the mouth of the Congo River; is a commercial station of some importance, where the goods required for all the surrounding stations are received, stored, and sent out by caravans and carriers. Mission station American Baptist Missionary Union; 4 missionaries (2 married), 2 female missionaries, 1 church, 8 church-members, 2 schools, 127 pupils, 1 Sunday-school, 25 scholars.

**Palmanur,** town in North Arcot, Madras, India, near the summit of the Magli Pass, 2,247 feet above the sea, 26 miles west of Chittoor. A healthy station, 10° cooler than the rest of the district. Population, 1,931. There is a busy trade. Mission station Reformed (Dutch) Church in U. S. A.; 1 missionary and wife, 5 native helpers, 11 church-members, 1 school, 22 scholars, 1 theological seminary.

**Palamcotta,** town in Tinnevelli, Madras, India, 45 miles north-northeast of Cape Comorin, 2½ miles east of Tinnevelli. Climate healthy. Population, 17,964, Hindus, Moslems, Christians. Mission station C. M. S. Is the seat of a bishop since 1877, and has very large educational institutions, especially the Sarah Tucker Institute, a normal school, male and female, established 1860. The Palamcotta Church council includes 132 villages with 9 native pastors, 2,185 communicants, 69 schools, 1,963 scholars. The Salvation Army has here its headquarters for South India.

**Palestine,** see Syria.

**Palghat,** city in the Malabar district, Madras, 30 miles south-southwest of Coimbatoor, 68 miles east of Calicut, in a famous pass of the Western Ghats. Has a large trade and active manufactures. Population, 36,339, Hindus, Moslems, Christians. Mission station Basle Missionary Society; 2 missionaries (1 married), 19 native helpers, 4 out-stations, 5 schools, 2,060 scholars.

**Pali Version.**—The Pali belongs to the Indic branch of the Aryan family of languages. It is the sacred and learned language of the Buddhists in Ceylon, the Burman Empire, Siam, Laos, Pegu, Ava, and the eastern peninsula of India. Messrs. Don Abraham de Thomas, Mohandiram of the governor's gate, and Tolfray of the Colombo Bible Society, translated the New Testament, which, after having been revised by the Rev. Benjamin Clough of the Wesleyan Missionary Society, was published in Burmese characters at Colombo in 1835.

*(Specimen verse.* John 3: 16.)

ကသ္သာတံသ္ဂုဟ ့ ၊ သ္ဂေ့ အပိ္ဂာသေတ္ဂ ၊
အ့ ့ ့ ြ့ ့်လ္ ့ ့ ့်  ေ ၈ော သ္ လ္ လ ၊ ်
ု ့ ့ ် ့ ် ့ ့ ့ ့ ့ ့ ့ ့ ် ့ ့ ့

**Palnur,** town in Northwest Provinces, India, half-way between Secunderabad and Kurnool, 63 miles southwest of Hyderabad. Hot, but quite healthy. Population of town and adjacent country included in the mission field, 1,000,000, Hindus, Moslems. Languages, Telugu, Hindustani, Tamil, Marathi, Kanarese. Mission station American Baptist Missionary Union (1885); 1 missionary and wife, 1 other lady, 13 native helpers, 5 out-stations, 1 church, 303 church-members.

**Palnadu,** a district along the lower course of the Godaveri, Madras, India, where the Evangelical Lutheran General Synod, U. S. A., began a mission in 1842, and now has 11 missionaries, 2,986 communicants, 2,358 pupils, and a theological seminary with 23 students.

**Palpa Version.**—The Palpa belongs to the Indic branch of the Aryan family of languages, and is spoken in the small states north of Oudh, below the Himalayas. The New Testament was translated by the late Dr. Carey, aided by some pundits, and published at Serampore in 1832, but never republished.

**Pamban,** a town in the Madura district, Madras, India. Population, 4,833. Half the year the Ceylon Government have their immigration depot fixed here, and this, with the conflux of pilgrims from every part of India, gives the place an appearance of great activity. Mission station S. P. G.; 8 villages, 99 communicants, 8 schools, 226 scholars.

**Panditeripo,** a town in the Jaffna district, Ceylon, 9 miles northwest of Jaffnapatam. Mission station of the A. B. C. F. M.; 1 native pastor, 21 native workers, 1 out-station, 1 church, 74 church members, 8 schools, 531 scholars.

**Pangaloan,** a town in Northwest Sumatra, on the East Batang River, southeast of Sigompulan. Mission station of the Rhenish Missionary Society; 1 missionary, 1 female missionary, 3 salaried and 7 volunteer native helpers, 285 members, 19 communicants.

**Pangasina Version.** — The Pangasina belongs to the Malaysian languages, and is spoken by 1,000,000 persons in the isle of Luzon, Philippine Islands. In 1885 the British and Foreign Bible Society published an edition of 500 copies of the Gospel of Luke. The manuscript of the version was presented to the Society in 1873 by Señor Alonzo of Seville, who was for a considerable time in the Philippine Islands. Chiefly through the interest taken in the version by a gentleman long resident in Luzon, it has been thoroughly revised and rewritten by Señor Alonzo, who also carried the edition through the press. Señor Alonzo also translated for the British Bible Society the other three Gospels and the Acts, and one of the Epistles of John, which he also carried through the press in 1887. The whole of the New Testament is now translated, except Revelation.

Thus far 8,508 portions of the Scriptures have been disposed of.

**Pang-chuang,** a town in Shantung, China, 13 miles from Tung Cho, 185 miles south-southwest of Tientsin, and 6 miles southeast of Grand Canal. Natives poor, low, crowded for room in which to live. Mission station A. B. C. F. M. (1880); 3 missionaries, 2 missionaries' wives, 2 other ladies, 10 native helpers, 9 out-stations, 350 church-members, 1 school, 15 students. The opening of this station was the immediate result of the benevolence of the mission to the starving people during the famine of 1878.

**Pangkoh,** a station of the Rhenish Missionary Society in Borneo, East Indies, on the Kahayan; 1 missionary, 4 native helpers, 100 members, 62 communicants, and 30 pupils.

**Panhala,** a town in Bombay, India, 14 miles north of Kolhapur. Mission station of the Presbyterian Church (North), 1877; 1 missionary and wife, 1 female missionary, 6 native helpers, 3 out-stations.

**Panncivilei,** a town in Madras, India; a station of the Tinnevelly Mission, C. M. S., containing in the church council 12 Pukka churches, 55 villages, 4 native pastors, 942 communicants, 28 schools, 988 scholars.

**Pannikulam,** a station of the C. M. S. in the Tinnevelly district, Madras, India. In the church council here are included 104 villages, 5 Pukka churches, 5 native pastors, 1,141 communicants, 41 schools, 976 scholars.

**Pantjur na pitu,** a town in Northwestern Sumatra, in Butakland, on the upper course of the Bantang River. Mission station of the Rhenish Missionary Society; 2 missionaries, 2 female missionaries, 7 native helpers, 825 members, 171 communicants, 57 school-children.

**Pao-ning,** a prefectural city of Szchuen, China. Mission station of the China Inland Mission (1886); 1 missionary and wife, 13 native helpers, 1 out-station, 1 church, 14 communicants.

**Pao-ting-fu,** a city in Chihli, China, 100 miles southwest of Pekin, on the Honan and Shansi road. Mission station of the A. B. C. F. M. (1874); 3 missionaries and wives, 1 female missionary, and an important medical work.

**Papiti,** the capital of Tahiti, the largest of the Society Islands, Polynesia, situated on the northwest coast, and is the chief town and port. Mission station of the Paris Evangelical Missionary Society. The population of Tahiti is Protestant; the whole of the island was converted in 1819, and Queen Pomare was baptized. After the French protectorate was established in 1872 the missionaries of the L. M. S. were withdrawn, and Protestant work was carried on by the Paris Society, which has its headquarters at Papiti, with 2 missionaries, 2 female missionaries, 22 congregations, and 19 pastors in the whole district.

**Papua, or New Guinea,** is the largest island on the globe, except Australia. It is very irregular in its outline, but extends for about 1,300 miles, between latitude 0° 30' to 10° 40' south, and longitude 131° to 150° 30' east, and contains an estimated area of 300,000 square miles. Very little is known about Papua, as it has not been fully explored and surveyed. In general it is a mountainous country in the northern part, while the southern coasts are low and wooded. Vegetation is very luxuriant, tropical fruit-trees are found in abundance, while the woods of the interior produce fine timber-trees. In the cultivated portions sugar-cane, tobacco, and rice are raised. The climate is healthy, though great changes in temperature occur during a very short time. The inhabitants, so far as they have been classified, belong to the Negro race (q.v.), though there are several varieties of Polynesians represented. In number they are estimated at 800,000. Of their language the only knowledge we have is gained from the researches of the Dutch missionaries, who collected a vocabulary of the Myfore language containing 1,200 words. This seems to show that the Papuan languages belong to a separate class from the Malayo-Polynesian languages. The western part of the island to 141° east longitude is under the Dutch Government, and belongs to the Residency of Ternate, Molucca Islands. The southeastern part of the island was proclaimed a possession of the Queen of England in September, 1888, and is governed by an administrator, but little has yet been done to develop the resources of the island. Port Moresby, with a population of 1,500, is the principal settlement.

Mission work in New Guinea was commenced at Port Moresby by the L. M. S. (1871), and there are now 6 missionaries at work in Port Moresby, Kerepunu, Motumotu and Fly River, and Suau. In the Dutch portion of the island the Rhenish Missionary Society has a station at Bojadjin, and the Utrecht Missionary Society has 5 stations.

**Paraguay,** one of the South American republics, is situated between 22° and 27° 35′ south latitude, and 54° 35′ and 61° 40′ west longitude, southwest of Brazil and northeast of the Argentine Republic. Area, 91,970 square miles. The country in general consists of a series of plateaus with wooded slopes and grassy plains. The climate is very fine, though at times the heat is excessive. Summer lasts from October to March, and May, June, July, and August are the coldest months. The mean temperature for winter is 71°, and for summer 81°.

According to the Constitution of November, 1870, the government consists of a president, and a Congress of two Houses, a Senate, and a House of Deputies. The senators and deputies are elected directly by the people, and the president holds office for four years.

The population is 329,645, according to an imperfect census of 1887, besides 60,000 semi-civilized and 70,000 uncivilized Indians. There are twice as many females as males. The prevailing language is Spanish, but large numbers speak the Guarani; the mixture of Indian blood is stronger in Paraguay than in other states.

The principal cities are Asuncion (24,838), the capital, rapidly growing in population and importance; Concepcion (11,000); Villa Rica (11,000); San Pedro (12,000); and Luque (8,000). One third of the inhabitants live in the central districts, containing the capital, one third in the districts of Villa Rica and Cuasapa, and the remainder in the cultivated portion of the country. Agriculture and the raising of cattle are the principal occupations of the people, and Italians, Spanish, and German colonists are

developing its resources in both these directions. There is a railway from Asuncion to Villa Rica, and telegraph and telephone lines are in operation. Roman Catholic is the established religion of the state, but other religions are tolerated. Education is free and compulsory. In 1888, 28,526 pupils attended 160 primary schools. Asuncion has a national college. The only Protestant mission in Paraguay is that of the Methodist Episcopal Church (North), which has in the Asuncion circuit 5 foreign teachers, 1 native preacher, 106 church-members, 1 day-school, 80 scholars, 1 Sabbath-school with 60 scholars.

**Paramaribo** is the chief town of Surinam, South America. Population, 22,000. In the year 1835 the first Moravian missionaries landed in Surinam. The object was at first to commence a mission in Berbice, making Paramaribo the headquarters. Here a company of five brethren worked at their trades in order to support themselves and the mission in Berbice. Their attention was soon directed to the negroes in Paramaribo. At first they had to face a good deal of opposition, but they gradually overcame ill-grounded prejudice, and were permitted to purchase a piece of land in the town. For a considerable time their missionary work continued very limited, but gradually it expanded and Paramaribo became a genuine mission station, which prospered so greatly that in 1882 it numbered nearly 10,000 souls. Has 20 missionaries, 18 missionaries' wives, 1 other lady.

**Parey-chaley,** a town in Travancore, India, 32½ miles northwest of Cape Cormorin. Climate good, moist, 80°–85° F. Race, Dravidian. Languages, Tamil, Malayalam. Social condition good. Mission station L. M. S. (1845); 1 missionary, 124 native helpers, 77 out-stations, 8 churches, 1,264 church-members, 59 schools, 3,772 scholars.

**Paris Evangelical Society,** headquarters, 102 Boulevard Arago, Paris, France.— The Paris Society for Evangelical Missions among non-Christian Nations (Society des Missions Évangéliques chez les Peuples non-chrétiens, établie à Paris) was formed in November, 1822. Before this time several missionary committees had been organized in Alsace, the "Midi," and in Paris, which now joined the Paris Society as auxiliary associations. Among the founders of the Society were some of the most prominent of the French Protestants. Its first president was Admiral Count Verhuël; Jean and Frederick Monod, Baron A. de Staël, and other celebrated men were on this first committee. Its first general assembly was held in 1824, and in the same year an institution for training future missionaries was established at Paris. It is interesting to note that in this, its first year, the income of the Society amounted to 13,061 francs.

Until 1840 the work of the Society went steadily forward; from this time its funds began to diminish, and after the Revolution of 1848 the want of money forced the Society to close the training institute. Of the 82 pupils who had joined it, 34 were laboring as missionaries in heathen countries, 17 as pastors in France, and 6 as teachers; the mission work in Basutoland, South Africa, was still carried on in spite of difficulties.

One of the Society's first missionaries, the Rev. E. Casalis, returned to France in 1849. His missionary addresses delivered in most of the churches all over the country were crowned with most remarkable success, and a new love for missions seemed to spring up everywhere. The yearly income soon amounted to 180,000 francs. In 1856 the Training Institute was re-opened with M. Casalis at its head, and new spheres of labor were soon added to that in South Africa. Missionaries were sent to China (1859), to Senegambia (1862), and to Tahiti (1863). From the year 1866 the annual income was always more than 200,000 francs, except-ing during the Franco-Prussian War. In 1879 it rose to 300,000 francs. In 1885 additional work was undertaken among the Kabyles, a Berber tribe living in North Africa, and in 1886 a long hoped for mission was begun on the Up-per Zambesi (Evangelical Mission to Upper Zambesi, q.v.). In 1889 mission work was begun in the French territories on the Ogove and Congo Rivers. Until 1887 the training-school, being dependent on hired rooms, had migrated from one end of Paris to the other; in that year a mission-house admirably adapted to its pur-pose was erected at 102 Boulevard Arago.

The Paris Society is undenominational. Its management is in the hands of a council com-posed of a president, two vice-presidents, two secretaries, two auditors, a treasurer, and twelve assessors. This council makes its own laws, and also the regulations to be followed by the auxiliary committees formed outside of Paris. The services of the council are rendered gratuitously. A general assembly of the whole membership of the Society is held annually.

*Mission Fields.*—The first three mission-aries, Revs. Bisseux, Lemue, and Rolland, trained by the Society were, by the advice of Dr. Philips of Cape Town, sent to South Africa in 1829. One of them, Mr. Bisseux, settled in Wagen-maker's Valley, about 40 miles northeast of Cape Town, and preached the gospel to the slaves of the farmers, the first one of whom was baptized in 1835. Eight years afterward the mission removed to Wellington, from which centre the work developed. In 1875 there were in the church at Wellington 350 members, and 200 children in the schools. This faithful missionary labored on for a few years more, completing fifty years of work, the results of which cannot be told. Then, on ac-count of Mr. Bisseux's age, the mission was made over to the Cape Dutch Church, Mr. Bisseux holding the position of honorary pastor. Mr. Lemue and Mr. Rolland went to Kuruman to take for a time Dr. Robert Moffat's place, and to learn the Bechuana tongue. In 1831 work was attempted among several Bechuana tribes, but progressed slowly, because of the opposition of the chiefs of neighboring tribes, and the nomadic habits of the people. In 1832 a station was established at Motito, and two years afterwards the first baptism took place. In 1848 there were four out-stations around Motito, and a station had been established in what is now the Transvaal. On account of the diminished revenue of the Paris Society, the mission at Motito was resigned to the Lon-don Missionary Society, and that in the Trans-vaal to the Berlin Society in 1866, while the efforts of the Paris Society were concentrated upon Basutoland.

The first station was planted in Basutoland in 1833. The first convert was baptized in 1839. At the station of Morijah Christian refugees collected from all points, and the re-port of 1840 shows already 378 Christians at the station. In 1848 there were in this mission 10 stations, with many out-stations or preach-ing-places, and the mission staff consisted of 10 ordained missionaries, 1 medical missionary, and 4 lay European teachers or helpers. The total number of native communicants was 1,216. The series of wars between the British troops, the Boers, and native tribes hindered the progress of the work. Many of the converts returned to their old pagan customs, and the missionaries were beset with trials and difficulties of every description; but after 10 years of patient, persevering effort they found their reward in seeing the mission begin to flourish once more. Between 1858 and 1864 six new missionaries were sent out, and for some years the work progressed rapidly until again interrupted by wars. In 1883 Basutoland became a crown colony, and from that time the mission has prospered. There is now at Morijah a training-school for teachers, and a Bible-school for preparing evangelists and preachers. There is also an in-dustrial school at Leloalong.

Tahiti.—The French occupation of Tahiti in 1845 induced the Paris Missionary Society, at the request of the London Missionary Society, to send some workers thither. The whole work was taken by the Paris Society in 1865. The Society Islands are Christianized, and therefore this mission is now rather a "home" than a foreign work to the heathen.

The Society began work in Senegambia, west coast of Africa, in 1862. The deadly climate and other trials have held back this mission; but in spite of all the difficulties, the station at St. Louis has been maintained, and a new one established 80 miles inland, on the Senegal River, and it is hoped that the work may soon take a real start and make rapid progress.

In 1887 the American Presbyterian Board of Missions asked from the Paris Missionary So-ciety some French teachers to help in their school work on the Gaboon and Ogove Rivers, the French Government having forbidden the instruction of the natives in any language but French. Accordingly three teachers and one industrial assistant were sent out in 1888. In 1889 two young ordained missionaries were sent to the Ogove River to visit the American stations. Their report will be submitted to the Council, and work will probably be undertaken in what is now called the French Congo.

The entire number of ordained missionaries now in the field is about 41.

**Parker, Benjamin,** b. Reading, Mass., U. S. A., October 13th, 1803; graduated at Am-herst College 1829; Andover Theological Seminary 1832; sailed November 21st, the same year, as a missionary of the American Board, for the Sandwich Islands. Soon after his arrival he sailed for the Marquesas Islands with Messrs. Armstrong and Alexander. Re-turning with them from the unsuccessful at-tempt to establish a mission on those islands, he was stationed at Kaneohe, on Oahu, where he labored as a missionary of the Board until the change which placed the Hawaiian churches under the care of native pastors, when he re-moved to Honolulu, and was principal of the

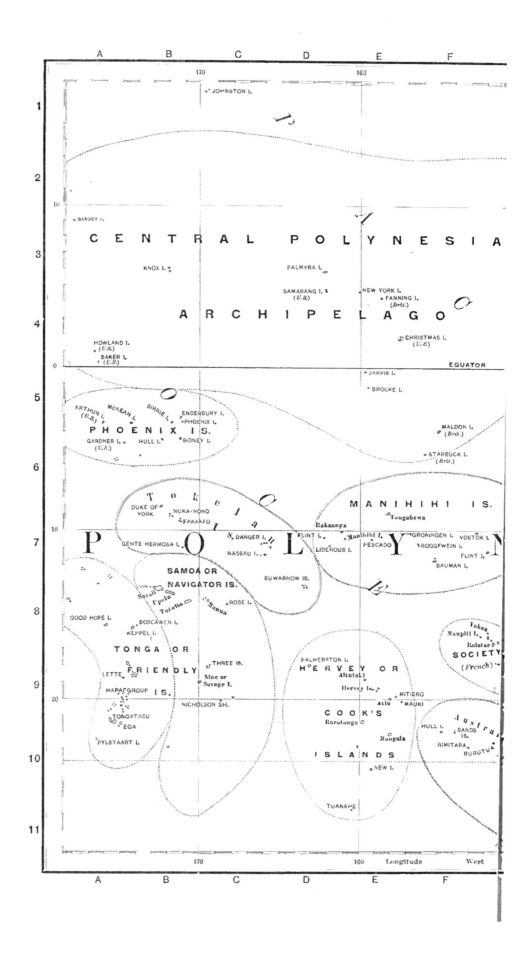

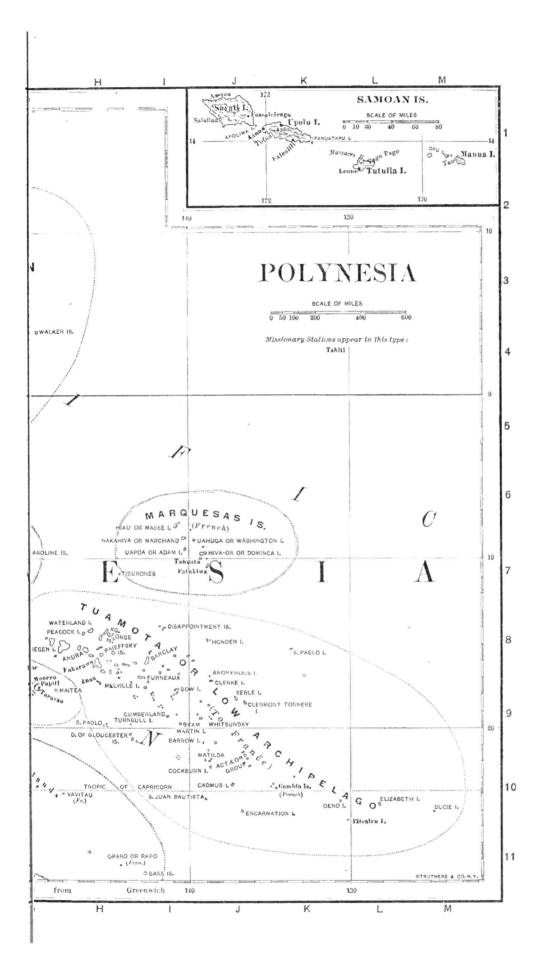

# POLYNESIA

SCALE OF MILES

0  50 100   200        400        600

*Missionary Stations appear in this type :*
Tahiti

SAMOAN IS.

SCALE OF MILES

0  10  20    40    60    80

Savaii I.
Salailua   Fasaalelanga
Apolima I.   Upolu I.
Anna   Apia
Falenlill   Tofoa   FANUATAPU I.
Massacre B.   Pago Pago
Leone   Tutuila I.
OFU I.   Manua I.

MARQUESAS IS.

(French)

HIAU OR MASSE I.
NAKAHIVA OR MARCHAND   UAHUGA OR WASHINGTON I.
UAPOA OR ADAM I.   HIVA-OA OR DOMINCA I.
Tahuata
TIBURONES   Fatuhiwa

AROLINE IS.

TUAMOTA OR LOW ARCHIPELAGO (to France)

WATERLAND I.
PEACOCK I.
KG.
GEORGE I.
IEGEN I.
ANURA
PAIEFFSKY IS.
BARCLAY
DISAPPOINTMENT IS.
HONDEN I.
S. PABLO I.
Fakarava
Moorea
Papiti
Taraytao   MAITEA
Anna   MELVILLE I.   FURNEAUX
ANONYMOUS I.
CLERKE I.
BOW I.
SERLE I.
CLERMONT TONNERE
CUMBERLAND
TURNBULL I.
BYAM   WHITSUNDAY
S. PADLO   MARTIN I.
D. OF GLOUCESTER IS.   BARROW I.
MATILDA
COCKBURN I.   ACTÆON GROUP
TROPIC OF CAPRICORN   CADMUS I.   Gambila Is. (French)
VAVITAU (Fr.)   S. JUAN BAUTISTA   OENO I.   ELIZABETH I.   DUCIE I.
ENCARNATION I.   Pitcairn I.
OPARO OR RAPO (Fren.)
BASS IS.

from   Greenwich   140

STRUTHERS & CO. N.Y.

O WALKER IS.

Native Hawaiian Theological School. In 1876, after an absence of forty-four years, he revisited his native land. He died at Honolulu March 23d, 1877, aged 73.

**Parker, Peter,** b. Framingham, Mass., U. S. A., June 18th, 1804. In his youth he worked on his father's farm, and when of age began to study for the ministry, teaching to earn money for his expenses. He entered Amherst College in 1827; graduated at Yale College in 1831; spent two years in Yale Divinity School, and took a course of medical study, receiving the degree of M.D. in 1834. He was appointed medical missionary to China by the American Board; was ordained at Philadelphia May 26th, 1834, and sailed the next month for Canton. In 1835 a hospital was opened for the gratuitous relief of the sick, which contributed greatly to disarm prejudice, and furnished opportunities for making known religious truth. In 1836 his Eye Infirmary had received 1,912 patients at a cost of $1,200, all of which was given by resident foreigners. In 1838 Dr. Parker had four Chinese students in medicine and surgery, one of whom became an expert operator. They were supported by the Medical Missionary Society, organized in February, whose president was the British surgeon at Canton. He visited the United States to promote its objects. The outbreak of the opium war with the English in 1840 making it necessary to close the dispensary, Dr. Parker visited the United States, reaching New York December 10th. In 1841 he was married in Washington to Miss Harriet C. Webster, and the next year returned to Canton, Mrs. Parker being the first foreign lady to reside in Canton. In 1844, with the hope thereby of aiding the missionary work, he accepted the appointment of Secretary and Interpreter to the United States Legation to China, and his connection with the American Board was soon after dissolved, though he did not cease missionary work, and his labors in the hospital continued till he resigned his secretaryship on his return to America in 1855. He often acted during these years as chargé d' affaires *ad interim.* Soon after his return he was appointed United States Commissioner to China, with plenipotentiary powers for the revision of the treaty of 1844. This service being completed in two years, he returned to America with health impaired, owing to the effects of a sunstroke. He resided in Washington, and in 1868 was elected Regent of the Smithsonian Institution. He died in Washington January 10th, 1888, aged 83. He published "A Statement respecting Hospitals in China," and an account of his visit to Loo-Choo Islands and Japan.

**Parral,** a town in Northern Mexico, 200 miles east-southeast of Chihuahua. Climate even, healthy. Population, 11,000, Spanish, Indian. Language, Spanish. Religion, a corruption of Roman Catholic. Mission station A. B. C. F. M. (1883-84); 1 missionary and wife, one other lady, 2 native helpers, 2 schools, 55 scholars.

**Parras,** a town in the State of Coahuila, Mexico, near Saltillo. Mission station of the Southern Baptist Convention; 1 missionary and wife, 1 single lady, 1 native pastor, 18 church-members, 15 Sabbath-scholars.

**Parsi-Gujarati Version.**—A dialect of the Gujarati is the Parsi, which belongs to the Indic branch of the Aryan family of languages, and is used by the Parsis in the Bombay presidency. A translation of the New Testament was made by the Rev. Dunjeebhoy Nouroji, and published under the editorship of Dr. Wilson, at Bombay, in 1864. For the educated natives the British and Foreign Bible Society also issued polyglot editions of the Gospel of Matthew, viz., Parsi-Gujarati with English, Marathi, and Sanskrit, and Parsi-Gujarati with English, Marathi, and Hindustani.

(*Specimen verse.* John 3 : 16.)

કેમકે ઓદાએ દુનીઆ પર એવો પીઆર કીધો કે તેણે પોતાનો એકાકીજનીત બેટો એ વાસતે આપીઓ કે, જે કોઇ તેના ઉપર એતકાદ લાવે તેહુલાક નથાએ, પણ હુમેરાની ઇંદગી પામે.

**Parsons, Justin Wright,** b. Westhampton, Mass., U. S. A., April 26th, 1824; graduated at Williams College 1848; sailed April 24, 1850, as a missionary of the A. B. C. F. M., for Turkey. He was stationed at Nicomedia and Bardezag doing general missionary work in Northern Bithynia. For thirty years he labored with unflagging zeal, " never so well contented as when upon those tours among the hills and valleys of the district he traversed so often, that he might preach Christ to those who knew Him not." " Brave enough and cool enough to lead an army, he carried with him no weapon save the gospel of peace, and with this he had successfully disarmed, through a long series of years, all the opposition he met." He was on his return from a missionary tour with Dudukian, a church-member, when they stopped near an encampment of Yuruks, a nomadic tribe of herdsmen. While Mr. Parsons and his companion were asleep they were attacked by three Yuruks and shot. The men were arrested, and the leader sentenced to imprisonment for life; it was found to be impracticable to secure the execution of a Moslem for the murder of a Christian. Mr. Parsons died August, 1880, leaving a wife and four children. The scene at the funeral bore witness to the power of the man, and the success of his methods of resisting evil. In a region where a few years ago the missionaries were hooted and stoned, there was at his burial an outpouring of the whole population. The immense crowd listened, amid their tears, to tender words of eulogy spoken by native Christians. The vicar of the Armenian patriarch, a native of Bardezag, was present from Constantinople, and made an address, bearing witness, after a friendship of more than twenty years, to his "spotless life."

**Parsons, Levi,** b. at Goshen, Mass., U. S. A., July 18th, 1792, graduated at Middlebury College 1814, sailed November 3d, 1819, with Pliny Fisk for the East, under the American Board. He arrived at Jerusalem February 17th, 1820, the first Protestant missionary who ever entered that city to make it the permanent field of his labors. He sailed with Mr. Fisk from Smyrna for Egypt, for the restoration of his impaired health, but died at Alexandria, February 10th, 1822. Great respect was shown him at his funeral by many persons from different nations.

**Pascoe, James.**—Work in Mexico: or The Gospel in Mexico. An individual mission, carried on in Toluca and other towns of Mexico, by James Pascoe from 1868 till his death in 1888, and then entrusted to a son and daughter. Present headquarters: San Telmo. It has no regular organization, but receives funds through Mr. John Mercer, Clitheroe, Lancashire, England.

James Pascoe, b. in Hellston, Cornwall, England, 1841, was educated in the Nautical Academy, where he was converted. In 1858 he went as midshipman on a sailing-vessel to Madras and Burmah, and through his efforts the ship, which left England, "a very floating hell," so vile and blasphemous were captain, crew, and passengers, was so changed that it returned "a floating Bethel."

In 1865 he went to Mexico in connection with a silver-mining company, hoping that this would prove the long-desired opening for missionary work. After various vicissitudes he was able to sow, in 1868, the first gospel seed by giving to his employees, in turn, a Spanish Bible, furnished him by Mr. John Mercer, an old friend in England. The depressing effect on business of the Franco-Prussian war gave him opportunity for evangelical work, which aroused the hostility of his employers, and resulted, in 1873, in the commencement of his distinctive mission work. His first public service was held in Toluca, February, 1873. Three years later there were hundreds of Protestants there, active in spreading the gospel. Mrs. Pascoe gave her husband invaluable help. Printing-presses were set up at Toluca and San Telmo, and tract-publishing was begun. In adjoining towns and villages many persons received the truth in the face of great perils. In November, 1875, Mrs. Pascoe died under the intentional maltreatment of a Mexican doctor. The Mission to the Indians was started at San Telmo in 1878.

There are now thousands of Protestants where, when Mr. Pascoe began his work, there was not one. Toluca and San Telmo, by means of the printing work, have become household words throughout the republic. Mr. Pascoe died November, 1888, and the work inaugurated by him is continued under the general superintendence of Mr. John Mercer.

**Pashtu** or **Afghan Version.**—The Pashtu belongs to the Iranic branch of the Aryan family of languages, and is spoken in Afghanistan, where it is also called Afghani. A translation of the New Testament was published at Serampore as early as in 1818. In 1832 the historical books of the Old Testament were also published at Serampore. A new translation was undertaken by the Rev. R. Clark, but only the Gospel of John was published in 1857, at Agra. In 1863 a new translation of the New Testament, made by the Rev. I. Loewenthal, a convert from Judaism, was published by the British and Foreign Bible Society. He was about to commence a translation of the Old Testament when he was killed in 1864. The work of translation was resumed by the Revs. T. P. Hughes and T. J. L. Mayes of the Church Missionary Society. The latter, who is aided by Quazi Abdur Rahman, translated considerable portions of the Old Testament, and his version of the Psalms was issued by the British and Foreign Bible Society in 1881. In 1883 a revision committee was formed under the presidency of the Bishop of Lahore; and in 1888 the New Testament, translated by Mr. Mayer and revised by the Revs. W. Jukes and W. Thwaites, was published by the above Society by the photo-lithographic process.

*(Specimen verse. John 3 : 16.)*

خلره چه خداي دنیاله دارنك مینه كړي
ده چه هغه خپل یوه پیدا شوی زوی لره
ورکړه چه هر یوسری چه یهغه باند یقین
کوی هغه دهلاك نشی لیکن بی نهایته
ژوندون دموی ۰

**Pasumalai,** a city in Madras, British India, 3 miles southwest of Madras City, on the railway to Tuticorin. Climate healthy; average annual temperature, 85° F.; rainfall, 35 inches. Population of city and district, 85,000 (including out-stations), Hindus, Moslems, Roman Catholics, Protestants. Languages, Tamil, Telugu, Hindustani. Natives poor, illiterate farmers, slowly improving. Mission station A. B. C. F. M. (1845); 1 ordained missionary, 1 unordained, 1 missionary's wife, 22 native helpers, 2 out-stations, 1 church, 146 church-members, 1 printing establishment, 1 theological seminary, 10 students, 5 schools, 419 scholars.

**Patagones** or **El Carmen,** a town in the Argentine Republic, South America, on the Rio Negro, 18 miles from its mouth; a medical mission of the South American Missionary Society (1864), with a church and dispensary under the care of an ordained physician. The work is carried on among the Patagonians, and also among the Spanish-speaking races.

**Patna,** a city in Bengal, India, on the Ganges, 326 miles northwest of Calcutta. The town is extensive, but its streets are narrow and crooked, its houses irregularly built, of many materials. It is on the East Indian R. R., and is the centre of the opium trade. Climate said to be unhealthy, but the natives are strong and well. Population, 158,900, Hindus, a few Moslems. Languages, Hindi, Urdu, Bengali. Mission station Baptist Missionary Society (1808–1810); 4 ordained missionaries, 3 single ladies, 11 native helpers, 9 out-stations, 4 native, 2 European churches, 68 native church-members, 1 girls' day-school, 25 scholars.

**Patrasburdsch,** a station of the Gossner Missionary Society among the Kols, Bengal, India (1869), with 12,775 church-members.

**Patterson, Alexander,** a native of Leith, Scotland; sent out by the Scottish Missionary Society to explore Tartary 1802, accompanied by Henry Brunton. On arriving at St. Petersburg he met so many discouragements that he felt inclined to turn back, when he unexpectedly found a friend in the lord of the emperor's bedchamber, M. Novassilgoff. Passports were given him, and full liberty granted to travel through the empire, and select any place as a residence agreeable to him. The government also gave them a large grant of land, and permission to keep under their care and instruction any of the Tartar youths they might ransom from the Tartars, until they were twenty-three years of age.

They chose a Mohammedan village called Karass as the place for the commencement of their mission, which contained over 500 inhabitants. Both the missionaries studied the Tartar language. As soon as they began circulating some tracts they had written in the language great interest was excited, and discussions arose as to the merits of Christ and Mohammed, and many persons of rank became interested in the teachings of the gospel.

In 1805 Mr. Patterson had the joy of seeing several of the ransomed youths embrace Christianity and be baptized. They also went with him on his journeys, acting as interpreters. In 1810 the mission was making such progress among the people that the Mohammedan priests became alarmed, and aroused the bitterest opposition. The Mohammedan tribes south of Karass were so zealous that they threatened to kill all who bore the Christian name. The Mohammedan schools were crowded with scholars, who were taught to read that they might defend the faith.

In 1813 the missionaries were obliged to move to the fortified town Georghievisk, about 30 miles from Karass, on account of the constant irruptions of hostile Tartars. While here the translation and binding of the New Testament were finished. In 1814 the missionaries again went back to Karass. In 1816 Mr. Patterson took with him one of the ransomed slaves and made a tour through the Crimea, distributing tracts and Tartar Testaments. The journey almost cost him his life, but he felt amply repaid in the reception he met from all classes of people. In 1825, on account of the anti-biblical revolution in Russia and restrictions by the government, the mission was transferred to other fields.

**Patteson, John Coleridge,** the missionary bishop and martyr of Melanesia, b. London, England, April 2d, 1827. His father was Sir John Patteson, a distinguished English judge, and his mother a niece of Samuel Taylor Coleridge, the poet. He was educated at Ottery St. Mary, Devonshire, 1835–37; at Eton 1838; Baliol College, Oxford, graduating B.A., 1845. In 1849 he obtained a scholarship in Merton College. Through his schooldays he took high rank as a linguist. After graduating he travelled in 1851 in Switzerland, Rome, and Germany as tutor to an English family. In 1852 he became a Fellow of Merton College. In 1853 he was curate of Alfington, and in 1854 was ordained. In 1855, March 29th, he sailed with Bishop Selwyn to the Melanesian Islands, in the South Pacific. During the voyage he acquired the Maori language. For five years he was assistant to the bishop in conducting a training school for native assistants. In 1861 he was made bishop of the Melanesian Islands. Possessing great linguistic talent, he translated the Bible, and reduced to writing and grammar several languages which before had only been spoken. His headquarters after being appointed bishop were at Mota, from which he made frequent excursions, and voyages to the other islands of his diocese in the mission ship, "The Southern Cross," exerting himself in

various ways for the good of the people. He not only preached, but taught the natives useful arts. In time of sickness he was their physician, watching and nursing them, and by love and kindness striving to lead them to the knowledge and worship of the true God. After one of these visits to Nackapu, an island of the Santa Cruz group, some traders having painted their ship in imitation of the bishop's ship, had through this artifice been able to kidnap some of the natives for the purpose of sending them to the plantations of Queensland and Fiji. When the missionary ship, as it cruised among the islands, again approached Nackapu, some of the islanders mistaking it for the kidnapping craft, determined to avenge themselves. The bishop, unsuspicious, lowered his boat, and went to meet them coming in their canoes. According to their custom, they asked him to get into one of their boats, which he did, and was taken to the shore. He was never seen alive again. Immediate search was made, and his body found, pierced with five wounds and wrapped in a coarse mat, with a palm leaf laid over the breast. When Parliament met next the Queen made touching reference to his untimely end. He is described as being in early life "gentle and refined in manner, scholarly in his tastes, devout, at the same time brave, earnest, vigorous, full of enthusiasm, being a leader and favorite at school in all athletic sports by reason of his elastic strength of body and skill in manipulation." All these qualities were needed, and all brought to his aid, when in later years he was at once friend, preacher, navigator, teacher, and exemplar in the useful arts to the Melanesian tribes.

**Payne, John,** was appointed by the Foreign Committee of the Protestant Episcopal Missionary Society in the United States to Africa, August 11th, 1836, and sailed May, 1837, reaching Cape Palmas, West Africa, on the 4th of July following. He was consecrated missionary bishop July 11th, 1851, and resigned the office in 1871. During this period of thirty-four years he was a faithful and laborious worker, both as a missionary and bishop. In his last report but one he said: "For myself, I fear that little ability remains to aid directly this glorious work. Thirty-three years' connection with one of the most unhealthy portions of the globe has left me the mere wreck of a man. But I claim that in devoting myself to preaching among the Gentiles the unsearchable riches of Christ, I was no fool. On the contrary, I did obey literally the command of my Lord. I did follow the very footsteps of apostles, martyrs, and prophets." He died at Oak Grove, Westmoreland Co., Va, October 23d, 1874, aged 60. The Foreign Committee in a minute adopted say: "Through thirty-three years he labored and suffered, ofttimes in great bodily weakness, yielding never until his powers were exhausted, ofttimes amid the deepest affliction of sickness and death in his own household or in the household of his fellow-missionaries. To him as the head of the mission all these things came as a great weight of sorrow on his heart. The Committee desire to record this minute of affectionate regard, and to join in a tribute of praise and thanksgiving to God for the grace which led His departed servant to consecrate to Him in untiring devotion all his powers of soul and body, and for the measure of success which attended his life-long labors." At the time of his resignation the House of Bishops recognized his long, faithful, and arduous services.

**Pea-Radja** (Paja-radja or Pea Ridge), a small town in Batukland, Northwest Sumatra, on the upper course of the East Butang River. Mission station of the Rhenish Missionary Society; 2 missionaries, 3,983 members, 1,060 communicants, 294 school-children.

**Pease, Lorenzo Warriner,** b. Hinsdale, Mass., U. S. A., May 20th, 1809; graduated at Hamilton College 1828; studied law three years; graduated at Auburn Theological Seminary 1833; embarked as a missionary of the American Board August 20th, 1834; explored Cyprus, and commenced a station at Larnaca. He was attacked with bilious remittent fever, and on the twenty-first day of the disease, after an agonizing convulsion, died August 28th, 1839. "Preaching was his most delightful employment. He had acquired a facility in the Greek language, and an acquaintance with its grammar and idioms, which were most accurate and valuable. This rare and rapid progress in the language had been facilitated by his labor in composing an extended grammar of the Modern Greek language, which he had nearly finished and translated into Greek before his sickness. He had projected the preparation of a 'Life of Christ,' which was approved by his missionary brethren of the Levant. The last work he completed was a valuable treatise on the Christian Sabbath."

**Pedi** or **Sepedi Version.**—The Pedi belongs to the Bantu family of African languages, and is the common dialect of the North Transvaal. The tribes who speak the language are Bakatla, Belobedu, Bakanoa, and some others, numbering from 140,000 to 160,000, of whom about 7,000 people are able to read. At the request of the Rev. C. Krothe, superintendent of the Berlin Mission in North Transvaal, the British and Foreign Bible Society published a version of the New Testament in 1889 at London.

**Peet, Lyman Bert,** b. Cornwall, Vt., U. S. A., March 1st, 1809; graduated at Middlebury College 1834, Andover Theological Seminary 1837; was accepted as a missionary of the A. B. C. F. M., but detained on account of the lack of funds, and labored over a year in its service at home; sailed July 6th, 1839, reaching Bankok May 28th, 1840. There he labored over six years among the Chinese who had immigrated thither, speaking the Amoy language. In August, 1846, he was transferred from Siam to China, and was stationed at Foo Chow. As a pioneer in that field, where peculiar difficulties were encountered, he was very successful in his efforts to reach the people by means of schools, preaching, preparation, and distribution of books. In July, 1856, Mrs. Peet died, and he returned with his two children to the United States. Having again married, he re-embarked October, 1858, for China. In addition to his other labors he held for several years an early morning service daily at the Nantai Church. His health failing, he returned home again in 1871, and resided at West Haven, Conn., where his death occurred January 11th, 1878. Several days before his death he dictated messages to his fellow-laborers at Foo Chow, saying: "My heart is with the dear missionaries at Foo Chow,

and the native Christians, and with all missionaries throughout the world."

**Pegu,** a town in Burma, Farther India; the former capital of the kingdom of Pegu, 40 miles northeast of Rangoon, on the railroad to Mandalay. The inhabitants are largely Talaings (Telugus) or Peguans. Mission station of the American Baptist Missionary Union; 1 female missionary, 4 native helpers, 4 out-stations, 2 self-supporting churches, 129 church-members, 3 schools, 128 scholars.

**Pegu Version.**—The Pegu belongs to the Mon-Anam family of Indo-China languages, and is spoken in the province of Pegu. A translation of the New Testament, made by the Rev. Haswell of the Baptist Missionary Society, was published at Moulmein in 1847, for the American and Foreign Bible Society.

(*Specimen verse.* Gal. 5 : 1.)

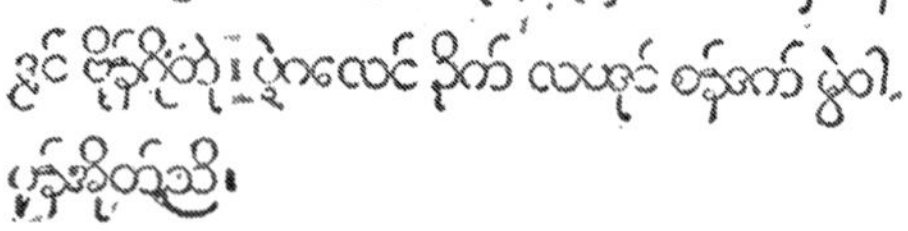

သ၎ တ်ၡ်ဃဃ း �်ဥ္ၫ း တုံ၎ ၢ ၊ၩ်ဖ္ ်ဃဃ း ႃ်တ၎ၣ
ၣၣ ႃိၣၨၪ်ဖ္ၣ ၩၢ်ဃဃၣ �်ၣ်တ ဃဃ္ၣ တ်ႃတ် ၍ဝ ၊
ၡ်ဒၣ်ၒ်တ္ဥ္ၣ ၊

**Peking,** the capital of China, situated on a plain about 12 miles southwest of the Pei-ho, in latitude 39° 54' 36" north, longitude 116° 27' east, is an ancient and historic city. Its name means Northern Capital, in opposition to Nanking, which was the capital for a time, and it became the seat of government under Kublai Khan in 1264 A.D., and has continued to be the capital ever since, except during the years when the emperors held their court at Nanking (q.v.). The city is divided into two parts, each with a retaining wall. There is the inner or Manchu city, where the palace, government buildings, and barracks are, surrounded with a wall of an average height of 50 feet and a circumference of 14 miles; added on to this at the south is the outer or Chinese city, surrounded by one of the finest walls around any city of the world—10 miles in circuit, 30 feet high, 15 feet broad at the top and 30 feet at the ground, pierced with 16 gates, each one surmounted with a many-storied tower 100 feet high, with embrasures for cannon. Within both walls is inclosed about 26 square miles, and with the numerous public buildings, the palaces, pagodas, temples, with its broad avenues, the lofty gates and massive wall, Peking has challenged the wonder of all visitors since the stories of Marco Polo gave him an unjust reputation as a second Munchausen. Within the Manchu city a smaller inclosure, the Prohibited city, of three miles in circuit, surrounds the palaces of the emperor and his consort. The age of the city is not definitely known. It has been built and rebuilt many times, and now is not at the zenith of its magnificence, which it attained at the time of the Emperor Kanghi. It is the best example of an Asiatic city now extant. The population is of a most varied character. Chinese predominate, but Manchus are numerous, and Kalmucks, Tartars, Koreans, Russians, and representatives of almost every country of Central Asia are found in the crowds that throng its streets, and add much to the picturesqueness of its appearance by their motley garb and diversified colors in dress. The number of inhabitants has been variously estimated from 1,000,000 to 3,000,000 —the mean between these two estimates is probably correct. By reason of the lack of any tall spires or buildings, the view from a distance is not imposing, the only prominent buildings being the Clock Tower, where a water clock measures the time, and the Bell Tower, whose ancient bell (cast A.D. 1406), the largest suspended bell in the world (120,000 lbs. weight), tolls forth the watches of the night. Of the many noteworthy buildings, none are of such interest to the missionary as the altars where the emperor offers worship to Heaven and to the Earth. (See Confucianism.) The Altar to Heaven stands to the left of the south gate, within the Chinese city; the Altar to Earth is without the walls, to the north of the Manchu city. Separated only by a wall from the Altar to Heaven, is the "Altar of Prayer for Grain," often wrongly called the Temple to Heaven, which was one of the most beautiful buildings of the East. Its triple, dome-shaped roofs towered 100 feet high, and were covered with blue porcelain tiles. Its base was a triple terraced altar of white marble. Large teakwood pillars arranged in circular rows supported its roofs, and it was inclosed with windows, shaded with blinds of blue-glass rods. The destruction of this temple by fire in the fall of 1889 was regarded by the Chinese as a visitation of the wrath of Heaven upon the emperor himself. Not only is worship paid to Heaven, but the temples of almost every form of religious belief are found here. Islam is represented by the mosque outside of the southwestern angle of the Imperial city, in the midst of a number of Mohammedan Turks who came from Turkestan over a hundred years ago. Not far from the mosque, to the southwest, is an old Portuguese church, and inside of the Manchu city, west of the Forbidden city, is the Roman Catholic cathedral. The Greek Church, Protestantism, Buddhism, and all the pantheon of Chinese gods and deified heroes have their respective houses of worship.

In the limited space at the disposal of this article no more than a mere mention can be made of the Sacrificial Hall to Confucius; the monument to the lama who died, some say was murdered, at Peking; the examination hall; and the parks and artificial lakes with which successive emperors have beautified the city. The ruins of the Summer Palace, which was destroyed by the allied French and English forces during the occupation of the city in 1860, lie to the northwest of the city, about 7 miles away. Here small hills with intervening vales had been beautified with pleasure houses and bowers in the best of Chinese style, and in the various buildings were collected the treasures of many dynasties and monarchs; a rich booty they proved to the wanton pillage of the soldiers.

The streets of Peking are in general wide and spacious. The centre is sometimes paved and is somewhat higher than at the sides. In summer the dust from the unpaved portion, and in winter the mud, make them intensely disagreeable to the passer-by. No foreign merchants are allowed to carry on business in Peking, and the aspect of the city is entirely different from that of the other Chinese cities where commerce brings a distinctive European element and settlement. The climate is healthy, but subject to great extremes of heat and cold, and the dryness for ten months of the year is hard to bear. Peking Mandarin, as the language of the capital

is called, is the standard language of the empire. (For an account of this dialect, and for the history of missionary work at Peking, see article on China.)

Mission station of the Presbyterian Church (North), 1863; 5 missionaries (3 married), 2 missionary physicians (1 married), 1 female physician, 3 female missionaries, 22 native helpers, 3 churches, 183 communicants, 7 boys' schools, 60 scholars, 2 girls' schools, 34 scholars, 2 boarding-schools, 64 scholars, 180 Sabbath-scholars, 18,640 out-patients (1888–89) in the hospital, and 155 in-patients. A. B. C. F. M. (1864); 3 missionaries (1 married), 2 female missionaries, 2 boys' schools, 1 girls' boarding-school, 36 pupils. Protestant Episcopal Church, U. S. A.; mission house and 2 chapels. Methodist Episcopal Church (North); 10 missionaries, 9 assistant missionaries, 4 female missionaries (in the district 500 members), 2 theological schools, 40 students, 2 high-schools, 180 students, 7 day-schools, 44 students, 3 Sabbath-schools, 400 scholars. L. M. S. (E. 1861, W. 1878); 4 missionaries, 3 female missionaries, 217 members, 2 Sabbath-schools, 130 scholars, 4 day-schools, 58 scholars. S. P. G. (1880); 1 missionary, 180 Chinese members.

**Pekyi,** capital of Krepeland, Slave Coast, West Africa; was in 1851 the starting-point of the North German Mission in this region, and has still a small congregation.

**Penang** or **Prince of Wales' Island** lies at the north entrance of the Straits of Malacca, and is one of the Straits Settlements belonging to England. It contains 106 square miles, and has a rich, fertile soil, where tropical fruits and spices are cultivated. The climate is healthy, and rain falls every month in the year. Georgetown, the capital, at the northeastern end of the island, is the seat of government for Malacca and Singapore as well. The province of Wellesley, on the peninsula opposite Penang, together with the Dindings, are included in its administrative district. Population (1881), 84,724 Malays, 67,820 Chinese, 12,058 natives of India, and 674 whites. Mission station of the S. P. G.; 1 missionary, 50 communicants.

**Penfield, Thornton Bigelow,** b. Alden, N. Y., U. S. A., October 2d, 1834; was converted at the age of eight, and his early consecration to the missionary work is traceable primarily to an address of Dr. Scudder, of which is found this memorandum: "Dr. Scudder asked me to become a missionary, and go to India and help him; and I intend to. T. B. Penfield, April 19th, 1846." He graduated at Oberlin College in 1856, and studied two years in Union Theological Seminary, New York. While there he was active in city-mission work, devoting to it a portion of each day. Returning to Oberlin he spent part of a year in theological study, and graduated in 1858. The way not being open to go to India, his chosen field, he went to Jamaica, W. I., under the American Mission Association, to labor among the emancipated negroes. There two daughters were born, the elder surviving him. His wife, returning in ill-health to Oberlin, died in 1863. Having labored for seven years in Jamaica, he returned to the United States in 1866, again married, and November 7th, the same year, sailed as a missionary of the American Board for the Madura Mission. In 1870, the cholera raging violently, he spent much time in administering medicine to the sick, when he was himself slightly attacked. His health having somewhat improved by a visit to the sanitarium, he resumed his missionary labors. In July he returned from a tour very much exhausted, and for several days his sufferings were severe. He died August 19th, 1870. Mr. Washburn, quoting the memorandum respecting Dr. Scudder from a scrap of paper much worn and tattered, says: "This record (written when Mr. Penfield was a boy of twelve) is the key to his whole subsequent life. He was diligent and active to the full limit of his strength; his judgment was trustworthy, and he was careful most faithfully to administer the funds of the churches committed to his hands. Though he had been with us but little more than four years, his diligence in acquiring the language, his active habits, and his generous assumption of the work put upon him, gave promise of a future of great usefulness."

**Penguin,** a town in Tasmania (Australia), 81 miles northwest of Launceston. Climate very mild, genial, and healthy. Population, 5,000, English, Germans, and Chinese. Language, English. Religion, Protestant, Catholic. People moral, prosperous. Mission station United Methodist Free Churches (1878); 2 ordained missionaries, 1 missionary's wife, 11 native helpers, 9 out-stations, 3 churches, 120 church-members.

**Pentecost Bands** of the Free Methodist Churches in the United States. Headquarters, 104 Franklin Street, Chicago, Ill., U. S. A.— The Pentecost Bands were organized at Parma, Mich., July 25th, 1885, by Rev. V. A. Dake, an elder belonging to the Free Methodist Church. He had been preaching on circuits and travelling districts as chairman (presiding elder), but feeling the responsibility upon him, laid down his regular duties and began this work. A Free Methodist Society was organized at Parma, and turned over to the proper authorities of the church. The work was started on account of the many young people in the church who felt led to gospel work, but were not called to preach. At first the intention was only to do home-mission work,—going to new towns and localities where there were no Free Methodist societies, and organizing, building churches, and establishing the church. But in this intense, essential mission work the foreign branch of the work developed, until to-day the home work has become simply a training-school for foreign-mission work. In Michigan they have organized 8 new societies, and in Illinois 25, in which are 19 church enterprises.

There are now 23 bands: 2 in Africa, 1 in Norway, 1 in Germany, 17 in the United States, and 2 in Canada. The missionaries in both home and foreign fields are about 70 in number.

In connection with the Pentecost Bands has been started an institution which is called "The Reapers' Home." Here it is calculated to train the children of foreign missionaries, and also to gather in orphan and dependent children to train for mission work. It is started on the principle of having the children "born again" while from four to six years of age, and then keeping them by careful watch-care in the fear of God. The various enterprises will all be separate, as the whole work is started on the cottage system. The "Reapers' Home" is temporarily located now, but may be addressed at 104 Franklin Street, Chicago, Ill. The leader of the Reapers' Home work is Mrs. Ida M. C. Dake. There is also a Mission Training work in St. Louis, Mo., under the charge of Mrs. C. W. Sherman. The object of this work is the especial training of those about to start for foreign fields.

The officers of the band are: a leader in charge, two assistant leaders in charge, one male and one female, a foreign-mission treasurer, a general book-agent, a secretary, and leaders of the Reapers' Home and Mission Training work. Each band has a leader and assistant leader. When several bands work together they are called a Division, and one worker is called the Divisional Leader. When work is opened in a foreign nation an overseeing leader is appointed, who is called the National Leader.

The first foreign field opened by the bands was near Colmar, in Elsass, Germany. The leader in charge went there in the summer of 1889, and organized a Free Methodist class and sent a Pentecost Band to continue the work. They stayed a few months and returned, and the work has since been in the charge of local leaders.

Monrovia, Liberia, was also opened in the fall of 1889 by Band No. 3, Elder George W. Chapman and his wife Mary W. Chapman, and C. S. Kerwood. The wife is the divisional leader. During the year Brother Kerwood has died, and his place has been filled by Band No. 9, Miss Matie North and Mrs. Jennie Torrence, making four workers on that field. They have an iron house costing $1,500, and are well equipped for work.

In the fall of 1890 Band No. 12, Mr. S. V. Ulness and wife, Lillian M. Burt Ulness, and Hans Fass, went to Norway and opened up work there. The work in Canada is under the leadership of Thomas H. Nelson. At present Miss Gracie Toll and Laura Douglass are getting ready for India, Edward Cryer for England, and Harvey D. Brink for Australia. The work in England and Australia will be mainly for training missionaries.

The special work before the missionaries is the salvation of souls and the sanctification of believers. They all dress plainly, use very plain food, object to all worldly entertainments, and find their pleasure in prayer and obedience to God. While not opposed to educational work, this is only used as supplementary, and not primary. They believe the all-powerful factor in the conversion of the heathen is the "Holy Ghost and Fire."

A band is composed of four workers, of whom one is a leader and another an assistant leader. They enter into a field where work is needed, hold street-meetings, visit from house to house, hold public services in church, tent, or hall, and throw everything else aside in desperate efforts to "pluck brands out of the burning." They are earnest, enthusiastic, and noisy. Their methods may all be called short-cuts to win souls.

The "Vanguard," published at St. Louis, Mo., is the organ of the Pentecost Bands. It has about 5,000 subscribers, and is in quite a prosperous state.

During the winter holidays is held in each division, home and foreign, the Semi-annual Ingathering. In the summer, at the date of organization, July 25th, is held the Annual Harvest Home Camp-meeting, when all workers are expected to be present. The whole movement is intensely missionary. A favorite song is "We'll girdle the Globe with Salvation." The home-work is for the purpose of training workers and raising money for the foreign work. The Bands are in their infancy. Only five years of effort, and yet they are constrained to say, What hath God wrought! From many lands comes the cry for Pentecost Bands to come and help in the battle against sin.

**Periodical Literature.**—When the missionary enters on his work he learns the number and power of the obstacles to its success. If he had pictured the heathen as calling on him to come to their help, he finds hard practical facts in sad contrast to such a dream; not that there are no heathen longing for the light, but the number of such is exceedingly small. One may labor for years among large masses of idolaters without finding one. The writer can never forget his surprise on first entering the missionary field to find a shrine of the Virgin Mary under the roof of good "Father Temple," as we called him in Smyrna; but the old servant to whom it belonged could not see the unscripturalness of such worship, and his employer was too wise to exercise authority in the matter. He preferred to wait for truth to lead the man to put it away himself, rather than to require it on the ground of his master's views of duty. The missionary finds men as mad upon their idols as he is loyal to Christ; many who welcome him as a man oppose him as a missionary. The worldly minded would receive him heartily if he brought some kind of merchandise on which they could make good profits. The unspiritual take scant interest in his most earnest setting forth of Christ and his salvation. The timid shrink from the persecution that is sure to follow their acceptance of the truth. The number who consent to listen to the preaching of the gospel is small, and the field extends in all directions beyond his reach. How can he fill it with the truth? If he prints it in volumes, however well reasoned and persuasive, they will not be read; but he can print the latest news from distant lands, and men who have not had access to it before are eager to hear that. He can set forth interesting facts in natural science or mechanics, and men read them also with avidity; and along with these he can sift in, not abstract dogmas, but truth in its practical applications; truth set at that angle which sheds light on their daily life, meets their wants, answers their questions, and brings the Word of God in contact with their hearts. Then each week the lesson is changed; some new aspect of truth equally timely and no less adapted to their needs is set before them. The lesson which needs reiteration is reiterated. The unexpressed longing is satisfied; the illusion that made error seem truth, and truth to look like error, is dexterously dispelled; and men are led on step by step till by the grace of God they know the truth, and the truth makes them free.

It may be questioned whether our churches at home are aware how much they owe to our own religious periodicals. In Mosul in 1844 the missionaries used to lend their "New York Observers" to the French consul, Mons. P. E. Botta, son of the Italian historian of our own revolution. He was a decided Romanist, yet genial and friendly, and not only expressed admiration for the religious feeling that created and sustained such a paper, but affirmed that such a one could not possibly find support in Papal France. The religious periodical is the outgrowth of the Bible religion of the present century. It reaches a larger number than any one pulpit can touch, and it speaks the word for the hour simultaneously in many places, and on a great variety of themes. It is essential to the unity and vigor of every advance of the kingdom; and just as the needs of the home field have called it into existence there, so the needs of the foreign field called it into being almost from the first. As early as 1818 the Baptist Mission at Serampore issued the "Samarchar Darpan," or "Mirror of Intelligence." In 1834 our missionaries in the Hawaiian Islands established the "Lama Hawaii," a weekly quarto of four pages, and another was commenced in 1835. In all, ten have made their appearance at different periods in the islands. The pioneer periodical in Turkey was the old *ΑΠΟΘΗΚΗ ΤΩΝ ΩΦΕΛΙΜΩΝ ΓΝΩΣΕΩΝ*, "Magazine of Useful Knowledge," published in Greek by Rev. D. Temple in 1837–1843. It also appeared in Armenian, and in 1854 became the "Avedaper" (Messenger), a semi-monthly quarto of eight pages, and afterwards a weekly folio of four pages. It was issued also in Armeno-Turkish in 1857.

Newspapers were unknown in Turkey till 1834. The first, edited by a native Christian, appeared in 1840. Still even in 1860 a paper was rarely seen in the hands of the thousands that thronged the decks of steamers in the Golden Horn; but six years later the newsboys were as busy in Constantinople as with us. The fifty papers of that city, however,—thirty of them dailies,—were generally hostile to spiritual piety. The Turks allowed no printing for two centuries after the discovery of the art.

In 1872 the Greco-Turkish "Angeliophoros" was added to the Armenian and Armeno-Turkish. The first page of each was devoted to brief moral and religious articles. The second to education, religious intelligence, and general topics. The third was given up to the natives, and current events. They were taken by one in five of adult Protestants, and were highly prized and carefully preserved. At the low rate of a dollar, postage included, they were very popular. In 1874, 1,800 copies of the weekly and 4,000 of the monthly were issued. As an evangelizing agency they went into hundreds of families not Protestant, and each copy was read by about four persons.

Besides these were four illustrated monthlies for children. Three of them, in the same languages as the weeklies, were established in 1871, and the fourth in Bulgarian, 1874, with 2,000 subscribers. These are the first periodicals for children printed in Turkey, and there has been great demand for them. The "Bulgarian Zornitza" was also issued as a weekly in 1877, and has proved one of the most important agencies in educating Bulgarians.

In Syria the "Neshera" (The Unfolding) has been issued for many years by the mission. It is a religious weekly, edited by Rev. Samuel Jessup. The "Koukab es Soobah" (Morning Star) is a monthly for the children, edited by Rev. H. H. Jessup, D.D. The "Lisan el Hal" (The Voice of the Condition, i.e., an object is better known from the sight of it than from any description) is a semi weekly Protestant paper. The "Beirût" is a Moslem weekly. The Beirût "Official" is a government weekly. "El Musbah" (The Lamp) is a Maronite weekly. "El Beshir" (Good News; or, The Bearer of Good News) is a Jesuit weekly. "El Hadiyeh" (The Present, or Gift) is the weekly paper of the orthodox Greeks, and the "Hadikut el Akhbur" (Garden of News) is a government weekly in Arabic and French. The "Muktatif" and several other monthly journals once published in Beirût, have now been transferred to Cairo, Egypt. The number of these publications indicates great literary activity, as well as denominational rivalry among the Arabic-speaking population of Syria.

In Persia "The Rays of Light," a monthly in the Nestorian vernacular, commenced to shine in 1848, and still sheds its radiance over the plains of Northwestern Persia, and far up into the secluded valleys of Koordistan. It is an 8vo, and in 1866 contained 384 pages. The edition was 400 copies; each number containing a department of religion, education, science, missions, and poetry, not forgetting something to interest the children. In late years it deals more with practical missionary work, and the present social, moral, and religious condition of the people. It gives notices of religious meetings, also accounts of them when held. It publishes communications from the native brethren, and even in Persia has a page of political intelligence. Since Syriac scholarship has improved in both Europe and America, some copies are subscribed for in Christian lands. The whole number of paying subscribers is about 500; but this by no means gives the number who read it, for every copy is not only perused by the readers in the family of the subscribers, but by others also. It is much prized by the Nestorians.

In India, a monthly Marathi periodical, with the fitting name of "Dnyanodaya" (Rise of Knowledge), was commenced at Ahmednagar in 1842, and in 1845 was transferred to Bombay. For eight years it was edited by Rev. R. W. Hume. The people were so eager for it that it soon made its appearance every fortnight, and then once a week. It is still published as an Anglo-vernacular paper, and has a circulation among Hindus as well as Christians, and the "Balbodhmena," a monthly periodical for children, illustrated by engravings, also enters many Hindu homes.

The Bombay "Witness," a religious paper in English, commenced in 1844; also the Bombay "Temperance Advocate." Rev. G. Bowen, who went out in 1848, established the Bombay "Guardian," also in English. At Madras, "The Aurora," a Tamil semi-monthly, made its appearance in 1844; and in 1869 Rev. G. T. Washburn established a monthly called "The True Newsbearer," which was then the only distinctively religious paper in Tamil. He also edited "The Satthia Warttamani," in Tamil and English. In Ceylon, "The Morning Star," a semi-monthly, in the same language, commenced about 1850; and "The Children's Friend," in Tamil, appeared in 1868.

The Rev. C. W. Park established at Bombay in 1873 "The Indian Evangelical Review." A specimen of the topics discussed in its pages for six years may be found in the Ely volume (p. 218). The "Review" was then transferred to Calcutta.

As early as 1845 ("Missionary Herald," p. 30)

there were in Bombay three weeklies and one monthly opposing Christianity; also a paper at Poona, and a Gujerati monthly, with three weeklies in the same tongue, besides two in Persian and one in Hindustani, all retailing the writings of English enemies of the gospel so that there was need enough for something on the other side.

In China the writer has not met with any notice of a missionary periodical. The well-known "Chinese Repository" (English) was established in 1832 by Dr. Bridgman, and edited by him and Dr. S. Wells Williams for twenty years. Its object was to diffuse information concerning China. A partial list of the topics discussed in it may be found in the Ely volume, pp. 32–35. It may be doubted whether Dr. Williams would have written the admirable account of China contained in his "Middle Kingdom" had he not been editor of the "Repository" for so many years. After that ceased to be issued, "The Chinese Recorder and Missionary Journal," commenced at Foochow in 1868 by Rev. S. L. Baldwin, took its place in the missionary department, and "The China Review" in literary matters. "The Chinese Evangelist," edited in New York in Chinese and English, by Mr. J. Stewart Happer, son of Dr. Happer, President of the Christian College, Canton, China, has been issued monthly, for the Chinese in our own country.

From Japan, Buddhists sent an agent to this country to gather together everything he could find against Christianity, and several of their periodicals deal out the result to their readers. The missionaries established "The Shichi Ichi Zappo" (Weekly Messenger) in 1876, giving a résumé of the scientific, political, and religious progress of the world. It is met with in the cars and steamboats, and men who have never seen a missionary have been led by it to Christ. It contains also papers on social science, such as the principles of hygiene, sanitary arrangements of the home, vaccination, and the like.

"The Morning Star" was issued among the Zulus in 1861, and has been succeeded by "The Torch Light."

Among the Dakotas "The Tapi Oaye" (Word-Carrier) commenced its rounds in 1871, edited by Rev. J. P. Williamson, and after his death by Dr. S. R. Riggs and Rev. A. L. Riggs. It receives an enthusiastic welcome. The Indians not only pay for it; they also write for it, and its circulation continually increases.

The periodicals referred to are only those issued by the missionaries of one or two of our large societies, but besides these are many more that have not been mentioned; and in view of so many published in so many languages, it is a privilege to pray that their editors may be so filled with the Spirit, that the truth they set forth may be blessed to the advancement of the kingdom of our Lord Jesus Christ.

**Perkins, Justin,** b. West Springfield, Mass., U. S. A., March 12th, 1805; graduated at Amherst College 1829; studied theology at Andover; embarked September 21st, 1833, as a missionary of the A. B. C. F. M., and established the Nestorian Mission at Oroomiah, Persia. His teacher in Syriac was Mar Yohannan. Schools established by Dr. Perkins and Dr. Grant are now flourishing seminaries. Dr. Perkins translated the Scriptures and several religious books into Syriac. He visited the United States in 1842, accompanied by the Nestorian bishop Mar Yohannan, whose presence and addresses awakened a deep interest in the mission. Returning to Persia in 1843, he labored successfully at his post, and ably defended Protestantism against misrepresentation and persecution. In 1869 impaired health compelled him to relinquish the work, in which he had been engaged for thirty-six years. He died at Chicopee, Mass., in the same year.

**Perm Version.**—The Perm belongs to the Finn branch of the Ural-Altaic family, and is spoken by the Permians in the Perm, Wiatka, and Archangel governments, Russia. They are composed of 50,000 souls, partially Christianized, but till recently without the Scriptures in their language, except the Gospel of Matthew, which was executed in 1866 by P. A. Popon, for Prince Louis Lucien Bonaparte, not with the view to circulation, but to aid in linguistic studies. In the year 1880 the British and Foreign Bible Society published an edition of the Gospel of Matthew, which has been revised and transcribed into the Russ character by the academician Wiedemann from the text prepared for Prince Bonaparte.

**Pernambuco,** a city on the northeast coast of Brazil, north of Bahia. Climate hot, but healthy. Population, 100,000, Portuguese, Africans, Indians. Language, Portuguese. Religion, Roman Catholic. Natives poor, ignorant, immoral, irreligious. Mission station of the Presbyterian Church (South), 1873; 2 ordained missionaries, 1 missionary's wife, 8 native helpers, 5 out-stations, 6 churches, 172 church-members. South American Missionary Society; 1 missionary and wife (conduct a Seaman's Mission). Southern Baptist Convention; 1 native pastor.

**Perry, John M. S.,** b. Sharon, Conn., U. S. A., September 7th, 1806; graduated at Yale College 1827; taught the Academy in Sharon 1827–28; graduated at the Yale Divinity School 1831; was ordained and installed pastor of the Congregational Church, Mendon, Mass., November 9th, 1831; married Harriet Joanna Lathrop, youngest sister of Mrs. Myron Winslow; relinquished his charge May 13th, 1835, to go to Ceylon; sailed the same year as a missionary of the A. B. C. F. M., arriving in Jaffna, Ceylon, in September.

In 1838 it was found necessary to reduce the number of students in the Batticotta Seminary from 150 to 100, and to disband nearly all the village schools. Mr. Perry, in behalf of the mission, addressed an earnest letter, March 1st, to the committee, in which he told of the 5,000 children of heathen parents deprived of Christian instruction, the discouragement of friends, the loss of influence and confidence caused by the want of funds, entreated the churches to repair the damage as far as possible, and to send no more missionaries till the means of usefulness were restored to those already in the field. Within ten days the writer of the letter died of cholera, after a few hours of severe suffering.

**Persia or Iran.**—The modern kingdom of Persia, called by the natives Iran, occupies, roughly speaking, that part of Western Asia lying between the Caspian Sea on the north and the Persian Gulf on the south, Afghanistan and Baluchistan on the east and Turkey on the west. Its exact boundaries have not as yet been definitely located, but starting from Mount Ararat at the northwest, the river Aras forms the greater part of its boundary line between that part of Russia lying west of the Caspian Sea, though there is a small strip of country extending south of the river Aras along the Caspian Sea, which does not belong to Persia. East of the Caspian, Russian Turkestan bounds it on the north, though the exact limits of Persian territory have not been accurately settled, Russian authorities claiming more than is allowed by other European powers. On the east the boundary lines between Afghanistan and Baluchistan have been determined by British commissioners at different times, although some parts of it are still disputed. Its southern and southwestern boundary is the coast-line of the Arabian Sea and the Persian Gulf. Its western boundary from Mount Ararat in a general southwesterly direction to the Persian Gulf is the disputed Perso-Turkish frontier for the settlement of which a mixed commission, appointed in 1843, labored for 25 years, with the result that the disputed territory has been defined rather than the exact boundaries delimited.

Persia extends for about 700 miles from north to south, and 900 miles from east to west, and includes an area estimated at 628,000 square miles. The greater part of this region is an elevated plateau, almost a perfect table-land in the centre and on the east, but cut up by mountain chains on the north, the west, and the south. More than three fourths of its entire surface is desert land, but many of the valleys between the high mountain ranges are wonderfully fertile and exceedingly beautiful. Rare flowers, luscious fruits, valuable timber, and mountain brooks and torrents make the land a scene of picturesque beauty which is celebrated in history and song, and indissolubly connected with the ideas of Persia. With such a diversity of physical characteristics there is of necessity a diversity of climate. On the plateau the climate is temperate; at Ispahan summer and winter are equally mild, and regular seasons follow each other. At the north and the northwest severe winters are experienced, while the inhabitants of the desert region in the centre and on the east of it are scorched in summer and frozen in winter. Along the Caspian Sea the summer heat is intense, while the winters are mild, and heavy and frequent rainfalls make the low country marshy and unhealthy. In the southern provinces, though the heat in autumn is excessive, winter and spring are delightful; and summer, though hot, is not unpleasant, since the atmosphere of Persia in general is remarkable for its dryness and purity.

The population of Persia is usually divided into three distinct classes, those inhabiting the cities estimated at 1,963,800, the wandering tribes 1,909,800; and the inhabitants of villages and country districts 3,780,000. The latter are engaged mainly in agriculture, and the best wheat in the world, together with other cereals, is raised, and cotton, sugar, rice, and tobacco are produced in the southern provinces. The wandering tribes dwell in tents, and move about with their flocks and herds as the seasons succeed each other, spending the spring and summer on the mountain slopes and the winter on the plains. The two principal races are the Turks and the Persians, the latter of whom belong to the Mongol race. Besides these, 260,000 are Arabs, 675,000 Koords and Leks, 207,000 Baluchis and Gypsies, and 234,000 Lurs. These last are sometimes classed with the Koords.

The principal cities of Persia, with their population, are Teheran 210,000, Tabriz 165,-000, Ispahan and Meshed each with 60,000, Kurman and Yezd each with 40,000. It is estimated that 6,860,600 of the population belong to the Shiah faith, 700,000 are Sunnis, 8,500 Parsis, 19,000 Jews, 43,000 Armenians, and 23,000 Nestorians.

The Government of Persia is similar to that of Turkey. It is a kingdom whose king, Nusred-din, is called the Shah. He is the absolute ruler and the master of the lives and goods of all his subjects; but though his power is absolute, he must not act contrary to the accepted doctrines of the Mohammedan religion as laid down by the prophet and interpreted by his descendants (Syeds), and the highpriesthood. The laws are based on the precepts of the Koran, and the Shah is regarded as vicegerent of the prophet. A ministry divided into several departments, after the European fashion, assists him in the executive department of the government. A governor-general is appointed over each one of the 27 provinces, who is directly responsible to the central government. The nomad tribes are ruled over by their chiefs, who are responsible to the governors.

The only instruction of the bulk of the population is from the teachings of the Koran, but there are a great number of colleges supported by public funds, where students are instructed not only in religion, and Persian and Arabic literature, but also in scientific knowledge.

Internal communication is difficult, as there are only 26 miles of railway,—Teheran to Shah Abdul-azim (6 miles); Mahmudabad to Barfurush and Amol, 20 miles; and but two good carriage roads,—Teheran to Kom and Teheran to Kasvin, each about 94 miles, though large wagons are used, especially between Tabriz and the Caucasus. The greater part of its telegraph system of 38,024 miles is worked by a European company and the English Government.

*History.*—It is not the province of this article to give any sketch of the history of the country of Persia, but the following dates of the principal epochs in its history may be of service. From the earliest records, dating back to about 2,000 B.C., the first rulers of Persia were the Medes, who conquered Babylonia, and established a Medo-Persian empire, which lasted, under the rule of famous kings,—Cyrus, Cambyses, Darius, Xerxes, and Artaxerxes,—until the conquest by Alexander the Great, 331 B.C., when the Greek and Parthian Empire was established, which ended about the middle of the 2d century. The Sassanian Empire, from the beginning of the 3d century lasted until about the end of the 7th, when the period of Arabian domination commenced, and gradually grew in extent and influence. Mohammedanism completely captured the life and permeated the thought of the people to the very core. Persia was at times a province, and the centre of the Arabian Empire, under successive rulers of Arab, Turk, or Mongol origin. The sway of the Timurides and Turkomans lasted from 1405 to 1499. From 1499 to 1736 the Sufi or Sufawi

dynasty ruled the country. Its founder, Ismail Sufi, was the originator of Sufism, which made a broad division in the world of Islam. With the downfall of the Sufi, and the accession of Nadir Shah, 1736, the last native Persian dynasty passed away. At the death of Nadir Shah in 1747 a period of anarchy, followed by short reigns of various despots, ensued, until in 1794 Agha Mohammed ascended the throne,—the first of the reigning dynasty of the Kajars. The present Shah succeeded to the throne in 1848.

*Missions in Persia.*—I. UNDER THE OLD COVENANT.—The Persians or Medes were descendants of Japhet, and were the first Aryan race brought into close relation to the kingdom of God under the Old Covenant. For a time the religious hope of the world was bound up in the handful of Jewish captives, of whom Daniel was the chief. As twelve hundred years earlier the hope of the world was centred in one man, Abraham, who came from the same far East,—so on Daniel and the few thousand faithful Jews in that same land of the East depended the true religion in the world. Hence no event in ancient times was so important and central to the kingdom of God as the overthrow of Babylon, and the restoration of God's ancient people, and the preservation of the true faith. No one figure was so central and so closely related to the providential events in the restoration as Cyrus, the king of the Persians. One reason of the friendship of the Persians to the Jews is found in the fact that both nations were Monotheists. The Medes and Persians were never idolaters in the grosser sense of setting up images and worshipping them. " No images profaned the severe simplicity of the Iranic temple. It was only after a long lapse of ages and in connection with foreign worship that idolatry crept in. The Old Zoroastrianism was in this respect as pure as the religion of the Jews, and thus a double bond of sympathy united the Hebrews and the Aryans" (Rawlinson).

The Jews, so impatient generally under a foreign yoke, never rebelled against the Persians; and the Persians, so intolerant of other nations, respected and protected the Jews. This great fact related the Persians very closely to the Old Covenant. Their fidelity, though so imperfect, was acknowledged of God. The Prophets foretold the desolation and complete destruction of all the surrounding idolatrous nations. Not one is left. But Persia is not thus denounced, and Persia is still a nation, holding in her bosom not the Persian stock alone, but the Jewish colonies that were planted in exile more than twenty-five centuries ago in Mesopotamia and in the cities of the Medes. The people of God were thus in most intimate relation to Persia before the coming of Christ.

2. THE EARLY CHRISTIAN AGE.—A person standing on the hills of Palestine can see the Great Sea to the west. His eye also discerns the bluish outline of the mountains beyond Jordan bounding the eastern horizon. That outline was practically the bound of the Roman Empire. Beyond it were the desert and the plains of Mesopotamia and Assyria, extending 700 miles eastward from Palestine, and bounded by the Zagros or Koordish Mountains. The traveller who crosses this range traverses nearly a hundred miles, climbing up and winding his way among the steep valleys and passes, with snow-

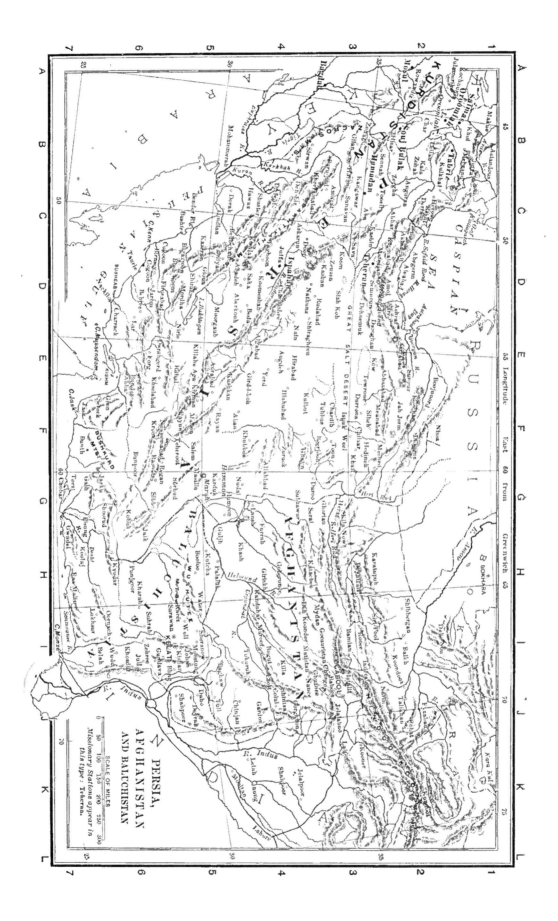

PERSIA,
AFGHANISTAN
AND BALUCHISTAN

SCALE OF MILES

Missionary Stations appear in
this type: Teheran.

covered peaks on every hand. The descent on the eastern side is less difficult, and opens on the plateau or upland regions of the Medes and Persians. We have reached the East in Mesopotamia and Babylon, and the Far East in Persia, whence came the Magi to Jerusalem to welcome the infant Redeemer. The regions of the East and Far East—all beyond the Roman Empire—were until A.D. 225 under the Parthian rule. From thence there were present at the day of Pentecost, Parthians, Medes, and dwellers in Mesopotamia. If we possessed an account of all the acts of the Apostles it would no doubt be clear that some of the twelve were missionaries in that Eastern land. Peter may have visited the Asiatic churches, as Origen and Eusebius assert, and 1 Peter 5:13 seems to convey the salutations of the church of the literal Babylon, the true centre of the East, where Peter and Mark were at the time, and not of the mystical Babylon of the West. Special traditions point to Bartholomew and Thomas as apostles in the Parthian dominions and eastward. Still more circumstantial is the mission of Thaddeus, one of the seventy, to Edessa (Oorfa) in Mesopotamia. Eusebius the historian is confirmed by Syriac documents of great antiquity. It should be remembered that eastward over Syria to the Persian Gulf the Aramaic was the common language, the vernacular of Christ and His apostles. Dr. Curiton says: "I have found among the MSS. in the British Museum a considerable portion of the original Aramaic documents which Eusebius cites as preserved in the archives of Edessa, and various passages from it quoted by several authors, with other testimonies which seem to be sufficient to establish the fact of the early conversion of the inhabitants of that city, and among them the king himself." These documents record that Abgar, King of Edessa, hearing of the fame of Jesus, and that He was persecuted of the Jews, sent Him a letter inviting Him to Edessa to live, and to heal the king of his malady. The reply of Christ was that His mission to the Jews was not complete, but after His ascension a disciple would come and teach the people of Edessa. This disciple was Thaddeus. He reached Edessa, saw the king, healed and converted, and thus planted the mother-church of the East. The king's son refused the Christian faith and persecuted the Christians. Following Thaddeus was Agghens, his disciple, and then Maris from about A.D. 90, under whom 360 churches were founded in the valley of the Euphrates and the plains and mountains of Assyria. There are documents recording the acts of the martyrs at Edessa in the same year (A.D. 115) that Trajan conquered the Parthian territory, of which Edessa was a part. The Christians were numerous at that time, and the conversion of the king is proved by the coins as early as A.D. 165.

The evidence is that under the Parthians there was an open door to the eastward. They were tolerant in religious matters. The missionary activity of the church and the progress of the gospel under the Parthian rule of the East was as great as under the Roman rule of Europe in the same period.

3. THE PERSIAN RULE OF THE SASSANIANS, (A.D. 226–641).—At the time when this purely Persian dynasty arose many religious forces were in conflict. The Jews had grown powerful under the Parthians, and had their great schools of tradition and Talmudic learning. The old heathenism in Mesopotamia was still prevalent. The claims of Christianity were pressed by growing numbers, but were paralyzed or retarded by the Gnostic sects, so prevalent in the East. Dominant over all, as the state religion, was the old faith of Zoroaster. There was a revival of this faith, with a fierce intolerance equal to any in the West. Some of the Persian kings were favorable to Christianity, but the national feeling always clung to the ancient faith. Many thousands of Persians became Christians, but the stronghold of Zoroastrianism never yielded, and there never arose an indigenous Persian church, worshipping in the Persian language and leavening the whole nation. The Persians refused to follow their wise men, as the Jews refused to follow their prophets, in accepting Jesus as the Christ. In fact the immense number of Jews in Persia had much to do in arraying the Magi against the Christians. When the religion of Christ was accepted by Constantine (A.D. 312) it was stigmatized by the rival empire of the East as the religion of the Romans. Religious zeal and national feeling united against it, and bitter persecutions continued in Persia for a century after they had ceased in the Roman Empire. The sufferings of the Christians under Shapûr II. were as terrible as any experienced under Diocletian.

In the face of these obstacles it is clear that the Christian faith had a harder mission field in Asia than in Europe. The 3d century saw Christian missions there advancing generally in peace. The 4th century was full of conflict and persecution, with an open door and many adversaries. The pious and zealous monks of Egypt and Syria were the leading missionaries, and their labors are still attested by the many churches that bear their names in Mesopotamia and among the Nestorians. The Armenians were largely converted, and the Georgians. In this century also strong heretical sects took shape, that have left relics to the present day. The disciples of John near Bagdad, calling themselves Mandean and numbering some hundreds of families, are such. Their literature and ritual are in the Aramaic dialect, and exceedingly complicated. They resemble the Manicheans. This sect was begun by Manes, a Persian, who formed an eclectic system from the doctrines of the Christians, Zoroastrians, and Buddhists, and gave himself out as the Paraclete promised by Christ. His disciples showed great activity in the spread of his doctrine, and, notwithstanding persecution, the sect increased and continued. It seems probable that a large section of the Persians to day, called Ali Illahees or Dawoodees, are connected with this doctrine.

In the 5th century the bitter controversies within the church resulted in the separation of the Eastern Christians from the West. The Nestorian controversy at the Council of Ephesus (A.D. 431) resulted in a schism which was carried thence to Edessa, and thence to Persia. The separation of the main body of Christians under the Persian rule was completed in a council held at Seleucia A.D. 499. There were political reasons for this separation as well as theological. It gave satisfaction to the Persian Government to have its Christian subjects break their connection entirely with the Romans, and thus it gave rest from persecution. In the 6th and 7th centuries there was much missionary activity by the Persian Church. Says Mosheim: "In the East the Nestorians, with incredible industry and perseverance, labored to propagate their religion beyond its former bounds among the barbarous and savage nations inhabiting the deserts and remotest shores of Asia." It appears from unquestioned documentary proofs that numerous missions were extended not only into but beyond Persia, to the Turkish tribes, and even to China. "Their zeal," says Gibbon, "overleaped the limits which confined the ambition and curiosity of the Greeks and Romans, and they pursued without fear the footsteps of the roving Tartar."

4. THE MOSLEM CALIPHS, A.D. 641–1258.— The dominant religion of Persia from the primeval days had been the faith of Zoroaster. Christianity failed to overthrow it. To this mighty religion, which once seemed likely to supersede all others and be proclaimed in the edicts of the great king over Europe as well as Asia, the fatal blow came suddenly, and from a quarter least expected. The Persian emperor received a letter one day from "the camel-driver of Mecca," bidding him abjure the faith of his ancestors and confess that "there is no God but God, and Mohammed is the prophet of God." The indignant monarch tore the letter in pieces, and drove the camel-drivers who brought it from his presence. But before ten years had passed the Arab hordes had driven the Persian from his throne. Persia, defeated in two decisive battles, reluctantly gave up the contest. The whole system fell with a crash, and the only remnants left to perpetuate its rites are some 5,000 souls in Yezd, a city of Persia, and 100,000 Parsis in Bombay.

The faith of Mohammed from that day to this has ruled in Persia. It is the only Aryan race that accepted Islam. One peculiarity should be noticed—the Mobeds of Magism became the Mollahs of Islam. These ecclesiastics were the bitter enemies of early Christian missionaries, and they are the bitter enemies of modern missions to-day. The rule of the Saracen caliphs at Bagdad did not destroy Christianity. The Christians were liable to excessive exactions, and to persecutions at times, but they were recognized as the people of the Book; and the Nestorians had special privileges, and held many offices of trust. The missionary work was prosecuted and expanded. It could not take much root in Persian soil after the Persians became Moslems, but it gained more and more influence in Tartary and China, beyond the Mohammedan conquest. There were ages of comparative peace in those regions, also of the greatest missionary zeal and enterprise on the part of the Nestorians. Their churches were planted in Transoxiana as far as Kashgar, in the regions of Mongolia, and throughout Northern China. To attest this fact there are extensive Christian graveyards containing memorials of the Turkish race on the borders of China, and the monument of Si-nganfu, in Shensi, giving the history of the Nestorian Mission in China for 145 years (A.D. 636–781). Timotheus, a patriarch of the church for forty years, was zealously devoted to missionary work, and many monks traversed Asia. What might have been the result if they had but taught the pure faith of the gospel, instead of fasts and formalism, and if they had but possessed an open Bible, and had relied on God's Spirit instead of trusting to intrigue and carnal weapons, we cannot say. But there was enough of the Christ-like spirit and doctrine to lead multitudes to the Christian profession, and, we may hope, to eternal life. In the eleventh and twelfth centuries there were large Christianized communities. A Mogul prince, Unkh Khan, gave the name to the celebrated Prester John, and his successors were nominal Christians till overthrown by Genghis Khan. The names of 25 metropolitan sees, from Cyprus on the west to Pekin on the east, are on record. The schools are almost as widely extended. When shall modern missions speak of training-schools and literary centres not only in the regions of Edessa, Nisibis, Seleucia, and Azerbijan, but also among the Elamites and Arabs, and in Khorassan, and far east in Tartary?

5. UNDER THE MOGUL TARTARS, A.D. 1258–1430.—The Moguls arose in Chinese Tartary. The last of the race of Christian kings—Christian in name, doubtless, more than in reality—was slain by Genghis Khan about A.D. 1202. Genghis had a Christian wife, the daughter of this king, and he was tolerant toward the Christian faith. In fact the Mogul conquerors were without much religion, and friendly toward all. The wave of carnage and conquest swept westward and covered Persia, and overwhelmed the Caliph of Bagdad in 1258. This change was for a time favorable to the Christians, as the rulers openly declared themselves Christians, or were partial to Christianity. The patriarch of the Nestorians was chosen from people of the same speech and race as the conquerors—a native of Western China. He ruled the church through a stormy period of seven reigns of Mogul kings; had the joy of baptizing some of them, and of indulging for a time the hope that they would form such an alliance with the Christians of Europe against the Moslems as would render all Asia, across to China, a highway for the Christian faith. But the period of such hope was brief, and soon ended in threatened ruin. The church of both East and West was too degraded in ignorance and superstition, too low in doctrine and life, to avail itself of the opportunity. After a time of vacillation the Moguls found Islam the more suited to their rough and bloody work. The emperor having decided in favor of the Moslems, flung his sword into the scale, and at his back were 100,000 warriors. The Christian cause was lost. The whole structure of the Nestorian Church, unequal to the day of trial, fell before the persecutions and wars of the Tartars. With Timourlane (A.D. 1379–1405) came their utter ruin. He was a bigoted Moslem, and put to the sword all who did not escape to the recesses of the mountains. Thus the fair field of Central Asia, once open to Christian missions, closed in the utter extermination of the Christians, leaving not a vestige of them east of the Koordish Mountains. The Christian faith was thrown back upon its last defences, and became a hunted and despised faith, with only a remnant of adherents, clinging with a death grip to their churches and worship.

6. THE PERIOD OF GREATEST DEPRESSION (A.D. 1400–1830).—Persia was torn by factions and wars for a century. As France rejected the Reformation and reaped her reward in anarchy and blood, so Persia suffered on a larger scale. The Christian Church was lost,—a buried and apparently lifeless seed only remaining, and the Christian name became a by-word.

In 1492 the confusion began to clear. The national religion underwent a change from the orthodox or Sunnee to the heterodox or Shiah system of Mohammedanism. The distinction between these sects runs back to the days of Mohammed and to his son-in-law Ali. It was through the accession to the throne of Persia of a lineal descendant of Mohammed and Ali that the Shiah system became the established creed of Persia. Since that time the Persians and Turks have indulged in mutual hatred, and regarded each other as worse than infidels. This schism has led to as bloody wars between Moslems and Moslems, as the divisions of Catholic and Protestant have among Christians.

The Suffavean kings (A.D. 1492–1722) ruled over large populations of Armenians and Georgians, Nestorians and Jacobites, in what is now Russian and Turkish territory. Meanwhile the Reformation came to Europe, and the revival of the spirit of propagandism in the Romish Church. Toward the close of the 16th century occurred some events bearing on Persian missions, especially during the reign of Shah Abbas the Great (A.D. 1582–1627), the contemporary of Queen Elizabeth. One was diplomatic intercourse between England and Persia. The first attempt was a failure, for in 1561 Anthony Jenkinson arrived in Persia with letters from Queen Elizabeth for Tamasp Shah. At their interview the Shah's first question was, " Are you a Moslem or an infidel ?" He replied that he was not a Moslem, nor was he an infidel. But the Shah expressed his dissatisfaction, and the Englishman retired, and every step of his was immediately sprinkled with sand and swept to remove the defilement of his contact with the royal court. But in 1598 Sir Anthony and Robert Shirley had better success, for they arrived in Persia with a numerous retinue, and for many years were intimately associated with Shah Abbas, and laid the foundation of English influence in the East.

Another event was in 1603 the forcible deportation of thousands of Armenians from the base of Mount Ararat to the central provinces. The descendants of these captives now form communities in Hamadan and Ispahan, and in many intervening districts and villages. This dispersed Christian population is the basis for missionary effort, the more important as the number of Armenians in Persia is small.

The aggressions of the Church of Rome upon the Nestorian Church began in the 13th and 14th centuries, when they competed with the Nestorians for the favor of the Grand Mogul. Nearly a hundred Papal monks perished in the massacres of Timourlane. In 1551 a dissension arose as to the succession of the patriarch, and an appeal was made by one of the parties to the Pope. This opened the way for a secession of a large party to Rome, and the setting up of a rival patriarch.

Following upon the Suffavean kings was an Afghan invasion of Persia, lasting through seven years of massacre and misrule. Then arose Nadir Shah, who extended the Persian frontier far eastward and westward, and pillaged India. A generation of anarchy and civil war followed, until the rise of the present line of kings, called the *Kajar* line, from the ancestral tribe from which they spring. Since the opening of this century these kings have ruled, and an era of peace has come. For twelve centuries Mohammedanism, in one form or another, has controlled the government, and moulded the laws and morals and destinies of the millions of Persia.

7. THE BEGINNING OF MODERN PROTESTANT MISSIONS.—Manifestly the ancient and mediæval missions in Persia have failed to Christianize the nation. The way for modern Protestant missions began to open with the opening of this century. The Persian language, through the Mogul emperors and the conquests of Nadir Shah, became the polite language of a large part of India, and the *lingua franca* of all Western Asia. The East India Company required their officials to study the Persian, until the time of Lord Macaulay, when English became the official language. Persia also from its position has an importance as a political power that was courted by Napoleon, by Russia, and by England. Thus it came to pass that splendid embassies were sent to Persia early in the century, and English influence most of all controlled affairs for several decades. Henry Martyn was a chaplain in India, and there acquired the Persian language. He came to Persia in 1811 to complete and improve the Persian translation of the New Testament. No one can read his memoir covering the eleven months that he spent in Shiraz, and not marvel at his boldness in confessing Christ and his deliverance from the bigoted Mollahs. In June, 1812, his translation was completed, and he proceeded to the king's camp with the intention of laying the work before the king. Here he was called to a severe trial of his faith, and witnessed a good confession in opposition to the Mollahs before the prime-minister. Both his witness and his book were rejected with scorn. The devoted missionary left the country without knowing of a single convert, and on his way to his native England entered into rest at Tocat, in Asia Minor. His translation of the New Testament and the Psalms was the lasting fruit of his labors. He wrote on completing it this prayer: " Now may the Spirit who gave the word, and called me, I trust, to be an interpreter of it, graciously and powerfully apply it to the hearts of sinners, even to gathering an elect people from the long-estranged Persians." Many wonderful facts in later years show that this prayer is being answered.

The next laborer was the Rev. C. G. Pfander of the Basle Missionary Society. He visited Persia in 1829, and at intervals for a few years sojourned there, passing part of his time in Shusha, Georgia, where his brethren from Germany then had a flourishing mission. This learned and devoted man came near sealing his testimony with his blood at Kermanshah, in Western Persia, but was preserved for protracted labors. He died at Constantinople in 1869. His great work for Persia is "The Balance of Truth," a book comparing Christianity and Mohammedanism. This work and several other treatises on the controversy with Islam were published in India, and are doing a great deal secretly in Persia to direct the thousands whose faith in their religion is shaken. The same works, perhaps unwisely published in Turkey before Dr. Pfander's death, led to severe persecution, and to a strict suppression of all books aimed at the system of Islam. But the books still live, and have their work to do, for they are exhaustive and unanswerable.

In 1833 the Rev. Frederic Haas, another German missionary, with his colleagues, on being obliged to leave Russia entered Persia, and for a time they made their headquarters in Tabriz. Mr. Haas especially was eminently fitted for the peculiar work among Persian Moslems, and he gained extensive influence and respect among them. Had the mission been sustained by the Society of Basle, the light of the gospel might have spread. Dr. Perkins in 1837 met them as they were leaving the country, and says: "They retired, not from choice, but from necessity. Their Society decided not to continue operations unless the gospel could be openly proclaimed to the Mohammedans. This is impracticable; life would be the price of the attempt." Mr. Haas was pastor until recent years in his native Wurtemberg, and has done much for Persia in times of famine, and in his efforts to establish an orphan asylum.

In 1838 Rev. Wm. Glen, D.D., a Scottish missionary, entered Persia. He had spent many years in Astrachan in Russia, on a translation of the Old Testament. He spent four years, from 1838 to 1842, in Tabriz and Teheran in revising the work with the help of native scholars. Dr. Glen's version of the Old Testament and Henry Martyn's of the New formed a handsome edition of the whole Bible, complete in 1847. Dr. Glen, at nearly seventy, returned to Persia to circulate the Scriptures, and had the pleasure of sowing the seed, but did not live to see any large harvest gathered.

8. MISSION OF THE A. B. C. F. M., 1834 TO 1871.—About the year 1827 the erratic adventurer and converted Jew, Dr. Joseph Wolf, in travelling through the East made a short visit to the Nestorians of Persia. A paragraph from his writings led Dr. Anderson of the American Board to direct Messrs. Smith and Dwight in exploring the Armenian field to extend their tour to Oroomiah, Persia. In the spring of 1831 they spent a week among the Nestorians, and reported their visit as the most satisfactory and interesting of the whole tour. (See "Researches of Smith and Dwight.") The liberal views of these Christians, their love of the Scriptures, their rejection of image-worship, auricular confession, and other errors of the Papal Church, marked them as in some sense the Protestants of the East. As the wasting remnant of the once great Syriac-Persian Church they awakened a peculiar sympathy, and started also the hope that with the candlestick replaced and the flame rekindled they would again be the light-bearers to the regions of the Far East.

The A. B. C. F. M. determined to establish a mission to the Nestorians. Rev. Justin Perkins and his wife embarked in the fall of 1833. They reached Tabriz about a year later, and in the summer of 1835 were joined by Dr. and Mrs. Grant. This little company of two missionaries and their wives arrived at Oroomiah formally to occupy the place as a station in November, 1835. Meanwhile the A. B. C. F. M. in 1834 sent out the Rev. J. L. Merrick, who had specially prepared himself to explore the Mohammedan field of Persia and Central Asia. He continued a missionary till 1843. He travelled extensively in company with Mr. Haas, and both came near losing their lives in an encounter with the Mollahs in Ispahan. Mr. Merrick's labors resulted only in teaching some Persian youths the English language and science, and in translating the Sheah traditional Life of

Mohammed. It became evident that Providence had not yet opened the way to labor directly for the Mohammedans, and the effort was abandoned.

Thus in 1835 there were three men and two women on the field, and the A. B. C. F. M. Mission was fairly begun. The roll of this mission counts fifty-two missionaries, men and women, sent out previous to 1871. Time would fail to tell of all these. The pioneers, Messrs. Perkins and Grant, were enthusiastic and apostolic men. One of them, Dr. Grant, finished his career in 1845. Thousands in America and England became familiar with his work through his letters and his book on the "Mountain Nestorians," and his "Memoir," written by a colleague in the mountain work, Dr. Laurie. His grave is by the shores of the Tigris, while the account of his labors has passed into the annals of the church's heroes.

Justin Perkins, D.D., was spared to labor for more than thirty-six years, dying on the last day of 1869. His eminent services were seen in pioneer work, and in making known the Nestorians, especially through his volume called "Eight Years' Residence in Persia," published in 1843; also in beginning the system of education; in translating and carrying through the press the Scriptures in modern Syriac; in preparing a religious literature, and in fostering and encouraging every good work of missionaries and native Christians, and the patrons in America and England. In his later days he was a real patriarch, with all the venerable bearing and deep piety of the best fathers of old.

The force of missionaries was steadily increased from time to time by the arrival of several able men,—Messrs. Holladay and Stocking in 1837; Dr. Wright and Mr. Breath, the printer, in 1840; Mr. Stoddard in 1843; Mr. Cochran in 1848; Mr. Coan in 1849; Mr. Rhea in 1851—most with their wives; and Miss Fiske in 1843, and Miss Rice in 1847. These were men and women of marked piety and character. Four of the men and two of the women furnished subjects for missionary biography, and exerted a greater reflex influence upon the life and spirituality of the church at home than their direct influence could have exerted if they had never become missionaries. The second generation of missionaries came in 1858–1860. Five young ministers, one physician, two single ladies, and five married ladies then joined the mission. This large company soon faded away through death and ill-health, so that in 1864 of the whole company only two ministers, Messrs. Shedd and Labaree and their wives, and Mrs. Rhea, were left on the field. Dr. Van Norden and his wife joined the mission in 1866 and Miss Dean in 1868. Of the missionaries of the A. B. C. F. M. there remain in the work at this date (1890) five persons, Messrs. Shedd and Labaree and their wives, and Miss Dean.

The average missionary life of the seventeen men who died or left the work previous to 1870 was nine years and two months. The average of the women was higher.

The work of the A. B. C. F. M. was almost entirely for the Nestorians, numbering about 100,000 souls, partly in Persia and partly in Koordistan, under Turkish rule.

The stages of progress at Oroomiah may be noticed.

(1) *The Preparatory Work.*—When Messrs. Perkins and Grant reached Oroomiah they

found a people entirely accessible. In fact, their arrival was one general welcome from the ecclesiastics and the people. The bishops gave them cordial co-operation in the prosecution of their missionary labors, regarding them not as rivals, but as teachers and coadjutors in the work of instruction and improvement of their people. The influence of Dr. Grant as a physician was very great with the governor and leading men of the Moslems, and the King of Persia sent a special firman to express his pleasure that teachers had come from the New World to instruct his subjects, and also to command their protection.

The first formal work was to prepare a series of cards in the common language, that had not till then been reduced to writing. The first school was begun in a basement in January, 1836, with seven small boys. This was the germ of the training-school on Mount Seir that has sent out scores of preachers and teachers, and that is now continued as Oroomiah College. About two years later Mrs. Grant succeeded in collecting a few little girls, the germ of the female seminary. In the first year three village schools were opened. This number increased till over seventy schools in less than ten years were in successful operation. In 1840 the printing-press arrived, and the Scriptures were so far translated that portions were at once struck off. Preaching was soon begun in the station chapel, in various village churches and in the schools. Privately and publicly, by teaching, preaching, and printing, the seed was sown broadcast. Hundreds had learned to read; the people were friendly, and scores of the ecclesiastics had been under instruction. The missionaries prophesied to the dry bones; but there were few if any signs of spiritual movement or life.

(2) *The Ingathering.*—After the lapse of ten years of faith and toil the harvest came in the two mission schools. Says Mr. Stoddard: "On December 19th, 1845, the Spirit came in both schools in wonderful power. From that time the interest rapidly increased, until two days after, as I was going to preaching service with one of the brethren, we heard the voice of prayer intermingled with sobs on every side. After exercises of the deepest solemnity we closed the meeting; but not one moved from his seat. When at last they left, they flocked to my study, and it was filled to overflowing with anxious inquirers. Then, with emotions that I can never describe, I unfolded with faltering tongue the gospel of Jesus Christ to one company after another, till near midnight. The morning light brought with it a repetition of similar scenes. Rising very early I found inquirers waiting to be guided to Jesus." Thus the work with deepening power continued for about two months in the two schools. At the close of that time fifty of the pupils had been hopefully converted. Thence the work spread throughout the mission premises and to several of the villages with something like pentecostal power and results, entirely changing the face of the missionary work, as the outgushing of a stream of water changes a Persian desert into a garden of flowers and fruits. Other similar revivals followed, and no year has passed since then without some portion of the field being blessed. A general enlightening and elevating influence went forth among the Nestorian

people. Nearly a thousand had been received to the communion previous to 1870.

(3) *Organizing and Training.*—The revivals brought some hundreds of converts to be trained and organized under difficult circumstances. The missionaries did not seek to form a new church, but to see a revival of pure religion in the old church. For many years an honest effort was made to reform the old body without destroying its organization. This effort failed. One reason was that the patriarch did his utmost, by his threats and persecutions, to alienate the spiritual-minded. Also, the converts could no longer accept the unscriptural practices and rank abuses that prevailed, and it became evident that there was no method to do away with these abuses and practices. The converts also asked for better care, and purer and better instruction and means of grace, than they found in the dead language and rituals and ordinances of the old church. The training began, something as Wesley's classes in England began, with no intention of disturbing the old establishment. The converts were invited to join with the missionaries in their communion, and the missionaries examined the candidates and exercised needed discipline. As the number became too large and widely scattered to come all to one place, it was divided, and after a time the native ordained preachers became pastors, and local churches arose and assumed their duties and responsibilities. In time these pastors and elders from the churches and the other preachers, including bishops, presbyters, and deacons, all of whom had received ordination in the old church, met in conference with the missionaries. The first conference was in 1862. This conference adopted very simple rules of order and discipline, and a brief confession of faith. Thus the separation took place in no spirit of hostility or controversy. There was no violent disruption, no bitter words were spoken of the old church or its ecclesiastics. Some things were taken from the canons and rituals of ancient usage, others from the usages of Protestant churches. The patriarch in office at the time was at first very friendly to Dr. Grant and the Mountain Mission, and personally aided in superintending the building of mission houses; subsequently he did all in his power to break up the mission. His most able brother, however, Deacon Isaac, accepted the evangelical doctrines, and till his death in 1865 was the foremost man in the reformed communion. Of the bishops, three united with the reform, and died in the evangelical communion,—Mar Elias of Geogtapa, Mar Yohannan of Gavalan, and Mar Joseph of Bohtan. A large majority of the presbyters of the old church in Persia joined the reform movement, and as large a proportion of the deacons; and the same is true of the Maleks or leading men.

The work accomplished under the A. B. C. F. M. was to establish an enterprise with all the appliances and parts of an aggressive reformation in this old church a thousand miles east of Constantinople, in the heart of Islam—the press, the training-schools for young men and young women, a band of over fifty native pastors and evangelists, an aggregate of over eighty schools and congregations. The results were great in themselves, and greater in their bearing upon the future.

The aggregate of appropriations made by the

A. B. C. F. M. for the nearly 38 years of its superintendence was about $580,000—an average of $15,470 per annum. The long inland journey renders Persia difficult of access, and one of the most expensive in the outlay for travel of the missions undertaken from America, while it is one of the cheapest in the employment of native agencies and expenses on the field.

9. MISSIONS OF THE PRESBYTERIAN BOARD. 1871 to 1890.—By the union of the two great branches of the Presbyterian Church in 1870, the New School body ceased its support of the A. B. C. F. M., and claimed a portion of the mission as its heritage. "The Mission to the Nestorians" changed its name, and since 1870 is called "The Mission to Persia," and the field was transferred to the care of the Presbyterian Board in 1871. The missionaries at the time of the transfer were 4 ordained missionaries and their wives, one physician and his wife, and one single lady. To these have been added since 1871, 18 ordained men and their wives, 4 physicians and their wives, 21 single ladies (two of whom are physicians), and 4 single gentleman (one of them a physician): in all 26 men and 43 women. Some of these have been removed by death; a larger number have failed in health and returned to America. The mission staff of workers at present in Persia is 16 men and 27 women.

The expansion of effort has been great in these years. In 1870 the mission considered it an urgent duty to embrace at once within their efforts the Armenians and Moslems of Central Persia. This effort was seconded by the Board. Teheran was occupied as a station in 1872; Tabriz in 1873; Hamadan in 1882; Salmas in 1886; and the station for Mountain Nestorians was revived in Turkish territory in 1889. The area of country brought within evangelizing labor has been greatly enlarged. The eleven missionaries in 1870 are now four times as many. The one station has become six. The territory was too extended for annual meetings of missionaries separated by twenty days of caravan travel, and speaking several languages. In 1883 the mission was divided into West Persia and East Persia. A glance at the first fifty years of this American Mission shows that the American Church has sent to Persia—a far off and inland nation, with which our country has few commercial or political relations—nearly a hundred of her chosen sons and daughters, at an expense of nearly $1,200,000 of free contributions for these missionaries and for evangelizing and educating the people. Such is the record in honor of Christ and for the benefit of the souls of men in a land so far away. The present annual expenditure of this mission is far in advance of former times, as the work and number of stations have increased. But in a great measure the work is still preparatory.

*The Western Mission* embraces the province of Azerbaijan, and a large portion of Koordistan, the lands of ancient Assyria and Media, and indirectly a much larger region in the Caucasus and in Turkey. The work is first for the nominal Christians, and then for Jews, Moslems, and others. Among the Syrian or Nestorian Christians there is the old work, continued in Oroomiah and the mountains.

The Oroomiah station continues to flourish. The reform among the Nestorians shows: communicants in 1857, 216; in 1877, 1,087; and in 1889 over 2,000. The Reformed Evangelical Church: the roll of ministers shows 40 fully ordained men, and 30 others, licentiates; also 87 elders, and 91 deaconesses of the congregations. The Reformed Church has its synod; also a native board of missions that meets monthly with the missionaries. By combining funds and counsels with the missionaries, a system of pastoral care and itinerant labors is in operation, which aims as fast as possible to reach all the Christian population, and to carry the gospel to all the other populations. The people are generally very poor in worldly goods, but are able to do much for their own support and for the spread of the gospel—averaging about a dollar a year to a communicant, when wages are but ten and twelve cents a day for work. The missionary spirit is embodied in their creed as well as the history of ancient times, and is seen in daily efforts of many men and women, especially the young laymen. There is a growing zeal to preach to Jews, Koords, Persians, and Moslems; and as the fields are ripening for the sickle, these native Christians are to be the reapers. They have already gathered the first-fruits among all these classes.

The first and highest call in a growing native church is for a native ministry, and here this field compares with any other in Western Asia. The college is at the head of the educational work, with a theological class, a scientific course, an industrial department, and a few medical students. New buildings have been erected in the same yard with the hospital, and thus the two agencies form a centre of great influence. In the city of Oroomiah is the Fidelia Fiske Female Seminary, with new buildings erected in 1888, for educating girls. During the winter in the villages far and near are over 100 parochial schools, giving education to 2,500 children. The Sabbath-school is the auxiliary in all the congregations attended by young and old to the number of about 5,000. These agencies are aided by the printing-press and small monthly papers, by colporteur work, and still more by the medical arm of the service. There are other schemes of benevolence in an orphanage conducted by Deacon Abraham, a native brother, and in relief for sufferers in time of famine. Two severe famines have passed over the region in the last twenty years, in which the mission has been the means of relieving thousands. The poor and oppressed and persecuted and unfortunate come to the missionary for assistance and help.

A notable event was the celebration of the jubilee of this work in 1885, followed by prevailing revivals in many of the congregations. The hope of the work is in the gift of the Holy Spirit in its convincing and renewing power. Thousands of hearts are more or less convinced, and there is opportunity for the work to grow manyfold before it is completed. There is the beginning of the end in several self-supporting churches. There can be no doubt that the great Head of the church has owned and blessed the work among the Nestorians; multitudes of souls have been saved, and the foundations of a new and lasting reformation laid. The hope is certainly cherished that the Nestorians may be rapidly enlightened and won to living Christianity, not only through the station at Oroomiah, but from the renewed activity in the mountains of Koordistan.

10. ARCHBISHOP'S MISSION TO THE ASSYRIAN

CHRISTIANS.—For account of the work of this Society among the Nestorians, see article on the Society.

*Work among the Armenians in Persia.*—Many Armenians dwelt in Northern Persia in ancient times. The communities of Central Persia date from the time of Shah Abbas, when 40,000 were led into captivity from Trans-Caucasia and settled near Ispahan. In the war of 1830 with Russia the Armenians were accused of wishing to betray Tabriz into their hands, and their massacre was planned. They were saved by the English residents, who placed guards at the entrances of the Armenian quarters. At that time 9,000 families of Armenians fled from Persia. Afterwards Abbas Mirza secured the priests in his service by presents, and induced Armenians to return by granting them special privileges.

Small communities of Armenians are scattered throughout Persia. In the fertile plains of Salmas and Oroomiah, under the shadow of Ararat, on the northern slopes of the Elburz in Karadagh, through the valleys of Bakbtiari, on the shores of the Caspian, in the cities of Tabriz, Teheran, Hamadan, Ispahan, Maragha, Khoi, and their surrounding districts, are these communities of Armenians, wonderfully preserved by God in the midst of thousands of Mohammedans. There is certainly a grand purpose in this providence. Their presence enables missionaries and evangelists to occupy as preaching stations all these places, and not only to labor for them, but for the Mohammedans. The Armenians themselves, too, will become a leaven among the surrounding peoples when their Christianity is revived. They are like a metallic mirror which once reflected the light, but is now rusted, and needs repolishing to reflect Christ's glory round about.

The efforts to reach the Armenians of Persia are of recent origin compared with work for Nestorians. The missionaries living in Armenian communities have given most of their time to Mussulman work. Only very recently has the mission taken action that they should learn the Armenian language. The intolerance of Islam has driven them more to work for Armenians. Now the stations of the Presbyterian Mission at Tabriz, Teheran, Hamadan, and Salmas, and of the Church Missionary Society at Ispahan, are chiefly engaged in work for Armenians. At each of these places is a prosperous girls' boarding-school. At Ispahan is a large and flourishing boys' school, with several hundred pupils. In Hamadan almost all the Armenian children of school age are in Protestant schools. In Teheran and Tabriz the schools meet much opposition and competition. In the latter place the Armenians have two graded schools with seven rooms, and liberally paid, well-trained teachers. The mission school has 50 pupils, and a fine class of young men just ready for a theological course. There are six organized churches in Persia, which are composed chiefly of Armenians, with perhaps 325 members. the largest congregation being in Julfa, near Ispahan. A lack of Armenian teachers and preachers has been greatly felt, but it is now on the point of being supplied, and we can anticipate greater progress in the future.

Every forward step is contested by the Armenians and their ecclesiastics. The validity of Protestant marriage, the purchase of houses, the establishment of new out-stations and schools, the entrance to new places—each advance is the occasion of a burst of opposition which frequently is not quieted until settled by the government. Sometimes they resort to the boycott. Mussulman work has been disturbed and persecution brought on by their instigation. Their belief that by dividing their race we weaken them politically is a great hindrance. The prospects are that the work among the Armenians will be slow.

**Persian Version.**—The Persian belongs to the Iranic branch of the Aryan family of languages, and is used in Persia, India, etc. Translations into the ancient Persian of single books of the Old and New Testament only are known : (*a*) Of the Old Testament, the Pentateuch, Proverbs, Ecclesiastes, and Song of Songs were slavishly translated from the Hebrew,—the Pentateuch by Jacob ben Joseph Tawus, and the other books by an unknown Jew. The former was published in Constantinople in Hebrew characters in 1546, and again in the London Polyglot in Persian characters with a Latin translation : the latter are still extant in a MS., No. 519, at the Paris National Library. (*b*) Of the New Testament there are two versions of the Gospels, one made from the Greek, the other from the Peshito. The former was edited according to two MSS. by Whelock and Pierson (London, 1657); the latter is contained in the London Polyglot, and was published in a Latin translation by Ch. Bode (Helmstadt, 1751). All these versions are prepared in the modern Persian ; even the translation of the Pentateuch was made at a late period, as may be seen from the rendering of "Babel" in Gen. 10.10, by "Bagdad," which was built in the year 772. An attempt to procure a version of the Scriptures in Persian was made by Nadir Shah, and a translation of the Gospels was prepared by the Jesuits Duhan and Desvignes in 1740. It was edited by Professor Dorn, Petersburg, 1848.

In the present century different translations into Persian were made. The New Testament was published by the Calcutta Auxiliary Society in 1816, and at London in 1825, according to a version made by Sabat ; Henry Martyn's version was printed at St Petersburg 1815, Calcutta 1826, and after. The Psalms, too, as translated by Henry Martyn, were published in 1816 at Calcutta; and republished at London, under the superintendence of Dr. Lee, in 1824. The Book of Genesis, translated by Mirza Jaffier, was printed at London in 1827; and Isaiah, as rendered by Mirza Ibrahim, was also published at London in 1834. At last the entire Old Testament, translated by the Archdeacon T. Robinson, was issued in 1838, after fourteen years had been spent on the work of translation. Another translation of the Old Testament, made by the Rev. W. Glen, of the Scottish Mission at Astrakhan, was published between 1830 and 1847, at Edinburgh. Henry Martyn's New Testament, which had been in use for more than half a century, was published in a revised form in 1877, the revision having been made by the Rev. N. R. Bruce, a Scottish missionary stationed at Julfa, near Ispahan. In the same year a revision committee, consisting of the Rev. R. Bruce of the Church Missionary Society, and the Revs. J. Bassett and J. L. Potter of the American Presbyterian Missions, has been formed for the purpose of revising the Persian

Scriptures. A revised edition of Mr. Bruce's revision of Henry Martyn's New Testament was published at London in 1881, the edition consisting of 6,000 copies; another edition was issued in 1885. The revision of the Old Testament has also been commenced by Dr. Bruce, and Genesis, Exodus, and the Psalms were published in 1888.

(*Specimen verses.* John 3 : 16.)

زیرا که خدا آنقدر جهان را دوست داشت که فرزند یکانه خود را ارزانی فرمود تا که هر کس که بر او ایمان آورد هلاک نشود بلکه زندهگانی جاوید یابد

Hebrew character.

זירא כה כדא אן קדר גהאן רא דוסת דאשת כה פרזנד־יכאנה' כּד רא ,ארזאני פרמוד כה תא הר כס כה בר ,אן אימאן אורד הלאך נשוד בלכה זנדגאני גאויד יאבד

**Peru,** a republic of South America, which lies between the Pacific Ocean on the west and Brazil and Bolivia on the east, Ecuador on the north, and Chili on the south. It contains three distinctive physical divisions—the coast region, the region of the Andes, and the tropical forests within the valley of the Amazon. Its area is 463,747 square miles, divided into nineteen departments. Every variety of climate is found in Peru, on account of the difference in elevation in various parts. The population (1876) is 2,621,844, besides 350,000 uncivilized Indians. Twenty-three per cent of the population are mixed races, Cholos and Zambos. There are 18,000 Europeans, and 50,000 Asiatics, chiefly Chinese. The principal cities, with their population, are: Lima, the capital (101,488); Callao, the principal seaport (33,502); Arequipa (29,237); and Cuzco (18,370). The constitution, proclaimed in 1856 and revised 1860, provides that a president and a congress of two houses shall be elected every four years. The constitution prohibits the public exercise of any other religion than the Roman Catholic, though in reality there is a certain amount of tolerance, since Anglican churches and Jewish synagogues are found in Callao and Lima. Education is compulsory, and is free in the municipal public schools. In 1889 there were 16,025 miles of railway, and Peru is in communication by cable with the telegraphic system of the world.

The American Bible Society through its colporteurs prosecutes the only Protestant work so far in Peru, by distributing the Bible translated into Spanish. The principal agent of the Bible Society is an Italian minister, who has been holding church services in Callao, where he gathered a congregation of over a hundred, to whom he preached in Spanish. His success in making converts roused the opposition of the priests, who viewed with unconcern the services in English, but saw that preaching in Spanish was likely to prove a potent means of enlight-

ening the people, and on the 25th of June, 1890, Mr. Penzotti, the minister, was arrested and put in prison, charged with offending the law, which has been practically a dead letter. At present writing (January, 1891) he is still in prison. The United States Government cannot interfere officially, since Mr. Penzotti is an Italian, but the consul has been instructed to use his personal influence to secure the release of the prisoner. The Italian Government has been strangely apathetic. In the mean time much popular indignation has been aroused in Peru, and several public meetings have been held to agitate the question of freedom of religion. Over 2,000 people, among them many of the most prominent citizens, attended such a meeting in Lima recently; the press have come out strongly in favor of freedom of religious belief and worship, and it is not unlikely that the prohibition of the Protestant religion will be removed ere the close of this year.

**Peshawar,** a city and military post in Punjab, India, 276 miles from Lahore, 190 miles from Kabul; the outpost against Afghanistan. The modern city has but slight architectural pretentions, the houses being generally built of small bricks of mud, held together by a wooden framework, and except the principal thoroughfare all the streets are narrow and crooked. The sanitary arrangements are good, and water plenty. Outside of the city are lovely fruit gardens, which form a favorite pleasure-ground of the people. Population of city and suburbs, 59,292, Moslems, Hindus, Sikhs, Christians, Jains, etc. Mission station C. M. S. (1855); 1 native pastor, 42 communicants, 18 native helpers, 4 schools, 656 scholars. An Afghan mission is conducted from this place. Kafiristan has also been reached from here.

**Petchaburee,** a city in Siam, on the west side of the Gulf of Siam, 85 miles southwest of Bangkok. Has 10,000 inhabitants. Mission station (1861) of the Presbyterian Church (North); 3 missionaries, 2 missionaries' wives, 2 single ladies, 17 native workers, 4 principal out-stations. There are 5 churches located in Petchaburee and its province, 153 communicants, 12 day-schools, 232 pupils, 60 Sabbath-scholars, boys' boarding-school, 28 boys, girls' industrial school, 37 girls. At the dispensary 4,327 patients were treated in 1889.

**Petersburg,** a town in Central Kaffraria, South Africa, west of King William's Town. Mission station of the Berlin Evangelical Missionary Society (1856); 1 missionary, 5 native helpers, 42 church-members, 5 schools, 37 scholars.

**Philadelphia Medical Mission** was the first established in the United States. Dr. A. B. Kirkpatrick, now (1890) a missionary in Burmah, founded this mission in 1879. Headquarters, 519 South Sixth Street; Henry R. Fox, Superintendent. The Advisory Board consists of a chairman, secretary, superintendent, four physicians (including the chairman), seven clergymen, eleven laymen, and seven women. In 1889 there was also a dispensary on Front Street below Christian, and one at 973 Frankford Avenue. Mr. John B. Stetson, a large manufacturer, has founded a "medical department" to meet the wants of those needing medical treatment in the neighborhood of the mission rooms, especially the employees of

Stetson & Co. The payment of one dollar entitles one to medical treatment for three months, the medicines being provided at cost, and no one is turned away for lack of means to meet the stipulated requirements. The rooms are open daily except on the Sabbath; a clergyman is superintendent, with whom a physician is associated, and there is also a staff of eminent practitioners and specialists.

*The Design* of the mission is to reach men and women who otherwise would never hear the gospel; it seeks to rescue the perishing who are not sought out by any other agencies. Germans, Russians, Arabs, Turks, Indians, Chinese, and Negroes make up the crowds which stand and listen with interest as the good news of salvation is proclaimed in their hearing. Special effort is also made to reach the fallen women.

*Method and Means Employed.*—Every Thursday evening a lunch is given for women immediately after the gospel service; visits are made to those who are known in the various hospitals, homes, and prisons; tracts are distributed, the Bible read, and prayers offered with and for the sick, and situations are sought in which to place wandering women who have proved that they are thoroughly renewed by the gospel's power. Services are held for the patients immediately before being waited upon by the doctor. After the reading of a passage from the Bible, followed by a hymn and prayer, the gospel is briefly presented to all who are in waiting. The interest of these meetings is greatly enhanced and the attendance increased by delegations of young people who attend, in turn, from different churches in order to lead the music, imparting their zest and skill to this division of the service.

Twice a week, before the evening meetings, visits are paid to a number of the houses in the vicinity by the superintendent, accompanied by a co-laborer; invitations are given to attend the meetings, and tracts, especially adapted to the class being sought, are distributed. Carefully selected story-books, containing the gospel, are also loaned upon these occasions.

The work is well-nigh foreign in its character. Jews and Italians, Armenians, Arabs, and mongrel Orientals find their way to the free distribution of medicine with gratuitous attendance, and in seeking to recover health for the body often secure the salvation of their souls. A Christian Armenian from the Berber country has been a preacher and interpreter in the work of the mission.

*Results.*—Many are the touching testimonies of those who speak of the higher good attained while they were in search of temporal healing. "The cloud is lifted, I see the light;" "Out of my tears, and away from my self-trusting, I now see *Him* as my Saviour;" "Hearing John 8 : 12 explained, I saw my mistake; now I am looking to Christ, who is the Light—I return home, though sick, a happy man;" "Thank God, I am saved! how I bless Him for bringing me here!" And like expressions often fall from the lips of those who have found joy and peace in believing.

The following figures will convey some idea of the general results attained:

Number of meetings (at three dispensaries) 756; persons present, 1,915; at evening gospel meetings, 10,886; at open-air meetings, 3,830; at Sunday-school, 1,015—total, 17,646. Number of inquirers, 913; in previous years, 9,253; total number in eleven years, 10,166. Tracts distributed (English, German, Hebrew, and Italian), 35,000; Bibles and Testaments given, 81; visits to hospitals, prisons, etc., 112; houses of prostitution visited, 140; visits to, 1,693; conversions of inmates, 8,465; women taken to reformatory homes, 17; received in the mission, 9; number furnished with clothing, 18; total number of dispensary cases in eleven years, 25,821; total number of home and dispensary cases in eleven years, 45,365; total number of home cases, 19,154; total number of prescriptions put up, 45,250. And all this work has been done at an average annual expense of about $1,100, which includes from $610 to $660 for rent.

**Philip, John,** b. in England; studied at Hoxton Academy; was appointed as a Deputation with Rev. John Campbell to visit the stations of the L. M. S. in South Africa; sailed December 10th, 1818, reaching Cape Town February 26th, 1819. Accompanied by Mr. Moffat and Mr. Evans, the Deputation visited the stations within the colony, but were prevented by the Kafir war from proceeding beyond. Mr. Philip returned to Cape Town. In 1820 he received from Princeton College, New Jersey, U. S. A., the degree of Doctor of Divinity. The Deputation having completed their work, Dr. Philip was appointed permanent superintendent of the Society's Missions in South Africa. He was also pastor of an English congregation at Cape Town. In 1826 he visited England by invitation of the directors, his place as superintendent being supplied by Rev. R. Miles. While at home he published his work "Researches in South Africa." Certain representations made by him respecting the condition of the Hottentots led the Directors to present a memorial to the government, which secured certain regulations for the amelioration of the civil condition of that tribe among the people. Dr. Philip returned to the Cape July 18th, 1829, and resumed his office as superintendent of the Society's missions. Soon after his return he was called as defendant in an action for libel in the Supreme Court at the Cape on account of a passage in his work, "Researches in South Africa." The action was decided against him, and the damages and costs amounted to £1,200. This was generously paid by friends in England. On February 28th, 1836, he left Cape Town with Rev. James Read, a Kafir chief, and a Hottentot, reaching London May 14th. With these he gave evidence before a Parliamentary Committee respecting the aborigines in South Africa and the causes of the Kafir war. Having accomplished the object of this visit he re-embarked for Africa, arriving at Cape Town February 6th, 1838. He made repeated visits to the various stations, and also undertook the education of several young men, to prepare them for missionary work. In 1844 Rev. J. C. Brown having taken his place as pastor of the English church at Cape Town, he went, December, 1846, on account of Mrs. Philip's ill-health, to Port Elizabeth. Thence he proceeded to Hankey, where she died October 23d, 1847. Dr. Philip died at Hankey, South Africa, August 27th, 1851. His "Researches in South Africa" were published in 2 vols. in London, 1828.

**Philippine Islands,** a group lying in the Indian Archipelago, extending almost due north and south from Formosa to Borneo and the Moluccas, embracing 16° of latitude and 9° of longitude, containing 114,326 square miles, with a population estimated at 7,500,000. Of the 400 islands many are small and of no importance. The two largest are Luzon and Mindanao. The climate is hot, but tempered by ocean breezes and great moisture; and the vegetation is luxurious.

The majority of the inhabitants are of the Malayan race. The resident Spaniards are few in number. There are a great many Chinese, and some tribes of Negritos.

The islands were discovered and conquered by the Spaniards in the 16th century, and they are now under the charge of a governor-general, under whom the 43 provinces are ruled by governors, alcaldes, or commandants, according to their importance. The capital, Manila, on the island of Luzon, has a population of 270,000 (1880). Other towns are Lavag, 36,639; San Miguel, 34,672; Banang, 33,106; Cabecera, 29,057. Missions: British and Foreign Bible Society, with a depot at Luzon. Scriptures: Psalms, Gospels, Acts, and New Testament in Pangisauen.

**Philippopolis,** a city of Bulgaria, the most important city of the southern province (Eastern Roumelia). Population, 45,000, Bulgarians, Turks, Greeks, etc. It suffered a great deal during the Bulgarian insurrection, but since the establishment of peace and its connection by rail with Europe it has grown in importance. Mission station of the A. B. C. F. M.; 2 missionaries and wives, 1 female missionary, 22 native helpers, 12 out-stations, 6 churches, 223 church-members, 2 schools, 188 scholars. There is also a large school for girls, carried on by Mrs. Mumford as a "faith" mission. A medical mission and hospital under the auspices of the Friends [of England] is carried on by Mr. Tonjoroff, formerly a preacher under the A. B. C. F. M.

**Phillips, Jeremiah,** b. Plainfield, N. Y., U. S. A., January 5th, 1812; attended Madison (now Colgate) University, but did not complete his course of study, the Committee of the Missionary Society desiring that he should accompany Dr. Sutton on his return to India. He was ordained at Plainfield, and embarked for Calcutta in company with Dr. E. Noyes, September 22d, 1835, under the Free Baptist Missionary Society. His field of labor was Orissa, a region of country hitherto wholly untouched by missionary effort, and was occupied in 1836. Balasore was first occupied in 1840 with a boarding-school of six native children. The same year Mr. Phillips commenced a new station at Jellasore' with some of the Balasore boarding scholars and native converts. He was the first to discover the Santals, a rude and numerous race of aborigines previously unknown to missionaries. He reduced their wild language to writing, prepared and published a grammar and dictionary, and established schools among them—for the first time in their existence, so far as known. As a result of his correspondence and published articles in the papers of India and America, seven missions have been established, and are successfully working among them. He translated the Gospels and other portions of the Bible into their language, and also prepared schoolbooks. The degree of doctor of divinity was conferred upon him by Bates College, Maine. The India Government officially thanked Dr. Phillips for his great work among the Santals. "The Indian Evangelical Review," in a notice of his leaving India in impaired health, says: "When he arrived in Orissa all was one unbroken expanse of Hinduism. And after 44 years of faithful toil he left five congregations, 478 communicants, 453 pupils in Sunday-schools, many day-schools with a large force of native teachers and preachers, a press sending out a stream of Bibles and Christian books, some of them in a dialect which but a few years ago existed only in the unwritten speech of savages, and a Biblical school with seventeen Hindu young men preparing for the Christian ministry." He left for home in 1855, sailed again for India December 17th, 1864, and his health failing he took his final departure, June, 1879. He died at Hillsdale, Mich., December 9th, 1879.

**Pieter Maritzburg,** the capital of Natal, Africa, is situated in a fertile plain, 2,000 feet above the sea, surrounded by a circle of hills. It has an excellent climate, especially curative of pulmonary complaints, and the rich vegetation of its gardens and surrounding woods makes it one of the most delightful cities of Africa. Its population, numbering 15,769, is most cosmopolitan in character, consisting of Zulus, Kafirs, Europeans, Hindus, Chinese, and Arabs; and English, Dutch, Tamil, and Zulu are the prevailing tongues. Mission station of the Free Church of Scotland (1865), taken over from the Wesleyan Methodists; 1 missionary and wife, 1 female missionary, 22 native helpers, 1 church, 163 church-members, 3 schools, 136 scholars. S. P. G. (1851); 2 missionaries.

**Pinalap,** one of the Caroline Islands, Micronesia, has a population of 800. Mission work is under the Hawaiian Evangelical Association; 1 native pastor, 100 scholars, 238 church-members.

**Pinetown,** a town in Natal, Africa, near Pieter Maritzburg. Mission station of S. P. G. (1857); 1 missionary, 43 communicants.

**Ping-yang,** a prefectural city in Shansi, China, on a tributary of the Yellow River, in the southern part of the province. Mission station of the C. I. M. (1879); 1 missionary, 1 church, 81 church-members.

**Pinkerton, Myron Winslow,** b. Boscawen, N. H., U. S. A., July 18th, 1843; graduated at Ripon College 1868, and Chicago Theological Seminary 1871. His mother was deeply interested in missions, especially in the labors of Myron Winslow, and named her first-born son after him, expressing the hope that he would be a missionary. She died when he was three years of age, but having heard of her desire, he said that when in college it often came to his mind. He was ordained July 14th, 1871. He said: "Perhaps there will be men who would wish to go to Turkey or Japan, while few will go to Africa. I would rather go where the laborers are few." He sailed August 9th, 1871, as a missionary of the A. B. C. F. M. for Africa, arriving at Natal October 9th, and was stationed among the Zulus at Umpwalumi. In 1875 he went 125 miles inland towards the Koplamba Mountains, and founded the station of Inundama, to which he removed with his family in 1876. Here, besides his pastoral and evangelistic work, he assisted in the translation of the Scriptures. Committing the station to the native helper, he pushed still further inland. A committee appointed by the mission to consider the matter of an inland mission, after due inquiry reported that desirable places could be found for mission stations, especially among the large Zulu-speaking tribes under the chief Umzila, and it was decided that such a mission be established. Mr. Pinkerton offered to engage in this enterprise, saying that if the mission desired it, he would make it his life-work. In 1879 he prepared to depart for Umzila's kingdom, distant by land a thousand miles. Before starting he took his family to America, "because," he wrote from Natal, "of the probably long time I shall be engaged, and the possibility of my being removed by death while I am away." Leaving his family at home, he sailed by way of England for Natal, reaching Durban July 2d, 1880. Associating with himself Mr. E. Jourdan, an American ship-officer, who had been five years in Senegambia, and more recently had labored in the mission at Adams, and John Pohleni, a Zulu convert, Mr. Pinkerton sailed from Natal July 9th, for Umzila's coast, by the way of Delagoa Bay and Inhambane. A severe storm having prevented the steamer's stopping at Inhambane, he was taken to Zanzibar, 1,400 miles north. After much delay he started, and on the way commenced a letter to his wife, dated October 18th, which he finished at Bazaruto, 90 miles from Inhambane. In his letter he said: "Let us patiently hold on, and bear a brave but humble part in our peculiar work. My expedition to Umzila's has been very popular among the natives, as well as the Portuguese. The Lord is giving me a fine start. Different dialects are spoken, but Zulu is everywhere understood. I am preaching and teaching Christ in the uttermost parts of the earth now as never before. The natives here are even in denser darkness than those about Indundama. If no special hindrance occurs, we expect to reach the king's kraal in three weeks." But, alas! the hindrance did occur. His attendant Jourdan wrote from Inhambane, December 3d, saying that they had reached Bakot's kraal November 5th, when Mr. Pinkerton was taken ill of fever. He told Jourdan to take him out of the hut to the bush, saying, "If I die in this hut the natives will murder you." These were the last words he spoke. They put him in a hammock and started, crossing the Gabuln River in canoes, November 10th, and in half an hour after crossing, he died. He was buried by Jourdan the same day on the east bank of the river, under a large moss-covered tree. John Pohleni read the funeral service in Zulu. Only a week before his death everything was hopeful, and Mr. Pinkerton wrote at different dates on his journey in the most enthusiastic terms of the prospect of establishing a mission in Umzila's country.

**Pipli,** a town in Bengal, India, 27 miles from Cuttack, on the road taken by the pilgrims on their way to the Jagannath festival at Puri. Mission station of the General Baptist Missionary Society, visited from Cuttack; 1 native pastor, 1 chapel, 102 church-members, 52 day-scholars, 57 Sunday-scholars.

**Pirrie,** a town in Kaffraria, South Africa, northwest of King William's Town. Mission station of the Free Church of Scotland; 1 missionary, 4 European teachers, 11 native helpers, 9 out-stations, 1 church, 280 communicants, 7 Anglo-vernacular schools, 340 scholars.

**Pithoragarh,** military outpost in Kumaon district, Northwest Provinces, India. Population, 438. Elevation, 5,334 feet. Mission station of the Methodist Episcopal Church (North); 1 medical missionary and wife, 1 assistant missionary, 28 native helpers, 16 schools, 578 scholars.

**Pogue, John Fawcett,** b. Wilmington, Delaware, U. S. A., December 29th, 1814; graduated at Marietta College 1840, Lane Theological Seminary 1843; sailed as a missionary of the A. B. C. F. M. for the Sandwich Islands December 4th the same year, reaching Honolulu July 10th, 1844. He was stationed 1845-48 at Koloa. There he came near losing his life from an extraordinary rise of waters in the night. Awaked by their rush past his dwelling, and attempting to reach the house of Dr. Smith near by, he was borne by the flood half a mile towards the sea, and when near perishing was thrown upon a heap of stones, where he remained till morning and the subsiding of the waters. He was associated with Mr. Alexander in the Lahaina Seminary, and succeeded him as principal, holding the position 1852-66. In 1870 he was elected secretary of the Hawaiian Board of Missions, and filled the office for seven years. Returning from a visit to the United States, he stopped at Laramie City, Wyoming Territory, on Saturday to avoid travelling on the Sabbath, was taken suddenly ill, and died at the hotel, December 4th, 1877. His labors, whether as pastor or teacher, were arduous. He was highly esteemed in the mission.

**Pohlman, William John,** born Albany, New York, U. S. A., 1812, of pious parents who belonged to the Lutheran Church; was converted at the age of 16, and united with the First Reformed Church at Albany. Devoting himself to the Christian ministry, he studied three years at the Albany Academy, graduated at Rutgers College 1834, and studied theology at the seminary in New Brunswick. While there he consecrated himself to the foreign missionary work. In August, 1836, he offered himself to the American Board, was ordained by the Classis of Albany, and with his wife, a sister of Dr. John Scudder, sailed for Borneo May 25th of the same year. After a brief sojourn at Singapore, he went to Batavia, where he was compelled to remain a year before the Dutch governor would permit him to go to Borneo. Meanwhile he studied the Malay language. Permitted to proceed, he settled at Pontianak, Borneo. Mrs. Pohlman died in 1845, a devoted, intelligent missionary. In 1844 he was transferred to China with Rev. Elihu Doty, to establish the Amoy Mission in connection with Dr. Abeel. Having studied the Chinese language in Borneo he was prepared to begin work at once in his new field. A church-building was erected with funds furnished from America, when there were but three communicants. Three other churches were established, native preachers and catechists raised up, and the mission has long been regarded as a model of evangelizing work in China. Mr. Pohlman's life was suddenly ended at Breaker's

Point by the wreck of the vessel on which he was bound from Hong Kong to Amoy, January 5th, 1849. Pirates attacked the sinking ship, but he sprang into the sea and was drowned. He is described as "amiable, buoyant, frank, tenacious to the last degree in prosecuting his good purposes, with practical common-sense and intense energy laboring for the kingdom of Christ."

**Point Pedro,** a town in Jaffna district, Ceylon. Mission station of L. M. S.; 2 missionaries, 148 communicants, 16 Sabbath-schools, 1,003 scholars, 16 day-schools, 1,214 scholars.

**Poklo,** a town in Kwangtung, China, near the coast, east of Canton. Mission station of the L. M. S. (1860); 1 missionary, 5 out-stations, 6 native preachers, 119 church-members, 2 schools, 21 scholars.

**Polfontein,** a station of the Wesleyan Methodist Missionary Society in the Transvaal, Africa. Has 1 chapel, 37 church-members, 1 Sabbath-school, 30 scholars. The Hermannsburg Missionary Society have also a station.

**Poles.**—The Poles form the most numerous branch of the Western Slavs. They number about 10,000,000, distributed by the division of Poland among Russia, Prussia, and Austria. They are all Catholics, except 500,000 Protestants, and they use the Latin alphabet, modified so as to express the sounds peculiar to their language. Their language belongs to the western branch of Slavic languages, and is divided into four or five dialects, which, however, are not very different from each other. The Polish language has been influenced more than any other Slavic language by the Latin,—which in olden time was the literary and church language of Poland,—the German, and the French. Its distinctive characteristics are that it has retained the nasal expression or *rhinesmus* of *a* and *b*, peculiar to the ancient Bulgarian or ancient Slovenic, but which has disappeared from common use now among the Slavs, and that it always accents the penultimate syllable of words. The Polish language bears quite a close resemblance to the language of the Bohemians and the Lusatian Serbs.

The history of the ancient settlements of the Poles is uncertain. Their history becomes more trustworthy with the introduction of Christianity among them, which took place in 965 or 966. It is deemed probable that orthodox Christianity was sown among them in the time of Sts. Cyril and Methodius, the Slavic apostles, long before this date; but it was soon supplanted by Latin Christianity, and so thoroughly extirpated that it has left no traces in their literature. Along with the introduction of Latin Christianity through German preachers, the Latin language acquired a firm footing in Poland, and was the language of the learned and higher classes, as well as of the courts. Luther's reformation penetrated into Poland, where it found zealous and ardent defenders and followers; but in spite of all the earnestness with which it was defended, it was overcome by the Catholic reaction. The political history of Poland is too long to be treated in details here. We can characterize it in a few words by saying that it was a history full of political vicissitudes, of glorious deeds, and of internal insta-

bility of government. The *shlahta* or nobility was the class that had the upper hand in the government of the country, while the common people had very little share in the government. The jealousies and the arrogance of the nobles was always a hindrance to the regular administration of the kingdom, and on more than one occasion the king's authority was set at naught. So the internal condition of Poland grew worse and worse, internal dissensions and strifes tended to weaken the government, and Poland fell a prey to her more powerful neighbors, who resolved upon her partition, and thus put an end to her independent political existence.

**Polish Version.**—The Polish belongs to the Slavonic branch of the Aryan family, and is spoken in Poland proper, and in parts of Prussia formerly belonging to Poland. The oldest manuscript extant of a translation into Polish is the "Psalter of Queen Margaret," preserved in the library of St. Florian at Linz, and edited by Count Borkowski, Vienna, 1834. A MS. of a Polish Bible from the second half of the 18th century is preserved in the college library at Saros-Patsk, Hungary, which was edited, at the expense of Prince George Lubomirski, by Prof. Anton Malecki in 1872, under the title "Bible of Queen Sophie." She was the daughter of Prince Andreas of Kiew, and fourth wife of King Ladislaus Jagello. The first complete Polish Bible was published in 1561 at Cracow (reprinted 1574–1577). As this edition did not answer all the requirements of the Church of Rome, the Jesuit Jacob Wujek, or Wuyk, prepared a new translation after the corrected Vulgate, and this edition was published at Cracow in 1593, 1617, 1647; Posen, 1594; Chelm, 1772; St. Petersburg, 1815; Moscow, 1819. Pope Clement VIII. highly praised his translation, and the National Synod held at Piotskow in 1607 recommended it for use in all Roman Catholic churches. It was therefore often reprinted (Breslau, 1740, 1771, 1804; Warsaw, 1821; Lemberg, 1839–1840; Leipzig, 1846). The British and Foreign Bible Society also circulated Wuyk's version of the New Testament, besides a new edition of the New Testament in Roman character, published at Vienna in 1881, revised after the Greek.

Of the Protestant translations we mention the version of the Socinians, published at the expense of Prince Radziwill, Cracow, 1863. When his son joined the Church of Rome he burned all the copies he could buy. A second translation, made for the Unitarians by Simon of Budug, from the original text, was published at Czaslau, Lithuania, in 1572. An edition for the adherents of the Reformed Lutheran churches was published at Dantzig in 1632 by Paul Paljurus, Daniel Mikolojewski, and Thomas Wengierski, and republished at Amsterdam, 1660; Halle, 1726; Konigsberg, 1779; and Berlin, 1810. An edition of the Dantzig version, revised by Jakowski, was published by the Society for Promoting Christian Knowledge in 1853. The British and Foreign Bible Society also published the Dantzig version in Roman and Gothic types.

*(Specimen verses. John 3 : 16.)*

Albowiem tak Bóg umiłował świat, że Syna swego iednorodzonego dał, aby każdy, kto weń wierzy, nie zginął, ale miał żywot wieczny.

Hebrew character.

וָאַרין נָאט הָאט דיא וֶועלְט אַזוֹ גִלִיבְּט, דאַש עֶר
הָאט גִיגֶעבֶּן זיין אַיינְצִיגֶן זֶהן, אַז אִיטְלִיכֶר
וָואש גְלֵיבְּט אָן איהם זָאל נִיט פַר־לוֹרין וֶוערין,
נֵיישֶרְטַ עֶר זָאל הָאבֶּן דָאש אֵייבִּיגֶי לֶעבֶּן:

**Ponape,** the principal island of the Carolines, Micronesia, is high and fertile, with good harbors. Its population of 2,100 speak a language of their own. Mission work is under the A. B. C. F. M., whose missionaries take charge of the work on several adjacent small islands as well. The recent Spanish occupation of the island has proved hurtful to the work; but the natives look up to the missionaries as their best friends, and the Spanish officers have been friendly since the first arrest of one of the missionaries. In the district are 1 missionary and wife, 3 female missionaries, a training-school for teachers, a girls' boarding-school, 5 native pastors, and 18 churches.

**Ponape Version.**—The Ponape belongs to the Micronesian languages, and is spoken in Ponape, one of the Caroline Islands. Missionary work began in 1852 by Messrs. Sturges and Gulick, American missionaries. In 1859 the first eight chapters of Matthew, translated by Dr. L. H. Gulick, were printed on the island. In 1862 the Gospel of John, translated by Rev. A. A. Sturges, was printed; in 1866, Luke and the Acts; in 1870, Matthew and Mark. The complete New Testament, prepared by Messrs. Sturges and E. T. Doane, was published in 1887 by the American Bible Society in New York. Mr. Doane also translated parts of the Old Testament, of which Genesis was published in New York in 1875, Exodus in 1876, followed by Joshua, Judges, and Ruth. The books of Samuel and Kings were published in 1889.

*(Specimen verse.* John 3 : 16.)

Pue Kot me kupura jappa ie me a ki to ki Na teroj eu, pue me pojon la i, en ter me la, a en me maur jo tuk.

**Pongo Adongo,** a great trading-place in Loando, South Guinea, Africa, 89 miles from Dondo. Population, 1,500. Station of Bishop Taylor's Mission; 2 Europeans (1 married), house and chapel, and a farm of 300 acres.

**Poo,** a town in Little Tibet, Central Asia, where since 1865 the Moravian Brethren have had a station, waiting for the opening of Tibet proper. The station is 9,400 feet above sea-level, and is about as isolated a post as can be found. The missionary and wife who now live there pass years without seeing a European, and the nearest post-office is fourteen days' journey over Himalayan mountain paths. Work is carried on among the Lamas and Tibetans who are met on the border, and tracts and books have been translated into Tibetan.

**Poona,** the capital of a district of the same name in Bombay, India, is situated in a plain, on the Moota River, 80 miles southeast of Bombay. It was formerly the capital of the Maratha power. The seven quarters of the city are named after the days of the week. Its climate is very pleasant and salubrious, making it a favorite place of resort during the rainy season. Population, 129,751, not including the garrison in the cantonment about two miles northeast of the city. Marathi, Gujarati, and Hindustani are the languages of the various races included in its mixed population.

Mission station of the Baptist Mission Society (1857); 2 missionaries (one married), 2 out-stations, 1 church, 10 members, 1 school, 30 scholars. Free Church of Scotland (1830); 1 missionary and wife, 2 female missionaries, 21 native helpers, 1 out-station, 1 church, 130 church-members, 8 schools, 284 scholars.

**Poor, Daniel,** b. Danvers, Mass., U. S. A., June 27th, 1789; graduated at Dartmouth College 1811; studied theology at Andover, and having been ordained, sailed as a missionary of the A. B C. F. M. for Ceylon October 23d, 1815. He lived and labored at the station of Tillipally till 1823, when he took charge of the boys' seminary at Batticotta. While instructing his class in astronomy he had occasion to calculate an approaching eclipse, and when the native astronomers, who also had predicted it, but inaccurately, found that his calculations were more correct than theirs, they were profoundly impressed, and in consequence listened with more deference when he spoke to them of Christ. He remained at Batticotta till March 9th, 1836. Desiring to be engaged more fully in evangelistic work among the people, he then went to Madura, where a mission had been established two years before. Returning to Jaffna in 1841, he was stationed at Tillipally till 1848, when he sailed for the United States. His earnest addresses in behalf of missions were heard with great interest. Returning to Jaffna in 1851 he resided at Manepy till his death by cholera in 1855, aged 66, after thirty-nine years of mission service. He had no fear of death. His last words, pronounced in a whisper, were: "Joy! Joy! Hallelujah!" the word joy spoken in Tamil. Dr. Poor was a clear thinker, dignified and courteous in debate. His familiarity with the colloquial Tamil, his knowledge of Hindu works, his self-command and quickness of repartee, enabled him to meet the arguments and sophistries of learned disputants with effect. He received the degree of D.D. from Dartmouth College in 1835.

**Popo** or **Dahomey Version.** — The Popo is a dialect of the Ewe, belonging to the Negro group of African languages, and is used by the people of Dahomey, between the Volta and Lagos, as their vernacular. The Rev. J. Milum, who was on a visit to the Western Mission in South Africa, brought to England a version of the Gospels of Matthew and Mark, which the Rev. T. J. Marshall, a native minister of Porto Novo, had made, and the British and Foreign Bible Society published an edition in 1888, at London, under the title "O Wen-Dagbe le St. Matiu Po St. Mâki Po Ton Lo Ogunû Gbe-Me." In addition to these Gospels the Popo Translation Committee at Lagos have completed the translation of the Book of Psalms, the Gospels of Luke and John, and the Acts, which were also issued by the British and Foreign Bible Society in 1888.

**Port-au-Prince,** capital of Haiti, West Indies, on the west coast, at the head of the Bay of Gonaives. The town is on rising ground, with wide though ill-paved and very filthy streets, and dilapidated houses. The surrounding country is marshy. Though the Bay of Gonaives is large and beautiful, the roadstead of Port-au-Prince is small and shallow. Climate hot, unhealthy for foreigners; average, 81° F. Population, 21,000. Mission station of the African Methodist Episcopal Church; 1 missionary.

Protestant Episcopal Church, U. S. A. This mission was started independently in 1862 by a colored preacher from America, who devoted himself entirely to the utterly degraded negroes in Port-au-Prince and its vicinity. In 1874 he was consecrated Bishop of Haiti, and has now charge of 18 congregations with 14 pastors. In the capital are 102 communicants and 50 scholars.

**Port Lokkoh,** a town in Sierra Leone, west coast Africa, 60 miles east of Sierra Leone town. Climate tropical. Race and language, Timne. Religions, Fetichism, Mohammedanism. Social condition very low; domestic slavery prevalent. Mission station C. M. S. (1876). For statistics see Sierra Leone.

**Port Louis,** the capital of Mauritius Island, on the northwest coast, at the head of a bay, is open on one side to the sea, and enclosed on the other three by picturesque mountains. Of late years its prosperity has declined, fevers having become so prevalent that many have deserted it for other villages. Population 40,000. Mission station of the C. M. S.; 1 native missionary, 2 native helpers.

**Port Moresby,** a town on the west coast of the southeastern extremity of New Guinea, northwest of Kerepunu. Mission station of the L. M. S. (1871); 4 missionaries, 14 native preachers, 314 church-members, 13 schools, 927 scholars.

**Port of Spain,** the capital of Trinidad, West Indies, is one of the handsomest towns of the West Indies, with a good harbor and an active trade. Temperature, 70°-93° Fahrenheit. Population, 31,900, English, English and French creoles, Indian coolies, Chinese, and Spanish. Each race speaks its own language. Religions, Protestant, Roman Catholic, Hindu, Moslem. Social condition, though far from good, is better than in most of the West Indies. Government, British crown colony. Mission station of the Baptist Missionary Society (1843); 1 missionary and wife, 1 native helper, 15 outstations, 3 churches, 750 church-members. United Presbyterian Church of Scotland; 1 missionary, 175 church-members, 285 Sabbath-scholars.

**Porto Novo,** a town in Dahomey, West Africa, under French authority. Mission station of the Wesleyan Methodist Missionary Society; 2 missionaries, 162 church-members, 275 Sabbath-scholars, 211 day-scholars.

**Porto Rico,** an island of the West Indies, lies east of Haiti. It is a Spanish colonial possession, containing an area of 3,550 square miles, and a population of 784,709, of whom over 300,000 are Negroes or of Negro blood. It is described as "the healthiest of all the Antilles." Slavery was abolished by the National Assembly on March 23d, 1873. The principal towns with their population are: San Juan, 23,414; Ponce, 37,545; San Germain, 30,146.

**Portuguese Version.**—The Portuguese belongs to the Græco-Latin branch of the Aryan family of languages, and is spoken in Portugal and South America. Of Portuguese versions only two have become especially known. A Catholic version, with annotations by Anton Ferara de Figueiredo, was published in Lisbon 1778-1790, in 23 volumes. The third edition, in 7 volumes, and greatly improved, was published 1804-1819. A Protestant version is the translation of John Ferreira d'Almeida. The New Testament was published at Batavia in 1693, Amsterdam 1712, Tranquebar 1765; the Old Testament between 1719 and 1732, also at Tranquebar. A version based on Almeida's translation was made by the Rev. Thomas Boys, and published at the expense of the Trinitarian Bible Society, London, 1843-47. Almeida's version was often republished by the British and Foreign Bible Society, but because the style and language are so stiff and antiquated that it repels readers instead of attracting them, this edition was not so favorably received as was anticipated. From time to time this Society issued revised editions, especially of the New Testament, in a modernized style and idiom, which appeared to give great satisfaction. In 1874 the same Society issued at Lisbon a thoroughly revised edition of Almeida's version. Another edition followed in 1877. The same Society, which since 1819 published Figueiredo's Bible, published in 1878 an edition with alternative readings from the Hebrew and Greek, under the care of the Rev. Robert Stewart. Besides the British Society, the American Bible Society published, in 1859, an edition of the New Testament after a version made in London from the Greek. In spite of the many revisions, the need of a better and more accurate translation of the Bible in the Portuguese language is generally recognized by the Protestant missionaries and laborers in Portugal and Brazil, and the American and British Bible Societies have taken steps for the formation of translation committees in Spain and Brazil, for the production of a new version of the Scriptures, which will be acceptable on both sides of the Atlantic. The committee, representing the Episcopalian, Presbyterian, Baptist, and Wesleyan churches, have prepared, under the presidency of Rev. R. Stewart, the Gospel of Matthew, which was published in 1886, and that of Mark in 1887. As an interesting item we remark that the editor of a newspaper has asked and obtained leave to publish the new version in his paper.

(*Specimen verse.* John 3 : 16.)

Porque de tal maneira amou Deos ao mundo, que deo o seu Filho unigenito; para que todo aquelle que nelle crê, não pereça, mas tenha a vida eterna.

**Potscheffstroom,** a town in Southwest Transvaal, South Africa, southwest of Pretoria. Mission station of the Berlin Evangelical Missionary Society (1872); 1 missionary, 8 native workers, 2 out-stations, 4 other preaching places, 364 members, 156 communicants.

**Powers, Philander O.,** b. Phillipston, Mass., U. S. A., August 19th, 1805; graduated at Amherst College 1830, and Andover Theological Seminary 1834; sailed November 10th the same year as missionary of the A. B. C. F. M.

arriving at Smyrna, January 12th, 1835; released from the service of the Board 1862; reappointed in 1864, and again in 1866. He was stationed at Broosa, Trebizond, Sivas, Antioch, Kessab, Oorfa, and Marash. Dr. Schneider remarks: "A distinguished trait of his character was his sound judgment, by which he was successful in reconciling two parties at variance in the church and congregation for a long time. His self-sacrificing spirit appeared in his readiness to leave one missionary field for another, never allowing the comforts of home to interfere with or keep him from his work at a distance. On account of the illness of his wife he was obliged to return home, and was happily settled as a pastor in East Windsor, Conn., when the proposal was made to him to return to Antioch. Though he and his people were mutually attached, he accepted the call, and returned to the East alone, his wife having previously died. He had a fine taste for music. This talent, together with his skill in versification, made him an excellent hymnologist. Many of the best hymns in the Armeno-Turkish are from his pen. He had been requested by the mission to revise, and by the addition of new hymns to enlarge, the present Armeno-Turkish Hymn-book." Dr. Nutting says: "During all his sickness he manifested unwavering faith and cheerful hope." He died October 2d, 1872, at Kessab, an out-station of Antioch, in the house he had built, and the funeral services were held in the large and pleasant chapel, the erection of which he had superintended. His remains rest at the foot of Mount Cassius.

**Prague,** a city in Bohemia, Austro-Hungary, on the Moldau River, 155 miles northwest of Vienna. Climate temperate. Population, 300,000. Race, Slavic. Languages, Bohemian, German. Religion, Roman Catholic; 2 per cent Protestant. Social condition corrupt, very poor. Mission station Free Church of Scotland Jewish Mission (1864); 1 missionary and wife, 2 native workers, 30 church-members.

**Pratt, Andrew T.,** b. Black Rock, near Buffalo, N. Y., U. S. A., February 22d, 1826; graduated at Yale College 1847; studied one year at Union Theological Seminary, New York, and two in New Haven; pursued medical studies at the New York College of Physicians and Surgeons; ordained August 6th, 1852; sailed December 22d the same year as a missionary of the A. B. C. F. M. for his mission field in Turkey. His first station was Aintab, but he removed to Aleppo in 1856, and to Marash in 1859. In 1868 he was transferred to the Western Turkey Mission, and removed to Constantinople, there to be connected with the literary department for the three American missions, and engaged especially with Dr. Riggs in the work of translating and revising the Scriptures, in the hope of "securing a correct and uniform translation of the Word of life in three of the languages of the Turkish Empire." He died December 5th, 1872. Dr. Schneider says: "He had not only an aptness in general for acquiring languages, but a special love for the Turkish. Often have I heard him expatiate on its beauties and power. His mind seemed to delight in its peculiar idioms and forms; his utterance in it was marked by a very pleasing flow of words. It is not surprising, therefore, that he became one of the best Turkish scholars in the field. His grammar of the Turkish, partly a translation of a work by two Turkish gentlemen and partly his own, is proof of this. The mission committed to him the revision of the Armeno-Turkish Bible, and on this work he was engaged when death ended his career. He possessed a very active mind, and ranked high as a scholar, with extensive general information. His judgment was remarkably sound. He was fond of music, and had a poetic taste. He was therefore an excellent hymnologist, and wrote some original hymns, and translated more from the English. Many of the best hymns in the Armeno-Turkish are from his pen, and when a hymn was wanted for a special occasion he was expected to furnish it. He was a good physician, and trained several native Armenians as physicians, who are now usefully employed in the medical profession."

**Presbyterian Church in Canada,** Home and Foreign Missions of. Headquarters, Toronto, Canada.—In June, 1875, the four existing Presbyterian churches of Canada, of which two were in the Maritime Provinces and two in the Western Provinces, met in Montreal, to consider the question of union, solemnly declared their belief that it would be for the glory of God and the advancement of the cause of Christ that they should unite, and then and there constituted the first "General Assembly of the Presbyterian Church in Canada," which pledged itself to take up and prosecute the Home and Foreign Missionary operations of the several Churches. Since the union the church has greatly prospered: the communicants have increased from 90,000 to 171,987; the annual contributions for Home Missions from $27,339 to $99,987; for Foreign Missions from $25,272 to $103,915; and for all church purposes from $982,671 to $2,054,951.

*Foreign Missions.* — The Foreign Missions of the Presbyterian Church in Canada are six in number, and are very widely separated from each other. This is less the result of design than of a necessity laid upon the church at the time of the union in 1875, when it was expressly stipulated that all the missions to the heathen then in existence in the several churches were to be continued by the united church. So intense was the interest that had been created in missions consecrated by the prayers and contributions, aye, and the lives of members of these churches, that to abandon any one of them would have been considered paying too dearly for the union. This accounts for a mission in the South Seas, one in the West Indies, one in India, two in China, and one to the Indians in the Northwest Territories of Canada. The staff of missionaries consists at present of thirty-five ordained ministers, of whom five are native converts to Christianity. These missionaries are assisted by twenty-five Canadian ladies variously employed as matrons of industrial schools, teachers, zenana visitors, etc. Three of the ladies are duly qualified doctors of medicine. The number of native assistants is about two hundred and fifty.

NEW HEBRIDES MISSION.—For full account of this mission, as carried on conjointly by this Board and other Presbyterian Boards, see article New Hebrides.

TRINIDAD MISSION.—This mission to the coolies of Trinidad originated with the Rev. John Morton, D.D., in 1869. He was also a minister of the Presbyterian Church of Nova Scotia, who, having visited Trinidad for the benefit of his health, noticed the deplorable condition of the imported laboring people, and on his return home offered his services to go and establish a mission for their benefit. In 1871 he was joined by the Rev. Kenneth J. Grant, who is now at San Fernando, a considerable town on the island, and from time to time the mission has been reinforced by other Canadians. There are now five Canadian ordained missionaries, two native pastors, five native catechists, and three Canadian lady teachers. The number of coolies in Trinidad is about 60,000. They are chiefly Hindus, brought from India under contract to labor on the sugar estates, with the option of returning to their native country at the expiration of a specified term of service. Many of them do return, but, as many more are coming still, their numbers have been increasing rapidly for some time past. The work carried on in their behalf is largely educational. The number of schools in operation last year was thirty-eight, having on the rolls 2,060 scholars, with an average daily attendance of 1,433. Thirty-five couples were married, 110 adults and 101 children were baptized, and there are 412 communicants in good standing.

CENTRAL INDIA.—Previous to the union of 1875 two of the Canadian churches had broken ground in India, by sending thither female missionaries who were attached in some form to a mission of the Presbyterian Church of the United States. In 1875 Rev. James Fraser Campbell of Nova Scotia was sent to Madras. About the same time, the Rev. James Douglas of Ontario was sent to Indore, Central India, situated about four hundred miles west by north from Bombay.

The city of Indore, having a population of some 70,000 inhabitants, was selected as the headquarters of the Canadian mission. Rev. John Wilkie was sent out in 1879. Other appointments followed, and now there are seven ordained ministers and ten Canadian ladies on the staff—three of the ladies being doctors of medicine. There are also about seventy native assistants employed in the work of the mission. The time for making an exhibit of results is not yet, for until within the last two or three years there has been one continuous struggle with the local authorities for the right even of existence, or to acquire any property for the purposes of a Christian mission. This having been at length conceded, the work has begun to assume an aspect at least of hopefulness. The Word is now preached without let or hindrance in many of the towns and villages. Day-schools and Sunday-schools have been established at a number of points, with a fair attendance of scholars. Medical dispensaries have been opened and a vast deal of suffering has been relieved through them: 17,979 patients were treated last year by the two doctors—Misses Beatty and Oliver. Now that the way is clear, the importance of providing higher education for the youth of the middle and upper classes is becoming every year more apparent. In view of this, a high-school and college, in affiliation with the University of Calcutta, have been opened at Indore with encouraging prospects of success,—the more that the field of higher education seems to be almost entirely unoccupied in that part of India, and that many of the more intelligent people appear to be willing to avail themselves of the advantages the mission is prepared to offer them in this direction. During his recent furlough Mr. Wilkie received from friends in Canada the sum of twelve thousand dollars towards the erection of suitable college buildings, in the expectation that the people of Indore and neighborhood would contribute a like sum. He also received donations of a very considerable number of valuable books as the nucleus of a college library.

The expenditure on account of this mission last year by the Canadian Board was $22,681.69. The Mission Council of Indore in its last report to the General Assembly records its "thankfulness for the past and hope for the future," and renews its pleading that the staff of missionaries may speedily be doubled.

FORMOSA, CHINA.—The mission in Northern Formosa has been one of the church's most successful enterprises. It was commenced in 1872 by Rev. George Leslie Mackay, a native of Oxford County, Ontario. In 1875 he was joined by Rev. J. B. Fraser, M.D., subsequently by Rev. Kenneth F. Junor, now of New York. At present the Rev. John Jamieson of Ontario is associated with Dr. Mackay. Dr. Mackay married a Chinese lady, who has been very helpful to him in gaining the attention of the women, and in superintending the girls' school. His opinion from the first was that the work of evangelizing the Chinese must be done through a native agency. So soon, therefore, as he had acquired a sufficient knowledge of the language himself he sought out young men with a view of training them to become teachers and preachers. He was fortunate in his first convert,—now the Rev. Giam Chheng Hôa,—through whose instrumentality a number of young men were brought under Dr. Mackay's influence. These were formed into a class, or band, rather, and were thoroughly drilled in a course of study which included the elements of theology, astronomy, geology, botany, geography, history, physiology, anatomy, medical practice, surgery, etc. Dr. Mackay having, meanwhile, adopted the itinerant method of preaching, he took his class with him wherever he went, and availed himself of such opportunities as he could for continuing his instructions.

In this way the students had the further advantage of observing Dr. Mackay's methods of working among the people, and had the opportunity afforded them from time to time of taking part in evangelistic services as they were qualified to do so. When a certain point had been reached in the student's curriculum he had a given district assigned to him, and he went to work as a local preacher; a chapel, with house accommodation for the preacher, and sometimes a prophet's chamber besides, was erected, and by and by a regular congregation was organized, with elders and deacons. In this way the work has spread over the whole of Northern Formosa, where Dr. Mackay has now the superintendence of 50 churches and congregations, 51 native preachers (including two native ordained pastors), a well-equipped college with 24 students, two large hospitals, and a girls' school. The number of baptized members—including adults and children—is 2,833, of whom 146 were baptized last year. There are 83 elders and 71 deacons. It is hoped that in the near future the mission will become an independent self-supporting church. Last year the people contributed $1,143.85 for church purposes. The draft upon the Canadian Committee was only $13,967.94. The amount of work done, in so short a time, and chiefly through the marvellous energy and zeal of one man, surely justifies the exclamation, " What hath God wrought!"

HONAN, CHINA. (See China, Protestant Missions.)—This mission was begun so recently as 1888, by the appointment of the Rev. Jonathan Goforth and Rev. Donald Macgillivray, graduates of Knox College, Toronto, the Rev. James Smith, M.D., of Queen's College, Kingston, and Mr. William M'Clure, M.D., who was ordained as an elder and designated as a medical missionary to this field. The year following three students of the Presbyterian College, Montreal, were ordained and set apart as missionaries to Honan, viz., Messrs. Murdoch Mackenzie, John Macdougall, and John H. MacVicar, a son of the principal of the college. The General Assembly of 1889 authorized the formation of a Presbytery in Honan, which was accordingly constituted on the 5th of December in that year. This is, perhaps, the first instance of a Presbytery being formed before its constituent members had even reached the field of their prospective labors. This unique Presbytery held its first meeting, not in Honan, but in the adjoining province of Shantung, and then and there fixed upon desirable points in Honan at which to commence missionary operations.

Honan is one of the inland provinces of China (q.v.). It has been visited by agents of the China Inland Mission, but this Canadian enterprise is probably the first attempt to obtain a permanent lodgment for missionary purposes; and as the movement has already met with undisguised opposition on the part of the local authorities, the issue is regarded with no small degree of interest. While the common people have gladly submitted themselves to the healing art of the medical missionaries in their tours of exploration, and have even thereby been led to listen to the preaching of the gospel, the upper classes have intimated their wish that the missionaries should leave the country as quickly as possible. The missionaries, however, have gone there to stay, and will not be easily moved from their determination. As yet their efforts have been chiefly to obtain a requisite knowledge of the language, and in this they have all been reasonably successful.

Two circumstances connected with this incipient mission are worthy of a passing notice: (1) Much has been said during the last few years about the number of theological students in different countries who have intimated their willingness to engage in foreign-mission work, but here is an instance of a well-equipped mission, composed entirely of young men fresh from college, planted in a new and very difficult field, far away from their base of supplies, and almost entirely cut off from intercourse with other missionaries from whose experience in similar fields they might have hoped to derive advantage. (2) Another singular feature of the mission is that while these seven missionaries are the recognized agents of the General Assembly and are to carry on their work under the authority and supervision of its foreign-mission committee, their salaries are all provided for in a manner that indicates a new departure in missionary finance. Three of the seven have a guarantee for their support from single congregations, with the understanding that these congregations shall continue their usual contributions to the general missionary fund of the church. Two are supported by the students comprising the missionary societies of Knox College, Toronto, and Queen's College, Kingston. The remaining two are each supported by private individuals. A statement like that would, in Canada at least, have been considered incredible a few years ago; and it goes without saying that when a like recognition of stewardship shall pervade the whole Christian Church one of the chief hindrances to the speedy evangelization of the world will have been removed. The disbursements on account of the Honan Mission for the year 1889-90 were $13,534.79.

NORTH AMERICAN INDIANS.—This mission to heathen tribes in our own country was begun in 1866 by the late Rev. James Nesbit and has been carried on ever since with a fair measure of success. It has, of course, claims on our practical sympathies such as no other mission to the heathen can have. We have taken possession of the Red man's hunting-ground. By exterminating the buffalo we have deprived him of a chief source of his subsistence. We have restricted the former occupant of the boundless prairie to a few paltry acres of " reserves;" and, worst of all, we have exposed the whole race to contamination, if not to utter extinction, from the vices of civilization. The State receives the Indian into citizenship, makes him such compensation as the nature of the case admits of, protects his person and property, makes him a few presents, say of blankets, bacon, or seed-corn, and votes a few dollars annually for the education of his children. The church recognizes, to some small extent at least, her duty to the poor Indian by offering him Christianity as a substitute for his pagan rites, and teaching him how to provide food and clothes for his children. " Here again," our missionaries tell us, " it is in the school, and especially in the industrial school, that the great work of the church for the elevation of the Indian must be done." Accordingly their efforts have of late been largely directed to the extension of the industrial boarding-school system. By this means the children are withdrawn for lengthened periods from the degrading surroundings of their pagan homes, and brought into close and continuous contact with Christian civilization. They are taught the elementary branches of an English education; the boys are trained to agricultural and mechanical pursuits, and the girls to housekeeping and all the domestic accomplishments implied in that term.

The total Indian population of Canada is about 121,000, of whom about 3,500 are connected with the Presbyterian Mission at eleven different stations. There are seven ordained missionaries, who carry on the work on nineteen reserves. They are assisted by nine teachers, besides other helpers whose services are very valuable as matrons, interpreters, and assistant teachers. There are 187 Indian communicants, of whom 24 were added during the past year and 68 infants and 31 adults were baptized. In the six or seven industrial schools there are enrolled 222 pupils, with an average attendance of 154. The expenditure on account of the mission for the past year was $15,544.87.

The total expenditure for the six missions above-named during the year ending 1st May,

1890, was $103,915.33. The expenses of management only amounted to about $2,000—the onerous duties of the chairman and secretary of the Foreign Mission Committee having hitherto been performed gratuitously. The time has now come, however, when it is necessary to appoint a convener of the Foreign Mission Committee, whose whole time and services shall be given to this department of the church's work.

Important aid has been rendered in the providing of means for carrying on the Foreign Mission work by the Women's Missionary Societies. The amount collected by the ladies last year reached $36,568.59, the greater part of which was handed over to the General Assembly's Committee. "The women who publish the tidings are a great host," nearly 20,000 being enrolled in their auxiliaries and Mission Bands.

*Home Missions.*—It may seem enough to say that the home missions of this church are co-extensive with the Dominion; but the vast extent of the field will be better understood by stating that the Presbytery of Newfoundland embraces a larger area than Ireland; the Synod of the Maritime Provinces is larger than Great Britain; the province of Quebec is nearly as large as France; Ontario is nearly as large as Spain; Manitoba, small as it is in comparison with its sister provinces, is yet much larger than Holland; British Columbia is much larger than Austria; while the great "Fertile Belt" east of the Rocky Mountains—known as yet only as the "Northwest Territories"—is said to be capable of maintaining a population as large as Russia in Europe. The Presbyterian Church has followed the immigrant and the settler into the remotest parts of the Dominion. Her missionaries are to be found amid the fogs and storms of Newfoundland and Cape Breton, on the barren and inhospitable shores of Labrador, in the backwoods settlements of New Brunswick, Quebec, and Ontario, in the mining regions and lonely ranches of the Northwest, at the gold diggings of British Columbia, and amid the wilds of Vancouver Island. The machinery for overtaking this great work is necessarily somewhat complicated. For home missions proper there are two Central Boards of Management—east and west. Each of these has a sub-committee for supplementing the salaries of ministers in the weak and struggling congregations—the aim of the church being that none of its ministers should receive a smaller stipend than $750 a year, with a manse.

The number of mission fields—i.e., groups of stations—in the 32 western Presbyteries is 276, and of preaching places 820. In the eastern section there are 45 fields and 170 preaching stations, making in all 321 distinct fields and 990 preaching stations. The total number of missionaries employed last year, for longer or shorter periods, was 329, of whom 121 were ordained ministers and licentiates; 208 were students and catechists. The number of families connected with these missions was 11,701, and of communicants, 13,997. The direct receipts by the Boards of Management were $66,475.60; adding, however, the amounts received for the augmentation of stipends above referred to, say $33,571.82, the whole amount is $99,987.42. This does not include sums expended by individual churches on town and city missions, nor the amounts contributed by the people belonging to the mission stations. For some years past by far the largest expenditure has been in Manitoba and the Northwest, where, owing to the opening up of the country by railways, the increase of population has been greatest. When the Presbytery of Manitoba was formed, nineteen years ago, the city of Winnipeg had only 421 inhabitants: now it has 25,000. The province of Manitoba had then 19,000 inhabitants: now it has 150,000. There are now six Presbyteries within the bounds of the original one. Vancouver, in British Columbia, had no existence five years ago: now it is a flourishing city of 18,000 inhabitants.

FRENCH EVANGELIZATION.—This branch of the work of the Church has for its specific object the spread of the gospel among the French-speaking Roman Catholics of Canada.

The Board of Management expended last year $53,000 on the various departments of its work—preaching, colportage, and education. The number of missionaries employed by it at the present time is 63, of whom 30 are able to preach in both French and English. Sixteen colporteurs were employed last year in selling and distributing Christian literature in the French language. It is estimated that upwards of 150,000 French copies of the Scriptures have been distributed during the past fifty years; during the past year 2,796 copies, and 23,800 French tracts and pamphlets were put into the hands of the people, notwithstanding the precautions of the priests in forbidding them to purchase or to accept gratuitously a copy of God's Word. There are 36 mission schools under the Board, with 1,020 pupils, of whom 423 are from Roman Catholic homes. There are in connection with the French Mission 26 churches, 92 stations, 1,337 communicants, 1,067 families, and 1,187 scholars in the Sabbath-schools and Bible-classes. The estimate of the current year calls for $70,000,—about forty per cent more than last year, indicating that the work is yearly assuming larger proportions.

Before passing from the Home Mission work of the church, it should be stated that there are six theological colleges, situated as follows: (1) The Presbyterian College, Halifax, N. S.; (2) Morrin College, Quebec; (3) The Presbyterian College, Montreal; (4) Queen's University and College, Kingston, Ont.; (5) Knox College, Toronto; (6) Manitoba College, Winnipeg. There are in all 19 theological professors, besides lecturers and teachers in the preparatory departments. The number of students last year having the ministry in view was 321, of whom 44 completed their theological curriculum. About two thirds of the students are usually employed during the summer months in the Home Mission fields of the church, where their services have been extremely valuable. In earlier years the churches in Canada were mainly dependent on the mother-country for the supply of ministers. But that is all changed now. Not only is Canada furnishing her own ministers of all denominations, but many trained in Canadian institutions are to be found in different parts of the world. The Presbyterian theological colleges are all aiming at permanent endowments for their support, but in the meantime the General Assembly authorizes an annual collection in all the congregations towards defraying the ordinary expenses of these institutions.

**Presbyterian Church of England, Foreign Missions.** Headquarters, 14 Paternoster Square, London.—The Presbyterian Church of England was virtually founded in 1570, when Cartwright opposed episcopal intolerance, and it promised during the period preceding the civil war to color the religious life of England, where it was the legal form of doctrine in 1641. After the time of Cromwell it gradually became the mere representative of the divided Presbyterian Church in Scotland, till 1776, when the congregations (in England) of the Free and United Presbyterian Churches united and formed the Presbyterian Church of England.

*Development of Work.*—CHINA.— The Rev. Wm. C. Burns was sent out as the first missionary, and Dr. James Young was his medical colleague in Amoy.

For the first four years after Mr. Burns's arrival in China he worked at Hong Kong, Canton, and the neighborhood, but in 1851 he visited Amoy on business, and was so much impressed with the needs of this city and the opening it gave for missionary work, that he transferred his work there, and made it the first centre of the organized work of the Presbyterian Church of England. As the work grew, the Society sent out in 1853 the Rev. James Johnson to join Mr. Burns; but in 1855 he was obliged to return home, and his place was filled by the Rev. Carstairs Douglas, who with Rev. David Sandeman was sent out by the Scottish branch of the mission (which contributes a fifth of the Society's income), and who at the time of Mr. Johnson's return was already on his way to China. These two men did efficient work both as evangelists and scholars before death stopped their labors. Dr. Douglas, it is said, was "a great power in China, remarkable for his evangelistic zeal and for his high literary attainments. To him is mainly due the organizing of the mission work in its several departments—Evangelistic, Medical, and Educational." His plan was to have a fixed centre from which steady and persevering efforts should be made for the redemption of the surrounding country. His plan has proved a good one, and the great aim of this mission, to build up a self-supporting native church, has been steadily kept in view.

The spheres of labor are: (1) The Evangelistic and Pastoral, carried out on the usual methods. (2) Medical, begun 1860; the medical missionaries also taking part in evangelistic work. (3) Educational, begun 1855, consisting of schools and colleges for the instruction of the children and training native youths for preachers and teachers. (4) Voluntary work by natives, which is of much value and of various sorts. (5) Woman's Work, begun 1879, chiefly carried on by the Woman's Association in connection with the Presbyterian Church of England, which aims to elevate and to help the women by means of schools and visiting in their homes.

This plan of work has also succeeded in India. In China proper this mission has three fields,—Amoy, Swatow, and the Hakka country,—in all of which a great and ever-increasing work is being done.

Also, the Society has extensive work in Formosa, begun in 1865, with its headquarters at Tai-wan-fu, the capital of the island. The conditions under which the missionaries entered Formosa were, and still are, peculiar and trying. The Chinese colonists are driving back and overrunning the aboriginal inhabitants, and the struggle between these races makes the work more difficult. Still, however, the work is growing, and a hospital opened a few years ago extends its healing influence over a wide area. In Singapore, in the Straits Settlements, a station has been opened and has grown wonderfully, and five branch stations are now in full working order, where four Chinese workers are regularly employed.

INDIA.—A mission to India was begun in 1878, when the Rev. D. Morrison, D.D., settled at Rampore-Bauleah, Bengal. He is still at the head of this work, and reports that last year was a year of progress and increased hopefulness at his station. There are several schools and dispensaries connected with the mission, and a new hospital is being opened which will greatly increase the influence of the missionaries among the natives. For the Jewish Mission of the Presbyterian Church of England see article "Jews."

**Presbyterian Church of Ireland, Foreign Missions.** Headquarters, 12 May Street, Belfast, Ireland.—In 1840 the "Synod of Ulster" and the "Secession Synod" became united under the name of the "General Assembly of the Presbyterian Church in Ireland." The society thus formed immediately resolved to begin missionary operations, and led by Dr. Duff's eloquence and by a missionary survey which Dr. John Wilson of Bombay (both of the Free Church of Scotland) had made of the feudatory states of Kathiawar, they chose India for their first field and sent out as their first missionaries the Revs. A. Kerr and J. Glasgow. These men had not offered themselves for the service, but had been chosen and called upon by the Assembly's Committee to undertake it. As this mode of obtaining missionaries was deemed by them preferable to the ordinary practice of receiving voluntary offers of service, they recorded it, "that it may serve to be a precedent in all time to come."

The missionaries proceeded to Kathiawar in Gujarat, and located in Rajkot, one of the principal towns. Mr. Kerr was attacked by a fever, and survived his arrival by only a few weeks. This was a severe blow to the mission, but before long four other missionaries—the Revs. A. Glasgow, J. McKee, R. Montgomery, and J. H. Spears—were sent to strengthen the mission, and on their arrival two new stations were opened—one at Purbundet on the west coast, the other at Gogo to the eastward. These, in addition to Surat, which was transferred to them by the L. M. S., who had carried on work there for several years, gave them quite a large field for work. In Kathiawar, especially at Purbundet, from the Mohammedans, the missionaries met with opposition unusual even for India; but by patient effort they began to gain a considerable influence over the people, and many applied for and received baptism. The most prominent and influential convert has been a Mohammedan "munshe," who had the reputation of being the most learned man in the district, and his baptism made a deep impression. At present the mission has stations at Rajkot (occupied 1841), Gogo (1844), Surat (1846), Borsad (1860), Ahmadabad (1861), Anand (1877), Broach (1887), where work is carried on by 8 missionaries, 8 zenana agents, and

166 native agents. Total number of communicants, 315.

The work of this mission at these different stations is of the most varied kind. There are regular Sabbath and week-day services for the instruction of the native Christians. There are large numbers of day-schools and orphanages in which instruction is given in both the vernacular and English, and the Word of God is carefully taught. Each station is the centre for extensive evangelistic work, the missionaries and evangelists touring in all directions. Native congregations have been formed, several of which are now prepared to call their own pastors, and to a large extant to support them. The mission press in Surat is circulating through colporteurs a large amount of Christian literature. The Gujarati version of the Scriptures is being carefully revised and reprinted, and the Gospels, neatly bound, are being sold at a price so low that no one, however poor, need be without them. In connection with the zenana missions dispensaries are open daily in Surat and Ahmadabad, and many women while receiving medical aid are also being taught the Bible truth. The natives are being taught to contribute largely, and do much towards the support of a native ministry. Last year their contributions amounted to about $453.

CHINA.—The work of the Irish Presbyterian Church in China was begun in 1879 in the province of Manchuria, North China. Their earliest station is Newchwang, a seaport town near the mouth of the Liao River; but in common with the agents of other societies, the Irish Presbyterian missionaries found that a Chinese seaport is a most unfavorable centre for operations. Still the station was held, and from Newchwang as a centre itinerating journeys were made and still are made over all the province to the far north, and the missionaries are making plans for occupying several large towns in the interior. The present mission staff consists of three ordained missionaries and one medical missionary and their wives, who are located at the three stations: Newchwang, Jinjow, and Kirin.

Jewish Missions.—The Assembly has Jewish missions in Syria and in Germany; Colonial missions in Canada, Australia, and New Zealand; and Continental work in Spain, Belgium, France, Switzerland, Bohemia, and Italy, which have been treated of under their respective heads: Jewish Missions; Colonial and Continental Missions.

## Presbyterian Church of Scotland.
*1. Established Church: Committee for the Propagation of the Gospel in Foreign Parts, especially in India.* Headquarters, 22 Queen Street, Edinburgh.

*2. Free Church: Committee on Foreign Missions.* Headquarters, 15 North Bank Street, Edinburgh.

*History, antecedent to the separation of the Free Churches from the Established Church.*—The foreign missionary enterprise of the Church of Scotland dates further back than is generally supposed. In 1699, shortly after the founding of the Scotch colony in Darien, the General Assembly sent out four missionaries to the isthmus to supply the vacant places of the two ministers who had accompanied the colonists but had died, one on the way out, the other shortly after his arrival.

In 1709 the Society for Promoting Christian Knowledge was incorporated, and in the years between 1741 and 1748 sent five missionaries to the American Indians. Between the years 1744 and 1814 several grand old preachers were preparing Scotland to become a missionary country. In 1818 Dr. Inglis caught the inspiration and began to urge the necessity of the Church of Scotland sending missionaries to the heathen; and in 1823 Dr. Bryce, a chaplain of the East India Company, sent home a memorial from Calcutta urging entrance on the work. In 1825 Dr. Inglis, then its convener, induced the General Assembly to appoint its first foreign mission committee, consisting of ten able men belonging to no one particular party in the church. At the first call for a collection the response was not enthusiastic, but when in 1829 Alexander Duff embarked for Calcutta as head-master of an educational institution which Dr. Inglis had proposed and the Society decided to attempt, the interest in missions increased. With the help of other missionaries, among them Dr. W. S. Mackay, Dr. D. Ewart, Rev. J. Macdonald, and Dr. Th. Smith, Dr. Duff during his service of thirteen years shaped the educational future of India. His aim was to raise up a body of well-disciplined Christian teachers, and of well-qualified native ministers; and to accomplish this end the missionaries resolved that educational seminaries of the highest character and on the most approved basis should be opened in the great centres of civilization. The institution at Calcutta, commenced by Dr. Duff in 1830 and carried on with the enthusiasm which he had himself and imparted to his colleagues, attained a pre-eminent degree of excellence and commanded general admiration. The whole course of education, even the literary and scientific parts of it, was brought to have a bearing on the religious improvement of its pupils, and although it was originally doubtful whether the Hindus would allow their children to attend an institution so decidedly Christian, yet the high education given in it made them not only willing but anxious to have their sons admitted, and the complete triumph of the institution over the prejudices of the natives has conferred an inestimable benefit on all future missions.

In 1835 the second great mission of the church was taken over by the General Assembly from the old Scottish Missionary Society, by which it had been founded in 1822. In Bombay and Poona Rev. John Wilson, D.D., F.R.S., Mr. Nesbit, Mr. James Mitchell, and Rev. Dr. J. Murray Mitchell had been since 1828 attempting the same work in Western as Dr. Duff was doing in Eastern India, with the difference that whereas the necessities of the Bengali Society made them fight for the use of English in the schools in Bengal, the use of Oriental languages, both classical and vernacular, was recommended. The first thing accomplished by the transfer of Bombay and Poona from the old to the newer Scottish Church Society was the development of the English school at Bombay into a missionary college, in which the first Parsi converts were won and many educated Brahmans convinced of the truth of Christianity. Of these converts two, the Rev. Dhanjibhai Naoroji, a Parsi, and Rev. Narayan Sheshadri, D.D., are among the most efficient workers in the mission field.

Dr. Duff's eloquent appeal in the General Assembly roused up the Rev. John Anderson to found, in 1837, a mission at Madras, South India. There, with the assistance of Rev. R. Johnston and Rev. J. Braidwood he soon developed a vigorous Christian institution out of a school. Very soon large towns or centres, both Tamil and Telugu speaking, were supplied with teachers and preachers, among them the Rev. A. Venkataramiah and Rev. P. Rajahgopaul, educated in the Madras College. In places such as Chingleput and Nellore, where the caste prejudice was not strong, many schools for girls were commenced, and good work done among the women.

In 1843 occurred the Disruption of the Church of Scotland and the formation of the Free Church, and from this point the history becomes twofold, embracing the work (1) of the Established Church, (2) of the Free Church.

1. *The Established Church of Scotland.*—This body found itself after the Disruption with a large amount of mission property, chiefly located in India, but without any missionary force, all the missionaries, with the exception of one lady, having joined the Free Church on its formation. Dr. Duff in withdrawing had made a proposition for an equitable arrangement regarding the property, but this was not accepted; and in 1845 Rev. Dr. Ogilvie was sent out to occupy the buildings, and take up the work left by Dr. Duff. Other missionaries filled the vacant places in Bombay and Madras, and as speedily as possible the institutions of all three presidencies were re-established on the same basis on which they had been conducted before. They were numerously attended, particularly that at Calcutta, and appear to have been carried on in a very efficient and successful manner. The whole instrumentality of the mission was after a time in operation—the girls' schools, including refuges for orphans; the branch stations, and the lectures on the subject of religion; and although the success of the Church of Scotland has not been great as regards the conversion of Hindus to the Christian faith, yet the high order of education they are offering India is undermining the Hindu religion slowly but steadily, and preparing the way for the future progress of the gospel in that country. In 1857 the church opened a new mission in the Punjab, their first station being Sialkot. Wazirabad was occupied in 1863 and Chumba in 1865.

GUJARAT.—This mission has been a very successful one, and has made steady progress, with the exception of one misfortune during the mutiny of 1857, when the missionary martyr Thomas Hunter of Sialkot was shot, with his wife and infant child. The Church of Scotland in 1870 sent out several missionaries to the British Lepchas of the Darjeeling district, who occupied first Darjeeling and afterwards Kalimpong (in 1873), now supported by the Young Men's Guild, whose first missionary, Rev. John A. Graham, sailed for India February, 1889; and Independent Sikkim, founded in 1886, and supported by the Missionary Association of the four Scottish Universities. "Great blessing has rested on this threefold mission." There is a monthly mission newspaper, the "Masik Patrika," in the vernacular, and the magazine "Life and Work" circulates with an English local supplement, linking the European residents with the mission. Both Europeans and natives contribute liberally to the mission.

2. AFRICA.—The Africa Mission of the Established Church, begun in 1874, owes its existence to the impulse given by the news of Livingstone's death and by Mr. Stanley's letter from Uganda. The Established Church and the Free Church of Scotland naturally took the territories most closely associated with Livingstone's memory, the Zambezi and Lake Nyassa. The Free Church Mission has an important station at the south end of that lake, while the Established Church Mission is at Blantyre, near Lake Shirwa. At present the East Africa Mission has 3 ordained, 2 medical, and 6 unordained missionaries, and 1 female missionary. Its two other stations are at Domasi and Chirazula. At Blantyre the native church is prospering, and it is hoped that some of the young men who have been baptized will hereafter be ordained missionaries. The mission has the advantage of most of those in Africa, in the fact that all its stations are elevated, and for Central Africa very healthy. The whole mission is full of promise, but it is at present struggling very hard against the attacks of cruel Arab invaders and treacherous Mohammedans, who are using all their wily strength to drive out the white men and hold the land for the slave-trade; and also from the threats of the Portuguese to annex Blantyre and Nyassaland.

In 1877, a mission was started at Ichang, China, where the Church of Scotland has now 2 ordained missionaries, 1 unordained medical missionary, and several native helpers at work.

The Society has also Jewish Missions in Egypt, Beirut, Smyrna, Salonica, and Constantinople. For full particulars of this work see articles on the Jews and those places. In 1878 Dr. Norman Macleod of the Barony Parish, Glasgow, visited the missions, and on his return, by his eloquence and work as Convener of its Foreign Mission Committee, did much to stir up the church to do its duty in foreign lands.

2. *Free Church of Scotland.*—In 1843, under the great advantage of beginning her career with a mission (except the buildings), and a mission staff, well trained by years of experience, ready to her hand, the Free Church commenced missionary operations in India and the East. New premises and various means necessary for carrying on the several institutions were speedily provided for the missionaries who had joined her cause, at considerable inconvenience in consequence of their resignation of the mission buildings, libraries, and philosophical apparatus belonging to the mission of the Established Church. Funds in aid of the mission also came in most liberally in both Scotland and India. When the Calcutta institution was reopened in the new premises after the usual vacation, the number of pupils was larger than ever, and the whole operations went on with the same regularity and efficiency as if nothing had happened. The school at Tahi established by the Church of Scotland was removed, on account of the unhealthiness of the place, to Baranagur, a village on the Hugli, a few miles above Calcutta; but afterwards, for some reason not generally known, Baranagur was also given up. In 1864 the congregation at Calcutta founded a most fruitful branch mission among the Santals in the rural districts of Upper Bengal, and about the same time flourishing schools were established at three other places, Chinsurah, Bansberia, and Culna. These schools were all of a superior

class, although of course not equal to the institution at Calcutta, on the model of which they were formed. In Bombay, Poona, and Madras the institutions and various schools, including those for girls which had recently been established by the women of the mission, were carried on as formerly, and with similar results. In Bombay the Wilson Missionary College, lately transferred to a new and splendid edifice, is the centre of a wonderful educational work; and from this city the mission, whose native converts give all their leisure time to assist the missionaries, work among the Jewish community as well as among the Parsis, Hindus, Mohammedans, and Africans. In Madras, under the Rev. W. Miller, C.I.E., L.L.D., the Institute has become the United Christian College for all South India. At Madras and Conjevaram there are medical missions, where the native youth are being educated for physicians and nurses. Two Scottish ladies are at present in London studying medicine, to work among the women of India.

At the Assembly in 1844 (although the Free Church of Scotland began with only £372 in its treasury) it was resolved to take two forward steps—to take over the Kafir Missions offered by that portion of the Glasgow Missionary Society which was in sympathy with the Free Church, and to respond to the invitation of Sir William Hill, of the Church of England, to open a mission in the Nagpur state, in the heart of India. Accordingly, in 1845, Rev. Stephen S. Hislop was appointed to found a station at Nagpur. Here he found already in the field three pious laymen, the surviving members of the German Mission among the Gonds, who had resided in the neighborhood of Nagpur since they left the forests of the interior, and were now received into the service of the Free Church. On the arrival of the Rev. Robert Hunter a second station was begun at Kampti, a British cantonment in the then native state of Nagpur, situated about ten miles from the capital. The missionaries met with determined opposition on the part of men of note among the Hindus; and many vexatious difficulties and disappointments arising from the "irregularity of attendance, which it was exceedingly difficult to correct, and the withdrawal of the best and most promising pupils at the very stage of their studies when it was most desirable they should continue them," because their parents, influenced in sending them only by love of gain, withdrew them as soon as they were able to earn money. Yet in spite of all this several prosperous institutions were established, of which Hislop Missionary College is the centre, and its splendid work adds greater lustre to the name of Dr. Hislop, a man worthy to be ranked with Duff, Wilson, and Anderson, the founders of India's three other great colleges. At Bhandara a prosperous medical mission has been established, while in Sitabuldi the schools and evangelistic work are making excellent progress. In 1864 the Rev. Narayan Sheshadri, a graduate of the Wilson College while it was still under the auspices of the Established Church, founded the Dekkan Mission, chiefly in the Mohammedan state of Haidarabad. The stations now occupied by this mission are Calcutta, Bombay, Poona, Jalna, Bethel and villages, Amraoti, Madras, Nagpur, and Indapur.

All the colleges of India are affiliated with the universities, and train Christian converts to be vernacular as well as English preaching missionaries, and pastors of native congregations established on the Presbyterian system.

2. AFRICA.—*Kaffraria.*—This mission was not started by the Free Church. In 1821, at a time when the Rev. John Brownlee of the L. M. S. was the only missionary working in the whole country, the Glasgow Missionary Society, a union formed of members of the Established Church of Scotland and Dissenters, sent out Rev. W. R. Thompson as missionary and Mr. John Bennie as catechist, to accompany a Scotch colony of people from Glasgow, who intended to settle on the borders of Kaffraria, and thus perhaps open a door for missionary work among the natives. The greater part of the company was lost at sea, but the missionaries escaped, and immediately upon their arrival opened missionary operations at a little village on the Chumie River, where the friendly attitude of the native chief made their work very successful, and in June, 1823, five Kafirs were baptized. In December, 1823, the Rev. John Ross and his wife arrived as reinforcements. At this time the schools were well attended by pupils of both sexes, and the progress of the children was most encouraging. A printing-press was in operation, and from the chiefs of different tribes the missionaries received warm invitations to come and be their instructors. In 1830 the mission was in a most thriving condition. The natives were fast becoming orderly and civilized in their habits, and showed a great desire for instruction. A church had been built, and the rude huts of the natives replaced by more substantial dwellings. A new station was now formed at Lovedale, twelve miles from Chumie, to which Messrs. Ross and Bennie were assigned. In 1833, another station, Balfour, had been occupied, where the work was progressing favorably; and during the next few years many other places were being evangelized. In 1838 the union between the Established Church and Dissenters was amicably dissolved, the members of the Established Church retaining the old name, and the Dissenters taking the name of the Glasgow African Missionary Society, and retaining the stations of Chumie, Izzibigha, Glenthorn, and Kirkwood, (the last three stations more recently occupied), while the old society took Lovedale, Burnshill, Pirrie, and Kwelcha, at all of which stations the work was carried on with most encouraging success. In 1843, when the Disruption of the Church of Scotland occurred, the Glasgow Society at Lovedale, etc., offered to hand over their mission to the Free Church of Scotland, and the offer being accepted, the transfer was made in 1844. At the time of the transfer there was a missionary seminary at Lovedale, under Rev. W. Gowan, valued at £2,000 to £3,000, free from debt, with twelve or fourteen native theological students, and some graduates already engaged in evangelistic work among their countrymen. The work went on smoothly, and in the hands of the Free Church continued to prosper greatly until 1846, when the breaking out of the Kafir war compelled the missionaries to flee. Mr. Gowan returned to Scotland. Mr. and Mrs. Gorrie, who were among the latest missionaries sent out, went to Cape Town to labor among the colonists, and some of the other missionaries barely escaped with their lives. Burnshill station was destroyed, and several others burned. Lovedale seminary and mission

houses had been turned into a garrison, and were occupied by 200 soldiers, with their military stores. But peace being restored, in 1848 the missionaries all returned to their posts, and at Lovedale soon everything was full of hope; and in 1849 the seminary was reopened with all its former success. At the other stations, however, the prospect was dreary enough. Much had been lost in the way of mission property and personal effects of the missionaries which for a time it was impossible to replace; but before the close of 1850 the mission had been restored to its former peaceful prosperity, and the fruits of the patient work of its earlier years began to be apparent. In 1852 Mr. Ross and his assistant were compelled to leave Pirrie for the fifth time on account of war, but they returned as soon as possible, and the work went on

The mission field is now in two parts—the South and North Kafir Missions, divided by the Great "Kei" River. At Alice, near King William's Town [South Kafir Mission], in the Lovedale Institution, with its annex for girls, under the Rev. J. Stewart, M.D., successor of Mr. Gowan, large numbers of native boys are taught farming, carpentering, wagon-making, printing, and book-binding; and the girls are trained in various domestic and culinary arts, while both sexes are given a broad general education, and are made thoroughly familiar with the Word of God. (See also Lovedale.)

In connection with the Lovedale Institution is the Lovedale Kafir Church, with a native pastor and board of elders. The work of the mission is progressing, and extending eastward towards Pondoland. The centre of population has come to be in the diamond fields, and these and the gold fields have drawn away many of the converts, for whom—although they are followed as well as possible under the difficult circumstances—the lack of money and men prevents the mission from providing. Other churches are growing up in the neighboring towns, and the general aspect of the field is very encouraging. The North Kafir division, founded in 1868, has its centre at the Blythes-wood Institution, under the Rev. James M'Laren, M.A. The work of this mission is chiefly among the Fingoes, and although, being younger, it is far less advanced than that of the Southern, yet it is growing rapidly throughout all the field, which now stretches north on the main road to Natal as far as Tsolo, and has stations besides Blytheswood, at Cunningham, Nain, Duff, and Somerville. "This Kafir Mission held its jubilee locally in 1871, amid great rejoicings and thanksgivings to God on the part of 2,000 natives and 1,000 Europeans. The one station of Kafir huts has grown into ten great evangelistic centres, with over 70 out-stations." These are cared for by 14 ordained missionaries, of whom 3 are native pastors of large congregations.

*Natal.*—Dr. Duff's visit to South Africa, and his eloquent appeals in its behalf when he returned to Scotland, brought about in 1867 the establishment of a new mission of the Free Church among the Zulu Kafirs of Natal. The first stations occupied were Pieter Maritzburg and Impolweni, for a long time under the charge of the Rev. James Allison, who proved himself a good and faithful missionary of Christ. At present Rev. John Bruce with several European and native assistants, has charge of Pieter Maritzburg, while Impolweni is superintended by Rev. James Scott and a number of helpers. The work at both stations is progressing nicely in spite of the difficulty in keeping some of the schools open, owing to the attractions of the gold-fields. Most faithful and fruitful work is being done by the native preachers and their wives in all parts of the mission. Medicine and medical advice are given free to all who apply at the dispensaries.

In 1874 the Dowager Countess of Aberdeen offered Dr. Duff a large sum if he would establish a station as a memorial of her son, Hon. J. H. Gordon, who had been removed by death before he could carry out his cherished plans of opening a mission to the heathen. A capital sum of £6,000, increased by gifts of £4,500, was vested in a trust, of which three of the noble Gordon family were members, and Gordon Memorial in Natal, a few miles from the frontier of Zululand, was occupied. The site had been selected by the Rev. J. Dalzell, who went out as its first missionary, and who still is at the head of the work. When schools and a native church were first being formed the Ketchawayo war broke out, and for some time mission work was obliged to cease. But when peace was restored the work increased and spread in all directions from Gordon Memorial as a centre.

East Central Africa forms the most self-sacrificing and interesting African mission field. The Free Church answered the appeal of Dr. Livingstone to the churches of Scotland, by sending out in 1875, the year after his death, missionaries to occupy the lands around Lake Nyassa, and half-way north to Lake Tanganyika. The work thus begun took the name of the Livingstonia Mission, as a memorial of the great explorer. "The enterprise is managed in detail by a sub-committee in Glasgow, and its secular affairs by the African Lakes Company."

The first settlement was made at Cape Maclean, at the south end of the lake, by Rev. James Stewart, C.E., who sacrificed his East India career and his life for the mission, and who was succeeded by Rev. Robt. Laws, the present missionary. From this centre have grown the stations of Bandawe, with its surrounding villages, along the west shore of Nyassa, also under Dr. Laws; the stations in North and South Agoniland, among the Agoni, a marauding tribe of Zulu origin on the western uplands, with Chinyera as an out-station, all under Dr. Elmslie; Chaenji, on the Stevenson road, between lakes Nyassa and Tanganyika, with Chinga to the northeast, under Rev. A. Bain, Dr. Kerr-Cross, and Rev. A. C. Murray; and Chikusi, in the uplands southwest of Cape Maclean, from which it has been very recently occupied as an out-station. Dr. Laws, at Bandawe, has been a long time in the country, and has thoroughly won the confidence of the people. On one recent occasion some five or six thousand people assembled in his schools, in which large numbers of children are taught daily. At present the prosperity and peace of the mission is threatened by two great dangers. First, by the effort on the part of the Portuguese to blockade the Zambesi and cut off the African Lakes Company from entrance to the lakes, and to subject them to many hindrances upon the same; and, secondly, by another danger which has lately shown itself in acute form—the trouble which arises from the impatience of the Arabs at the presence of Europeans and their influence on the lake. For years back the Arabs have been accustomed to visit this region for the sake of obtaining slaves, and have kept the people in hourly terror of their lives; and although for some time there seems to have been an abatement of those horrors which Dr. Livingstone describes as witnessed by him and perpetrated by Arab slave-dealers, yet recent occurrences show that the Arabs are only biding their time to repeat on the shores of Lake Nyassa the murderous raids which have always marked their course. The missionaries are in great straits, and an active struggle is now being carried on between the English consuls and the missionaries of the Scotch Free Church and the Arab traders. "The consuls advised the missionaries to leave the country for six months and return with more guns and ammunition; others felt that any absence would mean the abandonment of the mission, and would encourage the Arabs, with the consequent discouragement of the native allies. It was finally agreed that the members of the African Lakes Company and Dr. Cross should fortify themselves at Chiringe, and that the consuls should go to the coast and send to the besieged men such reinforcements as were needed. This was done. The native chiefs all adhere to the mission, and are bitterly hostile to the Arabs. Hitherto Dr. Cross and the missionaries have taken no part in the fighting, but have offered their services as surgeons to all, showing thus that the mission desires peace. But it seems improbable that they will be able to maintain this position long, for though there is now more quiet, the Arabs are still most hostile, and an attack at no late date is expected. Yet in spite of all these dangers and interruptions the missionaries have succeeded in keeping the schools open, and in carrying on the regular evangelical work among the natives, who have learned, by the way the missionaries share their troubles and dangers, that they are indeed true friends. In return the natives have shown great bravery and fidelity to the Europeans during the recent disturbances."

3. Syria.—*The Lebanon.*—The Free Church of Scotland resolved to carry on the work commenced in 1839 by their countrymen, M'Cheyne, Keith, Black, and A. Bonar, and followed in 1860 by the efforts of the Lebanon Schools' Society, a catholic agency in Scotland for the Christian education of the people of the Lebanon. Accordingly Dr. Duff and Principal Lumsden visited the mountains, and their visit resulted in the appointment in 1872 of the late Rev. John Rae, M.A., as an ordained, and in 1876 of the Rev. Dr. William Carslaw as a medical missionary. They chose the Metan as the district in which they should commence work, and occupied Shweir as their first station. They united in their work with the Lebanon Schools' Society, which has now 6 out-stations about Shweir, where a congregation of the Syrian Evangelical Church has been formed and a church built.

4. New Hebrides Mission is conducted by nine Presbyterian churches in harmonious co-operation under a local synod. For full particulars of the work of the Free Church, see the article on the New Hebrides Mission.

5. South Arabia.—In February, 1885, the Hon. Ion and Mrs. Keith-Falconer formed plans for a mission to the Mohammedans and Somalis around Aden. These volunteer founders of the mission, who themselves met the entire cost of the enterprise, surveyed all the district about Aden as far as El Hauta, the capital of the Sultan of Lahej, and resolved to settle at Sheikh-Othman, a pleasant little village and British outpost 10 miles from Steamer Point. A grant of two garden-plots of land was made by the British Government, and Hon. and Mrs. Keith-Falconer, after having returned to England in 1886, again went out to Arabia, accompanied by Dr. B. Stewart Cowan as a medical missionary. While in England, Mr. Keith-Falconer, whose father, the Earl of Kintore, was an elder of the Scottish Free Church, asked the Foreign Mission Committee to recognize him and to appoint his medical colleague as its representative. This the Committee and the General Assembly at once agreed to, but although the mission in this way became connected with the Free Church, it is still strictly undenominational in its principle. In the first week of 1887 the Medical and Bible Mission at Sheikh-Othman was begun, in a native house, and was carried on with remarkable success until May 11th, when the beautiful life of the much-loved founder, Hon. Ion-Grant Neville Keith-Falconer suddenly and peacefully ended, and his body was buried in the cemetery of Aden Camp. Immediately the Countess Dowager of Kintore and Mrs. Keith-Falconer each offered to guarantee £300 a year for the support of two missionaries.

The Keith-Falconer Mission is at last fully equipped. Dr. Paterson, the new medical missionary, is in charge, with Mr. Lochhead as his assistant. The committee asked the Rev. W. R. W. Gardner, who had volunteered for Africa, to go to Aden as an ordained missionary; and Mr. Gardner, with great self-denial, gave up long-formed plans for service in Africa to carry on Mr. Keith-Falconer's work. Sheikh-Othman, the headquarters of the mission, forms the natural centre of mission operations amongst a group of small villages within a few miles radius. Some of these have been visited, and the reception has always been friendly, but this is, on the whole, a most difficult field, owing to the low moral and religious tone of the people, and to the fluctuating character and the sparseness of the surrounding population. The medical work done by the mission is large enough to warrant their desire to establish a small hospital near the town, and conversations with the better class have proved that they are interested in the establishment of a school, and in the subjects to be taught—such as Arabic, English, etc. This is very encouraging, although it remains to be seen what success will at first attend a school where the Bible must avowedly be taught in place of the Koran.

Besides the work among the Arabs and Somalis, much good is being done among the rescued Galla captives, and two houses (one for boys and one for girls) are being built for the accommodation of the children and their teachers.

(6) Jewish Missions and (7) Continental Missions will be separately treated under these heads.

General View. (From the Free Church of Scotland Year-Book.)—"The Free Church of Scotland's foreign missions are now consolidated in seven well-defined fields, and are extended among certain great races of marked individuality and influence, in the two great continents of Asia and Africa. In and to the south of Asia the fields are: (1) India, and these especially among the educated Brahmanical Hindus, numbering 17,000,000, and the simple aboriginal demon-worshippers, numbering 7,000,000; (2) South Arabia, from Aden to Sheikh-Othman, as a base for work among the Mohammedan Arabs and Somalis; (3) The New Hebrides group of thirty islands in the Pacific Ocean, to the south of eastern Asia, containing 100,000 cannibals of the Malay or Polynesian, and the Negrillo or Papuan races; (4) Syria, where, on Lebanon, twenty miles to the northeast of Beirut, there is a medical and educational mission to the quasi-Mohammedan Druses, and to the ignorant Christians of the Greek and Latin churches. In Africa the missions are at work among the three principal varieties of the great Bantu race of fetich-worshippers, termed by their Mohammedan oppressors 'Kafirs.' These varieties are: (1) The Kafirs of Cape Colony, with whom we have fought seven cruel wars, but who are now peaceful, because largely Christianized and civilized around the provincial capital of King William's Town. In this great work the United Presbyterian and the Free Churches are practically, and will be corporately, united: (2) the Zulus of Natal are evangelized from Maritzburg, the capital; from Impolweni estate, where a girls' institution is being built like Lovedale, for Kaffraria proper; and from Gordon Memorial, on the borders of purely native Zululand; (3) the Kafir-Zulu tribes of Lake Nyassa region, farther north, are cared for by the Livingstonia Mission, begun by Rev. Dr. Stewart, and now under the Rev. Dr. Laws, who again illustrates the blessedness of union, being a United Presbyterian Missionary in the service of the Free Church of Scotland. The Free Church has in all 82 foreign missionaries in India, Africa, the New Hebrides, and Syria, besides 521 native agents who assist the missionaries."

New Hebrides: see New Hebrides Mission.

**Presbyterian Church (North), U. S. A., Board of Foreign Missions.** Headquarters, 53 Fifth Avenue, New York City.—"Foreign Missions" were undertaken by the Presbyterian Church in the United States at a very early date. The "Society for Propagating Christian Knowledge," which was formed in Scotland in 1709, established in 1841 a "Board of Correspondents" in New York, by whom the Rev. Azariah Horton, a member of the Presbytery of New York, was appointed to labor as a missionary among the Indians on Long Island. The second foreign missionary of the Presbyterian Church was David Brainerd, who was ordained by the Presbytery of New York, then meeting at Newark, N. J., June 12th, 1744, and immediately commenced his labors at the forks of the Delaware, on the Susquehanna, and at Crosswicks, near the centre of New Jersey. After his death in 1747, his brother, the Rev. John Brainerd, a member of the same Presbytery, took up the work among the Indians, which he carried on successfully for many years. These three missionaries to the heathen tribes of America maintained a correspondence with the parent society in Scotland, and derived a part of their support from that country. Mr. Horton

and David Brainerd received about two hundred dollars a year from that source, but John Brainerd was supported principally, if not wholly, by contributions from the Presbyterian churches in this country. In 1763 the Synod of New York ordered a collection to be made in all its churches for the support of the Indian missions, which now included work among the Oneidas. In 1766 the synod sent the Rev. Chas. Beatty and the Rev. George Duffield upon a mission to the Indians on the Muskingum River in Ohio; their report being very favorable, two missionaries were appointed to labor in the region. After the death of Mr. John Brainerd in 1780, on account of the many changes which, owing to the Revolutionary war and other causes, had occurred among the Indians, the foreign missionary work, which had been prosecuted for nearly forty years, was, to a considerable extent, abandoned, but was resumed in 1796, upon the formation of the "New York Missionary Society," a body independent of any presbyterial supervision, although it consisted principally of members of the Presbyterian Church. A considerable amount of funds was collected, and three Indian missions were established among the Chickasaws, the Tuscaroras, and the Senecas. In 1797 the "Northern Missionary Society," which, like its predecessor, was an independent body, and composed in part of Presbyterians, was instituted, and prosecuted missions to the Indian tribes for several years. In the year 1800, however, the General Assembly of the Presbyterian Church took up the work of foreign missions in a systematic manner. In 1802 the General Assembly's Standing Committee on Missions addressed a circular to all the Presbyteries under its care, urging collections for the support of missions, and making inquiries for suitable men to be employed. In 1803 a suitable person was found in the Rev. Gideon Blackburn, who offered himself for the work, and a mission was established among the Cherokee Indians, then residing within the limits of the chartered State of Georgia. The work was prosecuted with zeal and devotedness until, after eight years' labor, Mr. Blackburn's health failed. The General Assembly not being able to fill his place, the Rev. Mr. Kingsbury, acting under the American Board, established himself in the Cherokee country and built up a flourishing mission. From 1805 to 1818 the General Assembly carried on work among the Indians in various directions, and with some degree of success; but in 1818, a new society, consisting of the Presbyterian, Reformed Dutch, and Associate Reformed churches, was formed, called the "United Foreign Missionary Society," whose object was "to spread the gospel among the Indians of North America, the inhabitants of Mexico and South America, and other portions of the heathen and anti-Christian world," and until 1826 all the existing missionary interests of the Presbyterian Church were merged in this society. In 1826, when the Society had under its care nine missions, with a force of 60 missionaries, the whole work was transferred to the A. B. C. F. M., and the "United Foreign Missionary Society" ceased its operations.

Many Presbyterians desiring to prosecute foreign missions through the church of their preference, the Synod of Pittsburgh, which from its organization in 1802 had shown great missionary zeal, formed in 1831 the "Western

Foreign Missionary Society," intended not for that synod alone, but for all others which might wish to unite with it.

Operations were at once commenced, and the Society, organized for the purpose of "conveying the gospel to whatever parts of the heathen and antichristian world the providence of God might enable it to extend its evangelical exertions," had succeeded in planting missions among the American Indians, in India and Africa, and was contemplating work in China, when in June, 1837, a Board of Foreign Missions was established by the General Assembly, to which the work of the Society was surrendered. At this point (in 1838) the Presbyterian Church was divided, and the "Old School" Assembly carried on its work through the "Board of Foreign Missions," while the General Assembly of the "New School" continued to prosecute its missions by its "Committee on Foreign Missions" through the A. B. C. F. M. Upon the reunion of the Old and New School Assemblies in 1870, the Persian, Syrian, Gaboon, and several Indian missions were transferred from the American Board, and since that period all the missions of the Presbyterian Church, with the exception of those carried on by the Southern churches, which withdrew from the General Assembly of the Old School with the breaking out of the civil war, have been prosecuted through the "Board of Missions of the Presbyterian Church."

*Organization.*—The Board of Foreign Missions is simply a Permanent Committee of the General Assembly, and the title of "Committee" would have more clearly indicated its relation to that court. For convenience in holding real estate, a charter has been obtained in the State of New York, with the same title as designated by the General Assembly, "The Board of Foreign Missions of the Presbyterian Church in the United States of America." The members of the incorporated body are the same persons who are appointed as members of the Board by the General Assembly, which possesses exclusively the general authority, supervision, and control of the work of missions, the Board being but a form of its executive agency. From 1838 to 1870 the Board was composed of 120 members, from whom an Executive Committee was appointed of persons residing in or near New York City, the Board's headquarters. At the reunion, when the Board was reorganized, the membership was reduced to fifteen, and the Executive Committee was dispensed with. The Board has been presided over successively by Drs. James W. Phillips and J. M. Krebs, Mr. James Lenox (who was re-elected at the reorganization), Dr. William Adams, Dr. Wm. M. Paxton, and the present incumbent, Dr. John D. Wells. The first Corresponding Secretary of the Board was the Hon. Walter Lowrie, 1837-69. In 1838 the Rev. John C. Lowrie was chosen Assistant Secretary, and in 1850 became a full co-ordinate Secretary with his father. Dr. John Leighton Wilson was chosen third Secretary in 1853, continuing until 1861, when he resigned and became the first Corresponding Secretary of the "Foreign Mission Board of the Presbyterian Church in the Southern States." This vacancy was filled in 1865 by Dr. David Irving. In 1871, after the reunion, Dr. Frank F. Ellinwood was chosen third Secretary, to represent the New School churches. In 1883 the Rev. Dr. Arthur Mitchell became

the fourth Secretary, and in 1885 the vacancy caused by the death of Dr. Irving was filled by Dr. John Gillespie. The present (1890) Corresponding Secretaries are, in the order of their appointment, Drs. Lowrie, Ellinwood, Mitchell, and Gillespie, who divide the work of the Mission House among themselves, each having the correspondence with certain missions, and conducting such a share of the home correspondence as may fall to him. The Secretaries and Treasurer constitute the "Executive Council," which meets on the Friday preceding the meetings of the Board and carefully considers all business to be presented, formulating, on the various subjects, an opinion which is submitted to the Board, and adopted, rejected, or modified at its pleasure. In all business pertaining to the several missions the Board attaches great importance to the opinion of the missionaries on the field, and especially to the recommendations of the missions, which are the Board's business agencies, to which are committed the interests of the Presbyterian Church in the region covered by the mission. Local details are left as far as possible in the hands of the men on the ground, the general supervision being reserved to the Board. In its methods of work the Board has always assigned the chief place to the preaching of the Word as an evangelizing agency, while putting due emphasis upon the school, the press, the hospital and dispensary, with here and there an experimental effort in the line of the industrial arts.

Because of the many advantages for sending forth missionaries, remitting funds, foreign correspondence, etc., New York City was early chosen as the business headquarters of the Board, but for the first five years of its sojourn in that city it had no abiding-place, but was shifted from office to office, to the great inconvenience of all concerned; but in 1842, by the liberality of a few friends, in addition to collections made in some of the churches, the Mission House at 23 Centre Street was provided. With its ownership came the nucleus of a library, now increased to 7,000 volumes, and a museum of curios, illustrative of the customs of heathen nations, especially their idol-worship. The house on Centre Street continued to be occupied by the Board until in 1887 the "Lenox Mansion," 53 Fifth Avenue, was placed at its disposal.

*Missions of the Board.*—MISSIONS TO NORTH AMERICAN INDIANS.—The missions of the Presbyterian Board to the American Indians are treated of under the article Indians, but the following summary is here given:

*Chippewas and Ottawas.*—Station founded at Grand Traverse Bay, Michigan, 1839; church organized, 1843; Grand Traverse Bay station moved, Little Traverse Bay station opened, 1852; Middle Village station, 1853; manual-labor school opened at Grand Traverse Bay, 1853; church of 18 members organized at Little Traverse Bay, 1856. In 1867 the mission was discontinued, and the churches were placed under the care of the presbytery in 1871. During the 33 years of its existence about 200 members were received into the churches.

*Seneca Mission.*—Received from A.B.C.F.M., in 1870; placed under presbytery of Buffalo, 1880.

*Lake Superior Chippewas.*—Received from A. B. C. F. M. in 1870; boarding-school opened at Odanah; out-station and day-school started at Ashland, Lac Court d'Oreilles Reserve, 1878; school opened at Round Lake, 1884. Over 100 members have been received into the church since 1870.

*Iowa and Sac Mission.*—Missionaries sent out, 1837; boarding-school opened near Highland, 1845, from which in 25 years 500-600 children received education. Mission abandoned, 1860; resumed, 1881.

*Sac and Fox Mission.*—Under the care of the W. B. F. M. of the U. W. The work is difficult, but a few have been converted.

*Dakota Mission.*—Received from A.B.C.F.M., 1870. Stations: Yankton Agency, Flandreau, Poplar Creek, Wolf Point, and Pine Ridge.

*Omaha and Otoe.*—Commenced at Bellevue (now in Sarpy County, Neb.), 1846; Otoes received, 1855. Present station is on the new reservation at Blackbird Hills, Northwest Nebraska, on the Missouri, 70 miles above Omaha.

*Winnebago Mission.*—School started among these Indians on the Omaha reservation, 1865, but soon after given up; work resumed, 1881. Twenty Christians have been organized into a church.

*Choctaws.*—Spencer Academy, to which $6,000 was annually appropriated by the Indians, was offered to and accepted by the Board in 1845; great revival in 1854; boarding-school opened for girls, 1855; services held at seven different places. Statistics in 1859: 213 communicants, 171 scholars; received from the A. B. C. F. M. in 1860; 6 native preachers, 10 stations, 12 churches, 1,467 members, 3 day-schools, 3 boarding-schools, 445 scholars. Station and church organized at Jack's Forks, 1860; work discontinued on account of the civil war, 1861, and resumed by the Board of Home Missions, 1882.

*Creek Mission.*—Work commenced in 1841; boarding-school for 20 pupils built, 1845; larger school built at Koweta, 1848; school built at Tullahassee; work interrupted by the war, 1861; resumed at Tullahassee, 1866; school removed to Wealaka, 1882.

*Seminole Mission.*—Settlement of Seminoles on Creek reservation, 1832; unsuccessful attempt to establish a mission, 1845; work commenced at Oak Ridge, 1848; Seminoles removed and new station established at Wewoka, 1859; interrupted by the civil war, 1861; boarding-school reopened, 1870.

*Nez Percés Mission.*—Received from A. B. C. F. M., 1871. Stations occupied: Lapwai, Kamiah; church placed in close connection with presbytery of Oregon, and Spokane church organized with 92 members, 1878; Deep Creek, Wyoming Territory, church organized with 89 members, 1880; church on Umatilla Reserve, Oregon, with 28 members, and church among the Spokanes, 1882. Statistics for 1889 give 7 churches, 792 communicants. Joseph's Band have recently returned to their native place from their exile in Indian Territory.

*Chickasaw Mission.*—Work commenced, 1851; discontinued, 1861.

*Wea Mission.*—Work commenced, 1833; discontinued, 1838.

*Otoe Mission.*—Work commenced, 1856; discontinued, 1860.

*Kickapoo Mission.*—Work commenced, 1856; discontinued, 1860.

MISSION TO MEXICO.—*Southern Mexico Mis-sion.*—Miss Rankin's work in Mexico, which was the means of directing Bishop Riley towards that country, also influenced the Presbyterian churches of the United States, and in 1872 the General Assembly took action in regard to the establishment of a mission there, and in September of that year the first band of missionaries for Mexico sailed for New York. They went directly to Mexico City, where they found a large body of dissenters from the Catholic religion, embracing nine congregations, who at once solicited their guidance, and the organization of churches was begun, and in January, 1873, the mission of the capital was formed. The education of the native ministry was at once undertaken, and a hymn-book was prepared which has since been adopted by many of the other branches of the church in Mexico, and schools for girls and young men were opened. From Mexico City advances were made into the surrounding country, as the way was opened; much opposition was encountered, especially among the ignorant and bigoted population of the more remote districts, and at Acapulco a violent outbreak occurred in 1875, resulting in the death of several persons. This put an end for some years to all public effort in the state of Guerrero, but after a time a humble Christian woman, Mathilde Rodriguez, was employed to distribute Bibles and tracts in that region, and to converse with the people in their homes; and in 1884 Rev. J. Milton Greene, accompanied by Rev. Procopio Diaz, one of the sufferers by the violence of the mob in 1875, ventured to revisit Guerrero, where they were eagerly received. In seven weeks they held 32 services, established 13 congregations, baptized 280 persons, and formed 6 churches, with elders regularly organized.

In 1887, when a missionary was sent to Zitacuaro in the state of Michoacan, he was greatly surprised to find the way all prepared for the preaching of the gospel; six years before, a Mexican had opened a book-store there, and had sold or given away 400 Bibles and a large box of tracts, which during these six years had been doing their silent work. At the present time there are within a radius of 35 miles more than 16 congregations, with a membership exceeding 4,000.

In Tabasco, in the extreme southeast, a large number of Bibles had been scattered by the colporteurs of the American Bible Society; and four years after the commencement of their work, a young graduate of the theological seminary in Mexico City (now removed to San Luis Potosi) volunteered to serve in Tabasco. He was gladly received, and two churches were at once organized. The Southern Mexican Mission now embraces 56 churches, in addition to 15 stated preaching places, and the total membership of the churches is 3,224. The work has been extended from Tabasco into Yucatan, and at Merida there is a church with native pastor.

*Northern Mexico.*—This mission includes the stations of Zacatecas (occupied 1873), San Luis Potosi (1873), San Miguel del Mezquital (1876), and Saltillo (1884). At Zacatecas it has a flourishing church, and also various schools for grown people and children. Zacatecas, like Mexico City, has been the centre of influence for the surrounding country, and the work has extended in many directions. In addition to the principal station in the city there are two stations in the suburbs. In San Luis Potosi the theological seminary forms a very important part of the mission; the number of native students preparing for the ministry is 19; many have already gone forth from it to various parts of Mexico. At San Luis Potosi, also, is a boarding-school for girls, which is doing excellent work in training a large number of Mexican girls to be teachers among their own people. The school for girls which has been long in operation at Monterey is to be removed to Saltillo, on account of its more salubrious climate and other advantages. In Northern Mexico, as well as in the southern mission, the Protestants have met with much persecution, and in some places a good deal of fanaticism and opposition still exists, not, however, seriously affecting the work. The work of the mission press is of great interest and importance to the whole mission, the different sections of which have been brought into much closer contact since the building of railroads in the country.

*Guatemala Mission.*—Mission work in Guatemala has been thus far carried on exclusively by the Presbyterian Board, whose attention was called to it in 1882. The Jesuits had been expelled, religious liberty prevailed in the republic, and assurances were given of the sympathy of President Barrios with Protestant missions. These facts, and the consideration that there was not in the country one Protestant service, while in the capital were many Europeans and Americans who might be expected soon to make an English service self-sustaining, led to the appointment by the Board of Rev. John C. Hill and his wife as the first Protestant missionaries to Guatemala. The plan adopted was to gather an English-speaking congregation and organize a Protestant church. Services were held for a time in private residences, but very soon a house was rented from the President at a merely nominal sum, and furnished by the contributions of the English-speaking people. The missionaries were soon fully established, and were especially encouraged by the attendance of natives, the young men seeming to be particularly attracted. The patronage of leading citizens, both English and native, was offered if schools should be opened, and in January, 1884, upon the arrival of Miss Hammond and Miss Ottaway, a school was organized and received with great favor by the people. The Sunday-school was attended by the children of the President, and by others in high positions; and the new chapel was soon filled, mainly by intelligent citizens, who came notwithstanding the fact that their business was thereby endangered. Work among the Spaniards was taken up by Mr. Hill, in connection with a licentiate preacher from Mexico, whose ministrations attracted large numbers, some of whom gave evidence of conversion, and a church was organized in December, 1884. President Barrillos, President Barrios' successor, is most favorable to the mission, and the work in all its departments is making good progress.

Mission in South America.—The first mission of the Board in South America was the Buenos Ayres Mission, commenced in 1853, but discontinued in 1859.

*United States of Colombia.*—In 1856 a mission to "New Granada," now the United States of Colombia, was commenced at Bogota. The government interposed no hindrances, and when the services in Spanish called out bitter opposition from the priests, the disturbance was quelled by the authorities, and for some time the rights of toleration were vindicated, the priests however, threatening all Catholics who should attend any Protestant services with excommunication and its terrible consequences. The civil war which broke out in 1860 materially interfered with missionary work, the Romish party for a while holding the capital; afterwards the Liberal party gained possession of it, the Jesuits were banished, monastic orders restricted, and other means taken to reduce the political power of the papal party. The missionaries organized a church in 1868; a day-school and boarding-school were also established. For many years the work was carried on, against opposition, and the progress was very slow indeed. The difficulties still besetting the mission are so great as to prevent rapid growth; the opposition of the priesthood and the apathy and infidel tendencies of the people—who love Protestantism for political reasons, but hate its claims for a devoutly religious life—are among the greatest drawbacks to work in Bogota. A new station was opened at Barranquilla in 1888.

*Chili.*—The Chili Mission was transferred to the Presbyterian Board by the American and Foreign Christian Union in 1873, and occupies the whole republic, though operating from three centres, viz., Santiago, Valparaiso, and Concepcion. Santiago, situated on a plain 2,000 feet above the sea, is 120 miles inland from Valparaiso, and is connected with it by a railroad. It was first occupied by Rev. N. P. Gilbert in 1861, who, in the midst of many discouragements from foreigners and natives, persevered until he was able to organize a church and erect a building. The mission in Chili has had a most generous and efficient friend in Alexander Balfour, Esq., of Liverpool, and the training school and theological seminary at Santiago for five years received its support from him. The "Instituto Internacional," a boys' school for boarding and day pupils, is conceded to be far ahead of the Romish schools in curriculum and thoroughness, though in the erection and equipment of schools carried on in her interest the Romish Church expends large sums. At Valparaiso the Chilian church receives much help from the co-operation of the "Union Church," supported by English-speaking people. Its congregation numbers about 300. In addition to Sunday-schools the "Escuela Popular" for boys and girls has been established, and a "Shelter-home" for needy children is carried on under the supervision of the missionary, but is mainly supported by subscriptions in Valparaiso and receipts for board and lodging. The Valparaiso Bible Society is doing most efficient work.

Concepcion is the centre of a district containing nine towns and villages, which is in the charge of a native minister who received his theological training from this mission. Salea, Constitution, and Linares are other points of work in Chili, and in connection with this mission, work is carried on in Callao, Peru.

*Brazil.*—In June, 1859, the Rev. Ashbel Green Simonton sailed from New York as the Board's first missionary to Brazil. He landed at Rio Janeiro in August, and while acquiring the Portuguese language he gave lessons in English; but soon finding himself able to speak with some facility, he opened a place for preaching. His first audience consisted of two men whom he had taught English, three attended his second service, and the number gradually increased until full congregations attended his ministrations. Other missionaries were sent to aid in the work, and in 1862 the first Presbyterian Church in Brazil was organized at Rio; in 1875 two hundred converts had been added to the number received in 1862. This church is now the centre of much work carried on in the surrounding country; regular worship is maintained at Praia Grande, the capital of the province of Rio de Janeiro, and evangelistic tours to Rezende and Petropolis have been made. São Paulo was occupied as a mission station in 1863; in 1865 a church was organized, consisting of several converts who had been received on profession of their faith, and steady, though not rapid, progress was made; a noticeable fact in its history is the great number of its members who have removed to other places, often carrying the blessing with them. Funds for a preaching hall and accommodations for training schools were obtained by Mr. Chamberlain, who joined the mission in 1865, and ground and materials for building were purchased. The boarding-school for girls—now so well known—was established in 1867; there are now on the roll 264 pupils, not including those in the kindergarten, which is independent of the Board. The value of the educational work in Brazil cannot be estimated, for the influence of the schools extends into many homes throughout the various provinces, and the Bible, a new book to all, and full of interest, is thus brought within the reach of many outside of the missionary circuit. A weekly journal, the "Imprensa Evangelica," whose publication was begun in 1864, is also widely circulated through the provinces, and exerts a silent but very great influence. Through this influence churches have grown up in places never visited by a minister of the gospel. Rio Claro, the centre of a large German population, was also occupied in 1863. In 1867 a school for girls was established which is most highly recommended, even Romanists approving it openly. In connection with the work are many preaching stations, where services are held regularly. At Bahia, 735 miles northeast of Rio de Janeiro, at Campos, and at Larangeiras, and their out-stations, much energetic missionary work is carried on, and at Sorocaba, Caldas, Campanha, and Botucatu native churches have been organized, with native pastors in charge. Within the past year the church at São Paulo has become self-supporting and the pastoral charge put into the hands of a native minister, who had been trained in the theological school in that city. A station has been established at Corytiba, the chief town of the province of Parana, about 500 miles southwest of Rio de Janeiro.

The year 1889 was marked by the consolidation of the missions of the Board in Brazil with those of the Southern Presbyterian Church. The synod of the Presbyterian Church in Brazil thus formed has a total of 61 churches, with an aggregate membership of 3,000. By this union the Presbyterian Church now occupies 12 of the 20 provinces of Brazil; but as 34 of its churches are in the province of São Paulo and 9 in the province of Minas, it is plain that only a beginning has been made in many of the 12 provinces named. The synod of Brazil has asked for large reinforcements to

its missionary staff; and this appeal is all the more urgent by reason of the vast tide of emigration which has turned toward Brazil since the abolition of slavery in 1888, and which, owing to the establishment of the republic, will now be greatly augmented.

WESTERN AFRICA.—*Liberia Mission.*—The first settlement on the coast which now contains the republic of Liberia was by 89 free colored people who sailed from New York in 1820. Two years later a colony of manumitted slaves from the United States was planted by the American Colonization Society, under whose supervision they remained for twenty-five years, until the erection of the republic, with its capital at Monrovia, in 1847. Various missionary boards, representing all the evangelical Christian Churches, followed with their agents their members who had thus gone as colonists. The colonists, with re-captives from slave-ships, landed at Liberia, and the aborigines make now a population estimated at about 600,000. Mission work in Liberia was begun by Lot Cary, a slave, who, having bought his freedom, was sent out by Baptist aid in 1821; upon his death in 1828 the governor obtained Swiss missionaries from Basle, who were, however, afterward transferred to Sierra Leone. The Presbyterian Mission was commenced in 1833 at Monrovia, its more special object being work among the natives, and only incidentally for the colonists. Stations were extended to the Kroo coast near Cape Palmas. The six missionaries who were sent out very soon died from the effects of the climate. The Board then, in 1842, tried the experiment of sending only colored ministers, and Settra Kroo, Sinoe ("Greenville"), and Monrovia were occupied. The presbytery of Western Africa was constituted in 1848, and attached to the synod of Philadelphia. It was found that American Negroes were not exempt from fever, and, by their slave origin, lacked skill for the conduct of affairs; accordingly white men were again sent out. The Alexander High School, established at Monrovia in 1849, and also a school under the care of a very able colored teacher, did excellent work. After many discouragements, there came a year of blessing in 1857. Reinforcements were sent to the mission, and in 1859 two new stations were opened. At present the work is carried on from eight centres, viz., Monrovia, Brewerville and Clay-Ashland, Careysburgh, Schieffelin, Grassdale and Greenville; also at Ghina, in the Vey country, and among the Bassa tribe; all the missionaries of the present staff are Americo-Liberians, with the exception of two, one of whom is a Vey, the other a Bassa.

*Gaboon-Corisco Mission.*—In 1834 the American Board sent a missionary to Liberia, who located at Cape Palmas. A large missionary force followed him. There, work at first was successful, but after some reverses, and collisions with the neighboring American Negro colony from Maryland, it was in 1843 removed to Gaboon, about 1,000 miles distant. The great mortality among the missionaries of the Presbyterian Board on the Liberian coast led to the inquiry whether a more healthy locality could not be discovered elsewhere, and the comparative freedom from fever enjoyed by the missionaries of the American Board on the Gaboon River turned the attention of many to the equator. Accordingly two missionaries and their wives were sent to form a new mission; aided by the counsels of the American Board, and after making full examination of various places, they selected the island of Corisco as their station, hoping that its insular position might assure exemption from fever, and that natives of the island, after careful education, could undertake the danger and exposure of carrying the gospel to distant regions. Neither hope was realized. Four stations were established on the island—Evangasimba, Ugobi, Elongo, and Maluku; but the island proving quite as malarious as the mainland, and chronic tribal quarrels making it impossible to go any distance from their own tribe, the four Corisco stations were reduced to the single one of Elongo, and the work was extended to the mainland. In 1870 the Gaboon Mission was transferred to the Presbyterian Board, and since that time the work has been known as the "Gaboon and Corisco Mission," and now includes the stations of Baraka, on the Gaboon River, 10 miles from the sea, and Angow, higher up the same river; Corisco, with outstation at Mbiko, on the mainland opposite Corisco; Benita, Batanga, 75 miles north of Benita; Kangwe, on the Agowe River, 165 miles from the sea; and Talaguga, 50 miles above Kangwe. There are no roads in this part of Africa, the narrow forest-paths being trodden single file in hunting, or in emigrating from the bank of one river to another; the beach on the coast can be traversed by horse or hammock-bearer, but almost the entire travel and trade is done in native canoes and boats dug from the single tree-trunk, and by small foreign sloops, schooners, and steam-launches. The missionaries had always travelled by small open boats, with sails for the ocean and oars for the inland rivers, until 1871, when a rapid-sailing yacht was purchased for them; two years later this vessel was lost on the Corisco rocks, and her place was taken by the "Hudson;" this, again, has been replaced by the "Nassau," light enough for river service and large enough to take the place of sailing vessels for the coast stations.

The Mpongwe, Benga, and Fangwe dialects have been reduced to writing, and the entire New Testament and parts of the Old, with hymn-book, catechism, etc., have been translated into them. Churches have been organized on Corisco, at Benita, Gaboon, and on the Agowe; and schools for boys and girls at these points, and also at the other stations mentioned before and their out-stations. Owing to the fact that different sections of the territory occupied are under German, French, and Portuguese control, the missionaries have had many political difficulties to contend with. In the French territory French is now taught in the schools, and, so long as German and not English is taught within the German limits, no trouble need be apprehended from the German Government. Cannibalism still exists on the Agowe, and the custom of flinging sick children and aged parents into the river is openly followed. Polygamy is practised; this and the intemperance and indolence of the people, tribal wars, and slavery render the work of the mission most difficult; the people are, however, affectionate, hospitable, and docile, and the missionaries are encouraged by seeing the old customs constantly changing. Witchcraft murders are less frequent, houses and dress are more civilized, and education is being sought for its own sake, and paid for. Native licentiates and candidates for the ministry have rapidly increased, and a disposition to self-support has been shown in a remarkable manner. During the past year a rich blessing has rewarded the long-tried and patient workers; 253 names were added to the church rolls, and religion in several of the churches was greatly quickened.

SYRIA.—Missionary work in Syria was undertaken by the American Board in 1818, and conducted by it until the reunion of the Old and New School branches of the Presbyterian Church in 1870, when the members of the New School body, who had constituted a very considerable portion of the supporters of the American Board, gave up their relation to it and became constituents of the Presbyterian Board of Foreign Missions. As it would have been unjust that the American Board with its diminished number of contributors should continue to bear the same burden, and also unjust that those who had so long contributed to its work should be required to renounce all their rights therein, an arrangement was made whereby the missions in Syria, Persia, and West Africa, and—as has been already explained—certain missions to the North American Indians, were transferred to the Presbyterian Board. A slight sketch of the whole period, 1818–1890, follows (see also article on A. B. C. F. M.):

The history of the Syrian Mission begins with the appointment of Pliny Fisk and Levi Parsons as missionaries to Palestine. Mr. Parsons reached Jerusalem in February, 1821, and began the work of distributing the Scriptures, but was before long obliged to withdraw on account of the disturbing influence of the war in Greece. He died in Egypt in 1822. Mr. Fisk, with Jonas King, afterwards so well known as a missionary to Greece, reached Jerusalem in 1823, where they preached and taught until 1825. Their work was broken up by the arrival of the Pasha of Damascus, who came with an armed force to collect tribute. Mr. King soon afterward left Syria, Mr. Fisk died, and the station at Jerusalem was suspended for nine years. Subsequent efforts to revive it were not successful, and in 1844 it was finally abandoned. In the mean time a new station had been established at Beirut, where Messrs. Bird and Goodell were the first missionaries. They occupied themselves with the circulation of the Scriptures, the preparation of useful books, and the education of the young. Eli Smith joined the mission in 1827, but the unsettled state of all the East at that time led the missionaries in the following year to remove for a time to Malta. In 1830 the work was taken up again, and with the exception of another short period of suspension, for a similar cause, has been prosecuted ever since. Notwithstanding the many difficulties, and perils by the plague, cholera, and war, and the intolerance and bitter hatred of the Moslem magistrates and populace, new efforts were put forth and new stations formed. New missionaries arrived, and the work went on through times of quiet and of persecution—seasons of great promise and times when what seemed opportunities for expanded work and permanent growth vanished. But the work as a whole has prospered, and within the last few years especially abundant fruit has been gathered. The press, the school, and the pulpit have been the means employed. The first printing in connection with the mission was done at Malta, where the A. B. C. F. M. had an establishment in full operation as early as 1826. In 1834 the Arabic portion of the establishment was transferred to Beirut, where its issues have steadily increased in number and value. The Arabic translation of the Bible, prepared by Dr. Eli Smith and Dr. Van Dyck, is now on sale throughout the Mohammedan world.

Educational work has been especially prominent in the Syrian Mission. Schools were begun in Beirut in 1824, when a class of six Arab children was taught by the wives of the missionaries. In 1827 six hundred pupils (of whom one hundred were girls) were in attendance in thirteen schools, established in Mount Lebanon, the interior, and in various cities on the coast. At first only reading and writing were taught, there being no demand for higher instruction, but the great body of readers thus formed caused a demand for books and thus prepared the way for higher schools. Many taught in the common schools became converts to Christianity; Protestantism gained ground, and the other sects were roused to rivalry; the standard of intelligence was raised and knowledge diffused. It was part of the degradation of woman in Syria that it was thought unnecessary, or even dangerous, that she should be taught; but the missionaries received girls into their families; induced them to attend the common schools; and, finally, schools were opened for them. Some of the most important are the boarding-school at Beirut, the Missionary Institution at Sidon, and the school at Tripoli. The total number of schools now in operation is 80, with an attendance of 3,509 pupils, of whom 819 are girls.

At a meeting of the mission in 1861 the project for a Syrian Protestant College was discussed and the plan sketched. This college was opened in 1866. Although an outgrowth of the mission, "missionary instruction having created a demand for it, the plans and prayers of missionaries having established it, and the friends of missions having endowed it," it has been from the first entirely independent of the Board of Missions. A course of medical instruction was soon added to the academic, and medical work is now one of the most important branches of missionary work in Syria. The physicians of the Medical Department of the college have been appointed by the Order of St. John in Berlin, as the Medical Attendants of the "Johanniter Hospital" in Beirut, which is supported by the Order, and served also by the deaconesses of Kaiserswerth. Within the past year about 11,000 cases have been treated by the medical faculty of the college.

The Theological Seminary at Beirut was dedicated in 1883; this institution is under the sole charge and support of the Board of Foreign Missions.

The chief centres of missionary effort are at Beirut, Abeih, Tripoli, Sidon, and Zahleh. In connection with the first are four preaching places, with 2,000 children in the Sunday-schools; in Abeih are 4 churches, 22 preaching places, and 18 Sunday-schools. Tripoli has 15 preaching places and 22 Sunday-schools; Sidon, 25 preaching places and 17 Sunday-schools; and Zahleh, entered in 1872, three churches.

PERSIA.—In 1829 Rev. Messrs. Smith and Dwight were sent by the American Board to explore the regions of Northwest Persia. They became especially interested in the oppressed Nestorians on the plains about Lake Oroomiah, and upon their representations a mission to Persia, which for many years was known as the "Nestorian Mission," was resolved upon, and in September, 1833, the first missionaries, Justin Perkins and his wife, sailed from Boston, and about a year later reached Tabriz; in 1835 they were joined by Dr. and Mrs. Grant, and the little company formally occupied Oroomiah as a station in November of that year. A few years later Dr. Grant died, but Dr. Perkins was spared to labor with great vigor and usefulness for 36 years. With the help of one of the most intelligent of the Nestorian bishops, Mr. Perkins gave himself to the study of the common language, and, when he had mastered it to some extent, undertook the work of reducing it to writing (which had never yet been done), and the preparation of a series of cards. The first school was opened in January, 1836, in a cellar, with 7 small boys in attendance. This school was the germ of Oroomiah College, and has sent forth scores of devout and scholarly preachers and teachers among the people. During the past year 13 have been graduated from the course of theological study, and have gone out as pastors and evangelists; six have been graduated from the academic course. The school for girls, founded by Mrs. Grant in 1838, has increased to the proportions of a seminary, and is steadily growing in numbers and efficiency. As in the Syrian Mission, educational work was from the first employed as one of the chief auxiliaries, but the preaching of the Word was also regarded as of prime importance, and was at once instituted, the missionaries preaching in their own dwellings, in the homes of the people or in school-houses, until the Nestorian churches were opened to them. Much of the time of the missionaries was given to the villages, utterly ignorant and degraded, in the neighborhood of Oroomiah, and in these places the college students spent the long vacation, conducting schools and pursuing evangelistic labors.

In 1837 a printing-press was sent to the mission by the Board. It proved too unwieldy to be taken over the mountains, and was sent from Trebizond back to Constantinople. Two years later a press which could be taken to pieces had been invented, and one of these, in charge of Mr. Breath, a printer, was at once sent to Oroomiah, and was regarded with great interest and wonder by the people. Since that time many books have been published, and for many years a monthly periodical has been issued. Medical work very early became and continues to be an important feature of the mission. Tabriz, Teheran, Hamadan and Salmas have since been occupied, and new work has lately been taken up among the mountain Nestorians on the borders of Persia and Turkey. For a more extended account of the Persian Mission, see article "Persia."

INDIA.—In May, 1833, the Western Foreign Missionary Society sent the Rev. John C. Lowrie and the Rev. Wm. Reed to India to lay the foundations of missionary work. The selection of the particular field in which work should be commenced was left to their judgment after consultation with friends in India. Reaching Calcutta in November of 1833, they decided, after getting the best information available, to begin work in Lodiana, a frontier town of the Northwest Provinces, bordering upon the Punjab, which was at that time under the control of Ranjit Singh, a Sikh chief. While Messrs. Lowrie and Reed were detained at Calcutta Mrs. Lowrie died. Mr. Reed's health failed, and the conclusion was reached that he and his wife should return to America; in July, 1834, they took passage in a ship bound for Philadelphia, but three weeks after leaving Calcutta Mr. Reed died. Mr. Lowrie reached Lodiana in November, 1834. From failure of health he was soon obliged to return to America, but the work which he inaugurated has been successfully established in the Northwest Provinces, in the Punjab, and in the Kolhapur Mission, Southern India.

The Lodiana and Furrukhabad missions now comprise the stations of Rawal Pindi, Lahore, Ferozepore, Hoshyarpore, Jalandhar, Lodiana, Ambala, Sabathu, Dehra, Woodstock, Saharanpur, Mazaffarnagur, Furrukhabad, Futtehgurh, Mainpuri, Etah, Etawah, Gwalior, Jhansi, Futtepore, and Allahabad. These stations are given in geographical, not chronological, order. From Rawal Pindi in the northwest to Allahabad the distance by railroad is 900 miles. Throughout these provinces the same languages are spoken, and missionary work in them is conducted on the same methods; but for convenience of local and general administration the mission is divided as above indicated. The Kolhapur Mission comprises the stations of Kolhapur, Panhala, and Sangli. Lahore, the capital of the Punjab, was regarded as the objective point by the first of the missionaries sent to India, and for many years much of the work done at Lodiana was in preparation for the time when an advance might be made in this direction. This time came in 1849, when the death of Ranjit Singh left the country without a ruler, and the people soon fell into a state of anarchy under the leaders of the army which he had trained, who were so elated with mistaken views of their own power as to resolve on the overthrow of the British dominion in India. For this purpose they crossed the Sutlej into British territory. The conflict which ensued was terrible, and the issue for a long time doubtful; but in the end the Punjab was annexed to the Anglo-India Empire, and the whole of that interesting country was now open to the missionary. Missionary work in all the stations of these missions is carried on in the usual lines; the truth is preached in the chapel and on the highway, books and tracts are circulated, and schools established. Special educational advantages are offered at Lahore, in the college, which, under the usual policy of the church, may soon be separated from the Board and placed on the same footing as the Anglo-vernacular colleges at Beirut and Canton, and in the other excellent schools for boys and for girls. At Dehra is a large boarding-school for Christian girls, in which a training-class for work in the zenanas has recently been formed. There are day-schools also for boys and girls, which have been well attended. Zenana visiting is an important feature of the work at Dehra, 96 zenana pupils having been taught during the last year. The school at Woodstock, of which a fuller account will be found in articles on the Woman's Societies, is well

established, and may be regarded as one of the permanent agencies for the extension of Christ's kingdom in Northern India.

Of the mission stations of the Presbyterian Board, Lodiana, Futtehgurh, and Allahabad were the greatest sufferers in the Mutiny of 1857. The missionaries from Futtegurh and the adjoining station of Furrukhabad endeavored to reach Cawnpur, were captured on the way, forced to march eight miles to Cawnpur, were detained for a night in the house of their captor, and the following morning, on the parade-ground of the station, fell before the fire of their murderers.

*Kolhapur Mission.*—Kolhapur was selected by the Rev. R. G. Wilder, in 1853, as a centre of missionary operations. His work had been supported for years by friends in the United States and in India, and after he had severed his connection with the American Board it remained independent of any church until its transfer to the Presbyterian Board in 1870. Ratnagiri, on the coast, and Panhala have been occupied as mission stations within a few years. Work was suspended at the former for two years, but is to be resumed as soon as reinforcements can be sent out. The same agencies employed in Northern India are in operation in this mission. Zenana visiting and the work of the medical missionary are prominent features. The Kolhapur Mission being far distant from the Northwest Provinces suffered but little during the Mutiny.

SIAM AND LAOS MISSION.—The first visit made to Siam by any representative of the Presbyterian Church was for the same purpose which had already brought other visitors there, namely, to find some door of access to the Chinese; but the Rev. R. W. Orr, having spent a month at Bangkok in 1838, recommended the Board of Foreign Missions to take Siam as a field of effort, not only for the Chinese, but for the Siamese themselves. Accordingly Mr. and Mrs. Buell were sent to Bangkok, arriving there in 1840. After laying a good foundation for future work, Mr. Buell was compelled by the illness of his wife to return home in 1844, and for various reasons it was not until 1847 that his place was filled by others. From that time until the present, continuous work, addressed directly to the native Siamese, has been maintained, although for several years after the arrival of the Rev. Stephen Mattoon and his wife and the Rev. S. R. House, M.D., its foothold seemed very precarious, on account of the active, though secret, opposition of the king, whose despotic influence was so exerted upon the slavish people that none of them could be induced to sell or rent any house to the missionaries. Other difficulties of the same general nature were put in their way, until it seemed certain that they would be prevented from establishing themselves in the country, when the death of the king, in 1851, brought about a change in the whole situation and in all the succeeding history of the country, a change which is directly traceable to the influence of Protestant missions. The man whom the nobles elected to fill the throne was not an ignorant, unmanageable barbarian like his predecessor, but a man who could appreciate civilization, and who claimed to be himself quite a scholar even by European standards. This came from the fact that while still in private life he had been under the instruction of a missionary of the American Board, which maintained a mission in Siam from 1831 to 1850.

The policy of the new king proved to be very liberal; and during all the years which have intervened since his accession, Protestant missionaries have been accorded very noticeable influence with the government. For many years very slight results appeared, to gladden the hearts of the faithful workers in this field. The first convert was baptized in 1859, twelve years after the arrival of the missionaries, since which time members have been steadily gathered into the churches, and the work, though it may be regarded as largely in its preparatory stage, gives many a token of encouraging success. All the usual forms of Christian effort are employed with diligence and effectiveness; the press affords an agency of especial importance in a country where four-fifths of the men and boys are able to read, and the mission press at Bangkok is constantly sending forth copies of the Scriptures in Siamese,—printed in separate portions, for a complete copy, even in the smallest Siamese type, would make a volume larger than Webster's Unabridged Dictionary,—"Pilgrim's Progress," tracts, etc.; the "Siamese Hymnal" also proves very serviceable to this music-loving race. Medical work here exerts a twofold influence; as in every land, it opens a way to the hearts of men by its self-denying beneficence, and affords many an opportunity of pointing the sin-sick soul to the Great Physician; it also has the further effect of undermining the native confidence in the efficacy of spirit-worship. The mere fact of finding malaria healed through the use of quinine by one of the native assistants is mentioned as producing a marked impression of this kind, and the employment of incantations and witchcraft for the sick is proven to be false and useless by the scientific medical practice introduced by the missionaries. The opportunities for such service are abundant, Dr. House having in the first eighteen months of his practice treated 3,117 patients. The Siamese are now taking up this work for themselves. In 1881 a hospital for 60 patients was erected and given for public use by a native nobleman, being placed in charge of a native physician who had graduated first from the missionary boarding-school at Bangkok and afterwards from the Medical School of the University of New York. The very existence and operation of such a hospital is a living argument against Buddhism, of unceasing and ever-widening operation. The work of proclaiming the Word is always regarded as of the first importance, and educational work is vigorously prosecuted, with great encouragement to the missionaries because of the interest and approbation manifested by the government. Dr. MacFarland of the mission has been for some years, by appointment of the king, principal of King's College and superintendent of public instruction. In 1843 Petchaburee, 100 miles from Bangkok, was visited by a missionary, who was repulsed by the authorities in the most uncompromising manner; but in 1861, at the urgent request of the governor, a station was formed at this point; two years later a church was organized, which has been steadily growing ever since. School-work is very prominent, and the native ministry began to receive its development at this station. Medical work is also important, and the hospital

is so near the chapel that all patients physically able attend the daily morning service, as well as the preaching of the gospel on Sabbath afternoon. Within the past year 5,500 cases have come under the doctor's care, many of his patients coming from far-distant provinces.

The prime minister of Siam offered three years ago to furnish suitable buildings for a new mission station at Ralburee if the Board would undertake work at that point. Just before the new recruits arrived, the prime-minister died; but he had left in writing the expression of his desire that his plans in behalf of the missionaries might be fulfilled, and through the good-will of the king his wishes were met, and the station was established in 1889.

*Laos Mission.*—Chieng-Mai, the capital of the Laos country, was visited by a deputation from the Siam Mission in 1863. In 1867 and 1868 the Rev. Messrs. McGilvary and Wilson opened a station there, and were soon encouraged by the conversion of a man who had thoroughly studied Buddhism and was dissatisfied with it, while knowing of nothing to replace it; he began to study eagerly the spiritual truths of Christianity, and was soon able to make an intelligent confession of his faith in Christ. Seven other converts were baptized within a few months, but at this point the infant church was brought to a season of persecution and martyrdom. Exercising full control over his own people, though tributary to Siam, the king began to manifest the hostility he had thus far concealed. Two of the converts were arrested, and, on being brought before the authorities, confessed that they had forsaken Buddhism. They were tortured all night, and again examined in the morning, but steadfastly refused to deny their Saviour, even in the face of death. They prepared for execution by praying to Him, closing with the words: "Lord Jesus, receive my spirit!" They were then taken to the jungle and clubbed to death by the executioner; one of them was also thrust through the heart by a spear. The persecution was checked by the death of the king, and the mission was resumed. Another crisis was encountered in 1878, and an appeal was at once made to the king of Siam, which brought for reply a "Proclamation of Religious Liberty for the Laos," which entirely changed the conduct of the officials.

*Siamese Mission.*—Medical work has received especial attention. The Bethlehem Church was organized in 1880, at a point 9 miles above Chieng-Mai, as the result of an interesting awakening of inquiry among the natives, who had heard of Christianity from relatives visiting the capital. A station has been established at Lakawu, 90 miles from Chieng-Mai, where a very encouraging work is in progress. Maa Dok-Dang Church was organized in 1881, and the four churches of the mission were formed into a Presbytery in 1883. The number of churches at present is 5; membership, 600; number of schools, 6, with an attendance of 195.

CHINA MISSION.—Three months after its organization, in December, 1837, the Presbyterian Board sent two missionaries, Revs. J. A. Mitchell and R. W. Orr, to the Chinese Mission at Singapore. Mr. Mitchell died soon after reaching Singapore, and Mr. Orr was compelled by failure of health to return home. Mr. McBride, sent out in 1840, returned for the same reason in 1843. In the same year Dr. Hepburn and Mr. Walter Lowrie were sent out. They transferred the mission from Singapore to China, reinforcements were sent to them, and a most important agency, the mission press, was established. A special appeal for funds was made by the Board, and as a result a large force of workers was sent to strengthen the mission, and Macao, Amoy, and Ningpo were occupied as stations. The work as at present organized comprises the Canton, Shantung, Peking, and Central missions. Canton was occupied in 1845, and the agencies at first employed were chapel preaching, distribution of the Scriptures, teaching and ministering to the sick. In 1846 a boarding-school for boys was established, and a dispensary was opened in 1851. The first church was organized with seven members in January, 1862. A second was organized in 1872, and a third in 1881. A girl's school was opened in 1872, to which has since been added a preparatory school for younger girls, and a training-school for women. Each pupil in this school commits to memory the entire New Testament, and, in addition to the Chinese classics, the course of study embraces all branches commonly taught in a girl's seminary. The day-schools now established throughout the mission number 32, a large proportion being in Canton itself. The theological school has an attendance of from 15 to 20 students. The remaining stations of this mission are at Macao, on the island of Hainan, and at Yeung Kong; nearly 400 cities and villages have been visited by the Canton missionaries, and in a large number out-stations have been opened. The mission staff is assisted by 3 native pastors, 17 unordained evangelists, 24 native assistants, 37 teachers, and 11 Bible-women. Six medical missionaries, three of them ladies, are on the staff, and medical work constitutes a very important part of the mission; two hospitals and four dispensaries are maintained, in which, and through the visits of the physicians, nearly 50,000 patients have this year been treated. The Canton College, although not sustained by the funds of the Board, is an important adjunct and auxiliary to its work.

*The Central Mission* includes Ningpo (1845), Shanghai (1850), Hangchow (1859), Suchow (1871), and Nanking (1876).

Ningpo, one of the five ports opened in 1842, was entered in 1844 by Dr. McCartee. A few months later he was joined by a large force of missionaries, among them the Rev. W. M. Lowrie, who was in 1847 killed by pirates. The first convert was baptized in 1845, and a church was organized later in the same year. The girls' boarding-school dates from 1846, the industrial school for women from 1861, and the Presbyterial Academy, for the sons of native Christians, and almost wholly supported by the tuition fees and the native churches, from 1881. The boys' boarding-school, organized early in the mission, was removed to Hangchow in 1877. The field covered by the Ningpo station, 200 miles long and from 20 to 100 miles wide, embraces a population of several millions. There are several out-stations, at one of which is a self-supporting church of 111 members. Members of several churches have this year gone out at their own charges to tell the story of Christ's love to their fellow-countrymen. The number of churches connected with the station is 10; number of day-schools, 8. The three centres of missionary effort at Shanghai are at the Missionary Press, the South

Gate, and Hongkew. The first, within the city limits, in addition to the great printing-press, which has become historic, has closely connected with it a church, organized in 1882, and a day-school. The printing work of the mission, begun at Macao in 1844, was removed to Ningpo in 1845; in 1856 the use of separate characters instead of cut blocks was begun, the sum of $15,000, needed to secure the manufacture of matrices for the type, being furnished by King Louis Philippe, the British Museum, and the Presbyterian Board. After this a typefoundry and electrotyping department were added, and the institution was removed to Shanghai, which possessed superior commercial advantages, in 1860. Since 1876 the press has not only paid its way, but has also brought a large surplus into the mission treasury. Eight presses are constantly running, and 75 men are employed. Much printing is done for other societies in addition to that for the mission of the Board. At the "South Gate," outside the city limits, but in the midst of a dense population, uncared for by any other Society, there are boys' and girls' boarding-schools, a church, and a number of day-schools. Hangchow has two organized churches and a boarding-school, with an industrial department for boys. The work at Soochow is largely that of city evangelization, but five day-schools are kept up by the small missionary force, and itinerating tours are made. At Nanking educational work continues to be the most encouraging feature.

*The Shantung Mission* comprises the stations of Tungchow (1861), Chefoo (1862), Che-nan-foo (1872), Wei Hein (1882), and Chining Chow and Ichowfoo (1889). The people of Tungchow having been found willing to listen to the truth, a station was opened there in 1861, and a native church was organized in 1862. A boys' school was established in 1866. At the close of the twelfth year 31 boarders were reported, 21 of whom were professed Christians. In that year the name was changed to Tungchow High School, and it is now regularly organized as a college. Its religious tone has always been high, and nearly all the students are Christians. Much faithful work is carried on in the out-stations and in the neighboring villages. The boys' boarding-school at Chefoo is an important agency, as are also the girls' school and industrial school for children, and numerous day-schools. Many have been received to the church who became interested in Christianity through what they heard from the children in these schools. In a theological class helpers and preachers receive instruction; and Bible-women, specially trained for their work, are constantly employed in teaching from house to house. During the past year 24 preachers and 4 Bible-women have been employed under the supervision of Dr. Corbett, their work covering a district more than 300 miles in extent. The work in Che-nan-foo has been carried on in the face of much opposition from the higher classes, which has during the past year been more than usually violent. The chapel and dispensary work have been carried on daily; the boys' school has also had its usual number of scholars. Much time and labor are given to the out-station, and to the establishment of village day-schools. At Wei Hein work on the usual lines is prosecuted. The Christians here have met with much persecution, which is gradually diminishing.

Dr. Hunter's dispensary work has been encouraged by good attendance, many of the patients showing interest in religious truth. Connected with Wei Hein are 60 out-stations, where also there is less persecution, and greater respect is shown to foreigners than formerly.

*Peking Mission.*—The hospital at Peking and the medical training-school are doing a very important work. The women's department of the hospital is under the charge of a lady physician and trained nurse sent out this year by the Board. The lady missionaries at Peking, as at other stations, are doing much for the Chinese women, visiting from house to house, and conducting a training-school for them, which it is hoped may result in fitting many of them to be Bible-women. Two churches have been organized; the second, organized in 1888, is under the care of a native pastor, supported by the members. In addition to his support, this little handful of believers, numbering at the beginning of 1889 only 25, has contributed $100 to benevolent purposes; the greatness of their generosity can be measured only by the depths of their poverty.

MISSION IN JAPAN.—The Christian Church was watching with intense interest the steps by which Japan was opened to the civilized world. In 1853 Commodore Perry succeeded in opening the long-sealed gates, and in 1855 the Presbyterian Board requested Dr. McCartee, one of its missionaries in China, to visit Japan to prepare the way for missions to that country. Dr. McCartee went at once to Shanghai, but was unable to obtain a passage thence in any vessel to the Japanese Islands, and returned to his work at Ningpo. After three years of waiting, favorable indications were seen, and the new mission was undertaken. Dr. James C. Hepburn and his wife, formerly missionaries in China, and Rev. J. L. Nevius and wife, of the Ningpo Mission, were appointed to commence the work. The latter were prevented from permanently joining the mission by the state of their health and the urgent call for their services in China. Dr. Hepburn and his wife arrived in Japan early in November, 1859, and settled at Kanagawa, a few miles from Yedo (now Tokyo). Here a Buddhist temple was soon obtained as a residence, the idols were removed, and the heathen temple was converted into a Christian temple and church. Public service was established in the home and mission work begun, Dr. Hepburn availing himself of his medical practice to speak to the suffering of Christ, whose gospel he was not permitted to preach. Not being allowed to engage in direct mission work, the missionaries devoted themselves, until further opportunities might arise, to dispensary work, the acquisition of the language, and the distribution of Chinese New Testaments among a small portion of the people who could read that language. On account of the opposition of the Japanese authorities to the residence of foreigners in Kanagawa, Dr. Hepburn in 1862 purchased property for the mission in Yokohama, and removed thither. Soon after Rev. David Thompson joined the mission, and the study of the language and the rough preliminary translation of the Scriptures was pushed forward with great energy and success, and opportunities for other work began to appear. Dr. Thompson was asked to instruct a company of young Japanese in mathematics and chemistry, and was able to connect with this instruction lessons in Christian doctrines and duties. These young men were soon called away to fill posts in the army, but most of them took with them copies of the Bible in English and Chinese. Though not allowed to open public schools, they were invited to teach in the government schools, and in these and other ways laid the foundation on which they and others might afterwards build. The first edition of Dr. Hepburn's Japanese and English dictionary was published in 1867. Reinforcements joined the mission in 1868, and in 1869 the first converts were baptized. In 1870 the translation of the four Gospels was completed. Up to January, 1872, there had been no regular stated preaching of the gospel to a native audience. At that time, when all the missionaries at Yokohama and the English-speaking residents of all denominations united in the observance of the week of prayer, some Japanese students connected with the private classes taught by the missionaries also were present. For their benefit the Scripture of the day—the Book of Acts was read in course day by day—was extemporaneously translated. The meetings grew in interest, and were continued until the end of February. After a week or two the Japanese were on their knees entreating God that he would give His Spirit to Japan as to the early church and to the people around the apostles. These prayers were characterized by intense earnestness. Captains of men-of-war, English and American, who were present said: "The prayers of these Japanese take the heart out of us." The missionary in charge often feared he would faint away, so intense was the feeling. Such was the first Japanese prayer-meeting, and soon after a church consisting of eleven members was organized by the Rev. S. R. Brown, a missionary of the Reformed Church, who had labored side by side with the Presbyterian missionaries; they now rejoiced in the fruits of their common toil, as the church increased in numbers. From this time rapid progress was made. The year (1872) was also marked by the entrance of the woman's societies into this field. For account of their work see articles on Woman's Societies. In 1874 two churches were organized in Tokyo and Yokohama, which increased in numbers and manifested a readiness to engage in every Christian work. Through their influence many other churches were formed in other cities and towns. In 1877 the "United Church of Japan" was formed, which has established a theological seminary in which many Japanese have been trained for the ministry, and has, through its strong missionary spirit, extended the knowledge of Christianity. In all, 61 churches (with a membership of nearly 10,000) have been organized, of which 22 are entirely self-supporting. The total number of pupils in the schools is 2,260.

MISSION IN KOREA (see also article on Korea).—This mission was established in 1884 at Seoul, the capital. The work has prospered from the first; the church already has a membership of over seventy. Eight young men are under theological instruction; four native helpers are employed at out-stations, and four native teachers are under the direction of the mission, which has now a force of 4 ordained missionaries (three of them married), and 1 unmarried lady missionary teacher. The boys' boarding-school has an attendance of 36. Steps have been taken toward opening a new station at Fusan.

Missions to the Chinese and Japanese in the United States are carried on in San Francisco (1852), Oakland (1877), and Los Angeles, California; in Portland, Oregon; and New York City. Work for the Chinese is also carried on by volunteer workers in nearly all the principal cities of the Atlantic coast.

The Board has for many years extended some aid to the Protestant churches of the Presbyterian faith and order in Continental Europe, and within the past year action has been taken to render this aid more systematic and efficient.

## Presbyterian Church in the United States (South), Foreign Mission Committee. Headquarters, Nashville, Tennessee, U. S. A.

The history of the missionary work of the Presbyterian Church of the southern portion of the United States runs parallel with that of the northern portion up to the year 1861. At that time, in consequence of the civil war, the Synods of the Southern States united in the formation of a separate body, known as the General Assembly of the "Presbyterian Church in the Confederate States of America," which title, subsequent to the war, was changed to the "Presbyterian Church in the United States."

Immediately on the organization of the Southern Assembly, at Augusta, Ga., in December, 1861, a committee was chosen to conduct the work of foreign missions, with the Rev. J. Leighton Wilson, D.D., as Secretary, and the Rev. Jas. Woodrow, D.D., Treasurer. Dr. Wilson had labored nearly twenty years as a missionary in Africa, but for some time previous to the outbreak of the war had been connected with the Foreign Mission Office of the Presbyterian Church in New York. Dr. Woodrow was a Professor in the theological seminary at Columbia, South Carolina. The Committee was located at Columbia, with the Rev. Jas. H. Thornwell, D.D., as Chairman. Among other distinguished members of that committee were the Rev. Geo. Howe, D.D., and the Rev. Jno. B. Adger, D.D., also Professors, as was Dr. Thornwell, in the theological seminary. The first efforts of the committee were directed to the Choctaws, the Chickasaws, and other tribes of the Indian Territory. During the continuance of the war more than a dozen faithful laborers were sustained in this field; the more prominent of these being the well-known missionaries Drs. Kingsbury and Byington. A number of Presbyterian missionaries, natives of the Southern States, were laboring in foreign lands, and invitations were extended to these, who had originally been sent out by the Presbyterian Board in New York, to become the representatives of the Southern Church in their respective fields. Some of these labored in Africa, others in China, Japan, and Siam. As the outcome of these negotiations, the Rev. Elias B. Inslee of Hangchow, China, entered into a correspondence with the committee, which resulted in the establishment of its first mission in foreign lands. This, however, was not until the close of the war. Mr. Inslee, who was a member of the Synod of Mississippi, returned to the United States in 1866, was formally appointed, and sailed for his field in China in June, 1867.

In August of the same year the committee appointed Miss Christine Ronzone, a missionary under its care, to Italy, of which country she was a native. She labored first in the city of Naples, but subsequently removed to Milan, where she has ever since conducted a very interesting work. At the meeting of the General Assembly that year the committee was directed to publish a monthly magazine in the interest of the work. The first number of this periodical, "The Missionary," was issued from Columbia, South Carolina, in January, 1868. In the summer of that year the Rev. G. Nash Morton was sent to Brazil with a view to the establishment of a mission; and in September the Rev. Messrs. M. H. Houston, J. L. Stuart, and Benjamin Helm joined the mission in China.

Missions were established in Mexico and Greece in 1874, in Japan in 1875, and in the Congo Free State in 1890. In 1889 the Indian Mission was transferred to the Home Mission Committee. The total number of missionaries now (1891) under the care of the committee is 82; the number of stations established, 18; out-stations, 98; the number of communicants, 2,072; pupils in day-schools, 845; Sabbath-schools, 1,207; number of native ministers, 19; contributions from the native churches, $4,317. The contributions of the home churches in the support of this work have steadily increased from $15,000 in 1862, to $107,000 in 1890.

*Administration.*—The office of the Executive Committee was first established in Columbia, S. C., in 1862. In 1875 it was removed to Baltimore, Md., for increased commercial and financial facilities. In 1889 it was removed to its present location, Nashville, Tenn. The first Secretary was the Rev. J. Leighton Wilson, D.D., who remained in office until his death, in July, 1886. In 1872 the Rev. Richard McIlwaine, D.D., became co-ordinate Secretary, and also succeeded Professor Woodrow as treasurer, the latter having held that office from the establishment of the Committee in 1862. In 1882 Dr. Wilson became sole Secretary, and Dr. McIlwaine (who became President of Hampden Sidney College at that time), was succeeded as treasurer by Mr. L. C. Inglis. In 1884 the Rev. M. H. Houston, D.D., who had for many years been connected with the China Mission, was elected Assistant Secretary. He became full Secretary in 1887, after the death of Dr. Wilson. In 1888 the Rev. D. C. Rankin was elected as Assistant Secretary, to which office that of the retiring Treasurer, Mr. Inglis, was added on the removal of the office to Nashville in 1889.

*Missionary Societies.*—Children's Missionary Societies were first suggested by the Assembly in 1873. Contributions from missionary societies were first reported in 1874, the sum at that time being $2,100. In the annual report of the committee for that year these missionary societies were specially referred to, and again in 1875, at which time 58 societies were mentioned as in existence, contributing that year, $4,500. In 1890 there were 440 Ladies' Missionary Societies, 180 Children's Missionary Societies, and 15 Men's Societies, making 635 missionary societies in all. The total contributions from these societies in 1889 amounted to $27,855. There are also four Presbyterial Unions, including, for more effective work, all the Ladies' Missionary Societies in a given Presbytery. These Unions exist in the Presbyteries of East Hanover, Wilmington, Lafayette, and West Lexington.

*Missions.*—INDIAN MISSION. (See article Indians, American.)

CHINA MISSION.—This mission, as has already been stated, was organized in 1867. It includes 4 stations in the cities of Hangchow, Soochow, Chinkiang, and Tsing-Kiang-pu, and 7 out-stations.

Hangchow.—The work at Hangchow, conducted by 10 foreign workers, assisted by native helpers, includes preaching and teaching in the city and in the three out-stations, with much itinerant work among neighboring villages and in the country districts. An important feature of the Hangchow work from its inception, more than twenty years ago, has been the excellent school for girls, which now has about 50 boarding pupils. Recently great interest has been awakened in the Linwu district, some thirty miles northwest of Hangchow; and in many other portions of this field there are tokens of rich harvest in store for the laborer. Medical work is a very valuable aid here, as everywhere in China. The church in the Mission Compound has a membership of 60, and there are nearly one hundred members in the out-stations.

Soochow.—At this station, opened in 1872, there are 7 foreign missionaries. An important adjunct of the work here has been "The Woman's Home," under the care of Miss A. C. Safford, who died in August last. Regular preaching services are held in the street chapels of the city, and much itinerant work is done along the Grand Canal and in neighboring villages. The missionaries at Soochow have also done valuable work at Wuseih, a city thirty miles north of Hangchow, on the Canal. In Soochow Miss Safford had done a valuable work as an author and a translator of books into Chinese. Her death was a heavy loss to the mission. There are 3 day-schools attended by 60 pupils. The church is yet small, numbering only 6 communicants.

Chinkiang.—This city is a treaty port on the river Yangtsz, where it is crossed by the Grand Canal, about one hundred miles north of Soochow. The fruits here are yet small, this station having only been opened in 1883, but much evangelistic work has been done in the street chapels, among the boatmen who frequent this large commercial city; and in the towns and villages that line the Grand Canal.

Tsing-kiang-pu.—This station was opened in 1887, and its field extends through the northern part of the province of Kiangsu and into the southern portion of Shantung. It includes the district formerly occupied by the English Baptists. As a result of their seed-sowing, many inquirers and native Christians are found throughout this section by the missionaries. At Tsing-kiang-pu resides the only medical missionary of the Southern Committee, Dr. Edgar Woods. His services have been invaluable in the work of the mission.

ITALIAN MISSION.—This mission is prosecuted through the boarding and day school conducted by Miss Christine Ronzone, and assisted by Madame Rivoir. Miss Ronzone began her work in the city of Naples in 1867. In 1869 her school was transferred to Brodighiera, near Genoa, and in 1871 to Milan, where it has remained to the present time. All the pupils in the school, a number of whom are Roman Catholics, study the Bible and attend the Sabbath-school of the Waldensian church. This modest mission has done an excellent work, the fruits of which are found in many portions of Southern Italy and Switzerland.

BRAZIL MISSIONS.—On account of the great distances in Brazil, the work of the Southern Presbyterian Church is conducted there through three distinct missions, viz., those of Southern, Northern, and Interior Brazil.

*Southern Brazil Mission.*—One station, Campinas, with 12 flourishing out-stations. Campinas is a city of 25,000 inhabitants, and the mission was opened here in 1869. From the first an important feature of the Campinas work has been the International College, which now has an attendance of about 140 pupils, many of them boarding pupils. Besides the Campinas church, there are organized churches at Jundiahy, Itatiba, Branganca, and other places. This is a fine and encouraging field, and the work makes steady progress. The condition of the churches is good, and the members generally live in a manner that would make them examples to many professing Christians at home. From this important station as a centre the gospel has been preached and the Scriptures put in circulation over a large extent of country. Members of the mission have assumed the task of putting into circulation, either by translation or original composition, at least one book or treatise annually for the support and defence of the gospel in South America. The mission publishes "Pulpito Evangelico," a monthly magazine, which is doing great good. Recently a new printing-press has been given to the mission for this work.

*Northern Brazil Mission.*—This mission includes three separate stations: Pernambuco, Ceara, and Maranhao.

Pernambuco.—This station was opened in 1873, and now has a church with 60 members and 35 baptized children. An important part of the work of Dr. Smith, one of the missionaries at this station, has been the training of native ministers, a number of whom are now laboring most acceptably in the out-stations of this mission. Not only in Pernambuco, which is a city of 140,000 inhabitants, but in many of the surrounding towns, such as Goyanna, Parahyba, and Pao de Assucar, the work is full of encouragement. In these smaller towns there are more than 100 communicants who lead exemplary Christian lives. They also contribute liberally of their substance for the support of the gospel.

Ceara.—This station was opened in 1882. Ceara, which is the capital of the state of Ceara, has a population of 40,000 inhabitants. A church building has been commenced in the city, where the membership is about 50, with some 40 baptized children. There are also four other preaching places in this field, at one of which (Mossoro) there are 23 communicants. At this station there are six foreign missionaries, two of whom (ladies) have recently opened a day-school with encouraging prospects.

Maranhao.—This station was opened in 1885, and has proved to be one of the most inviting in Brazil. There are four foreign missionaries and a good church-building in the city of Maranhao, and a membership of about 40. Dr. Butler, in addition to his evangelistic labors, has enhanced his usefulness by his medical skill. An interesting work has been done in Alcantara, a town on the opposite side of the bay from Maranhao. Good use has been made of the press, and articles published weekly in the principal papers of Maranhao have added materially to the usefulness of the missionary.

*Interior Brazil Mission.*—This mission was opened in 1887, its only station being the town of Bagagem, in the State of Minas-Geraes. This place is 360 miles north of Campinas. From it as a centre the missionaries have made repeated and extended tours, especially up the San Francisco River and into the State of Goyaz. In these journeys thousands of miles have been travelled. The missionaries have preached in towns and communities never before visited by a missionary, and large numbers of copies of the Scriptures have been circulated. Everywhere the missionaries have been received most cordially by the people. Their preaching has been largely attended, and many have united with the Protestant church during these evangelistic tours. In no part of Brazil is the field so white to the harvest. One of the most interesting features in the work of interior Brazil has been the publication of "O Evangelisto," a semi-monthly paper edited by the Rev. Jno. Boyle. On these uplands of interior Brazil an old French atheist had owned and published a little paper called "The Echo of the Backwoods," in the prosecution of which work he had trained as his printers two orphan boys. In the course of time Mr. Boyle purchased the old editor's press, and with the aid of the two youthful printers sent forth the first numbers of "O Evangelisto." The paper at once met with such a cordial reception, that from time to time it was enlarged. It now has an extensive circulation in several of the states, and is doing great good. The Executive Committee of Foreign Missions has recently made an appropriation for the purchase of a new press for Mr. Boyle, and will hereafter make annual appropriations for its running expenses.

The Synod of Brazil.—The progress of Protestant missions in Brazil had been so encouraging, that in 1889 the Synod of Brazil was organized, composed of the four Presbyteries of Rio, São Paulo, Campinas and Western Minas, and Pernambuco. This Synod has no ecclesiastical connection outside of Brazil, and includes the churches of both the Northern and Southern Presbyterian missions.

In connection with work in South America, it should be mentioned that in 1869 the Southern church established a mission in the United States of Colombia, with stations at Baranquilla and Socorro. The missionaries at these stations were the Rev. H. B. Pratt and wife, the Rev. J. G. Hall and wife, and Mr. A. H. Irwin. This mission was discontinued in 1878, and Mr. and Mrs. Hall were transferred to the Mexico Mission.

MEXICO MISSION.—This mission was undertaken in 1874, and has proved one of the most prosperous and interesting under the care of the Southern church. This work is carried on in the States of Nuevo Leon and Tamaulipas, with Brownsville, Matamoras, and Linares as bases for evangelistic work. There are now 7 organized churches in this field, which have been constituted a Presbytery, bearing the name of Tamaulipas. The work in Brownsville and Matamoras has been both educational and evangelistic. In both places there are good schools under the care of lady missionaries. All the churches throughout the Presbytery are now supplied by competent native pastors. The foreign missionaries have chiefly the general direction of the work. This involves extended tours among the ranches throughout the Sierra Madre Mountains. The opening of new railroads in these states has added to the encouraging features of this work. One of these roads, branching off from the Mexican National at Monterey, runs in the direction of Tampico, passing through the towns of Montemorelos, Linares, and Victoria, in all of which towns there are growing churches. The work at Linares has been especially full of encouragement and promise. The native ministry of this mission forms a fine body of faithful men, full of promise for the church in this portion of Mexico. The work has not been prosecuted without its difficulties, and at times the missionaries and their assistants, as well as the church-members, have suffered persecution.

CUBA MISSION.—In response to an earnest appeal from Protestant Christians in Havana, the Executive Committee sent Mr. Graybill of the Mexico Mission to Cuba in the summer of 1890. This visit resulted in the organization of two Presbyterian churches, one in Havana and one in Santa Clara, a town in the interior of the island. Mr. Graybill also licensed and ordained to the work of the gospel ministry Sr. Earisto Collazo of Havana. So full of encouragement is this work, that again in the early part of the present year (1891) the committee sent Mr. Hall to visit these young churches. The result of this visit is not yet known.

GREEK MISSION.—The headquarters of this mission, which was begun in 1874, are at Salonica in Macedonia. The annual report for 1890 says: "The work among the Greeks, which had languished for forty years, began about ten years ago to show some symptoms of life, and within the last five years has advanced more than in forty-five years before. It now shows steady progress: some in Greece, more in Macedonia, more still on the western coast of Asia Minor, and a great deal on the Black Sea. The evidences of this change in the hopefulness of the Greek work are varied. Although so few in numbers and although so recently organized, the Greeks already lead all other natives in the matters of self-support and self-government. The special circumstances which are most encouraging to the thoughtful observer are such as the following: The general reading of the New Testament in the schools and the churches, as well as among the people generally; the increase in the number and quantity of preachers in the old church, as well as the growing dissatisfaction with the services and practices of the ignorant priest; a disposition to recognize evangelicals as not only not traitors, but as patriotic Greeks; the almost hearty welcome given by leaders of influence to missionaries, where a few years ago they were bitterly opposed. There is now an opportunity in Macedonia and Epirus and Asia Minor such as never existed there before. The work there can only be done by Americans, who are not mixed up with politics abroad or embarrassed by state establishments at home. The republican principles of our church are peculiarly acceptable to the infant liberties of Europe. In 1885, when the work in the Greek field was redistributed, there were two church-members in Salonica; in 1887 a church was organized with 10 members. There are now more than 25 regular members, besides 10 who commune with us regularly. There are a Bible depot and 3 colporteurs who help disseminate the truth. We are urged to open schools, and have no difficulty in obtaining houses, which was once almost impossible. Mr. Sampson is a member of the Literary Club, composed entirely of Greeks. in this city (Salonica), and Mrs. Sampson of the Ladies' Society for the Poor,—both by election. Monthly meetings of Christian workers, organized in 1889, have succeeded admirably, and done more than anything else to awaken and sustain an interest in the work generally. The members of the church all attend prayer-meeting regularly, and take active part in praying and speaking. They all contribute with commendable liberality to the church, and all have family worship. They have taken upon themselves the whole responsibility of the Sabbath-school, leaving the evangelist free for other work in the city and out of it."

JAPAN MISSION. Stations, Kochi, Nagoya, Tokushima, Okazaki.—This mission was established near the end of the year 1885, by Messrs. Grinnan and McAlpine. The Presbyterian missions of Europe and America act jointly in a council known as "The Council of United Missions." By the advice of this council the new missionaries settled at Kochi, an important city on the island of Shikoku.

Kochi.—This city is in the province of Tosa, one of the leading provinces of the empire, and the one which through her liberty-loving citizens has played an important part in the marvellous changes that have taken place in Japan in the last twenty years. Leading statesmen, such as Count Itagaki, warmly welcomed the new missionaries and patronized their schools. With such auspicious surroundings this mission (named the "McPheeters Mission" in memory of the Rev. Dr. S. B. McPheeters) was opened, and its success has surpassed even the most sanguine hopes of its friends. In January, 1886, active work was begun in Kochi, where a small body of native Christians already existed. In one year this band was more than doubled, and the membership of this vigorous young church has now grown to about 600. The congregation has built, without foreign aid, a commodious house of worship, capable of seating 700 persons, and supports its own native pastor. From Kochi as a centre the missionaries visit some twenty places in the surrounding country, where they preach the gospel to large and attentive audiences. In most of these out-stations there is now preaching once a month. When there is no evangelist present, the Christians gather for Bible-study on the Sabbath. At Susaki, the second city of the province, and at Aki, on the road from Kochi to Tokushima, the work is specially encouraging, and strong churches are being gathered.

Nagoya.—This is a large city of 250,000 inhabitants. It is situated on the Bay of Owari, on the southeastern coast of the island of Nippon. This important field having been transferred to the Presbyterians by the Reformed (Dutch) Board in the autumn of 1887, Mr. McAlpine at once began work there. The plain of Nagoya teems with a vast population, and is studded with numerous villages and towns yet unreached by Christian influences. The stringency maintained by Japanese officials in reference to passports has prevented the missionaries from laboring in this extensive field as effectively as they could wish.

Nevertheless, at Midzuno, seven miles from Nagoya, a church with 50 members was organized in October, 1889. In the city of Nagoya itself the obstacles to progress have been many, since this city is a great Buddhist stronghold. Nevertheless, after three years of faithful and patient seed-sowing, the missionaries are beginning to reap the harvest. Here also, as in most other Japanese missions, successful school work is done by members of the mission.

Tokushima.—This city of 60,000 inhabitants is the largest and most important on the island of Shikoku. The gospel had never been preached to these thousands prior to the establishment of this station by Messrs. Brown and Cumming in 1889. A church has been organized with encouraging prospects. (See Tokushima.)

Okazaki.—In the beginning of 1890 Mr. Fulton of the Nagoya station opened a new station at Okazaki, a city of 25,000 inhabitants, situated in the great plain of Nagoya, and some 30 miles distant from that city. He reports the work here as full of promise.

AFRICA MISSION. — For many years the Southern Presbyterian Church had cherished a desire to plant a mission in Africa. During the latter part of his life, the Rev. Dr. J. Leighton Wilson, the father of the mission work of his church, and who had himself labored nearly twenty years in Africa, earnestly laid this matter before the General Assembly; but various obstacles prevented the accomplishment of his heart's desire until he had passed to his rest. In the mind of the Southern Church there was an abiding conviction that because of the large Negro population within her own bounds she was specially called of Providence to undertake this work. Accordingly, at the meeting of the General Assembly in 1889, the Executive Committee of Foreign Missions was directed to take steps looking to the opening of the long-contemplated mission in the "Dark Continent." Early in 1890 the Rev. Samuel N. Lapsley (white), of the Synod of Alabama, and the Rev. W. H. Sheppard (colored), of Atlanta, Ga., were commissioned and sent forth with instructions to found a new mission in the Congo Free State. The appointment of Mr. Sheppard (who has already proved to be a most valuable worker) was of special interest, since he was the first fruits of a long-cherished desire on the part of many in the Southern Church to see some of this race bearing the gospel to the land of their forefathers. He was also the first-fruits, in this direction, of the Theological Seminary in Tuscaloosa, Alabama, which had been established some years before by the Southern Presbyterian Church exclusively for the purpose of training a colored ministry. Proceeding first to England, and then to Brussels in Belgium, they received every encouragement and assistance in preparation for their work. King Leopold himself granted Mr. Lapsley a personal interview, in which he expressed the deepest interest in his mission. They have gone as pioneers, with instructions that their station be sufficiently separated from other missions to give it the character of a thoroughly independent work. They were instructed to seek a locality as healthy as possible, on some highlands removed from the coast, and yet not too distant from the bases of supplies. The lives of these young missionaries have been graciously preserved thus far, and they have done a successful work in prospecting on the Upper Congo and its large tributary, the Kassai. At last accounts they had not yet found a suitable location for their mission. They have been most kindly received by the English and American missionaries already laboring on the Congo. The Executive Committee contemplates sending a considerable reinforcement to this mission during the year 1891.

**Presidency** (in British India), one of the chief administrative divisions of British India, of which there are three: Bengal, Bombay, and Madras. In the two latter the government is conducted by a governor, appointed by the crown, who is assisted by an executive council in matters of administration, and by a legislative council in making laws and regulations. The local government, thus constituted, is under the general supervision of the governor-general and viceroy of India. The Bengal presidency, much the largest of the three, has no governor and executive council, but is subdivided into several provinces, each with a lieutenant-governor or chief commissioner at its head, who is appointed, not by the crown, but by the governor-general of India. See under the titles Bengal Presidency, Bombay Presidency, and Madras Presidency.

**Pretoria**, a town in Central Transvaal, South Africa, northwest of Wakkerstroom. Mission station of the Berlin Evangelical Missionary Society (1866); 1 missionary, 11 native helpers, 3 out-stations, 665 church-members. S. P. G., 1 missionary. Wesleyan Methodist Missionary Society; 4 missionaries, 2 native helpers, 3 chapels (1 English), 120 native church-members, 3 schools, 97 scholars.

**Primitive Methodist Missionary Society.** Headquarters, Primitive Methodist Book Room, Sutton Street, Commercial Road, George's-in-the-East, London. — The Primitive Methodists are a body which arose in England in 1810. Finding themselves gaining strength, they organized in 1843-44 a foreign missionary society, adopting Canada, New Zealand, and Australia as their fields of labor. Since that time they have strengthened their mission in New Zealand and Australia, and their work has met with success; but some years after it was started they transferred their Canadian stations to the Methodist Church of the Dominion, which has since carried on the work. These home and colonial missions were the only ones carried on by this Society until 1869. In that year a vessel named the "Elgiva," trading between Liverpool and the west coast of Africa, touched at Fernando Po, a Spanish colony in the Gulf of Guinea. The captain and carpenter of this ship were good men, members of the Primitive Methodist Church of Liverpool, and during their short stay at the island, Mr. Hands, the carpenter, called together as many people as he could, and held a prayer-meeting with them. He found a few converts who had joined the English Baptist Church, before the Spanish authorities had expelled Mr. Saker, the missionary, from the island, and these people welcomed Mr. Hands most eagerly, and begged him to stay and teach them, since a change in the Spanish law now made this possible. He could not do this, of course, but promised to try and send them a missionary

when he should have returned home. Upon his having submitted the appeal of these people to the Missionary Committee of the Primitive Methodist Connexion, that body, after careful consideration, granted the request, and in 1870 sent two missionaries, Revs. R. W. Burnett and H. Roe, with their wives, to open a station at Santa Isabel, the chief town of the island. They met with a hearty welcome, and at once began work. In 1871 Rev. D. T. Maylott joined them, and an attempt was made to open a new station along the west coast. The plan met with some difficulties, but in 1873 George's (or San Carlos) Bay was occupied.

Associated with Mr. Maylott in this mission was the Rev. W. N. Barleycorn, one of the first converts of Santa Isabel, and his work among the Bubis was very successful, the first convert of the west mission being baptized in 1874.

The work at Santa Isabel had grown so much that several new missionaries had been sent out and a station had been opened at Banni on the northeast coast of that island, and thither in 1884 Mr. Barleycorn was removed, and remained for a short time; but difficulties with the Spanish authorities made his return to George's Bay necessary. No new stations have recently been occupied, but a steam-launch has been started, which runs between Fernando Po and the mainland, and along the coast of the island, touching at various points, and carrying, besides the passengers, all the mail and freight of the mission and of the government officials. At present there are in the mission 3 foreign missionaries, 1 native missionary, 3 other helpers, 3 chapels, 120 communicants, 3 schools, 13 teachers, 138 scholars. These missions have been steadily growing, although the hostility of the Roman Catholic priests and trouble with the civil authorities have often caused serious annoyance. But of late a better understanding with Spain has been established, and arrangements for increased educational advantages have been made, and the work bids fair to increase both in extent and usefulness.

SOUTH AFRICA.—In 1869 an appeal for help came to the Missionary Committee from Aliwal, North, a town and district in Cape Colony, bordering on the Orange Free State. The committee decided to send a missionary to that locality, and in 1870 Rev. H. Buckenham sailed for Port Elizabeth, Cape Colony, and travelled overland to Aliwal. Here he settled, at first conducting his services in a Dutch church which had been placed at his disposal; but in 1871 he opened a Sunday-school in a room fitted up for that purpose, and later commenced first an evening and then a day school for native pupils. Before long a church and parsonage were built, and Mr. Buckenham remained until 1875, when the Rev. John Smith succeeded him. In 1883 Rev. John Watson was sent out, but both he and Mr. Smith returned to England, and the present missionary, Rev. G. E. Butts, took charge of the work at Aliwal and its branch station, Jamestown. A native pastor, the Rev. John Msikinya, a graduate of the Lovedale Institution (see Lovedale), is associated with the missionary in the work at Aliwal, and his labors are proving most successful. A new training-school for native youths has been opened, which it is the purpose of the mission to make, as far as possible, self-sustaining.

Zambezi Mission.—It had long been a wish of the Missionary Committee to send a missionary party to the Upper Zambesi, but owing to the expense of pioneer work in such a difficult region, they had not been able to collect funds sufficient for the purpose.

In April, 1889, however, the Rev. H. Buckenham (formerly missionary at Aliwal, North) and Mrs. Buckenham, with Rev. A. Baldwin and Mr. J. Ward, sailed for Africa, and a few months later had gone from Cape Town to Aliwal, where they at once began to make preparations for their journey to their new field. Probably several of the native preachers at Aliwal will accompany them, and before the close of 1890 a new mission of the connexion will be begun at some station on the Zambezi.

**Princestown,** a town of South Central Trinidad, almost due east of San Fernando, and southeast of Concord. Mission station of the Presbyterian Church in Canada; 2 missionaries, 1 female missionary, 63 communicants, 138 school-children.

**Probbolingo,** a town in Central Java, southeast of Cheribon and southwest of Sumarang. Mission station of the Christian Reformed Missionary Society (of Holland), 1867; 690 church-members.

**Prome,** a city in the district of Pegu, Burma, India, on the Irrawaddy, 166 miles north-northwest of Rangoon. Climate temperate, healthy. Population, 28,000 Buddhists. Language, Burmese. Mission station of the American Baptist Missionary Union (1854); 1 missionary and wife, 1 other lady, 16 native helpers, 6 out-stations, 4 churches, 243 church-members, 3 schools, 300 scholars.

**Protestant Episcopal Church in the United States, Domestic and Foreign Missionary Society.** Headquarters, 21–26 Bible House, New York City.—The American Protestant Episcopal Church is indebted for its existence, under God, to the Church of England. Being a mission itself, generations passed before it felt strong enough to found missions on a large scale either within or without its own borders; its advancement being hindered by the expense and trouble of sending men to England to be ordained, and the prejudices following the Revolutionary war. However, in the beginning of this century interest in missionary work became manifest in the American Church, one of the prime movers in the cause being Bishop Griswold, who in correspondence with the Secretary of the Church Missionary Society suggested that an American clergyman be sent out by that Society into the foreign field. The English Society, however (1817), urged the formation of an American Board, and offered pecuniary aid. This advice was acted upon, and the Domestic and Foreign Missionary Society was instituted in 1820, the Rev. J. R. Andros being the first of the American clergy to offer himself for the foreign field.

Although organized in 1820 as a Society it was not until 1835 that it assumed its present character, and became but another name for the Church herself. Previous to that time the administration of the Society's work had been committed to a Board of Directors, who through its Executive Committee had made several attempts to found missions in heathen lands, but had only succeeded so far as to appoint a lay

teacher in Africa and two clergymen to China. They had, however, sent two clergymen to Greece in 1830, to labor among the nominal Christians in that country. In 1835 a change was made in the organization of the Society, which provided that the Society should be considered as "comprehending all persons who are members of this church." This action placing general mission work immediately under the direction of the church, was hailed with enthusiasm, the newly awakened interest being particularly manifested in the marked increase in the contributions.

Such were the beginnings of the Foreign Missions of the Protestant Episcopal Church of America. The first missionaries of the church were the Rev. J. J. Robertson and the Rev. J. H. Hill, and their wives, who were sent to Greece in 1830; but upon the reorganization of the Society in 1835 the work immediately began to assume greater proportions, and now is carried on in five foreign lands, where the work increases yearly in magnitude and importance, while the home interest is continually manifested in the generous contributions and general missionary enthusiasm.

*Constitution and Organization.*— The Board of Missions, which meets triennially, consists of all the bishops, and the members for the time being of the House of Deputies to the General Convention, the delegates from the Missionary jurisdictions, the Board of Managers, and the Treasurers of the Domestic and Foreign Committees. The bishops and the treasurers are members of the Board of Managers by virtue of their respective offices. There are, besides, fifteen clergymen and fifteen laymen elected by the Board of Missions. Of these, seven clergymen and eight laymen serve as the Committee for Foreign Missions.

*Development of Foreign Work.*— The first field chosen by the Society immediately on its organization was Africa, the field being one of great promise, and opportunities being offered for labor, due to the efforts of the American Colonization Society. The first missionary was appointed in 1822, but did not go; a second, appointed in 1828, died after his passage was engaged; and it was not until 1830 that work was actually begun there, in Monrovia, where the American Colonization Society had founded a colony of free colored people.

In 1830 Greece was chosen as a field for the work of the Society, since it was a nominally Christian country, but one where general Christian intelligence and education were sorely needed. Athens was decided upon as the most favorable point for location, for by its central position in regard to the whole Greek population, its facilities for communication with them, and its healthy climate, it promised to be an eligible missionary station.

The cause of missions in China, which under the guidance of the Church has assumed such important proportions, was indebted for its initial impulse to the devoted zeal of the Rev. Augustus Foster Lyde, who, though prevented by his early death from carrying into effect the one great longing of his life, to bear the gospel to the Chinese, inspired others with the enthusiasm which gave rise to the Chinese mission. In 1834 the Society voted to make China a field for missionary labor, and in 1835 Rev. F. R. Hanson and the Rev. H. R. Lockwood were accepted as laborers for that field.

The expedition of Commodore Perry in 1852, followed by the treaty between the United States and Japan in 1854, and the opening of the ports of Hakodati and Simoda, opened Japan to the introduction of Christianity Through the firmness of the United States consul-general, Townsend Harris, permission to teach Christian doctrine and hold Christian service was secured, and in 1858 the first Christian worship in Japan for nearly two and a half centuries was held at Consul Harris's house. In 1859 Rev. Messrs. C. M. Williams and J. Liggins, the first Protestant missionaries to Japan, were sent there by the Society of the Protestant Episcopal Church of America.

The work in Haiti was due to the interest and labor of the Right Rev. James Theo. Holly, a bishop of the church, of African descent. While in deacon's orders he obtained permission of the Foreign Committee to examine the field in Haiti, and having been ordained a priest, in 1861 sailed with a missionary colony for Port-au-Prince. In 1865 the mission was transferred to the Society of the Protestant Episcopal Church, and became one of their fields of active labor.

CHINA.—The China Mission dates from the landing at Canton of the Rev. Messrs. Hanson and Lockwood in 1835. They proceeded, however, to Java, to labor there, at Batavia, among the Chinese. The third missionary, the Rev. W. J. Boone, M.D., reached Batavia in 1837. In February, 1840, he really began work on Chinese soil, by the opening of a station at Amoy. Four years later he was consecrated as the first bishop of the Anglican communion in China. In 1845 the mission moved from Amoy to Shanghai, and in 1846 Mr. Kong Chai Wong, afterward a clergyman, was baptized, the first convert, on Easter Day. Since his baptism the work has spread marvellously, gradually gaining ground along the coast and in the interior. In 1860 the plan of opening the work in the interior was carried into effect, and two missionaries and their wives, after some difficulty, succeeded in fairly establishing a station at Chefoo. In 1868 another station was opened in Wuchang, capital of the province of Hupeh, in the very heart of the empire, from which point a population of 1,200,000 could be reached. The work now carried on in thirty-one stations is educational, evangelistic, and medical, and is scattered over the northern and central part of the vast empire.

JAPAN.—This mission was established in 1859 by the Rev. Messrs. C. M. Williams and J. Liggins, who were the first Protestant missionaries to settle in the empire. The first baptism was reported in 1866. The work for the first fifteen years of the mission was little more than learning the language, so great was the opposition experienced from the government and the bitter feeling on the part of the people. But in 1872 occurred the removal of the edicts against the Christians, and the release from imprisonment and the return from banishment of thousands of native Christians; and from this time the work has been carried on without danger or interruption. Until 1874 the Japan Mission was under the jurisdiction of the Bishop of China, but in that year, owing to the increased extent of both fields, it was decided to separate them into two dioceses. Rev. C. M. Williams, then Bishop of China, was appointed Bishop of Japan, and a new bishop set over China. The

work is carried on in Tokyo and Osaka, and the towns in the vicinity of each. Japan is a promising field, and there is great need of workers, the principal difficulty the mission has had to contend with being the lack of a sufficient staff of capable missionaries.

HAITI.—The Board's connection with Haiti dates from 1865, when the financial responsibility for the work at Port-au-Prince, carried on by Rev. J. Theodore Holly, was transferred by the American Church Missionary Society. It was conducted from that time until 1874 as a mission, when the church in Haiti was recognized under certain conditions by the General Convention, and Dr. Holly consecrated as its first bishop. The work has been constantly hindered by fire, war, pestilence, and famine; yet, considering the very limited resources at any time at the command of the bishop, the work has been exceedingly successful. By action of the House of Bishops taken in 1885, the church in Haiti was reorganized as an independent church, but nevertheless regular assistance is given by the Society to it as a church in communion with the Protestant Episcopal Church.

AFRICA.—The mission work of this church in Africa is confined to the Republic of Liberia. Mr. and Mrs. J. M. Thompson (colored), residing at Monrovia, were the first persons employed by the Society. They were appointed as missionary teachers in 1835, and in 1836 Rev. Thomas S. Savage, M.D., the first foreign missionary, landed at Cape Palmas. During the early years of the mission frequent difficulties occurred between the colonists and the native "bushmen," and the missionaries and mission property were often in danger. In 1843 troubles arose which compelled the missionaries at Cape Palmas to abandon the town and take refuge on a U. S. ship, and the school at Cavalla, an out-station, had to be closed. The next year found the work going on quietly, but in 1845 the disturbances again threatened the mission; still in spite of the political troubles there were substantial proofs of the progress of the mission. In 1849 the cornerstone was laid of the first Episcopal church edifice of Liberia, and in 1850 Rev. John Payne was appointed Missionary Bishop of Cape Palmas and the parts adjacent. The work gradually extended its borders from this time, with the exception of the years of financial trouble at home during the civil war, when, owing to the reduced support, the mission was obliged to discontinue work at some of the stations and curtail it at others. The principal native tribes with whom the missionaries come in contact are the Grebos in the northern, the Bassas in the central, and the Veys in the southern section of the country. The work is now carried on in Cape Mount, Monrovia, St. Paul's River, Bassa, Sinoe, Cape Palmas, and Cavalla.

GREECE.—The work in Greece was begun at Athens in 1830 by the Rev. J. J. Robertson and the Rev. J. H. Hill and their wives. The principle on which the mission was established was that of not attempting to make proselytes, or to withdraw the people from their own church, but simply to spread scriptural truth among them in the expectation that this would lead eventually to the reformation of the church by the Greeks themselves. The work was begun by establishing schools, and a printing-press set up at Athens, which last, how ever, had to be given up on account of the expense. In 1837 a station was begun on the island of Crete, which had to be given up at the end of a few years. In 1839 the Rev. Dr. Robertson removed to Constantinople with a view to working specially among the Greeks, but the object of the mission was afterward extended to the other Eastern churches. The mission in Greece is wholly educational; for fifty years the average attendance on the schools has been five hundred, and it is worthy of remark that more than half of these have been girls. The work is now confined to the city of Athens, and is carried on by Miss Marion Muir, assisted by 11 Greek teachers and 3 Greek student teachers, the number of scholars being 510, 136 of whom are boys and 374 girls.

**Provençal Version.** — The Provençal belongs to the Græco-Latin branch of the Aryan family of languages, and is a dialect of Southern France. Towards the close of the twelfth century a version of the Scriptures into this dialect was made by Waldo and his disciples. A copy of his version was presented to the Pope at the Lateran Council of 1179, but the work was condemned and prohibited by the Council of Toulouse in 1229, because it was written in the vernacular. Many copies were in consequence destroyed, but one copy was conveyed to England, and deposited by Cromwell in the library of the University of Cambridge. It now appears to be lost. There are, however, MSS. extant at different libraries, which may be traced back to one archetype, from which all seem to have been made. Such MSS. are the Dublin, the Grenoble, the Zurich, Lyons, and Paris. An edition of the Gospel of John, prepared after these MSS., was published by Dr. Gilly in 1848. The report of the British and Foreign Bible Society for 1884 makes the following statement: At the request of a liberal supporter interested in the peasantry of Cannes, the same Society agreed to publish one Gospel in the Cannes patois, to which the country people are attached. The work of translating the Gospel of Luke was committed to Mons. Amouretti, a student of the University of Paris. As the translation, however, was found incomplete and unsatisfactory, a version of the Gospel of Mark was prepared by Pastor Fesquet in the Languedoc dialect of the Canton La Salle St. Pierre, Gard. The translation, which was examined and revised by the Rev. Dr. Duncan Craig of Dublin, was issued by the British Bible Society in 1887.

**Province Wellesley,** a strip of territory on the west coast of the Malay peninsula, opposite Penang, 45 miles in length with an average width of about 8 miles, including a total area of 270 square miles. It forms part of the settlement of Penang (q.v.), and with it is a part of the British Colony of Straits Settlements (q.v.). The S. P. G. has a station among the 71,000 people, mostly Malays.

**Pudukattai** (Poodoocottah, Puducotta), a town in Madras, India, 28 miles southeast of Trichinopoly; is unusually clean, airy, well built; small, but having a fine mosque, a palace, and several temples. Population, 15,384, Hindus, Moslems, Christians. Mission station S. P. G. (1858); 2 native pastors, 1,547 church-members.

**Puebla,** a city in Mexico, 76 miles east-southeast of Mexico City, 25 miles northeast of the volcano Popocatapetal. The sacred city of Mexico, containing many religious and charitable institutions. Mission station Methodist Episcopal Church (North); 2 missionaries, 2 female missionaries, 8 native helpers, 243 church-members, 136 scholars. Methodist Episcopal Church (South); 1 missionary, 1 native pastor.

**Puerta Plata,** a seaport town of San Domingo, West Indies, on the north coast, 100 miles north-northwest of Santo Domingo City. Population, 3,000. It lies on the slope of a mountain by the shore of a crescent-shaped bay. The harbor has good anchorage, but shallows rapidly towards the shore. Mission station of the Baptist Missionary Society; 1 missionary, 77 church-members, 37 day-scholars, 149 Sabbath-scholars.

**Punjab** (British India), one of the five provinces going to make up the presidency of Bengal, in India. It is the most northerly of all the territories of Hindustan; its highest northern point is in latitude 35°, its most southern, 27° 39'. Its limits of east longitude are 69° 35' and 78° 35'. The area of that portion of it under British administration is 106,632 square miles; population (1881), 18,850,437. But there are 34 native states whose territory is intermingled with that of the British possessions — all of which are under the political supervision of the Punjab Government, though each has its own native chief (see article Native States, where these relations are explained more at length), and the area of these swells the total area of the Punjab to 142,449 square miles, and its aggregate population to 22,712,120. The Punjab is governed by a lieutenant-governor, under the general supervision of the governor-general and viceroy of India. The province — British and native together — comprises one tenth of the territorial extent and furnishes one eleventh of the whole population of all India. It contains one fourth of the Mohammedan population, but only one twentieth of the Hindu. The name means "Five Waters," and is derived from the fact that its territory is intersected by five great Himalayan rivers; these are the Sutlej, the Beas, the Ravi, the Chenab, and the Jhelum. The Indus River, into which these all flow, and which runs near the western (political) boundary, and the Jumna, which forms a part of the eastern (political) boundary, describe a course outside the territory to which the name was originally given; but that name has recently been made to cover the entire province placed under the administration of the local government. On the north the Punjab extends to the great range of the Himalayas, and on its northwestern corner extends into that area where the Himalayas unite in vast mountain masses with the other immense ranges of Central Asia. North and northeast it touches the independent kingdom of Cashmir, and also the frontier of Chinese Tibet. South it touches Sind and Rajputana; and on the west it comprises a part of the Trans-Indus territory extending to the Suleiman Mountains, which run north and southwest of that river, and form the boundary between British possessions and those of Afghanistan in the north, and Baluchistan in the south. The famous Khyber Pass extends through these mountains and is the natural door-way from India into Afghanistan, or from the countries of the northwest into India, and it was through this pass that the early Aryan invaders must have entered India, from whom are descended the present Hindu race, and whose earliest religious system has developed into the surprising and cumbrous growth of Hinduism and Buddhism. Later, through that same pass, came Alexander the Great and his armies. In the 10th and 11th centuries of our era, and later, the Mohammedan invaders, who in time extended the sway of Islam over the whole of India, and founded great dynasties whose ruins exist at Delhi, at Agra, at Haidarabad, at Bijapur and elsewhere, threaded the same defile; but the English—the last and greatest conquerors of India—came through another entrance, even by the gateways of the sea.

Thus the history of the Punjab is of exceeding variety and interest. So extensive and so various is it, that it must here be left almost wholly untouched. Suffice it to say that here was the original Indian home of the Aryans; here the Vedic rites were first practised, and here probably the Vedas written; here Hinduism began its development; and hence did the Hindu race, as it swelled to larger size and power, emerge for the conquest first of the great Gangetic valley, and then of all the Deccan and Southern India. The beginning of this Hindu history cannot be later than 1500 B.C., and may be earlier. Here also the Mohammedan power in India first took root. Lahore was the first Mohammedan capital; after a time Delhi was occupied as their imperial city, and later still Agra, by a few of the Mogul emperors in the 16th and 17th centuries.

The city of Delhi, which indeed lies outside of the natural area of the Punjab, though now within its political area, stands on the site of Indraprastha, a prehistoric Hindu capital, the foundation of which is said to go back to the 15th century B.C. Lahore, which is now the capital of the Punjab (population in 1881, 149,369), was founded probably early in our era, but became the capital of the early Mohammedan emperors, and grew greatly in size and importance under their sway. Amritsar is the chief city of the Sikh religion (population 151,896). Early in the 16th century there flourished one Baba Nanak, who was born near Lahore, and who taught a pure form of Monotheism—devotion was due to God alone; forms were of small account; both Hindu and Mohammedan worship was acceptable. He gained a large following, and a succession of teachers or *gurus* perpetuated his leadership among the people. Their power became so great that it drew the attention of the Mohammedan emperors, who undertook to quell the rising sect. Meantime Amritsar had been founded, and the temple—the sacred centre of Sikhism—had been built. The Sikhs—as they were called, meaning "Disciples" of Nanak, their first *guru*—suffered greatly for several generations, and were several times defeated in battle; but in the last century, as the Moslem power grew weaker, theirs grew stronger, and during the last quarter of the last century they were virtually masters of the Punjab. Early in the present century Ranjit Singh, an able adventurer of this sect, assumed the headship, and consolidated the power of his people into a strong kingdom, with Lahore as its capital. He made a treaty with the British, whose power by that time had crept up near to the confines of the Punjab. But his successors made inroads on British territory, with the inevitable result of war, defeat, and finally annexation. It was in 1849 that the Punjab was finally made a part of the English dominions. The treaty was signed by the young king of the Punjab, the Maharaja Dhulip Singh. Among other things, it was stipulated that the famous diamond Kohinur should be given up to the Queen, and it has since reposed peacefully among Her Majesty's crown jewels. The Maharaja received a pension, and retired to England, where he settled down as an English nobleman. Latterly he has engaged in intrigues against the government, of which he now professes himself repentant. After the mutiny the Punjab was made a lieutenant-governorship. The history of its connection with the great mutiny need not here detain us. It must be enough to say that, through the exertion of the chief English officials, the rebellion was promptly quelled and it was possible to send effective aid from that province to the assistance of the English army operating against the mutineers at Delhi.

Classifying the people by religions, nearly 56 per cent are Mohammedans; about 38 per cent Hindus; nearly 6 per cent Sikhs. In round numbers, there are 10,500,000 Mohammedans, 7,000,000 Hindus, and 1,000,000 Sikhs. These were the figures of 1881. There are nearly 36,000 Jains, and over 33,000 Christians, of whom less than 4,000 in 1881 were natives. The number is considerably greater now. The preponderance of Mohammedans is explained partly by the fact of early and long Mohammedan possession of the Punjab by rulers of that faith (as just described), and partly by its propinquity to the Mohammedan countries on the northwest, whence immigration is so easily accomplished. Peshawar is the city of next importance to those already named. It stands west of the Indus, in that part of the Punjab which was once Afghan territory. Its population was nearly 80,000 in 1881. It is the chief station on the northwest frontier, and its proximity to the territory of Afghanistan, peopled with its wild and violent mountain clans, makes it one of much importance.

The people of the Punjab are largely agriculturists. A sixth of the population of British Punjab is thus returned—over 3,000,000. The commercial and artisan classes number nearly 1,500,000. The rainfall is slight; in some parts of the province artificial irrigation is resorted to with good results. The rivers swell with the melting of the mountain snows, and when they subside leave well-watered strips of alluvial land enriched with the fresh deposits of each season. Education is in a tolerably forward state. It is stimulated somewhat by the existence of the Punjab University, which dates only from 1882, with which a number of colleges are affiliated. In 1883-4 there were 2,227 schools of all grades in operation, with 125,906 pupils; 348 of these schools were for girls, and the attendance at them was 10,588. The language of the Hindus is Punjabi—allied to Hindi. Hindustani and Persian are used by the Mohammedans. The Afghans speak Pashtu.

Missionary work in this province began in 1834. The American Presbyterians were first on the ground, and their earliest station was at Lodiana, where, besides the usual work of preaching, schools were at once begun, and a printing-press established, from which have since issued multitudes of books and tracts, including Bibli-

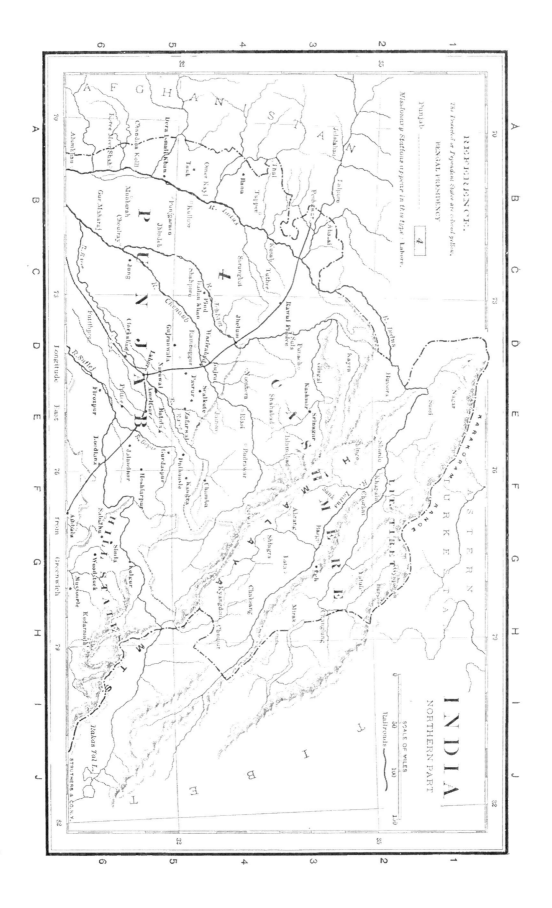

REFERENCE.

The Districts in Feudatory States are coloured yellow.

BENGAL PRESIDENCY

Punjab

Missionary Stations appear in this type Lahore.

4

INDIA
NORTHERN PART

SCALE OF MILES
Railroads

cal translations. Many other places have since been occupied. The Church Missionary Society occupied Amritsar in 1851. In 1870 that Society began a theological school at Lahore for training native preachers, which was the first school of the sort in India, it is said, to include Hebrew and New Testament Greek in the curriculum of study for native Christian students. Rev. T. Valpy French, afterwards the first Bishop of Lahore, was the first principal of the school, which he conducted with great success for several years. The same Society has occupied several stations in the Trans-Indus territory, as near the line as possible, with a view to using them as bases of movement upon the unevangelized regions of Afghanistan and Beluchistan. Peshawar was occupied in 1855 as a centre of Afghan missionary work. The United Presbyterians of America have a mission in the Punjab, in Sialkot, and adjoining districts. The Church of Scotland has a station at Chamba. Several leper asylums have been founded in connection with one and another of these missions, but these are now managed by the "Mission to Lepers in India"—a society founded in 1874 by Mr. W. C. Bailey, formerly connected with the Church of Scotland's mission, whose sympathy for these unfortunates was profoundly stirred, and who has devoted himself to the work of ameliorating their condition, both bodily and spiritual. His Society has asylums in many other parts of India besides the Punjab. The Moravians, true to their instincts of selecting the most difficult, laborious, and apparently unpromising fields, started a mission in 1855 at Kyelang, far up among the Himalayas, though in British territory, among the Tibetan mountaineers. Their work has involved severe hardship and unusual self-denial, but it has not been without its direct results. Circumstances have impelled the Punjab missionaries to labor among Mohammedans probably to a greater extent than has been attempted elsewhere in India. More than half the population being Mohammedans, opportunities have been constantly presented for meeting them, which it has not seemed right to disregard, although there has not been hope of great success. Several of the missionaries of the Punjab have studied the religion of Mohammed profoundly, and have published scholarly works in elucidation of it, while not neglecting the preparation of other works designed to commend Christianity directly to the Moslems themselves. Their labors have resulted in the conversion of many Mohammedans, some of whom have become able and fearless preachers of the gospel. The literary labors of Dr. Pfander, one of these missionaries, whose controversial works against Islam have won him renown in India as well as without its borders, deserve special mention; and among the living, Rev. T. B. Hughes, formerly at Peshawar, and Rev. E. M. Wherry, late of Lodiana, are among those who have contributed through their writings greatly to the comprehension of Mohammedanism, and added to the facilities of missionaries who undertake to cope with it.

**Punjabi** or **Sikh Version.**—The Punjabi belongs to the Indic branch of the Aryan family of languages, and is spoken in the province of Punjab, North India. A translation of the Bible into this language was undertaken by Serampore missionaries at a very early period, and was published in 1811. In 1832 a second edition was undertaken. Of the Old Testament only Genesis to Ezekiel was translated and published since 1820. A new translation was undertaken by the Rev. J. Newton in connection with American missionaries, and in 1850 Genesis, Exodus, the Psalms, and the New Testament were published by the British and Foreign Bible Society at Lodiana.

*(Specimen verse. John 3 : 16.)*

ਕਿਉਂਕਿ ਪਰਮੇਸੁਰ ਨੈ ਜਗਤ ਨੂੰ ਅਜਿਹਾ ਪਿਆਰ ਕੀਤਾ, ਜੋ ਉਸ ਨੈ ਆਪਣਾ ਇਕਲੌਤਾ ਪੁੱਤ੍ਰ ਦਿੱਤਾ; ਤਾਂ ਹਰੇਕ ਜੋ ਉਸ ਪਰ ਪਤੀਤ, ਤਿਸ ਦਾ ਨਾਸ ਨਾ ਹੋਵੇ, ਸਗਵਾਂ ਸਦੀਪਕ ਜੀਉਣ ਪਾਵੇ।

**Pure Literature Society.** Headquarters, 11 Buckingham Street, Adelphi, Strand, London, W. C.—This Society was established in 1854 for the purpose of increasing the circulation of pure literature throughout the United Kingdom and its colonies. This it endeavors to effect (1) by the publication of a catalogue of periodicals, books, and prints which the committee consider useful and good; (2) by grants from this catalogue of libraries at half-price; (3) by acting as an agency for the selection and distribution of desirable publications in order to supply persons, schools, and institutions, at home and abroad; and (4) by correspondence with managers of publications, either in praise or kindly remonstrance.

The Society's catalogue now contains the names of 4,548 books, each of which was carefully examined before being placed on the list. Library grants have been made to soldiers, sailors, policemen, mutual-improvement societies, etc., and to the English in France, Germany, Belgium, Switzerland, Italy, Holland, Denmark, Egypt, Turkey, Austria, and Jerusalem. Similar grants have been made to the Channel Islands and the British colonies. Books at half-price have been granted, to the value of £63,176, to 7,762 libraries.

**Puri,** the chief town of the district of the same name in Bengal, India, is situated on the coast, covers an area of 1,871 acres, and is a city of lodging-houses. Its ordinary population (22,000) is almost entirely Hindu, but during the great festivals of Jagannath, which are held here, there are 100,000 pilgrims added to the ordinary residents.

Mission station of the General Baptist Missionary Society, together with Pipli (q.v.). The work is carried on principally in the time of the festivals, by means of colporteurs and street-preachers.

**Purulia,** capital of the Manbhum district, Bengal, India. Population, 5,695. It has good public buildings, a hospital, and considerable trade. Mission station of the Gössner Missionary Society; 606 church-members.

# Q.

**Queenstown,** a town in Northeast Kaffraria, South Africa, northeast of Engotini and west of St. Mark's (Transkei). Mission station of the S. P. G.; 1 missionary.

**Queretaro,** a town 110 miles northwest of Mexico City, Central Mexico, situated on a plateau among hills 6,000 feet high, and separated from its suburbs by a small stream. The streets are well laid out, the houses regular, and the whole city one of the finest in the republic. Mission station M. E. Church (North); 1 missionary and wife, 1 school.

**Quetta,** a town in the western part of the Punjab, India, west of Dera Ghazi Khan and southwest of Dera Ismail Khan. Mission station of the C. M. S. among the Afghans; 1 missionary, 1 physician, 12 church-members.

**Quichua Version.**—The Quichua belongs to the South American languages, and is used in the interior of the Argentine Republic. A translation of the Gospel of John was undertaken by the Rev. J. H. Gybbon-Spilsbury of the South American Missionary Society, which was published at Buenos Ayres in 1880 for the British and Foreign Bible Society, in an edition of 1,000 copies. Another edition was issued after that time, and up to March 31st, 1889, 2,000 copies were disposed of.

(*Specimen verse.*   John 3 : 16.)
Pachacamackca chicatami ruuacunata munaica, chay Zapallay-Churinta kokcuïca, tucuy paypi ylïllc, mana huañunanpac, uiñay cauzaytari apinanpac.

**Quillota,** a town of Chili, South America, on the railroad connecting Valparaiso and Santiago. Population, 1,500. Mission station of the Presbyterian Church (North); 1 missionary and wife, 1 native preacher.

**Quilon,** a town and historic port in Travancore, India; is one of the oldest towns on the Malabar coast, from whose re-foundation in 1019 A. D. Travancore reckons its era. It was long one of the great ports of Malabar, and its ancient history goes back to the record of the primitive Syrian Church in India. Population, 13,588. Mission station L. M. S. (1821); 20 out-stations, 1 missionary and wife, 10 native helpers, 279 church-members, 28 boys' schools, 531 scholars, 2 girls' schools, 181 scholars.

**Quitta,** formerly a Danish, now a British, fort and town on the sea near the east point of the Gold Coast, Africa. Mission station of the North German Missionary Society.

**Quop,** a town in North Borneo, a little southeast of Sarawak, near the northern coast. Population, 700. Mission station of the S. P. G.; 2 missionaries, 150 communicants.

# R.

**Ra,** one of the Banks Islands, New Hebrides, Melanesia; has a Melanesian mission station since 1884, with 31 church-members.

**Rabai** or **Kisulutini,** a station of the C. M. S. (1846) in equatorial Africa, not far to the northwest of Mombasa, on the east coast. Has 1 missionary, 2 female missionaries, 190 communicants, 201 scholars.

**Rabinowich, Joseph,** a Jewish evangelical preacher in Kishinew, Russia. (See article Jews.)

**Ragharapuram,** a town among the Telugus, in East Madras, British India, on the Krishna River, south of Dummagudiem and northwest of Masulipatam. Mission station of the C. M. S.; 1 missionary, 2 native pastors, 347 church-members, 8 schools, 112 scholars.

**Rahuri,** a town in Ahmadnagar district, Bombay, India, 25 miles north of Ahmadnagar City. It has a railroad station and a weekly market. Population, 4,304. Mission station of A. B. C. F. M.; 1 missionary and wife, 37 native agents, 23 out-stations. S. P. G. (including Sangamner); 120 communicants, 1 boarding and 13 day schools, with a total of 311 pupils.

**Raiatea,** a pretty town in the Society Islands, extending for two miles along the margin of a bay. Agriculture and mechanical arts have been introduced by the missionaries with happy effect. Mission station L. M. S. (1816); 1 missionary. As the western group of the Society Islands, to which Raiatea belongs, is not under the French protectorate, the Protestant mission has not been disturbed here.

**Rai Bareli** (Roy Bareilly), a town in Oudh, Northwest Provinces, India, 48 miles southeast of Lucknow; possesses many interesting specimens of architecture, the principal being a strong, spacious fortress. Population, 11,781 Hindus, Moslems, Christians, etc. Mission station Methodist Episcopal Church (North); 1 missionary and wife, 5 other ladies, 10 native helpers, 40 church-members, 14 day-schools, 347 scholars, 29 Sabbath-schools, 800 scholars.

**Rajamahendri** (Rajahmundry), a historic town in Madras, India, on the bank of the Godaveri River. Population about 20,000. The surrounding country is rich and the people are prosperous. A mission station was opened here in 1844 by the North German Missionary Society, but the work was transferred to the General Council of the Evangelical Lutheran Church (U. S. A.) in 1851. Has 1 missionary, 91 scholars.

**Rajasingamangalam,** a town in Madras, India. Mission station of the S. P. G.; 9

native workers, 27 out-stations, 142 church-members, 6 schools, 169 scholars.

**Rajkot,** a city in Gujarat, India, a little north of the peninsula of Kathiawar. Climate tropical, 115° F. Population, 20,000, Hindus, Moslems. Language, Gujarati. Mission station Irish Presbyterian Church (1841); 1 missionary and wife, 13 native helpers, 1 church, 12 church-members, 5 schools, 249 scholars.

**Rajputana,** a vast territory in the north-west of India, which derives its name from the Rajput clans who inhabit it. The word "Rajput" means "son of a king;" and the Rajputs trace their origin from the princely families among the original Aryan invaders of India. Some of these clans have had their abodes here from time immemorial. The invading armies of Mohammedans, after the 11th century, shut them up within its borders, where, owing to the desert and difficult character of a great part of the territory, they were safe from further intrusion. The exact boundaries of Rajputana it is difficult to give. In a general way it may be said to lie between Sind on the west, the Punjab on the northwest, the Northwest Prov-inces on the northeast and the Maratha states of the Gaikwar, Sindhia, and Holkar on the south. Its limits of north latitude are 23° and 30°, and of east longitude 69° 30′, and 78° 15′. Its area is supposed to be about 132,000 square miles, containing a population of over 10,500,000 peo-ple. Within this area lies the British Commis-sionership of Ajmere-Merwara (q.v.), of which both area and population are included in the totals just given, and 20 native states (mostly Rajput—though at least one is Mohammedan) all under the general supervision of the para-mount British power, though each is ruled by its own chief. (See article on Native States, where the relations between these states and the British Government are more fully explained.) The population is prevailingly Hindu, only about nine per cent being Mohammedan, and about half as many Jains—who are more nearly Hindus than anything else. Those of other faiths furnish a mere sprinkling in the total mass. There are many wild jungle tribes—especially Bhils, of which any exact enumera-tion is well nigh impossible; the Bhils, how-ever, are supposed to number nearly 170,000, in-cluded mostly among the Hindus, whose relig-ion they follow. These figures are those of 1881.

Much of the territory of Rajputana, espe-cially in the western part, is mere desert. The southeastern portion is more fertile. The chief city is Jaipur (population in 1881, 142,578), capital of the native state of the same name. This is said to be the finest of modern Hindu cities, and is laid out on a regular plan, with streets of different widths crossing each other at right angles, with sewers, street lights and water, a college, hospitals, and other appliances of civilization. The Raja of Jaipur is a very intelligent ruler, who takes pride in the prog-ress of his people and the adornment of his chief town. Missionary work in Rajputana is in the hands of the United Presbyterian Church of Scotland, and dates from 1860. The sta-tions are Jaipur, Ajmere (q.v.), Nasirabad, Deoli, Beawr, Todgarh, Udaipur, Alwar, and Jodhpur. Much attention has been given to medical work; and the diligence of the mis-sionaries in relieving distress during a famine in 1869 gave them a firm hold upon the hearts of the people. There is a mission press at Aj-mere, and a strong corps of missionaries.

Education is said to be making fair progress, though female education is neglected. The Rajputs, who have given their name to the country and who constitute its aristocracy, fur-nish only about half a million of the popula-tion.

**Ramah,** a town on the northeast coast of Labrador, west of Zoar. The most northerly of the mission stations of the Moravian Breth-ren (1871); 2 missionaries. There are as yet no native preachers, but good work is being done in building up the native church.

**Ramah,** or **Ramah Key,** a small island in the lagoon, fifteen miles south of Blewfields, Mosquito coast, Central America. Mission sta-tion of the Moravian Brethren.

**Ramahyuck** (i.e. Ramah—our home), a town on the southeast coast of Victoria, Aus-tralia, 120 miles east of Melbourne. Mission station of the Moravians (1862); 1 missionary and wife. The success of this mission in civi-lizing, educating, and Christianizing the blacks has been more marked even than in Ebenezer (q.v.), and the work is steadily progressing. The sewing-machine and the harmonium may be found in the huts.

**Ramaliane,** a Hermannsburg station in the Mariko circle, Transvaal, South Africa, with 232 church-members.

**Ramapatam,** a town on the Bay of Ben-gal, India, between Nellore and Ongole. Climate not unhealthy, but generally debilitat-ing. Mission station of the American Baptist Missionary Union (1870); 1 missionary and wife, 1 other lady, 25 native helpers, 1 church, 470 church-members, 1 theological seminary, 110 students, 1 school, 45 scholars.

**Ramnad,** a town in Madura, Madras, In-dia, 125 miles northeast of Cape Comorin. Population, 10,519. Mission station of the S. P. G.; 2 missionaries, 6 native pastors, 16 native helpers, 1 church, 7 schools, 260 scholars.

**Rampur-Beauleah,** a town in Bengal, India. Mission station of the Presbyterian Church of England; 1 medical missionary, 2 female missionaries.

**Rangiora,** a town in New Zealand. Mis-sion circuit of the United Methodist Free Churches; 1 itinerant, 3 local preachers, 92 church-members, 182 Sunday-school scholars.

**Rangoon** (Rangun), the capital of Lower Burma, is situated on the left bank of the Rangoon River, 26 miles from the sea. It was annexed by Great Britain after the war of 1852. Large sums of money have been expended in improving the city, and the European quarter contains many fine buildings, though the na-tive town is not much improved. Population (1881), 134,176, Burmese, Mohammedans, Chris-tians, and others. Buddhism has here its strong-hold, and the city is noted for the number and splendor of its temples and dagobas or shrines. The most magnificent and venerated one is the Shoay Dagon, or Golden Dagon dagoba, said to be 2,300 years old. It is heavily decorated with gold, and is the receptacle of relics of the last four Buddhas, including eight hairs of Gautama.

Much internal and foreign commerce is carried on in Rangoon, as it has communication by rail and by water with the upper provinces. An English newspaper is published here. Mission station of the A. B. M. U. (1813; see article on A. B. M. U.); Burman department: 2 missionaries and wives, 7 female missionaries; Sgau-Karen, 2 missionaries and wives, 1 female missionary; Pwo-Karen, 1 missionary and wife. Shan Mission, 1 missionary and wife; Theological Seminary, 2 missionaries and wives; College, 1 missionary and wife; Eurasian boys' school, 1 female missionary; Mission Press, 1 superintendent; total, 28 missionaries and assistants; Burman Mission, 7 out-stations, 9 native preachers, 4 churches, 451 church-members, 5 Sunday-schools, 231 scholars, 7 schools, 231 pupils; Karen Mission, 23 out-stations, 70 native preachers, 80 churches (76 self-supporting), 4,434 church-members, 2 Sunday-schools, 150 pupils, 51 schools (49 self-supporting), 1,622 pupils.

S. P. G. (1862); 4 missionaries, 4 churches, 561 Burmese church-members, 511 natives of India, 23 Karens, 20 Chinese, 2 boys' boarding-schools, 350 boys, 5 boys' day-schools, 1,136 boys, 1 girls' school, 35 girls. 2 mixed schools.

Methodist Episcopal Church (North), 1878; 3 missionaries, 3 female missionaries; English work—1 chapel, 132 members, 1 high-school, 175 pupils, 2 Sunday-schools, 200 scholars; Tamil and Telugu—49 members, 1 Sunday-school, 31 scholars, 1 day-school, 45 scholars; Burmese, 5 members.

Leipsic Missionary Society (1878), 172 members.

**Raniganj,** a town in Bengal, India. Mission station of the Wesleyan Methodist Missionary Society; 2 missionaries, 2 chapels, 15 church-members, 45 Sabbath-scholars, 208 day-scholars.

**Ranikhet,** a town and military sanitarium in the Northwest Provinces, India, on the southern slope of the Himalayas, a little west of Almora. Climate temperate. Population, Hindus, Moslems. Language, Hindi. Natives prosperous, uneducated as yet, but honest and loyal. Mission station L. M. S. (1869); 1 missionary and wife, 14 native helpers, 3 out-stations, 2 churches, 26 church-members, 2 schools, 95 scholars, an asylum for lepers.

**Rankin, Henry,** b. Newark, N. J., U. S. A., September 11th, 1825. He was the eighth of ten children, religiously trained by godly parents, converted while in his junior year in Princeton College, and there, in his seventeenth year, resolved to be a missionary to the heathen. After his graduation in 1843 he studied theology for six months with Dr. Todd at Pittsfield, Mass. The following year he spent in the theological seminary at Auburn, and then entered the seminary at Princeton, graduating in 1847. He was ordained in 1848 by the Presbytery of Elizabeth; sailed October 7th, the same year, for China as a missionary of the Presbyterian Board, reaching Ningpo early the following year. In that city, containing a population of 300,000, and among the villages, with tens of thousands more, he labored with success until 1856, when Mrs. Rankin's failing health compelled him to return

to the United States. While at home he visited almost every State in the Union, presenting in the churches, seminaries, colleges, and schools the claims of the foreign missionary work. Mrs. Rankin's health being restored, they returned to China. But in 1860 her health again made a return to America necessary, while he remained for two years at his work, alone. Civil war then raging in China, and the Taiping rebels approaching the city of Ningpo, the missionaries, who knew their hostility to idolatry, deputed two of their number, one of them Mr. Rankin, to seek an interview with the commander-in-chief in behalf of the Christians in the city and suburban villages. He was promised safety from death and pillage for all the Christian Chinese. This promise was kept when the city was captured, and the idols were destroyed, and many of the people perished. In 1862 Mrs. Rankin returned to find her husband greatly prostrated from his continued work in the unhealthy climate of Ningpo. Though suffering much, he labored on till April, 1863, when he was advised to return home. Unwilling to leave China, he was persuaded by Dr. McCartee to go to Tungchow, in the healthy province of Shantung. He arrived there in May, and lingered till July 2d, 1863, when, among loving friends, he passed away.

**Ranchi,** a town in Bengal, India, with a population of 12,000; was made a mission station of the Gössner Missionary Society in 1844. Their work was mainly among the Kols, some of whom came to the town and asked to see Christ in person before they took any decisive stand. In 1869 a division took place in the mission, and a great part of the mission force left Gössner and took service under the S. P. G., which now has a bishop of Chota Nagpur resident at Ranchi, which is the head-quarter for its Chota Nagpur Mission (see Nagpur, Chutia). The two societies are now working in harmony.

**Rarotonga:** see Hervey Islands.

**Rarotonga Version.**—The Rarotonga belongs to the Polynesian languages, and is vernacular to the people of Hervey or Cook's Islands, numbering somewhat less than 10,000. The islanders speak seven dialects, but the Rarotongan language alone has been used by the missionaries in printing. In 1827 the Rev. John Williams, the discoverer of the island, accompanied the Rev. C. Pitman to Rarotonga, and remained with him a year. These two missionaries translated the whole of the New Testament (except two books by Rev. A. Buzacott, who had joined Mr. Pitman in 1828). The first complete edition of 5,000 copies of the New Testament was carried through the press in England at the expense of the British and Foreign Bible Society by Mr. Williams during his visit to England (1835–38). The first edition of the entire Bible was carefully edited by Mr. Buzacott during his stay in England (1847–51), at the request of the British Bible Society and 5,000 copies were printed and disposed of in three years. In 1855 the Rarotongan Bible was reprinted with a few alterations, under the care of Revs. William Gill and Thomas Metter. The edition consisted of 5,000 copies. In 1872 the British Bible Society issued a third and greatly improved edition of 5,000 copies. It was edited by the Revs. E. R. W. Krause and

George Gill. A thoroughly revised edition of the Bible in 8vo, with marginal references and stereotyped, was issued for the British Bible Society by the Rev. W. Gill during his stay in England in 1886. This revised standard version is in a great measure a return to the original translation made by Williams, Pitman, and Buzacott, with this difference—that thousands of foreign words in native dress have given place to native equivalents, thus rendering the book more intelligible. The edition consisted of 4,000 copies. Up to March 31st, 1889, there were 22,973 portions of the Scriptures disposed of.

(*Specimen verse.* John 3 : 16.)

I aroa mai te Atua i to te ao nei, kua tae rava ki te oronga anga mai i tana Tamaiti anau tai, kia kore e mate te akarongo iaia, kia rauka ra te ora mutu kore.

**Ratnapura,** a town in Ceylon, on a navigable river, 45 miles east of Colombo. Mission station of the Baptist Missionary Society; 1 missionary and wife, 5 native helpers, 8 out-stations, 21 church-members, 109 scholars.

**Rauch, Henry,** a missionary of the United Brethren to the North American Indians in 1740. Soon after his arrival in New York he heard that a delegation of the Mohican Indians had arrived in the city to treat with the government. On visiting them he found them in such a state of inebriety that he could not converse with them; but waiting patiently till they were sober, he inquired of two of them, named Tschoop and Shabash, whether they wished a teacher to settle among them and teach them the way of salvation. He agreed to go with them to their village (Shekomeko) on the borders of Connecticut, about 25 miles from the Hudson River. For a long time he persevered in his work, only to meet defiance and ridicule. After twelve months the two Indians he had met in New York were converted, and the white Christians at once became interested in his work on account of this wonderful circumstance, and Rauch was invited to preach to them. These encouraging prospects continued only a short time. Soon some unfriendly whites instigated the savages to threaten his life if he did not leave the place. He withdrew for a time to the house of a farmer, where he held the position of a teacher. He could not give up the work among the Indians, and often returned to Shekomeko to see them. His persistent efforts, patience, and fortitude at last gained for him the respect of the savages, and many true conversions followed. The regeneration of Tschoop was remarkable, as he had been one who had done most to alienate the affections of the Indians from their teacher, but now did all he could to restore harmony, and express to others his earnest belief in the truths he had heard.

Count Zinzendorf visited this station in 1742, and witnessed the baptism of Tschoop and Shabash. The mission was strengthened, new workers were sent to its aid, and the conversions were many. In 1743 ten of the Indians at Shekomeko were converted, and partook of the communion. A chapel was built for public worship, and at the close of the year sixty-three had been baptized in this mission alone. Up to this time the missionaries had experienced very

few difficulties; but in 1746 the white people in the neighborhood, who had failed in their efforts to draw the Indians away from their teachers, now began enlisting their own countrymen in the overthrow of the mission. Numerous persecutions now followed the missionaries, compelling them to serve in the militia, from which service they were exempt as ministers, and at last an act was passed forbidding them to instruct the Indians on pretence that they were connected with the French. All efforts to improve this state of affairs proved fruitless, and the Brethren with sorrowful hearts retired to Bethlehem.

**Rawal Pindi,** a city in Punjab, India. Because of its broad, straight, handsome streets, and its excellent drainage and sanitary arrangements, it is said to present a cleaner appearance than any other town in Northern India. Trees have been freely planted, and give the place a very pleasing appearance. Population, 26,735; Moslems, Hindus, Sikhs, Jains, Christians, Parsis. Mission station Presbyterian Church (North); 2 missionaries, 1 female missionary, 2,257 school-children.

**Read, Hollis,** b. Newfane, Vt., U. S. A., August 26th, 1802; graduated at Williams College 1826; taught a year after graduation in the Academy of Bennington; studied theology at Princeton Seminary; was licensed by the Franklin Association, Massachusetts, May 13th, 1829; spent a short time at Andover Seminary; was ordained at Park Street Church, Boston, September 24th, 1829; married Caroline Hubbell, of Bennington, Vt. Sailed August 2d, 1830, as a missionary of the A. B. C. F. M., for India, reaching Calcutta December 25th, and Bombay March 7th. His field of labor was Ahmadnagar. Failure of Mrs. Read's health caused his return in 1835, and prevented his again engaging in mission work abroad. He spent two years as agent of the Board, and preached and taught in a number of places. He died at his son's residence in Somerville, N. J., April 7th, 1887, and was buried in Bennington, Vt. One thus speaks of him: "Of great industry and perseverance, in earnest on all moral questions, he had also an inquisitive mind which ever delighted in the progress of the arts and sciences. He was full of interest in new things until the last."

**Rebmann, John,** b. Germany; was appointed in 1846 by the C. M. S. to the East African Mission. On his arrival at Mombasa arrangements were made by him and Dr. Krapf for commencing a mission among the Wa-Nikas, and Kisulutini (Rabai), fifteen miles inland, was selected for the station. The people gave their consent for a mission, assuring the missionaries of their friendship and protection. They found the place more healthful than Mombasa, but the people exceedingly ignorant, superstitious, intemperate, sensual, and cruel. They now began the journeys in the interior which led to the remarkable East and Central African explorations. They found a new country highly favorable for missionary labor, and three groups of mountains from 4,000 to 5,000 feet high, enclosing the Taita country, containing 170,000 people. In 1847 Mr. Rebmann made a journey to Kadiaro in the Taita country, 100 miles from the coast. In 1848 he explored the country beyond the Taita, called Jagga or Chagga, 300 miles inland, the Switzerland of East Africa, travelling on foot for seven days in a thorny jungle infested by wild beasts. On May 11th he discovered Kilima Njaro, a mountain as large as the Bernese Oberland, and proved since to be 18,700 feet high. He was reminded of the air and scenery of the Jura Mountains in the Canton of Basle. In his second journey he found King Mamking friendly, but when he went again in 1849 he found him very treacherous, plundering him and his native attendants of almost everything, so that he was obliged to return. The object of these journeys is thus explained by Rebmann: "We wished to pave the way for evangelizing Eastern Africa by making ourselves acquainted with its unexplored countries, their manners, modes of thought, languages, government, etc., by at least naming the name of Christ where it had never been named before, and by explaining to the natives the general character of our objects." Dr. Krapf having gone to Europe, Rebmann was left alone at Kisulutini. In 1856 he was driven from the place by an incursion of the Mosai, who destroyed the station, and dispersed the Wa-Nika people under instruction. Retiring to Zanzibar, he continued his linguistic studies for two years, and then returning to his old station, resumed his labors. For many years he was there alone, and in 1873 Sir Bartle Frere found him, quite blind, with a dozen converts, absorbed in his dictionaries and translations, which he prepared with the help of his faithful native attendant, Isaac Nyondo, son of Abe Gunga, the first convert of the mission. When the mission was reinforced in 1875 he returned home. An attempt to restore his sight was unsuccessful. He took up his abode near Dr. Krapf in Konthal, and died October 4th, 1876, after a missionary service of twenty-nine years. He translated Luke's Gospel into Ki-Swahili, and compiled also Ki-Nika and Ki-Nyassa dictionaries. Rebmann and his associate Krapf, though much occupied in exploring and discovering, were, above all, missionaries. "We came to Africa," wrote Rebmann, "without a thought or wish of making geographical discoveries. Our grand aim was but the spreading of the kingdom of God." Yet their labors led to great results. Their remarkable journeys into the interior contributed to all subsequent geographical and missionary enterprises in Eastern Africa. After discovering the two snow-capped mountains Kilima Njaro and Kenia, a map was prepared from native information, showing a great inland sea two months' journey from the coast, which led to the journeys of Burton, Speke, and Grant, later to the travels of Livingstone, and the expeditions of Stanley and Cameron. Their investigations into the languages of East Africa laid the foundation of our present knowledge of them, and their dictionaries and translations have been of great value to subsequent scholars.

**Reeve, William,** b. England, 1794; studied at Gosport; sailed April 22d, 1816, as a missionary of the L. M. S. to India; stationed first at Bellary. In January, 1821, accompanying Mrs. Reeve to Madras, on her way to England for health, he remained in Madras, occupied in the revision of the Kanarese version of the Old Testament. He returned in October to Bellary, leaving again for Madras in January, 1824, to arrange for printing his Kanarese and English

dictionary. The same year he sailed for England; re-embarked for India in 1827, and was stationed at Bangalore. In 1831 he went to Madras to superintend the printing of his Kanarese and English dictionary, which being completed, he returned to Bangalore. In 1834, on account of ill-health, he left with his family for England. In 1836 he became pastor of the Congregational Church in Oswestry. He died at Bristol February 14th, 1850.

**Reformed (Dutch) Church in America, Board of Foreign Missions.** Headquarters, 26 Reade Street, New York, N.Y., U. S. A.—This Board was organized in 1832 by the act of the General Synod of the "Reformed Protestant Dutch Church," as it was then called. This was not, however, the beginning, but rather the outgrowth, of its interest in missionary work, and of its effort and prayer for the conversion of the heathen. As early as 1643 missionary work was carried on by several of its ministers among the Mohawk Indians, many of whom were converted and baptized.

In 1816 the church united with the Presbyterian and Associate Reformed churches in forming the United Missionary Society, which sent missionaries to the Indians, until 1826, when it was merged in the A.B.C.F.M. In 1832 the General Synod elected "The Board of Foreign Missions of the Reformed Protestant Dutch Church," which, though operating through the American Board, was allowed to conduct its missions according to the ecclesiastical polity of the church. It continued its connection with the American Board until 1857, when an amicable separation took place, which was due to no dissatisfaction, but to a growing conviction that more would be accomplished for the salvation of souls and the glory of Christ if the two Boards acted independently. In the same year the American Board transferred to this Board the mission at Amoy in China, and the Arcot Mission in India, with the individual missionaries composing them. The contributions, which were in 1857 but $10,076, rose the next year to $25,034; and have since gone on increasing, till in 1887–8 they reached the sum of $155,381, of which about $50,000 were given to endow a theological seminary connected with Arcot Mission in India.

In 1875, in accordance with a recommendation of the General Synod, "The Woman's Board of Foreign Missions of the Reformed Church in America" was organized. Its objects were to awaken a deeper interest in the work of foreign missions among the women of the church, and to act as an auxiliary to the Board of the church. In 1880 it assumed the support of the work of that Board for women and girls in all the mission fields, including the maintenance of the several seminaries for girls in China, India, and Japan. Its contributions have steadily risen as the work has increased, and have always been more than sufficient for the purpose named. In 1875 it received $2,891; in 1889, $17,437; and in the fifteen years of its existence, $161,741.

*Development of Foreign Work.—* The foreign missions of the Reformed Church have been five in number, of which four are now maintained. The earliest mission was established on the island of Borneo in 1836. Four missionaries, with their wives and a single lady, sailed for Borneo in that year, and after spending a year at Batavia, by direction of the government, were allowed to proceed to their destination. Two stations were established at Sambas and Pontianak, with schools and preaching services in three languages. The first missionaries were joined at different times by five others, and part of the force began work among the Chinese colonists in Borneo. In 1844 two of the missionaries, Messrs. Pohlman and Doty were transferred to the more promising field of Amoy; others were obliged, from ill-health, to return home, and the mission was abandoned.

CHINA.—The Mission of the Reformed Church in Amoy was the first in that field. It was commenced by Rev. David Abeel, D.D., in 1842, when Amoy, at the close of the opium war, became an open port, and was reinforced in 1844 by Messrs. Pohlman and Doty, who had been laboring among the Chinese colonists in Borneo.

The district occupied by the Amoy Mission is about sixty miles square, and has a population of 3,000,000. In this district are three stations and nineteen out-stations and preaching places. There are at present in the mission six ordained missionaries and one unordained, and nine ladies (two unmarried). The first church was organized with eleven members in 1851, and there are now (1889) in the field eight churches, of which five are self-supporting, with a total of 861 communicants. The contributions from these churches during the year amounted to $2,367.66.

Medical and educational mission work is carried on by the missionaries. During the year past a hospital and dispensary has been built in the new station of Sio-ke. Connected with the hospital force is a native helper, and to all who come for treatment and medicine the gospel is preached. The educational work of the mission is represented by nine day-schools with 120 scholars, a Bible-school where native women are fitted to become Bible-women, three seminaries, one male and two female, and a union theological seminary, which is carried on by the American Reformed and English Presbyterian Missions conjointly. The London and the English Presbyterian missions are closely associated with that of the Reformed Church, with which they are in perfect harmony.

INDIA.—The Arcot Mission was organized in 1853 by Revs. Henry M., William W., and Joseph Scudder, three sons of Rev. John Scudder, M.D., one of the pioneers of American missions among the Tamils. A member of the Reformed Church, he was sent out under the American Board while the two Boards were still connected, and continued under it until his death in 1854. Of eight sons of Rev. John Scudder, seven, together with their sister, have been at some time connected with the Arcot Mission, and three are now on the field, together with six of the third generation.

The Arcot Mission occupies chiefly the Arcot district of the Madras Presidency, with an area of about 10,000 square miles, and a population of about 3,000,000, nearly equally divided between Tamils and Telugus. The people are divided into three general classes or castes, and the intense caste feeling forms one of the great difficulties of the mission work. The Brahmins, although but four per cent of the population, are by far the most influential section,

the duties of the priesthood and the intellectual professions being largely in their hands.

The Sudras form 75 per cent of the population, and are virtually the people. They were rude and ignorant when the Brahmins first came among them, but from them they have learned the arts and sciences. They are, like the Brahmins, tenacious caste-holders.

The Pariahs, or outcastes, form 20 per cent of the population, and are in a most pitiable condition, being little more than slaves. Much of the success of mission effort has been among this class.

The mission has 8 stations and 98 out-stations. These out-stations are placed under the care of native pastors and catechists, who also preach in the surrounding villages. The catechists are unordained helpers, but perform the same labors as a pastor, with the exception of administering the offices of the church. There are now on the field 8 ordained missionaries, 4 of whom are physicians, and 1 unordained, together with 11 ladies (3 unmarried). The number of churches is 23, forming the Classis of Arcot; of congregations 93, and of communicants 1,696, of which number 68 were received last year. There are in the mission 6 boarding-schools (4 male and 2 female), 8 caste girls' schools, and 97 day-schools.

There is also at Palmanair a theological seminary, opened March, 1888, for which a special endowment fund of about $50,000 was raised by Rev. Jacob Chamberlain, D.D., of the mission, while in the United States in 1887. The mission has also a hospital and dispensary at Ranipet, near Arcot, where about a hundred patients are treated daily.

JAPAN.—The Japan Mission was established in 1859, three missionaries and their wives being sent out in that year, of whom one, Rev. Guido F. Verbeck, D.D., is still on the field. He was at one time President of the Imperial College, which brought the mission into most friendly intercourse with the official Japanese. The number of missionaries now on the field is 11, of whom 2 are engaged in teaching and are unordained. There are also 16 ladies, 6 unmarried and engaged in teaching.

In 1874 the United Presbyterian Church of Scotland, the Presbyterian Church (North), and the Reformed Churches of America united in forming the "Union Church of Christ in Japan," and the general work has since then been carried on conjointly. There are 68 churches on the roll of the United Church, with a total membership of 8,954. Eighteen of these churches were established by this Board. The Kaigan church of Yokohama, organized in 1872 with 11 members, was the first, and is now the largest, having a membership of 649 adults and 39 children. The Japan Mission had three stations, Nagasaki, Tokyo-Yokohama, and Morioka, with 20 out-stations. In 1889 this mission was divided into the North Japan Mission, with the stations of Tokyo-Yokohama and Morioka; and the South Japan Mission, on the southern island of Kiu Shiu, with its station at Nagasaki. In educational work the Reformed Church, in conjunction with the Presbyterian Church, maintains the Meiji-Gakuin at Tokyo, which consists of a theological and academical department.

It is worthy of note that of the 219 students in 1889, 129 were professing Christians. Under its own special care the Board has the Ferris Seminary, a school for girls of a high grade, at Yokohama, with 144 scholars; the Sturges Seminary for girls, and the Steele Memorial School for boys and young men, at Nagasaki. A precious work of grace in 1877 in the Ferris Seminary brought 45 of the pupils to a confession of Christ.

*Special Features.*—The missionaries of the Board have borne an honorable part in the work of translating the Scriptures into the languages of the peoples to whom they have been sent. The Scriptures have already been translated entire in Tamil and Japanese, and in part in Telugu and the Amoy dialect.

Each mission of the Board is regularly organized with its appropriate officers. It was doubtless the original intention of the Reformed Church, as expressed in the constitution of its Board of Foreign Missions, that Classes or ecclesiastical bodies similar to those in the United States and having organic relation to the Synod, should be organized at as early a date as possible in each of its mission fields. This purpose has been carried out only in the Arcot Mission in India. The Classis of Arcot was organized in 1854, and includes the missionaries, native pastors, and representatives of the native churches, of which there are 23. This organization is entirely distinct from that of the mission, though composed in part of the same members. To the Classis belongs the spiritual care and oversight of the churches. To the mission is reserved all control of the funds appropriated by the Board, and of the educational work.

The attempt to secure a similar organization at Amoy was made in 1857. It was met, however, with earnest remonstrance by the members of the mission, who were closely associated in sympathies and labors with the missionaries of the English Presbyterian Church. Their view finally prevailed, and the missionaries of both churches, together with their native pastors and elders, now form the "Tai-hoey."

It is now proposed, as one result of the conference held at Shanghai in May, 1890, to unite all the Presbyterian and Reformed churches of Amoy, Swatow, and Formosa in one organization.

In 1876 the union of the missionaries of the Reformed Church in Japan with those of the United Presbyterian Church of Scotland and the Presbyterian Church (North) of the United States in the "Council of United Missions," and the formation of the "United Church of Christ in Japan," embracing the churches organized under these missions, was approved by the Synod.

In 1886 the General Synod formally approved the stand taken by its Board of Foreign Missions "on the important subjects of Union and Co-operation in Foreign Missions, etc.," and "permitted and advised" the Classis of Arcot "to initiate such measures as shall tend to bind together the churches of the Presbyterian polity in India." It further resolved "That this Synod will indorse the union of the Classis of Arcot with such a Union Church of Christ in India, composed of those holding the Reformed faith and Presbyterian polity."

A movement was inaugurated in 1890, at the meeting of the Presbyterian Alliance in Calcutta, looking to the formation of such a Union Church in India, with fair prospect of success.

The Reformed Church therefore occupies advanced ground in relation to the principle of co-operation in mission work, and the establishment in each mission field of a national, self-governing, self-supporting, and self-propagating church, "that shall grow from its own root."

*Constitution and Organization.*—The Board of Foreign Missions of the Reformed Church in America consists of 24 members, ministers and laymen, of whom at least one half shall be ministers, chosen by the General Synod, and regularly incorporated under the laws of the State of New York. Its members are chosen for three years, and are divided into three classes, so that one third of the membership is elected each year. The regular meetings of the Board are held at Synod's rooms, now at 26 Reade Street, N.Y. City, once in three months; and in addition to these, special meetings may be called at any time by order of the Executive Committee, or by a written request of three members of the Board. Its officers are, President, Vice-President, Recording Secretary, Honorary Secretary, Corresponding Secretary, and Treasurer, whose duties are such as are usually connected with those offices. In addition to these, at the regular meeting of the Board immediately following that of the General Synod, in June of each year, an Executive Committee is chosen, consisting of five ministers and five laymen. This committee meets in regular session once a month, and as much oftener as is necessary, and has the general oversight of all operations of the Board in the interval between its regular quarterly meetings, at which all its acts are reported. Upon this committee devolves the selection of candidates for active work in the missions, whether as missionaries, physicians, or teachers. The application of the candidate is accompanied by testimonials from his instructors, pastor, teachers, or others who are qualified to speak as to his fitness for the post applied for. If the candidate is a minister, the approval of his Classis is required in every case, and this is received as evidence of his theological training and acquirements and soundness in doctrine, without further examination by the Board. If, after consideration of the application and testimonials, they are accepted by the committee, a personal interview with the candidate is sought, and that proving satisfactory, the appointment is made.

The Finance Committee, which consists of three members chosen by the Executive Committee from its own body, is charged with the management of all financial interests pertaining to the work of the Board. It receives the estimates from the missions, from which it prepares the schedule of appropriations for each year, which is then submitted to the Board for approval. It also audits the accounts of the treasurer. In addition to the regularly constituted Board, each Classis nominates from its own members a missionary agent, subject to the approval of the General Synod, for the purpose of advancing the interests of foreign missions within the bounds of the Classis. These agents are, by act of General Synod, authorized to attend any or all meetings of the Board, and to participate in its proceedings by voice and vote. This agency serves a very useful purpose as a medium of communication between the Board and the churches, and in developing and fostering a greater interest in missions throughout the churches.

For several years past the General Synod has directed that apportionments of the whole amount needed for the work of each year be made by the Board among the various Classes of the church. The further distribution devolves upon the missionary agent in each Classis, with or without the advice and consenting action of the Classis.

For several years, beginning in 1880, a General Missionary Conference has been held, usually in October or November of each year. These meetings have been occasions of deep interest and great spiritual power, and have greatly helped to swell the tide of enthusiasm, which has been steadily rising throughout the denomination. During the years 1832–89 the Board has sent out a total of 132 missionaries, including 50 ordained (8 physicians), 6 unordained men, 51 missionaries' wives, and 25 unmarried female missionaries, and has organized 51 churches, with an aggregate of 3,719 members, in India and China.

## Reformed (German) Church in the United States.

Headquarters, Pottsville, Pa., U. S. A.—The Board of Commissioners for Foreign Missions of the Reformed Church in the United States was organized on the 29th day of September, in the year 1838, at Lancaster, Pa., during the sessions of the Synod. It is an interesting fact that the suggestion to organize a Foreign Missionary Board came from the Home Missionary Society. There was no opposition to it on the part of the delegates. The Synod made a good beginning. Immediately five ministers arose and signified their willingness to sustain a missionary of the cross in heathen lands. Rev. Dietrich Willers, D.D., was the first president, and a very sincere friend of the cause. Rev. Elias Heiner, D.D., of Baltimore, Md., an officer of the Board for a quarter of a century, was one of the most active ministers, taking a deep interest in the work and giving to its support his fervent prayers and constant labors to the last hour of his life. Elder Rudolph F. Kelker, the venerable treasurer, is the only link that unites the past with the present. His zeal and fidelity are well known throughout the Christian Church. Among the many faithful servants of the Board was the late secretary, the Rev. Thomas S. Johnston, D.D., who died at his residence in Lebanon, Pa., June, 1887.

Although the Board had no foreign missionary of its own, yet the Reformed Church in the United States was a regular contributor to the A. B. C. F. M., towards the support of Rev. Benjamin Schneider, D.D., from October 13th, 1840, to October 9th, 1865, just twenty-five years.

Beginning with 1860, the Synod became dissatisfied with this way of evangelizing the heathen, and in 1865 it decided to establish its own mission and to cease contributing to the American Board. From this time on the Board applied its funds to the East India Mission, and to the work among the Winnebago Indians in Wisconsin. In the year 1873 the Board was reorganized. This was a very significant meeting, for it marks a new era in the foreign-mission history of the Reformed Church in the United States. The Board then laid the foundation for its present flourishing mission in Japan. In the year 1878 there began a most gracious work in the General Synod at Lancaster, Pa., which among other precious results gave a new impetus to the Board of Foreign Missions. It was a happy coincidence that in the same church where the Foreign Mission Board was originally organized it should receive new life from the God of Missions.

The Board of Commissioners for Foreign Missions consists of 12 members, 8 ministers and 4 elders, elected by the General Synod. The Executive Committee consists of the officers of the Board and an additional member elected by the Board. This committee has the general oversight of all the work of foreign missions; and when impracticable to secure a meeting of the Board, it has all the powers of the same to meet any emergency which may occur and which requires immediate action, in which case it may appropriate necessary moneys. The regular meetings of the Board are held annually immediately before and after the annual session of the General Synod, and at such other times as the Board shall appoint. Special meetings may be called at any time by the Executive Committee.

JAPAN MISSION.—The Reformed Church in the United States has a very prosperous mission in Japan. It is only ten years old, but during this brief period the Board has sent out three male and three female missionaries. The first missionaries, the Rev. A. D. Gring and his wife, settled in Yokohama, but it was thought best to remove to Tokyo. In May, 1884, he organized the first church, in connection with this branch of the Reformed Church, at Nihon Bashi.

The large and flourishing Bancho church is the fruit of the Rev. J. P. Moore's work, the second missionary sent out by the Board, in 1883. In 1887, in reponse to a call from Yamagata for a teacher in an English-Japanese boys' school, Mr. Moore undertook the work, and while teaching there for two years laid the foundation of a strong congregation.

In 1885 another missionary went to the field and settled in Sendai, in response to a call from that field, and laid there the foundations of the Sendai Theological Seminary. In the year 1886 the foundation was laid for the flourishing girls' school at Sendai.

Besides the theological seminary and the girls' school at Sendai, the mission of the Reformed Church has paid much attention to evangelistic work. It has three centres of operation, Tokyo, Sendai, and Yamagata, comprising twelve stations and seventeen out-stations. Rev. Mr. Oshikawa, who was one of the first Christians in the empire, is identified with this mission. To him belongs the honor of being the pastor of the congregation which purchased in 1887 a large Buddhist temple at Sendai. This is the first instance in the history of the mission work in Japan where a heathen temple became a Christian church.

## Reformed Presbyterian (Covenanter) Church in North America, Foreign Missions.

Secretary Rev. R. M. Sommerville, D.D., 126 W. 45th St., New York, N. Y., U.S.A.—At a meeting of the Synod of the Reformed Presbyterian Church in North America held in 1818, a committee was appointed to inquire into the expediency of establishing a foreign mission. Nothing was accomplished then, however, and it was not until 1841 that the question was really considered and plans for foreign work proposed. In 1843 a committee was chosen to select a field for operation, and the island of St. Thomas in the West Indies was chosen. In 1846 this spot was abandoned in favor of Haiti, and in the fall of that year the Rev. J. B. Johnson was sent out by the Board to inspect the field. In the following year the Rev. J. W. Morton with his family was sent by the Board to Port-au-Prince, which had been designated by Mr. Johnson as the best place to begin operations, and, after preparing some books in French, the language of Haiti, he opened a school, which was very successful. While laboring at Port-au-Prince, Mr. Morton changed his views in regard to the Christian Sabbath, denying that the first day of the week was such. He returned to the United States to lay his case before the synod, and was suspended in May, 1849. The mission to Haiti was then abandoned.

At a meeting of Synod held in 1856 interest in missions was revived, and it was resolved to recommence foreign work. Syria was chosen as the field of operations. The Rev. R. J. Dodds and Joseph Beattie were chosen missionaries, and with their families sailed for Syria in October, 1856. After spending some time in Damascus in the study of Arabic, Mr. Dodds settled at Zahleh, a large town at the foot of Mount Lebanon, Mr. Beattie meanwhile continuing his studies at Damascus. In May, 1858, Mr. Dodds was compelled to abandon Zahleh on account of the threats of the Catholic priests, and, joined by Mr. Beattie, spent the following year in Bhamdun and Beirut. After several explorations, Latakia, a city on the Mediterranean, was selected in October, 1859, where the mission was permanently established.

In 1867, the United Presbyterian Church of Scotland having abandoned its mission to Aleppo, Dr. R. J. Dodds took charge of it until his death in 1870. The work was extended to Suadea on the river Orontes in 1875, and to Tarsus in Cilicia in 1882. The Latakia Mission has also undertaken work on the island of Cyprus, which has so increased that the Board has appointed a missionary to take charge of it. Within recent years a Chinese mission has been in progress in Oakland, Cal., and Indian missions have been established at several points in the United States.

LATAKIA MISSION.—As has been said, the Rev. Messrs. R. J. Dodds and Joseph Beattie were sent out by the Board in 1856 to open a mission among the Jews in Syria and Palestine. They went first to Damascus, intending to make that the headquarters of the work, but finding the Jewish field occupied they removed to Zahleh in Mount Lebanon. From Zahleh too, for reasons stated elsewhere, they were obliged to remove, and while looking for another field they met the Rev. S. Lyde of London, who was searching for the right persons to take up his work among the Nusairiyeh, which on account of failure of health he was obliged to lay down. While travelling in 1854 Mr. Lyde had come upon these strange people of Northern Syria, and, seeing their degradation and vice, had commenced a mission among them, which for several years he carried on at his own expense at Bahamrat. This work he now requested Mr. Dodds to undertake. Feeling that Providence must have brought about their meeting, Mr. Dodds agreed to do so, and with Mr. Beattie commenced operations at Latakia, with Bahamrat as an out-station. The Nusairiyeh, to whom

they attempted to bring the gospel, while nominally Moslem, are really a pagan people. They are the lineal descendants in race and religion of the Cannanites who fled before Joshua, and are as yet almost absolutely inaccessible to any Christian influence. Holding to their ancient faith with a pertinacity that is wonderful, yet compelled by a relentless oppression to cover their belief under the forms of a hated religion, they have developed a power of deceit and dissimulation probably not equalled in the history of any race. Defying all investigation, punishing treachery or apostasy with instant death, they seem impregnable to approaches of any kind, and have repelled in their gloomy isolation all Christian workers "except the sturdy Scotch Covenanters, who with persistency not less dogged than their own, but with a faith which lays hold on the power of the highest, have commenced their attack." Mr. Lyde during his life among the Nusairiyeh learned many of their customs and secured some of their religious books. From his published account of them we quote the following facts in regard to their history and religion.

Politically they are divided into many tribes or clans, each with its own chiefs or sheikhs, who are continually at war with each other. These wars are caused by the old custom of avenging the blood of the slain by his next of kin; only the custom has been broadened by the Nusairiyeh; so that it is not the next of kin that takes vengeance on the murderer, but the whole clan of the murdered man becomes the avenger, and the whole clan of the murderer, the party on whom vengeance is to be taken. Occasionally the matter is settled by paying the "price of blood."

In religion they are divided into two sects, the Shamaleiyeh and the Kalazeiyeh, the main difference between them being that the former reverence or worship the moon, and the latter the sun, as the dwelling-place of Ali. The former are the stricter in the practice of their religion, and it is almost impossible to open a school or do any mission work among them. Their condition socially and morally is of the lowest, and the government, although counting them as a Mohammedan sect and drawing soldiers from them, considers them so unclean that it will neither allow them to enter the mosques, nor eat any meat which has been killed by them. Much more might be said, but enough has been told to show the exceeding difficulty of the Latakia Mission, and also that, notwithstanding, a remarkable work has already been accomplished (see article Nusairiyeh). In the field of Latakia are now two regularly organized congregations, besides the one at Latakia. The total number of communicants is 190. Medical work in connection with the mission was begun in 1865 by the Rev. David Metheny, and carried on by him at Latakia until 1882, when he removed to Mersine. Dr. Archibald Dodds taking up his work in Latakia. In 1885 Dr. Dodds was lost in the wreck of the steamer "Sidon," off the coast of Spain, and during the two years following no medical work was carried on at Latakia. In 1887 Dr. I. M. Balph was appointed to conduct the medical work of the mission, which had become, and continues to be, a very important feature.

The present working force of the mission is: 2 married missionaries, 1 physician, as above mentioned, 3 lady missionaries, 4 native licentiates, who are also ruling elders, and 34 teachers. The total number of pupils under instruction in the schools is 730.

Since the year 1874 the mission at Latakia has had charge of work at Suadea, the ancient Seleucia, which was begun in 1846 by Dr. Holt Yates of London, and carried on by him, or by an agent placed there by him, until 1874, when he gave the property to the Reformed Presbyterian Mission. After his death Mrs. Yates supplied the funds for carrying on the work until the spring of 1890, when her own death took place. Six hundred dollars per annum suffices to carry on the boarding and day school, and the Board is making an effort to supply this sum by some other means, so that the work need not be stopped.

MERSINE, ASIA MINOR.—After the mission at Latakia had been established, it was found that a large number of Nusairiyeh were living in the cities of Mersine, Tarsus, and Adana, and surrounding villages, in Asia Minor, and it was decided to open a station among them; and accordingly, in the fall of 1882, Dr. Metheny and Miss Sterrett went there and established a mission, of which the city of Mersine is the headquarters. Here too, notwithstanding very great difficulties and obstacles, the work has made progress. The working force is 2 ministers, 3 female missionaries, and 6 native teachers in charge of six schools, with an aggregate attendance of 153 pupils.

CYPRUS.—Some years ago, to put him beyond the reach of persecution, a native teacher was sent from Latakia to Larnaca, on the island of Cyprus. While there he gathered together some children and taught them, thus beginning a work which was continued by the Latakia Mission until 1890, when the school had to be closed. The work was, however, only relinquished for a time, not abandoned; and the Board has now under appointment a missionary to Cyprus, under whose care it is hoped a successful mission may be developed.

**Reformed Presbyterian Church of North America, General Synod, Board of Missions.** Headquarters, Philadelphia, Pa.—The foreign missionary work of the General Synod of the Reformed Presbyterian Church was commenced in 1836, in the Northwest Provinces of India. In that year Dr. James Campbell was sent to Saharanpur. In the following year Rev. Joseph Caldwell and family and Mr. James Craig were sent out to join Dr. Campbell, and a Presbytery was organized in connection with the General Synod. A large orphanage was gathered at Saharanpur, the principal station, and sub-stations were formed at Roorkee and Dehra. In 1868 the Presbytery of Saharanpur, which had derived its support partly from the Reformed Presbyterian Board and partly from the Presbyterian Board, withdrew from the General Synod, and the mission stations passed under the control of the Presbyterian Board. In 1883 the mission at Roorkee, by mutual arrangement, reverted to the control of the General Synod, and in the same year the Rev. George W. Scott was sent thither by the Synod. Mr. Scott now has under his care a congregation at Roorkee, eight sub-stations, with a catechist at each, and four zenanas in or near Roorkee. At two of these

stations schools have been established and are in successful operation. Preaching services, Sabbath-schools, and prayer-meetings are held regularly at Roorkee. Preaching services are also held in the adjacent villages, in eight of which, as has been said, sub-stations have been formed.

In 1884, Mr. Charles G. Scott, formerly of Sialkot, was brought to the United States by the General Synod. After passing through the Synod's Theological Seminary in Philadelphia, Mr. Scott entered the medical department of the University of Pennsylvania, from which he was graduated in 1889, and in the same year was sent by the General Synod to India to join his brother at Roorkee. He has since organized a congregation of thirteen members at Muzaffarnaggar, and a church building and mission house are in course of erection at Patala, where the medical department will be an important feature of the work. Just before Mr. Scott's departure for India he was instrumental in leading to Christ a young man from India who belonged to the Society of Arya Somaj, and who is now being educated in Philadelphia by the General Synod for work among his countrymen.

**Reformed Presbyterian Church in Scotland ; Foreign Mission.**—From the year 1852 up till 1863 the Reformed Presbyterian Church of Scotland had mainly confined its foreign mission operations to the New Hebrides. In the latter year the church was divided over questions bearing upon the distinctive principles and position hitherto held and maintained by the church. The missionaries in the foreign field adhered to the majority of the Synod, who, in 1876, united with the Free Church of Scotland. Since that date the work in the New Hebrides, formerly carried on by the Reformed Presbyterian Church, has been under the direction of the Free Church of Scotland. The minority, who still continued to adhere to the principles and position of the church, found themselves so much weakened, numerically and financially, by the disruption of 1863, that they felt it impossible to continue to carry on work in the foreign field, alone. In these circumstances, an approach was made in 1865 to the Irish Reformed Presbyterian Synod, then contemplating entrance upon work in the foreign field, with a view to the establishment of a joint mission. An arrangement of this kind was subsequently entered into by the two Synods. Appeals were made for missionary agents, and, after some disappointments, Mr. James Martin, M.A., M.D., offered himself for service in the foreign field and was accepted. Syria, where the Reformed Presbyterian Church in the United States of America had already established a mission, was selected as the sphere of operations, and Dr. Martin was ordained and sent out in 1871. In 1875 Dr. Martin fixed on Antioch as a field and centre for his missionary labors, and up till the present he has continued vigorously to prosecute the work in that place and in surrounding districts. For a time both the preaching of the gospel and the educational work in the schools had to be conducted in rented premises; and those obtainable were not always of a suitable and satisfactory kind. After some delay a plot of ground was secured and a building for mission purposes was erected at a cost of nearly two thousand pounds sterling. This building furnishes accommodations for public worship, for dispensary purposes, and serves as a residence for the missionaries.

In 1884 a branch mission was established at Idlib, a village between forty and fifty miles distant from Antioch, and recently a mission school for girls has been opened in Suadea, the ancient Seleucia. In 1883 Miss Martha Cunningham, who had been under special training for some time, was designated and sent out to Syria as a female missionary to strengthen the mission staff there. Mr. Thomas Kirkwood, M.A., Greenock, Scotland, has offered his services as a missionary to Syria, and he is at present prosecuting medical studies in order to go out as a fully qualified medical missionary. The work is carried on by the stated preaching of the gospel to the congregation that assembles in the mission premises; open air preaching among the Fellaheen; religious instruction in the mission schools; visiting, Bible reading and religious conversation by European female missionaries; Bible reading and exposition by a native colporteur; and Bible reading by two native women converts. The members of the mission congregation are mostly drawn from the Greek church; but efforts are made to reach the other sections of the population—Moslems, Jews, and Nusairiyeh—as opportunity offers, and some of all these classes have been reached either through the preaching of the gospel, instructions in the mission schools, or by means of private personal dealing with the individuals.

The present statistics of the mission are: 1 ordained medical missionary, 2 female missionaries, 5 native teachers; 1 colporteur; and 2 native Bible women. The number of members gathered in is about 40. The ordinary expenditure on the mission will amount to over £600 sterling annually. The mission secretary for the Synod in Ireland is Rev. J. D. Houston, B.A., Coleraine; and Rev. Robert Dunlop, Paisley, is the secretary for the Synod in Scotland.

**Rehoboth,** a town in Great Namaqualand, West South Africa, celebrated for its hot springs. Mission station of the Rhenish Missionary Society; 1 ordained missionary, 1 female missionary, 5 native helpers, 244 communicants, 117 school-children.

**Relation of Missionaries to Governments.**—This is a matter of great perplexity, difficulty, and importance. The missionary is in one sense a man without a country. In another sense he is a man of many countries. He does not renounce his nationality or citizenship. As Paul at times fell back on his high position as a Jew and Pharisee, so the missionary must often assert his privileges of birth and country. At the same time he is a resident of foreign lands and inevitably related to foreign governments, on his own account, as an individual; in behalf of the property and other local interests acquired by his mission, and in behalf of converts and adherents, who rely on him for justice and protection in secular as well as sacred things. As Paul appeared now before Ananias, the high-priest; now before Felix and Festus, Roman governors; now before Agrippa, and finally appealed to Cæsar: so the missionary may find himself tossed between different, often conflicting, sources of authority, seeking to reach some supreme Cæsar, often finding only Herods and Pilates who will make friendship over his defeat.

The relation which he sustains to various governments may be one of defiance, of alliance, or of independence. These occur in all degrees and in all combinations. They may apply to the home government, the foreign governments, or to both. Ever since the Apostles met the prohibition of their persecutors by saying, "We ought to obey God rather than men," and rejoiced "that they were counted worthy to suffer dishonor for His name," the first preachers of the gospel have encountered in most countries the hostility of the powers that be. From Stephen to Bishop Hannington they have found hostile peoples and rulers arrayed against them, and yet have persisted in gentle defiance of threat and command and force. The first Protestant work in Japan was in quiet disregard of hostile laws, proclamations, and penalties. And for years before, Catholic priests had been at work sustaining suppressed Christianity, "sleeping," as one of them expressed it, "by day, working by night." Long have they also done the same in Korea, where, at last, our own missionaries are to-day, having come for the understood purpose of establishing a prohibited religion. Their position at Seoul, the capital, affords a most interesting instance of the curious intermingling of possible relations with different governments. As foreigners at an open port they are under the diplomatic protection of their home governments. As court physicians, heads of hospitals, asylums, schools, etc., they are under the protection of the Korean government, receive distinct appointment as Korean officials of a certain rank, and have a kind of private policemen assigned them for protection and service. In private they are also recognized as missionaries. Yet in all this public capacity, mission labor is prohibited; in any capacity it is liable to be stopped at any moment. The situation is one full of complications both for the judgment and the conscience. But Christianity is taking root in Korea; it has made progress more rapidly than in Japan at the start; churches are already organized, one of which has grown in three years from twenty members to over one hundred.

Even in Japan one restriction yet remains which involves the question of the true relation of the missionaries to the Japanese government. Outside of the open ports, passports are still required. These may be procured for residence by teaching in a Japanese school. For travel they can be had only for purposes of health and science. It is still a question among missionaries whether it is legitimate to use such travelling passports for evangelistic purposes, and whether the truer policy would not be to refuse to take out such ambiguous permits, casting all the evangelistic work on the native Christians until the whole country is thrown open to foreigners.

The first missions to India were in defiance not so much of heathen, as of Christian, government. The history of the East India Company's friendship with heathenism and hostility to Christian effort is one of disgrace, happily relieved, however, by noble exceptions, and steadily improved by the pressure of the better sentiment of England until, with the assumption of rule by the British government in 1857, the present policy of friendly neutrality was adopted. At the time, however, there was often nothing for the deported or prohibited missionaries to do but seek some other country, like Burma, or cast themselves on the help of a friendly government like that of Denmark at Serampore, or wait in quiet and disguise for reluctantly extorted permission to go on with work.

In Turkey the Christian laborer stands under the protection of his own government, with explicit recognition of his character as a missionary. Yet so far as his work touches Mohammedanism, he is engaged in an endeavor to lead persons to violate by a change of religion the most stringent provisions of their sacred law. This change only the most persistent pressure on the part of Christian governments has induced the Turkish government to permit in theory. Practically it is still bitterly opposed. The relation of a missionary to a government thus compelled against its will is of necessity strained. He must avow purposes utterly repugnant to the authorities. Yet he must claim rights and privileges secured for him and his work by treaty obligations. And he must have constant dealings with lower and higher officials who on the most flimsy pretext, or with no pretext at all, seek to close his schools and chapels, stop his printing-press, and silence his native preachers, while the unthinking multitude are stirred up to riot against Protestants, and wildest excesses are committed, until the diplomatic screws force the powers at Constantinople to interfere. The censorship of the press exercised in Turkey and especially directed against the missionaries is in many cases only more ignorant than it is severe.

School-books are claimed for inspection. Months pass. A decision is entreated. At last some official, who may know little or nothing of the contents of the book, gives or refuses the permit. Hamlet, Macbeth, Richard the Third, and Julius Cæsar are prohibited because they portray the death of kings. A pamphlet was recently published by a Greek benevolent society in Constantinople which bore on the title-page a quotation from Paul's Epistle to the Galatians. Shortly after an officer appeared in the printing-office with instructions to arrest one Paul, who had been writing letters to the people of Galata, a section of Constantinople, and to secure a copy of these presumably seditious letters. It was of no use to tell him that Paul died centuries ago, and that Galatia was a province of the old Roman Empire. In default of Paul, the editor was arrested and put in prison, where he might have been to-day had not the Greek patriarch come forward with a New Testament and shown the officials Paul's letter. At present the Turkish law prohibits the importation of all books reflecting on the government or religion of the empire. The worst of these are burned, the others returned to their native land at the expense of the owners. To keep in communication with hostile officials, to avert, evade, or endure oppressive laws, to contend for old-time rights and privileges, to press important cases on the attention of the American consul or minister—these are among the great embarrassments and hardships of a missionary's life, not only in Turkey, but in China, Korea, and, to some extent, still in Japan. Such are also some of the great difficulties in Austria and other papal countries. And a large part of the time of the American minister at Constantinople, even though he be a Hebrew, must be and has been spent in protecting the interests of

missionaries against the assaults and intrigues of those who are opposed to their work.

How a man shall be at once just and wise and true and Christian is often a most difficult question to answer. To specify but one point: How far may a missionary yield to the corrupt practices which prevail in Turkey and China, and secure his ends by a "proper" consideration?

Backsheesh is expected, and demanded. In most instances it is practically nothing more than a fee imposed by custom instead of being sanctioned by law. Yet its influence is demoralizing. How far shall the missionary sanction the prevailing corruption? how far must he resist it? This most practical question repeatedly recurs.

The missionary's relations to the government in India are also embarrassing in much the same way, though from a very different cause, as there it is help rather than hindrance that he receives from the state. Subject to official inspection, the government makes large grants of aid to all schools which fulfil certain conditions. The mission schools are largely sustained by these grants. But to conform to the minute and ever-changing requirements, to prepare scholars for the numerous examinations, to secure and retain the favor of the inspector and other officials, involves such an amount of time, delay, labor, annoyance, and secularization of the school, that many missionaries are of the opinion that it would be better, once for all, to dispense with all financial help from the government.

Much more entangling, however, are the relations of the missionary who enters into alliance with governments of any kind. It is as harmful to his work as the alliance of Church and State has ever been from the time of Constantine. The failings of Roman Catholic missions in this respect, whether in North and South America, in Japan, China, India, or other countries, are too well known to be told. They form a most instructive part of the history of missions. France and Germany to-day are eager to offer such alliance to missionaries. France, in particular, has sought to advance its diplomatic and colonial interests through claiming to be the protector of the missions. It has long sought to gain political power in China by posing as the patron of all Roman Catholic missionaries of whatever nationality. It has regarded and treated both Catholic and Protestant missionaries as its own emissaries in pushing its colonial schemes. The Legion of Honor has been recently conferred upon M. Casalis, an old French Protestant missionary, for "extending the influence of France in Basutoland," in the sphere of British influence in South Africa.

Germany, too, has the colonial fever, and the interest in missions has been increased all over the land because it is believed that even if missionaries are not successful as Christianizers of heathendom, they can be used wisely as Germanizers of certain parts of it. As a veteran missionary friend in Germany puts it: 'The opinion of the German African Society with regard to missionary societies is that they are not unselfish attempts to spread the gospel, but merely handmaids to colonial politics—a cow to give milk to the mother-country."

But this very alliance of the government with missionaries gives rise to a new set of hostile relations. France wants only French, Germany only German, missionaries. The language and sentiments of each country must be exclusively taught in the colonies of that country. Missionaries of other nationalities must be excluded, for they neither could nor would enter into such alliances for political and national schemes. This policy has been working with most harmful effect on many missions. It only just failed of breaking up the work of the A. B. C. F. M. in the Caroline Islands, now claimed by Spain. It has driven from Tahiti the British missionaries who converted that island, and in pursuance of it France is now endeavoring to annex the lesser islands of the Society group, to the vast harm of English mission work.

The work of the Presbyterian Board in its Gaboon and Corisco missions in West Africa has been seriously interfered with by the edict of the French Government which substitutes French not only for English, but even for the vernacular. The attempt has been made to transfer the work to the French Protestant Society, but so far without success. In the Cameroon country the English Baptists have been driven out by the Germans.

One of the most conspicuous instances of this baneful nationalization of missions occurred at the close of 1887 in the Loyalty Islands. The London Missionary Society had labored there so successfully, that "the whole of the people, so lately wild and savage cannibals, had embraced Christianity." There was left no trace of heathenism. There were self-supporting churches with over 3,000 members. There was but one missionary, with 40 native pastors. Then came the blow which Rev. John Jones thus describes : "I, the only English missionary on the island, while doing nothing more in religious work than revising the Maré Scriptures, was, on the morning of the 9th of December, 1887, expelled by the French Government, at half an hour's notice, from the island, where, with my wife, I had labored to elevate the natives for more than 34 years." Here the French Protestants have established a state church, and regard the native Christians as rebels because they will not attend it.

The whole matter of colonies and missions has become a burning question, and the energetic protest of German mission magazines against all mingling of the missionary interests with national movements stands in strong contrast with the position of most French Protestants.

Whatever profit may accrue to the government from such alliances as this, there can be no question as to their harm to missions. The Dutch Government long ago established religion on an official basis in Ceylon, requiring from all native office-seekers assent to its church creed as a condition of appointment. It has left the opprobrious epithet of "Government Christian" as a warning against all similar attempts to do spiritual work by secular bribes. The missionary is the ambassador of the King of kings. He is the herald of the Prince of Peace. He denies and betrays his Lord if he allows himself to be entangled in worldly schemes which, under cover of a Christian name and purpose, seek political aggrandizement. This danger of alliances with rulers and powers of this world is nowhere greater to-day than in Africa. Petty potentates of every tribe are only too happy to avail themselves of the resources and science and

prestige of a European or American to overcome a rival or to regain a throne. Not all missionaries are as wise as those of the Church Missionary Society on Lake Victoria Nyanza, who refused their services for this purpose to King Mwanga, and sought to prevent their native converts from joining his army. It was an old scandal which declared, especially of China, "With the missionary there is always the inevitable gunboat." The scandal will be as great in Africa, if with the missionary there is always the inevitable gunpowder. "What are we to think," writes Dr. Cust, "of rifles, revolvers, and one thousand rounds of ball-cartridges being part of the outfit of a Christian missionary to Africa in 1880?" Whether for resistance or succor to the native chiefs, such appeal to arms, to armies, and home governments back of them, is not of the true spirit of missions. There is frequent call from Africa to England that it should interfere by force in behalf of endangered missionaries. Lord Salisbury in 1888, however, clearly declined to interfere in territory beyond the sphere of British influence. "I will not use any language," he said, "to encourage the belief that the government will make any attempt by military action to support the commercial and religious efforts of the missionaries there. . . . We are certain that we should only injure, instead of promoting the great civilizing and missionary efforts if we were to convert them into a cause of war—of war the most exhausting, the most terrible, the least remunerative, in any sense ; war with the countless savages who fill these territories." That is perfectly true, and should lead missionaries to avoid all militant relations with their own or any other government.

But another large class of questions is added to those which perplex the missionary when he is appealed to by native Christians to secure government aid or interference in behalf of them and their interests. The expectation and hope of such aid and protection from the missionary is one of the motives most damaging to the sincerity of new converts. It harms the missionary, too, by filling his time and thoughts with civil matters, lawsuits, appeals, etc.

The temptation to such reliance on the arm of flesh to secure the rights and promote the interests of native Christians is strongest in British India and its protected states, where British law has modified many old customs in favor of humanity and religious equality. In Travancore, for instance, the question of the caste privileges of Christians comes up. They are said to be low caste, which would shut them off from much. They claim to be no caste. One typical case decides many. The privileges of entire communities are at stake; the courts must decide, the missionaries must make up, present, and push the case. That may keep them in the courts for years. Anywhere in India the right of Christians to use the village well or fountain may be denied. But the government has declared the wells free to all. The missionary must bring the case before the collector.

Lands of Christians are involved in lawsuits, perhaps brought on as part of a petty persecution by their heathen neighbors, perhaps independent of all religious cause. The influence of the missionary is incessantly invoked to help his adherents. Natural sympathy for those in distress and the desire to see fair play have made some men allow most of their time for years to be consumed by such lawsuits, whose result, of whatever sort, was sure to be harmful to their spiritual work.

There is another connection with the local government, however, which often works for good. From their superior education and ability missionaries are often appointed to some official position. Dr. Verbeck was for some time a state official of Japan. President Martin, of Pekin, at the head of the Imperial College, was appointed by the Government of China. Dr. Allen and Mrs. Bunker were the court physicians of the King and Queen of Korea. Dr. McKenzie at Tientsien was closely related to the Viceroy Li Hung Chang. Others have served for a time as diplomatic agent of the home government, like S. Wells Williams. Dr. Whitney, of Tokyo, as Secretary of the American Legation, is in a position to use his official as well as medical services for the benefit of Christianity. Such positions often prepare the way for the gospel, and commend it to strangers.

Yet as a rule, contrasting the high calling of a simple missionary with any other position, one might say of some who turn aside from the mission to official work what Dr Carey wrote regretfully of his son, "Felix has shrunk to an ambassador."

It is not strange, when one sees what a snare is spread in all such dealings with magistrates and civil authorities, that many of those who are most consecrated and experienced should decide that the only safe and desirable plan for missionaries is that of entire neutrality in all such matters. The best they can ask from any government is to be let alone, and regarded with friendly neutrality. The best they can do for the mission is to eschew the sword and the rifle, to lean on no arm of flesh, invoke no aid of consul or magistrate, but rely on God and what he may do for his servants. They are not the foes of any people, they should not be the political engines of any government, nor should they make any government their engine.

Alone, unarmed, and uninjured Mr. McCarthy of the China Inland Mission walked through the whole of China. "I am persuaded," writes the secretary of a leading society, "that official remonstrances do not help in the long-run. Patience is our strength when we are in the right." And another says: "During the whole course of the mission's history our agents have made their way and found safety and acceptance among savage tribes, quite independently of any aid from gunboats or otherwise from government. . . . Treaty rights involve treaty wrongs, to the injury of the people, and the hindrance in the most fatal manner of missionary effort."

When the German Government had discharged the British Baptists from the Cameroon country they asked the Basle Missionary Society, as one related to and sympathetic with Germany, to undertake the work in their place. The Society made the grand response that it had always maintained a position above all political considerations, and would never depart from it, all that was asked being liberty of action.

An experiment in this line of freedom from all reliance on government is now being tried in the Soudan. The "Church Missionary Intelligencer" (June, 1890), says: "Mr. Brooke is anxious that no missionary should seek safety from peril by virtue of being a British subject, and so looking to the British authorities for protection. He wishes to go to the Moslem and say, ' You and I are both in equal peril of life and liberty; nothing will be done for me that would not be done for you; if you have to suffer for Christ, so have I.' In the Turkish Empire a missionary could scarcely say this; in the Soudan he can if he will. . . . All that Mr. Brooke and Mr. Robinson really asked for was, (1) that no protection should be invoked for them which could not equally be invoked for any converts from Mohammedanism that God might give them; and (2) that neither for them nor for the converts should force or threats, involving the possible use of force, be employed. At a large and enthusiastic meeting of the committee it was resolved that the committee . . . would be thankful to welcome and send out at once a band of earnest, devoted men, who, with full knowledge of the risks involved, are prepared to carry on a vigorous mission on such methods as have been above indicated." Three weeks later the following explanatory resolution was added: "That while they heartily approve of the desire expressed by Mr. G. Wilmot-Brooke and his brethren to go among Mohammedans with exactly the same liabilities and perils as would attach to Christian converts from Mohammedanism in the same countries, they cannot pledge themselves, and do not understand that the resolutions of the committee of correspondence were intended to pledge them, never under any circumstances to interpose in any way to secure the safety or deliverance of the Society's missionaries or converts who may be in peril of life or liberty; but they put on record their conviction that the use of force, or of threats implying its possible use, in behalf of missions is a line of action which, as a missionary society, they could not take any steps to promote."

The general rule of the Church Missionary Society, as published among its regulations, is as follows: "Every missionary is strictly charged to abstain from interfering in the political affairs of the country or place in which he may be laboring;" "Never assume a position of hostility to the ruling powers;" "Stand aloof from all questions of political leadership and political partisanship;" "Tribute to whom tribute is due, custom to whom custom, fear to whom fear, honor to whom honor."

But the instructions of the China Inland Mission to its missionaries are still more strict. Under the head of "Relations to Governments" it says: "Too great caution cannot be exercised by all missionaries residing or journeying inland to avoid difficulties and complication with the people, and especially with the authorities. All the agents of the mission must fully understand that they go out depending for help and protection on the LIVING GOD, and not relying on an arm of flesh. While availing themselves of any privileges offered by the British or Chinese Governments, they must make no claim for their help or protection. Appeals to our consuls to procure the punishment of offenders, or to demand the vindication of real or supposed rights, or indemnifications for losses, are to be avoided. Should trouble or persecution arise inland, a friendly representation may be made to the local Chinese officials, failing redress from whom, those suffering must be satisfied to leave their case in God's hands. Under no circumstances must any missionary on his own responsibility make any appeal to the British authorities. As a last resource the injunction of the Master can be followed: 'If they persecute you in this city, flee ye into another.'"

Of that independence of all earthly government which must often become defiance, no one has spoken better than Dr. Duff in his letter in 1841 to Lord Auckland, Governor-General of India. In a question "affecting the interests of eternity not less than those of time, the Christian missionary must not, dares not, be silent, even if his voice should be uplifted against kings and governors and all earthly potentates. When the honor and glory of his Divine Master and the imperishable destinies of men are involved, the ambassador of Jesus can brook no dalliance with mere human greatness or rank or power. In the spirit of Basil in the presence of the Roman prefect, he is ever ready to exclaim: 'In all other things you will find us the most mild, the most accommodating among men; we carefully guard against the least appearance of haughtiness, even towards the obscurest citizen, still more so with respect to those who are invested with sovereign authority; but the moment that the cause of God is concerned, we despise everything.'"

**Religious Tract Society.** Headquarters, Paternoster Row, London, Eng' nd.— This Society was established in London in May, 1799, at the instance of Rev. G. Burder and Rowland Hill with some associates. Its first secretary was the Rev. Joseph Hughes. From the first, the Society has been unsectarian in principle, always selecting its committee from Churchmen and Nonconformists equally. Its special work is the publication and dissemination of Christian tracts and books, both at home and abroad. It carries on its work both by special agents and colporteurs, and by means of grants to Missionary and Tract Societies throughout the world. The accompanying statement of the general character of its work is from one of the officers of the Society, and indicates very clearly the nature of the work carried on by all the different Tract and Publication Societies of both Great Britain and America.

Towards the close of the last century and the beginning of the present there came that great outburst of missionary enterprise to which all the most powerful societies owe their origin, and the blessed influences of which are yearly widening and deepening over the whole heathen world. At this very epoch, viz. in 1799, a few earnest, devout, practical Christian men met together in St. Paul's Churchyard, and founded a society, then scanty in numbers and weak in resources, for the production and the sale of religious books and tracts. But the little society was a seed. It had within it some portion of the divine life, and it grew; and now "it has become a tree, and the fowls of the air come and lodge in the branches thereof." Out of the Religious Tract Society sprang almost immediately the Bible Society, and in less than a hundred years the work of the Tract Society has so developed that it is now carried on in two hundred languages, and the publications fostered, and in many cases rendered possible only by its aid, are now coextensive with the whole mission field. It is no exaggeration to say that there is scarcely a society or a missionary laboring for the salvation of the heathen who is not aided materially, directly or indirectly, by its work.

It was not until the year 1818 that the Society made its first grant for foreign work. In that year it voted $550 to aid French Protestants in their efforts to counteract infidelity and irreligion by a wide circulation of tracts. This work developed into the foundation of the Paris Tract Society in 1820, and of the Toulouse Book Society in 1835. From this beginning, close to her own shores, the circles of beneficent influence have widened out decade by decade until they now embrace the habitable globe.

The original method of foreign translation work was to do it in the main, if not wholly, at the central office in London. Such tracts and books as were deemed suitable for the localities assisted were prepared in London, and then forwarded to the distributing agencies. In the beginning of the great enterprise it was hardly possible to do otherwise. Means of communication were slow and uncertain, laborers were few and far between, knowledge of special districts and special needs was necessarily imperfect. But the principle on which the work has been pursued from the first is to do the best possible at any given time, although it may not be the ideally perfect.

In process of time experience indicated defects in the method of centralization. It was found, for example, that many tracts prepared in London for French readers had one radical defect—they were not truly French. The words and phrases were those of our volatile, light-hearted, attractive brethren, but the subtler modes of thought, the national point of view, the knowledge of French life, were not there, and hence the tracts only very imperfectly did their work. And so it came to pass that a new principle emerged, viz., that of trying to work wherever possible through local scholars and translators. The enormous advantage of this method can easily be seen. The worker on the spot, in close touch with those whom the tract, or book, or newspaper is intended to benefit, familiar with local coloring, and modes of thought and peculiarities of language, must of necessity know—other gifts being equal—how best to put the truth into the language and form desired.

Hence the bulk of the work for France was transferred at an early date to Paris and Toulouse, the Society in London stipulating that the workers in these places should first determine what in their judgment was best suited for the needs of France, should then put their proposals in a clear and business-like form, and thus render them suitable for consideration by the London Committee. When this was done, if, in accordance with their prayerful judgment, the scheme was one the Committee could approve, the Tract Society did all in its power to carry it into practice. For many years past, in addition to special grants for special publications, the Dépôt Centrale, Paris, has received $1,000 annually, the Paris Tract Society $1,000 or $1,500, and the Toulouse Book Society $2,000.

The most interesting recent extension of this principle in the foreign field has taken place in China. In no country is the circulation of

Christian literature easier or more fruitful in the most blessed results. From the time of Morrison onwards the missionaries have labored unceasingly in the effort to give the millions of China pure Christian literature. Special conditions have rendered the work exceptionally difficult. Missionaries are but human, and differences of opinion—carried sometimes to a point where they have been positively hurtful—have not been unknown. In 1882 the Society made a resolute effort, so far as their translation work was concerned, to bring about closer union and fuller co-operation among all their helpers. As regards translation work, the day for the solitary worker has almost passed. Hence Dr. Murdoch visited all the chief centres of Chinese Christian literary production, held conferences with the brethren, and finally formulated a scheme which has since, to a very large extent, been accomplished. This was to map out China into well-defined districts, to secure a thoroughly representative committee for each district, to lay down as an axiom that the chief literary enterprises of each district must be carefully considered by its committee, and that only upon their recommendation could tracts and books be sanctioned for publication. Three such committees are now at work: the North China Tract Society, having its headquarters at Tientsin; the East China Tract Society, with its centre at Shanghai; and the Mid-China, located at Hankow. The South China Committee has not yet been formally constituted.

The benefits of this system are: The Committee does not repress but encourages individual effort. It gets the best literary workers to take seats at its board. The various projects are discussed, the literary achievements criticised by the men best competent to form an accurate judgment; while a unanimous request from such a body comes to the home Society with a force which only one consideration—lack of funds—is able to resist.

One constant effort on the part of the Society is to get larger funds for China. Sums varying from $1,250 to $2,000 are granted annually to these committees; the constant effort being made to use these grants as stimulants to the liberality of others. For example, it has become a common practice for the Society to bear a part only of the expense of an undertaking. The proportion varies between one-quarter and three-quarters of the whole outlay. In this way others are influenced to give, and many a useful book, such as the Bulgarian Bible Dictionary, or the Japanese Pilgrim's Progress, or "More about Jesus," in the Congo language, has been thus sent on its useful way. The great missionary societies have always admitted the need for and the benefit of Christian literature in the foreign field; but it is not always possible, and sometimes it is not even deemed needful, to get the very best and ablest men to devote themselves to this department of work. Much, however, has already been accomplished, and still greater results are possible in the near future.

A few examples of what has been done will illustrate the work of the Society. The New Testament part of the well-known Annotated Paragraph Bible has been translated into eleven languages, and of these, special mention may be made of the renderings into Urdu, Marathi, Tamil, Kanarese, Sinhalese, Burmese, and Arabic. The recent visit of Dr. Wright to China, and the great conference held at Shang-

hai early in 1890, emphasized the need in China for not only the Word of God, without word and comment, in such Chinese renderings as the ripest Christian scholarship can give it, but also of editions containing such explanations as will remove difficulties peculiar to Chinese modes of thought and habits of life, and also equip the native convert with the best and latest aids to Bible study. The preparation of such editions as these will, in all probability, fall to the lot of the Tract Society.

Next to the Bible the Pilgrim's Progress is the book that has done most for the evangelization of the human race. This book has now been translated into no less than eighty-five languages, and in almost all of these editions the Society has had a hand, sometimes bearing the whole, sometimes only a fraction, of the cost. In its committee room in Paternoster Row stands a case containing specimens of nearly all these editions, and it would be hard to select a better object-lesson upon the spread of the gospel in our days than a careful inspection of these shelves. The Englishman, the Welshman, the Highlander, the Irish Erse-speaking peasant can there find the book in his native tongue; the Finn, the Russian, the Czech, the Greek, and the Armenian can delight his eye with familiar words and phrases; all the chief languages of India and China are represented; the Cree Indian, the Maori, the Kafir, the Malagasy, the Mexican, the dweller in Eastern or Western Africa, and the whilom cannibal from the islands of the Pacific can there follow the stages of the journey to Mount Zion by the aid of the only language he knows; and as the Japanese or the Chinese sees the Pilgrim struggling in the Slough of Despond, or passing through Vanity Fair, or crossing the cold dark river with the golden gates beyond, his feeling of national pride is gratified by illustrations executed by his own countrymen, representing exclusively costumes and habits familiar to him, and yet showing by the admirable way in which they illustrate the text that the life and the heart of the Oriental are subject to the same sins and need the same Saviour as the dweller in the west.

As illustrations of the scope and variety of foreign translation work, reference may be made to the new publications of 1888 and of 1889. In the former year there were prepared and issued in the way indicated above a Bible Dictionary for Spain, a Hymn-book for Portugal, a Church History for Bohemia, a Book of Prayers and Meditations for Hungary, a Commentary for Bulgaria, Bible Stories and "Come to Jesus" for Poland, a Church History for Samoa, the Pilgrim's Progress in Fanti (East Africa), a Hymn-book for Bechuanaland, the Pilgrim's Progress in Chinese (Swatow), a Hymn Book for Foochow, "More about Jesus" for the Congo, a Concordance for the Loyalty Islands, and a tract by John Williams, the martyr of Eromanga, for the Hervey Group, Polynesia. In 1889 the chief productions were a second edition of the Japanese Pilgrim's Progress and a volume on the "Evidences of Christianity" in the same tongue; a series of four-page tracts in Arabic consisting exclusively of Scripture passages bearing on the fundamental doctrines of Christianity, for circulation among Mohammedans, and at Cairo an Arabic edition of "The Silent Comforter" was published; for Abyssinia the Pilgrim's Progress in Amharic; a new edition of the same book, a Bible Dictionary and a large handsome hymn-book with tonic sol-fa notation for Basutoland; for the Congo "Peep of Day," "Line upon Line," and "More about Jesus;" for Madagascar a "Life of Luther," a volume of Sermons, and a Catechism; for India special schemes have been under consideration, first to secure there a much larger circulation for the "Present Day Tracts," and secondly by the appointment of a special agent to superintend the production of Christian literature by the ablest man.

Great efforts are being made in many parts to preach the gospel by means of newspapers and magazines. In these it is very rare for the Society to take any direct literary part. But it is hardly too much to say that if the aid given by the Society were withdrawn a very large part of this work would be either stopped at once, or else permanently crippled. By money grants, by either free gifts of electrotypes of engravings, or else by supplying them at a merely nominal charge, and above all by free grants of enormous quantities of printing paper, the Society develops this branch of missionary literature. In this way the now very extensive Christian literature of Madagascar has been created; in this way such literary centres as Madras, Calcutta, Hankow, Beirut, and Constantinople have been doubled or quadrupled in power; and although at first the statement may sound somewhat novel, it is yet nevertheless true that the gospel reaches many a family and many a heart because of this power to give clean white printing paper to the chief centres of missionary periodical and literary production.

Some conception of the present scale of this and the other forms of literary effort may be formed from the fact that the total foreign issues of all kinds in 1889 were 15,000,000, and the total expenditure on foreign missionary literary work was as follows: money grants, $50,000; printing paper, $12,500; publications of various kinds, $27,500; electrotypes and engravings, $7,500,—making a grand total of $97,-500 for the year. And these figures give the work of the largest but still only one society among the many that are enlisting the press in the ministry of the gospel to the heathen.

**Rendall, John,** b Halifax, Nova Scotia, January 21st, 1821; lived in Utica, N.Y.; studied at Quincy, Ill.; was ordained at Roxbury, Mass., October 13th, 1845; sailed as a missionary of the A. B. C. F. M. the same year for India. He was connected with the Madura Mission. Mr. Herrick thus writes: "Mr. Rendall's love for the natives, shown by a readiness to deny himself in their behalf, his excellent advice to them when in trouble, led them in great numbers, heathen as well as Christians, to trust and love him. The brotherly love and absence of self-interest, always apparent in him, together with the rare ability shown by him in the discharge of difficult duties, caused his associates to love him in return, to honor him, and to depend on him with peculiar confidence." For more than twenty-five years he was called to fill the offices of secretary and treasurer. His standing as a clergyman, and a man called to the frequent discharge of duties demanding peculiar qualifications, led officers of the government and other gentlemen with whom he came in contact, to regard him with great re-

spect. Mr. Rendall had for some time suffered from a disease which required surgical treatment. Dr. Chester of the mission accompanied him to Bombay to assist in the operation. The operation was not successful, and he died June 13th, 1883, at the house of Rev. E. S. Hume, after thirty-eight years of mission service.

**Rhea, Samuel Audley,** b. Blountville, Tenn., U. S. A., January 23d, 1827; graduated at Knoxville University 1847; Union Theological Seminary, New York, 1850; spent some weeks in visiting the churches in Tennessee, presenting the subject of missions; ordained February 2d, 1851; sailed as a missionary of the A.B.C.F.M. March 4th, same year, for the Nestorian Mission, in company with Mr. Stoddard, who was on his return to Persia. In 1851 Mr. Rhea went to the new station at Gawar, among the Koordish Mountains. His associates having died or left, he had the entire charge of the mission field, which was one of much hardship. His health being impaired, he spent the winters of 1858 and 1859 at Oroomiah, and in the latter year was obliged to return to his native land. He re-embarked July 3d, 1860, for Persia, and was stationed at Oroomiah till his death. Mr. Rhea was a close student, a thorough and accurate scholar. He was well versed in Hebrew and Syriac; spoke the modern Syriac with great accuracy and fluency; was able to preach in Azerbijan-Turkish with acceptance to the Armenians and others. His last public discourse in that language was delivered in Tabriz a fortnight before his death to a congregation of deeply-interested hearers. While at Tabriz he pursued his investigations in the Tartar-Turkish with the view of translating the Scriptures into that tongue, having already rendered in it the Sermon on the Mount. While in Koordistan he prosecuted the study of Koordish, and wrote out a small synopsis of the grammar. He was treasurer of the mission, and its business agent in general. He also had the charge of fifteen villages, some of them very large. His travels among the wilds of Koordistan were often protracted and perilous. He embraced every opportunity to preach Christ among Nestorians, Armenians, Mohammedans and Jews, high and low. He had long desired to visit Tabriz, for the purpose of settling difficulties in the church and removing prejudices from the mind of the foreign minister. The first week of his arrival there he took a severe cold in a sudden change of temperature, which brought on a fever. The next day he appeared convalescent, and started on his journey homeward. Reaching the village of Mnian he passed the night in great suffering. The next day he set out for Ali Shah, where in a few hours he passed away. He died September 2d, 1865. The mission thus testifies concerning his worth: "We are called to deplore the removal of one of the most amiable of men, one of the most single-minded and devoted of Christians, one of the most gifted, indefatigable, and devoted of missionaries, and one of the most eloquent and effective of preachers that ever adorned and blessed the missionary cause." Dr. Perkins remarks: "Mr. Rhea is one of the finest preachers I ever heard, whether in the English or in the Nestorian language. The Nestorians denominate him Chrysostom, from his remarkable powers as a preacher."

**Rhenish Mission Society,** Headquarters. Barmen, Germany.—A small mission society was formed at Elberfeld in 1799, and another at Barmen in 1815. They kept closely connected with the Society of Basle and had their missionaries educated there or in Berlin. But in 1825 an independent mission seminary was founded at Barmen, and in 1828 delegates from the societies of Elberfeld, Barmen, Cologne, and Wesel met at Mettmann and formed the Rhenish Mission Society, which was confirmed, June 24th, 1829, by Friedrich Wilhelm II.

In the same year the new Society sent out its first missionaries. They went to South Africa and landed at Cape Colony in October, 1829. In that region 40 missionaries under the direction of the Moravian Brethren, the London Society, the Wesleyans, and the Free Scotch Society, were already at work at 30 stations among the Hottentots, Katirs, Negroes, Bastards, etc., and the Rhenish missionaries hesitated where to go. Finally, in the beginning of 1830, they founded their first station at Wupperthal, and in 1832 they built and consecrated their first church at Unterbarmen, after which the South African Mission progressed steadily and safely. In 1834 the Society found that they had more missionaries ready for work than could be employed in Africa, and moved by what they had heard from the American missionary, Abeel, and the Dutch missionary, Medhurst, they decided to open a new field in Borneo, to which they afterwards added two other places in the Dutch colonies of the East Indies, Sumatra in 1862, and Nias in 1865. In 1846 they had also begun a Chinese mission.

Meanwhile difficulties arose at home. In 1881 the trade company of the Society failed and left it in debt for 204,966 marks. It was compelled to transfer parts of its Chinese mission to the societies of Basle and Berlin, but the interruption of its activity was only short, and it has recently been able to start a new mission in New Guinea. Thus it works at present in four different fields: South Africa, Dutch East Indies, China, and New Guinea. In 1888 its revenue amounted to 382,968 marks; its expenses to 384,762 marks. The whole body of converts under its care was 32,870, among whom were 10,475 communicants, contributing 49,752 marks. It maintained 53 stations, 75 out-stations, 69 ordained missionaries, and 166 salaried native helpers.

*South Africa.*—This field comprises three distinct divisions: Cape Colony, Namaqua, and Herero. Cape Colony is the best developed of these divisions. It is financially completely self-supporting, though it is very far from being morally able to govern itself. The population consists of European settlers, imported Negroes, native Hottentots, and a mixed people of all possible combinations and degrees. Such a population has, of course, no national religion and no national priesthood, a circumstance which cannot but be of some advantage to the Christian missionary. On the other side, however, the old saying that a half-breed is more likely to inherit the parents' vices than their virtues, is not altogether without truth, and the inborn levity, supercilliousness, and frivolity of the half-breeds, together with those remnants of old superstitions which still linger among them, and those new-fangled vices which they are only too ready to adopt, present grave difficulties. Complaints of drunkenness and lewd-

ness are loud enough in almost every report from the individual stations, and only in one case, Schietfontein or Carnavon, the remark has been added, that however lamentable those vices may be, they cannot be said to be on the increase but rather on the decrease. Another circumstance causes considerable embarrassment. When the first Rhenish missionaries arrived, the Hottentots, Negroes, and half-breeds were slaves, and the gulf between the slave and the master cannot at once be filled up by an emancipation edict. On the contrary, the situation becomes for a time more strained. The former slave naturally looks to the missionary as a protector, and the former master is apt to see in him a kind of seducer. The Cape Colony Government gives a land grant to every school which has a certain number of pupils and the official school inspector's certificate for the standard of those pupils. The schools are consequently crowded. The settlers complain of the impertinence and laziness of the working-class, and the missionaries complain of the havoc which the excitement of a discovery of new diamond or gold fields plays in their congregations. The state of affairs is somewhat peculiar, when, as for instance at Saron, the station owns considerable landed estates, and the missionary is not only the pastor, but also the employer.

In Namaqua the mission meets great difficulties. The country is by no means sterile, but it is dry, and the climate is rainless. Without artificial irrigation—something which, of course, in the present state of civilization cannot be thought of—the soil is unfit for agriculture, and the inhabitants are nomads. The bulk of the population consists of a Hottentot tribe, the Namaquas, who were gradually forced by their stronger neighbors to leave Cape Colony, where they originally belonged. They brought firearms with them, took a fancy for hunting, neglected their herds, and when game began to grow scarce they robbed their northern neighbors, the Hereros, who had large and fat herds and no fire-arms. Soon, however, the Hereros came into possession of the necessary weapons. Their defence was successful. The raids were thrown back upon the Namaquas, and in the war, still raging, some of the northern mission stations were utterly destroyed, and consequently had to be abandoned. Only the five northern stations have been able to continue their work in peace. Moreover, while in Cape Colony everybody is able and willing to speak Dutch, the Namaqua understands nothing but Namaqua, and that language is so uncongenial to the white man's ear and tongue, that even missionaries who for all scientific or literary purposes were complete masters of it, could not preach without an interpreter. On account of the unpromising prospects of the country and the people, the Germans have been the sole workers of the field, and at Walfisch Bay, which is the inlet not only to Namaqua, but also to Herero, they celebrate service in German.

In Herero, he who comes from the south comes into contact for the first time with a genuine African Negro tribe. They are herdsmen; the milk of their cows is their daily food. They have something like a national religion, and national organization. They are dull and slow to impress, but what they once grasp they hold tightly. The language proved an almost insurmountable barrier, but the mission has tried with considerable success to educate native helpers. Then came the raids with the Namaquas, and finally the rivalries between the Germans and the English. The German agents were overbearing in their demands, and reckless with respect to the promises they gave. The English agents saw the opportunity and improved it by the introduction of whiskey. By these squabbles the position of the missionary was, of course, greatly embarrassed.

*Dutch East Indies.*—This also comprises three distinct fields, Borneo, Sumatra, and Nias. Borneo is a huge, hot, forest-covered swamp, so thinly peopled that one may make a day's journey up a river without meeting a single village, and so unsteadily settled that the village of to-day may next week have been moved hundreds of miles away. The inhabitants are agricultural nomads. When a rice-field turns out less fertile than was expected or becomes exhausted, the farmers take their houses on their backs and go to another place. The missionaries landed in the southeastern portion of the island among the Dyaks, a tribe belonging to the Malayan race but occupying a very low stage of savagery.

In that country and among those people the missionaries labored for eight years before they could baptize the first convert. And even then they found they 'had accomplished nothing. They adopted two measures, both of which miscarried: i.e., the ransoming of "pandelings" or slaves for debt, and compulsory attendance at their schools. The Dyak is either very poor or very rich: one has not a rice-seed to eat, and another has a gold crown so heavy that he cannot bear it. Then the poor man borrows of the rich, but the rate of interest is so outrageous that a very small debt will in a very short time make a man a pandeling. He likes, of course, to be ransomed, but that ransom cannot make him a Christian. By the agency of the Dutch government the Dyak children were driven to the mission school, but that was not the true entrance to Christianity either. In 1859 the whole fabric suddenly tumbled down. The Dyaks rose in rebellion, seven missionaries were killed, the rest fled to to Bendjermasin, the seat of the government, and all the stations were burnt down and destroyed. In reality, the rebellion was raised against the Dutch government, but the missionaries were the sufferers, and they were not able to resume work until 1866. From that time, however, the work has progressed steadily and surely. It is principally carried on through the medium of native preachers and evangelists. The first were educated in the Malayan Evangelical Seminary at Depok, Java; but that method proved a failure. When the Dyak returned home from Depok, he felt discontented and confused. There is now a small seminary at Kwala Kapnas, and it succeeds.

Sumatra has rapidly developed into the most important field of the Rhenish mission. Circumstances were propitious. The climate is much better than that of Borneo, as most of the stations are situated at an altitude of 2,000 feet or more. The country is well filled up, and the Battas, the Malayan tribe among which the mission works, are possessed of some civilization. They have themselves reduced their language to writing, and they like to read. Dutch missionaries have long ago mastered the language for all scientific and literary purposes, and the whole Bible is

translated into Batta. Very fortunate also it was that the Rhenish missionaries came in contact with the Battas as early as, in some cases even earlier than, the Dutch government, whence it followed that the peculiar sympathy which the statesmen of Amsterdam apparently feel for Islam was not allowed free play. At any rate, not long ago the Mohammedans of Sumatra petitioned the king of the Netherlands for the expulsion of the Christian missionaries, but the request was refused.

Nias is the largest of the chain of islands which stretches along the western coast of Sumatra. It is inhabited by about 170,000 people, who maintain a very lively intercourse with the main island. Opium-smoking and whiskey-drinking are common among them, and polygamy is the prevailing custom. Nevertheless, the mission is very promising, as the statistics show.

*The Chinese Mission* works among the Puntis in the province of Kwantung. It maintains 3 stations, 5 out-stations, 6 missionaries, 6 salaried native helpers, and has gathered 265 members, among whom are 155 communicants. The Rhenish missionaries, like all other missionaries working in China, are forced to contend with the curious pride of the natives and their peculiar antipathy to all foreigners.

But they trust that the better mutual understanding which generally results from a fuller acquaintance will in due time correct whatever of mistake there may be at this point on either side. The greatest trouble is that while truth is the fundamental principle of all our morals, the Chinese cultivate lying as one of the fine arts; and when they are caught, they are simply ashamed of their own awkwardness and lack of elegance, but they have no feeling of baseness and depravity. The most discouraging feature of their religion is their ancestor-worship, and here Christianity finds itself face to face with a phenomenon which it can neither recognize nor reject, and which, as yet, it does not know how to treat. Until this is overcome, however, Christianity can make but comparatively small progress. Still the latest statistics from China give ground for encouragement.

*Kaiser William's Land* in New Guinea did not became a German possession until 1885, and missionary work did not begin there, among the Papuans, until 1887. One station has been founded, at Bojadjim, and the reports are encouraging.

**Rhenius, Charles Theophilus Ewald,** b. November 5th, 1790, at the fortress of Gaudens, West Prussia; attended the Cathedral School of Marienwerder till his fourteenth year. At the age of seventeen, after many spiritual conflicts, he found peace, and devoted himself wholly to Christ. Reading the missionary publications of the Moravians, he was led to inquire whether he should not preach the gospel to the heathen. Having decided that this was his duty, he entered in 1811 a seminary at Berlin, established for preparing young men for the missionary work. He was ordained August 7th, 1812, at Berlin as a minister of the Lutheran Church, to be a missionary to the heathen. Proceeding to England, he spent eighteen months, by direction of the Church Missionary Society, with the Rev. Thomas Scott in further preparation for his future work. The court of directors of the East India Company having given permission for missionaries to go to India, he embarked as a missionary of the C. M. S., February 22d, reaching Madras July 4th. He soon proceeded to Tranquebar, his appointed station. At the end of five months he was sent to Madras to establish a new mission. He was the first to labor there under the C. M. S. Having been appointed in 1816 to revise Fabricius' translation of the Scriptures, he found it so defective that he began a new translation. In two years a regular congregation of nineteen, or five families, was formed. During the five years of his residence in Madras he was constantly employed preaching the gospel in public meetings, conversing with individuals, holding discussions with Brahmans or other learned men, studying the Tamil and Telugu, and making frequent tours to various cities and temples. In 1817 Mr. Schmid joined him, to be his colleague for many years in mission work. In 1819 the corner-stone of a church in Black Town was laid, with impressive services. After laboring nearly six years in Madras, it was decided by the committee that Mr. Rhenius should establish a mission in Tinnevelly district, and in June, 1820, he removed to Palamcotta, the chief city of the district. Here he found Mr. Hough, the chaplain of the station, who was much interested in the people, and had established several schools. The schools and the heathen, the translation of the Scriptures, and the preparation of a pamphlet, "The Essence of the True Veda," occupied Mr. Rhenius' time. He was joined by his beloved friend, Mr. Schmid. He prepared a "Harmony of the Gospels," which has had extensive circulation in Southern India. Mr. Hough having left Palamcotta in 1821, Mr. Rhenius held an English service on the Sabbath for English residents until the arrival of another chaplain. In 1822 a seminary was established for the education of youth, which has furnished catechists and schoolmasters for the mission. The Madras Bible Society requested Mr. Rhenius to continue the translation or revision of the Bible. In 1824 he visited the missions in North Ceylon, and was delighted with what he saw and heard. The foundation of a church within the mission premises was laid January 3d, 1826. Previous to this the services had been held in a building with mud walls, thatched with palmyra leaves, and now too small to accommodate the worshippers. Besides subscriptions from Europeans, resident and elsewhere, and a liberal grant from the C. M. S., a wealthy heathen moodeliar contributed to its erection. The services at the dedication were in Tamil and English, and it was a memorable day for the mission. The differing opinions and discussions among Tamil scholars as to the principles of translation led Mr. Rhenius to publish early this year a valuable pamphlet of 60 pages, entitled "An Essay on the Principles of translating the Holy Scriptures, with critical remarks on various passages, particularly in reference to the Tamil language." The translation of the New Testament, begun 12 years before, was printed in 1828, but the Old Testament was left unfinished at his death. A distinguishing feature of this mission encouraged by Mr. Rhenius was the formation and settlement of Christian villages. In order to withdraw the converts from the influence of heathenism, pieces of land were purchased, those who forsook idolatry were located on them, and formed into a Christian congregation. A catechist was appointed, a school established, and a small chapel erected. But when in 1826 and the following years the Christian villages had increased in number, to relieve the missionary of the burden of their management an association of natives was formed in 1830, called "The Native Philanthropic Society," having for its object "the settling of native Christians in villages, the building of schoolhouses, the acquisition of grounds, etc., for these purposes, and the rendering of other assistance to the native Christians in their external affairs." In 1832 the congregations of Mr. Rhenius consisted of 2,519 families, containing 8,780 souls.

In 1832 an unhappy controversy arose between the C. M. S. and Mr. Rhenius regarding the ordination of natives, some having declined ordination because they could not subscribe to the articles, homilies, and canons. Mr. Rhenius proposed that the missionaries be allowed to use the German mode of ordination, to which the natives would not object. That the committee might know exactly his views in regard to the church, he sent them a "review" of a book by Mr. Harper entitled "The Church, her Daughters and Handmaidens." The Committee charged him with impugning in this the government, ritual, formulas, and discipline of the Episcopal Church, and dissolved the connection between him and the Society. He replied that the Home Committee had long been aware that he held the sentiments on church forms advanced in the review, and that the mission had been conducted without disapproval in accordance with those sentiments. He said also that he never promised to submit to the English bishops, nor even to observe the Church of England forms; that the C. M. S. had followed the example of other English societies, whose missions in India were conducted by Germans according to the form of the German church, and which authorized their German missionaries to ordain native priests according to the German ritual. The Committee adhered to its resolution that the connection between them must be dissolved, and also that he must leave the district of Tinnevelly. Admitting that the property belonged to the Society, he maintained that he had a strong claim to the congregations; yet for the sake of peace he would leave. Against the protests of the catechists he went to Madras, and fixed upon Arcot as the field of his future labors. While there he received numerous letters from Tinnevelly signed by a large number of catechists urging him to return. They wrote also to the Committee expressing their dissatisfaction. He returned, and finding the situation as represented, he decided to remain. In October, 1835, he was again in his chosen field. Separated from the C. M. S., and not connected with any organized body of Christians, he was dependent on the offerings of the friends of missions. Liberal donations came from England, Scotland, Germany, America, and India, so that he was able to go on with his work without embarrassment. In 1836 he published a "Grammar of the Tamil Language," 8vo, 300 pages, a work of high merit, and he intended to begin the preparation of a Tamil dictionary. Just before his illness he finished "The Summary of Divinity" in Tamil, for the use especially of catechists. His "Harmony of the Gospels" is in general use. He was struck with apoplexy, and died June 5th, 1836.

In the death of Mr. Rhenius India lost one of its greatest missionaries. In unremitting labors he was not surpassed by any, and as a Tamil scholar he had no superior. The following estimate of his character and work is from the "Madras Budget:" "Since the days of Schwartz there has been no missionary in Southern India equal to Rhenius. The happy union of such cheerful piety, masculine talent, strength and activity of mind, promptitude of action and decision of character, high acquirements in the native language, with a bodily constitution capable of great and sustained exertion, entirely consecrated to the Saviour's service, has not appeared in the missionary field. It was not merely or perhaps most by his preaching and teaching of the gospel that he has been the instrument in the hand of God for enlightening and saving men; his Tamil writings are both numerous and valuable, and will long delight and instruct both Christians and heathen. His piety and worth drew men's hearts to him. He had an extraordinary power over those who came under his personal influence. There was something winning in his manner and address; and few remained long with him, or came often under his ministrations without being brought under an influence which led them to vital religion. He was an honored instrument for bringing many to a knowledge and love of the Saviour, and his memory will long be cherished in the Indian church."

**Richards, James,** b. Abington, Mass., U. S. A., February 23d, 1784. He was converted at the age of thirteen, and early expressed a strong desire to devote himself to the ministry. He graduated at Williams College in 1809, where he excelled in mathematical studies. He was the class-mate of Samuel J. Mills, was with him at the haystack prayer-meetings, and between them a very endeared friendship was early formed. He was among the first in his native land who devoted themselves to the cause of foreign missions, at a time when the subject had excited little attention in America, and before any except the little band of brethren (see biographical sketch of Mills) had thought of making it a personal concern. At Andover Seminary, where he graduated in 1812, he labored with Mills and others to promote a spirit of missions among the students, and in the Christian public, by distribution of books and pamphlets. His name was one of the six who drew up the memorial to the Massachusetts General Association that led to the formation of the A.B.C.F.M. But his name and that of Hall were withdrawn lest the Association should be alarmed at the expense of supporting so many missionaries. He was licensed to preach in 1812, and studied medicine two years in Philadelphia, preaching while there to destitute congregations, and also employed as a city missionary. Ordained 1815 at Newburyport with Mills, Warren, Meigs, Poor, and Bardwell, he sailed the same year, October 22d, for Ceylon. On leaving his native land he said: "I have been waiting with anxiety almost eight years for an opportunity to go and preach Christ among the heathen. I have often wept at the long delay; but the day on which I now bid farewell to my native land is the happiest day of my life." He reached Ceylon March 22d, 1816. His health having soon failed, he took a voyage to the Cape of Good Hope, but returned without much benefit. He continued however

to perform missionary work and to render important service as a physician for four years. He died, after intensely painful sufferings, in Jaffna, Ceylon, August 3d, 1822, and was buried at Tillipally.

**Richards, William,** b. Plainfield, Mass., U. S. A., August 22d, 1792; graduated at Williams College 1819, Andover Theological Seminary 1822; sailed November 29th, same year, as a missionary of the A.B.C.F.M., for the Sandwich Islands, accompanied by four natives educated in the United States. He was stationed at Lahaina, on Maui. In 1837 he visited his native land with his wife and six children, arriving in May and returning in November. In 1838 the king and chiefs requested him to become their teacher in the science of government and laws, and also their chaplain and interpreter in their intercourse with foreigners. As he was well fitted for the position, and had the entire confidence of the king, chiefs, and people, the mission and the Prudential Committee approved of his compliance with their request. He was accordingly released from the mission and his connection with the Board, "that he might guide the infant steps of the government as it went onward, relaxing the bands of despotism, and forming relations with the great Christian world." The government up to this time was an absolute despotism, the chiefs sole proprietors of the soil, and the people virtually slaves. Dr. Anderson, who knew Mr. Richards well, having been his class-mate in the theological seminary, testifies to his "intelligence, his sound judgment, and utmost disinterestedness." In 1840 the king conferred upon the people a constitution, recognizing the three divisions of king, legislature, and judges, and defining the duties of each. The code of laws adopted by the nobles and people was translated into Hawaiian by Mr. Richards, occupying 228 pages. From 1842 to 1845 he was absent on a mission to secure the acknowledgement of the independence of the islands by Great Britain, France, and the United States. After this recognition by foreign powers, he was sent as embassador to England and other courts. On his return in 1845 he was appointed minister of public instruction, which office he held till his death, November 7th, 1847. His influence with the king and government was very great. The mission thus speak of him: "For many years he was an efficient and self-denying missionary. He always displayed a deep and cordial sympathy with our work, and was wholly devoted to the instruction of the Hawaiian race. As the advisor of the king and chiefs, he was often embarrassed by the opposition of foreigners; but he enjoyed the confidence of the government to the end, and when he died the grateful nation decreed a pension to his widow.

**Ribe,** a town on the east coast of Africa, in Masai-land, northeast of Freretown. Mission station of the United Methodist Free Churches; 7 native preachers, 1 chapel, 108 church-members, 54 Sunday scholars.

**Richmond** (1), an out-station of the S. P. G. Mission at Grahamstown, Cape Colony, Africa. (2) Mission station of the United Free Churches in New Zealand; 70 church-members, 1 chapel, 230 Sunday scholars.

**Rietfontein,** a town in Great Namaqualand, South Africa, near Keetmanshoop. Mission station of the Rhenish Missionary Society; 1 missionary and wife, 1 female missionary, 75 communicants, 100 scholars.

**Rifi Version.**—The Rifi is a dialect of the Shilha, and belongs to the Hamitic group of the languages of Africa. It is spoken by the wild tribes in the mountains in the north part of Morocco. Mr. William Mackintosh, agent of the British and Foreign Bible Society, at Tangiers, translated nine chapters of the Gospel of Matthew, which were tentatively printed in Arabic type in 1883. As these few chapters of Mr. Mackintosh's version were much admired by the natives, the translator proceeded with his version, and the entire Gospel was published in 1888. Mr. Mackintosh is continuing his translation work, and is preparing the Gospel of John.

**Riggs, Stephen R.,** b. Steubenville, Ohio, U. S. A., March 25th, 1812; graduated at Jefferson College; studied theology at Alleghany Seminary; ordained April 6th, 1837; went at once, with Mrs. Riggs, under appointment of the A. B. C. F. M. to the mission among the Dakotas. Here he labored with great zeal and success in missionary and literary work at various places till the Sioux outbreak of 1862, when, barely escaping with his life, he fled to St. Paul, returning soon as chaplain of the military forces sent to suppress the outbreak. For three years he dwelt at St. Anthony, making frequent and important visits to the Dakota prisoners at Fort Snelling and other posts. In 1865 he removed to Beloit, Wisconsin, where he resided till his death, engaged in winter in translating the Scriptures, and spending the summer in active missionary service, retaining his connection with the Board till the transfer in 1882 of the Indian Mission to the care of the American Missionary Association. After a long and painful illness he died, August 24th, 1883, aged 71, having spent over 45 years in active and successful work among the Indians. Dr. Riggs reduced the Dakota language to a written form, organizing and adapting it to religious expression, and translated into it nearly the entire Bible. He prepared also a Dakota dictionary of more than 16,000 words, which was published by the Smithsonian Institute. Upwards of 50 volumes, religious and literary, partly translated, partly original, were prepared by him for the use of the Dakotas in their language. He lived to see ten churches organized and efficient, under native pastors. Of his eight children, five entered the missionary field, four among the Indians and one in China. "Dr. Riggs," says the editor of the "Missionary Herald," "was an uncommon man, and was ordained and strengthened to an uncommon work. It has fallen to the lot of few to do a more important work for the triumph of the gospel." Dr. Riggs received the degree of D.D. from Beloit College, Wis., and that of LL.D. from Jefferson College, Penn.

**Ringeltaube, William Tobias,** b. Scheidelwitz, Prussia; educated at the University of Halle; sailed 1797 for India as a missionary of the S. P. C. K., and was stationed at Calcutta. Suddenly without any adequate reason he resigned and sailed for England. He was afterwards employed by the L. M. S. and went to India in 1804. He labored to some extent in Tinnevelly, and preached the gospel along the coast from Tuticorin to Cape Comorin. There was a scattered community of Christians brought into the fold through catechists sent by Schwartz, but they were very ignorant and their lives inconsistent. Ringeltaube earnestly set himself to correct their abuses, and impart sound religious instruction. He was very eccentric, but wholly devoted, and endured much privation and persecution. His work was a genuine work of usefulness among Christians and natives. Before settling in Travancore he spent a year in Madras in the study of Tamil. At the end of this period he had not only acquired a knowledge of the language so as to be able to write it, but had also completed a small dictionary in English and Tamil. Early in 1806 he went from Tranquebar to Tuticorin, where he found a congregation of fifty Christians, to whom he at once began to preach. He travelled more than a thousand miles, preaching everywhere, and baptizing many adults and children. He went also to Trichinopoly, where he baptized thirty-six adults. Through the kind offices of Col. C. Macauley, British resident at the court of Travancore, he received permission from the rajah to reside at Malâdi, to the south of the Ghauts, and to erect a church there. This was the first station of the L. M. S. in that province. Here he trained two young men for the ministry. He lived in a most primitive fashion. He occupied a small native hut, his only articles of furniture a rude table, two stools, and a cot. His habits were of the simplest character. "Scarcely an article of his dress," says Mr. Hough, "was of English manufacture. He seldom had a coat to his back, except when furnished with one by a friend in his occasional visits to Palamcotta. Expending his stipend on his poor people, his personal wants seem never to have entered into his thoughts." By the end of 1812 there were 677 communicants at all the stations. It was his custom to visit each congregation twice a month. In 1815, in the midst of his useful labors, he suddenly left his people, no one knew why. He called on Rev. Mr. Thompson of Madras, with whom he spent an evening, without a coat, though about to undertake a voyage to sea, and with a hat of native manufacture. No one ever knew whither he went, nor was he ever heard of again.

**Rio Claro,** a town in São Paulo, South Brazil. Climate temperate. Population 12,000. Language Portuguese. Religion Roman Catholic. Natives civilized but uncultured. Mission station Presbyterian Church (North) 1873; 2 married missionaries, 1 single lady, 9 native helpers, 3 out-stations, 4 churches, 227 church-members.

**Rio de Janeiro,** commonly called Rio, the capital of Brazil, is the most important commercial city of South America. It is situated on one of the finest harbors of the world, 75 miles west of Cape Frio. The bay is land-locked, and is entered from the south, and extends inland 17 miles, with a greatest breadth of 12 miles, and is said to be the most secure and spacious bay in the world. The city itself, like Rome, is built on seven hills, and the houses with their white walls and red roofs, clustering in the valley or extending along the sides of the green slopes, present a most picturesque appearance as one approaches from the sea. The old part of the town lies nearest the bay, while the elegantly built new town is situated on the west of it. Here are fine streets, handsome public buildings, hospitals, asylums, over fifty chapels and churches, and many convents and nunneries. A national college, academy of medicine, theological seminary, and a national library meet the literary and educational wants of the people. A splendid aqueduct conveys pure spring-water from a mountain three miles southwest of the city. The climate is tropical, ranging from 54° in August to 97° in December. The annual rainfall is about 60 inches, one-fifth of that falling in February. The commerce of Rio de Janeiro is great and steadily increasing. As Brazil is the greatest coffee-producing country in the world, Rio is the largest coffee-exporting city. The population is estimated at 357,332, consisting largely of Portuguese, with a mixture of Negro blood.

Mission station of the Methodist Episcopal Church (South); 2 missionaries. Southern Baptist Convention; 3 missionaries and wives, 1 female missionary. South American Missionary Society; 1 missionary to the seamen. Presbyterian Church (North); 2 missionaries and wives, 1 church, 230 communicants, 67 Sunday-scholars, 1 school, 19 pupils.

**Riversdale,** a town in Cape Colony, South Africa, 150 miles east of Cape Town, 22 miles from the sea. Mission station of the Berlin Evangelical Missionary Society (1868); 2 missionaries, 2 female missionaries, 17 native helpers, 10 out-stations, 451 communicants. S. P. G. (1857); 1 missionary.

**Robbins, Elijah,** b. Thompson, Conn., U. S. A, March 12th, 1828; graduated at Yale College 1856, and East Windsor Theological Seminary 1859; ordained August 3d; sailed as a missionary of the A. B. C. F. M. September 29th, the same year, for the Zulu Mission, where he and his wife labored for nearly thirty years, Mrs. Robbins dying October 20th, 1888. He was stationed first at Umzumbi, but the latter portion of his life was spent in connection with the Mission Training School at Adams. He died there June 30th, 1889. Mr. Tyler writes: "He had spoken of the deep interest he felt in the theological department at Adams, and his gladness that I could give to the students a course of lectures on pastoral duties. The seminary for training Zulu men for the mission is in a great measure the fruit of Mr. Robbins' zeal and perseverance. The native laborers now in the field are ready to testify to the diligence and thoroughness of their teacher."

**Robertson,** a town in Cape Colony, South Africa, near Cape Town. Population, 12,000. Mission station of the S. P. G.; 1 missionary, 300 church-members.

**Rock Fountain,** a town in Ixopo, Natal, East South Africa, where Mr. and Mrs. E. S. Clarke (Friends) have worked among the Zulu Kafirs since 1879. These natives are a fine race, but very degraded, although they gladly welcome the missionary, and are especially glad to have their children educated.

**Rodosto,** a town on the coast of Roumelia, West Turkey, 80 miles west of Constantinople, on the Sea of Marmora and the great route west of Constantinople. It has large caravansaries and khans, and is the seat of important trade by sea. Mission out-station A. B. C. F. M., worked from Constantinople.

**Rolwein,** an out-station of the Moravian Mission at Elukolweni between that town and Bethesda in Griqualand, East South Africa. The chief of the Kafir tribe occupying this district has given the mission a favorable site for a school-house, and has promised that 24 children will attend the school.

**Roma,** one of the southern Moluccas, East Indies, under Dutch authority, has about 1,000 inhabitants, of whom 280 are Christians. But these Christians offer sacrifices to the idols and have never seen that "assistant pastor" which the Dutch government is supposed to pay for since it compelled the missionaries to go.

**Roman Catholic Missions.**—By this we do not mean the mediæval missions appertaining to the yet undivided Western Church, but those which have been undertaken since the Reformation, by the Roman Catholics as distinct from the Protestants.

It is often said that the Roman Catholic missions among the heathen were undertaken to make good the losses of Rome from the great Protestant defection. No doubt this was a powerful motive. As Canning said of his patronage of the Spanish-American revolts, Rome desired "to call a new world into existence to redress the balance of the old." But, as pointed out by Dr. Warneck, the prime motive was the sudden enlargement of opportunity offered by the Spanish and Portuguese discoveries. Mr. Mackenzie, in his history of Spanish-America, states that from the very first a pure zeal glowed in the bosom of the Spanish Church, and of the Spanish State, both to convert the newly-discovered natives, and to protect them against the rapacious adventurers who poured out from the Iberian peninsula, and that both efforts were unremitting and slowly effective, though not until great multitudes had been swept away. Of both efforts Las Casas was the illustrious exemplification.

Rome has never claimed the right to compel unbelievers to receive baptism. Thomas Aquinas distinctly disavows this right for the Church, and even in Spain the bishops at various times rebuked the zeal of the princes for forcible proselytism. But as the rebukes of Alcuin did not deter Charles the Great from his policy of forcing Christianity upon the Saxons, so those of the Spanish bishops were often equally ineffective to prevent the forcible proselytizing of Jews and Moors. In the south, as in the north, religious unity was rightly esteemed by the rulers the only certain foundation of civil unity, and the State did not allow itself to be deterred by the inconsistency of forcible proselytism with the gospel from applying it where it was likely to avail. And the Roman Church, which maintains her own right to compel the baptized to remain, thereby broke the force of her protest against compelling the unbaptized to enter. Latin Christianity indeed being so predominantly an institute, cannot possibly be quite so sincerely disinclined to the ruder forms of conquest as Protestant Christianity, which emphasizes the necessity of inward appropriation of the gospel.

SPANISH-AMERICA.—Here there appears to have been but little forcible proselytism. The conquerors, indeed, prohibited the pagan worship, for Rome holds that the worship of the true God, as practised by Christians or Jews, has alone a right to demand toleration of a Christian government.* It is doubtful how far she would extend this allowance, even to Mohammedanism. But the actual incorporation of the American natives into the Christian Church was essentially the work of persuasion. The conquered Indians, indeed, except where they retreated as untamable tribes into the Andes or the Sierras, had little reluctance to accept the forms of the conquering religion. A French priest, however, declares that the Mexicans are Catholics, but are not Christians, as Southey says of the common people of England before the Wesleys, who had gone through two religions, but were not yet evangelized. The Spanish-American Wesley, it is to be feared, is yet to come.

The first Mexican missionaries were Franciscans. They are charged with having afterwards, at least in Northern Mexico, become hard slaveholders, who brought back their runaway Indians with the lasso. But it does not appear that any shadow rests on the name of the early missionaries. They came first in 1522 from Ghent. One of them, as Kalkar relates, Pedro de Musa, a simple lay-brother, who devoted fifty years of unwearied activity to the spiritual and temporal interests of his Indians, reports in 1529 to his Provincial, that in six years they had incorporated 200,000 souls with the Church of Christ; in eight years the archbishop of Mexico is said to have been metropolitan of a million Christians. This splendid see was refused by Musa, and also by the Emperor Charles the Fifth's near relative, Pedro of Ghent, likewise a simple lay-brother. He writes to his imperial kinsman: "Because the people possess a peculiar skilfulness, I can truly say that there are among them good copyists, preachers, and singers, who might well be cantors in Your Majesty's chapel. In a school and chapel built here there are every day 600 boys instructed. A hospital has been put up near our cloister, which is a great comfort, and a means of conversion." "Most heartily, and in the true evangelical temper, he raised his voice to plead against all oppression of the natives." The Mexican Indians, however, unlike the West Indian and the Peruvian, were treated mildly, or at least with comparative mildness, except in the mountain mines.

In 1526 appeared the first Dominicans, who henceforth furnished most of the bishops. Then came Augustinians, Antony de Roa being the most distinguished. In 1572 came Jesuits, who went into New Mexico, where they have always remained the chief influence. By their skilful kindness they allured the natives from the cliffs and cañons, and established them in villages.

The baneful Inquisition was soon transplanted. The Indians, however, were not so much exposed to it as the whites, partly from their simplicity, partly from the contempt in which their intellects were held as hardly capable of heresy (though sometimes of pagan practices), and partly from repeated royal edicts of exemption, lest haciendas and mines should be deprived of their peons.† The devotion of

the natives to the sacrament of Penance was most edifying, confession of sin being a main element of the Aztec religion. On the other hand, it is said that up to this century few of them were thought mentally competent to be admitted to the communion, although a rite analogous to this was also found in their old religion. That this estimate was too disparaging is beyond all question. It is even said that the pure Indians of Mexico commonly lead their classes in the schools.

Mexico, converted, became in her turn a basis of missions. From her the Philippines and Ladrones were Christianized, perhaps we should rather say, laid waste. Yet Sir John Bowring, it appears, regards the present condition of the Philippines as testifying to the judicious kindness of the Jesuits.

The Indians of the West Indies, a gentle and pleasing race, but of singular vileness of morals, who turned their memorial visits to the tombs into veritable orgies of lewdness, met the first wave of Spanish adventure, fierce, cruel, and rapacious, as yet unchecked by the slower steps of civil justice or religious benevolence, and were almost at once swept away. We lament the cruelty, but cannot think that the world lost much in the disappearance of so depraved a race.

Peru was conquered in 1533, and after twenty years of disturbances was brought to tranquillity in 1555 by the viceroy Mendoza, who took care to provide the natives with priests of good conduct. The Indians passed easily from the mild paganism of sun-worship into a nominal and formal Catholicism. Throughout Spanish and Portuguese America little pains seems to have been taken to build up an intelligent Christianity that shall deeply influence the heart and life. Yet that may have been true of South America which a missionary of the American Board states of Mexico, namely, that the Catholic Church seems there to have been mainly concerned about the shell of Christianity, but has by no means altogether withheld the substance, and that now and then there is a preacher of enlightened and energetic apprehensions of evangelical truth. Some one remarks of the Indians of California that they are devoted to Catholicism with all their hearts, and that all their highest feelings and ideas are intertwined with it.

The famous Jesuit mission of Paraguay was established in 1586, after the intolerable tyranny of the Spaniards had long rendered fruitless all the attempts of the Franciscans and some lesser orders to secure the conversion of the Indians. The Jesuits wisely judged that the Spaniards needed reconverting first, and turned their efforts towards their reformation with so good effect, that before long the Indians, believing at length that there must be something in a religion which could change the conduct of the whites, began to return to Christianity, or to seek baptism for the first time. The Jesuits were indefatigable. There was no tropical wilderness too intricate or wide-stretching for them to traverse, no water too wide for them to cross in their hollow logs, no rock or cave too dangerous for them to climb or enter, no Indian tribe too dull or refractory for them to undertake. "Their only weapons were the Word of God and the language of love." The Jesuit, like a Christian Orpheus, would often go up and down the rivers drawing the savages

---

* Indeed, it is doubtful whether she allows the public worship even of Jews.

† It raged, however, terribly, notwithstanding.

to him by the force of music and sacred song.

The missionaries, apparently becoming convinced that the reformation among the Spaniards, though sufficient to set the good work of Indian conversion in motion, was neither extensive nor deep enough to make them, on the whole, desirable neighbors for their converts, obtained from the King of Spain authority to govern their 200,000 or 300,000 neophytes with entirely independent authority. Under their mild control, resting purely on persuasion, the Guaranis (as these Indians were called) enjoyed a hundred and sixty years of simple happiness until the Jesuits were expelled in 1767. "The social system established in Paraguay," says the Encyclopædia Britannica, "was the most effectual ever contrived for reclaiming the Indians from their savage mode of life; but even its success shows how hopeless is the attempt to raise the American tribes to the rank of thoroughly civilized nations. The Jesuits were able to introduce settled habits and a slight knowledge of religion and the arts among the Indians only by means of the personal ascendancy they acquired over them. It was a few superior minds gaining the respect and confidence of a horde of savages, then employing the influence they acquired to lead them as children, giving them such portions of instruction as taught them to trust implicitly in their guides, working alternately on their fears, their pride, their kind affections, but never fully revealing to them the springs of the machinery by which they were governed. The incurable indolence of the savages rendered it necessary to prescribe the labor as task-work, and to carry it on under the constant inspection of the missionaries. The plan of cultivating the ground in common and of storing the produce in magazines, out of which the wants of each family were supplied, was resorted to as a check upon their improvident habits. In short, the eye and the hand of the missionaries were everywhere, and the social system was held together entirely by their knowledge and address. When these were withdrawn the fabric soon fell into ruins, and the Indians relapsed into their idolatry and savage habits."

According to the "Handbook of Foreign Missions," the whole number of Catholic Indians in all America, outside of those who were once subject to Spain or Portugal, is to be estimated at about 40,000. Of course the Spanish-American states are no longer properly mission ground.

CANADA.—Jesuit missions in Canada have been most fascinatingly described by Mr. Parkman. The heroism, both natural and regenerate, the humbleness and unswervingness of devotion to the most dreary and unfruitful field of labor, the patience and sweetness of temper of these heroes of the faith, form one of the noblest chapters of church history. Almost or quite all the original missionaries died as martyrs, commonly under atrocious torments, which they always had in view, but from which they never shrank. The heroic Brébeuf, before his martyrdom, which he suffered conjointly with Père 'Lallemont, had baptized 7,000 Hurons. The Huron Mission, says Kalkar, was the most brilliant point of the Jesuit labors in Canada; but the fierce Iroquois, destroying the tribe, destroyed the mission. Kalkar rightly laments the measure in which the Jesuits accommodated

themselves, never to Indian fierceness or immorality, but too often to the grossness of Indian superstition. But he remarks that the blind hatred with which the English followed them up in the inhospitable regions in which they bore every hardship for the love of God and men, makes it harder for us to resent the persecutions which our missions have so often suffered at the hands of Roman Catholic nations.

The most triumphant fields of Roman Catholic missions have been India and China, and for awhile Japan. Here too, unhappily (that is, in India and China), the dark shadow of Jesuit accommodation to heathenism has been the deepest.

INDIA.—The first Christians from Europe were the Portuguese, who landed, under the lead of Vasco da Gama, in 1498, at Calicut, on the southwest coast. The dissensions of the many independent states opened the way for their conquests, of which, in 1510, Goa became the capital. Here a bishopric was established, which was then raised into an archbishopric, whose incumbent bore and still bears the title of Primate of the East.* His metropolitan authority formerly extended from Southern Africa to China. The Inquisition, unhappily but inevitably, was also established in Goa, in all its baneful rigor. But neither Archbishop nor Inquisition could accomplish much amid the flood of sheer ungodliness which poured in from Europe. The reputed wealth of India brought an innumerable company of adventurers, whose unrestrained profligacy moved the indignation and incurred the indignant rebukes of the Hindus themselves. Meanwhile the uncertain endeavors of Diego de Borba and of Miguel Vaz, Vicar-General of Goa, to extend the gospel accomplished little. They established a school in Goa, it is true, for the Christian training of young people from India, China, and Abyssinia, which did good service for many years. "But still," says Kalkar, "there was lacking to the work of conversion anything like a fixed plan, and a rule of orderly proceeding." At last the right men appeared in the Jesuits.

May 6th, 1542, there landed in Goa the illustrious Francis Xavier. Of the high nobility of Spain, distinguished for learning and for eloquence, he had, in Paris, been brought over by his fellow-Spaniard and fellow-Basque, Ignatius Loyola, from visions of earthly glory to a burning zeal for the cause of Christ and of Rome, which in his mind were so absolutely one that there is no reason to suppose that even the shadow of a suspicion of any possible divergence between them ever fell upon the simple loyalty of his mind. Of Jesuit astuteness and accommodation to a worldly standard, as they afterwards developed themselves both abroad and at home, there does not appear to have been a trace in Xavier. Sunny frankness was the essence of his character. Himself one of the original Jesuits, he followed the wise temperance of its policy, and neither affected nor shunned privations and austerities. For the most part, however, he trod the way of hardship. He watched through the night with the sick; visited the prisons; trod half-shod the glowing sands of the Indian coast to care for the spiritual and the temporal wants of the oppressed pearl-fishers; met their savage op-

---

* He has lately been raised to the rank of a Patriarch.

pressors with dauntless courage, with only the cross in his hand, and in the might of the spirit, by the simple power of his rebuke, inspired them with such terror that they fled. No wonder that, himself as it were a visible Christ, he soon counted so many thousands of converts from among the heathen that his voice often failed for weariness, and his arms sank exhausted in the act of baptizing. He had, indeed, in these rapid and myriad conversions to submit to the necessity of leaving the greater part of his neophytes very ignorant of Christianity, although he took care to have the catechism translated into Tamil, and to supply the new congregations with priests as fast as possible, leaving them meanwhile in the care of his most trusty laymen. It does not appear, however, that Xavier, whose labors were spread over so wide a field, both in India and Japan, laid the foundations of any very thorough instruction of his converts. He might have done more had he stayed longer. But popular instruction has never been the strong point of Catholicism in general or of Spanish Catholicism in particular. Sir William Hunter, however, says that the elder missionaries of the Roman Catholic Church in India were far too indifferent to popular instruction, but that the modern missionaries have at last become convinced that they can only break up heathen superstition by a more thorough education, and that they are now behind none in their zeal for it.

Eminent Roman Catholic authorities, and such as are thoroughly friendly to the Jesuits, remark, nevertheless, that the results of their early labors in India hardly answered to their zeal and wisdom in them. Of course they found the same enormous difficulties that still exist—the strong solidity of Mohammedanism, at that time the imperial though not the prevailing creed of India, and the immovable prejudices of Brahminical caste. We are sorry to say that in Goa itself it was an act of persecution that opened the way to a somewhat greater extension of Christianity. In 1560 the Portuguese viceroy banished certain leading Brahmins from Goa, whereupon the Jesuits were soon after able to baptize some 13,000 converts.

The immovable barrier presented by Brahmin supremacy, and the divisions of caste, finally led the Jesuits into a system of accommodation —it would be well if we could say nothing worse—which met for a while with a brilliant outward success, but in the end showed its hollowness by its collapse. A Jesuit, Robert de Nobili, of one of the most illustrious families of Tuscany, and who therefore had all the aristocratic habitudes which fitted him to play his new part to perfection, gave himself out for a Brahmin of the west allied to princes (the last assumption being the truth); perfected himself in Sanskrit, Telugu, and Tamil; performed the usual Brahminical ceremonies; suffered only men of high caste to approach him, and received these seated on a throne; produced a Sanscrit book which he declared to be a recovered fifth Veda, and produced the sworn attestation of his fellow-Jesuits that this audacious forgery had been received by them from the god Brahma, as containing a mysterious wisdom which alone could give life. The result of this unscrupulous falsehood and accommodation to the ways of heathenism was, that in three years he had gained over seventy leading Brahmins, who of course had accepted the

Christian doctrine of God, creation, immortality, atonement, and the general teachings of Christian morality, and had abandoned their idols, but who retained all the haughtiness of caste, and were permitted to sign themselves with the sacred ashes, interpreted, of course, as having only a social significance. That they were allowed to baptize their children by the old heathen names does not signify so much, as in the early church no one scrupled to use such names as Phoebe, Demetrius, Diotrephes, Apollos, Hermas, and the like.

The accommodations of de Nobili and his followers did not disguise from the Brahmins at large that the sages of Rome proposed to them a fundamentally new religion. Angry oppositions arose, but before long 30,000 converts had been gathered. Separate churches were built for the higher and lower castes, the latter being rigorously forbidden to join with the former in their worship, while the Pariahs or outcastes were forbidden even to approach the priests. Even the last sacraments were administered to them at the end of a staff, so that the administrator might not be defiled.

One of Robert de Nobili's chief associates was Juan de Brito, son of the viceroy of Brazil. He brought great numbers to the faith in the kingdom of Marava, and died a martyr in 1693. Another associate, Veschi, was equally able, learned, successful, and heroic, and barely escaped martyrdom. He lived to become a mortal antagonist of the more enlightened Danish missionaries, dying in 1747.

The accommodations of Robert de Nobili and the Jesuits to heathenism could not fail to arouse great scandal at home. The rumor even spread that de Nobili had apostatized. His kinsman, the great Cardinal Bellarmine, himself a Jesuit, though better informed than to suppose this, expressed his grief over such principles of proceeding, saying (to quote from Kalkar): "The gospel needs no such false coloring: that Brahmins are not converted is of much less account than that Christians should not preach the gospel with joyful openness. The preaching of Christ crucified was once to the Jews a scandal, and to the Greeks foolishness; but St. Paul did not therefore cease to preach Christ, and Him crucified. I will not," he continues, " argue as to individual points, but cannot refrain from declaring that the imitation of Brahminical haughtiness is sadly at variance with the humility of our Lord Jesus Christ, and that the observance of their usages has something exceedingly dangerous to the faith." It is sad to reflect that the pressure of his order brought this great and good man at length to something very much like a retractation of these sound and evangelical principles.

The other orders were naturally scandalized over the Jesuit policy. While as yet it was represented at Rome that nothing was intended beyond an allowance of certain harmless national usages, Gregory XV., in 1623, had issued a bull not unfavorable to the Jesuits. But these took occasion thereby, it is said, to push their compliances farther and farther, until at last Roman Catholic Christendom at large was in a ferment. Finally, in 1703, the Pope sent Cardinal Tournon to India, where, after thorough investigation, he suggested the decree by which, in 1710, Clement XI. rigorously forbade all accommodations whatever to heathen usages.

The Jesuits, however, paid scarcely the least

attention to the decree, and soon obtained from a later Pope, Clement XII., a virtual revocation. But at last Father Norbert, of the Capuchins, came to Rome, and there opened the matter with so much insight and unreservedness, that the wise and upright Benedict XIV., in the bull *Omnium sollicitudinum*, of October 7th, 1744, condemned and forbade the Jesuit practices in the most peremptory terms. Norbert's life, however, was held to be in such danger from Jesuit revenge that the Pope gave him leave to lay aside his habit for better disguise. He fled from land to land, taking refuge even in Protestant countries. At last, when the Jesuits were banished from Portugal, he sought a safe harbor there. "Meanwhile in India," says Kalkar, "things remained on the old footing: the order founded for the vindication of the Papacy became its antagonist, mocked at and scorned the other orders, engaged in mercantile and other secular undertakings, until these things also did their part in hastening its fall."

These conversions around Goa, proceeding from Robert de Nobili as a centre, are to be distinguished from those in the more southern parts of the peninsula, and among the humbler classes, who did not provoke so much disingenuousness. No such stain, happily, rests on the memory of Xavier. He had his share of Spanish imperiousness, but nothing of de Nobili's Italian craftiness.

The result of this collapse of Jesuit missions in India was, that more than half a century passed during which the Roman Catholic Christians of India were almost wholly abandoned to themselves. Rome does not seem, in Hither India, to be much inclined to encourage the formation of a native priesthood. The development of subject energies generally is something of which she is rather jealous than zealous. Nevertheless, when Catholic missions were resumed in India, Mr. Marshall says that over a million converts were found to have remained steadfast to the great truths of creation and incarnate redemption, though, of course, their minds had become greatly obscured as to all secondary Christian doctrine, and overspread with many heathenish superstitions. Mr. Marshall's numbers, however, must be a good deal too large, as the official statements of the church make the present number of Roman Catholic Christians to be only 1,185,142, having 996 European and 93 native priests, 2,677 churches and chapels, 1,566 elementary schools, and 64,357 scholars. For the last five years the annual rate of increase has been 3½ per cent. Sir William Hunter gives the present general rate of Christian increase in India as 64 per cent in nine years. It appears therefore that under a Protestant government Christianity in India is chiefly advancing in the Protestant form. About 100,000 of these Roman Catholics are proselytes from the Syrian Church of India, not from heathenism. There are also 300,000 so-called Goa Christians—Catholics who have fallen out of communion with Rome during the long disputes between Portugal and the Pope over the right of nomination to the Indian bishoprics, and over the prerogatives of the Archbishopric of Goa. As these disputes are said to have been lately accommodated on very favorable terms for Portugal and Goa, which latter appears to have been advanced to patriarchal jurisdiction throughout India, the schism will probably now disappear.

In *Farther India* Roman Catholic missions were established about two centuries ago. They are, according to the "Handbook," divided into five nationalities, including 13 vicariates apostolic. *Burma* has 3, with 147 churches and chapels, 38 European and 11 native priests, and 25,808 Catholics. *Cambodia* has 74 churches and chapels, 23 European and 16,280 Catholics. *Cochin China* has 3 vicariates, 536 churches and chapels, 94 European and 94 native priests, and 124,267 Catholics. *Siam* has 2 vicariates, 67 churches and chapels, 43 European and 10 native priests, and 24,438 Catholics. *Tonkin* has 5 vicariates, 820 churches and chapels, 82 European and 258 native priests, and 437,483 Catholics. In all, 628,276 Catholics in an estimated population of about 45,000,000.

Tonkin and Cochin China have been eminently a land of martyrs. The "Handbook" remarks: "We cannot withhold our sincere admiration of the spirit which has animated both the European missionaries and the native converts of these missions. We may question some of the methods of the former and the customs of the latter; but in the presence of the courage and devotion of the missionaries, and the spirit of true martyrs manifested by both, in repeated and fiery persecutions, we have no desire to detract from their noble example. The converts in these missions have shown a manhood and constancy worthy of apostolic times.

"The difference between these missions and those of India is worthy of remark. The number of native priests in Tonkin is three times as great as in the whole of India, and as the number of converts is only about a third, the proportion is really eight or nine times greater in Tonkin, while the number of European priests is very small in proportion. This indicates much more of manly and independent spirit in the inhabitants, or of better management in the church, or it may be both."

AFRICA.—The Roman Catholic Mission in the kingdom of Congo, near the mouth of the great river, began as early as 1491. A vast number of negroes were baptized, so that, as with Xavier, the missionaries could hardly hold up their hands for weariness. Père Labat puts the number of the baptized at 100,000! Of preliminary instruction there had been none; an enemy at hand moved the missionaries to enroll as many as possible of those who might soon fall in battle in the ranks of the regenerate. The people had followed the example of their king and queen. Soon, however, the scene changed. "The mysteries of the faith," says one of the Dominican Fathers, "were something of which they were very willing to hear. But when we began to preach the moral virtues to them—that was another matter." A persecution even unto death, and headed by the newly baptized king, broke out. But the crown prince Alphonso, soon coming to the throne, displayed a steadfast zeal for Christianity. He even became, though not a priest, yet a zealous preacher. It appears, however, that he did not demand that his subjects should forsake their polygamy, but did demand, on pain of death, that they should forsake their idolatry. That rude mixture of superstition, gospel, and force, which is characteristic of Catholic mediævalism, was shown here in its perfection.

Portugal, with the profound selfishness which distinguishes all her early dealings abroad, took advantage of this new influence in Congo to secure enormous supplies of slaves. Dependent as they were on Portuguese protection, the priests made faint opposition to this iniquity, and even became accomplices in it. Soon they declined in zeal, and the princes and people in interest; " the shepherds became plunderers;" it is said they quarrelled with their bishop, and went back to Portugal with great substance. Yet baptisms went on, and soon Congo was proclaimed " wholly Catholic "! A very heathenish kind of Catholicism, it appears. The court relapsed into the deepest dissoluteness, which remained proof against the efforts of the few Jesuits who came to Congo about 1550, although these did a good deal, temporarily, for religion and education among the people. Unhappily, however, they could not resist their inborn propensity to intrigue for Portuguese sovereignty, and soon, neglecting their flocks, became little else than agents to secure the King of Portugal a large supply of slaves. Scandalized at this, their superiors recalled them. The next two Jesuits were of a purer zeal, and preached vigorously against polygamy and unchastity (of which the native clergy seem to have taken little account), but soon had to shake off the dust of their feet against the king, the court, and the people. After some alternations of persecution and apparent repentance, Christianity in Congo began to decay. Then matters passed into Spanish hands. But after 150 years Christianity is little more than a shadow. This closes the first period of the Congo Mission.

The second period opens in 1640, when the Capuchin friars arrived. Meanwhile the heretical Hollanders had diffused their opinions, which, however, were easily rooted out, with the help of a little persecution. It is hard to say which was the more pious or the more rapacious—Portugal or Holland. The new missionaries now preached against polygamy, but only stirred up a persecution against themselves. They gained a victory, but soon learned to be very tolerant towards such vices "as are to be expected in men of that color." When the kings apostatized, the people did; when they came back, the people professed to do so. The Capuchins made far too much use of royal edicts, but declared that there was no hope of accomplishing anything without them! The missionary Zucchelli in 1698 declares: " Assuredly the misery is great! Here is neither honor nor reputation, neither knowledge nor conscience, neither Word of God nor faith, neither state nor family, neither government nor civility, neither discipline nor shame, neither polity nor righteousness, neither fear of God nor zeal for the welfare of souls, nor anything. And great as are the sins, scandals, and vices which they commit every day, yea, every hour and moment, yet you can never bring them to any shame for them. . . . You can say nothing of these people when you see them, except that they are in fact nothing else than baptized heathen, who have nothing of Christianity about them but the bare name without any works."

Finally, everything went into ruin together. Says Zucchelli:

" Utter ruin impends over the land, the people, the mission. For there is no wisdom, reason, counsel, policy; no one troubles himself about the common weal. Civil wars, enmity, murder, robbery, superstition, devilish arts, incest, and adultery are the people's and the prince's virtues. Deceit in word and deed is in full vogue. As there is in the land no fortified place of refuge, men hide themselves in the wilderness."

Various subsequent attempts were made, some by the Capuchins, some by the Benedictines, to stay the rapidly advancing tide of temporal and spiritual ruin, but to no purpose. " Captain Tuckey, who in the year 1816 was sent by the English Government to explore the Congo, found during his stay on the left bank of the Congo no trace of Catholicism except some crucifixes and relics, which were strangely intermingled with the amulets and fetiches of the country. Of civilization not a trace was to be discovered; the visitors of the ship were one and all impudent, dirty vagabonds, full of vermin. With the people of Sogno the other inhabitants of the West Coast contrast to their own advantage. Among them a man presented himself on board as a priest, exhibiting a certificate; but he was wholly uncultivated, and so ignorant of the principles of the church which he pretended to represent, that he shamelessly confessed to having a wife and five concubines." Whose and what was the fault of this great ruin ?

CHINA.—Christianity was preached here as early as the eighth century by Nestorian missionaries. As early as 782 it was flourishing in the two widely distant provinces of Shensi and Fokien. This appears from the celebrated inscription in Shensi, discovered by the Jesuits in 1625, whose genuineness has been established. Even as late as 1300, under Kublai Khan, Nestorian Christians were numerous and powerful in China, and in Pekin itself, then called Cambalu. In 1294 the Pope sent the Franciscan John de Monte Corvino to Pekin, of which Rome afterwards appointed him archbishop. Neander says of him: " This distinguished man, displaying the wisdom of a genuine missionary, spared no pains in giving the people the Word of God in their own language, and in encouraging the education of the children, as well as training up missionaries from among the people themselves. He translated the New Testament and the Psalms into the Tartar language, and had these translations copied in the most beautiful style, and made use of them in preaching. . . . He had, during his residence in this place, baptized from five to six thousand; and he believed that, had it not been for the many plots laid against him by the Nestorians, he would have succeeded in baptizing above thirty thousand." Unhappily, however, says Neander, the Nestorians ultimately succeeded in bringing his labors to naught. His sainted memory, however, remains, and the souls whom he has been the means of saving. The Nestorians naturally resented being called heretics, but cannot be acquitted of deep blame, as Monte Corvino appears to have been a man of mild and pure spirit. Finally, however, the reassertion of Chinese independence, under the Ming dynasty, and the overthrow of the friendly Mongols, drew after it the destruction of Christianity, of which every trace seems to have disappeared.

In 1517 the Europeans, in the persons of the Portuguese, re-entered China,—this time by way of the sea. In 1556, for services rendered against the pirates, who have always been so formidable on the waterways of China, the Portuguese received the islands of Sancian and

Macao. It was on Sancian that, in 1552, Francis Xavier closed his heroic and consecrated life. "Rock, rock, when wilt thou open?" expressed the spirit of his last sighs, though the words were those of an earlier missionary, in front of the frowning seclusion of the great heathen empire.

The first Roman Catholic missionary who came to China in this second era was the Provincial of India, Nuñes Barreto, S.J., who, travelling to Japan in 1555, twice spent a short time at Canton. Neither he nor his immediate Jesuit, Franciscan, and Spanish successors, however, were permitted to remain long. At last, in 1582-3, the Jesuit Michael Roger, after some five or six fruitless visits to China, obtained with Paes and Matthias Ricci, who was afterwards so notable in China, leave to remain, and many privileges from the viceroy of Canton. The first public baptism was given in 1584. In 1586 there were 40 Christians, but then persecution broke out. After the Jesuits had adopted the dress of the mandarins, they were less annoyed. In 1598 Ricci, already in high repute for his scientific attainments, and now the head of the independent Chinese Mission, was received in Pekin, and established himself permanently there in 1601, dying in 1610. He is accused of having carried the conformity to Chinese usages to such a length as to have dispensed himself from his vow of celibacy, and to have married a Chinese woman, who bore him two sons. But the animosity of the other orders towards the Jesuits had become so great, that we are not to be too sure of the justice of any particular accusation against these. This animosity, which seems to have been strongest in the Dominicans, had various grounds. Jesuitism had an alertness and flexibility that contrasted very favorably with the lumbering mediævalism and rigid orthodoxy of the Dominicans. Their attainments in literature and science were also very much greater, and drew public favor to them. They showed also a wise consideration of circumstances, to which the rather stupid stiffness of the Dominicans was not adequate. Thus, when the Dominicans asked the Jesuits how soon they intended to introduce the discipline of fasting for their converts, the latter replied, "Not until Providence relieves them from the continual fasts imposed by their poverty." Yet, on the other hand, the Dominicans seem to have been essentially in the right, and the Jesuits essentially in the wrong, as to the great question of accommodation. The controversy turned especially upon the custom of ancestral worship. The Jesuits argued—and the emperor, in a public edict, confirmed their position—that this, in China, is only a civil and social act, implying nothing in the nature of religious homage. The Pope, however, and the Protestant missionaries, after full investigation of the opposing arguments, have decided that the Dominicans and the other protesting orders were right, and the Jesuits wrong. Herr Faber, who has given a very thorough exposition of the controversy in the "Allgemeine Missionszeitschrift," gives as his judgment, that, had Rome taken the Jesuit side, it would have reduced Christianity in China to the position of Buddhism—a mere luxury of private sentiment, entirely subject in all practical matters to the rigorous civic secularism of Confucianism.

Mr. Marshall, in his eulogy on Catholic Missions, gives glowing accounts of the wonderful successes which attended the Jesuit efforts in every class of Chinese society, and how, when persecution broke out, brothers and sisters of a former emperor—one of whom had even been viewed as a possible successor—cheerfully underwent for Christ's sake banishment, imprisonment, chains, and other maltreatment, under which several sank in martyrdom. The slight allusion to this family in Wetzer and Welte's great Roman Catholic encyclopedia confirms the belief that there were such imperial converts, and that they did exhibit this example of cheerful Christian faithfulness unto death. If we had nothing but the "Lettres Edifiantes" to depend upon, we should not know what to think. These princes and princesses, therefore, may be likened to the husband and wife, Clement and Domitilla, cousin and niece of the Emperor Domitian, who, in the first century underwent, the one death, the other banishment, for the name of Christ.

In 1617 the Jesuits had about 13,000 converts; in 1650 about 150,000; in 1664, 257,000. The Franciscans and Dominicans together had hardly more than 10,000. The conversions went on increasing until towards the end of the century, when the papal decisions against the accommodations allowed by the Jesuits, and the bitterness with which the other orders and the papal legates enforced them, led to violent persecutions. One of the legates, Cardinal Tournon, was sent to Macao, and died in prison there. Some even say that the Jesuits poisoned him. Many Christians were martyred; much greater numbers fell away, partly under the terror of death, and partly under the exasperation of national feeling. Compromises were for awhile admitted by the representatives of the Pope, which somewhat stayed the desolation. But Rome at last, in 1742, in the pontificate of Benedict XIV., issued a peremptory and irrevocable decision, forbidding every accommodation that could be interpreted as a concession to paganism. Then the persecutions broke out more violently than ever, and according to Wetzer and Welte, the Christian faith was almost rooted out. The Papacy is certainly highly to be commended for its immovable faithfulness to the essential principles of Christianity, even at the cost of losing almost all that had been won. Even Clement XI., so servile to the Jesuits in France, was immovable here. It is much to be regretted, however, as Herr Faber thinks, that Rome could not exhibit this Christian faithfulness without at the same time alloying it with so much of her own characteristic haughtiness, with such a contempt of the imperial representations, and such a determination to carry through the right position by overbearing will, that the emperor, the mandarins, and the people gathered the deep impression, that if they would become Christians they must cease to be Chinese.

At various times the devoted Roman Catholic missionaries in China underwent various persecutions, banishment, imprisonment, scourging and even death. The first actual martyr was the Jesuit Francis Martinez, murdered in 1606. The Dominican Francis de Capillas was beheaded in 1648. In 1665 five Christian mandarins were beheaded. The regent who commanded this was, however, soon after punished by the young emperor with death. During the exasperation caused by the decree of Benedict XIV., the Dominicans Peter Sanz, Serrano, Royo, Alcober Diaz, and the catechist Ko (Sanz being a bishop), and the Jesuits Anthemis and Henriquez, suffered death in 1747.

Only obscure accounts are accessible as to the subsequent resuscitation of Roman Catholic missions in China. There were still hundreds of families in which Christianity had become hereditary, and there have doubtless been many conversions in this century. In 1805 there was a cruel persecution; also in 1816 and in 1820. In these later persecutions three or four priests suffered death, one of them being Vicar Apostolic and Bishop *in partibus*. The present estimated number of Roman Catholic Christians in China is 483,403; European priests, 471; native priests, 281; scholars, 25,219.

The controversy which has raged so violently among Protestant missionaries in China as to the true name of God,—whether it should be Shang-ti, Shin, or Tien,—had previously rent the Roman Catholic ranks. They have finally decided on Tien-chu, Lord of Heaven.

It is to be feared that the Jesuits, as commonly, have finally tired out the Holy See, so that it connives at a good many practical infractions of the edict of Benedict XIV. It is, moreover, greatly to be deplored that two excellent edicts, rendered from Rome as early as 1615, for the celebration of the sacred offices in Chinese, and for a vernacular translation of the Scriptures, have both remained ineffective; yet the incidental notices of Abbé Huc show among the Roman Catholic converts a good deal of moral purity and genuine Christian piety.

JAPAN.—Japan, say Wetzer and Welte, had scarcely been opened to Europeans, when St. Francis Xavier, with some companions, hastened thither to plant the standard of the cross. Japan, it is known, until after the revolution induced by the American interposition, was divided into a number of feudal states governed by Daimios, who were subject in theory to the divine Mikado, but in fact had their lord paramount in the intensely human Shogun or Tycoon, the Imperator or General-in-chief of the realm. This feudal looseness of cohesion facilitated the spread of the gospel, as in Germany of the Reformation. Unhappily the Mikado had no such practical power of interfering with his military mayor of the palace as the Pope had of interfering with the emperor; so that when the Imperator made up his mind, his vassals had finally to yield. For a long while, however, the preaching of the missionaries was undisturbed, and in 1582 there were more than 200,000 Japanese Christians, with 250 churches. Even three Daimios were baptized. At last, however, the Shogun Taiko, or Taikosama, gradually became jealous of the missionaries, suspecting them of being agents of Portugal, and after the temporary union of the two Iberian crowns, agents of Spain for reducing Japan to dependence. It is customary for Protestant narrators to assume that of course these suspicions were well grounded. But our disposition to think ill of the Jesuits sometimes overshoots itself. As the details of their asserted intrigues seem to have been given out a good many years after the persecutions had begun, they were probably manufactured in order to justify the persecutors. At the same time there is reason to suppose that the Jesuits did inspire their converts with a habit of looking to Spain and Portugal

which might have injured the national instinct of independence. The Jesuits at this time were zealous partisans of the Spanish supremacy throughout Europe, and could hardly have been entirely relieved of their Iberianism by going to the East. Whatever the immediate occasion of Japanese suspicion may have been, Taiko began to persecute the Christians about 1582. The steadfast chastity of Christian maidens is said to have been one of the causes which inflamed the wrath of the imperial voluptuary. The inconsiderate zeal of some Franciscans, also, who persisted in public preaching after the Jesuits had discontinued it, is said to have increased his displeasure. On the 5th of February, 1597, 6 Franciscans, 3 Jesuits, and 17 other Christians were crucified. With the sound of psalms these heroes and followers of Christ breathed out their souls. From 1598 till 1611, under a new Shogun, there was a respite. But then a fearful revolution of sentiment in the Shogun's mind brought him and his three successors to that persevering and concentrated cruelty towards the Christians, which finally rooted out their religion. The guilt of this is laid by the Catholics on the Dutch, who revenged the cruelties of Spain towards them by stirring up all the terrors of heathen ferocity against the innocent converts of Iberian missionaries. We can well believe the charge, for Holland, in her Oriental policy, has always shown and still shows a cold-blooded indifference to everything but the pure love of gain, which, according to a Dutch missionary in Java, renders the very name of a white man odious to her subjects there. The Hollanders stirred up afresh the slumbering jealousies of the government towards Spain and Portugal, and towards the Jesuits, until its rage was so great, that all common forms of torment being too little for the wrath of the rulers, they exhausted their ingenuity in devising new tortures.

It has well been said that the Roman amphitheatres never witnessed, in men, women, or children, more resolute heroism of martyrdom. Here again, for a good while, the blood of the martyrs was the seed of the church. From Taikosama's death in 1598 to 1614, the Jesuits baptized 100,000 converts, and for many years afterwards they baptized several thousand yearly. Some apostasies took place, but in general all the Christians, princes, nobles, men, women, and children, went joyfully to their doom. "Children endured the most terrible deaths, without giving a sign of suffering." When any were conducted to the crown of martyrdom so greatly desired, they would be accompanied by many thousand Christians, who followed in triumphal procession, praying, praising, and bearing lighted tapers in their hands. But persecution raged incessantly, and finally outstripped the increase of the church. At last, in desperation, 37,000 Christians seized the fortified place Simbara, since known as the Mount of Martyrs, and there, after a long defence, were, shameful to tell, with the help of the Dutch, at length slain almost to the last man. Then were published the edicts forbidding "the God of the Christians, on pain of death, to re-enter Japan." Then too was introduced the requirement, maintained till within a few years, that all the subjects of the realm should, once a year, trample on the crucifix. With this requirement the cold-blooded Dutch merchants infamously complied, doubtless excusing the profanation under the pretext that the crucifix was a superstitious emblem. Until our own generation the real Christianity of Holland does not appear to have overflowed into the eastern world. Now, however, we are glad to say, it begins to show an undaunted and belligerent front towards the soulless ungodliness of Dutch government abroad. And the government itself is beginning to be ashamed of its apathy, and to promise its best support to the teachers of a living Christianity in the East Indies.

When Japan was reopened by the Americans, it was discovered that there were hundreds of concealed Roman Catholics in one province. A number of martyrdoms have taken place even since then, but are now, of course, discontinued. The Rev. Edward A. Lawrence, who has lately visited Japan, informs us that in the absence of Bibles, which unhappily Rome, as usual, had neglected to provide, these secret Christians had even forgotten the baptismal formula, and used to baptize their children " in the name of the Holy Jerusalem!" Mr. Lawrence asked a Jesuit missionary there whether such a formula would be valid. "No," he answered, " the Church must have her rules. But," he added most justly, " God is very much kinder than the Church."

The present number of Roman Catholic Christians in Japan is 30,230, with 84 churches, 78 priests, a good many being natives, and a number of schools. The missionaries are described by a native Japanese preacher as good men of irreproachable lives, humble, laborious, and sympathetic, sharing willingly in the poverty and the toils of their people, who belong almost altogether to the poorer classes. Among the more influential classes they make no headway, and their numbers increase much more slowly than those of the Protestants. He is of the opinion that they are doing a good and lasting work, but that the future of Japan does not rest with them. The superstitions, servility, and anachronistic forms of thought which weigh down their system, find no acceptance with the cultivated mind of Japan. There seems to be, however, a vitality and solidity in their work utterly lacking to the missionary work of the Russo-Greek Church, which appears to be fading away. As Dean Stanley says, the whole Western Church, from pope to presbyter, as compared with the Eastern Church, is full of the vigorous movement of thought and life.

The missionary operations of the Roman Catholic Church in most other regions of the world not yet noticed, especially in the Pacific, and in Madagascar, are so complicated with the Protestant work, and are so largely a simple proselytism from Protestantism, that they can hardly be put on the same level with her properly missionary labors, as already described. In Madagascar, however, they have 84,000 adherents. In Africa as a whole (including Madagascar) they reckon 210,000 converts. In Oceanica, about 75,000. In the regions adjacent to China, 78,000. The noble witness rendered to Christ by the martyrs of Uganda is fresh in memory. Of these some 20 were Protestants, and about 180 Catholics. Their numbers were doubtless greater, and the young tyrant Mwanga raged most fiercely against them, being himself an apostate Catholic catechumen. The fortunes of the Protestant and the Catholic Mission of Uganda have been so intertwined, that their history must be treated as one. Père Lourdel thinks that the Christians might have maintained their ground* there if they had not, after Mwanga's dethronement, against the admonitions of their guides, shown an inordinate zeal to fill the higher offices with their own men, and thereby awakened the jealousy of the Moslems, who had joined them in resisting the pagan tyranny. All Christendom, Catholic and Protestant, is now engaged to withstand the flood of Moslem fanaticism which is advancing from the Soudan towards the Mediterranean and towards the Lakes.

*Missionary Organization of the Roman Catholic Church.*—Rome divides the whole world into two great sections, *terra catholica* and *terra missionis*. Within the former her missionary organization has, properly and ordinarily, no application; within the latter it controls all ecclesiastical persons and processes whatever, archbishops and bishops themselves being subject to it.

*Terra catholica* (perhaps more properly *terrae catholicae*) is definable as including all those countries whose governments lend the support of the secular arm for the coercion of all baptized persons, whether Catholics, heretics, or simple schismatics, into obedience to the Holy Roman Church; that is, to the Roman Bishopric, which claims a maternal superiority to all other churches, that is, bishoprics, and claims the right to instruct them, and by inference to govern them. All schismatics or heretics, therefore, within the limits of any bishopric, may (it is held by the prevailing opinion) be lawfully compelled to yield obedience to their Catholic bishop, and in him to the Supreme Bishopric of Rome, which possesses throughout the Church both an ordinary and an appellate authority. The latter is chiefly in use, but the former may at any time be exercised. Wherever, then, the civil government, being apprised by the Holy Office of the Inquisition, a commission of Cardinals of which the Pope himself is the Prefect, that heresy or schism is prevailing within its jurisdiction, lends its authority to crush it, there, and there only, is *terra catholica*. All the rest of the world, Christian, Moslem, and Heathen, is *terra missionis*.

But as at present scarcely a government in the world subordinates itself to the Holy Office, which has now no tribunals outside the Vatican, and as almost every government of a Roman Catholic country has formally declared liberty, not only to Jewish worship, which Rome herself protects,† but to every variant form of Christian worship, does it not follow that there is now no *Terra catholica*—that the whole world is *Terra missionis?* There is still, however, a noticeable distinction between the two regions, as in the former the popular and even legal presumption commonly recognizes Roman Catholicism as the predominant religion. And in the hope that Catholic countries may even yet come to a better mind, and restrain the "madness" of freedom of conscience, Rome still thinks it prudent to maintain the distinction *dissimulando*.

Rome has no different agencies for proselytism of Christians and for conversion of unbelievers. Any country which does not, through its government, give effect to its spiritual subjection

---

* Which they have since recovered.
† At least if private.

to her, is indiscriminately included in the *Terra missionis*. Even the Eastern churches, although their ordinations are acknowledged, and although the prevailing Roman theory concedes to them spiritual jurisdiction, are nevertheless subject to the activity of the Propaganda, which, however, does not appear in fact to extend its operations among them except so far as they are in Moslem or pagan countries.

Rome, however, makes very important distinctions, within the *Terra missionis*, between *infideles*, *schismatici*, and *heretici*. The former term includes all who have never embraced the faith. For the conversion of these, it is held, the only lawful means is Persuasion, as they have never been subject to the jurisdiction of the church. *Heretics*, being baptized, are subject to her jurisdiction. For the restoration of these the lawful means are Persuasion and Coercion, the former being preferable. *Schismatics*, who are orthodox, but disobedient to Rome, may likewise, as occasion serves, be either persuaded or coerced into returning. Perhaps the only simple *schismatics* are the members of the Greek Church, which is not impeached by Rome of heresy, though she impeaches Rome of heresy, and sometimes speaks dubiously of her orders, and even of her baptism. The Greek and even the Monophysite and Nestorian bishops appear to be often recognized by Rome as the legitimate bishops of their sees, and the few Greek bishops, at least, who chose to admit the papal supremacy were received without difficulty to an equal suffrage in the Vatican Council. But in the Levant, if Rome spies an advantage, she is very apt to forget her concessions, and to thrust in her own nominees where she cannot secure the submission of the actual incumbents. Her policy here, it appears, is peculiarly odious and violent, and the examples given by her agents are often the reverse of reputable. Reordination, however, of the Eastern clergy she does not permit, even where, as in Abyssinia, the rites are extraordinarily irregular and defective. The succession, she says, is unquestioned, and the sacramental intention is sound, and sufficiently expressed.

In the Protestant world, however, she is not embarrassed by any question of orders or of jurisdiction. Only as to the Anglican communion is there with her even a pause of thought as to the former: and since the accession of Elizabeth she has always treated the Anglican orders as null, maintaining that the probabilities against their valid transmission are so overwhelming as to leave her under no obligation to pursue remote considerations and abstract possibilities. And as to jurisdiction, she declares even the Old Catholics of Holland, Germany, and Switzerland to be void of this, although she acknowledges the validity of their episcopal succession.

Protestants, therefore, are held to be destitute of all the ordinary means of grace except the sacraments of Baptism and Matrimony. She pursues her missions among them almost as if they were heathen. She does not, however, as often supposed, designate Protestant countries as *partes infidelium*. *Infideles*, as noted above, is the technical term of Rome and of Trent for all human beings who are neither baptized nor catechumens. Its application to cover heretics is casual, and seldom, if ever, official. *Partes infidelium* are those Mohammedan regions whose ancient Christian cities now give a titular dignity to some three hundred Roman Catholic bishops who have no actual dioceses. As they are largely employed in Protestant countries, their former style of "Bishops *in partibus*" was often mistaken as referring to the place of their residence, and not, as it did refer, to the location of their nominal sees. To obviate this not unnatural misunderstanding, the present Pope has courteously directed that they shall henceforth be known as *episcopi titulares*.

All ecclesiastical activity of the Roman Catholic Church within the *terra missionis*, whether of proselytism, conversion, or ordinary administration, is subject to the control of the *Congregatio de Propaganda Fide*. This great and powerful commission, which—subject, of course, to the Pope's intervention at any point —exercises papal authority over all Roman Catholics throughout the Protestant, Oriental, Moslem, and Pagan world, was instituted by Pope Gregory XV. in the year 1622. This Pope was the first pupil of the Jesuits who had ascended the chair, and therefore was naturally interested in missions. The Congregatio de Propaganda—familiarly called The Propaganda, and by Roman Catholics simply Propaganda— has permanent authority within regions yet extra-Christian, and within Christian regions until they become again *terrae catholicae*, subject in its modes of proceeding to the distinction laid down in a brief of Pius VI. of the year 1791: *Discrimen intercedit inter homines, qui extra gremium Ecclesiae semper fuerant, quales sunt Infideles atque Iudaei, atque inter illos, qui se Ecclesiae ipsi per susceptum baptismi sacramentum subjecerunt. Primi etenim constringi ad catholicam obedientiam praestandam non debent, contra vero alteri sunt cogendi.* So soon as this *coactio* is feasible, a region would cease to be a *terra missionis*, and would become a *terra catholica*, the yet unevangelized populations, however, remaining still the objects of missionary activity, and not becoming subject to the Holy Office, so long as they do not act offensively toward the Church.

The *Congregatio de Propaganda Fide*, which, of course, has its seat at Rome, is composed of a varying number of cardinals, at present 31, some being non-resident correspondents, and of a Secretary and Protonotary, on whom the practical business mainly devolves. There are also consultors and a large force of officials. It has also a training college for pupils from almost every nation under heaven. There are also in Rome various national colleges and monastic training houses for missionaries. Yet the whole number of pupils appears to be small compared with those that are trained for the priesthood in Protestant countries and other missionary jurisdictions.

Where the Roman Catholics in a country, being few, have never been organized into a diocese, or where the bishoprics have fallen under Mohammedan or heretical control, there the Pope, as having ordinary jurisdiction throughout the Church, is sole diocesan. The first stage of organization is the appointment of a priest as papal representative, with the title of Prefect Apostolic. He has almost unbounded authority (under the Propaganda), being empowered to station priests at discretion within his prefecture, and to grant dispensations almost *ad libitum* from every ecclesiastical precept not included in the *jus divinum*, from which last, of course, the Pope himself cannot dispense. If the mission flourishes, and there is a call for a superintendent with power to ordain to the priesthood, the Prefecture Apostolic becomes a Vicariate Apostolic. The distinction does not appear to be a hard-and-fast one, as there are occasionally Vicars Apostolic that are simply priests, who have to send elsewhere for new clergymen.

Almost all, however, are bishops *in partibus*, or, as they are now called, Titular Bishops. Both prefects and vicars are movable at pleasure.

If the Church has won or recovered such a following (especially in Protestant countries) as to warrant it, the Pope proceeds to organize a regular hierarchy of diocesan bishops, usually arranged in metropolitan provinces, each under the presidency of an Archbishop, who, besides his ordinary diocesan authority, has a certain right of determining appeals from his suffragan bishops, and always presides in the Provincial Council, whose decrees, when ratified by the Pope, have binding force. The bishops of the United States, moreover, have three times been convoked by Rome in Plenary Council, the Archbishop of Baltimore, the bishop of the eldest national see, having been each time appointed to preside as Apostolic Delegate. The decrees of these councils, of course, when papally ratified, are binding for the whole country.

The diocesan bishops of England and America are not, like mere Vicars Apostolic, remarkable *ad nutum*, but are understood to enjoy fixity of tenure, like those of Catholic lands. The cardinal's rank enjoyed by the present Archbishop of Baltimore greatly increases his influence, but adds nothing to his episcopal or metropolitan authority. As Cardinal he has no jurisdiction outside the city of Rome. And as belonging to a missionary jurisdiction, he, and all other American bishops, are still controlled by the Propaganda, due regard, of course, being had to the more developed character of their sees. The bishops enjoy the same powers with Vicars Apostolic, of dispensing from ordinary canonical restrictions. These powers, granted from Rome for terms of five years, are known as the Quinquennial Faculties.

Previous to the institution of the Propaganda missions were pursued in a somewhat disconnected way. Each order sent out its missionaries for itself, who rendered account of their activity only to their own provincials and generals, these latter, doubtless, frequently communicating with the Holy See, and obtaining from it such suggestions, exemptions, consecrations, pecuniary subventions, and other aids as it might be inclined to grant and they to receive. But since 1622 the control of all missions, among heretics, schismatics, and pagans, has lain in the hands of the Propaganda. Yet the bonds of connection within each monastic order are so strict, the authority of its superiors so unbounded, its policy and spirit, and even its doctrinal tenor, so specific, and the character attributed to each of the elder orders so sacred, that the comparatively new Congregatio de Propaganda Fide has doubtless to accommodate itself largely to this distinctness of action. The Jesuits, above all, though willing enough to accommodate themselves in form to the Papacy and its delegations, have, in fact, as is very well known, been much more disposed to govern Church, Pope and all, than to submit to any of them. In what way, and how far, the missionary operations of this overbearing society, or of the other orders, have been actually subordinated to the Propaganda, is something which it would require a profound interior knowledge of the workings of Roman Catholicism to decide. It must suffice us to know that every missionary, Jesuit, Benedictine, Franciscan, Dominican, of whatever order or of the secular priesthood, is subject to the supreme and universal episcopate of the Pope as ordinarily exercised through the Propaganda.

The orders, especially the Dominicans and Capuchins over against the Jesuits, have carried on their missions, especially in India and China, with far more bitterness of controversy against each other, than has prevailed between Protestant denominations the most widely remote. The Jesuits indeed long seemed disposed, both among Pagans and Protestants, almost to claim a monopoly of conversions, and if any one of another order, especially among the heretics, was guilty of a success, Pascal has described to what extremities their animosity would sometimes go. It was these internecine wars that finally came so near to ruining Roman Catholic missions in the far East. But since the suppression and restoration of the society, which has now an almost uncontested right of control in the church, and which in its turn has doubtless learned wisdom by its tribulations, we hear no more of these scandalous dissensions. The Jesuits doubtless take whatever fields of activity they wish, and leave the rest to others. There appear to be among the missionaries but few secular priests, that is, priests who, like the ordinary parish clergy, are subject only to the general authority of the church, and not to that of any monastic order. The native clergy from among the heathen are probably for the most part seculars.

The Roman Catholic laity appear to have just the same privileges in regard to missions that they have in regard to every other ecclesiastical interest, namely, the privilege of contributing of their substance for them and of being absolutely passive as to the disposal of it. The consequence is what might be expected. Assuming 100,000,000 as the number of active Roman Catholics, which almost equals the largest estimate of ostensible Protestants, it is estimated, as has been stated by Cardinal Lavigerie, that the Protestants contribute about twenty times as much for foreign missions. Whether lay associations, contributing to foreign missions, have a right to designate the objects* to which their gifts shall be applied, and to enter into correspondence, say with converted pagans, does not appear by examining the *Annals of the Propagation of the Faith*, or by a somewhat hasty reference to *Les Missions Catholiques*. Such an intervention of the laity would, indeed, be quite out of keeping with the general spirit of the Church.

France is the great centre of Roman Catholic zeal for missions among the heathen. The cheerfulness and kindly sympathy of the French character, when purified and elevated by Christian faith, make French priests and nuns by far the best missionaries. The Society

---

* It appears that some lay societies send their gifts to particular regions.

for the Propagation of the Faith, the seat of which is at Lyons, raises far more money for this end than any other similar Roman Catholic association. How the vast extent of Roman Catholic missions outside Christendom is maintained, it is difficult to say. The converts doubtless do much; the Propaganda has large means; the Pope makes ample contributions; and missionary bishops and priests may not unfrequently supply their own modest support from their private resources. The orders also, it may be presumed, have a natural interest in maintaining the efficiency of such missionaries as belong to them. The Jesuits especially are popularly supposed to be an exceedingly, even an inordinately, wealthy society.

It thus appears, from the somewhat vague lines in which we are able to portray the missionary activity of the Roman Catholic Church, that outside Christendom, while allowing ample play to the peculiarities of individual habit and devotion, and to the specific activities of various monastic institutes (some of which, like the brethren of the Christian schools, and various female orders, are devoted exclusively to education), it reserves an undisputed and all-pervasive control to Rome. Voluntary societies are welcome as a means of procuring money, but the missions themselves are through prefects apostolic, vicars apostolic, and more developed sees, at every point in the hand of the Church.

**Romansch Versions.**—The Romansch belongs to the Graeco-Latin branch of the Aryan family of languages, and consists of three dialects, the Upper and Lower Engadine (so called because spoken in the Engadine, Switzerland), and the Oberland.

(a) *The Upper Engadine.*—A translation of the New Testament into this dialect was published by Jachiam Bifrun (Basle, 1560; Püschlaff, 1607), Griti da Zuoz (Basle, 1640), and Menni (Coire, 1862). The latter's version is that circulated since 1882 by the British and Foreign Bible Society. The Psalms were published by Lorenz Witzel (Basle, 1661).

(b) *The Lower Engadine.*—The Psalms were translated by Ciampel (1562, Lindau, 1606); parts of the Old Testament were published by J. Pitscher Saluz, 1657 seq., and the entire Bible by Jac. Ant. Vulpio and Dorta a Vulpera (Basle, 1679, based on Diodati's Italian Version). Later editions, Basle, 1743. The New Testament was again published in 1812; the Old Testament of T. Gaudenz by the Coire Bible Society in 1815. An edition of the entire Bible was published at Cologne, 1867–1870.

(c) *The Oberland.*—In this dialect, which is spoken in the Grisons of Switzerland, Luis Gabriel published the New Testament at Basle, 1648. J. Grass edited the Psalms at Zurich, 1683. A version of the entire Bible was published at Coire in 1718, 1818–20, in 2 vols., and by the British and Foreign Bible Society at Frankfort in 1870. The Coire Bible Society published in 1856 an edition of the New Testament, made by Otto Carisol.

(*Specimen verse.* John 3 : 16.)

Engadine.

Perche chia Deis ha taunt amâ 'l muond; ch'el ha dat seis unigenit Filg, aclo chia scodün chi craja in el nun giaja à perder, mo haja vita eterna.

Oberland.

Parchei Deus ha teniu il mund aschi-car, ca el ha dau siu parsulnaschiu figl, par ca scadin, ca crei en el, vomi bue á perder, mo hagi la vita perpetna.

**Rosario,** a city of Argentine Republic, South America, in the province of Santa Fé, on the right bank of the Paraná, 170 miles northwest of Buenos Ayres. Population, 40,000. It is the second commercial city of the republic, is well laid out, with neatly-paved gas-lighted streets, traversed by cars. Climate temperate, healthy; average, 78° F. Mission station of the M. E. Ch. (North); 3 missionaries. South American Missionary Society; 1 missionary.

**Rotuma,** an island north of the Fiji Islands; has 2,500 inhabitants. In 1841 some evangelical missionaries landed from Tonga, in 1846 the French Jesuits, and in 1869 began the war between the two parties. But in 1879 the English Governor of the Fiji Islands annexed Rotuma, and the Jesuits left. Mission of the Wesleyan Methodist Church under the Australian Conference; 1 native preacher.

**Rotuma Version.**—The Rotuma belongs to the Melanesian languages, and is spoken in Rotuma Island. The first portions of Scripture which were translated into this language were the Gospel of Matthew, the 19th Psalm, and the 13th chapter of 1st Corinthians, made by the Rev. Joseph Waterhouse, with the assistance of a Fijian teacher named Eliezer, in 1857. They were printed at Hobart Town, Tasmania. In 1864 the Rev. William Fletcher of the Wesleyan Missionary Society settled at Rotuma and translated the entire New Testament, which was printed in 1870 at Sydney, at the expense of the British and Foreign Bible Society. The edition consisted of 2,500 copies. A second and revised edition was carried through the press by the Rev. James Calvert in 1885. Thus far 4,020 portions of the Scriptures have been disposed of.

(*Specimen verse.* John 3 : 16.)

Ne e fuamamau no hanfs on Oiitu se rantei, ia na on Lee eseama, la se raksa teu ne lelea ne maa se ia, la iris po ma ke mauri seesgataaga,

**Roumania** is the name given to the kingdom formed in 1861 by the union of the two principalities, Wallachia and Moldavia. Its independence from Turkey was proclaimed by its people in 1877, and was confirmed by the congress of Berlin in 1878. Its area is estimated at 48,307 square miles. On the northeast it is separated from Russia by the river Pruth and the Kilia mouth of the Danube, which latter river forms its southern boundary west of Silistria. The Transylvanian Alps and the Carpathian Mountains form its western and northwestern boundaries. That portion which lies between the Danube and the Black Sea is called the Dobrudja, and differs greatly from the rest of the kingdom. The climate has great extremes of temperature: in winter the cold northeast winds are very trying, while in the summer the southwest wind is scorching in its intense heat. The rainfall is not abundant. Agriculture is the principal occupation of the people, though not a few cattle and sheep are raised. The government is a constitutional monarchy, and the king is assisted by a senate of 120 members and a chamber of deputies of 183 members, all of whom must be Roumanians by birth or naturalization. The population of Roumania is of very mixed origin, including 4,500,000 Roumanians, 300,000 Jews, 200,000 Gypsies, 100,000 Bulgarians, 50,000 Germans, 50,000 Magyars, 15,000 Armenians, 2,000 French, 1,000 English, besides 3,000 Italians, Turks, Poles, and Tartars. The population of the Dobrudja is estimated at 106,943, and contains a larger Russian element than the other part of Roumania. The Orthodox Greek Church is the ruling Church, but Roman Catholics, Protestants, Armenians, Lipovani (Russian heretics), Jews, and Mohammedans are also found. Education is supposed to be compulsory, but there are very few schools, so that only about two per cent of the population are able to avail themselves of the free instruction. The principal cities, with their population, are: Bucharest, the capital (221,805), Jassy (90,125), Galatz (80,763), Botochani (39,-941).

Mission work in Roumania is carried on only by the colporteurs of the B. F. B. S. The entire Bible has been translated into the Roumanian language (a Latin dialect with a large Slavonic element), besides the Psalms and Isaiah into Polish for the Jews.

**Roumanian Version.**—The Roumanian belongs to the Græco-Latin branch of the Aryan family of languages, and is divided into the Roumanian proper and Macedonian-Roumanian. The former is spoken in Roumania and part of Transylvania, the latter in Macedonia.

1. The *Roumanian.*—A translation of the Scriptures was published at Bucharest in 1668 and 1714, and again at Blaje, Transylvania, in 1795. A New Testament was published as early as 1648. The Russian as well as the British and Foreign Bible Society issued editions of the Scriptures at different times. The latter especially published the New Testament and the Psalms in various characters; but in 1867 this Society brought out a New Testament and Psalms in the ancient Cyrilian character for use in churches and schools, and for those who can read in no other character. Another edition was issued in 1877. The same Society issued in 1869 a new version of the Roumanian Bible. The translation was made by Professor Jerome and others, and was edited in a uniform style of orthography by the Rev. W. Mayer of Jassy. In 1874 an edition of the Bible in revised orthography was issued at Jassy and Pesth.

2. *Macedonian-Roumanian.*—As there are a great many in Macedonia who cling to the mother-tongue, although pure Wallachian is being taught in the schools, the British and Foreign Bible Society issued in 1886 an edition of 500 copies each of Matthew and Mark in the Macedonian dialect. The version was made by Dimitri Athanasius, the director of a school at Monastir. It was printed in the modified Roman character now employed in Roumania.

(*Specimen verses.* John 3 : 16.)

Cyrilian.

Кэл ама а избит Думнезеŭ лŭмеа, кэ а дат пе Фііль сэŭ чел бŭланэскŭт, ка тот чел чо крѐде ѫн ел сі нŭ се пиерде, чи сі аіба вієца вечникъ.

Roman.

Cacĭ aşa a iubit Dumnedeu lumea, încât a dat pre Fiiul seu cel unul-nascut, ca tot cel ce crede în el sĭ nu se pierde, ci sĭ aiba vieţa eterna,

**Roumelia, or Eastern Roumelia,** is a part of the Principality of Bulgaria (q. v.), Turkey. It lies just south of the Balkan Mountains, is inhabited mainly by Bulgarians and Greeks, and by the Berlin Congress of 1878 its administration was made autonomous, though the Governor-General, necessarily a Christian, was to be nominated by the Porte. It was united with Bulgaria in 1885, and is now under the administration at Sofia. In 1888 the population was 960,441. Philippopolis, the former capital, is now merely the centre of a prefecture, and has a population of 33,442. Mission work is carried on by the A. B. C. F. M., with a station at Philippopolis (q. v.), and the British and Foreign Bible Society colporteurs. Since the union with Bulgaria there is properly speaking no province of Eastern Roumelia.

**Ruatan,** one of the Bay Islands, off the coast of Honduras, Central America; 30 miles long by 8 broad. It has 22 harbors, of which Port Medina is the chief. Population, 3,000, mostly Negroes. Mission station of the Wesleyan Methodist Missionary Society; 1 missionary, 8 chapels, 510 church-members, 10 Sunday-schools, 512 scholars, 3 day-schools, 215 scholars.

**Ruk,** a small island in the Caroline group, Micronesia, 31 miles west of Ponape. Mission station of the A. B. C. F. M.; 3 missionaries, 1 missionary's wife, 7 native agents, 15 churches.

**Rurki** (Roorkee), a town in Saharanpur district, Punjab, India, 22 miles east of Saharanpur City. Population, 15,953. Hindus, Jains, Moslems, Christians. Mission station of the Methodist Episcopal Church (North); 1 missionary and wife, 9 native helpers, 4 out-stations, 1 church, 60 members, 1 school, 25 scholars. S. P. G. (1871); 1 missionary, industrial school and 250 church-members.

**Russ Version.**—The Russ belongs to the Slavonic branch of the Aryan family of languages, and is spoken in the vast empire of Russia. Toward the end of the tenth century, Vladimir, Prince of the Russians, joined the Greek Church at Constantinople, and from that time on Cyril's Bible translation was introduced among the Russians. The first edition of Cyril's Bible was published at Ostrog, 1581. The editors of this edition state in the preface that they based their work on a codex now no more extant, belonging to the time of Vladimir (1000 A.D.). Many reprints of this edition were published at Moscow, 1663, 1727, and after. At the command of the Empress Elizabeth a new revision of this version was undertaken. The editors corrected the Ostrog edition according to the text of the Septuagint, published by Grabe (Oxford, 1707–1709), and corrected the Old Slavonic language in many passages according to the modern Russian language. A new version of the New Testament was made by the Archimandrite Philaret, under the auspices of the religious academy of St. Petersburg, and printed by the St. Petersburg Bible Society in 1819–23, with the Slavonic text in parallel columns. In

1822 the Psalms were published by the Holy Synod, the translation having been made by the Rev. Dr. Paosky, of the Cathedral of St. Petersburg. Editions of the New Testament, as well as of the Psalter, were printed and published at Leipsic, 1838, 1853, and at London, 1862. The Psalms were the only part of the Old Testament which was published by the Russian Bible Society. To supply the people of Russia with the entire Old Testament, the British and Foreign Bible Society engaged Prof. Dr. Levisohn to undertake the work, but he was cut off suddenly in the midst of his career in 1868. The work was taken up by Prof. Chwolson, and in 1876 the Old Testament in modern Russ, as translated by Levisohn and Chwolson, was printed at Vienna. In the mean time the Holy Synod had also issued the Russ Bible, and an edition of the Bible was printed by that body for the British and Foreign Bible Society in 1881, with the Apocryphal Books omitted, and the Septuagint readings in the Canonical Books expunged. Prof. Astafieff read the final proofs of this edition, in order to secure a pure text, and the Authorized Russ Bible can now be circulated by the British Bible Society. The edition consisted of 20,000 copies. For the Russian blind, who number from 160,000 to 200,000 souls, the British Bible Society issued the Gospel of John, and the Sermon on the Mount, according to Moon's system, in 1880.

*(Specimen verse.* John 3 . 16.)

Ибо такъ возлюбилъ Богъ міръ, что отдалъ Сына своего единороднаго, дабы всякій, вѣрующій въ Него, не погибъ, но имѣлъ жизнь вѣчную.

**Russelkonda,** a town of Madras, India, in the mountainous district of Gumsar. Population, 2,631. Mission station of the Geneva Baptist Missionary Society (1861); 1 missionary, 69 church-members.

**Russia.**—Mission work has been attempted at different times in different parts of this empire by the Basle and Moravian Missions, the London Missionary Society, the Scotch Free Church, etc., but it has never been successful, owing to the repressive action of the Russian government, whose laws forbid any subject to change his religion except as he becomes a member of the State Church, a branch of the Oriental Greek Church. The American and British and Foreign Bible Societies have accomplished a good deal in the form of Bible distribution (see articles on those societies).

*Russians.*—The Russians are the most numerous Slavic nation, numbering over sixty millions. They are divided into three chief branches : Great Russians, Little Russians, and White Russians. The Ruthenians or Red Russians, living in Austria, are also classed as a branch of the Russians. The distinctions between these various branches are rather linguistic than national. The great mass of the Russians belong to the Eastern Church, while 3,108,000 are *Uniats* or Unionists, 500,000 Catholics, and the number of the dissenters (*Raskolniks*) is variously estimated from 3 to 11 and even 15 millions.

The orthodox Russians use the Slavonic language in their church services; so also do the *Uniats* and the Dissenters, while the Catholic Russians use the Latin liturgy. In their literature all the Russians use the *Kyrillitza* alphabet. The Russian language belongs to the southeastern branch of Slavic languages, and is related to the Bulgarian and the Servian. It is divided into three dialects: the Great-Russian, the Little-Russian, and the White-Russian. The first of these dialects forms the Russian literary language of the present day; the Little-Russian may be considered as a distinct language, though related to the Great-Russian, while the White-Russian occupies a middle place between Great-Russian and Little-Russian, and contains elements of both these and of the Polish language. The language of the Ruthenians in Austria is Little-Russian.

The origin of Russia has been traced back to a group of Slavic tribes who inhabited the country around Kieff. They lived in separate communities, and were united into one government when Rurik, with his Variugian companions, came to rule over them. During the reign of Prince Vladimir (972–1015) Christianity was introduced into Russia from Byzantium, and with it the productions of Byzantine literature found their way into the country. Owing to the very close proximity then existing between the Bulgarian and Russian languages, the Russians copied also several of the productions of the ancient Bulgarian literature. The most ancient monument of this literature is "Ostromirov's Gospel," of 1053. In 1224 the Tartars invaded Russia and ruled over her for more than two centuries; and although their rule did not denationalize the people, it left its imprint upon the civil administration of the country, upon the social condition of the people, and upon their language. The Tartar dominion retarded the onward progress of Russia, and it was only in the reign of Peter the Great (1689–1725) that Russia began its emancipation from its semi-Asiatic, semi-barbaric condition, and became fit to take a rank amongst the European powers.

The reforms of Peter the Great could not be executed without producing discontent in the land. Before him the Patriarch Nikon, one of the greatest men on the patriarchal throne in Russia, roused the indignation of the people by attempting to revise the Bible and the liturgical books, and to purge them from the errors that had crept into them through the ignorance of the transcribers. Nikon was denounced as a heretic, his corrections were deemed sacrilegious, and a great many people refused to accept the revised books, and seceded from the Church. These were and are still called Dissenters (*Raskolniks*), and although the points on which they originally disagreed with the Church were puerile, they have clung and do still cling to their notions with an astonishing pertinacity. In their eyes the present Russian Church is not a true Church, the Tzar is an antichrist, and they only are the true Christians, because they hold to the old faith. The Russian Dissent has given rise to a great many sects, some of which profess the wildest vagaries. Nikon's revision of the church books is the one used now in the Russian, Bulgarian, and Servian churches, and its language, modified according to the Russian orthography, is known as the Church-Slavonic.

The Russian was governed originally by archbishops or metropolitans, who were ordained by the Greek Patriarch of Constantinople, and several of whom were Greeks. But after the capture of Constantinople in 1453 the metropolitans were consecrated by a council of bishops, and in 1589 the chief metropolitan was raised to the rank and dignity of a Patriarch. The Patriarchate lasted till the time of Peter the Great, who, in order to curb the opposition of the clergy to his reforms, abolished it and replaced it by a Synod, whose head was to be the Tzar. This reform has lasted till now, and the Russian Church is governed by it. But though the Tzar is the real president of the Synod, he never takes any part in its deliberations, but is represented by a substitute, usually a layman, who bears the title of *ober-prokuror*. The Synod can do nothing without the sanction of the *prokuror;* in fact. he is the Synod. The Tzar's prerogatives, however, are limited to the administration of the Church; his authority does not extend to matters purely spiritual, and he cannot interfere with the dogmas of the Church. The constitution of the Synod and of the Russian Church in general is such that it places the clergy under the authority and supervision of the government and makes it subservient to the interests of "the powers that be."

**Russ-Lapp Version.**—For the people of Russian Lapland, Magister Genetz translated the Gospel of Matthew. The work, after having been examined and approved by Prof. E. Lönnrott, was printed in 1877 by the British and Foreign Bible Society. The people who speak that dialect number about 4,000 or 5,000.

(*Specimen verse.* John 3 : 16.)

Тэн гудӥк што Имжель нит шабэшӥй тап альме, што иджес Альге, эхтушэитма эпдӥй, тэн варас што юкьянъ, Ӥӥе Сонне вӥер, ӥй майкьяхъ, а лехъ сонне агееалмуш.

**Rustchuk,** a city in Bulgaria on the Danube, 187 miles by rail northwest of Varna. Population, 30,000. Mission station of the Methodist Episcopal Church (North); 2 missionaries, 3 native helpers, 1 theological seminary, 24 students, 1 other school, 14 scholars.

**Rust en Vrede,** a station of the Moravians in Surinam, Dutch Guiana, South America. It was organized as a separate congregation in order to relieve to some extent the work in the large church of Paramaribo, and is situated in a suburb on the southwest side, in which during the last few years a great number of Negroes belonging to the Moravian Church had settled,

having migrated thither from the plantations. This suburb is divided into numerous squares by streets running at right angles. One looking down a street sees only what looks like a pathway leading through a wood far away into the dense forest. This seeming forest is inhabited throughout, Negro huts being hidden beneath the tall mangoes, cocoa-palms, and other fruit-trees. Two plots of ground were purchased, and the church from the abandoned station Annaszorg was brought and re-erected here, receiving the name Rust en Vrede (Rest and Peace).

**Rust en Werk,** a station of the Moravians in Dutch Guiana, established in the year 1821, at the request of the owners of an estate which lies on the north bank of the river Comewyne, not far from its junction with the Surinam, about ten miles below Paramaribo. The owners of this estate gave a large house as a residence for the missionary, the upper story of which served as a church. On the day upon which it was opened the first four Christians of this neighborhood were baptized. Many Chinese and coolies now live upon the adjoining estates, some of whom have united with the congregation.

**Ruthenian Version.**—The Ruthenian belongs to the Slavonic branch of the Aryan family of languages, and is spoken in Little Russia. In 1874 the British Bible Society published at Vienna the Gospel of Luke, as translated by Mr. Kobylanski. Being in the Cyrilian type, it was well received, and proved a success, because a part of the Divine Word was thus given to the Ruthenians for the first time in their vernacular. During the year 1877 the same Society published the Gospel of John, translated by the same author, after it had been critically examined by Professor Micklovich. A translation of the New Testament into Ruthenian was prepared from the Greek by Dr. Puley, with the assistance of Mr. Kulisch. The British and Foreign Bible Society bought in 1882 500 copies of this version for circulation, but in 1885 purchased the copyright of the translation, and published an edition in Cyrilian character, of 5,000 copies, in 1886.

(*Specimen verse.* Luke 15 : 18.)

Ѣставши пойдѫ до о҃тца моѥго, і зкажѫ ѥмѫ: Отче, згрішив ѥм протів неба і перед тѡбѡѵ.

# S.

**Sabathu** (Subathu), a town in Simla district, Punjab, India, 23 miles from Simla, 110 miles northwest of Lodiana. Mission station of Presbyterian Church (North), 1836; 1 missionary, 2 native helpers, 16 church-members, 44 school-children, and a hospital for lepers, several of whom are church-members.

**Safed,** a town, formerly of considerable note, on a hill overlooking the western coast of the Lake of Tiberius, Asiatic Turkey, 65 miles

west of Damascus. Mission station of the L. S. P. C. among the Jews; 2 missionaries, 2 native helpers, also a medical mission.

**Sagaing,** a populous town in Burma, on the west side of the Irawadi River, fifteen miles below Mandalay. It lies just opposite Ava, the scene of Judson's imprisonment, which is now an out-station of the work at Sagaing. Mission station of the A. B. M. U.; 2 missionaries and wives, 1 church, 23 communicants, 1 Sunday-school, 20 scholars, 3 schools, 78 scholars.

**Saharanpur,** a town in Northwest Provinces, India, 90 miles northeast of Delhi, 130 southeast of Lodiana. A large town, rather substantially built, and steadily improving in appearance and increasing in importance. Owing to its low, moist situation, it was very unhealthy, but recent sanitary improvements have somewhat remedied this evil. Mission station Presbyterian Church (North), 1836; 1 missionary and wife, 8 native helpers, 57 church-members, 429 scholars.

**Saibai Version.**—The Saibai belongs to the Melanesian languages, and is vernacular in Torres Straits. A translation of the Gospel of Mark into this dialect was made by Mr. Elia, a teacher who has been fifteen years engaged in the work, and revised by the Rev. S. Macfarlane of Murray Island. It was published at Sydney in 1883 under the care of the Auxiliary of the British and Foreign Bible Society. Besides the Gospel of Mark, that of Matthew has also been published.

**Saint Albans.**—A town in northeast Kaffraria, South Africa, near St. John's. Mission station of the S. P. G.; 1 missionary and wife, 250 communicants.

**Saint Barnabas,** a town in Norfolk, Melanesia: is the chief seat of the Melanesian Mission and its bishop since 1867. The mission consists of 8 native missionaries, 130 male and 35 female students. In the cool season, March to December, the bishop sails from island to island inspecting the various stations, and in the mean time he keeps school on board the steamer. The printing establishment, from which books in 35 different languages are issued, is also at St. Barnabas.

**Saint Croix,** one of the West Indies, is a Danish possession since 1716. It has an area of 74 square miles, and a population of 18,430 (1880). The inhabitants are mostly free Negroes, and are engaged in the raising of sugar-cane and the manufacture of rum.

The Moravian Brethren commenced their mission to the Danish West Indies at this island in 1754, and now have three stations: Friedensthal, Friedensberg, and Friedensfeld, with 3 missionaries, 1,363 communicants, 3 Sunday-schools, 825 scholars. The Danish Lutheran Church has also quite a membership here.

**Saint Eustache** is one of the Dutch West Indies, and forms part of the colony of Curaçoa. It contains a population of 2,335 in its area of 7 square miles. Mission station of Wesleyan Methodist West Indian Conference.

**Saint Helena,** an island belonging to Great Britain, in the Atlantic Ocean, 1,200 miles west of Africa and 2,000 miles east of South America. Area, 47 square miles. Population (1886), 4,500, Negroes and half-breeds. Mission field of the S. P. G.; 3 stations—St. Paul's, Jamestown, Longwood; 355 communicants. There are also 1 Roman Catholic and 2 Baptist chapels.

**Saint Jan** or **Saint John,** one of the Dutch possessions in the West Indies, has an area of 21 square miles, and a population (1880) of 944, among whom the Moravian Brethren commenced work in 1754, with stations at Bethany and Emmaus (see St. Thomas). Mission field of the Danish Missionary Society.

**Saint John's.**—1. The chief town on the island of Antigua, West Indies. Population, 10,000, chiefly pure Negroes and mulattoes. A station of the Moravian Brethren, opened in 1756 by a missionary from the Danish islands, who was moved by the miserable spiritual condition of the Negro population in Antigua to come to their assistance. He accomplished much, and his work is now being carried on by 1 missionary and his wife, 1 unmarried man, and 1 single lady. A training-school for women is carried on at this station, and the church has a congregation of over 1,000.

2. A diocese of the S. P. G. in South Africa, founded 1873, containing 10 stations, 2,523 communicants.

**Saint Kitt's,** or **Saint Christopher,** is one of the Leeward Group of the British West Indies. Its greatest length is 23 miles, and it contains an area of 65 square miles, with a population of 45,000. The island is of volcanic origin, the scenery is rich and beautiful, and the soil is fertile and well-watered. Basseterre, with a population of 7,000, is the capital. Mission field of the Moravian Brethren, with stations at Bethesda, Basseterre, Bethel, and Eastbridge, with a total of 3 missionaries, 1,480 communicants, 7 day-schools, 854 scholars, 6 Sunday-schools, 2,000 scholars. S. P. G. (1877); 1 missionary, 285 communicants. (For the work of the Wesleyan Methodists, see West Indies.)

**Saint Louis,** a town on an island at the mouth of the Senegal River, West Africa, is the chief town of the French possession, Senegambia, with a population of 20,000. Mission station of the Paris Evangelical Missionary Society (1863); 2 missionaries, 1 medical missionary.

**Saint Lucia,** one of the Windward Islands, British West Indies, has an area of 122 square miles, with a population (1888) of 42,504, principally Negroes and half-breeds. Chief town, Castries, 4,555. There are 26 schools (14 Protestant, 12 Roman Catholic), 3,351 pupils.

**Saint Mark's,** a station of the S. P. G. diocese of St. John's, in the Transkei, South Africa, was the first station (1859) occupied in the diocese; has 1 missionary, 746 communicants.

**Saint Mary's Island,** a large island off the coast of Gambia, West Africa, at the mouth of the Gambia River, east of Cape St. Mary. The principal city on the island is Bathurst. Mission station of the Wesleyan Missionary Society; 4 missionaries, 23 native helpers, 3 chapels, 2 schools, 358 scholars.

**Saint Matthew's,** a station of the S. P. G. in the diocese of Grahamstown, South Africa, near King William's Town; was occupied in 1859, and has 1 missionary and 370 communicants.

**Saint Paul de Loanda,** the capital of the province of Loanda, in the Portuguese colony Angola, on the west coast of Africa, is situated on a beautiful landlocked harbor, sixty miles by sea north of the mouth of the Coanza. Its population, estimated at 5,000, consists of a few hundred Portuguese, and the rest are Negroes. It was the starting-point in 1884 for the mission of Bishop Taylor to Central Africa, and is a station of that mission.

**Saint Paul's,** a station of the S. P. G. in Natal, South Africa, not far from the coast; has 1 missionary and 30 communicants.

**Saint Peter's,** a town in Cape Colony, South Africa, on the border of Kaffraria, north-west of King William's Town. Mission station of the S. P. G. in the diocese of Grahamstown; 1 missionary and wife, 110 communicants.

**Saint Thomas,** one of the West India islands belonging to Denmark (1716); has an area of 23 square miles, and a population of 14,389, mostly Negroes. Sugar and rum are the products. Mission field of the Moravian Brethren, with stations at New Herrnhut, Nisky, and St. Thomas. Including St. Jan (q.v.), there were in 1886 5 stations, 2 missionaries, 1,289 communicants, 7 schools, 388 pupils, 5 Sunday-schools, 1,000 scholars.

**Saint Thomas,** a town on the above island, is picturesquely situated on three hills on the south coast, overlooking a fine harbor. For many years it was the terminus of several steamship lines, a depot for the surrounding islands, and a port of call for vessels of all nations; but the laying of West India telegraph cable greatly changed these conditions, and its commercial importance is rapidly declining. In 1843 the Moravian Brethren, who had hitherto confined their labors to the sugar plantations, found it necessary to provide instruction for the many converts who had come out to the town to live, and a place of worship was procured near the centre of the town, where a school and preaching services were held. In 1882 a fine new building was completed, and was a memorial church of the 150th anniversary of the beginning of Moravian missions. The Danish Government provided schools and churches for the people at a very early date in their occupancy of the island.

**Saint Thomé,** a suburb of Madras, India, is a mission station of the S. P. G. for 16 villages, with 4 native preachers, 241 communicants, 3 mixed schools, 196 boys and girls.

**Saint Vincent,** one of the Windward Islands, West Indies, is a British colonial possession (1763), under an administrator and colonial secretary. Its area is 122 square miles. Population (1888), 46,872, mainly Negroes and half-breeds. Kingston is the capital; population, 5,393. Mission work is carried on by both the Wesleyan Methodists (W. I. Conference) and the S. P. G., the latter having 2 missionaries, 2 stations, 620 communicants.

**Salem.**—1. A town in a district of the same name in Madras, India. Its climate is dry and hot. Population, 50,667. Hindustani and Tamil are the languages spoken. Mission station of the London Missionary Society (1824), with 15 out-stations, 2 missionaries, 185 church-members, 3 Sunday-schools, 120 scholars, 9 boys' schools, 478 boys, 2 girls' schools, 178 scholars.

2. A town in the Coronie district, Surinam, South America, on the coast west of Paramaribo. Mission station of the Moravian Brethren, started in answer to the appeal of several English proprietors of estates in this district. A large congregation has been gathered into the church.

3. A town in Jamaica, West Indies, formerly called New Hope, lies near the seashore at Parker's Bay. A congregation was organized here and the place made a regular mission station of the Moravian Brethren in 1838.

**Salmas,** a district in West Persia, north of Lake Oroomiah, half-way betweeen Tabriz and Oroomiah, and near the eastern boundary of Turkey. (It is spoken of as a city, though there is really no city of that name.) Climate unusually pleasant and equable. Population, 30,000, Moslems, Armenians, Nestorians, Jews, and Koords—each speaking its own language, and generally Turkish also. Social condition of Moslems low, but of other classes a little better. Mission station of Presbyterian Church (North), 1884, chiefly among the Armenians; 2 missionaries and wives, 2 single ladies, 75 native helpers, 1 out-station, 1 church, 30 church-members, 6 schools.

**Salonica,** a seaport city in European Turkey, at the northeastern extremity of the Gulf of Saloniki. Population, 80,000. Greeks, Bulgarians, Wallachians, Turks, Spaniards. Religions, Greek Orthodox and Islam. Mission station of Presbyterian Church (South), 1876; 1 missionary and wife, 3 native helpers, 3 out-stations, 1 church, 35 church-members.

**Saltillo,** a city in North Central Mexico, in the frontier state of Coahuila, 239 miles southwest of Laredo, Texas, 60 miles west of Monterey. Climate mild, temperate, and healthy. Population, 15,000, mixed Spanish and Indian, speaking Spanish and Indian dialects. Social condition of two thirds of the people very degraded; class lines are closely drawn. Mission station of the Southern Baptist Convention; 2 missionaries and wives, 4 female missionaries, 3 colporteurs. Presbyterian Church (North), 1884: 2 female missionaries, 10 out-stations, 580 church-members, 363 Sabbath-scholars, 9 day-schools, 194 scholars.

**Salvador,** a republic of Central America, borders on the Pacific coast for 160 miles from the mouth of the Rio de la Paz to the mouth of the Goascoran, in the Gulf of Fonseca. Its inland boundaries are Guatemala on the west and Honduras on the north and east. It is the smallest of the Central American republics, having an area of 7,225 square miles. Except along the coast, where there are low alluvial plains, the country consists of a high plateau 2,000 feet above the sea, with many volcanic mountains. The volcanic forces are still at work, as shown by the frequent earthquakes.

Since 1853, when the union with Honduras and Nicaragua was dissolved, the government is that of a republic, with a president elected for four years by suffrage of all citizens, and a congress of 70 deputies. The population (1886) is 651,130, an average of 89 to the square mile, which is twenty times the average of the other Central American States. The bulk of the inhabitants are of aboriginal or mixed races; only 10,000 are whites, or descendants of Europeans. The natives are engaged principally in agriculture, though there is much mineral wealth as yet undeveloped. The climate is mild and pleasant. Roman Catholicism is the state religion, but there is tolerance of other religions. Education, which is under the care of the government, is carried on in free schools, attendance upon which is obligatory. In 1888 there were 732 primary schools with 27,000 pupils, and 18 high-schools with 1,293 students. Railways are being built; there are 1,440 miles of telegraph; telephones connect San Salvador, the capital, with Santa Anna, and the resources of the country are rapidly being developed. There is no organized mission work in Salvador.

**Salvation Army.** Headquarters. 101 Queen Victoria Street, London, E. C., England. —The Salvation Army is the largest and most powerful evangelizing agency in existence. It may be said to have been founded on July 5th, 1865, when Rev. Wm. Booth, who had shortly before left the Methodist New Connexion, held alone the first open-air meeting of what was then called the "Christian Mission." The meeting took place on Mile End Waste, in the heart of one of the most disreputable neighborhoods of London. The Christian Mission became the Salvation Army in 1878. It now occupies 34 countries and colonies, and its 4,000 corps are officered by some 10,000 men and women, to none of whom is any salary guaranteed, and none of whom receive anything more than the supply of their actual wants. These officers speak 29 languages. The total number of meetings held weekly is estimated at 50,000.

The Army publishes in 15 languages 27 weekly and 15 monthly journals, having a total annual circulation of 33,500,000 copies. The annual circulation of books and other pamphlets is put at 4,000,000 more. The total sum raised annually by the Army is reckoned at $2,250,000. Balance-sheets are issued every year from all the headquarters in the different countries, and quarterly in all the corps or local bodies. The balance-sheets of the various headquarters are audited by independent accountants.

The form of government is military throughout. The General for the time being is, under a deed-poll enrolled in the British High Court of Chancery, the trustee of the entire funds and property of the Army. General Booth has never drawn any salary or allowance whatever (except out-of-pocket expenses) from the Army funds, his private income being derived from other sources.

The General's representatives in charge of the work in the different countries may be of any rank, but have the power and, frequently, the title of Commissioner. There are six other grades of responsibility and power on the staff of the Army. Then come the field officers—those who conduct the work of the local corps, and then the local officers who assist those last mentioned.

The soldiers are converts or members who, having given satisfactory evidence of conversion for at least a month, have signed the Articles of War, and have been sworn in as members of the corps. In these they avow their determination to serve God, by His help, all their lives; to be true soldiers of and in the Army for life; to renounce the world with all its sinful pleasures, companionships, and objects, and to boldly confess Christ at all costs; to abstain not only from all intoxicating liquors, but opium, morphia, and all other baneful drugs, except when ordered by a doctor in sickness; to abstain not only from all low and profane language, but also from all falsehood, dishonesty, and fraud; that they will "never treat any woman, child, or other person in an oppressive, cruel, or cowardly manner;" to spend all the time, strength, money, and in-

fluence possible in supporting and carrying on the operations of the Army; to be obedient to all the lawful orders of superior officers; and to do all these things for the love of Christ.

The theology of the Army is most analogous to that of the Methodist Church.

Among features sufficiently striking to be distinctive of the Army are: 1. The prominence given to women, who form about one half of the total number of officers, and are not barred by their sex from any position in the whole organization. 2. The use (in theory at any rate) of every individual member as an active worker, and that as soon as he professes conversion. 3. Its adaptation of system and methods to particular tastes or needs of peoples, times, and circumstances. 4. The activity and energy shown in the meetings held every day of the week the year round. 5. The number and variety of its branches or offshoots. 6. The application of unusual means to attract the people to its meetings, etc. 7. The principle of self-support applied to every corps, division, and territory. 8. The self-denial of the whole Army in all lands, not only displayed by its officers and soldiers as such, but more especially by the "self-denial week" every year for the extension of the work generally, especially outside the territory raising the money. 9. The wearing of a distinctive uniform by all members of whatever rank. 10. The implicit, unquestioning obedience rendered by all to those next above them in rank. 11. The prominence given to teaching and testimony with regard to entire sanctification or complete deliverance not only from the guilt of sin, but also from its power. 12. The numerous opportunities afforded to every member not only for dealing with sinners by many different means, but also to rise to any position in the Army itself. 13. The mutual personal love and affection felt by Salvationists of all ranks, in all nations, and the solidarity of the whole organization. 14. The time and energy bestowed upon open air work. 15. The raising up everywhere of native soldiers and officers for the salvation of their own fellow-citizens or countrymen.

The principal officers are: William Booth, the General; W. Bramwell Booth, Chief of the Staff (this gentleman, by the way, has been aptly described as "the Von Moltke of the Salvation Army"); Commissioner Booth-Clibborn, Paris; Commissioner Ballington Booth, New York; Commissioner Booth-Tucker, Bombay; Mrs. Bramwell Booth, the head of the Rescue Work; Commissioner Railton, Berlin; Commissioner Howard, London; Commissioner Coombs, Melbourne; Commissioner Estill, Kimberley; Commissioner Adams, Toronto; Commissioners Carleton and Cadman, London: of these last the former is at the head of the gigantic trade operations of the Army, and the latter is in charge of the Social Reform wing. Of the same rank is Kommendor Hanna Ouchterloney of Stockholm, commanding the forces in Sweden, Norway, and Finland.

The respective numbers of corps and officers in the different countries are as follows: Great Britain, 1,514 and 4,652; the United States, 445 and 1,120; Canada and Newfoundland, 391 and 1,056; Australia (Victoria, South Australia, New South Wales, Tasmania, Queensland), 756 and 991; New Zealand, 170 and 193; France and Switzerland, 167 and 397; India and Ceylon, 158 and 423; Sweden, 150 and 373; South Africa (Cape Colony, Natal, Orange Free State, Transvaal), 61 and 160; Holland, 51 and 155; Norway, 48 and 142; Denmark, 36 and 100; Germany, 21 and 75; Finland, 5 and 19; Belgium, 4 and 26; Argentine Republic, 4 and 20; St. Helena, 1 and 2. Grand total, 3,834 corps and outposts and 9,904 officers. There are in all 33 Rescue Homes, 10 Prison-gate Brigades, and 35 Slum Posts, and about 60 garrisons for the training of officers.

In India and Ceylon the officers wear a dress similar to that worn by the natives, live in native huts, and beg their food from door to door, after the manner of the religious devotees so numerous in Oriental lands. In South Africa officers have been set apart to live among the Zulus and Swazies, following similar lines as to food and manner of life; and in New Zealand the Maoris are receiving attention of a similar character—in all four countries the Army officers even abandoning their own names and taking others from the people they seek to benefit.

The general lines of work are much the same everywhere. The Army does not so much try to teach doctrine as to bear witness to the power of God to deliver from the power as well as from the guilt of sin. Hence the comparative lack of education of some of its officers is not so great an obstacle to success as some might think, because their lives bear out the statements they make. The positiveness with which the Army speaks of many things which to not a few professed Christians are matters only of belief, is often startling; but the poverty, hard work, and self-sacrifice of the officers are everywhere proved to be powerful arguments in favor of the religion taught by them. The Army universally insists not only on a complete separation from the world and abandonment of even doubtful things, but upon a bold confession of Christ and His religion in every possible way—notably by public testimony and the wearing of uniform. It has little faith in religion that produces no change in a man that can be seen by his neighbors, and therefore every possible means is used to transform every convert into an active evangelist as quickly as possible. It also makes heavy demands upon the time and means of all its adherents, and is continually urging them on to a higher platform of devotion and self-sacrifice for the sake of the perishing.

The Army never attacks other religious, nor does it enter into discussions about its own. It conceives its mission to be to proclaim to all men the possibility of salvation through faith in Christ for every man who will accept it and renounce his sins, and it always aims to deal with the heart and conscience rather than with the intellect.

Every effort is put forth to make the meetings pleasant and attractive, music and singing being usually given great prominence. The chief object of every Salvationist in going into a meeting is usually rather to benefit others than to perform acts of adoration or to receive personal instruction for himself, and this principle has a great effect on the character of the services.

The positive, aggressive, and, as some consider, extreme character, not only of the religious theories but the practices of the Army on the one hand, and its bold and uncompromising hostility to every form of sin, vice, and hypocrisy on the other, have made the history of the Army a long record of opposition, slander, misrepresentation, and persecution of every conceivable kind. General Booth boasts of being at the head of the only religious body that always has some of its members in prison for conscience' sake. It is a curious fact with respect to imprisonment, that while the authorities of the United States, Canada, Great Britain, India, Sweden, South Africa, and Switzerland have all done their share in this direction, the avowedly atheistic French Government has never yet laid hands on a single Salvationist on account of his religion. Among those who have been imprisoned for conscience' sake are the General's eldest daughter and second son; the eldest son, as the result of action taken in concert with others to deal with peculiarly horrible vice, has been in the dock, charged with an offence of which he was subsequently acquitted; the third daughter has been arrested for street-preaching, though not imprisoned; and the third son has appeared before the Court of Queen's Bench, charged with inciting to riot. Commissioners Booth-Tucker and Booth-Clibborn, the husbands of two of the General's daughters, have also been to jail for Christ's sake—one in Bombay, the other in Switzerland.

As might be expected, the fiercest opposition—and that which most frequently finds expression in mob-violence—comes from the representatives of the liquor interest; and this is true everywhere, although in some instances, as in Switzerland, the authorities have also added their oppression to the action of the mob. It is not so easy to account for the active opposition of professedly Christian people and leaders—almost equally widespread—except on the theory that the practical sacrifice and self-denial demanded by the Army from others and practised by itself are considered to involve a reflection upon their own religious teaching and lives. In all forms of opposition and persecution it is a somewhat singular fact that Great Britain has always led the way: in no land have the attacks upon the Army been more bitter or fierce, and nowhere has it had to contend with more prejudice, contempt, secret enmity, and cruel hostility.

The Salvation Army's first landing in the United States took place in 1881, when Commissioner Railton and a small company of female evangelists arrived. It will be seen on looking at the figures for the whole world that the United States field stands next to that of Great Britain, with 445 corps and 1,120 officers. These extend all across the continent, and from Washington State in the north to Texas and Florida in the south; and not only is the whole country belted with corps, but also with training garrisons at the following cities: New York, Brooklyn, Boston (2), Detroit, Grand Rapids, Englewood, Ill., Des Moines, Omaha, Oakland, and San Francisco. There are Rescue Homes at Grand Rapids and San Francisco, and besides two Slum Posts in New York, work of the same kind is carried on by the Golden Gate. Prison work is done, though not on any large scale as yet, at Auburn, N.Y.; Minneapolis, Minn.; Kansas City, Mo.; and San Francisco. The National Headquarters is at 111 Reade Street, New York City, where Commissioner Ballington Booth, the General's son, can usually be found. The headquarters of the different divisions into which the country is divided for purposes of oversight are at Portland, Me.; Boston, Mass.; Syracuse, N.Y.; Baltimore, Md.; Homestead and Harrisburg, Pa.; Cleveland, O.; Springfield,

Ill.; Detroit, Mich.; Chicago, Ill.; Minneapolis, Minn.; Des Moines, Ia.; Kansas City, Mo.; Topeka, Kan.; Denver, Col.; Helena, Mont.; Sacramento and San Francisco, Cal.; Portland, Ore.; Los Angeles, Cal.; Austin, Tex.; and Jacksonville, Fla. There are 12 corps in Chicago, 8 in Brooklyn, 6 in New York, 5 in Detroit, 4 each in Boston, San Francisco, Kansas City, Minneapolis; 3 each in St. Paul and Baltimore; 2 each in Philadelphia, Buffalo, Cleveland, Nashville, St. Louis, Grand Rapids, Saginaw City, Omaha, and Los Angeles. There are Swedish corps in New York, Brooklyn, Perth Amboy, Chicago, Des Moines, and San Francisco, and a Danish corps at Omaha.

That the labors of the Army here have not been without visible result is shown by the fact that during the past twelve months (1890) no fewer than 22,550 persons professed conversion at its penitent forms. During the month of October no fewer than 1,070,000 persons attended the indoor meetings of the Army in this country, and a careful calculation shows that its open-air meetings during the past year were attended by 4,000,000 persons. This total is the more remarkable, because the municipal authorities in not a few cities either forbid open-air work altogether, or place restrictions upon it either so numerous or of such a character as to render it of little value compared with what the Army considers that it might be. It is estimated, however, that, taking both forms of meeting together, no fewer than 12,000,000 persons have, during the past year, listened to religious truth from the Army.

Of course these large figures are partly due to the immense number of the meetings. At every corps there are, or should be, ten indoor meetings per week, and, where there is liberty to do so, there should be at least six held in the open air. The Army is the only Protestant body with whom a devotional meeting at 7 A.M. on Sundays is a regular thing, and the attendance at, and character of, this meeting is judged to afford a fairly accurate index as to the spiritual condition of the corps. The meetings on Sunday morning and Friday evening are usually devoted to the inculcation of the Army views on holiness, and one evening in the week is given to spiritual dealing, by the officers, with the soldiers only. The other meetings are held chiefly with a view to reaching the godless and unconverted.

The officers responsible for the conduct of these meetings are the captain and lieutenant, but they are assisted in the management of the affairs of the corps by a treasurer, secretary, and sergeants, if the corps be large enough to need the services of all these. Every corps is supposed to raise its own income and pay its own expenses—usually week by week, and the officers are not supposed to draw their allowance until all the expenses for the week are paid. Male captains and lieutenants can then draw $7 and $6 respectively per week, and female officers of the same rank draw one dollar less. When the receipts are not equal to paying everything and leaving enough for the officers, the soldiers and friends usually give the latter articles of food. Over a number of corps is placed a divisional officer, who is supported by a small percentage from each of his corps on their receipts. It is his duty to visit all the corps in his charge as often as possible, to commence the work in new places, and to see to the

welfare of his officers and soldiers. He is responsible to headquarters for the prosperity of his division, and he has to report there both weekly and monthly on forms provided. The National Headquarters is supported largely by the profits accruing from the sale of the "War Cry" and other Army literature; also of uniform, musical instruments, and other things needed for the use of the Army. In this building are usually the offices where is conducted the business connected with property, candidates, the "War Cry" and other literature, the appointments of the field officers, and the financial arrangements. The number of departments and offices varies in different countries, according to the strength of the particular contingent. All officers are liable to removal at any moment, although commissioners under ordinary circumstances remain some four or five years in a command, divisional officers about a year, and field officers from four to six months. In theory every officer is ready and willing to go to any part of the globe at a moment's notice, and in the great majority of cases this is literally true; and where it does not so apply to individuals, it is because of family or other circumstances beyond their control.

The principal books published by the Army are: "Orders and Regulations for Field Officers" (700 pp.), "Salvation Soldiery," "The Training of Children," "Holy Living," and "In Darkest England and the Way Out," by the General; "Popular Christianity," "Aggressive Christianity," "Life and Death," "Godliness," "Practical Religion," "The Salvation Army in relation to the Church and the State," by the late Mrs. General Booth; "Heathen England," "Twenty-one Years Salvation Army," and "Apostolic Warfare," by Commissioner Railton; "The Doctrines and Discipline of the Salvation Army;" "The Soldier's Manual," by Commissioner Ballington Booth, and "Beneath Two Flags," by Mrs. Ballington Booth. There are two "War Crys" (one in Swedish) published in New York and another in San Francisco. "All the World" is the best and largest monthly, although the "Deliverer," the organ of the Rescue Work, is rapidly increasing in influence and circulation. The "Musical Salvationist" (monthly) is in its fifth year of publication; the contributions are furnished by officers and soldiers of the Army, although a few national and other tunes are to be found among them with Salvation Army words. The first volume of the "Musical Pioneer," recently published by the New York Headquarters, was the cheapest volume of music issued by the Army at the time of its appearance.

One feature of Salvation Army literature is that there are no "outside" advertisements in any book, journal, or magazine. When the enormous circulation of these is considered, it will be seen that the Army by this course sacrifices large sums of money every year. On the other hand, nearly every "War Cry" contains a column or so of advertisements for missing relatives and friends for which nothing is charged. No other religious papers are pushed as are the various "War Crys." In London and Melbourne, Cape Town and Bombay, Paris and Toronto,—to name typical cities,—Salvationists take their journals into saloons, beer-halls, concert-rooms, brothels, slums, and other places of ill-savor, and not only take them there, but sell them there. No issue of any "War Cry" in any language ever appears that does not contain in some form or other plain directions by which any person can learn the way and conditions of salvation, and the first attack on any person or society has yet to appear.

One of the ablest journalists in England, and a man whose personal experience of the world is such as to make his words worthy of attention, says, in referring to the Army's educating and elevating influence upon the masses: " It has trained thousands whose energies would have been wasted in tap-rooms and at street-corners, to do the practical work of teaching, ruling, and administering. It has done more to spread a real, rough, but genuine culture among the lowest than both our universities. It is easy to sneer at its ' War Crys,' but as a rough-and-ready school of journalism they have no rival. They are the natural expression of the common man, who, but for the Salvation Army, would never have learned to write grammatically, to express himself concisely, and to report succinctly what he sees. The Army hymnology may not be as polished as that of the Anglican Church, but regarded as the spontaneous utterance of the aspiration of the English poor towards an ideal life, it is one of the most remarkable literary and devotional growths of our time. Then, again, in music the Army has done great things. To teach every one to sing, to accustom the poorest and the most ignorant to the most inspiriting music of the day, to rear up in almost every village men and women who will spend hours learning to play musical instruments—all this is foundation work which must not be despised."

Among its more distinctive methods of work may be mentioned : 1. *Open-air Parades.* In addition to the evangelistic services in the open air, the Army, wherever practicable, has "marches." The soldiers form a procession, four deep, if there is a sufficient number, and as they march they sing songs, usually to stirring or popular tunes, calculated to direct the attention of all hearers to vital religious truths. At the head is carried the Army flag, and frequently the national colors also ; then come the officers in command, then the band, followed by the rank and file. The utility of this method is not only abundantly proved by the number of strangers who follow to the building,—a tap-room or bar very frequently being emptied by the music—but in hundreds of instances the words of the songs sung have been used to the conversion of those who would not have brought themselves under any religious influence whatever, but could not help hearing the street singing. The practical value of this mode of evangelization cannot be over-estimated. 2. *Bands of Music.*—These are greatly owned of God. The greatest care is taken to keep out from these any element of selfishness or vainglory. No member of any band receives any payment whatever, and when it is remembered that the great majority of the musicians never touched an instrument before their conversion, it is evident that disinterested love for souls is the sole incentive to a large amount of self-denying effort at a cost of much time and labor. Much of the music played by these bands is composed by officers and soldiers of the Army. 3. *Distinctive Titles and Phraseology.*—Not only are the holders of different positions in the Army designated by military titles, but most of the meetings are described in terms different to those used by most churches. The early morn-

ing prayer-meeting is " knee-drill ;" the Sunday-afternoon meeting usually given to testimony and song for the benefit of the godless crowd is a " free-and-easy ;" the commencement of the work in a city is an " attack " or " bombardment ;" the building used is frequently referred to as " the Hallelujah Factory," if that has been the character of the building rented ; and so on : the object of this being to avoid the dislike and contempt of the " masses " in most countries for churches. Hundreds who do not and would not go to church on any account can be found in the Army halls every night in the week, and the use of these terms has much to do with this. 4. " *Demonstrations" of Various Kinds.*—These are usually arranged where there are several corps near together, and are held with several objects in view. The most usual of these is, in the first place, to make an impression upon the public mind as to the existence of the Army in that city, and the success of its work ; in the second, to encourage and create love, unity, and solidarity among the soldiers themselves ; and in the third, to promote the advancement of the local work generally by giving special prominence to some particular feature, such as the reclamation of drunkards, the swearing-in of soldiers, the introduction of some new officer of rank, or some new plan for local work. 5. *The Slum Work.*—This is carried on by female officers, who take rooms in the most vicious and degraded neighborhoods that can be found, and live there. They dress as nearly as possible like the people among whom they labor, and spend much of their time in introducing the gospel of Christ to those most in need of it, by means of the gospel of soap and hot water. They nurse the sick and bedridden, wash dirty children, and perform many kind offices for those who have no other helper. They also visit low saloons and dives, and deal with the people they find there. There are two posts in New York, the first having only been established a few months. The officers have averaged about five in number, but in that time they have visited about 7,500 families, independently of visits made to individuals. They have had a *crèche* running for two or three months, at which 1,700 children have been nursed, fed, washed, and attended to during the day while their mothers were out at work.—6. *The Rescue Work.* This is carried on very successfully by the Army, the figures comparing very favorably with those of other organizations. In Victoria and other Australian colonies the Army receives grants of money for this special branch of work. In the United States there are Homes at Grand Rapids and San Francisco.—7. *The Prison-gate Work.* This branch deals with criminals when they leave jail, and, where the authorities are sufficiently sympathetic, while they are prisoners. It has been most conspicuously successful in Australia, South Africa, India, and Ceylon. The colony of Victoria gives an annual grant of money also to help this form of labor, and the Minister of the Interior gave the officer in charge of it, Colonel Barker, a most complimentary letter testifying to the value of this work to the State, when he returned to England to push it forward there. At Kimberley, in South Africa, there is quite a little corps of Salvationists among the prisoners, who have been " saved " through the exertions of the Army officers. At Colombo, in Ceylon, the prison-gate officers are furnished with lists of the prisoners leaving jail, with particulars about them and their offences for guidance in dealing with them.

The motto of the Army is the phrase "Blood and Fire," the former word referring to the blood of Christ, and the latter to the fire of the Holy Ghost. The expression has, however, come into frequent use as an adjective, especially in reference to the Flag of the Army, often spoken, sung, and written about as the "Blood and Fire Colors." This flag consists of a crimson field with a blue border. In the centre of the red is a yellow star bearing the words "Blood and Fire," and usually the number of the local corps in the territory. This flag is probably the only ensign in the world that flies after nightfall, and in all kinds of weather, but day and night, summer and winter, these colors are leading the soldiers of the Army all round the world—out in the streets and highways and byways of their cities seeking the lost, and advertising the Salvation of God.

This brief summary would not be complete without a reference to the late Mrs. General Booth, in many respects the most remarkable woman of the century. She died of cancer on October 4th, 1890, after two years' illness. For forty years she had been such an inspirer, companion, counsellor, and helpmeet as it falls to the lot of few men, either public or private, to possess. She was an eloquent preacher, an able advocate, a most convincing exponent of doctrine, and an unceasing worker both with voice and pen on behalf of the cause and the organization that she and the General had so much at heart. Her reasoning powers were developed to a remarkable degree, and her foresight, sound judgment, and almost unerring mental instincts made her labors in the cabinet as valuable to the Army as her sermons, speeches, and writings in public. Her funeral took place on the 10th of October, and the afternoon previous no fewer than 36,000 persons gathered in the great hippodrome known in London as Olympia, for her funeral service. On the following day the streets were for five miles thronged with people, traffic being completely suspended, while her coffin, followed by two or three thousand officers, was borne to the cemetery. It was doubtless mainly through her personal influence and example that what may be called female ministry has been so prominently brought to the front in the Army, and that many other of its distinctive features became part of its system. In addition to all the labor referred to, she brought up a family of eight children, every one of whom is engaged in the work of the Salvation Army in some form, all of them (except one, who has been an invalid from childhood) adorning prominent positions in the Army.

A fortnight after Mrs. Booth's death appeared the General's book, "In Darkest England and the Way Out" (370 pp). The first edition was sold in three hours, and it produced a tremendous sensation throughout the world. This was because it contained a scheme for dealing with all forms of social evil that, although gigantic in its scope, seemed practicable as coming from a man who had such a force at his disposal as the Salvation Army with which to carry it out. The book goes on the startling calculation that no less than 10 per cent of the population of England is in a chronic condition of vice, pauperism, or crime, forming what the General calls the "Submerged Tenth." After giving several chapters to graphic description of the condition of different classes of these people, it is shown that any scheme that will be of any permanent or practical service must combine within itself all of the following essentials: (*a*) Where a man is in his present circumstances because of his own character, influences must be brought to bear upon him that will change that character. (*b*) Where a man is in those circumstances either altogether or partly through no fault of his own, those circumstances must be modified. (*c*) The scheme must be large enough to cope with an evil of such great magnitude. (*d*) It must be permanent. (*e*) It must be immediately practicable. (*f*) It must not demoralize those whom it seeks to benefit. (*g*) It must not benefit one class by injuring another. The plan set forth in the book meets all these needs, and, speaking broadly, consists of three parts—the "City Colony," the "Farm Colony," and the "Over-the-Sea Colony." The first of these is really a combination of several agencies now in active operation, and that have been worked successfully for longer or shorter periods. Chief among these are the Food and Shelter depots, where supper, bed, breakfast, a Salvation Army meeting, and facilities for washing can be obtained for eight cents. These places are self-supporting, and not assisted by charity, except possibly in the matter of the first expense of altering buildings and fitting them up for this special purpose; the Labor Factory, where temporary work can be given those willing to do it, and the Labor Bureau for placing employers and laborers in communication with each other. The Rescue Work and the Prison-gate Brigade would doubtless also be channels by which many individuals would reach the City Colony. From the City Colony the members are transferred to the Farm or Country Colony, and from thence to the Over-Sea Colony. There are many details connected with the plan that can only be named here—the Household Salvage Brigade, the Poor Man's Metropole (a kind of glorified tenement-house run by Salvationists), the Bureau for finding lost people, industrial schools, asylums for moral lunatics, model suburban villages, a poor man's Long Branch or Newport for the benefit of the inhabitants of city slums, a poor man's bank, and even a matrimonial bureau. Of course every detail of the whole scheme is to be worked by Salvationists, and through the whole book as through the whole plan the General continually reminds the reader that his sole reliance for success is on God and Him alone, and that these various schemes are only devised as making it easier for certain people to find and retain salvation. The "Farm" and "Over-Sea" colonies are still in the future. At the end of the book the General estimates the sum needed to put the whole scheme into working order as five million dollars, but that half a million would be sufficient to start it. Of this latter amount the largest part was given or promised before Christmas. Few who have any intimate knowledge of the Army itself, its spirit, discipline, and the men and women of whom it is composed, can have any doubt as to the ultimate successful execution of the plan, although, of course, in respect of time, much will necessarily depend upon the amount of money forthcoming from outside its ranks. The poverty of the Army itself is, while a source of weakness in some respects, an advantage in others, as it either excludes self-seeking or ambitious people altogether, or speedily drives them out if they do manage to get in for a time. Among the many " credentials," as the General calls them, that the Army can present in order to justify its being intrusted with the execution of the plan are: 1. Its willingness to do it. 2. Its reliance upon, and experience of, the power of God. 3. The wonders that God has wrought by, for, and in it in all countries where it works. 4. Its acquaintance with, and past experience in, discipline exercised both within itself and over others. 5. The extent and universality of the Army. 6. The fact that the great majority of the officers of the Army have had considerable experience of the outer world before reaching their present positions. 7. The fact that among the officers are to be found men and women representing probably every trade, profession, and industrial occupation, who can bring their practical experience to bear upon all such present or future details of the scheme as they may be personally conversant with. Some idea of the tremendous influence that this new scheme is likely to produce upon the world may be obtained from the fact that General Booth—a man given to carefully weighing his words—has declared publicly that should it be carried out in England, in twenty years' time there would not be a man or woman in the land willing to work for whom there would not be employment. We close this sketch with two testimonies to the success and value of the operations of the Army from sources of a diametrically opposite character.

The editor of the " Review of Reviews" writes:

"I remember, as it were but yesterday, a remark made to me by a leading freethinker and eminent politician when we were discussing the work of the Salvation Army before its immense development over sea had more than begun. ' We have all been on the wrong tack,' he said, emphatically, ' and the result is that the whole of us have less to show for our work than that one man, Booth.' ' Whom do you call "we"? I asked.' ' Oh, we children of light,' he said, laughing; ' Herbert Spencer, Matthew Arnold, Frederic Harrison, and the rest of us who have spent our lives in endeavoring to dispel superstition, and to bring in a new era based upon reason and education and enlightened self-interest. But this man Booth has produced more effect upon this generation than all of us put together.' I suppose I must have seemed pleased, for he went on hastily, ' Don't imagine for a moment that it is his religion that has helped him. Not in the least. That is a mere drivelling superstition. What has enabled him to do this work is his appeal to the social nature in man. He has evoked the potent sentiment of brotherhood. He has grouped together human beings in associations, which make them feel that they are no longer alone in the world, but that they have many brethren. That is the secret of what he has done—that, and not his superstition, which is only a minus quantity.'"

Then, to go from the atheistic extreme to the organ of the High-Church party in the Anglican Establishment, we find the " Church Times" saying, only last May:

" When we compare the so-called ' Catholic advance' of the Pope in England with the Salvationist advance of the other international commander, the General, in England and all the world, the Pope has to be content with a very much lower place. What a very poor story is the glowing chronicle of the ' Tablet' in comparison with the glowing chronicle of the ' War Cry.' In the vulgar and imposing category of mere quantity the Pope lags far behind the General.. In the spiritual category of quality, if the Kingdom of Jesus Christ be especially the Commonwealth of the Poor, the victories of the General are more stupendously brilliant in every way than the triumphs attributed by the ' Tablet' to the last two Popes. None are more ready to do honor than we are to the devotion of so many Roman clergy and sisters to the service of the poor. They have done, as Calvinists and Methodists have done, much *for* the poor. But the Pope cannot boast in his ' Tablet's' triumph-song, as the General can boast in his ' War Cry,' that he has done almost everything for the poor *by* the poor."

On Friday, the 30th January, 1891, at St. James's Hall, London, General Booth publicly signed a deed of trust for the half-million dollars above referred to. He was inaugurated as director-general, but can make no change in the provisions of the deed without the consent of two-thirds of a consultative committee of which he controls or nominates only six members. The other twelve are nominated in pairs by the Archbishop of Canterbury, the President of the Wesleyan Society, the Chairman of the Congregational Union, the Chairman of the Baptist Union, the Attorney-General, and the Chairman of the London County Council, all of whom can, if they choose, serve on the committee themselves.

**Samarang,** a commercial centre of great importance, near the mouth of the Samarang River, Java. Population, 60,000, including many Chinese. Mission station of the Netherlands Missionary Society (1849); 230 church-members. Ermelo Missionary Society (1857).

**Sambalpur,** a district in the chief commissionership of the Central Provinces, India. The town of the same name is situated on the north bank of the Mahanuddi, which during the rainy season becomes a mill-brook, but at other times is a small stream fifty yards wide. The population of the district (1881) was 1,655,960. Mission station of the General Baptist Missionary Society. A very encouraging work among the Kols is being carried on, and there are in the town and district 1 chapel, 55 church-members, 39 day-scholars, and 25 Sunday-scholars.

**Samoa,** a group of islands in the South Pacific, 14 in number. Area, 1,701 square miles. The principal islands and the population of each are: Upolu, 36,000; Savaii, 12,500; and Tutuila, 3,750. The climate is equable and pleasant. Rain falls throughout the year, and in January, February, and March heavy storms with rain are frequent.

At the conference at Berlin in 1889, between the powers of Great Britain, Germany, and the United States, an act was signed (June 14th) by which the neutrality of the islands was guaranteed, and the rights of the citizens of the three signatory powers were declared to be equal in respect to trade, residence, and personal protection. Samoa is governed by a king, whose independence was recognized, and he was restored to power November 9th, 1889, and the natives are left in possession of their right to elect the king and legislate according to their own customs. A supreme court is established, to be presided over by one judge, the chief-justice of Samoa, who is to be appointed by the three powers, or, in case of disagreement, by the King of Norway and Sweden. To this court must be referred all civil suits concerning real property in Samoa, and rights affecting the same; all civil suits of any kind between natives and foreigners, or between foreigners of different nationalities; all crimes committed by natives against foreigners, or committed by such foreigners as are not subject to consular jurisdiction.

The natives are Polynesians, one of the finest races in the Pacific. The men are above the average height, with straight, well-rounded limbs and erect bearing. The women are slight, symmetrical, and graceful in their movements. The inhabitants of the islands are now all nominally Christians—Protestants and Roman Catholics. Nearly all the children of over seven years of age can read and write, and so can most of the adults. The Bible has been translated and printed. Mission work is carried on by the L. M. S., with stations in Tutuila, Manna, Upolu, Savaii, Tokelau, Ellice and Gilbert groups; 7 missionaries, 6 missionaries' wives, 175 native helpers. The B. F. B. S. have a depot on Navigator's Island.

**Samoa Version.**—The Samoan belongs to the Polynesian languages, and is spoken in Navigator's Island by about 40,000 people. The gospel was first conveyed to its shores by the Rev. John Williams and Rev. Charles Barff of the London Missionary Society. The first portion of the Scriptures which was printed was the Gospel of John, in 1841, and in 1846–50 the entire New Testament was completed at the mission press at Samoa. In 1849–50 a second and revised edition of the New Testament, consisting of 15,000 copies, was published at London by the British and Foreign Bible Society. In 1855 the Old Testament was printed at the mission press, and in 1861 a revised edition of 10,000 copies of the entire Bible, with marginal references, was published at London, under the Rev. Dr. Turner. In 1868 an edition of 5,000 copies of the New Testament and Psalms in large type was published at London; and a thoroughly revised edition of the entire Bible, prepared by the Revs. G. Pratt, Henry Nisbet, Dr. Turner, and A. W. Murray was published, under the care of Dr. Turner, at London, in 1872. The edition, which was stereotyped, consisted of 15,000 copies. A third edition, still further improved, corrected in about 1,378 places, was issued again under the care of Dr. Turner, at London, and in 1886 another edition of the Bible in small size was issued at the same place and by the same editor. Up to March 31st, 1889, 75,637 portions of the Scriptures were disposed of.

(*Specimen verse.* John 3: 16.)

Auā ua faapea lava ona-alofa mai o le Atua i le lalolagi, ua ia au mai ai lona Atalii e toatasi, ina ia le fano se tasi e faatuatua ia te ia, a ia maua e ia le ola e faavavau.

**Samogitian Version.**—The Samogitian belongs to the Lithuanic branch of the Aryan family of languages, and is spoken in the province of Kovno, Russia. In 1816 the Bible Society published at St. Petersburg a translation of the New Testament, made by the Bishop of Samogitia, Prince Giedrayti. In 1866 the British and Foreign Bible Society published an edition of the New Testament at Wilna and Berlin, and in 1885 a revised edition of the same. Up to date 5,200 copies have been disposed of.

(*Specimen verse.* John 3 : 16.)

Nesa taipo Diewas numilejo swieta,-jog Sunu sawo wiengimust bawe: idant fictwienas, furs ing ji tit, ne prajutu, bet turetu amjina giwata.

**Samokov,** a city of Bulgaria, European Turkey. Climate temperate. Population chiefly Bulgarians, though there are some Greeks, Turks, Albanians, etc. Its position is quite elevated, and the climate very healthy. Mission station A. B. C. F. M. (1869); 4 missionaries and wives, 2 other ladies, 24 native helpers, 10 out-stations, 3 churches, 347 church-members, 1 theological seminary, 20 students, 7 schools.

**Samsoon,** a city on the Black Sea, Turkey, 500 miles east of Constantinople. Population, Turkish, Greek, and Armenian. It is the port through which passes the greater part of the trade between Constantinople and northern and eastern Asia Minor. A carriage road has been built connecting it with all the mission stations of the Western and Eastern Turkey missions, except Erzroom, and the missionaries for those stations as a rule pass through it. It is very malarious, and continued residence has been impracticable for the missionaries. There is a native church under the care of the Marsovan station.

**Samulkota** (Chamarlakota), a town of Madras, India, in the Godaveri district, 7 miles north of Cocanada. Mission station of the Evangelical Lutheran General Council, which has out-stations in 7 villages, presided over by 1 missionary. There are in the mission district 41 scholars, 104 communicants.

**Sanders, Marshall D.,** b. Williamstown, Mass., U. S. A., July 3d, 1823; graduated at Williams College 1846; Auburn Theological Seminary 1851; ordained at Williamstown; sailed as a missionary of the A. B. C. F. M., for Ceylon, October 31st, 1851. In 1868 Mrs. Sanders died, and the next year he returned to the United States. After laboring to raise funds for a college in Ceylon, he re-embarked with his second wife May 10th, 1871. In apparently good health when he arrived, he died of apoplexy August 29th, only eight days after his arrival at Batticotta. Mr. De Riemer says: "The loss of any two other men would not have crippled and involved matters as the loss of Brother Sanders does. He was our strong tower. We thought him equal to any burden. Then the starting of the college was looked upon as the *summum bonum* for our field of labor. Our standard-bearer has fallen. He was admirably adapted to mission work. He had indomitable energy and foresight to arrange for his labor far in the future. He was a model of promptness and precision, as dependent upon his watch as upon his feet. He visited with happy effect every family of his out-stations, speaking a word with every person who showed any interest in Christianity." Dr. Hastings says: "I have been intimately associated with him for eighteen years, in missionary work, and have always found him a genial companion, an efficient co-laborer. He was systematic in his plans, prompt in meeting appointments, most persevering in his labors, not easily deterred by obstacles, nor easily discouraged. He possessed largely the confidence and affection of the native Christians, and the respect of the heathen. The training-school, over which he presided with great efficiency for many years, will feel his death deeply."

**Sandoway,** a very ancient town in Arakan, Lower Burma, on the Sandoway River, 15 miles from its mouth. Climate, except in town proper, unhealthy, owing to mangrove swamps. Population, 1,508, Ch'ins, Kemmees, other hill-tribes, Burmans, Arakanese, etc. Language, Burmese. Religions, Buddhism, Moslemism, demon-worship. Before the Pegu province of Burma was taken by the English, Sandoway was the headquarters of the Bassein Sgau Karen mission, and thousands were baptized there. Mission station American Baptist Missionary Union (1885); 1 missionary and wife, 1 other lady, 25 native helpers, 11 out-stations, 11 churches, 238 church-members, 3 schools, 126 scholars.

**San Fernando,** a town in Trinidad, West Indies, on the west coast, south of Conra. Mission station of the Presbyterian Church in Canada; 1 missionary, 1 female missionary, 1 native pastor, 2 other helpers, 7 out-stations, 261 communicants, 16 schools, 877 scholars. United Presbyterian Church of Scotland (1850); 1 missionary, 60 church-members, 4 Sabbath-schools, 89 scholars.

**Sangi Islands,** a group of islands, composed of Great Sangi and several smaller islands, in the East Indian Archipelago, south of Mindanao, Philippine Islands, between latitude 3° and 5° north. The Gossner Missionary Society has stations on Great Sangi and Sijauw.

**Sangi Version.**—The Sangi or Sanguir belongs to the Malaysian languages, and is used in the island of Sangi. A translation of the New Testament was made by the Rev. F. Kelling of the Gossner Mission, and for more than twenty-five years a missionary on the island of Tagulandang. The translator was assisted by an intelligent native, and at the request of the Moravian Mission in Germany and London the British and Foreign Bible Society published in 1879 an edition of 4,000 copies of the Gospels of Luke and John in the Siamo dialect. In 1882 the same Bible Society published an edition of 2,000 copies of the New Testament, made by Mr. Kelling, and intended for a people numbering 80,000 souls, of whom 10,000 have been baptized. As the New Testament was well received and purchased by the natives, the British Bible Society published Mr. Kelling's translation of the Psalms in 1885, and in 1888 an edition of 2,000 copies of his version of the Book of Proverbs, edited by his son, Paul Kelling.

**Sangli,** a town in South Bombay, India, 30 miles east of Kolhapur. Mission station of the Presbyterian Church (North), 1884; 3 missionaries and their wives, 3 native helpers.

**San Luis Potosi,** a city in Central Mexico. Climate semi-tropical; elevation, 6,000 feet. Population, 60,000, Mexicans, Indians, Spaniards. Language, Spanish. Religion, Roman Catholic. Natives poor, ignorant, priest-ridden. Mission station Presbyterian Church (North), 1887; 1 missionary and wife, 8 native helpers, 7 out-stations, 4 churches, 130 church-members, 3 schools, 75 scholars. Methodist Episcopal Church (South); 1 missionary.

**San Salvador.**—1. One of the Bahamas Islands, West Indies (q.v.). Mission station of the S. P. G. (1884); 2 missionaries, 34 communicants.

2. Mission station of the Baptist Missionary Society, in the Lower Congo region, West Central Africa. This was the first station of the Society in Central Africa, and was opened in 1879; it has now 2 missionaries, 1 out-station, 33 church-members, 108 day-scholars, 118 Sabbath-scholars.

3. The capital of Salvador (q.v.), Central America, is an old city (founded 1528), which has often been destroyed by earthquakes and volcanic eruptions. It has 16,327 inhabitants.

**Sanskrit Version.**—The Sanskrit belongs to the Indic branch of the Aryan family of languages, and is the learned language of the Brahmins. The late Dr. Carey utilized this language in the production of a New Testament in the Sanskrit, which was published at Serampore in 1809. The entire Bible was completed at press in 1818. A second edition of the New Testament was published in 1820. A new and more improved translation of the Bible made by Drs. Carey and Yates, and completed by Dr. Wenge, was issued in 1873.

Besides translations into the Sanskrit proper, there were published in (a) *Sanskrit-Bengalee*, i.e., in Bengalee characters, Genesis (1855–60), Proverbs (1855), Luke's Gospel (1855), and the Psalms (1857); (b) *Sanskrit-Devanagari*, i.e., in Sanskrit popularized, the Psalms (1876), Proverbs and the New Testament (1877); (c) *Sanskrit-Uriya*, i.e., in Uriya or Orissa characters, Genesis, Proverbs, and Luke (1855), and the Psalms (1858).

(*Specimen verses.* John 3 : 16.)

ईश्वर इत्थं जगद्दयत यत् स्वमद्वितीयं तनयं प्रादद्यात् यतो यः कश्चित् तस्मिन् विश्वसिष्यति सोऽविनाश्यः सन् अनन्तायुः प्राप्स्यति ।

(*Sanskrit-Uriya.*)

ଇଶ୍ୱର ଜଗତକୁ ଏପରି ପ୍ରେମ କଲେ ଯେ ଆପଣା ଅଦ୍ୱିତୀୟ ପୁତ୍ର ଦାନ କଲେ ଯେ କେହି ତାଙ୍କଠାରେ ବିଶ୍ୱାସ କରେ ସେ ନଷ୍ଟ ନ ହୋଇ ଅନନ୍ତ ଜୀବନ ପାଏ ।

**San Sebastian,** a city on the Bay of Biscay, Spain, 210 miles north-northeast of Madrid, is the headquarters of the Spanish Mission of the A. B. C. F. M. (q.v.) Population, 10,000, chiefly Spanish Basques. The work is educational and evangelistic, though churches are being organized in various out-stations. At San Sebastian a girls' boarding-school is a means of much good. The chief strength of Protestantism is found in the many groups of Christians who are found scattered throughout the country, where in small communities their life is more noticed, and makes a stronger protest against the surrounding Papacy. The present (1890) force in San Sebastian is: 1 missionary and wife, 1 female missionary, 1 church, 51 communicants, 41 boarding pupils, 100 pupils. Churches have been organized at each of the 17 out-stations, and there are in all 298 communicants and 504 scholars.

**Santa Barbara,** a town in Southeast Brazil, in the province and near the city of São Paulo. Mission station of the Methodist Episcopal Church (South), which works chiefly among American emigrants—not, however, to the exclusion of native Brazilians.

**Santa Cruz Islands,** a group of Melanesia, lying southeast of the Solomon Islands and north of the New Hebrides, between longitude 165° and 170° east, and latitude 8° and 12° south. Santa Cruz is the largest island. Mission work is carried on by the Melanesian Mission (q.v.).

**Santa Isabel,** mission station of the Primitive Methodists in West Africa, on the island of Fernando Po (q.v.).

**Santalia,** a name sometimes applied to that portion of Bengal, India, which is inhabited by an aboriginal tribe, the Santals, who speak a distinct language, called Santali. (See Santals under article Bengal.) The Free Church of Scotland has a Santal Mission (1871), with stations at Toondi, Pachamba, and Chakai. The C. M. S. mission to Santalia, commenced in 1860, includes the districts of Taljhari, Barharwa, Hirampur, Bhagaya, and Godda. There is also a Santal district church-council in connection with this mission, which has eight pastorates. (See also Bethel Santal Mission.)

**Santali Version.**—The Santali, which belongs to the Kolarian group of the non-Aryan languages, is spoken by the aborigines of Northwest Bengal. A translation of the Gospel of Matthew and of the Psalms was made by the Rev. E. L. Puxley of the Church Missionary Society. The former was published by the Calcutta Auxiliary Bible Society in 1868 (revised edition 1876), the latter in 1875. The character used was the Roman. In 1876 and 1877 the Gospels of Mark, Luke, and John were published, while the Acts were added in 1879. During the year 1880 a Translation and Revision Committee, consisting of three members of the Church Missionary Society, was formed; and in 1881 a revised edition of 1,000 copies of Matthew's Gospel was published by the Calcutta Auxiliary, with the sanction of the British and Foreign Bible Society. The Revision Committee, unable to determine which of the rival terms for *God* and *Holy Ghost* should be exclusively used, printed half the edition with the terms *Cando* and *Sonat*, and half with *Isor* and *Dharm Atma*, and a note is added to each part explanatory of the terms. A translation of the New Testament, made by the Rev. Skrefsrud, and offered to the British and Foreign Bible Society in 1881, seems not to have been accepted. In 1884 a representative committee was formed to carry out the translation of the New Testament. To meet the demand for the

book until the version now being prepared by the Rev. E. T. Cole and the Santal Revision Committee is ready, the Calcutta Auxiliary published in 1888 for the first time a complete edition of the New Testament, made up of the portion of the New Testament completed by the Revision Committee and Mr. Cole's translation of the rest unrevised by the Committee. The edition consisted of 1,000 copies, and is printed in Roman type. In 1886 the Calcutta Auxiliary published also an edition of 1,000 copies of the Gospel of Luke in Bengali characters, for the benefit of those who know the Santali languages, and only the Bengali character. The transliteration was made by Mr. Cole, one of the Revision Committee, who also edited the same. The demand for the portion was such that a second edition of 5,000 copies had to be published in 1887.

*(Specimen verse.* Matt. 5 : 16.)

Nonká báṛe ápe hoṇ horko samángre marsál gṇel ochoitápe jemon unko hoṇ ápeá· bugi kámi gṇelkáte áperen sermáren jaːnámi: ko sarhaue.

**Santander,** a town in Spain, 95 miles west of San Sebastian (q.v.). Together with Bilbao, Pamplona, Roa, Logrono, Pradejon, etc., it is an out-station of the A. B. C. F. M. mission to Spain. The work is carried on mainly by means of schools, which are attended with great eagerness on the part of the children. Church services have been greatly hindered by the difficulty of securing rooms; the parlors of the Christians were often the only available meeting-places.

**Santiago,** the capital and principal city of Chili, South America, has a beautiful location on a plain 1,830 feet above the sea, between the Andes and a lesser range, distant 115 miles by rail from Valparaiso. The streets are laid out with great regularity, but owing to the frequency of earthquakes the houses are usually of one story. The water-supply is brought in an aqueduct five miles long. The rainfall is not great, and is usually in the summer months. Snow and hail are rarely seen. As many as thirty earthquake shocks have occurred in one year. Population (1885), 200,000. Mission station of the Presbyterian Church (North); 3 missionaries and wives, 6 out-stations, 161 boys attending the *Institutio Internacional,* of whom 50 are boarders.

**Santo Domingo.**—1. A republic which occupies the eastern portion of the island of Haiti, West Indies (q.v.).—2. The capital of the above republic, situated at the mouth of the Ozama River; was founded in 1494, and has 25,000 inhabitants, according to the official statement. Mission station of the African Methodist Episcopal Church, which has the only Protestant church in the city, with a membership of 86 under the care of 1 missionary.

**Santo Espiritu,** the most northerly of the New Hebrides Islands (q.v.), is now (1890) a station of the Canada Presbyterian Church. A missionary and his wife have recently occupied this heretofore neglected island, and the reports from this most difficult field state that the work is encouraging and hopeful, and the mission is already a centre for much good.

**San-ui,** a city, the capital of the district of the same name, in Kwangtung, China, about 40 miles south of Canton and west of Hong Kong. From this and the adjoining districts of Sinning and Hokshan go forth the immigrants to other countries. Many of these returning have been of good service in mission work, and a chapel has been built not far from San-ui City, by contributions from Chinese Christians in America. Mission station of the Wesleyan Methodist Missionary Society; 1 missionary, 1 chapel, 63 church-members. Members of the mission of the Presbyterian Church (North) make tours throughout this whole region, and recently a member of the Canton Mission has been stationed at Macao, from which place he superintends the work in San-ui, where there is a church with 26 communicants.

**São Paulo** (San Paulo), the capital city of a province of the same name in Brazil, is quite an important city, and has developed very much within recent years. It is the centre of the railway system of the province, and is distant only 86 miles from Santos and 220 miles southwest from Rio de Janeiro. Though the streets are narrow, they are well paved, and are lighted with gas. Sewers and water-mains have been constructed. Population (1883), 40,000. Mission station of the Methodist Episcopal Church (South); 2 missionaries. Presbyterian Church (North); 1 missionary, 1 physician, 1 female missionary. South American Missionary Society; 1 missionary. Work is carried on at Santos from this point.

**Sarawak,** a town on the island of Borneo, East Indies, consisting of a native and European town, the former built on each side of two branches of a river; many of the houses are built on piles, and are very respectable in appearance. Trade with Singapore is considerable. Population, 18,000. Mission station of the S. P. G. (1851); 1 missionary.

**Sarawak,** district on northwest coast of Borneo, governed by Rajah Brooke, under the protection of the British; has an area of 35,000 square miles, with a population of about 30,000.

**Sarepta,** a town in Cape Colony, South Africa, near the west coast, south of Durban, northeast of Cape Town. Mission station of the Rhenish Missionary Society; 1 missionary, 2 native workers, 72 school-children, 102 communicants.

**Sargeant, John,** b. Newark, N. J., U. S. A., 1710; graduated at Yale College 1729; was tutor 1731-1734. He was contemporary with David Brainerd, and taught him the Algonquin language. The Commissioners for Indian Affairs having found that the Indians living at Skatekook and Unahktukook, on the Housatonic River, were disposed to receive a missionary, and having learned that Mr. Sargeant, a graduate of Yale, and then a tutor in the college, was willing to devote himself to labor among the Indians after his engagement as tutor had expired, selected him for that post. In October, 1734, he went to inspect the field, and preached his first sermon through an interpreter. Leaving a teacher, he returned to Yale, taking with him two natives, sons of the principal chiefs, to teach them English and to learn their vernacular. In July, 1735, he was settled as their missionary, and the next month ordained at Deerfield in presence of the governor and council and a large number of English and Indians. Among his first converts were the two sachems and their wives. These Indians, the wandering Mohicans, he collected from three localities at Stockbridge. A township six miles square was laid out for them and incorporated, a church and schoolhouse were erected, and a dwelling for the missionary, at the expense of the province.

Mr. Sargeant acquired the native language with facility, and so well that the people said he spoke it better than themselves. He translated into their language parts of the Old Testament, and all the New except the Book of Revelation. He introduced many of the arts of civilized life, interested them in singing, taught them Biblical history and doctrine, and brought into the mission school many Mohawk and Oneida children from the province of New York. Regarding the education of the youth as essential to his success, he had formed the plan of a manual-labor school, in which the pupils should contribute to their own support. Provision had been made for the education of several boys, land procured, a schoolhouse built, and some boys were collected; but the death of Mr. Sargeant prevented the consummation of the plan. He died July, 1749, aged 39, mourned by the Indians, who loved him as a father and friend. Their improvement through his labors had been great. He found them but 50 in number, living miserably and viciously in wigwams, widely scattered, and roving from place to place. He left them 218 in number, settled in a thriving town, with twenty families in frame houses, and many having farms cultivated, fenced, and well stocked. He had baptized 182, and 42 were communicants. At his death Mr. Woodward took charge of the mission, and was succeeded by Jonathan Edwards, afterwards President of Princeton College.

**Sargent, Edwin,** b. Paris, France, 1815; spent the early part of his life at Madras; went in 1835 to Palamcotta, Tinnevelly, as a missionary of the Church Missionary Society; in 1839 he went to England, and studied three years in the Church Missionary College at Islington; was ordained in 1842, and the same year returned to his work in Tinnevelly. The first eight years he was located at Suviseshapuram, having charge of a missionary district. In 1850 he was transferred to Palamcotta, and two years later appointed principal of the Preparandi Institution, which had a high character for proficiency while he was at the head of it. More than 500 young men were instructed by him, many of whom are now pastors of native Christian churches in the towns and villages, and many more are catechists and schoolmasters. In 1874 he was nominated a suffragan or coadjutor bishop to the Bishop of Madras, and on March 11th, 1877, consecrated in Calcutta by Bishop Johnson, assisted by the bishops of Madras, Bombay, and Colombo. He had charge of eight of the ten districts into which the Society's Tinnevelly Mission was divided. In these districts were 51,000 Christians, 66 native pastors, and many catechists and schoolmasters, all under his care. During the first fifty years of the bishop's missionary service, the number of villages containing Christians in the Church Missionary Society's portion of

Tinnevelly rose from 224 to 1,018, the Christians and catechumens from 8,693 to 56,287, and the native clergy from 1 to 68. In the earlier period native Christians did nothing for the support of the gospel among themselves; at the later period their contributions for church work amounted to over 33,000 rupees annually. The affairs of the church are now managed to a very large extent by the Christians themselves, and no native clergyman draws his stipend from the Foreign Missionary Society. The success of church work is due very largely, under God, to the practical wisdom, untiring zeal, and loving labor of Bishop Sargent.

In 1885 his jubilee was celebrated at Palamcotta. It was a day of great joy. A pundal or shed, capable of holding 2,000 persons, was erected adjacent to the bishop's house, adorned with numerous emblems of festivity. At the first service, which was held in the mission church, were upwards of 1,400, including sixty native clergymen, and hundreds more were outside. In the P.M. the pundal was crowded with representatives of all classes of the Christian community from all parts of the province. The native Christians presented to the bishop a beautifully bound English Bible with a suitable inscription. An address also was read reviewing the work of the preceding fifty years. Not the least gratifying part of this service was an address of a Brahmin in behalf of the leading members of the Hindu community in Tinnevelly district, in which they acknowledged his invariable courtesy and benevolence, his wise counsel, and his unwearied efforts for the public good, and assured him of the esteem in which he was held by all Hindus who had had the privilege of making his acquaintance.

During his long mission service Dr. Sargent made three visits to England—in 1854, 1872, and the last in 1888, when he went to attend the Lambeth Conference. He was too ill to be present at any of its meetings. He returned to Tinnevelly in October, 1888, very much enfeebled, and gradually grew weaker. He bore his long and painful illness with great patience, and died at Palamcotta October 10th, 1889, having been engaged fifty-four years in the mission service. The coffin, covered with flowers, was borne on the shoulders of the mission agents to the Tamil church.

Bishop Sargent had a marvellous knowledge of the vernacular. Mr. E. B. Thomas, of the Madras civil service, knew him well, and says: "I was struck with his untiring energy, kindly sympathy, and earnest love toward his native converts, who had constant and ready access to him at all times. I occasionally heard him preach in Tamil, when the church would be full, the open windows and doors being often thronged with heathen listeners."

The "Madras Mail" thus speaks of him: "He was blessed with a sanguine and cheerful temperament, and an all-embracing benevolence. There was an almost child-like simplicity in the faith that was within him, and which he eloquently preached from the heart to others, and allied with it was a habit of taking broad views of men and things. He loved his work for its own sake, and refused to be discouraged by any alleged slowness in its progress. He had a fine presence, a ready eloquence, a well-cultivated mind, and a retentive memory. He had also a keen sense of humor, and as a *raconteur* of good stories he was always a welcome guest at the houses of his countrymen."

**Saron.**—1. A small town near the west coast in Cape Colony, Africa, west of Tulbagh and north of Cape Town. Mission station of the Rhenish Missionary Society, with 1 missionary, 12 native helpers, 500 communicants, 345 scholars.

2. A station of the Hermannsburg Missionary Society in Basutoland, South Africa, having 583 members.

**Satara,** a town of Bombay, 56 miles south of Poona, near the confluence of the Kistna and the Yena, among the hills of the Deccan. The town is clean and the streets are broad, but there are few large or ornamental buildings; and though still a large place, it has greatly decreased in importance since occupation of the country by the British. Population, 28,601, Hindus, Moslems, Jains, Parsis, etc. Mission station A. B. C. F. M.; 1 female missionary, 25 native helpers, 7 out-stations.

**Savaii,** an island of the Samoan group, Polynesia, northwest of Tutuila and west of Upolu. Mission station of L. M. S. (1836); 2 ordained missionaries, 41 female missionaries, 67 native preachers, 2 stations, 1,889 church-members, 104 schools, 2,840 scholars.

**Savas,** an island of the East Indies, southwest of Timor Island, southeast of Java; has 15,000 inhabitants, more than half of whom are nominally Christians. They are visited twice a year by the Dutch Government's assistant pastor residing at Kupang, Timor.

**Sawyerpuram,** a mission station of the S. P. G. (1844) in Madras, India, with 4 native pastors, 672 communicants, boys' boarding-school, 153 scholars.

**Schauffler, William Gottlieb,** born in Stuttgart, Germany, August 22d, 1798. In 1804 his father led a colony of Germans to improve their condition, to Odessa, in Russia. There being no schools for Germans, the educational advantages for the son were scanty. His father's clerk taught him the first principles of arithmetic, the reading and writing of German, Scripture selections, and Luther's catechism, while he himself read history, travels, novels, copied pictures and poetry, played the flute, mastering also the French, Italian, and Russian. He also began the study of Latin and English. At the age of fourteen he worked at his father's trade, the turning-lathe. Dancing, billiards, and the theatre were his favorite amusements, but his chief passion was music, especially the flute. At the age of twenty-two he confessed his faith in Christ. He early became interested in foreign missions; and in 1826, meeting the famous missionary Dr. Joseph Wolff, his enthusiasm was further kindled. Finding, however, the plans of Dr. Wolff impracticable, he went to Constantinople and thence to Smyrna, where he met Rev. Jonas King, who induced him to go to America for an education. He entered the Andover Theological Seminary, where he remained five years, studying often fourteen and sixteen hours a day. He says: "Aside from the study of Greek and Hebrew, and general classical reading, I studied the Chaldee, Syriac, Arabic, Samaritan, Rabbinic, Hebrew-German,

Persian, Turkish, and Spanish; and, in order to be somewhat prepared for going to Africa, I extracted and wrote out pretty fully the Ethiopic and Coptic grammars. For some years I read the Syriac New Testament and Psalms for my edification, instead of the German or the English text." He also aided the professors in their translations. He was ordained November 14th, 1831, a missionary of the A. B. C. F. M. to the Jews; studied Arabic and Persian with De Sacy, and Turkish with Prof. Kieffer in Paris, and then went to Constantinople. There he preached in German, Spanish, Turkish, and English. In 1838 he visited Odessa, chiefly on Mrs. Schauffler's account, and was much engaged in evangelistic work, resulting in many conversions. He translated the Bible into Hebrew-Spanish, that is, Spanish with a mixture of Hebrew words and written with Hebrew characters, for the Jews in Constantinople, descendants of those who had been driven from Spain. Dr. Schauffler, besides being a translator, was an earnest evangelical preacher, his Sunday services in English and German for local residents being greatly blessed. He delivered in Constantinople a series of discourses, which were published in a volume by the American Tract Society, entitled "Meditations on the Last Days of Christ." In 1835 the first Jewish convert, a German whom he had known sixteen years before in Russia, not being allowed by the government to profess Christianity except as a member of the Greek Church, went to Constantinople, and was by him baptized. In 1839 he went to Vienna to superintend the printing of the Hebrew-Spanish Old Testament. There he resided three years, and many striking conversions occurred through his labors. He presented to the emperor in a private interview his printed Bible, on which he had bestowed great labor. The Jews having pronounced a favorable verdict upon it, a second and larger edition was printed. Journeying from Vienna he spent ten days in Pesth, where many of the better class of Jewish families embraced the Christian faith. The Jewish Mission having been relinquished in 1855, he was requested by the Scotch Free Church, to which it had been transferred, to take charge of the work, but he declined. He declined also the proposal to enter the American field. About this time he was appointed by the mission to lay before the Evangelical Alliance, soon to meet at Paris, the "great question of religious liberty in Turkey, including the Mohammedans," and to "urge the Alliance to memorialize the sovereigns of Europe to use their influence with the Sultan to secure the abolition of the death-penalty for Moslem converts to Christianity." The result was seen in the triumph of Sir Stratford Canning. The morning he left Paris the news of Sebastopol's fall was proclaimed on the streets, and in Stuttgart, his native city, he addressed an immense audience on the Crimean war. After this war the way seemed open for missionary work among the Turks, and Dr. Schauffler, with the approval of the mission, decided to enter the Islam field. To fit himself for this new work, he applied himself to the Turkish language anew. In 1857 a paper on the Turkish and Bulgarian work, prepared by Drs. Schauffler and Hamlin, was sent to the Prudential Committee, and Dr. Schauffler was deputed by the mission to present, in America and England, the claims of the new mission to the Turks.

After thirty-one years of absence he set sail for home. His appeals met with a generous response. The Prudential Committee, however, decided, after some years, not to continue the Turkish Mission as a separate work, but to have the Armenian Mission cover the whole field. This decision, and the entrance of the English Propagation Society into Turkey, led Dr. Schauffler to resign as a missionary of the Board, but he pursued his Bible translation in the employ of the American and British and Foreign Bible Societies. His great work was the translation of the whole Bible into Osmanli-Turkish, the language of the educated Turks. This occupied him eighteen years. He published an ancient Spanish version of the Old Testament, revised by himself, with the Hebrew original in parallel columns, a popular translation of the Psalms into Spanish, a grammar of the Hebrew language in Spanish, a Hebrew-Spanish Lexicon of the Bible. He contributed also articles in Spanish to a missionary periodical in Salonica. He was a remarkable linguist, able to speak ten languages, and read as many more. His rare scholarship, and especially his translation of the Bible into Osmanli-Turkish led the Universities of Halle and Wittenberg to confer upon him the degrees of D.D. and Ph.D., and Princeton College the degree of Doctor of Laws. For his great services to the German colony of Constantinople the King of Prussia sent him a valuable decoration. He left Constantinople in 1874, and after residing three years with his son Henry, a missionary of the A. B. C. F. M. in Moravia, he went to New York with his wife to live with the two youngest sons. After a brief and painless illness, he passed away, January 26th, 1883, aged 85, having been in active missionary service nearly fifty years.

Dr. Schauffler was a man of rare qualities, not only as a missionary and translator, but as a friend. His love of music, in which he was a great proficient, his wonderful memory, and kindly interest in persons made his home a delightful one to visit; and his rich imagination gave a marked vividness to the Bible scenes which, both in his sermons and private conversations, he was very fond of illustrating. It was his habit, as it was that of his friend and associate Dr. Elias Riggs, at morning worship at home to read from the original Hebrew and Greek, and the quaint comments that always attended the reading often brought out the meaning with a force that no one who ever heard them could forget.

**Sheitswa Version.**—The Sheitswa belongs to the languages of Africa, and is spoken by the natives in Gasaland and vicinity, to the number of 200,000 or 300,000 (estimated). Among these people the Rev. B. F. Ousley of the A. B. C. F. M. has labored for many years, and his translation of Matthew, Mark, Luke, and Acts has recently (January, 1890) been accepted by the American Bible Society for publication. The translator is in the United States, and will superintend the printing of his work.

**Schemachi** (Shamaka), a large and important city of Eastern Transcaucasia. Population about 25,000, of whom a large number are Armenians. As a result of the work of the Basle Missionary Society (q.v.), a congregation of evangelical Armenians was started here, which did not lose its power after the missionaries were obliged to leave. Its leader, Pastor Serkis, received some education at Basle Seminary, and by his rare skill and earnest piety succeeded in keeping his little band together. Notwithstanding the oppressive laws of Russia, they grew in numbers and in strength, until they became one of the most influential communities in that section of the Caucasus. From Schemachi the work spread to Shusha, Nucha, and Baku, in each of which places congregations were formed. Schemachi suffered severely from an earthquake, 1872 (*circa*), and many of the Protestants removed to Baku on the Caspian, where there is now a flourishing church. Foreign pastors are not allowed, but young men of the community have at different times been selected and sent to Basle for education, and then have returned to their homes to do good work.

**Schiali,** a town in the Tanjore district, Madras, India, between the Coleroon River and the coast, northwest of Nangoor and Manikramam. Mission station of the Evangelical Lutheran Society of Leipsic; 1 missionary, 473 communicants, 336 scholars.

**Schietfontein,** a town in Central Cape Colony, Africa, northwest of Victoria. Mission station of the Rhenish Missionary Society; 2 missionaries (1 married), 1 female missionary, 110 scholars, 440 communicants.

**Schiffelin,** a town in Liberia, West Africa, not far from Monrovia. Mission station of the Presbyterian Church (North); 1 female missionary, 35 church-members, 56 school-children.

**Schmelen, John Henry,** missionary of L. M. S. to South Africa 1811-1848. Stationed at Namaqua Mission, Stienkoff, and Pella. While there he was sent to explore the mouth of the Orange River and the Great Namaqua and Damara countries, which occupied three months. In 1814 he was invited by the Namaquas to Bethany, in Great Namaqualand, where he began a new station. In 1824 he visited Cape Town to arrange for the printing of his Namaqua version of the Gospels. In 1825 he spent several months exploring the sea-coast near Koeisy. In 1829 he formed a new station at Komaggas. In 1830 he again visited Cape Town, and having finished the printing of the Namaqua Gospels, he returned in 1831 to his new station. He died at Komaggas July 26th, 1848, aged 71.

**Schmidt, George,** a missionary of the Moravian Brethren to South Africa. See account of South African Mission in article on Moravian Missions.

**Schneider, Benjamin,** b. New Hanover, Penn., U. S. A., January 18th, 1807; graduated at Amherst College 1830; Andover Theological Seminary 1833; ordained October 2d; sailed for Turkey as a missionary of the A. B. C. F. M. December 12th, 1833, though supported by Reformed (German) Churches. He was stationed first at Broosa, where he preached the first evangelical sermon ever preached in the Turkish language. In 1849 he removed to Aintab, where he laid the foundation of two flourishing churches. After the death of his wife in 1856 he visited the United States; returned to Turkey with his second wife in 1858, and was again stationed in Broosa. His health failing, he

made a second visit home in 1872. A call for help in Turkish and Greek work in the theological seminary at Marsovan induced him, though advanced in years and in feeble health, to return, reaching Marsovan March, 1874. But from nervous prostration he was compelled to relinquish the work, and in 1875 he left first for Switzerland, thence for his native land. He died in Boston September 14th, 1877.

Dr. Crane, who was his associate at Aintab from 1850 to 1853, says: "For more than forty years he was connected with the work, laboring in almost every department of missionary service—preaching, translating, preparing young men for the ministry. Few have travelled more extensively as pioneers; few have labored in more places in Turkey; few have more cheerfully endured the privations of the service; few are the native churches in Turkey where his name is not known and revered. Even amid the intense sufferings of the last two years of his life his eye would brighten and glow with delight at the bare mention of the missionary life." He acquired languages with great facility. He spoke German, Greek, and Turkish, "almost as if each were his vernacular, the latter with an ease and fluency seldom equalled by foreigners. Even natives wondered at his marvellous flow of thought in idiomatic phrases, easily understood by all; for he chose simplicity of style, though at home in the higher and more complicated forms of expression. His preaching was almost exclusively extemporaneous, from brief notes, but rarely was he confused in thought, or at a loss for an expression in either language. Words flowed from his lips in those difficult Oriental tongues with a freedom that was the admiration of fellow-missionaries and the delight of native listeners." Mr. Tracy, with whom Dr. Schneider was associated in the theological seminary at Marsovan, says: "He entered at once into the affections of the students and of all the people. No one else so satisfied them as a preacher. His Turkish was almost perfect—simple in style, pure in idiom, and his accent such that no Turk would imagine that the language was not vernacular. In the school his labors were very useful. There seemed to be nothing but good in his example or his talk. He was as child-like as he was wise."

He received the degree of D.D. from Franklin and Marshall College, Lancaster, Penn., 1850.

**Scottish Episcopal Church. Foreign Mission Agency.** Secretary, Rev. C. R. Teape, Findhorn Place, Grange, Edinburgh, Scotland.—Formerly the Scottish Episcopal Church of Scotland collected funds for the Church of England Missionary Societies, but upon the consecration of Bishop Cotterill as Bishop of Edinburgh the contributions of the churches in the seven Scottish dioceses were devoted to missions in India and South Africa through their own Society,—"The Board of Foreign Missions of the Scottish Episcopal Church," the new form of their "Association for Foreign Missions." Bishop Cotterill having labored as a missionary of the C. M. S. in India for twelve years, and for another twelve in South Africa,—Kaffraria,—where he had been consecrated bishop, felt a peculiar interest in those two fields of his former efforts, and organized a permanent union with them. In addition to providing the income of the Bishop of Independent Kaffraria, the Board sends out contributions every year to Kaffraria for the general purposes of the diocese, and also many sums to be devoted to special objects in connection with the various churches and schools there. The Board also provides the funds necessary for the maintenance of the missionary schools at Chanda, in Central India, which are under the direction of the Bishop of Calcutta, and forwards sums entrusted to it for any mission work being carried on by the Church of England, or any church in communion with her.

**Scudder, John,** b. Freehold, N. J., U. S. A., September 13th, 1798; graduated at the College of New Jersey in 1811, and at the College of Physicians and Surgeons of New York City in 1815. While in professional attendance on a lady in New York he took up in the anteroom and read the tract "The Conversion of the World, or Claims of Six Hundred Millions." Deeply impressed, he was led to give his life to the missionary work. He sailed June 8th, 1819, under the A. B. C. F. M., for Ceylon. He was ordained in 1821 by the brethren of the mission, Baptist and Wesleyan missionaries taking part in the service. In 1836 he was transferred to Madras to found a new mission with Dr. Winslow. From 1842 to 1846 he was in the United States. In 1854, his health having failed, he went by medical advice to the Cape of Good Hope. When on the point of returning to Madras he was stricken with apoplexy, and died at Wynberg, South Africa, January 13th, 1855, having been in the missionary work 36 years. He was constant in labors, devoting much time to evangelistic itinerary. In his visit to America in 1843 he addressed a hundred thousand children. Mrs. Scudder died three years previous—a devoted woman, honored and beloved by all. Their eight sons, two grandsons, and two granddaughters have been members of the mission in Arcot.

**Schwartz, Christian Friedrich,** was born in Sonnenburg, Prussia, October 26th, 1726. His mother, dying in his childhood, consecrated him to the Lord. He says that at the age of eight he often, leaving his schoolmates, retired to a solitary place for prayer, and that in prayer to God he found much comfort. At the age of twenty he went to the Halle University, where he became established in the faith of Christ, and resolved to devote himself wholly to Him. Dr. Schultz, who had left India from failure of health, was at this time preparing to print the Bible in Tamil, and advised Schwartz to learn that language in order to assist him. Professor Francke hearing of his great success in acquiring the language, proposed to him to go as a missionary to India. He decided to go, declining an advantageous position in the ministry at home. He was ordained at Copenhagen, with the view of joining the Danish Mission at Tranquebar, where he arrived July 30th, 1750. In four months he preached his first sermon in Tamil in the church of Ziegenbalg. From the first he devoted much time and attention to the religious instruction of the young. In the following year 400 persons, adults and youth, whom he had carefully instructed, were added to the church by baptism. In 1760 he spent three months in Ceylon preaching to heathen and Christians. While

war was at this time raging between England and France, he continued his work around Tranquebar, and so much did the heathen respect him that, of their own accord, they contributed to his support. Two years later he went on foot to Tanjore, and obtained leave to preach in the city and even in the palace. After laboring fifteen years at Tranquebar he was sent to Trichinopoly. So great was his success here that, with the aid of the commandant and the English garrison, a church accommodating two thousand was opened in 1766. During this year the mission was adopted by the "Christian Knowledge Society," and this became his special field of labor. Here, in a room in an old Hindu building just large enough for himself and his bed, having for his "daily fare a dish of boiled rice with a few other vegetables," and "clad in a piece of dark cotton cloth woven and cut after the fashion of the country," he gave himself to his work. To assist him in his extensive labors he employed in 1772 eight of the promising converts as catechists, among whom was Sattianadden, who was afterwards ordained to the ministry, in which he labored with great eloquence and success.

In twelve years Schwartz had baptized 1,238 in the city. He labored also faithfully for the English garrison, for which no religious instruction was provided. The salary of £100 which he received as chaplain of the garrison from the Madras Government he devoted the first year to the building of a mission house and an English Tamil school, and afterwards gave a large part of it in charity.

In 1776 he went to Tanjore to found a new mission, and here he spent the remaining twenty years of his life. Even in this favorite abode of the Hindus, where was the most splendid pagoda of India, he had great success, two churches having been established in 1780. He won the high esteem of the English Government, which employed him in important political transactions with the native princes. When the powerful and haughty Hyder Ali of Mysore refused to receive an embassy from the English, whom he distrusted, he said he would treat with them through Schwartz. "Send me the Christian," meaning Schwartz; "he will not deceive me." Urged by the government, he consented to undertake the mission. Through his intercession Cuddalore was saved from destruction by the savage hordes of the enemy. On his return a present of money was forced upon him by Hyder, which he gave to the English Government, requesting that it be applied to the building of an English orphan asylum in Tanjore. Though a Mohammedan, Hyder's regard for Schwartz was so great that he issued orders to his officers, saying: "Let the venerable padre go about everywhere without hindrance, since he is a holy man, and will not injure me." While Hyder was ravaging the Carnatic with an army of a hundred thousand, and multitudes were fleeing in dismay to Tanjore, Schwartz moved about unmolested. In the famine caused by the war more than 800 starving people came daily to his door. He collected money and distributed provisions to Europeans and Hindus. He also built there a church for the Tamil congregation. The rajah a few hours before his death requested Schwartz to act as guardian to his adopted son Serfogee. The trust was accepted and faithfully discharged.

After a protracted and severe illness, during which he delighted to testify of Christ and to exhort the people, he expired in the arms of two of his native converts. At his funeral the effort to sing a hymn was suppressed by the noise of the wailing of the heathen who thronged the premises. Serfogee lingered, weeping, at the coffin, covered it with a cloth of gold, and accompanied the body to the grave. The small chapel in which he was interred outside of the fort has been demolished, and a large one erected. The grave is behind the pulpit, covered with a marble slab bearing an English inscription—

To the memory of the
REV. CHRISTIAN FRIEDRICH SCHWARTZ,
Born Sonnenburg, of Neumark, in the kingdom of
Prussia,
The 28th October, 1726,
And died at Tanjore the 13th February, 1798,
In the 72d year of his age.
Devoted from his early manhood to the office of
Missionary in the East,
The similarity of his situation to that of
The first preachers of the gospel
Produced in him a peculiar resemblance to
The simple sanctity of the
Apostolic character.
His natural vivacity won the affection
As his unspotted probity and purity of life
Alike commanded the reverence of the
Christian, Mohammedan, and Hindu,
For sovereign princes, Hindu and Mohammedan,
Selected this humble pastor
As the medium of political negotiation with
The British Government:
And the very marble that here records his virtues
Was raised by
The liberal affection and esteem of the
Rajah of Tanjore,
Maha Rajah Serfogee.

Another beautiful monument was erected to his memory by the East India Company in the Church of St. Mary, Madras, part of the inscription on which is as follows:

"On a spot of ground granted to him by the Rajah of Tanjore, two miles east of Tanjore, he built a house for his residence, and made it an Orphan Asylum. Here the last twenty years of his life were spent in the education and religious instruction of children, particularly those of indigent parents—whom he gratuitously maintained and instructed; and here, on the 13th of February, 1798, surrounded by his infant flock, and in the presence of several of his disconsolate brethren, he closed his truly Christian career in the 72d year of his age."

**Seamen, Missions to.**—Rev. John Flavel (England, 1627–91) and English contemporaries (Ryther, Janeway, et al.), as also a few clergymen of the English Established Church in the eighteenth century, preached occasional sermons, special and serial, some of which were printed, on behalf of seamen; but the second half of the eighteenth century witnessed the first organized efforts for their evangelization. An association, styled at first "The Bible Society," was organized in London in 1780, to supply English troops in Hyde Park with the Holy Scriptures, whose field of labor was speedily enlarged to embrace seamen in the British Navy. The first ship supplied with Bibles by this Society was "The Royal George," sunk off Spithead, England, August 29th, 1782. The Society's name was soon changed, becoming "The Naval and Military Bible Society." It is still in operation, confines itself to its original specific object—the diffusion of the Word of God, and has been of immense service to the army and navy of Great Britain. This Society had influence in originating the British and Foreign Bible Society, and the work of the latter led eventually to the formation of the American (U. S. A.) Bible Society. (Cf. art. "Bible Societies," Encyc. Brit., 9th ed., vol. iii. p. 649.)

The need for Christian work among seamen was urgent. Destitute, as a class, of any access to the Bible, to preaching, or to any Christian service, their lives passed, for the most part, without knowledge of the gospel of Christ. "It would be difficult," says a well-informed writer, "to conceive of a deeper moral night than that which, for centuries, had settled upon the sea."

THEIR BEGINNINGS AND HISTORY IN ENGLAND.—Early efforts in England, however, to furnish sailors with the gospel met with serious opposition from Christian people, as well as from unchristian officers in the Royal Navy. So late as 1828, the king was petitioned to abrogate an order, then recently issued by the Lord High Admiral, prohibiting the free circulation of tracts in the navy. But in 1814 the pioneers of the movement for this end—Rev. George Charles Smith, a dissenting clergyman, once a sailor, and Zebulon Rogers, a shoemaker, of the Methodist persuasion—established prayer-meetings for seamen on the Thames, at London, the first being held on the brig "Friendship," June 22d of that year, by Mr. Rogers. These were multiplied and sustained upon the shipping in the river. March 23d, 1817, the first Bethel Flag (a white dove on blue ground) was unfurled on the "Zephyr," Captain Hindulph, of South Shields, England.

The Port of London Society was organized March 18th, 1818, to provide for the continuous preaching of the gospel to seamen in London, upon a floating chapel (ship) of three hundred tons burden, and Rev. Mr. Smith ministered upon it with success during the next ensuing year. November 12th, 1819, the Bethel Union Society was formed, at London, which, in addition to the maintenance of religious meetings on the Thames, established correspondence with local Societies that had been organized through Mr. Smith's exertions in various parts of the kingdom. These two Societies were subsequently united to form what is now known as the British and Foreign Sailors' Society.

"The Sailors' Magazine" (London), merged, after publication for seven years by Rev. Mr. Smith, into "The New Sailors' Magazine," also issued by him, was established in 1820. "The Monthly Magazine," now issued by the British and Foreign Sailors' Society, is "Chart and Compass" (pp. 32), established in January, 1879.

In 1825 the London Mariners' Church and Rivermen's Bethel Union was organized, to provide a church for seamen on shore, Rev. Mr. Smith becoming its pastor. This church was for years the centre of an extensive system of Christian labor, including a Sabbath-school, Bethel prayer-meetings, tract and book distribution, magazine publishing, and open-air preaching to seamen on the wharves. Rev. Mr. Smith died at Penzance, Cornwall, England, in January, 1863.

Existing seamen's missionary societies in the empire of Great Britain, distinct from local organizations which limit the prosecution of work to their own ports, are: (1) The British and Foreign Sailors' Society (at Sailors' Institute, Shadwell, London, England), with receipts from April 1st, 1888, to April 18th, 1889, of £14,975

2s. 4d., and expenditures for the same period of £14,519 8s. 0d., which in its seventieth annual report (1887-8) names the ports of Rotterdam, Hamburg, Antwerp, Genoa, Naples and Malta, outside England; and London, Milford-Haven, Falmouth, and Barrow-in-Furness (English), as occupied more or less effectively by persons having entire or partial support from its treasury, and devoting themselves to the spiritual and temporal welfare of seamen. (2) The London Missions to Seamen (Established Church of England), whose operations are, for the most part, carried on afloat. Its chaplains are at fifty-two English and eight foreign seaports. Local English societies for seamen are at Liverpool (formed in 1821), Glasgow, and at other ports.

MISSIONS WITH HEADQUARTERS IN SCANDINAVIA.—Evangelical Lutheran missions to seamen are prosecuted by societies with headquarters in Scandinavian countries, whence come in our day the larger number of sailors for the world's mercantile marine. The Norwegian Society,—Foreningen til Evangeliets Forkyndelse for Skandinaviske Sömend i fremmede Havne (or, in English, The Society for the Gospel's preaching to Scandinavian Seamen in Foreign Harbors), was organized at Bergen, Norway, August 31st, 1864, and now (1890) has stations at Leith, Scotland; North Shields, London, and Cardiff, England; at Antwerp, Belgium; Havre, France; Amsterdam, Holland; New York City, U. S. A.; Quebec, Canada; at Pensacola, Fla., U. S. A.; and at Buenos Ayres, S. A. Mission work is also carried on by this Society at Montrose, Scotland. Its aggregate foreign working force consists of twelve ordained pastors with five or six assistant missionaries, unordained. The Society owns churches at its stations and publishes a monthly paper, "Bud og Hilsen," now in its twenty-fourth year of issue. Its receipts from 1864 to 1889 were 991,566 Kröner;* expenditures for the same period 963,606 Kröner.

*The Danish Seamen's Mission Society* (Danske Forening til Evangeliets Forkyndelse for Skandinavieke Söfolk i fremmede Havne (or, in English, The Danish Society for the Gospel's Preaching to Scandinavian Seamen in Foreign Ports) has stations at Hull and Grimsby, London, Newcastle and Hartlepool, Eng., and at New York City, U. S. A., with an aggregate of four ordained pastors. Three other ordained pastors perform some labor for sailors at Frederickstadt and Christianstadt, St. Croix, W. I., and at St. Thomas and St. Jan. At Brisbane, Australia, an ordained pastor gives a portion of his time to the interests of Scandinavian sailors in connection with this organization. Its bi-monthly paper is "Havnen," published at Copenhagen, Denmark. In the autumn of 1889 a seamen's pastor was sent from Denmark, by private contribution, to labor at Sydney, Australia. Some Christian labor is also now (1890) performed among Danish seamen, by ordained Danish pastors, at Portland, Me., and at Boston, Mass., U. S. A.

*The Swedish Society for Home and Foreign Missions* (Fosterlands-stiftelsen) has sustained missionary work for seamen since 1869, and has the following stations where such labor is per-

formed by its agents: Constantinople, Turkey; Alexandria, Egypt; Liverpool, Grimsby, and Gloucester, England; Boston, Mass., U. S. A.; Marseilles, France; Hamburg and Lübeck, Germany; and St. Ubes, Portugal,—with six ordained pastors.

The state church in Sweden has four ordained pastors laboring for seamen at London and West Hartlepool, Eng.; at Kiel, Russia; and at Calais, France.

*The Finland Seamen's Mission Society* (Föreningen for Beredande of Sjaleward at Finska Sjöman i Utlandska Hamnar), organized in 1880, has stations at London, Grimsby, and Hull, Eng., and at New York City, and San Francisco, Cal., U. S. A.

*The Swedish Evangelical Lutheran Augustana Synod in America* has a station for Scandinavian seaman, with one ordained pastor, at Philadelphia, Pa., U. S. A.

*The Synod for the Norwegian Evangelical Lutheran Church in America* has a Seamen's Mission in Australia, with one ordained pastor.

The total of stations occupied by the Scandinavian (Lutheran) Societies is thirty-eight, with thirty-four ordained pastors and seven unordained pastors as laborers.

AMERICAN MISSIONS FOR SEAMEN.—No organizations exist in North or South America, outside the United States, for the sole purpose of prosecuting religious labor among seamen, with the exception of the local Society at Halifax, N. S., established in 1887. At Boston, Mass., the first Society for this object was formed in May, 1812, but soon suspended operations. The first religious meeting on behalf of sailors in New York City (N. Y.) is believed to have been held in the summer of 1816, at the corner of Front Street and Old Slip. The Marine Bible Society of New York City was organized March 14th, 1817, to furnish sailors with the Holy Scriptures. The Society for Promoting the Gospel among Seamen in the Port of New York, commonly known as the New York Port Society, a local organization, was formed June 5th, 1818. This Society laid the foundations of the first mariner's church erected in the United States, in Roosevelt Street, near the East River, which was dedicated June 4th, 1820, Rev. Ward Stafford preacher and pastor. In 1823 the New York Port Society set at work in that city the first missionary to seamen, the Rev. Henry Chase. This Society sustains a church at Madison and Catherine Streets, in New York City, and a reading-room for sailors in the same edifice, with meetings during the week, and other evangelistic work, employing in the year ending May 1st, 1889, five missionaries. Receipts for 1888-9 were $9,073.71; expenditures, $9,129.98.

*The New York Bethel Union*, for the establishment and maintenance of religious meetings on vessels in the port, organized June 3d, 1821, had but a brief existence.

The movements noted—that at Boston, Mass., resulting in the formation of the earliest Society of its kind in the world—led to similar action for the performance of local work for seamen at Charleston, S. C. (1819); Philadelphia, Pa. (1819); Portland, Me., and New Orleans, La., (1823); at New Bedford, Mass. (1825), and elsewhere. In the latter year there were in the United States seventy Bethel Unions, thirty-three Marine Bible Societies, fifteen churches and floating chapels for seamen. There had

---

* A Kröner is about twenty-six cents, United States currency.

been many conversions to Christ among sailors, and their evangelization was recognized as among the most prominent and important of Christian enterprises.

Accordingly, after its formal establishment in the city of New York January 11th, 1826, succeeded by a new organization in its Board of Trustees May 5th, 1828,—from which time its birth is dated,—the American Seamen's Friend Society (76 Wall Street, New York) came into being. Its publications accredit Rev. John Truair as chiefly instrumental in bringing about its organization. Its first President was Hon. Smith Thompson, Secretary of the United States Navy; Rev. C. P. McIlvaine, afterwards Protestant Episcopal Bishop of Ohio, was its Corresponding Secretary; and Rev. Joshua Leavitt its General Agent. Article II. of its Constitution provides: "The object of this Society shall be to improve the social and moral condition of seamen by uniting the efforts of the wise and good in their behalf, by promoting in every port boarding-houses of good character, savings-banks, register-offices, libraries, museums, reading-rooms and schools, and also the ministration of the gospel and other religious blessings."

Its first foreign chaplain was Rev. David Abeel, who reached his field of labor at Whampoa, the anchorage for ships trading at Canton, China, February 16th, 1830. In its fortieth year (1867–68) its laborers, chaplains, and sailor-missionaries were stationed at twenty foreign and thirteen domestic sea-ports as follows: At Caribou Island on the Labrador coast, N. A.; at St. John, N. B.; in Norway, at Christiansand, Kragero, and Porsgrund; in Denmark, at Copenhagen and Odense; in Sweden, at Gottenberg, Warberg and Wedige, Wernersberg, and Stockholm; in Belgium, at Antwerp; in France, at Havre and Marseilles; in the Hawaiian Islands, at Honolulu and Hilo; at the Chincha Islands, in Peru; at Valparaiso and at Buenos Ayres, S. A.; and in the United States, at the following seaports: San Francisco, Cal.; Norfolk and Richmond, Va.; Charleston, S.C.; Mobile, Ala.; Boston and Gloucester, Mass.; and at New York, N. Y. Its missionary work was prosecuted in 1888–89 in the countries of Sweden, Norway, and Denmark; at Hamburg in Germany; at Rotterdam in Holland; at Antwerp in Belgium; at Genoa and Naples in Italy; at Yokohama in Japan; in the Madeira Islands; at Valparaiso, S. A.; at Bombay and Karachi, in India; and in the United States, at Portland and Astoria, Oregon; Tacoma, Seattle, and Port Townsend, W. T.; Galveston, Texas; Mobile, Ala.; Savannah, Ga.; Charleston, S. C.; Wilmington, N. C.; Norfolk, Va.; as well as in the cities of New York; Jersey City, N. J.; and Brooklyn, N. Y.; including the United States Navy Yard, numbering thirty-two laborers at twenty-nine seaports (fifteen foreign and fourteen domestic), supported in whole or in part by the Society.

Its receipts in the first decade of its existence were in round numbers, $91,000; in the second decade, $165,000; in the third, $229,000; in the fourth, $375,000; in the fifth, $655,000. Receipts for the year ending March 31st, 1889, with balance from previous year, $34,004.19; expenditures for same period, $34,972.05.

*The Church Missionary Society for Seamen in the City of New York*, (Protestant Episcopal) in its forty-sixth Annual Report (1889–90) states that the Society sustains three chapels and mission-houses, with reading and lecture rooms, oversight being in the hands of clergymen, with the assistance of a colporteur at one station. Its total services for the year were 585; visits to reading-rooms, 30,889; Seamen supplied with Bibles, 343; with Testaments, 533; with the Book of Common Prayer, 343. The Bishop of the Diocese is its president.

Beginning with the year 1888 the Boston, Mass., Seamen's Friend Society (organized in 1828),which had been an auxiliary of the American Seamen's Friend Society from 1865 to that date, has again prosecuted local Christian work for seamen, on an independent basis. Efficient local organizations for the evangelization and befriending of sailors have wrought to good purpose during recent years, at Baltimore, Md.; at Washington, D. C.; and at Cleveland, Ohio; the last Society concerning itself with river-boatmen and sailors on western lakes in the United States.

Methods.—Missionary Force, Sailors' Homes, Loan Libraries, Periodicals, Charitable Aid, Seamen's Savings-banks, Asylums, Rests, etc.

Besides the employment of chaplains resident at seaports, and serving as Christian ministers, of Bible and tract distributors, Scripture-readers, colporteurs and helpers, whose titles declare their functions, the Missionary Societies for Seamen have usually wrought for their welfare by establishing, and in part sustaining (temporarily), Sailors' Homes in various ports. In them are resident missionaries, who besides their services in religious meetings, devote portions of their time to spiritual and charitable visitations among sailors on shipboard and shore, at sailor boarding-houses and in hospitals, and in some cases to such service for the families of seamen. The Wells Street Sailors' Home, at London, Eng., Docks, was established by Mr. George Greene in 1830, was opened in 1835, and enlarged in 1865. In one year it admitted 5,444 boarders, who, besides a home, had evening instruction, the use of a savings-bank, etc. The Liverpool, Eng., Sailors' Homes were opened in 1844. The Sailors' Home at 190 Cherry Street, New York City, U. S. A., is the property and is under the direction of the American Seaman's Friend Society. It was opened in 1842, reconstructed, refurnished, and reopened in 1880, and is probably unsurpassed by any Sailors' Home in the world. During the year 1888–89 it accommodated 1,351 boarders. The whole number of its boarders since the Home was established is 112,677, and the amount saved by it to seamen and their relatives, during the forty-eight years since its establishment, has been reckoned at between $1,000,000 and $2,000,000.

The systematic supply of carefully selected libraries, to be loaned to vessels for use by their officers and crews at sea, is now largely counted on by these organizations, especially by the American Seamen's Friend Society. Its shipments of such libraries from 1858–59 to March 31st, 1889, were 9,221, and the reshipments of the same 10,074; the total shipments aggregating 19,295. The number of volumes was 482,800, accessible by original shipment to 350,304 seamen. Of the whole number sent out, 993 libraries, with 35,742 volumes, were placed upon United States naval vessels and in naval hospitals, and were accessible to 114,267 men; 117 libraries were in 117 stations of the United States Life-saving Service, containing 4,220 volumes, accessible to 819 keepers and surfmen.

The "Sailors' Magazine" (monthly, 32 pp.), organ of the American Seamen's Friend Society, is now the oldest of the periodicals issued on behalf of seamen. It was established in September, 1828, is in its sixty-second volume, and of its issues for 1888–89 56,400 copies were distributed. In the same twelve months 20,000 copies of "The Seamen's Friend" (annually, 4 pp.), established in 1858, were issued by the same Society for sailors, and 124,200 copies of the "Life Boat" (monthly, 4 and 8 pp.) for the use of Sabbath-schools.

Varied help is habitually extended to shipwrecked and destitute sailors by all these organizations. The establishment of savings-banks for seamen has ordinarily been due to their influence. The Seamen's Savings-bank in New York City (76 Wall Street) went into operation May 11th, 1829. Sailors' Asylums, Orphanages, and "Rests" (the last being houses of entertainment conducted upon temperance principles, with more or less of religious instruction and service) are open in many seaports, as the fruit of their existence. In January, 1888, the "Sailors' Magazine" (New York) published a list of fifty-seven sailors' "Rests" and "Homes" then accessible to seamen in various seaports throughout the United States, Great Britain, the European continent, Asia, Africa, South America, and on several islands. Miss Agnes Weston has distributed gratis, by voluntary contributions, many thousands of monthly "Blue Books" (8 pp., temperance and religious tracts) in the English tongue, in the British and American navies, which have been regularly translated into Dutch and German for the navies of Holland and Germany.

GENERAL SUMMARY OF RESULTS.—It is impracticable to present accurate detailed statistics as to the results of Christian labor for seamen. The best general estimate, however, fixes the number of Christianized sailors as not far from thirty thousand. But to say that during the last sixty years these men have been gathered into the Church of Christ by thousands, and that, as a class, English-speaking and Scandinavian sailors in the naval and largely in the mercantile (sailing) marine of England and America are manifestly being lifted, in our day, from the ignorance and degradation in which they lived at the opening of the nineteenth century, and to attribute these changes in great degree to the exertions of these Societies, is to speak with truthful moderation. The corporate and individual efforts of those connected with them have often originated and made effective beneficent public legislation for sailors, in Great Britain and in the United States.

It is in place to state that, with some exceptions, Seamen's Missionary Societies are administered upon a non-denominational basis, and that, so far as known, all are of the Protestant faith.

**Secunderabad,** a city in the Hyderabad state, Nizam's Dominions, India, 6 miles north of Hyderabad City, 358 miles northwest of Madras. The largest military station in India. Climate during rainy season very unhealthy;

at other times hot, but not insalubrious. Population, 74,124. Mission station of the American Baptist Missionary Union; 2 missionaries and wives, 11 native helpers, 3 out-stations, 1 church, 2 schools, 42 scholars. Methodist Episcopal Church (North); 1 missionary, 28 church-members, 1 Sunday-school, 50 scholars. S. P. G. (1840); 1 missionary, 14 native helpers, 853 members. Wesleyan Methodist Missionary Society; 1 missionary, 3 native helpers, 36 church-members, 1 Sunday-school, 30 scholars, 6 day-schools, 331 scholars.

**Secundra,** a town in Rajputana, India, near Agra and Aligarh. Mission station of the C. M. S.; 1 missionary, 147 communicants, 540 scholars. Large orphanages for girls and boys are located here, and the ladies of the Berlin Ladies' Missionary Society assist in the work of the village and zenana schools.

**Seir,** a suburb of the city of Oroomiah, Persia, long occupied by the missionaries of the A. B. C. F. M. and the Presbyterian Church (North) among the Nestorians as a health resort, Oroomiah itself being, especially in summer time, very malarious and unhealthy. It is here that the theological seminary was located for many years. Its distance from the city rendered residence there somewhat difficult, and since the establishment of the college on an advantageous site nearer the city, Seir has not been so continuously occupied.

**Selwyn, George Augustus,** b. Hampstead, England, 1809; studied at Eaton; graduated at Cambridge University 1831; ordained Deacon 1833, and took the curacy of Boveney; ordained Priest 1834, and became curate of Windsor 1839; was consecrated Bishop of New Zealand 1841; received the degree of D. D. the same year from both Cambridge and Oxford; sailed for his see December 26th, 1841. On the voyage he spent much of the time in compiling from the Rarotonga, Tahiti, and New Zealand translations of the New Testament a comparative grammar of these three dialects, and also studied navigation under the captain, in order to be his own master in his visitation voyages. He reached Auckland May 30th, 1842. Besides attending to the spiritual wants of his colonial diocese, he extended his operations to the South Seas, navigating his own vessel, the "Southern Cross." In 1843 he established a Polynesian college for the different branches of the Maori family, scattered over the Pacific. Connected with it was an industrial department, in which all were required to spend a definite portion of time in some occupation. In 1844 a site for the college was selected near Auckland. Three natives from the college were ordained as deacons. In 1854 he visited England, after twelve years' absence. In that period he had made seven voyages through the southern part of Melanesia, and visited 50 islands. From ten of these fifty youths had been received into the college. While at home he preached four remarkable discourses, which did much to increase the interest in foreign missions. In one of his sermons he said to the students: "Offer yourselves to the Archbishop of Canterbury as 1,200 young men have recently offered themselves to the Commander-in-chief for service in the Crimean war." When he preached his farewell sermon in 1841, John C. Patteson, a youth of fourteen, was present, and was much impressed. When the Bishop re-embarked in 1855, Patteson accompanied him as a missionary, and to him was committed the charge of the college. In 1857 his diocese was divided, and Mr. Patteson was consecrated Bishop of Melanesia. In 1867 Bishop Selwyn again visited England to attend the Lambeth Conference. His talents, character, and services placed him at the head of the colonial bishops, and his views and counsel were highly esteemed. While at home he was offered the bishopric of Lichfield, but declined, preferring to labor in New Zealand. But at the earnest request of the Archbishop he was induced to accept. After a brief visit to the island, he was made Bishop of Lichfield, January 9th, 1868, having spent twenty-seven years among the heathen. In 1871 he visited the United States to attend the Triennial Convention of the Episcopal Church, held at Baltimore. He was very cordially received, and preached at the consecration of Bishop Howe. At the Jubilee meeting of the Board of Missions he delivered an address of great power. In 1874 he again visited America, and was present at the General Convention of the Episcopal Church of the United States, held in New York. He also visited Canada. Returning to England in 1878, he was taken ill, was soon partly paralyzed, and continued to fail until April 11th, when the end came. He died in great peace, saying: "It is all light." He was buried, according to his expressed desire, in a grave dug out of the rock on which the cathedral of St. Chad is built. Five hundred who had held the foremost positions in the state and church followed him to the tomb.

Dr. Inglis, a missionary of the Scotch Church in the New Hebrides, says: "Bishop Selwyn was avowedly a High Churchman, but his heart was largely imbued with the spirit of apostolic love and charity. Had we been missionaries of his own Society he could not have been kinder to us or more attentive. He was a great favorite among the Scotch in New Zealand. As a missionary he was unsurpassed for self-denial, energy, and enterprise. While from his social position, talents, and acquirements he might have commanded the highest ecclesiastical appointments in the national church, he cheerfully resigned these advantages, and chose the obscurity, privations, perils, and drudgery of missionaries to the most degraded savages. His example awakened great enthusiasm among the students of both the two great English Universities."

**Sendai** (Xenday), a town in Japan, near a bay of the same name, on the east coast of Hondo. Population (1884), 55,321. A public moral movement has recently been inaugurated in Sendai. After public debate in the Prefectural Assembly, to which Christian women as well as men were invited, it was resolved to abolish legalized prostitution after three years from that time (1889). The credit of this moral victory belongs to the zeal and courage of the Christians of Japan. Mission station of the American Baptist Missionary Union; 1 missionary and wife, 2 single ladies, 19 native helpers, 7 out-stations, 2 schools, 1 church, 156 church-members. Methodist Episcopal Church (North); 1 native preacher, 63 church-members, 1 Sab-

bath-school, 63 scholars. A. B. C. F. M.; 2 missionaries and wives, 2 female missionaries, 2 churches, 223 church-members. The Reformed (German) Church, U. S. A., also conducts some work here.

**Seneca Version.**—The Seneca, which belongs to the languages of America, is vernacular to the Iroquois, one of six tribes whose original seat was in the province of New York. A translation of the Gospel of Luke was made by the Rev. T. S. Harris, a missionary of the American Board, and published at New York by the American Bible Society in 1830. In 1867 the same Society published the Gospels, and another translation of the Gospels made by the Rev. Ashe Wright, in 1874–75.

*(Specimen verse. John 3 : 16.)*

Neh săh'găh ne' sòh jih' ha nŏ'ọh gwah Na' wĕn ni yòh' he'yọ ăn ja deh, Neh No'a wak neh'' sho' kuh sgat ho wi'yă yăh tot gah wăh' ha ọ'. gweh da wiib heh yọ ăn'ja deh'; neh neh, Sọn'- dib gwa'nah ot ă ọ wạ'i wa gwĕn ni yòs, tăh ăh' ta ye'i wah dọb', neh gwaa', nă yò'i wa da dyeh' ă ya'go yăn daht' ne' yọh heh̦'o weh.

**Senegambia** (Senegal and Rivières du Sud), a district on the West Coast of Africa, a French colony, whose boundaries, according to French claims, extend from Cape Blanco in the north to Liberia on the south, with the exception of the English colonies Sierra Leone and Gambia, and the territory belonging to Portugal. The territory inland is claimed as far as the Upper Niger, and south to the limits of the Gold Coast colonies. The limits of the French territory and that of Gambia and Sierra Leone were defined by an arrangement signed at Paris August 10th, 1889. Since January 1st, 1890, a portion of Senegambia has been detached and formed into an autonomous administrative division, called Rivières du Sud. The total area is not definitely known. Including both divisions, the settled portion covers about 140,000 square miles, with a population in Senegal of 181,600, and 43,898 in the Rivières.

The surface is level, and in the north mostly open, low, sandy, and barren; but south of the Gambia there is a rich forest region and luxuriant vegetation. The two principal rivers are the Senegal and the Gambia. The climate is said to be the most continuously hot of any known. The people are Negroes, Moors, and half-breeds of every description. The principal town is St. Louis. Population, 20,000.

The Mohammedan religion prevails, along with Roman Catholicism. Missionary societies: Wesleyan Methodist; (see Sierra Leone, with which is included Gambia.) French Evangelical Missionary Society; stations at St. Louis and Kerbala; 4 missionaries.

**Seoni**, a town in Central Provinces, India, on the road from Nagpur to Jabalpur, half-way between the two places, 30 miles southwest of Hoshangabad. Seoni contains large public gardens, a fine market-place, and a handsome tank. Climate healthy; temperature moderate. Population, 10,203, Hindus, Moslems, Jains, Kabirpanthis, Satnamis, Christians, Parsis, and non-Hindu aboriginal tribes. Mission station of the Original Secession Church of Scotland

(1871), with a mission school and evangelistic work.

**Seoul, or Soül,** is the common appellation of the capital of Korea, and is a common noun meaning capital, like the Japanese *miako* or *kio*, or the Chinese *king*. The proper name of the chief city and seat of government is Han-yang, which means China's Sunshine. It was founded in 1392 by the first king and founder of the present ruling dynasty of Korea, who chose the site for the beauty and strength of its situation. Seoul is situated in the central home province, in N. lat. 37° 34′ and E. long. 127° 05′, on the north side of the Han River, about 35 miles from its mouth as the crow flies, or, as measured by the winding of the current, about 50 miles. The city in shape is an irregular oblong, and lies lengthwise in a valley whose trend is from northeast to southwest. The dimensions of the city are, roughly stated, 3 by 2½ miles. On the north is a succession of magnificent granite hills, culminating in granite peaks 3,500 feet high. On the south side is a chain of hills reaching the height of 1,500 feet. The most striking work of art in the landscape is the city wall, which crosses river, plain, and hills, and climbs the mountains on the south, encircling the whole city proper. At intervals are massive and imposing gates, all appropriately named, and through the largest of which the great high-roads starting from the royal palace run to all parts of the kingdom. In the military system of the country this walled city is the centre of a group of fortresses which, before the days of rifled cannon, were strong and trustworthy. The scenery from the walls of the city, and indeed from many points within the city, is magnificent, and the natural situation is one of the best for health and safety. An affluent of the Han River, with branches that run into nearly every part of the city, traverses Seoul from east to west, and is utilized as a drain and for washing clothes.

To most travellers the aspect of Seoul is uninteresting, shabby, and squalid. Nevertheless, the gay costumes, full of varied color, clean and brilliant with starch, and the peculiar gloss which the Korean women contrive to confer upon the male garments, make the streets in fair weather wear a very bright and animated appearance. The houses are about 8 or 9 feet high, built of stone and mortar, and mostly roofed with tiles. The windows are under the eaves. A long street, about 200 feet wide, divides the city into nearly two equal portions. In the northern half are the walled enclosure containing the king's palace and the more important public buildings. The main entrance gates face the south, and are three in number. From the central and principal gate runs a street 60 feet wide into the main street, intersecting it at right angles, and dividing the northern section of the city into eastern and western quarters. This point of meeting of these two streets is regarded as the centre of the city. Here stands an imposing pavilion, the *Chong-kah*, or belfry, in which is hung a large bell over seven feet in height, which is rung every morning as the signal for opening and shutting the three great gates of the city, at the eastern and western ends of the long main streets, and the Great South Gate. The street leading from the bell to the latter gate is as wide as the main street. It was at the corner of this bell-tower

that the regent in 1866 erected an inscribed stone denouncing as traitors to their country all Koreans who were friendly to European intercourse. Another feature in this centre of the city is the rows of large warehouses, two stories in height, the lower portions of which are divided into small shops opening into a central court, instead of into the streets. These large storehouses are not private property, but are owned by the great trading guilds, which enjoy a notable monopoly. Along most of the main streets there are thousands of pedlers' booths erected, at which most of the retail trade of the city is done. These shabby-looking, temporary structures greatly mar the effect and narrow the space of the great thoroughfares. Outside of the buildings in the royal enclosure there are three palaces—two belonging to the king and one to his father. The dignity of the several mansions is shown in the relative amount of land occupied. The offices of the six ministries, or government departments, are small houses, differing but slightly from the better sort of dwellings. The city gateways are imposing specimens of native architecture. The city gates are shut every evening at 8 o'clock in the winter and 9 o'clock in the summer, at the sound of the city bell. The gates open at 1 A.M. in the morning. Few horses or vehicles are seen, but bulls laden with brushwood for fuel and with country produce are numerous. Since the residence of foreigners in Seoul a number of the native dwellings have been altered into good-looking houses, the Korean house lending itself more easily to the convenience of western people than the Japanese. The Protestant missionaries obtained a foothold in Seoul through a liberal construction of the treaties, in autumn, 1884, and have since steadily resided there. Since the treaty with France, French Roman Catholic missionaries, hitherto in disguise, have openly appeared, and have not only purchased ground, but have erected attractive buildings. Several hundred Japanese, apart from the legation people, and probably a larger number of Chinese, live in Seoul, engaged in commercial pursuits. No other city in Korea has so large a number of natives of the official class, including retainers of the nobles and office-holders. The Japanese legation buildings and the edifices of the missionary societies are in modern western style, more or less adapted to the Korean. China, Japan, Great Britain, the United States, Russia, and France are represented by envoys, and their official residences, and the flags of these nations flying at the mastheads, lend color and variety to the low mass of thatch and tile built up in the dirtiest of cities. The population within and without the walls is variously estimated at from 200,000 to 400,000, the latter figure being probably the nearest to the facts. In the semi-millennium of its history, now nearly completed, Seoul has had many vicissitudes. Laid out at the end of the 14th century, it was here, in the new capital, that the Chinese costume and coiffure of the Ming period (1368–1628) was introduced, and became the still fashionable and national Korean dress. In June, 1592, Seoul was evacuated by the king and court, and occupied during parts of several years by the Japanese during the war from 1592–97. In 1637 the Manchiu Tartars captured Seoul, compelled the king and his ministers to perform *kow-tow*, or the nine prostrations, and to have set up a great memorial stone commemorating the clemency of the Manchiu general. In 1653 Hamel and his fellow-Dutchmen visited Seoul as shipwrecked prisoners, finding other Hollanders there. In 1777 Christianity entered Seoul through some members of the embassy to and from Peking; in 1794 the first Chinese Jesuit priest, who was beheaded in 1801; in 1836 the first French priest, Maubant, followed by Bishop Imbert, who in 1839 shepherded 9,000 believers, and was decapitated September 21st. In March, 1866, nine French priests were executed on the river flats in front of the city, and on March 25th from the French war-vessels, "Déroulède" and "Tardif," piloted by an escaped French bishop and native Christians, the flag of France floated, causing a cessation of all business for several days. The French invasion took place in October, when two native Christians were beheaded and their blood poured into the river over the place of the anchorage of the French ships. The riot and attack on the Japanese Legation July 23d, 1882, the *coup d'état* and battle of the Chinese and Japanese troops December 4th to 7th, 1884, and the funeral of the ex-queen, a spectacle of unprecedented magnificence of the Korean sort, on an autumn day of 1890, are among the notable historic events in Seoul. The addresses of foreigners now resident in Seoul, numbering less than a hundred, are published annually in Meiklejohn's Japan Directory. A map and guide-book of the city, constructed in modern style, are greatly needed.

**Serampur,** a city in Bengal, British India, on the banks of the Húglí, some 13 miles above Calcutta, though on the opposite (west) bank of the river. Population in 1881, 25,559; over 90 per cent Hindus. Serampur was long a Danish station, but in 1845 all the possessions held by the Danes in India were ceded to the East India Company. It was to Serampur that Carey, Marshman, and Ward, the great Baptist missionaries of the early part of this century, retreated; and there, under the Danish flag, they found an asylum from the opposing zeal of the English authorities at Calcutta, who until the new charter was granted to the East India Company by Parliament in 1814, were unwilling that missionaries should find a foothold in their possessions. The new charter contained a clause legalizing the residence in India of missionaries and philanthropists. The Baptist missionaries not only worked diligently in preaching the gospel in Serampur and surrounding towns, but established a press, printed books and tracts, assembled their translators from many parts of India, prepared and published versions of the Bible in the principal languages of Hindustan, and even in Chinese. These versions were afterwards found to be of comparatively small value, owing to the haste with which they were prepared, and the inadequate facilities enjoyed for correct translation into the idiom of the various Indian tongues; but nothing can better illustrate the diligence, zeal, and energy which have made the Baptist Mission at Serampur famous in the annals of modern missions, than the fact that they were made at all. A church, college, schools of lower grade, and a good library were established at Serampur, and the mission is still in active and successful operation. Adoniram Judson and others of the first American missionaries, whom the English au-

thorities would not allow to land at Calcutta, were received for a time by the Serampur missionaries. A newspaper, the "Friend of India," was started by the Baptist missionaries many years ago, and for a long time discussed public affairs with ability, and from a lofty standpoint. It had great influence in India. In 1874 it was removed to Calcutta. On the whole the history of Indian missions has few names of greater interest than Serampur.

**Servia,** a kingdom in Europe, bounded by Austria on the north, Roumania (Wallachia) and Bulgaria on the east, Bosnia and Eastern Roumelia (South Bulgaria) on the south, and Bosnia on the west. In general, the surface is mountainous, and covered with dense forests. The Danube and several other large rivers drain the country. Its total area is 18,855 square miles, of which over half is under cultivation. Cereals and grapes are the principal products.

The independence of Servia was secured by the treaty of Berlin (1878), and since January, 1889, the executive power is vested in a king, assisted by a council of eight ministers. The legislative authority is exercised by the king, together with the National Assembly, which is composed of deputies elected by the people, indirectly and by ballot. Personal liberty, liberty of the press and conscience, are guaranteed. Population (1884), 1,937,172, including in round numbers 150,000 Roumanians, 34,000 Gypsies, 3,000 Armenians and Turks, 4,000 Jews, 7,000 Bulgarians, 11,000 other foreigners. The Servians, or Serbs, belong to the most spirited of the Slavonic races, and are noted for the love of freedom and bravery. Poverty is rarely seen, for even the poorest have some sort of freehold property. Thus 97 per cent of the country population are engaged in agriculture. The principal cities, with their population, are: Belgrade, the capital (35,483), Nish (16,178), Leskovatz (10 870), Pozarevatz (9,083). The Greek Church is the state religion of Servia, but according to the census of 1884 there were 8,092 Catholics, 741 Protestants, 4,160 Jews, and 14,569 Mohammedans. Education is conducted in elementary schools, maintained by the municipalities, and various technical schools and schools for higher education, which are supported entirely by the State. Attendance is compulsory, and no fees are required from the pupils. In 1889 there were 52,538 pupils in attendance on the elementary schools, and 7,540 at the various institutions for higher education. The proportion of the population that are able to read and write has increased from 4 per cent in 1874 to 10 per cent in 1884. The only mission work in Servia is that which is carried on by the colporteurs of the B. F. B. S.

*Servians.*—The Servians form an important branch of the Eastern Slavs, or as they are sometimes called, the South Slavs. They inhabit the kingdom of Servia, Bosnia, and Herzegovina, and part of Hungary. They number about 4,000,000, and belong to the Eastern or Orthodox Church, with the exception of about half a million Mohammedan Servians in Bosnia.

The Servians settled in the first half of the 7th century in the Balkan Peninsula, and their settlements spread over an extensive tract of land, comprising the present Servia, Montenegro, Herzegovina, Bosnia, and the Dalmatian coast. These various communities were ruled over by separate independent rulers called

"Cans" or "Zhoopans," who were under the nominal authority of the "Great Zhoopan" residing at Rassa (Novi-Bazar), and all of whom originally were vassals to the Byzantine Emperor. Christianity was first introduced among the Servians by the Roman Church in the middle of the 7th century, but this first introduction did not succeed; and it was only in about 868–870 that the Orthodox Church was established by Greek ecclesiastics sent by the Emperor Basil. The political situation of Servia for a long while was one of dependence upon either the Byzantine emperors or the Bulgarian kings, who found it easy to rule over the Servians owing to the civil dissensions and wars of the various petty Zhoopans. In 1120 the princely authority was assumed by Bela Onrosh, who is considered as the progenitor and founder of the Nyemanitch dynasty, that ruled over Servia for more than two centuries. Stephen Nemanya succeeded in uniting the various petty "Zhoopanyas" in one, and thus laid the foundation of a united Servian principality, which after his death became a kingdom. His son Rastko, better known by his monkish name Sava, is one of the most important and famous men in Servian history. Abandoning all worldly goods and honors, he fled to Mount Athos, and there took the vows as a simple monk. Ordained as an archbishop in Nicæa (Asia Minor) by the Greek Patriarch in 1219, he returned to Servia and founded an independent or autocephalous Servian church. By his pious deeds, his zeal for the propagation of the gospel, and the great services he rendered his country in elevating and civilizing it, he has earned the name of "Servia's Enlightener," and is to this day honored as a saint by the Servian church. He died in 1237. Under the reign of King Stephen Dooshan (1336–1355) Servia reached its largest expansion and its greatest glory. Besides its proper territories, Servia comprised Albania, Ætolia, Epirus, Thessaly, and Macedonia, and even Bosnia acknowledged King Dooshan's rule. But after his death all this great kingdom which he had established crumbled to pieces, and internal quarrels and dissensions prepared the way for the final overthrow of Servia's political status. In Dooshan's time the Servian church was raised to the rank of a Patriarchate, with residence at Petch, or Ipek (in Albania), which lasted for more than four centuries (1346–1766). In 1389 took place the famous battle of Kossovo-Polye, between Servians and Turks, in which the latter routed completely the Servian forces, and put an end to Servia's independence. Up to 1459, six years after the capture of Constantinople, Servia was ruled over by princes called "Despots," who acknowledged the supreme authority of the Sultan, paid him tribute, and were obliged to aid the Turks in their wars; but in 1459 Servia lost even this shadow of political independence, and became a province of Turkey. In 1463 Bosnia was conquered, and in 1483 the same fate befell Herzegovina. The country had to suffer terribly from the constant wars of the Turks with Hungary and Austria, and thousands of Servians had to abandon their homes and emigrate to Hungary. In 1690 Patriarch Arseny Tchernoevitch, at the head of 37,000 Servian families, went over to Austria, which gave them lands to settle on, and promised them religious and social rights. Not wishing to have Servia and the Servians under their rule to be governed by a Patriarch from Austria, the Turks allowed the Servians to elect a new Patriarch, but it was soon after abolished, and all the Servians were subjected to the direct authority of the Greek Patriarch at Constantinople. In the beginning of the present century the Servians rose up against the Sultan to regain their political independence, and after a great many vicissitudes and struggles, they succeeded in establishing a semi-independent principality, under the suzerainty of the Sultan.

In 1882 this principality was raised to the rank of a kingdom, and by the Treaty of Berlin (1878) the territory of Servia was enlarged at the expense of Bulgaria, while Bosnia and Herzegovina were annexed to Austria.

The Servian church is ruled over by a Metropolitan residing at Belgrade, and bearing the title of "Metropolitan of all Servia." He is also the president of the Synod, who act as his councillors and advisers; but the power of the Metropolitan and the Synod does not extend beyond the limits of the Servian kingdom. Bosnia and Herzegovina are under the jurisdiction of bishops nominated by the Greek Patriarchate, subject to the approval of the Austrian Government. The Servians living in Austria-Hungary, and who also belong to the Orthodox Church, have a Patriarch residing at Carlovitz, who is chosen by a council and approved by the Austrian Government. He bears the title of Patriarch as an honorable title in continuation of the Patriarchs of Ipek, who ruled over the Servians in former days. All the Servians belonging to the Orthodox Church use the Church-Slavonic language in their churches, and the Kyrillitza alphabet in their literature. Their language belongs to the Eastern branch of Slavic languages, and is akin to the Bulgarian, from which it differs, however, considerably in its vocal sounds. Many Turkish, Greek, and Albanian words have entered into the formation of the modern Servian language. Under the influence of their ecclesiastics and their ecclesiastical literature, the Servians in the beginning of the present century used in their literature a language called Slavonico-Servian, a mixture of Church-Slavonic, and Servian, with the elements of the former predominating. But thanks to the genius and efforts of Verk Karadjiteh, a self-made man, the Servian alphabet was modified to a certain extent, to suit the pronunciation of the spoken language of the people, which was raised to the dignity of a literary language. In this way the Servian orthography became the most phonetic of all Slavic orthographies, and in spite of the opposition the reforms of Karadjitch met with, they were officially sanctioned by the government in 1868, and accepted by all the Servians who use the Kyrillitza alphabet. Karadjiteh translated also the New Testament into the common language of the people, while some years later Danitchiteh, a well-known Servian philologian, and a follower of Karadjitch, did the same thing for the Old Testament; and both these versions have been accepted and are used by the British and Foreign Bible Society.

**Servian Version.**—The Servian, which belongs to the Slavonic branch of the Aryan family, is spoken in Servia, Bosnia, Herzegovina, Montenegro, Croatia, Slavonia, Dalmatia, etc., and is more akin to the Russ and Wend than to the Bohemian and Polish languages. It is rich in vowels, and free from the accumulation of consonants which render the other Slavonic tongues so harsh to the ear of a foreigner. Its sound is very soft, and one of the best Slavic scholars of our age, Prof. Schafarik, in comparing the different dialects of the Slavonic family, makes the following remark: "Servian song resembles the tone of the violin; Old Slavonic that of the organ; Polish that of the guitar. The Old Slavonic in its psalms sounds like the loud rush of the mountain stream; the Polish like the bubbling and sparkling of a fountain; and the Servian like the quiet murmuring of a streamlet in the valley."

A translation of the New Testament into Servian was made by Due Stephanovitch, and printed at St. Petersburg in 1824. Another version made by Prof. Stoikovitch, which proved more acceptable, was published by the British and Foreign Bible Society at Leipsic in 1830, and republished at different times. In 1865 the same Society published the Psalms, which Prof. Danicii* had translated. The entire Old Testament, translated by Danicii, was published by the same Society, together with the New Testament in one volume in 1868. Upon the appearance of the Bible, the Bishop of Pakras, in Slavonia, the most talented of the Servian hierarchy, and formerly a strong opponent, wrote to the translator: "I am more pleased with your translation of the Bible than with any other. I only regret that I cannot express my approbation of your generous work as freely as you deserve, and as I wish." The Archbishop of Belgrade, on the other hand, denounced the translation as being corrupt and unfaithful, but his opposition soon made a second edition of the Servian Bible necessary. Indeed a Roman Catholic periodical publicly declared that "it is not worthy of praise that, with so many bishops of both (Greek and Roman) churches, it should have been left to the British and Foreign Bible Society to produce a more popular translation than we have had hitherto. If things are allowed to remain as they are now, no prohibition will be of any avail. The people will grasp at this translation unless an authentic one be provided for them." That the writer in that journal was correct in his anticipation may be seen from the fact that up to March 31st, 1889, 173,385 portions of the Scriptures, as a whole or in parts, have been distributed.

(*Specimen verse.* John 3 : 16.)

Јер Богу тако омиље свијет да је и сина својега јединороднога дао, да ни један који га вјерује не погине, него да има живот вјечни.

### Seventh Day Adventist Foreign Missionary Society.

Headquarters, Battle Creek, Michigan.—The foreign work of this Society is carried on in the following fields, according to the last report (1890):

EUROPE. *Switzerland.*—The centre of the work is in the printing-house at Basle, from which a large amount of literature has been circulated. There are twelve churches with a membership of 370, and an increase in the past

year of 56. After much difficulty the question of holding camp-meetings has been decided favorably, and the success of one in one of the most difficult places in Switzerland gives encouragement for the future.

*France.*—There are four churches and four companies of Sabbath-keepers in France, with a membership of 65. Some colportage work has been done, and two courses of meetings have been held.

*Algeria.*—Some three or four years ago a baker living at Realizani received a copy of the paper published in French, became interested in it, embraced its truths, as he understood them, and began to labor for others. Quite a number of Spaniards accepted the faith, and a society called the Apostolic Seventh Day Adventists was formed.

*Russia.*—The Seventh Day Adventist Church in this empire was organized in the Krimea in 1886, and during the same year labor was begun on the river Volga. One church of seven members was organized north of Saratow, and there are now about 100 Sabbath-keepers in this part of the empire. In the Caucasus there is one church of more than 100 Sabbath-keepers, and another of 17 members. The difficulty of sending books into Russia has been very great, and has hindered the spread of the work not a little.

*Germany.*—From 1876-79 two churches were organized in Rhenish Prussia, but the work then ceased, to be taken up again in 1888, since when eight or ten canvassers have labored in several provinces with good success. Work has also been carried on in Stuttgart, Hamburg, and Barmen.

*Scandinavia.*—A church has been organized with 15 members in Karlscrona, Sweden, and there are now 12 churches with 360 members. In Norway there are 3 churches with 301 Sabbath-keepers. Considerable canvassing has been done along the western border of Norway, and a church school has been opened at Christiania with 50 children. In Denmark there are 5 churches with 265 members.

The tour of P. W. B. Wessels among the mission stations of South Africa has led to the establishment of a community of about 40 in number near Cape Town, and a church is to be built at Kimberly. Two tents have been purchased—one to be used in the eastern district along the coast, the other in the western district.

*Australia.*—The work of the Society has been started in three colonies, namely, South Australia, Tasmania, and in Melbourne. In Adelaide a church of 25 members has been formed. In Hobart Town there are 65 members. The publishing work of the Society has been carried on with great difficulty. The Australian Conference is composed of six churches, with a membership of 362.

*New Zealand.*—During the past year a conference has been formed of three churches, with 155 members; also a Tract Society and a Sabbath-school Association.

### Seventh-Day Baptist Missionary Society.

Headquarters, Westerly, R. I., U. S. A.—The Seventh-Day Baptist Missionary Society, founded in 1842, aims to disseminate the gospel in America and in other parts of the world, and to promote religious and benevolent work. In 1847 its "Mission to

China" was established in Shanghai. There are at present at this station 4 American missionaries, with 6 native assistants, to carry on the preaching, teaching (in boys' and girls' boarding-schools), and medical work of the station. The number of patients at the dispensary in 1889 was 2,822. The Holland Mission, with principal station at Haarlem, is accomplishing great good by means of temperance work and " Midnight Missions." From Haarlem the work is extending throughout Holland and Belgium. The principal work of its "Mission to the Jews" is carried on in Galicia, Austria.

**Seychelles,** a group of islands in the Indian Ocean, are a dependency of the British colony of Mauritius (see, under Africa, West African Islands). Mission work is carried on by the S. P. G. and C. M. S., and not by the Scottish Presbyterian Societies, as stated in the article Africa. The C. M. S. (1875) has a station at Capucin, and has 47 children under instruction. The S. P. G. has 1 missionary resident at Praslin.

**Shaingay,** a town in the Sherbro district, West Africa, which gives name to a mission district of the United Brethren in Christ. Together with the Mendi Mission (q.v.) there are 266 communicants, 13 day-schools, 443 scholars, 11 Sunday-schools, 451 scholars. There is a training-school at Shaingay, whose 8 students assist in itinerating.

**Shahjahanpur,** a city in the Northwest Provinces, India. Population, 77,936. It gives name to a circuit of the M. E. Church (North). In the city are two stations—Shahjahanpur and East Shahjahanpur. The former has one missionary and wife, 152 church-members, 33 day-schools, 450 scholars, 22 Sunday-schools, 1,756 scholars; the latter, 1 missionary and wife, 124 church-members, 7 day-schools, 262 scholars, 8 Sunday-schools, 305 scholars.

**Shan States,** the name given to some of the hill provinces which lie on either side of the boundary between Burma and Siam, and are tributary to the one or to the other. They are inhabited by the Laos and other tribes. (For amount of mission work, see Burma and Siam.)

**Shan Version.**—The Shan belongs to the Tai family of the Indo-China languages, and is spoken by the natives of the Shan States, Burma. The Burma Bible and Tract Society published in 1882, at Rangoon, a translation of the New Testament by Mr. Cushing.

**Shanghai,** the most important emporium in China, and the city which shows more of western civilization than any other settlement of Europeans, except Hong Kong, is in Kiangsu, on the Woosung River, about 12 miles from its junction with the Yangtsz-kiang, in lat. 31° 10' N. and long. 121° 30' E. There are two entirely distinct parts to the city: (1) The Native City; (2) The Foreign Settlement.

(1) *The Native City* is very old. The first mention of it is found to be in A.D. 1015. In 1360 it became a district city. The British captured it in June, 1843, and it was the fifth of the treaty ports thrown open to foreign commerce. During the Taiping rebellion it was captured by the insurgents and occupied them for 17 months, and when they were driven out in 1860 the eastern and southern suburbs were almost entirely destroyed. By virtue of its position it is the outlet for a vast territory. The Wusung and Hwangpu rivers, the latter emptying into the Wusung at Shanghai, give it communication with Suchow, Sungkiang, and all the region of the Grand Canal; while the Yangtsz, only a few miles distant, makes it the outlet for the great Yangtsz valley. The city, walled, three miles in circuit, stands in a large and fertile plain. Along the water front are vessels which carry goods to and from the interior. The streets are narrow and paved, the houses built of brick; and shops, eating-houses, and the usual temples and Buddhist shrines common to all Chinese cities are found here in abundance, and none of the public buildings or temples are peculiar to this city any more than to other cities of the empire. The population is estimated at 200,000, but probably the estimate is low. The climate varies greatly—from an intense heat in summer to freezing cold in winter, and great changes of temperature in 24 hours are common in the spring and autumn. The mean temperature, like that of Rome, is 59° (F.). Heavy rainfalls occur in the summer, but from September to May the climate is delightful.

(2) *The Foreign Settlement* is a municipality, and is divided into the English (and American) and French concessions; is governed by municipal officers; and there is a mixed court where cases involving natives and foreigners are tried before both Chinese and English officials. Spacious docks line the river front for three miles. The streets are broad, overhung with trees, lighted with electric light, and nearly all the comforts of modern civilization are to be found. Jinrikshas, together with the native sedan chairs and wheelbarrows, provide abundant means of transportation; and horses and equipages of the latest European style are to be seen on the streets, especially along the Bubbling Well Road—the fashionable drive. Hundreds of native boats ply for hire on the river, and with the shipping, the steam-tugs, and small boats, the water presents a most animated appearance. The land of the concessions belongs really to the Emperor of China, to whom a mere nominal rental is paid. The domestic and foreign mails are handled at seven post-offices,—at the consulates,—in connection with the Chinese customs. Clubs, libraries, museums, in addition to the various mission establishments, present attractions to the visitor. Telephone service is provided. The great northern line of telegraph was connected with the settlement in 1871, and it is now in cable communication with the rest of the world. The first railroad in China was opened in 1876 between this city and Wusung, at the mouth of the river; the Chinese Government bought it the ensuing year, tore it up, and sent the material to Formosa, where it is now rotting.

From this port is carried on the most important trade in China, the value of it having risen from 65,000,000 taels in 1868 to 145,000,000 taels in 1889. It is the centre for the export of tea and silk.

According to the census of 1890, the population of the municipality exclusive of the French concession, was 168,129; on the French concession, 34,722; the foreigners numbered only 4,265, of whom 444 were in the French quarter. The death rate in 1888 was 18.5 per thousand. Such a wide range of nationality is seldom found in any Oriental settlement; while the bulk of the foreign population is British, American, French, and German, yet twenty-one other nationalities are represented in varying numbers. Together with the estimated population of the native city, the total population of Shanghai is 408,000.

Shanghai is the literary centre of the foreigners in China. Here is published the best English daily paper, together with the majority of the missionary publications. At the Presbyterian Mission Press books are printed in Chinese—not only religious, but scientific; and the Chinese Religious Tract Society issue from here their periodicals in Chinese, and the "Chinese Recorder" and "The Messenger" are published in English. On account of its central location, the beauty of its situation, the hospitality of the foreign community, it has been the place of meeting for the great Missionary Conferences (q.v.).

Its importance as a centre for religious work was early appreciated, and a larger force of missionaries, or representatives of more denominations, are probably not met with elsewhere in China. (See article China for development and history of mission work in Shanghai.) Mission societies now represented at Shanghai, with the last available statistics, are:

London Missionary Society (1843); 1 missionary and wife, 2 female missionaries, 7 out-stations, 5 churches, 250 communicants, 7 preaching places, 6 native preachers, 2 girls' schools, 2 day-schools, 100 scholars.

American Presbyterian Church (North), 1850; 4 missionaries and wives, 1 female missionary, 3 out-stations, 2 churches, 6 preaching places, 4 native preachers. 6 Sabbath-schools, 465 scholars, 6 theological students, 1 girls' school, 30 girls; 23,820,000 pages were issued from the Mission Press in 1889.

Southern Baptist Convention; 2 missionaries and wives, 1 female missionary, 3 churches, 95 members, 30 scholars.

Seventh-Day Baptist Missionary Society; 2 missionaries and wives, 1 medical missionary, 2 female missionaries, 30 communicants, 35 Sabbath-scholars, 33 day-scholars.

Methodist Episcopal Church (South); 4 missionaries (1 President of Anglo-Chinese College).

Protestant Episcopal Church (U. S. A.); 2 missionaries and wives, 2 missionary physicians and wives, 2 female missionaries, 3 churches, 2 chapels, 1 college, 1 medical school, 1 hospital, 264 communicants, 716 scholars.

C. M. S. (1845); 3 missionaries, 43 communicants. 3 schools, 71 scholars.

United Presbyterian Church of Scotland; Rev. A. Williamson, D.D., was for some time engaged in literary work, but since his death in August, 1890, the Society has no representative in the city.

The British and Foreign Bible Society have at Shanghai a centre for work, and it is the headquarters of the American Bible Society.

**Shanghai Colloquial.**—Into this dialect of the Chinese, which is spoken at Shanghai, the Revs. Medhurst and Milne translated the Gospels of Matthew and John, which were published at Shanghai in 1847. In 1872 the New Testament was published by the American Bible Society, translated by Bishop Boone, Revs. J. S. Roberts, E. H. Thomson, J. M. W. Farnham; in 1880 the same Society published a revised edition of the four Gospels; in 1885,

Genesis, Exodus, and Deuteronomy; in 1886, the Psalms, translated by the Revs. J. W. Lambuth and E. H. Thomson; in 1888, Isaiah and Daniel. In behalf of the British and Foreign Bible Society, the Rev. W. Muirhead of Shanghai is now engaged in translating portions of the Scriptures into this dialect for the untrained people, to whom the literary and even the Mandarin styles are not familiar. He will not adopt a low or commonplace colloquial, but such as would be appreciated by well-read native Christians, and understood by the common people when read to them.

(*Specimen verse.* John 3:16.)

因為 神愛世界上人造於實蓋拿伊獨
養兒子，賞撥伊拉以致凡係相信兒子个
人，勿滅脫咾得着永生。

*Roman.*

Iung-wæ' Zung juk æ' s'-ka loñg' kuk niung lau, soong' peh ye kuk dok 'yang Nie-'ts, s' feh kiû sa' niung, siang-sing' ye mæh, feh mih-t'eh lau, tuk-dzak 'loong-'yö wæh la'.

**Shangpoong,** a district in the Khasia and Jaintia Hills, Assam, which contains seven small governments or Dolloiships, in five of which the gospel, preached by the missionaries of the Welsh Calvinistic Methodist Missionary Society, has already secured a footing. In the district there is 1 missionary, with 17 preaching places, 126 communicants, 751 Sunday-scholars.

**Shaohing,** a city in Chehkiang, China, on the south side of the Bay of Hangchow. Its climate is warm and somewhat malarious. Surrounded by a fertile and prosperous country, with a population of 150,000, it is one of the important cities of Chehkiang. Mission station of the A. B. M. U. (1869); 1 missionary and wife, 2 churches, 55 church-members; theological seminary with 7 students. C. M. S. (1870); 13 communicants, 16 scholars. C. I. M.

(1866); 3 missionaries, 5 out-stations (including Sinchang), 6 churches, 208 communicants.

**Shao-tien-tzee,** a city of Northern China, in the province of Shansi, near Tai-yuen-fu. Mission station of the Baptist Missionary Society; 3 missionaries.

**Shao-wu,** a city in Fuhkien, China. A station of the Foochow Mission of the A. B. C. F. M. Mission houses and a hospital have been built, and the opportunities for medical and evangelistic work are very great. The station has 2 missionaries and wives, 1 medical missionary.

**Sharon,** the first permanent station of the Moravians in Barbadoes, West Indies. It is pleasantly situated on a rising ground 4 miles from Bridgetown. It was opened in 1794, but the labors of the missionaries have met with only a moderate degree of success, and there never has been any great awakening among the Moravian congregations on the Barbadoes, such as has been experienced in other West Indian islands. The work is now in the care of a missionary and his wife.

**Sheik Othman,** a town in the southwest part of Arabia, 10 miles from Aden. Mission station of the Free Church of Scotland, occupied in 1885 by the Keith-Falconer Mission (see Presbyterian Church of Scotland).

**Shella,** a small town of 5,000 people in the Khasia and Jaintia hills, Assam, which gives name to a district of the mission of the Welsh Calvinistic Methodists, under the oversight of 1 missionary. In the district are 25 churches, 196 communicants, 1,037 Sunday-scholars.

**Sherbro,** an island off the southwest coast of Sierra Leone, Africa, opposite the mouth of the Sherbro River; is about 30 miles long and 10 miles broad. Mission field of the former Mendi Mission, now United Brethren of Christ, with stations at Bonthe, Victoria, and Good Hope; also of the Wesleyan Methodists, with headquarters at Bonthe, and 14 preaching places, 1 missionary, 189 church-members, 154 Sabbath-scholars, 215 day-scholars; the Sierra Leone Native Church, in connection with the C. M. S., has 4 pastorates—Bonthe, Bendoo, Victoria, and York Island.

**Sherring, Matthew Atmore,** b. Halstead, Essex, England, September 26th, 1826; studied at University College, London, and Coward College; ordained December 7th, 1852; sailed as a missionary of the L. M. S. the same year for Benares. He took the superintendence of the Central School and soon engaged in vernacular work. A missionary tour which he made in 1853 with some of his brethren served early to introduce him to varied forms of Indian life. In 1856 he married the daughter of Rev. Dr. Cotton Mather, and in November the same year removed to Mirzapore to take charge of the station in the absence of Dr. Mather in England. Mrs. Sherring was active in efforts for native female improvement. In 1861 they returned to Benares, Mr. Sherring taking charge of the Central School, engaging in bazaar preaching and itinerating, Mrs. Sherring conducting the female school. In 1866 he left with his family for England, *via* America; reembarked for India alone, January 7th, 1869;

resumed charge of the Central School and took the pastorate of the native church. In the absence of Dr. Mather at Almora he supplied his station for nine months. In 1875 he visited the Nilgiri Hills for his health, but not regaining it, he made a second visit to England in 1876. Having recovered his health, he returned to India with Mrs. Sherring in 1878. On Sunday, August 8th, he went through his usual services in Hindustani and English, in apparently good health. At 2 o'clock Monday morning he was attacked with cholera, and on the 10th, 1880, passed gently away. The same evening native Christians carried his body to the grave, among them his first convert, baptized twenty-four years before, a Brahmin, and now vernacular headmaster in the institution at Benares. "Combining high culture and strong commonsense with a gentleness of disposition almost womanly, Mr. Sherring endeared himself to all with whom he came in contact." "I make it my rule," he would say, "to try to please every one if possible." In the twofold work of high-class education and of preaching in the vernacular, which devolved on him at Benares and Mirzapore, he found ample scope for his superior talents.

**Shidzuoka,** a city on the southern coast of Central Japan, 120 miles from Tokyo. Climate pleasant and healthy. Population, 36,838. People industrious, comfortable; the use of liquors and tobacco general, but not excessive. Mission station Methodist Episcopal Church, Canada (1873); 3 missionaries and wives, 2 single ladies, 22 native helpers, 27 out-stations, 9 churches, 720 church-members, 1 school, 50 scholars.

**Shillong,** the administrative headquarters of Assam, India; has a high location, from which there is a beautiful view of the valley of the Bramaputra. It gives name to a district of the Welsh Calvinistic Methodist Mission among the Khasia and Jaintia Hills, and in the town and district there are 13 stations, under the oversight of 1 missionary, with 36 preaching places, 689 communicants, 2,137 Sunday-scholars.

**Shimoga,** a town in Mysore, India. Mission station of the Wesleyan Methodist Missionary Society (1863); 2 missionaries, 34 church-members, 115 Sabbath-scholars, 399 day-scholars.

**Shimonoseki,** a city of Japan, of considerable commercial importance. It is situated on the southwestern extremity of Nippon, on the strait which connects the Inland Sea with the Yellow Sea. Mission station of the A. B. M. U. (1886); 1 missionary and wife, 4 native preachers, 36 church-members.

**Shimshi,** or **Zimshi.**—The Shimshi belongs to the languages of North America, and is used in Metlakatla. A translation of the Gospel of Matthew was published by the Society for Promoting Christian Knowledge in 1885, which was followed by the publication of the Gospels of Mark, Luke, and John in 1886-87.

**Shintoo.**—The origin of Shintoo is involved in more or less obscurity, but the translation of the Kojiki, which may be looked upon as the sacred record and exposition of the system, has thrown much light upon its doctrines. It is an embodiment of the crude superstitions of the early Japanese, their nature-worship, spirit-worship, ancestor-worship, and hero-worship, in fantastic combination. It is dimly monotheistic in its very earliest references. It presents the idea of one supreme being, from whom all things spring, but of whom nothing beyond this can be known. He was not a real Creator. This mysterious and unrevealed being is known in Shintoo as the "Central and Supreme God of Heaven."

Tradition relates that when the heaven and the earth separated from that confused relation in which they had been intermingled in the original chaos, this supreme God came forth and appeared uplifted between them, but he had existed, though unrevealed, from all eternity. This system also presents the idea of a second and a third deity, subordinate to the first but self-existent. From these deities two emanations proceeded, namely, Isaname (female), and Isanagi (male); from the fecundity of these sprang all things. They were the Adam and Eve of Shintoo. Several other subordinate gods were produced.

The process of creation ascribed to the divine pair was very unique: standing on a bridge of heaven and looking earthward, they stirred the ocean with a long spear. From the end of the spear dropped some fecund substance, from which sprang up the islands of Japan, and in the islands thus composed was the potency of all things; vegetable and animal life sprang up spontaneously. Shintoo does not recognize a real creation out of nothing. It claims only a development. The universe is regarded as eternal. God and man and all things are of one essence. The system, therefore, is in a sense Pantheistic.

The development of the sun myth appears in Japan as in so many other countries. The male and female deities above named produced a daughter of most resplendent beauty, represented by the sun. While this fair maiden was embroidering beautiful textures—thus, perhaps, symbolizing the beautiful work of nature in verdure and in flowers—her churlish brother spoiled her work by covering it with defilement; the brother representing the principle of evil, and thus establishing a dualism which has been found in so many nations. The maiden, thus insulted, is represented as having withdrawn herself in sulkiness to a dark cave, leaving the world in gloom. The legends represent the forlorn inhabitants of the world as having resorted to various expedients to bring her forth from the cave. Three of these appear to have been successful. One was to gather as many cocks together as possible, from all quarters, and place them near the cave's entrance, that at the proper hour of cock-crowing their clamor might excite her womanly curiosity, and bring her out. A second expedient was to institute a dance of beautiful goddesses before the cave. Becoming jealous of the praises which she heard lavished on them, she would certainly come out and reveal her charms.

Another plan, quite as successful, was that of constructing a mirror, which was so placed before the mouth of the cave as to reflect to the goddess her own beautiful form. This three-fold appeal to her curiosity, her jealousy, and her vanity succeeded. She came forth; whereupon means were immediately taken to prevent her return. The sunlight of her presence again bathed the world, and filled all nature with delight. This sun goddess married at length, and became the mother of the whole line of mikados, and from her to the present incumbent of the throne there has never been a break; the succession for thousands of years is claimed to be complete.

There are imposing ceremonies connected with the worship of this goddess, almost wholly of a cheerful tone; and it may be said in general, that of all races, perhaps the Japanese, before the advent of Buddhism, had the most light-hearted type of faith. In the springtime there are still festivals designed to hail the springing of the fruits and flowers, and ceremonies in imitation of planting and sowing are performed. Here is a vocation for the Shintoo priests, and one far more grateful than offering bloody sacrifices or in any way striving to appease gloomy deities. This sun-goddess, the ancestor of the mikados, is a genial being, and she is symbolized, not by cruelty and death as in the case of Moloch, the fiery sun-god of the Phœnicians, but by all benign influences, and her only sacrifices are offerings of rice and fish and flowers. It is scarcely necessary to say that the original supreme deity, who never revealed himself, and of whom nothing is known, is removed very remotely from the practical interests of life, and that the great mother of the mikados is the really supreme object of worship.

Shintoo can scarcely be called a religion. It has little moral earnestness. As a system, it is a vast Pantheon of demigods. It embraces the modified worship of ancestors and heroes. Its temples are full of heroes of Japanese history, fierce warriors, and successful Shoguns and Daimios, and the number is ever increasing. Even in modern times governmental decrees frequently confer semi-divine honors on dead statesmen and heroes. Every Shintoo temple is a sort of Westminster Abbey, in which the images of honored Shoguns are placed.

The literature of Shintoo is not extensive. Such as it is, it found its source in the fables and folk-lore of the earliest and rudest times. These were preserved by minstrels. In the third century A.D. Chinese legends were introduced, and some of these myths were committed to writing. It was in 712 A.D. that the Kojiki, or "ancient record," was compiled. This is the sacred Bible of Shintoo priests. It is also the earliest Japanese history. It is most unique in its style, resembling nothing else that has ever been published in any land. It is remarkable for the agglutination of long compound names and expressions. But although Shintoo cannot compare with Buddhism in its literature, or in its intellectual influence, yet it does not wholly neglect the instruction of the people. There is more or less preaching on ethical subjects, and the ethics thus presented are pure and salutary. Even this custom may have been borrowed from Buddhism. During the long centuries in which Shintoo and Buddhism have coexisted side by side, or rather have been more or less intermingled, the Buddhist influence has done most to promote the intellectual growth of the people, very little effort having been made by the Shintoo priests to emulate the Buddhist culture. Buddhism has not only proved educational in its influence: it has inculcated a higher moral feeling, and especially in the direction of benevolence and humanity.

It is difficult to decide whether or not Shintoo is to be regarded as idolatrous: no idols appear in the temples, even of the sun-goddess. Statues of heroes are not invoked in prayer, and yet undoubtedly they receive something akin to worship; and the Japanese temples are never closed against any object which seems even to approach the idea of the supernatural. In every Shintoo temple a mirror is seen, which is supposed to symbolize the divine man that is in us, at the same time that it is a vivid representative of one's conscience and his judge. The thought is that a man within the sacred temple precincts is brought face to face with himself, and that in one sense what it most concerns him to know is himself as he really is. It cannot be denied that this is a forcible conception. Next to the prayer of the Psalmist that the Spirit of God may search the petitioner and try his heart, is that means, whatever it be, which brings a man face to face with himself in the solemn presence of real or supposed deity. Shintoo is a religion in so far as it recognizes the relations of man to a higher power, as is shown in the fact that prayer is a resource constantly resorted to. It is offered to a supreme something, which is supposed to cherish an interest in all creatures. At funerals and elsewhere prayers are offered for the dead as well as for the living. There is in Shintoo a resemblance to the cult of the Aryans, both in its dread of death and of all that belongs to death. A corpse is looked upon as polluting, and one should have as little as possible to do with it; no people except the Zoroastrians carried this matter so far. It is closely connected with sun-worship in both cases.

*Relations of Shintoo to Buddhism.—* Buddhism entered Japan in the year 552, A.D. The Shintoo levity and thoughtlessness opened the way for a system which was of a more melancholy tone and spirit, and which took a more earnest hold upon the future life. For a thousand years, according to Kodera, there existed a strange partnership between the two religions. By common consent the Shintoo priests officiated at all marriages (with which Buddhist monks were supposed to be little in sympathy), while Buddhist priests took charge of the funerals, from which Shintoo priests were only glad to be exempt. At the present time marriage is a civil rite only. So intimately interwoven did these two systems become, that the Government at length began to dread the influence of Buddhism, which had proved the stronger element. And in order that Shintoo, with its traditions of imperial descent and the prestige which it thus afforded, might not lose its supreme place, a decree was passed declaring it to be the religion of the state; and this is still the theory of the Government. Yet so closely had the two systems been blended, and that for so long a time, that it is said that nine tenths of the people consider themselves as belonging to both. Like other Oriental systems, Shintoo is easygoing, and in a negative sense charitable toward Buddhism; both have long been accustomed to represent their position by the maxim: "Men may ascend Fujiama on any one of many sides, but when once on the summit the same glorious moon is visible to all. So with the religions."

There can be little doubt that the early mythology of Shintoo exerted a disastrous influence upon the morality of the people. The legend which represents the goddess as dancing in an almost nude condition before the cave in which the sun-goddess was hidden has presented a poor example to the generations of Japanese peasants, and one cannot greatly wonder that indecency and vice have known less restraint than in almost any other land. The Japanese have many attractive elements of charter, but immorality has, under the influence of Shintoo, been scarcely considered a vice.

The late Dr. S. R. Brown, after years of observation, could scarcely find any element of moral restraint in the system, and was slow to accord to it the name of religion. Rev. Drs. Hepburn and Griffiths have expressed similar opinions.

There can be no doubt that in comparison with this childish system of nature-worship and mere natural impulse Buddhism has been a blessing to Japan. Rev. K. C. Kurahara has summed up the beneficial influences of Buddhism in Japan as follows:

(1) It has taught the people a vivid realization of future rewards and punishments—thus ministering both inspiration and restraint, and giving to life a higher dignity and solemnity.

(2) It has presented a high conception of our common humanity, without caste or slavery.

(3) It has enjoined a higher grade of ethics, and much more of self-restraint.

(4) It taught the people temperance, even prohibition.

(5) It has emphatically enjoined benevolence and pity to all beings.

(6) It has stimulated an intellectual activity not known before. It has introduced philosophy and poetry and all literature.

(7) From the 12th century until the year 1868 Buddhist priests were the only educators. All schools were due to their influence.

(8) The Buddhist doctrines have greatly enkindled the powers of imagination, pathos, and lofty aspiration.

(9) The introduction of Buddhism has led to increased foreign intercourse, and has brought in its train the literatures not only of China, but of India.

(10) Buddhism has given great impulse to architecture, landscaping, gardening, and all ornamental arts. Of this the peerless bronzes, lacquers, and the sweet toned temple bells are proofs.

(11) By its support of a priestly and yet a thoughtful class, Buddhism furnished many men of leisure, who gave themselves to literature and were promoters of a higher national culture. Were the Buddhist element eliminated from Japanese literature there would be but little left.

(12) Although Buddhism weakened the divine autocracy of the Mikado, and thus perhaps facilited the introduction of the rival power of the Shoguns, yet nevertheless it exerted a powerful restraint upon cruelty and oppression.

(13) It taught rulers the duty of respecting the claims of the people and of promoting their good.

Rev. Mr. Ibuka of the Tokyo Christian College gives credit to Confucianism for imparting to the Japanese nation a higher degree of moral earnestness than either Shintoo or Buddhism. To the ethics of Confucius is due whatever of loyalty to government and to country have been found in public officials and all the higher classes of men.

A new cultus has now appeared in Japan. The gospel of Jesus Christ has imparted more of noble impulse, secured a greater degree of moral and intellectual advancement, in twenty-five years than all the other religions have realized in the centuries of their dominion.

**Shin-kwan,** an important station of the Wesleyan Methodist Mission in the Canton, China, district. It is south of Canton City, not far from San-ui, and like it, is in the region whence Chinese emigrants go forth to the United States and other countries. Land has been bought in the city, on which a school, a hospital, and two houses are to be erected. A dispensary in "Great Street" afforded medical treatment to 1,015 new patients during the year. There are 2 local preachers and 294 members.

**Sholapur,** a town in Bombay, India, 200 miles southeast of Bombay, on the Bombay and Madras Railroad. Temperature 50 to 110° F. Population, about 60,000, Hindus, Moslems. Languages, Marathi, Hindustani, Kanarese. Natives poor, degraded. Mission station A. B. C. F. M. (1861); 2 missionaries and wives, 37 native helpers, 13 out-stations, 6 churches, 295 church-members, 18 schools, 355 students.

**Shonai,** a town on the northwest coast of Nippon, Japan. Climate damp, healthy. Population, 20,000. Mission station Foreign Christian Missionary Society (1888); 2 missionaries and wives, 1 native helper, 20 church-members.

**Shurman, John Adam,** b. Westphalia, Germany, 1810; studied at Berlin; sailed for India July 9th, 1833, as a missionary of the L. M. S.; stationed at Benares February 17th, 1834. He devoted himself to the educational and Scripture-translation department. With others he labored in preparing the Urdu and Hindustani versions of the Scriptures. In April, 1842, he went to Calcutta to superintend the printing of the Urdu version of the Old Testament. Returned to Benares in June, 1843, and left in October for England. Re-embarked for India by the way of New York, without his family, in 1844, and reached Benares February 20th, 1846. He died at Benares October 1st, 1852. Mr. Sherring, who was associated with him, says: "He was a distinguished translator of the Bible into Hindustani."

**Shwe-gyin,** a town in Lower Burma, on the Sitang River, south of Toungoo, 100 miles northeast of Rangoon. Climate tropical. Population, 7,519. Race and language, Burmese. Religion, Buddhism. Mission station American Baptist Missionary Union (1853–55): 1 missionary and wife, 4 native helpers, 1 out-station, 1 church, 17 church-members, 1 school, 44 scholars.

**Shweir,** a town in Northern Syria, northeast of Beirut. Mission station of the Free Church of Scotland; 6 out-stations, 1 missionary, 2 churches, 61 communicants. The Lebanon School Society supports the school work.

**Shweybo,** a mission station of the S. P. G. in the Rangoon diocese, Burma, with 2 missionaries, 28 communicants among the Burmese of the five surrounding villages, 3 schools, 38 scholars.

**Sialkot,** a town in Punjab, British India, on the Aik River, 72 miles northeast of Lahore. The town is very extensive, steadily increasing in size and commercial importance; it is very handsome, well built, and clean, containing many shrines, schools, and public buildings worthy of note. Population, 26,000, Moslems, Hindus, Sikhs, Jains, and Christians. Mission station of the U. P. Church of Scotland (1857); 2 missionaries and wives, 3 female missionaries, 18 native helpers, 68 communicants, 42 theological students, 962 scholars. U. P. Church of America (1885); 3 missionaries and wives, 3 female missionaries, 101 communicants, 327 Sabbath-scholars, 544 day-scholars.

**Siam.**—The kingdom of Siam lies at the southeast corner of Asia, occupying the central and principal portion of the peninsula of Indo-China. It has Burma on the west, Cambodia, Cochin-China, and Tonkin on the east. It stretches along the Malay Peninsula to within four degrees of the equator. Its northern boundary lies between the 20th and 21st parallels of north latitude, and separates it from the independent Shan states. It has a total length from north to south of 1,350 miles, a maximum width of 450 miles, and an estimated area of 190,000 square miles,—or about that of New England and the four Middle states.

*Physical Features.*—The physical contour of the country may be best understood by remembering that both its mountain chains and its rivers have a general north and south direction. Of river systems there are two—that of the Mehan in the west, and that of the Mekong in the east. In their lower courses the rivers traverse immense alluvial plains which are to a large extent overflowed during a portion of the year. In the upper country the mountain walls on either side approach each other in some places so closely as to leave only a narrow gorge, while in others they recede, enclosing fertile plains varying in width from 10 to 50 miles. Nearly all the navigable streams are broken by rapids, which render water communication between the lower and upper courses difficult.

*Climate.*—Although Siam lies wholly within the tropics, the climate is not so hot as that of Southern India. The temperature at Bangkok ranges between 57° and 99° F., with a mean annual temperature of 80°.

The periodical monsoons of the Indian Ocean divide the year into two seasons of about equal length—the rainy season extending from May until October, and the dry season covering the rest of the year.

Owing to the tropical heat, the abundant rainfall, and the annual overflow of the rivers, Siam is a very fertile country.

*Vegetable Products.*—The great staple crops are rice, sugar-cane, cotton, and tobacco. Even under the primitive methods of agriculture in vogue, the yield of rice is sufficient to supply the needs of the people and leave large quantities for export to China and Japan. Considerable silk of excellent quality is produced.

Tropical fruits of all kinds grow in great profusion, and need scarcely any cultivation. The cocoa-nut and betel palms are found everywhere, as also the indispensable bamboo. The forests furnish teak-wood, dye-woods, and valuable gums and resins. The export of teak timber for shipbuilding is a large source of revenue to the kingdom.

*Minerals.*—The mineral wealth of Siam is

largely undeveloped. Gold, silver, iron, copper, antimony, and lead are worked to some extent. Limestone is plentiful, and coal is known to exist, but is not mined. Precious stones—notably rubies, sapphires, and emeralds—abound in certain districts.

*Domestic Animals.*—The domestic animals are the elephant, the water-buffalo, and the Indian bullock. The elephant is used for working timber, for journeying, and on ceremonial occasions. The water-buffalo is the dependence for all agricultural operations, and the bullock is the chief means of transporting goods, away from the watercourses.

*Population.*—The population of Siam is variously estimated at from six to twelve millions. The Siamese and their near kinsmen, the Laos, make up three fourths of the whole; the other fourth is composed of Chinese, Malays, Peguans, and Burmese, the first named being the most numerous and important. The Siamese and Laos are alike members of the Shan race, which at one time (14th century A.D.) dominated the greater part of Indo-China. Outside of Siam the principal seat of the Shans at present is in the independent Shan states, which lie between Siam on the south and Yunnan, the southwest province of the Chinese Empire, on the north.

*Physical Characteristics and Disposition.*— The Siamese are a people of medium stature, well formed, with brown skins, straight, black hair, which is worn short, except by the Laos women; and slightly flattened noses. Their eyes are not set obliquely, as in the Chinese and Japanese. In disposition they are gentle, lively, hospitable, kind to children and to the aged, fond of amusements, but lacking in energy, deceitful, unstable, and conceited. The Laos and Independent Shans are superior to the Siamese proper in strength of body and stability of character. The civilization of the Siamese strongly resembles that of China, but is of a lower grade, as they have not the patient industry, the inventive skill, nor the literary taste of the Chinese. Much of the trade of the country falls into the hands of the Chinese and Burmese. The Chinese in many cases marry Siamese women, and the children of such unions make one of the most promising elements in the population, combining the superior energy of the Chinese with the vivacity and quickness of the Siamese.

*Language.*—The Shans have a common language, broken into several local dialects— e.g., the Siamese, the Laos, and the Shan proper. This tongue is properly a monosyllabic language, and, like the Chinese, has an elaborate system of *tones*, by which words otherwise identical are given different meanings. There are six tones in common use. Thus, for example, the monosyllable *pa* means, according to the tone or inflection given to it, "fish," "jungle," "aunt," "to lead." Words otherwise similar are also distinguished by the value of the initial consonant, whether aspirated or unaspirated. Thus *pha*, with the same inflections as those given in the examples just mentioned, would mean "rock," "to cleave," "cloth," "to unite." Besides the distinction into aspirates and non-aspirates, the mutes and liquids have each two characters assigned to them,—one of which we may call strong, the other weak,—so that the number of consonants is swelled to forty-three. The system of vowels is also

elaborate. The Siamese use a written character entirely distinct from that in use by the Laos. It is thought to have been derived from the Cambodian. The Laos character is of the same type as that used by the Burmese and by the Shans, and in common with them appears to have been derived from the Pali, a dialect of the Sanskrit. Both Siamese and Laos are written from left to right. Vowels are written, some on the line after the consonant, some on the line before the consonant, some under the consonant, and some over it; while some diphthongs, as *au* and *ai*, have one element written before the consonant and one after. Besides the original stock of monosyllables there are many polysyllabic words introduced from the Pali. These are to a large extent *formal* words, used in reference either to religion or to government. Thus the Indian *rajah* appears as *racha*, "royal," in such combinations as *racha-bút*, "king's son;" *rachawong*, "king's palace." With reference to its grammar, Siamese may be said to be an uninflected language. There is no distinction of form to represent person, number, mood, or tense. There is no article; its place must be supplied when necessary by *ni*, "this," or *nan*, "that." There is no distinction of singular and plural: *all* or *many* or a numeral must be added to the singular to mark the plural. There is no conjugation of the verb except by auxiliaries, which are also in use as independent words: e.g., *yu*, "to be," "to dwell," present; *dái*, "to have," and *lao*, "finished," past; *ch* or *cha*, "also," future. There is no declension of the noun. The nominative precedes its verb, the objective follows it; the genitive and the adjective follow their noun; the other cases must be expressed by prepositions. There is also a notable lack of connective particles, as of cause, inference, purpose, etc.; even the simple conjunction "and" is but sparingly used. The chief difficulties of the language for the foreigner lie in the recognition and accurate reproduction of the tones. The chief obstacles to be overcome in translation are the lack of connective particles, the native love for multiplying synonyms, and the observance of a proper mean between the simplicity of the vernacular and the stilted style adopted in the sacred books of Buddhism. It should be added that besides the difference in written character between Siamese and Laos dialects, there are also slight but important differences of vocabulary, of tone, and of idiom—e.g., so common a word as "not" is in Siamese *mi*, in Laos *baw*. Missionaries to the Laos have not hitherto been agreed upon the question whether these differences justify a separate Bible for the Laos; but now (1890) type has been prepared in the Laos character, and it is intended to print at least portions of the Word of God in it.

*Social Customs.*—In their social customs the Siamese present several points of interest to the student of missions. The position of woman is high for an Oriental people. No attempt is made to seclude her, but she moves freely among men, engages in business, holds property in her own name, and is in general the equal of man. Monogamy is the rule, except among the nobility; and even among them the principle of monogamy is recognized in the pre-eminence given to one, generally the first wife. Child marriage is not practised; widows may remarry; divorce is easy. The position of woman is due

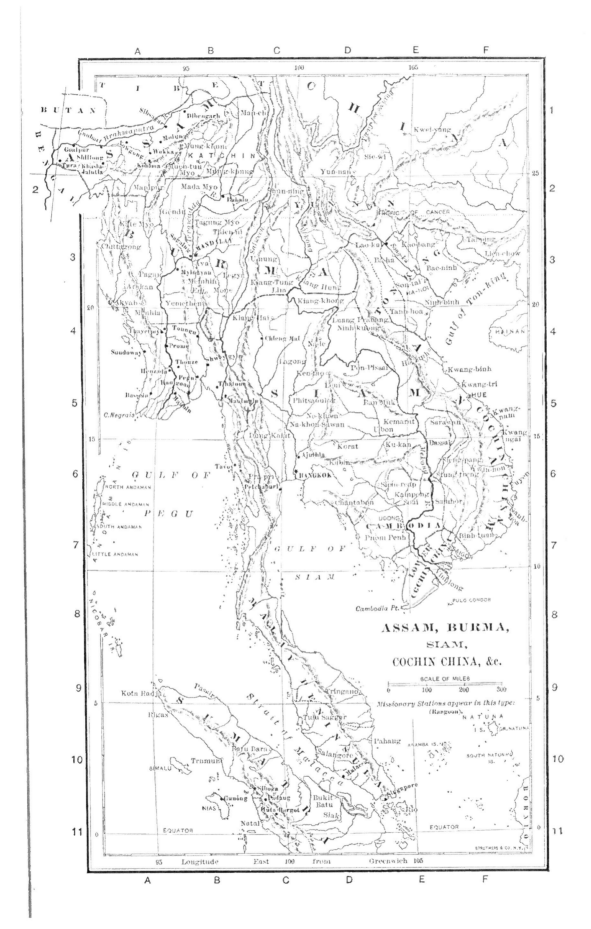

ASSAM, BURMA,
SIAM,
COCHIN CHINA, &c.

SCALE OF MILES

Missionary Stations appear in this type:
(Rangoon).

in part, doubtless, to the beneficent teachings of Buddhism, and in part to the social custom which ordains that a man on marriage shall become a member of his wife's family. Children are kindly treated, and the adoption of children by childless couples is common. Great respect is paid to distinctions of age and rank. There are separate sets of pronouns which must be used with regard to superiors, inferiors, and equals.

*Religions.*—Two religions obtain among the Siamese peoples—Buddhism and the worship of evil spirits. The one is a historic religion, with ancient, sacred books, costly temples, and a numerous priesthood; the other is an unorganized worship, without literature, priesthood, or temples, but in many portions of the country, particularly among the Laos tribes, it rivals, if it does not exceed, Buddhism in its hold upon the popular mind and its influence over the affairs of life.

BUDDHISM.—Buddhism, as understood and practised by the Siamese, revolves about a few leading ideas. The first of these is the wretchedness of existence. Human life from the Buddhist point of view is essentially unhappy. Strong emphasis is laid upon the pains, sorrows, failures, disappointments, and unsatisfied longings. The end to be sought is deliverance from these evils. Not holiness, but happiness, is the goal. But because Buddhism knows nothing of God and the satisfaction of the soul in fellowship with God, it looks for nothing more than a negative happiness, to be attained by the extinction of desire. Only when desire in all its forms—even the desire for existence itself—is done away with, can the soul be emancipated from its wretchedness. When desire is quenched, the soul will enter upon that state of existence without self-consciousness which constitutes Nirvâna, the Buddhist heaven. But this must be a slow process—too slow to be attained within the limits of a single lifetime, but requiring an indefinite course of ages. And this brings us to the second great idea in practical Buddhism—the transmigration of the soul. It is true, indeed, that according to theoretical Buddhism there can be no transmigration of the soul, because the soul is not an entity, but only a relation of unity between the various powers and faculties exhibited by man. As it has no separate existence, it cannot survive the death of the body. Death snaps the bond by which the faculties and feelings are held together, and suffers all to fall apart, or rather would do so, but that instantly, in a way entirely obscure, there arises a new set of powers and faculties in connection with a new body, but in character precisely what the old ones would have been had death not intervened. This is the philosophical tenet of *Karma*. It need scarcely be said, however, that this is too subtle for popular comprehension. For the great majority of Siamese Buddhists the truth is expressed by the common doctrine of the transmigration of the soul, according to which the present life is but one in a long series of existences, some past, some still to come. In each past existence the soul has inhabited a different body, sometimes that of a man, sometimes that of some animal; and so must it continue to do in future existences.

And here intervenes a third leading idea—that of merit and demerit. The state of the man in each new existence, the character of the body of which he will become the inmate, the environment in which he will move, the proportion of pleasure to pain in his experience, will depend upon the amount of merit or demerit resultant from his conduct in previous existences. The constant effort of the Buddhist, therefore, is to acquire merit, and to avoid the incurring of demerit. But it must not be supposed that "merit and demerit" are terms synonymous with "holiness and unholiness," or even with "righteousness and unrighteousness." They are equivalent rather to "profit and loss." Merit is the result of conformity to the precepts of Buddhism, and these are directed, as already noted, not to holiness, but to happiness: not to the overcoming of sin, but to the eradication of the principle of misery—desire. And while in these precepts are included the prohibitions of the second table of the Decalogue, and the command to universal charity, the vast majority of them are of a ceremonial rather than a moral or spiritual character. Merit is to be acquired by kindness, justice, truth, it is true; but far more stress is laid in the popular teaching upon the building, decoration, and maintenance of temples, the support of the priests, the giving of fêtes, and the observance of ceremonial usage. Indeed, if one will only be sufficiently diligent in these latter directions he may safely be somewhat reckless in regard to loss of merit through violations of the moral law. Hence Siam is a land of many temples. Scarce a village but has one, while in the larger cities the number rises into scores, or even hundreds. Each temple has a monastery attached to it, and a number of resident priests, and young men and boys in training for the priesthood. To become a priest is the most effective way of making merit for a man; for a woman the best thing is to have many sons, who may acquire merit for her by becoming priests. The majority of men in Siam and the Laos country spend at least a few years in the priesthood.

It will readily be seen from this brief account of Buddhism, as held and practised in Siam, that it constitutes a formidable barrier to the progress of Christianity. Simply as the ancient religion of the country, it is strongly intrenched in the popular regard. "It is not the custom of our ancestors" is often considered a sufficient reply to the best-constructed argument for Christianity. Buddhism, too, is interwoven with the whole social life of the people—scarcely a family but has or has had a member in its priesthood. Its fêtes furnish the principal opportunity for social pleasures. Vast sums of money have been invested in its temples, pagodas, and monasteries, and in the support of its priests. It makes strong appeal to the self-righteous tendencies of the human heart. It operates powerfully to deaden the conscience, and to discredit the possibility of a vicarious atonement for wrong-doing.

WORSHIP OF EVIL SPIRITS.—Side by side with Buddhism, and to a large degree intermingled with it, is the religion of demon-worship. This is but one form of that Shamanism which prevails so largely in Asia and Africa. What gives it interest is the extent to which it affects the lives of the people. The spirits or demons, some of which may be said to correspond to the elves and fairies of western superstitions, but the majority of which are believed to be in greater or less degree malevolent, are of several different kinds. Some are local genii,—spirits of the forests, the mountains, the streams, the caves. Others preside over certain natural phenomena,—as thunder, rain, wind; or over particular operations,—as ploughing, sowing, reaping, house-building; or certain situations in human experience,—notably birth, marriage, sickness, death. A vast multitude also are spirits of deceased persons. It would be easy to draw out these general statements into detail, but enough has been said to make it apparent how a superstition so elastic may be brought into connection with every event of life, and how it may cast the shade of fear over the whole of earthly existence. And this is the actual result. With every day and every turn in life the spirit-worshipper must consider how his conduct will be regarded by these invisible and for the most part malignant powers. His constant effort is to propitiate them. For this purpose he relies upon offerings, sometimes of animals, more frequently of food and flowers, and upon charms, spells, and incantations. In the more difficult questions he must have recourse to the professional medium or exorcist. This burdensome superstition finds its natural climax in the belief that in many instances sickness or misfortune is due to witchcraft. Severe injuries are not infrequently inflicted upon the supposed victim of such evil influence with the purpose of making the possessing spirit reveal the identity of the witch. Persons adjudged to be witches are driven from their homes, their houses burnt, and their gardens uprooted. There are in the Laos provinces cities where the whole population consists of such persons and their families.

Potent as this demon-worship is in its influence upon the people of Siam, and especially of the Laos provinces, it is less serious than Buddhism as a hindrance to the progress of the gospel. Since disease in its various forms is largely attributed to the influence of demons, medical missionary practice does much to weaken this superstition. So does the mission school, with its rational explanations of natural phenomena. And so heavy is the incubus of fear which this belief lays upon its adherents, that they are prepared to hail as good tidings a religion that promises relief.

*History of Missions.*—EARLY EFFORTS. —It was as a possible door of entrance to China that Siam first attracted the attention of Protestant Christians. In the year 1828, Dr. Karl Gutzlaff, who had gone to Singapore under the Netherlands Missionary Society, accompanied by Rev. Mr. Tomlin of the London Missionary Society, visited Bangkok. Convinced that here was an open door for missionary effort, these brethren sent an appeal to the American churches for men to occupy the field. This appeal was brought to America by the same trading vessel which brought the famous "Siamese Twins." In response the American Board instructed the Rev. David Abeel, then stationed in Canton, to visit Siam, with a view to the establishment of a mission there. Meanwhile Gutzlaff and Tomlin had been earnestly at work. While their attention was principally given to the Chinese, whom they found numerous in Bangkok, Dr. Gutzlaff prepared a tract in Siamese, and made a translation of one of the Gospels. But the death of his wife and the collapse of his own health compelled him to leave Siam for China. Mr. Tomlin also was shortly called away to take charge of the Anglo-Chinese College at Malacca; and Mr. Abeel, who had arrived just after Dr. Gutzlaff's departure, was, after fifteen months' stay, compelled by ill-health to abandon the field (November, 1832).

BAPTIST MISSIONS.—Besides the appeal to the American churches, Gutzlaff and Tomlin had sent one also to the American Baptist Mission in Burmah. It is interesting to note in this connection that the very earliest effort on the part of a Protestant for the evangelization of the Siamese was made by Mrs. Ann Hasseltine Judson, who had, by the help of a Siamese resident in Rangoon, learned something of the Siamese tongue, and had translated into it the catechism just prepared by Dr. Judson for the Burmans, also a tract and the Gospel of Matthew. The catechism was printed (1819) on the mission press at Serampore, and is believed to be the first Christian book ever printed in Siamese. In response to the appeal made to them, the American missionaries in Burma commissioned Rev. J. T. Jones, one of their own number, a missionary to Siam. He arrived in March, 1833, and was permitted to continue in the work until his death in 1851. (See article A. B. M. U., Siam Mission.)

MISSIONS OF THE A. B. C. F. M.—The attempt of the American Board to establish a mission in Siam, which had come to an end with the departure of Mr. Abeel (1832), was renewed by the sending out of Messrs. Johnson and Robinson, who reached Bangkok in 1834. They were joined a year later by Daniel B. Bradley, M.D., who arrived in the same vessel with Mr. Dean of the Baptist Mission. These two men were destined to enjoy long periods of missionary service. Dr. Dean continued his labors for the Chinese, with sundry interruptions, until 1885. Dr. Bradley was ordained to the ministry in 1838. He was a man of versatile powers, and left an abiding mark on the Siamese nation. As preacher, teacher, physician, author, translator, and printer, he labored with untiring devotion for thirty-eight years, when he was removed by death (1873). He still lives, however, not only in the influence of his own life, but in the persons of his widow, and of his children and grandchildren, six of whom have had an active share in missionary work for the Siamese. Like the Baptists, the missionaries of the American Board at first carried on missions both to the Chinese and the Siamese, but with the opening of China proper the laborers engaged among the Chinese were withdrawn. The mission to the Siamese was maintained until 1849, when it was brought to a close by the departure of Rev. Asa Hemenway, the Board's only remaining missionary, Dr. Bradley having previously withdrawn his connection with it.

As yet but slight results had been obtained, either by the missionaries of the American Board or by their Baptist brethren, in the conversion of the Siamese. But much had been accomplished in other directions. The missionaries by their blameless and self-denying lives, and especially by their success in healing the sick, had won the esteem of the native community. By preaching and teaching, and by translating, printing, and distributing portions of the Scriptures and Christian tracts, they had brought the truth into contact with a multitude of minds; and especially ought we in estimating their labors to be mindful of the influence which one of their number was permitted to exercise.

*Influence of Rev. Jesse Caswell.*—This was the Rev. Jesse Caswell, a missionary of the American Board, who arrived in Bangkok in 1840. The king who then ruled Siam was a usurper. At the death of the preceding king he had seized the government, compelling his nephew, the rightful heir to the throne, to seek safety by becoming a Buddhist priest. While pursuing his studies the young prince made the acquaintance of Mr. Caswell, with whom he was so much pleased that he invited the missionary to become his private tutor. The invitation was accepted, and for eighteen months this future king of Siam was under the daily instruction of Mr. Caswell. In this way the prince gained a knowledge of English, some acquaintance with Western civilization, and an introduction to the natural sciences, astronomy in particular. He learned, too, to put a high estimate upon the missionaries and their work, especially in its educational features. When, on the death of the usurper in 1851, he was raised to the throne, the results of these enlightening influences were at once felt. His predecessor had been a despotic and narrow-minded ruler, opposed to foreigners and all foreign innovations. He had rebuffed the overtures made by England and the United States for commercial treaties, and had used such rudeness toward Sir James Brooke, the English ambassador, that war with England seemed imminent. The new king at once instituted a more liberal policy. In 1855 treaties were consummated with England and the United States. The king also took frequent opportunity to show the favor with which he regarded the missionaries. Mr. Caswell having died in 1848, his Majesty erected a monument over his grave, and sent his widow presents amounting to $1,500. He afterward invited the wives of several of the missionaries to act as teachers to the ladies of his household, and at a still later time employed an English lady, Mrs. A. H. Leonowens, as governess for his children, among whom was the present king of Siam. From 1851 until the present time the missionaries have been treated with great kindness and marked respect. On several occasions the king has made liberal contributions to the educational and medical departments of the work. Upon the conclusion of the treaty with the United States (1856) the Siamese Government requested that one of the missionaries (Rev. Stephen Mattoon) should be appointed consul. In 1878 another missionary (Rev. S. G. McFarland) was placed in charge of the newly opened "Royal College" in Bangkok, with the office of Superintendent of Public Instruction. The son of a missionary, himself an active Christian, he for many years held a high position in the Foreign Office. In 1882 the present king gave an audience to a newly arrived party of missionaries, on which occasion he made use of language in the highest degree commendatory of the influence exerted upon his people by their predecessors. Within the last year (1890) a medical missionary has been placed in charge of two hospitals, and a dispensary opened in Bangkok by the Siamese Government, and this with the understanding that no restriction is to be put upon his work as a Christian missionary. Such favor shown the missionaries by the rulers of the land has had marked effect in giving the gospel free course among the people, and this advantage is due in large measure to the influence exerted by Mr. Caswell upon the late king.

PRESBYTERIAN MISSIONS.—One other of the American churches was to have a share in the work of missions in Siam. This was the Presbyterian Church (North). In 1848 the Presbyterian Board of Foreign Missions sent to Bangkok the Rev. William Buell and his wife. After three years of service they were compelled by the ill-health of Mrs. Buell to leave the field. The work was then suspended until 1847, when it was renewed by Rev. Stephen Mattoon and Samuel R. House, M.D. This mission continues until the present, and is now the only Protestant agency for the evangelization of the Siamese. Some points in its history may be briefly outlined. The first convert, Nai Chune, was baptized in 1859,—twelve years after the permanent establishment of the mission. What progress has been made since then may be judged from the statement taken from the last annual report of the Presbyterian Board, that at one station (Chieng Mai) "there have been adult accessions to the membership (of the church) at each monthly communion for the last twenty-two months, and in fifty-five out of the last sixty-one months, or since October, 1884."

In 1861 the mission opened a new station in Petchaburee, an important city, 85 miles southwest of Bangkok, and capital of a flourishing province of the same name. It was first occupied by Rev. Messrs. Daniel McGilvary and S. G. MacFarland. This station has been a prosperous one. It has now in connection with it 5 churches, numbering 267 communicants. It also maintains 12 day-schools, a boarding-school for boys, and an industrial school for girls. In 1882 a mission hospital was opened, and has since been carried on with marked success. The Petchaburee station has now become a centre of Christian influence not only for the province in which it is situated, but also for the provinces lying to the south, along the Gulf of Siam.

*Mission to the Laos.*—Another important step was taken in 1867 in the establishment of a mission to the Laos tribes. These are the inhabitants of the six provinces tributary to the King of Siam, which constitute the northern half of his dominions. Interest in the evangelization of these tribes was first awakened through the presence in the neighborhood of Petchaburee of a large colony of Laos, whose ancestors in a time of political disturbance had put themselves under the protection of the King of Siam, who had assigned them a residence in the province of Petchaburee. In 1863 Messrs. McGilvary and Wilson of the Petchaburee Mission made a tour of exploration to Chieng Mai, the capital of the most powerful Laos province. This important city is situated on the river Maa Ping, about 500 miles north of Bangkok. In 1867 Mr. McGilvary removed thither with his family, and Mr. Wilson and his wife followed him a year later. The courage exhibited in this undertaking may be seen in the fact that, owing to the rapid current of the river and the numerous rapids which break its course, the boat journey from Bangkok to Chieng Mai requires from six to ten weeks. The labor of the missionaries was soon rewarded by the baptism of their first convert, Nan Inta, a man of more than usual ability, and learned in the Buddhist religion. His faith in Buddhism was first seriously shaken by the verification of the prediction made by the missionaries of the eclipse of August 18th, 1868. His conversion was followed within a few months by that of six others.

Martyrdom of Laos Christians.—These successes aroused the fanaticism of the king of Chieng Mai, who had at first welcomed the missionaries. Having failed in an attempt to secure their recall to Bangkok by charging upon them a scarcity of rice, which had prevailed about the time of their arrival, he suddenly caused the arrest of two of the converts (Noi Soonya' and Nan Chai). The arrest was made upon the false pretext that they had failed to perform public work assigned to them. But when they were brought before the king, he demanded that they renounce their connection with Christianity. Upon their refusal they were tortured by means of cords made fast in the holes in the lobes of their ears, and then drawn tightly over a beam. In this position they spent the night. The next day (September 12th, 1869) they were again examined, and upon their renewed avowal of their steadfastness were clubbed to death. The remaining church-members took refuge in flight, and for a time the missionaries themselves were in extreme peril. But at this juncture the persecuting king was called to Bangkok to attend the obsequies of his master, the King of Siam, who had died from a fever contracted during a scientific expedition to a southern province for the purpose of observing that eclipse which had been used of God for the conversion of Nan Inta', the first Laos convert. While in Bangkok the king of Chieng Mai fell ill, and died before he could reach his capital. Since his death the missionaries and their converts have enjoyed a fair degree of toleration. This has been due in part to the act of the present enlightened King of Siam in issuing, in 1878, a "Proclamation of religious liberty for the Laos." This he did in response to an appeal from the missionaries in Chieng Mai, on behalf of two native Christians who wished to be married in Christian fashion, without making the offerings to spirits customary on such occasions. Their heathen relatives attempted to prevent the marriage, and were supported in their attempt by the authorities; so there was nothing left for the missionaries but to appeal to Bangkok. The resulting "proclamation" has since proved an effective instrument for holding the persecuting spirit in check.

Medical missionary work was begun in Chieng Mai in 1875 with the opening of a dispensary, since developed into a hospital. A boarding-school for girls was opened in 1878, and one for boys in 1888. The former now (1890) has 91 pupils, the latter 94.

In 1885 a new station was established in the city of Lakawn, capital of the province of the same name. Lakawn is situated on the river Maa Wang, and is 75 miles southeast from Chieng Mai. The first missionaries were Rev. S. C. Peoples, M.D., and his wife. Here also there is a mission hospital. An industrial school for boys is just being put into operation, and it is probable that the Laos press will be set up here. The Laos Mission has vigorous churches also in three other provinces—Lapon, which joins Chieng Mai on the south; and Chieng Hai (Chieng Rai) and Chieng San (Khiang Hsen) to the northwest of Chieng Mai.

The Presbyterian Board of Foreign Missions has in Siam and the Laos provinces five stations—Bangkok, Petchaburee, Ratburee (on river Maaklong, half-way between Bangkok and Petchaburee; opened 1889), Chieng Mai, and Lakawn. In connection with these stations there are now (1890) 13 ordained missionaries; 21 lay missionaries, of whom 4 are physicians; 33 native helpers, 20 of them ordained; 12 churches; 1,114 communicants; 21 schools with 641 pupils; 4 hospitals, and 2 mission presses. The missionaries have translated, revised, and published the whole Bible in Siamese. They have prepared also a hymn-book and many other religious works, besides text-books for use in the mission schools.

It will thus be seen that the time has come when the speedy evangelization of Siam may be looked for. The whole land is open to missionary effort. Prejudice has been overcome, and the missionaries are held in high esteem. Important centres have been seized. The Bible has been translated. Schools and hospitals have been established, and a substantial church has been gathered. These are broad foundations; it only needs that the present generation of Christians should be worthy of their opportunity, and the walls will rise apace.

**Siamese Version.**—The Siamese belongs to the Tai family of the Indo-China languages, and is spoken in the kingdom of Siam. A translation of the New Testament into Siamese was commenced by Messrs. Gutzlaff and Tomlin, and after a careful revision by the Rev. J. T. Jones, one of the Baptist missionaries at Burma, it was printed in two vols. at Bangkok, 1843, aided by a grant from the American Baptist Bible Society. A second of 1,000 copies was issued at Bangkok, 1850. Another translation of the New Testament was made by the Rev. M. Mattoon of the American Mission, but this version needs revising. The work of revision was undertaken by the American missionaries N. A. McDonald and Van Dyke, who in connection with other missionaries undertook a translation of the Old Testament also. The first edition was published in 1881, a second in 1886.

(*Specimen verse.* John 3 : 16.)

ด้วยว่าพระเจ้าเท้าทรงรักษ์โลกนั้น, จนถึง ประทานบุทรชเศก์เกียวขอร พระองค์, เพื่อทุกคนที่ไว้เชื่อถือในบุทร นั้น, ชะมิได้ฉิบทาย, แต่จะมีชีวิกรอยู่ชั่วนินิศก์.

**Sibogu,** a town of Sumatra, East Indies, on the coast, northwest of Pakenten. Mission station of the Rhenish Missionary Society; 2 missionaries, 1 lady, 16 native workers, 460 adherents, 54 communicants, 79 school-children.

**Sibsagar,** a town of Assam, India, on the Dikhu River, nine miles from the Brahmaputra; the seat of the river trade; once a very important place, as proved by the ruins of a magnificent tank, with temples and palaces along its border, and still interesting on account of its tea-gardens. Population, 5,868, Hindus, Moslems, Christians. Mission station American Baptist Missionary Union (1874); 2 missionaries and wives, 5 native helpers, 7 out-stations, 3 churches, 147 church-members, 3 schools, 14 scholars. In 1889 a missionary was sent here to commence work among the Kols; the former missionary had been working only among the Assamese.

**Sidon** (Saida), a city on the coast of Syria, 20 miles south of Beirut, on the site of the ancient Zidon. Population about 11,000. Mission station of the Presbyterian Church (North), 1851; 1 missionary and wife, 2 female missionaries in charge of a female seminary, 1 academy with 140 scholars.

**Sierra Leone,** a rich and fertile peninsula on the west coast of Africa (Sierra Leone proper), which, with the island of Sherbro and much adjacent territory, forms a crown colony of Great Britain. It extends from the Scarcies River on the north to the border of Liberia, 180 miles, with an area of 3,000 square miles, of which only one tenth belongs to Sierra Leone proper. The shore is low, but back of it rise rugged mountains 3,000 feet in height. It was originally (1787) a settlement for the "liberated Africans" who were set free from the slave ships; sometimes 2,000 slaves were settled here in a year. Coming from almost every part of Africa, many languages were spoken, but English became the common tongue. The moral condition of the natives was most degraded; barbarism, immorality, and superstition reigned supreme. The population in 1888 numbered 75,000, and through the influence of the missions there were in 1881 39,048 Protestants and 369 Catholics. The climate is most unhealthy, so that it has been called the "white man's grave."

Freetown, with a population of 4,930 inhabitants, is the capital. Missionary societies: S. P. G.; stations, Domingia and Farringia: 3 missionaries. Wesleyan Methodist, including Gambia; stations at Freetown, Wellington, Hastings, Waterloo, York, Wilberforce, Sherbro, Limbah; 18 missionaries and assistant missionaries, 5,821 communicants. C. M. S. (1816); 2 missionaries, 2 lady teachers, Fourah Bay College, Anna Walsh Institute, 12 stations. United Methodist Free Church; 6 stations; 1 missionary, 7 native helpers. United Brethren (U. S. A.); 12 stations, 5 missionaries, 154 members, 234 day-scholars, 236 Sunday-scholars; all in the Sherbro district. African Methodist Episcopal Church; stations at Freetown and interior; 2 missionaries. The mission of the C. M. S. has resulted in the establishment of a native church, with numerous pastorates and out-stations, 59 lay teachers, 41 female teachers, 12,929 members, 5,777 communicants, 43 schools, 4,750 pupils. Seventy years ago Sierra Leone was a heathen land: to-day it is filled with places of worship.

**Sigompulan,** a town of Northwest Sumatra near the west coast and north of Sipirok. Mission station of the Rhenish Missionary Society; 1 ordained missionary, 1 female missionary, 10 native workers, 50 communicants, 96 school-children.

**Sih-chau,** a town in Shansi, North China, southwest of Tai-yuen. Mission station of the China Inland Mission (1885); 1 missionary and wife, 2 single ladies, 2 churches, 14 church-members.

**Sihanaka,** a town in Madagascar near Tamatave. Mission station of the L. M. S. (1875); 2 missionaries, 48 native helpers, 188 church-members, 3,352 school-children.

**Silo** (Shiloh), a town among the Kafirs in Tambuki, East South Africa, on the Klipplaat River, 700 miles northeast of Cape Town. Mission station of the Moravians, opened in 1828, from the station Gnadendal (in accordance with a request of Lord Somerset that they should commence work on the northeast frontier of the colony), by three missionaries with some twenty Hottentots and a remarkable Kafir woman, who shortly after saved the mission from destruction by her bravery and eloquence, during an attack of the hostile chief of Tambuki. (See Moravian Missions, Eastern Province.) Silo has often suffered during the Kafir wars, once being laid in ruins, but it was rebuilt, and is now in a very flourishing condition, under the care of 3 missionaries and their wives.

**Simla,** a city of the Punjab, India, 170 miles north of Delhi. Chief sanitarium and summer capital of India. A very pleasant place, except for its inadequate water supply. Climate cool, exhilarating, healthy, though for several reasons the difficulties of drainage are considerable. Population, in summer 17,000, in winter 8,000, Hindus, Moslems, Sikhs, Jains, Christians. Mission station of the Baptist Missionary Society; 1 missionary, 10 native helpers, 3 out-stations, 160 church-members. C. M. S.; 1 missionary, 5 native helpers, 1 school, 63 scholars, 157 church-members.

**Simonton, Ashbel Green,** b. West Hanover, Penn., U. S. A., January 20th, 1833; graduated at Princeton College 1852; taught two years, and graduated at Princeton Theological Seminary 1858; ordained by the Presbytery of Carlisle; appointed the first missionary of the Presbyterian Board to Brazil, and reached Rio de Janeiro August 12th, 1859. While acquiring the language he preached in English to Americans and other foreigners. He soon became an effective preacher in Portuguese, and his ministry was remarkably blessed. In 1862 a church was organized in Rio, to which at almost every communion additions were made, mostly from the Church of Rome. He employed the press as an important auxiliary. He translated the Shorter Catechism and other works into Portuguese. He edited also the "Imprensa Evangelica," a religious monthly, sustained chiefly by his own articles, which were often of rare value, and attracted the attention of readers among the educated classes. His strength being overtaxed by his incessant labors, he took a journey to São Paulo, was attacked with fever at the house of his brother-in-law, Rev. Mr. Blackford, and died December 9th, 1867.

One of Mr. Simonton's colleagues has thus referred to him: "He was looked upon by all the members of the mission as our leader and chief stay, as he had been our pioneer. We took no important step, save from absolute necessity, without first hearing his counsels. The most talented, most learned, and best-formed of our members; master of the language, and possessing in unusual degree tact and prudence for planning and executing,—we have no one left to fill his place." Resolutions were drawn up by the United States consul, and adopted at a meeting held in the consulate, expressing the esteem of his countrymen and of many Brazilians.

**Simorangkir,** a town of Northwest Sumatra, northwest of Pantjurnapitti. Mission station of the Rhenish Missionary Society; 1 ordained missionary, 1 female missionary, 15 native workers, 103 communicants, 102 school-children.

**Sind** (British India), the most northwestern province of the Bombay Presidency. It occupies the lower part of the Indus valley, including the delta of that river. North of it lies the Punjab; west, Baluchistan; east, Rajputana; and south the Arabian Sea and the Rann of Kachchh. Its limits of north latitude are 23° and 28° 40´, and of east longitude 66° 50 and 71°. Including a small native state occupying a part of the territory, the area is 54,123 square miles, and the population 2,542,976, giving an average density of only 47 to the square mile; this sparsity of population is accounted for by the sterile nature of much of the soil. The country is largely destitute of trees, flat, and uninteresting in appearance. Its soil is in many places strongly impregnated with salt. Mohammedans preponderate, over three quarters of the population being of that faith. Hindus constitute only an eighth; Sikhs (members of a sect originating in the Punjab) about 5 per cent, aboriginal tribes about 3 per cent, Christians over 6,000, Jains and Parsis a thousand or more each. The Sindis represent the original Hindu population, but are now Mohammedans, having been converted under the reign of early Mohammedan rulers. The history of the province is complicated, and not of special interest. For many centuries it was ruled now by Hindu and now by Mohammedan dynasties. As English power on the west coast became stronger, entanglements with outlying native rulers were inevitable. At times the use of armed force against them was necessary for self-defence or for retaliation; and at other times treaties for trade and commerce would be made, and very likely broken, which again was supposed to render necessary military measures. As a result of such relationships, Sind was conquered in 1843 by an army under Sir Charles Napier, and formally annexed to British dominions. It is administered by a commissioner under the governor of Bombay. Karachi is the capital and chief town; it lies at the northern end of the Indus delta, and by the erection of elaborate harbor works it has been made one of the most important sea-ports in Western India. Its population (according to the census of 1881, the authority for all these statistics) is 73,560. The other large towns are Haiderabad, 48,153; Shikarpur, 42,496. There is constant communication between Karachi and Bombay by steamer; and the province is connected by rail with the railway system of Upper India.

The Church Missionary Society occupied Karachi in 1850, and Haiderabad in 1857. The success has been small. The American Methodists began work in Karachi, largely among unevangelized Europeans, in 1872 or 1873. Education has made rapid progress since the advent of British power. In 1859-60 there were only 20 government schools; in 1883-84 there were 340, with 23,273 pupils. There are also private schools, not included in the government figures. The census of 1881 returned over 27,000 males and over 2,000 females as under instruction, and nearly 77,000 males and over 2,800 females as able to read and write. The language in principal use is Sindhi, one of the Sanskrit family, to which Marathi, Hindi, Bengali, etc., belong.

**Sindhia's Dominions** (British India), a native state protected by the paramount power of British India (see article Native States). Otherwise known, from its chief city, as Gwalior State. Ruled over by the Maharaja Sindhia, descendant of one of the great Maratha princes of the last century. The situation of Gwalior is north latitude 26° 13´ and east longitude 78° 12´, 65 miles south of Agra. Sindhia's territories consist of blocks or masses of country intermingled with other areas belonging to other chieftains or to the British Government. Thus any attempt at defining his boundaries is impossible. The population numbers (1881) a little over 3,100,000. These are mostly Hindus; Mohammedans constitute a little more than a twentieth of the whole. Few native states in India exceed Sindhia's in size and importance. His chief city, Gwalior, is renowned as containing some of the finest specimens of Hindu architecture extant, and as the site of a famous rock fortress. There is also a very old Jain temple here.

Gwalior has been occupied by the American Presbyterians as a mission station. There are 92 schools with nearly 3,000 pupils in the state—rather a small showing for so large and important a state.

**Sindhi Version.**—The Sindhi belongs to the Indic branch of the Aryan family of languages, and is spoken in the province of Sind, belonging to the Bombay Presidency. A translation of the Gospel of Matthew was issued in 1825 at Serampore, in Arabic characters. Between the years 1859 and 1868 the Gospels and the Acts were prepared by the Rev. A. Burn of the Church Missionary Society, and published in 1868 at London under the care of Mr. A. Burn by the British and Foreign Bible Society. The work of translation was continued by the Revs. Burn, C. W. Isenberg, and G. Shirt, and a complete edition of the New Testament was published under the care of the Rev. Joseph Redman, in 1889. Besides the New Testament, the following parts of the Old Testament were published: Genesis, translated by the Rev. A. Burn, and the Psalms, translated by the Rev. G. Shirt, both published in 1882; Isaiah, also translated by Mr. Shirt, published in 1888. Besides the Sindhi version in Arabic, the same Society published at Oxford the Gospel of Luke in the Hindi, and that of John in the Gurmukhi character, as prepared by Mr. Burn.

(*Specimen verses.* John 3 : 16.)

Arabic.

جا کان ذ خُداءِ جهان کِی اِهڙو پيارو رکيو
جو پهنجو هِڪڙوئي جَڱَلَ پُت ڏِناءَ ذ
جيڪوڪو تنهِ نِي وِساهَ آڱي سو چِت
ذ نِئِي وِتر هميشه جِڱَلَ لهي

Gurmukhi.

ਛਾ ਧੀ ਤਈੇਸ਼ੁਰ ਜਗਤ ਖੇ ਇਤ੍ਰੇ ਪਿਆਰੇ ਰੁਖੇ ਜੋ ਪਨ੍ਜੇ
ਹਿਕੜੇ ਈ ਜਲਯਲ ਪੁਤ੍ ਡਿਨਾਈਂ ਤ ਜੇਕੋ ਕੋ ਤਨਿ ਤੇ ਦੇਸਾਲੁ
ਆਏੇ ਸੇ ਨਾਸੁ ਨ ਥਿਏ ਵੇਤਰਿ ਸਰਾ ਜਿਅਲ ਲਹੇ ॥

**Si-ngan,** a city in the province of Shensi,
China, has 8 mosques, 3 Roman Catholic chapels, and the famous Nestorian monument of A. D.
781. In 1881 the China Inland Mission established a station here, which was destroyed in
1883; and so far, (1889) no work has been recommenced in the city itself, but three missionaries
and assistants are working in the surrounding
plain.

**Singapore,** an island about 27 miles long,
by 14 wide, containing an area of 206 square
miles, is situated at the southern extremity of
the Malay peninsula, from which it is separated
by a strait about three quarters of a mile wide.
It is a part of the crown colony of Great Britain named the Straits Settlements. A number
of small islands adjacent to it are also included
in its territory. The inhabitants of the island
are Europeans (2,769), Malays (22,155),
Chinese (86,766), and natives of India (12,058)
according to the census of 1881. Singapore
town, at the southeastern part of the island, is
the seat of government for the Settlements,
has a well-defended harbor, and has 12¼ miles
of tramway. The climate is warm, but not unhealthy. Mission work is carried on by the S.
P. G., with 1 missionary at the town of Singapore. Presbyterian Church of England, 1 missionary and wife; and in 1889 the Methodist
Episcopal Church (North) made this a starting-point and prospective headquarters of their
Malaysia Mission—see account under Methodist Episcopal Church (North),—and have already
a large force of 5 missionaries, 3 assistants, 1
female missionary, working among the Chinese,
the Malays, and the Tamils, together with an
Anglo-Chinese school and a medical work.
The report shows 107 members, 380 pupils in
Anglo-Chinese school, 50 day-scholars, 160
Sabbath-scholars.

**Singhana,** a town in the Shaikhawati district of the Jaipur state, Rajputana, India, 95
miles southwest of Delhi, 80 miles north of
Jaipur City. Population (1881), 5,259, Hindus
and Moslems. It is said to be a handsome town,
built of stone, on the skirts of a hill of purplish
rocks, 600 feet high. Station of the Gossner
Missionary Society.

**Sinhalese Version.**—The Sinhali belongs to the Indic branch of the Aryan family
of languages, and is spoken in the southern part
of Ceylon, from Batticaloa on the east to the
river Chilaw on the west, and in the interior.
In the year 1739 the four Gospels, translated
by the Rev. W. Konjim, a Dutch minister,
were published at Colombo, under the care of
the Rev. J. P. Wetzel, and in a revised and
corrected form in 1780 under the care of the
Revs. Fybrands and Philipsz. The Acts were
published in 1771, and in 1776 the New Testament was issued from the press. In 1775 a metrical version of the Psalms was published at
Colombo, and republished in 1778. In 1783
the Books of Genesis, Exodus, and Leviticus, as
translated by Mr. Philipsz, were also published.
When, in 1812, the Colombo Auxiliary Bible
Society was formed, the existing translation

underwent a thorough revision; and in 1823 the
Bible, as prepared by Messrs. Armour, Tolfrey,
Chater, and Clough, was published at Colombo.
A new translation, which the Rev. Lambrick of
the Church Mission at Cotta, near Colombo
(whence it is called the "Cotta Version"), had
undertaken, was published at the expense of
the Church Missionary Society at Cotta, 1834.
As both these versions had their merits, and as
it was deemed important to have one standard
translation of the Scriptures, a revision committee was appointed in 1853, with a view of reconciling the Colombo and Cotta versions. The
Bible thus revised was issued in 1856, and
adopted by all the Protestant communities. In
1885 the British Bible Society, in response to a
resolution of the Kandy Auxiliary, supported
by the Colombo Auxiliary, agreed to undertake
a revision of the Bible. The Rev. S. Coles of
the Church Missionary Society has undertaken
the chief labor of revision, but he will be
assisted by a committee in Ceylon, appointed
by the Auxiliaries of Colombo and Kandy, who
will finally revise the work.

(*Specimen verse.* John 3 : 16.)

මක්නිසාද් ලෙවඟන්තේ අඟ්ගා තන්තා පිත-
ලෙඟ්ම විනාය හොාම බඩනාල් ඉිවනාල ලඬිහ
ිනාය දෙවිඳවිහන්තේ තමවිහන්තේගේ ඒක
රසාපුත්ගා දෙමින් ලොවට පරම්නා කරන්ා කළ
ෙඬ්ක.

**Si-ning,** a prefectural city in the western
part of Kansuh, China, northwest of Lanchau.
Mission station of the C. I. M. (1885); 4 missionaries, wives, and assistants.

**Sinnoris,** a town in Upper Egypt, in the
province of Fayoum, not far from that city.
Mission out-station of the United Presbyterian
Church, U. S. A. (1868); 4 native workers, 96
church-members, 2 schools, 116 scholars.

**Sinoe** (Greenville), a town in Liberia, West
Africa, 150 miles southeast of Monrovia.
Warm, but healthy. Population, 500 to 700,
chiefly Negroes. Language (at Sinoe) English.
Religion (at Sinoe) Christian, of adjacent tribes
paganism. Mission station Presbyterian
Church (North), 1846; 2 missionaries, 1 missionary's wife, 1 out-station, 1 church, 100
members, 1 school, 17 scholars. Protestant
Episcopal Church (U. S. A.); 1 missionary and
wife, 32 communicants, 66 scholars. Methodist
Episcopal Church (North); 1 missionary.

**Sio-ke,** a station of the Amoy, China,
mission of the Reformed (Dutch) Church, with
6 out-stations and 193 church-members.

**Sipirok,** a town in Northwestern Batakland, Sumatra, on the west coast, south of
Sigompulan. Mission station of the Rhenish
Missionary Society; 1 ordained missionary, 1
female missionary, 17 native workers, 7 out-stations, 450 communicants, 140 school-children.

**Sipoholon,** a station of the Rhenish Missionary Society in Sumatra, East Indies, with 1
ordained missionary, 15 native helpers, 56
communicants, 110 school-children.

**Sipohuttar**, a town in North Sumatra, northeast of Pantjurnapitti. Mission station of the Rhenish Missionary Society; 1 ordained missionary, 1 female missionary, 1 out-station, 70 communicants, 100 school-children.

**Sirier** (Ghodnadi), a town in Poona district, Bombay, India, on the Ghod River, 36 miles northeast of Poona, 34 miles southwest of Ahmaduagar. The country around is hilly and uncultivated. At one of the town's suburbs is held yearly a Hindu fair, attended by 3,000 persons. Population, 4,372. Mission station A.B.C.F.M.; 1 missionary and wife, 27 native helpers, 11 out-stations, and an industrial school.

**Sistof** (Sistova), a town in Bulgaria, on the Danube, 30 miles east-southeast of Nicopolis. Population 12,000. Mission station of the Methodist Episcopal Church (North); 1 missionary and wife, 1 female missionary, 3 native ordained preachers, 7 other helpers, 28 church-members, 50 Sabbath scholars. Here also there were printed in the year 2,000 volumes, 45,000 pages.

**Sitapur**, a town, in the district of Oudh, Northwest Provinces, India. Mission station of the Methodist Episcopal Church (North), 1861, 1 missionary and wife, 1 single lady, 48 native helpers, 40 church-members, 16 schools, 453 scholars.

**Sivas**, a city in Central Asia Minor, at quite a high altitude and with a cool climate. Population of city and out-stations 128,450: Turks, Armenians, Greeks, Koords. Mission station of the A. B. C. F. M. (1855); 2 missionaries and wives, 32 native helpers, 12 out-stations, 3 churches, 200 members, 22 schools, 1,043 students.

**Slave Trade and Missions.** The time has been when "The Slave Trade" suggested the unspeakable horrors of the middle passage, when in the stifling hold of a small vessel human beings were packed like dead freight that neither ate nor drank nor breathed. It needs no specially vivid fancy to paint the misery that filled such a prison-house under the most favorable circumstances. Even while still under tropic skies, the festering mass was thinned by the death of those not strong enough to endure such misery and live. But when storms required the cutting off of the slight ventilation ordinarily allowed, or when a contagious disease broke out, then death held high carnival, and the covetous wretches who, for the sake of gold, inflicted such misery on their fellow-men, were not led by their great losses in such cases to deal very mercifully with survivors. But that, thanks to the diffusion of a free gospel, has all passed away. It could exist at all only while the brotherhood of man set forth in the gospel was ignored by a hierarchical church that would not allow the Word of God to have free course and be glorified, and itself always sided with those who promised the largest help in its attainment of its own end. The old African slave trade could not live in the advancing light of the gospel any more than its victims could in their cramped and stifling prisons.

Gradually the extirpation of slavery in America closed that market for slaves and rendered the trade unprofitable. But the system was not dead, and the Arab slave trade across the Dark Continent from Central to Northeastern Africa and the adjoining lands of the Levant took the place of that across the Atlantic Ocean.

The missionary, at least the Protestant missionary (we cannot say as much for former Papal missionaries in the valley of the Congo. See Wilson's Western Africa, * p. 334) has always been the decided enemy of the slave trade, whether with American or Moslem countries, and it is to him more than to others that we are indebted for our knowledge of its horrors and abominations. In this connection the name of David Livingstone will never be forgotten, and lately we are happy to add to it that of Cardinal Lavigerie.

We learn something of the slave trade now carried on by Moslem Arabs from the pages of modern travellers. November 24th, 1883, H. M. Stanley was steaming up the Congo on his way to Stanley Falls, not far from the mouth of the Werre as it comes in from the north; he looked for the town of Mawembe, which he had passed in his first voyage down the river. The site was there, the clearing in the forest, and the white paths up the banks, but not a house or living thing was to be seen. The palisade had disappeared. The leaves of the banana trees were scorched and their stems blackened, showing the effects of the fire that had wiped out the town a few days before. Three days later he sent a boat to ascertain what slate-colored object was floating down stream, and found the bodies of two women bound together with cords. This tragedy had taken place only twelve hours before. Soon after he came in sight of the horde of banditti, 300 strong, with a like number of domestic slaves and women. Sixteen months had they been engaged in their work of slaughter. They had desolated a region of 34,570 square miles, just 2,000 square miles larger than Ireland; 118 villages in 43 districts had been destroyed, containing at least 118,000 people, and all they had to show as the result of these sixteen months of slaughter over so extensive a region was a wretched, ragged, and starving crowd of 2,300 women and children, with not one grown-up man among them. Five expeditions in all had already carried as many captives away as these possessed. To obtain these 2,300 they must have shot 2,500 men, while 1,300 more had perished by the way from hunger and despair. On an average, six persons had been killed to obtain each puny child in the encampment. The slaves were fettered in groups of twenty chained together; such fruits as could be found were thrown down before each gang, to fight for as they might, and the odors and abominations of the crowded camp were simply horrible. The bones of many stared through the skin that hung in flabby wrinkles. He adds, "How small a number of them will see the end of their journey, God only knows!"

* The substance of his testimony is that they not only held slaves, which might have been done at the request of the slave himself, as the best arrangement possible, but they participated in the traffic. Those who practised heathen rites were sold by them to the slave ships and the proceeds given to the poor, and the number of these was so large that slavers could always depend on them to complete their cargoes. Father Merolla tells that he once gave a slave to a captain in consideration of a flask of wine furnished him at the sacrament. Indeed the missionaries thought it not wrong to sell negroes into slavery if only they were first baptized and not sold to heretics; and though, knowing the horrors of the slave trade, they ought to have been the first to oppose it, yet when Cardinal Cibo toward the close of the seventeenth century wrote, complaining that "the pernicious and abominable abuse of selling slaves was still continued," the missionaries thought it impossible to do anything because the natives had very little to trade save slaves and ivory.

The process of their capture is as horrid, as their condition, when Mr. Stanley saw them, was full of misery. The Arab steals up stealthily at midnight through the darkness to the doomed town; no sound save the chirping of insects disturbs the sleepers, till suddenly the torch is applied on all sides, and in the light of the flames of the grass roofs of the houses, the deadly musket shoots down the men as fast as they appear. Many succeed in reaching the shelter of the woods, but the women and children are seized and carried off. Mr. Stanley estimated that the result of the slaughter was only two per cent of the previous population, and that even that was reduced to one per cent before they reached their destination (The Congo, II. 138–151).

This account of the great explorer is confirmed by the following from a letter of Rev. J. A. Bain ("Missionary Review of the World," 1889, 679). His station is in Ukukwi at Maindu, 35 miles northwest of Lake Nyassa, on the Kiwira River. He writes: "At daybreak, March 15th, we were awoke by a number of shots fired in rapid succession; we were told it was Mereri with two bands of Arabs. The surprise was complete. More than thirty women with babes and several girls were captured. The men, only half awake, tried to defend their wives and children, but were driven back by the murderous firing. The Arabs entrenched themselves in a bamboo stockade, then glutted their lust on their captives. Two children, whose weeping over the dead bodies of their mothers disturbed the orgies, were flung into the flames of a burning house. The two following days were spent in plundering and destroying the villages. The cattle are Mereri's. The women are claimed by the Arabs, who will sell them when they tire of them. They left, after burning everything that could be burned."

An English missionary at Kibanga on Lake Tanganyika writes in 1888 ("Missionary Herald" 1888, 562): "At night we could see the villages everywhere in flames, the people fleeing for refuge to the lake, and the brigands leading away the women and children in long files. A poor old woman as she was led away caught hold of the clothing of the missionary, and begged him to save her, but she was hauled away by the rope that was round her neck; another received a wound from the butt end of a pistol. Where yesterday we sought to impart instruction and comfort, now reigns the silence of a desert."

The Rev Chauncey Maples, of the Universities Mission, says that during a residence of six or seven years he had never gone 70 miles from Masasi without meeting a caravan of slaves. One of them numbered 2,000, and according to Mr. Stanley that number must represent an amount of butchery and an extent of territory turned from populous villages into a desert that is appalling to think of ("Missionary Herald" 1885, 135).

Dr. Kerr Cross writes from Karonga in April, 1889 ("Missionary Herald" 1889, 413): "For five weeks the Arabs have harassed us constantly. They hide in the woods and murder men as they pass to and from their gardens. A few days since a party of Wankondè were thus attacked; one was killed and another wounded. The Arabs cut off the head of their victim and fled home, and it is now stuck on a pole in their stockade. Another was in the woods cutting

trees for a house, when Arabs fired on him, piercing his shoulder. Again a band of our men were fired on by Arabs hidden in the long grass; only one was shot, and he was brought in carrying a piece of his intestines in his hand, and of course he soon died. A week ago we were awoke at midnight by a volley fired quite near our home. In a few minutes every man was at his post on the stockade, but only one old woman was killed; three bullets had gone through her body, and yet she lived till yesterday. What would be the fate of these poor villagers should the missionaries be driven off?"

Livingstone, in his "Last Journals" (59-63), gives some account of the brutalities on the road. June 19th, 1866, he passed a woman tied by the neck to a tree and dead; she could not keep up with the rest, and in order that she should not become the property of another she was thus despatched. Dr. Livingstone saw others tied up in the same way, and one lying in the path in a pool of blood. June 26th he passed another woman lying dead in the road. Bystanders told how an Arab had killed her early that morning, in anger that he must lose the money paid for her, because she was too exhausted to walk any further. His "Last Journals," pp. 383–386, gives an account of a merciless and unprovoked massacre of hundreds of native women and others.

On the borders of the Red Sea the regular price for girls from 10 to 15 years of age is from $80.00 to $100.00; boys from 7 to 11, $60.00 to $80.00; young women from 16 to 22, $50.00 to $70.00; and young men from 15 to 26, $30.00 to $50.00. They rarely sell a man over 25 years old. These slaves are carried to various Moslem countries by pilgrims returning from Mecca. The trade is carried on by Moslems alone in the open market under the shadow of the mosque of the prophet at Mecca ("Missionary Herald" 1888, 93).

As to the guilt of Mohammedans in connection with the slave trade, Cardinal Lavigerie is very outspoken, and for thirty years he has been in constant intercourse with them. He says ("Missionary Herald" 1888, 561):

1. "I do not know in Africa a Moslem state whose ruler does not permit, and often himself practise on his own subjects, and in ways barbarously atrocious, the hunting and sale of slaves.

2. "It is only Moslems who ravage Africa by slave raids and slave trading.

3. "Where the slave trade is prohibited by Christian powers, I do not know a Mohammedan who does not advocate slavery and declare himself ready to buy or sell Negro slaves.

4. "I know personally in Asiatic Turkey, and in that part of Africa under the Ottoman Sultan, many places where the slave trade and the passage of the sad caravans take place with the complicity of Turkish authorities.

5. "Never to my knowledge has any mufti or teacher of the Koran protested against this infamous traffic. On the contrary, in their conversation they recognize it as authorized by the Koran for true believers as regards infidels.

6. "Never to my knowledge has any cadi or Moslem judge pronounced a judgment which implied the condemnation of slavery, but all have sided with the teachers and expounders of the Koran."

In conclusion, we cannot more than barely

allude to the unutterable beastliness, as well as cruelty, of these Moslem slave traders, in connection with the mutilation of boys; for though the vast majority die after the operation, yet, as the market value of the survivors is greater on account of it than would have been the price of the whole, the horrid work goes on; to say nothing of another hardly less cruel operation performed on girls, to certify to their purchasers that they have not been outraged after its performance.

The following summary of an official paper, read in the Anti-slavery Conference at Brussels, and printed in the London "Times" concerning the Trade in Circassian Women, gives an idea of the difficulty of uprooting the system in Moslem communities. "The Porte cannot see its way (clear) to enter into any practical engagements affecting the time-honored and deep-rooted usages essentially connected with the domestic conditions of the Mussulman social fabric. All the conventions and treaties on the slave trade refer to African slaves; but as regards white Circassians, it would be impossible, short of a radical social revolution, to prevent the existing traffic, which is quite an ordinary thing, forming part of the domestic institutions of the country, and having a close connection with its religious tenets and usages."

**Slavé Version.**—The Slavé belongs to the languages of North America, and is spoken by the Indians of the station on the Mackenzie River, Canada. A translation of the four Gospels was made by Bishop Bompas, which, at the request of the Rev. W. S. Reeve, Archdeacon of Fort Chipewayan, supported by the Church Missionary Society, was published at London in 1863 by the British and Foreign Bible Society. The work of printing was commenced in 1881, but was considerably delayed by the necessity of sending proofs to Mr. Reeve. This edition was printed in the Roman character. In 1884 the same Society also published an edition of the same Gospels in syllabic characters for the greater benefit of the Indians themselves, under the editorship of the Rev. E. A. Watkins. Thus far 1,268 portions were disposed of.

**Slavonic Version.**—The Slavonic belongs to the Slavonic branch of the Aryan family of languages. The different tribes speaking this language were converted to Christianity through the labors of Methodius and Cyril, "who, contrary to the course pursued by Xavier, but anticipating the labors of modern and Protestant Missions and Bible Societies, conferred on those half-savage nations the inestimable blessing of a valuable translation of the Bible." Cyril, who understood the Slavic language, succeeded in making it available for literary purposes by inventing a suitable alphabet. He translated not only the liturgy and the pericopes into Slavic, but also commenced a translation of the Bible, which after his death (February 14th, 869) was completed by Methodius. The Old Testament was made from the Septuagint, the New after the Greek text of the so-called Constantinopolitan version. Passing over minor codices still extant, we only mention that a complete Bible codex of 1429 is at Oxford, and three others of 1499 at Moscow.

After the invention of the art of printing, the Psalter was published first (Cracow, 1481–1491; Cetynia, 1495); the four Gospels were published

in 1512 at Ugrowallachi; and the complete New Testament, together with the Psalms, at Ostrog, in 1580. In the year following, the entire Bible was published at the instance of the Ruthenian prince, Constantine Ostrogski (Ostrog, 1581). This edition was often reprinted (Moscow, 1663, 1727; Kief, 1758, 1779, 1788, etc.; St. Petersburg, 1730–39, 1751, 1756, 1757, 1759, 1762, 1763, 1778, 1784, 1797, 1802, 1806, 1811, 1815, 1822, 1862, 1863). The British and Foreign Bible Society, which also circulates the Slavonic version, disposed, up to March 31st, 1889, of 876,918 portions of the Scriptures.

(*Specimen verse.* John 3 : 16.)

Та́кѡ бо̀ возлюби̑ Бг҃ъ мі́ръ, я҆́кѡ и҆ Сн҃а своего̀ є҆диноро́днаго да́лъ є҆́сть, да вся́къ вѣ́руѧй въ о҆́нь, не поги́бнетъ, но и҆́мать живо́тъ вѣ́чный.

**Slavs.**—The Slavs belong to the Aryan or Indo-European family of nations, and the group in which they are classed is commonly called the Slavo-Germano-Lithuanian group. Comparative philology has proved the intimate connection and relationship existing between these three members of the group and Latin, Greek, and Sanskrit.

The primitive history of the Slavs and date of their immigrations into Europe are covered with the veil of darkness, like those of many other nations. It is generally supposed that they appeared in Europe after the Germans, and that their original settlements extended between the sources of the rivers Don and Dnieper, and beyond the Dnieper towards the eastern shores of the Baltic Sea and the river Vistula, and towards the south not farther than the river Pripet. But between the 3d and 4th century A.D. they are found occupying a district the approximative boundaries of which were: from the river Niemen as far as the mouth of the river Duna; from the Gulf of Riga over the Valdai Heights as far as the mouth of the Oka; on the east, a line stretching from the Oka to Kieff and from there to the river Boog, while on the west the line extended to the Carpathian Mountains and the upper Vistula. Towards the end of the 5th or beginning of the 6th century the Slavs occupied the northern banks of the Danube; they soon crossed over and took possession of its southern banks, whence they spread themselves as far down as Albania, Thessaly, Epirus, and even the Peloponnesus.

According to some, these immigrations of the Slavs into the Balkan Peninsula began in the 3d or 4th century and lasted till the 7th. In the 7th century A.D. the Servians and Croats, moving from the Carpathian Mountains, occupied the present Servia, Bosnia, Herzegovina, and pushed on into Croatia and Dalmatia. The region around the rivers Elbe and Oder were likewise occupied by Slavs, who, however, like the Baltic Slavs, were swallowed up in and amalgamated with the Germans; but the Slavs in Upper Austria, Styria, Carinthia, and Kraina have maintained their own ground, though the Germans have considerably encroached upon them.

The introduction of Christianity among the Slavs is the turning-point in their history; and with it their history takes a more definite shape and course. This momentous event was brought about by the combined efforts of two brothers, Cyril and Methodius, natives of Salonica, whom all the Slavs venerate as their apostles and "illuminators," and whom they worship as saints. Cyril, the younger brother, was a man well versed in all the learning that Byzantium at that time could impart, and on account of his erudition he was honored with the title of "philosopher." Giving up all the honors and emoluments to which they might have easily attained, the two brothers went to Pannonia at the request of Prince Rostislav, to preach Christianity among the Slavs of Pannonia.

Here they devoted themselves to the spreading of the gospel, and the translation of the Scriptures and the most essential liturgical books. Cyril revised a Slavic alphabet, constructed on the basis and model of the Greek, which is still known by the name of "Kyrillitza" (Kyrill's alphabet). It consisted of 38 letters, 24 of which were the 24 letters of the Greek alphabet, while 14 others were devised by Cyril to express sounds peculiar to the Slavic speech, and for which there were no corresponding Greek letters. In spite of the opposition of the German clergy, Cyril and Methodius succeeded in obtaining the approbation of the Pope, and he allowed them to use the Slavonic language in the church services. During a visit to Rome, in 869, Cyril died, aged 43 years; while Methodius returned to Moravia, having been appointed its bishop by the Pope. But he soon found his position shaken by the virulent opposition of the German clergy, was dispossessed of his bishopric, and died, it is said, in prison in 885.

The total number of the Slavs is estimated at about 90,000,000, distributed in round numbers as follows: Russians, over 60,000,000; Bulgarians, 4,000,000; Serbo-Croats and Slovenes about 7,000,000; Tchekho (czech) Moravians and Slovaks, 7,000,000; Poles about 10,000,000; and Serbo-Lansatians about 150,000. According to their religious denominations, about 68,000,000 Slavs belong to the Eastern or Orthodox Church; 20,000,000 to the Catholic; 1,500,000 to the Protestant; and about 800,000 are Mohammedans. To the Eastern Church belong the Russians, the Bulgarians, and the Servians; to the Catholic Church belong the Poles, the Tchekho-Moravians and Slovaks, the Croats, and the Slovenes. The Protestant Slavs are distributed as follows: Slovaks, 640,000; Poles, 500,000; Tchekho-Moravians, 150,000; Serbo-Lansatians, 130,000; Slovenes, 15,000; Servians, 13,000; Bulgarians, 5,000. The Mohammedan Slavs are found chiefly in Bosnia and Herzegovina (500,000), and Bulgaria (about 250,000), who, however, have retained and speak their respective Slavic dialects.

According to their geographical distribution, the Slavs are divided into (1) Southeastern Slavs, comprising the Russians, the Servians, the Croats, the Slovenes, and the Bulgarians; (2) Western Slavs, comprising Bohemians or Tchekhs (with their subdivisions, proper Tchekhs, Moravians, and Slovaks), Lansatian Serbs (divided into upper and lower Lansatians), and Poles. Accordingly the Slavic languages are also divided into two branches: (1) Southeastern, including the Russian, the Bulgarian, the Servian, the Croat, and the Slovene, with all their local dialects. (2) Western, including the Bohemian, the Polish, and the Serbo-Lansatian, with all their local dialects. The Catholic Slavs use the Latin language in their church services and the Latin alphabet in their literatures, while the Orthodox Slavs use the "Kyrillitza," with some partial modifications, in their writing, and the "Church-Slavonic" in their churches. This "Church-Slavonic" language is the Palæo-Slovenic of Cyril's translation of the Scriptures, changed and modified according to the orthography and grammatical construction or forms of the Russian. The most ancient manuscript of the Kyrillitza which bears a certain date, is the "Ostromirov's Gospel," written in 1053 for a Russian prince named Ostromir. There are other manuscripts, written in another alphabet, known as the "Glagolitza," which date probably as far back as this, and perhaps are older.

There can be no doubt that even in the ninth and the tenth centuries there existed various Slavic dialects, just as we find them now; but these dialects were nearer and much more intelligible to each other than at present. The differences did not relate so much to lexicological distinctions, as to distinctions in sound and pronunciation. Thus, for example, the ancient Bulgarian word *punt* or *pont* (road, way) was written and pronounced *poot* in Russian just as it is to-day. This explains how the work accomplished by Cyril and Methodius was accessible to all the Slavs in the ninth century, and how the literary productions of one Slavic tribe could be very easily transcribed and appropriated by another. But in the course of time these various Slavic dialects have tended to diverge more and more from each other, until at the present time they form quite distinct languages. The use of the Latin alphabet by the Catholic Slavs and of the Kyrillitza by the Orthodox tends to make this divergence still wider, as it makes their literatures unintelligible to each other. The common Bulgarian or Servian of to-day can hardly understand the spoken or literary language of the Pole or the Bohemian; nor can the Slovak or the Slovene comprehend the Russian. Then the foreign linguistic elements that have entered into the lexicological formations of the respective dialects have increased the differences. German and Latin have had a great influence over the Western Slavs, while Greek, Turkish, and other foreign languages have exerted a similar influence upon the Bulgarian, the Servian, and the Russian. In grammatical forms and construction all the modern Slavic dialects, with the exception of the Bulgarian, have retained a close resemblance to the Palæo-Slovenic language, and one well acquainted with the latter will not find much difficulty in mastering and understanding the various Slavic dialects.

In conclusion, we must say that many fanciful derivations and explanations of the word "Slav" have been given. The most probable one is that the word is derived from Slovo, which means "word" or "speech," and the name in its ancient orthography is "Slovyanin," which the Russians have converted into "Slavyanin" and the Europeans into "Slavs." So Slovyanin means the "man of speech," while the Germans, the nearest neighbors of the Slavs in olden time, were and are still called by the Slavs, Nyemtzi, from "nyem," meaning "dumb."

**Slovaks.**—The Slovaks are, strictly speaking, only a branch of the Bohemian race, and their language may be considered as a dialect of the Bohemian language. But of late years a separatist movement has risen among them, and they are trying to form a literature of their own and to be treated as a nation apart from the Bohemians, which is rather a sad comment upon the much-vaunted theory of panslavism. The Slovaks inhabit the northwest of Hungary, and number over two millions. The greater mass of them (1,583,000) belong to the Roman Catholic Church and 640,000 are Protestants. They settled in the present territory they occupy towards the end of the 5th century, and shared the fate of the Bohemians and Moravians in many historical events. Christianity was introduced among them before the first half of the 9th century by German preachers; and later on in the same century Methodius, the Slavic apostle, introduced among them orthodox Christianity, together with the Slavic liturgy. But this orthodox Christianity could not be maintained for a long time, and after the death of Methodius (885) it was replaced by Latin Christianity and the Latin liturgy. In 907 A.D. the Hungarians put an end to the existence of the great Moravian kingdom, which had united under one sceptre the Slavs of Bohemia and Moravia and the Slovaks. In 999 the country of the Slovaks was conquered by the Poles, but soon after they fell again under the Hungarians, who practically put an end to their political independence. They preserved, however, their local liberties and national immunities for a long time, and in the 15th century the doctrines of Huss found warm adherents and followers among them. The dispersion of the Hussites and the emigration of the Bohemian and Moravian brethren strengthened still more the Slovakian reformed party, and the Bohemian language along with Bohemian books was established among them. Luther's reformation likewise found an entrance among the Slovaks—not only among the common people, but also among the nobility. But a Catholic reaction, which manifested itself as far back as the 16th century, gradually recovered its ascendancy, and though it could not entirely put down Protestantism, it spread among the larger part of the Slovaks. The efforts of the Hungarians to impose upon the Slovaks the Hungarian language about the end of the last century provoked a counter-movement on the part of the Slovaks, who defended their nationality and language against the encroachments of the Hungarians by developing a national literature of their own. Although the lot of the Slovaks under the stern rule of the Hungarians is not a very enviable one, still the national sentiment among them is so strong that the efforts of the Hungarians to keep them down and to denationalize them will prove vain.

**Slovak Version.**—The Slovak belongs to the Slavonic branch of the Aryan family of languages, and is spoken by the Slovaks, who live in the northwest of Hungary, and who are either Protestants or Roman Catholics. The former read the Bohemian Bible, and number about 500,000; the latter, whose number is 1,300,000, had only the dominical Gospels and epistles, published in their language at Buda in 1818–1822. In the year 1831 an entire Bible was published for their benefit at Grau. The translation originally made by Bernolak was edited by Canon Georg Palkowicz, in two volumes. In the year 1883 the British and Foreign Bible Society published an edition of Palkowicz's New Testament, with approved and alternative readings in Roman characters, instead of the Gothic, as originally published by the editor. Up to March 31st, 1889, about 20,000 copies of the New Testament were disposed of.

**Slovenes.**—The Slovenes inhabit the districts of Carinthia, Kraina, Styria, and Istria in Austria, and number about one and one-third millions. They are classed among the Southeastern Slavs, and their language forms a branch of the South Slavic dialects. It bears a strong relationship to the Serbo-Croatian language, and in its lexicology has a great resemblance to the Bulgarian. The Slovenes belong to the Roman Catholic Church, with the exception of about 15,000 Protestants, and they all use the Latin alphabet, with some slight modifications, in their literature. The Slovenes settled in these parts of Europe in the 6th century; and about the end of the 8th they fell under the dominion of the Franks in the reign of Charles the Great. Their petty princes were allowed to rule over them as vassals of the Franks until, in the course of time, the country was entirely subjugated to German rulers, and ever since has formed a part of Austria. Christianity was introduced among the Slovenes in the 7th century by preachers who came to them from Aquilea (in Italy) and from Salzburg; but in the second half of the 8th century, and especially after the Frankish conquest of the country, the Catholic Archbishop of Salzburg, Virgilius (known as the apostle of the Slovenes), succeeded in establishing Catholic Christianity among the Slovenes through his German preachers. That the Slavic apostles Cyril and Methodius ever labored among the Slovenes is doubtful, still there are some very high authorities on the Slavic languages who claim that the language in which the original translation of the Scriptures was made by St. Cyril and Methodius was the language of the Slovenes, and not that of the Bulgarians. Hence they call it Palæo-Slovenic in distinction from the Neo-Slovenic. The most ancient linguistic remains of this old Slovenic language are the so-called "Freisinger Extracts," found in an old Latin manuscript, and referred to the 9th century. Up to the 16th century the Slovenic language seems to have been almost lost, and to have been replaced by the Latin and German. This was due to the fact that literature was exclusively in the hands of the clergy. But when the Reformation found its way among the people a movement was made to bring to notice the vernacular of the people as a means of their enlightenment and instruction. Primus Truber (1508–1586) was the most active laborer for the spread of the new ideas among his people and for the elevation of the national idiom. He found many followers and adherents, and, thanks to his labors and theirs, a translation of the whole Bible, the first one in Slovenic, was published in 1584, the New Testament having been translated by Truber himself. Unfortunately this reformatory movement did not last long, and in the first half of the 17th century it was suppressed by a Catholic reaction, which violently raged against the reformed party, banishing all those who refused to return to Catholicism, confiscating their property, and burning all the books and publications of Truber and his followers with such zeal that they are now seldom to be found. This persecution put a stop to all religious and literary progress among the Slovenes, so that all literary activity remained at a standstill till the end of the last century. The literature remained in the hands of the Catholic priests and the Jesuits. But in the general revival of the Slavic dialects and nationalities that began in the beginning of the present century the Slovenes also have begun to cultivate a national literature in their national tongue, and this movement has gone on increasing, especially since 1860.

**Slovenian Version.**—The Slovenian is a language of the Slavonic family, and is spoken in Illyria. The first who published a translation of Matthew for the Protestant Slovenians was Canon Truber, Tübingen, 1555, and the New Testament in 1577. A complete Bible prepared by Georg Dalmatyn was published at Wittemberg 1584. A New Testament was also published by St. Kuzmicz, Halle, 1771, Presburg 1818. For the Catholic Slovenians, Thomas Krön, bishop of Graz, translated the dominical Gospels and Epistles (Graz 1612); Ludwig Schonleben (ibid. 1672, 1678); Paglowic (Laibach 1764); Marcus (ibid. 1777). A translation of the New Testament by Japel and Kumerdy was published at Laibach 1784–86, and a complete translation of the Bible in ten vols. was issued 1791–1804. None of these translations were regarded by the British and Foreign Bible Society as suitable for circulation. At last the Society succeeded in finding a suitable translator (1869), who translated the Gospels of Matthew and Mark into the Sloveniau dialect, taking the original as his basis. As was to be expected, the publication of these Gospels awakened a violent opposition; but the success which attended their circulation encouraged the Bible Society to go on, and in 1882 the New Testament and the Psalms, translated and edited by Professor Stritar, was published for a million of Roman Catholics, among whom there is not a single Protestant community, or a single Protestant, except the Bible colporteurs. In 1888 the book of Isaiah, also translated by Professor Stritar, was published, Genesis having been issued in 1885. Up to March 31st, 1889, 72,650 portions of the Scriptures were disposed of.

(*Specimen verse.* John 3 : 16.)

Kajtl tako je Bog ljubil svet, da je sina svojega edinorojenega dal, da kdorkoli veruje va-nj, ne pogine, nego da ima večno življenje.

**Smith, Azariah,** b. Manlius, N. Y., U. S. A., February 16th, 1817; graduated at Yale College 1838. At the time of his conversion in college he became interested in missions, and decided to be a missionary. After graduating, he studied medicine at Geneva, N. Y., with Professor Spencer, attending six lectures daily. In 1839 he went to Philadelphia, where he had access to the Pennsylvania hospital and dispensary. In October of that year he entered the Divinity School, New Haven; received from the medical school connected with the college the degree of M.D. January 24th, 1840. He attended also lectures of the Law School on Blackstone's Commentaries. He was ordained at Manlius August 30th, 1842, and embarked for Western Asia November 17th, as a missionary of the A. B. C. F. M. After residing a few months at Broosa and Constantinople, he went to Trebizond, spending five months in studying Turkish and practising medicine. In 1844 he visited Smyrna, Rhodes, Cyprus, and Beirut, and made a tour in the interior to Aleppo, Oorfa, Diarbekir, and Mosul. He travelled for a time with Mr. Layard. He was present at the death of Dr. Grant at Mosul. This year he made a dangerous tour in the mountain Nestorian districts of Koordistan. In 1845 he travelled extensively, after visiting Constantinople, including a visit to Trebizond and Erzeroom, remaining a year and a half. He was attacked by robbers for affording protection to au Armenian priest who had fled to his house; but by his courage and perseverance the offenders were punished, and damages recovered from the Turkish Government. His travels were extensive, and he often took long journeys to prescribe for cholera patients at different missionary stations. "Dwight's cholera mixture," widely used in the United States in 1849 for the cholera, was his preparation. Once he was attacked with the disease in the wilderness, his attendant forsaking him through fear; but after two days of suffering he recovered so as to proceed on his journey. On account of his peculiar adaptation to different fields, he labored for longer or shorter periods in many places; but Aintab, to which he was sent in 1848, and which he made his missionary home, he loved most of all. There he had seen the most wonderful displays of divine grace, and there he wished to close his earthly career. He returned to America in 1848, was married, and went back to his field. Dr. Smith was a thorough scholar. He published valuable papers on meteorology, Syrian antiquities, and natural history in the "American Journal of Science." He died June 3d, 1851, at Aintab.

**Smith, Eli,** b. Northford, Conn., U. S. A., September 13th, 1801; graduated at Yale College 1821; taught in Putnam, Georgia, for two years; graduated at Andover Theological Seminary 1826; ordained May 10th same year; left for Malta under appointment of the A. B. C. F. M., May 23d, 1826, as superintendent of a missionary printing establishment. In 1827 he went to Beirut to study Arabic. The missionaries being obliged to leave Syria on the general outbreak of the war after the battle of Navarino, Mr. Smith in 1828 returned to Malta. He was subsequently transferred to the Syrian mission; travelled through Greece in 1829 with Rev. Dr. Anderson, and with Rev. H. G. O. Dwight 1830–31 in Armenia, Georgia, and North Persia, thus opening the way for the establishment of the Nestorian Mission at Oroomiah. Returning to the United States in 1832 he published "Missionary Researches in Armenia" (2 vols., Boston, 1833), also a small volume of "Missionary Sermons and Addresses." In 1833 he embarked for Syria, accompanied by Mrs. Smith, formerly Sarah Lanman Huntington, whose brief but bright missionary career of only three years was terminated by her death at Smyrna, September 30th, 1836. In 1836 Mr. Smith was wrecked on the coast of Asia Minor. In 1837–38 and 1852 he was the companion and coadjutor of Prof. E. Robinson in his extensive explorations of Palestine. "By his experience as an Oriental traveller, his tact in eliciting information, and his intimate knowledge of Arabic he contributed largely to the accuracy, variety, and value of the discoveries of Biblical Geography recorded in Dr. Robinson's celebrated 'Researches.'" In 1838 he again visited the United States. In passing through Europe he prosecuted inquiries concerning Arabic topography, and other details necessary to render the printing establishment as complete as possible. During this visit he travelled extensively in the United States, speaking and preaching to great acceptance. He returned to Beirut with his second wife, who died in a year. His health being greatly impaired, he made his last visit to the United States in 1845. With health restored he reembarked for Syria in 1847. He now devoted himself in earnest to the work of preparing a new translation of the Bible into Arabic, to which he had made all his plans subservient. Intending originally to be connected with the press, he was led to pursue the study of Arabic and kindred languages. Among his qualifications for a translator as well as editor was his ripe scholarship. His learning was extensive and accurate. To the ancient classics he added an acquaintance with French, Italian, German, and Turkish. With the Hebrew he was very familiar, and the Arabic, the most difficult of all, was to him a second vernacular. Not only did his learning fit him for the difficult office of editor, but by long practice and close attention to the business of printing in all its branches he acquired an unusual skill in managing the minutest details. He not only wrote himself for the Arabic press, but devoted much time and labor to correcting and properly editing works written or translated by others. For many years he carefully read the proofsheets of nearly everything that went through the mission press. He spent also much time and intense labor in superintending the cutting, casting, and perfecting of various fonts of new type made from models which he had himself drawn with the utmost accuracy. This work was done at Leipsic in the celebrated establishment of Tauchnitz. After eight years of incessant toil he completed the translation of the New Testament, the Pentateuch, the Minor Prophets from Hosea to Nahum, and the greater part of Isaiah. The degree of D.D. was conferred upon him by Williams College in 1850. With all his qualifications for the literary department, and his devotion to the work of translating, Dr. Smith was still a missionary of Christ, entering with his whole heart into all plans for the spread of divine truth. "By diligent effort he early became a fluent speaker in the vernacular, and ever after it was his delight to preach the gospel in the family, by the wayside, and in public assemblies." He had a strong desire to recover, and had prayed often and earnestly that he might be spared to complete the translation of the Bible. But God's plans, he said, were best, and he was grateful that he had been allowed to labor thirty years as a foreign missionary. His death was very peaceful. He died at Beirut, January 11th, 1857.

His work was taken up by his associate, Rev. C. V. A. Van Dyck, D. D., and carried to its completion on the basis furnished by Dr. Smith, and the Arabic Bible is to-day one of the finest of monuments to missionary scholarship (see article Arabic Version).

**Smithfield,** a town in Orange Free State, Southeast Africa, north of Bapatli, northwest of Aliwal, North. Mission station of the Paris Evangelical Society; 1 missionary, 100 communicants, 30 scholars.

**Smyrna** (Turkish, Ismir), a city of Turkey, at the head of the Gulf of Smyrna, about 200 miles southwest of Constantinople. Population about 150,000, of whom a little more than half are Turks and the remainder Greeks (40,000), Armenians (10,000), Jews (15,000), and Europeans. The climate is hot and trying, the summer being very oppressive. The general appearance of the city from the sea and also from the Acropolis is very attractive, many of the houses, especially in the Christian quarters and along the quay, being of stone, and well built. As a business centre Smyrna has grown rapidly in importance, especially since the establishment of two lines of railway connecting it with the interior of Asia Minor. European customs and influence have also been largely predominant, and the intimate connection of the large Greek population with Greece and the islands of the Ægean, has helped to make it a centre of far greater commercial activity even than Constantinople. It has also derived considerable importance from the fact that it is the only Turkish city where the fleets of Europe and America can visit, and during the cooler months there is seldom a time when one or more war-ships are not anchored in the roadstead.

As a station for missionary work Smyrna has been prominent from the earliest times. The interest of its name as the home of Polycarp, and the only remaining one of the Seven Churches addressed by the Apostle John, naturally drew attention to it; but even more was probably due to the fact that at the commencement of the present century it was the only city of Turkey that was really open to missionaries, and with which there was direct communication from European and American seaports. The British and Foreign Bible Society (q.v.) early established an agent here, and the first missionaries of the A. B. C. F. M. to the Levant were located here (see A. B. C. F. M. and **Armenia**).

At present the missionary work is carried on among the Greeks and Armenians by the Western Turkey Mission of the A. B. C. F. M., with 3 ordained missionaries and their wives and 4 female missionaries. There are 9 outstations, 28 native helpers, 3 churches, and 162 church-members. There is a large and successful girls' boarding-school and a kindergarten establishment.

Work among the Jews is carried on principally by the Established Church of Scotland, with 1 ordained and 1 medical missionary, 1 female missionary, 2 schools, 1,828 scholars (1,040 Jews, 698 Greeks, etc., 90 British); 220 communicants (18 Jews, 167 British, 35 Greeks, etc.).

The London Society for the Promotion of Christianity among the Jews also have a missionary and 2 colporteurs.

The Smyrna Rest is an establishment managed by some English ladies, though started by Miss Maria A. West, for many years a missionary of the A. B. C. F. M. in Constantinople and Harpoot. Its prime object is to reach the sailors of different nationalities that throng the port of Smyrna, and are easily led astray by the liquor-saloons, that are very numerous. A central and commodious room was hired and fitted up as a café and reading-room. Coffee, tea, chocolate, etc., with other light refreshments, were served; reading-matter was supplied in the form of newspapers and periodicals; and in the evening there was a gospel service, in which singing held a prominent place. Later on another room also was hired for Sabbath services. An English sailor was engaged to go among the seamen, and every steamer and sailing-vessel was visited for the purpose of inviting the sailors to "The Rest." While attention was especially given to the sailors, work was done for all, and the numbers of all nationalities and every condition who were reached was very large.

One of the most interesting developments of missionary work has been the formation and the growth of the Greek Evangelical Alliance. It originated in the effort of Rev. Geo. Constantine, D.D., a native Greek, educated in America, to place the work among the Greeks on a firm basis of self-support. For many years work for that people had seemed almost hopeless. The Greek spirit seemed antagonistic to Protestantism, and hostile to any reform in the church itself. The distractions of a seaport also proved great obstacles, and there seemed no way of reaching the people. Dr. Constantine commenced a series of sermons in the hall connected with "The Rest," and by his eloquence drew large crowds. A profound impression was made, and the hierarchy saw that they were in danger of losing their power. The volatile nature of the Greeks rendered it easy to stir a tumult. Threats were uttered, stones were thrown at the windows of the hall, and on one Sunday a mob attacked the place, seeking especially for Dr. Constantine. Not finding him, they turned and went to his house, which they assaulted. Mrs. Constantine, a lovely American lady in feeble health, succeeded in drawing the bolt to the iron door, and the mob was forced to content itself with what damage it could effect from the street. So great was the shock to Mrs. Constantine that she never recovered from it, but a few months later died, undoubtedly from the effects of the nervous strain at that time.

The priests soon saw that they had overdone the thing. The American consul took prompt measures, and the result was a greater interest in Christian life than at any time before. The Alliance grew until it has become a most potent influence, not only in Smyrna, but in many other Greek communities of Asia Minor. (See article A. B. C. F. M., Western Turkey Mission.)

**Snow, Benjamin Galen,** b. Brewer Maine, U. S. A., October 4th, 1817; graduated at Bowdoin College 1846, and Bangor Theological Seminary 1849; ordained September 25th, 1851, and sailed November 18th, 1851, a missionary of the A. B. C. F. M., for Micronesia. He was stationed at Kusaie and Ebon. From failure of health he returned home in 1868, re-embarked in 1871. In 1877 his health again failed, and he returned to the United States. "Among a people sunk in the lowest degradation, isolated from the world, long dependent for all communication with home friends on the yearly visit of the 'Morning Star,' he began and carried forth his work with unshaken faith in the promises of God. He lived to see Christian communities established on islands that had been the habitations of cruelty, to see men that had been the dread of the hapless mariners cast away on the coral reefs that girded their island-homes, the humble followers of Christ." He died at Brewer, Me., May 1st, 1880.

**Society for Promoting Christian Knowledge.** Headquarters: Northumberland Avenue, London, W. C., England.—This Society is the oldest organization for Christian work of the Church of England. It was founded in 1698, and has since carried on its work in ever-widening spheres of activity, and with ever-increasing expenditure of funds. Its history has not been furnished us, and the meagre facts which can be gained from its report must suffice instead of the lengthy notice which is its due both on account of its age and its widespread usefulness.

*Organization.*—The Society is composed of persons who must of necessity be members of the Church of England or some church in full communion with it. New members are received on recommendation of the existing members, after which they are elected, and on payment of a certain annual sum are entitled to full privileges. Persons who make subscriptions are entitled to some privileges in the form of receiving books and tracts; thus the Society is a close, self-perpetuating organization, with intimate connection with the Church of England, though apparently responsible to no one except its own elected authorities.

*Officers.*—Her Majesty, the Queen of England, is the patron of the Society. The Archbishop of Canterbury is the president, and there are numerous vice-presidents, comprising mainly the other archbishops and bishops of the Church of England, together with like dignitaries of any church in full communion with the Church of England, who may be members of the Society. There are four treasurers, two general secretaries, and two who are designated organizing secretaries. A general committee of administration called the Standing Committee, is assisted by special committees, such as the Committee of Finance, of Foreign Translation, of General Literature, the Tract Committee, etc.

Under one broad comprehensive title, the Society combines the work of many departments, each of which might well be the work of a single society. In its endeavor to aid Christian work of any kind throughout the world, it is:

1. The Bible and Prayer-book Society of the Church of England.—In this branch of the work is included the producing and circulating of these books or portions of them not only in England but throughout the world. The publication is in seventy-five or more different languages. By grants of money or books; by supplying these publications at cost or less; by assisting translation and publication committees in various foreign lands, the work is carried on, and during the year 1889-90 over 600,000 books or portions have been circulated.

2. A Tract and Pure Literature Society.

—It produces and circulates distinctively religious works, together with works by able writers, on science, history, and general literature, including fiction of a pure and elevating character. In connection with this branch of the work, grants of books are made to churches, reading-rooms, missions of every kind, deserving seamen, sailors, etc.

3. A Home Church Mission and Education Society.—In addition to the general Home Missionary work carried on along the lines already mentioned, there are the following distinctive objects of its care:

(a) A college (St. Katherine's) at Tottenham, England, where school-mistresses are trained. It has a capacity for 100, with the highest records for any such institution in England. (b) A training college for lay-workers was founded and is maintained in the east of London. (c) Money is given towards the building and fitting up of church institutes, and the building and renting of Sunday-schools, together with other purposes in connection with church education, such as the providing of lecturers on church history, the preparation of lectures and magic-lantern slides, to be rented out at low rates to churches or districts desiring such means of educating the masses, and many other plans along the same general lines.

4. A Foreign and Colonial Missionary Society.—This work is accomplished in various particular ways:

(a) Churches, chapels, mission-rooms are built or aided in being built in the dioceses of the church the world over. Over £7,000 were granted for this work during the year 1889-90. (b) Native clergy and lay mission agents are taken under its care and trained for their future work. During the year 26 such students were in training for holy orders, and 68 for lay work. (c) Medical missions are maintained or established, and medical missionaries, both men and women, are trained for the work. The sum expended for this purpose during the year was £500. (d) Bishops and clergy are endowed. For this object £500 were spent during the year. (e) As mentioned above, Bible translation and other work of similar character has been aided, and books of many varieties have been donated or the work of publication assisted. In connection with this work, the Translation Committee is assisted by vernacular sub-committees in Madras (Tamil and Telugu), Punjab Sind, Bombay, and Calcutta. Depots for the Society's publications have been established at 25 places on the continent of Europe.

5. Emigrants' Spiritual Aid Society.—An important and in some respects unique feature of the work of the Society is the care which it exercises over the many emigrants who annually leave the shores of Great Britain for other lands. These emigrants are watched over both spiritually and temporally in the following ways:

Chaplains attend them on their departure, and letters are given to the Society's representatives in foreign lands who meet the emigrants on their arrival, often give them substantial aid in locating in their new homes, besides protecting them from the wiles of those who are ready to take advantage of their ignorance and strangeness. In many cases chaplains are deputed to accompany a shipload of emigrants, and a matron is sent to look after the single women. During the voyage—a long one when Australia, New Zealand, or South America is the objective point—the gospel is preached, church ordinances are administered, and the weary days whiled away by lectures which deal with the country of their destination, in regard to which many of the emigrants are sadly ignorant. At the principal cities, especially the ports of the United States, the Society has its representatives, who meet the emigrants on arrival whether they bear letters of recommendation or not; and in Canada, Tasmania, Australia, South Africa, South America, and New Zealand the emigrant receives like attention.

These, briefly stated, are the various branches of the important work of the Society. During the year 1889-90 the total value of the grants made to these various objects, partly in books, was £42,397. To meet this expenditure, the Society depends on its annual subscriptions, on donations, and legacies, from all of which sources its income during the year mentioned amounted to £44,215.

**Society for the Propagation of the Gospel in Foreign Parts.** Headquarters, Society's Office, 19 Delahay Street, Westminster, London, England.—The Society for the Propagation of the Gospel in Foreign Parts received its first charter in 1701 from King William III., upon application of Archbishop Tenison, one of a committee appointed by the Lower House of the Convocation of Canterbury to consider what was to be done for "The Promotion of the Christian Religion in the Plantations and Colonies beyond the Seas." The Society, as incorporated by the king, consisted of ninety-six members, the charter providing that the two Archbishops of Canterbury and York, the Bishops of London and Ely, the Lord Almoner, the Deans of St. Paul's and of Westminster, the Archdeacon of London, and the two Regius and the two Margaret Professors of Divinity at Oxford and Cambridge should always belong to the Society, which was founded for the "receiving, managing, and dispensing of funds contributed for the religious instruction of the queen's subjects beyond the seas; for the maintenance of clergymen in the plantations, colonies, and factories of Great Britain, and for the propagation of the gospel in those parts." Work was commenced at once among settlements of English people engaged in trade in Moscow and Archangel, and was rapidly extended to North America, the West Indies, and other colonies; but the Society did not become a distinctly missionary agency until 1821.

India had been opened to the gospel in 1813, and in 1818 the S. P. G. undertook the foundation of a Missionary College at Calcutta. Its funds being pledged to colonial missions already existing, vigorous efforts were made to increase its income, and a memorial was addressed to the Prince Regent, praying that a royal letter, authorizing a general collection, might as, in former times, be issued. The proceeds from this letter, amounting to £45,747, were devoted to the Missionary College, which was designed to meet not only the present wants of the mission, but also all the requirements of a growing church. The plan combined chapel, hall, library, and printing-press; and instruction was to be given in the principal languages and dialects of India, as well as in the sacred and classical languages. The original object of the college was the education of native East Indian and European young men for the service of the church; but some years after its foundation it was enlarged for the reception of law-students. The practical working of the college was in many respects unsatisfactory; nevertheless, within a few years missions, in charge of the college graduates, were established in some of the larger villages south of Calcutta. Among the first were Tollygunge, Howrah, and Barripur. These missions, before many years had passed, extended over an area of 40 miles north to south, by from 12 to 20 east to west, embracing 113 villages, with 26 chapels and 7 schools. The college is regarded as the key of missions of Bengal, and the present reports show that after a long series of disappointments and failures it is at last fulfilling the purposes for which Bishop Middleton (first Bishop of Calcutta) founded it. It is not only doing its proper work by training and sending forth students representing eight distinct races, but has evidently become the centre of the Christian education of Bengal, and also of such evangelistic work as is being carried on in its immediate locality.

In 1841 a mission was commenced at Cawnpur, and in 1852 the Delhi Mission was established; both suffered severely in the Mutiny in 1857, and the latter was entirely swept away, but was recommenced in 1860, and in 1877 was given fresh life by an organized effort of the University of Cambridge to maintain a body of men who should live and labor together in some Indian city. Delhi was chosen for this venture, the S. P. G. becoming responsible for the larger part of the maintenance of the Cambridge contingent. In 1869 the Chutia Nagpur Mission of Pastor Gossner was transferred, with its 17,000 Kol converts, to the S. P. G. The district within the sphere of this mission comprised 300 villages, divided into 35 circles, in each of which a reader was placed, who read prayers, instructed inquirers, and was visited periodically by the chief missionary.

In 1826 the work which had hitherto been carried on in Madras by the Christian Knowledge Society, was undertaken by the S. P. G., which in 1835 constituted Madras a bishopric, comprising three circles—(1) Madras itself, with a few isolated stations and the missions in the Telugu country and Hyderabad; (2) Tanjore and Trichinopoli, including the various stations connected with them, together with Cuddalore; and (3) Tinnevelli and Ramnad.

The connection of the Society with Bombay (1836) was until recent years very slight. In 1869, when Bishop Douglas arrived at Bombay, he found that the entire missionary staff was laboring in the city itself and its immediate neighborhood. He proposed to commence a chain of mission stations, of which Poona, Kolhapur, and Ahmadnagar should be the chief. This plan was carried out, and the work has become so great that "Ahmadnagar itself could absorb all the S. P. G. staff in the diocese."

Burma was entered in 1859; the See of Rangoon now includes work in (1) the city of Rangoon, with St. John's College (which has 636 scholars), and the training institution at Kemmendine; (2) the general work of the missionaries at Moulmein, with a considerable Tamil Mission; (3) Toungoo, among the Karens; and (4) in Upper Burma, at Mandalay and Shweybo. The work in Burma has always been largely educational, but among the Karens is also distinctly evangelistic.

The Society commenced work in Ceylon in 1838, and late reports from Colombo speak of great missionary activity, which has roused the Buddhist priests from their usual lethargy into violent opposition.

The work of the diocese of Singapore, Sarawak, and Labuan falls into several divisions; Singapore itself, the care of English congregations, and the heathen in the scattered portions of the Straits Settlements; and the missions in Borneo, including new work in the territory of the North Borneo Company.

JAPAN.—The mission to Japan was commenced in 1873, and the North China Mission in 1874: in the former the missionary force has been increased from two to six, and from Osaka, Tokyo, and Kumamoto the work is progressing with encouraging rapidity. In China, work is carried on in Chefoo, Peking, and Yung Chang, and a mission to Korea was undertaken in 1889.

AFRICA.—The work of the S. P. G. in South Africa was begun in 1820, when a chaplain was sent to Cape Town: it now comprises the dioceses of Cape Town, Graham's Town, St. John's, Zululand, Maritzburg, Bloemfontein, Pretoria, and St. Helena. In addition to pastoral labors for English colonists, much missionary work is carried on among the native tribes, and the Kafir and other converts are now numbered by thousands, and the foundation is laid of a native ministry fund supported entirely by themselves. Much attention is given to school and industrial work in the South African stations, and five branches of industry are regularly taught; in the boys' department, carpentry, wagon-making, blacksmithing, tinsmithing, and gardening, while the girls are instructed in the usual branches of household work. The Bishop of St. John's has asked permission of the Society to begin work in Pondoland, occupying one quarter of his diocese, but quite unevangelized. The Pondowise are the least civilized of the native races, and all work hitherto attempted among them has been unsuccessful. The diocese of Mauritius includes not only that island, but its many small dependencies, embracing Diego, Garcia, Rodrigues, the Seychelles Archipelago, and many small islands of the Indian Ocean. The population of these islands is about 376,000, of whom a large proportion are creoles, coolies from India, and children of liberated slaves.

The S. P. G. commenced work in Madagascar in 1864, and obtained the consecration of a bishop to lead the missions in 1874. The present reports show reasons for encouragement in the various stations. The West Indian Mission to the Pongas (on the western coast of Africa) has for several years been assisted by the S. P. G.

AUSTRALIA, entered in 1795, shows the result of the Society's labors in twelve dioceses, ten of which are now independent of aid, and are co-operating with the S. P. G. in opening a mission to New Guinea.

THE NEW ZEALAND MISSION was commenced in 1837. The single See of New Zealand has now grown into six, all of which are independent of England.

From 1853 until 1880 the Society contributed annually to the Melanesian Mission, and upon the death of Bishop Patteson raised £7,000 for the perpetuation of his memory. This sum was devoted to the erection of a memorial church on Norfolk Island, to the building of the missionary ship, the "Southern Cross," and to the endowment of the mission.

The S. P. G. now assists in the maintenance of clergymen in Fiji, in Norfolk Island, and in the Sandwich Islands.

**Society** or **Tahiti Islands** are a group in the South Pacific, between latitude 16° and 18° south, and longitude 148° to 155° west. There are 13 islands and several small islets, divided by a channel, 60 miles wide, into two groups, originally called the Georgian Islands and the Society Islands. The principal islands are Tahiti, Moorea or Eimeo, Titiaroa, Meetia, Raratea, Tubuai, Moru, Huahine, Tahaa, and Bora-Bora. Tahiti, by far the largest of these islands, has an area of 412 square miles. Moorea has 50 square miles. The general physical characteristics are the same for nearly every one of the group. There is a mountainous interior, with low, rich plains sloping down to the coast. Coral reefs surround them. The water-supply is abundant, tropical fruits and vegetables grow in great abundance, and a salubrious, temperate climate is universal. The natives belong to the Malay race, and resemble the Marquesans and Rarotongans in appearance, but differ greatly from them in their customs. The dialect is one of the softest languages in Oceanica. Agriculture is in a rather backward state, except in Tahiti and Moorea, where 7,000 acres are under cultivation, producing cotton, sugar, and coffee. The population of Tahiti is 11,200, of Moorea 1,600, with perhaps 12,000 inhabitants in all the other islands. The chief town and port is Papeete, in Tahiti.

The Society Islands, together with the Marquesas, Tuamotu, Gambier, Tubuai, the island of Rapa, the Wallis or Uea, and Howe Islands, form what is called the French Establishment in Oceania, under the control of a Commandant-General, who resides in Tahiti. Tahiti was taken possession of in 1844, and the various other islands were gradually encroached upon by the French, until in 1880 they became French possessions.

*Missions in the Society Islands.*—In 1797 the L. M. S. sent out its missionary ship "Duff," and the missionaries arrived at Tahiti in March of that year. From that time until the French occupation in 1844 great success attended the labors of the missionaries, whose influence over the converted islanders was exerted for their best temporal and spiritual good. In 1818, the anniversary of the L. M. S., the Christian king Pomare originated and formed a Tahitian Missionary Society. In 1839, just previous to the introduction of the French Protectorate, the following testimony to the good effects of missionary labor was given by the captain of a whaling vessel: "This is the most civilized place that I have been at in the South Seas. It is governed by a dignified young lady, about 25 years of age. They have a good code of laws, and no liquors are allowed to be landed on the island. It is one of the most gratifying sights the eye can witness on a Sunday to see in their church, which holds about 5,000, the queen, near the pulpit, with all her subjects around her, decently apparelled, and in seemingly pure devotion." With the institution of the French Protectorate the floodgates of iniquity were opened. The people were corrupted by the combined influence of rumsellers and other foreigners. The L. M. S. Mission was embarrassed and broken up, and withdrew from Tahiti and Moorea in 1852. At that time there were 1870 church-members in those two islands. Huahine was first reached by the missionaries in 1808, and the history of the mission there is similar to that of Tahiti and Moorea. The islands were practically Christianized, missionary societies were organized, and in 1852 there were 962 church-members in Huahine, Raratea, Bora-Bora, and Maupiti. Since the French occupation of the islands the work in Tahiti and Moorea has been under the care of the Paris Evangelical Society, which has continued the good work done by the L. M. S. in the face of two great difficulties—"the traffic in liquors and the Romish Propaganda" (Report of 1889). The report of 1889 states that their parishioners show profound attachment to the Word of God, there is a general celebration of the Sabbath, and a practice of liberal Christianity. Tahiti is divided into two sections—North and South. In the former, which includes the town of Papeete, there are nine other missionary stations, which are under the care of a native pastor, with 1,063 communicants and over a thousand scholars. In the southern division are Matiea and seven other stations, each with a native pastor, with 600 church-members and about 500 school-children, all under the supervision of three European missionaries, two residing at Papeete and one at Matiea. In Moorea there are 4 stations, with 1 missionary, 3 native pastors, 360 church-members, and 300 school-children. A missionary was sent out in 1888 to Raratea to take the place of the sole remaining missionary of the L. M. S., who died before his successor arrived. The people of that island, however, have utterly refused to have anything to do with a French missionary, and the people of Huahine seem determined to resist the French and to provoke a conflict. The missionary of the L. M. S. remained on Huahine during 1889 to prevent, if possible, the utter wreck of Christian work, until the Christians were ready to accept the new condition of things. Bora-Bora and Maupiti have each one native ordained pastor under the L. M. S.

**Sohagpur**, a town in Central Provinces, India, on the high-road from Bombay, 30 miles east of Hoshangabad, 72 miles east northeast of Mandla. It is a station on the Great Indian Peninsula Railroad, but is a place of small importance, commercially or generally. Population, 7,027, Hindus, Moslems, Kabirpanthis, Christians, Jains, Parsis, non-Hindu aborigines. Mission station of Friends' Foreign Missionary Society; 1 missionary and wife, 30 scholars.

**Solomon Islands**, a group in the South Pacific, consisting of a double chain extending from northwest to southeast, between 5° and 10° 54′ south latitude, and 154° 40′ and 162° 30′ east longitude. They were first discovered in 1567, but as yet have not been explored to any great extent. Since 1886 the northerly part of the group, including the islands of Bougainville, Choiseul, Isabel or Mahaga, together with various smaller islands, with a total area of 57,000 square miles, has been seized by Germany. The population of this part is estimated at 80,000. The principal other islands are San Christoval, Guadalcanal, and Malanta. The climate is damp; unhealthy on the coasts, though the highlands are probably more salubrious.

The natives belong to the Melanesian race, and the language is of Melanesian type, with many dialects. Of their religion, habits, and customs little is known, though they resemble the other Melanesians in most things, and are known to be cannibals to some extent. Mission work is carried on in these islands by the Melanesian Mission (q. v.).

**Somerset, East,** a town in Cape Colony, Africa, 80 miles northwest of Grahamstown. Population, 2,231. Mission station of the United Presbyterian Church of Scotland (1869); 1 missionary, 6 out-stations, 102 church-members, 66 Sabbath scholars.

**Somerville,** a town in East Griqualand, Transkei, South Africa, 30 miles from Umlata. Climate, sub-tropical. Population, Kafirs, Fingoes, Pondomisis, and Gunbus. Language, Bantu and Kafir. Religion, fetichism and heathen superstitions. Mission station of the Free Church of Scotland (1884); 1 missionary and wife, 30 native helpers, 14 out-stations, 1 church, 317 church-members, 6 schools.

**Sonapur,** a town in India, in the Bombay district, not far from Dapoli. Race, Maratha. Mission station of the S. P. G.; 1 missionary, 2 schools, 119 scholars, 57 church-members.

**Sonora,** a large town in Hermosillo, northwest Mexico. Climate, tropical. Population, 10,000, Mexicans, Indians. Language, Spanish. Religion, Roman Catholic. Natives degraded, poor. Mission station of the A. B. C. F. M. (1886); 1 missionary and wife, 3 out-stations, 1 church, 15 church-members, 1 school, 12 scholars.

**Soudan, Historical Sketch of.—** Taken in its broader dimensions, or as spoken of by the Arabs and earlier European geographers, together with the additions claimed by Egyptian rulers in late years, Beled-es-Soudan, or the "Country of the Blacks," extends from west to east along the southern border of the Great Desert, from the Atlantic and Senegambia to the Red Sea and Abyssinia, and southward from the Desert to Upper Guinea on the west, and to the equatorial and lake regions on the east, being some 3,500 miles in length from west to east, and in its broader parts on the east some 1,600 in width, and comprising a population estimated at 50,000,000. It is thus almost a fourth of Africa, both in extent of country and in the number of its inhabitants. But Eastern or Egyptian Soudan, to which the eyes of the world have been chiefly turned the last few years, and which will attract yet greater attention in the near future, lies along each side of the Nile from Assouan or the first cataract to the equator, and, according to some, even beyond, some 1,600 miles or more from north to south, while its width, from Massowah on the Red Sea to the western limits of Darfur, is from twelve to fourteen hundred miles. It thus comprises the provinces of Nubia, Dongola, Sennaar, Kordofan, Darfur, the districts watered by the Bahr-el-Ghazelle and the Bahr-el-Arab, the lands of the Dinka, Shilluk, and of others in the Lake region on the equator. The extensive additions which the distinguished viceroy of Egypt, Mehemet Ali, made, more than half a century since, included all the country on the Blue and White Niles, for great distances east and west of them, and for several degrees south of the equator; and in after-years his grandson, Ismail, the first Khedive of Egypt, claimed that he had a right to extend his borders as far as the Juba River on the Indian Ocean. Khartoum, the capital of this vast region, is situated at the junction of the two Niles, Blue and White; and Suakim, on the Red Sea, is its chief seaport.

This section of Africa is chiefly inhabited by two distinct races. From the eleventh degree of latitude northward, the people are almost wholly Arab in their origin. They are chiefly nomads, and are professedly Mohammedan. Being exceedingly emotional and superstitious, they have the greatest regard for their fakirs or spiritual guides, ascribe to them a kind of supernatural power, and venerate them almost more than they do the Prophet himself. The country south of the eleventh degree of latitude is peopled by Negroes, chiefly of a sedentary and agricultural mode of life, who, while classed as Mohammedans, are in reality pagans. The mingling of Arab and Negro blood has produced a third hybrid, Arab-speaking, class, who are found in the more fertile parts of the Soudan, especially in Darfur. A small yet very distinct race, said to have descended from the ancient Nubians, is found in the northern province of Darsola; and between the Nile and the Red Sea, not far from Suakim, there is still another distinct and ancient tribe, who speak a language of their own.

Until the middle of the 7th century the present Soudan was under native rule, while Egypt was under the rule of the Romans. But in 638 the Saracens, led by the famous warrior Amrou, one of the generals of the caliph Omar, began to invade Egypt, and soon subjugated it. The Copts agreed to pay tribute to the Caliph, and the whole of Egypt as far south as Syene, the present Assouan, was made a province of the caliphate. For about five hundred years Egypt suffered from a frequent change of dynasty, until the reign of the heroic Sultan, Saladin, a Koord in origin, under whose vigorous rule she became in 1173 an independent empire. In 1250 the government was seized by the Mamelukes, who were brought from Turkey, Tartary, and Circassia as slaves, and were made soldiers, and some of them advanced to office in the state. They continued in power till 1517, when Selim I., Sultan of the Turks, overthrew the Mameluke dynasty, and reduced the country to a Turkish province under the rule of a pasha. The Mamelukes were still turbulent, and were not completely subdued till 1798, when the French conquered the country under the pretence of freeing it from the cruel Mameluke yoke. The English then came to the aid of the Turk, 1801, expelled the French, and restored the pasha appointed by the Sultan.

At this time Mehemet Ali, a poor fisherman of Greek descent, a shrewd and active leader, who, with a band of followers, had aided the English and Turks in expelling the French, succeeded in securing the appointment from the Porte, in 1806, as viceroy of Egypt. He proved himself to be a general, a statesman, and a man of affairs, and met with great success for many years. Finding the Mamelukes, whom he had used as a stepping-stone to power, a hindrance to his rule and a plague to the country, he massacred great numbers of them in 1811; others escaped and fled to New Dongola, but they were followed and finally exterminated in 1820. Mehemet then made himself master of Upper Egypt, and by him the Egypt of to-day was virtually founded. By his great genius and diplomacy he eventually obtained power in perpetuity, shook the throne of the Sublime Porte, and wrested from the Sultan the highest dignity ever conferred on a subject—the dominion of a practically independent empire. His rule extended from the Mediterranean to the equator, and hereditary succession was established forever, according to Mohammedan law, in the eldest of his blood. But success did not always attend his plans, and the expedition which he sent into Nubia and Sennaar, 1821, to take military possession of those provinces, ended in the murder of the leader, Ismail Pasha, his youngest son. Ahmet Bey, whom Mehemet had sent to take possession of Kordofan and other Soudan provinces, hastened to avenge the death of Ismail, and put thousands of the people to the sword and applied the torch to their villages.

Mehemet Ali was succeeded by his son Ibrahim, then by his grandson Abbas Pasha, then by his son Said Pasha, and then, in 1863, by his grandson Ismail, son of Ibrahim. Ismail was the fifth viceroy of Egypt. In 1867 the Sultan bestowed upon him the title of Highness and Khedive, with important additions to his authority. In 1868–9 the Khedive enlarged his army, extended his sway southward over regions which Mehemet Ali had nominally taken, so as to recover and include the Upper and White Nile together with the Equatorial and Lake provinces. In 1874 he pushed his victories into the Darfur regions. But in levying enormous taxes upon the people he laid the train for revolt; and by borrowing vast amounts of money from the English and other Europeans both he and the nation became bankrupt, and were completely in the power of bondholding foreigners under a debt of $500,-000,000; though it is said that not more than half of this amount was ever received by Egypt. The interest on these loans, the annual tribute of $3,600,000 to Turkey, together with all the running expenses of the land, which were now enormous, made Egypt and her Soudan territories the worst taxed country in the world, while the income thus derived was still inadequate to the heavy demands upon it. England and France were jealous of the interests of their bondholders, and England felt the supreme importance of keeping open her communications with India. They thus compelled the Khedive to receive foreign officials to supervise the revenue and look after foreign claims. Numerous other officials from England and France were appointed, at most extravagant salaries, to fill places from which natives were turned out. The growing arrogance of the foreigners increased the discontent of the cruelly taxed people, till at length the masses, including the Arabs and the ill-paid army, united into a "national party." The Khedive, under pressure of foreign influence, was compelled in 1879 to abdicate in favor of his son, Tewfik Pasha, who was generally looked upon as a mere creature of the foreign bondholding interest. The people, still cruelly taxed, began to resent the administration by foreigners, and the appropriation of much of the national income to pay interest on loans which had been made to Ismail, an utter spendthrift, for his personal benefit.

This resentment became so common and strong that Tewfik was compelled to appoint one of its foremost representatives, Arabi Pasha, as his minister of war. Arabi was an army officer and the head of the nationalist party, with the training received when he was practically at the head of the government. He was resolved to overthrow European influence, peaceably if possible, yet by arms if necessary. As minister of war, when he found a British fleet menacing Alexandria, he began to strengthen the forts which commanded the harbor; and his refusal to cease work on these forts was the nominal occasion of the bombardment which soon followed. The English had seen that Tewfik, who had been faithful to them, was in danger; his authority was gone; and deeming it necessary that he should be re-established as their ally, their ironclads appeared at Alexandria in spite of the Sultan's protest. The city was bombarded and burnt, June 11th, 1882, and thousands of Egyptians were killed. Meanwhile Tewfik, the nominal head of the government, had hidden himself in the palace at Ramleh.

The problem that confronted the English was a gigantic one and involved many conflicting elements. The other great powers would be jealous of a permanent occupation. The people of Egypt distrusted and disliked the Khedive, while they hated the foreigners. Thus it seemed utterly impossible to institute any system of government which should be strong and lasting, and yet satisfy Europe while securing England a predominant power. In the mean time a vigorous insurrection broke out in Soudan, where the turbulent people resented Egyptian oppression, as the Egyptians resented English interference. With all the fire of religious fanaticism, added to the wrath of the slave dealers; taking advantage of the smouldering wrath of the oppressed Egyptians, led by an ambitious adventurer, Mohammed Achmet or Ahmed, an Arab of African blood, the revolt began in June, 1881. An air of mystery surrounded Mohammed, and he styled himself El Mahdi (i.e. one who is spiritually guided), the Guide, and he claimed to be that Prophet of Islam whose coming had been awaited for 1,300 years. Emerging from seclusion, he and his army vowed to sweep every Egyptian soldier from the land, and free the people from any yoke, whether financial, religious, or political. When the revolt commenced, the Khedive was too much occupied with anarchy and Arabi Pasha at home to be able to cope with a distant rebellion. The Mahdi took several large towns before Egypt fell into the hands of the English. But these were petty successes as compared with the great victory he gained in July, 1882,—the same month in which Alexandria was bombarded,—when a force of about 6,000 Egyptian soldiers, nearly all the army, together with the commanders, were overpowered and massacred. In his efforts to take El Obeid, the capital of Kordofan, he was three times repulsed; but in January, 1883, he succeeded, and made the town henceforth his place of residence and base of operations. An English officer, General Hicks, was now sent to take command of the Egyptian forces in the service of the Khedive at Khartoum. In April he succeeded in defeating a rebel force of 5,000 in Sennaar; in May he defeated El Mahdi near Khartoum. In September he went from Khartoum in pursuit of El Mahdi with an Egyptian force of about 10,000 men, commanded by both English and Egyptian officers. In about two months, through the treachery of a guide, he was led into a defile not far from El Obeid, where the Mahdi fell upon him and left "not a man" of all his army to tell the tale.

While these events were transpiring in the Soudan, the English troops were preparing to withdraw from Egypt and leave that country to try the experiment of a semi-constitutional government. The orders for withdrawal had actually been given when the massacre at El Obeid occurred. As the massacred army was officered in part by Englishmen, it was feared the event would be looked upon as an English defeat; and being so interpreted, as it surely would be by the revolted tribes, would cause all the greater exultation among them. The English troops remained in Egypt, but did not enter the Soudan until they were in a sense forced to do so by the turn things had now taken at Khartoum, Sinkat, and Tokar.

The fate of General Hicks's expedition gave a new turn to Anglo-Egyptian affairs. England began now to take a deep interest in the Soudan war. She saw many Egyptian garrisons, and some of them in the command of English officers, hemmed in by hostile tribes, and in danger of being massacred. She saw Khartoum in danger. She heard a call for English troops to "vindicate English honor," and to this extent at least she was now willing to have a part in the war. But to send out troops to conquer the Mahdi would be to commit England to a policy of conquest and annexation, and surrender the conviction of the English Government that Soudan should be left to the Soudanese. The Khedive was first advised, then commanded, to abandon the Soudan, when the Khedive's ministers demurred; but a new ministry was appointed with Nubar Pasha at their head. Meantime affairs grew steadily worse. The report that Egypt would abandon the Soudan gave new strength to the revolt, and tribe after tribe joined the Mahdi's standard. Osman Digna, a courageous chief in Eastern Soudan, and one of the foremost of the Mahdi's lieutenants, raised an army of 20,000, laid siege to Sinkat and Tokar, not far from the Red Sea, and threatened the seaport Suakim, and thus threatened England's route to India. To protect this English ships were dispatched to Suakim, and marines landed there to protect the town. There, too, an Egyptian force was collected and marched thence, under General Baker, to the relief of Tokar. But they were too late. Ere they had reached the town they were attacked by Osman Digna, and half their number slain. The rest fled and took refuge in Khartoum, to which the Mahdi now laid siege. This was soon followed by a massacre of the whole force at Sinkat. Stung to action by these disasters, the British Government dispatched troops to Suakim, and was preparing to send an expedition, under General Graham, for the relief of Tokar, when news came that the garrison had surrendered. England, having now become concerned for the safety of Egypt, involving her connections with India and the protection of the bondholders, proposed to abandon the Soudan and encounter the Mahdi, if need be, farther north. She would begin by tranquillizing the hostile tribes, by relieving Khartoum, and by opening a way by which the 20,000 English and Egyptian troops and a still larger number of non-combatants, civil officers and others, might retreat and leave the country. To this end General "Chinese" Gordon, who had formerly been for five years governor and governor-general of the Soudan, was sent almost alone, nominally by the Khedive, but really by English pressure and out of regard to popular clamor, to commence operations at the capital.

This action was late, but Gordon was hopeful. On the 24th of January, 1884, he arrived on his peaceful mission at Cairo. His route was up the Nile by railway to Assiout, thence by steamer to Korosko. A four days' ride on a camel took him across the Nubian Desert to Abu Hamed, and on the 18th of February, by way of the Nile, he reached Khartoum. He began his mission by promising the people relief from the oppressions which had provoked the revolt, especially from the extortions of the tax-gatherers; he tried to conciliate the natives by conceding their rights, promising release from the Bashi-Bazouk system of government, and telling them they were henceforth to govern themselves. He tried also to appease the wrath of the slave-traders by saying he "had decided to permit the traffic. Every one having domestic servants," said he, "may consider them his property and dispose of them." By threats and bribes, and by taking advantage of mutual jealousies and rivalries among the Sheiks, he endeavored to weaken the Mahdi's power and to obtain a foothold for a successful shaping of the political future. In answer to the surprise generally felt, and the many inquiries that came in from different quarters, when these promises became generally known, General Gordon explained that the English and Egyptian governments had decided to evacuate the Soudan and leave the people to be governed in their own way, by chiefs or sultans, as they were before they became an Egyptian dependency, which would preclude his interfering with slave-holding; that to liberate slaves without compensating their masters would be robbery; that he made a distinction between slave-holding and slave-hunting; and that as for the latter he would never cease to do all in his power to prevent it. In attempting to restore and establish native rule, one of his first acts was to send El Mahdi a commission as Sultan of Kordofan, of which El Obeid was the capital; which the prophet was said to receive with an ecstasy of delight. Gordon proposed that the British government make Zebehr Pasha governor-general of the Soudan; but the government declined because of his reputation as a great slave-dealer. Gordon insisted that Zebehr was the only man to carry out his programme, and that without him a peaceful solution of the question was impossible. But his request was not granted. The Mahdi, seeing that Gordon was taking no active measures, made hostile demonstrations. Gordon abandoned the policy of reconciliation for one of a more vigorous character, and asked that 200 English soldiers might be sent to Wady Halfa for the sake of showing that he had the support of European power and influence at his command; but that, too, was denied him. By the 1st of March Gordon began to feel that his chances of success were rapidly diminishing; and at last he offered to resign his commission. His resignation not being accepted, he continued to struggle on as best he could, deserted by the government that sent him out, and beleaguered by the enemy. With these he fought several damaging battles as the months went by. On the 12th of May, 1884, the government was arraigned in the House of Commons for its inefficient, vacillating Egyptian policy, and charged with deserting Gordon. The motion to censure was lost; but it was not long before the government began to prepare an expedition to start in August for the relief of Gordon. On the 7th of August, $1,500,000 was voted by the House of Commons to pay the expenses of the expedition. But it was not till early in September (9–12) that Lord Wolseley arrived in Egypt and assumed command of the enterprise, in which something more than 10,000 troops were to participate. Early in December these troops, divided into three forces, were formed at different points scattered along the Nile, south of Korosko. On the 16th Lord Wolseley, having journeyed 1,200 miles from Cairo, had reached Korti, just above Old Dongola, on the Nile, where the advance, under General Herbert Stewart, was awaiting his arrival. On his way up the Nile Lord Wolseley heard of the assassination of Colonel Stewart, Gordon's associate, a little above Merawe, where one of the three or four Khartoum steamers, with which he had been sent with despatches down the Nile by Gordon to meet the coming expedition, had been wrecked on a rock. On the 30th of December, General Stewart, with a force of 1,000 men, started from Korti for Metemneh across the desert. Having been reinforced with 500 more men, on the 16th of January, 1885, he had a hard fight with about 6,000 Arabs at the Abu Klea wells, in which, after great loss, he came off victor. Three days later he fought and won another desperate battle, in which he was severely wounded, at Gubat, three miles west of the Nile, near Metemneh, some 75 miles below Khartoum. Colonel Wilson having now been sent, January 26th, with a flotilla of three steamers found at Metemneh, to communicate with Gordon, General Stewart remained at Gubat till he heard of the fall of Khartoum, and then retraced his steps, with much difficulty, to Korti. Meantime General Earle, who had been sent up the river to Berber, had been killed in an assault upon an Arab fortification, before he reached Abu Hamed; and his column, hearing that Khartoum had fallen, returned also to Korti. It was here at Korti that the last boat-load of reinforcements arrived, February 2d, from down the river. Colonel Wilson arrived at Khartoum on the 28th of January, 1885. Reaching the confluence of the Blue and the White Niles, he was surprised to find the Arabs opening fire upon him from the fortifications on the banks. Reaching Omdurman, Gordon's stronghold, the fusillade of the rebels was continued. It was discovered that the enemy was in possession of the island of Tuti, just outside of the city. Pushing ahead, the garrison commenced firing upon them. No flag, save the green banner of the Mahdi, floated from the public buildings. The palace where Gordon had held out so long was deserted.

Everything seemed to be in the undisputed possession of the enemy. The Mahdi, having sixty thousand men in the vicinity of Khartoum, had introduced a number of his emissaries into the city, who, mingling fully with the native troops under Gordon, using bribes and threats, and working on their religious feelings, had induced them to mutiny. Seven thousand of the garrison are said to have deserted to the rebels, leaving General Gordon only 2,500 that were faithful. With this small force he attempted to hold the city, but was finally compelled to surrender. Rumors as to just the time, place, and manner in which an end was put to the life of Gordon were many and varied. Dr. Fricke, who went out with him to Khartoum, and remained with him until his death, and who, as a merchant, has since travelled much in Africa, says: "He was speared by his own soldiers when he came to inspect them." Dr. Fricke, being a Mussulman, managed to escape, and with great difficulty made his way down the Nile. All reports were agreed, at the time, in saying that the Mahdi captured Khartoum on the 26th of January, 1885, through treachery; and most of these reports point to one Farez Pasha as the traitor. It is said that, having charge of the ramparts on that fatal day, he betrayed his trust, opened the gates, and so gave the foe the freest admission. Another report of the fate of Gordon was that he was "shot down under the acacias of the government buildings, on his way to the Austrian consul's, to take his last farewell of his good friend Hansal."

The great object of the costly work the government had undertaken in attempting to relieve Gordon and the beleagured garrisons having proved an utter failure, the expedition was recalled. Upon this the Arabs were much emboldened, and the Prophet seemed to be left well-nigh free to carry out his assumed mission, make the Soudan independent, and hasten the final triumph of Islam. The retiring troops were greatly harassed; the few garrisons required to remain were threatened; and some of the Sheiks who favored the English were put to death. But deeds of violence, and the hostile advance of the Arabs northward with an eye on Egypt, were presently somewhat checked by the small-pox that had now begun to rage, and of which the Mahdi himself died in June, 1885. But the lull was of short duration. Mohammed Achmet was soon succeeded by a new Mahdi, Khalifa Abdullah. Egypt, being again threatened, sought the continued aid of the English, who ordered Suakim and all the east coast of Egypt from Suez to Massowah to be blockaded. This brought increasing distress upon the Soudanese, and the new Mahdi sent Osman Digna to lay siege to Suakim and drive the Egyptians into the sea; but towards the end of the year 1888 the British government sent war-ships and troops and relieved the city. But the repulse was only local and temporary.

The Mahdism of Abdullah evidently took on more of the religious element than did that of his predecessor. His great aim and that of his dervishes was to extend and establish the triumphs of the Mohammedan faith, till Islam should be made universal. To this end they would drive the English alike out of the Soudan, out of the equatorial regions, out of East Africa, and push their conquests to the Atlantic on the west coast. To this end they would invoke the aid of all classes in the Soudan, assail Christian missions in Uganda, intrigue with tribes on the Congo, and claim, indeed, nothing less than all that part of Africa which lies north of the Zambesi as Mohammedan territory. Worsted at Suakim, they undertook the invasion of Egypt. Under the lead of his general, Wad-El-Njumi, several thousand of his dervish followers, some with heavy guns and gun-boats, were stationed at important points, as Wady Halfa and Assouan, along the Nile, and other places on the borders. To aid the Egyptian army in meeting them, fresh regiments were dispatched in July, 1889, from England, together with a squadron of the 20th Hussars, all under command of General Grenfell, to whom, in asking the foe to surrender, Wad-El-Njumi replied: "Your force is nothing to me. I have been sent to conquer the world. Remember Hicks and Gordon." On the 3d of August, 1889, General Grenfell engaged the dervishes near Toski, and completely routed them after a gallant defence, during which 1,500 of them were killed and wounded, and a thousand of them, together with fifty standards, were captured. But any further movement was deemed useless, unless the government would assent to the views of the British generals that Berber should be held as the true key of the Soudan.

It is more than sixty years since Mehemet Ali began to take at least nominal possession of extensive provinces, such as Nubia, Dongola, Sennaar, Faka, and Berber in the Soudan. Some fifty years ago, 1838, he passed through the land and tried to give the teeming millions there some good idea of commerce and agriculture, and turn the trade of the country down the Nile. But he was himself too much interested in the fruits of the slave-trade to hold his semi-savage officials back from the iniquitous traffic. And so it is that, from that time on to the present, the interest and enterprise of that country have centred in these inhuman pursuits. Abbas Pasha did nothing to counteract the evil. Said Pasha tried to advance the interests of Egypt in the Soudan, and gave orders to have all abuses stopped, especially the odious traffic in slaves. But his orders were never honored; and at the close of his reign the revenue Egypt was getting from that country through onerous taxation amounted to a million and a half dollars, aside from large amounts from the slave trade. Upon Ismail's accession, earnest efforts were made to extend the limits of Egyptian Soudan still farther southward and along all the tributaries of the Nile; and to this end in 1869, the Khedive set the renowned equatorial African traveller, Sir Samuel Baker, in command as governor-general over all that vast region. But at the end of four years, 1873, finding himself unable to continue his fight with the slave dealers and their Egyptian accomplices, he gave up, and fought his way out as best he could. And yet, after all the enormous expenditure of nearly $6,000,000, which this attempted four years' rule in equatorial Soudan had cost him, the Khedive could not give up the idea of holding the wild and lawless realm as an Egyptian dependency. And now a second arrangement was made with another distinguished Englishman, "Chinese" Gordon, who came to the Khedive recommended as just the man for the service he required. General Gordon entered upon the enterprise early in 1874, rich in experience, full of enthusiasm, having at his command a goodly number of able, scientific, and accomplished men, both English and American, and an infantry escort of 200 troops. The capital of his realm was, at first, Gondo-

koro, then Lado. At the end of three years, having recommended Emin Pasha to succeed him as governor of the Equatorial Provinces, in 1877 he was made Governor-general of all Soudan, the equatorial regions included. The plenary powers of his commission set him virtually above the Khedive's authority, while the indirect part which England had in the matter was a virtual pledge of his having the support of the Queen. Virtually independent, with much experience, and ample means at command, it was natural that much should be expected from his government. Upon his taking command, he found the country not only self-supporting, but paying more than half a million per annum into the Egyptian treasury. Egypt was, therefore, not a little surprised to hear, at the end of some two or three years of his administration, that he had determined to abandon the field, assigning as his chief reason that he hadn't money enough to carry on his government, there being now, in 1879, a deficit of nearly half a million dollars. Finding the Soudan, as he did, out of debt and with a surplus in the treasury, he left it heavily encumbered and with diminished boundaries. One great hindrance to Gordon's success was the determined opposition of the slave dealers. To their influence, direct or indirect, it was chiefly due that he too was so speedily compelled to withdraw and leave the country to their control.

As governor-general of the Soudan, Gordon was succeeded, in 1879, by Raouf Pasha. "He had three Europeans as his subordinates—Emin Bey, who, before Gordon left, had been placed in charge of the province of the Equator; Lupton Bey, an Englishman, who had followed Gessi as governor of the Bahr-el-Ghazelle; and Slatin Bey, an Austrian, in command at Darfur. Raouf had barely been two years at Khartoum when the Mahdi appeared on the scene."

Egypt was now too much occupied with her own direct home affairs, the revolt under Arabi and the incoming of the English, to admit of her doing anything for her dependencies. This gave the Mahdi and the slave-dealing Arabs a good opportunity to come to the front, out of which came the Soudan War; and with this, a long-continued entanglement of England with the affairs of Egypt and the Soudan provinces, over which Egypt claimed control. Nor is it yet plain to see what, or when, shall be the end of the strife and struggle still going on. Meantime the Mahdists, backed by the slave-dealing Arabs, have pushed their way up the Nile into the provinces over which Emin Pasha was set, until he has felt compelled to withdraw, little by little, southward, and finally, under the wing of Stanley's Relief Expedition, has been induced to give up the field and leave it to the undisputed sway of the Moslem and slave-hunting powers.

There have been several attempts to plant mission work in the Egyptian Soudan. Swedish and German missionaries have looked with hungry eyes toward it, and some of its towns were stations on the famous *Apostelstrasse* which was to connect Cairo with Abyssinia.

The most important effort, however, was made by the American Missionary Association in response to the generous offer of a large sum of money by Mr. R. Arthington, of Leeds, England. An expedition under the lead of Rev. Henry M. Ladd, D.D., made a long and extended exploration of the country in 1881 preparatory to its regular occupation. The coming on of the troubles mentioned above put a stop to the enterprise, and it has not been renewed. The Soudan Mission mentioned in the article on the Congo Free State is distinctively a Western Soudan mission and has no intimate relations with the Eastern or Egyptian Soudan.

As European interests and influence in Africa are increasing, great efforts are being made in England to bring the Soudan, or at least all the upper Nile regions, under British rule. Men who have seen and studied the country through and through, such as Baker and Loring, tell us that in all parts of the Soudan, but especially in the southern portions of it, " there are vast tracts of rich lands filled with untouched treasures, lying fallow, and covered with millions of human beings, who can easily be brought under the influence of that higher western civilization in which it is our privilege to live,"—to say nothing of the many millions of acres and people beyond Gondokoro or in the equatorial regions, and nothing about Harrar and the Somali country,—all indicating what a mighty and glorious future the gospel might bring to the Soudan and to all its fertile and populous borders, could it have sway over them.

## Soul-Winning and Prayer Union.

Headquarters, Newport-on-Tay, Scotland.—The Soul-Winning and Prayer Union was formed in 1880, and has now a membership from all parts of the world of more than 4,600. It supports missionaries and Bible-women in China, and India; in Morocco, Congo Free State, and Old Calabar, in Africa; and in Jerusalem, Bethany, and Beyrout, in Syria. Gospel work is carried on in Great Britain by means of tent-meetings, circulation of tracts, etc. The tenth day of each month is observed by members everywhere as a time of united prayer for success in all undertakings of the mission, and for means to carry on the work.

## South American Missionary Society.

Headquarters, 1 Clifford's Inn, Fleet Street, London, E. C.—Captain Allen Gardiner, the founder of the South American Missionary Society, first visited South America with a view of establishing a mission in 1838. For years the great aim of his life had been to become "the pioneer of a Christian Mission to the most abandoned heathen." With this object steadily in view, he went through a constant succession of travels and adventures for some years, taking his wife and children with him on long, perilous journeys. After repeated disappointments in other countries, he was led to direct all his efforts towards the natives of South America. His attempts to reach the mountain tribes were defeated by the jealousy of the Roman Catholic priests. At last he thought that not even the Spanish priesthood would consider it worth while to interfere with anything he might attempt among the poor savages at the desolate southern corner of the great continent, and by beginning with them he hoped to reach in time the nobler tribes.

In 1830 Captain (afterwards Admiral) Fitzroy had been sent by the British Government to survey the coasts of Tierra del Fuego. On his return to England he took with him, for a visit, three native lads and a girl of nine years. They were kindly treated, and found capable of learning a good deal. When, a year later, Captain Fitzroy took them back to their own land, he was accompanied by a Mr. Williams, who hoped to remain in Tierra del Fuego as a missionary. A very few days sufficed to show the danger of this attempt: he returned to the vessel, and all thought of missionary work in this region was abandoned until Captain Gardiner took it up. His hope was that the natives who had visited England might be still alive, and that one of them,—called "Jemmy Button,"—if he had not forgotten all his English, might act as interpreter and friend. But he found great difficulties in the way. England, while warmly supporting missions to other parts of the world, seemed utterly indifferent to the fate of South America. After much effort he succeeded, in 1844, in forming a society called the Patagonian Missionary Society; soon after, he, with a few companions, attempted to establish a mission in Tierra del Fuego. Owing to the hostility of the natives it was a complete failure. The Society in England was much discouraged; "not so the brave captain." The sum of £1,000, which the Committee declared necessary to the starting of another expedition, was secured, £700 being given by a Christian lady of Cheltenham, the remaining £300 by Captain Gardiner himself; and on September 7th, 1850, Captain Gardiner again sailed from England. With him were Mr. Richard Williams, a surgeon in good practice, who gave up all earthly hopes in order to carry the glad tidings to the heathen ; Mr. Maidment of the Church of England Y. M. C. A.; a ship-carpenter who had gone on the previous expedition, and who volunteered his services for this second attempt, saying that to be with Captain Gardiner was "like a heaven upon earth;" and three Cornish fishermen, Christian men, who readily offered themselves for the "forlorn hope," though plainly warned of its dangers. The seven brave men sailed from Liverpool, after a farewell service in Bristol, in the "Ocean Queen," a vessel bound for San Francisco, which promised to land them with their boats* and stores at Tierra del Fuego. They took with them provisions for six months, and arranged that more should be sent by the first opportunity.

On the 5th of December, the "Ocean Queen" anchored in Banner Cove, Tierra del Fuego, and on the 18th she sailed away with many cheerful messages to friends at home from the brave men left behind. The journals of Gardiner and Williams, preserved almost by miracle, tell the painful story of the next nine months. Misfortunes and disasters rapidly succeeded one another. In a heavy storm an anchor and both small boats for landing were lost; in repairing a leak in the "Pioneer" the terrible discovery was made that by an oversight almost the whole supply of powder and shot had been left on board the "Ocean Queen," leaving them without the means of obtaining game, upon which they had counted to help out their supplies, which contained very little animal food, and also without power to defend themselves from the attacks of the natives, by which many

---

* Living in a house upon land had been proved impracticable from the thieving and plundering habits of the natives; accordingly, for this attempt, two vessels, 26 feet long, to carry the stores, and to be a "floating home" for the missionaries, together with two smaller boats, to enable them to go on shore at any time, had been provided.

times their lives were in peril. Later, a terrible gale made a complete wreck of the " Pioneer." At Garden Island they buried several bottles, placing above them boards of wood on which were written, "Look underneath." Each bottle contained a written paper, "We are gone to Spaniard Harbor; we have sickness on board. . . . . Our supplies are nearly out, and if not soon relieved we shall be starved." They also painted on the rocks in two places, "You will find us in Spaniard Harbor." Then, with the " Speedwell" they succeeded in reaching this last place of refuge—Spaniard Harbor. The frightful Fuegian winter began in April, and from the terrific storms of wind and snow the deep caverns in the rocks formed their best refuge. Their efforts to catch game and fish met with little success; they grew weaker and weaker; the sailor, John Badcock, was the first to die. Mr. Williams seems to have realized that the still expected "ship" would arrive too late for his relief, and his journal contains many farewell messages to beloved friends at home. One by one the little band passed away; it is probable that the brave Gardiner himself was the last survivor. The last entry in his diary is September 5th; a little note was also found, dated September 6th. The long-looked-for vessel, owing to strange mistakes and delays, did not reach the coast until the end of October. Following the directions written on the rocks, the "Speedwell" was found, with one dead body on board, and another on the shore, while books, papers, etc., lay scattered around. "The captain and sailors cried like children at the sight." A violent gale arising, they dared not remain longer, but put out to sea at once, carrying the sad news to Montevideo. By this time friends in England, greatly alarmed, had applied to government for aid, and the frigate " Dido" was sent to search for the lost missionaries, reaching the coast in January. Guided by the writings on the rocks, the officers soon completed the sorrowful discoveries. In Spaniard Harbor they saw on a rock the verses from Psalm lxii. 5-8, "My soul, hope thou in God, for my expectation is from Him," etc., with the drawing of a hand pointing to the spot where the wreck of the " Pioneer" and the bodies of Maidment and Gardiner were found. All the remains of the martyrs were reverently collected, and after the reading of the beautiful burial-service of the Church of England, were buried in one grave beside the " Pioneer." The colors of the " Dido" were lowered, and three volleys fired, as in honor of an officer's funeral. The heroic death of Gardiner and his companions accomplished what in life they had failed to do. The Christian public of England, almost stunned at first by the sad tidings received, soon resolved that the dying wishes and prayers of the martyrs should not have ascended to heaven in vain. The last directions of Captain Gardiner, so wonderfully preserved from plundering natives and raging winds, were acted upon; the Society was re-formed according to his plan, and now a Christian Mission is firmly established in Tierra del Fuego, and the South American Missionary Society is rapidly extending its agencies over many regions of the great continent, where generations yet unborn may bless the name of Allen Gardiner.

According to the plan of Captain Gardiner, the South American Missionary Society should have the threefold object of supplying the spiritual wants of "his own fellow-countrymen," the Roman Catholics, and the heathen in South America; these directions the Society endeavors to carry out by missionary effort among the numerous native tribes, by ministerial work in the many communities of English-speaking people scattered throughout the continent, and among the sailors who frequent its harbors; and by evangelistic labors among the native people speaking Spanish and Portuguese, and among persons of other nationalities, by means of special services and, above all, by the distribution (by sale) of the Bible in the native languages.

The first attempt to carry out Gardiner's wishes was in 1854, when the missionary schooner "Allen Gardiner" sailed for Keppel Island, one of the West Falklands, which was selected as a station from which, by means of the schooner, missionaries might communicate with Tierra del Fuego, and to which natives might be brought for instruction. The Rev. G. P. Despard became the superintendent of this mission in 1856. Its further history will be found under the head of "The Fuegian Mission."

In 1860 the Rev. Allen Gardiner, the only son of Captain Gardiner, having first served under Mr. Despard at the Falklands, in Tierra del Fuego, and in Patagonia, went to Lota, in Chili, as chaplain to the English and Scotch residents; from whence he made many expeditions among the Araucanian Indians.

In 1864 a great enlargement of the work took place by the establishment of chaplaincies in Panama, Callao, and other places, and the opening of a medical mission in Patagones, Argentine Republic. During succeeding years the work was extended to Uruguay, Paraguay, and Brazil, and in 1867 the three departments of Captain Gardiner's plan, the English, the Spanish, and the heathen, were in full operation.

*The Fuegian Mission.*—As already stated, this mission was commenced by the formation of a station on the Falkland Islands. From thence, in 1856, a cautious intercourse was commenced with the Fuegians, and they were encouraged to visit the mission station at Keppel in small parties. After much toil of preparation a Fuegian family from one of the larger islands near Cape Horn was brought to Keppel by Mr. Allen Gardiner in 1858. The man was Jemmy Button; he was still able to speak broken English, and from him, at this early date, the missionaries learned something of the Fuegian language. On the return of that family to their own country, other natives visited Keppel. Mr. Despard visited Tierra del Fuego, and remained with the schooner a month on the coast, bringing back three men and their wives, together with two lads as visitors. Much pains were taken to gain the confidence of these natives, and to impart to them some religious knowledge. So friendly did they seem that in 1859 the missionaries thought they might venture to take the first step towards the establishment of a missionary station in their island home. Forming their judgment partly from their own visitors at Keppel and partly from others on the Fuegian coast, they believed that the ferocity of the natives had been overstated. Accordingly, they sailed for Woolya, in Navarin Island. Mr. Philips was the leader of the little band of missionaries, and he was fearlessly supported by Captain Fell of the "Allen Gardiner." Their first reception was friendly, and on Sunday, the 6th of November, they went ashore to conduct divine worship. While thus engaged they were attacked and massacred. One young Fuegian, who had been at the mission station, so earnestly implored to be taken back to Keppel in the ship which came in search of the missionaries that he prevailed over the scruples and hesitation of the captain. His arrival with his wife at the station enabled the surviving missionaries to go on with the difficult work of learning the Fuegian language; for, though bowed down with the weight of a great calamity, their courage never wavered, and they maintained their determination to go on with the work with unflinching constancy. For three years after the murder of the missionaries no visit was made to Tierra del Fuego. In January, 1863, the Rev. W. H. Stirling (now the Right Rev. W. H. Stirling, D.D., bishop of the Falkland Islands) was sent out as superintendent of the mission, and as soon as possible intercourse with Tierra del Fuego was resumed. Forty or fifty of the islanders were brought in successive groups of eight or ten to the station at Keppel, were fed, clothed, taught, and conducted back to their wild homes. They became accustomed to divine worship in their own language, and they also made rapid progress in acquiring English.

In 1868 a small settlement was commenced at Liwya, on Navarin Island, on the southern shore of the Beagle Channel. Four young natives who had had special training at Keppel were placed there, among others. A log-house was built for them, and they were provided with goats and sheep, also implements and seeds for the cultivation of the ground. When Mr. Stirling visited them some months later he found them still in possession of house and goats. Mr. Stirling then resolved to try a residence on shore himself, and accordingly in January, 1869, established himself at Ooshooia, on the north shore of the Beagle Channel, and opposite to Liwya, on the south shore. Ooshooia has good harborage, plenty of wood and water, with land available for tillage and pasture. The party at Liwya removed to Ooshooia, and became a body-guard to their new chief. The "Allen Gardiner" sailed away on 11th January, and Mr. Stirling was left to face the dangers of his position alone. For seven months he remained, proving that a mission station on Tierra del Fuego had at length become a possibility. Other missionaries with their wives bravely ventured over, and Ooshooia is now a Christian village, with cottages,—not wigwams,—a church, a school-house, and an orphanage. The present divisions of the work in South America are:

1. *The Southern Mission*, including the Falklands and Tierra del Fuego.

(a) Keppel Island.—West Falklands has been occupied as a station since 1855, and forms a valuable missionary settlement, where natives of Tierra del Fuego, brought over at their own request, are boarded, instructed in Christian doctrine, trained in husbandry, etc. There are also a very productive industrial farm, workshop, and school, together with the numerous flocks and herds which afford abundant means of educating the natives to lead Christian lives,

and to follow peaceful pursuits on their return to their own country.

(b) Ooshooia, first missionary station on Tierra del Fuego, founded in 1869. About 300 natives have here received the rite of baptism.

(c) Wallaston Islands.—A promising beginning has already made in the station established upon one of the islands of this group.

The mission vessel "Allen Gardiner" is employed in keeping open communication between these stations, conveying missionaries and natives to and from the coast, carrying farm produce, supplies, etc.

2. The "*East Coast*" *Mission*, including the Argentine Republic, Uruguay, Paraguay, and Brazil.

(a) The work of the Society—including ministration to English and Spanish speaking people, and natives in the Argentine Republic, is carried on at Patagones (El Carmen), Rosario, Cordoba and Tucuman, Canada De Gomez, Alexandria Colony, Gran Chaco, Chuput (Welsh) Colony, and Concordia.

(b) In Uruguay at Fray Bentos, Salto, and Paysandu.

(c) In Paraguay, the Chaco: and

(d) In Brazil, at Rio de Janeiro, San Paulo and Santos, and Pernambuco.

3. *The West Coast Mission*, with stations in Chili, at Lota and Coronel, Chanaral and Araucania.

**Southern Baptist Convention.—** Headquarters, Richmond, Va., U. S. A. The Southern Baptist Convention was organized in the city of Augusta, Georgia, in May, 1845. It originated in a withdrawal of the Southern churches from union and co-operation with "the General Convention of the Baptist Denomination in the United States," popularly known as the Triennial Convention. (See article on American Baptist Missionary Union.) The constitution of this convention, as well as the history of its proceedings from the beginning, conferred on all the members in good standing of the Baptist denomination, whether at the North or the South, eligibility to all appointments emanating from the convention of the Board. Unmistakable indications, however, led the Alabama Baptist State Convention in 1844 to adopt a preamble and resolutions which were submitted to the Board of Foreign Missions of the Triennial Convention, to which a frank and explicit answer was returned, that "if any one having slaves should offer himself as a missionary, and insist on retaining them as his property, we could not appoint him. One thing is certain, we can never be a party to any arrangement that would imply approbation of slavery."

When this reply was made known, the Board of the Virginia Foreign Missionary Society addressed a circular to the Baptist churches of Virginia, suggesting that a convention be held at Augusta, Georgia, for conference as to the best means of promoting the Foreign Mission cause, and other interests of the Baptist denomination in the South. Both at the North and the South a separation seemed inevitable. At the North it was desired by many, regretted by a few, and expected by all.

Before the proposed convention in Augusta could meet, the Home Mission Society at its meeting in Providence, in April, had virtually declared for a separation, and recommended that as the existing Society was planted in the North, and had there its Executive Board and charter, which it seemed desirable to preserve, it be retained by the Northern churches, and those sympathizing with them as to the appointment of slave-holders.

At the call of the Board of Managers of the Virginia Foreign Mission Society, there assembled in Augusta May 8th, 1845, 310 delegates from the states of Maryland, Virginia, North and South Carolina, Georgia, Alabama, Louisiana, Kentucky, and the District of Columbia. Owing to the short notice of the meeting, other states were represented only by letter. The Committee appointed for the purpose presented a resolution, "That for peace and harmony, and in order to accomplish the greatest amount of good, and for the maintenance of those scriptural principles on which the General Missionary Convention of the Baptist Denomination of the United States was formed, it is proper that this convention at once proceed to organize a society for the propagation of the gospel." Then followed the adoption of a constitution which was "precisely that of the original union; that in connection with which, throughout his missionary life, Adoniram Judson lived, under which Ann Judson and Boardman died. We recede from it no single step. We use the very terms, and we uphold the true spirit and great object of the late General Convention."

Thus the Southern Baptist Convention claims to be the real and proper successor and continuator of that body, which "at a special meeting held in New York November 19th, 1845, was 'dissolved,' and the American Baptist Missionary Union, with an entirely new constitution and a different basis of membership, was organized in its stead."

A Board of Foreign Missions was appointed to be located in Richmond, Virginia, and one for Domestic Missions, to be located in Marion, Alabama. The new Convention gathered around itself the enthusiastic support of the Baptist churches of the South; and the wisdom of its formation is evidenced by the fact that while Southern Baptists contributed to the Triennial Convention in 31 years, from 1814–1845, $212,000, during the 34 years, from 1845–1879 (covering the period of the war), their contributions for Foreign Missions alone were $939,377.

*Development of Work.*—Immediately after the organization of the Board they were instructed to correspond with the Boston Board with regard to mutual claims; and were authorized to make any equitable and prudent arrangement with that Board, to take a portion of its missions under the patronage of the convention. At the suggestion of the Boston Board, through Dr. Francis Wayland, it was agreed that "the property and liabilities of the General Convention should remain with that body," and that "the missionaries should have the choice of the associations with which they would be connected."

Under this arrangement Rev. J. L. Shuck, the first American Baptist missionary to China, and Rev. I. J. Roberts, who had followed Mr. Shuck in 1836, gave in their adherence to the Southern Convention. Rev. S. C. Clopton and Rev. George Pearcy were commissioned to join them, and the missions of the new Board were fairly inaugurated.

Coincident with the establishment of the China mission, it was determined to commence work on the coast of Africa, where missions of the Northern Board were already in operation, and in 1847 stations were formed in Liberia and in Sierra Leone, and in 1850 in Central Africa.

As early as 1850 the attention of the Board was directed to South America as an important field, but it was not until 1860 that the opportunity was afforded for carrying out the plans of the Board. The Rev. T. J. Bowen, who had been obliged to leave Africa on account of ill-health, volunteered for the South American field; he was gladly sent, and a station was founded at Rio de Janeiro, from which point the work has rapidly spread.

In 1859 the needs of Japan attracted the attention of the Board, and in 1860 four missionaries, two ministers and their wives, were sent. All were lost at sea before reaching their field of labor. The enterprise, though deferred, was never abandoned, and definite steps are now being taken to establish a station in that country.

The duty of Baptists to send the pure gospel into the Catholic countries of Europe was felt by the Board from the very beginning, and France was chosen as a field for missionary labor; but the occupation of Rome by Victor Emmanuel in 1870 opened Italy to missionary work, and drew attention thither, and in 1871 Rome became a centre of operations which have spread throughout the peninsula.

*Statement of the Missions.*—CHINA.— The work of the Southern Convention in China is carried on under three missions, Canton, Shanghai, and Shantung. In 1846 the work was begun in Canton by the Rev. George Pearcy and Rev. Samuel Clopton. The work has progressed since that time with little or no interruption, and Canton has been the centre of the work in China. The mission now includes 13 stations, in which labor 11 foreign missionaries and 28 native helpers; the church-membership is 207.

Shanghai was chosen as a station at the same time as Canton, being situated in a central position on the coast. It is a city of great importance for missionary operations, since the Chinese come here from all parts of the empire, the number of transient inhabitants being estimated at about 100,000. During the Tai-ping rebellion in 1854 the mission property was destroyed, but on the seizure of the city by the imperialists full restitution was made and the work renewed. The Tai-ping movement was strictly religious and iconoclastic in its origin, and proved in the end a benefit to the mission, for it roused the moral sense of the people and offered a blow at the great curse, idolatry, and the preaching of the missionaries was decidedly more effective after than before the insurrection. The Shanghai mission has now 2 stations, 2 out-stations, 4 ordained missionaries, 4 churches, and 107 members.

The mission in Shantung, a northern province of China, was begun in 1860, immediately on the conclusion of the treaty of Tien-tsin, the stations chosen being Tung-Chow and Chefoo. Some opposition was experienced at first from the gentry of Tung-Chow, but the common people showed great interest. At the outset the Shantung reports and statistics were included in those of the Shanghai mission, although the fields were 500 miles apart; but in 1866 Tung-Chow was set off as an independent mission, and has continued to be so regarded. There are now in Shantung 2 stations, 22 out-stations, 11 foreign missionaries, 2 churches, 127 church-members.

AFRICA.—One of the first fields chosen by the Southern Convention was Africa. In 1846 work was begun by Rev. John Day in Liberia, where the Northern Board had already established a mission, but in 1856 they withdrew and the Southern Board alone carried on the work of Baptists in the Dark Continent. The field was found to be one of great promise, and in 1850 the work was extended by the formation of a mission in the Yoruba country, and in 1855 a station was opened in Sierra Leone in connection with the Liberian mission. For four years, from 1860 to 1864, war raged among the native tribes of Central Africa, and the missionaries of the Yoruba country were driven to the coast and the mission had to be suspended. Soon after this, the money pressures and panics attendant upon the civil war at home rendered it necessary to withdraw support from the African mission for a time, and from 1866 to 1874 the work was carried on by the missionaries without aid from the Board. In 1875, the native war being terminated and the Yoruba country again opened to missionary operations, and the finances of the Board by this time permitting, laborers were sent to occupy that field. The Liberian mission was closed and Lagos chosen as a centre from which work could be extended to Central Africa. The report of the Board for 1889 gives the following statistics: 5 stations, Lagos, Abbeokuta, Ogbomoshaw, Gaun, and Hausser Farm; 13 foreign missionaries, 8 native assistants, 165 pupils in schools, and 79 church-members.

SOUTH AMERICA.—The mission in South America was begun in 1860 at Rio Janeiro by the Rev. T. J. Bowen and his wife. The health of the former, which had caused his transfer from Central Africa, compelled him to again give up his work, and with his return the mission in South America was suspended. For twelve years nothing was done, at the end of which time, at the urgent request of a church of settlers in Brazil from the Southern United States, the Board again renewed its operations. The Board has five stations in Brazil: Rio de Janeiro, on the coast, in the southeast; Pernambuco, on the coast, in the northeast; Bahia, midway between Rio de Janeiro and Pernambuco; Maceio, south of Pernambuco; and one in the city of Juiz de Froa in the mining district of Minas Geraes, in the southeastern part of the country. There are 13 foreign missionaries at work, 3 native preachers, 1 native assistant, and 229 church-members.

ITALY.—In 1850 the Board began deliberations with regard to work in the Catholic countries of Europe, but no mission was begun until 1870, when Rev. Wm. N. Cote, M.D., who was secretary of the Y. M. C. A. of France, was appointed missionary of the Southern Convention. On the opening of Italy for evangelistic work, by the victory of Victor Emmanuel, operations were immediately begun in that city, and from thence have spread throughout Italy. There are now 10 stations of the Southern Convention on the peninsula—Rome, Pinerolo, Milan, Venice, Bologna, Modena, Carpi, Bari, Naples, and Torre Pellice,—besides two,—Cagliari and Iglesias—on the island of Sardinia. There are 5 foreign missionaries, 11 native workers, and a total membership of about 350.

MEXICO.—The missions of the Convention are now established in the following states of Mexico: Coahuila, Zacatecas, Aguas Calientes and Jalisco. Saltillo, in Coahuila, is the headquarters of the mission, and there are in all 7 stations, occupied by 7 married missionaries and 5 female missionaries, with 800 church-members, organized into 19 churches. The churches are better organized, more liberal in their contributions, and more anxious after self-support than at any previous time in their history. A Mexican National Foreign Missionary Society has been organized, and a missionary has been sent to Central America.

JAPAN.—In 1860 the Board appointed three missionaries to Japan: two of them were prevented by the outbreak of the war from going out. The third, J. Q. A. Rohrer, with his wife, set sail from New York in the "Edwin Forrest" on August 3d, 1860. The vessel was never heard of afterwards, and the mission to Japan was then abandoned until November, 1889, when two missionaries and their wives were sent out. They are to be located at Kobe, and as soon as the language is acquired will enter upon active, aggressive work.

**Southon Ebenezer John,** b. Gosport, England, August 23d, 1850; studied medicine at Edinburgh; sailed April 18th, 1879, as a medical missionary of the L. M. S. to the Central African Mission, arriving at Zanzibar May 27th. Accompanied by Dr. Mullens and Mr. Griffiths, he reached Mpwapwa July 11th, and settled in Urambo October 25th, the same year. He was shot in the arm by the accidental discharge of a gun in the hands of an attendant. Mr. Coppleston, a missionary at Myui, being sent for, though not a surgeon, successfully amputated the arm, under directions from Dr. Southon. But there was not strength to rally from the shock to the system, and amid intense pain his life passed away. He died July 26th, 1882.

By having a board held in place for him, after he was wounded, he wrote two letters, closing the first in these words: "Who shall lay anything to the charge of the Master-builder if He removes one workman who has finished his portion, and sends others to carry on the work? If He calls me to help Mullens, Thomson, and others gone on before, how gladly will I respond, and joyfully 'knock off work here'!" The second was a letter to his brother in England in the view of approaching death, dated Urambo, July 22d, 1882, in which he says: "My sufferings during the last five weeks have been awful. Tell everybody, if I die, that my most earnest wish was to die at my post, and nothing short of death could make me leave it."

**Spalding, Henry H.,** b. Bath, N. Y., U. S. A., 1804; graduated at Western Reserve College 1833, and Lane Theological Seminary 1835; ordained August the same year; appointed by the A. B. C. F. M. in 1836 missionary to the Nez Percés Indians, with his wife, Dr. and Mrs. Whitman, and William B. Gray. In a company of fur-traders they travelled on horseback nearly 2,200 miles beyond the Missouri River, to Fort Walla-Walla, a trading-post of the Hudson's Bay Company, which they reached September 3d, 1836, being four months and six days on the journey from Liberty, Mo., to that place. The mission was broken up by the massacre of Dr. Whitman and others in 1847. (See article on **Dr. Whitman**.) Mr. Spalding, who was in the vicinity, providentially escaped. The murderers were on his track. Hiding by day, he made his way night after night, barefooted, over sharp rocks and thorns, until, almost dead, he reached a place of safety. Then, with his family, he left the mission field for a time. In 1862 he resumed his work, but remained only a few years. In 1871 he renewed his labors under the Presbyterian Board of Foreign Missions, in which he continued till his death, which occurred at Lapnor, Idaho, August 3d, 1874, after a long and useful life as a missionary among the Indians and a home-missionary among the whites. Though his labors were so much interrupted, he accomplished a great work among the Indians. "From savagehood they have been raised to a good degree of civilization. From knowing nothing of the gospel, a large proportion of the tribe have become its professed followers." Over 900 of the Nez Percés and Spokanes were added by him to the church. He prepared and gave to the people a translation of the Gospel of Matthew, and a collection of Nez Percés hymns. He had proceeded also far in the translation of the Book of Acts.

**Spanish Evangelization Society.** Secretary and Treasurer, Mrs. Robert Peddie, 8 Granville Terrace, Edinburgh.—The Spanish Evangelization Society, formed 1855, has done much to aid in establishing in Spain a native Protestant church. In its three long-established centre stations (Huelva, Cadiz, and Seville) are congregations of Spaniards, with resident missionary pastors, and well-attended day and Sabbath schools: from these centres itinerating work is done in the neighboring villages, and there is a wide-spread distribution of Scriptures and tracts among the outlying population. Minor stations having no resident pastors are at Escornar, Villafranca, Puerto-Real, El Carpio, and Tharsis. In the early days of its history the Society did much interesting work among the *Emancipados*—Spanish Negro slaves who had purchased their freedom; and also among the Gypsies, whom even the Catholic priests neglect.

The Society reports for 1888, 5 churches and 11 schools. Testaments, portions of Scripture, tracts, etc., have been distributed during the year to the number of 16,533.

**Spanish and Portuguese Church Aid Society.** Headquarters, 8 Adam Street, Adelphi, London, W. C.—In 1867 the Rev. L. S. Tugwell, a clergyman of the Church of England, was appointed to the British chaplaincy at Seville, Spain. Finding that the priest-ridden classes around him were eager to hear the gospel, he inaugurated a movement, which in 20 years has grown into a fully organized native church, comprising 16 organized congregations, and many mission stations not yet provided with pastors. To supply the needed funds to carry on this work, Mr. Tugwell founded the Spanish and Portuguese Church Aid Society, which had the warm support of the Earl of Shaftesbury and other prominent men, and which is now presided over by the Archbishop

of Dublin. The churches in Spain to which aid is given are in (1) Seville, where there are 2 churches, with boys' and girls' schools and free dispensary; (2) Madrid, 1 church, with 240 members, and schools. "La Luz," a fortnightly journal, is published here and circulated throughout Spain and Spanish America; (3) Malaga, 2 churches, mission stations, and schools; (4) Monistrol, church, schools, and mission stations; (5) San Vicente, carrying on work, notwithstanding bitter persecutions from the Jesuits; (6) Salamanca; (7) Villaescuso and (8) Valladolid; churches and mission stations. Aid is granted in Portugal to churches in Lisbon, Rio de Mouro, and Oporto.

**Spanish Version.**—The Spanish belongs to the Græco-Latin branch of the Aryan languages, and is spoken in Spain and her colonies, and South American republics. Nicolo Antonio (*Bibl. Hisp. vetus*, ii. 214) mentions many manuscripts of a translation into the Lemosinian dialect, which do not go beyond the year 1470. This text was printed (Valencia, 1478), and ascribed to the General of the Carthusians, Boniface Ferrer, who had died in 1417. The National Library of Paris has two manuscripts in the Lemosinian dialect, a complete Bible and an incomplete Old Testament, which are said to be older than the 15th century. (J. M. Guarda, *Revue de l'Instruction publique*, Avril, 1860.) In the same dialect there is also extant a manuscript containing a metrical version of the Bible by Romerus de Sabrugera, which Antonio (p. 273) mentions as *Biblia en Catalan*. A Castilian translation made by a rabbi in 1430 is also mentioned, and, as Antonio (p. 214) states, among other books the Escurial Library contained a *Hispania versis sacri textus IV evangg. et XIII epp. Pauli, interprete doctore Martius Lucena cognomine El Machabeo.*

The translations of the 16th century are almost exclusively made into the Castilian dialect of the present Spanish. To this period belongs the New Testament translated from the Greek, by Francisco de Enzina, Antwerp, 1543. This edition was presented to the Emperor Charles at Brussels by the translator. In 1556 a New Testament was published at Venice, the translation having been made by J. Perez. About the same time a translation of the Old Testament, made by Spanish Jews, was published at Ferrara, 1553 (Amsterdam, 1611, 1630, 1656, and after). This version was of service to Cassiodoro de Reyna, who published his translation of the entire Bible at Basle in 1569. Copies of this volume appeared with a new date on the title-page in 1586 and again in 1622. After the death of De Reyna his translation was revised and adopted as his own by Cipriano de Valera, by whose name it is generally known. In its revised form the New Testament appeared in 1596 and the Bible in 1602, but no subsequent edition of the Bible is noted until 1861.

Towards the end of the 18th century Felipe Scio de San Miguel, bishop of Segovia, published a classical translation of the Bible into Spanish (10 vols., Valencia, 1790-93; 20 vols., Madrid, 1794-97), with a commentary. It was often reprinted. A more recent translation, having respect to the sacred originals, was published by Felix Torres Amat, bishop of Astorga; Madrid, 1824-29, 9 vols.; 1832-35, 6 vols. (reprinted at Paris, 1835, 17 vols.). The British and Foreign Bible Society republished Valera's and

Scio's versions of the entire Bible and Enzina's version of the New Testament. The Society for Promoting Christian Knowledge published in 1853 a corrected edition of Amat's version, prepared with the assistance, and printed under the care, of Señor Calderon. A new version of the entire Scriptures, prepared by Mexican priests, was printed by Ribera in 1831–33. This was the first Bible ever printed in Spanish America. The present diffusion of the Bible in Spain and Spanish America is owing chiefly to the efforts of the British and Foreign and the American Bible Societies. The first editions of the former were printed only from Enzina's edition of 1708. At length, in 1820, in consequence of the representations and example of the American Bible Society, an edition of Scio's New Testament was printed in London, followed in 1821 by an edition of the entire Bible of this version. An edition of the New Testament from Valera's version was issued by the same Society in 1857. The Old Testament from the same version followed in 1861.

The style of the Reina-Valera version is harsh and antiquated, and it has been repeatedly revised, with but partial success. The editions published by the British and Foreign Bible Society in Madrid are, for the most part, conformed to a revision made about 1867 by the Rev. L. Lucena, Professor of Spanish at Oxford. Marginal references have been appended. In 1885 the Society printed tentatively a revision of the Gospel of Luke, made by its agent in Spain, the Rev. E. Reeves Palmer. At the present time a committee in Madrid is co-operating with the Rev. J. Jameson in preparing another revision of the New Testament. Pastor Fliedner of Madrid has also been publishing independently a translation of his own.

The American Bible Society's revision of Valera, prepared by Messrs. De Mora and H. B. Pratt, first appeared in 1865. Mr. Pratt had already at that time devoted much time to the study of Spanish, and the fruits of his life-long work are soon to appear in a new translation of the entire Bible, which may be looked for in the year 1892. His edition of the Psalms, first printed in Bucaramanga in 1876, was reproduced by the Society in 1879, and has also been printed in Barcelona. Since 1885, when his version of Genesis was published, he has been in the employ of the Society, devoting his whole time to the work, in which he has been materially aided by missionary and native scholars in Mexico, among whom he has resided.

An independent version of the New Testament was published by the American Bible Union in 1857. For the blind, too, the British and Foreign Bible Society issued a small edition of the Gospels of Mark and John.

(See also Judæo-Spanish.)

(*Specimen verse.* John 3 : 16.)

Porque de tal manera amó Dios al mundo, que haya dado á su Hijo unigénito; para que todo aquel que en él creyere, no se pierda, mas tenga vida eterna.

Hebrew character.

פורקי אינסי אמו איל דייו. אה איל מונדו קסטה־דקר אה סו חיג. רינאלאלו כארה קי טודו איל קי קריאין אין סיל, נו סי דיפיידרה סינו קי טיננה נידה די סיימפרי.

Spaulding, Levi, born Jaffrey, N. H., U. S. A., August, 22d, 1791; graduated at Dartmouth College 1815, and Andover Theological Seminary 1818; sailed for Ceylon June 8th, 1819. He occupied the station of Manepy for several years. In 1833 he removed to Oodooville, and with Mrs. Spaulding took charge of the girls' boarding-school, which was under their care for nearly forty years. He visited the United States in 1844 and returned in 1846. He was one of the most accurate Tamil scholars in Southern India, having so mastered the language as to use it with great facility, and often power. He performed a large amount of literary labor. More than twenty Tamil tracts were prepared by him, and many of the best lyrics in the vernacular hymn-book were from his pen. He prepared two dictionaries, one Tamil, the other English and Tamil, and took a prominent part in the revision of the Scriptures. He furnished an excellent translation of Pilgrim's Progress, and compiled a Scripture History, which is used in the schools. School-books, hymn-books, tracts, and Gospels passed through his hands for revision and proof-reading. But he was far from being chiefly occupied with these tasks. In season and out of season, to moodeliars and odigars, in their verandas, or seated with wayfarers under the hedge, to the poor and the maimed in lanes and highways, and to the children in the school or the street, wherever he met a native he ceased not to preach and to teach Jesus Christ. His fluency in the colloquial language, his apt quotations from Hindu books, his original illustrations, and ready and racy sallies, combined with his genial humor, gave him great influence with the natives. He died at Oodooville June 18th, 1874, fifty-four years and eleven days from his embarkation. The native converts throughout the district loved him as a father, and many of the heathen mourned his death.

Spaulding, Mary Chrystie, died at Batticotta in 1875. She had been over fifty-five years connected with the mission, and about forty years in charge of the girls' boarding-school at Oodooville. Her sympathetic services, rendered not only to the natives but to the mission families on all occasions of suffering or sorrow, richly entitled her to the appellation, which was universally accorded, of "Mother Spaulding."

Spezia Mission for Italy and the Levant. Funds supplied by individual contributions in England and Scotland. Secretary, Eliot Howard, Esq., Walthamstow, Essex, England.—In 1863 the Rev. Edward Clarke, an English pastor, published a paper on the importance of Italy as a mission field, which met with opposition from many sources, but finally resulted in the formation of "The Spezia Mission for Italy and the Levant," the object of which is to supply every necessitous part of Italy with the gospel.

In 1866 Mr. Clarke went to Italy as superintendent of the mission. Obstacles bristled at every point. The problem of Bible-school work proved a most difficult one to solve, but Mr. Clarke at length began it with one child. There are now nine schools with hundreds of scholars, superintended by earnest Italian teachers, some of whom were early scholars. The Bible-schools are a principal feature of the work, but through the religious services held weekly at thirty different points, and by the circulation of Bibles and tracts, there is a widely extending influence among men and women. Many who have been converted are actively engaged in evangelistic work. Other departments of the work are, work among soldiers and sailors, and the orphan home at La Spezia, which had its beginning during the terrible outbreak of cholera in 1883, and is now firmly established.

The mission is conducted by 3 English missionaries, with 30 native assistants. There are 19 day and Bible schools, with nearly 600 scholars, in the 20 stations and 21 sub-stations, on the Gulf of La Spezia, Tuscany, and the province of Venezia.

**Srinagar,** the capital of Kashmir, India, is the headquarters of the C. M. S. Mission in the valley of Kashmir, in which missionary tours have been made as far north as the Zaji La Pass, which leads to Little Tibet. The present staff consists of 1 missionary and 2 medical missionaries. Mrs. Bishop (better known as a traveller and writer by her maiden name of Isabella Bird) has given money to build a woman's hospital here, as a memorial to her late husband, Dr. John Bishop. The Maharajah gave an excellent site. Thirty patients will be accommodated, and the ladies of the Church of England Zenana Missionary Society are to have control of it.

**Srivillipatur,** a city in the Tinnevelli district, Madras, India, and centre of the local traffic of the state. It has a temple with an annual car procession attended by about 10,000 people. Population, 18,256, Hindus, Moslems, Christians. Mission station of the C. M. S.; 2 missionaries, 43 native helpers, 495 church-members, 24 schools, 593 scholars.

**Stack, Matthew,** b. Maukendorf, Moravia, Austria-Hungary, March 4th, 1711. In his early youth he had deep religious impressions, and leaving Moravia he went to Herrnhut in Saxony. Soon after his conversion he received from Count Zinzendorf an impression of the condition of the Greenlanders which led him to devote himself to work among the heathen. He set out with his cousin Christian Stack and Christian David for Copenhagen January 19th, 1733. On their arrival they found that the mission under Egede was about to be abandoned, communication with Greenland closed, and their project was regarded as romantic and ill-timed. They applied to Count Von Pless, the king's chamberlain, who fully stated the difficulties. "How will you live?" he asked. "We will cultivate the soil, and look for the Lord's blessing." "There is no soil to cultivate—nothing but ice and snow." "Then we must try to live as the natives do." "But in what will you live?" "We will build ourselves a house." "But there is no wood in that country." "Then we will dig holes in the ground, and live there." "No," said the count, seeing their faith, "you shall not do that. Here are $50 to help you: take wood with you." Other persons aided them. The king decided to reopen communication with Greenland, and gave them a letter to Egede, commending them to his kind attention.

Matthew Stack embarked with his two friends April, 1733, and after six weeks' voyage reached Ball's River, and selected a place for a mission, and called it New Herrnhut. In commencing his work Matthew Stack encountered great obstacles. The language was difficult of acquisition; the natives not only refused to listen to him, but were positively hostile, in various ways annoying and persecuting him. They mimicked his reading, praying, and singing; interrupted his devotions by hideous howling and beating of drums. They stoned him, destroyed his goods, attempted to send his boat out to sea, and even sought to take his life. He was often in straits for provisions, and obliged to buy seals from the Greenlanders, who sometimes refused to sell them at any price. Often he had to live on shell-fish and sea-weed, a little oatmeal mixed with train-oil, and even old tallow-candles. But, nothing daunted, he toiled on, when, after five years of privation and suffering, he had the reward of his patient endurance. As one of his associates was copying a translation of the Gospel of Matthew some natives from South Greenland passing by stopped, and asked what was in that book. On the missionary's reading the story of God's love and the sufferings of Christ to save us, Kajarnak, one of the savages, said with much earnestness, "How was that? Tell me that once more, for I too would fain be saved." He became a Christian, was baptized, labored faithfully for Christ, and died in faith the following year. His companions through his efforts were converted, and soon three large families pitched their tents near the missionary that they might hear more of the gospel. In his seventh year Stack baptized the wife, son, and daughter of Kajarnak. The wife became as active and useful as the husband. In 1741 Stack visited Germany, married, returned to Greenland in 1742, and found the work progressing and the mission established on a sure footing. In 1747 he had more than a hundred Greenlanders at the Lord's Table. After forty years spent in the Greenland Mission, he went in 1771 to Wachovia in North Carolina, and for years devoted himself to teaching the children in Bethabara, N. C. In 1783 he united with the Salem Congregation in celebrating the semi-annual centennial jubilee of the Greenland Mission. In 1785 he was rendered helpless by a fall. When told that the Master would soon come and call for him, he raised his clasped hands, and said with deep emotion, "Yes, dearest Saviour, come soon, come soon." He died December 21st, 1787, in the 77th year of his age.

**Stallybrass, Edward,** a missionary of the L. M. S. to Siberia from 1817–1839. His first station was Irkutsk. In 1819 he commenced a station at Selenghinsk. The early time of his residence here was spent in exploring the southeast of Lake Baikal with Mr. Rhamn, and later with Mr. Swan among the Chorinsky Buriats. On his return from a visit to England he made his home at St. Petersburg, and for some time was engaged in the revision of the Mongolian Scriptures. In 1840 the Siberian Mission was suppressed by the Russian Government, and he returned to England, arriving July 13th, 1841. He died at Shooter's Hill, Kent, July 25th, 1884, aged 91.

**Steinkopff,** a town in Cape Colony, Africa, a little south of the Orange River, east of Port Nolleth. Mission station of the Rhenish Missionary Society; 1 ordained missionary, 1 female missionary, 6 native workers, 2 outstations, 220 communicants, 200 school-children.

**Stellenbosch,** a town in Cape Colony, South Africa, 25 miles by rail east of Cape Town. Population, 3,173. Mission station of the Rhenish Missionary Society; 4 missionaries, 2 ladies, 15 native workers, 1,000 communicants, 310 day-scholars.

**Stendal,** a town in North Natal, Africa, on a branch of the Uhikela River, southeast of Ladysmith and northwest of Hermannsburg. Mission station of the Berlin Evangelical Society (1860); 1 missionary, 1 native helper, 104 church-members, 28 scholars.

**Stewart, Charles Samuel,** b. Flemington, N. J., U. S. A., October 16th, 1795; graduated at Princeton College 1815, where he was converted in the great revival. He first studied law and afterwards theology, graduating at Princeton Seminary, and sailed as a missionary of the A. B. C. F. M. for the Sandwich Islands in 1823. On account of the ill-health of his wife he returned home in 1825. He lectured extensively in the Northern States in behalf of missions. In 1828 he was appointed chaplain in the United States navy. This position enabled him to visit nearly all parts of the world, and furnished material for the works afterwards published. He was stationed for many years at New York, and in 1836-7 edited the U. S. "Naval Magazine." In 1862, on account of failing health, he was retired, and at his death he was the senior chaplain in the navy. In 1863 he received the degree of D.D. from the University of New York. He died at Cooperstown, N. Y., December 15th, 1870, aged 75.

**Stoddard, David Tappan,** b. Northampton, Mass., U. S. A., December 2d, 1818. His early education was at Round Hill Academy. He studied at Williams College; graduated at Yale College 1838, taking high rank as a scholar, especially in the physical sciences. Having consecrated himself to the work of the ministry, he declined an invitation to go on an exploring expedition with Captain Wilkes. After graduating he became tutor at Marshall College, Pa. While there he was offered a professorship in Marietta College, Ohio, but declined it, and entered the Theological Seminary, Andover. Before completing his course he was appointed tutor in Yale College, and accepted the position. Impressed with the conviction that he ought to be a missionary, he was licensed and ordained, and having offered himself to the A. B. C. F. M., was appointed to the Nestorian Mission. In 1843 he embarked for Smyrna. Before going to Oroomiah he visited several mission stations in Turkey. After learning Turkish he on reaching his station commenced Syriac, that he might preach and also might assist Dr. Perkins in his translation of the Scriptures into modern Syriac. In five months he was able to instruct a class of Nestorian youths, and the male seminary was reorganized and committed to his care. In 1846 a revival occurred, of which he gave an interesting account to the Board. In 1847 the cholera raged fearfully in Oroomiah. Mr. Stoddard's health being impaired, he went, by medical advice, to Erzeroum. He returned an invalid. The death of his wife in 1848 at Trebizond depressed him. With consent of the Board he took his orphan children home, intending to return as soon as they were provided for. He devoted his time to travelling through the country and presenting the claims of the missionary work. His labors were arduous and incessant. He re-embarked in 1851. Soon he began to instruct his older pupils in theology, to prepare them for preaching to their countrymen. Besides his other work, he prepared a grammar of Modern Syriac, published in the "Journal of the American Oriental Society" in 1855. Having taken his telescope with him, he pursued the study of astronomy, and furnished Sir John Herschel observations on the zodiacal light. He also prepared an extended notice of the meteorology of Oroomiah, published in "Silliman's Journal." His theological lectures, embracing a full course of doctrinal theology, were delivered in Syriac. After a visit to Tabriz to consult with the Russian consul in regard to plans for averting a threatened attack on the missions by the Persian Government, he was attacked with typhus-fever, and died January 22d, 1857. He had been connected with the Nestorian Mission fourteen years. "His talents, his varied acquirements, his energy and activity in the midst of weakness, his humility, his devoted piety, his kindly sympathy and warm affection, his winning gentleness, meekness, simplicity, and godly sincerity, made him decidedly 'a man of mark,' and secured from all who knew him high respect, and from very many ardent attachment."

**Stone, Seth Bradley,** b. Madison, Conn., U. S. A., April 30th, 1817; graduated at Yale College 1842, Union Theological Seminary 1850; embarked as a missionary of the A. B. C. F. M. for Africa, October 14th, 1850; was stationed among the Zulus. His health having failed, he returned to the United States in 1875, and died in New York June 27th, 1877. The mission say of him: "He was a faithful, hard-working missionary for twenty-four years among the Zulus. A close student of the Zulu language, he translated portions of the Old and New Testaments. He published an edition of church history in Zulu, also a summary of general history. Thirty-nine of the hymns in our new hymn-book were translated or composed by him."

**Straits Settlements,** a crown colony of Great Britain, comprises Singapore, Penang (with Province Wellesley), and Malacca, all of which are treated of in separate articles. In 1886 the Keeling or Cocos Islands, a small group 1,200 miles southwest of Singapore, owned by an English family, were placed under the government of the Straits Settlements, and in 1888 an uninhabited island 200 miles southwest of Java, named Christmas Island, was also added to the Straits Settlements.

**Strict Baptist Mission.**—Hon. Secretaries: Josiah Briscoe, 58 Grosvenor Road, Highbury New Park, London, N., England; I. R. Wakelin, 33 Robert Street, Hampstead Road, London, N. W., England.

The Strict Baptist Mission was established in 1861 simply as a church institution, with but one missionary, but has since become a denominational society supported by more than 50 churches. Its work was commenced in 1861 at Talleygaum, a populous village between Bombay and Poona. In 1866 this work was relinquished, a station having been in the meantime opened at St. Thomas' Mount (9 miles south of Madras). Here a church with a native pastor was formed in 1870. A Bible-woman and 5 school-teachers are now employed at this station. In 1871 a church was formed at Poonamallee, Madras; here there are also three schools.

In 1882 application was made to the committee to take under its care a station at Tinnevelly, left vacant by the death of Mr. Arnlappen. There were at this station in 1888 56 baptisms.

The mission to Ceylon was commenced in 1868. There are now six stations under the Society's care, in all of which there are day and Sunday schools; at Jaffna a church has been formed with 16 members.

**Stronach, Alexander,** b. Edinburgh, Scotland, April 15th, 1800; was an evangelist of the Irish Evangelical Society; ordained August 1st, 1837; sailed August 7th the same year as missionary of the L. M. S. for Singapore, arriving March 5th, 1838. In 1839 he took the place for a time of Mr. Davies at Penang. In August, 1843, he attended the conference of the L. M. S.'s missionaries at Hong Kong, and also the general convention of missionaries held from August 22d to September 4th, to discuss the subject of Scripture translation. He then returned to Penang, and, on the removal of the missionaries to China, he returned June, 1844, to Singapore, and conducted the Chinese department of that mission. Leaving that place May 1st, 1846, he went to Hong Kong, where he superintended the type-foundry, and also assisted in the mission. In August he went to Amoy, where, assisted by Mrs. Stronach, he conducted a boarding-school for Chinese boys. His health failing, he returned to England in 1869, retired from the service of the Society in 1870, and died in London February 6th, 1870.

**Stronach, John,** b. Edinburgh, Scotland, March 7th, 1810; studied at Edinburgh University and Theological Academy, Glasgow; was ordained August 10th, 1837, with his elder brother Alexander, and sailed as a missionary of the L. M. S. for China, reaching Malacca March 2d, 1838. He attended the Hong Kong conference (see above), and on the opening of the ports of China he went to Amoy and commenced a mission there. Mrs. Stronach sailed for England November 10th, 1845, for her health, but died at sea near England, March 7th, 1846. In May, 1847, Mr. Stronach removed to Shanghai, having been appointed one of the delegates for the revision of the Chinese version of the New Testament. On the completion of that work he returned to Amoy in 1853. On March 17th, 1876, he left Amoy, and, after visiting Japan, proceeded via America to England, arriving January 6th, 1877. In 1878 he retired from foreign missionary service. He died in Philadelphia, U. S. A., October 30th, 1888, after forty years' uninterrupted labor in China. Mr. Sadler, his colleague, says: "His powers of a literary and intellectual kind were of no common order. He stood well in his university, and made a great mark in the translation of the Bible into Chinese, known as the Delegates' Version. It was a charm to hear him speak Chinese. He was a most idiomatic speaker. His literary ability did not cease with Bible translation, but could be directed to the making of tracts. One of these, called the 'Hek bun' (or Inquirer), was a masterly setting forth of the difficulties felt by a literary Chinaman, and the answers of the missionary. He assisted also in revising Dr. Douglas' dictionary of the Amoy language. He was greatly blessed as an evangelist in Amoy, and labored indefatigably in starting stations, appointing native ministers and working with them. His strength and high spirits, as well as his fund of knowledge, made him very attractive to the Chinese, and to all who wished to become Chinese in their power of speaking the language. He was thoroughly at home in street-preaching, and would hold an audience in a remarkable way. His fund of humor was bewitching. And his good-nature in bearing abuse without resenting it won the heathen to the Saviour."

**Sturges, Albert A.,** b. Granville, Ohio, U. S. A., November 5th, 1819; graduated at Wabash College 1848; Yale Divinity School 1851; embarked January 11th, 1852. as a missionary of the A. B. C. F. M. for Micronesia, reaching Ponape the following September.

He labored most happily for thirty-three years at his missionary station on Ponape. He showed great tact in his relations with the natives, and skill in drawing out the activities of the church-members. Much of his time was given to the translation of the Scriptures, and he had the joy of seeing the New Testament completed, and in the hands of the people. In his last letter, written from Ponape, just before a paralytic stroke which he had in 1885, he says: "I cannot tell how thankful I am to be here, and to have so much strength given to me to preach the gospel to these needy people. Especially on the Sabbath is my heart full of gratitude to the Master and to the Board for sending me to help these infant churches into a better life." In 1885 his health required him to return home, where, though in much physical weakness, he carried on the work of translation. He died at Oakland, California, September 4th, 1887.

**Suchau** (Soochow) is regarded by the Chinese as one of the richest and most beautiful cities in China. It is situated on a cluster of islands in Ta hu, "Great Lake," 70 miles northwest of Shanghai, with which it is connected by a network of streams and canals. Its walls are 10 miles in circuit, and the suburbs extend for many miles around, while an immense population lives in boats. The rebels captured it in 1860, and left it, when recaptured, in 1865, a ruined city. But it is rapidly recovering from that calamity. The beauty of the women, and the picturesqueness of its location, with the many fine buildings, cause it to be celebrated in proverb and poetry. Its silk manufactures are of especial note, but all Chinese manufactures are produced in great abundance and of superior quality. Several channels connect it with the Yangtsz, and small steamers at high-tide reach the many important villages and towns in the surrounding districts. The population is estimated at 500,000, and from the top of one of the high pagodas can be seen an area containing a population of 5,000,000.

Mission station of the Southern Baptist Convention; 1 missionary and wife. Methodist Episcopal Church (South); 2 missionaries, 2 female missionaries (1 a physician), 1 hospital, and 1 high-school. Presbyterian Church (North); 2 missionaries and wives, 25 members, 72 day-scholars. Presbyterian Church (South); 2 missionaries and wives, 2 female missionaries.

**Suchau,** a city in Szchuen, China, on the Yangtsz River, 1,600 miles from Shanghai; has recently been occupied by the A. B. M. U., two missionaries leaving for that region early in 1890.

**Sukkur,** a town in Upper Sindh, India, 200 miles from Haiderabad and nearly 300 from Karachi. Mission station of the C. M. S. (1887); 1 missionary, 27 communicants.

**Sulu Islands,** an archipelago lying between Mindanao, the southern island of the Philippines, and the northeast extremity of British Borneo. By a protocol, signed at Madrid in 1885, Spanish protection is recognized over this archipelago. There are over fifty islands, the largest of which is 36 miles long and 12 broad. No Protestant mission work is carried on in these islands.

**Sumatra,** one of the largest and richest islands of the East Indian Archipelago, extends 1,047 miles from northwest to southeast, lying between latitude 5° 40' north, and latitude 5° 59' south. Its area is estimated at 160,000 square miles, and the greater part of the island belongs to the Dutch Government, though many of the interior districts have not been brought under complete subjection. Throughout the whole length of the island extends a range of lofty mountains, which lies nearer the western coast than the eastern, hence on the eastern slope there are several large rivers, but the watercourses on the western slope are comparatively short. Sugar-cane, coffee, rice, and spices are the principal products, though much fine timber and many tropical fruits are found in abundance. The greater part of the population belong to the Malay race, but it is probable that they have absorbed many aboriginal tribes, a few remnants of which are found in the interior, such as the Kubus, who seem to have a mixture of Negrito blood, and the Battaks. These latter differ in many points from the Malay type. They are somewhat undersized, with broad shoulders and rather muscular limbs. Their eyes are large and black, with heavy brown eyebrows. These people inhabit the country around Tobah Lake, about midway between the east and the west coast, near latitude 3° north. Their language contains words of Sanskrit origin, and has evidently been affected by Javanese, Malay, Macassar, Sundanese, and Tagal influence. Another peculiar tribe are the Redjangers, who use distinctive characters, which they cut on bamboo with their short kreeses or daggers. The possessions of the Dutch Government in the island of Sumatra are divided into the residencies of the West Coast, the East Coast, Benkulen (the extreme southwestern coast), Lampongs (southeastern coast), Palembang (southeastern and central), and Atjeh, the northern extremity. The principal towns are: Pedang, on the west coast, about latitude 1° south, the residence of the governor, with a population of 15,000, including a Chinese settlement and a European quarter; Benkulen, the capital of the Residency of that name, with 12,000 inhabitants; Palembang, in the Residency of Palembang, has 50,000 inhabitants, with barracks, hospitals, one of the finest mosques in the Dutch Indies, and a tomb, said to be that of Alexander the Great. Included

in the Dutch possessions of Sumatra are various islands which are contiguous to it. On the west coast, under the Residency of that name, are the Banyak Islands, Nias Islands (q.v.), Battu Islands, Nassau Islands, and Engano. On the east are Bengkalis, Reau-Lingga Archipelago, and Banca. The latter is separated from Palembang by Banca Strait, and has an area of about 5,000 square miles, and a population of about 7,000.

The Missionary Societies at work in Sumatra are: (1) The Rhenish Missionary Society, with stations at Sipirok, Bungaboudar, Pranserat, Panguloan, Csigonpulan, among the Battaks; (2) The Java Comité, with stations at Sinnapitapil and Haranbaru, near the west coast; (3) The British and Foreign Bible Society, with colporteurs in the seaports and along the coasts of Sumatra. Scriptures—New Testament and parts of the Old Testament in Malay; New Testament and Psalms in Nicobar for the Battaks of North and South Sumatra.

**Sundanese Version.**—The Sunda belongs to the Malaysian languages, and is spoken by about 4,200,000 of the 18,000,000 inhabitants of Java. Of these about 2,000 are Christians, and their numbers are increasing. There is as yet no complete Bible in the Sundanese, and this fact must be ascribed to the great difficulties in mastering the language. In 1870 the British and Foreign Bible Society published an edition of the Gospel of Luke, translated by the Rev. G. J. Grashius. In the mean time Mr. Cooloma, of the Netherlands Missionary Society, had undertaken a translation of the New Testament into the Sundanese, which was published by the Netherlands Bible Society at Leyden in 1878, in Roman characters. The same Society also published in the same year an edition of the Gospel of Luke in Arabic characters, also prepared by Mr. Cooloma. In 1877 the Netherlands Missionary Society requested the British and Foreign Bible Society to undertake the publication of Mr. Cooloma's translation of the Old Testament. It published in 1878 the Book of Genesis, and in 1882 the New Testament.

*(Specimen verse. Luke 15 : 18.)*

Ajeuna mah dek indit ngadeuheusan ka bapa, sarta rek oendjoekan kijeu : Noen ama, simkoering geus tarima migawe dosa ka sawarga saréng di pajoeneum ama.

**Sunday-Schools.** — Christianity is preeminently the religion which takes special interest in the young. Ever since childhood was ennobled by the example and teachings of Christ, it has been a well-known truth that the child or the youth is more susceptible to Christian teaching than the adult; what might be called the chance of Christian life diminishes in an increasing ratio as the years increase. The Sunday-school is thus one of the most important agencies for the spread of the gospel, and at times it is the only means which can be employed. The character of the work and its relation to the church varies greatly in point of time and influence, and may be divided, as is other mission work (see Methods of Missionary Work), into two great classes: 1. Evangelistic; 2. Pastoral.

The latter division may be dismissed with but a few words. The character of the work, the necessity for it, the methods used, are exemplified in all Christian communities, and are substantially the same in all lands, and among all people, where a church has been gathered together. In this work the Sunday-school is the nursery of the church, from which come the future fathers and mothers in Israel; and the church that ignores this important work will rapidly feel the effect on its stability and future usefulness.

As an evangelistic agency, the Sunday-school differs from the ordinary Sunday-school of Christian communities in that it becomes the parent of the church, and is thus the reverse of the preceding. Where bigotry, ignorance, superstition, and prejudice rule the natives of foreign countries; where immorality, scepticism, and sin in all its bold, defiant forms, flourish openly in the wilder sections of so-called Christian countries—the Sunday-school is ofttimes the only evangelistic agency that can be employed. The nature of children—unsuspecting, frank, innocent, and trustful—will aid in the work of interesting and instructing them; the instinct of parental love will lead people to welcome such efforts in behalf of their children, even when ignorant themselves, or seemingly hopelessly depraved; and by first reaching the children an entrance can be gained into homes whose doors would otherwise be closed. Then gratification at the kindness done the child will remove prejudice and disarm opposition, which otherwise would be an insurmountable obstacle to the missionary.

Under this head of evangelistic or missionary agencies the account of the following societies will fairly present the work which has been done and is now in progress along the lines thus briefly defined.

*Sunday-School Union, The American.*—The American Sunday-School Union was organized in Philadelphia in 1824; and the Philadelphia Sunday and Adult School Union, formed in 1817, some other Sunday-School societies being merged in it. It had two principal objects: *First*, to establish and maintain Sunday-schools for the benefit of neglected children and communities, and to aid in improving existing schools. *Second*, to publish and circulate moral and religious literature. Its first purpose is accomplished by the employment of Sunday-school missionaries, who devote their entire time to exploring destitute settlements and neighborhoods in the newer States and Territories, and in the older States, especially in the Central, Southern, and Southwestern States. Each missionary visits from house to house, consulting with persons representing different views; secures their approval and sympathy; holds religious meetings; persuades the people to establish a Bible-school where none exists; shows them how to conduct it; aids them in procuring Bibles and other suitable books; watches over each new school to secure its growth and permanence, and revives and aids other feeble schools, whether denominational or Union. He thus successively canvasses each neighborhood and district in the county, and then passes on to those of another county, until the entire field to which he is appointed is supplied with successful schools. In this effort all evangelical denominations unite, and the schools thus organized and maintained become *nuclei* for the formation of churches of the denomination which is the majority in the vicinity; sometimes two or more churches are formed from a single school.

The money for the support of these missionaries is contributed by Christian people of all denominations, who are interested in the moral and religious welfare and prosperity of the youth of our country. The number of these missionaries is large, and is constantly increasing; 95 are now employed. The greatest difficulty encountered is the procuring of men in every way qualified, by intelligence, industry, patience, perseverance, a pleasing address, and unquestioning faith in God, for the work. Some of these now in the field are veterans of many years' service. One, Rev. B. W. Chidlaw, D.D., has taken out his commission in 1890 for his fifty-fifth year of continuous labor in the cause. Another, a layman, Stephen Paxson, of blessed memory, went to his reward, after forty years of such labor as very few men could have performed. And Rev. John McCullagh of Kentucky died in June, 1888, after about fifty years' service. In 1890 the outlay for the prosecution of the missionary work was $106,186.24.

The amount of good accomplished by this faithful band of workers can never be known in this life. Their record is on high, and will be declared before an assembled universe. But a few figures gleaned from the records of the Union will indicate its vastness:

| | From 1824–1890. | Year end'g Mar. 1, 1890 |
|---|---|---|
| Schools organized | 85,896 | 1,685 |
| Teachers in these schools | 518,201 | 7,353 |
| Scholars " " " | 3,554,958 | 59,432 |
| Schools aided by missionaries | 158,265 | 1,852 |
| Teachers in the schools aided | | 12,788 |
| Scholars in these schools | 9,712,218 | 120,792 |
| Schools previously reported aided, and aid continued | | 4,461 |
| Containing teachers | | 22,685 |
| " scholars | | 210,527 |
| Bibles distributed in 1889–90 | | 6,788 |
| Bibles distributed in the thirteen years 1876–1889 about | | 53,000 |
| Testaments distributed in 1889–90 | | 9,337 |
| Testaments distributed in the thirteen years 1876–89, about | | 105,000 |
| Visits to families in 1889–90 | | 42,222 |
| Sermons and addresses delivered | | 12,020 |
| Miles travelled by missionaries, about 18½ times round the globe | | 463,243 |

About $8,300,000 worth of the Union's publications have been circulated by donation and sale, through this missionary agency, in the sixty-six years of the existence of the Union.

The aim of the Union, from its first organization, has been to call into Christian activity and usefulness the lay members of the churches, and induce them to consecrate themselves to Christ's work. The president, vice-presidents, the thirty-six managers, the corresponding and recording secretary and treasurer, are all laymen; but ministers may be employed as editors, secretaries, and missionaries. Yet very many of the missionaries are laymen.

But the aims of the Sunday-School Union extend farther than the employment and maintenance of Sunday-school missionaries and the establishment and aid of Sunday-schools, important as these objects are. It seeks also to impart to adults as well as to children such religious instruction and knowledge as will lead them to Christ and make them wise unto salvation. While it avoids all those doctrines which are matters of controversy, it aims to give to all whom it can reach a better knowledge of the Scriptures and of the plan of redemption, and attempts by its books and periodicals to develop a taste for a pure and Christian literature, and to attract both youths and adults to good books, and induce them to abandon the many vile and infidel works, and the foul and unwholesome issues of the secular press, which are leading them to destruction. It has published more than 2,300 books, and now issues 12 periodicals, semi-monthly, monthly, and quarterly, all devoted to religious and Sunday-school instruction. These papers and periodicals are ably edited, finely illustrated, and very interesting, and they have a wide circulation. The books and publications of the Union may be divided into three classes : 1. The Question Books, Graded Lessons, Lesson Helps, Scholars' Guides, Records, Hymn and Tune Books, and Maps, Charts, and other appliances for direct Sunday-school instruction. These number over 200. 2. Practical aids for Sunday-school and Bible-class workers, as well as for pastors and others. There are about 75 volumes of these, all of moderately large size, including Schaff's and other Bible Dictionaries, Bissell's Biblical Antiquities, Rice's People's Commentaries, Biblical Geography, Allibone's Bible Companion, Nicholl's Introduction to the Scriptures, Scripture Biographical Dictionary, etc. 3. About 2,000 Sunday-school books, carefully examined and edited, and of great interest. Narratives, biographies, historical and descriptive works, stories, inculcating temperance, purity, a Christian life, and philanthropic sacrifice for others. Every writer whose books have been examined and accepted has been scrupulously careful to send forth " no page, which, dying, he might wish to blot." And these books are sold, donated or distributed through the missionary and other agencies of the Union by scores and often hundreds of thousands of copies. They go on the frontiers, in the new States and Territories of the West, Southwest, and South; reaching families and communities, where books, except the vile, obscene, and infidel publications and newspapers, are not found, and furnish to the young the only wholesome reading to be obtained. This powerful agency for good, both in its publication and missionary departments, should be greatly enlarged and increased. The Union has also done a great and good work in aiding by money grants the translation and circulation in foreign tongues of some of its best books by missionaries and missionary societies. Many of these have been put in circulation in India, China, Japan, and Burmah, and not a few in France, Italy, Germany, and Greece.

The action of the Union toward all other publishing and missionary societies has been uniformly kind and helpful; many denominational Sunday-schools have been aided, and many libraries donated to these schools, and hundreds of vigorous churches have started from the Union schools. They have demonstrated that unity of action and Christian love could coexist with the largest charity, and that by this unity of action the cause of the Redeemer would. be greatly benefited and God would be glorified.

**Sunday-School Association, The Foreign.** Headquarters, 130 State Street, Brooklyn, N. Y.—This association is composed of a number of men and women voluntarily united for the purpose of establishing and aiding Sunday or Bible-schools in all non-English-speaking countries. It was incorporated in 1878, but its work practically began in 1856.

The working force of the Association consists of a president, A. Woodruff, 130 State Street, Brooklyn, N. Y., a recording secretary, a corresponding secretary, a treasurer, eleven trustees, and a corps of forty or fifty letter-writers. Its plan of work is to secure correspondence in foreign countries, and by means of systematic letter-writing to become acquainted with the spiritual condition of those lands, the need of religious instruction, the best method of supplying their need, and then suggestion are given, plans for the establishment of Sunday-schools are formulated, and, if necessary, money or books are donated, and the schools are inaugurated. The correspondents are sought out by means of reports of the various religious societies ; through magazines, missionaries, colporteurs, Bible agents, government officials, travellers, and personal friends. The vast amount of correspondence rendered necessary is conducted by the corps of letter-writers, who are divided into four committees : Spanish, Italian, German, French, one of which meets every week to read the letters received from its particular countries, and to recommend applications. A general meeting is held once a month, at which letters are read and supplies voted.

The principle which underlies the methods of the Association is that the Sunday-school is particularly adapted to those fields which are untilled from want of laborers and means, by reason of the following facts : 1. It has a capacity for utilizing any number of Christians too small for the work or support of a preacher, and gives them an opportunity for individual work and growth. 2. It is economical, as compared with the cost of preaching services. 3. It avoids national and ecclesiastical prejudice by making each nation self-evangelizing. 4. It reaches the mind of the pupil at an age most impressionable, and least blinded by superstition, prejudice, or scepticism.

The various committees donate their services, and the work is thus conducted with a minimum expenditure of money for a maximum diffusion of influence. The various countries reached by this methodical correspondence are: *Spanish :* Spain, Portugal, Mexico, Brazil and other South American States. *German :* Germany, Austria, Russia, Bulgaria. *Italian :* Italy. *French :* France, and all countries not included in the work of the other committees, such as China, Japan, and Africa. The Association aims also to supply literature suitable for the young. From the report for 1889 the results of the work of the Association are given as follows :

*Distribution of Christian Literature.*—Six illustrated papers for children have been aided in their establishment and distribution. "Glad Tidings," in Japanese; "El Amigo," in Spanish; "O Amigo," in Portuguese; "La Feuille du Dimanche," in French; "Die Sonntag Schule," in German ; and "Il Amico," in Italian. Last year 13,000 subscriptions were paid for these papers. Several books have been published. One, "Christie's Old Organ," will illustrate the diffusion of this work. First published in 1877, it has been translated into sixteen different languages, and previous to October, 1888, 21,500 copies were circulated in Germany, Hungary, Bulgaria, Belgium, Portugal, Greece, Syria, Japan, Bombay, Ceylon, Bohemia, France, Italy, Asia Minor, China.

Besides the publications of the Association, it also sends out copies of the "Sunday-school Times," "Peloubet's Notes," and the "Westminster Teacher," besides various helpful leaflets, tracts, and cards.

In Germany the 25th anniversary of the work was celebrated in 1888, at which time there were 3,000 schools, 30,000 teachers, and 300,000 pupils.

In Holland the last reports gave the number of schools as 1,291; teachers, 3,800; scholars, 141,640. The reports from other countries show a like gratifying progress in the work. The result of individual efforts is shown by one instance out of many, where a gentleman opened correspondence with Spain, and fifty flourishing Sunday-schools have already been organized, and fifty more have been started.

*Receipts.*—The Association receives donations from all sources, but especially from the Sunday-schools. Its work is carried on at a cost of less than six thousand dollars a year, no debt is incurred, and with the exception of a small sum for clerical work at headquarters, every cent of the money received is expended directly on the work. In addition to the annual report, a quarterly leaf is distributed, which is edited gratuitously by ladies chosen from the committees, and thus the claims of the foreign fields are presented.

The Association bases its claims for the efficacy of letter-writing on the example given by the apostles, and the precedent and authority of the New Testament, which is composed so largely of letters.

*Sunday-School Union's Continental Mission.* Headquarters, 55 and 56 Old Bailey, London., E. C., England.—The Sunday-School Union was formed in 1803. Until 1864 its efforts were confined to the improvement of methods of instruction in the Sunday-schools already established in Great Britain, the organization of new schools in destitute places, and to supplying these schools with books at reduced prices. These objects have been attained by means of a library and reading-room, containing 7,000 volumes for circulation, and 1,000 for reference, which is open daily, except Sundays, and is accessible to all teachers upon the annual payment of one shilling; training classes; a biblical and educational museum; Normal, Greek, Hebrew, and correspondence classes; college lectures, illustrated lectures for teachers and senior pupils, etc. In connection with the Union are Bands of Hope, Christian Endeavor Societies, Reading Circles, etc. The report for 1889 shows 18 Metropolitan Auxiliaries and 210 Country Unions.

In 1864 Mr. Albert Woodruff of New York, who had just completed a tour through the principal countries of Europe, pressed upon the committee so earnestly the needs of children in those lands that the Continental Sub-Committee was formed, to endeavor to extend among the nations across the Channel the blessings which the Sunday-school system had conferred upon the English people. At that time there were very few Sunday-schools in any part of Europe; now, owing in great measure to the efforts of this committee, there are about 3,000 in Germany, 1,500 in Holland, 400 in Switzerland, and large numbers in France and Sweden. During the past year (1889) 17 missionaries have been employed in this work in the countries above named.

The International Bible Reading Association, connected with the Sunday-School Union, has a membership of 232,000: 203,000 of these members reside in the United Kingdom, 6,200 in the United States, 2,500 in Canada, 2,350 in the West Indies, 450 in British Guiana, 16,000 in Australia, and 400 in South Africa. Branches of the Association have also been formed in India, Ceylon, Gibraltar, and Newfoundland, in China, Japan, Persia, Nicaragua, and other countries.

**Surat,** a town in Gujarat Province, Bombay, India. Climate hot, unhealthy, malarious. Population, 107,149, Hindus, Moslems, Parsis, Christians. Language, Gujarathi, Hindustani, English. Natives well-to-do, prosperous. Mission station Irish Presbyterian Church (1846); 1 ordained missionary and wife, 5 others, 16 helpers, 1 church, 53 church-members, 15 schools, 1,565 scholars, a high-school, and an orphan-asylum.

**Suri,** (Soory), the administrative headquarters of the Birbhum district, Bengal, India; has a population of 9,000, and is a mission station of the Baptist Missionary Society; 1 missionary, 53 church-members, 307 day-scholars, 44 Sabbath-scholars.

**Surinam:** see Dutch Guiana, under Guiana.

**Surinam,** or **Negro-English.**—The Surinam or Negro-Dutch is spoken in Surinam, Dutch Guiana, and is a compound mainly of English and Dutch. A translation into this dialect was made by Moravian missionaries, and published at London in 1829. A revised edition of the New Testament, prepared by Hans Wied, together with the Psalms, was also published at London in 1846; and another edition of the New Testament was published in the same year by the Netherlands Bible Society at Bantzen. In 1865 the British Bible Society published a third edition of the New Testament and Psalms, and a fourth revised edition was published in 1888.

The edition, consisting of 3,000 copies, was issued under the care of the Rev. E. Langerfield of the Moravian Mission, with which about 25,000 souls are connected, of whom over 8,000 are communicants.

(*Specimen verse.* John 3:16.)

Bikasi na so fasi Gado ben lobbi kondre, va a gi da *wan* Pikien va hem, va dem allamal, dissi briebi na hem, no sa go lasi, ma va dem, habi da Liebi vo tehgo.

**Susu Version.**—The Susu belongs to the Negro group of the languages of Africa, and is spoken on the coast of Senegambia.

The Rev. Duport, a West Indian Negro, has translated the Gospels of Matthew, Mark, and John into the Susu, and they were published by the Society for Promoting Christian Knowledge about the year 1858. The New Testament was published by the same Society in 1883.

**Suto,** or **Lesuto.**—The Lesuto belongs to the Bantu family of African languages, and is spoken in Basutoland by the Bapeli, Migwamba, and other tribes of the Transvaal, Cape Colony, and Orange Free State. French missionaries translated the Scriptures into the Suto. As early as 1837 the Gospel of Matthew was published, and since that time detached portions were added. In 1849 the British and Foreign Bible Society published the Psalms, the translation having been made by the Rev. E. Casalis of the French Protestant Missionary Society. In 1857 the New Testament was printed at Cape Town, and republished by the British and Foreign Bible Society at Paris in 1868, under the care of the Rev. E. Casalis. A revised edition, prepared by Mr. Ellenberger, was issued in 1875. Parts of the Bible, translated by Mr. Knothe of the Berlin Missionary Society, were issued at Berlin in 1870. In 1873 a revised edition of the New Testament was published at Morija, and in 1881 the entire Bible, prepared by Messrs. Pelissier, Arbousset, Ellenberger, and Mabille, French missionaries, was published at London under the care of the Rev. A. Mabille, who had brought the MS. from Basutoland to England. A new edition of the New Testament, with a few corrections and emendations, was published in 1867 by the British and Foreign Bible Society. The edition, which was in 32mo, consisted of 3,000 copies.

(*Specimen verse.* John 3 : 16.)

Gobane Molimo o ratile lefatsé hakãlo, o *le* nelle Mora oa oona a tsuetseng a 'notsi; gore e mong le e mong a lumelang go éena, a sé ke a fêla, a mpe a be le bophélo bo sa feleng.

**Sutton, Amos,** b. Sevenoaks, Kent, England, 1798. His early history is interesting. A lady, one Sunday morning on her way to Sunday-school, saw some boys playing, and invited them to go to the school. They all refused but one, who said he would go if she would give him a shilling. She consented; he came with her, and continued to attend. That boy was Amos Sutton, who was for thirty years a missionary in India. Having studied theology with Rev. J. G. Pike, he was ordained at Derby, and sailed in 1824 for Orissa, India, as a missionary of the General Baptist Missionary Society. He was stationed most of the time at Cuttack. He preached in Oriya and in English, taught in the mission academy and was superintendent of the orphan asylums. He translated the whole Bible into Oriya, and made a second revision of the New Testament. He visited England and America. He returned to his mission from America in 1835, in company with Rev. Dr. Phillips, who was sent to the same field by the American Free Baptist Missionary Society. Dr. Sutton, besides translating the Scriptures, published an Oriya dictionary, grammar, and lesson-book, wrote three volumes of tracts in that language, and translated many English books for his scholars and converts. He died at Cuttack, Orissa, August 17th, 1854.

**Suvisheshapuram,** a town in the Tinnevelli district, Madras, India. Mission station of the C. M. S. for 61 villages, with 4 native pastors, 54 other workers, 828 communicants, 942 scholars.

**Swahili Version.**—The Swahili belongs to the great Bantu family of languages, and is greatly affected by contact with the Arabic language. It is the *lingua franca* of Equatorial Africa. A translation into this language was undertaken by the Rev. Edward Steere (died 1882), who had been connected with the Central African Mission since 1863. The first portion of

the Bible, the Gospel of Matthew, was printed by the British and Foreign Bible Society in 1869, and the Psalms followed in 1870. In 1874 the Gospel of John was published, and in 1875 a reprint of the Gospel of Matthew under the editorship of Bishop W. G. Tozer, at Zanzibar. The Gospel of Luke, as translated by the Rev. J. Rebmann of the Church Missionary Society, was printed at the Crischona Press, near Basle, in 1876, the same Gospel having also been published in 1872 at Zanzibar, as translated by Abdul Aziz and Pennel. A revised edition of John's Gospel was issued in 1878, under the editorship of the Rev. T. H. Sparshott. The portions of the New Testament which were issued from time to time at Zanzibar were revised, including the Gospel of Luke as translated by Mr. Rebmann and Bishop Steere, and the New Testament as a whole was published in 1884, at London.

Of the Old Testament, the Book of Genesis was issued in 1883 by Archdeacon Hodgson, of the Universities Mission to Central Africa. The translation was the work of the late Bishop Steere. In 1884 the British and Foreign Bible Society published the Book of Joshua, which was translated by Archdeacon Hodgson, aided by a native of Zanzibar, once a slave, but at the time of publication a student at St. Augustine's College, Canterbury. This version, which was the first translation of the Book of Joshua in any East African language, was revised by the Rev. H. Geldart and Miss Thackeray. In 1890 the whole Bible was published, after twenty years' labor, in the Roman character. Besides the edition in Roman, the British and Foreign Bible Society issued in 1886 an edition of 500 copies of the Gospel of John in Arabic character, intended for those who know the Swahili language and only the Arabic character. The version has been transliterated by Miss Allen, who also carried the edition through the press.

(*Specimen verse.* John 3 : 16.)

Kwani ndivyo Muungu anvyoupenda ulimwengu, akatoa na Mwana wake wa pekee, illi wote wamwaminio waupate uzima wa milele wala wasipotee.

**Swan, William,** b June 21st, 1791. at Balgonie, New Brunswick; studied at the Theological Academy of Glasgow; sailed July 1st, 1818, for Siberia as a missionary of the L. M. S. His chief work was among the Tartars of the Buriat and Mongolian race on the frontiers of Siberia and Chinese Tartary, southeast of Lake Baikal. For eight years he itinerated with Mr. Stallybrass, but in 1828 made his permanent home at the Ona. During these years he, in conjunction with Mr. Stallybrass, completed the Mongolian version of the Scriptures. On its completion he visited St. Petersburg, and after a stay of ten weeks he obtained permission from the government to print it. He then went to England, married, and returned to St. Petersburg. In 1837 he returned to his station on the Ona. In 1840 the Siberian Mission was repressed by the government, and he went back to Scotland in 1841. His connection with the Society was then dissolved. He died at Edinburgh January 1st, 1866.

**Swatow,** a seaport of Kwangtung, China, is situated on the estuary of the Han River, 5 miles from the sea, 225 miles east of Canton and 180 northeast of Hong Kong. It is a treaty port, with quite an active foreign commerce and large manufactories. Population, 300,000. Mission station of the A. B. M. U. (1846); 2 missionaries and wives, 1,085 members, 7 schools, 132 pupils. The missionaries' premises are at Kak-chieh, a suburb opposite Swatow proper, across a channel of the river a mile wide. Presbyterian Church of England: 8 missionaries, 2 medical missionaries, 981 communicants.

**Swedish-Lapp.**—The Laplanders scattered throughout Sweden cannot understand the Bible published in Lapponese, and accordingly the Gospel of Matthew has been translated into this form or dialect of the Lapp language. The translation was made by a Swedish missionary in Lapland of the name of Laestadius, whose father worked among the poor Laplanders. The British and Foreign Bible Society published this Gospel at Stockholm in 1880, with the Swedish in parallel columns, and up to March 31st, 1889, disposed of 2,000 copies.

**Swedish Missions.**—The first missionary work undertaken by Protestant Sweden was among the Lapps, or, as they are more properly called, the Finns, who in scattered nomadic tribes occupy the whole northern part of the country. That mission has on its records several names, as for instance that of Peer Fjellström, 1697–1764, which are still remembered with gratitude; but unorganized and unsystematized as it was, all its exertions and sacrifices were of no avail for a thorough success.

In 1638 a Swedish colony, "Nya Svearike," afterwards called "Vinland," now Pennsylvania, was founded on the Delaware in North America, and the Swede Campanius, who in 1642 began to preach to the Delaware Indians and compiled a dictionary of their language, was the first Protestant missionary to enter the New World. The colony was afterwards transferred to Holland, then to England, and finally to William Penn; but up to 1831 it continued to be served by Swedish pastors.

Meanwhile the powerful impulse which the Protestant mission received from England in the beginning of the present century made itself felt also in Sweden. In 1818 a mission paper was established, and in 1829 the first small mission society was founded at Göteborg. It was followed in 1835 by the Swedish Mission Society, and in 1845 by the Mission Society of Lund. In 1855 the latter was absorbed by the former, and in 1876 the Swedish Mission Society united with the Swedish Church Mission (founded in 1874), though, as will be seen, it was not wholly absorbed by it. Two other large societies were organized—the Evangelical National Institution in 1856 and the Swedish Mission Union in 1878. Besides these four great associations, quite a number of minor ones, still in their infancy, have sprung up and will be enumerated below.

I. *The Swedish Mission Society* (*Svenska Missionssälskapet*). Headquarters, Stockholm, Sweden.—Very soon after its foundation, January 6th, 1835, the Society was able to send out its first missionary to the Finns, Carl Ludwig Tellström, an artist, a painter. During his summer visits to their camps it had gradually grown upon him that though it might be well enough to paint their portraits, tents, flocks, etc., for the Swedish public, it would be better

if he could speak Christ down into their own hearts, and he became a missionary. Next year he was joined by two other young men, and the field proved fruitful to them. Their methods were: visits to the tents, preaching of the gospel, and some general instruction.

But an entirely new departure of singular efficacy was taken by a young Finnish girl, Marie Magdalene Mads-daughter, in 1864. By the preaching of the missionaries she had come to see and understand the misery in which her race lived. Then she learned Swedish that she might be able to speak to the king. She then walked two hundred miles down to Stockholm. Nothing daunted by suddenly finding herself in the midst of a great, rich, exceedingly elegant and exceedingly gay city, she picked out in the street the first lady who to her eyes seemed to look trustworthy, and in a short conversation she made that lady her patroness. Next day she had an audience with the king, and after talking with a number of influential men during a stay of a few days, she walked back to her native place with money enough to build a house or an asylum, or, as it is called, a "Children's Home," to which she could invite the children of her race to come and stay for some time and be instructed in that which is necessary, and also in something of that which is useful. The Society provided her "Home" with teachers, and so successfully did the plan work that it has now five such institutions established among the Finns, and several more in preparation.

A considerable portion of its annual revenue, which, in all, amounts to 21,487 kronor, the Society draws from the so-called Five-cents Circles. A person belonging to a certain social circle undertakes to collect five cents every week from every member of that circle who is willing to contribute, and pays over the sum every month to the Society. The trouble is very little to any one person in comparison with the result attained. Besides its annual revenue the Society owns invested funds to the amount of about 150,000 kronor, and by these means it supports its missions to the Finns, which it also directs independently, while, since its union with the Swedish Church Mission in 1876, it pays the surplus of its income into the coffers of that Society, and partakes proportionally in the direction of its mission to the heathen. The Society has its seat in Stockholm.

II. *The Evangelical National Society* (*Den Evangeliska Fosterlandsstiftelsen*). Headquarters, Stockholm, Sweden.—The Evangelical National Institution was founded in 1856 by Pastor H. I. Lundborg, as a consequence of a strong and widespread revival within the pale of the Swedish church, produced by the lay-preacher Rosenius. Propositions of union were made to it in 1875 by the Swedish Church Mission, but declined. It is the object of the institution, on the ground of the Evangelical Lutheran Confession and in harmony with the church of Sweden, to make itself the organ of all such free and spontaneous mission movements which may arise among the Swedish people. It consists of a great number of minor societies, generally called "Ansgar Societies" or "Evangelical Lutheran Societies," having a common head in their annual conference, which assembles in Stockholm and decides all important questions, and in their common board of directors, which consists of twelve members elected by the conference, which has its seat in Stockholm. In 1887-88 the revenue of the institution amounted to 137,800 kronor, its expenses to 91,069 kronor. It also owns an invested fund from which old or sick missionaries are pensioned.

Since 1861 the institution issues a weekly paper, "Missionstidning," founded by Rosenius and edited by him until his death in 1869. In 1863 it established a missionary seminary at Johannelund, on Lake Mälar, a little outside of Stockholm. The seminary has at present eleven scholars, who, according to their educational advantages before their entrance, remain there from one to six years before they are sent out to the stations. Originally the institution undertook only home-mission work, and its labor was essentially evangelistic. But in 1861 it extended its activity also to foreign missions, and it now works in two different fields—among the Gallas in Eastern Africa, and among the Gonds in Hither India.

The mission to the Gallas was begun in 1865, on the advice of Dr. Krapf and Bishop Gobat, but the great sacrifices and enormous exertions it has cost do not seem to have brought proportional results. The difficulties do not arise from the character of the people. The Gallas, numbering between eight and ten millions, and inhabiting an inland region of Eastern Africa from latitude 3° south to latitude 8° north, have for centuries stood as a wall against Mohammedanism, but for Christianity they have on many occasions showed some sympathy. The difficulty is, how to reach them. From the north, through Abyssinia, the door is closed. Abyssinia is nominally a Christian land, with churches, monasteries, monks, and priests. But its Christianity is a petrified perversion, which makes the people utterly hostile to anything which looks like missions. To the east, along the coast, live the Somalis, and they and the Gallas are instinctively enemies. The first Swedish missionaries did not reach the Gallas at all, and up to date the principal result of the mission has been the establishment of 13 stations at Tendar, Ogauna, Frida, Kulluko, Massana, Amberderho, Eilet, Geleb, Godjam, McKullo, Djumma, Keren, and Arkeka, with 11 Swedish missionaries, 11 native helpers, 99 members, and 108 children in the schools.

The Mission to the Gonds, on the contrary, begun in 1877 on the advice of Dr. Kalkar, is very promising. The Gonds, inhabiting the forest-clad plateaus in the Central Provinces of India, belong to the old Dravidian population of India, but have in course of time become very much mixed up with and influenced by the surrounding Hindus. The Swedes have here 7 stations.—Sangor, Narsingpur, Chindwara, Nimpani, Betul, Amarvara,—with 20 male and female teachers, 64 members, 453 children in their day-schools, and 261 grown-up pupils in their Sunday-schools.

III. *The Swedish Church Mission* (*Svenska Kyrkans Mission*). Headquarters, Stockholm, Sweden.—In 1868 the General Assembly of the Swedish Church (*Kyrkomötet*) laid before the king a petition that the whole missionary activity should be organized by law as a function of the church, the state institution; and September 11th, 1874, the king authorized the establishment of the Swedish Church Mission, under a board of seven di-

rectors, with the Archbishop of Upsala as its permanent president. As above mentioned, the negotiations for a union with the other mission societies already existing did not succeed, but the Church Mission, nevertheless, immediately began work. It draws its revenue, amounting in 1888-89 to 46,406 kronor, with an expense of 58,060 kronor, from a general collection taken up on a certain day in all Swedish churches, and maintains a mission among the Zulus in Africa, and a mission among the Tamils in the southern part of Hither India.

The Zulu Mission was begun in 1876, on the advice of Bishop Schreuder, who had long wished to see the whole energy of all Scandinavian mission societies united into one common effort, made possible by the close relation between the languages and the fundamental unity of the confessions. An estate, "Rorke's Drift," was bought in Natal, just on the boundary of Zululand; and the mission has now 4 stations in Natal and 1 in Zululand, with 9 missionaries, 71 members, 68 children in the schools, and 326 heathen settlers on its grounds.

The Tamil Mission was also begun in 1876, in close connection with the Leipsic Tamil Mission, which has its central station in Tranquebar. The Swedish central station was located at Madura, and has now 9 out-stations, with 4 missionaries and 545 members.

IV. *The Swedish Mission Union* (*Svenska Missionsförbundet*). Headquarters, Christinehamn, Sweden.—The Swedish Mission Union was formed August 2d, 1878, in Stockholm, as the representative of the Waldenström faction, which separated from the Evangelical National Society because the latter clung rigorously to the Augsburg Confession, while there were certain minor details of said confession by which the separating faction would not be bound. The Union consists of 465 minor associations, with a membership of 53,688 persons. In 1888-89 its revenue amounted to 110,096 kronor, its expenses to 113,106 kronor. At its head stands a committee of seven, which has its seat in Stockholm, and is elected by the annual assembly of delegates from the associations.

The Union maintains a mission school at Christinehamn with 34 pupils, who generally remain there three years, and of whom 10 are preparing for missionary work among the heathen. It has stations in five different fields —Finn-marken, Russia, Congo, Alaska, and North Africa.

Among the Finns the mission was begun in 1880, and is now carried on by three missionaries at three stations—Wilhemina, Sorfeli, Malu. In the same year it was also begun in Russia, where at present seven missionaries are at work in five different places. The mission there, however, has principally the character of revival work, though at the station on the southeastern frontier the missionaries come in close contact with heathendom. The Congo Mission was started in 1881 and labored for some time in connection with the Congo Inland Mission, but has now 3 independent stations— Mukimbungu, Kibunfi, Dindia,—with 13 missionaries and helpers. The Alaska Mission works since 1886 among the Yakutats at St. Michel and Yakutat, with 5 missionaries; and the North Africa Mission since 1887, with 2 missionaries among the Jews in Algeria.

Among the minor mission societies, most of

whom simply support other societies with their money, we mention those which carry on independent missions.

V. *The Friends of the Finns* (*Lapska Missionens Vänner*). Headquarters, Stockholm, Sweden.—This Society was founded March 17th, 1880, by the Princess Eugenie, and is supported by a number of royal ladies. It has a revenue of 9,910 kronor, and supports two itinerant preachers.

VI. *East Gothland's Ansgarius Union* (*Öster-Göthland's Ansgariiförening*). Headquarters, Jönköping, Sweden.—With an annual revenue of 4,521 kronor the Society sent out in 1887 one missionary to the Gallas in East Africa.

VII. *The Swedish Mission in China* (*Svenska Missionen i Kina*).—This mission was begun in 1887 by Erik Falke, and labored for sometime in connection with the China Inland Mission, but its three missionaries are now preparing for the establishment of an independent station in the province of Shansi.

VIII. *Jönköping's Society for Home and Foreign Mission* (*Jönköping's Förening for inre och ytre Mission*).—The Society sent in 1887 one missionary to Honan, China.

IX. *Swedish Women's Mission among North Africa's Women* (*Svenska Kvinnors Mission blandt Nord Afrikas Kvinnor*).—The Society has since 1887 sent Swedish ladies to work among the Mohammedan women at Bona, Algeria.

**Swedish Version.**—The Swedish belongs to the Teutonic branch of the Aryan family of languages, and is spoken throughout Sweden. In the life of St. Bridget (died 1373), which was written shortly after her death, we are told that she had a translation of the Bible in her vernacular. This translation is said to have been prepared by her confessor, Canon Magnus Matthias of Linköping. King Magnus Erikson disposed in his will (about 1340) of "unum grossum librum biblic in swenico." In the "Swenska Bibelarbeten," which the librarian Klemming published at Stockholm 1848-55, 2 vols., we find a Pentateuch, probably from King Magnus' Bible; Joshua and Judges by Nils Ragwald or Ragevaldson, confessor at Wadstena (died 1514); Judith, Esther, Ruth, and the books of the Maccabees, by Jöns Budde of the Nädendal Monastery, Finland (died 1491); and the Apocalypse, and Gospel of Nicodemus, from the 15th century. In 1526 Laurentius Anderson, Chancellor of Sweden, published in connection with Olof Person, the New Testament at Stockholm, and the entire Bible, prepared after Luther's version, by the Archbishop Lars Person, was published, under the patronage of Gustavus Vasa, at Upsala, in 1541. A revised edition of this Bible was published at Stockholm 1617-1618, and often reprinted. A new revision undertaken by Johannes Gezchius, senior and junior, Bishops of Albo, was published in 1679 and 1728; and still another, undertaken at the command of Charles XII., appeared at Stockholm 1703. The most recent version of the New Testament is the translation by the Archbishop Lundberg of Upsala, and by the Professors Thorén and Johansen, which was published in 1882, and sanctioned by the church authorities and the king. This translation is now regarded as the authorized version of the Swedish Church. An excellent translation of the Old Testament has been published by Prof. Melin (1865-1869). The British and Foreign Bible Society adopted the text of the edition of the Swedish Bible Society, and published its first edition, which was stereotyped, at London in 1828. The Society circulated the Scriptures in Swedish till the year 1884, when it withdrew, leaving the field to home organizations. Its circulation up to March 31st, 1889, was 3,258,441 portions of the Scriptures in Swedish, and 5,122 Swedish-English New Testaments.

*Specimen verse.* John 3 : 16.)

Ty så älstade Gud werldena, att han utgaf sin enda Son, på det att hvar och en, som tror på honom, stall, icke förgås, utan få ewinnerligit lif

**Syria and Palestine.**—*The Name.*—The geographical term "Syria" seems to have originated with the early Greek traders, who designated by it the land whose chief commercial city was Tsur, Sur, or Tyre. When the Arabs came into the land in the 7th century A.D. they called Damascus, Dimishk esh-Sham, and named the provinces of which they made it the capital Bar esh Sham. The Christian inhabitants of the land still call it "Suriyeh." The term "Palestine" comes from Pelesheth (פְּלֶשֶׁת—"land of wanderers"), and refers probably to the nomadic tendencies of the early inhabitants. No form of the word "Palestine" (Philistia, Palestina, etc.) is at present in common use in the country. The term is historical rather than political, and defines that part of Syria which stretches from Dan (near Mt. Hermon) to Beersheba, and from the Mediterranean to the Syrian desert.

*Geography.*—Syria (Turk. *Suristan*) extends about 400 miles,—from the Taurus mountains on the north (latitude 37°) to Egypt (latitude 28°), and from the Mediterranean to the Syrian desert, an average width of less than 200 miles,—and contains 70,000 square miles. It is nearly conterminous with the "Promised Land" and the kingdom of David. It is about the size of New England, Palestine east and west of the Jordan being of the size of Vermont and New Hampshire, and very similarly situated. Mountains on the north, the sea on the west, and deserts south and east give the land a somewhat remarkable geographical unity. The mountain ranges and river basins run parallel with the coast, rendering access easy from north to south. The Taurus Mountains send a spur off to the south not far from the coast. This is broken by the deep gorge of the Orontes (El-'Asi) River. The range takes a new start in the beautiful peak of Mount Casius near Antioch, and stretches down along the coast, receiving various names at different points. Between Antioch and Tripoli it is called from the people who inhabit its slopes the "Nusairiyeh" range, which terminates in Jebel el Husn. A low saddle in the hills comes next, and then the Lebanon range springs suddenly up to the height of over 10,000 feet; and twenty miles across the plain to the east the almost equally massive Anti-Lebanon starts off to follow its mate down the coast for a hundred miles. Lebanon gradually tapers down from 10,000 feet to 8,000, to 5,000, to 2,000, until it drops into the hills of Galilee, and reaches almost sea-level in the Esdraelon plain. Anti-Lebanon holds its own for over half its length, then drops; but gathering in power, as a final effort, throws up its southern peak of

Mount Hermon (Jebel esh Shaykh) 10,000 feet into the air. Between these two magnificent ranges runs the fertile valley of Cælo Syria (El Bukaa), from ten to twenty miles in breadth and averaging over 2,000 feet above sea-level. The Orontes drains the northern part of the Bukaa, while the Litany (rising not far from the sources of the Orontes) flows southward and breaks through to the sea in the latitude of Mount Hermon. At the foot of this mountain rises the Jordan ("the descender'). This strange stream is delayed in the great marsh called El Huleh (Lake of Merom) at about sea-level. Breaking away from this it tumbles down in a few miles over 600 feet below sea-level into the sea of Galilee (Bahr Tabariyeh). After lingering for 16½ miles at this level it next plunges down 667 feet in a distance (as the crow flies) of 66 miles, but winding about 200 miles until it throws its muddy waters into the Dead Sea (Bahr Lut), 1,300 feet below the Mediterranean. To this phenomenal sea (46 miles long and 5 to 15 miles broad) there seems to be no outlet. Although there is a geological depression from its southern end to the Akabah Gulf of the Red Sea, and although there are indications that its waters were once on a higher level, the Dead or Salt Sea could not have been connected with the ocean, because there is a rise of ground of 781 feet above sea-level in its way.

West of the Jordan and south of the Esdraelon valley the hills of Ephraim slowly rise, forming the great backbone of Palestine. A sharp spur is thrown off to the northwest, which ends in the rocky headland of Mount Carmel. But to the south the trend is continually upward past Samaria, Nablous, Shiloh, Bethel, Jerusalem, Bethlehem, until Hebron is reached. From thence the hill-country of Judea falls away into the Sinaitic desert. Deep wadies run off gradually to the Mediterranean, but to the east sharp gorges plunge precipitately down into the Jordan valley a thousand or so feet below sea-level.

South of Mount Hermon and to the east of the Jordan, Anti-Lebanon gives place to a moderately high mountain wall, for the most part precipitous on its western side, but sloping away into the Hauran region and toward the desert beyond. The mountains of Gilead merge into the mountains of Moab and are continued southward to the Arabian border. The Hauran has indications of volcanic action, and has a number of interesting mountain peaks. A few oases in the desert—such as Tadmor (Palmyra) —belong geographically to Syria.

*Population.*—The population of Syria has been variously estimated, and as no accurate census has been taken, no definiteness can be attained. Just at present (1891) the population seems to be waning. There are probably 2,000,000 inhabitants in the country who have been roughly divided as follows:

| | |
|---|---|
| Mohammedans (Sunnites and Metawileh) | 1,000,000 |
| Nusairiyeh | 250,000 |
| Maronites | 250,000 |
| Orthodox Greeks | 235,000 |
| Papal sects | 80,000 |
| Jews | 30,000 |
| Ismaïlïyeh, Gypsies, etc. | 30,000 |
| Armenians | 20,000 |
| Jacobites | 15,000 |
| Druzes | 100,000 |
| Protestants | 6,300 |
| Bedouin Arabs | 60,000 |
| | 2,076,300 |

Such is the estimate of 1881. Since then the Jews have increased in number, notably at Jerusalem. The cities have grown, while in every direction the rural population is declining. The larger cities are Damascus (200,000), Aleppo (120,000), Beyrout (100,000), Jerusalem (35,000), Tripoli (with its port, 25,000), Homs (20,000), Hamath (20,000), Zahleh (15,000), Nablous (15,000), Sidon, Nazareth, Acre, Hebron, and Jaffa (each 10,000), Antioch (6,000), Bethlehem (5,000), Haifa (5,000), and Tiberias (3,000). The western slopes of Mount Lebanon are the most densely populated parts of the country outside of cities.

*Race.*—From the earliest times there has been a notable mixture of races in Syria, yet all along the Semitic type has prevailed with a persistence truly remarkable. Flood-tides of Egyptians, Greeks, Romans, Koords, Armenians, Persians, Teutons, and Mongols have swept the country repeatedly, only to be as repeatedly driven out. The bad blood of many nations has soaked into the soil, and reappears in many channels; but the original race type, though modified, has absorbed the remnant of many nationalities so effectively that there is a typical Syrian resultant, which differs widely from the surrounding peoples. With the exception of the Bedouin Arab of the southeast, the Koordish Bedouin of the northeast, the Turkish officials, the Armenian merchants, and the so-called Franks or foreign residents, the Syrian type is universal, modified, it is true, by hereditary religious customs and convictions, but holding its own through the centuries. It is characterized by a certain calculating shrewdness covered with an exterior of extreme politeness. The race-type is saturated with the despotic idea, which appears in every grade of society. Manual labor is counted ignoble. Religious differences have bred a mutual suspicion. Credit is almost unknown. Trade is a matter of sharp haggling over prices. The typical Syrian is proud, ambitious, loves display of ornament, cannot be trusted to obey to the letter, has a temerity of action on the basis of slight information, quickly yields to fear in the face of real calamity, and is thoroughly immersed in a gross materialism. A millennium of Moslem dominion and centuries of Turkish oppression have accentuated these faults. But wherever an opportunity has been given, a native force of character has come to the surface, so that even the precipitous slopes of Lebanon have been terraced thousands of feet above sea-level, and a restless desire to better their condition has sent whole colonies of Syrians across the oceans to Australia, South America, and to the United States. Common-school and higher education is having a marked effect upon the country, but the seeds of disunion and mutual hatred were planted too long ago to be materially affected during the short period, comparatively, in which western Christian influences have been brought to bear on Syria.

*Languages.*—With the Arabs in the 7th century came the Arabic tongue, which immediately became the language of trade. It was thus inevitable that it should become universal in the land. The older Syriac, a closely allied Semitic dialect, slowly succumbed, leaving behind broad marks of influence in the colloquial Arabic, so that a man's speech betrays the locality from which he comes. To the extreme north of Syria, in the region of Aleppo, the

Armenian (Aryan) language is frequently heard. The official language for the whole country is Turkish, while everywhere Moslems of all nationalities use Arabic as their religious language. Syriac remains the liturgical language of the Maronites and the Jacobites. North of Damascus there are several villages in which Syriac is still the vernacular. Hebrew is heard frequently in Jerusalem. Linguistically, then, Syria is a unit and is closely allied in this particular with the Euphrates region, Arabia, and Egypt.

*Commercially.*—The centres of commerce in Syria are Damascus (which means "seat of trade"), Aleppo, Alexandretta, Tripoli, Beyrout, Haifa, Nablous, and Jaffa. Homs, Hamath, and Jerusalem might also be mentioned. Railways have been projected, but the line running from Jaffa to Jerusalem is the only one in operation, unless the road in Cilicia running from Mersina to Adana should be counted as within the limits of Syria. A fine diligence road connects Damascus with its seaport Beyrout. Other roads, such as those connecting Tripoli and Homs, Homs and Hamath, Jaffa and Jerusalem, Jerusalem and Hebron, Haifa and Nazareth, Beyrout and Ain Zehalteh, and Beyrout and Brumana, are in operation, while other roads are in process of construction. Otherwise the highways of Syria are little better than bridle-paths, and transportation is expensive. The Hauran is the granary of the country. Olives, figs, licorice, oranges, grapes, and apricots are important crops. Maize, tobacco, and white potatoes are freely raised—America's gift to Syria. Soap from olive oil is made in quantities at Haifa and elsewhere. The silk-worm is busy all over. Mt. Lebanon, and the villages on the eastern slopes are alive with domestic weaving establishments. Bethlehem is the seat of work in olive-wood and pearl utensils (souvenirs). Jerusalem is now, as it always has been, a caravansery for pilgrims from every clime.

*Politically.*—Syria (in its widest extent) is divided by the Turkish government into four vilayets—Adana, Aleppo, Syria (proper), and Jerusalem. Since 1860 the Lebanon region has been under the protection of foreign powers and is governed by a Christian mutassarif under special foreign oversight. The result has been that this part of Syria is the best governed and most progressive section of the land. The seat of government is at Btedin. Roads have been constructed bringing the scattered sections of this region together. The centre of political danger to the Turk in Syria is in the Hauran district, where the Bedouin Arabs, settled and nomadic, have never consented to do military service in the Turkish army and are exceedingly jealous of official interference. However the telegraphic service has been extended everywhere, even to these remote districts, and Turkish soldiers have easily put down incipient revolts. The Porte has ruled Syria by skilfully playing off one religious sect against another, so that there is not the remotest danger of Nusairiyeh and Maronite and Druze striking hands. French influence since 1860 has been pervasive in the land. Trade has been opened, schools have been fostered, and religion has been watched by the French officials in the land with a care that betokens a desire at some time to control the country. Russia is jealous of this French propaganda, and under Moscovite auspices Jerusalem is being surrounded by towers,

churches, and hospices. The Turkish method of governing the Christian sects in Syria is to use the church organization in administering justice. Each sect commits its affairs into the hands of the head man of the body, who intermediates between the people and the Turkish officials. Woe to a man who falls out with his church! In effect he becomes an outlaw. Hence when the missionaries entered the country in the first half of this century, hoping to regenerate the decayed Christian churches, they were compelled to start a new sect so that those who accepted evangelical truth could have the protection of the law, such as it was. For when a Maronite was led to accept the gospel statement of redemption through Christ alone he was not allowed to remain in that communion. He was driven forth. His neighbors could wantonly take his property and maltreat him without let or hindrance. Consequently an evangelical communion was established under the Turkish law, and a Protestant is appointed to represent it before the law.

*Socially.*—The feudal system has not entirely disappeared from Syria, and princely families have until lately exercised great influence. The prince is patriarchal in his relations to his house, and thus many of the evils of the system are mitigated. But the mass of the people are plebeian. The clergy exercise great social power, as would be gathered from the preceding paragraph. The marriage of the secular clergy is almost universal among the Oriental Christian sects; and in the cases where these sects have been won over to the Roman Catholic faith this custom has, by special stipulation, been retained. The status of woman has been low. In the Moslem harem she has been denied all active connection with society. The Bedouin women, as well as those of the Nusairiyeh and Metawily, have a greater freedom and are more nearly on the level of men. The Druze women were of a higher grade and often could read. In this respect they were ahead of the women of the Christian sects, who have always been exceedingly ignorant and superstitious. Syrians are polite in the extreme, love neighborly chat, have joyous feast-days, and live a happy, careless, and rather indolent life. Drunkenness is common at certain seasons of the year among certain of the Christian sects. Instrumental and vocal music, mostly in the minor key, is constantly heard. Shepherd boys still picturesquely play the simple reed as they wander with their flocks. There are a great many home comforts among the middle and upper classes, and foreigners soon acquire a taste for many native dishes. The reverence of son for father, and many other Syrian characteristics, are truly admirable. At a later point in this article the great advance of Syria in education will be emphasized in its relation to social affairs. Syria is a land of homes, and in this centre lie the hopes for the country.

*Religiously.*—The statistics of the population of Syria are classified on a religious basis, and are given in a preceding paragraph. The orthodox Moslem faith (Sunnite) dominates the country. The Metawileh, Nusairiyeh, Ismailiyeh, and Druzes are Mohammedan sects more or less removed from orthodoxy. Until lately some of these sects were secret organizations, and even now we have a very limited knowledge of some of them. The Christian sects are found largely in the middle and northern parts of the land. The section of Mt. Lebanon under foreign oversight is very largely Christian in population. The Maronites (q. v.) are massed on the northerly slopes of this range. The Greek orthodox votaries are scattered about very evenly, but are especially numerous along the coast. The Jacobites are few in number, and are found mostly in the region of Homs and along the edge of the desert. The Armenian churches are more numerous in Northern Syria. While there is this great diversity in religious affairs in Syria, it is a diversity which is found everywhere, and so the same conditions prevail everywhere. Thus, whether we discuss the country religiously, socially, linguistically, commercially, racially, politically, or geographically, it is a unit.

*History.*—Syria has been from time immemorial the battle-field of nations, and it will be impossible to give in this statement even a chronicle of the great events that have taken place within its boundaries. It and its people have had a mission to perform for the civilized world, second to the mission of no other land and people. The Phœnician and the Hebrew stand for the two important elements in all civilization, commerce, and religion. As history dawns, the Phœnicians were the traders of the world, and had a strong rule along the coast. Innumerable warring tribes divided up the rest of the land among themselves. The Hebrews appeared as a nation in the 15th century B.C., and in the 11th century, under David, conquered the whole of the territory called Syria to-day, with the exception of Phœnicia. After the division of the Hebrew kingdom (975 B.C.) the new power of Syria arose, with its capital at Damascus. In the 8th century (721 B.C.) Assyria conquered Northern Syria and overwhelmed the northern tribes. Later Jerusalem fell before the Babylonian power (583 B.C.) and Judah went into captivity. Persia absorbed Babylon, and, until the conquests of Alexander the Great (323 B.C.), controlled the land along the eastern Mediterranean. After the death of the great conqueror, Ptolemy and the Seleucidæ were rivals in Syria, the power of the latter from their capital of Antioch being finally successful. The Jews rose in rebellion against the attempt to Hellenize their nation, and the heroic era of the Maccabees resulted (168–37 B.C.). The Romans were irresistibly being pushed eastward, and were obliged to add Syria to their growing empire. The country was ruled by native kings and Roman governors until it was thoroughly amalgamated in the Eastern or Byzantine empire. The grand duel between Byzantine and Persian (Sassanidæ) under the Emperor Heraclius weakened the Roman power so that in the 7th century A.D. the armies of Islam made easy work in conquering the land. The Ommeiad dynasty from Damascus ruled the Moslem world from 661 A.D. to 750. Several centuries later, as the Abbasside dynasty was breaking up at Baghdad, Syria was a prey to factions. The Seljuk Turk appeared, reversing the mild treatment the Christians had received at the hands of the Saracens hitherto, and persecution, imprisonment, and butchery aroused the knighthood of Christian Europe to undertake the Crusades (1095–1291). After the failure of the Crusades, Syria was again the scene of Moslem misrule at the hands of the Mameluke sultans of Egypt, and of fiercer raiders from Tartary. Early in the 15th century Tamerlane carried his annihilating hordes as far south as Damascus. In 1517 the whole land was conquered by Selim I., the Ottoman Turk, and, with the exception of the brief time during which Ibrahim Pasha held Syria (1832–1841), has been controlled successfully by the Porte.

The first Christian church was at Jerusalem, and at Antioch the name "Christian" arose. The Apostles and their followers carried the gospel to every portion of Syria, and the faith took root everywhere. The scattering of the Jews, as a result of the great rebellions against Roman dominion in 70 and 130 A.D., changed the type of Christianity in Syria materially; but it went on so successfully, that at the time of Constantine we find the land honeycombed with Christian churches.

Some of the greatest church fathers either were born or lived in Syria,—Ignatius, Justin Martyr, Eusebius, and Jerome,—missionary influences went out on every side, the Bedouin Arabs were reached, and Frumentius, a Syrian, was the apostle of the Abyssinians. Constantine and his mother, Helena, were drawn to the land made sacred by so many associations. Jerusalem became attractive to pilgrims. The ascetic spirit, so widespread in those days, took possession of this veneration for the sacred places. Monasteries sprang up all over the land. Hermits swarmed among the wild gorges of the Judean desert, and when Chosroes, the Persian conqueror, swept over the country, he slaughtered Christian monks by the thousand. Then came the Arab, who treated the Christians mildly. The Church of St. John in Damascus, it is true, was converted into a mosque; but Omar at Jerusalem left the Church of the Holy Sepulchre to the Christians, as well as the Church of the Nativity at Bethlehem. But Christianity dwindled. Islam attracted many Syrians into its ranks. At the time of the Crusades the whole number of Christians in the land was probably not more than half a million. The Roman pontiff had long been desirous to win the Oriental churches, which for the most part refused to acknowledge the universal supremacy of the Pope. During the Crusades, the Maronites (q v.) threw in their lot with the western Christians, and formed an alliance with the Church of Rome which has grown closer every century. The Roman Catholics have utilized these 250,000 Maronites as a centre for mission enterprises. The work has been pushed with vigor for three centuries, and has resulted in an addition to that communion of between 80,000 and 90,000 Syrians. The Greek Catholic Church is the most important outcome of this movement. It allows the marriage of the secular clergy, the retention of the Arabic service, the Oriental calendar and communion in both kinds. The Papal, Jacobite, and Armenian churches in Syria come next in importance. There are, in all, at least 350,000 (quite probably 400,000) of the inhabitants in Syria who acknowledge the papacy. The country is divided by the Roman Catholics into two parts—the patriarchal mission of Jerusalem (centred at Jerusalem and embracing Palestine and Cyprus) and the apostolic vicariate of Aleppo (embracing Northern Syria, centred at Beyrout). In the patriarchate mission in Palestine (including Cyprus) there are reported 28 stations (3 being in Cyprus), 20 churches, 22 secular European priests and 18 native clergy, 90 Franciscans and 10 Carmelite priests, 13,000 Latin Catholics and 11,000 in the Oriental churches subject to Rome, 58 schools with 3,900 pupils, and 7 orphanages with 429 pupils. In the vicariate of Aleppo there are 15 stations and 9 out-stations, 3,000 Latin Christians, with 344,500 of the Oriental rites, two seminaries, 280 elementary schools with 15,197 pupils, 1 university at Beyrout with 570 students, 12 intermediate schools with 1,674 pupils. The Capuchins, Carmelites, Jesuits, Lazarists, Trappists, Sisters of Charity, Sisters of St. Joseph, Dames de Nazareth, and Sisters of the Sacred Heart are the chief workers in this field.

*Protestantism.*—Into this seething little world of fierce religious propaganda—Mohammedan, Oriental, and Papal—the new force of Protestantism came in the third decade of this century. The Turkish Government rather favored it than otherwise,—considering it a new tool by which it could work confusion to its enemies. Rev. Pliny Fisk and Rev. Levi Parsons (Middlebury College, Vt.) landed at Smyrna in 1819. In 1821 Mr. Parsons went to Jerusalem to make that the headquarters for the work in Syria. In 1823 Mr. Fisk and Dr. Jonas King summered on Mt. Lebanon, and later made Beyrout the centre for work. In the same year Rev. Wm. Goodell, Rev. Isaac Bird, and their wives landed at that city. Shortly after both Mr. Parsons and Mr. Fisk died, but the work moved on. In 1828 violent persecution (ending in the death of Asaad Esh Shidiak, "the martyr of Lebanon"), political and warlike agitations, the forcible closure of schools at Beyrout, Tripoli, and elsewhere, led the missionaries to go to Malta and wait until the storm should blow over. In 1830, however, they returned and took up their labors with redoubled energy. A printing-press was established at Beyrout by Rev. Eli Smith, tracts and books were published and a translation of the Bible undertaken, and the land was more fully explored for favorable stations. Reinforcements came from America—Revs. Wm. M. Thomson, Nathaniel A. Keys, Samuel Wolcott, L. Thomson, Mr. Whiting, Mr. Sherman, Dr. C. V. A. Van Dyck, and their wives. In 1843 it appeared that greater concentration would make the work more effective, and Jerusalem was handed over to the Church Missionary Society of England. As already stated, the missionaries were compelled to organize a separate church to give protection to their followers under Turkish laws. Abeih and Hasbeiya were special centres for work. Other helpers came from America—Messrs. W. A. Benton, J. A. Ford (Aleppo), David M. Wilson, Horace Foote (Tripoli), and later still Messrs. Daniel Bliss, H. H. Jessup, W. W. Eddy, Simeon H. Calhoun, and Geo. E. Post. The translation of the Bible into Arabic (see Arabic Version) went on. The Syrian Protestant College was founded at Beyrout in 1865, having been incorporated in 1863 by the legislature of New York. A medical class was formed in 1867. In 1873 the present buildings, situated on Ras Beyrout, were first occupied.

But before this, in 1870 when the Old and New School Presbyterians of the United States were united, the Syrian Mission was handed over in a spirit of great magnanimity by the American Board to the Presbyterian Board, because up to this date the New School Presbyterians had contributed largely to the A. B. C. F. M. The missionaries found that the work would not be materially affected by the change. In fact a new impetus came to the mission, and the progress since 1870 has been very great, in twenty years more than trebling the resources of the mission as well as the number of native adherents. Other workers came, among whom may be mentioned Messrs. Samuel Jessup, James S. Dennis, Gerald F. Dale, Theo. S. Pond, O. J. Hardin, F. W. March, W. K. Eddy, Geo. A. Ford, Ira Harris, Harvey Porter, Frank Hoskins, with their wives, and Misses Emilia Thomson, E. D. Everett, Harriet La Grange and Harriet Eddy. The translation of the Bible was carried on to completion by Dr. Van Dyck after the death of Dr. Eli Smith. The college, under the wise leadership of Dr. Daniel Bliss, has grown constantly in efficiency and influence. It has three departments—preparatory, collegiate, and medical (with pharmaceutical)—with over 200 students from all parts of Syria, Egypt, and Cyprus. The theological seminary of the mission was built and equipped under the leadership of Dr. James S. Dennis, who is its president. The mission press at Beyrout has from the first printed nearly half a billion pages and has over four hundred publications on its catalogue, all of them with the government approval printed on the title-page. In 1889 24,569,167 pages were printed and 52,203 volumes sent forth.

During these years a large number of native Syrian Protestants have arisen who have done a great work for their land. Among them, besides the martyr Asaad Esh Shidiak, may be mentioned Gregory Wortabed, Butrus Bistany, Dr. Meshakah of Damascus; and a large number of men are to-day taking the places of these good and learned men whose names will never be forgotten.

The Church Mission Society took up the work in Palestine, with its headquarters at Jerusalem, in 1843. It occupies the field from Acre to Hebron and Gaza, and from Mt. Hermon to Moab east of the Jordan. It has pushed forward under great discouragements, but has made steady progress. It has stations at Jerusalem, Nablous, Jaffa, Gaza, Ramleh, Nazareth, Haifa, and Es Salt, etc. It has a number of successful schools. The work of this Society in the Hauran was stopped by the Turkish Government, and considerable opposition has developed of late throughout their territory.

The particulars of the work at Acca, Gaza, Jaffa, Jerusalem, Haifa, Nablous, and Nazareth are given in the articles on those stations. At Salt (the ancient Ramoth Gilead) there are substantial church and school buildings under the care of one missionary, with 4 out-stations and 30 communicants; girls' school, with 25 scholars, and 70 other scholars in the day-schools. Ramallah is occupied by 1 missionary and wife, with 3 out-stations, 55 communicants, 55 scholars,

The London Jews' Society has missions at Jerusalem, Jaffa, Damascus, Aleppo, and other places. The Established Church of Scotland has a mission to the Jews at Beyrout. At Tiberias there is another Scotch mission to the Jews.

The Irish Presbyterian Mission in Damascus (q.v.) was founded in 1843. The United Presbyterian Church of the United States was interested in this work for many years, but has of late concentrated its mission endeavors in Egypt. Dr. Crawford and his partners in the mission live at Damascus and occupy the territory around the city and in the southern sections of Anti-Lebanon.

The British Syrian schools and Bible Mission were established in 1860 by Mrs. Bowen Thompson. Since her death her sister, Mrs. Mott, has had charge of the work. It embraces about 30 schools, mostly for girls, in which over 3,000 pupils are gathered. The principal schools are at Beyrout, Damascus, Zahleh, Baalbec, Hasbeiya and Tyre. The Free Church of Scotland has a mission in the Metn district of Mt. Lebanon under the care of Rev. W Carslaw, M.D.

The Society of Friends in England and America has mission work at Brumana, on Mt. Lebanon, and at Ramallah, northwest from Jerusalem. The German Evangelical Missions include the German Deaconesses of Kaiserswerth, the Jerusalem Verein of Berlin, and the work of German chaplains in Beyrout and Jerusalem. The Kaiserswerth Deaconesses came to Syria after the terrible Druze massacres in 1860, and established orphanages in Jerusalem and Beyrout, and soon became connected as nurses with the Johanniter Hospital in the last-named city. The Jerusalem Verein (see article) has work in that city and also in Bethlehem. There are girls' schools at Bethlehem, Nazareth, and Shimlan under the care of a society of English ladies. Miss Taylor's (Scotch) school at Beyrout for Druze and Moslem girls is very successful.

There are also a number of special societies or private enterprises. *The Jerusalem Mission of Mercy.* Mr. T. J. A Alley arrived in Jerusalem in December, 1889, and since that time has conducted a work which can best be described in his own words: "In view of the unexampled poverty on all sides, I saw that to preach Christ (though I am not a minister) and the Golden Rule with its many parallels, and yet decline to illustrate those plain Scriptures by relieving the helpless poor, would be vain mockery." With this feeling Mr. Alley lives in the plainest possible manner, and spends his time and the money given him in answer to his solicitations and prayers in relieving the temporal wants of the poor, especially the Jews, so many of whom come to the land of their fathers in great want and distress to end their days among the scenes which remind them of past glories of Israel. By gifts of money, clothing, and other necessities his friends in England and America aid him in his life of self denial and ministration to those among whom he walks and labors as did his Saviour, with a like disregard of the comforts of life, and a warm heart for the poor and suffering.

*The Jerusalem Faith Mission and Home* is under the care of two ladies from New York, who represent the International Christian Alliance. They carry on a mission to the Jews and a Faith Home. The latter is a resort, resting-place, or home for missionaries or any Christians who seek the advanced Christian life without regard to any sectarian or denominational peculiarities. The ladies have won the highest esteem and earnest good wishes of missionaries of all denominations.

*Evangelical Mission to Israel* is the name of a mission under the care of an Israelite, Mr. D. C. Joseph, who has a reading-room where he conducts meetings, assisted by his wife and a Bible-woman. An assistant conducts an out-station at Hebron. The work is independent of any society, and relies on the gifts which come in answer to prayer and personal appeals.

*The Jerusalem Presbyterian* is another independent mission, similar to the above, conducted by the Rev. Abraham Ben Oliel, who, after forty years of missionary work along the Mediterranean, has recently moved from Jaffa to Jerusalem, and works among the Jews. Mr. Lethaby's mission has already been treated of under the title Moab Mission.

*The Bethany Home* is an independent mission started by Miss Crawford in 1887. A stone building was completed in 1889. She has gathered a school of thirty, both boys and girls, from among the Moslems. Assisted by a Bible-woman, she works also among the sick and poor around her. In addition to the work of the Jerusalem Union at Bethlehem, already spoken of under Bethlehem, the Society for Promoting Female Education in the East have at Bethlehem a mission with 2 medical missionaries, 3 female missionaries, and a girls' school with 60 scholars. Preaching service is attended by an average of 50, and the Sabbath-school numbers 48 scholars. At Nazareth Miss Hannah Kawar, the daughter of an educated native minister, is conducting a school for little girls at her own expense; the attendance numbers 36. A hospital for women and children, named Marienstift after its founder, H. R. H. the Grand Duchess of Mecklenburgh-Schwerin, is located at Jerusalem. It has no fixed income, and the labors of the doctor and his wife are given gratuitously.

The Reformed Presbyterian Church of the United States has a mission in northern Syria, with stations at Latakia, Antioch, and Mersine, Asia Minor. It deals more especially with the strange race of the Nusairiyeh (q.v.).

Besides these societies we find in Syria a number of very useful institutions such as Miss Arnott's school, the Mary Baldwin Memorial School, Miss Mangan's medical mission at Jaffa, as well as a large number of similar undertakings scattered about the country.

Bible work is carried on in Syria by the American Bible Society, with its headquarters at Beyrout, whence it sends Arabic scriptures over the whole world. Palestine is occupied by the British and Foreign Bible Society. The Tract Societies of America and England have given most substantial help to the mission in its effort to supply the whole Arabic reading world with Christian literature. The interesting item about all these numerous Protestant societies at work in Syria and Palestine is the fact that they are all working in substantial harmony. There is no more difficult mission field in the world. Jerusalem is the worst city in the world, not because of gross licentiousness, but because of spiritual pride; and the whole land partakes of the same spirit. Syria is at present in a most depressed state, agriculturally and commercially. The last fifty years have seen a leap ahead intellectually, and roads and the telegraph are binding the country together. In the end the simple gospel must prevail in the land that gave it birth, but many generations must come and go before Islam will yield, and before the stubborn oriental rites, as well as the papal votaries, will give up the meaningless and injurious human elements that have entered into their worship.

**Syriac Version.**—The Syriac belongs to the Semitic family of the languages of Asia. The oldest and most important version is the Peshito, or Peshita (i.e., the correct or simple), because confined to the text. The period at which this version was made has been much disputed, but there are reasons for believing that the whole version was completed by the close of the first or beginning of the second century; at any rate it was in common use in the year 350 A.D. The translation of the Old Testament seems to have been made immediately from the Hebrew, but with occasional reference to the Septuagint. This version is more particularly valuable on account of its being more ancient than any Hebrew manuscript now in existence. The Peshito version of the New Testament was made from the original text. The Old Testament was published first in the Paris Polyglot (1645), and then in Walton's (1657), and in an improved edition by the British and Foreign Bible Society (in 1823), under the care of Samuel Lee, Professor of Arabic at Cambridge. The New Testament was first published at Vienna in 1555, at the expense of the Emperor Ferdinand I., edited by Albert Widmanstadt, the imperial chancellor. This edition is the basis of all its European successors, and is not inferior to any. In 1816 the British Bible Society published the New Testament, edited by Dr. Lee, which was republished in 1826, together with the Old Testament as published in 1823. In 1829 the New Testament was edited by the late Dr. William Greenfield, and published by Bagster at London. The American Bible Society published the New Testament at Oroomiah, 1846, and New York, 1874; the Old Testament at Oroomiah, 1852. A critical edition of the New Testament and Psalms was published by the American Bible Society at New York in 1886. An edition of the Syriac New Testament in Hebrew, for the benefit of the Jews in the East, was published in 1837 by the London Society for Promoting Christianity among the Jews. Besides the Peshito version, there exist also various other versions in the Ancient Syriac, which we can pass over.

(*Specimen verse.* John 3 : 16.)

ܐܝܟܢܐ ܓܝܪ ܐܚܒ ܐܠܗܐ ܠܥܠܡܐ : ܐܝܟܢܐ ܕܠܒܪܗ ܝܚܝܕܝܐ ܝܗܒ :

ܕܟܠ ܡܢ ܕܡܗܝܡܢ ܒܗ ܠܐ ܢܐܒܕ : ܐܠܐ ܢܗܘܘܢ ܠܗ ܚܝܐ ܕܠܥܠܡ .

**Syriac—Modern, or Chaldaic, Version.**—The Modern Syriac language, a much-corrupted form of the venerable Ancient Syriac, is the spoken tongue of the Nestorian or Syrian Christians who reside in Persia and Turkey and are variously estimated at from 75,000 to 100,000 souls. By reason of their widely scattered tribal conditions for ages, the language presents many dialects, some with very marked peculiarities of their own. The late Dr. Joseph

Wolff, during his travels in 1826, purchased of the Nestorians several MSS. of various portions of the Bible and brought them to London, where they became the property of the London Jews' Society. From these MSS. the British Bible Society printed an edition of 2,000 copies of the Gospels, under the editorship of T. P. Platt. The edition left the press in 1829. With this exception little was known of the Modern Syriac to Western scholars, until the American missionaries began their labors among the Syrian Christians in Oroomiah in 1834. At that time no literature was known to exist in this language, and Dr. Perkins with his colleagues proceeded to reduce it to writing and to issue from the press religious and educational works. Later on a few manuscripts were discovered, dating a hundred years back, written in the Elkosh dialect spoken in the vicinity of Mosul, and proved to be unscholarly paraphrases of the Gospels, or rude poetical renderings of gospel history. These possess little interest save as throwing light on the development of the language.

The efforts of the missionaries were early directed to giving the people a translation of the New Testament from their Ancient version, for which the Syrian Christians have great reverence. In antiquity none exceeds it; in fidelity to the Greek it scarcely has an equal. It well deserves its name—Peshito, the "plain" or "simple" word. The first edition of this translation, with the Ancient Syriac in parallel columns, and the variations from the Greek, was published in 1846. Some few years later, when a pocket edition of the Modern Syriac version was issued from the press of the American Bible Society in New York, the text was emended to conform to the Greek. An edition with references was published in 1860. The translation of the Old Testament, with the Ancient Syriac in parallel columns, was issued from the Oroomiah press in 1852. An edition of the Modern followed in 1858. A careful revision of this translation is now in progress. There have been various issues of parts of the Scriptures from time to time. An edition of the Gospels in the Elkosh dialect was printed a few years ago, for which there was never much demand. The Roman Catholic missionaries have published an edition of the Gospels in Ancient and Modern Syriac with annotations.

(*Specimen verse.* John 3 : 16.)

ܗܟܢܐ ܓܝܪ ܡܚܒ ܗܘܐ ܐܠܗܐ ܠܥܠܡܐ : ܩܕܘܗܝ ܕܝܗܒܠܗ ܠܒܪܗ ܝܚܝܕܝܐ : ܕܟܠ ܡܢ ܕܗܝܡܢ ܒܝܗ ܠܐ ܐܒܕ : ܐܠܐ ܗܘܝ ܠܗ ܚܝܐ ܕܠܥܠܡ .

# T.

**Taba Mossegu,** a town in South Transvaal, South Africa. Mission station of the Berlin Evangelical Lutheran Society (1880); 1 missionary, 11 native helpers, 11 out-stations, 234 church-members, 93 scholars.

**Tabriz,** one of the oldest and most important cities of Persia, is the capital of the province of Azerbijan, and is situated in a val-

ley 4,000 feet above the sea. A large commerce is carried on here, as it is the centre of the trade between Persia, Russia, and Turkey, and it is on the line of the Indo-European telegraph from London to Bombay. There are few noteworthy public buildings, though numerous mosques, baths, and shops are found throughout the city, and one mosque is especially noted. The population is 165,000, chiefly Turks and

Armenians, the Persians being very few in number. Mission work is carried on by the Presbyterian Church (North), 1873, in the city itself and throughout the province, which is one of the most fertile and populous sections of Persia, specially at Maragha, Miandab (famous for the massacre during the Koordish insurrection in 1879), and Ilkahee. There is a boys' school, with 20 boarding and 47 day scholars; a girls' school with 30 day and 25 boarding scholars. The medical missionary, Dr. G. W. Holmes, was appointed court physician to the governor of the province, who is also heir-apparent to the throne of Persia, and was able to exert not a little influence towards mitigating the severity of the treatment of Protestants by the Persian Government. The present force is 2 missionaries and wives, 1 medical missionary, 3 female missionaries.

**Tahiti:** see Society Islands.

**Tahiti Version.**—The Tahiti belongs to the Polynesian languages, and is spoken in Tahiti, Society Islands. The Gospel of Luke, the first part of the Scripture published, was translated by the Rev. Henry Nott of the L. M. S. It was issued from the press at Tahiti in 1818. In 1830 the New Testament was completed, and five years later the complete Bible was printed. Mr. Nott was sent to England in 1836, and in 1838 the British and Foreign Bible Society issued an edition of 3,000 copies of the entire Bible and an equally large edition of the New Testament. A second edition of the Tahiti Bible was printed by the same society in 1845-6, after being revised by Rev. Messrs. William Howe and Thomas Joseph. This edition was soon exhausted, and a careful revision was made, preparatory to the printing of a new edition, by the Rev. Messrs. Howe, Alexander Chisholm, and John Barff, the latter supplying the marginal references. The edition was carried through the press in 1863 by the Rev. Joseph Moore, and 5,000 copies were printed. In 1877 a new edition of 5,000 copies was printed in London under the superintendence of the Rev. A. T. Saville; a few corrections were inserted and maps were supplied. In 1883 a school edition of 4,000 copies of the Bible was carried through the press in London by the Rev. J. L. Green. Up to March 31st, 1889, 57,579 portions of the Scriptures were disposed of.

(*Specimen verse.* John 3:16.)

I aroha mai te Atua i to te ao, e ua tae roa i te horoa mai i ta'na Tamaiti fanau tahi, ia ore ia pohe te faaroo ia 'na ra, ia roaa râ te ora mure ore.

**Tai-chair,** a town in Chehkiang, China, 75 miles southwest of Ningpo. Mission station of the China Inland Mission (1867); 1 missionary and wife, 12 native helpers, 6 out-stations, 7 churches, 191 church-members.

**Tai-ku,** a town in Shansi, China, 60 miles northwest of Fenchau-fu. Mission station of the A. B. C. F. M. (1883); 1 missionary and wife, 1 physician and wife, 1 out-station, 1 school, 15 scholars.

**Taiwan,** the capital and treaty port of Formosa (q.v.), China. The Presbyterian Church of England has here the headquarters of its mission in Formosa, which numbers 7

missionaries, 2 female missionaries, 17 stations among the Chinese, 1 Hakka station, 16 stations among the Pepohoans, and 21 organized, 14 unorganized congregations.

**Tai-yuen,** the capital of Shansi, China, lies on the bank of a branch of the Yellow River, in a fertile plain 3,000 feet above the level of the sea, 250 miles southwest of Peking. The climate is healthy, but subject to great extremes of heat and cold. Population, 80,000. Mission station of the C. I. M. (1877); 11 missionaries, wives, and assistants, 1 church, 20 communicants. Baptist Missionary Society (1879); 6 missionaries (4 married), 3 out-stations, 2 churches, 25 communicants.

**Takow,** a treaty port of Formosa (q.v.), China; is a mission station of the English Presbyterian Church, in the Tong Soa district, where they have 11 stations, 1 being for the Hakkas.

**Ta-ku-tang,** a market town in the extreme northern part of Kiangsi, China, on Lake Poyang, a little south of the Yangtsz-kiang. Mission station of the C. I. M. (1873); 1 missionary and wife, 1 female missionary, 1 chapel, 3 communicants.

**Talaguga,** a town in the Gaboon and Corisco district, West Africa, on the Ogowe River, 50 miles above Kangwe. Mission station of the Presbyterian Church (North); 1 ordained missionary, 1 female missionary, 1 native helper.

**Talaing Version,** the oldest of the versions made into any of the languages of Burma. Mrs. Sarah Boardman commenced the work of translation. After her marriage to Dr. Judson she continued the work, and in 1837 she had published several tracts and small books in the Talaing, and completed the translation of the New Testament, which she transferred to Mr. Haswell, who issued portions of the New Testament in 1838 and an edition of 3,000 copies of the whole New Testament in 1847. (See Pegu Version.)

**Ta-li,** a prefectural city in the northern part of Yunnan, China, northwest of Yunnan City. Mission station of the C. I. M. (1881); 2 missionaries, 1 chapel.

**Taljhari,** a native pastorate and district in Bengal, India, among the Santals, in the region sometimes called Santalia (q.v.), with 795 Christians, who support an evangelist in a neighboring district.

**Tamatave,** the principal port of Madagascar, is situated on the east coast, on a point about 350 yards wide. It is quite cosmopolitan in its character, as representatives of some of the principal European and Asiatic nationalities live within its limits. A low estimate of the foreign residents makes their number 1,200. Most of them are creoles from Mauritius, and natives of India of various religions and castes. Not more than 50 are pure British and French. French influence prevails, as there is a French Resident, controller of customs, and Roman Catholic priests, who teach and preach in French. The native population of about 4,000 is composed of Hovas from the interior, Taimoro from the south, Tanosy from St. Marie and Betsimisaraka from the surrounding districts. The latter are an exceptionally ignorant, superstitious tribe, who have been further debased by contact with the cargoes and crews of the various trading-vessels from Mauritius and Réunion which stop at the small ports. The town gives name to a district of the L. M. S., which has little political or administrative unity. It comprises the strip of country along the east coast of Madagascar, from the extreme north down to Mahanoro, a length of 480 miles, with a breadth of from 5 to 30 miles. This large district is under the charge of but 1 missionary. There are 51 congregations (9 in Tamatave town) with 448 church-members, 91 preachers, and 1,500 scholars in the mission schools. The Hova governors and soldiers, by their life and work, do much to keep the Christian spirit from dying out among the lower tribes. The S. P. G. have a station at Tamatave town, but find great difficulty in the work, since the majority of the creoles are Roman Catholics.

**Tameau-lajang,** a town on the upper course of the Burite River, Central Borneo. Mission station of the Rhenish Missionary Society; 1 missionary (ordained), 3 native helpers, 80 church-members, 30 school-children.

**Tamil Version.**—The Tamil belongs to the Dravidian family of the non-Aryan languages, and is spoken in the South and Central Karnatic and North Ceylon. The honor of producing the first translation of the New Testament into Tamil belongs to the Danish missionary Ziegenbalg, who was sent to Tranquebar in 1706 by Frederick IV., King of Denmark. The New Testament was published in 1714, the Society for Promoting Christian Knowledge having generously contributed towards its cost. Ziegenbalg had commenced the translation of the Old Testament, but left his task unfinished, as he died in 1719. In the same year Benjamin Schultze, also a Danish missionary, was sent to India. Having mastered the Tamil, he undertook the translation of the Old Testament, which was published in 1727. He then betook himself to a revision of Ziegenbalg's New Testament, and afterwards undertook a second revision, in which he was assisted by other missionaries. Schultze returned to Europe in 1742, and died in 1760. Schultze was followed by Fabricius, another Danish missionary. His version of the whole Bible was published at Tranquebar in 1782. Altogether there were fourteen editions of Fabricius' New Testament, and two of the Old, brought out by the Danish Mission before the close of the last century, aided by liberal grants made by the Society for Promoting Christian Knowledge, and some Continental missionary societies. A revision of the Tamil Scriptures was undertaken by Rhenius, of the Church Missionary Society, but he only lived to complete the New Testament, which was printed by the Madras Auxiliary of the British and Foreign Bible Society in 1820. Another revision was executed by a representative committee of the various missionary societies in the Tamil-speaking provinces, and was published in Madras in 1850. But in the opinion of many competent judges, it had serious defects, and a still further revision was demanded. In 1857 six missionary societies entered into the alliance for revision—the Society for the Propagation of the Gospel, the Church Missionary Society, the London Missionary Society, the Wesleyan Missionary Society, the American Board of

Missions, and the Scottish Free Church Mission. The only Tamil missionaries who held aloof were those of Ceylon. The Rev. H. Bowen was appointed principal reviser, and Fabricius' translation was taken as basis. The work of revision was completed in 1868. After a careful examination by members of the Jaffna Auxiliary, who had, as before stated, declined to take part in the revision, but afterwards cordially accepted it, the whole Bible was published in 1871. It went by the name of "The Union Version," and continues to this day the only version used in the Tamil missions, with the solitary exception of the Leipsic Evangelical Lutheran Mission, which uses the version of Fabricius. An edition of the Tamil Bible, with references and marginal readings, was published in 1882. A revised New Testament, with references and marginal readings, was also issued in 1887. Up to March 31st, 1889, the British and Foreign Bible Society disposed of 2,549,150 portions of the Scriptures, besides 32,000 portions in Tamil and English.

*(Specimen verse.* John 3 : 16.)

தேவன், தம்முடைய ஒரேபேறான குமாரன விசுவாசிக்கிறவன் எவனோ அவன் கெட்டுப்போகாமல் நித்தியசீவன உடைய ம்படிக்கு, அவனாத் தந்தருளி, இவ்வளவாய் உலகத்தில் அன்புகூர்ந்தார்.

**Tampico,** a town in the state of Tamaulipas, on the river Paranco, 5 miles from the Gulf of Mexico. Population, 5,000, Indians, Spaniards, Creoles. Language, Spanish. Religion, Roman Catholic. Social condition civilized, prosperous. Mission station Associate Reformed Synod Southern Presbyterians (1881); 2 missionaries and wives, 1 other lady, 13 native helpers, 12 out-stations, 6 churches, 226 church-members, 1 theological seminary, 2 students, 4 other schools.

**Tamsui,** a treaty port of Formosa (q. v.), China, in the northern part of the island; is headquarters and principal station of the mission of the Presbyterian Church of Canada. A missionary and a missionary physician are located at Tamsui, and from there visit and direct the work in the surrounding districts, in which there are 50 congregations, 51 native preachers, 2,833 church-members, 25 students in the college at Tamsui, 30 girls in the girl's school, and 1 hospital.

**Tandur,** a station of the Methodist Episcopal Church (North) in Madras, India, near Secunderabad; 1 missionary and wife, 4 native helpers, 2 church-members, 2 schools, 55 scholars.

**Tanganyika,** a large lake in Central Africa, 480 miles in length from northwest to southeast, and from 10 to 60 miles broad. It occupies a long depression in a region of considerable elevation, south of Victoria and Albert lakes, and northwest of Nyassa. Beautiful scenery borders the lake, and many parts of its shores are thickly inhabited. Ujiji on the east shore is the largest settlement.

Lake Tanganyika was discovered by Speke, 1867, and visited by Livingstone (1867) and Stanley (1874).

The L. M. S. has two stations on the lake: Niumkorlo, at the south end of the lake, with

3 missionaries (1 married); and Fwambo (q.v.), 2 missionaries (1 married).

**Tangier,** a seaport of Morocco (q.v.), is situated on the south shore of the Strait of Gibraltar, 38 miles southwest of the Rock. Population, 10,000. Mission station of the North Africa Mission (see article); 9 missionaries.

**Tanjore,** a town of Madras, India, 180 miles southwest of Madras City, 45 miles from the Bay of Bengal. It contains two forts, the rajah's palace, and a pagoda, considered one of the finest in India. Tanjore is also noted for its artistic manufactures, including silk carpets, jewelry, répoussé work, copperware, and curious models in pith, etc. Population, 54,745, Hindus, Christians, Moslems, etc. Mission station of the S. P. G.; 1 missionary, 23 native helpers, 7 schools, 268 scholars. Wesleyan Missionary Society; 1 native pastor, 1 chapel, 1 school, 22 scholars.

**Tanna Version.**—The Tanna belongs to the Melanesian languages, and is spoken in Tanna, New Hebrides. Before the year 1869 no portion of God's Word appears to have been printed in Tanna. In that year, the Rev. J. G. Paton from Scotland, who had been driven from Tanna in 1862, printed a portion of the Gospel of Mark in Auckland. In 1878 the Gospel of Matthew was printed at the mission press at Tanna, followed in 1881 by the Acts of the Apostles; in 1883 by the Book of Genesis; and in 1884 by the first 19 chapters and part of the 20th chapter of Exodus. In each case the edition consisted of 200 copies. With the exception of the portion of Mark, the other parts were translated by the Rev. William Watt. The New Testament, translated by Mr. Watt, was published in 1890 by the National Bible Society of Scotland.

**Taouism.**—Laotze is said to have been born in the year 604 B.C., though there has been some question whether he was or was not a real character. The fact that the names of his village and county and state or province seem to be allegorical, like the names in Pilgrim's Progress, has led to a doubt on this subject. But some allowance should be made, probably, for the tendency among the Chinese to deal in allegorical names. Even the shops of the chief cities sometimes bear upon their signs names which excite a smile in a foreigner.

Laotze's history, all things considered, seems real. It is said that he left a son, who won distinction in public office.

Laotze's birth occurred about a half-century before the birth of Confucius: they were therefore contemporaries. Both are said to have been the sons of very old men.

The condition of China, or of that particular province in which Laotze lived, corresponding to a portion of the present Shantung province, was greatly disturbed by border wars and intestine revolts and intrigues. There was scarcely a vestige of morality, and the political condition of the country was chaotic. Both Laotze and Confucius aimed at reform. Both appear to have been disinterested and high-minded. Both were rather impatient, however, with the stolidity and degradation of the people, and with the vices and corruption of the reigning princes.

Laotze appears to have held for a time an office as keeper of the archives, as the old records express it; but his mind drifted toward philosophy and political reform, and the position he held was far from meeting his ambition: political engagements were irksome to him.

Comparatively little is known of this truly profound thinker or reformer. He is supposed to have been poor, and for that reason perhaps the more keenly conscious that his nation and his age failed to appreciate him. He was, in short, too morbid in spirit to make the best use and secure the greatest results of his rare gifts. He formed no school of followers, and wrote no books. On the contrary, he withdrew himself from men, was too proud to teach or write, disliked display of any kind, and was in fact a recluse.

Confucius, on arriving at manhood and entering upon his career, sought an interview with Laotze, with a hope of profiting by his great ability, his observation, and his experience. He was received coldly, however, and with severe criticism instead of sympathy. Much as the two men were alike, they had wide differences of character, and these were increased by the fact that Laotze was already an old man when Confucius appeared before him. He was in no attitude of mind to approve or even tolerate what he considered the gushing enthusiasm and crudity of Confucius. He looked upon him as an ambitious, blustering agitator, sounding brass and a tinkling cymbal, and he predicted the failure of his pretentious efforts at reform.

Confucius, on the other hand, was astonished at the churlishness of the old reformer, was perplexed at his involved and incomprehensible theories and mystical speculations, and he could only compare him to the "incomprehensible Dragon."

At last, in old age, Laotze's despair at the condition of the country became overmastering. He had dire forebodings of calamity, revolution, bloodshed, political chaos, and destruction. He had become more and more unpopular as he had grown more and more reproachful toward his countrymen.

He dreaded to witness the ruin which he was sure was coming upon the land, and he fled into voluntary exile, passing westward through the Hankow Pass into the province of Honan. He was induced to stop for a time with the Keeper of the Pass, and instruct him in the principles of his philosophy. This gate-keeper seems to have realized that no ordinary person was before him, and he was unwilling that a man who was too morbid and impracticable to write any book or organize any class of disciples should pass from the knowledge of men without leaving some substantial results of his thinking. He appears to have taken down from dictation the main principles of the reformer's teaching. This record is known as the Taou Teh King. It embraces all that is known of Laotze's doctrines.

After leaving the Hankow Pass for the west, Laotze passed into obscurity, and, so far as is known, nothing was ever heard of him afterward. Many legends sprang up around the history of Laotze like the young shoots at the root of a dying tree. One of these relates that upon leaving the Pass for his voluntary exile he parted with his servant. The latter, learning the plan of his master, was unwilling to accompany him, and in the settlement charged an exorbitant sum as back wages; but as Laotze had by a spell kept him alive far beyond his appointed time, he withdrew the spell, and the servant became a dry skeleton. However, at the request of the gate-keeper, who interceded for the servant, he restored him to life, and then found him reasonable in his price. Other absurd legends are preserved, one of which is that Laotze was miraculously born at the age of eighty, and that he was known as the "Old Boy." He was gray-haired at birth. Certain legends similar to those which are related of Gautama, and which may have been copied, are also given—as that Laotze leaped into the air as soon as he was born. Some of his followers have claimed that he was a spiritual being, and not an actual, ordinary man.

*The Character of Laotze.*—Laying aside all legends, and contemplating the actual life of Laotze, so far as scanty materials enable us to do, we find him a man above reproach in morals, though living in a dissolute age. The parallels between his severe type of philosophy and that of the great names of Greece are quite remarkable. He was uncompromising and exacting in his standards of right and wrong, morose and despondent in temperament, proud and impracticable in his relations to men, and having little tact in approaching them. He was too much of a quietist to be a successful reformer. He had been soured by disappointment and he died in despair. His system had brought him no comfort; he had seen no improvement in the condition of society. He regarded his life as a failure, and yet he seems to have come very near to the truth in many respects.

He approached the sublime ethics of our Saviour more nearly than any of his contemporaries, though they were among the greatest names in history, for Laotze, Confucius, Pythagorus, Gautama, and, according to Monier Williams, Zoroaster, are supposed to have lived within a century of each other. Laotze taught that real virtue is a spiritual and interior excellence, and not outward doing or speaking. In this respect he fought much the same battle with the objectivity of mere formal and immovable customs as our Saviour did in His dealings with the Pharisees; and like Him he urged the law that is written within, and of which the outward world knows nothing. He taught also that he who foregoes and yields up and forbears is the one who really finds and succeeds, and that he who humbles himself is really exalted.

In general, like our Saviour, he exalted the quiet and passive virtues, and he taught the duty of doing good even to those who injure us. In this respect he stood in strong contrast with Confucius, whose position more nearly resembled that of the old Jewish dispensation, which required "an eye for an eye, and a tooth for a tooth." The justice of that dispensation was as high as Confucius felt called to go in his dealings with men; no one placed greater emphasis than he upon justice, but he could not understand the duty of doing good in return for evil. Some terse expressions from the lips of Laotze show the deep subjectivity of character as he conceived it. "It is not necessary," he said, "even to peep through the window to see the celestial Taou." At another time he said, "There is a purity and quietude by which one may rule the world." Again, "Lay hold of Taou (wisdom) and the whole world will come to you." Again, "One pure act of resignation is worth more than one hundred thousand exercises of one's own will." The moral elevation of character that is set forth in these utterances is certainly remarkable. It is worthy of a place in Christian ethics.

There were some points in which Laotze seemed to be at one with Gautama. He taught that even in this life it is possible to completely possess Taou, and that thus the creature may become one with the creator by the annihilation of self, it being understood that to possess Taou is in another sense to be possessed by Taou as an indwelling principle or life, all of which implies a near approach to the Pantheistic absorption in deity which Hinduism also teaches. A general difference between the spirit of Laotze's teaching and that of Confucius may be expressed thus: Confucius would say, "Practise virtues, and call them by their right names." Laotze would say, "Practise them, and say nothing about it." Although he had great reverence for the ancients, he did not idolize them as did Confucius, and as he has led the Chinese nation to do.

There seems to have been in the interviews of the two sages some little controversy on this point, in which Laotze told Confucius, by way of subduing his romantic enthusiasm, that the "ancients were only so many bundles of dry bones; wisdom did not die with them." He illustrated the grace of quietness and the safety which it secures by saying that "the leopard by his brilliant colors, and the monkey by his frivolous activity, only draw the arrows of the archer," and to the loud-mouthed reformer he would say, "You are like a man who beats a drum while hunting for a truant sheep."

One point in which Laotze was far in advance of his age, and abreast with some of the best political thinking of whatever age, was his maintenance of the theory that kings exist for the good of the people and not for their own selfish ends, which ends the people, like so many dumb beasts, are designed to subserve. "Kings," according to Laotze, "should rule so quietly, and holds the reigns so lightly, that the people may forget them as kings, and only think of them as superiors." There should in all government, as he insisted, be a minimum, and not a maximum, of government. Surely these practical and lofty political principles stamped Laotze as a man of prophetic genius.

Confucius said much more than he concerning government: more, certainly, in the number of details; but no counsels of his are so laden with sublime principles as those of his rival, and none of his teachings are more in accord with the truth.

*The Philosophy of Laotze.*—It is as a philosopher that Laotze most inspires our respect and honor. Taou, which was his ideal of the all-comprehending and eternal essence of things, means Reason, as nearly as it can be translated; but it means more than that word represents to us. It is the Infinite Reason, in such a sense that it embraces all excellence and glory; it corresponds very nearly to the word Wisdom as it is used in the Book of Job and the Ecclesiastes. Taou was deified by Laotze, though in no superstitious sense; and yet it was impersonal; it was apprehended by him in a pantheistic sense. Thus he says: "All things originate with Taou, conform to Taou, and return to Taou."

Taou exerts its influence in a very quiet manner; its influence is still and void, and yet it "encircles everything and is not endangered;" it is ever inactive, and yet leaves nothing undone; nameless, it is the origin of heaven and of earth. It is not strange, perhaps, that with so vague a conception of the supreme force in the world the Chinese mind should have lapsed into a mere general conception of Deity, and that the prayers of the emperors have for ages been addressed to Heaven.

Professor Douglas, of the London University, has summarized the elements of Taou as follows: (1) "It is the Absolute, the Totality of Being and Things. (2) The Phenomenal world and its order. (3) The ethical nature of the good man, and the principle of his action." One is reminded of various philosophic schools of ancient and modern times. The "totality of being and things" is about equivalent to the pantheistic conception of the Indian Vedanta. It does not differ materially from the "absolute substance" of Spinosa or the "absolute intelligence" of Hegel. It must be confessed that Laotze was a profound philosopher. He has rarely been excelled in the history of philosophy, for in view of his comparatively isolated position we must regard him as eminently original. His system was wholly his own; he was the father of Chinese philosophy. In profundity of thought he far exceeded Confucius, though he was less practical. Confucius was not a philosopher in the strictest sense: he was only a skilful and eminently practical compiler of ancient wisdom. He did not claim to be more than this, and with laudable modesty he spoke of himself as only an editor. But the Taou Teh King of Laotze came from his own brain.

There is a seeming contradiction in the teachings of Laotze in reference to the past. While Confucius carried his reverence for ancient authorities to an extreme which scarcely seemed to admit the possibility of anything new in the world, Laotze took issue with him sharply, and even poured a degree of contempt upon his extreme reverence. At the same time, though he admitted no age of antiquity as necessarily authoritative, he looked back, in a general way, to a golden age of simplicity and virtue which had passed away, and his whole idea was to return from the complex wisdom and civilization which he regarded as only a curse, to the better days when men had few wants and lived quietly.

He was in accord with Confucius on one point, namely, the uprightness and dignity of man's original nature. They recognized no doctrine of human apostasy which assumed hereditary form. In logical consistency they both maintained that every man is born without evil bias, and is sound at the core. The continued influences of demoralizing example were supposed to account for the evils which these great sages found in the world about them.

Like the ancient Druids Laotze propounded his great principles of life in triads, and the three precious virtues which he cherished were compassion, economy, and humility, all of a quiet type. He did not believe in intellectual brilliancy of any kind, much less in any show and pomp of conscious power, and he had little to say of prowess; his ideals were not the great and ambitious and mighty as men are reckoned to be mighty, but those, rather, who represented the passive virtues, the gentle and retiring graces of human life.

There is a difference of opinion as to Laotze's idea of God. Professor Douglas thinks that he had no conception of a personal divine being, at least that he recognized no such being; but, on the other hand, Professor Legge of Oxford seems confident that the supreme "heaven" or God in heaven was involved in his idea of Taou. He maintains that Laotze often spoke of heaven in a non-material sense, and that in one instance he calls the name of God itself.

One thing is certain: whether Laotze regarded Taou as personal or not, he assigned to it providential oversight and care and all forms of beneficent interest. Says Professor Legge: "Taou does more than create. It watches over its offspring with parental interest. It enters into the life of every living thing. It produces, nourishes, feeds, etc."

Laotze's doctrine of creation seems a little vague. He says: "That which is nameless is the beginning of heaven and earth. Taou produced One, the first great cause; One produced Two, the male and female principles of nature; Two produced Three, and Three produced all things, beginning from heaven and earth." This strikingly resembles the Shintoo notion of the origin of all things, according to which there is one absolute though unknown being, from whom emanated two, male and female, and from these the world of beings was produced. Both Confucius and Laotze speak of heaven both as material and as personified.

According to Professor Douglas, Laotze would agree with the Darwinians as to the creative indifference of the Deity or deified influence which is characterized as heaven. "It has," he says, "no special love, but regards all existing beings as 'grass dogs' made for sacrificial purposes." "Yet," he adds, "it is great, and compassionate, and is ever ready to become the Saviour of men."

If the question whether Laotze was really religious in his thought were dependent on such statements as this, we should be compelled to answer in the affirmative, for the being or power which is regarded as "great and compassionate and ever ready to become the Saviour of men" is an object of religious contemplation, surely.

As to the physical laws of the world, Laotze maintained that the earth is held together, not by gravitation, but by Taou. In a sense this was true, supposing Taou to represent the infinite force, for gravitation is but a second cause. The expression "the earth is held together by Taou" is nearly equivalent to the declaration that "God holdeth the earth in His right hand." Something like the Buddhist idea of an eternal round of life and death seems to be intended by Laotze's doctrine that existence and nonexistence constantly originate each other.

We have alluded to some similarities between the teachings of Laotze and those of Christ, especially in the gentle virtues of kindness, humility, forbearance, etc. The differences, however, which appear are more striking than the resemblances.

Christ showed a balance of truth. He taught the passive virtues, but also the active ones which Laotze did not. He commended modesty and secrecy in prayer, and yet the duty of active influence. "Let your light so shine," etc. This was not for self, but for others. Confucianism was active, Taouism passive, Christianity was both. The fatal defect in Taouism was its lack of divine recognition and divine power. Its ethics were high, but it had no love for God and therefore none for man.

*The Taou Teh King.*—This is a short treatise, already referred to, embracing the sayings of Laotze which were recorded by the Keeper of the Hankow Pass as the great teacher was about to go into exile. It is very brief, only about the length of the Sermon on the Mount. In its general character it is exceedingly intricate, and often obscure. The best scholars feel little confidence in their interpretations of it. Here is a specimen. "There was something chaotic and complete before the birth of heaven and earth. How still it was and formless, standing alone and undergoing no change, proceeding everywhere, and in no danger of being exhausted. It may be regarded as the mother of all things." In its real spirit and meaning this passage corresponds remarkably with one found in the Rig Veda, in which the original chaos is described as being brooded over by the infinite Brahm, the "Only Existing One," breathing quietly. The vagueness of the philosopher's conception is well set forth in this passage: "I do not know the name, but designate it the Taou (the way), and forcing myself to frame a name for it, I call it the Great. Great, it passes on in constant flux; so passing on it becomes remote; when remote it comes back."

*Modern Taouism.*—There could hardly be a stronger contrast than that which is presented between the ancient and the modern Taouism. Laotze was virtually rationalistic, but the present system is the most irrational of the great existing religions; it is a mass of superstitions of the lowest type. It is only the name of Taouism applied to a mixture of Buddhism and the ancient nature-worship and other superstitions of China. Speculation seems to have spent itself in the few centuries which followed the life of Laotze. Having first run wild in theories, it degenerated into low superstitions. The principle in Laotze's teaching which seems to have suggested the prevalence of spirits and ghosts in all nature, animate and inanimate, was his declaration that the presence of Taou is universal. He gave it a pantheistic omnipresence and indwelling in all beings and things. He little thought, probably, that this would lead to the notion that every object in nature is haunted, and thus cause the land to swarm with polytheism. A Taouist is afraid of his shadow. In the woods or in dark ravines he imagines he is about to be pounced upon by sprites or demons. The trees have souls, the very air is laden with a mysterious influence. Telegraph wires cannot pass through the open spaces nor steeples be reared without disturbing "fungschuay," nor can the earth be excavated for the purpose of mining or the introduction of any modern improvement without great risk that this omnipresent something shall be disturbed.

Taouism continued to be a philosophy for some time after the death of Laotze, but it was a changed and ever-varying series of speculations. In the opinion of Dr. Legge, it did not become a religion, strictly speaking, until after the introduction of Buddhism in the first century A.D. It had a priesthood and abundant superstitions, but it was sorely in need of being reinforced by something higher. So far as history informs us, no successor of Laotze seemed to correctly interpret or propagate his teachings.

His standard was too high, his theories were above the reach of his successors, his ethics and his transcendentalism alike failed to be appreciated. Professor Douglas has a very different estimate of the followers of Laotze from that ascribed to the immediate successors of Confucius. While the latter drew multitudes of the best men of the age about him, Laotze's camp was a Cave of Adullam to which the discontented and erratic resorted. His teachings, therefore, were left in the worst of hands.

Among the most influential Taouists in the next generation was Leitsze, who argued Laotze's quietism into a general Epicurean license. "Lay aside aspiration, and live for to-day; live in the freedom of the beast," would express his general view. Laotze had said: "Lay aside pomp and circumstance, live simply and with little pretence." Leitsze carried the idea to extremes. He also gave a licentious interpretation to the pantheism of Laotze, assuming that "if Deity lives and acts in us, then we are Deity, and are above restraint; we are as free as the gods."

The development of this extreme logical sequence of pantheism has not been confined to Taouists or to any particular country. The Upanishad pantheism of the Hindus led to the same results by the same logical process; men came to regard the soul as beyond the reach of sin or stain. Even in the extreme fanaticism which sometimes attaches to Christian doctrine, notions of liberty and perfection lead to the abandonment of law, and to general laxity of life.

Leitsze attached great importance to dreams. They constituted one mode of his teaching. He represented the emperor Hwangte as dreaming that he was in a world where men lived in the freedom of perfect indifference; nothing troubled them. These wonders led to the art of conjuring, and Leitsze wrung from Yin He, the Hankow Gate-keeper, his assent to these arts, and his endorsement of them on the alleged authority of Laotze. In all this Leitsze wholly misrepresented the great philosopher and his principles. As a result of these frauds there swept in that flood-tide of juggleries which swamped the principles of Taouism, and opened the way for the old national superstitions.

Leitsze did not fail to encounter the rising Confucianism. He tried the old tactics of his master Laotze; he endeavored to put down Confucianism with ridicule. He had no better weapons than those of borrowed sarcasm. As it seemed necessary to his prestige that he assume the rôle of a philosopher, he developed a theory of the universe, but it was puerile and failed to win respect. His favorite method of argument was that of dialogue in which his view was always made to triumph. He was forever fighting men of straw of his own manufacture. In one of these the superior wisdom of pursuing sensual enjoyments while one can is shown to the best advantage. Yet this man, by his intellect and vigor, won great influence for a time.

He was followed by Chwangtsze. He was inclined to return from Leitsze to a position more like that of Laotze. He discoursed on the vanity of life, and bitterly opposed the superfluous homilies and showy benevolences of Confucianism. "Sages," he said, "turn round and round to be benevolent and kick and struggle to become righteous, and the people suspect their very earnestness. They bow and distort themselves in their endeavors to act with propriety, and the empire begins to break up." The satire which underlies all this is keen, and has a measure of truth.

There are some resemblances between the theories of Chwangtze and the Vedanda philosophy of India. He treated wakeful and conscious life as an illusion, and doubted the substantial reality of all things. And to this day there is a belief among Taouists that there is an inner and invisible soul in all objects; the unseen appears to be quite as real as the visible. As an illustration of this doubt as between the tangible and the invisible, he related a dream in which he seemed to be a butterfly, flitting about in the air, and he felt no little surprise on waking to find that he was no butterfly, but Chwangtze. "But then," he says, "the thought came to me, on the other hand, was that really a dream, or am I now dreaming that I am Chwangtze and not a butterfly?"

In the third century before Christ, Taouism had gained such influence that the reigning emperor ordered a general conflagration of all sacred books except those of the Taouists, but the doctrine as then held was not that of Laotze. It had undergone successive changes until it had become a system of childish superstitions. It was believed that immortality might be gained by charms and spells. The emperor Chwangtze believed this, and also that in the western seas there were happy isles where genii dispensed the elixir of immortality to all who came. This emperor sent expeditions to these imaginary isles to bring back the elixir. The period of his reign was a great harvest-time for all Taouist frauds. The priests claimed the most astonishing of occult arts.

Taouism was now neither a philosophy nor a religion; it was a system of jugglery. Under the reign of the emperor Woo of the Han dynasty, who also became an implicit believer, the system still flourished, even down to about 100 B.C. This emperor also sent expeditions to the happy islands; alchemy and the quest for the elixir of life were at their height. It will be remembered that in Europe also similar fanaticisms have at various times been rife; but the wildest of them never equalled that of the Taouists of China in the reign of Woo. From the emperor down, all classes were seeking this elixir. Business of every kind was for a time neglected and the fields were untilled. Only the astrologists and priests were thrifty. The emperor lavished fortunes on their wild schemes.

Under these fanatical emperors Confucianism was bitterly persecuted. Many distinguished Confucian philosophers were burned alive, and all their books were burned (see Prof. Legge's "Religions of China"). But at the death of Woo a great reaction took place and Confucianism was revived and reinstated.

In the first century A.D. the first high-priest or pope of the Taouists was appointed, and the office has descended in his clan to this day. He is elected by the priests of the clan; he is not bound by rules of celibacy or any particularly ascetic requirements.

Taouism became a religion, strictly speaking, soon after the advent of the Buddhists, somewhere about the close of the first century A.D. Like Buddhism it had great powers of absorption, and from having been at first a philosophy and then a system of jugglery it now borrowed certain religious elements from Buddhism. The two systems, both of which were rather absorbent than catholic and charitable, entered into kindly relations with each other. They at length came to have so much in common that their priests united in the same services, and it is stated by Prof. Legge that an emperor of the Chi dynasty strove to unite them by ordering Taouist priests to adopt the practice and the habit of the Buddhists. Some were put to death for refusing to conform. Taouists have persistently refused to submit to the full ritual of Buddhism, and their monks have withstood the requirement of celibacy. Low and degraded as Taouism had long been, it never sank into idol-worship until it came into contact with Buddhism. Neither had the followers of Confucius or Laotze ever worshipped an image until the custom was borrowed from the Buddhists. Now the temples of Taouists vie with those of the Buddhists in this respect.

One of the most noticeable effects of Buddhism upon the Taouist system is seen in the adoption by the latter of a trinity. Buddhism had images in its temples representing Buddha, the Law and the Sangha, though at a later day they came to be regarded as representing Buddha past, present and to come. At length there appeared in the Taouist temples a trinity of colossal images, representing the Perfect Holy One, the Highest Holy One, and the Greatest Holy One. Monasteries and nunneries were unknown among the Taouists until after the introduction of Buddhism; the doctrine of transmigration was also derived from the same source. The Buddhist notion that women distinguished for virtue and character shall be rewarded at the next birth by being born as men, was also adopted by Taouists (see Prof. Legge's Religions, etc., page 192).

In one view a doctrine of eschatology seems out of place in Taouism, since it maintains that rewards and punishments are received in the present life. For example: the so-called "Book of Rewards" makes punishments consist almost invariably in shortening the period of the present life; immortality is spoken of, but it is something treated as of little account. Nevertheless, in each provincial temple of the Taouists may be seen what is called a Chamber of Horrors—a Purgatory. This, doubtless, is an esoteric conception, and is borrowed from Buddhism.

The real spirit of Taouist superstition is seen in the writings of an old author of the fourth century A.D. named Ko Hung. He says that "mountains are inhabited by evil spirits who are more or less powerful, according to the size of the mountain. If a traveller has no protection he will fall into some calamity. He will see trees move though not by the wind, and stones will fall from impending rocks without any apparent cause; he will be attacked by sickness or pierced by thorns, etc." A mirror should be carried, since the mischievous elves are afraid to approach him thus equipped, lest their true character should be discovered.

Taouism has experienced great vicissitudes. During the reign of the emperor Whan, 147–165 A.D., great favor was shown to this system, and the custom of offering imperial sacrifices to Laotze at Kocheen, his birthplace, was begun. Many attempts were made to save life by charms, and in order to increase their power, legends borrowed from Buddhism were assigned to Laotze. Among other things it was claimed that after he left the Hankow Pass he spent three nights under a mulberry tree under temptation of the Evil One; lovely women, also, were his tempters.

The system again sank into neglect in the reign of Taikeen, 569–583 A.D. Orders were issued against both Taouist and Buddhist monasteries, and no doctrine could be taught but Confucianism. Again, under the Wei dynasty, Buddhism and Taouism were reinstated. In the reign of Tai Wute there was a return to the notion of an elixir of life, and the emperor became a Taouist. In this reign Buddhist asceticism began to be copied by Taouists. The emperor Tai Ho, 477–500 A.D. built temples and monasteries for this sect.

The emperor Woo, 566–578 A.D., abolished Buddhism and Taouism because their jealousies and strifes created disturbance, but Tcing, 580–591, reinstated the two religions on equal grade. Under the Tang dynasty Taouism again held for a century the ascendency over Buddhism, and Laotze was canonized. In A D., 625–627, the Taouists, having become insolent, were banished to the provinces of Quangtung and Quangsi, but under Hwuy Chang they were reinstated and Buddhism was stigmatized officially as a foreign religion. Under the Sung dynasty, 960–976, Taouist priests were forbidden to marry. Hweitsung ordered the Buddhist priests to adopt Taouist names for their orders. The Manchu dynasty, following next in order, persecuted the Taouists, but Jenghis Khan promoted them; also Kublai Khan, in the 13th century A.D. Hung Che, 1488–1506, was very hostile. The present Manchu dynasty has also been hostile, and has passed various edicts against Taouist jugglery.

The sacred book of Taouism, known as the "Book of Rewards," inculcates ethics which are on the whole commendable. The precepts are generally in negative form, but notwithstanding the morality of the "Book of Rewards," the moral grade of modern Taouism is extremely low.

Among the virtual deities at the present time are first of all, Laotze, who is supremely reverenced. But a god of providence having general charge of human affairs is found to be necessary, and accordingly Yunwang Shangti, or the Precious Imperial God, is assigned to that place. The constellation of the Great Bear is also worshipped as a representative of the sidereal powers, also various forces of nature, as the Mother of Lightning, the Spirit of the Sea, the Lord of the Tides, etc. The dragon is a great object of worship with Taouists. His images are everywhere; serpents are his living representatives. Even Li Hung Chang, great statesman as he is, worshipped a serpent which crept into a temple in Tiensin in time of a flood in 1874. Chang Chun, a disembodied sage of the past, is now worshipped as a god of literature; a great hero of the past is worshipped as the god of war, and a third deity is the god of medicine. But altogether the most popular is Tsaichin, the god of wealth. Every store and shop has a little altar for burning incense to him. This suits the average Chinaman better than the transcendentalism of Laotze, or the lofty ethics of Confucius, or the nirvana of Buddhism. The boasted millions of Buddhists in China all believe supremely in Tsaichin.

The polytheism of China is still further ramified under the influence of Taouism, embracing gods of the sea, of the village, of the hearth, of the kitchen, and demigods to represent all virtues; in other words, deified men, heroes, scholars, etc.

A remarkable influence has been produced by these superstitions upon the Buddhism of China, as shown in the fact that the Buddhist temples are full of the same images of ideals, of virtues, and of heroic men. In the great Buddhist temple of Honan in Canton there are hundreds of full-sized figures of deified men.

**Tapiteua,** one of the Gilbert Islands (q.v.); mission station of the Hawaiian Evangelical Association; 2 native pastors, 174 church-members.

**Tarsus,** a city of Southern Asia Minor, 20 miles from Mersine. The birthplace of the Apostle Paul. Population, Turks, Armenians, and Nusairiyeh. Mission out-station of the A. B. C. F. M. worked from Adana. Occupied also by the Reformed Presbyterian (Covenanter) Church, U. S. A., for its work among the Nusairiyeh. A movement was started in 1889 for establishing an institute called St. Paul's Institute, which should combine several departments of evangelistic and educational work. The unhealthiness of the climate, due to the great heat in summer and the prevalence of malaria, together with the difficulty of securing the necessary permits from the Turkish Government, have, however, so far delayed the accomplishment of the plan.

**Tartar,** or **Tatar,** is a name which has been loosely applied to the inhabitants of Central Asia, and does not carry with it any ethnological or political significance. The various races which inhabit Central Asia belong to the Aryan and Turanian races—the former predominating in the Russian provinces, the latter more numerous towards the confines of China. In the Russian Empire there are three large groups:

(1) Those in European Russia and Poland. These are: The Kazan Tartars, who speak a pure Turkish dialect, and are followers of Mohammed; the Astrakhan Tartars; and the Crimean, or Nogai, who are perhaps the best type of the Tartar race.

(2) Those inhabiting the Caucasus: The nomadic Nogai; the Karatschi; the Mountain Tartars, who are of very mixed origin, and practically consist of tribes who are not included in any other classification.

(3) The Siberian Tartars, who are mixed with Finnish blood, and are the most difficult to classify. Some of them have been named as follows: Baraba Tartars, who live in Tobolsk; the Teholym, on the Teholym River, who present many Mongolian characteristics; the Altai-Teleutes, and numerous other tribes.

In Turkestan the intermixture of the Mongol and the Turkish races is so indiscriminate and complete, that it is perhaps convenient to designate the various tribes by this provisional term until further research will enable correct subdivisions of the races to be determined. (See Mongol.)

**Tasmania,** formerly Van Diemen's Land, is a British colony of Australasia, including the island of that name, and several smaller ones lying, for the most part, in Bass Strait. Area, 26,215 square miles. The estimated population (1889) is 151,470, composed of Tasmanians, English, Australasians, Chinese, and Germans.

The island is traversed by mountain ranges with fertile valleys. The climate is mild, and not subject to extremes. It was made a penal settlement in 1804, but transportation of criminals ceased in 1853. The aborigines are entirely extinct. Hobart, the capital, had a population of 21,118 in 1881, and Launceston had 12,752.

The people are now nominally Christian, the majority belonging to the Church of England, the remainder being Roman Catholics, Wesleyan Methodists, Presbyterians, and others.

The S. P. G. has 1 missionary. The Wesleyan Methodist Missionary Society have 602 churches in Victoria and Tasmania together.

**Ta-tung,** a prefectural city in Shansi, China, is occupied by the C. I. M. (1886); 3 missionaries and assistant missionaries.

**Taung,** a town in Bechuanaland, South African Republic, near a branch of the Orange River. Mission station of the L. M. S. (1868); 1 missionary, 5 out-stations, 8 native preachers, 391 church-members.

**Tavoy,** a town in Lower Burma, India, on the Tavoy River, 30 miles from its mouth. The town lies low, and its northwestern and southern portions are flooded at high tide, and swampy during the rains. It is laid out in straight streets, and the houses are generally built of timber or bamboo, thatched with palm-leaves. Its trade is of little importance. Population, 13,372, Moslems, Hindus, Christians. It is the place where the Karen Mission of the A. B. M. U. was commenced in 1828. In the Burman department there are now 1 missionary and wife, 1 church, 15 church-members, 1 Sunday-school, 1 school, 75 scholars; Karen work, 1 missionary and wife, 17 out-stations, 14 native preachers, 17 self-supporting churches, 984 church-members, 3 Sunday-schools, 14 day-schools, 440 scholars

**Taylor, Bishop William: Self-Supporting Mission Work.**—William Taylor is a clergyman of the Methodist Episcopal Church in the United States who in about 1850 commenced a work which has identified his name with missions in many countries. At first a street-preacher in San Francisco, Cal., he afterwards visited other countries, and became impressed with the idea that the existing system of missionary societies was not the best. That missions should be self-supporting, and in a sense indigenous to the soil. He has worked in India, South America and Africa, with good results in each country, but at present his labors are chiefly confined to Africa. He is now Missionary Bishop of the M. E. Church (North) for Africa, where he remains most of the time. In his absence he is represented in New York City by a few non-salaried men and women, who administer the home business, take entire charge of the South American work, and of the African work, so far as to respond to Bishop Taylor's calls for men and equipments.

His custom is to go in advance of his missionaries, select a locality, open the way and station the men, and then consider himself responsible for nothing additional. There is also a Transit and Building Fund Society of Bishop Taylor's Self-Supporting Missions which pays the transportation fares of accepted candidates (where they are unable to bear their own expenses) from New York to the mission fields, with such outfit as is deemed necessary to start the mission, but assumes no further obligation.

Nor does the Society deem itself justified in paying the outgoing expenses entire, where less than five years' service is rendered.

All applications must be accompanied by testimonials from the pastor and presiding elder as to religious character and general fitness for the work. A certificate as to health from a reliable physician, and a statement from a principal, professor, or other intelligent person, as to education, are required.

In South America three kinds of laborers are in demand: 1. Well-qualified teachers (graduates); those who have had some experience in teaching being preferred. Some first-class music-teachers required. 2. Preachers and teachers—men who can teach through the week and do evangelistic work on the Sabbath. 3. Missionaries pure and simple, who will devote their entire time to soul-saving. The same literary qualifications are required for each class. Both married and single men can be employed in each of these departments, and all will be expected to labor in Sunday-schools and gospel-meetings.

The qualifications necessary are good health, sound mind, holiness of heart and life, entire consecration to the self-supporting work, willingness to live among the people, fare as they fare, and, if need be, die among them.

As appears by the report, dated March, 1888, within three years about 100 missionaries have been secured and sent to the field; and from February 5th, 1886, to March 24th, 1888, there was expended for transit, outfits, furnishings, Congo steamer ($16,301), Santiago College building mortgage ($46,600), etc., the total sum of $109,000.

The great departments of the work are: Educational, Industrial, and Evangelical, and of early self-sustentation; later, absolute self-support, and then self-propagation,—founding new missions without help from home.

*Work in South America.* — CHILI. Concepcion.—Here there are (1888) two schools and a church organization. On a large lot frouting the best street in the city has been erected a building (90 by 35) for the boys' school.

Santiago.—A large and magnificent school building is located here on one of the best streets. It is doubtful whether there is anywhere in the United States a school structure with better appointments. It is three stories in height, having about 100 rooms, besides a large gymnasium detached from the main building.

Coquimbo.—This station is the oldest and perhaps the most flourishing of their stations. There is here a Methodist Episcopal church-building, a parsonage, a church organization, and school-buildings for both boys and girls,—instruction given separately,—and all in prosperous condition.

Iquique.—This place is the chief city taken by Chili from Peru as a war indemnity, and the transfer has proved a benefit. The mineral products are reported to be inexhaustible. A lot has been purchased on the corner of two principal streets. On this a building has been erected containing two apartments for schools, for boys and girls respectively. There is also a commodious parsonage, a neat chapel-room, and a revived organization of a Methodist Episcopal church.

PERU.—Callao, the most northern station in South America, is the chief seaport town of Peru, only seven miles from Lima, the capital. Romanism is dominant here, and the country is in almost every respect more than a century behind the age. Callao is the only place in Peru where there has been any attempt at missionary work. Here there is a school of 35 pupils and religious services are held.

At Colon there is a mission house, and a Methodist Episcopal church has been organized. Other preaching places are at San Pablo, Tabernilla, and Panama.

From July, 1878, to July, 1889, there came to the western coast of South America, under the auspices of the "Self-Supporting Mission," 26 preachers, 18 of them married; 9 male teachers, 3 of them married; and 46 female teachers. Most of the wives assisted in the schools. Of the entire number 27 are still in the field; of the 26 preachers 6 remain.

In BRAZIL there are three stations—Para, Pernambuco, and Manaos. These are served by 5 persons. There is at Para (March, 1888) a church organization with a membership of 29. The station at Manaos has just been opened.

*Work in Africa.*—Within three years (preceding March, 1888) about 100 missionaries have been secured and sent into the field.

*West Coast Stations.*—It was understood from the beginning that the mission should not take boarding-scholars or open school-work regularly until enough food could be produced from the soil for their sustenance. Bishop Taylor arranged for building 14 houses in the missions on the west coast this year (1888-9), for chapel and school purposes.

*Cavalla River District.*—This includes the following stations : Wisika Station, about 40 miles up from the mouth of the river. Its king, chiefs, and people received a missionary, built him a good native house, and supported him for several months. Eubloky, on the west bank. Yahky. Tateka, on the east bank. Beabo, on the west bank, has adequate resources of self-support. Bararoba, on the east bank. Gerribo, west bank, has a mission house. Wallaky, a large town of the Gerribo tribe, on the west bank. Plebo. Barreky.

At eight of these stations there are frame, weather boarded, shingle-roofed houses, the floors elevated about six feet above the ground, the whole set up pillars of native logs from the forest. In all these places schoolhouses are being built. Each station is in a tribe distinct and separate from every other tribe, and each river town represents a larger population far back in the interior of the wild country.

*Cape Palmas District.*—Pluky (across Hoffman River from Cape Palmas) is the beginning of the Kroo coast line of stations. Here Miss McNeal's school-house is crowded; besides teaching during the week, she preaches on the Sabbath. Garaway, 20 miles northwest of Cape Palmas. Here enough of food is produced on the farm to feed two or three stations. Piquinini Sea, 30 miles northwest of Cape Palmas, has a school and a school-farm. Grand Ses. Sas Town; a church organized. Niffoo. Nanna Kroo. Settra Kroo; farming, teaching, and preaching carried on. On each of these Kroo stations, except Pluky, there is a well-built mission house. Excepting the missionaries, there is not a Liberian or foreigner of any sort in any of the stations named on Cavalla River or Kroo

coast. Ebenezer, west side of the Sinoe River. The king of the tribe has proclaimed Sabbath as God's Day, and ordered his people not to work on that day, but to go to church. Benson River, in the Grand Bassa country.

At Mamby, on an inland lake, which can only be reached by a journey of many days' length by steamer and boat, the French have recognized and registered the native title given to the mission to 100 acres of land. While professedly friendly, the French have limited the work of the mission by forbidding the giving of instruction in any language save French.

Kabindu, near the mouth of the Congo.

St. Paul de Loanda, a beautiful landlocked harbor, has a mission which has been self-supporting from the Portuguese patronage of the schools, but an adequate corps of teachers is needed.

Dombo, 180 miles up the Coanza River,—which is as large as the Hudson,—is a noted trading centre and the head of steamboat navigation. The property of the mission here is worth $5,000. The school-work and machine-shop were self-supporting from the beginning.

Fifty one miles overland from Dombo, over hills and valleys, reached by way of an old caravan trail, lies Nhanguepepo, with $6,000 worth of mission property. Originally intended to be a receiving station for new missionaries, where they could be acclimatized, it has become specially a training-school for native agency. There is here an organized Methodist Episcopal church. A great variety of work is carried on by converts. This station yields ample sustentation for all these workers, and is continually making improvements, which are paid for from their profits.

Pongo Andongo is reached by a march of 38 miles easterly. It is wedged in between stupendous mountains. There is a large adobe house here, including chapel and store-room, nearly an acre of ground with fruit-bearing trees in the town, and a good farm of about 300 acres a mile out—all worth about $4,000. Pongo Andongo has passed the line of self-support, and is making money to open new stations in the regions beyond.

Malange, a town of about 2,000, and noted for its merchandise, is 62 miles from Pongo Andongo. Here is a mission store; school-work and preaching are sustained. The property here is worth about $6,000, and the big farm pays, and two pit saws, run by four natives, turned out $1,500 worth of lumber last year, which sells for cash at the saw-pits. A two-story mission house has lately been completed.

Luluaburg, in the Bashalanga country, discovered by Dr. Pogge and Lieut. Weismann in 1883, is reached by a journey of a "thousand miles" toward the northeast. Here Dr. Summers founded a station, built a couple of houses, and was making good progress when, worn out by disease, he died.

Lueba, at the junction of the Lulua and Kassai rivers.

Kimpopo, near the northeast angle of Stanley Pool, was opened in 1886 as a way-station on the line of transportation to the countries of the Upper Kassai. Here was dug an irrigating ditch a mile long, drawing an abundant supply of water from a mountain creek, and the mission farm of 10 acres supplies plenty of food, and is a source of revenue.

South Manyanga is 100 miles from Leopoldville and Matadi is 230 miles distant on the Lower Congo. A launch of three or four tons burden is used in traversing the 88 miles from this station to Isangda, which has been a station for over two years, with good native houses built by the mission.

Vivi, 55 miles distant, is one of the most beautiful stations on the Congo, and will soon be self-supporting, as the soil is fertile and game is plenty. The mission raises live-stock, in addition to vegetables and fruits.

Banana is reached by steamer 100 miles down the Congo, and is within one hour and a half, by oars, of the station at Natombe. Here there is a school-house 22×24 ft., with 20 scholars; also a fruit orchard.

Two years ago were started, between Vivi and Isangila, three stations,—Vumtomby Vivi, Sadi Kabanza, and Matamba,—where pretty good houses were built. The aim this year has been to supply the guarantees for self-support. Besides fruits and vegetables, the most reliable resource for the new Liberian stations in marketable values is coffee.

Provision has been made to supply the stations with ploughs and oxen, and coffee scions, which after five years will produce two crops annually in Liberia for fifty years.

The Steamer.—A steamer is needed on the Lower Congo much more than upon the Upper. With it on the Lower Congo, and a steel boat on the middle passage, to carry freights from Isangila to Manyanga, the mission will have an advantage in the freight business to the upper countries, and it will cut expenses down more than one-half of the present rate, and they will be able to do work for other missions as well. Except in leadership and superintendency, all this heavy work will be done by natives, whom the missionaries wish to employ and train to habits of industry, as that is part of their mission plan.

From March 25th, 1888, to October 31st, 1889, there was expended $71,219.38.

**Taylor, Horace S.,** b. West Hartland, Conn., U. S. A., October 31st, 1814; received his collegiate and theological education at Western Reserve College 1844; ordained Milan, Ohio; sailed May 6th the same year under the A. B. C. F. M. for the Madura Mission; stationed first at Tirupuvanum, removed in 1850 to Mandapasálai, which he occupied till his death, except during a visit to the United States 1865-7. Letters from his associates show how he was esteemed. Mr. Capron says: "With the exception of Mr. Tracy, Mr. Taylor was our oldest missionary. He was active, laborious, and successful. No other member of our mission had the privilege of gathering so many congregations and receiving so many converts to the church. He lived near to Christ by prayer and the study of the Scriptures." Mr. Rendall says: "Mr. Taylor leaves behind a very precious memory. His heart was full of love for his Master and for his work. He had a kind, loving word for all, both Christians and heathen. I never knew him to be discouraged in all these twenty-five years. During my eighteen years in Madura I received nearly a hundred notes from him every year, and I never received one in which he showed the least depression or the slightest indication of discouragement. He was remarkably active in mind and labors, ever planning

to advance Christ's cause among the people. In the Mandapasálai station he gathered from the heathen into Christian congregations about 1,800 souls, of whom nearly 300 are communicants, and he organized nine village churches." Mr. Taylor had been declining in health for some time; and though he went to Madura to attend the annual meeting of the mission, he was not able to leave his room. He visited the sanitarium on the hills, but failed rapidly, and died February 3d, 1871.

**Tchermiss Version.**—The Tchermiss belongs to the Finn branch of the Ural-Altaic family of languages, and is spoken by a tribe on the Volga and Kama, in the governments of Kazan and Simbersk. During the reign of the emperor Alexander I. the Russian Bible Society printed at St. Petersburg in 1820 the New Testament in the Tchermiss language, under the care of the archbishop of Kazan. Since the dissolution of the Russian Bible Society nothing further has been done for this people.

(*Specimen verse.* John 3 : 16.)

Теньгӗ ярашıӑнъ Юма сапда́ıпкамъ, шша́ ıкъ шкӗ эргажамъ. пушъ, са́каı инӑньша : шыдалапъ йнже-ямъ, а пˌлеже вара́ мучӑшдэма ку́румъ му́чка.

**Tchuvash Version.**—The Tchuvash belongs to the Turki branch of the Ural-Altaic family of languages, and is spoken by a tribe of 670,000, partially Christianized and living in the mountains of Kazan, Nijni-Novogorod, and Orenburg. In 1820 the Russian Bible Society published at St. Petersburg an edition of the four Gospels, which were translated by a committee at Simbersk. When the Russian Bible Society was dissolved the work of translation came to an end. Of late the British and Foreign Bible Society has engaged Prof. Jacobliff, the government inspector of the Tchuvash schools in and around Simbersk, to prepare a translation into the Tchuvash dialect.

(*Specimen verse.* John 3 : 16.)

Сяпла̀ ıӧра́дре Тӧра Эдемя, што барза́ ху у́вылне пӗрь сюра́дпыне, штобы порь инӑнягга́нь она̀ апъ пю́дтаръ, а о́сра́даръ ıу́нюрьгı бу́рпаза.

**Teheran** (Tehran), the capital of Persia, is situated in latitude 35° 40' north, longitude 51° 25' east. It is a walled city, with narrow, ill-paved streets, though here and there Parisian boulevards and European houses present striking contrasts to the native quarters. The water supply is good and abundant, and public baths are numerous. The population of 210,000 consists of Turks, Persians, and Armenians, and a few Jews and Parsis. The king's college is established here, with 250 students who receive a liberal education.

Mission station of the Presbyterian Church (North) ,1872; 4 missionaries and wives (1 medical missionary), 4 female missionaries (1 medical missionary), 2 out-stations, 48 communicants, 3 day-schools, 120 pupils, girls' boarding-school, 81 scholars, boys' school, 34 day and 46 boarding scholars, and a dispensary.

**Teh-ngan,** a city in the province of Hupeh, Central China, on an affluent of the Yang-tsz River. Mission station of the Wesleyan Missionary Society; 1 missionary, 1 native pastor, 2 chapels, 84 church-members, 1 school, 1 teacher, 10 scholars.

**Telang,** a town in Borneo, on the upper course of the Kahajair River, north of Raive. Mission station of the Rhenish Missionary Society; 1 missionary, 1 native helper, 40 church-members, 14 school-children.

**Tellicherri,** a port on the Malabar Coast, Madras, India, 43 miles north-northwest of Calicut. A healthy and picturesque town built upon a group of wooded hills running down to the sea, protected by a natural breakwater of rock. It has a good harbor and an excellent trade. Population, 26,410, Hindus, Moslems, Christians. Mission station of the Basle Missionary Society; 3 missionaries (2 married), 37 native helpers, 3 out-stations, 415 church-members.

**Telugus,** a race occupying a section of the Madras Presidency, India. (See India, Madras, A. B. M. U., C. M. S., etc.)

**Telugu Mission.**—Conducted by Rev. C. B. Ward. Supported at first by contributions, at present mainly by its own earnings.

The Telugu Mission had its start in a prayer-meeting held in Goolburga, a railway station about 300 miles from Bombay, India, in February, 1879. The great famine of 1876–78 was just over, and the actual work of the mission began in March, 1879, by taking from a famine poorhouse, which had been kept up by private charity for over a year, 5 boys and girls, who were cared for by Mr. Davis, a Methodist missionary, at his house in Goolburga; to this number were soon added 14 waifs from a famine camp at Adoni, and 2 from Goolburga, making 21 Telugu, Kanarese, and Mohammedan children. By the 1st of October, 1879, 180 orphans had been gathered at Mr. Davis's house, the bulk of the care of all these little ones falling on Mr. Davis. At a later period Rev. C. B. Ward, of Chicago, U. S. A., was put in charge of the work, which is not now an "Orphan Home," but a Christian colony of 50 adults and 40 children.

The insurmountable difficulties in the way of acquiring any land under the Mohammedan Government has made a "two-house" arrangement a necessity—one at Secunderabad for Mrs. Ward, her own and the native children; the other at Dothan, or wherever Mr. Ward can find employment in railroad construction or mining, for his whole field force. The last four years have been thus spent in camp by the greater part of the colony.

The mission has lately succeeded in renting about 2,000 acres of land; its migratory life will therefore soon cease, and the colony will become the basis of supply for evangelistic workers in all the region around.

The mission has from the first been conducted on the "faith" principle, contributions towards its support never having been solicited; it is now in large measure self-supporting, one half of the $35,000 which have been expended during its ten years of existence having been earned by the mission. For the last four years the earnings have far exceeded the contributions.

Work has been begun on the mission village, and it is hoped that vigorous evangelizing labors may be entered upon from this centre.

**Telugu Version.**—The Telugu belongs to the Dravidian family of non-Aryan languages, and is spoken in Northern Circars, Cuddapah, Nellore, and the greater part of Hyderabad or Telingana. A translation into the Telugu, or Telinga as it is also called, was undertaken by the famous missionary, Benjamin Schultze, which, however, was never published. Of the translation undertaken by Serampore missionaries, the New Testament was published in 1818, and the Pentateuch in 1820.

A translation known as the *Vizagapatam Version,* commenced by the Rev. Augustus Desgranges of the London Missionary Society, aided by Mr. Anunderayer, a Telugu Brahmin of high caste, but a convert to Christianity, and continued by the Revs. J. Gordon and Pritchett of the London Missionary Society, was published at Madras, 1812–55. The Telugu Bible is at present undergoing a careful revision by a revision board under the presidency of the Rev. Dr. J. Hay. Of the revised version, thus far the Pentateuch, Job, Psalms, Proverbs, Jeremiah, and Lamentations have been published. In the mean time interim editions of the Bible made up of revised parts and portions of the old version are printed to satisfy the necessary demand.

Portions of the New Testament were also published with English and Sanscrit.

(*Specimen verse.* John 3 : 16.)

మెందుకంటే దేవుడు లోకము ప్రేమించుట
యేలాగంటే—ఆయన యందు విశ్వసమంచే
ప్రతిపాదుస్నన నశించక నిత్యజీవము పొందేలా
రకు తన జనిత్తైక కుమారుని యిచ్చెను

**Temne Version.**—The Temne belongs to the negro group of African languages, and is spoken by the Temnes, who are a small and destitute tribe in Quiah Country, in the neighborhood of Sierra Leone, West Africa. The Rev. C. F. Schlenker of the Church Missionary Society translated the New Testament and the Book of Genesis, which were published by the British and Foreign Bible Society in 1867. In 1869 the same society published the Psalms at Stuttgart, prepared by the same translator. In 1888 the same society published the Book of Exodus, translated by the Rev. J. Markah and J. A. Alley of Port Lokkoh. The latter also read the proof.

(*Specimen verse.* John. 3 : 16.)

*Téa yọ K'úru ọ pọ̀t bọ̀tạr ara-rū, lā ọ sọnd Qw'án-
Pọ̀n ọ kom gbo sön, káma w'úni ô w'úni, qwọ́ láng-kọ̀,
ọ tẽ dinnẹ; kẹrẹ káma ọ sọlo a-ñêsạm atabána.*

**Temple, Daniel,** b. December 23d, 1789, at Reading, Mass., U. S. A. The perusal of Dr. Buchanan's "Christian Researches in India" at his conversion led him to the decision to become a missionary to the heathen. He studied at Phillips Academy, Andover; Dartmouth College; and Andover Theological Seminary. While in the seminary he offered himself to the

A. B. C. F. M., and was appointed a missionary to Palestine. After spending a year in the service of the Board, he was ordained October 3d, 1821, and embarked January 2d, 1822, reaching Malta February 22d. Here he remained till 1833, the political condition of Turkey and Syria rendering it unsafe for a missionary family to settle there. He prepared books and tracts for circulation in Italy, Greece, and Turkey, which were printed on the press he took with him, widely distributed, and well received. In 1828, by invitation of the Prudential Committee, he visited the United States, and engaged in an agency for the Board till his return to the East. He embarked for Malta January 18th, 1830, taking his children with him. In addition to the superintendence of the press, he had during almost his whole residence here two services on the Sabbath in English in his own house, a Sabbath-school which he taught himself, and also a lecture Friday evening. In 1833, December 7th, he left Malta for Smyrna, the place selected by the Committee as the most eligible for the press. From 1822, when the press was established in Malta, to the time of its removal, were issued 350,000 volumes containing 21,000,000 pages. Nearly the whole had been circulated, and additional supplies of some of the works were urgently demanded. The arrival at Smyrna of a vessel with presses and printing materials, and an ordained missionary, created great opposition, and Mr. Temple was ordered by the governor to leave the city in ten days. But after some correspondence with the consul the storm passed away. The Greek Ecclesiastical Committee broke up eight schools, containing from six to eight hundred children, and forbade the teachers to remain with the missionaries, threatening them with imprisonment or banishment if they refused to obey. In 1837 Mr. Temple commenced the publication of a monthly magazine in Greek, "The Repository," of a mixed character, which met with much favor. The Greek patriarch forbade all his subjects to read any of the missionaries' translations of the Scriptures in Turkish, Arabic, Servian, Bulgarian, or Slavonian dialect. During this year the plague, of which Mrs. Dwight died at Constantinople, raged with terrific violence at Smyrna. In 1839 the famous edict known as the "Hatti Sherif" was promulgated by the Sultan, placing all the subjects of his empire on an equality. An imperial order also was issued restoring the Armenians who had been banished for embracing the gospel. During the visit of Drs. Anderson and Hawes to the mission it was decided to abandon the Greek department in Greece and Turkey. This made it necessary for Mr. Temple to leave the missionary field. He embarked for the United States June 7th, 1844. He preached in Concord, N. H., and at Phelps, N. Y., but resigned his pastorate on account of ill-health December 27th, 1849. A voyage to Chagres, and in 1851 to Liverpool, did not benefit him, and he rapidly failed, and died August 9th, 1851. Dr. Goodell, his associate at Smyrna, in his funeral sermon thus spoke of him: "His study of the Bible, his familiarity with the very language of the Bible, the copiousness and pertinency of his prayers, the perfect ease with which he would introduce religious conversation, even of the most personal kind, and the truly Christian courteousness of his manner under the contradic-

tions of cavillers, were all wonderful. His labors were blessed wherever he went, and soldiers and sailors, as well as many others, look up to him as their spiritual father."

**Tetuan,** a seaport of Morocco (q.v.). The province of the same name has an area of 914 square miles, with a population of 17,900. Mission station of the North African Mission (see article); 3 missionaries.

**Tezpur,** a town of Assam, India, on the Brahmaputra, 75 miles above Gauhati. The town is built on a plain between two low ranges of hills, upon which the houses of the European residents are built. It is an important seat of trade, where the river steamers touch to take on board tea, and to leave stores of various kinds to be distributed among the neighboring tea-gardens. Of late years the character of the houses and sanitary condition of the town have been much improved. Population, 2,910. Mission station S. P. G.; 2 missionaries, 3 native helpers, 26 out-stations, 207 school-children.

**Thaba-Bosiou,** a town in the Orange Free State, Africa, northeast of Hermon. Mission station of the Paris Evangelical Society (1837); 1 ordained missionary, 1 female missionary, 460 communicants.

**Thatun** (Thatone), a town in Amherst district, Tenasserim division, Burma, India. Population, 3,218. Now a place of little importance, but formerly capital of an independent kingdom, and one of the earliest places mentioned in Talaing history. The town contains several pagodas, most of them mutilated and in ruins. Mission station of the American Baptist Missionary Union; 1 female missionary, 7 native helpers, 26 church-members, 1 school, 32 scholars.

**Thayetmyo,** a town on the Irrawaddy River, Burma, 25 miles from Prome. In the rains the place looks fresh and green, but during the dry season it presents a dreary appearance. Climate healthy, but excessively hot. Population, 8,379. Race and language, Chinese. Religion, spirit-worship. Social condition barbarous. Mission station A. B. M. U. (1888); 1 missionary and wife, 11 native helpers, 3 out-stations, 3 churches, 61 church-members. S. P. G. (1867); 1 native missionary.

**Thlotse Heights,** a town in the northeast of Orange Free State, South Africa, on the Caledon River, south of Ebenezer. Mission station of the S. P. G.; 1 missionary, 63 communicants.

**Thongze** (Thoungzai), a town in Burma, India, on the Prome and Thongzai Railroad, midway between the two places. Mission station of the American Baptist Missionary Union (1855); 1 female missionary, 12 native helpers, 7 out-stations, 2 churches, 397 church-members, 3 schools, 145 scholars. (See American Baptist Missionary Union.)

**Thurston, Asa,** b. Fitchburg, Mass., U. S. A., October 12th, 1787; graduated at Yale College 1816, Andover Theological Seminary 1819; embarked as a missionary of the A. B. C. F. M. October 23d, 1819, with others, who formed the first band of missionaries for the Sandwich Islands. In an obituary notice in the

" Honolulu Friend" it is stated: "As a missionary Mr. Thurston ever labored with great usefulness and success. His knowledge of the native language and character was most thorough; and as a preacher he was much beloved by the native Hawaiians. In the early years of the mission his labors as a translator were arduous and successful." In an address at his funeral, March 12th, 1868, Mr. Corwin said: " This day is just one month less than 48 years from the day when he and the still surviving companion of his earthly pilgrimage were stationed at Kailua, the ancient residence of the Hawaiian kings. And there for more than 40 years he continued to reside and to labor as the honored pastor of a large and very important parish. He was the instructor for a time of both Kamehameha II. and Kamehameha III., and his influence over them, especially the latter, was great. Never once leaving the islands for 48 years, he was honored by natives and foreigners alike as a faithful, patient, persistent worker. Only when advanced age and repeated strokes of paralysis had rendered him incapable of service did he consent to resign his pastorate at Kailua, that he might spend the closing years of his life in this city." He died at Honolulu March 11th, 1868, aged 81.

**Tiberias,** a town in Western Palestine, on the upper course of the Jordan River. Population, 6,000, Jews, Moslems, and Syrian Christians. Languages, Arabic, a Jewish jargon, and Hebrew. Mission station of the Free Church of Scotland Jewish Mission (1884); 2 missionaries (1 married), 1 female missionary, 7 native helpers, 1 out-station, 1 school, 60 scholars, 2 preaching places, 20 to 50 average attendance.

**Tibet,** one of the possessions of China, comprising a great division of the Chinese Empire, is a country of which very little is definitely known. Surrounded by high mountains, it has been to a great degree isolated from the rest of the world. Tibet is a corruption of the Chinese name; the people themselves call it the "land of Bod." The Kwanlun Mountains bound it on the north; on the east are the Chinese provinces of Szchuen and Yunnan; Assam, Buhtan, Nipal, and Gurhwal separate it from Burma and India on the south; while on the west its boundaries are not sharply defined from the territory of Kokonor. Little Tibet does not properly belong to Tibet, though it is claimed by Chinese geographers. The greater part of the surface consists of high tableland (elevation 11.510 ft.), divided into three parts by mountain ranges: the valley of the Indus on the west, between the Hindu Kush and Himalaya Mountains; the high desert land, almost uninhabitable and wholly unknown, lying between the Kwanlun and Himalaya Mountains; and the basin of the Yaru-tsangbu on the east, consisting of high ridges and deep gorges, mountains and valleys. Numerous peaks of perpetually snow-capped mountains are here found, of which Mt. Kailasa (26,000 ft.) is the highest.

The principal river, the Yaru-tsangbu. drains the whole of Southern Tibet between the first and second ranges of the Himalayas, and is supposed to empty into the Brahmaputra, though explorations have not yet been extensive enough to decide the truth. All the large rivers of Southern and Eastern Asia find their source in Tibet. In the central part are numerous lakes. The climate is varied, but in general the air is pure and excessively dry. Snow and ice last for most of the year, but in the middle of summer the valleys, even between the snowy mountains, are excessively hot. In the southern part moisture and vegetation are found, and sheep, goats, and yaks are raised.

The government is conducted by two high commissioners appointed at Peking, but these confer with and are guided by the two grand officers of the Tibetan hierarchy, the Dalai-Lama and the Teshu-Lama: the former is known generally as the Grand Lama. The power is practically in the hands of the priests or lamas (see Lamaism, under Buddhism), whose number is so great as to give Tibet the name of the " kingdom of priests." The southern frontier is strongly fortified, and communication with the states intervening between Tibet and India is forbidden. On the Chinese frontier the same strictness is exercised, for the policy of exclusion is fostered alike by the Lamas and the Chinese— the one because they wish to preserve their religious supremacy and fat offices, the other because they wish to retain their political power, faint though it be. L'hassa, the capital, has only once been visited by an Englishman,— Mr. Manning, in 1811,—and its location has but recently been agreed upon to be approximately in lat. 29° 39′ 17″ N. and long. 91° 05′ E. It stands in a fertile plain, at an altitude of 11,700 feet, encircled by mountains. It is noted for the number of its monasteries, bonzes and lamas, filthy streets and mean buildings. The population is estimated at from 40,000 to 80,000, and the population of the whole of Tibet is estimated by Russian authorities at 6,000,000. The people belong to the Mongol race. They are not so highly civilized as the Chinese, but are more so than the Mongols. Physically they are of somewhat slender build, with brown hair, slightly oblique eyes, swarthy, and beardless. They are a mild-tempered, genial, kind and friendly people, and intensely religious. In no other country is so much deference paid to the priests; the proportion of believers in the religion is also greater than in most countries. Their religion consists of two kinds: the old original religion called the " Bon," of which little or nothing definite is known; and that form of Buddhism called Lamaism. The social customs of the people differ greatly from that of their neighbors on the east and south, particularly in the position which women hold. Here polyandry is the custom instead of polygamy, the wife being usually espoused by brothers. In general education is restricted to the priests, but the women, who conduct most of the traffic, learn writing and arithmetic. In some of the northern provinces the chieftainship is held by the women.

The language of Tibet is derived from the Sanskrit. It is alphabetical, and reads from left to right. Thirty consonants are recognized, with four additional vowel signs. Their literature, as well as many of their customs, has been influenced to a great degree by China.

Missions are not permitted in Tibet. In former times the Roman Catholic Church made noble efforts to enter the forbidden land, and was for a time successful. In 1330 the apostle of Tartary, Odoric Forojuliensis, travelled in Tibet and found missionaries already in the city of L'hassa, who had gone there, it is supposed, early in the preceding century. In the 17th century a mission was commenced from India, and the reigning prince was favorable to the new religion; but his apostasy was made the pretext for his overthrow. Various attempts at evangelization have been made since that time. The most noteworthy one was in 1845, when Fathers Gabet and Huc penetrated to L'hassa after a journey of eighteen months, only to be arrested by the Chinese officials, who sent them prisoners to Canton. From that time the Société des Étrangères has made numerous attempts both by way of India and China to enter the kingdom; but after suffering persecution and the massacre of their priests they have given up the effort, and occupy now only the confines of Tibet, where they work among the Chinese and such Tibetans as are there found.

The Moravian Brethren occupy three stations in Little Tibet (see Leh, Poo, and Kyelang), where they are waiting for opportunity to enter Tibet. One or two attempts have been made at great risk, but have proved ineffectual. They have studied the Tibetan language, and there are now several works which will aid the future missionaries to Tibet when the country is opened. A Tibetan-English grammar, a Tibetan grammar, and a New Testament in Tibetan have all been published. The missionaries of the C. I. M. in Szchuen and Yunnan are also waiting to possess the land. A prayer union has been formed among the Moravians, whose object is to pray for the opening of the land of priests to the preaching of the gospel.

**Tibetan Version.**—The Tibetan belongs to the Tibeto-Burma group of non-Aryan languages, and is spoken in Tibet. The Gospels of Mark and John have been translated into the Tibetan language, and lithographed by Moravian missionaries, who have found their way into the immediate vicinity of this vast country, from which visitors and foreigners are rigidly excluded. Prior to 1868 the Rev. H. A. Jaeschke of the Moravian Missionary Society had translated the New Testament (save Luke, Hebrews, and Revelation), which was published at Lahore 1859-1865. A new effort was made by the British and Foreign Bible Society in 1880 to publish, at the request of the Moravian Missionary Society, a revised edition of the New Testament, made by Mr. Jaeschke, who was to complete the translation and edit the edition at Berlin, where he was carrying through the press for the India Government a Tibetan dictionary. In 1881 an edition of 5,000 copies of each of the four Gospels was published, which was much admired by Tibetan scholars. They were printed in the square form common to Tibetan books, and revised by Messrs. Heyde and Redslob of Kyelang, and aided by Nathaniel, a baptized lama. As Mr. Jaeschke died in 1883, the British and Foreign Bible Society agreed that Mr. Reichelt who worked many years on Jaeschke's dictionary, read the first proof, while Dr. Malan of Broadwindsor read the second proof. Under this arrangement the New Testament was completed in 1884. In 1887 the Psalms, translated by the Revs. F. A. Redslob and A. W. Heyde, and in 1889 the Pentateuch and Isaiah, were published. Up to March 31st, 1889, there were disposed of 30,023 portions of the Scriptures.

(*Specimen verse.* John 3 : 16.)

[Tibetan script specimen verse]

**Tieling,** a city in Manchuria, China, not far from Moukden, with a population of 30,000. Mission station of the United Presbyterian Church of Scotland (1875); 1 missionary, 73 church-members.

**Tientsin,** one of the most important cities of North China, is situated at the junction of the Grand Canal with the Pei Ho, 30 miles from the sea and 80 miles southeast of Peking. It is the port of and "key to the capital," and is famous as the place where in 1858 the treaties were made. Climate healthy and pleasant; maximum temperature 100° F. Population, 500,000. Religions, Confucianism, Buddhism, Taouism, Moslemism. Natives not very elevated, distrustful, untruthful. Mission station of the A. B. C. F. M. (1860); 2 ordained missionaries, 1 unordained, 2 missionaries' wives, 1 female missionary, 4 native helpers, 2 out-stations, 1 church, 79 members, 2 schools, 37 scholars. It is the financial headquarters of the mission. Methodist New Connexion (1859); 2 missionaries and wives, 1 single lady, 10 native helpers, 2 out-stations, 3 churches, 105 members, 1 theological seminary, 10 students, 2 schools, 40 students. A work for women has recently been commenced under the care of a lady missionary, and is progressing rapidly. L. M. S. (4 missionaries and wives, 2 female missionaries) has a large medical mission here, with a hospital and dispensary, and the work of the mission has been vigorous along the usual lines of boys' schools and theological schools. The country work of the mission has also developed into a new station of the mission at Hsiao-Chang, 150 miles southwest of Tientsin. A beautiful church-building, in the form of an elaborate temple, adorns the main road to the native city; a conspicuous object to thousands who pass its busy location upon the river. In the Tientsin district of the Methodist Episcopal Church (North) Mission there are 6 circuits and stations, 4 of which find their centre in the city. The present force consists of 2 missionaries and wives, 3 female missionaries, with 2 churches, 150 members, 4 day-schools, 81 scholars, 2 Sabbath-schools, 150 scholars, in the city itself. C. I. M. (1888); 3 missionaries and associates. (For further account of Tientsin Missions, see article on China.)

**Tierra del Fuego,** an archipelago at the extremity of South America, separated from the mainland by the Strait of Magellan. The islands are divided into three groups: East Fuegia, including one large island 200 miles long from north to south; South Fuegia, a triangle of numerous small islands, with Cape Horn at the apex; and West Fuegia. The climate of most of the archipelago is cold and disagreeable, and fogs and high winds make navigation difficult. A line from Cape Espiritu Santo due south to Beagle Channel divides the archipelago between the Argentine Republic on the east and Chile on the west. Three races are recognized among the inhabitants: the Onas, the Alacalufs, and the Yaghans. They are all on a low scale of mental and moral life; they wear little or no clothing, kill the old women and eat them, throw their children overboard to propitiate the storm spirits, and indulge in other barbaric customs. The language has been reduced to writing by the missionaries, and is said to contain 30,000 words. The South American Missionary Society (q.v.) works among the Yaghans almost exclusively, from Ooshooia, a station on Beagle Channel, on both sides of which this race is found. There are in all 6 missionaries (3 married), 1 female missionary, 5 native helpers, 3 stations, 4 outstations, 2 churches, 35 church-members, 3 schools, 60 scholars.

**Tiflis,** the capital of Transcaucasia, on the Kur River. It is a mixture of Asiatic and European architecture, the old part being built of sun-dried brick, and containing all the bazaars and business life of Tiflis, the modern part resembling any European city. Climate hot and unhealthy, but the place is popular on account of the warm mineral springs in the vicinity. Population, 104,024, Russians, Georgians, Armenians, Persians, Jews, Germans, and French. Mission work has been attempted at different times by different societies (see Caucasus; Basle Missionary Society), but none with success, on account of the oppressive laws of the Russian Government. The American Bible Society had a Bible depot there, but that was withdrawn, and now the only evangelical work is that of the British and Foreign Bible Society.

**Tigré Version.**—The Tigré belongs to the Semitic family of African languages, and is spoken throughout Eastern Abyssinia. A translation of the four Gospels, made by the Revs Isenburg and Kügler, and revised by Dr. Krapf, was published by the British and Foreign Bible Society in 1865, at the Crischona Press, near Basle.

(*Specimen verse.* John 3 : 16.)

�baፈዘውዓ፡ ፈተው፡ አዘ.አብሐር፡ ንዓ
ለቀ፡ ክሳብ፡ ዝሀቦ፡ ብሕተ፡ ንዝተወልደ፡
ወደ፡ ክ.ይaጠኣ፡ ጐ-ለው፡ ዘ.አቀነ፡
ብኣ.ዱ፡ ዘፈ፡ላ.ደ፡ አቀብc፡ ሕይወተ፡
ዘዓለቀ፡።

**Tillipally,** a large town in Ceylon, East Indies, on the north shore of the peninsula of Jaffna, at the northern extremity of the island. Climate tropical, damp. Temperature, 80° F.; very healthy for young children. Population, 21,698, Hindus, Tamil. Dravidian. Religions, Hindu and Dravidian demonology. Language, Tamil. Christians do not lose caste here. Mission station of the A. B. C. F. M. (1816); 1 missionary and wife, 68 native helpers, 4 out-stations, 2 churches, 167 church-members, 1 theological seminary, 137 students, 18 schools, 1,013 scholars.

**Tinana,** the principal station of the Moravians in East Griqualand, South Africa, on the Tinana River, 3,000 to 4,000 feet above the sea. It was chosen on account of the plentiful supply of wood and water in the neighborhood, and for the great fertility of the soil. The surrounding country consists of high table-lands, intersected by ravines and rivers, and at the time of the opening of the station (1869) it was inhabited by about 5,000 heathen, Fingoes and Kafirs. The missionaries here have been compelled to undergo many and great hardships, owing to the frequent Kafir wars; but the work has prospered, and the present missionary and his wife are accomplishing much in and about the station, and the out-stations Muari and Xotshan.

**Tindivanam,** a town in Madras, India. Station of the Reformed (Dutch) Church, U. S. A. (1875); 1 medical missionary, 29 out-stations, 451 communicants, 27 schools, 627 scholars, 1 boys' boarding-school, 34 boys, 1 caste-girls' school, 49 girls.

**Tinné Version.**—The Tinné belongs to the languages of North America, and is spoken in the Hudson's Bay Territory, near Fort Simpson, and over a vast tract of country east of the Rocky Mountains. The Rev. W. W. Kirkby of the Church Missionary Society translated the Gospels of Mark and John, which were printed in the syllabic character by the British and Foreign Bible Society, and circulated among those for whom they were designed since 1871. In 1873 the same Bible Society published an edition of the Gospel of Mark in the Roman character. The version was prepared by the Rev. W. C. Bompar, Bishop of Athabasca.

(*Specimen verse.* John 3 : 16.)

ᒡᐅᑯ ᐅᑊᐧᐳ ᒧᐟ ᐧᑌᑕᑊ ᐧᑊᐳᑊ ᑌᑊᐅᑏ ᒐᑊᒧᑖᑊ, ᑔᑊ ᑌᑐᐳ ᐁ ᐧᐁ ᒐᑊᑌᐳ ᑌᑊ ᐧᐅᑊ ᑯᐧᑌ ᐃᐅ ᐅᑎᑎ, ᐧᐁᐅᐅᒐ ᐃᑊᑌᑊ ᐁᐳᓄ ᐅᑎᑎ.

**Tinnevelli,** a district and town in the southern part of the Madras presidency, in India. The town is located in N. lat. 8° 44′, and E. long. 77° 44′, about 350 miles south-southwest of Madras, with which it is connected by rail. The population in 1881 was 23,221, almost wholly Hindu, Mohammedans numbering 1,538, and Christians 425. The district of Tinnevelli, of which the town is the capital, contains an area of 5,381 square miles, at the southeastern point of Hindustan, bounded on the south and east by the sea, on the west by the Ghats, which separate it from Travancore, and on the north by the district of Madura. The history of the district is involved with that of Madura. After centuries of Hindu rule the Mohammedans came, and after them came a half-century of anarchy, which was ended in 1801 by the cession of the whole region to the English. The population of the district was (1881) 1,699,747; 86½ per cent were Hindus, 8⅓ per cent (140,946) Christians, 5⅓ per cent Mohammedans. Christianity has taken firmer root here than in any other district in India. Statistics show that between 1871 and 1881 the Hindus lost 2½ per cent, while the Mohammedans gained nearly 6 and the Christians over 37 per cent. The converts to Christianity are chiefly among the Paravars, who are all Roman Catholics, and constitute a fishing caste, occupying the shore villages; and the Shanans, a low caste, who live by cultivating the Palmyra palm, and who have furnished most of the converts to the Protestant missions. The number of Protestant native Christians was returned as nearly 80,000 in 1881. Protestant missionary work was begun in the town of Tinnevelli about 140 years ago, by the Danish missionaries at Tranquebar, who with their native preachers made occasional tours to the south. But no Christian preacher seems to have resided there permanently before 1771, when a native preacher took up his residence at Palamcotta, three miles from the town of Tinnevelli; no European missionary was stationed there until the year 1788, when Rev. J. D. Joenicke was sent there. He died in 1800. The missionary Schwartz also travelled in the district. The S. P. C. K. maintained the mission at Palamcotta until 1816 when it was passed over to the Church Missionary Society, and in 1829 transferred its work in the town of Tinnevelli to the S. P. G. These two societies have since divided the work in the district between them. Christianity had begun to exert no small degree of influence at the time the work was transferred to the societies that now conduct it, and since then the work of conversion has proceeded with great vigor. About the year 1877 Rev. R. Caldwell, D.D., of the S. P. G., and the Rev. E. Sargent, D.D., of the C. M. S., were consecrated bishops assistant to the Bishop of Madras, for the purpose of affording better episcopal supervision to the work of their respective societies in that district.

The C. M. S. carries on an itinerant mission from this place under 5 missionaries. A college, with an attendance of 226, is under the care of 2 missionaries. A female institute with 185 boarders and 39 branch schools are under the care of 2 missionaries of the Church of England Zenana Missionary Society. In the native church there are 10 councils in the district.

**Tiruvalure,** a town in the Negapatam district, Madras, India. Mission station of the Wesleyan Methodist Missionary Society; 2 out-stations, 24 native workers, 18 church-members, 8 schools, 283 scholars.

**Tiruvella,** a town in the Travancore district, India, near Alleppie. Mission station of the C. M. S. under the missionary at Alleppie; 1 native pastor, 29 other workers, 753 communicants, 3 churches, 22 schools, 390 scholars.

**Tobago Island,** one of the Windward Group, West Indies. It is a mass of rocks, which rise abruptly to the height of 900 feet at its steepest point. There are several good harbors. Area, 120 square miles. Population, 17,054. Mission field of the Moravians (1790–1827); 1 missionary, 3 stations, 3,071 church-members.

**Tobase,** a town in British Kaffraria, E. South Africa. Mission station of the Moravians, occupied in 1869 as an out-station of Buziyia. At first it was not successful, but since the Kafir war of 1881 the work has progressed most encouragingly. A native minister is in charge, and the station is visited by the missionaries at Buziyia.

**Tocat,** a city in Western Turkey, 60 miles north-northwest of Sivas. Mission sub-station of A. B. C. F. M., worked from Sivas, although for many years also the residence of a missionary of the Foreign Christian Missionary Society. It was here that Henry Martyn died, and his grave is marked by a stone in the Armenian cemetery.

**Tokelau Islands,** a group of small islands in Polynesia, north of Samoan Islands, southeast of the Ellice Group. These islands, together with the Ellice and Gilbert Groups, are visited annually by missionaries of the L. M. S. at Samoa. The statistics for the three groups are: 23 native ministers, 2,051 church-members, 23 Sunday-schools, 2,659 scholars, 23 boys' schools, 1,443 scholars, 23 girls' schools, 1,216 scholars.

**Tokushima** is the largest and most important city on the island of Shikoku, Japan. It is situated on the northeast coast, and is connected with Osaka by a daily line of steamers, the trip to Osaka occupying only eight hours. It has a population of 60,000, and in the province of Awa, of which it is the capital, there are 800,000 people in the many towns and villages. Mission station of the C. M. S. (1884); 1 native pastor, 25 church-members, 1 school, 28 scholars, Presbyterian Church (South), 1885; 3 missionaries.

**Tokyo,** formerly called Yeddo, the capital and principal city of Japan, is built in the centre of a great plain, which extends back from the water to the mountains for a distance varying from twenty to sixty miles, and borders the shores of the Bay of Tokyo for about a hundred miles. There is thus no want of land over which the city may extend. Already it occupies about 28 square miles, and as far as the extent is concerned, it is second only to London. It is situated at the northwest end of the Bay of Tokyo, in latitude 35° 26′ 30″ north, and longitude 139° 39′ 24″ east. Through the city runs the O-gawa, or Great River, dividing it into an eastern and a western part. Numerous canals penetrate the city at various points, and on the east is another river, Naka-gawa. The city is divided into various sections for purposes of government and postal delivery. Here are found the numerous palaces and public buildings of the government; the temples of Buddha, Confucius, and various Japanese deities representing the old civilization and the old religion; but side by side with these stand the distinctively Christian buildings, together with the Imperial University, School of Engineers, and the numerous other institutions of learning, whose influence is rapidly lessening the number of worshippers at the ancient shrines, so that a few years from now they will probably be museums of antiquities rather than temples to which worshippers are drawn through fear and superstition. The rapid strides which European civilization is making in Japan can be seen nowhere better than in this city. Alongside the old stone wall, surrounding the palace grounds, with its moat,—one tortuous ribbon of variegated colors from the lotus-flowers which bloom there in summer-time,— are seen the electric wires for the telegraph and telephone. The puffing smoke of the railway-engine overcomes the pungent odor of the incense in the temples; gas is used for lighting streets and shops, and each year civilization, with its attendant conveniences and luxuries, is thoroughly permeating the life and habits of the citizens. Not only is Tokyo within easy reach of Yokohama, 10 miles away by rail, but it is the centre of many important railway systems, some already completed and others in course of construction. One of the numerous bridges which span the watercourses of the city is considered the topographical centre of the empire, from which all distances are reckoned. The population is estimated at 1,165,048.

Missionary societies commenced their work in Tokyo almost as soon as the empire was opened to the outside world. A fuller, more detailed account of the occupation of this city by the missionaries will be found under the articles treating of the various missionary societies, and also in the article on Japan. At present the societies represented in Tokyo are: A. B. C. F. M.; 1 missionary and wife (for residence only). A. B. M. U. (1874); 3 missionaries (2 married), 4 female missionaries, 3 native preachers, 3 churches, 192 members, 1 school, 88 scholars. Methodist Episcopal Church (South); Biblical institute, 3 European professors, Anglo-Japanese college, publishing department, 1 European superintendent,—total, 9 foreign missionaries (6 married), 7 female missionaries, 2 churches, 700 members, 1 day-school, 130 scholars. Protestant Episcopal Church; 6 missionaries and wives, including missionary bishop, 5 female missionaries, 7 chapels, 60 church-members, a young ladies' seminary, a boys' school, a girls' school, and a divinity school. Presbyterian Church (North), 1869; 7 missionaries and wives, 2 unmarried missionaries, 12 female missionaries, 1 university with preparatory college and theological department, 213 students, 1 female seminary, 77 pupils. The work of this church is combined with the seven other missions who have united to form the United Church of Christ in Japan. The Reformed (Dutch) Church co-operates in the work of the Presbyterian Church (North) in the *Meiji-gakuin* or University at Tokyo, and together with the other missions has united in the Union Church of Christ in Japan. The Methodist Church of Canada has 6 missionaries at Tokyo, 4 employed in the academy and theological school, and 2 in a self-supporting mission, which reports 101 members. S. P. G. (1873); 2 missionaries (one the Bishop of Japan), 198 communicants. C. M. S. (1874); 1 missionary, 54 native communicants, 2 schools, 87 scholars. Baptist Missionary Society; 1 missionary, 157 church-members, 58 day-scholars, 102 Sabbath-scholars. United Presbyterian Church of Scotland (1874); 2 missionaries. Their work is united with the other missions in the Union Church.

**Tolligunge** (Tollygunge), a town in the district of Calcutta, Bengal, India. Mission station of the S. P. G. (1887); 2 missionaries, 14 native helpers, 2 churches, 850 church-members.

**Tomlin, Jacob,** b. near Clitheroe, Lancashire, England, 1793; was a Fellow of St. John's College, Cambridge; sailed as a missionary of the L. M. S. for Malacca June 20th, 1826. Leaving Malacca in April, 1827, he went to Singapore, whence he took a voyage to Batavia. In January, 1828, he returned to Singapore. In March he removed to Malacca, and aided in the work of the college. In August he went with Mr. Gutzlaff to Bankok in Siam. In May, 1829, on account of ill-health, he returned to Singapore. In the

autumn he sailed for Batavia. From November to January, 1830, he accompanied Mr. Medhurst to the island of Bali. On June 17th, 1831, he sailed from Singapore with Dr. Abeel for Siam, returning to Singapore January 14th, 1832. In that year his connection with the Society was dissolved. In 1834 he commenced a seminary at Malacca, called "The Benevolent Institution." In 1836 he returned to England. Mr. Tomlin was an earnest worker, and highly esteemed. He died in England, but the date and place of his death are not known to the Society.

**Tonga,** a dialect of East Central Africa. Reduced to alphabetic form by Rev. E. H. Richards, a missionary of the A. B. C. F. M. at Inhambane. The New Testament was prepared and printed, most of the press-work being done by the natives at Inhambane. The Book of Revelation, however, was brought to New York to be printed. Mr. Richards, at present (1890) in America, intends on his return to Africa to take up the translation of the Old Testament, and to make further revision of the present work. The work is done under the auspices of the American Bible Society.

**Tonga Islands:** see Friendly Islands.

**Tonga Version.**—The Tonga belongs to the Polynesian languages, and is spoken on the Friendly Islands by about 22,000 people. The work of translating the Scriptures into this language commenced in the year 1831, when a strong reinforcement of missionaries arrived at Tonga. The New Testament was printed at the mission press in 1849, and after undergoing another revision it was sent to London, and an edition consisting of 10,000 copies was printed by the British and Foreign Bible Society in 1851. In 1860 the same Society published an edition of 10,000 copies of the entire Bible, under the superintendence of Rev. Thomas West, of the Wesleyan Missionary Society. In 1873 the Rev. James Egan Moulton was sent, by a resolution of the Wesleyan District Meeting in Tonga, to England to revise the New Testament, and to carry it through the press. Owing to the reviser's failing to comply with the rules of the Bible Society, his version was printed by a private firm in 1880. It was warmly welcomed by the natives, and by them pronounced superior to all former versions. The Old Testament is now undergoing a thorough revision. Up to March 31st, 1889, the British and Foreign Bible Society had disposed of 35,276 parts of the Scriptures.

(*Specimen verse.* John 3 : 16.)

He nae ofa behe ae Otua ki mama ni, naa ne foaki hono Alo be taha nae fakatubu, koeuhi ko ia kotoabe e tui kiate ia ke oua naa auha, kae ma'u ae moui taegata.

**Tongareva,** or **Penrhyn,** a small island in Polynesia, east of the Tokelau Islands, west of the Marquesas, and north of the Society Islands. It is visited from Raratonga.

**Tonkin** (Tonquin), is a French colony in Asia on the borders of the Gulf of Tonkin, lying between the Chinese provinces of Kwangtung and Yunnan on the north, and Annam on the south and west. It was annexed by France in 1884, and is divided into fourteen provinces, with an estimated population of

9,000,000. Hanoi, the chief city, is a union of many villages, with an aggregate population of 150,000. The Roman Catholics are at work in Tonkin, and claim 400,000 members.

**Toungoo** (Taung-ngu), one of the principal cities of Burma, India, 170 miles from Rangoon by land, 295 miles by water, 37 miles in a direct line from the frontier of Upper Burma (see Burma). Mission station of the A. B. M. U. (see article), which carries on here work among the (1) Burmese—1 missionary, 31 members; (2) Paku-Karen—1 missionary and wife, 51 native preachers, 65 churches, 2,723 church-members, 65 schools, 890 scholars; (3) Bghai Karens—1 missionary and wife, 2 female missionaries, 91 native preachers, 75 churches, 2,689 members, 50 schools, 932 scholars, (4) Red Karens—1 missionary and wife; (5) Shans—1 missionary and wife, 2 female missionaries, 3 native preachers, 1 church, 27 church-members, 18 scholars.

S. P. G. (1873); 3 missionaries, 1,094 communicants (nearly exclusively Karens), 3 boarding-schools, 157 scholars, 15 other schools, 434 pupils.

**Toy, Robert,** a missionary of the L. M. S. to Madagascar from 1862 to 1880; stationed at Antananarivo. In 1863 he took charge of the native church at Ambohipotsy, in the capital, and of the connected country churches. He visited the eastern part of Vonizongo in 1868, and with Mr. Jukes made a tour of the Betsileo provinces. In November of this year the Memorial Church at Ambohipotsy was opened, of which he took charge, and in connection with his other duties was occupied in a revision of the Malagasy version of the Bible and other literary work in the Malagasy language. He started a training-class for native preachers in 1869, assisted by Mr. G. Cousins, which afterwards became a theological seminary. His health failing, he went to England in 1870. Returning in 1873, he resumed his work in the theological institution, and in addition assisted in the revision of the Malagasy Bible. In 1877 the church at Faravohitra and its surrounding districts was added to his college work. In 1879, his health having seriously failed, he started for England, and died on the voyage, April 19th.

**Translation and Revision of the Bible.**—The Bible is God's Message to all His children; but the children of the One great Father and the one great family speak many tongues, mutually unintelligible to each other, and the object of Bible translation is to enable all the children to hear and understand their Father's words and purpose of love. The Bible reveals God's thoughts in men's words. The bookless savage hears in it a message and summons from his true home—just as the Christian scholar who breaks through conventional crusts recognizes in it the Father's voice speaking words of comfort to His child.

When God revealed Himself in the flesh He did not come in the intolerable splendors of Deity to alarm men, but in the guise of a simple, plain, homely man, who shared in their common labors, sufferings, sorrows, joys. In like manner God's message is humanized in coming to men in their own common, homely tongue. It is God's will that every man should hear His voice in the familiar speech of his own home.

In the early days of the Christian Church a great assemblage came together in Jerusalem. It was fifty days after the Passover Sabbath, and the event of the festival looked for was the presentation of the first-fruit loaves of wheat harvest. "The day of Pentecost was fully come;" but a different event awaited the multitude "The feast of harvest" was gladdened by the first-fruit of that great work of enabling all men to hear the gospel in their own common speech. There were "Parthians, and Medes, and Elamites, and the dwellers in Mesopotamia, and in Judea, and Cappadocia, in Pontus, and Asia, Phrygia, and Pamphylia, in Egypt, and in the parts of Libya about Cyrene, and strangers of Rome, Jews and proselytes, Cretes and Arabians;" and the Spirit of God worked great miracles, and the Galilean disciples were enabled to proclaim the gospel in the divergent tongues of the vast heterogeneous crowd of three continents. "We do hear them speak in our tongues the wonderful works of God."

What the Spirit of God did on the day of Pentecost for fifteen or sixteen peoples, that are the translators of the Bible doing for all the peoples of the world. God worked a miracle, as there was no other way on that occasion of making His will known to the people. But God never works a miracle to do for us what we can do for ourselves or others. He has left it to His church to continue the work begun at Pentecost; not by miracle, but by patient labor, faith, and prayer, under the guidance of the same Spirit that touched with flame the tongues of the disciples on the day of Pentecost. The translator aims at doing by incessant practical hard work, by learning, by zeal, by energy, what was done by divine and gracious miracle in the early days of the infant church. The end in view is that every man may hear in his own tongue the wonderful works of God. For such a work special gifts, graces, acquirements, and instruments are needed, and of these we proceed to speak in the following sections.

*Qualifications Necessary for a Translator.*—The translator should be deeply conscious of the gravity of his work as well as of its importance. The man who enters on such work in a frivolous spirit will fail, like the general who entered on a great war with a light heart. Perfection in translation is unattainable, but it should be aimed at. Translation at best bears pretty much the same relation to the original that the wrong side of velvet bears to the right side. In the wrong side of the texture you may have all the material of the original; the warp and woof may be skilfully shot, all the weight and color may be in the piece, but the glossy pile is wanting. In translation the artistic touch which each author gives to his work, independent of the substance matter, can never be caught or transferred by another hand. If this be so in ordinary translation, it is still more applicable to Bible translation.

The original languages of the Bible constitute great difficulties. The Semitic Old Testament—Hebrew and Aramaic—is full of perplexities. The language is archaic, the idioms are Oriental, the transitions are abrupt, the allusions are uncertain; the words thrown together in juxtaposition give little cue, by form or relation, to their exact meaning. Many passages are vague, and capable of several interpretations, and all passages have alliteration and play upon words which cannot possibly be reproduced in translation.

The original of the New Testament is Semiticised Greek, and the old Hellenic forms are filled with new ideas, like the new wine in the old bottles. The Hellenic words had to be emptied of their old meanings before being dedicated to the new service, and they are often inadequate expressions of the fresh gospel thought. The translator will have to trace the Hebrew conception in the Greek form.

In both Old and New Testaments there are many hands visible. The Holy Ghost, who inspired the men that wrote as they were moved, did not interfere with their individuality or style of expression. Paul does not write like Luke, nor John like James. The prophets are distinct from each other in thought and style, and immeasurably removed from the feeling and form of our exact, metallic age. Taking into account the composite character of the book, from the simplest narrative to the most flowing rhapsody, one cannot but recognize how ill-equipped a modern scholar is for translating right through the Bible. The man who would successfully reproduce this Holy Book must himself be under the influence of the Holy Spirit who inspired and guided the various authors. Purvey, in his prologue to Wickliffe's Bible, says: "He hath need to live a clean life, and be full of devout prayers, that the Holy Spirit, Author of wisdom, knowledge, and truth, dress him in his work, and suffer him not to err. . . . By this manner, with good living and great travail, men may come to true and clear translating, and true understanding of Holy Writ." God's Spirit is needed to help in any work undertaken for His glory or for the elevation of man; but His presence is indispensable in understanding and reproducing in another language the book that proceeded from Himself. The author of a book understands it best, and the Spirit of God will help all who seek His aid to the right comprehension of His word. Without the Spirit the translator must and should fail.

Faith in the Bible is absolutely essential to the translator. He must have an assured conviction that the Bible is the veritable Word of God—the word that has gone forth out of His mouth, and which is destined to accomplish that which He pleases, and to prosper in the thing whereto He sent it. It is not necessary that he pin his faith to any special theory of inspiration. A clear conviction that the Bible is what it professes to be—the Word of God—will save him from perplexity and panic on the issue of new theories from the Sceptic Ring. It is not desirable that he should have to take down all his beliefs from the shelf and re-examine them whenever a new hypothesis regarding the Bible makes its appearance. The hypothesis will doubtless come from a professed believer, with regrets as to the unsettling tendencies of the times. A fixed faith on reasonable grounds will save him much trouble. The hypothesis will stand till the next theory is elaborated, and then it will be ground to powder, like its predecessors. Their

> . . . "little systems have their day,
> They have their day, and cease to be."

'But the Word of the Lord endureth forever."

The translator should not only have a reasonable intellectual belief in the Word of God, but he should be a man who has tried and tested it, and found in it his own strength and joy.

Loyalty to the Bible always accompanies a living faith in the Book. As God's Word, he will reverence it; as his strength in weakness, his guide in perplexity, his light in darkness, he will love and trust it. He will not treat it as a common or secular thing, but as a precious and sacred treasure. Having felt its power himself, he will be careful that none of its meaning is lost in passing through his hands. Having been blessed by it, he will do all that is in his power to make it the bearer of blessings to others. Every phrase, word, letter, mood, and tense will have due weight with him, and nothing will be slurred over or dealt with in a careless or slovenly manner.

A sound judgment is indispensable to a translator of the Bible. No matter how great his attachment and loyalty to the Bible, if he has an ill-balanced mind he is in danger of getting entangled with biblical fads; and the biblical fadist is always discovering things in the text of the Bible that have no existence, giving prominence to parts that are of no more importance than other parts, and unconsciously using the book to support his own whimsical opinions. The translator should know the Bible in the unity of its truth, and be able to see individual passages in the light of surrounding truth. He should be able to divest himself of the prejudices of the religious or philosophical school in which he has been brought up, and to cast aside all prepossessions in favor of even the venerable readings of his own Authorized Version. He should avoid controversy as much as possible, for most advocates are in danger of being carried by their own arguments into extreme positions. Controversy is seldom fair, and when a little heat is engendered, the simple truth, between the two extremes, is overlooked. The biblical fadist should not be encouraged to undertake translation. The reproduction of his fancies may do incalculable harm.

Sound scholarship must be based on sound judgment. A liberal education, especially in languages, is a good groundwork for biblical scholarship. The miraculous linguist is to be avoided. The man who professes to know twenty or thirty or a hundred languages is a deceiver. None of the phenomenal linguists ever did any work that lived, and never will. The translator should concentrate his chief attention on a few languages, and leave large professions to people who wish to be wondered at. A good knowledge of the original languages of the Bible is requisite to a good translator. If he has an opportunity of learning Arabic, he will be well rewarded. Besides the help it will give him in understanding the Hebrew Old Testament, the Arabic language will introduce him to Semitic thought, in the length and breadth of a splendid living literature. Moreover, Van Dyck's Arabic version of the Bible is one of the best in existence, and often, by the modern living idiom, supplies the key to the obscure Hebrew idiom. The Syriac version was one of the first made from the original, after the writing of the New Testament—perhaps the very first, and a knowledge of the Peshito will be useful to the translator; but Syriac has little literature worth reading, and the time spent on it might more profitably be devoted to Arabic. The Latin Vulgate should also be at the side of the translator for consultation, and also the Septuagint; and of living versions the English Revised and Segond's French will be found useful and suggestive. The latter need not be followed blindly. The translator should be thoroughly acquainted with the manners and customs of Bible lands, and with all modern discoveries bearing on the Bible.

The translator should be thoroughly acquainted with the literature of the language into which he is to render the Scriptures. He should read its classics, and especially the poetry, in order to enrich his vocabulary with choice words, and to learn to pack them close with concentrated thought. He should read the newspapers, and converse with the people, until he is able to think in their language, without the intrusion of auxiliary words from other languages. Most languages have corresponding idioms, and by constant watchfulness and practice approximations may be found. If the language is foreign to the translator, he should employ a trustworthy native to accompany him as much as possible. He should be constantly composing in the language, and employing his native assistant to correct his compositions, and he should get by heart a choice specimen of the language daily. Dr. Van Dyck, the translator of the Arabic Bible, like his predecessor in the work, Dr. Eli Smith, made himself thoroughly acquainted with the poetry, proverbs, history, and indeed the whole range of Arabic literature. He spoke the language faultlessly, and knew all the niceties of Arab speech better than the Arabs themselves. His perfect mastery of the Arab tongue nearly cost him his life. During the fearful massacres of 1860, in the Lebanon, Dr. Van Dyck was mistaken for a native Christian. He protested that he was an American, but the Mohammedans told him no foreigner ever spoke Arabic as he did. He escaped with difficulty by establishing his identity. Dr. Van Dyck began to learn Arabic when he was young. He had an ear for delicate shades and tones of sound; an intense thirst for knowledge regarding the Arab race, which he loved; unwearied perseverance in study; a retentive memory, always strengthened by exercise; the art of conversation, which not only charmed the natives as they listened to the poetry of their tongue flowing from his lips, but also inspired them to pour out at his feet their choicest stores of jewelled thought; and above all, with his strong American head was allied a large, warm, loving heart, and a simple, living faith that made him a prince of Bible translators. The result has been perhaps the best version of the Bible in existence.

Patience, in abundant measure, is a necessary endowment of a translator. Haste is the fruitful author of ill-done work. The student in a hurry will never be a scholar. The impatient translator will turn out crude and unfinished copy. The translator's best equivalents for the original words which he wishes to translate will be only approximations. He will have to weigh and balance every word, feel its rhythm on his tongue, and mark its cadence in relation to other words. He will require to examine, with much expenditure of time, the use made of the same word in other places in the Bible. In many instances he will have to forget the classical usage of Hellenic Greek, and seek new meanings for familiar words in the Septuagint and in the Hebrew idiom. He must never be too indolent to turn up his lexicon or concordance. There will doubtless be many influences drawing and pushing him forward at headlong speed. It may be that he is called to work for a bookless people, who have never had the Scriptures. Their need is an urgent call, and he is anxious to get the New Testament into their hands. Or he finds an imperfect version in the hands of the people, and by the help of a presumptuous native he hastens to improve the version, *currente calamo*. It not infrequently happens that Bible Societies expect impossibilities, and, with inadequate knowledge of the difficulties to be overcome, urge translators forward with inconsiderate haste. Many translators in their early impatience, or through the impatience of others, have rushed versions to their own discredit, and to the injury of the cause which they sought to serve.

Patience is an attribute of strength, and the translator requires firm moral fibre to resist the influences that would hinder patience from having her perfect work.

Bishop Steere of Zanzibar spent five years in completing his version of the Gospel of St. Mark, which he first took in hand, into the Swahili tongue. He made a first draft of the portion, and taught his freedmen to print it. This he revised, and his freedmen printed it again. Then he read it, and discussed it with his converts, and re-revised it; and again they printed it. This process was repeated many times before he sent his work as copy to the Bible Society to have it set up in permanent form. By this patient procedure with one Gospel he acquired facility in translation, and he had the joy of giving the New Testament to that great people before being taken home to his reward. The memorable words of the revisers of the Authorized Version should never be forgotten by translators: " We did not disdain to revise that which we had done, and to bring back to the anvil that which we had hammered; but having and using as great helps as were needful, and fearing no reproach for slowness, nor coveting praise for expedition, we have at length, through the good hand of the Lord upon us, brought the work to that pass that you see."

So in the translation of Luther's Bible. The scholars who aided Luther revised with him every line with patient care, and sometimes they returned fourteen successive days to the revision of a single line, several days being given to the consideration of the fitness of a troublesome word. On one of these occasions Luther said to Melancthon, " It is not easy to make the old prophets speak German."

The English and German translators and revisers were rendering the Scriptures into their mother tongues, but the majority of translators and revisers are called upon to translate into tongues which are foreign to them, and which they are obliged to learn. The wise translator will always work by the assistance of native scholars, and this will necessitate patience in many respects. He will have to bear with the inaccurate and self-satisfied ways of the unmethodical natives. He will not be able to take renderings on trust, but must lead his helper round the idea until the exact point is reached. Sometimes, when engaged on languages which have no literature, and which have never been written, he will have to catch the words alive, and fix them as best he can on paper. He will have to fish up his nouns and verbs and prepositions with the patience of a perfect angler, and when he has got his parts of speech, he will only be able to string them with unwearied practice. Moffat used to assemble the natives around him, and listen to their discussions, noting their accents, shades of inflexion, structure of sentences, and all their processes of word-building. Others gather a few natives together as friends or converts, and by their aid construct vocabularies and grammars while building up a new version. In all such operations it is only patience that has her perfect work. There is nothing, perhaps, which tries a translator's patience so much as having his work revised by others. It is never pleasant to have one's composition found fault with, and every correction made by a reviser assumes imperfect work on the part of the author. If the translator has the grace of patience when he first sees the work that has cost him so much pulled to pieces, he will soon come to appreciate the suggestions of men much inferior to himself. For all these things patience and Christian courtesy are absolutely necessary.

The translator should cultivate a simple, easily understood style. Very often first translations, made into a literary language, are cast in too lofty a style. The native helper is a scholar, generally proud of his native literature in which he has been educated, and his aim will be to translate the Scriptures in accordance with high classical models. He is ambitious to do his best, and his best will be a style understood only by scholars like himself. When Bishop Steere reached Zanzibar he found some portions of Scripture in a poetic, stilted style, and he began at once with simpler aims. The Turkish version was also at first rendered in the form pleasing only to the educated, but it has been brought down by a revision committee of missionaries to the comprehension of the people. It is not the business of a translator to render a version in a language as the language ought to be, but as the language is. The common plain language of the people as used in commerce and in everyday life will be the victorious form of speech, and into this form, avoiding all vulgarisms and low expressions, the Scriptures should be translated.

When the proper standard has been reached another question of great difficulty will arise. The translator should strive to convey the meaning while remaining as faithful as possible to the letter of the text. Jerome's dictum, " to translate after the sense, rather than after the word,"—" *magis sensum e sensu quam ex Verbo Verbum transferre*,"—is the rule for translators. The sense must be given whether the passage be rendered literally or not, but pains should be taken to transfer the sense by giving due weight to every word.

In China a corps of delegates, consisting of English and Americans, were appointed to make a version of the Scriptures in the classical script. The Americans and English had diametrically opposite notions as to how the work was to be done. The American leading idea was faithfulness, and the American delegates attempted to carry their idea into practice by literal translation. The English aimed at conveying the sense with idiomatic polish. The delegates did not work harmoniously, and after the completion of the New Testament they separated. In the end two versions were produced, an English and an American. Both had striking merits and striking defects. The American was literal, but unidiomatic and harsh. The English was idiomatic and polished, but somewhat paraphrastic. Up to the present time most of the Americans have stood by their faithful version, and the English have held by their classical version. The two translations will afford rich material for the committee now engaged on a new Union Bible, and the various versions, which were a source of division, will be blended in the book which is to be the authorized version of China.

COMMITTEES.—Translators of the Scriptures should, whenever practicable, carry out their work by committees. The general rule of the British and Foreign Bible Society on this subject is as follows: " That whenever it is practicable to obtain a board of competent persons to translate or revise a version of the Scriptures, it is undesirable to accept for publication the work of a single translator or reviser."

The language of Scripture, like the truths of Scripture, is many-sided, to meet the necessities of many-sided man. Like the diamond, it must be looked at from many points and angles before the full effect of its light is realized. The most learned and most intelligent missionary should be chairman of the committee, which should be as representative as possible of the different denominations and nationalities concerned, competent scholarship for the work being the paramount consideration.

The chairman, by the assistance of native scholars, should make the first draft. When he has made it as perfect as he can, clean copy with wide margins should be submitted to each member of the committee for revision. These copies, with revisions and criticisms, should be returned to the chairman within a given time, and when he has had sufficient opportunity to examine and collate the suggested emendations, the committee should be convened for what may be called the first revision. Carefully drawn up rules should be formulated and agreed upon before beginning the work. One of the most important revisions of modern times was that of the Malagasi Bible. The chief reviser was in the pay of the British and Foreign Bible Society. Of the other members, three belonged to the London Missionary Society, one to the Norwegian Missionary Society, one to the Society for the Propagation of the Gospel, and one represented the Friends' Foreign Mission.

In the meetings of committee for the first revision, when the copy prepared by the chief reviser was under discussion, he, as chairman, had simply a casting vote; but at the second or final revision he had a personal vote in addition to the casting vote as chairman. The entire revision occupied a little over eleven years. During the first revision there were 771 meetings of committee of three hours' duration each. In the second revision the chief reviser had the assistance of three native scholars, and the members of committee sent their suggestions to the chief reviser, and met once a month to settle doubtful points. In carrying out the final revision on these lines, the chief reviser and his native helpers spent 89 days together, and the committee held seven sessions, occupying twelve days. The changes made in the second revision were to give harmony to all the parts, and from the native standpoint, to render the translation more easily understood, and more pleasant to the ear.

The first great version of the Old Testament takes its name, Septuagint, from the supposition that the translation into Greek was the work of seventy scholars. It was certainly the work of a large revision committee, and hence its great value and permanence. The revision of the English Bible which resulted in the Authorized Version of 1611 was the work of many scholars. The Dutch version was the production of twelve translators and sixteen revisers. The Manx Old Testament was the work of twenty-four translators and two revisers.

The recent revision of the English Bible by two companies of revisers, one for the Old Testament and one for the New, with the co-operation of two committees of American scholars, has been one of the events of our time. A full statement of the origin, aim, and accomplishment of that great undertaking may be read in the revisers' preface to the Old and New Testaments, and the result of their labors is in our hands. One of the rules of procedure which guided the revisers was as follows :

" To make or retain no change in the text on the second final revision by each Company, except two thirds of those present approve of the same, but on the first revision to decide by simple majorities."

The guidance of one strong scholarly man as chief reviser secures to some extent unity of style, purpose, and plan in a version. The assistance of a number of patient, courteous, fellow-workers guarantees the due consideration of different shades of meaning and expression. Some of the revisers may be well up in the Hebrew and critical literature of the Old Testament; some may be acquainted specially with the Greek and textual criticism of the New Testament; there may be some who may not have had the advantages of an early liberal education, and who may not know much or anything of the original languages of the Bible, but who have thoroughly mastered the native language into which the translation is to be made, and who know their own Bibles; and the assistance of all such members on a committee will be of inestimable value. There are some minds which delight in unravelling the mazy and involved composition of St. Paul; some which will feel more pleasure in the narratives of St. Luke; and there are some whose minds have an affinity to the minds of the old Hebrew prophets and seers, and who will be best fitted for rendering the poetic parts of the Bible. The cold, matter-of-fact scholar who has been drilled in the exact and literal rendering of the classics is, by the very precision of his scholarship, to a certain extent unfitted to translate Hebrew poetry, which is always richer in thought than in words. The Hebrew poet always projected his theme beyond the formal expression of it.

In the translation and revision of the Japanese Bible many hands were employed. The different books were committed to those best able to deal with them, and when translated were revised by committees, aided by accomplished and scholarly native Christians. In this way the style of the Old Testament has been made to conform to that of the New, and the work of various translators has been harmonized so that there is as complete uniformity in the entire version as if the different books had been the individual work of a single translator. Of individual translators one of the earliest and one of the latest are brilliant examples. Jerome gave the Bible to the Latin world. His version was for many centuries the only Bible used in the West, and directly or indirectly it is the real parent of all the vernacular translations of

Western Europe, not taking into account the Gothic and Slavonic. The crisis in which the version was produced and the man who produced it were alike exceptional. Referring to both, Westcott writes: "In the crisis of danger the great scholar was raised up who probably alone for 1,500 years possessed the qualifications necessary for producing an original version of the Scriptures for the use of the Latin churches."

For many years the late Professor F. Delitzsch, D.D., employed all his learning and skill as a specialist in Hebrew on the translation of the Greek New Testament into Hebrew. He took counsel with many Hebrew friends during the preparation of the work. The first edition was published by the British and Foreign Bible Society in 1877. The version was at once admitted to be the best translation of the New Testament into Hebrew ever produced. The first edition of 5,000 copies was immediately exhausted. With a view to the publication of a revised edition interleaved copies were placed in the hands of all prominent British and American Hebraists for revision and suggestion. Similar copies were submitted to the leading German Hebraists. The world's great Semitic scholars were unanimous in acknowledging the excellence of the version, and most of them sent elaborate criticisms and revisions. These Dr. Delitzsch collated with great care by the aid of several Jewish scholars, and a second edition of 5,000 was exhausted in 1879. Again a number of Hebrew scholars were appealed to for suggestions with a view to a third edition, and again they responded by elaborate criticisms. Dr. Delitzsch, with humility equal to his profound scholarship, revised his work in the light of every suggestion, and spared no pains to make the version worthy of the message which it carried. The same course was followed in preparing the fourth and stereotyped edition in 1880. Again many Hebrew scholars contributed suggestions, and again Dr. Delitzsch devoted all his learning to the perfecting of what he then considered the final revision.

The printing of the fourth edition was exceedingly slow, owing to the extraordinary care taken by the author to have it not only faultless, but as perfect an expression of the original as possible. When Dr. Delitzsch had examined and collated all the suggestions submitted to him he settled the copy and sent it to press. The first proof was read by a Jewish scholar on the Rhine, who corrected it, making suggestions, and returned it to Dr. Delitzsch, who revised it and returned it to press. The second revise was read by the same Jewish scholar, and by Dr. Delitzsch as before. The third revise was sent to Canon Driver of New College, Oxford, and by him returned direct to Dr. Delitzsch, who examined all Canon Driver's corrections and suggestions before marking it "for press." It was now supposed that the text was fixed, and that Dr. Delitzsch, by paying back to the Jews the Christian's obligation for the Hebrew Scriptures, had placed the Christian Church under an incalculable debt of gratitude to him; but the final touches had not yet been given. In 1883 he was again preparing the text for a fifth edition of 5,000 copies, and proceeding in the same methodical, thorough, and elaborate manner. In 1884 he was unremittingly occupied in the improvement of his version, and in constant exchange of thought with

Hebrew professors, in view of the publication of a large octavo edition to be bound up with the Hebrew Old Testament. In 1885 he was busy with the text by the help of a number of Hebrew scholars, revising and collating for a fifth edition 32mo. Thus year after year found the greatest of modern scholars turning anew to the perfecting of his great work; and in 1889, when over 76 years of age, he was still unwearied in his correspondence with the leading Hebrew scholars in preparing for the eleventh edition of 5,000 copies, his one desire being to leave the most splendid achievement of his mature scholarship as faultless as possible. In 1890, when confined to bed, feeble and helpless in body, but clear in mind, he continued his beloved task. On the 7th of March he went home to his reward, leaving his friend, Dr. Dalman of Leipsic, to carry the edition through the press. Never in the history of translation was such splendid scholarship, united with unstinted labor, so lavishly bestowed on a version of the Scriptures. And in the entire range of the world's versions there is nothing to compare with Delitzsch's Hebrew New Testament. The world is richer for this matchless work of faith and labor of love.

Single translators, without any pretensions to Delitzsch's scholarship, have frequently produced useful versions of the Scriptures. Moffat translated from the English Authorized Version into the language of the Bechuana and Matebele tribes. While following the Authorized Version he consulted the Dutch version, and occasionally Luther's German version. The translation was a faithful reproduction of the 1611 text, with a few deviations in accordance with the Dutch. Moffat declared that he was conscious of the imperfection of his version, but that he knew it had brought many into the fold of Christ. He did the best he could in translating, and the Committee of the Bible Society did the best they could in publishing his translation, and the Spirit of God accepted the work, and blessed it to the salvation of souls. In these as in other matters our gracious heavenly Father accepts our best. An imperfect version is better than no version. When a perfectly equipped scholar cannot be found for translation or revision work, we must be content with less than perfection. When a committee cannot be got together for the work, it must be entrusted to individuals. De Sacy's Vulgate version in French has been greatly honored, and Lasserre's translation of the Gospels has made the fourfold story of Jesus live in the hands of Frenchmen. Segond also has given the French a living Bible in their own tongue. But all these "one-man versions" have the distinct defects of "one-man versions."

THE TEXT TO BE FOLLOWED is of primary importance in Bible translation. Up to 1881 the work of translation for the British and Foreign Bible Society was carried on in accordance with the following instructions:

"Whenever practicable, a version should be a direct translation from the Hebrew and Greek originals. For the Hebrew Bible, the edition of Van der Hooght is considered the standard; and in the use of this the translator is at liberty to follow either the *ketib* or the *keri*; but not to adopt any rendering which is not sanctioned by the Massoretic vowel-points, or the *keri*, or the English Authorized Version, or the marginal readings of this last. In the

Greek Testament the Elzevir edition of the 'Textus Receptus' of 1633, and reprinted by the British and Foreign Bible Society, is considered the standard; but in cases where the Authorized Version differs from this, either in the text or in the marginal reading, the translator is at liberty to adopt a rendering which may agree with any one of these three; and if a translator or editor think it better to omit the subscriptions of the epistles, the insertion of these is not required."

As far as the Old Testament is concerned these instructions still hold good. Hebrew manuscripts of the Old Testament are of no great antiquity, dating only from A.D. 916. No doubt there are ancient readings preserved in such versions as the Septuagint, the Samaritan Pentateuch, the Syriac, and the Latin Vulgate. And there are doubtless previous readings of the old Hebrew preserved in quotations in the New Testament. Collations of such readings have been made with much labor and some skill; but nothing has been discovered or done to warrant the Bible Society in adopting a new text. The English revisers did not consider the present state of knowledge on the subject of versions and manuscripts sufficient to justify them in any reconstruction, and they agreed to abide by the Massoretic text as the basis of their work. The Common Hebrew Bible of the British and Foreign Bible Society was followed by the revisers, and they were guided in their procedure on lines practically similar to those laid down for translators by the Bible Society. They only departed from the Hebrew text in exceptional cases, as had been done by the Authorized translators. Alternatives to all such variations are placed in the margins, the most authoritative readings standing in the text.

The case of the New Testament is widely different from that of the Old. Numerous ancient and important Greek manuscripts of the New Testament, in whole or in part, have been discovered in recent years. Enormous learning and pains have been bestowed on the collation and classification of these manuscripts, and on the investigation of early versions and quotations. Sufficient material has been accumulated for the substantial restoration of the Greek Testament of the fourth century. Textual critics have made the results of their patient labor known in many ways. Many critical editions of the Greek Testament have been published, some of them accompanied by commentaries in which the weight and bearings of the various readings have been set forth, and the process by which they have been appraised. Different schools of critics have dealt with the subject, and have followed slightly different methods in settling the text. All have not been able to agree on exactly the same results. One result, however, of importance to Bible societies was clear, namely, that the "Textus Receptus" was of little critical value, and could not be imposed on translators or revisers as the sole text to be followed. The adoption or construction of a text that would fairly represent the best *consensus* of sound critical scholarship became a necessity, but a necessity almost impossible of accomplishment. Textual criticism, as applied to the Greek New Testament, forms a study of much intricacy and difficulty, and, with the soundest and most candid workers, still leaves room for considerable latitude of opinion. It was suggested that the Bible Society should form a text of the New Testament that would unite alike the timorous and the reckless. A critical text formed by the Bible Society would have simply added another edition of the Greek Testament to the numerous editions already in existence. It might have met the wants of translators, but it would have been rejected by extreme men of the different schools. The Committee were urged to take up one of the many good editions, and give it the stamp of the Society's *imprimatur*, but this counsel they wisely declined to follow.

A more practicable proposal was that a Greek text should be formed, giving the readings in all cases where Tischendorf, Tregelles, Lachmann, and Scrivener were agreed, and in all other places abiding by the "Textus Receptus." Such an edition could have been produced with great ease, but it is doubtful if it would have given satisfaction; and as the matter-of-fact Tregelles and the more speculative Tischendorf would have been often at variance, as well as the others, the edition would have been almost the same as the "Textus Receptus."

No proposal was made that was not beset with difficulties for the Bible Societies, but the difficulties of inaction were also great; for some of the many translation and revision committees at work for the Society—the Malagasi for instance—declined to reproduce the "Textus Receptus" in all its parts, and in proceeding with the translation left all passages of questionable authority untranslated till such time as the Bible Society should modify the instructions binding translators to follow an imperfect text.

Under these circumstances it was resolved to await the text of the English revisers. The New Testament Company was composed of experts who had made a special study of the Greek New Testament. The members were chosen for eminence in textual criticism, and they represented the different schools of thought. It was not in their commission to provide a new text of the Greek Testament, but by their rules they were to follow the text "for which the evidence was decidedly preponderating." Such a company of revisers had never been brought together before, and it was believed that the text agreed upon would meet the wants of the Bible Society. In any case it would go forth with a weight of authority possessed by no other version. The result has in a large measure justified expectation, and while many objections have been raised against the English of the revisers, the text that underlies the revision has been pretty generally accepted as bearing the stamp and authorization of the leading masters in textual criticism—the most cautious as well as the most conservative. The Committee of the British and Foreign Bible Society in 1881 issued the following revised instructions to translators and revisers:

"The question, what Greek text ought to be the basis of translations and revisions of translations of the New Testament, has long engaged the anxious consideration of the committee. They have watched with deepening interest the gradual accumulation of manuscript evidence, and the vast amount of learning and skill brought to bear upon it during recent years. They were by no means unaware of the defects of the Elzevir edition of the 'Textus Receptus,' reprinted by the Bible Society, and hitherto recommended as the standard; but they felt, amongst the multiplication of editions in the present day, the difficulty of suggesting a satisfactory alternative.

"The revisers of the English New Testament having now completed their labors, the subject has again claimed the attention of the committee; and they thankfully avail themselves of the opportunity thus afforded of acting, as they trust, with proper caution, and yet with a due regard to the requirements of sound Biblical knowledge, in this important matter. The committee have accordingly resolved to authorize missionaries and others engaged on behalf of this Society in the work of translation or revision to adopt such deviations from the 'Textus Receptus' as are sanctioned by the text of the Revised English Version of 1881. The committee are not prepared to authorize any deviation from the 'Textus Receptus' not sanctioned by the text of the Revised English Version.

"In transmitting this resolution the committee would offer the following suggestions:

"Two editions of the Greek Testament have been published simultaneously with the Revised English Version—one at Oxford, the other at Cambridge. Neither of these has the direct sanction of the Company of Revisers; but each in its way gives the result of their decision.

"The Oxford edition gives in the text the readings followed by the revisers; the old readings, or those not followed, being, so far as was thought material, placed at the foot of the page.

"The Cambridge edition is a reprint of the text from which the English Authorized Version is presumed to be taken, and which, for practical purposes, may be treated as nearly identical with the Elzevir text, the variations adopted by the revisers being carefully noted at the foot of the page; attention being called to variations or omissions from the old text by a marked difference in the Greek type.

"It will be open to translators or revisers to use either of these editions.

"Neither of these editions gives any clue to the varying degrees of weight attached by the Company of Revisers to the readings adopted by them. For this we are obliged to turn to the marginal notes in the Revised English Version. The careful attention of translators is invited to the observations of the Company of Revisers on the revision of the Greek text in their preface, and to the caution suggested by their emphatic words: 'Many places still remain in which for the present it would not be safe to accept one reading to the absolute exclusion of others.' 'In these cases,' the revisers add, 'we have given alternative readings in the margin, whenever they seem to be of sufficient importance or interest to deserve notice.' These alternative readings should, therefore, be carefully studied before any change is adopted from the 'Textus Receptus;' and whilst the committee would not desire to control the conscientious judgment of translators or revisers, they would suggest that where the marginal note in the English version indicates that there are ancient authorities in support of the Elzevir text, there would be safety in adhering for the present to the Elzevir text.

" With regard to omissions from the Elzevir text, the committee believe it will be found that in nearly all cases in which words and sentences are omitted from the text, and are unnoticed in the margin of the English revision, they may be safely rejected as spurious.

" It is possible that in some cases a translation or revision may admit of alternative marginal readings. The committee would not discourage their introduction where thought necessary; but the circumstances attending translation so greatly vary, that the introduction of such must be largely left to the judgment and discretion of translators and revisers. In any difficulty the editorial superintendent will render any assistance in his power.

" The Committee feel how much of sound judgment, and heavenly wisdom and skill, is needed in the important and responsible work of translation and revision; but they rejoice to know that, as they who are called to it labor in faith and prayer, in an habitual dependence upon the illumination and direction of the Holy Spirit, they will find it a work which the Great Inspirer of Scripture in an especial manner loves to honor and bless."

The same regulations substantially have been adopted by the American Bible Society, and thus far the two great societies have proceeded on the same lines in the work of translation and revision.

Translators and revisers will find useful guidance in the Revised English Bible in the matter of uniformity and consistency. In this matter the Authorized Version was very misleading. It was a principle with the Authorized revisers to vary their translations and phrases as much as possible, even when rendering the same words and phrases, and in the same passages. In this way literary elegance was secured at the expense of strength and faithfulness. The English revisers aimed at translating the same Greek word by the same English word, but they did not carry out this principle with inflexible rigidity. Varieties of rendering compatible with the true meaning of the text have to some extent been preserved, but varieties suggestive of differences which have no existence in the Greek have been excluded. The exact shade of meaning of words and phrases is generally to be reached from the context. All important names and terms should be uniformly translated. The names for the Divine Being and His attributes, for man and his faculties, theological terms, ceremonial and Christian ordinances, and all such expressions as become the common currency of the Christian Church, should be maintained at one uniform standard. When versions are completed, and almost ready for the press, it is desirable that the whole should be gone over with a concordance, for the purpose of harmonizing all the parts.

The Names for the Divine Being require special attention. The difficulty of finding any Supreme Being among the heathen is sometimes very great. Sometimes the gods are so numerous that the difficulty consists in making a proper selection. Sometimes there are no gods at all; but the translator's chief difficulty will be to find any name among the heathen associated with the ideas of reverence or worship. In this matter as in many others the translator will have to do the best he can. In the Septuagint and Greek Testament, Theos

is substituted for Elohim, and Lord (Kurios) for Jehovah and Adonai promiscuously. The terms were not equivalents, but apostles and martyrs preached the gospel meanings into the names until they became expressive of the true gospel thoughts now associated with each. Every care should be taken to select the best word, but it must be remembered that in all countries the truth about God is gathered not so much from the name as from what is taught concerning Him who bears it. The translator in a heathen tongue must select the best term or name he can find. Though he may be obliged to take the name of a false god, he will find that by degrees, through reading the Bible, the false meaning will disappear, and the true meaning assert itself. It might be possible to transfer the original names of God by transliteration, as the name Jehovah is transferred in a few places into the English Bible, but in that case the names would, in themselves, be absolutely without significance when first introduced.

Great difficulties have arisen in China regarding the Divine name. When the delegates began to make a union version for China they did not like to take the names for God and Spirit that they considered had been degraded by some of the Roman Catholics. They were also unwilling to take the names of Chinese gods whose characters and appearances were most ungodlike. It was suggested that the divine names should be transliterated, but the Delegates' Version was made on the condition that every evangelical denomination in China should have liberty to publish editions for itself, employing whatever name it thought best for God, Spirit, and Baptize. The Committee of the British and Foreign Bible Society, in accordance with almost the unanimous opinion of British scholarship, came to the conclusion that the most appropriate terms for God and Spirit, in China, were Shang-ti and Shin, and they only published editions of the Scriptures with such terms. The American Bible Society published editions of the Scriptures with such names for God and Spirit as were demanded. At present there are nine possible forms and combinations of the names for God and Spirit in use in China, but there is reason to believe that the native Christians will decide the question, throughout China, in favor of Shang-ti and Shin, as they have already done in several localities where they have had power.

In the Revised English Version the word Jehovah is transliterated in a few places more than in the Authorized Version, but only in places where a proper name seemed to the revisers to be absolutely required. In many versions the word Jehovah occurs wherever it is found in the Hebrew. This is sometimes a disadvantage. The British and Foreign Bible Society was requested to withdraw Valera's Version from Spain, owing to the frequent occurrence of the word Jehovah, which the natives declared was a new Protestant God. The name when translated and not transliterated should be printed in small capitals, as is done in English, or in some other way which will distinguish the word.

Translators will find it difficult to render the word *Baptizo* in a manner satisfactory to all. If translating for a non-denominational society which is supported by all denominations, they cannot be expected to translate the word by a term which supports the views of one denomination and condemns the usage of almost all other denominations. In versions made for the British and Foreign Bible Society the word *Baptizo* and its cognates are transliterated or transferred, as is done in the English Bible, unless it can be translated by some native word signifying sacred washing, without limiting the form to either dipping or sprinkling. An attempt has been made to get over the difficulty by placing the neutral term in the text, and the denominational term in the margin, with the words "some translate immerse"—which is simply the statement of a fact. Where the version is Baptist, it would be better that the difficulty should be got over by an alternative reading, than that a rival version should be issued. These matters require to be dealt with on both sides in a spirit of mutual forbearance.

Translators should be careful to choose the central language in commencing versions, and to resist all pressure to undertake translations in insignificant and dying dialects. Many versions produced in local *patois* have led to considerable waste of Christian money. At first it may not be possible, with limited experience, to say which branch of a group of languages is the best vehicle for reaching the most people; but first editions should be tentative and small, and the second editions should be revised into the dominant form. Prince L. L. Bonaparte has made versions of the Scriptures into more than a hundred languages, dialects, and *patois*, for linguistic purposes. These his Highness has handed over to the Bible Society, with permission to revise them for evangelistic purposes; but there are only a few of them on which the Society would be at all justified in spending funds.

The translator should be careful to mark in some distinctive way words translated to make the sense complete, but which have no equivalents in the originals. Such words are marked in our English Bibles by being printed in italics. This is somewhat unfortunate, as in all other forms of English literature italics are used to give emphasis and prominence to words. In our old black-letter English Bibles the understood words were marked in Roman characters, which were smaller, and somewhat insignificant, and hence more suitable. In the modern Greek Bible the supplied words are printed in a smaller character. The italics should be as few as possible. A great many in the Authorized Version are superfluous. In foreign languages the supplied words, when necessary, should be printed in type similar to the body of the text, but somewhat smaller. In preparing chapter and page headings only simple summaries should be given. In our English Bibles the chapter headings are printed in such small italics that they are seldom consulted, and they form an undesirable wedge between chapter and chapter. The British and Foreign Bible Society has long had a paragraph English Bible prepared by Canon Girdlestone, and it has begun to print foreign versions in paragraphs, with sectional headings which simply announce the subjects of the sections. The headings are simple summaries, such as "The Creation," "The Flood," "The Temptation," "The Fall," etc. Versions so arranged, well printed, and accompanied by maps have been published in Italian, Sesuto, Malagasi, French, and Dutch, and they have been well received.

For the present distress, in China, the committee have agreed to publish summaries, sectional headings, and simple explanations of words and terms not likely to be understood by the Chinese.

The ordinary chapter and verse form in which most of our English Bibles are printed has certain advantages in facilitating the finding of passages and for reading verses about, but the Scriptures can be read much more intelligently in the paragraph form. Much can be done by artistic printing, by proper spacing, and the arrangement of parallelisms to encourage the reading of the Scriptures. Lasserre's Gospels in paragraph form are so arranged that every page says "read me;" and Frenchmen for the first time read the gospel with pleasure. There are many additional considerations, and necessary conditions, and infinite details, which might be advanced with regard to Bible translation, but these will be best learned in the practical work of translation. As in preparing sermons, writing books, and public speaking, each worker reaches his own style by his own methods, so translators must be left to find out the lines within certain limitations on which they can best accomplish the sacred work entrusted to them; and in the matter of details, common sense and scrupulous conscientiousness will be the best guides.

Dr. Cust's contribution to this encyclopedia (see Appendix B) enables one to judge of the immense work already accomplished in Bible translation.

The Bible is the greatest of all the classics, and its importance may be judged in contrast with them. Versions of the classic masterpieces of Greece, Rome, and the far East are few, and are found on the shelves of libraries and in the homes of learning. The versions of the Bible are for the people, and no sooner have they fallen from the press than they are taken up in such quantities by the missionaries, by the colporteurs, by the zenana women, and by all who wish the divine message made known, that the average circulation of the British and Foreign Bible Society alone is over four million copies a year.

Plato was perhaps the most spiritual, the most elevated, teacher that the heathen world produced. Excellent translations of Plato's works have been published in English, German, French; but no one can imagine an attempt being made to translate them into three or four hundred languages, as has been done with the sacred Scriptures. There are at the present time over a thousand philologists busied with Bible translation and revision, and wherever the living missionary goes he takes with him the living word. What a grand work this is when regarded merely from the standpoint of literature and science, but how glorious when it is remembered that the Book is the living Word of God, dowered with the gifts of civilization and salvation.

**Tracy, William,** b. Norwich, Conn., U. S. A., June 2d, 1807; studied at Williams College; graduated at Princeton Theological Seminary 1835; was ordained April 12th, 1836; sailed November 23d, 1836, and after spending a few months at Madras, reached Madura October 9th, 1837. He visited the United States in 1851 and 1867. At Tirumungalam he opened a boarding-school for boys. From that day he was largely engaged with the educational work of the district. By 1842 the boarding-school had grown to a high-grade seminary, and in 1845 it was removed to Pasumalai. Here the next twenty-two years of his life were spent, except when at home in 1850. More than 250 young men passed through the course of study. Few classes left him in which nearly all were not Christians, a large number of them engaging in evangelistic work, and others occupying honorable posts in government service. He was an efficient member of the Revision Committee of the Tamil Bible. A short time before his death he had the joy of welcoming his youngest son with his wife to the mission work in the land of his birth. He died at Tirupuvanam, South India, November 28th, 1877, aged seventy, and in the forty-first year of his missionary service.

**Tranquebar,** a town in British India, on the shore of the Bay of Bengal, about 150 miles south of Madras. It is situated in the delta of the Caveri River, in north latitude 11° 2′, and east longitude 79° 54′. The town, with a small area of country, was obtained by the Danish East India Company in 1616, and held by the Danes until 1845 (with the exception of a few years), when, with Serampur in Bengal, it was sold by them to the English. Under Danish rule it was a place of some political and commercial importance, which in recent years, by the diversion of business to other centres, it has almost wholly lost. The population in 1881 was only 6,189, of whom 4,916 were Hindus, Mohammedans 820, and Christians 453. The great interest which Tranquebar possesses for us consists in the fact that it is the place where Protestant missionary effort first began in India. Here Bartholomew Ziegenbalg and Henry Plutschau, the pioneers of the great army of Protestant evangelists, came from Denmark in 1706 and founded the first Protestant mission station. They labored under the greatest difficulties, and yet within three and a half years a Christian community had been gathered, numbering 160 persons, which rapidly grew. The publication of books was begun at once. Ziegenbalg completed the translation of the New Testament in 1711, and when he died in 1719 he left behind him a translation of the Old Testament as far as the Book of Ruth. A church was built by his efforts, which is no longer in existence, its site having been undermined by the sea. The mission was manned for many years by men of superior attainments and character, among whom was the great Schwartz, and exerted a profound influence in South India. For a long time it received pecuniary aid from England through the Society for Propagating Christian Knowledge. In 1847 the mission passed into the hands of the Leipsic Evangelical Lutheran Mission, and is still vigorously maintained by that body, who have 418 communicants. Protestants at and near Tranquebar numbered 2,000 several years ago. There are in the same area about 1,200 Roman Catholics. The S. P. G. have a work there also, conducted by 4 native workers, with 1 school and 18 scholars.

**Trans-Caucasian Turki** (Azerbijan Turkish) **Version.**—The Trans-Caucasian belongs to the Turki branch of the Ural-Altaic family, and is spoken in Trans-Caucasia, Russia, and Northwest of Persia. In 1843 the Gospel of Matthew was published by the British and Foreign Bible Society, the translation having been made by Dr. Pfander. The work of translation continued with the aid of Mirza Ferookh, who translated the New Testament, save the Epistle to the Romans. The manuscript version, after being revised by his son, the Rev. A. Amirkhanianz, was published in 1878, together with the Epistle to the Romans, which the reviser had translated, under the superintendence of Dr. Sauerwein and Mr. Amirkhanianz. Some years ago Messrs. Rhea, Labaree, and Van Norden, American missionaries in Persia, undertook a translation of the Bible into this dialect. After Mr. Amirkhanianz completed the translation of the Bible in 1883, the American missionaries gave up their version, and united with the translator in a final revision of the Old Testament, so that there should be but one version of the Bible in the Trans-Caucasian language. After all dialectical and orthographical differences between the language as spoken in Northern Persia and other Turki-speaking districts had been satisfactorily adjusted, the British and Foreign Bible Society commenced the publication of an octavo edition of the whole Bible, consisting of 2,500 Old Testaments and 5,000 New Testaments, one half to be bound up with the Old Testament, and one half to be issued separately. The printing was commenced at Leipsic in 1886, proofs being read by the translator at Orenburg (whither he had been exiled by the Russian Government) and Dr. Sauerwein at Banteln, and completed in 1888.

**Transvaal,** is a term which is often used to designate the territory also called the South African Republic, which is described under the article on Africa.

**Travancore,** a native state in India, occupying the extreme southwestern portion of the peninsula. Its limits of north latitude are 8° 4′ and 10° 22′, and of east longitude 76° 12′ and 77° 38′. Its boundaries are: on the north the native state of Cochin; on the east the British districts of Madura and Tinnevelli, belonging to the Madras presidency, from which districts it is separated by a mountain range; on the south and west the Indian Ocean. The length of Travancore from north to south is 174 miles, and its greatest breadth 75. It embraces an area of 6,730 square miles, with a population of 2,401,158 in 1881; 73 per cent were Hindus, about 21 per cent (498,542) Christians, and a trifle over 6 per cent were Mohammedans. The Christian population includes a large number of adherents of the old Syrian Church of Malabar,—more than half of the whole; nearly a third are Romanists, and the remainder Protestants. As to language, Malayalim—a Dravidian tongue allied to Tamil—is used by about four fifths of the people, and Tamil by the rest. The chief town and capital is Trivandrum, with a population of 41,173. Travancore has been ruled from time immemorial by Hindu princes of approved orthodoxy. It has never—like all the rest of India—come at any time under the sway of the Mohammedans. In the latter part of the last century it was attacked by Tippu, Sultan of Mysore, but, with the aid of the English, successfully resisted him. Treaties, made early in this century with the English, have firmly cemented this old connection, and made English influence powerful within its borders, though there was armed opposition in 1809. The relation between the Anglo-Indian Government and the native states like Travancore has been sufficiently explained in the article "Native States." An English resident is maintained at the court of the Maharajah (king) of Travancore, and an annual tribute is paid to the "paramount power." The Government of Travancore, though Hindu, is intelligent, efficient, and progressive. Its native rulers have studied to good advantage the example set them by the English rulers of adjacent regions. There is a good system of education in vogue, as a result of which the people of Travancore show about as high an average of intelligence and as large a proportion of persons able to read and write as many British provinces in India. The people are chiefly agricultural; rice, the cocoanut palm, and pepper are the principal productions, and the exports are largely derived from the cocoanut tree, though pepper, ginger, cardamom, timber, and some other articles are included among them.

The forms of Hindu worship usual throughout India are practised in Travancore, mingled, however, to a greater or less extent, with the rites of demon-worship, which prevails extensively in South India and Ceylon, especially among the aboriginal tribes. This demon-worship was that originally practised by the early tribes of India; and when advancing waves of Aryan conquest drove these primal settlers to the mountains, or pushed them far to the south, their religion was with them concentrated, as it were, in those localities, and has since lingered in them. To a large extent the Aryans (or Hindus) incorporated the aborigines into their own system, assigning to them the low social status of laborers, or Shudras; and many of their demon-deities were received into the Hindu pantheon, and their old rites made permissible for Hindus. Thus the Hinduism of Travancore, and indeed of all South India, became mingled and corrupted with these aboriginal notions and rites to a degree not noticed elsewhere. Missionaries in Travancore have had to encounter among their converts far more of the degrading power of these old habits and associations, rooted in this ancestral demonolatry, than their fellow-laborers among Hindus in other regions.

Travancore, and its sister kingdom, Cochin, which adjoins it in the north, are famous as the home of an exceedingly ancient branch of the Christian Church, usually known as the "Syrian Church of Malabar," Malabar being the name applied for many centuries to the strip of coast embracing the kingdoms named and the British district just north of them. The origin of this church is doubtful. The traditions current among the people go back to the preaching of Thomas, in the middle of the 1st century; but scholars suppose that a small colony from Antioch (Syria) may have landed here in the 4th century. The church is Syrian in doctrine and ritual, maintaining the Nestorian type of Christology, and is subject to the Patriarch of Antioch, though the Romanists have tried hard to subject it to the Pope, and did succeed, in 1599, in detaching some 80,000 members from the patriarch, and in thus forming a Romo-Syrian community, which is still allowed, however, to retain the Syrian ritual and language. The remainder of the Roman Catholic population represents chiefly the results of Francis Xavier's missionary activity in the 16th century. The existence of this ancient Syrian Church attracted the attention of Rev. Dr. Buchanan (then chaplain to the East India Company at Tinnevelli), and at his urgent suggestion the Church Missionary Society, in 1816, sent missionaries to labor among its members. At first the Syrian priests co-operated with them, but in 1838 signs of hostility appeared, which culminated in the Syrian *Metran* (or Metropolitan) dissolving all connection with the English missionaries. Since then the Church Mission has devoted its attention to the people at large, with the most gratifying results, drawing their converts from the old church in part, but very largely from Hindus, and especially from certain low castes.

The London Missionary Society's operations in Travancore began in 1806. Rev. Mr. Ringeltaube, a German, joined one of the first companies which this Society sent to India. He resided first at Tranquebar, under the protection of the Danish Government, at a period when the East India Company frowned on all missionary operations within their own territories. His attention was drawn to Travancore by seeing two or three persons from that country, one of whom evinced great interest in Christianity, and begged for the services of a missionary to teach his people. Ringeltaube accepted the invitation, and was greatly assisted in getting a foothold in Travancore by Col. Macaulay, then British resident at Trivandrum. The first station was at Meiladi. Ringeltaube labored until 1816, when, having baptized some 900 persons, he left his work in the hands of a native catechist, and retired from India with broken health. Nothing is known of the end of his life. In 1818 other missionaries arrived. Col. Munro was then resident, and continued the aid of the mission which his predecessor had begun; without such aid from the representative of British power it is hard to see how the mission could have started in the face of Hindu opposition on the part of the Brahmans and the Hindu Government. The converts rapidly increased—largely from among the low-caste Shanars. From 1827 to 1830 violent persecution was experienced; and the low-caste people in Travancore have never, unless perhaps recently, been admitted to the privileges of the public schools maintained by the government. The progress of the mission in late years has been rapid, and its usefulness great. In 1838 it was allowed to begin a station at Trivandrum, the capital; and since 1844 it has drawn many converts from the higher castes. Rev. Samuel Mateer, one of its most distinguished members, published, in 1871, a full account of the country and people of Travancore, with historical sketches of missionary work within its borders, under the title "The Land of Charity."

**Trebizond**, a city on the Black Sea, in Asiatic Turkey, is, by reason of its location, an important centre for the trade from Persia and Central Asia to Europe. The climate is temperate, and its location is picturesque. The city is divided into the old quarter, inhabited by Turks; the more modern, or Christian quarter; and the commercial quarter. The harbor is not very deep, nor is it well protected. Caravans start from here for Persia and Central Asia. The population is estimated at 45,000, Turks, Armenians, and Greeks. Mission station of the A. B. C. F. M.; 1 medical missionary and wife.

**Trevandrum,** a town in the Travancore district, South India, near Cape Comorin; has 60,000 inhabitants. Mission station of the L. M. S; 1 missionary and wife, 4 native pastors, 4 other preachers. 46 out-stations, 1,690 scholars, with an institute for girls of the higher castes.

**Trichinopoli,** a city in Madras, India, on the Caveri River, 56 miles from the sea; 186 miles southwest of Madras City. It is a place of much historic interest, having been the scene of many well-known sieges, etc., of which the fortifications are interesting evidences. It is well known for its cigars, and for its peculiar and beautiful gold jewelry. Population, 84,449, Hindus, Moslems, Christians. Heber, the Protestant Bishop of Calcutta, is buried here (1826), and the place is the scene of great missionary activity. Mission stations: S. P. G.; 2 missionaries, 1 missionary's wife, 1 female missionary, 84 native helpers, 29 schools, 1,118 scholars. Leipsic Evangelical Lutheran Society; 261 communicants, 193 scholars. Wesleyan Missionary Society; 3 missionaries, 5 native helpers, 100 church-members, 6 Sunday-schools, 315 scholars, 9 day-schools, 570 scholars.

**Trichur,** an ancient town in the Travancore district, Madras, South India. A station of the C. M. S. together with Kunnankulam, under the charge of 1 missionary. There are 338 communicants, 5 schools, 229 scholars.

**Trinidad,** a colony belonging to Great Britain, in the West Indies, at the mouth of the Gulf of Paria, off the northeast coast of Venezuela, north of the mouth of the Orinoco. Area, 1,754 square miles. Population, 189,566 (1888). Temperature, 70° to 86° Fahrenheit. Soil fertile. Capital, Port-of-Spain. Mission field of United Presbyterian Church of Scotland; 3 missionaries,—with stations at Port-of-Spain, Arouca, and San Fernando,—3 churches, 379 church-members, 600 scholars. There are 191 schools, 16,000 pupils, under the Government grant of £16,783. The Queen's Royal College has 65 students. The Roman Catholics have also a college with 220 students. Tobago (area, 114 square miles) is included in the administration of Trinidad.

**Trinitarian Bible Society.** Headquarters, 7 St. Paul's Churchyard, London, E. C., England.—The Trinitarian Bible Society was organized in 1831, for the circulation of the Word of God, translated from the originals only, to the exclusion of all versions from the Vulgate. The term "Trinitarian" expresses the religious views of all its members. No person is admitted to the management of the Society who denies the doctrines of the Trinity and the Atonement. The work of the Society is chiefly in those countries in which the Vulgate or Romish versions most abound. It has prepared a Spanish Bible in several editions, and a Portuguese Bible with references. The first translation of the Bible into the Breton language (see Breton Evangelical Mission) was printed by the Society; also Salkinson's Hebrew translation of the New Testament, of which 100,000 copies have already (within three

years) been distributed among Jews in all countries.

The Society avoids colportage as far as possible, its work of distribution being mainly carried on by agents of other societies. In the year 1888 its grants and sales of Bibles, New Testaments, and portions (in 21 different languages) amounted to 93,829.

**Tripatur** (Tirupatur), a town in the Salem district, Madras, India, 137 miles southwest of Madras. Climate dry, hot. Population, Hindus, Moslems. Languages, Tamil, Hindustani, Telugu. Natives prosperous; occupation, agriculture. Mission station L. M. S. (1861); 1 missionary, 18 native helpers, 4 out-stations, 1 church, 42 church-members, 2 schools, 144 scholars.

**Tripoli.**—1. A seaport town of Syria, on the Mediterranean, 40 miles north-northeast of Beirut, 70 miles northwest of Damascus. It is one of the neatest towns of Syria, and is surrounded by many gardens and groves of orange and other fruit trees, but the ground in the neighborhood is marshy, and the climate is unhealthful at certain seasons. Population, 16,000, one half Greek Catholics. Mission station of the Presbyterian Church (North); 3 missionaries and wives, 2 female missionaries, 1 school, 106 pupils.

2. The capital of the Turkish possession of same name in Africa (see Tripoli under Africa); has a population of 30,000. Mission station of the North Africa Mission (1887), with two missionaries, who do evangelistic and medical work. Living is cheap and the climate "splendid; not at all hot, rarely above 87°, never above 90°, Fahrenheit," and more laborers are greatly needed. (See North Africa Mission.)

**Trowbridge, Tillman Conklin,** b. Michigan, U. S. A., January 28th, 1831; studied at Romeo, Mich.; the University of Michigan, Ann Arbor; and Union Theological Seminary. Appointed missionary of the A. B. C. F. M. 1856, and sailed for Constantinople. He made a long tour with Rev. Mr. Dunmore through Northern Armenia. Returning to Constantinople in 1861, he married a daughter of Dr. Elias Riggs. He had charge of the city work of Constantinople for over six years, and in 1868 was transferred to Marash to assist in the instruction of the Theological Seminary. In 1872 he visited England and America to raise funds for the Central Turkey College decided upon for Aintab. Having prosecuted this work with vigor and success, he returned in 1876 to Aintab, and was appointed president of the college. From that time to his death, with the exception of a brief visit to England to solicit funds for the college, he devoted himself with energy to promoting its interests, as well as to the material, moral, and religious improvement of the people of Turkey. Having completed the college examinations and commencement exercises, he attended in July the annual meeting of the Central Turkey Mission at Marash in his usual health, and took part in the celebration of the Lord's Supper with apparent ease. In attempting to leave the room soon after the service, he found it difficult to walk, rapidly grew worse, and in less than half an hour his left side was wholly paralyzed, and he could utter only half-articulated mono-syllables. He died four days after, July 20th, 1888. The remains were taken to Aintab. "An immense congregation of all nationalities and religions listened attentively to the words spoken, and with many expressions of grief followed the body to the grave in the corner of the college grounds." Mr. Fuller of Aintab, speaking of his connection with the college, says: "In this work his wide acquaintance with influential, wealthy, and philanthropic men and women, his well-known integrity and good judgment, his quick and contagious sym-pathies, his unfailing cheerfulness and hope, his ready and tireless pen, and his persuasive voice have given him a wide and effective influ-ence; and it is not too much to say that the college owes a large share of its present position and hopeful prospects to the efforts he has made in its behalf." *

He received the degree of LL.D. from Michi-gan University.

**Tsakoma,** a town in North Transvaal, South Africa. Mission station of the Berlin Evangelical Lutheran Society (1874); 1 mis-sionary, 4 native helpers, 4 out-stations, 94 church-members, 31 scholars.

**Tschoutshun,** a town in Kwangtung, China, northwest of Swatow. Mission station of the Basle Missionary Society; 1 missionary and wife, 8 native helpers, 2 out-stations, 4 schools.

**Tsin-chau,** a prefectural city in the prov-ince of Kansuh, China, between Han Chung and Lan-chau. Mission station of the China Inland Mission (1878); 1 missionary and wife, 4 female missionaries, 1 native helper, 1 church, 28 church-members, 1 school, 20 scholars.

**Tsing-chau** (Tsing-chew-fu), a prefectural city in Shantung, China, east of the Hoang Ho, southwest of Cheefoo. Mission station of the Baptist Missionary Society; there are in the district 13 missionaries, 55 sub-stations, 1,023 communicants.

**Tsing-kiang-pu,** a station of the Presby-terian Church (South) in the northern part of Kiangsu, China, not far from the Yellow Sea. Medical work, evangelistic work in the country along the Grand Canal as far north as Shantung, and school work are energetically carried on by the 2 missionaries and their wives, 1 medical missionary, and 1 female missionary.

**Tsun-hua,** a city of the second class in Northeast China, in the province of Chihli, 60 miles east of Peking, on the great road to Man-churia. The city is reached by a railroad from Tien-tsin to the Kai-Ping Mines. Mission station of the Methodist Episcopal Church (North), opened in 1882; 3 missionaries and their wives, 1 female missionary, 4 native workers, 35 church-members, 1 school, 21 scholars. Be-

sides the evangelistic work, which extends over a large area, the medical work forms a prom-inent feature of this mission.

**Tuamotu,** a cluster of small islands east of the Society Islands, Polynesia; is visited by missionaries from the other islands of Polynesia. They were acquired by France in 1880, together with the Gambier Islands, and form part of the French establishments in Oceania. The two groups have an area of 390 square miles and a population of 5,946.

**Tukudh Version.**—The Tukudh belongs to the languages of North America, and is spoken by the Tukudh or Loucheux Indians, on the Yukon River, Alaska. The Rev. R. McDonald of the Church Missionary Society, for many years a missionary among these people, undertook a translation of the New Testament into their vernacular, of which the four Gospels with St. John's Epistles were published by the British and Foreign Bible Society at London in 1874. The printed parts were revised by the translator, and the remaining books of the New Testament translated, and an edition of the New Testament was issued by the same Society in 1885. Mr. McDonald is now engaged on a ver-sion of the Old Testament. As for the Indians who speak the language, and for whom the version is made, it may be stated that they are scattered over 100,000 square miles of a desolate region on the confines of the Arctic Circle. They have all been brought under Christian in-fluence, and baptized. Other tribes speak a cognate language, and the version will circulate among them. Up to March 31st, 1889, 4,886 portions of the Scriptures were disposed of.

*(Specimen verse. John 3 : 16.)*

Kwugguh yoo Vittukoochanchyo nunh kug kwikyit kettinizhin, tih Tinji chihthlug rzi kwuntlantshi chootyin tte yih kyinjizhit rsyet-tetgititelya kkwa, ko sheggu kwundui tettiya.

**Tulbagh,** a town in West Cape Colony, Africa, 75 miles northeast of Cape Town. Population, 548. Mission station of the Rhenish Missionary Society; 2 missionaries, 1 single lady, 8 native workers, 395 church-members, 184 day-scholars.

**Tulu Version.**—The Tulu belongs to the Dravidian family of non-Aryan languages, and is spoken in part of South Kanara, in the Ma-dras presidency, by about half a million of people. Till recently there was no literature in the Tulu language, except some legends, written on palm-leaves in the Malayalam char-acter. Mr. Grainer, one of the Basle mission-aries who landed at Bangalore in 1834, began a translation of the New Testament. He was afterwards aided by Messrs. Ammann and Bührer. An edition of the four Gospels was lithographed as soon as completed. The re-mainder of the New Testament was completed in 1847. Mr. Ammann revised his version in 1850, but the MS. was destroyed by fire. His subsequent version was printed in 1858. Inac-curacies in the edition made a revision necessary, and a revision committee was formed in 1884.

---

* Since the above was written news has been received of the destruction of a large portion of the buildings of Aintab College by fire. It is to be hoped that they will soon be rebuilt, as the college exerts a most important influence in that section of the Turk-ish Empire.

In 1888 the revised version was published, under the auspices of the Madras Auxiliary.

(*Specimen verse.* John 3 : 16.)

ರಾಯೆಗಂದಂದಾಳ್ಾ ಯತ ನಂಬನಾಯೆ ಯೆಕ್ಕಲ್ಲ
ನಾಕನಾರಮೋಂವಂಠೆ ನಿರ್ತ್ಯ ಜಿಟವಯ್ಯುತಾ ಯೆಲ್ಾರು.
ಮ್ಯಳ್ಕಿಕ್ಷ್ಣೇಲಿರಕೆನ ಭೂಂಿಯಾಂ ಡ ಮಟಿಮಗನ ಶಾಂಿಯೆ.
ಶಿಬಾಕ್ಾಳಕಯಂಚ್ೕ ಪ್ರೇಲಿಮಕೆ.

**Tumkur,** a town in Mysore district, Madras, India. Mission station of the Wesleyan Methodist Missionary Society (1857); 1 missionary, 1 assistant, 147 church-members, 5 Sunday-schools, 142 scholars, 17 day-schools, 1,048 scholars.

**Tunapuna,** a town in Northwestern Trinidad, due east from Port-of-Spain. Mission station of the Presbyterian Church of Scotland; 1 missionary, 65 scholars. (See Trinidad.)

**Tungcho.**—A city in Chihli, China, at the head of navigation on the Peiho, 13 miles east of Peking. Mission station of the A. B. C. F. M. (1867): 2 missionaries and wives, 1 physician and wife, 2 female missionaries, Gordon Memorial theological school, high school, 37 scholars, hospital and dispensary, 1 church, 110 church-members, 2 out-stations.

**Tungchow.**—A city in Shantung, China, on the coast of the Gulf of Chihli, 55 miles northwest of Chefoo. This city is one of the most healthy places for Europeans in China. Mission station of the Presbyterian Church (North), 1861; 5 missionaries and wives, 1 medical missionary and wife, 4 out-stations, 5 churches, 238 members, theological seminary, 15 students, 6 schools, 198 scholars. Southern Baptist Convention (1860), 3 female missionaries.

**Tuni,** a town and tract of country in Madras, India. Mission station of the Baptist Convention of Ontario and Quebec; 1 missionary and wife, 8 native preachers, 3 teachers, 5 Biblewomen, 1 church, 75 church-members, a girls' boarding-school.

**Tunis,** the capital of the country of the same name in Africa (see article on Africa), is situated on the western side of a lake which separates it from its port, Goletta. The population is estimated at from 100,000 to 145,000, of whom 20,000 are Europeans, the rest Moors, Arabs, Negroes, and Jews. Mission station of the North Africa Mission (1884); 2 missionaries and wives, 3 female missionaries. London Society for Propagating the Gospel among the Jews; 1 missionary, 1 school, 108 scholars.

**Tura,** a town among the Garo Hills, Assam, on the Brahmaputra River. Climate hot and unhealthy; 90° to 51° F. Population, 109,548. Race and language, Garo. Mission station American Baptist Missionary Union (1877); 2 missionaries and wives, 2 female missionaries, 17 native helpers, 40 out-stations, 10 churches, 1,168 church-members, a seminary for native teachers, 50 schools, 1,670 scholars.

**Turkestan,** or **Tartary,** are terms which have been loosely applied to all that part of Central Asia which lies east of the Caspian Sea, south of Siberia, west of Manchuria or China, and north of Tibet, India, Afghanistan, and Persia. These names are gradually falling into disuse as the formerly unknown plateaus and steppes of Central Asia are being more thoroughly explored, but the term Turkestan can still be retained as applying to that part of Central Asia which includes three divisions; (1) West Turkestan, (2) East Turkestan, and (3) Jungaria.

West Turkestan includes in its territory the highlands of Thian Shan, the plains of the Balkash, and the lowlands between the Aral and the Caspian Sea. It is divided into Russian Turkestan, including the provinces of Samarcand, Ferganah, Semirichensk, Syr-Daria, Khiva, Bokhara, and Kokhand; the Chinese oases of Kulja, and some parts of Afghan Turkestan. It includes an area of about 1,600,000 square miles, with a population estimated at 8,500,000, of which 793,032 square miles are in the Russian provinces or dependencies, having a population of over 3,500,000. The physical features of this large area vary greatly—from mountain peaks of perpetual snow, to deep gorges and valleys with every variety of climate and vegetation. Prairies and lowlands alternate with deserts, over which the dry winds, at times scorching hot, and then again icy cold, blow sand or snow, and blight all vegetation. The population of this territory is very mixed. Aryans and Mongols are both found, the former principally in the cities, while the latter are wandering tribes. To the Turanian group belong the Turcomans, Kirghiz, Uzbegs, and Sarts. The Mongolians include the Kalmucks and Torgoutes. To the Aryan race belong the Tajaks, who are Sunnite Mohammedans, Persians, British Indians, and Russians. The principal cities are Kokhand, Marghilan, Tashkend, Khojend, Bokhara, and Khiva. The two latter have each from 30,000 to 100,000 inhabitants.

East Turkestan includes that large depression in the plateau of Eastern Asia which lies between Western Turkestan and those parts of Asia which have received distinctive names, and whose boundaries have been defined. Its boundary on the northwest is the Thian Shan range; on the southwest and south the Kuenlun mountains; on the southeast to Lake Lob-nor, the Altyn-Dagh; and on the northeast the mountains which run east-northeast from the Thian Shan range. It includes a territory of about 465,000 square miles, with a population of 1,000,000, of which 431,800 square miles, with a population of 580,000, is part of the Chinese Empire. The climate is severe; there is no great fertility of the soil, and consequently the whole district is very sparsely populated. The few inhabitants are representatives of both the Aryan and Turanian groups of the human race. The Mongol element predominates towards the northeast. Turkish mixed with Chinese is the prevailing tongue. Yarkand and Kashgar are the chief towns.

Jungaria or Songaria lies to the north of East Turkestan, and is a deep valley leading from the lowlands to the central plateau. It includes 147,950 square miles, with a population of 600,000, and is a dependency of the Chinese Empire.

There are no missionary societies at work in Turkestan. The only Protestant work that is carried on is that by the B. and F. B. S. The Scriptures in whole or in part have been translated into the Kazan-Turki, Kazak-Turki, and Karass-Turki.

**Turkey,** or the Ottoman Empire, covers extensive territories of Southeastern Europe, Western Asia, Northern Africa, and the islands of the Eastern Mediterranean and Ægean Seas. In Europe and Africa, however, there are certain tributary states which are only nominally a part of the Empire, being either autonomous, or under the general supervision of European governments.

*Geographical Extent.* Taking first the Empire in its fullest sense, we notice,—

TURKEY IN EUROPE. This covers the extent of country stretching from the Adriatic Sea on the west, across the Balkan Peninsula, to the Black Sea on the east, and includes the districts of Albania, Macedonia, and Adrianople, and the Principality of Bulgaria, with Eastern Roumelia.

TURKEY IN ASIA is bounded on the north by the Black Sea, on the east by Russia (Trans-Caucasia) and Persia, on the south by the desert of Arabia, and on the west by the Mediterranean and Ægean Seas, and the straits of the Dardanelles and Bosphorus. Both eastern and southern boundaries are somewhat vague, the former because the two empires have not succeeded in drawing a satisfactory line through the mountains of Koordistan, the latter because of the very shadowy nature of the Sultan's authority over the tribes that roam the border land of Syria and Arabia.

TURKISH POSSESSIONS IN AFRICA. There is no definite Turkey in Africa, as in Asia and Europe, the Sultan's authority being limited to two countries, each quite distinct from the rest of his dominions: Egypt and Tripoli, including Barca and Fezzan.

ISLANDS IN THE EASTERN MEDITERRANEAN include the islands of the Archipelago, Crete and Cyprus. Crete and all the islands of the Archipelago, except Samos, are included in the tables among the Asiatic possessions. Samos is a tributary principality, with an area of 210 sq. miles. Cyprus, with 3,670 sq. miles, is under the British Government, which, however, pays an annual tribute to the Turkish Government, so that the island is fairly included in the Turkish Empire, using that term in its fullest sense.

Tabulating the whole we have the following:—

IMMEDIATE POSSESSIONS OF THE EMPIRE:

| | |
|---|---|
| Europe, | 63,850 |
| Asia, | 729,170 |
| Africa, | 398,873 |

1,191,893 sq. miles

TRIBUTARY STATES:

| | |
|---|---|
| Europe, | 37,860 |
| Africa, | 400,000 |
| Mediterranean, | 3,880 |

441,740

Total, 1,633,633 sq. miles

It should be remembered that estimates as prepared by different authorities differ very widely, owing partly to the diverse views held in regard to the political relations of the various sections, and partly to the absence of absolutely accurate measurements. In this article the figures are taken in the main from the Statesman's Year Book for 1890.

*Population.* Following the same general divisions as above, we find the totals as follows:

IMMEDIATE POSSESSIONS OF THE EMPIRE:

| | |
|---|---|
| Europe, | 4,790,000 |
| Asia, | 16,133,900 |
| Africa, | 1,000,000 |

21,923,900

TRIBUTARY STATES:

| | |
|---|---|
| Europe, | 3,154,375 |
| Africa, | 6,817,265 |
| Mediterranean, | 276,156 |

10,247,796

Total, 32,171,696

Here, too, mere estimates are possible. A census in the East is in a great degree an anomaly, and although the Turkish Government has taken two, its efforts have not been crowned with the greatest success. The fact that in some provinces, especially in Asiatic Turkey, the males were reported as 20–50% in excess of the females, indicates the great difficulty of the census taker. For a division of these totals among the different races and religions, see below.

*Divisions.* Albania, Arabia, Armenia, Bulgaria, Egypt, Koordistan, and Syria are described under their several heads.

EUROPEAN TURKEY comprises the provinces of Macedonia and Adrianople, the former being really a continuation of Albania, while the latter includes the great plains extending from the Rhodope to Constantinople.

ASIA MINOR, or Anatolia, consists almost entirely of high plateaus, varying from 150 to 300 miles in width, and about 4,000 feet above the level of the sea, extending from the Black Sea on the north to Armenia on the east, and Syria and Mesopotamia on the south.

*General Characteristics.* The natural barriers are rendered the stronger by the facts that the coast lines furnish almost no harbors, the mountains few passes, and those mostly difficult, while the deserts are practically unlimited. In the European and Northern Asiatic provinces, the country is mostly a high tableland, broken by ranges of mountains, and interspersed with alluvial river basins. South from the Taurus lie the great Mesopotamian and Syrian plains, following the course of the Euphrates and Tigris, while the Lebanon helps to raise the western coasts to a higher level. Egypt is one unbroken plain, and in Tripoli the rocks and desert seem to vie with each other as to which shall possess the land.

*Climate.* The Turkish Empire has every variety of climate, from the severe cold of the Balkans and the highlands of Armenia, to the almost equatorial heat of the Dead Sea and Bagdad. In the greater portion, however, it is temperate, not varying very much from that of corresponding sections of the United States. In general, Mesopotamia and Syria may be called hot, and the sections bordering upon them are affected in a great degree by the winds that blow over their plains. Northern and Eastern Asiatic Turkey feel the cold from the Black Sea and the snow-capped peaks of the Zagros. Central Asia Minor is temperate, its great plains being warm in summer and cold in winter, but day and night generally equal-

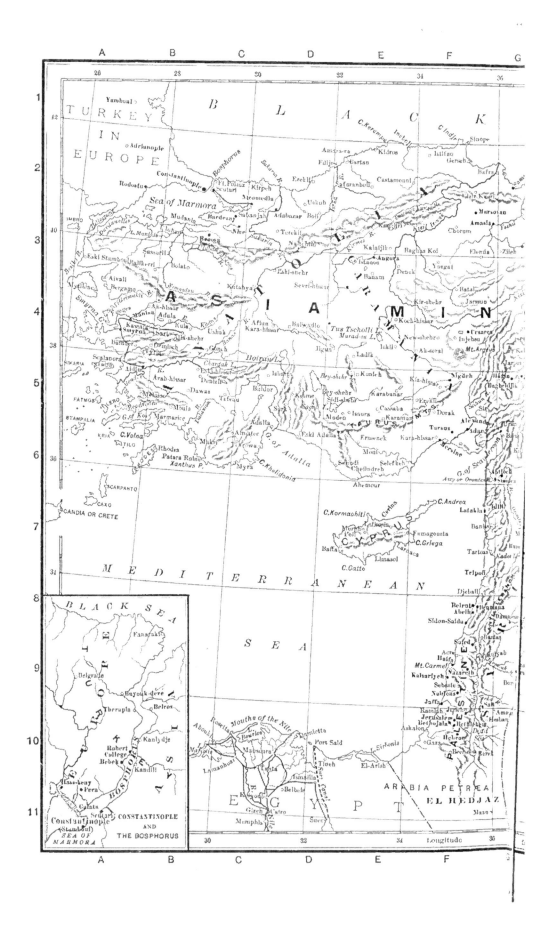

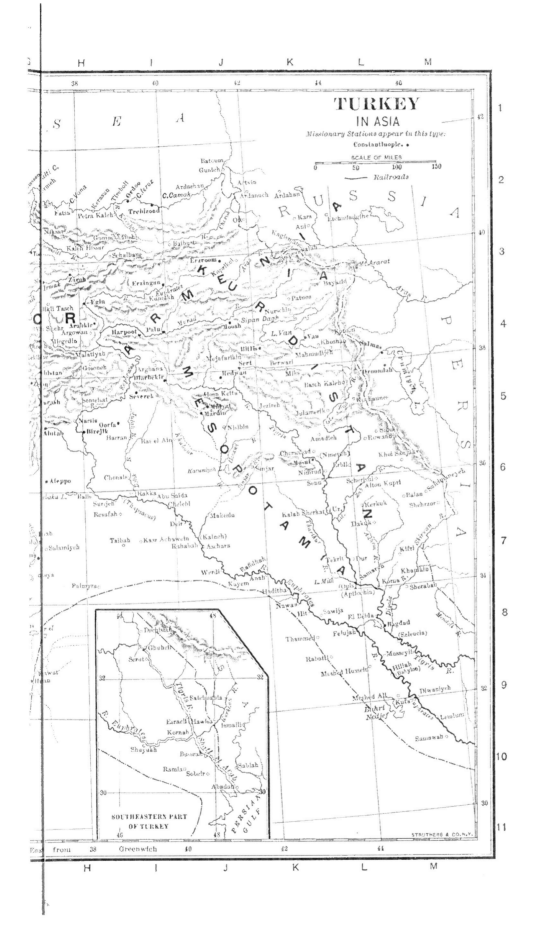

# TURKEY
## IN ASIA

Missionary Stations appear in this type:
Constantinople. •

SCALE OF MILES
0    50    100    150

⌣ Railroads

STRUTHERS & CO. N.Y.

SOUTHEASTERN PART
OF TURKEY

East from 38 Greenwich

izing the temperature. The same is true of European Turkey, where Salonica is the only city that can be called hot.

The climate is undoubtedly greatly affected by the almost entire absence of trees over the great plains and even most of the mountains. The soil having to a great degree been washed down into the plains and valleys, the hills and mountain sides are barren, and the reflection of the sun from them in summer is intense. Especially is this true in some places, as Aintab, Oorfa, Mardin, and Erzroom, where the summers are very hot. Wherever there is cultivation about the cities as at Van, Harpoot, Marsovan, Cesarea, there the climate is more equable. Constantinople is temperate, Smyrna is hot.

*Soil and Productions.* The Turkish Empire includes probably some of the most fertile land on the globe. From the plains of Bulgaria to the valleys of the Nile and the Tigris the soil is wonderfully rich. The people of a section of the great central table land of Asia Minor near Cesarea have a proverb: "If the world is hungry, Bozuk can satisfy it, but if Bozuk is hungry the world is not sufficient." The wheat of Bulgaria and Roumelia is well known in the markets of Europe, and America is finding dangerous rivals in Asia Minor and Mesopotamia, as means of communication make it profitable to bring their grain to the sea shore. Mesopotamia is especially rich, and any one who goes down the Tigris by raft and watches the line that marks the depth of the rich loam in the river banks will not wonder that empires succeeded each other with such rapidity in that whole section, or that the mountaineers of Persia looked with such longing eyes on the fields of Assyria. Aside from wheat there is a large amount of barley raised, and in Eastern Turkey a good deal of millet. Near the coast in northern Syria, and within Asia Minor, cotton is raised to some extent, and on the plains of Central Asia Minor there are large fields of poppies for the opium trade. The common vegetables are rice, cabbage, onion, turnip, and okra, but the potato is being largely introduced. Tobacco is cultivated everywhere, the best coming from northern Syria and European Turkey.

Turkey is especially rich in fruits. Grapes, melons, figs, olives, peaches, pears, quinces, pomegranates, dates, etc. are of the finest.

In European Turkey and the western parts of Asiatic Turkey there are large vineyards, and a considerable amount of wine is made. This is generally pure, and is very largely exported to Italy, France, and Austria, where it is fortified, and exported again as French and Italian wines.

Olive groves are especially abundant along the shores of the Mediterranean, and the fig orchards of Smyrna are famous. The dried fig of commerce is a somewhat different variety from the fresh fig that is so largely used by the people of the land. Dates are not found in numbers north of Egypt.

The only sections of forest in Turkey are on the Rhodope and Balkan Mountains in Europe, the shores of the Black Sea, the Zagros about Bitlis and Van, and a portion of the Taurus, and the valleys leading down to Alexandretta. In these forests there is still much fine timber, oak, walnut, and sycamore, but elsewhere almost the only trees, aside from the fruit trees, are the cypresses of the Moslem cemeteries, and the poplars and willows that line the streams and water courses near cities and villages.

By far the greater part of Asiatic Turkey is pasture-land, and wherever one goes he sees large flocks of sheep and goats generally making their way slowly towards the sea-coast, from the mountains of Koordistan and the plains of Mesopotamia.

The mineral wealth of Turkey is very great, but has never been developed, so that it remains still an unknown, scarcely even an estimated, quantity. Iron, copper, silver, baryta, coal, etc., are mined to a greater or less degree, but mostly in a crude, imperfect way. Foreign capital would gladly take up the business, but the hostility not only of the government, but of the people, is an almost insurmountable obstacle.

*Means of Communication.* Previous to the Crimean war, almost the only roads in Turkey were bridle paths, trodden smooth by the caravans of several centuries. In a few places remnants could be seen of old Roman causeways, but the huge blocks of stone, and the intervening pitfalls were shunned by all, except as the mire by the side was so deep as to be really impassable. In a few instances the Sultans, both Seljuk and Ottoman, made some efforts to repair these causeways, but they were seldom successful, and caravans were forced to find their own way over plains and mountain passes as best they might. Everything was carried on horses, mules, or camels, and such a thing as a cart or carriage was unknown. As the country, however, was opened up to foreign enterprise, one of the first things attempted was the building of roads over the great routes of travel. Of these there were five, four connecting the western coast with Bagdad, and one from Trebizond on the Black Sea, to Persia. The course they took was 1. Constantinople, via Nicomedia, Angora, Sivas, Diarbekir, Mardin, and Moosul. 2. Samsoon (on the Black Sea) via Amasia, Sivas, etc. 3. Smyrna, via Konia, Cesarea, Diarbekir. 4. Alexandretta, via Aleppo, Oorfa, Diarbekir. 5. Trebizond, via Erzroom and Van, to Khoi, and Tabriz. There were numerous other routes, and these varied somewhat, but in general they kept a straight course, and were those followed by caravans and travellers. Along all of these lines work was commenced in sections, but the sections seldom connected. There was little regard paid to culverts on the mountain roads, and the result was that the paths remained. Then a new element came in. After the overthrow of Schamyl (1859), the great Circassian leader, multitudes of Circassians found their way into Asia Minor, bringing with them the rough carts they had used in the Caucasus. These made roads for themselves, and gradually, as renewed pressure was brought to bear upon the Turkish government, road building was recommenced, so that now there are fairly good carriage roads from Trebizond to Erzroom, and from Samsoon to Diarbekir and Mardin; while in not a few places there are branches from these to important cities.

The first railroad in Asiatic Turkey, was from Smyrna to Aidin. That was followed by one from Smyrna to Manisa, and from Constantinople to Nicomedia, and one from Mersine to Adana. All of them have been somewhat extended, but not as yet to any great length.

In European Turkey the first railroad connected the Danube with the Black Sea at Kusteudji; that was followed by one between Varna and Roustchuk connecting with one to Bucharest and Vienna; one from Constantinople to Adrianople and Philippopolis, now extended to Sofia, Pirot, Alexinatz, Belgrade, Pesth, and Vienna; and one from Salonica to Uscup.

*Postal and Telegraph Arrangements:*—These are entirely in the hands of the Turkish Government as far as the interior is concerned, the mails being carried on horseback, under the escort of an armed guard. Considering the method of carriage the rates are not excessive. The telegraph bureau is fairly well managed.

The foreign postal service is a curious anomaly resulting from the peculiar treaty relations between Turkey and the various powers. According to the "Capitulations," each foreign community in the Empire has the right to its own postal communication with its own lands. So long as there was no regular Turkish service this was an absolute essential, and the English, French, Austrian, Russian, Italian, and Greek Governments established post-offices of their own in the various seaports, and sent their own bags of mail-matter. Previously this communication was simply with their own countries, but as the international postal system came into vogue, each post-office took mail-matter for every country in the Postal Union. By that time the Turkish Government also had organized a complete postal system, and as it had been admitted to the Postal Union it pressed its claim that the foreign post-offices should retire. Some of them did, but the majority have not as yet done so.

**Social Condition.** To describe in detail the mode of life of the people of Turkey is scarcely within the province of this work. The city life, approaching so nearly in its buildings, its customs, its dress, and food to that of Europe; the country life with its adobe houses, sometimes with a single room, sometimes more pretentions with its upper chambers; the tent life of the Koords,—have all been described over and over again. A few general statements will suffice here.

Except in the poorest parts of the Koordish mountains and in some of the villages of northern Syria, or Mesopotamia, the people live in comparative comfort. To be sure, what is ample for them seems to the foreigner a very meagre supply, but it is still true as a rule that they are in comfort so far as the supply of bodily needs is concerned. Their food is simple, but it is wholesome, and there is ordinarily enough of it. It is rarely the case that they suffer from hunger, except as drought and poor transportation cause famine. It is very seldom that the traveller fails to find bread, rice, milk, and some meat in even the smallest hamlet, or the poorest hut. Their houses are rough, their furniture scanty, their bedding and clothing coarse, but they serve usually to keep them warm. It is when sickness and old age bring weakness and distress that the discomforts principally appear. Taken as a class the Turkish peasant, whether Moslem or Christian, probably fares as well as the peasant class of any non-Christian land; in some respects he is better off. There are few if any in Turkey, even in the great cities, as wretched as are the miners of Europe or many of the poor of London.

If we look now to the relations of the different classes, we find them exceedingly democratic. There is no aristocracy in Turkey. There is absolutely nothing to hinder a farm-hand or a pedler from becoming Grand Vizier, if he be a Moslem, or Patriarch, if he be Armenian or Greek; and should he thus rise he will never find his low birth a cause of shame or regret. The castes of India are unknown, and equally so are the ceremonial laws of Persia, which forbid a Moslem to eat from the same dish as a Christian. In every part of the Empire there is the freest inter-communication between the different races, and between the different parts of the same race. Not that this inter-communication involves good feeling. The Turk despises the "dog of a Christian;" the Armenian hates the Greek; and the Jew, Nusairiyeh and Yezidee, are the contempt of all. Intermarriage between Moslems and Christians is unknown, except as a Christian girl is drawn into the harem of a wealthy Turk. There is no social intercourse of the families of different races, yet business relations and social courtesies between the men are common, and in that one is in most cases just as good as any other.

*Races.* The population of the Turkish Empire presents some very interesting features to the student and especially to the missionary. To trace back through the centuries the influences that have converged from all the surrounding countries, and have resulted in the races of to-day, would be beyond the limits of this article. We can only give a sketch of them as they exist.

In a general sense, the inhabitants of Turkey are either Mohammedan or Christian, and if we assume the population of the direct possessions of the empire to be about 22,000,000, we shall have about 16,000,000 Mohammedans and 6,000,000 Christians. Both Mohammedans and Christians, however, include widely different races. Greeks and Armenians are hardly more diverse than are Turks and Albanians; Jacobites and Bulgarians, are as little alike as are Koords and Kabyles. This great diversity gives rise to much of the misconception in regard to the country, its history, and its political relations. We note now these different races very briefly.

I. MOHAMMEDANS. 1. The Turks proper, or Ottomans or Osmanlis, as they call themselves. The word Turk is a general term applied almost indiscriminately to the general Tartar races, that from different sections of Central Asia, and at different periods have poured in upon the richer countries of Asia Minor and south-eastern Europe. They include the Ottomans, Seljuks, Turkomans, etc. We have to do now with that particular tribe of Ottomans or Osmanlis, so called from their leader Ottoman or Osman, who first established them in power, and whose tomb is one of the sacred places of the city of Broosa. As has been said, only estimates are possible, but if the number of Ottoman Turks be put at 9,000,000, it is probably not far from the truth. They are found chiefly in Asia Minor, comparatively few living in European Turkey, or in Koordistan, Mesopotamia, or Syria. The so-called Turks of European Turkey are mostly Albanians or Slavs who have accepted Islam, of Koordistan Koords, of Syria Syrians or Arabs. This fact should be distinctly kept in mind in forming an estimate of the Ottoman Turk. "The unspeakable Turk" of the Batak massacres in

Bulgaria was a Pomak, Moslem Bulgarian; of the Druze massacres of Syria an Arab. The Ottoman peasant of Asia Minor is a man far different from the ordinary conception. As a rule quite peacefully inclined, a hard worker, a faithful servant, courteous and dignified in his bearing, rather proud of his assumed superiority to the "meannesses of his Christian fellows," there is still an inherent element of ferocity in his nature, and when religious fanaticism is roused, his fatalism makes him a most dreaded enemy. The Ottoman of the city is, however, quite a different man; with as much Christian as Tartar blood in his veins, and influenced by the strife of Western with Eastern civilization, studiously polite, easily adapting himself to the circumstances of his associates, he develops a power of intrigue, a facility for deception, an unblushing delight in bribery that makes him the scorn of his sturdy compatriot of Anatolia. There are notable exceptions, but as a rule, and this is the testimony of those who have travelled most in the interior of Asiatic Turkey, the native unadulterated Ottoman Turk is a man with many noble characteristics, and presenting great possibilities for Christian influence. Of the other elements making up the Moslem population the most important races in Asia are the Arabs and Koords, in Europe the Albanians. They are spoken of more fully in the articles on Syria, Koordistan, and Albania. As a rule they are hostile to the Turks, feeling that the latter are oppressors, and even their recognition of the Sultan or Caliph is weakened by the race enmity and the sense of subjection. Next to them in importance are the Circassians, including the Circassians proper and the Lazes who have been driven by Russian rule from the Caucasus to Asia Minor. They furnish the most turbulent element of the population, and by far the greater amount of the depredations committed in Asia Minor are by them. There are also large numbers of Turkomans (another Turkish race), chiefly found in northern Syria. The Druzes and Nusairiyeh of Syria and the Yezidees of Mesopotamia are especially described under those headings. They probably represent the small remnant of the ancient paganism of the Levant which has accepted the form though not the spirit of Mohammedanism. The original races of Asia Minor are represented among the Mohammedans by a number of tribes, of somewhat uncertain extent and character, found chiefly in the mountains of the western part. Such are the Yuruks (or Nomads) of Bithynia, and the Xeibecks of the region of Smyrna. The Kabyles of Tripoli in Africa, of the Berber race (q.v.), are scarcely recognized as Turkish subjects.

II. CHRISTIANS. These include the Armenians, Greeks, Syrians, Jacobites, Copts, Bulgarians and Protestants. The Armenians are a race by themselves, as distinct to-day as at any time in their history. Formerly occupying the northeastern part of Asiatic Turkey, they have spread until they are found all over Asia Minor (see Armenia). The Greeks are found chiefly in western Asia Minor and along the shores of the Black Sea. They too have kept their race distinction very sharp, and retain many of the characteristics of their ancestors who founded the Euxine and Doric colonies. Sharp, keen in enterprise and speculation, the commerce of Turkey is largely in their hands,

while the traders and bankers are chiefly Armenians. Those in the interior are of a higher grade of character than those at the seaboard. The term Jacobite is distinctive of the remnants of the Monophysite Church found in northern Syria about Oorfa (Edessa) and through Mesopotamia. The term Syrian is often a very indefinite one, applied generally to all the Christians of Syria and Mesopotamia. Specifically it refers to those churches in communion with the Roman Catholic Church, such as the Maronites (q.v.), the United Greeks, and sometimes the Chaldeans, who are Jacobites that have left their old communion for the Romish Church. The term Syrian is also applied, though incorrectly, to the Assyrians or Nestorians who are found in the mountains of Koordistan. The Copts are found only in Egypt. The Bulgarians are a distinct race, occupying European Turkey. They belong to the Orthodox or Greek Church, but are independent of the Patriarch. Of these, the only ones whose race distinctions have been preserved are the Armenians, Greeks, and Bulgarians. The rest are not races, properly speaking, but religio-political divisions of the descendants of those of the original inhabitants who accepted Christianity under the rule of the Byzantine Empire.

The Protestants of Turkey can hardly be spoken of as a race, and would not be were it not for the peculiar system of government, which identifies religious and civil authority (see below). They number perhaps 50,000, and include members of all the races mentioned above, though the Armenian element is the largest. Other elements of the population are the Jews, found chiefly in the cities by the seaboard, the gypsies, and the Europeans. Of these there are large numbers, chiefly in Constantinople and Smyrna, though scattered more or less throughout the Empire.

*Languages.*—The languages of Turkey are Turkish, Arabic, Armenian, Greek, Koordish, Bulgarian and Albanian. The Turkish is the official language throughout the empire and is vernacular in Asia Minor and Southeastern European Turkey.

Arabic is spoken in Mesopotamia, Syria and Palestine, Northern Africa, and somewhat on the southern border of Asia Minor.

Armenian is used commonly by the Armenians wherever found except in some sections of Asia Minor, especially in the region of Cesarea, Konia and Adana, and in Northern Syria, Aintab and Marash, where Turkish is the language of every-day life, the Armenian being used only in the church services and schools. Even there, however, as education is progressing, Armenian is rapidly taking the place of the Turkish in the homes. Their use of the Turkish in conversation, together with the preservation of the Armenian as the literary and liturgical language, has given rise to what is often called Armeno-Turkish. This is simply Turkish written in the Armenian character, and differs from Osmanli-Turkish (Turkish as used by the Osmanlis and written in the Arabic character) merely in the use of certain distinctive names and phrases preserved from the Armenian, especially among the uneducated.

The Greeks of the Turkish Empire who live in the interior use chiefly the Turkish, employing however the Greek character in the same way that the Armenians use their own character. This Greco-Turkish, or Caramanlija (q.v.), as it is sometimes called, differs in practical use from the Osmanli-Turkish more than does the Armeno-Turkish, but is rapidly giving place to the use of the Greek language itself. The Greeks of the seaboard cities use Greek, though with varying inflections, so that one who is conversant with the language of Athens would find it difficult to understand or be understood in many of the towns and villages. In Turkey as well as in Greece there is, however, a constant tendency towards the ancient Greek, except in the intricacies of its syntax.

Koordish is spoken by the Koords in the mountains of Koordistan and wherever they are found in Asia Minor. (See Koordistan.)

Bulgarian is used in Bulgaria, and Albanian in Albania. (See those articles.)

In the seaports of the Mediterranean a great deal of Italian is spoken, and in the commercial and official world French is almost universal. German is often heard, and English is increasing in use everywhere.

The only one of these languages needing special mention here is the Turkish.

*The Turkish language* is a leading member of the Turanian or Ural-Altaic family, which is characterized by the preservation of the roots of words intact through all the changes of inflection and word-building effected by the addition of suffixes, and by a rigid rule of euphony which requires the quality of sound in the suffixes to agree with the quality of the sound of the root to which they are added. It is the language of Central Asia, whose origin is hidden in the misty past. But the Chinese annals of a time 2,500 years before Christ are said to contain the name Turk, while the Turkish vocabulary contains some words that can be identified as Chinese. The less developed character of the dialects of Turkish found in the far East, as well as the refinements of grammatical system which become more visible as the student moves westward, would seem to show that the language had its origin in the most eastern parts of Tartary and found growth and progress by means of that westward rush of the tribes which introduced the Turks to the knowledge of the European peoples.

The Turkish dialects of the present day may be roughly classed in three great groups: the Eastern or Ouighour, the Central or Jagatai, and the Western or Osmanli. While the dialects of these groups differ from each other materially in grammar and vocabulary, the names of mountains and rivers found on the map of Asia from China to the Black Sea, and from the Arctic Ocean to the Himalayas, often carry meaning to the mind of one who knows any one of the Turkish dialects. In fact it has been said, almost without exaggeration, that one may travel with the Turkish language from the Adriatic Sea to the Chinese frontier, and be sure of making his ordinary wants everywhere understood.

The alphabet now used for writing the Turkish language is the Arabic-Persian alphabet, to which the Western Turks have added one modified character peculiar to themselves. The earliest Turkish manuscripts are written in the Ouighour alphabet, now obsolete, which by some is supposed to have been derived from the Syriac through the Nestorian missionaries of the ninth and tenth centuries. The Arabic-Persian alphabet does not satisfy the Turkish need for the expression of vowel sounds, and

Turkish scholars sometimes use its characters for this purpose in ways quite unacceptable to the Arabic writers. In Russia some Turkish tribes write their language with the Russian characters, while in Asiatic Turkey, Greeks and Armenians who have lost their own vernacular and use the Turkish language alone, write it with the Greek and Armenian alphabets respectively.

The Turkish vocabulary is of limited extent, suggesting the limited range of ideas of pastoral peoples. All the dialects borrow freely from the Persian and Arabic languages. In the Osmanli Turkish, used in the Turkish Empire, this appropriation of Persian and Arabic words and even phrases has been carried to a degree which has raised its classical literature far above the comprehension of the unlearned, and has even sometimes threatened to destroy the very basis of the language. Of late years, however, the revival of the use of purely Turkish words by the best writers has brought the literary language back within the grasp of the masses. The words adopted by the Osmanli Turkish from European languages have a close relation to the history of the Ottoman Empire. Names of winds, currents, fishes, etc., often come from the Greeks who had possession of the coasts seized by the Turks; those of whatever relates to the sailor's craft commonly have an Italian origin, the Genoese and Venetians having been the instructors of the Turks in naval enterprise; words relating to the fine arts and to etiquette often come from the French, while names of machinery bear the impress of English origin.

In etymology the Turkish is remarkable for the regularity of its declensions and conjugations, and for the abundance of the forms of the verb, especially in the Osmanli Turkish. There is, properly speaking, but one conjugation of verbs. In the Eastern Turkish dialects there is no auxiliary verb and hence the compound tenses lack. But in the Osmanli Turkish the verb is conjugated in great fullness of moods and tenses, with great abundance of participial forms and verbal nouns. Moreover, by the incorporation of certain particles the simple verb may give rise to new verbs signifying a reflexive and a reciprocal quality of action. Each of these verbs, whether simple or reflexive or reciprocal, may take another particle and form a second series of new verbs signifying the causing of the action implied by the verbs of the first series. A second causative particle may still be incorporated in the verbs of the second series, giving a third series of new verbs with the signification of the causing another to cause the action implied by the verbs of the first series. And finally, by use of the appropriate particle with each of the verbs of the three series, each one is made to produce a new verb with a negative and one with an impossible signification. Each simple verb may thus give rise to 26 new verbs, each of which can be conjugated in all the moods and tenses, and in the active and passive voices exactly on the model of the simple verb. The variety and compactness of expression thus secured is extraordinary. For instance, the sentence "I was not able to have [them] made to love each other" can be expressed in Turkish by the one word *sevishtirtemedim*, formed from the simple verb *sevmek* [to love] by a rule so regular that any one knowing the rule and the root *sev* [love] can understand with precision the meaning of the word even if he has not previously met with it.

The principle of agglutination here illustrated has its application also in the formation of adjectives, adverbs, and nouns, giving great breadth of expression in the use of the somewhat limited vocabulary. Most pronouns and all prepositions in Turkish are used in accordance with the same principle, following the noun which they limit as suffixes and having a regular place in the building of the word.

The Turkish language lacks the relative pronoun and the article. It has neither gender nor declension of adjectves, and is also defective in the comparison of adjectives.

In syntax the characteristic of the Turkish is that while the subject occurs at or near the commencement of a sentence, the sense is held in long suspense while qualifying phrases and sentences giving particulars of the most diverse description are brought in, the verb of the predicate, which stands at the very end of all, serving as the key to the whole enigma.

*Religions.*—The religions of the Turkish Empire have been specially noticed under the articles Albania, Armenia, Bulgaria, Koordistan, Maronites, Mohammedanism, Nusairiyeh, Yezidees. It remains here to note merely the Greek, Roman Catholic, and Protestant churches.

The Greek, or Orthodox, church is the direct descendant of the Byzantine church. In general doctrine, as found in the creeds and confessions, it is in sympathy with the Protestant church, and only separated from the Armenian by a distinction so shadowy that it is claimed by some Armenians that the theological difference was a pretext, rather than an occasion, for the separation, the real reason lying in the effort of the Byzantine church to compel the Armenians to use the Greek liturgy. However that may be, it is certain that the age of theological controversy between the different Oriental churches has passed. The question now is not of "one Nature or two," "one Will or two," but of nationality. Under the rule of the Moslem Caliph every Christian sect has become a native, and every apostate is also a traitor, (see paragraph—"The Government of Turkey"—below). The position of the Greek church in Turkey is thus primarily political. In its religious aspect it is practically on a par with its fellows, and a stranger could hardly tell the difference between the services of each.

Ecclesiastically the Patriarch of Constantinople is the head of the Church in all its different branches, but the Holy Synods of Russia, Greece, and Servia practically ignore him, while the Patriarch of Jerusalem and the Exarch of Bulgaria render a very shadowy reverence to his precedence. In fact the Greek church of to-day is split up into fragments, each fragment claiming absolute independence, and each characterized by the same formalism and absence of spiritual life.

The Roman Catholics of Turkey, aside from the Maronites (q.v.), include sections of the Armenians, Greeks (Uniats), and Syrians (Chaldeans), who, chiefly for political reasons, have made their peace with the Papacy. They have succeeded, by special dispensation from the Pope, in preserving the use of their national language in their liturgy, in return for

their political support, and, except in the dress of their priests, are not distinguishable from their fellows of the old faiths.

The Protestantism of Turkey needs no special description, following as it does closely in the lines of the churches of America and England. Except in rare cases there is little emphasis laid upon creeds. Of the doctrines, perhaps the one that is most prominent is the one that Luther pressed so hard—Justification by Faith—and for the same reason. There has been no effort to establish new dogmas. The new church was a civil even more than a religious necessity. In most cases every effort has been made to avoid antagonism to the old churches, in the belief that the emphasis laid upon truth would crowd out the error. The Protestant churches of Turkey are distinguished from the old churches rather by their conception of sin, its character and heinousness, the absolute necessity of a change of life, and the idea of individual communion with Christ, as a personal Redeemer and Saviour, than by elaborate creeds or confessions. Church services take on the non-liturgical form, partly because that has been the habit of the missionaries, partly because of the natural repulsion of the soul, awakened to a sense of its personal need, to a ritual where personality was lost in forms that had practically lost their meaning.

*Government.*—The Government of Turkey is often called "Theocratic." In the sense that the Sultan as Caliph is the head of the Moslem religion, as well as of the Turkish Empire, and that all civil authority centres in the ecclesiastical, this is correct. Mohammed claimed to derive his power from God by special dispensation through the Archangel Gabriel, and committed his authority to the Caliphs, whose descendant or representative is the Sultan. But as for any personal relations between the Sultan and Deity, they are no more than those of the meanest of his subjects. He is the representative of divine authority, but by no means its medium. To apply the term "theocratic" to it as to the Mosaic government is incorrect.

Both theoretically and practically the Sultan is the head of the government. He has the usual number of Ministers, each responsible for the minutiæ of his special department of Foreign Affairs, The Interior, Finance, Commerce, War, Marine, Public Instruction, and Evkaf, all presided over by the Grand Vizier; but any question may be referred to him, and he keeps his eye on all the different lines of governmental policy. So too the Sheik ul Islam and the Ulema guide the affairs of the church, under his supervision, and, whether in civil or ecclesiastical affairs, the Palace is constantly a most potent factor, liable at any moment to interfere with the best-laid plans of subordinates, and assume direct control even of the minutiæ of administration. That administration, in its civil department, is in general on much the same plan as that of the European governments, at least in the cities of the seaboard. The interior is divided into provinces, whose boundaries are indefinite and constantly modified to suit political exigencies of many kinds.

Side by side with the civil administration are the judicial and ecclesiastical, and the three are often so intermingled that it is impossible to separate between them. The judicial is based in some respects upon the Code Napoleon, but in others on the Che'ri or law of the Koran, and where one ends and the other begins it is impossible to decide. Especially does this intermingling become manifest in questions affecting real estate. All landed properties in Turkey are in general divided into two parts, *mulk* and *vacouf*. The former corresponds very nearly to freehold, the latter pays rent to some mosque, or "pious foundation" of some sort, either directly or indirectly through some beneficiary. The former is transferable in full, the latter only on condition of payment of the vacouf tax, which also carries with it certain restrictions, imposed by the ecclesiastico-judicial laws of the empire. Mulk can be made vacouf at any time by the act of the owner, but vacouf can be made mulk only by securing an exchange with some other piece of equally valuable property or by the payment of a sum of money which shall represent the continued payment of the tax. It will be readily seen what an opportunity is thus offered to those who would hinder or prevent the erection of buildings for missionary purposes, or even the building of a church or school for native Protestants, in places where the local authorities, whether Moslem or Christian, are opposed. That so much has been accomplished in this line is a great tribute to the wisdom and patience of both missionaries and natives.

The peculiar relations between the Moslem Government and the Christian communities, and between the different Christian communities themselves, offer special perplexities. When the Moslem conquered Constantinople, the question arose of his relations to his Christian subjects who refused his faith. To put them to the sword was not only practically impossible, but would deprive the government of much income. It was the natural way for the Moslem to consider that he must deal with them through their religious chiefs, and hence the ecclesiastical rulers of the different sects were appointed their civil representatives. At the same time the special right to judge concerning all relations in any way coming under ecclesiastical jurisdiction was committed to their representatives, and the result was that, except for purposes of general taxation, the Turkish Christian subjects formed nations as distinct from each other as from their Moslem rulers. These distinctions it has been the constant effort of the government to gradually obliterate, and to bring all alike under the full control of the distinctively Turkish courts.

The position of foreigners in Turkey has been somewhat peculiar. When the first treaties were made between Christian governments and the Sublime Porte, the question of jurisdiction over foreign residents was solved by clauses appended to the treaties making such residents amenable solely to their own consular courts. Special privileges of introduction of articles for personal use, of the enjoyment of certain customs, etc., were allowed, and in general the foreigner was absolutely independent in his person and personal property of the Turkish officials. No police officer could lay hands on him, or even enter his door, except as he received special authorization from the consul of the country to which he belonged, and no Turkish court could summon him to its bar. During the first part of the present century the "capitulations," as these clauses were called, continued in full force, but of late they are

gradually being either disregarded or repealed, the Turkish Government claiming that foreigners in its land have the same rights, and no others, that a Turk has in other lands.

*History.*—The history of Turkey is of the utmost importance to the student of Christian missions. Only by a careful survey of it from the time when the Byzantine Empire commenced to decay can he understand how the present condition is but the crystallization of conditions that existed many centuries ago. The capture of Constantinople by the Turks, and the establishment of the internal regulation of the empire on the basis of an absolute union of church and state, or rather of an absorption of the state by the church, for not only the Moslem but the Christian, acted upon the social, civil, and religious condition of the land like a sudden petrifying power, and when the present century opened it found a country which had practically slept for nearly four centuries. The modern era of Turkish history, which is all that space and the general purpose of this article will allow, commences with the reign of Mahmoud II. (1808). More than any, perhaps, of his predecessors, Mahmoud realized the trend of modern progress, and he understood very clearly the situation in which he found his empire. Napoleon had just uttered his famous prediction that Europe was destined to be either all Cossack or all Republican. The French Revolution on the west, Russian aggression on the east, were stirring influences that he felt must be fatal unless they could be checked. Internally there was commotion. The Janissaries had ruled so long that the upturning of their kettles was a more serious affair than a death in the Palace. The feudal chiefs of Asia Minor were growing more and more restive, and the army was in danger of disorganization, through their refusal to send recruits to the order of the Sultan. Greece was feeling the impulse of the strife for freedom. Mohammed Ali was laying the foundation of his power in Egypt, while Albania was practically independent under Ali Pasha of Janina. A less vigorous, indefatigable, progressive man would have succumbed, and the Cossack would have carried the day. Mahmoud set himself to his task with courage, but the forces against him were too strong. He succeeded in overpowering the Janissaries, reorganized his army, and successfully withstood an attack from Russia; but England and France interfered and forced upon him the Treaty of London, 1827, and the Treaty of Adrianople, 1829. Greece was declared free, and the Danubian Principalities were placed under the protection of Russia. Meanwhile Mohammed Ali was increasing in power. The traditional hostility of England and France manifested itself more and more in the Mediterranean. France espoused the cause of the Pasha, while England supported the Sultan. The rivalry became open war, and the Albanian leader threatened the very existence of the Turkish Empire. Just at this crisis Mahmoud died (1839), leaving the Caliph's sword to his oldest son Abd ul Medjid, an amiable but weak and irresolute man. England and France saw at once that the danger foreseen by Napoleon was upon them. The "Cossack" was an immediate probability, the "Republican" (Louis Philippe was then reigning) a remote possibility. Accordingly they united their forces, and by the treaty of 1841 confirmed Mohammed Ali in the possession of Egypt as vassal to the Sultan, and assumed a European protectorate over the Turkish Empire.

No sooner was this settled than intrigues opened again. England, realizing the necessity of the situation as affecting her relations with India, placed one of her strongest men at Constantinople. Sir Stratford Canning (afterwards Viscount Stratford de Redcliffe) was an able, far-sighted, truly Christian man. Not only did he comprehend the general political bearings of the situation, but he understood clearly their social, civil, and religious relations. He realized that for the Christian races of Turkey it was in a sense a choice between two evils—the despotism of a weak Sultan amenable to influence and under obligation to Christian nations, or that of the Czar, secure in his position and utterly beyond the reach of any motives except those of aggrandizement of empire. With marvellous patience and skill he set himself to his task of strengthening his hold upon the Sultan. French and Russian ambassadors alike had to yield to the great "Elchi," as he was called. One after another, reforms were introduced. The Hatti Sherif of Gulhané announced the speedy establishment of institutions "which should insure to all the subjects of the Sultan perfect security for their lives, their homes, and their property, a regular method of collecting the taxes, and an equally regular method of recruiting the army and fixing the duration of service." But proclamation was one thing, enforcement another. Palace intrigues supplemented those of Russia. The Turkish officials saw their opportunities for oppression and bribery disappearing, and offered to the new reforms an Oriental shrug when they did not positively refuse obedience. Genuine advance was, however, made. Torture and the death-penalty for apostasy from Islam were abolished, and the bastinado was forbidden in the schools and finally in the army. Christian evidence in courts of law was rendered legal, if not always actual, and there appeared possibilities for the future where hitherto there had been absolutely no hope. Then came the stirring scenes of 1848 and 1849. Kossuth and some associates took refuge with the Porte, which refused to give them up to the power that had crushed the Magyar government. Nicholas, flushed with his victory, looked forward to the speedy extinction of Turkey, and in 1853 proposed to the British ambassador at St. Petersburg a plan for the division of "the Sick Man's" inheritance as soon as he should expire, and claimed the right of a protectorate over the (then 12,000,000) Christian subjects of the Sultan. This was naturally objected to by the Porte, and was followed by the entrance of the Russian army into the Danubian principalities. England took up the side of Turkey, and France, angered by the Russian claims in a contest between Latin and Greek priests in Jerusalem, added her forces to those of the Sultan, while Sardinia took her place for the first time as one of the allied powers. Austria also entered the Danubian principalities with her army, and hostilities were transferred to the Crimea. The victory of the allied powers resulted in the Treaty of Paris, which affirmed the neutrality of the Black Sea, the independence and integrity of Turkey, abolished the

Russian protectorate over the Danubian principalities, closed the Bosphorus and Dardanelles to foreign ships of war while the Porte was at peace, and emphasized the principles of the Hatti Humayoun, guaranteeing complete religious liberty and the carrying out of the reforms already promulgated, but leaving the administration entirely to the Porte, and forbidding all foreign interference.

In 1858 Lord Stratford was replaced by Sir Henry Bulwer, and English influence at the Porte rapidly lessened. Then commenced a time of national extravagance. Hitherto Turkey had been an almost unknown factor in the markets and Bourses of Europe, but now investors began to crowd in. The adoption of the Code Napoleon in civil courts, and the introduction of customs revenues, etc., necessitated the employment of vast numbers of Europeans, who looked upon the Turks as legitimate prey. Financial propositions of every sort were made; bonds were offered for sale, and the government was fairly launched upon a course of financial management to which it was an utter stranger. When Abd ul Medjid came to the throne he had reversed the usual custom of his ancestors, and spared the life of his brother, Abd ul Aziz; and he on the death of Medjid, in 1861, became Sultan. A morose, selfish man, bent upon gratifying every whim of the moment, he lent a ready ear to the adventurers that thronged Constantinople. Palaces, public buildings of various kinds, sprang up on every hand. A fleet was necessary and it was furnished, while contractors in every department grew rich at the expense of the government, which, elated by the hitherto unheard-of possibility of borrowing unlimited sums of money, on which only interest was payable, went into the wildest extravagancies. Meanwhile the Druze massacres of 1860 had resulted in the French occupation of Syria. Wallachia and Moldavia united in the kingdom of Roumania, and Servia became independent. The Russian Embassy was practically supreme, Sir Henry Bulwer, Sir Henry Austin Layard, and Sir Henry Elliott being utterly unable to cope with Count Ignatieff. The year 1869 saw the completion of the Suez Canal, intensifying England's interest in keeping her connections with India clear, and the collapse of France in the war of 1870 made it possible for Lord Beaconsfield to secure from the feeble Khedive a controlling interest in that great water-way. The abuses rife on every side increased. Internal politics developed two parties, Old Turkey and New Turkey, the former entirely under Russian influence, the latter siding with England. The leader of the latter, Midhat Pasha, an energetic, shrewd man, contrived a plot to replace Abd ul Aziz by his nephew Murad (eldest son of Abd ul Medjid). A deliverance (*fetwah*) was secured from the Sheik ul Islam to the effect that a Caliph who ceased to be capable of reigning could be deposed. There was no question about the incapability of Abd ul Aziz, and the revolution was easily carried through. But Murad was even less capable, and in three months gave place (May, 1876) to his brother, Abd ul Hamid II., the present Sultan. Midhat and his associates were exiled, and Old Turkey remained in the ascendency. Numerous efforts were made to secure genuine reform, but in vain. Revolt in Bosnia and Herzegovina spread to Bulgaria, and the Bulgarian massacres gave Russia the pretext for entering the Balkans in 1877. England held aloof, stipulating the neutrality of Egypt. Austria had received her price in Bosnia and Herzegovina, and Russia met Turkey alone. The campaign of the Balkans resulted in placing Constantinople at the mercy of the Czar, and the Treaty of San Stefano made Russia supreme in the Balkan peninsula, and gave her a strong hold on eastern Turkey. This was more than England and Austria could stand. The British fleet entered the Marmora, covering with its guns the Russian camp at San Stefano. Austria gave tokens of hostility, and Russia, ill prepared for a general European war, consented to the Conference of Berlin. This granted the independence of Bulgaria (q. v.), assured Bosnia and Herzegovina to Austria, enlarged the borders of Greece, regained a portion of Eastern Turkey for the Sultan, and guaranteed internal reforms, especially for the Armenians.

Since then there have been no great changes except that Eastern Roumelia was joined to Bulgaria in 1885, and Prince Alexander, who proved not as amenable to Russian influence as was desired, was seized, forced to abdicate, and was replaced by Prince Ferdinand. (See Bulgaria.)

The present (March, 1891) condition of the "Eastern Question," which is still voiced by the famous prophecy of Napoleon, may be briefly summed up.

1st. Internal. The ruling influences among the Turks represent neither of the parties of a few years ago. Taking as his motto "Turkey for the Turks," the Sultan, with a patience, skill, and persistence that mark him as a most important factor in the politics of the day, is endeavoring by every means in his power to strengthen the Turkish as distinct from the Christian element. Christian officials are less and less in favor. Advances are made wherever they seem likely to strengthen Islam, or when they are so vigorously pressed that refusal is unsafe. Little by little the concessions wrung by early treaties, or guaranteed by arrangements many centuries old, are being quietly forgotten or slipped aside in an unnoticeable way. Recognizing that the time of rule in Europe may be limited, and that Asiatic Turkey must be their home, everything is made to tend toward the development of distinctive Moslem rule in that section. Sections that have been distinctively Christian are being occupied by Moslems. The Koords are extending until they are found all through the mountainous regions even of Asia Minor. Circassians and Lazes are located on the plains, and all are suffered with little or no hindrance to persecute, hamper, and distress the Christians, with the evident desire of making them as weak an element in the country as possible. These disturbing forces, however, are by no means always under the control of the government. There is no love lost between the Ottomans and their subject Moslems, not a few of whom are looking forward to a time when the Turk shall be forced to recognize them at least as equals. Of these the Koordish element is undoubtedly the most vigorous. It has representatives high in office in Constantinople, who are ambitious not merely for Islam but for their own race.

The Christians are in a state of turmoil and unrest. Naturally exasperated by the continued refusal or failure of the government to grant the reforms that have been promised, feeling more keenly the oppression they suffer (even though it be no worse than of old, if indeed as bad), watching with envious eyes the success that has crowned the efforts of Bulgaria, the Armenians besiege Europe with claims for protection. Regardless of the fact that there is scarcely a section of the empire where they are not in an actual minority, certain agitators, for the most part outside of the country, keep up the demand for an autonomous Armenia. Most of the people, feeling the impossibility of this, are content with improving their condition as best they can, protesting against real abuses, of which there is a full supply, and deprecating the conflicts which invariably end in the weakening those who are already weak, and strengthening the strong. Among the Greeks there is less of commotion, though a no less careful and jealous watch is kept upon the efforts of the Turkish Government to deprive them of rights accorded to their church when Mohammed II. captured Constantinople, and assured to them repeatedly by his successors. The Protestants, both Armenian and Greek, recognize the importance to them of the changes that may take place at any time, but hold themselves quiet, not undertaking the impossible; strengthening themselves, careful to accord to law and to avoid every appearance of hostility, while claiming in full the rights that belong to them. Meanwhile certain influences are at work among every class, modifying each, sometimes silently, but not the less surely; often unnoticed, yet which at no distant day may be most potent factors in the political situation.

Of these the most prominent perhaps is Education. The presence of Robert College on the Bosphorus, the American College for Girls in Scutari, the Syrian Protestant College at Beirut, and the many others through Asia Minor, have had a mighty influence in stirring the popular demand, until there is not a city in the empire, scarcely a town or village, where there is not a certain amount of education. This education is not always thorough or complete, but it is opening the eyes of the people to truths that have hitherto been unrecognized, and no efforts of ecclesiastics or government officials can close them. The wide use of the French language has occasioned a great influx of French literature and French phrases, and it is not infrequent to hear some Armenian Greek, or even Turk, boast of being a "libre penseur." Free-thinking is spreading, and with it the ideas of modern socialism. As yet confined chiefly to the cities of the seaboard, they are spreading into the cities and towns of the interior, and are exerting an influence which it is impossible to measure but which is not less potent.

Next to education as a very positive element in influencing the political condition of all classes of the empire is the introduction of European modes of life. The change in this respect is most marked; and though detailed notice is out of place here, the fact that the Oriental simplicity of manners, from which has come in no small degree the vigor of the Ottoman race, is fast becoming a thing of the past, is of most practical import. Parallel with these is the growth of infidelity. This will be especially noticed below, under the head of

Mission Work, but it should be mentioned here as a most important element in politics. The condition of the Turkish Empire, both Moslem and Christian (except the Protestant), is rapidly assuming the complexion of the late Roman Empire. Religion is a good thing for the masses, but for the educated, the leaders, it really has no existence. It continues only as a political bond. In the consciousness of this among the more sincere Mohammedans of Koordistan, Arabia, and Africa lies the ground for such movements as those of the Mahdi, declaring that the Caliph has fallen from his high estate and no longer deserves to hold his position. But not only of the Turk is this true, it is true also of the members of the so-called Oriental churches, Armenians, Greeks, Jacobites, etc. The spirit of nationalism that has grown up within their church life has crowded out in a great measure the spirit of religion, but has brought with it a feeling of contempt for all spiritual life. Thus there is little or no power of real patriotism. They are glad to get outside help if they can, but have in the past been willing to do little or nothing for themselves.

The internal aspect of the Eastern Question then is practically this. The dominant race is straining every nerve to strengthen its hold upon the country, but has largely lost those elements of strength that formed the basis of its early growth, without replacing them by others.

The subject races, divided among themselves, grasping at anything that seems to offer them any help, are waiting, sometimes patiently, sometimes impatiently for the action of the European Powers.

2d. External or European. The Eastern Question as it affects the European Powers has always presented many phases, somewhat complicated, and not infrequently contradictory, according as they are regarded from different standpoints or at different times, which, however, need not be remotely apart. Indeed so shifting are these phases that a statement which is true one day may be very incomplete and unsatisfactory a week later.

The most important single factor is unquestionably Russia. The intentions of the Czar have always been a matter of much discussion. It has been positively affirmed and as vehemently denied that he meditates absorbing the whole Turkish Empire, and cutting off England's connections with India by the Red Sea, while he proposes to make Afghanistan a passage-way to the Punjab. Whatever may be said of these ultimate designs, there has been little doubt of his desire to hold Constantinople, make the Black Sea an inland lake, and utilize the power thus gained to dominate the Mediterranean. The course of events in Bulgaria, Servia, Montenegro, and Greece indicate very clearly that what he failed to secure at Berlin he is striving hard to accomplish by other means. The officering of the Bulgarian army with Russians, and the sudden withdrawal of them all just as Servia had commenced an unprovoked attack; the abduction of Prince Alexander; the repeated snubs to Prince Ferdinand, and the numerous plots against his life; the support of the claims of Karageorgevitch in Servia, indicate very clearly the desire of the Russian Government. It is also claimed, and is positively believed by many, that the repeated disturbances in Erzroom, Con-

stantinople, and Crete have been fomented, if not immediately by Russian agents, at least by committees of Armenians and Greeks acting in concert with Russians. That Russia would at any time within the past five years (1886-1891) have made war had she felt that the time was propitious, and for the purpose of capturing Constantinople and extending her boundaries in Eastern Turkey, hardly admits of a question with most. Russia may thus be considered the radical element.

The conservative elements are England, Austria, Germany, Italy, and Bulgaria.

(1) England. The interest of England in the Eastern Question is primarily occasioned by her commercial relations. For Russia to hold the Bosphorus and the Dardanelles would be a most serious menace to English commerce. Even supposing that Russia cares nothing for India, should any difficulty arise between the two Powers, Russia would be able within thirty-six hours, without any warning, to completely paralyze all passage through the Suez Canal, and render even Malta useless for defence. The far-reaching effects of this need not be detailed. There are other elements—British investments in Turkish securities; interest in the people of Turkey, especially the Christians, whom she would most unwillingly see under the thrall of the Czar; there is also the general importance of not allowing such a preponderance in the counsels of Europe to any one government.

(2) Austria. With Austria it is a life and death struggle. The peculiar composition of the political family over which the House of Hapsburg reigns is such that to seriously disturb the balance kept with such difficulty would destroy the whole. Any one who has read the accounts of the Czech movement, centring in Prague in Bohemia, will easily see that to bring a great Slav Power to the very border of the empire would produce a disturbance that would break the empire to pieces. But not only is there the Czech element in the North. There are other kindred races—the Lansatian-Serbs, Slovaks, etc.—that would inevitably be drawn in. Hungary would be almost alone, and the Magyars would feel again the iron heel of the Czar.

(3) Germany. While Germany would not be affected immediately in her territorial possessions by the Czar's conquest of Constantinople, she would feel very much the overwhelming power that such occupation would give. With Austria gone, Germany could hardly hold her own against Russia in any case of rival interests, while liable more than ever to French reprisals. Her interest is a general rather than a specific one.

(4) Italy's interest in the Eastern Question is occasioned by her great coast-line, which would be entirely at the mercy of a Power that could mass a great navy securely behind the Dardanelles, and could hurl it in a few hours at almost any portion of her coast.

(5) Bulgaria. With Bulgaria even more than with Austria it is a question of life or death. When the Treaty of Berlin was signed, Russia was looked upon by the Bulgarians as their national benefactor, and there was no feeling but of profound gratitude. With the course of events, however, that feeling has changed to one of bitter hostility. As it has become evident that, however much the people of Russia may have desired the freedom of the Bulgarian from the Turkish yoke for their own sake, the

Russian government looked upon it simply as a means to an end, and that a purely selfish end, the Bulgarians felt outraged and resolved that they would not give up their independence, no matter what it cost. They have quietly, firmly held their own, refused all bribes, evaded all enticements, repelled all attacks. To them the Eastern Question is simply one of national existence.

There remain two countries directly interested—Greece and France. Greece is divided. She dreads the Colossus of the North, yet has a feeling that even Russia will find it hard to absorb Greece, and watches with divided interest the course of other Powers, glad to avail herself of whatever advantages may fall to her share in a general mêlée. France, alone, appears to have anything to gain by Russia's conquest of Constantinople. Too far removed to have any fear of territorial loss, she feels that there is a possibility that a Russian alliance, under such prestige as that conquest would give, might help her to secure revenge for provinces lost to Germany. Still there are some Frenchmen who realize that a nation's life is not benefited by repeated reprisals, that peace is better than strife, and that such a power as the Czar would then wield might be a constant menace to the peace of Europe. Externally, then, the Eastern Question is summed up in this: When will Russia feel herself strong enough to strike for the prize she covets, and what price will the rest of Europe pay to prevent her success?

As to the solution of the problem, it is scarcely wise to hazard a conjecture. The most popular proposal is to make Constantinople a free city under international guarantees, and leave the Turk to establish himself in Asia Minor with his capital again at Broosa or Konia.

Meanwhile a new element is entering into the question. Mission work is spreading over the empire, carrying in its train education, moral quickening, a growth in the sense of individual responsibility and self respect, and a clearer conception of human rights.

*Mission Work.*—The general history of missions in the Turkish Empire is sufficiently noted elsewhere (see articles on the societies mentioned below, and also Albania, Armenia, Bulgaria, Koordistan, Nusairiyeh, and Yezidees). It is needful here to give merely an outline of the work as a whole, and show its relations to the peculiar problems, political, social, and religious, of this interesting field of foreign missions.

The territory of the Turkish Empire is well covered by the mission societies. The A. B. C. F. M., the oldest in the field, also occupies the largest territory—the whole of European Turkey, together with Bulgaria south of the Balkans, Asia Minor, Eastern Turkey, and Mesopotamia. The Presbyterian Church (North) occupies Syria and a portion of Eastern Turkey, where Nestorians are found in Koordistan. The Methodist Episcopal Church (North) has its work in Bulgaria, north of the Balkans. The Reformed Presbyterian (Covenanter) Church of America has its stations in Northern Syria and Southern Asia Minor, and the Presbyterian Church (South) holds a portion of Macedonia. There are also some congregations under the care of the Foreign Christian Missionary Society (Disciples) in Asia Minor, and a few Baptist Churches, at one time under

the care of the American Baptist Publication Society. The Church Missionary Society has considerable work in Palestine, the Friends of England have a mission in Syria, and a single medical missionary among the Armenians of Constantinople. The Free Church of Scotland has a station at Shweir in Syria, the Reformed Presbyterian Church of Ireland one at Idlib, near Antioch, and the North Africa Mission one at Hums in Syria. There are also a number of schools in Syria supported by the Lebanon Schools Committee and British Syrian Schools Association. The missions to the Jews of the various English and Scotch societies at Constantinople, Smyrna, Adrianople, and in Palestine are specially noted in the article on the Jews.

The Bible work of the empire is carried on by the American and the British and Foreign Bible Societies, and the National Bible Society of Scotland. The American Bible Society occupies the territory covered by the American mission societies, except Bulgaria, while the B. and F. B. S. works Bulgaria, the western coast of Asia Minor, and Palestine. Constantinople and Smyrna are shared by the two societies. The National Bible Society of Scotland has a depot at Salonica in European Turkey.

If we turn now to the population, we find that the work for the Armenians is carried on chiefly by the A.B.C.F.M.; for the Greeks by the A. B. C. F. M. and the Presbyterian Church (South); for the Bulgarians by the A. B. C. F. M. and the Methodist Episcopal Church (North); for the Maronites and Syrians by the Presbyterian Church (North) and the various English and Scotch societies and committees; while the Nusairiyeh are the chosen field of the sturdy Scotch Covenanters. The Turks, Arabs, Koords, Yezidees, etc., have been the care of all the societies, though the C. M. S. is the only one that has made a special effort to establish mission work distinctively for Moslems, if we except an effort commenced but not developed under the auspices of the A. B. C. F. M.

Not merely is the territory thus provided for as a whole, but it is well covered in its different parts. True to the best policy, the missionaries have from the beginning sought the centres. Not always the largest cities on the basis of a census, but those which for one reason or another furnish most opportunities for reaching the widest circle of people. Thus, in Asiatic Turkey, from Trebizond on the Black Sea to Port Said in Egypt there is not an important seaport that has not either a force of missionaries or an established congregation with its pastor or preacher. These include Trebizond, Ordoo, Kerasunde, Samsoon, Constantinople, Banderma, Dardanelles, Smyrna, Mersine, Latakia, Tripoli, Beirut, Sidon, and Jaffa. Other less important places, such as Sinop, Imboli, Edremid (Adramyttium), Adalia, Alexandretta, receive the regular visits of evangelists or colporteurs. In the interior, Erzroom, Van, Bitlis, Harpoot, Sivas, Cesarea, Broosa, Aintab, Marash, Mardin, Mosul, Bagdad, Damascus, Zahleh, Jerusalem, are full mission stations, while Erzingan, Moosh, Sert, Diarbekir, Arabkir, Malatia, Amasia, Yuzgat, Angora, Konia (Iconium), Afion Kara Hissar, Kutahya, Aleppo, are fully equipped with native churches. These are all centres, and around many of them are grouped numerous smaller places where there is a successful work being carried on.

If we turn to European Turkey and Bulgaria we find the same true. Salonica, Monastir, Seres, Samakov, Philippopolis, Loftcha, Sistof, Rustchuk, Varna, are mission stations, while Sofia is in special charge of the Bulgarian Evangelical Society. Uscup, Bansko, Yambol, Plevna, Adrianople, Rodosto, are among the most important out-stations.

In all there are over 400 stations and out-stations, with 102 ordained missionaries, 150 organized churches with a membership of 15,128, while nearly 30,000 pupils are enrolled in the various schools, and there is an average annual sale of about 60,000 copies of the Scriptures in whole or in part.

There are of course sections where there is comparatively little accomplished, but these are few. In the main the Turkish Empire is well covered, and it may be truly said that there is scarcely a village, except in the mountains of Koordistan and some parts of Mesopotamia and Syria bordering on Arabia, that does not have at least occasionally the opportunity to hear the gospel, while in some cities, notably Aintab, Marash, Harpoot, the evangelical element is so strong as to be a very important factor in the general life of the people. Mission work in the Turkish Empire thus has passed the exploring introductory stage and reached that of development. It is no longer experimental; it has settled down to the same problems that meet the church in other lands, affected yet by the fact that it is still rejected totally by the immense majority of the people, and looked upon with varying degrees of distrust by the greater part of the remainder.

We will look now at the relations that mission work in Turkey holds to the different classes of people whom it seeks to influence.

I. THE JEWS.—When the first missionaries entered the Levant in 1819, their special message was to the Jews. Not many years passed, however, before that branch of the work was given up by them as manifesting less opportunity for success than others. At present it is chiefly educational. Large schools are supported by the Scotch and English societies, especially in Constantinople, Smyrna, Salonica, and Jerusalem. There are also numerous preaching services, and there is enough of success manifested in the Christian life of converts to keep the laborers from being discouraged in their work or giving up the hope of a redeemed Israel, apart from their faith in the promises of the Scriptures. Mission work among the Jews is, however, so distinctively sectional, and confined to them as a race, that it enters as a comparatively unimportant factor into the question of the conversion of the empire as a whole.

II. THE ORIENTAL CHURCHES.—When missionaries first turned their attention to the Christian churches of Turkey, their one idea was to secure reform within the churches themselves. So close to the creeds and confessions of the Reformation were those of the Armenians, Greeks, Nestorians, that it seemed to them a comparatively easy task to show the incompatibility between those confessions and the actual practices of the church. Thus every effort was made to come into cordial relations with the people, and all idea of a separate communion was specially disclaimed. This course was favored also by the eagerness with which these churches looked for foreign sympathy and aid in their bitter struggles with their Moslem rulers.

It was not long, however, before the ecclesiastics saw that the new ideas would inevitably result in loosening and ultimately destroying their control over their followers. Thus they massed their power against the new doctrines. An excommunicated man had no rights that a Turkish court could recognize. He was nobody; could neither marry, nor be buried; could not buy, sell, or employ. He had absolutely no status as a citizen. The result was that the formation of a Protestant civil community became absolutely essential to the very life of Protestants. Then other influences began to come in. The introduction of Europeans into the commercial and governmental affairs of the empire, brought with it the introduction of French and German thought. With increased ease of access to Europe more and more of Armenian and Greek youth sought education in Paris and Vienna. Returning they brought with them the free-thinking of the day, and the grip of the church, not only on their belief but their life, began very perceptibly to loosen, and the ecclesiastics began to think that perhaps they had not been absolutely wise in their repulsion of evangelicalism. In the mean time it became evident that these Protestants were no less national in their feeling than the orthodox, indeed had an even clearer conception of what a true national life was. The experiences of Bulgaria assisted in this, and the graduates of Robert College and the Home School (now the American College for Girls) gave very clear proof that the study of the Bible did not make a man or woman less capable of good work for his people. General intercourse also had its advantageous results, and the chasm between the two was less and less marked. The result has been that in very many sections of the empire there is a constantly growing cordiality between the evangelical and the orthodox communities. Bishops, vartabeds, and priests are preaching gospel sermons, in some cases Sunday-schools and Bible classes are started, in order to satisfy the growing desire for religious instruction. With infidelity staring them in the face the leaders of the old churches are coming more and more to look upon the missionaries and the native evangelical churches as allies rather than enemies.

The problem of missions in Turkey in their relations to the old orthodox churches is, on the one hand, so to establish the evangelical churches in faith and life that when a reunion with the others comes they shall not be borne away and swallowed up, on the other, to convince the old churches that their one aim is to establish the kingdom of God, not a temporal organization, and at the same time to set forth in the evangelical churches as clear and accurate an idea as possible of what constitutes a true church life.

III. MOHAMMEDANISM.—The general relations of evangelical missions to Mohammedanism are fully set forth in the article on that subject. It is needful here to note only such points as are specially brought out in the Turkish Empire.

The first feeling of the Moslems of Turkey toward the new sect was one of amused and rather tolerant indifference. Indeed, in not a few instances Turks who saw the simplicity of the evangelical worship, the absence of ritual, of pictures and priestly rule, the stress laid upon spiritual worship, said: " Why, these are Moslems." The use of the Bible in distinction from the creeds of the church compared favorably in their eyes with the position they accorded to the Koran, and a Koordish chief once said: " Why do not the Bible Societies print and bind the two books together? then we should have the complete revelation." For a while this cordial feeling for Protestants as distinct from the Orthodox rather increased, except when the influence of ecclesiastics (either personal or pecuniary) secured special hardships for those who had dared to brave the power of the church. The missionaries had great influence, both because of their means of access to Lord Stratford and because the Turkish officials recognized, in many cases, their freedom from political motives. Little by little, however, this changed. Shrewd Mollahs saw, as Armenian and Greek bishops had already seen, that these new people were exerting an influence that would in time cut the ground entirely from under their whole system of belief and government. Then commenced a most determined and bitter opposition. Not in appearance,—that was in most cases friendly, —but in the form of hindrance. Censorship of publications was made increasingly stringent. Customs regulations were made more and more onerous. The necessary permits for buildings, churches, schools, and even private dwellings were refused or delayed as long as was possible. Any Turks who manifested a leaning toward or an interest in the Bible were quietly spirited away or arrested on some fictitious charge. Spies were everywhere. Occasionally some one more bold than his fellows, or feeling more secure in his position and relations with Porte or Palace, would give expression to his feeling that the work of the missionaries was really a good thing for the empire, but means were generally found to neutralize the effect of such a statement. In not a few instances laws were promulgated especially directed against the missionaries. Vexations upon vexations were put upon them. The result has been that there have been very few conversions of Moslems to Protestant Christianity. There have come, however, from every side constantly increasing testimonies to the hold that Christianity is getting upon the people of the land. The number of Scriptures sold to Moslems indicates a profound interest in the Bible, which cannot fail to bring forth fruit in Christian life.

Islam in its historic inception was in a great degree a protest against a devitalized polytheistic Christianity. If Moslems are to be brought to Christ, it must be largely through the example and influence of a living Christian church. The problem of missions in Turkey in their relation to Mohammedanism is to develop a native church freed from the errors of the old churches, strong in its belief in the unity of God, manifesting in its daily life an educated Christian faith.

In meeting these problems, missions in Turkey rely upon five special agencies: 1. Evangelical preaching; 2. Bible distribution; 3. Education; 4. Publication; 5. Social influence.

1. *The Evangelical preaching* of Turkey is very largely, in most cases almost entirely, in the hands of the native pastorate. These men, educated in the different seminaries and colleges under such men as Cyrus Hamlin, George F. Herrick, H. N. Barnum, George Washburn, T. C. Trowbridge, C. H. Wheeler, S. H. Calhoun, Daniel Bliss, J. H. House, and many others, are taking a position of constantly increasing importance. Men of large views, earnest Christian spirit, they have done much, not only to build up the native evangelical churches, but to convince others that Protestant Christianity is a genuine power in the world for good. Not only in the larger cities but in the smaller places they are doing a great though often unheralded work, laying foundations in Christian character for future building.

2. *Bible Distribution.*—There is probably no mission field where this department of mission work is more thoroughly organized so as to reach periodically every portion of it than the Turkish Empire. This has been already spoken of in the articles on the American and the British and Foreign Bible Societies.

3. *Education* in connection with the missionary work has been a normal growth. Free primary schools were first started. Schools, called theological, to educate native ministers and teachers soon followed, and were free to the class for which they were designed. Girls' boarding-schools were also established early, the first in 1840. All this work was rudimentary. In 1863 Robert College was opened on the Bosphorus, and, almost simultaneously, the Syrian Protestant College at Beirut. These institutions mark the beginning of serious educational work in Turkey on the basis of requiring pupils to pay reasonably for their instruction, and on a plan of thorough training with an ample and well-prepared curriculum.

They had much to contend against in the as yet feebly developed desire among even the people of the seaboard for a college education. They had also to meet the opposition of many Christian men, missionaries and supporters of missions, who, in their zeal for the largest development of the evangelistic work, were jealous of an elaborate course of collegiate training. The first years of those colleges were marked by a slow growth. Classes of five, three, two, in one case of only one, were graduated.

In the course of a decade of years the increase was abnormal. There was a plethora of raw material which had to be in part eliminated that what remained might be assimilated.

The institution at Scutari, Constantinople, now known as the American College for Girls, was started at this time, and struggled, in its inception, through difficulties and limitations similar to those from which the College on the Bosphorus had emerged.

Between 1871 and 1875 two colleges in the interior of the country were projected, and in the latter year were opened, viz., the Central Turkey College at Aintab, south of the Taurus Mountains, and the Armenia—now Euphrates —College, at Harpoot, east of the Euphrates River. These colleges show points of resemblance and of unlikeness to each other and to Robert College. Their course of study is not quite so full as that of the colleges on the seaboard. German and Italian are not needed in the interior, and much better work is done at Robert College in the physical sciences and in chemistry than is yet possible in an interior college. But the colleges of the interior have the advantage of being in closer touch with the races to be reached and moulded by them. Moreover, Robert College has had the unique opportunity of exerting one of the controlling forces in the birth of free Bulgaria.

The colleges of the interior are available to a very large number of youth who could not meet the much greater expense of education at the capital, an expense about fourfold greater.

The Syrian Protestant College at Beirut is specially spoken of in the article on Syria.

In the year 1875 began that remarkable advance movement in female education, undertaken by the Woman's Boards, which has already resulted in sixteen colleges or girls' boarding-schools within the bounds of the three Turkey missions, viz., at Constantinople, Marsovan, Smyrna, Adabazar, Broosa, Cesarea, and Sivas in the western Turkey mission, at Aintab, Marash, Adana, and Hadjin in the Central Turkey mission, and at Harpoot (a department of Euphrates College), Mardin, Erzroom, Bitlis, and Van in the Eastern Turkey mission. This movement, conducted in great quiet, without noise or ostentation, marks a new era, a veritable revolution in education, in Turkey.

In September, 1886, the school at Marsovan formally became known as Anatolia College, and took its place beside the other two interior colleges. This college has the unique advantage of location in the heart of a large Greek and Armenian population and educates the two races together. It has also, as yet,—in 1890,—the unique disadvantage of being obliged to do its work without permanent resources.

In other missions the work has been carried on on a smaller scale. In Bulgaria, Samakov, with its college, seminary, girls' school, and department for manual training, has exerted a marked influence upon Bulgaria, not less potent, if less prominent, than that of Robert College. In Syria, the theological seminary at Abeih paved the way for the Syrian Protestant College at Beirut, with its full collegiate and medical departments. The graduates of both, especially of the latter, are finding their way not only through Syria and Egypt, but through North Africa as well, and will be among the most efficient workers as the Soudan is opened and the great Arabic-speaking world of Africa comes within reach of the Gospel. There are also the numerous English and Scotch schools mentioned above and in the article on Syria. In Egypt there are two centres of educational influence—the College of the United Presbyterian Mission at Assiout, and the schools of the same Board at Cairo. At Assiout there are two departments, for young men and young women, distinct in organization yet really one in influence.

This growth of education, especially within the last seven or eight years, has developed the following noteworthy results:

*a.* The youth of Turkey *can pay* for their education, where terms are made light, according to location of the college, and such proportion of aid is given, through scholarships, and by furnishing work, as is done in the colleges of this country.

*b.* This securing of the privilege of Christian education through strenuous exertion on the part of pupils and their friends is one of the most essential conditions of realizing that growth in manly, self-reliant, aspiring character, and that establishment of a vital, self-propagating Christianity, without which education is nowhere a blessing. The plan of education now adopted has already yielded excellent results in this way. The more men, or races of men, are held down by the incubus of poverty, the more urgent is the necessity of rousing the will-power to self-help, by every right device and pressure.

*c.* It is the stand taken and the work done by Americans in recent years, in the matter of education, which has won the confidence of the best men of all races in Turkey.

*d.* It is this influence alone which can fit the several races for their future and hold in harmonious relation one to another, all those whose vital interests are identical.

*e.* These American colleges furnish in large part the models in education for all races, and train large numbers of the teachers. It was after Americans gave the signal that Armenians, Greeks, Bulgarians established for themselves any schools worthy of the name. The Turks have ideal capacity for establishing excellent schools on paper, and ideal incapacity for establishing them in any other way. They also are already recognizing the American leadership, and will, it may be hoped, profit by the example set them.

*f.* All discussion among missionaries and their supporters relative to the utility of education and to the *comparative* value of educational and evangelistic work has ceased.

4. *Publication.*—There are two centres of missionary publication in the Turkish Empire, Constantinople and Beirut. The work at Beirut is entirely Arabic, that at Constantinople includes Turkish, Armenian, Greek, Bulgarian, Judæo-Spanish, Koordish, etc. In each place some of the best of missionary strength has gone into the work of providing not only the Bible and religious books, but periodical literature, educational works, and such general literature as a growing Christian community is constantly demanding, and in ever-increasing quantity. Aside from the work of Bible translation in these different languages, the work done in Turkey by Geo. W. Wood, Edwin E. Bliss, I. F. Pettibone, J. K. Greene, H. O. Dwight, T. L. Byington, R. Thomson, and in Syria by W. W. Eddy, H. H. Jessup, C. V. A. Van Dyck, G. E. Post, and many others is work that is telling all over the empire in the correction of erroneous views, not by antagonizing their errors, but by presenting the truth. (See also article Periodical Literature.)

5. *Social Influence.*—This is an ever-increasing power in Turkey. The ready access gained to all classes of people, the power of personal presence and actual acquaintance has done and is doing a great deal towards preparing the way for the entrance of the Gospel. Many old-time prejudices against those that "having turned the world upside down, are come hither also," have quietly but absolutely disappeared before the presence in an Armenian, Greek, Maronite, and Turkish home of a simply dressed, unassuming Christian lady. Many an ecclesiastic has found it impossible to harangue against one whom he knew from personal acquaintance to be a Christian gentleman.

In the Turkish Empire the bars are down, the gates are open. It is only necessary to hold the vantage-ground gained and to make steady advance, in order to solve the deepest problems of the Eastern Question by building up the kingdom of God in the lands where it was first established.

**Turkish Missions' Aid Society.**
Headquarters, 32 The Avenue, Bedford Park,
Chiswick, London, Eng.

In 1853-4 Rev. C. G. Young, a minister in
the North of England, travelling in the East,
came into contact with missionaries of the
American Board engaged in work among the
Armenians in Constantinople, and was greatly
impressed with their devotedness and zeal.
Much spiritual success had been achieved, and
the educational efforts of Dr. Hamlin and
others filled him with admiration. He studied
the work in all its branches with the utmost
care, and returned to England with a burning
desire to do something effective toward the
support of a mission which was full of promise
for the evangelization of the Turkish Empire.
He took every opportunity of telling what he
had seen, and of urging that an endeavor should
be made to associate Christians of all the
churches in an effort to co-operate with those
already in the field. Other circumstances contributed to awaken interest in the subject. The
Eastern question was assuming an acute phase.
The Sultan was looking to Britain for support
against Russia, and public opinion was ripening
in favor of intervention. Sir Stratford de Redcliffe, the astute and able English ambassador
at the Porte, had shown himself friendly to
the educational efforts of the American missionaries, and sought to influence the Sultan in
the direction of a policy of toleration in religious matters. For several years Christians in
Britain had watched with sympathy the converts among the Armenians, who had been
grievously persecuted. The moment was favorable for an effort of some kind. Mr. Young
sought to interest Christian men of various denominations in the matter which lay so near his
own heart, and to a large extent he succeeded.
In response to an invitation by circular, a large
meeting was held to consult how best to take
advantage of openings for spreading the gospel
among the Armenians and Greeks of the Ottoman Empire. Other meetings followed; and at
last, on the 3d of July, 1854, the Turkish Missions' Aid Society was fairly launched at a
public meeting held in the Lower Room of
Exeter Hall, at which the Earl of Shaftesbury,
who had been elected president, took the chair,
One of the resolutions adopted at that meeting
was as follows: "That the facilities now providentially afforded for circulating the Holy
Scriptures and preaching the gospel in the
Turkish Empire, and the cheering tokens of
success which continue to attend existing missions there, especially that of the American
Board, and also the peculiar circumstances of
the country at the present crisis, call for special
efforts by British Christians to furnish the
pecuniary aid required in order to the wider
extension of missionary operations." On that
resolution the Society was based, and it is entirely undenominational, both in respect of the
fact that its supporters and subscribers may belong to any and every branch of the Christian
Church, and in respect of its funds being expended without taking account of the ecclesiastical relations of the societies or individuals assisted. The first rule of its constitution
runs thus: "The object of this Society is not to
originate a new mission, but to aid in the extension of gospel work in Bible lands, especially
that carried on by the Americans."

It will thus be observed that the founders deliberately preferred to establish an agency for
providing pecuniary help to those on the field,
then chiefly American, and, by implication, to
all such evangelical churches and societies as
should at any time thereafter undertake gospel
work within that region.

This plan of operations has been faithfully
carried out, and the T. M. A. S., although
not now so largely supported as formerly, continues to work on the same lines. It makes its
special province the assistance of truly Christian
work all over the Bible lands, and missionaries in
Greece, Bulgaria, Constantinople, Asia Minor,
Eastern Turkey, Persia, Syria, and Egypt have
borne grateful witness to its importance and
value as a factor in the evangelization of the
East. During the civil war in America, when
the resources of the foreign missionary societies
were so seriously crippled, the aid afforded by
this Society was particularly helpful, and acknowledged as such.

The organ of the Society is "The Star in the
East," published quarterly.

The president is The Earl of Aberdeen; the
treasurer, Lord Kinnaird; and the secretary,
Rev. T. M. Brown, D.D.

**Turkish Versions.**—The earliest translations of the Holy Bible into Turkish appear
to have been two, which were made about the
middle of the 17th century. One of these, in
one of the Eastern Turkish dialects of Central
Asia, was made by the Englishman Seaman
about 1666. The other, in the Western or
Osmanli dialect, was executed at Constantinople
about the same time, by Ali Bey, chief interpreter at the court of Sultan Mohammed IV.
This scholar was a Pole, captured by the Turks
in childhood, and educated as a Moslem among
the slaves of the Sultan's palace. He seems to
have made his translation of his own accord;
but when it was done he handed over the manuscript to the Dutch Ambassador at Constantinople, who sent it to Leyden to be printed.
The manuscript remained in the library of the
University in that city a century and a half,
when it was unearthed by Baron Von Diez,
once Russian Ambassador at Constantinople.
Baron Von Diez agreed with the British and
Foreign Bible Society to superintend the printing of the book, thus providentially preserved,
against the time of the formation of a Society
which would take an interest in its publication.
He died, however, before he had completed the
collation of the manuscript. Professor Kieffer of
the University of Paris was then entrusted with
the work, and in 1819 he at length brought out the
New Testament, which was published on the
plan of exact conformity to the ancient manuscript of Ali Bey.

This idiomatic and simple version of the
Scriptures might have answered for the need of
the different classes of the population of Turkey,
had it not been deficient in accuracy of rendering the original. The edition published
under the circumstances related above was
promptly suppressed on account of this defect,
and the British and Foreign Bible Society
caused a revision to be made by Professor
Kieffer, which was published in 1827. Ali
Bey's version, again revised in 1853 by Turabi
Effendi, and in 1857 by the lexicographer
Redhouse, was freely circulated in Turkey until
1866. The various revisions to which it had
been subjected had modified the native sim-

plicity of the style of Ali Bey, under the influence of the theory that the language of such a work ought to be modelled on that of works of the Turkish classical period. At the same time the work had not been entirely recast by any one of the revisers. The result was unsatisfactory: the style was not smooth, and too often the meaning of the word was obscured to the intelligence of the common people by the introduction of Arabic or Persian phrases prized by Turkish writers mainly for their sonorous cadences.

In the meantime contributions of material for a Turkish version of the Scriptures had been made on an entirely different line by missionaries of the American Board. With a view to placing the Scriptures in the hands of the large section of the Armenians of Turkey who use the Turkish language but write it with the characters of the Armenian alphabet, Rev. W. Goodell in 1831 published at Malta, in the Armenian characters, his translation of the New Testament into Turkish. He afterwards revised this work, and completed a translation of the whole Bible, which was published in the Armenian character at Constantinople in 1857, a newly revised edition of the same being published in 1863. This Armeno-Turkish version of the Scriptures was notable for the simplicity of its style. It has been for nearly thirty years in the hands of the Armenians of Turkey, and is beloved of multitudes as the very Word of Life, notwithstanding its too evident imperfections in the matter of idiomatic expression. Owing to these imperfections no edition of this version has ever been printed in the Turkish (Arabic*) characters.

After the Crimean War, with its assistance to Turkey rendered by Christian troops, a strong interest in the Christian Scriptures appeared among the Moslems of Turkey. The version of the Scriptures accessible to them, as has been seen, was a sort of patchwork, which imperatively demanded improvement in the presence of the many Turkish inquirers seeking to examine the teachings of Christ. The British and Foreign Bible Society, with which was afterwards associated in this good work the American Bible Society, appointed Rev. W. G. Schauffler, D.D., formerly of the American Board's Mission at Constantinople, to make an entirely new translation of the Bible into Turkish. Dr. Schauffler brought tried and eminent abilities to this task, which he completed in 1873.

The New Testament of this version was published in 1866; and tentative editions afterwards issued, of the Pentateuch, the Psalms, and the Prophecy of Isaiah, are the only parts of the Old Testament of this version which have been published. The reception given to these parts was not satisfactory. While scholars praised the beauty of its diction, the common people were not moved by its words. The version was a specimen of good classical Turkish; but aside from the Gospels, which were simpler in style, it was unintelligible to people whose education was only moderate in degree. The difficulty lay in the fact that the canons of Turkish literary style required all serious works to be composed upon a level attained only by the learned. The idea of a book which could be understood by the common people could not exist in Turkey; for the language of books was a separate language, spoken nowhere in the empire save in the ceremonious circles of public official life. The official and literary classes themselves rarely used in social privacy any of those sounding phrases with which they loved to prove their erudition in the artificial atmosphere of the court. And since the highest authorities deemed it impossible to depart from the classical standards, especially in such a work as the translation of the sublime poetry of the Bible, the problem of providing for Turkey a version of the Scriptures that should be respected by the small literary class and fairly comprehended by the illiterate multitude, seemed to be insoluble.

But God was preparing the solution of this difficult problem. The great popular uprising against the Persian and Arabic rhetoricians, which within the last thirty years has completely revolutionized Turkish ideas of literary style, had already begun. A few bold writers among the Turks were already proving that an intelligible style, which should honor simple "Turkish" words much as good English writers honor the Saxon, could possess both grace and dignity. Under the influence of these circumstances, the Rev. A. T. Pratt, M.D., of the Mission of the American Board, made an attempt, with the assistance of the Rev. A. Constantian, pastor of an Evangelical Armenian church in Marash, to improve the style of the Goodell Armeno-Turkish version. This work, begun under the auspices of the American Bible Society, Dr. Pratt did not live to complete; but the success of his revision of the New Testament, tentatively published in 1870, justified the decision of the Bible Societies to delay the publication of Dr. Schauffler's translation until it had been revised by a competent committee in the hope of securing greater simplicity. Upon this committee the two Bible Societies associated together Rev. Dr. Schauffler, Rev. Dr. Riggs, and Rev. G. F. Herrick of the American Mission, Rev. R. H. Weakley of the Church Missionary Society's Mission, and Rev. A. Constantian, they having the aid of two Turks of known literary ability. Dr. Schauffler early withdrew from this committee, which proceeded to make what was practically a new translation, with free use of the work not only of Dr. Schauffler but of that of Drs. Goodell and Pratt.

The committee's version was published in both the Armenian and the Turkish characters in the year 1878. In order to keep pace with the rapid progress of the new school of Turkish writers in the direction of simplicity and strength of style, a revision of this version was made by the same committee, assisted by a score or more of corresponding members in various parts of the empire, and was published in Turkish characters in 1884, and in Armenian characters in 1888. This version is marked by precision in rendering of the original, and by strength and clearness in its Turkish style; ranking in this respect with the best of contemporary literature, and affording at last a version which the literary can enjoy and the illiterate can understand to a large degree. While changes still in progress in the Osmanli Turkish language will naturally call in time for some further

---

* The Arabic character is used in a large number of versions, the Persian, Turkish, Hindustan. etc., but varies somewhat in style. The fonts used at Beyrout differ somewhat from those of Constantinople, Teheran or Bombay. Hence it is not as incorrect as it appears to speak of the Persian or Turkish characters, although they are virtually the same as the Arabic.

revision of the text, it seems probable that the two Bible Societies, by placing the work in the hands of this committee, have completed the labor of preparing the Osmanli Turkish version of the Scriptures—a labor commenced almost 250 years ago by the slave Ali Bey.

A version of the Bible for the Greeks of Asia Minor who use the Turkish, writing it in the Greek characters, was prepared under the auspices of the British and Foreign Bible Society in 1856 by Mr. C. Philadelpheus. A revision of this version, executed by two native gentlemen, was published by the Society in 1884. This Greco-Turkish version unhappily leaves much to be desired in accuracy of rendering the original.

A version of the Scriptures in the Azerbijan (or Trans-Caucasian) dialect of Turkish, spoken in the Caucasus and north-western parts of Persia, was undertaken by the American Bible Society, which published a New Testament in 1881, prepared by the Rev. B. Labaree of the American Presbyterian Mission in Persia. A version of the whole Bible in this dialect, under the British and Foreign Bible Society, has been made by Rev. A. Amirkhanianz of Tiflis, and Rev. Mr. Wright of the American Presbyterian Mission. The printing of this version is now (1890) proceeding at Leipsic; a curious and interesting detail of its publication being the fact that the proofs are read in Siberia, Mr. Amirkhanianz having been sent into exile by the Russian Government.

Translations of parts of this Bible have also been made, under the auspices of the British and Foreign Bible Society, into the Kazan, Kirghiz, Uzbek, Jagatai, and Kumuki Turkish dialects in Central Asia, and into the Krim dialect in the Crimea. (See articles.)

(*Specimen verses.* John 3 : 16.)

*Arabic.*

زيرا الله دنياثى بو قدر سودى كه
كندى ابن وحيدينى ويردى تا كه آكا
هر ايمان ايدن هلاك اوليوب انجق حيات
ابديه يه مالك اوله.

*Greek.*

Ζίρα Ἀλλὰχ τϐνγιαγιὴ ποὺ κατὰρ σεϐτί κι, κεντὶ πιριτζὶκ Ὀγλουνοὺ βερτί, τάκι χὲρ ὀνὰ ἰναυὰν, ζάϊ ὀλμαγια, ἴλλα ἐπέτι χαϊατὰ μαλὶκ ὀλά.

*Armenian.*

Օրքա կ՚աւս տրեսնայբ դես գատար սեմրի րի բեսնի իսկն ի վահինքի մերկ, թա բի ասա չեր ինան եստն չեսար ոյնարմ, ասանգ հայաթ ը եգեներկեն մասիս ոդա.

**Turton, William,** a native of Barbadoes, who after conversion came to reside at St. Bartholomew in 1785. He had formerly been a preacher in America, and on settling in St. Bartholomew made application to the governor for the use of the church, which belonged to the Swedes. At about this time the colony had been ceded to Sweden, and it was the only one in the West Indies belonging to that country. Mr. Turton also opened a school in connection with the church. Mr. David Nesbit, an English gentleman, was much interested in this work, and as it was more convenient to meet the Negroes in the evening on account of their employments, he advised Mr. Turton to build a chapel. In 1797 the latter had received such encouragement from those to whom he applied for assistance that he was able to build a chapel, and dwelling-house connected with it. The governor was his friend, and when some inhabitants of St. Eustatius and St. Martin's, who had come there to live, opposed Mr. Turton and appealed to the governor to sustain them, he silenced them by saying, "Every man is at liberty to worship God according to his own conscience." After the completion of the house of worship, the congregation, which at first numbered thirty, was increased to one hundred and ten. On application of Mr. Turton to the British Conference of the Wesleyan Methodists, St. Bartholomew was put on the list of missionary stations. In 1801 Mr. Turton went to Providence, one of the Bahama Islands. Some unfaithful missionaries had been there before him, and had done so much injury to the cause of missions that a law had been passed that no one should preach to the slaves. The governor granted him permission to labor among the slaves, but he had only commenced his work when the clergy objected to his administering the sacrament, and he was obliged to desist. They also tried to prevent his preaching during church hours. He went on with his work, however, and soon, under the patronage of some influential friends, he built another chapel for his now overflowing congregation. The people on the eastern part of the island had been living a long time without the knowledge of God, but under the administrations of Mr. Turton many became true followers of Christ. While the outlook in the country was so encouraging, the ministers of the Established Church in the town had not discontinued their opposition. Mr. Turton's health was much impaired, and he could not on account of this prosecute his work with the vigor the circumstances demanded. In 1804 Mr. Rutledge was sent out from England to help him. He continued to labor, principally in the Bahamas, till his death. Laws were finally passed in 1816 prohibiting the Negroes from attending meetings at all, but after a few years they were repealed. In 1853 the members of the Methodist societies in the Bahamas numbered 2,800.

**Tuticorin,** a large town on the coast of Tinnevelli, Madras, India, 65 miles northeast of Cape Comorin. The appearance of the place and its neighborhood is very unattractive, since in parts the subsoil is so shallow that no plants or trees will grow, and elsewhere there is nothing but heavy sand with palmyra palms and a few bushes. During the southwest monsoon the dust is intolerable. In value of its foreign trade Tuticorin is second in Madras and sixth in all India. Its harbor, though shallow, is secure. Population, 16,281. Mission station S. P. G.; 2 missionaries, 18 out-stations, 11 schools, 383 scholars.

**Tutuila,** one of the Samoan Islands, South

Pacific. High and mountainous, of volcanic origin; its west end is covered with luxurious vegetation, and thickly settled. Area, 50 square miles. Population, 4,000. Mission station of the L. M. S.; 35 native pastors, 19 other helpers, 550 church-members, 66 schools, 1,067 scholars.

**Tuwon,** a trading-post for the lower Niger valley, West Africa, at the mouth of the Brass River, on the Bight of Biafra. Mission station of the C. M. S. (1868); 1 missionary and wife, 2 native helpers, 1 church, 262 communicants, 1 school, 107 scholars.

# U.

**Udayagiri,** a town in Nellore district, Madras, India. Formerly a place of importance, strongly fortified, and containing temples and palaces, the ruins of which still remain. Climate hot, dry. Population, 3,885, Hindus, Moslems. Race and language, Telugu. Social condition poor. Mission station American Baptist Missionary Union (1885); 1 missionary and wife, 25 native helpers, 6 out-stations, 2 churches, 150 church-members, 12 schools, 109 scholars.

**Udipi** (Udapy), a town in South Kanara district, Madras, British India. Considered by the Hindus to be the most sacred spot in Kanarese territory, and much frequented by pilgrims from Mysore. Population, 4,449, Hindus, Moslems, Christians. Mission station Basle Missionary Society; 5 missionaries, 4 missionaries' wives, 29 native helpers, 1,081 church-members, 32 out-stations, 9 schools.

**Udipuri Version.**—The Udipuri belongs to the Indic branch of the Aryan family of languages, and is spoken in the province of Mewar, or Udipur. A translation of the Gospel of Matthew was published at Serampore in 1815, but was never reprinted.

**Ujaini Version.**—The Ujaini also belongs to the Indic branch of the Aryan family, and is spoken in the province of Malwa. A translation of the New Testament into this dialect was made by Dr. Carey, and published at Serampore 1824, but never again issued.

**Ulwar** (Alwar), a city in Rajputana, India, nearly in the centre of the state, 90 miles southwest of Delhi. Climate hot, unhealthy. Population, 52,000, Hindus, Moslems. Language, Urdu. Natives poor, indolent, irreligious. Mission station United Presbyterian Church of Scotland (1877); 2 missionaries and wives, 33 native helpers, 1 out-station, 1 church, 27 church-members, 9 schools, 532 scholars.

**Umanak,** a town in Greenland, on an island at the mouth of the Baals River, 42 miles from New Herrnhut. Mission station of the Moravians (1861); 1 missionary and wife. Formerly an out-station of New Herrnhut, but finding that periodical visits were not sufficient to supply the religious wants of the people, a full station was afterwards organized.

**Umbala** (Ambala), a town of the Punjab, India, 120 miles north-northwest of Delhi, on the route to Lahore. Climate of city dry, healthy. Population, 26,777, Hindus, Moslems, Sikhs, Christians. Language Urdu, Punjabi. Social condition rather low. Mission station Presbyterian Church (North), 1848; 2 ordained missionaries, 1 missionary's wife, 1 female mission-

ary, 19 native helpers, 6 out-stations, 3 churches, 70 church-members, 7 schools, 807 scholars.

**Umtata,** a town in Tembuland, Africa, northwest of Buntingville. Mission station of the S. P. G. (1873); 2 foreign missionaries, native preacher, 203 communicants.

**Umtwalume,** a town in Cape Colony, South Africa, 75 miles south of Port Natal, 8 miles from the sea. Climate unusually healthy. Population, 12,000, Zulus or Bantus. Language, Zulu. Religion, worship of ancestors. Mission station of the A. B. C. F. M. (1852); 1 missionary and wife, 23 native helpers, 3 out-stations, 2 churches, 184 church-members, 2 schools, 150 scholars.

**Umvote** (Groutville), a town in Natal, Africa, 40 miles north of Port Natal, on the Umvote River. It is situated in a well watered and wooded district, with good arable and pasture lands. Mission station of the A. B. C. F. M.; 1 lay missionary, 1 out-station.

**Umzumbe,** a town of Southeast Natal, Africa, southeast of Umtwalume. Mission station of A. B. C. F. M.; 2 missionaries and wives, 1 female missionary, 1 out-station, 60 pupils.

**Undop** (Undup), a town in West Borneo, northeast of Banting and east of Quop. Population, 6,000. Mission station of S. P. G. (1864); 1 missionary, 350 communicants.

**United Brethren in Christ.** The Home, Frontier, and Foreign Missionary Society. Headquarters, Rooms of the Society, Dayton, Ohio, U. S. A.—The first missionary work undertaken by the United Brethren in Christ was located in the home field. For this collections were taken, and expended by the Annual Conferences. The missionary spirit increased until in 1853 a society was organized for the prosecution of home, frontier, and foreign work. Its first foreign mission field was Shaingay, among the Sherbro people, on the west coast of Africa. Work was begun here in 1855. The territory occupied by the Society covers about 7,000 square miles, and its missionaries visit nearly 400 towns. Seven stations have been established: at Rhnbee, Shaingay, Manoh, and Boompehtook, on the coast; Mambo, on the Mambo River; Mo-fuss, on the Cargbror River; and Touchohlop, on the Yaltucker River. At Shaingay is located the "Rufus Clarke Training-school," from which it is hoped that many native missionaries may proclaim the gospel to destitute tribes around them. The Women's Board of the church, organized in 1876, maintains 3 stations,—at Geemah, Samah, and Palla, on the Boomphe River. In these stations are now about 5,000 native Christians, and a large number of pupils in the day and Sunday schools.

A mission to China was entered upon in 1889. Work among the Chinese is also carried on in Portland, Oregon, and Walla Walla, Washington; and the Society hopes at an early day to extend this work to San Francisco and Sacramento, California.

A mission has been established in Naila, Bavaria, and among the Freedmen in Virginia.

### United Methodist Free Churches Foreign Missions.
Headquarters, 17 Wharncliff Road, Sheffield, England.—The Missionary Society of the United Methodist Free Churches was formed in 1857, by a union of the Wesleyan Association with certain churches of the Wesleyan Reformers. The Wesleyan Association had, at the time of the union, several missions in Jamaica and the Australian colonies, carried on by the united body, which also opened in a few years missionary operations in the new fields of New Zealand, East and West Africa and China.

In the West Indies, the Wesleyan Association had been strengthened by the action of an ex-Wesleyan minister, Rev. Thomas Pennock, who brought certain churches under his care into that body. In 1838, two missionaries had been sent to Jamaica, who made little progress until after the time of the liberation of the people from slavery; but since that period up to the present time the work has made steady progress in spite of some trying circumstances, which have only served to prove the loyalty and faith of its ministers and people.

(a) *Australia*, and (b) *New Zealand.*—(a) This mission had been commenced in 1849 by the Rev. J. Townsend, and its growth has been very slow. At the time of the union very little progress had been made. Of late, however, the Australian churches have advanced a little. New stations are being opened, with new missionaries; and the time is slowly approaching when the hope of this mission's becoming self-supporting will be realized. The present work in this field is divided into the two districts of (1) Victoria and Tasmania, (2) New South Wales and Queensland. The present missionary staff is composed of 33 ordained ministers, 88 lay-workers, 71 churches and chapels, with 2,343 communicants.—(b) New Zealand was entered in 1864 by the Rev. J. Tyerman. No incidents of special note have checked the slow progress of this work, but of late the mission has suffered from the temporary adverse circumstances of the colony. The numerical loss has been the result of many people having changed their places of residence, but the natural advantages of the country, and the enterprise of the people give good ground for the expectation of a favorable change. There are now in this field 11 ordained ministers, 37 lay-workers, 946 church-members, 22 schools, 2,503 scholars.

*West Africa.*—The admission in 1859 of a body of native Christians of Sierra Leone into the missionary connection turned the attention of the Society to that field. Accordingly the Rev. Joseph New was sent out, and shortly afterwards Rev. Charles Worboys. The work of these two men was of short duration, but of great success. The former died, and the latter was obliged to return home to recover his fast-failing health. Their places in the mission

were not long left vacant, and many noble men have been found willing to risk the climate, so unfavorable to Europeans, and have carried on the work with much success. Churches are being erected, schools opened; and at the Sierra Leone Ministerial Institute two young natives, Messrs. Nichols and Thompson, are fitting themselves for work among their countrymen. The native communicants in this mission now number 2,809.

*East Africa.*—The Christian missionary enterprise in Eastern Equatorial Africa can be traced upward to a most interesting origin, and downward through a most interesting history. To Rev. Dr. Krapf, the enthusiastic missionary, East Africa owes most of its Christian missions, and to the Rev. Chas. Cheetham of Heywood, this particular mission of the United Methodist Free Churches; for Mr. Cheetham brought before his denomination the necessities of this field as represented by Dr. Krapf and so interested his brethren in the object of his own attention, that in 1861 the Methodist Free Churches, who were then seeking to send out missionaries to a heathen field, applied to Dr. Krapf for advice as to a sphere of labor. He promptly replied, recommending East Africa, and volunteered to conduct thither and establish firmly there four young missionaries, if the church would send them; and so in that same year, the Revs. Thomas Wakefield and James Woolner, accompanied by two young Swiss, sailed for Africa. Ere long the failing health of Drs. Krapf and Woolner made their return home necessary, and the two Swiss shortly followed them. Thus Dr. Wakefield was left alone until the latter part of 1862, when he was joined by the Rev. Chas. New. Together these patient missionaries held the ground under those vicissitudes of experience which all pioneers must pass through. In 1868 Mr. Wakefield visited England, and in 1872 Mr. New, and their stirring addresses and eloquent appeals roused much interest in their work. When Mr. New returned to Africa in 1874 he attempted to open a new mission; but he was cruelly treated by a savage chief, and died alone, when trying to return to Ribe, before any one could come to his assistance. He was a missionary of the finest type, and his Society owed much to his life and lost much by his death.

Mr. Wakefield, again alone, continued his work among the Wa Nyika race, dwelling along the coast about twelve miles from the Indian Ocean. In 1886 Revs. John Baxter, John Houghton, and Rev. W. H. During, a colored minister from West Africa, joined the mission, but after a short period Mr. Baxter broke down and was obliged to return home, and the Rev. John Houghton and his wife were murdered, along with a number of native converts, during a sudden rush of raiding savages at a new station on the river Sana, where Mr. Wakefield had recently opened a mission to the Gallas. Rev. W. H. During, however, has proved himself a most successful agent of the Society.

In 1887 Mr. Wakefield retired, and his place was filled by the Revs. F. J. Heroe, T. H. Carthew, and W. G. Howe, who were located respectively at Ribé, Jomvu, and Goldbanti in the Galla country, where Mr. During is also at work. The very unsettled state of society in East Africa, and the contests which have arisen during the past year, in the Galla country especially, have hindered the progress of the mission to a serious extent. It is, however, a cause for gratitude that the stations of the Society have not been assailed, nor their people scattered. The work is steadily and most hopefully increasing, and is one of the best and strongest of the United Methodist missions. An important feature of its work is the successful way in which it has come into contact with slavery.

*China.*—This mission was opened in 1864 by the Rev. Wm. Fuller, at Ningpo. Here he was joined after a short time by Rev. John Mara, and in 1868 the Rev. F. W. Galpin arrived in China, and for ten years served his church most faithfully. For two years of this time, from 1869 to 1871, Mr. Galpin was alone, but at the latter date Rev. Robert Swallow went out as his colleague, and located in Ningpo suburb. A little later a third missionary, Rev. R. I. Exley of Leeds joined them; but his earnest work was ended in a very few years, for he died of consumption before he could carry out his plans for increased usefulness. His place was supplied by the Rev. Wm. Soothill, who was sent to take charge of Wenchow, the opening of which new station was the result of a visit of Mr. Galpin's to England, where his representations of China's need roused the missionary committee to new efforts in its behalf. The work at this place was at first held in great dislike by the Chinese, whom the war with France had made distrustful of all foreign influence. At one time during a riot the mission premises were destroyed, and all missionary operations interrupted and discontinued; but when peace was once more restored the Chinese Government made full compensation for all losses, and work was resumed and grew more successful than ever. In 1886 Mr. Swallow visited England, in order that he might, by acquiring some knowledge of medicine, fit himself more fully for his work, and also to interest the churches in his mission. At the expiration of the time necessary to accomplish both these objects he and his wife returned to Ningpo, where they have carried on their work with ever increasing success, and the efforts prove what three men are able to do among so many millions of heathen, even though they are restricted and their work limited for want of larger means and more helpers. The native converts of this mission number 365.

## United Original Secession Church of Scotland, South India Mission.

Headquarters, Shawlands, Glasgow, Scotland.— The United Original Secession Church had its origin in 1733 in a secession from the Established Church of Scotland, and for a few years the entire seceding body was known by this name; but in 1761 another secession from the Scottish Church took place, which resulted in 1847 in the union of these two sections, giving rise to the United Presbyterian Church of Scotland. A small remnant of the Secession Church, however, did not join the United Presbyterians, but when that church took up their missions in the West Indies (see article on the United Presbyterian Church of Scotland) after a little time commenced new missions in the Central Provinces of India, where the Rev. and Mrs. Anderson are now doing much good work at the town of Seoni. Evangelistic work progresses, and native children are being cared for and instructed at the orphanage and schools.

## United Presbyterian Church of

**Scotland.** Headquarters, United Presbyterian Church Offices, Castle Terrace, Edinburgh.—The United Presbyterian Church of Scotland had its origin in a secession from the Established Church in 1733, and was at that time, and for a long time afterwards, known as the "Secession Church." Another secession took place in 1761, those seceding at that time being called the "Relief Church." These were united in 1847, and since then the church has been known as the United Presbyterian Church. Early in this century two missionary societies were formed—the Scottish Missionary Society, for the purpose of sending missionaries to the West Indies; and the Glasgow Missionary Society, for work in South Africa. A large number of the missionaries connected with these two societies were ministers of the Secession and Relief Churches, so that by the secession of 1733 the United Presbyterian Church has the honor of having kept evangelical truth alive, and the first Scottish missionary to the heathen, Peter Greig, was of this church, although another society sent him out.

*Development of Work.*—1. WEST INDIES. (*a*) *Jamaica* and (*b*) *Trinidad.*—(*a*) The first mission undertaken by the United Secession Church as a body was in Jamaica, where the Scottish Missionary Society had already five missionaries, Revs. George Blyth, James Watson, Hope M. Waddel, John Cowan, and John Simpson, engaged in active work. In 1835 Revs. James Paterson and William Niven, the first missionaries of the United Secession Church to Jamaica, were sent out; and in 1836 the missionaries of both societies united and formed the Jamaica Presbytery. Under the harmonious co-operation in work which this union brought about, the mission prospered wonderfully, and between 1836 and 1840 three new stations, at Friendship (1837), Goshen (1837), and Mount Olivet (1839), had been occupied, with constantly increasing success. In 1846 the negroes in Jamaica had been entirely raised from their degradation, and were so interested in Christianity that they sent some of their own esteemed missionaries to their less fortunate brothers in West Africa, thus commencing the Old Calabar Mission of the United Presbyterian Church.

In 1847 the complete union of the Secession and Relief Churches was consummated. The Relief Church, in anticipation of this union, had undertaken no denominational mission, but it is well known, however, that the Glasgow African Missionary Society was almost exclusively sustained by the Relief Church. The first work of the United Presbyterian Church, formed in May, 1847, was to accept the transference of the stations and agents of the Scottish Missionary Society in Jamaica, and of the Glasgow African Society in Kaffraria.

The stations formerly under the care of the Scottish Society have been greatly strengthened since their adoption by the United Presbyterian Church, though of late years the mission has been subjected to very heavy trials, and for a time disasters swept over it in close and appalling succession.

In 1846 the Rev. Mr. Niven, who had gone to the Great Caymans with a view of seeing Mr. Emslie, a new missionary settled at Georgetown, on that island, perished at sea in a great storm which came upon the ship in which he was returning to Jamaica. He was followed in a few weeks by his young wife, to whom he had been married less than a year. In the course of a few months the Rev. W. P. Young, Rev. J. Scott and his wife, the Rev. J. Caldwell, and Mrs. Winton, the wife of another of the missionaries, all of whom had been but a short time on the island, were successively laid in the grave; and they were afterwards followed by the Rev. W. Turnbull and Mr. J. Drummond, who had been for some years a very useful teacher at Hampden. The burning of the West Indies steam-packet "Amazon" deprived the mission of the Rev. J. Winton and his newly-wedded wife. Other missionaries suffered in health, and were obliged to leave the country, so that in 1849 very few workers of all the large mission staff were left to carry on the mission. It was some time before new missionaries were sent out to supply the vacant places, and in the meanwhile some of the congregations suffered greatly in their spiritual interests. Things had hardly begun to be settled before, towards the close of 1850, cholera made its appearance, and wrought fearful ravages. At Port Maria about two thirds of the population perished, and the disease, which was of the most malignant form, quickly spread to Kingston and other parts of the island. There was a great want of medical men and medicines in the island, and it was utterly impossible to stay the progress of the disease, and although business was suspended and every precaution taken to prevent its spread, the effort was of no avail, until after some days the force of the disease had spent itself. Strange to say, while the pestilence was sweeping off hundreds, only one of the entire mission staff perished—the wife of the Rev. Adan Thompson, who had been only about a year on the island.

For a time after the panic was over unusual seriousness prevailed. The chapels were thronged, and although many returned to their old life, yet not a few were brought by their trouble to seek comfort of God.

Before long new missionaries arrived, and the work was again in a state of prosperous activity. A first-class seminary was opened in Montego Bay, and is doing successful work. To this seminary a theological branch is attached for the training of native ministry, and this graduates yearly several students of much promise. There are now in Jamaica 31 ordained missionaries (of whom 14 are natives), 16 native evangelists, 46 congregations with 9,131 members.

(b) Trinidad was occupied in 1835 by the Rev. Alexander Kennedy, who settled at Port-of-Spain. The progress of the mission has been uneventful, though steadily increasing in its influence and successful work. In 1842 a station at Arouca was opened, and a little later one at San Fernando. At present there are in this island 2 European and 1 native ordained missionaries, and 3 congregations with 379 members, by whose aid extensive work is carried on among the coolies.

2. *Africa.*—(a) *Old Calabar.*—In 1846, sent out by the Jamaica Negroes, the Rev. Hope M. Waddell, accompanied by Mr. Samuel Edgerly, Andrew Chisholm, a brown man, and Edward Miller, a pure Negro, began the Old Calabar Mission and the study of the Efik language. It was originally hoped that this West African Mission would be chiefly prosecuted by the Negroes when educated in the Jamaica field, and to some

extent this hope has been realized. Mr. Waddell and his company, on arriving in Old Calabar in 1846, were welcomed heartily by the kings of Duke Town and Creek Town, with both of whom a correspondence had previously been opened on the subject of the mission. They found both the kings and people somewhat advanced in civilization. Many of the people spoke English quite well, and some of the chiefs could also write and read a little in that language, although unable to read a printed book. They were anxious to have their children educated according to English methods, and were willing to be taught the Christian religion, for already both the existence of God and of a future state was generally believed by them. They carried on considerable trade with England and with the neighboring regions about them, and thus obtained large quantities of foreign goods, and the handsome furniture and mirrors with which the houses of the kings were crowded.

Yet in spite of this, ignorance, superstition, and cruelty everywhere prevailed. Under these circumstances the missionaries opened stations at Creek Town, Duke Town, and Old Town, and at each place suitable buildings were erected, schools opened and largely attended in which the elements of a good English education were given, and in a very short time the Efik or Calabar language was reduced to writing by the missionaries, and, by the means of a printing-press, school-books and the Bible soon appeared in the vernacular. The missionaries also preached to the people, at first through an interpreter, and afterwards without one. To facilitate this part of their work, a galvanized-iron church, made in London, was sent out and erected at Creek Town. Some time after its beginning the mission was reinforced by the arrival of the Rev. Wm. Jameson, Rev. Wm. Anderson, and Rev. Hugh Goldie. The first of these, Mr. Jameson, died very soon after his arrival in Africa, but the other two are still at work. Later the arrival of Rev. R. M. Beedie, Rev. A. Cruickshank, Rev. E. W. Jarett, Rev. John Gartshore, Rev. James Luke, and Mr. John Morrison, all of whom are now in the field, raised the number of ordained missionaries to nine. There are at present in Old Calabar 8 stations—at Duke Town, Creek Town, Ikorofiong, Ikunetu, and Adiabo, and the new stations at Ikotana, Umvana, and Emovra-movra; 24 out-stations, 22 native agents, 3 unordained Europeans, 311 church-members, 19 day-schools with 564 scholars. The printing-press is still at work, and a steamer has been provided for working in the interior, where it is expected that other stations will soon be opened.

(b) *Kaffraria.*—This mission was begun by the Glasgow Missionary Society, and in 1837 it was divided, one section joining the Free Church in 1844, and the other joining the United Presbyterian in 1847. Notwithstanding the wars that had ravaged that land, the work of the mission has been steadily carried on. The first missionary was the Rev. Wm. Chalmers. Tiyo Soga, a son of one of Yaika's chief councillors, was trained under Mr. Chalmers, and having completed his education in Scotland, was ordained as a native missionary, but after a brilliant career died at the age of forty-four. The mission has now 4 stations in the Colonial District and 7 in the Transkei; 76 out-stations; 12 ordained missionaries, of whom one is the Rev. Dr. W. A. Soga, eldest son of Tiyo Soga; 60

native agents, 2,307 church-members, 43 day-schools with 1,735 scholars.

3. *Asia.* (*a*) *India.*—The events of the Mutiny in India in 1857 led this church to open the first mission among the millions of Rajputana and its feudatory states in the heart of Northwestern India, acting in this on the advice of Dr. John Wilson of Bombay. The Rev. Dr. Williamson-Shoolbred, an able student of the Edinburgh University, founded the mission at Beawar in 1860, and it has greatly prospered. Other agents followed him, and stations were opened in rapid succession at Musseerabad (1861), Ajmere (1862), Todgarh (1863), Jaipur (1866), Deoli (1871), Oodeypore (1877), Ulwar or Alwar (1880), Jodhpur (1885). "During the great famine of 1869 two of the missionaries, William and Gavin Martin, devoted themselves with self-sacrificing energy to the help of the sick and dying, and specially to the gathering in of hundreds of orphans who were left in destitution. This had a marvellous effect upon the people, and gave the missionaries generally a firm place in their confidence. The two brothers, first Gavin and then, a few years afterwards, William, were removed by death in the very midst of their usefulness; but their memory is still a power throughout Rajputana." At present the missionaries, ordained and medical, number 16, and the native agents 40. The work is being very successfully carried on by the 85 day-schools of the mission, which have an average attendance of 4,839 scholars. The church-members number 456. A mission press is successfully at work in Ajmere.

(*b*) *China.* Manchuria.—From 1862 to 1870 the only mission work of the U. P. Church in China was that of a medical missionary in Ningpo, but in 1870 Rev. Dr. Alexander Williamson was sent out, and a station was opened at Chefoo. In 1873 work was begun in Manchuria by the Rev. John Ross and Rev. John Macintyre, and their work was so successful that the Society decided to remove the entire mission to this field, which was done in 1885. Dr. Williamson, however, remained at Shanghai in China proper, and devoted himself to the preparation of Christian literature for the Chinese. The work in Manchuria is largely increasing; nine out-stations have now been opened from the stations of Newchwang, Haichung, and Liaoyang (occupied 1872); Moukden, Tieling, Kaiyeren, and Saiping-Kow (occupied 1875). The desire of the mission is to open work in Korea, and in anticipation of this the Rev. Mr. Ross has prepared a translation of the New Testament in Korean. The mission staff at present employed in this mission includes 5 ordained foreign missionaries, 3 medical missionaries, and 19 native helpers. There are four congregations, with 795 members and 100 candidates.

(*c*) *Japan.*—The opening up of Japan in 1863 induced the United Presbyterian Church to send out several missionaries to engage in work there. Shortly after the establishment of the work they united with the American Presbyterian Church (North) and the Reformed (Dutch) Church of America in forming the Union Church of Christ in Japan. The missionaries connected with this United Church now number eighty-two. The church-membership is 7,551, and in no previous year has the increase been so great. A large amount of evangelistic and educational work is being done every year. Fifty-nine young men are now in training for

the ministry. The growth of self-support in the Japan Mission is very noticeable, and very soon the work of the Christian church will be largely in the hands of the Japanese themselves. Meanwhile the work advances, and there is every reason to hope that at no distant day the whole land will be won for Christ.

The Society has, besides its home and foreign missions, considerable continental and colonial work (the former devoting most of its interest to Spain), and also a Jewish mission in Morocco, carried on under the superintendence of the Presbyterian Church of England, which is treated under the general head of "Jewish Missions," q.v.

**United Presbyterian Church, Board of Foreign Missions.** Headquarters, Philadelphia, Pa., U. S. A.—The Board of Foreign Missions of the United Presbyterian Church dates from the organization of that church by the union of the Associate and Associate Reformed Churches in the city of Pittsburg, Pa., May 26th, 1858. It had its beginnings in the Board of Foreign Missions which each of these churches had before the above union. Its constitution was issued by the General Assembly in May, 1859. It was formally organized in Philadelphia, June 15th of that year, and was incorporated by the Legislature of the State of Pennsylvania April 12th, 1866, under the title of "The Board of Foreign Missions of the United Presbyterian Church of North America."

This Board consists of nine members, each elected by the General Assembly of the church for a term of three years. The Corresponding Secretary, who is also appointed by the Assembly for a term of four years, is a member of the Board *ex officio*. To this Board is entrusted everything pertaining to the foreign missionary work of the church in the interval of the meetings of the Assembly, and to that body it must every year make a full report of its proceedings, its appointments of missionaries, its fields of operation, its receipts and expenditures, and its general condition and prospects of all the foreign work of the church. Its officers are a president (Rev. W. W. Barr, D.D.), a recording secretary (Rev. D. W. Collins, D.D.), a corresponding secretary (Rev. J. B. Dales, D.D.), and a treasurer (Jos. D. McKee). It is located in Philadelphia, and holds its stated meeting on the second Monday of each month.

For a number of years this Board had under its care missions in Trinidad, Syria, China, Egypt, and India. At length it concentrated, under the direction of the General Assembly, its whole foreign work upon the latter two of these fields—Egypt and India.

The first missionary of the Board in India was the Rev. Andrew Gordon. He embarked for the field with his wife and sister on September 28th, 1854, under the appointment of the Board of the Associated Church, and fixed his first station at Sialkot in the Punjab. In 1856 he was joined by the Revs. E. H. Stevenson and R. A. Hill, and thus the mission was organized and manned as it came under the Board of the United Presbyterian Church in 1858.

From the beginning it had two special methods of operation—evangelistic and educational. Its first effort in the spirit of the great commission, "Go preach the gospel to every creature," has ever been to make the gospel known; and so it has sought to reach men in the mission stations, in bazaars, in itinerating from village to village, in the zenanas and in every place and way in which the missionary could by any proper means do the work.

Next to this, and almost coexistent with it, has been educational work. Schools have been opened both for males and females wherever opportunity offered and the mission had the ability. These schools have gradually risen in grade from the primary to the collegiate and theological institute, whence young men in increasing numbers are already coming to form a well-trained and able native ministry. For the girls also boarding-schools as well as others are opened, and many are thus in training for the forming and carrying on of Christian homes in their after lives. In all the schools, from the lowest to the highest, and for both sexes, the Bible is daily read, and the way of life is constantly made known.

MISSION TO INDIA.—This mission was commenced at Sialkot in 1855 by Rev. Andrew Gordon. The work now occupies 8 districts: Sialkot, Pasrur, East and West Gujranwala, Gurdaspur, Pathankot, Jhelum, and Zafarwal. The work is carried in four great divisions: 1. Evangelistic. Besides the regular services at the churches, preaching tours are made throughout the villages, in the bazaars, and street corners. Churches have been organized in each of the districts, and in the Pasrur district there are three congregations. The total figures for this branch of the work are: 8 mission districts, 10 congregations, 51 stations, 511 villages containing 6,597 communicants.—2. Educational. At Sialkot there is a theological seminary, a Christian training-institute with 125 students, and a girls' boarding-school with an average attendance of 45. Christian primary schools, boys' and girls' day-schools, and Sabbath-schools are conducted at all the stations and in many of the villages of the districts. In all there are 60 schools, 2,553 male pupils, and 3,164 female pupils.—3. Zenana work. This is carried on in both the city and the villages. In Sialkot, Gujranwala, Gurdaspur, and Jhelum many houses are open to the visits of the faithful women.—4. Medical work. A lady physician has charge of the Memorial hospital at Sialkot City, which was opened with appropriate ceremonies December 30th, 1889. The work among the women is thus made practical and efficient. During the year over 5,000 patients were treated at the dispensary alone. The force of workers for the India Mission is composed of 12 ordained missionaries (11 married), 11 female missionaries, 1 female medical missionary. (See also articles on Punjab and the above-mentioned stations.)

MISSION IN EGYPT.—The mission was begun by the arrival in Cairo of the Rev. Thomas McCague and his wife, on November 15th of the year 1854. They were young and zealous, but they had no knowledge of the language at first, and therefore actual work for the first year or more was done by Rev. James Barnet, who joined them on December 5th of the same year, and who had been laboring in Damascus for several years in connection with the same church. It was a favorable time for establishing a mission in Egypt, as Said Pasha, the chief ruler at that time, was favorably disposed towards European civilization, and seemed not the least afflicted with that

jealousy and hatred of Europeans so common among Mohammedan officials. For some years little was accomplished in mission work, except the opening of a school for girls and another for boys, and the observance of regular divine services on the Sabbath, at which, however, very few attended. All the difficulties of beginning such a work were experienced. It was next to impossible to find a suitable building, and few were willing to rent their houses to the propagators of a "new religion;" yet it was some time before the persecutions of the spiritual rulers began. In 1856 Rev. G. Lansing also removed from Damascus to Egypt, taking up his residence first in Cairo and then in Alexandria, in 1857. About the same time Miss S. B. Dales also changed her place of missionary labor from Damascus to Alexandria. Subsequently the work carried on by Dr. Philip at Alexandria, under the United Presbyterian Church of Scotland, and Miss Pringle's girls' school, to the support of which the Ladies' Society of Paisley, Scotland, contributed so long and so liberally, both passed over to the American United Presbyterian Mission, and Mr. John Hogg, then a student of theology, and assisted by Dr. Philip, joined the same mission, and was in May ordained by the Presbytery of Egypt, soon after its organization. Up to the year 1860 the missionary operations of the United Presbyterian Mission were, for the most part, confined to Cairo and Alexandria, in each of which cities were a school for boys and another for girls, in which the missionaries sought to fill the minds of the children with Bible knowledge, and touch their hearts with the love of the Saviour. There were also preaching services, at which however few attended, not more than 15 or 20, in addition to those pupils who could be induced to come. A few evangelistic trips for the sale of Scriptures and other religious books, and for preaching the gospel in an informal way, had been made both north and south of Cairo, and unsuccessful attempts had been tried to open regular mission work at Benisouef, Luxor, and Assiout. At Assiout, Moslem hatred broke out against the mission's native agent there, and thirteen Moslems were imprisoned a year for beating him in open court; and the Coptic hierarchy had begun to traduce and malign the missionaries and decry their labors; while excommunication was threatened against any Copts who were disposed to read Protestant books, or meet with those who had joined the little Protestant church, and all who had professed openly their belief in Protestant principles were made the subjects of the church's anathemas. All this meant not only that truth had been disseminated and had taken root in the minds and hearts of the people, but also that it had begun to exert an influence on their daily life. In 1860 Rev. S. C. Ewing and wife and Miss C. J. McKown, and from that time onward for several years other recruits from America, joined the mission. Revs. Drs. Lansing and Hogg, and their families, and also Miss Dales, were transferred to Cairo station in the autumn of 1861 and the following winter, making a strong missionary force in the capital. From that time the work began to prosper, the schools grew in the number of pupils and in efficiency; the attendance at divine service on Sabbath steadily increased; the property at the "mouth" of the Mooski, given by Said Pasha, was repaired and fitted up as mission premises, containing residences for the missionaries and rooms for the schools, and a comfortable and commodious place for religious services. The central position of these premises, separated but not distant from the Coptic quarter, and in the very line of traffic and travel, helped to swell the number of visitors and inquirers. The truth began to exert a mighty power: persons from all parts of the country visited the mission book-depot on the Mooski on week-days, and the mission chapel on the Sabbath. Additions by profession of faith were made every few months. A commencement was made in training young natives for mission service. Sabbath-school work was prosecuted with vigor and success, and the organization of the first native Protestant church was effected in Cairo in the year 1863.

From this time the work prospered more than ever before. Assiout was occupied by Dr. Hogg and family and Miss McKown in 1865; Koos, near Luxor, was opened in 1865; Modeenet, El Fayoom, and Mansura in the Delta, in 1866; Sinoris El Fayoom, in 1868; Mooteea and Nakhaileh, near Assiout, in 1869; Bagore, Fahta, Rhoda, Luxor, and Suft Meedoom, in 1873; Goorneh, near Luxor, and Jawily, north of Assiout, in 1874; Ahnoob, near Assiout, and Sinhore, on the Fayoom, in 1875; Esneh and Erment south of Luxor, Kosair on the Red Sea, and Zerabi near Assiout, in 1876; Dweir, Moosera, Beezadeeza, Marees, and Boolac, in 1877; Beni-Adi and Manfaloot in 1878; Akhmeem and Sanalio, in 1879; Minich, Deir Aboo-Hinnis, and Tanta, in 1880; Azaimeh near Esneh, Kinneh, Tameeyah, and El Kome El Akhdar, in 1881; Wasta, Moir, Tanda, and Benisouef, in 1882; Tima, Abooteeg, and Furkus, in 1883; Edfos, Aboo-Kerkas, and Daminhoor, in 1884; Deir El-jenadily, Kome-espaht Busra, Menharg, Mahalla, Kafr-Bilmisht, Zagazig, and Mist Ehamr, in 1885; Deir-Birsha, Nezlet-Rooman, Fesh, Gerobeea, in 1886; Assouan at the First Cataract, Hammam, Serokina, Nezlet-Nahkly, Dakoof, Tanbody, Safaneezah, and Atf-Haider, in 1887; Girgeh, Sidfeh, Mas'oodeh, Shamee'a, Beni-Aleig, Deiroot, Beni-Korah, Hore, Beshoda, Boorzain, Nezlet Aboo-Hamis, Supt El-Khumar, Aboo-Girgeh, Maidoom, Teeh El-Barood, and Fam El Bohr, in 1888; Deir Mawas, Roda in Assiout Province, Nezlet-Hamzamee, Nezlet-Sultan Pasha, Hilma, Kome Matai, El-Idwa, Fiddameen, Shiblenza, Dronka, and Kome Bedar, in 1829. These places are found all along the Nile valley up as far as Assouan. In many of them meetings for prayer, singing, reading, and study of the Word are held every night in the week. The methods and means employed in the U. P. Mission are those generally employed by American missionaries—school work, book distribution, evangelistic work, zenana work. It has been the policy of the mission to leave to the natives themselves the primary education of their children, and in consequence a large number of parochial or free schools have been established, supported entirely, superintended, and taught by them. The mission restricts its operations in the line of education for the most part to the training of teachers, and to giving instruction in the higher branches. Most of the teachers in the parochial schools were taught in the Mission Training-school or College at Assiout. There are also academies and seminaries for boys and girls at Alexandria, Mansura, Cairo,

and Assiout, where instruction and training are given sufficient to enable pupils to prepare for school-teaching, or for taking positions in the government service. In these, as in all the mission schools, an hour every day is devoted to religious instruction in addition to the opening exercises in the morning. More than 800 Mohammedan boys and girls are on the roll of the schools, and are receiving a Christian education. The Training-school or College at Assiout has a good corps of American and native professors, and has fine premises and a healthy location. The theological classes are taught in Cairo, and are steadily increasing in the numbers, character, and ability as well as piety of the students. Over 6,000 pupils were under instruction in the various schools during 1889.

Having great faith in the power of the Word read in the homes of the people, the mission has given a good deal of attention to the distribution of religious literature, educational, practical, and controversial, and to this end has opened depots for the sale of books in Alexandria, Mansoora, Cairo, Tanta, Zagazig, Assouan, and Luxor, and employs a large number of colporteurs, who carry the books to the towns and villages. Over 35,000 volumes are thus distributed yearly in the Nile valley, many of these being Scriptures and other religious books, and all being of a useful character.

Special attention has been given to the instruction of women, because it was seen that they were ignorant and superstitious and oppressed to a degree not understood in civilized countries; and their instruction and elevation are not only needed for themselves and their salvation, but also for the sake of the men, who cannot be enlightened and evangelized without the women.

Opportunities for acquiring knowledge at public meetings are much fewer in the case of the women than of the men. On the Sabbath there is the custom among the men of visiting one another, and the women are expected to stay at home during the day and prepare the dinner for the company; while it is not considered proper for a woman to go out at night, even to religious meetings, unless accompanied by a male attendant. None of the women could read when the mission was established, and at the present time (1890) not more than one in 700 can read understandingly, while a much smaller proportion can write. Under these circumstances the distribution of books among them is of little profit, and therefore it has become necessary to visit them personally in their homes, and read to them out of the Scriptures in order to give them a knowledge of God, themselves, and the way of salvation. This is the necessity for the large and increasing force of unmarried ladies in the Egyptian Mission, in addition to the wives of the male missionaries. With the Bible in hand they go to the houses of the people, sometimes to teach them the art of reading, and always to read to them, and often accompanying the reading with prayer.

Of course direct evangelistic work has produced the best results, especially where the natives themselves have earnestly taken a part in it. It has been the endeavor of the missionaries to enlist the natives in this work, whether in the zenana department or in the wider field of missionary effort among men and women indiscriminately. This has been done by encouraging them to take an interest in the nightly meetings for prayer and the study of the Word, at which very often the natives are the leaders, and by adopting a system of local preachers something similar to that adopted by the Methodists. In many places an earnest Christian who can read intelligently can do good work among his own people in giving them a knowledge of the way of salvation, even though he may never have been inside of a school-house. Men, however, who intend to be permanent pastors are required to pass through a course of training similar to young men in the church at home, except that during their vacations they are sent out as local teachers and preachers to sow the precious seed and use their talents and learning. The missionaries themselves make frequent tours through the valley, visiting new places as well as old stations and organized churches, for the purpose of encouraging the workers, aiding in solving difficulties, stimulating the people, and leading them onward and upward in the Christian life. Curiosity, as well as other motives, generally secures for them large audiences, and great good is always accomplished by these tours. No other means is more blessed than this in rousing the people from their religious indifference and formalism, bringing them to see their need of a Saviour, and leading them to declare themselves on the side of the Lamb of God who takes away the sin of the world. This, with the liberal use of the native talent in all the departments of the work, has been the chief cause of the success of the U. P. Mission in Egypt. If ever Egypt is to be fully brought to Christ, it will be done largely by itinerant evangelists, both foreign and native; both are needed to secure, by the blessing of God, the best results in the salvation of souls and the dissemination of the truth.

The chief difficulties with which the missionaries have to contend in Egypt are: 1st. *The language.* No doubt the Arabic language is difficult. With time and application all may so far learn it as to be able to communicate their thoughts in it, but it will generally be with some faults of pronunciation and many of diction. Few can become fluent in the use of it. It is only by patient study, continual practice, and constant mingling with the people that a person, even with a natural talent for languages, will be able to acquire the easy and effective use of this language. In not a few instances inaccuracy in the use of the language on the part of the missionary grates harshly on the ears of the people, and in the case of Mohammedans acts as a strong hindrance to their willingly listening to the gospel. They say that a man who uses bad grammar cannot have a good religion. 2d. *The formalism of the religions of the people.* All have a religion, but it is only a form. Prayer, repentance, faith, obedience, are all mere forms. There is no life, no reality—at least few persons among the Egyptians are in dead earnest in religion. Religion is a covering, a means of livelihood, an inheritance; and its rites are mere outward ceremonies, and its technical terms are lifeless, meaningless, except for outward effect. The truth preached to such a people is at first a mere sound: pleasant it may be to the ear—indeed sometimes they smack their lips in expression of their admiration; but they have no idea that the preacher means what he says, or that he expects the hearer to accept and live in accordance with gospel precept. At first they regard the gospel as another religion like their own. 3d. *The character of most of the so-called Christians residing in Egypt.* Frenchmen, Italians, Greeks, Maltese, Germans, British, all bear the Christian name; but, alas! their lives are for the most part in direct contrast with the lives of true Christians, while the character of the Copts is equally bad. It is no wonder that the Moslem deridingly replies, "If these be Christians, I want nothing of Christianity; and if these be not Christians, why do not you convert them first?" 4th. *Add to these the customs and manners of the Egyptians,* formed apparently in direct opposition to the principles and requirements of the gospel of Jesus Christ. The manner of doing business among the various trades; the conditions of government service, requiring work on the Sabbath; and the constant habit of lying and deceit in all the relations of life, render it difficult for a Christian to find employment or earn a livelihood. Such are a few of the many obstacles met with in conducting missionary work in Egypt, but by the Spirit of God quickening the converted soul, and by the grace of God strengthening the powers of the new life, the true Christian can overcome them all; and the gospel is, notwithstanding these obstacles, the power of God to the salvation of souls in Egypt to-day as heretofore.

**United States of America.**—This is one of the greatest mission fields of the world. Ever since the days when the discovery of the New World and the condition of the savage Indians stirred up the Christians of the Old World to send missionaries, the history of Christian effort in the United States has been one of continual and almost unabated zeal and earnestness. The work has gone through the various stages of evangelistic and pastoral agencies in the older and more settled districts of the country, but there are always new regions to be cared for and new people to evangelize.

The urgency, diversity, and magnitude of the work of Christian missions in the United States can best be understood by looking at the different elements which compose the population, and the influences which affect the efforts of the church.

1. *Work for the Native Population.*—Under this head we can consider the term "native" as including that part of the people who are native born or who have been located in the country for a period long enough to be naturalized: the Indians, the Negroes, as well as the native Americans. The work for the Indian has already been treated of in a separate article; the work for the Negro, as well as for others, will be shown in the detailed account of the various Home Missionary societies which follows. The general facts in regard to this element of the population may be dwelt upon but briefly.

The development of the great Territories in the West, and the consequent migration of the inhabitants of the older and more settled States, has caused the growth of mission work and the division of Christian work into two heads, pastoral and evangelistic (see Missionary Methods). Pastoral work is carried on in the settled States; in the large cities it is combined with the work of city missions (q.v.) in order that the poor and the rich may have an equal chance to hear and profit by the teachings of the gospel. But as has been well said, man is kept in the right path as much from fear of the censure of the surrounding community as by the desire and purpose to do right for right's sake; and when the adventurous ones leave the well-ordered communities to go where they will be pioneers of civilization, they too often forget to take their religion with them; amid the freedom and license of the new life the ungodly become more so, while the nominal Christian soon loses even the name. Then the evangelistic methods of the church must be brought to bear upon these migratory multitudes, and the parent churches send out missionaries to look after the stray sheep as well as to claim those who have belonged to no fold. The rapidity with which the Western States are increasing in population may be shown by a few instances from the figures of the census of 1890. The percentage of increase in the population of the North Atlantic States for the decade 1880-90 was 19.95; for the Northern Central States, among which are Michigan, the Dakotas, Kansas, and Nebraska, the percentage of increase was 23.78; and of the Western States, 71.27. The greatest percentage of increase was in the States of North Dakota (385.05), South Dakota (234.60), Montana (237.49), and Washington (365.13). The growth of the latter is phenomenal, as it is almost entirely during the last five years that the increase has taken place. How great a proportion of this increase is due to migration, and how much is properly referred to the arrival of emigrants from other countries, cannot be determined without more data than have yet been furnished by the Census Bureau; but the lessening rate of increase in many of the older States, such as Ohio, Indiana, Idaho, Missouri, and Illinois, is distinctly traced to the migration of the people. Hence a great proportion of the rapidly increasing population of the Western Territories and States is made up of those who have severed family, social, and religious ties by moving into the new districts. Must these ties be left with no new objects around which to cling, until they shrivel up and respond but slowly to any stimulus? Or shall the church keep pace with the world and supply new church ties as soon as the old ones are severed ; new places of worship, ere the habit of church-going ceases to exist; new influences for good before the careless or seared conscience fails to respond? These questions indicate the nature of home mission work in so far as it concerns what might be called the peculiar objects of the church's care—her own wandering sons and daughters.

2. *Work for the Immigrants.*—Attracted by the visions of liberty, wealth, freedom ; driven out from their home-lands , by poverty, increase of population, tyranny, and misrule; aided by cheapness of travel and the short time required for the journey, the emigrants of European countries have poured in upon the United States in a steady stream. According to the tenth census (1880) the total foreign-born population numbered 6,679,943. In "Our Country" Dr. Strong states that at a rate of emigration which the history of the past would give as a basis for the future, the total foreign population in 1900 will be 43,000,000. This influx of foreigners is regarded as the most dangerous element which threatens the civil and religious life of the country. The time is past when the immigrant was hailed with joy. There is now no great urgency for his labor. His morals,

his socialistic, anarchistic tendencies, his conception of liberty as license, his inability to appreciate the honor and responsibility which go with the right of franchise,—all these make the average European emigrant one of the most objectionable of strangers. The results of this immigration are seen distinctly upon the statistics of crime, and these foreigners compose a formidable element to be looked out for and opposed by the church. Many of these immigrants come from Christian communities, but they are influenced in the same way as the native American is when he changes his home; but by far the greater number belong to the bilge-water of the various ships of state in the old countries. Here is a herculean task thrown upon the state and the church. The state is devising means to escape the conflict which is imminent by stopping the inroads; but with strange lack of the sense of proportion, the immigration of the few thousand Chinese has been prohibited, while during the year ending June 30th, 1890, of the total of 455,302 immigrants, 443,225 came from Europe. The church has the greater task, for many of these immigrants come from countries where they have had little religious instruction; and in addition to the difficulties which arise from the nature of the case,—the known character of the people, the isolation of their life,—there are added other factors which complicate still further the problem. These are, as ably set forth in "Our Country," Romanism, intemperance, Mormonism, wealth, and the collection of people into cities. Mormonism has officially abolished polygamy, but it is still the foe to all that is for the best interests of the individual and the state; of the papacy this is not the place to speak; intemperance is so well recognized as an enemy to the church and the commonwealth that it needs no words of description; city life and its dangers are seen on all sides; and the influence of the chase after, or the possession of, wealth is keenly felt by all.

This, in brief outline, is the condition of affairs which makes the field of the Home Missionary societies one of paramount importance by reason of the enormous extent of territory, the number of the people, the interests at stake, and the conviction that the future of this nation, the greatest example of a republican form of government, will depend upon the success with which the church fulfils the obligations thus imposed upon her.

Home missions is the name given to the work of the church for those in her own country, whether it be among freedmen, immigrants, or frontier settlers; and every denomination is actively engaged in this work, whether it is made a separate department or not, and it may or may not be classified and reported separately from the general work of the church. The ways are many but the end is the same, and the means adopted substantially agree. Some of the denominations have a Board of Home Missions, just as they have a Board of Foreign Missions, where the work is put under the charge of a special set of officials chosen by the church to administer this important part of the work. Thus there is the Board of Domestic Missions of the Protestant Episcopal Church, the Missionary Society of the Methodist Episcopal Church (North), and the Board of Home Missions of the Presbyterian Church, and there are special Boards of Church Election and of Education. Some churches organize special departments, etc., of Home Missions under separate boards or committees; thus the Freedmen are under the care of a special Board in the Presbyterian Church. In some cases the work for the Chinese and Japanese is under the care of the Foreign Board; in others it is part of the Domestic Missions. Sometimes, in addition to or in place of the general society, there are local or State societies which carry on independent work. Individual churches support their missionaries, women's societies or bands support schools and teachers. Thus the total work which is done it is hard to trace or to tabulate, from the fact that the dividing line between home missions and parent-church work is so often vague, impalpable, and constantly shifting.

It has been impossible to give space for a full statement of each of the different organizations. The similarity, too, of their history and work is so great that it has been deemed most satisfactory to give a slight sketch of a few only, and those the older and larger societies.

AMERICAN BAPTIST HOME MISSION SOCIETY, THE.—The Baptist churches in some of the Northern and two or three of the Southern States had formed associations or societies about the commencement of the present century, for aiding feeble churches on the frontiers, and for carrying the gospel to the pioneer settlers, who occupied the States and Territories between the Alleghanies and the Mississippi River. Prominent among these were: the Massachusetts Domestic Missionary Society, founded in 1802, which occupied after a time Maine, Lower Canada, Western New York, Pennsylvania, Ohio, Illinois, and Missouri. The Lake Baptist Missionary Society, founded in 1807, afterwards the Hamilton Missionary Society, and eventually in 1825, with other societies, forming the Baptist Missionary Convention of the State of New York. This organization sustained missionaries in New Jersey, Pennsylvania, Ohio, Michigan, Canada, and Wisconsin. The Triennial Convention of the Baptists in the United States for Foreign Missions in 1817 altered its constitution so as to include Home Missions; but the low state of the treasury, the demands of Foreign Missions for immediate help, and other cases, led to the relinquishment of this work by the Triennial Convention to other organizations. Between 1820 and 1836 eighteen State Conventions were in existence, all of them more or less active in Home Mission work, either within their own bounds, or "in the regions beyond." The time was favorable for a combined national movement. At this time there were in all the States and Territories about 5,322 Baptist churches, with a membership of 385,000, distributed as follows: New England, about 65,000; New York, New Jersey, and Pennsylvania, about 75,000; the Southern States, about 213,000; and the Western States, perhaps 32,000.

Such was the condition of the denomination when two men, Rev. John M. Peck, of Rock Spring, Illinois, and Rev. Jonathan Going, of Worcester, Mass., undertook the work of founding the American Baptist Home Mission Society. The convention for this purpose met in the Mulberry Street Baptist Church, in New York City, April 27, 28, 1832, adopted a constitution, and elected officers, and an executive commit-

tee of five clergymen and five laymen. The former, John M. Peck, became its exploring missionary for the West. The field before the Society was vast. The Society was new, and, owing to the poverty of many of the churches the responses to the appeals for funds were not so large or prompt as they were expected to be. There was also a difficulty in obtaining the best men for missionaries, but in 1837 the Society was in a sound condition. Its receipts had risen to $13,438 per annum; the number of missionaries was 105. They had organized 29 new churches and had supplied 237 churches and stations. At first their work was wholly east of the Mississippi River, but as the great flood of immigration commenced in 1839, the Society's field extended westward to the Pacific coast, including the fast growing Territories, California and the Pacific States, and Texas. The gold discoveries in California were causing an immense home emigration across the continent; railroads were extending in all directions with great rapidity; the Mormon delusion had gathered a host of adherents; there were conflicts with the Indians at many points; the anti-slavery agitation constantly increased in volume, and involved the disruption of churches and benevolent societies, and threatened the dissolution of the Union; the disastrous financial panic of 1857 crippled the resources of all business-men, and the civil war of 1861–5 brought about what seemed the culmination of woes. The growth of the Society was not rapid. The average of the twenty-two years (1840–1862) of Dr. Benjamin Hill's service was only about $31,000; but during them a large force of missionaries, had been kept in the field, 830 churches had been organized—almost 40 a year—an average of 450 churches had been supplied, and about 950 baptisms per year administered. In 1846, missionary work among the Germans had been commenced, and subsequently enlarged. Aid to the French Mission at Grande Ligne, Canada, had been given from 1849, and in 1848 the first missions among the Scandinavians of the Northwest had been commenced. Missionary work in the Spanish language commenced in New Mexico in 1849, and preparation was made for labor among the Chinese in San Francisco in 1852 and the following years. But amid financial disasters, war, and the languid interest of the people in Home Missions from 1852–62, the treasury of the Society was seriously crippled, and not only were new enterprises abandoned, but many of the old ones were given up. In 1861–62 the receipts of the society had fallen to $31,144.28, and the number of missionaries to 84.

It was a critical time. The war was in full progress; the expansion of the currency by the great national loans had made money plenty, and the country was ripe for greater enterprises than had hitherto been attempted. The emancipation proclamation of January, 1863, threw a new burden upon Christian men and women of the North. The rapid growth of the new States and Territories necessitated help to the new and feeble churches of the frontiers, not only in the support of missionaries but in aid in erecting houses of worship. Germans, Scandinavians, the Canadian French in New England, and the Indian tribes, were looking to them for instruction and religious care. In the distance, other missionary work, among the Chinese on the Pacific coast, and the

Mexicans, just throwing off the imperial yoke of Maximilian, and rising to the dignity of a free and genuine republicanism, were stretching forth their hands for help. All these calls were coming to the ears of the managers of a society whose receipts had never averaged over $40,000, and were now but little over $30,000. But Dr. Backus the new secretary was equal to the emergency. In that twelve years he raised the annual receipts from $31,000 to $221,000; the number of missionaries from 84 to 435; the annual number of churches organized from 30 to 166; the baptisms from 473 to 7,236, and the churches supplied each year from 215 to 500.

While the war was yet raging, the Society sent missionaries to gather the members of the colored Baptist churches in the South, to instruct, comfort, and strengthen them, and to bring the unconverted to the truth. Then came the necessity of a native ministry. The Society pledged itself, in May, 1866, to continue its work among freedmen, and declared itself especially in favor of established institutions. Under these instructions, grounds and buildings for training-schools were procured in Washington, D. C., and Nashville, Tenn., and good accommodations for a high school at New Orleans, and schools were opened in a number of cities, and soon the whole training of colored Baptist preachers and teachers came into the hands of the American Baptist Home Mission Society. $350,000 were secured for this work in the five years 1869-74 ; and a plan was formed for raising $500,000 for the permanent endowment of these schools and institutions. The statistics as given in 1889 show that the Society have 13 incorporate institutions, including an Indian university, now at Muskogee, Ind. Territory; 7 unincorporated institutions, of which two are in the Indian territory, and one at Monterey, Mexico. In these there are 137 teachers and 3,741 students enrolled. The Society has also 15 schools, supported wholly or in part for the colored people. These have 131 teachers, 3,106 scholars. The expenditures of the society for educational and missionary work among the colored people in twenty-five years was over two million dollars.

But the Board found themselves confronted by a new difficulty, growing out of the rapid development of new churches in the West, and their need of help in building houses of worship. Rev. E. E. L. Taylor was appointed in 1866 to undertake to raise a permanent fund of $500,000 for this purpose, as a secretary for the Church Edifice Department. He labored zealously and successfully till his death in 1874, raising nearly $300,000. Present amount of Loan Fund, 1889, $119,720; Church Edifice Benevolent Investment Fund, $88,000. Total amount paid to churches since 1866, $296,000.

In 1870 the Board took up a mission enterprise inaugurated in Mexico, in 1864, by Rev. James Hickey and Rev. T. M. Westrup. At that time, there were 7 Baptist churches in that State, with about 120 members; there were 4 ordained ministers, three of them native Mexicans. In 1889 there were 44 stations, 25 missionaries, 533 members of the churches ; 20 schools, 479 pupils. The fields occupied are in the State and City of Mexico, where there has been recently erected a substantial and extensive building in which are a chapel, the offices necessary for the work, a dwelling for the superintendent, a printing establishment and depository. There are a church and offices at Monterey, for the numerous stations in Nueva Leon and Tamaulipas, and a new interest in the City of Leon, and another at San Luis Potosi. The annual expenditure was in 1889 about $11,000.

The transfer of the missions to the Indians, previously belonging to the Missionary Union, to the Home Mission Society, was made in 1865.

The mission to our foreign population distinctively began in 1846, with the calling of a young German minister to labor among the Germans of New York, and Newark, N. J., and were promoted in 1856 and 1858 by the active labors of Prof. A. Rauschenbusch, who, in addition to his services as Professor of Theology in the Rochester Theological Seminary, was appointed by the Board in 1863, 1866, and 1871, to act as a missionary superintendent in the German work.

The missions among the Scandinavians began in 1853, with the Swedes in Illinois, but were successfully continued by Prof. J. A. Erdgren, for the Swedes, from 1858 to 1866; by Hans Valder for the Norwegians in Illinois, in 1848-9; and among the Danes, from 1856 to 1886, in Wisconsin, by Rev. Lewis Jargensen and Rev. P. H. Dau. The whole Scandinavian missionary movement was organized and unified in 1866-69. In 1871 Prof. Edgren was made professor in the Scandinavian Department in the Chicago Baptist Theological Seminary. In 1889 the Germans represented in the Society numbered about 14,000 members, the Swedes about 10,500, and the Danes and Norwegians 4,000.

The missions among the Canadian French in the United States were commenced in 1869 in New England and New York by Rev. N. Cyr. Their success has been great; but desiring to make their converts good and patriotic *American* Christians, the missionaries, as in their Scandinavian and Bohemian work, have not organized distinct French churches, but have encouraged them to unite with the American churches.

The mission to the Chinese on the Pacific coast, though beginning as early as 1854 with the Southern Baptist Convention, first took an organized form in 1870, and was continued with good prospects of success for several years; subsequently it was carried on with the co-operation of the Southern Home Mission Board, and the cordial aid of the Baptist churches in San Francisco, and Portland, Oregon. It is now in a flourishing condition, having 13 stations, and is marked by very zealous labor on the part of the missionaries and the Chinese converts.

In 1879 Dr. H. L. Morehouse was elected secretary, and since then every department of the work has been quickened into new life, and new ones have been added.

Work was begun in Arizona in 1880 ; resumed in New Mexico and Mexico in 1881 ; begun in Utah, Montana, and Idaho in 1881 ; in the City of Mexico in 1883; in Alaska in 1886 ; co-operation with the Western States conventions since 1879-82 ; with colored Baptist conventions in the Southern States, in part since 1884, generally in 1888. In the Educational Department the co-operation with the Women's Home Mission Societies had become most thorough and complete.

The mission work among foreign populations. has been greatly extended and enlarged, and work among the Bohemians, Poles, Hungarians, and Russian Jews has been commenced.

BOARD OF HOME MISSIONS OF THE PRESBY-TERIAN CHURCH IN THE UNITED STATES OF AMERICA. Headquarters, 53 Fifth Avenue, New York City.—The history of this Board is almost identical with the history of the Presbyterian Church of America, for at the same time that scattered congregations were formed in the colonies during the last decade of the seventeenth century, the ministers were actuated with a desire to follow the adventurous spirits who left the settled portions and sought homes in the surrounding wilderness. About the time of the founding of the first Presbytery (1700–1705), the ministers of the early church followed the colonists wherever they went, and the gospel was preached along the Atlantic coast, up to the foot of the Alleghanies and beyond, not only to English but to all settlers, of whatever tongue or faith. Missions to the Negroes and the Indians were established. David and John Brainerd to the Indians in New Jersey and Pennsylvania; Occum to the tribes on Long Island and to the Oneidas, Mohawks, Senecas, Cayugas, and other Iroquois; Gideon Blackburn to the Cherokees, Choctaws, Sanduskies, and others,—are all examples of the zealous men who were thus early carrying on the work of home missions under the Presbyterian Church. Education was also needed, and the first presbytery and synod founded colleges and schools, notably Princeton College. Records of the synod show that continual demands were made upon it for means to support missionaries and to open missions in destitute places. These "supplications" were met by the proceeds of collections which were ordered to be taken up in the churches. An interesting item is the fact that the first recorded grant of missionary money was made to the First Presbyterian Church of New York City. The synods of Scotland and Ireland were sent to for additional means when the American church felt unable to meet all the demands in the rapidly growing country.

At the first meeting of the General Assembly which was organized in 1789, it was resolved to send forth missionaries to the frontiers to organize churches and attend in general to the religious and educational needs of the people. To meet the expenses to be incurred, the presbyteries were enjoined to take up collections. Books and Bibles were bought or donated, and were distributed by these missionaries.

In 1802 the work had grown to such dimensions that the first regularly constituted Board was formed under the name of the Standing Committee of Missions. Nominations of missionaries were made by it and presented to the General Assembly for confirmation. During the years of revival which marked the beginning of the present century great success attended the labors of its missionaries.

After the War of 1812 the Committee felt unable to cope with the increased needs and opportunities of the work, and the General Assembly in 1816 organized a larger and more comprehensive body to take up the work, called "The Board of Missions." Its power was such as to enable it to conduct the missions and decide all questions as to the appointment of missionaries and the payment of salaries, without waiting for the approval of the Assembly; it was further empowered to organize branch societies, and the church was urged to co-operate in such organizations.

Under the increased facilities which this Board presented the work grew rapidly. In the mean time the colleges of Hamilton and Auburn had already been established to supply the demand for an educated ministry. Central and Western New York were rapidly growing in population and importance in consequence of the opening of the Erie Canal, and the tide of emigration set in with a strong current toward the Central and Western States. Other churches besides the Presbyterian Church had felt the need of evangelizing these masses thus cut loose from home ties and restraining influences, and in 1826 the American Home Missionary Association was formed. In its directorship were many Presbyterians, and Presbyterian churches contributed to its support and benefited by its aid.

When the division took place in the Presbyterian Church in 1839, the Board of Missions remained in connection with the old-school branch, and in 1857 underwent a change in name, being called "The Trustees of the Board of Domestic Missions of the General Assembly of the Presbyterian Church in the U. S. A."; the new-school threw in its allegiance for a time with the A. H. M. S. (q.v.), but gradually separated from it. The first step in departure was the organization in 1855 of a Church Extension Committee, which carefully disclaimed all intention of interfering with the work or support of the A. H. M. S.; but the differences grew, until finally in 1861 the new-school Presbyterian Church withdrew entirely from the A. H. M. S., organized a Presbyterian Committee of Home Missions, which superseded the Church Extension Committee and which conducted the home-mission work of that branch of the church, until finally in 1870 the glorious reunion of the two assemblies took place, and the two bodies, the Presbyterian Committee of Home Missions and the Board of Domestic Mission, were merged into the Board whose title is given at the head of this article. At the time of reunion the new-school committee had the names of 530 missionaries on its roll, and the old-school Board 613. The new Board was incorporated in New York in 1872.

Organization.—The members of the Board are appointed by the General Assembly, and number 7 ministers and 8 laymen; one of the ministers is the president of the Board. In addition there are two corresponding secretaries, a treasurer, and a recording secretary. The Board reports annually to the General Assembly, to which it is responsible for its actions, though it has absolute jurisdiction in the interim between the meetings of the General Assembly, but appeal can be had to the General Assembly. Its administrative offices are at 53 Fifth Avenue, New York City, together with the other offices of the various Boards.

*The Work of the Board* is in general the establishment of churches where there are none, whether this object be attained directly, or by the gradual process of first establishing a Sunday-school or street services. Within the last few years the Board has assisted in the organization of churches in the cities. This step was taken in view of the fact that about one fourth of the entire population is found in cities of not less than eight thousand people each, and the local churches or societies were unable to keep pace with the increasing demand. During the year 1890 there were 1,701 missionaries employed, distributed over 48 States.

Among the Mexicans, the Mormons, the Southern whites, teachers have been employed to start and conduct schools which are nuclei from which, in time, churches may be organized. Among the two millions of illiterate whites in the South the work has been most hopeful. The White Hall Seminary at Concord, N. C., the boarding-school for girls at Asheville, N. C., and other institutions of higher education are meeting the urgent demand of the South for education. In 1889 all the missions among the Indians where instruction is given in the English language were turned over to the care of the Home Mission Board. The following tribes of Indians are now under the care of this Board: the Nebraska Omahas, the Sacs, the Foxes, and the Chippewas. Among these Indians there are 164 teachers.

Among the Mormons there are 99 teachers in 37 schools with 2,374 scholars. The Mexicans are reached by 67 teachers, 32 schools, and 1,627 scholars. This school work is under the charge of the Woman's Executive Committee.

RESULTS.—The growth of the church has in the main been steady. From 177 ministers in 1879 there are now, in 1890, 6,158 ministers, 6,894 churches, with a membership of 775,903. The direct work of the Board has grown from a total force of 1,566 missionaries and teachers in 1885-6 to a total of 2,064 in 1889-90, and the funds expended from $660,000, in round numbers to $900,000. The magnitude of the work can easily be seen from the following general summary for the year 1890:

| | |
|---|---:|
| Number of missionaries, | 1,701 |
| " " missionary teachers. | 308 |
| Additions on profession of faith. | 9,795 |
| " " certificate. | 7,091 |
| Total membership | 100,778 |
| " in congregations. | 151,366 |
| Adult baptisms. | 3,844 |
| Infant baptisms. | 5,031 |
| Sunday-schools organized. | 578 |
| Number of Sunday-schools. | 2,516 |
| Membership of Sunday-schools. | 160,111 |
| Church edifices (value of same, $4,657,027), | 1,751 |
| " " built during the year (cost of same, $397,681). | 151 |
| " " repaired and enlarged, (cost of same, $65,178). | 321 |
| Church debts cancelled. | $161,838 |
| Churches self-sustaining this year | 30 |
| " organized. | 200 |
| Number of parsonages (value $446,684). | 261 |

DOMESTIC MISSIONS, PROTESTANT EPISCOPAL CHURCH. Headquarters 21-23 Bible House, Astor Place, New York City.—Previous to the year 1820 some efforts had been made, notably by the diocese of Pennsylvania, to establish outposts of the church beyond the Alleghanies. In the year mentioned a project was formed to establish a general society to be known as "The Domestic and Foreign Missionary Society of the Protestant Episcopal Church in the United States of America." In the following year this project took form and a Board of Directors was appointed. The beginnings were small, but such work as was undertaken was altogether in the home field up to the year 1829, when the first missionaries were appointed for Greece, and with that exception so continued until 1834 and 1835, when appointments of missionaries were made for Africa and China. Under this first organization of the Society, membership was secured by the payment of an annual amount, or life-membership and patronage by the payment at one time of respectively larger sums. For this period the Society was practically a voluntary association within the church.

At the time of the General Convention of 1835, which was held in Christ Church, Philadelphia, there was a very strong feeling that the underlying principle of the Society was wrong, and upon the 20th day of August of that year a special committee, which had been appointed two days earlier, brought in a report to the "Board of Directors" of the Missionary Society recommending that "the Church herself, in dependence upon her Divine Head, and for the promotion of His glory, undertake and carry on in her character as the Church, and as the Domestic and Foreign Missionary Society, the work of Christian missions," and that "the appeal of the Church through the Board for the support of missions is made expressly to all baptized persons, as such, and on the ground of their baptismal vows." Upon this report was based the reorganization of the Missionary Society by the General Convention then in session.

By the constitution as amended it was declared that "this Society shall be considered as comprehending all persons who are members of this church." For fifty years thereafter this one Society worked through two committees, one of which had the care and oversight of missions established within, and the other of missions established without, the territory of the United States, known respectively as the Domestic and the Foreign Committees.

At the General Convention held in Boston in 1877 the old Board of Missions, meeting annually and to some degree representative of the church at large, was superseded by the General Convention itself becoming such Board, and the appointment of a Board of Managers, to consist of fifteen clergymen and fifteen laymen, all the bishops being *ex-officio* members. In 1886 this arrangement was further modified by the addition of fifteen elected bishops to the Board of Managers, the other bishops still remaining *ex-officio* members. In the previous year the Domestic and Foreign Committees had been discontinued, the Board of Managers itself assuming immediate care of all the work at home and abroad, and meeting more frequently than it had previously met. The principles of the Society as reorganized in 1835 are well expressed by the motto which appeared for many years upon the title-page of "The Spirit of Missions," its official publication: "It belongs to the calling of a Church of Christ to preach the gospel, not only in Christendom, but to all mankind, for the purpose of leading men to their Saviour."

This paper, however, is to speak particularly of the Society's work in the home field. In 1835 the Rev. Dr. Jackson Kemper, rector of St. Paul's Church, Norwalk, Connecticut, was consecrated as the first of the long and honored line of missionary bishops, with the title of "Bishop of Missouri and Indiana," but his jurisdiction was practically without limit, stretching as it did over so vast a tract of new country devoid of facilities or internal improvements. Dr. Kemper lived until 1870, dying as the diocesan of Wisconsin. In those thirty-five years he travelled 300,000 miles, many thousands of them on horseback, hundreds of them on foot, through snow and mud, under cold and burning skies, exposed to all vicissitudes. For the first twelve years he was never at home except on Christmas Day. He ordained more than two hundred clergymen and confirmed about ten thousand persons. His original jurisdiction was divided and subdivided. At the time of his death seven dioceses had been formed out of it, and missionary jurisdictions had been erected one after another until every portion of the whole country, from the Atlantic to the Pacific, so far as this church was concerned, was under the immediate supervision of some bishop.

From the moment that the church declared herself to be a divinely appointed Missionary Society, she began to grow in a manner that was surprising even to the most sanguine of her members. Statistics cannot easily be compiled which would show the full measure of this growth, decade by decade, for the reason that each new diocese, immediately that it was set up, became itself a missionary society for work within its own limits and all the older dioceses (organized previous to 1835) were greatly stimulated in carrying on the work of diocesan missions, as well as in contributing for the regions beyond. Some idea of the growth of which we speak will be gained from the following facts:

The receipts for Domestic Missions for the fiscal year 1839-40 were $25,000, and the number of Domestic Missionaries was 71.
For 1859-60 the receipts were $66,304, and the number of Missionaries 140.
For 1879-80 the receipts were $165,273, and the number of Missionaries 370.
For 1889-90 the receipts were $251,502, and the number of Missionaries 640.

At the time of the last report it was estimated that a full computation of all the sums given for missionary work in the United States (exclusive of charities) by members of the Protestant Episcopal Church, including what are technically known as Diocesan Missions and the aid given by the Woman's Auxiliary of the Board of Missions, would exceed three-quarters of a million dollars.

While this work at home has been carried on for the most part as a unit, it has had many phases. At one time, for instance, the Board addressed itself to the Jews. This department has long since been in the hands of a separate society, now a recognized auxiliary, and the contributions for it do not appear in the foregoing figures. Work in later years has been carried on in our large cities among the Chinese population, but this for the most part has not been immediately under the General Board.

Since the close of the Civil War, missions to the colored people of the South have been a definite feature of the Society's labors. In the beginning there was a commission especially created for this duty. In 1877 this was discontinued. Ten years later the present Commission on Work among Colored People, having its centre in Washington, D. C., was appointed by the Board of Managers. The work is now larger than ever before.

From the very earliest history of the Society work has been prosecuted among the Indians. This assumed larger proportions in 1870, and one year later was placed under charge of a commission similar to that created for the Colored work. In 1879 the care of this sub-department was relegated to the Board of Managers. There has been very great vigor in the prosecution of this work afield under the able management of

the Right Rev. Dr. Henry B. Whipple, known as the apostle to the Indians of this generation, the Right Rev. Dr. Robert H. Clarkson, late bishop of Nebraska, the Right Rev. Dr. William Hobart Hare, and others. Bishop Hare was specifically consecrated for the work among the Indians in the Niobrara River district, although in course of time his jurisdiction was changed to include the whole population of what is now the State of South Dakota, together with an Indian reservation in Nebraska.

It is safe to say that no religious body has accomplished more valuable and permanent spiritual results among the Indians than has this church. This has been recognized and publicly acknowledged by independent witnesses not of its communion.

The work among people of our own race, by reason of immigration from all the nations of the civilized world, is most varied. In some of the dioceses the Prayer Book is used in three or more tongues.

There are at present employed in the domestic field twelve missionary bishops and 459 other ordained men, among whom is the bishop-elect of Alaska. Eighty-nine of these are employed in work among the colored people of the South—forty-three being colored men—and thirty-one among the Indians—eighteen being Indians. Sixty-six laymen and women are engaged in educational and other work among the Indians in five boarding-schools and at seventy-five stations—thirty-three of them being Indians. One hundred laymen and women—eighty of them being of the colored race—are employed as teachers in colored schools and otherwise at 132 stations. Eight of the missionary bishops and a large number of the bishops of the newer dioceses are giving earnest and successful attention to the work of Christian education in well-established schools, the training of young men of the soil for the ministry being especially cared for. Among the colored people of the South there are 117 Sunday-schools and seventy-seven day and industrial schools, in which about 9,000 children are being educated.

Looking back to 1835 and comparing it with the present, we may note the increase which, humanly speaking, is directly attributable to missionary work, by the following brief statistics:

In 1835 the Episcopal Church in the United States had 15 bishops, 763 other clergymen, with 36,500 communicants. The population of the country was then about 13,000,000. In 1890 there were 75 bishops and 4,000 other clergymen, with 510,000 communicants; and the population 62,000,000. Thus while the population of the country has increased four and one-half times, and that largely by reason of immigration, which has not, in the first generation at least, very greatly increased the membership of this church, the number of communicants has increased fourteen times. In 1840 the ratio was one communicant in each 308 of the population; in 1890, one in each 122 of the population.

**AMERICAN HOME MISSIONARY SOCIETY.** Headquarters, Bible House, New York, N. Y.—When this Society was organized, in 1826, several local organizations for home-missionary work were in operation, some of which originated in the last century. The Society for Propagating the Gospel among the Indians and others in North America was founded in 1787; the Missionary Society of Connecticut, and the Berkshire and Columbia Missionary Society, in 1798; the Massachusetts Missionary Society in 1799. Others of a later origin existed in the other New England States and in New York. Some of them confined their operations within their own geographical limits. Others sent missionaries to the destitute in the new settlements of Northern New England, and the remoter wilderness, even to the banks of the Mississippi. But as these societies acted independently of each other, some sections were over-supplied with laborers and others were left in utter destitution. Moreover, the laborers sometimes came into competition and conflict with each other, and the funds contributed for their support were worse than wasted. It was evident that a more comprehensive and effective system must be devised to supply the destitute portions of the country with gospel ministrations; but no direct steps were taken toward the solution of this problem till 1825, when plans were formed which resulted in the organization of the American Home Missionary Society.

The United Domestic Missionary Society, undenominational in its principles and spirit, was formed in 1822. At an important meeting, composed of eminent New England ministers, held in Boston January 11th, 1826, a resolution was adopted recommending that the United Domestic Missionary Society of New York become the American Domestic Missionary Society. The Executive Committee of the U. D. M. S. cordially responded to the overture from the Boston meeting and issued a circular to friends of Home Missions in all parts of the United States, inviting them to meet in New York to form an American Home Missionary Society. One hundred and twenty-six individuals, representing thirteen States and four denominations, responded to this invitation, and met in New York (Brick Church) on May 10th, 1826. On May 12th the United Domestic Missionary Society, in responding to the proposition made by the convention meeting in the Brick Church, adopted the following resolution:

"*Resolved*, That the recommendation of the convention be adopted, and the U. D. M. S. now become the American Home Missionary Society, under the constitution recommended by the convention."

Officers were at once elected and the work begun.

*Its Constituency.*—Of the churches co-operating, the Associate Reformed shared but little either in its labors or benefactions. The Reformed Dutch churches withdrew when their own Board was organized in 1832. The New School Presbyterian churches continued to co-operate until 1861, when the General Assembly instituted its Presbyterian Committee on Home Missions. Thus the A. H. M. S., without any change either in its constitution or principles of action, became the organ of Congregational churches only.

Its *object* was "to assist congregations that are unable to support the gospel ministry, and to send the gospel to the destitute within the United States." It was to supply the destitute everywhere, but especially those in the new settlements on the Northern and Western and Southern frontiers, with the privileges of the gospel through the ministry of the Word and the Church of God.

Its *method* has been to supplement the former plan of mere missionary tours, pursued by the Domestic Missionary Societies, by providing permanent churches and a permanent ministry, entering into partnership with each church in sustaining its minister, stipulating that it shall bear its full share of the burden, an annually increasing share, until the church shall become self-supporting. The stimulating effect of this system is seen in the fact that, during the last ten years, more than 50 churches have been annually brought to self-support; and the average annual expenditure for a year of missionary labor has been but $263.

Its *Educational Department* was added in 1880, a clause being inserted in the constitution enabling it "to send the means of Christian education to the destitute." Experience has shown that some intellectual training under Christian auspices is essential to the best success of evangelical effort, and should be associated with it.

Through the *Woman's Department* no inconsiderable portion of revenue has been obtained.

The estimated value of gifts sent in "missionary boxes" during the last twenty years has exceeded $50,000 annually.

Its *Children's Department* has within a few months reported the organization in ten States of 50 Home Missionary Circles of children.

Its *Foreign Department.*—When the Society was organized, our population was being increased by only 10,000 immigrants annually. In 1882 no less than 788,992 immigrants reached our shores, increasing our foreign-born population to more than 8,000,000, and adding the children, the number was increased to 17,000,000, or about one third of our whole white population. In view of the peril to our country involved in this vast increase of foreign immigration, the Society in 1883 entered upon a more distinct systematic effort in behalf of this class of our population. In these four years the work has made rapid progress, and the number of missionaries who have preached in foreign languages during last year (1888) is 136.

*Summary.*—Of the 4,689 Congregational churches in the United States, 3,824, or more than four fifths of the whole, were planted, and many more have been fostered by the American Home Missionary Society and its auxiliaries. Since the organization of the American Home Missionary Society in 1826, 376,961 members have been added to churches under its care.

In 1889-90 1,879 home missionaries were employed, 7,211 hopeful conversions were reported, 10,650 members were received into home-missionary churches, 3,251 churches and stations were regularly supplied with the gospel, 56 churches reached self-support, 184 new churches were organized, 169 houses of worship were built, 86 parsonages were erected, 311 Sunday-schools were organized, 142,000 Sunday-school scholars were cared for, 97 young men connected with home-missionary churches were preparing for the ministry; 181 home missionaries labored among the Germans, Welsh, French, Swedes, Norwegians, Danes, Bohemians, Spanish, Indians, Mexicans, and Chinese.

Total expenditures in 45 States and Territories, $604,000.

The work of church erection is carried on by a distinct organization, the Congregational Union.

MISSIONARY SOCIETY OF THE METHODIST

EPISCOPAL CHURCH. Headquarters, Fifth Avenue and Twentieth Street, New York, N. Y.

The origin of Domestic Missions in the M. E. Church was in 1812. Bishop Asbury about this date began soliciting funds for the support of ministers upon missionary circuits. This was the period of vigorous aggressive work in the Far West and in the New England States.

In 1819 the Missionary Society of the M. E. Church was formed, and in the autumn of 1820 it actively began its operations, sending Rev. Ebenezer Brown of the New York Conference to labor among the French people of Louisiana. In the preacher's meeting of New York, held April 5th, 1819, in the Forsyth Street Church, it was

"*Resolved*, That it is expedient for this meeting to form a Missionary and Bible Society of the M. E. Church in America."

Article XIII. of the Constitution provided that the Society should be established "wherever the Book Concern may be located," and the General Conference was authorized to insert articles into the Constitution for such purpose, and to make the book-agents treasurers, and also to provide for the appropriation of funds within the object specified.

The plan of procedure was to organize auxiliaries in all the principal cities. The first auxiliary formed was the Female Missionary Society of New York, about ninety days after the parent Society was instituted, and anticipating all other missionary organizations of woman in the land. The Young Men's Missionary Society of New York was the next in order.

The Conferences of Baltimore, Virginia, Genesee, next in order formed auxiliaries, and the Boston Domestic Missionary Society became an auxiliary. These, with one each at Cortland, N. Y., Columbia, S. C., and Stamford, Conn., constituted all the auxiliaries reported the first year.

The General Conference in Baltimore May, 1820, adopted the report of a committee on organization, and gave the Society and the missionary cause a great and effectual impulse. The existence of the Society really dates from this General Conference of 1820.

The field embraces Arizona with 11 circuits or stations, Black Hills with 14 circuits or stations, Nevada with 25, New Mexico (English) with 10, New Mexico (Spanish) with 22, Utah (English) with 14, Utah (Norwegian and Danish) with 7, Wyoming with 13. Among the Indians there are (1889) 31 circuits or stations.

*Missions Administered by Conferences.*— American Indians; commenced in 1814. Central New York Conference has under its charge the Onondaga Indian Mission; the Columbia River Conference has the Simcoe Indian Mission; Genesee Conference has the church on the Indian Reservation; Puget Sound Conference has under its care the mission in Whatcom County; Wisconsin Conference has the Oneida Mission.

Welsh Missions, began in 1828, are conducted in Northern New York, Rock River, and Wyoming.

Chinese Missions, commenced in 1868, are conducted in San Francisco, Sacramento, San Jose, and Oakland. In addition to these fields the New York Conference opened (May 13th, 1888) a Chinese Mission at Seventh Avenue and Twenty-third Street, New York; and the Oregon Conference founded a similar mission in Portland, Oregon.

Missions to the Germans.—In September, 1835, a missionary began laboring among the Germans in Cincinnati. In 1836 the field was extended to a circuit of 300 miles, having about twenty-five appointments.

In the next year the work was extended to Wheeling, Va.; then to Marietta and Miami, Ohio; and Pittsburgh, Pa. In 1840 a mission was begun in Louisville, Ky., and much fruit was gathered in. In 1841 the Chester Mission had its beginning, and the same year work was extended to Maysville, Ky.

Work now extended to the entire northern half of Ohio, and steps were taken to enter upon missions in the East. The New York Conference (1841) decided to open a mission in New York City, and in May, 1843, a larger edifice succeeded a small one, which had proved insufficient to accommodate the numbers in attendance.

In the South, work commenced at New Orleans in 1841. Stations were successively established in Indiana (Evansville), in Baltimore, in Newark, in Bloomingdale, in the vicinity of Pittsburg, and in Iowa in 1844. The work extended to Detroit, and to Northern Ohio, embracing Delaware (1846), Galion, and Lower Sandusky, Cleveland and Liverpool also becoming stations. The same year missions were multiplied in Indiana, and begun in Booneville, Charleston, Madison, Rockford, Indianapolis, Laughery, and Brookville. Missionaries to the Germans also began their labors in Milwaukee, in Chicago, in Galena, and in Dubuque; also in Buffalo, in Rochester, in Schenectady, in Poughkeepsie, and in Williamsburgh, Long Island.

In 1874 the work, in fact, covered the land, extending to the Pacific coast, in San Francisco, Oakland, San José, Stockton, Los Angeles, and Portland, and has gone on increasing with the opening up of new sections from that time till the present.

*Institutions of Learning.*—A Normal School was opened (November 23d, 1868) at Galena, Ill., whose aim is to furnish Anglo-German teachers for schools, and to fit students for college. The most important schools are at Berea, Ohio, a German department having been opened (1858) in connection with Baldwin University, and it is rapidly expanding into a college.

Another German college was organized (1872) in connection with the Iowa Wesleyan University at Mount Pleasant, Iowa. A nucleus for a fifth (German) institution has been formed in Texas.

Summary by the Report of 1889: Missionaries, 3,325 (in 1888, 3,632); local preachers, 3,594 (in 1888, 3,102); members, 261,981 (in 1888, 242,386); Sabbath-schools, 4,571 (in 1888, 4,977); scholars, 281,157 (in 1888, 241,610); churches and chapels, 4,569 (in 1888, 3,953). Estimated value, $6,477,095 (in 1888, $6,017,545).

Appropriations for home-mission work among foreigners, English-speaking and Indians, $605,511 (in 1888, $604,189).

REFORMED (DUTCH) CHURCH IN U. S. A., BOARD OF DOMESTIC MISSIONS OF THE. Headquarters, 26 Reade Street, New York.—Until the independence of the American Reformed churches in 1772, they were themselves missionary ground. At the close of the Revolution the list of Dr. Livingston shows 85 churches, 32 ministers serving 53 of these churches, and two licentiates.

In 1786 the old Synod took the first action on the subject of church extension, and appointed Messrs. Westerlo D. Romeyn, H. Schoonmaker, and H. Meyer a committee to devise some plan for sending the gospel to destitute localities, and they reported to the next Synod, and recommended that voluntary collections be taken up in all the congregations, to aid in the extension of the church. This was the first effort made. The moneys collected were to be transferred through the Classes to the Synod.

The subject of church extension is found inserted as an item, in the regular business of each Classis, as early as 1790, and moneys began to come in for this cause. A Classis at this time would collect from £10 to £20 annually. At the close of the century all the Classes were forwarding money (most of the churches contributing), except the Classis of Kingston, for the cause of church extension.

The Synod in 1800 formally appointed the Classis of Albany to take charge of all the missionary operations of the North.

1806-1822. The Synod now appointed a committee of four ministers and four elders, with plenary powers, to whom should be confided all her missionary operations. They were located in Albany till 1819, when, on the final abandonment of the Canadian Missions, they were directed to locate henceforth in New York. They were known as the "Standing Committee of Missions for the Reformed Dutch Church in America."

The committee began their operations on the old plan,—short tours by settled pastors; but such efforts proved unsatisfactory. Settled ministers were wanted.

With the transfer of the committee to New York the Canadian churches were quietly abandoned. Some of the Classes now began to retain their money for their own missionary necessities. At the suggestion of Paschal N. Strong, a number of individuals in January, 1822, organized themselves into a society, to be known as "The Missionary Society of the Reformed Dutch Church." This act was made known to the Synod, and the matter was referred to the Committee on Missions. The birth of the Society was hailed with joy. Its board of managers was made Synod's Committee on Missions, and all the churches were exhorted to form auxiliary societies, both for domestic and foreign operations.

1822-32. The policy of the new Society was to employ as many of the graduates of the seminary as were willing to undertake mission work; to have auxiliary societies in every congregation, and to take up collections at the monthly concerts for prayer. During the ten years of its existence the Society collected more than $30,000, aided about 100 churches or stations, and 130 missionaries. It also started, in 1826, the "Magazine of the Reformed Dutch Church," which, four years later, was transformed into the "Christian Intelligencer."

The old Missionary Society consented in 1833 to become auxiliary to the Board, and for nine years the Board depended on Classical agents. At this time (1837) the first church of the denomination was formed in the West, at Fairview, Ill. In 1841 there were enough churches to organize the Classes of Illinois and Michigan, and ten years later the Classis of Holland. The name of the Board was in 1842 changed from the "Board of Missions" to the "Board of Domestic Missions of General Synod."

The Board was reorganized in 1849, was incorporated in 1867, and now holds its own funds, which were previously held by the Board of Corporation. In 1854 the plan of a Church Building Fund was proposed. The aim was to raise funds to aid feeble churches by loans, to enable them to build places of worship.

The Fifty-seventh Annual Report to the General Synod (May, 1889) presents the following facts:

In the two departments there are 120 churches and missions, 93 missionary pastors; $41,244 given for the support of pastors; $1,975 to home missions, and $4,144 to other benevolent objects.

Total receipts for the year, $32,367.60.

BOARD OF MISSIONS OF THE METHODIST EPISCOPAL CHURCH (SOUTH). Headquarters, Nashville, Tenn.—In the charter of incorporation it is declared: "The object of said corporation is to provide for the support of public worship, the building of schools, churches, and chapels, and the maintenance of all missionary undertakings; to provide for the support of superannuated missionaries, and the widows and orphans of missionaries who may not be provided for by any Annual Conference; to print books for the Indian, German, Mexican, and other foreign missions, under the direction and according to the law of the said Methodist Episcopal Church (South.)"

Its charter was obtained according to the laws of the State of Tennessee on the 8th day of April, 1881.

In 1846 the Mission Board reported 24,430 members, while the general minutes gave a total of 124,931. Many of the leading ministers of the South were noted for their devotion to the religious welfare of the slaves, and at an annual conference the presiding elder could pronounce no higher encomium on a pastor than to say: "He is a good Negro preacher." In 1860, when the war disturbed the labors among these people, the Methodist Episcopal Church (South) reported a colored membership of 207,766.

*Indian Missions of the Methodist Episcopal Church (South).*—In 1844 the Indian Mission Conference was organized. It included the Indian Territory and Indians in the Missouri Conference. At its session held in October of that year the work was divided into three districts, with 25 men, several of whom were Indians, and 85 whites, 33 colored members, and 2,992 Indian members.

In the division of the church in 1844 the Indian Mission Conference remained with the Methodist Episcopal Church (South). In 1846 the work was divided into the Kansas River, the Cherokee, and Choctaw districts, with 22 missions, 32 missionaries, 3,404 members, 9 churches, 18 Sunday-schools, and 7 literary institutions. Missions were established among the Pottawattamie, Chippewa, Peoria, Wea, Kansas, Wyandotte, Shawnee, Kickapoo, Quapaw, Seneca, and other tribes or fragments of tribes located on reservations in the Indian Territory.

The cloud of war for several years obscured the missions, and there were no reports. The records of the Board from 1861 to 1870 remain undiscovered. From the statistical report of 1871 we find the following from the Indian Mission Conference: Itinerant preachers, 17; local, 54; white members, 139; colored, 437; Indian, 3,833. Total, 4,480. Sunday-schools, 12; scholars, 372. Expenditures, $5,674.30.

Since the last date the work has been carried on steadily through itinerant and local preachers with their helpers, until the report of 1888 shows the following results: Travelling preachers, 45; supplies, 31; local preachers, 129; white members, 3,514; colored, 21; Indian, 5,246. Total, 8,781. Expenditures, $17,874.60.

The Indian Mission Conference (Indian Territory) furnishes the following summary: Local preachers, 147; Indian members, 4,954; white, 3,616; colored, 17. Total, 8,587. Sunday-schools, 129; officers and teachers, 661; scholars, 4,301. Churches, 90; value, $36,475. Parsonages, 24; value, $10,025. Money expended for church purposes, $4,164.73. Collections for domestic missions, $1,000; foreign, $1,171.62.

*Institutions.*—The Board has under its care the following institutions: *Galloway College* (Vinita, Indian Territory); *Pierce Institute* (Indian Territory); *Andrew Marvin Institute; Collins Institute* (near Stonewall, Indian Territory), a manual-labor school; *Harrell International Institute* (at Muskogee, Indian Territory) is under the control of the Woman's Board of Missions of the Methodist Episcopal Church (South), having five departments—collegiate, academic, primary, music, and art.

The Oklahoma country is now open for occupation by the Indian Mission Conference.

*German Missions.*—No record is found of the German missions of this church prior to 1846. The records of that year report missions at New Orleans, Mobile, Charleston, and Galveston, with 5 missionaries, 139 members, 2 Sunday-schools, and 80 scholars. In 1861 there were: Missionaries, 23; members, 1,078; Sunday-schools, 11; scholars, 461.

The war greatly disorganized the German work. A number of the preachers and many members left for the Northern Methodist Church, which in the days of depression following the war was able to contribute more liberally than the South for their support. A number of preachers were true to their mother church.

*Western Work.*—In 1836 Texas gained her independence, and in 1837 the bishops of the Methodist Episcopal Church, in conjunction with the Missionary Society, commissioned Dr. Littleton Fowler superintendent of the Texas Mission. At the division of the church the mission had grown into two annual conferences. These adhered to the Methodist Episcopal Church (South). In 1846 they reported 61 missionaries; 6,817 white and 1,005 colored members. In 1888 they had expanded into five annual conferences, with 564 itinerant preachers, 961 local preachers, 117,652 members. The German Mission Conference and the Mexican Border Mission Conference are also the outgrowth of the old Texas Mission.

October 9th, 1849, three missionaries were appointed to California, who departed in 1850. In 1888 there were reported 108 itinerant preachers, 99 local preachers, and 7,957 members. July 19th, 1870, saw the beginning of that work which now includes the Denver, Montana, and Western Conferences. In 1888 there

were reported 100 itinerant, 64 local preachers, and 6,635 members.

*Columbia Conference* has three districts: (1) Oregon, which reports (1888) 19 charges supplied by 13 itinerant and 2 local preachers, and a membership of 869; (2) Washington, which reports 108 accessions, and a school (at Weston) with 36 students; (3) Spokane, which reports four churches and districts enjoying revivals.

MISSIONS TO THE CHINESE.—To give a full account of the work of home missions among all the different classes of foreigners that have come to the United States would be far beyond the limits of this work, originally designed especially for foreign missions. The work among the Chinese, however, is so distinctive and so important that it has been treated below somewhat fully.

Chinese immigrants came to America soon after the discovery of gold in 1848, attracted as were other men by the visions of wealth which that discovery excited in the minds of all. No large numbers came till 1852 and afterward, and at that time the Chinese Government was hostile to emigration. After the "Burlingame" treaty in 1868 the inalienable right of man to change his habitation was officially recognized by China as well as by the United States, and from that time till the first restriction act in 1882 the tide of immigration was a steady stream, and the number annually ran up to the hundred thousand. Since 1882, and especially since the exclusion act of 1888, the number has lessened, until the last census will probably show not more than 80,000 Chinese in the United States; a large decrease as compared with the figures for 1880—105,613. At first the advent of the Chinese was hailed with joy; now, denied the rights of citizenship, hooted at, persecuted, imposed upon, maltreated in many ways at the instigation of prejudice and ignorance, they still remain among us, with a pluck, a perseverance, an endurance worthy of admiration, and figure so little in the police courts, still less in the saloons, that one is ofttimes tempted to think that therein lies their lack of power for assimilation.

Christian work among this class of our immigrant population is fraught with peculiar hindrances for many reasons. (1) They are a migratory people, and return home as soon as they have secured a competence. (2) They know little of our language, and still less of our modes of thought; they ask but to be let alone. (3) The prejudice which they excite in the minds of most people has had its effect in making them doubly suspicious, especially when the man who stones them and the one who offers them Christian instruction is alike a "Christian" to their indiscriminating minds; and too often even those who are Christians refuse to have them baptized into the same church, and to allow them to sit at the same table with themselves. The people who sometimes are willing to send the gospel are very unwilling to have it shared by these strangers at their own doors. (4) The nature of their occupations and the mental capacity of the men, who are of the peasant class, render them somewhat dull to hear and slow to understand the truth given them. But the greatest impediments to the acceptance of the gospel by the Chinese are the inconsistencies which they see in the lives of those whom they consider Christians.

In spite of these hindrances, an important and growing work is carried on among the Chinese which demands particular mention. It is carried on in two ways, and by somewhat varying methods. There is regular missionary work, which is under the care of organized Boards or branches of some Board, and is conducted in the usual manner of all mission work, with missionaries who speak the language, and with preaching, teaching, and other evangelistic work, to which is added rescue work for the girls who are brought over to pander to the lusts of depraved Americans as well as Chinese. Then there is the great work which is carried on by individual churches, which partakes almost entirely of the nature of Sunday-school work, and is undertaken by faithful workers wherever the Chinaman is found. The methods adopted differ materially from those of the former in that English is the only medium of communication, and there is first instruction in English and then in gospel truth.

*Organized Missions.*—These are found mainly on the Pacific coast. The earliest effort of this nature was commenced in San Francisco in 1852 by Rev. W. M. Speer, at one time a missionary of the Presbyterian Board to China. He called the attention of the Presbyterian Church to the need of the Chinese in this country, and labored as their missionary for five years, when, his health failing, Rev. A. W. Loomis came back from China and took up the work. In 1870 the mission was reinforced by the return from China of the Rev. I. M. Condit. In 1877 work was begun in Oakland, and now there are the following stations on the Pacific coast: San Francisco, Los Angeles, Oakland, in California; and Portland, Oregon. Mr. and Mrs. Loomis, Mr. and Mrs. Kerr, are stationed at San Francisco, together with three female missionaries. A home for rescued Chinese women and girls has been in existence for fifteen years, during which time it has sheltered 260 persons, many of whom were saved from a life of the most dreadful slavery, at the risk of danger to the persons of the missionaries, and at the cost of much effort and appeal to the courts of law.

In the church at San Francisco there are 78 members, and much work is done by means of street-preaching, and house-to-house visitation of the women. At Oakland there is a church with 44 members, under the care of a native. One missionary and his wife, together with native helpers, have charge of the work at Sacramento, where there is a church, and Sunday and day schools are conducted. Missions are also conducted under the care of Chinese at Santa Rosa, San José, Napa, and Alameda. Los Angeles has a church of 65 members under the care of a missionary, and the school work is carried on both day and evening, for women and girls as well as for men. The mission at Santa Barbara has ten Christian Chinese, and a female missionary conducts the schools. The work in Portland is under the care of a returned China missionary. There are nineteen Christians, a home for girls (under the care of the North Pacific Woman's Board), and various schools. Two new schools have been opened during the last year—at Ashland and at Salem. The only work in the East under the care of the Board, is the mission in New York. It is the successor of work which was commenced by the Rev. Lycurgus Railsback in the Five Points House of Industry in 1869, and carried on for many succeeding years by a faithful woman, Miss Goodrich. There is now a commodious mission room at University Place, where a Chinese assistant holds services and takes charge of Sunday-school work. Every Sunday evening a prayer-meeting is held, at which the Chinese Christians take part. Several Chinese have joined the church, and money is contributed toward the support of a church in the native district from which these immigrants come.

*The Methodist Episcopal Church (North)* commenced a mission to the California Chinese in 1868, under the superintendence of Rev. Otis Gibson, D. D. The mission is now under the care of Rev. F. J. Masters, formerly stationed at Canton, China. Since the establishment of the mission up to 1890, 352 were admitted to the church, 230 Chinese women and girls were rescued from slavery, and upwards of 4,000 Chinese have received religious and secular instruction in the schools. There are missions at San Francisco (105 church-members), Sacramento (19 members), Oakland (19 members), and San José (12 members). In Oregon the work is under the care of a missionary and his wife who reside at Portland, and there are 15 church-members. The Society also has a mission in New York, which was opened May 13th, 1888. It was the combination of Sunday-schools which had been carried on in the Eighteenth-street and Seventh-street churches. The rooms are always open for the use of the Chinese, and Sunday-school and prayer-meetings are held weekly. Several Chinamen have been baptized from among the students.

*The American Baptist Home Missionary Society* commenced its work in San Francisco in 1870, at which time there were 3 missionaries. The mission at Portland was opened soon afterward. At present the work is carried on in California with headquarters at San Francisco, and in Oregon. A returned China missionary is the superintendent of the missions. In San Francisco there is a Chinese church of 41 members, under the care of a Chinese pastor. In Portland there is also a Chinese church and pastor, with 41 members, and a Chinese missionary, who works among the Chinese in other places in Oregon. There are in addition 6 mission schools. The first church built for the Chinese was dedicated in San Francisco in connection with this mission in August, 1887. The greatest harmony exists in San Francisco between all these missions, and a service is held in the streets, at which the different missionaries preach in turn. The United Brethren have a mission in Walla Walla, Washington.

*The American Missionary Association* carries on a widely extended work among the Chinese on the Pacific coast. Its methods are those which characterize the second division of the work, the Sunday-school system, rather than those of the above-mentioned missions. In addition to the Sunday-school, day and evening schools are held, whose teachers are engaged in teaching English and then the gospel. Indeed, it is claimed that the first school work of this kind was undertaken by Mrs. L. L. Lynde, of the Congregational Church in Oakland, in 1867. The mission of the Association was commenced at San Francisco in 1870, under the superintendency of the Rev. John Kimball with 329 scholars. Since 1875 the care of the mission has been placed in the hands of the Rev. W. C. Pond, pastor of the Bethany Congregational Church of San Francisco. In 1875 the General Association of the Congregational churches in California organized the California Chinese Mission, auxiliary to the A. M. A., with Rev. J. K. McLean, D.D., as president, and Dr. Pond as secretary. During 1889 the auxiliary raised $4,299,55 for the expenses of the mission, in addition to the $7,100 which was appropriated by the A. M. A. for the work. The missions are: 3 in San Francisco—the Central, the Barnes, and the West; and 14 at Oakland, Santa Cruz, Los Angeles, San Diego, Riverside, Fresno, Stockton, Sacramento, Oroville, Marysville, Petaluma, Santa Barbara, San Buenaventura, in California; and Tucson, Arizona. There are 21 lady-teachers, and 10 Chinese, with a total of 1,380 in attendance on instruction. Over 750 conversions are the result of these missions, of which 150 were the gain during one year. At Marysville and Oroville there are Chinese churches; at the other missions the converts join the American Congregational churches. In 1871 the "Congregational Association of Christian Chinese" was organized in San Francisco, and now has a branch at each of the missions. It is a Christian association, to which every Chinese must belong for six months of probation before he is admitted to the church. It is also a missionary organization, and it was in direct response to their contribution of $500 that the A. B. C. F. M. sent out in 1883 the missionary who has charge of its work in Hong Kong and part of the Canton province. In 1890 these Christian Chinese, together with those of other denominations, raised a sum of money to build a chapel and start a mission in their native district, near San-ui, Kwangtung. One Christian Chinaman has paid the salary of a Christian Chinese physician, and another Christian Chinese supplies the medicines which are dispensed. In all $2,500 was raised in 1890 by this Association.

*Unorganized Work.*—After the school was started in New York which was afterwards handed over to the care of the Presbyterian Board, it was many years before the churches awoke to the responsibility which was imposed upon them by the presence of these strangers within our gates. The work was so difficult; it seemed such a hopeless task to teach a Chinaman his letters for an hour or two a week; there was no romance of missions, no display of self-denial, in teaching the heathen at home; and it was difficult to overcome the distrust of the Chinese sufficiently to insure their attendance. But godly women took up the arduous work. At first by inviting the Chinese to their own homes one at a time, then gathering them into a secluded corner of the church Sunday-school room, until finally a Sunday-school would be organized—in this way schools were started in the principal cities. In 1876 such a school was started in connection with the Mt. Vernon Church of Boston, which is now the largest school in the country. In 1878 the Trinity Baptist Church in New York City commenced a Sunday-school for the Chinese, and within the last decade such schools have been started in nearly all the large cities along the Atlantic coast, and inland, and also in many small places devout women have gathered the two or three Chinese together for instruction. In the spring of 1890 a monthly magazine was published in New York City for the purpose of establishing communication between the scattered and unorganized workers, as well as for publishing Christian teaching in Chinese.

The "Chinese Evangelist," as it was called, was published in both Chinese and English by Guy Maine, a Christian Chinaman, and J. Stewart Happer, son of the China missionary. It was partially self-supporting with the aid of donations for two years, but had to be relinquished in April, 1890, on account of the lack of sufficient remuneration for the labors of the editors, which had been gratuitous for two years. During its existence a list of the schools was published, together with statistics which, though incomplete, were more full than anything that had yet been compiled. Its subscription books gave a good idea of the extent of the work for the Chinese in the United States. It went to 31 States and Territories and 145 different post-offices. The schools given on the incomplete list numbered 123, with an average attendance, as far as could be ascertained, of 1,600, exclusive of the mission schools on the Pacific coast. There were 217 Christians in connection with these schools.

*Indirect Results.*—In addition to the direct results which the above account shows for the work among the Chinese, there is a result of the work which is no less important, though not so generally recognized. This is the reflex influence on China. It is a notable fact that the mission schools in this country have by disarming prejudice, by the power of kindness, been the direct means of opening fields in Kwangtung province to the labors of the foreign missionary. Men who have never shown any signs of a change of heart under instruction abroad have been so impressed with the spirit of kindness shown by Christians, that they have in many instances made the way easy for the foreigner who comes to their native village after they have returned to their homes, and the opposition of their neighbors has been overcome by words such as these: "The Christians were kind to me in America; these men are Christians; let them come; they intend to do you good." In this way several preaching places have been opened in districts which would otherwise have been inaccessible, and very often the itinerant missionary in the San-ui and Sinning districts in Kwangtung is greeted with a "How d'ye do" in English from a returned immigrant, and an invitation to come and spend the night with him has been the means of opening the way to the preaching of the gospel in that village. The results of the work, which is carried on in faith, though in darkness, can never be adequately represented by any figures save those which are kept in the book of the recording angel.

Some mention should be made of the work of the "St. Bartholomew's Chinese Guild" in New York City. This is an organization in connection with the mission rooms of St. Bartholomew's P. E. Church. On payment of a nominal fee, Chinese of good character may become members; and in addition to the privileges of the reading and meeting rooms at 23 St. Mark's Place, they are at liberty to call on the manager, Mr. Guy Maine, before mentioned, who will act as interpreter for them in any matters of legitimate business, and the services of the Guild's lawyer are available to protect them from impositions, or to defend them from malicious persecution. This Guild was opened in 1889, and during the year 1890 there were 466 members; 776 cases were attended to. A Sunday-school is held every Sunday afternoon, and 6 Chinese have united with the church. One rescue case was successfully undertaken by the lawyer and manager of the Guild, and the rescued Chinese girl is now under Christian instruction.

The work in Vancouver, B. C., is not strictly within the scope of this article; but mention may be made that the Methodist Church of Canada has there quite a flourishing work under the care of a missionary of Chinese birth, who preaches and teaches in the Chinese language. The Presbyterian Church of Canada is also contemplating commencing work for the Chinese in Victoria in the near future.

**Universalist General Convention.** Secretary, Rev. G. L. Demarest, Manchester, N. H.—The Universalist churches of the United States are organized for missionary work, as well as for legislation, into State Universalist Conventions, of which there are twenty-five, and the Universalist General Convention. The work of the former is mainly home-missionary work; the latter has recently inaugurated a mission to Japan.

The General Convention is under a Board of Trustees, consisting of twelve members, of whom John D. W. Joy of Boston is chairman. They represent an organized strength of 934 parishes with about 41,000 families, who during the year 1889 contributed for missionary purposes $43,000. In April, 1890, a band of missionaries was sent to Japan, and Tokyo was chosen as the field, but the work is as yet in the preparatory stages. For the support of this mission a special contribution of more than $60,000 for five years was made. The care of the mission is with a standing committee of the Board of Trustees.

Women's Auxiliary Societies have also been formed in several places, one of which supports a mission in Glasgow, Scotland.

**Universities' Mission to Central Africa.** Headquarters, 14 Delahay Street, Westminster, London, S. W., England—The Universities' Mission to Central Africa was proposed by David Livingstone in 1857, and undertaken in 1859, after a second appeal by Robert Gray, Bishop of Cape Town. In 1861 Charles Frederick Mackenzie, Archdeacon of Natal, was consecrated bishop of the mission, and by him, under the guidance of Livingstone, the mission was started at Magomero, south of Lake Nyassa, a colony of released slaves forming the nucleus of the mission. The place chosen being found impracticable on account of the climate, the site was twice changed, but both places proving too unhealthy for the European missionaries, Bishop Tozer, who succeeded Bishop Mackenzie in 1862, then resolved to settle in Zanzibar, and there to devote himself to the training of released slave children, in the hope of forming with them Christian settlements on the mainland at a later date.

About ten years of quiet preparatory work was carried on in Zanzibar, under Bishop Tozer and Dr. Steere, in the education of rescued slaves, the preparation of grammars and dictionaries, and the translation of portions of the Scriptures.

In 1874 Bishop Steere succeeded Bishop Tozer, and in 1875 a station was opened at Magila, on the mainland northwest of Zanzibar, by a colony of released slaves trained by the mission. With a view to the formation of stations in the interior, a half-way station was made at Masisi in 1876, and in 1879 the Rev. W. P. Johnson settled alone on the south shore of Lake Nyassa, but was expelled in 1881 by the chief of the district. In 1882 a station was opened on the east shore of Lake Nyassa, at Chitiji's, and was maintained for eighteen months under great danger, owing to the repeated attacks of the natives.

In 1883 Charles Alan Smythies was appointed bishop of the mission. In 1884, owing to the efforts of the Rev. W. P. Johnson, a steamer was purchased for the use of the mission on Lake Nyassa, and in 1885 a station was begun on the island of Lukoma, in the lake, where are now the headquarters of the Nyassa Mission.

The work is now carried on from three centres: Zanzibar Island, Lake Nyassa, and stations on the mainland between. There are in the field 26 English clergymen, 25 laymen, 20 ladies, 2 African clergy, and 32 native teachers and readers; about 420 children are supported by the mission, and 300 Africans are assisted by it and are under its care. The cost of the work in 1888 was upwards of £17,000; the funds are sent out to and are managed by the bishop himself.

**Unwana,** a town in Old Calabar, West Africa, near the Cross River. Climate tropical. Population, 4,000. Race and language, Ibo. Religion, idolatry. People peaceful, agricultural; polygamy common. Mission station United Presbyterian Church of Scotland (1888); 1 missionary and wife, 1 native helper, 1 Sabbath-school.

**Upolu Island,** one of the Samoan Group, South Pacific. Surface mountainous, covered with luxuriant vegetation. Area, 335 square miles. Chief town, Apia. Population, 300, of which 100 are Europeans. Mission station London Missionary Society; 5 missionaries, 104 native pastors, 4 stations, 209 schools. (See Samoa.)

**Urambo,** a town in East Central Africa, between Lakes Tanganyika and Victoria Nyanza. Mission station of the London Missionary Society (1849); 2 missionaries. The missionaries at this station have enjoyed fairly good health, have had the friendship of the native chief; the confidence of the people has been won, and good preparatory work has been accomplished. A medical missionary was added to the force during 1890.

**Uriya Version.**—The Uriya, also called Orissa, belongs to the Indic branch of the Aryan family of languages, and is used in the province of Orissa, the greater part of which is attached to Bengal. Serampore missionaries translated the New Testament, which was published in 1811. The first translation of the Old Testament was made by Dr. Carey, and published in 1819. Shortly afterwards the first Baptist missionaries commenced this work at Cuttack, and as the whole Bible had been translated into the languages of the people, they could in this sense take to themselves the whole armor of God. A revision of the Bible, or rather of the Old Testament, soon became necessary, and Messrs. Sutton, Noyes, and Buckley betook themselves to the work of translation or revision. The work was published under the care of Dr. Sutton at Calcutta by the Bible Society in 1844, in three volumes. A third was undertaken by the Rev. Dr. Buckley, which was published at Cuttack in 1872. In his work Dr. Buckley was aided by Jagoo Roul, a native minister, who had a more accurate acquaintance with the niceties of the Uriya language than any other native. A fourth edition of the Old Testament was also prepared by Dr. Buckley. His object was to make Dr. Sutton's version something better, and to achieve this, Dr. Buckley availed himself of native opinion on questions of idiom and diction. He had carried on his revision up to the 83d Psalm, when he was suddenly called to rest in 1886. Up to March 31st, 1889, the British and Foreign Bible Society had disposed of 40,000 portions of the Bible.

**Uruguay,** the smallest republic of South America, is situated on the east coast, and is bounded by Brazil on the northeast, the Atlantic Ocean and the La Plata River on the south, and on the west by the Uruguay River, which separates it from the Argentine Republic. The country is divided into 19 provinces, with a total area of 72,110 square miles, and a population of 687,194. Seven per cent of the population are native-born, consisting principally of half-breeds; the remainder are Spanish, Italians, French, Brazilians, and Argentines. Montevideo, the capital, situated at the entrance of the river La Plata, has a good harbor and roadstead, and a population of 134,346. Uruguay was formerly a part of the vice-royalty of Spain, then became a province of Brazil, but declared its independence in 1825, which was recognized by the treaty of Montevideo (1828). By the terms of the constitution adopted 1830, a president, elected for four years, and a parliament, composed of two houses, constitute the government of the republic.

The territory is one vast pasture-land. On the rolling plains great numbers of cattle and sheep are raised, and the principal wealth and exports of the country consist of live-stock, and the resulting products. Agriculture is carried on to a limited extent. The climate is in general healthy. In the coast districts there are no great extremes of heat and cold; in the interior the thermometer ranges from 86° in summer to 35° in winter.

The state religion is Roman Catholic, but there is complete toleration, and the general condition of education is very satisfactory.

Missionary societies at work in Uruguay are: the Methodist Episcopal Church (North), with stations at Montevideo, Colonia, Tacuarembo, and Trinidad, under the charge of 1 missionary and wife, 2 female missionaries, 3 native ordained preachers; 6 chapels with 350 members, 11 day-schools, 700 scholars, 10 Sabbath-schools, 424 scholars. The South American Missionary Society, with stations at Fray Bentos and Salto, and 1 missionary.

**Usambiro,** a station of the C. M. S. on the south shore of Lake Nyanza, Eastern Equatorial Africa. Here it was that the intrepid missionary Alexander M. Mackay, after fourteen years of work, died. One missionary was left in charge, and reinforcements left England in April, 1890, to continue the work in this district.

**Utrecht Missionary Society.** Headquarters, Utrecht, Holland.—The object of this Society was to send the gospel to the Dutch East Indies. It was founded in 1859, and its first missionaries were sent out to Dutch New Guinea, or Papua, in 1863, when Mansinam and Doueh were occupied. In 1865 two more stations were opened—Andai and Rhoon. These stations have now each a resident married missionary, a church, and a school.

In 1865 work was commenced at Almahera, with two stations, Duma and Soakonora. At the former station there is a Christian village, and each station has a married missionary, with church and school work. A mission was begun in 1884 at Boeroe, with one station, Kawiri, under the care of a married missionary.

**Uvea,** one of the Loyalty Islands (q.v.), Melanesia.

**Uzbek-Turki** or **Sart Version.**— To the Turki branch of languages included in the Russian Empire belongs the ancient Uigur, which covers the varieties of Trans-Caspian Turki spoken by the Uzbek nation scattered over Central Asia southward from Tashkend to near Afghanistan, and westward from Ferghana to the Caspian. Of these varieties the Jaghatai Turki of the Tekkes and of Central Turkestan has been treated already. Another variety is the Uzbek Turki or Sart, and into this dialect Mr. Osbrunoff, a Russian inspector of schools, undertook a translation of the New Testament, of which the four Gospels were published by the British Bible Society at St. Petersburg, in 1888. The translator, who is acquainted with the different Turki dialects of Central Asia, believes that the Uzbek, which is used by the more settled and civilized portions of the inhabitants, is certain to become the dominant language of Central Asia. The version, which is in the Sart dialect, was amended by the Rev. A. Amirkhanianz, and printed under the care of Dr. Sauerwein, and Messrs. Radloff and Amirkhanianz.

# V.

**Valparaiso,** an important city of Chili, is situated on a bay of the same name. It has many institutions of learning; the streets are narrow, but usually well paved, and the houses present a gay appearance with their bright colors and overhanging balconies. A railroad connects it with Santiago. Population estimated at 212,810 (1889).

Mission work is carried on by the Presbyterian Church (North); 2 missionaries and wives, 7 out-stations, 90 communicants.

**Van,** a city in Armenia, East Turkey, on the east shore of Lake Van, 145 miles southeast of Erzroom, 350 miles southeast of Trebizond. Climate mild, healthy; elevation

5 500 feet. Population, 50,000, Christians, Moslems Races, Armenians, Koords, Turks. Mission station A. B. C. F. M. (1872); 1 missionary and wife, 2 other ladies, 15 native helpers, 2 out-stations, 1 church, 37 church-members, 6 schools, 228 scholars.

It is now, as it always has been, the centre of Armenian influence in Eastern Turkey. On the picturesque castle of the city are a large number of inscriptions in Armenian cuneiform, dating back even earlier than many of the Assyrian inscriptions. Near Van is the island of Aghtamar, the seat of an Armenian Catholicos, whose spiritual rank is equal to that of the Catholicos of Etchmiadzine. His influence however is small.

**Vanderkemp, John T.,** b. 1747, Rotterdam, Holland, where his father was pastor of the Dutch Reformed Church; studied at the University in Leyden; spent 16 years in the army, where he was captain of horse and lieutenant of the dragoons. After leaving the army he went to Edinburgh, where he became distinguished for his attainments in the natural sciences and modern languages. He then returned to Holland and practised medicine with great success. The accidental death of his wife and child, caused by a sudden storm which capsized the boat in which he was sailing with them, was the means of his genuine conversion, for though a nominal member of his father's church, he had become strongly influenced by infidel opinions. During the war with France he served in the hospital. Hearing of the appeal of the London Missionary Society, he offered himself to the directors, was accepted, and on the 3d of November, 1797, was ordained missionary to South Africa. Before leaving he organized two missionary societies, one at Rotterdam and one at Friesland, in his native country, to co-operate with the L. M. S. In 1798 he sailed with three others for Africa, taking passage in a convict ship. On the voyage he and his companions administered to the spiritual as well as the temporal wants of the convicts. Arriving at Cape Town in March, 1799, Dr. Vanderkemp commenced at once to labor among the natives, while at the same time he awakened a deep interest in missions among the Europeans. In May he left Cape Town for the interior. After a wearisome and dangerous journey he reached Graaf Reinet in June; and though the surrounding country was in a state of anarchy and strife, he pushed farther inland to the Great Fish River, at that time the southern limit of Kaffraria. After a month of waiting he secured an audience with the king, Geika, who gave him permission to pitch his tent, but advised him to leave on account of the unsettled state of affairs. Permission was finally given to start the mission near the Keiskamma River, where in October a station was founded. A school was opened, and in spite of messages from the governor at the Cape entreating him to return, left alone by the departure of his colleague, the doctor labored on for over a year, when the king, growing jealous of the advance which Christianity had already made, ordered the missionary to leave. Accompanied by his people to the number of about sixty, some English, some Hottentot, some Kafirs, some Tambookees, and some of mixed race, Dr. Vanderkemp started across the country, and for more than four months the caravan moved about from place to place, while the faithful missionary continued the instruction of the people. In May, 1801, he arrived again at Graaf Reinet, and, declining a call to take charge of the church there, continued to give himself to mission work, especially among the Hottentots, of whom he soon collected a congregation of over 200. His efforts in behalf of this despised race aroused the enmity of the colonists, but by his wise conciliatory policy they were pacified, and he continued his work unmolested. Buildings were erected and Graaf Reinet was made a permanent station, but the privileges afforded to the natives at that station bade fair to stir up another rebellion, and Dr. Vanderkemp saw the necessity of removing the Hottentots to a place of safety, where they would form a colony by themselves. The plan was approved by the government, and a grant of land near Algoa Bay was made to the mission. This was occupied early in 1802 by a part of the congregation (160 in all), and though the movement was not attained with complete success, in September, when the governor visited them, he was so impressed with the good they were doing and the dangers they incurred, that he advised them to take up their quarters in Fort Frederick, from which the garrison had been removed, and the missionaries deemed it wise to take his advice. For the next few months the work was most encouraging, and several Hottentots applied for baptism. The doctor was at this time quite ill with rheumatism, so that he was obliged to perform the ceremony while lying on a couch. The country then passed from the rule of the English to that of the Dutch, and the governor, though prejudiced at first, soon became convinced of the good done by the missionaries, and offered assistance in the forming of a new station. In June, 1803, the missionaries and their people moved to a place seven miles north of the Bay, which they named Bethelsdorp, where a flourishing village soon sprang up, and a church and schoolhouse were built. From this time on, until the reoccupation of the colony by the English, the work was carried on with great vigor and success by the doctor. In 1807 great religious interest was manifested among the Kafirs, and the following year an out-station of Bethelsdorp was formed at Stuerman's Kraal. In 1810 the population of Bethelsdorp had become a thousand, and many who had been enemies to the mission had been won over.

The cruelties which the Hottentots had so often suffered at the hands of their Boer masters excited the deepest pity in the heart of the doctor, and it is said that in the course of three years he paid no less than $5,000 for the redemption of slaves from bondage, and by his exertions, with the help of other missionaries, the Hottentots were finally delivered. Almost the last public service which the doctor was able to render that people was in testifying in the courts at the Cape to the wrongs practised upon the Hottentots.

He died on the 15th of December, 1811, in the midst of active preparation to enter upon a new field of work in Madagascar. One well acquainted with his life, character, and labors says that, "for combining natural talents, extensive learning, elevated piety, ardent zeal, disinterested benevolence, unshaken perseverance, unfeigned humility, and primitive simplicity, Dr. Vanderkemp has perhaps never been equalled since the days of the Apostles." Well does the venerable Moffat say of him: " He came from a university to teach the alphabet to the poor, naked Hottentot and Kafir; from the society of nobles, to associate with beings of the lowest grade of humanity; from stately mansions, to the filthy hovel of the greasy African; from the army, to instruct the fierce savage in the tactics of a heavenly warfare, under the banner of the Prince of Peace; from the study of medicine, to become a guide to the Balm of Gilead and the Physician there; and finally, from a life of earthly honor and ease to be exposed to perils of waters, of robbers, of his own countrymen, of the heathen, in the city, in the wilderness."

**Van Lennep, Henry John,** b. Smyrna, Asia Minor, April 18th, 1815. His ancestors on the banks of the Rhine took part in the Thirty Years' War for religious liberty, and later engaged in business in the East. At the age of fifteen Henry was sent to America for an education. At seventeen the reading of the Memoirs of Levi Parsons, missionary in Palestine, and a letter from his mother led him to seek his own salvation "and that of as many others as possible." He graduated at Amherst College in 1837, and Andover Theological Seminary 1839; was ordained at Amherst; and embarked for Turkey the same year as a missionary of the A. B. C. F. M. He was stationed first at his native city, removed in 1844 to Constantinople, and in 1854 was sent as a pioneer missionary to Tokat, Asia Minor. In 1863 he was again stationed at Smyrna, where he remained till his final departure for America. His main work was preaching and education. He was distinguished as a linguist, preaching acceptably in four foreign languages—French, Armenian, Greek, and Turkish. He was a proficient in music, drawing, and painting, which were his favorite sources of recreation. He excelled as an instructor of youth. "Numbers of the most successful professional men among the evangelical Armenians and Greeks of Constantinople and Asia Minor—ministers, physicians, and instructors of youth—were his pupils." After retiring from his work abroad he secured to twenty-five Asiatics facilities for education in the United States. A prominent Armenian gentleman, a native of Constantinople and once a pupil of Dr. Van Lennep, says: "One of his best qualifications as a missionary was that he understood the people among whom he was working, and loved them. In the Bebek Seminary, where he taught for a while, the students looked to him not merely as a teacher and respected him, but also as their companion and friend, and loved him accordingly."

In 1869, blindness coming on and strength failing, he returned home, after thirty years of mission service, and resided at Great Barrington, Mass. He died January 11th, 1889.

Dr. Van Lennep was honored with the degree of D.D. by his "Alma Mater," Amherst College, in 1862.

**Varna,** a city on the east coast of Bulgaria, 160 miles north-northwest of Constantinople. Climate temperate. Population, 261,000, Bulgarians, Greeks, Armenians, Jews, Gypsies. Social condition quite low. Mission station Methodist Episcopal Church (North), 1884; 1 missionary and wife, 1 native helper, 1 out-station, 1 church, 13 church-members.

It is the terminus of the Varna-Rustchuk Railroad, and until the recent opening of the railroad from Constantinople to Vienna direct, all travellers from Vienna by the Danube passed through it.

**Vaudois Version.**—The Vaudois is a dialect of the French, belonging to the Græco-Latin branch of the Aryan languages of Europe. It is spoken in Piedmont. At a very early period the Vaudois, or Waldenses, as they are sometimes called, had a translation of the Scriptures made into their dialect, at the instance of Waldo, or Waldensis, which was greatly blessed to them, and supported them in the endurance of many cruel persecutions. In 1831 the British and Foreign Bible Society published an edition of the Gospels of Luke and John in the Vaudois dialect, the translation having been made by Mr. Berte, pastor of La Tour. As the French is now the medium of instruction in all the schools, the French version is more generally read by the people than the Vaudois Gospels.

(*Specimen verse.* John 3 : 16.)

Perqué Diou ha tant vourgù bén ar mount, qu'a l ha dounà so Fill unic, per que quiounqué cré en el perissé pâ, mà qu'a l abbia la vita éternella.

**Vediarpuram,** a city in India, in the Trichinopoli district, Madras. Mission station of S. P. G.; 1 missionary, 9 native workers, 166 communicants, 2 schools, 98 scholars.

**Vellore,** a city in North Arcot, Madras, India, 15 miles west of Arcot, 89 miles westsouthwest of Madras City. Tolerably clean and well built, containing many ancient buildings of interest. Climate very hot, but healthy. Population, 37,491, Hindus, Moslems, Christians. Mission station Reformed (Dutch) Church in America; 1 missionary and wife, 1 female missionary, 16 native helpers, 19 outstations, 515 communicants, 742 scholars, 1 girls' boarding-school, 66 scholars. Established Church of Scotland (1860); 19 native helpers, 1 school, 343 scholars.

**Velpur,** a town in the Godaveri district, Madras, India. Population, 6,282, chiefly Hindus; a few Christians and Moslems. Mission station of the Evangelical Lutheran General Council; 1 native missionary, 2 other workers, 1 school, 12 children.

**Venezuela,** the most northerly of the South American republics, lies between British Guiana on the east and Colombia on the east and west, with Brazil to the south and the Carribbean sea to the north. It has an area of 632,695 square miles, which is divided politically into eight large states, two national settlements, and eight territories. In 1888 the estimated population was 2,234,385, of whom the native Indians numbered 326,000. The government is modelled after that of the United States of America, with more freedom given to the provincial and local governments. Education is compulsory and gratuitous, and illiteracy is fast decreasing. In 1888 over 100,000 attended the primary schools. Higher education is applied by 2 universities, 20 federal colleges, 9 colleges for girls, etc. The state religion is Roman Catholic, and though other religions are tolerated, they are not permitted any external manifestations. The people are engaged in agriculture, cattle and sheep raising, and mining; there are very rich deposits of gold and silver, copper, and iron.

Caracas, the capital, has a population of 70,466. Protestant mission work is carried on solely by the American Bible Society, with the circulation of the Bible in Spanish.

**Venyane,** a town of Griqualand, East South Africa, 40 miles from Tinana. Mission out-station of the Moravian Brethren's station at Bethesda. The people are Kafirs of the Hlubi tribe, who are so eager for a minister that whenever the missionary from Bethesda comes there, they tell him they would like to detain him by force; and a small number of Hottentots, who moved there from Silo, who exert a good influence, and have been largely instrumental in making arrangements for a station.

**Vepery,** a town in the Mutyalapad district, Madras, India. Mission station of the S. P. G.; 2 missionaries, 10 native helpers, 373 church-members.

**Victoria.**—1. The principal city and capital of the colony of Hong Kong (q. v.).—2. A town in Tamaulipas, East Mexico, southwest of Ciudad. Hot, but healthy. Race and language, mixed Spanish and Indian. Religion, Roman Catholic. An out-station of the Matamoras Mission of the Presbyterian Church (South), with 1 native preacher.—2. Capital of Vancouver, British Columbia. The Methodist Church of Canada has quite a flourishing work among the Chinese immigrants; 1 missionary and wife, rescue home for girls, 67 church-members.— 4. A town in Isupu, West Africa, at the foot of the Cameroon Mountains; has a small Baptist congregation, started in 1860 by Negro missionaries from Jamaica.

**Villupuram** (Wilupuram), (Belpore of the old maps, etc.,) a town in South Arcot, Madras, India, 25 miles west of Pondicherri. Population, 8,241, Hindus, Moslems, Christians. Mission station Evangelical Lutheran Society of Leipsic; 177 communicants, 98 scholars.

**Vinuconda,** a hill and town in the Kistna district, Madras, India. Population, 5,638, Hindus chiefly; a few Moslems and Christians. It contains an interesting hill fort, around which a number of legends cluster. Mission station A. B. M. U. (1883); 1 missionary, 13 native preachers, 6 churches, 3,616 church-members, 34 schools, 250 scholars.

**Vinton, Justus Hatch,** b. Willington, Conn., U. S. A., February 17th, 1806; graduated at Hamilton Literary and Theological Institution, 1828; appointed in 1832 missionary to Burma by the A. B. M. U.; studied with Dr. Wade and two native converts, a Burman and a Karen, who were then in the United States; sailed with Mrs. Vinton July, 1834, reaching Moulmein in December. Having studied the language at home and on the voyage, they began their work at once. Within a week they left the jungles, travelling for three months from village to village, making known the gospel of Christ. At first they went together, but many calls coming from distant villages, they separated, each taking a band of native assistants: she going in her little boat, with a few of her school-girls, to the villages along the rivers, telling the story of redemption to the crowds who gathered about her; he visiting the mountain villages and places more difficult of access. They were

often in danger from robbers and wild beasts. But they had great success in their work. His labors were not confined to the Karens. He studied the Burmese that he might preach to the Burmans. During the rainy season, when travel is impossible, he labored among the English soldiers in garrison, preaching and distributing tracts among the Burmans, and translating the New Testament into Karen, or writing his commentary. In six weeks he distributed 8,000 tracts, and his labors among the troops resulted in the conversion of many, both among the common soldiers and the officers. In Moulmein Mrs. Vinton had in her school pupils who had come 200 miles for the sake of learning to read God's Word in their own language, threading the forests by night, not daring to travel by day.

The complete failure of Mrs. Vinton's health made a return home in 1847 necessary. Partly for his own health, and partly to arouse the missionary spirit in the churches, he accompanied her. By his earnest addresses and his sweet singing of "Rock of Ages" in Karen and English, and Dr. Brown's "A Missionary Call," he made a deep impression. His labors in Burma between 1834 and 1848 had been confined mostly to the Moulmein district, but on his return in 1850 Rangoon was to be the centre of missionary operations by the providential opening of the Pegu provinces to the gospel. In 1852 the English Government sent an armed vessel from Calcutta to Rangoon to demand redress from the Burman governor for outrages inflicted upon English residents in the Burmese dominions. The Burmans in defiance began preparations for resistance, repairing old fortifications, and erecting batteries on the river-banks. Enraged by the successes of the English, they treated the Karens, whom they considered the cause of their misfortunes, with extreme cruelty. The imploring cry for relief from the seventeen suffering Karen churches in Rangoon reached Mr. Vinton, and, urged by Dr. Kincaid and other missionaries in Moulmein, he went to their help. He found that three native preachers had been crucified, and 5,000 refugee Karens were living in carts and under trees. The Burmese part of the city being in ruins, he and Dr. Kincaid obtained permission to occupy the deserted monastery inside of the stockade, and six weeks after the capture of the city their families joined them from Moulmein. As soon as it was known that "Teacher Vinton" had come, the refugees, who had been driven from their burning homes, and who had been living secreted in the forests and jungles, subsisting on roots and herbs, flocked to the city, filling the monastery occupied by the Vintons, or camping out under the trees. They were not only hungry, but diseased. Mr. Vinton built a hospital for the small pox patients, to whom Mrs. Vinton ministered day and night. During most of the first year, besides the labors of the hospital, she had a school of 200 pupils, men, women, and children, mothers with babes in their arms, fathers and sons sitting on the same bench, learning to read the Word of God. Scarcely a day but many came in from the jungles—some for books and medicine, many for advice and consolation. In 1857 many were converted; 250 Karens, during the rains, learned to read the Bible; and 30 young men received Biblical instruction to fit them to work in the distant villages as preachers or school-teachers. The English army in its advance having threatened Ava, the king yielded, a treaty was made, and peace proclaimed. An order being issued by the English Government for the vacation of all the religious buildings occupied during the war, the Vintons left the old monastery which had sheltered them, and moved to Kemmendine, two miles from the fort. Here Mr. Vinton put up buildings for his family, and the large school which followed to his new home. Teachers were trained to take charge of the village schools, which were established when quiet was restored. A new trial now fell upon the Karens. War and pestilence were followed by famine. Mr. Vinton, by his earnest efforts to supply the wants of the suffering people, so won their hearts that they gathered about him in crowds, hailing him as their deliverer, and declaring that his religion was the one they wanted. "Thousands were baptized, churches organized, chapels and school-houses built, and the hearts of both Burmans and Karens turned toward God as never before." In 1854, at Mr. Vinton's suggestion, the Karens of the Rangoon district organized the Karen Home Missionary Society, the first of the kind ever formed in Burma, designed for aggressive work among the heathen, the natives already supporting their own pastors and schools. In May, 1855, the corner-stone of a church was laid by Mr. Vinton in the presence of a large assembly of native and English friends. A substantial church of brick was erected, with funds contributed in America, England, and Burma, at Kemmendine, on the Rangoon River, on land given to the mission by Lord Dalhousie, Governor-General of India.

In the mission now settled at Kemmendine Mrs. Vinton had the entire charge of the Pegu High School, numbering from 200 to 250 pupils. Mr. Vinton had during the rains a theological class of young men preparing for the ministry. News having come from the mountains that many villages in a region never yet reached by missionaries, on account of its being difficult of access, were ready to receive the gospel, he went to survey the field and select the most eligible site for a station. He returned March 24th, complaining of being "very tired." The next day he was ill; fever set in, which was succeeded by dysentery, and he gradually failed, when, on the 31st of March, 1858, he passed away. "He is regarded as one of the most zealous and successful missionaries ever sent to heathen lands by the Baptists of the United States."

Mrs. Vinton remained, doing efficient work in Rangoon. Her daughter Calista, who, when the news of her father's death was received, was about to graduate at Suffield, at once prepared to sail for Burma, and joined her mother on Christmas Day, 1858. In 1861 Brainerd Vinton, having graduated at Madison University, married the daughter of Rev. Dr. Haswell of Moulmein, and sailed in September for Burma, to become the missionary of the Karen churches of the Rangoon district. The health of Mrs. Vinton and her daughter failing, they both embarked for America by the way of England, October, 1862, reaching New York June, 1863. Mrs. Vinton's health being partially restored, she returned to Rangoon, arriving March, 1864, followed soon by her daughter and her husband, Rev. R. M. Luther. Mrs. Vinton was suddenly attacked with an acute form of the disease which had long afflicted her, and died December 18th, 1864.

**Vizagapatam,** a town in Madras, India, situated on a small bay near a remarkable hill, bold and rocky, 1,500 feet in height. It is a military station with considerable trade. Population, 30,291, Hindus, Moslems, Christians, etc. Mission station L. M. S. (1806); 2 foreign missionaries, 1 native missionary, 58 church-members, 5 Sunday-schools, 375 scholars, 5 boys' schools, 481 scholars, 3 girls' schools, 197 scholars.

# W.

**Wadali,** an ancient capital city in Bombay, India, 26 miles northeast of Ahmadnagar. Mission station of A. B. C. F. M.; 1 missionary and wife, 41 native agents, 19 out-stations.

**Wade, Jonathan,** b. Otsego, N. Y., U. S. A., December 10th, 1798; graduated at Hamilton Literary and Theological Institution 1822; ordained February, 1823; embarked as a missionary of the A. B. M. U. for Burma June 22d, 1823; reached Rangoon December 5th following. At the commencement of the first Burmese war, soon after his arrival, he and Mr. Hough were arrested, imprisoned, and put in irons, then dragged to the place of execution, and compelled to kneel before a Burmese executioner, who had received orders to smite off their heads at the discharge of the first British gun on Rangoon. Panic-stricken at the sound of the cannon, the executioner, alarmed for his own safety, left his prisoners and fled. They were afterwards seized by the Burmese officials, but rescued by the advancing British troops. They went to Calcutta, remaining till the close of the war. Mr. Wade resided at Doorgapore, near Calcutta, occupied in the study of the language, the translation of books, and in superintending the printing of useful works. He preached also in English in the Circular Roads Baptist Chapel, and many persons were converted. At the close of the war he returned to Burmah, making Amherst his home until the transfer of the mission to Moulmein, where he was stationed from 1827 to 1830. In that year he returned to Rangoon. In 1831 he visited Kyouk Phyoo in Arrakan, and began the work which was continued by Mr. Comstock and others. In 1832, on account of the failure of Mrs. Wade's health, he visited the United States, accompanied by a Burman and a Karen convert, returning to Burma in 1834. In December, 1847, he made a second visit to his native land, being threatened with total blindness. He re embarked for Burma July 25th, 1850, resuming his work in Moulmein in January, 1851. He received the degree of D.D. in 1852 from Madison, now Colby, University. In the absence of Dr. Binney in the United States he had charge of the theological seminary for Karens at Moulmein. In addition to preaching the gospel, he performed much literary labor. He reduced to writing the two Karen dialects, Sgau and Pwo, and prepared several important literary, theological, and educational works—among them a Karen Thesaurus, a work in 5 vols., the last volume completed in 1850. This he designed to be for the Karen language what Dr. Judson's Dictionary was for the Burman, and to its revision he devoted his powers as long as he was able to work. Though suffering greatly from an incurable malady, he continued his literary work for the mission with untiring assiduity until six days before his decease. After the death of Mrs. Wade he resided in the families of Mr. Bennett and Dr. Binney. Dr. Binney says that for months, after the labors of the day were ended, he was accustomed to spend an hour in the evening in conversation with him "on the missionary enterprise, the methods of missionary work, the necessities and modes of supply for the Karen field, and the great doctrines of that divine system on which his soul rested." Dr. Binney testifies that he was "edified and delighted with his broad and discriminating views, his ripe judgment, his practical wisdom, and his sound theology." He died at Rangoon June 10th, 1872, of cancer on the lip, after nearly forty-nine years of mission service, aged 73.

**Wakkerstroom,** a town in the Pretoria district, Transvaal, Africa, between Utrecht and Pretoria, north of the Orange River. Mission station of the S. P. G. (1880); 1 missionary, 159 church-members.

**Wallisch Bay,** a harbor of Namaqualand, South Africa, in British territory. (See Africa.) Mission station of the Rhenish Missionary Society; 1 missionary, 1 female missionary, 2 out-stations, 120 church-members, 40 school-children.

**Walker, Augustus,** b. Medway, Mass., U. S. A., October 30th, 1822; graduated at Yale College 1849; studied theology one year at Bangor, two years at Andover Seminary, graduating in 1852; ordained October 13th; sailed as a missionary of the A. B. C. F. M. January 7th, 1853, for the Assyrian Mission, and was stationed at Diarbekir on the Tigris—the field of his labors, his success, and his death. In 1864 he visited the United States for his wife's health, and sailed again with her August 19th, 1865, reaching Diarbekir November 21st. The cholera raging there, he spent some time over one stricken with that disease. He was soon himself attacked, and died September 13th, 1866. "Diarbekir," it is said, "was filled with mourning. Not Protestants alone, but Moslems and Armenians, all were stricken. Such a funeral, as of one who was a father to all, was never witnessed there before." "Mr. Walker had a clear head, a ready understanding, and very correct views of the way the work should be prosecuted. He helped to shape the policy of the mission, and was a strong pillar in it." "It was touching to witness the deep grief of this orphaned people, and to learn how heartfelt was the tie that bound them to a stranger from the far off-West. Singing the hymns he had taught them, they carried his bier on their shoulders two and a half miles."

**Walmannsthal,** a town in the Transvaal, Africa, on one of the sources of the Limpopo, northwest of Botchabelo, and northeast of

Pretoria. Mission station of the Berlin Evangelical Missionary Society (1869); 1 missionary, 8 native helpers, 5 out-stations, 420 church-members, 172 scholars.

**Ward Faith Mission in India.**—In 1880 Rev. Ernest F. Ward, of the United States, went to India with his wife, following a conviction that they must establish a mission there. They located the mission first at Burhanpur, in Berar, where land was purchased and a bungalow built. In 1884 the property was sold and the mission was moved to Ellichpur, where the property of another mission was purchased. There is now in connection with the mission a sanitarium among the hills, where the workers can retire in the hot season.

The property of the mission was purchased with money belonging to the founders. Since that time the work has been well sustained, although a rule of the mission is that no member of it shall ask any person for money or support in any way. Prayer to God is their sole reliance. Additional workers have joined the mission from America and England. Mr. Ward has assisted in reducing the language of the Korkoos to writing. He spends much time in visiting from village to village, and all of the workers carry on bazaar visitation, selling tracts and engaging in personal conversations. A school is conducted in the mission house.

**Warren, Edward,** b. Marlborough, Mass., U. S. A., August 4th, 1786; graduated at Middlebury College 1808, and after studying law entered Andover Seminary; graduated in 1812, and sailed as a missionary of the A. B. C. F. M. for Ceylon October 23d, 1815. His health soon failed from pulmonary disease, and April 25th, 1816, he sailed with Mr. Richards for the Cape of Good Hope, where, August 11th, he passed away. His body was interred by the side of a man supposed to be the first convert from Mohammedanism in Africa, who had died a few days before, aged seventy-seven, in the triumph of faith.

**Wanganui** (Whanganui), a town in New Zealand, on the southwest coast, at the mouth of a river of the same name. Mission station of the Church Missionary Society; 2 missionaries, 2 native pastors, 25 other native workers, 250 church-members.

**Ward, William,** b. Derby, England, October 20th, 1769. After learning the printers' trade, he studied for the ministry, and in 1798 was appointed missionary printer by the Baptist Missionary Society; sailed May, 1799, for Calcutta, but, owing to the opposition of the East India Company to missions in its territory, settled at Serampore, a Danish settlement on the Hoogly, 16 miles above Calcutta. In 1800 he printed Dr. Carey's translation of the Bengâli New Testament and afterwards other translations, performing also faithfully other missionary labors. His health being impaired, he visited in 1819 England, Holland, and America, returning to Calcutta in 1821. He died at Serampore March 7th, 1823.

**Warmbad,** a town in Namaqualand, West South Africa, on a short northern branch of the Orange River, northeast of Steinkopf and northwest of Pella. Mission station of the Rhenish Missionary Society; 1 missionary, 1 single lady, 6 native workers, 360 church-members, 100 school-children.

**Warsaw,** a city of Polish Russia, on the Vistula River. Most of the city is well built, and recently many new structures have been erected. Population (1884), 454,898, Catholics, Jews, German Protestants, Greek Catholics. Mission station London Society for Propagation of the Gospel among the Jews; 2 missionaries, 1 native helper.

**Wartburg,** a town in Kaffraria, South Africa, north of Bethel. Mission station of the Berlin Evangelical Lutheran Society (1855); 1 missionary, 5 native helpers, 7 out-stations, 276 church-members, 96 scholars.

**Waterberg** (Waterburg), a town in the South African Republic (Transvaal), the same as Modimolle (q.v.). Mission station of the Wesleyan Methodist Missionary Society; 1 missionary, 1 chapel, 55 communicants, 42 Sabbath-scholars, 35 day-scholars.

**Waterloo.**—1. A town in Surinam, South America, is situated in Nickerie, the most western district, on the east bank of the Corentyn River. Mission station of the Moravian Brethren, commenced at the request of several planters, one of whom gave the plot of ground on which the station is built, and another presented the church. One missionary is stationed there.
2. A town in Sierra Leone, West Africa. Mission station of the Wesleyan Methodist Missionary Society; 1 missionary, 3 chapels, 352 communicants, 167 Sabbath-scholars, 110 day-scholars. There is also a native pastorate of the C. M. S.

**Wathen,** a district on the Congo River, West Africa, 80 miles west of Stanley Pool, 220 miles from the river's mouth. Climate tropical. Elevation, 2,000 feet. Race, Bantu. Language, Kikongo. Religion, Fetichism. Social condition low, but improved and improving to some extent, owing to their active trade Government practically patriarchal, each town being a petty state, but all more or less subject to the Congo Free State. Mission station of the Baptist Missionary Society (1884); 4 missionaries, 1 married, 1 church, 10 church-members, 1 school, 38 scholars.

**Wa-ting,** a town in Shantung, China, north of the Yellow River. Language, Mandarin. Mission station Methodist New Connexion (1867); 2 ordained missionaries, 1 missionary's wife, 27 native helpers, 31 out-stations, 15 churches, 950 church-members, 10 schools, 109 scholars.

**Wazirabad,** a large town in the Punjab, India, 64 miles northwest of Lahore, 21 miles north of Gujranwala. The town is comparatively new, and has only recently risen to importance. It is much better and more regularly built than most native towns, although the houses are mostly made of sun-dried or kiln-burned bricks. Population, 16,462, Moslems, Hindus, Sikhs, Christians, Jains. Mission station Established Church of Scotland (1863); 1 native missionary, 5 helpers, 15 communicants, 9 schools, 480 scholars.

**Weasisi Version.**—The Weasisi, which belongs to the Melanesian languages, is spoken in Tanna, New Hebrides. In October, 1882, the Rev. W. Gray, from South Australia, opened a missionary station at Weasisi, and translated the first six chapters of St. John's Gospel. These chapters were printed as a tentative edition by the Adelaide Auxiliary Committee, at the request of the Foreign Missions Committee of the Presbyterian Church of Australia in 1888.

**Wei-Hien,** a town in the province of Shantung, China. 150 miles southwest of Tungchow. Mission station of the Presbyterian Church (North), 1882; 4 missionaries (3 married), 2 physicians, 4 female missionaries (2 medical), 29 out-stations; 23 native helpers.

**Wei-hui,** a city in Honan, China, on the north side of the Yellow River. The Presbyterian Church of Canada has selected this place as one of the stations for their mission in Honan, which was commenced in 1889 (see article Presbyterian Church of Canada).

**Weligama,** a town in the Galle district, Ceylon. Mission station of the Wesleyan Methodist Missionary Society; 1 missionary, 1 chapel, 3 Sabbath-schools, 210 scholars, 3 day-schools, 593 scholars.

**Wellington.**—1. A town in Sierra Leone, West Africa. Mission station of the Wesleyan Methodist Missionary Society; 1 missionary, 3 chapels, 360 communicants, 113 Sabbath-scholars, 210 day-scholars. There is also a native pastorate of the C. M. S.
2. Town in New Zealand. Mission station of the United Methodist Free Churches; 1 missionary, 73 church-members, 180 Sabbath-scholars. The Diocese of Wellington of the C. M. S. in New Zealand has at present (1890) two stations—Whanganui and Otaki.

**Welsh Presbyterians, or Calvinistic Methodists of Wales, Foreign Missions.** Headquarters, 28 Breckfield Road South, Liverpool, Eng.—The Calvinistic Methodists of Wales began to take an interest in missionary work at the time when the London Missionary Society was established. They contributed liberally to its funds, and several of the most useful missionaries of that Society had been trained in their churches. But the growing desire that the connection should have a mission of its own led ultimately to the Welsh Calvinistic Methodist Foreign Missionary Society, which was established in Liverpool in January, 1840. The first field, chosen immediately on the formation of the Society, was Bengal; and in 1842 operations in the foreign field were further extended by the opening of a mission among the Bretons in Western France.

The work of the Society is under the direction of an Executive Committee, twenty-one in number, appointed by the General Assembly of the church. This committee meets once a month to consider applications from missionary candidates, make arrangements for the sending out of missionaries, fixing their salaries, etc., to invest the funds of the Society, and prepare reports.

DEVELOPMENT OF FOREIGN WORK. *India Mission*—In 1834 the British Government completed a treaty with the kings of Khasia, a group of small states in the extreme northeastern part of Hindustan, and a military post was to be established at Cherrapoonjee, and a road made across the Khasia Hills to the British territory in Assam. When the Welsh Foreign Mission was established in 1840 the attention of the directors was called to Khasia as a new and promising field. Accordingly, the plan seeming wise, the first missionary of the Society, the Rev. Thomas Jones, left for Cherrapoonjee in November, 1840. Missionaries were also sent out in 1842 and again in 1845; but at times, owing to various circumstances, defection, illness, and death, only one or two men were left to carry on the work, and the progress for some years was but small, if reckoned by the number of converts, which reached but fourteen in the first decade.

In 1846 a new station was established at Jiwai, the chief village in the Jaintia Hills, and in subsequent years the work was extended to various other parts of the hills. In 1849 the Rev. W. Pryse commenced operations at Sylhet, in the plains of Bengal. Though the work was carried on vigorously, and not without some degree of success, circumstances occurred which made it advisable to limit the operations of the mission to the hills, and until 1887 the large district around Sylhet was left unoccupied, when in that year the mission was again enabled to resume its work there. The mission field in India is divided into seven districts: Cherra, Shillong, Shella, Mawphlang, Khadsawphrah, Jiwai, and Shangpoong. Dayschools, evangelistic work, publishing in the Khasi language, and medical work are all features of the mission, and the beneficial results of the Christian teaching are strongly manifested in the general improvement of the domestic and social life of the entire district in which the mission works. Places for stated preaching, 136; Sabbath-schools, 140; Sundayschool scholars, 7,294; theological seminary, 1; theological students, 8.

*Brittany.*—The work in Brittany is carried on at the three stations, Quimper, Pont l'Abbé, and Douarnenez, with regular meetings at Peu-ar-bout and Treboul, and occasional visits to other villages on the coast of Finisterre.

**Welsh Version.**—The Welsh, which is spoken in Wales, belongs to the Keltic branch of the Aryan family of languages. The earliest reliable reference to a Welsh version of any portion of Holy Writ is contained in a letter of Dr. Richard Davies, Bishop of St. David's, prefixed to the first printed edition of the Welsh New Testament, published in 1567, in which the Bishop states that there was extant about the year 1527 a Welsh version of the Pentateuch, a copy of which he himself saw. The first edition of the New Testament, prepared by William Salesbury, was published at London in 1567. The edition consisted of 500 copies, quarto size, and was printed in black letter. The first edition of the Bible with the Apocrypha was printed in 1588, in one volume folio, and numbered 500 copies. The translation was executed by Dr. William Morgan, Bishop of St. Asaph. He undertook a second revision of the New Testament, which he completed in readiness for the press in 1604, when death put an end to his labors. Dr. Morgan's successor, Dr. Richard Perry, in conjunction with his chaplain, Dr. John Davies, undertook an entire revision of the Old and New Testaments. This revision was made so carefully that it became in fact the standard version of the Welsh Bible. It was first printed at London in 1620, folio size, and dedicated to King James I. In 1630 a small octavo edition was published at the expense of some Christian philanthropists, citizens of London. From the time of the publication of this edition to the establishment of the British and Foreign Bible Society, nearly 20 editions of the Welsh Bible were printed. Most of the editions were supported by the Society for Promoting Christian Knowledge. The edition published in 1799 was scarcely dry from the printer's hand before it was all sold, and this before a quarter of the demand had been satisfied. The most urgent appeals from all parts of the Principality reached the Christian Knowledge Society for further supplies of the Scriptures, but the state of the finances prevented this society from making any adequate response to the repeated cries for help. At this crisis in the history of the Welsh Bible, the Rev. Thomas Charles of Bala suggested the idea of establishing a large printing society, for the purpose of keeping Wales well supplied with Bibles. He was successful in securing the hearty co-operation of both Churchmen and Dissenters. The original plan was so ordered and developed that it ultimately eventuated in the institution of the British and Foreign Bible Society, which was established in 1804. The Bible Society's first edition left the press in 1800, following the text of the version of 1752 published by the Christian Knowledge Society (the first edition, known as the "Moses Williams" Bible, having been issued in 1718). Ever since, editions have been issued, and up to March 31st, 1889, the British Bible Society had disposed of 2,534,335 portions of the Scriptures, besides 105,994 New Testaments with English in parallel columns. Portions of the New Testament for the blind have also been issued by the same Bible Society.

(*Specimen verse.* John 3 : 16.)

Canys felly y carodd Duw y byd, fel y rhoddodd efe ei unig-anedig Fab, fel na choller pwy hynnag a gredo ynddo ef, ond caffael o hono fywyd tragywyddol.

**Wen-chau** (Wen-chow), a city on the coast of Chehkiang, China, southwest of Ningpo, 300 miles from Shanghai. Climate subtropical. Mission station United Methodist Free Churches (1878); 1 missionary and wife, 8 native keepers, 8 out-stations, 5 churches, 129 churchmembers.

**Wen-chau Colloquial Version.**—The Wen-chau belongs to the colloquial languages of China, and is used in Wen-chau, Mid-China. In 1888 the British and Foreign Bible Society published an edition of 500 copies of the four Gospels and Acts. The version was made by the Rev. W. E. Scothill of Wenchow, and revised by his fellow-missionaries. The style is that adopted by all the missionaries in Wen-chau. The edition is printed in Roman character.

**Wendish Versions.**—There are three dialects of the Wendish, which belongs to the Slavonic branch of the Aryan family of languages, viz., the Upper, the Lower, and the Hungarian. Before the Reformation the Wends had neither written nor printed books in their language. Rome had kept them in intellectual as well as spiritual bondage. But when the true light shone upon them, this darkness, both of mind and soul, was dispelled, and, like so many other races, they became indebted for their literature and mental development to the publication of the Scriptures in their mother tongue.

1. *Upper Wendish.*—This dialect is spoken in Saxon Lusatia, and in it some portions of the Scriptures were published in the early part of the 17th century. The whole was first published in 1728, at Bautzen; a second and amended edition was issued in 1742, and a third in 1797. The Prussian Bible Society published an edition in 1820; the British and Foreign Bible Society issued one in 1860; and the Saxon Bible Society issued an edition, translated by Immisch, Siebert, and others, in 1879 at Bautzen.

2. *Lower Wendish.*—This dialect is spoken in Prussian Lusatia, and in it the Psalms, translated by Albin Moller, were published in 1574. The Old Testament, translated by Friedrich Fritze, was published in 1796, and the New Testament, prepared by Gottlieb Fabricius, was issued in 1709, and reprinted in 1728 and 1775. An edition of the entire Bible was published by the British and Foreign Bible Society in 1818; the Prussian Bible Society published a revised edition at Berlin in 1822–25.

3. *Hungarian Wendish.*—For the Protestants in Hungary and Carniola Stephen Kugnitz translated the New Testament, which was published by the British and Foreign Bible Society in 1817, together with the Psalms, translated by the Rev. Trplan. In 1882 the same Society issued an edition with a slight revision, limited to orthographical and syntactical errors, prepared by Pastor Berke.

(*Specimen verses.* John 3 : 16.)

*Upper.*

‚Pſchetoj tak je Boh tan Sŏwĕt lubowal, ſo won ſtwojeho jenicżtѕho narodżeucho Sŏyua dal je. ſo bychu ſchityy, liż do ujeho wjerja, ſhubeni nebyli, ale wjeczne ѕhiweuſe mjeli.

*Lower.*

Pſchetr tak lo Bohg ten ſtwet lubowal. aſ won ſtwojogo ѕabnoporojonego ſhynna dal lo, abu ſchytne do nogo ѕwĕreѕe, ѕgubone nebuli, ale to ſilmerne ѕhiweuſe méll.

*Hungarian.*

Ar je tak lübo Bôg ete szvèt, da je Szlná szvojega jeđinorodjenoga dáo, dá vszáki, kí vu nyem verjè, sze ne szkvari, nego má zítek vekivecsni.

**Wen-li,** is the term applied to the classical or book language of China, as distinguished from the colloquial. To write in the same natural way as one would talk is contrary to Chinese teaching and practice; and the classical book style so abounds in stilted, condensed, epigrammatic phrases, that a man who has not mastered the literary style is unable to understand the sense, even though he may be able to recognize the characters or ideograms. A variation of the Wen-li is the Easy Wen-li, which is not so severely classical. For further information see Chinese Versions, and the Book Language under China.

**Wesleyan Methodist Missionary Society.** Headquarters, Centenary Hall, Bishopsgate Street Within, London, England.

*History.*—To find the real starting-point of the Wesleyan Methodist Missionary Society, it is necessary to travel backward for a long distance,—to Wycliffe, from whom we trace it to John Huss, Wycliffe's disciple; thence to Zinzendorf and Francke; from them to Whitefield and John and Charles Wesley; and finally to the first distinctively foreign missionary of Wesleyan Methodism, Dr. Coke. As early as 1744, through the efforts of Whitefield, special hours of prayer for the outpouring of the Spirit of God upon all Christian churches and upon the "whole inhabited earth" were observed, and John Wesley went to North America to preach. From that time onward missions in the British possessions in North America were carried on, and numerous preachers were sent out. These missions, however, were mainly intended for the benefit of British colonists; and distinctively foreign work, i.e., missions to the heathen, was not undertaken until 1786, when Thomas Coke, destined by the Methodists in England for Nova Scotia, was providentially driven to the British West Indies, where a mission to the Negro slaves was at once commenced. In Dr. Coke's hand the conduct of the Wesleyan missions was mainly placed until 1804, when, upon his departure for America, a committee of three was appointed by the Conference to undertake the management of the work. It was at Dr. Coke's instigation that a mission to West Africa was undertaken in 1811, and after crossing the Atlantic eighteen times, when he was 76 years old, he again sailed with six other missionaries, December 31st, 1813, to Ceylon to found there the third Methodist Mission. His death, early in the following year, made necessary other arrangements for carrying on the work; the Society was accordingly reorganized, and in the course of a few years was placed on its present permanent footing.

*Organization of the Society.*—The object of the Wesleyan Methodist Missionary Society is to combine the exertions of the societies and congregations of the Wesleyan Methodists, in the support and extension of the foreign missions established by the Rev. John Wesley, the Rev. Thomas Coke, and others; and any additional enterprises which are now, or shall be from year to year, carried on under the direction of the people called Methodists.

The management of the missions and the collection and disbursement of funds are entrusted to a committee appointed annually by the Conference. The general secretaries of the Society, and two treasurers, a minister and a layman, are also appointed annually by the Conference, in accordance with any regulations which from time to time may be in force touching such appointments.

The committee meets in London once a month or oftener, for the transaction of business; and at its first meeting after the Conference appoints a Finance and General Purposes Sub-committee, to meet weekly to consider and report upon any matter, financial or otherwise, which may be submitted to it, and generally to prepare business for the committee. An annual public meeting for the members and friends of the Society is held in London in May. Missionary societies for the several districts into which the connection is divided in Great Britain, or elsewhere, are entitled Auxiliary Wesleyan Methodist Missionary Societies for the districts in which they are formed; and Societies in the several circuits of any district are entitled Branch Societies for the circuit, or for the cities, towns, or villages in which they are established.

***Development of Work.***—Before the death of John Wesley, his teachings had been extended into Ireland, Scotland, the Shetland Isles, and the Channel Islands; and the first years of the new century saw the Methodists at work among the French prisoners in England and in the French prisons. As early as 1807 a society of seventy persons was reported at Arras, France, and Methodism rapidly extended to other parts of the country. Work was begun in Germany in 1830 by Christopher Gottlob Müller, who had been converted through the instrumentality of a Wesleyan minister; in Switzerland in 1839, by the Wesleyan missionaries already at work in the south of France; at Gibraltar in 1809, from whence Spain and Portugal were reached; and in Italy in 1860, after the revolution in the civil government had allowed a measure of religious liberty to the people. At an early period of the Society's history several mission stations were commenced at different points on the islands and shores of the Mediterranean, but after a few years were relinquished. In 1766 the first Methodist sermon was preached in America by a Mr. Embury at his house in New York City. In 1780 Methodism was carried to Canada by a local preacher; and not long after, missions were established among the Indians in Canada, and, later, work was commenced in Hudson Bay Territory and British Columbia. Nova Scotia, New Brunswick, Prince Edward's Island, and Newfoundland were early fields of work, and as has been said, it was to the first named that Dr. Coke was appointed by the Conference, when he was providentially driven to the West Indies. Upon Dr. Coke's recommendation a missionary was sent to the Bermudas in 1799. The mission to India at Ceylon was undertaken by Dr. Coke in 1813. The first scheme for the establishment of a mission to West Africa, devised by Dr. Coke in 1769, proved a failure; but in 1811 a second attempt was made at Sierra Leone, which was eventually successful; in 1821 a second station was opened on the river Gambia, and in 1834 a mission to the Gold Coast was undertaken. In the year 1814 the Society sent the Rev. John M'Kenny to Southern Africa as its first missionary. A little later a station was established in Little Namaqualand, and from this point the work extended by degrees throughout Southern Africa. In 1812 the committee received an appeal from two schoolmasters who were teaching in New South Wales, by order of government, to send out Wesleyan preachers to undertake a mission among the, at that time, desperately and shamelessly wicked inhabitants. Although the funds of the Society were hardly equal to such an undertaking, yet the committee began to look for a suitable missionary, with the hope that their friends would stand by them and provide the necessary money. The right man was soon found in the Rev. Samuel Leigh, who reached Sydney in August, 1815. Missionaries were sent to Tasmania in 1821, to Victoria in 1838, and to Queensland in 1850. The Mission to the cannibals of New Zealand was commenced in 1822; in the same year a missionary was also sent to the Friendly Islands, but it was not until 1826 that a mission was established there. As soon as this work

was on a firm basis, the missionaries endeavored to do something for Fiji, but some years elapsed before the mission to Fiji became an actual fact. Work in China was undertaken in 1853.

***Missions of the Society.***—THE WEST INDIES. *Antigua.*—In January, 1758, Mr. Wesley preached in the house of Nathaniel Gilbert, Esq., the Speaker of the House of Assembly in Antigua, who was at that time residing in England. At Mr. Wesley's service several of Mr. Gilbert's Negro servants were also present and appeared much affected by the sermon. Later on two of these slaves were baptized by Mr. Wesley. Mr. Gilbert, too, became identified with the Methodist people, and upon his return to Antigua commenced at once to hold religious meetings for his own people and those of the surrounding estates, and in every possible way labored for their good until his death. There was no one qualified to take his place, but the society he had formed was kept alive by the faithful labors of two Negro slaves named Mary Alley and Sophia Campbell, who were unwearied in their efforts to do good. They held prayer-meetings and other religious services until John Baxter, a shipwright, was sent to Antigua in 1778 on the king's service. Baxter was a Methodist local preacher, and when he found the remnants of Mr. Gilbert's society he immediately began to preach to them, with the most encouraging results. To meet the urgent demands for religious instruction he soon extended his labors to other parts of the island. At the same time he supported himself by his trade.

As the work expanded, application was continually made to Mr. Wesley and Dr. Coke for missionaries for the West Indies, but at that period every available laborer was required to assist in reclaiming deeply degraded populations in England and America. Consequently Mr. Baxter was left to toil alone for eight years, having under his care a congregation of 1,569 members, all black but ten, when help was sent in a way which has few parallels even in the history of missions. About five o'clock on the morning of Christmas Day, 1786, when the lonely preacher was on his way to the rude chapel he had built, he was met by a group of four weather-beaten travellers who had just landed from a half-wrecked vessel in the harbor. The principal person in the group inquired for Mr. Baxter, and his eyes sparkled when he found that he was speaking to the man himself, and understood where he was going at that early hour. This "little clerical-looking gentleman" was Dr. Coke, and his companions were Messrs. Hammett, Warrener, and Clarke, three missionaries with whom he had embarked at Gravesend for Nova Scotia, just three months before, and who had been driven by the violence of the tempest to the West Indies. The whole party went at once to the chapel, where Dr. Coke preached with all his wonted zeal and fire to a large and attentive congregation; and his loving heart overflowed with emotion as he gazed upon the upturned faces of a thousand Negroes anxiously listening to the Word of Life. It was afterwards arranged that Mr. Warrener should continue in Antigua, and that the others of the party should be stationed where their labors appeared to be most urgently needed, several of the West India colonies having already asked for missionaries.

During his stay Dr. Coke preached twice a day to crowded congregations, and on the 5th of January, 1787, accompanied by Mr. Baxter and the missionaries, he set out on a tour among the islands. They visited Dominica, St. Vincent's, Nevis, St. Christopher's, and St. Eustatius, collecting information, and embracing every opportunity to preach to the people. In all the islands but St. Eustatius there seemed to be openings for mission work; Messrs. Hammett and Clarke were left at St. Christopher and St. Vincent's, and Dr. Coke embarked for America February 10th, promising to send missionaries to the remaining islands as soon as possible. From year to year new stations were occupied and the number of laborers was increased, until almost every colony was brought under the influence of the gospel. In Antigua out-stations were formed at English Harbor, Parham, Sion Hill, Freetown, and other other places, in addition to the headquarters at St. John's, where the work commenced.

For Dominica nothing could be done until two years later, when the Rev. W. McCormick commenced a mission there. Within a few months Mr. McCormick died of fever, and Dr. Coke came a third time, leaving more missionaries. Notwithstanding the unhealthy climate and other drawbacks, the mission prospered. Chapels were built and societies formed in Roseau, the capital of the colony, in Lasoye, Prince Rupert's, and in other villages and towns. The little island of Montserrat was also visited several times by Dr. Coke, and in 1820 a regularly organized mission was established there and three stations formed.

A missionary was sent to Nevis in 1787, and from the beginning the work prospered in the stations of Charlestown, Gingerland, Combermere, etc. St. Christopher's (named for Columbus, its discoverer), where Mr. Hammett was left in 1787, soon had spacious and substantial chapels in Basseterre, the capital, at Old Road, Sandy Point, Half-way Tree, and other towns and villages. At St. Eustatius, owing to the determined opposition of the governor and other civil authorities, no mission was begun until 1811, when Rev. M. C. Dixon was appointed to the island, and all resistance having ceased, a flourishing station was soon established, which has now the cordial support of the authorities (Dutch), who have no mission of their own on the island. At St. Bartholomew's (belonging to Sweden) a mission was begun in 1796, which has never been relinquished, though emigration has reduced the population. Upon Anguila (Snake Island) the gospel was first preached by a converted native, who was afterwards ordained as a minister. A missionary afterwards occupied the station, but owing to the smallness of the population and the pressing demands of other places it has of late years shared a minister with St. Martin's. Tortola, the largest and most important of the Virgin Islands, was visited by Dr. Coke in 1789, and the results of the labors of Mr. Hammett and his successors were such that it is now the head of a circuit. From here the missionaries extend their labors to West End, East End, Spanish Town, Road Town, and other places. The above mentioned islands are all included in the *Antigua District.* The *St. Vincent's District* includes the islands of (1) St. Vincent's, where Mr. Clarke was left in 1787. Many things hindered the work here, and the

Mission to the Caribs failed. After much bitter persecution from the authorities, religious liberty was at length restored to the land, and the work of the mission extended till the whole island was encircled with a chain of stations. (2) Grenada, originally a French colony, also presented many difficulties, notwithstanding which the work has been attended with a considerable measure of success. (3) Trinidad formerly belonged to Spain, and the prevalence of Roman Catholicism placed great obstacles in the way of the missionaries. For a time it was necessary to close the chapels, but an appeal to the Imperial Government brought relief, all restrictions were removed, and the mission was extended from Port-of-Spain to Diego Martin, Couva, San Fernando, and other places.

*Barbadoes.* The Wesleyan mission to Barbadoes was commenced in 1788, but for several years was less prosperous than the missions to the other islands. In 1822 signs of improvement appeared, upon which a storm of persecution burst forth, which culminated in the entire demolition of the chapel and mission-house, and the banishment of the missionary. In 1826 the mission was recommenced, and Barbadoes ultimately became a very important station. Tobago, the only remaining island of the St. Vincent's District, was repeatedly visited before arrangements were made, in 1817, for a permanent settlement. The labors of the missionaries met with varied success until the years immediately following the emancipation of the slaves, when a great revival of religion took place. In Scarborough, at Mt. St. George, Mason Hall, and other places chapels have been built, societies formed, and schools established.

*British Guiana.* Demerara.—In 1815 the Wesleyan Society succeeded in establishing a mission in Demerara, after a previous attempt (1805) had been frustrated by the expulsion of the missionary from the colony. It was with difficulty that the work was recommenced by Rev. T. Talboys, with the aid of two native converts from Nevis. Gradually the zealous efforts of the missionaries were crowned with success, culminating in 1868 in a great revival. From Georgetown the work extended to Mahaica, an ancient village on the coast, about twenty-five miles distant, and from here to many other places on the coast and inland. At a subsequent period a missionary was appointed to Victoria and Golden Grove, new villages formed soon after the emancipation. A mission to Essequibo was commenced in 1836. Out-stations with chapels and schools have been formed at Borg, Queen's Town, Ebenezer, Anna Regina, and other places, including the Island of Wakenaam. Berbice is a comparatively new station, which owes its origin to the removal of a considerable number of Wesleyan converts from the Leeward Islands. In conjunction with the Dutch Reformed Church in that place, the work has prospered, and several out-stations have been formed. A very important feature of this mission is the work among the Coolies, who are brought from the East Indies to supply the lack of agricultural laborers occasioned by the emancipation of the negro slaves (1838), many of whom then became mechanics and shopmen. The principal stations in British Guiana have for many years been entirely self-supporting, and have contributed liberally towards the funds of the parent society to help send the gospel to other lands.

*Jamaica.*—When Dr. Coke had succeeded in establishing Methodist missions in several of the smaller islands of the West Indies, he hastened to Jamaica, the largest and most important of the islands belonging to the British Crown. He preached several times, finding that the Negroes heard him gladly, and receiving from four or five wealthy white families promises of a warm welcome to any missionaries who might be sent to them. Upon his return to England the Doctor sent the Rev. William Hammett. Others were sent later, and Dr. Coke himself paid two more visits to Jamaica. Several of the missionaries fell victims to the climate, and much persecution was endured from the planters and white people generally. Nevertheless the efforts for the good of the Negroes were not relaxed, and the work spread from Kingston to Spanish Town, Morant Bay, Falmouth Bay, St. Ann's Bay, Bath, Clarendon, and other places far away in the interior of the island.

*Honduras,* although in North America, is, like British Guiana, usually classed with the West Indies. The population comprises a strange mixture of Europeans, Spanish creoles, Negroes, and Indians, and all classes were in a fearful state of degradation before Christian missionaries were sent among them. The Wesleyan Mission was commenced in 1825, in the town of Belize and among the scattered settlements of wood-cutters on the banks of the rivers. The climate is very trying, more so than that of the West Indies, to the European constitution, and a few months after his arrival the first missionary died; the second also died within a year from his appointment; but others followed whose lives were spared for a longer period, and the foundation was laid of a good work, which has steadily increased up to the present time. In 1868 a revival of religion took place, and the mission was then extended to Freetown and other places, which are now important stations. To supply as far as possible the spiritual needs of the mixed population, preaching and teaching are carried on in English, Spanish, and Maya, the language of a considerable tribe of Indians. Into the latter, portions of Scripture and other books have been translated, and it is hoped that by means of them access may be obtained to native populations which have not yet been brought under the influence of the gospel. In 1829 a mission was attempted to the wandering Indians inhabiting the Mosquito Coast, but the difficulties were so numerous and the prospect so discouraging that the undertaking was at length relinquished. The Honduras mission was formerly attached to Jamaica, but is now a separate mission.

*The Bahamas.*—The Rev. William Turton, a native of the West Indies, converted in the Wesleyan missions, was appointed to labor at New Providence, in the Bahamas, in 1803. He afterwards went to other islands in the group as openings presented themselves, being assisted by missionaries sent out from England. The gospel was thus carried to Eleuthera, Harbor Island, Abaco, Turk's Island, and other places, and great success attended the work.

*Haiti.*—In the year 1817 the Wesleyan Society sent two missionaries to Haiti to commence a mission. They were kindly received, and for some time labored without opposition; but when their efforts to evangelize the people

began to produce a powerful impression, a spirit of persecution was excited by the Romish priests which resulted in the passing of laws entirely subversive of religious liberty. The following year the missionaries were obliged to leave the country; but the people endured persecution with a patience and steadfastness that were remarkable, meeting together whenever possible for prayer and praise and keeping up communication with their banished pastors. At length it seemed possible to re-establish the mission, and in 1835 the Rev. John Tindall was appointed to Haiti, in conjunction with a converted native who had been instrumental in keeping the people together. For a time the work was prosecuted with cheering prospects of success, and various parts of the country were visited, and stations were established at Jérémie, Cayes, Cape Haytien, and other towns and villages of the republic, in addition to that at Port-au-Prince, the capital; but, in consequence of the instability of the government, the intolerance of popery, and the trying climate, this mission has always been a most difficult one, and, owing to these and other adverse circumstances, is now reduced to one station, although at one time constituting a separate district. In 1869, in the great fire at Port-au-Prince, the entire mission premises, consisting of chapel, school-house, and minister's residence, were entirely destroyed by fire.

WEST AFRICA. *Sierra Leone.*—The first British settlement on the west coast of Africa—the avowed objects of which were the suppression of the slave-trade, the encouragement of legitimate commerce, and the moral and religious improvement of the natives—received the name of Sierra Leone, from a river so called, on the southern bank of which the first town, appropriately named Freetown, was built. To this place a large number of slaves captured by British men-of-war were brought from time to time, for the purpose of settling them upon land bought for their use, so that the population consisted chiefly of liberated Africans, brought from different parts of the continent, and speaking different languages or dialects, who soon became industrious, learned to speak at least broken English, and attended to the instructions given them. A good work has been carried on among them for many years by several missionary societies, the results of which are encouraging. The capacity of the Negro race to receive instruction, and the perfect adaptation of the gospel to meet their case and to raise them in the scale of being, has been proved beyond the possibility of successful contradiction. As has been said, Dr. Coke's first scheme for the civilization of the Fulas, in the neighborhood of Sierra Leone, proved a failure. Some of the company sent out died of fever before reaching their destination, others absconded, and the rest returned home. In the year 1811 the Rev. George Warren and three school-teachers were sent to Sierra Leone. Upon their arrival in the colony they found about one hundred persons who were in the habit of meeting together for religious worship, and who called themselves Methodists. These people were chiefly free blacks from Nova Scotia, who had received the gospel at the hands of the missionaries there. They had already built a chapel, and had sent repeatedly to England for a missionary. After eight months of labor Mr. Warren died of fever—the first of a long line of Wesleyan missionaries who fell victims to the climate. Many times reinforcements were sent out, many times the same sad story was repeated; nevertheless the faithful, though brief labors, brought forth abundant fruit, assistance was at length afforded by native converts, and after 1840 the European missionaries and their families endured the climate with less suffering from illness and bereavement than formerly. From one point of view the whole history of the Sierra Leone Mission seems but a mournful record of the sacrifice of young lives. There is a brighter side; and they did not labor in vain. Important circuits and out-stations were formed, congregations gathered, churches organized, and schools established, not only in Freetown, but also in Gloucester, Regent, Wellington, Rissey, York, Kent, Russell, Wilberforce, Hamilton, and at other villages. At King Tom's Point, near Freetown, a seminary for the training of native ministers is in successful operation.

*River Gambia Mission.*—In 1866 an English settlement was formed on the island of St. Mary, near the mouth of the river Gambia, on the same principle as that at Sierra Leone. Nothing was done, however, for the religious instruction of the people until 1821, when the Wesleyan Society opened a station at a place called Mandanaree, on the mainland, but the dangers and difficulties here were so numerous that the missionaries resolved to remove to St. Mary's, where they might obtain medical aid in sickness, and where the people seemed more willing to attend to their instructions. In 1824, after the death of several devoted workers, the Gambia Mission was placed on a permanent footing. Buildings were erected and a girls' school established. Though suffering greatly from repeated bereavements, the work prospered, and after some native assistants had been trained an attempt was made to reach the Upper Gambia. War interfered; but as soon as peace was restored and the river was consequently open, a piece of land on Macarthy's Island was secured, and a chapel and schoolhouse were erected, a number of little wild, naked children were collected, partially clothed, and put into a mission school. The experiment was a somewhat novel and amusing one, but with patience and perseverance succeeded better than was expected. The missionaries some time later returned to their station at St. Mary's, leaving in charge of the work at Macarthy's a native teacher, who did most faithful and noble work. Subsequently it was strengthened by the appointment of European missionaries, and from this point the Gambia Mission branches out into two divisions, each with a separate history. Important educational and translating work were undertaken at Macarthy's, but up to 1848 the mortality among the European missionaries and their families was so great, that it was deemed advisable to supply the station with native ministers, to act under the direction of a European minister at St. Mary's. These native preachers, who were brought from Sierra Leone, where they had received special training for their work, by their piety, zeal, and intelligence gave general satisfaction, and were very useful. The hope that the Fulas might be benefited by the Macarthy Mission has not been realized to any great extent; but to the multitudes of liberated Africans who settled there, and to the Mandingoes, the mission has been of untold value. Meanwhile the Mission at St. Mary's made remarkable progress, but, like all missions to West Africa, was subject to many and sad vicissitudes, and for years the record of the mission is one of repeated sickness and death. But, as at Sierra Leone, the work made progress, and from the headquarters at St. Mary's spread throughout the island and to many points on the mainland, where stations were formed, chapels built, and schools established.

*Gold Coast.*—It was at a comparatively recent period that the Wesleyan Society commenced its mission to the "Gold Coast." At the principal British settlement, Cape Coast Castle, a few native youths had learned to read the Bible in the government school. They became so much interested in it that they formed themselves into a little society for its more careful reading and study, sending to England, through Captain Potter, the master of a British merchant vessel, for a supply of Bibles. The captain not only secured the Bibles, but also called at the Wesleyan Mission House, and generously offered to take out a missionary to the Cape Coast free of charge, and if the attempt to introduce the gospel there were not successful, to bring him home again. The committee appointed the Rev. J. Dunwell to sail with Captain Potter, and to commence a mission on the Gold Coast. He was received with kindness by the Governor, and with rapture by the youths who were so anxious for instruction. At Cape Coast and other parts of New Guinea which he visited his labors were greatly blessed, but in a few months he died of fever, the first of a long list who laid down their lives for the sake of the people inhabiting this unhealthy region. In 1845, the Rev. Henry Wharton, a native of the West Indies, offered himself for service in this mission, and about the same time several native missionaries were ready to assist in the work. It was still necessary to send out some European missionaries, but in consequence of some improvement in the the sanitary condition of the country, and the assistance given by the native helpers, they were almost all spared to fill their term of service. Of the later reinforcements, some died very soon after their arrival, but others were permitted to labor through the allotted time, and important circuits were formed at Cape Coast Town, Dix Cove, James Town, Lagos, Badagry, Abeokuta, and other places along the coast and far away in the interior. For some time Coomassie, the capital of Ashanti, was occupied by the missionaries, and the gospel was faithfully preached to the king and his people, who delight in human sacrifices. At all the stations congregations have been gathered, places of worship erected, and schools established.

In the course of fifty years sixty-three missionaries had lost their lives through the climate of West Africa, or had died at sea when proceeding to or from their appointments; yet there was no lack of laborers: as one fell another volunteered to take his place, and so the work has gone on. As now organized, the Mission to West Africa comprises (1) the *Sierra Leone* and *Gambia district*, and (2) the *Gold Coast* and *Lagos district*, containing the Cape Coast, Aburah, Accra, Apollonia, Yoruba, Porto Novo, and Popo (Dahomey) sections.

SOUTH AFRICA.—In the year 1814 the Wesleyan Society put forth its first efforts for the evangelization of South Africa. Its first missionary was not permitted to preach in the colony, and was therefore instructed to proceed to Ceylon, but did not. The following year the Rev. Barnabas Shaw was appointed to commence a Wesleyan Mission in Cape Colony. Permission to preach was refused him, but Mr. Shaw took matters into his own hands and preached without the governor's sanction. His congregations, however, were composed principally of soldiers, and his greatest desire being to preach Christ to the heathen, he gladly availed himself of an opportunity which offered, through Mr. Schmelen of the London Missionary Society, to go to Great Namaqualand. In September, 1815, Mr. Schmelen and Mr. Shaw, with their families, attendants, and supplies, set out on their long journey. On the 4th of October, after crossing the Elephant River, Mr Shaw unexpectedly found his sphere of labor, in meeting the chief of Little Namaqualand, accompanied by four men, on his way to Cape Town to seek for a Christian teacher, so that his tribe, like others, might have the advantages which he had seen follow the introduction of the gospel. Mr. Shaw agreed to go with the chief to his mountain home and to remain with him and his people, while Mr. Schmelen continued his journey to his own station in Great Namaqualand. About three weeks later the chief and his party reached Lily Fountain, on Khamiesberg, the principal home of the chief of the tribe of Little Namaquas. As the wagon ascended the mountain, and long before it reached the chief's "great place," they were met by a party of more than twenty natives mounted on oxen, and riding at full gallop, who had heard the good news and had thus come to welcome their teacher, and especially to have a good look at the missionary's wife, whom they surveyed with reverence and awe, never having seen a white woman before. On reaching the end of the journey, a council was held by the chief and his head men, when they all entreated Mr. Shaw to remain with them and teach them, promising to assist him in every possible way in establishing a mission. Mr. Shaw therefore began at once to lay the foundations of a mission which, from that day to this, has continued to exercise a most beneficial influence on all around. He preached in the open air, and taught both young and old the elements of religion, and the use of letters, by which they might read for themselves the Word of God. It was hard and trying work, and required much patience; but labor, prayer, faith, and perseverance were at length crowned with success. A number of children and young people learned to read, and a church was formed. As the civilizing influences of Christianity were brought to bear upon the people from year to year, their temporal condition also greatly improved. Among Mr. Shaw's labor-saving inventions were a cross-cut saw and a plough, the latter made chiefly by himself. As the old chief stood upon a hill and watched the plough "tear up the ground with its iron mouth," he exclaimed, "If it goes on so all day, it will do more work than *ten* wives !!" Thus was ushered in a new era in agricultural pursuits, as well as in the moral condition of the people. The rapid growth of garden seeds amused them very much, but when they saw the use to which lettuce and other salads were put, they laughed

heartily, saying, "If the missionaries and their wives can eat grass, they need never starve." When the mission was fully organized, the Rev. Edward Edwards came from England to join Mr. Shaw, and arrangements were made to extend the work to various places in the Unterveldt, and in the Bushmanland. Journeys were also made through Great Namaqualand and a part of Damaraland, with a view to the establishment of permanent missions in those countries, while the work in Little Namaqualand, through the faithful efforts of Mr. Shaw, Mr. Edwards (whose period of labor covered a half-century), and others who were sent out, made good progress in all its branches, notwithstanding difficulties which beset it from time to time. In 1855 a beautiful stone chapel, accommodating six hundred people, the cost of which was £1,000, was erected by the united efforts and contributions of the people, without foreign aid, with the exception of a gift of a pulpit from a few friends in Cape Town. At its opening services the chapel was filled with an attentive and well-dressed congregation, and the collections amounted to £16 4s. 0d. There were at that time 184 communicants and 300 children in the mission schools.

In 1825 the way seemed to open for the extension of work to Great Namaqualand, and the Rev. Mr. Threlfall and two native teachers were sent thither on a tour of observation. When some distance beyond the Orange River, they were met by a party of Bushmen, who, while pretending to guide them to a place of safety, murdered them, that they might take possession of their effects. This put an end, for the time, to any attempt to establish a mission north of the Orange River. Requests that teachers might be sent there were several times received from chiefs of tribes in this region, and in 1832 another attempt was made at "Warm Bath," now called Nisbit's Bath, and this time with success. This work was nobly carried on, but the migratory habits of the people and other drawbacks prevented as much advance in religious instruction and civilization as had been made in Little Namaqualand. In 1842 the work was extended to Damaraland, and the stations of "Concordville," "Elephant Fountain," and "Wesley Vale" were formed. There were for a time pleasing prospects of success at these places; but afterwards the restless, wandering, and warlike habits of the people, and the great difficulty of obtaining supplies from the Cape for the support of the mission, made the work very discouraging. In the meantime a number of German missionaries connected with the Rhenish Missionary Society had established themselves in Great Namaqualand and Damaraland, and the Wesleyan Society ultimately thought it best to transfer their stations on the southwest coast of Africa, beyond the Orange River, to the Rhenish Society.

*Cape Colony.*—In the year 1820 a second attempt was made to start a Wesleyan Mission in Cape Colony, and Mr. Edwards was directed to proceed thither from Little Namaqualand. With the cordial permission of the governor to preach to and instruct the slave population of the town and neighborhood, he began his work, which he for some time prosecuted with success, and in which he was succeeded by other missionaries sent out from England. Chapels were built in various parts of Cape Town, with which were connected prosperous day and Sunday schools. In connection also with this mission are the out-stations established in country places in the neighborhood of Cape Town, and the stations at Simon's Town, Stellenbosch, Somerset, and Robertson, the last a new station, situated in the midst of a dense population, and about one hundred miles from Cape Town. Here a large congregation has been gathered, a prosperous native church formed, and out-stations have been opened in the villages of Lady Gray, Montague, and Newmanville.

Graham's Town District. The work of the Wesleyan Society in the eastern province of the Cape Colony began in 1820, and was at first carried on for the benefit of a band of Wesleyans; it was soon extended to all colonists and natives, both Kafir and Hottentot, who could be reached by the missionaries. The work was commenced in Graham's Town, and from thence extended in many directions.

Salem became an important station at an early period, where evangelical and educational work for both Europeans and natives was vigorously prosecuted, but owing to Kafir wars has fluctuated according to circumstances. Fort Beaufort, Seymour, and Alice are out-stations. At Heald Town there was established in the early days of the mission an industrial school under government auspices, for the training of natives in the knowledge of religion and the arts of civilized life. Some years later, when the government grant was withdrawn, the school was converted into an institution for training native missionaries and teachers. The work here has now extended to various parts of the eastern province as well as to Kafirland. At Port Elizabeth (formerly "Algoa Bay") and at Uitenhage, a village eight miles distant, the Wesleyan Society labors for the Fingoes, who collect there in large numbers for the sake of employment. Higher up in the country are the stations of Craddock, Somerset (East), Peddie, and Newton Dale. In connection with some of these, extensive circuits have been formed, in which the missionaries itinerate among the scattered farms and villages, preach to natives and settlers, superintend the schools which have been established, and exert themselves in every possible way for the benefit of the people, who are in many instances entirely dependent upon them for religious instruction. Their journeys extend over scores, sometimes hundreds, of miles, and involve much danger and personal discomfort in crossing rivers, deserts, and mountains. At King William's Town the work of the Society has been repeatedly interrupted by Kafir wars, but is now in a prosperous condition; an out-station has been formed at Berkely. Mount Coke and the native station of Annshaw are also included in the Graham's Town district, although geographically related to Kafirland. At the former is the mission press, from which have issued countless numbers of school-books, portions of Scripture, and other publications, in English, Dutch, Kafir, and the Lesuto languages, to the great advantage of the work in all its departments. The Annshaw circuit is very populous and extensive, embracing 60 villages and 80 preaching places. At the respective stations and outposts 102 class-meetings are held each week.

Queen's Town District.—The mission stations of the Society comprised in this district are chiefly in Kafirland, and, with the exception of Queen's Town itself, where a number of Europeans reside, the work is entirely among natives, and is not of the mixed character which is necessary where British settlers reside in considerable numbers. The Rev. William Shaw, who accompanied the before-mentioned colony for East Africa, introduced the gospel into Kafirland, with the further design of establishing, as soon as help should arrive from England, a chain of stations to connect the Cape Colony with Natal. In 1823 he removed with his family to Kafirland, and formed the first station, which he called Wesleyville. In 1825 the second station was established, and named Mount Coke. The third, Butterworth, which now has about 40 preaching places, was formed in 1827. In 1829 a fourth station, Morley, was established for the benefit of a remarkable tribe of people, who seem to have descended from a number of Europeans cast away upon the shores of Kafirland many years before. This station, afterward removed to a healthier locality and called New Morley, is a centre of light to thousands of once degraded natives. The fifth station was commenced in 1830, and called Clarkeburg. Two of the laborers at this station were murdered by the Kafirs, but, notwithstanding this and other adverse circumstances which for a time threatened to impede the work, it has gradually advanced to a very encouraging degree of prosperity. Several important churches have been formed in various directions, and at many additional places the gospel is faithfully preached in the language of the natives. The sixth Kafir station was commenced about the same time as Clarkeburg, by the Rev. W. B. Boyce, who named it Buntingville. Although this station is the most isolated in the list, it is the only one which has never been devastated by wars; all the others have been laid waste at one time or another, and some of them repeatedly. Two more stations have grown out of Buntingville,—Shawbury and Palmerton,—which are on the borders of Natal, and thus complete the "chain of stations," on which the zealous pioneer missionary set his heart when first he penetrated the wilds of Kafirland. Other stations farther inland which have developed from these are: Osborn, Mt. Arthur, Lessey Town, Queen's Town, and others of recent origin.

*Bechuanaland District.*—The first attempt of the Wesleyan Society to carry the gospel to Bechuanaland was made in 1822. This attempt, owing to the sickness of the missionary and the unsettled state of the country, partially failed; and after being many times thwarted in their plans by tribal wars, the missionaries were at length enabled to commence a promising mission at Makwassi, in the upper region of the Vaal River. But from this place also they were driven away by the Matebele, a powerful and hostile tribe who made war upon the country from the north. As soon as possible they and their scattered people rallied, and finally settled at a place called Thaba Unchu, to the north of the Orange River. Here the Baralongs, with a few remnants of other scattered tribes who have joined them from time to time, have become a comparatively happy and prosperous people, through the instrumentality of the faithful missionaries who have labored among them for so many years. The Bechuana district includes several other stations, some for the benefit of English, Dutch, and colored people; others for natives alone. Among the latter are

Witteberge and Bensonville. At Bloemfontein and Fauresmith, in the Orange Free State, Wesleyan missionaries are stationed and it is hoped that the work of evangelization may rapidly extend to all classes of the people.

*Natal.*—Wesleyan missions were not undertaken in the colony of Natal until 1841, when a Wesleyan missionary accompanied a detachment of British troops sent from Cape Colony through Kaffraria to Natal, to keep order in the country. He preached to English, Dutch, and natives, being regarded as "the friend of all and the enemy of none," until peace was restored to the land, when a permanent mission was established by missionaries sent out from England. These were after a time assisted by native teachers, and important stations sprang up in many places. At Dunbar, Maritzburg, and Ladysmith, at Verulam and Umhali, the work is of a mixed character; but at Edendale, Kwangubeni, Indaleni, and Inanda it is conducted chiefly for the benefit of the natives. A more recent feature of the work in Natal is the mission to the coolies, begun in 1861.

Much valuable linguistic work has been accomplished in the Wesleyan missions of South Africa; the Scriptures, wholly or in part, hymn-books, catechisms, and other religious publications have been translated into five or six different languages, some of which had never been written before the missionaries undertook the difficult task of reducing them to grammatical form. To the Rev. W. B. Boyce belongs the honor of compiling the first Kafir grammar, and of unravelling the intricacies of one of the most difficult languages of Southern Africa.

Within recent years the missions have been reorganized, and the South African is now comprised in the districts of Transvaal and Swaziland, and Bechuanaland and Zululand.

AUSTRALIA.—It is perhaps doubtful whether a mission was ever commenced in any part of the world under more discouraging circumstances than was that of the Wesleyan Society to Australia. With a few exceptions, the colony of New South Wales was a vast community of convicts, with wandering tribes of savage natives on its borders. The free settlers and squatters were widely scattered over a large section of the country, and being entirely destitute of the means of religious instruction, their moral condition was only a few degrees above that of the convict population. Up to the time of the arrival of the first Wesleyan missionary the government had been occupied in erecting jails, barracks, and other public buildings necessary for the civil, military, and convict establishment, but very little had been done for the religious and moral improvement of the people. Indeed, the whole aspect of affairs—the state of society, the mode of government, the discipline adopted in the management of convicts, and the temper and spirit of everything and everybody—appeared cold, cruel, and repulsive in the extreme. Nevertheless, Mr. Leigh, having secured the countenance and protection of the Colonial Government, began to arrange his plans for a vigorous and systematic attack upon the mass of ignorance and immorality by which he was surrounded, and mapped out for himself a wide circuit in which to itinerate. Beginning at Sydney, the capital of the colony, which he made his headquarters, he extended his labors to Paramatta, where he met the Rev. Samuel Marsden, one of the four chaplains appointed by the government to minister to the troops and convicts, and now widely known as one of the founders of missions in the southern world, who gave him a cordial welcome to his station. Windsor, Liverpool, Castlereagh, Prospect, Concord, Burkham Hills, Castle Hill, and other places were also visited, and never was the transforming power of the gospel more gloriously manifested than in the early history of this mission, in the administration of which Mr. Leigh was from the first assisted by several zealous Methodists who had previously settled in New South Wales, one of whom had been converted in the Wesleyan Mission in the West Indies. Reinforcements were sent from England at various periods, and the mission from its commencement in 1814 made steady progress. At its jubilee, held in Sydney in 1864, £12,000 was subscribed for the purpose of founding a Wesleyan college and for the relief of church property. In Queensland, Victoria, Tasmania, and South and Western Australia missions were also established, which were carried on chiefly for the benefit of the colonists. In Victoria a mission to the aborigines was also undertaken, and carried on for nearly ten years, when, in view of the fact that the efforts put forth were almost fruitless, it was given up. A mission to the Chinese, who came in large numbers to the gold-diggings, was also established some years ago in connection with the Victoria Mission.

NEW ZEALAND.—In 1818 the Rev. Samuel Marsden, who had been laboring in New Zealand for several years, persuaded Mr. Leigh, then in Australia as above told, to take a trip thither. While there Mr. Leigh visited many of the native villages, and received from the people assurances that if "white teachers" should be sent to them they would attend to their instructions. Some time after Mr. Leigh went to England, and laid before the committee a proposal for the commencement of a mission to the cannibals of New Zealand. The Society was at that time laboring under a heavy debt, but Mr. Leigh, by forcible appeals to the friends of missions in many parts of England, obtained contributions of goods of various kinds which in New Zealand would be more valuable than money itself, and the Society undertook to commence the new mission without delay. About this time two Maori chiefs arrived in London with Mr. Kendall of the Church Missionary Society; their appearance gave a new impetus to the plans for New Zealand; the necessary preparations were soon completed, and the party of missionaries—consisting of Mr. and Mrs. Leigh, Mr. and Mrs. Horton, appointed to Tasmania, and Mr. Walker—sailed from England on April 28th, 1821. Work was commenced at Wangaroa in 1822. In 1823 Mr. and Mrs. Leigh left on account of failing health to seek restoration to strength in New South Wales, and Mr. and Mrs. Turner, Rev. Wm. White from England, and two colonists from New South Wales arrived and took charge of the work. The subsequent attack on the mission, the enforced flight of the missionaries, the abandonment and re-establishment of the mission, and the ultimate success of the work are treated of under New Zealand (q.v.).

THE FRIENDLY ISLANDS.—The Wesleyan Society, seeing that, after a long and gloomy night of toil, the missions of the London Missionary Society in the Society and Marquesas

Islands were beginning to bear fruit, sent a missionary to the Friendly Islanders, in the hope that they too might now be ready to receive the gospel. In June, 1822, about twenty-two years after the last surviving agent of the L. M. S. had escaped from Tonga, the Rev. Walter Lawry, with his family, sailed from Sydney, and in the following August anchored off Tonga. Among the hundreds of natives who came off from the shore in their canoes was one Englishman, named Singleton, who had lived sixteen years on the island, being one of the survivors of the ill-fated "Port-au-Prince," whose crew had been massacred in 1806. He had become a thorough Tonga man in manners and language, but became very useful to Mr. Lawry as an interpreter and in other ways, and before long himself accepted the gospel. Mr. Lawry was kindly welcomed by chiefs and people, and for two or three months such a desire for instruction was manifested that when the "St. Michael," which had brought Mr. Lawry, sailed again for home, it carried a request for more missionaries, a surgeon, a printer, teachers, books, and articles for barter. Soon after the departure of the ship, the characteristic fickleness and superstition of the people were shown. One chief, however, remained friendly; and notwithstanding the disadvantages under which Mr. Lawry labored, there were occasions when he had reason to hope that he had made an impression on the minds of some of the natives, and it seemed a matter for regret that, after laboring for about fourteen months, Mr. Lawry was obliged, on account of his wife's health, to return to New South Wales, leaving the work in charge of assistants. In 1826 more missionaries were sent out by the Society. They found that the chief who had befriended Mr. Lawry had turned against and threatened to kill his assistants. Securing the protection of another chief, they endeavored amid many and peculiar trials to build up a mission, and were at length rewarded by seeing some improvement in the people; and as a more general desire for instruction began to be manifested, an earnest request for help was forwarded to England. In 1828 the Revs. Nathaniel Turner (from New Zealand) and William Cross, with their wives, arrived at Tonga, and a second station was commenced at Nukuolofa. Messrs. Thomas and Hutchison continued at Hikifo, the first station. Schools were established at both stations, which were attended by hundreds of children, who were taught chiefly from manuscript translations, but who made rapid progress in learning to read, as well as in committing to memory hymns, prayers, and lessons from the Scriptures. At the Sabbath services there were sometimes over two hundred natives present. Open opposition almost entirely disappeared, and the missionaries were enabled to devote themselves fully to preaching, teaching, and translating, and the acquisition of the language. Urgent calls for their services came in from other islands in the group—from Vavau, Haabai, and from Man, where the chief and his people spontaneously abolished idol-worship and built a neat Christian place of worship in anticipation of the coming of a missionary. These and other remarkable indications of the readiness of the people to receive the gospel induced the missionaries at Tonga to unite in a very urgent appeal to the Committee to send out more missionaries. The request was readily granted, but from the great distance and the difficulty of finding suitable men for the work a considerable time elapsed before those sent out reached their destination. In the mean time places of worship were erected, schools established, the gospel was faithfully preached, and multitudes of people were turned from the worship of dumb idols to the fear of God. While waiting anxiously for communication from home, not daring to add to the financial burden of the Society by further outlay without the express permission of the Committee, a small box or packet was washed on shore and handed to Mr. Turner. It was found to contain a letter authorizing the missionaries to commence a mission on Haabai without delay. The vessel that bore that letter, a schooner from Sydney, had foundered at sea and all on board were lost. It is said that neither the vessel, nor crew, nor any of the cargo were ever seen or heard of again; that letter alone escaped the general wreck, and was cast on shore just at the right place and time. Mr. and Mrs. Thomas immediately started for their new sphere of labor, and reached Lifuka, one of the Haabai Islands, after a stormy and dangerous voyage, January 30th, 1830. A native teacher had been previously sent to this group to instruct the people as best he could in the truths which he himself had just learned. Mr. Thomas was glad to find that the efforts of this pioneer evangelist had not been in vain. Out of eighteen inhabited islands, all but three had embraced Christianity. Many houses, formerly sacred to idol gods, were either used as common dwellings or set apart for the worship of Jehovah. The king took five of the principal idols and hung them up by the neck in one of the principal houses, that the people might see that they were "all dead." The people were anxious to learn to read and write, as well as to worship God, and the work was becoming too much for poor Peter, when the first English missionary opportunely arrived. There was a great work for him to do; the people were absolutely ignorant and required instruction. All that they knew was that they were wrong, and there was one among them who could set them right. On the day following his arrival (the Sabbath) Mr. Thomas preached to about three hundred persons, and from that time on the work prospered. Schools were opened, and Mr. and Mrs. Thomas and Peter were constantly engaged in teaching the crowds of people who came together for instruction—no easy task, even with the aid of books and other school requisites, but, in a country where letters were previously unknown, and where every book had to be written with the pen, the difficulties were increased a hundred-fold. Still they toiled on, preaching, teaching, and translating. Hundreds of young people soon learned to read their own language with fluency, and native teachers were trained to take part in the work, which flourished in all its departments.

In 1831 three missionaries arrived from England, and through their united labors the mission was greatly strengthened; many were added to the church, and the work of education still further advanced among the people. Many of those educated in the mission schools became teachers, and with their aid the work was extended to the islands of the group which had not yet received Christianity.

*Vavau.*—As has been stated, the chief of this island requested that a missionary might be sent to them early in the history of the mission Finding that he could not be supplied with a teacher, he turned again to his idols; but in 1831 King George of Haabai, a man of remarkable intelligence and strong Christian character, visited Vavau, and after much persuasion the chief, Finan, agreed to give up his idols. His manner of doing so was unique. Having given orders that seven of his principal idols should be brought out of their house and placed in a row, he stood in front of them and addressed them thus: "I have brought you here to prove you, and I tell you beforehand what I am about to do, that you may be without excuse." Then to the first one he said: "If you are a god, run away, or I shall burn you in the fire I have prepared!" The god made no attempt to escape, nor did the others, when spoken to in the same way. As none of them ran, the king gave orders that the sacred houses should be set on fire. His commands were promptly obeyed, and eighteen temples with their gods were burned to ashes. Many of the people, greatly troubled at the king's impious conduct, as they considered it, sat trembling and silent to watch the result. The expected awful calamity not occurring, they came to the conclusion that their gods must be liars after all, and they too joined the "praying people." Two native teachers were immediately sent to Vavau, and Mr. and Mrs. Cross were appointed to take charge of the work. Upon the voyage thither their vessel was shipwrecked; Mrs. Cross was drowned, and her husband was cast upon a desolate island, from which he was rescued by a canoe from Tonga. Embarking a second time, he reached Vavau in safety. His labors and the unwearied exertions of those who joined or succeeded him were richly blessed, and a wonderful change was effected in the whole group. Idol-worship was totally abandoned, native churches were organized, and schools established. The progress of the mission here and in all the Friendly Islands was greatly aided by the arrival of a printing-press from England. Great were the surprise and delight of the natives of Tonga when they saw with what rapidity and neatness copies of school-books and other publications were multiplied by the mysterious machine. Crowds of people eager to get a glimpse of the press in motion besieged the printing-office, and to gratify their curiosity the first sheets which were struck off were distributed. In 1833 Finan died, leaving the government of Vavau to King George of Haabai. To Haabai and Vavau was soon added the dominion of Tonga, and George thus became king of the Friendly Islands—a circumstance very favorable to the development and establishment of Christianity, as he was a man of superior judgment and ability, and of unwavering Christian principle. By his Christian forbearance and the pacific influence of the missionaries the last enemies of Christianity —a band of men in the remote parts of Tonga, who were encouraged in their bitter opposition to the king and the missionaries by abandoned Europeans who had settled among them—were overcome, and in a few years the whole group of the Friendly Islands became at least nominally Christian. Seeing the danger that Christianity might become a mere profession, the

missionaries most earnestly desired a special baptism of the Spirit, and their prayers were answered in 1834 by one of the most remarkably revivals ever known, in which thousands of persons were truly converted, as was shown in their after life. From this period the history of the stations in Vavau and Haabai, and very soon after in Tonga also, was that of regularly organized Christian churches, the whole of the population professing Christianity. For many years the mission depended for its supplies upon the precarious and uncertain visits of trading-vessels from the Australian colonies, or upon the occasional charter of boats to convey goods to the stations. To improve this very trying condition of things the committee provided a vessel expressly for the service of the missions, and in September, 1839, the "Trixton," fitted out for a four years' voyage among the islands, sailed from England, having on board twenty-six persons, chiefly missionaries and their families, appointed to stations in South Africa, New Zealand, the Friendly Islands, and Fiji. After four years of useful service, the "Trixton" was succeeded by the more commodious "John Wesley," whose periodical visits to the different stations were occasions of great joy to the missionaries and their people, great comfort to the mission families, and great saving to the Society's funds. A second "John Wesley" afterwards took the place of the first, which was wrecked on Haabai.

At all the stations on the Friendly Islands special attention is given to educational work. High-schools are numerous, and the training institution at Nukuolofa has developed into Tubou College,—in honor of King George Tubou,—whose course of study embraces arithmetic, algebra, geometry, trigonometry, chemistry, history, geography, Scripture history, and theology.

The liberality of these islanders has always been remarkable, and in 1870 the mission had become not only self-supporting, but also a large contributor to the funds of the Wesleyan Society. A second revival was experienced at Haabai in 1869, and in 1870 it was confidently asserted that there was not one heathen remaining on any of the Friendly Islands.

SAMOA.—The Wesleyan Society undertook work in Samoa in 1835; its early efforts were attended with great success and the work has continued to prosper, comprising now several stations, which are carried on, as are the other missions of the South Seas, under the direction of the Australian Conference.

FIJI.—One of the results of the revival in the Friendly Islands in 1834 was the commencement of a mission to Fiji, which was undertaken by the missionaries (one of whom, Mr. Watkin, went to England to plead there the cause of "poor Fiji"), seconded by King George and some other zealous disciples from Tonga. The Fijians at that time were atrocious cannibals. Instances of this most appalling and barbaric feature of heathenism, shocking and revolting enough, have been known to occur in New Zealand, the New Hebrides, and other islands, but Fiji earned for itself the greatest notoriety for this abomination; and, in addition, war, polygamy, adultery, murder, suicide, deception, fraud, theft, and many other crimes which cannot be named, were prevalent among the natives. To these people a mission was commenced in October, 1835, when Messrs. Cross and Cargill, with their families, several converted Friendly Islanders, and a few Fijians returning to their own country, embarked in a small schooner, the "Blackbird," for whose arrival from Australia they had been waiting since March. Landing at Lukemba, they commenced the work destined to be so hard and perilous, but also so blessed. Many and fierce were the conflicts which these brave missionaries and those who came after them had to encounter from the prevalence of war, cannibalism, and superstition. Perhaps there never was another such struggle between light and darkness, truth and error, as that which took place in the course of the Fiji Mission; but the missionaries persevered and pushed forward their noble enterprise with a moral heroism beyond all praise, and they had their reward in the victory which crowned their efforts at last. From point to point, from island to island, they extended their work, the results of which are indicated in the following extract from a recently published account of Fiji as it now is: "Strange indeed is the change which has come over these isles since first Messrs. Cargill and Cross, Wesleyan missionaries, landed here in the year 1835, resolved at the hazard of their lives to bring the gospel to these ferocious cannibals. Imagine the faith and courage of the two white men, without any visible protection, landing in the midst of these bloodthirsty hordes, whose unknown language they had in the first instance to master, and day after day witnessing such scenes as chill one's blood even to hear about. Many such have been described to me by eye-witnesses.

"Slow and disheartening was their labor for many years; yet so well has that little leaven worked that, with the exception of the Kai Tholos, the wild highlanders who still hold out in their mountain fastnesses, the eighty inhabited isles have all abjured cannibalism and other frightful customs, and have *lotued* (i.e. embraced Christianity) in such good earnest as may well put to shame many more civilized nations.

"I often wish that some of the cavillers who are forever sneering at Christian missions could see something of their results in these isles. But first they would have to recall the Fiji of ten years ago, when every man's hand was against his neighbor, and the land had no rest from barbarous intertribal wars, in which the foe, without respect to age or sex, were looked upon as so much beef, the prisoners deliberately fattened for the slaughter; dead bodies dug up that had been buried ten or twelve days, and that could only be cooked in the form of puddings; limbs cut off from living men and women, and cooked and eaten in the presence of the victim, who had previously been compelled to dig the oven and cut the firewood for the purpose; and this not only in time of war, when such atrocity might be deemed less inexcusable, but in time of peace also, to gratify the caprice or the appetite of the moment.

"Think of the sick burned alive; the array of widows who were deliberately strangled on the death of any great man; the living victims who were buried beside every post of a chief's new house, and must needs stand clasping it, while the earth was gradually heaped over their devoted heads; or those who were bound hand and foot, and laid on the ground to act as rollers when a chief launched a new canoe, and

thus doomed to a death of excruciating agony;—a time when there was not the slightest security for life and property, and no man knew how quickly his own hour of doom might come; when whole villages were depopulated simply to supply their neighbors with fresh meat! Just think of all this, and of the change which has been wrought, and then just imagine white men who can sneer at missionary work the way they do. Now you may pass from isle to isle, certain everywhere to find the same cordial reception from kindly men and women. Every village on the eighty inhabited isles has built for itself a tidy church, and a good house for its teacher or native minister, for whom, also, the village provides food and clothing. Can you realize that there are nine hundred Wesleyan churches in Fiji, at every one of which the frequent services are crowded by devout congregations; that the schools are well attended; and that the first sound which greets your ear at dawn, and the last at night, is that of hymn-singing, and most fervent worship, rising from each dwelling at the hour of family prayer?

"What these people may become after much contact with the common run of white men we cannot, of course, tell, though we may unhappily guess. At present they are a body of simple and devout Christians, full of deepest reverence for their teachers and the message they bring, and only anxious to yield all obedience. . . . It is painfully suggestive to know that the thing chiefly deprecated by all who have the welfare of the people at heart is their acquiring English, or being thrown in the way of foreigners."

The thrilling story of how this mighty work was accomplished—than which no part is more thrilling than the share taken in it by the natives of the Friendly Islands who came as missionaries to the Fijians—we are compelled, from want of space, to leave untold; but surely in the whole history of Christianity there is nothing more wonderful than the transformation of these savages through the power of the gospel, nothing more touching than their readiness to receive, and their eagerness to make known, that gospel to those who know it not.

MISSION TO NEW BRITAIN.—As the mission to Fiji was the outgrowth of the work for the Friendly Islands, so from Fiji has gone forth the first effort to carry the gospel to the desperate cannibals of New Britain. In June, 1875, the idea of this mission was first suggested; and the missionary, Mr. Brown, after fully explaining to all the native teachers the imminent dangers it involved, asked if there were any among them who would volunteer for the work. The response was most cordial; and nine brave, determined men (seven of whom were married, and their wives true helpmeets in this great work) announced their wish to undertake it. On hearing of this the English consul considered it his duty to summon these teachers and lay before them in darkest colors the dangers they were about to incur from the climate and cannibals, and the almost inevitable fate that awaited them should they persist in their rash determination. They replied that they had counted the cost and were ready to accept all risks. One, acting as spokesman for all, said: "We are all of one mind. We know what those islands are. We have given ourselves to this work. If we get killed, well; if we live, well. We have had everything explained to us, and know the danger. We are willing to go." They added that all dangers had been fully set before them by the missionaries, and that they had determined to go because of their own wish to make known the gospel of Christ to the people of other isles. The native teachers in Fiji receive a salary of £10 per annum, and are supplied with food by the scholars. These men resigned all claim to any definite salary, giving themselves as volunteers, without even the certainty of daily bread, resolved to face whatever hardships might lie before them. With something more than the zeal of the early saints (for we never hear that they went to live amongst cannibals), this band of brave men set sail in the "John Wesley," Mr. Brown having left his wife and children in New Zealand. Some time after, just as a fresh detachment of teachers was about to start for New Britain, the distressing tidings reached Fiji that four of the first party had been treacherously murdered and eaten by the cannibal people of the Duke of York Island, on which they with their wives and little ones had settled in the hope of forming a separate mission. The murderers threatened also to kill and eat the widows and orphans, and urged the natives of New Britain likewise to dispose of their teachers, especially the white missionary. The latter, being a Christian of the muscular type, deemed it wise, once for all, to teach these murderers that the shedding of blood involves punishment in kind; so mustering his little force of Fijians and Samoan catechists, he crossed over to the offending isle, rescued the widows and orphans, and routed the horde of savages. But notwithstanding all this, the determination of the new teachers was unshaken. One of the wives was asked whether she still intended to accompany her husband to a scene of so great danger. She replied: "I am like the outrigger of a canoe—where the canoe goes, there you will find the outrigger." Later on Mr. Brown returned to New Zealand to announce that the mission was fairly established, and to see his family; his wife, being of one mind with him, resolved to return with him. Placing the elder children at school, and taking only their little baby with them, they stopped at Fiji to enlist fresh volunteers, and then quietly sailed away on their errand of mercy—their departure hardly exciting a passing comment; but there is small doubt that their work will leave an enduring mark on the history of the Pacific Isles. In 1888 missionary meetings were held for the first time in the history of the mission, and £50 were contributed to the funds of the Wesleyan Society. A small seed, from which greater things will surely grow. Portions of Scripture, gospel lessons, hymn-books, and catechisms have been prepared in the Duke of York and the New Britain language, and have given a great impetus to the work. Loud and urgent are the calls for help. None but those who met and handled it, lived in its midst, and have seen its working, can know how fearful, how dark, how repulsive, cruel, and wretched is heathenism; and none but those can fully understand the earnestness of this cry for help.

INDIA.—The origin of the mission to Ceylon has been already indicated. It was not until Dr. Coke had offered himself for this mission, and had promised to defray the necessary expenses of its commencement to the amount of £6,000, that the conference which assembled in Liverpool in 1813 consented to undertake the enterprise, and to send out at the close of the year Dr. Coke and six young missionaries. As is well known, Dr. Coke died on the voyage, and was buried at sea. His young colleagues, thus left without their head, had a difficult task before them, but upon reaching Ceylon they were kindly received by the governor, and several places were named to them as greatly in need of the gospel, and of schools for the training of native children. It was decided to open stations at Colombo, Galle, and Matura, in the south among those of the native population who speak Sinhalese, and at Jaffna and Batticaloa in the north, where the Tamil language was in common use. In a very short time, such was their zeal in studying the language, the missionaries were able to preach to the natives, and also to Dutch and Portuguese colonists. Schools were organized, a printing-press was set up at Colombo, a Sinhalese grammar and dictionary were prepared, and the work flourished in all its departments, literary, evangelical, and educational. In addition to those already mentioned, important stations were established in Southern Ceylon at Negombo, Kandy, Caltura, Pantura, Seedua, Morotto, Wellewatta, and other places; while in North Ceylon, where the Tamil language had been conquered and several native teachers trained for the work, chapels and schools were established not only in the villages adjacent to Jaffna, but also at places at a considerable distance, which were afterwards occupied as separate stations. As the work required, missionaries were sent from England, and the unwearied efforts put forth were rewarded with abundant success.

*Madras.* In 1817 a Wesleyan mission was commenced at Madras, which has ever since been zealously maintained, and has been a great blessing to the people through its evangelical and educational departments. A very important and useful feature of the latter is the girls' school. Other stations of the Society in India are at St. Thomas Mount, Negapatam, Manaragoody, Trichinopoly, Melnattam, Warriore, Trivaloor, and Caroor. A very important Indian Mission has its headquarters at Bangalore. It embraces many chapels, schools, and a fine printing establishment. Seringapatam and the city of Mysore are included in the Mysore District. At Calcutta and Lucknow Wesleyan missions have been established, for the benefit of English soldiers and also the native population. At Bombay, the Mauritius (included in the India Missions), and some other points, missions were commenced and hopefully carried on for a time, but were afterwards relinquished.

CHINA.—In 1852 Mr. Piercy, who had for some time labored in China at his own expense, offered his services to the Wesleyan Society, was accepted by them, and appointed to Canton, where he remained until the war between England and China forced him, with other missionaries, to take refuge in Macao. During the two years spent there he continued the study of the language with unabated zeal, and upon the restoration of peace, in 1858, reoccupied Canton as a station of the Society. In 1860, upon the receipt of a legacy intended expressly for the India and China missions, the Committee was enabled to largely extend its work. The staff of workers was increased in numbers, and a new station was commenced at Fatshan. In 1862 a mission for North China was established at Hankow. In addition to the usual departments of evangelical and educational work, a medical mission has been commenced, and is proving itself a most important factor in the success of the enterprise. As at present constituted, the China Mission includes the districts of Canton ("East" and "West") and Wuchang, both comprising many out-stations. Dispensary work is now an important element of the Canton District also.

With the mention only of one more very important enterprise, its "Army and Navy Work," carried on in all parts of the world, we close our account of the Wesleyan Missionary Society.

**West, Henry S.,** b. Binghamton, N. Y., U. S. A., January 21st, 1827; studied at Yale College, and the College of Physicians and Surgeons, New York City; practised medicine for some years in Binghamton; sailed as a missionary of the A. B. C. F. M. January 17th, 1859, for the mission to the Armenians of Turkey. He spent most of his missionary life at Sivas, but his influence was widely extended. He visited the United States in 1868 for the health of his family, but returned to Turkey the following year. While attending one of the poor families in Sivas he contracted from them the typhus fever, which, complicated with pneumonia, resulted in his death. Dr. Barnum of Harpoot wrote: "Dr. West was a noble, cheerful, kind, unselfish man. He was a man of rare skill in his profession. I presume it is no disparagement to others to say that there is probably no physician in the Turkish Empire who enjoyed an equal reputation among the people. He was withal, and best of all, an humble, sincere, and earnest Christian. In addition to his professional services, he trained quite a body of native physicians in a region cursed with ignorant quacks. One of his students is a physician in Harpoot. He is equal to the average of his profession in America, and is the only trustworthy doctor within a hundred miles. When he was examined in Constantinople by the faculty of the Government Medical College for a diploma, his examiners said: 'The Turkish Government is greatly indebted to Dr. West for educating so many young men, and so well, for the medical profession.'" "He attained an eminence reached by comparatively few in his profession. The almost unprecedented number of surgical operations which he has performed have given him celebrity, not only in the East, but also in Europe and America. His lithotomic operations reached the number of 150 or more, of which scarcely half a dozen resulted unfavorably; and other operations were numerous in proportion. The blind eyes he has opened are past counting; the crippled, the deformed, the sick from various diseases, who have been relieved by him, if all assembled would make a great host. Much the larger portion of these cases were attended without pay, and all earnings from patients able to pay were turned over to the treasury of the Board. He received personally nothing but his regular salary, yet many a case which he attended would, in America, have brought him hundreds, even thousands, of dollars. Wherever he went, the diseased, the halt, the lame, the blind thronged him. The natives remarked, 'He is like Jesus.' Pashas and great men would humble themselves to secure the help of this plain, un-

pretending physician. The ignorant would get his prescriptions and hang them about their necks as charms, or dissolve the papers in water and drink them, hoping for healing efficacy. His simplicity and faithfulness were admirable. Without hesitation he would lay his ear for auscultation on chests so foul and squalid that native doctors shrank from them. He never flinched in duty, and never showed a nervous hand in the most difficult operations. When ether was about to be administered before the operation, the doctor would call upon some gray-headed native in the company to offer prayer, then coolly give the ether, take the knife and proceed.

"Dr. West's special duty was the care of the missionaries in sickness, and he never shrank from any hardship, making long and perilous journeys on horseback. All Asia Minor became familiar to him on account of these travels. The mission felt bereaved and downcast at his loss.—Who now will brave storm and wind and winter snow, wolf, Circassians, and Koords, on wild mountain and desolate plain, to minister to our sick, bringing such love and skill to the work?" Mr. Hubbard says: "During the meetings of the Week of Prayer, in addition to his medical practice, he did more than any one of us in pastoral work and conversation. His hard day's work was seldom followed by refreshing sleep at night." He died April 1st, 1876.

**West Indies.**—This group of islands extends in a rude bow-like form from the coast of Florida, U. S. A., to the coast of Venezuela in South America. The larger and more important islands belong to one or other of the great European nations, with the exception of two republics, and this political division will be followed in the more detailed account of the islands, while some facts which are true of all will serve as a preface to the specific description of them as English, Danish, Dutch, Spanish, or French possessions.

The population of these islands is composed of Europeans and Americans, together with Negroes and other Africans, Hindus and Chinese. Diversity of tongue, of character, and of life is consequently so great that there is little attempt at cohesion or federation even where the islands are under the same flag.

From the second visit of Columbus until within the present century these islands have been the scene of sorrow and oppression. In the years just subsequent to their discovery, evil of the most pronounced character was the business of the men who invaded these shores, and all that selfish greed and fiendish cruelty could suggest was done to exterminate the mild aborigines. Hardly a trace of them is now to be found.

Then the islands became the battlefields of the rival powers of Europe. The waters were dyed red with human blood; many an earthly paradise was changed to a scene of desolation, grim and bare. In the early times of British occupancy the streets of London, as well as the wilds of Ireland, were the scenes of many crimes peculiar to that age, for women were stolen and sent to the West Indies to supply the profligate Europeans. So common was the practice that the term "Barbadosed" had a terrible significance, and political enemies and many others were forced against their will to spend their remaining days in a second Botany

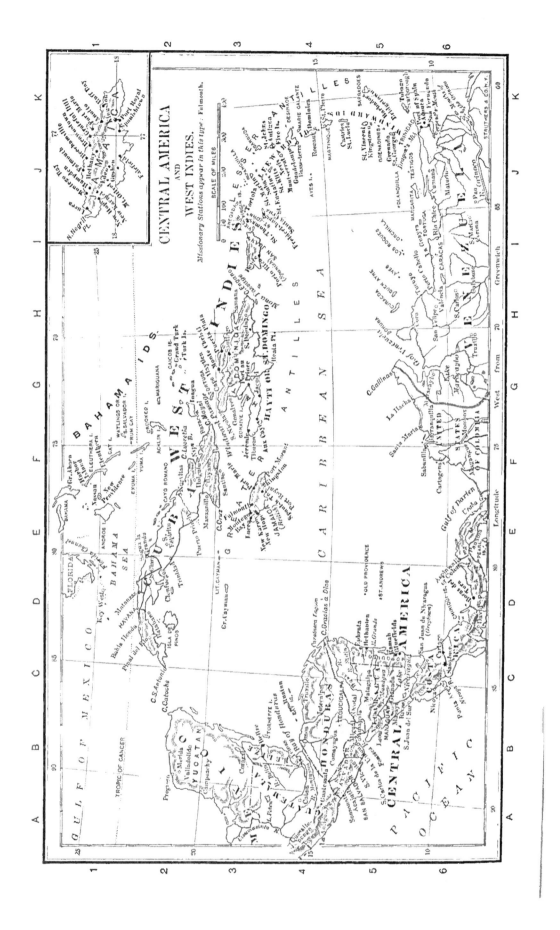

CENTRAL AMERICA
AND
WEST INDIES.

Missionary Stations appear in this type.—Falmouth.

SCALE OF MILES

Bay in the western seas. Piracy was rife, and the commerce of Europe suffered from the marauding buccaneers, who smarted from the wrongs they suffered and retaliated on the innocent as well as the guilty. The slave trade had its origin here, and the hardly less cruel importation of coolies has left its curse on the lands. The occupation of the West Indies has afforded the material for a black chapter in the history of the conquests of European nations. Harmless savages were put to death in the name of Christ. Into this moral sewer was swept the refuse of Europe. Hundreds of Hindus and Chinese were lured to this land of faithless promises. The African was dragged here only to die of pestilence. Is it strange that these lands should have been sunk in the lowest depths of sin and degradation? No wonder that the burden of debt which weighs down the different administrations is the despair of statesmen.

Patient and heroic hands early planted the gospel in this miry soil. From the earliest time when Christians saw the image of God in the sable body, to the present day, the conflict between the forces of good and the powers of evil has been fierce and bitter. Prejudices of the white and superstitions of the black races united to render the work excessively difficult. The faithful preacher of Christ was never free from all the persecutions that malignity and hatred could devise or ignorance and superstition suggest. Even his own race insulted, beat, and imprisoned the missionary, and the people he came to succor betrayed him into the hands of his enemies.

The results which are now seen in the islands are but additional proof that the gospel is suited alike to the moral and the immoral, to the wise and the foolish, to the black as well as to the white man.

*British West Indies.*—THE BAHAMAS.—These are nineteen inhabited and many uninhabited islands off the southeast coast of Florida. The total area is 5,450 square miles. The principal islands are: New Providence, which, with the capital, Nassau (q.v.), is well known as the home of buccaneers, pirates, and blockade-runners, and San Salvador, which is supposed to be the island first discovered by Columbus, but that honor is disputed in favor of Watlings. On the west side of the island are quite a number of intelligent Africans. Eleuthera (q.v.) is over 200 miles long. Abaco is the most northerly island, and has a length of 90 miles. Andros is the largest of the group, with a length of 90 miles, and 40 miles across at its widest part. The remaining islands are: Great Bahama, Harbor Island, Long Island, Mayaguana, Great Inagua, Ragged Island, Rum Cay, Fortune Island, Exuma, Crooked Island, Biminis, Acklin's, and Berry. The total population in 1881 was 43,521, of whom 11,000 were whites. In 1888 it was 48,000. The government is in the hands of a governor assisted by an Executive Council of 9, a Legislative Council of 9, and an Assembly of 29 representatives.

*Missions.*—Soon after the occupation of the islands by the English, the Church of England formed each island into a parish, and a bishop was appointed in 1861. There are now about 20 clergymen. The Wesleyan Methodist Missionary Society (see article) took up the work in these islands in 1825. Five islands are occupied:—*San Salvador*—station, Arthur's Town; *New Providence*—Nassau, with 3 chapels

and the superintendent of missions, and Fox Hill; *Eleuthera*—Current Island, East End, Governor's Harbor; *Harbor Island; Biminis*—Alice Town and Bayley Town; and *Abaco.* The total statistics for the Bahamas are: 9 missionaries, 28 stations, 3,016 members. 3,000 Sunday scholars. (See also articles Harbor Island and Eleuthera.)

The Baptist Missionary Society commenced work in the islands in 1833, by opening a mission to the slaves. It has now 1 missionary in charge of the whole work, which is carried on in all of the nineteen islands with 81 stations, 14 native assistants, and 4,320 members. There is a native Baptist church numbering about 1,600 members under the care of native pastors. The Roman Catholics built a chapel at Nassau in 1888, and have opened a school. There is one Presbyterian church in the whole colony; it is at Nassau.

JAMAICA.—The island of Jamaica is about 140 miles long, with an average width of 50 miles. On account of its mountainous character the scenery is beautiful, and there is abundance of fresh water. The sagacity of Oliver Cromwell saw the future value of this island, and secured it to the British Government. Its area is 4,200 square miles, with a population (1881) of 580,804, of whom 444,186 were blacks. The capital is Kingston (40,000). and some of the other principal towns are Spanish Town (5,689), Montego Bay (4,651), and Port Maria (6,741). Attached to Jamaica for administrative purposes are the following smaller islands. Turk's and Caicos Islands, area 224 square miles, population 4,778; Cayman Islands—Grand Cayman, Little Cayman, and Cayman Brae—with a total population of 4,000; the Morant Cays and Pedro Cays.

*Missions.*—The Church of England early divided the island into parishes, and its adherents number now 38,945, though its work is more for the owners of the plantations than for the natives. The first missionaries to the natives were the Moravian Brethren, who commenced their work in 1754, and now have in Jamaica 20 stations, 27 missionaries, and 5,792 communicants. In the early part of the present century the Wesleyan Methodist mission was commenced. The members now number 20,700, and Jamaica has been divided into the following districts: Kingston, Montego Bay, Saint Ann's, and Morant Bay. The Baptist Missionary Society followed soon after the Wesleyan Methodist, and after 30 years of missionary work the Baptist churches formed a union, which now has 86 churches in the south side parishes and 63 in the north, which are wholly self-supporting. There are 35,000 church-members. A Jamaican Baptist Missionary Society has also been formed which has stations and missionaries on Turk's Island, Haiti, San Domingo. the Caymans, Cuba, Santa Croix, and Central America. The only branch of the work which is supported by the parent society in England is the Calabar College for the training of ministers and school-teachers. The work of the various Presbyterian churches was consolidated in 1847, and the United Presbyterian Church of Scotland has the direction of the missionary work. There are 46 stations, 14 out-stations, and 9,131 members. The Colonial and Continental Church Society has its agents in the island, and has assisted the Episcopal churches since 1870, when they were thrown on their own resources. There are 86 clergymen, 95 churches, 52 chapels, 242 day-schools, and 30,000 communicants.

BARBADOS lies to the east of the Windward Islands, and has an area of 166 square miles. It abounds in varied and beautiful scenery, and almost the entire island is under cultivation. Population (1881), 171,860, of whom 113,302 were blacks. Bridgetown, the capital, has a population of 25,000, and is beautifully situated on the shores of the bay. The English began to exercise authority here in 1645. Since 1885 it has been separated from the Windward Islands, to which administration it formerly belonged, and has now a government of its own.

*Missions.*—The Church of England has 151,-038 communicants, and there is a training college for clergymen, under control of the S. P. G. The Moravian Brethren have 4 stations, 4 missionaries, 7,000 communicants, and 2,362 day-scholars. The Wesleyan Methodist work is organized under the West Indian Conference, with 13,000 church-members. The Roman Catholics also have congregations in Barbados.

LEEWARD ISLANDS lie to the north of the Windward Group, and southeast of Porto Rico. The islands, together with their area and population, are: Antigua, 170 square miles, 35,000; Barbuda and Redonda, 62 square miles; Virgin Islands, 58 square miles, 5,000; Dominica, 291 square miles, 29,500; St. Kitt's or St. Christopher, 65 square miles, 45,000; Nevis, 50 square miles, 11,864; Anguilla, 35 square miles, 9,000; Montserrat, 32 square miles, 10,083. Only part of the Virgin Islands belongs to Great Britain; the remainder belongs to Denmark, except Crab Island, which is Spanish. The principal cities are: St. John, Antigua (10,000); Basseterre, St. Christopher (7,000).

Mission work is carried on by the Church of England, 49,000 members; Wesleyan Methodists, 30,000 members; Moravian Brethren, 8 stations in Antigua and 4 in St. Kitt's (q.v.), 4,962 communicants, 2,473 day-scholars. There are also 29,000 Roman Catholics.

WINDWARD ISLANDS.—These islands, with their area and population, are: Grenada, 120 square miles, 490,337; St. Vincent (q.v.), 122 square miles, 46,872; and the Grenadines. The principal cities are: Kingston, the capital of St. Vincent, population 5,393; Castres, the chief town of St. Lucia, population 4,555; and St. George, the capital of Grenada, with 5,000 inhabitants.

*Missions.*—S. P. G. (1885), 3 stations on St. Vincent and 1 in Grenada. There are 1,000 communicants under the care of 4 missionaries. The Roman Catholics and the Wesleyan Methodists have also large churches.

TRINIDAD lies immediately north of the mouth of the Orinoco. It is an island of extreme beauty and great fertility. In 1802 it was finally handed over to British rule by the peace of Amiens. Its area is 1,754 square miles, with a population of 139,566. Port-of-Spain is the capital (31,900). Tobago was annexed to Trinidad on January 1st, 1889. It has an area of 114 square miles, with a population of 19,937.

*Missions.*—S. P. G., 1 catechist for the coolies. The Moravian Brethren have 3 stations in Tobago, with 2 missionaries 1,144 communicants, 5 schools, and 437 scholars. Baptist Missionary Society has 2 missionaries stationed at Port-of-Spain and San Fernando, 15 preaching stations,

with 8 evangelists, 862 church-members, and 320 Sabbath-scholars. The U. P. Church of Scotland has 3 stations in Trinidad—at Port-of-Spain, Arouca, and San Fernando; 3 ordained missionaries, 3 congregations, 387 communicants, 9 Sabbath-schools, 567 scholars. The Wesleyan Methodists' work is carried on in connection with the West Indian Conference. There are numerous Roman Catholic churches.

*Danish West Indies.*—These are: St. Thomas, St. Croix, and St. Jan (see separate articles). Part of the Virgin Islands also belong to Denmark.

*Dutch West Indies.*—Curaçao is the name given to the colony, which consists of the following islands: Curaçao, 210 square miles, population 25,567; Bonaire, 95 square miles, 4,259; Aruba, 69 square miles, 6,990; the southern part of St. Martin, 17 square miles, 4,198; St. Eustache, 7 square miles, 2,335; and Saba, 5 square miles, 2,505. The colony is administered by a governor, assisted by a council, and all are nominated by the king.

*Missions.*—The Wesleyan Methodists carry on work in these islands in connection with the West Indian Conference. There are 35,676 Roman Catholics.

*French West Indies*, consist of Guadaloupe and dependencies, and Martinique. Guadaloupe is one of the Lesser Antilles, and has an area of 360 square miles, with a population of 182,182, in which administration are included several islands, which make a total area of 720 square miles. These islands were acquired by France in 1634. Point-à-Pitre is the principal town. Martinique was acquired in 1635, and has an area of 380 square miles, and population of 170,391. St. Pierre is the chief commercial town, and has a population of 20,000. The only missions are those of the Roman Catholic Church.

*Spanish West Indies.*—CUBA is the largest and one of the richest of the islands in its natural resources. It has an area of 43,222 square miles. It was discovered by Columbus, and afterwards taken possession of by Spain. Of the original inhabitants, whose name for the island, Cuba, has outlived all the various Spanish names, not a trace is left. The country possesses every variety of mountain, valley, and plateau scenery, and the rivers are navigable, and empty into the ocean in the midst of large and beautiful harbors. The population (1877) was 1,521,684, of whom the majority are Spaniards, and the remainder Negroes, Chinese, and Europeans. The moral and spiritual condition of the inhabitants is worse than in any other section of the West Indies, with the exception of Haiti and Santo Domingo. Pride, insolence, and cruelty are the normal instincts of the people of the higher rank, and the sufferings which the enslaved Negroes and the imported coolies have endured are almost incredible. Slavery was abolished absolutely by a law passed in 1886. Havana, the capital, is a city of great beauty, containing many places of historic interest. The cathedral contains the tomb of Columbus. Population, 198,271. Other important towns with their populations are: Matanzas, 87,760; Santiago, 71,307; Cienfuegos, 65,067. Those contain the great proportion of the educated classes, and are gay with theatres and bull-rings for the national sport. There is freedom of worship in Cuba.

*Missions.*—The Jamaica Baptist Missionary

Society carries on some work in the islands, but the principal work is under the superintendence of a Señor Diaz, who is assisted by the Southern Baptist Convention of the United States. Working from Havana, he has now in all 7 stations, 20 missionaries, and 1,493 members. The American Bible Society also has an agency here.

PORTO RICO, area 3,550 square miles, 784,709. It is considered the healthiest of the Antilles. The religion of the island is Roman Catholic, but since the abolition of slavery in 1853 an attempt has been made to introduce other forms of faith. Under the care of the Colonial and Continental Church Society of England there is one clergyman with a congregation.

*Independent Republics.*—The island of Haiti is divided between the two republics of Santo Domingo and Haiti. The republic of SANTO DOMINGO was founded in 1844, and includes the eastern portion of the island, containing 18,045 square miles, with a population of 610,000, composed mainly of Negroes and mulattoes. The capital is the city of Santo Domingo (25,000), and Puerto Plata (15,000) is the chief port. The religion of the state is Roman Catholic, but other forms of worship are permitted.

HAITI became a republic in 1867. It occupies the western portion of the island, with an area of 10,204 square miles. The inhabitants, nine tenths of whom are Negroes, and the rest mulattoes, are variously estimated from 500,000 to 900,000. The capital, Port-au-Prince, has a fine harbor. The religion is nominally Roman Catholic, but the moral and intellectual condition of the people both of Haiti and San Domingo is low in the extreme.

The Wesleyan Methodists and the Jamaican Baptist Missionary Society have a few stations in each of these republics, but the work is hampered, and has not met with very great success. The Protestant Episcopal Church of the United States has quite a flourishing mission in Haiti. During the year 1888–89 it was retarded greatly by the civil war which raged during that year. The missionary staff consists of 1 bishop, 9 presbyters, 4 deacons, 17 lay-readers. The stations or parishes are: Port-au-Prince, Leogane, Gros Morne, Jeremie Aux Cayes, Torbeck, Petit Fond, Trianon; in all there are 382 communicants, 181 day-scholars, 124 Sabbath-scholars.

**Whately, Mary L.,** second daughter of Archbishop Whately, b. Halesworth, in Suffolk, Eng., 1824. After the father's appointment to the See of Dublin the family removed thither. She received the highest educational training, mental, moral, and religious, by her parents, and from her childhood was distinguished for uncommon activity, energy, and intelligence. She early gave herself to the service of Christ in works of kindness to the needy. After the Irish famine, she and her mother and sisters spent most of their time in the ragged schools in Dublin. Subsequently, having acquired Italian, she was much occupied with teaching and visiting the poor Italians, who were numerous in that city. In 1858 she visited Cairo and the Holy Land, and in 1860 was ordered by her physician for her health to a southern climate. In Cairo she opened a school for neglected Moslem girls, the first attempt of the kind in Egypt. Taking

with her a Syrian Protestant matron, she went into the streets and lanes near her home, and persuading the mothers to let their girls come to learn to read and sew, she gathered nine little ones into her school. Later, home duties required her return, and while at home she read to her father the proof-sheets of her second volume of "Ragged Life in Egypt." Her father having died, she returned to Cairo. She soon opened a boys' school also. In 1869, at the suggestion of the Prince of Wales, Ismail Pasha gave her a site just outside the city walls, and friends in England aided her in the erection of a spacious building. The school increased to six hundred, half the boys and two thirds of the girls being Moslems, the rest Copts, Syrians, and Jews. All were taught to read and write Arabic, and all learned the Scriptures and Christian doctrine. In addition the boys received an excellent secular education, and the girls were taught plain and fancy needle-work. Two branch schools have also been established. Pupils of the boys' school are found all over the country, filling important positions in the railway and telegraph offices, mercantile houses, places under government, and in other situations of trust. In 1879 a medical mission was added to the schools, and with her own private means Miss Whately built a dispensary and patients' waiting-room, where several thousands of sick and suffering poor have been treated gratuitously, and where she herself daily read and expounded the Scriptures to such as were willing to listen. Often she was cheered by overhearing the exclamations: "We never heard such words before; they are sweeter than honey." In addition to this varied work, she spent a few days yearly on a Nile boat, which she had hired, and distributed copies of the Scriptures in the villages along the shore to such as could read. These efforts were at first opposed by the ignorant and bigoted, but soon the arrival of the boat was hailed at many a village, and a crowd came to the shore to meet "the people with the book." Women grouped around her to listen to the gospel story. In one of these expeditions a cold which she had taken developed into congestion of the lungs, which resulted in her death March 9th, 1889. Friends had tried to dissuade her from going on this trip on account of her cold, but she said she had hired the boat and must go. For years she had wished to purchase a boat for the mission work, but could not raise the money needed. It is painful to reflect that but for this her highly useful life might have been prolonged.

**Whiting, George B.,** b. Canaan, N. Y., U. S. A., August 30th, 1801; graduated at Union College 1824; taught one year; graduated at Princeton Theological Seminary 1828; sailed in 1830 as a missionary of the A. B. C. F. M. for Syria. There he labored for twenty-five years, with the exception of brief visits to Constantinople and Switzerland for his health, and to the United States in 1837 on account of the protracted illness of his wife. He was stationed at Beirut till the autumn of 1834, when he was transferred to Jerusalem. After laboring there nine years he returned to Beirut in 1843. He died at Beirut of cholera November 8th, 1856.

**Whitney, Samuel,** b. Branford, Conn., U. S. A., April 28th, 1793; entered Yale College 1817, remaining two years; offered his services in 1819 to the A. B. C. F. M. as a missionary to the Sandwich Islands, purposing to pursue his theological studies after reaching his field of labor; embarked October 23d, 1819, with the pioneers and founders of the mission, arriving at Hawaii March 30th, 1820. He was licensed to preach February 28th, 1823, by the Hawaiian Association, and ordained by the same November 30th, 1825. He spent most of his missionary life on the island of Kauai, and was a faithful laborer. He was taken ill and died September 21st, at the house of Mr. Alexander, at Lahainaluna.

**Whitman, Marcus**, b. Rushville (Gorham), N. Y., U. S. A., September 4th, 1802; studied with private tutors and at Berkshire Medical College; appointed by the A. B. C. F.M. missionary physician to Oregon. He left home February, 1835, on an exploring tour with Rev. Samuel Parker, arriving at St. Louis in April, Council Bluffs May 30th; crossed the Rocky Mountains, reaching Green River, a branch of the Western Colorado, a rendezvous of the fur-traders, previous to August 17th. The prospect for missionary labor among the Nez Percés and Flathead Indians seemed so favorable, that it was deemed expedient for Dr. Whitman to return and procure associates before establishing a mission among them. For this purpose he directed his way homeward August 27th. In March, 1836, he set out with his wife, Mr. Henry Spalding and his wife, and Mr. Gray, for Liberty, Mo., 1,700 miles mostly by water, then 2,200 miles all by land, and on horseback to Walla Walla, arriving September 3d. Mrs. Whitman and Mrs. Spalding were the first white women that ever crossed the Rocky Mountains. Dr. Whitman established himself at Waiilatpu, among the Kayuses, 25 miles from Walla Walla. The Indians manifested lively interest in their religious instruction. Having frequent occasion to visit the post of the Hudson's Bay Company at that place, he perceived that it was designed to hold that immense and valuable territory as a British possession. To forestall that design in part, and in compliance with a resolve of the mission, he, in October, 1842, crossed the Rocky Mountains in mid-winter on horseback, arriving at St. Louis February, 1843, with fingers, nose, ears, and feet frost-bitten, in spite of furs and buffalo robes. He visited Washington, called on Mr. Webster, Secretary of State, and President Tyler, and by his earnest representations prevailed upon them not to cede Oregon to the British Government (which they were about to do). A personal friend of Mr. Webster remarked: "It is safe to say that our country owes it to Dr. Whitman and his associate missionaries that all the territory west of the Rocky Mountains, and as far south as the Columbia River, is not now owned by England, and held by the Hudson's Bay Company." Dr. Whitman wrote from Fort Walla Walla November 1st, 1843: "I do not regret having visited the States, for I feel that this country must be either American or foreign, and mostly papal. If I never do more than to establish the first wagon-road to the Columbia River, and prevent the disaster and reaction which would have followed the breaking up of the present emigration, I am satisfied." While at the East he published a pamphlet describing the climate and soil of the

western region, and its desirableness for American colonies. After a hurried visit to Boston, he was back again on the Missouri in March, and conducted more than a thousand emigrants in wagons over the Rocky Mountains.

Dr. Whitman, Mrs. Whitman, two adopted children, and ten other persons, American emigrants, who had stopped at the station to winter there, were cruelly murdered by the Kayuse Indians November 29th, 1847. Mr. Spalding narrowly escaped. Forty-eight women and children were made slaves by the murderers, and treated with great barbarity. The mission was broken up. Dr. Whitman was a "diligent and self-denying laborer in the work to which he consecrated his time and energies." In his last letter he described his plans and hopes in regard to the Indians.

**Wilder, Hyman Augustine**, b. Cornwall, Vt., U. S. A., February 17th, 1822; graduated at Williams College 1845, East Windsor Theological Seminary 1848; ordained February same year; sailed as a missionary of the A. B. C. F. M. April 7th, 1849, for the Zulu Mission in South Africa. In 1868 he visited the United States for his health, but returned to his mission field in 1870. Continued ill-health obliged him to retire from his work, and in January, 1877, he arrived home. "For a short time after his arrival in 1849 he had charge of the mission press. He then went to Umtwalumi and commenced a new station, where he was very successful in winning souls to Christ. He was our secretary nearly all the time he was in the mission, and was very successful in obtaining funds from the government for the support of our mission schools. He was highly esteemed by his brethren and the natives, as well as by the colonists generally."

**Wilder, Royal Gould**, b. Bridport, Vt., U. S. A., October 27th, 1816; graduated at Middlebury College 1839; taught in Mississippi and Vermont; graduated at Andover Theological Seminary 1845; sailed for India as a missionary of the A. B. C. F. M. in 1846. He was stationed for six years at Ahmadnagar. The seminary, containing from 50 to 80 boys, was put under his care by the mission. In 1852 he went to Kolhapur. On his arrival the Brahmans petitioned for his banishment, but he continued at his post, and after five years had one convert. When he went there he found in a population of 44,000 only one school, in a back street, with twelve boys. When he left in 1857 there was a government college costing $200,000, and he was requested to make the opening address. In the years 1854–56 occurred the controversy between Dr. Anderson and the missionaries concerning mission schools. Mr. Wilder, in common with all his associates, was a strong advocate of schools for the Hindus; was in favor of employing even heathen teachers, if Christians could not be obtained; and refused to abandon his schools, or curtail school work, as required by Dr. Anderson. Mr. Wilder's health having utterly failed from the severe labor and exposure involved in founding a new mission, he embarked in 1857 for America, the day after the Sepoy mutiny broke out. His health having improved, he offered in 1858 to return to his station, but was informed by Dr. Anderson that the Prudential Committee had voted to discontinue the Kolhapur Mission. His Presbytery and friends approving his course, he returned to Kolhapur in 1861, and established an independent mission. There he continued to labor for twelve years, receiving no aid from any Society, but sustained by voluntary gifts, Sir Bartle Frere, Governor of Bombay, and other English people, as well as natives, contributing to the work. From 1861 to 1869 he contributed many articles to the Bombay "Times" and "Gazette" on the subject of the system of national education. He also took a prominent part in memorializing Parliament, and inducing the Indian Government to establish the present system. In the "Times of India" appeared from his pen anonymous letters, which were said by those in high official position to have influenced Parliament in adopting measures for the education of the masses. He was offered an influential position in the educational department. When his schools were suspended by Dr. Anderson he had 500 boys and 100 girls under instruction. Before he left Kolhapur in 1857 the schools were reopened. On reaching his Indian home he found his beautiful church had been sold, and turned into a mosque. He received generous aid for a second church. In 1871 he transferred the Kolhapur Mission to the Presbyterian Board of Foreign Missions, and was a missionary of that Board till 1875, when, partly for his health, and partly to educate his children, he left India and returned home, having been engaged in mission work for thirty-two years. During that time he had preached in 3,000 cities, towns, and villages, had distributed 3,000,000 pages of tracts, had gathered into schools 3,300 pupils, of whom 300 were girls. Besides this, he had served on committees for the translation and revision of the Bible, and had written and published commentaries on three Gospels, and had edited and translated many books. The vessel which brought his luggage by sea was wrecked off the Cape of Good Hope, and among his goods that were lost was his manuscript of the Kolhapur kingdom, with full diary of his missionary work. His later years were spent at Princeton, N. J. In 1877 he started the "Missionary Review," which he edited with ability and success. He longed to return to India; and when the "Review" was provided for, he determined, though a great sufferer from an internal malady, to sail for Kolhapur. But his work was done, and on the day when the "Review" was transferred to other hands, and he had sent to the printers proof of the closing number of the last volume, he was called away. He died in New York October 8th, 1887.

**Williams, John,** b. Tottenham, near London, England, June 29th, 1796. At the age of fourteen, while an apprentice to an ironmonger, he showed great taste for mechanics, and acquired considerable experience in mechanical work. At the age of twenty he offered himself to the London Missionary Society as a missionary, and, after some special training, was ordained, and sent with his wife, November, 1816, to the South Sea Islands. He was first stationed at Eimeo, one of the Society Islands, where he soon acquired a knowledge of the native language. Thence he went to Huahine, where he found the natives had generally renounced idolatry. At the invitation of the King of Raiatea, the largest of the Society Group, he went to that island, which became his permanent headquarters. His success here was remarkable, not only in Christianizing the people, but with Christianity introducing the arts and habits of civilization. In 1823 he visited with six native teachers the Hervey Islands, and after several days' search discovered Rarotonga, the largest of this group. Remaining here for some time, he founded a mission, which was greatly successful; not only Rarotonga, but the whole group of the Hervey Islands being Christianized. He helped the people at their own request to draw up a code of laws for civil administration. He made great use of native teachers whom he had trained. The work accomplished by him on both of these islands for the secular as well as the religious welfare of the natives was useful and permanent. He reduced the language of Raiatea to writing, translated with Pitman and Buzacot the New Testament into it, and prepared books for the schools he had established. Rarotonga being out of the way of vessels, he determined to build one in which he might visit other islands. With the aid of the natives he made the necessary tools, and within four months completed a vessel 60 feet long, 18 wide, the sails of native matting, the cordage of the bark of the hibiscus, the oakum of cocoanut husks and banana stumps, the sheaves of iron-wood, the rudder of "a piece of a pickaxe, a cooper's adze, and a long hoe." The boat was named "The Messenger of Peace." In this vessel, during the next four years, he explored nearly all the South Sea Islands, and several times visited Tahiti, Raiatea, and Rarotonga. In 1830 he set out in his vessel to carry the gospel to the Samoan Islands, which he had planned to do in 1824, but was deterred by the great distance—2,000 miles—and the ferocious character of the people. In 1832 he made a second visit to the Samoans, and found the people waiting for the gospel. "In less than twenty months an entire change had taken place in the habits and character of the Samoans. Chapels had been built, and everywhere the people seemed waiting to receive instruction." Having completed the object of his voyage, and visited all the islands of the Samoan Group, he returned to his family. With health impaired after seventeen years of toil and hardship, he sailed in 1833 for England, where he remained four years. During this time he had the Rarotongan New Testament published by the Bible Society, £4,000 raised for the purchase and outfit of a missionary ship for Polynesia, wrote and published a "Narrative of Missionary Enterprises in the South Sea Islands, with Remarks on the Natural History of the Islands, Origin, Languages, Traditions, and Usages of the Inhabitants," and prepared plans for the establishment of a college for the education of native teachers, and for a high-school at Tahiti. In 1838 he and his wife again embarked, accompanied by ten other missionaries. After visiting the stations already established by him, and several new groups, he proceeded with one companion to the New Hebrides with the view of establishing a mission, but was met by hostile natives of Erromanga, by whom he was killed, after he had landed, November 20th, 1839. A portion of his bones was recovered from the cannibals. It is supposed they were provoked to the deed by the ill treatment they had received from the crew of a vessel which a short time before had landed there.

**Williams, Samuel Wells,** b. Utica, N. Y., U. S. A., September 22d, 1812; graduated at the Rensselaer Institute in Troy 1832. While there, he was, at the age of twenty, invited by the A. B. C. F. M. to join a mission about to start for China, as superintendent of the press, having learned to some extent the art of type-setting in his father's publishing house. He accepted the invitation, and June 15th, 1833, sailed in the ship "Morrison" for Canton, China. Drs. Abeel and Bridgman were the only Americans to welcome him. He rapidly gained a knowledge of the Chinese language, and published several standard works. He became editor of "The Chinese Repository," begun the year before by Dr. Bridgman, to which many able writers contributed, he himself furnishing 140 distinct articles. The "Celestial Empire," published in Shanghai, says: "The Repository, extending through 20 volumes, is looked upon as of priceless worth, and the name of the editor will be long and honorably remembered by sinologues in connection with it." In 1835 he completed at Macao Medhurst's "Hokkeen Dictionary." In 1837 he was one of a party sent to Japan to restore seven shipwrecked seamen to their home. They were fired upon from batteries of two ports, and returned with the men to Canton. Taking some of these sailors into his own house, he learned their language, translated for them the Book of Genesis and the Gospel of Matthew, and had the joy of seeing them embrace Christianity. This knowledge of the language thus providentially acquired, led to his being appointed interpreter for Commodore Perry, who was sent by our government to Japan fifteen years later. Soon after the press was established at Canton, Chinese interference with his native helpers compelled him to remove it to Macao; thence, later, it was transferred to Hong Kong, and established again afterwards in Canton, where, in December, 1856, his own dwelling and the entire establishment, comprising three presses and many fonts of type, with 7,000 printed books, were destroyed by fire. In 1844 he returned to the United States, passing through Egypt, Syria, and Europe. During the three years spent at home he delivered a course of lectures on Chinese subjects, which were afterwards enlarged and published under the title of "The Middle Kingdom." With the proceeds of the lectures he secured from Berlin a font of movable Chinese type. Soon after the publication of "The Middle Kingdom" the trustees of Union College conferred upon him the degree of LL.D.

Restrictions forbidding foreigners to bring their wives to Canton having been by the treaties removed, he was married, and with his wife sailed in 1848 for Canton, taking with him the new font of type. On arriving at Canton he found to his great joy regular public services in Chinese. His remarkable success as an interpreter led to his appointment to the diplomatic service of the United States from 1858 to his resignation in 1876. In 1857 he was Secretary of the United States Legation in Japan. In 1858 he aided William B. Reed in negotiating the treaty of Tientsin. In 1860–61 he revisited the United States, and delivered lectures before the Smithsonian Institution and elsewhere, returning to China in 1862 as Secretary of the United States Legation at Pekin. Besides the "Chinese Repository," which for twenty years

occupied much of his time, he published "Easy Lessons in Chinese" (1841); "An English and Chinese Vocabulary in the Court Dialect" (1843); "The Chinese Commercial Guide" (1844); "A Tonic Dictionary of the Canton Dialect" (1856); "A Syllabic Dictionary of the Chinese Language" (1874), containing 12,527 characters. On this dictionary, a work of great philological value, he spent eleven years. His "Middle Kingdom," the best work extant on Chinese government, geography, religion, and social life, reappeared in 1883 in a revised and enlarged edition. Retiring from the service of the government in 1876, he returned to the United States, took up his residence in New Haven, was appointed professor of Chinese at Yale College, and in 1881 was elected president of the American Bible Society. He died February 16th, 1884.

"Few men," says President Porter, "were better fitted in temperament, intellectual tastes and habits, moral energy and spiritual self-consecration for the constant and unsparing drudgery involved in such a life. He was by himself and in his words a living and speaking witness of the dignity and inspiration of the missionary calling."

**Williams, William Frederic,** b. Utica, N. Y., U. S. A., January 11th, 1818; studied at Yale College, and was subsequently engaged in various employments, mostly in engineering, till 1844, when he entered Auburn Theological Seminary to prepare for the ministry. In November, 1846, he offered himself to the A. B. C. F. M. for the missionary work, in which his elder brother, Samuel Wells Williams, was engaged in China. Was ordained in 1848; sailed January 3d, 1849, for the Syria Mission. In the summer of 1850 he was designated to Mosul, which soon became a station of the "Assyrian Mission." There he remained till 1859, when he commenced the station at Mardin. He died at Mardin, Eastern Turkey, February 14th, 1871.

"There was in Mr. Williams an undue tendency to distrust his own powers and judgment, and to look on the dark side of things, but aside from this he was a rare man. He had great power of self-control. He possessed genuine refinement, and with the marvellous fund of information which he had in almost all departments of knowledge, his fine command of language, his good nature and enthusiasm, he was in his more cheerful moods a fascinating member of the social circle. His clear mind had been carefully cultivated, and his acquisitions were very exact. However much he distrusted his own judgment, his associates confided in it largely. He was enthusiastic in his zeal for the policy of self-support in the missionary work. His students held him in the highest admiration, and very few missionaries have secured the affection of the people for whom they labor, to so great an extent as he. He was withal a devoted Christian."

He was in a sense the mainstay of the mission work among the Arabic-speaking peoples of Northern Mesopotamia during years of trial and perplexity when it seemed often as if the mission would be compelled to withdraw, and to his patient, wise perseverance is very largely due the success that is now attending the labors of the missionaries in that field.

**Williamson, Alexander,** b. Falkirk, Scotland, December 5th, 1829; studied at Glasgow; ordained April, 1855; sailed as a medical missionary of the L. M. S. May 21st, for China, arriving at Shanghai September 24th; was stationed for two years at Shanghai and Pinghoo. His health failing, he returned to England in 1858, and his connection with the Society soon terminated. After some years spent in Scotland, he returned to China as the agent of the Scottish Bible Society, and in connection with the United Presbyterian Mission. He was at first stationed at Chefoo, and travelled extensively, making adventurous journeys into unknown and distant regions. Much valuable information was obtained, which in 1879 was published in two volumes. He was afterwards settled in Shanghai, where he established a Society for the Diffusion of Christian and General Knowledge among the Chinese. He was a frequent contributor to the "North China Daily News." Dr. Williamson was attacked with fever, and died August 28th, 1890.

**Williamson, Thomas S.,** b. Union District, S. C., U. S. A., March, 1800. His ancestors on both the father's and mother's side were slaveholders, but not from choice, and in 1805 his parents removed to Ohio for the purpose of liberating the slaves in their possession. Dr. Williamson inherited a practical sympathy with the colored people. He graduated at Jefferson College, Penn., and at Yale Medical School, and practised medicine for ten years in Brown County, Ohio. After spending one year in Lane Theological Seminary, he was licensed and ordained by the Presbytery of Chillicothe, and April 1st, 1835, left Ripley, O., as a missionary of the A. B. C. F. M., with his family, reaching Fort Snelling, in the country of the Dakotas, in May. He remained in connection with the A. B. C. F. M. for thirty-six years, until 1871, when he and his son, Rev. John P. Williamson, transferred themselves to the care of the Presbyterian Board. He died at St. Peter, Minn., June 24th, 1879.

He fully believed in the capability of Indians to become civilized and Christianized, and also that God had by special providences called him to this work. His great life-work—that of translating the Bible into the language of the Sioux Nation—was continued through more than twoscore years, and was only completed in 1889. In this, as in most things, he worked slowly and carefully. He lived to read the plate-proofs of all, and to know that the Scriptures of the Old and New Testaments were in the language of the Dakotas."

**Wilson, John,** b. Lauder, in Berwickshire, Scotland, December 11th, 1804. At the age of fourteen he went to the Edinburgh University, where he graduated in 1828, taking a high place in the classes of physical science, and in the last two years studying anatomy, surgery, and the practice of physic. The reading of the reports of the Bible Society, he said, first awakened him to the importance of missions, and led him to resolve to devote himself to a foreign field. He was ordained in 1828, and sailed August 30th of the same year for India, under the Scottish Missionary Society, reaching Bombay February, 1829. Remaining there a month, he left for the comparative seclusion of Bankote and then Hurnee, that he might, aided by his brethren, and in the midst of country-people, learn Ma-

râthi thoroughly. In the eight months of the first hot and rainy season he laid the foundation of his Orientalism "with a rapidity, thoroughness, and breadth, due alike to his overmastering motive, his previous training, and his extraordinary memory." In March, 1832, was established an English school, afterwards known as the General Assembly's Institution, and under the immediate superintendence of Dr. Wilson. He gave himself to the acquisition of the vernaculars of a varied population—the Marâthi, Gujarati, Hindustâni, Hebrew, Portuguese, with Persian, Arabic, and Sanskrit in reserve for the learned classes, which he acquired and fluently used. Though aware that for some time and to a great degree his must be the toil of preparation, he from the first expected and worked for baptized converts. So, in February, 1831, two years after landing, he formed a native church in Bombay with eight members, who chose him as their minister. Almost his earliest work in Bombay was the preparation of a Hebrew and Marâthi grammar for the Jews, known there as Ben Israel. He also spoke the Portuguese with fluency. He was thus able early to influence the Hindu, Mohammedan, Parsi, Jewish, and Portuguese communities. His advance in Sanskrit was parallel with his acquisition of Marâthi, so that he was able to confute the Brahmans out of their own sacred books. He soon commenced a series of discourses on Christianity with Hindus, Mohammedans, and Parsis. Having mastered the languages, he mingled with the people who spoke them, and made many tours to Nasik, Poona, the caves of Ellora, and other prominent places. In 1833 was established in Bombay an English college for the Christian education of native youth among Parsis and Hindus, and Dr. Wilson threw the whole weight of his culture and energy into the new institution. He lectured to the students on the Evidences of Christianity, Biblical Criticism, and Systematic Divinity. In 1835, April 19th, his devoted and talented wife died. In 1836 he received the degree of Doctor of Divinity from Edinburgh University. In 1839 he baptized two Parsi youths,—the first proselytes from the faith of Zoroaster,—who are now ordained ministers in the Free Church of Scotland and the Baptist Church. In 1842 he resigned the Presidency of the Bombay branch of the Royal Asiatic Society, which he had filled for seven years. In 1843, after fourteen years of hard work in India, Dr. Wilson left for his native land. Every community vied with each other in its demonstrations of respect, and the government furnished him with letters to the authorities of the countries through which he wished to pass; but he valued none more highly than the honor paid him by the native and non-Christian students of the institution established in 1833. On the way he intended to visit Egypt, Syria, Palestine, and Eastern Europe, not only for scholarly and biblical research, but to report to his church the condition of the Jews, Samaritans, and Eastern Christians.

In the Disruption of the Scotch Church he joined the Free Church, and on his arrival was received with great honor. He addressed large audiences of all the evangelical churches on the missionary claims of India. At Oxford he preached to the *élite* of the university and of the Church of England. At the General Assembly of the Presbyterian Church of Ireland in 1844 he was received with "loud acclamations" as the co-founder of the mission to the two millions of Kathiawar. In 1846 he again married, and in September, 1847, re-embarked for India. In 1857 he was appointed by the government Vice-Chancellor of the University of Bombay, and was examiner in Sanskrit, Persian, Hebrew, Marâthi, Gujarati, and Hindustani. He was twelve years secretary to the different translation committees of the Bombay Bible Society. In 1869, when about to return to Scotland, the leaders of all the communities in Bombay, European and Asiatic, resolved to honor him on the fortieth anniversary of his arrival in Western India. The sum of £2,100 was subscribed, and presented to him on a silver salver wrought by native artists, and bearing the inscription in Sanskrit: "This salver was presented to Rev. John Wilson, D.R.S., F.R.S., at a meeting of the inhabitants of Bombay, as a mark of esteem for his high personal character, and in acknowledgment of his great services to India in the cause of education and philanthropy." The governor presided at a great meeting held in the Town Hall February 15th, 1869, and made the presentation. The Chief Justice assisted, and a loving letter from Sir Bartle Frere was read. The names of the subscribers on the parchment were in many languages, and represented all races, creeds, and classes in the East, and all varieties of Christian sects. Dr. Wilson determined to use the interest only in his philanthropic and literary labors, designating the capital sum to aid the higher studies of the youth of Bombay. The fund was used by the University of Bombay to found the John Wilson Philological Lectureship. The citizens of Bombay in general also presented him with an address, and the Asiatic Society reviewed, with high commendation, his great services for India. While at home he was elected Moderator of the General Assembly of the Free Church. In his closing address before the Assembly on the foreign-mission work, he said that notwithstanding his forty-one years' connection with India, if he lived to the age of Methuselah, he would consider it a privilege to devote his life to its regeneration. He returned to India in 1871. Frequent attacks of fever after his return ended in 1875 in a chronic breathlessness from weakness of the heart. On attempting to reach Mahableshwar he was forced by an alarming attack to stop twelve miles short of the sanitarium. To Mr. Bowen, American missionary, he said the day before he died : "I have perfect peace, and am content that the Lord should do what seems good to Him.' He died December 1st, 1875. "Governor, council, judges, the vice-chancellor of the university, missionaries, chaplains, and Portuguese Catholics, the converts, students and school-children, Asiatics and Africans, of every caste and creed, reverently followed the remains of the venerated missionary for two hours, as the bier was borne to the last resting-place."

The Rev. George Bowen, who saw much of Dr. Wilson's life and work for thirty years in Bombay, says: " Dr. Wilson was among missionaries *sui generis*, and a law unto himself. There was a many-sidedness about him that made it easy for him to enter into relations with men who cared little for the gospel, and who were perhaps led to regard with more favor the work of missions, because of the wide range of thought and investigation to which Dr. Wilson lent himself. His capacities determined his spheres. His Orientalism, his archæology, his philosophy, his relations with the rulers or with the university, doubtless interfered with a more direct and simple evangelism, but never suffered him to lose sight of the fact that he was a missionary; he doubtless believed, and the readers of his biography will believe, that he made these things tributary to the advancement of Christ's cause."

**Wilson, John Leighton,** b. Sumter Co., S. C., U. S. A., March 28th, 1809; graduated at Union College 1829, and Theological Seminary of Columbia, S. C., 1833; ordained the same year by Harmony Presbytery, and set apart as a missionary to Africa. In the summer of 1833 he studied Arabic at Andover Seminary, and in the autumn went to Western Africa to explore the coast, returning in the spring. He decided on Cape Palmas as the most favorable place for the mission. In May, 1834, he was married to Miss Bayard of Savannah, and on the 24th of November following sailed as a missionary of the A. B. C. F. M. for Cape Palmas, arriving in December. He was received with demonstrations of joy by the natives, and found the frame house which he had taken out on his first visit erected on the spot he had selected. In 1836 he made three tours of exploration in the interior, journeying mostly on foot. He had while at Cape Palmas, where he remained seven years, a boarding-school numbering fifty, a fourth of whom were females; a church of forty members; 180 youths had been educated, the Grebo language reduced to writing, a grammar and dictionary of the language published, the Gospels of Matthew and John translated and printed, besides several other small volumes. In 1842 he removed to the Gaboon River on the Gulf of Bahia, 1,200 miles south of Cape Palmas, and commenced a new station among the Mpongwe people. This language also was reduced to writing, a grammar and vocabulary published, and portions of the Bible translated and printed. In 1853 he returned home on account of failing health, and became Secretary of the Presbyterian Board of Foreign Missions in New York, editing also the foreign department of the "Home and Foreign Record." He served as Secretary till the commencement of the civil war, when, returning to his Southern home, he organized for the Southern Church a Board of Foreign Missions, of which he was appointed secretary, holding the office till 1885. He established and edited " The Missionary," a monthly magazine. He organized also the Board of Sustentation. In 1854 he published a volume of 500 pages on Western Africa, its history, condition, and prospects, which was pronounced by Dr. Livingstone the best work on that part of Africa ever published. He published also many articles in the " Southern Presbyterian Review." He received the degree of D.D. from Lafayette College 1854. He died at his home near Mayesville, S. C., July 13th, 1886.

**Winslow, Miron, D.D., LL.D.,** b. Williston, Vt., U. S. A., December 11th, 1789; in the sixth generation from Kenelm Winslow, brother of Gov. Edward Winslow, of Plymouth Colony. Having acquired a good English education, at the age of twenty-one he engaged in mercantile pursuits at Norwich, Ct., and two years later he became so deeply impressed with the importance of foreign missions, that he consecrated himself to the work of a missionary; studied in Middlebury College, Vt.; then pursued special studies in languages at Yale, and graduated at Andover Theological Seminary. For six months he preached on behalf of the A. B. C. F. M., raising large sums of money for its work, and displaying that rare combination of intellectual, business, and religious gifts which so distinguished his subsequent career.

At his ordination on November 4th, 1818, in the Salem Tabernacle, in company with Messrs. Spaulding, Woodward, and Fisk, Professor Moses Stuart preached the sermon, which was widely circulated among the churches. In the same edifice, February 6th, 1812, had been ordained the initial band of American foreign missionaries—Messrs. Judson, Hall, Newell, Nott, and Rice. On January 11th, 1819, he married Harriet W. Lathrop, of Norwich, Ct., and with Messrs. Spaulding, Woodward, and Scudder sailed for India June 8th, 1819; arriving at Oodooville, Ceylon, on July 4th. He remained there till 1833, conducting the boarding and day school, laboring and preaching in the neighborhood, and performing a large amount of literary work. His contributions to the "Missionary Herald" alone would fill, if collected, several large volumes. His observation taught him that education must go hand-in-hand with the missionary chapel and preaching. In this respect he was the pioneer American missionary of his day, and so late as 1856 he advocated his views at the meeting of the A. B. C. F. M. in Albany. His interest in the Batticotta Seminary, established 1823, was great. " The plan—which, seven or eight years later, was adopted in Calcutta by the Rev. Dr. Duff and his colleagues "—was, as he wrote, that "of giving the pupils a good knowledge of English and Western science, in connection with their own vernaculars, instead of Sanskrit." He adds: "The institution had great influence in raising the standard of education in North Ceylon, and affected even the continent." The Madras University conferred its first degrees of B.A. on the seminary graduates. Mrs. Winslow died January 14th, 1833, at Oodooville. The following October he sailed for the United States, where his missionary addresses created a wide and deep interest in India as a mission field. He married April 23d, 1835, in New York, Mrs. Catherine Waterbury Carman, and sailed November 16th, 1835, for Oodooville. On August 18th, 1836, he established the A. B. C. F. M. Mission in Madras, the scene of his labors for the remaining twenty-eight years of his life. Mrs. Winslow died of cholera, September 23d, 1837, and September 12th, 1838, he married Annie Spiers, daughter of Hon. Archibald Spiers of the East India Board, and granddaughter of Lord Dundas. She died June 20th, 1843.

At an early period of his labors in Madras Mr. Winslow was engaged in translating the Bible into Tamil; and as late as 1850 he was much occupied with improvements and revisions of portions of the translations. When not thus engaged, he was occupied three hours daily with a moonshee on the Tamil and English dictionary. In November, 1850, he announced that the printing of the new version of the Tamil

Scriptures was completed. ("Missionary Herald," March, 1865.) He published "occasional reports" of the Madras Mission.

On March 12th, 1845, Mr. Winslow married Mrs. Mary W. Dwight, widow of Rev. Robert O. Dwight, D.D., of the Madura Mission ; she died April 20th, 1852. He received from Harvard College the degree of D.D., which his Alma Mater supplemented with LL.D. upon the reception in this country of copies of his Tamil Lexicon.

Dr. Winslow's great literary work requires special notice. Its title-page reads thus : " A Comprehensive Tamil and English Dictionary of High and Low Tamil, by the Rev. Miron Winslow, D.D., etc., assisted by competent Native Scholars : in part from manuscript materials of the late Rev. Joseph Knight and others. Madras : Printed and Published by P. R. Hunt, American Mission Press." The splendid quarto of 976 pages, three columns to a page, with 11 additional pages, attested the capacity of the mission press to execute the highest grade of printing. With the exception of Wilson's Sanskrit Lexicon, it is the most elaborate and complete dictionary of the languages of India, containing 67,452 words with definitions, of which 30,551 for the first time take their place in Tamil lexicography. Said the "Round Table" (N. Y.): " It thus appears that nearly half of all the words in the Tamil language owe their English lexicographic birth and position to the labors of our American Orientalist. The work before us includes both the common and poetic dialects, and the astronomical, astrological, mythological, botanical, scientific, and official terms, together with the names of authors, poets, heroes, and gods. It thus initiates the learner not only into the language, but into its literature, and makes him acquainted with the philosophies, mythologies, sciences, traditions, superstitions, and customs of the Hindus. . . . The learned author has adopted an original arrangement of the verbs. He says that all the other parts of the verbs flow naturally from the imperative singular, and that he finds this the most simple and natural arrangement. He thus makes an important advance on all preceding steps, not only in this but other languages, in the grammatical analysis of this most difficult part of speech. The original introduction of nearly half of the classical words in Tamil literature, in connection with translations of peculiar idioms and phrases, and the scholarly and philosophical arrangement of the whole work, make this the first and only comprehensive and complete Tamil and English dictionary ever published. It is a great honor to American scholarship that one of our own number should have produced this work." The publication of the dictionary elicited the gratitude of scholars and missionaries, as well as the government officials of India.

On the eve of his departure from Madras in rapidly failing health, Dr. Winslow received a formal letter from " The Madras Missionary Conference" (composed of over 40 members from the missionaries of all denominations), in which they said : " The brethren feel that in you they lose one whose place can never be supplied." The native church also expressed its feelings of regret in a lengthy scroll. Dr. Winslow sailed with Mrs. Winslow August 29th, 1864 ; was landed October 20th, at Cape

Town, South Africa, and died two days later. His body lies in the Cape Town Cemetery, near that of Scudder, with whom he had so long been associated in the missions of India.

**Winslow, Harriet Lathrop,** first wife of Miron Winslow, b. Norwich, Ct., U. S. A. April 9th, 1796; d. at Oodooville, Ceylon, Jan. 14th, 1833, where her body lies by the side of her two sisters, both devoted missionaries, Mrs. Charlotte H. Cherry and Mrs. Harriet Joanna Perry. Distinguished for her lofty missionary spirit and efficient educational labors. Her memoir contains an interesting mass of missionary intelligence, and two poetical tributes from Mrs. Lydia H. Sigourney.

**Wittewater,** a town in South Africa, in West Cape Colony, north of Malmesbury and near Goederwacht. Mission station of the Moravians, with 1 missionary and wife, occupied for the purpose of having a base of operations from which to reach the estate of Goederwacht, where it was impossible for the missionaries to obtain a permanent title to any property (for the reason of this see Goederwacht). From Wittewater Goederwacht was regularly visited until it became a separate station.

**Wittkleibosch,** a village inhabited by Fingoes, 10 or 12 miles from Clarkson, in the Zitzekamma district, Cape Colony, South Africa. Mission station of the Moravians, who began work in this place from their station Clarkson soon after Governor Lord Napier had set it apart for the Fingoes freed by the Kafir war of 1835-36. All their efforts, however, were of no effect until a native Fingo was stationed in the neighborhood as a teacher; and his earnest, patient, faithful work for his people has been wonderfully blessed, so that now there is in this station a large and prosperous congregation, of which he is the pastor.

**Wolff, Joseph,** b. Bavaria, Germany, 1795, of Jewish parentage, the son of a rabbi; early became a Christian; was baptized in 1812 at Prague by a Benedictine monk, taught Hebrew for a time at Frankfort and Halle, studied at Munich, Weimar, and Vienna; went to Rome in 1815, to be educated as a missionary. He entered first the Collegio Romano, and in 1817 the College of the Propaganda. While in Rome he spent his time in studying the Oriental languages. Suspected by the Inquisition of heresy on account of some liberal views he had expressed, he was sent in 1818 to Vienna, then to the monastery of Val Saint in Switzerland, and finally dismissed as incorrigible. He went to London, joined the Church of England, and through the influence of Charles Simeon and others, who perceived his fitness for mission work among the Jews, he entered Cambridge University, where for two years he continued his Oriental studies under Professor Lee. He then commenced his career as a traveller, visiting Malta, Egypt, Palestine, Mesopotamia, Armenia, Bassorah, and Persia, and returning home by the way of Circassia, Constantinople, and the Crimea, reached Dublin, May, 1826. In these travels he became acquainted with learned men of all ecclesiastical relations, everywhere professing Jesus as the Christ, and although he had been imprisoned, and his life

often endangered, showing in all undaunted courage and great presence of mind. In 1827 he married Lady Georgiana Walpole, daughter of the Earl of Oxford, who accompanied him on his second missionary tour as far as Malta. In April he proceeded to Smyrna, the Ionian Islands, and Jerusalem, where he was poisoned by some Jews, and just escaped death. On recovering, he set out for Bokhara by way of Persia, encountering on the journey the plague; was repeatedly robbed, taken prisoner, and sold as a slave, but finally reached Bokhara. After laboring there three months in mission work among the Jews, he went to India, visited the Punjab, Lahore, Lodiana, Simlah, Delhi, Benares, Lucknow, and reached Calcutta March, 1833. He preached everywhere in different languages, distributed the Scriptures, and interested the most prominent men and women in his behalf. From Calcutta he went to Haidarabad, visited the Jews at Cochin and Goa, proceeded to Bombay, whence he sailed for Arabia, and returned to England in 1834. In 1836 he made a second visit to Abyssinia, whence he sailed for Bombay, and there embarked for America, reaching New York August, 1837. He was ordained as deacon in the Protestant Episcopal Church by Bishop Doane of New Jersey, visited the principal cities, preached before Congress, and returned to England January 2d, 1838. Having received priest's orders, he was settled as curate in Lengthwaite, and then for his wife's health he went to York, where he remained five years. In 1843, the news of the imprisonment of Colonel Stoddart and Captain Conolly at Bokhara having reached England, Dr. Wolff, means being furnished by individuals, set out to attempt their release or ascertain their fate. Before reaching Bokhara he learned that they had been beheaded. He himself was made a prisoner and condemned to death, but through the intervention of the Persian Ambassador he made his escape. Reaching England in 1845, he was settled in the parish of Isle Brewers, Somersetshire, where he labored till he died, May 2d, 1862. The most interesting of his publications are "Travels and Adventures of Rev. Joseph Wolff, D.D., LL.D." (2 vols. 1861).

**Wogul Version.**—The Wogul belongs to the Finn branch of the Ural-Altaic family of languages, and is spoken in Western Siberia, Russia. The Gospels of Matthew and Mark were translated in 1820, and were entrusted to the Russian Bible Society for publication. They do not appear to have been printed. The Gospel of Matthew, prepared by G Popoo, was printed phonetically for Prince L. L. Bonaparte in 1868. But this was not intended for circulation, but for linguistic purposes. In 1882 the British and Foreign Bible Society published at Helsingfors the Gospel of Matthew, and in 1883 that of Mark; both were prepared by Professor Ahlquist.

(*Specimen verse.* John 3 : 16.)

Тн-саувт Торим ērептиста мермаˇсто еле-мнста äкутēлнм пувта, нстоˇ сокнн-карˇ; кон аггта тäве,ˊ ат нн колнп,ˊаˊ нпра лнлма.контнтä.

**Woman's Work for Woman.**—The modern uprising of women in behalf of foreign missions had its motive in the social systems of the East. It was primarily the *purdah* and the latticed window, the zenana and the harem, that roused the women of Christendom to attempt an errand of mercy to their sister-women of the heathen world. Experience proved that no nation can be elevated until its women are regenerated; also that no man, whether clerical missionary or even physician, could carry the gospel to the jealously-guarded women of Oriental households. When the degradation and sufferings of Asiatic women and the darkness of their future were revealed to the western world, the conscience of Christian women was aroused. The gospel had developed them and set them in honor; given them security and moral power; made them intellectually free, and queens of happy homes; and English-speaking women recognized the claim of their less happy sisters to the same blessings. They undertook to carry the gospel where without them it could not go.

David Abeel, missionary of the American Board, was the first to suggest a movement of this kind. On his way home from China in 1834 Mr. Abeel told the people of England the facts, which had hitherto been imperfectly known, concerning the condition of women in India and China. He showed that missionaries' wives, who had always done what they could for women and children about them, were neither sufficient in numbers nor sufficiently free to assume the burden of lifting up their sex. Efforts so strenuous and continuous would be necessary as to demand the entire consecration of many lives, and he urged that single ladies should volunteer in Christ's name for this new form of service, and that women of the church at home should organize to secure a base of supplies and to render their labors permanent. Little did Mr. Abeel know what a force he was evoking. The Spirit of God winged his words. That same year the first society was formed in England. It is still in operation,—"The Society for Promoting Female Education in the East;"—and upon whatever others, in the progress of years and under divine control, the burden of leadership may seem to fall, this society is ever to be had in reverence, as the one that ventured first and led the way. Others followed speedily in Great Britain: those connected with the Free Church and the Established Church of Scotland in 1837, the Indian Female Normal School and Instruction Society in 1852, and the Wesleyan Auxiliary in 1859; but none of these were much known across the Atlantic.

Meanwhile Mr. Abeel had brought his plea to America, but hearts were not ready for it. At last, in 1861, Mrs. Doremus of New York City was able to carry out her cherished longing, and the Union Missionary Society was launched. Women of six denominations composed its membership, and it stood alone in America for eight years. This was the period of the civil war in the republic, and in the absorbing demands of that struggle Christian women had no leisure to undertake new departures in missions, but at the same time they were acquiring a training for it in the future. By combining as they did, on a large scale, for work in soldiers' hospitals and in the Sanitary Commission, they learned the possibility of working through organizations, how to handle them, and their value above that of individual efforts. The end of the war found many women developed in executive ability and at the same time empty-handed, stripped of their dearest cares and plans. Then missions came to the front.

The Woman's Board in Boston was formed in 1868, not like her predecessor, the "Union," to stand alone, but to co-operate with the Church Board already in existence. In the next three years four denominational societies had undertaken their share in the world's conversion. Time has proved the wisdom of this separation of forces for the accomplishment of one end.

Instead of the one society of 1834 there are now in Great Britain, Canada, and America more than sixty such boards and societies, each under its own management; or societies which contribute to forty-nine separate treasuries, besides many others which resemble them more or less in aim and method. Not less than 1,468 English-speaking women, of whom more than 50 are physicians, were maintained in the missionary field in 1889-90 by women's societies, and more than a million and a half dollars were gathered and disbursed by them. If in all these years there have been times when individual societies have halted or stood still, there has never been a day when there was not progress somewhere along the line

***Organization at Home.***—All the main features of organization necessary in each separate Woman's Board of Missions may be included in three, and in England two are often made to answer.

*First.* There is the local or parish society, made up of individuals from a single local church, or, as often occurs in America, women of two or more churches of the same denomination in one large town unite to form one Missionary Society. This local society is usually called an Auxiliary. It has its own constitution and officers, and is independent in its management; but when it undertakes to carry out its purpose of sending forth missionaries and funds to sustain various forms of missionary work at a distance, it does not try to act alone, but under its Woman's Board, of which it thus becomes an "auxiliary," or helper. An annual fee is the usual requisite for membership.

*Second.* These auxiliaries are grouped, and thus constitute what are usually called Branches. This relation is sectional. Adjacent auxiliaries, sometimes to the number of not more than 20, sometimes covering a county, sometimes a whole State containing 800 auxiliaries, combine with a set of officers elected from the whole territory represented by the branch. This stands between the Board and its auxiliaries. It voices the wishes of the Board to the auxiliaries, and expresses the sentiment of the latter to the Board. A branch assumes the responsibility for some missionary enterprise, and its auxiliaries share it among themselves proportionally.

*Third.* The Board includes all the branches, and requires its own officers. A legal charter is requisite for a Board, but not for auxiliaries and branches. Auxiliaries usually hold their meetings monthly, or oftener; branches quarterly; but the Board meets annually, or, at most, two or three times a year. Business of the Board is transacted throughout the year by its officers, who are elected by the delegates of annual meeting. The delegates are chosen, not from auxiliaries, but from branches. The

Board, or Society (whichever name is given to the inclusive organization), has supervision over an area which varies according to circumstances. If the Society is undenominational, like the English Society for Promoting Education in the East, or the Union Missionary Society in America, it may have its constituency in any part of the country. If the Society co-operates with a Board of some Church, its territory will depend upon the essential organization of that Church. The Society within the Protestant Episcopal Church in America, for reasons which are apparent, is indivisibly one, all over the country. That within the Methodist Episcopal Church has jurisdiction over all the Northern and Western United States. But the geographical spaces are so great in America that in many cases it is found more practicable to have several co-ordinate Boards in one Church. The area of each Board is geographically determined. The Congregational women are massed distinctly under Eastern, Middle, and Western Boards; the Baptist women under the East, the West, and two Pacific Coast Boards.

The advantage of one great undivided Board is offset in the case of several co-ordinate Boards by the following results:

a. A far greater number of responsible, official workers are secured.

b. The work of each Board does not become unmanageably large for its officers.

c. Interest throughout the constituency is augmented by nearness to headquarters.

d. It is possible for a vastly greater number of members to afford the expense and take the journey to attend annual meetings of several Boards than of one Board.

While organization always begins at the top, with the Board the real germ is the auxiliary, and this is the place of growth. Enlargement of an auxiliary by addition of members, one at a time; an auxiliary formed in a local church by gathering a few picked individuals into a little monthly meeting,—this is the unobtrusive way in which Boards grow. Societies of Young Ladies, and Children's Bands, are regarded as only phases of the auxiliary. The former may be wholly or in part independent in management and share delegates to annual meeting with the senior auxiliary, but the branch officers are responsible for the work undertaken both by young ladies and children within its domain.

The existence of more than 30,000 auxiliaries and bands in America, with a membership of several hundreds of thousands, speaks volumes for the patient, persevering, enthusiastic efforts of the women of the church for foreign missions; but it after all represents the efforts of only a fraction of them. The Woman's Board in Boston, Mass. (Congregational Church), having its constituency in New England and the Middle States,—where traditions in favor of foreign missions are exceptionally strong, and where the intelligence of the people and conditions of society would be more advantageous for such an enterprise than in new States,—had in 1889 only 1,182 auxiliaries out of 1,921 churches, and of 190,000 women church-members, about 50,000 belonged to the auxiliaries. There are 600 churches in the borders of the largest Presbyterian Society which are not yet reached by its efforts. Many

other societies cover not more than one fifth of the church-membership.

TERMS EMPLOYED.—In Great Britain the name "Ladies' Society" or "Ladies' Association" is common, while in America the phrase "Woman's Board," or "Society" is preferred. Also many societies in Great Britain dispense with the "auxiliary," and appoint "collectors" of funds from the churches; others do not use the term "Branch," but "District Auxiliary" instead. "Presbyterial Secretaries" and "Associations" and a variety of other terms take the place of those explained above.

In the Presbyterian Church in America "Presbyterial Society" corresponds to the term "Branch," and a fourth feature, the "Synodical Society," is introduced in places. The Protestant Episcopal Society is itself called, not Board, but "Auxiliary;" and its constituent societies, not auxiliaries, but branches, diocesan and parish respectively.

In Great Britain, societies often have long lists of honorary officers. Such are scarcely known in America, where names heading the official list are those of the actually responsible leaders, who conduct public meetings and control the affairs of their societies. The committees of gentlemen which some societies in the old country appoint are also unknown in America, the office of Auditor of Accounts being the only one among them ordinarily filled by a man.

INCOME.—The total income of all these Woman's Societies for 1889–90 was not less than one million six hundred and ninety-two thousand dollars. Whence and how was it gathered, and, above all, does it represent so much gain to foreign missions, or is it only taken out of one treasury and put into another?

1. Some of it came from legacies. A moiety was the income of schools, the gifts of visitors, the profits of publications, the fees of women physicians. Some Sunday-schools made contributions. The large proportion of it was the offerings of women and children of the organized societies. It represents annual fees, or monthly and weekly pledges; the occasional thank-offerings of praise-meetings; the tithing of incomes; earnings for the sake of giving; the results of fairs and other inventions; the superfluities of some, the self denials of others.

2. Little copper or silver offerings from the auxiliary and band were gathered by the branch treasurer, who sent the sums to the treasury of the Woman's Board, which, if independent, disbursed it for its missions, or, if acting with a Church Board, handed it over outright, thus saving that Board infinite labor of collecting, recording, and acknowledging microscopic sums from little children and the mites of the poor.

3. From the beginning of all this woman's work it has been the pronounced aim to gather funds which would not otherwise be given, for the prosecution of foreign missions. At the annual meeting of the Ladies' Committee of the London Missionary Society in 1888, their Hon. secretary said the satisfaction of the committee in seeing the advance in their own contributions during the year was marred by noticing a falling off in those of the parent society, and she recalled to the audience the purpose of the committee not to make their treasury a side-

channel into which to divert contributions from the General Fund.

There would always be devout women in the church who would sustain foreign missions. Some of them still regularly contribute to the general Board alone; some to both its treasury and that of the Woman's Society: but the mass of women would never, without the methods now in use, be sufficiently informed upon missions, nor sufficiently in touch with them, to make many sacrifices for them. Secretaries of influential Missionary Boards in America say without hesitation that a very large proportion of the funds collected through the Woman's Societies are a clear gain to foreign missions.

MEETINGS. —Under the auspices of a single one of many of these Woman's Societies hundreds of meetings are held every year. Meetings for both business and prayer are convened at the headquarters of most Boards, at stated times, besides farewell meetings upon the occasion of departure of missionaries, and other meetings specially called; and an annual public meeting is universal. But in both the character and conduct of them great diversity exists.

Breakfast and Tea Meetings, and Working Parties for the purpose of making clothing for native children in orphanages and schools, for filling Christmas boxes and preparing embroidery patterns for classes,—all these are much mentioned in English reports, but are comparatively infrequent in America. There, a limited number of Christmas boxes are sent to the missions, but the general purpose of meetings, in America, is either for the transaction of business, or to impart information and arouse interest in missions, and, whichever its object, it is always partly a devotional service and sometimes strictly such. Many societies have a by-law requiring the opening of all meetings with devotional exercises; and although many printed reports make no allusion to prayer-meetings, it is not supposable that societies often exist without them. When the organization extends to parishes the number of meetings is vastly multiplied. An "auxiliary" is generally understood in America to mean a company of ladies who, among other things, hold a meeting for prayer and deliberate study of missions every month, in the morning, in cities; in the afternoon, in the country; and, perhaps, on Sunday, in rural districts where people live widely scattered.

A Branch, or Presbyterial, meeting means a quarterly meeting, often lasting all day, and which moves from town to town, by invitation. This brings it at some time within reach of every lady in the branch. Those of adjacent towns who can conveniently attend go by carriage or train to the quarterly meeting, and a hearty sight it is, on a pleasant day, in a country town, to see the ladies driving up from every direction, all their horses' heads pointed toward the church. There they spend the day. A little Branch business, Scripture reading, and frequent prayer and song, wide-awake practical papers, inspiring talks, often from missionary ladies on furlough, with a hospitable lunch between morning and afternoon sessions,—these are quarterly meetings. Perhaps their place is most nearly filled in Great Britain by "deputation meetings," where some speaker is sent out to a certain locality by the secretary and holds an appointed meeting, generally in connection with one managed by the parent society.

In the old country, also, annual meetings are often, but not always, presided over by gentlemen, and sometimes no ladies speak on their own platforms. Such a thing is unknown in America. It is there very exceptional for a gentleman to preside, although occasionally one is invited to speak; and while in the early days of the societies they were rigorously excluded from the audience, gentlemen are now absent chiefly because there is not room for them. Annual meetings of the stronger Boards now occupy two or three days, and attendants upon them are quite familiar with the sight of a large church packed with women.

In October, 1889, one of these woman's meetings was held in New York City, where in a morning service of three hours, in a crowded church, besides devotional exercises, there were short addresses from twelve missionary ladies, all in active service—among them three missionary mothers, each with her grown missionary daughter. All of these ladies were heard to the church door.

LITERATURE. —Dr. Arthur T. Pierson has said that "the Woman's Societies are doing a wonderful amount of good by scattering missionary literature broadcast, in light, condensed, and cheap forms." His language well describes those little two to eight page leaflets, given away, or sold for two, three, and five cents apiece, and ten cents per dozen, which have been sent out from the rooms of the Woman's Societies in recent years. Many of them have gone through two editions, and at least one, the popular "Mrs. Pickett's Missionary Box," has passed through four editions. One American society has published a series of "Missionary Annals" in eight or ten small volumes. Others have printed valuable "Historical Sketches" of their missions. They get up missionary calendars, they furnish a column of missionary intelligence regularly for a number of the weekly newspapers. They all publish annual reports and ten years' histories, and most societies on both sides of the Atlantic, issue some monthly or quarterly publication in which to represent their work continuously, both at home and abroad. Of such in Great Britain "The Quarterly News of Woman's Work" appears to have the widest circulation (10,000), while in America there are four monthly publications, each with more than 15,000 subscribers. Two of these are papers, "The Helping Hand" and "The Heathen Woman's Friend," the latter of which issues a German edition of 3,000 additional; the other two, "Life and Light for Women," and "Woman's Work for Woman," are magazines, and all four are fully self-supporting. Two children's papers, also, "Children's Work for Children" and "The Dayspring," have about 20,000 subscribers each, and are monthlies. Besides all that is done with the printing-press, there is frequently a Bureau of Exchange at society headquarters, and a regular business is made of supplying hektograph and type-writer copies of thousands of mission reports and letters yearly, to be read in society meetings. In these and similar ways a great amount of fresh information from the field is constantly kept in circulation.

CHILDREN'S SOCIETIES. —Beyond occasional mention of contributions from "pupils" of some lady, or "from a Bible-class" or Sunday-school, the reports of woman's societies in the old country seldom have anything to say of the children's part in the modern missionary crusade. But in America they are a great factor—both in the United States and in Canada. They are organized into Bands, of which they are themselves officers, although superintended by some skilful leader; and they read their little reports with quite as much gravity, accumulate their offerings with equal enthusiasm, and, in general, march to the music, if with a somewhat broken step, as happily as their seniors. There were 10,162 accredited bands in the United States in 1888, for which a membership of 200,000 would be a low estimate.

One of the first momentous duties of a Band is to name itself, and the English language has been explored for the purpose. There are the Carrier Doves and Lookout Guards, Snowflakes and Mayflowers, Busy Bees, Steady Streams, Mustard Seeds, King's Cadets, Up and Readys, Little Lights, Pearl Seekers, Acorns, The Drum Corps, Do What You Can Band, and so on, in endless variety. As one has said, "Each dainty or suggestive name looks out from the record like the glowing face of a child." And no mean sum in hard cash do these children send to the foreign-mission treasury. The American Board is enriched by $15,000 a year from them.

And what have the children not done to fill their mite-boxes? They have tithed what was given them for Christmas and Fourth of July; they have hemmed towels by the mile, and practised scales by the half-day; they have foregone sweets and even butter; they have picked blackberries in the sun; they have "minded" baby, and submitted to have their teeth drawn, and "buttoned papa's boots, who can't stoop over because he's so fat;" they have bunched flowers and shovelled snow; raised vegetables and chickens; and, after earning their money, some of them have divided with little brother so that he might share the glory of giving. One little girl kept her music-box "which plays with a handle, right by my bank, and I play a tune whenever I put some money in, so I like to put the pennies in oftener than before."

Band meetings are held stately, and the inventiveness of the most skilful leader is taxed to arrange programmes which are at once instructive and entertaining. The children are taught numerous hymns and Scripture passages and many learn to pray in the meetings. They draw maps, recite dialogues, hold African palavers and Indian pow-wows in costume, and give facts about missions and missionary lands in one-minute reports or five-minute papers. They quiz their parents and teachers, and ransack the library and search the atlas for information, because they are "on the committee." Sometimes exercises take a different turn, and they make scrap-books or dress dolls for a mission school, or pick lint and roll bandages for a hospital. In a great variety of ways their childish energies and sympathies are directed into missionary channels, and they are becoming both grounded in principles of giving, and through graphic stories and letters, exhibitions of curios, and talks from missionaries, they are growing up in the churches of America, familiarized with missions as their parents never were; so that, much as the little people now accomplish, it is as nothing compared with what may be expected from them when they come to years of maturity.

*Organization in the Foreign Field.*—The departments of missionary labor for which women ordinarily enlist are Educational, Medical, Evangelistic.

They do not go forth to preach, and are not ordained to that form of ministry, although one occasionally finds herself, like Miss Adele Fielde, "foreordained" to it. An American lady in Siam has so often lent her nimble tongue to the freshly arrived brother that she is quite at home in all of his ministerial functions except that of the marriage ceremony. Some ladies, especially in Turkey, North China, and Japan, preach, as the Master most frequently preached, by the wayside, in the boat, on the mountain,—everywhere but in the pulpit. Some possessing special linguistic endowment engage in important literary labors. Of such more than one has been a "silent partner" in translating the Scriptures. Others have been accredited translators.

One American lady has translated the New Testament into Muskokee for the Creek Indians. Another has assisted upon the Burmese Bible and hymn-book, and edited for a time a Christian newspaper, "The Burmese Messenger," at Rangoon. Another aided the translation of the Bible into the Swatow dialect; another, a missionary daughter, born in Siam and having spent her life there, has an advantage above other members of the mission in idiomatic use of the languages of the peninsula, and, accepting the text of the Revised English New Testament, has put the Gospel of Matthew and Book of Acts into the Laos tongue.

A lady of the Gaboon Mission, West Africa, translated Pilgrim's Progress into Benga; another is doing the same in a Congo tongue, and a considerable number have edited children's papers, prepared instructive books, and translated or aided translations of hymns and text-books for schools.

EDUCATION.—But the great majority of missionary women devote themselves to teaching. The schools are of all grades, from the kindergarten up to the high-school and college. Wherever missions are sufficiently developed, foreign teachers confine their direct instruction to institutions of higher grade while superintending groups of village schools in charge of girls who have been trained in the grades above. All these teachers, as a rule, acquire the vernacular and teach in it; the majority confine themselves, as was formerly the case with all, to the tongue or several tongues of their locality. But in the last years, the English language has made such strides in parts of India, Turkey, and the port cities of China and Japan that it is used more or less in teaching advanced pupils. The advantages chiefly urged for the use of English are, that—

It opens the door to a rich and pure literature.

It provides text-books without the expense and labor of translation.

It harmonizes and equalizes pupils of different races, religions, and tongues in such polyglot cities as Constantinople, Beirut, Singapore, Bombay, and Calcutta.

*Boarding schools.*—Of all educational instrumentalities, missionaries have long looked with special favor upon the boarding-school for girls. The intimate oversight which it permits; the absolute separation of the pupils for a period from the unwholesome, if not vile and idolatrous, surroundings of their homes; the contact which it affords with society at many and its most sensitive points—all these offer rare opportunities for permanent impress upon character, and some of the best and most lasting work in missions has been wrought through this channel.

Day-schools disarm prejudice and opposition to Christianity, but it is in the boarding-school that girls become Christians. An experienced Methodist missionary in Japan has estimated that while only one to three per cent of day-students in their mission have become open Christians, 25 to 30 per cent of those in boarding-school have been won. The teacher in such a school has a place of great laboriousness and responsibility. Her school-room is a theatre for exercise of all her ingenuity and for unlimited activity. She is at once mother, nurse, counsellor and guardian, as well as instructor and often lifelong ideal to her pupils. It is hers to see them the first thing in the morning and stand by their pillow the last thing at night; to quiet their superstitious fears in thunder-storm, eclipse, and earthquake shock; to transport the games of western childhood to their dull school-yard; to wrestle for them in prayer and, in the hour when they struggle with an accusing conscience, to lead them into the way of peace; to give them in suitable marriage; to create in them the sense of home-making and the sanctities of a Christian woman's life. Such work has been done. Such schools have been pioneers in a country, and their graduates were marked women among their people.

When to the character of their labors is added the length of service which many of these teachers have rendered, the girls' boarding-school may well be considered a choice weapon in the armory of the church for the evangelization of the world.

Miss Agnew taught her school in Oodooville, Ceylon, forty-four years without returning to her native land. A number of teachers have kept their "silver wedding;" and there were in 1890 six ladies in the Turkish Empire who had been teaching there for more than twenty years, and were receiving the children of their earlier pupils. One such teacher at Marsovan, Asia Minor, had six spiritual grandchildren in her school that year. In missions of the Presbyterian Church (North) in America there are 16 ladies in boarding-schools who have given already ten years or more to this work. Six of them have given as many as fifteen years and three over twenty years.

While the influence of the boarding-school has drawn a great number into obedience to the Lord Jesus Christ, and often worked a transformation in the social habits of a community, it has always affected the personal elevation, appearance, and manners of the individual. Even a traveller might divide the women of a Syrian village, from their personal appearance alone, into those who have been to school and those who have not. Let a European light down upon any village in the Turkish or Chinese empires, and choose a place in which to spend the night: the tidiest house in that village, with the cleanest table-cloth, the picture on the wall, the most inviting bed, is the home of a mission-school graduate.

If there are disgraceful exceptions, the rule prevails; and in every field a teacher who has been any considerable time in the service may take up her pilgrim staff and travel from home to home of her pupils, and it is like going from one green oasis to another in the desert. Gentlemen of the missions are thankful to avail themselves of the home-like comforts of these houses when on touring expeditions. The tenth annual report (1889) of the Women's Association of the Presbyterian Church in England observes with regard to country tours made by their ladies in China: "There is one thing that always cheers them—the visible difference in the homes of their old school-girls, and the women who have not been with them. Both homes and children stand in strong contrast in their neatness and cleanliness to those of the heathen."

*Day-schools.*—In some missions there are day or village schools, without the home schools; but any mission which sustains boarding-schools will soon have a supporting column of the humbler order radiating in all directions from its centre. They are usually taught by a graduate of the boarding-school, and afford a good testing-place of her ability and worth. They are superintended by the missionary at great cost of fatigue in going from one to another. Some of these schools are composed of the children of Christian parents, others are wholly or in part from heathen homes. In the former case they are taught the rudiments, and the brightest and most promising children are taken on farther in the boarding-school; in the latter case they are often the only bit of gospel light in a whole village, and the Scripture verses committed by a single child, or the pure Christian hymn which she sings at home, or her peaceful deathbed, is the starting-point for the introduction of the gospel into a new place. They seem a weak instrumentality, with their lowly buildings, their primitive furnishings, their young "slip of a girl" for teacher, and the crowd of rude children in motley attire; but governments know they are a power, and according as they are favorable or not to the missionary's religion, they, as in the case of the King of Siam, bestow royal patronage upon the children's schools; or, as in the case of the Sultan of the Turkish Empire, they close them by imperial firman, whenever they dare.

Very often the day-schools have justified the saying of the Brazilian mother, who, in withdrawing her little daughter of five years, explained, "If she were older I could leave her in your school—she would forget this Bible teaching; but at her age she will never forget."

Eight English societies reported in 1888, 796 day-schools, with an aggregate of more than 40,000 children.

*Tuition and Industrial Education.*—It has been commonly the case in unevangelized lands that parents would pay something for the education of their sons long before they would do the same for their daughters, so that any tuition received for the latter in mission schools indicates the stage of progress reached by the whole country. In Japan, where Christians support their churches with great readiness, and schools are so popular that the Japanese themselves establish schools for girls, more tuition is received than in most countries; still, the first entirely self-supporting school in Japan is yet to be heard from.

In Asia Minor, where there is an extensive system of mission schools and learning is popular, and Protestant communities have been trained to self-support, there are 15 or more schools for girls of the higher grades, in all of which there is a fixed price of tuition. Those in provincial towns, where people handle but little money, sometimes receive payment in farm produce. At the college for girls in Constantinople the income from tuition has averaged $8,000 annually ever since 1879. In that college it is rare to give the value of an entire scholarship to a single pupil, but it is divided between several, and the number of scholarships is limited to twelve. Scholarships are a feature of all mission schools, and it is the business of many little home societies to gather enough money to pay the variable but generally small amounts at which they are rated.

As to industrial education in these schools, the widest divergence obtains among Missionary Boards, and there is almost equal absence of uniformity of practice among different missions of the same Board. It may be said, as a rule, that girls in English mission schools are taught more handicraft than in the American missions. Where government grants are given, as to English schools in India and South Africa, industrial education is especially cultivated, and the most complete experiment in this direction is at Lovedale, in Kaffraria. So, in America, the earliest mission schools among the North American Indians made industrial education a feature, because the Federal Government paid the costs. But where there is no such secular backer, missionary Boards have usually drawn a clear distinction between humanitarian and gospel work. The object in the mission school (especially where education is free) is to send out a girl educated above, but not away from, her people. Accordingly she is generally kept in touch with her home surroundings, by practising in school the characteristic household duties which she will perform all her life. Many glimpses of mission girls at their work are given by travellers' pens.

One went to the Baptist School in Delhi, where "every girl is brought up to use the fan of the country for cleaning every kind of grain." He saw the three large sets of millstones "where nine girls every morning grind flour for the school," and when they go to Agra to take their normal or medical examination these girls "stand head and shoulders above those who never grind at the mill." In a school at the other end of Delhi, in connection with the Society for the Propagation of the Gospel, it was work-day, and the girls were spinning cotton at their wheels, sewing, cutting out, and making garments for the boys. At Sialkot, at the United Presbyterian Mission, the traveller saw the copper boiler for washing, the bucket and well, and the washing drying on the lines—all the work of the school-girls.

A great amount of needle-work is taught in English schools at Lahore and other cities of India, and the dressmaker has been introduced into some schools in Japan since western dress has been adopted, and knitting classes are fashionable.

At the Bridgman Memorial Home, Shanghai, the embroidery class were taking the fine straight stitches which would give them a means of support if need be. "Another class was making shoes for the school, substantial and comfortable."

Through Asia Minor the girls all clean and dry wheat for *bulgoor*. In South Africa, the Zulu girls. who have been accustomed to open-air life, would pine in the school-room were it not for the trees to be planted and the garden-digging.

A Spanish pastor of Madrid visited the American school at San Sebastian, and wrote of it: "Especial care is given to educate the scholars in the life of a well-organized home. They are taught to do for themselves to-day what to-morrow they will have to do in their own homes. That is to say, they are taught to be good housekeepers—not mere señoritas of the drawing-room."

Nor should Bishop Crowther's story be omitted, for it shows how industrial education induced the payment of tuition.

At Bonny, in the Niger Mission, it was agreed by the chiefs that £2 a year should be paid for each boy and girl who attended the school. When the time came the chiefs objected to pay for the girls, as they could not afterwards earn moneylike boys. The bishop himself then agreed to pay for the girls, who were trained to read, sew, knit, and make bread. A certain day came when the chiefs were entertained, and Miss Susan Jumbo, daughter of Oko Jumbo, made the bread which her father praised without knowing who had made it. When informed, he was greatly pleased, and from that time native scruples as to the utility of investing money on the education of girls disappeared in that mission.

MEDICAL WORK.—This agency of mission work is newer than the school, but its importance is universally acknowledged, and its efficiency becomes more and more apparent.

The woman physician is called for on the same grounds as the man: To remove barriers for the gospel; to be a safeguard for the life of the mission; to bear a kind of testimony which the followers of Christ neither have the right to withhold nor the missions can afford to do without. Not only so, but in countries like India and China, there is an additional demand for her service. All those sufferings in illness which are universal from ignorance of medicine, barbarous malpractice of native doctors, and slavery to superstitious fears, dire as they are among people of all ages and stations, bear upon the women with tenfold weight. Whatever alleviation the foreign doctor may be permitted to bring to the enlightened Hindu Babu, it is not for his high-caste wife when she is ill, certainly not in the hour of maternity, when every sentiment of humanity would insure to her consideration and pity. The customs of ages are not to be brushed aside. All the laws of social etiquette which prevent millions of Eastern women from ever hearing the gospel from the ordained missionary apply with equal rigor to his brother physician. "We would rather die," they say, "than go to his hospital, or be seen by him." An incident of the well-known Dr. Valentine's experience in India has been often told: "A curtain was hung between him and his patient. Inside this curtain the lady sat with a slave-girl at her side, and outside the curtain sat the doctor with a slave-girl by his side. Any question the doctor wished to ask had to be put to the slave-girl outside, who repeated it to the slave-girl inside, who in her turn repeated it to her mistress: and the answer came back in the same way."[*]

---

[*] Medical Work of the W. F. M. S. of the M. E. Church (Mrs. J. T. Gracey), p. 27.

The medical woman goes under the banner of the missions to these sufferers to save countless lives, to relieve untold and unnecessary pains, and to point the dying to the home beyond.

The practice in America has been to send out only fully qualified women physicians, with, occasionally, a trained nurse to assist. Such a pair are at the Margaret Williamson Hospital, Shanghai; another pair at the woman's pavilion of the An Ting Hospital, Peking; and another two in the city of Madura, South India. But, ordinarily, the number of physicians at the disposal of Boards has not been sufficient to warrant this method, and the doctor has often been unsupported even by a person able to compound her drugs.

In Great Britain a somewhat different course has been pursued. While some thoroughly qualified women have gone out to their missions, others who have taken only a partial course in medicine have often been commissioned. It is common among all societies which send out physicians to aid suitable candidates to obtain their medical education.

Besides her house-visiting, the physician generally has a dispensary, and, often, what is still more satisfactory, a hospital, larger or smaller, where she can secure the treatment necessary for her patients' recovery. There is always Christian teaching in the woman's ward and provision for instructing the patients while waiting their turn in the dispensary. A sample picture is this from Tabriz, Persia: The account of one of our Saviour's miracles of healing is first read in the midst of the waiting company of women, and prayer offered for a blessing on the day's efforts, after which the doctor proceeds to her inner room and the assisting missionary stays with the outsiders to further open to them the Scriptures, while the clinic goes on all the morning.

Sometimes tickets are distributed from the dispensary each with a passage of Scripture on the back, and a lady in Moradabad mentions another device. "Religion is taught," she says, "at every opportunity. I have printed upon small white envelopes, in Hindi and Urdu, texts or sentences of Scripture, and every dose of medicine carried out of the dispensary is enclosed in one of these envelopes, and these messages have found their way into thousands of heathen families." Many, both hospital assistants and patients, have been converted under these varied influences, and have carried the new doctrine back to their homes and neighbors.

The first physician is yet to be heard from who lacked patients. From the time she first appears upon the scene, when she is obliged to hide away to learn the language, till long strain compels her to take refuge in a furlough, the doctor is always in demand; and the proverbial ingratitude of the heathen has had more striking refutation in her experience than in that of any other who tried to do them good. The poor have offered her their best; the rich have made substantial additions to the dispensary funds; and rank has stepped down from its place to do her honor. The poetry of the Orient has been drawn upon to find phrases worthy to inscribe upon a tablet and when it was prepared, people of all conditions in life carried it with processions and fireworks, music and banners and arches, to erect it above their benefactor's door.

English and Scotch medical women have made their mark in Lucknow, Peshawar, Amritsar, Benares, Madras, Haidarabad, in India; in Hankow, China; at Bethlehem, and other places. Their reports for 1889-90 mention altogether twenty-six such workers. One of the most recent very interesting medical missions opened is that of the Church of England Zenana Society in Kashmir.

The woman's missionary societies in America have 50* physicians in the service, distributed in eight different countries. Of these, eleven represent the Presbyterian Church (North). One is at Allahabad, where, with but two brief furloughs in her native land, she has labored unremittingly for eighteen years. The same Church has sent the first woman-physician, also a second, to Persia, and the first also to Korea, in the capacity of physician to her majesty, the queen.

The societies of the Congregational churches have seven physicians in the service, two of them at peculiarly isolated outposts—the one at Kalgan on the border of Mongolia, the other at Ponape in Micronesia. The Baptist societies furnish five physicians and the Union has four; the Disciples and the United Presbyterian, two each; the Methodist Episcopal (South), Free Baptist, Protestant Episcopal, Friends, and Lutheran, each have one. But of all societies the Methodist Episcopal (North) has the glory of taking the lead in this department of missionary work. They sent the first regularly graduated medical woman to the continent of Asia; they have sent in all 29 women, and now* have 14 in the field.

Nearly all of these 50 women physicians conduct one or more dispensaries, and 17 of them have charge of either an entire hospital, or, what is nearly equivalent, a woman's ward, or annex. They are located in the following cities: Bareilly, Allahabad, Madura, and Sialkot in India; Canton, Foochow (2), Peking, Tientsin, Wei Hien, Wuchang, Amoy, and Shanghai in China; Kyoto, Japan; Seoul, Korea; and Oroomiah and Teheran, Persia. Presbyterian women in Canada have also one in progress at Indore, India. Several of these hospitals have been mainly endowed by a single lady, as the Isabella Fisher Hospital, Tientsin, by a Baltimore lady ($5,000); the woman's pavilion in Peking, by an Albany lady ($3,000); the woman's ward at Teheran, by a Detroit lady ($2,000); the fine hospital of the Union Society at Shanghai, where land, building, furnishing, wire-beds, instruments, and salary of a physician and nurse for seven years, were all provided, at an expense of $35,000, by Mrs. Margaret Williamson of New York (deceased), for whom the hospital is named. A maternity ward is about to be added, at a cost of $17,000, by two sisters of Princeton, N. J., as well as another ward through a legacy from Dr. Wells Williams.

Some of these hospitals have been largely aided by the population surrounding them, and in others the annual running expenses are largely defrayed (in one case in India, one half) by the voluntary thank-offerings of the in-patients. The first of all, that at Bareilly, was built, together with a dispensary and doctor's house, upon an estate given to the Methodist Mission for the purpose by the Nawab of Rampore, and

---

* January, 1891.

valued at $15,000, the Society meeting the additional cost of $10,000.

A lady of the United Presbyterian Mission in India has named some reasons for building mission hospitals. One is the economic reason. She says a missionary can do twice the amount of work with a hospital that she could otherwise. She mentions a physician whose "daily attendance at her hospital was from fifty to seventy patients. If she had to visit this number at their homes it would require two days' hard work; but in her hospital she treats them, both physically and spiritually, during the morning hours, and in the afternoon she goes out into the zenanas and does the same work."

"Another advantage of the mission hospital is as a field for training Christian nurses. The government hospital is not such a field, and caste prejudice is never eradicated there. The supreme advantage is, to have a place "where the Great Physician is honored and the grand work of healing body and soul go hand in hand."

The same competent observer urges that, when possible, two physicians should be associated to relieve one another, and that opportunity be secured to the physician for evangelistic work. Upon this point she says: "When, for want of help, a medical missionary's time is occupied in compounding medicines, washing bottles, or in the wards dressing simple wounds, or in the kitchen looking after the meals of the patients, and a hundred other things,—all of which a good nurse and a well-trained compounder could do,—she has not much time, if any, to speak to her patients about the one thing needful."

Brief extracts from the certified reports of some of these hospitals indicate what the labors of the physician are, although no figures can include all her cases, or indeed accurately measure her work.

Shanghai, China.   Margaret Williamson Hospital; Dr. Elizabeth Reifsnyder and assistant.

"More than 60,000 patients were treated from 1886-1888, and more than 80,000 prescriptions filled; 100 cases every day during the month of May, 1887."

Madura City, India.   Mission Dispensary; Dr. Pauline Root and assistant. During the year 1888:

| | |
|---|---:|
| Total, new and old cases | 20,551 |
| New cases | 12,709 |
| In-patients | 518 |
| Surgical cases | 4,832 |
| Europeans and Eurasians | 235 |
| Native Christians | 3,181 |
| Mohammedans | 1,492 |
| Under 6 years of age | 2,500 |
| Villages from which patients have come | 216 |

Canton, China. Mission Hospital; Dr. Mary West Niles and assistant. During the year 1889:

| | |
|---|---:|
| Out-patients, 4,286 ⎫ total | 4,679 |
| In-patients,     393 ⎭ | |
| Surgical operations | 683 |
| Professional house visits | 275 |

Besides their practice, some physicians in addition to their other duties, by no means light, have been able to train a few students in medicine. Several such from a class at Bareilly have done valuable work in India. The Government Medical School, founded at Agra in 1884 under Dr. Valentine's direction, has classes for women, which girls from English, Scotch, and American mission schools have already entered. In Kyoto, Japan, a training-school for nurses, in charge of two American ladies, had a class of 14 in 1888.

EVANGELISTIC DEPARTMENT.—This includes the personal hand-to-hand work for souls which may come to any missionary: house visitation; Sunday-school teaching; mothers' meetings; church prayer-meetings; wayside meetings with heathen women, gathered by accident or purposely sought at the threshing-floor, the well, the *mela*; temperance work; superintendence of Bible-women; and zenana visitation.

Some societies are formed for one special department of effort. In Great Britain the name commonly indicates the particular aim, and five large societies indicate by their names that they are established chiefly for evangelistic labor.

In America, it is more customary to go out under a missionary charter simply, but lend a hand in whatever departments of work providentially open.

The evangelistic department often requires touring over a large area, and as it is done, particularly in Japan, North China, Persia, and Eastern Turkey, it involves much hardship of travel from long hours in the saddle or in jolting carts or by jinrikisha, from fording rivers, nights spent in rude *khans* or country inns, inferior food, the vicissitudes of weather, insects, and other exposures. Such work is fatiguing, and demands health and endurance. On the other hand, it is full of incident, and those who have the tact and power for the spiritual work and vigor for the hardships, are among the happiest missionaries.

English societies have, in some cases, established itinerating village missions around a city station, and make the circuit of them with their travelling tents, magic lantern, and other equipment. In all societies considerable work that is never reported is done by the wives of missionaries, who accompany their husbands more or less in itinerations, and gather the women for instruction at the same time the men are at the preaching service.

Ladies of the American missions in Japan are often called to places where there are enough Christian men to form a church, but no women are instructed, because it is improper for them to assemble in public promiscuous meetings. The missionary accordingly takes a Christian Japanese woman for her companion and goes forth. She is absent from ten days to three weeks at a time; her farthest point perhaps several hundred miles away, taking in many places between. She hesitates not to stop and teach in a town of thousands of Buddhists, where there may be not more than one Christian family.

A Methodist lady, making a trip in 1888 through the Tokyo district, in about three weeks, "visited nine places, held nineteen meetings for women, attended thirty-five services, and found much cause for gratitude and encouragement in many places." Another of the American Board ladies in Okayama is accustomed to take no table comforts with her on these country trips, except coffee, sugar, and salt, and to average not more than six hours nightly sleep during her absence. She travels all day and arrives at evening, and, the message having gone in advance, the meeting with the women is appointed for nine o'clock the same night; it lasts till 11.30. If she stays a day in a place, callers come before breakfast, and, unless she interrupts them with a service, they continue to come till near midnight; and no matter how late she retires, if she is to depart the following day, horsemen arouse her at early dawn. In towns where there is neither church nor school, a common place of meeting is the upper story of a *sakè* storehouse. One of her by-the-way episodes is given in this missionary's own language:

"We went on by a cross-road and through occasional showers to the house of an official, the mother, wife, and daughter being Christians, but long isolated from Christian society, in a lonely place. The house was full of silk-worms, but the women were delighted to see us. We were seven Christians altogether, and after a little visit we read John 16th, sang 'There is a fountain,' and prayed together. This visit introduced the evangelist to the leading family in a large township."

BIBLE-WOMEN.—As soon as a missionary or native pastor has gathered a little church in a new place, he wants a Bible-woman to go about and impart elementary instruction to the women. Or, a missionary lady trying to bring the gospel to bear upon the homes of a great city wants her Bible-women to take her instruction and multiply it manyfold. "Our efforts," wrote a missionary in Travancore, "would amount to comparatively little in such a climate had we not a band of native Christian women to go forth under our direction to labor from day to day." "I am more and more convinced that we must repeat ourselves in our Christian women that our work may live on when we are gone," wrote another.

These Bible-women have generally passed through the mission schools and become wives of teachers or catechists; or, they are widows; or, occasionally, blindness or other personal disfigurement has permitted a girl to step aside from the Oriental woman's lot of early marriage and obtain a better education than others, and make herself a very ornament of grace to the mission that she serves. It is especially difficult to find women suitable for this work, and those not drawn to it from worldly motives, out of the *first* generation of Christians. But many have proved themselves true in life and death.

Training-schools for women evangelists are conducted by American ladies in Japan, at Kobè, Yokohama, Tokyo, and Nagasaki. All Bible-women make regular reports to some missionary, and are under her guidance.

It was estimated that the Bible-women connected with one mission in the Bombay district reached an aggregate of 85,000 persons, by reading the Scriptures or discourse upon them, in the year 1888.

Of American societies, the Methodist has the largest number of Bible-women—308. The Church of England Zenana Society employs 139. A lady wrote from Yokohama: "At a Japanese prayer-meeting in Mrs. Pierson's room about thirty Bible-women offered prayer and expounded the Bible. It is a pleasure to see the young girls so neat and graceful, learning the way of life; but it is a joy to know that these poor, sad-looking women are having opened to them all the consolations of the gospel."

ZENANA WORK.—Strictly zenana work is limited to parts of India. And what is a zenana? That part of a native gentleman's house where the women live separate and secluded. The

following description of such a place is published by the Church of England Zenana Society: "These apartments are generally situated in the most secluded and inaccessible part of the building, approached by narrow stairs, dark and dull, with scarcely any windows and these grated and so small and high up in the wall that it is impossible for those inside to look out or for any outsider to look in. The room within is as bare and comfortless as possible, entirely without furniture, except, perhaps, a mat and a *charpai*, or native bedstead, in one corner. In this dreary prison the poor Hindu girl of the upper classes is shut up as soon as she is eight years old; for by Hindu law she ought, if possible, to be married at that age, and certainly before she is ten.

"So rigidly is this seclusion of women of the upper classes maintained, that when a Hindu lady travels or goes to visit her relatives, as she is sometimes allowed to do, she is carried from one house to another in a palanquin, which is closely shut up and entirely covered with a cloth covering, so that it is impossible for her even then to obtain a glimpse of the outer world."

A contrast is furnished by the same pen in a description of a Calcutta zenana, whose occupant was the wife of a wealthy gentleman, holding an appointment under government, and who had been taught in an English mission school: "The lady's boudoir, or study, was a small but pleasant room, well lighted, and containing a sofa, table, and book-shelves filled with English books, against the wall. There was also a piece of wool embroidery, which had been worked by the lady herself, framed and glazed, hanging on the wall, which she pointed out to us with much satisfaction. The lady, who had a gentle, intelligent countenance, received us with evident pleasure, and none of the *mauvaise honte* which is characteristic of Bengali uneducated women. As she was learning English, she read a little very fairly. She also showed us her copy-book, in which her husband was in the habit of setting her a copy, before leaving for his office in the morning. Very remarkably, that morning, without knowing of our visit, the copy he had written for his wife was the text: 'What shall it profit a man if he shall gain the whole world and lose his own soul?' and we were delighted to hear that he had told our friend that he was only waiting till his wife was sufficiently instructed in the Christian religion to come out from Hinduism with her and be baptized—and this, we are thankful to add, he afterward did." (From "Inside the Zenana.")

The method of zenana visitation is partly indicated by this quotation from an English missionary's letter: "The plan of our work is this: A certain number of houses in a fixed locality is appointed for each teacher, who is expected to have about thirty-five women on her list. A daily register is kept, showing the names and number learning, and the lessons taught. These registers are carefully examined at the end of every month when a general review of the work is taken. All women well able to read the Bible are specially visited and conversed with." What zenana visiting really is, Miss Rainy of the Free Church of Scotland has told in graphic language: "The drive through the dusty streets in the heat of the day, ending often in a walk through lanes too narrow for a carriage and full of evil odors; the climb up steep, narrow stairs; the time spent in close, untidy rooms, trying to teach through the medium of a foreign language, and amid endless interruptions; the exuberance of insect life, which the natives of India seem to regard with nonchalance, but which is a real trial to a white woman,—all these are but the outward difficulties. And there are others of a spiritual kind—the unbelief begotten of anguish and cruel bondage, the frivolity and fickleness of some, the rooted prejudices of others; the national want of straightforwardness, and readiness to agree with you merely from politeness; the necessity of dealing with objections, scruples, doubts, and perplexities, with no aid from minister or elder. These constitute a formidable list; and when we remember that our agents are generally young and comparatively inexperienced, that they are far from many of the helpful influences of home, and that the climate is exhausting and trying, how earnestly we should pray that God's strength may be perfected in their weakness." (From "Our Jubilee," by C. Rainy [A tract], p. 27.)

Opposition to zenana teaching still proceeds from the quarter whence it might be expected. A native gentleman passing the door of a house and hearing some women singing, said: "As we see and hear such things in these days, the world must be coming to an end. A queen is now ruling the whole of this country, therefore women are much cared for." "There is no rain in the country, because women have begun to learn," complained another. But instruction of women goes on, and is destined to honeycomb the fanaticism of India.

The first entrance to what is popularly called a "zenana" was gained in 1851 to the royal household of the thirty wives of the King of Siam. The first true zenana entered was in Calcutta in 1855, and it was accomplished, as was also the case in Siam, at the point of a lady's embroidery needle. In 1881 it was ascertained that between 9,000 and 10,000 zenana pupils were under instruction throughout India, and there have been gains every year since.

In 1889 a single society, the "Union" of America, had 1,000 pupils in Calcutta and 320 zenanas in Allahabad. The Church of England Zenana Society averaged 170 pupils in Amritsar and visited in all India 3,118 zenanas. The Ladies' Committee of the London Missionary Society had 2,209 pupils, and the Zenana Bible and Medical Mission 1,994,—all in 1888. Numbers of zenana pupils are constantly fluctuating, and figures are therefore unsatisfactory except in the mass. The dulness and monotony of teaching in zenanas is enlivened very much by the *bhajan* or Christian hymn set to a native air—a style of music which wins access to the people universally. Several zenana papers are published by different missions. The London Mission Committee prints one in Tamil. The American Methodist women have established an illustrated Christian paper by means of an endowment fund of $25,000, and it is now printed in four of the dialects of India.

Such efforts and effects as are outlined in the foregoing statements could never have been realized by a host of independent pickets. Organization was needful, and that after a new pattern; for there had been woman's missionary societies before this modern movement.

Of them it may be said in general, certainly of those in America, they were circumscribed and local in character. Most of them had declined, if they had not altogether died out, before 1861, owing to the absence of those very motives which give power to our present organizations.

1. The early societies lacked centralization and provision for perpetuating themselves.

2. They lacked the stimulus of responsibility. They pledged no amounts, assumed neither missionaries nor schools.

3. There was no expectation of large service from them on the part of Churches and Church Boards.

4. Especially, there was no such access for them among the nations, as in these later years has called upon Christian devotion with an ever-increasing volume of appeal.

*Outline of Women's Foreign Missionary Societies' Operations in America previous to 1861:*

1800 "Boston Female Society for Missionary Purposes." (Baptist and Congregational.)

1801 "Boston Female Society for Promoting the Diffusion of Christian Knowledge." (Congregational.)

1808 "Female Mite Society," Beverly, Mass. (Baptist.)

1811 "Salem Female Cent Society," Massachusetts. (Baptist.)

About this time, 1808–1812, "Cent a Week" societies were common among women of different denominations in Eastern Massachusetts.

1812 The "Female Foreign Missionary Society" of New Haven, Conn., contributed to the American Board $177.09.

1813 First legacy to the American Board. $345.83 out of an estate of $500, left by Sally Thomas, of Cornish, N. H., a domestic, whose wages had never exceeded fifty cents a week.

1814 April 11th, a woman's missionary society was organized in the Fayette Street Baptist Church in New York City.

1815 Legacy from Mrs. Norris of Salem, Mass., was realized to the American Board—$30,000, the largest received up to that time or for many years thereafter.

1816 "Female Charitable Society" of Tallmadge, Ohio, contributed $20 to the American Board—the first received by the Board from west of the Alleghenies, save one dollar from a pastor's pocket.

1818 Woman's Missionary Society formed in Derry, Pa. (Presbyterian.)

1819 July 5th, a society was formed in the Wesleyan Seminary, Forsyth Street, New York City. It issued its last annual report in 1861. During forty years it had contributed to the missionary treasury of the Methodist Episcopal Church the sum of $20,000.

1821 There were 250 societies in existence (formed from 1812–1820), all contributing to the American Board; many of them were composed exclusively of women.

1823 A society "For the Support of Heathen Youth" was organized in Philadelphia, Pa., and existed until 1874. (Presbyterian.)

1835 A society "For the Evangelization of the

World" was organized in the First Presbyterian Church, Newark, N. J. During the first ten years it contributed $2,344.76 to the American Board. The Society still lives (having joined the new movement), and celebrated its Jubilee in 1885, one of its original members and 20 descendants of members participating on that occasion.

1838    A society was formed in the First Church, Allegheny, Pa. (United Presbyterian), and has celebrated its Jubilee. The original secretary still holds the position.

1839    More than 680 "Ladies' Associations," having nearly 3,000 local agents of their own membership, were collecting funds for the American Board. One of these Associations met in Brookline, Mass., at the house of Mr. Ropes, and made regular contributions for Japan, although that empire was then sealed against foreigners. The amount which they forwarded expressly for Japan was $600, which with the accruing interest became $4,104.23 before the American Board opened its Mission to Japan, of which the first expenses were paid from the Brookline fund.

1847    "The Free Baptist Female Mission Society" was formed in Sutton, Vermont. It continued in operation for over twenty years, and was never formally dissolved.

1848    The "Ladies' China Missionary Society" (Methodist) of Baltimore, Md., was formed. It was a thriving Society in 1871, when it merged itself as a Branch of the wider organization of the Methodist Episcopal Church.

The separate accounts of the various societies are arranged in the order in which they are given in Appendix C.

## Boards working Independently.

### UNITED STATES.

**The Woman's Union Missionary Society of America, for Heathen Lands. Organized in 1861.** Headquarters, 41 Bible House, Astor Place, New York City.—The first meeting called to consider organizing a society was gathered in a private parlor in New York, January 9th, 1861, and addressed by a returned missionary from Burma. At a subsequent meeting, January 15th, the organization was effected, with Mrs. Doremus as president.

The basis of the Society was undenominational, and ladies from six divisions of the church were of its first membership. It proposed to send out only single ladies, and the converts to be gathered would naturally unite with such Churches as nearness and fellowship made practicable. So, from the first, the Society undertook to be a helper of many Churches, rather than to establish a monument in its own name.

The original plan was to secure a hundred collectors, who would each be responsible for twenty dollars for five consecutive years. In a twelvemonth from the time of organization the 100 collectors were pledged, and the subscriptions received amounted to more than $2,000. The Society immediately began to issue a publication, which at first was called "Missionary Crumbs,"

but with the eighth issue was changed to "Missionary Link,"—the name it has carried ever since. It is a monthly; price 50 cents per year. One of the original auxiliaries of the "Union" had formed as an independent society in Boston in 1860. Other auxiliaries have sprung up until they now number 26, and 178 Bands, which are found in fifteen different States and in New Brunswick. A unique feature of this Society is its "Invalids' Auxiliary," to which 91 members were added in 1888, and whose contributions for that year were $100. Up to 1886 the total receipts of the Society were about a million dollars. They stood for 1890 at $60,026.88. The Society lost its honored leader in Mrs. Doremus' death, but will never cease to be identified with her memory and name.

The first missionary was sent out in November, 1861, Miss Marston, to Burma. In July, 1863, Miss Brittan (Episcopalian) went to zenana work in Calcutta. At the end of four years the Society had 2 missionaries, 7 Bible-women, and another serving in hospitals in Calcutta.

In 1890 their force had become 63 missionaries, of whom 4 are physicians. All these ladies were located in Calcutta, Allahabad, and Cawnpur, India; Shanghai, China; and Yokohama, Japan.

*India.*—Zenana work has been the strongest feature of this Society's labors from the beginning. In Calcutta it is known as "The American Doremus Zenana Mission." There are the superintendent (always one of the missionary ladies); 16 missionaries; 55 native teachers; zenana pupils, 1,000; schools, 50; suburban schools, in Rajpore, 12; and Entally, 2. In Calcutta is also the orphanage, with superintendent, zenana teacher, Bible-class teacher, and 112 pupils.

The mission has no school-houses in Calcutta, but its 50 schools are taught in rooms which are rented in the houses of Babus. There are 1,500 children in these schools, who learn faster than their mothers, whose solitary lessons are received behind the purdah, as these children's will be as soon as they are married.

Great pains is taken to provide Christian literature for circulation in the zenanas.

"Every month there are 500 copies of the 'Child's Friend' given away, of the 'Christio Bandab' 300, and of the 'Mahila Bandab' 210; part of the last are subscribed for. Besides these, throughout the year, between 6,000 and 7,000 Bengali tracts, and some 3,000 English tracts have been distributed; many are given to the Babus at the stations, on the route to Rajpore, and have been received so pleasantly as to render it an agreeable work."

The children of the orphanage, all girls, divide their time between study, work, and play. Their ages range from two years to eighteen. The youngest have no school. Those above them are taught and trained for teaching in their vernacular,—either Bengali or Hindustani,—with a little English besides. The older girls constitute a higher department, and their work is done wholly in English, with one language of the country also. The most advanced of all are put into a normal training-class and study for the entrance examinations of the University of Calcutta. Several of these upper-class girls are suitable candidates for a medical course, and the superintendent hopes to see them trained physicians. All these girls receiving such advanced instructions are thoroughly trained in the Bible.

Allahabad. — Superintendent, zenana missionary, 16 missionaries, 6 native assistants, 1,398 pupils, 1,000 in 47 schools, 398 pupils in 320 zenanas.

Cawnpur.—A superintendent, zenana missionary, 13 missionaries, 5 native assistants, 968 pupils, 623 in 37 schools, 345 pupils in 184 zenanas. Among the schools is one for high-caste Hindus taught by a Pundita. It contained 38 girls, in 1889, who were learning Bible verses, catechism, and Scripture lessons. There are also Mohammedan schools in the city.

*China.*—Shanghai. Medical missionary, medical assistant, missionary teacher, 5 Chinese teachers, 5 hospital helpers.

The Margaret Williamson Hospital (see below) is a fine stone building, which probably has not its superior on mission ground. Patients come 15 miles by boat or wheelbarrow to the dispensary, or walk there from 5 to 10 miles on their bound feet. It is open every day except Sundays. Every new patient is registered, and all who are able pay 28 cash or 2½ Mexican cents; sufficient medicine is given for five or more days. The doctor sees 160 in a day, 175, once even 196; and her assistant, the nurse, stands and puts up 250 prescriptions in one day.

All patients in the hospital are expected, if possible, to pay for their rice 80 cash (about eight cents) a day. Many cannot afford even this. Private patients can be received at $1.00 (Mexican) per day. Work begins at 8 A.M. with prayer, and a Bible-class meets on Friday evening.

Interesting conversions have taken place at the hospital, a recent case being a nun who has been connected with a temple since her eighth year. She was baptized, and much is hoped for from the good that she may do in her own village. A Chinese woman, who is an hospital assistant, was also baptized in 1888.

The Bridgman Memorial Home contains forty or more girls from five to sixteen years old. Ten were received into the church in February, 1888, and in the summer of 1889 twelve more were preparing for baptism.

Public examinations of the school open with prayer and a hymn. The singing is well spoken of. The girls are not taught English; all are from poor homes, and are trained in sewing, mending, darning, and knitting. They are also taught to wash and iron, and take turns in the kitchen to learn cooking.

There are several day-schools in the city, numbering 70 or more scholars, who join the girls from the Home in Sunday-school, and with women also, bring the attendance up to 150–180. The children are well drilled in both behavior and the Scriptures, and one of the oldest missionaries in China said of it: "In all my forty years of service I have seen nothing so good in the way of a Sabbath-school."

*Japan.* Yokohama.—The staff includes the superintendent, missionary teacher and evangelist, superintendent of Children's Home, 2 missionary teachers, physician, 6 Japanese teachers, 6 Japanese medical assistants, 21 Bible-women, 140 scholars, 200 in Sunday-school.

Seven girls, all Christians, were graduated from the school in the English course in June, 1888. The music of this school is celebrated among all those of Japan. On public occasions the girls render such choruses as "The Heavens are Telling" from the "Creation," and Mozart's "Hallelujah Chorus." In all, thirty-five girls had passed the English department up to 1889, some of whom are teaching in mission schools, and others are married to evangelists and pastors.

Morning worship at the school is divided into two services—that for servants and Bible-women conducted in Japanese, and for the students in English.

There is a corps of 21 Bible-women, three of them self-supporting. None of them understand a word of English. They are all under Mrs. Pierson's constant instruction, and, with her, hold 26 weekly meetings. During vacations, besides their city work, two by two, they go out on country trips in different directions, some of them accompanying their leader herself, and going a distance of 200 miles or more from Yokohama. In 1889 the women went to 21 places; 83 persons gave known evidence of conversion through their instrumentality.

The Woman's Foreign Missionary Union of Friends was consummated in 1890. The "Union" was formed from ten independent societies corresponding to as many yearly meetings. The first Society was organized in 1881, the last in 1887. Their contributions for 1888–89 amounted to $16,703.58. Then came into the Union between 200 and 300 auxiliaries with a membership of over 4,000, but this does not include half the women of any yearly meeting, unless it be that of Canada. Two important standards were set up by the unanimous vote of the first Union conference in resolutions to the effect that:

"We recommend our public meetings be carefully guarded from the introduction of anything that would tend to foster a love for the dramatic; and that

"We will unitedly seek to promote systematic giving, and use our influence to prevent the introduction of methods of raising money for our work upon which we cannot invoke the Divine blessing."

The formation of Mission Bands was a feature of 1889.

The "Friends' Missionary Advocate," formerly a private enterprise, became the property of the Union in 1890. It is published at Center Valley, Indiana. A monthly paper. Price, 50 cents.

The Union is represented abroad by two men and ten women, who are distributed in missions among the Kickapoo Indians; in Jamaica; in Matamoras, Mexico; the Ramallah Mission, Palestine; at Tokyo, Japan; and Nanking, China. The last is but just begun. Land is bought, and buildings will go forward as rapidly as practicable for an orphanage and training-school for Chinese Bible-women, to be under the care of two ladies who have already gone out for the purpose.

The societies co-operate at several points with English Friends. From one of these, Brumana, Mount Lebanon, after fifteen years of mutual work, the Union withdraws to concentrate itself upon Ramallah, ten miles north of Jerusalem. Here a large school-building has been put up at a cost of $7,000, a house rented for worship, a medical mission opened, and a girls' training-home is projected. Day-schools are also established. Three ladies joined this mission in the autumn of 1889, of whom one is a physician.

In Tokyo there is a girls' school with a three years' course of study; four of the pupils were recently "savingly converted."

In Matamoras a home for girls has about 25 in training, and Hussey Institute enrolled 150 Mexican girls in 1889.

### CANADA.

***Canadian Woman's Board of Foreign Missions.*** Organized 1871.—This was the first Society of the kind in Canada, and undenominational; but as, one after another, denominational societies have been established, its constituency has gradually withdrawn until the mother society is now chiefly represented by the American and St. Andrew's (Presbyterian) and Emmanuel (Congregational) Churches in Montreal. The receipts for 1888 were $958.42.

The Society has given at least one of her own daughters to missions in recent years, and contributes towards her salary at Smyrna in connection with the American Board. Contributions have recently been made to Presbyterian missions in India, the Telugu (Baptist) to Labrador, and the China Inland missions. Two noble schools for girls—one at Woodstock, India, the other at Constantinople—have both received gifts from this Society, which has always been known for its intelligent and catholic interest in missions.

### GREAT BRITAIN AND IRELAND.

***The Society for Promoting Female Education in the East.***—This Society was founded in 1834, and is sustained jointly by Church-women and Nonconformists. All officers, except the treasurer, are ladies. The annual income is about $35,000. "The Female Missionary Intelligencer," 16 pp., is published monthly, at 48 Paternoster Row, London, E. C.

The number of missionaries, 40; missionary correspondents, 43; schools in connection or correspondence with the Society, 275; scholars, 17,624; zenanas visited, 382; pupils in zenanas (returns imperfect), 2,354.

Seven missionaries of this Society received dismissal at a farewell meeting in the autumn of 1889, of whom some were returning to their fields and some were going out at their own charges. The Society is represented in the Levant, Persia, India, Singapore, China, Japan, and Egypt. The forms of work in which its missionaries chiefly engage are: Orphanages, schools, Bible and sewing classes, mothers' meetings, and zenana visiting. Considerable medical work is also carried on, although not, usually, by graduated physicians.

*Palestine.*—Several institutions are located at places associated with our Lord's earthly life. At Bethlehem is a fine school for girls, a class for the blind, and a dispensary. At Nazareth is an orphanage of "80 lively, healthy girls." Sewing-class record for 1888 showed: "3,967 articles mended, 1,157 marked, 550 altered; 182 pinafores made, also 400 under-garments, 130 dresses; 168 collars were crocheted; caps and pockets, with aprons for the bigger girls."

There are schools in the Galilee Village Mission about Nazareth, one of which, at Shefamer, was opened in 1889.

At Shemlan in the Lebanon is a training-school, of which an American missionary said: "No training-school in Syria, except that of the American Mission in Sidon, has turned out more pupils who have actually engaged in the work

of gospel instruction in elementary and high schools."

*Persia.*—Single ladies have only recently been sent to Julfa.

*India.*—At Agra the zenana workers have a "home," and (in 1889) 250 pupils, mostly Hindus. Thirty villages are open to evangelistic teaching from this centre, and there are eleven girls' schools in the district, for both Hindu and Mohammedan children.

At Delhi are schools and zenana visitation, and near the city is a Christian girls' boarding-school of 40 pupils, in which the teaching includes arithmetic, Urdu, Hindi, and Persian. New work was begun in Faizabad in 1889.

At Mooltan is a small *purdah* hospital. The special feature at Lodiana is village work, and the missionaries here are versed in tent life, sitting on *charpais*, and drinking sweetened milk with straws floating on the surface. They are able to write, "We are often well received and listened to."

At Singapore the Society's work is in its early stages. It is confined to the Chinese population, and depends largely upon native district visitors.

*China.*—This was the first of all Women's Societies to enter Foochow, and the first missionary sent here is still superintending the boarding-school of 50 girls from 10 to 19 years of age. "They are taught to read and write their own language, to do every kind of household work, to make and mend their own clothes; also arithmetic, geography, astronomy, and singing. But the Bible is their chief and constant study." Two small day-schools for heathen children are at Foochow, and the missionaries regularly visit and teach patients in the woman's hospital.

*Japan.*—At Osaka there is some school-work, a small training-class for Bible-women, and especially evangelistic work. Country trips are made, occupying several weeks together; the missionary and her Bible-woman constantly address audiences of 150 to 200 women, and hold afternoon meetings for children. Bible pictures and the little organ are a part of the equipment for these tours. In the city, knitting, English, and Bible classes are conducted.

*Egypt.*—The Society was lately called upon to mourn the loss of their representative for nearly thirty years—Miss Mary Whately. She had taught generations of Egyptian girls at Cairo, and established a medical mission, which at the time of her death in 1889 was in full operation under a Syrian doctor. Miss Whately's reputation is world-wide.

***Indian Female Normal School and Instruction Society.***—This Society was founded in 1852. It originated within the Church of England and is largely supported by its members, but has also a Nonconformist constituency, and co-operates abroad with all orthodox missionary societies. The offices of treasurer and finance committee are filled by gentlemen, and the annual meetings are presided over by gentlemen. The by-laws require a stated Wednesday prayer-meeting, and set apart Monday morning for private prayer on behalf of the interests of the Society.

The home constituency is represented by 170 Associations, of which about 30 are in Scotland and 13 in Ireland.

The income for 1889 was £13,054.

"The Indian Female Evangelist," 52 pp., is published quarterly. Price, 1s. Tracts and leaflets are issued from time to time from head-quarters, at 2 Adelphi Terrace, London, W. C.

The efforts of the Society are confined to India. Three new missionaries were sent out in 1889. During the years 1881–1888 the number of stations, missionaries, and native teachers was about doubled. The Society is represented abroad by 38 European missionaries, of whom 5 are physicians; Eurasian assistants, 23; native teachers and nurses, 125; Bible-women, 58.

The agencies of the Society are:

I. Normal Schools.—These are located at Bombay, Poona, Ahmadnagar, and Allahabad. The "Shaftesbury Memorial," in the latter city, is the largest, having 12 pupils—all Eurasians. A fee is charged, but by means of scholarships is put very low. The Society also supplies teachers for a normal school of 100 pupils, at Benares, belonging to the C. M. S.

II. Zenana Visitation.—Number of zenanas visited, 1,353; zenana pupils, 1,994.

Instances are given in recent reports of baptisms of Mohammedan women at Bombay. Patna, where this Society sent the first lady missionaries, has come into recent prominence through the "Lachmin Case." The zenana missionary here fought a good fight to save two of her pupils who had voluntarily fled to her from a life of degradation. In the case of the younger she was defeated by the mother and the courts, but the other was openly baptized, and has since engaged in Christian work. The "first-fruits" of sixty houses at Ajodhya was a Begum, who was obliged to fly from her husband in order to confess Christ. She was sheltered in the converts' home at Allahabad at the close of 1889. The Lucknow Zenana Mission completed its twenty-second year with the opening of 1890. Of more than 600 pupils, about 400 are Mohammedans, 100 Bengalis, and the remainder Hindus. They learn to read, each her own vernacular, a few learn English, and more, writing, arithmetic, and fancy-work. No houses are entered in Lucknow except by special request. One of the visitors in Nasik says: "In some of the houses the women only care to hear the Scripture lesson. In others they want to learn how to make caps, baby socks, comforters, gloves, stockings, embroidery, besides learning to read and to write."

A varying number of zenanas are visited in other cities, as Jaunpur, Lahore, and Faizabad.

III. Medical Work.—The staff consists of five ladies, of whom four are fully qualified practitioners, and their assistants. Two of these physicians are at Lucknow, where they have temporary hospital accommodations, until a permanent hospital, which was begun in 1890, in memory of the late President, Lady Kinnaird, is completed. The medical report here for 1888 was: In-patients, 94; dispensary attendance, 5,338; patients in their homes, 102. The largest number of in-patients of one class were Mohammedans.

At Benares are two more medical women, and the foundations of the Victoria Hospital were laid at the close of 1889. Funds for its erection have been provided by a lady. A dispensary has been in progress here for over two years, and a temporary hospital for one year, during which 54 in-patients were received. The last physician sent out by the Society is preparing to initiate medical work in Patna.

The Society proposes to increase its facilities in this department sufficiently to require an addition of £2,000 to its annual income, and they hope to train nurses in India, at a cost of £8 per annum.

IV. Hindu and Mohammedan Girls' Schools.—"One of the primary objects of the Society is the promotion of education in India based upon the Bible. Secular instruction is important, but religious instruction is all-important, and in the schools this principle has the first place." Annual Report, July, 1889. Total number of schools, 66; total number of pupils, 2,162.

In Bombay a Beni-Israel school of nearly one hundred calls for a new building, which would require £1,000.

Poona is a strong school centre. The corner-stone of a new building for the Victoria High School was laid in 1888. It receives children of five races, and will accommodate two hundred. No English lady superintends this school, both it and the ragged school for poor children having been for years in charge of Mrs. Sorabji. Thirteen girls have passed out of the Victoria as teachers.

In Lucknow, in addition to zenana teaching, the Society sustains six day-schools, four of which are for Mohammedan *purdah* girls. The pupils receive instruction in Urdu, Hindi, Persian, arithmetic, geography, and Scripture.

At Lahore the Lady Dufferin Native Christian Girls' School is strictly undenominational. Religious instruction is given daily from the Bible. There are about fifty pupils. Rev. E. A. Lawrence, a Presbyterian minister of the United States, visiting Lahore, said: "Nowhere in travelling over India have I seen a finer, more intelligent, more promising class of girls than in this school." The Society maintains also ten day-schools for Mohammedan girls in the city, and one for Hindus. The Society has schools in other cities also.

V. Bible-women.—Of 59 Bible-women connected with the Society, the larger number are at 13 different centres in the Bombay presidency. Thirteen are at Jalna, superintended by Rev. Narayan Sheshadri of the Free Church of Scotland. Support for seventeen of these agents is furnished by the British and Foreign Bible Society.

*British Syrian Mission Schools and Bible Work.*—Founded 1860 by the late Mrs. Bowen Thompson, and since carried on by her sisters, sustained by an influential council in England. Annual income, £5,000.

In the year 1860 Damascus and the towns and villages of the Lebanon and Anti-Lebanon became the scene of fearful massacres. The Druzes rose against the Maronites and Greeks, and having put to death about 11,000 men, they turned adrift 20,000 widows and orphans, who fled to the seaport towns. Their tale of woe called forth sympathy and contributions from many countries, and Mrs. Bowen Thompson, leaving her English home, hastened to Beirut in October of that same year, stirred with desire to supply a deeper than temporal need of the sufferers. Mrs. Bowen Thompson was the widow of a physician, and had spent most of her married life in Syria, where she had learned the Arabic tongue and had acquainted herself with the absolute ignorance and degradation of the women of that country. With the determination to bring the knowledge of the gospel to these neglected women, she first opened an industrial refuge, where 200 women and children gathered around her the first week. Schools followed in Beirut, one of which has become a training institution, where about 80 girls are now fitting to be teachers. Within a few years the work had spread to other stations; schools were opened in Hasbeiya, Ainzahalteh, Mokhtara, Zahleh, and Damascus, which were attended not only by children of various Christian denominations, but also by Druzes, Moslems, and Jewesses. Mrs. Bowen Thompson was soon joined by her sisters, Mrs. Smith, Miss Lloyd, and Mrs. Mentor Mott, with her husband. With their aid and that of a small staff of native Bible-women and Scripture-readers, the mission was well organized before Mrs. Thompson's death, which occurred in 1869.

The mission now sustains about 30 schools, extending from Damascus to Tyre, and containing more than 3,000 pupils. There are: a night-school, which has a large work for Lebanon soldiers; and 28 day-schools, which include 4 for boys, 4 for the blind of both sexes, 2 specially for Moslem girls, and 1 specially for Jewesses; the remaining 17 are attended by girls, who mingle without distinction of creed or rank, princesses and peasants sitting side by side. Every one receives thorough instruction in the Holy Scriptures. Women's classes are held on Sundays and week-days, and attended by large numbers, and Sunday services are conducted in several of the schools.

The corner-stone of a memorial school-building was laid in Baalbec in 1889, and the mission has established a medical work in the same place. "Daughters of Syria" is a quarterly, price 1s., published in the interests of the schools by Messrs. Seeley & Co., Essex Street, Strand, London, W. C. The foreign workers in the British Syrian schools number 3 laymen and 18 women; the native helpers are 20 laymen and 100 women.

*The "Net" Collections.*—The "Net" is a monthly magazine established in 1864. It is self-supporting (address, 22 Upper Montagu Street, Montagu Square, London, W.), and collections are received in its name for any missions mentioned in its pages, and are disbursed without expense. But while other missions are thus regarded, the "Net" is now particularly the organ of the Mackenzie Memorial Mission in the diocese of Zululand, South Africa. This mission was established and its bishopric endowed as a memorial of the lamented Bishop Mackenzie of the University Mission in East Central Africa.

There is an influential body of administrators of the "Net" fund in England, which includes both ladies and gentlemen, and they pledge £1,000 annually for the mission, which is also aided by the Society for the Propagation of the Gospel.

The missionary force consists of the bishop, ten priests, several deacons, and nine lay helpers, of whom one is a lady. They occupy eight stations, and report in 1889: communicants, 488; catechumens on the roll, 77; average number at day-school, 280; confirmed in 1888, 107; total average congregations on Sunday, 1,000.

*The Helping Hands Association.*—This Association, organized by young ladies, is in its eighth year (1891), and publishes monthly "Indian Jewels," price 1s. 6d. There are over 40 branches of the Association, and they raise between £600 and £700 annually.

The object of the members is not to inaugurate or conduct missions themselves, but to be "the handmaidens of larger societies." In 1888 they disbursed their funds through five separate societies, all but one connected with the Church of England.

Each associate is required to pay an annual fee of 1s., and they add to their resources by sales from their Helping Hands Depot, 42 A, Fulham Road, London, S. W. Each associate must contribute once every three months for these sales, in one of the following departments, or send a donation of money in lieu of such contribution: art, music, gardening, wood-carving, wood-engraving, bees, needlework, cooking, waste-paper and scraps.

A "Nurses' Association" and "Sixpenny Scheme" are departments of the Helping Hands.

*The Tabeetha Mission.*—This mission is confined to Jaffa, and includes three schools which are carried on by Miss Walker-Arnott, with the co-operation of committees in England, both gentlemen and ladies.

The boarding-school in Jaffa, now in its twenty-ninth year, has about sixty girls resident—Christians, Jewesses, and Moslems. The twenty-fifth anniversary, in 1887, was happily celebrated. Three hundred old pupils sat down to dinner at the school, of whom 70 were Jewesses. About one fifth of the school pay their expenses, and a few provide clothing and beds. The annual cost of food and clothing is £10 for each child.

Two day-schools aggregate 100 children. The mission is undenominational.

### Boards working in connection with other Boards.

#### UNITED STATES.

*Woman's Boards of the Congregational Church.*—Woman's Board of Missions; organized 1868; No. 1 Congregational House, Boston, Mass. Woman's Board of the Interior; organized 1868; No. 59 Dearborn Street, Chicago, Ill. Woman's Board of the Pacific; organized 1873; San Francisco, Cal. Woman's Board of the Pacific Islands; organized 1871; Honolulu, Hawaii, S. I.

The first three Boards co-operate with the A. B. C. F. M. in Mexico, Spain, the Turkish Empire, India, Ceylon, China, Japan, Africa (East, West, and South), and the Micronesian Islands. The fourth Board co-operates in the Hawaiian Islands and in Micronesia. Several facts indicate the results of this co-operation. Twenty years ago there was a great disparity in the church-membership of all the A. B. C. F. M. Missions in favor of men; now the number of men and women is very evenly divided. Then their schools for girls (exclusive of those taken by the Presbyterian Church in 1870) numbered: boarding-schools 11, pupils 350; common-schools 352, pupils 3,103. To-day the corresponding facts are: boarding-schools 53, pupils 3,300; common-schools 930, pupils 34,694. Twenty years ago such a thing as a dispensary for women was not heard of, and the few higher school buildings were inadequate; now the largest of these Boards has more than $200,000 invested in such Christian monuments.

Then the American Board had 43 single ladies in missionary service—a larger number than had the ten other leading societies of America and Great Britain combined. During its 57 years of previous history it had sent out 170 single ladies. Now it enrolls 173 in a single year.

I. *The Woman's Board* (Boston).—It aims, by extra funds, efforts, and prayers, to co-operate with the American Board in its several departments of labor for the benefit of women and children; to disseminate missionary intelligence and increase a missionary spirit among Christian women at home; to train children to interest and participation in the work of missions.

The initial step in its organization was taken by a handful of women, in a half-day meeting called in Boston (1868). Twelve churches of the vicinity were represented, and they began that day, without a dollar, without an auxiliary, without a missionary.

At the first anniversary of this meeting more than 600 ladies were present and they reported 129 life members, two auxiliaries, an income of $5,033.13, and seven missionaries in the field, four of whom are still there.

This Board now requires three days for its annual meeting. Its first president held the office till January, 1890, when she resigned. Home force: branches, 23; auxiliaries 1,182, out of 1,921 churches; bands, 549; total 1,731.

The income for 1889 was $123,218.50, a gain of $8,000 on the previous year. There are about 15,000 children in its Mission Bands, who have in some years contributed $10,000.

Abroad, the Board sustains: missionaries 111, of whom 3 are physicians; boarding-schools, 32; day-schools, 228; pupils in all, 10,000; Bible-women, 143.

II. *The Board of the Interior.*—This was constituted only nine months later than the Board in Boston, and its beginning was fostered directly by Secretaries of the American Board acting with pastors in Chicago. The first auxiliary to enroll was a veteran society of Rockford, Ill., dating back to 1838. At the end of four months the Board forwarded $1,200 to the treasury of the A. B. C. F. M. At the first annual meeting the record ran: 70 auxiliaries, 52 life-members, 6 missionaries, $4,096.77 received. At the end of twenty years they had given more than half a million dollars, had 70 missionaries in the service, and had multiplied their auxiliaries twenty times, or once for every year.

Home force: Senior Societies, 997; Junior Societies, 355; Juvenile Societies, 648; total, 2,000. Added in 1889, 271; contributions in 1889, $56,685.26,—a gain of $7,000 on the previous year. The children of the "Interior" gave over $6,000 in 1889.

Abroad, the force is represented by: missionaries 82, of whom 4 are physicians (6 went out in 1889); boarding-schools, 12; Bible-readers, 34.

III. *Board of the Pacific.*—The territory covered by this Board is scarcely more than the State of California, which in 1887 contained but 115 Congregational churches, 81 of them being aided by the Home Missionary Society. The Board has 67 auxiliaries, supports 5 missionaries, and contributed in 1889, $4,490.05.

IV. *Woman's Board of Missions for the Pacific Islands.*—This originated in the efforts of one of the missionaries to Micronesia while she tarried on her way for a visit at Honolulu. Its members are European and American ladies residing at the Hawaiian Islands, and it is almost entirely

officered by descendants of the early missionaries there. Regular societies are established on several islands. Their contributions in the year ending June, 1889, amounted to $1,015.52. Up to June, 1888, the total amount expended by this Society on the foreign field (chiefly Micronesia) was $4,510.57. During the same seventeen years there was also expended on the home field (Hawaiian Islands) $5,598.51.

The Board sustains a missionary in a girls' boarding-school on Ponape, and another among Hawaiian women of the islands, and shares in efforts for the Chinese among them. Its supervision is exercised over schools, Bible-women (6), a hospital, a home, a prison.

Work done by this Board is extended by two juvenile societies: "The Helping Hand," and "Missionary Gleaners." The latter contributed $200 in 1888 toward the salary of a second lady in Micronesia.

Missionary effort for the Chinese at Honolulu has developed a very interesting society, viz., the *Kituk Nui To Ui*—a Woman's Christian Association of Chinese Women.

"Life and Light for Woman," the joint publication of the three Boards in the United States, is published monthly in Boston, at 60 cents per annum, and has about 16,000 subscribers. "The Mission Dayspring," for children, is published jointly by the American Board and the Women's Boards. Each of the latter issues annually a variety of leaflets and reports from its own headquarters, and the Board of the Interior, in addition, prints monthly a twenty-page paper, "Mission Studies," and furnishes a column for a weekly paper in Chicago.

While these three Boards are geographically separated and entirely independent in their home management, their relations to the American Board are the same, and their interests and labors abroad are side by side, not only in the same mission, but it may be in the same school.

Their missionary enterprises will therefore be considered in this place as a unit, without reference to that particular Board under whose direction any one enterprise in any particular field may be.

Educational Work.—While not neglecting other departments, these societies, in the outset, gave their first strength to schools, and consequently have a fine array of institutions of all grades. Of fifty-three boarding-schools for girls, several rank as colleges. Such are the American College for Girls at Constantinople, the woman's department of Euphrates College at Harpoot in Eastern Turkey, the College at Marash in Central Turkey, and the Kyoto School, Japan. Courses of study in these institutions are equivalent to those pursued in high schools at home. No Latin is taught, but the classic Greek is, in cases where there are Greek students; and from the circumstances of the case the language department is often the strongest; young children in the entering class, at Constantinople for instance, often speaking three or four languages. Visiting that college on a day of the regular rhetorical exercises, one may listen in turn to essays from young girls, in English, French, Armenian, Greek, Bulgarian, and possibly Turkish. In interior cities like Marash three or four tongues will be in use. In schools in Japan, like the Kobe Home, Japanese, Chinese, and English studies are pursued. In all these institutions, Bible-teaching is made prominent, and public examinations are conducted in the Scriptures, as in mathematics; while daily prayers, meetings, Sunday-school and church service, are a part of the curriculum that must be accepted by every parent. Musical instruction is usually afforded, and its full cost required. It has become customary to give the students some gymnastic exercises, and they always are kept in practice of such domestic duties as are thought proper in the families from which they come.

Tuition is not free in these higher schools beyond a limited number of part scholarships for those who are to become teachers. The school in Oodooville, Ceylon, is wholly self-supporting. All those in Japan are largely supported by the Japanese, and several, as at Osaka and Niigata, are wholly or in part under their control. That at Adabazar, Western Turkey, is the only one of its kind in that country, and has been a successful experiment for a number of years. It is directed and supported by the Evangelical Armenian community, there being no Americans in the place, except the ladies who teach the school, co-operating with the people, whose confidence they have. The salaries of these ladies are paid in America.

The boarding-schools and colleges are distributed as follows:

South Africa, 2; European Turkey, 2; Asia Minor, 17; India and Ceylon, 11; China, 6; Japan, 7; Micronesia, 2; Mexico, 3; Spain, 1; Austria, 2.

The general style of living in these schools varies with the country and social condition of the pupils. Some of the Zulu girls arrive at school in their blankets directly out of heathen kraals, while those in Smyrna may come from the hands of a French dressmaker. In none of these schools do they sit on the floor at lessons; in several they have pianos, as at Marash College, whither one was carried 90 miles swung between mules. The aim is to develop wants in the lowest, but not to lift any too far above their people to be useful among them.

Industrial Training.—At Inanda, in Zululand, the school-girls in 1888 harvested potatoes, corn, beans, pumpkins, and other vegetables and fruits sufficient to supply one third of the table necessities for a whole year, and planted 138 trees on Arbor Day. A few years ago a teacher on her way to South Africa, upon visiting the Intercolonial Exhibition in London, saw a shirt made by the girls of the Umzumbe Home, to which she was going, bearing the mark " First Prize."

In Turkey, at Sivas, Armenian girls pulled down small barns and assisted in putting up a building. At Van there was a furore over white embroidery; "they do it beautifully—quite equal to the nuns's work at home." At Marsovan the girls cook, wash, clean house, cleanse the wheat and rice, pickle, dry beef and fruits. In Madura City, India, they pound their rice, cook their food, cut and make their own garments, and sometimes for the catechists' families as well. In all the schools in Japan foreign sewing and knitting have been introduced.

As specimens of the numbers of house pupils in these different schools, the following recent figures may be considered representative:

Africa—Inanda, 60-70 (some of whom walk more than 70 miles to reach the school); Umzumbe, 43. India—Bombay, 35; Ahmadnagar, 84; Battalagundu, 40–50; Otis School, Madura, 75. Ceylon—Oodooville, 105. China—Foochow, 33; Peking, 25. Turkey—Bitlis, 40; Harpoot, 48; Constantinople, 60; Monastir, 43. Japan—Kyoto, 75; Osaka, 100. Micronesia—Kusaie, 26.

Besides these boarding-pupils, all the schools have so many day-scholars as often to double the numbers, as at Sirur, India, where the whole number is 94, as against 42 boarders. Otis school, 143; at Kyoto, 214; and at Osaka, 420, with 27 classes in English daily.

Not every stone has been polished into a gem, but the whole record of these schools makes a history of elevation and piety. The teachers of elementary mission schools and many invaluable assistants in higher grades, the Sunday-school workers, wives of helpers and pastors, the female church-membership, and the Christian motherhood of the country around the missions, have come out of these schools.

It is the common experience in all of them to have some uniting with the church year by year, and few are those which have not enjoyed precious revivals. Very rare are the graduates who are not confessing Christians. A few statistics of conversions may be given from the reports of 1888.

Received to the church: in Turkey: Adabazar, 6, " all the boarders Christians;" Broussa, 7; Euphrates College, 35 conversions. In China: Foochow, over 30 conversions; Bridgman School, Peking, all Christians but two who were " so small and new they couldn't understand;" Pao-ting-fu, 4 confessors. In Japan: received to the church at Kyoto, 26; Osaka, 32; in Niigata, 25 were Christians.

In 1889, at Okayama, 21 girls united with the church. Every girl was hopefully converted at Osaka, and over 60 at Kobe.

The school in the city of Madura was opened in 1837. Up to 1867 more than 300 girls had been educated there. From 1845 to 1866, 77 from it united with the church. In 1886-87 it (now called the Otis School) was visited by a powerful revival, in which " only five or six out of 78 appeared to receive little benefit." The after history proved this a genuine work of God.

A day of prayer has been set apart many times in some schools, and at Harpoot, at the Hadjin Home at Aintab and other places, it has been followed by outpourings of the Holy Spirit.

*Village and Day Schools.*—These are not taught by American ladies but by trained pupils under their superintendence. An exceptional case is at Oorfa, Northern Syria, an interesting city of 30,000 people, where the mission has a church, but no resident missionary. A lady went there temporarily from Aintab in 1888, and aided by an Armenian girl, gave a part of her day directly to a school which, beginning with only 12 pupils, has not only developed a large school, but an efficient gospel work through the city.

Tuition in day-schools is nominal. In the city of Adana, Asia Minor, it is 86 cents per term. In Marsovan it is one piastre ($4\frac{4}{5}$ cents) per week. In the Kindergarten at Mardin the charge is three piastres a month, and more than 50 little people attend. Societies in America are asked to supplement the income of these day-schools at such rates as the following:

Boys' school, Cesarea, Turkey, $25 per year; village school, Madura district, India, $40 per year; village school, Sholapur district, India, $50 per year; village school, Ahmadnagar district, India, $46 per year; village school, Sirur district, India, $43 per year.

Attendance at day-schools fluctuates with persecution and good or bad harvests. Ten high-schools on the plains of Cilicia had an aggregate of 356 pupils in 1889. One public school in Marsovan had over 200 pupils. Young business men paid 80 cents a term in the same city for tuition at a night-school.

Five day-schools in the Spanish Mission have a total of 117 scholars; 16 in the Foochow Mission have 240.

*Evangelistic Department.*—Bible Women.—There is no strictly zenana visiting done by the missionaries of these churches, because there are no zenanas proper within the fields of their missions; but in India house visitation among high-caste women is done by 24 Bible-women in the Maratha Mission, and 35 in the large district of Madura, Southeast India, among the Tamil people. The following outline indicates the development of such Bible-work in Madura:

1850.—No special work for women outside of girls' schools in Madura district of two millions of people.

1867.—A woman of respectable caste, educated at the mission-school, daily visited a rich man's house to teach his wife and daughter to read. This opened the door in the city. The same year, at Mana Madura, Mrs. Capron began her first systematic efforts for high-caste Hindu women. The same year, also, a Hindu gentleman, a pleader in the courts, appealed to educated women to visit and instruct in heathen homes of the higher classes.

1875.—Fourteen Bible-women, of whom none deserted their posts during the cholera. Annual report of the mission for the first time has a heading "Work for Women and Work by Women." It states that 250 women in the mission now have a fair education, and more than 100 are capable of conducting a religious meeting among their own sex. At Battalagundu the church chose a deaconess. Some women deterred by ridicule from learning to read.

1885.—Ten Bible-women in Madura City; 915 pupils, of whom 362 read the Bible. Christian Hindu women contributed to the support of one Bible-woman, of whom there were 24 in the district.

1889.—In the district 35 Bible-women; in the city 12; hundreds under the instruction of the latter, and 10,000 hearers of the Word for the first time.

These women devote their time to Hindu, Roman Catholic, and Mohammedan houses. They are not engaged among the coarse and rough, but generally in homes of the better class, where intelligence, tact, and good breeding are requisite. They visit with Bibles and tracts in their hands, teaching the ignorant to read, and leading the lost to Christ; sometimes reaching even the husbands, who listen to the reader, perhaps from behind a curtain.

In the Ceylon Mission 22 Bible-women are employed, in Asia Minor 58, and smaller numbers in other countries. Their wages are sometimes rated at $5 per month in Bulgaria; in Mardin, Eastern Turkey, they receive $35 a year; in places in India about $30.

In Mexico missionaries take the high ground that they want voluntary workers and not paid women, and they have Christian women at Chihuahua who call themselves "Willing Workers," and pledge an afternoon or more a week to a Bible-woman's proper labors, and their missionary says of them, "I do not know a drone in the hive."

*Touring.*—Some missionaries combine teaching and touring. Two ladies at Harpoot, Turkey, after teaching for years, are devoting themselves to the arduous life of itinerating among the sixty out-stations of that field. Of them a missionary wrote in 1888: "We have had to hold them back all winter. They have done grand service in schools, women's societies, house-to-house and hand-to-hand work, and not less in evangelistic meetings with women, with audiences of a hundred and fifty to three hundred, and in the superintendence of Bible-women. If they should be compelled to give up, what would become of the work out in the field?"

Of the "woman's societies" referred to above, one of these very ladies reports: "They are accomplishing a quiet work. It is theirs to make the pulpit-seat comfortable with a cushion, to buy carpets for the church, help support the girls' school, buy a communion service, whitewash the chapel, etc." Of the spiritual work she says:

"Daily preaching services and women's meetings are crowded, and the noon-day meetings at stables are of deep interest. Inquirers come to us at all hours, the sunrise prayer-meetings are tender and solemn, and we hope that souls are added to the church of such as shall be saved."

In Central Turkey touring is extensively carried on. In European Turkey one lady gives herself exclusively to evangelistic labors. In Stamboul two carry on city missions in the form of Sunday-schools, coffee-house tract-distribution, mothers' meetings, prayer-meetings, and night school.

In North China, at Kalgan, Tung-cho, Pang Chuang, and Pao-ting-fu, the whole missionary work is in that stage of development when hand-to-hand evangelistic labor is demanded, and several ladies give themselves to it exclusively, and with large success. One of them recalls how timidly the first few women came to Sunday-school in Tung-cho sixteen years ago, and now she sees 158 crowd into the chapel in a morning.

In Japan, evangelistic work is many-sided. It is close at hand in the city; or, it carries ladies on trips hundreds of miles from home, visiting isolated Christians and country churches, and preaching among the heathen. Miss Dudley of Kobe on one such tour met 350 Christian Japanese women, and talked with the majority personally. Listeners are so eager that the missionary's stay is never quite long enough, and her mind and body are kept on a stretch from morning till late at night. Or, evangelistic work is special and unique, as that of Miss Colby at Osaka, who has had classes of men—teachers, policemen, merchants. Referring to her experience of men crowding into her woman's meetings, she says: "A missionary is very much like firemen during a conflagration—each one is on the ground to save as much as possible." Another lady in Kobe taught English to a class of 60 women, preceding the lesson with a half-hour of Bible. The class soon petitioned to make the Bible lesson an hour long; within this class grew up, besides, a weekly Bible-class.

The Christian Japanese woman who accompanies the missionary on her tours is a very important person. One is thus described: "She has a gift for addressing audiences; she is self-poised, clear, and almost eloquent. We spoke in three places before students of high-schools—in all to 800 young people." Of another, at a time when 80 out of an audience of 100 proved to be men: "My helper is a spirited little woman, and rises to the occasion beautifully. She spoke on temperance wisely and pointedly."

*Medical Department.*—There are three medical centres in China. At Kalgan, under the shadow of the great wall, Dr. Virginia Murdock has a hospital (which is equally an opium refuge), and a dispensary, and teaches women to read, even to embroider.

She "goes off into the country on tours, staying sometimes twenty days. She takes a servant or Chinese helper with her, medicines, books, bedding, cooking uteusils and foreign food, and puts in three weeks of as hard work and as much discomfort as can be imagined.

"When opium patients come to the hospital she has a plain talk with them. If they are not frightened away, she makes them deposit a sum of money, which she keeps if they run away before the treatment is over; but if they have pluck to stick it out, she gives it back when they go home. For three days, sometimes four, they are in fearful misery, and keep up a series of howls and groans. To go into the hospital in the evening is like stepping into Pandemonium itself. Her patients seldom give out during the process."

A second hospital, at Foochow, is nearly completed. In 1888 Dr. Kate Woodhull treated 3,398 cases, 1,000 being new patients. She took $246 in fees, and has received unqualified confidence and praise from the Chinese. She is training a class of young women in medicine.

There is also a dispensary at Tung-cho, China.

In Kyoto, Japan, a hospital and training-school for nurses constitute a branch of the Doshisha University. The land was purchased with the gifts of 553 Japanese, and the buildings provided by friends in America, especially young ladies of the "Interior." There is a general ward for 12 patients, an obstetrical ward for 8, a house to accommodate 30 nurses, and other buildings. All were formally dedicated November, 1887. The head of the training-school is Miss Richards, who left the post of superintendent in the Boston Hospital to assume these duties, and the clinics are divided between Dr. Berry and Dr. Sara Buckley. There were five nurses in the first class, all earnest Christians.

Other institutions under care of these Boards are training-schools in Kobe for women evangelists and kindergarten teachers.

An object of special effort in 1889 was an improved school-building for Bombay, for which $10,000 were contributed.

*Woman's Foreign Missionary Society of the Methodist Episcopal Church.*—On a stormy day in March, 1869, a few Methodist women met in the Tremont Street Church, Boston, Mass., and organized the Society bearing the above name. In May following, at a special meeting, it was voted to send out their first missionary. In November two ladies were sent to India, and have done distinguished service for missions ever since.

The constitution of the Society provides for a General Executive Committee, composed of delegates from each Branch, who have general management of the affairs of the Society.

It is now composed of ten associated branches, stretching from the Atlantic to the Pacific, and from New England and the Lakes as far as Virginia and Arkansas on the south. Unlike most Woman's Societies, it disburses its own funds, and chooses missionaries without direction of the General Board of the Church. The few salaries paid at home are remarkably small, while those of missionaries are thought to average higher than in other denominations.

The method adopted for raising funds to prosecute the work of the Society was the usual plan of Woman's Boards, viz., every Christian woman to lay aside two cents a week, or pay one dollar a year as a membership fee.

When the first missionary departed there was not money enough in the treasury to provide the entire expense. "Shall we lose Miss Thoburn," said one of the committee, "because we have not the money in our hands to send her? Rather let us walk the streets of Boston in our calico dresses." So they borrowed the money, and in their history of twenty years since have never been in debt, nor has one of their branches failed to meet its obligations.

The twentieth annual meeting of the Society was held in Detroit, Mich., in October, 1889. Its sessions occupied nine days, and the business was transacted in presence of large audiences by three delegates from each of the ten Branches.

The rate of progress within the Society may be indicated by the figures following:

At the end of the first year the number of auxiliaries was 100, money raised $4,546.86; fifth year, auxiliaries 1,839; $64,309.25; tenth year, 2,172 auxiliaries; $66,843.69; twentieth year (1889), 5,531 auxiliaries; $226,496.15. The total membership is 138,950.

The auxiliaries include 501 societies of young ladies and 748 Children's Bands, which last began to be organized in 1879.

The contributions of 1889 were the largest in the history of the Society, and an advance of $20,000 over the previous year. The money raised in 1890 amounted to $220,329.00.

Since 1883 a German constituency has also been growing up, which includes 52 auxiliaries in Europe and 141 in the United States, having a total membership of 4,082. And yet the committee are obliged to report that only one woman in eleven connected with the Methodist Church is a member of the Foreign Missionary Society.

"The Heathen Woman's Friend," issued in 1869, had a subscription list of 4,000 the first year, and paid expenses. It has remained in the same editorial hands ever since, and having been enlarged from time to time, became in 1875 a paper of 24 pp., at fifty cents. It is illustrated, has 19,800 subscribers, and pays, besides its own expenses, for nearly all the miscellaneous literature issued by the Society, which amounts to more than 2,000,000 of pages annually. The paper is published at 36 Bromfield Street, Boston, Mass. A German edition is also published, and has 1,776 subscribers.

An illustrated eight-page zenana paper, "The Woman's Friend," is also printed in four of the dialects of India, and reaches 25,000 women readers. It is carried by an endowment fund of $25,000. The recent death at Madras of the editor of the Tamil edition was a great loss. The "Child's Friend" appeared in 1890, a small monthly, fifteen cents per year.

The Society has sent into the foreign field 137 missionaries in all, of whom about 100 are still in active service. Some at home on leave are hoping to return, and 9 have died; 23 went out in 1889. These missionaries are located in India (33), China (22), Japan (20), Korea, Bulgaria, South America, and Mexico. The following outline indicates the order in which different branches of work have been assumed:

1870 Third missionary to India.
1871 Two ladies to China.
1873 Beginnings in Mexico and South America.
1874 Beginnings in Japan and Africa; the latter afterwards abandoned.
1877 Bible-readers in Italy and Bulgaria.
1879 A school for Eurasians opened in Calcutta.
1882 Chungking occupied in West China, and a hopeful work carried on until all the mission property was destroyed by a mob in 1886.
1884 Chinkiang, on the Grand Canal, occupied.
1885 Missionary to Korea.
1886 Nanking, China, entered.
1887 A lady sent to Singapore.
1888 Beginnings in the great heathen city of Muttra, India.

Property held by the Society in its several missions is rated at about $300,000.

*Schools.*—There are some 250 schools of all kinds connected with the missions, of which the most important boarding-schools are as follows:

In Japan: At Tokyo, where 34 were baptized in 1888; Aoyama high-school, where all but two were Christians in 1889; Nagasaki, which has the finest building in the city, and where 85 were converted in 1889; Hakodate, which allows 55 scholarships, though only 19 pupils are wholly supported; and Nagoya, which had 86 pupils, all self-supporting, and a number converted during 1889.

In Korea: At Seoul.

In China: At Foochow, Chinkiang, Kiukiang, Nanking, and Peking.

In India: Five in the Rohilkund district, of which that at Moradabad has 150 girls from more than 50 villages. There are over 300 intelligent Christian women in this province, more than 500 girls in higher-grade schools, and about 900 in schools of all grades. Fifty young women, students' wives, are in the training-school at Bareilly. In the Oudh district are 4 boarding-schools, including that at Lucknow—the oldest and most notable of all. About half the pupils here are Eurasians, all pay their entire expenses, and the school itself became a chartered woman's college in 1890. In the Kumaon district are four schools, of which Pithoragarh and Naini Tal are the largest. In the former there is scarcely a girl, with the exception of the little ones, who has not become a Christian. They "sew two hours, study four, work in the fields two, and do all their own grinding, cooking, and washing." The Calcutta school is the largest under care of the Society, and occupies one of the largest buildings in India used for a girls' school. It is self-supporting, and requires 13 teachers besides the American ladies. The pupils are of eight or nine races, and out of 200 members 77 have

united with the church. Bombay, Singapore, and Rangoon in Burma, each have a school.

In Mexico: At Puebla, where in 1888 nearly every scholar became a Christian; Mexico City, where was a revival in 1889.

In South America: At Rosario, in Buenos Ayres, where is a "Home."

The number of house-pupils varies from 20 in Puebla and Seoul, to 78 at Cawnpur, 90 at Calcutta, and over 100 in some of the Japanese schools. In all cases day-scholars bring the number much higher. The Bareilly Orphanage has nearly 200 girls. The schools are arranged to reach all classes. There are more than 4,000 children in city and day schools in the North India Conference alone, and 935 girls in the Society's schools in Mexico.

*Evangelistic Department.*—Direct evangelistic work is done in all the missions. From the 70 centres in the North India Conference, 220 Bible-women regularly visit 4,000 houses, and more than 6,000 women are receiving religious instruction. A large itinerating work is prosecuted in the villages of Rohilkund, and about Gonda, in Oudh; and at a camp-meeting held near Moradabad, in the summer of 1889, 300 intelligent and neatly dressed "King's Daughters" were present.

A large evangelistic work is also carried on in the Foochow district, China, where one Bible-woman reported for the year: "There came to me to hear the gospel about 1,700 women," and where one of the missionaries in the spring of 1889 thus summed up a single itinerating trip: "This is a hurried recital of 45 days' work, in which 1,442 heathen women were told 'in all your afflictions He was afflicted,' and men unnumbered; 16 schools were visited, 32 meetings attended, 36 visits made, and 500 miles travelled in Chinese boats and sedan-chairs."

There are seven Bible-women employed in Italy.

Other Evangelistic agencies are: The Sunday-school, which is universal, and established at 67 points in Oudh alone; women's meetings, having regular attendance of 58 in Tokyo, sometimes 90 at Seoul; refuges at Lucknow and other places; a widows' home at Lodipore; industrial classes; a women's workshop in Rangoon, where over 30 women are employed in sewing under direction of a forewoman; orphanages at Mexico City, Madras, and other places; and instruction in leper asylums.

A new feature is Deaconess Homes at Calcutta, Lucknow, and Muttra. At the latter evangelists are trained. There are also training-classes for women at several places—notably Yokohama, Japan, and Peking, China.

*Medical Department.*—The Society has a notable record in this line. Its medical women are stationed in four cities of India, four of China, and one in Korea. Medical work is also in progress under other instrumentalities, e.g., at Bithoor, near Cawnpur, where one of the Christian native women who took a medical certificate in India treated successfully nearly 1,000 Mohammedan and Hindu women in one year. Twelve Christian girls are studying medicine at Agra.

Of two physicians of this Society, special mention is appropriate—of Dr. Clara A. Swain, because she was the first of all, and of Dr. Leonora Howard, because it was given to her to be connected with a great providential opportunity, one of the most marked in all the history of modern missions.

The urgent representation of the wife of a missionary at Bareilly, India, led the Society to inaugurate a medical mission there, at its very start, and one of the first two missionaries sent out was Dr. Clara Swain, a graduate of the Woman's Medical College in Philadelphia. She reached Bareilly in January, 1870, and during the first six weeks had 108 patients; during the first year 1,225 were received at the mission house; the second year they built a dispensary, the third year a hospital. The fourth year there were 3,000 dispensary patients with 150 out-door patients; and woman's medical missions were no longer an experiment.

It had been hoped the doctor might unlock zenana doors; 38 new zenanas were opened through the hospital at Bareilly in 1874, and four Bible-women became necessary to the mission. It was faintly hoped that women would emerge from the zenanas to consult the doctor at her dispensary. They came, shut up in their doolies, which were carried into the dispensary, and inside which they stayed, one curtain only thrown aside, while they received their prescription. To quote one instance from a letter from Dr. Swain at the close of 1874: "This morning a Mohammedan lady came in a conveyance which could not be brought into the room. She was young and pretty, and her husband seemed quite perplexed, as there were several men at work on the road in front of the dispensary. I assured him that an umbrella was quite sufficient to protect her from their sight, but he was not satisfied until he got the second one and held it over her while she came in." *

After fifteen years of valuable labors bestowed at Bareilly, Dr. Swain severed her connection with her Society for the sake of entering what seemed a Providential door to wider usefulness. The Rajah of Rajputana called her to attend his wife at Khetri, and her success led to her remaining as permanent physician there. No restrictions are placed upon her, or the Christian women with her; and they have been for four years scattering Christian books, teaching Christian hymns, talking among the women of the palace and establishing schools,—all at the expense of the rajah.

Dr. Leonora Howard, a graduate of Michigan University, Ann Arbor, reached Peking in 1877, and in the latter part of the next year, while in the full tide of very onerous and useful labors, she was interrupted by a call to Tientsin. Lady Li, wife of the distinguished statesman Li Hung Chang, then governor of the province, was seriously ill, and the viceroy, who was very fond of her, had gone so far as to call in a foreign physician of the London Missionary Society. But the doctor could not overstep the bounds of Chinese tradition to give her suitable care, and the lady from America was suggested. So the man next to the emperor despatched a special courier and a steam-launch, and Dr. Howard was brought to Tientsin. Her remedies were effective, and Lady Li gradually recovered. Dr. Howard was then pressed to remain permanently at Tientsin, which she did by advice of all the mission. Apartments in one of the finest temples in the city were placed at her disposal for a dispensary, the expense of which Lady Li herself defrayed. During

the first five months, 810 cases were treated there, and 1,000 more at a second dispensary in another part of the city. A hospital was built in 1881 under the auspices of the Society, and Dr. Howard continued in charge of it, while also making professional visits in families of the highest officials, and combining religious instruction and medical labors without restraint, until her marriage in 1884, to a member of the London Mission. During all that time her relations with Lady Li remained most cordial, and she had the pleasure of warmly commending to the viceroy one of the treaty commissioners from the United States—the man whose name was on her medical diploma, President Angell of Ann Arbor.

The hospital has been ably carried on by Dr. Howard's successors.

Two things in recent reports from the mission are specially suggestive of the broad results: First: The large number of missionary societies and bands of King's Daughters among the converted women and school-girls. They are to be found in Mexico, Italy, Bulgaria, Japan, China, and there are twenty in India.

Second: The conferences held, composed of native women who have been trained in the missions. Of one such at Foochow, in 1886, a Chinese brother exclaimed, "This is wonderful, and we never thought to see it here; but last year the telegraph came, and this year the woman's conference!"

The women attending read carefully prepared papers on such subjects as, "The importance of the Holy Spirit's aid in preparing for work;" "Can Christian women be admitted to schools?" "The importance of attending prayer-meetings." At Lucknow as many as 600 have met for a day in such a conference.

Some of the events of 1889 were the establishment of a home and orphanage in the city of Rome; purchase of new property at Foochow and Peking; and opening a new school-building, with 50 pupils, at Hirosaki. The Society is making an effort to raise $50,000 for the college at Lucknow.

**The Woman's Missionary Society of the Methodist Episcopal Church (South)** was organized by General Conference at Atlanta, Georgia, May, 1878. It is composed of thirty-four conference societies. The corresponding secretary of each conference, together with five officers and six managers, constitute the Woman's Board, which is the executive body of the Society.

The Home force consists of: Auxiliary societies 1852, membership 38,203; young people's and children's societies 890, membership 27,263. Total receipts for year ending May, 1890, $75,486.54.

"The Woman's Missionary Advocate" is published monthly at Nashville, Tenn. Price, 50 cents. It is self-supporting, with a circulation of more than 11,000.

The Society also in 1889 printed and distributed without charge 1,500,000 pages of leaflets.

Abroad the force is represented (January, 1891) by: Missionaries, 32, of whom 14 are in China; assistants, 27; native teachers, 27; boarding-schools, 10; day-schools, 24; pupils, 1,248; hospital, 1.

The value of property held by the Board is $181,000.

China was the first field entered, in 1878; and the following stations were occupied in the

---

* "Medical Work," published by W. F. M. S. of the M. E. Church, p. 59.

order given: Shanghai, Nantziang, Soochow, and Kahding.

Boarding-schools are carried on in all of these cities. There are nine church-members in the Clopton School, Shanghai. The teacher at Soochow says in a late report that her school had read the entire New Testament during the year, the older girls were neat and patient needlewomen, and 14 out of a school of 21 were probationers.

At Soochow Dr. Mildred Philips has charge of a woman's hospital in China, whose whole cost—building, site, and equipment—was $10,000. It comprises a two-storied home for the medical missionary and others, a dispensary, two wards, and an operating ward, with cheap buildings for servants, kitchen, etc. The hospital was opened in October, 1888.

Several schools in the mission are Anglo-Chinese, and two ladies at Shanghai give their entire time to teaching in the Anglo-Chinese College for young men.

Work at Kahding was opened by a lady of ten years' experience in China, who went, with Chinese assistants only, to make a beginning in that large, walled city. At the end of a year she had six day-schools with 76 pupils, with five Chinese teachers and a Bible-woman at work.

The Society entered Brazil in 1880, and occupies stations at Piracicaba and Rio de Janeiro. They have boarding-schools at both places, with about 100 girls in the former, although only 20 are house-pupils; the latter school receives children from two to thirteen years old. A school for young boys in Rio is also under care of the ladies. The language of all the Brazilian schools is Portuguese.

In 1881 the Society entered Mexico, where it has stations at Laredo and Saltillo. The girls' school in the former place enrolls 144, and a boys' school of 39 is self-supporting. The Laredo Band is a missionary society in the church, which has contributed from $40 to $60 in a year. The school for girls at Saltillo closed its first year in December, 1888, having received $282.15 (Mexican) for tuition, which, aside from the missionary's salary, was sufficient to cover expenses. Instruction is given at both stations in day-schools and Sunday-schools.

Harrell Institute, in the Osage Nation, Indian Territory, is also under care of this Society.

**The Woman's Foreign Missionary Society of the Methodist Protestant Church** was organized in Pittsburg, Pa., in 1879. Before that date moneys raised by local societies had been sent to the foreign field through others, especially the Woman's Union Society of New York.

Administration of the affairs of the Society is vested in a General Executive Board, to represent all the branches, and to meet annually—a plan in harmony with the government of the church.

The first representative of the Society abroad died on her way to Japan.

The home force consists of 20 branches, 320 auxiliaries, 60 mission bands, 3,000 to 4,000 membership. Contributions for 1889-90 were $3,566.07.

"The Woman's Missionary Record" is a monthly paper, published at headquarters in Pittsburg, at 50 cents.

Abroad.—This Society has five missionaries, all in Japan. They have a prosperous girls' school at Yokohama, which lately moved into a new and improved home, built at a cost of nearly $6,000, and said to be capable of housing 150 pupils. They have also a station at Nagoya.

The secretary says: "Besides our regular teachers, we have Bible-readers and assistants among the older pupils, who render good service as interpreters and teachers of primary classes. Our Society is one of the youngest, but it is hopeful. With faith and courage we have entered the 'open door,' and in obeying the last command of our blessed Master, we can confidently claim His promise, 'Lo, I am with you alway, even unto the end of the world.'"

**Women's Mite Missionary Society, African Methodist Episcopal Church.** Organized 1874.—The object of this Society is to aid in "the evangelization of the world, and especially the island of Haiti." It is auxiliary to the Missionary Board of the Church, and is centred in Philadelphia, where the officers hold a quarterly meeting.

The Society enrolls 200 auxiliaries. Annual income is about $1,000.

The general work is managed by the missionary secretary of the church, and the funds are chiefly expended on the salaries of missionaries.

**Woman's Boards of the Presbyterian Church (North).**—Woman's Foreign Missionary Society; organized 1870; 1334 Chestnut Street, Philadelphia, Pa. Woman's Board of Missions of the Northwest; organized 1870; Room 48, McCormick Block, Chicago, Ill. Women's Board of Foreign Missions; organized 1870; 53 Fifth Avenue, New York City, N. Y. Woman's Foreign Missionary Society, Northern New York; organized 1871; 232 State Street, Albany, N. Y. Woman's Board of Missions of the Southwest; organized 1877; 1107 Olive Street, St. Louis, Mo. The Occidental Board; organized 1872; 933 Sacramento Street, San Francisco, Cal. Woman's Board of the North Pacific; organized 1888; headquarters, Portland, Ore.

The last of these Boards is constituted for both home and foreign missions, and its territory is Oregon, Idaho, and Puget Sound. Its third contribution sent to the Mission House for the Board of Foreign Missions was in 1889-90, and amounted to $944.92. In the general statements following, this Board only, of the seven named, is not included.

All of these Boards and Societies originated in the enlarged life of the Presbyterian Church after the reunion in 1870. They bear a uniform relation towards the Assembly's Board of Foreign Missions, and though they are "sometimes more aggressive in their enterprise than the Assembly's Board, the first instance is yet to be known in which its decisions have not been cheerfully acceded to. Names and testimonials of missionaries are presented, but no appointment is ever made, no salary is fixed, no field assigned, no apportionment of work adopted, except by the central Board in New York, and this uniform policy is cheerfully acquiesced in."

So the president of one of these Boards, referring to the same relation, has said: "Recognition, co-operation, and courtesy from our 'fathers and brethren' we do indeed desire, and we can truly say 'we have all and abound.' The deliverances of every General Assembly in regard to our work have been uniformly favorable and eulogistic. . . . Our loyalty to the Assembly's Board is unquestioned."

The constituency of these Boards in 1891 is not less than 6,500 auxiliaries and bands. Their united contributions sent to the Mission House in 1889-90 were $280,285.51, besides many special disbursements.

While independent of one another in their home management, these societies unite in the publication of two monthly magazines, both illustrated, and both fully self-supporting.

"Woman's Work for Woman" is a 32-page magazine published from the Mission House at 53 Fifth Avenue, New York, at 60 cents per year. It has a subscription list of 16,000 to 17,000. It publishes the receipts of every auxiliary and band of these Boards, reports their annual meetings, serves as a means of communication between their several headquarters and the auxiliaries, and, especially, keeps the thread of history of the women missionaries of the church and their varied work abroad.

"Children's Work for Children" is a 20-page paper published at 1334 Chestnut Street, Philadelphia, at 35 cents single copies, or 25 cents club rates.

Each of the larger boards publishes thousands of copies of leaflets annually.

Abroad these societies are represented at the opening of 1891 by 305 missionary ladies in active service, besides many missionary wives who co-operate with them as they are able. Of these missionaries eleven are physicians.

The missions are among North American Indians; in Mexico and Guatemala; in Brazil, Colombia, and Chili; in West Africa; in Syria, Persia, India (three missions), Siam and Laos, China (three missions), Japan, and Korea.

I. THE PHILADELPHIA SOCIETY.—At a meeting called in Calvary Church, Philadelphia, May, 1870, a committee was appointed to draft a constitution and submit it to the Assembly's Board of Foreign Missions. This having been duly presented and accepted, "The Woman's Foreign Missionary Society" was formally organized in October of the same year. The president then chosen retained her position until 1890. The aim was to send out and sustain women in the foreign mission field, and support the work which they might be able to develop. At the end of six months the Society enrolled 48 auxiliaries and 30 mission bands, had raised $6,870.35, and assumed the care of 14 missionaries.

The income for 1871 was: $10,000; for 1889-90, "twentieth year," $141,487.88.

The home force in 1890 was: Presbyterial societies, 48; auxiliaries, 1,233; bands, 1,190; total membership (about) 65,000.

Abroad: Missionaries, 141 (of whom 2 are physicians); on furlough, 18; missionaries added during the year, 10; missionaries transferred, 2; missionaries self-supporting, 5; native assistants, 82; missionary teachers, 10; boarding-schools, whole or in part, 33; day schools, 153.

Seven young women are studying medicine preparatory for service under this Society.

The territory covered by this Society is Pennsylvania, New Jersey, Delaware, Maryland, District of Columbia, West Virginia, Tennessee, and all of Ohio except four presbyteries.

II. THE BOARD OF THE NORTHWEST.—This was organized in Chicago by a few ladies, who,

for reasons of expediency alone, withdrew from their Congregational sisters, with whom they were happily associated in labor. At the end of five months the report stood: Auxiliaries, 50; life-members, 24; paid to the treasury, $2,545.85; missionaries adopted, 7.

The home force in 1890 was: Synodical societies, 10; presbyterial societies, 66; auxiliaries, including young people's societies and bands: 1661. Income for 1889-90, $80,643.93.

Abroad: Missionaries, 69, of whom 6 are physicians; hospitals, 4.

"El Faro," an illustrated Christian newspaper in Mexico, is supported.

The name of this Board indicates the territory which it covers. Its eastern boundary is in Ohio.

III. THE NEW YORK BOARD.—This was organized in New York City, under the name of "Ladies' Board of Missions of the Presbyterian Church." Its beginnings were fostered by aid and encouragement from secretaries of the Assembly's Boards of Home and Foreign Missions, to both of which it was at first auxiliary.

At the end of the first year it had 22 auxiliaries in New York City, and 25 in other places; its contributions had amounted to $1,164; and it had assumed the care of eight missionaries, six of whom were abroad.

In 1883 the devoted and honored president, Mrs. Jas. Lorimer Graham, died. To her more than any other was owing the success of the thirteen years previous, and advantageous changes which she had already contemplated were carried into effect that same year. The Home Missions Department was, as a measure of expediency, transferred to the Woman's Synodical Committee of Home Missions, and the original name was changed to Women's Board of Foreign Missions.

Contributions to the Central Treasury, aside from independent disbursements, stood as follows, in the years specified: 1875, $9,907.74; 1880, tenth year, $19,099; 1890, twentieth year, $58,305.27.

The home force in 1890 was: Auxiliaries, 504; young people's societies, 121; bands and contributing Sunday-schools, 358.

The force abroad is represented by 55 missionaries, of whom one is a physician.

Of 100 foreign missionaries who have been for a longer or shorter time connected with this Board, one of the first year, another of the second, and three others of the third year are still in active service. The first treasurer is still gratuitously serving, but the Board was deeply bereaved in 1887 by the death of the second president, Mrs O. P. Hubbard.

The Board occupies the most of New York State and Kentucky, and has certain societies in New Jersey and in New England.

IV. THE BOARD OF NORTHERN NEW YORK.—This covers four presbyteries in the northeastern part of New York State, viz., Albany, Champlain, Columbia, and Troy. Its contributions to the central treasury were as follows, for the years specified: 1872, $1,180.00; 1875, $4,750.00; 1880, $5,740.35.

The home force in 1890 was: Auxiliaries, 96; bands, 100; income for the year, $9,692.35.

Abroad: Missionaries, 4; native pastors, 5; other native assistants, 21; schools and scholarships, 64; besides miscellaneous work.

V. THE BOARD OF THE SOUTHWEST.—This is constituted for both home and foreign missions, and its name denotes the part of the country from which it draws its constituency.

The home force in 1890 was: Auxiliaries, 191; bands, 123. Total membership, 5,461.

They report out of 15,000 Presbyterian Church women in the State of Kansas only 3,016 in their auxiliaries. Receipts for the foreign fund for 1889-90 were $7,102.00. Missionaries, 12 in the foreign field and 12 in the home field.

The event of the year is raising $1,000 for a medical scholarship fund, by which to aid young women to a medical training for the foreign field.

VI. THE OCCIDENTAL BOARD.—This was organized in connection with the Philadelphia society, and maintained the relation until 1889, when they separated in the belief that greater efficiency would result.

The Board has 65 auxiliaries and 70 bands, all within 6 presbyteries. The income for 1889-90 was $9,555.73, an advance of nearly $3,000 upon the year before. An important charge of this Board is a Mission for the Chinese in San Francisco. It includes four departments—a school; a Mission Home at 933 Sacramento Street; the families of girls who have married from the Home—61 in number; and house-to-house visitation, which has been carried on by the same efficient lady for ten years. The Board is represented abroad by 6 missionaries.

Work abroad.—All these Boards and Societies move side by side upon the mission field, and share each new enterprise. They have together built and are running a schooner in West Africa; they have kindergartens at Canton (China), Kanazawa (Japan), São Paulo (Brazil), and other points; they have orphanages at Futtehgurh, Hoshyapore, and Saharanpur (India), and Seoul (Korea); they meet all the expenses connected with their work at home, and pay unappropriated into the treasury of the Assembly's Board five per cent of their receipts, for contingent expenses connected with their special departments. Societies in one Western State contributed $1,000 in 1889 to prevent retrenchment in schools. Several individual ladies support a substitute upon mission ground. The largest legacy ever given to Presbyterian foreign missions was given by a lady, and the total contributions of these societies since the beginning (outside of legacies) have been about four million dollars. Their heaviest responsibilities, however, have not yet been named. They are in the usual departments of woman's work—educational, evangelistic, medical.

*Medical Department.*—China.—Six of the eleven physicians representing the societies are in China, where are also three hospitals for women and children. One of the latter is the Mateer Memorial at Wei Hien, in Shantung, where two ladies have lately taken charge. Another is the Douw Pavilion in Peking, built by one lady; a physician and trained nurse have been in charge here since 1887. The third is a woman's ward in the large Mission Hospital at Canton. Dr. Mary Niles has had charge for about eight years, and has also shared with Dr. Mary H. Fulton the care of several dispensaries. The latter lady has repeatedly tried with her medicine case to open the door for her brother (an ordained missionary) into the unoccupied province of Kwong Sai. They were mobbed out in 1886, but have persevered, and are likely to be rewarded with success.

Persia.—At Teheran there is an annex for women in connection with the Mission Hospital, and a physician went out in the fall of 1889 to assume charge. The Howard Annex for Women, also a lady's gift, has been added to the hospital at Oroomiah. In Tabriz another physician is crowded with dispensary and house visits, aiding surgeons in operations, studying Turkish, and teaching boys to compound drugs.

India.—Dr. Jessica Carleton, unassisted, has a dispensary in the heart of Ambala City in the Punjab, and is medically caring for a leper hospital as well. At Allahabad the dispensary used for 18 years has been replaced by a new building. The physician is ably aided by assistants.

Korea.—In Seoul the lady physician has won goodwill for the mission through her attendance upon the queen, and has practised in country tours.

In several cases societies contribute towards the running expenses of general mission hospitals—as the Westminster at Oroomiah.

There is also a graduated physician among the missionary ladies in Japan, but the jealousy of Japanese doctors has prevented her kind services even among the poor. There are in all the missionary fields other ladies, whose natural gifts and experience make them, though without medical training, useful in administering simple remedies. To one such, in a country-place near Peking, the people knocked their heads on the ground, offering worship as before their idols. Another in Vaga, near Lahore, treated 5,000 cases during ten months of the year 1889.

*Evangelistic Department.*—Bible-women. All missionary ladies living in large cities have opportunity to conduct meetings, teach Sunday-school classes, visit and receive the people in connection with the mission churches. Some of them in addition superintend Bible-women, who are supported from America by salaries of from $36 annually in Canton to $50 or $60 in cities of India. Bible-work is specially developed in Yokohama and Tokyo, where Christian Japanese women presented a Bible to the empress last year; in Petchaburi, Siam; in West Africa; in Central China, especially at Ningpo; at Canton, where are employed twenty Bible-women; but most of all in India.

The memory of one Bible-woman in the Gaboon Mission, Africa, will long be cherished. She could not read, but had a store of Bible-knowledge which she imparted in a quaint and impressive way. She could not write, so she kept a string in which she put knots to indicate the number of meetings held. She died in 1885 "without a stain upon her character."

Mrs. Wilder, a veteran missionary in South India, gives herself to house-to-house visiting, colporteur work, preaching among women, and establishing week-day and Sunday schools. During eight months of 1889 she paid fifty-two visits to villages about Kolhapur City.

About forty Bible-women are employed in the missions in North India.

*Zenana Visiting.*—A young missionary fell heir to 80 zenanas at her entrance upon service at Futtehgurh a few years ago. It was well she was a missionary child, with an Indian tongue already acquired. One of the evangelists of the Furrukhabad Mission, Miss Belz, has been in service 17 years. "In eleven months," said her last report, "I have paid 309 visits to villages, been in 106 zenanas, superintended zenana schools in towns and villages, attended 12 *mèlas*, and 107 days I devoted to work in the city of Etawah.

In North India there are four strictly "zenana visitors," and many ladies who give more or less time to such work in Lahore, Mainpuri, Furrukhabad, Lodiana, Jhansi, Dehra, and other cities. At Vaga, near Lahore, Miss Thiede, who has given 17 years to India, does itinerant work chiefly among a great group of surrounding villages. The Lodiana Mission lately called for 15 women to devote themselves to evangelistic work alone.

Itinerating is a form of labor in which many wives engage with their husbands, and many teachers devote a part of their vacations in this way.

Miss Cort, who has been 15 years in Petchaburi, is the only lady in the Siam Mission sent expressly for evangelistic work. She oversees 12 day-schools, builds school-houses, directs Bible-women, makes systematic country trips, keeps Sunday-school and temperance and missionary societies going, and is ready to hold a meeting with women any time and anywhere.

In Japan, while over 20 ladies are devoting themselves to schools, none are appointed particularly to the department under consideration, but here and there one has made some time for it. At Takata, 250 miles from Tokyo, a school for girls, two large Sunday-schools, and other means have been used to open the city to the gospel, and it has been done by lady teachers of Tokyo, who have exiled themselves for months together from sight of a European face, for the sake of what they could do in Takata.

In Africa several ladies give their entire time to such labors, and boat journeys and visits to the river towns are a prominent feature in their reports.

One lady at Tabriz, Persia, one at Oroomiah, a third at Salmas (having 30 villages), each give their attention to superintending schools, to visits among out-stations, or to classes of women and children.

In South China but few ladies have taken tours into the provinces. The largest share of itinerant work in China is done in Shantung. A number of ladies living in Chefoo, Che-nan-foo, Tungchow, and Wei Hien have devoted a great deal of time and strength in touring with their husbands. One of the number spent the first three months of 1889 in unremitting labor among the heartrending scenes of the famine district. She and her husband alone administered relief to 6,000 persons on their regular list, besides special cases. Other ladies shared the same work for a shorter period. The large number of Chinese women who are members of the country churches of this mission have generally heard the glad tidings from the lips of missionary ladies.

*Schools.*—The societies maintain scholarships in a large number of boys' schools; build some school-houses for them; pay the salaries of many teachers in their day-schools; and a few missionary ladies teach only boys and young men, as Miss McBeth, who trains a theological class of Nez Percés in Idaho.

But by far the largest item of expenditure in the Society's accounts is girls' schools. A hundred missionaries are devoting their lives to the boarding-school. In most cases it is carried on by two together; in some instances several teachers are required.

A background of time is necessary in order to mark the influence of an institution upon a whole people, and this condition is supplied in the history of the Oroomiah Seminary in Persia. Fidelia Fiske opened it in 1844 with six wild little girls. After sixteen years of labor, just before returning to America, 93 women sat down with her at the table of our Lord. Fifty years ago there was not a woman in Oroomiah who could read. When this mission celebrated its semi-centennial in July, 1885, an eye-witness said: "The attendance of nearly 800 Nestorian women, the most quiet and attentive part of the audience, was the most impressive feature of the occasion. In response to the request that the readers among the women should rise, fully three fourths of them rose to their feet." Contrast the "decorum" and "suitable modest dress" of that multitude of women" with their appearance thirty years before, as described by one who lived among them: "If they [the missionary ladies] met the women in large companies they acted like unruly mobs or herds of Bashan, violent enough to frighten gentle ladies; and there was never one single thing attractive or lovely in these coarse women."

Of the first two untutored little girls whom Mar Yohanan led to Miss Fiske's knee with the words, "They are your daughters: no man shall take them out of your hand," one, now a woman of dignified presence and gifted pen, the wife of priest Oshana, was in that jubilee audience.

These Nestorian women, who have been educated in the seminary, hold large quarterly meetings in villages on Oroomiah Plain, when several hundred of them, with a chairman of their own and a literary and devotional programme before them, spend a day together in prayer and worship and discussion, with original essays and evangelistic plans. At such a meeting Oshana's wife gave reminiscences which another present reported for "Rays of Light" (a fortnightly publication to which Nestorian women often contribute), and which filled several columns, closing with the simple words, "These things said our sister Sarra."

Thirty-three boarding-schools for girls are maintained by the societies, in each case occupying property owned by them, and generally in buildings erected for the purpose.

Three of these schools are for Spanish-speaking girls—at Bogotá in Colombia, Mexico City, and Saltillo, Mexico. The latter took possession of a new building in 1890, and that at Mexico City was enlarged and re-dedicated in 1889, when it had forty house-pupils, all over twelve years of age.

A school for Portuguese-speaking girls at São Paulo, Brazil, is limited by its accommodation to thirty house-pupils, but "we could easily double the number." Writing in September, 1889, of the graduates, their teacher says: "Four have charge of departments, eight are assistant teachers, and several more are teaching evangelical schools in the country."

The pupils here recite in connection with large day-schools of both boys and girls under superintendence of a gentleman of the mission.

In Syria are three important boarding-schools for Arabic speaking girls—at Beirut, Tripoli, and Sidon. In the first of these there are 75 in the upper department, two thirds of whom pay full tuition, or $60 per year. In religion they are Greeks, Greek Catholics, Maronites, Moslems, Armenians, Jews, Druzes, and Protestants.

At Tripoli, with but about 20 house-pupils there are 100 day-scholars. Income for tuition in 1888 was $200. Six girls united with the church in May, 1889. Sidon school has nearly 50 boarders, and a good record of contributions and graduates at work.

In Persia, the oldest school is for Nestorians or Syriac-speaking girls, at Oroomiah. At Tabriz and Salmas they are chiefly Armenian-speaking. The children, as they come in their raw state to the latter and smaller of the schools, are described:

"Little girls would come without the remotest idea of sitting still: one minute they would be quiet, book in hand; the next they would be out in the yard or part way home. When we closed, all had learned to sit still and seldom even whispered. Advertising cards should have the credit of most of this, for the children would often cry if they had not been good enough to get a picture."

At Teheran six languages are spoken; the nationalities being represented by Armenians, Jewesses, Mohammedans, and Fire-worshippers. Early Sunday-morning prayer-meeting, woman's meeting at sunset on Saturday, and school-girls teaching in Sunday-school are prominent features here. Equally prominent is the industry cultivated. Besides all kinds of housework, to which the girls are trained, 900 articles of clothing or housekeeping outfit, including some 2,500 button holes, were all the product of their needles during two summer months of 1889.

At Hamadan the Faith Hubbard School, with 40 house-members, is swelled to more than 100 by day-scholars. The girls are Armenian, Jew, and Moslem, speaking chiefly the former tongue. Three learned the whole Gospel by Mark in 1889. The school is a centre of evangelistic influences. Conversions take place in all the Persia schools. More is done for Jews at Oroomiah and Hamadan than at any other stations in the Presbyterian Missions.

In India there is a flourishing school called Woodstock, near Landour, among the Himalayas. It is not for native girls, but for missionary children, American or European, and for Eurasians. The school supports current expenses, aside from missionary salaries. Five American ladies are teachers, and the standard is high. The language is English. At Dehra and Allahabad are large schools, and at Kolhapur, in the south, a smaller one, for native Christian girls. At the latter they speak Marathi; in the others, Hindustani. Eight native teachers assist the missionary in charge at Dehra. At the close of 1888 the teacher said: "During the last four and a half years we have put 24 girls into mission work. Some of them are married; all are doing well."

In the Siamese Peninsula there are two schools, conducted wholly in Siamese. At Bangkok the needle department brings in favor and money, and they have ceased to give clothes to pupils, and are trying to require tuition. In 1888 the girls contributed about $76 for benevolent purposes.

At Petchaburi the girls grind the rice in the mill, and the governor sends his daughters. At Chieng Mai, in the Laos, both Siamese and Laos are spoken. They have about 50 house-pupils, and the year 1889 was marked by a delightful work of grace, 18 joining the church during one term.

In China the principal schools are at Canton, Ningpo, Shanghai, Nanking, Chefoo, Tungchow, Wei Hien, and Peking. There is general difficulty with bound feet, and some children are sent home, as from Shanghai, because they will not consent to unbind them. The children in these schools commit to memory with facility, and get a store of chapters and hymns. At Nanking a class of eight little girls lately could each recite 2,000 verses of Scripture. Many of the pupils have become Christians.

At Ningpo, eight united with the church in 1888-89, four at Shanghai, and eight at Nanking. There are four departments at Canton: woman's training-school, upper class of girls, primary grade, and kindergarten—about 125 pupils in all, of whom 22 united with the church in 1889. Thirty day-schools cluster about this institution.

In Japan the schools are at Tokyo, Osaka, Kanazawa, and Sapporo. At the last-named, one lady alone has kept her school, and taught besides in a government school for young men. In 1889 she saw 13 of her girls confess Christ. From Kanazawa "all the boarding-scholars went home Christians" in 1889. At Osaka 15 were baptized the same year, making 43 in the seven years' history of the school. It asks for no scholarships, and pays current expenses outside the salaries of two American and two Japanese teachers. Two schools in Tokyo were consolidated in 1890, and erected several new buildings. More than 500 children in two day-schools under Japanese control (at Yokohama and Tokyo) are under the instruction and influence of the missionaries.

There is a school for girls also in the capital of Korea, and several schools among the North American Indians.

Except in Korea, where missions are yet new, and in Japan, where the common-schools are under control of government, all the missions of these societies embrace day-schools. There are many in India and China, but the number is proportionally greatest in Syria and Western Persia, each of which has more than 100. The cost of maintaining one in Syria is from $100 to $200 annually, and in the village schools of Persia a scholarship runs from $10 to $32. In those cases where they are supported by the Woman's Boards, these sums are raised, not necessarily by apportioning an entire school to an auxiliary, but the salary of a teacher will be assigned to one, the rent of school-room to another, a pupil's tuition to a third, so as to bring a share of the good work within the reach of even weak societies and bands of young children. These missions have now so many branches, and the business of subdividing the expense of each into shares and assigning them to societies has become so taxing, that a special secretary has been appointed at the Mission House in New York to have it in charge. The sum which the Assembly's Board asks of these societies, and which they aim to raise in 1890-91, is $310,000.

***The Woman's Board of Foreign Missions of the Reformed (Dutch) Church in America*** was organized in New York City in 1875. Its business is conducted by thirty managers elected annually, and from them the officers and executive committee are taken. The president first elected still holds the position.

At the end of three years the Board had 52 auxiliaries, and had raised over $10,000.

At the end of seven years there were 129 auxiliaries, and in that year alone receipts were $10,000. In 1889 there were 263 auxiliaries. Contributions amounted in 1890 to $27,932.37. The "Mission Gleaner" is self-supporting, a bi-monthly of sixteen pages, published at 25 cents per year, from headquarters, 26 Reade Street, New York.

Abroad.—There are 35 missionaries, of whom 12 are unmarried. They are in Japan; at Amoy, China; and in the Madras presidency, India.

The oldest and most distinguished institution of the Board is Ferris Seminary for Girls, at Yokohama, Japan. The principal here, one of the gentlemen of the mission, is assisted by his wife and several young lady teachers. In 1889 there were 134 house-pupils, of whom 47 were baptized Christians, and half as many more waited their parents' consent to be baptized. In June the same year an enlargement of the building was dedicated. It is called Van Schaick Hall, and includes chapel, reception-room, dining-room, class rooms, and general accommodation for 120 pupils. The Japanese subscribed $1,200 towards the cost of this hall, $750 of it having been obtained through the indefatigable efforts of the Japanese matron of the school.

It is the endeavor to make Ferris Seminary, as far as possible, self-supporting, and a fee of $3.50 per month covers the Japanese part of the expense.

The girls have sewing-classes, the older ones making their own and their little sisters' clothing, and the younger ones darning beautifully.

The first graduate of the school became one of its valued teachers, until her recent marriage to a gentleman of Tokyo, who has long been interested in the higher education of his country-women.

At Nagasaki is a new boarding-school, Sturges Seminary. Of 20 house-pupils in 1889, 14 were Christian workers. All the pupils study Japanese and Chinese, and receive regular instruction in cooking and sewing.

At Morioka, Japan, one of the ladies, assisted by a young Japanese, edits a monthly paper, "Glad Tidings," which requires an edition of 3,000 copies.

At Amoy, China, is a boarding-school for girls connected with Christian families. The average annual expense for a pupil, outside salaries of American teachers, is brought within $15. The girls are all taught needlework and cooking.

The Charlotte Duryea Bible School for Women, also in Amoy, has twenty-four women in attendance; and both Amoy schools are in care of two ladies, who by relieving each other are able to also teach patients in the hospital, itinerate among country churches, and supervise several Bible-women.

A monthly newspaper, the "Church Messenger," is edited in the Romanized colloquial by a lady of the mission, and has a circulation of about 700, at a cost of a cent per copy.

The nine missionaries of the Arcot Mission in India are at six different stations; eight of the ladies are named Scudder. Girls' boarding-schools are at Vellore and Madanapalle, at each of which five pupils united with the church in 1889. There are 9 high-caste girls' schools in the India Mission, and the numbers of pupils are generally large, as at Vellore, 119; at Chittoor, 120. Parents who pay to send their boys to school in this district will object to pay for their girls. "It is only with a great amount of persuasion that we can get them to give even as much as ten or fifteen cents a month for the education of their girls." There are 97 village schools in the mission. A late report mentions a Bible-reader at Chittoor, who explained the Scriptures to over 1,600 of her sisters in the year. Zenana visiting is done at different stations. The Board employs about fifty native assistants. The societies have been recently raising funds to assist a mission hospital at Sio-khe, sixty miles from Amoy.

*The Woman's Board of Foreign Missions of the Cumberland Presbyterian Church* was not organized until 1880, but already the complaint is made that the church as a whole is far behind the women of the church in zeal and offerings. In 1889 from twenty-nine presbyteries more money was sent to the Woman's Board of Foreign Missions than to the Church Board of Missions—both home and foreign. Those who have taken pains to find out these facts publish them in no spirit of rebuke to the societies, for they say at the same time : "Not that the women did too much, but the church did not do enough."

The home force in 1890 was : Auxiliaries 793, membership 9,770 ; young ladies' societies 8, membership 130 ; children's bands 138 ; membership 1,741.

Their contributions for the year amounted to $9,117.35.

Headquarters are at Evansville, Indiana, and work of the Board is represented in a department of "The Missionary Record," published monthly at St. Louis. They also print a child's paper, "The Missionary Banner."

Abroad.—The Board has eight missionaries in Japan, located at Osaka, Nagoya, Shingu, and other places.

The Wilmena Girls' School at Osaka was opened in 1885; the building was destroyed by fire in 1888, but immediately replaced by a better. The boarding-pupils reported in 1889 were 22, of whom 10 were supported by foreign funds.

Nagoya was opened to the mission through one of the ladies who is teaching Bible and industrial classes there. Another lady itinerates between the stations, and was at Wakayama when the flood wrecked the church there in the summer of 1889. Two sisters joined the mission at the opening of 1890.

The Board has contributed to the Mexico Mission at different times, and recently appropriated $1,500 to that field, and is now asked by the mission to assume charge of a school at San Pedro. It also has Hogan Institute in Indian Territory. The pupils are whites and half-breeds.

*The Woman's General Missionary Society of the United Presbyterian Church* was organized in 1883, and the same year attained to 335 congregational societies, some of which had already been in existence for fifty years.

In 1889 their home force stood : Presbyterial societies, 45; congregational societies, 737; membership, 18,687. The Society is constituted for both home and foreign missions. The contributions to the latter were as follows for the years named : 1883, $7,546 ; 1885, $10,177 ; 1888, $15,619 ; 1889, $16,704.

WOMAN'S WORK FOR WOMAN

"The Women's Missionary Magazine" is published monthly at Xenia, Ohio. Price, 60c.

Abroad there are twenty missionaries, all single ladies, besides co-operating missionary wives. The missions of this church are in Egypt, and in Sialkot, India, and the missionaries are all located among five stations in each mission.

The recent event in India is the establishment of a Memorial Hospital at Sialkot, for which the societies raised $5,000 in 1888. The institution is in charge of Dr. Maria White, who during her first three years in India treated 12,000 patients at her dispensary and paid more than 900 visits to houses, and dispensed medicine in thirty different villages. "These poor, suffering ones," she says, "constantly ply me with questions: 'What did you come to India for?' 'Who sent you?' Then I tell them of the love of Christ, who can see how they suffer, and that He has commanded us to come and help them. This answer almost always brings forth the remark: 'Your God must be a very kind, good God to send a doctor to the women; none of our gods ever sent us a doctor. Tell us more about your God.' And so the way before us opens up, and we try to make them feel that it is God alone who makes the medicine give them relief."

The societies are asked to raise $600 annually for current expenses of the hospital. There is a girls' boarding-school of about 50 at Sialkot, of whom less than a dozen are supported by their friends. The rest depend on scholarships provided in America at $25 apiece. There is room for zenana work and itinerating in this mission. At Jhelum a Bible-woman has 100 houses, and "plenty to do. We have to coax them to make them hear us. It is all by hard persuasion."

The ladies of the mission have entreated the Society to send them three missionaries at once as an absolute necessity. The mission has been lately affected by the approaches of Roman Catholics upon their fold.

The missionaries in Egypt are located at four stations, and there are excellent boarding-schools in their care at Assiout, Cairo, and Alexandria. In the latter are many Jewesses, and the pupils are praised for their pronunciation of Arabic. At a prize-giving both Mohammedans and Copts will lend their presence. In accordance with the principles of the mission, the girls of these schools "are not only daily taught a Bible lesson, but to use the needle in both plain sewing and fancy-work, to cut and make clothes of all kinds used by their people, to wash and iron, scrub and cook, make beds and clean house. In fact, it is the purpose of the ladies in charge to teach them home work and economy." It is also the purpose to train teachers and zenana visitors.

Women's missionary societies among the Christians in Cairo and Assiout have taught the people to give for the Lord's work. In 1888 four such societies had an aggregate membership of 217, and had contributed the previous year $165 for missions. Of one Society, that at Boulak, in Cairo, the missionary wrote: "We have many young children who contribute two and a half cents per month. Some of them earn money by sale of fancy-work, or by money saved from the amount allowed them for luncheon. One of our contributors was a slave-woman, but has obtained her freedom. She takes in sewing in addition to daily labor as a servant, and contributes five cents per month."

The schools between Alexandria and the first cataract of the Nile number about 70, and include from 5,000 to 6,000 pupils. More than 50 of these schools are entirely supported by the Coptic people. The ladies of the mission long for additions to their force in order to permit the more experienced of them to itinerate among villages of the Nile valley. They repeat the inquiry of one woman: "Is it God's will that we must live on year after year, and no one to preach to us or show us how to live?" The missionary asked intelligent women in Upper Egypt if they went to hear the helper preach, to which they replied, "The meetings are held in a room where there is no place for us. On Sabbaths we go and sit on the roof of an adjoining house, from which we can hear the preaching."

The name of Mrs. Sarah B. Lansing, who lately went to her reward, has been for thirty years inseparably associated with the good work of this mission.

*Woman's Work of the Presbyterian Church (South).*—There is no Woman's Board of Missions in this church, but congregational societies directly auxiliary to the Foreign Missions Committee of General Assembly have been quietly forming for fifteen years. There were 537 such societies in 1889, being 78 more than contributed the year before. Two presbyterial societies have also been organized. In 1888 there were reported 150 children's societies, whose contributions aggregated $5,179.41.

The General Assembly of 1889 recommended the formation of foreign missionary societies in all the churches, although an overture was presented from one presbytery offering arguments against their formation, and deprecating "ladies' presbyterial unions." The Executive Committee of Foreign Missions informally approves the societies, and the women of the church are further heartened to go forward by the outspoken confidence of the secretaries. "For our part," says the organ of the church, "The Missionary," "we think the ladies deserve all encouragement. Let a society be organized in every church; let the representatives of these societies come together in presbyterial unions to devise means by which the life and enterprise of the societies may be best maintained. We are not afraid the ladies will do too much."

The contributions of the auxiliaries were, from January, 1890, to January, 1891, $30,567.61.

There are about 1,800 churches in which no auxiliary as yet exists.

Abroad the missionary ladies number 39, of whom about half are unmarried. They are in Mexico, Brazil, China, Japan, Greece, and Italy. The Brazil Mission was afflicted in 1889 with the yellow-fever pestilence, especially at Campinas, the largest of the six stations. Schools and evangelistic work were much interrupted, the health of several ladies suffered so as to compel a furlough, and, for the first time in 18 years, death visited the station, taking a little child and a gifted ordained young man, "the flower of the mission." Ten missionaries in China are in four cities of a chain of stations on the Grand Canal, of which Hangchow is the southern terminus. It is also the oldest station, having been opened in 1867. There is a boarding-school here of about fifty girls, besides day-schools, in charge of one lady. Another itinerates in many villages and towns outlying, walking to some of them and going by boat to others. She directs Bible-women, also visits in the city, and dispenses medicine. By the last means she has won admission to many homes otherwise closed against her. "She has been encouraged in finding that the truth taught to a class of fifty girls some eight or ten years ago has not been entirely forgotten. She has come across them in different parts of the city, in the suburbs and villages, and finds that many of them still know the Ten Commandments, can tell the miracles and parables of Christ, and above all they remember that "there is none other Name under heaven given among men whereby we must be saved." One of these fifty girls within the last year made hopeful profession of faith in Christ, and died trusting in Him as her only Saviour."

In the temporary absence of this missionary in America, another, borrowed from Soochow to fill her place, writes urgently for physicians, "both men and women," for this field.

At Soochow the central feature of woman's work is the Woman's Home, which was occupied by missionaries at the close of 1888. On the same lot with the Home is a chapel, reception-room, and school-room for use of Chinese women.

Miss Safford, who had been connected with this station for seventeen years, died in 1890. She spent the greater part of the last two years of her life in revising and superintending the printing of her series of Chinese books. She also added two new works to the series, viz., "Talks about Anatomy and Physiology," and a "Primer of Physiology," translated from the Mandarin. These raise the number of volumes in the series to ten. They are popular books, not only in the schools of this mission, but in other missions, and have been requested for publication in several dialects.

In the midst of the riot which occurred in 1889 at Chinkiang, 120 miles above Soochow, while property of other missions was destroyed, that of this mission was left undisturbed, owing in part to its location.

The newest station is Tsing-kiang-fu, 140 miles north of Chinkiang. The wife of a missionary here received 700 visits from Chinese women during the year, to all of whom she told something of the Saviour before they left. It is hoped to have a Woman's Home here, and through it open a channel of influence to the crowds of burdened women.

There are but two stations occupied in Japan, Nagoya and Kochi, in both of which there is teaching done in day-schools and in classes of women.

One lady has long aided her husband in Salonica, in Macedonia, a city of 130,000, where the only evangelical preaching for the Greeks is in the little mission chapel.

Another lady has taught a school in Milan, Italy, for twenty years, under the auspices of this church committee.

Information about these missions is to be obtained from the headquarters at Nashville, Tenn., and through the pages of "The Missionary," which devotes a department to woman's work.

**Woman's Baptist Foreign Missionary Society (North).**—Woman's Foreign Missionary Society; organized 1871; Tremont Temple, Boston, Mass. Woman's Foreign Missionary Society of the West; organized 1871; 122 Wabash Avenue, Chicago, Ill. Woman's Foreign Missionary Society of California; organized 1875. Woman's Foreign Missionary Society of Oregon; organized 1888.

The appeals contained in letters written in 1869 and 1870 by a missionary wife in Bassein, Burma, led directly to the organization of the first of these societies. These letters pictured the missionary and his wife sinking under their burdens; the sacrifices of Karen Christians to provide school facilities; the large number of girls at Bassein, and the tempting opportunities to teach the women. The writer begged for unmarried women, of whom there were only four in the Burma Missions; and "I am not sure," she wrote, "that you have not a work to do in forming women's societies, auxiliary to the Missionary Union. I believe that is the true course."

A few ladies in Newton Centre, Mass., acted upon this suggestion and called a general meeting of Baptist women in Boston, April, 1871. Two hundred responded, and accepted the constitution which was presented; and in the following December their first missionary was on her way to Burma. At the end of the first year they had: Missionaries, 6; auxiliaries, 141; receipts, $9,172.63. Fifth year: Missionaries, 18; schools, 20; auxiliaries, 750; mission bands, 80; receipts, $33,260.69. Tenth year: Missionaries, 40; Bible-women, 47; schools, 78; receipts, $50,010.91. Report for 1889, the eighteenth year: Income, $70,666.83; circles or contributing churches from ten States and the District of Columbia, 1,377; children's bands, 644. Total membership about 42,000.

Abroad: Missionaries, 51, of whom 2 are physicians; Bible women, 56; schools, 154; pupils, 5,212.

THE SOCIETY OF THE WEST was organized in Chicago only one month later than that in Boston, and they too had a missionary for Burma the next December. This lady met the committee the very day of the great Chicago fire, and her outfit was burned up at the depot. The Society at the East immediately provided for the loss, and the lady went her way with joy. Receipts for the first year were $4,244.69; auxiliaries, 131. Fourth year, receipts reported were $11,105.

Record for 1889.—Home force: Circles, 1,321; young people's guilds, 209; bands, 294; total, 1,824; receipts, $33,722.09.

Abroad: Five new missionaries during the year, making in all 30, of whom 2 are physicians; Bible-women, 43; and 1,500 pupils in schools.

Both the Eastern and Western Societies aid in supporting a Home for Missionary Children at Newton, Mass. "The Helping Hand" is the organ of these two societies. It is published monthly in Boston. Price, 35 cents. "The King's Messengers" is a children's paper, at 25 cents.

THE SOCIETY OF CALIFORNIA was organized in San Francisco, and receipts for the first ten months were nearly $300.

In 1889 they sent contributions to the treasury of the Union amounting to $1,012.20. They maintain three missionaries.

THE SOCIETY IN OREGON sent to the central treasury in 1889 $1,599.83, and is represented by one missionary.

Total number of missionaries under care of

all these societies is eighty-five. The following facts regarding the missions are given without reference to the separate societies, as their work is all part and parcel of one whole.

The missionaries are located in the fields of the A. B. M. U.: in Burma, Assam, Southeast India, Siam, China, Japan, and Africa. The six missions in Burma are conducted in six languages, and 90 per cent of the missionary force are women.

Of the schools, 26 are for the Burmans. One of the largest is a girls' boarding-school at Rangoon with 160* pupils, of whom their teacher says that though all do not become witnessing Christians, they lose faith in idols after a year in school. They are not baptized without their parents' consent, but baptisms take place from time to time.

At Moulmein is a similar school of 110 girls: "No free pupils admitted; all furnish their own books and clothes." There are also an Eurasian and a Karen school, for girls, in each of these cities.

In a day-school at Myingyan, "the boys, besides buying their books, pay one rupee per month tuition; girls, eight annas."

Mandalay has recently passed through great trials, in the death of a missionary at the head of her prosperous school and the destruction of property by fire.

The largest of the Karen schools is at Bassein, where nearly 400 pupils were in the midst of a prosperous term (in 1888-89) when an epidemic scattered them to their homes. Of 72 house-pupils most are professing Christians. One of the teachers here has been 22 years in the service. The teacher at Maubin says: "In accordance with our custom, all boarders have regularly devoted two hours daily to manual labor. The girls, besides doing the necessary work about the house, have woven many yards of cloth. The boys have completed a new fence, and rendered assistance in the erection of their new dormitory."

The missionary lady at Toungoo reports: "We have one Red Karen village on the plains near town, which is composed almost entirely of heathen families that have come down from Karenee to avoid persecution for witchcraft, and to be allowed to worship the true God. We have a large school in this village, and my husband reports the Sunday-school wide-awake, and very much interested. In the day-school grown men and women sit beside the little tots, all learning their letters together."

Among the Karens "jungle schools" are much heard of. Their teachers have been trained in the boarding-schools. Some of the missionaries alternate teaching school with jungle trips, when their work presents all the evangelistic elements known in other lands. One of these ladies is mentioned in the last report, who spent a vacation of two months in this way, visiting fifteen villages, and her helpers nine or ten others. "In most places we were well received, and had interesting meetings every evening when the people were at leisure to attend, sometimes the crowd remaining late after the regular meeting to hear the singing and glad tidings. Many of these Karens said they never heard God's Word before, never saw a white woman, nor even a Christian Karen before. Some begged me to come again so they could learn more, and be able to enter this religion, which seemed so good."

It is said of the Bghai Karen pupils in the schools, that 85 per cent have been converted. At Henzada is a Karen school of 165 pupils, where 15 girls kept their pledge to abstain from smoking. In a village sixteen miles out, the first day-school was opened in 1889, and the young Karen woman teaching it was paid a monthly salary of seven rupees ($2.50) by the Henzada Karen Woman's Missionary Society. "This devoted young woman has done such good work, that the children and young people are urging their parents not to work on Sunday, and not to observe heathen practices, but to become Christians."

There are also schools for Shans and Ch'ins, and at Bhamo, the most northern station of Upper Burma, a neat little bamboo school-house, and a school for Kach'ins, where they teach English and sewing, and read Burmese books, as there are none in Kach'in.

Two ladies in Burma have been correcting proof—the one of the revised Burmese Bible, the other of the recent Shan translation.

Among the Telugus in India is one of the largest and best known missions of the Baptist Church, and many missionaries' wives are very active; but at the opening of 1890 the force of unmarried ladies was reduced to five. One of these, a physician at Ramapatam, reports more evangelistic than medical work.

At Nellore one lady superintends several schools and translates hymns into Telugu for the children; another directs an industrial work, which brought in (last report) 1,100 rupees for sewing, knitting, and crocheting. She has charge of six Bible-women. One of these she describes as an "earnest worker and fearless talker." "She forgets herself entirely, and the other women complain that when they are all out she often forgets the time, and they go without food till very late. The preachers recognize the good the women do, and often ask for them." Bible-women are a feature at all the Telugu stations.

At Ongole are caste schools; at Madras, caste schools again, and zenana visitation; at Kurnool, 300 miles from Madras, in a population of 20,000, there is no mission work for women. A lady from Madras describes her first approaches to these women, who were shy, and ran away from her: "One evening it was to a dozen women, who were bringing home great loads of firewood, and sat down to rest by the roadside; . . . another evening we walked down a street, and talked to the people as they were weaving mats at their own doors. . . . Every Sunday since we have been here, from thirty to fifty have come in, most of them from a village nine miles distant, but quite a number as far as eighteen miles, and they walked. Two Sundays, twenty came from a place called Atmakur, forty miles away. Seven of these were women, two of whom carried infants in their arms. The Christians here, and even some who have not been baptized, every Sunday brought a quarter or half anna each. Some who had no money brought vegetables or grain."

Village schools swarm around Cumbum and Udayagiri, and at the latter place parents are more willing to send their girls to school than the boys—a singular exception to the rule in India.

---

* These figures, and all those given by these societies, include day-scholars.

In Assam woman's work is emphasized at Nowgong, Gauhati, and Tura. In the girls' boarding-school at the latter place all but six out of thirty-seven Garo pupils were confessing Christians at the date of the last report. Nearly all are of the second generation of Christians. One lady here devotes herself to the normal school for young men.

At Gauhati the missionary reported a woman's meeting which she conducted in connection with the Association of Native Christians held in that city. "Fifty-eight were present. I called for reports of the mission circles organized last year, and all said they had enjoyed their prayer-meetings and given their pice, and all expressed a desire to continue the circles."

Very difficult touring is done in the Assam field.

In China the societies have a history chiefly at Swatow and Ningpo. Two young ladies were sent in 1889 to Kinhwa-fu, 250 miles from Ningpo, where they use the Mandarin dialect.

A leading spirit for the last twenty years at Swatow has been Miss Adele M. Fielde, with her trained Bible-women, of whom fourteen are mentioned in the last report. They are not selected from those offering themselves, but are sought out and invited for their adaptation and Christian character, and then trained and superintended with remarkable thoroughness. The annual report of the Missionary Union for 1874 says: "Miss Fielde has a cottage for her own use, and a house for her Bible-women, which will contain good class-rooms and accommodations for thirty persons while they are studying here." These women are sent out two by two from 50 to 60 miles from Swatow, to the country stations, at each of which there are rooms provided for them in connection with the chapel. From the stations they go forth to pagan hamlets, of which there are always 20 or 30 within a few miles. Sometimes they stay several days in a village, lodging with a friendly heathen. "Once a year," says their instructor, "all the Bible-women return to the school-house in Swatow for about three months' continuous study of the Bible. Perpetual contact with heathenism benumbs their conscience, and they need the quickening influence of a new view of their Lord." These Bible-women receive $2.00 per month and travelling expenses. They eat and dress as poorly as the women to whom they go, and suffer much exposure and fatigue.

Miss Fielde's literary labors have been important. She assisted in the translation of the Scriptures into the Swatow dialect, and prepared a time-saving dictionary, besides other undertakings. Failure in health obliged her to retire from Swatow and return to America in the summer of 1890.

The educational work around Swatow is carried on vigorously. From the two departments of the boys' boarding-school fees were received for 1887–1890 respectively, $32.00, $68.00, $83.50.

The features at Ningpo are a boarding-school of 40 girls, day-school, Bible-women, and country work. A glimpse of the latter is given in the last report: "The usual three boats left our jetty to scatter the seed broadcast amidst the heathen devotees, thirteen native women in two boats, while I occupied the third. All the

women did excellent work. It did my heart good to see them witness for Christ, though but a handful amongst the crowds. It is a hard trip, and on the following Sunday many of the women told me they were in bed two days after it."

In Japan the societies have seven missionaries, some of whom are fresh arrivals, while one lady has given thirteen years of service there. The stations are Yokohama and Tokyo, and the ladies are occupied with girls' schools and Bible instruction. "All the ladies regretted that our Society had not been more aggressive in the matter of schools, and thought it a great pity that we had not a single boys' school in the country." (From "Helping Hand," January, 1890.)

The first missionaries of the societies, to the Congo, went in 1887. Seven are on the field—at Lukungu and Palabala. They have had the experiences of pioneers. "One morning they took the tent down before I got my hair combed, and when I turned round, all the carriers of one caravan were drawn up in a circle, watching me with awe-struck faces. I believe they were afraid of my hair. I am the only woman up country with long hair."

The name of the hill on which their house at Palabala was built meant "hill of death"—a reminiscence of the time when condemned witches suffered here; but in the new state of things, the king, though not a good man, has requested to have the name changed, "as it is no more a hill of death, but life." One of the missionaries, from whom the people in a new place at first ran away, stayed a few days among them, and "they flocked to her tent to hear more of the 'wonderful words of life.' When she first read God's Word to them in their own language, some ran screaming away, greatly alarmed to know that their own language could be talked from a book. They had never heard such a thing before. They plead with her to remain with them, and teach them."

The ladies at Lukungu are sheltering the nucleus of a girls' home, and teaching 75 children in three classes. Some of the boys have been already received into the church.

The societies support Bible-women in France, Sweden, and Russia.

At the meeting of the Boston Board of Directors in December, 1889, the secretary announced that she had requests "for ten ladies and six medical missionaries, all of which must wait until a deeper consecration in our churches shall greatly enlarge our resources."

*The Woman's Missionary Society of the Free Baptist Church.*—In 1873 the missionaries of this church in India, sadly weakened by sickness and death, appealed to the women at home. Before they called, the answer had been framed, at the yearly meeting held in Sandwich, New Hampshire, in June, that same year. They had met in convention and organized the Woman's Missionary Society. The Board selects and supports its own missionaries.

Home work is carried on among the freedmen at Harper's Ferry and on the frontier.

The home force reported in December, 1889, was: Auxiliaries, 273, besides about 30 quarterly meetings which gave no report of auxiliaries. Receipts, $5,686.57.

Abroad.—The Board has stations at Midnapore, and Balasore, near Calcutta, India, and supports four missionaries in full, besides aiding other ladies sent out by the church.

The Sinclair Orphanage at Balasore was the gift of one gentleman and his wife in New Hampshire. It shelters about forty girls. There is also a day-school here for Christian girls, and seven Hindu girls' schools in the city and its suburbs. Eleven zenana teachers are employed.

Seven Bible-women itinerate through the region about Balasore. They visited 178 villages in 1888-89, and through them a number of women have been received into the church. As one of these said, it was " the love in the hearts of the teachers" that first led her to think about Christianity. The support of most of these Bible-women is given by the Indian Female Normal School and Instruction Society of England.

A large ragged school is located at Midnapore, and a girls' English school; while Bible-women and zenana visitation are features at this station.

***Woman's Missionary Union Auxiliary to Southern Baptist Convention.***—The first Woman's Mission Societies were organized in 1884. They were congregational only, and adopted no common constitution until the appointment of the executive committee, who held their first meeting in Memphis, Tenn., in 1889. The societies are auxiliary to both the Home and Foreign Boards of the Convention, and in their constitution expressly disclaim " all intention of independent action." In their " plan of work" they recommend raising money by " setting apart a certain proportion of earnings or spendings," and " deprecate the employment of any method that would put the cause of Christ before the world as a beggar."

The headquarters of the committee are at Baltimore, Maryland.

The constituency are in twelve States, from which a total of 1,259 societies was reported in 1889. Aggregate receipts for the same year were $30,773.69, of which $18,716.28 were appropriated to the foreign field.

There are 600,000 women in this church.

While the committee sends out no missionaries, there are 18 unmarried ladies in the foreign service of the church. Of these, 12 are in North, Central, and Southern China; 5 in Mexico, and one in Rio de Janeiro. A society in Virginia has also undertaken the support of a lady missionary in Rome.

The societies also aid work of the Board in Cuba and Africa; and a new mission having been lately opened in Japan, bands and young people are urged to support a missionary in that country.

The Committee, true to their position, proffer no reports of foreign work, which must be looked for in the annals of the Board; but publications of the Board admit monthly reports from the committee to their columns, and the ladies publish a monthly paper, " The Baptist Basket," at Louisville, Ky. Price, 50 cents.

***Woman's Executive Board Seventhday Baptist Church.*** Organized 1884. Headquarters, Milton, Wisconsin. Besides the ordinary officers, there are five associational secretaries. The Board acts for both home and foreign missions.

The church has mission work in China, Holland and amongst the Jews; and the Auxiliary Board sent out its first missionary in November, 1889, to have charge of school work in Shanghai, China.

The woman's societies are not fully in running order, but their secretary says their work "has already proved a spiritual blessing to us all."

The contributions to the missionary fund of the church for 1889 were $724.76.

***The Woman's Auxiliary to the Board of Missions of the Protestant Episcopal Church of the U. S. of America*** was organized by order of the Board October, 1871. It has become organized, on ecclesiastical lines, into diocesan and parochial branches, each responsible only to its own bishop or rector. It had in July, 1889, 54 diocesan branches, 10 of which are in missionary jurisdiction. There are 1,000 to 2,000 parochial, besides juvenile, branches.

Officers of the Auxiliary are called together for conference monthly at headquarters, 21 Bible House, New York, and triennially, with all members of the Auxiliary, at the time and place of meeting of the General Convention. At the last triennial meeting in New York City, October, 1889, there were 371 delegates present.

The Auxiliary is constituted for both domestic and foreign missions. The contributions in 1889 for foreign missions were about $30,000, besides boxes valued at $3,456.

" The Spirit of Missions " (published at the Bible House, New York City) is the organ of the Board of Missions, and devotes a department to woman's work. " The Young Christian Soldier " is for the juvenile branches. Besides these, " The Church Mission News " is unofficially published monthly by the ladies in New York: price, 30 cents. Catechisms upon the missions of this church have been prepared for instruction of the children.

The Auxiliary aims to aid the general missionary work of the church through the support of women serving as missionaries, scholarships in foreign and Indian mission schools, contributions for general missions (undesignated) through mite-boxes and regular subscriptions, and by special effort at the close of each working year.

This church is represented abroad by 60 ladies in all, of whom 31 are unmarried. Twelve of these have been sent to Japan during 1887-1890. Several ladies have gone out at their own charges. One is a physician. They are connected with the missions of their church in Greece, West Africa, China, and Japan. Those in China are stationed at Shanghai, Hankow, and Wuchang. At Shanghai one lady teaches English classes in St. John's College for boys, and another with a missionary's wife cares for an orphanage of children and St. Mary's Hall, a school for girls who are received young, and kept in training sometimes as many as eight years together.

A letter written from them at Christmas-time 1888 said: " We opened the new building for St. Mary's School, which has just been completed. It is substantially built, much more roomy than the old one, and a palace compared with it." Scholarships are $40 per annum.

The Bridgman Memorial and the Emma Jones Schools are both aided by the Auxiliary, and there are also many day-schools in Shanghai. At Wuchang the Jane Bohlen Memorial School cared for fifteen girls in 1889. In this city, Dr. Marie Haslep (wrote Bishop Boone in the autumn of 1889), "besides the study of the language, has been teaching medicine in English to her one very exceptional pupil, Miss Wong, and has also had her dispensary open for several months past, and seen hundreds of patients."

The ladies in Japan live in Osaka and Tokyo. At Osaka they have the Woman's Institute, comprising three departments—a primary, a school for girls, and women's classes. The ladies teach English extensively here; music also, and foreign sewing. There is interesting evangelistic work in Osaka, and also St. Agnes School of about fifty house-pupils, nearly all of them Christians. Six were baptized and eight confirmed in 1889. Scholarships are $40.

In Tokyo a school for the higher classes was opened in March, 1889, and in the course of a few months had twenty pupils. The dining-room is ordered in foreign style, to suit the parents of the girls; and a Steinway piano has been sent them by a lady of Tarrytown-on-the-Hudson.

Several ladies are connected with the Cape Palmas Mission, West Africa. One has a primary school of about ninety children at Cape Mount and has organized a Ministering League among them.

The last Sunday of 1888 the bishop baptized 24 persons in St. Mark's Church, of whom nine adults and four children were the fruits of efforts put forth by the Woman's Auxiliary of that church. In 1889 occurred the thirtieth anniversary of the Ladies' Church Aid Society of Trinity Church, Monrovia. Their contributions for the year were $312.63. The Auxiliary has recently put up a new building for Hoffman Institution of this mission.

Some of the largest gifts made through the Auxiliary have been in behalf of missions to the North American Indians. Among the converted women of South Dakota many societies have been formed, which make regular and large offerings for church work, and even for foreign missions.

**The Woman's Foreign Missionary Society of the Reformed Episcopal Church.**—This Society was organized in Boston, May, 1889. A constitution was adopted, and the usual officers elected. Responsibility for the conduct of business rests with an executive committee, which has met regularly during the first year of the Society's existence. The formation of auxiliaries in different churches has begun. The Society will co-operate with the general council committee of the church to put forth missionary effort for some particular field, which may be chosen by the council.

It is announced that "one of the younger clergy of the church has consecrated himself, with his wife, to work in China," and two ladies from western parishes have gone to India. One of these went at her own charges to Calcutta, where she is engaged in evangelistic work in connection with the Union Society. The other is a zenana missionary at Cawnpur, and is sustained by the Young People's Conference. Both these ladies have received aid for their work from the Society, and a grant has also been made for a training-school in Sierra Leone, Africa. About $1,500 in all is accounted for by the corresponding secretary in her report for the year. "As a church," she says, "we dare not lag behind our sister churches. Though we are small in numbers we can be great in

faith. Most earnestly do we desire to labor in the Master's service, and to obey His last command."

**The Woman's Missionary Association of the United Brethren in Christ** was organized in 1875. It is under direction of General Conference, and submits quadrennial reports to that body. Business is directed by a Board of Managers, composed of delegates elected annually by the Conference branches. Branches hold annual meetings; local societies and children's bands meet quarterly. The home force in 1890 was: Branch societies, 44; membership, about 10,000; income for 1889-90, $13,230.90. The "Woman's Evangel" is published monthly at Dayton, O. Price, 50 cents.

The first work abroad was undertaken in Sierra Leone, West Africa, where the General Board had been operating for years, but, by their advice, in a new and unbroken field. The station was located at Rotofunk on the Bompeh River, and a single lady was the pioneer in 1877. She held religious services and opened two schools. Her successor, another lady, doubled the number of schools and superintended building a house. Rotofunk was a slave-traders' station when the mission was opened, but ceased to be within five years after.

In 1882 a man and his wife were sent to the lonely station, and others followed in 1887.

Native chiefs made grants of land to the Association, and the buildings which have been erected, with other improvements, give the property a present valuation of $15,000.

In 1888 the Mary Sowers Home for Girls was completed at an expense of $2,000. It is a substantial building, and attracts a great deal of attention in those parts. There are about one hundred pupils, who are taught to wash, bake, cook, and everything pertaining to housekeeping, besides their school-training.

Wars and pestilence have interrupted the progress of the mission, and in 1888 it became necessary for such reasons to consolidate all the schools outside of Rotofunk at Bompeh. This school is fortunate in having the services of Mrs. Thompson, daughter of Bishop Crowther of the Niger. The number of full communicants here at the opening of 1889 was 37; seekers, 813. Three Sunday-schools had 156 pupils enrolled.

Itinerating is done, under direction of the missionaries, by converts who go two by two through the country, preaching and singing gospel songs, reaching many towns in a single day.

A mission to the Chinese in Portland, Oregon, was assumed in 1882. In 1884 property was purchased at a cost of $8,000. In 1888 there were 72 converts brought into church-membership out of about 600 who had received instruction. Pupils have paid $2,700 for tuition, and for church purposes over $750.

The interest of these converted Chinamen for their people led the Association to project a mission to China, and in 1889 the missionary from Portland, accompanied by two young ladies and a Chinese assistant, sailed for Canton to locate a mission in some destitute part of that province.

The entire foreign force representing the Association is: American missionaries, 10; native assistants, 18; church-membership, 1,484.

**Christian Woman's Board of Missions (Disciples).**—Several local societies having led the way, a mass meeting of the women of the church was called at the suggestion of one of its ministers. It was held in connection with the General Convention at Cincinnati, O., in 1874, and resulted in the organization of the "Christian Woman's Board of Missions." "Headquarters were located at Indianapolis, Ind., and the general officers chosen with reference to that vicinity."

The annual convention has never been held east of Cleveland, O. The management is in the hands of an executive committee. Twenty-nine States furnish auxiliaries to the Board.

Ever since 1884, bands of children have been organized, under the name of "Little Builders of the Christian Woman's Board of Missions," and to them is assigned erection of chapels, mission homes, and the like. The Board is constituted for both home and foreign missions. The contributions of the first year amounted to $1,000. In 1890 they were $45,166.81, of which about one third was expended upon foreign missions.

The home force reported at the fifteenth annual meeting, October, 1890, was: Auxiliaries, 882, a gain of 156 during the year; membership, 15,000; young people's societies, 49; mission bands, 380.

"Missionary Tidings" is published monthly at Indianapolis, Ind. Price, 50 cents.

Home work of the Board is carried on both east and west of the Mississippi.

The first undertaking abroad was the revival of the Jamaica Mission, which had fallen into decay. The Board sustains five men in Jamaica, with day-schools, Sunday-schools, and churches having a membership of over 13,000. Their property is valued at about $20,000.

A mission to India was begun in co-operation with the Church "Foreign Society" in 1882. Three stations are occupied in the Bilaspur district in the Bombay Presidency. Four missionary ladies are in this field, two of whom are physicians. A new bungalow for the ladies was built in 1889. They have an orphanage in charge, Sunday-schools, a school which opened with 31 girls in October, 1889, and zenana visiting. The event of 1889 was the opening of a medical mission in Bilaspur. Two women physicians who went for that purpose, although chiefly occupied with studying the language, gave out 1,000 prescriptions during the first two months after their arrival. They ask for a hospital, and the $6,000 proposed for that object was nearly raised in 1890.

A second "Woman's Board for Foreign Missions" of this Church is also reported from New Bedford, Mass. Its specific work is the support of Bible-women in connection with a mission in Japan, undertaken by the convention in 1887.

### Woman's Home and Foreign Missionary Society of the Lutheran Church.

—The first impulse toward united woman's missionary work in this church was given by a Swedish pastor in 1874, when he urged upon two Lutheran women to take the initiative in organizing such a society. A year or two later a letter in the "Lutheran Evangelist" called attention to the desire of an eminently fit young woman to go out as a missionary, and to the fact that the Foreign Missionary Board of the church had no money to send her. Inquiry revealed that several worthy women had been refused the same request for the same reason. Women now began in earnest to consider their

duty in the matter. They were blocked, as their first president afterwards expressed it, by "a difficulty so perverse as to seem amusing in retrospect." "We could gain no footing in the churches unless we were willing to become auxiliary to the Home Mission Board as well as the Foreign, and the Home Mission Board did not feel justified in suggesting any work for us."

In 1877 General Synod appointed a committee of gentlemen to forward the organization of such a society. They called a woman's missionary convention at Canton, Ohio, in June, 1879, and in "a spirit of unity and harmony of devotion to the work in hand, with an irresistible conviction that we were called to a life service," the large assembly of women, encouraged by "many well-wishing pastors," launched the Woman's Missionary Society.

The management is in the hands of the church officers, and an executive committee of thirteen ladies, nearly all of whom live in Springfield, Ohio. A general convention is held every two years, at which all societies are represented by delegates. Synodical societies meet every year; auxiliaries monthly.

At the convention in Baltimore, Maryland, 1889, the secretary reported 20 synodical societies, 507 auxiliaries, 13,801 members. Contributions, $32,331.35. As this was the tenth year in the history of the Society, thank-offerings were invited, which added over $6,000 to the amount reported by the treasurer. There are about 900 congregations in which is no auxiliary.

The "Missionary Journal" devotes a department to woman's work, which is edited under direction of the ladies.

The Literature Committee of seven ladies reside in Baltimore. They publish tracts, and "Mission Studies," a quarterly, containing readings on the subject of study for each month.

Abroad.—The first missionary was sent out in 1880. The four now sustained by the Society, one of them a physician, are all in Guntur, Madras presidency, India. The Lutheran Church founded a mission here in 1842.

There are 16 high-caste Hindu schools here, with 700 to 800 girls in them. An industrial-school for Mohammedan girls was opened in 1888, and a *gosha* department, having 30 women, added the following year. The day-schools are not confined to Guntur, but spread into the surrounding district. Lastly there is a boarding-school, accommodating about 40, for the daughters of Christian converts. The pupils are supported from America at a cost of $25 per year. "All the work of the school, cooking, carrying water, cleaning, sewing, is done by them. They are given a good common education, and as much knowledge of Bible truth as possible. We do not change the food, dress or habits of life of these girls, except when necessary for the sake of morality or health. They live on rice and curry in the district. In school we give them rice and curry, or *chollum* (a sort of grain) and curry. We do not Anglicise their dress. They eat with their hands, sitting on the floor, but they sit in an orderly row, and the older ones take turns in asking a blessing.

Zenana helpers to the number of 14 have been employed. The physician of the mission, after six years' labor, is on furlough, but her return is hoped for by the Society and by the people of Guntur, whose confidence she won to a remarkable degree. The report for her last year abroad is as follows : Number of patients treated at dispensaries, 3,175; number of patients treated at their homes, 302; number of attendances at dispensaries, 7,081; number of visits at homes, 1,295; number of prescriptions compounded, 11,211. The Society raised funds to build a hospital in 1890.

A request for a matron from the mission house at Muhlenberg, Africa, will be granted as soon as the Society can find a suitable person.

*Woman's Board of the Evangelical Association of North America* (German Churches).—In the year 1839, when the Evangelical Association numbered but 8,000 members, a Woman's Missionary Society was organized in the city of Philadelphia, Pa., numbering 60 members, who met once a week for work and prayer; from that time on, women of the Association have been actively engaged in the mission work of the church.

In 1876, when the first missionaries of the Association went to Japan, there went with them the awakened sympathy of the entire church; and women especially felt a new inspiration for missions, since two ladies were of the party.

In 1878 a petition was sent to the Board of Missions from Cleveland, Ohio, for permission to organize a Woman's Foreign Missionary Society. The Board deprecated organization for one branch of church work, and said, "We cannot comply with this request."

In 1880 another petition, sent up from Lindsay, Ohio, met with a partial assent; but societies did not organize rapidly, and a corresponding secretary was appointed who sent letters of appeal throughout the church.

These efforts resulted in forty societies in 1883. The same year a woman's convention was called, and for the third time the Board was petitioned to allow a general woman's society. Permission was now granted on condition: (a) That all local Societies be under supervision of a preacher. (b) That the Society be auxiliary to the Board of Missions, and submit its proceedings to that body.

In 1889 its home force was: Auxiliaries, about 135; membership, 2,400; receipts, $2,187.67.

"The Missionary Messenger" contains a Woman's Work department. Published monthly at Cleveland, Ohio. Price, 25c.

For a time a missionary was supported in Japan, but at present the Society reports none.

### CANADA.

*Woman's Foreign Missionary Society of the Presbyterian Church in Canada.* Organized 1876. Western Division: Headquarters, Toronto. Eastern Division: Headquarters, Halifax. Montreal Women's Missionary Society. Organized 1882.

Definite interest in woman's foreign mission work began in the Presbyterian Church of Canada in 1874, when two ladies offered themselves for service in India. The church not having at that time an established mission in India, these ladies were temporarily employed in the American Mission near Futtehgurh, though supported by Canadian funds.

In April, 1877, at the request of the Foreign Missions Committee of the church, the Western Division of the Woman's Society was formed, with a membership of 50. During the first year 18 auxiliaries and 3 mission bands were organized, which in the second year were increased to 28 auxiliaries and 6 bands. The re-

port for 1890 gives the numerical strength as follows: Presbyterial societies, 25; auxiliaries, 437; mission bands, 176; total membership, 15,312.

The first presbyterial society was formed in 1879, and ten years after every presbytery in Ontario had its organization, including one composed of 13 auxiliaries in the far Northwest Territory. The Society aims to establish a branch in every Presbyterian congregation throughout the land.

The offerings since the beginning have been, speaking roughly, one, two, three, four, five, six, seven, eight, ten, thirteen, eighteen, twenty-five, twenty-nine thousand dollars, and in 1890 $31,999.28. These sums, however, are but a faint indication of the real growth of the organization or its direct results for good to the church.

Abroad.—The Society sustains twelve missionaries, of whom two are physicians (and all but two in Central India), besides missionaries' wives. Four ladies went out in 1889. Seven missionaries are also on the Indian reserves in the Northwest.

THE EASTERN DIVISION has a constituency of, auxiliaries, 91; mission bands, 25, and contributed in 1889 $4,296. The Society has six missionaries in the field.

THE MONTREAL SOCIETY is successor of the "Ladies' French Evangelization Society," and conducts city mission work, French evangelization, and aids foreign missions. Its income for 1889-90 was $1,615, of which $700 was devoted to city missions.

The bulk of the revenue of these societies is obtained from voluntary offerings made through envelopes and mite-chests. "In few cases are 'sales' or entertainments resorted to as a means of raising money. Collecting is not included in our methods." The publications of the societies are leaflets, and a monthly letter composed of letters from missionaries; notices from the Board of Management to the branches, and items of special interest to members. The Eastern and Western Divisions are strictly auxiliary to the Assembly's Foreign Missions Committee, and co-operate with them among the Indians of 13 reserves in the Northwest and Manitoba, in the West Indies, British Guiana, China, India, and the New Hebrides.

Indian Reserves.—Connected with this oldest missionary work of the church are five industrial and boarding schools, and two smaller schools, in which day-pupils are received; all largely supported by the societies. The girls in these schools learn to knit, sew, cook, bake bread, and do all kinds of household work. In one, every girl over eight years of age wears stockings of her own knitting, and every girl of sixteen is required to make each year a suit of clothes for herself and one for her brother. The children also show great aptitude for music.

Sending bales of half-worn or new clothing to these reserves has constituted an important factor in the work of the societies for several years. Without this aid the schools could not have been carried on, as the Indians are miserably poor. The supplies are designed chiefly for children at the schools, and for the aged, feeble, and sick.

Central India.—Since 1877 the Western Division of the Society has sent twelve single ladies to India, of whom ten are still in the service. Two of them have gone distinctively for zenana work.

Five large centres are occupied,—Indore, Mhow, Rutlam, Neemuch, and Ujjain,—all located under the government of native princes, with British garrisons of occupation.

Medical work at Indore, conducted by Dr. Elizabeth Beattie and Dr. Marion Oliver, has been most successful. In 1889 they treated 16,678 out-patients and 67 in-patients, besides 1,192 house-visits paid. A dispensary has been established, and a temporary hospital, which is soon to be replaced by a permanent one. There are schools at all the stations, and where a regular lady missionary is not available, wives of the missionaries have collected the children and taught them very efficiently. A deposit sufficient to cover the cost of erecting a girls' boarding-school stands to the credit of the W. F. M. S., to be applied as soon as local conditions are favorable to begin.

China.—A handsome and complete girls' school-building was erected in Tamsui, Formosa, in 1884. It is under the management of the wife of Dr. G. L. Mackay, missionary of the Canadian Church in Formosa, and herself a Chinese woman.

In Honan, North China, it is proposed to establish hospitals at two centres, and two trained nurses were sent out from Toronto in 1889

Trinidad.—Mission work is conducted in Trinidad among Hindu coolies, of whom there are about 60,000 on the island. Much attention is given to education, and the schools have been a great means of good. Daily attendance of children is now verging upon 2,000. This mission belongs more especially to the Eastern Division of the Canadian Church, as does also the interesting field of the

New Hebrides.—Women have borne a heroic share in the fortunes of this mission, and one was martyred with her husband. No single ladies have been sent here, but the Society has three married ladies at the islands.

## Woman's Boards of the Baptist Church in Canada.
—Women's Foreign Missionary Society of Ontario; organized 1876. Women's Foreign Mission Society of Eastern Ontario and Quebec; organized 1876. Woman's Missionary Union of the Maritime Provinces; organized 1870.

The Ontario Society is the largest of these, comprising in itself 13 associational societies and about 250 circles and bands.

The "Union" was formed in 1883, by combining aid societies of thirteen years' standing in Nova Scotia, New Brunswick, and Prince Edward Island. At first few in numbers, banded together to support one sister who desired to carry the Gospel of the Redeemer to the perishing heathen, they found that union has strength, and have had the joy of helping a large number of ladies in the work in the foreign field, while their contributions have also secured some most valuable buildings. It is constituted for both home and foreign mission work. Both societies and the Union act in direct connection with their general church boards, to whose treasurers their funds are sent. The receipts reported for the year ending October, 1889, were, respectively: Ontario Society, $4,924.36; E. Ontario and Quebec Society, $1,255.90; Maritime Union (for foreign missions), $3,500.00. Total, $9,680.26.

These organizations are represented by "The Canadian Missionary Link," a self-supporting monthly paper published at Toronto; price, 25 cents per annum.

Abroad.—There are ten unmarried ladies representing these societies, of whom three went out in 1889. One is a trained nurse, and there is loud call for a woman physician. There are, besides, several missionary wives, who are actively in charge of regular departments of work.

The foreign field of this church is entirely among the Telugus of the Madras presidency, India. The oldest station is Cocanada, where woman's work is developing in several directions.

One lady has charge of the boarding-school for Christian girls. The tuition fee is four annas a month. The records of the school show that, of former pupils, 11 are wives of Telugu pastors, 6 are teachers, 1 is a Bible-woman. One missionary devotes herself to the Bible department, numbering 75 young men, in Samulcotta Seminary, besides doing evangelistic work in vacations.

Instead of 99 zenanas on the visiting list at the beginning of 1889, there were 132 in August of the same year; 14 villages had been visited during the year, and 1,955 visits made in all. Among the mission buildings in Cocanada are a Zenana Home, and a Rest House for missionaries coming from out-stations for medical treatment.

The second station of this mission was Tuni, "dark as night," and "40 miles from English faces and comforts." There is a girls' boarding-school here, of which the brief report runs as follows: "Opened August 1st, 1889, with 12 boarders, big and little, all glad to come and anxious to learn. The little school-house, ready to receive the classes, while the shady church veranda affords a good place for beginners to trace their letters in the sand; 3 teachers, and an old lady to care for them when out of school. Bible lessons, overseeing sewing-classes, and a great many smaller but not less important tasks fall to the lot of the missionary; but it is a pleasure to be busy with such neat little black-eyed girls, who wear little skirts right down to their toes, and sit on the floor." Akidu, 75 miles southwest from Cocanada, was opened in 1881; but ladies have been here so little, that in 1889, as one walked the streets, it was discussed on the verandas whether she were "man or woman." A school for girls, and evangelistic efforts, will soon enlighten the Akidu people in new directions.

Four stations belong to the Board of the Maritime Provinces, viz., Bobbili, Bimlipatam, Chicacole, and Vizianagram. The purchase of the latter property from the London Missionary Society was the financial event of 1889. Two thirds of the cost was paid by the Woman's Union. The features of each station are much alike. Day-school and Sunday-school supervising, taking children into their families, visiting from house to house and touring with their husbands, are all done by the married ladies. A young lady at Bimlipatam went on a tour of 63 days in the summer of 1889, travelling in a bandy, accompanied by a Telugu preacher and his family, a Bible-woman, and one of her pupils. In 50 villages, reached from five centres, she preached and sang the gospel to the women, whom she found more accessible than in the towns. Another young lady at Chicacole reports touring among 30 villages, and superintends 7 Bible-women, who make over 2,000 visits annually, and went steadfastly on their way through the last cholera season.

### The Woman's Missionary Society of the Methodist Church in Canada.

—Through the recommendation of the General Conference of 1878, and after some preliminary steps, this Society was organized in Hamilton, Ontario, November, 1881. There had previously existed in Montreal a Ladies' Association for the Evangelization of the French, which subsequently united with this Society, their work being incorporated with its other plans.

The administration is vested in the general officers of the Society and the board of managers, consisting of the president and corresponding secretary, and delegates from each branch. An unusual feature of the Society is that the funds are gathered one year and disbursed the following. While in frequent consultation with the parent missionary society of the church, and in perfect harmony with it, the ladies remit money directly to their own agents.

At the first annual meeting (1882), reports were received from 20 auxiliaries, showing a membership of nearly 800, with 34 life-members, and an income of $2,916.78.

In October, 1889, there were reported 224 auxiliaries, with about 5,000 members, and 73 missionary bands. The income for the year was $22,306.28

Auxiliaries exist from St. John's, Newfoundland, to Victoria, British Columbia, stretching across the continent.

Japan.—The only foreign field occupied is Japan, the missionaries there having sent a request for ladies to come to their help, even before the Society was formed. The first representative landed in Japan, December, 1882. It was soon discovered that a school for girls would contribute more than anything else to the success of the mission, and accordingly she opened one in Tokyo in 1884. In 1885 the school was strengthened by a second teacher. The building facilities have been repeatedly improved. The present accommodation limits the number to 150 boarders, and 100 day-pupils. The fees pay expenses outside of missionaries' salaries, only six girls being supported by the Society.

Over one hundred pupils and some of the Japanese teachers have been converted, and some of them have in turn led their friends to Christ. The general secretary of the parent Society after a trip to Japan reported this as "one of the very best mission schools in the country," and an American lady has called it "a model institution."

Another branch of work in Tokyo is that of training and employing Bible-women under supervision of Japanese pastors. Seven earnest women are thus occupied. A school was opened in 1887 in Shidzuoka, Japanese gentlemen providing the building and assuming the running expenses, the Society being responsible only for salaries of the ladies in charge. This city is in a province of over a million of people, and has been occupied by no other church than the Methodist of Canada. The same may be said of the province of which Kofu is the chief city. Here another school for girls has just been opened. The articles of agreement with the Japanese founders hold it to a strictly Christian standard.

The Society had twelve missionaries in active service in Japan at the opening of 1890.

French Work.—A school for girls has been carried on since 1885 at Actonvale, amidst the concentrated Romanism of the province of Quebec, and a small mission school also in Montreal.

A special effort is being made in connection with the French Institute erected in the west end of Montreal for the education of boys and girls. During 1890 there were 43 pupils (25 male and 18 female), ranging in age from ten to twenty-six.

Indian Work.—There are two Indian Homes to which the Society contributes: the one at Port Simpson, British Columbia; the other near Mosley, Northwest Territory, named The McDougall Orphanage and Training Institution. Each of these shelters from twenty to twenty-five children. The Society has also put up a fine building for a home and school for Indian children at Chilliwhack, in the beautiful valley of the Fraser River, British Columbia.

Chinese Work.—In 1877 a rescue work for Chinese girls was undertaken at Victoria. Of nine in residence in the summer of 1889, six gave evidence that they had passed from death to life.

"To summarize," says the secretary, "we are working among four nationalities: Japanese, French, Indians, and Chinese. Our funds go to nine different homes and schools, in which we have eighteen representatives, besides native teachers, and we minister to over four hundred children."

### The Woman's Board of Missions of the Congregational Church in Canada

was organized in 1886, and constituted for both home and foreign missions.

In 1889 it reported: auxiliaries, 28; bands, 11. Receipts for previous year for foreign missions, $1,281.56.

The Board has one missionary teaching in Bombay in connection with the A. B. C. F. M. They have also contributed for a memorial school-building in West Central Africa, where the early death of one of their ladies caused heavy mourning.

The Board coöperates with the Missionary Society of the Church in Canada, and is not auxiliary to the American Board, although its missionaries serve under that charter. One of its officers writes that they aim "to awaken interest in woman's work from the Atlantic to the Pacific."

"The Canadian Independent," published monthly at Newmarket, Ontario, allows a "Woman's Board Column" in its pages. Price, $1.50 per year.

### The Woman's Auxiliary to the Board of Diocesan, Domestic, and Foreign Missions of the Church of England in Canada

was organized in 1886. In 1889 it reported, Diocesan branches (of which the largest is Toronto), 6; Parish branches, about 200. Total receipts for the previous year, $18,675.81. This has been chiefly expended upon domestic missions.

Diocesan branches hold annual meetings, and the first triennial meeting of the Auxiliary was held in September, 1889.

The Auxiliary has one missionary among the Blackfeet Indians.

"The Canadian Church Magazine and Mission News," Hamilton, Ontario, devotes a space to the Auxiliary. Price, $1.00. The Toronto branch publishes a monthly letter leaflet; price, 15 cents.

*Coral Missionary Magazine and Fund.* For aiding missions at home and abroad.

Besides the Societies organized and conducted by women primarily in behalf of women and children, and doing work which would be nobody's work should the Society withdraw, there are other valuable missionary organizations which equally deserve to be recorded in this connection. Some of these are not strictly "societies;" others support no specific missionaries, but help societies that do; others are either not working expressly for women, or have not a constituency of women.

The oldest of these admirable institutions goes by the name of the "Coral Fund."

The foreign work of this association is in connection with the Church Missionary Society, and its home efforts in aid of London City Missions.

The "Coral Missionary Magazine" (first known as the "Children's Magazine") was founded in 1838, and the "Fund" ten years later; both taking their name from the coral insects, which produce useful results from multiplied small efforts.

The association has raised over £40,000 from the beginning, its average income at the present time being about £1,000 annually.

The "Fund" is under trustees, the editor of the magazine acting as treasurer, and conducting correspondence with mission stations aided by it. It has several working parties and other co-helpers, who collect subscriptions, copy reports, and if possible pack a box annually for the schools.

The chief work of the "Fund" is support of children in the C. M. S. schools and orphanages, and thousands have been maintained by its agency, many of them through contributions of Sunday-schools and Bible-classes, or the proceeds of missionary baskets or sales.

The asociation has always been ready to provide some special want of a station—a magic lantern, or a harmonium, or an extra catechist's salary; and repeatedly it has come to the rescue in an emergency. Such instances were the store of provisions for the Bishop of Moosonee, when only one uncertain ship a year brought his supplies; the relief of slaves rescued at Freetown, East Africa; and of famine in India.

The Magazine is published monthly, price 1d., by Wells, Gardner, Darton & Co., London. A. L. O. E. is one of the many contributors to the pages of its fifty-three volumes.

*The Ladies' Auxiliary of the Wesleyan Methodist Missionary Society.* —This Society was formed at the close of the year 1858, in response to appeals from wives of missionaries in India, for help in commencing and carrying on schools for girls, and in instructing women. It is managed by a president who is also treasurer, four honorary secretaries, and a committee of thirty ladies. The committee works in harmony with, and to a certain extent under the direction of, the Wesleyan Missionary Society of England.

The home force is represented by: Auxiliaries, 200; working-meetings, 150; busy bees. 82.

The income for 1889-90 was £8,138 7s. 5d.— the largest ever received.

The "Quarterly Paper" is published at the Mission House, Bishopsgate Street Within, London, E. C., England. Price, 4d.

The force abroad includes: Missionaries, 37; native assistants, 58. Twelve Bible-women (all in India) are supported by the British and Foreign Bible Society. Missionaries' wives (about 40) superintend schools and visit zenanas, but without salary.

*Medical Work.*—Five missionaries are medical visitors, and some of these are full physicians. One of the latter, Dr. Sugden, has charge of a woman's hospital in Hangkow, China, which having been erected at a cost of £1,000, was opened amidst much rejoicing at the close of 1888. At a meeting of the Auxiliary in London the July following, a gentleman of the mission reported that Dr. Sugden "during two and a-half years' work had seen over 13,000 patients, and visited 308 who were unable to attend the dispensary. There had never been such a demand on any foreign medical man. Many a life had been saved, and he trusted many a soul. People came ten, twenty, thirty, even in some cases two hundred, miles to the hospital. Many were now brought to attend the chapel. When it was built one third of the space was allotted to the women, and that was usually nearly empty. Now they were pushing the men out of their places, and the medical work was bringing about freer access to the homes of the people."

There are also hospitals at Madras and in Uva, Ceylon.

*Educational Work.*—The Auxiliary has connected with its missions about 12,000 pupils distributed in some 15 boarding-schools; 6 orphanages; 260 day-schools. The greater number of pupils are in India. One of the Wesleyan missionaries in the Madras presidency wrote to the Auxiliary ("Quarterly Paper," 1889, p. 159):

"In every village, side by side with the boys' school, I want a girls' school. Side by side with the catechist and boys' school-teacher there must be an intelligent, godly woman to work among the women, to teach them to sew and keep themselves tidy and clean, and to instruct them in the simple truths of Christianity. We have a great deal of civilizing work to do."

In the Calcutta district are 24 schools containing about 800 girls. In Mysore there are 3,500 in school. At Bangalore about 50 house-pupils, many of them small, are in the boarding-school. The missionary says ("Quarterly Paper," January, 1890):

"We intend to weed out girls whose friends pay no fees, though we cannot of course turn away destitute children We have some girls who have been in school for many years, and for whom scarcely anything has ever been paid We want to raise the school and get a better class of children. I hope we shall get the parents to supply all the children's clothing. I find the girls take so much more care of their 'house clothes,' as they call their own things, than they do of things that I give them."

There are schools in Madras City (sometimes 350 girls in 6 schools), in Lucknow, Faizabad, Haidarabad, Benares, and other cities.

The Ceylon Mission is also strong in schools in the Jaffna, Batticaloa and Kalmunai districts in the north. In 1889 there were 1,470 boys and 353 girls in Kalmunai schools. In South Ceylon there are large schools in Colombo, Uva, Kandy, and the Galle and Matora districts. An industrial school for girls at Badulla demands low fees.

In China the lack of a boarding-school at Canton, and the early removal of pupils at Hankow, are the great hindrances to be overcome.

Africa.—The missions in Africa are at Lagos, on the west coast, and in the south. In the latter they have large schools at three stations, and from one of these, Peddie, nearly 20 day-schools are worked. One of the ladies recently had a catechumen class of 35 out of 106 enrolled pupils.

The Auxiliary also aids Wesleyan missions in Syria, Italy, and Spain.

*Ladies' Association for the Promotion of Female Education among the Heathen.* In connection with the missions of the Society for the Propagation of the Gospel. Organized 1865.—The home organization consists of a committee of ladies meeting monthly at 19 Delahay Street, London, and several sub-committees. The constituency furnish funds through branch associations. The committee appoint a lady in each archdeaconry to be correspondent. She aids in organizing branch associations, and transmits their collections to London. There are 73 correspondents. Funds are also raised by sales of work, which is furnished by some 300 working parties. By the same means about forty valuable boxes are annually sent to the missions. The funds are administered by a committee of ladies aided by two members of the Standing Committee of the S. P. G., and by the Secretary of the Society.

The income of the Association for 1888 was £6,351.

"The Grain of Mustard Seed" is published monthly at 2 Paternoster Buildings, London. Price, 1d.

The missions are in India, Burma, Madagascar, South Africa, and Japan.

The force abroad is represented by: English missionaries, 61, of whom 12 are honorary (at their own charges); foreign assistants, 104; zenana pupils, 3,000; schools, 18; pupils in schools, 1,250.

The oldest and strongest mission is that at Delhi, in the Punjab. The forms of work here carried on by the Association are: Zenana missions in Delhi and seven other towns; Bible-women; the native female normal school; the European normal school; the industrial school (which sometimes supports itself by embroidery); the Christian girls' boarding-school (£10 will cover all expenses for a girl, one year); the Refuge (for women of all religions).

The industrial school is for Mohammedan women, and has become in part a shop as well as school. The Christian girls' school has about 50 boarders. An American visitor there thus describes what he saw: "We entered the school by surprise. It was work-day. Young girls with their native spinning-wheels were spinning cotton; others were sewing; others, larger girls, were cutting out and making garments for the boys' boarding-school. The lady in charge took us to the cook-rooms, where she showed us 160 pounds of extra fine flour that the girls had made from the wheat bought in the bazaar." The standard of the school includes a middle department and the full complement of eight classes. The Mission Report says of it: "There is perhaps no more useful institution in the mission."

There are five day-schools in Delhi, two for Mohammedans and three for Hindus.

There is a woman's medical mission in the Lahore diocese, having two centres. The one is at Delhi, where there is a hospital and dispensary in charge of a medical woman and her

assistant. The in-patients in 1888 numbered 137, and the total number of patients was 12,688.

At Karnal, 75 miles north of Delhi, is the other medical centre, with dispensary and lying-in hospital.

In the summer of 1889 the Delhi Mission appealed for six English women,—"if possible, those having private means." Two were particularly called for to establish a village mission, and two for a girls' school in the town of Hissar, for which a Hindu gentleman had promised to give twenty rupees a month if it were in charge of a Christian lady.

Other important stations in India are in the Calcutta district, Bombay and Madras presidencies. In all, zenana visiting and schools are prosecuted. In the city of Madras about 90 girls, over 60 being orphans, are cared for in a boarding-school. The Lady Napier Caste School at Tanjore, according to a late report, had but 25 Brahman girls out of 135 children, so that "it is not yet patronized by the class for whom it was intended." At Trichinopoly there has been a training-school for teachers for nine years. In the Mahratta country there are 100 girls in boarding-school at Ahmednagar, and at Kolhapur 400 high-caste women and girls in eight schools, and a teachers' training-class, the fruit of six years' effort.

Burma.—The mission has schools at Rangoon, Prome, Moulmein, Toungoo (Karen).

Madagascar.—Six or more missionaries are on the island. At the capital they are in schools, where "it is so difficult to make girls that have never seen a train or even a carriage understand geography." At Mahanoro, a child said she would go a fortnight without food, except a little dry rice, in order to possess a doll.

South Africa.—There are several schools for Kafir children at Cape Town, Graham's Town, and Maritzburg; and in 1888 a new school was opened at Durban for Indian girls, the daughters of coolies from India, who have come in large numbers to work on the plantations in Natal.

Japan.—The mission has two ladies at Tokyo, and a third at Kobe.

*Ladies' Association for Support of Zenana Work and Bible-women in India in connection with The Baptist Missionary Society.*—The Association was formed in 1867 as an auxiliary to the B. M. Society, but is independent in general management and disposition of its income. The home constituency is organized into auxiliaries only in rare cases, and funds are obtained by means of "collectors," who are appointed in connection with chapels and churches all over the kingdom, and solicit from men as well as women. The income for 1889 was £9,641.

"Our Indian Sisters," a quarterly magazine, price 8d., and leaflets, may be obtained from headquarters, Furnival Street, Holborn, London.

An annual breakfast meeting is held in London in May, where gentlemen are invited to speak.

Abroad.—The Association has nineteen mission stations, all in India, stretching from Calcutta to Madras. Its missionary staff consisted in 1889 of: Lady zenana visitors, 42; assistants, 30; native Bible-women, 55; native school-teachers, 59. About 50 schools are cared for, with 1,700 children. About 700 zenanas are regularly visited, where 1,200 pupils are taught.

The largest boarding-school, of 60 girls, is at

Delhi, where they are trained to clean and grind the grain daily, as well as to such habits of study that some of them have excelled in the medical classes at Agra. There are also several purdah and other day schools at Delhi.

The Rajghat School in Benares has about 100 children (one fourth of them boys) from twenty-one distinct castes.

Evangelistic work in the villages is the branch of mission work which has most increased of late. During the cold season some of the missionaries have tented for weeks together in the vicinity of their city stations, and moved about within reach of numerous villages, where, in many cases, an English lady has not been seen before. A boat has been built at Barisal, for use in itinerating.

Some special expenditures in 1889 were: the purchase of a piece of land at Delhi, on which a hospital for women and children has since been erected; purchase of a house to accommodate the lady workers in Barisal; houses for Bible-women, and a normal school in Calcutta.

*Ladies' Committee of the London Missionary Society.* Organized 1875.—The constituency of the Committee, like that of the Society with which it co-operates, is unde-nominational, but largely derived from the churches of the Congregational order.

The secretary of the Committee thus explains their relation to the Society: "Our Committee is entirely subject to control of the Board of Directors, who, however, treat us with full consideration, and almost invariably accept and sanction our recommendations." Candidates apply to the Ladies' Committee, and are selected by them and "recommended" to the Society, and although the Committee does not disburse funds, it "recommends" grants.

No stated meetings are held in London, except the annual meeting in May, which is conducted by ladies; but "deputation work" is done throughout the year, in provincial towns, in connection with the Society.

The total contributions received in 1888-89 were £6,471 4s. 2d.

The Committee publish the "Quarterly News of Woman's Work." Headquarters, 14 Blomfield Street, London, E. C. Price, 4d. Circulation, 10,000.

The force abroad is represented by: Missionaries, 36, besides missionaries' wives, who co-operate as they are able; girls' boarding-schools, 6 or more; day-schools for girls, 133; zenana pupils, more than 2,000; pupils in schools, about 8,000.

The missionary ladies are located in the missions of the Society in India, China, and Madagascar, but no single ladies have yet been sent to the missions in Central Africa, to British Guiana, nor, with but one exception, to Polynesia.

North India.—Thirteen of the missionaries are distributed in the centres of this mission. At Calcutta, where zenana work is specially strong, not less than 2,000 houses receive religious instruction only, from the Bible-women. At 60 or 70 more houses secular teaching is also given, and for this a fee is usually paid.

Schools comprising 250 caste girls pay annual fees of more than a thousand rupees. A boarding-school for native Christian girls, day-schools, and work among Mohammedan women are all features at Calcutta.

At Berhampur the baptism of a Hindu lady

at the opening of 1889 resulted in closing most of the zenanas. Other centres are Benares; Mirzapur, where there is an orphanage; Bangalore; and Almora, where a "Home" for women was lately erected.

South India.—There are 39 schools for girls in this mission, of which several centre at Madras. Among them are two caste-schools, and a Christian girls' boarding-school. In the latter domestic work is taught, and nearly all pay a fee. Some zenana pupils in Madras buy their own Bibles. Ten Bible-women visit in the suburbs.

Travancore.—Woman's work is largely developed here, although the missionary ladies are few. The death of Mrs. Knowles in 1889 was a heavy loss to the mission.

An illustration of the great changes which have taken place in public opinion in Travancore during the last twenty-five years was given by a missionary in a paper presented to the annual meeting in London, May, 1889.

One Sunday morning, soon after she had started a Hindu girls' school, her husband was addressed by a man who passed the door. "All this is quite a new thing," he said. "It may seem good to Europeans to educate girls, but our opinion is just the reverse. No woman of respectability amongst us would ever dream of learning to read—only Temple women stoop to that. And, besides, if women are to be taught such arts as reading, writing, and arithmetic, we men will be ruined." "How so?" "Oh!" said he, "if my wife were to know arithmetic I certainly should soon be a ruined man. It is in this way. As things now are, I send her to the bazaar to buy certain articles, giving her so much money in hand. When she returns from the market I make her lay down the various articles bought. She tells me the price of each. I add up the account, and the exact balance is duly handed over. You see, my wife has not got it in her power to cheat me; but if you teach her arithmetic, see what it will be. She will go to the bazaar, pay five *coslo* for an article and write it down seven; for another, ten *coslo* will be given, but she will put it down fifteen. Before she comes to the house all will be fair and square, and the wrong balance she will be ready to hand over to me, retaining ever so much in her own possession. I should be a ruined man. No, no. It is very needful for men and boys to have book knowledge, but women and girls must learn to cook, to stay at home, and obey their husbands."

Four Hindu girls' day-schools, a fifth for Christian girls in a fine building, and a prosperous boarding-school for the outlying districts, all now stand within a radius of a mile from that doorway. There is a band of 18 Bible-women in Nagercoil, the most southerly mission station in India.

China.—The stations occupied are Hong-Kong, Amoy, Shanghai, Tientsin, and Peking. Visits are made to hospital patients in the first two cities, and some medical work among women is done in the last two cities. Boarding-schools are at Amoy, where are 34 house-pupils and a fine new building; and at Peking, where the industry of the girls, their aptitude in handiwork, and interest in the Scriptures are all manifest. A Ladies' Home, recently built at Tientsin, has a hall accommodating 60 to 70, for the use of the Chinese women.

Madagascar.—There are girls' boarding-schools at Antananarivo and Fianarantsoa. In the latter the pupils, to the number of 40, are wives of students in the normal school. Much attention is given here to needle and domestic work. At the beginning of 1889 two pupils were known to be Christians; at the close of the year 29 were members of the church. Hundreds of girls in Madagascar attend mixed schools.

The event of 1889 was sending out a lady to establish a training-school for women and girls at Samoa, in the South Seas.

The secretary says of this step: "Work in the South Seas has been more or less at a standstill during the past few years, from marked inferiority, intellectual and spiritual, of the women to the men. Education of the women has been too much neglected, while that of the men has made rapid strides; the home life of native pastors has suffered."

*Woman's Committee on Christian Work in France.* Under the care of Friends.—The work of the Committee was instituted in 1871. They have collectors in the different monthly meetings of Great Britain and Ireland, and even receive contributions from America. The collections of 1888 amounted to £587.

The Committee sustain meetings in Paris (several stations), Marseilles, and nine other cities of France. Their special instrumentality is mothers' meetings. They have also evangelical industrial schools for girls, Bible-nurses, meetings for children, and tract distribution. At a Sunday-meeting for young washerwomen, in Paris, all being Roman Catholics, seven out of twenty-two had never heard the word "Bible."

Other aids employed are lending libraries, savings-banks, clothing-clubs, and Bible-depots.

*The Woman's Missionary Association of the Presbyterian Church of England* was founded in 1878, Synod having previously expressed its conviction of the desirability of some such action. It is in immediate connection with the Foreign Missionary Committee of the church, and its appointments of missionaries are subject to the approval of that committee. Membership requires a minimum subscription of one shilling per annum.

There are 11 presbyterial secretaries, and 148 congregational associations, representing as many churches; but nearly 150 churches have not yet joined the Association. The income for 1889–90 was £2,603 15s.

"Our Sisters in Other Lands" is published quarterly, at 14 Paternoster Square, London, E. C. Price, 6d. per year.

"The work undertaken abroad is girls' boarding-schools, country visiting, and day-schools, Sunday-schools, visits to women in their homes and in the hospitals, Bible-classes, training Bible-women, and preparation and distribution of gospel leaflets in Chinese character."

The missionaries of the Association number 17, of whom 10 are in China, 3 in India, 2 in North Africa, and 2 in Singapore; Bible-women, 12 or more; boarding-schools, 4; day-schools, 6. The principal centres in China are Swatow, Amoy, and Formosa, in each of which there is a girls' boarding-school; the largest, of over forty, at Amoy. Here there is also an orphanage.

At Swatow there is a training-class for Bible-women, and a boat belonging to the mission carries the ladies to their country stations. In the seven day-schools about the city the girls are taught sewing and knitting along with their books.

The first missionary of the Association was sent out here in 1878, and has been laboring ever since. Writing from Swatow of the progress she has noted, she says:* "I have been pleased to see the increasing cleanliness of the Christian homes, notably the pastor's house at P—— and the chapel at N——. In the pastor's study a shelf of books, all carefully dusted and neatly arranged, gives the room a comfortable air, contrasting happily with the chaos and filth which distinguish most heathen dwellings. The pastor's daughter is married to a nice young student. Their house is spotlessly clean, and a foreign clock encourages punctuality, being a better guide to the time of day than the cat's eye at noon, or a guess how many bamboos high or low the sun is in the heavens."

The missionaries at Formosa include 15 villages within their field. One lady with medical training has opened a new centre for woman's work at Chin-Chew, and another is, with missionaries of the general society, laboring in the Hakka country.

The only station in India is Rampore Bauleah, among four millions of people whom no other society is helping, and where the Association sent its first "agent" in 1881. The ladies divide their time between schools and zenanas.

Through the aid of one gentleman there are two ladies in Singapore; one devoting herself to Malay-speaking women, the other to the Chinese.

A new work was entered upon by two ladies in November, 1890, at Rabat, Morocco, where a physician and his wife, of the general society, have been conducting a medical mission for some time.

*The Church of England Zenana Missionary Society,* in co-operation with the Church Missionary Society, was founded in 1880, upon the separation of the zenana workers from the Indian Female Normal School and Instruction Society. The president, vice-presidents, and most members of the committee are ladies, but treasurers, finance committee, and some other officers are gentlemen. The constituency of the Society is represented by 842 associations, and many working parties and sales of work also add to the income.

In 1888–89 the total income amounted to £27,653, the largest received in any year up to that time.

"India's Women" is published bi-monthly. Price, 1s. 6d. Leaflets are also issued from headquarters, 9 Salisbury Square, London, E. C.

Abroad.—The Society originally withdrew from the I. F. N. S. 31 missionaries and 17 stations, all in India. The plan of development has been to accept calls to new stations, as they have been made from time to time by local conferences or the committee in London, according as funds of the Society warranted enlargement. In conformity with this plan, missionaries were sent to China in 1883, to Japan in 1885, and to Ceylon in 1889. The mission staff in 1890 was as follows. Missionaries in home connection 117, of whom 18 are honorary (i.e. at their own

---

* See "Our Sisters in Other Lands," April, 1889.

charges); assistants in local connection, 57; Bible-women, 139; native teachers, 368.

*Medical Work.*—There are hospitals and dispensaries at Amritsar and Peshawar, in the Punjab; at Haidarabad and Trichur in South India; and at Srinagar in Kashmir, where the valued physician died in 1889, after nine years' service with the Society. The report in 1889 mentioned that 32,469 patients were seen at the St. Catherine's Hospital in Amritsar the previous year, and 205 in-patients had been received. Five English ladies are connected with this hospital. At both Peshawar and Trichur over 4,000 patients were recorded in the register, and at the former place 84 received hospital treatment, of whom 58 were Afghans. At many other points much suffering is relieved by missionaries who have had some medical training.

Educational Department.—The Society occupies 46 stations in India, 3 in China, 2 in Japan, and 1 in Ceylon, and some form of school-work is prosecuted at almost every station. The total number of schools is 183.

Calcutta.—A normal school here for European and Eurasian girls has connected with it a training-class of about 30 Bengali girls. The "Central School" has over 100 Hindu girls, and there are not less than 13 other day-schools in the city and its suburbs. Some are attended by girls from families of high social position, while one is exclusively for sweepers.

A widows' training-class at Chupra, and a convert's home at Barrackpore, 15 miles from Calcutta, are noticeable institutions.

Amritsar.—The Alexandra School for girls, here, has had a record of 13 years, and numbers about 80 pupils, one of whom won the prize of a gold medal conferred by the lieutenant-governor in jubilee year. A school for the blind, with a blind Christian teacher, is a branch of St. Catherine's Hospital. Other schools are: in North India at Peshawar; at Sukkur in Sindh; and Haidarabad, the latter said to be "one of the best of its kind in India." In the south there are schools in the Madras presidency and in Travancore. In and about Masulipatam more than 1,200 children are gathered into 20 schools.

*Evangelistic Department.*—The Society aimed at zenana visitation from the first, and has always given its chief strength to that. Village missions are also coming into prominence of late. This claims to be the only zenana society for Mohammedans in the Calcutta district. In addition to the Moslem branch, they have many Hindu houses and purdah schools. Zenana pupils in Bengal sometimes pay a tuition fee. There is a large zenana work at Peshawar, where "the ladies have the *entrée* of every zenana in the city;" in Amritsar and Batala, in the Punjab; but a still larger in Tinnivelly in the Madras presidency, and at Trevandrum in Travancore. There are about 900 houses visited in these two places.

Village missions are strongest in the Punjab about Jandiala, Narowal, and Ajnala; within a day's visit of the latter are 85 villages. The staff here includes more than a dozen persons.

At Taru Taran the people themselves contributed 600 rupees towards buildings required by the ladies.

The only stations belonging to the Society in China are Foochow, Shanghai, and Ningpo. In some places of the Foochow field 90 per cent of the Christians are men.

The Society sent two ladies to Osaka, Japan, in 1888, where they engage in evangelistic work.

The committee during 1889 accepted the following calls for new work, to be taken up as soon as suitable workers and sufficient means are available, viz., a normal school for female teachers at Amritsar; a boarding-school for village girls in the Krishnagar district; a boarding-school for Christian girls at Kandy, in Ceylon; the establishment, in conjunction with the C. M. S., of the Buchanan Institution for training female workers in the diocese of Travancore and Cochin.

*Woman's Societies of the Church of Scotland (Established).*—Ladies' Association for Foreign Missions, including zenana work. Organized 1837. Ladies' Association for the Christian Education of Jewish Females. Organized 1845. The Fellow-workers' Union for Jewish and Foreign Missions. Headquarters, Edinburgh. Organized 1889.

The last of these is composed of young ladies. It affiliates with the Associations, to whose treasuries the Union contributed £10 during the first year of its existence.

THE ASSOCIATION FOR FOREIGN MISSIONS has a home constituency of 32 presbyterial auxiliaries and 482 contributing congregations. The income reported for the year ending July, 1889, was: Income in Scotland, £6,690 13s.; income in India, £967 11s. Total, £7,658 4s.

The "News of Female Missions" is published quarterly, at 8d. per annum. A quarterly leaflet, "Fellow-workers," is also issued; and tracts and leaflets may be had from headquarters, 22 Queen Street, Edinburgh. The office-bearers, except the treasurer, are all ladies.

The force abroad is: Missionaries appointed in Scotland, 15; missionaries appointed in India, 11; native Christian agents, 82; non-Christian agents, 24; pupils enrolled in schools, 2,500.

The methods of work adopted by the Association are five in number, viz., orphanages and training institutions, schools, zenana-visiting, village teaching, medical work. There are two kinds of zenana work: (1) In fee-paying zenanas, where instruction in ordinary subjects of education is given, as well as the Bible-lesson; (2) in zenanas where no fees are paid, and the Bible only is taught. There were 283 zenanas of the first class, paying fees of 1,632 rupees, and 160 of the second class, mentioned in the last report.

The chief difficulty in school-work is to secure regular attendance. This the missionaries in India are trying to overcome by enforcing fees, so that parents may use authority to make their children attend. In Africa the parents think they should receive payment for sending their children to school. The lady missionary has charge of the industrial training as well as elementary education of the girls in the Blantyre Mission. The scale of salaries to native teachers in India varies from 7 rupees to 35 rupees per month. Young teachers trained in the mission, board in the institutions.

Work of the Association is located at Calcutta, Madras, Poona, Darjeeling, Gujrat, Sialkot, and Chamba, in India; and Blantyre, East Africa.

The largest share of school-work is in Calcutta, where are 890 pupils in 12 schools, viz, one institution for Christian girls, comprising orphanage, boarding-school, and normal class; ten

Hindu schools, and one Chamar. The superintending missionary spends one day a week in each school.

Of four schools in Poona, one in the most bigoted part of the city has 80 to 90 girls, mostly Brahmins. In each day-school there is a Sunday-school, in which a treat is allowed but once a year. In the Sialkot district three schools are for Mohammedans only, and one for Sikhs. In Chamba, one school is for high-caste Hindus, and another for both Mohammedans and Christians.

*Medical Work.*—The only undertaking as yet in this department is at Poona, where there has been one physician for several years. She has a dispensary in the city open on certain days of the week, and on other days dispenses in neighboring villages. Total attendance in the city in 1889 was 4,348. The greater number of cases were Hindus, of the middle and trading castes, with a proportion of Jews, Mussulmans, and a few Christians. The following picture of country dispensing is taken from Dr. Lettice Bernard's report :

"That in Bamboorda is held in the veranda of the school and a small room opening out of it. This is very convenient. I sit in the little room, and the patients come in turns and stand in the doorway ; and when I have seen them all, I can just shut the door and make up the medicines quietly, while my sister speaks and sings to the women outside. Lately she has had a little American harmonium, which proves a great help in keeping their attention."

A hospital was opened in Poona in 1889.

East Africa.—The only lady at present in Blantyre went from Aberdeen in 1889.

THE ASSOCIATION IN BEHALF OF THE JEWS has five stations : Alexandria, Beirut, Constantinople, Salonica, and Smyrna. Of 950 girls taught in the schools, 778 are Spanish Jewesses. A nurse is called for in Smyrna.

At Alexandria there are two schools—one of them for the poor alone. The missionaries are called upon to teach a variety of subjects—English, Italian, needlework, besides reading German with German Jewesses. Bible lessons are given in Arabic and other tongues. The receipts of the Association for 1889 were £524 10s. 2d.

*Woman's Societies of the Free Church of Scotland.*—Ladies' Society of the Free Church of Scotland for female education in India and South Africa. Founded 1837. Ladies' Association in connection with the Free Church Mission to the Jews. Ladies' Continental Association in correspondence with the Free Church.

Appointments for India are made by an Edinburgh committee of ladies, and for Africa by a Glasgow committee, while the presidents and secretaries of the Society are all gentlemen.

The constituency of the Society was represented in 1889 by: contributing congregations, 627; contributing Sunday-schools, 77. Over 300 congregations did not aid the Society.

The income covered fifteen months, and amounted to a little above £9,000.

The publications of the Society are reports and quarterly papers, and "Woman's Work in Heathen Lands," a small quarterly, price 1d. J. & R. Parlane, Paisley, publisher.

The force abroad: European and Eurasian agents in India, 21; European and Eurasian agents in Africa, 13; native Christian agents 181; total pupils under instruction, 6,738.

India.—The work of the Society in India is conducted in eight different languages, and at five large centres: Calcutta, Madras, Bombay, Poona, and Nagpore.

*Schools.*—There is a boarding-school for Christian girls in each of these cities, in which "they are brought up as much as possible in native style." "They are all trained to household work, and to habits of cleanliness, punctuality, modesty, truthfulness, and kindness to one another. . . . They are all educated in their own vernacular, and almost all learn English also." The Madras and Calcutta schools are the largest, each numbering over 90 pupils. Several graduates of the latter school have taken University degrees, and hold influential positions. There is a boarding-school in Pachamba (Bengal) for girls from the jungle whose arrangements are accordingly primitive; numbers, about 50. Caste day-schools are in all the cities, those of Madras (including a day normal school) having a special reputation. Of both city and village day-schools the Society maintains fifty, with an attendance of 4,000 pupils. Most of them are held in hired houses. The great majority of pupils are from well-to-do Hindu families, but there are small schools for Mohammedans at Poona and Madras, and Beni-Israel schools in Poona and the Madras presidency. A training-home for widows was opened with two members, at Calcutta, in 1889.

*Zenana Visitation.*—A new zenana home, accommodating fourteen workers, was erected at Calcutta in 1888. The number of pupils in the city that same year, in houses and zenana schools, was 727. In Madras, where the mission is 52 years old, the house-pupils are about 170, with four visitors. One of the latter recently retired, to the great regret of the mission, after 33 years of service. A Jubilee bungalow for zenana workers was built at Bombay, where a few of the pupils visited are Parsis. The common experience at all the stations is described by one of the workers at Nagpore: "The zenana teacher has disappointment as well as encouragement in her daily rounds. . . . When the application of the [Bible] lesson is being gone through, we notice that attention flags; but at other times, again, the interest is kept up to the end, and the questions that follow show real desire to know more of Christ." Secular as well as religious instruction is given.

*Medical Work.*—Several stations have called for fully qualified medical women, and a beginning has been made in this department, with the intention of developing it as soon as practicable. Two medical ladies fully qualified are stationed at Madras.

South Africa.—At Lovedale, in Kaffraria, the girls' boarding and training school has over 100 pupils, and carries on both the educational and industrial departments, which have been features of that well-known institution. A class for musical drill was an innovation of 1888.

In Transkei a great many sewing-schools are reported, and mending, darning, knitting, and cutting out clothes. One of the missionaries says: "I know some people give the things sewn in these schools to the pupils. I do not in any case, for I do not wish to spoil these people or their children. Many of them are better off than most of the people that keep up the funds of our foreign missions. . . . I do not believe in letting the ladies' money go to pay for work that should be paid for by government."

In Natal, there are "Homes" for Zulu girls at Pietermaritzburg, Impolweni, and in the Gordon Memorial Mission, all of which furnish interesting reports. At the first, we hear of weeping and praying girls, and a children's Bible and singing class; at the second, there is now and then "a wild Maria;" but most of the fifteen girls are interested in the Bible: one of them made the bread for a social meeting of the temperance society. At the Gordon Mission women are coming on faster than the men. The 30 members of the Home go to day-school in the forenoon, and in the afternoon learn sewing, household and garden work. Some of the girls are refugees from heathen homes.

The New Hebrides.—The Society has never sent single ladies to the South Seas, but has a married missionary on both Aneityum and Futuna. They train a few girls at a time in their own homes, and lead church-singing, superintend schools as they can, and bear up many parts of the general work, while making a Christian home, forty miles from another white family and six months from the post-office.

The Jewish Association has had a school for German Jewesses in Constantinople for forty years. In 1889 there were 250 pupils, and "as many tokens of the Lord's blessing." While this school is under care of the Edinburgh Association, another at Tiberias is supported by Glasgow ladies.

The Continental Association contributes £100 per annum to the funds of the general society.

The Scottish Episcopal Church. The Central Committee and Church-women's Association for Foreign Missions.—This Committee was formed in accordance with a resolution of the Board of Missions in 1875. The management consists of a central committee of ladies, a convener, general secretary, and treasurer. The aim is to have a correspondent in every diocese, and a congregational correspondent in every congregation. The Committee meets once a month. Membership of the Association is over 3,000. An annual fee of 2s. 6d. is required of each member. The annual income amounts to about £750, and boxes and needlework of as much value are also sent abroad.

The Association publishes the "Mission Chronicle." Office, 122 George Street, Edinburgh.

Efforts abroad are in aid of the church missions in the diocese of St. John's, Kaffraria, and in Chanda, Calcutta district, India.

A juvenile guild is a branch of the association.

Zenana Mission of the United Presbyterian Church of Scotland. Organized 1880.—A Missionary Prayer Union was formed in 1889, with purpose to pray daily for the zenana missions. There are now congregational committees (corresponding to auxiliaries), 200 to 300; presbytery and district committees (corresponding to presbyterial societies), 33. The income in 1889 was £4,307 12s. The "Quarterly Record" is published at College Buildings, Castle Terrace, Edinburgh; price, 4d.

The mission has 18 agents abroad, of whom 1 is a physician. Of the whole number, 11 are in Rajputana, India; 1 in Manchuria, China; and 6 in Old Calabar, West Africa. The na-

tive assistants are about 50, schools for girls 12.

India.—The stations are Ajmere, Nusseerabad, and Jeypore, in all of which many zenanas are visited. In Ajmere are the only physician and hospital of the society. The largest of the Christian girls' boarding-schools is at Nusseerabad, and numbers over 50 boarders. There is an industrial department, and the girls can make all their clothes without help.

Manchuria.—The only agent of the mission here is the wife of the missionary physician at Hai-chung, who, while the doctor treats the patients medically, herself imparts religious instruction in a small woman's ward fitted up in her apartments.

Old Calabar.—The stations are Creek Town, Duke Town, and Ikorofiong. One of the missionaries, who has taken hospital training, has charge of a dispensary at Duke Town. The teaching at all these stations is very elementary.

Ladies' Kaffrarian Society.—Three missionary agents (one of them unsalaried) are laboring at two stations in Kaffraria as representatives of this Society. Their most important undertaking is a girls' boarding-school at Emgwali. The school is supported by local contributions as well as funds of the Society, but is under joint management of the Ladies' Society and the Foreign Mission Board.

Female Association of the Presbyterian Church of Ireland for Promoting Christianity among the Women of the East. Organized 1873.—The management of the Association is in the hands of secretaries, treasurer, and a large general committee (all ladies), consulting and examining committees (gentlemen), and an executive committee (ladies and gentlemen).

The income for 1890, including offerings from Sunday-schools, was £3,906.

"Woman's Work," a small quarterly, is printed at 16 Howard Street, Belfast; price, 2d.

Abroad.—The force in 1889 was represented by: missionaries, 9, of whom 1 is a physician; native helpers, 56; schools, 19; pupils, about 1,100. Three stations are occupied in Western India,—Surat, Borsad, and Ahmadabad,—from each of which the district is worked.

In Surat are a normal class for training Christian teachers, an orphanage, an Anglo-vernacular school, and 5 heathen day-schools. In one of the latter the majority of the girls are Parsis, who, having fewer holidays than the Hindus, make greater progress. At Ahmadabad Dr. Mary M'George had an average daily attendance of 50 at her dispensary during the year 1888, of whom more than 600 were under three years of age. Some patients came 25 miles for treatment, and four came from a village where the year previous every woman had fled from the missionary. Four girls' schools are connected with Ahmadabad station, one containing many daughters from Jain families, one for Mohammedans, and one for Christian girls. A medical work has been opened at Borsad.

The Association has one missionary doing Evangelistic work in Newchang, China, and sent its first lady to join the new mission in Manchuria in 1889.

GERMANY.

Berlin Woman's Missionary Association.—This has been in existence nearly fifty years. It is represented by six missionaries in India, at Secundra and Benares. It also pays the salary of the superintending sister at an orphanage, the Talitha Kumi, in Jerusalem.

*The Berlin Woman's Mission for China.*—This operates entirely by itself, has an annual income of about $4,000, and sustains one or two missionaries.

Other women's societies, among which is one at Stockholm, Sweden, send grants in aid for China through the Basle Mission, and to North Africa through the North Africa Mission.

**Woodstock.**—(1) Mission station of the S. P. G. (1855) in Cape Colony, South Africa, near Cape Town, with 1 missionary.

(2) A town in Landour, Punjab, India, 15 miles east of Dehra. A seminary for girls, both foreign and native, was commenced here in 1874 by the Presbyterian Church (North). Five missionary ladies are now in charge of the work, which is almost self-supporting.

**Worcester,** a town in Cape Colony, South Africa, 80 miles by rail northeast of Cape Town. Population, 3,788. Mission station of the Rhenish Missionary Society; 1 ordained missionary, 1 female missionary, 2 native workers, 2,568 church-members, 633 day-school children; S. P. G. (1885); 1 missionary.

**Worcester, Samuel Austin,** b. Worcester, Mass., U. S. A., January 19th, 1798; graduated University of Vermont, 1819; Andover Theological Seminary, 1823; ordained August 25th, 1825; left as a missionary of the A. B. C. F. M., August 31st, for the Cherokees, reaching Brainerd October 21st, 1825. Through his labors and those of other missionaries, the Indians had made great progress in Christian knowledge and the arts of civilized life. They had become largely a nation of farmers and artisans, had organized with the advice of the United States Government a regular and creditable government, were to a considerable extent supplied with schools and religious institutions, and many were members of Christian churches.

Georgia had long coveted the lands of the Indians. Some had been relinquished by the owners, some had been obtained from them by artifice, and the Indians removed beyond the Mississippi. But those who remained at this time were utterly unwilling to leave their comfortable homes, their cultivated fields, and the graves of their fathers, and remove to a distant and unknown wilderness. In spite of repeated treaties which recognized them as a nation, and which were declared to be "binding on the State of Georgia, her government and citizens, forever," the legislature in 1830 passed a law extending complete jurisdiction over the Cherokee nation, forbidding any white man residing within the limits of the Cherokee nation without a license or permission from the governor, and requiring an oath to submit to and support the jurisdiction of Georgia, declaring also that whoever violated this law should be considered guilty of a high misdemeanor, and imprisoned in the penitentiary at hard labor for four years. The law also disqualified the Cherokees from testifying in any court of justice. Copies of this law were sent to the missionaries at the four stations. They, considering this unconstitutional law not only against their rights, but the rights of their people, resolved to seek protection from the Supreme Court of the United States, and con-

tinued their work. On March 12th, 1831, Mr. Worcester, Mr. Thompson, and Mr. Proctor had been arrested and made prisoners by a detachment of the "Georgia Guard," consisting of 25 armed and mounted men. They were released by the judge on the ground that they were agents of the general government. The governor, on May 6th, wrote to Mr. Worcester and Dr. Butler requiring them to leave the country "with as little delay as possible," under the penalty of arrest. Both replied that they could not in conscience obey the law enacted for their expulsion. On July 7th they were arrested and treated with great indignity. The details of the shocking treatment they received from the military, both on the march and in the filthy prison where they were kept for eleven days, are given in a letter written by Mr. Worcester, and published in the Annual Report of 1831. They were released on a writ of *habeas corpus* under bonds to appear for trial before the court in September. On September 25th they were tried, and Mr. Worcester, Dr. Butler, with eight others, were sentenced to four years in the penitentiary with hard labor. On arriving at the prison they were offered a pardon by the governor if they would take an oath to support the government in its measures against the Cherokees, or abandon their missionary work and leave the Cherokee country. Mr. Worcester and Dr. Butler, believing that obedience to such laws would be treason against God, refused, and were shut up in prison with felons. The case was brought before the Supreme Court of the United States in 1832, and Chief Justice Marshall declared that the laws of Georgia extending her jurisdiction over the Cherokee country were repugnant to the Constitution, to treaties, and to the laws of the United States, and therefore null and void. The court issued a mandate ordering all the proceedings against the prisoners to cease, and that the missionaries be dismissed. Georgia refusing to obey the mandate, the missionaries gave notice that they would move the Supreme Court for further proceedings in their case. Owing to the excitement in South Carolina over the revenue law of the United States, and the fear that if the missionaries should persevere in their suit, and the Supreme Court endeavor to enforce its decision in their favor, not only Georgia but Alabama and Mississippi would join the South Carolina nullifiers; as the governor had promised that if they withdrew their suit they should be unconditionally discharged; as, moreover, the decision of the Supreme Court established the right of the missionaries to a discharge from confinement, and the right of the Cherokees to protection by the President from the aggressions of Georgia; and finally as the law under which they had been imprisoned had been repealed, they, acting under advice of friends, in which the Prudential Committee concurred, withdrew their suit. After sixteen and a half months' imprisonment, they were released, January 14th, 1833, returned to their stations, and resumed their missionary work. While in prison they were permitted to read the Scriptures and pray with the prisoners confined in the same building; and during the last six months Mr. Worcester preached every Sabbath to the prisoners. A spirit of inquiry was awakened, and many, it is believed, were savingly benefited.

Mr. Worcester removed, in April, 1835, with the press to Dwight, and spent the summer among the Cherokees of Arkansas, mostly in making arrangements for printing. He afterwards was stationed at Park Hill among the Cherokees in the Indian Territory, to which they had been removed, and here he died April 20th, 1859.

**Wotyak Version.**—The Wotyak belongs to the Finn branch of the Ural-Altaic family of languages, and is spoken in the provinces of Wiakta and Orenburg, Russia. The Wotyaks profess adherence to the Russian Church. The four Gospels were translated in 1823, or soon after, by a learned Wotyak, and the printing of St. Matthew was begun by the Russian Bible Society. But the work was broken off and left unfinished through the suspension of that Society. A version of Matthew was published by Prince Lucien Bonaparte in phonetic type in 1863. In the year 1878 the British Bible Society authorized Dr. Aminoff to prepare a version of Matthew. With the assistance of a Wotyak teacher he executed the work, which, after a careful revision by the Academician Wiedermann, was published in 1882.

(*Specimen verse.* Matt. 5 : 16.)

Озй медъ пыштозъ югытъ-ты тилядъ адямпїосъазйнъ, собсъ медъ адзїозы дзёць уждэсь тилядъ, сй-но мёдъ сїотозы Анлы, кудызъ ип вылынъ.

**Woyenthin,** a station of the Berlin Missionary Society in South Transvaal, Africa (1884); 1 missionary, 240 communicants.

**Wray, John,** missionary of the L. M. S. to British Guiana, South America, from 1807 to 1837. Sent to Demerara in 1808, at the request of a wealthy planter, and made his home on the plantation. Here his labors were so much blessed that a great reformation took place among the Negroes, not only on this estate, but also on the surrounding ones. They changed their ways of living, and became earnest and attentive listeners to his preaching. He married in 1809. It soon became apparent that the local government of Demerara was not in sympathy with the religious work among the Negroes, and it placed so many obstructions in the way of the missionaries that Mr. Wray was sent to England to obtain, if he could, a modification of the laws of the country. He partially succeeded, and returned to Demerara in 1811, where he continued his work for two years, when he was succeeded by Mr. John Smith.

After this he divided his time among the crown Negroes at the stations of Georgetown and Berbice. The laws which he had secured for the amelioration of the condition of the Negroes being misunderstood and not carried out, he found it necessary to go a second time to England in their behalf. Although the mission work progressed, the Negroes were very much hindered in their religious worship. Their books were taken from them, and overseers accompanied some of them to their meetings "to judge of the doctrines held forth to the Negroes."

Their persecutions irritated them beyond endurance, and a serious insurrection broke out, many of them leaving the plantations and going into the back country. On Mr. Wray's return to Berbice he was requested by the governor to explain to the slaves the new laws, so that there might be no further trouble. He seems to have succeeded, and quiet was restored in his mission, where he remained for 13 years, when, worn out with his work, he with his wife sought rest and health in England. In 1832 he returned to Berbice and continued his work for eight years longer, when he died of yellow-fever at New Amsterdam. In 1834 the emancipation of the Negroes removed the obstacles to the progress of the mission work, and many stations and schools became self-supporting.

**Wright, Alfred,** b. Columbia, Conn., U. S. A., March 1st, 1798; graduated Williams College 1812; Andover Theological Seminary 1814; ordained, December 17th, 1819, at Charleston, S. C.; and appointed by the A. B. C. F. M. as a missionary among the Choctaw Indians, arriving at Elliott, Choctaw Nation, December, 1820. For more than thirty years he labored among the Choctaws, and died at Wheelock, March 31st, 1853. He held meetings for prayer or preaching at different places, though feeble in frame, never without pain, and for twenty years unable to walk more than a few rods, or raise with his hands more than a few pounds' weight without bringing on severe distress from heart-disease. He was emphatically a man of prayer. This was the secret of his success. After a long day's ride of ten hours, staying at a miserable hut, wearied and sick, he would call all the family together, read a chapter in the Bible by firelight, sing a hymn from memory, and offer a prayer. "Few ministers of Christ," says one, "have labored more faithfully or more successfully."

**Wright, Asher,** b. Hanover, N. H., U. S. A., September 7th, 1803; studied one year at Dartmouth College and three in Andover Theological Seminary; ordained October 12th, 1831; joined the Mission to the Senecas, November 9th, 1831, and continued to labor faithfully for that people till his death at Upper Cattaraugus Station, April 13th, 1875, in connection with the A. B. C. F. M. till 1870, and then in connection with the Presbyterian Board. "He was a transparently good man, and gained in a remarkable degree the confidence of the red men and the high esteem of the whites in this vicinity. The Indians feel that they have lost a wise counsellor and true friend."

**Wright, Austin H.,** b. Hartford, Vt., U. S. A., November 11th, 1811; studied at Dartmouth College, and Union Theological Seminary, N. Y., and in the medical department of the University of Virginia, Charlottsville, preaching during his term of study to the destitute population of the "Ragged Mountains;" sailed March 9th, 1840, as a missionary of the A. B. C. F. M. for Smyrna, to join the Nestorian mission and take the place in Oroomiah of Dr. Grant, whose impaired health and large plans for the Mountain Nestorians led him to seek a residence in one of the mountain districts of Koordistan. His perfect acquaintance with the Turkish, Syriac, and Persian languages, coupled with his knowledge of medicine and his kind, gentle courtesy of manner, gave him much influence among all classes of the people, and the business connected with the authorities, and intercourse with the higher classes, was to a great extent in his hands, or carried on through him. The Persian officials and other gentlemen appreciated very highly the courteous, dignified, yet simple ease and grace with which he met them, so that, as a Nestorian preacher said, "the Khâns used to love to see him."

In 1860 he returned to the United States, but, though feeble, he engaged in labors for the Nestorians. In the early part of 1863 he began the revision of the New Testament in Syriac, preparatory to its being electrotyped and printed by the A. B. S. in pocket form. To this the Psalms were added, and he took back with him on his return in 1864 the first few copies, which were hailed with delight by the people. A short time before this it was determined to undertake the translation of the Bible into Tartar-Turkish for the Mohammedan population of Azerbaijan. This work was assigned to Dr. Wright in conjunction with Mr. Rhea, and he entered upon it "with great zest, amounting to enthusiasm." But in three months he was called to a higher service. He died January 14th, 1865, of typhoid fever, after an illness of twelve days.

"The long period of his service, and the great amount of labors which he performed during that time as a preacher, physician, coadjutor in the department of the mission press, and last, not least, as an effective shield to succor the poor oppressed Nestorians,—standing as a daysman between them and the Mohammedans, by whom he was profoundly respected,—as well as the scrupulous fidelity, the marked ability and almost unerring judgment, though so modest. in his bearing, and the untiring energy and endurance with which he cheerfully met and discharged all his multifarious and arduous duties, rendered his death a loss to the mission which seemed to them entirely irreparable."

**Wuchang,** the capital of Hupeh, China (see article), is situated on the south bank of the Yangtsz River, near Hankow (q.v.). Mission station of the Protestant Episcopal Church (1867); 2 missionaries (1 married), 1 female physician, 100 communicants, 77 day-scholars, 40 boarding-scholars. L. M. S. (1865); 1 missionary, 2 native preachers, 90 church-members, 20 Sunday-scholars, 24 day-scholars. Wesleyan Methodist Missionary Society; 1 missionary, 1 chapel, 75 church-members, 35 Sabbath-scholars, 2 day-schools, 35 scholars. C. I. M. (1874); 3 missionaries and assistants, 11 communicants.

**Wuhu,** a city in Nganhwui, China, on the Yangtsz River, 50 miles above Nanking. Mission station of the Methodist Episcopal Church (North, 1884; 2 missionaries and wives, 2 female missionaries, 1 out-station, 2 churches, 36 members, 3 schools, 40 scholars. Protestant Episcopal Church; 2 native pastors, 15 communicants, 46 scholars.

**Wupperthal,** a town in Western Cape Colony, South Africa, near the coast, on the Olifant River, a little southeast of Clan-William. Mission station of the Rhenish Missionary Society; 1 missionary, 1 female missionary, 8 native workers, 750 church-members, 150 school-children.

# Y.

**Yahgan Version.**—The Yahgan belongs to the languages of South America, and is spoken by the inhabitants of Tierra del Fuego, about 3,000 in number. The Rev. Thomas Bridges of the South American Missionary Society, who has been working for more than a decade among the Fuegians, translated the Gospel of Luke, which was published in an edition of 1,000 copies by the British and Foreign Bible Society. printed according to Ellis' phonetic system, in 1880. The Acts of the Apostles were published by the same society in 1883. and in 1884 the Gospel of John was issued. Up to March 31st, 1889, 2,529 portions of the Scriptures were disposed of.

**Yang-Chow,** a prefectural city in Kiangsu, China, 75 miles southeast of Nanking. Mission station of the China Inland Mission (1868); 1 missionary and wife, 5 female missionaries, 87 church-members, 1 girls' school, 23 scholars.

**Yao Version.**—The Yao belongs to the Bantu family of African languages, and is spoken by the Yaos, who occupy the country to the east and south of Lake Nyassa, including the Scotch stations of Blantyre and Livingstonia. A translation of the Gospel of Matthew was made by the Rev. Chauncey Maples, of the Universities' Mission, who has been laboring several years at Masasi, in Africa, with Bishop Heere. On the recommendation of the latter, the British and Foreign Bible Society published in 1879 an edition of the Gospel of Matthew under the editorship of the translator, who had gone to England to read the proofs. As Mr. Maples' translation contained many Swahili words, the British Bible Society published in 1888 a version of the four Gospels and the Acts, made by the Rev. A. Hetherwick of the Blantyre Mission of the Presbyterian Church of Scotland, in pure Yao. The translator carried the translation through the press in England.

**Yates, William,** b. Loughborough, Leicestershire, England, December 15th, 1792; educated for the ministry at Bristol College; ordained August, 1814, and sailed for Calcutta as a missionary of the Baptist Missionary Society April 16th, 1815. He joined the mission at Serampore, devoting himself to preaching and assisting Dr. Carey in the translation of the Scriptures. After Dr. Carey's death he gave himself to translation and preparation of textbooks. He visited England and the United States 1827–29, re-embarking for India in 1829. After his return he was stationed at Calcutta. He translated the whole Bible into Bengâli, the New Testament into Hindi and Hindustani, and the New Testament and large portions of the Old Testament into Sanskrit. He was engaged in preparing the latter for the press, and a large part had been already printed. He hoped by the close of another year to complete the translation of the Scriptures into this sacred and learned language of the East. But his health failing he sailed for England in 1845, but died on the passage up the Red Sea, July 3d. A few years before his death the East India Company offered him a salary of $6,000 if he would enter their service, and prepare books for the government schools. On his declining it, he was offered $3,000 for half of his time, but he refused this also, preferring the work of a missionary on less than half the salary offered.

**Yezidees, The.**—ORIGIN.—The Arabs who accepted Mohammed called those who did not "el johaleen," i.e., the ignorant ones. Among the latter was Yezeed ben M'âwe, who refused to accompany M'âwe his father, who, as an attendant upon his person, followed the fortunes of Mohammed. Many of "the ignorant ones" rallied around Yezeed, and he became the nucleus of the sect which appropriated his name. The Yezidees possess a lineage tree by means of which they trace their religious origin back to him.

They seem to have existed as a very loose organization until about 1106 A.D., when there arose among them one called Sheikh Hâdi (elderly guide), from the region of Damascus. He removed to the district of Hakkari in Koordistan, and dwelt in Mount Lalish, which is eleven hours from Mosul. He died in 1162 A.D. (558 A.H.), and his tomb, called Sheikh Âdi, is hard by the village of Ba'adri, where also is the temple of the Yezidees. This place, as their religious centre, is by them esteemed superior to Mecca.

Sheikh Hâdi gave more consistency to their religious system,—still very confused and illogical,—and greater stability to its organization, by committing to writing its tenets and traditions. His work, which is the authority for their belief, is named "El Jilweh," i.e. "The Revelation." The original is the only copy existing, and it is esteemed as most holy, and is guarded at Sheikh Âdi with the most scrupulous care. It is in the Arabic language and character, and speaks in this wise of the origin of the Yezidees: "'O angels!' said the great God, 'I am going to create Adam and Eve. They will become mankind, and from the lines of Adam's palm (?) shall proceed Shehr ben Jebr, and of him a separate community will appear upon the earth, that of Azazâel, i.e., of Tâoos Melek, which is the sect of the Yezidees.' Then He sent Sheikh Hâdi ben Musaffer from the land of Damascus, and he came and dwelt in Mount Lalish." Sheikh Hâdi was an Arab, and was held in high repute for his piety and devotion. He holds among the Yezidees the same place that is given to Moses by the Jews, and that is claimed by the Moslems for Mohammed.

NUMBER AND LANGUAGE.—This degraded yet interesting people number probably about 200,000 souls, but they are scattered over a belt of territory 300 miles wide, extending in length from the neighborhood of Aleppo in northern Syria to the Caucasus in southern Russia. The mass of them, however, are to be found in the mountains of Northern and Central Koordistan, and among the Sinjar hills of Northern Mesopotamia.

While it originated with the Arabs, this religion was not confined to them, but in the course of centuries received adherents from Koords and the nominally Christian sects. We cannot otherwise account for their wide dispersion.

Though the mysteries of their religion are in the Arabic language, Koordish is more generally spoken by the Yezidees than Arabic; while those about Mosul and in the Sinjar hills use both.

GENERAL CHARACTERISTICS.—They are an agricultural people and live in fixed abodes. As a rule they are neater and cleaner in their homes, and in respect to person and dress, than either Arab or Koord; while their style of dress follows the fashions of the people by whom they are surrounded, except that the shirt has a square-cut opening in front.

Generally speaking they are quiet and industrious, but in the regions of Redwan and Midyat they are given to house-breaking and highway robbery, and also hire themselves to Moslems and Christians for the commission of deeds of blood, so that they are the terror of those districts. In the Sinjar hills, where they constitute almost the entire population, they are restive and refractory. Everywhere they entertain a deep-seated hatred of Moslems, whether Arabs or Koords, who treat them in return with contempt and oppression. Polygamy is allowed among them to the limit of six wives, but its practice is not so general as with the Moslems, who are limited to four wives. The drinking of raki (a mild alcohol) is enjoined as a religious rite in connection with the worship of Melek Tâoos, and accordingly intemperance is common.

CIVIL ORGANIZATION.—They are recognized by the Turkish Government as a distinct religious community. Their civil head is an Emir whose title is hereditary, and who is of kingly origin,—if "El Jilweh" is to be believed. It says: "Then Melek Tâoos came down to earth for our sect, i.e., the Yezidees, the disturbed, and appointed kings for us, besides the kings of ancient Assyrians, Nisroch, etc. . . . And after that we had two kings,—Shâboor (Sapor) First and Second,—who reigned 150 years; and our Emirs, until this day, have descended from their seed."

The Emir never marries outside of this royal line. He is lord of the persons and affairs of the Yezidees, and his power over them is absolute. His person is considered holy, and all his acts are regarded as righteous. To him belongs administrative power and dignity, as well as ecclesiastical, and all the dealings of the Turkish Government with the Yezidees are through him. For this reason he resides most of the time in Mosul. The present Emir is Meerza Beg.

The Yezidees have written laws and statutes which are read and interpreted only by the members of one family—that of Mella Haider, the Bussovahite. The secretary of the Emir is always chosen from this family.

RELIGIOUS SYSTEM.—*Doctrine.*—They believe in God as the supreme deity and the first cause of all things; but they have nothing to do with Him either in the way of worship or service.

They believe in one Melek Tâoos, or King Peacock, who is eternal, an emanation from God, became incarnate as Lucifer, deceived Adam and Eve as Satan, is one of the seven gods who in turn rule the world for 10,000 years (some affirm 7,000) and who, having now governed it for the last 6,000 years, has yet 4,000 years in which to reign.

They believe in one Sheikh Hâdi, called also in "El Jilweh" 'Abd Tâoos (servant of Tâoos). They call him the god of that which is good, of day and of life; say that he is descended from the divine nature, or, at least, is so honored of God that whatever Sheikh Hâdi wills comes to pass; and that when upon the earth he revealed to his disciples revelations, secrets, a knowledge of the unseen and of prophecies. In his book he claimed to be sent both of God and of Melek Tâoos. The second assertion of "El Jilweh" is: "He (Melek Tâoos) sent 'Abd Tâoos to this world that he might separate truth from error and make it known to his people; and the first step to that is by tradition, and afterward by this book 'El Jilweh' which the uninitiated must neither read nor behold." His claim to have been sent of God is made farther on in the sentence quoted at length when stating the origin of this sect. They say also of him, "The Yezidees' god descended in this era and both taught and established us." Sheikh Hâdi associated himself with God in stating farther on in his book that "He afterwards came and dwelt in Lalish." Is there in Sheikh Hâdi an effort at the reconciliation of God and Melek Tâoos, or the union of the two eternal principles (according to Zoroaster) of good and evil, in order to secure a reconciliation of man with each, and with both together, through worship at the shrine of one who stood for both?

They believe in six other gods. "El Jilweh" says: "He created six gods from himself and from his light; and their creation was as one lights a light from another light." (Compare the Parsi doctrine of Ahura Mazda and his six gifts.)

They accept of Christ as the "Light of God," and say that He cannot die; also that He is a Saviour and will come again. But all these are evidently accommodations to the Christian sects with whom they are brought into contact. In the same way the Yezidees about Redwan have attempted to accommodate their tenets to the Christian doctrine of the Trinity.

They hold to the Transmigration of Souls, but subject to the caprice of Melek Tâoos, for "El Jilweh" says: "I (Melek Tâoos) will not allow one in this wretched world longer than the time determined by me; and if I desire it I send him a second or a third time into this world, or some other, by the transmigration of souls." When righteous souls return they enter into men, but wicked spirits are sent back to reside in the beasts. Yet along with this they hold to a Resurrection, when Sheikh Hâdi will carry all the Yezidees to paradise on a tray borne upon his head. They hold to a future judgment and punishment for all—except the Yezidees. "El Jilweh" says: "I (Melek Tâoos) punish in other worlds those who do contrary to my laws." They have Islamic notions of paradise as a place of eating and drinking, together with the pleasures of physical love. They claim to receive the Old Testament, the New Testament, and the Koran, but reverence the Old Testament more than either of the others. This acceptance is, however, a qualified one, for "El Jilweh" says: "The books of those who are without I accept in a sense; i.e., those that agree with and conform to my statutes. Whatsoever is contrary to these they have altered."

*Ecclesiastical Polity.*—This has the form of a religious oligarchy, is composed of six orders besides the Emir, which are chiefly hereditary and confined to as many distinct families. These orders are:

(1) The Sheikh.—He is called Sheikh Mengah, which is the name of a district comprising the regions of Mosul, Amadieh, and Zakho. He is the chief ecclesiastic of the sect, and corresponds to the Sheikh ul Islam. He ranks next to the Emir, who is the religious as well as political head, even as the Sheikh ul Islam to the Sultan, who is also the Caliph. He is the guardian of the tomb of Sheikh Hâdi. The insignia of his office are a kind of girdle which is worn about the body, and a netting of catgut which is carried in the hand. He is supposed to prophesy, and has paradise in his flowing sleeves, sections of which he disposes to purchasers according to the sums received. Whenever the Sheikh appears among the people they submit themselves to him in lowly reverence and humility. The last Sheikh was named Nâsur, but he died recently, and the name of his successor has not yet been ascertained.

(2) Sheikhs.—This order was founded by Sheikh Hâdi. Every Sheikh traces his lineage back through a regular succession to a Patriarch who is regarded not only as the bestower of the office of Sheikh, but also as the assistant and advocate of those in his line who exercise the office, and as the avenger of all injuries inflicted upon them. For this reason no Yezidee dares to return the smiting of an ecclesiastic. Each Sheikh has the privilege of doctoring a special disease. The Sheikhs frighten their followers into giving presents and alms according to their will by threatening to punish them, upon refusal, with pestilence, fever, distress, sickness, and pains, or the control of their enemies over them,—such power being supposed to reside in them.

From this order comes the Mella, who is the instructor of youth, the guardian of "the book," of religious mysteries, and of the interests of the sect. He is also the secretary of the Emir, and in his family alone are reading and writing allowed. The office is hereditary, and the present incumbent is Mella Haider.

(3) Peers.—They are the Nazarites who take vows of celibacy and devote themselves and their property to Sheikh Hâdi. To them appertains the conduct of hair-dressing and of the fasts and feasts. They are also intercessors, and perform their function upon certain heaps of stones in the neighborhood of Sheikh Âdi, where they continually reside.

(4) Koochiks.—The word is Koordish and signifies dancer. These attend to the service of the tambourines, praises and songs. They order and conduct the sacred dance upon the feast-days. They praise the gods Hâdi and Tâoos with tambourine and fife until they swoon in a trance, when they utter strange sounds and language. They declare what is revealed to them in dream, trance, and vision, and are reckoned as prophets. They are said to have the power of life and death,—probably through the influence of magic.

(5) Kowals—"speakers." These are the priests proper, to whom pertain the duties of imparting religious instruction to the people, and of sepulture. All instruction is oral, in which they profess to be guided by an "inner light" to which all, even the Emir, must give

heed. Whenever a Yezidee is about to die he is visited by a Kowal, or his agent, who removes the dying man's sins by transferring them to himself. They divide with the Peers the function of intercessors, and to them belongs the privilege, each year, of bidding for the concession of conducting the "Sanjak Tâoos" (see Worship) among the Yezidee villages. They never use a razor upon their heads.

(6) Fakirs.—These constitute the lowest order of the priesthood. They are entrusted with the assembling of boys and girls and the instruction of them in the tambourine, in dancing and religious evolutions. They are married, have a salary, live in Sheikh Âdi, and are the janitors of that holy place.

*Worship*—Objects of. Melek Tâoos through his "Sanjak," or symbol, which is a sacred brazen cock one eye of which is marked over by a cross.

Sheikh Hâdi, who is still a god though his body be dead, and who receives divine honors at his tomb in Sheikh Âdi. Forasmuch as he was also sent of Melek Tâoos, the sacred cock stands for him also, so that he is worshipped at the same time with Melek Tâoos; and at his tomb the "Sanjak" of Melek Tâoos is revered equally with the tomb. The two eternal principles have thus equal honor, and by this arrangement no one can worship the one without equally worshipping the other. Here again there seems to be an attempt to accommodate something to their needs from the Parsi religion. In the Vendidad the cock is a sacred bird—the bird of Sraosha, who is Obedience to the law of Mazda and chief of the Yazatas and their leader against the leader of the demon host, Æshna Dæva. The Yezidees seem to combine the two principles and so make the cock represent both.

These two gods are the chief objects of their worship, and the tomb of one and the sanjak of the other are the symbols employed to bring them before the worshippers.

The sun is regarded as an exalted spirit without whom there would be no stability to the universe, and therefore worthy of respect and worship.

Fire, more especially as lightning and flame, is considered a sacred element, and is worshipped by adoration.

They have also a bronze image of an ox which they worship at a festival in November.

The tombs of departed Sheikhs are regarded as holy, and in religious rites conducted at them the assistance of those entombed therein is specially invoked.

*Forms of Worship.*—The "Sanjak Tâoos" when carried to a village is accompanied by Kowals, who march before it with timbrel and pipe. It must remain in the village over night, and the Yezidees must drink "raki" in its presence. Its worshippers approach it upon their knees, kiss it, mutter prayers, deposit their contributions in a box by its side, rise and walk away with their face toward it. Meanwhile a candle burns on either side of the holy bird.

Prayer.—They have no liturgy, nor do they pray audibly, believing that all prayer should be with the heart only.

Fasts.—They say God does not require them to fast, save during Ramazan, when they fast three days instead of thirty. This fast must be begun and ended in the presence of either Sheikh or Peer. It is ended by a participation in holy wine that is considered to be the blood of Christ. The cup containing it is held in both hands, after the sacrificial manner of the East, and if a drop should fall it is gathered with religious care.

Feasts.—These are the following: 1. On the first Wednesday in April, which is the beginning of their year. 2. August 1st, and continuing three days, in honor of Melek Fukhr ed Deen. 3. September 22d, and continuing eight days, to Sheikh Hâdi, and called "et towafat" —i.e. the floods. 4. November, called the Naheevi. (This feast is especially observed by the Yezidees of Jebel Toor, at which the sacred ox is worshipped in connection with Babylonian orgies.) 5. January 1st, and lasting three days, in honor of Shems ed Deen. At all these feasts there is much singing in connection with the religious dances. They have a hymn-book called "Zemboor," the hymns of which are in Arabic. They have also songs which are in Koordish and are sung to Koordish tunes.

RELATION TO MISSIONARY WORK.—So long as the Turkish Government continues to draft Yezidees into the army it will not allow them to be Christianized. Another formidable obstacle is found in a requisition of their religion that no one shall learn to read or have any dealing with books except the family of Sheikh ul Bussowi, as stated above, the custodians of the sacred book.

An attempt to teach a young man from this sect was frustrated by his relatives. An agha of influence among them in the vicinity of Wevan Sheho has been induced by Protestants to learn to read. He now refuses to worship "Sanjak Tâoos," and asks for a teacher for his village. An English lady has just sent a small sum for a tentative effort among them, and the Mardin station of the Eastern Turkey Mission, in whose field the most of the Yezidees reside, has accordingly sent out a young man for that effort. We have faith that the Yezidees will yet come forth from their darkness and ignorance, and walk in the light and knowledge of Him who is the "Light of the World."

**Yokohama** is one of the most important of the treaty ports of Japan. It is situated on a plain by the side of the Bay of Tokyo, and is shut in by hills. It occupies an area of a square mile, about one fourth of which is a foreign settlement. The climate is variable, the thermometer ranging from 95° to 43° F., and the rainfall is quite great. The population is 119,783, and there are large numbers of Chinese and Europeans. The harbor is a wide and commodious one, well protected by a breakwater. Yokohama is the port of call for the lines of steamers between San Francisco and Hong Kong, and other lines connect it with Shanghai, as well as numerous steamers which run from it to points in Japan and China. A line of steamers from Vancouver to Hong Kong stop there regularly. A railway connects it with Tokyo, and was the first railway opened in Japan (1872). It is also the terminus of a railroad which runs to Kyoto.

Mission station of the Presbyterian Church (North), 1859; 1 missionary and wife, 1 female missionary. A. B. M. U. (1872); 2 missionaries and wives, 2 female missionaries, 3 churches, 327 church-members, 2 schools, 90 pupils,

Methodist Episcopal Church (North); 2 missionaries and wives, 1 female missionary, 178 members, 4 day-schools, 372 scholars. Reformed (Dutch) Church U. S. A.; 2 missionaries and wives, 4 female missionaries, Ferris Seminary, 102 scholars. (For development of mission work, see article Japan.)

**Yonezewa,** a station of the Methodist Episcopal Church (North) in the Tokyo district, in the southeastern part of the island of Nippon, Japan; 1 missionary and his wife, 2 foreign teachers, 2 native workers, 56 church-members, 1 school, 35 scholars.

**Yoruba,** a section of the slave coast, West Africa. See Africa.

**Yoruba Version.**—The Yoruba belongs to the Negro group of the languages of Africa, and is spoken by several Yoruba tribes,—Yoruba proper, Egba, Ijebu. Ijesa, Effon, Ondo,—extending from Dahomey to the tribes on the west bank of the Niger, and said to number 3,000,000. A version was undertaken by the Revs. C. Crowther, T. King, and others, and between the years 1850 and 1878 there were issued at London, besides the New Testament, Genesis to Ruth, Psalms and Daniel. In 1879, at the request of the Church Missionary Society, a new edition of the New Testament and Psalms, slightly revised, especially as to the spelling of certain words agreed upon at a conference of Europeans and natives convened at Lagos, was published under the care of the Rev. Dr. Hinderer, the reviser. During the year 1880 the Yoruba Scriptures, the main part of which was translated by the Rev. (afterwards Bishop) Crowther, were completed at press in London under the care of Dr. Hinderer. In the same year a translating and revising committee, consisting of natives and Europeans, at Lagos, began the revision of the entire work, and a revised edition of the entire Bible was published in 1884, under the care of the Rev. Dr. Hinderer. The first edition of the New Testament being almost exhausted, a revision committee, in which the Wesleyan missionaries joined the Church Missionary Society missionaries, was formed in 1886 to revise the New Testament, with a view to the publication of an edition of 10,000 copies. In 1888 the edition passed through the press under the care of the Rev. N. Johnson. In the same year the British Bible Society also published an edition of 6,000 copies of the revised Old Testament, under the care of the Rev. J. B. Wood. Up to March 31st, 1889, 70,123 portions of the Scriptures in the Yoruba Version were disposed of.

(*Specimen verse.* John 3 : 16.)

Nitori ti Olorun fę araiye tobę ge, ti o fi Omo bibi rę nikansoso fun ni pe, ęnikęni ti o ba gbà a gbő ki yio sęgbé, sugbou yio ni iye ti ko nipekun.

**Young Men's Association in Aid of the Baptist Missionary Society.** Headquarters, Baptist Mission House, Furnival Street, London.—The Young Men's Missionary Association was organized in 1848. Its object is to increase in every way possible interest in missions among the young. Many members of the Association have gone as missionaries to one or another of the mission fields of the Baptist Missionary Society. Ten of the native schools of that society in India are supported by the Association, and in various other ways its influence is felt by the parent society. By means of its "Missionary Journal," published monthly, much interest in missions has been awakened in the Baptist Sunday-schools of Great Britain. Annual income, £193 18s. 10d.

**Young Men's Christian Association.**—Organizations of Christian young men for mutual improvement, and for more or less of religious activity, have probably existed in almost every age of the church. There is historical record of such societies in Great Britain and Ireland as early as the reign of Charles I. They maintained a continuous existence for nearly one hundred years, through the revolutions under Cromwell and King William, attaining their highest prosperity in the reign of the latter. The chief object of these societies was the promotion of personal piety among their members, but they gave rise in 1691 to the "Societies for the Reformation of Manners," which had for their aim the suppression of vice through legal means. These were called into being by the low state of public morals, which, notwithstanding the better attitude of the court of William and Mary, had little mended since the dissolute reign of Charles II. The early efforts of these reform societies were favored by the civil courts, and they flourished for about forty years. They had become extinct, however, in 1757, and an effort to revive them by members of Wesley's and Whitefield's congregations was defeated through the indifference if not actual hostility of the authorities. In the present century, between 1823 and 1838, David Nasmith, of Glasgow, formed about seventy Young Men's Societies in as many cities of the United Kingdom, France, and America. In Germany, as early as 1832, similar associations of young men were formed, closely connected with the established churches and their pastors. But while all these were societies for young men, with a distinctively Christian purpose and activity, still they were very far from measuring up to the present organization. They did not as individual societies seek broadly to promote the physical, intellectual, and social as well as the spiritual welfare of young men. They did not develop or train a special class of executive officers employed to devote to this comprehensive work their entire time and energies. They did not acquire property in the form of buildings, making themselves permanent institutions in their respective communities. They did not band themselves together in district, national, international, and world's conferences, each with an executive committee employing executive officers for correspondence and visitation. They did not produce a literature stating in periodical and more permanent form the important mission and distinctive features of their Christian institution. It is true that some of these pre-existing organizations, notably those of Germany, are now part of the brotherhood forming the World's Conference of the Associations. The present Glasgow Association traces its origin to a Nasmith Society formed in 1824, and the Cincinnati Association claims also to have originated, under another name, in 1849, quite independently of suggestion from London. But it seems beyond dispute that it was not until the life of the new movement, with the fuller conception of work for young men developed along its path, touched and modified these older organizations that they became, or are becoming, in any real sense what are now recognized as Young Men's Christian Associations. The movement which has resulted in the present world-wide brotherhood can be traced to the parent English-speaking Association which was organized in London by George Williams, June 6th, 1844, and of which that gentleman, still in vigorous manhood, is now the honored president.

But while the origin and early growth of the movement took place in London and other cities of Great Britain, the larger development and expansion of the work has been wrought out by the American Associations, which have for many years greatly exceeded any other group of these societies in numbers, strength, and usefulness. A knowledge of the London Association and its work led to the formation of Associations in Montreal (Canada), December 9th, 1851, and in Boston the 29th of the same month, neither city having any knowledge of the other's action. Other cities followed, till some twenty-five similar organizations were known to be in existence at the date of the first convention, which met in Buffalo, June 7th, 1854. By the action of this body a confederation was formed, a central committee appointed, and an annual delegated meeting of the Associations of the United States and British Provinces authorized. The first World's Conference met in Paris August 19th, 1855. Here the following declaration, since known as the Paris Basis, or the Basis of 1855, was adopted: "The Young Men's Christian Associations seek to unite those young men who, regarding Jesus Christ as their God and Saviour, according to the Holy Scriptures, desire to be His disciples in their doctrine and in their life, and to associate their efforts for the extension of His kingdom among young men." Upon this rests the affiliation of the Associations of all lands, represented since 1855 by a triennial World's Convention, and since 1878 by a Central International Committee, with headquarters at Geneva, Switzerland. This declaration was ratified by the American International Convention at Montreal in 1856, and at Detroit in 1868 was added what is known as the "active membership test," by which in the American Associations only those in full communion with an evangelical church are admitted to voting and office-bearing membership. At the Portland Convention the following year this action was unanimously reaffirmed, the meaning of the term "evangelical" was defined, and representation at the International Convention, from all Associations thereafter organized, made conditional upon this test being embodied in their constitutions.

In April, 1860, the Associations of North America had about 25,000 members. At the breaking out of the civil war large numbers of their young men entered the armies on both sides, and the Associations naturally followed them with efforts for their welfare and that of their comrades. At the instance of the New York Association a special convention was called November 14th, 1861, which resulted in the organization of the United States Christian Commission, the work of which largely absorbed the energies of the Northern Associations during the remainder of the war. With the return of peace, however, the Associations took up their old work with renewed zeal, advanced ideas, and better methods. From about this time dates the beginning of that unparalleled growth which has marked the past two decades. The formal adoption of the evangelical test secured the active sympathy of the churches; a clearer conception of the work, as distinctively for and by young men, focalized thought and effort, and rapidly developed both methods and men; this called for better facilities, which were readily furnished as the practical character of the work was recognized; the work demanded systematic supervision, and the paid secretaryship was developed; the Associations increased in number, spread over the country, and grew multiplex in their departments of work, and State organization and a comprehensive general supervision became a necessity; broadened methods and appliances in the local work asked for larger, better adapted and permanent quarters, and buildings sprang up by the score; till to-day the Associations are a universally acknowledged force in the religious, educational, and social life of the country.

In government the individual Associations are independent, except as to the single item of the active-membership test, each society conducting its business affairs through a board of directors as the corporate management, and with a paid executive officer styled a general secretary; but they are united in a thorough system of general organization, embracing delegated conventions, executive committees, and visiting agents, the decisions and advice of which, though in the main only advisory, are very generally accepted and followed. With the Associations of the United States and Canada this system embraces:

1. A BIENNIAL CONVENTION (annual previous to 1878), composed of delegates from all the Associations, representation being based upon the active membership. The *ad interim* powers of this convention are vested in an executive board, the members of which are elected by classes at the biennial sessions. Since 1866 the headquarters and a working quorum of this body have been located in New York, and in 1883 it was incorporated as the International Committee, a name by which it had for years been known. The present executive force of the committee consists of a general secretary, with fourteen office and travelling secretaries in the home and two in the foreign field. The scope of the committee's work is broad, including (a) supervision and extension—generally of all the work, in full when there is no State organization, and very largely of such special departments as the college, railroad, German, and foreign work; the State organizations owe their existence and early nurture to the act and care of the International Convention and its committee; (b) securing, training, and recommending general secretaries; (c) advising, and assisting regarding the plans, location, and methods of building and the management of property; (d) securing funds for its own work and aiding State and local Associations in raising money for State work for new buildings, to place secretaries in new fields, and in special financial emergencies; (e) arranging for the International meetings, assisting in planning many State and special conventions, and sending official representatives to all; (f) conducting

an extensive correspondence—200,000 letters and circulars being sent out and received in a year; (g) besides a publication list of nearly one hundred tracts and books, several annuals and other periodicals are issued, including the "Year-Book" of 200 pages, which contains, besides many valuable statistical tables, the reports of the officers and secretaries of the committee, and of its corresponding members located in every State and Province at home and in many foreign lands; (h) through the systematic efforts of the committee, the American Associations have observed annually, since 1866, a day and week of prayer in November, and since 1875, by act of the World's Conference, the Associations of other lands have joined in this observance; (i) in times of overwhelming calamity by fire, flood, fever, or disaster, the Associations have often rendered communities effective help through this committee, as their agent, in gathering and distributing such relief.

2. STATE ORGANIZATIONS, modelled after the international, and doing a like work, so far as needed, in their respective fields. First authorized by the International Convention at Albany in 1866, and first called together in each State and Province by the International Committee, these organizations have increased until in 1890 there were 34, embracing 45 States and Provinces, with 66 travelling and office secretaries. For the year ending March 1st, 1890, there were held 34 State Conventions, with an attendance of 7,295 delegates, and representing 987 Associations. The organization of a State is perfected by a subdivision into districts, of three to six counties each, with an executive committee, containing usually a member from each Association, and with a corresponding member in every non-Association town. A district convention is held at least annually, and a system of inter-visitation maintained among the several Associations. The various delegated gatherings, district, state, national, international, and world's conventions, with the conferences of general secretaries, are very helpful; not only in the social and religious contact of the workers, but the close comparison of views and methods in the various papers and discussions results in a better understanding and a more intelligent preference of the best plans and agencies developed. The instruction and advice of the travelling secretaries, and the teachings of official publications purpose to harmonize with the deliverances of the conventions, and tend to uniformity of aim and action through the organizations at large. The amount expended by the International and State Committees in the work of general supervision and extension for 1889 was $162,000, being one tenth of the total annual expenditure of the American Associations for that year.

The organization and work of the typical American Association may be thus described: (a) A dual membership: (1) Active—men who are members of evangelical churches, and who constitute its voting, office-bearing, and working force; (2) Associate—young men of good moral character, who join usually for the secular privileges. The total membership of the 1,208 Associations reporting in 1890 is 212,000, more than half being associate members. (b) A business organization, with constitution, legal incorporation, officers, board of management, and well-ordered system of committees. Ordinarily the work is arranged under five or more depart-

ments, namely, business, religious, educational, social, physical, etc. The membership of these boards and committees, through whom the work is largely carried on, aggregates 32,000. The solidarity of the work in the larger cities is promoted by the metropolitan plan, as it is termed, by which the several organizations in a city, each under a board of management, are on an equal footing as branches, while the general control is vested in a central directorship. This body, relieved of detail work, and with its own executive officer, is able to devote its energy to a general supervision of the field and a wise extension of the work. (c) A paid secretary, with such assistants as are needed. The general secretaryship demands a person fitted for its duties by natural tact, love for the work, and more or less of technical training. His province is to supervise and direct, under the local board, and to develop workers, rather than to attempt too much detail work himself; yet his personality should touch for good the largest possible number in the sphere of his daily work. The total number of general secretaries, physical directors, and assistants in the various departments of the local work is 891, with 116 temporary vacancies. A school devoted chiefly to the training of young men as general secretaries and gymnasium instructors was opened in Springfield, Mass., in 1885, since which time it has been in successful operation, having 11 instructors in its general and special courses, with a present enrolment of over 60 students. A school of like character is in process of organization at Chicago, and there are several well-constituted summer schools. (d) A building of its own, adapted to its manifold work. A distinguishing feature in its construction is a central reception or social room, adjoining the business offices, and through which access must ordinarily be had to all other departments. These usually comprise reading-room, library, parlors, recreation-room, offices for secretaries and directors, large and small lecture-rooms, class rooms, gymnasium, including bowling-alley, baths, and dressing-rooms, a kitchen, and janitor's quarters. Two hundred and five associations have buildings, many of which are large and elegant, complete in their appointments. The total value of Association real estate is $10,149,410—a good index of the estimate put upon the work by Christian business men, and a strong guarantee of its permanency. (e) An organized work: (1) Religious—consisting of Bible-classes, evangelistic and for Christian young men; workers' training-classes; evangelistic and devotional; meetings for young men; special work in the interests of personal purity, temperance, etc.; systematic invitation work; the distribution of religious literature; and a directly personal work, which is specially emphasized. (2) Educational—reading-rooms; circulating and reference libraries; evening classes in practical and liberal branches, book-keeping, penmanship, stenography, mathematics, drawing, languages, history, literature, political science, music, etc.; literary societies, and educational lectures. (3) Social—attractive rooms for resort, with companionable supervision, music, recreative games, and a variety of social gatherings and entertainments. (4) Physical—facilities for artificial exercise of every description, and under instructors competent, from both a scientific and practical training, to make physical examinations and prescribe safe and helpful work; baths, and often athletic grounds for field-sports, and clubs for boating, swimming, rambling, etc. (5) Economics—employment bureau, boarding-house register, savings-bank, medical club, visitation of the sick, and similar service. (6) Junior department, in which, under special supervision and with separate rooms, a more or less full line of work is carried on for boys, and from which they graduate into the senior departments. The following are some statistics of the local work of the American Associations for 1889, about 90 per cent of the whole number of organizations reporting:

*Religious.*—Three hundred and forty-nine report 487 Bible-classes, 470 with a total average attendance of 6,005; 389 report 544 training-classes for special study of the Bible, 536 with a total average attendance of 4,206; 580 report 798 weekly prayer-meetings, 742 with a total average attendance of 18,030, 628 report 684 gospel meetings, 644 with a total average attendance of 33,000.

*Secular.*—Six hundred and eleven report a total average daily attendance at the rooms of 50,970; 731 report reading-rooms; 511 report libraries, containing 422,912 volumes; 490 libraries are valued at $426,796; 277 report educational classes, with from 1 to 15 different branches of study, 247 reporting 17,143 different students in attendance; 145 report literary societies, 127 with a total average attendance of 3,377; 592 report 4,949 lectures; 691 report 3,269 sociables; 499 report attention to physical culture, 368 through gymnasiums and 240 through athletics and other means. The amount expended in the local work of the Associations for 1889 was $1,700,000. Full statistics may be found in the "Year-Book," published by the International Committee, 40 East Twenty-third Street, New York. The financial management of the Associations is in the hands of representative Christian business men in the various communities, and is generally conceded to be exceptionally economical, exhibiting a very large return in labor and results for the amount invested and expended.

As has been clearly shown, a leading feature of the Young Men's Christian Association is its power of adaptation. With the young man as the focal centre, the radius of its helpfulness touches every point in the circle of his needs. Its gymnasium and athletic sports afford recreation and make his body strong; its reading-room, library, classes, lyceum, and lectures train his mind, advance him in social and business position, and broaden his whole life; its pleasant rooms and social companionship take the place of the distant or lost home; its relief agencies come to the stranger, the destitute, and the sick with aid and comfort in time of need; and its religious meetings, Bible study, and personal work win to faith and the Christian life, build up moral character, and train in active work for the best welfare of others; while the spirit and principles of Christianity pervade and vitalize the entire work.

This arm of the church is stretched down into the busy centre of the city, with its hand of shelter and helpfulness open 365 days in the year. But some of the more distinct and isolated classes of young men have been reached by the use of means specially adapted to the sphere of each. There are 302 college associations in as many institutions of learning, with a total membership of 19,000 students, and knit together by a system of intercollegiate correspondence and visitation. This work has also given rise largely to such offshoots as: (*a*) the Northfield Summer School, where some 400 students from over 100 colleges spend part of their annual vacation in studying the Bible and methods of Christian work, under the instructions of eminent scholars and workers of this and other lands; (*b*) the great Student Volunteer Movement, through which several thousand students are pledged to foreign missionary work; (*c*) the Inter-Seminary Missionary Alliance; (*d*) the later and important movement of the Young Women's Christian Association; (*e*) the introduction of the college association into schools of heathen lands; (*f*) the recent foreign mission work for young men of the International Committee, by which, at the solicitation and with the co-operation of the church missionary boards, experienced men are being placed in the great centres of the foreign mission field to organize associations after American models, and to train native Christian young men as general secretaries and workers. In this interest a travelling agent is now visiting the Asiatic countries; secretaries of the Committee have been located at Tokyo, Japan, and Madras, India, and will follow at other places as soon as the men and means can be obtained. Railroad branches are in operation at 82 terminal points, and so acceptable is their work to both employers and employed, that railroad corporations are appropriating more than $100,000 annually to their support. Branches exist for German-speaking young men in cities having a large population of this character, and for colored young men, especially in educational and city centres of the South. Some beginning of effort has also been made to reach the commercial traveller on the road and at his hotel, the men on the fire and police departments of the cities, the lumbermen and the miners in their western camps, the soldier and the sailor, and as has already been said, the boys, who are recognized as the young men of to-morrow.

The parent London Society at its beginning sought only the spiritual welfare of young men in a limited sphere and by the simplest means. But like everything destined to life and usefulness, it began to grow, slowly at first, adding one by one the lines of effort that have since been characteristic of the work, especially the reading-room, library, and other means of mental improvement. Through the entire history of the Associations, their methods and agencies have been a development, never forced, but wrought out gradually, and only as clearly demanded. A study of these agencies shows them to be twofold—the directly religious, and the so-called secular. The latter are employed with a double purpose—for the direct mental and physical benefit they confer, and to attract young men within the sphere of the religious influences. Neither of these objects must be lost sight of. The secular agencies are the means of largely augmenting the membership, especially from the fact that because of much generous volunteer labor and the gifts of friends the Association membership fee can be made much smaller than would be charged elsewhere for similar privileges. Aside from these paid-for privileges, however, are the directly moral and religious agencies, whose scope is broader.

Their benefits enumerated reach: (1) the active members, who in connection with their systematic duties receive a practical training in Christian work unexcelled in any other field; (2) the associates, to whose welfare the efforts of the first are specially directed; and (3) nonmembers who avail themselves of the readingroom, the employment bureau, the boardinghouse register, and other hospitalities open to all young men, including the religious meetings. Of this threefold constituency the first and second classes are about equal, while the third largely outnumbers both the others, greatly extending the reach of the Association's influence. The institution has distinct aims as it touches men of various classes and characters. It seeks by aggressive effort to rescue those who have fallen under the power of vice, to shield and restrain those still free from evil habit and association by providing healthful recreation and good companionship, and to instruct and build up in true manliness all with whom it comes in contact; yet it constantly relies upon the gospel of Christ, and expects little permanent result except as young men commit their lives to His keeping. Those Associations are judged the most successful in which the largest percentage of active workers is developed and the greatest number of young men led into church-fellowship.

As peculiarly a lay movement, and in a sense independent of existing ecclesiastical organizations, the Associations were not at once received into favor and confidence; neither were they free from mistakes, especially in the earlier years of the work; but their loyalty and sustained usefulness long since won them recognition as thoroughly legitimate and helpful auxiliaries of the church, and on a par with such interdenominational institutions as the various missionary, Sunday-school, and publication societies. In fact they hold in some respects a closer relation to the evangelical body than some of its organic connections, as each active member must be in communion with and under the disciplinary control of one of its recognized branches, and the moment such relations cease his vital connection with the Association is severed. In compensation for the general secretaries, who are to a considerable degree withdrawn from distinctively denominational effort, the number of lay workers has been largely increased, young men are rendered more efficient through the peculiar training received, and the hearty testimony of pastors is that those most active in the Association are the best workers in the several churches. It is a well-defined principle of the Associations, that the church has paramount claim upon its young men which must in no wise be interfered with, and that success can only be expected as the work is conducted in general harmony with the pastors and general Christian sentiment of a community.

The transatlantic Associations have developed less rapidly than in America, and the work of the individual societies is much narrower in scope, especially along the line of the secular agencies. The most advance has been made in Great Britain and its colonial dependencies. In Great Britain and Ireland there are 600 Associations, with 61,000 members. In England and Ireland 49 own buildings valued at $1,100,000; 219 report 306 weekly Bible-classes, and 385 weekly devotional meetings;

206 report libraries, 207 reading rooms, 118 educational classes, 42 gymnasiums.

In Australia, at Melbourne, Sydney, and Adelaide, buildings are owned, as well as at Cape Town, Africa; Honolulu, Hawaii; at Osaka, Japan; and Bombay, India.

Associations have been recently organized on the American plan in Berlin, Geneva, Zürich, Amsterdam, Paris, and other cities of the Continent. In Berlin an admirable Association building has been erected, and the movement promises to spread from these centres. The recent improvements in the methods of general organization and supervision are largely the result of contact with Western ideas through the World's Conferences, at which, beginning with 1878, the American Associations have been very fully represented. At the Geneva Conference in this year 41 American delegates were present, being one fifth of the entire number, and chiefly owing to their influence the Central International Committee was appointed. To the Conferences of 1881, 1884, and 1888 this committee reported a work of visitation and correspondence which has greatly promoted the brotherhood of Associations in all lands. A general organization, with representative conventions and travelling secretaries, has followed in England, Scotland, Ireland, and other countries, in every instance greatly stimulating and advancing the entire work.

The number of Associations in the world is now 4,107; they are grouped as follows: United States, 1,259; Dominion of Canada, 82; Bermuda, 1; Argentine Republic, 1; British Guiana, 1; Chili, 2; West Indies, 5; England and Wales, 278; Ireland, 56; Scotland, 249; France, 61; Germany, 836; Holland, 457; Denmark, 93; Switzerland, 383; Norway, 73; Sweden, 85; Italy, 41; Spain, 8; Belgium, 27; Austria, 5; Hungary, 3; Russia, 9; Bulgaria, 1; European Turkey, 1; India, 15; Ceylon, 10; China, 6; Japan, 10; Asiatic Turkey, 11; Persia, 3; Syria, 1; Madagascar, 2; Africa, 11; Australia, 11; Tasmania, 2; New Zealand, 4; Hawaii, 4.

Widely as the organization has spread, it is evidently but in its infancy. In the larger cities, its earlier and more important field, only a good beginning has yet been made; the demand is immensely greater than the supply of either money or men. The extent and usefulness of the institution when the Christian faith of the world shall be fully roused to the wisdom of its methods, and the gifts of multitudes who have started in life under its helpful influences shall flow back to it, is open only to prophecy.

**Young Men's Foreign Missionary Society.** Headquarters, Y. M. C. A., Needless Alley, Birmingham, England.—This Society was organized by young men belonging to the Y. M. C. A of Birmingham, England, in 1876, with the following objects: To promote among Christian young men a direct personal interest in foreign mission work by sending out and entirely supporting one or more missionaries chosen by the Society; to receive and circulate regular reports from missionaries who shall be in every way the representatives of the Society. The only mission, so far, of this Society is in Alfred County, Natal, South Africa. The station is named Ikwezi Lamaci, and is 4 miles distant from Harding, a military and postal station. One missionary and his wife are at the station. They went out in 1877, and now there is a commodious mission house, a church, and a school. In addition, a building has been put up at Harding, where services are held for the police and the Griqua Kafirs. Industrial education is also conducted in the mission school. A preaching station and school has been established at Ithluku, and a mission near the coast has been opened, called Malan Cliff. Several natives have been baptized, and the outlook is most promising.

**Yuh-shan,** a county town in Kiangsi, China, in the northeast part, near the source of the Kung King River. It has an important transit trade. Mission station of the China Inland Mission (1877); 2 female missionaries, 1 native pastor, 65 communicants.

**Yung-Ping,** a town in Chihli, North China, 135 miles due east of Peking. Opened in connection with the Kaiping mines, at the eastern terminus of the railroad from Tientsin. Climate dry, with marked alternations of heat and cold. Population, 120,000. Language, Mandarin. Social condition fairly good. Mission station of the Methodist New Connexion (1884); 1 missionary and wife, 7 native helpers, 4 out-stations, 2 churches, 33 church-members, 1 school, 8 scholars.

**Yunnan,** the capital of the province of Yunnan, China. An important manufacturing and trading place. Mission station of the China Inland Mission (1882); 3 missionaries, 4 female missionaries, 3 associate missionaries, 5 communicants.

# Z.

**Zacatecas,** a city of Mexico, in the inland State of the same name. The place is not attractive in its appearance, owing to its wild, arid surroundings, and the streets are uneven and badly paved. Population, 60,000, pure-blood Indians, mixed Indians, and Spanish. Mission station of the Southern Baptist Convention; 1 missionary and wife, 1 single lady, 1 native unordained preacher, 3 churches, 73 church-members, 1 school, 20 scholars. Mission station of the Presbyterian Church (North); 1 missionary, 17 out-stations, 1,090 communicants, 597 Sabbath-scholars, 61 day-schools, 2 native pastors, 1 Bible-woman.

**Zafarwal,** a station of the U. P. Church of U. S. A. (1866), in the Punjab, India, near Sialkot. There are 5 native workers, 107 church-members, 3 schools, 95 scholars.

**Zahleh,** a town in Syria, 35 miles northwest of Damascus. Population, 10,000. It was nearly destroyed during the Druse insurrection. Mission station of the Presbyterian Church (North); 1 missionary.

**Zanzibar.**—The territory under this name included the strip of the east coast of Africa between Warsheikh, latitude 3° north, and Delgado Bay, latitude 10° 42' south, with an indefinite extent inland, until in 1886 the extent was limited to 10 miles inland, from Cape Delgado to Kipini on the Ozi River; and that territory, together with the islands of Zanzibar, Pemba, and other small islands, constitutes the dominions of the Sultan. The German East African Association have secured the rights of the mainland, and with the lease of the northern part of the coast to the Imperial British East Africa Company, the Sultan's dominion is limited almost to the islands of Zanzibar and Pemba. Zanzibar island has an area of 625 square miles, with a population of 200,000. The town of Zanzibar has a population estimated at 100,000. Mohammedanism is the religion of the country. Mission work is carried on by the Universities' Mission, with three stations on the island, Mkunazini, Mbweni, and Kiungani, with schools, hospital and dispensary work, industrial school, theological school and home, a printing-press, under the charge of 2 clergy and 8 laity. For additional information in regard to the mainland and mission work, see Zanzibar under Africa.

**Zaragoza,** a most important city of Spain, on the Ebro River, 170 miles northeast of Madrid. It is gloomy and antiquated, with narrow, ill-paved, irregular streets, and, except charitable and religious edifices, few fine buildings. Population, 92,407 (1887). Mission station of the A. B. C. F. M.; 1 native pastor, 5 native helpers, 1 church, 66 school-children.

**Zenana Work :** see Women's Boards.

**Ziegenbalg, Bartholomew,** was born June 24th, 1683, in Pullsnitz, Saxony. King Frederick IV. of Denmark, aroused to his duty to give the gospel to those under his sway in India by his chaplain, Dr. Lütken, directed him to seek men suitable for missionary service. Ziegenbalg and Plutschau, then students at Halle, young men of talent, learning, and Christian zeal, were appointed, and embarked at Copenhagen 1705. After a long and dangerous voyage, they arrived, July, 1706, at Tranquebar, a Danish possession on the Coromandel coast of Hindustan. After several days' delay the governor received them with great harshness. Ziegenbalg obtained a room near the heathen and Portuguese quarters, and began his work not only among hostile heathen, but with a government openly opposed, and a European population absorbed in business, addicted to vice, and determined at all hazards to be rid of these earnest men. Ziegenbalg having no grammar or dictionary to help in learning the language, persuaded a native schoolmaster to bring his school to the mission room, and sitting down with the children he imitated them in making the letters in the sand till he had become familiar with their form. He then found a Brahman who knew a little of English, and with his help was able in eight months to speak Tamil intelligibly. The teacher, however, was loaded with irons by the rajah and thrown into prison. Some of the Europeans owning slaves, Ziegenbalg obtained their consent that "these poor outcasts might meet for two hours daily for instruction." In less than a year five slaves were baptized. A native built a church at his own expense, and at the dedication Ziegenbalg preached in Tamil and Portuguese to a large congregation of Christians, Hindus, and Mohammedans, and in it within a month nine natives were baptized. In the second year he made extensive preaching tours. In 1708 he visited Negapatam, and the Dutch magistrate invited the most learned Brahmans, sunjasces, etc., to a friendly conference with the missionary on religious subjects. The discussion lasted five days, and much information concerning the origin, history, and doctrines of Christianity was diffused among the native population.

Ziegenbalg had so far mastered the language that in two years after his arrival he began Scripture translation, and a year later could speak Tamil with as much facility as his native German. He soon began the preparation of a grammar and two lexicons—one of prose, the other of poetical words. In 1711 he finished the translation of the New Testament—the first into any language of India—and a large part of the Old Testament. Not only to the Hindus, but to the half-breed Portuguese and to the slaves of Tranquebar he preached the gospel. He had also a German service weekly, which was largely attended

The European residents, who regarded his enterprise as visionary and absurd; the trading companies, who regarded missions as detrimental to their commercial interests—all did what they could to molest and hinder him. The Danish East India Company had sent secret instructions to their agents in Tranquebar that a missionary was going to India, and that he must be driven from the country. The governor charged him with rebellion, and when Ziegenbalg vindicated his divine commission, he not only in his rage struck him, but had him taken to the fortress, where he was kept in close confinement four months, suffering greatly from the intense heat, and forbidden the use of pen and paper to communicate with his friends. When released he found the converts scattered by persecution and terror. Some were in prison, others banished; some had been violently beaten, some put to death. Though he had regained his liberty he was still persecuted, and nothing but royal authority secured him from violence at the hands of his own countrymen. He was often in straits, money sent from home having failed to reach him.

In 1714 his translation of the New Testament, the Danish Liturgy, and German hymns, with thirty-three Tamil works, including a dictionary which he had prepared, were printed. His health failing, he returned to his native land in 1715. His account of the Hindus and his missionary work created great interest in Germany and England, vast crowds being moved by his glowing appeals, kings, princes, and prelates giving liberally to the cause. He returned to India in 1719, but died soon after, at the early age of thirty-six, having in the brief period of thirteen years as the pioneer of modern missions in India accomplished a remarkable work. Three hundred and fifty converts and a large body of catechumens mourned his death. He was buried in the large mission church opened two years before his death at Tranquebar, and a marble slab in the wall bears an inscription to his memory.

**Zeisberger, David,** b. Zauchtenthal, Moravia, April 11th, 1721. His progenitors be-

longed to the ancient Church of the Bohemian Brethren, founded sixty years before the Reformation, by the followers of John Huss. When David was five years old, his parents fled to Herrnhut in Saxony, which had been founded by a colony of Moravian emigrants on the estate of Count Zinzendorf. In 1736 his parents joined the colony in Georgia, which James Oglethorpe had established three years before, leaving their son at Herrnhut to be educated by the Moravians. From this he went to Holland, and lived in a Moravian settlement called Herrendyk. Thence he went to England, where General Oglethorpe met him, and with his aid he joined his parents in 1738. In 1740 he went North, and with others founded Bethlehem and Nazareth in Pennsylvania. In 1745 he began his work among the Indians, and was soon arrested as a spy of the French by the colonial government of New York, and was imprisoned for seven weeks. Released by Governor Clinton, he labored till 1750 among the Delawares at Shamokin (Sunbury, Pa.) and the Iroquois at Onondaga, where the Six Nations made him a sachem, and "keeper of their archives." In 1750 he visited Europe in behalf of the mission. In 1752 he returned to Onondaga, but was compelled to retire to Bethlehem at the opening of the French and Indian war. Between 1755 and 1762 he visited North Carolina and the New England provinces, labored among the Indians of Canada, and acted as interpreter for Pennsylvania in the treaty with Teedyuseung and his allies. In the time of the Pontiac conspiracy he ministered to the Christian Indians who had found refuge in Philadelphia, and at the close of the war he led the survivors of the converts to Wyalusing, Bradford County, Pa., on the Susquehanna. In 1767 he established a mission among the Monsey Delawares on the Alleghany River, Venango County, and three years later began the station which he called Friedenstadt, on Beaver Creek, in what is now Lawrence County. In 1772 he went to Central Ohio, and commenced a town called Schoenbrunn, on the Tuscarawas, ten miles from the site of Canal Dover, where he was soon joined by all the Moravian converts from Pennsylvania. He built two more towns, other missionaries came, and many converts were added. Early in the Revolution the Delawares were accused of favoring the American side, and the converts were forced to leave their towns and come within the British lines. In 1781 the settlements were destroyed by a band of Wyandotte warriors at the instigation of the commandant of the British post at Detroit, the missionaries were tried as spies, and the Christian Indians removed to Sandusky. The next year ninety-six of them returned from Sandusky to the Tuscarawas to gather their corn, and were massacred at Gnadenhütten by a party of colonial militia. Disheartened by this catastrophe, Zeisberger in 1782 led a small remnant to what is now Michigan, and built an Indian town on the Clinton River; in 1786 he went back to Ohio, and founded New Salem, one mile from Lake Erie. Thence the hostility of other Indians, after four years' rest, compelled them to emigrate to Canada, where they founded Fairfield. In 1798 he returned to the Tuscarawas valley, where Congress had granted to his Indians their former lands, and built a town, calling it Go-hen. There he labored for ten years, to the close of his life. He died November 17th, 1808, aged 87, having been a missionary among the American Indians for sixty years. He established thirteen Christian towns, and though scarcely one remained, yet he had many converts, and his character, motives, and efforts are "an honor to the Moravian Church, and to our common humanity."

Zeisberger was a thorough scholar. He mastered several native tongues, especially the Delaware and Onondaga. He left in manuscript a German and Onondaga Lexicon in seven volumes quarto; a Grammar of the Onondaga language in German and English, a Delaware Grammar and Dictionary, and several vocabularies. All of these are deposited in the Library of Harvard College, and in the Library of the American Philosophical Society in Philadelphia. His Diary, translated by Eugene H. Bliss, was published in two octavo volumes in 1885.

**Zirian** or **Siryinian Version.** — The Zir or Syrjen belongs to the Finn branch of the Ural-Altai family of languages, and is spoken by a race living in the government of Vologda, Russia, who number about 70,000. For their benefit the Russian Bible Society published the Gospel of Matthew in 1823. The British and Foreign Bible Society published in 1881 an edition of the same Gospel in Russ character, the transcription from the Slavonian character having been made by M. Luitkins, a native teacher, under the direction of the academician Wiedemann.

(*Specimen verse.* Matt. 5: 16.)

Сыдзн медъ югъаласъ тíанъ югыадъ мортъасъ водзнiъ, медъ адзасны тíанлыcь бэръ керöмъасъ, и ошкасны Батесъ тíанлысь, коди небесаасъ вылынъ.

**Zoar.** — 1. A town in Cape Colony, South Africa, southwest of Amalienstein, east of Worcester, north of Riversdale. Mission station of the Berlin Evangelical Missionary Society; 1 ordained missionary, 3 native helpers, 448 church-members, 102 school-children.

2. A settlement in Labrador, on the northeast coast, between Hebron and Ramah; mission station of the Moravian Brethren (1865). It was opened for the benefit of the Eskimo, who come from Nain and elsewhere for the fishing, and spend a large part of the year here. The European settlers as well as the Eskimo have also been benefited. Zoar presents a more pleasing appearance than most of the settlements in Labrador, for trees are numerous, and afford a pleasant change to the eye. One missionary is now in charge of the work.

**Zoroastrianism,** the form of religion supposed to have been inculcated by Zoroaster (Persian, *Zardusht*), long the state religion of Persia, but now professed by a mere handful of followers in two districts in Persia (Kirman and Yezd), and by the Parsis of India, whose name bears witness to their Persian origin. If Zoroaster was a historical character, as seems to have been the case, he probably lived in the east of Iran, in the region known as Bactria, now sometimes called Balk. His date cannot

be ascertained; some Greek writers put him 5,000 years before the siege of Troy! Modern scholars place him some 1,000 years before Christ, and some 1,500; at the best all is conjecture, but he certainly lived before Cyrus. That he was the leader of a schism in the old Aryan race seems to many probable, as the result of which the religion of one branch of the race developed into Vedism and Hinduism in India, and that of the other, which settled in Persia, into the dualistic system which still bears the name of Zoroaster.

According to this system, the world is the battle-field of two contending spirits, eternal in their origin and possessing the power of creation. The one is Ahuro-mazdao (the wise god); who is the source and author of all that is good, the other is Angro-mainyush (the spirit enemy), who, evil in his nature, ever strives to neutralize the beneficent activities of the first. These two names have become corrupted by long use into the shorter forms now common, Ormuzd and Ahriman. But the conflict between these two powers, though now conducted on terms which are apparently pretty nearly equal, is not hopeless, and is not destined to be perpetual. In due time Ormuzd is to summon all his power, and enter upon the last and decisive phase of the struggle. The might of Ahriman is to be broken forever, and the supremacy of the good established; Ahriman with his defeated followers is to be cast into hell, and to remain there, destitute of power to disturb the progress and enjoyment of the good, who are to be rewarded and to prosper, unvexed by evil, as citizens of the good kingdom.

Modern Zoroastrianism recognizes the existence of vast hierarchies of good and evil spirits, doing the will and fulfilling the purposes respectively of Ormuzd and of Ahriman. To what extent these elaborate systems of angelology and demonology influenced Jewish thought, and through them Christian thought, is a question still undetermined. The sacred books of Zoroastrianism are spoken of collectively as the Zend-Avesta. The term is not wholly accurate, the proper designation is *Avesta*, the word *Zend* signifying "interpretation," with reference to the commentaries on the original books. The Avesta itself is written in an ancient form of Aryan speech, allied to the Sanskrit, known popularly as the *Zend*, and possessing no other extant literature. The "interpretation" is in Pahlavi, a more modern (though ancient and now dead) language, which prevailed formerly in Persia. The Avesta, as at present known, is but a fragment, and not a large fragment, of the original sacred literature of Zoroastrianism. Like the Old Testament, it is not a book, but a collection of books—a literature developing in and with the life of the people. Parts of it may date back to Zoroaster, but much of it consists of the accretions of later ages. A collection of hymns or "Gâthâs" is the oldest part of it, and may be said to form the kernel of the whole; these alone claim to be the *ipsissima verba* of Zoroaster. The remainder consists of liturgical matter, and what is called by some (borrowing a phrase from Old Testament scholarship) the "priestly code" of Zoroastrianism.

The light, the sun, the fire, are considered by the Zoroastrians the symbol of Ormuzd. Therefore in their temples the sacred fire is continually burning, night and day, year after year. For this reason at evening, when they recite the prayers of the Avesta, the faces of Zoroastrian worshippers are turned westward, towards the setting sun. Hence they are often spoken of as "sun-worshippers" and "fire-worshippers," though they themselves reject the imputation which is thus involved: they do not pray to the sun or to the fire, they say, but to that good and shining one whose presence and character are symbolized by the light, and the sources of it.

The Zoroastrian religion developed and flourished in Persia, through the vicissitudes of declension and revival incident to all religious history, from the time of its origin to the Mohammedan invasion During that time it saw and survived the political changes and dynastic revolutions to which Persia was subject, but which need not be recounted here. Mohammed died in 632. It was but a few years after his death that Persia was invaded by armies of his followers, who, under the fierce lead of the early caliphs, were just beginning that astonishing career of conquest which within a century carried the crescent over Western Asia, Northern Africa, into Spain, across the Pyrenees, and almost to the shores of the British Channel. The Persian army was ignominiously defeated, the king dethroned, and his realms taken possession of in the name of the Prophet. The people embraced the new religion. The fire went out on the Zoroastrian altars, and the Avesta was dropped for the Koran. A handful merely of the Persians refused to be converted, and sought refuge among the mountains. There for a time they were suffered to remain. But soon after the year 700 they were subjected to such a violence of Moslem persecution that many of them were constrained to abandon Persia, and look for a refuge beyond the sea. The story of the wanderings and sufferings of this company of Zoroastrians forms a pathetic episode in the religious history of the race.

Through all their wanderings and shipwrecks the sacred fire was studiously kept alive. About the year 720 of the Christian era they landed on the western coast of India near the city of Surat, some 150 miles north of where Bombay now stands, and craved permission from the Hindu prince then ruling in that region to settle among his people, and to practise the religion of their fathers. The permission was granted,—so tradition says,—with a few easily observed conditions, among which were these, that they should adopt the dress and language of the country where they were to make their home. These conditions were accepted, and ever since the language of this Indian branch of the race has been the Gujarati, the vernacular of the district where they landed, with such dialectic variations as would naturally arise in the use of a new tongue by foreigners whose customs and religion differed so greatly from those of the land where the language had developed. The Parsis—as these Persian dwellers in India came in course of time to be called—do not appear prominently in Indian history until the English era. They faithfully maintained the practice of their religion, jealously guarded the sacred fire, and preserved inviolate the purity of their race. When, under English rule, the city of Bombay grew from a cluster of fishermen's huts into a great commercial mart, the Parsis appear as keen-eyed men of business, and founded great commercial houses. Much of the business and of the wealth of the city of Bombay at the present time is in their hands. They have extended their operations not only into other large places in India, so that in most of the chief Indian cities at least a few Parsi merchants will be found, but even throughout the East, as far as China. Yet no large settlement of them exists outside of the Bombay presidency. The total Parsi population of British India in 1881 was 73,760; to this a small number may be added on account of the Parsi residents in native states not included in British India; the entire number being about 83,000. Of this number over 72,000 are found in the presidency of Bombay, and nearly 50,000 of them in Bombay City. Surat has also a large Parsi population (over 5,000), and the town of Nawsari, in the native state of Baroda, about 15 miles from Surat, one still larger. There are said to be about 8,500 Zoroastrians in Persia, in the districts named above.

Thus existing as a community by themselves in the midst of the composite mass of the Indian population, separated from others by their peculiar religion and customs, and with their own social organism, the Parsis are everywhere well-to do, intelligent, and thrifty. The average degree of wealth is probably higher among them than among any other class in India. A Parsi beggar is never seen; the Parsi community always attends to the wants of its own poor, and suffers no member of its race to become a public burden. Their method of disposing of the dead is their most commonly known peculiarity. According to their belief, a dead body, the result of the working of the powers of evil, is unclean, and must not be allowed to contaminate by its presence any of the elements; it can neither be buried nor burnt nor thrown into the water, for in that way one of the elements would be defiled. It is therefore exposed in a circular structure without a roof, round the interior of which runs a shelf slightly sloping towards an opening at the centre. After being deposited in this place the vultures make swift work with it, and the bones, stripped of flesh, are afterwards swept down through the central aperture into a cavity below. These structures are called "towers of silence." Their outward life and demeanor is always respectable and decorous. It is to be feared that their religion exerts but small influence over them, and that it has deteriorated to the level of a merely perfunctory formalism. Practically they are materialists—or at least secularists, given up to the enjoyment of the good things of this world, and satisfied with the practice of the ordinary secular virtues. The Parsis have contributed the merest handful of converts to the Christian Church. No mission especially for them has ever been undertaken; but many Parsi youths are found in the missionary schools of the Bombay presidency. The few converts that have been gained from among them, however, have become men of mark and influence in the native churches of India; several of them have done and are doing most excellent work as missionaries and pastors in different parts of the Bombay presidency.

They take a prominent part in public as well as in business affairs, in modern India. Their wealthy men are liberal and public-spirited. Besides various charitable institutions supported by them for the benefit of their own race, the Parsis have not been wanting in acts of general philanthropy. A great hospital in Bombay was founded by and bears the name of Sir Jamsetji Jijibhai, who was the first native of Hindustan to be created a baronet by the sovereign of Great Britain.

**Zoutpansberg,** a town in Transvaal, South Africa. Mission station of the Wesleyan Methodist Missionary Society; 3 missionaries work among several of the neighboring tribes, and among the English colonists in the vicinity.

**Zulus, Missions among the.—1. American.**—The Zulus being a part of the Bantu race, their general history, race characteristics, and language are treated of in the article "Bantu." The mission work among them being so identified with the term Zulu, it has been placed under this head.

In 1833 the Rev. Dr. Philip of Cape Town, superintendent of the London Society in South Africa, called the attention of American Christians to the great need and encouragement for Christian effort in behalf of the Zulus. The A. B. C. F. M. took up the appeal, and sent out six men with their wives to labor there. Three of these, Rev. D. Lindley, H. J. Venable, and A. E. Wilson, M.D., with their wives, were to labor for a branch of the Zulu race in what was called the "Interior," the Matabele and others, under the chieftain Umzilikazi, at Mosiga.

The other three missionaries, Rev. Messrs. Aldin Grout, George Champion, and Newton Adams, M.D., appointed to labor among the Zulus, and constituting what was called the "Maritime Mission," were detained for some five months at the Cape by reason of a war then raging in Kaffraria, through which the overland route of the missionaries would take them. Waiting in vain for these hostilities to cease, in July they left the Cape for Port Elizabeth. Here they remained till the 7th of December, then took ship, and in two weeks, December 21st, 1835, they cast anchor in Port Natal. Landing the next day, they purchased a span of oxen for the wagons which they had brought with them from the old colony, and started at once on a trip of a hundred and fifty or sixty miles, to visit the Zulu chieftain Dingan, at his residence in Zululand, and get permission to labor as missionaries among his people. Two weeks brought them to the capital. Here they were received and treated with kindness, though the king was slow to comply with their wishes in respect to the people just about him. He proposed that they take up their abode and open their school in the vicinity of the port, being allowed, however, to spend some time with him, or among the people in his more immediate neighborhood, till he should know more of the character of their labors. They remained six days at the capital, and then Mr. Champion was left in the country to make arrangements; while the other two, Grout and Adams, returned to Algoa Bay for their families and effects. Mrs. Grout, however, died of consumption, at Bethelsdorp, February 24th, 1836, before they were ready to start. The rest of the company soon set off, in ox-wagons, for Natal; and after about two months' travelling, in a new land, without roads, and through many rivers, all without a bridge, on the 21st of May they reached the Umlazi River, where Mr. Champion had prepared a

house for their reception. During the absence of his brethren Mr. Champion explored the country as far southwest as the Ilovu, and selected a site for their first station, on the Umlazi, eight miles west of the Bay. Here he set about building a temporary house on the 22d of February. On the 7th of March he opened a school for the natives, using the shade of a large tree for a school-room, and the earth—the letters written in the sand—for an a-b-c book. The first day he had about a dozen scholars, some of them nurses with infants tied, as usual, to their backs. On the 21st of March he began, with about thirty people, to clear a spot for the mission house at that place. Thus commenced the first mission station among the Zulu Kafirs in the region of Natal.

The other members of the mission having returned from Algoa Bay, the brethren now made a second visit to the king, when he gave them permission to commence a station in Zululand. The site chosen was eight or ten miles north of the river Tugela, and about the same distance from the sea, on a stream called—as two others in Natal are called—the Umsunduzi. The name *Ginani*, which was given to the station, is composed of three Zulu words, in which it was designed to embody the promise of our Saviour: "Lo, I am with you."

Mr. Champion had now made such proficiency in the language as to be able to tell the people about God in their own tongue. His audience on the Sabbath numbered about two hundred. The king also sent him ten or a dozen pupils, boys and girls, to be taught, which, with others, at the end of eight or nine months made a school of ten boys and twenty girls. The day-school under Dr. Adams' instruction at Umlazi now numbered fifty; and his Sabbath audience amounted to some five or six hundred, most of whom were also gathered into a Sabbath-school. Meantime the printing-press was set up at Umlazi, and a few elementary books printed in the native language for the schools.

The mission to the interior having been broken up by an attack of the Boers upon the natives, in January, 1837, the missionaries left that field to join their brethren in Natal. Their journey thither was long, and they were about six months on the way. Their arrival at Natal, however, was a speedy response to the request which their brethren of the mission had just made to the Board in Boston for a reinforcement.

Mr. Lindley now at Ifumi, and Messrs. Venable and Wilson on the Umhlatuzi in Zululand, more than a hundred miles northeast from the Bay, had hardly more than begun work before they were interrupted again by the incoming of the Boers, by whose attack upon the people for whom they were laboring in the "Interior" they had but recently been moved to leave that field and come to the coast.

Many of the Dutch farmers, Boers, of the Cape Colony, being greatly offended at the small compensation allowed them by the British Government in setting their slaves, "apprentices," free, in 1837 left their homes, went north, crossed the Orange River, and settled here and there among the native tribes. Some of them came into collision with Umzilikazi, chief of the people among whom the missionaries for the Interior had attempted to establish a Boer station. In 1838 great numbers of these found their way into Natal, and began at once to negotiate with Dingan, king of the Zulus, to whom it belonged, to get possession of it. Claiming to have complied with the king's conditions by recovering the cattle the king required, a deputation was sent to deliver the cattle and have the cession ratified. Before the messengers were allowed to leave the capital the king managed to have them all massacred. Having slain the Dutch, the king sent for Mr. Venable to come with his interpreter and see him, which he did. The king told him of the massacre, but assured him that the missionaries had nothing to fear. Mr. Venable went, with the king's permission, to consult with Mr. Owen of the Church Missionary Society, who was living near the capital, and who, having heard of the fate of the Boers, was now in great distress. The missionaries were not long in deciding to leave that part of the district, assured as they were that the end was not yet. With apparent reluctance the king allowed them to go.

As soon as news of the slaughter at Dingan's kraal had reached Dr. Adams on the Umlazi, well knowing that the circumstances of his brethren in Zululand were anything but desirable, he lost no time in attempting to aid their escape. The swollen rivers and terrified natives rendered the task by no means an easy one, but eventually all were enabled to reach the Bay in safety. In like manner those who were farther away—Venable and Wilson—having complied with the monarch Dingan's request to give him the greater part of their goods, made their preparations quickly, and in due time found themselves in the company of their brethren at Umlazi and the Bay.

Thinking it best to withdraw, at least for the present, the missionaries sailed for Port Elizabeth. It was not long before the Zulus undertook to avenge the attacks that had been not long since made upon them by white residents, and swept the entire region as with the besom of destruction. Mr. Grout had already gone to America. Mr. and Mrs. Champion also returned, and Mr. Champion died of pulmonary consumption at Santa Cruz December 17th, 1841. Dr. Wilson went also to America, and thence, in 1839, to Cape Palmas in West Africa. After two years of faithful service in this field he fell sick, and died October 13th, 1841.

Dingan's power had now been broken by the Boers and his kingdom divided; Zululand was put under the rule of Dingan's brother, Umpande, and Natal was claimed by the Boers. Then the English came in and claimed the Dutch as British subjects, and took possession of Natal. The affairs of the district beginning to betoken peace and safety, Dr. Adams came up from Graham's Town to see what encouragement there might be to resume labor. Carrying back a good report, he soon returned again with Mrs. Adams and Mr. Lindley, reaching Natal in June, 1839. Mr. Lindley now gave himself to labor as teacher and preacher among the Dutch. Dr. Adams returned to his old station at Umlazi, and had, at the end of a year's labor, a Sabbath audience of about 500, a Sabbath-school of 200, a large day-school, and an out-station 6 miles away. Mrs. Adams held meetings for the women, and taught them to read, sew, and do other work in a civilized manner. Soon at least one woman was converted. The printing-press was now set **up, and** by the end of 1840

more than 50,000 papers had been printed at Umlazi.

Mr. Grout, having now returned from America, recrossed the Tugela, May, 1841, and commenced a new station at Empangeni, an Eastern branch of the Umhlatusi, calling it Inkanyeri, a star. The country around was thickly inhabited, and for a time the station seemed to prosper. The attendance upon Sabbath worship was large, and the day-school well attended. But the new king, Umpande, soon became jealous of the missionary's influence, and sent a force to destroy some of his adherents. Upon this, Mr. Grout and some of his followers fled across the Tugela to the Natal side of the river, where the missionary preached for a time to a large audience on the Umgeni.

These reverses, together with the prospect that the field would be cared for by English missionaries, as the district was now becoming a British colony, decided the A. B. C. F. M. to discontinue the mission, and on the 31st of August, 1843, the Board wrote the missionaries to bring it to a close. On the receipt of the orders in the early part of 1844, Mr. Grout went to Cape Town, on his way to America. Dr. Adams resolved to remain at his post, hoping to be able to support himself, if necessary, by his profession. Thus ended the first nine years of the mission. Before the mission was finally closed, the affairs of the country seemed likely to be so peaceful and orderly that the missionaries and the Board agreed to continue the mission and have it reinforced. Dr. Adams's steadfast, hopeful, diligent work had prevented any absolute break in the mission work, and when Mr. Grout arrived at Cape Town he was encouraged to return to Natal, instead of to the United States. Ministers of the gospel, the American consul, the governor of the colony, and others, showed a deep interest in the mission. A public meeting was held, addresses were made, and money was raised to defray Mr. Grout's expenses while he should report the present aspect of the field and wait for further instructions. In the mean time Mr. Grout returned to Natal with an appointment from the governor of the Cape, Sir P. Maitland, as government missionary on a salary of £150, and, resuming his work in June, 1844, began and established a prosperous station on the Umvoti River, some 40 miles from the Port and 6 from the sea-coast, where he labored till 1870, making meantime a visit to America, and finally, at the age of 67 years, he withdrew from active service, returned home, and took up his abode in Springfield, Mass., where he still resides.

Toward the close of the year 1844 Dr. Adams made a visit to the Cape, and received ordination as a minister of the gospel from clergymen there. The offer of an appointment as government missionary was made to Dr. Adams, but he declined to receive it. On his return from the Cape he resumed his labors at Umlazi and throughout the new colony. His Sabbath audiences were large, varying from five hundred to a thousand; their attention to the preaching was good, often earnest and solemn, and their general deportment was quiet and orderly. His Sabbath-school numbered from three hundred to five hundred, and his day-school about a hundred. In the summer season he held services at an out-station six miles away, and made occasional tours among the tribes at a distance. Here his arrival at a kraal was a signal for the people in that and the neighboring kraals to assemble for worship. Having addressed them for half an hour, more or less, he rode to another settlement; and when night came his hut would be filled with men, women, and children, all glad to hear as long as his strength would allow him to speak.

More than ten years elapsed, after the missionaries first set their feet on the shores of Natal, ere they began to see any very manifest or important results of their labors. But during the year 1846 not only were the Sabbath audiences and day-schools large and flourishing, but a few of their hearers profited by the truths of the gospel and became Christians.

In the early part of the year an old woman, Umbalazi by name, once the wife of a distinguished chief, expressed to the missionary a wish to be baptized, and to make a public profession of her faith in Christ. For many months her life had been such as to induce the belief that she had been born of the Spirit. Accordingly, in June of that year, she was permitted to sit down with the missionary and his wife at the table of the Lord, to commemorate with them His dying love. On the 19th of August, two men, then living at Umlazi, came out from their heathenism and polygamy; and, in presence of a sinful and adulterous generation, took each a wife in accordance with the teachings of the gospel and the forms of a civilized, Christian government. These men having had two wives each, one of them was now married to the woman who was first taken; the other to the one who was taken last, inasmuch as the first was opposed to his embracing the gospel and had no desire to remain with him longer. Near the close of the year, another couple were married in a Christian manner at Umvoti, who also, in a few months, made a profession of the Christian faith.

In 1847 Dr. Adams transferred his station from Umlazi to Amanzimtote, some ten miles further from Durban, the new site being more centrally situated in regard to the people among whom he wished to labor. Here he labored till his death on the 16th of September, 1851. He was a pioneer missionary, whose zeal, faith, and patience never failed. In September, 1847, a new station was commenced by Rev. J. C. Bryant at Ifumi, where Mr. Lindley began labor ten years before. Mr. Bryant remained here for two years, but owing to an affection of the lungs, he, after the arrival of Mr. Ireland in 1849, devoted his strength until his death in 1850, chiefly to the preparing of books for the natives.

In the early part of 1847 Mr. Lindley resumed his connection with the mission, and began a station some twenty miles northwest from the Bay near the mountain of Inanda, from which the station took its name. In 1858 he transferred his station to a new site a few miles nearer the Bay, and remained here till his return to America in 1873. (See biographical sketch.)

In 1847 a new station was started on the Umsunduzi, some thirty miles north of the Port, by Rev. Lewis Grout, who remained here for fifteen years, teaching, preaching, studying the language and preparing a grammar of it, travelling, translating portions of the Bible, and gathering a church, till his health began to decline

and finally made it necessary for him to return to America in 1862, when he closed direct connection with the Board.

During the next two years the mission was much enlarged and encouraged by the incoming of six new missionaries, Rev. Messrs. Marsh and Rood with their wives in 1848, and Rev. Messrs. Ireland, Abraham, and Wilder with their wives in 1849.

Rev. J. L. Dohne, a German in the employ of the Berlin society, joined the mission in 1849, and had charge of a station near Table Mountain for some ten years, where he died, leaving a Zulu-Kafir Dictionary of more than ten thousand words, a monument of his scholarship, industry, and perseverance.

At the annual meeting of the mission held in September, 1850, at Umsunduzi, all the members of the mission, fourteen families, numbering forty-six souls, were present; and though nearly fifteen years had elapsed since the mission was commenced, no member of the mission had died in the field. The first grave for any of the number was dug in the following December, when Mr. Bryant died at Inanda. A nucleus of nine churches had now been formed, containing a hundred and twenty-three members, thirty-six of whom were received during the current year.

The need of competent native helpers was so apparent that a training school was opened in 1853 at Amanzimtote, and put under the care of Mr. Rood till his health failed, when others had it in charge. For want of funds this department of Christian work was eventually given up, though not till it had done much towards furnishing the mission with some of the most efficient native pastors it has ever had.

During the years 1855 and '56 much discussion arose concerning the practice of polygamy, whether it should be tolerated or allowed in converts to the Christian faith, or suffered in the church of Christ. In this Bishop Colenso took an active part in favor of sufferance and in opposition to the principles by which the American missionaries were governed in their treatment of it. The discussion resulted in confirming the mission more than ever in the importance and rightfulness of their rule. It was now also that Sir George Grey, governor of Cape Colony, High Commissioner, etc., came to Natal, and made arrangements for having five hundred acres of land set apart at each station for mission purposes, and for having a reserve of some eight or ten thousand laid off round each station for the people. Out of these reserves the station people might have a village lot of an acre and a rural allotment of fifteen or twenty acres each, on certain conditions, such as paying survey fees, etc. He also provided for having a first-class sugar-making mill erected at one of the stations at a cost of £9,000 to the government.

In the early part of 1859 the printing-press was set up at Umsunduzi; and in a little more than six months half a sheet of easy lessons, a translation of the Acts of the Apostles, and a grammar of the Zulu language were printed,—the whole number of pages amounting to nearly three hundred thousand, all large octavo; which, considering the size of the pages and other circumstances, was really more than twice as much as had been done on the presses of the colony during the seven previous years. These three works were printed in Dr. Lepsius's "Standard Alphabet," which the mission had resolved to adopt.

Between the years 1855–1870, the mission was reinforced by the incoming of eleven new workers, Rev. Messrs. Pixley, Robbins, Bridgman, Lloyd and their wives, with Miss Hance and Miss Day. Meantime death made many inroads upon the working force already in the field. To aid in meeting the depletion, something was done by a native home missionary society, which was organized in 1860, by setting native workers apart, with a formal license and a small salary, to preach the gospel and do other mission work. Many of the people began also to take a deeper interest in education, and to unite with the mission in a desire for better educational facilities. This led to the reviving or reorganizing of schools that had been already founded, and to the establishing of new ones. In place of the seminary at Amanzimtote, which had been given up, efforts were now made to start a new one on a broader, better basis. In this the Colonial Secretary of Education took a deep interest, and secured "grants-in-aid" from the local government. Mr. Ireland was appointed in charge of the institution. In 1871 a new building was erected. In 1882 the management of the school came into the hands of Rev. H. D. Goodenough, who is still in charge. In 1869 a prosperous boarding-school for girls was opened, under the care of Mr. Edwards, at Inanda. In 1873 a home for the education of "kraal girls" was opened at Umzumbe. In this way, by these schools and other means, some eight or ten of the more promising young men were selected from those under instruction for ministry among the Zulus. Meantime, between the years 1871–80, other helpers went out from America,—Rev. Messrs. Pinkerton and Kilbon with their wives, also the Misses Pinkerton, Price, and Morris.

Some of the more troublesome native customs—such as polygamy, beer-drinking, and the selling of daughters for cattle, in marriage, against all which the missionaries had from the first found it necessary to contend—began now to reassert themselves, and to find tolerance, if not virtual approval, and sometimes an advocate, among some of the native Christians, and thus called for a firm expression of opinion, together with a decided effort to check and eradicate the evil. At a meeting of the missionaries and delegates of the churches, held at Umsunduzi in 1879, a series of "rules" was adopted, the sum of which was: that polygamy should not be allowed in any church; that no church-member should be allowed to *lobolisa;* nor should any such member be allowed to participate in any way in the making of beer-drinks, or use intoxicating drinks of any kind as a beverage; nor should any such member be allowed to smoke the *isangu.*

From the year 1880 to 1885 the mission was again reinforced by five new missionaries, Rev. Messrs. G. A. Wilder, Richards, Goodenough, Wilcox, Holbrook, and their wives; also Miss Phelps and Miss Gilson. This made the whole number of men from the beginning till 1885 30, of whom 13 had now died and 5 had retired from the mission, leaving 12 in the field. Half a century had now expired since the mission was begun, and the year 1885 was honored as a year of "Jubilee," and the last week of the year given to a series of religious festivities at Amanzimtote, now called the "Adams" station.

The presence of invited guests, among whom were the governor and a goodly number of other officials, clergymen, ladies and gentlemen of the colony, added much to the interest of the occasion.

From that time on to the present the progress, development, and fruitage of mission work have been rapid and gratifying, notwithstanding the repeated removals of one and another from the working force which death or advanced age has caused. A fitting close of this sketch of the Zulu Mission is found in a paper read by one of the secretaries of the Board at their annual meeting in New York, October 15th, 1889, as follows: "The development of Christian work here has been slow, but shows steady gains and substantial results. The entire Bible has been translated into the Zulu language; a hymn and tune book has been provided; text books for schools and something of a Christian literature are in the hands of the people. The native churches, numbering 1,097 members, some of them served by native pastors, show the deepening hold of the gospel. A theological school and a normal and industrial school for boys at Adams, girls' boarding-schools at Inanda and Umzumbi, besides day-schools on all the stations, provide for the Christian education of the young and for the suitable training of preachers and teachers. The field covered by this mission is fairly reached by Christian teaching; the Christian life is gaining in breadth, intelligence, and reality; temperance principles prevail in these churches; and there is a growing interest in carrying the gospel to the regions beyond. For this missionary activity wide fields are open: Zululand to the north, and all the country from Delagoa Bay northward to the Zambesi, and stretching inland more than a third of the way across the continent. The work in the Zulu Mission was never in a more promising condition, and if the force can be duly maintained this mission may soon be in the way of realizing in good degree its original aim of reaching the peoples inland as well as on the coast."

***Inland or Interior Mission.***—Of the six men and their wives whom the American Board sent out to Africa in December, 1834, one half, namely, Rev. Messrs. D. Lindley, H. J. Venable, and A. E. Wilson, M.D., were appointed to what was called an "Interior" field. Arriving at Cape Town February 5th, 1835, they soon provided themselves with the needful means of travel. Seven months of journey brought them to Griqua Town, six hundred miles on their way to Umzilikazi's country and people. After remaining here for some time, another hundred miles of travel brought them to the missionary Moffat at Kuruman. In the early part of 1836 Messrs. Lindley and Venable went on before the rest of the band, to select a mission site and prepare for the coming of the rest. The site chosen was called Mosign, near the chief's residence, a hundred miles west of what is now called Pretoria, the capital of the Transvaal Republic, and not far from the Kashan or Kemehane Mountains. The Paris Missionary Society had made an attempt to plant a station here in 1832, but were hindered by the jealousy and strifes of the tribes around them, especially of Umzilikazi, chief of the Matabele, against the Bahurutse, whom the former claimed as tributaries. These Matabele and their chief were of Zulu origin, having come in not long before from the northwest part of Zululand, or from the sources of the Black Folosi, where they were called Kwakumulo. Being there harassed by a powerful neighbor, Umzilikazi sought to obtain the aid of Chaka, and so became a subordinate of the great monarch. But when his brother Dingan came to be king, not being satisfied with Umzilikazi's allegiance, he sent an army to chastise him, whereupon Umzilikazi fled with his people to the westward till he reached the vale of Mosiga, where they were called Matabele, or those who hide behind their shields.

These Matabele, then, with their chief Umzilikazi, were the people for whom the missionaries Lindley, Venable, and Wilson, with their wives, went to labor when they commenced operations in the valley of Mosiga, on the 15th of June, 1836. Three months' work, with such native help as they could obtain, enabled the missionaries to prepare a dwelling; but, moving into it while the floors were yet damp, all save Dr. Wilson were soon seized with a most distressing and obstinate fever. After eight days' suffering, one of their number, Mrs. Wilson, yielded to the disease. Her body was laid uncoffined in the ground hard by. The rest recovered, though not until the fever, together with distressing rheumatic affections, had preyed upon them for several months. Indeed, some of them were still confined to the house, some to their beds, when they were startled one morning in January, 1837, by the guns of the Boers, who were now making a sudden attack upon the people by whom the missionaries were surrounded. So unexpected and vigorous was the onslaught, that the greater portion of the dwellers in the vale of Mosiga were shot down on that one bloody morning ere the sun could reach the meridian.

Having destroyed fourteen or fifteen villages, and recovered six or seven thousand head of cattle, together with the wagons which Umzilikazi had taken from them, the Boers prepared to return,—not, however, till they had persuaded the missionaries to go back with them. Fearing that the infuriated Matabele would follow them, neither the Boers nor the missionaries made any halt for twenty-three hours. Nor did the sick seem to suffer from the ride. Such a journey, however, as that was until they judged themselves to be beyond the reach of Umzilikazi's vengeance!

To their fear of being followed by a host of exasperated savages, to the unceasing cry of cattle, and to all the tumult of an irregular, excited soldiery, add the want of proper food, especially for the sick; the absence of a road, save such as the open field affords; the want of a bridge or a boat on the now swollen streams; the want of a dry suit for the women and children, who had to be floated across the Orange on a bundle of reeds, keeping only head and shoulders above water; then, forthwith, out of the river, add a night of Egyptian darkness, through all the hours of which no sleep can be had, save that which comes in spite of torrents of rain, thunder, lightning, and all the noise of the motley group by which they are surrounded,—and you have some idea of what fell to the lot of the missionaries Lindley, Venable, Wilson, and their families,

on this journey. From this place, the banks of the Ky Gariep, a few days' travel brought them to the station of a Wesleyan missionary at Thaba 'Nchu, where they were kindly received. After resting for a time, they passed on to Graham's Town, and thence overland to Natal, where they arrived the last of July, 1837.

Here, in Natal, they joined their brethren of the "Maritime" or Zulu Mission, as described in a sketch of that mission. Umzilikazi and his people eventually went north and settled in the Zambezi region, where they became powerful, and other missionaries are now laboring among them.

*European Missions among the Zulus.*—Of the eight or nine missionary societies doing mission work in Natal and Zululand, all but one, the American Board, are of European origin.

THE ENGLISH WESLEYAN METHODIST SOCIETY is the oldest and largest of these, aside from the Board. It labors for all classes, colored and white, heathen or otherwise. Its work in South Africa was begun in Cape Colony in 1814. Extending its operations by degrees, it has reached Kaffraria, Natal, and the Bechuana regions, and now numbers about forty stations, sixty missionaries, and more than 6,000 church-members. Natal was occupied in 1841. Their first missionary, Rev. Mr. Archbell, was followed by Rev. Mr. Davis. At the end of the first ten years they had among the heathen or colored population of Natal 150 communicants, 4 day-schools, and 300 scholars. At the end of forty years they had 20 missionaries in this field, 63 preaching places, and a membership of 2,496. (See Wesleyan Methodist Missionary Society.)

THE NORWEGIAN MISSIONARY SOCIETY.— The mission of this Society in Natal was commenced by Rev. Mr. Schreuder in 1845. In 1847 he had two preaching places—one on the Umhloti near Verulam, the other on the Umtongati. He then went to China, but soon returned and bought a large farm, with a view of devoting it to mission purposes. But the natives did not like the soil or situation of it, and few accepted the invitation to settle there and come under instruction. In 1850 he sold his farm, and went to labor in the upper part of Mapumulo region, on an inland branch of the Umvoti. From this he soon went to undertake mission work in the Zulu country, being invited there by the king, Umpanda, who was now desirous of his medical aid. The place chosen for the mission was called Echowe, on the Umlazi. His time was now divided between this and his other station at Mapumulo, till the next year, when three co-laborers arrived, two of whom, Larsen and Oftebro, were put in charge of the Natal station, while Mr. Schreuder and the other, Udland, devoted themselves to the Zulu field. The mission continued to grow and prosper till the great English and Zulu war in 1879, when their work was much hindered and some of the stations broken up. But in 1882 the mission had so far recovered from interruption as to be able to report one station in Natal, and no less than seven of its former ten in Zululand, with nine pastors and a church-membership of 270. Since then Mr. Schreuder has died; two or three new men have been sent out from Norway, and their stations in Natal have come to number four. In Zululand their six or seven stations are occupied by eight or nine men.

THE BERLIN MISSIONARY SOCIETY commenced its work in South Africa in 1834. In 1847 two or three of its missionaries, of whom were Messrs. Dohne and Posselt, were driven by war from their stations in Kafirland, and came and commenced work in Natal. The former, Dohne, labored for a time among the Dutch, and then joined the American Mission. The other founded two stations, one on the sources of the Tugela, called Emmaus, the other near Pine Town, called at first New Germany and then Christianaburg. The mission was reinforced, other stations were planted in Natal, and two men sent to work among the Amaswari, north of Zululand. Not being allowed to remain there, they passed on farther north, and commenced operations at Lydenberg, in the upper part of the Transvaal Republic, where, as in other parts of South Africa, their Society has had great success. In Natal they now number four stations, and have a white missionary at each station.

THE HERMANNSBURG MISSION was commenced in 1854, when the attempt to enter Gallaland by way of Mombasa had failed. The first station, called Hermannsburg, was a large farm of 6,000 acres, on the sources of the Inhimbiti, one of the branches of the Umvoti. In 1856, 1857, and 1860 reinforcements arrived, and in 1860 their mission consisted of 120 souls, eighty of whom were colonists, and the rest missionaries, catechists, or teachers. Among the colonists they could reckon men of almost every kind of handcraft—agriculturists, carpenters, joiners, wheelwrights, shoemaker and tailor, mason and miller, tanner and turner, shepherd and dyer.

Their first labor at Hermannsburg was to build a house 130 feet in length, by 40 in width, containing a large dining and sitting room, a large kitchen, 12 dwelling-rooms, and 16 sleeping-rooms, all opening into a common hall through the centre, and all looking out upon the veranda by which the building was encompassed. A missionary visitor found that this dwelling was the abode of thirteen families, who took their meals all at one table in one of the central rooms. Here, too, they all met, morning and evening, for family-worship. At a little distance, less than half a mile, was another company of seven families, living in a similar manner in one house; nor was there anything but order and harmony in each house.

Rev. Mr. Hardeland, Doctor of Theology and Philosophy, and at one time missionary among the Dyaks in Borneo, being invited to take charge of the Harms Mission in Natal, consented to do so on condition that the mission should be brought in some measure into connection with the Lutheran Church of Hanover, so far at least as to require that church to examine and ordain all the missionaries who might be sent to this field by the Hanoverian Society. To this Mr. Harms assented.

The baptized natives lived in cottages arranged in a row near the houses and shops of the Germans. Previous to Mr. Hardeland's taking charge of the mission, as he did in 1859, these natives were accustomed to receive much aid of a secular kind from the mission, especially in the building of their houses, the ploughing of their land, the grinding of their meal, and other things of a like character. No baptized person was allowed to marry a heathen, or one who had not been baptized; and if any who had been baptized should leave the station and church, or give occasion to be dismissed, they were required to leave their children in the care of the mission, that being one of the conditions on which they were baptized and received into the church.

Having established Hermannsburg as a head-station, the mission went on to plant others, some in Natal, some in Zululand, and then some in regions beyond, among the Bechuana, the Bamangwato in the Transvaal, and Sechele's people, not far from Mosiga. In 1870 they reported at their annual Home festival thirty-seven stations, of which seven were in North Zululand, five in South Zululand, eight in Natal, two in Alfred's-land, ten in Bechuana-land, and five in Little Moriko District.

CHURCH OF ENGLAND.—Certain Episcopalians, acting as private individuals, undertook mission work among the Zulus at an early date; though the Church of England Mission can hardly be said to have had a beginning in Natal till the 20th of May, 1855, at which time Bishop Colenso arrived in the colony, on his return from England, having made a visit of ten weeks in the early part of the preceding year.

Previous to this movement of the Church of England, Captain A. F. Gardiner of the Royal Navy visited Natal for the purpose of planting a mission. He reached the district in 1835, a little before the arrival of the American missionaries. Going at once to Dingan to get permission to commence missionary operations in the Zulu country, he succeeded only in part, being allowed to settle in Natal, at the Bay.

The enthusiastic missionary at length succeeded in getting Dingan to make him a grant of all Natal; whereupon he set off for England to have the act approved by the British Government, and also to procure men and means for prosecuting the great work on which his heart was set among this heathen people. In the former he failed; in the latter he succeeded, —in part at least, returning to Natal in May, 1837, accompanied by the Rev. Mr. Owen of the Church Missionary Society.

The captain soon took final leave of the country and returned to England. He afterwards went on a mission to the Patagonians, where he and his followers eventually died of starvation.

Mr. Owen was allowed to take up his residence near Dingan's Great Kraal, Unkungunhlovu, where he commenced his labors October 10th, 1837. Here he remained till the following February, when the troubles between Dingan and the Boers obliged him to leave his work. On his return from England he labored for a time at Mosiga.

In 1850 Bishop Gray of the Cape, regarding Natal as a part of his diocese, made it a visit, and drew up a scheme for mission work by the Church of England among the heathen. Supposing that ten locations were to be formed here for the exclusive use of the natives, each to contain ten thousand souls, he proposed that one or more institutions be founded in each of these, to convert the heathen to the faith of Christ, to educate the young, to form industrial habits, and to relieve the sick and afflicted. Each institution was to be under the care of a clergyman, who should be aided in the industrial and educational part of the work by teachers. In addition to the ordinary instruction of schools, the pupils were to be taught: the males, gardening, farming, and mechanical arts; the females, sewing, cooking, washing, etc. Each institution was to exhibit a model farm and garden, and to have a guarantee of aid from government to the amount of three hundred pounds sterling per year, so long as such aid should be needed. The whole scheme and all the institutions were to be under the direction of the bishop of the diocese; though their accounts would be open to the inspection of the government, so long as its aid should be continued; and it was hoped that each of these institutions, the cost of which was put at five hundred pounds per annum, would be self-supporting in five years from the time they should be commenced. The school at each place was to consist of fifty Zulu children, who were to be under the charge of four missionaries,—a clergyman, a catechist, a mechanic, and a farmer,—and be content with shelter, food, and raiment.

On Dr. Colenso's arrival in the colony, 1855, he seemed to approve this plan, and to be ready to act upon it, and was himself made Bishop of Natal, when the colony became a separate diocese. But instead of entering at once upon the forming of ten stations, he thought it better to begin with establishing one, as a general centre of operations, a parent and model for others. Upon this he entered, on his return from England, about the middle of 1855, the government having granted him a farm of 6,000 acres for the purpose. These lands were contiguous to another grant of 2,500 acres, an endowment for a bishopric, not far from the capital of the colony. But the bishop evidently found it difficult to carry his plan into successful operation, though he never showed any lack of resolution, zeal, or perseverance in his mission work. In the course of a year, with the aid of the colonial secretary for native affairs, he succeeded in having thirty-three children, all but two of them being sons of chiefs or headmen, brought to his station, *Ekukanyeni*, "in the light," for instruction. In 1860 a girls' school was opened. Meantime half a dozen native houses of an upright fashion were built, also several native huts, and the number of baptized persons under the bishop's charge amounted to about two dozen. In this work he had the aid of three assistants and one native teacher. Other stations were now attempted, one especially at Maritzburg, under the care of Dr. Callaway, where they built a fine stone chapel for the natives, and had a printing-press. Rev. Mr. Robertson labored for a time at Umlari, then went to Zululand. Archdeacon Mackenzie labored for a time in Natal, and then received ordination and was appointed Missionary Bishop for Central Africa, and went to the Zambezi, where he soon died of African fever.

Bishop Colenso was deeply interested in his mission work, a diligent student of the Zulu language, and author of many books in that tongue. Many of the English Church, not pleased with his views on certain points, tried to have him deposed. Failing in this, they had another bishop appointed in the same field, and called Bishop of Maritzburg. Bishop Colenso's station, Ekukanyeni, became the prey of a prairie fire; he died, and his work for the most part collapsed, or passed into other hands; though it is understood that Mrs. Colenso and one of her daughters still reside at the station, keep up a school for the natives, and have a small school in the city. The other bishop, he of Maritzburg, has charge of the two stations which Dr. Callaway established, at each of which he employs a white missionary. He has also two schools in charge—one at the capital and one at the seaport. The Bishop of Zululand, now some five or six years in the field, and a zealous worker, has his head station at Isandhlwana, the site of the famous battle in which the English were defeated and their Twenty-fourth Regiment utterly annihilated. Aside from this they have some six or more other stations in Zululand, with a white missionary resident at each station.

THE FREE CHURCH OF SCOTLAND MISSION IN NATAL.—Rev. James Allison, who labored for a time under the auspices of the Wesleyan Methodist Society, began his work in the Griqua country in 1832. He then labored for a time among the Mantatees of Basutuland; then among the Amaswari and Bahurutsi on the sources of the Pongolo. Driven thence by war and famine, he came in 1847, with 400 natives, to Natal, and settled at Indaleni, 25 miles south of Maritzburg. Separating here from the Wesleyan Society, he went with a portion of his church and people, 450 souls, and founded a new station at Edendale, 6 miles west of Maritzburg, where he and his people bought a farm of 6,000 acres. In 1857 the population numbered 600 souls, of whom 170 were church-members. At a later date the station was made over to the Wesleyan Society, and Mr. Allison eventually joined the Free Church of Scotland Mission, and put the work he was doing at Maritzburg and Empolweni into their hands, having his abode at the latter station, Empolweni, near the Umgeni. Aside from these two stations, where the Scotch are doing a prosperous work, they have a "Gordon Memorial Mission" at Umsinga, in the upper part of the colony. Here they combine industry with education. Aside from the missionary in charge, they have a white teacher, a farmer and assistant, and a girls' boarding-school in charge of a lady.

THE SWEDISH CHURCH began mission work in Natal not many years since, planting their first and central station on the Natal side of Rorke's Drift, not far from where the Zulus annihilated the English in battle a few years since. They now have two other stations, one in Natal and one in Zululand. They have three missionaries, and promise to do good work.

THE ROMAN CATHOLICS have three stations in Natal, one of which is under the Trappists, an order of Jesuits who have recently begun mission work on a large scale in South Africa. In Griqualand they have an estate of 50,000 acres, and in Natal another of 20,000. They are spending much money in buildings and work, and making earnest efforts to get a hold upon the natives. Their plan is to civilize them first, then make Trappists of them. The monks at Marianhill, a monastery near Pine Town, number 170, and the nuns at a convent half a mile away number 120. The station numbers already many large buildings. The church will hold 2,000 people. Another large building is the St. Joseph's Industrial School. Activity abounds in all the shops. They have 300 native boys and girls under instruction, chiefly industrial. The boys become good tradesmen, masons, carpenters, blacksmiths, printers. The girls are taught to sew, knit, cook. They publish papers in English, Zulu, German, and Polish. But the government is not altogether satisfied with their teaching and influence.

THE DUTCH BOERS (farmers), who have in former years been thought indifferent if not opposed to mission work in behalf of the natives, are, many of them, now showing a warm, substantial interest in their spiritual well-being. The genuineness of the deep religious awakening they experienced some four years since is seen in their efforts to bring the Zulus with and around them into a saving knowledge of the same gospel grace of which they are happy partakers. They have their own way of carrying on the work, taking hold of it, not through any organized missionary society, but as individuals, families, committees, ministers, and laymen. Most of their preaching places are but farm-houses, sometimes the wagon-houses of the Boers, where both they and their native employés and others meet for prayer, praise, and religious instruction. Rev. James Scott speaks of being on a visit among them and "seeing eighty Boers and three or four hundred Zulus gather together for worship. The Zulus came from kraals and villages, both old and young, some clothed, but most of them heathen in their blankets. Over one hundred in Greytown have been formed into a native church in connection with the Dutch church. This work is now being carried forward under the direction of a committee of Dutch farmers, employing three native evangelists."

**Zulu Version.**—The Zulu belongs to the Bantu family of the languages of Africa, and is spoken in Zululand.

To supply the Zulu Kafirs with the Word of Life various endeavors were made at different periods and from different quarters. In the year 1857 the New Testament, as translated into Zulu by Messrs. Annamm and Greiner of the Basle Missionary Society, was published at Mangalore, at the joint expense of the Wurtemberg and Basle Missionary Societies. In 1865 the American Bible Society issued likewise a New Testament at Natal, as translated by Mr. Wilder, while parts of the New Testament, translated by Mr. Dohne of the Berlin Missionary Society, had been published the previous year (1864) at Pietermaritzburg. In 1872 the British and Foreign Bible Society published the New Testament as translated by American missionaries; and in 1879 a slightly revised edition was issued by the American Zulu Mission, at the joint expense of the British and American Bible Societies. An edition of the entire Zulu Bible was published by the American Bible Society in 1883. In 1889 the British and American Bible Societies issued a corrected edition of the New Testament, prepared by the Rev. I. Rood.

(*Specimen verse.* John 3 : 16.)

Ngokuba uTixo wa li tanda kangaka izwe, wa li nika inDodana yakē ezelweyo yodwa, ukuba bonke aba kolwa 'kuyo ba nga bubi kodwa ba be nobomi obungapeliyo.

# APPENDIX B.

## *BIBLE VERSIONS.*

### INTRODUCTION.

THE accompanying lists of Bible versions are based upon those compiled by R. N. Cust, LL.D., of London, whose long labors in connection with the Church Missionary Society and British and Foreign Bible Society have placed him in the front rank of writers on missionary subjects. Languages and Bible versions have been his special study, and these tables are the result of many years of patient and careful research. The advance sheets came with the inscription, " To be placed at the disposal of the editor of the Missionary Encyclopædia, for any purpose that he may wish," and the editor has felt that the best use that could be made of them was to give them as fully as possible.

The original tables are three in number: 1. Alphabetical, 2. Geographical, 3. Linguistic. Consideration of space compelled the condensation of these into two: 1. Alphabetical, 2. Geographical and Linguistic.

The Alphabetical list is an exact reprint of the original, except that the dialects are introduced into the column of the languages, and the locality is given a little more fully, in accordance with the corresponding column in the original Geographical list.

The Geographical list in the original included the columns Language, Region, Diglott, Dialect, Written Character, and Number in Linguistic List. In this the dialect has been placed with the language, the region has been omitted, as sufficiently given in the first list, and their places have been taken by two columns from the Linguistic list, giving the Family and Branch, and the source of translation. The numbering of the Geographical list has also been made consecutive, instead of being divided into groups as in the original, and the number in the Alphabetical list has taken the place of the number in the Linguistic list.

One difficulty met the editor at the outset: What system of spelling should be adopted? It would require great temerity to criticise Dr. Cust's spelling, and besides there is no common usage. At the same time there were so many instances where the ordinary reader would find it difficult to trace a particular version, that it was decided to make an index giving the common spelling, and indicating by numbers the corresponding names in the lists. There are also quite a number of versions in dialects that are not ordinarily recognized as such, and the index includes all the dialects in alphabetical order with the languages. For assistance in this the editor is greatly indebted to Rev. J. Y. Leonard, of New Haven, Conn., U. S. A., for many years a missionary of the A. B. C. F. M., in Western Turkey.

With this general preface we give below a portion of Dr. Cust's introduction in his own words:

" In 1886 I published a List of Bible Translations actually accomplished, arranged according to the Linguistic Families, and indicating the source of each translation. In 1889 I published a List of Bible Translations actually accomplished, arranged according to the Geographical Distribution of the populations using such translations, and indicating the form of written character used for each translation.

In 1890 I now publish a third List of Bible Translations actually accomplished, arranged:

1. Alphabetically according to the Language, with the Dialects of each, if any exist. The following columns indicate (1) the locality; (2) the amount of population of speakers; (3) probable duration of the language; (4) and amount of translation work done.

547

The following principles of these lists are brought to special notice:

(1) The work is actually done, or in course of doing.

(2) The versions are in actual or approximate circulation.

(3) Obsolete and useless versions are excluded.

(4) The object of the version is Evangelization.

(5) The record includes all Bible Societies.

(6) No notice is taken of plurality of versions, if they exist.

(7) All names are entered on one uniform principle of transliteration and terminology, with stress accent to help the pronunciation.

(8) Languages are discriminated scientifically from dialects of the same language on certain understood principles, and no other terms but Language and Dialect are used.

2. The Geographical list shows where the language is spoken, and in what written character it appears.

3. The Linguistic list is to satisfy those who wish to obtain scientific information, not of practical value for purposes of Evangelization, but of surpassing interest to the scholar and student, who is informed in the last column of the name of the society which has published each translation.

Certain appendices are added for further illustration.

*a.* Table of languages (exclusive of dialects), spoken by populations grouped in classes according to their importance, as possible vehicles of Divine Truth.

*b.* Table of obsolete translations which are of no evangelizing value.

*c.* Table of versions in existence before the British and Foreign Bible Society led the way in the glorious career of giving the Bible to the world at large.

My object is to shut out for the future all the vagueness and uncertainty which surrounded Bible work. We ought to know whether a language is worthy of a translation, by how many it would be read, in what part of the world, what is the proper name of that language, whether it is only a dialect of another language or a jargon, whether it is a dead language, or, if a living language, what prospect of vitality it has. The word "jargon" has crept into use; it is something better than an illiterate patois, and something worse than a recognized literary dialect. Bible translations in jargons exist only for the use of the Jews in Europe or Negroes in America. It is a waste of money to spend it on translations into languages which are doomed to extinction in a short period by an inexorable law; in each case, therefore, it is a question of sound judgment whether a translation should be accepted, the work of an unduly sanguine translator: it is also wise to reflect whether the translation of the whole Bible is necessary for a small population in a low state of civilization. Appendix A shows the languages grouped in classes according to their relative importance; a study of these classes will enable an opinion to be formed, whether the translation of the whole Bible should be pressed forward; as a fact the great "conquering" languages of the world have been provided for, and the majority of the second or "permanent" class. Year by year languages will die out, and the translations must be removed from the efficient list and placed away with the honored dead and the worthies who have outlived their usefulness. Some, though dead, like the Ethiopic, Hebrew, Koptic, Latin, Mongol (literary), Pali, Sanskrit, Slavonic, and Syriac Peshito, are still kept on the active list out of deference to the wishes of those who desire to purchase them for educational, exegetical, or liturgical purposes, though on a strict application of my fourth principle above stated they ought to be excluded, and I am almost inclined to exclude them.

The population of the earth is thus distributed roughly: (1) Europe, 312,500,000; (2) Asia, 800,000,000; (3) Africa, 200,000,000; (4) America, 86,000,000; (5) Oceanica, 4,500,000. Total, 1,403,000,000.

The total number of mutually unintelligible forms of speech, whether carelessly called "tongues" or scientifically differentiated as languages, dialects of languages, or jargons, is certainly more than two thousand. No finality has been attained, or is likely in this generation to be attained, as the face of the earth has not yet been fully explored. Many of these languages are not likely to attain the honor of being intrusted with the oracles of God; they will perish before their turn comes.

In filling up the column "Population of Speakers" I became aware how extremely imperfect our data are. Where I could find no entry in an esteemed work which at the same time commended itself to my judgment, I have preferred to enter the word "Unknown." Those who have accurate information can make their own entries, and no doubt attention will be called to the subject. English is unquestionably the great leading language of the world, and deserves the honor, being free from the useless bondage of Gender, Number, Case, and Tense.

In filling up the column "Probable Duration of Language" I have been guided by my own observations, and am quite prepared to reconsider any entry for cause shown.

Many considerations occur. Some populations are bilingual: in which language shall the Bible be supplied to them? It is not a matter in which the prejudices of the priesthood or the blind policy of a ruler should be allowed to interfere; nor is it possible to forejudge the wishes of a people.

Nor should the reader blame the compiler of these lists, or the compiler be vexed, if within a very few years after he has sent forth his work, additions and emendations are required, as the work of translation is yearly progressive, and new names appear; and it is hoped that those into whose hands these lists fall, the result of much labor, will care to keep them corrected up to the mark until the time when a new and revised edition is required.

As regards the Geographical List No. II., the primary division of the five portions of the globe is by "regions," formed for convenience of the subject. The second subdivision is by "languages." From a language is differentiated a dialect by phonetics, word-store, and structure.

Ex. gr., Venetian and Neapolitan are dialects of Italian; Spanish and Portuguese, Swedish and Danish, are separate languages.

A language is entered but once. French appears under France, but the third column tells us that the language called French is the vernacular in part of Belgium, part of Switzerland, part of Italy, part of Great Britain, viz., the Channel Islands, in Canada and Mauritius, and so on. The same column tells us in what countries, and, as far as possible, in what provinces of that country, the language is spoken. This has been a most laborious task, and it cannot be pretended that the inquiry has been exhausted. It has required a very serious amount of labor, an accumulation of general knowledge, and a great deal of leisure to accomplish what has been done, for innumerable references had to be made to geographical and linguistic books. (Note. This column is transferred in these tables to the Alphabetical list.)

As the scope of the work is catholic, translations published by all Bible Societies and other associations are entered. Notice is made of the three forms in which a translation can appear, in addition to the original form in which it left the hand of the translator: (1) as a diglott, (2) in a particular dialect, and (3) a particular form of written character.

A difficulty has occurred in the grouping of some dialects. Take for instance the Lapp language; it has three dialects: the language is entered under Russia, where the main dialect is spoken; two dialects are shown, as Norse and Swedish, necessarily entered under Russia, but in the enumeration they count under Norway and Sweden. The same remark applies to Mongol; one dialect counts under China.

To secure precision the nature of the written character of every version is stated; the following are represented:

I. Ideograms. Some of the translations of languages current in China.

II. Syllabaries. North American, Japan.

III. Alphabets. 1, Roman; 2, Gothic; 3, Irish; 4, Cyril; 5, Greek; 6, Syriac; 7, Arabic; 8,; Hebrew; 9, Armenian; 10, Georgian; 11, Mongol; 12, Manchu; 13, Gurmúkhí; 14, Deva-Nágari; 15, Nágari; 16, Pahári; 17, Bangáli; 18, Úriya; 19, Modhi; 20, Gujaráti; 21, Tamil; 22, Télugu; 23, Karnáta; 24, Malayálam; 25, Sinháli; 26, Pali; 27, Barma; 28, Pegu; 29, Siam; 30, Tibet; 31, Java; 32, Batta; 33, Bugi; 34, Macassar; 35, Koréa; 36, Koptic; 37, Amháric; 38, Ethiopic.

Care has been taken to get rid of all the adjectival suffixes which have been fastened on to the root-word. For instance, the words Ehst, Rouman, Liv, etc., take the place of Esth-onian, Rouman-ian, Liv-onian. There can be no good reason for adding final syllables to the root-words. The well-known Greek, Swiss, Russ, Dutch, are not long words, but are familiarly used. Why then coin such words as Ruthen-ian, Croat-ian, Wend-ish, Piedmont-ese, Bulgar-ian, Kurd-ish, Sinhal-ese, Assam-ese, Mongol-ian, Bali-nese, Osset-inian, Cheremisi-an, and Lapp-onese? In the Russ language another set of adjectival suffixes are attached to the names in the Russian catalogue. In the German language another set of adjectival suffixes are attached to the names in the German and Austrian catalogues. This creates difficulties, and gives rise to errors, which are avoided by the maintenance of one uniform terminology in scientific catalogues. In the Arian languages of Northern India there is one linguistic suffix, which is used with a few exceptions, and that has been preserved, but there is no reason for adding the Arian suffix to the non-Arian languages, such as Sontal-i, Gond-i, unless the name is an Arian name superimposed, as the Malto or Maler is called geographically Rajmahál-i, because the tribe resides in that political division, and Pahár-i, because their residence is in the hills.

The use of some terms is out of date, such as Orenburg-Turki for Kirghíz, because the original translator resided at Orenburg; Karass-Turki, for Nogai-Turki, because the translator resided at the obscure village of Karass. The word Tartar should never be used at all. It is a tribal, not a linguistic, term, and is synonymous with Turki. Why, again, should the languages of China be grouped under the general term of "Chinese"? The languages of India are not grouped under the general term of "Indian." The terms "Indian" and "Chinese" have no occasion to be used at all, as each language of those great countries has its own name.

Then, again, the entering of the same language a second time, because an edition has been struck off in a different "written character," is confusing. If the English Bible were printed for the convenience of a class of the English-reading world in an alphabet used by people in India, it would still be English, and an Urdu translation is still Urdu, whether it appears in the Roman, Arabic, or Nágari alphabet. Judeo-German, long entered as a separate language, is only pure German in the Hebrew alphabet. Such expressions as Armeno-Turki, Judeo-Persian, Judeo-Arabic, suggest something very different from the fact. The uninstructed reader would suppose that they were dialects, when they are only the Osmánli-Turki in the Armenian alphabet, the Persian in the Hebrew alphabet, and the Arabic in the Hebrew alphabet. The use of the word "type," or letters, is objectionable when some form of written character is intended. Obviously the English language can be printed in many different types, such as pica, pearl, etc., but it is the same "alphabet." The use of the word "alphabet" as a general term is inaccurate, as some translations are in ideograms, or syllabaries, which are totally distinct from an alphabet. (This word, thus formed from the first two letters of the Phenician and Greek alphabets, is now applied to all connections of symbols, so organized as to represent accurately the sounds of each language.) An alphabet consists of consonants and vowels separate; a syllabary is composed of syllables necessarily composed of consonants and vowels united. Therefore the general term of the subject is "written character;" the three subdivisions are ideograms, syllabaries, alphabets. The word "letter" is only used when discussing the interior organization of an alphabet; the word "type" is a technical term of the printing-office.

The spelling of names should be on one uniform system, as settled by the Royal Geographical Society, the Ordnance Department of the Admiralty, and the government of British India; and an attempt has been made to introduce an accurate system.

The words "Roman alphabet" cover a great variety of forms of that alphabet, which it would be impossible to express in a statement such as the one now prepared. This alphabet has been adapted to express a great variety of sounds by diacritical marks, additional symbols, new combinations of letters, and new values given to the symbols. The same remark applies to the Arabic alphabet, which has been enlarged to express the sounds of the Persian language, and still further enlarged to express the sounds of the Urdu language. In some cases syllabaries have been devised by translators, and the ideographic symbols proper to the book-language and Mandarin-language in China, have been adapted for expressing the sounds of provincial vernaculars. It is sufficient for my purpose to indicate generally what form of "written character" has been used.

A careful distinction must be made betwixt languages that are "dead" and "extinct." When a language like Latin, Sanskrit, Hebrew, and Slavonic ceases to live on the lips of men as a vernacular, it is "dead," though perfectly intelligible and useful as a medium of oral or written communication. But when the power to read and understand a language has faded away from the knowledge even of scholars, it is "extinct," though possibly it may be resuscitated as a curiosity or for purposes of antiquarian research. Instances of resuscitated "extinct" languages offer themselves in the Egyptian, Babylonian, and Assyrian. Instances of the languages still hopelessly "extinct" are the Etruscan, Cypriot, and Hittite. It is a glad fact that no language to which has been committed the oracles of God has ever become "extinct," or passed away from the reservoir of human knowledge.

As regards the obsolete translations, under principle 3 I have omitted them. It is throwing dust into the eyes to retain them. A certain number of the names entered as dialects of the Hindi language are palpably of no use, and never were. The New England Indian translation in North America is useless, because the speakers of that language have all died out. The Narinyéri translation in Australia is useless, although the tribe exists, for the edition is exhausted, and no second edition has ever been called for. I was unable to secure a copy for my private library.

The third or linguistic list requires some remark. The languages of the world have been provisionally divided into families, or groups, but nothing like finality or exhaustion of the subject has been attained. Every portion of the world is represented on the lists of the Bible Society, except unhappy Australia. It is a marvellous surprise to a scholar who has never left Europe to have a translation of a Gospel handed to him, of the genuineness and the approximate accuracy of which there can be no doubt, in a language unprovided with scientific works or literary helps. From this text the scholar, by a reverse process to the translator, works out the linguistic features of the new language, the phonetics, the word-store, and the structure, discovers affinities with known languages, notes the variation, and makes a provisional classification. Thus the Bible Societies have mightily contributed to the expansion of knowledge. I myself receive constant application for copies or references on certain subjects, standing, as I try to stand, as an intermediary betwixt the translators in the field and the scholars of Europe at home.

TABLE OF ABBREVIATIONS.

| | | | |
|---|---|---|---|
| B. | Bible. | B. F. B. S. | British and Foreign Bible Society. |
| O. T. | Old Testament. | A. B. S. | American Bible Society. |
| N. T. | New Testament. | N. B. S. S. | National Bible Society of Scotland. |
| Pent. | Pentateuch. | B. T. S. | Bible Translation Society (Baptist). |
| Gen. | Genesis. | R. B. S. | Russian Bible Society. |
| Ex. | Exodus. | Ba. B. S. | Basle Bible Society. |
| Lev. | Leviticus. | N. B. S. | Netherlands Bible Society. |
| Psl. | Psalms. | Br. B. S. | Bremen Bible Society. |
| Is | Isaiah. | C. B. S. | Coire Bible Society. |
| Gos. | Gospel. | D. B. S. | Danish Bible Society. |
| Epis. | Epistle. | No. B. S. | Norwegian Bible Society. |
| Matt. | Matthew. | P. B. S. | Prussian Bible Society. |
| N. S. E. W. | North, South, East, West. | B. M. S. | Baptist Missionary Society. |
| N. W. | Northwest. | M. M. S. | Moravian Missionary Society. |
| Cent. | Central. | C. M. S. | Church Missionary Society. |
| U. S. | United States. | L. M. S. | London Missionary Society. |
| Gt. | Great. | A. B. M. S. | American Baptist Missionary Society. |
| Brit. | Britain, British. | A. B. C. F. M. | American Board of Commissioners for Foreign Missions |
| Isl | Island. | A. P. M. S. | Board of Foreign Missions, Presbyterian Church (North). |
| Equat. | Equatorial. | M. M. | Melanesian Mission. |
| Di. | Dialect. | U. M. | Universities' Mission. |
| C. | Conquering. | W. M. S. | Wesleyan Missionary Society. |
| P. | Permanent. | B. B. T. S. | Burma Bible and Tract Society. |
| I. | Isolated. | U. M. S. | United Methodist Society. |
| U. | Uncertain future. | F. C. S. M. | Free Church of Scotland Mission. |
| M. | Moribund. | C. P. M. | Canada Presbyterian Mission. |
| D. | Dead. | | |
| Cap. | Chapter. | | |
| Lit. | Liturgical. | | |
| O. V. | Old Version. | | |
| S. P. C. K. | Society for Promoting Christian Knowledge. | | |

## I. ALPHABETICAL LIST OF LANGUAGES WITH THEIR DIALECTS.

| No. | Language. Dialect. | Locality. | Population. | Probable Duration of Language. | Amount of Translation done. | No. in Geog. List. |
|---|---|---|---|---|---|---|
| 1 | Akra, or Ga. | W. Equat. Africa, Basin of Volta. | 100,000 | P. | B. | 186 |
| 2 | Aimará. | South America, Bolivia. | 370,000 | U. | Luke. | 230 |
| 3 | Ainu. | Japan. | 15,000 | M. | Jonah, Matt. | 140 |
| 4 | Akkawáy. | South America, Dutch Guiana. | Unknown | U. | Gen., Matt., parts. | 227 |
| 5 | Alban: 1. Tosk, or S. 2. Gheg, or N. | Turkey, Albania. | 1,750,000 | P. | N. T. N. T., Psl. | 46 |
| 6 | Aliout. | North America, Aleutian Islands. | Unknown | U. | Matt. | 199 |
| 7 | Alfuor. | Malaysia, Celebes Island. | Unknown | U. | Matt. | 119 |
| 8 | Amhára. | Africa, Abyssinia. | 2,000,000 | P. | B. | 144 |
| 9 | Amoy. | China, Fuh-Kien. | 15,000,000 | P. | B. | 128 |
| 10 | Aneityum Island. | Melanesia, New Hebrides. | 3,600 | I. | B. | 246 |
| 11 | Aniwa Island. | Melanesia, New Hebrides. | 500 | I. | N. T., parts. | 248 |
| 12 | Annam. | Indo-China. | 10,500,000 | P. | Luke. | 110 |
| 13 | Api, or Baki. | Melanesia, New Hebrides. | Unknown | I. | Mark. | 254 |
| 14 | Arabic: 1. Standard. | Turkey, Syria, Mesopotamia Arabia. Egypt, Tripoli; Algeria; Morocco; Zanzibar; | 50,000,000 | C. | B. | 68 |
|  | 2. Malta. | Malta. |  | M. | Matt., John, Acts. |  |
| 15 | Arawák. | S. America, Dutch Guiana. | 2,000 | U. | Acts. | 228 |
| 16 | Armenian: 1. Ancient. 2. Ararat (E.). 3. Modern (W.). | Trans-Caucasia. Turkey (Asia Minor). | Lit. 4,000,000 | P. P. P. | B. B. B. | 66 |
| 17 | Asámi. | N. E. Brit. India, Assam. | 2,000,000 | P. | B. | 88 |
| 18 | Ashánti: 1. Fanti. 2. Akwapem. | W. Africa, Cape Coast Castle Col., Ashanti. | 3,000,000 | P. P. | 4 Gos., Gen. B. | 187 |
| 19 | Azerbijáni, or Trans-Caucasian Turki. | Russia (Asia), Trans-Caucasia, Persia, Azerbiján. | 3,000,000 | C. | B. | 62 |
| 20 | Bali. | Malaysia, Java. | 1,000,000 | P. | parts. | 115 |
| 21 | Balúchi. | N. Brit. India, Balúchistan. | 1,500,000 | P. | 3 Gos. | 73 |
| 22 | Bangáli: 1. Standard. 2. Mahometan. | Cent. Brit. India, Bangál. | 39,000,000 | C. U. | B. O. & N. T., parts. | 80 |
| 23 | Barma. | N. E. Brit. India, Barma. | 6,000,000 | C. | B. | 101 |

| No. | Language. Dialect. | Locality. | Population. | Probable Duration of Language. | Amount of Translation done. | No. in Geog. List. |
|---|---|---|---|---|---|---|
| 24 | Basque: | France, Spain; | 600,000 | | | 8 |
| | 1. French. | Prov. of Pyrenees (France): | | P. | N. T. | |
| | 2. Spanish. | Prov. of Biscay; | | P. | Luke. | |
| | 3. Guipuscóa. | " " Guipuscóa. | | U. | Luke. John. | |
| 25 | Batta: | Malaysia, | 3,500,000 | | | 112 |
| | 1. Toba. | Sumatra. | | P. | N. T., Psl. | |
| | 2. Mandailing. | | | P. | N. T. | |
| 26 | Beaver. | Canada, Athabasca. | Unknown | U. | Mark. | 207 |
| 27 | Benga. | W. Equat. Africa, Gabún Col. | Unknown | P. | 4 Gos., Acts. | 174 |
| 28 | Bilin, or Bogos. | Africa, Abyssinia. | 10.000 | P. | Mark. | 147 |
| 29 | Blackfoot. | Canada, Prov. Alberta. | 7,000 | U. | Matt. | 209 |
| 30 | Bohemian, or Czech. | Austria, Bohemia. | 5,000,000 | P. | B. | 15 |
| 31 | Bondei. | E. Equat. Africa: U. Sambára (Germany). | Unknown | P. | Matt. | 152 |
| 32 | Breton. | France, Brittany. | 3,000,000 | P. | N. T., Psl. | 7 |
| 33 | Bugi. | Malaysia, Celebes Island. | 1,000,000 | P. | 3 Gos., Acts. | 117 |
| 34 | Bulgár. | Turkey (Europe), Bulgaria. | 4,500,000 | P. | B. | 47 |
| 35 | Bullom. | W. Equat. Africa, Sierra Leone Col. | 1,000 | M. | Matt. | 191 |
| 36 | Bunda, or Mbunda, or Ki-Mbunda. | W. Equat. Africa, Angóla Col. | Unknown | P. | Luke, John. | 170 |
| 37 | Chau-Chau, or Swatau. | China, Kwang-Tung. | 15,000,000 | P. | 3 Gos., Acts, Gen. | 127 |
| 38 | Cheroki. | U. S. A., Mississippi Region. | 15,000 | U. | O. & N. T., parts. | 220 |
| 39 | Cheremisi | N. Russia (Europe), Kazán and Simbirsk. | 200,000 | U. | N. T. | 37 |
| 40 | Chipewán. | Canada, Athabasca. | Unknown | U. | N. T. | 206 |
| 41 | Choktau. | U. S. A., Mississippi Region. | 18,500 | U. | O.T., parts, N.T. | 219 |
| 42 | Chuana. | S. Africa, Bechuanaland and Matabeleland. | Unknown | P. | B. | 162 |
| 43 | Chuvash. | Russia (Europe), Kazán, Nijni-Novgorod, and Orenburg. | 670,000 | U. | 4 Gos. | 39 |
| 44 | Cree: | | 40,000 | | | 208 |
| | 1. E., or Hudson Bay. | Canada, | | P. | N. T., parts. | |
| | 2. W., or Moosonee. | Hudson's Bay Ter. | | P. | B. | |
| 45 | Dakóta, or Sioux. | U. S. A., Dakota. | 50,000 | U. | O.T., parts, N.T. | 217 |
| 46 | Delaware, or Munsée. | U. S. A., Delaware. | Unknown | U. | Matt., John. | 215 |
| 47 | Dualla. | W. Equat. Africa, Kamerún Col. | Unknown | P. | B. | 176 |
| 48 | Duke of York's Isl. | Melanesia, Bismarck Archipelago Col. | Unknown | I. | Matt., Acts. | 264 |

| No. | Language. Dialect. | Locality. | Population. | Probable Duration of Language. | Amount of Translation done. | No. in Geog. List. |
|---|---|---|---|---|---|---|
| 49 | Dutch. | Holland and Cape of Good Hope Col. | 3,500,000 | C. | B. | 10 |
| 50 | Dyak:<br>1. Standard.<br>2. Sea. | Malaysia,<br>Island of Borneo. | Unknown<br><br> | <br>P.<br>U. | <br>N. T.<br>Psl. | 120 |
| 51 | Ebon Island. | Mikronesia,<br>Marshall Islands. | Unknown | U. | Gen., N. T. | 267 |
| 52 | Efík. | W. Equat. Africa,<br>Old Calabar. | 90,000 | P. | B | 177 |
| 53 | English:<br>1. Standard.<br><br><br>2. Negro of Súrinam. | Gt. Brit. and Ireland,<br>Brit. Subject-Do-<br>minions.<br>U. S. of N. America.<br>West Indies. | <br><br>200,000,000<br><br>Unknown | <br><br>C.<br><br>M. | <br><br>B.<br><br>N. T., Psl. | 1 |
| 54 | Eromanga Islands. | Melanesia,<br>New Hebrides. | 5,000 | I. | 3 Gos., Acts, Gen. | 250 |
| 55 | Eskimó:<br>1. Greenland.<br>2. Labrador.<br>3. Hudson's Bay. | Denmark, Greenland,<br>Labrador, and Provs.<br>of Hudson's Bay. | <br>9,500<br>3,000<br>Unknown | <br>P.<br>P.<br>P. | <br>O.T., parts, N.T.<br>B.<br>Luke. | 197 |
| 56 | Ehst:<br>1. Dorpat, or Werro.<br>2. Reval. | Russia (Europe),<br>Provs. Esthonia<br>and Livonia. | <br>100,000<br>Unknown | <br>P.<br>P. | <br>N. T., Psl.<br>B. | 29 |
| 57 | Ethiopic, or Giz. | Africa,<br>Abyssinia. | Lit. | D. | N. T., Psl. | 145 |
| 58 | Ewé:<br>1. Anlo.<br>2. Popo. | W. Equat. Africa,<br>Dahomi. | Unknown<br><br> | <br>P.<br>P. | <br>O.T., parts, N.T.<br>4 Gos., Psl. | 185 |
| 59 | Falasha-Kara<br>(Di. of Agau). | Africa,<br>Abyssinia (Jews). | 200,000 | P. | Mark. | 146 |
| 60 | Faté Iands.<br>1. Erakar.<br>2. Havannah Harbor. | Melanesia,<br>New Hebrides. | 3,000<br><br> | <br>I.<br>I. | <br>N. T., parts, Gen.<br>N. T. | 251 |
| 61 | Fiji Islands. | Melanesia,<br>Fiji Islands. | 146,000 | I. | B. | 241 |
| 62 | Finn. | Russia (Europe),<br>Finland. | 2,250,000 | P. | B. | 27 |
| 63 | Flemish. | Belgium. | 4,000,000 | P. | B. | 9 |
| 64 | Flórida Islands. | Melanesia,<br>Solomon's Islands. | Unknown | I. | Luke, John. | 256 |
| 65 | Formósa. | China,<br>Formosa. | 1,500,000 | P. | Luke, John. | 123 |
| 66 | French:<br>1. Standard.<br>2. Vaudois.<br>3. Provençál.<br><br><br><br><br>4. Mauritius. | France, French Cols.<br>Channel Isl., Can-<br>ada, Belgium,<br>Switzerland<br>(FrenchCantons),<br>Italy (Submon-<br>tane Prov.).<br>Mauritius Isl. | 40,000,000<br><br><br><br><br><br><br>Unknown | <br>C.<br>U.<br>U.<br><br><br><br>U. | <br>B.<br>Luke, John.<br>Mark.<br><br><br><br>Matt., Mark. | 6 |
| 67 | Fris. | Holland. | Unknown | M. | Matt. | 11 |
| 68 | Fuh-Chau. | China,<br>Fuh-Kien. | 8,000,000 | P. | O. T., parts, N. T. | 129 |
| 69 | Fútuna. | Melanesia,<br>New Hebrides. | 500 | U. | Mark, Acts. | 247 |
| 70 | Gaelic. | Gt. Britain.<br>Highlands of Scot-<br>land. | Unknown | U. | B. | 3 |
| 71 | Galla:<br>1. Shoa.<br>2. Ittu.<br>3. Bararetta. | E. Africa,<br>Galla-land. | Unknown<br><br><br> | <br>P.<br>P.<br>P. | <br>N.T., O.T., parts.<br>Matt.<br>John. | 149 |

| No. | Language. Dialect. | Locality. | Population. | Probable Duration of Language. | Amount of Translation done. | No. in Geog. List. |
|---|---|---|---|---|---|---|
| 72 | GANDA. | E. Equat. Africa, U-Ganda. | Unknown | P. | Matt. | 153 |
| 73 | GARO. | N. E. Brit. India, Assam. | Unknown | P. | 4 Gos., 3 Epis. | 89 |
| 74 | GEORGIAN. | Russia (Asia), Trans-Caucasia. | 3,000,000 | P. | B. | 65 |
| 75 | GERMAN: 1. Standard. | Germany, Austria, Switzerland, Russia, France. | 45,000,000 | C. | B. | 12 |
|  | 2. Judæo. |  | 500,000 |  |  |  |
| 76 | GILBERT ISLANDS. | Mikronesia. | 30,000 | I. | N. T. | 265 |
| 77 | GITÁNO, or SPANISH GYPSY. | Spain. | Unknown | U. | Luke. | 51 |
| 78 | GOGO. | E. Equat. Africa, U-Gogo. | Unknown | P. | Matt. | 154 |
| 79 | GOND. | Brit. India, Cent. Provs. | 1,500,000 | P. | 3 Gos., Gen. | 85 |
| 80 | GREBO. | W. Africa, Liberia. | Unknown | P. | O. & N. T., parts. | 188 |
| 81 | GREEK : 1. Ancient. |  | Lit. | P. | B. | 45 |
|  | 2. Modern, or Romaic. | Greece, Turkey. | 3,000,000 | D. | B. |  |
| 82 | GÚARANI. | S. America, Paraguay. | 500,000 | U. | Matt., part. | 231 |
| 83 | GUJARATI : 1. Standard. | Brit. India, Bombay. | 9,000,000 | P. | B. | 99 |
|  | 2. Parsi. |  |  | P. | N. T. |  |
| 84 | GWAMBA. | S. Africa, Transvaal. | Unknown | P. | 4 Gos. | 165 |
| 85 | HAI-NAN. | S. China Hai-Nan. | Unknown | P. | Matt. | 124 |
| 86 | HAKKA. | S. China, Kwang-Tung. | 1,000,000 | P. | N. T. | 126 |
| 87 | HAUSA. | W. Equat. Africa, Upper basin of the Niger. | Unknown | C. | N. T., Gen., Ex., Ps., Is. | 178 |
| 88 | HAWÁII. | Sandwich Islands. | 49,000 | I. | B. | 236 |
| 89 | HEBREW. |  | Lit. | D. | B. | 69 |
| 90 | HERERÓ. | W. Equat. Africa, Damara-land Col. | Unknown | P. | N. T., Psl. | 168 |
| 91 | HINDI : 1. Standard. | N. Brit. India. | 82,000,000 | C. | B. | 78 |
|  | 2. Hindustáni, or Urdu. |  |  | C. | B. |  |
|  | 3. Dákhani, or S. |  |  | U. | N. T., Gen., Ex. |  |
|  | 4. Kumáoni, or Pahári. |  |  | U. | N. T. |  |
|  | 5. Marwári, or Central. |  |  | U. | N. T. |  |
|  | 6. Guhrwáli. |  |  | U. | N. T. |  |
| 92 | HYDAH. | N. America, Pacific Coast, Queen Charlotte's Island. | Unknown | L | Matt. | 203 |
| 93 | IBO. | W. Equat. Africa, Lower basin of Niger. | Unknown | P. | N. T., parts. | 180 |
| 94 | ICELANDIC, or Old NORSE: | Iceland. |  |  |  | 54 |
|  | 1. Standard. |  | 72,500 | P. | B. |  |
|  | 2. Faroe Islands. |  | 11,000 |  | Matt. |  |

| No. | LANGUAGE. DIALECT. | LOCALITY. | POPULATION. | PROBABLE DURATION OF LANGUAGE. | AMOUNT OF TRANSLATION DONE. | No. IN GEOG. LIST. |
|---|---|---|---|---|---|---|
| 95 | IDZO. | W. Equat. Africa, Estuary of Niger. | Unknown | P. | John, part. | 181 |
| 96 | IGÁRA. | W. Equat. Africa, Estuary of Niger. | Unknown | P. | N. T. | 182 |
| 97 | I'GBIRA. | W. Equat. Africa, Estuary of Niger. | Unknown | P. | 4 Gos., O.T., parts. | 183 |
| 98 | IRISH, or ERSE. | Gt. Britain, Ireland. | Unknown | M. | B. | 4 |
| 99 | IROQUOIS. | N. America, Quebec and Ontario. | Unknown | U. | 4 Gos. | 213 |
| 100 | ISABEL, or BOGOTU ISL. | Melanesia, Solomon's Islands. | Unknown | I. | John. | 257 |
| 101 | ITALIAN : 1. Standard. | Italy; the Levant; Ionian Islands; Island of Malta; Adriatic Provs.(Austria.) | 28,500,000 | C. | B. | 48 |
| | 2. Piedmont. | Italian Cantons (Switzerland); | | U. | N. T., Psl. | |
| 102 | JAGHATAI-TURKI, or TRANS-CASPIAN. | Russia (Asia), Prov. of Trans-Caspia, or Tekke-Turkoman. | Unknown | U. | Matt. | 63 |
| 103 | JAPAN. | Japan Islands. | 28,000,000 | P. | B. | 139 |
| 104 | JAVA. | Malaisia, Java Islands. | 13,000,000 | P. | N. T., O. T., parts. | 113 |
| 105 | JOLOF. | W. Equat. Africa, Senegambia. | Unknown | P. | Matt. | 194 |
| 106 | KABÁIL. | N. Africa, Algeria. | Unknown | P. | John. | 196 |
| 107 | KÁFIR, or XOSA. | S. Africa, Kaffraria. | 210,000 | P. | B. | 161 |
| 108 | KAGÚRU. | E. Equat. Africa, U-Sagára. | Unknown | P. | Luke. | 155 |
| 109 | KARA-KIRGHIZ-TURKI, or BURUT. | N. Russia (Asia), E. Siberia. | 66,000 | P. | N. T. | 58 |
| 110 | KARÉL. | N. Russia (Asia), Prov. of Tver. | Unknown | U. | Matt. | 33 |
| 111 | KARÉN: 1. Bghai. 2. Sgau. 3. Pwo. | N. E. Brit. India, Barma. | 50,000 | P. P. P. | O. & N. T., parts. Pent. O. T., 4 books. | 103 |
| 112 | KARÍB. | S. America, Dutch Guiana. | 20,000 | U. | Matt. | 226 |
| 113 | KARNÁTA: 1. Standard. 2 Bádaga. | S. Brit. India, Madras. | 9,250,000 | P. U. | B. Matt., Luke. | 94 |
| 114 | KASHMÍRI. | N. Brit. India, Kashmir. | 500,000 | P. | N.T., O.T., parts. | 75 |
| 115 | KAZÁK-KIRGHIZ-TURKI. | N. Russia (Europe), Prov. Orenburg. | 1,500,000 | P. | N. T., O. T., part. | 41 |
| 116 | KAZÁN-TURKI. | N. Russia (Europe), Prov. Kazán. | 1,000,000 | P. | 3 Gos. | 40 |
| 117 | KELE. | W. Equat. Africa, Gabún Col. | | P. | John. | 173 |
| 118 | KHASI. | N. E. Brit. India, Assam. | 200,000 | P. | N. T., O.T., parts. | 90 |
| 119 | KINH-WHA. | Cent. China, Prov. Che-Kiang. | Unknown | P. | John. | 132 |

| No. | LANGUAGE. DIALECT. | LOCALITY. | POPULATION. | PROBABLE DURATION OF LAN- GUAGE. | AMOUNT OF TRANS- LATION DONE. | NO. IN GEOG. LIST. |
|---|---|---|---|---|---|---|
| 120 | KOI. | S. Brit. India, Madras. | 100,000 | P. | Luke, John, 1st Epis. | 97 |
| 121 | KONGO. | W. Equat. Africa, Kongo Ter. | Unknown | P. | parts. | 171 |
| 122 | KOPTIC. | Africa, Egypt. | Lit. | D. | 4 Gos., Psl. | 142 |
| 123 | KORÉA. | N. China, Korea. | 9,000,000 | P. | N. T. | 138 |
| 124 | KROAT. | Austria, Provs. Kroatia and Dalmatia. | 2,360,000 | P. | B. | 21 |
| 125 | KÚMUKI-TURKI. | S. Russia (Europe), Daghestán. | 25,000 | P. | Matt. | 43 |
| 126 | KURD. | Turkey (Asia), Persia. Trans-Caucasia. | 10,000 | D. | N. T. | 67 |
| 127 | KUSAIE. | Mikronesia, Strong Island. | 1,200 | I. | Matt.,Luke,John. | 268 |
| 128 | KWAGUTL. | N. America, Pacific Coast, Vancouver's Isl. | Unknown | U. | Matt., John. | 202 |
| 129 | KWANG-TUNG, or CANTON. | S. China, Kwang-Tung. | 20,000,000 | P. | N. T., Gen., Psl. | 125 |
| 130 | LAOS. | Indo-China, Siam. | 1,000,000 | P. | parts. | 107 |
| 131 | LAPP: 1. Norse, or Quán. 2. Russ. 3. Swedish. | Lapland, Norway, and Sweden. | 17,000 5,000 6,700 | I. I. I. | Gen., Is. Matt. B. | 28 |
| 132 | LATIN. | Roman Cath. Ch. | Lit. | D. | B. | 49 |
| 133 | LEPCHA. | Cent. Brit. India, Sikim. | 7,000 | P. | 2 Gos., Gen., Ex. | 82 |
| 134 | LETT. | N. Russia (Europe), Livonia and Cour- land. | 3,000,000 | U. | B. | 30 |
| 135 | LIFU ISL. | Melanesia, Loyalty Islands. | 6,000 | I. | B. | 244 |
| 136 | LITHU: 1. Standard. 2. Samoghít, or Zemait. | Russia, Germany, Baltic Prov. | 2,500,000 | P. U. | B. N. T. | 31 |
| 137 | LIV. | N. Russia (Europe), Prov. W. Courland. | 4,500 | U. | Matt. | 32 |
| 138 | LÚCHU. | Japan, Luchu Islands. | 167,000 | P. | N. T., part. | 141 |
| 139 | MACASSAR. | Malaisia, Celebes Islands. | 120,000 | P. | 3 Gos., Acts. | 118 |
| 140 | MAFÚR. | Melanesia, Island of New Guinea. | Unknown | I. | | 262 |
| 141 | MÁGHADI. | Cent. Brit. India, Prov. Behár. | Unknown | P. | Matt. | 81 |
| 142 | MAGYAR, or HUNGAR- IAN. | Austria Hungary. | 6,500,000 | P. | B. | 18 |
| 143 | MAKÚA. | E. Equat. Africa, Mozambik. | Unknown | P. | Matt., 7 caps. | 156 |
| 144 | MALAGÁSI. | S. Africa, Madagascar Island. | 2,500,000 | P. | B. | 159 |

| No. | Language. Dialect. | Locality. | Population. | Probable Duration of Language. | Amount of Translation done. | No. in Geog. List. |
|---|---|---|---|---|---|---|
| 145 | MALAY: 1. Standard. 2. Low Malay, or Surabaya. | Malaisia, Pen. of Malacca, Isl. of Sumatra. | 10,500,000 . | C. U. | B. N. T., Ex. | 111 |
| 146 | MALAYÁLAM. | S. Brit. India. Madras. | 3,750,000 | P. | B. | 95 |
| 147 | MALISEET. | Canada, New Brunswick. | Unknown | U. | John. | 212 |
| 148 | MALLIKOLLO ISLAND. | Melanesia, New Hebrides. | Unknown | I. | Matt. | 253 |
| 149 | MALTO, PAHÁRI, or RAJMAHÁLI, or MALER. | Cent. Brit. India, Hill tribes of Rajmahal, Bengál. | 400,000 | P. | 4 Gos., Acts, Psl. | 83 |
| 150 | MANCHU. | N. China, Manchúria. | Unknown | P. | N. T. | 137 |
| 151 | MANDÁRI, or KOL. | Cent. Provs. India. | 850,000 | P. | 4 Gos., 2 Epis. | 86 |
| 152 | MANDARIN: 1. N., or Peking. 2. S., or Nanking. | N. China. | 200,000,000 | C. | B. N. T. | 135 |
| 153 | MANDÉ, or MANDINGO. | W. Equat. Africa, Mandingo. | 8,000,000 | P. | 4 Gos. | 193 |
| 154 | MANIPÚR. | Cent. Provs. India. | Unknown | P. | N. T. | 91 |
| 155 | MANX. | Gt. Britain, Isle of Man. | Very few | M. | B. | 5 |
| 156 | MAORI. | Polynesia, New Zealand. | 45,000 | P. | B. | 240 |
| 157 | MARÁTHI: 1. Standard. 2. Konkani. | S. Brit. India, Bombay. | 17,000,000 1,000,000 | P. P. | B. N. T., Pent. | 98 |
| 158 | MARE, or NENGÓNE ISLAND. | Melanesia, Loyalty Islands. | 4,000 | I. | N.T.,O.T., parts. | 243 |
| 159 | MARQUÉSAS ISLAND. | Polynesia, Marquesas Isl. | 8,000 | U. | John, part. | 235 |
| 160 | MAYA. | Cent. America, Yucatan. | 500,000 | U. | Luke, John. | 222 |
| 161 | MENDÉ. | W. Equat. Africa, Sierra Leone. | Unknown | | 4 Gos., Romans. | 189 |
| 162 | MEXICAN, or AZTEK. | Cent. America, Mexico. | 1,250,000 | U. | Luke. | 223 |
| 163 | MIK-MAK: 1. Standard. 2. Abenaqui. | N. America, Nova Scotia. | 3,000 Unknown | U. U. | O. & N. T., parts. parts. | 211 |
| 164 | MOHAWK. | U. S. America. New York | 7,000 | U. | Luke, John, Is. | 214 |
| 165 | MON, or PEGU. | N. E. Brit. India, Burma. | Unknown | M. | N. T. | 102 |
| 166 | MONGOL: 1. Literary. 2. N. (Buriat). 3. S. (Kalkhas). 4. W. (Kalmuk). | Russia (Europe). Basin of Volga; Russia (Asia), China, Provs. Mongolia. | Lit. 150,000 6 000 12,000 | D. P. P. P. | B. Matt.,John,Acts. Matt. Matt.,John,Acts. | 60 |
| 167 | MORDWIN: 1. Erza. 2. Moksha. | Russia (Europe), Provs. of Nijni-Novgoród and Kaján. | 480,000 Unknown | U. U. | N. T. 1 Gos. | 36 |
| 168 | MORTLOCK ISLAND. | Mikronesia, Mortlock Islands. | 3,000 | I. | N. T. | 266 |
| 169 | MOSKÍTO. | Cent. America, Moskito Coast. | Unknown | U. | 4 Gos., Acts. | 225 |

| No. | LANGUAGE. DIALECT. | LOCALITY. | POPULATION. | PROBABLE DURATION OF LANGUAGE. | AMOUNT OF TRANSLATION DONE. | NO. IN GEOG. LIST. |
|---|---|---|---|---|---|---|
| 170 | MOTA ISLAND. | Melanesia, Banks' Islands. | Unknown | P. | N. T. | 255 |
| 171 | MOTU. | Melanesia, New Guinea. | Unknown | P. | 4 Gos. | 261 |
| 172 | MURRAY ISLAND. | Melanesia, Torres Strait. | 700 | I. | Mark, John. | 258 |
| 173 | MUSKÓKI, or CREEK. | U. S. America, Mississippi Region. | Unknown | U. | N. T. | 221 |
| 174 | NAHUATL. | Central America, Mexico. | Unknown | U. | parts. | 224 |
| 175 | NAMA, or KHOI-KHOI, or HOTTENTOT. | S. Africa, Cape of Good Hope, and Namaqualand. | Unknown | U. | N. T., Psl. | 167 |
| 176 | NEPÁLI. | N. Brit. India, Nepál. | Unknown | P. | N. T. | 79 |
| 177 | NEW BRITAIN ISLAND. | Melanesia, Bismarck Archipelago. | 10,000 | I. | Matt. | 263 |
| 178 | NEW GUINEA, SOUTH CAPE. | Melanesia, New Guinea. | Unknown | P. | Mark. | 260 |
| 179 | NEY-PERCES, or SAHAPTIN. | U. S. America, Idaho. | Unknown | U. | parts. | 216 |
| 180 | NGUNA ISLAND. | Melanesia, New Hebrides. | 4,500 | I. | 4 Gos., Acts. | 252 |
| 181 | NIAS ISLAND. | Malaisia, Nias Island. | 80,000 | I. | Luke. | 116 |
| 182 | NICOBÁR ISLAND. | Brit. India, Nicobár Island. | 5,000 | I. | Matt. | 104 |
| 183 | NING-PO. | Cent. China, Che-Kiang. | 5,000,000 | P. | N. T. | 131 |
| 184 | NIUE, or SAVAGE ISLAND. | Polynesia, Savage Island. | 5,000 | I. | N. T., O. T., part. | 238 |
| 185 | NISHKAH. | N. America, Pacific Coast. Basin of R. Naas. | Unknown | I. | John. | 201 |
| 186 | NOGAI-TURKI: 1. E. 2. Krim, or W. | S. Russia (Europe), Prov. Cis-Caucasia, Krimea. | 25,000 | P. U. | N. T., Pent. Gen. | 42 |
| 187 | NORWEGO-DANISH. | Norway and Denmark. | 4,000,000 | P. | B. | 53 |
| 188 | NUBA. | Africa, Soudan, Nubia. | 1,000,000 | P. | Mark. | 143 |
| 189 | NUPÉ. | W. Equat. Africa, Quarrah Branch of Niger. | Uncertain | P. | 4 Gos. | 179 |
| 190 | NYANJA. | E. Equat. Africa, Basin R. Shiré. | Unknown | P. | parts. | 158 |
| 191 | NYIKA. | E. Equat. Africa, Wa-Nyika Tribe. | 50,000 | P. | Luke. | 150 |
| 192 | OJIBWA, or CHIPPEWA. | Canada, W. of Lake Superior, and United States. | 25,000 | U. | O.T.,N.T., parts. | 210 |
| 193 | OSSÉT | S. Russia (Asia), Prov. Cis-Caucasia. | 27,000 | P. | Epis. of James, 4 Gos., Psl. | 64 |
| 194 | OSTYAK. | Russia (Asia), Provs. Tobolsk, Tomsk. | 25,000 | I. | 1 Gos. | 56 |
| 195 | PALI. | India. Ceylon. | Lit. | D. | N. T. | 106 |

| No. | LANGUAGE. DIALECT. | LOCALITY. | POPULATION. | PROBABLE DURATION OF LANGUAGE. | AMOUNT OF TRANSLATION DONE. | No. IN GEOG. LIST. |
|---|---|---|---|---|---|---|
| 196 | PANGASÍNAN. | Malaisia, Philippine Islands. | Unknown | P. | 4 Gos., Acts, Psl. | 121 |
| 197 | PANJÁBI, or SIKH: | N. Brit. India, Prov. Panjab. | 14,000,000 | | | 76 |
| | 1. Standard. | | | U. | N. T., O. T., part. | |
| | 2. Dogri. | | | U. | N. T. | |
| | 3. Chambáli. | | | U. | Matt., John. | |
| | 4. Multani, or Jatki. | | | U. | N. T. | |
| 198 | PASTÚ. | N. Brit. India; Afghanistan. | 5,000,000 | P. | N.T., O.T., part. | 72 |
| 199 | PEDI. | S. Africa, Transvaal. | Unknown | U. | N. T. | 166 |
| 200 | PERM. | N. Russia (Europe), Provs. Perm, Viatka, and Archangel. | 50,000 | U. | Matt. | 35 |
| 201 | PERSIAN. | Persia; Afghanistan. | 5,000,000 | C. | B. | 70 |
| 202 | POLE. | Polish Provinces of Russia, Germany, and Austria. | 13,500,000 | P. | B. | 17 |
| 203 | PONAPÉ ISLAND. | Mikronesia, Caroline Islands. | 10,000 | I. | O. & N. T., parts. | 269 |
| 204 | PONGWÉ. | W. Equat. Africa, Gabún Col. | Unknown | P. | N. T., Psl., Is. | 175 |
| 205 | PORTUGUESE: | | | | | 52 |
| | 1. Standard. | Portugal; Brazil; | 5,000,000 | C. | B. | |
| | 2. Indian. | Ceylon. | Unknown | U. | N. T., Psl. | |
| 206 | QUICHÚA. | S. America, Peru. | 1,000,000 | P. | John. | 229 |
| 207 | RAROTONGA ISLAND. | Polynesia, Hervey Islands. | 10,000 | I. | B. | 234 |
| 208 | ROMANSCH, or LADIN: | Switzerland, Engadine. | 10,000 | | | 14 |
| | 1. Upper. | | | U. | N. T. | |
| | 2. Lower. | | | U. | B. | |
| | 3. Oberland. | | | U. | B. | |
| 209 | RÓTUMA ISLAND. | Melanesia, Rótuma Island. | 3,000 | I. | N. T. | 242 |
| 210 | ROUMÁN: | Roumania; | | | | 19 |
| | 1. Standard. | Austria, Hungary, | 7,500,000 | P. | B. | |
| | 2. Macedon. | Transylvania, and Bukowina. | | P. | Matt. | |
| 211 | RUSS. | N. Russia (Europe). | 75,000,000 | C. | B. | 24 |
| 212 | RUTHÉN. | N. Russia (Europe); Austria, Galicia, Bukowina, Transylvania. | 9,500,000 | P. | B. | 26 |
| 213 | SAIBAI ISLAND. | Melanesia, Torres Straits. | Unknown | I. | Matt., Mark. | 259 |
| 214 | SÁMOA ISLANDS. | Polynesia, Navigator's Islands. | 34,000 | I. | B. | 237 |
| 215 | SANGÍR ISLAND. | Malaisia. | 80,000 | I. | N.T., Psl., Prov. | 122 |
| 216 | SANSKRIT. | N. Brit. India. | Lit. | D. | B. | 74 |
| 217 | SÉNEKA. | N. America, Borders of Lake Erie. | 2,700 | U. | 4 Gos. | 218 |
| 218 | SERB. | Austria, Hungary, Bosnia, Herzegovina; Servia; Montenegro. | 2,250,000 | P. | B. | 20 |

| No. | Language. Dialect. | Locality. | Population. | Probable Duration of Language. | Amount of Translation done. | No. in Geog. List. |
|---|---|---|---|---|---|---|
| 219 | SHAN. | Indo-China, Ind. Shan States. | Unknown | P. | parts. | 109 |
| 220 | SHANG-HAI. | Cent. China, Kiang-Su. | 8,000,000 | P. | Matt., John. | 133 |
| 221 | SHILHA, Riff. | N. Africa, Morocco. | Unknown | P. | Matt. | 195 |
| 222 | SHIMSHI. | Canada, Prov. Metlakatla. | Unknown | I. | 4 Gos. | 200 |
| 223 | SIAM. | Siam. | 6,500,000 | P. | Luke, John. | 107 |
| 224 | SINDHI: 1. Standard. 2. Katchi. | N. W. Brit. India, Prov. of Sindh. | 1,750,000 | P. P. | N. T., Psl., Is. Matt. | 100 |
| 225 | SINHÁLI. | India, Ceylon. | 750,000 | P. | B. | 105 |
| 226 | SLAVÉ. | Canada, MacKénzie R. | Unknown | P. | 4 Gos. | 205 |
| 227 | SLAVONIC. | Greek Church, Russia, Austria, Northern Balkan Peninsula. | Lit. | D. | B. | 25 |
| 228 | SLOVÁK. | Austria, Hungary. | 1,900,000 | P. | N. T. | 16 |
| 229 | SLOVÉN. | Austria, Provs. Karniola and Karinthia. | 2,361,000 | P. | N. T., Psl., Is. | 22 |
| 230 | SONTÁL. | Cent. Brit. India, Sontalia. | 1,000,000 | P. | N. T., Psl. | 84 |
| 231 | SPANISH: 1. Standard. 2. Catalan. 3. Judæo. 4. Curacao | Spain; Cent. and S. America (except Brazil); W. Indies. | 16,000,000 Unknown Unknown Unknown | C. P. U. U. | B. N. T. N. T. | 50 |
| 232 | SUNDA. | Malaysia, Java Island. | 4,000,000 | P. | N. T., Gen. | 114 |
| 233 | SUSU. | W. Equat. Africa, Senegambia. | Unknown | P. | 3 Gos. | 192 |
| 234 | SU-CHAU. | Cent. China, Kiang-Su. | 3,000,000 | P. | N. T. | 134 |
| 235 | SUTO. | South Africa, Ba-Suto-land. | Unknown | P. | B. | 164 |
| 236 | SWAHÍLI. | E. Equat. Africa. | Unknown | C. | B. | 151 |
| 237 | SWEDISH. | Sweden. | 4,000,000 | P. | B. | 55 |
| 238 | SYRIAC: 1. Peshito, or Ancient. 2. Syro-Chaldaic, or Modern | Syria. Persia. | Lit. Unknown | D. P. | B. B. | 71 |
| 239 | SIRYIN, or ZIR. | N. Russia (Europe), Vologda. | 70,000 | U. | Matt. | 84 |
| 240 | TAHÍTI ISLAND. | Polynesia, Society Islands. | 18,000 | I. | B. | 233 |
| 241 | TAMIL. | S. Brit. India, Madras, Ceylon. | 13,000,000 | D. | B. | 92 |
| 242 | TANNA ISLAND: 1. Kwaméra. 2. Weasísi. | Melanesia, New Hebrides. | 7,000 | I. I. | Matt., Acts. John. part. | 249 |
| 243 | TEKÉ. | W. Equat. Africa, Kongo. | Unknown | U. | Mark. | 172 |
| 244 | TÉLUGU. | S. Brit. India, Madras. | 17,000,000 | P. | B. | 93 |

| No. | LANGUAGE. DIALECT. | LOCALITY. | POPULATION. | PROBABLE DURATION OF LAN- GUAGE. | AMOUNT OF TRANS- LATION DONE. | No. IN GEOG. LIST. |
|---|---|---|---|---|---|---|
| 245 | TEMNÉ. | W. Equat. Africa, Sierra Leone. | 200,000 | P. | N. T., Gen., Ex., Psl. | 190 |
| 246 | TIBET. | China, Tibet; N. Brit. India, Lahúl. | Unknown | P. | N.T., Pent., Psl., Is. | 77 |
| 247 | TIGRÉ. | Africa, E. Abyssinia. | See No. 8 | P. | 4 Gos. | 148 |
| 248 | TINNÉ. | Canada, Hudson's Bay. | Unknown | U. | Mark, John. | 204 |
| 249 | TONGA, or FRIENDLY ISLANDS. | Polynesia, Friendly Islands. | 25,000 | I. | B. | 239 |
| 250 | TONGA, or SIGA. | S. E. Africa, Amatonga-land. | Unknown | U. | Revelation. | 163 |
| 251 | TUKUDH, or LOUCHEUX. | N. America, Alaska. | Unknown | I. | Gen., Ex., Lev. | 198 |
| 252 | TULU. | S. Brit. India, Madras. | 300,000 | P. | N. T. | 96 |
| 253 | TURKI-OSMANLI, or TURKISH. | Turkey, (Europe and Asia). | 5,000,000 | P. | B. | 44 |
| 254 | UMBUNDU. | W. Equat. Africa, Benguella. | Unknown | P. | Mark, John. | . 169 |
| 255 | URIYA. | Cent. Brit. India, Prov. Orissa. | 8,000,000 | P. | B. | 87 |
| 256 | UVEA ISLAND. | Melanesia, Loyalty Islands. | 2,000 | I. | N. T., Psl. | 245 |
| 257 | UZBEK-TURKI, or CENTRAL ASIA, or KHIVA. | N. Russia (Asia); Khiva; Bukhara; Turkistan. | 500,000 | P. | 4 Gos. | 59 |
| 258 | VÓGUL. | N. Russia (Asia), W. Siberia. | 6,000 | U. | Matt., Mark. | 57 |
| 259 | VOTYAK. | N. Russia (Europe), Provs. Viatka and Orenburg. | 200,000 | U. | Matt. | 38 |
| 260 | WELSH. | Great Britain, Wales. | 1,000,000 | P. | B. | 2 |
| 261 | WEN-LI, or BOOK-LANGUAGE OF CHINA: 1. Standard. 2. Easy. | China generally. | Unknown | P. P. | B. N. T. | 136 |
| 262 | WEND: 1. Saxon. 2. Prussian. | Germany, Prov. Lusatia. | Unknown Unknown | U. U. | B. B. | 13 |
| 263 | WIND, or ANCIENT SLOVÉN. | Austria, Hungary, Styria. | Unknown | U. | N. T., Psl. | 23 |
| 264 | WUN-CHAU. | Cent. China, Prov. Che-Kiang. | Unknown | P. | 4 Gos., Acts. | 130 |
| 265 | YAHGÁN. | S. America, Argentine Rep., Tierra del Fuego | Unknown | I. | Luke, John, Acts. | 232 |
| 266 | YAKÚT. | N. Russia (Asia), N. Siberia. | 100,000 | I. | 4 Gos. | 61 |
| 267 | YAO. | E. Equat. Africa, Yao-land. | Unknown | P. | Matt. | 157 |
| 268 | YÁRIBA. | W. Equat. Africa, Yáriba-land. | 3,000,000 | C. | B. | 184 |
| 269 | ZULU. | S. Africa, Zulu-land, Natal. | 270,000 | C. | B. | 160 |

## II. GEOGRAPHICAL AND LINGUISTIC LIST.

| No. | LANGUAGE DIALECT. | WRITTEN CHARACTER. | FAMILY, BRANCH. | SOURCE OF TRANSLATION. | DIGLOTT. | No. IN ALPHABETIC LIST. |
|---|---|---|---|---|---|---|
| | | | **EUROPE.** | | | |
| | | | *GREAT BRITAIN.* | | | |
| | ENGLISH: 1. Standard. 2. Negro of Surinam. | Roman. | Arian, Teuton. | O. V. B. F. B. S. | E.—Arabic, E.—Bangáli, E.—Bullom, E.—Dutch, E.—French, E.—German, E.—Greek, E.—Gujaráti, E.—Hebrew, E.—Italian, E.—Karnáta, E.—Malayalám, E.—Maráthi, E.—Norwégo-Danish, E.—Osmanli-Turki, E.—Spanish, E.—Swedish, E.—Tamil, E.—Télegu, E.—Urdu, E.—Welsh. | 53 |
| 2 | WELSH. | Roman. | Arian, Kelt. | O. V. | W.—English. | 260 |
| 3 | GAELIC. | Roman. | Arian, Kelt. | O. V. | | 70 |
| 4 | ERSE. | Roman. Irish. | Arian, Kelt. | O. V. | | 98 |
| 5 | MANX. | Roman. | Arian, Kelt. | O. V. | | 155 |
| | | | *FRANCE.* | | | |
| 6 | FRENCH: 1. Standard. 2. Vaudois. 3. Provençal. 4. Mauritius. | Roman. | Arian, Greco-Latin. | O. V. B. F. B. S. B. F. B. S. | F.—Arabic, F.—Breton, F.—English, F.—Flemish, F.—German, F.—Greek, F.—Hebrew, F.—Malta, F.—Osmanli-Turki, F.—Piedmont, F.—Romaic, F.—Vaudois, | 65 |
| 7 | BRETON. | Roman. | Arian, Kelt. | B. F. B. S. | B.—French. | 32 |
| 8 | BASQUE. 1. French. 2. Spanish. 3. Guipuscóa. | Roman. | Arian, Isolated. | B. F. B. S. B. F. B. S. B. F. B. S. | | 24 |
| | | | *BELGIUM.* | | | |
| 9 | FLEMISH. | Roman. | Arian, Teuton. | O. V. | F.—French. | 63 |
| | | | *HOLLAND.* | | | |
| 10 | DUTCH. | Roman. | Arian, Teuton. | O. V. | D.—English. | 49 |
| 11 | FRIS. | Roman. | Arian, Teuton. | B. F. B. S. | | 66 |

| No. | Language, Dialect. | Written Character. | Family, Branch. | Source of Translation. | Diglott. | No. in Alphabetic List. |
|---|---|---|---|---|---|---|
| | *GERMANY, SWITZERLAND, ETC.* | | | | | |
| 12 | GERMAN: | | Arian, | | G.—English, | 75 |
| | 1. Standard. | { Gothic. { Roman. | Teuton. | O. V. | G.—French, G.—Hebrew, | |
| | 2. Judæo. | Hebrew. | | B. F. B. S. | G. in Hebrew Character—Hebrew. G.—Italian. | |
| 13 | WEND: | Gothic. | Arian, Slav. | | | 262 |
| | 1. Saxon. | | | P. B. S. | | |
| | 2. Prussian. | | | P. B. S. | | |
| 14 | ROMANSCH: | Roman. | Arian, Greco-Latin. | | | 208 |
| | 1. Upper. | | | O. V. | | |
| | 2. Lower. | | | C. B. S. | | |
| | 3. Oberland. | | | C. B. S. | | |
| | *AUSTRIA, ETC.* | | | | | |
| 15 | CZECH, or BOHEMIAN. | { Gothic. { Roman. | Arian, Slav. | O. V. | | 30 |
| 16 | SLOVÁK. | Roman. | Arian, Slav. | B. F. B. S. | | 228 |
| 17 | POLE. | { Roman, { Gothic. | Arian, Slav. | O. V. | P.—Hebrew. | 202 |
| 18 | MAGYAR, or HUNGARIAN. | Roman. | Ural-Altaic, Finn. | O. V. | M.—Hebrew. | 142 |
| 19 | ROUMÁN: | | Arian, Greco-Latin. | | | 210 |
| | 1. Standard. | { Roman. { Old Cyril. | | B. F. B. S. | | |
| | 2. Macedon. | Mod. Cyril. | | B. F. B. S. | | |
| 20 | SERB. | Cyril. | Arian, Slav. | B. F. B. S. | | 218 |
| 21 | KROÁT. | Roman. | Arian, Slav. | B. F. B. S. | | 124 |
| 22 | SLOVÉN. | Roman. | Arian, Slav. | B. F. B. S. | | 229 |
| 23 | WIND, or ANCIENT SLOVÉN. | Roman. | Arian, Slav. | B. F. B. S. | | 263 |
| | *RUSSIA.* | | | | | |
| 24 | RUSS. | Cyril. | Arian, Slav. | O. V. | R.—Slavonic, R.—Hebrew. | 211 |
| 25 | SLAVÓNIC. | { Old Cyril. { Cyril. | Arian, Slav. | O. V. | S.—Bulgár, S.—Russ. | 227 |
| 26 | RUTHÉN. | { Cyril. { Roman. | Arian, Slav. | O. V. | | 212 |
| 27 | FINN. | Gothic. | Ural-Altaic, Finn. | O. V. | | 62 |
| 28 | LAPP: | | Ural-Altaic, Finn. | | | 131 |
| | 1. Norse or Quán. | Gothic. | | { No. B. S. N. L.—Norwego- { B. F. B. S.   Danish, | | |
| | 2. Swedish. | Gothic. | | B. F. B. S. | S. L.—Swedish, | |
| | 3. Russ. | Cyril. | | O. V. | R. L.—Swedish. | |
| 29 | EHST: | | Ural-Altaic, Finn. | | | 56 |
| | 1. Dorpat, or Werro. | Gothic. | | B. F. B. S. | | |
| | 2. Reval. | Gothic. | | O. V. | | |
| 30 | LETT. | Gothic. | Arian, Lithuanic. | O. V. | | 134 |
| 31 | LITHU: | | Arian, Lithuanic. | | | 136 |
| | 1. Standard. | { Roman. { Gothic. | | O.V.,P. B. S. R. B. S. | | |
| | 2. Samoghít, or Zemait. | | | | | |

| No. | Language, Dialect. | Written Character. | Family, Branch. | Source of Translation. | Diglott. | No. in Alphabetic List. |
|---|---|---|---|---|---|---|
| 32 | Liv. | Gothic. | Ural-Altaic, Finn. | B. F. B. S. | | 137 |
| 33 | Karél. | Cyril. | Ural-Altaic, Finn. | R. B. S. | | 110 |
| 34 | Siryin (Zir). | Cyril. | Ural-Altaic, Finn. | R. B. S. | | 239 |
| 35 | Perm. | Cyril. | Ural-Altaic, Finn. | R. B. S. | | 200 |
| 36 | Mordvin: 1. Erza. 2. Moksha. | Cyril. | Ural-Altaic, Finn. | R. B. S. | | 167 |
| 37 | Cheremísi. | Cyril. | Ural-Altaic, Finn. | R. B. S. | | 39 |
| 38 | Votyak. | Cyril. | Ural-Altaic, Finn. | R. B. S. | | 259 |
| 39 | Chuvásh. | Cyril. | Ural-Altaic, Turki. | R. B. S. | | 43 |
| 40 | Turki-Kazán. | Arabic. | Ural-Altaic, Turki. | B. F. B. S. | | 116 |
| 41 | Turki-Kazak-Kirghiz. | Arabic. | Ural-Altaic, Turki. | R. B. S. | | 115 |
| 42 | Turki-Nogai: 1. E. 2 Krim, or W. | Arabic. | Ural-Altaic, Turki. | B. F. B. S. O. V. | | 186 |
| 43 | Turki-Kúmuki. | Arabic. | Ural-Altaic, Turki. | B. F. B. S. | | 125 |

*TURKEY, ETC. (EUROPE).*

| No. | Language, Dialect. | Written Character. | Family, Branch. | Source of Translation. | Diglott. | No. in Alphabetic List. |
|---|---|---|---|---|---|---|
| 44 | Turki-Osmanli. | { Arabic. Greek. Armenian. | Ural-Altaic, Turki. | { B. F. B. S. A. B. S. B. F. B. S. A. B. S. | O.—English, O.—French, O.—Hebrew, O.—Italian. | 253 |
| 45 | Greek: 1. Ancient. 2. Modern, or Romaic. | { Greek. Roman. | Arian, Greco-Latin. | O. V. B. F. B. S. | G.—English, G.—French, G.—German, G.—Latin, G.—Tosk. | 81 |
| 46 | Alban: 1. Tosk, or S. 2. Gheg, or N. | { Greek. New Roman. { Roman. New Roman. | Arian, Isolated. | B. F. B. S. B. F. B. S., | Tosk-Greek. | 5 |
| 47 | Bulgár. | Cyril. | Arian, Slav. | B. F. B. S. | B.—Slavonic, B.—Hebrew. | 34 |

*ITALY.*

| No. | Language, Dialect. | Written Character. | Family, Branch. | Source of Translation. | Diglott. | No. in Alphabetic List. |
|---|---|---|---|---|---|---|
| 48 | Italian: 1. Standard. 2. Piedmont. | Roman. | Arian, Greco-Latin. | O. V. B. F. B. S. | I.—English, I.—French, I.—German, I.—Hebrew, I.—Latin, I.—Malta, I.—Osmanli-Turki. | 101 |
| 49 | Latin. | Roman. | Arian, Greco-Latin. | O. V. | L.—Italian, L.—Osmanli-Turki, L.—Spanish. | 132 |

*SPAIN.*

| No. | Language, Dialect. | Written Character. | Family, Branch. | Source of Translation. | Diglott. | No. in Alphabetic List. |
|---|---|---|---|---|---|---|
| 50 | Spanish: 1. Standard. 2. Catalan. 3. Judæo. 4. Curacao. | Roman. | Arian, Greco-Latin. | O. V. B. F. B. S. B. F. B. S. N. B. S. | S.—English, S.—Latin, Judeo-Hebrew, S.—Aimara. | 231 |

| No. | Language, Dialect. | Written Character. | Family, Branch. | Source of Translation. | Diglott. | No. in Alphabetic List. |
|---|---|---|---|---|---|---|
| 51 | Gitano, or Spanish Gypsy. | Roman. | Arian, Isolated. | B. F. B. S. | S.—Guarani. | 77 |
| | *PORTUGAL.* | | | | | |
| 52 | Portuguese: 1. Standard. 2. Indian. | Roman. | Arian, Greco-Latin. | O. V. B. F. B. S. | | 205 |
| | *DENMARK.* | | | | | |
| 53 | Norwégo-Danish. | Gothic. Roman. | Arian, Teuton. | O. V. | N. D.—English, N. D.—Norse-Lapp. | 187 |
| 54 | Icelandic. or Old Norse: 1. Standard. 2. Faroe Islands. | Roman. | Arian, Teuton. | O.V.,D.B.S. D. B. S. | | 94 |
| | *SWEDEN.* | | | | | |
| 55 | Swedish. | { Gothic. { Roman. | Arian, Teuton. | O. V. | S.—English, S.—Swedish-Lapp, S.—Russ-Lapp. | 237 |
| | ASIA. | | | | | |
| | *N. RUSSIA.* | | | | | |
| 56 | Ostyak. | Cyril. | Ural-Altaic, Finn. | B. F. B. S. | | 194 |
| 57 | Vógul. | Cyril. | Ural-Altaic, Finn. | B. F. B. S. | | 258 |
| 58 | Turki-Kara- Kirghiz, or Burut. | Arabic. | Ural-Altaic, Turki. | B. F. B. S. | | 109 |
| 59 | Turki-Uzbék. | Arabic. | Ural-Altaic, Turki | B. F. B. S. | | 257 |
| 60 | Mongol: 1. Literary. 2. N. (Buriat). 3. S. (Kalkhas) 4 W. (Kalmuk). | { Mongol. { Manchu. Mongol. Mongol. Mongol. | Ural-Altaic, Mongol. | B. F. B. S. B. F. B. S. B. F. B. S. B. F. B. S. | | 166 |
| 61 | Yakút. | Cyril. | Ural-Altaic, Turki. | Moscow. | | 266 |
| | *S. RUSSIA.* | | | | | |
| 62 | Turki-Azerbijáni, or Trans-Cau- casian. | Arabic. | Ural-Altaic, Turki. | { B. F. B. S. { A. B. S. | | 14 |
| 63 | Turki-Jaghatái, or Trans-Caspian. | Arabic. | Ural-Altaic, Turki. | B. F. B. S. | | 102 |
| 64 | Ossét. | Cyril. | Arian, Iran. | R. B. S. | | 193 |
| 65 | Georgian. | { Liturgical { Civil. | Ural-Altaic, Caucasus. | O. V. | | 74 |
| 66 | Armenian: 1. Ancient. 2. Ararat (E.). 3. Modern (W.) | Armenian. | Arian, Iran. | O. V. B. F. B. S. { B.F. B. S. { A. B. S. | Ancient-Ararat, Ancient-Modern. | 16 |
| 67 | Kurd. | Armenian. | Arian, Iran. | { B. F. B. S. { A. B. S. | | 126 |

| No. | Language, Dialect. | Written Character. | Family, Branch. | Source of Translation. | Diglott. | No. in Alphabetic List. |
|---|---|---|---|---|---|---|
| | *SYRIA AND ARABIA.* | | | | | |
| 68 | Arabic: 1. Standard. | Roman. Arabic. Hebrew. Syriac, or Kárshun. | Semitic. | B. F. B. S. A. B. S. | A.—English, A.—Ethiopic, A.—French, A.—Hausa, A.—Koptic, A.—Syriac, | 14 |
| | 2. Malta. | | | B. F. B. S. | M.—French. | |
| 69 | Hebrew. | Hebrew. | Semitic. | O. V. (Old Test.) B. F. B. S. (New Test.) | H.—English, H.—German, H.—German in Hebrew Character, H.—Judeo-Spanish, H.—Russ, H.—Bulgár, H.—French, H.—Osmanli-Turki, H.—Magyar, H.—Italian, H.—Pole. | 89 |
| | *PERSIA.* | | | | | |
| 70 | Persian. | Arabic. Hebrew. | Arian, Iran. | O. V. | | 201 |
| 71 | Syriac: 1. Peshito, or Ancient. 2. Syro-Chaldaic, or Modern. | Syriac. Arabic. Hebrew. | Semitic. | O. V. A. B. S. | S.—Arabic in Syriac or Karshun Character. | 238 |
| | *BRITISH INDIA.* | | | | | |
| 72 | Pastú. | Arabic. | Arian, Iran. | B. F. B. S. B. M. S. | | 198 |
| 73 | Balúchi. | Arabic. | Arian, Iran. | B. F. B. S. | | 21 |
| 74 | Sanskrit. | Deva-Nágari. | Arian, Indic. | B. T. S. | S.—Bangáli, S.—Úriya, S.—Télugu, S.—Malayálam, S.—Maráthi, S.—Gujaráti. | 216 |
| 75 | Kashmíri. | Arabic. | Arian, Indic. | B. F. B. S. | | 114 |
| 76 | Panjábi, or Sikh: 1. Standard. 2. Dogri. 3. Chambali. 4. Multani, or Jatki. | Gurmúkhi Nágari. Pahári. | Arian, Indic. | B. F. B. S. B. F. B. S. B. F. B. S. B. F. B. S. | | 197 |
| 77 | Tibet. | Tibet. | Non-Arian, Tibeto-Barman. | B. F. B. S. | | 246 |
| 78 | Hindi: 1. Standard. 2. Hindustani, or Urdu. 3. Dákhani, or S. 4. Kumáoni, or Pahári. 5. Marwári, or Central. 6. Guhrwáli. | Arabic. Nágari. Roman. Nágari. | Arian, Indic. | B. F. B. S. B. M. S. B. F. B. S. B. F. B. S. B. F. B. S. A. B. S. B. F. B. S. | Urdu-English, Urdu-Maráthi and Gujaráti. | 91 |

| No. | Language, Dialect. | Written Character. | Family, Branch. | Source of Translation. | Diglott. | No. in Alphabetic List. |
|---|---|---|---|---|---|---|
| 79 | Nepáli. | Nágari. | Arian, Indic. | B. F. B. S. | | 176 |
| 80 | Bangáli: 1. Standard. 2. Mahometan. | { Bangáli. { Roman. | Arian, Indic. | B. T. S. B. F. B. S. | B.—English. | 22 |
| 81 | Mághadi. | Nágari. | Arian, Indic. | B. F. B. S. | | 141 |
| 82 | Lepcha. | Pahári. | Non-Arian, Tibeto-Barman. | B. T. S. | | 133 |
| 83 | Malto, Pahári, or Rajmaháli, or Maler. | Roman. | Non-Arian, Dravidian. | B. F. B. S. | | 149 |
| 84 | Sontál. | { Roman. { Bangáli. | Non-Arian, Kolarian. | B. F. B. S. | | 230 |
| 85 | Gond. | Nágari. | Non-Arian, Dravidian. | B. F. B. S. | | 79 |
| 86 | Mandári, or Kol. | Roman. | Non-Arian, Kolarian. | B. F. B. S. | | 151 |
| 87 | Úriya. | Úriya. | Arian, Indic. | B. F. B. S. | | 255 |
| 88 | Asámi. | Bangáli. | Arian, Indic. | B. T. S. | | 17 |
| 89 | Garo. | Bangáli. | Non-Arian, Tibeto-Barman. | { B. T. S. { B. F. B. S. | | 73 |
| 90 | Khasi. | Roman. | Non-Arian, Khasi. | B. F. B. S. | | 118 |
| 91 | Manipúr. | Bangáli. | Non-Arian, Tibeto Barman. | B. F. B. S. | | 154 |
| 92 | Tamil. | Tamil. | Non-Arian, Dravidian. | { B. F. B. S. { D. B. S. | T.—English. | 241 |
| 93 | Télugu: | Télugu. | Non-Arian, Dravidian. | B. F. B. S. | T.—English, T.—Sanskrit. | 244 |
| 94 | Karnáta: 1. Standard. 2. Bádaga. | Karnáta. | Non-Arian, Dravidian. | B. F. B. S. B. F. B. S. | K.—English. | 113 |
| 95 | Malayálam. | Malayálam. | Non-Arian, Dravidian. | { B. F. B. S. { Ba. B. S. | M.—English, M.—Sanskrit. | 146 |
| 96 | Tulu. | Karnáta. | Non-Arian, Dravidian. | Ba. B. S. | | 252 |
| 97 | Koi. | Roman. | Non-Arian, Dravidian. | B. F. B. S. | | 120 |
| 98 | Maráthí: 1. Standard. 2. Konkáni. | { Nágari, or { Balbodh. { Modhi. { Roman. | Arian, Indic. | { A. B. S. { B. F. B. S | M.—English, M.—Gujaráti and Sanskrit, M.—Nágari and Modhi, M.—Gujaráti and Urdu. | 157 |
| 99 | Gujaráti: 1. Standard. 2. Pársi. | Gujaráti. | Arian, Indic. | B. F. B. S. B. F. B. S. | G.—English, G.—Maráthi and Sanskrit, G.—Maráthi and Urdu. | 83 |
| 100 | Sindhi: 1. Standard. 2. Katchi. | { Nágari, { Arabic, { Gurmúkhi. | Arian, Indic. | B. F. B. S. B. F. B. S. | | 224 |
| 101 | Barma. | Barma. | Non-Arian, Tibeto-Barman. | A. B. M. S. | | 23 |

| No. | Language, Dialect. | Written Character. | Family, Branch. | Source of Translation. | Diglott. | No. in Alphabetic List. |
|---|---|---|---|---|---|---|
| 102 | Pegu, or Mon. | Barma. | Indo-China, Mon-Anam. | B. F. B. S. | | 165 |
| 103 | Karén: 1. Bghai. 2. Sgau. 3. Pwo. | Barma. | Non-Arian, Tibeto Barman. | A. B. M. S. A. B. M. S. A. B. M. S. | | 111 |
| 104 | Nicobár. | Roman. | Malayan. | B. F. B. S. | | 182 |

*CEYLON.*

| 105 | Sinháli. | Sinháli. | Arian, Indic. | B. F. B. S. | | 225 |
| 106 | Pali. | Pali. | Arian, Indic. | B. F. B. S. | | 195 |

*INDO-CHINA.*

| 107 | Siam. | Siam. | Indo-China, Tai. | B. F. B. S. | | 223 |
| 108 | Laos. | Siam. | Indo-China, Tai. | A.P.M.S. A.B.M.S. | | 130 |
| 109 | Shan. | Roman | Indo-China, Tai. | B. B. T. S. | | 219 |
| 110 | Annam. | Roman. Annam. | Indo-China, Mon-Anam. | B. F. B. S. | | 12 |

*INDIAN ARCHIPELAGO.*

| 111 | Malay: 1. Standard. 2. Low Malay, or Surabáya. | Arabic. Roman. | Malayan. | O. V. B. F. B. S. B. F. B. S. | | 145 |
| 112 | Batta: 1. Toba. 2. Mandailing. | Batta. Roman. | Malayan. | N. B. S. B. F. B. S. B. F. B. S. | | 25 |
| 113 | Java. | Java. Roman. | Malayan. | N. B. S. B. F. B. S. | | 104 |
| 114 | Sunda. | Roman. | Malayan. | N. B. S. | | 232 |
| 115 | Bali Island. | Roman. | Malayan. | N. B. S. | | 20 |
| 116 | Nias Island. | Roman. | Malayan. | B. F. B. S. | | 181 |
| 117 | Bugi. | Bugi. | Malayan. | N. B. S. | | 33 |
| 118 | Macassar. | Macassar. | Malayan. | N. B. S. | | 139 |
| 119 | Alfuor: | Roman. | Malayan. | N. B. S. | | 7 |
| 120 | Dyak: 1. Standard. 2. Sea. | Roman. | Malayan. | N. B. S. S. P. C. K. | | 50 |
| 121 | Panjasinán. | Roman. | Malayan. | B. F. B. S. | | 196 |
| 122 | Sangír Island. | Roman. | Malayan. | B. F. B. S. | | 215 |

*CHINA.*

| 123 | Formósa. | Roman. | Malayan. | C P. M. | | 65 |
| 124 | Hai-Nan. | Roman. | China. | B. F. B. S. | | 85 |
| 125 | Kwang-Tung, or Canton. | Ideograms Roman | China. | B. F. B. S. A. B S. | | 129 |
| 126 | Hakka. | Ideograms Roman. | China. | B. F. B. S. | | 86 |

| No. | LANGUAGE, DIALECT. | WRITTEN CHARACTER. | FAMILY, BRANCH. | SOURCE OF TRANSLATION. | DIGLOTT. | No. IN ALPHA-BETIC LIST. |
|---|---|---|---|---|---|---|
| 127 | CHAU-CHAU, or SWATAU. | { Ideograms { Roman. | China. | B. F. B. S. | | 37 |
| 128 | AMOY. | Roman. | China. | A. B. S. | | 9 |
| 129 | FUH-CHAU. | Ideograms. | China. | B. F. B. S. | | 68 |
| 130 | WUN-CHAU. | Roman. | China. | B. F. B. S. | | 264 |
| 131 | NING-PO. | Roman. | China. | B. F. B. S. | | 183 |
| 132 | KINH-WHA. | Roman. | China. | | | 119 |
| 133 | SHANG-HAI. | { Ideograms { Roman. | China. | { B. F. B. S. { A. B. S. | | 220 |
| 134 | SU-CHAU. | Ideograms. | China. | B. F. B. S. | | 234 |
| 135 | MANDARÍN. 1. N. or Peking. 2. S. or Nanking. | { Ideograms { Roman. | China. | { B. F. B. S. { A. B. S. { B. F. B. S. { A. B. S. | | 152 |
| 136 | WEN-LI. or BOOK LANGUAGE: 1. Standard. 2. Easy. | Ideograms. | China. | { B. F. B. S. { B. M. S. { A. B. S. | Wen-Li Japan. | 261 |
| 137 | MANCHU. | Manchu. | Ural-Altaic, Tungus. | B. F. B. S. | | 150 |
| 138 | KORÉA. | Koréa. | Extreme Orient. | B. F. B. S. | | 123 |

*JAPAN.*

| 139 | JAPAN. | { Syllabary. { Roman. | Extreme Orient. | { A. B. S. { B. F. B. S. { N. B. S. S. | J.—Wen-Li. | 103 |
|---|---|---|---|---|---|---|
| 140 | AINU. | Roman. | Extreme Orient. | B. F. B. S. | | 3 |
| 141 | LÚCHÚ. | Syllabary. | Extreme Orient. | { S. P. C. K. { B. F. B. S. | | 138 |

AFRICA.

*EGYPT.*

| 142 | KOPTIC. | Koptic. | Hamitic. | O. V. | K.—Arabic. | 122 |
|---|---|---|---|---|---|---|
| 143 | NUBA. | { Roman. { Arabic. | Nuba-Fulah. | B. F. B. S. | | 188 |

*ABYSSINIA.*

| 144 | AMHÁRA. | { Amháric. { Roman. | Semitic. | B. F. B. S. | A.—Ethiopic. | 8 |
|---|---|---|---|---|---|---|
| 145 | GIZ, or ETHIOPIC. | Ethiopic. | Semitic. | O. V. | E.—Amhara. | 57 |
| 146 | FALÁSHA-KARA (Di. of Agau). | Amháric. | Hamitic. | B. F. B. S. | | 59 |
| 147 | BOGOS, or BILIN. | Amháric. | Hamitic. | B. F. B. S. | | 28 |
| 148 | TIGRÉ. | { Amháric. { Roman. | Semitic. | B. F. B. S. | | 247 |

*EAST EQUATORIAL.*

| 149 | GALLA: 1. Shoa. 2. Ittu. 3. Bararetta. | { Amháric. { Roman. | Hamitic. | B. F. B. S. B. F. B. S. B: F. B. S. | | 71 |
|---|---|---|---|---|---|---|
| 150 | NYIKÁ. | Roman. | Bántu. | B. F. B. S. | | 191 |

| No. | Language, Dialect. | Written Character. | Family, Branch. | Source of Translation. | Diglott. | No. in Alphabetic List. |
|---|---|---|---|---|---|---|
| 151 | Swahíli. | { Arabic. { Roman. | Bántu. | B. F. B. S. | | 236 |
| 152 | Bondei. | Roman. | Bántu. | B. F. B. S. | | 31 |
| 153 | Ganda. | Roman. | Bántu. | B. F. B. S. | | 72 |
| 154 | Gogo. | Roman. | Bántu. | B. F. B. S. | | 78 |
| 155 | Kagúru. | Roman. | Bántu. | B. F. B. S. | | 108 |
| 156 | Makúa. | Roman. | Bántu. | U. M. | | 143 |
| 157 | Yao. | Roman. | Bántu. | B. F. B. S. | | 267 |
| 158 | Nyanja. | Roman. | Bántu. | N. B. S. S. | | 190 |
| | | | *SOUTH.* | | | |
| 159 | Malagási. | Roman. | Malayan. | B. F. B. S. | | 144 |
| 160 | Zúlú. | Roman. | Bántu. | { A. B. S. { B. B. S. | | 269 |
| 161 | Xosa, or Káfir. | Roman. | Bántu. | { B. F. B. S. { B. B. S. | | 107 |
| 162 | Chuána. | Roman. | Bántu. | B. F. B. S. | | 42 |
| 163 | Tonga, or Siga. | Roman. | Bántu. | A. B. C. F. M. | | 250 |
| 164 | Suto. | Roman. | Bántu. | B. F. B. S. | | 235 |
| 165 | Gwamba. | Roman. | Bántu. | B. F. B. S. | | 84 |
| 166 | Pedi. | Roman. | Bántu. | B. F. B. S. | | 199 |
| 167 | Nama, Hottentot, or Khoikhoi. | Roman. | Hottentot. | B. F. B. S. | | 175 |
| | | | *WEST EQUATORIAL.* | | | |
| 168 | Hereró. | Roman. | Bántu. | B. F. B. S. | | 90 |
| 169 | Umbundu. | Roman. | Bántu. | A. B. C. F. M. | | 254 |
| 170 | Bunda, or Kimbunda, or Mbunda. | Roman. | Bántu. | B. F. B. S. | | 36 |
| 171 | Kongo. | Roman. | Bántu. | B. M. S. | | 121 |
| 172 | Teké. | Roman. | Bántu. | A. B. M. S. | | 243 |
| 173 | Kele. | Roman. | Bántu. | A. B. S. | | 117 |
| 174 | Benga. | Roman | Bántu. | A. B. S. | | 27 |
| 175 | Pongwé. | Roman. | Bántu. | A. B. S. | | 204 |
| 176 | Dualla. | Roman. | Bántu. | B. T. S. | | 47 |
| 177 | Efík. | Roman. | Negro. | N. B. S. S. | | 52 |
| 178 | Hausa. | Roman. | Negro. | B. F. B. S. | | 87 |
| 179 | Nupé. | Roman. | Negro. | B. F. B. S. | | 189 |
| 180 | Ibo. | Roman. | Negro. | B. F. B. S. | | 93 |
| 181 | Idzo. | Roman. | | | | 95 |
| 182 | Igára. | Roman. | Negro. | C. M. S. | | 96 |
| 183 | Igbira. | Roman. | Negro. | B. F. B. S. | | 97 |
| 184 | Yáriba. | Roman. | Negro. | B. F. B. S. | | 268 |
| 185 | Ewé. | Roman. | Negro. | | | 58 |
| | 1. Anlo. | | | { B. F. B. S. { Br. B. S. | | |
| | 2. Popo. | | | B. F. B. S. | | |
| 186 | Akrá, or Gá. | Roman. | Negro. | B. F. B. S. | | 1 |

| No. | Language, Dialect. | Written Character. | Family, Branch. | Source of Translation. | Diglott. | No. in Alphabetic List. |
|---|---|---|---|---|---|---|
| 187 | Ashánti: 1. Fanti. 2. Akwapem. | Roman. | Negro. | B. F. B. S. | | 18 |
| 188 | Grebo. | Roman. | Negro. | A. B. S. | | 80 |
| 189 | Mendé. | Roman. | Negro. | B. F. B. S. | | 161 |
| 190 | Temné. | Roman. | Negro. | B. F. B. S. | | 245 |
| 191 | Bullom. | Roman. | Negro. | B. F. B. S. | B. with English. | 35 |
| 192 | Susu. | Roman. | Negro. | S. P. C. K. | | 233 |
| 193 | Mandé, or Mandingo. | Roman. | Negro. | B. F. B. S. | | 153 |
| 194 | Jolof. | Roman. | Negro. | B. F. B. S. | | 105 |
| 195 | Shilha: Riff. | Roman. | Hamitic. | B. F. B. S. | | 221 |
| | *NORTH.* | | | | | |
| 196 | Kabáil. | Roman. | Hamitic. | B. F. B. S. | | 106 |

## AMERICA.
### North.

*ARCTIC COAST.*

| No. | Language, Dialect. | Written Character. | Family, Branch. | Source of Translation. | Diglott. | No. in Alphabetic List. |
|---|---|---|---|---|---|---|
| 197 | Eskimó: 1. Greenland. 2. Labrador. 3. Hudson's Bay. | Roman. { Roman. } Syllabary. | North American, Arctic Coast. | D. B. S. B. F. B. S. B. F. B. S. | | 55 |
| 198 | Tukudh, or Loucheux. | Roman. | North American, Arctic Coast. | B. F. B. S. | | 251 |
| 199 | Aliout. | Roman | North American, Arctic Coast. | R. B. S. | | 6 |

*PACIFIC COAST.*

| 200 | Shimshi. | Roman. | North American, Pacific Coast. | C. M. S. | | 222 |
|---|---|---|---|---|---|---|
| 201 | Nishkah. | Roman. | North American, Pacific Coast. | C. M. S. | | 185 |
| 202 | Kwagutl. | Roman. | North American, Pacific Coast. | B. F. B. S. | | 128 |
| 203 | Hydah. | Roman. | North American, Pacific Coast. | C. M. S. | | 92 |

*CANADA AND UNITED STATES.*

| 204 | Tinné. | { Roman. } Syllabary. | North American, Cent. Prov. | B. F. B. S. | | 248 |
|---|---|---|---|---|---|---|
| 205 | Slavé. | { Roman. } Syllabary. | North American, Cent. Prov. | B. F. B. S. | | 226 |
| 206 | Chipewán. | { Roman. } Syllabary. | North American, Cent. Prov. | B. F. B. S. | | 40 |
| 207 | Beaver. | Syllabary. | North American, Cent. Prov. | { B. F. B. S. } S. P. C. K. | | 26 |
| 208 | Cree: 1. E., or Hudson's Bay. 2. W., or Moosonee. | Roman. | North American, Cent. Prov. | B. F. B. S. B. F. B. S. | | 44 |
| 209 | Blackfoot. | Roman. | North American, Cent. Prov. | B. F. B. S. | | 29 |

| No. | Language, Dialect. | Written Character. | Family, Branch. | Source of Translation. | Diglott. | No. in Alphabetic List. |
|---|---|---|---|---|---|---|
| 210 | Ojibwa. | Syllabary. | North American, Cent. Prov. | A. B. S. S. P. C. K. B. F. B. S. | | 192 |
| 211 | Mik-Mak: 1. Standard. 2. Abenáqui. | Roman. | North American, Cent. Prov.; Montreal. | B. F. B. S. A. B. S. | | 163 |
| 212 | Maliséet. | Roman. | North American, Cent. Prov. | B. F. B. S. | | 147 |
| 213 | Iroquois. | Roman. | North American, Cent. Prov. | B. F. B. S. | | 99 |
| 214 | Mohawk. | Roman. | North American, Cent. Prov. | B. F. B. S. | | 164 |
| 215 | Delaware. | Roman. | North American, Cent. Prov. | A. B. S. | | 46 |
| 216 | Ney-Perces, or Sahaptin. | Roman. | North American, Cent. Prov. | A. B. S. | | 179 |
| 217 | Sioux, or Dakóta. | Roman. | North American, Cent. Prov. | A. B. S. | | 45 |
| 218 | Séneka. | Roman. | North American, Cent. Prov. | A. B. S. | | 217 |
| 219 | Choktau. | Roman. | North American, Cent. Prov. | A. B. S. | | 41 |
| 220 | Cheróki. | Syllabary. | North American, Cent. Prov. | A. B. S. | | 38 |
| 221 | Muskóki, or Creek. | Roman. | North American, Cent. Prov. | A. B. S. | | 173 |

CENTRAL.

| No. | Language, Dialect. | Written Character. | Family, Branch. | Source of Translation. | Diglott. | No. in Alphabetic List. |
|---|---|---|---|---|---|---|
| 222 | Maya. | Roman. | S. American. | B. F. B. S. | | 160 |
| 223 | Aztek. | Roman. | S. American. | B. F. B. S. | | 162 |
| 224 | Nahuatl. | Roman. | S. American. | A. B. S. | | 174 |
| 225 | Moskíto. | Roman. | S. American. | M. M. S. | | 169 |

SOUTH.

| No. | Language, Dialect. | Written Character. | Family, Branch. | Source of Translation. | Diglott. | No. in Alphabetic List. |
|---|---|---|---|---|---|---|
| 226 | Karíb. | Roman. | S. American. | Edinburgh. | | 112 |
| 227 | Akkawáy. | Roman. | S. American. | S. P. C. K. | | 4 |
| 228 | Arawák. | Roman. | S. American. | A. B. S. S. P. C. K. | | 15 |
| 229 | Quichúa. | Roman. | S. American. | B. F. B. S. | | 206 |
| 230 | Aimará. | Roman. | S. American. | B. F. B. S. | A.—Spanish. | 2 |
| 231 | Gúarani. | Roman. | S. American. | B. F. B. S. | G.—Spanish. | 82 |
| 232 | Yahgán. | Roman. | S. American. | B. F. B. S. | | 265 |

OCEANIA.
*POLYNESIA.*

| No. | Language, Dialect. | Written Character. | Family, Branch. | Source of Translation. | Diglott. | No. in Alphabetic List. |
|---|---|---|---|---|---|---|
| 233 | Tahiti Island. | Roman. | Polynesian. | B. F. B. S. | | 240 |
| 234 | Rarotonga Island. | Roman. | Polynesian. | B. F. B. S. | | 207 |
| 235 | Marquésas Islands. | Roman. | Polynesian. | A. B. S. | | 159 |
| 236 | Hawáii Island. | Roman. | Polynesian. | A. B. S. | | 88 |
| 237 | Sámoa Island. | Roman. | Polynesian. | B. F. B. S. | | 214 |
| 238 | Niue, or Savage Island. | Roman. | Polynesian. | B. F. B. S. | | 184 |

| No. | LANGUAGE DIALECT. | WRITTEN CHARACTER. | FAMILY, BRANCH. | SOURCE OF TRANSLATION. | DIGLOTT. | No. IN ALPHA-BETIC LIST. |
|---|---|---|---|---|---|---|
| 239 | TONGA, or FRIENDLY ISLANDS. | Roman. | Polynesian. | B. F. B. S. | | 249 |
| 240 | MAORI. | Roman. | Polynesian. | B. F. B. S. | | 156 |

*MELANESIA.*

| No. | LANGUAGE DIALECT. | WRITTEN CHARACTER. | FAMILY, BRANCH. | SOURCE OF TRANSLATION. | DIGLOTT. | No. IN ALPHA-BETIC LIST. |
|---|---|---|---|---|---|---|
| 241 | FIJI ISLANDS. | Roman. | Melanesian. | B. F. B. S. | . | [ 61 |
| 242 | RÓTUMA ISLAND. | Roman. | Melanesian. | B. F. B. S. | | 210 |
| 243 | MARE, or NENGÓNE ISLANDS. | Roman. | Melanesian. | B. F. B. S. | | 158 |
| 244 | LIFU ISLAND. | Roman. | Melanesian. | B. F. B. S. | | 135 |
| 245 | UVEA ISLAND. | Roman. | Melanesian. | B. F. B. S. | | 256 |
| 246 | ANEITYÚM ISLAND. | Roman. | Melanesian. | B. F. B. S. | | 10 |
| 247 | FÚTUNA ISLAND. | Roman. | Melanesian. | B. F. B. S. | | 69 |
| 248 | ANÍWA ISLAND. | Roman. | Melanesian. | B. F. B. S. | | 11 |
| 249 | TANNA ISLAND: 1. Kwaméra. 2. Weasísi. | Roman. | Melanesian. | B. F. B. S. | | 242 |
| 250 | EROMANGA ISLAND. | Roman. | Melanesian. | B. F. B. S. | | 54 |
| 251 | FATÉ ISLAND: 1. Erakar. 2. Havannah Harbor. | Roman. | Melanesian. | B. F. B. S. | | 60 |
| 252 | NGUNA ISLAND. | Roman. | Melanesian. | B. F. B. S. | | 180 |
| 253 | MALLICOLLO ISLAND. | Roman. | Melanesian. | | | 148 |
| 254 | API, or BAKI. | Roman. | Melanesian. | B. F. B. S. | | 13 |
| 255 | MOTA ISLAND. | Roman. | Melanesian. | S. P. C. K. | | 170 |
| 256 | FLORIDA. | Roman. | Melanesian. | S. P. C. K. | | 64 |
| 257 | ISABEL, or BOGÓTU. | Roman. | Melanesian. | S. P. C. K. | | 100 |
| 258 | MURRAY ISLANDS. | Roman. | Melanesian. | B. F. B. S. | | 172 |
| 259 | SAIBAI ISLAND. | Roman. | Melanesian. | B. F. B. S. | | 213 |
| 260 | NEW GUINEA, S. CAPE. | Roman. | Melanesian. | B. F. B. S. | | 178 |
| 261 | MOTU. | Roman. | Melanesian. | B. F. B. S. | | 171 |
| 262 | MÁFUR. | Roman. | Melanesian. | N. B. S. | | 140 |
| 263 | NEW BRITAIN ISLAND. | Roman. | Melanesian. | B. F. B. S. | | 177 |
| 264 | DUKE OF YORK'S ISLAND. | Roman. | Melanesian. | W. M. S. | | 48 |

*MIKRONESIA.*

| No. | LANGUAGE DIALECT. | WRITTEN CHARACTER. | FAMILY, BRANCH. | SOURCE OF TRANSLATION. | DIGLOTT. | No. IN ALPHA-BETIC LIST. |
|---|---|---|---|---|---|---|
| 265 | GILBERT ISLANDS. | Roman. | Mikronesian. | A. B. S. | | 76 |
| 266 | MORTLOCK ISLANDS. | Roman. | Mikronesian. | A. B. S. | | 168 |
| 267 | EBON ISLAND. | Roman. | Mikronesian. | A. B. S. | | 51 |
| 268 | KUSAIE. | Roman. | Mikronesian. | A. B. S. | | 127 |
| 269 | PONAPÉ ISLAND. | Roman. | Mikronesian. | A. B. S. | | 203 |

AUSTRALIA.

*(Nothing.)*

## III. ALPHABETICAL INDEX OF LANGUAGES AND DIALECTS INTO WHICH THE HOLY SCRIPTURES OR INTEGRAL PORTIONS THEREOF HAVE BEEN TRANSLATED.

# APPENDIX C.

## *FOREIGN MISSIONARY SOCIETIES.*

A number of efforts have been made to compile an accurate list of the various organizations for foreign mission work of the Protestant churches of England, Europe, and America. The most complete was that prepared by Rev. John Mitchell, B.D., a Presbyterian minister in Chester, England, and which was published in "The Christian" of December 14th, 1888. Another was made by Dr. R. N. Cust in connection with the Mildmay Conference, and various modifications of these have appeared at different times and in different places. The number of difficulties to be overcome is greater than one would perhaps imagine, the greatest being that of determining what shall be included. Many societies do foreign work in connection with or supplemental to their home work; there are also many organizations which only in their indirect results have any relation to foreign lands; again, within the past few years a large number of individual efforts have been inaugurated which certainly deserve mention; where to draw the line it is not easy to determine.

In the preparation of the following list, circulars were sent to every organization of which any trace could be gained which had even a remote connection with foreign missionary work. In almost every case, those directly connected with foreign work responded most cordially. Some others replied that they were not foreign societies, while others still gave no answer at all.

Acting upon the basis of these replies, together with whatever of additional information could be gained by indirect queries, the following list has been prepared. The headings of the different sections will substantially indicate its scope, and these will be found further described in the article "Organization of Missionary Work," vol. ii. pp. 195–201.

That the list is absolutely complete is not claimed; but it is believed that it includes all organizations of prominence and most, if not all, of those that give hope of permanence.

The arrangement adopted has conformed in general to that of Mr. Mitchell's list, such changes having been introduced as seemed to be required by the modifications in his plan.

The numbers on the left correspond to those used in Appendix D, list of mission stations, spaces having been allowed for the introduction of new societies. The dates are those of the organization of the societies. The addresses of secretaries of societies or representatives of individual missionaries have been corrected to date (February, 1891) as carefully as possible. The figures following the addresses indicate the volume and page of the Encyclopædia on which the account of the society is to be found.

## I.—*SOCIETIES ENGAGED DIRECTLY IN GENERAL FOREIGN MISSIONARY WORK.*

### AMERICA.

#### UNITED STATES.

No. Date. CONGREGATIONAL.
1. 1810. American Board of Commissioners for Foreign Missions. The Secretary, Congregational House, 1 Somerset Street, Boston, Mass. I. 66.

#### BAPTIST.

3. 1814. American Baptist Missionary Union. Secretary, Rev. J. N. Murdock, D.D., LL.D., Tremont Temple, Boston, Mass. I. 43.
4. 1836. Free Baptist Foreign Mission Society. Secretary, Rev. Th. H. Stacy, Auburn, Me. I. 378.
5. 1845. Southern Baptist Convention. Secretary, Rev. H. A. Tupper, D.D., Richmond, Va. II. 358.

6. 1847. Foreign Mission Society of Seventh-Day Baptists. Secretary, Rev. A. E. Main, D.D., Ashaway, R. I. II. 325.
7. 1881. Home and Foreign Mission Society of the German Baptist Brethren Church. Secretary, Rev. G. B. Royer, Mount Morris, Ill. I. 388.
8. 1884. Consolidated American Baptist Missionary Convention. Secretary, Rev. R. L. Perry, D.D., Ph.D., 999 St. Mark's Avenue, Brooklyn, New York. I. 321.
9. 1886. Board of Foreign Missions, Baptist General Association. Secretary, Rev. R. De Baptiste, D.D., 118 E. S. Street, Galesburg, Ill. I. 133.
10. 1886. Baptist Convention of the United States. Secretary, Rev. J. E. Jones, D.D., 520 St. James Street, Richmond, Va. I. 132.

#### METHODIST.

13. 1819. Missionary Society of the Methodist Episcopal Church (North). The Secretaries, 150 Fifth Avenue, New York, N. Y. II. 66.

14. 1844. Foreign Missionary Society of the African Methodist Episcopal Church. The Secretary, Room 61, Bible House, Astor Place, New York, N. Y. I. 32.

15. 1845. Board of Foreign Missions in the Methodist Episcopal Church (South). Secretary, Rev. I. G. John, D.D., Nashville, Tenn. II. 80.

16. 1880. Board of Foreign Missions of the Methodist Protestant Church. Secretary, Rev. F. T. Tagg, Easton, Md. II. 84.

17. 1880. Wesleyan Methodist Missionary Society of America. Secretary, Rev. A. W. Hall, Syracuse, N. Y. I. 85.

18. 1882. General Missionary Board of the Free Methodist Church. Secretary, Rev. W. W. Kelley, 104 Franklin Street, Chicago, Ill.

EPISCOPALIAN.

20. 1835. The Domestic and Foreign Missionary Society of the Protestant Episcopal Church in the United States of America. Secretary, Rev. William S. Langford, D.D., 21–26 Bible House, Astor Place, New York, N. Y. II. 259.

PRESBYTERIAN.

22. 1836. Reformed Presbyterian General Synod, Board of Missions. President, Rev. D. Steele, D.D., 2102 Spring Garden Street, Philadelphia, Pa. II. 273.

23. 1836. Reformed (German) Church in the United States, Board of Foreign Missions. Secretary, Rev. S. N. Callender, D.D., Mt. Crawford, Rockingham Co., Va. II. 271.

24. 1837. Board of Foreign Missions of the Presbyterian Church (North). The Secretaries, 53 Fifth Avenue, New York, N. Y. II. 243.

25. 1858. Board of Foreign Missions of the Reformed (Dutch) Church in America. Secretary, Rev. Henry N. Cobb, D.D., 26 Reade Street, New York, N. Y. II. 269.

26. 1858. Board of Foreign Missions of the United Presbyterian Church of North America. Secretary, Rev. J. B. Dales, D.D., 136 N. 18th Street, Philadelphia, Pa. II. 431.

27. 1859. Board of Missions of the Reformed Presbyterian (Covenanter) Church. Secretary, Rev. R. M. Sommerville, D.D., 126 W. 45th Street, New York, N. Y. II. 271.

28. 1862. Board of Foreign Missions of the Presbyterian Church (South) in the United States. Secretary, Rev. M. H. Houston, D.D., Nashville, Tenn. II. 254.

29. 1875. Associate Reformed Synod Southern Presbyterians. Secretary, Rev. W. L. Pressly, D.D., Due-West, S. C. I. 111.

30. 1876. Board of Missions of the Cumberland Presbyterian Church. Secretary, Rev. J. V. Stephens, 904 Olive Street, St. Louis, Mo. I. 328.

31. 1883. German Evangelical Synod of North America. Secretary, Rev. J. Huber, Attica, N. Y. I. 388.

LUTHERAN.

34. 1839. Board of Foreign Missions of the General Synod of the Evangelical Lutheran Church. Secretary, Rev. George Scholl, D.D., 1005 W. Lanvale Street, Baltimore, Md. I. 363.

35. 1869. Board of Missions of the General Council of the Evangelical Lutheran Church. English Secretary, Rev. William A. Schaeffer, 4784 Germantown Avenue, Philadelphia, Pa. I. 363.

OTHER DENOMINATIONS.

36. 1849. Foreign Christian Missionary Society (Disciples of Christ). Secretary, Rev. A. McLean, Box 750, Cincinnati, O. I. 376.

37. 1853. Home, Frontier and Foreign Missionary Society of the United Brethren in Christ. Secretary, Rev. B. F. Booth, D.D., Dayton, O. II. 427.

38. 1878. Missionary Society of the Evangelical Association. Secretary, Rev. S. Heininger, 265 Woodland Avenue, Cleveland, O. I. 363.

39. 1880. Mennonite Mission Board. Secretary, Rev. A. B. Shelly, Milford Square, Pa. II. 64.

40. 1880. Foreign Missionary Society of the Church of God. Secretary, Professor J. R. H. Latchaw, Findley, O. I. 279.

41. 1886. Foreign Missionary Society of the American Christian Convention. Secretary, Rev. J. P. Watson, Dayton, O. I. 83.

42. 1889. Board of Foreign Missions of the Seventh-Day Adventist Church. Secretary, W. C. White, 229 West Main Street, Battle Creek, Mich. II. 325.

43. 1890. Committee on Foreign Missions, Universalist Churches Secretary, Rev. G. L. Demarest, Manchester, N. Y. II. 447.

INTERDENOMINATIONAL.

47. 1849. American and Foreign Christian Union. President, Rev. Wm. M. Taylor, D.D., New York, N. Y. I. 43.

CANADA.

50. 1824. Missionary Society of the Methodist Church (Canada). Secretary, Rev. A. Sutherland, D.D., Methodist Mission Rooms, Toronto. II. 65.

51. 1844. Foreign Mission Committee (Western Division) of the Presbyterian Church in Canada. Secretary, Hamilton Cassels, Esq., 8 Manning Arcade, Toronto II. 233.

52. 1866. (a) The Foreign Mission Board of the Baptist Convention of Ontario and Quebec. Secretary, Rev. John McLaurin, Woodstock, Ontario.

(b) Foreign Mission Board of the Baptist Convention of Nova Scotia, New Brunswick and Prince Edward Island (Maritime Provinces Board). Secretary, Rev. G. O. Gates, St. John, N. B. I. 130.

53. 1881. The Canada Congregational Missionary Society. Secretary, Rev. John Wood, 88 Elgin Street, Ottawa. I. 230.

54. 1888. Foreign Missionary Society of the Church of England in Canada. Secretary. Rev. C. H. Mockridge, D.D., Windsor, Nova Scotia. I. 280.

### GREAT BRITAIN.

### ENGLAND.

#### INTERDENOMINATIONAL.

61. 1649. New England Company. Secretary, Mr. William M. Venning, 1 Furnival's Inn, Holborn, London, E. C. II. 167.

62. 1795. The London Missionary Society. Secretary, Rev. Edward H. Jones, Mission House, Blomfield Street, London Wall, London, E. C. I. 554.

63. 1856. Mildmay Mission. Secretary, Mr. James E. Mathieson, Conference Hall, Mildmay Park, London, N. II. 102.

64. 1858. Christian Vernacular Education Society for India. Secretary, Rev. James Johnston, F.S.S., 7 Adam Street, Strand, London, W. C. I. 278.

65. 1865. China Inland Mission. Secretary, Mr. B. Broomhall, 4 Pyrland Road, Mildmay, London, N. I. 271.

66. 1880. The Salvation Army. The Secretaries, International Headquarters, 101 Queen Victoria Street, London, E. C. II. 303.

67. 1881. North Africa Mission. Secretary, Mr. E. H. Glenny, 21 Linton Road, Barking, Essex. II. 179.

#### EPISCOPALIAN.

71. 1701. The Society for the Propagation of the Gospel in Foreign Parts. Secretary, Rev. H. W. Tucker, M.A., 19 Delahay Street, Westminster, London, S. W. II. 348.

72. 1799. Church Missionary Society for Africa and the East. The Secretaries, Church Missionary House, Salisbury Square, London, E. C. I. 280.

73. 1844. South American Missionary Society. Secretary, Captain E. Poulden, R. N., 1 Clifford's Inn, Fleet Street, London, E. C. II. 356.

74. 1860. Universities' Mission to Central Africa. Secretary, Rev. Duncan Travers, 14 Delahay Street, Westminster, London, S. W. II. 447.

75. 1886. The Archbishop's Mission to the Assyrian Christians. Secretary, Rev. R. M. Blakiston, M.A., F.R.G.S., 2 Dean's Yard, Westminster, London, S. W. I. 95.

#### BAPTIST.

77. 1792. Baptist Missionary Society. Secretary, Mr. Alfred H. Baynes, F.R.A.S., Mission House, 19 Furnival Street, Holborn, London, E. C. I. 133.

78. 1816. General Baptist Missionary Society. Secretary, Rev. William Hill, Mission House, 60 Wilson Street, Derby. I. 387.

79. 1861. Strict Baptist Mission. Secretary, Mr. Josiah Briscoe, 58 Grosvenor Road, Highbury New Park, London, N. II. 364.

#### METHODIST.

81. 1814. Wesleyan Methodist Mission Society. The Secretaries, Wesleyan Centenary-Hall and Mission-House, Bishopsgate Street Within, London, E. C. II. 456.

82. 1858. United Methodist Free Churches Foreign Mission. Secretary, Rev. G. Turner, 17 Wharncliffe-road, Sheffield. II. 428.

83. 1859. Methodist New Connexion Missionary Society. Secretary, Rev. W. J. Townsend, Richmond Hill, Ashton-under-Lyne. II. 83.

84. 1862. Central China Wesleyan Methodist Lay Mission. Secretary, Rev. W. F. Moulton, D.D., Cambridge. I. 239.

85. 1870. Primitive Methodist Missionary Society. Secretary, Rev. James Travis, 71 Freegrove Road, Holloway, London, N. II. 258.

86. 1885. Bible Christian Home and Foreign Mission Society. Secretary, Rev. I. B. Vanstone, 73 Herbert Road, Plumstead, Kent. I. 162.

#### PRESBYTERIAN.

89. 1841. Welsh Calvinistic Methodists' Foreign Missionary Society. Secretary, Rev. Josiah Thomas, M.A., 28 Breckfield Road South, Liverpool. II. 454.

90. 1847. Foreign Missions of the Presbyterian Church of England. Secretary, Mr. John Bell, 13 Fenchurch Avenue, London, E. C. II. 237.

#### FRIENDS.

93. 1867. Friends' Foreign Mission Association. Secretary, Mr. Charles Linney, Hitchin. I. 381.

94. 1869. Friends' Syrian Mission. Hon. Secretary, R. Hingston Fox, M.D., 23 Finsbury Square, London, E. C. I. 382.

### SCOTLAND.

#### PRESBYTERIAN.

101. 1829. Church of Scotland (Established) Committee for the Propagation of the Gospel in Foreign Parts. Secretary, Mr. J. T. Maclagan, 6 N. St. David Street, Edinburgh. II. 239.

102. 1842. Scottish Reformed Presbyterian Synod, Syrian Missions (also Irish Synod). Secretary, Rev. Rob-

ert Dunlop, Blackhall, Paisley, N. B. II. 273.

103. 1843. Foreign Mission Committee of the Free Church of Scotland. Secretary, Dr. George Smith, C.I.E., 15 N. Bank Street, Edinburgh. II. 239.

104. 1847. United Presbyterian Church of Scotland Foreign Mission. Secretary, Rev. James Buchanan, College Buildings, Castle Terrace, Edinburgh. II. 429.

105. 1871. United Original Secession Church of Scotland, South India Mission (also Irish Synod). Secretary, Rev. W. B. Gardiner, Shawlands, Glasgow. II. 429.

### EPISCOPAL.

108. 1872. Scottish Episcopal Church, Central Board of Foreign Missions. Secretary, Rev. C. R. Teape, D.D., Findhorn Place, Grange, Edinburgh. II. 315.

### IRELAND.

109. 1840. Presbyterian Church of Ireland Foreign Mission. Secretary, Rev. George MacFarland, 12 May Street, Belfast, Ireland. II. 237.

*Note.*—Several Irish churches act in connection with the corresponding churches in Scotland.

### CONTINENTAL EUROPE.

### DENMARK.

115. 1721. Danish Mission Society (Det Danske Missionsselskab). Secretary, Rev. Provost I. Vahl, North Olslu. I. 332.

116. 1869. Indian Home Mission to the Santals. Treasurer, Rev. V. Jacobson, Copenhagen. I. 334.

117. 1872. Loventhal's Mission. President, Rev. A. S. Lund. Vium. I. 333.

118. 1884. The Red Karen's Mission. Secretary, L. Schreuder, Askof. I. 334.

### NORWAY.

121. 1842. Norwegian Mission Society (Det Norske Missionsselskab). Secretary, Rev. L. Dahl, Stavanger. II. 184.

122. 1873. The Schreuder Mission (Den norske Kirkes, Mission ved Schreuder). Secretary, Dr. G. Kent, Christiania. II. 185.

123. 1888. Norwegian Mission among the Finns (Finnemissionen). Secretary, Rev. L. Dahl, Stavanger. II. 183.

### SWEDEN.

126. 1835. Swedish Missionary Society (Svenska Missionssäls-kapet). Secretary, Rev. Prof. H. W. Tottie, Stockholm. II. 371.

127. 1856. Evangelical National Society (Den evangeliska Fosterlandsstiftelse). Secretary, Rev. H. B. Hammar, Stockholm. II. 371.

128. 1861. Jönköping Society for Home and Foreign Missions (revived 1887) (Jönköping Förening forinne ock ytre Mission). Secretary, J. Peterson, Jönköping. II. 373.

129. 1865. Orebro Province Ansgarius Union (Orebro Läus Ansgariiförening). Secretary, Rev. H. B. Hammar, Stockholm.

130. 1874. Swedish Church Mission (Svenska Kyrkans Mission). Secretary, Rev. Prof. H. W. Tottie, Stockholm. II. 372.

131. 1878. Swedish Missionary Union (Svenska Missionsförbundet). President, Mr. E. J. Ekman, Kristineham. II. 372.

132. 1880. Laplander's Mission's Friends (Lapska Missionen's Vänner). Secretary, A. U. Holmgren, Stockholm. II. 373.

133. 1885. Congo Children's Friends (in Göteborg) (Kongobarnen's Vänner). Secretary, F. A. Petersen, Göteborg.

134. 1886. Oster Götland's Ansgarius Union (Oster Götland Ansgariiförening). Secretary, E. J. Lindblom, Jönköping. II. 373.

135. 1887. Swedish Mission in China (Eric Falke Mission) (Svenska Missionen, Kina). Secretary, Josef Holmgren, Stockholm. II. 373.

### FINLAND.

138. 1859. Finland Mission Society. Director, Pastor C. G. Töttermann, Helsingfors. I. 371.

### GERMANY.

141. 1732. Foreign Missions of the Church of the United Brethren (Moravians). Secretary, Rev. B. La Trobe, 29 Ely Place. London, E. C., England. II. 129.

### LUTHERAN.

142. 1815. Basle Evangelical Mission Society. Secretary, Herr Th. Öhler, Basle, Switzerland. I. 137.

143. 1819. Leipsic Evangelical Lutheran Missionary Society. Secretary, D. J. Hardeland, Leipsic. I. 543.

144. 1824. Berlin Evangelical Missionary Society. Secretary, Rev. Dr. Wangeman, Berlin. I. 154.

145. 1829. Rhenish Missionary Society. Secretaries, Rev. Drs. Fabric and Schreiber. Barmen. II. 280.

146. 1836. Gossner's Missionary Society. Secretary, Rev. Paul Gerhard, 31 Potsdamer Strasse, Berlin. I. 392.

147. 1836. North German Missionary Society. Secretary, Rev. F. M. Zahn, 26 Ellhorn Street, Bremen. II. 179.

148. 1840. St. Chrischona Pilgrim Missionary Society (Switzerland). Secretary, Rev. C. F. Spittler, Basle, Switzerland.

149. 1849. Hermannsburg Evangelical Lutheran Mission. Secretary, Rev. Egmont Harms, Hermannsburg. I. 413.

150. 1882. Breklum Missionary Society. Secretary, A. Fiensch, Breklum, Schleswick. I. 191.

## HOLLAND.

155. 1797. Netherlands Mission Society, Evangelical Church. Secretary, Rev. J. C. Neurdenburg, Rotterdam. II. 166.

156. 1846. Ermelo Missionary Society. Secretary, Fr. Fries, Ermelo. I. 358.

157. 1849. Mennonite Missionary Society. Secretary, Rev. T. Kniper, Amsterdam. II. 63.

158. 1856. Java Comité. Secretary, J. C. Groeuewegen, Amsterdam. I. 503.

159. 1858. Dutch Missionary Society. Secretary, Rev. B. F. Gerretson, Rotterdam. I. 344.

160. 1859. Utrecht Missionary Society, Evangelical. Secretary, Rev. Mr. Looyen, Utrecht. II. 448.

161. 1859. Dutch Reformed Missionary Society. Secretary, Rev. F. Lion Cachet, Rotterdam. I. 344.

162. 1860. Christian Reformed Missionary Society. Secretary, Rev. Mr. Donner, Leyden. I. 278.

## FRANCE.

165. 1822. Paris Society for Evangelical Missions among non-Christian Nations. French Protestant. (Société des Missions Evangeliques.) Secretary, M. E. De Pressensé, Rue Val-de-Grace; Director, M. A. Begner, Maison des Missions, 102 Boulevard Arago, Paris. II. 207.

166. 1874. Foreign Mission Board of the Free Churches of French Switzerland (Missions des Eglises libres de la Suisse Romande). French Protestant. Secretary, Rev. Paul Leresche, Lausanne, Switzerland. I. 379

## SANDWICH ISLANDS.

169. 1853. Hawaiian Evangelical Association. Secretary, Rev. O. P. Emerson, Honolulu. I. 412.

## NEW ZEALAND.

170. 1850. Melanesian Mission. Secretary of the English Committee, Rev. William Selwyn, Bromfield Vicarage, R.S.O., Shropshire, England, or Rt. Rev. John R. Selwyn, D.D., Auckland, New Zealand. II. 58.

## II.—WOMAN'S MISSIONARY SOCIETIES.

### 1. Engaged Directly in Missionary Work.

### UNITED STATES.

180. 1861. Union Missionary Society. Undenominational. Secretary, Miss S. D. Doremus, 41 Bible House, Astor Place, New York, N. Y. II. 489.

181. 1881. Woman's Foreign Missionary Union of Friends. Secretary, Eliza C. Armstrong, Center Valley, Ind. II. 490.

### CANADA.

183. 1871. Canadian Woman's Board of Foreign Missions. Secretary, Miss Mary E. Baylis, 55 McGill College Avenue, Montreal. II. 491.

## ENGLAND.

185. 1825. Ladies' Society for Promoting Education in the West Indies. Episcopalian. Secretary, Miss A. M. Barney, 16 Lupus Street, St. George's Square, London, S. W.

186. 1834. Society for Promoting Female Education in the East. Undenominational. Secretary, Miss Webb, 267 Vauxhall Bridge Road, London, S. W. II. 491.

187. 1852. Indian Female Normal School and Instruction Society, or Zenana Bible and Medical Mission. Undenominational. Secretary, Mrs. Gilmore, 8 York Terrace, Regent's Park, London, N. W. II. 491.

188. 1860. British Syrian Schools and Bible Mission. Undenominational. Secretary, Miss A. Poulton, 18 Homefield Road, Wimbledon, S. W. II. 492.

189. 1866. The Net Collections. Episcopalian. Secretary, Miss E. Wigram, 22 Upper Montagu Street, Montagu Square, London, W. II. 493.

190. 1881. Church of England Women's Mission Association. Secretary, Miss M. A. Lloyd, 143 Clapham Road, London, S. W.

191. 1883. Helping Hands' Association. Secretary, Miss Beynon, 423 Fulham Road, London, S. W. II. 493.

## SCOTLAND.

197. 1863. Tabitha Mission at Jaffa. Undenominational. Secretary, Miss E. Walker-Arnott, 24 St. Bernard's Crescent, Edinburgh. II. 493.

### 2. Those working through Other General Societies.

## UNITED STATES.

201. 1868. Woman's Board of Missions, in connection with A. B. C. F. M. Secretary, Miss A. B. Child, No. 1 Congregational House, 1 Somerset Street, Boston, Mass. II. 493.

### Associate Boards.

a. Of the Interior. Secretary, Miss M. D. Wingate, 59 Dearborn Street, Chicago, Ill.

b. Of the Pacific. Secretary, Mrs. J. H. Warren, 1316 Mason Street, San Francisco, Cal.

c. Of the Pacific Islands. Secretary, Mrs. George P. Castle, Honolulu, S. I.

### Methodist.

203. 1869. Woman's Foreign Mission Society, Methodist Episcopal Church (North). Secretary, Mrs. J. T. Gracey, 161 Pearl Street, Rochester, N. Y. II. 497.

204. 1878. Woman's Board of Missions, Methodist Episcopal Church (South). Secretary, Mrs. D. H. McGavock, Nashville, Tenn. II. 499.

205. 1879. Woman's Foreign Missionary Society, Methodist Protestant Church. Secretary, Mrs. M. A. Miller, Box 1,065, Pittsburg, Pa. II. 500.

206. 1874. Mite Society, African Methodist Episcopal Church. Secretary, Mrs. L. J. Coppin, 631 Pine Street, Philadelphia, Pa. II. 500.

### PRESBYTERIAN.

210. 1870. Woman's Foreign Mission Society of the Presbyterian Church (North). Secretary, Mrs. H. R. Massey, 1334 Chestnut Street, Philadelphia, Pa. II. 500.

### ASSOCIATE BOARDS.

*a.* Woman's Board of Foreign Missions of the Presbyterian Church. Secretary, Miss H. W. Hubbard, 53 Fifth Avenue, New York, N. Y.

*b.* Woman's Presbyterian Board of Missions of the Northwest. Secretary, Mrs. George H. Laflin, 48 McCormick Block, Chicago, Ill.

*c.* Woman's Foreign Mission Society of Northern New York. Secretary, Mrs. Archibald McClure, 232 State Street, Albany, N. Y.

*d.* Woman's Board of Missions of the Southwest. Secretary, Miss Agnes H. Fenby, 1107 Olive Street, St. Louis, Mo.

*e.* Occidental Board of Foreign Missions of the Presbyterian Church. Secretary, Mrs. J. G. Chown, 933 Sacramento Street, San Francisco, Cal.

*f.* Woman's North Pacific Presbyterian Board of Missions. Secretary, Mrs. A. W. Stowell, 275 Clay Street, Portland, Ore.

211. 1875. Woman's Board of Foreign Missions of the Reformed (Dutch) Church. Secretary, Mrs. A. L. Cushing, 933 Park Avenue, New York, N. Y. II. 504

212. 1879. Woman's Board of Missions, Cumberland Presbyterian Church. Secretary, Mrs. J. C. McClurkin, Evansville, Ind. II. 505.

213. 1884. Woman's Foreign Missionary Society, United Presbyterian Church. Secretary, Mrs. J. C. Doty, Bellevue, Pa. II. 505.

N.B.—There is no organized Woman's Board connected with either the Presbyterian Church (South) or the Reformed Presbyterian (Covenanter) Church. The ladies work directly in connection with the General Boards.

### BAPTIST.

221. 1870. Woman's Baptist Foreign Mission Society (Northern Convention). Secretary, Mrs. O. W. Gates, Tremont Temple, Boston, Mass. II. 507.

### ASSOCIATE BOARDS.

*a.* Woman's Baptist Foreign Mission Society of the West. Secretary, Mrs. A. M. Bacon, 3032 South Park Avenue, Chicago, Ill.

*b.* Woman's Baptist Foreign Mission Society of California. Secretary, Mrs. L. P. Huntsman, 2221 California Street, San Francisco, Cal.

*c.* Woman's Foreign Mission Society of Oregon. Secretary, Mrs. E. S. Latourette, Oregon City, Ore.

222. 1873. Free Baptist Woman's Mission Society. Secretary, Mrs J. A. Lowell, Danville, N. H. II. 509.

223. 1884. Woman's Missionary Union Auxiliary to the Baptist Southern Convention. Secretary, Miss Annie W. Armstrong, 10 East Fayette Street, Baltimore, Md. II. 510.

224. 1884. Woman's Executive Board of the Seventh-Day Baptist General Conference. Secretary, Miss Mary F. Bailey, Milton, Wis. II. 510.

### OTHER DENOMINATIONS.

231. 1872. Woman's Auxiliary Board of Missions, Protestant Episcopal Church. Secretary, Miss Julia C. Emery, 21 Bible House, Astor Place, New York, N. Y. II. 510.

233. 1875. Woman's Foreign Mission Association, United Brethren. Secretary, Mrs L. R. Keister, Dayton, O. II. 511.

234. 1875. Christian Woman's Board of Missions (Disciples of Christ). Secretary, Miss Lois A. White, 160 N. Delaware Street, Indianapolis, Ind. II. 512.

235. 1879. The Woman's Home and Foreign Missionary Society of the General Synod, Lutheran Church. Secretary, Miss Mary Hay Morris, 406 N. Greene Street, Baltimore, Md. II. 512.

236. 1884. Woman's Mission Society, Evangelical Association. Secretary, Eliza C. Armstrong, Centre Valley, Ind. II. 513.

### CANADA.

251. 1870. *a.* Woman's Baptist Missionary Union of the Maritime Provinces of Canada. Secretary, Mrs. John March, St. John, N. B. II. 514.

1876. *b.* Woman's Foreign Mission Society, E. Ontario and Quebec. Secretary, Miss Nannie E. Green, 478 St. Urbain Street, Montreal.

*c.* Woman's Foreign Mission Society of Ontario. Secretary, Miss J. Buchan, 125 Bloor Street, E. Toronto.

252. 1876. *a.* Woman's Foreign Mission Society, Presbyterian Church of Canada, Western Division. Secretary, II. 513.

Mrs. A F. Robinson, Toronto.

*b.* Woman's Foreign Mission Society, Presbyterian Church of Canada, Eastern Division. Secretary, Mrs. Burns, Kent Street, Halifax, Nova Scotia.

*c.* Montreal Woman's Mission Society of the Presbyterian Church in Canada. Secretary, Miss Sarah J. McMaster, 2672 St. Catherine Street, Montreal.

253. 1881. Woman's Mission Society, Methodist Church in Canada. Secretary, Mrs. E. S. Strachan, 113 Hughson Street, Hamilton, Ont. II. 515.

254. 1886. Canadian Congregational Woman's Board of Missions. Secretary, Miss H. Wood, Ottawa, Ont. II. 515.

255. 1886. Woman's Auxiliary to Board of Missions of the Church of England in Canada. Secretary, Mrs. Roberta E Tilton, Ottawa. II. 515.

### ENGLAND.

260. 1848. Coral Missionary Magazine and Fund of the C. M. S. Publishers, Wells, Gardner & Co., London. II. 516.

261. 1859. Ladies' Auxiliary of the Wesleyan Methodist Mission Society. Secretary, Mrs. Mary W. Farrar, Wesleyan Mission House, Bishopsgate Street Within, London, E. C. II. 516.

262. 1865. Ladies' Association in connection with S. P. G. Secretary, Miss Louisa Bullock, 19 Delahay Street, Westminster, London, N. W. II. 517.

263. 1867. Ladies' Association for the Support of Zenana Work and Bible Women in India, in connection with Baptist Mission Society. Secretary, Mrs. Angus, The College, Regent's Park, London, N. W. II. 517.

264. 1875. Ladies' Committee of the London Missionary Society. Secretary, Miss Bennett, 14 Blomfield Street, London, E. C. II. 518.

265. 1877. Christian Work in France, under the care of Friends. Secretary, Mary S. Pace, 5 Warwick Road, Upper Clapton, London, N. II. 519.

266. 1879. Women's Missionary Association of the Presbyterian Church of England. Secretary, Mrs. Carruthers, 44 Central Hill, London, S. E. II. 519.

267. 1880. Church of England Zenana Missionary Society in co-operation with C. M. S. Secretary, Miss Mulvaney, 6 Park Villas, Charlton Road, Blackheath, London, S. E. II. 519.

### SCOTLAND.

275. 1838. Church of Scotland (Established) Ladies' Association for Foreign Missions. Secretary, Miss H. C. Reid, 22 Queen Street, Edinburgh. II. 520.

276. 1843. Ladies' Society of the Free Church of Scotland for Female Education in India and South Africa. Secretary, Rev. William Stevenson, M.A., Free Church Offices, Edinburgh. II. 521.

277. 1875. The Central Committee and Church Woman's Association for Foreign Missions of the Scottish Episcopal Church. Secretary, Miss E. M. Hope, 122 George Street, Edinburgh. II. 522.

278. 1880. United Presbyterian Church of Scotland Zenana Mission. Secretary, Mr. John Cochran, College Building, Castle Terrace, Edinburgh. II. 522.

### IRELAND.

283. 1874. Presbyterian Church of Ireland, Female Association for Promoting Christianity among the Women of the East. Secretary, Mrs. Park, Fort William Park, Belfast. II. 522.

### CONTINENTAL EUROPE.

285. Berlin Woman's Association. II. 522.

286. Berlin Woman's Mission for China. II. 522.

295. 1850. Ladies' Committee at Stockholm for Furtherance of the Gospel among the Women of China. Lutheran. II. 522.

296. Stockholm Woman's Missions to North Africa. II. 373.

### III.—SPECIAL SOCIETIES.

### I.—AID.

*(Not sending out special missionaries, but giving aid to other societies.)*

### ENGLAND AND SCOTLAND.

301. 1691. Christian Faith Society. Episcopalian. Secretary, Rev. H. Bailey, D.D., West Tarring Rectory, Worthing, Sussex. I. 278.

302. 1818. London Association in Aid of the Moravian Missions. Undenominational. Secretary; Rev. B. La Trobe, 29 Ely Place, London, E. C. I. 554.

303. 1839. Foreign Aid Society. Undenominational. Secretary, Rev. H. Joy Browne, M.A., Barnet, Herts.

304. 1848. Young Men's Association in Aid of Baptist Missionary Society. Secretary, Mr. C. Holliday, Mission House, 19 Furnival Street, Holborn, London, E. C.

305. 1855. China Mission in connection with Presbyterian Church of England. Secretary, Mr. R. R. Simpson, 22 Hill Street, Edinburgh, Scotland.

306. 1855. Turkish Missions Aid Society. Undenominational. Secretary, Rev. T. W. Brown, D.D., 32 The Avenue, Bedford Park, Chiswick, London. II. 424.

307. 1866. Indian Home Mission to the Santals, Undenominational. Secretary, Archibald Graham, M.D., 1 Chamberlain Road, Edinburgh, Scotland. I. 334.

308. 1868. Missionary Leaves Association, Auxiliary to C. M. S. Secretary, Mr. H. G. Malaher, 20 Compton Terrace, Upper Street, Islington, London. N. II. 110.

309. 1869. Spanish, Portuguese, and Mexican Church Aid Society. Episcopalian. Secretary, Rev. L. S. Tugwell, 8 Adam Street, Adelphi, London, W. C. II. 361.

310. 1874. Association for the Free Distribution of the Scriptures. Secretary, Mrs. A. E. Robertson, Chesils, Christ Church Road, Hampstead, London, N. W. I. 111.

311. 1883. Central Agency for Foreign Missions, Special Funds. Episcopalian. Secretary, Mr. G. Haynes, 54 Gresham Street, London, E. C. I. 239.

*b.—BIBLE AND PUBLICATION SOCIETIES.*

*(Engaged directly in foreign work by employing colporteurs and distributing agents.)*

### UNITED STATES.

321. 1816. American Bible Society. Undenominational. The Secretaries, Bible House, Astor Place, New York, N. Y. I. 61.

322. 1826. American Tract Society. Undenominational, The Secretary, 150 Nassau Street, New York, N. Y. I. 83.

323. 1824. Baptist Publication Society. The Secretary, the Times Building, New York, N. Y. I. 59.

### ENGLAND.

325. 1698. Society for Promoting Christian Knowledge. Episcopalian. Secretary, Rev. W. H. Grove, M.A., Northumberland Avenue, Charing Cross, London, S. W. II. 347.

326. 1799. Religious Tract Society. Undenominational. The Secretaries, 56 Paternoster Row, London, E. C. II. 278.

327. 1804. British and Foreign Bible Society. Undenominational. The Secretaries, Bible House, 146 Queen Victoria Street, London, E. C. I. 194.

328. 1830. Trinitarian Bible Society. Undenominational. Secretary, Rev. E. W. Bullinger, D.D., 7 St. Paul's Churchyard, London, E. C. II. 409.

329. 1840. Bible Translation Society. Baptist. Secretary, Rev. Philip G. Scorey, East Dulwich, London.

330. 1841. Baptist Tract and Book Society. Secretary, Rev. George Simmons, Malden Villa, Granville Road, Sidcup, Kent.

331. 1854. Pure Literature Society. Undenominational. Secretary, Mr. Richard Turner, 11 Buckingham Street, Adelphi, London, W. C. II. 263.

332. 1880. Church of England Book Society. Secretary, Mr. John Shrimpton, 11 Adam Street, Strand, London, W. C. I. 279.

### SCOTLAND.

335. 1709. Society in Scotland for Promoting Christian Knowledge. Presbyterian. Secretary, Mr. C. Nisbet, 23 York Place, Edinburgh.

336. 1793. Religious Tract and Book Society of Scotland. Undenominational. Secretary, Rev. George Douglas, 99 George Street, Edinburgh.

337. 1860. National Bible Society of Scotland. Undenominational. Secretary.

Rev. W. H. Goold, D.D., 224 W. George Street, Glasgow. II. 159.

338. 1884. Book and Tract Society of China. Undenominational. Secretary, Mr. A. Cuthbert, 14 Newton Terrace, Glasgow. I. 177.

### C.—MISSIONS TO SEAMEN.

*(Not including many local organizations.)*

### UNITED STATES.

351. 1828. American Seamen's Friend Society. Secretary, Rev. W. C. Stitt, D.D., 76 Wall Street, New York, N. Y. II. 319.

### ENGLAND.

355. 1803. British and Foreign Sailors' Society. Secretary, Rev. Edward W. Matthews, Sailors' Institute, Shadwell, London, E. II. 317.

356. 1821. The Missions to Seamen. Commander W. Dawson, R.N., 11 Buckingham Street, Strand, London, W.C. II. 318.

### CONTINENTAL EUROPE.

361. 1864. Society for the Preaching of the Gospel among Scandinavian Sailors in Foreign Ports. (Foreningen til Evangeliets Forkyndelse for Skandinaviske Sömænd i fremmede Havne.) Secretary, Candidatus Theologiæ Niels Aars, Nicolaüsen, Bergen, Norway. II. 318.

362. Danish Society for the Preaching of the Gospel among Scandinavian Sailors in Foreign Ports. (Danske Forening til Evangeliets Forkyndelse for Skandinaviske Söfolk i fremmede Havne.) Secretary, Pastor D. C. Prior, R.A.D., Copenhagen, Denmark. II. 318.

363. 1869. Swedish National Society. (Fosterlands-stiftelsen.) Secretary, Pastor H. B. Hammar, Stockholm, Sweden. II. 318.

364. 1880. Society for Preaching the Gospel among Finnish Sailors in Foreign Ports. (Förenningen for Beredande of Sjaleward at Finska Sjörman i Utlandska Hamnar.) Secretary, Pastor Elis Bergooth, Helsingfors, Finland. II. 318.

### D.—MEDICAL MISSIONS.

### UNITED STATES.

371. 1879. Philadelphia Medical Missions. Superintendent, Dr. A. B. Kirkpatrick, 519 South Sixth Street, Philadelphia, Pa. II. 226.

372. 1881. International Medical Missionary Society. Secretary, William S. Stuart, 131 West Seventieth Street, New York, N. Y. I. 476.

373. 1885. American Medical Missionary Society. Secretary, Dr. H. M. Scudder, Chicago, Ill. II. 57.

## ENGLAND AND SCOTLAND.

391. 1840. Edinburgh Medical Missionary Society. Secretary, Rev. John Lowe, F.R.C.S.E., 56 George Square, Edinburgh. I. 351.

392. 1874. Children's Medical Mission. Undenominational. Secretary, Miss Annie R. Butler, 104 Pentherton Road, London, N. I. 246.

393. 1877. Jaffa Medical Mission. Secretary, Miss Cooke, 68 Mildmay Park, London, N. I. 480.

394. 1878. Medical Missionary Association. Undenominational. Secretary, Dr. James L. Maxwell, M.A., 104 Pentherton Road, London, N.

395. 1881. Medical Mission among Armenians. Secretary, Mrs. W. C. Braithwaite, 312 Camden Road, London, N.

396. 1887. Tonjoroff Cottage Hospital and Mission at Philippopolis, Bulgaria. Secretary, Mr. M. Braithwaite, 312 Camden Road, London, N.

### E.—SUNDAY-SCHOOL SOCIETIES.

411. 1803. Sunday-School Union's Continental Mission. Secretary, 55 and 56 Old Bailey, London, E. C., England. II. 369.

412. 1824. The American Sunday-School Union. Secretary of Missions, Rev. James M. Crowell, D.D., Philadelphia, Pa., U.S.A. II. 367.

413. 1856. The Foreign Sunday-School Association. President, Albert Woodruff, 130 State Street, Brooklyn, N. Y., U. S. A. II. 368.

### F.—INDIVIDUAL AND MISCELLANEOUS.

#### UNITED STATES.

421. 1874. Ellichpur Faith Mission. Secretary, Rev. J. W. Sibley, Ellichpur, Berar, C. P. India. II. 453.

422. 1877. Telugu Mission (Rev. C. B. Ward). Secretary, Rev. C. B. Ward, Secunderabad, India. II. 391.

423. 1884. Akola Mission, India. Secretary, Rev. M. B. Fuller, Akola, Berar, C. P. India. I. 34.

424. 1885. Inhambane Mission. Secretary, Rev. H. Agnew, Inhambane, South Africa.

425. 1885. Bassa Mission. Africa. Secretary, Rev. William Allan Fair, Bassa, West Africa. I. 142.

426. 1885. Pentecost Bands of the Free Methodist Churches of the United States. Secretary, Rev. Vivian A. Dake, 104 Franklin Street, Chicago, Ill. II. 214.

#### ENGLAND.

441. 1792. Sierra Leone Mission Society for the Spread of the Gospel at Home and Abroad (in connection with C. M. S.). Secretary, Rev. Thomas Dodd, Worcester. I. 283.

442. 1834. German Baptist Mission. Secretary, Rev. F. Horace Newton, 11 Bismarck Road, Highgate Hill, London.

443. 1862. Bible Stand, Crystal Palace. Undenominational. Secretary, Mr. W. Hawke, Bible Stand, Crystal Palace, Sydenham, London, S. E. I. 167.

444. 1866. Children's Special Service Mission. Undenominational. Secretary, Rev. Henry Hankinson, 13 Warwick Lane, Paternoster Row, London, E. C. I. 246.

445. 1866. Spezia Mission for Italy and the Levant. Secretary, Mr. Eliot Howard, J. P., Walthamstow, Essex. II. 362.

446. 1871. Evangelical Mission, known as Mr. Pascoe's Work in Mexico. Representative in England, Mr. John Mercer, 29 Queen's Road, Southport. II. 210.

447. 1871. Evangelistic Mission to France, known as McAll Mission to France. Undenominational. Secretary, Mr. Robert McAll, 17 Tressillian Crescent, St. Johns, London, S. E. II. 42.

448. 1871. Belleville Mission, Paris. Secretary, Miss de Broën, 3 Rue Clavel, Belleville, Paris. I. 146.

449. 1871. Mission to Italian Soldiers. Secretary, Miss Annie M. Stoddard, 36 Dennington Park, West Hampstead, London, N. W. I. 365.

450. 1872. East London Institute for Home and Foreign Missions. Secretary, Dr. H. Grattan Guinness, Harley House, Bow, London, E. I. 346.

451. 1873. Foreign Evangelization Society. Undenominational. Secretary, Hon. Rev. Horace Noel, Woking-Surrey. I. 376.

452. 1874. The Cowley Brotherhood, associate with the S. P. G. Secretary, Rev. Father Superior Cowley, St. John, Oxford.

453. 1875. Bethel Santhal Mission. Secretary, Miss M. C. Gurney, Granville Road, Eastbourne. I. 161.

454. 1875. Highway and Hedges Mission, Cuddalore, India. Secretary, Miss C. M. S. Lowe, 12 Dafforne Road, Upper Tooting, London, S. W. I. 417.

455. 1876. Birmingham Young Men's Foreign Missionary Society. Secretary, Mr. W. H. Silk, Needless Alley, New Street, Birmingham. II. 533.

456. 1876. Pastor Lopez Rodriguez Mission in Figueras, Northeastern Spain. Secretary, Rev. J. C. S. Matthias, Adringham Vicarage, Saxmundham, Sussex. I. 369.

457. 1876. The Kolar Mission, Mysore, India. Secretary, Miss Helen James, Fair View, Seven Oaks, Kent. I. 529.

458. 1879. Oxford Mission to Calcutta, associate with S. P. G. Secretary, Rev. J. O. Johnstone, Principal of St. Stephen's House, Oxford. II. 204.

459. 1879. Mission to Kafirs. Rock Fountain, Natal. Secretary, Mrs. E. Fothergil, Pierremont Crescent, Darlington. II. 286.

460. 1882. The Church Army, India, associate

with S. P. G. Secretary, Rev. W. Carlile, 128 Edgware Road, London, W.

461. 1883. Methodist Mission to Palestine. Secretary, Rev. G. Piercy, 276 Burdett Road, London, E. II. 111.

462. 1885. Breton Evangelical Mission. Undenominational. Secretary, Mr. J. Wates, 4 Princess Road, Lewisham, Kent. I. 192.

463. 1885. Normandy Protestant Evangelical Mission. Secretary, Rev. Randolph E. Healey, B.A., Lower Crumpsall Rectory, Manchester.

464. 1887. Joyful News Foreign Mission. Secretary, Rev. Thomas Champness, "Joyful News" Home, Rochdale.

465. 1887. Gopalgunge Evangelical Mission, India. Secretary, Rev. N. M. Bose, Gopalgunge, India.

### SCOTLAND.

471. 1854. Spanish Evangelization Society. Secretary, Mrs. Maria D. Peddie, 8 Granville Terrace, Edinburgh. II. 361.

472. 1868. Association for the Support of Miss Taylor's Moslem Girls' School, Beirut. Undenominational. Secretary, Mr. William Ferguson, Kinmundy House, Mintlaw, Aberdeenshire. I. 111.

473. 1872. Lebanon Schools for Children of Mohammedans, Druses, Maronites, and Greeks. Secretary, Andrew Scott, Esq., C.A., 2 York Buildings, Edinburgh. I. 542.

474. 1874. Mission to the Lepers in India. Undenominational. Secretary, Mr. Wellesley C. Bailey, 17 Glengyle Terrace, Edinburgh. I. 545.

475. 1877. Evangelical Mission to Upper Zambesi. Undenominational. Secretary, Mr. Richard H. Hunter, 27 Jamaica Street, Glasgow. I. 365.

476. 1880. Soul Winning and Prayer Union. Secretary, Mr. J. C. Smith, Newport-on-Tay, N. B. II. 356.

477. 1881. F. S. Arnot Mission to Central Africa. Representative in England, Mr. John Mercer, 29 Queen's Road, Southport, England. I. 107.

478. 1887. Mission to the Chinese Blind. Undenominational. Secretary, Mr. William J. Slowan, 224 West George Street, Glasgow. I. 275.

## IV.—MISSIONS TO THE JEWS.

### GENERAL ARTICLE. I. 595–515.

### ENGLAND.

500. 1809. London Society for Promoting Christianity among the Jews. Secretary, Rev. W. Fleming, LL.B., 16 Lincoln's-Inn-Fields, London, W. C.

501. 1842. British Society for Propagation of the Gospel among the Jews. Secretary, Rev. John Dunlop, 96 Great Russell Street, Bloomsbury, London, W. C.

502. 1856. Mildmay Mission to the Jews. Secretary, Rev. J. Wilkinson, 79 Mildmay Road, London, N.

503. 1856. Mission to Jews in Paris. Secretary, Mr. Alexander Donaldson, 6 Rue Malhar, Paris, France.

504. 1867. Jewish Mission of the Presbyterian Church of England. Secretary, Rev. John Edmond, D.D., 60 Beresford Road, Highbury, London, N.

505. 1876. Parochial Mission to the Jews' Fund. Episcopalian. Secretary, Rev. John Schor, Arundel House, Victoria Embankment, London, W. C.

506. 1888. Rabinowich Council in London. Undenominational.

### SCOTLAND.

511. 1842. Church of Scotland Committee for the Conversion of the Jews. Secretary, Mr. John Tawse, W.S., 21 St. Andrew's Square, Edinburgh.

512. 1843. Free Church of Scotland Committee for Conversion of the Jews. Secretary, Rev. William Affeck, D.D., Auchtermuchty, N. B., Scotland.

513. 1846. Church of Scotland Ladies' Association for the Christian Education of Jewish Females. Presbyterian, Scotland.

514. 1885. Jewish Mission of the United Presbyterian Church.

515. 1885. Scottish Home Mission to Jews. The Edinburgh Society for Promoting the Gospel among Foreign Jews, Seamen, and Emigrants.

### IRELAND.

518. 1842. Presbyterian Church of Ireland Jewish Mission. Secretary, Rev. George McFarland, 12 May Street, Belfast, Ireland.

### GERMANY.

521. 1667. Edzard Stiftung (Edzard Fund). Hamburg.

522. 1822. Die Gesellschaft zur Beförderung des Christenthums unter den Juden (Society for Promoting Christianity among the Jews). Berlin.

523. 1822. Der Evangelisch-Lutherische Sächsische Haupt-Missionsverein (Chief Society for Evangelical Lutheran Mission in Saxony). Dresden.

524. 1842. Der Rheinische Westfälische Verein für Israel (The Rhenish-Westphalian Society for Israel). Cologne.

525. 1871. Der Evangelisch-Lutherische Central-verein für die Mission unter Israel (Central Society for Evangelical Lutheran Mission among the Jews). Leipzig.

### SWITZERLAND.

531. 1830. Der Verein der Freunde Israels in Basle (The Society of Friends of Israel in Basle). Basle.

### THE NETHERLANDS.

535. 1844. De Netherlandsche Vereeniging hot medewerking aan de uitbreiding van het Christendon, onder de Juden (The Netherland Society for the Promotion of Christianity among the Jews). Amsterdam.

536. 1863. De Nederlandsche Vereenigung voon Israel. (The Netherland Society for Israel). Amsterdam.

537. 1875. Christelojke Gereformeerde Zending onder Israel (Christian Reformed Mission to Israel). Alblasserdam.

### FRANCE.

541. 1888. Société française pour l'Évangélisation d'Israel (French Society for the Evangelization of Israel). Paris.

### NORWAY, SWEDEN, DENMARK.

545. 1856. Evangeliske Fosterlands Stiftelsen (Evangelical National Society). Stockholm.

546. 1865. Central Komiteen for Israelsmissionen (The Central Committee for the Jewish Missions). Christiania.

547. 1877. Svenska Missions forbundet (Swedish Mission Society). Stockholm.

### RUSSIA.

551. 1870. The Baltic Mission among the Jews. Riga.

552. 1883. Joseph Rabinowitsch's Mission in Kishénew.

### UNITED STATES.

555. 1878. The Church Society for Promoting Christianity among the Jews. New York.

556. 1878. Zions foreningen for Israelsmissionen blandt norske Lutheranere. Amerika (The Norwegian Lutheran Zion Society in America for Mission to Israel). Chicago.

557. 1882. The Hebrew Christian Work in New York.

558. 1883. The Jewish Mission of the Evangelical Lutheran Synod of Missions. St. Louis.

559. 1886. The Methodist Mission to the Jews. Galena, Ill.

560. 1886. The Wesleyan Mission to the Jews. Oxford, Ga.

561. 1887. The Hebrew Christian Work in Chicago.

----

# ABBREVIATIONS.

A. B. C. F. M......American Board of Commissioners for Foreign Missions.
A. B. M. U........American Baptist Missionary Union.
A. B. S..........American Bible Society.
B. F. B. S........British and Foreign Bible Society.
B. M. S...........Baptist Missionary Society (England).
C. I. M...........China Inland Mission.
C. M. S...........Church Missionary Society.
Evan..............Evangelical.
Herrm.............Herrmansburg.
I. F. N. S........Indian Female Normal School and Instruction Society.
L. M. S...........London Missionary Society.
Luth..............Lutheran.
M. E..............Methodist Episcopal.
Med...............Medical.
Melan.............Melanesian.
Miss..............Mission.
Pres..............Presbyterian.
Prot. Epis........Protestant Episcopal.
Ref...............Reformed.
R. T. S...........Religious Tract Society.
Rhen..............Rhenish.
S. P. C. K........Society for the Propagation of Christian Knowledge.
S. P. G...........Society for the Propagation of the Gospel.
Unit. ............United (Meth. and Pres.).
Wes. Meth.........Wesleyan Methodist (England).
W. B. M...........Woman's Board of Missions.
W. F. M. S........Woman's Foreign Missionary Society.
Y. M. C. A........Young Men's Christian Association.

# APPENDIX D.

## *LIST OF MISSIONARY STATIONS.*

The word "station" is used by different societies in widely different ways. In this list it includes any place where there is permanent missionary work carried on either with the residence or under the immediate superintendence of a missionary. It thus includes a number of places that are by some called out-stations.

This list was based upon one prepared by W. E. Blackstone, Esq., of Oak Park, Ill., and kindly furnished by him to the editor, and has been compared with the published reports of the different societies and whatever other sources were available. It is aimed to include every place mentioned in the reports when the accompanying statements seemed to imply a work of permanent value. To include every name mentioned would in not a few cases, be misleading. It will inevitably happen that some names have been omitted which should have been inserted, and some inserted which might well have been omitted. In the European missions of the Baptist and Methodist Societies only those places have been retained where there are foreign missionaries either resident or in immediate charge. The table has been arranged on the following plan: Immediately succeeding the name of the station are indicated the volume and page of the Encyclopedia where there is a special account of the place. (Reference in other articles will be found in the general index.) Then comes the geographical section; then the number of the society at work, as per Appendix C, immediately preceding; and last, the number and section of the Map where the place is located. A star indicates that the location is not exact, but is estimated. Thus: Agra is described in vol. 1, page 33, of the Encyclopedia; is located in Rajputana, India; is occupied by the Methodist Episcopal Church (North), 13; the Church Missionary Society, 72; the Baptist Missionary Society, 77; and the Edinburgh Medical Missionary Society, 391; and will be found on Map No. VIII., section J. 4. Maps I. to XV. are in Vol. I.; XVI. to XXVI. in Vol. II.

Absolute accuracy in such a work is almost impossible, and although great care has been taken mistakes will undoubtedly appear.

| | | | |
|---|---|---|---|
| Aana (I. 1), | Samoan Isl., Pac. | 62 | (XXI. J. 1) |
| Aangeleken (I. 1), | Natal, Africa, | 126 | (IV. J. 8) |
| Ababa (I. 1), | Banks Isl., Pac. | 170 | (XIX. I. 9). |
| Abaco (I. 1), | Bahamas, | 77, 81 | (XXVI. E. 1) |
| Abeih (I. 1), | Syria, | 24 | (XXV. G. 8) |
| Abeokuta (I. 2), | Yoruba, Africa, | 72, 81 | (V. I. 9) |
| Abetifi (I. 2), | Ashanti, Africa, | 142 | (V. G. 9) |
| Abokobi (I. 2), | Gold Coast, Afr., | 142 | (V. G. 9) |
| Abome (I. 2), | Dahomey, Africa, | 81 | (V. I. 9) |
| Aburi (I. 2), | Gold Coast, Afr., | 142 | (V. H. 9) |
| Accra (I. 4), | Gold Coast, Afr., | 81 | (V. H. 10) |
| Ada (I. 5), | Gold Coast, Afr., | 142 | (V. H. 10) |
| Adabazar (I. 5), | Asia Minor, | 1 | (XXV. D. 2) |
| Adachi (I. 5), | Japan, | | (XV.) |
| Adalia (I. 5), | Asia Minor, | 327 | (XXV. D. 6) |
| Adams, see Amanzimtote. | | | |
| Adamshoop (I. 5), Orange Free State, | | | |
| | Africa, | 144 | (IV. G. 8) |
| Adana (I. 5), | Asia Minor, | 1, 27 | (XXV. F. 5) |
| Addington (I. 5), | New Zealand, | 82 | |
| Adelaide (I. 5), | Kaffraria, Africa, | 71, 104 | (IV. H. 10) |
| Adelaide (I. 5), | Australia, | 83, 85, 86 | |
| Aden (I. 6), | Arabia, | 72, 103 | (IL. K. 9) |
| Adiabo (I. 6), | Old Calabar, Afr., | 104 | (V. K. 10) |
| Admiralty I. (I.6), | South Pacific, | | (XIX. F. 6) |
| Adrianople (I. 6), | European Turkey, | 1 | (XI. I. 7) |
| Agarpara (I. 32), | Bengal, India, | 72 | (VII. I. 6) |
| Agra (I. 33), | Rajputana, Ind., | 13, 72, 77, 391 | (VIII. J. 4) |
| Aguascalientes | | | |
| (I. 33), | Mexico, | 5, 15, 30 | (XX. E. 4) |
| Agune (I. 33), | Japan, | 13 | (XV. D. 6*) |
| Ahmadabad(I.33), | Bombay, India, | 109 | (VIII. E. 8) |
| Ahmadnagar(I.33), | Bombay, India, | 71 | (XVII. B. 1) |
| Aidin (I. 33), | Asia Minor, | 1 | (XXV. B. 5) |
| Aintab (I. 34), | Asia Minor, | 1 | (XXV. H. 5) |
| Aitutaki (I. 34), | Hervey Isl., Pac., | 62 | (XXI. E. 9) |
| Aiyonsh (I. 34), | British Columbia, | | |
| | Canada, | 72 | (XIV. D. 5*) |
| Ajimadidi (I. 34), | Celebes, E. Ind., | 155 | (XVIII. L. 7) |
| Ajmere (I. 34), | Rajputana, India, | 13,71,104 | (VIII.G. 4) |
| Ajuthia (I. 34), | Siam, | 24 | (XXIV. C. 6) |
| Akamagasika, | Japan, | | (XV. D. 5) |
| Akasa (I. 34), | Niger, Africa, | 72 | (V. J. 10) |
| Akashi (I. 34), | Japan, | 1 | (XV. F. 5) |
| Akidu (I. 34), | Madras, India, | 52 | (VII. B. 12) |
| Akita (I. 34), | Japan, | 36 | (XV. I. 3) |
| Akola (I. 35), | Cent. Prov., Ind., | 13 | (VIII. I. 10) |
| Akra, | Bengal, India, | 72 | (VII. H. 7*) |
| Akropong, | Gold Coast, Afr., | 142 | (V. H. 9) |
| Albany (I. 39), | James Bay, Can., | 72 | (XIV. I. 5) |
| Alenso (I. 39), | Niger, Africa, | 72 | (V. J. 9) |
| Aleppo (I. 39), | Asia Minor, | 1 | (XXV. H. 6) |
| Alert Bay (I. 39), | British Columbia, | | |
| | Canada, | 72 | (XIV. D. 5) |
| Alexandretta(I.40),Syria, | | 1 | (XXV. G. 6) |
| Alexandria (I. 41), | Egypt, | 26,542 | (II. E. 1) |
| Algiers (I. 41), | Algiers, | 511 | (VI. G. 1) |
| Aligarb (I. 41), | N. W. Provinces, | | |
| | India, | 72 | (VIII. J. 3) |
| Alipur (I. 41), | Bengal, India, | 77 | (VII. H. 6*) |
| Aliwal, North | | | |
| (I. 41), | Kaffraria, Afr., | 85 | (IV. H. 9) |
| Allahabad (I. 41), | N. W. Provinces, | | |
| | India, | 13,24,72,77 | (VII.B.4) |
| Alleppi (I. 42), | Travancore, Ind., | 72 | (XVII. C. 10) |
| Almora (I. 42), | N. W. Provinces, | | |
| | India, | 62 | (VIII. K. 1) |
| Alwar (Ulwar) | | | |
| (I. 42, II. 427), | Rajputana, India, | 104 | (VIII. I. 4) |
| Alway (I. 42), | Madras, India, | 72 | (XVII. D. 9*) |
| Amabei (I. 42), | Ceram, E. Ind., | 155 | (XVIII. A. 2) |
| Amalapuram(I.42),Madras, India, | | 72 | (VII. C. 12) |
| Amalienstein(I.42),CapeColony,Afr., | | 144 | (IV. E. 10) |
| Amanzimtote | | | |
| (Adams) (I. 42), | Natal, Africa, | 1 | (IV. J. 8) |
| Amraoti (I. 42), | Cent. Prov., Ind., | 103 | (VIII. J. 10) |
| Amasia (I. 42), | Asia Minor, | 1 | (XXV. G. 3) |
| Ambala (Umbala) | | | |
| (I. 43), | Punjab, India, | 24 | (XXII. F. 6) |
| Ambato (Manam- | | | |
| bato?), | Madagascar, | 121 | (XVI. D. 10) |
| Ambatoharanana | | | |
| (I. 43), | Madagascar, | 71 | (XVI. D. 6*) |
| Ambatonakanga | | | |
| (I. 43), | Madagascar, | 62, 93 | (XVI. D. 6*) |
| Ambohibeloma | | | |
| (I. 43), | Madagascar, | 62 | (XVI. D. 6) |
| Ambobimandroso | | | |
| (I. 43), | Madagascar, | 62 | (XVI. D. 9) |
| Ambositra (I. 43), | Madagascar, | 62 | (XVI. D. 7) |

NOTE.—The first figures indicate the vol. and page of the Encyclopedia: the third column corresponds to the numbers in Appendix C; the last column shows number and section of Map.

NOTE.—The first figures indicate the vol. and page of the Encyclopedia; the third column corresponds to the numbers in Appendix C; the last column shows number and section of Map.

| | | | |
|---|---|---|---|
| Benita (I. 152), | Corisco, Africa, | 24 | (III. B. 3) |
| Benoob (I. 152), | Egypt, | 26 | (II. E. 3) |
| Berea (I. 154) | Orange FreeState, Africa, | 141,165 | (IV. H. 8) |
| Berg-en-Dal(I.154), | Dutch Guiana, South America, | 141 | (IX. J. 2*) |
| Berhampore (I. 154), | Madras, India, | | 13,62,78(VII.E.10) |
| Beroa, | Cape Colony, Afr., | 141 | (IV. D. 10) |
| Beroa, | Basuto-land, Afr., | 165 | (IV. I. 8*) |
| Bersaba (I. 160), | Namaqua-land, Africa, | 145,149 | (IV. D. 6) |
| Betafo (I. 160), | Madagascar, | 121 | (XVI. D. 7) |
| Bethania, | Mosquito Coast, Cent. Am., | 141 | (XXVI. C. 5) |
| Bethanien (I. 160), | Namaqua-land,Afr., | 145 | (IV. C. 6) |
| Bethanien (I. 160), | Orange Free State, Africa, | 144 | (IV. H. 8) |
| Bethanien (I. 160), | Gt. Namaqualand, Africa, | 149 | (IV. C. 6) |
| Bethany (I. 160), | Jamaica, W. Ind., | 141 | (XXVI. J. 1) |
| Bethel (I. 160), | Alaska, | 141 | (XIV. A. 2) |
| Bethel, | Bengal, India, | | Beth. Santhal Miss. (VII. G. 5*) |
| Bethel (I. 161), | Cent. Prov., Ind., | 103 | (VIII. H. 11*) |
| Bethel (I. 161), | Cameroons,Africa, | 77 | (III. B. 2*) |
| Bethel (I. 161), | Kaffraria, Africa, | 144 | (IV. I. 10) |
| Bethel (I. 161), | St. Kitts, W. Ind., | 141 | (XXVI. J. 3) |
| Bethelsdorp, | Cape Colony, Afr., | 62 | (IV. G. 10) |
| Bethesda (I. 161), | Kaffraria (Orange Free State), Afr., | 141, 149, 165 | (IV J. 9) |
| Bethlehem (I.161), | Palestine, | 542 | (XXV. G. 10) |
| Bethjala (or Beth-ala), (I. 161), | Syria, | 542 | (XXV. F. 10) |
| Betigeri (I. 161), | Bombay, India, | 142 | (XVII. C. 4) |
| Betul (I. 161), | Cent. Prov., Ind., | 127 | (VIII. J. 9) |
| Bezuki (I. 161), | Java, East Indies, | 158 | (XVIII. H.11) |
| Bezwada, | Madras, India, | 72 | (VII. A. 12) |
| Bhagalpur(I.161), | Bengal, India, | 72 | (VII. G. 4) |
| Bhaghaya (I.161), | Bengal, India, | 72 | (VII. G. 4) |
| Bhandara (I. 161), | Cent. Prov.,India, | 103 | (VIII. K 10) |
| Bhimpore (I.161), | Bengal, India, | 4 | (VII. F. 9) |
| Bhudruck (Bhad-rak) (I. 161), | Bengal, India, | 4 | (VII. F. 8) |
| Bida (I. 168), | Niger, Africa, | 72 | (V. J. 8) |
| Bihe (I. 168), | Benguela, Afr., | 1 | (III. D. 9) |
| Bijnaur (I. 168), | N. W. Provinces, India, | 13 | (VII. B. 3*) |
| Bilaspur (I. 168), | Cent. Prov., Ind., | 36 | (VII. C. 7) |
| Bilbao (I. 168), | Spain, | 1 | |
| Bimlapatam, | Madras, India, | 52 | (VII. D. 11) |
| Bishtopore, | Bengal, India, | 77 | (VII. H. 6*) |
| Bisrampur, | Cent. Prov., Ind., | 23 | (VIII. K. 9) |
| Bitlis (I. 169), | Koordistan, Ty., | 1 | (XXV. J. 4) |
| Blantyre (I. 169), | Mozambique (Lake Nyassa), Africa | 101 | (III. L. 10) |
| Blauberg (I. 169), | Transvaal, Africa, | 144 | (IV. J. 4) |
| Blewfields(I.169), | Mosquito Coast, Cent. Am., | 141 | (XXVI. C. 5) |
| Bloemfontein (I. 169), | Orange Free State, Afr., | 71,144 | (IV. H. 8) |
| Bloemhof (I. 170), | Swaziland, Afr., | 71, 81 | (IV. H. 7) |
| Blytheswood(I.170), | Kaffraria, Afr., | 103 | (IV. J. 9) |
| Bobbili, | India, | 52 | (VII. D. 11) |
| Bocas-del-Toro (I. 172), | Cent. America, | 82 | (XXVI. D. 6) |
| Bogota (I. 172), | U. S. of Colombia, So. America, | 24 | (IX. C. 3) |
| Boli I. (see Bauro) (I. 144), | Solomon's I., Pac., | 170 | (XIX. I. 8) |
| Bolobo (I. 174), | Congo, Africa, | 77 | (III. D. 5) |
| Bologna, | Italy, | 5, 13, 81 | |
| Bombay (I. 174), | Bombay, India, | | 1,13,71,72.77,103,etc. (XVII.A.1) |
| Bompehtook(I.177), | Sherbro,W. Afr., | 37 | (V. C. 9*) |
| Boudo (I. 177), | Java, | 157 | (XVIII. 11*) |
| Bonjongo, | Cameroons, Afr., | 77 | (V. K. 10) |
| Bonny, | Niger Valley, Afr., | 72 | (V. J. 10) |
| Bonthe, | Sherbro Isl., Afr., | 37 | (V. C. 9) |
| Borasit(Barasat), | India, | 77 | (VII. H. 6) |
| Borga (I. 178), | Finland, | 131 | |
| Borsad (I. 178), | Bombay, India, | 109 | (VIII. E. 8) |
| Botschabelo(I.178), | S. African Rep. (Transvaal),Afr., | 144 | (IV. J. 6) |
| Botucatu (I. 178), | Brazil. So. Am., | 24 | (IX. H. 8) |
| Bowen (I. 178), | Australia, | 71, 86 | |
| Brass (I. 179), | Niger Valley, Afr., | 72 | (V. J. 10) |
| Brewerville(I.193), | Liberia, Africa, | 13, 14, 24 | (V. B. 9*) |
| Bridgetown(I.194), | Barbadoes, W. Indies, | 13 | (XXVI. K. 5) |
| Broach (I. 205), | Bombay, India, | 109 | (VIII. F. 9) |
| Brokie (I. 205), | N. W. Provinces, India, | 13 | (VIII. J. 1*) |
| Broosa (I. 205), | W. Turkey, | 1 | (XXV. C. 3) |
| Brotas (I. 205), | Brazil, | 24 | (IX. H. 7) |
| Brownstown, | Jamaica, W. Ind., | 77 | (XXVI. J. 1) |
| Brumana (I. 207), | Syria, | 93 | (XXV. G. 8) |
| Brussels, | Belgium, | 81 | |
| Buchanan (I.207), | Liberia, Africa, | 13 | (V. E. 9*) |
| Buchanan (I.207), | E. Africa, | 104 | (IV. I. 10*) |
| Bucharest (I.207), | Roumania, | 511 | (XI. H. 4) |
| Budapest (I. 207), | Hungary, | 526 | (XI. C. 1) |
| Buenos Ayres (I. 215), | Argentine Rep., | 13 | (IX. F. 10) |
| Buitnezong (Buit-enzorg?)(I.215), | Java, | 159 | (XVIII. E. 10) |
| Bukaboka, | Tokelau Isl., Pac., | 62 | (XXI. B. 7*) |
| Bukunda, | Cameroons, Afr., | 77 | (V. K. 10) |
| Buleling, | Bali Isl., E. Ind., | 145 | (XVIII. H.11) |
| Bungabondar (I. 218), | Sumatra, | 145 | (XVIII. B. 7) |
| Burhanpur(I.218), | Cent. Prov. Ind., Faith Miss., | | (VIII. I. 10) |
| Burkujanna, | S. Australia, | 149 | |
| Burnshill (I. 223), | Kaffraria, Africa, | 103 | (IV. I. 10*) |
| Burrows, | Australia, | 69 | |
| Butaritari(I.223), | Gilbert Isl., Pac., | | (XIX. L. 5) |
| Cabanburi, | British Guiana, So. America, | 141 | (IX. H. 1) |
| Cabruang (I.225), | Talaut Isl.,E. Ind., | 156 | (XVIII. M. 6) |
| Cairo (I. 225), | Egypt, | | 26, 72, 81, 542 (II. E. 2) |
| Calao, | Peru, | | 13, 24 (IX. C. 5) |
| Calcutta (I. 227), | Bengal, India, | | 13, 62, 71, 72. 77, 81, 101, 103 (VII. H. 6) |
| Caldas (I. 229), | Brazil, | 24 | (IX. H. 7) |
| Caldwell (I. 229), | Liberia, Africa, | 13 | (V. D. 9) |
| Caledon (I. 229), | Cape Colony,Afr., | 71 | (IV. E. 11) |
| Calicut (I. 230), | Malabar, India, | 142 | (XVII. C. 8) |
| Caliub, | Egypt, | 156 | (II. E. 2) |
| Calsapad (Kal-sapad) (I. 520), | Madras, India, | 71 | (XVII. E. 3*) |
| Caltura, | Ceylon, India, | 81 | (VII. I. 13) |
| Camargo (I. 230), | Mexico, | 15 | (XX. F. 3) |
| Campanha, | Brazil, | 24 | (IX. I. 7) |
| Campinas (I.230), | Brazil, | 15, 28 | (IX. H. 7) |
| Campos, | Brazil, | 24 | (IX. I. 7) |
| Cana (I. 230), | So. African Rep. (Transvaal),Afr,. | 165 | (IV. I. 6) |
| Canada-de-Gomez (I. 232), | Argentine Rep., | 79 | (IX. E. 9) |
| Canan-da-goody, | Madras, India, | 71 | (XVII. F. 9*) |
| Candawu (I. 232), | Tonga Isl., Pac., | 81 | (XXI. B. 9*) |
| Cannanore, | Madras, India, | 142 | (XVII. C. 8) |
| Canton (I. 232), | China, | | 5, 24, 62, 72, 81, 144 (X. H. 10) |
| Cape Coast(I.234), | Gold Coast, Afr., | 81 | (V. G. 10) |
| Cape Maclear, | Lake Nyassa, Afr., | 103 | (III. K. 9) |
| Cape Mount(I.234), | Liberia, Africa, | 20 | (V. D. 9) |
| Cape Palmas (I. 234), | Liberia, Africa, | 20 | (V. E. 10) |
| Cape Town, | Cape Colony, Afr., | | (IV. C. 11) |
| Capuchin, | Seychelles Isl., | 72 | |
| Carata, | Mosquito Coast, Cent. America, | 141 | (XXVI. C.*) |
| Careysburgh (I. 235), | Liberia, Africa, | 13, 24 | (V. D. 9) |
| Carisbrook (I.235), | Jamaica, W.Ind., | 141 | (XXVI. J. 1*) |
| Carmel (I. 235), | Alaska, U. S. A., | 141 | |
| Carmel (I. 235), | Jamaica, W. Ind., | 141 | (XXVI. J. 1*) |
| Caroline Islands, (I. 235), | Pacific, | 1 | (XIX. D. 5) |
| Carozal (I. 236), | Yucatan, Cent. America, | 81 | (XXVI. B. 3) |
| Cashmir (I. 236), | Punjab, India, | 72 | (XXII. E. 3) |
| Caserta, | Italy, | 77, 81 | |
| Catania, | Sicily, | 81 | |
| Catanzaro, | Italy, | 81 | |
| Catharina Sophia (I. 237), | Dutch Guiana, South America, | 81,141 | (IX. J. 2) |
| Catwa, | Bengal, India, | 77 | (VII. H. 5) |
| Cavalla (I. 238), | Maryland, Africa, | 20 | (V. E. 10) |
| Cawnpur (I. 238), | N. W. Provinces, India, | 13, 71 | (VII. A. 3) |
| Cayman's Isl., | West Indies, | 104 | (XXVI. E. 3) |
| Ceara (I. 238), | Brazil, | 28 | (IX. J. 4) |
| Ceres, | Cape Colony. Afr., | 71 | (IV. D. 10) |
| Cesarea (I. 239), | Turkey, | 1 | (XXV. F. 4) |
| Chai-basa (I. 243), | Bengal, India, | 146 | (VII. F. 7) |
| Chamba (I. 243), | Punjab, India, | 101 | (XXII. F. 4) |
| Chanaral (I. 244), | Chili, | 73 | (IX. D. 8) |
| Chandausi(I.244), | N. W. Provinces, India, | 13 | (VIII. K. 3*) |
| Chandbali(I.244), | Bengal, India, | 4 | (VII. E. 10*) |
| Chang-Chin, | China, | | 25, 62 (X. J. 9) |
| Chaput (Chuput), | Argentine Rep., | 73 | (IX. F. 11) |
| CharlestonWorks, | Africa, | 14 | (V. D. 9*) |
| Charlottenburg (I. 245), | Dutch Guiana, South America, | 141 | (IX. J. 2) |
| Chau-kia-keo (I. 245), | China, | 65 | (X. I. 5) |

NOTE.—The first figures indicate the vol. and page of the Encyclopedia; the third column corresponds to the numbers in Appendix C; the last column shows number and section of Map.

| | | | |
|---|---|---|---|
| Chavagacherry (I. 245), | Ceylon, | 1 | (VII. J. 10) |
| Chefoo (I. 245), | China, | 24,65,71 | (X. K. 3) |
| Chengku, | China, | 65 | (X. G. 4) |
| Chen-tu (I. 245), | China, | 65 | (X. E. 6) |
| Cheribon (I. 245), | Java, | 159 | (XVIII. F. 10) |
| Cherra (I. 245), | Assam, | 89 | (XXIV. A. 1*) |
| Chhota Nagpur district, | Cent. Prov., Ind., | 71,146 | (VII. E. 5) |
| Chiang Chiu(I.245),China, | | 25, 62 | (X. J. 9) |
| Chiang Hoa(I.245),Formosa, China, | | 90 | (X. K. 9) |
| Chicacole, | Madras, India, | 52 | (VII. D. 11) |
| Chichow (I. 246), | China, | 62, 65 | (X. J. 6) |
| Chiconchilio(I.246),Mexico, | | 29 | (XX. G. 4*) |
| Chieng Mai, | North Siam, | 3, 24 | (XXIV. C. 4) |
| Chihuahua(I.246),Mexico, | | 1, 15 | (XX. D. 2) |
| Chin-an-fu(I.275),China, | | 24, 34, 71 | (X. J. 3) |
| Chinga, | East Cent. Afr., | | (III. K. 7) |
| Ching-cho-fu (see Tsing-cho-fu). | | | |
| Chinhua (see Kin-wha) (I. 277), | China, | 65 | (X. K. 7) |
| Chin Kiang(I.277), | China, | 5,13,28,90 | (X. K. 6) |
| Chin Kong, | Formosa, China, | | (X. K. 9) |
| Chittagong(I.277), | Bengal, India, | 77 | (VII. K. 7) |
| Chitangali(I.277),East Cent. Africa, | | 74 | (III. M. 8*) |
| Chitesi (I. 277), | Lake Nyassa,Afr., | 74 | (III. K. 8) |
| Chittoor (I. 277), | Madras, India, | 25 | (XVII. F. 6) |
| Chombala (Tsjom-bala) (I. 278), | Madras, India, | 142 | (XVII. C.10*) |
| Chota (see Chhota), | Cent.Prov.,Ind., | 71 | |
| Christianagaram,Madras, India, | | 71 | (XVII.F.11*) |
| Christiansborg, (I. 278), | Africa, | 144 | (V. H. 10) |
| Christianenberg (I. 278), | Natal, Africa, | 144 | (IV. J. 8) |
| ChungKing(I.279), | China, | 13, 65 | (X. F. 7) |
| Chuprah (I. 279), | Bengal, India, | 146 | (VII. E. 4) |
| Clan William(I.304),Cape Colony, Africa, | | 71 | (IV. D. 9) |
| Claremont(I.304),Natal, Africa, | | 71 | (IV. K. 8*) |
| Clarkabad(I.304), | Punjab, India, | 72 | (XXII. D. 6) |
| Clarkeburg, | Kaffraria, Afr., | 81 | (IV. I. 9) |
| Clarkson (I. 304), | Cape Colony, Afr., | 141 | (IV. G. 11) |
| Clay Ashland (I. 304), | Liberia, Africa, | 13, 20, 24 | (V. D. 9) |
| Clevia, | Dutch Guiana, South America, | 141 | (IX. J. 2) |
| Clydesdale(I.304),Natal, Africa, | | 71 | (IV. J. 9) |
| Cocanada(I. 306), | Madras, India, | 52 | (VII. C. 12) |
| Cochin (I. 306), | Madras, India, | 72 | (XVII. C. 10) |
| Codacal (Kodakal) (I. 306), | Malabar, India, | 142 | (XVII. C. 9) |
| Cohima(Kohima,Assam, India, | | 3 | (XXIV. A. 1) |
| Coimbatore(I.306),Madras, India, | | 62,126,143 | (XVII. D. 9) |
| Colar (Kolar) (I. 307), | Madras, India, | 457 | (XVII. E. 7) |
| Colesburg, | Cape Colony, Afr., | 81 | (IV. H. 9) |
| Colombo (I. 307), | Ceylon, | 71,72,77,81 | (VII.I.12) |
| Colonia (I. 307), | Uruguay, | 13 | (IX. F. 9) |
| Comaggas (Ko-maggas)(I.308), | Little Namaqua-land, Africa, | 145 | (IV. C. 8) |
| Combaconum (I. 308), | Madras, India, | 71,143 | (XVII. F. 8) |
| Combe (Morao) Dutch Guiana, (I. 308), | South America, | 141 | (IX. J. 2*) |
| Comilah (I. 312), | Bengal, India, | 77 | (VII. K. 5) |
| Concepcion(I.312),Chili, | | 24 | (IX. D. 10) |
| Concordia(I.312),Argentine Rep., | | 73 | (IX. G. 9*) |
| Concordia (I.312), Namaqua-land, Africa, | | 145 | (IV. D. 8) |
| Condah, | Australia, | 72 | |
| Constantia, | Cape Colony, Afr., | 71 | (IV. D. 11) |
| Constantine, | Algeria, | 67 | (VI. H. 1) |
| Constantinople (I. 321). | Turkey, | 1, 36, 93, 511, 512 | (XI. J. 7) |
| Constitucion (I.324), Chili, | | 24 | (IX. D. 10) |
| Coonoor (I. 324), | Madras, India, | 25, 81 | (XVII. C. 9*) |
| Copay (I. 324), | Ceylon, India, | 72 | (VII. I. 10*) |
| Copiapo (I. 324), | Chili, | 13 | (IX. D. 8) |
| Copperamana (I. 324), | South Australia, | 141 | |
| Coquimbo (I. 324), | Chili, | 13 | (IX. D. 9) |
| Coranderk, | South Australia, | 72 | |
| Corapat (Korapat) (I. 325), | Madras, India, | 150 | (VII. C. 10*) |
| Cordoba (I. 325), | Argentine Rep., | 73 | (IX. E. 9) |
| Cordova, | Mexico, | 13 | (XX. G. 5) |
| Corfu (I. 325), | Ionian Islands, | | (XI. D. 9) |
| Corientes, | Brazil, | 13 | (IX. F. 10) |
| Corisco (I. 325), | West Africa, | 24 | (III. A. 3) |
| Corytiba (I. 325), | Brazil, | 24 | (IX. H. 8) |
| Cosihuiriachic (I. 325), | North Mexico, | 1 | (XX. D. 2) |
| Cotagiri (see Kotagiri) (I. 325), | Madras, India, | 142 | (XVII. D. 8) |
| Cotta (I. 325), | Ceylon, India, | 72 | (VII. I. 12*) |
| Cottayam (I.325), | Travancore, Ind., | 72 | (XVII. C. 10) |
| Cowwa, | Trinidad, W. Ind., | 51, 77 | (XXVI. K. 6*) |
| Cradock, | Cape Colony, Afr., | 62 | (IV. H. 9) |
| Cranmer (I. 326), | Keppel Isl., Falkland Isl., S. Am., | 73 | (IX. F. 13*) |
| Creek Town(I.326), | Old Calabar, Afr., | 78 | (V. K. 10) |
| Cuddalore (I. 328), | Madras, India, | 71,143 | (XVII. F. 8) |
| Cuddapah (I.328), | Madras, India, | 62 | (XVII. F. 6) |
| Culattur (see Kulathur), | Madras, India, | 71 | (VIII. F. 7*) |
| Cumberland, | Canada, | 72 | (XIV. G. 5*) |
| Cumbum (Kambam) (I. 328), | Madras, India, | 3 | (XVII. F. 4) |
| Cumelembuai(Komelemboai), | Celebes, | 155 | (XVIII. L. 7) |
| Cunningham (I. 328), | Kaffraria, Africa, | 103 | (IV. I. 10) |
| Cupang (I. 328), | Timor I., E. Ind., | 155 | (XVIII. L. 11) |
| Curallaya, | Mosquito Coast, Cent. America, | 141 | (XXVI. C. 5*) |
| Cuttack, | Bengal, India, | 78 | (VII. F. 9) |
| Dacca (I. 329), | Bengal, India, | 77 | (VII. J. 5) |
| Dahana (I. 329), | Nias, E. Indies, | 145 | (XVIII.A.7*) |
| Dalhousie (I. 330), | Punjab, India, | 101 | (XXII. F. 5) |
| Damascus (I. 330), | Syria, | 109, 391, 511 | (XXV. G. 8) |
| Daraletta, | Egypt, | 26 | (II. F. 1) |
| Dammer Island, | Moluccas, E. Ind., | | (XVIII. M. 7) |
| Danzig, | Germany, | 511 | |
| Dapoli (I. 335), | Bombay, India, | 71 | (XVII. A. 2) |
| Darjeeling (I. 335), | Bengal, India, | 101 | (VII. G. 2) |
| Dehra (I. 336), | N. W. Provinces, India, | 24, 72 | (VIII. J. 1) |
| De Kaap Valley, | Natal, Africa, | 71 | (IV. K. 8*) |
| Delhi (I. 336), | Punjab, India, | 72, 77 | (VIII. I. 2) |
| Demerara (I. 336), | British Guiana, South America, | 62,141 | (IX. I. 1) |
| Deoband (I. 337), | N. W. Provinces, India, | 13 | (XXII. D. 3*) |
| Deoli (I. 337), | Rajputana, India, | 104 | (VIII. H. 5) |
| Depoh (I. 337), | Java, E. Indies, | 155 | (XVIII. E. 10) |
| Dera Ghazi Khan (I. 337), | Punjab, India, | 72 | (VIII. D. 1) |
| Dera Ismail Khan (I. 337), | Punjab, India, | 72 | (XXII. B. 5) |
| Devon (I. 338), | Canada, | 72 | (XIV. G. 5) |
| Dharwar (I. 338), | Bombay, India, | 142 | (XVII. B. 4) |
| Dhurbhanga (see Durbhanga)(I.343),India, | | 146 | (VII. F. 3) |
| Diarbekir (I. 338), | Koordistan, Ty., | 1 | (XXV. I. 5) |
| Dibrugarh (Dibengarh), | Assam, India, | 72 | (XXIV. B. 1) |
| Dinajpore (Dinajpur) (I. 338), | Bengal, India, | 77 | (VII. H. 4) |
| Dinapur (I. 338), | Bengal, India, | 71, 77 | (VII. E. 4) |
| Dindigul (I. 338), | Madras, India, | 1 | (XVII. E. 9) |
| Djemmaa Sahridj, | Algeria, | 67 | (VI. G. 1) |
| Djimma (I. 339), | Abyssinia, | 127 | (II. H. 10) |
| Dober, | Jamaica, W. Ind., | 141 | (XXVI. J. 1*) |
| Dohnavur (I. 340), | Madras, India, | 72 | (XVII. E. 11) |
| Domasi (I. 340), | East. Equat. Afr., | 101 | (III. K. 10) |
| Domburg (I. 340), | Surinam, So. Am., | 141 | (IX. J. 2*) |
| Domingia (I. 340), | Sierra Leone, Afr., | 71 | (V. B. 8) |
| Dominica (I. 340), | Leeward Islands, West Indies, | 81 | (XXVI. J. 4) |
| Dondo (I. 340), | Guinea Coast,Afr., | 13 | (III. C. 8) |
| Dordrecht, | Cape Colony, Afr., | 71 | (IV. H. 9) |
| Dowlaishvaram (I. 340), | Madras, India, | 35 | (VII. B. 12*) |
| Dudhi (I. 341), | N. W. Provinces, India, | 62 | (VII. D. 5) |
| Duff (I. 341), | Kaffraria, Africa, | 103 | (IV. I. 10) |
| Duke of York's Islands (I. 342), | Tokelau Isl., Pac., | 81 | (XXI. B. 7) |
| Duke Town(I.342), | Old Calabar, Afr., | 104 | (III. A. 2)(V. J. 10) |
| Duma (I. 343), | Moluccas, E. Ind., | 160 | (XVIII. M. 7) |
| Dumagudiem (I. 343), | Madras, India, | 72 | (VII. A. 10) |
| Dundedin, | New Zealand, | 71 | |
| Durban (I. 343), | Natal, Africa, | 71 | (IV. J. 8) |
| Durbhanga(I.343),Bengal, India, | | 146 | (VII. F. 3) |
| Dwarahat (I.345), | N. W. Provinces, India, | 13 | (VIII. K. 1*) |
| Eakehnd, | Denmark, | 13 | |
| East Harbor, | Turk's I.W. Ind., | 77 | (XXVI. G. 2*) |
| Ebenezer (I. 350), | Bengal, India, | 121 | (VII. G. 4*) |
| Ebenezer (I. 350), | Sinoe River, Afr., | 13 | (V. D. 10*) |
| Ebenezer (I. 350), | British Guiana, South America, | 62 | (IX. I. 1) |
| Ebenezer (I. 350), | Australia, | 141 | |
| Ebenezer (I. 350), | Cape Colony, Afr., | 145 | (IV. D. 9) |
| Ebenezer (I. 350), | S. African Rep. (Transvaal),Afr., | 149 | (IV. J. 6) |
| Ebenezer (I. 350), | Natal, Africa, | 145 | (IV. J. 9) |

NOTE.—The first figures indicate the vol. and page of the Encyclopedia; the third column corresponds to the numbers in Appendix C; the last column shows number and section of Map.

NOTE.—The first figures indicate the vol. and page of the Encyclopedia; the third column corresponds to the numbers in Appendix C; the last column shows number and section of Map.

NOTE.—The first figures indicate the vol. and page of the Encyclopedia; the third column corresponds to the numbers in Appendix C; the last column shows number and section of Map.

| | | | |
|---|---|---|---|
| Hazelton, | British Columbia, | 72 | (XIV. D. 5) |
| Hebron (I. 413), | Labrador, | 141 | (XIV. K. 3) |
| Hebron (I. 413), | S. African Rep. (Transvaal),Afr., | 149 | (IV. I. 6) |
| Hebrou, | Syria, | 542 | (XXV. F. 10) |
| Hector's River, | Jamaica, | 93 | (XXVI. J. 1*) |
| Heerendyk(I.413), | British Guiana, South America, | 141 | (IX. J. 2*) |
| Heidelberg(I.413), | S. African Rep. (Transvaal),Afr., | 71, 144, 149 | (IV. J. 6) |
| Helena Creek (I. 413), | Dutch Guiana, South America, | 141 | (IX. J. 2*) |
| Henzada (I. 413), | Burmah, | 1, 3 | (XXIV. B. 5) |
| Herbertsdale (I. 413), | Cape Colony, Afr., | 144 | (IV. F. 11) |
| Heretaunga, | New Zealand (see Haretaunga) | | |
| Hermannsburg (I. 413), | Natal, Africa, | 149 | (IV. J. 8) |
| Hermannsburg (I. 413), | South Australia, | 149 | |
| Hermon (I. 416), | Basuto-land, Afr., | 165 | (IV. H. 8) |
| Hermosillo(I.416),Mexico, | | 1 | (XX. C. 2) |
| Herrnhut (see New Herrnhut)(II.171b), | West Indies, | 141 | (XXVI. I. 3) |
| Herschel, | Cape Colony, Afr., | 71 | (IV. I. 9) |
| Hervey I. (I. 416), | Cook's Isl., Pacif., | 62 | (XXI. E. 9) |
| Highflats, | Natal, Africa, | 71 | (IV. J. 8) |
| Hikone, | Japan, | 1 | (XV. G. 5) |
| Himeji, | Japan, | 12 | (XV. F. 5) |
| Hindmark, | Victoria,Australia,72 | | |
| Hinghwa (I. 426), | China, | 13 | (X. J. 8) |
| Hiogo (I. 426), | Japan, | 1, 15 | (XV. G. 5) |
| Hirampur(I.426), | Bengal, India, | 72 | (VII. G. 4) |
| Hirosaki (I. 426), | Japan, | 13 | (XV. I. 2) |
| Hiroshima(I.426),Japan, | | 15, 24 | (XV. E. 5) |
| Ho (Wegbé) (I. 436), | Slave Coast, Afr., | | (V. H. 9) |
| Hoachanas (I.436), | Namaqua-land, South Africa, | 145 | (IV. C. 5) |
| Hoffenthal(I.436), | Natal, Africa, | 144 | (IV. I. 8) |
| Hoffenthal, | Labrador, | 141 | |
| Hokchiang(I.437), | China, | 13, 72 | (X. J. 8) |
| Holsteinborg, | Greenland, | 115 | |
| Hong Koug(I.437),China, | | 1, 62, 72, 81, 142 | (X.J.10) |
| Honjo, | Japan, | 13, 36 | (XV. I. 5*) |
| Honolulu (I. 438), | Sandwich Islands, | 71,169 | (XII. E. 1) |
| Honor, | Canara, India, | 142 | (XVII. A. 6) |
| Honoyeke, | Japan, | 38 | (XV.) |
| Hopedale (I. 438), | Labrador, | 141 | (XIV. J. 4*) |
| Hope Fountain, | Matabeleland, Africa, | 62 | (IV. I. 3) |
| Hoputalé (I. 438), | Ceylon, | 81 | (VII. J. 12*) |
| Hoshangabad (I. 438), | Cent. Provs., Ind., | 93 | (VIII. I. 8) |
| Hoshiarpur(I.438), | Punjab, India, | 24 | (XXII. F. 5) |
| Hsin Chow (Tsin?), | China, | 77 | (X. F. 4) |
| Huahine (I. 441), | Society Isl., Pac., | 165 | (XXI. G. 8) |
| Hubli (I. 441), | Bombay, India, | 142 | (XVII. B. 5) |
| Huchow (I. 441), | China, | 3 | (X. K. 6) |
| Hurda (I. 442), | Cent. Provs., Ind., | 36 | (VIII. I. 8) |
| Huta Bargot (I.442), | Sumatra, E. Ind., | 158 | (XVIII. B. 7) |
| Huta Rimbaru (I. 442), | Sumatra, E. Ind., | 158 | (XVIII. B. 7) |
| Hwaughien, | China, | 15 | (X. K. 3) |
| Hwuy-chau, | China, | 65 | (X. J. 6) |
| Iarindrano(I.442),Madagascar, | | 62 | (XVI. D. 9*) |
| Ibadan (I. 443), | West Africa, | 72 | (V. I. 9) |
| Iboina, | Madagascar, | 62 | (XVI. D. 6*) |
| Ichang, | China, | 65,101 | (X. H. 5) |
| Ida, | Niger, Africa, | 72 | (V. J. 9) |
| Ifumi (I. 443), | Natal, Africa, | 1 | (IV. J. 8) |
| Igatpuri, | Bombay, India, | 13 | (VIII. F. 9*) |
| Igdlorpait(I.444), | Greenland, | 141 | |
| Iida, | Japan, | 13 | (XV. G. 4) |
| Ikoroflong, | West Africa, | 104 | (V. K. 9) |
| Ikenetu, | West Africa, | 104 | (V. K. 9) |
| Ilalangina(I.444), | Madagascar, | 62 | (XVI. E. 8) |
| Imabari, | Japan, | 1 | (XV. E. 5*) |
| Imandandriana (I. 444), | Madagascar, | 62 | (XVI. C.8*) |
| Imfule, | Natal, Africa, | 121 | (IV. J. 8*) |
| Impolweni, | Natal, Africa, | 103 | (IV. J. 8) |
| Inagua (I. 444), | Bahamas, W. Ind., | 71, 77 | (XXVI. G. 2) |
| Inanda (or Lindley) (I. 444), | Natal, Africa, | 1 | (IV. J. 8) |
| Ingehung (Inching) (I. 476), | China, | 13 | (X. J. 8) |
| Indaleni, | Natal, S. Africa, | 81 | (IV. J. 8) |
| Indore (I. 476), | Cent. Provs., Ind., | 51 | (VIII. H. 8) |
| Indramadja (see Indramazne), | Java, | 155 | (XVIII. E. 10) |
| Indunduma, | Zululand, Africa, | 1 | (IV. I. 8*) |
| Inhambane, | East. Equat., Afr., | 1 | (IV. M. 5) |
| Injezane, | Zululand, Africa, | 149 | (IV. K. 7*) |
| Intlasakie (Inklazatga), | Transvaal, Afr., | 121 | (IV. I. 9*) |
| Inyaki (I. 478), | Matabele-land, Africa, | 62 | (IV. J. 3) |
| Iquique, | Chile, | 13 | (IX. D. 7) |
| Irandrano (Iarindrano ?), | Madagascar, | 62 | (XVI. C. 8*) |
| Irwin Hill, | Jamaica, W. Ind., | 141 | (XXVI. J. 1*) |
| Isle of Batjam, | Ceram, E. Indies, | 155 | (XIX. A. 6*) |
| Islington, | Rupert's Land, Canada, | 72 | (XIV. H. 6) |
| Isoavina (Soavina) (I. 479), | Madagascar, | 62 | (XVI. D. 7) |
| Isotry (I. 479), | Madagascar, | 62 | (XVI. D. 7*) |
| Ispahan (I. 479), | Persia, | 72 | (XXIII. D. 4) |
| Itafamasi, | Zululand, Africa, | 1 | (IV. K. 8) |
| Italangina, | Madagascar, | 62 | (XVI. E. 8) |
| Itoomoorl, | Amboina, E. Ind., | 155 | (XVIII. M. 9) |
| Iwakuni, | Japan, | 15 | (XV. E. 6) |
| Iwami, | Japan, | 72 | (XV. D. 5*) |
| Jabalpur (Jubbulpore) (I. 480), | Cent. Provs., Ind., | 13, 72, 81 | (VII. A. 6) |
| Jacmel, | Haiti, W. Indies, | 77 | (XXVI. G. 3) |
| Jacobshavn, | Greenland, | 115 | |
| Jaffa (I. 480), | Syria, | 72,511 | (XXV. F. 9) |
| Jaffna (I. 481), | Ceylon, India, | 1, 72, 81 | (VII. J. 10) |
| Jagurapad, | India, | 85 | (VII. B. 12*) |
| Jaipur (see Jeypore) | | | |
| Jalandhar(I.481), | Punjab, India, | 24 | (XXII. F. 5) |
| Jalna (I. 481), | Deccan, India, | 103 | (VIII. H. 11) |
| Japara, | Java, | 157 | (XVIII G. 10) |
| Jarez, | Mexico, | 24 | (XX. E. 4) |
| Jaunpur, | N. W. Provinces, India, | 72 | (VII. C. 3) |
| Jawalli (El Jawily) (I. 355), | Egypt, | 26 | (II. E. 3) |
| Jehlam (Jhelum) (I. 503), | Punjab, India, | 26 | (XXII. D. 4) |
| Jellasore, | Bengal, India, | 4 | (VII. G. 7) |
| Jema Sahridsch (see Djemma), | Tunis, Africa, | 67 | (VI. G. 1) |
| Jérémie (L. 503), | Haiti, W. Indies, | 20 | (XXVI. F. 3) |
| Jericho (I. 503), | S. African Rep. (Transvaal),Afr., | 149 | (IV. I. 6) |
| Jericho (I. 503), | Jamaica, W. Ind., | 77 | (XXVI. J. 1) |
| Jerusalem (I.503), | Syria, | 72,148,511,542 | (XXV. G. 10) |
| Jessore (I. 505), | Bengal, India, | 77 | (VII. L. 6) |
| Jeypore (Jaipur) (I. 481), | Rajputana, India, | 104 | (VII. C. 10) |
| Jhansi (I. 515), | N. W. Provinces, India, | 24 | (VIII. J. 5) |
| Jhelum (see Jehlam) | | | |
| Jiminez (I. 515), | Mexico, | 28 | (XX. G. 3*) |
| Jiwai (I. 515), | Assam, India, | 89 | (XXIV. A.1*) |
| Jodhpur (Marwar) (I. 515), | Rajputana, India, | 104 | (VIII. F. 5) |
| Johannesburg, | Transvaal, Afr., | 144 | (IV. J. 8*) |
| Jokkmokk, | Lapland, | 132 | |
| Juiz de-Fora, | Brazil, | 15 | (IX. H. 8*) |
| Julfa (I. 519), | Persia, | 72 | (XXIII. D. 4) |
| Jundihy, | Brazil, | 28 | (IX. H. 8) |
| Junnar (Junir), | Bombay, India, | 72 | (XVII. A. 1) |
| Kagi (I. 520), | Formosa, China, | 90 | (X. K. 9) |
| Kagoshima(I.520),Japan, | | 13, 72 | (XV. D. 7) |
| Kaitaia, | New Zealand, | 72 | |
| Kaiyuen, | Manchuria,China,104 | | (X. K. 1*) |
| Kajiki, | Japan, | 13 | (XV. D. 7) |
| Kalastry (Kalahasti)(I. 520), | Madras, India, | 149 | (XVII. F. 6*) |
| Kalgan (I. 520), | Chihli, China, | 1 | (X. I. 2) |
| Kalimpong(I.520), | Bhutan, India, | 101 | (VII. H. 2) |
| Kalutara (see Caltura), | Ceylon, India, | 71 | (VII. I. 13) |
| Kamalapuri(I.521),Madras, India, | | 71 | (XVII. E. 5) |
| Kambini (I. 521), | East. Equat. Afr., | 1 | (IV. M. 5*) |
| Ka-Mende, | Sierra Leone, Afr., | 37,141 | (V. C. 9) |
| Kamondongo(Bihe),West Central Africa, | | 1 | (III. E. 9) |
| Kana, | S. African Rep. (Transvaal),Afr., | 149 | (IV. I. 6) |
| Kanagawa (I.521), Japan, | | 13 | (XV. I. 5) |
| Kanazawa (I.521), Japan, | | 24 | (XV. G. 4) |
| Kandy (Candy) (I. 521), | Ceylon, India, | 72,77,81 | (VII. J. 12) |
| Kangwe (I. 521), | Gaboon, Africa, | 24 | (III. B. 4) |
| Kangra (Cangra) (I. 521), | Punjab, India, | 72 | (XXII. F. 5) |
| Kanye, | Bechuana-land, Africa, | 62 | (IV. H. 5) |
| Karachi (Kurrachee) (I. 521), | Bombay, India, | 72 | (VIII. A. 6) |
| Karakal (Karkal), (I. 521), | Madras, India, | 142 | (XVII. B. 6) |
| Karessnando, | Lapland, | 132 | |
| Karnaul (Carnal), | Punjab, India, | 71 | (VIII. I. 1) |

NOTE.—The first figures indicate the vol. and page of the Encyclopædia; the third column corresponds to the numbers in Appendix C; the last column shows number and section of Map.

Kars (I. 523), Caucasus, Russia, 1 (XXV. K. 2)
Karur (I. 523), Madras, India, 81 (XVII. E. 9)
Katka, Russia, 131
Kavala I. (I. 523), Lake Tanganyika, Africa, 62 (III. I. 6)
Kawakawa(1.523), New Zealand, 72
Kaylug-chau (Kia-ying) (I. 523), China, 142 (X. H. 9*)
Kediri, Java, East Indies, 155 (XVIII. H.11)
Kedoeng-pendjalin, Java, E. Indies, 157 (XVIII. H. 11*)
Keetmanshoop, Great Namaqua-land, Africa, 145 (IV. D. 7)
Kelakarai (I. 521), Madras, India, 71 (XVII. E.10*)
Keppel I. (I. 524), Falkland Islands, 73 (IX. F. 12*)
Kerepunu, New Guinea, 62 (XVIII. F. 3*)
Kessab, Asia Minor, 72 (XXV. G. 5*)
Keti (I. 524), Madras, India, 142 (XVII. D. 8*)
Khalatlolu (I.524), S. African Rep. (Transvaal), Afr., 144 (IV. J. 5)
Khamierberg, Little Namaqua-land, S. Africa, (IV. D. 8)
Khandwa (I. 524), Bengal, India, 13
Kherwan (I.525), Cent. Provs., Ind., 72 (VIII. F. 7)
Khitshung, Kwangtung, China,142 (X. I. 10)
Khodsawphrah, Assam, India, 89 (XXIV. A. 7*)
Khulna (Koolna, Culna) (I. 525), Bengal, India, 72 (VII. I. 6)
Khurda, Bengal, India, 78 (VII. F. 9)
Kilanjani, Madras, India, 71 (XVII. E.10*)
Kimberly (I. 525), Orange Free State, Africa, 71,144 (IV. G. 8)
Kinchau (Jin-jou, Manchuria, Chin-chau) (I.526), China, 109 (X. K. 1)
Kincolith, British Columbia, Canada, 72 (XIV. D. 5)
Kingston (I. 527), Jamaica, W. Ind., 77, 82, 104 (XXVI. K. 1)
King William's Town (I. 527), Cape Colony (Kaffraria), Africa, 62, 71, 90 (IV. I. 10)
Kin-hwa (I. 527), China, 3, 65 (X. K. 7)
Kioto (Kyoto) (I. 538), Japan, 1 (XV. G. 5)
Kipo Hill, Niger, Africa, 72 (V. J. 8)
Kirin, Manchuria, China, 109 (X. K. 1*)
Kischineff, Russia, 511
Kishengurh, Rajputana, India, 104 (VIII. G. 4)
Kisulutini, East, Equat. Afr., 72 (III. M. 5)
Kitwanga, British Columbia, Canada, 72 (XIV. D. 5*)
Kiu-chau (I. 528), China, 65 (X. J. 7)
Kiu-kiang (I. 528), China, 13, 20, 65 (X. I. 7)
Kiungani (I. 528), Zanzibar, Africa, 74 (III. M. 6)
Kiungchow(I.528),Hainan, China, 13 (X. G. 11)
Kjibi (I. 529), Gold Coast, Afr., 142 (V. G. 9)
Kladno, Bohemia, Austria, 81
Klaushavn, Greenland, 115
Klerksdorp(I.529),Transvaal, Africa, 81 (IV. G. 7*)
Knapp's Hope, Kaffraria, Africa, 62 (IV. I. 10*)
Kneisna, Cape Colony, Afr., 71 (IV. G. 11)
Kobe (I. 529), Japan, 1.3, 15, 71 (XV. F. 5)
Kochi (I. 529), Japan, 28 (XV. E. 6)
Kochannes, Asia, Minor, 75 (XXV. L. 5)
Kofu, Japan, 50 (XV. H. 5)
Kohima (I. 529), Assam, India, 3 (XXIV. A. 2)
Kolhapur (I. 529), Bombay, India, 24, 71 (XVII. B. 3)
Komefembooai, Celebes, E. Indies, 155 (XVIII. L. 7)
Kommagas(I.530),Little Namaqua, Africa, 145 (IV. C. 8)
Konigsburg, Natal, Africa, 144 (IV. J. 7)
Konigsburg, Germany, 144, 511, 512
Kopay, Ceylon, India, 72 (VII. I. 10*)
Koskstad (I. 529), Natal, Africa, 71 (IV. J. 8*)
Kotagiri (I. 535), Madras, India, 142 (XVII. D. 8)
Kotahena, Ceylon, India, 71 (VII. I. 13*)
Kotgur (I. 535), Himalayas, India, 72 (XXII. G. 6)
Krabschitz, Austria, 1
Krian, Borneo, E. Indies, 72 (XVIII. H. 5*)
Krishnagar(I.537),Bengal, India, 72 (VII. H. 6)
Kronstadt, Austria, 131
Kroondal, Transvaal, Africa, 149 (IV. K. 7*)
Kucheng (I. 537), China, 13, 72 (X. J. 8)
Kuching (I. 537), Borneo, E. Indies, 71 (XVIII. H.5*)
Kuhwu, North China, 65 (X. H. 3*)
Kumamoto(I.537),Japan, 1, 13, 72 (XV. D. 5)
Kumagaye, Japan, 13 (XV. I. 5)
Kummamett (Kam- Nizam's Dom., amet) (I. 537), India, 72 (XVII. F. 2)
Kunnankulam (I. 537), Madras, India, 72 (XVII. D.10*)
Kundapur (Condapore), Madras, India, 142 (XVII. B. 6)
Kurreem-Nuggar (I. 537), Haidarabad, Ind., 81 (XVII. E. 3*)
Kurnul (Kurnool) (I. 537), Madras, India, 3 (XVII. E. 4)

Kuroishi, Japan, 13 (XV. I. 2*)
Kuruman (I. 537), Bechuanaland, Africa, 62 (IV. F. 7)
Kusaie (I. 537), Caroline Group, Melanesia, 1 (XIX. I. 5)
Kwalakapnas, Borneo, E. Indies, 145 (XVIII. II. 8)
Kwa (Kwa-Ma- Victoria Nyanza, kolo ?), Africa, 72 (III. K 5)
Kwangchi (I.538), Central China, 81 (X. H. 6*)
Kwei-hwa-cheng (I. 538), China, 65 (X. H. 3*)
Kwei-yang (I.538), China, 65 (X. F. 8)
Kyelang (I. 538), Little Tibet, 141 (XXII. F. 1*)
Kyoto (Kioto) (I. 538), Japan, 1 (XV. G. 5)
La Barca, Mexico, 1 (XX. D. 2*)
Lac Seul, Rupertsland, Canada, 72 (XIV. G. 6*)
Ladysmith(I.540),Cape Colony, Afr., 144 (IV. E. 10*)
Ladysmith(I.540), Natal, Africa, 144 (IV. J. 7)
La Fère, France, 3
Lagos (I. 540), Dahomey, Africa, 5, 72, 81 (V. I 9)
Lagu Boti, Sumatra, E. Ind., 145 (XVIII. )
Lahaina (Lahain-aluna), Hawaii Islands, 71 (XII. G. 3)
Lahore (I. 540), Punjab, India, 13, 24, 72 (XXII. D. 5)
Laingsburg (I. 540), Cape Colony, Afr., 144 (IV. F. 11*)
Lakawn (Lagong) (I. 540), Siam, 24 (XXIV. C. 5)
Lakemba (I. 540), Tonga Isl., Pac., 81 (XXI. A. 9)
Lake Tanganyika, East Cent. Africa, 62 (III. L. 5)
Lanchau (I. 540), China, 13, 65 (X. E. 4)
Langowan, Celebes, E. Ind., (XVIII. L. 7)
Laohokeo (I. 541), China, (X. H. 6*)
Lao-ling (I. 541), China, 85 (X. I. 3*)
Lapptrask, Lapland, 132
Larangeiras(I.541),Brazil, 24 (IX. I. 5*)
Laredo, Texas, U. S. A., 15 (XX. F. 2)
Latakia (I. 541), Syria, Turkey, 27 (XXV. G. 6)
Leghorn, Italy, 77, 103
Leh (I. 543), Little Tibet, 141 (XXII. G. 3)
Leke, Yoruba, Africa, 72 (V. I. 9)
Leliendal (I. 543), Surinam, S. Am., 141 (IX. J. 2)
Lemberg (I. 544), Austria, 511, 512
Leogane (I. 544), Haiti, W. Indies, 20 (XXVI. G. 3*)
Leon, Mexico, 15 (XX. F. 4)
Leone, Tutuila, Samoan Isl., Pacific, 62 (XXI. L. 2*)
Leopoldville(I.544),Congo, Africa, 3, 22 (III. D. 6)
Leporo (I. 546), Transvaal, Afr., 149 (IV. J. 7*)
Lerdo, Mexico, 24 (XX. E. 3)
Leribe (I. 546), Orange Free State, Africa, 165 (IV. I 8*)
Letti, Moluccas, E. Ind., (XVIII. M. 7)
Levuka, Fiji Islands, Pac., 71 (XIX. L. 10*)
Leydensburg, Transvaal, Afr., 144 (IV. J. 6)
Liang-chau, China, 65 (X. D. 3)
Liaoyang, China, 104 (X. K. 1*)
Lichtenau(I.547), Greenland, 141
Lichtenfels(I.547),Greenland, 141
Lifu (I. 547), Loyalty Islands, Pacific, 62 (XIX. J. 11)
Lilong (I. 547), China, 142 (X. H. 9*)
Linares (I. 547), Mexico, 28 (XX. F. 3)
Linching (I. 547), China, 1 (X. I. 3)
Lindi, East. Equat. Afr., (III. M 8)
Lindley (see Inanda)
Lirang (I. 550), Talaut I., E. Ind., 146 (XVIII. M. 6)
Lititz (I. 550), Jamaica, W. Ind., 141 (XXVI. J. 1*)
Little Popo(I.550), Dahomey, Africa, 81 (V. H. 9)
Lobethal (I. 553), S. African Rep. (Transvaal), Afr., 144 (IV. J. 5)
Lobu Siregar, Sumatra, 145 (XVIII. B.7*)
Lodiana (I. 553), Punjab, India, 24 (XXII. F. 6)
Loftcha (I. 554), Bulgaria, 13 (XI. G. 5)
Loharano, Madagascar, 121 (XVI. D. 7)
Lohardagga, Bengal, India, 146 (VII. E. 6)
Lokoja (I. 554), Niger, Africa, 72 (V. J. 9)
Lomaloma, Fiji Islands, Pac., 81 (XIX. M. 10)
Lombok (I. 554), Java, E. Indies, 160 (XVIII. H.11)
Longhen, China, 142 (X. I. 10)
Lo-Ngwong(I.569),China, 72 (X. K. 8)
Lorenzo Marques, Gasaland, S. Afr., 166 (IV. K. 6)
Lota (I. 569), Chile, 73 (IX. D. 9)
Lotlokani, W. Bechuanaland, Africa, 81 (IV. E. 7*)
Lovedale (I. 569), Cape Colony, Afr., 103 (IV. H. 10)
Lucea (I. 572), Jamaica, W. Ind., 104 (XXVI. I. 1)
Lucknow (I. 572), N. W. Provinces, India, 13, 72, 81 (VII. B. 2)
Lufi-lufi, Samoan Islands, Pacific, 81 (XXI. K. 2*)
Lugan (I. 572), China, 65 (X. H. 4)
Lukanor (I. 572), Mortlock Isl.,Pac., 169 (XIX. G. 5)

NOTE.—The first figures indicate the vol. and page of the Encyclopedia; the third column corresponds to the numbers in Appendix C; the last column shows number and section of Map.

| | | | |
|---|---|---|---|
| Lukolela (I. 572), | Congo, Africa, | 77 | (III. D. 4) |
| Lukunga (I. 572), | Congo, Africa, | 3, 77 | (III. C. 6) |
| Lundu (I. 572), | Borneo, E. Ind., | 71 | (XVIII. F. 7) |
| Luxor (I. 572), | Egypt, | 26 | (II. F. 4) |
| Maboulela (II. 1), | Orange Free State, Africa, | 165 | (IV. I. 8) |
| Mabang (II. 1), | Sierra Leone, Afr., | 81 | (V. G. 1*) |
| Macarthy Island (II. 1), | Senegambia, Afr., | 81 | (V. B. 6*) |
| Macao (II. 1), | China, | 24 | (X. H. 10) |
| Maceio (II. 1), | Brazil, | 5, 28 | (IX. J. 5) |
| MacFarlan (II. 1), | Kaffraria, Africa, | 103 | (IV. H. 9*) |
| Macleag (II. 3), | South Australia, | 149 | |
| MacMillanpatna (II. 3), | India, | 78 | (VII. F. 8*) |
| Madampitiya (II. 18), | Ceylon, India, | 81 | (VII. I. 12) |
| Madanapalli (II.18), | Madras, India, | 25 | (XVII. F. 5*) |
| Madhepur (II. 19), | Bengal, India, | 81 | (VII. F. 5) |
| Madjalengka (II. 19), | Java, | 159 | (XVIII. E. 10) |
| Madras (II. 19), | Madras, India, | 3,13,62,71,79,81,101, 103, 143 | (XVII. F. 7) |
| Madrid, | Spain, | 81 | |
| Madura (II. 23), | Madras, India, 1, 126, 143 | | (XVII. E. 9) |
| Madurantakam (II. 24), | India, | 81 | (VII. F. 7*) |
| Mafeking (II. 24), | British Bechuanaland, Africa, | 81 | (IV. B. 7*) |
| Mafubé (II. 24), | Orange Free State, Africa, | 165 | (IV. I. 7*) |
| Magalle (II. 24), | Ceylon, India, | 81 | (VII. I. 13) |
| Magdala (II. 24), | Central America, | 141 | (XXVI. C. 5) |
| Magdala (II. 24), | Griqualand, South Africa, | | (IV. G. 8*) |
| Magila (II. 24), | East Equat. Afr., | 74 | (III. M. 6) |
| Magomero (II.24), | East Equat. Afr., | 74 | (III. L. 10) |
| Mahabeleshwar (II. 24), | Bombay, India, | 1 | (XVII. A. 2) |
| Mahaena (II. 24), | Tahiti Isl., Pac., | 165 | (XXI. G. 9) |
| Mahanad (II. 25), | Bengal, India, | 103 | (VII. H. 6*) |
| Mahanaim (II.25), | Transvaal, Africa, | 149 | (IV. J 8*) |
| Mahanoro (II.25), | Madagascar, | 71 | (XVI. E. 7) |
| Mahé (II. 25), | Seychelles, | 72 | |
| Mahraoli (II. 25), | Punjab, India, | 71 | (VIII. I. 2*) |
| Mai (II. 25), | New Hebrides, Melanesia, | 170 | (XIX. J. 10) |
| Maimansingh (see Mymensing; see Nasirabad) (II. 159), | | 77,104 | (VII. I. 4) |
| Main (II. 25), | Kaffraria, Africa, | 103 | (IV. I. 10) |
| Maiana (II. 25), | Gilbert Isl., Pac., | 169 | (XIX. K. 6) |
| Maiwo (II. 25), | New Hebrides, Pacific, | 169 | (XIX. J. 9) |
| Majaweram (II. 25), | Madras, India, | 143 | (XVII. F. 8) |
| Makchabeng (II. 25), | Transvaal, Africa, | 144 | (IV. I. 5*) |
| Makewitta (II.25), | Ceylon, India, | 77 | (VII. I. 12*) |
| Makhaleh (II.25), | Egypt, | 26 | (II. E. 3) |
| Makodweni (II.25), | East Cent. Africa, | 1 | (IV. L. 4*) |
| Mala (II. 25), | Lapland, | 132 | |
| Malan (II. 26), | E. Kaffraria, Afr., | 104 | (IV. I. 10*) |
| Malanha (II. 26), | Solomon Isl., Pac., | 170 | (XIX. H. 7*) |
| Malang (II. 26), | Java, E. Indies, | 155 | (XVIII. G. 11) |
| Malegam (Malegaon) (II. 28), | Bombay, India, | 72 | (VIII. G. 10) |
| Malekula (II. 28), | New Hebrides, Pacific, | 51 | (XIX. J. 10) |
| Malmesbury (II. 28), | Cape Colony, Afr., | 71 | (IV. D. 10) |
| Maloga, | Australia, | 141 | |
| Malokong (II. 28), | Transvaal, Afr., | 144 | (IV. J. 5) |
| Malua (II. 29), | Samoan Islands, Pacific, | 62 | (XXI. K. 2*) |
| Mambo, | Sherbro, Africa, | 37 | (V. C.*9) |
| Mamboia (II. 29), | Nyanza, Africa, | 72 | (III. L. 6) |
| Mamgaia (II. 29), | Hervey Isl., Pac., | 62 | (XXI. E. 10) |
| Mamre (II. 29), | Cape Colony, Afr., | 141 | (IV. D. 10) |
| Mamusa (II. 29), | S. Afr. Rep. (Griqualand), Afr., | 62 | (IV. H. 7) |
| Manaar (II. 29), | Ceylon, India, | 81 | (VII. I. 10*) |
| Manado (II. 29), | Celebes, E. Ind., | | (XVIII. L. 7) |
| Mana Madura (II. 29), | Madras, Ind., | 1 | (XVII. F. 10) |
| Manandaza, | Madagascar, | 121 | (XVI. C. 7) |
| Manargudi (II.29), | Madras, India, | 81 | (XVII. F. 9) |
| Manchentuduvy (II. 29), | Ceylon, India, | 81 | (VII. I. 10*) |
| Mandalay (II. 30), | Burma, India, | 3, 71, 81 | (XXIV. B. 3) |
| Mandapasalai (II. 30), | Madras, India, | 1 | (XVII. E. 10) |
| Mandaur (Mandawar) (II. 31), | N. W. Provinces, India, | 13 | (VIII. J. 2*) |
| Mandla (II. 31), | Cent. Provs., Ind., | 72 | (VIII. L. 8) |
| Mandomai (II.31), | Borneo, | 145 | (XVIII. H. 9) |
| Mandridrano (II. 31), | Madagascar, | 93 | (XVI. E. 4) |
| Manelmodu (II.31), | Madras, India, | 143 | (XVII. F. 8*) |
| Manepy (II. 31), | Ceylon, India, | 1 | (VII. I. 10) |
| Mangaia (Mamgaia) (II. 31), | Hervey Islands, Pacific, | 62 | (XXI. E. 10) |
| Mangalore (II.31), | Madras, India, | 142 | (XVII. B. 7) |
| Manihihi (II. 31), | Pacific, | 62 | (XXI. F. 7) |
| Manikramam (II. 31), | Madras, India, | 143 | (XVII. F. 8) |
| Manisa (II. 31), | Asia Minor, | 1 | (XXV. B. 4) |
| Mannheim, | Germany, | 13 | |
| Mannoh (II. 32), | Sherbro, Africa, | 37 | (V. C. 9*) |
| Mansinam (II. 32), | Manaswari, Pacific, | 160 | (XIX ) |
| Mansura (II. 32), | Egypt, | 26 | (II. E. 1) |
| Manua (II. 32), | Samoan Isl., Pac., | 62 | (XXI M. 2) |
| Mannane (II. 32), | Transvaal, Afr., | 149 | (IV. J. 8) |
| Maoobi, | Celebes, E. Ind., | 145 | (XVIII. L. 7) |
| Manpumulo (Mapumulo) (II. 33), | Natal, Africa, | 1 | (IV. K. 8) |
| Marakei (II. 33), | Gilbert Isl., Pac., | 169 | (XIX. L. 6) |
| Maran (II. 33), | Solomon's Islands, Pacific, | 170 | (XIX. H. 8*) |
| Maranhao (II. 33), | Brazil, | 28 | (IX. I. 4) |
| Marash (II. 33), | Asia Minor, | 1, 36 | (XXV. G. 5) |
| Marbach, | Germany, | 13 | |
| Marburg (II. 33), | Natal, Africa, | 149 | (IV. J. 9) |
| Mardin (II. 34), | Asia Minor, | 1 | (XXV. J. 5) |
| Maré (II. 34), | Loyalty Isl., Pac., | 62 | (XIX. J. 11) |
| Maripastoou (II. 34), | Surinam, S. Am., | 141 | (IX. J. 2) |
| Marshall Islands, (II. 36), | Pacific, | 1 | (XIX. J. 4) |
| Marsovan (II. 36), | Asia Minor, | 1 | (XXV. F. 2) |
| Maruthuvanibadi (II. 38), | Madras, India, | 25 | (XVII. F. 7*) |
| Masasi, | East Africa, | 74,126 | (III. M. 8) |
| Masindrano (II.38), | Madagascar, | 121 | (XVI. E. 8) |
| Massowa (II. 39), | Abyssinia, Africa, | 126 | (II. H. 8) |
| Massett (II. 39), | Queen Charlotte's Island, Canada, | 72 | (XIV. C. 5) |
| Massitissi (II. 39), | Cape Colony, Afr., | 165 | (IV. J. 10*) |
| Masulipatam (II. 39), | Madras, India, | 72 | (VII. B. 13) |
| Matale (II. 39), | Ceylon, India, | 71, 77 | (VII. J. 12) |
| Matamoras (II.39), | Mexico, | 15, 28 | (XX. G. 3) |
| Matara (II. 39), | Ceylon, India, | 71, 81 | (VII. I. 12*) |
| Matara (II. 40), | British Guiana, South America, | | (IX. I. 1*) |
| Matautu (II. 40), | Samoan Isl., Pac., | 62, 81 | (XXI. J. 1*) |
| Matehuala (II.40), | Mexico, | 5 | (XX. ) |
| Matsumoto (II.40), | Japan, | 13 | (XV. G. 4) |
| Matsushiro (II.40), | Japan, | 13 | (XV. H. 4) |
| Matsuyama (II.40), | Japan, | 15 | (XV. E. 6) |
| Matsuye (II. 40), | Japan, | 72 | (XV. E. 5) |
| Mattisudden (II. 40), | Lapland, | 132 | |
| Maubin (II. 41), | Burma, | 3 | (XXIV. B. 5) |
| Maui (II. 41), | Hawaiian Islands, | 169 | (XII. H. 3) |
| Maulmain (Moulmein), | Burma, | 3, 71 | (XXIV. B. 5) |
| Maupiti (II. 41), | Society Isl., Pac., | 62 | (XXI. F. 8) |
| Mauritius Island (II. 41), | So. Indian Ocean, | 72 | |
| Mavelikara (II.41), | Madras, India, | 72 | (XVII. C. 10) |
| Mawphlang (II. 41), | Assam, India, | 89 | (XXIV. A. 1*) |
| Mayaguana (Maraguana?) (II. 41), | Bahamas, W. Ind., | 77 | (XXVI. G. 2)? |
| Mazaffarnagur, | N. W. Provinces, India, | 24 | (VIII. J. 1) |
| Mazatlan (II. 42), | Mexico, | 15 | (XX. D. 3) |
| Mazino, | Nias, East Indies, | 145 | (XVIII. A.7*) |
| Mbau (Mbua) (II. 42), | Fiji Islands, Pac., | 81 | (XIX. L. 10) |
| Mbuiu (II. 42), | Cape Colony, Afr., | 104 | (IV. I. 10) |
| Mbweni (II. 42), | Zanzibar Coast, Africa, | 74 | (III. M. 6) |
| Mc'Kullo (II. 43), | Abyssinia, Afr., | 127 | (II. H. 8) |
| Medak (II. 43), | Cent. Provs., Ind., | 81 | (XVII. E. 2) |
| Medingen (II.57), | Transvaal, Afr., | 144 | (IV. J. 5) |
| Medino, | Mexico, | 15 | (XX. ) |
| Medjuro, | Rabak, Marshall Isl., Polynesia, | 169 | (XIX. J. 4*) |
| Meerut (see Mirat) (II. 58), | N. W. Provinces, India, | 13, 72 | (VIII. I. 2) |
| Meiktila (II. 58), | Burma, | 3 | (XXIV. B. *) |
| Meisei (II. 58), | Tokyo, Japan, | 25 | (XV. J. 5) |
| Megnanapuram (II. 58), | Madras, India, | 72 | (XVII. E. 11) |
| Mela Seithali (II. 62), | Madras, India, | 71 | (XVII. F. 11*) |
| Melbourne, | Australia, | 83, 132 | |

NOTE.—The first figures indicate the vol. and page of the Encyclopedia; the third column corresponds to the numbers in Appendix C; the last column shows number and section of Map.

| | | | |
|---|---|---|---|
| Melkavu, | Cochin, India, | 72 | (XVII. C. 9*) |
| Mellawi (II. 62), | Egypt, | 26 | (II. E. 3) |
| Melnattan (II.62), | Negapatam, Ind., | 81 | (XVII. F. 9*) |
| Melorane (II. 63), | S. African Rep. (Transvaal), Afr., | 149 | (IV. H. 5) |
| Melur, | Madura, India, | 1 | (XVII. E. 9) |
| Memikan (II. 63), | Persia, | 24 | (XXIII. B. 2*) |
| Mendi (II. 63), | Africa, | 37 | (V. C. 9) |
| Mendoza (II. 63), | Argentine Rep., South America, | 13 | (IX. D. 9) |
| Mercara (Merkara) (II. 64), | Madras, India, | 142 | (XVII. C. 7) |
| Mercedes, | Argentine Rep., South America, | 13 | (IX. F. 10*) |
| Mergaredja, | Java, E. Indies, | 157 | (XVIII.F.10*) |
| Mersine, | Asia Minor, | 1, 27 | (XXV. F. 5) |
| Messina, | Sicily, | 13, 81 | |
| Metaremba(II.65), | Ceylon, India, | 81 | (VII. I. 13*) |
| Metrapur, | Bengal, India, | 4 | (VII. F. 7*) |
| Metlakahtla (II. 90), | British Columbia, Canada, | 72 | (XIV. C. 5) |
| Mexico (II. 91), | Mexico, | 13, 15, 24 | (XX. F. 5) |
| Mhow (II. 99), | Cent. Provs., Ind., | 13, 51 | (VIII. H. 8) |
| Midnapur(II.101), | Bengal, India, | 4 | (VII. G. 7) |
| Midyat (II. 101), | East Turkey, | 1 | (XXV. J. 5) |
| Mier (II. 101), | Tamaulipas, Mexico, | 15 | (XX. G. 3*) |
| Milan, | Italy, | 5, 13, 28, 81 | |
| Mili, | Marshall Islands, Pacific, | 169 | (XIX. J. 4*) |
| Millsburg, | Liberia, Africa, | 35 | (V. D. 9) |
| Minas Geraes (II. 104), | Brazil, | 5 | (IX. I. 7*) |
| Minchinpatua (II. 104), | Bengal, India, | 78 | (VII. F. 9*) |
| Minnangoda (II. 104), | Ceylon, India, | 81 | (VII. J. 12*) |
| Mirzapore(II.104), | N. W. Provinces, India, | 62 | (VII. C. 4) |
| Mishima, | Japan, | 25 | (XV. G. 5*) |
| Misozwe, | Africa, | 74 | (III. M. 6) |
| Mitani, | Japan, | 30 | (X. ) |
| Mizpah (II. 110), | Jamaica, W. Ind., | 141 | (XXVI. J. 1*) |
| Mkunazini(II.111), | Zanzibar, Africa, | 74 | (III. M. 6*) |
| Mkusi, | East. Eqnat. Afr., | 74 | (III. M. 6*) |
| Moa, | Moluccas, E. Ind., | | (XVIII.M.7*) |
| Modena, | Italy, | 5, 13 | |
| Modinmolle(see Waterburg)(II.111), | Transvaal, Afr., | 144 | (IV. J. 6) |
| Modjovarno(Modjo-Warno)(II.111), | Java, | 155 | (XVIII.E 10*) |
| Mofuss (II. 112), | Sherbro, Africa, | 37 | (V. C. 9) |
| Mogadore(II.112), | Morocco, Barbary States, | 511 | (VI. C. 3) |
| Mograhat(II.112), | Bengal, India, | 71 | (VII. G. 7*) |
| Mogy Mirim (II. 112), | Brazil, | 28 | (IX. G. 7*) |
| Mokil, | Caroline Isl., Pac., | 169 | (XIX. H. 4) |
| Moknea, | Algiers, Africa, | 165 | (VI. G. 1*) |
| Mohaka, | New Zealand, | 72 | |
| Molepolole(II.125), | Transvaal, Afr., | 62 | (IV. H. 5) |
| Moletse (II. 125), | Transvaal, Afr., | 144 | (IV. H. 5) |
| Molung (II. 126), | Assam, India, | 3 | (XXIV. A. 1) |
| Mombasa(II.126), | Nyassa, Africa, | 72 | (III. M. 5) |
| Mombera, | Nyassa, Africa, | 103 | (III. K. 8) |
| Mombetsu, | Japan, | 23 | (XV. J. 1) |
| Monastir (II. 126), | European Turkey, | 1 | (XII. E. 7) |
| Monclova (II.126), | Mexico, | 15 | (XX. E. 2*) |
| Monghyr (II. 126), | Bengal, India, | 77 | (VII. F. 4) |
| Mongwe (II. 128), | East Cent. Africa, | 1 | (IV. L. 4*) |
| Monrovia (II.128), | Liberia, Africa, | 13, 20, 24 | (V. C. 9) |
| Monte Allegro (II. 128), | Brazil, | 28 | (IX. J. 4*) |
| Monte Christi (II. 128), | San Domingo, West Indies, | 77 | (XXVI. G. 3) |
| Montego Bay (II. 128), | Jamaica, W. Ind., | 104 | (XXVI. J. 1) |
| Montemorelos (II. 128), | Mexico, | 28 | (XX. F. 3) |
| Monterey (II.128), | Mexico, | 15 | (XX. F. 3) |
| Montevideo(II.129), | Uruguay, | 13 | (IX. G. 10) |
| Montgomery (II. 129), | Tobago, W. Ind., | 141 | (XXVI.K. 6*) |
| Montserrat (II. 129), | Leeward Islands, West Indies, | 77 | (XXVI. J. 4) |
| Mooreo, | Society Isl., Pac., | 62 | (XXI. G. 8*) |
| Moose Factory, | Moosonee,Canada, | 72 | (XIV. J. 5) |
| Moosh (II. 129), | Armenia, Turkey, | 1 | (XXV. J. 4) |
| Moosonee, | Manitoba,Canada, | 71 | (XIV. G. 6) |
| Moradabad (II. 129), | N. W. Provinces, India, | 13 | (VIII. J. 2) |
| Moratummulla (II. 129), | Ceylon, | 81 | (VII. I. 12*) |
| Moravian Hill (II. 129), | Cape Colony, Afr., | 141 | (IV. D. 11*) |
| Morelia, | Mexico, | 15 | (XX.) |
| Moresby (Port Moresby) (II. 147), | | | (XVIII. F. 3) |
| Moriah (II. 147), | West Indies, | 141 | (XXVI.K. 6*) |
| Moriaro (II. 147), | Bengal, India, | 146 | (VII. A. 6*) |
| Morija (II. 147), | Cape Colony, Afr., | 165 | (IV. E. 11*) |
| Morioka (II. 147), | Japan, | 3, 13 | (XV. I. 3) |
| Mortlock Islands (II. 148), | Pacific, | 1 | (XIX. G. 5) |
| Mose Island, | Bahamas,W. Ind., | 77 | (XXVI. F. *) |
| Mosetla (II. 149), | Transvaal, Afr., | 149 | (IV. J. 8*) |
| Mossel Bay (II. 149), | Cape Colony, Afr., | 71 | (IV. F. 11) |
| Mossoro, | Brazil, | 28 | (IX. I. 4*) |
| Mostaganem, | Algeria, Africa, | 67 | (VI. F. 2) |
| Mosul (II. 149), | Turkey, | 1 | (XXV. K. 6) |
| Mota (II. 149), | New Hebrides, Pacific, | 51 | (XIX. J. 9) |
| Motomotu, | New Guinea, | 62 | (XVIII. E. 3*) |
| Motupatti (II.149), | Madras, India, | 143 | (XVII. F. 9*) |
| Moukden (II. 149), | China, | 104 | (X. L. 1) |
| Moulmein (Maulmain) (II. 149), | Burma, | 3, 71 | (XXIV. B. 5) |
| Mount Olive (II. 150), | Liberia, Africa, | 13 | (V. D. 9) |
| Mount Olivet, | Jamaica, W. Ind., | 104 | (XXVI. J. 1) |
| MountScott(II.150), | Liberia, Africa, | 13 | (V. E. 10) |
| Mount Tabor (II. 150), | Barbadoes, West Indies, | 141 | (XXVI. K. 5) |
| Mphome (II. 150), | S. African Rep. (Transvaal),Afr., | 144 | (IV. J. 5) |
| Mpwapwa(II.150), | Nyanza, Africa, | 72 | (III. L. 6) |
| Mudalur (II. 150), | Madras, India, | 71 | (XVII. E. 11) |
| Muden (II. 150), | Natal, Africa, | 149 | (IV. K. 8*) |
| Muhlenberg (II. 150), | Liberia, Africa, | 34 | (V. D. 9*) |
| Mukimvika(II.150), | Congo, Africa, | 3, 9 | (III. B. 6) |
| Mulki (II. 150), | Madras, India, | 142 | (XVII. B. 7) |
| Multan (II. 150), | Punjab, India, | 13, 72 | (XXII. D. 5*) |
| Mundakayam (II. 151), | Madras, India, | 72 | (XVII. D 10) |
| Mungeli (II. 151), | Cent. Provs., Ind., | 36 | (VIII. K. 9*) |
| Mun-keu-liang (II. 151), | China, | 3 | (X. J. 9*) |
| Murakami, | Japan, | 25 | (XV. H. 3) |
| Murray I. (II.151), | New Guinea, | 62 | (XVIII. D. 3) |
| Musquiz, | Mexico, | 5, 15 | (XX. F. 2*) |
| Mussoorle(II.155), | N. W. Provinces, India, | 13 | (XXII. G. 6) |
| Mutyalapad (II. 155), | Madras. India, | 71 | (XVII. E. 3*) |
| Muttra (Mattra) (II. 155), | N. W. Provinces, India, | 13, 72, 77 | (VIII. I. 3) |
| Mutwal (II. 155), | Ceylon, | 71 | (VII. I. 12*) |
| Muzaffarnagur (II. 155), | N. W. Provinces, India, | 24 | (VIII. J. 2) |
| Muzaffarpur (II. 155), | Bengal, India, | 13,146 | (VII. F. 3) |
| Myingyan(II.155), | Burma, | 3 | (XXIV. B. 3) |
| Mymensingh(see Nasirabad)(II.155), | Bengal, India, | 77 | (VII. I. 4) |
| Mynpuri (II. 155), | Bengal, India, | 24 | (VII. G. 4*) |
| Mysore (II. 156), | Mysore State, South India, | 81 | (XVII. D. 8) |
| Nablous (II. 157), | Syria, | 72, 77 | (XXV. F. 9) |
| Nagalapuram (II. 157), | Madras, India, | 71 | (XVII. F. 6) |
| Nagasaki, | Japan, | 13, 25, 72 | (XV. C. 6) |
| Nagerkoil(II.157), | Madras, India, | 62 | (XVII. D. 11) |
| Nagore, | Madras, India, | 81 | (XVII. F. 9*) |
| Nagoya (II. 157), | Japan, | 13, 16, 28, 30 | (XV. G. 5) |
| Nagpur (Nagpore) (II. 157), | Cent. Provs, Ind., | 13,103 | (VIII. K. 9) |
| Naidupetta, | Cent. Provs., Ind., | 149 | (VIII.K. 9*) |
| Nain (II. 157), | Labrador, | 141 | (XIV. K. 3) |
| Naini Tal (II. 157), | N. W. Provinces, India, | 13 | (VIII. K. 2) |
| Nakabashi, | Japan, | | (XV. I. 5) |
| Nakamura, | Japan, | 23 | (XV. I. 3*) |
| Nakatsu, | Japan, | 25 | (XV. D. 6*) |
| Nakhaleh, | Egypt, | 26 | (II. E. 3) |
| Nallapalli (Mallapally), | Cochin, India, | 72 | (XVII. D. 10*) |
| Namerik, | Marshall Islands, Pacific, | 169 | (XIX. J. 5) |
| Namkyung (Nanbiung?) (II.158), | China, | | (X. I. 9) |
| Nan-chang(II.158), | China, | 13 | (X. I. 7) |
| Nandial (II. 158), | Madras, India, | 71 | (XVII. F. 5) |
| Nangoor (II. 158), | Madras, India, | 71 | (XVII. F. 8) |
| Nanjangud, | Mysore, India, | 81 | (XVII. D. 8*) |
| Nankang(II.158), | China, | 65 | (X. J. 7) |
| Nanking (II. 158), | China, | 13, 24, 36 | (X. J. 6) |
| Nantai (II. 159), | China, | 1 | (X. J. 8*) |
| Nantziang(II.159), | China, | 20 | (X. K. 6) |
| Naples, | Italy, | 5, 13, 77, 81, 103 | |

NOTE.—The first figures indicate the vol. and page of the Encyclopedia; the third column corresponds to the numbers in Appendix C; the last column shows number and section of Map.

| | | | |
|---|---|---|---|
| Narasaraopet (Nursarava- | | | |
| petta) (II. 159), | Madras, India, | 1, 3, 34 | (XVII. F. 4) |
| Narowal (II. 159), | Punjab, India, | 72 | (XXII. E. 5) |
| Nardupett | Nizam's Dominions, | | |
| (II. 159), | India, | 149 | (XVII. F. 3*) |
| Narsapur, | Madras, India, | 77 | (VII. B. 13) |
| Narsinghpur | | | |
| (II. 159), | Madras, India, | 127 | (VII. E. 9) |
| Nasa (II. 159), | Victoria Nyanza, | | |
| | Africa, | 72 | (III. K. 5) |
| Nasik (II. 159), | Bombay, India, | 72,149 | (VIII. G. 11) |
| Nasirabad (Mymen- | | | |
| singh) (II. 159), | Rajputana, Ind., | 104 | (VIII. G. 4) |
| Nassau (II. 159), | New Providence, | | |
| | West Indies, | 77, 81 | (XXVI. E. 1) |
| Nateta (II. 159), | Victoria Nyanza, | | |
| | Africa, | 72 | (III. K. 4) |
| Navapetta, | Jagurapad, Ind., | 35 | (VII. B. 12*) |
| Navuloa (II. 161), | Fiji Islands, | | |
| | Polynesia, | 81 | (XIX. L. 10*) |
| Nawalapitya, | Ceylon, | 72 | (VII. J. 12*) |
| Nazareth (II. 161), | Syria, | 72,391 | (XXV. F. 9) |
| Nazareth (II. 161), | Madras, India, | 71 | (XVII. E. 11) |
| Nazareth (II. 161), | Transvaal, Afr., | 149 | (IV. J. 7*) |
| Nazareth (II. 161), | Jamaica, W. Ind., | 141 | (XXVI. J. 1*) |
| Neemuch (II.161), | Cent. Provs., Ind., | 51 | (VIII. G. 6) |
| Negapatam | | | |
| (II. 162), | Madras, Ind., | 71, 81, 143 | (XVII. F. 9) |
| Negombo (II.162), | Ceylon, India, | 71, 81 | (VII. I. 12) |
| Nellore (II. 165), | Madras, India, | 3, 103 | (XVII. F. 5) |
| Nellore (II. 165), | Ceylon, India, | 72 | (VII. I. 10) |
| Nembe, | Niger, Africa, | 72 | (V. J. 10*) |
| Nemuro (II. 165), | Japan, | 3 | (XV. K. 1) |
| Nevis (II. 166), | Leeward Islands, | | |
| | West Indies, | 81 | (XXVI. J. 4) |
| New Bethlehem, | Jamaica, W. Ind., | 141 | (XXVI. J. 1*) |
| New Calabar | | | |
| (II. 167), | Niger, Africa, | 72 | (V. J. 10) |
| Newcastle, | Natal, Africa, | 71 | (IV. I. 8*) |
| New Carmel, | Jamaica, W. Ind., | 141 | (XXVI. J. 1) |
| Newchwang | | | |
| (II. 167), | Manchuria, China, | 104, 109 | (X. K. 1) |
| New Eden, | Jamaica, W. Ind., | 141 | (XXVI. J. 1) |
| New Fairfield | | | |
| (II. 167), | Canada, | 141 | (XIV. J. 7) |
| Newfield (II. 168), | Antigua, W. Ind., | 141 | (XXVI. J. 3*) |
| New Fulneck, | Jamaica, W. Ind., | 141 | (XXVI. J. 1*) |
| New Georgia, | Monrovia, Africa, | 13 | (V. D. 9) |
| New Halle (II.168), | Transvaal, Afr., | 144 | (IV. J. 5) |
| New Hanover | | | |
| (II. 168), | Natal, Africa, | 149 | (IV. J. 8*) |
| New Herrnhut, | Greenland, | 141 | (XIV. K. 1*) |
| New Herrnhut | St. Thomas, | | |
| (II. 171), | West Indies, | 141 | (XXVI. I. 3) |
| New Hope, | Jamaica, W. Ind., | 141 | (XXVI. J. 1) |
| New Providence | | | |
| (II. 171), | Bahamas, W. Ind., | 77, 81 | (XXVI. E. 1) |
| New Rotterdam | Surinam, | | |
| (II. 171), | South America, | 141 | (IX. I. 1*) |
| Neyoor (II. 175), | Madras, India, | 62 | (XVII. D. 11) |
| Ng-kang-phu | | | |
| (II. 175), | China, | 77, 90 | (X. H. 9*) |
| Ngombe (II. 175), | Congo, Africa, | 77 | (III. E. 4) |
| Ngu-cheng, | China, | 13 | (X. I. 8*) |
| Ngu-ka, | China, | 13 | (X. I. 8*) |
| Nguna (II. 175), | New Hebrides, | | |
| | Pacific, | 51 | (XIX. J. 11*) |
| Nicobar I. (II.176), | East Indies, | 115 | |
| Nicomedia (II.176), | Asia Minor, | 1 | (XXV. C. 3) |
| Niigata (II. 176), | Japan, | 1, 25 | (XV. H. 4) |
| Ning-hai, | China, | 65 | (X. I. 3*) |
| Ning-hsia (II.176), | China, | 65 | (X. F. 2) |
| Ningkwoh (Ning- | | | |
| kweh) (II. 177), | China, | 65 | (X. J. 6) |
| Ningpo (II. 177), | China, | 3, 24, 65, 72, 82 | (X. K. 6) |
| Ningtaik (II. 177), | China, | 72 | (X. J. 8) |
| Nishinomiya, | Japan, | 15 | (XV. F. 5*) |
| Nishiwo (II. 177), | Japan, | 13 | (XV. G. 5*) |
| Nisky (II. 177), | Virgin Isl., W.Ind., | 141 | (XXVI. I. 3*) |
| Niue (Savage I.), | | | |
| (II. 177), | Tonga Isl., Pac., | 62 | (XXI. C. 9) |
| Niutao | Tokelau Isl., Pac., | 62 | (XXI. B. 7*) |
| Njemo (II. 179), | Java, E. Indies, | 155 | (XVIII. F. 10) |
| Njen-hang-li | | | |
| (II. 179), | China, | 112 | (X. I. 9) |
| Nogales, | Mexico, | 15 | (XX. C. 1*) |
| Nombre de Dios, | Mexico, | 15 | (XX. E. 3*) |
| Nongbah, | Assam, India, | 89 | (XXIV. A. 1*) |
| Nongirri, | Assam, India, | 89 | (XXIV. A. 1*) |
| Nongkroh, | Assam, India, | 89 | (XXIV. A. 1*) |
| Nongkyllem | | | |
| (II. 179), | Assam, India, | 89 | (XXIV. A. 1*) |
| Nongrymai (II 179), | Assam, India, | 89 | (XXIV. A. 1*) |
| Nongsawlia | | | |
| (II. 179), | Assam, India, | 89 | (XXIV. A. 1*) |

| | | | |
|---|---|---|---|
| Nongspung, | Assam, India, | 89 | (XXIV. A. 1*) |
| Nongtalang, | Assam, India, | 89 | (XXIV. A. 1*) |
| Nongtrai, | Assam, India, | 89 | (XXIV. A. 1*) |
| Nongwah (II.179), | Assam, India, | 89 | (XXIV. A. 1*) |
| Nononti (II. 179), | Gilbert Islands, | | |
| | Pacific, | 169 | (XIX. L. 6) |
| Nonpareil (II.179), | British Guiana, | | |
| | South America, | 71 | (IX. I. 1*) |
| Nördlingen, | Germany, | 81 | |
| Norfolk Island | | | |
| (II. 179), | Pacific, | 71, 170 | |
| Nowgong (II. 186), | Assam, India, | 3 | (XXIV. A. 1) |
| Nui, | Tokelau Isl., Pac., | 62 | (XXI. B. 7*) |
| Nukufetu, | Tokelau Isl., Pac., | 62 | (XXI. B. 7*) |
| Nukuiselae, | Tokelau Isl., Pac., | 62 | (XXI. B. 7*) |
| Numadzu (II.187), | Japan, | 50 | (XV. I. 5) |
| Nunes, | New Caledonia, | | |
| | Pacific, | 5 | (XIX. I. 11); |
| Numpaul (II.187), | Bombay, India, | 127 | (XVII. B. 4) |
| Nuremberg, | Bavaria, Germ., | 512 | |
| Nusalant, | Moluccas, E. Ind., | | (XVIII. M. 7*) |
| Nusiloli, | St. Cruz Islands, | | |
| | Pacific, | 170 | (XIX. J. 8*) |
| Nyinaimu, | Cape Palmas Dist., | | |
| | Africa, | 20 | (V. E. 10*) |
| Nyrtiang, | Assam, India, | 89 | (XXIV. A. 1*) |
| Oamaru, | New Zealand, | 85 | |
| Oaxaca (II. 191), | Mexico, | 13 | (XX. G. 5) |
| Obama, | Japan, | 20 | (XV. F. 5) |
| Obotshi, | Niger, Africa, | 72 | (V. J. 9) |
| Odaiputty (II.191), | Madras, India, | 71 | (XVII. F. 7*) |
| Odawara, | Japan, | 13 | (XV. I. 5) |
| Odense, | Denmark, | 13 | |
| Ode-Ondo (II.191), | Yoruba, Africa, | 72 | (V. I. 9) |
| Odonga (II. 191), | Hereroland, Afr., | | (IV. C. 4*) |
| Odumase (II. 191), | Gold Coast, Afr., | 142 | (V. G. 9) |
| Oehringen, | Wurtemberg, | | |
| | Germany, | 13 | |
| Ogbomoshaw | | | |
| (II. 192), | Yoruba, Africa, | 5 | (V. I. 8) |
| Oghonoma, | Niger, W. Africa, | 72 | (V. K. 9*) |
| Oita (II. 192), | Japan, | 15 | (XV. D. 6) |
| Okahandya | Hereroland, | | |
| (II. 192), | W. Africa, | 145 | (IV. C. 4) |
| Okayama (II.192), | Japan, | 1 | (XV. E. 5) |
| Okombahe, | Hereroland, Afr., | 145 | (IV. C. 4*) |
| Okozondye, | Hereroland, Afr., | 145 | (IV. B. 4) |
| Okrika (II. 192), | Niger, Africa, | 72 | (V. J. 10) |
| Oldenburg, | Germany, | 13 | |
| Old-town, | Calabar, Africa, | 104 | (V. K. 9) |
| Omaruru, | Hereroland, Afr., | 145 | (IV. C. 4*) |
| Ombolata (II.192), | Sumatra, E. Ind., | 145 | (XVIII. A. 7) |
| Omburo (II. 192), | Hereroland, Afr., | 145 | (IV. B. 3) |
| Ondonga (Un- | | | |
| donga), | Ovambo, Africa, | 138 | (III. D. 10) |
| Ongole (II. 192), | Madras, India, | 3 | (VII. A. 13) |
| Oniop, | Mortlock I., Pac., | 169 | (XIX. G. 5*) |
| Onitsha (II. 192), | Niger, W. Africa, | 72 | (V. J. 9) |
| Onoatoa, | Gilbert Isl., Pac., | 62 | (XIX. L. 7) |
| Onomabo, | Gold Coast, | | |
| | West Africa, | 81 | (V. G. 9*) |
| Oodeypore (II.193), | Rajputana, Ind., | 104 | (VIII. F. 6) |
| Oodoopitty | | | |
| (II. 193), | Ceylon, | 1 | (VII. I. 10) |
| Oodooville | | | |
| (II. 193), | Ceylon, | 1 | (VII. I. 10*) |
| Oorfa, | Central Turkey, | 1 | (XXV. L. 5) |
| Ooshooia (II. 193), | Terra-del-Fuego, | | |
| | South America, | 73 | (IX. F. 13*) |
| Ootacamund (Uta- | | | |
| camund) (II.193), | Madras, India, | 72 | (XVII. D. 8) |
| Opa, | New Hebrides, | | |
| | Pacific, | 170 | (XIX. J. 10*) |
| Opotiki, | New Zealand, | 72 | |
| Opunake, | New Zealand, | 149 | |
| Orattur, | Madras, India, | 25 | (XVII. F. 7*) |
| Orchanie, | Bulgaria, | 13 | (XI. G. 5) |
| Orealla, | British Guiana, | | |
| | South America, | 71 | (IX. I. 2) |
| Orebro, | Sweden, | 13 | |
| Oregrund, | Sweden, | 13 | |
| Orizaba, | Mexico, | 13, 15 | (XX. G. 5) |
| Oroomiah (Urmia) | | | |
| (II. 203), | Persia, | 24 | (XXIII. B. 2) |
| Oruru, | New Zealand, | 72 | |
| Osaka (II. 203), | Japan, | 1, 15, 20, 24, 90, 72 | (XV. G. 5) |
| Oskarsburg, | Natal, Africa, | 126 | (IV. J. 8*) |
| Oskarshamn, | Sweden, | 13 | |
| Osomare, | Upper Niger, Afr., | 72 | (V. J. 9) |
| Ota, | Yoruba, Africa, | 72 | (V. I. 9) |
| Otaki (II. 204), | New Zealand, | 72 | |
| Otaru (II. 204), | Japan, | 13 | (XV. I. 2) |
| Otterbein, | Sherbro District, | | |
| | Africa, | 37 | (V. H. 1*) |
| Ottmarsheim, | Germany, | 13 | |

NOTE.—The first figures indicate the vol. and page of the Encyclopedia; the third column corresponds to the numbers in Appendix C; the last column shows number and section of Map.

| Station | Location | Enc. | Map |
|---|---|---|---|
| Otyikango, | Hereroland, Afr., | 145 | (IV. D. 3) |
| Otyimbengue (Otyi-moingue)(II.204), | Hereroland, Afr., | 145 | (IV. C. 4) |
| Otyizeva, | Hereroland, Afr., | 145 | (IV. D. 4) |
| Otyosazu (II.204), | Hereroland, Afr., | 145 | (IV. D. 3) |
| Oua (II. 204), | Ponape, Pacific, | 169 | (XIX. H. 4) |
| Oudtshoorn (II. 204), | Cape Colony, Afr., | 71 | (IV. F. 10) |
| Outing, | Basutoland (Orange Free State), S. Afr., | 165 | (IV. H. 9) |
| Owalou, | Fiji Islands, Pac., | 81 | (XIX. L. 10) |
| Oxford, | New Zealand, | 82 | |
| Oye, | Asaba, Upper Niger, Africa, | 72 | (V. J. 9*) |
| Oyo, | Yoruba, W. Afr., | 3, 72 | (V. I. 8) |
| Paarl, | Cape Colony, Afr., | 72 | (IV. D. 10*) |
| Pabalong, | Kaffraria, Africa, | 165 | (IV. J. 9) |
| Pachamba, | Bengal, India, | 103 | (VII. F. 5*) |
| Pachuca, | Mexico, | 13 | (XX. F. 4) |
| Padang (II. 205), | Sumatra, E. Ind., | 145 | (XVIII. B. 8) |
| Padre Polli(II.205), | Madras, India. | 78 | (VII. E. 10) |
| Pakenten, | Sumatra, E. Ind., | 147 | (XVIII. B. 7*) |
| Pakhoi (II. 205), | China, | 72 | (X. G. 10) |
| Pakur, | Bengal, India, | 13 | (VII. G. 5) |
| Palaballa (II.205), | Congo, Africa, | 3 | (III C. 6) |
| Palamainair, | Madras, India, | 25 | (XVII. F. 7*) |
| Palamcotta (II. 205), | Madras, India, | 72 | (XVII E. 11*) |
| Palani (Palni). | Madras. India, | 1 | (XVII. E. 9) |
| Palghat (II. 205), | Madras, India, | 142 | (XVII. D. 9) |
| Palli, | Sherbro. Africa, | 37 | (V. C. 9*) |
| Palmur(Palmoor) (II. 206), | N. W. Provinces, India, | 3 | (XVII. E. 3) |
| Pamban (II. 206), | Madras, India, | 71 | (XVII. E.10*) |
| Panagurishte, | Bulgaria, | 1 | (XI. G. 6) |
| Panapur, | N. W. Provinces, India, | 13 | (VIII. K. 3*) |
| Panchgani, | Bombay. India, | 1 | (XVII. A. 2) |
| Pandhapur, | Bombay, India, | 71 | (XVII. B. 2) |
| Panditeripo (II. 206), | Ceylon, | 1 | (VII. I. 10) |
| Pangaloan(II.206), | Sumatra, E. Ind., | 145 | (XVIII. B. 7) |
| Pang chuang (II. 206), | China, | 1 | (X. I. 3*) |
| Pang-koh (II.206), | Borneo, E. Indies, | 145 | (XVIII. G. 9) |
| Panhala (II. 206), | Bombay, India, | 24 | (XVII. B. 3) |
| Panneivilei(II.206), | Madras, India, | 72 | (XVII. E.10*) |
| Pannikulam (II. 206), | Madras, India, | 72 | (XVII. E. 16) |
| Pantjornapitu (II. 206), | Sumatra, E. Ind., | 145 | (XVIII. B. 7) |
| Pantura, | Ceylon, | | (VII. I. 13) |
| Panuco, | Mexico, | 29 | (XX. G. 4) |
| Paoning (II. 206), | China, | 65 | (X. F. 6) |
| Paori, | N. W. Provinces, India, | 13 | (VIII. K. 1) |
| Pao-teo, | China, | 65 | (X. G. 3) |
| Pao-ting-fu(II.206), | China, | 1 | (X. I. 3) |
| Papiti (II. 205), | Tahiti, Society I., | 165 | (XXI. G. 9) |
| Para, | Brazil, | 13 | (IX. H. 4) |
| Paramakudi, | Madras, India, | 71 | (XVII. F. 7*) |
| Paramaribo, | Surinam, S. Am., | 141 | (IX. J. 2) |
| Pareychaley, | Madras, India, | 62 | (XVII. D. 11) |
| Paris, | France, | 3, 36, 81. 511 | |
| Parral (II. 209), | Mexico, | 1 | (XX. D. 2) |
| Parras (II. 209), | Mexico, | 5 | (XX. E. 3) |
| Pasrur, | Punjab, India, | 26 | (XXII. E. 5) |
| Pasumalai(II.210), | Madras, India, | 1 | (XVII. F. 6) |
| Patagones(II.210), | Argentine Rep., | 73 | (IX. F. 11) |
| Pathankot, | Punjab, India, | 26 | (XXII. F. 5*) |
| Patna (II. 210), | Bengal, India, | 77 | (VII. E. 4) |
| Patos, | Mexico, | 5 | (XX. E. 3) |
| Patpara, | Cent. Provs., Ind., | 72 | (VIII. K. 9*) |
| Patrasburdsch (II. 210), | Bengal, India, | 146 | (VII. A. 11*) |
| Pattambakam, | Madras, India, | 115 | (XVII. F. 8) |
| Paysandu, | Uruguay, | 73 | (IX. F. 9) |
| Pea Ridge (Pea Radja)(II. 212), | Sumatra, E. Ind., | 145 | (XVIII. A. 7) |
| Peelton, | Kaffraria, Africa, | 62 | (IV. I. 10*) |
| Pegu, | Burma, | 3 | (XXIV. B. 5) |
| Pei-Su-Chu-Fu, | China, | 77 | (X. J. 5*) |
| Pekyi, | Slave Coast, Afr., | 147 | (V. I. 9*) |
| Peking (II. 212), | China, 1, 13, 20, 24, | 62, 71 | (X. I. 2) |
| Pella, | Little Namaqua-land, Africa, | 141 | (IV. E. 8) |
| Pella, | S. African Rep. (Transvaal),Afr., | 149 | (IV. H. 6) |
| Penang I. (II.213), | Malacca Straits, | 71 | (XVIII. B. 5) |
| Penguin (II. 214), | Tasmania, Australia, | 82 | |
| Periakulam, | Madras, India. | 1 | (XVII. E. 9) |
| Perlepe, | European Turkey, | 1 | (XI. E. 7) |
| Pernambuco (II. 217), | Brazil. | 5, 28, 73 | (IX. J. 5) |
| Peshawar (II.226), | Punjab, India, | 72 | (XXII. B. 3) |
| Petchaburee (II. 226), | Siam, | 24 | (XXIV. C. 6) |
| Petekajan, | Java, E. Indies, | 157 | (XVIII. F. 10) |
| Petersburg | Cape Colony (Kaf-fraria), Africa, | 144 | (IV. I. 10) |
| Philippopolis (II. 228), | Bulgaria, | 1 | (XI. G. 6) |
| Phokoane, | Orange Free State, Africa, | 71 | (IV. H. 8*) |
| Pietermaritzburg (II. 228), | Natal, Africa, | 103 | (IV. J. 8) |
| Pinalap (II. 228), | Caroline Islands, Pacific, | 169 | (XIX. H. 5) |
| Pind Dadan Khan, | Punjab, India, | 72 | (XXII. C. 5) |
| Pinerolo, | Italy, | 5 | |
| Pinetown (II 228), | Natal, Africa, | 71 | (IV. J. 8*) |
| Ping Nang, | China, | 72 | (X. J. 8*) |
| Pingyang (II.228), | China, | 65 | (X. H. 4) |
| Pinkol, | Java, East Indies, | 156 | (XVIII. F.10*) |
| Pipli (Piplee) (II. 229), | Bengal, India, | 78 | (VII. F. 9) |
| Piracicabo, | Brazil, | 15 | (IX. H. 8*) |
| Pirara, | British Guiana, South America, | 4 | (IX. F. 2*) |
| Pirrie (II. 229), | Cape Colony (Kaf-fraria), Africa, | 103 | (IV. H. 10) |
| Pitcairn, | Tuamotu, Pacific, | 170 | (XXI. L. 10) |
| Pithau, | Formosa, China, | 90 | (X. K. 9) |
| Pithoragarh (II. 229), | N. W. Provinces, India, | 13 | (VIII. K. 1) |
| Plevna, | Bulgaria, | 13 | (XI. G. 5) |
| Poelo, | Sumatra, E. Ind., | 156 | (XVIII. B. 7) |
| Point Pearee, | South Australia, | 149 | |
| Point Pedro (II. 230), | Ceylon, | 81 | (VII. I. 10*) |
| Poklo (Pak-hoi), | South China, | 62 | (X. G. 10) |
| Polfontein, | Transvaal, Afr., | 81 | (IV. I. 6*) |
| Polonia, | Transvaal, Afr., | 149 | (IV. I. 9*) |
| Ponape (II. 231), | Caroline Isl., Pac., | 1 | (XIX. H. 4) |
| Ponce, | Porto Rico, West Indies, | 69 | (XXVI. I. 3) |
| Pongo Adongo (II. 231), | Guinea, Africa, | 13 | (III. C. 8*) |
| Poo (II. 231), | Little Tibet, | 141 | (XXII. F. 2*) |
| Poona (II. 231), | Bombay, India, | 13, 71, 72, 77, 101, 103 | (XVII. A. 1) |
| Poonamallee (Punamalli), | Madras, India, | 72 | (XVII. F. 7*) |
| Poreiar, | Madras, India, | 143 | (XVII. F. 9) |
| Porto Alegre, | Brazil, | 13 | (IX. G. 9) |
| Port-au-Prince (II. 231), | Haiti, W. Ind., | 14, 20 | (XXVI. G. 3) |
| Port Blair, | Andaman Islands, East Indies, | 71 | |
| Port Darwin, | Australia, | 71 | |
| Port Douglas. | Australia, | 71 | |
| Port Elisabeth, | Cape Colony, Afr. | 62 | (IV. H. 10) |
| Port Lokka (or Lokkoh)(II.232), | Sierra Leone, Africa, | 72 | (V. C. 8) |
| Port Louis(II.232), | Mauritius Island, | 71 | |
| Port Maria. | Jamaica, W. Ind., | 104 | (XXVI. K. 1) |
| Port Moresby (II. 232), | New Guinea, | 62 | (XVIII. F. 3) |
| Port Nolleth, | Cape Colony, Afr., | 71 | (IV. C. 8) |
| Port of Spain (II. 232), | West Trinidad, | 77,104 | (XXVI. K. 6) |
| Porto Novo (II. 232), | Dahomey, Africa, | 104 | (V. I. 9) |
| Porto Rico(II.232). | West Indies, | 20 | (XXVI. I. 3) |
| Port Said. | Egypt, | | (II. E. 1) |
| Potaro River, | British Guiana, South America, | 71 | (IX. F. 3*) |
| Potscheffstroom (II. 232), | S. African Rep., Africa, | 71,144 | (IV. I. 7) |
| Prague (II. 233), | Austria, | 1, 526 | |
| Praslin, | Mauritius, | 71 | |
| Pretoria (II. 258), | S. African Rep. (Transvaal),Afr., | 71, 81, 144 | (IV. I. 6) |
| Prince Albert, | Canada, | 51, 72 | |
| Princestown (II. 259), | Trinidad, W. Ind., | 51 | (XXVI. K. 6*) |
| Probbolingo (II. 259), | Java, E. Indies, | 162 | (XVIII. G. 10) |
| Progresso, | Mexico, | 5 | (XX. I. 4) |
| Prome, | Burma, India, | 3 | (XXIV. A. 4) |
| Pudukattai (Pudu-cotta) (II. 261), | Madras, India, | 71 | (XVII. F. 9) |
| Puebla (II. 261), | Mexico, | 13, 15 | (XX. G. 5) |
| Pueblo Viego, | Mexico, | 29 | (XX. G. 4) |
| Puerta Plata, | San Domingo, West Indies. | 77 | (XXVI. H. 3) |
| Puiel, | Orange Free State, Africa, | 144 | (IV. I. 7*) |
| Punindie, | South Australia, | 149 | |

NOTE.—The first figures indicate the vol. and page of the Encyclopedia; the third column corresponds to the numbers in Appendix C; the last column shows number and section of Map.

Note.—The first figures indicate the vol. and page of the Encyclopedia; the third column corresponds to the numbers in Appendix C; the last column shows number and section of Map.

| | | | | | | | |
|---|---|---|---|---|---|---|---|
| Salt, | Syria, | 72 | (XXV. G. 9) | Shidzuoka(II.328), | Japan, | 50 | (XV. H. 5) |
| Sälta, | Uruguay, | 73 | (IX. F. 9) | Shietfontein, | Cape Colony, Afr., | 145 | (IV. F. 9) |
| Saltillo (II. 302), | Mexico, | 5, 24 | (XX. F. 3) | Shih-chia-tang, | China, | 1 | (X. I. 3*) |
| Salurpetta, | Madras, India, | 150 | (XVII. F. 6) | Shillong (II. 328), | Assam, India, | 89 | (XXIV. A. 2) |
| Samarang(II.308), | Java, E. Indies, | 155 | (XVIII. G. 10) | Shiloh (Silo), | Cape Colony, Afr., | 141 | (IV. I. 8) |
| Sambalpur (Sum- | | | | Shimoga (II. 328), | Mysore, India, | 81 | (XVII. C. 6) |
| bulpore) (II. 308), | Cent. Provs., Ind., | 78 | (VII. E. 8) | Shimonoseki | | | |
| Samokov (II. 309), | Bulgaria, | 1 | (XI. F. 6) | (II. 328), | Japan, | 3 | (XV. D. 6) |
| Sampit, | Borneo, E. Indies, | 145 | (XVIII. G. 9) | Shimosa, | Japan, | 13 | (XV. I. 5) |
| Samsoon (II. 309), | Turkey, | 1 | (XXV. G. 2) | Shinsakai, | Japan, | 25 | (XV. I. 5*) |
| Samulkota | | | | Shin-kwan(II.321), | China, | 81 | (X. H. 9*) |
| (II. 309), | Madras, India, | 35 | (VII. C. 12) | Shirakawa, | Japan, | 13 | (XV. I. 4) |
| San Antonio, | Mexico (Texas), | 15 | (XX. F. 2) | Shitaya, | Japan, | 50 | (XV. I. 5*) |
| San Buenaventura, | Mexico, | 15 | (XX. F. 3) | Shobara, | Japan, | 15 | (XV. D. 5*) |
| Sanda, | Japan, | 1 | (XV. F. 5) | Sholapur (II. 331), | Bombay, India, | 1 | (XVII. C. 2) |
| San Domingo, | Haiti, W. Indies, | 14 | (XXVI. H. 3) | Shouai (II. 331), | Japan, | 36 | (XV. I. 3*) |
| Sandoway(II.310), | Burma, | 3 | (XXIV. A. 4) | Shoshong, | Bechuanaland | | |
| San Fernando | | | | | (Transvaal), Afr., | 62 | (IV. H. 4) |
| (II. 310), | Trinidad, | 51,104 | (XXVI. K. 6) | Shweir, | Syria, | 103 | (XXV. G. 9*) |
| Sangi-Besar, | Sangi Isl., E. Ind., | 146 | (XVIII. L. 6) | Shweygyin(II.331), | Burma, | 3 | (XXIV. B. 5) |
| Sangli (II. 310), | Bombay, India, | 24 | (XVII. C. 3) | Shumla, | Bulgaria, | 13 | (XI. I. 5) |
| Sangor, | Cent. Provs., Ind., | 127 | (VIII. K. 7) | Sialkot(Sealkote), | Punjab, India, | 26,101 | (XXII. E. 5) |
| Sauhoor, | Egypt, | 26 | (II. B. 2*) | Siboga (II. 336), | Sumatra, E. Ind., | 145 | (XVIII. A. 7) |
| San Juan del Rio, | Mexico, | 15 | (XX. E. 3) | Sibsagar (II. 336), | Assam, India, | 3 | (XXIV. A. 1) |
| San Luis Potosi, | Mexico, | 15, 24 | (XX. F. 4) | Sidanabaram, | Madras, India, | 143 | (XVII. F. 8) |
| San Miguel del | | | | Sidon (Saida) | | | |
| Mezquital, | Mexico, | 24 | (XX. E. 3*) | (II. 337), | Syria, | 24 | (XXV. G. 8) |
| San Pedro, | Honduras, Cen- | | | Sigompulan | | | |
| | tral America, | 81 | (XXVI. B. 4*) | (II. 337), | Sumatra, E. Ind., | 145 | (XVIII. B. 7) |
| San Salvador | Bahama Islands, | | | Sigong (Zigon?), | Burma, | 3 | (XXIV. B. 5*) |
| (II. 310), | West Indies, | 71 | (XXVI. F. 2) | Sihchau, | China, | 65 | (X. H. 4) |
| San Salvador | Lower Congo, | | | Sihanaka (II. 337), | Madagascar, | 62 | (XVI. E. 6) |
| (II. 310), | Africa, | 77 | (III. C. 6) | Sijann, | Sangi Isl., E. Ind., | 146 | (XVIII. L. 6) |
| San Sebastian | | | | Silo (Shiloh) | | | |
| (II. 310), | Spain, | 1 | | (II. 337), | Cape Colony, Afr., | 141 | (IV. E. 10*) |
| Santa Barbara | | | | Siloam, | Madras, India, | 115 | (XVII. F. 7*) |
| (II. 311), | Brazil, | 15 | (IX. H. 7*) | Siloé, | Basutoland, Afr., | 165 | (IV. I. 8) |
| Santa Isabel | Fernando Po, | | | Simla (II. 337), | Punjab, India, | 72, 77 | (XXII. G. 6) |
| (II. 311), | West Africa, | 85 | (III. A. 2) | Simorangkir | | | |
| Santander(II.311), | Spain, | 1 | | (II. 337), | Sumatra, E. Ind., | 145 | (XVIII. A. 7) |
| Santa Rosalia, | Mexico, | 28 | | Si-ngan (II. 339), | China, | 65 | (X. G. 5) |
| Santiago (II. 311), | Chili, | 24, 73 | (IX. D. 9) | Singapore(II.339), | Malacca, | 13, 71, 90 | (XXIV. D. 11) |
| Santipur, | Bengal, India, | 4 | (VII. G. 8) | Singhana (II. 339), | Rajputana,N.Ind., | 146 | (VIII. H. 4*) |
| Santos, | Brazil, | 73 | (IX. H. 8) | Sining (II. 339), | China, | 65 | (X. D. 4) |
| San Ui (II. 311), | China, | 24, 81 | (X. H. 10) | Sinnoris (II. 339), | Egypt, | 26 | (II. E. 2) |
| Sao Paulo (II.312), | Brazil, | 15, 24, 73 | (IX. H. 8) | Sinoe (Greenville) | | | |
| Sarawak, | Borneo, E. Ind., | 71 | (XVIII. F. 7) | (II. 339), | Liberia, Africa, | 13, 20, 24 | (V. E 10) |
| Sarepta (II. 312), | Cape Colony, Afr., | 145 | (IV. D. 10) | Sio-ke (II. 339), | China, | 25 | (X. J. 9*) |
| Sarnia, | Canada, | 50, 71 | (XIV. J. 7) | Sipirok (II. 339), | Sumatra, E. Ind., | 145 | (XVIII. B. 7) |
| Saron (II. 313), | Cape Colony, Afr., | 142 | (IV. D. 10) | Sipoholon (II.339), | Sumatra, E. Ind., | 145 | (XVIII. B. 6) |
| Sarou (II. 313), | Transvaal, Afr., | 149 | (IV. I. 9*) | Sipohuttar | | | |
| Satara (II. 313), | Bombay, India, | 1 | (XVII. A. 2) | (II. 340), | Sumatra, E Ind., | 145 | (XVIII. B. 6) |
| Sault St Marie, | Canada, | 71 | (XIV. I. 6) | Sirabe, | Madagascar, | 121 | (XVI. D. 7) |
| Savaii Isl. (II.313), | Samoan Isl., Pac., | 62 | (XXI. J. 1) | Sirampur, | Bengal, India, | 77 | (VII. H. 6) |
| Savas Isl. (Sawu) | | | | Siroucha, | Nizam's Domin- | | |
| (II. 313), | Timor Isl., E. Ind., | 155 | (XVIII. K.11) | | ion, India, | 8 | (VII. A. 10) |
| Sawyerpuram | | | | Sirur, | Bombay, India, | 1 | (XVII. B. 1) |
| (II. 313), | Madras, India, | 71 | (XVII. E. 10) | Sistof (II. 340), | Bulgaria, | 13 | (XI. H. 5) |
| Schemachi(II.314), | Caucasus, Russia, | 131 | | Sitapur (II. 340), | N. W. Provinces, | | |
| Schiali (II. 315), | Madras, India, | 143 | (XVII. F. 8) | | India, | 13 | (VII. A. 2) |
| Schietfontein (Shiet- | | | | Sitka, | Alaska, | 24 | (XIV. C. 4) |
| fontein) (II.315), | Cape Colony, Afr., | 145 | (IV. F. 9) | Sivas (II. 340), | Turkey, | 1, 36 | (XXV. G. 3) |
| Schiffelin (II. 315), | Liberia, Africa, | 24 | (V. D. 9*) | Skarnug, | Malacca, | 71 | (XXIV.D.10*) |
| Sealkote (see Sialkot) | | | | Skein, | Norway, | 77 | |
| Secunderabad | Nizam's Domin- | 3, 13, 71, 81 | | Slevin (see Selvi) | | | |
| (II. 320), | ion, India, | | (XVII. E. 3) | Smithfield | Orange Free State, | | |
| Secundra (II. 320), | N. W. Provinces, | | | (II. 346), | Africa, | 165 | (IV. H. 8) |
| | India, | 72 | (VIII. J. 4) | Smyrna (II. 346), | Turkey, | 1, 36, 511 | (XXV. B. 4) |
| Seir (II. 320), | Persia, | 24 | (XXIII. B. 2*) | Soakanora, | Ternate, E. Ind., | 160 | |
| Selvi (Slevin), | Bulgaria, | 13 | (XI. G. 5) | Soatanana, | Madagascar, | 121 | (XVI. D. 7*) |
| Sendai (Xenday) | | | | Soavina, | Madagascar, | 121 | (XVI. D. 7) |
| (II. 321), | Japan, | 1, 3, 13, 23 | (XV. I. 3) | Soekaboemi, | Java, | 159 | (XVIII. E. 10) |
| Senehoo, | Sierra Leone, Afr.,82 | | (V. H. 1*) | Soemedang, | Java, | 159 | (XVIII. E. 10) |
| Seoni (II. 321), | Cent. Provs., Ind., | 105 | (VIII. K. 9) | Sofia, | Bulgaria, | 1 | (XI. F. 6) |
| Seoul (II. 322), | Korea, | 13, 24 | (XV. B. 4) | Sohagpur (II.350), | Cent. Provs., Ind., | 93 | (VII. B. 6) |
| Serampur(II.323), | Bengal, India, | 77 | (VII. G. 6) | Somerset, East | | | |
| Seychelles Isl. | Mauritius, | | | (II. 351), | Cape Colony, Afr., | 104 | (IV. H. 10) |
| (II. 326), | Indian Ocean, | 71, 72 | | Somerville | E. Griqualand, | | |
| Shaingay, | Sherbro, Africa, | 37 | (V. C. 9) | (II. 351), | Africa, | 103 | (IV. J. 10*) |
| Shajahanpur | N. W. Provinces, | | | Sonapur (II. 351), | Bombay, India, | 71 | (XVII. A. 2*) |
| (II. 326), | India, | 13 | (VIII. K. 3) | Sonder, | Celebes, E. Ind., | | (XVIII. L. 7) |
| Shanghai (II.326), | E. China, 5,6,15,20,24,62,72,104 | | (X. K. 6) | Sonora (II. 351), | Mexico, | 1 | (XX. C. 1) |
| Shangpoong | | | | Soori (Bheer- | | | |
| (II. 327), | Assam, India, | 89 | (XXIV. A. 1*) | bhum), | Bengal, India, | 77 | (VII. G. 5) |
| Shaohing (II.327), | China, | 3, 65, 72 | (X. K. 7*) | Soracaba, | Brazil, | 24 | (IX. H. 8) |
| Shao-tien-tzee | | | | Sorsele, | Lapland, | 131 | |
| (II. 328), | China, | 77 | (X. H. 3*) | South Kona, | Hawaii Isl., Pac., | 71 | (XXI. E. 1*) |
| Shaowu (II. 328), | China, | 1 | (X. J. 8) | Spanishtown, | Jamaica, W. Ind., | 77 | (XXVI. F. 3) |
| Sheik Othman | | | | Springfield, | Jamaica, W. Ind., | 141 | (XXVI. J. 1) |
| (II. 328), | Arabia, | 103 | | Springvale, | Natal, Africa, | 71 | (IV. J. 8*) |
| Sheila (II. 328), | Assam, India, | 89 | (XXIV. A. 1*) | Sriharikota, | Madras, India, | 149 | (XVII. F. 6) |
| Sheppmanusdorp, | Herero, Africa, | 142 | (IV. B. 4) | Srinagar (II. 363), | Ladakh, India, | 72 | (XXII. E. 3) |
| Sherbro I. (II.328), | West Africa, | 37, 72, 81 | (V. C. 9) | Srivillaputur | | | |
| Shiba, | Japan, | 25 | (XV. I. 5) | (II. 363), | Madras, India, | 72 | (XVII. E. 10) |

Note.—The first figures indicate the vol. and page of the Encyclopedia; the third column corresponds to the numbers in Appendix C; the last column shows number and section of Map.

| | | | |
|---|---|---|---|
| Stanley, | Canada, | 72 | (XIV. G. 6) |
| Stanley Pool, | Congo, Africa, | 77 | (III. D. 5) |
| Steinkopff(II.363), | Cape Colony, Afr., | 145 | (IV. D. 8) |
| Stillenbosch (II. 364), | Cape Colony, Afr., | 145 | (IV. D. 11) |
| Stendal (II. 364), | Natal, Africa, | 144 | (IV. J. 8) |
| Stockholm, | Sweden, | 13 | |
| Strasburg, | Germany, | 511 | |
| Stupitz, | Austria, | 1 | |
| Suchau (II. 365), | China, | 5, 15, 24, 28 | (X. H. 4) |
| Sukabumi, | Java, E. Indies, | 155 | (XVIII. E. 11) |
| Sukkerhoppen, | Greenland, | 115 | |
| Sukkur (II. 366), | N. W. Provinces, India, | 72 | (VIII. B. 3) |
| Suhrpetta, | Madras, India, | 149 | (XVII. F. 6) |
| Sumba, | Timor Isl., E. Ind., | 155 | (XVIII. L. 11) |
| Surabaya, | Java, E. Indies, | 155 | (XVIII. G. 10) |
| Surat (II. 369), | Bombay, India, | 109 | (VIII. F. 9) |
| Suri (Soory; Sooree) (II. 369), | Bengal, India, | 77 | (VII. G. 5) |
| Suva, | Fiji Islands, Pac., | 71 | (XIX. L. 10*) |
| Suvisheshapuram (II. 370), | Madras, India, | 72 | (XVII. E. 11) |
| Swatow (II. 370), | China, | 3, 90 | (X. J. 9) |
| Swellendam, | Cape Colony, Afr., | 71 | (IV. E. 10) |
| Sydney, | Australia, | 85 | |
| Taba Mossegu (Thaba Massegu)(II.379), | Africa, | 144 | (IV. H. 8) |
| Table Cape, | New Zealand, | 304 | |
| Tabor, | Bohemia, Austria, | 1 | |
| Tabriz (II. 379), | Persia, | 24 | (XXIII. B. 2) |
| Tagal, | Java, E. Indies, | 162 | (XVIII. F. 10) |
| Tagulandang, | Sangi Isl., E. Ind., | 146 | (XVIII. L. 6) |
| Tahaa, | Society Isl., Pac., | 62 | (XXI. G. 8) |
| Tahiti (II. 380), | Society Isl., Pac., | 165 | (XXI. G. 9) |
| Tahuata, | Marquesas Isl., Pacific, | 169 | (XXI. I. 7) |
| Tai-chau (II. 380), | China, | 65 | (X. J. 7*) |
| Tai-ku (II. 380), | China, | 1 | (X. J. 3) |
| Tai-wan (II. 380), | Formosa, | 90 | (X. K. 10) |
| Tai-yuen (II. 380), | China, | 65, 77 | (X. H. 3) |
| Takaruna, | Bengal, India, | 146 | (VII. A. 11*) |
| Takato, | Japan, | 13 | (XV. H. 4) |
| Takow (II. 380), | Formosa, China, | 90 | (X. K. 9*) |
| Ta-ku-tang (II.380), | China, | 65 | (X. J. 7) |
| Talaguga (II. 380), | Gaboon, Africa, | 24 | (III. B. 4) |
| Talaut Islands, | East Indies, | 156 | (XVIII. M. 6) |
| Ta li (II. 380), | China, | 65 | (X. D. 9) |
| Taligandsch, | Bengal, India, | 71 | (VII. H. 6*) |
| Taljhari (II. 380), | Bengal, India, | 72 | (VII. G. 5) |
| Tallapudi, | Madras, India, | 35 | (VII. B. 12*) |
| Tamana, | Gilbert Isl., Pac., | 62 | (XIX. L. 6) |
| Tamatave (II. 380), | Madagascar, | 62, 71 | (XVI. E. 6) |
| Tameau-lajang (II. 381), | Borneo, E. Indies, | 145 | (XVIII. I. 8) |
| Tampico (II. 381), | Mexico, | 29 | (XX. G. 4) |
| Tanisui (II. 381), | Formosa, China, | 51 | (X. K. 8) |
| Tanna, | New Hebrides, Pacific, | 103 | (XIX. J. 10) |
| Tanawanko, | Celebes, E. Ind., | 155 | (XVIII. L. 7*) |
| Tandur (II. 381), | Madras, India, | 13 | (XVII. E. 3*) |
| Tanjore (II. 382), | Madras, India, | 71 | (XVII. F. 9) |
| Tank, | Punjab, India, | 72 | (XXII. B. 4) |
| Tapitena (II. 387), | Gilbert Isl., Pac., | 169 | (XIX. K. 6) |
| Tapitenam, | Gilbert Isl., Pac., | 169 | (XIX. K. 6*) |
| Taravao, | Tahiti, Society I., | 103 | (XXI. G. 6*) |
| Tarkastad, | Cape Colony (Kaffraria), Africa, | | (IV. H. 10) |
| Tarna, | Lapland, | 132 | |
| Tarsus (II. 387), | Turkey, | 1, 22 | (XXV. F. 5) |
| Tatung (II. 388), | China, | 65 | (X. H. 2) |
| Taung (II. 388), | S. African Rep., Africa, | 62 | (IV. H. 7) |
| Tauranga, | New Zealand, | 72 | |
| Tavoy, | Burma, | 3 | (XXIV. C. 6) |
| Teheran (II. 390), | Persia, | 24 | (XXIII. D. 3) |
| Teh Ngan (II.391), | China, | 81 | (X. H 6) |
| Telang (II. 391), | Borneo, E. Indies, | 145 | (XVIII. H. 8) |
| Tellicherri (Talalschiri) (II.391), | Malabar, India, | 142 | (XVII. C. 8) |
| Telvek Dalam, | Nias, E. Indies, | 143 | (XVIII. A. 7) |
| Tembu, | Kaffraria, Africa, | 81 | (IV. H. 9) |
| Tempoeran, | Java, E. Indies, | 145 | (XVIII.F.10*) |
| Tezpur (II. 392), | Assam, India, | 71 | (XXIV. B. 1*) |
| Thaba-Bossigo (II. 392), | Orange Free State, Africa, | 165 | (IV. I. 8) |
| Thaba-Morena, | Basutoland, Afr., | 165 | (IV. I. 8) |
| Thaba Nchu, | Basutoland, Afr., | 71 | (IV. I. 8*) |
| Thakandrawi, | Tonga Islands, Pacific, | 81 | (XXI. B. 9*) |
| Thana, | Bombay, India, | 103 | (VIII. F. 11) |
| Thatun (II. 392), | Burma, | 3 | (XXIV. B. 5) |
| Thayetmyo (II. 392), | India, | 3, 71 | (XXIV. B. 4) |
| Thlotse Heights (II. 392), | Orange Free State, Africa, | 71 | (IV. I. 8) |
| Thougze (II. 392), | Burma, | 3 | (XXIV. B. 5) |
| Tiberias, Lake (II. 393), | Palestine, | 526 | (XXV. F. 8) |
| Tichi, | China, | 1 | (X. L. 3*) |
| Tieling (II. 394), | Manchuria, China, | 104 | (X. K. 1*) |
| Tientsin (II. 394), | N. China, | 1, 13, 62, 65, 83 | (X. I. 3) |
| Tierra del Fuego (II. 394), | South America, | 73 | (IX. E. 13) |
| Titlis (II. 395), | Caucasus, Russia, | 131 | |
| Tillipally (II. 395), | Ceylon, | 1 | (VII. I. 9) |
| Tinana (II. 395), | Kaffraria, Africa, | 141 | (IV. J. 9*) |
| Tindivanam (II. 395), | Madras, India, | 25 | (XVII. F. 8) |
| Tinnivelli (II.395), | Madras, India, | 72 | (XVII. E. 11) |
| Tippura, | Bengal, India, | 77 | (VII. J. 6) |
| Tirokukowilar, | Madras, India, | 115 | (XVII. E.10*) |
| Tirumangalam, | Madras, India, | 1 | (XVII. E. 10*) |
| Tirupati, | Madras, India, | 149 | (XVII. F. 6) |
| Tirupuvanam, | Madras, India, | 1 | (XVII. E. 10) |
| Tiruvalure(II.396), | Madras, India, | 81 | (XVII. E. 9) |
| Tiruvannanalei, | Madras, India, | 115 | (XVII E.10*) |
| Tiruvella (II. 396), | Madras, India, | 72 | (XVII. D. 10) |
| Tittuvilei, | Madras, India, | 62 | (XVII. C. 10*) |
| Tjandvara, | Java, E. Indies, | 127 | (XVIII.E.10*) |
| Tjandver, | Java, E. Indies, | 159 | (XVIII.E.10*) |
| Tjemee, | Java, E. Indies, | 156 | (XVIII.E.10*) |
| Tobago (II. 395), | Windward Islands, West Indies, | 141 | (XXVI. K. 5) |
| Tobase (II. 396), | Kaffraria, Africa, | 141 | (IV. I. 10*) |
| Tocat (II. 396), | Turkey, | 1, 36 | (XXV. G. 2) |
| Todgarh, | Rajputana, India, | 104 | (VIII. G. 5) |
| Tokelau Isl.(II.396), | Pacific, | 62 | (XXI. B. 7) |
| Tokushima(II.396), | Japan, | 15, 28, 72 | (XV. F. 6) |
| Tokyo (II. 396), | Japan, | 1, 3, 13, 28, 24, 25, 39, 50, 71, 72, 77, 104 | (XV. I. 5) |
| Toledo, | British Honduras, Cent. America, | 81 | (XXVI. B. 4*) |
| Tollingnge(II.397), | Bengal, India, | 71 | (VII. H. 7*) |
| Toluca, | Mexico, | 15 | (XX. F. 5) |
| Tombou, | Celebes, E. Indies, | 155 | (XVIII. L.7*) |
| Tomohou, | Celebes, E. Indies, | 155 | (XVIII. L. 7) |
| Tondano, | Celebes, E. Indies, | 155 | (XVIII. L. 7) |
| Tondo, | Philippines, East Indies, | 155 | (XVIII.) |
| Tonganewa, | Manihihi Islands, Pacific, | 62 | (XXI. F. 7) |
| Tonga Isl. (II. 397), | Pacific, | 81 | (XXI. B. 9) |
| Ton Rohloh, | Sherbro, Africa, | 39 | (V. C. 9*) |
| Tortola, | Windward Islands, West Indies, | 71, 81 | (XXVI. K. 5*) |
| Toucara, | Terneke Island, East Indies, | 180 | |
| Toungkohloh, | Sherbro, Africa, | 37 | (V. C. 9*) |
| Toungoo (Taungngu) (II. 398), | Burma, | 3, 13, 71 | (XXIV. B. 4) |
| Tourr, | Skena River, Canada, | 50 | (XIV. D. 5*) |
| Towara, | Ternate, E. Ind., | 160 | |
| Toyohashi, | Japan, | 13 | (XV. G. 5) |
| Tranquebar (II. 407), | Madras, India, | 71,143 | (XVII. F. 9) |
| Trebizond(II.408), | Turkey, | 1 | (XXV. I. 2) |
| Trevandrum (II. 409), | Travancore, Ind., | 62 | (XVII. D. 11) |
| Trianon, | Haiti, W. Indies, | 20 | (XXVI.G. 3*) |
| Trichinopoli (II. 409), | Madras, India, | 71, 81, 143 | (XVII. E. 9) |
| Trichur (II. 409), | Madras, India, | 72 | (XVII. C. 9*) |
| Trincomalai, | Ceylon, India, | 81 | (VII. J. 11) |
| Trinidad, | West Indies, | 51, 81, 104 | (XXVI. K. 6) |
| Tripati, | Nellore, Madras, India, | 149 | (XVII. F. 6*) |
| Tripatur (II. 409), | Madras, India, | 62 | (XVII. E. 9) |
| Tripoli (II. 409), | Syria, | 24 | (XXV. G. 8) |
| Tsakoma (II. 410), | S. African Rep. (Transvaal), Afr., | 144 | (IV. J. 4) |
| Tsaraindrana, | Madagascar, | 121 | (XVI. D. 7*) |
| Tschoutshun (II. 410), | China, | 142 | (X. I. 9) |
| Tsiafahy, | Madagascar, | 62 | (XVI. D. 7*) |
| Tsin-chan (Tsing-chow-fu?)(II.410), | China, | 65 | (X. J. 4) |
| Tsing-chew-fu (II. 310), | China, | 77 | (X. J. 4) |
| Tsing-kiang-pu (II. 410), | China, | 28 | (X. J. 5) |
| Tsunhua (II. 410), | China, | 13 | (X. I. 2) |
| Tuamotu Isl. (see Paumotu)(II.410), | Pacific, | 62 | (XXI. I. 8) |
| Tulbagh (II. 410), | Cape Colony, Afr., | 145 | (IV. E. 10) |

NOTE.—The first figures indicate the vol. and page of the Encyclopedia; the third column corresponds to the numbers in Appendix C; the last column shows number and section of Map.

| | | | |
|---|---|---|---|
| Tumkur (II. 411), | Madras, India, | 81 | (XVII. D. 6*) |
| Tunapuna(II.411), | Trinidad, W. Ind., | 51 | (XXVI. K.6*) |
| Tundi, | Bengal, India, | 103 | (VII. F. 5*) |
| Tung-chow(II.411), | China, | 1, 5, 24 | (X. K. 3) |
| Tuni (II. 411), | Madras, India, | 52 | (VII. C. 11) |
| Tunis (II. 411), | Africa, | 67,511 | (V. I. 1) |
| Tura (II. 411), | Assam, India, | 3 | (XXIV. A. 2) |
| Tuticorin (II. 426), | Madras, India, | 71 | (XVII. F. 10) |
| Tutuila (II. 426), | Samoan Isl., Pac., | 62 | (XXI. L. 1) |
| Uajima, | Japan, | 15 | (XV. E. 6) |
| Udayagiri(I 427), | Madras, India, | 3 | (XVII. D. 5) |
| Udipi (II. 427), | Madras, India, | 142 | (XVII. B. 6) |
| Ueda (Iida), | Japan, | 25 | (XV. G. 5) |
| Uganda, | Africa, | 72 | (III. J. 4) |
| Uitenhage, | Cape Colony, Afr., | 71 | (IV. H. 10) |
| Ujain, | Cent. Provs., Ind., | 51 | (VIII. H. 8) |
| Ujiji, | Lake Tanganyika, Africa, | 62 | (III. J. 6) |
| Ulawa, | Solomon's Islands, Pacific, | 170 | (XIX. I. 8) |
| Umanak (II. 427), | Greenland, | 141 | (XIV. K. 1*) |
| Umba, | East Equat. Afr., | 74 | (III. M. 6) |
| Umbonambi, | Zululand, Africa, | 126 | (IV. K. 8) |
| Umpumulo, | Kaffraria, Africa, | 121 | (IV. I. 9*) |
| Umsunduzi, | Zululand, Africa, | 1 | (IV. J. 8*) |
| Umtata (II. 427). | Temba-land, South Africa, | 71 | (IV. I. 10*) |
| Umtwalume (II. 427). | Cape Colony, Afr., | 1 | (IV. J. 9*) |
| Umvote (Groutville) (II. 427), | Nat l, Africa, | 1 | (IV. J. 8*) |
| Umzinto, | Natal, Africa. | 71 | (IV. J. 9) |
| Umzumbe(II.427), | Natal, Africa. | 1 | (IV. I. 9*) |
| Underhill, | Congo, Africa, | 77 | (III. E. 5*) |
| Undup (Undop) (II. 427), | Borneo, E. Indies, | 71 | (XVIII. G. 7*) |
| Ungoji, | Natal (Zululand), Africa, | 121 | (IV. K. 8) |
| Unitata (see Umtata) (II. 427), | Africa, | 71 | (IV. I. 10*) |
| Unwana (II. 447), | Old Calabar, Afr., | 104 | (V. K. 9) |
| Uole, | Caroline Isl., Pac., | 4 | (XIX. E. 4) |
| Upernavik, | Greenland, | 115 | (XIV. K. 1*) |
| Upolu (II. 447), | Samoan Isl., Pac., | 62 | (XXI. K. 2) |
| Upper Paarl (Paarl), | Africa, | 71 | (IV. D. 10) |
| Ural, | Russia, | 131 | |
| Urambo (II. 447), | E. Cent. Africa, | 62 | (III. J. 6) |
| Urbanville, | Cape Colony, Afr., | 71 | (IV. D. 10) |
| Usambiro (II.448), | Victoria Nyanza, Africa, | 72 | (III. K. 5) |
| Ushigome, | Japan, | 50 | (XV. I. 5*) |
| Utsunomiya, | Japan, | 13 | (XV. I. 4) |
| Uvea (II. 448), | Loyalty Isl., Pac., | 62 | (XIX. J. 10) |
| Uyui, | Nyanza, Africa, | 72 | (III. K. 6) |
| Vadaku, | Madras, India, | 149 | (XVII. E. 10) |
| Vaitupu, | Tokelau Islands, Pacific, | 62 | (XXI. D. 7*) |
| Vakin Ankaratou, | Madagascar, | 93 | (XIV. D. 7*) |
| Valdesia, | S. African Rep. (Transvaal),Afr., | 166 | (IV. J. 5) |
| Valparaiso(II.448), | Chile, | 13, 24 | (IX. D. 9) |
| Van (II. 448), | Turkey, | 1 | (XXV. K. 4) |
| Varna (II. 450), | Bulgaria, | 13 | (XI. I. 5) |
| Veckoski, | Finland, | 131 | |
| Vediarpuram (II. 450), | Madras, India, | 71 | (XVII. F. 9) |
| Vellore (II. 450), | Madras, India, | 25,101 | (XVII. F. 7) |
| Velpur (II. 450), | Madras, India, | 35 | (VII. C. 12*) |
| Venkatageri, | Madras, India, | 149 | (XVII. E. 7) |
| Venyane (II. 451), | Griqualand, South Africa, | 141 | (IV. G. 8*) |
| Vepery (II. 451), | Madras, India, | 71 | (XVII. E. 8*) |
| Verulam, | Natal, Africa, | 71 | (IV. J. 8) |
| Victoria (II. 451), | Mexico, | 28 | (XX. F. 4) |
| Victoria (II. 451), | Vancouver's Isl., | 50 | (XIV. D. 6) |
| Victoria (Hongkong) (II. 451), | China, | | (X. I. 10) |
| Vienna, | Austria. | 103, 511, 512 | |
| Vilhemina, | Lapland, | 131 | |
| Villupuram (Willupuram) (II. 451), | Madras, India, | 143 | (XVII. F. 8) |
| Vinuconda(II.451), | Madras, India, | 3 | (XVII. F. 4) |
| Vitangi (Wittangi), | Lapland, | 132 | |
| Vizagapatam (II. 452), | Madras, India, | 62 | (VII. D. 12) |
| Vizianagram, | Madras, India, | 62 | (VII. D. 11) |
| Volo, | Greece, | 28 | (XI. F. 9) |
| Waai, | Amboina, E. Ind., | 155 | (XVIII. M. 9) |
| Wadale (II. 452), | Bombay, India, | 1 | (VIII. H. 11) |
| Wadomura, | Japan, | 25 | (XV.) |
| Wageikulam, | Madras, India, | 72 | (XVII. E. 10) |
| Wai, | Bombay, India, | 1 | (VIII. G. 11) |
| Waikokara, | New Zealand, | 149 | |
| Waimate, | New Zealand, | 85 | |
| Wairoa, | New Zealand, | 72 | |
| Waitara, | New Zealand, | 72 | |
| Wakkerstroom (II. 453), | S. African Rep. (Transvaal),Afr., | 71 | (IV. J. 7) |
| Walfisch Bay (II. 453), | Namaqualand, Africa, | 145 | (IV. B. 4) |
| Walmannsthal (II. 453), | S. African Rep. (Transvaal),Afr., | 144 | (IV. J. 6) |
| Wanganui(II.453), | New Zealand, | 72 | |
| Wanikoro, | St. Cruz Islands, Pacific, | 170 | (XIX. J. 8*) |
| Wanua-Lawa, | Banks Islands, Pacific, | 170 | (XIX. J. 9) |
| Warmbad(II.453), | Namaqualand, Africa, | 145 | (IV. D. 8) |
| Warsaw (II. 454), | Poland, | 511, 512 | |
| Wartburg (II.454), | Cape Colony (Kaffraria), Africa, | 144 | (IV. I. 10) |
| Waterburg (Modimolle) (II. 454), | Transvaal, Afr., | 81,144 | (IV. J. 5) |
| Waterloo (II. 454), | Surinam, S. Am., | 141 | (IX. I. 2) |
| Waterloo (II. 454), | Sierra Leone, Afr., | 72, 81 | (V. C. 8) |
| Wathen (II. 454), | Congo River, Afr., | 77 | (III. C. 5*) |
| Wa-ting (II. 454), | China, | 83 | (X. I. 3) |
| Wayentheim, | Transvaal, Afr., | 144, 149 | (IV. I. 7) |
| Wazirabad(II.454), | Punjab, India, | 101 | (XXII. D. 5) |
| Wegbe Ho (see Ho and Ho Wegbe), | Africa, | | (V. H. 9) |
| Weida, | Dahomey, Africa, | 147 | (V. I. 9) |
| Wei-Hien (II.454), | China, | 24 | (X. I. 4) |
| Wei-hui (II. 454), | China, | 51 | (X. I. 4)? |
| Weligama(II.454), | Ceylon, | 77, 81 | (VII. I. 13*) |
| Wellington(II.454), | Sierra Leone,Afr., | 72, 81 | (V. B. 8) |
| Wellington(II.454), | New Zealand, | 72, 82 | |
| Wenchau (II.455), | China, | 82 | (X. K. 7) |
| Westport and Charleston, | New Zealand, | 82 | |
| Wetter, | Moluccas, E. Ind., | | (XVIII. M. 7) |
| Whang Hien (Hwang-hien), | China, | 3 | (X. K. 3) |
| William's River, | Australia, | 71 | |
| Winnebah, | Gold Coast, Afr., | 81 | (V. G. 10) |
| Winterburg, | Cape Colony, Afr., | 71 | (IV. H. 10) |
| Witkliebosch (II. 478), | Cape Colony, Afr., | 141 | (IV. G. 11) |
| Witsiehock, | Orange Free State, Africa, | 81 | (IV. I. 7) |
| Wittewater (II. 478), | Cape Colony, Afr., | 141 | (IV. D. 10) |
| Wiwa, | Fiji Isl., Pacific, | 81 | (XIX. L. 10) |
| Wokka, | Assam, India, | 3 | (XXIV. A. 1) |
| Wonoredyo, | Java, E. Indies, | 156 | (XVIII.) |
| Woodstock (II. 523), | Cape Colony, Afr., | 71 | (IV. D. 10*) |
| Woodstock(II.523), | Punjab, India, | 24 | (XXII. G. 6) |
| Woodville, | New Zealand, | 82 | |
| Worcester(II.523), | Cape Colony, Afr., | 71,145 | (IV. E. 10) |
| Woureli, | Amboina, E. Ind., | 155 | (XVIII. M. 9) |
| Woyeutin (II.524), | S. African Rep. (Transvaal),Afr., | 144 | (IV. J. 7) |
| Wuchang (II.525), | Hupeh, China, | 20, 62, 65, 81 | (X. H. 6) |
| Wuhu (II. 525), | Ngan Hwui, East China, | 13, 20 | (X. J. 6) |
| Wupperthal (II. 525), | Cape Colony, Afr., | 145 | (IV. D. 10) |
| Würtemberg, | Germany, | 13, 512 | |
| Wu-sutch, | China, | 81 | (X. I. 6) |
| Wuting, | China, | 129, 134 | (X. J. 3) |
| Yaba, | Yoruba, Africa, | 81 | (V. I. 9*) |
| Yamagata, | Japan, | 13, 23 | (XV. I. 4) |
| Yamaguchi, | Japan, | | (XV. D. 6) |
| Yambol, | European Turkey, | 1 | (XI. H. 6) |
| Yanagawa, | Japan, | 13 | (XV. D. 6) |
| Yangchow(II.525), | China, | 65 | (X. J. 5) |
| Yanina (Janina), | European Turkey, | | (XI. E. 8) |
| Yap, | Caroline Islands, Pacific, | 169 | (XIX. D. 4) |
| Yatsushiro, | Japan, | 13 | (XV. D. 6) |
| Yeung-kong, | China, | 24 | (X. H. 9*) |
| Yokohama(II 528), | Japan, | 3, 13, 16, 24, 25 | (XV. I. 5) |
| Yokosuka, | Japan, | 3, 25 | (XV. I. 5) |
| Yonezewa(II.529), | Japan, | 13 | (XV. I. 4) |
| York Castle, | Jamaica, W. Ind., | 81 | (XXVI. J. 1*) |
| York, | Canada, | 71 | (XIV. H. 4) |
| Ysabel, | Solomon's Islands, Pacific, | 170 | (XIX. H. 7) |
| Yuh-shau (II.534), | Kiangsi, China, | 85 | (X. J. 7) |
| Yulu, | Mosquito Coast, Honduras, | 141 | (XXVI. C. 5*) |
| Yung-ping(II.534), | China, | 83 | (X. J. 2) |
| Yun-nan-fu, | China, | 65 | (X. D. 9) |

NOTE.—The first figures indicate the vol. and page of the Encyclopedia; the third column corresponds to the numbers in Appendix C; the last column shows number and section of Map.

| | | | |
|---|---|---|---|
| Zacatecas (II. 534), | Mexico, | 5, 24 | (XX. E. 4) |
| Zafarwal (II. 534), | Punjab, India, | 26 | (XXII. E. 5) |
| Zahleh (II. 534), | Syria, | 24 | (XXV. F. 8*) |
| Zaragoza (II. 534), | Spain, | 1 | |
| Zeerust, | S. African Rep., Africa, | 71 | (IV. H. 6) |

| | | | |
|---|---|---|---|
| Zigon (Sigong?), | Burma, India, | 3 | (XXIV. B. 5*) |
| Zoar (II. 536), | Cape Colony, Afr., | 144 | (IV. F. 10) |
| Zoar (II. 536), | Labrador, | 141 | |
| Zoutpansburg (II. 538), | Transvaal, Afr., | 81 | (IV. J. 4) |
| Zundee, | Borneo, E. Ind., | 71 | (XVIII. F. 7) |
| Zuurbraak, | Cape Colony, Afr., | 71 | (IV. D. 10) |

NOTE.—The first figures indicate the vol. and page of the Encyclopedia; the third column corresponds to the numbers in Appendix C; the last column shows number and section of Map.

# APPENDIX E.

## *STATISTICAL TABLES.*

### 1. *SOCIETIES.*

THE preparation of the statistics has been perhaps the most perplexing part of the work of this Encyclopædia. Many times the editor has been upon the point of giving them up. Yet that seemed impossible, and he has done the best he could. If he has failed to fairly represent the work of the societies, he must crave their kindly judgment. When the Encyclopædia was commenced, blanks were sent to every mission station asking for statistics of its work. A large number of answers were received, but the immense majority failed entirely to respond. Then when a comparison was made between these and the published reports of the societies, not a few discrepancies appeared, due chiefly, as was evident, to different dates and methods of statement. The published reports themselves presented difficulties that seemed insuperable. To quote the language of the editor of the "Missionary Herald" (A. B. C. F. M.), in the Almanac for 1891, "Missionary organizations make their statistical reports in a great variety of ways, some of them making no detailed reports at all. For instance, many make no report of the wives of missionaries; some report only ordained men; many count adherents as converts; others make no report of stations occupied; some include in contributions the amount given at mission stations. For these and other reasons no exact summary is possible." Still, aided by the kind replies of the secretaries of the different societies to the questions sent to them, the following tables have been prepared, and are presented as the best that the editor can do under the circumstances.

The tables are arranged in three parts: I. By societies, giving the work in each country. These are derived in almost every case from the published reports. II. By countries, giving the work of the different societies. These are collated from the preceding table. III. A general summary, based chiefly upon blanks filled out in the offices of the societies.

## AMERICA.
### UNITED STATES.

No 1. AMERICAN BOARD OF COMMISSIONERS FOR FOREIGN MISSIONS. YEAR ENDING AUGUST 31ST, 1890.

| MISSIONS. | Stations and Out-stations. | MISSIONARIES. | | | | NATIVE WORKERS. | | | Preaching Places. | Sabbath-school Scholars. | Churches. | Communicants. | Additions. | Schools for Higher Education. | Pupils. | Common Schools. | Pupils. | Native Contributions for all purposes. |
|---|---|---|---|---|---|---|---|---|---|---|---|---|---|---|---|---|---|---|
| | | Ordained. | Lay. | Wives. | Other Women. | Ordained. | Teachers. | Other Helpers. | | | | | | | | | | |
| **AFRICA:** | | | | | | | | | | | | | | | | | | |
| EAST CENTRAL.... | 4 | 2 | .. | 2 | 1 | .... | .... | .... | 2 | 22 | .... | 45 | .... | .... | ..... | 2 | 86 | |
| ZULU.......... | 26 | 11 | .. | 10 | 10 | 1 | 36 | 97 | 81 | 1,480 | 16 | 1,155 | 86 | 4 | 187 | 31 | 1,425 | $1,151 |
| WEST CENTRAL.... | 7 | 7 | 1 | 6 | 3 | ... | .. | 3 | 3 | 45 | 1 | 19 | 2 | ... | ..... | 5 | 103 | 58 |
| **TURKEY:** | | | | | | | | | | | | | | | | | | |
| EUROPEAN.... | 31 | 10 | .. | 9 | 4 | 8 | 19 | 28 | 31 | 1,497 | 9 | 729 | 82 | 4 | 161 | 14 | 395 | 4,533 |
| WESTERN.... | 116 | 24 | 1 | 23 | 27 | 32 | 183 | 66 | 120 | 7,571 | 34 | 3,118 | 275 | 15 | 872 | 141 | 4,953 | 20,337 |
| CENTRAL. ... | 51 | 6 | 1 | 6 | 13 | 17 | 115 | 25 | 57 | 9,500 | 33 | 5,055 | 793 | 13 | 467 | 99 | 4,077 | 7,150 |
| EASTERN.... | 132 | 18 | 1 | 19 | 15 | 29 | 178 | 91 | 135 | 6,982 | 41 | 2,807 | 217 | 22 | 728 | 156 | 6,237 | 11,454 |
| **INDIA:** | | | | | | | | | | | | | | | | | | |
| MARATHA ... | 114 | 13 | 1 | 11 | 8 | 18 | 182 | 77 | 130 | 4,747 | 33 | 2,115 | 192 | 13 | 924 | 110 | 2,050 | 1,755 |
| MADURA. ........ | 271 | 13 | .. | 13 | 8 | 17 | 221 | 210 | 404 | 4,628 | 36 | 3,562 | 254 | 11 | 975 | 144 | 4,435 | 6,192 |
| CEYLON.... | 32 | 4 | .. | 4 | 2 | 13 | 247 | 68 | 37 | 3,160 | 15 | 1,477 | 80 | 5 | 473 | 133 | 8,416 | 4,878 |
| **CHINA:** | | | | | | | | | | | | | | | | | | |
| HONG KONG....... | 4 | 2 | .. | 1 | .. | .. | 6 | 3 | 3 | ...... | .. | 26 | 6 | .. | ..... | 6 | 328 | 896 |
| FOOCHOW.......... | 27 | 7 | 2 | 9 | 4 | 2 | 25 | 23 | 19 | ...... | 16 | 484 | 88 | 4 | 81 | 19 | 334 | 1,081 |
| NORTH CHINA..... | 35 | 18 | 5 | 22 | 12 | 3 | 14 | 35 | 37 | ...... | 7 | 1,042 | 127 | 8 | 146 | 8 | 107 | 267 |
| SHANSI.... | 3 | 6 | 1 | 6 | .... | .. | ..... | 1 | 4 | ...... | 1 | 10 | 2 | 1 | 19 | ... | ...... | 72 |
| **JAPAN:** | | | | | | | | | | | | | | | | | | |
| NORTH JAPAN..... | 82 | 26 | 4 | 26 | 32 | 26 | 43 | 100 | 190 | 6,920 | 61 | 9,146 | 1,615 | 21 | 2,633 | ... | ...... | 50,841 |
| MICRONESIA....... | 52 | 5 | .. | 4 | 10 | 17 | 57 | 12 | 85 | ...... | 51 | 4,475 | 496 | 8 | 182 | ... | ...... | 1,785 |
| **MEXICO:** | | | | | | | | | | | | | | | | | | |
| WESTERN.......... | 7 | 2 | .. | 2 | .. | 1 | ...... | 7 | ... | ...... | 2 | 68 | 18 | 1 | 12 | 2 | ...... | 843 |
| NORTHERN......... | 12 | 5 | .. | 4 | 2 | .. | 7 | 4 | 13 | 415 | 8 | 255 | 74 | 1 | 13 | 6 | 168 | |
| SPAIN.... | 18 | 1 | .. | 1 | 1 | 5 | 18 | 10 | 18 | 556 | 18 | 349 | 55 | 1 | 41 | 13 | ...... | 3,471 |
| AUSTRIA.......... | 32 | 1 | .. | 1 | .. | 3 | 2 | 12 | 33 | ...... | 3 | 364 | 92 | 3 | 99 | ... | ...... | 800 |
| HAWAIIAN ISLANDS.. | 2 | 2 | .. | 2 | .. | ... | ...... | ...... | ...... | ...... | ...... | ...... | ...... | 1 | 14 | ... | ...... | |
| **Total** ...... ... | 1,058 | 183 | 17 | 181 | 152 | 192 | 1,353 | 872 | 1,402 | 47,523 | 387 | 36,256 | 4,554 | 136 | 8,027 | 889 | 33,114 | $117,494 |

| Missions | Stations and Out-stations | Missionaries | | | | Native Workers | | | Preaching Places | Sabbath-school Scholars | Churches | Communicants | Additions | Schools for Higher Education | Pupils | Common Schools | Pupils | Native Contributions for all purposes |
|---|---|---|---|---|---|---|---|---|---|---|---|---|---|---|---|---|---|---|
| | | Ordained | Lay | Wives | Other Women | Ordained | Teachers | Other Helpers | | | | | | | | | | |
| **No. 3. American Baptist Missionary Union. Year ending December 31st, 1889.** | | | | | | | | | | | | | | | | | | |
| INDIA: | | | | | | | | | | | | | | | | | | |
| Burma | 614 | 42 | 93 | | 143 | | 436 | 494 | .... | 3,895 | 520 | 29,689 | 2,039 | .... | .... | 444 | 12,669 | $52,633 |
| Assam | 71 | 11 | 14 | | 7 | | 84 | 69 | .... | 1,441 | 30 | 1,937 | 185 | .... | .... | 87 | 1,900 | 740 |
| Telugus | 648 | 20 | 27 | | 67 | | 520 | 354 | .... | 2,577 | 72 | 33,838 | 3,340 | .... | .... | 460 | 4,934 | 564 |
| CHINA | 67 | 18 | 23 | | 7 | | 25 | 56 | ... | 330 | 17 | 1,535 | 61 | .... | .... | 23 | 325 | 521 |
| JAPAN | 35 | 15 | 26 | | 4 | | 16 | 42 | .... | 605 | 10 | 905 | 158 | .... | .... | 6 | 216 | 311 |
| AFRICA: Congo | 11 | 23 | 16 | | ... | | 6 | 5 | .... | 124 | 5 | 386 | 156 | .... | .... | 10 | 471 | 75 |
| Total | 1,446 | 129 | 199 | | 228 | | 1,087 | 1,020 | .... | 8,972 | 654 | 68,290 | 5,939 | .... | .... | 1030 | 20,515 | $54,844 |
| **No. 4. Free Baptist Foreign Missionary Society. Year ending March 31st, 1890.** | | | | | | | | | | | | | | | | | | |
| INDIA: Bengal | 11 | 9 | 1 | 9 | 6 | 5 | .... | 12 | .... | 2,721 | 11 | 699 | 55 | 1 | 28 | 104 | 3,591 | Rs. a. p. 788 9 3 / $394.27 |
| **No. 5. Southern Baptist Convention. Year ending April 30th, 1890.** | | | | | | | | | | | | | | | | | | |
| CHINA | 41 | 13 | | 12 | 8 | 11 | .... | 23 | ... | ... | 13 | 806 | 83 | .... | .... | 18 | 308 | $728.34 |
| JAPAN | | 2 | | 2 | | ... | | | ... | ... | | | | | | | | |
| AFRICA | 5 | 5 | | 4 | 1 | ... | ... | 7 | ... | ... | 4 | 58 | 1 | .... | .... | 3 | 150 | 24.00 |
| BRAZIL | 13 | 4 | | 4 | 1 | 4 | ... | 8 | ... | ... | 8 | 312 | 53 | .... | | ... | ... | 760.00 |
| MEXICO | 34 | 7 | | 7 | 5 | 1 | ... | 14 | ... | ... | 24 | 782 | 213 | .... | .... | 6 | 182 | 1,430.53 |
| ITALY | 68 | 2 | | 1 | | 13 | ... | 5 | ... | ... | 13 | 255 | 59 | .... | .... | 2 | 35 | 1,738.00 |
| Total | 161 | 33 | | 30 | 15 | 29 | .... | 57 | .... | .... | 62 | 2,213 | 409 | .... | .... | 29 | 675 | 4,680.87 |
| **No. 6. Seventh-Day Baptist Missionary Society. Year ending June 30th, 1890.** | | | | | | | | | | | | | | | | | | |
| CHINA | 3 | 2 | | 2 | 2 | 2 | .... | 7 | 3 | .... | 1 | 30 | 5 | .. | | 2 | 29 | ........ |
| **No. 7. German Baptist Brethren Church. Year ending April 8th, 1890.** | | | | | | | | | | | | | | | | | | |
| SCANDINAVIAN MISSIONS | | | | | | | | 9 | | | | 5 | 131 | 16 | | | | | $33.00 |
| **No. 8. Consolidated American Baptists.** | | | | | | | | | | | | | | | | | | |
| HAITI | | | | | | | 1 | | | | | | | | | | | |
| **No. 9. Baptist General Association. Year ending September, 1890.** | | | | | | | | | | | | | | | | | | |
| AFRICA: Congo | 1 | 1 | 1 | 1 | | | | | 6 | | | | | | | | | |
| **No. 10. Baptist Foreign Mission Convention for Year Ending September, 1890.** | | | | | | | | | | | | | | | | | | |
| AFRICA: Congo | | 2 | | | | 1 | | | | | | | | | | | | |
| **No. 13. Missionary Society of the Methodist Episcopal Church (North). Year ending December 31st, 1890.** | | | | | | | | | | | | | | | | | | |
| AFRICA | 37 | | | | | 22 | | 58 | 36 | 2,614 | 36 | 3,179 | 227 | | | | | $4,835 |
| SOUTH AMERICA | 17 | 11 | | 11 | 7 | 12 | 21 | 42 | 56 | 2,113 | 23 | 1,865 | 105 | 2 | 49 | 21 | 1,358 | 28,279 |
| CHINA: | | | | | | | | | | | | | | | | | | |
| Foochow | 59 | 7 | 1 | 8 | 8 | 62 | 75 | 30 | 123 | 2,735 | 81 | 4,172 | 597 | 2 | 60 | 79 | 1,211 | 1,845 |
| Central China | 29 | 13 | 1 | 14 | 7 | 2 | 37 | 36 | 37 | 745 | 15 | 536 | 55 | 7 | 224 | 28 | 454 | 1,362 |
| North China | 20 | 13 | 2 | 14 | 13 | 6 | 27 | 38 | 32 | 907 | 14 | 1,644 | 30 | 6 | 318 | 27 | 332 | 665 |
| West China | 1 | 3 | 1 | 2 | | | 4 | 1 | 2 | .... | .... | 45 | 28 | .... | | 3 | 70 | 20 |
| INDIA: | | | | | | | | | | | | | | | | | | |
| North India | 57 | 28 | | 25 | 20 | 67 | 724 | 81 | 117 | 30,823 | 64 | 13,421 | 2,402 | 14 | 1,782 | 655 | 15,951 | 6,099 |
| South India | 15 | 25 | | 22 | 8 | 2 | 76 | 54 | 36 | 7,719 | 21 | 879 | 202 | 3 | 365 | 70 | 2,557 | 13,204 |
| Bengal | 20 | 24 | | 22 | 11 | 6 | 57 | 48 | 37 | 3,881 | 18 | 2,240 | 1,057 | 2 | 281 | 74 | 2,412 | 16,732 |
| MALAYSIA | 1 | 5 | 3 | 4 | 1 | | 2 | 5 | 3 | 160 | 1 | 107 | 35 | 1 | 380 | 1 | 50 | 4,220 |
| BULGARIA | 12 | 4 | | 4 | 2 | 10 | 11 | 5 | 9 | 229 | 3 | 163 | 10 | 2 | 64 | 5 | 97 | 553 |
| ITALY | 23 | 4 | | 2 | 2 | 19 | 4 | 39 | 25 | 436 | 9 | 941 | 158 | 1 | 8 | 3 | 136 | 1,854 |
| JAPAN | 49 | 19 | | 18 | 32 | 22 | 76 | 12 | 61 | 4,022 | 25 | 3,532 | 492 | 12 | 1,326 | 14 | 1,159 | 19,290 |
| MEXICO | 32 | 10 | | 10 | 10 | 10 | 25 | 38 | 48 | 1,648 | 22 | 2,430 | 349 | 4 | 120 | 42 | 2,725 | 9,012 |
| KOREA | 1 | 3 | 2 | 4 | 5 | 2 | 4 | 6 | 2 | 43 | 2 | 45 | ...... | 3 | 88 | .... | .... | ...... |
| Total | 573 | 169 | 10 | 160 | 126 | 242 | 1,143 | 493 | 624 | 58,075 | 334 | 35,200 | 5,747 | 59 | 5,065 | 1022 | 28,512 | $107,970 |

**No. 14. FOREIGN MISSIONARY SOCIETY OF THE AFRICAN METHODIST EPISCOPAL CHURCH. YEAR ENDING MAY, 1890.**

| Missions. | Stations and Out-stations. | MISSION-ARIES. | | | | NATIVE WORKERS. | | | Preaching Places. | Sabbath-school Scholars. | Churches. | Communicants. | Additions. | Schools for Higher Education. | Pupils. | Common Schools. | Pupils. | Native Contributions for all purposes. |
|---|---|---|---|---|---|---|---|---|---|---|---|---|---|---|---|---|---|---|
| | | Ordained. | Lay. | Wives. | Other Women. | Ordained. | Teachers. | Other Helpers. | | | | | | | | | | |
| AFRICA: | | | | | | | | | | | | | | | | | | |
| SIERRA LEONE | 2 | 1 | 1 | 1 | 1 | ... | 2 | ... | 4 | 73 | 2 | 139 | 39 | ... | ... | 1 | 67 | $900 |
| LIBERIA | 3 | 2 | 3 | 4 | 2 | ... | 1 | ... | 5 | 54 | 3 | 68 | 18 | ... | ... | 1 | 44 | 100 |
| WEST INDIES: | | | | | | | | | | | | | | | | | | |
| HAITI | 4 | 4 | 3 | 3 | ... | ... | 2 | ... | 4 | 50 | 3 | 69 | 9 | ... | ... | 1 | 84 | 360 |
| SAN DOMINGO | 3 | 2 | 2 | 4 | ... | ... | 2 | ... | 4 | 75 | 2 | 80 | 10 | ... | ... | 2 | 62 | 280 |
| Total | 12 | 9 | 9 | 12 | 3 | .. | 7 | ... | 17 | 258 | 10 | 356 | 76 | ... | ... | 5 | 257 | $1,640 |

**No. 15. BOARD OF FOREIGN MISSIONS IN THE METHODIST EPISCOPAL CHURCH (SOUTH). YEAR ENDING MARCH 31ST, 1890.**

| Missions. | Stations and Out-stations. | Ordained. | Lay. | Wives. | Other Women. | Ordained. | Teachers. | Other Helpers. | Preaching Places. | Sabbath-school Scholars. | Churches. | Communicants. | Additions. | Schools for Higher Education. | Pupils. | Common Schools. | Pupils. | Native Contributions for all purposes. |
|---|---|---|---|---|---|---|---|---|---|---|---|---|---|---|---|---|---|---|
| CHINA | 14 | 15 | 1 | 12 | 14 | 21 | 9 | 45 | 14 | 742 | 8 | 345 | 50 | 2 | 220 | 4 | 141 | $265.33 |
| MEXICO: | | | | | | | | | | | | | | | | | | |
| CENTRAL MEXICO | 56 | 5 | 1 | 5 | ... | 43 | ... | ... | 39 | 1,394 | 33 | 1,989 | 98 | 1 | 20 | 28 | 955 | 834.19 |
| MEXICAN BORDER | 59 | 8 | ... | 7 | 7 | 38 | ... | 20 | 43 | 1,860 | 14 | 1,819 | 179 | ... | ... | 6 | 372 | 3,873.00 |
| BRAZIL | 18 | 9 | ... | 7 | 9 | 11 | ... | 8 | 18 | 356 | 4 | 470 | 103 | 1 | 31 | 4 | 135 | 3,053.00 |
| JAPAN | 22 | 11 | 1 | 9 | 5 | 8 | ... | ... | 22 | 617 | 1 | 318 | 86 | 1 | 7 | 5 | 110 | 3,116.01 |
| Total | 169 | 48 | 3 | 40 | 35 | 121* | 9 | 73 | 136 | 4,969 | 60 | 4,941 | 516 | 5 | 278 | 47 | 1,719 | 11,141.53 |

\* Ordained and unordained.

**No. 16. BOARD OF FOREIGN MISSIONS OF THE METHODIST PROTESTANT CHURCH. YEAR ENDING MAY 1ST, 1890.**

| Missions. | Stations and Out-stations. | Ordained. | Lay. | Wives. | Other Women. | Ordained. | Teachers. | Other Helpers. | Preaching Places. | Sabbath-school Scholars. | Churches. | Communicants. | Additions. | Schools for Higher Education. | Pupils. | Common Schools. | Pupils. | Native Contributions for all purposes. |
|---|---|---|---|---|---|---|---|---|---|---|---|---|---|---|---|---|---|---|
| JAPAN | 3 | 5 | .. | 5 | 4 | ... | 5 | 7 | 4 | 350 | 2 | 203 | ... | 2 | 7 | 4 | 249 | $460 |

**No. 17. AMERICAN WESLEYAN METHODIST CONNECTION. YEAR ENDING MAY (?), 1890.**

| Missions. | Stations and Out-stations. | Ordained. | Lay. | Wives. | Other Women. | Ordained. | Teachers. | Other Helpers. | Preaching Places. | Sabbath-school Scholars. | Churches. | Communicants. | Additions. | Schools for Higher Education. | Pupils. | Common Schools. | Pupils. | Native Contributions for all purposes. |
|---|---|---|---|---|---|---|---|---|---|---|---|---|---|---|---|---|---|---|
| AFRICA: | | | | | | | | | | | | | | | | | | |
| SIERRA LEONE | 2 | 2 | 2 | 2 | .. | 1 | ... | ... | 2 | ... | 1 | 300 | 12 | ... | ... | 1 | 300 | $300 |

**No. 20. FOREIGN MISSIONARY SOCIETY OF THE PROTESTANT EPISCOPAL CHURCH IN THE UNITED STATES OF AMERICA. YEAR ENDING SEPTEMBER 30TH, 1890.**

| Missions. | Stations and Out-stations. | Ordained. | Lay. | Wives. | Other Women. | Ordained. | Teachers. | Other Helpers. | Preaching Places. | Sabbath-school Scholars. | Churches. | Communicants. | Additions. | Schools for Higher Education. | Pupils. | Common Schools. | Pupils. | Native Contributions for all purposes. |
|---|---|---|---|---|---|---|---|---|---|---|---|---|---|---|---|---|---|---|
| GREECE | 1 | ... | ... | ... | 2 | ... | 10 | 2 | ... | ... | ... | ... | ... | ... | ... | 1 | 450 | ... |
| AFRICA | 69 | 1 | ... | ... | ... | 1 | 14 | 38 | 2 | 69 | 1,272 | 11 | 709 | 145 | 2 | 131 | 27 | 871 | $1990 57 |
| CHINA | 59 | 8 | 3 | 7 | 12 | 25 | 53 | 4 | 59 | 1,099 | 9 | 536 | 76 | 3 | 92 | 46 | 1,009 | 676.99 |
| JAPAN | 68 | 13 | 3 | 13 | 12 | 1 | 82 | ... | 68 | 876 | 5 | 994 | 129 | 1 | 63 | 7 | 274 | 2920.23 |
| HAITI | 23 | 1 | ... | ... | ... | 13 | 34 | ... | 23 | 150 | 11 | 405 | 20 | 1 | 13 | 4 | 205 | 1249.86 |
| Total | 220 | 23 | 6 | 20 | 27 | 53 | 217 | 8 | 219 | 3,397 | *36 | 2,644 | 370 | 7 | 299 | 85 | 2,809 | $6777.65 |

\* Buildings.

**No. 22. REFORMED PRESBYTERIAN GENERAL SYNOD, BOARD OF MISSIONS. YEAR ENDING MAY, 1890.**

| Missions. | Stations and Out-stations. | Ordained. | Lay. | Wives. | Other Women. | Ordained. | Teachers. | Other Helpers. | Preaching Places. | Sabbath-school Scholars. | Churches. | Communicants. | Additions. | Schools for Higher Education. | Pupils. | Common Schools. | Pupils. | Native Contributions for all purposes. |
|---|---|---|---|---|---|---|---|---|---|---|---|---|---|---|---|---|---|---|
| INDIA: | | | | | | | | | | | | | | | | | | |
| N. W. PROVINCES | 10 | ... | ... | ... | ... | 2 | ... | 18 | 10 | ... | .. | 2 | 117 | 5 | ... | ... | 1 | 30 | Rs. 700 ($350) |

**No. 23. REFORMED GERMAN CHURCH BOARD OF FOREIGN MISSIONS. YEAR ENDING JUNE 1ST, 1890.**

| Missions. | Stations and Out-stations. | Ordained. | Lay. | Wives. | Other Women. | Ordained. | Teachers. | Other Helpers. | Preaching Places. | Sabbath-school Scholars. | Churches. | Communicants. | Additions. | Schools for Higher Education. | Pupils. | Common Schools. | Pupils. | Native Contributions for all purposes. |
|---|---|---|---|---|---|---|---|---|---|---|---|---|---|---|---|---|---|---|
| JAPAN | 24 | 3 | .. | 3 | 2 | 7 | ... | 15 | 20 | 915 | 12 | 1,656 | ... | 1 | 26 | 1 | 40 | $2835.15 |

| SOCIETIES. | Stations and Out-stations. | MISSIONARIES. | | | | NATIVE WORKERS. | | | Preaching Places. | Sabbath-school Scholars. | Churches. | Communicants. | Additions. | Schools for Higher Education. | Pupils. | Common Schools. | Pupils. | Native Contributions for all purposes. |
|---|---|---|---|---|---|---|---|---|---|---|---|---|---|---|---|---|---|---|
| | | Ordained. | Lay. | Wives. | Other Women. | Ordained. | Teachers. | Other Helpers. | | | | | | | | | | |

**No. 24. BOARD OF FOREIGN MISSIONS OF THE PRESBYTERIAN CHURCH (NORTH). YEAR ENDING MAY 1ST, 1890.**

| SOCIETIES. | Stations and Out-stations. | Ordained. | Lay. | Wives. | Other Women. | Ordained. | Teachers. | Other Helpers. | Preaching Places. | Sabbath-school Scholars. | Churches. | Communicants. | Additions. | Schools for Higher Education. | Pupils. | Common Schools. | Pupils. | Native Contributions for all purposes. |
|---|---|---|---|---|---|---|---|---|---|---|---|---|---|---|---|---|---|---|
| AFRICA | 17 | 9 | 9 | 4 | 6 | 4 | ..... | 29 | ..... | 1,312 | 17 | 1,398 | 156 | .... | 8 | 18 | 579 | $504 |
| SOUTH AMERICA: | | | | | | | | | | | | | | | | | | |
| BRAZIL | 8 | 12 | 1 | 11 | 3 | 9 | ..... | 51 | ..... | 552 | 38 | 2,663 | 270 | .... | 3 | 15 | 718 | 12,640 |
| CHILI | 4 | 7 | .. | 7 | ... | 3 | ..... | 9 | ..... | 279 | 6 | 226 | 29 | .... | ..... | 3 | 409 | 962 |
| U. S. OF COLOMBIA. | 3 | 3 | .. | 3 | 1 | ... | ..... | 9 | .... | 116 | 2 | 104 | 25 | .... | 2 | 4 | 136 | ........ |
| MEXICO | 5 | 7 | . | 7 | 4 | 25 | ..... | 78 | .... | 1,795 | 90 | 5,165 | 388 | .... | 15 | 42 | 1,358 | 3,627 |
| GUATEMALA | 1 | 2 | .. | 2 | 2 | .. | ..... | 1 | .... | 50 | 1 | 4 | ..... | .... | 2 | 1 | 38 | 15 |
| INDIA (NORTH) | 19 | 37 | 4 | 35 | 36 | 22 | ..... | 185 | ..... | 4,590 | 4 | 1,093 | 81 | .... | ..... | 14 | 8,016 | ........ |
| CHINA | 13 | 4× | 12 | 47 | 21 | 22 | ..... | 265 | ..... | 2,969 | 45 | 4,084 | 446 | ... | 6 | 124 | 2,689 | 2,809 |
| JAPAN | 5 | 21 | 3 | 22 | 25 | 20 | ..... | 23 | ..... | ...... | 34 | 4,977 | 672 | ... | 17 | 15 | 1,409 | 6,750 |
| KOREA | 1 | 3 | 2 | 3 | 2 | .. | ..... | ..... | ..... | ...... | .. | 104 | 39 | ... | ..... | ... | ..... | ...... |
| SIAM | 3 | 7 | 3 | 8 | 3 | .. | ..... | 27 | ..... | 155 | 7 | 392 | 3 | ... | ..... | 17 | 412 | 269 |
| LAOS | 2 | 6 | 1 | 6 | 4 | 1 | ..... | 14 | ..... | 521 | 5 | 722 | 108 | ... | 14 | 4 | 229 | 35 |
| SYRIA | 5 | 14 | 1 | 14 | 10 | 4 | ..... | 197 | ..... | 4,966 | 20 | 1,619 | 98 | .... | 7 | 142 | 5,853 | 7,767 |
| PERSIA | 6 | 14 | 5 | 17 | 18 | 42 | ..... | 217 | ..... | 5,210 | 27 | 2,269 | 141 | .... | 18 | 147 | 3,069 | 2,200 |
| Total | 92 | 190 | 41 | 186 | 135 | 152 | ..... | 1,105 | ..... | 22,515 | 296 | 24,820 | 2,510 | .... | 92 | 546 | 24,915 | $37,578 |

**No. 25. BOARD OF MISSIONS OF THE REFORMED (DUTCH) CHURCH IN AMERICA. YEAR ENDING DECEMBER 31ST, 1890.**

| SOCIETIES. | Stations and Out-stations. | Ordained. | Lay. | Wives. | Other Women. | Ordained. | Teachers. | Other Helpers. | Preaching Places. | Sabbath-school Scholars. | Churches. | Communicants. | Additions. | Schools for Higher Education. | Pupils. | Common Schools. | Pupils. | Native Contributions for all purposes. |
|---|---|---|---|---|---|---|---|---|---|---|---|---|---|---|---|---|---|---|
| CHINA | 25 | 6 | 1 | 7 | 2 | 8 | ..... | 20 | 25 | ..... | 8 | 856 | 35 | 4 | 97 | 8 | 122 | $2,535 |
| INDIA (ARCOT) | 106 | 8 | 1 | 7 | 2 | 4 | ..... | 216 | 106 | ..... | 23 | 1,696 | 68 | 7 | 266 | 105 | 3,320 | 650 |
| JAPAN | 24 | 9 | 2 | 10 | 6 | 18 | ..... | 17 | 24 | ..... | 20 | 2,784 | 449 | 6 | 281 | ... | ..... | 4,818 |
| Total | 155 | 23 | 4 | 24 | 10 | 30 | ..... | 253 | 155 | ..... | 51 | 5,336 | 552 | 17 | 644 | 113 | 3,442 | $8,003 |

**No. 26. BOARD OF FOREIGN MISSIONS OF THE UNITED PRESBYTERIAN CHURCH. YEAR ENDING APRIL 30TH, 1890.**

| SOCIETIES. | Stations and Out-stations. | Ordained. | Lay. | Wives. | Other Women. | Ordained. | Teachers. | Other Helpers. | Preaching Places. | Sabbath-school Scholars. | Churches. | Communicants. | Additions. | Schools for Higher Education. | Pupils. | Common Schools. | Pupils. | Native Contributions for all purposes. |
|---|---|---|---|---|---|---|---|---|---|---|---|---|---|---|---|---|---|---|
| EGYPT | 100 | 14 | .. | 11 | 14 | 12 | ..... | 244 | ..... | 4,427 | 29 | 2,971 | 464 | 2 | 265 | 98 | 6,039 | $27,353 |
| INDIA (NORTH) | 85 | 12 | .. | 11 | 12 | 11 | .. .. | 192 | ..... | 2,824 | 10 | 6,597 | 1,258 | 2 | 110 | 166 | 4,273 | 1,022 |
| Total | 185 | 26 | .. | 22 | 26 | 23 | ..... | 436 | ..... | 7,251 | 39 | 9,568 | 1,722 | 4 | 375 | 264 | 10,312 | $28,375 |

**No. 27. BOARD OF MISSIONS OF THE REFORMED PRESBYTERIAN CHURCH. YEAR ENDING APRIL 30TH, 1890.**

| SOCIETIES. | Stations and Out-stations. | Ordained. | Lay. | Wives. | Other Women. | Ordained. | Teachers. | Other Helpers. | Preaching Places. | Sabbath-school Scholars. | Churches. | Communicants. | Additions. | Schools for Higher Education. | Pupils. | Common Schools. | Pupils. | Native Contributions for all purposes. |
|---|---|---|---|---|---|---|---|---|---|---|---|---|---|---|---|---|---|---|
| SYRIA | 8 | 4 | 1 | 4 | 4 | 4 | 34 | .... | 11 | 526 | 3 | 190 | 12 | ... | ...... | 25 | 730 | $33.91 |

**No. 28. BOARD OF FOREIGN MISSIONS OF THE PRESBYTERIAN CHURCH (SOUTH). YEAR ENDING MARCH 31ST, 1890.**

| SOCIETIES. | Stations and Out-stations. | Ordained. | Lay. | Wives. | Other Women. | Ordained. | Teachers. | Other Helpers. | Preaching Places. | Sabbath-school Scholars. | Churches. | Communicants. | Additions. | Schools for Higher Education. | Pupils. | Common Schools. | Pupils. | Native Contributions for all purposes. |
|---|---|---|---|---|---|---|---|---|---|---|---|---|---|---|---|---|---|---|
| BRAZIL | 30 | 10 | 1 | 8 | 5 | 5 | ..... | 10 | ..... | 224 | 21 | 670 | ...... | 1 | 50 | 3 | ..... | $1,400 |
| CHINA | 12 | 11 | 2 | 9 | 6 | ... | 3 | 15 | ..... | 245 | 3 | 180 | 23 | 1 | 47 | 14 | 160 | 60 |
| MEXICO | 51 | 2 | .. | 1 | 3 | 8 | ..... | 3 | ..... | 418 | ... | 450 | ..... | .. | ...... | 2 | 250 | 635 |
| GREECE | 4 | 2 | .. | 2 | ... | 1 | ..... | 4 | 2 | 20 | 1 | 33 | 2 | ... | ...... | ... | ...... | 30 |
| ITALY | 1 | .. | .. | ... | 2 | .. | ..... | ...... | ..... | ...... | ... | ...... | ..... | 1 | 40 | ... | ...... | ...... |
| JAPAN | 21 | 9 | .. | 5 | 5 | 2 | 10 | 2 | 48 | 520 | 4 | 796 | 142 | 1 | 50 | 3 | 100 | 600 |
| AFRICA (CONGO FREE STATE) | ...... | 2 | .. | ... | ... | ... | ..... | ...... | ..... | ...... | ... | ...... | ..... | .. | ...... | ... | ...... | ...... |
| Total | 119 | 36 | 3 | 25 | 21 | 16 | 13 | 34 | 50 | 1,427 | 29 | 2,129 | 167 | 4 | 187 | 22 | 510 | $2,725 |

**No. 29. ASSOCIATE REFORMED SYNOD SOUTHERN PRESBYTERIANS. YEAR ENDING SEPTEMBER 30TH, 1889.**

| SOCIETIES. | Stations and Out-stations. | Ordained. | Lay. | Wives. | Other Women. | Ordained. | Teachers. | Other Helpers. | Preaching Places. | Sabbath-school Scholars. | Churches. | Communicants. | Additions. | Schools for Higher Education. | Pupils. | Common Schools. | Pupils. | Native Contributions for all purposes. |
|---|---|---|---|---|---|---|---|---|---|---|---|---|---|---|---|---|---|---|
| MEXICO | 11 | 2 | .. | 1 | 1 | 2 | ..... | 2 | ..... | 159 | 6 | 226 | 32 | ... | ...... | 2 | 27 | $106.25 |

| Missions. | Stations and Out-stations. | Missionaries. | | | | Native Workers. | | | Preaching Places. | Sabbath-school Scholars. | Churches. | Communicants. | Additions. | Schools for Higher Education. | Pupils. | Common Schools. | Pupils. | Native Contributions for all purposes. |
|---|---|---|---|---|---|---|---|---|---|---|---|---|---|---|---|---|---|---|
| | | Ordained. | Lay. | Wives. | Other Women. | Ordained. | Teachers. | Other Helpers. | | | | | | | | | | |

### No. 30. Board of Foreign Missions of the Cumberland Presbyterian Church. Year ending April 30th, 1890.

| Missions. | Stations and Out-stations. | Ordained. | Lay. | Wives. | Other Women. | Ordained. | Teachers. | Other Helpers. | Preaching Places. | Sabbath-school Scholars. | Churches. | Communicants. | Additions. | Schools for Higher Education. | Pupils. | Common Schools. | Pupils. | Native Contributions. |
|---|---|---|---|---|---|---|---|---|---|---|---|---|---|---|---|---|---|---|
| JAPAN | 8 | 4 | .. | 4 | 6 | 1 | ..... | 4 | ..... | ..... | 8 | 521 | ..... | .. | ..... | 2 | 54 | ..... |
| MEXICO | 2 | 2 | .. | 2 | ... | ..... | ..... | 1 | ..... | ..... | 2 | 79 | ..... | .. | ..... | 2 | 146 | ..... |
| Total | 10 | 6 | .. | 6 | 6 | 1 | ..... | 5 | ..... | ..... | 10 | 600 | .. | ..... | ..... | 4 | 200 | ..... |

### No. 31. German Evangelical Synod of North America. Year ending May, 1890.

| Missions. | Stations and Out-stations. | Ordained. | Lay. | Wives. | Other Women. | Ordained. | Teachers. | Other Helpers. | Preaching Places. | Sabbath-school Scholars. | Churches. | Communicants. | Additions. | Schools for Higher Education. | Pupils. | Common Schools. | Pupils. | Native Contributions. |
|---|---|---|---|---|---|---|---|---|---|---|---|---|---|---|---|---|---|---|
| INDIA (CENTRAL) | 10 | 4 | ... | 4 | 1 | ... | .... | 15 | ..... | .... | ... | 3 | 234 | 34 | 1 | 70 | 3 | 180 |

### No. 34. Board of Foreign Missions of the General Synod of the Evangelical Lutheran Church. Year ending December 31st, 1889.

| Missions. | Stations and Out-stations. | Ordained. | Lay. | Wives. | Other Women. | Ordained. | Teachers. | Other Helpers. | Preaching Places. | Sabbath-school Scholars. | Churches. | Communicants. | Additions. | Schools for Higher Education. | Pupils. | Common Schools. | Pupils. | Native Contributions. |
|---|---|---|---|---|---|---|---|---|---|---|---|---|---|---|---|---|---|---|
| INDIA (MADRAS) | 11 | 4 | .. | 3 | 2 | 2 | ..... | 169 | 7 | 341 | 300 | 7,605 | 6,367 | 2,350 | 1 | 378 | 173 | 3,766 | $1,500 |
| AFRICA | 1 | 1 | .. | 1 | 1 | 2 | ..... | 7 | | 13 | +38 | ..... | 200 | +53 | . | ..... | 22 | 342 | +55 |
| Total | 12 | 5 | . | 4 | 3 | 4 | 212 | 176 | | 354 | 338 | 7,605 | *6,567 | 2,403 | 1 | 378 | 195 | 4,108 | $1,555 |

\* Total in Society's Report, $7,726. † Apportionment estimated.

### No. 35. Board of Missions of the General Council of the Evangelical Lutheran Church. Year ending September 30th, 1889.

| Missions. | Stations and Out-stations. | Ordained. | Lay. | Wives. | Other Women. | Ordained. | Teachers. | Other Helpers. | Preaching Places. | Sabbath-school Scholars. | Churches. | Communicants. | Additions. | Schools for Higher Education. | Pupils. | Common Schools. | Pupils. | Native Contributions. |
|---|---|---|---|---|---|---|---|---|---|---|---|---|---|---|---|---|---|---|
| INDIA (MADRAS) | 6 | 4 | .. | 3 | ... | 2 | 81 | 7 | 103 | ..... | 2 | 832 | 1 | .... | ..... | 89 | 1,073 | $50.03 |

### No. 36 Foreign Christian Missionary Society (Disciples of Christ). Year ending October 20th, 1889.

| Missions. | Stations and Out-stations. | Ordained. | Lay. | Wives. | Other Women. | Ordained. | Teachers. | Other Helpers. | Preaching Places. | Sabbath-school Scholars. | Churches. | Communicants. | Additions. | Schools for Higher Education. | Pupils. | Common Schools. | Pupils. | Native Contributions. |
|---|---|---|---|---|---|---|---|---|---|---|---|---|---|---|---|---|---|---|
| JAPAN | 3 | 4 | . | 4 | 2 | ... | ..... | 2 | ..... | 340 | ... | 168 | 51 | ... | . | ... | 2 | 53 | ..... |
| INDIA (CENTRAL) | 8 | 4 | . | 4 | 2 | ... | ..... | 8 | ..... | 650 | ... | 58 | 35 | ... | . | ... | 3 | 100 | ..... |
| CHINA | 3 | 8 | . | 3 | 0 | ... | ..... | 2 | ..... | 24 | ... | 4 | 3 | ... | . | ... | 1 | 24 | ..... |
| TURKEY | 14 | 3 | .. | 1 | 0 | ... | ..... | 11 | ..... | 130 | ... | 629 | 127 | ... | . | ... | 2 | 55 | ..... |
| Total | 28 | 19 | .. | 12 | 4 | ... | ..... | 23 | ..... | 1,144 | ... | 859 | 216 | ... | ..... | ..... | 8 | 232 | ..... |

### No. 37. Board of Missions of the United Brethren in Christ. Year ending March 31st, 1890.

| Missions. | Stations and Out-stations. | Ordained. | Lay. | Wives. | Other Women. | Ordained. | Teachers. | Other Helpers. | Preaching Places. | Sabbath-school Scholars. | Churches. | Communicants. | Additions. | Schools for Higher Education. | Pupils. | Common Schools. | Pupils. | Native Contributions. |
|---|---|---|---|---|---|---|---|---|---|---|---|---|---|---|---|---|---|---|
| AFRICA | 12* | 18 | 25 | 16 | 5 | 3 | 10 | 24 | 405 | 236 | 131 | 6,712 | 1,150 | 1 | 23 | 13 | 568 | $1484.18 |

\* Stations only.

### No. 38 Board of Missions of the Evangelical Association.

| Missions. | Stations and Out-stations. | Ordained. | Lay. | Wives. | Other Women. | Ordained. | Teachers. | Other Helpers. | Preaching Places. | Sabbath-school Scholars. | Churches. | Communicants. | Additions. | Schools for Higher Education. | Pupils. | Common Schools. | Pupils. | Native Contributions. |
|---|---|---|---|---|---|---|---|---|---|---|---|---|---|---|---|---|---|---|
| JAPAN | 15 | 3 | .. | 3 | ... | 5 | 2 | 22 | 18 | 441 | 5 | 333 | 128 | 1 | 18 | ... | ..... | $440.12 |

### No. 41. Foreign Missionary Society of the American Christian Convention. Year ending December 31st, 1890.

| Missions. | Stations and Out-stations. | Ordained. | Lay. | Wives. | Other Women. | Ordained. | Teachers. | Other Helpers. | Preaching Places. | Sabbath-school Scholars. | Churches. | Communicants. | Additions. | Schools for Higher Education. | Pupils. | Common Schools. | Pupils. | Native Contributions. |
|---|---|---|---|---|---|---|---|---|---|---|---|---|---|---|---|---|---|---|
| JAPAN | 37 | 2 | .. | 2 | ... | 6 | .... | .... | 37 | ..... | 3 | 93 | 34 | ... | ..... | ... | ..... | $73.80 |

| Missions. | Stations and Out-stations. | Missionaries. | | | | Native Workers. | | | Preaching Places. | Sabbath-school Scholars. | Churches. | Communicants. | Additions. | Schools for Higher Education. | Pupils. | Common Schools. | Pupils. | Native Contributions for all purposes. |
|---|---|---|---|---|---|---|---|---|---|---|---|---|---|---|---|---|---|---|
| | | Ordained. | Lay. | Wives. | Other Women. | Ordained. | Teachers. | Other Helpers. | | | | | | | | | | |

### No. 42. Foreign Missionary Society of the Seventh-Day Adventists. Year ending June 30th, 1890.

| Missions. | Stations and Out-stations. | Ordained. | Lay. | Wives. | Other Women. | Ordained. | Teachers. | Other Helpers. | Preaching Places. | Sabbath-school Scholars. | Churches. | Communicants. | Additions. | Schools for Higher Education. | Pupils. | Common Schools. | Pupils. | Native Contributions. |
|---|---|---|---|---|---|---|---|---|---|---|---|---|---|---|---|---|---|---|
| AFRICA (South).. | ...... | 2 | 2 | ... | 1 | ... | ...... | .... | .... | ...... | 5 | 120 | .... | .... | .... | .. | .. | ...... |
| AUSTRALIA and NEW ZEALAND.. | ...... | 2 | 1 | ... | 1 | ... | ...... | .... | .... | ...... | 2 | 107 | .... | .... | .... | .. | .. | ...... |
| PACIFIC ISLANDS.. | ...... | 5 | 2 | ... | 3 | 3 | ...... | .... | .... | ...... | 10 | 655 | .... | .... | .... | .. | .. | ...... |
| EUROPE............. | ...... | 9 | 6 | ... | 5 | 7 | ...... | .... | .... | ...... | 71 | 1,945 | .... | .... | .... | .. | .. | ...... |
| Total ........... | ...... | 18 | 11 | 10 | 10 | 10 | ...... | 135 | .. | .... | 88 | 2,827 | 431 | .... | .... | .. | .. | ...... |

### No. 50. Board of Foreign Missions of the Methodist Church in Canada. Year ending June 30th, 1889.

| Missions. | Stations and Out-stations. | Ordained. | Lay. | Wives. | Other Women. | Ordained. | Teachers. | Other Helpers. | Preaching Places. | Sabbath-school Scholars. | Churches. | Communicants. | Additions. | Schools for Higher Education. | Pupils. | Common Schools. | Pupils. | Native Contributions. |
|---|---|---|---|---|---|---|---|---|---|---|---|---|---|---|---|---|---|---|
| JAPAN............ .. | 13 | 9 | 2 | 8 | ... | 5 | ...... | 31 | 31 | 1,486 | 10 | 1,538 | 578 | 1 | 210 | 3 | 275 | $6491.35 |

### No. 51. Board of Foreign Missions of the Presbyterian Church in Canada. Year ending April 30th, 1890.

| Missions. | Stations and Out-stations. | Ordained. | Lay. | Wives. | Other Women. | Ordained. | Teachers. | Other Helpers. | Preaching Places. | Sabbath-school Scholars. | Churches. | Communicants. | Additions. | Schools for Higher Education. | Pupils. | Common Schools. | Pupils. | Native Contributions. |
|---|---|---|---|---|---|---|---|---|---|---|---|---|---|---|---|---|---|---|
| Total ........... | 130 | 25 | 4 | 22 | 24 | 6 | ...... | 214 | 130 | ...... | 65 | 3,881 | 71 | 1 | 22 | 98 | 3,750 | $3,038 |

(NOTE.—It was impracticable to divide these among the five missions of the Society, in China, India, Trinidad, New Hebrides, and Indians of Canada.)

### No. 52. Foreign Mission Board of the Baptist Convention of Ontario and Quebec. Year ending September 30th, 1889.

| Missions. | Stations and Out-stations. | Ordained. | Lay. | Wives. | Other Women. | Ordained. | Teachers. | Other Helpers. | Preaching Places. | Sabbath-school Scholars. | Churches. | Communicants. | Additions. | Schools for Higher Education. | Pupils. | Common Schools. | Pupils. | Native Contributions. |
|---|---|---|---|---|---|---|---|---|---|---|---|---|---|---|---|---|---|---|
| INDIA.............. | 9 | 16 | .. | 14 | 8 | 8 | ...... | 141 | ... | .. .... | 23 | 2,466 | 110 | 1 | 70 | .... | ...... | ........ |

### No. 53. The Canada Congregational Missionary Society. Year ending May, 1890.

| Missions. | Stations and Out-stations. | Ordained. | Lay. | Wives. | Other Women. | Ordained. | Teachers. | Other Helpers. | Preaching Places. | Sabbath-school Scholars. | Churches. | Communicants. | Additions. | Schools for Higher Education. | Pupils. | Common Schools. | Pupils. | Native Contributions. |
|---|---|---|---|---|---|---|---|---|---|---|---|---|---|---|---|---|---|---|
| AFRICA: West Central..... | 2 | 2 | .. | .... | 2 | ... | .... | .... | .... | .... | 1 | ..... | .... | .. | .... | .. | .. | ......... |

### No. 62. The London Missionary Society. Year ending March 31st, 1890.

| Missions. | Stations and Out-stations. | Ordained. | Lay. | Wives. | Other Women. | Ordained. | Teachers. | Other Helpers. | Preaching Places. | Sabbath-school Scholars. | Churches. | Communicants. | Additions. | Schools for Higher Education. | Pupils. | Common Schools. | Pupils. | Native Contributions. |
|---|---|---|---|---|---|---|---|---|---|---|---|---|---|---|---|---|---|---|
| AFRICA............. | 68 | 20 | 5 | 21 | ... | ... | .... | 103 | ..... | ..... | 420 | ... | 2,662 | ..... | .... | ...... | 19 | 1,545 | £ 349 |
| CHINA...... ........ | 98 | 23 | 8 | 24 | 13 | 9 | .... | 76 | ..... | 420 | ... | 4,272 | ..... | ... | ...... | 63 | 2,150 | 2,445 |
| INDIA: North...... | 33 | 16 | .. | 13 | 12 | 7 | ... | 32 | ...... | 1,838 | ... | 626 | ..... | .. | ...... | 110 | 6,648 | 3,389 |
| South .. ...... | 208 | 28 | .. | 18 | 6 | 16 | ... | 125 | ...... | 1,449 | ... | 1,458 | ..... | ... | ...... | 141 | 8,220 | 4,160 |
| Travancore.. | 279 | 7 | 1 | 5 | 1 | 18 | .... | 167 | ...... | ... | 5,659 | ..... | ... | ...... | 311 | 14,064 | 1,580 |
| MADAGASCAR..... | 1,218 | 23 | 4 | 23 | 3 | 827 | ... | 3,459 | ..... | 4,448 | ... | 39,984 | ..... | ... | ...... | 860 | 58,888 | 4,400 |
| WEST INDIES...... | 4 | 1 | .. | 1 | ... | ... | ... | 17 | ...... | 815 | ... | 481 | ... | .. | ...... | 5 | 611 | 475 |
| POLYNESIA ....... | 21 | 20 | .. | 16 | 1 | 347 | .... | 216 | ... | 13,445 | .. | 13,663 | ..... | ... | ..... | 483 | 13,848 | 3,499 |
| Total ........... | 1,929 | 138 | 18 | 121 | 36 | 1224 | .... | 4,195 | ...... | 22,415 | ... | 68,805 | ..... | .... | ...... | 1990 | 106,980 | £20,302 $101,510 |

(NOTE.—Statistics of schools include 12 schools for higher education with 3,684 students.)

### No. 64. Christian Vernacular Education Society for India. Year ending March 31st, 1890.

| Missions. | Stations and Out-stations. | Ordained. | Lay. | Wives. | Other Women. | Ordained. | Teachers. | Other Helpers. | Preaching Places. | Sabbath-school Scholars. | Churches. | Communicants. | Additions. | Schools for Higher Education. | Pupils. | Common Schools. | Pupils. | Native Contributions. |
|---|---|---|---|---|---|---|---|---|---|---|---|---|---|---|---|---|---|---|
| INDIA.............. | ...... | .. | .. | .. | ... | .. | 1,018 | .. | .. | ..... | ..... | .. | ...... | .... | .. | ..... | 211 | 8,555 | ........ |

### No. 65. China Inland Mission. Year ending December 31st, 1889.

| MISSIONS | Stations and Out-stations | Missionaries Ordained | Lay | Wives | Other Women | Native Workers Ordained | Teachers | Other Helpers | Preaching Places | Sabbath-school Scholars | Churches | Communicants | Additions | Schools for Higher Education | Pupils | Common Schools | Pupils | Native Contributions for all purposes |
|---|---|---|---|---|---|---|---|---|---|---|---|---|---|---|---|---|---|---|
| CHINA | 138 | 171 | .. | 70 | 142 | 14 | 18 | 200 | ..... | ...... | 88 | 2,839 | 536 | ... | | 24 | 276 | $676 |

### No. 67. North Africa Mission. Year ending December 31st, 1890.

| MISSIONS | Stations and Out-stations | Ordained | Lay | Wives | Other Women | Ordained | Teachers | Other Helpers | Preaching Places | Sabbath-school Scholars | Churches | Communicants | Additions | Schools Higher Ed. | Pupils | Common Schools | Pupils | Native Contributions |
|---|---|---|---|---|---|---|---|---|---|---|---|---|---|---|---|---|---|---|
| AFRICA: NORTH | 15 | 17 | .. | 9 | 28 | | | | | | | 17 | | | | 1 | 20 | |

### No. 71. Society for the Propagation of the Gospel. Year ending December 31st, 1889.

| MISSIONS | Stations and Out-stations | Ordained | Lay | Wives | Other Women | Ordained | Teachers | Other Helpers | Preaching Places | Sabbath-school Scholars | Churches | Communicants | Additions | Schools Higher Ed. | Pupils | Common Schools | Pupils | Native Contributions |
|---|---|---|---|---|---|---|---|---|---|---|---|---|---|---|---|---|---|---|
| Total | 470* | 198 | 30 | ... | 79 | 148 | | 2,300 | | | | 484† | | | | 25 | 2,650 | 800 · 39,000 (?) |

\* Stations only.     † Dioceses.

(NOTE.—The division into missions was found to be impracticable.)

### No. 72. Church Missionary Society. Year ending June 1st, 1890.

| MISSIONS | Stations and Out-stations | Ordained | Lay | Wives | Other Women | Ordained | Teachers | Other Helpers | Preaching Places | Sabbath-school Scholars | Churches | Communicants | Additions | Schools Higher Ed. | Pupils | Common Schools | Pupils | Native Contributions |
|---|---|---|---|---|---|---|---|---|---|---|---|---|---|---|---|---|---|---|
| **AFRICA:** | | | | | | | | | | | | | | | | | | |
| WEST | 48 | 14 | 4 | | 8 | | 46 | 274 | | | | 9,541 | 379 | 4 | 170 | 96 | 8,120 | £4,310 |
| EAST AND CENTRAL | 11 | 16 | 13 | | 7 | 2 | | 19 | | | | 285 | 66 | | | 8 | 521 | 13 |
| EGYPT AND ARABIA | 2 | 2 | 1 | | | | | 9 | | | | 12 | | | | 4 | 199 | 7 |
| **TURKEY:** | | | | | | | | | | | | | | | | | | |
| PALESTINE | 9 | 9 | 3 | | 7 | 8 | | 72 | | | | 455 | 3 | 1 | 22 | 43 | 2,013 | 4 |
| **PERSIA AND BAGDAD** | 2 | 5 | 2 | | 2 | 1 | | 26 | | | | 130 | 1 | | | 2 | 341 | ... |
| INDIA | 96 | 128 | 14 | | 15 | 144 | | 2,150 | | | | 26,942 | 1,577 | 5 | 224 | 1186 | 46,960 | 4,586 |
| CEYLON | 14 | 18 | | | 2 | 15 | | 446 | | | | 2,363 | 172 | 1 | 240 | 228 | 11,105 | 313 |
| MAURITIUS | 7 | 3 | 1 | | | 3 | | 51 | | | | 542 | 103 | | | 25 | 1,562 | 35 |
| CHINA | 23 | 27 | 8 | | 10 | 16 | | 309 | | | | 2,836 | 452 | 3 | 89 | 120 | 2,236 | 709 |
| JAPAN | 10 | 17 | | | 8 | 4 | | 36 | | | | 824 | 242 | 1 | 25 | 10 | 312 | 457 |
| NEW ZEALAND | 98 | 15 | 2 | | | 27 | | 378 | | | | 2,631 | 5 | 1 | | 18 | | 1,156 |
| Total | 260 | 254 | 48 | | 59 | 266 | | 3,770 | | | | 46,561 | 3,001* | 16 | 788 | 1722 | 73,369 | £11,590 · $57,950 |

\* Baptisms of adults.

(NOTE.—This table is made out from the tables in the reports, and does not include the missions in Canada.)

### No. 73. South American Missionary Society. Year ending December 31st, 1889.

| MISSIONS | Stations and Out-stations | Ordained | Lay | Wives | Other Women | Ordained | Teachers | Other Helpers | Preaching Places | Sabbath-school Scholars | Churches | Communicants | Additions | Schools Higher Ed. | Pupils | Common Schools | Pupils | Native Contributions |
|---|---|---|---|---|---|---|---|---|---|---|---|---|---|---|---|---|---|---|
| SOUTH AMERICA | 25 | 12 | 12 | 6 | 2 | | .... | | 6 | | | 14 | | | | | | £2,014 · $10,074 |

### No. 74. Universities Mission to Central Africa. Year ending December 31st, 1889.

| MISSIONS | Stations and Out-stations | Ordained | Lay | Wives | Other Women | Ordained | Teachers | Other Helpers | Preaching Places | Sabbath-school Scholars | Churches | Communicants | Additions | Schools Higher Ed. | Pupils | Common Schools | Pupils | Native Contributions |
|---|---|---|---|---|---|---|---|---|---|---|---|---|---|---|---|---|---|---|
| AFRICA: CENTRAL | 39 | 18 | 26 | | 24 | 3 | | 70 | | | 11 | 586 | | | 1 | 24 | 21 | 1,000 | |

### No. 75. Archbishop's Mission to the Assyrian Christians. Year ending June, 1888.

| MISSIONS | Stations and Out-stations | Ordained | Lay | Wives | Other Women | Ordained | Teachers | Other Helpers | Preaching Places | Sabbath-school Scholars | Churches | Communicants | Additions | Schools Higher Ed. | Pupils | Common Schools | Pupils | Native Contributions |
|---|---|---|---|---|---|---|---|---|---|---|---|---|---|---|---|---|---|---|
| PERSIA | 3 | 3 | | | | 1 | | | | | | | | | 1 | 58 | 28 | 762 | |

### No. 77. Baptist Missionary Society. Year ending March 31st, 1890.

| MISSIONS | Stations and Out-stations | Ordained | Lay | Wives | Other Women | Ordained | Teachers | Other Helpers | Preaching Places | Sabbath-school Scholars | Churches | Communicants | Additions | Schools Higher Ed. | Pupils | Common Schools | Pupils | Native Contributions |
|---|---|---|---|---|---|---|---|---|---|---|---|---|---|---|---|---|---|---|
| INDIA | 147 | 54 | | | | 94 | 160 | | | 2,132 | .. | 4,578 | 231 | | | | 3,998 | £5,475 |
| CEYLON | 104 | 3 | | | | 25 | 76 | | | 1,432 | ... | 1,017 | 64 | | | | 3,190 | 317 |
| CHINA | 60 | 21 | | | | 10 | | | | | | 1,049 | 108 | | | | | 482 |
| JAPAN | 20 | 1 | | | | 5 | 3 | | | 102 | ... | 157 | 8 | | | | 58 | ... |
| PALESTINE | 3 | 1 | | | | | 6 | | | 90 | ... | 75 | 2 | | | | 69 | ... |
| AFRICA | 10 | 25 | | | | 5 | 1 | | | 228 | ... | 43 | 12 | | | | 143 | ... |
| WEST INDIES | 111 | 7 | | | | 421 | 147 | | | 21,087 | ... | 39,869 | 3,005 | | | | 16,548 | 1,174 |
| Total | 455 | 112 | | | | 560 | 393 | | | 25,071 | ... | 46,788 | 3,425 | | | | 24,006 | £7,448 · $37,240 |

(NOTE.—Some natives are included among the missionaries. The sum total of native workers is 3,177, but to apportion all proves impracticable.)

| Missions. | Stations and Out-stations. | Missionaries. Ordained. | Lay. | Wives. | Other Women. | Native Workers. Ordained. | Teachers. | Other Helpers. | Preaching Places. | Sabbath-school Scholars. | Churches. | Communicants. | Additions. | Schools for Higher Education. | Pupils. | Common Schools. | Pupils. | Native Contributions for all purposes. |
|---|---|---|---|---|---|---|---|---|---|---|---|---|---|---|---|---|---|---|

### No. 78. General Baptist Missionary Society. Year ending March 31st, 1890.

| Missions. | | | | | | | | | | | | | | | | | | |
|---|---|---|---|---|---|---|---|---|---|---|---|---|---|---|---|---|---|---|
| INDIA : ORISSA.... | 21 | 8 | .. | 5 | 2 | 21 | 105 | ..... | ...... | 755 | 18 | 1,376 | 71 | ... | ...... | .... | 763 | Rs.6,585 $3,292 |

### No. 79. Strict Baptist Mission. Year ending December 31st, 1889.

| Missions. | | | | | | | | | | | | | | | | | | |
|---|---|---|---|---|---|---|---|---|---|---|---|---|---|---|---|---|---|---|
| INDIA : | | | | | | | | | | | | | | | | | | |
| MADRAS........... | 12 | 2 | .. | (?)2 | | 3 | 6 | 10 | ..... | .. ... | ... | 319 | ..... | ..... | .. | 15 | 359 | ....... |
| CEYLON.......... | 6 | 1 | .. | 1 | ... | .. | 7 | .... | ..... | ..... | .... | 34 | ..... | .. | | 4 | 150 | ....... |
| Total .... ....... | 18 | 3 | .. | 3 | ... | 3 | 13 | 10 | ..... | .. ... | ... | 353 | ..... | ..... | | 19 | 509 | ....... |

### No. 81. Wesleyan Methodist Missionary Society. Year ending December 31st, 1889.

| Missions. | | | | | | | | | | | | | | | | | | |
|---|---|---|---|---|---|---|---|---|---|---|---|---|---|---|---|---|---|---|
| CEYLON.......... | 75 | 16 | .. | ... | ... | 52 | 612 | 923 | 230 | 13,463 | 77 | 3,599 | 1,080 | ... | ... | 290 | 20,328 | £13,054 |
| INDIA: | | | | | | | | | | | | | | | | | | |
| MADRAS.......... | 30 | 14 | .. | ... | ... | 13 | 303 | 407 | 68 | 2,871 | 28 | 1,192 | 326 | ... | ..... | 115 | 5,876 | 7,805 |
| CENTRAL INDIA..... | 46 | 18 | .. | ... | ... | 12 | 433 | 217 | 87 | 1,361 | 33 | 1,468 | 398 | ... | ..... | 147 | 8,952 | 8,604 |
| CALCUTTA. ...... | 15 | 7 | .. | ... | ... | 7 | 94 | 99 | 44 | 619 | 10 | 360 | 71 | .... | ... | 72 | 2,965 | 3,290 |
| NORTHWEST PROV.. | 10 | 8 | .. | ... | ... | 2 | 76 | 93 | 30 | 1,792 | 7 | 418 | 17 | .... | ... | 30 | 1,726 | 4,172 |
| BURMA............ | 3 | 2 | .. | ... | ... | 2 | 6 | 2 | 8 | 62 | ... | 10 | 7 | .... | ... | 4 | 137 | 352 |
| CHINA : | | | | | | | | | | | | | | | | | | |
| CANTON AND WU-CHANG | 12 | 17 | .. | ... | ... | 5 | 14 | 27 | 14 | 94 | 12 | 1,166 | 163 | .... | ... | 14 | 223 | 472 |
| AFRICA: | | | | | | | | | | | | | | | | | | |
| SOUTH AFRICA.... | 50 | 12 | .. | ... | ... | 9 | 25 | 390 | 147 | 2,438 | 46 | 2,299 | 620 | ... | ... | 28 | 1,101 | 5,216 |
| WEST AFRICA..... | 26 | 8 | .. | ... | ... | 38 | 132 | 1,221 | 363 | 8,406 | 133 | 14,014 | 1,652 | ... | ... | 79 | 5,802 | 9,482 |
| WEST INDIES... .. | 12 | 15 | .. | ... | ... | 2 | 25 | 720 | 25 | 4,592 | 53 | 5,251 | 125 | .... | ... | 18 | 1,354 | 2,292 |
| NEW ZEALAND.... | ... | ... | .. | ... | ... | ... | ... | 2,769 | 520 | 19,742 | 213 | 7,778 | 395 | ... | .. | 23 | ..... | ..... |
| SOUTH SEAS...... | ... | ... | .. | ... | ... | ... | ... | 7,935 | 1,454 | 43,875 | 1049 | 28,757 | 4,330 | ... | ... | ... | ..... | ..... |
| Total .......... | 279 | 112 | .. | ... | ... | 142 | 1,720 | 14803 | 2,990 | 99,315 | 1661 | 66,312 | 9,184 | .... | ...... | 820 | 48,164 | £54,739 $273.695 |

### No. 82. United Methodist Free Churches. Year ending June, 1889.

| Missions. | | | | | | | | | | | | | | | | | | |
|---|---|---|---|---|---|---|---|---|---|---|---|---|---|---|---|---|---|---|
| AUSTRALIA........ | 29 | 35 | ... | ... | ... | ... | ... | ..... | 132 | 4,663 | 71 | 2,343 | 196 | ... | ... | ... | ... | ...... |
| NEW ZEALAND.... | 12 | 11 | ... | ... | ... | ... | ... | ..... | 24 | 2,216 | 23 | 898 | 21 | ... | ... | ... | ... | ...... |
| AFRICA : EAST ..... | 3 | 4 | ... | ... | ... | ... | ... | ..... | 5 | 226 | 5 | 223 | 36 | ... | ... | ... | ... | ...... |
| WEST ............ | 6 | ... | ... | ... | ... | 4 | ... | ..... | 16 | 1,386 | 15 | 2,809 | 80 | ... | ... | ... | ... | ...... |
| CHINA ............. | 3 | 3 | ... | ... | ... | ... | ... | ..... | 17 | 43 | 5 | 365 | 39 | ... | ... | ... | ... | ...... |
| JAMAICA.......... | 9 | 10 | ... | ... | ... | ... | ... | ..... | 46 | 2,176 | †26 | 3,470 | 94 | ... | ... | ... | ... | ...... |
| Total ........... | *62 | 63 | ... | ... | ... | 4 | ... | ..... | 250 | 10,710 | 145 | 10,108 | 466 | .... | ... | ... | ... | ...... |

     * Stations.      † Chapels.

### No. 83. Methodist New Connexion Missionary Society. Year ending May 30th, 1890.

| Missions. | | | | | | | | | | | | | | | | | | |
|---|---|---|---|---|---|---|---|---|---|---|---|---|---|---|---|---|---|---|
| CHINA........... | 55 | 7 | 1 | 5 | 1 | 3 | ..... | 36 | 60 | ..... | 42 | 1,301 | 33 | 1 | 10 | 15 | 230 | .... ... |

### No. 84. The Central China Wesleyan Methodist Lay Mission. Year ending December 31st, 1889.

| Missions. | | | | | | | | | | | | | | | | | | |
|---|---|---|---|---|---|---|---|---|---|---|---|---|---|---|---|---|---|---|
| CHINA............. | 3 | ... | 8 | 2 | ... | ... | ...... | 4 | 100 | ..... | ... | 12 | 12 | ... | ...... | 1 | 12 | ........ |

### No. 85. Primitive Methodist Connexion Missionary Society. Year ending March 31st, 1890.

| Missions. | | | | | | | | | | | | | | | | | | |
|---|---|---|---|---|---|---|---|---|---|---|---|---|---|---|---|---|---|---|
| AUSTRALIA........ | 40 | 31 | ... | ... | ... | ... | .... | 199 | 10? | 1,884 | ..... | .... | ... | ... | 94 | 4,625 | ....... |
| NEW ZEALAND.... | 7 | 4 | ... | ... | ... | ... | .... | 24 | 9 | 261 | ..... | .... | | 8 | 794 | ....... |
| AFRICA, SOUTH..... | 5 | 7 | ... | ... | 2 | 4 | 1 | 23 | 8 | 530 | 19 | .... | ... | 8 | 315 | £974 |
| Total .......... | 52 | 42 | ... | ... | 2 | 4 | 1 | 243 | ..... | 119 | 2,675 | 19 | .... | ...... | 110 | 5,734 | £974 $4.870 |

| Missions. | Stations and Out-stations. | Missionaries. | | | | Native Workers. | | | Preaching Places. | Sabbath-school Scholars. | Churches. | Communicants. | Additions. | Schools for Higher Education. | Pupils. | Common Schools. | Pupils. | Native Contributions for all purposes. |
|---|---|---|---|---|---|---|---|---|---|---|---|---|---|---|---|---|---|---|
| | | Ordained. | Lay. | Wives. | Other Women. | Ordained. | Teachers. | Other Helpers. | | | | | | | | | | |

**No. 86. Bible Christian Home and Foreign Missionary Society. Year ending July, 1890.**

| Missions. | Stations and Out-stations. | Ordained. | Lay. | Wives. | Other Women. | Ordained. | Teachers. | Other Helpers. | Preaching Places. | Sabbath-school Scholars. | Churches. | Communicants. | Additions. | Schools for Higher Education. | Pupils. | Common Schools. | Pupils. | Native Contributions. |
|---|---|---|---|---|---|---|---|---|---|---|---|---|---|---|---|---|---|---|
| AUSTRALIA | | 78 | | | | | 1,755 | 385 | 334 | 12,500 | 254 | 5,426 | 656 | | | | | £2,657 |
| NEW ZEALAND | | 7 | | | | | 80 | 32 | 38 | 600 | 8 | 294 | 60 | | | | | $13,285 |
| CHINA | | 6 | | | | | 2 | 1 | 3 | 24 | | 6 | | | | | | |
| Total | | 91 | | | | | 1,837 | 408 | 375 | 13,124 | 262 | 5,726 | 716 | | | | | |

**No. 89. Welsh Calvinistic Methodist Foreign Missionary Society. Year ending December 31st, 1889.**

| Missions. | Stations and Out-stations. | Ordained. | Lay. | Wives. | Other Women. | Ordained. | Teachers. | Other Helpers. | Preaching Places. | Sabbath-school Scholars. | Churches. | Communicants. | Additions. | Schools for Higher Education. | Pupils. | Common Schools. | Pupils. | Native Contributions. |
|---|---|---|---|---|---|---|---|---|---|---|---|---|---|---|---|---|---|---|
| INDIA, N. E. | *9 | 8 | 1 | 5 | 1 | 4 | | 564 | 163 | 6,611 | 72 | 1,869 | 285 | 1 | 9 | 142 | 4,131 | £400 ($2,000) |

\* Stations only.

**No. 90. Presbyterian Church of England Foreign Missionary Society. Year ending December 31st, 1889.**

| Missions. | Stations and Out-stations. | Ordained. | Lay. | Wives. | Other Women. | Ordained. | Teachers. | Other Helpers. | Preaching Places. | Sabbath-school Scholars. | Churches. | Communicants. | Additions. | Schools for Higher Education. | Pupils. | Common Schools. | Pupils. | Native Contributions. |
|---|---|---|---|---|---|---|---|---|---|---|---|---|---|---|---|---|---|---|
| CHINA | 130 | 20 | 11 | 20 | 13 | 8 | | 106 | 130 | | 43 | 3,572 | 164 | 4 | 41 | | | £525 |
| INDIA | | | 2 | 1 | 3 | | | 2 | | | | 30 | 10 | | | | | 24 |
| Total | 130 | 20 | 13 | 21 | 16 | 8 | | 108 | 130 | | 43 | 3,602 | 174 | 4 | 41 | | | £549 $2,745 |

**No. 93. Friends' Foreign Mission Association. Year ending December 31st, 1889.**

| Missions. | Stations and Out-stations. | Ordained. | Lay. | Wives. | Other Women. | Ordained. | Teachers. | Other Helpers. | Preaching Places. | Sabbath-school Scholars. | Churches. | Communicants. | Additions. | Schools for Higher Education. | Pupils. | Common Schools. | Pupils. | Native Contributions. |
|---|---|---|---|---|---|---|---|---|---|---|---|---|---|---|---|---|---|---|
| CHINA | 1 | 3 | | 1 | | | | | | | | | | | | | | |
| INDIA | 4 | 6 | | 9 | | 4 | | | 10 | | 5 | | | | | 2 | †75 | |
| TURKEY (Armenian Mission) | 4 | 1 | | 1 | | 4 | | 3 | 1 | | | | | | | | | |
| MADAGASCAR | 3 | 9 | | 13 | | 323 | | | | | 143 | | | 2 | 514 | 31 | †3,967 | |
| AFRICA: Zululand | 4 | 2 | | 1 | | | | | | | | | | | | | | |
| Total | 16 | 21 | | 25 | | 331 | | 3 | 11 | | 148 | *2,612 | | 2 | 514 | 33 | †4,042 | |

\* Total December, 1890.     † Estimated.

**No. 94. Friends' Mission to Syria and Palestine. Year ending December 31st, 1890.**

| Missions. | Stations and Out-stations. | Ordained. | Lay. | Wives. | Other Women. | Ordained. | Teachers. | Other Helpers. | Preaching Places. | Sabbath-school Scholars. | Churches. | Communicants. | Additions. | Schools for Higher Education. | Pupils. | Common Schools. | Pupils. | Native Contributions. |
|---|---|---|---|---|---|---|---|---|---|---|---|---|---|---|---|---|---|---|
| SYRIA | 7 | 2 | | 2 | 4 | 1 | | | 12 | | | | 1 | | | 2 | 50 | 10 | 330 | £431 ($2,155) |

## SCOTLAND.

**No. 101. Church of Scotland Committee for the Propagation of the Gospel in Foreign Parts. Year ending December 31st, 1889.**

| Missions. | Stations and Out-stations. | Ordained. | Lay. | Wives. | Other Women. | Ordained. | Teachers. | Other Helpers. | Preaching Places. | Sabbath-school Scholars. | Churches. | Communicants. | Additions. | Schools for Higher Education. | Pupils. | Common Schools. | Pupils. | Native Contributions. |
|---|---|---|---|---|---|---|---|---|---|---|---|---|---|---|---|---|---|---|
| INDIA: | | | | | | | | | | | | | | | | | | |
| CALCUTTA | 4 | 3 | | | | | 1 | 6 | 5 | 3 | | 3 | 82 | 9 | 1 | 326 | 1 | 516 | £2,865 |
| MADRAS | 3 | 2 | 2 | | | | 2 | 19 | 4 | 1 | | 1 | 135 | 6 | 1 | | 10 | 1,436 | 2,497 |
| BOMBAY | 1 | 1 | 1 | | | | | | | 1 | | | 17 | 3 | | | 1 | 201 | 354 |
| PUNJAB | 5 | 3 | 1 | | | | 4 | 32 | 20 | 4 | | 4 | 195 | 555 | 1 | 52 | 40 | 2,115 | 634 |
| DARJEELING | 15 | 2 | | | | | | 19 | 21 | 15 | | 15 | 176 | 45 | | 15 | 23 | 842 | 89 |
| GUILD MISSION | 4 | 1 | | | | | | 15 | 5 | 4 | | 4 | 209 | 23 | | 14 | 7 | 231 | 31 |
| UNIVERSITIES MISS. | 3 | 1 | | | | | | 6 | 1 | 2 | | 2 | 32 | | | | 7 | 221 | 14 |
| AFRICA, EAST | 1 | 3 | 10 | | | | | 7 | 4 | 11 | | 2 | 23 | 16 | | | 7 | 640 | *58 |
| CHINA | 1 | 1 | | | | | | 1 | 2 | 1 | | 1 | 26 | | | | 1 | 39 | 1 |
| Total | 37 | 17 | 14 | 18 | | 7 | 105 | 63 | 42 | | 33 | 825 | †657 | 3 | 407 | 97 | 6,241 | £5,943 $29,715 |

\* Including European collections.     † Baptisms of adults.

| Missions. | Stations and Out-stations. | Missionaries. | | | | Native Workers. | | | Preaching Places. | Sabbath-school Scholars. | Churches. | Communicants. | Additions. | Schools for Higher Education. | Pupils. | Common Schools. | Pupils. | Native Contributions for all purposes. |
|---|---|---|---|---|---|---|---|---|---|---|---|---|---|---|---|---|---|---|
| | | Ordained. | Lay. | Wives. | Other Women | Ordained. | Teachers. | Other Helpers | | | | | | | | | | |

**No. 102. Scottish Reformed Presbyterian Synod Syrian Mission. Year ending April 30th, 1890.**

| Missions. | | Ord. | | | | | | | | | | | | | | | | |
|---|---|---|---|---|---|---|---|---|---|---|---|---|---|---|---|---|---|---|
| Syria | 3 | 1 | .. | 1 | 1 | .. | .. | 9 | 3 | 120 | 1 | 37 | 2 | .. | .. | 3 | 200 | .. .. |

**No. 103. Foreign Mission Committee of the Free Church of Scotland. Year ending March 31st, 1890.**

| Missions. | | Ord. | Lay | Wives | O.W. | Ord. | Teach. | O.H. | P.P. | S.S. | Ch. | Comm. | Add. | S.H.E. | Pupils | C.S. | Pupils | Contrib. |
|---|---|---|---|---|---|---|---|---|---|---|---|---|---|---|---|---|---|---|
| INDIA: | | | | | | | | | | | | | | | | | | |
| Western India | 7 | 7 | 1 | ... | 5 | 4 | 31 | 7 | 7 | ..... | 4 | 243 | 26 | 1 | 221 | 26 | 2,715 | £2,141 |
| Madras | 13 | 10 | 4 | ... | 7 | 2 | 118 | 35 | 13 | ..... | 3 | 358 | 34 | 2 | 619 | 39 | 5,757 | 7,782 |
| Central India | 7 | 5 | 2 | ... | 4 | 2 | 24 | 12 | 7 | ..... | 4 | 173 | 6 | 1 | 60 | 16 | 2,507 | 268 |
| Deccan | 44 | .. | .. | ... | 1 | 1 | 1 | 31 | 44 | ..... | 6 | 1,035 | 1 | ... | .. | 16 | 400 | 10 |
| Calcutta | 4 | 6 | 2 | ... | 6 | 3 | 38 | 15 | 4 | ..... | 5 | 170 | 8 | 1 | 196 | 58 | 4,719 | 2,889 |
| Santalia | 4 | 2 | 1 | ... | .. | .. | 26 | 21 | 4 | ..... | 2 | 168 | ..... | ... | ..... | 55 | 1,200 | 71 |
| AFRICA: | | | | | | | | | | | | | | | | | | |
| Kafraria | 74 | 10 | 17 | ... | 9 | 2 | 95 | 32 | 74 | ..... | 9 | 2,293 | 75 | 1 | 51 | 58 | 4,189 | 4,191 |
| Natal | 25 | 8 | 6 | ... | 7 | ... | 13 | 48 | 25 | ..... | 3 | 621 | 1 | ... | ..... | 15 | 805 | 235 |
| Livingstonia | 17 | 5 | 8 | ... | .. | ... | 43 | 5 | 17 | ..... | 1 | 48 | ..... | ... | ..... | 21 | 3,080 | 1 |
| NEW HEBRIDES | 4 | 1 | 1 | ... | .. | ... | 37 | ... | 4 | ..... | 3 | 344 | ..... | ... | ..... | 14 | 241 | 13 |
| SYRIA | 7 | 1 | .. | ... | .. | ... | .. | 4 | 7 | ..... | 2 | 61 | ..... | ... | ..... | .. | ..... | 7 |
| ARABIA | 1 | 1 | 2 | ... | .. | .. | 3 | ... | 1 | ..... | .. | ..... | ..... | ... | ..... | 2 | 66 | .. .. |
| Total | 207 | 51 | 44 | 32 | 38 | 14 | 429 | 210 | 207 | ..... | 42 | 6,626 | 151 | 6 | 1,147 | 329 | 25,679 | £17,561 |
| | | | | | | | | | | | | | | | | | | $87,805 |

**No. 104. United Presbyterian Church of Scotland Foreign Mission. Year ending December 31st, 1889.**

| Missions. | | Ord. | Lay | Wives | O.W. | Ord. | Teach. | O.H. | P.P. | S.S. | Ch. | Comm. | Add. | S.H.E. | Pupils | C.S. | Pupils | Contrib. |
|---|---|---|---|---|---|---|---|---|---|---|---|---|---|---|---|---|---|---|
| WEST INDIES: | | | | | | | | | | | | | | | | | | |
| Jamaica | 50 | 16 | ... | .. | 15 | 79 | 17 | | 50 | 7,704 | *50 | 9,444 | 313 | ... | ..... | 79 | 7,196 | £7,150 |
| Trinidad | 3 | 2 | ... | .. | 1 | ..... | ... | | 3 | 567 | *3 | 387 | 8 | ... | ..... | .. | ..... | 1,063 |
| AFRICA, West | 27 | 7 | 4 | .. | 7 | 3 | 16 | 5 | 27 | 979 | *8 | 328 | 17 | ... | ..... | 23 | 781 | ....... |
| Kafraria | 108 | 12 | ... | .. | 3 | ... | 39 | 24 | 108 | 1,174 | +12 | 2,425 | 118 | ... | ..... | 37 | 1,641 | ....... |
| INDIA | 42 | 14 | 3 | .. | 11 | 2 | 169 | 108 | ..... | 1,526 | +11 | 485 | 29 | ... | ..... | 79 | 4,579 | ....... |
| CHINA | 18 | 5 | 3 | .. | 2 | ... | 2 | 32 | 18 | ..... | +5 | 956 | 161 | ... | ..... | 8 | 86 | ....... |
| JAPAN | 3 | 3 | ... | .. | 2 | ... | 2 | 2 | ..... | ..... | *7 | 874 | 174 | ... | ..... | .. | ..... | ....... |
| Total | 251 | 59 | 10 | 60 | 24 | 23 | 307 | 188 | 206 | 11,950 | 96 | 14,899 | 820 | ... | 80 | 226 | 14,283 | ‡10,470 |
| | | | | | | | | | | | | | | | | | | $52,350 |

      * Congregations.      † Stations.      ‡ Total.

**No. 105. United Original Secession Church, South India Mission. Year ending May 1st, 1890.**

| Missions. | | Ord. | Lay | Wives | O.W. | Ord. | Teach. | O.H. | P.P. | S.S. | Ch. | Comm. | Add. | S.H.E. | Pupils | C.S. | Pupils | Contrib. |
|---|---|---|---|---|---|---|---|---|---|---|---|---|---|---|---|---|---|---|
| INDIA: | | | | | | | | | | | | | | | | | | £62 |
| Central | ..... | 1 | 1 | 1 | ... | ... | .... | 9 | 2 | ..... | 1 | 16 | ..... | ... | ..... | 3 | 312 | $310 |

## IRELAND.

**No. 109. Presbyterian Church of Ireland, Foreign Mission. Year ending March 31st, 1890.**

| Missions. | | Ord. | Lay | Wives | O.W. | Ord. | Teach. | O.H. | P.P. | S.S. | Ch. | Comm. | Add. | S.H.E. | Pupils | C.S. | Pupils | Contrib. |
|---|---|---|---|---|---|---|---|---|---|---|---|---|---|---|---|---|---|---|
| INDIA | 16 | 8 | 3 | 7 | 8 | ... | 56 | *20 | ..... | ..... | 18 | 290 | ..... | 2 | 43 | 42 | 3,359 | ....... |
| CHINA | 8 | 4 | ... | 4 | 1 | 2 | ..... | 16 | ..... | ..... | .. | 130 | ..... | .. | .. | .. | 20 | ....... |
| Total | 24 | 12 | 3 | 11 | 9 | 2 | 56 | 36 | ..... | ..... | 18 | 420 | ..... | 2 | 43 | 42 | 3,379 | £1,836 |
| | | | | | | | | | | | | | | | | | | $9,180 |

      * Estimated.

## CONTINENTAL EUROPE.

### DENMARK.

**No. 115. Danish Mission Society (Det Danske Missionsselskab). Year ending December 31st, 1889.**

| Missions. | | Ord. | Lay | Wives | O.W. | Ord. | Teach. | O.H. | P.P. | S.S. | Ch. | Comm. | Add. | S.H.E. | Pupils | C.S. | Pupils | Contrib. |
|---|---|---|---|---|---|---|---|---|---|---|---|---|---|---|---|---|---|---|
| INDIA | 4 | 5 | 2 | 5 | 1 | 3 | ..... | 19 | 4 | ..... | 4 | 208 | ..... | .. | ..... | .. | ..... | ....... |

| Missions. | Stations and Out-stations. | Missionaries. | | | | Native Workers. | | | Preaching Places. | Sabbath-school Scholars. | Churches. | Communicants. | Additions. | Schools for Higher Education. | Pupils. | Common Schools. | Pupils. | Native Contributions for all purposes. |
|---|---|---|---|---|---|---|---|---|---|---|---|---|---|---|---|---|---|---|
| | | Ordained. | Lay. | Wives. | Other Women. | Ordained. | Teachers. | Other Helpers. | | | | | | | | | | |

**No. 116. Indian Home Mission to the Santals. Year ending March 31st, 1890.**

| Missions. | Stations and Out-stations. | Ordained. | Lay. | Wives. | Other Women. | Ordained. | Teachers. | Other Helpers. | Preaching Places. | Sabbath-school Scholars. | Churches. | Communicants. | Additions. | Schools for Higher Education. | Pupils. | Common Schools. | Pupils. | Native Contributions. |
|---|---|---|---|---|---|---|---|---|---|---|---|---|---|---|---|---|---|---|
| INDIA.... .......... | 14 | 6 | 2 | 5 | 5 | 5 | ..... | ..... | 142 | ..... | .... | 14 | 6,070 | 707 | 2 | 284 | ... | ..... | Rs 134 $67 |

**No. 117. Loventhal's Mission. Year ending December 31st, 1889.**

| INDIA : Madras.... | 1 | 1 | .. | 1 | ... | ... | ...... | | 3 | ...... | | ..... | 1 | 12 | ...... | ... | ...... | ... | ...... |

## NORWAY.

**No. 121. The Norwegian Missionary Society (Det Norske Missionsselskab). Year ending December 31st, 1889.**

| AFRICA (South).... | 11 | 14 | .... | ... | 2 | ... | ..... | 16 | ..... | ...... | | 500 | ..... | ... | ... | ..... | ... | 448 | ...... |
| MADAGASCAR...... | 29 | 25 | ... | ... | 10 | 16 | ..... | 900 | ... | .... | | 16,555 | ..... | | ... | ..... | | 37,500 | ........ |
| Total .... ........ | 40 | 39 | 5 | 37 | 12 | 16 | ..... | 916 | 379 | ..... | | 17,055 | ..... | | 2 | | 80 | 370 | 37,948 | ........ |

**No. 122. The Schreuder Mission. Year ending December, 1888 (?).**

| AFRICA (South)... | 2 | 3 | . | 1 | ... | 2 | ..... | | ...... | ..... | | ... | 130 | ..... | | ... | ...... | .. | 124 | .... ... |

## SWEDEN.

**No. 127. Evangelical National Association. Year ending December 31st, 1889.**

| AFRICA.... ........ | 4 | 3 | 4 | 3 | 3 | 3 | .... | 18 | ...... | ...... | 1 | 84 | 26 | .... | ... | | 2 | 111 | ... ..... |
| INDIA......... ..... | 6 | 8 | 3 | 6 | 2 | | .... | 8 | ...... | ...... | 4 | 24 | 24 | ..... | ... | | 8 | 342 | ........ |
| Total ........... | 10 | 11 | 7 | 9 | 5 | 3 | .... | 26 | ...... | ...... | 5 | ·108 | 50 | ... | .... | | 10 | 453 | ........ |

**No. 130. Swedish Church Mission.**

| AFRICA............ | 5 | 9 | ... | ... | ... | ... | ...... | | ...... | ..... | ... | 71 | ..... | | ... | ...... | .. | 68 | ...... |
| INDIA .............. | 9 | 4 | ... | ... | ... | ... | ...... | | ...... | ...... | ... | 545 | ..... | | ... | ...... | .. | | ...... |
| Total ........ ... | 14 | 13 | ... | ... | ... | ... | ...... | | ...... | ...... | ... | 616 | ...... | .. | | ...... | ... | 68 | ... ..... |

**No. 131. Swedish Mission Association (Svenska Missionsförbundet). Year ending December, 1890.**

| RUSSIA and FINN-MARK.... ...... | 10 | 0 | ... | ... | .. | ... | ..... | | ...... | ...... | | ...... | ..... | | ... | ...... | | ...... | ...... |
| AFRICA (Congo).... | 3 | 3 | ... | ... | ... | ... | ..... | 10 | ...... | ...... | | .. | ...... | | ... | ...... | | ...... | ...... |
| ALGIERS ......... | ... | 2 | ... | ... | ... | ... | ..... | | ...... | ...... | | .. | ...... | | ... | ...... | | ...... | ...... |
| ALASKA........... | 2 | 5 | ... | ... | ... | ... | ..... | | ...... | ...... | | .. | ...... | | ... | ...... | | ...... | ...... |
| Total ........... | 15 | 10 | .. | ... | ... | ... | ..... | 10 | ...... | ...... | | .. | ...... | | ... | ...... | | ...... | ...... |

**No. 135. Swedish Mission in China (Svenska Missionen, Kina). Year ending May, 1890.**

| CHINA............. | 8 | ... | 4 | 1 | 4 | ... | ..... | | ...... | ...... | | ... | 1 | 14 | 8 | ... | ...... | ... | ...... | ...... |

**No. 138. Finland Missionary Society. Year ending April 30th, 1890.**

| AFRICA (South).... | 4 | 5 | 1 | 5 | ... | ... | ..... | 10 | ... | ... | | | 2 | 87 | ...... | | ...... | 3 | 160 | £5 ($25) |

| MISSIONS. | Stations and Out-stations. | Missionaries Ordained. | Lay. | Wives. | Other Women. | Native Workers Ordained. | Teachers. | Other Helpers. | Preaching Places. | Sabbath-school Scholars. | Churches. | Communicants. | Additions. | Schools for Higher Education. | Pupils. | Common Schools. | Pupils. | Native Contributions for all purposes. |
|---|---|---|---|---|---|---|---|---|---|---|---|---|---|---|---|---|---|---|

## GERMANY.

### No. 141. UNITED BRETHREN OR MORAVIAN MISSIONS. YEAR ENDING DECEMBER 31st, 1888.

| MISSIONS. | Stations | Ord. | Lay | Wives | Oth.W | Ord. | Teach. | Oth.H | Preach | S.S.Schol | Ch. | Commun | Add | Sch.H.E | Pupils | Com.Sch | Pupils | Native Contrib |
|---|---|---|---|---|---|---|---|---|---|---|---|---|---|---|---|---|---|---|
| NORTH AMERICA: | | | | | | | | | | | | | | | | | | |
| GREENLAND | 6 | 16 | ... | ... | ... | ... | 32 | 10 | ... | ... | ... | 780 | ... | ... | ... | 32 | ... | ... |
| LABRADOR | 6 | 38 | ... | ... | ... | ... | 5 | 53 | ... | ... | ... | 496 | ... | ... | ... | 6 | ... | ... |
| ALASKA | 2 | 8 | ... | ... | ... | ... | ... | ... | ... | ... | ... | ... | ... | ... | ... | 2 | ... | ... |
| INDIAN MISSION | 5 | 10 | ... | ... | ... | ... | 2 | 8 | 135 | ... | ... | 201 | ... | ... | ... | 2 | ... | ... |
| WEST INDIES | 49 | 50 | ... | ... | ... | 33 | 145 | 471 | ... | ... | 6,371 | 10,251 | ... | ... | ... | 62 | ... | ... |
| MOSQUITO COAST | 14 | 20 | ... | ... | ... | 6 | 13 | 54 | ... | 755 | ... | 867 | ... | ... | ... | 11 | ... | ... |
| SURINAM | 22 | 74 | ... | ... | ... | 3 | 49 | 259 | ... | 270 | ... | 8,056 | ... | ... | ... | 13 | ... | ... |
| AFRICA (South) | 24 | 61 | ... | ... | ... | 9 | 66 | 302 | ... | 488 | ... | 3,206 | ... | ... | ... | 30 | ... | ... |
| AUSTRALIA | 2 | 5 | ... | ... | ... | ... | 1 | ... | ... | 22 | ... | 32 | ... | ... | ... | 2 | ... | ... |
| ASIA (Little Tibet) | 3 | 10 | ... | ... | ... | ... | 3 | ... | ... | ... | ... | 12 | ... | ... | ... | 5 | ... | ... |
| Total | 133 | 292 | 24 | 135 | 6 | 51 | 316 | 1,157 | ... | 8,041 | ... | 23,901 | ... | ... | ... | 165 | ... | ... |

### No. 142. BASEL EVANGELICAL MISSION SOCIETY. YEAR ENDING JUNE 30TH, 1890.

| MISSIONS. | Stations | Ord. | Lay | Wives | Oth.W | Ord. | Teach. | Oth.H | Preach | S.S.Schol | Ch. | Commun | Add | Sch.H.E | Pupils | Com.Sch | Pupils | Native Contrib |
|---|---|---|---|---|---|---|---|---|---|---|---|---|---|---|---|---|---|---|
| AFRICA: | | | | | | | | | | | | | | | | | | |
| GOLD COAST | 117 | 24 | 11 | 20 | 3 | 18 | 60 | 91 | 117 | 146 | ... | 3,662 | 849 | 1 | 38 | 107 | 2,607 | Francs. |
| KAMERUNS | 33 | 8 | 3 | 2 | ... | ... | 4 | 13 | 33 | 493 | ... | 149 | 15 | ... | ... | 12 | 284 | ... |
| CHINA | 45 | 18 | 1 | 14 | ... | 6 | 45 | 44 | 45 | ... | ... | 2,111 | 226 | 1 | 9 | 42 | 801 | ... |
| INDIA | 157 | 54 | 14 | 52 | 1 | 15 | 279 | 136 | 157 | 335 | ... | 5,160 | 219 | 2 | 29 | 117 | 6,343 | ... |
| Total | 352 | 104 | 29 | 88 | 4 | 39 | 388 | 284 | 352 | 974 | ... | 11,082 | 1,309 | 4 | 76 | 278 | 10,035 | +40-50,000 $8-10,000 |

*Details not given.*

### No. 143. LEIPSIC EVANGELICAL LUTHERAN MISSIONARY SOCIETY. YEAR ENDING DECEMBER 31st, 1889.

| MISSIONS. | Stations | Ord. | Lay | Wives | Oth.W | Ord. | Teach. | Oth.H | Preach | S.S.Schol | Ch. | Commun | Add | Sch.H.E | Pupils | Com.Sch | Pupils | Native Contrib |
|---|---|---|---|---|---|---|---|---|---|---|---|---|---|---|---|---|---|---|
| INDIA: | | | | | | | | | | | | | | | | | | |
| MADRAS | 612 | 25 | 1 | ... | ... | 13 | 295 | 187 | ... | ... | 140 | 13,442 | 227 | ... | ... | 176 | 4,414 | Rs 4,308 |
| BURMA | 5 | ... | ... | ... | ... | 1 | 5 | 4 | ... | ... | 1 | 117 | 1 | ... | ... | 1 | 78 | 327 |
| Total | 617 | 25 | 1 | ... | ... | 14 | 300 | 191 | ... | ... | 141* | 13,559 | 228 | ... | ... | 177 | 4,492 | 4,635 $2,317 |

*Gottesdienstlokale.*

### No. 144. BERLIN EVANGELICAL MISSIONARY SOCIETY. YEAR ENDING DECEMBER, 1889.

| MISSIONS. | Stations | Ord. | Lay | Wives | Oth.W | Ord. | Teach. | Oth.H | Preach | S.S.Schol | Ch. | Commun | Add | Sch.H.E | Pupils | Com.Sch | Pupils | Native Contrib |
|---|---|---|---|---|---|---|---|---|---|---|---|---|---|---|---|---|---|---|
| AFRICA | 134 | 56 | 5 | 53 | ... | ... | ... | 429 | 152 | ... | ... | 10,384 | 585 | ... | ... | ... | ... | ... |
| CHINA | 17 | 6 | ... | 6 | ... | ... | ... | 46 | 15 | ... | ... | 372 | 36 | ... | ... | ... | ... | ... |
| Total | 151 | 62 | 5 | 59 | 5 | 5 | ... | 475 | 167 | ... | ... | 10,756 | 621 | 3 | 28 | 52 | 430 | ... |

### No. 145. RHENISH MISSIONARY SOCIETY. YEAR ENDING DECEMBER 31st, 1888.

| MISSIONS. | Stations | Ord. | Lay | Wives | Oth.W | Ord. | Teach. | Oth.H | Preach | S.S.Schol | Ch. | Commun | Add | Sch.H.E | Pupils | Com.Sch | Pupils | Native Contrib |
|---|---|---|---|---|---|---|---|---|---|---|---|---|---|---|---|---|---|---|
| AFRICA: | | | | | | | | | | | | | | | | | | Marks |
| CAPE COLONY | 14 | 13 | 1 | 13 | ... | ... | 43 | 44 | ... | 1,864 | ... | 3,918 | 63 | ... | ... | ... | 2,373 | 38,749 |
| NAMAQUA | 11 | 9 | ... | 9 | ... | ... | 5 | 27 | ... | 245 | ... | 1,709 | 68 | ... | ... | ... | 651 | 1,985 |
| HERERO | 12 | 7 | ... | 6 | ... | ... | 13 | 29 | ... | ... | ... | 757 | 19 | ... | ... | ... | 552 | 1,730 |
| MALAYSIA: | | | | | | | | | | | | | | | | | | |
| SUMATRA | 69 | 16 | ... | 13 | ... | 3 | 78 | 202 | ... | 1,074 | ... | 3,192 | 1,244 | ... | ... | ... | 1,422 | 6,918 |
| BORNEO | 8 | 8 | ... | 4 | ... | ... | 16 | 10 | ... | 60 | ... | 583 | 72 | ... | ... | ... | 365 | 638 |
| NIAS | 5 | 5 | ... | 3 | ... | ... | 6 | 3 | ... | 52 | ... | 161 | 15 | ... | ... | ... | 46 | ... |
| NEW GUINEA | 1 | 4 | ... | 1 | ... | ... | ... | ... | ... | ... | ... | ... | ... | ... | ... | ... | ... | ... |
| CHINA | 8 | 5 | 1 | 2 | ... | 1 | 5 | 3 | ... | ... | ... | 155 | 8 | ... | ... | ... | 51 | 280 |
| Total | 128 | 67 | 2 | 51 | ... | 4 | *166 | 311 | ... | 3,295 | ... | 10,475 | 1,489 | ... | ... | ... | 5,460 | +50,300 $12,575 |

* Paid native helpers (unordained). Statistics received to close of 1890, but not so full as in the Report, and therefore the Report is given.
† Approximated.

### No. 146. GOSSNER'S MISSIONARY SOCIETY. YEAR ENDING DECEMBER 31st, 1889.

| MISSIONS. | Stations | Ord. | Lay | Wives | Oth.W | Ord. | Teach. | Oth.H | Preach | S.S.Schol | Ch. | Commun | Add | Sch.H.E | Pupils | Com.Sch | Pupils | Native Contrib |
|---|---|---|---|---|---|---|---|---|---|---|---|---|---|---|---|---|---|---|
| INDIA | 8 | ... | ... | ... | ... | 17 | ... | ... | ... | ... | 165 | 30,027 | ... | ... | ... | ... | ... | ... |

| Missions. | Out-Stations and stations. | MISSIONARIES. | | | | NATIVE WORKERS. | | | Preaching Places. | Sabbath-school Scholars. | Churches. | Communicants. | Additions. | Schools for Higher Education. | Pupils. | Common Schools. | Pupils. | Native Contributions for all purposes. |
|---|---|---|---|---|---|---|---|---|---|---|---|---|---|---|---|---|---|---|
| | | Ordained. | Lay. | Wives. | Other Women. | Ordained. | Teachers. | Other Helpers. | | | | | | | | | | |

### No. 147. North German Missionary Society. Year ending December 31st, 1889.

| Missions. | Out-Stations and stations. | Ordained. | Lay. | Wives. | Other Women. | Ordained. | Teachers. | Other Helpers. | Preaching Places. | Sabbath-school Scholars. | Churches. | Communicants. | Additions. | Schools for Higher Education. | Pupils. | Common Schools. | Pupils. | Native Contributions for all purposes. |
|---|---|---|---|---|---|---|---|---|---|---|---|---|---|---|---|---|---|---|
| AFRICA (WESTERN). | 14 | 11 | 4 | 6 | 2 | 1 | ...... | 24 | ...... | ...... | ... | 408 | 29 | 2 | 30 | 13 | 280 | Marks 615 ($153.75) |

### No. 149. Hermannsburg Evangelical Lutheran Mission. Year ending December 31st, 1889.

| Missions. | Out-Stations and stations. | Ordained. | Lay. | Wives. | Other Women. | Ordained. | Teachers. | Other Helpers. | Preaching Places. | Sabbath-school Scholars. | Churches. | Communicants. | Additions. | Schools for Higher Education. | Pupils. | Common Schools. | Pupils. | Native Contributions for all purposes. |
|---|---|---|---|---|---|---|---|---|---|---|---|---|---|---|---|---|---|---|
| AFRICA: TRANSVAAL | 80 | 60 | ... | ... | ... | ... | ... | 297 | ...... | ...... | ... | (?) 11,500 | (?) 1,735 | ...... | ...... | ...... | 2,567 | Marks 21,187 |
| INDIA | 10 | 9 | ... | ... | ... | ... | ... | 35 | ...... | ...... | ... | (?)871 | (?)25 | ...... | ...... | ...... | ...... | ...... |
| Total | 90 | 69 | ... | ... | ... | ... | ... | 332 | ...... | ...... | ... | 12,371 | 1,760 | ...... | ...... | ...... | 2,567 | 21,187 $5,297 |

### No. 150. Breklum Missionary Society. Year ending December, 1888 (?).

| Missions. | Out-Stations and stations. | Ordained. | Lay. | Wives. | Other Women. | Ordained. | Teachers. | Other Helpers. | Preaching Places. | Sabbath-school Scholars. | Churches. | Communicants. | Additions. | Schools for Higher Education. | Pupils. | Common Schools. | Pupils. | Native Contributions for all purposes. |
|---|---|---|---|---|---|---|---|---|---|---|---|---|---|---|---|---|---|---|
| INDIA (CENTRAL) ... | 6 | 11 | ... | ... | ... | ... | ... | ...... | ...... | ...... | ... | ...... | ...... | ...... | ...... | ...... | 6 | ...... |

## HOLLAND.

### No. 155. Netherlands Mission Society. Year ending December, 31st, 1889 (?).

| Missions. | Out-Stations and stations. | Ordained. | Lay. | Wives. | Other Women. | Ordained. | Teachers. | Other Helpers. | Preaching Places. | Sabbath-school Scholars. | Churches. | Communicants. | Additions. | Schools for Higher Education. | Pupils. | Common Schools. | Pupils. | Native Contributions for all purposes. |
|---|---|---|---|---|---|---|---|---|---|---|---|---|---|---|---|---|---|---|
| MALAYSIA. | *3 | 18 | ... | ... | ... | ... | ... | 184 | ...... | ...... | ... | 20,000 | ...... | ... | ...... | 136 | ...... | ...... |

*Stations.

### No. 156. Ermelo Missionary Society.

| Missions. | Out-Stations and stations. | Ordained. | Lay. | Wives. | Other Women. | Ordained. | Teachers. | Other Helpers. | Preaching Places. | Sabbath-school Scholars. | Churches. | Communicants. | Additions. | Schools for Higher Education. | Pupils. | Common Schools. | Pupils. | Native Contributions for all purposes. |
|---|---|---|---|---|---|---|---|---|---|---|---|---|---|---|---|---|---|---|
| JAVA | 6 | 6 | ... | ... | ... | ... | ... | 19 | ... | ... | 30 | 700 | ...... | ... | ...... | ... | ... | ... |

### No. 157. Mennonite Missionary Society. Year ending September, 1889.

| Missions. | Out-Stations and stations. | Ordained. | Lay. | Wives. | Other Women. | Ordained. | Teachers. | Other Helpers. | Preaching Places. | Sabbath-school Scholars. | Churches. | Communicants. | Additions. | Schools for Higher Education. | Pupils. | Common Schools. | Pupils. | Native Contributions for all purposes. |
|---|---|---|---|---|---|---|---|---|---|---|---|---|---|---|---|---|---|---|
| JAVA | 6 | 2 | ... | ... | ... | ... | ... | 12 | ...... | ...... | ... | 388 | 20 | 1 | ...... | 4 | 140 | ...... |
| SUMATRA | 2 | 2 | ... | ... | ... | ... | ... | 5 | ...... | ...... | ... | 123 | ...... | ... | ...... | 2 | 70 | ...... |
| Total | 8 | 4 | 2 | ... | ... | ... | ... | 17 | ...... | ...... | ... | 511 | 20 | 1 | ...... | 6 | 210 | ...... |

### No. 159. Dutch Missionary Society. Year ending December 31st, 1889.

| Missions. | Out-Stations and stations. | Ordained. | Lay. | Wives. | Other Women. | Ordained. | Teachers. | Other Helpers. | Preaching Places. | Sabbath-school Scholars. | Churches. | Communicants. | Additions. | Schools for Higher Education. | Pupils. | Common Schools. | Pupils. | Native Contributions for all purposes. |
|---|---|---|---|---|---|---|---|---|---|---|---|---|---|---|---|---|---|---|
| JAVA | 20 | 8 | 8 | ... | ... | ... | ... | 24 | 8 | ...... | ... | 1,013 | 143 | ... | ...... | 15 | 219 | ...... |

### No. 160. Utrecht Missionary Society.

| Missions. | Out-Stations and stations. | Ordained. | Lay. | Wives. | Other Women. | Ordained. | Teachers. | Other Helpers. | Preaching Places. | Sabbath-school Scholars. | Churches. | Communicants. | Additions. | Schools for Higher Education. | Pupils. | Common Schools. | Pupils. | Native Contributions for all purposes. |
|---|---|---|---|---|---|---|---|---|---|---|---|---|---|---|---|---|---|---|
| DUTCH EAST INDIES | 7 | 7 | 7 | ... | ... | ... | ... | ...... | ...... | ...... | ... | ...... | ...... | ... | ...... | ... | ...... | ...... |

### No. 161. Dutch Reformed Missionary Society (Nederlandsche Gereformeerde Zendingsvereeniging). Year ending December, 1889 (?).

| Missions. | Out-Stations and stations. | Ordained. | Lay. | Wives. | Other Women. | Ordained. | Teachers. | Other Helpers. | Preaching Places. | Sabbath-school Scholars. | Churches. | Communicants. | Additions. | Schools for Higher Education. | Pupils. | Common Schools. | Pupils. | Native Contributions for all purposes. |
|---|---|---|---|---|---|---|---|---|---|---|---|---|---|---|---|---|---|---|
| CENTRAL JAVA | ...... | 3 | 1 | 4 | ... | ... | ...... | 12 | ...... | ...... | 65 | 6,500 | 1,000 | 1 | ...... | 12 | ... | ... |

## FRANCE.

### No. 165. Paris Society for Evangelical Missions. Year ending March 31st, 1890.

| Missions. | Out-Stations and stations. | Ordained. | Lay. | Wives. | Other Women. | Ordained. | Teachers. | Other Helpers. | Preaching Places. | Sabbath-school Scholars. | Churches. | Communicants. | Additions. | Schools for Higher Education. | Pupils. | Common Schools. | Pupils. | Native Contributions for all purposes. |
|---|---|---|---|---|---|---|---|---|---|---|---|---|---|---|---|---|---|---|
| | | | | | | | | | | | | | | | | | | Francs |
| AFRICA : SOUTH | 17 | 19 | 1 | ... | ... | ... | ... | 206 | ...... | ...... | ... | 6,937 | 390 | 3 | 78 | ... | 1,426 | ...... |
| SENEGAL | 2 | 3 | 1 | ... | ... | ... | ... | ...... | ...... | ...... | ... | ...... | ...... | ... | ... | ... | ... | ...... |
| ZAMBEZI | 3 | 4 | 1 | ... | ... | ... | ... | ...... | ...... | ...... | ... | ...... | ...... | ... | ... | ... | ... | ...... |
| POLYNESIA : TAHITI | 23 | 4 | ... | ... | ... | ... | 19 | ...... | ...... | ...... | ... | 2,010 | (?) | ... | ...... | ... | 6,502 | ...... |
| Total | *45 | 30 | 3 | 27 | 6 | 19 | ...... | 206 | ...... | ...... | ... | 8,947 | 390 | 3 | 78 | ... | 7,928 | 69,226 $13,848 |

*Stations only.

| SOCIETIES. | Stations and Out-stations. | Missionaries. | | | | Native Workers. | | | Preaching Places. | Sabbath-school Scholars. | Churches. | Communicants. | Additions. | Schools for Higher Education. | Pupils. | Common Schools. | Pupils. | Native Contributions for all purposes. |
|---|---|---|---|---|---|---|---|---|---|---|---|---|---|---|---|---|---|---|
| | | Ordained. | Lay. | Wives. | Other Women. | Ordained. | Teachers. | Other Helpers. | | | | | | | | | | |

No. 166.  MISSIONS OF THE FREE CHURCHES OF FRENCH SWITZERLAND, CANTON DE VAUD.  YEAR ENDING DECEMBER 31ST, 1889.

| SOCIETIES. | Stations and Out-stations. | Ordained. | Lay. | Wives. | Other Women. | Ordained. | Teachers. | Other Helpers. | Preaching Places. | Sabbath-school Scholars. | Churches. | Communicants. | Additions. | Schools for Higher Education. | Pupils. | Common Schools. | Pupils. | Native Contributions for all purposes. |
|---|---|---|---|---|---|---|---|---|---|---|---|---|---|---|---|---|---|---|
| AFRICA (SOUTH) ... | 14 | 7 | ... | 7 | 1 | ... | .... | 18 | 14 | .... | 7 | 312 | 56 | 1 | 16 | 14 | 497 | Francs 1,288 $257.60 |

### THE PACIFIC.

No. 169.  HAWAIIAN EVANGELICAL ASSOCIATION.  YEAR ENDING MAY 31ST, 1890.

| SOCIETIES. | Stations and Out-stations. | Ordained. | Lay. | Wives. | Other Women. | Ordained. | Teachers. | Other Helpers. | Preaching Places. | Sabbath-school Scholars. | Churches. | Communicants. | Additions. | Schools for Higher Education. | Pupils. | Common Schools. | Pupils. | Native Contributions for all purposes. |
|---|---|---|---|---|---|---|---|---|---|---|---|---|---|---|---|---|---|---|
| HAWAIIAN ISL ... | 56 | | ... | ... | 36 | .... | .... | .... | | 2,769 | 62 | 5,049 | 282 | ... | .... | ... | .... | $20,133 |
| MICRONESIA...... | 45 | | ... | ... | 20 | 16 | ... | ...... | | | 20 | 2,599 | 415 | ... | .... | . | ... | 1,786 |
| Total ........ | 101 | ... | ... | ... | 56 | 16 | .... | ...... | | 2,769 | 82 | 7,648 | 697 | | ... | ... | .... | 21,919 |

No. 170.  MELANESIAN MISSION.  YEAR ENDING DECEMBER 31ST, 1889.

| SOCIETIES. | Stations and Out-stations. | Ordained. | Lay. | Wives. | Other Women. | Ordained. | Teachers. | Other Helpers. | Preaching Places. | Sabbath-school Scholars. | Churches. | Communicants. | Additions. | Schools for Higher Education. | Pupils. | Common Schools. | Pupils. | Native Contributions for all purposes. |
|---|---|---|---|---|---|---|---|---|---|---|---|---|---|---|---|---|---|---|
| MELANESIA........ | *9 | 9 | 4 | ... | ... | 5 | 192 | ... | ...... | .. | ..... | .. | ...... | .. | .... | 86 | 2,897 | ... .... |

\* Stations only.

## 2. COUNTRIES AND SOCIETIES.

| SOCIETIES. | Stations and Out-stations. | Missionaries: Ordained. | Lay. | Wives. | Other Women. | Native Workers: Ordained. | Teachers. | Other Helpers. | Preaching Places. | Sabbath-school Scholars. | Churches. | Communicants. | Additions. | Schools for Higher Education. | Pupils. | Common Schools. | Pupils. | Native Contributions for all purposes. |
|---|---|---|---|---|---|---|---|---|---|---|---|---|---|---|---|---|---|---|
| **AFRICA.** | | | | | | | | | | | | | | | | | | |
| 1. A. B. C. F. M. ...... | 37 | 20 | 1 | 18 | 14 | 1 | 36 | 100 | 86 | 1,547 | 17 | 1,174 | 88 | 4 | 187 | 38 | 1,614 | $1,209 |
| 3. A. B. M. U. ...... | 11 | 23 | ... | 16 | ... | ... | 6 | 5 | ... | 124 | 5 | 386 | 156 | ... | ... | 10 | 471 | 75 |
| 5. So. Bap. Conv ..... | 5 | 5 | ... | 4 | 1 | ... | ... | 7 | ... | ... | 4 | 58 | 1 | ... | ... | 3 | 150 | 24 |
| 9. Bap. Gen. Assoc.... | 1 | 1 | 1 | 1 | ... | ... | ... | ... | 6 | ... | ... | ... | ... | ... | ... | ... | ... | ... |
| 10. Bap. F. M. Conv... | ... | 2 | ... | ... | ... | 1 | ... | ... | ... | ... | ... | ... | ... | ... | ... | ... | ... | ... |
| 13. M. E. Ch. (North).. | 37 | ... | ... | ... | 22 | ... | 58 | 36 | 2,614 | 36 | 3,179 | 227 | ... | ... | ... | ... | ... | 4,835 |
| 14. Afr. M. E. Church... | 5 | 3 | 4 | 5 | 3 | ... | 3 | ... | 9 | 127 | 5 | 207 | 57 | ... | ... | 2 | 111 | 1,000 |
| 17. Wes. Meth. Con ... | 2 | 2 | 2 | 2 | ... | 1 | ... | ... | 2 | ... | 1 | 300 | 12 | ... | ... | 1 | 300 | 300 |
| 20. Pr. Ep. Church ... | 69 | 1 | ... | ... | 1 | 14 | 38 | 2 | 69 | 1,272 | 11 | 709 | 145 | 2 | 131 | 27 | 871 | 1,331 |
| 22. Ref. Pres. Gen. Syn. | 10 | ... | ... | ... | ... | 2 | ... | 18 | 10 | ... | 2 | 117 | 5 | ... | ... | 1 | 30 | 350 |
| 24. Pres. Ch. (North)... | 17 | 9 | 9 | 4 | 6 | 4 | ... | 29 | ... | 1,312 | 17 | 1,398 | 156 | ... | ... | 18 | 579 | 504 |
| 26. U. P. Church...... | 100 | 14 | ... | 11 | 14 | 12 | ... | 244 | ... | 4,427 | 29 | 2,971 | 464 | 2 | 265 | 98 | 6,039 | 27,353 |
| 28. Pres. Ch. (South)... | ... | 2 | ... | ... | ... | ... | ... | ... | ... | ... | ... | ... | ... | ... | ... | ... | ... | ... |
| 34. Ev. Luth. Ch. ..... | 1 | 1 | ... | 1 | 1 | 2 | ... | 7 | 13 | ... | 38 | 200 | 53 | ... | ... | 22 | 342 | 55 |
| 37. Un. Brethren ...... | *12 | 18 | 25 | 16 | 5 | 3 | 16 | 24 | 405 | 236 | 131 | 6,712 | 1,150 | 1 | 23 | 13 | 568 | 1,484 |
| 42. Sev. Day Adv...... | ... | 2 | 2 | ... | 1 | ... | ... | ... | ... | ... | 5 | 120 | ... | ... | ... | ... | ... | ... |
| 53. Canada Cong...... | 2 | 2 | ... | ... | 2 | ... | ... | ... | ... | ... | 1 | ... | ... | ... | ... | ... | ... | ... |
| 62. Lon. Miss. Soc..... | 68 | 20 | 5 | 21 | ... | ... | ... | 103 | ... | ... | ... | 2,662 | ... | ... | ... | 19 | 1,545 | 1,747 |
| 67. N. Africa Miss..... | 15 | 17 | ... | 9 | 28 | ... | ... | ... | ... | ... | ... | 17 | ... | ... | ... | 1 | 20 | ... |
| 72. C. M. S............ | 61 | 32 | 18 | ... | 15 | 48 | ... | 302 | ... | ... | ... | 9,838 | 445 | 4 | 170 | 108 | 8,840 | 21,650 |
| 74. Univ. Miss......... | 39 | 18 | 26 | ... | 24 | 3 | ... | 70 | ... | ... | 11 | 586 | ... | 1 | 24 | 21 | 1,000 | ... |
| 77. Bap. M. S......... | 10 | 25 | ... | ... | 5 | 1 | ... | 228 | ... | ... | ... | 43 | 12 | ... | ... | ... | 143 | ... |
| 81. Wes. Methodist..... | 76 | 20 | ... | ... | 47 | 157 | 1,611 | 510 | 10,844 | 179 | 16,313 | 2,272 | ... | ... | 107 | 6,908 | 73,489 | |
| 82. United Meth....... | 9 | 4 | ... | ... | ... | 4 | ... | ... | 21 | 1,612 | 20 | 3,032 | 116 | ... | ... | ... | 111 | ... |
| 85. Prim. Meth. Con... | 5 | 7 | ... | ... | ... | 2 | 4 | 1 | 22 | ... | 8 | 530 | 13 | ... | ... | 8 | 315 | 4,873 |
| 93. Friends' For. Miss.. | 4 | 2 | 1 | ... | ... | ... | ... | ... | ... | ... | ... | ... | ... | ... | ... | ... | ... | ... |
| 101. Ch. of Scot. (Estab.) | 1 | 3 | 10 | ... | 1 | ... | 7 | 4 | 11 | ... | 2 | 23 | 16 | ... | ... | 7 | 610 | †291 |
| 103. Free Ch. of Scot... | 116 | 18 | 31 | ... | 16 | 2 | 151 | 85 | 116 | ... | 13 | 4,068 | 75 | 1 | 51 | 94 | 8,074 | 22,133 |
| 104. U. P. Ch. Scotland. | 135 | 19 | 4 | ... | 10 | 3 | 55 | 29 | 135 | 2,151 | 20 | 2,753 | 135 | ... | ... | 60 | 2,822 | ... |
| 121. Nor. Miss. Soc .... | 11 | 11 | ... | ... | 2 | ... | ... | 16 | ... | ... | ... | 500 | ... | ... | ... | ... | 449 | ... |
| 122. Schreuder Miss ... | 2 | 3 | ... | 1 | ... | 2 | ... | ... | ... | ... | ... | 130 | ... | ... | ... | ... | 124 | ... |
| 127. Ev. Natl. Assoc ... | 4 | 3 | 4 | 3 | 3 | 3 | ... | 18 | ... | ... | 1 | 84 | 26 | ... | ... | 2 | 111 | ... |
| 130. Swed. Ch. Miss.... | 5 | 9 | ... | ... | ... | ... | ... | ... | ... | ... | ... | 71 | ... | ... | ... | ... | 68 | ... |
| 131. Swed. Miss. Assoc. | 3 | 5 | ... | ... | ... | ... | ... | 10 | ... | ... | ... | ... | ... | ... | ... | ... | ... | ... |
| 138. Finland Miss...... | 4 | 5 | 1 | 5 | ... | ... | ... | 10 | ... | ... | 2 | 87 | ... | ... | ... | 3 | 160 | 25 |
| 141. Moravian Miss.... | 24 | 61 | ... | ... | ... | 9 | 66 | 302 | ... | 488 | ... | 3,206 | ... | ... | ... | 30 | ... | ... |
| 142. Basle Miss. Soc.... | 150 | 32 | 14 | 22 | 3 | 18 | 64 | 104 | 150 | 639 | ... | 3,811 | 864 | 1 | 38 | 119 | 2,891 | ... |
| 144. Berlin Miss. Soc.... | 134 | 56 | 5 | 53 | ... | ... | ... | 429 | 152 | ... | ... | 10,984 | 585 | ... | ... | ... | ... | ... |
| 145. Rhenish Miss. Soc.. | 37 | 29 | 1 | 28 | ... | ... | 61 | 93 | ... | 2,109 | ... | 6,384 | 156 | ... | ... | ... | 3,576 | 10,619 |
| 147. N. Ger. Miss. Soc.. | 14 | 11 | 4 | 6 | 2 | 1 | ... | 24 | ... | ... | ... | 408 | 29 | 2 | 30 | 13 | 280 | 154 |
| 149. Hermannsburg..... | 80 | 60 | ... | ... | ... | ... | ... | 207 | ... | ... | ... | 11,500 | 1,735 | ... | ... | ... | 2,567 | 5,297 |
| 165. Paris Ev. Soc..... | 22 | 26 | 3 | ... | ... | ... | ... | 206 | ... | ... | ... | 6,939 | 390 | 3 | 78 | ... | 1,426 | ... |
| 166. Free Ch. French Sw. | 14 | 7 | ... | 7 | 1 | ... | ... | 18 | 14 | ... | 7 | 312 | 56 | 1 | 16 | 14 | 207 | 258 |
| **Total............** | 1352 | 611 | 170 | 234 | 153 | 209 | 665 | 4,226 | 1,767 | 29,730 | 565 | 101,212 | 9,489 | 22 | 1,021 | 839 | 53,235 | 179,650 |

\* Stations only.     † Including European collections.

### MADAGASCAR.

| SOCIETIES. | Stations and Out-stations. | Ordained. | Lay. | Wives. | Other Women. | Ordained. | Teachers. | Other Helpers. | Preaching Places. | Sabbath-school Scholars. | Churches. | Communicants. | Additions. | Schools for Higher Education. | Pupils. | Common Schools. | Pupils. | Native Contributions. |
|---|---|---|---|---|---|---|---|---|---|---|---|---|---|---|---|---|---|---|
| 62. Lond. Miss. Soc.... | 1218 | 23 | 4 | 23 | 3 | 827 | ... | 3,459 | ... | 4,448 | ... | 39,984 | ... | ... | ... | 860 | 58,888 | 4,400 |
| 93. Friends For. Miss.. | 3 | 9 | ... | 13 | ... | 323 | ... | ... | ... | 143 | ... | ... | 2 | 514 | 31 | 3,907 | ... | ... |
| 121. Norw. Miss. Soc... | 29 | 25 | ... | 10 | ... | 16 | ... | 900 | ... | ... | ... | 16,555 | ... | ... | ... | ... | 37,500 | ... |
| **Total............** | 1250 | 57 | 4 | 46 | 3 | 1166 | ... | 4,359 | ... | 4,448 | 143 | 56,539 | ... | 5 | 514 | 891 | 100,355 | 4,400 |

(Note.—Some societies, as the Soc. for the Prop. of the Gos., have been omitted from these tables because of the impossibility of distinguishing, in their statistics, between the different countries.)

| SOCIETIES. | Out stations and stations. | Ordained. | Lay. | Wives. | Other Women. | Ordained. | Teachers. | Other Helpers. | Preaching Places. | Sabbath-school Scholars. | Churches. | Communicants. | Additions. | Schools for Higher Education. | Pupils. | Common Schools. | Pupils. | Native Contributions for all purposes. |
|---|---|---|---|---|---|---|---|---|---|---|---|---|---|---|---|---|---|---|

### INDIA.

| SOCIETIES. | Stations | Ord. | Lay | Wives | Oth. W. | Ord. | Teach. | Oth. H. | Pr. Pl. | S.S. Sch. | Ch. | Commun. | Add. | Sch. H.E. | Pupils | Com. Sch. | Pupils | Contrib. |
|---|---|---|---|---|---|---|---|---|---|---|---|---|---|---|---|---|---|---|
| 1. A. B. C. F. M. | 417 | 30 | 1 | 28 | 18 | 48 | 650 | 355 | 571 | 12,735 | 84 | 7,154 | 526 | 29 | 2,372 | 387 | 14,900 | $12,825 |
| 3. A. B. M. U. | 1333 | 73 | | 134 | | 217 | 1,040 | 917 | | 7,913 | 622 | 65,464 | 5,564 | | | 991 | 19,503 | 53,937 |
| 4. Free Bap. F. M. S. | 11 | 9 | 1 | 9 | 6 | 5 | | 1 | | 2,721 | 11 | 699 | 55 | 1 | 28 | 104 | 3,591 | 394 |
| 13. M. E. Ch. (North) | 92 | 77 | | 60 | 39 | 75 | 857 | 183 | 190 | 42,423 | 163 | 16,540 | 3,661 | 19 | 2,428 | 799 | 20,120 | 36,035 |
| 22. Ref. Pres. Synod | 10 | | | | | 2 | | 18 | 10 | | 2 | 117 | 5 | | | 1 | 30 | 350 |
| 24. Pres. Ch. (North) | 19 | 37 | 4 | 35 | 36 | 22 | | 185 | | 4,590 | 4 | 1,093 | 81 | | | 14 | 8,016 | |
| 25. Ref. (Dutch) | 106 | 8 | 1 | 7 | 2 | 4 | | 246 | 106 | | 23 | 1,696 | 68 | 7 | 266 | 105 | 3,320 | 650 |
| 26. U. P. Church | 85 | 12 | | 11 | 12 | 11 | | 192 | | 2,824 | 10 | 6,597 | 1,258 | 2 | 110 | 106 | 4,273 | 1,022 |
| 31. Ger. Ev. Synod | 10 | 4 | | 4 | 1 | | | 15 | | | 3 | 234 | 34 | 1 | 70 | 3 | 180 | |
| 34. Ev. Luth. Ch. | 11 | 4 | | 3 | 2 | 2 | | 169 | 341 | 7,605 | 300 | 6,367 | 2,350 | 1 | 378 | 173 | 8,766 | 1,500 |
| 35. Ev. Luth. Gen. Con. | 6 | 4 | | 3 | | 2 | 81 | 7 | 103 | | 2 | 832 | 1 | | 89 | 1,073 | | 50 |
| 36. For. Chris. M. S. | 3 | 4 | | 4 | 2 | | | 8 | | 650 | | 58 | 35 | | | 3 | 100 | |
| 51. Pres. Ch. in Canada | 5 | 5 | 1 | 5 | 10 | 2 | 29 | 41 | 300 | | | 5 | | 1 | | 5 | 320 | |
| 52. Bap. Chs. Canada | 9 | 10 | | 14 | 8 | 8 | | 141 | | | 23 | 2,466 | 410 | 1 | 70 | | | |
| 62. Lon. Miss. Soc. | 510 | 54 | 1 | 31 | 19 | 41 | | 324 | | 3,287 | | 7,743 | | | | 562 | 28,932 | 45,670 |
| 64. Chr. Vern. Ed. Soc. | | | | | | | 1,018 | | | | | | | | | 211 | 8,555 | |
| 72. C. M. S. | 110 | 146 | 14 | | 17 | 159 | | 2,596 | | | | 29,305 | 1,749 | 6 | 464 | 1414 | 58,065 | 4,899 |
| 77. Bap. Miss. Soc. | 251 | 57 | | | | 119 | 236 | | | 3,564 | | 5,595 | 295 | | | | 7,188 | 28,960 |
| 78. Gen. Bap. Miss. Soc. | 21 | 8 | | 5 | 2 | 21 | 105 | | | 755 | 18 | 1,376 | 71 | | | | 763 | 3,293 |
| 79. Strict Baptist | 18 | 3 | | 3 | | 3 | 13 | 10 | | | | 353 | | | | 19 | 509 | |
| 81. Wes. Meth. | 179 | 60 | | | | 88 | 1,524 | 1,741 | 467 | 20,168 | 155 | 7,047 | 1,899 | | | 658 | 39,684 | 186,886 |
| 89. Welsh Calv. Meth. | 9 | 8 | 1 | 5 | 1 | 4 | | 564 | 163 | 6,611 | 72 | 1,869 | 285 | 1 | 9 | 142 | 4,134 | 2,000 |
| 90. Pres. Ch. Eng | | | 2 | 1 | 3 | | | 2 | | | | 30 | 10 | | | | | 122 |
| 93. Friends For. Miss. | 4 | 6 | | 9 | | 4 | | | 10 | | 5 | | | | | 2 | 75 | |
| 101. Ch. Scot. Commit. | 35 | 13 | 4 | | 15 | 7 | 97 | 57 | 30 | | 30 | 776 | 641 | 3 | 407 | 89 | 5,563 | 29,423 |
| 103. Free Ch. Scot | 79 | 30 | 10 | | 22 | 12 | 238 | 121 | 79 | | 21 | 2,147 | 75 | 5 | 1,096 | 210 | 20,898 | 67,075 |
| 104. U. P. Ch. Scot | 42 | 14 | 3 | | 11 | 2 | 169 | 108 | | 1,536 | 11 | 485 | 29 | | | 79 | 4,579 | |
| 105. Unit. Or. Sec. Ch. | | 1 | 1 | 1 | | | | 3 | 2 | | 1 | 16 | | | | 3 | 312 | 308 |
| 109. Pres. Ch. Ireland | 16 | 8 | 3 | 7 | 8 | | 56 | 20 | | | 18 | 290 | | 2 | 43 | 43 | 3,959 | |
| 115. Danish Miss. Soc. | 4 | 5 | 2 | 5 | 1 | 3 | | 19 | 4 | | 4 | 208 | | | | | | |
| 116. Ind. Home Miss. | 14 | 6 | 2 | 5 | 5 | 5 | | 142 | | | 14 | 6,070 | 707 | 2 | 284 | | | 67 |
| 117. Loventhal's Miss. | 1 | 1 | | 1 | | | | 3 | | | 1 | 12 | | | | | | |
| 127. Ev. Na'l Assoc. | 6 | 8 | 3 | 6 | 2 | | | 8 | | | 4 | 24 | 24 | | | 8 | 312 | |
| 130. Swed. Ch. Miss. | 9 | 4 | | | | | | | | | | | 545 | | | | | |
| 141. Moravian | 3 | 10 | | | | 3 | | | | | | 12 | | | 5 | | | |
| 142. Basle Ev | 157 | 54 | 14 | 52 | 1 | 15 | 279 | 126 | 157 | 835 | | 5,160 | 219 | 2 | 29 | 117 | 6,343 | 2,317 |
| 143. Leipsic Ev | 617 | 25 | 1 | | | 14 | 300 | 191 | | | 141 | 13,559 | 228 | | | 177 | 4,492 | |
| 146. Gossner's M. S. | 8 | | | | | 17 | | | | | 165 | 30,027 | | | | | | |
| 149. Hermannsburg | 10 | 9 | | | | | | 35 | | | | 871 | 27 | | | | | |
| 150. Breklum M. S. | 6 | 11 | | | | | | | | | | | | | | | | |
| Total | 4223 | 816 | 69 | 460 | 243 | 912 | 6,692 | 8,569 | 2,533 | 117,797 | 1855 | 222,283 | 20,850 | 83 | 8,051 | 6574 | 273,785 | 477,288 |

### SIAM.

| SOCIETIES. | Stations | Ord. | Lay | Wives | Oth. W. | Ord. | Teach. | Oth. H. | Pr. Pl. | S.S. Sch. | Ch. | Commun. | Add. | Sch. H.E. | Pupils | Com. Sch. | Pupils | Contrib. |
|---|---|---|---|---|---|---|---|---|---|---|---|---|---|---|---|---|---|---|
| 24. Pres. Ch. (North) | 5 | 13 | 4 | 14 | 7 | 1 | | 98 | | 676 | 42 | 1,114 | 174 | . | 14 | 21 | 641 | $304 |

### CHINA.

| SOCIETIES. | Stations | Ord. | Lay | Wives | Oth. W. | Ord. | Teach. | Oth. H. | Pr. Pl. | S.S. Sch. | Ch. | Commun. | Add. | Sch. H.E. | Pupils | Com. Sch. | Pupils | Contrib. |
|---|---|---|---|---|---|---|---|---|---|---|---|---|---|---|---|---|---|---|
| 1. A. B. C. F. M | 69 | 33 | 8 | 38 | 16 | 5 | 45 | 62 | 63 | | 26 | 1,562 | 223 | 13 | 246 | 33 | 769 | $2,246 |
| 3. A. B. M. U. | 67 | 18 | | 23 | | 7 | 25 | 56 | | 330 | 17 | 1,585 | 61 | | | 23 | 325 | 521 |
| 5. So. Bap. Conv. | 41 | 13 | | 12 | 8 | 11 | | 23 | | | 13 | 806 | 83 | | | 18 | 308 | 728 |
| 6. Sev. Day Bap | 3 | 2 | | 2 | 2 | 2 | | 7 | 3 | | 1 | 30 | 5 | | | 2 | 29 | |
| 13. M. E. Ch. (North) | 109 | 36 | 5 | 38 | 28 | 70 | 143 | 105 | 194 | 4,387 | 110 | 6,397 | 710 | 15 | 602 | 137 | 2,067 | 3,892 |
| 15. M. E. Ch. South | 14 | 15 | 1 | 12 | 14 | 21 | 9 | 45 | 14 | 742 | 8 | 345 | 50 | 2 | 220 | 4 | 141 | 265 |
| 20. Pr. Ep. Ch. | 59 | 8 | 3 | 7 | 12 | 25 | 53 | 4 | 59 | 1,099 | 9 | 536 | 76 | 3 | 92 | 46 | 1,009 | 677 |
| 21. Pres. Ch. (North) | 13 | 48 | 12 | 47 | 21 | 22 | | 265 | | 2,969 | 45 | 4,084 | 446 | | 6 | 124 | 2,689 | 2,809 |
| 25. Ref. (Dutch) | 25 | 6 | 1 | 7 | 2 | 8 | | 20 | 25 | | 8 | 856 | 35 | 4 | 97 | 8 | 122 | 2,535 |
| 28. Pres. Ch. (South) | 12 | 11 | 2 | 9 | 6 | | 3 | 15 | | 245 | 3 | 180 | 23 | 1 | 47 | 14 | 160 | 60 |
| 36. Chris. Miss. Soc. | 3 | 8 | | 3 | 6 | | | 2 | | 24 | | 4 | 3 | | | 1 | 24 | |
| 51. Pres. Ch. in Canada | 2 | 8 | 1 | 6 | 2 | 2 | | 50 | 50 | | 2 | 2,833 | 146 | | | 2 | 50 | 1,144 |
| 62. Lon. Miss. Soc. | 98 | 23 | 8 | 24 | 13 | 9 | | 76 | | 420 | | 4,272 | | | | 63 | 2,156 | 12,223 |
| 65. China In. Miss. | 158 | 171 | | 70 | 142 | 14 | 18 | 200 | | | 88 | 2,839 | 530 | | 24 | 276 | | 676 |
| 72. C. M. S. | 23 | 27 | 8 | | 10 | 16 | | 30 | | | | 2,896 | 453 | 3 | 89 | 120 | 2,236 | 3,545 |
| 77. B. M. S. | 60 | 21 | | | | 10 | | | | | | 1,049 | 103 | | | | | 482 |
| 81. Wes. Methodist | 12 | 17 | | | | 5 | 14 | 27 | 14 | 94 | 12 | 1,166 | 163 | | | 14 | 223 | 2,363 |
| 82. Un. Meth | 3 | 3 | | | | | | | 17 | 43 | 5 | 365 | 39 | | | | | |
| 83. Meth. New Connex. | 55 | 7 | 1 | 5 | 1 | 3 | | 36 | 60 | | 42 | 1,301 | 33 | 1 | 10 | 15 | 290 | |
| 84. Cen. China Wes. Mth. | 3 | | 8 | 2 | | | | 4 | 100 | | | 12 | 12 | | | 1 | 12 | |
| 96. Bible Christian | 6 | | | | | 2 | | 1 | 3 | 24 | | 6 | | | | | | |
| 90. Pres. Ch. England | 130 | 20 | 11 | 20 | 13 | 8 | | 106 | 130 | | 43 | 3,572 | 164 | 4 | 41 | | | 2,625 |
| 93. Friends' For. Miss. | 1 | 3 | | 1 | | | | | | | | | | | | | | |
| 101. Ch. of Scot. Com. | 1 | 1 | | | | 1 | 2 | 1 | | | 1 | 26 | | | 1 | 39 | | 4 |
| 104. U. P. Ch. Scotland | 18 | 5 | 3 | | 3 | | 2 | 32 | 18 | | 5 | 956 | 161 | | 8 | 86 | | |
| 109. Pres. Ch. Ireland | 8 | 4 | | 4 | 1 | 2 | | 16 | | | | 130 | | | | 20 | | |
| 135. Sw. Miss. in China | 8 | | 4 | 1 | 4 | | | | | | 1 | 14 | | | | | | |
| 142. Basle Ev. M. S. | 45 | 18 | 1 | 14 | | 6 | 45 | 44 | 45 | | | 2,111 | 226 | 1 | 9 | 42 | 801 | |
| 144. Berlin Ev. | 17 | 6 | | 6 | | | | 46 | 15 | | | 373 | 36 | | | | | |
| 145. Rhenish M. S. | 8 | 5 | 1 | 2 | | 1 | 5 | 3 | | | | 155 | 8 | | | | 51 | 70 |
| Total | 1071 | 537 | 78 | 353 | 208 | 247 | 362 | 1,277 | 871 | 10,377 | 439 | 40,350 | 3,803 | 47 | 1,459 | 700 | 13,823 | $36,865 |

| Societies. | Stations and Out-stations. | Mission-aries. Ordained. | Lay. | Wives. | Other Women. | Native Workers. Ordained. | Teachers. | Other Helpers. | Preaching Places. | Sabbath-school Scholars. | Churches. | Communicants. | Additions. | Schools for Higher Education. | Pupils. | Common Schools. | Pupils. | Native Contributions for all purposes. |
|---|---|---|---|---|---|---|---|---|---|---|---|---|---|---|---|---|---|---|

### KOREA.

| Societies. | | | | | | | | | | | | | | | | | | |
|---|---|---|---|---|---|---|---|---|---|---|---|---|---|---|---|---|---|---|
| 13. M. E. Ch. (North).. | 1 | 3 | 2 | 4 | 5 | 2 | 4 | 6 | 2 | 43 | 2 | 45 | .... | 3 | 88 | .... | .... | .... |
| 24. Pres. Ch. (North)... | 1 | 3 | 2 | 3 | 2 | .. | .. | .. | .. | .. | .. | 104 | 39 | .. | .. | .. | .. | .. |
| Total ............ | 2 | 6 | 4 | 7 | 7 | 2 | 4 | 6 | 2 | 43 | 2 | 149 | 39 | 3 | 88 | .. | .. | .. |

### JAPAN.

| Societies. | | | | | | | | | | | | | | | | | | |
|---|---|---|---|---|---|---|---|---|---|---|---|---|---|---|---|---|---|---|
| 1. A. B. C. F. M...... | 82 | 26 | 4 | 26 | 32 | 26 | 43 | 100 | 190 | 6,920 | 61 | 9,146 | 1,615 | 21 | 2,633 | ... | ... | $50,841 |
| 3. A. B. M. U. ...... | 35 | 12 | .. | 26 | .. | 4 | 16 | 42 | .. | 605 | 10 | 905 | 158 | .. | .... | 6 | 216 | 311 |
| 5. So. Bap. Conv ... | .. | 2 | .. | 2 | .. | | | | | | | | | | | | | |
| 13. M. E. Ch. (North).. | 49 | 19 | .. | 18 | 32 | 22 | 76 | 12 | 61 | 4,022 | 25 | 3,533 | 492 | 12 | 1,326 | 14 | 1,159 | 19,290 |
| 15. M. E. Ch. (South).. | 22 | 11 | 1 | 9 | 5 | 8 | .. | 22 | 617 | 1 | 318 | 86 | 1 | 7 | 5 | 116 | 3,116 | |
| 16. Meth. Prot. Ch. .. | 3 | 5 | .. | 5 | 4 | .. | 5 | 7 | 4 | 359 | 2 | 203 | .... | 2 | 7 | 4 | 249 | 460 |
| 20. Pr. Ep. Church... | 68 | 13 | 3 | 13 | 12 | 1 | 82 | .. | 68 | 876 | 5 | 904 | 129 | 1 | 63 | 7 | 274 | 2,920 |
| 23. Ref. German Ch... | 21 | 3 | .. | 3 | 2 | 7 | .. | 15 | 20 | 915 | 12 | 1,656 | .... | 1 | 26 | 1 | 40 | 2,835 |
| 24. Pres. Ch. (North) | 5 | 21 | 3 | 22 | 25 | 20 | .... | 23 | .. | .. | 34 | 4,977 | 672 | .. | 17 | 15 | 1,409 | 6,750 |
| 25. Ref. (Dutch)..... | 24 | 9 | 2 | 10 | 6 | 18 | .. | 17 | 24 | .. | 20 | 2,784 | 449 | 6 | 281 | .. | .. | 4,818 |
| 28. Pres. Ch. (South) | 21 | 9 | .. | 5 | 5 | 2 | 10 | 2 | 48 | 520 | 4 | 796 | 142 | 1 | 50 | 3 | 190 | 600 |
| 30. Cumb. Pres. Ch .. | 8 | 4 | .. | 4 | 6 | 1 | .. | 4 | .. | .. | 5 | 521 | .. | .. | .. | 2 | 54 | .. |
| 36. For. Chris.Miss.Soc. | 3 | 4 | .. | 4 | 2 | .. | .. | 2 | .. | 310 | .. | 108 | 51 | .. | .. | 2 | 53 | .. |
| 38. Ev. Association .. | 15 | 3 | .. | 3 | .. | 5 | 2 | 22 | 18 | 411 | 5 | 333 | 128 | 1 | 18 | .. | .. | 440 |
| 41. Am. Chris. Conv.. | 37 | 2 | .. | 2 | .. | .. | 6 | .. | 37 | .. | 3 | 93 | 31 | .. | .. | .. | .. | 74 |
| 50. Meth.Ch.in Canada. | 13 | 9 | 2 | 8 | .. | 5 | .. | 31 | 31 | 1,486 | 10 | 1,538 | 578 | 1 | 210 | 3 | 275 | 6,491 |
| 72. C. M. S. .... | 10 | 17 | .. | .. | 8 | 4 | .. | 36 | .. | .. | .. | 824 | 212 | 1 | 25 | 10 | 312 | 457 |
| 104. U. P. Ch. Scot ... | 3 | 3 | .. | .. | 2 | 2 | .. | 2 | .. | .. | 7 | 874 | 114 | .. | .. | .. | .. | .. |
| Total ............ | 422 | 175 | 15 | 160 | 139 | 131 | 236 | 315 | 529 | 17,092 | 207 | 29,653 | 4,948 | 48 | 4,663 | 72 | 4,257 | $99,103 |

### TURKEY, BULGARIA, AND SYRIA.

| Societies. | | | | | | | | | | | | | | | | | | |
|---|---|---|---|---|---|---|---|---|---|---|---|---|---|---|---|---|---|---|
| 1. A. B. C. F. M.... | 330 | 58 | 3 | 57 | 59 | 86 | 495 | 210 | 343 | 25,550 | 117 | 11,709 | 1,367 | 54 | 2,228 | 410 | 15,662 | $45,474 |
| 13. M. E. Ch. (North).. | 12 | 4 | .. | 4 | 2 | 10 | 11 | 5 | 9 | 229 | 3 | 163 | 10 | 2 | 64 | 5 | 97 | 553 |
| 24. Pres. Ch. (North).. | 5 | 14 | 1 | 14 | 10 | 4 | .. | 197 | .. | 4,966 | 20 | 1,619 | 98 | .. | 7 | 142 | 5,853 | 7,767 |
| 27. Ref. Pres. Ch.... | 8 | 4 | 1 | 4 | 4 | 4 | 34 | .. | 11 | 526 | 3 | 190 | 12 | .. | 25 | 730 | 34 | |
| 36. For. Chris. M. S... | 14 | 3 | .. | 1 | .. | .. | 11 | .. | 130 | .. | 629 | 127 | .. | 2 | 55 | .. | | |
| 72. C. M. S. ....... | 9 | 9 | 3 | .. | 7 | 8 | .. | 72 | .. | .. | .. | 455 | 3 | 1 | 22 | 43 | 2,013 | 4 |
| 77. Bapt. Miss. Soc .. | 3 | 1 | .. | .. | .. | .. | 6 | .. | 90 | .. | 75 | 2 | .. | .. | 69 | .. | | |
| 93. Friends' For. Miss. | 4 | 1 | .. | 1 | .. | 4 | .. | 3 | 1 | .. | .. | .. | .. | .. | .. | .. | | |
| 94. Friends' Miss. Syria | 7 | 2 | .. | 2 | 4 | 1 | .. | 12 | .. | .. | 1 | .. | .. | 2 | 50 | 10 | 390 | 2,155 |
| 102. Scot. Ref. Pres..... | 3 | 1 | .. | 1 | 1 | .. | .. | 9 | 3 | 120 | 1 | 37 | 3 | .. | .. | 3 | 200 | .. |
| 103. Free Ch. Scot...... | 7 | 1 | .. | .. | .. | .. | 4 | 7 | .. | 2 | 61 | .. | .. | .. | .. | 35 | | |
| Total............. | 402 | 98 | 8 | 84 | 87 | 117 | 516 | 523 | 374 | 31,611 | 147 | 14,938 | 1,622 | 59 | 2,371 | 640 | 25,009 | $54,682 |

### ARABIA.

| Societies. | | | | | | | | | | | | | | | | | | |
|---|---|---|---|---|---|---|---|---|---|---|---|---|---|---|---|---|---|---|
| 103. Free Ch. Scot..... | 1 | 1 | 2 | .. | .. | .. | 3 | .. | 1 | .. | .. | .. | .. | .. | .. | 2 | 66 | .. |

### EGYPT.

| Societies. | | | | | | | | | | | | | | | | | | |
|---|---|---|---|---|---|---|---|---|---|---|---|---|---|---|---|---|---|---|
| 26. U. P. Ch .......... | 100 | 14 | .. | 11 | 14 | 12 | .. | 244 | .. | 4,427 | 29 | 2,971 | 464 | 2 | 265 | 98 | 6,039 | $27,353 |

### PERSIA.

| Societies. | | | | | | | | | | | | | | | | | | |
|---|---|---|---|---|---|---|---|---|---|---|---|---|---|---|---|---|---|---|
| 24. Pres. Ch. (North).. | 6 | 14 | 5 | 17 | 18 | 42 | .. | 217 | .. | 5,210 | 27 | 2,269 | 141 | .. | 18 | 147 | 3,069 | $2,200 |
| 72. C. M. S. ........ | 2 | 5 | 2 | .. | 2 | 1 | .. | 26 | .. | .. | .. | 130 | 1 | .. | .. | 2 | 341 | .. |
| 75. Arch. Miss ........ | 3 | 3 | .. | .. | .. | 1 | .. | .. | .. | .. | .. | .. | .. | 1 | 58 | 28 | 762 | .. |
| Total .......... | 11 | 22 | 7 | 17 | 20 | 44 | .. | 243 | .. | 5,210 | 27 | 2,399 | 142 | 1 | 76 | 177 | 4,172 | $2,200 |

| Societies. | Stations and Out-stations. | Missionaries — Ordained. | Lay. | Wives. | Other Women. | Native Workers — Ordained. | Teachers. | Other Helpers. | Preaching Places. | Sabbath-school Scholars. | Churches. | Communicants. | Additions. | Schools for Higher Education. | Pupils. | Common Schools. | Pupils. | Native Contributions for all purposes. |
|---|---|---|---|---|---|---|---|---|---|---|---|---|---|---|---|---|---|---|
| **AUSTRALIA AND NEW ZEALAND.** | | | | | | | | | | | | | | | | | | |
| 42. Sev. Day Adv. | | 2 | 1 | | 1 | | | | | | 2 | 107 | | | | | | |
| 81. Wes. Meth. | | | | | | | | 2,769 | 520 | 19,742 | 213 | 7,778 | 395 | | | 23 | | |
| 82. United Meth | 41 | 46 | | | | | | | 166 | 6,879 | 94 | 3,241 | 217 | | | | | |
| 85. Prim. Meth. Con | 47 | 35 | | | | | | | 221 | | 111 | 2,245 | | | | 102 | 5,419 | |
| 86. Bible Chris. | | 85 | | | | | 1,835 | 207 | 372 | 13,100 | 262 | 5,720 | 716 | | | | | $3,285 |
| 141. Moravian | 2 | 5 | | | | | 1 | | | | | 22 | 3 | | | 2 | | |
| Total | 90 | 171 | 1 | | 1 | | 1,836 | 2,976 | 1,279 | 39,743 | 680 | 19,016 | 1,328 | | | 127 | 5,419 | 3,285 |
| **MALAYSIA.** | | | | | | | | | | | | | | | | | | |
| 13. M. E. Ch. (North) | 1 | 5 | 3 | 4 | 1 | | 2 | 5 | 3 | 160 | 1 | 107 | 35 | 1 | 380 | 1 | 50 | $4,220 |
| 145. Rheuish M. S. | 83 | 33 | | 21 | | 3 | 100 | 215 | | 1,186 | | 3,936 | 1,331 | | | 136 | 1,833 | 1,889 |
| 155. Netherlands M. S. | 3 | 18 | | | | | | 184 | | | | 20,000 | | | | | | |
| 156. Ermelo M. S. | 6 | 6 | | | | | | 10 | | | 30 | 700 | | | | | | |
| 157. Mennonite M. S | 8 | 4 | 2 | | | | | 17 | | | | 511 | 20 | 1 | | 6 | 210 | |
| 159. Dutch Miss. Soc | 20 | 8 | | 8 | | | | 24 | 8 | | | 1,013 | 143 | | | 15 | 219 | |
| 160. Utrecht M. S. | 77 | | 7 | | | | | | | | | | | | | | | |
| 161. Dutch Ref. M. S | | 3 | 1 | 4 | | | | 12 | | | 65 | 6,500 | 1,000 | 1 | | 12 | | |
| Total | 198 | 77 | 18 | 37 | 1 | 3 | 102 | 467 | 11 | 1,346 | 96 | 32,767 | 2,529 | 3 | 380 | 170 | 2,312 | 6,109 |

### PACIFIC.

#### MICRONESIA.

| Societies. | Stations and Out-stations. | Missionaries — Ordained. | Lay. | Wives. | Other Women. | Native Workers — Ordained. | Teachers. | Other Helpers. | Preaching Places. | Sabbath-school Scholars. | Churches. | Communicants. | Additions. | Schools for Higher Education. | Pupils. | Common Schools. | Pupils. | Native Contributions for all purposes. |
|---|---|---|---|---|---|---|---|---|---|---|---|---|---|---|---|---|---|---|
| 1. A. B. C. F. M | 52 | 5 | | 4 | 10 | 17 | 57 | 12 | 85 | | | 51 | 4,475 | 496 | 8 | 182 | | | $1,785 |
| 42. Sev. Day Adv | | 5 | 2 | | 3 | 3 | | | | | | 10 | 655 | | | | | | |
| 169. Haw. Ev. Assoc | 45 | | | | | 20 | 16 | | | | | 20 | 2,599 | 415 | | | | | 1,786 |

#### MELANESIA.

| Societies. | Stations and Out-stations. | Missionaries — Ordained. | Lay. | Wives. | Other Women. | Native Workers — Ordained. | Teachers. | Other Helpers. | Preaching Places. | Sabbath-school Scholars. | Churches. | Communicants. | Additions. | Schools for Higher Education. | Pupils. | Common Schools. | Pupils. | Native Contributions for all purposes. |
|---|---|---|---|---|---|---|---|---|---|---|---|---|---|---|---|---|---|---|
| 104. Free Ch. Scot | 4 | 1 | 1 | | | | 37 | | 4 | | 3 | 344 | | | | 14 | 241 | $65 |
| 170. Melanesia Miss | 9 | 9 | 4 | | | 5 | 192 | | | | | | | | | | 86 | 2,897 | |

#### POLYNESIA.

| Societies. | Stations and Out-stations. | Missionaries — Ordained. | Lay. | Wives. | Other Women. | Native Workers — Ordained. | Teachers. | Other Helpers. | Preaching Places. | Sabbath-school Scholars. | Churches. | Communicants. | Additions. | Schools for Higher Education. | Pupils. | Common Schools. | Pupils. | Native Contributions for all purposes. |
|---|---|---|---|---|---|---|---|---|---|---|---|---|---|---|---|---|---|---|
| 62. Lond. Miss. Soc | 21 | 20 | | 16 | 1 | 347 | | 216 | | 13,445 | | 13,663 | | | | | 489 | 13,848 | 17,495 |
| 81. Wes. Meth. Soc | | | | | | | | 7,935 | 1,454 | 43,875 | 1049 | 28,757 | 4,230 | | | | | | |
| 165. Paris Ev. Soc | 28 | 4 | | | | 19 | | | | | | 2,010 | | | | | | 6,502 | |

#### HAWAIIAN ISLANDS.

| Societies. | Stations and Out-stations. | Missionaries — Ordained. | Lay. | Wives. | Other Women. | Native Workers — Ordained. | Teachers. | Other Helpers. | Preaching Places. | Sabbath-school Scholars. | Churches. | Communicants. | Additions. | Schools for Higher Education. | Pupils. | Common Schools. | Pupils. | Native Contributions for all purposes. |
|---|---|---|---|---|---|---|---|---|---|---|---|---|---|---|---|---|---|---|
| 1. A. B. C. F. M | 2 | 2 | | 2 | | | | | | | | | | | 1 | 14 | | | |
| 169. Haw. Ev. Assoc | 56 | | | | | 36 | | | | 2,769 | 62 | 5,049 | 281 | | | | | | $20,132 |
| Total Pacific | 211 | 46 | 7 | 22 | 14 | 447 | 302 | 8,163 | 1,543 | 90,089 | 1195 | 57,552 | 5,522 | 9 | 196 | 589 | 23,488 | $41,263 |

| Societies. | Stations and Out-stations. | Missionaries. | | | | Native Workers. | | | Preaching Places. | Sabbath-school Scholars. | Churches. | Communicants. | Additions. | Schools for Higher Education. | Pupils. | Common Schools. | Pupils. | Native Contributions for all purposes. |
|---|---|---|---|---|---|---|---|---|---|---|---|---|---|---|---|---|---|---|
| | | Ordained. | Lay. | Wives. | OtherWomen. | Ordained. | Teachers. | Other Helpers. | | | | | | | | | | |

### GREENLAND.

| | | | | | | | | | | | | | | | | | | |
|---|---|---|---|---|---|---|---|---|---|---|---|---|---|---|---|---|---|---|
| 141. Moravian.......... | 6 | 16 | ... | .. | . | ... | 32 | 10 | .... | ...... | ... | 780 | ... | .. | | 32 | ..... | ..... |

### LABRADOR.

| | | | | | | | | | | | | | | | | | | |
|---|---|---|---|---|---|---|---|---|---|---|---|---|---|---|---|---|---|---|
| 141. Moravian.......... | 6 | 38 | .. | ... | ... | . | 5 | 53 | .... | ...... | ... | 496 | ..... | ...... | | 6 | ..... | ..... |

### WEST INDIES.

| | | | | | | | | | | | | | | | | | | |
|---|---|---|---|---|---|---|---|---|---|---|---|---|---|---|---|---|---|---|
| 8. Cons. Am. Bap..... | .. | . | . | . | . | . | 1 | .... | | | | | | | | | | |
| 14. A. M. E. Ch ...... | 7 | 6 | 5 | 7 | ... | ... | 4 | .... | 8 | 131 | 5 | 149 | 19 | ... | ..... | 3 | 146 | $640 |
| 20. P. E. Church...... | 23 | 1 | ... | ... | ... | 12 | 34 | .... | 23 | 150 | 11 | 405 | 20 | 1 | 13 | 4 | 205 | 1,250 |
| 51. Pres. Ch. Canada . | 21 | 4 | ... | ... | 3 | 2 | ... | 4 | | | | | | | | | | |
| 62. Lon. Miss. Soc.. | 4 | 1 | ... | 1 | ... | ... | ... | 17 | ... | 815 | ... | 481 | ... | ... | ..... | 3 | 611 | 2,876 |
| 77. B. M. S ......... | 111 | 7 | ... | ... | ... | 421 | 147 | ... | ... | 21,087 | ... | 39,869 | 3,005 | ... | ..... | ... | 16,548 | 5,870 |
| 81. Wes. Meth... | 12 | 15 | ... | ... | ... | 2 | 25 | 720 | 25 | 4,592 | 53 | 5,251 | 125 | ... | ..... | 18 | 1,354 | 11,461 |
| 82. Un. Meth. Free Ch. | 9 | 10 | ... | ... | ... | ... | ... | 46 | 2,176 | 26 | 3,470 | 91 | ... | | | | ..... | ..... |
| 104. U. P. Ch. Scot.. | 53 | 18 | ... | ... | ... | 16 | 79 | 17 | 53 | 8,271 | 53 | 9,831 | 321 | ... | ..... | 79 | 7,196 | 841,069 |
| 141. Moravians .. ..... | 49 | 50 | ... | ... | ... | 38 | 145 | 471 | ... | 6,371 | ... | 10,251 | ..... | ... | ..... | 62 | ..... | ....... |
| Total.. ...... ....... | 289 | 112 | 5 | 8 | 3 | 488 | 434 | 1,229 | 155 | 43,593 | 148 | 69,707 | 3,584 | 1 | 13 | 169 | 26,960 | $863,166 |

### MEXICO.

| | | | | | | | | | | | | | | | | | | |
|---|---|---|---|---|---|---|---|---|---|---|---|---|---|---|---|---|---|---|
| 1. A. B. C. F. M. | 19 | 7 | ... | 6 | 2 | 1 | 7 | 11 | 13 | 413 | 10 | 823 | 92 | 2 | 25 | 8 | 168 | $843 |
| 5. So. Bap. Conv..... | 34 | 7 | ... | 7 | 5 | 1 | ... | 14 | .... | ..... | 24 | 782 | 213 | ... | ..... | 6 | 182 | 1,430 |
| 13. M. E. Ch. (North). | 32 | 10 | ... | 10 | 10 | 10 | 25 | 38 | 48 | 1,648 | 22 | 2,430 | 549 | 4 | 120 | 42 | 2,725 | 9,012 |
| 15. M. E. Ch. South.... | 115 | 13 | 1 | 12 | 7 | 81 | ... | 20 | 82 | 3,254 | 47 | 3,808 | 277 | 1 | 20 | 34 | 1,327 | 4,707 |
| 24. Pres. Ch. (North).. | 5 | 7 | ... | 7 | 4 | 25 | ... | 78 | . | 1,795 | 90 | 5,165 | 388 | ... | 15 | 42 | 1,358 | 3,627 |
| 28. Pres. Ch. (South).. | 51 | 2 | ... | 1 | 3 | 8 | ... | 3 | ... | 418 | ... | 450 | ..... | ... | ..... | 2 | 250 | 635 |
| 19. A. R. P. Synod..... | 11 | 2 | ... | 1 | 1 | 2 | ... | 2 | ... | 159 | 6 | 226 | 32 | ... | ..... | 2 | 27 | 100 |
| 30. Cumb. Pres. Ch .. | 2 | 2 | ... | 2 | ... | ... | ... | 1 | ... | ..... | 2 | 79 | ..... | ... | ..... | 2 | 146 | ....... |
| Total ............. | 269 | 50 | 1 | 40 | 32 | 128 | 32 | 167 | 143 | 7,689 | 201 | 13,262 | 1,351 | 7 | 180 | 138 | 6,183 | $20,360 |

### CENTRAL AMERICA.

| | | | | | | | | | | | | | | | | | | |
|---|---|---|---|---|---|---|---|---|---|---|---|---|---|---|---|---|---|---|
| 24. Pres. Ch. (North)... | 1 | 2 | ... | 2 | 2 | ... | ... | 1 | .... | 50 | 1 | 4 | ..... | ... | ..... | 2 | 1 | 38 | $15 |
| 141. Moravian. ...... .. | 14 | 20 | ... | ... | ... | 6 | 13 | 54 | .... | 755 | ... | 867 | ..... | ... | ..... | 11 | ..... | ..... |
| Total............. | 15 | 22 | ... | 2 | 2 | 6 | 13 | 55 | ..... | 805 | 1 | 871 | ... | ... | ..... | 2 | 12 | 38 | $15 |

### SOUTH AMERICA.

| | | | | | | | | | | | | | | | | | | |
|---|---|---|---|---|---|---|---|---|---|---|---|---|---|---|---|---|---|---|
| 5. So. Bap. Conv..... | 13 | 4 | ... | 4 | 1 | 4 | ..... | 8 | ... | ..... | 8 | 312 | 53 | ... | ..... | ... | ..... | $760 |
| 13. M. E. Ch. (North)... | 17 | 11 | ... | 11 | 7 | 12 | 21 | 42 | 56 | 2,113 | 23 | 1,865 | 105 | 2 | 49 | 21 | 1,858 | 28,279 |
| 15. M. E. Ch. South.... | 19 | 9 | ... | 7 | 9 | 11 | ..... | 8 | 18 | 356 | 4 | 470 | 103 | 1 | 31 | 4 | 135 | 3,053 |
| 24. Pres. Ch. (North)... | 15 | 22 | 1 | 21 | 4 | 12 | ..... | 72 | ... | 947 | 46 | 2,992 | 324 | ... | 5 | 22 | 1,263 | 13,602 |
| 28. Pres. Ch. (South).. | 30 | 10 | 1 | 8 | 5 | 5 | ..... | 10 | ... | 224 | 21 | 670 | ..... | 1 | 50 | 3 | ..... | 1,400 |
| 73. So. Am. Miss. Soc.. | 25 | 12 | 12 | 6 | 2 | ... | ..... | 6 | ... | ..... | 14 | ..... | ..... | ... | ..... | ... | ..... | 10,074 |
| 141. Moravian ......... | 22 | 74 | ... | ... | ... | 3 | 49 | 259 | ..... | 270 | ... | 8,056 | ..... | ... | ..... | 13 | ..... | ..... |
| Total ......... ..... | 140 | 142 | 14 | 57 | 28 | 47 | 70 | 405 | 74 | 3,910 | 116 | 14,366 | 585 | 4 | 135 | 63 | 2,756 | $57,168 |

## 3. *GENERAL SUMMARY.*

| SOCIETIES. | No. of Ministers. | Congregations Contributing. | No. of Communicants. | Receipts at Home. | Per cent per Member. | Total Expenditures. | Native Contributions. | Per cent per Member. |
|---|---|---|---|---|---|---|---|---|

### AMERICA.

#### UNITED STATES.

| SOCIETIES. | No. of Ministers. | Congregations Contributing. | No. of Communicants. | Receipts at Home. | Per cent per Member. | Total Expenditures. | Native Contributions. | Per cent per Member. |
|---|---|---|---|---|---|---|---|---|
| 1. A. B. C. F. M. | 4,640 | 3,000 | 491,985 | $617,724 | 1.26 | $762,947 | $117,494 | 3.23 |
| 3. Am. Bap. Miss. Union | 6,138 | 7,786 | 717,640 | 559,528 | .78 | 440,557 | 224,269 | 1.62 |
| 4. Free Baptist | 1,598 | 1,613 | 86,297 | 25,497 | .29 | 21,476 | 894 | .61 |
| 5. Southern Bap. Convention | 8,518 | 15,894 | 1,194,520 | 109,174 | .09 | 108,007 | 4,681 | 2 11 |
| 6. Seventh Day Baptist | 100 | 100 | 9,000 | 4,500 | .50 | 12,000 | ...... | ..... |
| 7. German Baptist | 1 1,000 | ¹600 | 170,000 | ⁹7,936 | .11 | 6,196 | 33 | .25 |
| 9. Bap. General Association | 562 | ¹200 | 49,668 | 500 | .01 | ...... | ...... | ..... |
| 13. M. E. Ch. (North) | 12,914 | 22,833 | 2,283,967 | 590,000 | .25 | 607,032 | 107,970 | 3.06 |
| 14. African M. E. Ch. | 2,500 | 3,000 | 100,000 | 7,000 | .07 | 15,000 | 1,640 | ..... |
| 15. M. E. Ch (South) | 4,862 | 11,767 | 1,161,666 | 276,124 | .23 | 298,598 | 8,147 | 1.85 |
| 16. Meth. Prot. Ch. | 1,282 | ¹600 | 142,755 | 16,771 | .11 | 15,629 | 460 | 2.26 |
| 17. Wes. Meth. Connection | 275 | ...... | 1,700 | 2,000 | 1.17 | 1,500 | 300 | 1.00 |
| 20. Prot. Episcopal | 4,180 | 2,435 | 509,143 | 189,184 | .37 | 211,480 | 6,778 | 2.56 |
| 22. Ref. Pres. Gen. Synod | 40 | 48 | 5,000 | 4,500 | .90 | 3,500 | ¹350 | 2 99 |
| 23. Ref. German | 835 | 1,554 | 200,498 | 20,000 | .10 | 20,000 | 2,835 | ..... |
| 24. Pres. Ch. (North) | 6,158 | 6,894 | 775,903 | 794,066 | 1.02 | 907,972 | ...... | ..... |
| 25. Ref (Dutch) Church | ¹570 | 530 | 88,979 | 117,090 | 1.31 | 108,980 | 8,003 | 1.50 |
| 26. United Presbyterian | 774 | 705 | 103,921 | 100,539 | .97 | 100,539 | 28,375 | 2.96 |
| 27. Ref. Pres. (Covenanter) | 124 | 124 | 10,819 | 18,463 | 1.71 | 17,057 | 34 | .18 |
| 28. Pres. Ch. (South) | 1,200 | 1,544 | 161,742 | 107,627 | .66 | 105,293 | 4,317 | 2.08 |
| 29. Asso. Ref. South. Pres | 80 | 117 | 8,309 | 5,768 | .70 | 8,500 | 106 | .47 |
| 30. Cumberland Pres | 1,595 | 1,175 | 160,185 | 21,107 | .13 | 12,788 | ...... | ..... |
| 31. German Evangelical | 650 | 845 | ¹150,000 | 9,010 | .06 | 8,881 | ...... | ..... |
| 34. Evan Luth. Gen Synod | 979 | 1,437 | 151,404 | 41,292 | .27 | 41,000 | 1,555 | .20 |
| 35. Evan. Luth. Gen. Coun | 899 | 1,557 | 264,235 | 12,177 | .05 | 11,979 | 50 | .06 |
| 36. For. Chris. Miss. Society | 3,388 | 1,023 | 645,771 | 57,280 | .09 | 63,409 | ...... | ..... |
| 37. United Brethren | 1,455 | 4,265 | 200,000 | 26,224 | .13 | 44,759 | 1,484 | .22 |
| 38. Evan. Association | 1,845 | ...... | 145,603 | ⁹135,784 | ...... | ...... | 440 | ..... |
| 39. Mennonites | 150 | 75 | 8,000 | 6,191 | .77 | 9,502 | ...... | ..... |
| 41. Am. Chris. Conv | 1,500 | ...... | 100,000 | 3,000 | .03 | 3,423 | 74 | .79 |
| 42. Seventh Day Adventists | 354 | 930 | 27,031 | 47,000 | 1.73 | 60,000 | 21,000 | 7.42 |
| Total | 72,195 | 92,651 | 10,025,647 | 3,932,975 | ...... | 4,023,005 | 540,789 | .... |

#### CANADA.

| SOCIETIES. | No. of Ministers. | Congregations Contributing. | No. of Communicants. | Receipts at Home. | Per cent per Member. | Total Expenditures. | Native Contributions. | Per cent per Member. |
|---|---|---|---|---|---|---|---|---|
| 50. Methodist | 1,285 | 1,285 | 229,775 | 215,775 | .93 | 210,692 | ...... | ..... |
| 51. Presbyterian | 841 | 1,920 | 157,990 | 100,106 | .63 | 101,885 | 3,028 | .78 |
| 52. Baptist | 532 | ...... | 77,247 | 33,175 | .43 | 27,721 | ...... | ..... |
| 53. Congregational | 88 | 95 | 1,734 | 1,576 | .90 | 1,992 | ...... | ..... |
| Total | 2,746 | 3,300 | 466,746 | 350,632 | ...... | 342,290 | 3,028 | ..... |

¹ Estimated or approximate.    ² Incomplete returns.    ⁶ Exclusive of school fees.
⁷ School fees only.    ⁹ Including home missions.
† From all adherents.

## 3. GENERAL SUMMARY.

| SOCIETIES. | Stations and Out-stations. | Missionaries | | | | Native Workers | | Preaching Places. | Churches. | Communicants. | Additions. | Schools for Higher Education. | Pupils. | Common Schools. | Pupils. |
|---|---|---|---|---|---|---|---|---|---|---|---|---|---|---|---|
| | | Ordained. | Lay. | Wives. | Other Women. | Ordained. | Other Helpers. | | | | | | | | |

### AMERICA.

#### UNITED STATES.

| | | | | | | | | | | | | | | | |
|---|---|---|---|---|---|---|---|---|---|---|---|---|---|---|---|
| 1. A. B. C. F. M. | 1058 | 188 | 17 | 181 | 152 | 174 | 2,243 | 1,402 | 387 | 36,256 | 1,554 | 136 | 8,027 | 889 | 33,114 |
| 3. Am. Bap. Mis. Union | 2153 | 125 | 11 | 98 | 97 | 584 | 1,639 | ... | 1361 | 138,293 | 11,577 | 6 | ... | 1030 | $20,615 |
| 4. Free Baptist | 211 | 9 | 1 | 9 | 6 | 5 | 212 | ... | 11 | 646 | 55 | 1 | 28 | 104 | 3,591 |
| 5. Southern Bap. Convention | 161 | 33 | ... | 30 | 15 | 29 | 57 | 223 | 62 | 2,213 | 479 | 2 | 75 | 26 | 600 |
| 6. Seventh Day Baptist | 3 | 2 | ... | 2 | 2 | 2 | 7 | ... | 1 | 30 | 5 | ... | ... | 2 | 29 |
| 7. German Baptist | ... | 1 | 1 | 1 | ... | 9 | ... | ... | 5 | 131 | 16 | ... | ... | ... | ... |
| 9. Bap. General Association | ... | ... | ... | ... | ... | ... | ... | 6 | ... | ... | ... | ... | ... | ... | ... |
| 13. M. E. Ch. (North) | 373 | 169 | 10 | 160 | 126 | 242 | 1,696 | 624 | 334 | 35,000 | 5,747 | 59 | 5,065 | 1022 | 28,512 |
| 14. African M. E. Ch. | 12 | 9 | 9 | 12 | 3 | ... | 7 | 17 | 10 | 356 | 76 | ... | ... | 5 | 257 |
| 15. M. E. Ch. (South) | 169 | 48 | 3 | 40 | 35 | ³121 | 82 | 153 | 60 | 4,941 | 516 | 5 | 278 | 47 | 1,719 |
| 16. Meth. Prot. Ch. | 3 | 5 | ... | 5 | 4 | ... | 12 | 4 | 2 | 203 | ... | 2 | 7 | 4 | 249 |
| 17. Wes. Meth. Connection | 2 | 2 | 2 | 2 | ... | 1 | ... | 2 | 1 | 300 | 12 | ... | ... | 1 | 300 |
| 20. Prot. Episcopal | 220 | 23 | 6 | 19 | 27 | 52 | ... | 220 | 19 | 2,644 | 370 | 4 | ... | 85 | ⁵3,107 |
| 22. Ref.Pres.Gen.Synod | 10 | ... | ... | ... | ... | 2 | 18 | 10 | 2 | 117 | 5 | ... | ... | ... | 138 |
| 23. Ref. German | 24 | 3 | ... | 3 | 2 | 7 | 15 | 26 | 12 | 1,656 | ... | 1 | 26 | 1 | 40 |
| 24. Pres. Ch. (North) | 92 | 190 | 41 | 186 | 135 | 152 | 1,105 | ... | 296 | 24,820 | 2,516 | ... | 92 | 546 | 24,915 |
| 25. Ref. (Dutch Church) | 155 | 23 | 4 | 23 | 12 | 30 | 283 | 155 | 51 | 5,336 | 552 | 2 | 95 | 111 | 8,974 |
| 26. United Presbyterian | 185 | 26 | ... | 22 | 26 | 23 | 436 | ... | 39 | 9,508 | 1,722 | 4 | 375 | 208 | 10,687 |
| 27. Ref. Pres. (Covenanter) | 8 | 4 | 1 | 4 | 4 | 4 | 34 | 11 | 3 | 190 | 12 | ... | ... | 25 | 720 |
| 28. Pres. Ch. (South) | 116 | 35 | 2 | 53 | 18 | 19 | 31 | ... | 25 | 2,072 | 360 | 1 | 50 | 15 | 1,207 |
| 29. Asso. Ref. South. Pres | 11 | 2 | ... | 1 | 1 | 2 | 2 | ... | 6 | 226 | 32 | ... | ... | 3 | ... |
| 30. Cumberland Pres. | 10 | 6 | ... | 6 | 6 | 1 | 5 | ... | 10 | 600 | ... | ... | ... | 4 | 200 |
| 31. German Evangelical | 10 | 4 | ... | 4 | 1 | ... | 15 | ... | 3 | 234 | 34 | 1 | 70 | 3 | 180 |
| 34. Ev. Lutheran Synod | 12 | 5 | ... | 4 | 3 | 4 | 388 | 354 | 338 | 7,726 | 2,403 | 1 | 378 | 195 | 4,108 |
| 35. Ev. Luth. Gen. Conv. | 6 | 4 | ... | 3 | ... | 2 | 88 | 103 | 2 | 832 | 1 | ... | ... | 89 | 1,073 |
| 36. For. Chris. Miss. Soc. | 30 | 30 | ... | 12 | 4 | ... | 27 | ... | 26 | 2,990 | 617 | ... | ... | 8 | 232 |
| 37. United Brethren | ... | 18 | 25 | 16 | 5 | 3 | 40 | 405 | 131 | 6,712 | 1,150 | 1 | 23 | 13 | 568 |
| 38. Evan. Association | 15 | 5 | ... | 3 | ... | 5 | 24 | 18 | 5 | 333 | ... | 1 | 18 | ... | ... |
| 39. Mennonites | 5 | 3 | 3 | 3 | 6 | ... | 6 | 3 | ... | 21 | 12 | ... | ... | 3 | 125 |
| 41. Am. Chris. Conv | 37 | 2 | ... | 2 | ... | 6 | ... | 37 | 3 | 93 | 34 | ... | ... | ... | ... |
| 42. Seventh Day Adventists | ... | 18 | 11 | 10 | 10 | 10 | 135 | ... | 88 | 2,827 | 431 | ... | ... | ... | ... |
| Total | 4889 | 985 | 147 | 884 | 700 | 1439 | 8,347 | 3,773 | 3293 | 287,366 | 33,288 | 225 | 14697 | 4499 | 140,170 |

#### CANADA.

| | | | | | | | | | | | | | | | |
|---|---|---|---|---|---|---|---|---|---|---|---|---|---|---|---|
| 50. Methodist | 13 | 9 | 2 | 8 | ... | 5 | 31 | 31 | 10 | 1,538 | 578 | 1 | 210 | 3 | 275 |
| 51. Presbyterian | 130 | 25 | 4 | 22 | 24 | 6 | 214 | 130 | 65 | 3,881 | 71 | 1 | 22 | 98 | ⁵3,750 |
| 52. Baptist | 9 | 16 | ... | 14 | 8 | 8 | 141 | ... | 23 | 2,466 | 410 | 1 | 70 | ... | ... |
| 53. Congregational | 2 | 2 | ... | ... | 2 | ... | ... | ... | 1 | ... | ... | ... | ... | ... | ... |
| Total | 154 | 52 | 6 | 44 | 34 | 19 | 386 | 161 | 99 | 7,885 | 1,059 | 3 | 302 | 101 | 4,025 |

³ Ordained and lay.     ⁴ Total ladies.     ⁵ Total pupils.     ⁶ Dioceses.

| Societies | No. of Ministers. | Congregations Contributing. | No. of Communicants. | Receipts at Home. | Per cent per Member. | Total Expenditures. | Native Contributions. | Per cent per Member. |
|---|---|---|---|---|---|---|---|---|
| | | | | | | | | |

## GREAT BRITAIN.

### ENGLAND.

| Societies | No. of Ministers. | Congregations Contributing. | No. of Communicants. | Receipts at Home. | Per cent per Member. | Total Expenditures. | Native Contributions. | Per cent per Member. |
|---|---|---|---|---|---|---|---|---|
| 61. New England Company ... ... | ........ | ........ | ........ | 17,500 | ..... | 17,500 | ........ | ..... |
| 62. London Miss. Soc. ... ... ... | ........ | ........ | ........ | 517,896 | ..... | ........ | 89,380 | ..... |
| 64. Chris. Vernac. Ed. Soc. ... ... | ........ | ........ | ........ | 20,225 | ..... | 13,955 | ........ | ..... |
| 65. China Inland Miss ... ... ... | ........ | ........ | ... .. | 186,045 | ..... | 168,405 | ........ | ..... |
| 67. North Africa Miss ... ... ... | ........ | ........ | ........ | 23,250 | ..... | 22,500 | ........ | ..... |
| 71. Soc. for Prop. of Gospel ... ... | ...... | 8,347 | ........ | 625,195 | ..... | 556,829 | ........ | ..... |
| 72. Ch. Miss. Soc. ... ... ... | ¹7,000 | 5,876 | ........ | 1,301,410 | ..... | 1,122,925 | ¹100,000 | 2.04 |
| 73. So. American Miss. Soc. ... | ........ | .. | ........ | 51,736 | ..... | 55,831 | ¹10,075 | ..... |
| 74. Universities Miss. Cent. Africa. | ... ... | ........ | ........ | 76,427 | ..... | 85,080 | ........ | ..... |
| 75. Arch. Miss. Assyrian Christians | ........ | ........ | ........ | 7,000 | ..... | 7,000 | ........ | ..... |
| 77. Baptist Miss. Soc. ... ... | ¹1,500 | 1,725 | 220,000 | 373,573 | 1.69 | 399,842 | ¹45,000 | .95 |
| 78. Gen. Baptist Miss. Soc. ... ... | 110 | 152 | 26,700 | 28,371 | 1.06 | 43,713 | 1,300 | 1.00 |
| 79. Strict Baptist ... ... ... | ........ | ........ | ........ | 3,500 | ..... | 3,500 | ........ | ..... |
| 81. Wesleyan Methodist ... ... ... | 1,975 | 7,105 | 423,615 | 639,630 | 1.51 | 635,535 | 326,495 | 9.52 |
| 82. United Meth. Free Churches. ... | 345 | 1,339 | 67,510 | 49,953 | .73 | 52,261 | 58,147 | 5.63 |
| 83. Meth. New Connexion. ... ... | 196 | 449 | 29,508 | 22,283 | .75 | 23,581 | ........ | ..... |
| 84. Cent. China Wes. Lay ... ... | ........ | ........ | ........ | 3,585 | ..... | 4,574 | ........ | ..... |
| 85. Primitive Meth ... ... ... | ........ | ........ | ........ | 17,895 | ..... | 20,450 | ........ | ..... |
| 86. Bible Christian For. Miss. Soc. | ........ | ........ | ........ | ........ | ..... | ........ | ........ | ..... |
| 89. Welsh Calvinistic ... ... | 673 | 1,200 | 134,239 | 37,768 | .28 | 33,990 | 2,000 | 1.07 |
| 90. Pres. Ch. of England ... ... | 288 | 272 | 65,019 | 85,696 | 1.32 | 98,853 | 6,000 | 1.67 |
| 93. Friends' Association ... ... | ¹350 | ¹200 | ¹20,000 | 43,105 | 2.15 | 42,385 | ........ | ..... |
| 94. Friends' Miss. to Syria. ... | ... .. | ... .. | ... .. | 10,450 | ..... | 10,270 | ¹2,155 | ..... |
| Total ... ... ... ... | 12,437 | 26,659 | 986,591 | 4,142,493 | — | 3,418,977 | 640,552 | — |

### SCOTLAND.

| Societies | No. of Ministers. | Congregations Contributing. | No. of Communicants. | Receipts at Home. | Per cent per Member. | Total Expenditures. | Native Contributions. | Per cent per Member. |
|---|---|---|---|---|---|---|---|---|
| 101. Ch. of Scotland (Estab.) ... ... | 1,515 | 1,358 | 587,954 | 112,110 | .19 | 128,819 | 45,734 | 11.57 |
| 102. Ref. Pres. Ch. of Scotland ... | 40 | 45 | 5,552 | ¹3,750 | .68 | 4,000 | ........ | ..... |
| 103. Free Ch. of Scotland ... ... | 1,153 | 1,030 | 335,000 | 391,225 | 1.17 | 476,585 | 89,310 | 13.49 |
| 104. U. P. Ch. of Scotland ... | 615 | 567 | 184,354 | 202,460 | 1.09 | 186,000 | 52,350 | 3.51 |
| 105. Un. Or. Secession Ch ... ... | 26 | 29 | 4,678 | 4,895 | 1.05 | 4,651 | 308 | 19.26 |
| Total ... ... ... ... | 3,349 | 3,029 | 1,117,538 | 714,440 | .... | 800,055 | 187,702 | .... |

### IRELAND.

| Societies | No. of Ministers. | Congregations Contributing. | No. of Communicants. | Receipts at Home. | Per cent per Member. | Total Expenditures. | Native Contributions. | Per cent per Member. |
|---|---|---|---|---|---|---|---|---|
| 109. Pres. Ch. of Ireland * ... ... ... | 636 | 551 | 102,678 | 78,368 | .76 | 65,987 | 9,182 | 21.85 |

## CONTINENTAL EUROPE.

### DENMARK.

| Societies | No. of Ministers. | Congregations Contributing. | No. of Communicants. | Receipts at Home. | Per cent per Member. | Total Expenditures. | Native Contributions. | Per cent per Member. |
|---|---|---|---|---|---|---|---|---|
| 115. Danish Miss. Soc. ... ... ... | ........ | ........ | ........ | 19,626 | ..... | 22,312 | ........ | ..... |
| 116. Indian Home Miss ... ... .. | ... ... | ... ... | ... ... | ⁹ | ..... | 54,958 | 67 | .01 |
| 117. Loventhal's Mission ... ... .. | ... ... | ... ... | ... ... | 1,876 | ..... | 2,073 | ........ | ..... |
| Total ... ... ... ... | ........ | .. .. | ........ | 21,502 | .... | 79,343 | 67 | .... |

### NORWAY.

| Societies | No. of Ministers. | Congregations Contributing. | No. of Communicants. | Receipts at Home. | Per cent per Member. | Total Expenditures. | Native Contributions. | Per cent per Member. |
|---|---|---|---|---|---|---|---|---|
| 121. Norwegian Miss. Soc. ... ... | ... .. | ........ | ........ | ¹100,000 | ..... | ¹90,000 | ........ | ..... |
| 122. Schreuder Mission ... ... ... | ... ... | ........ | ........ | ... ... | ..... | .. .. | ... ... | ..... |
| Total ... ... ... ... ... | ... ... | ... ... | ........ | 100,000 | ..... | 90,000 | ........ | ..... |

¹ Estimated or approximate.    ² Incomplete returns.    ⁵ Exclusive of school fees.
⁷ School fees only.     ⁹ Including home missions.
\* Most of the churches of Ireland unite in their foreign mission
† From all adherents.

| SOCIETIES. | Stations and Out-stations. | Missionaries. Ordained. | Lay. | Wives. | Other Women. | Native Workers. Ordained. | Other Helpers. | Preaching Places. | Churches. | Communicants. | Additions. | Schools for Higher Education. | Pupils. | Common Schools. | Pupils. |
|---|---|---|---|---|---|---|---|---|---|---|---|---|---|---|---|

## GREAT BRITAIN.

### ENGLAND.

| SOCIETIES. | Stations and Out-stations. | Ordained. | Lay. | Wives. | Other Women. | Ordained. | Other Helps. | Preaching Places. | Churches. | Communicants. | Additions. | Schools for Higher Education. | Pupils. | Common Schools. | Pupils. |
|---|---|---|---|---|---|---|---|---|---|---|---|---|---|---|---|
| 61. New England Company............ | | | | | | | | | | 68,805 | | 12 | 3,684 | 1978 | 102,296 |
| 62. London Miss. Soc........... | 1929 | 188 | 18 | 121 | 36 | 1224 | 4,195 | .... | .... | 68,805 | .... | 12 | 3,684 | 1978 | 102,296 |
| 64. Chris. Vernac. Ed. Soc............ | | | | | | | 1,018 | | | | | | | 211 | 8,555 |
| 65. China Inland Miss............ | 158 | 171 | | 70 | 142 | 14 | 218 | .... | 88 | 2,839 | 536 | .... | | 24 | 276 |
| 67. North Africa Miss............ | 15 | ³17 | | 9 | 28 | | 1 | | 1 | 17 | .... | | | 1 | 20 |
| 71. Soc. for Prop. of Gospel............ | ²470 | 498 | 30 | .... | 79 | 148 | 2,300 | .... | ⁸48 | ........ | .... | 25 | 2,650 | 800 | ²38,000 |
| 72. Ch. Miss. Soc............ | 315 | 286 | 53 | .... | 59 | 286 | 3,835 | .... | .... | 49,016 | 1,252 | 16 | ¹350 | 1777 | ⁵74,785 |
| 73. So. American Miss. Soc...... | 25 | 12 | 12 | .... | 6 | 2 | | | | | .... | | | | |
| 74. Universities Miss. Cent. Africa ..... | 39 | 18 | 26 | .... | 24 | 3 | 70 | .... | 11 | 586 | .... | 1 | 24 | 21 | ¹1,000 |
| 75. Arch. Miss. Assyrian Christians...... | 3 | 2 | 3 | | | 1 | | | .... | | .... | 1 | 58 | 28 | 762 |
| 77. Baptist Miss. Soc............ | 496 | 128 | .... | 101 | 3 | 581 | 2,506 | .... | .... | 47,133 | 2,871 | .. | .... | .... | 16,381 |
| 78. Gen. Baptist Miss. Soc...... | 19 | 8 | .. | 4 | 3 | 21 | 28 | .... | 18 | 1,876 | 53 | .. | 641 | .... | |
| 79. Strict Baptist.. ..... | 18 | 3 | | 3 | | 3 | 23 | .... | | 358 | .... | | 19 | | 509 |
| 81. Wesleyan Methodist............ | ²357 | 159 | 20 | 109 | 91 | 216 | 5,990 | 1,588 | .... | 34,287 | 1,101 | .. | 634 | | 64,395 |
| 82. United Meth. Free Churches........ | 275 | 66 | 295 | .... | | 9 | .... | 275 | 275 | 10,335 | 227 | .. | 152 | | 11,367 |
| 83. Meth. New Connexion............ | 55 | 7 | 1 | 5 | 1 | 3 | 36 | 60 | 42 | 1,301 | 83 | 1 | 10 | 15 | 230 |
| 84. Cent. China Wes. Lay............ | 3 | .. | 8 | 2 | .... | | 4 | ²100 | .... | 12 | 12 | .... | | 1 | 12 |
| 85. Primitive Meth. .. ........ | 5 | | | | | 2 | 5 | .... | | 530 | 19 | | | | |
| 86. Bible Christian For. Miss. Soc...... | .... | 91 | | | | | 2,245 | 375 | 262 | 5,726 | 716 | .. | .... | .... | .... |
| 89. Welsh Calvinistic............ | | 9 | 3 | 5 | 1 | .... | 564 | 163 | 72 | 1,809 | 285 | 3 | .... | 140 | ⁵4,143 |
| 90. Pres. Ch. of England. ............ | 130 | 20 | 13 | 21 | 16 | 8 | 198 | 130 | 43 | 3,602 | 222 | 4 | 41 | ... | .... |
| 93. Friends' Association.. ...... | 8 | ³17 | | ⁴24 | | | 850 | 257 | 148 | 2,612 | .... | 2 | 510 | 140 | 2,945 |
| 94. Friends' Miss. to Syria............ | 7 | .. | 2 | 2 | 4 | .... | 13 | .... | 1 | .... | .... | 2 | 50 | 14 | ²350 |
| Total............ | 4327 | 1646 | 481 | 476 | 493 | 2521 | 2350⁸ | 2,944 | 1008 | 230,399 | 7,327 | 65 | 7,377 | 6590 | 345,966 |

### SCOTLAND.

| SOCIETIES. | Stations and Out-stations. | Ordained. | Lay. | Wives. | Other Women. | Ordained. | Other Helps. | Preaching Places. | Churches. | Communicants. | Additions. | Schools for Higher Education. | Pupils. | Common Schools. | Pupils. |
|---|---|---|---|---|---|---|---|---|---|---|---|---|---|---|---|
| 101. Ch. of Scotland (Estab.)............ | 37 | 17 | 14 | 18 | 29 | 7 | 168 | 42 | 33 | 3,952 | 1,146 | 3 | 407 | 97 | 6,241 |
| 102. Ref. Pres. Ch. of Scotland ......... | 3 | 1 | ... | 1 | 1 | .. | 9 | 3 | 1 | 37 | 3 | ... | 3 | ¹200 | |
| 103. Free Ch. of Scotland.... ......... | 207 | 51 | 46 | 32 | 38 | 24 | 600 | 207 | 42 | 6,629 | 647 | 6 | 947 | 320 | 25,679 |
| 104. U. P. Ch. of Scotland ............. | 251 | 59 | 11 | 60 | 24 | 23 | 495 | 251 | 155 | 14,899 | 820 | .. | 80 | 226 | 14,283 |
| 105. Un. Or. Secession Ch............... | | 1 | 1 | 1 | .. | | 3 | 2 | 1 | 16 | .. | .. | .... | 3 | 312 |
| Total............ | 498 | 129 | 72 | 112 | 92 | 54 | 1,275 | 505 | 232 | 25,524 | 2,616 | 9 | 1,434 | 649 | 46,715 |

### IRELAND.

| SOCIETIES. | Stations and Out-stations. | Ordained. | Lay. | Wives. | Other Women. | Ordained. | Other Helps. | Preaching Places. | Churches. | Communicants. | Additions. | Schools for Higher Education. | Pupils. | Common Schools. | Pupils. |
|---|---|---|---|---|---|---|---|---|---|---|---|---|---|---|---|
| 109. Pres. Ch. of Ireland* ............ | 24 | 12 | 3 | 11 | 9 | 2 | 92 | .... | 18 | 420 | 57 | 2 | .... | 48 | ⁵3,379 |

## CONTINENTAL EUROPE.

### DENMARK.

| SOCIETIES. | Stations and Out-stations. | Ordained. | Lay. | Wives. | Other Women. | Ordained. | Other Helps. | Preaching Places. | Churches. | Communicants. | Additions. | Schools for Higher Education. | Pupils. | Common Schools. | Pupils. |
|---|---|---|---|---|---|---|---|---|---|---|---|---|---|---|---|
| 115. Danish Miss. Soc... ............ | 4 | 5 | 2 | 5 | 1 | 3 | 19 | .... | 4 | 208 | .... | | | | |
| 116. Indian Home Miss. ............ | 14 | 6 | 2 | 5 | 5 | 5 | 142 | .... | 14 | 6,070 | 707 | 2 | 284 | | |
| 117. Loventhal's Mission. ............ | 1 | 1 | | 1 | .... | .. | 3 | .... | 1 | .... | .... | .. | .. | | |
| Total...... ............ | 19 | 12 | 4 | 11 | 6 | 8 | 164 | .... | 19 | 6,278 | 707 | 2 | 284 | | .... |

### NORWAY.

| SOCIETIES. | Stations and Out-stations. | Ordained. | Lay. | Wives. | Other Women. | Ordained. | Other Helps. | Preaching Places. | Churches. | Communicants. | Additions. | Schools for Higher Education. | Pupils. | Common Schools. | Pupils. |
|---|---|---|---|---|---|---|---|---|---|---|---|---|---|---|---|
| 121. Norwegian Miss. Soc............. | .... | 40 | 5 | 37 | 12 | 16 | ²1000 | 379 | ... | ¹2,500 | ¹4,000 | 2 | 80 | 370 | 30,500 |
| 122. Schreuder Mission............... | 2 | 3 | ... | 1 | .. | 2 | .... | ........ | | 130 | .. | .. | .... | .. | 124 |
| Total.. ............ | 2 | 43 | 5 | 38 | 12 | 18 | 1,000 | 379 | .... | 2,630 | 4,000 | 2 | 80 | 370 | 30,624 |

³ Ordained and lay.     ⁴ Total ladies.     ⁵ Total pupils.     ⁶ Dioceses.
work with the corresponding churches of England and Scotland.

| Societies. | No. of Ministers. | Congregations Contributing. | No. of Communicants. | Receipts at Home. | Per cent per Member. | Total Expenditures. | Native Contributions. | Per cent per Member. |
|---|---|---|---|---|---|---|---|---|

## SWEDEN

| Societies. | No. of Ministers. | Congregations Contributing. | No. of Communicants. | Receipts at Home. | Per cent per Member. | Total Expenditures. | Native Contributions. | Per cent per Member. |
|---|---|---|---|---|---|---|---|---|
| 127. Evan. National Association. ... | 245 | ........ | .......... | 48,959 | ...... | ¹ 51,883 | ............. | .... |
| 130. Swedish Ch. Miss. ........... | ........ | .... | ...... | .. | .. | ...... | ............. | .... |
| 131. Swedish Miss. Association . . . | 550 | 650 | 80,000 | 34,852 | ...... | 32,172 | ............. | .... |
| 135. Swedish Miss. in China ........ | 4 | ........ | .......... | 4,021 | ...... | 3,217 | ............. | .... |
| Total ..................... | 799 | 650 | 80,000 | 87,832 | ...... | 87,272 | ... ........ | ...... |

## FINLAND.

| Societies. | No. of Ministers. | Congregations Contributing. | No. of Communicants. | Receipts at Home. | Per cent per Member. | Total Expenditures. | Native Contributions. | Per cent per Member. |
|---|---|---|---|---|---|---|---|---|
| 138. Finland Miss. Soc. .......... | ....... | ....... | ....... | 20,000 | ...... | 19,290 | 25 | .28 |

## GERMANY.

| Societies. | No. of Ministers. | Congregations Contributing. | No. of Communicants. | Receipts at Home. | Per cent per Member. | Total Expenditures. | Native Contributions. | Per cent per Member. |
|---|---|---|---|---|---|---|---|---|
| 141. United Brethren ............. | 337 | 132 | 21,287 | 140,000 | 6.57 | 305,000 | 165,000 | 5.50 |
| 142. Basle Evangelical.............. | ........ | .......... | .......... | 209,273 | ...... | 222,310 | 19,000 | .81 |
| 143. Leipsic Ev. Lutheran ......... | ........ | .......... | .......... | 79,183 | ...... | 77,175 | ............. | .... |
| 144. Berlin Evangelical....... ..... | ........ | .......... | .......... | 76,539 | ...... | 76,370 | .. | .... |
| 145. Rhenish Miss. Soc .. ......... | ¹2,000 | ¹2,000 | .......... | 98,897 | ...... | 97,570 | 16,320 | 1.52 |
| 146. Gossner's Miss. Soc............ | .. .. | ...... | ......... | .. | .. | ...... | ...... | .... |
| 147. N. German Miss. Soc ......... | ........ | ....... | .......... | 20,472 | ...... | 25,825 | 154 | .98 |
| 149. Hermannsburg Ev. Luth....... | ...... | ..... | ......... | 48,630 | ...... | 68,958 | 5,327 | † .20 |
| 150. Breklum Miss. Soc............ | .... | ......... | ......... | 11,000 | .... | 11,000 | ......... | .... |
| Total ..................... | 2,337 | 2,132 | 21,287 | 684,294 | ...... | 884,208 | 195,801 | ...... |

## HOLLAND.

| Societies. | No. of Ministers. | Congregations Contributing. | No. of Communicants. | Receipts at Home. | Per cent per Member. | Total Expenditures. | Native Contributions. | Per cent per Member. |
|---|---|---|---|---|---|---|---|---|
| 155. Netherlands Miss. Soc. ...... ... | ........ | ....... | ........ | 5,000 | ....... | 5,000 | ......... | ...... |
| 156. Ermelo Miss. Soc ........... ... | ........ | ..... | ........ | 9,688 | .... | 9,705 | ......... | ...... |
| 157. Mennonite Miss. Soc ......... | ........ | ........ | ........ | 15,528 | .... | 18,434 | ......... | ...... |
| 159. Dutch Miss. Soc. ........... | 9 | 51 | .......... | ........ | .... | ........ | ......... | ...... |
| 160. Utrecht Miss. Soc ........ .... | ...... | ...... | ........ | .. | .. | .... | ......... | ...... |
| 161. Dutch Ref. Ch. Miss. Soc....... | 180 | 280 | .......... | 5,500 | .... | 7,750 | ......... | ...... |
| Total .......... ............ | 189 | 331 | .. .......... | 35,711 | .... | 40,889 | ......... | ..... |

## FRANCE.

| Societies. | No. of Ministers. | Congregations Contributing. | No. of Communicants. | Receipts at Home. | Per cent per Member. | Total Expenditures. | Native Contributions. | Per cent per Member. |
|---|---|---|---|---|---|---|---|---|
| 165. Paris Ev. Assoc. ......... | ........ | ........ | .......... | 48,315 | ...... | 77,535 | 13,846 | .... .. |
| 166. Free Ch's French Switzerland.. | 97 | 67 | 13,218 | 15,406 | 1.01 | 15,576 | 258 | ...... |
| Total ............ .............. | 97 | 67 | 13,218 | 63,721 | ...... | 93,111 | 14,104 | .... ... |

## THE PACIFIC.

| Societies. | No. of Ministers. | Congregations Contributing. | No. of Communicants. | Receipts at Home. | Per cent per Member. | Total Expenditures. | Native Contributions. | Per cent per Member. |
|---|---|---|---|---|---|---|---|---|
| 169. Hawaiian Ev. Association... | ........ | ... ... | .......... | 32,658 | ...... | 25,862 | ..........⁵...| ...... |
| 170. Melanesian Mission............ | ........ | ......... | ... ...... | 32,500 | ...... | 32,500 | ... .........| ...... |
| Total ..................... | ... ......... | .......... | 65,158 | ...... | 58,362 | ......... | ...... |

¹ Estimated or approximate.     ² Incomplete returns.     ⁶ Exclusive of school fees.
⁷ School fees only.     ⁵ Including home missions.
† From all adherents.

| SOCIETIES. | Stations and Out-stations. | MISSION-ARIES. | | | | NATIVE WORKERS. | | Preaching Places. | Churches. | Communicants. | Additions. | Schools for Higher Education. | Pupils. | Common Schools. | Pupils. |
|---|---|---|---|---|---|---|---|---|---|---|---|---|---|---|---|
| | | Ordained. | Lay. | Wives. | Other Women. | Ordained. | Other Helpers. | | | | | | | | |
| **SWEDEN.** | | | | | | | | | | | | | | | |
| 127. Evan. National Association | 10 | 11 | 7 | 9 | 5 | 3 | 26 | | 5 | 108 | 50 | | | 10 | 453 |
| 130. Swedish Ch. Miss. | 14 | 13 | | | | | | | | 616 | | | | | 68 |
| 131. Swedish Miss. Association | 12 | | 23 | 10 | 6 | | 6 | 16 | 6 | 200 | | 1 | 40 | 3 | 120 |
| 135. Swedish Miss. in China | 8 | | 4 | 1 | 4 | | | | 1 | 14 | 8 | | | | |
| Total | 44 | 24 | 34 | 20 | 15 | 3 | 32 | 16 | 12 | 938 | 58 | 1 | 40 | 13 | 641 |
| **FINLAND.** | | | | | | | | | | | | | | | |
| 138. Finland Miss. Soc. | 4 | 5 | 1 | 5 | | | 10 | | 2 | 87 | | | | 3 | 160 |
| **GERMANY.** | | | | | | | | | | | | | | | |
| 141. United Brethren | 139 | 127 | 24 | 135 | 6 | 19 | 1,691 | | 137 | 29,971 | 1,411 | 4 | 50 | 232 | 19,794 |
| 142. Basle Evangelical | 352 | 104 | 29 | 88 | 4 | 39 | 672 | | | 11,082 | 1,279 | 4 | 76 | 278 | 10,035 |
| 143. Leipsic Ev. Lutheran | 117 | 25 | 1 | | | 14 | 491 | | 141 | 13,559 | 228 | | | 177 | 4,492 |
| 144. Berlin Evangelical | 145 | 60 | 11 | 59 | 5 | 5 | 471 | 307 | | 6,971 | 2,011 | 3 | 28 | 52 | 4,130 |
| 145. Rhenish Miss. Soc. | 158 | 75 | 3 | 61 | 1 | 11 | 490 | | 134 | 10,735 | 360 | 5 | 76 | 120 | 5,460 |
| 146. Gossner's Miss. Soc. | 8 | | | | | 17 | | | 165 | 30,027 | | | | | |
| 147. N. German Miss. Soc | 14 | 11 | 4 | 6 | 2 | 1 | 24 | | | 408 | 29 | 2 | 30 | 14 | 280 |
| 149. Hermannsburg Ev. Luth | 59 | 69 | | | | | ¹332 | | | ¹26,000 | ¹1,770 | | | | ¹2,567 |
| 150. Breklum Miss. Soc. | 6 | 11 | | | | | | | | | | | | | 6 |
| Total | 992 | 482 | 72 | 349 | 18 | 106 | 4,171 | 307 | 577 | 128,753 | 7,088 | 18 | 260 | 873 | 46,764 |
| **HOLLAND.** | | | | | | | | | | | | | | | |
| 155. Netherlands Miss. Soc. | 3 | 18 | | | | | 184 | | | 20,000 | | | | 136 | |
| 156. Ermelo Miss. Soc. | 6 | 6 | | | | | 10 | | 30 | 700 | | | | | |
| 157. Mennonite Miss. Soc. | 8 | ³4 | | 2 | | | 17 | 8 | 8 | 511 | 220 | 1 | | 6 | 210 |
| 159. Dutch Miss. Soc. | 20 | 8 | | 2 | | | 24 | | | 1,013 | 143 | | | 15 | 219 |
| 160. Utrecht Miss. Soc | 7 | 7 | | 7 | | | | | | | | | | | |
| 161. Dutch Ref. Ch. Miss Soc. | | 3 | 1 | 4 | | | ¹112 | 65 | 65 | 6,500 | ¹1,000 | 1 | | ¹12 | |
| Total | 44 | 46 | 1 | 21 | | | 347 | 73 | 103 | 28,724 | 1,163 | 2 | | 169 | 429 |
| **FRANCE.** | | | | | | | | | | | | | | | |
| 165. Paris Ev. Assoc. | 261 | 30 | 3 | 27 | 6 | 19 | 206 | 19 | 19 | 8,947 | 390 | 3 | 78 | 113 | 7,928 |
| 166. Free Ch's French Switzerland | 14 | 7 | | 7 | 1 | | 18 | 7 | 7 | 312 | 56 | 1 | 16 | 14 | 407 |
| Total | 275 | 37 | 3 | 34 | 7 | 19 | 224 | 26 | 26 | 9,259 | 446 | 4 | 94 | 127 | 8,335 |
| **THE PACIFIC.** | | | | | | | | | | | | | | | |
| 169. Hawaiian Ev. Association | 101 | | | | | 56 | 16 | | 82 | 7,648 | 697 | | | 86 | 2,897 |
| 170. Melanesian Mission | 9 | 9 | 4 | | | 5 | 192 | | | | | | | | |
| Total | 110 | 9 | 4 | | | 61 | 208 | | 82 | 7,648 | 697 | | | 86 | 2,897 |

¹ Ordained and lay.　⁴ Total ladies.　⁵ Total pupils.　⁶ Dioceses.

| NAME OF SOCIETY. | Auxiliaries and Bands. | Income. | MISSIONARIES. | | | | SCHOOLS | | SCHOLARS. | | NAME OF GENERAL BOARD |
|---|---|---|---|---|---|---|---|---|---|---|---|
| | | | Teachers. | General Work. | Medical. | Native Helpers. | Boarding | Day. | Boarding | Day. | |

## WOMAN'S SOCIETIES AND BOARDS.

## INDEPENDENT.

| NAME OF SOCIETY. | Aux. | Income. | Teach. | Gen. | Med. | Nat. | Bd. | Day | Bd. | Day | NAME OF GENERAL BOARD |
|---|---|---|---|---|---|---|---|---|---|---|---|
| 180. Union Missionary Society. Year ending Dec. 31, 1890. New York, U. S. A. | ..... | $56,393 | 60 | .... | 4 | 109 | 3 | 155 | 280 | 4,037 | |
| 181. Woman's Foreign Missionary Union of Friends. Year ending May, 1890. Centre Valley, Ill., U. S. A. | 326 | 34,222 | 17 | .... | .... | 9 | 7 | .... | 52 | ..... | |
| 183. Canadian Woman's Board of Foreign Missions. Year ending Dec. 9, 1890. Montreal, Canada | 2 | 893 | 1 | ... | .... | .... | .... | .... | 1 | .... | |
| 186. Society for Promoting Female Education in the East. (1889.) London, England | 275 | 25,000 | 40 | .... | .... | .... | .... | .... | ...... | *19,978 | |
| 187. Indian Female Normal School and Instruction Society, or Zenana Bible and Medical Mission. Year ending Dec. 31, 1889. London, England | 200 | 65,270 | 38 | .... | 5 | 206 | 5 | 58 | 234 | 2,145 | British and Foreign Bible Society Grant for Bible Women, £187. Church Missionary Society for Bible Women, £9. |
| 188. British Syrian Schools and Bible Mission. Year ending June 30, 1890. Wimbledon, England | 76 | 17,435 | 103 | 27 | 1 | 31 | 1 | 28 | 74 | 2,922 | |
| 189. The Net Collections. (1889.) London, England | ..... | 5,000 | 1 | .... | ... | .... | .... | .... | ... | *280 | Work in connection with Mackenzie Memorial Mission, South Africa. |
| 191. Helping Hands Association. (1889.) London, England. | 40 | 3,500 | .... | .... | .... | .... | .... | .... | ..... | ..... | |
| 197. Tabeetha Mission at Jaffa. (1889.) Edinburgh, Scot. | ..... | ...... | ... | .... | .... | .... | 3 | .... | 60 | ..... | |
| Total | 919 | $207,714 | 260 | 27 | 10 | 349 | 19 | 241 | 701 | 29,362 | |

## IN CONNECTION WITH OTHER BOARDS.

## UNITED STATES.

| NAME OF SOCIETY. | Aux. | Income. | Teach. | Gen. | Med. | Nat. | Bd. | Day | Bd. | Day | NAME OF GENERAL BOARD |
|---|---|---|---|---|---|---|---|---|---|---|---|
| 201. Woman's Board of Missions in connection with A. B. C. F. M. Year ending Dec. 1890 | 1,800 | $96,000 | 33 | 79 | 2 | 135 | 28 | 277 | 1,000 | 10,000 | American Board of Commissioners for Foreign Missions. |
| 201a. Board of the Interior. Year ending Oct. 25, 1890. | 2,000 | 56,042 | 63 | 14 | 3 | 105 | 13 | 73 | ..... | ...... | |
| 201b. Board of the Pacific. Year ending Aug 31, 1890. | 45 | 4,222 | 3 | 1 | .... | .... | 2 | .... | ..... | ...... | |
| 201c. Board of the Pacific Islands Year ending Dec. 31, 1890. | 4 | 1,100 | 2 | 1 | .... | 5 | 1 | 3 | 17 | 200 | |
| 203. Woman's Foreign Missionary Society, Methodist Episcopal Church (North). Year ending Oct. 31, 1890. | 5,567 | 220,329 | 100 | 11 | 11 | 626 | 58 | 294 | 1,000 | 5,000 | Meth. Epis. Ch. (North). |
| 204. Woman's Board of Missions, Methodist Episcopal Ch. South. Year ending May, 1890. | 1,852 | 75,487 | 32 | .... | .... | 54 | 10 | 24 | ..... | *1,248 | Missionary Society in the M. E. Church South. |
| 205. Woman's Foreign Missionary Society, Methodist Protestant Church. Year ending Dec. 1, 1890. | 435 | 5,059 | 4 | 4 | ... | 5 | 1 | 1 | 40 | 10 | Meth. Prot. Church. |
| 206. Mite Society, African Methodist Episcopal Church. Year ending May, 1890. | 200 | 1,000 | .... | .... | .... | .... | .... | .... | ..... | ..... | Missionary Society of the African M. E. Church. |

* Total pupils.

| NAME OF SOCIETY. | Auxiliaries and Bands. | Income. | MISSIONARIES. | | | | SCHOOLS. | | SCHOLARS. | | NAME OF GENERAL BOARD |
|---|---|---|---|---|---|---|---|---|---|---|---|
| | | | Teachers. | General Work. | Medical. | Native Helpers. | Boarding. | Day. | Boarding. | Day. | |
| 210. Woman's Foreign Mission Society of the Presbyterian Church (North). Year ending May 1, 1890 | 2,500 | $141,488 | 139 | ... | 3 | 84 | 35 | 153 | ...... | ...... | |
| 210a. Woman's Board of Foreign Missions of the Presbyterian Church. Year ending April, 1890 | 983 | 58,190 | 60 | ... | 3 | 36 | 10 | 44 | ...... | ...... | |
| 210b. Woman's Presbyterian Board of Missions of the Northwest. Year ending April 29, 1890 | 1,661 | 80,679 | 24 | 44 | 7 | 61 | 7 | 93 | ...... | ...... | |
| 210c. Woman's Foreign Mission Society of Northern New York. Year ending April 29, 1890 | 196 | 9,692 | 4 | .. | ... | 17 | ... | ... | ...... | ...... | Board of Foreign Missions Presbyterian Ch. (North). |
| 210d. Woman's Board of Missions of the Southwest. (1889.) | 314 | 7,102 | 12 | ... | ... | ... | ... | ... | ...... | ...... | |
| 210e. Occidental Board of Foreign Missions of the Presbyterian Church. Year ending March 25, 1890. | 174 | 10,611 | 6 | 9 | 2 | 6 | 2 | 12 | ...... | ...... | |
| 210f. Woman's North Pacific Presbyterian Board of Missions. Year ending April, 1890 | 37 | 5,908 | 1 | ... | ... | ... | 1 | 1 | 1 | 1 | |
| 211. Woman's Board of Foreign Missions of the Reformed (Dutch) Church. Year ending May, 1890. | 267 | 27,932 | 28 | 11 | ... | 57 | 6 | 8 | 28 | 611 | Reformed (Dutch) Ch. |
| 212. Woman's Board of Missions, Cumberland Presbyterian Church. Year ending Dec., 1890. | 1,000 | 9,117 | 4 | 4 | ... | ... | 2 | 2 | 140 | ...... | Foreign Missionary Society, Cumberland Presbyterian Church. |
| 213. Woman's Foreign Missionary Society, United Presbyterian Church. Year ending March 31, 1890. | 782 | 16,705 | 19 | ... | 1 | ... | 3 | 265 | ...... | *2,793 | Board of Foreign Missions of the United Presbyterian Church. |
| 221. Woman's Baptist Foreign Mission Society (Northern Convention). Year ending April, 1890 | 2,142 | 90,637 | 52 | ... | 2 | 67 | 25 | 171 | 61 | 19 | |
| 221a. Woman's Baptist Foreign Mission Society of the West. Year ending March 31, 1890 | 1,785 | 29,803 | 18 | 16 | 2 | 63 | 11 | 66 | 1,192 | ..... | American Baptist Missionary Union. |
| 221b. Woman's Baptist Foreign Mission Society of California. Year ending March, 1890 | 85 | 2,300 | ... | ... | ... | ... | ... | ... | ... | .. | |
| 221c. Woman's Foreign Mission Society of Oregon. Year ending Oct. 25, 1890 | 50 | 1,500 | 1 | 1 | ... | ... | ... | ... | ...... | ...... | |
| 222. Free Baptist Woman's Mission Society. Year ending Oct., 1890 | 331 | 7,409 | .. | 5 | 1 | 94 | 1 | 39 | 35 | ...... | Free Bap. Ch. |
| 223. Woman's Missionary Union, Auxiliary to the Southern Baptist Convention. Year ending Dec. 31, 1889 | 1,259 | 18,716 | 18 | ... | ... | ... | ... | ... | ... | ... | Board of Foreign Missions of the Southern Baptist Convention. |
| 224. Woman's Executive Board of the Seventh Day Baptist General Conference. Year ending July 15, 1890. | 70 | 675 | 1 | ... | ... | 5 | 2 | 22 | ...... | ...... | Foreign Missionary Society of Seventh Day Baptists. |
| 231. Woman's Auxiliary Board of Missions, Protestant Episcopal Church. Year ending Sept. 1, 1890 | 59 | 36,838 | 39 | .. | 1 | 490 | 28 | 67 | 785 | 2,378 | Domestic and Foreign Missionary Society of the Protestant Episcopal Church. |
| 233. Woman's Foreign Mission Association, United Brethren. Year ending March 31, 1890. | 44 | 13,231 | 10 | ... | ... | 18 | ... | ... | ...... | ...... | Board of Missions of the United Brethren in Christ. |
| 234. Christian Woman's Board of Missions (Disciples of Christ). Year ending Sept. 30, 1890 | 1,329 | ...... | 4 | 22 | 2 | 2 | 2 | .... | 52 | ...... | Christian For. Miss. Society |
| 235. The Woman's Home and Foreign Missionary Society of the General Synod, Lutheran Church. Year ending March 31, 1890.. | 570 | 22,753 | 45 | ... | 1 | 2 | 1 | 19 | 50 | 943 | Board of Foreign Missions, Evangelical Luth. Church, General Synod. |
| 236. Woman's Mission Society, Evangelical Association. (1889.) | 135 | 2,188 | ... | ... | ... | ... | ... | .. | ...... | ...... | Foreign Missionary Society, Evan. Assoc. |
| Total | 27,676 | 1,060,932 | 721 | 222 | 41 | 1472 | 247 | 1634 | 4,657 | 23,903 | |

\* Total pupils.

| NAME OF SOCIETY. | Auxiliaries and Bands. | Income. | MISSIONARIES. | | | | SCHOOLS | | SCHOLARS. | | NAME OF GENERAL BOARD |
| --- | --- | --- | --- | --- | --- | --- | --- | --- | --- | --- | --- |
| | | | Teachers. | General Work. | Medical. | Native Helpers. | Boarding. | Day. | Boarding. | Day. | |

### CANADA.

| NAME OF SOCIETY. | Auxiliaries and Bands. | Income. | Teachers. | General Work. | Medical. | Native Helpers. | Boarding. | Day. | Boarding. | Day. | NAME OF GENERAL BOARD |
| --- | --- | --- | --- | --- | --- | --- | --- | --- | --- | --- | --- |
| 251a. Woman's Baptist Missionary Union of the Maritime Provinces of Canada (1889) | ..... | $5,700 | .... | 12 | .... | 44 | 3 | 10 | 34 | ..... | Foreign Missionary Society of the Maritime Provinces of Canada. |
| 251b. Woman's Foreign Mission Society. East Ontario and Quebec. Year ending Oct. 10, 1890. | 61 | 1,186 | 2 | ... | 1 | .... | 2 | .... | 32 | .... | |
| 251c. Woman's Foreign Mission Society of Ontario. Year ending Sept., 1890 | 254 | 6,167 | 2 | 3 | .... | 22 | 1 | 5 | 26 | 31 | |
| 252a. Woman's Foreign Mission Society, Presbyterian Ch. in Canada, Western Division. (1889.) | 638 | 31,999 | 10 | .... | 2 | .... | .. | .... | .... | .... | Foreign Missionary Society Presbyterian Ch. in Canada. |
| 252b. Woman's Foreign Mission Society, Presbyterian Ch. in Canada, Eastern Division. (1889.) | 116 | 4,296 | 6 | .... | .... | .... | .. | .... | .... | .... | |
| 252c. Montreal Woman's Mission Society of the Presbyterian Church in Canada. Year ending March 18, 1890. | 6 | 1,615 | .... | 2 | .... | ... | .. | .... | .... | .... | |
| 253. Woman's Mission Society, Methodist Church in Canada. Year ending Oct., 1890 | 511 | 25,561 | 24 | .... | .... | 11 | 8 | 5 | 269 | 150 | Meth. Church. |
| 254. Canada Congregational Woman's Board of Missions. Year ending May 31, 1890. | 57 | 1,606 | 1 | .... | .... | .... | .. | .... | .... | .... | A. B. C. F. M. |
| 255. Woman's Auxiliary to Board of Missions of the Church of England in Canada. (1889.) | 290 | 10,861 | .... | .... | .... | .... | .. | .... | .... | .... | Church of England. |
| Total | 1,849 | 88,991 | 45 | 17 | 3 | 77 | 14 | 20 | 361 | 181 | |

| Name of Society. | Auxiliaries and Bands. | Income. | Teachers. | General Work. | Medical. | Native Helpers. | Boarding. | Day. | Boarding. | Day. | Name of General Board |
|---|---|---|---|---|---|---|---|---|---|---|---|
| | | | | Missionaries. | | | Schools | | Scholars. | | |

## GREAT BRITAIN AND IRELAND.

| Name of Society. | Auxiliaries and Bands. | Income. | Teachers. | General Work. | Medical. | Native Helpers. | Boarding. | Day. | Boarding. | Day. | Name of General Board |
|---|---|---|---|---|---|---|---|---|---|---|---|
| 260. Coral Missionary Magazine and Fund of the W. C. M. S. (1889.) | ... | £1,000 | ... | ... | ... | ... | ... | ... | ... | ... | Church Missionary Soc. |
| 261. Ladies' Auxiliary of the Wesleyan Methodist Mission Society. Year ending Dec. 1889 | 432 | 8,138 | 32 | ... | 5 | 58 | 21 | 260 | ... | *12,000 | Wesleyan Methodist Missionary Society. |
| 262. Ladies' Association in connection with the Society for the Propagation of the Gospel. Year ending Dec. 31, 1889 | ... | 6,351 | 61 | ... | ... | 104 | ... | *18 | ... | *4,250 | Society for the Propagation of the Gospel. |
| 263. Ladies' Association for the Support of Zenana Work and Bible-Women in India in connection with the Baptist Missionary Society. Year ending March 31, 1890 | ... | 7,732 | ‡48 | ... | 2 | 161 | 2 | 49 | 95 | 1,800 | Baptist Missionary Society. |
| 264. Ladies' Committee of the London Missionary Society. Year ending March 31, 1890 | ... | 6,471 | 36 | ... | ... | ... | 6 | 133 | ... | *10,000 | London Missionary Soc. |
| 265. Christian Work in France, under the care of Friends. Year ending Dec. 31, 1890 | ... | 500 | ... | 15 | ... | 21 | ... | ... | 5 | ... | Friends' For. Miss. Soc. |
| 266. Women's Missionary Association of the Presbyterian Church of England. Year ending Dec. 31, 1890 | 160 | 3,333 | 19 | ... | ... | 19 | 4 | 10 | 102 | 171 | Pres. Ch. of England. |
| 267. Church of England Zenana Missionary Society in co-operation with C. M. S. Year ending March 31, 1890 | 961 | 25,817 | 7 | 112 | 1 | 650 | 6 | 186 | 162 | 7,649 | Church Miss. Soc. |
| 275. Church of Scotland (Established) Ladies' Association for Foreign Missions. Year ending Dec. 31, 1889 | †546 | 7,001 | 22 | 20 | 3 | 98 | 4 | 35 | 111 | 2,479 | Church of Scotland. (Established.) |
| 276. Ladies' Society of the Free Church of Scotland for Female Education in India and South Africa. Year ending March 31, 1890 | 608 | 19,272 | 29 | 13 | 2 | 232 | 10 | 60 | 448 | 6,906 | Free Church of Scotland Foreign Missionary Reports. |
| 277. The Central Committee and Church Woman's Association for Foreign Missions of the Scottish Episcopal Church. (1889.) | ... | 750 | ... | ... | ... | ... | ... | ... | ... | ... | Central Board Foreign Missions, Scottish Episcopal Church. |
| 278. United Presbyterian Church of Scotland, Zenana Mission. Year ending Dec., 1889 | 259 | 3,798 | 21 | ... | 2 | 75 | 3 | ... | ... | ... | United Pres. Ch. |
| 283. Presbyterian Church of Ireland, Female Association for Promoting Christianity among the Women of the East. Year ending March 31, 1890 | ... | 3,906 | 8 | ... | 1 | 56 | ... | *19 | ... | *1,100 | Presbyterian Church of Ireland, Board of Foreign Missions. |
| Total | 3,056 | £91,069 $470,345 | 283 | 160 | 16 | 1474 | 56 | 770 | 923 | 46,355 | |
| Grand Total | 33,500 | 1,827,982 | 1309 | 426 | 70 | 3472 | 336 | 2665 | 6,642 | 99,101 | |

* Total schools or pupils.     † Estimated.     ‡ Zenana workers.

# GENERAL INDEX.

*Italics indicate general articles.   For mission stations see also Appendix E.*

*Italics indicate general articles. For mission stations see also Appendix E.*

*Italics indicate general articles. For mission stations see also Appendix E.*

*Italics indicate general articles. For mission stations see also Appendix E.*

*Italics indicate general articles. For mission stations see also Appendix E.*

*Italics indicate general articles. For mission stations see also Appendix E.*

*Italics indicate general articles. For mission stations see also Appendix E.*

*Italics indicate general articles. For mission stations see also Appendix E.*

*Italics indicate general articles. For mission stations see also Appendix E.*

*Italics indicate general articles. For mission stations see also Appendix E.*

*Italics indicate general articles. For mission stations see also Appendix E.*

*Italics indicate general articles. For mission stations see also Appendix E.*

*Italics indicate general articles. For mission stations see also Appendix E.*

*Italics indicate general articles. For mission stations see also Appendix E.*

*Italics indicate general articles. For mission stations see also Appendix E.*

*Italics indicate general articles. For mission stations see also Appendix E.*

*Italics indicate general articles. For mission stations see also Appendix E.*

*Italics indicate general articles. For mission stations see also Appendix E.*

*Italics indicate general articles. For mission stations see also Appendix E.*

*Italics indicate general articles. For mission stations see also Appendix E.*

*Italics indicate general articles. For mission stations see also Appendix E.*

*Italics indicate general articles. For mission stations see also Appendix E.*

*Italics indicate general articles. For mission stations see also Appendix E.*

*Italics indicate general articles.  For mission stations see also Appendix E.*

*Italics indicate general articles. For mission stations see also Appendix E.*

Italics indicate general articles. For mission stations see also Appendix E.

*Italics indicate general articles. For mission stations see also Appendix E.*

*Italics indicate general articles. For mission stations see also Appendix E.*

*Italics indicate general articles. For mission stations see also Appendix E.*

*Italics indicate general articles. For mission stations see also Appendix E.*

*Italics indicate general articles. For mission stations see also Appendix E.*

*Italics indicate general articles. For mission stations see also Appendix E.*

*Italics indicate general articles. For mission stations see also Appendix E.*

*Italics indicate general articles. For mission stations see also Appendix E.*

*Italics indicate general articles. For mission stations see also Appendix E.*

*Italics indicate general articles.    For mission stations see also Appendix E.*

*Italics indicate general articles. For mission stations see also Appendix E.*

*Italics indicate general articles. For mission stations see also Appendix E.*

*Italics indicate general articles. For mission stations see also Appendix F.*

# X.

# Y.

*Italics indicate general articles. For mission stations see also Appendix E.*

*Italics indicate general articles. For mission stations see also Appendix E.*

CPSIA information can be obtained at www.ICGtesting.com
Printed in the USA
BVOW051406110412

287445BV00001B/4/A